THE OFFICIAL 2011 PRICE GUIDE TO BASKETBALL CARDS

Edited By: Keith Hower with the staff of
Beckett Basketball

Founder & Advisor: Dr. James Beckett III

TWENTIETH EDITION

HOUSE OF COLLECTIBLES
Random House Reference
New York

Important Notice: All of the information, including valuations, in this book has been compiled from reliable sources, and efforts have been made to eliminate errors and questionable data. Nevertheless, the possibility of error in a work of such scope always exists. The publisher will not be held responsible for losses which may occur in the purchase, sale or other transaction of items because of information contained herein. Readers who feel they have discovered errors are invited to write and inform us, so that they may be corrected in subsequent editions. Those seeking further information on the topics covered in this book are advised to refer to the complete line of *Official Price Guides* published by the House of Collectibles.

Please address inquiries about electronic licensing of any products for use on a network, in software, or on CD-ROM to the Subsidiary Rights Department, Random House Information Group, fax 212-572-6003
Visit the House of Collectibles Web site: www.houseofcollectibles.com

This book is available for special discounts for bulk purchases for sales promotions or premiums. Special editions, including personalized covers, excerpts of existing books, and corporate imprints, can be created in large quantities for special needs. For more information, write to:

Random House, Inc.,
Special Markets/Premium Sales
1745 Broadway, MD 6-2
New York, NY 10019

or e-mail specialmarket@randomhouse.com

Manufactured in the United States of America

ISSN: 1062-6980

ISBN: 978-0-375-723377

10 9 8 7 6 5 4 3 2 1

Twentieth Edition: November 2011

Table of Contents

Table of Contents

Table of Contents

MIGHTY
MOUSE
With more than 4.7 million prices available
at the click of a button,
every mouse is a super hero
BECKETT
B
MEDIA
www.beckett.com/opg
Online
PRICE
GUIDES

About the Author

Jim Beckett, the leading authority on sports card values in the United States, conducts a wide range of activities in the world of sports. He possesses one of the finest collections of sports cards and autographs in the world, has made numerous appearances on radio and television, and has been frequently cited in many national publications. He was awarded the first "Special Achievement Award" for Contributions to the Hobby by the National Sports Collectors Convention in 1980, the "Jock Jaspersen Award" for Hobby Dedication in 1983, and the "Buck Barker Spirit of the Hobby Award" in 1991.

Dr. Beckett is the author of *Beckett Baseball Card Price Guide, The Official Price Guide to Baseball Cards, The Sport Americana Price Guide to Baseball Collectibles, The Sport Americana Baseball Memorabilia and Autograph Price Guide, Beckett Football Card Price Guide, The Official Price Guide to Football Cards, Beckett Hockey Card Price Guide, The Official Price Guide to Hockey Cards, Beckett Basketball Card Price Guide, The Official Price Guide to Basketball Cards,* and *The Sport Americana Baseball Card Alphabetical Checklist.* In addition, he is the founder, publisher, and editor of *Beckett Baseball, Beckett Basketball, Beckett Football, Beckett Hockey,* and *Beckett Racing* magazines.

Jim Beckett received his Ph.D. in Statistics from Southern Methodist University in 1975. Prior to starting Beckett Publications in 1984, Dr. Beckett served as an Associate Professor of Statistics at Bowling Green State University and as a vice president of a consulting firm in Dallas, Texas. He currently resides in Dallas.

How to Use This Book

Isn't it great? Every year this book gets bigger and bigger with all the new sets coming out. But even more exciting is that every year there are more attractive choices and, subsequently, more interest in the cards we love so much. This edition has been enhanced and expanded from the previous edition. The cards you collect—who appears on them, what they look like, where they are from, and (most important to most of you) what their current values are —are enumerated within. Many of the features contained in the other Beckett Price Guides have been incorporated into this volume since condition grading, terminology, and many other aspects of collecting are common to card collecting in general. We hope you find the book both interesting and useful in your collecting pursuits.

The Beckett Guide has been successful where other attempts have failed because it is complete, current, and valid. This price guide contains not just one, but two prices by condition for all the basketball cards listed, which account for most of the basketball cards in existence. The prices were added to the card lists just prior to printing and reflect not the author's opinions or desires but the going retail prices for each card, based on the marketplace (sports memorabilia conventions and shows, sports card shops, hobby papers, Internet auctions, current mail-order catalogs, local club meetings, auction results, and other firsthand reports of actually realized prices).

What is the best price guide available on the market today? Of course, card sellers will prefer the price guide with the highest prices, while card buyers will naturally prefer the one with the lowest prices. Accuracy, however, is the true test. Use the price guide used by more collectors and dealers than all the others combined. Look for the Beckett name. I won't put my name on anything I won't stake my reputation on. Not the lowest and not the highest—but the most accurate, with integrity.

To facilitate your use of this book, read the complete introductory section on the following pages before going to the pricing pages. Every collectible field has its own terminology; we've tried to capture most of these terms and definitions in our glossary. Please read carefully the section on grading and the condition of your cards, as you will not be able to determine which price column is appropriate for a given card without first knowing its condition.

Introduction

Welcome to the exciting world of sports card collecting, one of America's most popular avocations. You have made a good choice in buying this book, since it will open up to you the entire spectrum of this field in the simplest, most concise way.

The growth of *Beckett Baseball, Beckett Basketball, Beckett Football, Beckett Hockey*, and *Beckett Racing* is another indication of the unprecedented popularity of sports cards. Founded in 1984 by Dr. James Beckett—the author of this price guide—*Beckett Basketball* contains the most extensive and accepted monthly Price Guide, collectible glossy superstar covers, colorful feature articles, a "Hot List," Convention Calendar, tips for beginners, "Readers Write" letters to and responses from the editor, information on errors and varieties, autograph collecting tips and profiles of the sport's hottest stars. Published every month, *BB* is the hobby's largest paid circulation periodical. The other five magazines were built on the success of *BB*.

So collecting sports cards—while still pursued as a hobby with youthful exuberance by kids in the neighborhood—has also taken on the trappings of an industry, with thousands of full- and part-time card dealers, as well as vendors of supplies, clubs, and conventions. In fact, each year since 1980 thousands of hobbyists have assembled for a National Sports Collectors Convention, at which hundreds of dealers have displayed their wares, seminars have been conducted, autographs penned by sports notables, and millions of cards changed hands.

The Beckett Guide is the best annual guide available to the exciting world of basketball cards. Read it and use it. May your enjoyment and your card collection increase in the coming months and years.

How to Collect

Each collection is personal and reflects the individuality of its owner. There are no set rules on how to collect cards. Since card collecting is a hobby or leisurely pastime, what you collect, how much you collect, and how much time and money you spend collecting are entirely up to you. The funds you have available for collecting and your own personal taste should determine how you collect. The information and ideas presented here are intended to help you get the most enjoyment from this hobby.

It is impossible to collect every card ever produced. Therefore, beginners as well as intermediate and advanced collectors usually specialize their collections in some way. One of the reasons this hobby is popular is that individual collectors can define and tailor their collecting methods to match their own tastes. To give you some ideas of the various approaches to collecting, we will list some of the more popular areas of specialization.

Many collectors select complete sets from particular years. For example, they may concentrate on assembling complete sets from all the years since their birth or from when they became avid sports fans. They may try to collect a card for every player during that specified period of time. Many others wish to acquire only certain players. Usually such players are the superstars of the sport, but occasionally collectors will specialize in all the cards of players who attended a particular college or came from a certain town. Some collectors are only interested in the first cards or Rookie cards of certain players.

Another fun way to collect cards is by team. Most fans have a favorite team, and it is natural for that loyalty to be translated into a desire for cards of the players on that particular team. For most of the recent years, team sets (all the cards from a given team for that year) are readily available at a reasonable price. *The Sport Americana Team Football and Basketball Card Checklist* will open up this aspect of the field to the collector.

Obtaining Cards

Several avenues are open to card collectors. Cards still can be purchased in the traditional way: by the pack at the local discount, grocery, or convenience store. But there are also thousands of card shops across the country that specialize in selling cards individually or by the pack, box, or set. Another alternative is the thousands of card shows held each month around the country, which feature anywhere from five to 800 tables of sports cards and memorabilia for sale.

For many years, it has been possible to purchase complete sets of cards through mail-order advertisers found in traditional sports media publications, such as *The Sporting News, Basketball Digest, Street & Smith* yearbooks, and others. These sets also are advertised in the card collecting periodicals. Many collectors will begin by subscribing to at least one of the hobby periodicals, all of which have good up-to-date information. In fact, subscription offers can be found in the advertising section of this book.

Most serious card collectors obtain old (and new) cards from one or more of several main sources: (1) trading or buying from other collectors or dealers; (2) responding to sale or auction ads in the hobby publications; (3) buying at a local hobby store; (4) attending sports collectibles shows or conventions; and/or (5) purchasing cards over the Internet.

We advise that you try all five methods since each has its own distinct advantages: (1) trading is a great way to make new friends; (2) hobby periodicals help you keep up with what's going on (including when and where the conventions are happening); (3) stores provide the opportunity to enjoy personalized service and to consider a great diversity of material in a relaxed sports-oriented atmosphere; (4) shows allow you to choose from multiple dealers and thousands of cards under one roof in a competitive situation; and (5) the Internet allows a collector to purchase cards from just about anywhere in the world.

Preserving Your Cards

Cards are fragile. They must be handled properly in order to retain their value. Careless handling can easily result in creased or bent cards. It is, however, not recommended that tweezers or tongs be used to pick up your cards since such utensils might mar or indent card surfaces and thus reduce those cards' conditions and values. In general, your cards should be directly handled as little as possible. This is sometimes easier said than done.

Although there are still many who use custom boxes, storage trays, or even shoeboxes, plastic sheets are the preferred method of many collectors for storing cards. A collection stored in plastic pages in a three-ring album allows you to view your collection at any time without the need to touch the card itself. Cards can also be kept in single holders (of various types and thicknesses) designed for the enjoyment of each card individually. For a large collection, some collectors may use a combination of the above methods. When purchasing plastic sheets for your cards, be sure that you find the pocket size that fits the cards snugly. Don't put your 1969-70 Topps in a sheet designed to fit 1992-93 Topps.

Most hobby and collectibles shops and virtually all collectors' conventions will have these plastic pages available in quantity for the various sizes offered. Also, remember that pocket size isn't the only factor to consider when looking for plastic sheets. Other factors such as safety, economy, appearance, availability, or personal preference also may indicate which types of sheets a collector may want to buy.

Damp, sunny, and/or hot conditions—no, this is not a weather forecast—are three elements to avoid in extremes if you are interested in preserving your collection. Too much (or too little) humidity can cause gradual deterioration of a card. Direct, bright sun (or fluorescent light) over time will bleach out the color of a card. Extreme heat accelerates the decomposition of the card. On the other hand, many cards have lasted more than 50 years without much scientific intervention. So be cautious, even if the above factors typically present a problem only when in the extreme. It never hurts to be prudent.

Collecting vs. Investing

Collecting individual players and collecting complete sets are both popular vehicles for investment and speculation. Most investors and speculators stock up on complete sets or on quantities of players that they think have good investment potential.

There is obviously no guarantee in this book, or anywhere else for that matter, that cards will outperform the stock market or other investment alternatives in the future. After all, basketball cards do not pay quarterly dividends and cards cannot be sold at their "current values" as easily as stocks or bonds.

Nevertheless, investors have noticed a favorable long-term trend in the past performance of sports collectibles, and certain cards and sets have outperformed just about any other investment in certain years. Many hobbyists maintain that the best investment is and always will be the building of a collection, which traditionally has held up better than outright speculation.

Some of the obvious questions are, Which cards? When to buy? When to sell? The best investment you can make is in your own education. The more you know about your collection and collecting in general, the more informed the decisions you will be able to make. We're not selling investment tips. We're selling information about the current value of basketball cards. It's up to you to use that information to your best advantage.

Glossary/Legend

Our glossary defines terms frequently used in card collecting. Many of these terms are also common to other types of sports memorabilia collecting. Some terms may have several meanings depending on use and context.

ABA—American Basketball Association.
ACC—Accomplishment.
ACO—Assistant Coach Card.
AL—Active Leader.
ART—All-Rookie Team.
AS—All-Star.
ASA—All-Star Advice.
ASW—All-Star Weekend.
AUTO/AU—Autograph.
AW—Award Winner.

B—Bronze.

BC—Bonus Card.

BRICK—A group or "lot" or cards, usually 50 or more having common characteristics, that is, intended to be bought, sold, or traded as a unit.

BT—Beam Team or Breakaway Threats.

CB—Collegiate Best.

CBA—Continental Basketball Association.

CL—Checklist Card. A card that lists in order the cards and players in the set or series. Older checklist cards in mint condition that have not been checked off are very desirable and command large premiums.

CO—Coach Card.

COIN—A small disc of metal or plastic portraying a player in its center.

COLLECTOR—A person who engages in the hobby of collecting cards primarily for his/her own enjoyment, with any profit motive being secondary.

COMBINATION CARD—A single card depicting two or more players (not including team cards).

COMMON CARD—The typical card of any set.

CONVENTION ISSUE—A set produced in conjunction with a sports collectibles convention to commemorate or promote the show. Most recent convention issues could also be classified as promo sets.

COR—Corrected Card. A version of an error card that was fixed by the manufacturer.

COUPON—See Tab.

CY—City Lights.

DEALER—A person who engages in buying, selling, and trading sports collectibles or supplies. A dealer may also be a collector, but as a dealer, he anticipates a profit.

DIE-CUT—A card with part of its stock partially cut for ornamental reasons.

DISC—A circular-shaped card.

DISPLAY SHEET—A clear, plastic page that is punched for insertion into a binder (with standard three-ring spacing) containing pockets for displaying cards. Many different styles of sheets exist with pockets of varying sizes to hold the many differing card formats. The vast majority of current cards measure 2 1/2 by 3 1/2 inches and fit in nine-pocket sheets.

DP—Double Print. A card that was printed in approximately double the quantity compared to other cards in the same series. Or, Draft Pick Card.

ERR—Error Card. A card with erroneous information, spelling, or depiction on either side of the card. Most errors are never corrected by the producing card company.

EXCH—A card that is inserted into packs that can be redeemed for something else—usually a set or autograph.

FIN—Finals.

FLB—Flashback.

FPM—Future Playoff MVPs.

FSL—Future Scoring Leaders.

FULL SHEET—A complete sheet of cards that has not been cut into individual cards by the manufacturer. Also called an uncut sheet.

G—Gold.

GQ—Gentleman's Quarterly.

GRA—Grace.

HL—Highlight Card.

HOF—Hall of Fame, or Hall of Famer (also abbreviated HOFer).

HOR—Horizontal pose on a card, as opposed to the standard vertical orientation found on most cards.

IA—In Action Card. A special type of card depicting a player in an action photo, such as the 1982 Topps cards.

INSERT—A card of a different type, e.g., a poster, or any other sports collectible contained and sold in the same package along with a card or cards of a major set.

IS—Inside Stuff.

ISSUE—Synonymous with set, but usually used in conjunction with a manufacturer, e.g., a Topps issue.

JSY—Jersey Card.

JWA—John Wooden Award.

KID—Kid Picture Card.

LEGITIMATE ISSUE—A set produced to promote or boost sales of a product or service, e.g., bubble gum, cereal, cigarettes, etc. Most collector issues are not legitimate issues in this sense.

LID—A circular-shaped card (possibly with tab) that forms the top of the container for the product being promoted.

MAG—Magic of SkyBox cards.

MAJOR SET—A set produced by a national manufacturer of cards, containing a large number of cards. Usually 100 or more different cards comprise a major set.

MC—Members Choice.

MEM—Memorial.

MINI—A small card or stamp (the 1991-92 SkyBox Canadian set, for example).

MO—McDonald's Open.

MVP—Most Valuable Player.

NNO—No Number on Back.

NY—New York.

OBVERSE—The front, face, or pictured side of tho card.

OLY—Olympic Card.

PANEL—An extended card that is composed of multiple individual cards.

PC—Poster Card.

PERIPHERAL SET—A loosely defined term that applies to any nonregular issue set. This term most often is used to describe food issue, giveaway, regional, or sendaway sets that contain a fairly small number of cards and are not accepted by the hobby as major sets.

PF—Pacific Finest.

POY—Player of the Year.

PREMIUM—A card, sometimes on photographic stock, that is purchased or obtained in conjunction with (or redeemed for) another card or product. This term applies mainly to older products, as newer cards distributed in this manner are generally lumped together as peripheral sets.

PREMIUM CARDS—A class of products introduced recently, intended to have higher-quality card stock and photography than regular cards, but with more limited production and higher cost. Determining what is and isn't a premium card is somewhat subjective.

PROMOTIONAL SET—A set, usually containing a small number of cards, issued by a national card producer and distributed in limited quantities or to a select group of people, such as major show attendees or dealers with wholesale accounts. Presumably, the purpose of a promo set is to stir up demand for an upcoming set. Also called a preview, prototype, promo, or test set.

QP—Quadruple Print. A card that was printed in approximately four times the quantity compared to other cards in the same series.

RARE—A card or series of cards of very limited availability. Unfortunately, "rare" is a subjective term sometimes used indiscriminately. Using strict definitions, rare cards are harder to obtain than scarce cards.

RC—Rookie Card.

REGIONAL—A card issued and distributed only in a limited geographical area of the country. The producer may or may not be a major, national producer of trading cards. The key is whether the set was distributed nationally in any form or not.

REVERSE—The back or narrative side of the card.

REV NEG—Reversed or flopped photo side of the card. This is a common type of error card, but only some are corrected.

RIS—Rising Star.

ROY—Rookie of the Year.

S—Silver.

SA—Super Action Card. Similar to an In Action Card.

SAL—SkyBox Salutes.

SASE—Self-addressed, stamped envelope.

SCARCE—A card or series of cards of limited availability. This subjective term is sometimes used indiscriminately to promote or hype value. Using strict definitions, scarce cards are easier to obtain than rare cards.

SERIES—The entire set of cards issued by a particular producer in a particular year, e.g., the 1978-79 Topps series. Also, within a particular set, series can refer to a group of (consecutively numbered) cards printed at the same time, e.g., the first series of the 1972-73 Topps set (#1 through #132).

SET—One each of an entire run of cards of the same type, produced by a particular manufacturer during a single season. In other words, if you have a complete set of 1989-90 Fleer cards, then you have every card from #1 up to and including #132; i.e., all the different cards that were produced.

SHOOT—Shooting Star.

SHOW—A large gathering of dealers and collectors at a single location for the purpose of buying, selling, and trading sports cards and memorabilia. Conventions are open to the public and sometimes also feature autograph guests, door prizes, films, contests, etc. (Or, Showcase, as in 1996-97 Flair Showcase.)

SKED—Schedules.

SP—Single or Short Print. A card that was printed in a lesser quantity compared to the other cards in the same series (also see Double Print). This term can be used only in a relative sense and in reference to one particular set. For instance, the 1989-90 Hoops Pistons Championship card (#353A) is less common than the other cards in that set, but it isn't necessarily scarcer than regular cards of any other set.

SPECIAL CARD—A card that portrays something other than a single player or team.

SS—Star Stats.

STANDARD SIZE—The standard size for sports cards is 2 1/2 by 3 1/2 inches. All exceptions, such as 1969-70 Topps, are noted in card descriptions.

STAR CARD—A card that portrays a player of some repute, usually determined by his ability, but sometimes referring to sheer popularity.

STAY—Stay in School.

STICKER—A card-like item with a removable layer that can be affixed to another surface. Example: 1986-87 through 1989-90 Fleer bonus cards.

STOCK—The cardboard or paper on which the card is printed.

STY—Style.

SUPERSTAR CARD—A card that portrays a superstar, e.g., a Hall of Fame member or a player whose current performance may eventually warrant serious Hall of Fame consideration.

SY—Schoolyard Stars.

TAB — A card portion set off from the rest of the card, usually with perforations, that may be removed without damaging the central character or event depicted by the card.

TC—Team Card or Team Checklist Card.

TD—Triple Double. A term used for having double-digit totals in three categories.

TEAM CARD—A card that depicts an entire team, notably the 1989-90 and 1990-91 NBA Hoops Detroit Pistons championship cards and the 1991-92 NBA Hoops subset.

TEST SET—A set, usually containing a small number of cards, issued by a national producer and distributed in a limited section of the country or to a select group of people. Presumably, the purpose of a test set is to measure market appeal for a particular type of card. Also called a promo or prototype set.

TFC—Team Fact Card.

TL—Team Leader.

TO—Tip-Off.

TR—Traded Card.

TRIB—Tribune.

TRV—Trivia.

TT—Team Tickets Card.

UER—Uncorrected Error Card.

USA—Team USA.

VAR—Variation Card. One of two or more cards from the same series, with the same card number (or player with identical pose, if the series is unnumbered) differing from one another in some aspect, from the printing, stock, or other feature of the card. This is often caused when the manufacturer of the cards notices an error in a particular card, corrects the error, and then resumes the print run. In this case there will be two versions or variations of the same card. Sometimes one of the variations is relatively scarce. Variations also can result from accidental or deliberate design changes, information updates, photo substitutions, etc.

VERT—Vertical pose on a card.

XRC—Extended Rookie Card. A player's first appearance on a card, but issued in a set that was not distributed nationally or in packs. In basketball sets, this term refers only to the 1983, '84, and '85 Star Company sets.

YB—Yearbook.

20A—Twenty Assist Club.

50P—Fifty point Club.

6M—Sixth Man.

!—Condition-sensitive card or set (see Grading Your Cards).

*****—Multisport set.

Understanding Card Values

Determining Value

Why are some cards more valuable than others? Obviously, the economic laws of supply and demand are applicable to card collecting, just as they are to any other field where a commodity is bought, sold, or traded in a free, unregulated market.

Supply (the number of cards available on the market) is less than the total number of cards originally produced, since attrition diminishes that original quantity of cards. Each year a percentage of cards is typically thrown away, destroyed, or otherwise lost to collectors. This percentage is much, much smaller today than it was in the past, because more and more people have become increasingly aware of the value of their cards.

For those who collect only mint condition cards, the supply of older cards can be quite small indeed. Until recently, collectors were not so conscious of the need to preserve the condition of their cards. For this reason, it is difficult to know exactly how many 1957-58 Topps cards are currently available, mint or otherwise. It is generally accepted that there are fewer 1957-58 Topps cards available than 1969-70, 1979-80, or 1992-93 Topps cards. If demand were equal for each of these sets, the law of supply and demand would increase the price for the least available sets.

Demand, however, is never equal for all sets, so price correlations can be complicated. The demand for a card is influenced by many factors. These include (1) the age of the card; (2) the number of cards printed; (3) the player(s) portrayed on the card; (4) the attractiveness and popularity of the set; and (5) the physical condition of the card.

In general, (1) the older the card, (2) the fewer the number of the cards printed, (3) the more famous, popular, and talented the player, (4) the more attractive and popular the set, and (5) the better the condition of the card, the higher the value of the card will be. There are exceptions to all but one of these factors: the condition of the card. Given two cards similar in all respects except condition, the one in the best condition will always be valued higher.

While those guidelines help to establish the value of a card, the countless exceptions and peculiarities make it impossible to develop any simple, direct mathematical formula to determine card values.

Regional Variation

Since the market for cards varies from region to region, card prices of local players may be higher. This is known as a regional premium. How significant the premium is—and if there is any premium at all—depends on the local popularity of the team and the player.

The largest regional premiums usually do not apply to superstars, who often are so well-known nationwide that the prices of their key cards are too high for local dealers to realize a premium.

Lesser stars often command the strongest premiums. Their popularity is concentrated in their home region, creating local demand that greatly exceeds overall demand.

Regional premiums can apply to popular retired players, and sometimes can be found in the areas where the players grew up or starred in college in addition to where they played.

A regional discount is the converse of a regional premium. Regional discounts occur when a player has been so popular in his region for so long that local collectors and dealers have accumulated quantities of his cards. The abundant supply may make the cards available in that area at the lowest prices anywhere.

Set Prices

A somewhat paradoxical situation exists in the price of a complete set versus the combined cost of the individual cards in the set. In nearly every case, the sum of the prices for the individual cards is higher than the cost for the complete set. This is prevalent especially in cards of the past few years. The reasons for this apparent anomaly stem from the habits of collectors and from the carrying costs to dealers. Today, each card in a set normally is produced in the same quantity as all others in its set.

Many collectors pick up only stars, superstars, and particular teams. As a result, the dealer is left with a shortage of certain player cards and an abundance of others. He therefore incurs an expense in simply "carrying" these less desirable cards in stock. On the other hand, if he sells a complete set, he gets rid of large numbers of cards at one time. For this reason, he generally is willing to receive less money for a complete set. By doing this, he recovers all of his costs and also makes a profit.

Set prices do not include rare card varieties, unless specifically stated. Of course, the prices for sets do include one example of each type for the given set, but this is the least expensive variety.

For some sets, a complete set price is not listed. This is due to sets currently not trading on the market as such. Usually, the sets that have low serial number print runs do not have complete set prices.

Scarce Series

Only a select few pre-1990 basketball sets contain scarce series: 1948 Bowman; 1970-71 and 1972-73 Topps; and 1983-84, 1984-85, and 1985-86 Star. The 1948 Bowman set was printed on two 36-card sheets, the second of which was issued in significantly lower quantities. The two Topps scarce series are only marginally tougher to aquire than the set as a whole. The Star Company scarcities relate to particular team sets that, to different extents, were less widely distributed.

We are always looking for information or photographs of printing sheets of cards for research. Each year, we try to update the hobby's knowledge of distribution anomalies. Please contact us at the address in this book if you have firsthand knowledge that would be helpful in this pursuit.

Grading Your Cards

Each hobby has its own grading terminology—stamps, coins, comic books, record collecting, etc. Collectors of sports cards are no exception. The one invariable criterion for determining the value of a card is its condition: The better the condition of the card, the more valuable it is. Condition grading, however, is subjective. Individual card dealers and collectors differ in the strictness of their grading, but the stated condition of a card should be determined without regard to whether it is being bought or sold.

No allowance is made for age. A 1961-62 Fleer card is judged by the same standards as a 1991-92 Fleer card. But there are specific sets and cards that are condition-sensitive (marked with "!" in the price guide) because of their border color, consistently poor centering, or other factors. Such cards and sets sometimes command premiums above the listed percentages in Mint condition.

Centering

Current centering terminology uses numbers representing the percentage of border on either side of the main design. Obviously, centering is diminished in importance for borderless cards such as Stadium Club.

Slightly Off-Center (60/40) — A slightly off-center card is one that upon close inspection is found to have one border wider than the opposite border. This degree once was offensive only to purists, but now some hobbyists try to avoid cards that are anything other than perfectly centered.

Off-Center (70/30) — An off-center card has one border that is noticeably more than twice as wide as the opposite border.

Badly Off-Center (80/20 or worse) — A badly off-center card has virtually no border on one side of the card.

Centering

Well-center

Slightly off-center

Off-center

Badly off-center

Miscut

Miscut — A miscut card actually shows part of the adjacent card in its larger border, and consequently a corresponding amount of its card is cut off.

Corner Wear

Corner wear is the most scrutinized grading criteria in the hobby. These are the major categories of corner wear:

Corner with a slight touch of wear — The corner still is sharp, but there is a slight touch of wear showing. On a dark-bordered card, this shows as a dot of white.

Fuzzy corner — The corner still comes to a point, but the point has just begun to fray. A slightly "dinged" corner is considered the same as a fuzzy corner.

Slightly rounded corner — The fraying of the corner has increased to where there is only a hint of a point. Mild layering may be evident. A "dinged" corner is considered the same as a slightly rounded corner.

Rounded corner — The point is completely gone. Some layering is noticeable.

Badly rounded corner — The corner is completely round and rough. Severe layering is evident.

Creases

A third common defect is the crease. The degree of creasing in a card is difficult to show in a drawing or picture. On giving the specific condition of an expensive card for sale, the seller should also note any creases. Creases can be categorized by severity according to the following scale:

Light Crease — A light crease is a crease that is barely noticeable upon close inspection. In fact, when cards are in plastic sheets or holders, a light crease may not be seen (until the card is taken out of the holder). A light crease on the front is much more serious than a light crease only on the back of the card.

Medium Crease — A medium crease is noticeable when held and studied at arm's length by the naked eye, but does not overly detract from the appearance of the card. It is an obvious crease, but not one that breaks the picture surface of the card.

Heavy Crease — A heavy crease is one that has torn or broken through the card's picture surface, e.g., puts a tear in the photo surface.

Alterations

Deceptive Trimming — This occurs when someone alters the card in order to (1) shave off edge wear, (2) improve the sharpness of the corners, or (3) improve centering. Obviously, the objective is to falsely increase the perceived value of the card to an unsuspecting buyer. The shrinkage is usually evident only if the trimmed card is compared to an adjacent full-size card or if the trimmed card is itself measured.

Obvious Trimming — Obvious trimming is noticeable and unfortunate. It is usually performed by non-collectors who give no thought to the present or future value of their cards.

Deceptively Retouched Borders — This occurs when the borders (especially on those cards with dark borders) are touched up on the edges and corners with Magic Marker or crayons of appropriate color in order to make the card appear to be in mint condition.

Categorization of Defects

Miscellaneous Flaws

The following are common minor flaws that, depending on severity, lower a card's condition by one to four grades and often render it no better than

Excellent-Mint (see Condition Guide): bubbles (lumps in surface), gum and wax stains, diamond cutting (slanted borders), notching, off-centered backs, paper wrinkles, scratched-off cartoons or puzzles on back, rubber band marks, scratches, surface impressions, and warping.

The following are common serious flaws that, depending on severity, lower a card's condition at least four grades and often render it no better than Good: chemical or sun fading, erasure marks, mildew, miscutting (severe off-centering), holes, bleached or retouched borders, tape marks, tears, trimming, water or coffee stains, and writing.

Condition Guide

Grades

Mint (Mt) — A card with no flaws or wear. The card has four perfect corners, 55/45 or better centering from top to bottom and from left to right, original gloss, smooth edges, and original color borders. A mint card does not have print spots, or color or focus imperfections.

Near Mint-Mint (NrMt-Mt) — A card with one minor flaw. Any one of the following would lower a mint card to near mint-mint: one corner with a slight touch of wear, barely noticeable print spots, or color or focus imperfections. The card must have 60/40 or better centering in both directions, original gloss, smooth edges, and original color borders.

Near Mint (NrMt) — A card with one minor flaw. Any one of the following would lower a mint card to near mint: one fuzzy corner or two to four corners with slight touches of wear, 70/30 to 60/40 centering, slightly rough edges, minor print spots, or color or focus imperfections. The card must have original gloss and original color borders.

Excellent-Mint (ExMt) — A card with two or three fuzzy, but not rounded, corners and centering no worse than 80/20. The card may have no more than two of the following: slightly rough edges, very slightly discolored borders, minor print spots, or color or focus imperfections. The card must have original gloss.

Excellent (Ex) — A card with four fuzzy but definitely not rounded corners and centering no worse than 80/20. The card may have a small amount of original gloss lost, rough edges, slightly discolored borders and minor print spots, or color or focus imperfections.

Very Good (Vg) — A card that has been handled but not abused: Factors may include slightly rounded corners with slight layering, slight notching on edges, a significant amount of gloss lost from the surface but no scuffing, and moderate discoloration of borders. The card may have a few light creases.

Good (G), Fair (F), Poor (P) — A well-worn, mishandled, or abused card: Factors may include badly rounded and layered corners, scuffing, most or all original gloss missing, seriously discolored borders, moderate or heavy creases, and one or more serious flaws. The grade of good, fair, or poor depends on the severity of wear and flaws. Good, fair, and poor cards generally are used only as fillers.

The most widely used grades are defined above. Obviously, many cards will not perfectly fit one of these definitions. Therefore, categories between the major grades known as in-between grades are used, such as Good to Very Good (G-Vg), Very Good to Excellent (VgEx), and Excellent-Mint to Near Mint (ExMt-NrMt). Such grades indicate a card with all qualities of the lower category but with at least a few qualities of the higher category.

This price guide book lists each card and set in two grades, with the bottom grade valued at about 40-45 percent of the top grade.

The value of cards that fall between the listed columns can also be calculated using a percentage of the top grade. For example, a card that falls between the top and middle grades (Ex, ExMt, or NrMt in most cases) will generally be valued at anywhere from 50 percent to 90 percent of the top grade.

Similarly, a card that falls between the middle and bottom grades (G-Vg, Vg, or VgEx in most cases) will generally be valued at anywhere from 20 percent to 40 percent of the top grade.

There are also cases where cards are in better condition than the top grade or worse than the bottom grade. Cards that grade worse than the lowest grade are generally valued at 5-10 percent of the top grade.

When a card exceeds the top grade by one—such as NrMt-Mt when the top grade is NrMt, or mint when the top grade is NrMt-Mt—a premium of up to 50 percent is possible, with 10-20 percent the usual norm.

When a card exceeds the top grade by two—such as mint when the top grade is NrMt, or NrMt-Mt when the top grade is ExMt—a premium of 25-50 percentis the usual norm. But certain condition-sensitive cards or sets, particularly those from the prewar era, can bring premiums of up to 100 percent or even more.

Unopened packs, boxes, and factory-collated sets are considered mint in their unknown (and presumed perfect) state. Once opened, however, each card can be graded (and valued) in its own right by taking into account any defects that may be present in spite of the fact that the card has never been handled.

History of Basketball Cards

The earliest basketball collectibles known are team postcards issued at the turn of the twentieth century. Many of those postcards feature collegiate or high school teams of that day. Postcards were intermittently issued throughout the first half of the twentieth century, with the bulk of them coming out in the 1920s and '30s. Unfortunately, the cataloging of these collectibles is sporadic at best. In addition, many collectors consider these postcards as more memorabilia than trading cards, thus their exclusion from this book.

In 1910, College Athlete felts (catalog number B-33) made their debut. Of a total of 270 felts, 20 featured basketball players.

The first true basketball trading cards were issued by Murad cigarettes in 1911. The "College Series" cards depict a number of various sports and colleges, including four basketball cards (Luther, Northwestern, Williams, and Xavier). In addition to these small (2-by-3-inch) cards, Murad issued a large (8-by-5-inch) basketball card featuring Williams College (catalog number T-6) as part of another multisport set.

The first basketball cards ever to be issued in gum packs were distributed in 1933 by Goudey in its multisport Sport Kings set, which was the first issue to list individual and professional players. Four cards from the complete 48-card set feature original Celtics basketball players Nat Holman, Ed Wachter, Joe Lapchick, and Eddie Burke.

The period of growth that the National Basketball Association experienced from 1948 to 1951 marked the first initial boom, both for that sport and the cards that chronicle it. In 1948, Bowman created the first trading card set exclusively devoted to basketball cards, ushering in the modern era of hoops collectibles. The 72-card Bowman set contains the Rookie card of HOFer George Mikan, one of the most valuable, and important, basketball cards in the hobby. Mikan, pro basketball's first dominant big man, set the stage for Bill Russell, Wilt Chamberlain, and all the other legendary centers who have played the game since.

In addition to the Bowman release, Topps included 11 basketball cards in its 252-card multisport 1948 Magic Photo set. Five of the cards feature individual players (including collegiate great "Easy" Ed Macauley), another five feature colleges, and one additional card highlights a Manhattan-Dartmouth game. These 11 cards represent Topps' first effort to produce basketball trading cards. Kellogg's also created an 18-card multisport set of trading cards in 1948 that was inserted into boxes of Pep cereal. The only basketball card in the set features Mikan. Throughout 1948 and 1949, the Exhibit Supply Company of Chicago issued oversized thick-stock multisport trading cards in conjunction with the 1948 Olympic games. Six basketball players were featured, including HOFers Mikan and Joe Fulks, among others. The cards were distributed through penny arcade machines.

In 1950-51, Scott's Chips issued a 13-card set featuring the Minneapolis Lakers. The cards were issued in Scott's Potato and Cheese Potato Chip boxes. The cards are extremely scarce today due to the fact that many were redeemed back in 1950-51 in exchange for game tickets and signed team pictures. This set contains possibly the scarcest Mikan issue in existence. In 1951, a Philadelphia-based meat company called Berk Ross issued a four-series, 72-card multisport set. The set contains five different basketball players, including the first cards of HOFers Bob Cousy and Bill Sharman.

General Mills issued an oversized six-card multisport set on the backs of Wheaties cereal boxes in 1951. The only basketball player featured in the set is Mikan.

In 1952, Wheaties expanded the cereal box set to 30 cards, including six issues featuring basketball players of that day. Of these six cards, two feature Mikan (a portrait and an action shot). The 1952 cards are significantly smaller than the previous year's issue. That same year, the 32-card Bread for Health set was issued. The set was one of the few trading card issues of that decade exclusively devoted to the sport of basketball. The cards are actually bread end labels and were probably meant to be housed in an album. To date, the only companies known to have issued this set are Fisher's Bread in the New Jersey, New York, and Pennsylvania areas and NBC Bread in the Michigan area.

One must skip ahead to 1957-58 to find the next major basketball issue, again produced by Topps. Its 80-card basketball set from that year is recognized within the hobby as the second major modern basketball issue, including Rookie cards of all-time greats such as Bill Russell, Bob Cousy, and Bob Pettit.

In 1960, Post cereal created a nine-card multisport set by devoting most of the back of the actual cereal boxes to full-color picture frames of the athletes. HOFers Cousy and Pettit are the two featured basketball players.

In 1961-62, Fleer issued the third major modern basketball set. The 66-card set contains the Rookie cards of all-time greats such as Wilt Chamberlain, Oscar Robertson, and Jerry West. That same year, Bell Brand Potato Chips inserted trading cards (one per bag) featuring the L.A. Lakers team of that year and including scarce, early issues of HOFers West and Elgin Baylor.

From 1963 to 1968 no major companies manufactured basketball cards. Kahn's (an Ohio-based meat company) issued small regional basketball sets from 1957-58 through 1965-66 (including the first cards of Jerry West and Oscar Robertson in its 1960-61 set). All the Kahn's sets feature members of the Cincinnati Royals, except for the few issues featuring the Lakers' West.

In 1968, Topps printed a very limited quantity of standard-size black-and-white test issue cards, preluding its 1969-70 nationwide return to the basketball card market.

The 1969-70 Topps set began a 13-year run of producing nationally distributed basketball card sets, which ended in 1981-82. This was about the time the league's popularity bottomed out and was about to begin its ascent to the lofty level it's at today. Topps' run included several sets that are troublesome for today's collectors. The 1969-70, 1970-71, and 1976-77 sets are larger than standard size, thus making them hard to store and preserve. The 1980-81 set consists of standard-size panels containing three cards each. Completing and cataloging the 1980-81 set (which features the classic Larry Bird RC/Magic Johnson RC/Julius Erving panel) is challenging, to say the least.

In 1983, this basketball card void was filled by the Star Company, a small company that issued three attractive sets of basketball cards, along with a plethora of peripheral sets. Star's 1983-84 premiere offering was issued in four groups, with the first series (cards 1-100) very difficult to obtain, as many of the early team subsets were miscut and destroyed before release. The 1984-85 and 1985-86 sets were more widely and evenly distributed. Even so, players' initial appearances on any of the three Star Company sets are considered Extended Rookie cards, not regular Rookie cards, because of the relatively limited distribution. Chief among these is Michael Jordan's 1984-85 Star XRC, the most valuable sports card issued in a 1980s major set.

Then, in 1986, Fleer took over the rights to produce cards for the NBA. Their 1986-87, 1987-88, and 1988-89 sets each contain 132 attractive, colorful cards depicting mostly stars and superstars. They were sold in the familiar wax pack format (12 cards and one sticker per pack). Fleer increased its set size to 168 in 1989-90, and was joined by NBA Hoops, which produced a 300-card first series (containing David Robinson's only Rookie card) and a 52-card second series. The demand for all three Star Company sets, along with the first four Fleer sets and the premiere NBA Hoops set, skyrocketed during the early part of 1990.

The basketball card market stabilized somewhat in 1990-91, with both Fleer and Hoops stepping up production substantially. A new major set, SkyBox, also made a splash in the market with its unique "high-tech" cards featuring computer-generated backgrounds. Because of overproduction, none of the three major 1990-91 sets have experienced significant price growth, although the increased competition has led to higher quality and more innovative products.

Another milestone in 1990-91 was the first-time inclusion of current rookies in update sets (NBA Hoops and SkyBox Series II, Fleer Update). The NBA Hoops and SkyBox issues contain just the 11 lottery picks, while Fleer's 100-card boxed set includes all rookies of any significance. A small company called "Star Pics" (not to be confused with Star Company) tried to fill this niche by printing a 70-card set in late 1990, but because the set was not licensed by the NBA, it is not considered a major set by the majority of collectors. It does, however, contain the first nationally distributed cards of 1990-91 rookies such as Derrick Coleman and Kendall Gill, among others.

In 1991-92, the draft pick set market that Star Pics opened in 1990-91 expanded to include several competitors. More significantly, that season brought with it the three established NBA card brands plus Upper Deck, known throughout the hobby for its high-quality card stock and photography in other sports. Upper Deck's first basketball set probably captured NBA action better than any previous set. But its value—like all other major 1990-91 and 1991-92 NBA sets—declined because of overproduction.

On the bright side, the historic entrance of NBA players to Olympic competition kept interest in basketball cards going long after the Chicago Bulls won their second straight NBA championship. So for at least one year, the basketball card market—probably the most seasonal of the four major team sports—remained in the spotlight for an extended period of time.

The 1992-93 season will be remembered as the year of Shaq—the debut campaign of the most heralded rookie in many years. Shaquille O'Neal headlined the most promising rookie class in NBA history, sparking unprecedented interest in basketball cards. Among O'Neal's many talented rookie companions were Alonzo Mourning, Jim Jackson, and Latrell Sprewell.

Classic Games, known primarily for producing draft picks and minor league baseball cards, signed O'Neal to an exclusive contract through 1992, thus postponing the appearances of O'Neal's NBA-licensed cards.

Shaquille's Classic and NBA cards, particularly the inserts, became some of the most sought-after collectibles in years. As a direct result of O'Neal and his fellow rookie standouts, the basketball card market achieved a new level of popularity in 1993.

The hobby rode that crest of popularity throughout the 1993-94 season. Michael Jordan may have retired, but his absence only spurred interest in some of his tougher inserts. Another strong rookie class followed Shaq, and Reggie Miller elevated his collectibility to a superstar level. Hakeem Olajuwon, by leading the Rockets to an NBA title, boosted his early cards to levels surpassed only by Jordan.

No new cardmakers came on board, but super premium Topps Finest raised the stakes, and the parallel set came into its own.

In 1994-95, the return of Michael Jordan, coupled with the high impact splash of Detroit Pistons rookie Grant Hill, kept collector interest high. In addition, the NBA granted all the licensed manufacturers the opportunity to create a fourth brand of basketball cards that year, allowing each company to create a selection of clearly defined niche products at different price points. The manufacturers also expanded the calendar release dates, with 1994-95 cards being released on a consistent basis from August 1994, all the way through June 1995. The super-premium card market expanded greatly as the battle for the best-selling five-dollar (or more) pack reached epic levels by season's end. The key new super premium products included the premier of SP, Embossed, and Emotion. This has continued through 1996 with the release of SPx, which contained only one card per pack.

The collecting year of 1996-97 brought even more to the table with a prominent motif of tough parallel sets and an influx of autographs available at lower ratio pulls. One of the greatest rookie classes in some time also carried the collecting season with players showing great promise: Allen Iverson, Kobe Bryant, Stephon Marbury, Antoine Walker, and Shareef Abdur-Rahim. Topps Chrome was also introduced, bringing about a rookie frenzy not seen since the 1986-87 Fleer set.

In 1997-98, Kobe Bryant was deemed the next Michael Jordan and his cards escalated in value throughout the year. In addition, a stronger than expected rookie class gave collectors some new blood to chase after, including Tim Duncan, Keith Van Horn, Ron Mercer, and Tim Thomas. Autographs and serial-numbered inserts were the key inserts to chase, featuring numbering as low as one of one.

The 1998-99 season brought about a huge change in basketball. The players' strike crushed a growing basketball market and sent manufacturers scrambling. On top of this, Michael Jordan decided to retire (again), sending another direct hit to the hobby. Many releases were cut back—or cut period. There was a bright spot once the season began though—a great rookie class led by Vince Carter. The hobby benefited by combining the great class with shorter print run products. The top of the class was the 1998-99 SP Authentic release, which serially numbered the rookies to 3500. The San Antonio Spurs were crowned NBA Champions, leading to a spike in Tim Duncan cards. The top hobby card of the season was the SP Authentic Vince Carter RC.

If the beginning of the 1998-99 season was at rock bottom, the 1999-00 season was one of transition. Vince Carter became the new hobby hero and the NBA Champion L.A. Lakers helped the state of the hobby with their two horses, Kobe Bryant and Shaquille O'Neal. Another solid rookie class emerged, led by Steve Francis and Elton Brand, who shared Rookie of the Year honors. The 1999-00 card releases all combined elements of short-printed or serially numbered rookies, autographs, and game-worn materials. SP Authentic again led the way for consumer dollars, but many other brands also did extremely well, including E-X, Flair Showcase, and SPx, which combined rookie serial-numbered cards with autographs. The top hobby card of the season was the SPx Steve Francis RC, which was autographed to 500.

The year of 2000-01 releases will definitely leave its mark on the face of basketball cards for years to come. Noteworthy points of interest include the first one-per-pack graded insert in Upper Deck Ultimate Collection, the first one-per-pack memorabilia release in SP Game Floor, and the first one-per-box autographed jersey in Fleer Legacy. While these concepts have become commonplace over the course of the last year and a half, more than two years ago, notions such as these were unheard of.

Rookie cards were all the rage this year, and were available in several different formats and pricing tiers. It looks as though the sequentially numbered rookie has worked its way in as a hobby staple, as have autographed and memorabilia rookie issues. The uniqueness of 2000-01's releases is both staggering and impressive, as it is comforting to know that our hobby is still pointed in the right direction.

It also appears that 2000-01 marks a changing of the guard as far as basketball heroes are concerned. It is rather unfeasible to compare anyone in today's basketball game to the stature and legend that Michael Jordan has built for himself throughout the past two decades, but several young heroes are working their way up into our daily sports repertoire. As Michael Jordan sales begin to slow, Kobe Bryant, the L.A. Lakers' cast and crew, and Allen Iverson continue to build steam and fill the derelict space left by our hobby idol.

The release year of 2001-02 followed in the footsteps of previous years, as nearly every set issued had some type of memorabilia and/or autographed element to it. The hobby was shaken into somewhat of a frenzy as Michael Jordan rose up out of retirement (again), this time as a mentor and a player of the young Washington Wizards squad. Base Michael Jordan card values dominated sets, and at one point, $10 to $12 was a common value on the high end; and the explosive volume of sales provided the biggest boost as far as hobby dollars is concerned. Notable releases this year include Topps Pristine for its pack-in-a-pack-in-a-pack concept, encased uncirculated cards, and the use of new playoff-related materials such as towels. Upper Deck followed the comeback of Michael Jordan with several commemorative issues such as MJ Jersey Collection, and MJ's Back Jerseys, which was inserted in several brands at the beginning of the release season. Fleer and Topps rejuvenated the market for parallel sets as Fleer issued two memorabilia parallels with its E-X release, and Topps made waves with the Topps Chrome Refractors Black Border set. A soft rookie crop as of the end of 2001-02 card releases had an impact on newer sales; the emergence of young stars such as Mike Bibby, Dirk Nowitzki, and Paul Pierce had collectors stammering for cardboard of players, who, since their rookie issues, had gone unnoticed, and dominated the market toward the end of the season.

2002-03 paved the way for the globalization of basketball trading cards. The 2002 NBA Draft boasts the highest number of foreign players drafted in the first round with ten, and the biggest push towards international card collecting was the number one draft choice, Yao Ming. Unlike most big men drafted, Ming had the ability to come in right away and put up good numbers for his Houston squad. Then, Ming coupled with Amare Stoudemire, a high-school draftee for Phoenix, provided the perfect one-two punch to breathe some life back into the hobby, which had died off after the retirement of Michael Jordan in 1997 and the NBA lockout in 1998.

The incredible success of the 2003-04 rookie class, namely LeBron James, Carmelo Anthony, and Dwyane Wade, brought basketball card collecting to new heights. More money was invested and made this year than any year since the mid-to late nineties and the Shaq craze back in 1992. Upper Deck signed an exclusive deal with LeBron at the beginning of the season for autographs and memorabilia, limiting his usage options for Fleer and Topps. The impact of LeBron James alone drove the high-end market, paving the way for some of the basketball hobby's highest priced super-premium sets. Upper Deck delivered Exquisite Collection ($500 per pack), which saw several sales above $30,000 for single cards. Topps answered with Contemporary Collection ($50 per pack), which delivered an array of autographs and memorabilia. Fleer issued Flair Final Edition (approximately $125 per pack), the only product where collectors had the opportunity to pull redemption cards for Draft Day memorabilia such as the team and player placards used on the actual NBA draft board and the Ping-Pong balls from the draft lottery. Shaq's trade at the end of the season rejuvenated his cardboard career and also pushed the sales of Miami rookie Dwyane Wade. As in the previous three seasons, the release year of 2003-04 points towards a healthier future for basketball cards.

2004-05 provided a solid rookie class where a sleeper, Ben Gordon, who started out as a middle-of-the-pack guy, ended the season as the most popular and expensive RC of the year. Other young and solid prospects from the class include Dwight Howard, Josh Smith, Josh Childress, and Shaun Livingston. As for manufacturer highlights, it's an unfortunate fact that the year will be remembered for the closing down of Fleer/Skybox International at the beginning of the 2005 summer. Upper Deck made an offer and won the intellectual rights of the company, and the hobby is looking forward to what UD has in store for the brand names and trademarks. Aside from the Fleer purchase, UD made headlines with an unannounced return of Exquisite Collection, which ruled the hobby for months. Topps highlights included the return of the autographed Bowman and Bowman Chrome rookies, which find themselves atop the hot list month in and month out, and introduced new brands Topps Luxury Box, which provided plenty of autographs and memorabilia along with Topps Total, a set that boasts the largest player roster of the year with a 440-card base set.

2005-06 releases continued to build on the reputation that the basketball card market has established itself as the high-end market for sports cards. LeBron James' 2003-04 Exquisite Collection broke the $10,000 barrier, a first for any rookie card over any sport in the modern era of sports cards. During the release year, Upper Deck again issued Exquisite Collection ($500 per pack), Ultimate Collection ($100 per pack), and Topps issued its first-time super premium product, Big Game ($75 per pack). Top rookies from the 2005-06 crop include Chris Paul, Deron Williams, and Andrew Bogut. Players from recent years' rookie classes made strong showings throughout the 2005-06 season such as Dwight Howard and Kevin Martin, both of whom have huge NBA potential and the chance to be superstars. Miami phenom Dwyane Wade won both his first NBA Title and first NBA Finals MVP, and dominated hot lists throughout the season and the summer of 2006. With Wade reaching these goals so early in his career and young players like LeBron James and Carmelo Anthony leading their teams to the playoffs, these young stars are setting the stage for another hobby boom.

While LeBron, Carmelo, and Wade continue to be popular, the hobby suffered a lackluster 2006-07 release year. The two rookies who received unheralded hype, Adam Morrison and J.J. Redick, both disappointed and devastated collectibles during the year. Both came out of the gate incredibly hot, but were met with nothing but down arrows in the price guides for most of the year. That said, a few youngsters stepped up and salvaged what has otherwise been an inadequate rookie class: Brandon Roy, LaMarcus Aldridge, Andrea Bargnani, and Tyrus Thomas. Product highlights include a fourth Exquisite Collection release, the return of Hoops Hot Prospects under the Upper Deck umbrella and Topps Triple Threads—one of the most expensive and nicest premium products Topps has ever released.

On the bright side, hoops hobbyists have been chomping at the bit for the 2007-08 rookie class as it is said to be one of the deepest basketball has ever seen. Players expected to make a big impact on the game are Kevin Durant, Greg Oden, Al Horford, and Mike Conley.

2008-09 Was marked by a top-notch rookie class headlined by Chicago's Derrick Rose and Memphis's O.J. Mayo. In the middle of the release year, the NBA announced that starting in 2009-10, Panini America will be the sole producer of basketball cards. With this announcement, the hobby waits and hopes for what the future might hold.

Additional Reading

Each year Beckett Publications produces comprehensive annual price guides for each of the five major sports: *Beckett Baseball Card Price Guide, Beckett Football Card Price Guide, Beckett Basketball Card Price Guide, Beckett Hockey Card Price Guide and Alphabetical Checklist*, and *Beckett Racing Card and Die Cast Price Guide*. The aim of these annual guides is to provide information and accurate pricing on a wide array of sports cards, ranging from main issues by the major card manufacturers to various regional, promotional, and food issues. Also, alphabetical checklists, such as *Beckett Basketball Card Alphabetical Checklist #1*, are published to assist the collector in identifying all the cards of a particular player. The seasoned collector will find these tools valuable sources of information that will enable him or her to pursue his or her hobby interests.

In addition, abridged editions of the Beckett Price Guides have been published for each of three major sports as part of the House of Collectibles series: *The Official Price Guide to Baseball Cards, The Official Price Guide to Football Cards*, and *The Official Price Guide to Basketball Cards*. Published in a convenient mass-market paperback format, these price guides provide information and accurate pricing on all the main issues by the major card manufacturers.

Prices in This Guide

Prices found in this guide reflect current retail rates just prior to the printing of this book. They do not reflect the FOR SALE prices of the author, the publisher, the distributors, the advertisers, or any card dealers associated with this guide. No one is obligated in any way to buy, sell, or trade his or her cards based on these prices. The price listings were compiled by the author from actual buy/sell transactions at sports conventions, sports card shops, buy/sell advertisements in the hobby papers, for-sale prices from dealer catalogs and price lists, and discussions with leading hobbyists in the U.S. and Canada. All prices are in U.S. dollars. Prices marked .00 are either not available or are not priced because of their rarity.

Acknowledgments

A great deal of diligence, hard work, and dedicated effort went into this year's volume. The high standards to which we hold ourselves, however, could not have been met without the expert input and generous amount of time contributed by many people. Our sincere thanks are extended to each and every one of them.

2009-10 Absolute

❑ 1 Kobe Bryant	6.00	15.00
❑ 2 Dwight Howard	2.50	6.00
❑ 3 Rajon Rondo	1.25	3.00
❑ 4 Samuel Dalembert	.75	2.00
❑ 5 LeBron James	6.00	15.00
❑ 6 Chris Andersen	1.25	3.00
❑ 7 Dwyane Wade	2.50	6.00
❑ 8 Chris Bosh	1.25	3.00
❑ 9 Steve Nash	1.25	3.00
❑ 10 LaMarcus Aldridge	1.25	3.00
❑ 11 Danilo Gallinari	1.25	3.00
❑ 12 Joakim Noah	1.25	3.00
❑ 13 Brook Lopez	.75	2.00
❑ 14 Tony Parker	1.25	3.00
❑ 15 Deron Williams	1.50	4.00
❑ 16 Marc Gasol	1.25	3.00
❑ 17 Joe Johnson	1.25	3.00
❑ 18 Dirk Nowitzki	1.50	4.00
❑ 19 Chris Paul	2.50	6.00
❑ 20 Chris Kaman	1.25	3.00
❑ 21 Kevin Love	1.00	2.50
❑ 22 Danny Granger	1.25	3.00
❑ 23 Antawn Jamison	1.25	3.00
❑ 24 Trevor Ariza	1.25	3.00
❑ 25 Carmelo Anthony	1.50	4.00
❑ 26 Monta Ellis	1.25	3.00
❑ 27 Al Horford	1.25	3.00
❑ 28 Kevin Durant	3.00	8.00
❑ 29 Brandon Roy	1.50	4.00
❑ 30 Corey Maggette	1.00	2.50
❑ 31 Andre Iguodala	1.25	3.00
❑ 32 Ray Allen	1.25	3.00
❑ 33 Shaquille O'Neal	2.50	6.00
❑ 34 Jamal Crawford	.75	2.00
❑ 35 Gerald Wallace	1.25	3.00
❑ 36 David West	1.25	3.00
❑ 37 Zach Randolph	.75	2.00
❑ 38 Rodney Stuckey	1.25	3.00
❑ 39 Derrick Rose	2.50	6.00
❑ 40 Tim Duncan	2.00	5.00
❑ 41 David Lee	1.00	2.50
❑ 42 Amare Stoudemire	1.50	4.00
❑ 43 Aaron Brooks	1.00	2.50
❑ 44 Lamar Odom	1.25	3.00
❑ 45 Ben Wallace	1.25	3.00
❑ 46 J.J. Barea	1.25	3.00
❑ 47 Emeka Okafor	1.25	3.00
❑ 48 Brendan Haywood	.75	2.00
❑ 49 Michael Beasley	1.50	4.00
❑ 50 Allen Iverson	1.50	4.00
❑ 51 Andrea Bargnani	1.00	2.50
❑ 52 Nene	1.00	2.50
❑ 53 Paul Pierce	1.50	4.00
❑ 54 Mo Williams	1.00	2.50
❑ 55 Jason Thompson	.75	2.00
❑ 56 Russell Westbrook	1.25	3.00
❑ 57 Andrew Bogut	1.25	3.00
❑ 58 Al Jefferson	1.25	3.00
❑ 59 Devin Harris	1.25	3.00
❑ 60 Vince Carter	1.50	4.00
❑ 61 Jason Kidd	1.25	3.00
❑ 62 Kevin Garnett	2.50	6.00
❑ 63 Rudy Gay	1.25	3.00
❑ 64 Stephen Jackson	1.00	2.50
❑ 65 Luol Deng	1.25	3.00
❑ 66 Carl Landry	.75	2.00
❑ 67 Baron Davis	1.25	3.00
❑ 68 Ben Gordon	1.25	3.00
❑ 69 Al Harrington	1.00	2.50
❑ 70 Carlos Boozer	1.25	3.00
❑ 71 Pau Gasol	1.25	3.00
❑ 72 Luke Ridnour	.75	2.00
❑ 73 Josh Smith	1.25	3.00
❑ 74 Raymond Felton	1.00	2.50
❑ 75 Kendrick Perkins	.75	2.00
❑ 76 Dahntay Jones	.75	2.00
❑ 77 Kevin Martin	1.25	3.00
❑ 78 Shawn Marion	1.25	3.00
❑ 79 Marcus Camby	.75	2.00
❑ 80 Jermaine O'Neal	1.25	3.00
❑ 81 Manu Ginobili	1.25	3.00
❑ 82 Richard Hamilton	1.00	2.50
❑ 83 Rashard Lewis	1.25	3.00
❑ 84 Jason Richardson	1.25	3.00
❑ 85 Jeff Green	1.00	2.50
❑ 86 Elton Brand	1.25	3.00
❑ 87 Mehmet Okur	.75	2.00
❑ 88 O.J. Mayo	1.50	4.00
❑ 89 Caron Butler	1.25	3.00
❑ 90 Rasheed Wallace	1.25	3.00
❑ 91 Jason Terry	1.00	2.50
❑ 92 Ron Artest	1.25	3.00
❑ 93 Jason Williams	1.25	3.00
❑ 94 Hedo Turkoglu	1.25	3.00
❑ 95 Yao Ming	1.50	4.00
❑ 96 Chauncey Billups	1.25	3.00
❑ 97 Nate Robinson	1.25	3.00
❑ 98 Mike Dunleavy	.75	2.00
❑ 99 Louis Williams	.75	2.00
❑ 100 Juwan Howard	.75	2.00
❑ 101 Jalen Rose	1.25	3.00
❑ 102 Chris Webber	1.25	3.00
❑ 103 David Robinson	2.00	5.00
❑ 104 Chuck Person	1.25	3.00
❑ 105 Alvan Adams	1.25	3.00
❑ 106 Larry Bird	4.00	10.00
❑ 107 Scottie Pippen	1.25	3.00
❑ 108 Connie Hawkins	1.25	3.00
❑ 109 Magic Johnson	2.50	6.00
❑ 110 Bill Laimbeer	1.25	3.00
❑ 111 Shawn Bradley	1.25	3.00
❑ 112 Kelly Tripucka	1.25	3.00
❑ 113 Robert Horry	1.50	4.00
❑ 114 Spud Webb	1.25	3.00
❑ 115 World B. Free	1.25	3.00
❑ 116 Tim Hardaway	1.25	3.00
❑ 117 Sean Elliott	1.25	3.00
❑ 118 Anfernee Hardaway	3.00	8.00
❑ 119 Paul Westphal	1.25	3.00
❑ 120 Pete Maravich	4.00	10.00
❑ 121 Willis Reed	1.25	3.00
❑ 122 Nate Thurmond	1.25	3.00
❑ 123 Mychal Thompson	1.25	3.00
❑ 124 Kenny Anderson	1.25	3.00
❑ 125 Jerry West	1.50	4.00
❑ 131 Serge Ibaka RC	2.50	6.00
❑ 137 Daniel Green RC	2.50	6.00
❑ 140 Patrick Mills RC	2.50	6.00
❑ 142 B.Jennings JSY AU/499 RC EXCH	25.00	50.00
❑ 143 J.Flynn JSY AU/349 RC EXCH	8.00	20.00
❑ 144 Stephen Curry JSY AU/499 RC	25.00	50.00
❑ 145 Omri Casspi JSY AU/499 RC	6.00	15.00
❑ 146 James Harden JSY AU/499 RC	8.00	20.00
❑ 147 Ty Lawson JSY AU/349 RC	8.00	20.00
❑ 148 Taj Gibson JSY AU/499 RC	8.00	20.00
❑ 149 Tyler Hansbrough JSY AU/499 RC	10.00	25.00
❑ 150 Chase Budinger JSY AU/499 RC	5.00	12.00
❑ 151 S.Young JSY AU/299 RC EXCH	5.00	12.00
❑ 152 DeJuan Blair JSY AU/499 RC	8.00	20.00
❑ 153 Terrence Williams JSY AU/499 RC	8.00	20.00
❑ 154 Darren Collison JSY AU/499 RC	10.00	25.00
❑ 155 Toney Douglas JSY AU/499 RC	5.00	12.00
❑ 156 Wayne Ellington JSY AU/499 RC	5.00	12.00
❑ 157 Jrue Holiday JSY AU/499 RC	8.00	20.00
❑ 158 Eric Maynor JSY AU/499 RC	6.00	15.00
❑ 159 R.Beaubois JSY AU/349 RC EXCH	8.00	20.00
❑ 160 Austin Daye JSY AU/499 RC	5.00	12.00
❑ 161 Jodie Meeks JSY AU/499 RC	5.00	12.00
❑ 162 Jeff Pendergraph JSY AU/499 RC	5.00	12.00
❑ 163 Jordan Hill JSY AU/499 RC	5.00	12.00
❑ 164 DeMarre Carroll JSY AU/499 RC	5.00	12.00
❑ 165 Jeff Teague JSY AU/499 RC	5.00	12.00
❑ 166 Tyreke Evans JSY AU/499 RC	35.00	75.00
❑ 167 J.Johnson JSY AU/349 RC EXCH	5.00	12.00
❑ 168 Earl Clark JSY AU/499 RC	5.00	12.00
❑ 169 Gerald Henderson JSY AU/499 RC	5.00	12.00
❑ 170 DaJuan Summers JSY AU/499 RC	5.00	12.00
❑ 171 Hasheem Thabeet JSY AU/499 RC	5.00	12.00
❑ 172 Blake Griffin JSY AU/499 RC	25.00	50.00
❑ 173 B.J. Mullens JSY AU/499 RC	5.00	12.00
❑ 174 Taylor Griffin JSY AU/499 RC	5.00	12.00
❑ 175 J.Taylor JSY AU/299 RC EXCH	5.00	12.00
❑ 176 D.DeRozan JSY AU/299 RC EXCH	15.00	30.00

2007-08 Artifacts

❑ COMP.SET w/o SP's (100)	15.00	40.00
❑ 1 Joe Johnson	.40	1.00
❑ 2 Josh Smith	.40	1.00
❑ 3 Marvin Williams	.40	1.00
❑ 4 Josh Childress	.30	.75
❑ 5 Al Jefferson	.40	1.00
❑ 6 Paul Pierce	.40	1.00
❑ 7 Gerald Green	.40	1.00
❑ 8 Adam Morrison	.40	1.00
❑ 9 Gerald Wallace	.40	1.00
❑ 10 Emeka Okafor	.40	1.00
❑ 11 Raymond Felton	.50	1.25
❑ 12 Ben Gordon	.50	1.25
❑ 13 Luol Deng	.40	1.00
❑ 14 Kirk Hinrich	.40	1.00
❑ 15 Andres Nocioni	.25	.60
❑ 16 LeBron James	2.00	5.00
❑ 17 Larry Hughes	.30	.75
❑ 18 Zydrunas Ilgauskas	.30	.75
❑ 19 Dirk Nowitzki	.60	1.50
❑ 20 Josh Howard	.40	1.00
❑ 21 Jason Terry	.40	1.00
❑ 22 Carmelo Anthony	.75	2.00
❑ 23 Allen Iverson	.75	2.00
❑ 24 J.R. Smith	.30	.75
❑ 25 Richard Hamilton	.30	.75
❑ 26 Tayshaun Prince	.40	1.00
❑ 27 Chauncey Billups	.40	1.00
❑ 28 Baron Davis	.40	1.00
❑ 29 Monta Ellis	.30	.75
❑ 30 Jason Richardson	.40	1.00
❑ 31 Yao Ming	1.00	2.50
❑ 32 Tracy McGrady	.75	2.00
❑ 33 Rafer Alston	.25	.60
❑ 34 Jermaine O'Neal	.40	1.00
❑ 35 Jamaal Tinsley	.25	.60
❑ 36 Mike Dunleavy	.30	.75
❑ 37 Elton Brand	.40	1.00
❑ 38 Cuttino Mobley	.30	.75
❑ 39 Corey Maggette	.30	.75
❑ 40 Kobe Bryant	2.00	5.00
❑ 41 Lamar Odom	.40	1.00
❑ 42 Jordan Farmar	.30	.75
❑ 43 Pau Gasol	.40	1.00
❑ 44 Rudy Gay	.30	.75
❑ 45 Mike Miller	.40	1.00
❑ 46 Shaquille O'Neal	1.00	2.50
❑ 47 Dwyane Wade	1.00	2.50
❑ 48 Jason Kapono	.25	.60
❑ 49 Alonzo Mourning	.50	1.25
❑ 50 Andrew Bogut	.40	1.00
❑ 51 Michael Redd	.40	1.00
❑ 52 Maurice Williams	.30	.75
❑ 53 Kevin Garnett	1.00	2.50
❑ 54 Ricky Davis	.40	1.00
❑ 55 Randy Foye	.40	1.00
❑ 56 Rashad McCants	.30	.75
❑ 57 Jason Kidd	.60	1.50
❑ 58 Vince Carter	.75	2.00
❑ 59 Richard Jefferson	.40	1.00
❑ 60 Peja Stojakovic	.40	1.00
❑ 61 Chris Paul	.75	2.00
❑ 62 David West	.40	1.00
❑ 63 David Lee	.30	.75

❑ 64 Stephon Marbury .40 1.00
❑ 65 Eddy Curry .25 .60
❑ 66 Jamal Crawford .25 .60
❑ 67 Dwight Howard .75 2.00
❑ 68 Grant Hill .40 1.00
❑ 69 Jameer Nelson .30 .75
❑ 70 J.J. Redick .40 1.00
❑ 71 Andre Iguodala .40 1.00
❑ 72 Andre Miller .30 .75
❑ 73 Samuel Dalembert .25 .60
❑ 74 Steve Nash .50 1.25
❑ 75 Amare Stoudemire .75 2.00
❑ 76 Shawn Marion .40 1.00
❑ 77 Leandro Barbosa .30 .75
❑ 78 Zach Randolph .40 1.00
❑ 79 Brandon Roy .60 1.50
❑ 80 LaMarcus Aldridge .50 1.25
❑ 81 Jarrett Jack .30 .75
❑ 82 Mike Bibby .40 1.00
❑ 83 Kevin Martin .40 1.00
❑ 84 Brad Miller .40 1.00
❑ 85 Tim Duncan .75 2.00
❑ 86 Manu Ginobili .40 1.00
❑ 87 Tony Parker .40 1.00
❑ 88 Rashard Lewis .40 1.00
❑ 89 Ray Allen .40 1.00
❑ 90 Chris Wilcox .30 .75
❑ 91 Chris Bosh .40 1.00
❑ 92 Andrea Bargnani .50 1.25
❑ 93 T.J. Ford .30 .75
❑ 94 Anthony Parker .25 .60
❑ 95 Deron Williams .60 1.50
❑ 96 Carlos Boozer .40 1.00
❑ 97 Mehmet Okur .30 .75
❑ 98 Gilbert Arenas .40 1.00
❑ 99 Caron Butler .40 1.00
❑ 100 Antawn Jamison .40 1.00
❑ 101 Greg Oden RC 3.00 8.00
❑ 102 Kevin Durant RC 15.00 40.00
❑ 103 Al Horford RC 2.50 6.00
❑ 104 Michael Conley RC 2.50 6.00
❑ 105 Jeff Green RC 2.50 6.00
❑ 106 Sun Yue RC 2.00 5.00
❑ 107 Corey Brewer RC 2.50 6.00
❑ 108 Brandan Wright RC 2.50 6.00
❑ 109 Joakim Noah RC 2.50 6.00
❑ 110 Spencer Hawes RC 2.00 5.00
❑ 111 Acie Law RC 2.50 6.00
❑ 112 Thaddeus Young RC 2.50 6.00
❑ 113 Julian Wright RC 2.50 6.00
❑ 114 Al Thornton RC 2.00 5.00
❑ 115 Rodney Stuckey RC 4.00 10.00
❑ 116 Nick Young RC 2.00 5.00
❑ 117 Sean Williams RC 2.00 5.00
❑ 118 Marco Belinelli RC 2.00 5.00
❑ 119 Javaris Crittenton RC 2.00 5.00
❑ 120 Jason Smith RC 2.00 5.00
❑ 121 Daequan Cook RC 2.50 6.00
❑ 122 Jared Dudley RC 2.00 5.00
❑ 123 Wilson Chandler RC 2.00 5.00
❑ 124 Morris Almond RC 2.00 5.00
❑ 125 Aaron Brooks RC 3.00 8.00
❑ 126 Arron Afflalo RC 2.00 5.00
❑ 127 Alando Tucker RC 2.00 5.00
❑ 128 Petteri Koponen RC 2.00 5.00
❑ 129 Carl Landry RC 2.00 5.00
❑ 130 Gabe Pruitt RC 2.00 5.00
❑ 131 Marcus Williams RC 2.00 5.00
❑ 132 Nick Fazekas RC 2.00 5.00
❑ 133 Glen Davis RC 4.00 10.00
❑ 134 Jermareo Davidson RC 2.00 5.00
❑ 135 Josh McRoberts RC 2.50 6.00
❑ 136 Chris Richard RC 2.00 5.00
❑ 137 Derrick Byars RC 2.00 5.00
❑ 138 Adam Haluska RC 2.00 5.00
❑ 139 Reyshawn Terry RC 2.00 5.00
❑ 140 Jared Jordan RC 2.00 5.00
❑ 141 Stephane Lasme RC 2.00 5.00
❑ 142 Dominic McGuire RC 2.00 5.00
❑ 143 Aaron Gray RC 2.00 5.00
❑ 144 JamesOn Curry RC 2.00 5.00
❑ 145 Taurean Green RC 2.00 5.00
❑ 146 Demetris Nichols RC 2.00 5.00
❑ 147 Herbert Hill RC 2.00 5.00
❑ 148 Ramon Sessions RC 2.50 6.00
❑ 149 Sammy Mejia RC 2.00 5.00
❑ 150 D.J. Strawberry RC 2.00 5.00
❑ 151 Bernard King 1.25 3.00
❑ 152 Bill Laimbeer 1.25 3.00
❑ 153 Bill Russell 2.00 5.00
❑ 154 Bill Sharman 1.25 3.00
❑ 155 Bill Walton 1.25 3.00
❑ 156 Billy Cunningham 1.25 3.00
❑ 157 Bob Cousy 2.00 5.00
❑ 158 Bob McAdoo 1.25 3.00
❑ 159 Bob Pettit 1.50 4.00
❑ 160 Chris Mullin 1.25 3.00
❑ 161 Clyde Drexler 1.50 4.00
❑ 162 Dave Bing 1.25 3.00
❑ 163 Dave Cowens 1.50 4.00
❑ 164 David Robinson 2.00 5.00
❑ 165 David Thompson 1.50 4.00
❑ 166 Dennis Rodman 1.25 3.00
❑ 167 Dolph Schayes 1.25 3.00
❑ 168 Earl Monroe 1.25 3.00
❑ 169 Elgin Baylor 1.25 3.00
❑ 170 Elvin Hayes 1.25 3.00
❑ 171 George Gervin 1.25 3.00
❑ 172 George Mikan 2.50 6.00
❑ 173 Hakeem Olajuwon 1.50 4.00
❑ 174 Hal Greer 1.25 3.00
❑ 175 Isiah Thomas 1.25 3.00
❑ 176 James Worthy 1.50 4.00
❑ 177 Jerry West 1.50 4.00
❑ 178 John Havlicek 1.25 3.00
❑ 179 John Stockton 2.00 5.00
❑ 180 Julius Erving 2.50 6.00
❑ 181 Karl Malone 1.50 4.00
❑ 182 Kevin McHale 1.50 4.00
❑ 183 Larry Bird 4.00 10.00
❑ 184 Lenny Wilkens 1.25 3.00
❑ 185 Magic Johnson 2.50 6.00
❑ 186 Michael Jordan 8.00 20.00
❑ 187 Moses Malone 1.25 3.00
❑ 188 Nate Archibald 1.25 3.00
❑ 189 Nate Thurmond 1.25 3.00
❑ 190 Oscar Robertson 1.25 3.00
❑ 191 Paul Arizin 1.25 3.00
❑ 192 Paul Westphal 1.50 4.00
❑ 193 Pete Maravich 4.00 10.00
❑ 194 Rick Barry 1.25 3.00
❑ 195 Robert Parish 1.25 3.00
❑ 196 Sam Jones 1.50 4.00
❑ 197 Walt Frazier 1.25 3.00
❑ 198 Wes Unseld 1.25 3.00
❑ 199 Willis Reed 1.25 3.00
❑ 200 Wilt Chamberlain 2.50 6.00
❑ 201 Yao Ming EX 1.50 4.00
❑ 202 Steve Nash EX .75 2.00
❑ 203 Chris Paul EX 1.25 3.00
❑ 204 Brandon Roy EX 1.00 2.50
❑ 205 Rudy Gay EX .75 2.00
❑ 206 Al Horford Uni EX .75 2.00
❑ 207 LaMarcus Aldridge EX .75 2.00
❑ 208 Tyrus Thomas EX .75 2.00
❑ 209 Julian Wright EX .75 2.00
❑ 210 Al Horford Suit EX .75 2.00
❑ 211 Corey Brewer EX .75 2.00
❑ 212 Joakim Noah EX .75 2.00
❑ 213 Mike Conley Jr. EX .75 2.00
❑ 214 Jeff Green EX .75 2.00
❑ 215 Kevin Durant Suit EX 5.00 12.00
❑ 216 Michael Jordan Red EX 4.00 10.00
❑ 217 Kobe Bryant Prpl EX 3.00 8.00
❑ 218 LeBron James Red EX 3.00 8.00
❑ 219 Kevin Durant Ball EX 5.00 12.00
❑ 220 Michael Jordan White EX 4.00 10.00
❑ 221 Kobe Bryant Yllw EX 3.00 8.00
❑ 222 LeBron James Blue EX 3.00 8.00
❑ 223 Kevin Durant Uni EX 5.00 12.00
❑ 224 Michael Jordan Red EX 4.00 10.00
❑ 225 Kobe Bryant Yllw EX 3.00 8.00
❑ 226 LeBron James White EX 3.00 8.00
❑ 227 Kevin Durant Back EX 5.00 12.00
❑ 228 Michael Jordan Black EX 4.00 10.00
❑ 229 Kobe Bryant White EX 3.00 8.00
❑ 230 LeBron James Orange EX 3.00 8.00

2003-04 Bazooka

❑ COMP.SET w/o RC's (220) 15.00 30.00
❑ COMMON CARD (1-220) .15 .40
❑ COMMON ROOKIE (221-275) .60 1.50
❑ COMMON BAZ.JOE (276-288) .50 1.25
❑ CARDS 1, 3, 23, 31, 66, 72, 90, 223, 226, 227
❑ 228, 240, 243, 244, 245, 250, 252, 260, 270,
❑ AND 275 HAVE HOME & AWAY VERSIONS
❑ B VERSION AWAY SAME VALUE AS A
❑ 1A Tracy McGady .50 1.25
❑ 1B Tracy McGrady .50 1.25

❑ 2 DaJuan Wagner .15 .40
❑ 3A Allen Iverson .50 1.25
❑ 3B Allen Iverson .50 1.25
❑ 4 Stromile Swift .15 .40
❑ 5 Jalen Rose .20 .50
❑ 6 Morris Peterson .20 .50
❑ 7 Lamar Odom .25 .60
❑ 8 Kobe Bryant 1.25 3.00
❑ 9 Chauncey Billups .25 .60
❑ 10 Jason Kidd .40 1.00
❑ 11 Yao Ming .50 1.25
❑ 12 Stephon Marbury .25 .60
❑ 13 Ricky Davis .20 .50
❑ 14 Andrei Kirilenko .25 .60
❑ 15 Courtney Alexander .15 .40
❑ 16 Brad Miller .20 .50
❑ 17 Bobby Jackson .15 .40
❑ 18 Rashard Lewis .25 .60
❑ 19 Juwan Howard .20 .50
❑ 20 Allan Houston .20 .50
❑ 21 Kevin Garnett .50 1.25
❑ 22 Jason Terry .20 .50
❑ 23A Jason Richardson .25 .60
❑ 23B Jason Richardson .25 .60
❑ 24 Jerry Stackhouse .20 .50
❑ 25 Tyson Chandler .20 .50
❑ 26 Drew Gooden .15 .40
❑ 27 Jason Williams .20 .50
❑ 28 Eddie Jones .20 .50
❑ 29 Quentin Richardson .20 .50
❑ 30 Rasheed Wallace .25 .60
❑ 31A Shawn Marion .25 .60
❑ 31B Shawn Marion .25 .60
❑ 32 Malik Rose .15 .40
❑ 33 Ben Wallace .20 .50
❑ 34 Paul Pierce .25 .60
❑ 35 Matt Harpring .20 .50
❑ 36 Eddie Griffin .15 .40
❑ 37 Toni Kukoc .20 .50
❑ 38 Mike Bibby .20 .50
❑ 39 Kwame Brown .15 .40
❑ 40 Kurt Thomas .15 .40
❑ 41 Dirk Nowitzki .40 1.00
❑ 42 Theo Ratliff .15 .40
❑ 43 Ray Allen .15 .40
❑ 44 Michael Finley .25 .60
❑ 45 Lucious Harris .15 .40
❑ 46 Anfernee Hardaway .25 .60
❑ 47 Christian Laettner .15 .40
❑ 48 Manu Ginobili .25 .60
❑ 49 Tayshaun Prince .20 .50
❑ 50 Shaquille O'Neal .60 1.50
❑ 51 Vladimir Radmanovic .15 .40
❑ 52 Calbert Cheaney .15 .40
❑ 53 Eric Snow .15 .40
❑ 54A Pau Gasol .25 .60
❑ 54B Pau Gasol .25 .60
❑ 55 Dikembe Mutombo .20 .50
❑ 56 Alvin Williams .15 .40
❑ 57 Corliss Williamson .15 .40
❑ 58 Kedrick Brown .15 .40
❑ 59 Jamaal Tinsley .20 .50
❑ 60 Chris Webber .25 .60
❑ 61 Donyell Marshall .15 .40
❑ 62 Darrell Armstrong .15 .40
❑ 63 Kenny Thomas .15 .40
❑ 64 Mehmet Okur .20 .50
❑ 65 Carlos Boozer .25 .60
❑ 66A Kenyon Martin .25 .60
❑ 66B Kenyon Martin .25 .60
❑ 67 Speedy Claxton .15 .40
❑ 68 Brent Barry .15 .40
❑ 69 Ron Artest .20 .50
❑ 70 Elton Brand .25 .60
❑ 71 Troy Hudson .15 .40

❑ 72A Steve Nash	.40	1.00
❑ 72B Steve Nash	.40	1.00
❑ 73 Tony Parker	.25	.60
❑ 74 Earl Boykins	.15	.40
❑ 75 Kerry Kittles	.20	.50
❑ 76 Shawn Bradley	.15	.40
❑ 77 Tony Delk	.15	.40
❑ 78 Zydrunas Ilgauskas	.20	.50
❑ 79 Doug Christie	.15	.40
❑ 80 Amare Stoudemire	.50	1.25
❑ 81 Rick Fox	.15	.40
❑ 82 Brian Skinner	.15	.40
❑ 83 Jamal Mashburn	.15	.40
❑ 84 Qyntel Woods	.15	.40
❑ 85 Rafer Alston	.15	.40
❑ 86 Derek Anderson	.20	.50
❑ 87 Andre Miller	.20	.50
❑ 88 Antoine Walker	.25	.60
❑ 89 Frank Williams	.15	.40
❑ 90A Vince Carter	.50	1.25
❑ 90B Vince Carter	.50	1.25
❑ 91 Donnell Harvey	.15	.40
❑ 92 Raef Lafrentz	.15	.40
❑ 93 Desmond Mason	.20	.50
❑ 94 Rodney Rogers	.15	.40
❑ 95 Juan DixonA•	.15	.40
❑ 96 Kareem Rush	.15	.40
❑ 97 Bryon Russell	.15	.40
❑ 98 Shandon Anderson	.15	.40
❑ 99 Gordan Giricek	.15	.40
❑ 100 Tim Duncan	.50	1.25
❑ 101 Zach Randolph	.25	.60
❑ 102 Malik Allen	.15	.40
❑ 103 Richard Hamilton	.20	.50
❑ 104 Maurice Taylor	.15	.40
❑ 105 Marko Jaric	.15	.40
❑ 106 Joe Smith	.15	.40
❑ 107 Peja Stojakovic	.20	.50
❑ 108 Othella Harrington	.15	.40
❑ 109 Anthony Carter	.15	.40
❑ 110 Wally Szczerbiak	.20	.50
❑ 111 Troy Murphy	.25	.60
❑ 112 Shareef Abdur-Rahim	.20	.50
❑ 113 Reggie Miller	.25	.60
❑ 114 Vin Baker	.15	.40
❑ 115 Brian Scalabrine	.15	.40
❑ 116 Eric Piatkowski	.15	.40
❑ 117 Cuttino Mobley	.20	.50
❑ 118 Erick Dampier	.15	.40
❑ 119 Walter Mccarty	.15	.40
❑ 120 Caron Butler	.20	.50
❑ 121 Keyon Dooling	.15	.40
❑ 122 Michael Redd	.25	.60
❑ 123 Kenny Anderson	.20	.50
❑ 124 P.J. Brown	.15	.40
❑ 125 Devean George	.15	.40
❑ 126 Joe Johnson	.25	.60
❑ 127 Adrian Griffin	.15	.40
❑ 128 Bonzi Wells	.15	.40
❑ 129 Rasual Butler	.15	.40
❑ 130 Baron Davis	.25	.60
❑ 131 Wesley Person	.15	.40
❑ 132 Shammond Williams	.15	.40
❑ 133 Tyronn Lue	.15	.40
❑ 134 Brian Grant	.15	.40
❑ 135 Elden Campbell	.15	.40
❑ 136 Glen Rice	.15	.40
❑ 137 Michael Olowokandi	.15	.40
❑ 138 Anthony Peeler	.15	.40
❑ 139 Steven Hunter	.15	.40
❑ 140 Eddy Curry	.20	.50
❑ 141 Jerome James	.15	.40
❑ 142 Travis Best	.15	.40
❑ 143 Nazr Mohammed	.15	.40
❑ 144 Tony Battie	.15	.40
❑ 145 Scot Pollard	.15	.40
❑ 146 Stanislav Medvedenko	.15	.40
❑ 147 Jim Jackson	.15	.40
❑ 148 Marcus Camby	.20	.50
❑ 149 Marcus Haislip	.15	.40
❑ 150 Glenn Robinson	.20	.50
❑ 151 Jerome Williams	.15	.40
❑ 152 Greg Ostertag	.15	.40
❑ 153 Stephen Jackson	.20	.50
❑ 154 David Wesley	.15	.40
❑ 155 Sam Cassell	.20	.50
❑ 156 Hedo Turkoglu	.20	.50
❑ 157 Al Harrington	.20	.50
❑ 158 John Salmons	.20	.50
❑ 159 Nikoloz Tskitishvili	.15	.40
❑ 160 Samaki Walker	.15	.40
❑ 161 Jake Tsakalidis	.15	.40
❑ 162 Tim Thomas	.15	.40
❑ 163 Ronald Murray	.15	.40
❑ 164 Alonzo Mourning	.25	.60
❑ 165 Chris Jefferies	.15	.40
❑ 166 Darius Miles	.20	.50
❑ 167 Kendall Gill	.15	.40
❑ 168 Lonny Baxter	.15	.40
❑ 169 Jonathan Bender	.15	.40
❑ 170 Antawn Jamison	.25	.60
❑ 171 Keon Clark	.15	.40
❑ 172 Chris Wilcox	.15	.40
❑ 173 Brendan Haywood	.15	.40
❑ 174 Predrag Drobnjak	.15	.40
❑ 175 Nene	.20	.50
❑ 176 Casey Jacobsen	.15	.40
❑ 177 Marcus Fizer	.15	.40
❑ 178 Howard Eisley	.15	.40
❑ 179 Damon Stoudamire	.20	.50
❑ 180 Gary Payton	.25	.60
❑ 181 Shane Battier	.20	.50
❑ 182 Desagana Diop	.15	.40
❑ 183 Antonio Davis	.15	.40
❑ 184 Keith Van Horn	.20	.50
❑ 185 Corey Maggette	.15	.40
❑ 186 Jarron Collins	.15	.40
❑ 187 James Posey	.15	.40
❑ 188 Latrell Sprewell	.20	.50
❑ 189 Aaron McKie	.15	.40
❑ 190 Vlade Divac	.20	.50
❑ 191 Pat Garrity	.15	.40
❑ 192 Eric Williams	.15	.40
❑ 193 Radoslav Nesterovic	.15	.40
❑ 194 Dan Gadzuric	.15	.40
❑ 195 Moochie Norris	.15	.40
❑ 196 Clifford Robinson	.15	.40
❑ 197 Richard Jefferson	.25	.60
❑ 198 Lorenzen Wright	.15	.40
❑ 199 Nick Van Exel	.20	.50
❑ 200 Gilbert Arenas	.25	.60
❑ 201 Robert Horry	.20	.50
❑ 202 Scottie Pippen	.40	1.00
❑ 203 Jon Barry	.15	.40
❑ 204 Derrick Coleman	.20	.50
❑ 205 Ron Mercer	.15	.40
❑ 206 DeShawn Stevenson	.15	.40
❑ 207 Ruben Patterson	.15	.40
❑ 208 Rodney White	.15	.40
❑ 209 Jamal Crawford	.20	.50
❑ 210 Jermaine O'Neal	.25	.60
❑ 211 Eduardo Najera	.15	.40
❑ 212 Dan Dickau	.15	.40
❑ 213 Antonio McDyess	.20	.50
❑ 214 J.R. Bremer	.15	.40
❑ 215 Dion Glover	.15	.40
❑ 216 Lamond Murray	.15	.40
❑ 217 Larry Hughes	.20	.50
❑ 218 Mike Miller	.20	.50
❑ 219 Mike Dunleavy	.20	.50
❑ 220 Karl Malone	.25	.60
❑ 221 David West RC	.75	2.00
❑ 222 Steve Blake RC	.75	2.00
❑ 223A LeBron James RC	8.00	20.00
❑ 223B LeBron James RC	8.00	20.00
❑ 224 Keith Bogans RC	.60	1.50
❑ 225 Josh Howard RC	.75	2.00
❑ 226A Chris Kaman RC	.75	2.00
❑ 226B Chris Kaman RC	.75	2.00
❑ 227A Marcus Banks RC	.60	1.50
❑ 227B Marcus Banks RC	.60	1.50
❑ 228A Chris Bosh RC	1.00	2.50
❑ 228B Chris Bosh RC	1.00	2.50
❑ 229 Troy Bell RC	.60	1.50
❑ 230 Luke Walton RC	.75	2.00
❑ 231 Francisco Elson RC	.60	1.50
❑ 232 Ndudi Ebi RC	.60	1.50
❑ 233 Maurice Williams RC	1.00	2.50
❑ 234 Kendrick Perkins RC	1.00	2.50
❑ 235 Dahntay Jones RC	.60	1.50
❑ 236 Jason Kapono RC	.75	2.00
❑ 237 Kyle Korver RC	.75	2.00
❑ 238 Josh Moore RC	.60	1.50
❑ 239 Travis Hansen RC	.60	1.50
❑ 240A Carmelo Anthony Blue RC	1.50	4.00
❑ 240B Carmelo Anthony White RC	1.50	4.00
❑ 241 Keith McLeod RC	.60	1.50
❑ 242 Zoran Planinic RC	.60	1.50
❑ 243A Jarvis Hayes RC	.60	1.50
❑ 243B Jarvis Hayes RC	.60	1.50
❑ 244A Mickael Pietrus RC	.75	2.00
❑ 244B Mickael Pietrus RC	.75	2.00
❑ 245A Mike Sweetney RC	.60	1.50
❑ 245B Mike Sweetney RC	.60	1.50
❑ 246 Jerome Beasley RC	.60	1.50
❑ 247 Zaza Pachulia RC	.75	2.00
❑ 248 Ben Handlogten RC	.60	1.50
❑ 249 Torraye Braggs RC	.60	1.50
❑ 250A Nick Collison White RC	.60	1.50
❑ 250B Nick Collison Green RC	.60	1.50
❑ 251 Reece Gaines RC	.60	1.50
❑ 252A Dwyane Wade Dribble RC	1.50	4.00
❑ 252B Dwyane Wade Layup RC	1.50	4.00
❑ 253 Devin Brown RC	.60	1.50
❑ 254 Leandro Barbosa RC	.75	2.00
❑ 255 Boris Diaw RC	.75	2.00
❑ 256 Aleksandar Pavlovic RC	.75	2.00
❑ 257 Udonis Haslem RC	.75	2.00
❑ 258 Brian Cook RC	.60	1.50
❑ 259 Maciej Lampe RC	.60	1.50
❑ 260A T.J. Ford RC	.75	2.00
❑ 260B T.J. Ford RC	.75	2.00
❑ 261 Matt Carroll RC	.60	1.50
❑ 262 James Jones RC	.60	1.50
❑ 263 Brandon Hunter RC	.60	1.50
❑ 264 Luke Ridnour RC	.75	2.00
❑ 265 Theron Smith RC	.60	1.50
❑ 266 Jon Stefansson RC	.60	1.50
❑ 267 Zarko Cabarkapa RC	.60	1.50
❑ 268 Marquis Daniels RC	.75	2.00
❑ 269 Willie Green RC	.60	1.50
❑ 270A Kirk Hinrich Left RC	.75	2.00
❑ 270B Kirk Hinrich Right RC	.75	2.00
❑ 271 Linton Johnson RC	.60	1.50
❑ 272 Travis Outlaw RC	.75	2.00
❑ 273 James Lang RC	.60	1.50
❑ 274 Slavko Vranes RC	.60	1.50
❑ 275A Darko Milicic RC	.75	2.00
❑ 275B Darko Milicic RC	.75	2.00
❑ 276 LeBron James BAZ	6.00	15.00
❑ 277 Darko Milicic BAZ	.60	1.50
❑ 278 Carmelo Anthony BAZ	1.25	3.00
❑ 279 Chris Bosh BAZ	.75	2.00
❑ 280 Dwyane Wade BAZ	1.25	3.00
❑ 281 Chris Kaman BAZ	.60	1.50
❑ 282 Kirk Hinrich BAZ	.60	1.50
❑ 283 T.J. Ford BAZ	.60	1.50
❑ 284 Mike Sweetney BAZ	.50	1.25
❑ 285 Jarvis Hayes BAZ	.50	1.25
❑ 286 Mickael Pietrus BAZ	.60	1.50
❑ 287 Nick Collison BAZ	.50	1.25
❑ 288 Marcus Banks BAZ	.50	1.25

2004-05 Bazooka

❑ COMP.SET w/o RC's (165)	10.00	25.00
❑ COMMON CARD (1-165)	.15	.40
❑ COMMON ROOKIE (166-220)	.60	1.50
❑ 1 Shaquille O'Neal	.60	1.50
❑ 2 Marquis Daniels	.15	.40
❑ 3 Ben Wallace	.20	.50
❑ 4 Jarvis Hayes	.15	.40
❑ 5 Gerald Wallace	.25	.60
❑ 6 Fred Jones	.15	.40
❑ 7 Pau Gasol	.25	.60
❑ 8 Latrell Sprewell	.20	.50
❑ 9 Steve Francis	.25	.60
❑ 10 Mike Bibby	.20	.50
❑ 11 Chris Bosh	.25	.60
❑ 12 Steve Nash	.40	1.00
❑ 13 Kirk Hinrich	.20	.50
❑ 14 Richard Jefferson	.25	.60
❑ 15 Zach Randolph	.25	.60
❑ 16 Willie Green	.15	.40
❑ 17 Al Harrington	.20	.50

❑ 18 Rashard Lewis	.25	.60
❑ 19 Ricky Davis	.20	.50
❑ 20 Dwyane Wade	.75	2.00
❑ 21 Tim Duncan	.50	1.25
❑ 22 Eddy Curry	.20	.50
❑ 23 Andre Miller	.20	.50
❑ 24 Chris Wilcox	.15	.40
❑ 25 Bobby Jackson	.15	.40
❑ 26 Stephen Jackson	.20	.50
❑ 27 Shane Battier	.20	.50
❑ 28 Antawn Jamison	.25	.60
❑ 29 Brent Barry	.15	.40
❑ 30 Stephon Marbury	.25	.60
❑ 31 Gordan Giricek	.15	.40
❑ 32 Jamal Mashburn	.20	.50
❑ 33 Allen Iverson	.50	1.25
❑ 34 Paul Pierce	.25	.60
❑ 35 Mike Dunleavy	.20	.50
❑ 36 Gary Payton	.25	.60
❑ 37 Brad Miller	.20	.50
❑ 38 Eric Snow	.15	.40
❑ 39 Theo Ratliff	.15	.40
❑ 40 Richard Hamilton	.20	.50
❑ 41 Dirk Nowitzki	.40	1.00
❑ 42 Elton Brand	.25	.60
❑ 43 Reggie Miller	.25	.60
❑ 44 Baron Davis	.25	.60
❑ 45 Jerome Williams	.15	.40
❑ 46 Stromile Swift	.15	.40
❑ 47 Andrei Kirilenko	.25	.60
❑ 48 Jason Richardson	.25	.60
❑ 49 Larry Hughes	.20	.50
❑ 50 Yao Ming	.60	1.50
❑ 51 Tim Thomas	.15	.40
❑ 52 Erick Dampier	.15	.40
❑ 53 Keith Van Horn	.20	.50
❑ 54 Grant Hill	.25	.60
❑ 55 Shareef Abdur-Rahim	.20	.50
❑ 56 Amare Stoudemire	.50	1.25
❑ 57 David Wesley	.15	.40
❑ 58 Chris Kaman	.20	.50
❑ 59 Caron Butler	.20	.50
❑ 60 Kenyon Martin	.25	.60
❑ 61 Ray Allen	.25	.60
❑ 62 Jerry Stackhouse	.20	.50
❑ 63 Jason Kapono	.15	.40
❑ 64 Mark Blount	.15	.40
❑ 65 Hedo Turkoglu	.20	.50
❑ 66 Carlos Boozer	.25	.60
❑ 67 Kenny Thomas	.15	.40
❑ 68 Manu Ginobili	.25	.60
❑ 69 Kobe Bryant	1.25	3.00
❑ 70 Vince Carter	.50	1.25
❑ 71 Troy Murphy	.25	.60
❑ 72 Maurice Taylor	.15	.40
❑ 73 Earl Boykins	.15	.40
❑ 74 Boris Diaw	.20	.50
❑ 75 Kerry Kittles	.20	.50
❑ 76 Jamaal Tinsley	.20	.50
❑ 77 Lamar Odom	.25	.60
❑ 78 Jamaal Magloire	.15	.40
❑ 79 Wally Szczerbiak	.20	.50
❑ 80 Tayshaun Prince	.20	.50
❑ 81 Mehmet Okur	.20	.50
❑ 82 Eddie Jones	.20	.50
❑ 83 Voshon Lenard	.15	.40
❑ 84 Jamal Crawford	.20	.50
❑ 85 Marko Jaric	.15	.40
❑ 86 Ron Mercer	.15	.40
❑ 87 Steve Smith	.20	.50
❑ 88 Antoine Walker	.25	.60
❑ 89 Kurt Thomas	.15	.40
❑ 90 Ron Artest	.20	.50
❑ 91 Luke Walton	.20	.50
❑ 92 Dajuan Wagner	.15	.40
❑ 93 Luke Ridnour	.15	.40
❑ 94 Nene	.20	.50
❑ 95 Josh Howard	.25	.60
❑ 96 Juwan Howard	.20	.50
❑ 97 David West	.25	.60
❑ 98 Jonathan Bender	.15	.40
❑ 99 Tony Parker	.25	.60
❑ 100 LeBron James	1.50	4.00
❑ 101 Chris Webber	.25	.60
❑ 102 Cuttino Mobley	.20	.50
❑ 103 Rasheed Wallace	.25	.60
❑ 104 Marcus Banks	.15	.40
❑ 105 Ronald Murray	.15	.40
❑ 106 Quentin Richardson	.20	.50
❑ 107 Antonio McDyess	.20	.50
❑ 108 Sam Cassell	.20	.50
❑ 109 Allan Houston	.20	.50
❑ 110 Leandro Barbosa	.25	.60
❑ 111 Joe Smith	.15	.40
❑ 112 Jason Kidd	.40	1.00
❑ 113 Aleksandar Pavlovic	.15	.40
❑ 114 Bruce Bowen	.15	.40
❑ 115 Carmelo Anthony	.75	2.00
❑ 116 Kwame Brown	.15	.40
❑ 117 Mickael Pietrus	.20	.50
❑ 118 Tony Battie	.15	.40
❑ 119 Joe Johnson	.25	.60
❑ 120 Damon Stoudamire	.20	.50
❑ 121 Kevin Garnett	.50	1.25
❑ 122 Michael Redd	.25	.60
❑ 123 Doug Christie	.15	.40
❑ 124 Darrell Armstrong	.15	.40
❑ 125 James Posey	.15	.40
❑ 126 Jim Jackson	.15	.40
❑ 127 Udonis Haslem	.20	.50
❑ 128 Drew Gooden	.15	.40
❑ 129 Rasho Nesterovic	.15	.40
❑ 130 Jermaine O'Neal	.25	.60
❑ 131 Shawn Marion	.25	.60
❑ 132 Samuel Dalembert	.15	.40
❑ 133 Marcus Camby	.20	.50
❑ 134 Devean George	.15	.40
❑ 135 Darius Miles	.20	.50
❑ 136 Michael Olowokandi	.15	.40
❑ 137 Mike Miller	.20	.50
❑ 138 Kareem Rush	.15	.40
❑ 139 Jalen Rose	.20	.50
❑ 140 Chauncey Billups	.25	.60
❑ 141 Jason Williams	.20	.50
❑ 142 Derek Fisher	.20	.50
❑ 143 Donyell Marshall	.15	.40
❑ 144 Alonzo Mourning	.25	.60
❑ 145 T.J. Ford	.20	.50
❑ 146 Tony Delk	.15	.40
❑ 147 Gilbert Arenas	.25	.60
❑ 148 Glenn Robinson	.20	.50
❑ 149 Peja Stojakovic	.20	.50
❑ 150 Tracy McGrady	.50	1.25
❑ 151 Rafer Alston	.15	.40
❑ 152 Nazr Mohammed	.15	.40
❑ 153 Corey Maggette	.20	.50
❑ 154 Michael Doleac	.15	.40
❑ 155 Zydrunas Ilgauskas	.20	.50
❑ 156 Troy Hudson	.15	.40
❑ 157 Vladimir Radmanovic	.15	.40
❑ 158 Jason Collins	.15	.40
❑ 159 Dikembe Mutombo	.20	.50
❑ 160 Bonzi Wells	.15	.40
❑ 161 Jason Terry	.20	.50
❑ 162 Tyson Chandler	.20	.50
❑ 163 Desmond Mason	.20	.50
❑ 164 Carlos Arroyo	.25	.60
❑ 165 Darko Milicic	.15	.40
❑ 166 Ben Gordon RC	.75	2.00
❑ 167 Kevin Martin RC	.75	2.00
❑ 168 Jackson Vroman RC	.60	1.50
❑ 169 Delonte West RC	1.00	2.50
❑ 170 Dorell Wright RC	.75	2.00
❑ 171 Erik Daniels RC	.60	1.50
❑ 172 Josh Childress RC	.60	1.50
❑ 173 Anderson Varejao RC	.75	2.00
❑ 174 Andre Emmett RC	.60	1.50
❑ 175 Chris Duhon RC	1.00	2.50
❑ 176 Bernard Robinson RC	.60	1.50
❑ 177 D.J. Mbenga RC	.60	1.50
❑ 178 Kirk Snyder RC	.60	1.50
❑ 179 Damien Wilkins RC	.60	1.50
❑ 180 Andre Iguodala RC	1.50	4.00
❑ 181 Nenad Krstic RC	.75	2.00
❑ 182 Pape Sow RC	.60	1.50
❑ 183 Maurice Evans RC	.60	1.50
❑ 184 John Edwards RC	.60	1.50
❑ 185 Andres Nocioni RC	.75	2.00
❑ 186 Arthur Johnson RC	.60	1.50
❑ 187 Beno Udrih RC	.75	2.00
❑ 188 Andris Biedrins RC	1.00	2.50
❑ 189 Kris Humphries RC	1.00	2.50
❑ 190 Trevor Ariza RC	.75	2.00
❑ 191 Devin Harris RC	1.25	3.00
❑ 192 J.R. Smith RC	1.25	3.00
❑ 193 Romain Sato RC	.60	1.50
❑ 194 Lionel Chalmers RC	.60	1.50
❑ 195 Al Jefferson RC	1.25	3.00
❑ 196 Josh Smith RC	1.50	4.00
❑ 197 Antonio Burks RC	.60	1.50
❑ 198 Tim Pickett RC	.60	1.50
❑ 199 Justin Reed RC	.60	1.50
❑ 200 Emeka Okafor RC	1.25	3.00
❑ 201 Sebastian Telfair RC	.60	1.50
❑ 202 Sasha Vujacic RC	.60	1.50
❑ 203 Royal Ivey RC	.60	1.50
❑ 204 Rafael Araujo RC	.60	1.50
❑ 205 Ibrahim Kutluay RC	.60	1.50
❑ 206 Matt Freije RC	.60	1.50
❑ 207 Jared Reiner RC	.60	1.50
❑ 208 Luis Flores RC	.60	1.50
❑ 209 Robert Swift RC	.60	1.50
❑ 210 Shaun Livingston RC	.60	1.50
❑ 211 Peter John Ramos RC	.60	1.50
❑ 212 Luke Jackson RC	.60	1.50
❑ 213 Luol Deng RC	.75	2.00
❑ 214 Jameer Nelson RC	.75	2.00
❑ 215 Tony Allen RC	.75	2.00
❑ 216 Josh Davis RC	.60	1.50
❑ 217 Yuta Tabuse RC	1.25	3.00
❑ 218 Donta Smith RC	.60	1.50
❑ 219 David Harrison RC	.60	1.50
❑ 220 Dwight Howard RC	2.00	5.00

2005-06 Bazooka

❑ COMPLETE SET (220)	15.00	40.00
❑ 1 Gilbert Arenas	.25	.60
❑ 2 Josh Smith	.25	.60
❑ 3 Carlos Boozer	.25	.60
❑ 4 Al Jefferson	.25	.60
❑ 5 Jalen Rose	.25	.60
❑ 6 Primoz Brezec	.15	.40
❑ 7 Rashard Lewis	.25	.60
❑ 8 Ben Gordon	.30	.75
❑ 9 Tony Parker	.25	.60
❑ 10 Drew Gooden	.20	.50
❑ 11 Mike Bibby	.25	.60
❑ 12 Josh Howard	.25	.60
❑ 13 Sebastian Telfair	.20	.50
❑ 14 Earl Boykins	.15	.40
❑ 15 Joe Johnson	.25	.60
❑ 16 Rasheed Wallace	.25	.60
❑ 17 Marc Jackson	.15	.40
❑ 18 Baron Davis	.25	.60
❑ 19 Dwight Howard	.50	1.25
❑ 20 Tracy McGrady	.50	1.25
❑ 21 Trevor Ariza	.20	.50
❑ 22 David Harrison	.15	.40
❑ 23 J.R. Smith	.20	.50
❑ 24 Chris Kaman	.15	.40
❑ 25 Richard Jefferson	.20	.50
❑ 26 Chris Mihm	.15	.40
❑ 27 Sam Cassell	.25	.60
❑ 28 Mike Miller	.25	.60
❑ 29 Joe Smith	.20	.50
❑ 30 Dwyane Wade	.60	1.50
❑ 31 Tony Allen	.15	.40
❑ 32 Antawn Jamison	.25	.60
❑ 33 Eddy Curry	.20	.50
❑ 34 Rafael Araujo	.15	.40
❑ 35 Jerry Stackhouse	.25	.60
❑ 36 Manu Ginobili	.25	.60
❑ 37 Antonio McDyess	.15	.40
❑ 38 Zach Randolph	.25	.60
❑ 39 Mike James	.15	.40
❑ 40 Chris Webber	.25	.60
❑ 41 Bobby Simmons	.15	.40
❑ 42 Jamal Crawford	.20	.50
❑ 43 Pau Gasol	.25	.60
❑ 44 Brian Scalabrine	.15	.40
❑ 45 Desmond Mason	.15	.40
❑ 46 Tyronn Lue	.15	.40
❑ 47 Andrei Kirilenko	.25	.60
❑ 48 Luke Ridnour	.20	.50

❑ 49 Gerald Wallace	.25	.60
❑ 50 LeBron James	1.25	3.00
❑ 51 Peja Stojakovic	.25	.60
❑ 52 Andre Miller	.20	.50
❑ 53 Quentin Richardson	.20	.50
❑ 54 Mike Dunleavy	.20	.50
❑ 55 Steve Francis	.25	.60
❑ 56 Stephen Jackson	.20	.50
❑ 57 P.J. Brown	.15	.40
❑ 58 Caron Butler	.25	.60
❑ 59 Keith Van Horn	.20	.50
❑ 60 Shaquille O'Neal	.60	1.50
❑ 61 Josh Childress	.20	.50
❑ 62 Michael Doleac	.15	.40
❑ 63 Lamar Odom	.25	.60
❑ 64 Stephon Marbury	.25	.60
❑ 65 Chris Duhon	.20	.50
❑ 66 Shaun Livingston	.15	.40
❑ 67 Eric Snow	.15	.40
❑ 68 Travis Outlaw	.15	.40
❑ 69 Ron Artest	.20	.50
❑ 70 Emeka Okafor	.25	.60
❑ 71 Chauncey Billups	.25	.60
❑ 72 Jason Williams	.20	.50
❑ 73 Jameer Nelson	.20	.50
❑ 74 Eduardo Najera	.25	.60
❑ 75 Speedy Claxton	.15	.40
❑ 76 Kirk Snyder	.15	.40
❑ 77 Rafer Alston	.15	.40
❑ 78 Kobe Bryant	1.25	3.00
❑ 79 Michael Redd	.25	.60
❑ 80 Tim Duncan	.50	1.25
❑ 81 Tayshaun Prince	.25	.60
❑ 82 Brendan Haywood	.15	.40
❑ 83 Kyle Korver	.25	.60
❑ 84 Tony Delk	.15	.40
❑ 85 Luol Deng	.25	.60
❑ 86 Elton Brand	.25	.60
❑ 87 Jason Richardson	.25	.60
❑ 88 Antoine Walker	.20	.50
❑ 89 Ray Allen	.25	.60
❑ 90 Yao Ming	.60	1.50
❑ 91 Damon Jones	.20	.50
❑ 92 Anderson Varejao	.20	.50
❑ 93 Kurt Thomas	.15	.40
❑ 94 Latrell Sprewell	.15	.40
❑ 95 Cuttino Mobley	.20	.50
❑ 96 Chris Wilcox	.15	.40
❑ 97 Devin Harris	.25	.60
❑ 98 Jared Jeffries	.15	.40
❑ 99 Nenad Krstic	.20	.50
❑ 100 Steve Nash	.30	.75
❑ 101 Reggie Evans	.15	.40
❑ 102 Ben Wallace	.25	.60
❑ 103 Allen Iverson	.50	1.25
❑ 104 Bruce Bowen	.15	.40
❑ 105 Paul Pierce	.25	.60
❑ 106 Shareef Abdur-Rahim	.25	.60
❑ 107 Vladimir Radmanovic	.15	.40
❑ 108 Michael Finley	.25	.60
❑ 109 Brent Barry	.15	.40
❑ 110 Carmelo Anthony	.50	1.25
❑ 111 Andre Iguodala	.25	.60
❑ 112 Shane Battier	.25	.60
❑ 113 Richard Hamilton	.20	.50
❑ 114 Kenny Thomas	.15	.40
❑ 115 Tyson Chandler	.25	.60
❑ 116 Jim Jackson	.15	.40
❑ 117 David Wesley	.15	.40
❑ 118 Grant Hill	.25	.60
❑ 119 Wally Szczerbiak	.20	.50
❑ 120 Dirk Nowitzki	.40	1.00
❑ 121 Udonis Haslem	.25	.60
❑ 122 Jason Hart	.15	.40
❑ 123 Marcus Camby	.20	.50
❑ 124 Kirk Hinrich	.25	.60
❑ 125 Jermaine O'Neal	.25	.60
❑ 126 Derek Fisher	.15	.40
❑ 127 Donyell Marshall	.15	.40
❑ 128 Darius Miles	.25	.60
❑ 129 Kenyon Martin	.25	.60
❑ 130 Jason Kidd	.40	1.00
❑ 131 Marquis Daniels	.20	.50
❑ 132 Kevin Garnett	.50	1.25
❑ 133 Juwan Howard	.20	.50
❑ 134 Shawn Marion	.25	.60
❑ 135 Morris Peterson	.20	.50
❑ 136 Kevin Martin	.25	.60
❑ 137 Gary Payton	.25	.60
❑ 138 Maurice Williams	.20	.50
❑ 139 Eddie Jones	.15	.40
❑ 140 Vince Carter	.50	1.25
❑ 141 Lorenzen Wright	.15	.40
❑ 142 Dan Dickau	.15	.40
❑ 143 Chucky Atkins	.15	.40
❑ 144 Mike Sweetney	.20	.50
❑ 145 Corey Maggette	.20	.50
❑ 146 Hedo Turkoglu	.20	.50
❑ 147 Jamaal Tinsley	.20	.50
❑ 148 Samuel Dalembert	.15	.40
❑ 149 Bob Sura	.15	.40
❑ 150 Amare Stoudemire	.50	1.25
❑ 151 Troy Murphy	.25	.60
❑ 152 Joel Przybilla	.15	.40
❑ 153 Carlos Arroyo	.25	.60
❑ 154 Brad Miller	.25	.60
❑ 155 Jason Terry	.25	.60
❑ 156 Beno Udrih	.15	.40
❑ 157 Zydrunas Ilgauskas	.20	.50
❑ 158 Nick Collison	.15	.40
❑ 159 Andres Nocioni	.15	.40
❑ 160 Chris Bosh	.25	.60
❑ 161 Brevin Knight	.15	.40
❑ 162 Mehmet Okur	.15	.40
❑ 163 Ricky Davis	.25	.60
❑ 164 Larry Hughes	.20	.50
❑ 165 Al Harrington	.15	.40
❑ 166 Chris Paul RC	2.00	5.00
❑ 167 Danny Granger RC	1.50	4.00
❑ 168 Jarrett Jack RC	.60	1.50
❑ 169 Wayne Simien RC	.75	2.00
❑ 170 Deron Williams RC	1.50	4.00
❑ 171 Ryan Gomes RC	.60	1.50
❑ 172 Daniel Ewing RC	.75	2.00
❑ 173 Sean May RC	.75	2.00
❑ 174 Alan Anderson RC	.60	1.50
❑ 175 Hakim Warrick RC	1.00	2.50
❑ 176 Francisco Garcia RC	.75	2.00
❑ 177 Nate Robinson RC	1.00	2.50
❑ 178 Luther Head RC	.75	2.00
❑ 179 Joey Graham RC	.60	1.50
❑ 180 Marvin Williams RC	1.00	2.50
❑ 181 Antoine Wright RC	.60	1.50
❑ 182 Andrew Bynum RC	2.00	5.00
❑ 183 Johan Petro RC	.60	1.50
❑ 184 Louis Williams RC	1.00	2.50
❑ 185 Andray Blatche RC	.75	2.00
❑ 186 Sarunas Jasikevicius RC	.75	2.00
❑ 187 Ike Diogu RC	.75	2.00
❑ 188 Channing Frye RC	.75	2.00
❑ 189 Julius Hodge RC	.75	2.00
❑ 190 Rashad McCants RC	.75	2.00
❑ 191 Yaroslav Korolev RC	.60	1.50
❑ 192 C.J. Miles RC	.60	1.50
❑ 193 Brandon Bass RC	.60	1.50
❑ 194 Travis Diener RC	.60	1.50
❑ 195 Monta Ellis RC	1.50	4.00
❑ 196 Linas Kleiza RC	.75	2.00
❑ 197 Gerald Green RC	.60	1.50
❑ 198 Jason Maxiell RC	.75	2.00
❑ 199 David Lee RC	1.25	3.00
❑ 200 Andrew Bogut RC	.75	2.00
❑ 201 Salim Stoudamire RC	.75	2.00
❑ 202 Raymond Felton RC	.75	2.00
❑ 203 Martell Webster RC	.60	1.50
❑ 204 Chris Taft RC	.60	1.50
❑ 205 Charlie Villanueva RC	1.00	2.50
❑ 206 Lawrence Roberts RC	.60	1.50
❑ 207 Ersan Ilyasova RC	.60	1.50
❑ 208 Martynas Andriuskevicius RC	.60	1.50
❑ 209 Bracey Wright RC	.60	1.50
❑ 210 Von Wafer RC	.60	1.50
❑ 211 Eddie Basden RC	.60	1.50
❑ 212 Dijon Thompson RC	.60	1.50
❑ 213 Robert Whaley RC	.60	1.50
❑ 214 Matt Walsh RC	.60	1.50
❑ 215 Ricky Sanchez RC	.60	1.50
❑ 216 Jay-Z	.75	2.00
❑ 217 Shannon Elizabeth	.75	2.00
❑ 218 Christie Brinkley	.75	2.00
❑ 219 Jenny McCarthy	.75	2.00
❑ 220 Carmen Electra	.75	2.00

1998-99 Black Diamond

❑ COMPLETE SET (120)	40.00	80.00
❑ COMPLETE SET w/o RC (90)	20.00	40.00
❑ COMMON MJ (1-13/22)	1.25	3.00
❑ COMMON CARD (14-90)	.10	.30
❑ COMMON ROOKIE (91-120)	.20	.50

❑ 1 Michael Jordan	1.25	3.00
❑ 2 Michael Jordan	1.25	3.00
❑ 3 Michael Jordan	1.25	3.00
❑ 4 Michael Jordan	1.25	3.00
❑ 5 Michael Jordan	1.25	3.00
❑ 6 Michael Jordan	1.25	3.00
❑ 7 Michael Jordan	1.25	3.00
❑ 8 Michael Jordan	1.25	3.00
❑ 9 Michael Jordan	1.25	3.00
❑ 10 Michael Jordan	1.25	3.00
❑ 11 Michael Jordan	1.25	3.00
❑ 12 Michael Jordan	1.25	3.00
❑ 13 Michael Jordan	1.25	3.00
❑ 14 Dikembe Mutombo	.25	.60
❑ 15 Steve Smith	.25	.60
❑ 16 Mookie Blaylock	.10	.30
❑ 17 Antoine Walker	.40	1.00
❑ 18 Kenny Anderson	.25	.60
❑ 19 Ron Mercer	.20	.50
❑ 20 Glen Rice	.25	.60
❑ 21 Derrick Coleman	.10	.30
❑ 22 Michael Jordan	1.25	3.00
❑ 23 Toni Kukoc	.25	.60
❑ 24 Brent Barry	.25	.60
❑ 25 Brevin Knight	.10	.30
❑ 26 Derek Anderson	.30	.75
❑ 27 Shawn Kemp	.25	.60
❑ 28 Shawn Bradley	.10	.30
❑ 29 Michael Finley	.40	1.00
❑ 30 Nick Van Exel	.40	1.00
❑ 31 Chauncey Billups	.25	.60
❑ 32 Antonio McDyess	.25	.60
❑ 33 Grant Hill	.40	1.00
❑ 34 Jerry Stackhouse	.40	1.00
❑ 35 Bison Dele	.10	.30
❑ 36 John Starks	.25	.60
❑ 37 Chris Mills	.10	.30
❑ 38 Scottie Pippen	.60	1.50
❑ 39 Hakeem Olajuwon	.40	1.00
❑ 40 Charles Barkley	.50	1.25
❑ 41 Antonio Davis	.10	.30
❑ 42 Reggie Miller	.40	1.00
❑ 43 Mark Jackson	.25	.60
❑ 44 Eddie Jones	.40	1.00
❑ 45 Shaquille O'Neal	1.00	2.50
❑ 46 Kobe Bryant	1.50	4.00
❑ 47 Rodney Rogers	.10	.30
❑ 48 Maurice Taylor	.20	.50
❑ 49 Tim Hardaway	.25	.60
❑ 50 Jamal Mashburn	.25	.60
❑ 51 Alonzo Mourning	.25	.60
❑ 52 Ray Allen	.40	1.00
❑ 53 Terrell Brandon	.25	.60
❑ 54 Glenn Robinson	.25	.60
❑ 55 Joe Smith	.25	.60
❑ 56 Stephon Marbury	.40	1.00
❑ 57 Kevin Garnett	.75	2.00
❑ 58 Kerry Kittles	.10	.30
❑ 59 Jayson Williams	.10	.30
❑ 60 Keith Van Horn	.40	1.00
❑ 61 Patrick Ewing	.40	1.00
❑ 62 Allan Houston	.25	.60
❑ 63 Latrell Sprewell	.40	1.00
❑ 64 Anfernee Hardaway	.40	1.00
❑ 65 Horace Grant	.25	.60
❑ 66 Allen Iverson	.75	2.00
❑ 67 Tim Thomas	.25	.60
❑ 68 Jason Kidd	.60	1.50
❑ 69 Danny Manning	.10	.30
❑ 70 Tom Gugliotta	.10	.30
❑ 71 Damon Stoudamire	.25	.60
❑ 72 Rasheed Wallace	.40	1.00
❑ 73 Isaiah Rider	.10	.30
❑ 74 Corliss Williamson	.25	.60
❑ 75 Chris Webber	.40	1.00

76 Tim Duncan	.60	1.50
77 David Robinson	.40	1.00
78 Sean Elliott	.25	.60
79 Gary Payton	.40	1.00
80 Vin Baker	.25	.60
81 John Wallace	.10	.30
82 Tracy McGrady	1.00	2.50
83 Jeff Hornacek	.25	.60
84 Karl Malone	.40	1.00
85 John Stockton	.40	1.00
86 Bryant Reeves	.10	.30
87 Shareef Abdur-Rahim	.40	1.00
88 Rod Strickland	.10	.30
89 Juwan Howard	.25	.60
90 Mitch Richmond	.25	.60
91 Michael Olowokandi RC	.75	2.00
92 Dirk Nowitzki RC	6.00	12.00
93 Raef LaFrentz RC	.75	2.00
94 Mike Bibby RC	2.00	5.00
95 Ricky Davis RC	1.50	4.00
96 Jason Williams RC	2.00	5.00
97 Al Harrington RC	1.25	3.00
98 Bonzi Wells RC	2.00	5.00
99 Keon Clark RC	.75	2.00
100 Rashard Lewis RC	2.00	5.00
101 Paul Pierce RC	4.00	10.00
102 Antawn Jamison RC	2.50	6.00
103 Nazr Mohammed RC	.25	.60
104 Brian Skinner RC	.50	1.25
105 Corey Benjamin RC	.50	1.25
106 Peja Stojakovic RC	2.00	5.00
107 Bryce Drew RC	.50	1.25
108 Matt Harpring RC	1.00	2.50
109 Toby Bailey RC	.20	.50
110 Tyronn Lue RC	.60	1.50
111 Michael Dickerson RC	1.00	2.50
112 Roshown McLeod RC	.25	.60
113 Felipe Lopez RC	.60	1.50
114 Michael Doleac RC	.50	1.25
115 Ruben Patterson RC	1.00	2.50
116 Robert Traylor RC	.50	1.25
117 Sam Jacobson RC	.20	.50
118 Larry Hughes RC	1.50	4.00
119 Pat Garrity RC	.25	.60
120 Vince Carter RC	4.00	10.00

1999-00 Black Diamond

COMPLETE SET (120)	25.00	50.00
COMPLETE SET w/o RC (90)	12.50	25.00
COMMON CARD (1-90)	.20	.50
COMMON ROOKIE (91-120)	.40	1.00
1 Dikembe Mutombo	.25	.60
2 Alan Henderson	.20	.50
3 Roshown McLeod	.20	.50
4 Kenny Anderson	.25	.60
5 Paul Pierce	.30	.75
6 Antoine Walker	.30	.75
7 Eddie Jones	.30	.75
8 Elden Campbell	.20	.50
9 David Wesley	.20	.50
10 Toni Kukoc	.30	.75
11 Randy Brown	.20	.50
12 Dickey Simpkins	.20	.50
13 Shawn Kemp	.30	.75
14 Zydrunas Ilgauskas	.25	.60
15 Brevin Knight	.20	.50
16 Michael Finley	.30	.75
17 Dirk Nowitzki	.50	1.25
18 Robert Pack	.20	.50
19 Antonio McDyess	.25	.60
20 Nick Van Exel	.25	.60
21 Ron Mercer	.20	.50
22 Grant Hill	.30	.75
23 Lindsey Hunter	.20	.50
24 Jerry Stackhouse	.30	.75
25 Antawn Jamison	.30	.75
26 John Starks	.30	.75
27 Donyell Marshall	.25	.60
28 Hakeem Olajuwon	.30	.75
29 Charles Barkley	.40	1.00
30 Cuttino Mobley	.25	.60
31 Reggie Miller	.30	.75
32 Rik Smits	.30	.75
33 Jalen Rose	.25	.60
34 Maurice Taylor	.25	.60
35 Tyrone Nesby RC	.30	.75
36 Michael Olowokandi	.20	.50
37 Shaquille O'Neal	.75	2.00
38 Kobe Bryant	1.50	4.00
39 Glen Rice	.30	.75
40 P.J. Brown	.20	.50
41 Tim Hardaway	.30	.75
42 Alonzo Mourning	.30	.75
43 Jamal Mashburn	.20	.50
44 Glenn Robinson	.25	.60
45 Ray Allen	.30	.75
46 Tim Thomas	.25	.60
47 Kevin Garnett	.60	1.50
48 Joe Smith	.25	.60
49 Terrell Brandon	.20	.50
50 Stephon Marbury	.30	.75
51 Jayson Williams	.25	.60
52 Keith Van Horn	.25	.60
53 Latrell Sprewell	.25	.60
54 Allan Houston	.25	.60
55 Patrick Ewing	.40	1.00
56 Marcus Camby	.25	.60
57 Darrell Armstrong	.20	.50
58 Bo Outlaw	.20	.50
59 Michael Doleac	.20	.50
60 Allen Iverson	.60	1.50
61 Theo Ratliff	.25	.60
62 Larry Hughes	.25	.60
63 Anfernee Hardaway	.30	.75
64 Jason Kidd	.50	1.25
65 Tom Gugliotta	.20	.50
66 Brian Grant	.20	.50
67 Damon Stoudamire	.30	.75
68 Rasheed Wallace	.30	.75
69 Jason Williams	.30	.75
70 Chris Webber	.30	.75
71 Vlade Divac	.30	.75
72 Tim Duncan	.60	1.50
73 David Robinson	.40	1.00
74 Avery Johnson	.25	.60
75 Sean Elliott	.30	.75
76 Gary Payton	.30	.75
77 Vin Baker	.30	.75
78 Brent Barry	.25	.60
79 Vince Carter	.60	1.50
80 Tracy McGrady	.60	1.50
81 Doug Christie	.25	.60
82 Karl Malone	.40	1.00
83 John Stockton	.40	1.00
84 Bryon Russell	.20	.50
85 Shareef Abdur-Rahim	.25	.60
86 Mike Bibby	.30	.75
87 Felipe Lopez	.20	.50
88 Juwan Howard	.25	.60
89 Rod Strickland	.20	.50
90 Mitch Richmond	.25	.60
91 Elton Brand RC	1.25	3.00
92 Steve Francis RC	1.25	3.00
93 Baron Davis RC	1.50	4.00
94 Lamar Odom RC	1.25	3.00
95 Jonathan Bender RC	.40	1.00
96 Wally Szczerbiak RC	1.25	3.00
97 Richard Hamilton RC	1.25	3.00
98 Andre Miller RC	1.25	3.00
99 Shawn Marion RC	1.25	3.00
100 Jason Terry RC	1.00	2.50
101 Trajan Langdon RC	.40	1.00
102 A.Radojevic RC	.40	1.00
103 Corey Maggette RC	1.25	3.00
104 William Avery RC	.40	1.00
105 Ron Artest RC	1.50	4.00
106 Adrian Griffin RC	.40	1.00
107 James Posey RC	.60	1.50
108 Quincy Lewis RC	.40	1.00
109 Dion Glover RC	.40	1.00
110 Jeff Foster RC	.50	1.25
111 Kenny Thomas RC	.40	1.00
112 Devean George RC	.60	1.50
113 Tim James RC	.40	1.00
114 Vonteego Cummings RC	.40	1.00
115 Jumaine Jones RC	.40	1.00
116 Scott Padgett RC	.40	1.00
117 Obinna Ekezie RC	.40	1.00
118 Ryan Robertson RC	.40	1.00
119 Chucky Atkins RC	.50	1.25
120 A.J. Bramlett RC	.40	1.00

2000-01 Black Diamond

COMP.SET w/o SP's (90)	8.00	20.00
COMMON CARD (1-90)	.08	.25
COMMON GEM (91-100)	1.25	3.00
COMMON GEM (101-110)	1.50	4.00
COMMON GEM (111-120)	1.50	4.00
COMMON JSY (121-126)	3.00	8.00
COMMON JSY (127-132)	4.00	10.00
1 Dikembe Mutombo	.25	.60
2 Alan Henderson	.20	.50
3 Jason Terry	.30	.75
4 Paul Pierce	.30	.75
5 Antoine Walker	.25	.60
6 Kenny Anderson	.25	.60
7 Jamal Mashburn	.25	.60
8 Derrick Coleman	.25	.60
9 Baron Davis	.30	.75
10 Elton Brand	.30	.75
11 Ron Artest	.30	.75
12 Ron Mercer	.20	.50
13 Lamond Murray	.20	.50
14 Andre Miller	.25	.60
15 Matt Harpring	.25	.60
16 Michael Finley	.30	.75
17 Dirk Nowitzki	.50	1.25
18 Steve Nash	.50	1.25
19 Antonio McDyess	.25	.60
20 Nick Van Exel	.25	.60
21 Raef LaFrentz	.20	.50
22 Jerry Stackhouse	.25	.60
23 Joe Smith	.20	.50
24 Chucky Atkins	.20	.50
25 Antawn Jamison	.30	.75
26 Larry Hughes	.25	.60
27 Chris Mills	.20	.50
28 Steve Francis	.30	.75
29 Hakeem Olajuwon	.40	1.00
30 Cuttino Mobley	.25	.60
31 Reggie Miller	.30	.75
32 Jalen Rose	.25	.60
33 Jermaine O'Neal	.30	.75
34 Austin Croshere	.20	.50
35 Lamar Odom	.30	.75
36 Corey Maggette	.25	.60
37 Jeff McInnis	.20	.50
38 Kobe Bryant	1.50	4.00
39 Shaquille O'Neal	.75	2.00
40 Ron Harper	.25	.60
41 Isaiah Rider	.25	.60
42 Eddie Jones	.25	.60
43 Tim Hardaway	.25	.60
44 Brian Grant	.20	.50
45 Glenn Robinson	.25	.60
46 Sam Cassell	.25	.60
47 Ray Allen	.30	.75
48 Kevin Garnett	.60	1.50
49 Terrell Brandon	.20	.50
50 Wally Szczerbiak	.25	.60
51 Stephon Marbury	.30	.75
52 Keith Van Horn	.25	.60
53 Kendall Gill	.20	.50
54 Latrell Sprewell	.25	.60
55 Allan Houston	.25	.60
56 Marcus Camby	.25	.60
57 Grant Hill	.30	.75
58 Tracy McGrady	.60	1.50
59 Darrell Armstrong	.20	.50
60 Allen Iverson	.60	1.50
61 Toni Kukoc	.25	.60

62 Theo Ratliff	.20	.50
63 Jason Kidd	.50	1.25
64 Shawn Marion	.30	.75
65 Anfernee Hardaway	.30	.75
66 Scottie Pippen	.50	1.25
67 Rasheed Wallace	.30	.75
68 Damon Stoudamire	.25	.60
69 Steve Smith	.25	.60
70 Chris Webber	.30	.75
71 Jason Williams	.25	.60
72 Peja Stojakovic	.25	.60
73 Tim Duncan	.60	1.50
74 David Robinson	.40	1.00
75 Derek Anderson	.25	.60
76 Gary Payton	.30	.75
77 Patrick Ewing	.40	1.00
78 Rashard Lewis	.30	.75
79 Vince Carter	.60	1.50
80 Mark Jackson	.25	.60
81 Antonio Davis	.20	.50
82 Karl Malone	.40	1.00
83 John Stockton	.40	1.00
84 Bryon Russell	.20	.50
85 Shareef Abdur-Rahim	.25	.60
86 Michael Dickerson	.20	.50
87 Mike Bibby	.25	.60
88 Mitch Richmond	.25	.60
89 Richard Hamilton	.25	.60
90 Juwan Howard	.25	.60
91 Eduardo Najera RC	1.25	3.00
92 Eddie House RC	1.25	3.00
93 Michael Redd RC	3.00	8.00
94 Ruben Wolkowyski RC	1.25	3.00
95 Dan Langhi RC	1.25	3.00
96 Mark Madsen RC	1.25	3.00
97 Speedy Claxton RC	1.25	3.00
98 Iakovos Tsakalidis RC	1.25	3.00
99 Dragan Tarlac RC	1.25	3.00
100 Donnell Harvey RC	1.25	3.00
101 Etan Thomas RC	1.50	4.00
102 Hedo Turkoglu RC	4.00	10.00
103 Mike Penberthy RC	1.50	4.00
104 Paul McPherson RC	1.50	4.00
105 Jason Collier RC	1.50	4.00
106 Hanno Mottola RC	1.50	4.00
107 A.J. Guyton RC	1.50	4.00
108 Daniel Santiago RC	4.00	10.00
109 Lavor Postell RC	1.50	4.00
110 Erick Barkley RC	1.50	4.00
111 Chris Porter RC	1.50	4.00
112 Mateen Cleaves RC	1.50	4.00
113 Marc Jackson RC	2.00	5.00
114 Joel Przybilla RC	1.50	4.00
115 Courtney Alexander RC	1.50	4.00
116 Khalid El-Amin RC	1.50	4.00
117 Keyon Dooling RC	1.50	4.00
118 Desmond Mason RC	2.00	5.00
119 Stephen Jackson RC	2.50	6.00
120 Morris Peterson RC	2.50	6.00
121 Jerome Moiso JSY RC	3.00	8.00
122 Jamal Crawford JSY RC	5.00	12.00
123 DeShawn Stevenson JSY RC	3.00	8.00
124 Quentin Richardson JSY RC	4.00	10.00
125 Marcus Fizer JSY RC	3.00	8.00
126 Mike Miller JSY RC	5.00	12.00
127 Jamaal Magloire JSY RC	4.00	10.00
128 Chris Mihm JSY RC	4.00	10.00
129 DerMarr Johnson JSY RC	4.00	10.00
130 Stromile Swift JSY RC	5.00	12.00
131 Darius Miles JSY RC	5.00	12.00
132 Kenyon Martin JSY RC	10.00	25.00

2003-04 Black Diamond

COMMON CARD (1-84)	.15	.40
COMMON CARD (85-117)	.25	.60
COMMON ROOKIE (118-126)	1.25	3.00
COMMON CARD (127-147)	.75	2.00
COMMON ROOKIE (148-168)	1.50	4.00
COMMON CARD (169-183)	1.50	4.00
COMMON ROOKIE (184-198)	4.00	10.00
KORVER AND KITTLES HAVE 2 CARDS		
1 Carlos Boozer	.30	.75
2 Dajuan Wagner	.20	.50
3 Steve Francis	.30	.75
4 Michael Finley	.30	.75
5 Jalen Rose	.25	.60
6 Kenyon Martin	.30	.75
7 Quentin Richardson	.25	.60
8 Antoine Walker	.30	.75
9 Drew Gooden	.20	.50
10 Mike Bibby	.25	.60
11 Zydrunas Ilgauskas	.25	.60
12 Dan Dickau	.20	.50
13 Steve Nash	.50	1.25
14 Eduardo Najera	.20	.50
15 Joe Smith	.20	.50
16 Pau Gasol	.30	.75
17 Anthony Mason	.20	.50
18 Lamar Odom	.30	.75
19 Sam Cassell	.25	.60
20 Marko Jaric	.20	.50
21 Marcus Fizer	.20	.50
22 Jay Williams	.20	.50
23 Jason Richardson	.30	.75
24 Richard Jefferson	.30	.75
25 Gerald Wallace	.30	.75
26 Reggie Evans	.20	.50
27 Jerome Williams	.20	.50
28 Grant Hill	.30	.75
29 Darrell Armstrong	.20	.50
30 Rasheed Wallace	.30	.75
31 Shane Battier	.25	.60
32 Richard Hamilton	.25	.60
33 Antonio Davis	.20	.50
34 Ray Allen	.20	.50
35 Terrell Brandon	.20	.50
36 Tim Thomas	.20	.50
37 Al Harrington	.25	.60
38 Brian Grant	.20	.50
39 Zeljko Rebraca	.20	.50
40 Kerry Kittles	.25	.60
41 Maurice Taylor	.20	.50
42 Jerry Stackhouse	.25	.60
43 Nikoloz Tskitishvili	.20	.50
44 Derrick Coleman	.25	.60
45 Raef LaFrentz	.20	.50
46 Dale Davis	.20	.50
47 Andrei Kirilenko	.30	.75
48 Melvin Ely	.20	.50
49 Speedy Claxton	.20	.50
50 Mike Miller	.25	.60
51 Scot Pollard	.20	.50
52 Popeye Jones	.20	.50
53 Wesley Person	.20	.50
54 Chris Wilcox	.20	.50
55 Dikembe Mutombo	.25	.60
56 Toni Kukoc	.25	.60
57 Eddie Griffin	.20	.50
58 Kedrick Brown	.20	.50
59 Eddie Jones	.25	.60
60 Jon Barry	.20	.50
61 Jonathan Bender	.20	.50
62 Larry Hughes	.25	.60
63 Rodney White	.20	.50
64 Eddy Curry	.25	.60
65 Theo Ratliff	.20	.50
66 Jamaal Tinsley	.25	.60
67 Zach Randolph	.30	.75
68 Alvin Williams	.20	.50
69 Derek Fisher	.25	.60
70 Vin Baker	.20	.50
71 Juan Dixon	.20	.50
72 Devean George	.20	.50
73 Damon Stoudamire	.25	.60
74 Joe Johnson	.30	.75
75 Jared Jeffries	.20	.50
76 Cuttino Mobley	.25	.60
77 Vladimir Radmanovic	.20	.50
78 Ron Mercer	.20	.50
79 Kenny Thomas	.20	.50
80 Nazr Mohammed	.20	.50
81 Donyell Marshall	.20	.50
82 Lorenzen Wright	.20	.50
83 Nick Van Exel	.25	.60
84 Jason Terry	.25	.60
85 Ben Wallace	.30	.75
86 Glenn Robinson	.30	.75
87 Gilbert Arenas	.40	1.00
88 Caron Butler	.30	.75
89 Marcus Camby	.30	.75
90 Jason Kidd	.60	1.50
91 Antawn Jamison	.40	1.00
92 Rashard Lewis	.40	1.00
93 Juwan Howard	.30	.75
94 Andre Miller	.30	.75
95 Hedo Turkoglu	.30	.75
96 Jason Williams	.30	.75
97 Chauncey Billups	.40	1.00
98 P.J. Brown	.25	.60
99 Tyson Chandler	.30	.75
100 Jamal Mashburn	.25	.60
101 Bonzi Wells	.25	.60
102 Brad Miller	.30	.75
103 Gordan Giricek	.25	.60
104 Nene	.30	.75
105 Mike Dunleavy	.30	.75
106 Kerry Kittles	.30	.75
107 Jamaal Magloire	.25	.60
108 Desmond Mason	.30	.75
109 Corey Maggette	.25	.60
110 Michael Olowokandi	.25	.60
111 Tayshaun Prince	.30	.75
112 Earl Boykins	.25	.60
113 Allan Houston	.30	.75
114 Morris Peterson	.30	.75
115 Ricky Davis	.30	.75
116 Keith Van Horn	.30	.75
117 Shareef Abdur-Rahim	.30	.75
118 Willie Green RC	1.25	3.00
119 Kyle Korver RC	1.50	4.00
120 Brandon Hunter RC	1.25	3.00
121 Keith Bogans RC	1.25	3.00
122 Maurice Williams RC	2.00	5.00
123 James Lang RC	1.25	3.00
124 Zaur Pachulia RC	1.50	4.00
125 Slavko Vranes RC	1.25	3.00
126 Theron Smith RC	1.25	3.00
127 Paul Pierce	.75	2.00
128 Alonzo Mourning	.75	2.00
129 Elton Brand	.75	2.00
130 Manu Ginobili	.75	2.00
131 Peja Stojakovic	.60	1.50
132 Latrell Sprewell	.60	1.50
133 Baron Davis	.75	2.00
134 Stephon Marbury	.75	2.00
135 Darius Miles	.60	1.50
136 Antonio McDyess	.60	1.50
137 Jermaine O'Neal	.75	2.00
138 Scottie Pippen	1.25	3.00
139 Wally Szczerbiak	.60	1.50
140 Chris Webber	.75	2.00
141 Reggie Miller	.75	2.00
142 Tony Parker	.75	2.00
143 Karl Malone	.75	2.00
144 David Robinson	1.25	3.00
145 Matt Harpring	.60	1.50
146 Shawn Marion	.75	2.00
147 Tim Duncan	1.50	4.00
148 Dwyane Wade RC	4.00	10.00
149 Chris Kaman RC	2.00	5.00
150 Chris Bosh RC	2.50	6.00
151 Mickael Pietrus RC	2.00	5.00
152 Boris Diaw RC	2.00	5.00
153 Marcus Banks RC	1.50	4.00
154 Troy Bell RC	1.50	4.00
155 Zarko Cabarkapa RC	1.50	4.00
156 David West RC	2.00	5.00
157 Zoran Planinic RC	1.50	4.00
158 Aleksandar Pavlovic RC	2.00	5.00
159 Jerome Beasley RC	1.50	4.00
160 Kyle Korver	2.00	5.00
161 Travis Hansen RC	1.50	4.00
162 Steve Blake RC	2.00	5.00
163 Leandro Barbosa RC	2.00	5.00
164 Kendrick Perkins RC	2.50	6.00
165 Kirk Penney RC	1.50	4.00
166 Maciej Lampe RC	1.50	4.00
167 Jason Kapono RC	2.00	5.00
168 Luke Walton RC	2.00	5.00
169 Gary Payton	1.50	4.00
170 Wilt Chamberlain	3.00	8.00
171 Tracy McGrady	3.00	8.00
172 Amare Stoudemire	3.00	8.00
173 Vince Carter	3.00	8.00

❑ 174 Shaquille O'Neal	4.00	10.00
❑ 175 Larry Bird	5.00	12.00
❑ 176 Julius Erving	3.00	8.00
❑ 177 Magic Johnson	3.00	8.00
❑ 178 Dirk Nowitzki	2.50	6.00
❑ 179 Yao Ming	3.00	8.00
❑ 180 Allen Iverson	3.00	8.00
❑ 181 Kevin Garnett	3.00	8.00
❑ 182 Kobe Bryant	8.00	20.00
❑ 183 Michael Jordan	10.00	25.00
❑ 184 LeBron James RC	40.00	100.00
❑ 185 Darko Milicic RC	4.00	10.00
❑ 186 Carmelo Anthony RC	8.00	20.00
❑ 187 T.J. Ford RC	4.00	10.00
❑ 188 Mike Sweetney RC	3.00	8.00
❑ 189 Kirk Hinrich RC	4.00	10.00
❑ 190 Nick Collison RC	3.00	8.00
❑ 191 Travis Outlaw RC	4.00	10.00
❑ 192 Jarvis Hayes RC	3.00	8.00
❑ 193 Luke Ridnour RC	4.00	10.00
❑ 194 Reece Gaines RC	3.00	8.00
❑ 195 Ndudi Ebi RC	3.00	8.00
❑ 196 Dahntay Jones RC	3.00	8.00
❑ 197 Brian Cook RC	3.00	8.00
❑ 198 Josh Howard RC	4.00	10.00

2004-05 Black Diamond

❑ COMP.SET w/o SP's (84)	8.00	20.00
❑ COMMON SINGLE (1-84)	.20	.50
❑ COMMON DOUBLE (85-126)	.30	.75
❑ COMMON TRIPLE (127-147)	.75	2.00
❑ COMMON QUAD (148-162)	2.50	6.00
❑ COMMON RC TRIPLE (163-183)	2.50	6.00
❑ COMMON RC QUAD (184-198)	3.00	8.00
❑ 1 Tony Delk	.20	.50
❑ 2 Boris Diaw	.25	.60
❑ 3 Chris Crawford	.20	.50
❑ 4 Ricky Davis	.25	.60
❑ 5 Jiri Welsch	.20	.50
❑ 6 Raef LaFrentz	.20	.50
❑ 7 Jason Kapono	.20	.50
❑ 8 Brevin Knight	.20	.50
❑ 9 Bernard Robinson RC	1.25	3.00
❑ 10 Jahidi White	.20	.50
❑ 11 Tyson Chandler	.25	.60
❑ 12 Antonio Davis	.20	.50
❑ 13 Andres Nocioni RC	1.50	4.00
❑ 14 Dajuan Wagner	.20	.50
❑ 15 Zydrunas Ilgauskas	.25	.60
❑ 16 Jeff McInnis	.20	.50
❑ 17 Josh Howard	.30	.75
❑ 18 Marquis Daniels	.20	.50
❑ 19 Jason Terry	.25	.60
❑ 20 Andre Miller	.25	.60
❑ 21 Earl Boykins	.20	.50
❑ 22 Carlos Delfino	.30	.75
❑ 23 Ben Wallace	.25	.60
❑ 24 Tayshaun Prince	.25	.60
❑ 25 Mickael Pietrus	.25	.60
❑ 26 Mike Dunleavy	.25	.60
❑ 27 Speedy Claxton	.20	.50
❑ 28 Jim Jackson	.20	.50
❑ 29 Juwan Howard	.25	.60
❑ 30 Maurice Taylor	.20	.50
❑ 31 Tyronn Lue	.20	.50
❑ 32 Jamaal Tinsley	.25	.60
❑ 33 Stephen Jackson	.25	.60
❑ 34 Fred Jones	.20	.50
❑ 35 Kerry Kittles	.25	.60
❑ 36 Marko Jaric	.20	.50
❑ 37 Chris Kaman	.25	.60
❑ 38 Caron Butler	.25	.60
❑ 39 Kareem Rush	.20	.50
❑ 40 Mike Miller	.25	.60
❑ 41 James Posey	.20	.50
❑ 42 Stromile Swift	.20	.50
❑ 43 Eddie Jones	.25	.60
❑ 44 Udonis Haslem	.25	.60
❑ 45 Matt Freije RC	1.25	3.00
❑ 46 T.J. Ford	.25	.60
❑ 47 Toni Kukoc	.25	.60
❑ 48 Joe Smith	.20	.50
❑ 49 Michael Olowokandi	.20	.50
❑ 50 Wally Szczerbiak	.25	.60
❑ 51 Troy Hudson	.20	.50
❑ 52 Aaron Williams	.20	.50
❑ 53 Alonzo Mourning	.30	.75
❑ 54 Nenad Krstic RC	1.50	4.00
❑ 55 Jamal Mashburn	.25	.60
❑ 56 David Wesley	.20	.50
❑ 57 Tim Pickett RC	1.25	3.00
❑ 58 Trevor Ariza RC	1.50	4.00
❑ 59 Tim Thomas	.20	.50
❑ 60 Grant Hill	.30	.75
❑ 61 Hedo Turkoglu	.25	.60
❑ 62 Kelvin Cato	.20	.50
❑ 63 Kenny Thomas	.20	.50
❑ 64 Aaron McKie	.20	.50
❑ 65 Joe Johnson	.30	.75
❑ 66 Quentin Richardson	.25	.60
❑ 67 Damon Stoudamire	.25	.60
❑ 68 Derek Anderson	.25	.60
❑ 69 Nick Van Exel	.25	.60
❑ 70 Doug Christie	.20	.50
❑ 71 Bobby Jackson	.20	.50
❑ 72 Malik Rose	.20	.50
❑ 73 Rasho Nesterovic	.20	.50
❑ 74 Romain Sato RC	1.25	3.00
❑ 75 Ronald Murray	.20	.50
❑ 76 Luke Ridnour	.20	.50
❑ 77 Pape Sow RC	1.25	3.00
❑ 78 Rafer Alston	.20	.50
❑ 79 Morris Peterson	.25	.60
❑ 80 Matt Harpring	.25	.60
❑ 81 Mehmet Okur	.25	.60
❑ 82 Larry Hughes	.25	.60
❑ 83 Jarvis Hayes	.20	.50
❑ 84 Kwame Brown	.20	.50
❑ 85 Antoine Walker	.50	1.25
❑ 86 Al Harrington	.40	1.00
❑ 87 Gary Payton	.50	1.25
❑ 88 Gerald Wallace	.50	1.25
❑ 89 Eddy Curry	.40	1.00
❑ 90 Kirk Hinrich	.40	1.00
❑ 91 Drew Gooden	.30	.75
❑ 92 Michael Finley	.50	1.25
❑ 93 Jerry Stackhouse	.40	1.00
❑ 94 Kenyon Martin	.50	1.25
❑ 95 Nene	.40	1.00
❑ 96 Chauncey Billups	.50	1.25
❑ 97 Richard Hamilton	.40	1.00
❑ 98 Derek Fisher	.40	1.00
❑ 99 Reggie Miller	.50	1.25
❑ 100 Ron Artest	.40	1.00
❑ 101 Corey Maggette	.40	1.00
❑ 102 Lamar Odom	.50	1.25
❑ 103 Karl Malone	.50	1.25
❑ 104 Jason Williams	.40	1.00
❑ 105 Bonzi Wells	.30	.75
❑ 106 Desmond Mason	.40	1.00
❑ 107 Sam Cassell	.40	1.00
❑ 108 Jamaal Magloire	.30	.75
❑ 109 Jamal Crawford	.40	1.00
❑ 110 Allan Houston	.40	1.00
❑ 111 Cuttino Mobley	.40	1.00
❑ 112 Glenn Robinson	.40	1.00
❑ 113 Shawn Marion	.50	1.25
❑ 114 Darius Miles	.40	1.00
❑ 115 Zach Randolph	.50	1.25
❑ 116 Chris Webber	.50	1.25
❑ 117 Mike Bibby	.40	1.00
❑ 118 Brad Miller	.40	1.00
❑ 119 Manu Ginobili	.50	1.25
❑ 120 Rashard Lewis	.50	1.25
❑ 121 Jalen Rose	.40	1.00
❑ 122 Chris Bosh	.50	1.25
❑ 123 Carlos Boozer	.50	1.25
❑ 124 Carlos Arroyo	.50	1.25
❑ 125 Gilbert Arenas	.50	1.25
❑ 126 Antawn Jamison	.50	1.25
❑ 127 Paul Pierce	1.00	2.50
❑ 128 Dirk Nowitzki	1.50	4.00
❑ 129 Rasheed Wallace	1.00	2.50
❑ 130 Jason Richardson	1.00	2.50
❑ 131 Jermaine O'Neal	1.00	2.50
❑ 132 Elton Brand	1.00	2.50
❑ 133 Pau Gasol	1.00	2.50
❑ 134 Dwyane Wade	3.00	8.00
❑ 135 Michael Redd	1.00	2.50
❑ 136 Latrell Sprewell	.75	2.00
❑ 137 Richard Jefferson	1.00	2.50
❑ 138 Baron Davis	1.00	2.50
❑ 139 Stephon Marbury	1.00	2.50
❑ 140 Steve Francis	1.00	2.50
❑ 141 Steve Nash	1.50	4.00
❑ 142 Shareef Abdur-Rahim	.75	2.00
❑ 143 Peja Stojakovic	.75	2.00
❑ 144 Tony Parker	1.00	2.50
❑ 145 Ray Allen	1.00	2.50
❑ 146 Vince Carter	2.00	5.00
❑ 147 Andrei Kirilenko	1.00	2.50
❑ 148 Larry Bird	8.00	20.00
❑ 149 Michael Jordan	10.00	25.00
❑ 150 LeBron James	10.00	25.00
❑ 151 Carmelo Anthony	5.00	12.00
❑ 152 Tracy McGrady	3.00	8.00
❑ 153 Yao Ming	4.00	10.00
❑ 154 Kobe Bryant	8.00	20.00
❑ 155 Magic Johnson	5.00	12.00
❑ 156 Shaquille O'Neal	4.00	10.00
❑ 157 Kevin Garnett	3.00	8.00
❑ 158 Jason Kidd	2.50	6.00
❑ 159 Allen Iverson	3.00	8.00
❑ 160 Julius Erving	4.00	10.00
❑ 161 Amare Stoudemire	3.00	8.00
❑ 162 Tim Duncan	3.00	8.00
❑ 163 Andris Biedrins RC	4.00	10.00
❑ 164 Robert Swift RC	2.50	6.00
❑ 165 Al Jefferson RC	5.00	12.00
❑ 166 Kirk Snyder RC	2.50	6.00
❑ 167 Dorell Wright RC	3.00	8.00
❑ 168 Pavel Podkolzine RC	2.50	6.00
❑ 169 Viktor Khryapa RC	2.50	6.00
❑ 170 Delonte West RC	4.00	10.00
❑ 171 Tony Allen RC	3.00	8.00
❑ 172 Kevin Martin RC	3.00	8.00
❑ 173 Sasha Vujacic RC	2.50	6.00
❑ 174 Beno Udrih RC	3.00	8.00
❑ 175 David Harrison RC	2.50	6.00
❑ 176 Anderson Varejao RC	3.00	8.00
❑ 177 Jackson Vroman RC	2.50	6.00
❑ 178 Peter John Ramos RC	2.50	6.00
❑ 179 Lionel Chalmers RC	2.50	6.00
❑ 180 Andre Emmett RC	2.50	6.00
❑ 181 Yuta Tabuse RC	5.00	12.00
❑ 182 Trevor Ariza RC	3.00	8.00
❑ 183 Chris Duhon RC	4.00	10.00
❑ 184 Dwight Howard RC	10.00	25.00
❑ 185 Emeka Okafor RC	6.00	15.00
❑ 186 Ben Gordon RC	4.00	10.00
❑ 187 Shaun Livingston RC	3.00	8.00
❑ 188 Devin Harris RC	6.00	15.00
❑ 189 Josh Childress RC	3.00	8.00
❑ 190 Luol Deng RC	4.00	10.00
❑ 191 Andre Iguodala RC	8.00	20.00
❑ 192 Luke Jackson RC	3.00	8.00
❑ 193 Sebastian Telfair RC	3.00	8.00
❑ 194 Kris Humphries RC	5.00	12.00
❑ 195 Josh Smith RC	8.00	20.00
❑ 196 J.R. Smith RC	6.00	15.00
❑ 197 Jameer Nelson RC	4.00	10.00
❑ 198 Rafael Araujo RC	3.00	8.00

1948 Bowman

❑ COMPLETE SET (72)	4000.00	6000.00
❑ COMMON CARD (1-36)	40.00	60.00
❑ COMMON CARD (37-72)	60.00	90.00
❑ 1 Ernie Calverley RC	75.00	150.00
❑ 2 Ralph Hamilton	40.00	60.00
❑ 3 Gale Bishop	40.00	60.00
❑ 4 Fred Lewis RC	50.00	75.00
❑ 5 Basketball Play	30.00	50.00

❑ 6 Bob Feerick RC	50.00	75.00
❑ 7 John Logan	40.00	60.00
❑ 8 Mel Riebe	40.00	60.00
❑ 9 Andy Phillip RC	50.00	100.00
❑ 10 Bob Davies RC	50.00	100.00
❑ 11 Basketball Play	30.00	50.00
❑ 12 Kenny Sailors RC	50.00	75.00
❑ 13 Paul Armstrong	40.00	60.00
❑ 14 Howard Dallmar RC	50.00	75.00
❑ 15 Bruce Hale RC	50.00	75.00
❑ 16 Sid Hertzberg	50.00	75.00
❑ 17 Basketball Play	30.00	50.00
❑ 18 Red Rocha	40.00	60.00
❑ 19 Eddie Ehlers	40.00	60.00
❑ 20 Ellis(Gene) Vance	40.00	60.00
❑ 21 Fuzzy Levane RC	50.00	75.00
❑ 22 Earl Shannon	40.00	60.00
❑ 23 Basketball Play	30.00	50.00
❑ 24 Leo(Crystal) Klier	40.00	60.00
❑ 25 George Senesky	40.00	60.00
❑ 26 Price Brookfield	40.00	60.00
❑ 27 John Norlander	40.00	60.00
❑ 28 Don Putman	40.00	60.00
❑ 29 Basketball Play	30.00	50.00
❑ 30 Jack Garfinkel	40.00	60.00
❑ 31 Chuck Gilmur	40.00	60.00
❑ 32 Red Holzman RC	125.00	225.00
❑ 33 Jack Smiley	40.00	60.00
❑ 34 Joe Fulks RC	90.00	150.00
❑ 35 Basketball Play	30.00	50.00
❑ 36 Hal Tidrick	40.00	60.00
❑ 37 Don(Swede) Carlson	60.00	90.00
❑ 38 Buddy Jeanette CO RC	80.00	135.00
❑ 39 Ray Kuka	60.00	90.00
❑ 40 Stan Miasek	60.00	90.00
❑ 41 Basketball Play	50.00	75.00
❑ 42 George Nostrand	60.00	90.00
❑ 43 Chuck Halbert RC	75.00	125.00
❑ 44 Arnie Johnson	60.00	90.00
❑ 45 Bob Doll	60.00	90.00
❑ 46 Bones McKinney RC	80.00	135.00
❑ 47 Basketball Play	50.00	75.00
❑ 48 Ed Sadowski	75.00	125.00
❑ 49 Bob Kinney	60.00	90.00
❑ 50 Charles(Hawk) Black	60.00	90.00
❑ 51 Jack Dwan	50.00	75.00
❑ 52 Connie Simmons RC	75.00	125.00
❑ 53 Basketball Play	50.00	75.00
❑ 54 Bud Palmer RC	100.00	150.00
❑ 55 Max Zaslofsky RC	125.00	200.00
❑ 56 Lee Roy Robbins	60.00	90.00
❑ 57 Arthur Spector	60.00	90.00
❑ 58 Arnie Risen RC	90.00	150.00
❑ 59 Basketball Play	50.00	75.00
❑ 60 Ariel Maughan	60.00	90.00
❑ 61 Dick O'Keefe	60.00	90.00
❑ 62 Herman Schaefer	60.00	90.00
❑ 63 John Mahnken	60.00	90.00
❑ 64 Tommy Byrnes	60.00	90.00
❑ 65 Basketball Play	50.00	75.00
❑ 66 Jim Pollard RC	125.00	250.00
❑ 67 Lee Mogus	60.00	90.00
❑ 68 Lee Knorek	60.00	90.00
❑ 69 George Mikan RC	1500.00	2250.00
❑ 70 Walter Budko	60.00	90.00
❑ 71 Basketball Play	50.00	75.00
❑ 72 Carl Braun RC	200.00	400.00

2003-04 Bowman

❑ COMP.SET w/o RC's (110)	15.00	40.00
❑ COMMON CARD (1-110)	.08	.20
❑ COMMON ROOKIE (111-146)	1.50	4.00
❑ COMMON AU RC (148-156)	15.00	40.00
❑ CARD 147 NOT RELEASED		
❑ 1 Yao Ming	.60	1.50
❑ 2 Glenn Robinson	.25	.60
❑ 3 Antoine Walker	.30	.75
❑ 4 Jalen Rose	.25	.60
❑ 5 Ricky Davis	.25	.60
❑ 6 Juwan Howard	.25	.60
❑ 7 Kwame Brown	.20	.50
❑ 8 Mike Bibby	.25	.60
❑ 9 Wally Szczerbiak	.25	.60
❑ 10 Allen Iverson	.60	1.50
❑ 11 Shareef Abdur-Rahim	.25	.60
❑ 12 Jamal Mashburn	.20	.50
❑ 13 Stephon Marbury	.30	.75
❑ 14 Desmond Mason	.25	.60
❑ 15 Gordan Giricek	.20	.50
❑ 16 Caron Butler	.25	.60
❑ 17 Jermaine O'Neal	.30	.75
❑ 18 Kenyon Martin	.30	.75
❑ 19 Andrei Kirilenko	.30	.75
❑ 20 Dirk Nowitzki	.50	1.25
❑ 21 Richard Hamilton	.25	.60
❑ 22 Troy Murphy	.30	.75
❑ 23 Shawn Marion	.30	.75
❑ 24 Allan Houston	.25	.60
❑ 25 Keith Van Horn	.25	.60
❑ 26 Brian Grant	.20	.50
❑ 27 Mike Miller	.25	.60
❑ 28 Chris Webber	.30	.75
❑ 29 Brent Barry	.20	.50
❑ 30 Elton Brand	.30	.75
❑ 31 Juan Dixon	.20	.50
❑ 32 Karl Malone	.30	.75
❑ 33 Darrell Armstrong	.20	.50
❑ 34 Rasheed Wallace	.30	.75
❑ 35 Michael Redd	.30	.75
❑ 36 Rashard Lewis	.30	.75
❑ 37 Ron Artest	.25	.60
❑ 38 P.J. Brown	.20	.50
❑ 39 Eddie Griffin	.20	.50
❑ 40 Tim Duncan	.60	1.50
❑ 41 Kurt Thomas	.20	.50
❑ 42 Raef Lafrentz	.20	.50
❑ 43 Ben Wallace	.25	.60
❑ 44 Lamar Odom	.30	.75
❑ 45 Vince Carter	.60	1.50
❑ 46 Derek Anderson	.25	.60
❑ 47 Stromile Swift	.20	.50
❑ 48 Bobby Jackson	.20	.50
❑ 49 Richard Jefferson	.30	.75
❑ 50 Shaquille O'Neal	.75	2.00
❑ 51 Calbert Cheaney	.20	.50
❑ 52 Troy Hudson	.20	.50
❑ 53 Ray Allen	.20	.50
❑ 54 Howard Eisley	.20	.50
❑ 55 Alonzo Mourning	.30	.75
❑ 56 Sam Cassell	.25	.60
❑ 57 Derrick Coleman	.25	.60
❑ 58 Andre Miller	.25	.60
❑ 59 Antawn Jamison	.30	.75
❑ 60 Kevin Garnett	.60	1.50
❑ 61 Steve Francis	.30	.75
❑ 62 Tyson Chandler	.25	.60
❑ 63 Drew Gooden	.20	.50
❑ 64 Scottie Pippen	.50	1.25
❑ 65 Pau Gasol	.30	.75
❑ 66 Steve Nash	.50	1.25
❑ 67 DaJuan Wagner	.20	.50
❑ 68 Jason Terry	.25	.60
❑ 69 Reggie Miller	.30	.75
❑ 70 Tracy McGrady	.60	1.50
❑ 71 Nene Hilario	.25	.60
❑ 72 Morris Peterson	.25	.60
❑ 73 Peja Stojakovic	.25	.60
❑ 74 Eddie Jones	.25	.60
❑ 75 Tony Parker	.30	.75
❑ 76 Corliss Williamson	.20	.50
❑ 77 Vladimir Radmanovic	.20	.50
❑ 78 Amare Stoudemire	.60	1.50
❑ 79 Tony Delk	.20	.50
❑ 80 Jason Kidd	.50	1.25
❑ 81 Gary Payton	.30	.75
❑ 82 Corey Maggette	.20	.50
❑ 83 Darius Miles	.25	.60
❑ 84 Cuttino Mobley	.25	.60
❑ 85 Eric Snow	.20	.50
❑ 86 Matt Harpring	.25	.60
❑ 87 Manu Ginobili	.30	.75
❑ 88 Latrell Sprewell	.25	.60
❑ 89 Alvin Williams	.20	.50
❑ 90 Paul Pierce	.30	.75
❑ 91 Anfernee Hardaway	.30	.75
❑ 92 Gilbert Arenas	.30	.75
❑ 93 Jerry Stackhouse	.25	.60
❑ 94 Tim Thomas	.20	.50
❑ 95 Nikoloz Tskitishvili	.20	.50
❑ 96 Doug Christie	.20	.50
❑ 97 Zydrunas Ilgauskas	.25	.60
❑ 98 Jamaal Tinsley	.25	.60
❑ 99 Theo Ratliff	.20	.50
❑ 100 Kobe Bryant	1.50	4.00
❑ 101 Chauncey Billups	.30	.75
❑ 102 Michael Finley	.30	.75
❑ 103 Jason Williams	.25	.60
❑ 104 Bonzi Wells	.20	.50
❑ 105 Voshon Lenard	.20	.50
❑ 106 Jason Richardson	.30	.75
❑ 107 Baron Davis	.30	.75
❑ 108 Radoslav Nesterovic	.20	.50
❑ 109 Eddy Curry	.25	.60
❑ 110 Michael Olowokandi	.20	.50
❑ 111 Josh Howard RC	2.00	5.00
❑ 112 Mario Austin RC	1.50	4.00
❑ 113 Rick Rickert RC	1.50	4.00
❑ 114 Tommy Smith RC	1.50	4.00
❑ 115 Dahntay Jones RC	1.50	4.00
❑ 116 Ndudi Ebi RC	1.50	4.00
❑ 117 Maurice Williams RC	2.50	6.00
❑ 118 Kendrick Perkins RC	2.50	6.00
❑ 119 Steve Blake RC	2.00	5.00
❑ 120 David West RC	2.00	5.00
❑ 121 Chris Kaman RC	2.00	5.00
❑ 122 Keith Bogans RC	1.50	4.00
❑ 123 LeBron James RC	20.00	50.00
❑ 124 Devin Brown RC	1.50	4.00
❑ 125 Jason Kapono RC	2.00	5.00
❑ 126 Zoran Planinic RC	1.50	4.00
❑ 127 Zaur Pachulia RC	2.00	5.00
❑ 128 Malick Badiane RC	1.50	4.00
❑ 129 Kyle Korver RC	2.00	5.00
❑ 130 Darko Milicic RC	2.00	5.00
❑ 131 Troy Bell RC	1.50	4.00
❑ 132 Luke Walton RC	2.00	5.00
❑ 133 Mike Sweetney RC	1.50	4.00
❑ 134 Jarvis Hayes RC	1.50	4.00
❑ 135 Leandro Barbosa RC	2.00	5.00
❑ 136 Carlos Delfino RC	2.00	5.00
❑ 137 Sofoklis Schortsanitis RC	1.50	4.00
❑ 138 Slavko Vranes RC	1.50	4.00
❑ 139 Travis Hansen RC	1.50	4.00
❑ 140 Carmelo Anthony RC	4.00	10.00
❑ 141 Reece Gaines RC	1.50	4.00
❑ 142 Maciej Lampe RC	1.50	4.00
❑ 143 Travis Outlaw RC	2.00	5.00
❑ 144 Jerome Beasley RC	1.50	4.00
❑ 145 Mickael Pietrus RC	2.00	5.00
❑ 146 Brian Cook RC	1.50	4.00
❑ 148 Kirk Hinrich AU RC	25.00	50.00
❑ 148B K.Hinrich Scribble AU RC		
❑ 149 Dwyane Wade AU RC	10.00	100.00
❑ 150 Marcus Banks AU RC	10.00	25.00
❑ 151 Nick Collison AU RC	10.00	25.00
❑ 152 Boris Diaw AU RC	10.00	25.00
❑ 153 Chris Bosh AU RC	15.00	30.00
❑ 154 T.J. Ford AU RC	8.00	20.00
❑ 155 Luke Ridnour AU RC	10.00	25.00
❑ 156 A.Pavlovic AU RC	12.50	30.00
❑ 157 Z.Cabarkapa AU RC	10.00	25.00

2004-05 Bowman

❑ COMP.SET w/o RC's (110)	15.00	40.00
❑ COMMON CARD (1-110)	.20	.50
❑ COMMON ROOKIE (111-146)	1.00	2.50
❑ COMMON AU RC (147-156)	5.00	12.00
❑ 1 Yao Ming	.75	2.00
❑ 2 Eddy Curry	.25	.60
❑ 3 Stephon Marbury	.30	.75
❑ 4 Chris Webber	.30	.75

❑ 5 Jason Kidd	.50	1.25
❑ 6 Cuttino Mobley	.25	.60
❑ 7 Jermaine O'Neal	.30	.75
❑ 8 Kobe Bryant	1.50	4.00
❑ 9 Tony Parker	.30	.75
❑ 10 Gary Payton	.30	.75
❑ 11 T.J. Ford	.25	.60
❑ 12 Tim Duncan	.60	1.50
❑ 13 Glenn Robinson	.25	.60
❑ 14 Jason Richardson	.30	.75
❑ 15 Carmelo Anthony	1.00	2.50
❑ 16 Pau Gasol	.30	.75
❑ 17 Kirk Hinrich	.25	.60
❑ 18 Kenyon Martin	.30	.75
❑ 19 Jamal Crawford	.25	.60
❑ 20 Elton Brand	.30	.75
❑ 21 Kevin Garnett	.60	1.50
❑ 22 Michael Redd	.30	.75
❑ 23 LeBron James	2.00	5.00
❑ 24 Andre Miller	.25	.60
❑ 25 Peja Stojakovic	.25	.60
❑ 26 Jarvis Hayes	.20	.50
❑ 27 David Wesley	.20	.50
❑ 28 Jason Kapono	.20	.50
❑ 29 Corey Maggette	.25	.60
❑ 30 Rasheed Wallace	.30	.75
❑ 31 Nene	.25	.60
❑ 32 Amare Stoudemire	.60	1.50
❑ 33 Allen Iverson	.60	1.50
❑ 34 Shaquille O'Neal	.75	2.00
❑ 35 Mike Dunleavy	.25	.60
❑ 36 Steve Nash	.50	1.25
❑ 37 Brad Miller	.25	.60
❑ 38 Chris Bosh	.30	.75
❑ 39 Boris Diaw	.25	.60
❑ 40 Steve Francis	.30	.75
❑ 41 Dirk Nowitzki	.50	1.25
❑ 42 Jason Williams	.25	.60
❑ 43 Gilbert Arenas	.30	.75
❑ 44 Keith Van Horn	.25	.60
❑ 45 Jamal Mashburn	.25	.60
❑ 46 Derek Fisher	.25	.60
❑ 47 Andrei Kirilenko	.30	.75
❑ 48 Ricky Davis	.25	.60
❑ 49 Gerald Wallace	.30	.75
❑ 50 Tracy McGrady	.60	1.50
❑ 51 Zach Randolph	.30	.75
❑ 52 Rafer Alston	.20	.50
❑ 53 Bobby Jackson	.20	.50
❑ 54 Desmond Mason	.25	.60
❑ 55 Tim Thomas	.20	.50
❑ 56 Jamaal Tinsley	.25	.60
❑ 57 Kwame Brown	.20	.50
❑ 58 Chauncey Billups	.30	.75
❑ 59 Brandon Hunter	.20	.50
❑ 60 Reggie Miller	.30	.75
❑ 61 Samuel Dalembert	.20	.50
❑ 62 James Posey	.20	.50
❑ 63 Erick Dampier	.20	.50
❑ 64 Carlos Arroyo	.30	.75
❑ 65 Reece Gaines	.20	.50
❑ 66 Darko Milicic	.20	.50
❑ 67 Sam Cassell	.25	.60
❑ 68 Dwyane Wade	1.00	2.50
❑ 69 Allan Houston	.25	.60
❑ 70 Ray Allen	.30	.75
❑ 71 Tyson Chandler	.25	.60
❑ 72 Bonzi Wells	.20	.50
❑ 73 Jalen Rose	.25	.60
❑ 74 Marquis Daniels	.20	.50
❑ 75 Zydrunas Ilgauskas	.25	.60
❑ 76 Tayshaun Prince	.25	.60
❑ 77 Lamar Odom	.30	.75
❑ 78 Luke Ridnour	.20	.50
❑ 79 Joe Johnson	.30	.75
❑ 80 Vince Carter	.60	1.50
❑ 81 Antoine Walker	.30	.75
❑ 82 Shareef Abdur-Rahim	.25	.60
❑ 83 Richard Jefferson	.30	.75
❑ 84 Maurice Taylor	.20	.50
❑ 85 Chris Kaman	.25	.60
❑ 86 Marcus Banks	.20	.50
❑ 87 Mike Bibby	.25	.60
❑ 88 Latrell Sprewell	.25	.60
❑ 89 Rashard Lewis	.30	.75
❑ 90 Baron Davis	.30	.75
❑ 91 Caron Butler	.25	.60
❑ 92 Michael Finley	.30	.75
❑ 93 Mike Miller	.25	.60
❑ 94 Al Harrington	.25	.60
❑ 95 Quentin Richardson	.25	.60
❑ 96 Jamaal Magloire	.20	.50
❑ 97 Darius Miles	.25	.60
❑ 98 Jeff Foster	.20	.50
❑ 99 Karl Malone	.30	.75
❑ 100 Shawn Marion	.30	.75
❑ 101 Antawn Jamison	.30	.75
❑ 102 Manu Ginobili	.30	.75
❑ 103 Ben Wallace	.25	.60
❑ 104 Paul Pierce	.30	.75
❑ 105 Mike Sweetney	.20	.50
❑ 106 Ron Artest	.25	.60
❑ 107 Michael Olowokandi	.20	.50
❑ 108 Jason Terry	.25	.60
❑ 109 Gordan Giricek	.20	.50
❑ 110 Carlos Boozer	.30	.75
❑ 111 Romain Sato RC	1.00	2.50
❑ 112 Chris Duhon RC	1.50	4.00
❑ 113 Ben Gordon RC	1.25	3.00
❑ 114 Matt Freije RC	1.00	2.50
❑ 115 Al Jefferson RC	2.00	5.00
❑ 116 Beno Udrih RC	1.25	3.00
❑ 117 Kirk Snyder RC	1.00	2.50
❑ 118 Anderson Varejao RC	1.25	3.00
❑ 119 Devin Harris RC	2.00	5.00
❑ 120 Tony Allen RC	1.25	3.00
❑ 121 Ha Seung-Jin RC	1.00	2.50
❑ 122 J.R. Smith RC	2.00	5.00
❑ 123 Blake Stepp RC	1.00	2.50
❑ 124 Jameer Nelson RC	1.25	3.00
❑ 125 Kris Humphries RC	1.50	4.00
❑ 126 Josh Childress RC	1.00	2.50
❑ 127 Tim Pickett RC	1.00	2.50
❑ 128 Delonte West RC	1.50	4.00
❑ 129 Dwight Howard RC	3.00	8.00
❑ 130 Luke Jackson RC	1.00	2.50
❑ 131 Rickey Paulding RC	1.00	2.50
❑ 132 Andre Emmett RC	1.00	2.50
❑ 133 Josh Smith RC	2.50	6.00
❑ 134 Antonio Burks RC	1.00	2.50
❑ 135 Ricky Minard RC	1.00	2.50
❑ 136 Lionel Chalmers RC	1.00	2.50
❑ 137 Shaun Livingston RC	1.00	2.50
❑ 138 Trevor Ariza RC	1.25	3.00
❑ 139 Sergei Lishouk RC	1.00	2.50
❑ 140 Pape Sow RC	1.00	2.50
❑ 141 Rashad Wright RC	1.00	2.50
❑ 142 Jackson Vroman RC	1.00	2.50
❑ 143 Luis Flores RC	1.00	2.50
❑ 144 Royal Ivey RC	1.00	2.50
❑ 145 Kevin Martin RC	1.25	3.00
❑ 146 Andre Iguodala RC	2.50	6.00
❑ 147 Andris Biedrins AU RC	8.00	20.00
❑ 148 Pavel Podkolzine AU RC	5.00	12.00
❑ 149 Luol Deng AU RC	6.00	15.00
❑ 150 Robert Swift AU RC	5.00	12.00
❑ 151 Sebastian Telfair AU RC	5.00	12.00
❑ 152 Emeka Okafor AU RC	10.00	25.00
❑ 153 Dorell Wright AU RC	6.00	15.00
❑ 154 Sasha Vujacic AU RC	5.00	12.00
❑ 155 Rafael Araujo AU RC	5.00	12.00
❑ 156 David Harrison AU RC	5.00	12.00

2005-06 Bowman

❑ COMP.SET w/o RC's (110)	15.00	40.00
❑ COMMON CARD (1-110)	.20	.50
❑ COMMON ROOKIE (111-146)	1.00	2.50
❑ COMMON CELEBRITY (147-151)	2.50	6.00
❑ COMMON AU RC (152-161)	4.00	10.00
❑ 1 Steve Nash	.40	1.00
❑ 2 Primoz Brezec	.20	.50
❑ 3 Baron Davis	.30	.75
❑ 4 Al Harrington	.20	.50
❑ 5 Caron Butler	.30	.75
❑ 6 Marcus Camby	.25	.60
❑ 7 Carlos Boozer	.30	.75
❑ 8 Ben Gordon	.40	1.00
❑ 9 Stephen Jackson	.25	.60
❑ 10 Dirk Nowitzki	.50	1.25
❑ 11 Nenad Krstic	.25	.60
❑ 12 Jason Richardson	.30	.75
❑ 13 Brendan Haywood	.20	.50
❑ 14 Chauncey Billups	.30	.75
❑ 15 Corey Maggette	.25	.60
❑ 16 Peja Stojakovic	.30	.75
❑ 17 Grant Hill	.30	.75
❑ 18 Pau Gasol	.30	.75
❑ 19 Vladimir Radmanovic	.20	.50
❑ 20 Jason Kidd	.50	1.25
❑ 21 Tim Duncan	.60	1.50
❑ 22 David Harrison	.20	.50
❑ 23 LeBron James	1.50	4.00
❑ 24 Udonis Haslem	.30	.75
❑ 25 Dan Dickau	.20	.50
❑ 26 Cuttino Mobley	.25	.60
❑ 27 Chris Bosh	.30	.75
❑ 28 Sebastian Telfair	.25	.60
❑ 29 Latrell Sprewell	.20	.50
❑ 30 Emeka Okafor	.30	.75
❑ 31 Mike James	.20	.50
❑ 32 Trevor Ariza	.25	.60
❑ 33 Larry Hughes	.25	.60
❑ 34 Desmond Mason	.20	.50
❑ 35 Tayshaun Prince	.30	.75
❑ 36 Manu Ginobili	.30	.75
❑ 37 Mike Bibby	.30	.75
❑ 38 Andre Iguodala	.30	.75
❑ 39 Jamaal Magloire	.20	.50
❑ 40 Amare Stoudemire	.60	1.50
❑ 41 Rafer Alston	.20	.50
❑ 42 Elton Brand	.30	.75
❑ 43 Steve Francis	.30	.75
❑ 44 Rashard Lewis	.30	.75
❑ 45 Lorenzen Wright	.20	.50
❑ 46 Kirk Hinrich	.30	.75
❑ 47 Andrei Kirilenko	.30	.75
❑ 48 Brad Miller	.30	.75
❑ 49 Jamal Crawford	.25	.60
❑ 50 Shaquille O'Neal	.75	2.00
❑ 51 Shaun Livingston	.20	.50
❑ 52 Troy Murphy	.30	.75
❑ 53 Drew Gooden	.25	.60
❑ 54 Paul Pierce	.30	.75
❑ 55 Vince Carter	.60	1.50
❑ 56 Wally Szczerbiak	.25	.60
❑ 57 Antawn Jamison	.30	.75
❑ 58 Marquis Daniels	.25	.60
❑ 59 Gerald Wallace	.30	.75
❑ 60 Ray Allen	.30	.75
❑ 61 Jamaal Tinsley	.25	.60
❑ 62 Shane Battier	.30	.75
❑ 63 Zydrunas Ilgauskas	.25	.60
❑ 64 Mehmet Okur	.20	.50
❑ 65 Rasheed Wallace	.30	.75
❑ 66 Maurice Williams	.25	.60
❑ 67 Josh Howard	.30	.75
❑ 68 Zach Randolph	.30	.75
❑ 69 Kobe Bryant	1.50	4.00
❑ 70 Tracy McGrady	.60	1.50
❑ 71 Luke Ridnour	.25	.60
❑ 72 Damon Jones	.25	.60
❑ 73 Tony Allen	.20	.50
❑ 74 Mike Miller	.30	.75
❑ 75 Sam Cassell	.30	.75
❑ 76 Ben Wallace	.30	.75
❑ 77 Mike Sweetney	.25	.60
❑ 78 Eddy Curry	.25	.60
❑ 79 Michael Redd	.30	.75
❑ 80 Carmelo Anthony	.60	1.50
❑ 81 Dwight Howard	.60	1.50
❑ 82 Josh Smith	.30	.75
❑ 83 Richard Jefferson	.25	.60
❑ 84 Richard Hamilton	.25	.60
❑ 85 Chris Webber	.30	.75
❑ 86 Shawn Marion	.30	.75
❑ 87 Jalen Rose	.30	.75
❑ 88 Bob Sura	.20	.50
❑ 89 Mike Dunleavy	.25	.60
❑ 90 Dwyane Wade	.75	2.00
❑ 91 Gary Payton	.30	.75
❑ 92 Luol Deng	.30	.75
❑ 93 Kenyon Martin	.30	.75
❑ 94 Beno Udrih	.20	.50
❑ 95 J.R. Smith	.25	.60

❑ 96 Lamar Odom	.30	.75
❑ 97 Andre Miller	.25	.60
❑ 98 Jermaine O'Neal	.30	.75
❑ 99 Yao Ming	.75	2.00
❑ 100 Allen Iverson	.60	1.50
❑ 101 Quentin Richardson	.25	.60
❑ 102 Gilbert Arenas	.30	.75
❑ 103 Stephon Marbury	.30	.75
❑ 104 Antoine Walker	.25	.60
❑ 105 Jameer Nelson	.25	.60
❑ 106 Joel Przybilla	.20	.50
❑ 107 Devin Harris	.30	.75
❑ 108 Tony Parker	.30	.75
❑ 109 Josh Childress	.25	.60
❑ 110 Kevin Garnett	.60	1.50
❑ 111 Chris Paul RC	3.00	8.00
❑ 112 Danny Granger RC	2.50	6.00
❑ 113 Antoine Wright RC	1.00	2.50
❑ 114 Joey Graham RC	1.00	2.50
❑ 115 Wayne Simien RC	1.25	3.00
❑ 116 Channing Frye RC	1.25	3.00
❑ 117 Charlie Villanueva RC	1.50	4.00
❑ 118 Francisco Garcia RC	1.25	3.00
❑ 119 Ike Diogu RC	1.25	3.00
❑ 120 Jarrett Jack RC	1.00	2.50
❑ 121 Robert Whaley RC	1.00	2.50
❑ 122 C.J. Miles RC	1.00	2.50
❑ 123 Ryan Gomes RC	1.00	2.50
❑ 124 Nate Robinson RC	1.50	4.00
❑ 125 Daniel Ewing RC	1.25	3.00
❑ 126 Andray Blatche RC	1.25	3.00
❑ 127 Luther Head RC	1.25	3.00
❑ 128 Julius Hodge RC	1.25	3.00
❑ 129 Lawrence Roberts RC	1.00	2.50
❑ 130 Jason Maxiell RC	1.25	3.00
❑ 131 Martynas Andriuskevicius RC	1.00	2.50
❑ 132 Ersan Ilyasova RC	1.00	2.50
❑ 133 Martell Webster RC	1.00	2.50
❑ 134 Andrew Bynum RC	3.00	8.00
❑ 135 Louis Williams RC	1.50	4.00
❑ 136 Johan Petro RC	1.00	2.50
❑ 137 Brandon Bass RC	1.00	2.50
❑ 138 Travis Diener RC	1.00	2.50
❑ 139 Bracey Wright RC	1.00	2.50
❑ 140 Marvin Williams RC	1.50	4.00
❑ 141 Eddie Basden RC	1.00	2.50
❑ 142 Von Wafer RC	1.00	2.50
❑ 143 David Lee RC	2.00	5.00
❑ 144 Linas Kleiza RC	1.25	3.00
❑ 145 Luke Schenscher RC	1.00	2.50
❑ 146 Yaroslav Korolev RC	1.00	2.50
❑ 147 Carmen Electra	2.50	6.00
❑ 148 Christie Brinkley	2.50	6.00
❑ 149 Shannon Elizabeth	2.50	6.00
❑ 150 Jenny McCarthy	2.50	6.00
❑ 151 Jay-Z	2.50	6.00
❑ 152 Raymond Felton AU RC	5.00	12.00
❑ 153 Gerald Green AU RC	5.00	12.00
❑ 154 Rashad McCants AU RC	6.00	15.00
❑ 155 Andrew Bogut AU RC	6.00	15.00
❑ 156 Chris Taft AU RC	4.00	10.00
❑ 157 Sarunas Jasikevicius AU RC	6.00	15.00
❑ 158 Hakim Warrick AU RC	6.00	15.00
❑ 159 Deron Williams AU RC	10.00	25.00
❑ 160 Sean May AU RC	4.00	10.00
❑ 161 Monta Ellis AU RC	15.00	30.00
❑ DSBS A.Bogut/A.Smith AU/100	60.00	120.00

2006-07 Bowman

❑ COMPLETE SET (165)	20.00	50.00
❑ 1 Gilbert Arenas	.30	.75
❑ 2 Delonte West	.25	.60
❑ 3 Gerald Wallace	.30	.75
❑ 4 Ike Diogu	.25	.60
❑ 5 Mike Miller	.30	.75
❑ 6 Kobe Bryant	1.50	4.00
❑ 7 Richard Hamilton	.25	.60
❑ 8 Vince Carter	.60	1.50
❑ 9 Elton Brand	.30	.75
❑ 10 Boris Diaw	.25	.60
❑ 11 Carmelo Anthony	.40	1.00
❑ 12 Jermaine O'Neal	.30	.75
❑ 13 Al Harrington	.20	.50
❑ 14 Dwight Howard	.60	1.50
❑ 15 Chris Bosh	.30	.75
❑ 16 Ben Gordon	.40	1.00
❑ 17 Josh Howard	.30	.75
❑ 18 Yao Ming	.75	2.00
❑ 19 David West	.30	.75
❑ 20 Tim Duncan	.60	1.50
❑ 21 Andre Iguodala	.30	.75
❑ 22 LeBron James	1.50	4.00
❑ 23 Channing Frye	.25	.60
❑ 24 Antoine Walker	.25	.60
❑ 25 Ricky Davis	.30	.75
❑ 26 Lamar Odom	.30	.75
❑ 27 Amare Stoudemire	.60	1.50
❑ 28 Mike Bibby	.30	.75
❑ 29 Allen Iverson	.60	1.50
❑ 30 Marvin Williams	.30	.75
❑ 31 Wally Szczerbiak	.25	.60
❑ 32 Ben Wallace	.30	.75
❑ 33 Nenad Krstic	.25	.60
❑ 34 Deron Williams	.50	1.25
❑ 35 Troy Murphy	.30	.75
❑ 36 Raymond Felton	.40	1.00
❑ 37 Jason Terry	.30	.75
❑ 38 Zach Randolph	.30	.75
❑ 39 Pau Gasol	.30	.75
❑ 40 Larry Hughes	.25	.60
❑ 41 Luol Deng	.30	.75
❑ 42 Steve Francis	.30	.75
❑ 43 Chauncey Billups	.30	.75
❑ 44 Smush Parker	.20	.50
❑ 45 Shareef Abdur-Rahim	.30	.75
❑ 46 Andrei Kirilenko	.30	.75
❑ 47 Shawn Marion	.30	.75
❑ 48 Darko Milicic	.30	.75
❑ 49 Shaquille O'Neal	.75	2.00
❑ 50 Kevin Garnett	.60	1.50
❑ 51 Michael Finley	.30	.75
❑ 52 Peja Stojakovic	.30	.75
❑ 53 Michael Redd	.30	.75
❑ 54 Desmond Mason	.20	.50
❑ 55 Luke Ridnour	.25	.60
❑ 56 Kenyon Martin	.30	.75
❑ 57 Morris Peterson	.25	.60
❑ 58 Chris Kaman	.20	.50
❑ 59 Jason Richardson	.30	.75
❑ 60 Jason Kidd	.50	1.25
❑ 61 Carlos Boozer	.30	.75
❑ 62 Rashad McCants	.25	.60
❑ 63 Nate Robinson	.30	.75
❑ 64 Devin Harris	.30	.75
❑ 65 Andrew Bogut	.30	.75
❑ 66 Chris Duhon	.20	.50
❑ 67 Drew Gooden	.25	.60
❑ 68 Manu Ginobili	.30	.75
❑ 69 Jameer Nelson	.25	.60
❑ 70 Corey Maggette	.25	.60
❑ 71 Charlie Villanueva	.30	.75
❑ 72 Shane Battier	.30	.75
❑ 73 Udonis Haslem	.30	.75
❑ 74 Tracy McGrady	.60	1.50
❑ 75 Bobby Simmons	.20	.50
❑ 76 Baron Davis	.30	.75
❑ 77 Zydrunas Ilgauskas	.25	.60
❑ 78 Danny Granger	.25	.60
❑ 79 Hakim Warrick	.25	.60
❑ 80 Josh Smith	.30	.75
❑ 81 Tayshaun Prince	.30	.75
❑ 82 Rashard Lewis	.30	.75
❑ 83 Luther Head	.25	.60
❑ 84 Andre Miller	.25	.60
❑ 85 T.J. Ford	.25	.60
❑ 86 Sebastian Telfair	.25	.60
❑ 87 Dirk Nowitzki	.50	1.25
❑ 88 Kwame Brown	.25	.60
❑ 89 Antawn Jamison	.30	.75
❑ 90 Ron Artest	.30	.75
❑ 91 Mehmet Okur	.20	.50
❑ 92 Emeka Okafor	.30	.75
❑ 93 Sam Cassell	.30	.75
❑ 94 Chris Paul	.60	1.50
❑ 95 Chris Webber	.30	.75
❑ 96 Richard Jefferson	.25	.60
❑ 97 Dwyane Wade	.75	2.00
❑ 98 Tony Parker	.30	.75
❑ 99 Paul Pierce	.30	.75
❑ 100 Marcus Camby	.25	.60
❑ 101 Ray Allen	.30	.75
❑ 102 Stephon Marbury	.30	.75
❑ 103 Rasheed Wallace	.30	.75
❑ 104 Brad Miller	.30	.75
❑ 105 Kirk Hinrich	.30	.75
❑ 106 Steve Nash	.40	1.00
❑ 107 Sarunas Jasikevicius	.25	.60
❑ 108 Darius Miles	.20	.50
❑ 109 Joe Johnson	.25	.60
❑ 110 Caron Butler	.30	.75
❑ 111 John Wooden CO	1.25	3.00
❑ 112 Ben Howland CO	1.00	2.50
❑ 113 Jim Calhoun CO	1.00	2.50
❑ 114 Jim Boeheim CO	1.00	2.50
❑ 115 Roy Williams CO	1.00	2.50
❑ 116 LaMarcus Aldridge RC	1.25	3.00
❑ 117 Marcus Vinicius RC	1.00	2.50
❑ 118 Sergio Rodriguez RC	1.00	2.50
❑ 119 Will Blalock RC	1.00	2.50
❑ 120 Paul Millsap RC	1.50	4.00
❑ 121 Leon Powe RC	1.00	2.50
❑ 122 Rudy Gay RC	1.00	2.50
❑ 123 Tyrus Thomas RC	1.25	3.00
❑ 124 Brandon Roy RC	2.50	6.00
❑ 125 J.R. Pinnock RC	1.00	2.50
❑ 126 Kevin Pittsnogle RC	1.00	2.50
❑ 127 Mile Ilic RC	1.00	2.50
❑ 128 Mardy Collins RC	1.00	2.50
❑ 129 Craig Smith RC	1.00	2.50
❑ 130 Jordan Farmar RC	1.25	3.00
❑ 131 Quincy Douby RC	1.00	2.50
❑ 132 James Augustine RC	1.00	2.50
❑ 133 Josh Boone RC	1.00	2.50
❑ 134 Shannon Brown RC	1.00	2.50
❑ 135 David Noel RC	1.00	2.50
❑ 136 Kyle Lowry RC	1.00	2.50
❑ 137 Ryan Hollins RC	1.00	2.50
❑ 138 Renaldo Balkman RC	1.00	2.50
❑ 139 James White RC	1.00	2.50
❑ 140 Damir Markota RC	1.00	2.50
❑ 141 Paul Davis RC	1.00	2.50
❑ 142 Alexander Johnson RC	1.00	2.50
❑ 143 Steve Novak RC	1.00	2.50
❑ 144 P.J. Tucker RC	1.00	2.50
❑ 145 Saer Sene RC	1.00	2.50
❑ 146 Bobby Jones RC	1.00	2.50
❑ 147 Cedric Simmons RC	1.00	2.50
❑ 148 Allan Ray RC	1.00	2.50
❑ 149 Solomon Jones RC	1.00	2.50
❑ 150 Ronnie Brewer RC	1.25	3.00
❑ 151 Thabo Sefolosha RC	1.25	3.00
❑ 152 Maurice Ager RC	1.00	2.50
❑ 153 Daniel Gibson RC	1.25	3.00
❑ 154 Shawne Williams RC	1.00	2.50
❑ 155 Dee Brown RC	1.00	2.50
❑ 156 Andrea Bargnani RC	1.50	4.00
❑ 157 Patrick O'Bryant RC	1.00	2.50
❑ 158 Shelden Williams RC	1.25	3.00
❑ 159 Hilton Armstrong RC	1.00	2.50
❑ 160 Adam Morrison RC	1.25	3.00
❑ 161 Rodney Carney RC	1.00	2.50
❑ 162 Randy Foye RC	1.00	2.50
❑ 163 Rajon Rondo RC	4.00	10.00
❑ 164 Marcus Williams RC	1.25	3.00
❑ 165 J.J. Redick RC	1.00	2.50

2007-08 Bowman

❑ COMP.SET w/o SP's (110)	15.00	30.00
❑ 1 Gilbert Arenas	.30	.75
❑ 2 Dwight Howard	.60	1.50
❑ 3 Dwyane Wade	.75	2.00

❑ 4 Chris Bosh	.30	.75
❑ 5 Josh Smith	.30	.75
❑ 6 Andrew Bogut	.30	.75
❑ 7 Ben Gordon	.40	1.00
❑ 8 Deron Williams	.50	1.25
❑ 9 Tony Parker	.30	.75
❑ 10 Mike Bibby	.30	.75
❑ 11 Yao Ming	.75	2.00
❑ 12 Raymond Felton	.40	1.00
❑ 13 Steve Nash	.40	1.00
❑ 14 Jameer Nelson	.25	.60
❑ 15 Carmelo Anthony	.60	1.50
❑ 16 Pau Gasol	.30	.75
❑ 17 Rashard Lewis	.30	.75
❑ 18 Eddy Curry	.20	.50
❑ 19 Luol Deng	.30	.75
❑ 20 Kevin Garnett	.75	2.00
❑ 21 Tim Duncan	.60	1.50
❑ 22 Michael Redd	.30	.75
❑ 23 LeBron James	1.50	4.00
❑ 24 Kobe Bryant	1.50	4.00
❑ 25 Al Jefferson	.30	.75
❑ 26 Mike Dunleavy	.25	.60
❑ 27 Tyson Chandler	.30	.75
❑ 28 Zach Randolph	.30	.75
❑ 29 Jason Richardson	.30	.75
❑ 30 Rasheed Wallace	.30	.75
❑ 31 Shawn Marion	.30	.75
❑ 32 Shaquille O'Neal	.75	2.00
❑ 33 Allen Iverson	.60	1.50
❑ 34 Paul Pierce	.30	.75
❑ 35 Adam Morrison	.30	.75
❑ 36 Mike Miller	.30	.75
❑ 37 Larry Hughes	.25	.60
❑ 38 Kevin Martin	.30	.75
❑ 39 Charlie Villanueva	.30	.75
❑ 40 Vince Carter	.60	1.50
❑ 41 Dirk Nowitzki	.50	1.25
❑ 42 Elton Brand	.30	.75
❑ 43 Ray Allen	.30	.75
❑ 44 Luke Walton	.25	.60
❑ 45 Chris Paul	.60	1.50
❑ 46 Marcus Camby	.20	.50
❑ 47 Andrei Kirilenko	.30	.75
❑ 48 J.J. Redick	.30	.75
❑ 49 Richard Hamilton	.25	.60
❑ 50 Emeka Okafor	.30	.75
❑ 51 Manu Ginobili	.30	.75
❑ 52 Monta Ellis	.25	.60
❑ 53 Jorge Garbajosa	.30	.75
❑ 54 Kyle Korver	.30	.75
❑ 55 Jason Kidd	.50	1.25
❑ 56 Randy Foye	.30	.75
❑ 57 Shane Battier	.30	.75
❑ 58 Shaun Livingston	.20	.50
❑ 59 Jason Terry	.30	.75
❑ 60 Joe Johnson	.30	.75
❑ 61 Lamar Odom	.30	.75
❑ 62 Tayshaun Prince	.30	.75
❑ 63 Chris Wilcox	.25	.60
❑ 64 Leandro Barbosa	.25	.60
❑ 65 Al Harrington	.25	.60
❑ 66 Jamal Crawford	.20	.50
❑ 67 Caron Butler	.30	.75
❑ 68 Chauncey Billups	.30	.75
❑ 69 Ricky Davis	.30	.75
❑ 70 Andrea Bargnani	.40	1.00
❑ 71 Samuel Dalembert	.20	.50
❑ 72 LaMarcus Aldridge	.40	1.00
❑ 73 Mehmet Okur	.25	.60
❑ 74 Marcus Williams	.30	.75
❑ 75 Andre Miller	.25	.60
❑ 76 Rudy Gay	.25	.60
❑ 77 Jermaine O'Neal	.30	.75
❑ 78 Boris Diaw	.25	.60
❑ 79 Ryan Gomes	.20	.50
❑ 80 Gerald Wallace	.30	.75
❑ 81 Udonis Haslem	.30	.75
❑ 82 Mo Williams	.25	.60
❑ 83 Jarrett Jack	.25	.60
❑ 84 Chris Webber	.30	.75
❑ 85 Trevor Ariza	.20	.50
❑ 86 Kirk Hinrich	.30	.75
❑ 87 Rafer Alston	.20	.50
❑ 88 Danny Granger	.25	.60
❑ 89 David West	.30	.75
❑ 90 Drew Gooden	.25	.60
❑ 91 Stephon Marbury	.30	.75
❑ 92 Antawn Jamison	.30	.75
❑ 93 Ron Artest	.30	.75
❑ 94 Richard Jefferson	.30	.75
❑ 95 Carlos Boozer	.30	.75
❑ 96 Hakim Warrick	.25	.60
❑ 97 T.J. Ford	.25	.60
❑ 98 Desmond Mason	.20	.50
❑ 99 Andre Iguodala	.30	.75
❑ 100 Amare Stoudemire	.60	1.50
❑ 101 Tracy McGrady	.60	1.50
❑ 102 Jason Kapono	.20	.50
❑ 103 Ben Wallace	.30	.75
❑ 104 Marvin Williams	.30	.75
❑ 105 Baron Davis	.30	.75
❑ 106 Andrew Bynum	.30	.75
❑ 107 Brandon Roy	.50	1.25
❑ 108 David Lee	.25	.60
❑ 109 Corey Maggette	.25	.60
❑ 110 Josh Howard	.30	.75
❑ 111 Kevin Durant RC	12.00	30.00
❑ 112 Al Horford RC	2.00	5.00
❑ 113 Michael Conley RC	2.00	5.00
❑ 114 Jeff Green RC	2.00	5.00
❑ 115 Corey Brewer RC	2.00	5.00
❑ 116 Joakim Noah RC	2.00	5.00
❑ 117 Julian Wright RC	2.00	5.00
❑ 118 Ramon Sessions RC	2.00	5.00
❑ 119 Sammy Mejia RC	1.50	4.00
❑ 120 Luis Scola RC	2.50	6.00
❑ 121 Yi Jianlian RC	2.50	6.00
❑ 122 Arron Afflalo RC	1.50	4.00
❑ 123 Carl Landry RC	1.50	4.00
❑ 124 Alando Tucker RC	1.50	4.00
❑ 125 Gabe Pruitt RC	1.50	4.00
❑ 126 Marcus Williams RC	1.50	4.00
❑ 127 Spencer Hawes RC	1.50	4.00
❑ 128 Acie Law RC	2.00	5.00
❑ 129 Thaddeus Young RC	2.00	5.00
❑ 130 Nick Fazekas RC	1.50	4.00
❑ 131 Al Thornton RC	1.50	4.00
❑ 132 Rodney Stuckey RC	3.00	8.00
❑ 133 Nick Young RC	1.50	4.00
❑ 134 Glen Davis RC	3.00	8.00
❑ 135 Jermareo Davidson RC	1.50	4.00
❑ 136 JamesOn Curry RC	1.50	4.00
❑ 137 Jason Smith RC	1.50	4.00
❑ 138 Daequan Cook RC	2.00	5.00
❑ 139 Jared Dudley RC	1.50	4.00
❑ 140 Derrick Byars RC	1.50	4.00
❑ 141 Josh McRoberts RC	2.00	5.00
❑ 142 Adam Haluska RC	1.50	4.00
❑ 143 Reyshawn Terry RC	1.50	4.00
❑ 144 Aaron Gray RC	1.50	4.00
❑ 145 Herbert Hill RC	1.50	4.00
❑ 146 Jared Jordan RC	1.50	4.00
❑ 147 Wilson Chandler RC	1.50	4.00
❑ 148 Morris Almond RC	1.50	4.00
❑ 149 Aaron Brooks RC	2.50	6.00
❑ 150 Petteri Koponen RC	1.50	4.00
❑ 151 Dominic McGuire RC	1.50	4.00
❑ 152 Greg Oden RC	2.50	6.00
❑ 153 Stephane Lasme RC	1.50	4.00
❑ 154 D.J. Strawberry RC	1.50	4.00
❑ 155 Sean Williams RC	1.50	4.00
❑ 156 Marco Belinelli RC	1.50	4.00
❑ 157 Javaris Crittenton RC	1.50	4.00
❑ 158 Demetris Nichols RC	1.50	4.00
❑ 159 Taurean Green RC	1.50	4.00
❑ 160 Brandan Wright RC	2.00	5.00

2008-09 Bowman

❑ COMPLETE SET (150)	30.00	60.00
❑ 1 Tracy McGrady	.40	1.00
❑ 2 Jason Kidd	.30	.75
❑ 3 LeBron James	1.50	4.00
❑ 4 Chris Bosh	.30	.75
❑ 5 Kevin Garnett	.60	1.50
❑ 6 Josh Smith	.30	.75
❑ 7 Richard Hamilton	.25	.60
❑ 8 Monta Ellis	.30	.75
❑ 9 Yi Jianlian	.30	.75
❑ 10 Danny Granger	.30	.75
❑ 11 Richard Jefferson	.30	.75
❑ 12 Elton Brand	.50	1.25
❑ 13 Rudy Gay	.30	.75
❑ 14 Andres Nocioni	.25	.60
❑ 15 Carmelo Anthony	.40	1.00
❑ 16 Pau Gasol	.30	.75
❑ 17 Corey Brewer	.25	.60
❑ 18 Hedo Turkoglu	.30	.75
❑ 19 Andre Iguodala	.30	.75
❑ 20 Raymond Felton	.25	.60
❑ 21 Tim Duncan	.50	1.25
❑ 22 Michael Redd	.30	.75
❑ 23 Chris Paul	.60	1.50
❑ 24 Kobe Bryant	1.50	4.00
❑ 25 Brandon Roy	.40	1.00
❑ 26 Carlos Boozer	.30	.75
❑ 27 Jeff Green	.25	.60
❑ 28 Luis Scola	.25	.60
❑ 29 Al Thornton	.30	.75
❑ 30 Gilbert Arenas	.30	.75
❑ 31 Brandan Wright	.25	.60
❑ 32 Shaquille O'Neal	.60	1.50
❑ 33 Allen Iverson	.40	1.00
❑ 34 Paul Pierce	.40	1.00
❑ 35 Ben Gordon	.30	.75
❑ 36 Jamal Crawford	.20	.50
❑ 37 Andrew Bynum	.30	.75
❑ 38 Gerald Wallace	.30	.75
❑ 39 Mike Conley	.25	.60
❑ 40 Ben Wallace	.30	.75
❑ 41 Dirk Nowitzki	.40	1.00
❑ 42 David Lee	.25	.60
❑ 43 Mo Williams	.25	.60
❑ 44 Al Jefferson	.30	.75
❑ 45 Tayshaun Prince	.30	.75
❑ 46 Jameer Nelson	.25	.60
❑ 47 Andrei Kirilenko	.30	.75
❑ 48 David West	.30	.75
❑ 49 Al Horford	.30	.75
❑ 50 Steve Nash	.30	.75
❑ 51 Ron Artest	.30	.75
❑ 52 Greg Oden	.30	.75
❑ 53 Sean Williams	.25	.60
❑ 54 Jamario Moon	.30	.75
❑ 55 Baron Davis	.30	.75
❑ 56 Udonis Haslem	.30	.75
❑ 57 Mike Dunleavy	.25	.60
❑ 58 Shane Battier	.25	.60
❑ 59 Andrew Bogut	.30	.75
❑ 60 Ray Allen	.30	.75
❑ 61 Nick Young	.20	.50
❑ 62 Manu Ginobili	.30	.75
❑ 63 Jason Richardson	.30	.75
❑ 64 Mike Miller	.30	.75
❑ 65 Leandro Barbosa	.25	.60
❑ 66 Luol Deng	.30	.75
❑ 67 Shawn Marion	.30	.75
❑ 68 Peja Stojakovic	.30	.75
❑ 69 Kevin Durant	.75	2.00
❑ 70 Corey Maggette	.30	.75
❑ 71 Chauncey Billups	.30	.75
❑ 72 Josh Howard	.30	.75
❑ 73 Kevin Martin	.30	.75
❑ 74 Anderson Varejao	.25	.60
❑ 75 Craig Smith	.30	.75
❑ 76 Antawn Jamison	.30	.75
❑ 77 Marcus Camby	.20	.50
❑ 78 Andre Miller	.25	.60
❑ 79 Zach Randolph	.30	.75
❑ 80 Deron Williams	.40	1.00
❑ 81 Devin Harris	.30	.75
❑ 82 Rashard Lewis	.30	.75
❑ 83 Damien Wilkins	.20	.50
❑ 84 LaMarcus Aldridge	.30	.75
❑ 85 Larry Hughes	.25	.60
❑ 86 Brad Miller	.30	.75
❑ 87 Jermaine O'Neal	.30	.75
❑ 88 Caron Butler	.30	.75
❑ 89 Tyson Chandler	.25	.60
❑ 90 Joe Johnson	.30	.75
❑ 91 Amare Stoudemire	.40	1.00
❑ 92 Dwight Howard	.60	1.50
❑ 93 Rajon Rondo	.30	.75
❑ 94 T.J. Ford	.20	.50

❑ 95 Rodney Stuckey	.40	1.00
❑ 96 Samuel Dalembert	.20	.50
❑ 97 Tony Parker	.30	.75
❑ 98 Vince Carter	.40	1.00
❑ 99 Yao Ming	.40	1.00
❑ 100 Dwyane Wade	.60	1.50
❑ 101 Dominique Wilkins	.40	1.00
❑ 102 Rick Barry	.30	.75
❑ 103 John Stockton	.50	1.25
❑ 104 Magic Johnson	.60	1.50
❑ 105 George Gervin	.40	1.00
❑ 106 Bill Russell	.50	1.25
❑ 107 David Robinson	.50	1.25
❑ 108 Dennis Rodman	.30	.75
❑ 109 Larry Bird	1.00	2.50
❑ 110 Jerry West	.40	1.00
❑ 111 Derrick Rose RC	3.00	8.00
❑ 112 Michael Beasley RC	1.50	4.00
❑ 113 O.J. Mayo RC	1.25	3.00
❑ 114 Russell Westbrook RC	2.00	5.00
❑ 115 Kevin Love RC	1.00	2.50
❑ 116 Danilo Gallinari RC	1.25	3.00
❑ 117 Eric Gordon RC	1.00	2.50
❑ 118 Joe Alexander RC	.75	2.00
❑ 119 D.J. Augustin RC	.75	2.00
❑ 120 Brook Lopez RC	1.50	4.00
❑ 121 Jerryd Bayless RC	.75	2.00
❑ 122 Jason Thompson RC	.75	2.00
❑ 123 Anthony Randolph RC	1.25	3.00
❑ 124 Robin Lopez RC	.75	2.00
❑ 125 Marreese Speights RC	.75	2.00
❑ 126 Roy Hibbert RC	1.00	2.50
❑ 127 JaVale McGee RC	.75	2.00
❑ 128 J.J. Hickson RC	1.25	3.00
❑ 129 Alexis Ajinca RC	.75	2.00
❑ 130 Ryan Anderson RC	.75	2.00
❑ 131 Courtney Lee RC	1.25	3.00
❑ 132 Kosta Koufos RC	.75	2.00
❑ 133 Donte Greene RC	.75	2.00
❑ 134 George Hill RC	1.25	3.00
❑ 135 D.J. White RC	.75	2.00
❑ 136 J.R. Giddens RC	.75	2.00
❑ 137 Joey Dorsey RC	.75	2.00
❑ 138 Mario Chalmers RC	1.00	2.50
❑ 139 DeAndre Jordan RC	.75	2.00
❑ 140 Chris Douglas-Roberts RC	1.00	2.50
❑ 141 Malik Hairston RC	.75	2.00
❑ 142 Sean Singletary RC	.75	2.00
❑ 143 Kyle Weaver RC	.75	2.00
❑ 144 Patrick Ewing Jr. RC	.75	2.00
❑ 145 Walter Sharpe RC	.75	2.00
❑ 146 Sonny Weems RC	.75	2.00
❑ 147 Shan Foster RC	.75	2.00
❑ 148 Nicolas Batum RC	1.00	2.50
❑ 149 Brandon Rush RC	.75	2.00
❑ 150 Darrell Arthur RC	.75	2.00

2009-10 Bowman 48

❑ 1 Al Horford	.30	.75
❑ 2 Joe Johnson	.30	.75
❑ 3 Josh Smith	.30	.75
❑ 4 Paul Pierce	.40	1.00
❑ 5 Kevin Garnett	.60	1.50
❑ 6 Ray Allen	.30	.75
❑ 7 Rajon Rondo	.30	.75
❑ 8 Gerald Wallace	.30	.75
❑ 9 Emeka Okafor	.30	.75
❑ 10 Ben Gordon	.30	.75
❑ 11 Derrick Rose	.60	1.50
❑ 12 John Salmons	.30	.75
❑ 13 Mo Williams	.25	.60
❑ 14 LeBron James	1.50	4.00
❑ 15 Anderson Varejao	.25	.60
❑ 16 Dirk Nowitzki	.40	1.00
❑ 17 Jason Kidd	.30	.75
❑ 18 Jason Terry	.25	.60
❑ 19 Chauncey Billups	.30	.75
❑ 20 Carmelo Anthony	.40	1.00
❑ 21 Richard Hamilton	.25	.60
❑ 22 Allen Iverson	.40	1.00
❑ 23 Rasheed Wallace	.30	.75
❑ 24 Monta Ellis	.30	.75
❑ 25 Corey Maggette	.25	.60
❑ 26 Anthony Randolph	.30	.75
❑ 27 Tracy McGrady	.40	1.00
❑ 28 Yao Ming	.40	1.00
❑ 29 Ron Artest	.30	.75
❑ 30 Danny Granger	.30	.75
❑ 31 T.J. Ford	.20	.50
❑ 32 Eric Gordon	.30	.75
❑ 33 Baron Davis	.30	.75
❑ 34 Marcus Camby	.20	.50
❑ 35 Pau Gasol	.30	.75
❑ 36 Kobe Bryant	1.50	4.00
❑ 37 Andrew Bynum	.30	.75
❑ 38 Rudy Gay	.30	.75
❑ 39 O.J. Mayo	.40	1.00
❑ 40 Michael Beasley	.40	1.00
❑ 41 Dwyane Wade	.60	1.50
❑ 42 Jermaine O'Neal	.30	.75
❑ 43 Michael Redd	.30	.75
❑ 44 Richard Jefferson	.30	.75
❑ 45 Al Jefferson	.30	.75
❑ 46 Kevin Love	.25	.60
❑ 47 Mike Miller	.30	.75
❑ 48 Vince Carter	.40	1.00
❑ 49 Devin Harris	.30	.75
❑ 50 David West	.30	.75
❑ 51 Chris Paul	.60	1.50
❑ 52 Nate Robinson	.30	.75
❑ 53 David Lee	.25	.60
❑ 54 Kevin Durant	.75	2.00
❑ 55 Russell Westbrook	.30	.75
❑ 56 Dwight Howard	.60	1.50
❑ 57 Jameer Nelson	.25	.60
❑ 58 Hedo Turkoglu	.30	.75
❑ 59 Andre Iguodala	.30	.75
❑ 60 Elton Brand	.30	.75
❑ 61 Andre Miller	.25	.60
❑ 62 Shaquille O'Neal	.60	1.50
❑ 63 Amare Stoudemire	.40	1.00
❑ 64 Steve Nash	.30	.75
❑ 65 Rudy Fernandez	.30	.75
❑ 66 Brandon Roy	.40	1.00
❑ 67 LaMarcus Aldridge	.30	.75
❑ 68 Spencer Hawes	.25	.60
❑ 69 Kevin Martin	.30	.75
❑ 70 Tony Parker	.30	.75
❑ 71 Tim Duncan	.50	1.25
❑ 72 Manu Ginobili	.30	.75
❑ 73 Jose Calderon	.25	.60
❑ 74 Chris Bosh	.30	.75
❑ 75 Shawn Marion	.30	.75
❑ 76 Carlos Boozer	.30	.75
❑ 77 Deron Williams	.40	1.00
❑ 78 Caron Butler	.30	.75
❑ 79 Antawn Jamison	.30	.75
❑ 80 Gilbert Arenas	.30	.75
❑ 81 Dominique Wilkins	.40	1.00
❑ 82 Bill Russell	.50	1.25
❑ 83 Bob Cousy	.50	1.25
❑ 84 Larry Bird	1.00	2.50
❑ 85 Rick Barry	.30	.75
❑ 86 Elgin Baylor	.30	.75
❑ 87 Jerry West	.40	1.00
❑ 88 Magic Johnson	.60	1.50
❑ 89 Oscar Robertson	.30	.75
❑ 90 George Mikan	.60	1.50
❑ 91 Pete Maravich	1.00	2.50
❑ 92 Patrick Ewing	.40	1.00
❑ 93 Willis Reed	.30	.75
❑ 94 Julius Erving	.60	1.50
❑ 95 Moses Malone	.30	.75
❑ 96 Wilt Chamberlain	.60	1.50
❑ 97 Bill Walton	.30	.75
❑ 98 Clyde Drexler	.40	1.00
❑ 99 Bob Pettit	.30	.75
❑ 100 Karl Malone	.40	1.00
❑ 101 Blake Griffin RC	3.00	8.00
❑ 102 Jonny Flynn RC	2.00	5.00
❑ 103 Hasheem Thabeet RC	1.25	3.00
❑ 104 James Harden RC	2.50	6.00
❑ 105 DeMar DeRozan RC	2.00	5.00
❑ 106 Stephen Curry RC	3.00	8.00
❑ 107 Brandon Jennings RC	3.00	8.00
❑ 108 Jordan Hill RC	1.50	4.00
❑ 109 Earl Clark RC	2.00	5.00
❑ 110 Gerald Henderson RC	2.00	5.00
❑ 111 Tyreke Evans RC	5.00	12.00
❑ 112 Jrue Holiday RC	2.00	5.00
❑ 113 Tyler Hansbrough RC	2.00	5.00
❑ 114 Terrence Williams RC	2.50	6.00
❑ 115 Play Card	1.25	3.00
❑ 116 Play Card	1.25	3.00
❑ 117 Play Card	1.25	3.00
❑ 118 Play Card	1.25	3.00
❑ 119 Play Card	1.25	3.00
❑ 120 Play Card	1.25	3.00
❑ 121 Play Card	1.25	3.00

2003-04 Bowman Chrome

❑ COMP.SET w/o RC's (110)	30.00	80.00
❑ COMMON CARD (1-110)	.30	.75
❑ COMMON ROOKIE (111-147)	3.00	8.00
❑ COMMON AU RC (148-157)	15.00	30.00
❑ 148-157 AU RC STATED ODDS 1:385		
❑ 148-157 AU PRINT RUN 250 SER.#'d SETS		
❑ CARD 147 NOT RELEASED		
❑ 1 Yao Ming	1.00	2.50
❑ 2 Glenn Robinson	.40	1.00
❑ 3 Antoine Walker	.50	1.25
❑ 4 Jalen Rose	.40	1.00
❑ 5 Ricky Davis	.40	1.00
❑ 6 Juwan Howard	.40	1.00
❑ 7 Kwame Brown	.30	.75
❑ 8 Mike Bibby	.40	1.00
❑ 9 Wally Szczerbiak	.40	1.00
❑ 10 Allen Iverson	1.00	2.50
❑ 11 Shareef Abdur-Rahim	.40	1.00
❑ 12 Jamal Mashburn	.30	.75
❑ 13 Stephon Marbury	.50	1.25
❑ 14 Desmond Mason	.40	1.00
❑ 15 Gordan Giricek	.30	.75
❑ 16 Caron Butler	.40	1.00
❑ 17 Jermaine O'Neal	.50	1.25
❑ 18 Kenyon Martin	.50	1.25
❑ 19 Andrei Kirilenko	.50	1.25
❑ 20 Dirk Nowitzki	.75	2.00
❑ 21 Richard Hamilton	.40	1.00
❑ 22 Troy Murphy	.50	1.25
❑ 23 Shawn Marion	.50	1.25
❑ 24 Allan Houston	.40	1.00
❑ 25 Keith Van Horn	.40	1.00
❑ 26 Brian Grant	.30	.75
❑ 27 Mike Miller	.40	1.00
❑ 28 Chris Webber	.50	1.25
❑ 29 Brent Barry	.30	.75
❑ 30 Elton Brand	.50	1.25
❑ 31 Juan Dixon	.30	.75
❑ 32 Karl Malone	.50	1.25
❑ 33 Darrell Armstrong	.30	.75
❑ 34 Rasheed Wallace	.50	1.25
❑ 35 Michael Redd	.50	1.25
❑ 36 Rashard Lewis	.50	1.25
❑ 37 Ron Artest	.40	1.00
❑ 38 P.J. Brown	.30	.75
❑ 39 Eddie Griffin	.30	.75
❑ 40 Tim Duncan	1.00	2.50
❑ 41 Kurt Thomas	.30	.75
❑ 42 Raef Lafrentz	.30	.75
❑ 43 Ben Wallace	.40	1.00
❑ 44 Lamar Odom	.50	1.25
❑ 45 Vince Carter	1.00	2.50
❑ 46 Derek Anderson	.40	1.00
❑ 47 Stromile Swift	.30	.75
❑ 48 Bobby Jackson	.30	.75
❑ 49 Richard Jefferson	.50	1.25
❑ 50 Shaquille O'Neal	1.25	3.00
❑ 51 Calbert Cheaney	.30	.75
❑ 52 Troy Hudson	.30	.75
❑ 53 Ray Allen	.30	.75

❑ 54 Howard Eisley	.30	.75
❑ 55 Alonzo Mourning	.50	1.25
❑ 56 Sam Cassell	.40	1.00
❑ 57 Derrick Coleman	.40	1.00
❑ 58 Andre Miller	.40	1.00
❑ 59 Antawn Jamison	.50	1.25
❑ 60 Kevin Garnett	1.00	2.50
❑ 61 Steve Francis	.50	1.25
❑ 62 Tyson Chandler	.40	1.00
❑ 63 Drew Gooden	.30	.75
❑ 64 Scottie Pippen	.75	2.00
❑ 65 Pau Gasol	.50	1.25
❑ 66 Steve Nash	.75	2.00
❑ 67 DaJuan Wagner	.30	.75
❑ 68 Jason Terry	.40	1.00
❑ 69 Reggie Miller	.50	1.25
❑ 70 Tracy McGrady	1.00	2.50
❑ 71 Nene Hilario	.40	1.00
❑ 72 Morris Peterson	.40	1.00
❑ 73 Peja Stojakovic	.40	1.00
❑ 74 Eddie Jones	.40	1.00
❑ 75 Tony Parker	.50	1.25
❑ 76 Corliss Williamson	.30	.75
❑ 77 Vladimir Radmanovic	.30	.75
❑ 78 Amare Stoudemire	1.00	2.50
❑ 79 Tony Delk	.30	.75
❑ 80 Jason Kidd	.75	2.00
❑ 81 Gary Payton	.50	1.25
❑ 82 Corey Maggette	.30	.75
❑ 83 Darius Miles	.40	1.00
❑ 84 Cuttino Mobley	.40	1.00
❑ 85 Eric Snow	.30	.75
❑ 86 Matt Harpring	.40	1.00
❑ 87 Manu Ginobili	.50	1.25
❑ 88 Latrell Sprewell	.40	1.00
❑ 89 Alvin Williams	.30	.75
❑ 90 Paul Pierce	.50	1.25
❑ 91 Anfernee Hardaway	.50	1.25
❑ 92 Gilbert Arenas	.50	1.25
❑ 93 Jerry Stackhouse	.40	1.00
❑ 94 Tim Thomas	.30	.75
❑ 95 Nikoloz Tskitishvili	.30	.75
❑ 96 Doug Christie	.30	.75
❑ 97 Zydrunas Ilgauskas	.40	1.00
❑ 98 Jamaal Tinsley	.40	1.00
❑ 99 Theo Ratliff	.30	.75
❑ 100 Kobe Bryant	2.50	6.00
❑ 101 Chauncey Billups	.50	1.25
❑ 102 Michael Finley	.50	1.25
❑ 103 Jason Williams	.40	1.00
❑ 104 Bonzi Wells	.30	.75
❑ 105 Voshon Lenard	.30	.75
❑ 106 Jason Richardson	.50	1.25
❑ 107 Baron Davis	.50	1.25
❑ 108 Radoslav Nesterovic	.30	.75
❑ 109 Eddy Curry	.40	1.00
❑ 110 Michael Olowokandi	.30	.75
❑ 111 Josh Howard RC	4.00	10.00
❑ 112 Mario Austin RC	3.00	8.00
❑ 113 Rick Rickert RC	3.00	8.00
❑ 114 Tommy Smith RC	3.00	8.00
❑ 115 Dahntay Jones RC	3.00	8.00
❑ 116 Ndudi Ebi RC	3.00	8.00
❑ 117 Maurice Williams RC	5.00	12.00
❑ 118 Kendrick Perkins RC	5.00	12.00
❑ 119 Steve Blake RC	4.00	10.00
❑ 120 David West RC	4.00	10.00
❑ 121 Chris Kaman RC	4.00	10.00
❑ 122 Keith Bogans RC	3.00	8.00
❑ 123 LeBron James RC	40.00	75.00
❑ 124 Devin Brown RC	3.00	8.00
❑ 125 Jason Kapono RC	4.00	10.00
❑ 126 Zoran Planinic RC	3.00	8.00
❑ 127 Zaur Pachulia RC	4.00	10.00
❑ 128 Malick Badiane RC	3.00	8.00
❑ 129 Kyle Korver RC	4.00	10.00
❑ 130 Darko Milicic RC	4.00	10.00
❑ 131 Troy Bell RC	3.00	8.00
❑ 132 Luke Walton RC	4.00	10.00
❑ 133 Mike Sweetney RC	3.00	8.00
❑ 134 Jarvis Hayes RC	3.00	8.00
❑ 135 Leandro Barbosa RC	4.00	10.00
❑ 136 Carlos Delfino RC	4.00	10.00
❑ 137 Sofoklis Schortsanitis RC	3.00	8.00
❑ 138 Slavko Vranes RC	3.00	8.00
❑ 139 Travis Hansen RC	3.00	8.00
❑ 140 Carmelo Anthony RC	8.00	20.00
❑ 141 Reece Gaines RC	3.00	8.00
❑ 142 Maciej Lampe RC	3.00	8.00
❑ 143 Travis Outlaw RC	4.00	10.00
❑ 144 Jerome Beasley RC	3.00	8.00
❑ 145 Mickael Pietrus RC	4.00	10.00
❑ 146 Brian Cook RC	3.00	8.00
❑ 148 Kirk Hinrich AU RC	40.00	80.00
❑ 149 Dwyane Wade AU RC	150.00	300.00
❑ 150 Marcus Banks AU RC	15.00	40.00
❑ 151 Nick Collison AU RC	12.50	30.00
❑ 152 Boris Diaw AU RC	15.00	30.00
❑ 153 Chris Bosh AU RC	60.00	120.00
❑ 154 T.J. Ford AU RC	25.00	50.00
❑ 155 Luke Ridnour AU RC	15.00	40.00
❑ 156 A.Pavlovic AU RC	15.00	40.00
❑ 157 Zarko Cabarkapa AU RC	12.50	30.00

2004-05 Bowman Chrome

❑ COMP.SET w/o RC's (110)	25.00	60.00
❑ COMMON CARD (1-110)	.30	.75
❑ COMMON ROOKIE (111-146)	2.00	5.00
❑ COMMON AU RC (147-156)	12.50	30.00
❑ 1 Yao Ming	1.25	3.00
❑ 2 Eddy Curry	.40	1.00
❑ 3 Stephon Marbury	.50	1.25
❑ 4 Chris Webber	.50	1.25
❑ 5 Jason Kidd	.75	2.00
❑ 6 Cuttino Mobley	.40	1.00
❑ 7 Jermaine O'Neal	.50	1.25
❑ 8 Kobe Bryant	2.50	6.00
❑ 9 Tony Parker	.50	1.25
❑ 10 Gary Payton	.50	1.25
❑ 11 T.J. Ford	.40	1.00
❑ 12 Tim Duncan	1.00	2.50
❑ 13 Glenn Robinson	.40	1.00
❑ 14 Jason Richardson	.50	1.25
❑ 15 Carmelo Anthony	1.50	4.00
❑ 16 Pau Gasol	.50	1.25
❑ 17 Kirk Hinrich	.40	1.00
❑ 18 Kenyon Martin	.50	1.25
❑ 19 Jamal Crawford	.40	1.00
❑ 20 Elton Brand	.50	1.25
❑ 21 Kevin Garnett	1.00	2.50
❑ 22 Michael Redd	.50	1.25
❑ 23 LeBron James	3.00	8.00
❑ 24 Andre Miller	.40	1.00
❑ 25 Peja Stojakovic	.40	1.00
❑ 26 Jarvis Hayes	.30	.75
❑ 27 David Wesley	.30	.75
❑ 28 Jason Kapono	.30	.75
❑ 29 Corey Maggette	.40	1.00
❑ 30 Rasheed Wallace	.50	1.25
❑ 31 Nene	.40	1.00
❑ 32 Amare Stoudemire	1.00	2.50
❑ 33 Allen Iverson	1.00	2.50
❑ 34 Shaquille O'Neal	1.25	3.00
❑ 35 Mike Dunleavy	.40	1.00
❑ 36 Steve Nash	.75	2.00
❑ 37 Brad Miller	.40	1.00
❑ 38 Chris Bosh	.50	1.25
❑ 39 Boris Diaw	.40	1.00
❑ 40 Steve Francis	.50	1.25
❑ 41 Dirk Nowitzki	.75	2.00
❑ 42 Jason Williams	.40	1.00
❑ 43 Gilbert Arenas	.50	1.25
❑ 44 Keith Van Horn	.40	1.00
❑ 45 Jamal Mashburn	.40	1.00
❑ 46 Derek Fisher	.40	1.00
❑ 47 Andrei Kirilenko	.50	1.25
❑ 48 Ricky Davis	.40	1.00
❑ 49 Gerald Wallace	.50	1.25
❑ 50 Tracy McGrady	1.00	2.50
❑ 51 Zach Randolph	.50	1.25
❑ 52 Rafer Alston	.30	.75
❑ 53 Bobby Jackson	.30	.75
❑ 54 Desmond Mason	.40	1.00
❑ 55 Tim Thomas	.30	.75
❑ 56 Jamaal Tinsley	.40	1.00

❑ 57 Kwame Brown	.30	.75
❑ 58 Chauncey Billups	.50	1.25
❑ 59 Brandon Hunter	.30	.75
❑ 60 Reggie Miller	.50	1.25
❑ 61 Samuel Dalembert	.30	.75
❑ 62 James Posey	.30	.75
❑ 63 Erick Dampier	.30	.75
❑ 64 Carlos Arroyo	.50	1.25
❑ 65 Reece Gaines	.30	.75
❑ 66 Darko Milicic	.30	.75
❑ 67 Sam Cassell	.40	1.00
❑ 68 Dwyane Wade	1.50	4.00
❑ 69 Allan Houston	.40	1.00
❑ 70 Ray Allen	.50	1.25
❑ 71 Tyson Chandler	.40	1.00
❑ 72 Bonzi Wells	.30	.75
❑ 73 Jalen Rose	.40	1.00
❑ 74 Marquis Daniels	.30	.75
❑ 75 Zydrunas Ilgauskas	.40	1.00
❑ 76 Tayshaun Prince	.40	1.00
❑ 77 Lamar Odom	.50	1.25
❑ 78 Luke Ridnour	.30	.75
❑ 79 Joe Johnson	.50	1.25
❑ 80 Vince Carter	1.00	2.50
❑ 81 Antoine Walker	.50	1.25
❑ 82 Shareef Abdur-Rahim	.40	1.00
❑ 83 Richard Jefferson	.50	1.25
❑ 84 Maurice Taylor	.30	.75
❑ 85 Chris Kaman	.40	1.00
❑ 86 Marcus Banks	.30	.75
❑ 87 Mike Bibby	.40	1.00
❑ 88 Latrell Sprewell	.40	1.00
❑ 89 Rashard Lewis	.50	1.25
❑ 90 Baron Davis	.50	1.25
❑ 91 Caron Butler	.40	1.00
❑ 92 Michael Finley	.50	1.25
❑ 93 Mike Miller	.40	1.00
❑ 94 Al Harrington	.40	1.00
❑ 95 Quentin Richardson	.40	1.00
❑ 96 Jamaal Magloire	.30	.75
❑ 97 Darius Miles	.40	1.00
❑ 98 Jeff Foster	.30	.75
❑ 99 Karl Malone	.50	1.25
❑ 100 Shawn Marion	.50	1.25
❑ 101 Antawn Jamison	.50	1.25
❑ 102 Manu Ginobili	.50	1.25
❑ 103 Ben Wallace	.40	1.00
❑ 104 Paul Pierce	.50	1.25
❑ 105 Mike Sweetney	.30	.75
❑ 106 Ron Artest	.40	1.00
❑ 107 Michael Olowokandi	.30	.75
❑ 108 Jason Terry	.40	1.00
❑ 109 Gordan Giricek	.30	.75
❑ 110 Carlos Boozer	.50	1.25
❑ 111 Romain Sato RC	2.00	5.00
❑ 112 Chris Duhon RC	3.00	8.00
❑ 113 Ben Gordon RC	2.50	6.00
❑ 114 Matt Freije RC	2.00	5.00
❑ 115 Al Jefferson RC	4.00	10.00
❑ 116 Beno Udrih RC	2.50	6.00
❑ 117 Kirk Snyder RC	2.00	5.00
❑ 118 Anderson Varejao RC	2.50	6.00
❑ 119 Devin Harris RC	4.00	10.00
❑ 120 Tony Allen RC	2.50	6.00
❑ 121 Ha Seung-Jin RC	2.00	5.00
❑ 122 J.R. Smith RC	4.00	10.00
❑ 123 Blake Stepp RC	2.00	5.00
❑ 124 Jameer Nelson RC	2.50	6.00
❑ 125 Kris Humphries RC	3.00	8.00
❑ 126 Josh Childress RC	2.00	5.00
❑ 127 Tim Pickett RC	2.00	5.00
❑ 128 Delonte West RC	3.00	8.00
❑ 129 Dwight Howard RC	6.00	15.00
❑ 130 Luke Jackson RC	2.00	5.00
❑ 131 Rickey Paulding RC	2.00	5.00
❑ 132 Andre Emmett RC	2.00	5.00
❑ 133 Josh Smith RC	5.00	12.00
❑ 134 Antonio Burks RC	2.00	5.00
❑ 135 Ricky Minard RC	2.00	5.00
❑ 136 Lionel Chalmers RC	2.00	5.00
❑ 137 Shaun Livingston RC	2.00	5.00
❑ 138 Trevor Ariza RC	2.50	6.00
❑ 139 Sergei Lishouk RC	2.00	5.00
❑ 140 Pape Sow RC	2.00	5.00
❑ 141 Rashad Wright RC	2.00	5.00
❑ 142 Jackson Vroman RC	2.00	5.00
❑ 143 Luis Flores RC	2.00	5.00
❑ 144 Royal Ivey RC	2.00	5.00
❑ 145 Kevin Martin RC	2.50	6.00

❑ 146 Andre Iguodala RC	5.00	12.00
❑ 147 Andris Biedrins AU RC	20.00	50.00
❑ 148 Pavel Podkolzine AU RC	12.00	30.00
❑ 149 Luol Deng AU RC	15.00	40.00
❑ 150 Robert Swift AU RC	12.00	30.00
❑ 151 Sebastian Telfair AU RC	12.00	30.00
❑ 152 Emeka Okafor AU RC	25.00	60.00
❑ 153 Dorell Wright AU RC	15.00	40.00
❑ 154 Sasha Vujacic AU RC	12.00	30.00
❑ 155 Rafael Araujo AU RC	12.00	30.00
❑ 156 David Harrison AU RC	12.00	30.00

2005-06 Bowman Chrome

❑ COMP.SET w/o RC's (110)	25.00	60.00
❑ COMMON CARD (1-110)	.40	1.00
❑ COMMON ROOKIE (111-146)	2.00	5.00
❑ COMMON CELEBRITY (147-151)	4.00	10.00
❑ COMMON AU RC (152-161)	6.00	15.00
❑ 1 Steve Nash	.75	2.00
❑ 2 Primoz Brezec	.40	1.00
❑ 3 Baron Davis	.60	1.50
❑ 4 Al Harrington	.40	1.00
❑ 5 Caron Butler	.60	1.50
❑ 6 Marcus Camby	.50	1.25
❑ 7 Carlos Boozer	.60	1.50
❑ 8 Ben Gordon	.75	2.00
❑ 9 Stephen Jackson	.50	1.25
❑ 10 Dirk Nowitzki	1.00	2.50
❑ 11 Nenad Krstic	.50	1.25
❑ 12 Jason Richardson	.60	1.50
❑ 13 Brendan Haywood	.40	1.00
❑ 14 Chauncey Billups	.60	1.50
❑ 15 Corey Maggette	.50	1.25
❑ 16 Peja Stojakovic	.60	1.50
❑ 17 Grant Hill	.60	1.50
❑ 18 Pau Gasol	.60	1.50
❑ 19 Vladimir Radmanovic	.40	1.00
❑ 20 Jason Kidd	1.00	2.50
❑ 21 Tim Duncan	1.25	3.00
❑ 22 David Harrison	.40	1.00
❑ 23 LeBron James	3.00	8.00
❑ 24 Udonis Haslem	.60	1.50
❑ 25 Dan Dickau	.40	1.00
❑ 26 Cuttino Mobley	.50	1.25
❑ 27 Chris Bosh	.60	1.50
❑ 28 Sebastian Telfair	.50	1.25
❑ 29 Latrell Sprewell	.40	1.00
❑ 30 Emeka Okafor	.60	1.50
❑ 31 Mike James	.40	1.00
❑ 32 Trevor Ariza	.50	1.25
❑ 33 Larry Hughes	.50	1.25
❑ 34 Desmond Mason	.40	1.00
❑ 35 Tayshaun Prince	.60	1.50
❑ 36 Manu Ginobili	.60	1.50
❑ 37 Mike Bibby	.60	1.50
❑ 38 Andre Iguodala	.60	1.50
❑ 39 Jamaal Magloire	.40	1.00
❑ 40 Amare Stoudemire	1.25	3.00
❑ 41 Rafer Alston	.40	1.00
❑ 42 Elton Brand	.60	1.50
❑ 43 Steve Francis	.60	1.50
❑ 44 Rashard Lewis	.60	1.50
❑ 45 Lorenzen Wright	.40	1.00
❑ 46 Kirk Hinrich	.60	1.50
❑ 47 Andrei Kirilenko	.60	1.50
❑ 48 Brad Miller	.60	1.50
❑ 49 Jamal Crawford	.50	1.25
❑ 50 Shaquille O'Neal	1.50	4.00
❑ 51 Shaun Livingston	.40	1.00
❑ 52 Troy Murphy	.60	1.50
❑ 53 Drew Gooden	.50	1.25
❑ 54 Paul Pierce	.60	1.50
❑ 55 Vince Carter	1.25	3.00
❑ 56 Wally Szczerbiak	.50	1.25
❑ 57 Antawn Jamison	.60	1.50
❑ 58 Marquis Daniels	.50	1.25
❑ 59 Gerald Wallace	.60	1.50
❑ 60 Ray Allen	.60	1.50
❑ 61 Jamaal Tinsley	.50	1.25
❑ 62 Shane Battier	.60	1.50
❑ 63 Zydrunas Ilgauskas	.50	1.25
❑ 64 Mehmet Okur	.40	1.00
❑ 65 Rasheed Wallace	.60	1.50
❑ 66 Maurice Williams	.50	1.25
❑ 67 Josh Howard	.60	1.50
❑ 68 Zach Randolph	.60	1.50
❑ 69 Kobe Bryant	3.00	8.00
❑ 70 Tracy McGrady	1.25	3.00
❑ 71 Luke Ridnour	.50	1.25
❑ 72 Damon Jones	.50	1.25
❑ 73 Tony Allen	.40	1.00
❑ 74 Mike Miller	.60	1.50
❑ 75 Sam Cassell	.60	1.50
❑ 76 Ben Wallace	.60	1.50
❑ 77 Mike Sweetney	.50	1.25
❑ 78 Eddy Curry	.50	1.25
❑ 79 Michael Redd	.60	1.50
❑ 80 Carmelo Anthony	1.25	3.00
❑ 81 Dwight Howard	1.25	3.00
❑ 82 Josh Smith	.60	1.50
❑ 83 Richard Jefferson	.50	1.25
❑ 84 Richard Hamilton	.50	1.25
❑ 85 Chris Webber	.60	1.50
❑ 86 Shawn Marion	.60	1.50
❑ 87 Jalen Rose	.60	1.50
❑ 88 Bob Sura	.40	1.00
❑ 89 Mike Dunleavy	.50	1.25
❑ 90 Dwyane Wade	1.50	4.00
❑ 91 Gary Payton	.60	1.50
❑ 92 Luol Deng	.60	1.50
❑ 93 Kenyon Martin	.60	1.50
❑ 94 Beno Udrih	.40	1.00
❑ 95 J.R. Smith	.50	1.25
❑ 96 Lamar Odom	.60	1.50
❑ 97 Andre Miller	.50	1.25
❑ 98 Jermaine O'Neal	.60	1.50
❑ 99 Yao Ming	1.50	4.00
❑ 100 Allen Iverson	1.25	3.00
❑ 101 Quentin Richardson	.50	1.25
❑ 102 Gilbert Arenas	.60	1.50
❑ 103 Stephon Marbury	.60	1.50
❑ 104 Antoine Walker	.50	1.25
❑ 105 Jameer Nelson	.50	1.25
❑ 106 Joel Przybilla	.40	1.00
❑ 107 Devin Harris	.60	1.50
❑ 108 Tony Parker	.60	1.50
❑ 109 Josh Childress	.50	1.25
❑ 110 Kevin Garnett	1.25	3.00
❑ 111 Chris Paul RC	6.00	15.00
❑ 112 Danny Granger RC	5.00	12.00
❑ 113 Antoine Wright RC	2.00	5.00
❑ 114 Joey Graham RC	2.00	5.00
❑ 115 Wayne Simien RC	2.50	6.00
❑ 116 Channing Frye RC	2.50	6.00
❑ 117 Charlie Villanueva RC	3.00	8.00
❑ 118 Francisco Garcia RC	2.50	6.00
❑ 119 Ike Diogu RC	2.50	6.00
❑ 120 Jarrett Jack RC	2.00	5.00
❑ 121 Robert Whaley RC	2.00	5.00
❑ 122 C.J. Miles RC	2.00	5.00
❑ 123 Ryan Gomes RC	2.00	5.00
❑ 124 Nate Robinson RC	3.00	8.00
❑ 125 Daniel Ewing RC	2.50	6.00
❑ 126 Andray Blatche RC	2.50	6.00
❑ 127 Luther Head RC	2.50	6.00
❑ 128 Julius Hodge RC	2.50	6.00
❑ 129 Lawrence Roberts RC	2.00	5.00
❑ 130 Jason Maxiell RC	2.50	6.00
❑ 131 Martynas Andriuskevicius RC	2.00	5.00
❑ 132 Ersan Ilyasova RC	2.00	5.00
❑ 133 Martell Webster RC	2.00	5.00
❑ 134 Andrew Bynum RC	6.00	15.00
❑ 135 Louis Williams RC	3.00	8.00
❑ 136 Johan Petro RC	2.00	5.00
❑ 137 Brandon Bass RC	2.00	5.00
❑ 138 Travis Diener RC	2.00	5.00
❑ 139 Bracey Wright RC	2.00	5.00
❑ 140 Marvin Williams RC	3.00	8.00
❑ 141 Eddie Basden RC	2.00	5.00
❑ 142 Von Wafer RC	2.00	5.00
❑ 143 David Lee RC	4.00	10.00
❑ 144 Linas Kleiza RC	2.50	6.00
❑ 145 Luke Schenscher RC	2.00	5.00
❑ 146 Yaroslav Korolev RC	2.00	5.00
❑ 147 Carmen Electra	4.00	10.00
❑ 148 Christie Brinkley	4.00	10.00
❑ 149 Shannon Elizabeth	4.00	10.00
❑ 150 Jenny McCarthy	4.00	10.00
❑ 151 Jay-Z	4.00	10.00
❑ 152 Raymond Felton AU RC	8.00	20.00
❑ 153 Gerald Green AU RC	10.00	25.00
❑ 154 Rashad McCants AU RC	10.00	25.00
❑ 155 Andrew Bogut AU RC	10.00	25.00
❑ 156 Chris Taft AU RC	8.00	20.00
❑ 157 S.Jasikevicius AU RC	8.00	20.00
❑ 158 Hakim Warrick AU RC	8.00	20.00
❑ 159 Deron Williams AU RC	30.00	60.00
❑ 160 Sean May AU RC	6.00	15.00
❑ 161 Monta Ellis AU RC	30.00	60.00

2006-07 Bowman Chrome

❑ COMP.SET w/o SP's (115)	35.00	70.00
❑ 1 Gilbert Arenas	.60	1.50
❑ 2 Delonte West	.50	1.25
❑ 3 Gerald Wallace	.60	1.50
❑ 4 Ike Diogu	.50	1.25
❑ 5 Mike Miller	.60	1.50
❑ 6 Kobe Bryant	3.00	8.00
❑ 7 Richard Hamilton	.50	1.25
❑ 8 Vince Carter	1.25	3.00
❑ 9 Elton Brand	.60	1.50
❑ 10 Boris Diaw	.50	1.25
❑ 11 Carmelo Anthony	.75	2.00
❑ 12 Jermaine O'Neal	.60	1.50
❑ 13 Al Harrington	.40	1.00
❑ 14 Dwight Howard	1.25	3.00
❑ 15 Chris Bosh	.60	1.50
❑ 16 Ben Gordon	.75	2.00
❑ 17 Josh Howard	.60	1.50
❑ 18 Yao Ming	1.50	4.00
❑ 19 David West	.60	1.50
❑ 20 Tim Duncan	1.25	3.00
❑ 21 Andre Iguodala	.60	1.50
❑ 22 LeBron James	3.00	8.00
❑ 23 Channing Frye	.50	1.25
❑ 24 Antoine Walker	.50	1.25
❑ 25 Ricky Davis	.60	1.50
❑ 26 Lamar Odom	.60	1.50
❑ 27 Amare Stoudemire	1.25	3.00
❑ 28 Mike Bibby	.60	1.50
❑ 29 Allen Iverson	1.25	3.00
❑ 30 Marvin Williams	.60	1.50
❑ 31 Wally Szczerbiak	.50	1.25
❑ 32 Ben Wallace	.60	1.50
❑ 33 Nenad Krstic	.50	1.25
❑ 34 Deron Williams	1.00	2.50
❑ 35 Troy Murphy	.60	1.50
❑ 36 Raymond Felton	.75	2.00
❑ 37 Jason Terry	.60	1.50
❑ 38 Zach Randolph	.60	1.50
❑ 39 Pau Gasol	.60	1.50
❑ 40 Larry Hughes	.50	1.25
❑ 41 Luol Deng	.60	1.50
❑ 42 Steve Francis	.60	1.50
❑ 43 Chauncey Billups	.60	1.50
❑ 44 Smush Parker	.40	1.00
❑ 45 Shareef Abdur-Rahim	.60	1.50
❑ 46 Andrei Kirilenko	.60	1.50
❑ 47 Shawn Marion	.60	1.50
❑ 48 Darko Milicic	.60	1.50
❑ 49 Shaquille O'Neal	1.50	4.00
❑ 50 Kevin Garnett	1.25	3.00
❑ 51 Michael Finley	.60	1.50
❑ 52 Peja Stojakovic	.60	1.50
❑ 53 Michael Redd	.60	1.50
❑ 54 Desmond Mason	.40	1.00
❑ 55 Luke Ridnour	.50	1.25
❑ 56 Kenyon Martin	.60	1.50
❑ 57 Morris Peterson	.50	1.25
❑ 58 Chris Kaman	.40	1.00
❑ 59 Jason Richardson	.60	1.50

❑ 60 Jason Kidd	1.00	2.50
❑ 61 Carlos Boozer	.60	1.50
❑ 62 Rashad McCants	.50	1.25
❑ 63 Nate Robinson	.60	1.50
❑ 64 Devin Harris	.60	1.50
❑ 65 Andrew Bogut	.60	1.50
❑ 66 Chris Duhon	.40	1.00
❑ 67 Drew Gooden	.50	1.25
❑ 68 Manu Ginobili	.60	1.50
❑ 69 Jameer Nelson	.50	1.25
❑ 70 Corey Maggette	.50	1.25
❑ 71 Charlie Villanueva	.60	1.50
❑ 72 Shane Battier	.60	1.50
❑ 73 Udonis Haslem	.60	1.50
❑ 74 Tracy McGrady	1.25	3.00
❑ 75 Bobby Simmons	.40	1.00
❑ 76 Baron Davis	.60	1.50
❑ 77 Zydrunas Ilgauskas	.50	1.25
❑ 78 Danny Granger	.50	1.25
❑ 79 Hakim Warrick	.50	1.25
❑ 80 Josh Smith	.60	1.50
❑ 81 Tayshaun Prince	.60	1.50
❑ 82 Rashard Lewis	.60	1.50
❑ 83 Luther Head	.50	1.25
❑ 84 Andre Miller	.50	1.25
❑ 85 T.J. Ford	.50	1.25
❑ 86 Sebastian Telfair	.50	1.25
❑ 87 Dirk Nowitzki	1.00	2.50
❑ 88 Kwame Brown	.50	1.25
❑ 89 Antawn Jamison	.60	1.50
❑ 90 Ron Artest	.60	1.50
❑ 91 Mehmet Okur	.40	1.00
❑ 92 Emeka Okafor	.60	1.50
❑ 93 Sam Cassell	.60	1.50
❑ 94 Chris Paul	1.25	3.00
❑ 95 Chris Webber	.60	1.50
❑ 96 Richard Jefferson	.50	1.25
❑ 97 Dwyane Wade	1.50	4.00
❑ 98 Tony Parker	.60	1.50
❑ 99 Paul Pierce	.60	1.50
❑ 100 Marcus Camby	.50	1.25
❑ 101 Ray Allen	.60	1.50
❑ 102 Stephon Marbury	.60	1.50
❑ 103 Rasheed Wallace	.60	1.50
❑ 104 Brad Miller	.60	1.50
❑ 105 Kirk Hinrich	.60	1.50
❑ 106 Steve Nash	.75	2.00
❑ 107 Sarunas Jasikevicius	.50	1.25
❑ 108 Darius Miles	.40	1.00
❑ 109 Joe Johnson	.50	1.25
❑ 110 Caron Butler	.60	1.50
❑ 111 John Wooden CO	2.50	6.00
❑ 112 Ben Howland CO	2.00	5.00
❑ 113 Jim Calhoun CO	2.00	5.00
❑ 114 Jim Boeheim CO	2.00	5.00
❑ 115 Roy Williams CO	2.00	5.00
❑ 116 LaMarcus Aldridge RC	2.50	6.00
❑ 117 Marcus Vinicius RC	2.00	5.00
❑ 118 Sergio Rodriguez RC	2.00	5.00
❑ 119 Will Blalock RC	2.00	5.00
❑ 120 Paul Millsap RC	3.00	8.00
❑ 121 Leon Powe RC	2.00	5.00
❑ 122 Rudy Gay RC	2.00	5.00
❑ 123 Tyrus Thomas RC	2.50	6.00
❑ 124 Brandon Roy RC	5.00	12.00
❑ 125 J.R. Pinnock RC	2.00	5.00
❑ 126 Kevin Pittsnogle B AU RC	5.00	12.00
❑ 127 Mile Ilic C AU RC	5.00	12.00
❑ 128 Mardy Collins B AU RC	5.00	12.00
❑ 129 Craig Smith C AU RC	5.00	12.00
❑ 130 Jordan Farmar B AU RC	8.00	20.00
❑ 131 Quincy Douby B AU RC	5.00	12.00
❑ 132 James Augustine B AU RC	5.00	12.00
❑ 133 Josh Boone B AU RC	5.00	12.00
❑ 134 Shannon Brown B AU RC	5.00	12.00
❑ 135 David Noel B AU RC	5.00	12.00
❑ 136 Kyle Lowry B AU RC	5.00	12.00
❑ 137 Ryan Hollins C AU RC	5.00	12.00
❑ 138 Renaldo Balkman B AU RC	5.00	12.00
❑ 139 James White C AU RC	5.00	12.00
❑ 140 Damir Markota C AU RC	5.00	12.00
❑ 141 Paul Davis B AU RC	5.00	12.00
❑ 142 Alexander Johnson C AU RC	5.00	12.00
❑ 143 Steve Novak B AU RC	5.00	12.00
❑ 144 P.J. Tucker B AU RC	5.00	12.00
❑ 145 Saer Sene B AU RC	5.00	12.00
❑ 146 Bobby Jones B AU RC	5.00	12.00
❑ 147 Cedric Simmons B AU RC	5.00	12.00
❑ 148 Allan Ray C AU RC	5.00	12.00
❑ 149 Solomon Jones B AU RC	5.00	12.00
❑ 150 Ronnie Brewer A AU RC	6.00	15.00
❑ 151 Thabo Sefolosha B AU RC	12.50	30.00
❑ 152 Maurice Ager B AU RC	5.00	12.00
❑ 153 Daniel Gibson C AU RC	10.00	25.00
❑ 154 Shawne Williams B AU RC	5.00	12.00
❑ 155 Dee Brown B AU RC	5.00	12.00
❑ 156 Andrea Bargnani A AU RC	15.00	30.00
❑ 157 Patrick O'Bryant A AU RC	5.00	12.00
❑ 158 Shelden Williams A AU RC	6.00	15.00
❑ 159 Hilton Armstrong A AU RC	5.00	12.00
❑ 160 Adam Morrison A AU RC	15.00	30.00
❑ 161 Rodney Carney B AU RC	5.00	12.00
❑ 162 Randy Foye A AU RC	10.00	25.00
❑ 163 Rajon Rondo B AU RC	30.00	60.00
❑ 164 Marcus Williams A AU RC	12.50	30.00
❑ 165 J.J. Redick A AU RC	15.00	30.00

2007-08 Bowman Chrome

❑ COMP.SET w/o SP's (110)	20.00	50.00
❑ 1 Gilbert Arenas	.60	1.50
❑ 2 Dwight Howard	1.25	3.00
❑ 3 Dwyane Wade	1.50	4.00
❑ 4 Chris Bosh	.60	1.50
❑ 5 Josh Smith	.60	1.50
❑ 6 Andrew Bogut	.60	1.50
❑ 7 Ben Gordon	.75	2.00
❑ 8 Deron Williams	1.00	2.50
❑ 9 Tony Parker	.60	1.50
❑ 10 Mike Bibby	.60	1.50
❑ 11 Yao Ming	1.50	4.00
❑ 12 Raymond Felton	.75	2.00
❑ 13 Steve Nash	.75	2.00
❑ 14 Jameer Nelson	.50	1.25
❑ 15 Carmelo Anthony	1.25	3.00
❑ 16 Pau Gasol	.60	1.50
❑ 17 Rashard Lewis	.60	1.50
❑ 18 Eddy Curry	.40	1.00
❑ 19 Luol Deng	.60	1.50
❑ 20 Kevin Garnett	1.50	4.00
❑ 21 Tim Duncan	1.25	3.00
❑ 22 Michael Redd	.60	1.50
❑ 23 LeBron James	3.00	8.00
❑ 24 Kobe Bryant	3.00	8.00
❑ 25 Al Jefferson	.60	1.50
❑ 26 Mike Dunleavy	.50	1.25
❑ 27 Tyson Chandler	.60	1.50
❑ 28 Zach Randolph	.60	1.50
❑ 29 Jason Richardson	.60	1.50
❑ 30 Rasheed Wallace	.60	1.50
❑ 31 Shawn Marion	.60	1.50
❑ 32 Shaquille O'Neal	1.50	4.00
❑ 33 Allen Iverson	1.25	3.00
❑ 34 Paul Pierce	.60	1.50
❑ 35 Adam Morrison	.60	1.50
❑ 36 Mike Miller	.60	1.50
❑ 37 Larry Hughes	.50	1.25
❑ 38 Kevin Martin	.60	1.50
❑ 39 Charlie Villanueva	.60	1.50
❑ 40 Vince Carter	1.25	3.00
❑ 41 Dirk Nowitzki	1.00	2.50
❑ 42 Elton Brand	.60	1.50
❑ 43 Ray Allen	.60	1.50
❑ 44 Luke Walton	.50	1.25
❑ 45 Chris Paul	1.25	3.00
❑ 46 Marcus Camby	.40	1.00
❑ 47 Andrei Kirilenko	.60	1.50
❑ 48 J.J. Redick	.60	1.50
❑ 49 Richard Hamilton	.50	1.25
❑ 50 Emeka Okafor	.60	1.50
❑ 51 Manu Ginobili	.60	1.50
❑ 52 Monta Ellis	.50	1.25
❑ 53 Jorge Garbajosa	.60	1.50
❑ 54 Kyle Korver	.60	1.50
❑ 55 Jason Kidd	1.00	2.50
❑ 56 Randy Foye	.60	1.50
❑ 57 Shane Battier	.60	1.50
❑ 58 Shaun Livingston	.40	1.00
❑ 59 Jason Terry	.60	1.50
❑ 60 Joe Johnson	.60	1.50
❑ 61 Lamar Odom	.60	1.50
❑ 62 Tayshaun Prince	.60	1.50
❑ 63 Chris Wilcox	.50	1.25
❑ 64 Leandro Barbosa	.50	1.25
❑ 65 Al Harrington	.50	1.25
❑ 66 Jamal Crawford	.40	1.00
❑ 67 Caron Butler	.60	1.50
❑ 68 Chauncey Billups	.60	1.50
❑ 69 Ricky Davis	.60	1.50
❑ 70 Andrea Bargnani	.75	2.00
❑ 71 Samuel Dalembert	.40	1.00
❑ 72 LaMarcus Aldridge	.75	2.00
❑ 73 Mehmet Okur	.50	1.25
❑ 74 Marcus Williams	.60	1.50
❑ 75 Andre Miller	.50	1.25
❑ 76 Rudy Gay	.50	1.25
❑ 77 Jermaine O'Neal	.60	1.50
❑ 78 Boris Diaw	.50	1.25
❑ 79 Ryan Gomes	.40	1.00
❑ 80 Gerald Wallace	.60	1.50
❑ 81 Udonis Haslem	.60	1.50
❑ 82 Mo Williams	.50	1.25
❑ 83 Jarrett Jack	.50	1.25
❑ 84 Chris Webber	.60	1.50
❑ 85 Trevor Ariza	.40	1.00
❑ 86 Kirk Hinrich	.60	1.50
❑ 87 Rafer Alston	.40	1.00
❑ 88 Danny Granger	.50	1.25
❑ 89 David West	.60	1.50
❑ 90 Drew Gooden	.50	1.25
❑ 91 Stephon Marbury	.60	1.50
❑ 92 Antawn Jamison	.60	1.50
❑ 93 Ron Artest	.60	1.50
❑ 94 Richard Jefferson	.60	1.50
❑ 95 Carlos Boozer	.60	1.50
❑ 96 Hakim Warrick	.50	1.25
❑ 97 T.J. Ford	.50	1.25
❑ 98 Desmond Mason	.40	1.00
❑ 99 Andre Iguodala	.60	1.50
❑ 100 Amare Stoudemire	1.25	3.00
❑ 101 Tracy McGrady	1.25	3.00
❑ 102 Jason Kapono	.40	1.00
❑ 103 Ben Wallace	.60	1.50
❑ 104 Marvin Williams	.60	1.50
❑ 105 Baron Davis	.60	1.50
❑ 106 Andrew Bynum	.60	1.50
❑ 107 Brandon Roy	1.00	2.50
❑ 108 David Lee	.50	1.25
❑ 109 Corey Maggette	.50	1.25
❑ 110 Josh Howard	.60	1.50
❑ 111 Kevin Durant RC	20.00	50.00
❑ 112 Al Horford RC	3.00	8.00
❑ 113 Michael Conley RC	3.00	8.00
❑ 114 Jeff Green RC	3.00	8.00
❑ 115 Corey Brewer RC	3.00	8.00
❑ 116 Joakim Noah RC	3.00	8.00
❑ 117 Julian Wright RC	3.00	8.00
❑ 118 Ramon Sessions RC	3.00	8.00
❑ 119 Sammy Mejia RC	2.50	6.00
❑ 120 Luis Scola RC	4.00	10.00
❑ 121 Yi Jianlian RC	4.00	10.00
❑ 122 Arron Afflalo RC	2.50	6.00
❑ 123 Carl Landry RC	2.50	6.00
❑ 124 Alando Tucker RC	2.50	6.00
❑ 125 Gabe Pruitt RC	2.50	6.00
❑ 126 Marcus Williams RC	2.50	6.00
❑ 127 Spencer Hawes RC	2.50	6.00
❑ 128 Acie Law RC	3.00	8.00
❑ 129 Thaddeus Young RC	3.00	8.00
❑ 130 Nick Fazekas RC	2.50	6.00
❑ 131 Al Thornton RC	2.50	6.00
❑ 132 Rodney Stuckey RC	5.00	12.00
❑ 133 Nick Young RC	2.50	6.00
❑ 134 Glen Davis RC	5.00	12.00
❑ 135 Jermareo Davidson RC	2.50	6.00
❑ 136 JamesOn Curry RC	2.50	6.00
❑ 137 Jason Smith RC	2.50	6.00
❑ 138 Daequan Cook RC	3.00	8.00
❑ 139 Jared Dudley RC	2.50	6.00
❑ 140 Derrick Byars RC	2.50	6.00
❑ 141 Josh McRoberts RC	3.00	8.00
❑ 142 Adam Haluska RC	2.50	6.00
❑ 143 Reyshawn Terry RC	2.50	6.00
❑ 144 Aaron Gray AU RC	2.50	6.00
❑ 145 Herbert Hill RC	2.50	6.00

❑ 146 Jared Jordan RC	2.50	6.00
❑ 147 Wilson Chandler RC	2.50	6.00
❑ 148 Morris Almond RC	2.50	6.00
❑ 149 Aaron Brooks RC	4.00	10.00
❑ 150 Petteri Koponen RC	2.50	6.00
❑ 151 Dominic McGuire RC	2.50	6.00
❑ 152 Greg Oden RC	4.00	10.00
❑ 153 Stephane Lasme RC	2.50	6.00
❑ 154 D.J. Strawberry RC	2.50	6.00
❑ 155 Sean Williams RC	2.50	6.00
❑ 156 Marco Belinelli RC	2.50	6.00
❑ 157 Javaris Crittenton RC	2.50	6.00
❑ 158 Demetris Nichols RC	2.50	6.00
❑ 159 Taurean Green RC	2.50	6.00
❑ 160 Brandan Wright RC	3.00	8.00

2008-09 Bowman Chrome

❑ COMP.SET w/o RC (110)	20.00	40.00
❑ 1 Tracy McGrady	.75	2.00
❑ 2 Jason Kidd	.60	1.50
❑ 3 LeBron James	3.00	8.00
❑ 4 Chris Bosh	.60	1.50
❑ 5 Kevin Garnett	1.25	3.00
❑ 6 Josh Smith	.60	1.50
❑ 7 Richard Hamilton	.50	1.25
❑ 8 Monta Ellis	.60	1.50
❑ 9 Yi Jianlian	.60	1.50
❑ 10 Danny Granger	.60	1.50
❑ 11 Richard Jefferson	.60	1.50
❑ 12 Elton Brand	1.00	2.50
❑ 13 Rudy Gay	.60	1.50
❑ 14 Andres Nocioni	.50	1.25
❑ 15 Carmelo Anthony	.75	2.00
❑ 16 Pau Gasol	.60	1.50
❑ 17 Corey Brewer	.50	1.25
❑ 18 Hedo Turkoglu	.60	1.50
❑ 19 Andre Iguodala	.60	1.50
❑ 20 Raymond Felton	.50	1.25
❑ 21 Tim Duncan	1.00	2.50
❑ 22 Michael Redd	.60	1.50
❑ 23 Chris Paul	1.25	3.00
❑ 24 Kobe Bryant	3.00	8.00
❑ 25 Brandon Roy	.75	2.00
❑ 26 Carlos Boozer	.60	1.50
❑ 27 Jeff Green	.50	1.25
❑ 28 Luis Scola	.50	1.25
❑ 29 Al Thornton	.60	1.50
❑ 30 Gilbert Arenas	.60	1.50
❑ 31 Brandan Wright	.50	1.25
❑ 32 Shaquille O'Neal	1.25	3.00
❑ 33 Allen Iverson	.75	2.00
❑ 34 Paul Pierce	.75	2.00
❑ 35 Ben Gordon	.60	1.50
❑ 36 Jamal Crawford	.40	1.00
❑ 37 Andrew Bynum	.60	1.50
❑ 38 Gerald Wallace	.60	1.50
❑ 39 Mike Conley	.50	1.25
❑ 40 Ben Wallace	.60	1.50
❑ 41 Dirk Nowitzki	.75	2.00
❑ 42 David Lee	.50	1.25
❑ 43 Mo Williams	.50	1.25
❑ 44 Al Jefferson	.60	1.50
❑ 45 Tayshaun Prince	.60	1.50
❑ 46 Jameer Nelson	.50	1.25
❑ 47 Andrei Kirilenko	.60	1.50
❑ 48 David West	.60	1.50
❑ 49 Al Horford	.60	1.50
❑ 50 Steve Nash	.60	1.50
❑ 51 Ron Artest	.60	1.50
❑ 52 Greg Oden	.60	1.50
❑ 53 Sean Williams	.50	1.25
❑ 54 Jamario Moon	.60	1.50
❑ 55 Baron Davis	.60	1.50
❑ 56 Udonis Haslem	.60	1.50
❑ 57 Mike Dunleavy	.50	1.25
❑ 58 Shane Battier	.50	1.25
❑ 59 Andrew Bogut	.60	1.50
❑ 60 Ray Allen	.60	1.50
❑ 61 Nick Young	.40	1.00
❑ 62 Manu Ginobili	.60	1.50
❑ 63 Jason Richardson	.60	1.50
❑ 64 Mike Miller	.60	1.50
❑ 65 Leandro Barbosa	.50	1.25
❑ 66 Luol Deng	.60	1.50
❑ 67 Shawn Marion	.60	1.50
❑ 68 Peja Stojakovic	.60	1.50
❑ 69 Kevin Durant	1.50	4.00
❑ 70 Corey Maggette	.60	1.50
❑ 71 Chauncey Billups	.60	1.50
❑ 72 Josh Howard	.60	1.50
❑ 73 Kevin Martin	.60	1.50
❑ 74 Anderson Varejao	.50	1.25
❑ 75 Craig Smith	.60	1.50
❑ 76 Antawn Jamison	.60	1.50
❑ 77 Marcus Camby	.40	1.00
❑ 78 Andre Miller	.50	1.25
❑ 79 Zach Randolph	.60	1.50
❑ 80 Deron Williams	.75	2.00
❑ 81 Devin Harris	.60	1.50
❑ 82 Rashard Lewis	.60	1.50
❑ 83 Damien Wilkins	.40	1.00
❑ 84 LaMarcus Aldridge	.60	1.50
❑ 85 Larry Hughes	.50	1.25
❑ 86 Brad Miller	.60	1.50
❑ 87 Jermaine O'Neal	.60	1.50
❑ 88 Caron Butler	.60	1.50
❑ 89 Tyson Chandler	.50	1.25
❑ 90 Joe Johnson	.60	1.50
❑ 91 Amare Stoudemire	.75	2.00
❑ 92 Dwight Howard	1.25	3.00
❑ 93 Rajon Rondo	.60	1.50
❑ 94 T.J. Ford	.40	1.00
❑ 95 Rodney Stuckey	.75	2.00
❑ 96 Samuel Dalembert	.40	1.00
❑ 97 Tony Parker	.60	1.50
❑ 98 Vince Carter	.75	2.00
❑ 99 Yao Ming	.75	2.00
❑ 100 Dwyane Wade	1.25	3.00
❑ 101 Dominique Wilkins	.75	2.00
❑ 102 Rick Barry	.60	1.50
❑ 103 John Stockton	1.00	2.50
❑ 104 Magic Johnson	1.25	3.00
❑ 105 George Gervin	.75	2.00
❑ 106 Bill Russell	1.00	2.50
❑ 107 David Robinson	1.00	2.50
❑ 108 Dennis Rodman	.60	1.50
❑ 109 Larry Bird	2.00	5.00
❑ 110 Jerry West	.75	2.00
❑ 111 Derrick Rose RC	6.00	15.00
❑ 112 Michael Beasley RC	3.00	8.00
❑ 113 O.J. Mayo RC	2.50	6.00
❑ 114 Russell Westbrook RC	4.00	10.00
❑ 115 Kevin Love RC	2.00	5.00
❑ 116 Danilo Gallinari RC	2.50	6.00
❑ 117 Eric Gordon RC	2.00	5.00
❑ 118 Joe Alexander RC	1.50	4.00
❑ 119 D.J. Augustin RC	1.50	4.00
❑ 120 Brook Lopez RC	3.00	8.00
❑ 121 Jerryd Bayless RC	1.50	4.00
❑ 122 Jason Thompson RC	1.50	4.00
❑ 123 Anthony Randolph RC	2.50	6.00
❑ 124 Robin Lopez RC	1.50	4.00
❑ 125 Marreese Speights RC	1.50	4.00
❑ 126 Roy Hibbert RC	2.00	5.00
❑ 127 JaVale McGee RC	1.50	4.00
❑ 128 J.J. Hickson RC	2.50	6.00
❑ 129 Alexis Ajinca RC	1.50	4.00
❑ 130 Ryan Anderson RC	1.50	4.00
❑ 131 Courtney Lee RC	2.50	6.00
❑ 132 Kosta Koufos RC	1.50	4.00
❑ 133 Donte Greene RC	1.50	4.00
❑ 134 George Hill RC	2.50	6.00
❑ 135 D.J. White RC	1.50	4.00
❑ 136 J.R. Giddens RC	1.50	4.00
❑ 137 Joey Dorsey RC	1.50	4.00
❑ 138 Mario Chalmers RC	2.00	5.00
❑ 139 DeAndre Jordan RC	1.50	4.00
❑ 140 Chris Douglas-Roberts RC	2.00	5.00
❑ 141 Malik Hairston RC	1.50	4.00
❑ 142 Sean Singletary RC	1.50	4.00
❑ 143 Kyle Weaver RC	1.50	4.00
❑ 144 Patrick Ewing Jr. RC	1.50	4.00
❑ 145 Walter Sharpe RC	1.50	4.00
❑ 146 Sonny Weems RC	1.50	4.00
❑ 147 Shan Foster RC	1.50	4.00
❑ 148 Nicolas Batum RC	2.00	5.00
❑ 149 Brandon Rush RC	1.50	4.00
❑ 150 Darrell Arthur RC	1.50	4.00
❑ 151 Derrick Rose AU A	75.00	150.00
❑ 152 Michael Beasley AU A	60.00	120.00
❑ 153 O.J. Mayo AU A	30.00	60.00
❑ 154 Russell Westbrook AU A	15.00	30.00
❑ 155 Kevin Love AU A	15.00	30.00
❑ 156 Danilo Gallinari AU A	10.00	25.00
❑ 157 Eric Gordon AU A	15.00	30.00
❑ 158 Joe Alexander AU A	10.00	25.00
❑ 159 D.J. Augustin AU B	5.00	12.00
❑ 160 Brook Lopez AU A	6.00	15.00
❑ 161 Jerryd Bayless AU A	15.00	30.00
❑ 162 Jason Thompson AU B	6.00	15.00
❑ 163 Anthony Randolph AU B	6.00	15.00
❑ 164 Robin Lopez AU B	5.00	12.00
❑ 165 Marreese Speights AU B	5.00	12.00
❑ 166 Roy Hibbert AU B	5.00	12.00
❑ 167 J.J. Hickson AU B	6.00	15.00
❑ 168 Ryan Anderson AU B	4.00	10.00
❑ 169 Courtney Lee AU B	5.00	12.00
❑ 170 Kosta Koufos AU B	4.00	10.00
❑ 171 George Hill AU B	8.00	20.00
❑ 172 D.J. White AU B	5.00	12.00
❑ 173 J.R. Giddens AU B	5.00	12.00
❑ 174 Joey Dorsey AU B	4.00	10.00
❑ 175 Mario Chalmers AU B	8.00	20.00
❑ 176 DeAndre Jordan AU B	4.00	10.00
❑ 177 Chris Douglas-Roberts AU B	4.00	10.00
❑ 178 JaVale McGee AU B	4.00	10.00
❑ 179 Kyle Weaver AU B	4.00	10.00
❑ 180 Patrick Ewing Jr. AU B	5.00	12.00
❑ 181 Sonny Weems AU B	4.00	10.00
❑ 182 Brandon Rush AU B	5.00	12.00
❑ 183 Darrell Arthur AU B	5.00	12.00

2006-07 Bowman Elevation

❑ COMP.SET w/o SP's (90)	25.00	60.00
❑ 1 Dwyane Wade	1.50	4.00
❑ 2 Elton Brand	.60	1.50
❑ 3 Dwight Howard	1.25	3.00
❑ 4 Chris Bosh	.60	1.50
❑ 5 Baron Davis	.60	1.50
❑ 6 Marcus Camby	.50	1.25
❑ 7 Rashard Lewis	.60	1.50
❑ 8 Paul Pierce	.60	1.50
❑ 9 Jermaine O'Neal	.60	1.50
❑ 10 Gilbert Arenas	.60	1.50
❑ 11 Larry Hughes	.50	1.25
❑ 12 Manu Ginobili	.60	1.50
❑ 13 Lamar Odom	.60	1.50
❑ 14 Ron Artest	.60	1.50
❑ 15 Carmelo Anthony	.75	2.00
❑ 16 Deron Williams	1.00	2.50
❑ 17 Gerald Wallace	.60	1.50
❑ 18 Peja Stojakovic	.60	1.50
❑ 19 Vince Carter	1.25	3.00
❑ 20 Kevin Garnett	1.25	3.00
❑ 21 Yao Ming	1.50	4.00
❑ 22 Josh Howard	.60	1.50
❑ 23 Michael Redd	.60	1.50
❑ 24 Eddy Curry	.50	1.25
❑ 25 Shawn Marion	.60	1.50
❑ 26 Luol Deng	.60	1.50
❑ 27 Ben Wallace	.60	1.50
❑ 28 Sam Cassell	.60	1.50
❑ 29 Steve Francis	.60	1.50
❑ 30 Ray Allen	.60	1.50
❑ 31 Andre Iguodala	.60	1.50
❑ 32 Shaquille O'Neal	1.50	4.00
❑ 33 Pau Gasol	.60	1.50
❑ 34 Jason Richardson	.60	1.50
❑ 35 Ricky Davis	.60	1.50

❑ 36 Joe Johnson	.50	1.25
❑ 37 Dirk Nowitzki	1.00	2.50
❑ 38 Richard Hamilton	.50	1.25
❑ 39 Troy Murphy	.60	1.50
❑ 40 Charlie Villanueva	.60	1.50
❑ 41 T.J. Ford	.50	1.25
❑ 42 Zydrunas Ilgauskas	.50	1.25
❑ 43 Andrei Kirilenko	.60	1.50
❑ 44 Chris Paul	1.25	3.00
❑ 45 Grant Hill	.60	1.50
❑ 46 Kobe Bryant	3.00	8.00
❑ 47 Tim Duncan	1.25	3.00
❑ 48 Raymond Felton	.75	2.00
❑ 49 Antawn Jamison	.60	1.50
❑ 50 Jason Kidd	1.00	2.50
❑ 51 Shareef Abdur-Rahim	.60	1.50
❑ 52 Shane Battier	.60	1.50
❑ 53 Kirk Hinrich	.60	1.50
❑ 54 Jason Terry	.60	1.50
❑ 55 Mehmet Okur	.40	1.00
❑ 56 Stephon Marbury	.60	1.50
❑ 57 Steve Nash	.75	2.00
❑ 58 Mike Bibby	.60	1.50
❑ 59 Sebastian Telfair	.50	1.25
❑ 60 Richard Jefferson	.50	1.25
❑ 61 Andre Miller	.50	1.25
❑ 62 Delonte West	.50	1.25
❑ 63 Tracy McGrady	1.25	3.00
❑ 64 Rasheed Wallace	.60	1.50
❑ 65 Al Harrington	.40	1.00
❑ 66 Emeka Okafor	.60	1.50
❑ 67 Caron Butler	.60	1.50
❑ 68 Andrew Bogut	.60	1.50
❑ 69 Tony Parker	.60	1.50
❑ 70 Zach Randolph	.60	1.50
❑ 71 Allen Iverson	1.25	3.00
❑ 72 David West	.60	1.50
❑ 73 Chris Webber	.60	1.50
❑ 74 Ben Gordon	.75	2.00
❑ 75 Corey Maggette	.50	1.25
❑ 76 Sarunas Jasikevicius	.50	1.25
❑ 77 Chauncey Billups	.60	1.50
❑ 78 Amare Stoudemire	1.25	3.00
❑ 79 Luke Ridnour	.50	1.25
❑ 80 LeBron James	3.00	8.00
❑ 81 Kenyon Martin	.60	1.50
❑ 82 Marko Jaric	.40	1.00
❑ 83 Antoine Walker	.50	1.25
❑ 84 J.R. Smith	.50	1.25
❑ 85 Mike Miller	.60	1.50
❑ 86 Channing Frye	.50	1.25
❑ 87 Smush Parker	.40	1.00
❑ 88 Wally Szczerbiak	.50	1.25
❑ 89 Morris Peterson	.50	1.25
❑ 90 Luther Head	.50	1.25
❑ 91 Randy Foye RC	2.00	5.00
❑ 92 Daniel Gibson RC	2.50	6.00
❑ 93 Hassan Adams RC	2.50	6.00
❑ 94 Hilton Armstrong RC	2.00	5.00
❑ 95 Marcus Williams RC	2.50	6.00
❑ 96 Paul Davis RC	2.00	5.00
❑ 97 Quincy Douby RC	2.00	5.00
❑ 98 Ronnie Brewer RC	2.50	6.00
❑ 99 Rodney Carney RC	2.00	5.00
❑ 100 Rudy Gay RC	2.00	5.00
❑ 101 Adam Morrison RC	2.50	6.00
❑ 102 Rajon Rondo RC	8.00	20.00
❑ 103 Steve Novak RC	2.00	5.00
❑ 104 Craig Smith RC	2.00	5.00
❑ 105 Leon Powe RC	2.00	5.00
❑ 106 James White RC	2.00	5.00
❑ 107 Josh Boone RC	2.00	5.00
❑ 108 J.J. Redick RC	2.00	5.00
❑ 109 Shelden Williams RC	2.50	6.00
❑ 110 Alexander Johnson RC	2.00	5.00
❑ 111 Guillermo Diaz RC	2.00	5.00
❑ 112 Maurice Ager RC	2.00	5.00
❑ 113 Jordan Farmar RC	2.50	6.00
❑ 114 Mardy Collins RC	2.00	5.00
❑ 115 Ryan Hollins RC	2.00	5.00
❑ 116 Kyle Lowry RC	2.00	5.00
❑ 117 James Augustine RC	2.00	5.00
❑ 118 Shawne Williams RC	2.00	5.00
❑ 119 LaMarcus Aldridge RC	2.50	6.00
❑ 120 Patrick O'Bryant RC	2.00	5.00
❑ 121 Cedric Simmons RC	2.00	5.00
❑ 122 P.J. Tucker RC	2.00	5.00
❑ 123 Brandon Roy RC	5.00	12.00
❑ 124 Tyrus Thomas RC	2.50	6.00
❑ 125 Andrea Bargnani RC	3.00	8.00
❑ 126 Dee Brown RC	2.00	5.00
❑ 127 Denham Brown RC	2.00	5.00
❑ 128 Saer Sene RC	2.00	5.00
❑ 129 Thabo Sefolosha RC	2.50	6.00
❑ 130 Shannon Brown RC	2.00	5.00

2007-08 Bowman Elevation

❑ COMPLETE SET (100)	25.00	50.00
❑ 1 Tracy Mcgrady	.75	2.00
❑ 2 Shaquille O'Neal	1.00	2.50
❑ 3 Allen Iverson	.75	2.00
❑ 4 Chris Bosh	.40	1.00
❑ 5 Jason Kidd	.60	1.50
❑ 6 Elton Brand	.40	1.00
❑ 7 Brandon Roy	.60	1.50
❑ 8 Tony Parker	.40	1.00
❑ 9 Luol Deng	.40	1.00
❑ 10 Gilbert Arenas	.40	1.00
❑ 11 Amare Stoudemire	.75	2.00
❑ 12 Dwight Howard	.75	2.00
❑ 13 Deron Williams	.60	1.50
❑ 14 Dirk Nowitzki	.60	1.50
❑ 15 Vince Carter	.75	2.00
❑ 16 Richard Hamilton	.30	.75
❑ 17 Baron Davis	.40	1.00
❑ 18 Pau Gasol	.40	1.00
❑ 19 Kevin Garnett	1.00	2.50
❑ 20 Lebron James	2.00	5.00
❑ 21 Tim Duncan	.75	2.00
❑ 22 Steve Nash	.50	1.25
❑ 23 Jason Richardson	.40	1.00
❑ 24 Kobe Bryant	2.00	5.00
❑ 25 Josh Smith	.40	1.00
❑ 26 Eddy Curry	.25	.60
❑ 27 Mike Bibby	.40	1.00
❑ 28 Ray Allen	.40	1.00
❑ 29 Andre Iguodala	.40	1.00
❑ 30 Chris Paul	.75	2.00
❑ 31 Yao Ming	1.00	2.50
❑ 32 Shawn Marion	.40	1.00
❑ 33 Dwyane Wade	1.00	2.50
❑ 34 Paul Pierce	.40	1.00
❑ 35 Carmelo Anthony	.75	2.00
❑ 36 Jermaine O'Neal	.40	1.00
❑ 37 Michael Redd	.40	1.00
❑ 38 Gerald Wallace	.40	1.00
❑ 39 Ben Gordon	.50	1.25
❑ 40 Carlos Boozer	.40	1.00
❑ 41 Larry Bird	2.00	5.00
❑ 42 Bill Walton	.60	1.50
❑ 43 Kareem Abdul-Jabbar	1.00	2.50
❑ 44 John Havlicek	.60	1.50
❑ 45 David Robinson	1.00	2.50
❑ 46 Bill Russell	1.00	2.50
❑ 47 Isiah Thomas	.60	1.50
❑ 48 John Stockton	1.00	2.50
❑ 49 Dominique Wilkins	.75	2.00
❑ 50 Magic Johnson	1.25	3.00
❑ 51 Nick Young RC	1.50	4.00
❑ 52 Greg Oden RC	2.50	6.00
❑ 53 Julian Wright RC	2.00	5.00
❑ 54 Dominic Mcguire RC	1.50	4.00
❑ 55 Acie Law IV RC	2.00	5.00
❑ 56 Luis Scola RC	2.50	6.00
❑ 57 Thaddeus Young RC	2.00	5.00
❑ 58 Rodney Stuckey RC	3.00	8.00
❑ 59 Jermareo Davidson RC	1.50	4.00
❑ 60 Daequan Cook RC	2.00	5.00
❑ 61 Josh McRoberts RC	2.00	5.00
❑ 62 Aaron Gray RC	1.50	4.00
❑ 63 Wilson Chandler RC	1.50	4.00
❑ 64 Chris Richard RC	1.50	4.00
❑ 65 Stephane Lasme RC	1.50	4.00
❑ 66 Kyrylo Fesenko RC	1.50	4.00
❑ 67 Taurean Green RC	1.50	4.00
❑ 68 Al Thornton RC	1.50	4.00
❑ 69 Corey Brewer RC	2.00	5.00
❑ 70 Ramon Sessions RC	2.00	5.00
❑ 71 Kevin Durant RC	12.00	30.00
❑ 72 Alando Tucker RC	1.50	4.00
❑ 73 Spencer Hawes RC	1.50	4.00
❑ 74 Nick Fazekas RC	1.50	4.00
❑ 75 Yi Jianlian RC	2.50	6.00
❑ 76 Juan Carlos Navarro RC	2.00	5.00
❑ 77 Jared Dudley RC	1.50	4.00
❑ 78 Adam Haluska RC	1.50	4.00
❑ 79 Herbert Hill RC	1.50	4.00
❑ 80 Kosta Perovic RC	1.50	4.00
❑ 81 JamesOn Curry RC	1.50	4.00
❑ 82 D.J. Strawberry RC	1.50	4.00
❑ 83 Javaris Crittenton RC	1.50	4.00
❑ 84 Al Horford RC	2.00	5.00
❑ 85 Mike Conley RC	2.00	5.00
❑ 86 Joakim Noah RC	2.00	5.00
❑ 87 Marco Belinelli RC	1.50	4.00
❑ 88 Arron Afflalo RC	1.50	4.00
❑ 89 Gabe Pruitt RC	1.50	4.00
❑ 90 Carl Landry RC	1.50	4.00
❑ 91 Jeff Green RC	2.00	5.00
❑ 92 Glen Davis RC	3.00	8.00
❑ 93 Jason Smith RC	1.50	4.00
❑ 94 Morris Almond RC	1.50	4.00
❑ 95 Cheik Samb RC	1.50	4.00
❑ 96 Brandon Wallace RC	1.50	4.00
❑ 97 Aaron Brooks RC	2.50	6.00
❑ 98 Brandan Wright RC	2.00	5.00
❑ 99 Sean Williams RC	1.50	4.00
❑ 100 Coby Karl RC	1.50	4.00

2002-03 Bowman Signature Edition

❑ COMMON CARD	.50	1.25
❑ COMMON ROOKIE	4.00	10.00
❑ SEAI Allen Iverson	1.50	4.00
❑ SEAJ Antawn Jamison	.75	2.00
❑ SEAK Andrei Kirilenko	.75	2.00
❑ SEAM Alonzo Mourning	.75	2.00
❑ SEAS Stoudemire JSY AU RC	40.00	80.00
❑ SEAW Antoine Walker	.60	1.50
❑ SEAKM Antonio McDyess	.60	1.50
❑ SEALM Andre Miller	.60	1.50
❑ SEBD Baron Davis	.75	2.00
❑ SEBN Bostjan Nachbar AU RC	4.00	10.00
❑ SEBW Ben Wallace	.60	1.50
❑ SECB Curtis Borchardt AU RC	4.00	10.00
❑ SECM Cuttino Mobley	.60	1.50
❑ SECO Chris Owens AU RC	4.00	10.00
❑ SECT Cezary Trybanski AU RC	4.00	10.00
❑ SECW Chris Wilcox JSY AU RC	5.00	12.00
❑ SECBO C.Boozer JSY AU RC	8.00	20.00
❑ SECBU Caron Butler JSY AU RC	8.00	20.00
❑ SECJA C.Jacobsen JSY AU RC	4.00	10.00
❑ SECJE C.Jefferies JSY AU RC	4.00	10.00
❑ SEDD Dan Dickau AU RC	4.00	10.00
❑ SEDN Dirk Nowitzki	1.25	3.00
❑ SEDW D.Wagner JSY AU RC	4.00	10.00
❑ SEDGA D.Gadzuric JSY AU RC	4.00	10.00
❑ SEDGO D.Gooden JSY AU RC	10.00	25.00
❑ SEDLM Darius Miles	.50	1.25
❑ SEEB Elton Brand	.75	2.00
❑ SEEC Eddy Curry	.60	1.50
❑ SEEG Manu Ginobili AU RC	20.00	40.00
❑ SEEJ Eddie Jones	.60	1.50
❑ SEER E.Rentzias AU RC	4.00	10.00
❑ SEFJ Fred Jones JSY AU RC	5.00	12.00
❑ SEFR Frank Williams AU RC	4.00	10.00
❑ SEGG Gordan Giricek AU RC	4.00	10.00
❑ SEGP Gary Payton	.75	2.00

❑ SEGR Glenn Robinson	.60	1.50
❑ SEJB J.R. Bremer AU RC	4.00	10.00
❑ SEJD Juan Dixon JSY AU RC	6.00	15.00
❑ SEJJ J.Jeffries JSY AU RC	4.00	10.00
❑ SEJK Jason Kidd	1.25	3.00
❑ SEJM Jamal Mashburn	.60	1.50
❑ SEJO Jermaine O'Neal	.75	2.00
❑ SEJP Jannero Pargo AU RC	4.00	10.00
❑ SEJS John Salmons JSY AU RC	6.00	15.00
❑ SEJT Jamaal Tinsley	.60	1.50
❑ SEJAW Jay Williams/1249 RC	2.50	6.00
❑ SEJDS Jerry Stackhouse	.60	1.50
❑ SEJOS John Stockton	1.00	2.50
❑ SEJWE Jiri Welsch AU RC	4.00	10.00
❑ SEJWI Jerome Williams	.50	1.25
❑ SEKB Kobe Bryant	4.00	10.00
❑ SEKG Kevin Garnett	1.50	4.00
❑ SEKM Karl Malone	.75	2.00
❑ SEKR K.Rush JSY AU RC	5.00	12.00
❑ SEKS Kenny Satterfield	.50	1.25
❑ SEKLM Kenyon Martin	.75	2.00
❑ SELS Latrell Sprewell	.60	1.50
❑ SEMB Mike Bibby	.60	1.50
❑ SEMD M.Dunleavy JSY AU RC	5.00	12.00
❑ SEME Melvin Ely JSY AU RC	4.00	10.00
❑ SEMH M.Haislip JSY AU RC	4.00	10.00
❑ SEMO Mehmet Okur AU RC	5.00	12.00
❑ SEMCW Chris Webber	.75	2.00
❑ SEMJA Marko Jaric AU	4.00	10.00
❑ SEMJJ Michael Jordan	5.00	12.00
❑ SENH N.Hilario JSY AU RC	10.00	25.00
❑ SENT N.Tskitishvili JSY AU RC	4.00	10.00
❑ SEPG Pau Gasol	.75	2.00
❑ SEPP Paul Pierce	.75	2.00
❑ SEPS Peja Stojakovic	.60	1.50
❑ SEPSA P.Savovic JSY AU RC	4.00	10.00
❑ SEQR Quentin Richardson	.60	1.50
❑ SERA Ray Allen	.75	2.00
❑ SERA R.Archibald JSY AU RC	4.00	10.00
❑ SERB Rasual Butler AU RC	4.00	10.00
❑ SERJ Richard Jefferson	.75	2.00
❑ SERL Rashard Lewis	.75	2.00
❑ SERW Rasheed Wallace	.75	2.00
❑ SERCH Richard Hamilton	.60	1.50
❑ SERHU R.Humphrey JSY AU RC	4.00	10.00
❑ SERMA R.Mason JSY AU RC	4.00	10.00
❑ SERMU R.Murray JSY AU RC	10.00	25.00
❑ SESA Shareef Abdur-Rahim	.60	1.50
❑ SESC Sam Clancy JSY AU RC	4.00	10.00
❑ SESF Steve Francis	.75	2.00
❑ SESM Stephon Marbury	.75	2.00
❑ SESN Steve Nash	1.25	3.00
❑ SESO Shaquille O'Neal	2.00	5.00
❑ SESCB Shane Battier	.60	1.50
❑ SESDM Shawn Marion	.75	2.00
❑ SETC Tyson Chandler	.60	1.50
❑ SETD Tim Duncan	1.50	4.00
❑ SETP T.Prince JSY AU RC	12.50	30.00
❑ SETP Tony Parker	.75	2.00
❑ SETS Tamar Slay AU RC	4.00	10.00
❑ SETLM Tracy McGrady	1.50	4.00
❑ SEVC Vince Carter	1.50	4.00
❑ SEVY V.Yarbrough JSY AU RC	4.00	10.00
❑ SEWS Wally Szczerbiak	.60	1.50
❑ SEYM Yao Ming AU RC	40.00	80.00

2003-04 Bowman Signature Edition

❑ COMP.SET w/o SP's (55)	25.00	60.00
❑ COMMON CARD (1-55)	.50	1.25
❑ SEMISTARS 1-55	.60	1.50
❑ UNLISTED STARS 1-55	.75	2.00
❑ COMMON ROOKIE (56-60)	2.50	6.00
❑ UNLESS NOTED BELOW		
❑ COMMON AU RC (61-76)	4.00	10.00
❑ COMMON JSY AU RC (77-105)	5.00	12.00
❑ COMMON AU RC (106-118)	3.00	8.00
❑ 1 Tracy McGrady	1.50	4.00
❑ 2 Baron Davis	.75	2.00
❑ 3 Allen Iverson	1.50	4.00
❑ 4 Bonzi Wells	.50	1.25
❑ 5 Tony Parker	.75	2.00
❑ 6 Morris Peterson	.60	1.50
❑ 7 Jerry Stackhouse	.60	1.50
❑ 8 Jason Terry	.60	1.50
❑ 9 Tyson Chandler	.60	1.50
❑ 10 Dirk Nowitzki	1.25	3.00
❑ 11 Nene	.60	1.50
❑ 12 Antawn Jamison	.75	2.00
❑ 13 Richard Hamilton	.60	1.50
❑ 14 Steve Francis	.75	2.00
❑ 15 Jermaine O'Neal	.75	2.00
❑ 16 Elton Brand	.75	2.00
❑ 17 Mike Miller	.60	1.50
❑ 18 Caron Butler	.60	1.50
❑ 19 Gary Payton	.75	2.00
❑ 20 Shaquille O'Neal	2.00	5.00
❑ 21 Kevin Garnett	1.50	4.00
❑ 22 Desmond Mason	.60	1.50
❑ 23 Jamal Mashburn	.50	1.25
❑ 24 Drew Gooden	.50	1.25
❑ 25 Eric Snow	.50	1.25
❑ 26 Shawn Marion	.75	2.00
❑ 27 Peja Stojakovic	.60	1.50
❑ 28 Karl Malone	.75	2.00
❑ 29 Shareef Abdur-Rahim	.60	1.50
❑ 30 Paul Pierce	.75	2.00
❑ 31 Dajuan Wagner	.50	1.25
❑ 32 Steve Nash	1.25	3.00
❑ 33 Ben Wallace	.60	1.50
❑ 34 Jason Richardson	.75	2.00
❑ 35 Yao Ming	1.50	4.00
❑ 36 Ron Artest	.60	1.50
❑ 37 Andre Miller	.60	1.50
❑ 38 Kobe Bryant	4.00	10.00
❑ 39 Pau Gasol	.75	2.00
❑ 40 Tim Duncan	1.50	4.00
❑ 41 Ray Allen	.50	1.25
❑ 42 Vince Carter	1.50	4.00
❑ 43 Andrei Kirilenko	.75	2.00
❑ 44 Chris Webber	.75	2.00
❑ 45 Rasheed Wallace	.75	2.00
❑ 46 Amare Stoudemire	1.50	4.00
❑ 47 Latrell Sprewell	.60	1.50
❑ 48 Kenyon Martin	.75	2.00
❑ 49 Wally Szczerbiak	.60	1.50
❑ 50 Jason Kidd	1.25	3.00
❑ 51 Eddie Jones	.60	1.50
❑ 52 Jalen Rose	.60	1.50
❑ 53 Ricky Davis	.60	1.50
❑ 54 Antoine Walker	.75	2.00
❑ 55 Allan Houston	.60	1.50
❑ 56 Lebron James RC	30.00	80.00
❑ 57 Darko Milicic RC	3.00	8.00
❑ 58 Chris Kaman RC	3.00	8.00
❑ 59 Kyle Korver RC	3.00	8.00
❑ 60 Willie Green RC	2.50	6.00
❑ 61 James Lang AU RC	4.00	10.00
❑ 62 Carl English AU RC	4.00	10.00
❑ 63 Devin Brown AU RC	4.00	10.00
❑ 64 Theron Smith AU RC	4.00	10.00
❑ 65 Rick Rickert AU RC	4.00	10.00
❑ 66 Z.Cabarkapa AU RC	4.00	10.00
❑ 67 D.Zimmerman AU RC	4.00	10.00
❑ 68 A.Pavlovic AU RC	5.00	12.00
❑ 69 Malick Badiane AU RC	4.00	10.00
❑ 70 Boris Diaw AU RC	5.00	12.00
❑ 71 Zaur Pachulia AU RC	4.00	10.00
❑ 72 Zoran Planinic AU RC	4.00	10.00
❑ 73 Carlos Delfino AU RC	4.00	10.00
❑ 74 Maciej Lampe AU RC	4.00	10.00
❑ 75 S.Schortsanitis AU RC	8.00	20.00
❑ 76 Mario Austin AU RC	4.00	10.00
❑ 77 C.Anthony/1170 JSY AU RC	40.00	80.00
❑ 78 Chris Bosh JSY AU RC	15.00	30.00
❑ 79 D.Wade JSY AU RC	80.00	160.00
❑ 80 Kirk Hinrich JSY AU RC	10.00	25.00
❑ 81 T.J. Ford JSY AU RC	6.00	15.00
❑ 82 D.West/1245 JSY AU RC	10.00	25.00
❑ 83 Marcus Banks JSY AU RC	5.00	12.00
❑ 84 Dahntay Jones JSY AU RC	5.00	12.00
❑ 85 Luke Ridnour JSY AU RC	8.00	20.00
❑ 86 Reece Gaines JSY AU RC	5.00	12.00
❑ 87 T.Outlaw/1075 JSY AU RC	6.00	15.00
❑ 88 B.Cook/1063 JSY AU RC	5.00	12.00
❑ 89 Troy Bell JSY AU RC	5.00	12.00
❑ 90 Ndudi Ebi JSY AU RC	6.00	15.00
❑ 91 K.Perkins/1238 JSY AU RC	8.00	20.00
❑ 92 L.Barbosa JSY AU RC	8.00	20.00
❑ 93 J.Howard/1111 JSY AU RC	8.00	20.00
❑ 94 Slavko Vranes JSY AU RC	5.00	12.00
❑ 95 Jason Kapono JSY AU RC	5.00	12.00
❑ 96 Luke Walton JSY AU RC	8.00	20.00
❑ 97 M.Williams/1172 JSY AU RC	10.00	25.00
❑ 98 M.Bonner/960 JSY AU RC	5.00	12.00
❑ 99 Travis Hansen JSY AU RC	5.00	12.00
❑ 100 Steve Blake JSY AU RC	5.00	12.00
❑ 101 Keith Bogans JSY AU RC	5.00	12.00
❑ 102 Mike Sweetney JSY AU RC	5.00	12.00
❑ 103 Jarvis Hayes JSY AU RC	5.00	12.00
❑ 104 Mickael Pietrus JSY AU RC	6.00	15.00
❑ 105 Nick Collison JSY AU RC	6.00	15.00
❑ 106 Jerome Beasley AU RC		
❑ 107 James Jones AU RC	3.00	8.00
❑ 108 Brandon Hunter AU RC	3.00	8.00
❑ 109 Tommy Smith AU RC	3.00	8.00
❑ 110 Marcus Hatten AU RC	3.00	8.00
❑ 111 Koko Archibong AU RC	3.00	8.00
❑ 112 Ime Udoka AU RC	5.00	12.00
❑ 113 Eric Chenowith AU RC	3.00	8.00
❑ 114 Stephane Pelle AU RC	3.00	8.00
❑ 115 Marquis Daniels AU RC	6.00	15.00
❑ 116 Paccelis Morlende AU RC	3.00	8.00
❑ 117 George Williams AU RC	3.00	8.00
❑ 118 Udonis Haslem AU RC	5.00	12.00

2004-05 Bowman Signature Edition

❑ COMP.SET w/o SP's (55)	25.00	60.00
❑ COMMON CARD (1-55)	.50	1.25
❑ COMMON JSY AU RC (58-86)	5.00	12.00
❑ COMMON AU RC (87-103)	3.00	8.00
❑ 1 Kevin Garnett	1.50	4.00
❑ 2 Eddy Curry	.60	1.50
❑ 3 Ben Wallace	.60	1.50
❑ 4 Cuttino Mobley	.60	1.50
❑ 5 Vince Carter	1.50	4.00
❑ 6 Bonzi Wells	.50	1.25
❑ 7 Jermaine O'Neal	.75	2.00
❑ 8 Kobe Bryant	4.00	10.00
❑ 9 Stephon Marbury	.75	2.00
❑ 10 Mike Bibby	.60	1.50
❑ 11 Yao Ming	2.00	5.00
❑ 12 Richard Jefferson	.75	2.00
❑ 13 Steve Nash	1.25	3.00
❑ 14 Luke Ridnour	.50	1.25
❑ 15 Carmelo Anthony	2.50	6.00
❑ 16 Pau Gasol	.75	2.00
❑ 17 Amare Stoudemire	1.50	4.00
❑ 18 Chris Webber	.75	2.00
❑ 19 Sam Cassell	.60	1.50
❑ 20 Tracy McGrady	1.50	4.00
❑ 21 Tim Duncan	1.50	4.00
❑ 22 Michael Redd	.75	2.00
❑ 23 LeBron James	5.00	12.00
❑ 24 Baron Davis	.75	2.00
❑ 25 Zach Randolph	.75	2.00
❑ 26 Peja Stojakovic	.60	1.50
❑ 27 Lamar Odom	.75	2.00
❑ 28 Michael Finley	.75	2.00
❑ 29 Zydrunas Ilgauskas	.60	1.50
❑ 30 Rasheed Wallace	.75	2.00
❑ 31 Mike Sweetney	.50	1.25
❑ 32 Elton Brand	.75	2.00
❑ 33 Steve Francis	.75	2.00
❑ 34 Paul Pierce	.75	2.00
❑ 35 Ray Allen	.75	2.00
❑ 36 Tony Parker	.75	2.00
❑ 37 Gerald Wallace	.75	2.00

❑ 38 Chris Bosh .75 2.00
❑ 39 Desmond Mason .60 1.50
❑ 40 Allen Iverson 1.50 4.00
❑ 41 Dirk Nowitzki 1.25 3.00
❑ 42 Antoine Walker .75 2.00
❑ 43 Ron Artest .60 1.50
❑ 44 Jamaal Magloire .50 1.25
❑ 45 Kirk Hinrich .60 1.50
❑ 46 Jason Richardson .75 2.00
❑ 47 Andrei Kirilenko .75 2.00
❑ 48 Kenyon Martin .75 2.00
❑ 49 Carlos Boozer .75 2.00
❑ 50 Shaquille O'Neal 2.00 5.00
❑ 51 Shawn Marion .75 2.00
❑ 52 Kwame Brown .50 1.25
❑ 53 Corey Maggette .60 1.50
❑ 54 Dwyane Wade 2.50 6.00
❑ 55 Jason Kidd 1.25 3.00
❑ 56 Dwight Howard JSY RC 6.00 15.00
❑ 57 Andre Iguodala JSY RC 5.00 12.00
❑ 58 Andre Emmett JSY AU RC 5.00 12.00
❑ 59 Al Jefferson JSY AU RC 10.00 25.00
❑ 60 A.Varejao JSY AU RC 6.00 15.00
❑ 61 Ben Gordon JSY AU RC 6.00 15.00
❑ 62 David Harrison JSY AU RC 5.00 12.00
❑ 63 Delonte West JSY AU RC 8.00 20.00
❑ 64 Devin Harris JSY AU RC 10.00 25.00
❑ 65 Dorell Wright JSY AU RC 6.00 15.00
❑ 66 Ha Seung-Jin JSY AU RC 5.00 12.00
❑ 67 J.R. Smith JSY AU RC 10.00 25.00
❑ 68 Jackson Vroman JSY AU RC 5.00 12.00
❑ 69 Jameer Nelson JSY AU RC 6.00 15.00
❑ 70 Kris Humphries JSY AU RC 8.00 20.00
❑ 71 Josh Smith JSY AU RC 12.00 30.00
❑ 72 Kevin Martin JSY AU RC 6.00 15.00
❑ 73 Kirk Snyder JSY AU RC 5.00 12.00
❑ 74 Trevor Ariza JSY AU RC 6.00 15.00
❑ 75 Lionel Chalmers JSY AU RC 5.00 12.00
❑ 76 Luke Jackson JSY AU RC 5.00 12.00
❑ 77 Luol Deng JSY AU RC 6.00 15.00
❑ 78 Rafael Araujo JSY AU RC 5.00 12.00
❑ 79 Rickey Paulding JSY AU RC 5.00 12.00
❑ 80 SebastianTelfair JSY AU RC 5.00 12.00
❑ 81 S.Livingston JSY AU RC 5.00 12.00
❑ 82 Tony Allen JSY AU RC 6.00 15.00
❑ 83 Josh Childress JSY AU RC 5.00 12.00
❑ 84 Emeka Okafor JSY AU RC 10.00 25.00
❑ 85 Ber.Robinson JSY AU RC 5.00 12.00
❑ 86 Chris Duhon JSY AU RC 8.00 20.00
❑ 87 Blake Stepp AU RC 3.00 8.00
❑ 88 Andris Biedrins AU RC 5.00 12.00
❑ 89 Donta Smith AU RC 3.00 8.00
❑ 90 Beno Udrih AU RC 4.00 10.00
❑ 91 Justin Reed AU RC 3.00 8.00
❑ 92 Pavel Podkolzine AU RC 3.00 8.00
❑ 93 Matt Freije AU RC 3.00 8.00
❑ 94 Pape Sow AU RC 3.00 8.00
❑ 95 Antonio Burks AU RC 3.00 8.00
❑ 96 Rashad Wright AU RC 3.00 8.00
❑ 97 Ricky Minard AU RC 3.00 8.00
❑ 98 Robert Swift AU RC 3.00 8.00
❑ 99 Romain Sato AU RC 3.00 8.00
❑ 100 Sasha Vujacic AU RC 3.00 8.00
❑ 102 Tim Pickett AU RC 3.00 8.00
❑ 103 Yuta Tabuse AU RC 10.00 25.00

2006-07 Bowman Sterling

❑ 1 Ben Wallace JSY 4.00 10.00
❑ 2 Jason Richardson JSY 4.00 10.00
❑ 3 Steve Nash JSY 6.00 15.00
❑ 4 Pau Gasol JSY 4.00 10.00
❑ 5 Carmelo Anthony JSY 6.00 15.00
❑ 6 Kevin Garnett JSY 5.00 12.00
❑ 7 Tim Duncan JSY 5.00 12.00
❑ 8 Chauncey Billups JSY 4.00 10.00
❑ 9 Chris Paul JSY 5.00 12.00
❑ 10 Kobe Bryant JSY 10.00 25.00
❑ 11 Tony Parker JSY 4.00 10.00
❑ 12 Shaquille O'Neal JSY 8.00 20.00
❑ 13 Allen Iverson JSY 6.00 15.00
❑ 14 Dirk Nowitzki JSY 5.00 12.00
❑ 15 Paul Pierce JSY 5.00 12.00
❑ 16 Tracy McGrady JSY 5.00 12.00
❑ 17 Channing Frye JSY 4.00 10.00
❑ 18 Amare Stoudemire JSY 5.00 12.00
❑ 19 Dwight Howard JSY 5.00 12.00
❑ 20 Dwyane Wade JSY 8.00 20.00
❑ 21 Yao Ming JSY 5.00 12.00
❑ 22 Andrei Kirilenko JSY 4.00 10.00
❑ 23 Gilbert Arenas JSY 4.00 10.00
❑ 24 Shawn Marion JSY 4.00 10.00
❑ 25 Bob Lanier JSY 4.00 10.00
❑ 26 Pete Maravich JSY 20.00 40.00
❑ 27 Bill Walton JSY 5.00 12.00
❑ 28 Dennis Rodman JSY 6.00 15.00
❑ 29 Magic Johnson JSY 8.00 20.00
❑ 30 John Stockton JSY 5.00 12.00
❑ 31 Larry Bird JSY AU 60.00 120.00
❑ 32 Rick Barry JSY AU 20.00 40.00
❑ 33 Isiah Thomas JSY AU 12.50 30.00
❑ 34 Dominique Wilkins JSY AU 20.00 40.00
❑ 35 Ben Gordon JSY AU 20.00 40.00
❑ 36 Raymond Felton JSY AU 8.00 20.00
❑ 37 T.J. Ford JSY AU 8.00 20.00
❑ 38 Josh Howard JSY AU 8.00 20.00
❑ 39 Dwyane Wade JSY AU 30.00 60.00
❑ 40 Andre Iguodala JSY AU 8.00 20.00
❑ 41 Tarence Kinsey RC 2.50 6.00
❑ 42 Mickael Gelabale RC 2.50 6.00
❑ 43 Kelenna Azubuike RC 3.00 8.00
❑ 44 Pops Mensah-Bonsu RC 2.50 6.00
❑ 45 Walter Herrmann RC 3.00 8.00
❑ 46 Tyrus Thomas RC 3.00 8.00
❑ 47 Lynn Greer RC 2.50 6.00
❑ 48 Leon Powe RC 2.50 6.00
❑ 49 Yakhouba Diawara RC 2.50 6.00
❑ 50 Jose Barea RC 2.50 6.00
❑ 51 Saer Sene JSY RC 3.00 8.00
❑ 52 Steve Novak JSY RC 3.00 8.00
❑ 53 Josh Boone JSY RC 3.00 8.00
❑ 54 James White JSY RC 3.00 8.00
❑ 55 Rudy Gay JSY RC 3.00 8.00
❑ 56 David Noel JSY RC 3.00 8.00
❑ 57 Allan Ray JSY RC 3.00 8.00
❑ 58 Paul Davis JSY RC 3.00 8.00
❑ 59 Shawne Williams JSY RC 3.00 8.00
❑ 60 LaMarcus Aldridge JSY RC 4.00 10.00
❑ 61 Mardy Collins JSY RC 3.00 8.00
❑ 62 Solomon Jones JSY RC 3.00 8.00
❑ 63 Craig Smith JSY RC 3.00 8.00
❑ 64 Rajon Rondo JSY RC 12.00 30.00
❑ 65 Jorge Garbajosa JSY RC 6.00 15.00
❑ 66 Patrick O'Bryant JSY RC 3.00 8.00
❑ 67 Dee Brown JSY RC 3.00 8.00
❑ 68 Brandon Roy JSY RC 8.00 20.00
❑ 69 Bobby Jones JSY RC 3.00 8.00
❑ 70 Kyle Lowry JSY RC 3.00 8.00
❑ 71 Paul Millsap AU RC 5.00 12.00
❑ 72 Vassilis Spanoulis AU RC 5.00 12.00
❑ 73 Daniel Gibson AU RC 6.00 15.00
❑ 74 Marcus Vinicius AU RC 5.00 12.00
❑ 75 Ronnie Brewer AU RC 6.00 15.00
❑ 76 Damir Markota AU RC 5.00 12.00
❑ 77 Hilton Armstrong AU RC 5.00 12.00
❑ 78 Shannon Brown AU RC 5.00 12.00
❑ 79 Mile Ilic AU RC 5.00 12.00
❑ 80 Alexander Johnson AU RC 5.00 12.00
❑ 81 Will Blalock AU RC 5.00 12.00
❑ 82 P.J. Tucker AU RC 5.00 12.00
❑ 83 Sergio Rodriguez AU RC 5.00 12.00
❑ 84 Jordan Farmar AU RC 6.00 15.00
❑ 85 Renaldo Balkman AU RC 5.00 12.00
❑ 86 Quincy Douby AU RC 5.00 12.00
❑ 87 Hassan Adams AU RC 6.00 15.00
❑ 88 Chris Quinn AU RC 5.00 12.00
❑ 89 James Augustine AU RC 5.00 12.00
❑ 90 Ryan Hollins AU RC 5.00 12.00
❑ 91 J.J. Redick JSY AU RC 5.00 12.00
❑ 92 Adam Morrison JSY AU RC 6.00 15.00
❑ 93 Maurice Ager JSY AU RC 5.00 12.00
❑ 94 Shelden Williams JSY AU RC 6.00 15.00
❑ 95 Marcus Williams JSY AU RC 6.00 15.00
❑ 96 Andrea Bargnani JSY AU RC 8.00 20.00
❑ 97 Thabo Sefolosha JSY AU RC 6.00 15.00
❑ 98 Randy Foye JSY AU RC 5.00 12.00
❑ 99 Cedric Simmons JSY AU RC 5.00 12.00
❑ 100 Rodney Carney JSY AU RC 5.00 12.00

2007-08 Bowman Sterling

❑ AA Arron Afflalo JSY AU/218 RC 5.00 12.00
❑ AB Andrea Bargnani JSY/385 2.50 6.00
❑ ABR Aaron Brooks JSY AU/218 6.00 15.00
❑ ABY Andrew Bynum JSY/385 4.00 10.00
❑ AG Aaron Gray AU/412 RC 4.00 10.00
❑ AH1 Al Horford RC 2.50 6.00
❑ AH2 Al Horford JSY/975 4.00 10.00
❑ AHA Al Harrington JSY/385 2.50 6.00
❑ AHK Adam Haluska JSY AU/218 RC 5.00 12.00
❑ AI Allen Iverson JSY/385 4.00 10.00
❑ AIG Andre Iguodala JSY AU/190 6.00 15.00
❑ AJ Al Jefferson JSY/385 2.50 6.00
❑ AJA Antawn Jamison JSY/385 2.50 6.00
❑ AL1 Acie Law IV JSY AU/113
❑ AL2 Acie Law IV AU/412 RC 4.00 10.00
❑ AS Amare Stoudemire JSY/385 4.00 10.00
❑ AT1 Alando Tucker JSY AU/218 4.00 10.00
❑ AT2 Alando Tucker AU/829 RC 5.00 12.00
❑ ATH1 Al Thornton JSY AU/21
❑ ATH2 Al Thornton AU/412 RC 5.00 12.00
❑ BD Baron Davis JSY AU/275 6.00 15.00
❑ BG Ben Gordon JSY/385 2.50 6.00
❑ BK Bernard King JSY/385 3.00 8.00
❑ BL Bill Laimbeer JSY/385 3.00 8.00
❑ BR Brandon Roy JSY/385 4.00 10.00
❑ BRU Bill Russell JSY AU/15 100.00 200.00
❑ BWR1 Brandan Wright JSY AU/21
❑ BWR2 Brandan Wright JSY/975 RC 3.00 8.00
❑ CA Carmelo Anthony JSY AU/15 25.0050.00
❑ CB1 Corey Brewer RC 2.50 6.00
❑ CB2 Corey Brewer JSY/975 3.00 8.00
❑ CBO Chris Bosh JSY AU/89 8.00 20.00
❑ CBZ Carlos Boozer JSY AU/340 8.00 20.00
❑ CD Clyde Drexler JSY/385 4.00 10.00
❑ CK Coby Karl AU/829 RC 5.00 12.00
❑ CL Carl Landry JSY AU/218 RC 6.00 15.00
❑ CM Corey Maggette JSY/385 2.50 6.00
❑ CP Chris Paul JSY/385 4.00 10.00
❑ CR Chris Richard RC 2.00 5.00
❑ CR2 Chris Richard JSY/975 2.50 6.00
❑ DC Daequan Cook JSY AU/113 RC 5.00 12.00
❑ DH Dwight Howard JSY AU/89 20.00 40.00
❑ DJS1 D.J. Strawberry JSY AU/218 5.00 12.00
❑ DJS2 D.J. Strawberry AU/829 RC 5.0012.00
❑ DM D.McGuire JSY AU/113 RC 5.00 12.00
❑ DN Dirk Nowitzki JSY/385 3.00 8.00
❑ DNI D.Nichols JSY AU/218 RC 5.00 12.00
❑ DR David Robinson JSY AU/15 75.00150.00
❑ DRO Dennis Rodman JSY AU/89 30.00 60.00
❑ DW Dwyane Wade JSY AU/15 40.00 80.00
❑ DWI D.Wilkins JSY AU/275 15.00 30.00
❑ EM Earl Monroe JSY/385 3.00 8.00
❑ GA1 Gilbert Arenas JSY/385 2.50 6.00
❑ GA2 Gilbert Arenas JSY AU/15
❑ GD1 Glen Davis JSY AU/218 6.00 15.00
❑ GD2 Glen Davis AU/829 RC 5.00 12.00
❑ GG George Gervin JSY/385 4.00 10.00
❑ GO1 Greg Oden JSY AU/21 100.00 200.00
❑ GO2 Greg Oden JSY/975 RC 4.00 10.00
❑ GP1 Gabe Pruitt JSY AU/218 5.00 12.00
❑ GP2 Gabe Pruitt AU/829 RC 5.00 12.00
❑ HH1 Herbert Hill JSY AU/218 5.00 12.00
❑ HH2 Herbert Hill AU/829 RC 5.00 12.00
❑ IT Isiah Thomas JSY AU/89 15.00 30.00
❑ JC1 J.Crittenton JSY/218 AU 5.00 12.00
❑ JC2 Javaris Crittenton AU/412 RC 5.0012.00
❑ JCN Juan Navarro AU/129 RC 5.00 12.00

❑ JD Jared Dudley JSY AU/218 RC	5.00	12.00
❑ JDA J.Davidson JSY AU/218 RC	5.00	12.00
❑ JG1 Jeff Green RC	2.50	6.00
❑ JG2 Jeff Green JSY/975	4.00	10.00
❑ JJ Joe Johnson JSY/385	2.50	6.00
❑ JK Jason Kidd JSY/385	2.50	6.00
❑ JMC J.McRoberts JSY AU/218 RC	5.00	12.00
❑ JN1 Joakim Noah RC	2.50	6.00
❑ JN2 Joakim Noah JSY/975	4.00	10.00
❑ JO Jermaine O'Neal JSY/385	2.50	6.00
❑ JOC J.Curry AU/412 RC EXCH	5.00	12.00
❑ JR Jason Richardson JSY/385	2.50	6.00
❑ JS Jason Smith JSY AU/113 RC	5.00	12.00
❑ JW1 Julian Wright RC	2.50	6.00
❑ JW2 Julian Wright JSY/975	4.00	10.00
❑ KB Kobe Bryant JSY/385	8.00	20.00
❑ KD Kevin Durant RC	15.00	40.00
❑ KG Kevin Garnett JSY/385	5.00	12.00
❑ KMA Karl Malone JSY/385	5.00	12.00
❑ LB Larry Bird JSY AU/15	75.00	150.00
❑ LD Luol Deng JSY/385	2.50	6.00
❑ LS Luis Scola RC	3.00	8.00
❑ MA Morris Almond JSY AU/113 RC	5.00	12.00
❑ MB Mike Bibby JSY/385	2.50	6.00
❑ MBE Marco Belinelli AU/129 RC	5.00	12.00
❑ MC1 Mike Conley RC	2.50	6.00
❑ MC2 Mike Conley JSY/975	4.00	10.00
❑ MCO Michael Cooper JSY/385	3.00	8.00
❑ MG Manu Ginobili JSY/385	3.00	8.00
❑ MG Marcin Gortat AU/829 RC	5.00	12.00
❑ MJ Magic Johnson JSY AU/15	75.00	150.00
❑ MM Mike Miller JSY/385	2.50	6.00
❑ MR Michael Redd JSY/385	2.50	6.00
❑ NF Nick Fazekas JSY AU/218 RC	5.00	12.00
❑ NTA Nate Archibald JSY/385	3.00	8.00
❑ NY1 Nick Young JSY AU/21		
❑ NY2 Nick Young JSY RC	4.00	10.00
❑ PG Pau Gasol JSY/385	2.50	6.00
❑ PP Paul Pierce JSY AU/190	15.00	30.00
❑ RA Ray Allen JSY AU/190	15.00	30.00
❑ RB Rick Barry JSY AU/340	10.00	25.00
❑ RH Richard Hamilton JSY/385	2.50	6.00
❑ RS Ramon Sessions RC	2.50	6.00
❑ RS R.Stuckey JSY AU/218 RC	20.00	40.00
❑ SH Spencer Hawes JSY AU/113 RC	5.00	12.00
❑ SM Stephon Marbury JSY/385	2.50	6.00
❑ SMA Shawn Marion JSY/385	2.50	6.00
❑ SN Steve Nash JSY/385	4.00	10.00
❑ SO Shaquille O'Neal JSY AU/15	100.00	200.00
❑ SW Sean Williams JSY AU/218 RC	5.00	12.00
❑ TD Tim Duncan JSY/385	4.00	10.00
❑ TG T.Green JSY AU/218 RC EXCH	5.00	12.00
❑ TM Tracy McGrady JSY/385	3.00	8.00
❑ TY T.Young JSY AU/21 RC	50.00	100.00
❑ VC Vince Carter JSY AU/89	25.00	50.00
❑ WC W.Chandler JSY AU/218 RC	5.00	12.00
❑ YJ Yi Jianlian AU/129 RC	10.00	25.00
❑ YM Yao Ming JSY	3.00	8.00

1996-97 Bowman's Best

❑ COMPLETE SET (125)	25.00	50.00
❑ COMMON CARD (1-80/TB1-20)	.15	.40
❑ COMMON ROOKIE (R1-R25)	.20	.50
❑ 1 Scottie Pippen	.75	2.00
❑ 2 Glen Rice	.30	.75
❑ 3 Bryant Stith	.15	.40
❑ 4 Dino Radja	.15	.40
❑ 5 Horace Grant	.30	.75
❑ 6 Mahmoud Abdul-Rauf	.15	.40
❑ 7 Mookie Blaylock	.15	.40
❑ 8 Clifford Robinson	.15	.40
❑ 9 Vin Baker	.30	.75
❑ 10 Grant Hill	.50	1.25
❑ 11 Terrell Brandon	.30	.75
❑ 12 P.J. Brown	.15	.40
❑ 13 Kendall Gill	.15	.40
❑ 14 Brent Barry	.15	.40
❑ 15 Hakeem Olajuwon	.50	1.25
❑ 16 Allan Houston	.30	.75
❑ 17 Elden Campbell	.15	.40
❑ 18 Latrell Sprewell	.50	1.25
❑ 19 Jerry Stackhouse	.60	1.50
❑ 20 Robert Horry	.30	.75
❑ 21 Mitch Richmond	.30	.75
❑ 22 Gary Payton	.50	1.25
❑ 23 Rik Smits	.30	.75
❑ 24 Jim Jackson	.15	.40
❑ 25 Damon Stoudamire	.50	1.25
❑ 26 Bobby Phills	.15	.40
❑ 27 Chris Webber	.50	1.25
❑ 28 Shawn Bradley	.15	.40
❑ 29 Arvydas Sabonis	.30	.75
❑ 30 John Stockton	.50	1.25
❑ 31 Anfernee Hardaway	.50	1.25
❑ 32 Christian Laettner	.30	.75
❑ 33 Juwan Howard	.30	.75
❑ 34 Anthony Mason	.30	.75
❑ 35 Tom Gugliotta	.15	.40
❑ 36 Avery Johnson	.15	.40
❑ 37 Cedric Ceballos	.15	.40
❑ 38 Patrick Ewing	.50	1.25
❑ 39 Joe Smith	.30	.75
❑ 40 Dennis Rodman	.30	.75
❑ 41 Alonzo Mourning	.30	.75
❑ 42 Kevin Garnett	1.00	2.50
❑ 43 Antonio McDyess	.50	1.25
❑ 44 Detlef Schrempf	.30	.75
❑ 45 Reggie Miller	.50	1.25
❑ 46 Charles Barkley	.60	1.50
❑ 47 Derrick Coleman	.30	.75
❑ 48 Brian Grant	.50	1.25
❑ 49 Kenny Anderson	.15	.40
❑ 50 Otis Thorpe	.15	.40
❑ 51 Rod Strickland	.15	.40
❑ 52 Eric Williams	.15	.40
❑ 53 Rony Seikaly	.15	.40
❑ 54 Danny Manning	.30	.75
❑ 55 Karl Malone	.50	1.25
❑ 56 B.J. Armstrong	.15	.40
❑ 57 Greg Anthony	.15	.40
❑ 58 Larry Johnson	.30	.75
❑ 59 Loy Vaught	.15	.40
❑ 60 Sean Elliott	.30	.75
❑ 61 Dikembe Mutombo	.30	.75
❑ 62 Clarence Weatherspoon	.15	.40
❑ 63 Jamal Mashburn	.30	.75
❑ 64 Bryant Reeves	.15	.40
❑ 65 Vlade Divac	.15	.40
❑ 66 Shawn Kemp	.30	.75
❑ 67 LaPhonso Ellis	.15	.40
❑ 68 Tyrone Hill	.15	.40
❑ 69 David Robinson	.50	1.25
❑ 70 Shaquille O'Neal	1.25	3.00
❑ 71 Doug Christie	.30	.75
❑ 72 Jayson Williams	.30	.75
❑ 73 Michael Finley	.60	1.50
❑ 74 Tim Hardaway	.30	.75
❑ 75 Clyde Drexler	.50	1.25
❑ 76 Joe Dumars	.50	1.25
❑ 77 Glenn Robinson	.50	1.25
❑ 78 Dana Barros	.15	.40
❑ 79 Jason Kidd	.75	2.00
❑ 80 Michael Jordan	3.00	8.00
❑ R1 Allen Iverson RC	3.00	8.00
❑ R2 Stephon Marbury RC	1.25	3.00
❑ R3 Shareef Abdur-Rahim RC	1.50	4.00
❑ R4 Marcus Camby RC	.75	2.00
❑ R5 Ray Allen RC	2.00	5.00
❑ R6 Antoine Walker RC	1.25	3.00
❑ R7 Lorenzen Wright RC	.20	.50
❑ R8 Kerry Kittles RC	.60	1.50
❑ R9 Samaki Walker RC	.20	.50
❑ R10 Tony Delk RC	.20	.50
❑ R11 Vitaly Potapenko RC	.20	.50
❑ R12 Jerome Williams RC	.60	1.50
❑ R13 Todd Fuller RC	.20	.50
❑ R14 Erick Dampier RC	.60	1.50
❑ R15 Derek Fisher RC	1.00	2.50
❑ R16 Donald Whiteside RC	.20	.50
❑ R17 John Wallace RC	.20	.50
❑ R18 Steve Nash RC	3.00	8.00
❑ R19 Brian Evans RC	.20	.50
❑ R20 Jermaine O'Neal RC	1.25	3.00
❑ R21 Roy Rogers RC	.20	.50
❑ R22 Priest Lauderdale RC	.20	.50
❑ R23 Kobe Bryant RC	20.00	40.00
❑ R24 Martin Muursepp RC	.20	.50
❑ R25 Zydrunas Ilgauskas RC	.40	1.00
❑ TB1 Avery Johnson RET	.15	.40
❑ TB2 Chris Webber RET	.50	1.25
❑ TB3 Sean Elliott RET	.15	.40
❑ TB4 Joe Dumars RET	.30	.75
❑ TB5 Grant Hill RET	.50	1.25
❑ TB6 Gary Payton RET	.30	.75
❑ TB7 Shawn Kemp RET	.15	.40
❑ TB8 S.O'Neal Lakers RET	.50	1.25
❑ TB9 Eddie Jones RET	.30	.75
❑ TB10 John Wallace RET	.30	.75
❑ TB11 Patrick Ewing RET	.30	.75
❑ TB12 Jerry Stackhouse RET	.20	.50
❑ TB13 Allen Iverson RET	.60	1.50
❑ TB14 Latrell Sprewell RET	.50	1.25
❑ TB15 Dino Radja RET	.15	.40
❑ TB16 David Wesley RET	.15	.40
❑ TB17 Joe Smith RET	.15	.40
❑ TB18 Damon Stoudamire RET	.30	.75
❑ TB19 Marcus Camby RET	.30	.75
❑ TB20 Juwan Howard RET	.15	.40

1997-98 Bowman's Best

❑ COMPLETE SET (125)	15.00	40.00
❑ COMMON CARD (1-100)	.08	.25
❑ COMMON ROOKIE (101-125)	.10	.30
❑ 1 Scottie Pippen	.50	1.25
❑ 2 Michael Finley	.30	.75
❑ 3 David Wesley	.08	.25
❑ 4 Brent Barry	.20	.50
❑ 5 Gary Payton	.30	.75
❑ 6 Christian Laettner	.20	.50
❑ 7 Grant Hill	.30	.75
❑ 8 Glenn Robinson	.30	.75
❑ 9 Reggie Miller	.30	.75
❑ 10 Tyus Edney	.08	.25
❑ 11 Jim Jackson	.08	.25
❑ 12 John Stockton	.30	.75
❑ 13 Karl Malone	.30	.75
❑ 14 Samaki Walker	.08	.25
❑ 15 Bryant Stith	.08	.25
❑ 16 Clyde Drexler	.30	.75
❑ 17 Danny Ferry	.08	.25
❑ 18 Shawn Bradley	.08	.25
❑ 19 Bryant Reeves	.08	.25
❑ 20 John Starks	.08	.25
❑ 21 Joe Dumars	.30	.75
❑ 22 Checklist	.08	.25
❑ 23 Antonio McDyess	.20	.50
❑ 24 Jeff Hornacek	.20	.50
❑ 25 Terrell Brandon	.20	.50
❑ 26 Kendall Gill	.08	.25
❑ 27 LaPhonso Ellis	.08	.25
❑ 28 Shaquille O'Neal	.75	2.00
❑ 29 Mahmoud Abdul-Rauf	.08	.25
❑ 30 Eric Williams	.08	.25
❑ 31 Lorenzen Wright	.08	.25
❑ 32 Shareef Abdur-Rahim	.50	1.25
❑ 33 Avery Johnson	.08	.25
❑ 34 Juwan Howard	.20	.50
❑ 35 Vin Baker	.20	.50
❑ 36 Dikembe Mutombo	.20	.50
❑ 37 Patrick Ewing	.30	.75
❑ 38 Allen Iverson	.75	2.00
❑ 39 Alonzo Mourning	.20	.50
❑ 40 Travis Knight	.08	.25
❑ 41 Ray Allen	.30	.75
❑ 42 Detlef Schrempf	.20	.50

❑ 43 Kevin Johnson	.20	.50
❑ 44 David Robinson	.30	.75
❑ 45 Tim Hardaway	.20	.50
❑ 46 Shawn Kemp	.20	.50
❑ 47 Marcus Camby	.30	.75
❑ 48 Rony Seikaly	.08	.25
❑ 49 Eddie Jones	.30	.75
❑ 50 Rik Smits	.20	.50
❑ 51 Jayson Williams	.08	.25
❑ 52 Malik Sealy	.08	.25
❑ 53 Chris Mullin	.30	.75
❑ 54 Larry Johnson	.20	.50
❑ 55 Isaiah Rider	.20	.50
❑ 56 Dennis Rodman	.20	.50
❑ 57 Bob Sura	.08	.25
❑ 58 Hakeem Olajuwon	.30	.75
❑ 59 Steve Smith	.20	.50
❑ 60 Michael Jordan	2.00	5.00
❑ 61 Jerry Stackhouse	.30	.75
❑ 62 Joe Smith	.20	.50
❑ 63 Walt Williams	.08	.25
❑ 64 Anthony Peeler	.08	.25
❑ 65 Charles Barkley	.40	1.00
❑ 66 Erick Dampier	.20	.50
❑ 67 Horace Grant	.20	.50
❑ 68 Anthony Mason	.20	.50
❑ 69 Anfernee Hardaway	.30	.75
❑ 70 Elden Campbell	.08	.25
❑ 71 Cedric Ceballos	.08	.25
❑ 72 Allan Houston	.20	.50
❑ 73 Kerry Kittles	.30	.75
❑ 74 Antoine Walker	.40	1.00
❑ 75 Sean Elliott	.20	.50
❑ 76 Jamal Mashburn	.20	.50
❑ 77 Mitch Richmond	.20	.50
❑ 78 Damon Stoudamire	.20	.50
❑ 79 Tom Gugliotta	.20	.50
❑ 80 Jason Kidd	.50	1.25
❑ 81 Chris Webber	.30	.75
❑ 82 Glen Rice	.20	.50
❑ 83 Loy Vaught	.08	.25
❑ 84 Olden Polynice	.08	.25
❑ 85 Kenny Anderson	.20	.50
❑ 86 Stephon Marbury	.40	1.00
❑ 87 Calbert Cheaney	.08	.25
❑ 88 Kobe Bryant	1.25	3.00
❑ 89 Arvydas Sabonis	.20	.50
❑ 90 Kevin Garnett	.60	1.50
❑ 91 Grant Hill BP	.30	.75
❑ 92 Clyde Drexler BP	.20	.50
❑ 93 Patrick Ewing BP	.20	.50
❑ 94 Shawn Kemp BP	.08	.25
❑ 95 Shaquille O'Neal BP	.30	.75
❑ 96 Michael Jordan BP	1.00	2.50
❑ 97 Karl Malone BP	.30	.75
❑ 98 Allen Iverson BP	.40	1.00
❑ 99 Shareef Abdur-Rahim BP	.25	.60
❑ 100 Dikembe Mutombo BP	.08	.25
❑ 101 Bobby Jackson RC	.40	1.00
❑ 102 Tony Battie RC	.25	.60
❑ 103 Keith Booth RC	.10	.30
❑ 104 Keith Van Horn RC	.60	1.50
❑ 105 Paul Grant RC	.10	.30
❑ 106 Tim Duncan RC	1.25	3.00
❑ 107 Scot Pollard RC	.20	.50
❑ 108 Maurice Taylor RC	.40	1.00
❑ 109 Antonio Daniels RC	.25	.60
❑ 110 Austin Croshere RC	.40	1.00
❑ 111 Tracy McGrady RC	1.50	4.00
❑ 112 Charles O'Bannon RC	.10	.30
❑ 113 Rodrick Rhodes RC	.10	.30
❑ 114 Johnny Taylor RC	.10	.30
❑ 115 Danny Fortson RC	.30	.75
❑ 116 Chauncey Billups RC	1.50	4.00
❑ 117 Tim Thomas RC	.75	2.00
❑ 118 Derek Anderson RC	.50	1.25
❑ 119 Ed Gray RC	.10	.30
❑ 120 Jacque Vaughn RC	.20	.50
❑ 121 Kelvin Cato RC	.25	.60
❑ 122 Tariq Abdul-Wahad RC	.20	.50
❑ 123 Ron Mercer RC	.40	1.00
❑ 124 Brevin Knight RC	.30	.75
❑ 125 Adonal Foyle RC	.20	.50

1998-99 Bowman's Best

❑ COMPLETE SET (125)	50.00	100.00
❑ COMPLETE SET w/o SP (100)	10.00	20.00
❑ COMMON CARD (1-100)	.08	.25
❑ COMMON ROOKIE (101-125)	.30	.75
❑ 1 Jason Kidd	.50	1.25
❑ 2 Dikembe Mutombo	.20	.50
❑ 3 Chris Mullin	.30	.75
❑ 4 Terrell Brandon	.20	.50
❑ 5 Cedric Ceballos	.08	.25
❑ 6 Rod Strickland	.08	.25
❑ 7 Darrell Armstrong	.08	.25
❑ 8 Anfernee Hardaway	.30	.75
❑ 9 Eddie Jones	.30	.75
❑ 10 Allen Iverson	.60	1.50
❑ 11 Kenny Anderson	.20	.50
❑ 12 Toni Kukoc	.20	.50
❑ 13 Lawrence Funderburke	.08	.25
❑ 14 P.J. Brown	.08	.25
❑ 15 Jeff Hornacek	.20	.50
❑ 16 Mookie Blaylock	.08	.25
❑ 17 Avery Johnson	.08	.25
❑ 18 Donyell Marshall	.20	.50
❑ 19 Detlef Schrempf	.20	.50
❑ 20 Joe Dumars	.30	.75
❑ 21 Charles Barkley	.40	1.00
❑ 22 Maurice Taylor	.15	.40
❑ 23 Chauncey Billups	.20	.50
❑ 24 Lee Mayberry	.08	.25
❑ 25 Glen Rice	.20	.50
❑ 26 John Stockton	.30	.75
❑ 27 Rik Smits	.20	.50
❑ 28 Laphonso Ellis	.08	.25
❑ 29 Kerry Kittles	.08	.25
❑ 30 Damon Stoudamire	.20	.50
❑ 31 Kevin Garnett	.60	1.50
❑ 32 Chris Mills	.08	.25
❑ 33 Kendall Gill	.08	.25
❑ 34 Tim Thomas	.20	.50
❑ 35 Derek Anderson	.25	.60
❑ 36 Billy Owens	.08	.25
❑ 37 Bobby Jackson	.20	.50
❑ 38 Allan Houston	.20	.50
❑ 39 Horace Grant	.20	.50
❑ 40 Ray Allen	.30	.75
❑ 41 Shawn Bradley	.08	.25
❑ 42 Arvydas Sabonis	.20	.50
❑ 43 Rex Chapman	.08	.25
❑ 44 Larry Johnson	.20	.50
❑ 45 Jayson Williams	.08	.25
❑ 46 Joe Smith	.20	.50
❑ 47 Ron Mercer	.15	.40
❑ 48 Rodney Rogers	.08	.25
❑ 49 Corliss Williamson	.20	.50
❑ 50 Tim Duncan	.50	1.25
❑ 51 Rasheed Wallace	.30	.75
❑ 52 Vin Baker	.20	.50
❑ 53 Reggie Miller	.30	.75
❑ 54 Patrick Ewing	.30	.75
❑ 55 Michael Finley	.30	.75
❑ 56 Bryant Reeves	.08	.25
❑ 57 Glenn Robinson	.20	.50
❑ 58 Walter McCarty	.08	.25
❑ 59 Brent Barry	.20	.50
❑ 60 John Starks	.20	.50
❑ 61 Clarence Weatherspoon	.08	.25
❑ 62 Calbert Cheaney	.08	.25
❑ 63 Lamond Murray	.08	.25
❑ 64 Zydrunas Ilgauskas	.20	.50
❑ 65 Anthony Mason	.20	.50
❑ 66 Bryon Russell	.08	.25
❑ 67 Dean Garrett	.08	.25
❑ 68 Tom Gugliotta	.08	.25
❑ 69 Dennis Rodman	.20	.50
❑ 70 Keith Van Horn	.30	.75
❑ 71 Jamal Mashburn	.20	.50
❑ 72 Steve Smith	.20	.50
❑ 73 David Wesley	.08	.25
❑ 74 Chris Webber	.30	.75
❑ 75 Isaiah Rider	.08	.25
❑ 76 Stephon Marbury	.30	.75
❑ 77 Tim Hardaway	.20	.50
❑ 78 Jerry Stackhouse	.30	.75
❑ 79 John Wallace	.08	.25
❑ 80 Karl Malone	.30	.75
❑ 81 Juwan Howard	.20	.50
❑ 82 Antonio McDyess	.20	.50
❑ 83 David Robinson	.30	.75
❑ 84 Bobby Phills	.08	.25
❑ 85 Scottie Pippen	.50	1.25
❑ 86 Brevin Knight	.08	.25
❑ 87 Alan Henderson	.08	.25
❑ 88 Kobe Bryant	1.25	3.00
❑ 89 Shawn Kemp	.20	.50
❑ 90 Antoine Walker	.30	.75
❑ 91 Tracy McGrady	.75	2.00
❑ 92 Hakeem Olajuwon	.30	.75
❑ 93 Mark Jackson	.20	.50
❑ 94 Bison Dele	.08	.25
❑ 95 Gary Payton	.30	.75
❑ 96 Ron Harper	.20	.50
❑ 97 Shareef Abdur-Rahim	.30	.75
❑ 98 Alonzo Mourning	.20	.50
❑ 99 Grant Hill	.30	.75
❑ 100 Shaquille O'Neal	.75	2.00
❑ 101 Michael Olowokandi RC	1.00	2.50
❑ 102 Mike Bibby RC	2.00	5.00
❑ 103 Raef LaFrentz RC	1.00	2.50
❑ 104 Antawn Jamison RC	3.00	8.00
❑ 105 Vince Carter RC	5.00	12.00
❑ 106 Robert Traylor RC	.60	1.50
❑ 107 Jason Williams RC	2.50	6.00
❑ 108 Larry Hughes RC	2.00	5.00
❑ 109 Dirk Nowitzki RC	6.00	15.00
❑ 110 Paul Pierce RC	5.00	12.00
❑ 111 Bonzi Wells RC	2.50	6.00
❑ 112 Michael Doleac RC	.60	1.50
❑ 113 Keon Clark RC	1.00	2.50
❑ 114 Michael Dickerson RC	1.25	3.00
❑ 115 Matt Harpring RC	1.00	2.50
❑ 116 Bryce Drew RC	.60	1.50
❑ 117 Pat Garrity RC	.40	1.00
❑ 118 Roshown McLeod RC	.40	1.00
❑ 119 Ricky Davis RC	2.00	5.00
❑ 120 Brian Skinner RC	.60	1.50
❑ 121 Tyronn Lue RC	.75	2.00
❑ 122 Felipe Lopez RC	.75	2.00
❑ 123 Al Harrington RC	1.50	4.00
❑ 124 Corey Benjamin RC	.60	1.50
❑ 125 Nazr Mohammed RC	.30	.75

1999-00 Bowman's Best

❑ COMPLETE SET (133)	30.00	60.00
❑ COMMON CARD (1-100)	.20	.50
❑ COMMON ROOKIE (101-133)	.40	1.00
❑ 1 Vince Carter	.60	1.50
❑ 2 Dikembe Mutombo	.25	.60
❑ 3 Steve Nash	.50	1.25
❑ 4 Matt Harpring	.25	.60
❑ 5 Stephon Marbury	.30	.75
❑ 6 Chris Webber	.30	.75
❑ 7 Jason Kidd	.50	1.25
❑ 8 Theo Ratliff	.25	.60
❑ 9 Damon Stoudamire	.30	.75
❑ 10 Shareef Abdur-Rahim	.25	.60
❑ 11 Rod Strickland	.20	.50
❑ 12 Jeff Hornacek	.25	.60
❑ 13 Vin Baker	.30	.75
❑ 14 Joe Smith	.25	.60
❑ 15 Alonzo Mourning	.30	.75
❑ 16 Isaiah Rider	.20	.50
❑ 17 Shaquille O'Neal	.75	2.00
❑ 18 Chris Mullin	.30	.75
❑ 19 Charles Barkley	.40	1.00
❑ 20 Grant Hill	.30	.75
❑ 21 Chris Mills	.20	.50
❑ 22 Antonio McDyess	.25	.60

❑ 23 Brevin Knight	.20	.50
❑ 24 Toni Kukoc	.30	.75
❑ 25 Antoine Walker	.30	.75
❑ 26 Eddie Jones	.30	.75
❑ 27 Tim Thomas	.25	.60
❑ 28 Latrell Sprewell	.25	.60
❑ 29 Larry Hughes	.25	.60
❑ 30 Tim Duncan	.60	1.50
❑ 31 Horace Grant	.25	.60
❑ 32 John Stockton	.40	1.00
❑ 33 Mike Bibby	.30	.75
❑ 34 Mitch Richmond	.25	.60
❑ 35 Allan Houston	.25	.60
❑ 36 Terrell Brandon	.20	.50
❑ 37 Glenn Robinson	.25	.60
❑ 38 Tyrone Nesby RC	.30	.75
❑ 39 Glen Rice	.30	.75
❑ 40 Hakeem Olajuwon	.30	.75
❑ 41 Jerry Stackhouse	.30	.75
❑ 42 Elden Campbell	.20	.50
❑ 43 Ron Harper	.20	.50
❑ 44 Kenny Anderson	.25	.60
❑ 45 Michael Finley	.30	.75
❑ 46 Scottie Pippen	.50	1.25
❑ 47 Lindsey Hunter	.20	.50
❑ 48 Michael Olowokandi	.20	.50
❑ 49 P.J. Brown	.20	.50
❑ 50 Keith Van Horn	.25	.60
❑ 51 Michael Doleac	.20	.50
❑ 52 Anfernee Hardaway	.30	.75
❑ 53 Rasheed Wallace	.30	.75
❑ 54 Nick Anderson	.20	.50
❑ 55 Gary Payton	.30	.75
❑ 56 Tracy McGrady	.60	1.50
❑ 57 Ray Allen	.30	.75
❑ 58 Kobe Bryant	1.50	4.00
❑ 59 Ron Mercer	.20	.50
❑ 60 Shawn Kemp	.30	.75
❑ 61 Anthony Mason	.20	.50
❑ 62 Tim Hardaway	.30	.75
❑ 63 Antawn Jamison	.30	.75
❑ 64 Mark Jackson	.30	.75
❑ 65 Tom Gugliotta	.20	.50
❑ 66 Marcus Camby	.25	.60
❑ 67 Kerry Kittles	.20	.50
❑ 68 Vlade Divac	.30	.75
❑ 69 Avery Johnson	.25	.60
❑ 70 Karl Malone	.40	1.00
❑ 71 Juwan Howard	.25	.60
❑ 72 Alan Henderson	.20	.50
❑ 73 Hersey Hawkins	.20	.50
❑ 74 Darrell Armstrong	.20	.50
❑ 75 Allen Iverson	.60	1.50
❑ 76 Maurice Taylor	.25	.60
❑ 77 Gary Trent	.20	.50
❑ 78 John Starks	.30	.75
❑ 79 Paul Pierce	.30	.75
❑ 80 Kevin Garnett	.60	1.50
❑ 81 Patrick Ewing	.40	1.00
❑ 82 Steve Smith	.20	.50
❑ 83 Jason Williams	.30	.75
❑ 84 David Robinson	.40	1.00
❑ 85 Charles Oakley	.25	.60
❑ 86 Bryant Reeves	.20	.50
❑ 87 Nick Van Exel	.25	.60
❑ 88 Reggie Miller	.30	.75
❑ 89 Chris Gatling	.20	.50
❑ 90 Brian Grant	.20	.50
❑ 91 Allen Iverson BP	.60	1.50
❑ 92 Tim Duncan BP	.60	1.50
❑ 93 Keith Van Horn BP	.25	.60
❑ 94 Kevin Garnett BP	.60	1.50
❑ 95 Kobe Bryant BP	1.50	4.00
❑ 96 Elton Brand BP	1.00	2.50
❑ 97 Baron Davis BP	1.25	3.00
❑ 98 Lamar Odom BP	1.00	2.50
❑ 99 Wally Szczerbiak BP	1.00	2.50
❑ 100 Jason Terry BP	.75	2.00
❑ 101 Elton Brand RC	1.25	3.00
❑ 102 Steve Francis RC	1.25	3.00
❑ 103 Baron Davis RC	1.50	4.00
❑ 104 Lamar Odom RC	1.25	3.00
❑ 105 Jonathan Bender RC	.40	1.00
❑ 106 Wally Szczerbiak RC	1.25	3.00
❑ 107 Richard Hamilton RC	1.25	3.00
❑ 108 Andre Miller RC	1.25	3.00
❑ 109 Shawn Marion RC	1.25	3.00
❑ 110 Jason Terry RC	1.00	2.50
❑ 111 Trajan Langdon RC	.40	1.00
❑ 112 A.Radojevic RC	.40	1.00
❑ 113 Corey Maggette RC	1.25	3.00
❑ 114 William Avery RC	.40	1.00
❑ 115 DeMarco Johnson RC	.40	1.00
❑ 116 Ron Artest RC	1.50	4.00
❑ 117 Cal Bowdler RC	.40	1.00
❑ 118 James Posey RC	.60	1.50
❑ 119 Quincy Lewis RC	.40	1.00
❑ 120 Dion Glover RC	.40	1.00
❑ 121 Jeff Foster RC	.50	1.25
❑ 122 Kenny Thomas RC	.40	1.00
❑ 123 Devean George RC	.60	1.50
❑ 124 Tim James RC	.40	1.00
❑ 125 Vonteego Cummings RC	.40	1.00
❑ 126 Jumaine Jones RC	.40	1.00
❑ 127 Scott Padgett RC	.40	1.00
❑ 128 Anthony Carter RC	.75	2.00
❑ 129 Chris Herren RC	.40	1.00
❑ 130 Todd MacCulloch RC	.40	1.00
❑ 131 John Celestand RC	.40	1.00
❑ 132 Adrian Griffin RC	.40	1.00
❑ 133 Mirsad Turkcan RC	.40	1.00

2000-01 Bowman's Best

❑ COMPLETE SET w/o RC (100)	15.00	30.00
❑ COMMON CARD (1-100)	.20	.50
❑ COMMON ROOKIE (101-133)	1.00	2.50
❑ 1 Allen Iverson	.60	1.50
❑ 2 Darrell Armstrong	.20	.50
❑ 3 Kendall Gill	.20	.50
❑ 4 Marcus Camby	.25	.60
❑ 5 Glen Rice	.25	.60
❑ 6 Eddie Jones	.25	.60
❑ 7 Wally Szczerbiak	.25	.60
❑ 8 Antawn Jamison	.30	.75
❑ 9 Raef LaFrentz	.20	.50
❑ 10 Steve Francis	.30	.75
❑ 11 Tracy McGrady	.60	1.50
❑ 12 Brian Grant	.20	.50
❑ 13 Vlade Divac	.25	.60
❑ 14 Gary Payton	.30	.75
❑ 15 Vince Carter	.60	1.50
❑ 16 John Stockton	.40	1.00
❑ 17 Mike Bibby	.25	.60
❑ 18 Derek Anderson	.25	.60
❑ 19 Juwan Howard	.25	.60
❑ 20 Allan Houston	.25	.60
❑ 21 Kevin Garnett	.60	1.50
❑ 22 Michael Olowokandi	.20	.50
❑ 23 Maurice Taylor	.20	.50
❑ 24 Jerry Stackhouse	.25	.60
❑ 25 Nick Van Exel	.25	.60
❑ 26 Andre Miller	.25	.60
❑ 27 Michael Finley	.30	.75
❑ 28 Jamal Mashburn	.25	.60
❑ 29 Ron Mercer	.20	.50
❑ 30 Jim Jackson	.20	.50
❑ 31 Kenny Anderson	.25	.60
❑ 32 Karl Malone	.40	1.00
❑ 33 Rod Strickland	.25	.60
❑ 34 Shaquille O'Neal	.75	2.00
❑ 35 Glenn Robinson	.25	.60
❑ 36 Keith Van Horn	.25	.60
❑ 37 Grant Hill	.30	.75
❑ 38 Eric Snow	.20	.50
❑ 39 Anfernee Hardaway	.30	.75
❑ 40 Scottie Pippen	.50	1.25
❑ 41 Jason Williams	.25	.60
❑ 42 Elton Brand	.30	.75
❑ 43 Stephon Marbury	.30	.75
❑ 44 David Robinson	.40	1.00
❑ 45 Antonio Davis	.20	.50
❑ 46 Michael Dickerson	.20	.50
❑ 47 Mitch Richmond	.25	.60
❑ 48 Rashard Lewis	.30	.75
❑ 49 Jermaine O'Neal	.30	.75
❑ 50 Tim Duncan	.60	1.50
❑ 51 Tom Gugliotta	.20	.50
❑ 52 Theo Ratliff	.20	.50
❑ 53 Joe Smith	.20	.50
❑ 54 Tim Thomas	.20	.50
❑ 55 Brevin Knight	.20	.50
❑ 56 Dale Davis	.20	.50
❑ 57 Cuttino Mobley	.25	.60
❑ 58 Cedric Ceballos	.20	.50
❑ 59 Christian Laettner	.20	.50
❑ 60 Dirk Nowitzki	.50	1.25
❑ 61 Paul Pierce	.30	.75
❑ 62 Derrick Coleman	.25	.60
❑ 63 Dikembe Mutombo	.25	.60
❑ 64 Lamond Murray	.20	.50
❑ 65 Antonio McDyess	.25	.60
❑ 66 Reggie Miller	.30	.75
❑ 67 Hakeem Olajuwon	.40	1.00
❑ 68 Corey Maggette	.25	.60
❑ 69 Lamar Odom	.30	.75
❑ 70 Larry Hughes	.25	.60
❑ 71 Anthony Mason	.20	.50
❑ 72 Sam Cassell	.25	.60
❑ 73 Terrell Brandon	.20	.50
❑ 74 Latrell Sprewell	.25	.60
❑ 75 Kobe Bryant	1.50	4.00
❑ 76 Tim Hardaway	.25	.60
❑ 77 Mark Jackson	.25	.60
❑ 78 Vin Baker	.25	.60
❑ 79 Jonathan Bender	.20	.50
❑ 80 Chris Webber	.30	.75
❑ 81 Rasheed Wallace	.30	.75
❑ 82 Shawn Marion	.30	.75
❑ 83 Toni Kukoc	.25	.60
❑ 84 Patrick Ewing	.40	1.00
❑ 85 Ray Allen	.30	.75
❑ 86 Isaiah Rider	.25	.60
❑ 87 Danny Fortson	.20	.50
❑ 88 Jerome Williams	.20	.50
❑ 89 Shawn Kemp	.30	.75
❑ 90 Ron Artest	.30	.75
❑ 91 P.J. Brown	.20	.50
❑ 92 Baron Davis	.30	.75
❑ 93 Antoine Walker	.25	.60
❑ 94 Jason Terry	.30	.75
❑ 95 Jalen Rose	.25	.60
❑ 96 Avery Johnson	.25	.60
❑ 97 Shareef Abdur-Rahim	.25	.60
❑ 98 Bryon Russell	.20	.50
❑ 99 Richard Hamilton	.25	.60
❑ 100 Jason Kidd	.50	1.25
❑ 101A Kenyon Martin RC	2.50	6.00
❑ 101B Kenyon Martin RC	2.50	6.00
❑ 101C Kenyon Martin RC	2.50	6.00
❑ 102A Stromile Swift RC	1.25	3.00
❑ 102B Stromile Swift RC	1.25	3.00
❑ 102C Stromile Swift RC	1.25	3.00
❑ 103A Darius Miles RC	1.25	3.00
❑ 103B Darius Miles RC	1.25	3.00
❑ 103C Darius Miles RC	1.25	3.00
❑ 104A Marcus Fizer RC	1.00	2.50
❑ 104B Marcus Fizer RC	1.00	2.50
❑ 104C Marcus Fizer RC	1.00	2.50
❑ 105A Mike Miller RC	1.50	4.00
❑ 105B Mike Miller RC	1.50	4.00
❑ 105C Mike Miller RC	1.50	4.00
❑ 106A DerMarr Johnson RC	1.00	2.50
❑ 106B DerMarr Johnson RC	1.00	2.50
❑ 106C DerMarr Johnson RC	1.00	2.50
❑ 107A Chris Mihm RC	1.00	2.50
❑ 107B Chris Mihm RC	1.00	2.50
❑ 107C Chris Mihm RC	1.00	2.50
❑ 108A Jamal Crawford RC	1.50	4.00
❑ 108B Jamal Crawford RC	1.50	4.00
❑ 108C Jamal Crawford RC	1.50	4.00
❑ 109A Joel Przybilla RC	1.00	2.50
❑ 109B Joel Przybilla RC	1.00	2.50
❑ 109C Joel Przybilla RC	1.00	2.50
❑ 110A Keyon Dooling RC	1.00	2.50
❑ 110B Keyon Dooling RC	1.00	2.50
❑ 110C Keyon Dooling RC	1.00	2.50
❑ 111A Jerome Moiso RC	1.00	2.50
❑ 111B Jerome Moiso RC	1.00	2.50
❑ 111C Jerome Moiso RC	1.00	2.50
❑ 112A Etan Thomas RC	1.00	2.50
❑ 112B Etan Thomas RC	1.00	2.50
❑ 112C Etan Thomas RC	1.00	2.50
❑ 113A Courtney Alexander RC	1.00	2.50
❑ 113B Courtney Alexander RC	1.00	2.50

- ❑ 113C Courtney Alexander RC 1.00 2.50
- ❑ 114A Mateen Cleaves RC 1.00 2.50
- ❑ 114B Mateen Cleaves RC 1.00 2.50
- ❑ 114C Mateen Cleaves RC 1.00 2.50
- ❑ 115A Jason Collier RC 1.00 2.50
- ❑ 115B Jason Collier RC 1.00 2.50
- ❑ 115C Jason Collier RC 1.00 2.50
- ❑ 116A Hedo Turkoglu RC 2.50 6.00
- ❑ 116B Hedo Turkoglu RC 2.50 6.00
- ❑ 116C Hedo Turkoglu RC 2.50 6.00
- ❑ 117A Desmond Mason RC 1.25 3.00
- ❑ 117B Desmond Mason RC 1.25 3.00
- ❑ 117C Desmond Mason RC 1.25 3.00
- ❑ 118A Quentin Richardson RC 1.25 3.00
- ❑ 118B Quentin Richardson RC 1.25 3.00
- ❑ 118C Quentin Richardson RC 1.25 3.00
- ❑ 119A Jamaal Magloire RC 1.00 2.50
- ❑ 119B Jamaal Magloire RC 1.00 2.50
- ❑ 119C Jamaal Magloire RC 1.00 2.50
- ❑ 120A Speedy Claxton RC 1.00 2.50
- ❑ 120B Speedy Claxton RC 1.00 2.50
- ❑ 120C Speedy Claxton RC 1.00 2.50
- ❑ 121A Morris Peterson RC 1.50 4.00
- ❑ 121B Morris Peterson RC 1.50 4.00
- ❑ 121C Morris Peterson RC 1.50 4.00
- ❑ 122A Donnell Harvey RC 1.00 2.50
- ❑ 122B Donnell Harvey RC 1.00 2.50
- ❑ 122C Donnell Harvey RC 1.00 2.50
- ❑ 123A DeShawn Stevenson RC 1.00 2.50
- ❑ 123B DeShawn Stevenson RC 1.00 2.50
- ❑ 123C DeShawn Stevenson RC 1.00 2.50
- ❑ 124A Dalibor Bagaric RC 1.00 2.50
- ❑ 124B Dalibor Bagaric RC 1.00 2.50
- ❑ 124C Dalibor Bagaric RC 1.00 2.50
- ❑ 125A Iakovos Tsakalidis RC 1.00 2.50
- ❑ 125B Iakovos Tsakalidis RC 1.00 2.50
- ❑ 125C Iakovos Tsakalidis RC 1.00 2.50
- ❑ 126A Mamadou N'Diaye RC 1.00 2.50
- ❑ 126B Mamadou N'Diaye RC 1.00 2.50
- ❑ 126C Mamadou N'Diaye RC 1.00 2.50
- ❑ 127A Lavor Postell RC 1.00 2.50
- ❑ 127B Lavor Postell RC 1.00 2.50
- ❑ 127C Lavor Postell RC 1.00 2.50
- ❑ 128A Erick Barkley RC 1.00 2.50
- ❑ 128B Erick Barkley RC 1.00 2.50
- ❑ 128C Erick Barkley RC 1.00 2.50
- ❑ 129A Mark Madsen RC 1.00 2.50
- ❑ 129B Mark Madsen RC 1.00 2.50
- ❑ 129C Mark Madsen RC 1.00 2.50
- ❑ 130A Khalid El-Amin RC 1.00 2.50
- ❑ 130B Khalid El-Amin RC 1.00 2.50
- ❑ 130C Khalid El-Amin RC 1.00 2.50
- ❑ 131A A.J. Guyton RC 1.00 2.50
- ❑ 131B A.J. Guyton RC 1.00 2.50
- ❑ 131C A.J. Guyton RC 1.00 2.50
- ❑ 132A Stephen Jackson RC 1.50 4.00
- ❑ 132B Stephen Jackson RC 1.50 4.00
- ❑ 132C Stephen Jackson RC 1.50 4.00
- ❑ 133A Michael Redd RC 2.50 6.00
- ❑ 133B Michael Redd RC 2.50 6.00
- ❑ 133C Michael Redd RC 2.50 6.00
- ❑ LCP1 Draft Picks 3.00 8.00

2009-10 Certified

- ❑ 1 Dirk Nowitzki 1.00 2.50
- ❑ 2 Jason Kidd .75 2.00
- ❑ 3 Jason Terry .60 1.50
- ❑ 4 J.J. Barea .75 2.00
- ❑ 5 Josh Howard .75 2.00
- ❑ 6 Shawn Marion .75 2.00
- ❑ 7 Luis Scola .50 1.25
- ❑ 8 Shane Battier .60 1.50
- ❑ 9 Tracy McGrady 1.00 2.50
- ❑ 10 Trevor Ariza .75 2.00
- ❑ 11 Yao Ming 1.00 2.50
- ❑ 12 Allen Iverson 1.00 2.50
- ❑ 13 Marc Gasol .75 2.00
- ❑ 14 O.J. Mayo 1.00 2.50
- ❑ 15 Rudy Gay .75 2.00
- ❑ 16 Zach Randolph .50 1.25
- ❑ 17 Chris Paul 1.50 4.00
- ❑ 18 David West .75 2.00
- ❑ 19 Emeka Okafor .75 2.00
- ❑ 20 James Posey .60 1.50
- ❑ 21 Peja Stojakovic .50 1.25
- ❑ 22 Manu Ginobili .75 2.00
- ❑ 23 Michael Finley .50 1.25
- ❑ 24 Richard Jefferson .75 2.00
- ❑ 25 Tim Duncan 1.25 3.00
- ❑ 26 Tony Parker .75 2.00
- ❑ 27 Carmelo Anthony 1.00 2.50
- ❑ 28 Chauncey Billups .75 2.00
- ❑ 29 Chris Andersen .75 2.00
- ❑ 30 J.R. Smith .60 1.50
- ❑ 31 Kenyon Martin .75 2.00
- ❑ 32 Nene .60 1.50
- ❑ 33 Al Jefferson .75 2.00
- ❑ 34 Kevin Love .60 1.50
- ❑ 35 Ramon Sessions .50 1.25
- ❑ 36 Ryan Gomes .50 1.25
- ❑ 37 Andre Miller .60 1.50
- ❑ 38 Brandon Roy 1.00 2.50
- ❑ 39 Greg Oden .60 1.50
- ❑ 40 LaMarcus Aldridge .75 2.00
- ❑ 41 Rudy Fernandez .75 2.00
- ❑ 42 Jeff Green .60 1.50
- ❑ 43 Kevin Durant 2.00 5.00
- ❑ 44 Nick Collison .50 1.25
- ❑ 45 Russell Westbrook .75 2.00
- ❑ 46 Andrei Kirilenko .60 1.50
- ❑ 47 Carlos Boozer .75 2.00
- ❑ 48 Deron Williams 1.00 2.50
- ❑ 49 Mehmet Okur .50 1.25
- ❑ 50 Paul Millsap .60 1.50
- ❑ 51 Andris Biedrins .50 1.25
- ❑ 52 Anthony Randolph .75 2.00
- ❑ 53 Corey Maggette .60 1.50
- ❑ 54 Devean George .60 1.50
- ❑ 55 Kelenna Azubuike .50 1.25
- ❑ 56 Stephen Jackson .60 1.50
- ❑ 57 Al Thornton .75 2.00
- ❑ 58 Baron Davis .75 2.00
- ❑ 59 Chris Kaman .75 2.00
- ❑ 60 Eric Gordon .75 2.00
- ❑ 61 Marcus Camby .50 1.25
- ❑ 62 Andrew Bynum .75 2.00
- ❑ 63 Derek Fisher .60 1.50
- ❑ 64 Kobe Bryant 4.00 10.00
- ❑ 65 Lamar Odom .75 2.00
- ❑ 66 Luke Walton .50 1.25
- ❑ 67 Pau Gasol .75 2.00
- ❑ 68 Ron Artest .75 2.00
- ❑ 69 Amare Stoudemire 1.00 2.50
- ❑ 70 Grant Hill .75 2.00
- ❑ 71 Jason Richardson .75 2.00
- ❑ 72 Leandro Barbosa .60 1.50
- ❑ 73 Steve Nash .75 2.00
- ❑ 74 Andres Nocioni .60 1.50
- ❑ 75 Francisco Garcia .60 1.50
- ❑ 76 Kevin Martin .75 2.00
- ❑ 77 Sean May .50 1.25
- ❑ 78 Kevin Garnett 1.50 4.00
- ❑ 79 Paul Pierce 1.00 2.50
- ❑ 80 Rajon Rondo .75 2.00
- ❑ 81 Rasheed Wallace .75 2.00
- ❑ 82 Ray Allen .75 2.00
- ❑ 83 Brook Lopez .50 1.25
- ❑ 84 Courtney Lee .60 1.50
- ❑ 85 Devin Harris .75 2.00
- ❑ 86 Yi Jianlian .75 2.00
- ❑ 87 Al Harrington .60 1.50
- ❑ 88 Chris Duhon .50 1.25
- ❑ 89 Danilo Gallinari .75 2.00
- ❑ 90 Darko Milicic .50 1.25
- ❑ 91 David Lee .60 1.50
- ❑ 92 Nate Robinson .75 2.00
- ❑ 93 Andre Iguodala .75 2.00
- ❑ 94 Elton Brand .75 2.00
- ❑ 95 Samuel Dalembert .50 1.25
- ❑ 96 Thaddeus Young .50 1.25
- ❑ 97 Andrea Bargnani .60 1.50
- ❑ 98 Chris Bosh .75 2.00
- ❑ 99 Hedo Turkoglu .75 2.00
- ❑ 100 Jarrett Jack .60 1.50
- ❑ 101 Jose Calderon .60 1.50
- ❑ 102 Derrick Rose 1.50 4.00
- ❑ 103 Joakim Noah .75 2.00
- ❑ 104 Luol Deng .75 2.00
- ❑ 105 Tyrus Thomas .60 1.50
- ❑ 106 Anderson Varejao .60 1.50
- ❑ 107 LeBron James 4.00 10.00
- ❑ 108 Mo Williams .60 1.50
- ❑ 109 Shaquille O'Neal 1.50 4.00
- ❑ 110 Zydrunas Ilgauskas .50 1.25
- ❑ 111 Ben Gordon .75 2.00
- ❑ 112 Ben Wallace .75 2.00
- ❑ 113 Charlie Villanueva .60 1.50
- ❑ 114 Richard Hamilton .60 1.50
- ❑ 115 Rodney Stuckey .75 2.00
- ❑ 116 Tayshaun Prince .75 2.00
- ❑ 117 Danny Granger .75 2.00
- ❑ 118 Jeff Foster .50 1.25
- ❑ 119 T.J. Ford .50 1.25
- ❑ 120 Troy Murphy .50 1.25
- ❑ 121 Andrew Bogut .75 2.00
- ❑ 122 Hakim Warrick .60 1.50
- ❑ 123 Luke Ridnour .50 1.25
- ❑ 124 Michael Redd .75 2.00
- ❑ 125 Al Horford .75 2.00
- ❑ 126 Jamal Crawford .50 1.25
- ❑ 127 Joe Johnson .75 2.00
- ❑ 128 Josh Smith .75 2.00
- ❑ 129 Mike Bibby .50 1.25
- ❑ 130 Boris Diaw .60 1.50
- ❑ 131 D.J. Augustin .60 1.50
- ❑ 132 Gerald Wallace .75 2.00
- ❑ 133 Raja Bell .60 1.50
- ❑ 134 Raymond Felton .60 1.50
- ❑ 135 Tyson Chandler .60 1.50
- ❑ 136 Dwyane Wade 1.50 4.00
- ❑ 137 Jermaine O'Neal .75 2.00
- ❑ 138 Mario Chalmers .75 2.00
- ❑ 139 Michael Beasley 1.00 2.50
- ❑ 140 Quentin Richardson .50 1.25
- ❑ 141 Udonis Haslem .60 1.50
- ❑ 142 Dwight Howard 1.50 4.00
- ❑ 143 J.J. Redick .75 2.00
- ❑ 144 Jameer Nelson .60 1.50
- ❑ 145 Mickael Pietrus .50 1.25
- ❑ 146 Rashard Lewis .75 2.00
- ❑ 147 Antawn Jamison .75 2.00
- ❑ 148 Caron Butler .75 2.00
- ❑ 149 Gilbert Arenas .75 2.00
- ❑ 150 Randy Foye .50 1.25
- ❑ 151 Isiah Thomas 1.50 4.00
- ❑ 152 Byron Scott 1.50 4.00
- ❑ 153 Frank Ramsey 1.50 4.00
- ❑ 154 Dikembe Mutombo 1.50 4.00
- ❑ 155 Alonzo Mourning 2.00 5.00
- ❑ 156 John Starks 1.50 4.00
- ❑ 157 Adrian Dantley 1.50 4.00
- ❑ 158 Bailey Howell 1.50 4.00
- ❑ 159 Al Attles 1.50 4.00
- ❑ 160 Walt Frazier 1.50 4.00
- ❑ 161 Tim Hardaway 1.50 4.00
- ❑ 162 Pat Riley 1.50 4.00
- ❑ 163 Paul Westphal 1.50 4.00
- ❑ 164 Bill Walton 1.50 4.00
- ❑ 165 Jack Sikma 1.50 4.00
- ❑ 166 Magic Johnson 3.00 8.00
- ❑ 167 Spud Webb 1.50 4.00
- ❑ 168 Wilt Chamberlain 3.00 8.00
- ❑ 169 Wes Unseld 1.50 4.00
- ❑ 170 James Worthy 2.00 5.00
- ❑ 171 Blake Griffin JSY AU RC 25.00 50.00
- ❑ 172 Hasheem Thabeet JSY AU RC 5.00 12.00
- ❑ 173 James Harden JSY AU RC 10.00 25.00
- ❑ 174 T.Evans JSY AU RC 40.00 80.00
- ❑ 175 Jonny Flynn JSY AU RC 8.00 20.00
- ❑ 176 Stephen Curry JSY AU RC 25.00 50.00
- ❑ 177 Jordan Hill JSY AU RC 5.00 12.00
- ❑ 178 Brandon Jennings JSY AU RC 25.00 50.00
- ❑ 179 T.Williams JSY AU RC EXCH 6.0015.00
- ❑ 180 Henderson JSY AU RC EXCH 5.00 12.00
- ❑ 181 Tyler Hansbrough JSY AU RC 15.00 30.00
- ❑ 182 Earl Clark JSY AU RC 5.00 12.00
- ❑ 183 Austin Daye JSY AU RC 5.00 12.00
- ❑ 184 Johnson JSY AU RC EXCH 5.00 12.00
- ❑ 185 Jrue Holiday JSY AU RC 6.00 15.00
- ❑ 186 Ty Lawson JSY AU RC 15.00 30.00

❑ 187 Jeff Teague JSY AU RC 5.00 12.00
❑ 188 Eric Maynor JSY AU RC 5.00 12.00
❑ 189 Darren Collison JSY AU RC 15.0030.00
❑ 190 Casspi JSY AU RC EXCH 6.00 15.00
❑ 191 B.J. Mullens JSY AU RC 5.00 12.00
❑ 192 Beaubois JSY AU RC EXCH 6.0015.00
❑ 193 Taj Gibson JSY AU RC 6.00 15.00
❑ 194 DeMarre Carroll JSY AU RC 5.00 12.00
❑ 195 Wayne Ellington JSY AU RC 5.00 12.00
❑ 196 T.Douglas JSY AU RC EXCH 5.0012.00
❑ 197 Jeff Pendergraph JSY AU RC 5.0012.00
❑ 198 Jermaine Taylor JSY AU RC 5.00 12.00
❑ 199 DeJuan Blair JSY AU RC 8.00 20.00
❑ 200 Jodie Meeks JSY AU RC 5.00 12.00

2006-07 Chronology

❑ 1 Slick Watts 2.50 6.00
❑ 2 Louie Dampier 2.50 6.00
❑ 3 Al Attles 2.50 6.00
❑ 4 Alvin Robertson 2.50 6.00
❑ 5 Detlef Schrempf 2.50 6.00
❑ 6 Artis Gilmore 2.50 6.00
❑ 7 Austin Carr 2.50 6.00
❑ 8 Avery Johnson 2.50 6.00
❑ 9 B.J. Armstrong 2.50 6.00
❑ 10 Dave Bing 2.50 6.00
❑ 11 Bingo Smith 2.50 6.00
❑ 12 Bob Dandridge 3.00 8.00
❑ 13 Bill Bradley 3.00 8.00
❑ 14 Bobby Jones 2.50 6.00
❑ 15 Brad Daugherty 2.50 6.00
❑ 16 Byron Scott 2.50 6.00
❑ 17 Cazzie Russell 2.50 6.00
❑ 18 Cedric Maxwell 2.50 6.00
❑ 19 Charles Oakley 2.50 6.00
❑ 20 Chet Walker 2.50 6.00
❑ 21 Chuck Share 2.50 6.00
❑ 22 Dan Majerle 3.00 8.00
❑ 23 Danny Ainge 2.50 6.00
❑ 24 Danny Manning 2.50 6.00
❑ 25 Darrell Griffith 2.50 6.00
❑ 26 Darryl Dawkins 2.50 6.00
❑ 27 Dennis Johnson 3.00 8.00
❑ 28 Gheorghe Muresan 2.50 6.00
❑ 29 Dick Barnett 3.00 8.00
❑ 30 Dick Van Arsdale 2.50 6.00
❑ 31 Dominique Wilkins 3.00 8.00
❑ 32 Don Buse 2.50 6.00
❑ 33 Don Ohl 2.50 6.00
❑ 34 Ernie DiGregorio 2.50 6.00
❑ 35 Fred Brown 2.50 6.00
❑ 36 Julius Erving 5.00 12.00
❑ 37 George McGinnis 2.50 6.00
❑ 38 Calvin Natt 2.50 6.00
❑ 39 Rick Mahorn 2.50 6.00
❑ 40 Gus Williams 2.50 6.00
❑ 41 Jack Sikma 2.50 6.00
❑ 42 Jamaal Wilkes 2.50 6.00
❑ 43 James Edwards 2.50 6.00
❑ 44 Jerry Sloan 2.50 6.00
❑ 45 Jim Loscutoff 3.00 8.00
❑ 46 Jo Jo White 2.50 6.00
❑ 47 John Johnson 2.50 6.00
❑ 48 Johnny Kerr 3.00 8.00
❑ 49 Karl Malone 3.00 8.00
❑ 50 Junior Bridgeman 2.50 6.00
❑ 51 Kiki Vandeweghe 2.50 6.00
❑ 52 Kurt Rambis 2.50 6.00
❑ 53 Larry Nance 2.50 6.00
❑ 54 Lonnie Shelton 2.50 6.00
❑ 55 Lou Hudson 2.50 6.00
❑ 56 Kevin McHale 3.00 8.00
❑ 57 Tree Rollins 2.50 6.00
❑ 58 George Karl 3.00 8.00
❑ 59 Maurice Lucas 2.50 6.00
❑ 60 Mel Daniels 2.50 6.00
❑ 61 Michael Cooper 2.50 6.00
❑ 62 Mitch Richmond 2.50 6.00
❑ 63 Joe Dumars 2.50 6.00
❑ 64 Mike Dunleavy Sr. 2.50 6.00
❑ 65 Moses Malone 2.50 6.00
❑ 66 Muggsy Bogues 2.50 6.00
❑ 67 Norm Nixon 2.50 6.00
❑ 68 Norm Van Lier 3.00 8.00
❑ 69 Oscar Robertson 2.50 6.00
❑ 70 Paul Arizin 2.50 6.00
❑ 71 Paul Westphal 2.50 6.00
❑ 72 Phil Chenier 2.50 6.00
❑ 73 Phil Ford 2.50 6.00
❑ 74 John Starks 2.50 6.00
❑ 75 Richie Guerin 2.50 6.00
❑ 76 Rolando Blackman 2.50 6.00
❑ 77 World B. Free 2.50 6.00
❑ 78 Rudy Tomjanovich 2.50 6.00
❑ 79 Sam Perkins 2.50 6.00
❑ 80 Sean Elliott 2.50 6.00
❑ 81 Ricky Pierce 2.50 6.00
❑ 82 Sidney Moncrief 2.50 6.00
❑ 83 Horace Grant 2.50 6.00
❑ 84 Spencer Haywood 2.50 6.00
❑ 85 Steve Kerr 2.50 6.00
❑ 86 Terry Dischinger 2.50 6.00
❑ 87 Mitch Kupchak 2.50 6.00
❑ 88 Tom Chambers 2.50 6.00
❑ 89 Tom Sanders 2.50 6.00
❑ 90 Michael Ray Richardson 2.50 6.00
❑ 91 Terry Cummings 2.50 6.00
❑ 92 Spud Webb 2.50 6.00
❑ 93 Walter Davis 2.50 6.00
❑ 94 Wayman Tisdale 2.50 6.00
❑ 95 Wayne Embry 2.50 6.00
❑ 96 Wilt Chamberlain 5.00 12.00
❑ 97 Jeff Hornacek 2.50 6.00
❑ 98 Eddie Johnson 2.50 6.00
❑ 99 Xavier McDaniel 2.50 6.00
❑ 100 Zelmo Beaty 2.50 6.00
❑ 101 Allan Ray JSY AU RC EXCH 6.00 15.00
❑ 102 A.Bargnani JSY AU RC EXCH 20.00 40.00
❑ 103 Bobby Jones JSY AU RC 6.00 15.00
❑ 104 Brandon Roy JSY AU RC 60.00 120.00
❑ 105 Cedric Simmons JSY AU RC 6.0015.00
❑ 106 Craig Smith JSY AU RC 10.00 25.00
❑ 107 Daniel Gibson JSY AU RC 20.00 40.00
❑ 108 Dee Brown JSY AU RC EXCH 6.00 15.00
❑ 109 D.Markota JSY AU RC EXCH 6.0015.00
❑ 110 Hilton Armstrong JSY AU RC 6.0015.00
❑ 111 James Augustine JSY AU RC 6.0015.00
❑ 112 James White JSY AU RC 8.00 20.00
❑ 113 H.Adams JSY AU RC EXCH 6.00 15.00
❑ 114 J.Garbajosa JSY AU RC EXCH 15.00 30.00
❑ 115 Josh Boone JSY AU RC 10.00 25.00
❑ 116 Kyle Lowry JSY AU RC 8.00 20.00
❑ 117 L.Aldridge JSY AU RC 20.00 40.00
❑ 118 David Noel JSY AU RC 8.00 20.00
❑ 119 M.Williams JSY AU RC EXCH 10.00 25.00
❑ 120 Mardy Collins JSY AU RC EXCH 6.00 15.00
❑ 121 Maurice Ager JSY AU RC 10.00 25.00
❑ 122 P.J. Tucker JSY AU RC 6.00 15.00
❑ 123 Patrick O'Bryant JSY AU RC 8.00 20.00
❑ 124 Paul Davis JSY AU RC 8.00 20.00
❑ 125 Paul Millsap JSY AU RC 15.00 30.00
❑ 126 Q.Douby JSY AU RC EXCH 6.00 15.00
❑ 127 Rajon Rondo JSY AU RC 40.00 80.00
❑ 128 Randy Foye JSY AU RC 10.00 25.00
❑ 129 Renaldo Balkman JSY AU RC 15.00 30.00
❑ 130 Y.Diawara JSY AU RC EXCH 10.00 25.00
❑ 131 Rodney Carney JSY AU RC 8.00 20.00
❑ 132 Ronnie Brewer JSY AU RC 5.00 12.00
❑ 133 Rudy Gay JSY AU RC 15.00 30.00
❑ 134 Saer Sene JSY AU RC 8.00 20.00
❑ 135 S.Rodriguez JSY AU RC EXCH 8.00 20.00
❑ 136 Shannon Brown JSY AU RC 10.0025.00
❑ 137 Shawne Williams JSY AU RC 8.0020.00
❑ 138 Shelden Williams JSY AU RC 10.00 25.00
❑ 139 Solomon Jones JSY AU RC 6.00 15.00
❑ 140 Thabo Sefolosha JSY AU RC 20.00 40.00
❑ 141 Tyrus Thomas JSY AU RC 20.00 40.00
❑ 142 Steve Novak JSY AU RC 6.00 15.00
❑ 143 Adam Morrison JSY RC
❑ 144 J.J. Redick JSY RC
❑ 145 Marcus Vinicius JSY RC
❑ 146 Vassilis Spanoulis JSY RC
❑ 147 Leon Powe JSY RC
❑ 148 Jordan Farmar JSY RC
❑ 149 Al Cervi JSY AU 15.00 30.00
❑ 150 Alex English JSY AU 10.00 25.00
❑ 151 Arnie Risen JSY AU 15.00 30.00
❑ 152 Bailey Howell JSY AU 15.00 30.00
❑ 153 Bill Sharman JSY AU 20.00 40.00
❑ 154 Don Nelson JSY AU 20.00 40.00
❑ 155 Bob Lanier JSY AU 15.00 30.00
❑ 156 Bob McAdoo JSY AU 25.00 50.00
❑ 157 Bob Pettit JSY AU 20.00 40.00
❑ 158 Bobby Wanzer JSY AU 15.00 30.00
❑ 159 Calvin Murphy JSY AU 10.00 25.00
❑ 160 Clyde Lovellette JSY AU 20.00 40.00
❑ 161 Bill Laimbeer JSY AU 25.00 50.00
❑ 162 Dave Cowens JSY AU 20.00 40.00
❑ 163 David Thompson JSY AU 15.00 30.00
❑ 164 Dick McGuire JSY AU 15.00 30.00
❑ 165 John Wooden JSY AU 125.00 250.00
❑ 166 Ed Macauley JSY AU 15.00 30.00
❑ 167 Elgin Baylor JSY AU 60.00 120.00
❑ 168 Elvin Hayes JSY AU 15.00 30.00
❑ 169 Frank Ramsey JSY AU 25.00 50.00
❑ 170 Gail Goodrich JSY AU 20.00 40.00
❑ 171 Hal Greer JSY AU 20.00 40.00
❑ 172 Adrian Dantley JSY AU EXCH 15.00 30.00
❑ 173 Jerry Lucas JSY AU 15.00 30.00
❑ 174 Reggie Theus JSY AU EXCH 15.00 30.00
❑ 175 Charlie Scott JSY AU 15.00 30.00
❑ 176 Nate Archibald JSY AU 20.00 40.00
❑ 177 Nate Thurmond JSY AU 15.00 30.00
❑ 178 Rick Barry JSY AU 20.00 40.00
❑ 179 Slater Martin JSY AU 25.00 50.00
❑ 180 Tom Heinsohn JSY AU 15.00 30.00
❑ 181 Vern Mikkelsen JSY AU 25.00 50.00
❑ 182 Walt Bellamy JSY AU EXCH 10.0025.00
❑ 183 Walt Frazier JSY AU 25.00 50.00
❑ 184 Rod Hundley JSY AU 20.00 40.00
❑ 185 Ralph Sampson JSY AU EXCH 20.00 40.00
❑ 186 Bill Russell JSY AU 150.00 300.00
❑ 187 Julius Erving JSY AU 125.00 250.00
❑ 188 Larry Bird JSY AU 125.00 250.00
❑ 189 James Worthy JSY AU 60.00 120.00
❑ 190 K.Abdul-Jabbar JSY AU 50.00 100.00
❑ 191 Clyde Drexler JSY AU 40.00 80.00
❑ 192 Magic Johnson JSY AU 80.00 160.00
❑ 193 Wes Unseld JSY AU 20.00 40.00
❑ 194 John Stockton JSY AU 60.00 120.00
❑ 195 George Gervin JSY AU 20.00 40.00
❑ 196 Chris Mullin JSY AU
❑ 197 David Robinson JSY AU 80.00 160.00
❑ 198 Sam Jones JSY AU 50.00 100.00
❑ 199 Bill Walton JSY AU 20.00 40.00
❑ 200 Earl Lloyd JSY AU 30.00 60.00
❑ 201 Mark Price JSY AU 40.00 80.00
❑ 202 John Havlicek JSY AU 50.00 100.00
❑ 203 Cliff Hagan JSY AU 25.00 50.00
❑ 204 Dolph Schayes JSY AU 25.00 50.00
❑ 205 Harry Gallatin JSY AU 20.00 40.00
❑ 206 Jerry West JSY AU 75.00 150.00
❑ 207 Connie Hawkins JSY AU 20.00 40.00
❑ 208 Lenny Wilkens JSY AU 20.00 40.00
❑ 209 Michael Jordan JSY AU 500.00 800.00
❑ 210 Hakeem Olajuwon JSY AU 50.00100.00
❑ 211 Dan Issel JSY AU 20.00 40.00
❑ 212 Robert Parish JSY AU 25.00 50.00
❑ 213 Dennis Rodman JSY AU 75.00 150.00
❑ 214 Pat Riley JSY AU 50.00 100.00
❑ 215 Maurice Cheeks JSY AU 20.00 40.00
❑ 216 Bob Houbregs JSY AU 20.00 40.00
❑ 217 Tracy McGrady JSY AU 50.00 100.00
❑ 218 Yao Ming JSY AU 40.00 80.00
❑ 219 Paul Pierce JSY AU 30.00 60.00
❑ 220 Ben Gordon JSY AU 75.00 150.00
❑ 221 Kobe Bryant JSY AU 250.00 500.00
❑ 222 Steve Nash JSY AU 100.00 200.00
❑ 223 LeBron James JSY AU 225.00 450.00
❑ 224 Carmelo Anthony JSY AU 50.00 100.00

❑ 225 Jason Kidd JSY AU 50.00 100.00
❑ 226 Chris Paul JSY AU 50.00 100.00
❑ 227 Bill Fitch AU EXCH 10.00 25.00
❑ 228 Jack Ramsay AU 15.00 30.00
❑ 229 John Kundla AU 50.00 100.00
❑ 230 Dean Smith AU 25.00 50.00
❑ 231 Pat Riley AU 15.00 30.00
❑ 232 Jerry Sloan AU 15.00 30.00
❑ 233 Don Haskins AU 20.00 40.00
❑ 234 Rick Pitino AU 20.00 40.00
❑ 235 John Chaney AU 15.00 30.00
❑ 236 Pete Carril AU
❑ 237 Jerry Tarkanian AU
❑ 238 Lenny Wilkens AU 10.00 25.00
❑ 239 Chuck Daly AU 25.00 50.00
❑ 240 George Karl AU 20.00 40.00
❑ 241 John Wooden AU 100.00 200.00
❑ 242 Digger Phelps AU 10.00 25.00
❑ 243 Jud Heathcote AU 20.00 40.00
❑ 244 Dick Motta AU 10.00 25.00
❑ 245 Gene Shue AU 10.00 25.00
❑ 246 Jim Calhoun AU 10.00 25.00
❑ 247 Greg Oden 60.00 120.00
❑ 248 Kevin Durant 80.00 160.00
❑ 249 Al Horford 15.00 30.00
❑ 250 Michael Conley 15.00 30.00
❑ 251 Jeff Green 15.00 30.00
❑ 252 Yi Jianlian 10.00 25.00
❑ 253 Corey Brewer 15.00 30.00
❑ 254 Brandan Wright 8.00 20.00
❑ 255 Joakim Noah 15.00 30.00
❑ 256 Spencer Hawes 8.00 20.00
❑ 257 Acie Law 10.00 25.00
❑ 258 Thaddeus Young 8.00 20.00
❑ 259 Julian Wright 10.00 25.00
❑ 260 Al Thornton 10.00 25.00
❑ 261 Rodney Stuckey 15.00 30.00
❑ 262 Nick Young 8.00 20.00
❑ 263 Sean Williams 8.00 20.00
❑ 264 Marco Belinelli 10.00 25.00
❑ 265 Javaris Crittenton 10.00 25.00
❑ 266 Jason Smith 8.00 20.00
❑ 267 Daequan Cook 10.00 25.00
❑ 268 Jared Dudley 6.00 15.00
❑ 269 Wilson Chandler 66.00 15.00
❑ 270 Morris Almond 6.00 15.00
❑ 271 Arron Afflalo 6.00 15.00
❑ 272 Aaron Brooks 6.00 15.00
❑ 273 Alando Tucker 6.00 15.00
❑ 274 Petteri Koponen 6.00 15.00
❑ 275 Carl Landry 6.00 15.00
❑ 276 Gabe Pruitt 6.00 15.00

2007-08 Chronology

❑ 1 Andrew Toney 2.50 6.00
❑ 2 Artis Gilmore 2.50 6.00
❑ 3 B.J. Armstrong 2.50 6.00
❑ 4 Bernard King 2.50 6.00
❑ 5 Bill Cartwright 2.50 6.00
❑ 6 Bill Laimbeer 2.50 6.00
❑ 7 Bill Russell 4.00 10.00
❑ 8 Bill Walton 2.50 6.00
❑ 9 Bill Wennington 2.50 6.00
❑ 10 Billy Cunningham 2.50 6.00
❑ 11 Bob Cousy 4.00 10.00
❑ 12 Bob McAdoo 2.50 6.00
❑ 13 Brad Davis 2.50 6.00
❑ 14 Byron Scott 2.50 6.00
❑ 15 Cedric Maxwell 2.50 6.00
❑ 16 Charles Oakley 2.50 6.00
❑ 17 Clyde Drexler 3.00 8.00
❑ 18 Clyde Lovellette 2.50 6.00
❑ 19 Dan Issel 2.50 6.00
❑ 20 Danny Ainge 2.50 6.00
❑ 21 Darrell Walker 2.50 6.00
❑ 22 Dave Bing 2.50 6.00
❑ 23 Dave Cowens 3.00 8.00
❑ 24 Dave DeBusschere 3.00 8.00
❑ 25 David Robinson 4.00 10.00
❑ 26 Dennis Rodman 2.50 6.00
❑ 27 Derrick Coleman 2.50 6.00
❑ 28 Dino Radja 3.00 8.00
❑ 29 Doc Rivers 2.50 6.00
❑ 30 Dominique Wilkins 3.00 8.00
❑ 31 Earl Monroe 2.50 6.00
❑ 32 Elgin Baylor 2.50 6.00
❑ 33 Freddie Lewis 2.50 6.00
❑ 34 George Gervin 2.50 6.00
❑ 35 George Mikan 5.00 12.00
❑ 36 Gheorghe Muresan 2.50 6.00
❑ 37 Gus Williams 2.50 6.00
❑ 38 Hakeem Olajuwon 3.00 8.00
❑ 39 Hal Greer 2.50 6.00
❑ 40 Harry Gallatin 2.50 6.00
❑ 41 Horace Grant 2.50 6.00
❑ 42 Isiah Thomas 2.50 6.00
❑ 43 Jack Sikma 2.50 6.00
❑ 44 James Worthy 3.00 8.00
❑ 45 Jay Vincent 2.50 6.00
❑ 46 Jerry Lucas 2.50 6.00
❑ 47 Jerry West 3.00 8.00
❑ 48 Jim Paxson 2.50 6.00
❑ 49 Jim Price 2.50 6.00
❑ 50 Joe Dumars 2.50 6.00
❑ 51 John Havlicek 2.50 6.00
❑ 52 John Paxson 2.50 6.00
❑ 53 John Salley 2.50 6.00
❑ 54 Julius Erving 5.00 12.00
❑ 55 Kareem Abdul-Jabbar 4.00 10.00
❑ 56 Karl Malone 3.00 8.00
❑ 57 Kenny Smith 2.50 6.00
❑ 58 Kermit Washington 2.50 6.00
❑ 59 Kevin McHale 3.00 8.00
❑ 60 Kurt Rambis 3.00 8.00
❑ 61 Larry Bird 8.00 20.00
❑ 62 Lenny Wilkens 2.50 6.00
❑ 63 Lionel Hollins 2.50 6.00
❑ 64 Luc Longley 2.50 6.00
❑ 65 Magic Johnson 5.00 12.00
❑ 66 Manute Bol 3.00 8.00
❑ 67 Mark Aguirre 2.50 6.00
❑ 68 Marques Johnson 2.50 6.00
❑ 69 Michael Jordan 15.00 40.00
❑ 70 Michael Ray Richardson 2.50 6.00
❑ 71 Moses Malone 2.50 6.00
❑ 72 Nate Archibald 2.50 6.00
❑ 73 Oscar Robertson 2.50 6.00
❑ 74 Paul Arizin 2.50 6.00
❑ 75 Paul Silas 2.50 6.00
❑ 76 Paul Westphal 3.00 8.00
❑ 77 Pete Maravich 8.00 20.00
❑ 78 Phil Jackson 3.00 8.00
❑ 79 Pooh Richardson 2.50 6.00
❑ 80 Reggie Miller 4.00 10.00
❑ 81 Rick Barry 2.50 6.00
❑ 82 Ron Harper 2.50 6.00
❑ 83 Joe Barry Carroll 2.50 6.00
❑ 84 Spencer Haywood 2.50 6.00
❑ 85 Stacey Augmon 2.50 6.00
❑ 86 Steve Kerr 2.50 6.00
❑ 87 Swen Nater 2.50 6.00
❑ 88 Lonnie Shelton 2.50 6.00
❑ 89 Thurl Bailey 2.50 6.00
❑ 90 Tom Chambers 2.50 6.00
❑ 91 Tom Sanders 2.50 6.00
❑ 92 Toni Kukoc 3.00 8.00
❑ 94 Vlade Divac 2.50 6.00
❑ 95 Walt Bellamy 2.50 6.00
❑ 96 Will Perdue 2.50 6.00
❑ 97 Reggie Theus 2.50 6.00
❑ 98 Willis Reed 2.50 6.00
❑ 99 Wilt Chamberlain 5.00 12.00
❑ 100 Xavier McDaniel 2.50 6.00
❑ 101 James Silas AU 10.00 25.00
❑ 102 Steve Nash AU 40.00 80.00
❑ 103 Yao Ming AU 20.00 40.00
❑ 104 Kevin Durant AU 125.00 250.00
❑ 106 Carmelo Anthony AU 15.00 30.00
❑ 108 Chris Paul AU 25.00 50.00
❑ 109 Dwight Howard AU 25.00 50.00
❑ 110 Vince Carter AU 25.00 50.00
❑ 111 Bill Laimbeer AU 15.00 30.00
❑ 113 Spencer Haywood AU 10.00 25.00
❑ 114 Paul Pierce AU 15.00 30.00
❑ 116 Wes Unseld AU 10.00 25.00
❑ 117 Artis Gilmore AU 10.00 25.00
❑ 119 David Robinson AU 30.00 60.00
❑ 121 Dennis Rodman AU 30.00 60.00
❑ 122 Pat Riley AU 15.00 30.00
❑ 124 LaMarcus Aldridge AU 10.00 25.00
❑ 125 Randy Foye AU 10.00 25.00
❑ 127 Brad Daugherty AU 10.00 25.00
❑ 128 Muggsy Bogues AU 15.00 30.00
❑ 130 Micheal Ray Richardson AU 10.0025.00
❑ 131 David Robinson AU 25.00 50.00
❑ 132 Kobe Bryant AU 100.00 200.00
❑ 133 Vince Carter AU 25.00 50.00
❑ 134 Kobe Bryant AU 100.00 200.00
❑ 135 Kevin Durant AU 125.00 250.00
❑ 136 Michael Jordan AU Blue 300.00 550.00
❑ 137 Magic Johnson AU 40.00 80.00
❑ 138 Michael Jordan AU 300.00 550.00
❑ 139 Jerry West AU 25.00 50.00
❑ 140 Tom Chambers AU 8.00 20.00
❑ 141 Bill Laimbeer AU 8.00 20.00
❑ 142 Julius Erving AU 30.00 60.00
❑ 143 Spud Webb AU 8.00 20.00
❑ 144 Clyde Drexler AU 15.00 30.00
❑ 145 Sean Elliott AU 8.00 20.00
❑ 146 Dominique Wilkins AU 15.00 30.00
❑ 147 Magic Johnson AU 40.00 80.00
❑ 148 John Wooden AU 75.00 150.00
❑ 150 Larry Bird/Magic Johnson AU 125.00 250.00
❑ 151 Steve Kerr AU 8.00 20.00
❑ 152 Rick Barry AU 10.00 25.00
❑ 153 James Worthy AU 20.00 40.00
❑ 154 John Paxson AU 10.00 25.00
❑ 155 Baron Davis AU 10.00 25.00
❑ 157 LeBron James AU 100.00 200.00
❑ 158 Kobe Bryant AU 100.00 200.00
❑ 159 Kevin Durant AU 125.00 250.00
❑ 160 Kevin Garnett AU 40.00 80.00
❑ 161 Bailey Howell AU 8.00 20.00
❑ 162 Bob Love AU 8.00 20.00
❑ 162a Bob Love #10 10.00 25.00
❑ 163 Norm Nixon AU 8.00 20.00
❑ 164 Horace Grant AU 15.00 30.00
❑ 165 Darrell Griffith AU 8.00 20.00
❑ 165a Darrell Griffith AU Dr. Dunk 20.0040.00
❑ 166 Dick McGuire AU 8.00 20.00
❑ 167 Chet Walker AU 8.00 20.00
❑ 168 Clyde Drexler AU 15.00 30.00
❑ 169 Gail Goodrich AU 8.00 20.00
❑ 170 Walt Frazier AU 8.00 20.00
❑ 171 George Gervin AU 10.00 25.00
❑ 172 Hal Greer AU 10.00 25.00
❑ 173 Sam Jones AU 10.00 25.00
❑ 174 Jerry Lucas AU 8.00 20.00
❑ 175 Hakeem Olajuwon AU 15.00 30.00
❑ 175a Hakeem Olajuwon AU 94 MVP 25.00 50.00
❑ 176 Robert Parish AU 8.00 20.00
❑ 177 Bob Pettit AU 10.00 25.00
❑ 178 Spud Webb AU 10.00 25.00
❑ 179 Pat Riley AU 10.00 25.00
❑ 180 Bill Sharman AU 8.00 20.00
❑ 180a Bill Sharman WW2 Vet 25.00 50.00
❑ 181 John Stockton AU 25.00 50.00
❑ 182 Nate Thurmond AU 8.00 20.00
❑ 183 Wes Unseld AU 8.00 20.00
❑ 184 Bill Walton AU 8.00 20.00
❑ 185 Sam Perkins AU 15.00 30.00
❑ 186 Lenny Wilkens AU 8.00 20.00
❑ 187 Rudy Tomjanovich AU 8.00 20.00
❑ 188 Artis Gilmore AU 8.00 20.00
❑ 189 Adrian Dantley AU 8.00 20.00
❑ 190 David Thompson AU 8.00 25.00
❑ 190a David Thompson AU Skywalker 15.00 30.00
❑ 190b David Thompson AU Wolfpack 15.00 30.00
❑ 191 Dominique Wilkins AU 10.00 25.00
❑ 192 Dennis Rodman AU 20.00 40.00
❑ 193 Kiki Vandeweghe AU 8.00 20.00
❑ 194 Bob McAdoo AU 10.00 25.00
❑ 195 Alex English AU 8.00 20.00
❑ 196 George McGinnis AU 8.00 20.00
❑ 198 Walt Bellamy AU 8.00 20.00
❑ 199 Bob Lanier AU 8.00 20.00
❑ 199a Bob Lanier AU MVP 25.00 50.00
❑ 200 Connie Hawkins AU 8.00 20.00
❑ 201 Bobby Wanzer AU 10.00 25.00
❑ 202 Tom Heinsohn AU 8.00 20.00

❑ 203 Slater Martin AU 10.00 25.00
❑ 204 Michael Cooper AU 8.00 20.00
❑ 205 Darryl Dawkins AU 8.00 20.00
❑ 206 Bobby Jones AU 8.00 20.00
❑ 207 Dolph Schayes AU 10.00 25.00
❑ 208 Louie Dampier AU 8.00 20.00
❑ 209 Don Nelson AU 8.00 20.00
❑ 210 Marques Johnson AU 8.00 20.00
❑ 211 Moses Malone AU 10.00 25.00
❑ 212 Dick Barnett AU 8.00 20.00
❑ 213 Cliff Hagan AU 10.00 25.00
❑ 214 Meadowlark Lemon AU 20.00 40.00
❑ 215 Kevin Durant AU RC 125.00 250.00
❑ 216 Al Horford AU RC 15.00 30.00
❑ 217 Corey Brewer AU RC 8.00 20.00
❑ 218 Mike Conley AU RC 15.00 30.00
❑ 218a Mike Conley AU Go Buckeyes 25.00 50.00
❑ 219 Joakim Noah AU RC 20.00 40.00
❑ 220 Julian Wright AU RC 10.00 25.00
❑ 220a Julian Wright AU Go Jayhawks 20.00 40.00
❑ 221 Jeff Green AU RC 15.00 30.00
❑ 222 Spencer Hawes AU RC 10.00 25.00
❑ 222a Spencer Hawes AU Go Huskies 15.00 30.00
❑ 223 Acie Law IV AU RC 8.00 20.00
❑ 224 Al Thornton AU RC 10.00 25.00
❑ 225 Rodney Stuckey AU RC 20.00 40.00
❑ 226 Sean Williams AU RC 10.00 25.00
❑ 226a Sean Williams AU Area 51 15.0030.00
❑ 227 Marco Belinelli AU RC 10.00 25.00
❑ 228 Javaris Crittenton AU RC 10.00 25.00
❑ 229 Jason Smith AU RC 10.00 25.00
❑ 230 Daequan Cook AU RC 10.00 25.00
❑ 231 Jared Dudley AU RC 10.00 25.00
❑ 232 Wilson Chandler AU RC 10.00 25.00
❑ 233 Morris Almond AU RC 10.00 25.00
❑ 234 Aaron Brooks AU RC 15.00 30.00
❑ 235 Arron Afflalo AU RC 10.00 25.00
❑ 235a Arron Afflalo AU Go Bruins 20.0040.00
❑ 236 Alando Tucker AU RC 10.00 25.00
❑ 237 Jermareo Davidson AU RC 10.00 25.00
❑ 230 Gabe Pruitt AU RC 10.00 25.00
❑ 240 Dominic McGuire AU RC 10.00 25.00
❑ 241 Glen Davis AU RC 15.00 30.00
❑ 241a Glen Davis AU Big Baby 20.00 40.00
❑ 242 Josh McRoberts AU RC 10.00 25.00
❑ 243 Luis Scola AU RC 10.00 25.00
❑ 244 Juan Navarro AU RC 10.00 25.00
❑ 245 Greg Oden RC 10.00 25.00
❑ 246 Yi Jianlian RC 5.00 12.00
❑ 247 Brandan Wright RC 5.00 12.00
❑ 248 Nick Young RC 4.00 10.00
❑ 249 Thaddeus Young RC 4.00 10.00
❑ 250 Kyrylo Fesenko RC 4.00 10.00
❑ 251 Derrick Rose EXCH 40.00 100.00
❑ 252 Michael Beasley EXCH 40.00 100.00
❑ 253 O.J. Mayo EXCH 25.00 60.00
❑ 254 Russell Westbrook EXCH 10.00 25.00
❑ 255 Kevin Love EXCH 12.00 30.00
❑ 256 Danilo Gallinari EXCH 12.00 30.00
❑ 257 Eric Gordon EXCH 12.00 30.00
❑ 258 Joe Alexander EXCH 10.00 25.00
❑ 259 D.J. Augustin EXCH 10.00 25.00
❑ 260 Brook Lopez EXCH 10.00 25.00
❑ 261 Jerryd Bayless EXCH 12.00 30.00
❑ 262 Jason Thompson EXCH 10.00 25.00
❑ 263 Brandon Rush EXCH 20.00 50.00
❑ 264 Anthony Randolph EXCH 10.00 25.00
❑ 265 Robin Lopez EXCH 10.00 25.00
❑ 266 Marreese Speights EXCH 10.00 25.00
❑ 267 Roy Hibbert EXCH 10.00 25.00
❑ 268 JaVale McGee EXCH 10.00 25.00
❑ 269 J.J. Hickson EXCH 10.00 25.00
❑ 270 Alexis Ajinca EXCH 10.00 25.00
❑ 271 Ryan Anderson EXCH 10.00 25.00
❑ 272 Courtney Lee EXCH 10.00 25.00
❑ 273 Kosta Koufos EXCH 10.00 25.00
❑ 274 Kyle Weaver EXCH
❑ 275 Nicolas Batum EXCH 10.00 25.00
❑ 276 George Hill EXCH 10.00 25.00
❑ 277 Darrell Arthur EXCH 10.00 25.00
❑ 278 Donte Greene EXCH 10.00 25.00
❑ 279 D.J. White EXCH 10.00 25.00
❑ 280 J.R. Giddens EXCH 10.00 25.00
❑ 281 Mario Chalmers EXCH 12.00 30.00
❑ 282 Walter Sharpe EXCH 10.00 25.00
❑ 283 DeAndre Jordan EXCH

2009-10 Classics

❑ 1 Kevin Garnett 1.00 2.50
❑ 2 Rasheed Wallace .50 1.25
❑ 3 Paul Pierce .60 1.50
❑ 4 Kendrick Perkins .30 .75
❑ 5 Brook Lopez .30 .75
❑ 6 Devin Harris .50 1.25
❑ 7 Chris Douglas-Roberts .30 .75
❑ 8 Al Harrington .40 1.00
❑ 9 David Lee .40 1.00
❑ 10 Danilo Gallinari .50 1.25
❑ 11 Andre Iguodala .50 1.25
❑ 12 Louis Williams .30 .75
❑ 13 Elton Brand .50 1.25
❑ 14 Chris Bosh .50 1.25
❑ 15 Andrea Bargnani .40 1.00
❑ 16 Hedo Turkoglu .50 1.25
❑ 17 Jose Calderon .40 1.00
❑ 18 Dirk Nowitzki .60 1.50
❑ 19 Shawn Marion .50 1.25
❑ 20 Drew Gooden .40 1.00
❑ 21 J.J. Barea .50 1.25
❑ 22 Shane Battier .40 1.00
❑ 23 Aaron Brooks .40 1.00
❑ 24 Trevor Ariza .50 1.25
❑ 25 Rudy Gay .50 1.25
❑ 26 Zach Randolph .30 .75
❑ 27 O.J. Mayo .60 1.50
❑ 28 Chris Paul 1.00 2.50
❑ 29 David West .50 1.25
❑ 30 Emeka Okafor .50 1.25
❑ 31 Tim Duncan .75 2.00
❑ 32 Tony Parker .50 1.25
❑ 33 Richard Jefferson .50 1.25
❑ 34 Manu Ginobili .50 1.25
❑ 35 Luol Deng .50 1.25
❑ 36 Derrick Rose 1.00 2.50
❑ 37 John Salmons .50 1.25
❑ 38 LeBron James 2.50 6.00
❑ 39 Mo Williams .40 1.00
❑ 40 Shaquille O'Neal 1.00 2.50
❑ 41 Anderson Varejao .40 1.00
❑ 42 Ben Gordon .50 1.25
❑ 43 Rodney Stuckey .50 1.25
❑ 44 Charlie Villanueva .40 1.00
❑ 45 Danny Granger .50 1.25
❑ 46 Mike Dunleavy .30 .75
❑ 47 Dahntay Jones .30 .75
❑ 48 Andrew Bogut .50 1.25
❑ 49 Michael Redd .50 1.25
❑ 50 Hakim Warrick .40 1.00
❑ 51 Carmelo Anthony .60 1.50
❑ 52 Chauncey Billups .50 1.25
❑ 53 Nene .40 1.00
❑ 54 Chris Andersen .50 1.25
❑ 55 Al Jefferson .50 1.25
❑ 56 Corey Brewer .30 .75
❑ 57 Ryan Gomes .30 .75
❑ 58 Brandon Roy .60 1.50
❑ 59 LaMarcus Aldridge .50 1.25
❑ 60 Andre Miller .40 1.00
❑ 61 Kevin Durant 1.25 3.00
❑ 62 Russell Westbrook .50 1.25
❑ 63 Jeff Green .40 1.00
❑ 64 Carlos Boozer .50 1.25
❑ 65 Deron Williams .60 1.50
❑ 66 Andrei Kirilenko .40 1.00
❑ 67 Joe Johnson .50 1.25
❑ 68 Josh Smith .50 1.25
❑ 69 Jamal Crawford .30 .75
❑ 70 Stephen Jackson .40 1.00
❑ 71 Raymond Felton .40 1.00
❑ 72 Gerald Wallace .50 1.25
❑ 73 Dwyane Wade 1.00 2.50
❑ 74 Jermaine O'Neal .50 1.25
❑ 75 Michael Beasley .60 1.50
❑ 76 Udonis Haslem .40 1.00
❑ 77 Vince Carter .60 1.50
❑ 78 Dwight Howard 1.00 2.50
❑ 79 Rashard Lewis .50 1.25
❑ 80 J.J. Redick .50 1.25
❑ 81 Antawn Jamison .50 1.25
❑ 82 Caron Butler .50 1.25
❑ 83 Randy Foye .30 .75
❑ 84 Monta Ellis .50 1.25
❑ 85 Corey Maggette .40 1.00
❑ 86 Anthony Randolph .50 1.25
❑ 87 Chris Kaman .50 1.25
❑ 88 Eric Gordon .50 1.25
❑ 89 Baron Davis .50 1.25
❑ 90 Kobe Bryant 2.50 6.00
❑ 91 Andrew Bynum .50 1.25
❑ 92 Lamar Odom .50 1.25
❑ 93 Ron Artest .50 1.25
❑ 94 Amare Stoudemire .60 1.50
❑ 95 Jason Richardson .50 1.25
❑ 96 Steve Nash .50 1.25
❑ 97 Grant Hill .50 1.25
❑ 98 Kevin Martin .50 1.25
❑ 99 Beno Udrih .30 .75
❑ 100 Jason Thompson .30 .75
❑ 101 Larry Bird 4.00 10.00
❑ 102 Gail Goodrich 1.25 3.00
❑ 103 Harry Gallatin 1.25 3.00
❑ 104 Chris Webber 1.25 3.00
❑ 105 Nate McMillan 1.25 3.00
❑ 106 George Mikan 2.50 6.00
❑ 107 Drazen Petrovic 2.50 6.00
❑ 108 Jalen Rose 1.25 3.00
❑ 109 Mitch Richmond 1.25 3.00
❑ 110 Mark Price 1.25 3.00
❑ 111 David Robinson 2.00 5.00
❑ 112 Rick Barry 1.25 3.00
❑ 113 Lenny Wilkens 1.25 3.00
❑ 114 Robert Horry 1.50 4.00
❑ 115 Walt Frazier 1.25 3.00
❑ 116 Buck Williams 1.25 3.00
❑ 117 Patrick Ewing 1.25 3.00
❑ 118 Danny Manning 1.25 3.00
❑ 119 Dennis Johnson 1.25 3.00
❑ 120 Rony Seikaly 1.25 3.00
❑ 121 Chris Mullin 1.25 3.00
❑ 122 Hakeem Olajuwon 1.50 4.00
❑ 123 George Gervin 1.25 3.00
❑ 124 Rex Chapman 1.25 3.00
❑ 125 Bob McAdoo 1.25 3.00
❑ 126 Dana Barros 1.25 3.00
❑ 127 B.J. Armstrong 1.25 3.00
❑ 128 Danny Roundfield 1.25 3.00
❑ 129 Oscar Robertson 1.25 3.00
❑ 130 Bill Russell 2.00 5.00
❑ 131 Doc Rivers 1.25 3.00
❑ 132 Clyde Drexler 1.50 4.00
❑ 133 Kareem Abdul-Jabbar 2.00 5.00
❑ 134 Bernard King 1.25 3.00
❑ 135 Don Nelson 1.25 3.00
❑ 136 John Salley 1.25 3.00
❑ 137 Jerry Sloan 1.25 3.00
❑ 138 Joe Dumars 1.25 3.00
❑ 139 Karl Malone 1.50 4.00
❑ 140 Magic Johnson 2.50 6.00
❑ 141 Dominique Wilkins 1.50 4.00
❑ 142 Jack Sikma 1.25 3.00
❑ 143 Wes Unseld 1.25 3.00
❑ 144 Sidney Moncrief 1.25 3.00
❑ 145 Sleepy Floyd 1.25 3.00
❑ 146 Spencer Haywood 1.25 3.00
❑ 147 Kevin McHale 1.25 3.00
❑ 148 Glen Rice 1.25 3.00
❑ 149 Isiah Thomas 1.25 3.00
❑ 150 Jerry West 1.50 4.00
❑ 151 Willis Reed 1.25 3.00
❑ 152 Bob Lanier 1.25 3.00
❑ 153 Elgin Baylor 1.25 3.00
❑ 154 Scottie Pippen 1.25 3.00
❑ 155 Elvin Hayes 1.25 3.00
❑ 156 Scott Skiles 1.25 3.00
❑ 157 Ed Macauley 1.25 3.00
❑ 158 Pete Maravich 4.00 10.00
❑ 159 Bob Cousy 2.00 5.00
❑ 160 Wilt Chamberlain 2.50 6.00
❑ 161 Blake Griffin AU/499 RC 25.00 50.00
❑ 162 Hasheem Thabeet AU/499 RC 5.00 12.00
❑ 163 James Harden AU/499 RC 8.00 20.00
❑ 164 Tyreke Evans AU/499 RC 40.00 80.00
❑ 165 Jonny Flynn AU/499 RC
❑ 166 Stephen Curry AU/499 RC 25.00 50.00
❑ 167 Jordan Hill AU/469 RC 5.00 12.00
❑ 168 B.Jennings AU/499 RC EXCH 25.00 50.00
❑ 169 Terrence Williams AU/499 RC 6.00 15.00
❑ 170 Gerald Henderson AU/499 RC 5.00 12.00
❑ 171 Tyler Hansbrough AU/499 RC 8.00 20.00
❑ 172 Earl Clark AU/571 RC 5.00 12.00
❑ 173 Austin Daye AU/598 RC 5.00 12.00

❑ 174 J.Johnson AU/199 RC EXCH 5.0012.00
❑ 175 Jrue Holiday AU/499 RC 6.00 15.00
❑ 176 Ty Lawson AU/599 RC 6.00 15.00
❑ 177 Jeff Teague AU/553 RC 5.00 12.00
❑ 178 Eric Maynor AU/599 RC 5.00 12.00
❑ 179 D.Collison AU/799 RC EXCH 8.0020.00
❑ 180 Omri Casspi AU/862 RC 6.00 15.00
❑ 181 B.J. Mullens AU/872 RC 5.00 12.00
❑ 182 Rodrigue Beaubois AU/199 RC 10.00 25.00
❑ 183 Taj Gibson AU/823 RC 6.00 15.00
❑ 184 DeMarre Carroll AU/864 RC 5.00 12.00
❑ 185 Wayne Ellington AU/575 RC 5.00 12.00
❑ 186 Toney Douglas AU/933 RC 5.00 12.00
❑ 187 DeJuan Blair AU/999 RC 6.00 15.00
❑ 188 Sam Young AU/249 RC EXCH 5.00 12.00
❑ 189 A.J. Price AU/999 RC 5.00 12.00
❑ 190 Chase Budinger AU/999 RC 5.00 12.00
❑ 192 Jonas Jerebko AU/999 RC 10.00 25.00
❑ 193 Marcus Landry AU/999 RC 5.00 12.00
❑ 194 Serge Ibaka AU/99 RC EXCH 40.00 80.00
❑ 195 Patrick Mills AU/99 RC EXCH 25.00 50.00
❑ 196 Wes Matthews AU/99 RC EXCH 6.00 15.00
❑ 197 Taylor Griffin AU/999 RC 5.00 12.00
❑ 198 Jermaine Taylor AU/999 RC 5.00 12.00
❑ 199 J.Meeks AU/249 RC EXCH 5.00 12.00
❑ 200 DaJuan Summers AU/999 RC 5.00 12.00

1994-95 Collector's Choice

❑ COMPLETE SET (420) 20.00 50.00
❑ COMPLETE SERIES 1 (210) 8.00 20.00
❑ COMPLETE SERIES 2 (210) 8.00 20.00
❑ 1 Anfernee Hardaway .20 .50
❑ 2 Mark Macon .05 .15
❑ 3 Steve Smith .05 .15
❑ 4 Chris Webber .20 .50
❑ 5 Donald Royal .05 .15
❑ 6 Avery Johnson .05 .15
❑ 7 Kevin Johnson .05 .15
❑ 8 Doug Christie .05 .15
❑ 9 Derrick McKey .05 .15
❑ 10 Dennis Rodman .15 .40
❑ 11 Scott Skiles UER .05 .15
❑ 12 Isiah Thomas .07 .20
❑ 13 Kendall Gill .05 .15
❑ 14 Jeff Hornacek .05 .15
❑ 15 Latrell Sprewell .07 .20
❑ 16 Lucious Harris .05 .15
❑ 17 Chris Mullin .07 .20
❑ 18 John Williams .05 .15
❑ 19 Tony Campbell .05 .15
❑ 20 LaPhonso Ellis .05 .15
❑ 21 Gerald Wilkins .05 .15
❑ 22 Clyde Drexler .07 .20
❑ 23 Michael Jordan BB 1.00 2.50
❑ 24 George Lynch .05 .15
❑ 25 Mark Price .05 .15
❑ 26 James Robinson .05 .15
❑ 27 Elmore Spencer .05 .15
❑ 28 Stacey King .05 .15
❑ 29 Corie Blount .05 .15
❑ 30 Dell Curry .05 .15
❑ 31 Reggie Miller .07 .20
❑ 32 Karl Malone .10 .30
❑ 33 Scottie Pippen .25 .60
❑ 34 Hakeem Olajuwon .10 .30
❑ 35 Clarence Weatherspoon .05 .15
❑ 36 Kevin Edwards .05 .15
❑ 37 Pete Myers .05 .15
❑ 38 Jeff Turner .05 .15
❑ 39 Ennis Whatley .05 .15
❑ 40 Calbert Cheaney .05 .15
❑ 41 Glen Rice .05 .15
❑ 42 Vin Baker .07 .20
❑ 43 Grant Long .05 .15
❑ 44 Derrick Coleman .05 .15
❑ 45 Rik Smits .05 .15
❑ 46 Chris Smith .05 .15
❑ 47 Carl Herrera .05 .15
❑ 48 Bob Martin .05 .15
❑ 49 Terrell Brandon .05 .15
❑ 50 David Robinson .10 .30
❑ 51 Danny Ferry .05 .15
❑ 52 Buck Williams .05 .15
❑ 53 Josh Grant .05 .15
❑ 54 Ed Pinckney .05 .15
❑ 55 Dikembe Mutombo .05 .15
❑ 56 Clifford Robinson .05 .15
❑ 57 Luther Wright .05 .15
❑ 58 Scott Burrell .05 .15
❑ 59 Stacey Augmon .05 .15
❑ 60 Jeff Malone .05 .15
❑ 61 Byron Houston .05 .15
❑ 62 Anthony Peeler .05 .15
❑ 63 Michael Adams .05 .15
❑ 64 Negele Knight .05 .15
❑ 65 Terry Cummings .05 .15
❑ 66 Christian Laettner .05 .15
❑ 67 Tracy Murray .05 .15
❑ 68 Sedale Threatt .05 .15
❑ 69 Dan Majerle .05 .15
❑ 70 Frank Brickowski .05 .15
❑ 71 Ken Norman .05 .15
❑ 72 Charles Smith .05 .15
❑ 73 Adam Keefe .05 .15
❑ 74 P.J. Brown .05 .15
❑ 75 Kevin Duckworth .05 .15
❑ 76 Shawn Bradley .05 .15
❑ 77 Darnell Mee .05 .15
❑ 78 Nick Anderson .05 .15
❑ 79 Mark West .05 .15
❑ 80 B.J. Armstrong .05 .15
❑ 81 Dennis Scott .05 .15
❑ 82 Lindsey Hunter .05 .15
❑ 83 Derek Strong .05 .15
❑ 84 Mike Brown .05 .15
❑ 85 Antonio Harvey .05 .15
❑ 86 Anthony Bonner .05 .15
❑ 87 Sam Cassell .07 .20
❑ 88 Harold Miner .05 .15
❑ 89 Spud Webb .05 .15
❑ 90 Mookie Blaylock .05 .15
❑ 91 Greg Anthony .05 .15
❑ 92 Richard Petruska .05 .15
❑ 93 Sean Rooks .05 .15
❑ 94 Ervin Johnson .05 .15
❑ 95 Randy Brown .05 .15
❑ 96 Orlando Woolridge .05 .15
❑ 97 Charles Oakley .05 .15
❑ 98 Craig Ehlo .05 .15
❑ 99 Derek Harper .05 .15
❑ 100 Doug Edwards .05 .15
❑ 101 Muggsy Bogues .05 .15
❑ 102 Mitch Richmond .07 .20
❑ 103 Mahmoud Abdul-Rauf .05 .15
❑ 104 Joe Dumars .07 .20
❑ 105 Eric Riley .05 .15
❑ 106 Terry Mills .05 .15
❑ 107 Toni Kukoc .10 .30
❑ 108 Jon Koncak .05 .15
❑ 109 Haywoode Workman .05 .15
❑ 110 Todd Day .05 .15
❑ 111 Detlef Schrempf .05 .15
❑ 112 David Wesley .05 .15
❑ 113 Mark Jackson .05 .15
❑ 114 Doug Overton .05 .15
❑ 115 Vinny Del Negro .05 .15
❑ 116 Loy Vaught .05 .15
❑ 117 Mike Peplowski .05 .15
❑ 118 Bimbo Coles .05 .15
❑ 119 Rex Walters .05 .15
❑ 120 Sherman Douglas .05 .15
❑ 121 David Benoit .05 .15
❑ 122 John Salley .05 .15
❑ 123 Cedric Ceballos .05 .15
❑ 124 Chris Mills .05 .15
❑ 125 Robert Horry .05 .15
❑ 126 Johnny Newman .05 .15
❑ 127 Malcolm Mackey .05 .15
❑ 128 Terry Dehere .05 .15
❑ 129 Dino Radja .05 .15
❑ 130 Reggie Williams .05 .15
❑ 131 Xavier McDaniel .05 .15
❑ 132 Bobby Hurley .05 .15
❑ 133 Alonzo Mourning .08 .25
❑ 134 Isaiah Rider .05 .15
❑ 135 Antoine Carr .05 .15
❑ 136 Robert Pack .05 .15
❑ 137 Walt Williams .05 .15
❑ 138 Tyrone Corbin .05 .15
❑ 139 Popeye Jones .05 .15
❑ 140 Shawn Kemp .10 .30
❑ 141 Thurl Bailey .05 .15
❑ 142 James Worthy .07 .20
❑ 143 Scott Haskin .05 .15
❑ 144 Hubert Davis .05 .15
❑ 145 A.C. Green .05 .15
❑ 146 Dale Davis .05 .15
❑ 147 Nate McMillan .05 .15
❑ 148 Chris Morris .05 .15
❑ 149 Will Perdue .05 .15
❑ 150 Felton Spencer .05 .15
❑ 151 Rod Strickland .05 .15
❑ 152 Blue Edwards .05 .15
❑ 153 John Williams .05 .15
❑ 154 Rodney Rogers .05 .15
❑ 155 Acie Earl .05 .15
❑ 156 Hersey Hawkins .05 .15
❑ 157 Jamal Mashburn .07 .20
❑ 158 Don MacLean .05 .15
❑ 159 Micheal Williams .05 .15
❑ 160 Kenny Gattison .05 .15
❑ 161 Rich King .05 .15
❑ 162 Allan Houston .10 .30
❑ 163 Hoop-it up .05 .15
❑ 164 Hoop-it up .05 .15
❑ 165 Hoop-it up .05 .15
❑ 166 Danny Manning TO .05 .15
❑ 167 Robert Parish TO .05 .15
❑ 168 Alonzo Mourning TO .07 .20
❑ 169 Scottie Pippen TO .10 .30
❑ 170 Mark Price TO .05 .15
❑ 171 Jamal Mashburn TO .05 .15
❑ 172 Dikembe Mutombo TO .05 .15
❑ 173 Joe Dumars TO .05 .15
❑ 174 Chris Webber TO .08 .25
❑ 175 Hakeem Olajuwon TO .07 .20
❑ 176 Reggie Miller TO .05 .15
❑ 177 Ron Harper TO .05 .15
❑ 178 Nick Van Exel TO .05 .15
❑ 179 Steve Smith TO .05 .15
❑ 180 Vin Baker TO .05 .15
❑ 181 Isaiah Rider TO .05 .15
❑ 182 Derrick Coleman TO .05 .15
❑ 183 Patrick Ewing TO .05 .15
❑ 184 Shaquille O'Neal TO .15 .40
❑ 185 Clarence Weatherspoon .05 .15
❑ 186 Charles Barkley TO .07 .20
❑ 187 Clyde Drexler TO .05 .15
❑ 188 Mitch Richmond TO .05 .15
❑ 189 David Robinson TO .07 .20
❑ 190 Shawn Kemp TO .07 .20
❑ 191 Karl Malone TO .07 .20
❑ 192 Tom Gugliotta TO .05 .15
❑ 193 Kenny Anderson ASA .05 .15
❑ 194 Alonzo Mourning ASA .07 .20
❑ 195 Mark Price ASA .05 .15
❑ 196 John Stockton ASA .07 .20
❑ 197 Shaquille O'Neal ASA .15 .40
❑ 198 Latrell Sprewell ASA .07 .20
❑ 199 Charles Barkley PRO .07 .20
❑ 200 Chris Webber PRO .08 .25
❑ 201 Patrick Ewing PRO .05 .15
❑ 202 Dennis Rodman PRO .07 .20
❑ 203 Shawn Kemp PRO .07 .20
❑ 204 Michael Jordan PRO .50 1.25
❑ 205 Shaquille O'Neal PRO .15 .40
❑ 206 Larry Johnson PRO .05 .15
❑ 207 Tim Hardaway CL .05 .15
❑ 208 John Stockton CL .07 .20
❑ 209 Harold Miner CL .05 .15
❑ 210 B.J. Armstrong CL .05 .15
❑ 211 Vernon Maxwell .05 .15
❑ 212 John Stockton .08 .25
❑ 213 Luc Longley .05 .15
❑ 214 Sam Perkins .05 .15
❑ 215 Pooh Richardson .05 .15

❑ 216 Tyrone Corbin	.05	.15
❑ 217 Mario Elie	.05	.15
❑ 218 Bobby Phills	.05	.15
❑ 219 Grant Hill RC	.40	1.00
❑ 220 Gary Payton	.10	.30
❑ 221 Tom Hammonds	.05	.15
❑ 222 Danny Ainge	.05	.15
❑ 223 Gary Grant	.05	.15
❑ 224 Jim Jackson	.05	.15
❑ 225 Chris Gatling	.05	.15
❑ 226 Sergei Bazarevich RC	.05	.15
❑ 227 Tony Dumas RC	.05	.15
❑ 228 Andrew Lang	.05	.15
❑ 229 Wesley Person RC	.07	.20
❑ 230 Terry Porter	.05	.15
❑ 231 Duane Causwell	.05	.15
❑ 232 Shaquille O'Neal	.40	1.00
❑ 233 Antonio Davis	.05	.15
❑ 234 Charles Barkley	.10	.30
❑ 235 Tony Massenburg	.05	.15
❑ 236 Ricky Pierce	.05	.15
❑ 237 Scott Skiles	.05	.15
❑ 238 Jalen Rose RC	.30	.75
❑ 239 Charlie Ward RC	.07	.20
❑ 240 Michael Jordan COMM	.50	1.25
❑ 241 Elden Campbell	.05	.15
❑ 242 Bill Cartwright	.05	.15
❑ 243 Armon Gilliam	.05	.15
❑ 244 Rick Fox	.05	.15
❑ 245 Tim Breaux	.05	.15
❑ 246 Monty Williams RC	.05	.15
❑ 247 Dominique Wilkins	.07	.20
❑ 248 Robert Parish	.05	.15
❑ 249 Mark Jackson	.05	.15
❑ 250 Jason Kidd RC	.75	2.00
❑ 251 Andres Guibert	.05	.15
❑ 252 Matt Geiger	.05	.15
❑ 253 Stanley Roberts	.05	.15
❑ 254 Jack Haley	.05	.15
❑ 255 David Wingate	.05	.15
❑ 256 John Crotty	.05	.15
❑ 257 Brian Grant RC	.20	.50
❑ 258 Otis Thorpe	.05	.15
❑ 259 Clifford Rozier RC	.05	.15
❑ 260 Grant Long	.05	.15
❑ 261 Eric Mobley RC	.05	.15
❑ 262 Dickey Simpkins RC	.05	.15
❑ 263 J.R. Reid	.05	.15
❑ 264 Kevin Willis	.05	.15
❑ 265 Scott Brooks	.05	.15
❑ 266 Glenn Robinson RC	.25	.60
❑ 267 Dana Barros	.05	.15
❑ 268 Ken Norman	.05	.15
❑ 269 Herb Williams	.05	.15
❑ 270 Dee Brown	.05	.15
❑ 271 Steve Kerr	.05	.15
❑ 272 Jon Barry	.05	.15
❑ 273 Sean Elliott	.05	.15
❑ 274 Elliot Perry	.05	.15
❑ 275 Kenny Smith	.05	.15
❑ 276 Sean Rooks	.05	.15
❑ 277 Gheorghe Muresan	.05	.15
❑ 278 Juwan Howard RC	.20	.50
❑ 279 Steve Smith	.05	.15
❑ 280 Anthony Bowie	.05	.15
❑ 281 Moses Malone	.07	.20
❑ 282 Olden Polynice	.05	.15
❑ 283 Jo Jo English	.05	.15
❑ 284 Marty Conlon	.05	.15
❑ 285 Sam Mitchell	.05	.15
❑ 286 Doug West	.05	.15
❑ 287 Cedric Ceballos	.05	.15
❑ 288 Lorenzo Williams	.05	.15
❑ 289 Harold Ellis	.05	.15
❑ 290 Doc Rivers	.05	.15
❑ 291 Keith Tower	.05	.15
❑ 292 Mark Bryant	.05	.15
❑ 293 Oliver Miller	.05	.15
❑ 294 Michael Adams	.05	.15
❑ 295 Tree Rollins	.05	.15
❑ 296 Eddie Jones RC	.40	1.00
❑ 297 Malik Sealy	.05	.15
❑ 298 Blue Edwards	.05	.15
❑ 299 Brooks Thompson RC	.05	.15
❑ 300 Benoit Benjamin	.05	.15
❑ 301 Avery Johnson	.05	.15
❑ 302 Larry Johnson	.05	.15
❑ 303 John Starks	.05	.15
❑ 304 Byron Scott	.05	.15

❑ 305 Eric Murdock	.05	.15
❑ 306 Jay Humphries	.05	.15
❑ 307 Kenny Anderson	.05	.15
❑ 308 Brian Williams	.05	.15
❑ 309 Nick Van Exel	.07	.20
❑ 310 Tim Hardaway	.07	.20
❑ 311 Lee Mayberry	.05	.15
❑ 312 Vlade Divac	.05	.15
❑ 313 Donyell Marshall RC	.07	.20
❑ 314 Anthony Mason	.05	.15
❑ 315 Danny Manning	.05	.15
❑ 316 Tyrone Hill	.05	.15
❑ 317 Vincent Askew	.05	.15
❑ 318 Khalid Reeves RC	.05	.15
❑ 319 Ron Harper	.05	.15
❑ 320 Brent Price	.05	.15
❑ 321 Byron Houston	.05	.15
❑ 322 Lamond Murray RC	.05	.15
❑ 323 Bryant Stith	.05	.15
❑ 324 Tom Gugliotta	.05	.15
❑ 325 Jerome Kersey	.05	.15
❑ 326 B.J.Tyler RC	.05	.15
❑ 327 Antonio Lang	.05	.15
❑ 328 Carlos Rogers RC	.05	.15
❑ 329 Wayman Tisdale	.05	.15
❑ 330 Kevin Gamble	.05	.15
❑ 331 Eric Piatkowski RC	.05	.15
❑ 332 Mitchell Butler	.05	.15
❑ 333 Patrick Ewing	.07	.20
❑ 334 Doug Smith	.05	.15
❑ 335 Joe Kleine	.05	.15
❑ 336 Keith Jennings	.05	.15
❑ 337 Bill Curley RC	.05	.15
❑ 338 Johnny Newman	.05	.15
❑ 339 Howard Eisley RC	.05	.15
❑ 340 Willie Anderson	.05	.15
❑ 341 Aaron McKie RC	.20	.50
❑ 342 Tom Chambers	.05	.15
❑ 343 Scott Williams	.05	.15
❑ 344 Harvey Grant	.05	.15
❑ 345 Billy Owens	.05	.15
❑ 346 Sharone Wright RC	.05	.15
❑ 347 Michael Cage	.05	.15
❑ 348 Vern Fleming	.05	.15
❑ 349 Darrin Hancock RC	.05	.15
❑ 350 Matt Fish	.05	.15
❑ 351 Rony Seikaly	.05	.15
❑ 352 Victor Alexander	.05	.15
❑ 353 Anthony Miller RC	.05	.15
❑ 354 Horace Grant	.05	.15
❑ 355 Jayson Williams	.05	.15
❑ 356 Dale Ellis	.05	.15
❑ 357 Sarunas Marciulionis	.05	.15
❑ 358 Anthony Avent	.05	.15
❑ 359 Rex Chapman	.05	.15
❑ 360 Askia Jones RC	.05	.15
❑ 361 Bo Outlaw RC	.05	.15
❑ 362 Chuck Person	.05	.15
❑ 363 Danny Schayes	.05	.15
❑ 364 Morlon Wiley	.05	.15
❑ 365 Dontonio Wingfield RC	.05	.15
❑ 366 Tony Smith	.05	.15
❑ 367 Bill Wennington	.05	.15
❑ 368 Bryon Russell	.05	.15
❑ 369 Geert Hammink	.05	.15
❑ 370 Eric Montross RC	.05	.15
❑ 371 Cliff Levingston	.05	.15
❑ 372 Stacey Augmon BP	.05	.15
❑ 373 Eric Montross BP	.05	.15
❑ 374 Alonzo Mourning BP	.07	.20
❑ 375 Scottie Pippen BP	.10	.30
❑ 376 Mark Price BP	.05	.15
❑ 377 Jason Kidd BP	.30	.75
❑ 378 Jalen Rose BP	.05	.15
❑ 379 Grant Hill BP	.15	.40
❑ 380 Latrell Sprewell BP	.07	.20
❑ 381 Hakeem Olajuwon BP	.07	.20
❑ 382 Reggie Miller BP	.05	.15
❑ 383 Lamond Murray BP	.05	.15
❑ 384 Eddie Jones BP	.20	.50
❑ 385 Khalid Reeves BP	.05	.15
❑ 386 Glenn Robinson BP	.10	.30
❑ 387 Donyell Marshall BP	.05	.15
❑ 388 Derrick Coleman BP	.05	.15
❑ 389 Patrick Ewing BP	.05	.15
❑ 390 Shaquille O'Neal BP	.15	.40
❑ 391 Sharone Wright BP	.05	.15
❑ 392 Charles Barkley BP	.07	.20
❑ 393 Aaron McKie BP	.05	.15

❑ 394 Brian Grant BP	.05	.15
❑ 395 David Robinson BP	.07	.20
❑ 396 Shawn Kemp BP	.07	.20
❑ 397 Karl Malone BP	.07	.20
❑ 398 Tom Gugliotta BP	.05	.15
❑ 399 Hakeem Olajuwon TRIV	.07	.20
❑ 400 Shaquille O'Neal TRIV	.15	.40
❑ 401 Chris Webber TRIV	.08	.25
❑ 402 Michael Jordan TRIV	.50	1.25
❑ 403 David Robinson TRIV	.07	.20
❑ 404 Shawn Kemp TRIV	.07	.20
❑ 405 Patrick Ewing TRIV	.05	.15
❑ 406 Charles Barkley TRIV	.07	.20
❑ 407 Glenn Robinson DC	.10	.30
❑ 408 Jason Kidd DC	.30	.75
❑ 409 Grant Hill DC	.15	.40
❑ 410 Donyell Marshall DC	.05	.15
❑ 411 Sharone Wright DC	.05	.15
❑ 412 Lamond Murray DC	.05	.15
❑ 413 Brian Grant DC	.05	.15
❑ 414 Eric Montross DC	.05	.15
❑ 415 Eddie Jones DC	.20	.50
❑ 416 Carlos Rogers DC	.05	.15
❑ 417 Shawn Kemp CL	.05	.15
❑ 418 Bobby Hurley CL	.05	.15
❑ 419 Shawn Bradley CL	.05	.15
❑ 420 Michael Jordan CL	.30	.75

1995-96 Collector's Choice

❑ COMPLETE SET (410)	17.50	35.00
❑ COMP.FACTORY SET (419)	25.00	35.00
❑ COMPLETE SERIES 1 (210)	7.50	15.00
❑ COMPLETE SERIES 2 (200)	10.00	20.00
❑ 1 Rod Strickland	.05	.15
❑ 2 Larry Johnson	.08	.25
❑ 3 Mahmoud Abdul-Rauf	.05	.15
❑ 4 Joe Dumars	.15	.40
❑ 5 Jason Kidd	.50	1.25
❑ 6 Avery Johnson	.05	.15
❑ 7 Dee Brown	.05	.15
❑ 8 Brian Williams	.05	.15
❑ 9 Nick Van Exel	.15	.40
❑ 10 Dennis Rodman	.08	.25
❑ 11 Rony Seikaly	.05	.15
❑ 12 Harvey Grant	.05	.15
❑ 13 Craig Ehlo	.05	.15
❑ 14 Derek Harper	.08	.25
❑ 15 Oliver Miller	.05	.15
❑ 16 Dennis Scott	.05	.15
❑ 17 Ed Pinckney	.05	.15
❑ 18 Eric Piatkowski	.08	.25
❑ 19 B.J. Armstrong	.05	.15
❑ 20 Tyrone Hill	.05	.15
❑ 21 Malik Sealy	.05	.15
❑ 22 Clyde Drexler	.15	.40
❑ 23 Aaron McKie	.08	.25
❑ 24 Harold Miner	.05	.15
❑ 25 Bobby Hurley	.05	.15
❑ 26 Dell Curry	.05	.15
❑ 27 Micheal Williams	.05	.15
❑ 28 Adam Keefe	.05	.15
❑ 29 Antonio Harvey	.05	.15
❑ 30 Billy Owens	.05	.15
❑ 31 Nate McMillan	.05	.15
❑ 32 J.R. Reid	.05	.15
❑ 33 Grant Hill	.20	.50
❑ 34 Charles Barkley	.15	.40
❑ 35 Tyrone Corbin	.05	.15
❑ 36 Don MacLean	.05	.15
❑ 37 Kenny Smith	.05	.15
❑ 38 Juwan Howard	.15	.40
❑ 39 Charles Smith	.05	.15
❑ 40 Shawn Kemp	.08	.25
❑ 41 Dana Barros	.05	.15

❑ 42 Vin Baker	.08	.25
❑ 43 Armon Gilliam	.05	.15
❑ 44 Spud Webb	.08	.25
❑ 45 Michael Jordan	1.00	2.50
❑ 46 Scott Williams	.05	.15
❑ 47 Vlade Divac	.08	.25
❑ 48 Roy Tarpley	.05	.15
❑ 49 Bimbo Coles	.05	.15
❑ 50 David Robinson	.15	.40
❑ 51 Terry Dehere	.05	.15
❑ 52 Bobby Phills	.05	.15
❑ 53 Sherman Douglas	.05	.15
❑ 54 Rodney Rogers	.05	.15
❑ 55 Detlef Schrempf	.08	.25
❑ 56 Calbert Cheaney	.05	.15
❑ 57 Tom Gugliotta	.05	.15
❑ 58 Jeff Turner	.05	.15
❑ 59 Mookie Blaylock	.05	.15
❑ 60 Bill Curley	.05	.15
❑ 61 Chris Dudley	.05	.15
❑ 62 Popeye Jones	.05	.15
❑ 63 Scott Burrell	.05	.15
❑ 64 Dale Davis	.05	.15
❑ 65 Mitchell Butler	.05	.15
❑ 66 Pervis Ellison	.05	.15
❑ 67 Todd Day	.05	.15
❑ 68 Carl Herrera	.05	.15
❑ 69 Jeff Hornacek	.08	.25
❑ 70 Vincent Askew	.05	.15
❑ 71 A.C. Green	.08	.25
❑ 72 Kevin Gamble	.05	.15
❑ 73 Chris Gatling	.05	.15
❑ 74 Otis Thorpe	.05	.15
❑ 75 Michael Cage	.05	.15
❑ 76 Carlos Rogers	.05	.15
❑ 77 Gheorghe Muresan	.05	.15
❑ 78 Olden Polynice	.05	.15
❑ 79 Grant Long	.05	.15
❑ 80 Allan Houston	.08	.25
❑ 81 Bo Outlaw	.05	.15
❑ 82 Clarence Weatherspoon	.05	.15
❑ 83 Tony Dumas	.05	.15
❑ 84 Herb Williams	.05	.15
❑ 85 P.J. Brown	.05	.15
❑ 86 Robert Horry	.08	.25
❑ 87 Byron Scott	.05	.15
❑ 88 Horace Grant	.08	.25
❑ 89 Dominique Wilkins	.15	.40
❑ 90 Doug West	.05	.15
❑ 91 Antoine Carr	.05	.15
❑ 92 Dickey Simpkins	.05	.15
❑ 93 Elden Campbell	.05	.15
❑ 94 Kevin Johnson	.08	.25
❑ 95 Rex Chapman	.05	.15
❑ 96 John Williams	.05	.15
❑ 97 Tim Hardaway	.08	.25
❑ 98 Rik Smits	.08	.25
❑ 99 Rex Walters	.05	.15
❑ 100 Robert Parish	.08	.25
❑ 101 Isaiah Rider	.05	.15
❑ 102 Sarunas Marciulionis	.05	.15
❑ 103 Andrew Lang	.05	.15
❑ 104 Eric Mobley	.05	.15
❑ 105 Randy Brown	.05	.15
❑ 106 John Stockton	.20	.50
❑ 107 Lamond Murray	.05	.15
❑ 108 Will Perdue	.05	.15
❑ 109 Wayman Tisdale	.05	.15
❑ 110 John Starks	.08	.25
❑ 111 John Salley	.05	.15
❑ 112 Lucious Harris	.05	.15
❑ 113 Jeff Malone	.05	.15
❑ 114 Anthony Bowie	.05	.15
❑ 115 Vinny Del Negro	.05	.15
❑ 116 Michael Adams	.05	.15
❑ 117 Chris Mullin	.15	.40
❑ 118 Benoit Benjamin	.05	.15
❑ 119 Byron Houston	.05	.15
❑ 120 LaPhonso Ellis	.05	.15
❑ 121 Doug Overton	.05	.15
❑ 122 Jerome Kersey	.05	.15
❑ 123 Greg Minor	.05	.15
❑ 124 Christian Laettner	.08	.25
❑ 125 Mark Price	.08	.25
❑ 126 Kevin Willis	.08	.25
❑ 127 Kenny Anderson	.08	.25
❑ 128 Marty Conlon	.05	.15
❑ 129 Blue Edwards	.05	.15
❑ 130 Danny Schayes	.05	.15
❑ 131 Duane Ferrell	.05	.15
❑ 132 Charles Oakley	.05	.15
❑ 133 Brian Grant	.15	.40
❑ 134 Reggie Williams	.05	.15
❑ 135 Steve Kerr	.08	.25
❑ 136 Khalid Reeves	.05	.15
❑ 137 David Benoit	.05	.15
❑ 138 Derrick Coleman	.05	.15
❑ 139 Anthony Peeler	.05	.15
❑ 140 Jim Jackson	.05	.15
❑ 141 Stacey Augmon	.05	.15
❑ 142 Sam Cassell	.15	.40
❑ 143 Derrick McKey	.05	.15
❑ 144 Danny Ferry	.05	.15
❑ 145 Anfernee Hardaway	.15	.40
❑ 146 Clifford Robinson	.05	.15
❑ 147 B.J. Tyler	.05	.15
❑ 148 Mark West	.05	.15
❑ 149 David Wingate	.05	.15
❑ 150 Willie Anderson	.05	.15
❑ 151 Hersey Hawkins	.05	.15
❑ 152 Bryant Stith	.05	.15
❑ 153 Dan Majerle	.08	.25
❑ 154 Chris Smith	.05	.15
❑ 155 Donyell Marshall	.08	.25
❑ 156 Loy Vaught	.05	.15
❑ 157 Reggie Miller	.15	.40
❑ 158 Hubert Davis	.05	.15
❑ 159 Ron Harper	.08	.25
❑ 160 Lee Mayberry	.05	.15
❑ 161 Eddie Jones	.20	.50
❑ 162 Shawn Bradley	.05	.15
❑ 163 Nick Anderson	.05	.15
❑ 164 Ervin Johnson	.05	.15
❑ 165 Walt Williams	.05	.15
❑ 166 Steve Smith FF	.05	.15
❑ 167 Dino Radja FF	.05	.15
❑ 168 Alonzo Mourning FF	.05	.15
❑ 169 Michael Jordan FF	.50	1.25
❑ 170 Tyrone Hill FF	.05	.15
❑ 171 Jamal Mashburn FF	.05	.15
❑ 172 Dikembe Mutombo FF	.05	.15
❑ 173 Grant Hill FF w/Jordan	.20	.50
❑ 174 Latrell Sprewell FF	.15	.40
❑ 175 Hakeem Olajuwon FF	.08	.25
❑ 176 Reggie Miller FF	.08	.25
❑ 177 Pooh Richardson FF	.05	.15
❑ 178 Cedric Ceballos FF	.05	.15
❑ 179 Glen Rice FF	.05	.15
❑ 180 Glenn Robinson FF	.08	.25
❑ 181 Isaiah Rider FF	.05	.15
❑ 182 Derrick Coleman FF	.05	.15
❑ 183 Patrick Ewing FF	.08	.25
❑ 184 Shaquille O'Neal FF	.15	.40
❑ 185 Dana Barros FF	.05	.15
❑ 186 Dan Majerle FF	.05	.15
❑ 187 Clifford Robinson FF	.05	.15
❑ 188 Mitch Richmond FF	.05	.15
❑ 189 David Robinson FF	.08	.25
❑ 190 Gary Payton FF	.08	.25
❑ 191 Oliver Miller FF	.05	.15
❑ 192 Karl Malone FF	.15	.40
❑ 193 Kevin Pritchard FF	.05	.15
❑ 194 Chris Webber FF	.15	.40
❑ 195 Michael Jordan PD	.50	1.25
❑ 196 Hakeem Olajuwon PD	.08	.25
❑ 197 Vin Baker PD	.08	.25
❑ 198 Grant Hill PD	.15	.40
❑ 199 Clyde Drexler PD	.08	.25
❑ 200 Chris Webber PD	.15	.40
❑ 201 Shawn Kemp PD	.05	.15
❑ 202 Shaquille O'Neal PD	.15	.40
❑ 203 Stacey Augmon PD	.05	.15
❑ 204 David Benoit PD	.05	.15
❑ 205 Rodney Rogers PD	.05	.15
❑ 206 Latrell Sprewell PD	.15	.40
❑ 207 Brian Grant PD	.08	.25
❑ 208 Lamond Murray PD	.05	.15
❑ 209 Shawn Kemp CL	.05	.15
❑ 210 Michael Jordan CL	.25	.60
❑ 211 Cory Alexander RC	.05	.15
❑ 212 Vernon Maxwell	.05	.15
❑ 213 George Lynch	.05	.15
❑ 214 Terry Mills	.05	.15
❑ 215 Scottie Pippen	.25	.60
❑ 216 Donald Royal	.05	.15
❑ 217 Wesley Person	.05	.15
❑ 218 Antonio Davis	.05	.15
❑ 219 Glenn Robinson	.15	.40
❑ 220 Jerry Stackhouse RC	.50	1.25
❑ 221 James Robinson	.05	.15
❑ 222 Chris Mills	.05	.15
❑ 223 Chuck Person	.05	.15
❑ 224 Duane Causwell	.05	.15
❑ 225 Gary Payton	.15	.40
❑ 226 Eric Montross	.05	.15
❑ 227 Felton Spencer	.05	.15
❑ 228 Scott Skiles	.05	.15
❑ 229 Latrell Sprewell	.15	.40
❑ 230 Sedale Threatt	.05	.15
❑ 231 Mark Bryant	.05	.15
❑ 232 Buck Williams	.05	.15
❑ 233 Brian Williams	.05	.15
❑ 234 Sharone Wright	.05	.15
❑ 235 Karl Malone	.20	.50
❑ 236 Kevin Edwards	.05	.15
❑ 237 Muggsy Bogues	.08	.25
❑ 238 Mario Elie	.05	.15
❑ 239 Rasheed Wallace RC	.40	1.00
❑ 240 George Zidek RC	.05	.15
❑ 241 Cedric Ceballos	.05	.15
❑ 242 Alan Henderson RC	.15	.40
❑ 243 Joe Kleine	.05	.15
❑ 244 Patrick Ewing	.15	.40
❑ 245 Sasha Danilovic RC	.05	.15
❑ 246 Bill Wennington	.05	.15
❑ 247 Steve Smith	.08	.25
❑ 248 Bryant Stith	.05	.15
❑ 249 Dino Radja	.05	.15
❑ 250 Monty Williams	.05	.15
❑ 251 Andrew DeClercq RC	.05	.15
❑ 252 Sean Elliott	.08	.25
❑ 253 Rick Fox	.08	.25
❑ 254 Lionel Simmons	.05	.15
❑ 255 Dikembe Mutombo	.08	.25
❑ 256 Lindsey Hunter	.05	.15
❑ 257 Terrell Brandon	.08	.25
❑ 258 Shawn Respert RC	.05	.15
❑ 259 Rodney Rogers	.05	.15
❑ 260 Bryon Russell	.05	.15
❑ 261 David Wesley	.05	.15
❑ 262 Ken Norman	.05	.15
❑ 263 Mitch Richmond	.08	.25
❑ 264 Sam Perkins	.08	.25
❑ 265 Hakeem Olajuwon	.15	.40
❑ 266 Brian Shaw	.05	.15
❑ 267 B.J. Armstrong	.05	.15
❑ 268 Jalen Rose	.20	.50
❑ 269 Bryant Reeves RC	.15	.40
❑ 270 Cherokee Parks RC	.05	.15
❑ 271 Dennis Rodman	.08	.25
❑ 272 Kendall Gill	.05	.15
❑ 273 Elliot Perry	.05	.15
❑ 274 Anthony Mason	.08	.25
❑ 275 Kevin Garnett RC	1.00	2.50
❑ 276 Damon Stoudamire RC	.30	.75
❑ 277 Lawrence Moten RC	.05	.15
❑ 278 Ed O'Bannon RC	.05	.15
❑ 279 Toni Kukoc	.08	.25
❑ 280 Greg Ostertag RC	.05	.15
❑ 281 Tom Hammonds	.05	.15
❑ 282 Yinka Dare	.05	.15
❑ 283 Michael Smith	.05	.15
❑ 284 Clifford Rozier	.05	.15
❑ 285 Gary Trent RC	.05	.15
❑ 286 Shaquille O'Neal	.40	1.00
❑ 287 Luc Longley	.05	.15
❑ 288 Bob Sura RC	.08	.25
❑ 289 Dana Barros	.05	.15
❑ 290 Lorenzo Williams	.05	.15
❑ 291 Haywoode Workman	.05	.15
❑ 292 Randolph Childress RC	.05	.15
❑ 293 Doc Rivers	.08	.25
❑ 294 Chris Webber	.20	.50
❑ 295 Kurt Thomas RC	.08	.25
❑ 296 Greg Anthony	.05	.15
❑ 297 Tyus Edney RC	.05	.15
❑ 298 Danny Manning	.08	.25
❑ 299 Brent Barry RC	.15	.40
❑ 300 Joe Smith RC	.25	.60
❑ 301 Pooh Richardson	.05	.15
❑ 302 Mark Jackson	.08	.25
❑ 303 Richard Dumas	.05	.15
❑ 304 Michael Finley RC	.40	1.00
❑ 305 Theo Ratliff RC	.20	.50
❑ 306 Gary Grant	.05	.15
❑ 307 Jamal Mashburn	.08	.25
❑ 308 Corliss Williamson RC	.15	.40

309 Eric Williams RC	.08	.25
310 Zan Tabak	.05	.15
311 Eric Murdock	.05	.15
312 Sherrell Ford RC	.05	.15
313 Terry Davis	.05	.15
314 Vern Fleming	.05	.15
315 Jason Caffey RC	.08	.25
316 Mario Bennett RC	.05	.15
317 David Vaughn RC	.05	.15
318 Loren Meyer RC	.05	.15
319 Travis Best RC	.05	.15
320 Byron Scott	.05	.15
321 Mookie Blaylock SR	.05	.15
322 Dee Brown SR	.05	.15
323 Alonzo Mourning SR	.05	.15
324 Michael Jordan SR	.50	1.25
325 Terrell Brandon SR	.05	.15
326 Jim Jackson SR	.05	.15
327 Dikembe Mutombo SR	.05	.15
328 Grant Hill SR	.15	.40
329 Joe Smith SR	.15	.40
330 Clyde Drexler SR	.08	.25
331 Reggie Miller SR	.08	.25
332 Lamond Murray SR	.05	.15
333 Nick Van Exel SR	.05	.15
334 Glen Rice SR	.05	.15
335 Glenn Robinson SR	.08	.25
336 Christian Laettner SR	.05	.15
337 Kenny Anderson SR	.05	.15
338 Patrick Ewing SR	.08	.25
339 Shaquille O'Neal SR	.15	.40
340 Jerry Stackhouse SR	.25	.60
341 Charles Barkley SR	.15	.40
342 Clifford Robinson SR	.05	.15
343 Brian Grant SR	.08	.25
344 David Robinson SR	.08	.25
345 Shawn Kemp SR	.05	.15
346 Damon Stoudamire SR	.20	.50
347 Karl Malone SR	.15	.40
348 Bryant Reeves SR	.08	.25
349 Juwan Howard SR	.08	.25
350 N.Anderson/D.Brown PT	.05	.15
351 Rik Smits PT	.05	.15
352 H.Williams/T.Tolbert PT	.05	.15
353 Michael Jordan PT	.50	1.25
354 David Robinson PT	.08	.25
355 T.Porter/K.Johnson PT	.08	.25
356 Clyde Drexler PT	.08	.25
357 Cedric Ceballos PT	.05	.15
358 Horace Grant/Group PT	.05	.15
359 Reggie Miller PT	.08	.25
360 A.Johnson/N.Van Exel PT	.08	.25
361 H.Olajuwon/R.Horry PT	.15	.40
362 Rik Smits PT	.05	.15
363 D.Rob/H.Olajuwon PT	.15	.40
364 Robert Horry PT	.05	.15
365 Kenny Smith PT	.05	.15
366 Stacey Augmon LOVE	.05	.15
367 Sherman Douglas LOVE	.05	.15
368 Larry Johnson LOVE	.05	.15
369 Scottie Pippen LOVE	.15	.40
370 Tyrone Hill LOVE	.05	.15
371 Jamal Mashburn LOVE	.05	.15
372 Mahmoud Abdul-Rauf LOVE	.05	.15
373 Grant Hill LOVE	.15	.40
374 Latrell Sprewell LOVE	.15	.40
375 Sam Cassell LOVE	.05	.15
376 Rik Smits LOVE	.05	.15
377 Terry Dehere LOVE	.05	.15
378 Eddie Jones LOVE	.15	.40
379 Billy Owens LOVE	.05	.15
380 Vin Baker LOVE	.05	.15
381 Isaiah Rider LOVE	.05	.15
382 Kenny Anderson LOVE	.05	.15
383 John Starks LOVE	.05	.15
384 Anfernee Hardaway LOVE	.08	.25
385 Sharone Wright LOVE	.05	.15
386 Charles Barkley LOVE	.15	.40
387 Clifford Robinson LOVE	.05	.15
388 Walt Williams LOVE	.05	.15
389 Sean Elliott LOVE	.05	.15
390 Gary Payton LOVE	.08	.25
391 Carlos Rogers LOVE	.05	.15
392 John Stockton LOVE	.15	.40
393 Greg Anthony LOVE	.05	.15
394 Chris Webber LOVE	.15	.40
395 Gary Payton PG	.08	.25
396 Mookie Blaylock PG	.05	.15
397 Charles Barkley PG	.15	.40
398 Grant Hill PG	.15	.40
399 Anfernee Hardaway PG	.08	.25
400 Kenny Anderson PG	.05	.15
401 Mark Jackson PG	.05	.15
402 Karl Malone PG	.15	.40
403 Avery Johnson PG	.05	.15
404 Larry Johnson 40	.05	.15
405 Nick Van Exel 40	.05	.15
406 Vin Baker 40	.05	.15
407 Jason Kidd 40	.15	.40
408 David Robinson 40	.08	.25
409 Shawn Kemp CL	.05	.15
410 Michael Jordan CL	.25	.60
NNO Bulls Fact.Set Comm.	2.50	6.00

1996-97 Collector's Choice

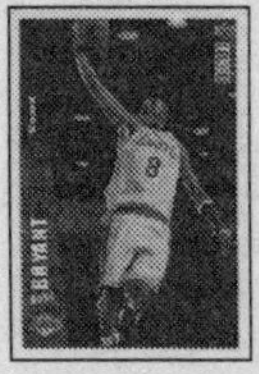

COMPLETE SET (400)	30.00	30.00
COMP.FACT.SET (406)	15.00	35.00
COMPLETE SERIES 1 (200)	7.50	15.00
COMPLETE SERIES 2 (200)	7.50	15.00
COMMON CARD (1-400)	.05	.15
COMMON PENNY! (113-117)	.10	.30
COMP.UPDATE SET (30)	6.00	12.00
COMMON UPDATE (401-430)	.15	.40
1 Mookie Blaylock	.05	.15
2 Grant Long	.05	.15
3 Christian Laettner	.08	.25
4 Craig Ehlo	.05	.15
5 Ken Norman	.05	.15
6 Stacey Augmon	.05	.15
7 Dana Barros	.05	.15
8 Dino Radja	.05	.15
9 Rick Fox	.05	.15
10 Eric Montross	.05	.15
11 David Wesley	.05	.15
12 Eric Williams	.05	.15
13 Glen Rice	.08	.25
14 Dell Curry	.05	.15
15 Matt Geiger	.05	.15
16 Scott Burrell	.05	.15
17 George Zidek	.05	.15
18 Muggsy Bogues	.05	.15
19 Ron Harper	.08	.25
20 Steve Kerr	.08	.25
21 Toni Kukoc	.08	.25
22 Dennis Rodman	.08	.25
23 Michael Jordan	1.00	2.50
24 Luc Longley	.05	.15
25 M.Jordan/V.Divac Bulls VT	.50	1.25
26 M.Jordan Bulls VT	.50	1.25
27 L.Longley Bulls VT	.05	.15
28 S.Pippen Bulls VT	.15	.40
29 T.Kukoc/J.Howard Bulls VT	.08	.25
30 Terrell Brandon	.08	.25
31 Bobby Phills	.05	.15
32 Tyrone Hill	.05	.15
33 Michael Cage	.05	.15
34 Bob Sura	.05	.15
35 Tony Dumas	.05	.15
36 Jim Jackson	.05	.15
37 Loren Meyer	.05	.15
38 Cherokee Parks	.05	.15
39 Jamal Mashburn	.08	.25
40 Popeye Jones	.05	.15
41 LaPhonso Ellis	.05	.15
42 Jalen Rose	.15	.40
43 Antonio McDyess	.08	.25
44 Tom Hammonds	.05	.15
45 Mahmoud Abdul-Rauf	.05	.15
46 Dale Ellis	.05	.15
47 Joe Dumars	.15	.40
48 Theo Ratliff	.08	.25
49 Lindsey Hunter	.05	.15
50 Terry Mills	.05	.15
51 Don Reid	.05	.15
52 B.J. Armstrong	.05	.15
53 Bimbo Coles	.05	.15
54 Joe Smith	.08	.25
55 Chris Mullin	.15	.40
56 Rony Seikaly	.05	.15
57 Donyell Marshall	.08	.25
58 Hakeem Olajuwon	.15	.40
59 Robert Horry	.08	.25
60 Mario Elie	.05	.15
61 Mark Bryant	.05	.15
62 Chucky Brown	.05	.15
63 Rik Smits	.08	.25
64 Derrick McKey	.05	.15
65 Eddie Johnson	.05	.15
66 Mark Jackson	.05	.15
67 Ricky Pierce	.05	.15
68 Travis Best	.05	.15
69 Rodney Rogers	.05	.15
70 Brent Barry	.05	.15
71 Lamond Murray	.05	.15
72 Eric Piatkowski	.08	.25
73 Pooh Richardson	.05	.15
74 Cedric Ceballos	.05	.15
75 Eddie Jones	.15	.40
76 Anthony Peeler	.05	.15
77 George Lynch	.05	.15
78 Vlade Divac	.05	.15
79 Rex Chapman	.05	.15
80 Sasha Danilovic	.05	.15
81 Kurt Thomas	.08	.25
82 Keith Askins	.05	.15
83 Walt Williams	.05	.15
84 Vin Baker	.08	.25
85 Shawn Respert	.05	.15
86 Sherman Douglas	.05	.15
87 Marty Conlon	.05	.15
88 Johnny Newman	.05	.15
89 Kevin Garnett	.30	.75
90 Andrew Lang	.05	.15
91 Terry Porter	.05	.15
92 Sam Mitchell	.05	.15
93 Tom Gugliotta	.05	.15
94 Spud Webb	.05	.15
95 Kendall Gill	.05	.15
96 Vern Fleming	.05	.15
97 Shawn Bradley	.05	.15
98 Yinka Dare	.05	.15
99 Jayson Williams	.08	.25
100 Kevin Edwards	.05	.15
101 Charles Oakley	.05	.15
102 Anthony Mason	.08	.25
103 John Starks	.08	.25
104 J.R. Reid	.05	.15
105 Hubert Davis	.05	.15
106 Gary Grant	.05	.15
107 Nick Anderson	.05	.15
108 Donald Royal	.05	.15
109 Brian Shaw	.05	.15
110 Brooks Thompson	.05	.15
111 Anfernee Hardaway	.15	.40
112 Dennis Scott	.05	.15
113 Anfernee Hardaway PEN	.10	.30
114 Anfernee Hardaway PEN	.10	.30
115 Anfernee Hardaway PEN	.10	.30
116 Anfernee Hardaway PEN	.10	.30
117 Anfernee Hardaway PEN	.10	.30
118 Derrick Coleman	.08	.25
119 Rex Walters	.05	.15
120 Sean Higgins	.05	.15
121 Clarence Weatherspoon	.05	.15
122 Jerry Stackhouse	.15	.40
123 Elliot Perry	.05	.15
124 Wayman Tisdale	.05	.15
125 Wesley Person	.05	.15
126 Charles Barkley	.20	.50
127 A.C. Green	.08	.25
128 Harvey Grant	.05	.15
129 Arvydas Sabonis	.08	.25
130 Aaron McKie	.08	.25
131 Gary Trent	.05	.15
132 Buck Williams	.05	.15
133 Billy Owens	.05	.15
134 Brian Grant	.15	.40
135 Corliss Williamson	.08	.25
136 Tyus Edney	.05	.15
137 Olden Polynice	.05	.15
138 Avery Johnson	.05	.15
139 Vinny Del Negro	.05	.15

❑ 140 Sean Elliott	.08	.25
❑ 141 Chuck Person	.05	.15
❑ 142 Will Perdue	.05	.15
❑ 143 Nate McMillan	.05	.15
❑ 144 Vincent Askew	.05	.15
❑ 145 Detlef Schrempf	.08	.25
❑ 146 Hersey Hawkins	.08	.25
❑ 147 Sharone Wright	.05	.15
❑ 148 Zan Tabak	.05	.15
❑ 149 Oliver Miller	.05	.15
❑ 150 Doug Christie	.08	.25
❑ 151 Damon Stoudamire	.15	.40
❑ 152 Jeff Hornacek	.08	.25
❑ 153 Chris Morris	.05	.15
❑ 154 Antoine Carr	.05	.15
❑ 155 Karl Malone	.15	.40
❑ 156 Adam Keefe	.05	.15
❑ 157 Greg Anthony	.05	.15
❑ 158 Blue Edwards	.05	.15
❑ 159 Bryant Reeves	.05	.15
❑ 160 Anthony Avent	.05	.15
❑ 161 Lawrence Moten	.05	.15
❑ 162 Calbert Cheaney	.05	.15
❑ 163 Chris Webber	.15	.40
❑ 164 Tim Legler	.05	.15
❑ 165 Gheorghe Muresan	.05	.15
❑ 166 Stacey Augmon FUND	.05	.15
❑ 167 Dee Brown FUND	.05	.15
❑ 168 Glen Rice FUND	.05	.15
❑ 169 Scottie Pippen FUND	.15	.40
❑ 170 Danny Ferry FUND	.05	.15
❑ 171 Jason Kidd FUND	.15	.40
❑ 172 LaPhonso Ellis FUND	.05	.15
❑ 173 Grant Hill FUND	.15	.40
❑ 174 Chris Mullin FUND	.08	.25
❑ 175 Clyde Drexler FUND	.08	.25
❑ 176 Rik Smits FUND	.05	.15
❑ 177 Loy Vaught FUND	.05	.15
❑ 178 Nick Van Exel FUND	.05	.15
❑ 179 Alonzo Mourning FUND	.05	.15
❑ 180 Glenn Robinson FUND	.08	.25
❑ 181 Isaiah Rider FUND	.05	.15
❑ 182 Ed O'Bannon FUND	.05	.15
❑ 183 Patrick Ewing FUND	.08	.25
❑ 184 Shaquille O'Neal FUND	.15	.40
❑ 185 Derrick Coleman FUND	.05	.15
❑ 186 Danny Manning FUND	.05	.15
❑ 187 Clifford Robinson FUND	.05	.15
❑ 188 Mitch Richmond FUND	.05	.15
❑ 189 David Robinson FUND	.08	.25
❑ 190 Shawn Kemp FUND	.05	.15
❑ 191 Oliver Miller FUND	.05	.15
❑ 192 John Stockton FUND	.20	.50
❑ 193 Greg Anthony FUND	.05	.15
❑ 194 Rasheed Wallace FUND	.15	.40
❑ 195 Michael Jordan FUND	.50	1.25
❑ 196 M.Jordan/M.Geiger CL	.15	.40
❑ 197 E.Jones/A.McDyess CL	.05	.15
❑ 198 A.Hardaway/K.Garnett CL	.15	.40
❑ 199 D.Stoudamire/A.Johnson CL	.05	.15
❑ 200 D.Robinson/C.Mullin CL	.05	.15
❑ 201 Alan Henderson	.05	.15
❑ 202 Steve Smith	.08	.25
❑ 203 Donnie Boyce RC	.05	.15
❑ 204 Priest Lauderdale RC	.05	.15
❑ 205 Dikembe Mutombo	.08	.25
❑ 206 Dee Brown	.05	.15
❑ 207 Junior Burrough	.05	.15
❑ 208 Todd Day	.05	.15
❑ 209 Pervis Ellison	.05	.15
❑ 210 Greg Minor	.05	.15
❑ 211 Antoine Walker RC	.40	1.00
❑ 212 Rafael Addison	.05	.15
❑ 213 Tony Delk RC	.15	.40
❑ 214 Vlade Divac	.05	.15
❑ 215 Anthony Goldwire	.05	.15
❑ 216 Anthony Mason	.08	.25
❑ 217 Dickey Simpkins	.05	.15
❑ 218 Randy Brown	.05	.15
❑ 219 Jud Buechler	.05	.15
❑ 220 Jason Caffey	.05	.15
❑ 221 Scottie Pippen	.25	.60
❑ 222 Bill Wennington	.05	.15
❑ 223 Danny Ferry	.05	.15
❑ 224 Antonio Lang	.05	.15
❑ 225 Chris Mills	.05	.15
❑ 226 Vitaly Potapenko RC	.05	.15
❑ 227 Terry Davis	.05	.15
❑ 228 Chris Gatling	.05	.15
❑ 229 Jason Kidd	.25	.60
❑ 230 George McCloud	.05	.15
❑ 231 Eric Montross	.05	.15
❑ 232 Samaki Walker RC	.05	.15
❑ 233 Mark Jackson	.05	.15
❑ 234 Ervin Johnson	.05	.15
❑ 235 Sarunas Marciulionis	.05	.15
❑ 236 Eric Murdock	.05	.15
❑ 237 Ricky Pierce	.05	.15
❑ 238 Bryant Stith	.05	.15
❑ 239 Stacey Augmon	.05	.15
❑ 240 Grant Hill	.15	.40
❑ 241 Otis Thorpe	.05	.15
❑ 242 Jerome Williams RC	.15	.40
❑ 243 Andrew DeClercq	.05	.15
❑ 244 Todd Fuller RC	.05	.15
❑ 245 Mark Price	.08	.25
❑ 246 Clifford Rozier	.05	.15
❑ 247 Latrell Sprewell	.15	.40
❑ 248 Charles Barkley	.20	.50
❑ 249 Clyde Drexler	.15	.40
❑ 250 Othella Harrington RC	.15	.40
❑ 251 Sam Mack	.05	.15
❑ 252 Kevin Willis	.05	.15
❑ 253 Erick Dampier RC	.15	.40
❑ 254 Antonio Davis	.05	.15
❑ 255 Dale Davis	.05	.15
❑ 256 Duane Ferrell	.05	.15
❑ 257 Reggie Miller	.15	.40
❑ 258 Jalen Rose	.15	.40
❑ 259 Reggie Williams	.05	.15
❑ 260 Terry Dehere	.05	.15
❑ 261 Bo Outlaw	.05	.15
❑ 262 Stanley Roberts	.05	.15
❑ 263 Malik Sealy	.05	.15
❑ 264 Loy Vaught	.05	.15
❑ 265 Lorenzen Wright RC	.08	.25
❑ 266 Corie Blount	.05	.15
❑ 267 Kobe Bryant RC	2.00	5.00
❑ 268 Elden Campbell	.05	.15
❑ 269 Derek Fisher RC	.25	.60
❑ 270 Shaquille O'Neal	.40	1.00
❑ 271 Nick Van Exel	.15	.40
❑ 272 P.J. Brown	.05	.15
❑ 273 Tim Hardaway	.08	.25
❑ 274 Voshon Lenard RC	.08	.25
❑ 275 Dan Majerle	.08	.25
❑ 276 Alonzo Mourning	.08	.25
❑ 277 Martin Muursepp RC	.05	.15
❑ 278 Ray Allen RC	.50	1.25
❑ 279 Elliot Perry	.05	.15
❑ 280 Glenn Robinson	.15	.40
❑ 281 Stephon Marbury RC	.40	1.00
❑ 282 Cherokee Parks	.05	.15
❑ 283 Doug West	.05	.15
❑ 284 Micheal Williams	.05	.15
❑ 285 Kerry Kittles RC	.15	.40
❑ 286 Ed O'Bannon	.05	.15
❑ 287 Robert Pack	.05	.15
❑ 288 Khalid Reeves	.05	.15
❑ 289 David Benoit	.05	.15
❑ 290 Patrick Ewing	.15	.40
❑ 291 Allan Houston	.08	.25
❑ 292 Larry Johnson	.08	.25
❑ 293 Dontae' Jones RC	.05	.15
❑ 294 Walter McCarty RC	.05	.15
❑ 295 John Wallace RC	.15	.40
❑ 296 Charlie Ward	.05	.15
❑ 297 Brian Evans RC	.05	.15
❑ 298 Horace Grant	.08	.25
❑ 299 Jon Koncak	.05	.15
❑ 300 Felton Spencer	.05	.15
❑ 301 Allen Iverson RC	.50	1.25
❑ 302 Don MacLean	.05	.15
❑ 303 Scott Williams	.05	.15
❑ 304 Sam Cassell	.15	.40
❑ 305 Michael Finley	.08	.25
❑ 306 Robert Horry	.08	.25
❑ 307 Kevin Johnson	.08	.25
❑ 308 Joe Kleine	.05	.15
❑ 309 Danny Manning	.08	.25
❑ 310 Steve Nash RC	1.25	3.00
❑ 311 John Williams	.05	.15
❑ 312 Kenny Anderson	.05	.15
❑ 313 Randolph Childress	.05	.15
❑ 314 Chris Dudley	.05	.15
❑ 315 Jermaine O'Neal RC	.50	1.25
❑ 316 Isaiah Rider	.08	.25
❑ 317 Clifford Robinson	.05	.15
❑ 318 Rasheed Wallace	.20	.50
❑ 319 Mahmoud Abdul-Rauf	.05	.15
❑ 320 Duane Causwell	.05	.15
❑ 321 Bobby Hurley	.05	.15
❑ 322 Mitch Richmond	.08	.25
❑ 323 Lionel Simmons	.05	.15
❑ 324 Michael Smith	.05	.15
❑ 325 Dominique Wilkins	.15	.40
❑ 326 Cory Alexander	.05	.15
❑ 327 Greg Anderson	.05	.15
❑ 328 Carl Herrera	.05	.15
❑ 329 David Robinson	.15	.40
❑ 330 Charles Smith	.05	.15
❑ 331 Craig Ehlo	.05	.15
❑ 332 Sherrell Ford	.05	.15
❑ 333 Shawn Kemp	.08	.25
❑ 334 Jim McIlvaine	.05	.15
❑ 335 Gary Payton	.15	.40
❑ 336 Sam Perkins	.08	.25
❑ 337 Eric Snow RC	.08	.25
❑ 338 David Wingate	.05	.15
❑ 339 Marcus Camby RC	.20	.50
❑ 340 Acie Earl	.05	.15
❑ 341 Carlos Rogers	.05	.15
❑ 342 Greg Ostertag	.05	.15
❑ 343 Bryon Russell	.05	.15
❑ 344 John Stockton	.20	.50
❑ 345 Jamie Watson	.05	.15
❑ 346 Shareef Abdur-Rahim RC	.50	1.25
❑ 347 Doug Edwards	.05	.15
❑ 348 George Lynch	.05	.15
❑ 349 Eric Mobley	.05	.15
❑ 350 Anthony Peeler	.05	.15
❑ 351 Roy Rogers RC	.05	.15
❑ 352 Juwan Howard	.08	.25
❑ 353 Harvey Grant	.05	.15
❑ 354 Tracy Murray	.05	.15
❑ 355 Rod Strickland	.05	.15
❑ 356 A.Hardaway/M.Jordan ONE	.50	1.25
❑ 357 H.Olajuwon/S.O'Neal ONE	.25	.60
❑ 358 J.Smith/S.Kemp ONE	.15	.40
❑ 359 D.Schrempf/T.Kukoc ONE	.08	.25
❑ 360 J.Jackson/Stackhouse ONE	.15	.40
❑ 361 Bryant/Abdur-Rahim ONE	.40	1.00
❑ 362 N.Anderson/M.Jordan AJ	.30	.75
❑ 363 J.Dumars/M.Jordan AJ	.30	.75
❑ 364 J.Starks/M.Jordan AJ	.30	.75
❑ 365 R.Miller/M.Jordan AJ	.40	1.00
❑ 366 G.Payton/M.Jordan AJ	.40	1.00
❑ 367 Mookie Blaylock PLAY	.05	.15
❑ 368 D.Radja/Fox/Wesley PLAY	.05	.15
❑ 369 Glen Rice PLAY	.05	.15
❑ 370 M.Jordan/S.Pippen PLAY	.50	1.25
❑ 371 Terrell Brandon PLAY	.05	.15
❑ 372 Jason Kidd PLAY	.15	.40
❑ 373 Antonio McDyess PLAY	.08	.25
❑ 374 Grant Hill PLAY	.15	.40
❑ 375 Joe Smith PLAY	.05	.15
❑ 376 Barkley/Olaj/Drexler PLAY	.30	.75
❑ 377 Reggie Miller PLAY	.08	.25
❑ 378 L.A. Clippers PLAY	.05	.15
❑ 379 Nick Van Exel PLAY	.05	.15
❑ 380 Alonzo Mourning PLAY	.05	.15
❑ 381 Ray Allen PLAY	.25	.60
❑ 382 Stephon Marbury PLAY	.25	.60
❑ 383 Shawn Bradley PLAY	.05	.15
❑ 384 Patrick Ewing PLAY	.08	.25
❑ 385 Anfernee Hardaway PLAY	.08	.25
❑ 386 Jerry Stackhouse PLAY	.15	.40
❑ 387 Danny Manning PLAY	.05	.15
❑ 388 Clifford Robinson PLAY	.05	.15
❑ 389 Tyus Edney PLAY	.05	.15
❑ 390 San Antonio Spurs PLAY	.05	.15
❑ 391 Shawn Kemp PLAY	.05	.15
❑ 392 Toronto Raptors PLAY	.05	.15
❑ 393 John Stockton PLAY	.20	.50
❑ 394 Greg Anthony PLAY	.05	.15
❑ 395 Gheorghe Muresan PLAY	.05	.15
❑ 396 Checklist	.05	.15
❑ 397 Checklist	.05	.15
❑ 398 Checklist	.05	.15
❑ 399 Checklist	.05	.15
❑ 400 Checklist	.05	.15
❑ 401 Henry James TRADE	.15	.40
❑ 402 Shawn Bradley TRADE	.15	.40
❑ 403 Sasha Danilovic TRADE	.15	.40
❑ 404 Michael Finley TRADE	.50	1.25
❑ 405 A.C. Green TRADE	.25	.60
❑ 406 Derek Harper TRADE	.15	.40

❑ 407 Khalid Reeves TRADE	.15	.40
❑ 408 Aaron McKie TRADE	.25	.60
❑ 409 Matt Maloney TRADE	.25	.60
❑ 410 Darrick Martin TRADE	.15	.40
❑ 411 Robert Horry TRADE	.25	.60
❑ 412 Travis Knight TRADE	.15	.40
❑ 413 Isaac Austin TRADE	.15	.40
❑ 414 Jamal Mashburn TRADE	.25	.60
❑ 415 Armon Gilliam TRADE	.15	.40
❑ 416 Chris Carr TRADE	.15	.40
❑ 417 Dean Garrett TRADE	.15	.40
❑ 418 Shane Heal TRADE	.15	.40
❑ 419 Sam Cassell TRADE	.40	1.00
❑ 420 Chris Gatling TRADE	.15	.40
❑ 421 Jim Jackson TRADE	.15	.40
❑ 422 Chris Childs TRADE	.15	.40
❑ 423 Rony Seikaly TRADE	.15	.40
❑ 424 Gerald Wilkins TRADE	.15	.40
❑ 425 Cedric Ceballos TRADE	.15	.40
❑ 426 Tony Dumas TRADE	.15	.40
❑ 427 Jason Kidd TRADE	1.00	2.50
❑ 428 Popeye Jones TRADE	.15	.40
❑ 429 Walt Williams TRADE	.15	.40
❑ 430 Jaren Jackson TRADE	.25	.60
❑ NNO Update Trade Card	6.00	15.00
❑ NNO Michael Jordan 5x7 MM		
❑ NNO Michael Jordan 5x7 DD		

1997-98 Collector's Choice

❑ COMPLETE SET (400)	15.00	30.00
❑ COMP.FACTORY SET (415)	25.00	40.00
❑ COMPLETE SERIES 1 (200)	7.50	15.00
❑ COMPLETE SERIES 2 (200)	7.50	15.00
❑ 1 Mookie Blaylock	.05	.15
❑ 2 Dikembe Mutombo	.08	.25
❑ 3 Eldridge Recasner	.05	.15
❑ 4 Christian Laettner	.08	.25
❑ 5 Tyrone Corbin	.05	.15
❑ 6 Antoine Walker	.20	.50
❑ 7 Eric Williams	.05	.15
❑ 8 Dana Barros	.05	.15
❑ 9 David Wesley	.05	.15
❑ 10 Dino Radja	.05	.15
❑ 11 Vlade Divac	.08	.25
❑ 12 Dell Curry	.05	.15
❑ 13 Muggsy Bogues	.08	.25
❑ 14 Tony Smith	.05	.15
❑ 15 Glen Rice	.08	.25
❑ 16 Anthony Mason	.08	.25
❑ 17 Dennis Rodman	.08	.25
❑ 18 Brian Williams	.05	.15
❑ 19 Toni Kukoc	.08	.25
❑ 20 Jason Caffey	.05	.15
❑ 21 Steve Kerr	.08	.25
❑ 22 Luc Longley	.05	.15
❑ 23 Michael Jordan	1.00	2.50
❑ 24 Chris Mills	.05	.15
❑ 25 Tyrone Hill	.05	.15
❑ 26 Vitaly Potapenko	.05	.15
❑ 27 Bob Sura	.05	.15
❑ 28 Robert Pack	.05	.15
❑ 29 Ed O'Bannon	.05	.15
❑ 30 Michael Finley	.15	.40
❑ 31 Shawn Bradley	.05	.15
❑ 32 Khalid Reeves	.05	.15
❑ 33 Antonio McDyess	.08	.25
❑ 34 Ervin Johnson	.05	.15
❑ 35 Dale Ellis	.05	.15
❑ 36 Bryant Stith	.05	.15
❑ 37 Tom Hammonds	.05	.15
❑ 38 Otis Thorpe	.05	.15
❑ 39 Lindsey Hunter	.05	.15
❑ 40 Grant Long	.05	.15
❑ 41 Aaron McKie	.08	.25

❑ 42 Randolph Childress	.05	.15
❑ 43 Scott Burrell	.05	.15
❑ 44 Bimbo Coles	.05	.15
❑ 45 B.J. Armstrong	.05	.15
❑ 46 Mark Price	.08	.25
❑ 47 Latrell Sprewell	.15	.40
❑ 48 Felton Spencer	.05	.15
❑ 49 Charles Barkley	.15	.40
❑ 50 Mario Elie	.05	.15
❑ 51 Clyde Drexler	.15	.40
❑ 52 Kevin Willis	.08	.25
❑ 53 Antonio Davis	.05	.15
❑ 54 Reggie Miller	.15	.40
❑ 55 Dale Davis	.05	.15
❑ 56 Mark Jackson	.08	.25
❑ 57 Erick Dampier	.08	.25
❑ 58 Pooh Richardson	.05	.15
❑ 59 Terry Dehere	.05	.15
❑ 60 Brent Barry	.08	.25
❑ 61 Loy Vaught	.05	.15
❑ 62 Lorenzen Wright	.05	.15
❑ 63 Eddie Jones	.15	.40
❑ 64 Kobe Bryant	.60	1.50
❑ 65 Elden Campbell	.05	.15
❑ 66 Corie Blount	.05	.15
❑ 67 Shaquille O'Neal	.40	1.00
❑ 68 Dan Majerle	.08	.25
❑ 69 P.J. Brown	.05	.15
❑ 70 Tim Hardaway	.08	.25
❑ 71 Isaac Austin	.05	.15
❑ 72 Jamal Mashburn	.08	.25
❑ 73 Ray Allen	.15	.40
❑ 74 Glenn Robinson	.15	.40
❑ 75 Armon Gilliam	.05	.15
❑ 76 Johnny Newman	.05	.15
❑ 77 Elliot Perry	.05	.15
❑ 78 Sherman Douglas	.05	.15
❑ 79 Doug West	.05	.15
❑ 80 Kevin Garnett	.30	.75
❑ 81 Sam Mitchell	.05	.15
❑ 82 Tom Gugliotta	.08	.25
❑ 83 Terry Porter	.05	.15
❑ 84 Chris Carr	.05	.15
❑ 85 Kevin Edwards	.05	.15
❑ 86 Jayson Williams	.05	.15
❑ 87 Kendall Gill	.05	.15
❑ 88 Kerry Kittles	.15	.40
❑ 89 Chris Gatling	.05	.15
❑ 90 John Starks	.08	.25
❑ 91 Charlie Ward	.05	.15
❑ 92 Larry Johnson	.08	.25
❑ 93 Charles Oakley	.08	.25
❑ 94 Chris Childs	.05	.15
❑ 95 Allan Houston	.08	.25
❑ 96 Horace Grant	.08	.25
❑ 97 Darrell Armstrong	.05	.15
❑ 98 Rony Seikaly	.05	.15
❑ 99 Dennis Scott	.05	.15
❑ 100 Anfernee Hardaway	.15	.40
❑ 101 Brian Shaw	.05	.15
❑ 102 Jerry Stackhouse	.15	.40
❑ 103 Rex Walters	.05	.15
❑ 104 Don MacLean	.05	.15
❑ 105 Derrick Coleman	.05	.15
❑ 106 Lucious Harris	.05	.15
❑ 107 Clarence Weatherspoon	.05	.15
❑ 108 Cedric Ceballos	.05	.15
❑ 109 Danny Manning	.08	.25
❑ 110 Jason Kidd	.25	.60
❑ 111 Loren Meyer	.05	.15
❑ 112 Wesley Person	.05	.15
❑ 113 Steve Nash	.15	.40
❑ 114 Isaiah Rider	.08	.25
❑ 115 Stacey Augmon	.05	.15
❑ 116 Arvydas Sabonis	.08	.25
❑ 117 Kenny Anderson	.08	.25
❑ 118 Jermaine O'Neal	.25	.60
❑ 119 Gary Trent	.05	.15
❑ 120 Michael Smith	.05	.15
❑ 121 Kevin Gamble	.05	.15
❑ 122 Olden Polynice	.05	.15
❑ 123 Billy Owens	.05	.15
❑ 124 Corliss Williamson	.08	.25
❑ 125 Cory Alexander	.05	.15
❑ 126 Vinny Del Negro	.05	.15
❑ 127 Sean Elliott	.08	.25
❑ 128 Will Perdue	.05	.15
❑ 129 Carl Herrera	.05	.15
❑ 130 Shawn Kemp	.08	.25

❑ 131 Hersey Hawkins	.05	.15
❑ 132 Nate McMillan	.05	.15
❑ 133 Craig Ehlo	.05	.15
❑ 134 Detlef Schrempf	.08	.25
❑ 135 Sam Perkins	.08	.25
❑ 136 Sharone Wright	.05	.15
❑ 137 Doug Christie	.08	.25
❑ 138 Popeye Jones	.05	.15
❑ 139 Shawn Respert	.05	.15
❑ 140 Marcus Camby	.15	.40
❑ 141 Adam Keefe	.05	.15
❑ 142 Karl Malone	.15	.40
❑ 143 John Stockton	.20	.50
❑ 144 Greg Ostertag	.05	.15
❑ 145 Chris Morris	.05	.15
❑ 146 Shareef Abdur-Rahim	.25	.60
❑ 147 Roy Rogers	.05	.15
❑ 148 George Lynch	.05	.15
❑ 149 Anthony Peeler	.05	.15
❑ 150 Lee Mayberry	.05	.15
❑ 151 Calbert Cheaney	.05	.15
❑ 152 Harvey Grant	.05	.15
❑ 153 Rod Strickland	.05	.15
❑ 154 Tracy Murray	.05	.15
❑ 155 Chris Webber	.15	.40
❑ 156 Mookie Blaylock/Hawks GN	.05	.15
❑ 157 A.Walker/Celtics GN	.15	.40
❑ 158 Glen Rice/Hornets GN	.08	.25
❑ 159 M.Jordan/Bulls GN	.50	1.25
❑ 160 Tyrone Hill/Cavaliers GN	.05	.15
❑ 161 Shawn Bradley/Mavericks GN	.05	.15
❑ 162 Antonio McDyess/Nuggets GN	.08	.25
❑ 163 G.Hill/Pistons GN	.08	.25
❑ 164 Latrell Sprewell/Warriors GN	.05	.15
❑ 165 H.Olajuwon/Rockets GN	.15	.40
❑ 166 Reggie Miller/Pacers GN	.08	.25
❑ 167 Loy Vaught/Clippers GN	.05	.15
❑ 168 E.Jones/Lakers GN	.15	.40
❑ 169 Tim Hardaway/Heat GN	.05	.15
❑ 170 Vin Baker/Bucks GN	.05	.15
❑ 171 K.Garnett/T'wolves GN	.25	.60
❑ 172 Kendall Gill/Nets GN	.05	.15
❑ 173 Patrick Ewing/Knicks GN	.08	.25
❑ 174 A.Hardaway/Magic GN	.08	.25
❑ 175 A.Iverson/76ers GN	.15	.40
❑ 176 J.Kidd/Suns GN	.15	.40
❑ 177 Rasheed Wallace/Trail Blazers GN	.08	.25
❑ 178 Mitch Richmond/Kings GN	.08	.25
❑ 179 Sean Elliott/Spurs GN	.08	.25
❑ 180 G.Payton/SuperSonics GN	.15	.40
❑ 181 D.Stoudamire/Raptors GN	.15	.40
❑ 182 Karl Malone/Jazz GN	.15	.40
❑ 183 S.Abdur-Rahim/Griz. GN	.10	.30
❑ 184 C.Webber/Wizards GN	.08	.25
❑ 185 M.Jordan/97 Finals GN	.50	1.25
❑ 186 Michael Jordan C23	.40	1.00
❑ 187 Michael Jordan C23	.40	1.00
❑ 188 Michael Jordan C23	.40	1.00
❑ 189 Michael Jordan C23	.40	1.00
❑ 190 Michael Jordan C23	.40	1.00
❑ 191 Michael Jordan C23	.40	1.00
❑ 192 Michael Jordan C23	.40	1.00
❑ 193 Michael Jordan C23	.40	1.00
❑ 194 Michael Jordan C23	.40	1.00
❑ 195 Michael Jordan C23	.40	1.00
❑ 196 Checklist #1	.05	.15
❑ 197 Checklist #2	.05	.15
❑ 198 Checklist #3	.05	.15
❑ 199 Checklist #4	.05	.15
❑ 200 Checklist #5	.05	.15
❑ 201 Steve Smith	.08	.25
❑ 202 Chris Crawford RC	.05	.15
❑ 203 Ed Gray RC	.05	.15
❑ 204 Alan Henderson	.05	.15
❑ 205 Walter McCarty	.05	.15
❑ 206 Dee Brown	.05	.15
❑ 207 Chauncey Billups RC	.75	2.00
❑ 208 Ron Mercer RC	.15	.40
❑ 209 Travis Knight	.05	.15
❑ 210 Andrew DeClercq	.05	.15
❑ 211 Tyus Edney	.05	.15
❑ 212 Matt Geiger	.05	.15
❑ 213 Tony Delk	.05	.15
❑ 214 J.R. Reid	.05	.15
❑ 215 Bobby Phills	.05	.15
❑ 216 David Wesley	.05	.15
❑ 217 Ron Harper	.08	.25
❑ 218 Scottie Pippen	.25	.60

❑ 219 Scott Burrell	.05	.15
❑ 220 Keith Booth RC	.05	.15
❑ 221 Bill Wennington	.05	.15
❑ 222 Shawn Kemp	.08	.25
❑ 223 Zydrunas Ilgauskas	.08	.25
❑ 224 Brevin Knight RC	.08	.25
❑ 225 Danny Ferry	.05	.15
❑ 226 Derek Anderson RC	.15	.40
❑ 227 Wesley Person	.05	.15
❑ 228 A.C. Green	.08	.25
❑ 229 Samaki Walker	.05	.15
❑ 230 Hubert Davis	.05	.15
❑ 231 Erick Strickland RC	.08	.25
❑ 232 Dennis Scott	.05	.15
❑ 233 Tony Battie RC	.15	.40
❑ 234 LaPhonso Ellis	.05	.15
❑ 235 Eric Williams	.05	.15
❑ 236 Bobby Jackson RC	.40	1.00
❑ 237 Anthony Goldwire	.05	.15
❑ 238 Danny Fortson RC	.08	.25
❑ 239 Joe Dumars	.15	.40
❑ 240 Grant Hill	.15	.40
❑ 241 Malik Sealy	.05	.15
❑ 242 Brian Williams	.05	.15
❑ 243 Theo Ratliff	.05	.15
❑ 244 Scot Pollard RC	.08	.25
❑ 245 Erick Dampier	.08	.25
❑ 246 Duane Ferrell	.05	.15
❑ 247 Joe Smith	.08	.25
❑ 248 Todd Fuller	.05	.15
❑ 249 Adonal Foyle RC	.08	.25
❑ 250 Othella Harrington	.05	.15
❑ 251 Matt Maloney	.05	.15
❑ 252 Hakeem Olajuwon	.15	.40
❑ 253 Rodrick Rhodes RC	.05	.15
❑ 254 Eddie Johnson	.05	.15
❑ 255 Brent Price	.05	.15
❑ 256 Austin Croshere RC	.10	.30
❑ 257 Derrick McKey	.05	.15
❑ 258 Chris Mullin	.15	.40
❑ 259 Rik Smits	.08	.25
❑ 260 Jalen Rose	.15	.40
❑ 261 Darrick Martin	.05	.15
❑ 262 Lamond Murray	.05	.15
❑ 263 Maurice Taylor RC	.10	.30
❑ 264 Rodney Rogers	.05	.15
❑ 265 James Robinson	.05	.15
❑ 266 Rick Fox	.08	.25
❑ 267 Nick Van Exel	.15	.40
❑ 268 Sean Rooks	.05	.15
❑ 269 Derek Fisher	.15	.40
❑ 270 Jon Barry	.05	.15
❑ 271 Robert Horry	.08	.25
❑ 272 Terry Mills	.05	.15
❑ 273 Charles Smith RC	.05	.15
❑ 274 Alonzo Mourning	.08	.25
❑ 275 Voshon Lenard	.05	.15
❑ 276 Todd Day	.05	.15
❑ 277 Ervin Johnson	.05	.15
❑ 278 Terrell Brandon	.08	.25
❑ 279 Michael Curry	.05	.15
❑ 280 Andrew Lang	.05	.15
❑ 281 Tyrone Hill	.05	.15
❑ 282 Stephon Marbury	.20	.50
❑ 283 Cherokee Parks	.05	.15
❑ 284 Stanley Roberts	.05	.15
❑ 285 Paul Grant RC	.05	.15
❑ 286 David Benoit	.05	.15
❑ 287 Lucious Harris	.05	.15
❑ 288 Don MacLean	.05	.15
❑ 289 Sam Cassell	.15	.40
❑ 290 Keith Van Horn RC	.20	.50
❑ 291 Patrick Ewing	.15	.40
❑ 292 Walter McCarty	.05	.15
❑ 293 Chris Dudley	.05	.15
❑ 294 Chris Mills	.05	.15
❑ 295 Buck Williams	.05	.15
❑ 296 Nick Anderson	.05	.15
❑ 297 Derek Strong	.05	.15
❑ 298 Gerald Wilkins	.05	.15
❑ 299 Johnny Taylor RC	.05	.15
❑ 300 Derek Harper	.08	.25
❑ 301 Anthony Parker RC	.15	.30
❑ 302 Allen Iverson	.40	1.00
❑ 303 Jim Jackson	.05	.15
❑ 304 Eric Montross	.05	.15
❑ 305 Tim Thomas RC	.25	.60
❑ 306 Kebu Stewart RC	.05	.15
❑ 307 Rex Chapman	.05	.15
❑ 308 Tom Chambers	.05	.15
❑ 309 Kevin Johnson	.08	.25
❑ 310 John Williams	.05	.15
❑ 311 Clifford Robinson	.05	.15
❑ 312 Antonio McDyess	.08	.25
❑ 313 Rasheed Wallace	.15	.40
❑ 314 Brian Grant	.08	.25
❑ 315 Dontonio Wingfield	.05	.15
❑ 316 Kelvin Cato RC	.15	.40
❑ 317 Mahmoud Abdul-Rauf	.05	.15
❑ 318 Lawrence Funderburke RC	.08	.25
❑ 319 Mitch Richmond	.08	.25
❑ 320 Tariq Abdul-Wahad RC	.08	.25
❑ 321 Terry Dehere	.05	.15
❑ 322 Michael Stewart RC	.05	.15
❑ 323 Tim Duncan RC	.40	1.00
❑ 324 Avery Johnson	.05	.15
❑ 325 David Robinson	.15	.40
❑ 326 Charles Smith	.05	.15
❑ 327 Chuck Person	.05	.15
❑ 328 Monty Williams	.05	.15
❑ 329 Jim McIlvaine	.05	.15
❑ 330 Gary Payton	.15	.40
❑ 331 Eric Snow	.08	.25
❑ 332 Dale Ellis	.05	.15
❑ 333 Vin Baker	.08	.25
❑ 334 Walt Williams	.05	.15
❑ 335 Tracy McGrady RC	.40	1.00
❑ 336 Damon Stoudamire	.08	.25
❑ 337 Carlos Rogers	.05	.15
❑ 338 John Wallace	.05	.15
❑ 339 Shandon Anderson	.05	.15
❑ 340 Jeff Hornacek	.08	.25
❑ 341 Howard Eisley	.05	.15
❑ 342 Jacque Vaughn RC	.08	.25
❑ 343 Bryon Russell	.05	.15
❑ 344 Antoine Carr	.05	.15
❑ 345 Antonio Daniels RC	.15	.40
❑ 346 Pete Chilcutt	.05	.15
❑ 347 Blue Edwards	.05	.15
❑ 348 Bryant Reeves	.05	.15
❑ 349 Chris Robinson RC	.05	.15
❑ 350 Otis Thorpe	.05	.15
❑ 351 Tim Legler	.05	.15
❑ 352 Juwan Howard	.08	.25
❑ 353 God Shammgod RC	.05	.15
❑ 354 Gheorghe Muresan	.05	.15
❑ 355 Chris Whitney	.05	.15
❑ 356 Dikembe Mutombo HP	.05	.15
❑ 357 Antoine Walker HP	.15	.40
❑ 358 Glen Rice HP	.05	.15
❑ 359 Scottie Pippen HP	.10	.30
❑ 360 Derek Anderson HP	.05	.15
❑ 361 Michael Finley HP	.08	.25
❑ 362 LaPhonso Ellis HP	.05	.15
❑ 363 Grant Hill HP	.08	.25
❑ 364 Joe Smith HP	.05	.15
❑ 365 Charles Barkley HP	.15	.40
❑ 366 Reggie Miller HP	.08	.25
❑ 367 Loy Vaught HP	.05	.15
❑ 368 Shaquille O'Neal HP	.15	.40
❑ 369 Alonzo Mourning HP	.08	.25
❑ 370 Glenn Robinson HP	.08	.25
❑ 371 Kevin Garnett HP	.20	.50
❑ 372 Kendall Gill HP	.05	.15
❑ 373 Allan Houston HP	.05	.15
❑ 374 Anfernee Hardaway HP	.08	.25
❑ 375 Tim Thomas HP	.10	.30
❑ 376 Jason Kidd HP	.10	.30
❑ 377 Kenny Anderson HP	.05	.15
❑ 378 Mitch Richmond HP	.05	.15
❑ 379 Tim Duncan HP	.20	.50
❑ 380 Gary Payton HP	.08	.25
❑ 381 Marcus Camby HP	.08	.25
❑ 382 Karl Malone HP	.15	.40
❑ 383 Shareef Abdur-Rahim HP	.10	.30
❑ 384 Chris Webber HP	.08	.25
❑ 385 Michael Jordan HP	.50	1.25
❑ 386 Michael Jordan MM	.40	1.00
❑ 387 Michael Jordan MM	.40	1.00
❑ 388 Michael Jordan MM	.40	1.00
❑ 389 Michael Jordan MM	.40	1.00
❑ 390 Michael Jordan MM	.40	1.00
❑ 391 Michael Jordan MM	.40	1.00
❑ 392 Michael Jordan MM	.40	1.00
❑ 393 Michael Jordan MM	.40	1.00
❑ 394 Michael Jordan MM	.40	1.00
❑ 395 Michael Jordan MM	.40	1.00
❑ 396 Checklist #1	.05	.15
❑ 397 Checklist #2	.05	.15
❑ 398 Checklist #3	.05	.15
❑ 399 Checklist #4	.05	.15
❑ 400 Checklist #5	.05	.15

2009-10 Donruss Elite

❑ 1 Joe Johnson	.50	1.25
❑ 2 Jamal Crawford	.30	.75
❑ 3 Josh Smith	.50	1.25
❑ 4 Mike Bibby	.30	.75
❑ 5 Paul Pierce	.60	1.50
❑ 6 Kevin Garnett	1.00	2.50
❑ 7 Ray Allen	.50	1.25
❑ 8 Rajon Rondo	.50	1.25
❑ 9 Gerald Wallace	.50	1.25
❑ 10 Boris Diaw	.40	1.00
❑ 11 Raymond Felton	.40	1.00
❑ 12 Derrick Rose	1.00	2.50
❑ 13 John Salmons	.50	1.25
❑ 14 Brad Miller	.50	1.25
❑ 15 Tyrus Thomas	.40	1.00
❑ 16 LeBron James	2.50	6.00
❑ 17 Shaquille O'Neal	1.00	2.50
❑ 18 Mo Williams	.40	1.00
❑ 19 Delonte West	.30	.75
❑ 20 Dirk Nowitzki	.60	1.50
❑ 21 Jason Kidd	.50	1.25
❑ 22 Jason Terry	.40	1.00
❑ 23 Shawn Marion	.50	1.25
❑ 24 Carmelo Anthony	.60	1.50
❑ 25 Chauncey Billups	.50	1.25
❑ 26 Kenyon Martin	.50	1.25
❑ 27 Nene	.40	1.00
❑ 28 Ben Gordon	.50	1.25
❑ 29 Richard Hamilton	.40	1.00
❑ 30 Charlie Villanueva	.40	1.00
❑ 31 Tayshaun Prince	.50	1.25
❑ 32 Stephen Jackson	.40	1.00
❑ 33 Monta Ellis	.50	1.25
❑ 34 Corey Maggette	.40	1.00
❑ 35 Kelenna Azubuike	.30	.75
❑ 36 Tracy McGrady	.60	1.50
❑ 37 Shane Battier	.40	1.00
❑ 38 Luis Scola	.30	.75
❑ 39 Trevor Ariza	.50	1.25
❑ 40 Danny Granger	.50	1.25
❑ 41 Mike Dunleavy	.30	.75
❑ 42 Troy Murphy	.30	.75
❑ 43 T.J. Ford	.30	.75
❑ 44 Eric Gordon	.50	1.25
❑ 45 Al Thornton	.50	1.25
❑ 46 Baron Davis	.50	1.25
❑ 47 Marcus Camby	.30	.75
❑ 48 Kobe Bryant	2.50	6.00
❑ 49 Ron Artest	.50	1.25
❑ 50 Pau Gasol	.50	1.25
❑ 51 Andrew Bynum	.50	1.25
❑ 52 Zach Randolph	.30	.75
❑ 53 Rudy Gay	.50	1.25
❑ 54 O.J. Mayo	.60	1.50
❑ 55 Marc Gasol	.50	1.25
❑ 56 Dwyane Wade	1.00	2.50
❑ 57 Michael Beasley	.60	1.50
❑ 58 Jermaine O'Neal	.50	1.25
❑ 59 Daequan Cook	.40	1.00
❑ 60 Quentin Richardson	.30	.75
❑ 61 Michael Redd	.50	1.25
❑ 62 Hakim Warrick	.40	1.00
❑ 63 Andrew Bogut	.50	1.25
❑ 64 Luke Ridnour	.30	.75
❑ 65 Al Jefferson	.50	1.25
❑ 66 Ryan Gomes	.30	.75
❑ 67 Kevin Love	.40	1.00
❑ 68 Devin Harris	.50	1.25
❑ 69 Brook Lopez	.30	.75
❑ 70 Yi Jianlian	.50	1.25

❑ 71 Rafer Alston	.40	1.00
❑ 72 Chris Paul	1.00	2.50
❑ 73 David West	.50	1.25
❑ 74 Peja Stojakovic	.30	.75
❑ 75 James Posey	.40	1.00
❑ 76 Emeka Okafor	.50	1.25
❑ 77 Nate Robinson	.50	1.25
❑ 78 David Lee	.40	1.00
❑ 79 Al Harrington	.40	1.00
❑ 80 Larry Hughes	.30	.75
❑ 81 Kevin Durant	1.25	3.00
❑ 82 Russell Westbrook	.50	1.25
❑ 83 Jeff Green	.40	1.00
❑ 84 Nenad Krstic	.40	1.00
❑ 85 Dwight Howard	1.00	2.50
❑ 86 Vince Carter	.60	1.50
❑ 87 Rashard Lewis	.50	1.25
❑ 88 Jameer Nelson	.40	1.00
❑ 89 Elton Brand	.50	1.25
❑ 90 Andre Iguodala	.50	1.25
❑ 91 Thaddeus Young	.30	.75
❑ 92 Amare Stoudemire	.60	1.50
❑ 93 Steve Nash	.50	1.25
❑ 94 Jason Richardson	.50	1.25
❑ 95 Grant Hill	.50	1.25
❑ 96 Brandon Roy	.60	1.50
❑ 97 LaMarcus Aldridge	.50	1.25
❑ 98 Steve Blake	.30	.75
❑ 99 Andre Miller	.40	1.00
❑ 100 Greg Oden	.40	1.00
❑ 101 Kevin Martin	.50	1.25
❑ 102 Andres Nocioni	.40	1.00
❑ 103 Francisco Garcia	.40	1.00
❑ 104 Spencer Hawes	.40	1.00
❑ 105 Tony Parker	.50	1.25
❑ 106 Tim Duncan	.75	2.00
❑ 107 Manu Ginobili	.50	1.25
❑ 108 Richard Jefferson	.50	1.25
❑ 109 Chris Bosh	.50	1.25
❑ 110 Jose Calderon	.40	1.00
❑ 111 Andrea Bargnani	.40	1.00
❑ 112 Hedo Turkoglu	.50	1.25
❑ 113 Deron Williams	.60	1.50
❑ 114 Mehmet Okur	.30	.75
❑ 115 Andrei Kirilenko	.40	1.00
❑ 116 Carlos Boozer	.50	1.25
❑ 117 Antawn Jamison	.50	1.25
❑ 118 Caron Butler	.50	1.25
❑ 119 Gilbert Arenas	.50	1.25
❑ 120 Randy Foye	.30	.75
❑ 121 Willis Reed	.75	2.00
❑ 122 Chris Mullin	.75	2.00
❑ 123 Kevin Johnson	.75	2.00
❑ 124 Spencer Haywood	.75	2.00
❑ 125 David Robinson	1.25	3.00
❑ 126 Phil Jackson	1.00	2.50
❑ 127 Magic Johnson	1.50	4.00
❑ 128 Paul Westphal	.75	2.00
❑ 129 Alex English	.75	2.00
❑ 130 Kareem Abdul-Jabbar	1.25	3.00
❑ 131 Glen Rice	.75	2.00
❑ 132 Nate McMillan	.75	2.00
❑ 133 Bob Cousy	1.25	3.00
❑ 134 Mitch Richmond	.75	2.00
❑ 135 Kelly Tripucka	.75	2.00
❑ 136 Cedric Maxwell	.75	2.00
❑ 137 Lenny Wilkens	.75	2.00
❑ 138 Bill Russell	1.25	3.00
❑ 139 Sean Elliott	.75	2.00
❑ 140 Hersey Hawkins	.75	2.00
❑ 141 Clyde Drexler	1.00	2.50
❑ 142 Larry Bird	2.50	6.00
❑ 143 Connie Hawkins	.75	2.00
❑ 144 Lou Hudson	.75	2.00
❑ 145 Oscar Robertson	.75	2.00
❑ 146 Jerry Lucas	.75	2.00
❑ 147 Kevin McHale	.75	2.00
❑ 148 Michael Cage	.75	2.00
❑ 149 Vlade Divac	.75	2.00
❑ 150 Jerry West	1.00	2.50
❑ 151 Bill Walton	.75	2.00
❑ 152 Rick Barry	.75	2.00
❑ 153 Artis Gilmore	.75	2.00
❑ 154 Earl Monroe	.75	2.00
❑ 155 Xavier McDaniel	.75	2.00
❑ 156 Jalen Rose	.75	2.00
❑ 157 Walt Frazier	.75	2.00
❑ 158 Isiah Thomas	.75	2.00
❑ 159 James Worthy	1.00	2.50
❑ 160 Karl Malone	1.00	2.50
❑ 161 Blake Griffin AU RC	25.00	50.00
❑ 162 Hasheem Thabeet AU RC	5.00	12.00
❑ 163 James Harden/479 AU RC	15.00	30.00
❑ 164 Tyreke Evans AU RC	40.00	75.00
❑ 165 Jonny Flynn AU RC	8.00	20.00
❑ 166 Stephen Curry AU RC	20.00	40.00
❑ 167 Jordan Hill AU RC	6.00	15.00
❑ 168 Daniel Green AU RC EXCH	2.00	12.00
❑ 169 Brandon Jennings AU RC	20.00	40.00
❑ 170 Terrence Williams AU RC	8.00	20.00
❑ 171 Gerald Henderson AU RC	5.00	12.00
❑ 172 Tyler Hansbrough AU RC	10.00	25.00
❑ 173 Earl Clark AU RC	6.00	15.00
❑ 174 Austin Daye AU RC	5.00	12.00
❑ 175 James Johnson AU RC	5.00	12.00
❑ 176 Jrue Holiday AU RC	5.00	12.00
❑ 177 Ty Lawson AU RC	10.00	25.00
❑ 178 Jeff Teague AU RC	5.00	12.00
❑ 179 Eric Maynor/199 AU RC EXCH	6.00	15.00
❑ 180 Darren Collison/199 AU RC	8.00	20.00
❑ 181 Omri Casspi AU RC	8.00	20.00
❑ 182 B.J. Mullens AU RC	5.00	12.00
❑ 183 Rodrigue Beaubois AU RC	8.00	20.00
❑ 184 Taj Gibson/199 AU RC	6.00	15.00
❑ 185 DeMarre Carroll AU RC	5.00	12.00
❑ 186 Wayne Ellington/199 AU RC	8.00	20.00
❑ 187 Toney Douglas AU RC	5.00	12.00
❑ 188 Jeff Pendergraph AU RC	5.00	12.00
❑ 189 Jermaine Taylor AU RC	5.00	12.00
❑ 190 D.Cunningham/199 AU RC	5.00	12.00
❑ 191 DaJuan Summers AU RC	5.00	12.00
❑ 192 Sam Young/199 AU RC EXCH	5.00	12.00
❑ 193 DeJuan Blair AU RC	6.00	15.00
❑ 194 Jon Brockman AU RC	5.00	12.00
❑ 195 A.J. Price AU RC	5.00	12.00
❑ 196 Derrick Brown/199 AU RC	5.00	12.00
❑ 197 Jodie Meeks AU RC	6.00	15.00
❑ 198 Marcus Thornton/199 AU RC	5.00	12.00
❑ 199 Chase Budinger AU RC	5.00	12.00
❑ 200 Taylor Griffin AU RC	5.00	12.00

1994-95 Emotion

❑ COMPLETE SET (121)	25.00	50.00
❑ 1 Stacey Augmon	.05	.15
❑ 2 Mookie Blaylock	.05	.15
❑ 3 Steve Smith	.10	.30
❑ 4 Greg Minor RC	.05	.15
❑ 5 Eric Montross RC	.05	.15
❑ 6 Dino Radja	.05	.15
❑ 7 Dominique Wilkins	.25	.60
❑ 8 Muggsy Bogues	.10	.30
❑ 9 Larry Johnson	.10	.30
❑ 10 Alonzo Mourning	.30	.75
❑ 11 B.J. Armstrong	.05	.15
❑ 12 Toni Kukoc	.40	1.00
❑ 13 Scottie Pippen	.75	2.00
❑ 14 Dickey Simpkins RC	.05	.15
❑ 15 Tyrone Hill	.05	.15
❑ 16 Chris Mills	.10	.30
❑ 17 Mark Price	.05	.15
❑ 18 Tony Dumas RC	.05	.15
❑ 19 Jim Jackson	.10	.30
❑ 20 Jason Kidd RC	2.50	6.00
❑ 21 Jamal Mashburn	.25	.60
❑ 22 LaPhonso Ellis	.05	.15
❑ 23 Dikembe Mutombo	.10	.30
❑ 24 Rodney Rogers	.05	.15
❑ 25 Jalen Rose RC	1.00	2.50
❑ 26 Bill Curley RC	.05	.15
❑ 27 Joe Dumars	.25	.60
❑ 28 Grant Hill RC	1.50	4.00
❑ 29 Tim Hardaway	.25	.60
❑ 30 Donyell Marshall RC	.25	.60
❑ 31 Chris Mullin	.25	.60
❑ 32 Carlos Rogers RC	.05	.15
❑ 33 Clifford Rozier RC	.05	.15
❑ 34 Latrell Sprewell	.25	.60
❑ 35 Sam Cassell	.25	.60
❑ 36 Clyde Drexler w/Hakeem	.25	.60
❑ 37 Robert Horry	.10	.30
❑ 38 Hakeem Olajuwon	.40	1.00
❑ 39 Mark Jackson	.05	.15
❑ 40 Reggie Miller	.25	.60
❑ 41 Rik Smits	.05	.15
❑ 42 Lamond Murray RC	.10	.30
❑ 43 Eric Piatkowski RC	.05	.15
❑ 44 Loy Vaught	.05	.15
❑ 45 Cedric Ceballos	.05	.15
❑ 46 Eddie Jones RC	1.25	3.00
❑ 47 George Lynch	.05	.15
❑ 48 Nick Van Exel	.25	.60
❑ 49 Harold Miner	.05	.15
❑ 50 Khalid Reeves RC	.05	.15
❑ 51 Glen Rice	.10	.30
❑ 52 Kevin Willis	.05	.15
❑ 53 Vin Baker	.25	.60
❑ 54 Eric Mobley RC	.05	.15
❑ 55 Eric Murdock	.05	.15
❑ 56 Glenn Robinson RC	.75	2.00
❑ 57 Tom Gugliotta	.10	.30
❑ 58 Christian Laettner	.10	.30
❑ 59 Isaiah Rider	.10	.30
❑ 60 Kenny Anderson	.10	.30
❑ 61 Derrick Coleman	.10	.30
❑ 62 Yinka Dare	.05	.15
❑ 63 Patrick Ewing	.25	.60
❑ 64 John Starks	.05	.15
❑ 65 Charlie Ward RC	.25	.60
❑ 66 Monty Williams RC	.05	.15
❑ 67 Nick Anderson	.05	.15
❑ 68 Horace Grant	.10	.30
❑ 69 Anfernee Hardaway	.60	1.50
❑ 70 Shaquille O'Neal	1.25	3.00
❑ 71 Brooks Thompson	.05	.15
❑ 72 Dana Barros	.05	.15
❑ 73 Shawn Bradley	.05	.15
❑ 74 B.J. Tyler	.05	.15
❑ 75 Clarence Weatherspoon	.05	.15
❑ 76 Sharone Wright RC	.05	.15
❑ 77 Charles Barkley	.40	1.00
❑ 78 Kevin Johnson	.10	.30
❑ 79 Dan Majerle	.10	.30
❑ 80 Danny Manning	.10	.30
❑ 81 Wesley Person RC	.25	.60
❑ 82 Aaron McKie RC	.40	1.00
❑ 83 Clifford Robinson	.10	.30
❑ 84 Rod Strickland	.10	.30
❑ 85 Brian Grant RC	.60	1.50
❑ 86 Bobby Hurley	.05	.15
❑ 87 Mitch Richmond	.25	.60
❑ 88 Sean Elliott	.10	.30
❑ 89 David Robinson	.40	1.00
❑ 90 Dennis Rodman	.50	1.25
❑ 91 Shawn Kemp	.40	1.00
❑ 92 Gary Payton	.40	1.00
❑ 93 Dontonio Wingfield	.05	.15
❑ 94 Jeff Hornacek	.10	.30
❑ 95 Karl Malone	.40	1.00
❑ 96 John Stockton	.25	.60
❑ 97 Calbert Cheaney	.05	.15
❑ 98 Juwan Howard RC	.60	1.50
❑ 99 Chris Webber	.60	1.50
❑ 100 Michael Jordan	5.00	12.00
❑ 101 Brian Grant ROO	.10	.30
❑ 102 Grant Hill ROO	.60	1.50
❑ 103 Juwan Howard ROO	.50	1.25
❑ 104 Eddie Jones ROO	.60	1.50
❑ 105 Jason Kidd ROO	1.50	4.00
❑ 106 Eric Montross ROO	.05	.15
❑ 107 Lamond Murray ROO	.05	.15
❑ 108 Wesley Person ROO	.10	.30
❑ 109 Glenn Robinson ROO	.40	1.00
❑ 110 Sharone Wright ROO	.05	.15
❑ 111 Anfernee Hardaway MAS	.30	.75
❑ 112 Shawn Kemp MAS	.25	.60
❑ 113 Karl Malone MAS	.25	.60
❑ 114 Alonzo Mourning MAS	.25	.60
❑ 115 Shaquille O'Neal MAS	.50	1.25
❑ 116 Hakeem Olajuwon MAS	.25	.60
❑ 117 Scottie Pippen MAS	.40	1.00
❑ 118 David Robinson MAS	.25	.60
❑ 119 Latrell Sprewell MAS	.25	.60

❑ 120 Chris Webber MAS	.30	.75
❑ 121 Checklist	.05	.15
❑ NNO Hill SkyMotion Exch.	20.00	40.00
❑ NNO Grant Hill David Robinson Promo	1.00	2.50

1995-96 E-XL

❑ COMPLETE SET (100)	20.00	50.00
❑ 1 Stacey Augmon	.15	.40
❑ 2 Mookie Blaylock	.15	.40
❑ 3 Christian Laettner	.30	.75
❑ 4 Dana Barros	.15	.40
❑ 5 Dino Radja	.15	.40
❑ 6 Eric Williams RC	.30	.75
❑ 7 Kenny Anderson	.30	.75
❑ 8 Larry Johnson	.30	.75
❑ 9 Glen Rice	.30	.75
❑ 10 Michael Jordan	3.00	8.00
❑ 11 Toni Kukoc	.30	.75
❑ 12 Scottie Pippen	.75	2.00
❑ 13 Dennis Rodman	.30	.75
❑ 14 Terrell Brandon	.30	.75
❑ 15 Bobby Phills	.15	.40
❑ 16 Bob Sura RC	.30	.75
❑ 17 Jim Jackson	.15	.40
❑ 18 Jason Kidd	1.50	4.00
❑ 19 Jamal Mashburn	.30	.75
❑ 20 Mahmoud Abdul-Rauf	.15	.40
❑ 21 Antonio McDyess RC	1.00	2.50
❑ 22 Dikembe Mutombo	.30	.75
❑ 23 Joe Dumars	.50	1.25
❑ 24 Grant Hill	.60	1.50
❑ 25 Allan Houston	.30	.75
❑ 26 Joe Smith RC	.75	2.00
❑ 27 Latrell Sprewell	.50	1.25
❑ 28 Kevin Willis	.30	.75
❑ 29 Sam Cassell	.50	1.25
❑ 30 Clyde Drexler	.50	1.25
❑ 31 Robert Horry	.30	.75
❑ 32 Hakeem Olajuwon	.50	1.25
❑ 33 Derrick McKey	.15	.40
❑ 34 Reggie Miller	.50	1.25
❑ 35 Rik Smits	.30	.75
❑ 36 Brent Barry RC	.50	1.25
❑ 37 Loy Vaught	.15	.40
❑ 38 Brian Williams	.15	.40
❑ 39 Cedric Ceballos	.15	.40
❑ 40 Magic Johnson	.75	2.00
❑ 41 Nick Van Exel	.50	1.25
❑ 42 Tim Hardaway	.30	.75
❑ 43 Alonzo Mourning	.30	.75
❑ 44 Kurt Thomas RC	.30	.75
❑ 45 Walt Williams	.15	.40
❑ 46 Vin Baker	.30	.75
❑ 47 Shawn Respert RC	.15	.40
❑ 48 Glenn Robinson	.50	1.25
❑ 49 Kevin Garnett RC	3.00	8.00
❑ 50 Tom Gugliotta	.15	.40
❑ 51 Isaiah Rider	.15	.40
❑ 52 Shawn Bradley	.15	.40
❑ 53 Chris Childs	.15	.40
❑ 54 Ed O'Bannon RC	.15	.40
❑ 55 Patrick Ewing	.50	1.25
❑ 56 Anthony Mason	.30	.75
❑ 57 Charles Oakley	.15	.40
❑ 58 Horace Grant	.30	.75
❑ 59 Anfernee Hardaway	.50	1.25
❑ 60 Shaquille O'Neal	1.25	3.00
❑ 61 Derrick Coleman	.15	.40
❑ 62 Jerry Stackhouse RC	1.50	4.00
❑ 63 Clarence Weatherspoon	.15	.40
❑ 64 Charles Barkley	.60	1.50
❑ 65 Michael Finley RC	1.25	3.00
❑ 66 Kevin Johnson	.30	.75
❑ 67 Clifford Robinson	.15	.40
❑ 68 Arvydas Sabonis RC	.60	1.50
❑ 69 Rod Strickland	.15	.40
❑ 70 Tyus Edney RC	.15	.40
❑ 71 Billy Owens	.15	.40
❑ 72 Mitch Richmond	.30	.75
❑ 73 Sean Elliott	.30	.75
❑ 74 Avery Johnson	.15	.40
❑ 75 David Robinson	.50	1.25
❑ 76 Shawn Kemp	.30	.75
❑ 77 Gary Payton	.50	1.25
❑ 78 Detlef Schrempf	.30	.75
❑ 79 Tracy Murray	.15	.40
❑ 80 Damon Stoudamire RC	1.00	2.50
❑ 81 Sharone Wright	.15	.40
❑ 82 Jeff Hornacek	.30	.75
❑ 83 Karl Malone	.60	1.50
❑ 84 John Stockton	.60	1.50
❑ 85 Greg Anthony	.15	.40
❑ 86 Bryant Reeves RC	.50	1.25
❑ 87 Byron Scott	.15	.40
❑ 88 Juwan Howard	.50	1.25
❑ 89 Gheorghe Muresan	.15	.40
❑ 90 Rasheed Wallace RC	1.25	3.00
❑ 91 Steve Smith UNT	.15	.40
❑ 92 Dikembe Mutombo UNT	.15	.40
❑ 93 Brent Barry UNT	.30	.75
❑ 94 Glenn Robinson UNT	.30	.75
❑ 95 Armon Gilliam UNT	.15	.40
❑ 96 Nick Anderson UNT	.15	.40
❑ 97 Gary Trent UNT	.15	.40
❑ 98 Brian Grant UNT	.30	.75
❑ 99 Bryant Reeves UNT	.30	.75
❑ 100 Checklist	.15	.40
❑ NNO Grant Hill Promo	1.00	2.50

2004-05 E-XL

❑ COMP.SET w/o SP's (70)	15.00	40.00
❑ COMMON CARD (1-70)	.25	.60
❑ COMMON ROOKIE (71-94)	2.50	6.00
❑ COMMON ROOKIE (95-107)	1.50	4.00
❑ 1 Dwyane Wade	1.25	3.00
❑ 2 Kobe Bryant	2.00	5.00
❑ 3 Mike Bibby	.30	.75
❑ 4 Michael Finley	.40	1.00
❑ 5 Jamal Mashburn	.30	.75
❑ 6 Carmelo Anthony	1.25	3.00
❑ 7 Jason Kidd	.60	1.50
❑ 8 Andrei Kirilenko	.40	1.00
❑ 9 Ron Artest	.30	.75
❑ 10 Peja Stojakovic	.30	.75
❑ 11 Yao Ming	1.00	2.50
❑ 12 Shawn Marion	.40	1.00
❑ 13 Desmond Mason	.30	.75
❑ 14 Paul Pierce	.40	1.00
❑ 15 Pau Gasol	.40	1.00
❑ 16 Tim Duncan	.75	2.00
❑ 17 Andre Miller	.30	.75
❑ 18 Allan Houston	.30	.75
❑ 19 Ben Wallace	.30	.75
❑ 20 Stephon Marbury	.40	1.00
❑ 21 Gilbert Arenas	.40	1.00
❑ 22 Luke Walton	.30	.75
❑ 23 Rashard Lewis	.40	1.00
❑ 24 Elton Brand	.40	1.00
❑ 25 Zach Randolph	.40	1.00
❑ 26 Eddy Curry	.30	.75
❑ 27 Richard Jefferson	.40	1.00
❑ 28 Kirk Hinrich	.30	.75
❑ 29 Jason Terry	.30	.75
❑ 30 Ray Allen	.40	1.00
❑ 31 Mike Dunleavy	.30	.75
❑ 32 Glenn Robinson	.30	.75
❑ 33 Darko Milicic	.25	.60
❑ 34 Steve Francis	.40	1.00
❑ 35 Antawn Jamison	.40	1.00
❑ 36 Jason Williams	.30	.75
❑ 37 Tracy McGrady	.75	2.00
❑ 38 Steve Nash	.60	1.50
❑ 39 Gary Payton	.40	1.00
❑ 40 Sam Cassell	.30	.75
❑ 41 Gerald Wallace	.40	1.00
❑ 42 Shaquille O'Neal	1.00	2.50
❑ 43 Tony Parker	.40	1.00
❑ 44 Richard Hamilton	.30	.75
❑ 45 Kenyon Martin	.40	1.00
❑ 46 Baron Davis	.40	1.00
❑ 47 Jarvis Hayes	.25	.60
❑ 48 Chris Kaman	.30	.75
❑ 49 Manu Ginobili	.40	1.00
❑ 50 Jermaine O'Neal	.40	1.00
❑ 51 Amare Stoudemire	.75	2.00
❑ 52 Latrell Sprewell	.30	.75
❑ 53 LeBron James	2.50	6.00
❑ 54 Michael Redd	.40	1.00
❑ 55 Chris Bosh	.40	1.00
❑ 56 Juwan Howard	.30	.75
❑ 57 Jason Richardson	.40	1.00
❑ 58 Allen Iverson	.75	2.00
❑ 59 Antoine Walker	.40	1.00
❑ 60 Eddie Jones	.30	.75
❑ 61 Carlos Arroyo	.40	1.00
❑ 62 Lamar Odom	.40	1.00
❑ 63 Chris Webber	.40	1.00
❑ 64 Drew Gooden	.25	.60
❑ 65 Jamaal Magloire	.25	.60
❑ 66 Dirk Nowitzki	.60	1.50
❑ 67 Kevin Garnett	.75	2.00
❑ 68 Vince Carter	.75	2.00
❑ 69 Reggie Miller	.40	1.00
❑ 70 Shareef Abdur-Rahim	.30	.75
❑ 71 Emeka Okafor RC	5.00	12.00
❑ 72 Pavel Podkolzine RC	2.50	6.00
❑ 73 Kirk Snyder RC	2.50	6.00
❑ 74 Ben Gordon RC	3.00	8.00
❑ 75 Devin Harris RC	5.00	12.00
❑ 76 Josh Childress RC	2.50	6.00
❑ 77 Dorell Wright RC	3.00	8.00
❑ 78 Dwight Howard RC	8.00	20.00
❑ 79 Andre Iguodala RC	6.00	15.00
❑ 80 Viktor Khryapa RC	2.50	6.00
❑ 81 Al Jefferson RC	5.00	12.00
❑ 82 Kevin Martin RC	3.00	8.00
❑ 83 Delonte West RC	4.00	10.00
❑ 84 Josh Smith RC	6.00	15.00
❑ 85 Luol Deng RC	3.00	8.00
❑ 86 Kris Humphries RC	4.00	10.00
❑ 87 Sebastian Telfair RC	2.50	6.00
❑ 88 Rafael Araujo RC	2.50	6.00
❑ 89 Jameer Nelson RC	3.00	8.00
❑ 90 Shaun Livingston RC	2.50	6.00
❑ 91 Andris Biedrins RC	4.00	10.00
❑ 92 Robert Swift RC	2.50	6.00
❑ 93 Luke Jackson RC	2.50	6.00
❑ 94 J.R. Smith RC	5.00	12.00
❑ 95 Tony Allen RC	2.00	5.00
❑ 96 Sasha Vujacic RC	1.50	4.00
❑ 97 David Harrison RC	1.50	4.00
❑ 98 Anderson Varejao RC	2.00	5.00
❑ 99 Jackson Vroman RC	1.50	4.00
❑ 100 Peter John Ramos RC	1.50	4.00
❑ 101 Lionel Chalmers RC	1.50	4.00
❑ 102 Donta Smith RC	1.50	4.00
❑ 103 Andre Emmett RC	1.50	4.00
❑ 104 Trevor Ariza RC	2.00	5.00
❑ 105 Tim Pickett RC	1.50	4.00
❑ 106 Bernard Robinson RC	1.50	4.00
❑ 107 Matt Freije RC	1.50	4.00

1996-97 E-X2000

❑ COMPLETE SET (82)	60.00	120.00
❑ COMMON CARD (1-82)	.25	.60
❑ COMMON ROOKIE	.75	2.00
❑ 1 Christian Laettner	.60	1.50

❑ 2 Dikembe Mutombo	.60	1.50
❑ 3 Steve Smith	.60	1.50
❑ 4 Antoine Walker RC	2.50	6.00
❑ 5 David Wesley	.25	.60
❑ 6 Tony Delk RC	.75	2.00
❑ 7 Anthony Mason	.60	1.50
❑ 8 Glen Rice	.60	1.50
❑ 9 Michael Jordan	7.50	15.00
❑ 10 Scottie Pippen	1.25	3.00
❑ 11 Dennis Rodman	.60	1.50
❑ 12 Terrell Brandon	.60	1.50
❑ 13 Chris Mills	.25	.60
❑ 14 Shawn Bradley	.25	.60
❑ 15 Michael Finley	1.00	2.50
❑ 16 Dale Ellis	.25	.60
❑ 17 Antonio McDyess	.60	1.50
❑ 18 Joe Dumars	.75	2.00
❑ 19 Grant Hill	.75	2.00
❑ 20 Chris Mullin	.75	2.00
❑ 21 Joe Smith	.60	1.50
❑ 22 Latrell Sprewell	.75	2.00
❑ 23 Charles Barkley	1.00	2.50
❑ 24 Clyde Drexler	.75	2.00
❑ 25 Hakeem Olajuwon	.75	2.00
❑ 26 Erick Dampier RC	1.00	2.50
❑ 27 Reggie Miller	.75	2.00
❑ 28 Loy Vaught	.25	.60
❑ 29 Lorenzen Wright RC	.75	2.00
❑ 30 Kobe Bryant RC	30.00	60.00
❑ 31 Eddie Jones	.75	2.00
❑ 32 Shaquille O'Neal	2.00	5.00
❑ 33 Nick Van Exel	.75	2.00
❑ 34 Tim Hardaway	.60	1.50
❑ 35 Jamal Mashburn	.60	1.50
❑ 36 Alonzo Mourning	.60	1.50
❑ 37 Ray Allen RC	4.00	10.00
❑ 38 Vin Baker	.60	1.50
❑ 39 Glenn Robinson	.75	2.00
❑ 40 Kevin Garnett	1.50	4.00
❑ 41 Tom Gugliotta	.25	.60
❑ 42 Stephon Marbury RC	2.50	6.00
❑ 43 Kendall Gill	.25	.60
❑ 44 Jim Jackson	.25	.60
❑ 45 Kerry Kittles RC	1.00	2.50
❑ 46 Patrick Ewing	.75	2.00
❑ 47 Larry Johnson	.60	1.50
❑ 48 John Wallace RC	.75	2.00
❑ 49 Nick Anderson	.25	.60
❑ 50 Horace Grant	.60	1.50
❑ 51 Anfernee Hardaway	.75	2.00
❑ 52 Derrick Coleman	.60	1.50
❑ 53 Allen Iverson RC	6.00	15.00
❑ 54 Jerry Stackhouse	1.25	3.00
❑ 55 Cedric Ceballos	.25	.60
❑ 56 Kevin Johnson	.60	1.50
❑ 57 Jason Kidd	1.25	3.00
❑ 58 Clifford Robinson	.25	.60
❑ 59 Arvydas Sabonis	.60	1.50
❑ 60 Rasheed Wallace	1.00	2.50
❑ 61 Mahmoud Abdul-Rauf	.25	.60
❑ 62 Brian Grant	.75	2.00
❑ 63 Mitch Richmond	.60	1.50
❑ 64 Sean Elliott	.60	1.50
❑ 65 David Robinson	.75	2.00
❑ 66 Dominique Wilkins	.75	2.00
❑ 67 Shawn Kemp	.60	1.50
❑ 68 Gary Payton	.75	2.00
❑ 69 Detlef Schrempf	.60	1.50
❑ 70 Marcus Camby RC	1.50	4.00
❑ 71 Damon Stoudamire	.75	2.00
❑ 72 Walt Williams	.25	.60
❑ 73 Shandon Anderson RC	1.00	2.50
❑ 74 Karl Malone	.75	2.00
❑ 75 John Stockton	.75	2.00
❑ 76 Shareef Abdur-Rahim RC	4.00	10.00
❑ 77 Bryant Reeves	.25	.60
❑ 78 Roy Rogers RC	.75	2.00
❑ 79 Juwan Howard	.60	1.50
❑ 80 Chris Webber	.75	2.00
❑ 81 Checklist	.25	.60
❑ 82 Checklist	.25	.60
❑ NNO Grant Hill Blow-Up/3000	6.00	15.00
❑ NNO G.Hill Emerald AU	100.00	200.00
❑ NNO Grant Hill Promo	1.00	2.50

1997-98 E-X2001

❑ COMPLETE SET (82)	25.00	60.00
❑ COMMON CARD (1-61)	.15	.40
❑ COMMON ROOKIE (62-80)	.30	.75
❑ 1 Grant Hill	.50	1.25
❑ 2 Kevin Garnett	1.00	2.50
❑ 3 Allen Iverson	1.25	3.00
❑ 4 Anfernee Hardaway	.50	1.25
❑ 5 Dennis Rodman	.30	.75
❑ 6 Shawn Kemp	.30	.75
❑ 7 Shaquille O'Neal	1.25	3.00
❑ 8 Kobe Bryant	2.50	6.00
❑ 9 Michael Jordan	3.00	8.00
❑ 10 Marcus Camby	.50	1.25
❑ 11 Scottie Pippen	.75	2.00
❑ 12 Antoine Walker	.60	1.50
❑ 13 Stephon Marbury	.60	1.50
❑ 14 Shareef Abdur-Rahim	.75	2.00
❑ 15 Jerry Stackhouse	.50	1.25
❑ 16 Eddie Jones	.50	1.25
❑ 17 Charles Barkley	.60	1.50
❑ 18 David Robinson	.50	1.25
❑ 19 Karl Malone	.50	1.25
❑ 20 Damon Stoudamire	.30	.75
❑ 21 Patrick Ewing	.50	1.25
❑ 22 Kerry Kittles	.50	1.25
❑ 23 Gary Payton	.50	1.25
❑ 24 Glenn Robinson	.50	1.25
❑ 25 Hakeem Olajuwon	.50	1.25
❑ 26 John Starks	.30	.75
❑ 27 John Stockton	.50	1.25
❑ 28 Vin Baker	.30	.75
❑ 29 Reggie Miller	.50	1.25
❑ 30 Clyde Drexler	.50	1.25
❑ 31 Alonzo Mourning	.30	.75
❑ 32 Juwan Howard	.30	.75
❑ 33 Ray Allen	.50	1.25
❑ 34 Christian Laettner	.30	.75
❑ 35 Terrell Brandon	.30	.75
❑ 36 Sean Elliott	.30	.75
❑ 37 Rod Strickland	.15	.40
❑ 38 Rodney Rogers	.15	.40
❑ 39 Donyell Marshall	.30	.75
❑ 40 David Wesley	.15	.40
❑ 41 Sam Cassell	.50	1.25
❑ 42 Cedric Ceballos	.15	.40
❑ 43 Mahmoud Abdul-Rauf	.15	.40
❑ 44 Rik Smits	.30	.75
❑ 45 Lindsey Hunter	.15	.40
❑ 46 Michael Finley	.50	1.25
❑ 47 Steve Smith	.30	.75
❑ 48 Larry Johnson	.30	.75
❑ 49 Dikembe Mutombo	.30	.75
❑ 50 Tom Gugliotta	.30	.75
❑ 51 Joe Dumars	.50	1.25
❑ 52 Glen Rice	.30	.75
❑ 53 Bryant Reeves	.15	.40
❑ 54 Tim Hardaway	.30	.75
❑ 55 Isaiah Rider	.30	.75
❑ 56 Rasheed Wallace	.50	1.25
❑ 57 Jason Kidd	.75	2.00
❑ 58 Joe Smith	.30	.75
❑ 59 Chris Webber	.50	1.25
❑ 60 Mitch Richmond	.30	.75
❑ 61 Antonio McDyess	.30	.75
❑ 62 Bobby Jackson RC	1.00	2.50
❑ 63 Derek Anderson RC	1.25	3.00
❑ 64 Kelvin Cato RC	.50	1.25
❑ 65 Jacque Vaughn RC	.40	1.00
❑ 66 Tariq Abdul-Wahad RC	.40	1.00
❑ 67 Johnny Taylor RC	.30	.75
❑ 68 Chris Anstey RC	.30	.75
❑ 69 Maurice Taylor RC	.75	2.00
❑ 70 Antonio Daniels RC	.50	1.25
❑ 71 Chauncey Billups RC	3.00	8.00
❑ 72 Austin Croshere RC	.75	2.00
❑ 73 Brevin Knight RC	.50	1.25
❑ 74 Keith Van Horn RC	1.25	3.00
❑ 75 Tim Duncan RC	3.00	8.00
❑ 76 Danny Fortson RC	.60	1.50
❑ 77 Tim Thomas RC	1.50	4.00
❑ 78 Tony Battie RC	.50	1.25
❑ 79 Tracy McGrady RC	2.50	6.00
❑ 80 Ron Mercer RC	1.00	2.50
❑ 81 Checklist (1-82)	.15	.40
❑ 82 Checklist (inserts)	.15	.40
❑ S1 Grant Hill SAMPLE	1.25	3.00

1998-99 E-X Century

❑ COMPLETE SET (1-90)	40.00	100.00
❑ COMMON CARD (1-60)	.10	.30
❑ COMMON ROOKIE (61-90)	.30	.75
❑ 1 Keith Van Horn	.40	1.00
❑ 2 Scottie Pippen	.60	1.50
❑ 3 Tim Thomas	.25	.60
❑ 4 Stephon Marbury	.40	1.00
❑ 5 Allen Iverson	.75	2.00
❑ 6 Grant Hill	.40	1.00
❑ 7 Tim Duncan	.60	1.50
❑ 8 Latrell Sprewell	.40	1.00
❑ 9 Ron Mercer	.20	.50
❑ 10 Kobe Bryant	1.50	4.00
❑ 11 Antoine Walker	.40	1.00
❑ 12 Reggie Miller	.40	1.00
❑ 13 Kevin Garnett	.75	2.00
❑ 14 Shaquille O'Neal	1.00	2.50
❑ 15 Karl Malone	.40	1.00
❑ 16 Dennis Rodman	.25	.60
❑ 17 Tracy McGrady	1.00	2.50
❑ 18 Anfernee Hardaway	.40	1.00
❑ 19 Shareef Abdur-Rahim	.40	1.00
❑ 20 Marcus Camby	.25	.60
❑ 21 Eddie Jones	.40	1.00
❑ 22 Vin Baker	.25	.60
❑ 23 Charles Barkley	.50	1.25
❑ 24 Patrick Ewing	.40	1.00
❑ 25 Jason Kidd	.60	1.50
❑ 26 Mitch Richmond	.25	.60
❑ 27 Tim Hardaway	.25	.60
❑ 28 Glen Rice	.25	.60
❑ 29 Shawn Kemp	.25	.60
❑ 30 John Stockton	.40	1.00
❑ 31 Ray Allen	.40	1.00
❑ 32 Brevin Knight	.10	.30
❑ 33 David Robinson	.40	1.00
❑ 34 Juwan Howard	.25	.60
❑ 35 Alonzo Mourning	.25	.60
❑ 36 Hakeem Olajuwon	.40	1.00
❑ 37 Gary Payton	.40	1.00
❑ 38 Damon Stoudamire	.25	.60
❑ 39 Steve Smith	.25	.60
❑ 40 Chris Webber	.40	1.00
❑ 41 Michael Finley	.40	1.00
❑ 42 Jayson Williams	.10	.30
❑ 43 Maurice Taylor	.20	.50
❑ 44 Jalen Rose	.40	1.00
❑ 45 Sam Cassell	.40	1.00
❑ 46 Jerry Stackhouse	.40	1.00
❑ 47 Toni Kukoc	.25	.60
❑ 48 Charles Oakley	.10	.30
❑ 49 Jim Jackson	.10	.30
❑ 50 Dikembe Mutombo	.25	.60
❑ 51 Wesley Person	.10	.30
❑ 52 Antonio Daniels	.10	.30
❑ 53 Isaiah Rider	.10	.30
❑ 54 Tom Gugliotta	.10	.30
❑ 55 Antonio McDyess	.25	.60
❑ 56 Jeff Hornacek	.25	.60
❑ 57 Joe Dumars	.40	1.00
❑ 58 Jamal Mashburn	.25	.60
❑ 59 Donyell Marshall	.25	.60
❑ 60 Glenn Robinson	.25	.60
❑ 61 Jelani McCoy RC	.30	.75
❑ 62 Peja Stojakovic RC	2.50	6.00

❑ 63 Randell Jackson RC .30 .75
❑ 64 Brad Miller RC 3.00 8.00
❑ 65 Corey Benjamin RC .60 1.50
❑ 66 Toby Bailey RC .30 .75
❑ 67 Nazr Mohammed RC .40 1.00
❑ 68 Dirk Nowitzki RC 6.00 15.00
❑ 69 Andrae Patterson RC .30 .75
❑ 70 Michael Dickerson RC 1.25 3.00
❑ 71 Cory Carr RC .30 .75
❑ 72 Brian Skinner RC .60 1.50
❑ 73 Pat Garrity RC .40 1.00
❑ 74 Ricky Davis RC 2.00 5.00
❑ 75 Roshown McLeod RC .40 1.00
❑ 76 Matt Harpring RC 1.00 2.50
❑ 77 Jason Williams RC 2.50 6.00
❑ 78 Keon Clark RC 1.00 2.50
❑ 79 Al Harrington RC 1.50 4.00
❑ 80 Felipe Lopez RC .75 2.00
❑ 81 Michael Doleac RC .60 1.50
❑ 82 Paul Pierce RC 5.00 12.00
❑ 83 Robert Traylor RC .60 1.50
❑ 84 Raef LaFrentz RC 1.00 2.50
❑ 85 Michael Olowokandi RC 1.00 2.50
❑ 86 Mike Bibby RC 2.00 5.00
❑ 87 Antawn Jamison RC 3.00 8.00
❑ 88 Bonzi Wells RC 2.50 6.00
❑ 89 Vince Carter RC 20.00 40.00
❑ 90 Larry Hughes RC 2.00 5.00

1999-00 E-X

❑ COMPLETE SET (90) 60.00 120.00
❑ COMPLETE SET w/o RC (60) 15.00 30.00
❑ COMMON CARD (1-60) .25 .60
❑ COMMON ROOKIE (61-90) .75 2.00
❑ 1 Stephon Marbury .40 1.00
❑ 2 Antawn Jamison .40 1.00
❑ 3 Patrick Ewing .50 1.25
❑ 4 Nick Anderson .25 .60
❑ 5 Charles Barkley .50 1.25
❑ 6 Marcus Camby .30 .75
❑ 7 Ron Mercer .25 .60
❑ 8 Avery Johnson .30 .75
❑ 9 Maurice Taylor .30 .75
❑ 10 Isaiah Rider .25 .60
❑ 11 Dirk Nowitzki .60 1.50
❑ 12 Damon Stoudamire .40 1.00
❑ 13 Alonzo Mourning .40 1.00
❑ 14 Jason Kidd .60 1.50
❑ 15 Juwan Howard .30 .75
❑ 16 Vince Carter .75 2.00
❑ 17 Tim Duncan .75 2.00
❑ 18 Paul Pierce .40 1.00
❑ 19 Tim Hardaway .40 1.00
❑ 20 Grant Hill .40 1.00
❑ 21 Keith Van Horn .30 .75
❑ 22 Shaquille O'Neal 1.00 2.50
❑ 23 Jason Williams .40 1.00
❑ 24 Shareef Abdur-Rahim .30 .75
❑ 25 Kobe Bryant 2.00 5.00
❑ 26 David Robinson .50 1.25
❑ 27 Anfernee Hardaway .40 1.00
❑ 28 Vin Baker .40 1.00
❑ 29 Hakeem Olajuwon .40 1.00
❑ 30 Michael Olowokandi .25 .60
❑ 31 Mike Bibby .40 1.00
❑ 32 Tracy McGrady .75 2.00
❑ 33 Antoine Walker .40 1.00
❑ 34 Larry Hughes .30 .75
❑ 35 Chris Webber .40 1.00
❑ 36 Ray Allen .40 1.00
❑ 37 Danny Fortson .25 .60
❑ 38 Shawn Kemp .40 1.00
❑ 39 Michael Doleac .25 .60
❑ 40 Gary Payton .40 1.00
❑ 41 Toni Kukoc .40 1.00
❑ 42 Kevin Garnett .75 2.00
❑ 43 Steve Smith .25 .60
❑ 44 Scottie Pippen .60 1.50
❑ 45 Allen Iverson .75 2.00
❑ 46 Latrell Sprewell .30 .75
❑ 47 Matt Harpring .30 .75
❑ 48 Lindsey Hunter .25 .60
❑ 49 Karl Malone .50 1.25
❑ 50 Michael Finley .40 1.00
❑ 51 Jerry Stackhouse .40 1.00
❑ 52 Cedric Ceballos .25 .60
❑ 53 Brent Barry .30 .75
❑ 54 Elden Campbell .25 .60
❑ 55 Glenn Robinson .30 .75
❑ 56 Eddie Jones .40 1.00
❑ 57 Reggie Miller .40 1.00
❑ 58 Mitch Richmond .30 .75
❑ 59 Raef LaFrentz .30 .75
❑ 60 John Starks .40 1.00
❑ 61 Elton Brand RC 2.50 6.00
❑ 62 William Avery RC .75 2.00
❑ 63 Cal Bowdler RC .75 2.00
❑ 64 Dion Glover RC .75 2.00
❑ 65 Lamar Odom RC 2.50 6.00
❑ 66 Richard Hamilton RC 2.50 6.00
❑ 67 Kenny Thomas RC .75 2.00
❑ 68 Shawn Marion RC 2.50 6.00
❑ 69 Baron Davis RC 3.00 8.00
❑ 70 Wally Szczerbiak RC 2.50 6.00
❑ 71 Scott Padgett RC .75 2.00
❑ 72 Jason Terry RC 2.00 5.00
❑ 73 Trajan Langdon RC .75 2.00
❑ 74 Andre Miller RC 2.50 6.00
❑ 75 Jeff Foster RC 1.00 2.50
❑ 76 Tim James RC .75 2.00
❑ 77 A.Radojevic RC .75 2.00
❑ 78 Quincy Lewis RC .75 2.00
❑ 79 James Posey RC 1.25 3.00
❑ 80 Steve Francis RC 2.50 6.00
❑ 81 Jonathan Bender RC .75 2.00
❑ 82 Corey Maggette RC 2.50 6.00
❑ 83 Obinna Ekezie RC .75 2.00
❑ 84 Laron Profit RC .75 2.00
❑ 85 Devean George RC 1.25 3.00
❑ 86 Ron Artest RC 3.00 8.00
❑ 87 Rafer Alston RC 1.50 4.00
❑ 88 Vonteego Cummings RC .75 2.00
❑ 89 Evan Eschmeyer RC .75 2.00
❑ 90 Jumaine Jones RC .75 2.00
❑ S16 Vince Carter PROMO 1.00 2.50

2000-01 E-X

❑ COMPLETE SET w/o RC (100) 20.00 40.00
❑ COMMON CARD (1-100) .25 .60
❑ COMMON ROOKIE (101-130) 1.50 4.00
❑ 1 Dikembe Mutombo .30 .75
❑ 2 Jim Jackson .25 .60
❑ 3 Jason Terry .40 1.00
❑ 4 Kenny Anderson .30 .75
❑ 5 Antoine Walker .30 .75
❑ 6 Paul Pierce .40 1.00
❑ 7 Jamal Mashburn .30 .75
❑ 8 Baron Davis .40 1.00
❑ 9 Derrick Coleman .30 .75
❑ 10 Elton Brand .40 1.00
❑ 11 Ron Artest .40 1.00
❑ 12 Andre Miller .30 .75
❑ 13 Brevin Knight .25 .60
❑ 14 Trajan Langdon .25 .60
❑ 15 Lamond Murray .25 .60
❑ 16 Dirk Nowitzki .60 1.50
❑ 17 Michael Finley .40 1.00
❑ 18 Nick Van Exel .30 .75
❑ 19 Antonio McDyess .30 .75
❑ 20 Raef LaFrentz .25 .60
❑ 21 Tariq Abdul-Wahad .25 .60
❑ 22 Cedric Ceballos .25 .60
❑ 23 Jerry Stackhouse .30 .75
❑ 24 Jerome Williams .25 .60
❑ 25 Larry Hughes .30 .75
❑ 26 Antawn Jamison .40 1.00
❑ 27 Mookie Blaylock .30 .75
❑ 28 Steve Francis .40 1.00
❑ 29 Hakeem Olajuwon .50 1.25
❑ 30 Maurice Taylor .25 .60
❑ 31 Jonathan Bender .25 .60
❑ 32 Reggie Miller .40 1.00
❑ 33 Austin Croshere .25 .60
❑ 34 Travis Best .25 .60
❑ 35 Jalen Rose .30 .75
❑ 36 Lamar Odom .40 1.00
❑ 37 Corey Maggette .30 .75
❑ 38 Shaquille O'Neal 1.00 2.50
❑ 39 Kobe Bryant 2.00 5.00
❑ 40 Horace Grant .30 .75
❑ 41 Isaiah Rider .30 .75
❑ 42 Brian Grant .25 .60
❑ 43 Eddie Jones .30 .75
❑ 44 Tim Hardaway .30 .75
❑ 45 Anthony Mason .25 .60
❑ 46 Glenn Robinson .30 .75
❑ 47 Ray Allen .40 1.00
❑ 48 Sam Cassell .30 .75
❑ 49 Tim Thomas .25 .60
❑ 50 Kevin Garnett .75 2.00
❑ 51 Terrell Brandon .25 .60
❑ 52 Joe Smith .25 .60
❑ 53 Wally Szczerbiak .30 .75
❑ 54 Chauncey Billups .40 1.00
❑ 55 Stephon Marbury .40 1.00
❑ 56 Keith Van Horn .30 .75
❑ 57 Kerry Kittles .30 .75
❑ 58 Allan Houston .30 .75
❑ 59 Latrell Sprewell .30 .75
❑ 60 Larry Johnson .30 .75
❑ 61 Glen Rice .30 .75
❑ 62 Grant Hill .40 1.00
❑ 63 Tracy McGrady .75 2.00
❑ 64 Darrell Armstrong .25 .60
❑ 65 Allen Iverson .75 2.00
❑ 66 Toni Kukoc .30 .75
❑ 67 Theo Ratliff .25 .60
❑ 68 Jason Kidd .60 1.50
❑ 69 Anfernee Hardaway .40 1.00
❑ 70 Tom Gugliotta .25 .60
❑ 71 Clifford Robinson .25 .60
❑ 72 Shawn Kemp .40 1.00
❑ 73 Scottie Pippen .60 1.50
❑ 74 Rasheed Wallace .40 1.00
❑ 75 Steve Smith .30 .75
❑ 76 Chris Webber .40 1.00
❑ 77 Jason Williams .30 .75
❑ 78 Peja Stojakovic .30 .75
❑ 79 Tim Duncan .75 2.00
❑ 80 David Robinson .50 1.25
❑ 81 Sean Elliott .30 .75
❑ 82 Derek Anderson .30 .75
❑ 83 Vin Baker .30 .75
❑ 84 Rashard Lewis .40 1.00
❑ 85 Gary Payton .40 1.00
❑ 86 Patrick Ewing .50 1.25
❑ 87 Vince Carter .75 2.00
❑ 88 Mark Jackson .30 .75
❑ 89 Antonio Davis .25 .60
❑ 90 Karl Malone .50 1.25
❑ 91 John Stockton .50 1.25
❑ 92 Bryon Russell .25 .60
❑ 93 Donyell Marshall .25 .60
❑ 94 Shareef Abdur-Rahim .30 .75
❑ 95 Mike Bibby .30 .75
❑ 96 Michael Dickerson .25 .60
❑ 97 Mitch Richmond .30 .75
❑ 98 Juwan Howard .30 .75
❑ 99 Richard Hamilton .30 .75
❑ 100 Rod Strickland .30 .75
❑ 101 DerMarr Johnson RC 1.50 4.00
❑ 102 Kenyon Martin RC 4.00 10.00
❑ 103 Marcus Fizer RC 1.50 4.00
❑ 104 Courtney Alexander RC 1.50 4.00
❑ 105 Stromile Swift RC 2.00 5.00
❑ 106 Darius Miles RC 2.00 5.00
❑ 107 Mike Miller RC 2.50 6.00
❑ 108 Jamal Crawford RC 2.50 6.00
❑ 109 Speedy Claxton RC 1.50 4.00
❑ 110 Quentin Richardson RC 2.00 5.00
❑ 111 Keyon Dooling RC 1.50 4.00

❑ 112 Desmond Mason RC	2.00	5.00
❑ 113 Mateen Cleaves RC	1.50	4.00
❑ 114 Morris Peterson RC	2.50	6.00
❑ 115 Hedo Turkoglu RC	4.00	10.00
❑ 116 Donnell Harvey RC	1.50	4.00
❑ 117 Jerome Moiso RC	1.50	4.00
❑ 118 Jason Collier RC	1.50	4.00
❑ 119 Jamaal Magloire RC	1.50	4.00
❑ 120 Erick Barkley RC	1.50	4.00
❑ 121 Etan Thomas RC	1.50	4.00
❑ 122 DeShawn Stevenson RC	1.50	4.00
❑ 123 Dan Langhi RC	1.50	4.00
❑ 124 Mark Madsen RC	1.50	4.00
❑ 125 Khalid El-Amin RC	1.50	4.00
❑ 126 Lavor Postell RC	1.50	4.00
❑ 127 Eddie House RC	1.50	4.00
❑ 128 Michael Redd RC	4.00	10.00
❑ 129 Chris Porter RC	1.50	4.00
❑ 130 Mike Smith RC	1.50	4.00

2001-02 E-X

❑ COMPLETE SET (130)	200.00	500.00
❑ COMP.SET w/o SP's (100)	25.00	50.00
❑ COMMON CARD (1-100)	.25	.60
❑ COMMON ROOKIE (101-130)	1.00	2.50
❑ 1 Shareef Abdur-Rahim	.30	.75
❑ 2 DerMarr Johnson	.25	.60
❑ 3 Jason Terry	.40	1.00
❑ 4 Paul Pierce	.40	1.00
❑ 5 Antoine Walker	.30	.75
❑ 6 Baron Davis	.40	1.00
❑ 7 Jamal Mashburn	.30	.75
❑ 8 Chris Mihm	.25	.60
❑ 9 Andre Miller	.30	.75
❑ 10 Dirk Nowitzki	.60	1.50
❑ 11 Michael Finley	.40	1.00
❑ 12 Raef LaFrentz	.25	.60
❑ 13 Antonio McDyess	.30	.75
❑ 14 Jerry Stackhouse	.30	.75
❑ 15 Antawn Jamison	.40	1.00
❑ 16 Steve Francis	.40	1.00
❑ 17 Jalen Rose	.30	.75
❑ 18 Elton Brand	.40	1.00
❑ 19 Darius Miles	.25	.60
❑ 20 Lamar Odom	.40	1.00
❑ 21 Mitch Richmond	.30	.75
❑ 22 Michael Dickerson	.25	.60
❑ 23 Stromile Swift	.25	.60
❑ 24 Alonzo Mourning	.40	1.00
❑ 25 Courtney Alexander	.25	.60
❑ 26 Ray Allen	.40	1.00
❑ 27 Glenn Robinson	.30	.75
❑ 28 Terrell Brandon	.25	.60
❑ 29 Wally Szczerbiak	.30	.75
❑ 30 Joe Smith	.25	.60
❑ 31 Jason Kidd	.60	1.50
❑ 32 Kenyon Martin	.40	1.00
❑ 33 Keith Van Horn	.30	.75
❑ 34 Grant Hill	.40	1.00
❑ 35 Tracy McGrady	.75	2.00
❑ 36 Mike Miller	.30	.75
❑ 37 Allen Iverson	.75	2.00
❑ 38 Speedy Claxton	.25	.60
❑ 39 Dikembe Mutombo	.30	.75
❑ 40 Tom Gugliotta	.25	.60
❑ 41 Penny Hardaway	.40	1.00
❑ 42 Stephon Marbury	.40	1.00
❑ 43 Shawn Marion	.40	1.00
❑ 44 Rasheed Wallace	.40	1.00
❑ 45 Peja Stojakovic	.30	.75
❑ 46 Mike Bibby	.30	.75
❑ 47 Chris Webber	.40	1.00
❑ 48 David Robinson	.50	1.25
❑ 49 Vin Baker	.30	.75
❑ 50 Rashard Lewis	.40	1.00
❑ 51 Desmond Mason	.30	.75
❑ 52 Gary Payton	.40	1.00
❑ 53 Vince Carter	.75	2.00
❑ 54 Antonio Davis	.25	.60
❑ 55 Hakeem Olajuwon	.50	1.25
❑ 56 Morris Peterson	.30	.75
❑ 57 Karl Malone	.50	1.25
❑ 58 DeShawn Stevenson	.25	.60
❑ 59 John Stockton	.50	1.25
❑ 60 Richard Hamilton	.30	.75
❑ 61 Corey Maggette	.30	.75
❑ 62 Steve Smith	.30	.75
❑ 63 Tim Thomas	.25	.60
❑ 64 Lindsey Hunter	.25	.60
❑ 65 Jermaine O'Neal	.40	1.00
❑ 66 Cuttino Mobley	.30	.75
❑ 67 Nick Van Exel	.30	.75
❑ 68 Juwan Howard	.30	.75
❑ 69 James Posey	.25	.60
❑ 70 David Wesley	.25	.60
❑ 71 Marcus Fizer	.25	.60
❑ 72 Jumaine Jones	.25	.60
❑ 73 Tim Hardaway	.30	.75
❑ 74 Danny Fortson	.25	.60
❑ 75 Jonathan Bender	.25	.60
❑ 76 Quentin Richardson	.30	.75
❑ 77 Eddie House	.25	.60
❑ 78 Kurt Thomas	.25	.60
❑ 79 Anthony Mason	.25	.60
❑ 80 Theo Ratliff	.25	.60
❑ 81 Allan Houston	.30	.75
❑ 82 Latrell Sprewell	.30	.75
❑ 83 Jason Williams	.30	.75
❑ 84 Eddie Jones	.30	.75
❑ 85 Damon Stoudamire	.30	.75
❑ 86 Sam Cassell	.30	.75
❑ 87 Cliff Robinson	.30	.75
❑ 88 Patrick Ewing	.50	1.25
❑ 89 Tim Duncan	.75	2.00
❑ 90 Marcus Camby	.30	.75
❑ 91 Brian Grant	.25	.60
❑ 92 Kobe Bryant	2.00	5.00
❑ 93 Ron Mercer	.25	.60
❑ 94 Reggie Miller	.40	1.00
❑ 95 Shaquille O'Neal	1.00	2.50
❑ 96 Kevin Garnett	.75	2.00
❑ 97 Scottie Pippen	.60	1.50
❑ 98 Michael Jordan	6.00	15.00
❑ 99 Steve Nash	.60	1.50
❑ 100 Derek Anderson	.30	.75
❑ 101 Kedrick Brown/1750 RC	1.00	2.50
❑ 102 Joseph Forte/1750 RC	1.00	2.50
❑ 103 Joe Johnson/1250 RC	3.00	8.00
❑ 104 Kirk Haston/1750 RC	1.00	2.50
❑ 105 Tyson Chandler/750 RC	4.00	10.00
❑ 106 Eddy Curry/1250 RC	2.00	5.00
❑ 107 D.Diop/1750 RC	1.00	2.50
❑ 108 T.Hassell/1250 RC	1.50	4.00
❑ 109 Z.Rebraca/1250 RC	1.25	3.00
❑ 110 Rodney White/1750 RC	1.00	2.50
❑ 111 Troy Murphy/1250 RC	2.50	6.00
❑ 112 J.Richardson/750 RC	4.00	10.00
❑ 113 Eddie Griffin/750 RC	2.00	5.00
❑ 114 Terence Morris/1750 RC	1.00	2.50
❑ 115 Oscar Torres/1250 RC	1.25	3.00
❑ 116 Jamaal Tinsley/750 RC	2.50	6.00
❑ 117 Pau Gasol/750 RC	8.00	20.00
❑ 118 Shane Battier/750 RC	3.00	8.00
❑ 119 B.Armstrong/1250 RC	1.25	3.00
❑ 120 R.Jefferson/750 RC	5.00	12.00
❑ 121 Steven Hunter/1250 RC	1.25	3.00
❑ 122 S.Dalembert/1750 RC	1.25	3.00
❑ 123 Z.Randolph/1250 RC	3.00	8.00
❑ 124 G.Wallace/1750 RC	2.50	6.00
❑ 125 Tony Parker/750 RC	8.00	20.00
❑ 126 V.Radmanovic/1250 RC	1.50	4.00
❑ 127 Michael Bradley/1750 RC	1.00	2.50
❑ 128 Jarron Collins/1750 RC	1.00	2.50
❑ 129 Andrei Kirilenko/750 RC	5.00	12.00
❑ 130 Kwame Brown/750 RC	2.50	6.00

2003-04 E-X

❑ COMP.SET w/o SP's (72)	20.00	50.00
❑ COMMON CARD (1-72)	.25	.60
❑ COMMON ROOKIE (73-102)	3.00	8.00
❑ 1 Shareef Abdur-Rahim	.30	.75
❑ 2 Ray Allen	.25	.60
❑ 3 Gilbert Arenas	.40	1.00
❑ 4 Ron Artest	.30	.75
❑ 5 Mike Bibby	.30	.75
❑ 6 Chauncey Billups	.40	1.00

❑ 7 Elton Brand	.40	1.00
❑ 8 Kwame Brown	.25	.60
❑ 9 Kobe Bryant	2.00	5.00
❑ 10 Caron Butler	.30	.75
❑ 11 Vince Carter	.75	2.00
❑ 12 Eddy Curry	.30	.75
❑ 13 Ricky Davis	.30	.75
❑ 14 Baron Davis	.40	1.00
❑ 15 Tim Duncan	.75	2.00
❑ 16 Michael Finley	.40	1.00
❑ 17 Steve Francis	.40	1.00
❑ 18 Kevin Garnett	.75	2.00
❑ 19 Pau Gasol	.40	1.00
❑ 20 Manu Ginobili	.40	1.00
❑ 21 Drew Gooden	.25	.60
❑ 22 Nene	.30	.75
❑ 23 Grant Hill	.40	1.00
❑ 24 Allan Houston	.30	.75
❑ 25 Juwan Howard	.30	.75
❑ 26 Zydrunas Ilgauskas	.30	.75
❑ 27 Allen Iverson	.75	2.00
❑ 28 Antawn Jamison	.40	1.00
❑ 29 Richard Jefferson	.40	1.00
❑ 30 Eddie Jones	.30	.75
❑ 31 Jason Kidd	.60	1.50
❑ 32 Andrei Kirilenko	.40	1.00
❑ 33 Rashard Lewis	.40	1.00
❑ 34 Corey Maggette	.25	.60
❑ 35 Karl Malone	.40	1.00
❑ 36 Stephon Marbury	.40	1.00
❑ 37 Shawn Marion	.40	1.00
❑ 38 Kenyon Martin	.40	1.00
❑ 39 Jamal Mashburn	.25	.60
❑ 40 Tracy McGrady	.75	2.00
❑ 41 Reggie Miller	.40	1.00
❑ 42 Mike Miller	.30	.75
❑ 43 Yao Ming	.75	2.00
❑ 44 Cuttino Mobley	.30	.75
❑ 45 Steve Nash	.60	1.50
❑ 46 Dirk Nowitzki	.60	1.50
❑ 47 Jermaine O'Neal	.40	1.00
❑ 48 Shaquille O'Neal	1.00	2.50
❑ 49 Tony Parker	.40	1.00
❑ 50 Gary Payton	.40	1.00
❑ 51 Morris Peterson	.30	.75
❑ 52 Paul Pierce	.40	1.00
❑ 53 Scottie Pippen	.60	1.50
❑ 54 Tayshaun Prince	.30	.75
❑ 55 Vladimir Radmanovic	.25	.60
❑ 56 Michael Redd	.40	1.00
❑ 57 Jason Richardson	.40	1.00
❑ 58 Glenn Robinson	.30	.75
❑ 59 Jalen Rose	.30	.75
❑ 60 Latrell Sprewell	.30	.75
❑ 61 Jerry Stackhouse	.30	.75
❑ 62 Peja Stojakovic	.30	.75
❑ 63 Amare Stoudemire	.75	2.00
❑ 64 Wally Szczerbiak	.30	.75
❑ 65 Jason Terry	.30	.75
❑ 66 Keith Van Horn	.30	.75
❑ 67 Dajuan Wagner	.25	.60
❑ 68 Antoine Walker	.40	1.00
❑ 69 Ben Wallace	.30	.75
❑ 70 Rasheed Wallace	.40	1.00
❑ 71 Chris Webber	.40	1.00
❑ 72 Bonzi Wells	.25	.60
❑ 73 Carmelo Anthony RC	8.00	20.00
❑ 74 Ndudi Ebi RC	3.00	8.00
❑ 75 Luke Ridnour RC	4.00	10.00
❑ 76 Josh Howard RC	4.00	10.00
❑ 77 Marcus Banks RC	3.00	8.00
❑ 78 Zarko Cabarkapa RC	3.00	8.00
❑ 79 Kendrick Perkins RC	5.00	12.00
❑ 80 Leandro Barbosa RC	4.00	10.00
❑ 81 David West RC	4.00	10.00

❑ 82 Boris Diaw RC	4.00	10.00
❑ 83 Carlos Delfino RC	4.00	10.00
❑ 84 Mickael Pietrus RC	4.00	10.00
❑ 85 Troy Bell RC	3.00	8.00
❑ 86 Reece Gaines RC	3.00	8.00
❑ 87 Brian Cook RC	3.00	8.00
❑ 88 Kirk Hinrich RC	4.00	10.00
❑ 89 Travis Outlaw RC	4.00	10.00
❑ 90 Dwyane Wade RC	8.00	20.00
❑ 91 Luke Walton RC	4.00	10.00
❑ 92 Chris Bosh RC	5.00	12.00
❑ 93 Jarvis Hayes RC	3.00	8.00
❑ 94 Maciej Lampe RC	3.00	8.00
❑ 95 Mike Sweetney RC	3.00	8.00
❑ 96 Sofoklis Schortsanitis RC	3.00	8.00
❑ 97 Dahntay Jones RC	3.00	8.00
❑ 98 Nick Collison RC	3.00	8.00
❑ 99 Chris Kaman RC	4.00	10.00
❑ 100 Darko Milicic RC	4.00	10.00
❑ 101 T.J. Ford RC	4.00	10.00
❑ 102 LeBron James RC	40.00	100.00

2006-07 E-X

❑ COMP.SET w/o RC's (40)	12.50	30.00
❑ 1 Joe Johnson	.40	1.00
❑ 2 Paul Pierce	.50	1.25
❑ 3 Emeka Okafor	.50	1.25
❑ 4 Michael Jordan	3.00	8.00
❑ 5 Ben Gordon	.60	1.50
❑ 6 LeBron James	2.50	6.00
❑ 7 Dirk Nowitzki	.75	2.00
❑ 8 Jason Terry	.50	1.25
❑ 9 Carmelo Anthony	.60	1.50
❑ 10 Chauncey Billups	.50	1.25
❑ 11 Ben Wallace	.50	1.25
❑ 12 Baron Davis	.50	1.25
❑ 13 Jason Richardson	.50	1.25
❑ 14 Yao Ming	1.25	3.00
❑ 15 Jermaine O'Neal	.50	1.25
❑ 16 Elton Brand	.50	1.25
❑ 17 Kobe Bryant	2.50	6.00
❑ 18 Pau Gasol	.50	1.25
❑ 19 Tracy McGrady	1.00	2.50
❑ 20 Shaquille O'Neal	1.25	3.00
❑ 21 Dwyane Wade	1.25	3.00
❑ 22 Andrew Bogut	.50	1.25
❑ 23 Kevin Garnett	1.00	2.50
❑ 24 Vince Carter	1.00	2.50
❑ 25 Jason Kidd	.75	2.00
❑ 26 Chris Paul	1.00	2.50
❑ 27 Stephon Marbury	.50	1.25
❑ 28 Dwight Howard	1.00	2.50
❑ 29 Allen Iverson	1.00	2.50
❑ 30 Steve Nash	.60	1.50
❑ 31 Shawn Marion	.50	1.25
❑ 32 Martell Webster	.40	1.00
❑ 33 Mike Bibby	.50	1.25
❑ 34 Ron Artest	.50	1.25
❑ 35 Tim Duncan	1.00	2.50
❑ 36 Manu Ginobili	.50	1.25
❑ 37 Ray Allen	.50	1.25
❑ 38 Chris Bosh	.50	1.25
❑ 39 Andrei Kirilenko	.50	1.25
❑ 40 Gilbert Arenas	.50	1.25
❑ 41 J.J. Redick/99 RC	8.00	15.00
❑ 42 Adam Morrison/99 RC	8.00	20.00
❑ 43 Jorge Garbajosa/99 RC	8.00	20.00
❑ 44 Saer Sene/99 RC	8.00	20.00
❑ 45 Renaldo Balkman/99 RC	10.00	25.00
❑ 46 Thabo Sefolosha/99 RC	8.00	15.00
❑ 47 Kevin Pittsnogle/899 AU RC	5.00	12.00
❑ 48 Daniel Gibson/899 AU RC	10.00	25.00
❑ 49 Dee Brown/899 AU RC	5.00	12.00
❑ 50 Sergio Rodriguez/899 AU RC	5.00	12.00
❑ 51 Bobby Jones/899 AU RC	5.00	12.00
❑ 52 Craig Smith/899 AU RC	5.00	12.00
❑ 53 David Noel/899 AU RC	5.00	12.00
❑ 54 Denham Brown/899 AU RC	5.00	12.00
❑ 55 James White/899 AU RC	5.00	12.00
❑ 56 Paul Davis/899 AU RC	5.00	12.00
❑ 57 P.J. Tucker/899 AU RC	5.00	12.00
❑ 58 Solomon Jones/899 AU RC	5.00	12.00
❑ 59 Steve Novak/899 AU RC	5.00	12.00
❑ 60 Allan Ray/899 AU RC	5.00	12.00
❑ 61 Jordan Farmar/899 AU RC	6.00	15.00
❑ 62 Josh Boone/899 AU RC	5.00	12.00
❑ 63 Mardy Collins/899 AU RC	5.00	12.00
❑ 64 Rodney Carney/399 AU RC	6.00	15.00
❑ 65 Quincy Douby/399 AU RC	6.00	15.00
❑ 66 Shannon Brown/399 AU RC	6.00	15.00
❑ 67 Rajon Rondo/399 AU RC	25.00	60.00
❑ 68 Maurice Ager/399 AU RC	6.00	15.00
❑ 69 Ronnie Brewer/399 AU RC	8.00	20.00
❑ 70 Marcus Williams/399 AU RC	8.00	20.00
❑ 71 Kyle Lowry/399 AU RC	6.00	15.00
❑ 72 Cedric Simmons/399 AU RC	6.00	15.00
❑ 73 Patrick O'Bryant/399 AU RC	6.00	15.00
❑ 74 Hilton Armstrong/399 AU RC	6.00	15.00
❑ 75 Rudy Gay/199 AU RC	15.00	30.00
❑ 76 Brandon Roy/199 AU RC	40.00	80.00
❑ 77 Shelden Williams/199 AU RC	8.00	20.00
❑ 78 Tyrus Thomas/199 AU RC	20.00	40.00
❑ 79 LaMarcus Aldridge/199 AU RC	20.00	40.00
❑ 80 Andrea Bargnani/199 AU RC	15.00	30.00

2003-04 Exquisite Collection

❑ COMMON CARD (1-42)	6.00	15.00
❑ COMMON ROOKIE (44-73)	15.00	30.00
❑ 1 Jason Terry	8.00	20.00
❑ 2 Paul Pierce	10.00	25.00
❑ 3 Michael Jordan	80.00	160.00
❑ 4 Kirk Hinrich RC	30.00	75.00
❑ 5 Dajuan Wagner	6.00	15.00
❑ 6 Dirk Nowitzki	20.00	40.00
❑ 7 Steve Nash	20.00	40.00
❑ 8 Andre Miller	6.00	15.00
❑ 9 Ben Wallace	8.00	20.00
❑ 10 Jason Richardson	8.00	20.00
❑ 11 Steve Francis	8.00	20.00
❑ 12 Yao Ming	25.00	50.00
❑ 13 Jermaine O'Neal	8.00	20.00
❑ 14 Elton Brand	8.00	20.00
❑ 15 Kobe Bryant	50.00	100.00
❑ 16 Gary Payton	8.00	20.00
❑ 17 Shaquille O'Neal	30.00	60.00
❑ 18 Pau Gasol	8.00	20.00
❑ 19 Lamar Odom	8.00	20.00
❑ 20 T.J. Ford RC	15.00	30.00
❑ 21 Kevin Garnett	25.00	50.00
❑ 22 Latrell Sprewell	8.00	20.00
❑ 23 Jason Kidd	15.00	30.00
❑ 24 Richard Jefferson	6.00	15.00
❑ 25 Baron Davis	8.00	20.00
❑ 26 Allan Houston	6.00	15.00
❑ 27 Stephon Marbury	8.00	20.00
❑ 28 Tracy McGrady	30.00	60.00
❑ 29 Allen Iverson	50.00	100.00
❑ 30 Shawn Marion	8.00	20.00
❑ 31 Amare Stoudemire	15.00	30.00
❑ 32 Shareef Abdur-Rahim	8.00	20.00
❑ 33 Mike Bibby	8.00	20.00
❑ 34 Chris Webber	10.00	25.00
❑ 35 Tim Duncan	30.00	60.00
❑ 36 Manu Ginobili	20.00	40.00
❑ 37 Ray Allen	8.00	20.00
❑ 38 Nick Collison RC	10.00	25.00
❑ 39 Vince Carter	25.00	50.00
❑ 40 Andrei Kirilenko	10.00	25.00
❑ 41 Gilbert Arenas	10.00	25.00
❑ 42 Jerry Stackhouse	6.00	15.00
❑ 43 Udonis Haslem JSY AU RC	80.00	160.00
❑ 44 Mo Williams JSY AU RC	50.00	100.00
❑ 45 Keith Bogans JSY AU RC	10.00	25.00
❑ 46 Travis Hansen JSY AU RC	10.00	25.00
❑ 47 Jason Kapono JSY AU RC	15.00	30.00
❑ 48 Zaza Pachulia JSY AU RC	20.00	40.00
❑ 49 Z.Cabarkapa JSY AU RC	10.00	25.00
❑ 50 Kyle Korver JSY AU RC	25.00	50.00
❑ 51 Luke Walton JSY AU RC	25.00	50.00
❑ 52 Maciej Lampe JSY AU RC	10.00	25.00
❑ 53 Josh Howard JSY AU RC	40.00	80.00
❑ 54 Leandro Barbosa JSY AU RC	40.00	80.00
❑ 55 Kendrick Perkins JSY AU RC	30.00	60.00
❑ 56 Ndudi Ebi JSY AU RC	10.00	25.00
❑ 57 Jarome Beasley JSY AU RC	10.00	25.00
❑ 58 Brian Cook JSY AU RC	10.00	25.00
❑ 59 Travis Outlaw JSY AU RC	40.00	80.00
❑ 60 Zoran Planinic JSY AU RC	10.00	25.00
❑ 61 Boris Diaw JSY AU RC	40.00	80.00
❑ 62 Steve Blake JSY AU RC	25.00	50.00
❑ 63 A.Pavlovic JSY AU RC	25.00	50.00
❑ 64 David West JSY AU RC	100.00	200.00
❑ 65 Mike Sweetney JSY AU RC	10.00	25.00
❑ 66 Troy Bell JSY AU RC	10.00	25.00
❑ 67 Reece Gaines JSY AU RC	20.00	40.00
❑ 68 Luke Ridnour JSY AU RC	20.00	40.00
❑ 69 Marcus Banks JSY AU RC	10.00	25.00
❑ 70 Dahntay Jones JSY AU RC	10.00	25.00
❑ 71 Mickael Pietrus JSY AU RC	30.00	60.00
❑ 72 Chris Kaman JSY AU RC	40.00	80.00
❑ 73 Jarvis Hayes JSY AU RC	10.00	25.00
❑ 74 Dwyane Wade JSY AU RC	2000.00	2500.00
❑ 75 Chris Bosh JSY AU RC	800.00	1000.00
❑ 76 C.Anthony JSY AU RC	1700.00	2100.00
❑ 77 Darko Milicic JSY AU RC	125.00	225.00
❑ 78 LeBron James JSY AU RC	8000.00	12000.00

2004-05 Exquisite Collection

❑ COMMON JSY AU RC LEV 2 (43-84)	8.00	20.00
❑ COMMON AU RC LEV 2 (43-84)	8.00	20.00
❑ 1 Al Harrington	4.00	10.00
❑ 2 Paul Pierce	4.00	10.00
❑ 3 Emeka Okafor RC	15.00	30.00
❑ 4 Michael Jordan	60.00	120.00
❑ 5 LeBron James	40.00	80.00
❑ 6 Dirk Nowitzki	6.00	15.00
❑ 7 Carmelo Anthony	6.00	15.00
❑ 8 Kenyon Martin	4.00	10.00
❑ 9 Richard Hamilton	4.00	10.00
❑ 10 Ben Wallace	4.00	10.00
❑ 11 Jason Richardson	4.00	10.00
❑ 12 Yao Ming	8.00	20.00
❑ 13 Tracy McGrady	8.00	20.00
❑ 14 Reggie Miller	4.00	10.00
❑ 15 Corey Maggette	4.00	10.00
❑ 16 Kobe Bryant	25.00	50.00
❑ 17 Lamar Odom	4.00	10.00
❑ 18 Pau Gasol	4.00	10.00
❑ 19 Dwyane Wade	10.00	25.00
❑ 20 Shaquille O'Neal	10.00	25.00
❑ 21 Michael Redd	4.00	10.00
❑ 22 Kevin Garnett	6.00	15.00
❑ 23 Vince Carter	8.00	20.00
❑ 24 Jason Kidd	6.00	15.00
❑ 25 Baron Davis	4.00	10.00
❑ 26 Jamaal Magloire	4.00	10.00
❑ 27 Stephon Marbury	4.00	10.00
❑ 28 Steve Francis	4.00	10.00
❑ 29 Allen Iverson	30.00	60.00
❑ 30 Amare Stoudemire	6.00	15.00

❑ 31 Shawn Marion 4.00 10.00
❑ 32 Shareef Abdur-Rahim 4.00 10.00
❑ 33 Peja Stojakovic 4.00 10.00
❑ 34 Mike Bibby 4.00 10.00
❑ 35 Tim Duncan 8.00 20.00
❑ 36 Tony Parker 4.00 10.00
❑ 37 Ray Allen 4.00 10.00
❑ 38 Chris Bosh 4.00 10.00
❑ 39 Andrei Kirilenko 4.00 10.00
❑ 40 Carlos Boozer 4.00 10.00
❑ 41 Gilbert Arenas 4.00 10.00
❑ 42 Antawn Jamison 4.00 10.00
❑ 43 Andre Emmett JSY AU RC 8.00 20.00
❑ 44 Jameer Nelson JSY AU RC 40.00 80.00
❑ 45 S.Livingston JSY AU RC 30.00 60.00
❑ 46 Delonte West JSY AU RC 40.00 80.00
❑ 47 Trevor Ariza AU RC 40.00 80.00
❑ 48 Tony Allen JSY AU RC 40.00 80.00
❑ 49 Luke Jackson JSY AU RC 10.00 25.00
❑ 50 Dorell Wright JSY AU RC 50.00 100.00
❑ 51 Nenad Krstic JSY AU RC 15.00 30.00
❑ 52 Al Jefferson JSY RC 150.00 275.00
❑ 53 J.R. Smith JSY AU RC 75.00 150.00
❑ 54 Rafael Araujo JSY AU RC 8.00 20.00
❑ 55 Andris Biedrins JSY AU RC 30.00 60.00
❑ 56 Josh Smith JSY AU RC 100.00 175.00
❑ 57 Ha Seung-Jin JSY AU RC 8.00 20.00
❑ 58 B.Robinson JSY AU RC 8.00 20.00
❑ 59 Kevin Martin JSY AU RC 50.00 100.00
❑ 60 David Harrison JSY AU RC 8.00 20.00
❑ 61 Kris Humphries JSY AU RC 10.00 25.00
❑ 62 A.Varejao JSY AU RC 30.00 60.00
❑ 63 Jackson Vroman JSY AU RC 8.00 20.00
❑ 64 Sebastian Telfair JSY AU RC 15.00 30.00
❑ 65 Chris Duhon JSY AU RC 20.00 40.00
❑ 66 Kirk Snyder JSY AU RC 10.00 25.00
❑ 67 Andres Nocioni AU RC 20.00 40.00
❑ 68 Antonio Burks AU RC 8.00 20.00
❑ 69 Beno Udrih AU RC 8.00 20.00
❑ 70 D.J. Mbenga AU RC 8.00 20.00
❑ 71 Lionel Chalmers JSY AU RC 8.00 20.00
❑ 72 Robert Swift AU RC 8.00 20.00
❑ 73 Sasha Vujacic JSY AU RC 40.00 80.00
❑ 74 Donta Smith AU RC 8.00 20.00
❑ 75 Peter John Ramos AU RC 8.00 20.00
❑ 76 Justin Reed AU RC 8.00 20.00
❑ 77 Pape Sow AU RC 8.00 20.00
❑ 78 Pavel Podkolzin AU RC 8.00 20.00
❑ 79 Viktor Khryapa AU RC 8.00 20.00
❑ 80 John Edwards AU RC 8.00 20.00
❑ 81 Royal Ivey AU RC 8.00 20.00
❑ 82 Damien Wilkins AU RC 8.00 20.00
❑ 83 Erik Daniels AU RC 8.00 20.00
❑ 84 Luis Flores AU RC 8.00 20.00
❑ 85 Andre Iguodala JSY AU RC 250.00 500.00
❑ 86 Josh Childress JSY AU RC 50.00 100.00
❑ 87 Devin Harris JSY AU RC 125.00 250.00
❑ 88 Ben Gordon JSY AU RC 150.00 300.00
❑ 89 Luol Deng JSY AU RC 150.00 300.00
❑ 90 Dwight Howard JSY AU RC 1800.002300.00

2005-06 Exquisite Collection

❑ 1 Joe Johnson 4.00 10.00
❑ 2 Paul Pierce 4.00 10.00
❑ 3 Emeka Okafor 4.00 10.00
❑ 4 Ben Gordon 5.00 12.00
❑ 5 Michael Jordan 60.00 120.00
❑ 6 LeBron James 30.00 60.00
❑ 7 Dirk Nowitzki 6.00 15.00
❑ 8 Carmelo Anthony 8.00 20.00
❑ 9 Kenyon Martin 4.00 10.00
❑ 10 Chauncey Billups 4.00 10.00
❑ 11 Ben Wallace 4.00 10.00
❑ 12 Jason Richardson 4.00 10.00
❑ 13 Tracy McGrady 8.00 20.00
❑ 14 Yao Ming 10.00 25.00
❑ 15 Jermaine O'Neal 4.00 10.00
❑ 16 Elton Brand 4.00 10.00
❑ 17 Kobe Bryant 20.00 50.00
❑ 18 Pau Gasol 4.00 10.00
❑ 19 Shaquille O'Neal 10.00 25.00
❑ 20 Dwyane Wade 20.00 40.00
❑ 21 Michael Redd 4.00 10.00
❑ 22 Kevin Garnett 8.00 20.00
❑ 23 Vince Carter 8.00 20.00
❑ 24 Jason Kidd 6.00 15.00
❑ 25 J.R. Smith 3.00 8.00
❑ 26 Stephon Marbury 4.00 10.00
❑ 27 Quentin Richardson 3.00 8.00
❑ 28 Steve Francis 4.00 10.00
❑ 29 Dwight Howard 8.00 20.00
❑ 30 Allen Iverson 25.00 50.00
❑ 31 Chris Webber 4.00 10.00
❑ 32 Steve Nash 5.00 12.00
❑ 33 Amare Stoudemire 8.00 20.00
❑ 34 Zach Randolph 4.00 10.00
❑ 35 Mike Bibby 4.00 10.00
❑ 36 Peja Stojakovic 4.00 10.00
❑ 37 Tim Duncan 8.00 20.00
❑ 38 Tony Parker 4.00 10.00
❑ 39 Ray Allen 4.00 10.00
❑ 40 Chris Bosh 4.00 10.00
❑ 41 Andrei Kirilenko 4.00 10.00
❑ 42 Gilbert Arenas 4.00 10.00
❑ 43 Andrew Bogut JSY AU/99 RC 125.00 225.00
❑ 44 M.Williams JSY AU/99 RC 100.00200.00
❑ 45 D.Williams JSY AU/99 RC 400.00750.00
❑ 46 Chris Paul JSY AU/99 RC 1800.002200.00
❑ 47 R.Felton JSY AU RC/99 60.00 120.00
❑ 48 C.Frye JSY AU/99 RC 60.00 120.00
❑ 49 M.Webster JSY AU RC 40.00 80.00
❑ 50 C.Villanueva JSY AU RC 40.00 80.00
❑ 51 Ike Diogu JSY AU RC 25.00 50.00
❑ 52 Andrew Bynum JSY AU RC 200.00 300.00
❑ 53 Sean May JSY AU RC 15.00 30.00
❑ 54 Rashad McCants JSY AU RC 30.0060.00
❑ 55 Antoine Wright JSY AU RC 15.00 30.00
❑ 56 Joey Graham JSY AU RC 10.00 25.00
❑ 57 Danny Granger JSY AU RC 100.00 200.00
❑ 58 Gerald Green JSY AU RC 20.00 40.00
❑ 59 Hakim Warrick JSY AU RC 20.00 40.00
❑ 60 Julius Hodge JSY AU RC 10.00 25.00
❑ 61 Nate Robinson JSY AU RC 30.00 60.00
❑ 62 Jarrett Jack JSY AU RC 25.00 50.00
❑ 63 Francisco Garcia JSY AU RC 25.0050.00
❑ 64 Luther Head JSY AU RC 20.00 40.00
❑ 65 Johan Petro JSY AU RC 10.00 25.00
❑ 66 Jason Maxiell JSY AU RC 25.00 50.00
❑ 67 Linas Kleiza JSY AU RC 10.00 25.00
❑ 68 Wayne Simien JSY AU RC 10.00 25.00
❑ 69 David Lee JSY AU RC 60.00 120.00
❑ 70 Salim Stoudamire JSY AU RC 20.00 40.00
❑ 71 Daniel Ewing JSY AU RC 10.00 25.00
❑ 72 Brandon Bass JSY AU RC 15.00 30.00
❑ 73 C.J. Miles JSY AU RC 20.00 40.00
❑ 74 Ersan Ilyasova JSY AU RC 40.00 80.00
❑ 75 Travis Diener JSY AU RC 10.00 25.00
❑ 76 Monta Ellis JSY AU RC 100.00 200.00
❑ 77 Chris Taft JSY AU RC 10.00 25.00
❑ 78 M.Andriuskevicius JSY AU RC 25.00 50.00
❑ 79 Louis Williams JSY AU RC 35.00 75.00
❑ 80 Andray Blatche JSY AU RC 50.00100.00
❑ 81 Ryan Gomes JSY AU RC 20.00 40.00
❑ 82 S.Jasikevicius JSY AU RC 10.00 25.00
❑ 83 Yaroslav Korolev AU RC 6.00 15.00
❑ 85 Von Wafer AU RC 6.00 15.00
❑ 86 Orien Greene AU RC 6.00 15.00
❑ 87 Robert Whaley AU RC 6.00 15.00
❑ 88 Dijon Thompson AU RC 6.00 15.00
❑ 89 Bracey Wright AU RC 6.00 15.00
❑ 90 Amir Johnson AU RC 20.00 40.00
❑ 91 Ronny Turiaf AU RC 30.00 60.00
❑ 92 James Singleton AU RC 6.00 15.00
❑ 93 Alex Acker AU RC 6.00 15.00
❑ 94 Chuck Hayes AU RC 6.00 15.00
❑ 95 Lawrence Roberts AU RC 6.00 15.00
❑ 96 Stephen Graham AU RC 6.00 15.00

2006-07 Exquisite Collection

❑ 1 Joe Johnson 3.00 8.00
❑ 2 Paul Pierce 4.00 10.00
❑ 3 Emeka Okafor 4.00 10.00
❑ 4 Adam Morrison RC 10.00 25.00
❑ 5 Michael Jordan 40.00 80.00
❑ 6 Kirk Hinrich 4.00 10.00
❑ 7 LeBron James 20.00 50.00
❑ 8 Dirk Nowitzki 6.00 15.00
❑ 9 Carmelo Anthony 5.00 12.00
❑ 10 Allen Iverson 8.00 20.00
❑ 11 Chauncey Billups 4.00 10.00
❑ 12 Richard Hamilton 3.00 8.00
❑ 13 Baron Davis 4.00 10.00
❑ 14 Yao Ming 10.00 25.00
❑ 15 Tracy McGrady 8.00 20.00
❑ 16 Jermaine O'Neal 4.00 10.00
❑ 17 Elton Brand 4.00 10.00
❑ 18 Kobe Bryant 20.00 50.00
❑ 19 Lamar Odom 4.00 10.00
❑ 20 Pau Gasol 4.00 10.00
❑ 21 Dwyane Wade 10.00 25.00
❑ 22 Shaquille O'Neal 10.00 25.00
❑ 23 Michael Redd 4.00 10.00
❑ 24 Kevin Garnett 8.00 20.00
❑ 25 Vince Carter 8.00 20.00
❑ 26 Jason Kidd 6.00 15.00
❑ 27 Chris Paul 8.00 20.00
❑ 28 Peja Stojakovic 4.00 10.00
❑ 29 Stephon Marbury 4.00 10.00
❑ 30 Dwight Howard 8.00 20.00
❑ 31 J.J. Redick RC 15.00 30.00
❑ 32 Andre Iguodala 3.00 8.00
❑ 33 Steve Nash 4.00 10.00
❑ 34 Amare Stoudemire 6.00 15.00
❑ 35 Jarrett Jack 2.50 6.00
❑ 36 Mike Bibby 3.00 8.00
❑ 37 Tim Duncan 6.00 15.00
❑ 38 Tony Parker 3.00 8.00
❑ 39 Ray Allen 3.00 8.00
❑ 40 Chris Bosh 3.00 8.00
❑ 41 Deron Williams 5.00 12.00
❑ 42 Antawn Jamison 3.00 8.00
❑ 43 A.Bargnani JSY AU/99 RC 80.00 160.00
❑ 44 L.Aldridge JSY AU/99 RC 150.00 250.00
❑ 45 Tyrus Thomas JSY AU/99 RC 60.00 120.00
❑ 46 Brandon Roy JSY AU/99 RC 400.00 600.00
❑ 47 Rudy Gay JSY AU/99 RC 125.00 225.00
❑ 48 S.Williams JSY AU/99 RC 30.00 60.00
❑ 49 Randy Foye JSY AU RC 20.00 40.00
❑ 50 Patrick O'Bryant JSY AU RC 8.00 20.00
❑ 51 Saer Sene JSY AU RC 8.00 20.00
❑ 52 Hilton Armstrong JSY AU RC 10.0025.00
❑ 53 Thabo Sefolosha JSY AU RC 10.0025.00
❑ 54 Ronnie Brewer JSY AU RC 25.00 50.00
❑ 55 Cedric Simmons JSY AU RC 8.00 20.00
❑ 56 Rodney Carney JSY AU RC 10.00 25.00
❑ 57 Shawne Williams JSY AU RC 8.00 20.00
❑ 58 Quincy Douby JSY AU RC 10.00 25.00
❑ 59 Renaldo Balkman JSY AU RC 10.00 25.00
❑ 60 Rajon Rondo JSY AU RC 225.00 325.00
❑ 61 Marcus Williams JSY AU RC 10.00 25.00
❑ 62 Josh Boone JSY AU RC 8.00 20.00
❑ 63 Allan Ray JSY AU RC 8.00 20.00
❑ 64 Shannon Brown JSY AU RC 20.00 40.00
❑ 65 Jordan Farmar JSY AU RC 25.00 50.00
❑ 66 Dee Brown JSY AU RC 10.00 25.00
❑ 67 Maurice Ager JSY AU RC 8.00 20.00

❑ 68 Mardy Collins JSY AU RC 8.00 20.00
❑ 69 James White JSY AU RC 8.00 20.00
❑ 70 Steve Novak JSY AU RC 8.00 20.00
❑ 71 Solomon Jones JSY AU RC 8.00 20.00
❑ 72 Paul Davis JSY AU RC 8.00 20.00
❑ 73 P.J. Tucker JSY AU RC 8.00 20.00
❑ 74 Craig Smith JSY AU RC 8.00 20.00
❑ 75 Bobby Jones JSY AU RC 8.00 20.00
❑ 76 David Noel JSY AU RC 8.00 20.00
❑ 77 Jorge Garbajosa JSY AU RC 8.00 20.00
❑ 78 Daniel Gibson JSY AU RC 15.00 30.00
❑ 79 Sergio Rodriguez AU RC 10.00 25.00
❑ 80 Paul Millsap AU RC 10.00 25.00
❑ 81 Will Blalock AU RC 8.00 20.00
❑ 82 Hassan Adams AU RC 8.00 20.00
❑ 83 Kyle Lowry AU RC 8.00 20.00
❑ 84 James Augustine AU RC 8.00 20.00

2007-08 Exquisite Collection

❑ 1 LeBron James 12.00 30.00
❑ 2 Yao Ming 6.00 15.00
❑ 3 Kobe Bryant 25.00 50.00
❑ 4 Dwyane Wade 6.00 15.00
❑ 5 Tracy McGrady 5.00 12.00
❑ 6 Allen Iverson 5.00 12.00
❑ 7 Shaquille O'Neal 6.00 15.00
❑ 8 Kevin Garnett 6.00 15.00
❑ 9 Steve Nash 3.00 8.00
❑ 10 Dwight Howard 5.00 12.00
❑ 11 Gilbert Arenas 2.50 6.00
❑ 12 Vince Carter 5.00 12.00
❑ 13 Tim Duncan 5.00 12.00
❑ 14 Carmelo Anthony 5.00 12.00
❑ 15 Dirk Nowitzki 4.00 10.00
❑ 16 Amare Stoudemire 5.00 12.00
❑ 17 Chris Bosh 2.50 6.00
❑ 18 Jermaine O'Neal 2.50 6.00
❑ 19 Jason Kidd 4.00 10.00
❑ 20 Ben Wallace 2.50 6.00
❑ 21 Paul Pierce 2.50 6.00
❑ 22 Shawn Marion 2.50 6.00
❑ 23 Michael Jordan 30.00 60.00
❑ 24 Manu Ginobili 2.50 6.00
❑ 25 Tony Parker 2.50 6.00
❑ 26 Chauncey Billups 2.50 6.00
❑ 27 Chris Paul 5.00 12.00
❑ 28 Andre Iguodala 2.50 6.00
❑ 29 Stephon Marbury 2.50 6.00
❑ 30 Ray Allen 2.50 6.00
❑ 31 Lamar Odom 2.50 6.00
❑ 32 Jason Terry 2.50 6.00
❑ 33 Josh Howard 2.50 6.00
❑ 34 Caron Butler 2.50 6.00
❑ 35 Emeka Okafor 2.50 6.00
❑ 36 Marcus Camby 1.50 4.00
❑ 37 Pau Gasol 2.50 6.00
❑ 38 Carlos Boozer 2.50 6.00
❑ 39 Baron Davis 2.50 6.00
❑ 40 Michael Redd 2.50 6.00
❑ 41 Ben Gordon 3.00 8.00
❑ 42 Richard Hamilton 2.00 5.00
❑ 43 Andrew Bogut 2.50 6.00
❑ 44 Tyson Chandler 2.50 6.00
❑ 45 Eddy Curry 1.50 4.00
❑ 46 Larry Hughes 2.00 5.00
❑ 47 LaMarcus Aldridge 3.00 8.00
❑ 48 Andrea Bargnani 3.00 8.00
❑ 49 Mike Bibby 2.50 6.00
❑ 50 Elton Brand 2.50 6.00
❑ 51 Al Harrington 2.00 5.00
❑ 52 Al Jefferson 2.50 6.00
❑ 53 Joe Johnson 2.50 6.00
❑ 54 Rashard Lewis 2.50 6.00
❑ 55 Kevin Martin 2.50 6.00
❑ 56 Andre Miller 2.00 5.00
❑ 57 Brandon Roy 4.00 10.00
❑ 58 Gerald Wallace 2.50 6.00
❑ 59 Rasheed Wallace 2.50 6.00
❑ 60 Deron Williams 4.00 10.00
❑ 61 Arron Afflalo JSY AU RC 10.00 25.00
❑ 62 Morris Almond JSY AU RC 10.00 25.00
❑ 63 Julian Wright JSY AU RC 20.00 40.00
❑ 64 Aaron Brooks JSY AU RC 40.00 80.00
❑ 65 Herbert Hill JSY AU RC 10.00 25.00
❑ 66 Wilson Chandler JSY AU RC 30.0060.00
❑ 67 Daequan Cook JSY AU RC 20.00 40.00
❑ 68 Javaris Crittenton JSY AU RC 15.0030.00
❑ 69 Jermareo Davidson JSY AU RC 10.00 25.00
❑ 70 Glen Davis JSY AU RC 25.00 50.00
❑ 71 Jared Dudley JSY AU RC 15.00 30.00
❑ 72 Corey Brewer JSY AU RC 15.00 30.00
❑ 73 Aaron Gray JSY AU RC 10.00 25.00
❑ 74 Taurean Green JSY AU RC 10.00 25.00
❑ 75 Nick Fazekas JSY AU RC 10.00 25.00
❑ 76 Spencer Hawes JSY AU RC 20.00 40.00
❑ 77 Al Horford JSY AU RC 60.00 120.00
❑ 78 Jeff Green JSY AU RC 50.00 100.00
❑ 79 Carl Landry JSY AU RC 20.00 40.00
❑ 80 Mike Conley JSY AU RC 30.00 60.00
❑ 81 Acie Law IV JSY AU RC 15.00 30.00
❑ 82 Dominic McGuire JSY AU RC 10.0025.00
❑ 83 Josh McRoberts JSY AU RC 15.0030.00
❑ 84 Demetris Nichols JSY AU RC 10.0025.00
❑ 85 Joakim Noah JSY AU RC 40.00 80.00
❑ 86 Gabe Pruitt JSY AU RC 10.00 25.00
❑ 87 Chris Richard JSY AU RC 10.00 25.00
❑ 88 Jason Smith JSY AU RC 10.00 25.00
❑ 89 D.J. Strawberry JSY AU RC 10.00 25.00
❑ 90 Rodney Stuckey JSY AU RC 60.00 120.00
❑ 91 Sean Williams JSY AU RC 15.00 30.00
❑ 92 Al Thornton JSY AU RC 60.00 120.00
❑ 93 Alando Tucker JSY AU RC 10.00 25.00
❑ 94 K.Durant JSY AU/99 RC 2000.00 3000.00
❑ 95 Marco Belinelli JSY AU/99 RC 40.00 80.00
❑ 96 Luis Scola JSY AU/99 RC 40.00 80.00
❑ 97 Louis Amundson JSY AU/99 RC 20.00 40.00
❑ 98 C.J. Watson AU RC 15.00 30.00
❑ 99 Cheikh Samb AU RC 15.00 30.00
❑ 100 Juan Navarro AU RC 15.00 30.00
❑ 101 JamesOn Curry AU RC 15.00 30.00
❑ 102 Ramon Sessions AU RC 40.00 80.00
❑ 103 Mario West AU RC 15.00 30.00
❑ 104 Coby Karl AU RC 15.00 30.00
❑ 105 Oleksiy Pecherov AU RC 15.00 30.00
❑ 106 Jamario Moon AU RC 30.00 60.00
❑ 107 Kyrylo Fesenko RC 15.00 30.00
❑ 108 Yi Jianlian RC 25.00 50.00
❑ 109 Brandan Wright RC 15.00 30.00
❑ 110 Thaddeus Young RC 15.00 30.00
❑ 111 Nick Young RC 15.00 30.00
❑ 112 Greg Oden RC 50.00 100.00

2008-09 Exquisite Collection

❑ 1 Kevin Garnett 6.00 15.00
❑ 2 LeBron James 15.00 40.00
❑ 3 Dwight Howard 6.00 15.00
❑ 4 Kobe Bryant 15.00 40.00
❑ 5 Carmelo Anthony 4.00 10.00
❑ 6 Tim Duncan 5.00 12.00
❑ 7 Yao Ming 4.00 10.00
❑ 8 Dwyane Wade 6.00 15.00
❑ 9 Dirk Nowitzki 4.00 10.00
❑ 10 Jason Kidd 3.00 8.00
❑ 11 Allen Iverson 4.00 10.00
❑ 12 Tracy McGrady 4.00 10.00
❑ 13 Steve Nash 3.00 8.00
❑ 14 Ray Allen 3.00 8.00
❑ 15 Amare Stoudemire 4.00 10.00
❑ 16 Vince Carter 4.00 10.00
❑ 17 Shaquille O'Neal 10.00 25.00
❑ 18 Chris Bosh 3.00 8.00
❑ 19 Gilbert Arenas 3.00 8.00
❑ 20 Chauncey Billups 3.00 8.00
❑ 21 Paul Pierce 4.00 10.00
❑ 22 Chris Paul 6.00 15.00
❑ 23 Michael Jordan 50.00 100.00
❑ 24 Carlos Boozer 3.00 8.00
❑ 25 Manu Ginobili 3.00 8.00
❑ 26 Shawn Marion 3.00 8.00
❑ 27 Tony Parker 3.00 8.00
❑ 28 Baron Davis 3.00 8.00
❑ 29 Kevin Durant 8.00 20.00
❑ 30 Josh Howard 3.00 8.00
❑ 31 Marcus Camby 2.00 5.00
❑ 32 Michael Redd 3.00 8.00
❑ 33 Caron Butler 3.00 8.00
❑ 34 Richard Hamilton 2.50 6.00
❑ 35 Andrea Bargnani 2.50 6.00
❑ 36 Tyson Chandler 2.50 6.00
❑ 37 Andrew Bogut 3.00 8.00
❑ 38 Joe Johnson 3.00 8.00
❑ 39 T.J. Ford 2.00 5.00
❑ 40 Rashard Lewis 3.00 8.00
❑ 41 Pau Gasol 3.00 8.00
❑ 42 David Lee 2.50 6.00
❑ 43 Andre Iguodala 3.00 8.00
❑ 44 Greg Oden 3.00 8.00
❑ 45 Corey Maggette 3.00 8.00
❑ 46 Andrew Bynum 3.00 8.00
❑ 47 Mo Williams 2.50 6.00
❑ 48 Elton Brand 5.00 12.00
❑ 49 Ben Gordon 3.00 8.00
❑ 50 Danny Granger 3.00 8.00
❑ 51 Richard Jefferson 3.00 8.00
❑ 52 Al Horford 3.00 8.00
❑ 53 Gerald Wallace 3.00 8.00
❑ 54 Rudy Gay 3.00 8.00
❑ 55 Deron Williams 4.00 10.00
❑ 56 Corey Brewer 2.50 6.00
❑ 57 Monta Ellis 3.00 8.00
❑ 58 Kevin Martin 3.00 8.00
❑ 59 Luol Deng 3.00 8.00
❑ 60 Brandon Roy 4.00 10.00
❑ 61 Kevin Love JSY AU RC 30.00 60.00
❑ 62 Joe Alexander JSY AU RC 15.00 30.00
❑ 63 D.J. Augustin JSY AU RC 20.00 40.00
❑ 64 Brook Lopez JSY AU RC 50.00 100.00
❑ 65 Jason Thompson JSY AU RC 25.0050.00
❑ 66 Brandon Rush JSY AU RC 20.00 40.00
❑ 67 Anthony Randolph JSY AU RC 125.00 250.00
❑ 68 Robin Lopez JSY AU RC 15.00 30.00
❑ 69 Marreese Speights JSY AU RC 15.00 30.00
❑ 70 Roy Hibbert JSY AU RC 20.00 40.00
❑ 71 Javale McGee JSY AU RC 20.00 40.00
❑ 72 J.J. Hickson JSY AU RC 25.00 50.00
❑ 73 Ryan Anderson JSY AU RC 15.00 30.00
❑ 74 Courtney Lee JSY AU RC 40.00 80.00
❑ 75 Kosta Koufos JSY AU RC 10.00 25.00
❑ 76 George Hill JSY AU RC 50.00 100.00
❑ 77 Darrell Arthur JSY AU RC 10.00 25.00
❑ 78 Donte Greene JSY AU RC 10.00 25.00
❑ 79 D.J. White JSY AU/55 RC 25.00 50.00
❑ 80 J.R. Giddens JSY AU RC 10.00 25.00
❑ 81 Walter Sharpe JSY AU RC 10.00 25.00
❑ 82 Joey Dorsey JSY AU RC 10.00 25.00
❑ 83 Mario Chalmers JSY AU RC 20.00 40.00
❑ 84 DeAndre Jordan JSY AU RC 15.0030.00
❑ 85 Kyle Weaver JSY AU RC 10.00 25.00
❑ 86 Sonny Weems JSY AU RC 10.00 25.00
❑ 87 Chris Douglas-Roberts JSY AU RC 20.00 40.00
❑ 88 Rudy Fernandez JSY AU RC 40.00 80.00
❑ 89 Marc Gasol JSY AU/150 RC 15.00 30.00
❑ 90 O.J. Mayo JSY AU/99 RC 200.00 400.00
❑ 91 Michael Beasley JSY AU/99 RC 250.00 500.00
❑ 92 Derrick Rose JSY AU/99 RC 1700.002200.00
❑ 93 Russell Westbrook JSY AU RC 150.00 300.00
❑ 94 Eric Gordon JSY AU RC 100.00 200.00

❑ 95 Nicolas Batum AU/99 RC	40.00	80.00
❑ 96 Mike Taylor AU/99 RC	10.00	25.00
❑ 97 Alexis Ajinca AU/99 RC	10.00	25.00
❑ 98 Luc Mbah A Moute AU/99 RC	10.00	25.00
❑ 99 Sean Singletary AU/99 RC	10.00	25.00
❑ 100 Danilo Gallinari AU/99 RC	75.00	150.00
❑ NNO Uncut Sheet EXCH	100.00	200.00

2009-10 Exquisite Collection

❑ 1 Dwight Howard	6.00	15.00
❑ 2 LeBron James	15.00	40.00
❑ 3 Kobe Bryant	15.00	40.00
❑ 4 Dwyane Wade	6.00	15.00
❑ 5 Yao Ming	4.00	10.00
❑ 6 Tim Duncan	5.00	12.00
❑ 7 Kevin Garnett	6.00	15.00
❑ 8 Allen Iverson	4.00	10.00
❑ 9 Yi Jianlian	3.00	8.00
❑ 10 Tracy McGrady	4.00	10.00
❑ 11 Chris Paul	6.00	15.00
❑ 12 Shaquille O'Neal	6.00	15.00
❑ 13 Carmelo Anthony	4.00	10.00
❑ 14 Vince Carter	4.00	10.00
❑ 15 Dirk Nowitzki	4.00	10.00
❑ 16 Chris Bosh	3.00	8.00
❑ 17 Manu Ginobili	3.00	8.00
❑ 18 Pau Gasol	3.00	8.00
❑ 19 Ray Allen	3.00	8.00
❑ 20 Paul Pierce	4.00	10.00
❑ 21 Jamal Crawford	2.00	5.00
❑ 22 Steve Nash	3.00	8.00
❑ 23 Michael Jordan	40.00	80.00
❑ 24 Gilbert Arenas	3.00	8.00
❑ 25 Luke Ridnour	2.00	5.00
❑ 26 Derrick Rose	6.00	15.00
❑ 27 Jose Calderon	2.50	6.00
❑ 28 Brandon Roy	4.00	10.00
❑ 29 Joe Johnson	3.00	8.00
❑ 30 Danny Granger	3.00	8.00
❑ 31 Greg Oden	2.50	6.00
❑ 32 Al Jefferson	3.00	8.00
❑ 33 Kevin Durant	8.00	20.00
❑ 34 Andre Iguodala	3.00	8.00
❑ 35 David Lee	2.50	6.00
❑ 36 Kevin Martin	3.00	8.00
❑ 37 O.J. Mayo	4.00	10.00
❑ 38 Zach Randolph	2.00	5.00
❑ 39 Gerald Wallace	3.00	8.00
❑ 40 Russell Westbrook	3.00	8.00
❑ 41 Deron Williams	4.00	10.00
❑ 42 Mo Williams	2.50	6.00
❑ 43 Blake Griffin RC	50.00	100.00
❑ 44 Ricky Rubio EXCH	60.00	120.00
❑ 45 James Harden AU RC	40.00	80.00
❑ 46 Tyreke Evans RC	125.00	225.00
❑ 47 Brandon Jennings RC	75.00	150.00
❑ 48 James Johnson AU RC	20.00	40.00
❑ 49 Earl Clark AU RC	40.00	80.00
❑ 50 Chase Budinger AU RC	15.00	30.00
❑ 51 DeJuan Blair RC	20.00	40.00
❑ 52 B.J. Mullens AU RC	8.00	20.00
❑ 53 Darren Collison AU RC	50.00	100.00
❑ 54 Tyler Hansbrough RC	20.00	40.00
❑ 55 Sam Young AU RC	10.00	25.00
❑ 56 Marcus Thornton AU RC	40.00	80.00
❑ 57 Jeff Teague AU RC	20.00	40.00
❑ 58 Jonny Flynn AU RC	40.00	80.00
❑ 59 Terrence Williams RC	15.00	30.00
❑ 60 Gerald Henderson AU RC	20.00	40.00
❑ 61 Hasheem Thabeet RC	8.00	20.00
❑ 62 Ty Lawson AU RC	30.00	60.00
❑ 63 Eric Maynor AU RC	20.00	40.00
❑ 64 Stephen Curry AU RC	100.00	200.00
❑ 65 DeMar DeRozan RC	25.00	50.00
❑ 66 Patrick Mills RC	15.00	30.00
❑ 67 Jordan Hill RC	8.00	20.00
❑ 68 Derrick Brown AU RC	10.00	25.00
❑ 69 Wayne Ellington AU RC	20.00	40.00
❑ 70 DaJuan Summers AU RC	10.00	25.00
❑ 71 Eric Maynor AU RC	20.00	40.00
❑ 72 Stephen Curry AU	100.00	200.00
❑ 73 Ricky Rubio EXCH	80.00	160.00
❑ 74 James Harden AU	30.00	60.00
❑ 75 James Johnson AU	20.00	40.00
❑ 76 Sam Young AU	10.00	25.00
❑ 77 Gerald Henderson AU	20.00	40.00
❑ 78 B.J. Mullens AU	8.00	20.00
❑ 79 Jonny Flynn AU	40.00	80.00

1993-94 Finest

❑ COMPLETE SET (220)	40.00	100.00
❑ 1 Michael Jordan	6.00	12.00
❑ 2 Larry Bird	1.00	2.50
❑ 3 Shaquille O'Neal	2.00	5.00
❑ 4 Benoit Benjamin	.08	.25
❑ 5 Ricky Pierce	.08	.25
❑ 6 Ken Norman	.08	.25
❑ 7 Victor Alexander	.08	.25
❑ 8 Mark Jackson	.15	.40
❑ 9 Mark West	.08	.25
❑ 10 Don MacLean	.08	.25
❑ 11 Reggie Miller	.30	.75
❑ 12 Sarunas Marciulionis	.08	.25
❑ 13 Craig Ehlo	.08	.25
❑ 14 Toni Kukoc RC	1.50	4.00
❑ 15 Glen Rice	.15	.40
❑ 16 Otis Thorpe	.15	.40
❑ 17 Reggie Williams	.08	.25
❑ 18 Charles Smith	.08	.25
❑ 19 Micheal Williams	.08	.25
❑ 20 Tom Chambers	.08	.25
❑ 21 David Robinson	.60	1.50
❑ 22 Jamal Mashburn RC	2.00	5.00
❑ 23 Clifford Robinson	.15	.40
❑ 24 Acie Earl RC	.08	.25
❑ 25 Danny Ferry	.08	.25
❑ 26 Bobby Hurley RC	.15	.40
❑ 27 Eddie Johnson	.08	.25
❑ 28 Detlef Schrempf	.15	.40
❑ 29 Mike Brown	.08	.25
❑ 30 Latrell Sprewell	1.00	2.50
❑ 31 Derek Harper	.15	.40
❑ 32 Stacey Augmon	.08	.25
❑ 33 Pooh Richardson	.08	.25
❑ 34 Larry Krystkowiak	.08	.25
❑ 35 Pervis Ellison	.08	.25
❑ 36 Jeff Malone	.08	.25
❑ 37 Sean Elliott	.15	.40
❑ 38 John Paxson	.08	.25
❑ 39 Robert Parish	.15	.40
❑ 40 Mark Aguirre	.08	.25
❑ 41 Danny Ainge	.15	.40
❑ 42 Brian Shaw	.08	.25
❑ 43 LaPhonso Ellis	.08	.25
❑ 44 Carl Herrera	.08	.25
❑ 45 Terry Cummings	.08	.25
❑ 46 Chris Dudley	.08	.25
❑ 47 Anthony Mason	.15	.40
❑ 48 Chris Morris	.08	.25
❑ 49 Todd Day	.08	.25
❑ 50 Nick Van Exel RC	2.50	6.00
❑ 51 Larry Nance	.08	.25
❑ 52 Derrick McKey	.08	.25
❑ 53 Muggsy Bogues	.15	.40
❑ 54 Andrew Lang	.08	.25
❑ 55 Chuck Person	.08	.25
❑ 56 Michael Adams	.08	.25
❑ 57 Spud Webb	.15	.40
❑ 58 Scott Skiles	.08	.25
❑ 59 A.C. Green	.15	.40
❑ 60 Terry Mills	.08	.25
❑ 61 Xavier McDaniel	.08	.25
❑ 62 B.J. Armstrong	.08	.25
❑ 63 Donald Hodge	.08	.25
❑ 64 Gary Grant	.08	.25
❑ 65 Billy Owens	.08	.25
❑ 66 Greg Anthony	.08	.25
❑ 67 Jay Humphries	.08	.25
❑ 68 Lionel Simmons	.08	.25
❑ 69 Dana Barros	.08	.25
❑ 70 Steve Smith	.30	.75
❑ 71 Ervin Johnson RC	.15	.40
❑ 72 Sleepy Floyd	.08	.25
❑ 73 Blue Edwards	.08	.25
❑ 74 Clyde Drexler	.30	.75
❑ 75 Elden Campbell	.08	.25
❑ 76 Hakeem Olajuwon	.60	1.50
❑ 77 Clarence Weatherspoon	.08	.25
❑ 78 Kevin Willis	.08	.25
❑ 79 Isaiah Rider RC	1.50	4.00
❑ 80 Derrick Coleman	.15	.40
❑ 81 Nick Anderson	.15	.40
❑ 82 Bryant Stith	.08	.25
❑ 83 Johnny Newman	.08	.25
❑ 84 Calbert Cheaney RC	.60	1.50
❑ 85 Oliver Miller	.08	.25
❑ 86 Loy Vaught	.08	.25
❑ 87 Isiah Thomas	.30	.75
❑ 88 Dee Brown	.08	.25
❑ 89 Horace Grant	.15	.40
❑ 90 Patrick Ewing AF	.15	.40
❑ 91 Clarence Weatherspoon AF	.08	.25
❑ 92 Rony Seikaly AF	.08	.25
❑ 93 Dino Radja AF	.08	.25
❑ 94 Kenny Anderson AF	.08	.25
❑ 95 John Starks AF	.08	.25
❑ 96 Tom Gugliotta AF	.15	.40
❑ 97 Steve Smith AF	.15	.40
❑ 98 Derrick Coleman AF	.08	.25
❑ 99 Shaquille O'Neal AF	1.25	3.00
❑ 100 Brad Daugherty CF	.08	.25
❑ 101 Horace Grant CF	.08	.25
❑ 102 Dominique Wilkins CF	.15	.40
❑ 103 Joe Dumars CF	.15	.40
❑ 104 Alonzo Mourning CF	.30	.75
❑ 105 Scottie Pippen CF	1.00	2.50
❑ 106 Reggie Miller CF	.15	.40
❑ 107 Mark Price CF	.08	.25
❑ 108 Ken Norman CF	.08	.25
❑ 109 Larry Johnson CF	.15	.40
❑ 110 Jamal Mashburn MF	.30	.75
❑ 111 Christian Laettner MF	.08	.25
❑ 112 Karl Malone MF	.30	.75
❑ 113 Dennis Hodman MF	.30	.75
❑ 114 Mahmoud Abdul-Rauf MF	.08	.25
❑ 115 Hakeem Olajuwon MF	.30	.75
❑ 116 Jim Jackson MF	.08	.25
❑ 117 John Stockton MF	.15	.40
❑ 118 David Robinson MF	.30	.75
❑ 119 Dikembe Mutombo MF	.15	.40
❑ 120 Vlade Divac PF	.08	.25
❑ 121 Dan Majerle PF	.08	.25
❑ 122 Chris Mullin PF	.15	.40
❑ 123 Shawn Kemp PF	.30	.75
❑ 124 Danny Manning PF	.08	.25
❑ 125 Charles Barkley PF	.30	.75
❑ 126 Mitch Richmond PF	.15	.40
❑ 127 Tim Hardaway PF	.15	.40
❑ 128 Detlef Schrempf PF	.08	.25
❑ 129 Clyde Drexler PF	.15	.40
❑ 130 Christian Laettner	.15	.40
❑ 131 Rodney Rogers RC	.75	2.00
❑ 132 Rik Smits	.15	.40
❑ 133 Chris Mills RC	.75	2.00
❑ 134 Corie Blount RC	.08	.25
❑ 135 Mookie Blaylock	.15	.40
❑ 136 Jim Jackson	.15	.40
❑ 137 Tom Gugliotta	.30	.75
❑ 138 Dennis Scott	.08	.25
❑ 139 Vin Baker RC	1.50	4.00
❑ 140 Gary Payton	.60	1.50
❑ 141 Sedale Threatt	.08	.25
❑ 142 Orlando Woolridge	.08	.25
❑ 143 Avery Johnson	.08	.25
❑ 144 Charles Oakley	.15	.40
❑ 145 Harvey Grant	.08	.25
❑ 146 Bimbo Coles	.08	.25
❑ 147 Vernon Maxwell	.08	.25
❑ 148 Danny Manning	.15	.40

❑ 149 Hersey Hawkins	.15	.40
❑ 150 Kevin Gamble	.08	.25
❑ 151 Johnny Dawkins	.08	.25
❑ 152 Olden Polynice	.08	.25
❑ 153 Kevin Edwards	.08	.25
❑ 154 Willie Anderson	.08	.25
❑ 155 Wayman Tisdale	.08	.25
❑ 156 Popeye Jones RC	.08	.25
❑ 157 Dan Majerle	.15	.40
❑ 158 Rex Chapman	.08	.25
❑ 159 Shawn Kemp UER 136	.60	1.50
❑ 160 Eric Murdock	.08	.25
❑ 161 Randy White	.08	.25
❑ 162 Larry Johnson	.30	.75
❑ 163 Dominique Wilkins	.30	.75
❑ 164 Dikembe Mutombo	.30	.75
❑ 165 Patrick Ewing	.30	.75
❑ 166 Jerome Kersey	.08	.25
❑ 167 Dale Davis	.08	.25
❑ 168 Ron Harper	.15	.40
❑ 169 Sam Cassell RC	2.50	6.00
❑ 170 Bill Cartwright	.08	.25
❑ 171 John Williams	.08	.25
❑ 172 Dino Radja RC	.08	.25
❑ 173 Dennis Rodman	.75	2.00
❑ 174 Kenny Anderson	.15	.40
❑ 175 Robert Horry	.15	.40
❑ 176 Chris Mullin	.30	.75
❑ 177 John Salley	.08	.25
❑ 178 Scott Burrell RC	.60	1.50
❑ 179 Mitch Richmond	.30	.75
❑ 180 Lee Mayberry	.08	.25
❑ 181 James Worthy	.30	.75
❑ 182 Rick Fox	.08	.25
❑ 183 Kevin Johnson	.15	.40
❑ 184 Lindsey Hunter RC	.75	2.00
❑ 185 Marlon Maxey	.08	.25
❑ 186 Sam Perkins	.15	.40
❑ 187 Kevin Duckworth	.08	.25
❑ 188 Jeff Hornacek	.15	.40
❑ 189 Anfernee Hardaway RC	5.00	12.00
❑ 190 Rex Walters RC	.08	.25
❑ 191 Mahmoud Abdul-Rauf	.08	.25
❑ 192 Terry Dehere RC	.08	.25
❑ 193 Brad Daugherty	.08	.25
❑ 194 John Starks	.15	.40
❑ 195 Rod Strickland	.15	.40
❑ 196 Luther Wright RC	.08	.25
❑ 197 Vlade Divac	.15	.40
❑ 198 Tim Hardaway	.30	.75
❑ 199 Joe Dumars	.30	.75
❑ 200 Charles Barkley	.60	1.50
❑ 201 Alonzo Mourning	.60	1.50
❑ 202 Doug West	.08	.25
❑ 203 Anthony Avent	.08	.25
❑ 204 Lloyd Daniels	.08	.25
❑ 205 Mark Price	.08	.25
❑ 206 Rumeal Robinson	.08	.25
❑ 207 Kendall Gill	.15	.40
❑ 208 Scottie Pippen	1.25	3.00
❑ 209 Kenny Smith	.08	.25
❑ 210 Walt Williams	.08	.25
❑ 211 Hubert Davis	.08	.25
❑ 212 Chris Webber RC	8.00	20.00
❑ 213 Rony Seikaly	.08	.25
❑ 214 Sam Bowie	.08	.25
❑ 215 Karl Malone	.60	1.50
❑ 216 Malik Sealy	.08	.25
❑ 217 Dale Ellis	.08	.25
❑ 218 Harold Miner	.08	.25
❑ 219 John Stockton	.30	.75
❑ 220 Shawn Bradley RC	.75	2.00

1994-95 Finest

❑ COMPLETE SET (1-331)	125.00	250.00
❑ COMP.SERIES 1 (165)	50.00	100.00
❑ COMP.SERIES 2 (166)	75.00	150.00
❑ COMMON CARD (1-165)	.25	.60
❑ COMMON CARD (166-331)	.10	.30
❑ 1 Chris Mullin CY	.50	1.25
❑ 2 Anthony Mason CY	.25	.60
❑ 3 John Salley CY	.25	.60
❑ 4 Jamal Mashburn CY	.50	1.25
❑ 5 Mark Jackson CY	.25	.60
❑ 6 Mario Elie CY	.25	.60
❑ 7 Kenny Anderson CY	.25	.60
❑ 8 Rod Strickland CY	.25	.60
❑ 9 Kenny Smith CY	.25	.60
❑ 10 Olden Polynice CY	.25	.60
❑ 11 Derek Harper	.25	.60
❑ 12 Danny Ainge	.25	.60
❑ 13 Dino Radja	.25	.60
❑ 14 Eric Murdock	.25	.60
❑ 15 Sean Rooks	.25	.60
❑ 16 Dell Curry	.25	.60
❑ 17 Victor Alexander	.25	.60
❑ 18 Rodney Rogers	.25	.60
❑ 19 John Salley	.25	.60
❑ 20 Brad Daugherty	.25	.60
❑ 21 Elmore Spencer	.25	.60
❑ 22 Mitch Richmond	1.00	2.50
❑ 23 Rex Walters	.25	.60
❑ 24 Antonio Davis	.25	.60
❑ 25 B.J. Armstrong	.25	.60
❑ 26 Andrew Lang	.25	.60
❑ 27 Carl Herrera	.25	.60
❑ 28 Kevin Edwards	.25	.60
❑ 29 Micheal Williams	.25	.60
❑ 30 Clyde Drexler	1.00	2.50
❑ 31 Dana Barros	.25	.60
❑ 32 Shaquille O'Neal	5.00	12.00
❑ 33 Patrick Ewing	1.00	2.50
❑ 34 Charles Barkley	1.50	4.00
❑ 35 J.R. Reid	.25	.60
❑ 36 Lindsey Hunter	.50	1.25
❑ 37 Jeff Malone	.25	.60
❑ 38 Rik Smits	.25	.60
❑ 39 Brian Williams	.25	.60
❑ 40 Shawn Kemp	1.50	4.00
❑ 41 Terry Porter	.25	.60
❑ 42 James Worthy	1.00	2.50
❑ 43 Rex Chapman	.25	.60
❑ 44 Stanley Roberts	.25	.60
❑ 45 Chris Smith	.25	.60
❑ 46 Dee Brown	.25	.60
❑ 47 Chris Gatling	.25	.60
❑ 48 Donald Hodge	.25	.60
❑ 49 Bimbo Coles	.25	.60
❑ 50 Derrick Coleman	.50	1.25
❑ 51 Muggsy Bogues CY	.25	.60
❑ 52 Reggie Williams CY	.25	.60
❑ 53 David Wingate CY	.25	.60
❑ 54 Sam Cassell CY	1.00	2.50
❑ 55 Sherman Douglas CY	.25	.60
❑ 56 Keith Jennings	.25	.60
❑ 57 Kenny Gattison	.25	.60
❑ 58 Brent Price	.25	.60
❑ 59 Luc Longley	.25	.60
❑ 60 Jamal Mashburn	1.00	2.50
❑ 61 Doug West	.25	.60
❑ 62 Walt Williams	.25	.60
❑ 63 Tracy Murray	.25	.60
❑ 64 Robert Pack	.25	.60
❑ 65 Johnny Dawkins	.25	.60
❑ 66 Vin Baker	1.00	2.50
❑ 67 Sam Cassell	1.00	2.50
❑ 68 Dale Davis	.25	.60
❑ 69 Terrell Brandon	.50	1.25
❑ 70 Billy Owens	.25	.60
❑ 71 Ervin Johnson	.25	.60
❑ 72 Allan Houston	1.50	4.00
❑ 73 Craig Ehlo	.25	.60
❑ 74 Loy Vaught	.25	.60
❑ 75 Scottie Pippen	3.00	8.00
❑ 76 Sam Bowie	.25	.60
❑ 77 Anthony Mason	.50	1.25
❑ 78 Felton Spencer	.25	.60
❑ 79 P.J. Brown	.25	.60
❑ 80 Christian Laettner	.50	1.25
❑ 81 Todd Day	.25	.60
❑ 82 Sean Elliott	.50	1.25
❑ 83 Grant Long	.25	.60
❑ 84 Xavier McDaniel	.25	.60
❑ 85 David Benoit	.25	.60
❑ 86 Larry Stewart	.25	.60
❑ 87 Donald Royal	.25	.60
❑ 88 Duane Causwell	.25	.60
❑ 89 Vlade Divac	.25	.60
❑ 90 Derrick McKey	.25	.60
❑ 91 Kevin Johnson	.50	1.25
❑ 92 LaPhonso Ellis	.25	.60
❑ 93 Jerome Kersey	.25	.60
❑ 94 Muggsy Bogues	.50	1.25
❑ 95 Tom Gugliotta	.50	1.25
❑ 96 Jeff Hornacek	.50	1.25
❑ 97 Kevin Willis	.25	.60
❑ 98 Chris Mills	.50	1.25
❑ 99 Sam Perkins	.50	1.25
❑ 100 Alonzo Mourning	1.25	3.00
❑ 101 Derrick Coleman CY	.25	.60
❑ 102 Glen Rice CY	.25	.60
❑ 103 Kevin Willis CY	.25	.60
❑ 104 Chris Webber CY	1.25	3.00
❑ 105 Terry Mills CY	.25	.60
❑ 106 Tim Hardaway CY	.50	1.25
❑ 107 Nick Anderson CY	.25	.60
❑ 108 Terry Cummings CY	.25	.60
❑ 109 Hersey Hawkins CY	.25	.60
❑ 110 Ken Norman CY	.25	.60
❑ 111 Nick Anderson	.25	.60
❑ 112 Tim Perry	.25	.60
❑ 113 Terry Dehere	.25	.60
❑ 114 Chris Morris	.25	.60
❑ 115 John Williams	.25	.60
❑ 116 Jon Barry	.25	.60
❑ 117 Rony Seikaly	.25	.60
❑ 118 Detlef Schrempf	.50	1.25
❑ 119 Terry Cummings	.25	.60
❑ 120 Chris Webber	2.50	6.00
❑ 121 David Wingate	.25	.60
❑ 122 Popeye Jones	.25	.60
❑ 123 Sherman Douglas	.25	.60
❑ 124 Greg Anthony	.25	.60
❑ 125 Mookie Blaylock	.25	.60
❑ 126 Don MacLean	.25	.60
❑ 127 Lionel Simmons	.25	.60
❑ 128 Scott Brooks	.25	.60
❑ 129 Jeff Turner	.25	.60
❑ 130 Bryant Stith	.25	.60
❑ 131 Shawn Bradley	.25	.60
❑ 132 Byron Scott	.50	1.25
❑ 133 Doug Christie	.50	1.25
❑ 134 Dennis Rodman	2.00	5.00
❑ 135 Dan Majerle	.50	1.25
❑ 136 Gary Grant	.25	.60
❑ 137 Bryon Russell	.25	.60
❑ 138 Will Perdue	.25	.60
❑ 139 Gheorghe Muresan	.25	.60
❑ 140 Kendall Gill	.50	1.25
❑ 141 Isaiah Rider	.50	1.25
❑ 142 Terry Mills	.25	.60
❑ 143 Willie Anderson	.25	.60
❑ 144 Hubert Davis	.25	.60
❑ 145 Lucious Harris	.25	.60
❑ 146 Spud Webb	.25	.60
❑ 147 Glen Rice	.50	1.25
❑ 148 Dennis Scott	.25	.60
❑ 149 Robert Horry	.50	1.25
❑ 150 John Stockton	1.00	2.50
❑ 151 Stacey Augmon CY	.25	.60
❑ 152 Chris Mills CY	.25	.60
❑ 153 Elden Campbell CY	.25	.60
❑ 154 Jay Humphries CY	.25	.60
❑ 155 Reggie Miller CY	.50	1.25
❑ 156 George Lynch	.25	.60
❑ 157 Tyrone Hill	.25	.60
❑ 158 Lee Mayberry	.25	.60
❑ 159 Jon Koncak	.25	.60
❑ 160 Joe Dumars	1.00	2.50
❑ 161 Vernon Maxwell	.25	.60
❑ 162 Joe Kleine	.25	.60
❑ 163 Acie Earl	.25	.60
❑ 164 Steve Kerr	.25	.60
❑ 165 Rod Strickland	.50	1.25
❑ 166 Glenn Robinson RC	4.00	10.00
❑ 167 Anfernee Hardaway	1.50	4.00
❑ 168 Latrell Sprewell	1.00	2.50
❑ 169 Sergei Bazarevich RC	.10	.30
❑ 170 Hakeem Olajuwon	.75	2.00
❑ 171 Nick Van Exel	.50	1.25
❑ 172 Buck Williams	.10	.30
❑ 173 Antoine Carr	.10	.30
❑ 174 Corie Blount	.10	.30
❑ 175 Dominique Wilkins	.50	1.25

❑ 176 Yinka Dare .10 .30
❑ 177 Byron Houston .10 .30
❑ 178 LaSalle Thompson .10 .30
❑ 179 Doug Smith .10 .30
❑ 180 David Robinson .75 2.00
❑ 181 Eric Piatkowski RC .10 .30
❑ 182 Scott Skiles .10 .30
❑ 183 Scott Burrell .10 .30
❑ 184 Mark West .10 .30
❑ 185 Billy Owens .10 .30
❑ 186 Brian Grant RC 2.00 5.00
❑ 187 Scott Williams .10 .30
❑ 188 Gerald Madkins .10 .30
❑ 189 Reggie Williams .10 .30
❑ 190 Danny Manning .25 .60
❑ 191 Mike Brown .10 .30
❑ 192 Charles Smith .10 .30
❑ 193 Elden Campbell .10 .30
❑ 194 Ricky Pierce .10 .30
❑ 195 Karl Malone .75 2.00
❑ 196 Brooks Thompson .10 .30
❑ 197 Alaa Abdelnaby .10 .30
❑ 198 Tyrone Corbin .10 .30
❑ 199 Johnny Newman .10 .30
❑ 200 Grant Hill CB 2.50 6.00
❑ 201 Kenny Anderson CB .10 .30
❑ 202 Olden Polynice CB .10 .30
❑ 203 Horace Grant CB .10 .30
❑ 204 Muggsy Bogues CB .10 .30
❑ 205 Mark Price CB .10 .30
❑ 206 Tom Gugliotta CB .10 .30
❑ 207 Christian Laettner CB .10 .30
❑ 208 Eric Montross CB .10 .30
❑ 209 Sam Cassell CB .50 1.25
❑ 210 Charles Oakley .10 .30
❑ 211 Harold Ellis .10 .30
❑ 212 Nate McMillan .10 .30
❑ 213 Chuck Person .10 .30
❑ 214 Harold Miner .10 .30
❑ 215 Clarence Weatherspoon .10 .30
❑ 216 Robert Parish .25 .60
❑ 217 Michael Cage .10 .30
❑ 218 Kenny Smith .10 .30
❑ 219 Larry Krystkowiak .10 .30
❑ 220 Dikembe Mutombo .25 .60
❑ 221 Wayman Tisdale .10 .30
❑ 222 Kevin Duckworth .10 .30
❑ 223 Vern Fleming .10 .30
❑ 224 Eric Mobley RC .10 .30
❑ 225 Patrick Ewing CB .25 .60
❑ 226 Clifford Robinson CB .10 .30
❑ 227 Eric Murdock CB .10 .30
❑ 228 Derrick Coleman CB .10 .30
❑ 229 Otis Thorpe CB .10 .30
❑ 230 Alonzo Mourning CB .50 1.25
❑ 231 Donyell Marshall CB .25 .60
❑ 232 Dikembe Mutombo CB .10 .30
❑ 233 Rony Seikaly CB .10 .30
❑ 234 Chris Mullin CB .25 .60
❑ 235 Reggie Miller .50 1.25
❑ 236 Benoit Benjamin .10 .30
❑ 237 Sean Rooks .10 .30
❑ 238 Terry Davis .10 .30
❑ 239 Anthony Avent .10 .30
❑ 240 Grant Hill RC 10.00 25.00
❑ 241 Randy Woods .10 .30
❑ 242 Tom Chambers .10 .30
❑ 243 Michael Adams .10 .30
❑ 244 Monty Williams RC .10 .30
❑ 245 Chris Mullin .50 1.25
❑ 246 Bill Wennington .10 .30
❑ 247 Mark Jackson .10 .30
❑ 248 Blue Edwards .10 .30
❑ 249 Jalen Rose RC 4.00 10.00
❑ 250 Glenn Robinson CB .60 1.50
❑ 251 Kevin Willis CB .10 .30
❑ 252 B.J. Armstrong CB .10 .30
❑ 253 Jim Jackson CB .10 .30
❑ 254 Steve Smith CB .10 .30
❑ 255 Chris Webber CB .60 1.50
❑ 256 Glen Rice CB .10 .30
❑ 257 Derek Harper CB .10 .30
❑ 258 Jalen Rose CB .75 2.00
❑ 259 Juwan Howard CB .50 1.25
❑ 260 Kenny Anderson .25 .60
❑ 261 Calbert Cheaney .10 .30
❑ 262 Bill Cartwright .10 .30
❑ 263 Mario Elie .10 .30
❑ 264 Chris Dudley .10 .30
❑ 265 Jim Jackson .25 .60
❑ 266 Antonio Harvey .10 .30
❑ 267 Bill Curley RC .10 .30
❑ 268 Moses Malone .50 1.25
❑ 269 A.C. Green .25 .60
❑ 270 Larry Johnson .25 .60
❑ 271 Marty Conlon .10 .30
❑ 272 Greg Graham .10 .30
❑ 273 Eric Montross RC .10 .30
❑ 274 Stacey King .10 .30
❑ 275 Charles Barkley CB .50 1.25
❑ 276 Chris Morris CB .10 .30
❑ 277 Robert Horry CB .25 .60
❑ 278 Dominique Wilkins CB .25 .60
❑ 279 Latrell Sprewell CB .50 1.25
❑ 280 Shaquille O'Neal CB 1.25 3.00
❑ 281 Wesley Person CB .25 .60
❑ 282 Mahmoud Abdul-Rauf CB .10 .30
❑ 283 Jamal Mashburn CB .25 .60
❑ 284 Dale Ellis CB .10 .30
❑ 285 Gary Payton .75 2.00
❑ 286 Jason Kidd RC 8.00 20.00
❑ 287 Ken Norman .10 .30
❑ 288 Juwan Howard RC 2.00 5.00
❑ 289 Lamond Murray RC .75 2.00
❑ 290 Clifford Robinson .25 .60
❑ 291 Frank Brickowski .10 .30
❑ 292 Adam Keefe .10 .30
❑ 293 Ron Harper .25 .60
❑ 294 Tom Hammonds .10 .30
❑ 295 Otis Thorpe .10 .30
❑ 296 Rick Mahorn .10 .30
❑ 297 Alton Lister .10 .30
❑ 298 Vinny Del Negro .10 .30
❑ 299 Danny Ferry .10 .30
❑ 300 John Starks .10 .30
❑ 301 Duane Ferrell .10 .30
❑ 302 Hersey Hawkins .25 .60
❑ 303 Khalid Reeves RC .10 .30
❑ 304 Anthony Peeler .10 .30
❑ 305 Tim Hardaway .50 1.25
❑ 306 Rick Fox .10 .30
❑ 307 Jay Humphries .10 .30
❑ 308 Brian Shaw .10 .30
❑ 309 Danny Schayes .10 .30
❑ 310 Stacey Augmon .10 .30
❑ 311 Oliver Miller .10 .30
❑ 312 Pooh Richardson .10 .30
❑ 313 Donyell Marshall RC 2.00 5.00
❑ 314 Aaron McKie RC 2.00 5.00
❑ 315 Mark Price .10 .30
❑ 316 B.J.Tyler RC .10 .30
❑ 317 Olden Polynice .10 .30
❑ 318 Avery Johnson .10 .30
❑ 319 Derek Strong .10 .30
❑ 320 Toni Kukoc .75 2.00
❑ 321 Charlie Ward RC 1.50 4.00
❑ 322 Wesley Person RC 1.50 4.00
❑ 323 Eddie Jones RC 4.00 10.00
❑ 324 Horace Grant .25 .60
❑ 325 Mahmoud Abdul-Rauf .10 .30
❑ 326 Sharone Wright RC .10 .30
❑ 327 Kevin Gamble .10 .30
❑ 328 Sarunas Marciulionis .10 .30
❑ 329 Harvey Grant .10 .30
❑ 330 Bobby Hurley .10 .30
❑ 331 Michael Jordan 6.00 15.00

1995-96 Finest

❑ COMPLETE SET (251) 120.00 220.00
❑ COMP.SERIES 1 (140) 100.00 180.00
❑ COMP.SERIES 2 (111) 20.00 40.00
❑ COMMON CARD (1-250/252) .30 .75
❑ COMMON ROOKIE .60 1.50
❑ 1 Hakeem Olajuwon 1.00 2.50
❑ 2 Stacey Augmon .30 .75
❑ 3 John Starks .60 1.50
❑ 4 Sharone Wright .30 .75
❑ 5 Jason Kidd 3.00 8.00
❑ 6 Lamond Murray .30 .75
❑ 7 Kenny Anderson .60 1.50
❑ 8 James Robinson .30 .75
❑ 9 Wesley Person .30 .75
❑ 10 Latrell Sprewell 1.00 2.50
❑ 11 Sean Elliott .60 1.50
❑ 12 Greg Anthony .30 .75
❑ 13 Kendall Gill .30 .75
❑ 14 Mark Jackson .60 1.50
❑ 15 John Stockton 1.25 3.00
❑ 16 Steve Smith .60 1.50
❑ 17 Bobby Hurley .30 .75
❑ 18 Ervin Johnson .30 .75
❑ 19 Elden Campbell .30 .75
❑ 20 Vin Baker .60 1.50
❑ 21 Micheal Williams .30 .75
❑ 22 Steve Kerr .60 1.50
❑ 23 Kevin Duckworth .30 .75
❑ 24 Willie Anderson .30 .75
❑ 25 Joe Dumars 1.00 2.50
❑ 26 Dale Ellis .30 .75
❑ 27 Bimbo Coles .30 .75
❑ 28 Nick Anderson .30 .75
❑ 29 Dee Brown .30 .75
❑ 30 Tyrone Hill .30 .75
❑ 31 Reggie Miller 1.00 2.50
❑ 32 Shaquille O'Neal 2.50 6.00
❑ 33 Brian Grant 1.00 2.50
❑ 34 Charles Barkley 1.25 3.00
❑ 35 Cedric Ceballos .30 .75
❑ 36 Rex Walters .30 .75
❑ 37 Kenny Smith .30 .75
❑ 38 Popeye Jones .30 .75
❑ 39 Harvey Grant .30 .75
❑ 40 Gary Payton 1.00 2.50
❑ 41 John Williams .30 .75
❑ 42 Sherman Douglas .30 .75
❑ 43 Oliver Miller .30 .75
❑ 44 Kevin Willis .60 1.50
❑ 45 Isaiah Rider .30 .75
❑ 46 Gheorghe Muresan .30 .75
❑ 47 Blue Edwards .30 .75
❑ 48 Jeff Hornacek .60 1.50
❑ 49 J.R. Reid .30 .75
❑ 50 Glenn Robinson 1.00 2.50
❑ 51 Dell Curry .30 .75
❑ 52 Greg Graham .30 .75
❑ 53 Ron Harper .60 1.50
❑ 54 Derek Harper .60 1.50
❑ 55 Dikembe Mutombo .60 1.50
❑ 56 Terry Mills .30 .75
❑ 57 Victor Alexander .30 .75
❑ 58 Malik Sealy .30 .75
❑ 59 Vincent Askew .30 .75
❑ 60 Mitch Richmond .60 1.50
❑ 61 Duane Ferrell .30 .75
❑ 62 Dickey Simpkins .30 .75
❑ 63 Pooh Richardson .30 .75
❑ 64 Khalid Reeves .30 .75
❑ 65 Dino Radja .30 .75
❑ 66 Lee Mayberry .30 .75
❑ 67 Kenny Gattison .30 .75
❑ 68 Joe Kleine .30 .75
❑ 69 Tony Dumas .30 .75
❑ 70 Nick Van Exel 1.00 2.50
❑ 71 Armon Gilliam .30 .75
❑ 72 Craig Ehlo .30 .75
❑ 73 Adam Keefe .30 .75
❑ 74 Chris Dudley .30 .75
❑ 75 Clyde Drexler 1.00 2.50
❑ 76 Jeff Turner .30 .75
❑ 77 Calbert Cheaney .30 .75
❑ 78 Vinny Del Negro .30 .75
❑ 79 Tim Perry .30 .75
❑ 80 Tim Hardaway .60 1.50
❑ 81 B.J. Armstrong .30 .75
❑ 82 Muggsy Bogues .60 1.50
❑ 83 Mark Macon .30 .75
❑ 84 Doug West .30 .75
❑ 85 Jalen Rose 1.25 3.00
❑ 86 Chris Mills .30 .75
❑ 87 Charles Oakley .30 .75
❑ 88 Andrew Lang .30 .75
❑ 89 Olden Polynice .30 .75
❑ 90 Sam Cassell 1.00 2.50
❑ 91 Todd Day .30 .75

❑ 92 P.J. Brown	.30	.75
❑ 93 Benoit Benjamin	.30	.75
❑ 94 Sam Perkins	.60	1.50
❑ 95 Eddie Jones	1.25	3.00
❑ 96 Robert Parish	.60	1.50
❑ 97 Avery Johnson	.30	.75
❑ 98 Lindsey Hunter	.30	.75
❑ 99 Billy Owens	.30	.75
❑ 100 Shawn Bradley	.30	.75
❑ 101 Dale Davis	.30	.75
❑ 102 Terry Dehere	.30	.75
❑ 103 A.C. Green	.60	1.50
❑ 104 Christian Laettner	.60	1.50
❑ 105 Horace Grant	.60	1.50
❑ 106 Rony Seikaly	.30	.75
❑ 107 Reggie Williams	.30	.75
❑ 108 Toni Kukoc	.60	1.50
❑ 109 Terrell Brandon	.60	1.50
❑ 110 Clifford Robinson	.30	.75
❑ 111 Joe Smith RC	2.00	5.00
❑ 112 Antonio McDyess RC	4.00	10.00
❑ 113 Jerry Stackhouse RC	6.00	15.00
❑ 114 Rasheed Wallace RC	6.00	12.00
❑ 115 Kevin Garnett RC	20.00	40.00
❑ 116 Bryant Reeves RC	1.00	2.50
❑ 117 Damon Stoudamire RC	2.50	6.00
❑ 118 Shawn Respert RC	.30	.75
❑ 119 Ed O'Bannon RC	.60	1.50
❑ 120 Kurt Thomas RC	.60	1.50
❑ 121 Gary Trent RC	1.25	3.00
❑ 122 Cherokee Parks RC	.60	1.50
❑ 123 Corliss Williamson RC	1.25	3.00
❑ 124 Eric Williams RC	.60	1.50
❑ 125 Brent Barry RC	1.00	2.50
❑ 126 Alan Henderson RC	1.25	3.00
❑ 127 Bob Sura RC	.60	1.50
❑ 128 Theo Ratliff RC	2.00	5.00
❑ 129 Randolph Childress RC	.60	1.50
❑ 130 Jason Caffey RC	.60	1.50
❑ 131 Michael Finley RC	5.00	12.00
❑ 132 George Zidek RC	.60	1.50
❑ 133 Travis Best RC	.60	1.50
❑ 134 Loren Meyer RC	.60	1.50
❑ 135 David Vaughn RC	.60	1.50
❑ 136 Sherrell Ford RC	.60	1.50
❑ 137 Mario Bennett RC	.60	1.50
❑ 138 Greg Ostertag RC	.60	1.50
❑ 139 Cory Alexander RC	.60	1.50
❑ 140 Checklist (1-110) UER misnumbered #111	.30	.75
❑ 141 Chucky Brown	.30	.75
❑ 142 Eric Mobley	.30	.75
❑ 143 Tom Hammonds	.30	.75
❑ 144 Chris Webber	1.25	3.00
❑ 145 Carlos Rogers	.30	.75
❑ 146 Chuck Person	.30	.75
❑ 147 Brian Williams	.30	.75
❑ 148 Kevin Gamble	.30	.75
❑ 149 Dennis Rodman	.60	1.50
❑ 150 Pervis Ellison	.30	.75
❑ 151 Jayson Williams	.30	.75
❑ 152 Buck Williams	.30	.75
❑ 153 Allan Houston	.60	1.50
❑ 154 Tom Gugliotta	.30	.75
❑ 155 Charles Smith	.30	.75
❑ 156 Chris Gatling	.30	.75
❑ 157 Darrin Hancock	.30	.75
❑ 158 Blue Edwards	.30	.75
❑ 159 Shawn Kemp	.60	1.50
❑ 160 Michael Cage	.30	.75
❑ 161 Sedale Threatt	.30	.75
❑ 162 Byron Scott	.30	.75
❑ 163 Elliot Perry	.30	.75
❑ 164 Jim Jackson	.30	.75
❑ 165 Wayman Tisdale	.30	.75
❑ 166 Vernon Maxwell	.30	.75
❑ 167 Brian Shaw	.30	.75
❑ 168 Haywoode Workman	.30	.75
❑ 169 Mookie Blaylock	.30	.75
❑ 170 Donald Royal	.30	.75
❑ 171 Lorenzo Williams	.30	.75
❑ 172 Eric Piatkowski	.60	1.50
❑ 173 Sarunas Marciulionis	.30	.75
❑ 174 Otis Thorpe	.30	.75
❑ 175 Rex Chapman	.30	.75
❑ 176 Felton Spencer	.30	.75
❑ 177 John Salley	.30	.75
❑ 178 Pete Chilcutt	.30	.75
❑ 179 Scottie Pippen	1.50	4.00
❑ 180 Robert Pack	.30	.75
❑ 181 Dana Barros	.30	.75
❑ 182 Mahmoud Abdul-Rauf	.30	.75
❑ 183 Eric Murdock	.30	.75
❑ 184 Anthony Mason	.60	1.50
❑ 185 Will Perdue	.30	.75
❑ 186 Jeff Malone	.30	.75
❑ 187 Anthony Peeler	.30	.75
❑ 188 Chris Childs	.30	.75
❑ 189 Glen Rice	.60	1.50
❑ 190 Grant Hill	1.25	3.00
❑ 191 Michael Smith	.30	.75
❑ 192 Sean Rooks	.30	.75
❑ 193 Clifford Rozier	.30	.75
❑ 194 Rik Smits	.60	1.50
❑ 195 Spud Webb	.60	1.50
❑ 196 Aaron McKie	.60	1.50
❑ 197 Nate McMillan	.30	.75
❑ 198 Bobby Phills	.30	.75
❑ 199 Dennis Scott	.30	.75
❑ 200 Mark West	.30	.75
❑ 201 George McCloud	.30	.75
❑ 202 B.J. Tyler	.30	.75
❑ 203 Lionel Simmons	.30	.75
❑ 204 Loy Vaught	.30	.75
❑ 205 Kevin Edwards	.30	.75
❑ 206 Eric Montross	.30	.75
❑ 207 Kenny Gattison	.30	.75
❑ 208 Mario Elie	.30	.75
❑ 209 Karl Malone	1.25	3.00
❑ 210 Ken Norman	.30	.75
❑ 211 Antonio Davis	.30	.75
❑ 212 Doc Rivers	.60	1.50
❑ 213 Hubert Davis	.30	.75
❑ 214 Jamal Mashburn	.60	1.50
❑ 215 Donyell Marshall	.60	1.50
❑ 216 Sasha Danilovic RC	.30	.75
❑ 217 Danny Manning	.60	1.50
❑ 218 Scott Burrell	.30	.75
❑ 219 Vlade Divac	.60	1.50
❑ 220 Marty Conlon	.30	.75
❑ 221 Clarence Weatherspoon	.30	.75
❑ 222 Terry Porter	.30	.75
❑ 223 Luc Longley	.30	.75
❑ 224 Juwan Howard	1.00	2.50
❑ 225 Danny Ferry	.30	.75
❑ 226 Rod Strickland	.30	.75
❑ 227 Bryant Stith	.30	.75
❑ 228 Derrick McKey	.30	.75
❑ 229 Michael Jordan	6.00	15.00
❑ 230 Jamie Watson	.30	.75
❑ 231 Rick Fox	.60	1.50
❑ 232 Scott Williams	.30	.75
❑ 233 Larry Johnson	.60	1.50
❑ 234 Anfernee Hardaway	1.00	2.50
❑ 235 Hersey Hawkins	.30	.75
❑ 236 Robert Horry	.60	1.50
❑ 237 Kevin Johnson	.60	1.50
❑ 238 Rodney Rogers	.30	.75
❑ 239 Detlef Schrempf	.60	1.50
❑ 240 Derrick Coleman	.30	.75
❑ 241 Walt Williams	.30	.75
❑ 242 LaPhonso Ellis	.30	.75
❑ 243 Patrick Ewing	1.00	2.50
❑ 244 Grant Long	.30	.75
❑ 245 David Robinson	1.00	2.50
❑ 246 Chris Mullin	1.00	2.50
❑ 247 Alonzo Mourning	.60	1.50
❑ 248 Dan Majerle	.60	1.50
❑ 249 Johnny Newman	.30	.75
❑ 250 Chris Morris	.30	.75
❑ 252 Magic Johnson	1.50	4.00

1996-97 Finest

❑ COMPLETE SET (291)	300.00	600.00
❑ COMPLETE SERIES 1 (146)	150.00	350.00
❑ COMPLETE SERIES 2 (145)	150.00	300.00
❑ COMP.BRONZE SET (200)	70.00	140.00
❑ COMP.BRONZE SER.1 (100)	50.00	100.00
❑ COMP.BRONZE SER.2 (100)	20.00	40.00
❑ COMMON BRONZE	.15	.40
❑ COMMON BRONZE RC	.50	1.25
❑ COMP.SILVER SET (54)	60.00	120.00
❑ COMP.SILVER SER.1 (27)	20.00	40.00
❑ COMP.SILVER SER.2 (27)	40.00	80.00
❑ COMMON SILVER	.50	1.25
❑ COMP.GOLD SET (37)	200.00	400.00
❑ COMP.GOLD SER.1 (19)	100.00	200.00
❑ COMP.GOLD SER.2 (18)	100.00	200.00
❑ COMMON GOLD	1.50	4.00
❑ 1 Scottie Pippen B	.75	2.00
❑ 2 Tim Legler B	.15	.40
❑ 3 Rex Walters B	.15	.40
❑ 4 Calbert Cheaney B	.15	.40
❑ 5 Dennis Rodman B	.30	.75
❑ 6 Tyrone Hill B	.15	.40
❑ 7 Christian Laettner B UER	2.50	6.00
❑ 8 Dell Curry B	.15	.40
❑ 9 Olden Polynice B	.15	.40
❑ 10 John Wallace B RC	.60	1.50
❑ 11 Martin Muursepp B RC	.50	1.25
❑ 12 Chuck Person B	.15	.40
❑ 13 Grant Hill B	.50	1.25
❑ 14 Shawn Kemp B	.30	.75
❑ 15 B.J. Armstrong B	.15	.40
❑ 16 Gary Trent B	.15	.40
❑ 17 Scott Williams B	.15	.40
❑ 18 Dino Radja B	.15	.40
❑ 19 Roy Rogers B RC	.50	1.25
❑ 20 Tony Delk B RC	1.00	2.50
❑ 21 Clifford Robinson B	.15	.40
❑ 22 Ray Allen B RC	3.00	8.00
❑ 23 Clyde Drexler B	.50	1.25
❑ 24 Elliot Perry B	.15	.40
❑ 25 Gary Payton B	.50	1.25
❑ 26 Dale Davis B	.15	.40
❑ 27 Horace Grant B	.30	.75
❑ 28 Brian Evans B RC	.50	1.25
❑ 29 Joe Smith B	.30	.75
❑ 30 Reggie Miller B	.50	1.25
❑ 31 Jermaine O'Neal B RC	2.50	6.00
❑ 32 Avery Johnson B	.15	.40
❑ 33 Ed O'Bannon B	.15	.40
❑ 34 Cedric Ceballos B	.15	.40
❑ 35 Jamal Mashburn B	.30	.75
❑ 36 Micheal Williams B	.15	.40
❑ 37 Detlef Schrempf B	.30	.75
❑ 38 Damon Stoudamire B	.50	1.25
❑ 39 Jason Kidd B	.75	2.00
❑ 40 Tom Gugliotta B	.15	.40
❑ 41 Arvydas Sabonis B	.30	.75
❑ 42 Samaki Walker B RC	.50	1.25
❑ 43 Derek Fisher B RC	1.50	4.00
❑ 44 Patrick Ewing B	.50	1.25
❑ 45 Bryant Reeves B	.15	.40
❑ 46 Mookie Blaylock B	.15	.40
❑ 47 George Zidek B	.15	.40
❑ 48 Jerry Stackhouse B	.60	1.50
❑ 49 Vin Baker B	.30	.75
❑ 50 Michael Jordan B	3.00	8.00
❑ 51 Terrell Brandon B	.30	.75
❑ 52 Karl Malone B	.50	1.25
❑ 53 Lorenzen Wright B RC	.50	1.25
❑ 54 S.Abdur-Rahim B RC	2.00	5.00
❑ 55 Kurt Thomas B	.30	.75
❑ 56 Glen Rice B	.30	.75
❑ 57 Shawn Bradley B	.15	.40
❑ 58 Todd Fuller B RC	.50	1.25
❑ 59 Dale Ellis B	.15	.40
❑ 60 David Robinson B	.50	1.25
❑ 61 Doug Christie B	.30	.75
❑ 62 Stephon Marbury B RC	2.50	6.00
❑ 63 Hakeem Olajuwon B	.50	1.25
❑ 64 Lindsey Hunter B	.15	.40
❑ 65 Anfernee Hardaway B	.50	1.25
❑ 66 Kevin Garnett B	1.00	2.50
❑ 67 Kendall Gill B	.15	.40
❑ 68 Sean Elliott B	.30	.75
❑ 69 Allen Iverson B RC	4.00	10.00
❑ 70 Erick Dampier B RC	1.00	2.50
❑ 71 Jerome Williams B RC	1.00	2.50
❑ 72 Charles Jones B	.15	.40
❑ 73 Danny Manning B	.30	.75
❑ 74 Kobe Bryant B RC	25.00	50.00
❑ 75 Steve Nash B RC	5.00	12.00

❑ 76 Sam Perkins B	.30	.75
❑ 77 Horace Grant B	.30	.75
❑ 78 Alonzo Mourning B	.30	.75
❑ 79 Kerry Kittles B RC	1.00	2.50
❑ 80 LaPhonso Ellis B	.15	.40
❑ 81 Michael Finley B	.60	1.50
❑ 82 Marcus Camby B RC	1.25	3.00
❑ 83 Antonio McDyess B	.30	.75
❑ 84 Antoine Walker B RC	2.50	6.00
❑ 85 Juwan Howard B	.30	.75
❑ 86 Bryon Russell B	.15	.40
❑ 87 Walter McCarty B RC	.50	1.25
❑ 88 Priest Lauderdale B RC	.50	1.25
❑ 89 C.Weatherspoon B	.15	.40
❑ 90 John Stockton B	.50	1.25
❑ 91 Mitch Richmond B	.30	.75
❑ 92 Dontae' Jones B RC	.50	1.25
❑ 93 Michael Smith B	.15	.40
❑ 94 Brent Barry B	.15	.40
❑ 95 Chris Mills B	.15	.40
❑ 96 Dee Brown B	.15	.40
❑ 97 Terry Dehere B	.15	.40
❑ 98 Danny Ferry B	.15	.40
❑ 99 Gheorghe Muresan B	.15	.40
❑ 100 Checklist B	.15	.40
❑ 101 Jim Jackson S	.50	1.25
❑ 102 Cedric Ceballos S	.50	1.25
❑ 103 Glen Rice S	1.00	2.50
❑ 104 Tom Gugliotta S	.50	1.25
❑ 105 Mario Elie S	.50	1.25
❑ 106 Nick Anderson S	.50	1.25
❑ 107 Glenn Robinson S	1.00	2.50
❑ 108 Terrell Brandon S	1.00	2.50
❑ 109 Tim Hardaway S	1.00	2.50
❑ 110 John Stockton S	1.50	4.00
❑ 111 Brent Barry S	.50	1.25
❑ 112 Mookie Blaylock S	.50	1.25
❑ 113 Tyus Edney S	.50	1.25
❑ 114 Gary Payton S	1.50	4.00
❑ 115 Joe Smith S	1.00	2.50
❑ 116 Karl Malone S	1.50	4.00
❑ 117 Dino Radja S	.50	1.25
❑ 118 Alonzo Mourning S	1.00	2.50
❑ 119 Bryant Stith S	.50	1.25
❑ 120 Derrick McKey S	.50	1.25
❑ 121 Clyde Drexler S	1.50	4.00
❑ 122 Michael Finley S	2.00	5.00
❑ 123 Sean Elliott S	1.00	2.50
❑ 124 Hakeem Olajuwon S	1.50	4.00
❑ 125 Joe Dumars S	1.50	4.00
❑ 126 Shawn Bradley S	.50	1.25
❑ 127 Michael Jordan S	10.00	25.00
❑ 128 Latrell Sprewell G	4.00	10.00
❑ 129 Anfernee Hardaway G	4.00	10.00
❑ 130 Grant Hill G	4.00	10.00
❑ 131 Damon Stoudamire G	4.00	10.00
❑ 132 David Robinson G	4.00	10.00
❑ 133 Scottie Pippen G	6.00	15.00
❑ 135 Jason Kidd G	6.00	15.00
❑ 136A Jeff Hornacek G	1.50	4.00
❑ 136B Patrick Ewing G UER	4.00	10.00
❑ 137 Jerry Stackhouse G	5.00	12.00
❑ 138 Kevin Garnett G	8.00	20.00
❑ 139 Mitch Richmond G	2.50	6.00
❑ 140 Juwan Howard G	2.50	6.00
❑ 141 Reggie Miller G	4.00	10.00
❑ 142 Christian Laettner G	2.50	6.00
❑ 143 Vin Baker G	2.50	6.00
❑ 144 Shawn Kemp G	2.50	6.00
❑ 145 Dennis Rodman G	2.50	6.00
❑ 146 Shaquille O'Neal G	10.00	25.00
❑ 147 Mookie Blaylock B	.15	.40
❑ 148 Derek Harper B	.15	.40
❑ 149 Gerald Wilkins B	.15	.40
❑ 150 Adam Keefe B	.15	.40
❑ 151 Billy Owens B	.15	.40
❑ 152 Terrell Brandon B	.30	.75
❑ 153 Antonio Davis B	.15	.40
❑ 154 Muggsy Bogues B	.15	.40
❑ 155 Cherokee Parks B	.15	.40
❑ 156 Rasheed Wallace B	.60	1.50
❑ 157 Lee Mayberry B	.15	.40
❑ 158 Craig Ehlo B	.15	.40
❑ 159 Todd Fuller B	.15	.40
❑ 160 Charles Barkley B	.60	1.50
❑ 161 Glenn Robinson B	.50	1.25
❑ 162 Charles Oakley B	.15	.40
❑ 163 Chris Webber B	.50	1.25
❑ 164 Frank Brickowski B	.15	.40
❑ 165 Mark Jackson B	.15	.40
❑ 166 Jayson Williams B	.30	.75
❑ 167 Clarence Weatherspoon B	.15	.40
❑ 168 Toni Kukoc B	.30	.75
❑ 169 Alan Henderson B	.15	.40
❑ 170 Tony Delk B	.30	.75
❑ 171 Jamal Mashburn B	.30	.75
❑ 172 Vinny Del Negro B	.15	.40
❑ 173 Greg Ostertag B	.15	.40
❑ 174 Shawn Bradley B	.15	.40
❑ 175 Gheorghe Muresan B	.15	.40
❑ 176 Brent Price B	.15	.40
❑ 177 Rick Fox B	.15	.40
❑ 178 Stacey Augmon B	.15	.40
❑ 179 P.J. Brown B	.15	.40
❑ 180 Jim Jackson B	.15	.40
❑ 181 Hersey Hawkins B	.30	.75
❑ 182 Danny Manning B	.30	.75
❑ 183 Dennis Scott B	.15	.40
❑ 184 Tom Gugliotta B	.15	.40
❑ 185 Tyrone Hill B	.15	.40
❑ 186 Malik Sealy B	.15	.40
❑ 187 John Starks B	.30	.75
❑ 188 Mark Price B	.30	.75
❑ 189 Elden Campbell B	.15	.40
❑ 190 Mahmoud Abdul-Rauf B	.15	.40
❑ 191 Will Perdue B	.15	.40
❑ 192 Nate McMillan B	.15	.40
❑ 193 Robert Horry B	.30	.75
❑ 194 Dino Radja B	.15	.40
❑ 195 Loy Vaught B	.15	.40
❑ 196 Dikembe Mutombo B	.30	.75
❑ 197 Eric Montross B	.15	.40
❑ 198 Sasha Danilovic B	.15	.40
❑ 199 Kenny Anderson B	.15	.40
❑ 200 Sean Elliott B	.30	.75
❑ 201 Mark West B	.15	.40
❑ 202 Vlade Divac B	.15	.40
❑ 203 Joe Dumars B	.50	1.25
❑ 204 Allan Houston B	.30	.75
❑ 205 Kevin Garnett B	1.00	2.50
❑ 206 Rod Strickland B	.15	.40
❑ 207 Robert Parish B	.30	.75
❑ 208 Jalen Rose B	.50	1.25
❑ 209 Armon Gilliam B	.15	.40
❑ 210 Kerry Kittles B	.50	1.25
❑ 211 Derrick Coleman B	.30	.75
❑ 212 Greg Anthony B	.15	.40
❑ 213 Joe Smith B	.30	.75
❑ 214 Steve Smith B	.30	.75
❑ 215 Tim Hardaway B	.30	.75
❑ 216 Tyus Edney B	.15	.40
❑ 217 Steve Nash B	.60	1.50
❑ 218 Anthony Mason B	.30	.75
❑ 219 Otis Thorpe B	.15	.40
❑ 220 Eddie Jones B	.50	1.25
❑ 221 Rik Smits B	.30	.75
❑ 222 Isaiah Rider B	.30	.75
❑ 223 Bobby Phills B	.15	.40
❑ 224 Antoine Walker B	.50	1.25
❑ 225 Rod Strickland B	.15	.40
❑ 226 Hubert Davis B	.15	.40
❑ 227 Eric Williams B	.15	.40
❑ 228 Danny Manning B	.30	.75
❑ 229 Dominique Wilkins B	.50	1.25
❑ 230 Brian Shaw B	.15	.40
❑ 231 Larry Johnson B	.30	.75
❑ 232 Kevin Willis B	.15	.40
❑ 233 Bryant Stith B	.15	.40
❑ 234 Blue Edwards B	.15	.40
❑ 235 Robert Pack B	.15	.40
❑ 236 Brian Grant B	.50	1.25
❑ 237 Latrell Sprewell B	.50	1.25
❑ 238 Glen Rice B	.30	.75
❑ 239 Jerome Williams B	.50	1.25
❑ 240 Allen Iverson B	1.00	2.50
❑ 241 Popeye Jones B	.15	.40
❑ 242 Clifford Robinson B	.15	.40
❑ 243 Shaquille O'Neal B	1.50	4.00
❑ 244 Vitaly Potapenko B RC	.50	1.25
❑ 245 Ervin Johnson B	.15	.40
❑ 246 Checklist	.15	.40
❑ 247 Scottie Pippen S	2.50	6.00
❑ 248 Jason Kidd S	2.50	6.00
❑ 249 Antonio McDyess S	1.00	2.50
❑ 250 Latrell Sprewell S	1.50	4.00
❑ 251 Lorenzen Wright S	.50	1.25
❑ 252 Ray Allen S	3.00	8.00
❑ 253 Stephon Marbury S	2.00	5.00
❑ 254 Patrick Ewing S	1.50	4.00
❑ 255 Anfernee Hardaway S	1.50	4.00
❑ 256 Kenny Anderson S	.50	1.25
❑ 257 David Robinson S	1.50	4.00
❑ 258 Marcus Camby S	1.50	4.00
❑ 259 S.Abdur-Rahim S	3.00	8.00
❑ 260 Dennis Rodman S	1.00	2.50
❑ 261 Juwan Howard S	1.00	2.50
❑ 262 Damon Stoudamire S	1.50	4.00
❑ 263 Shawn Kemp S	1.00	2.50
❑ 264 Mitch Richmond S	1.00	2.50
❑ 265 Jerry Stackhouse S	2.00	5.00
❑ 266 Horace Grant S	1.00	2.50
❑ 267 Kerry Kittles S	.50	1.25
❑ 268 Vin Baker S	1.00	2.50
❑ 269 Kobe Bryant G	40.00	80.00
❑ 270 Reggie Miller S	1.50	4.00
❑ 271 Grant Hill S	1.50	4.00
❑ 272 Oliver Miller S	.50	1.25
❑ 273 Chris Webber S	1.00	2.50
❑ 274 Dikembe Mutombo G	2.50	6.00
❑ 275 Antonio McDyess G	2.50	6.00
❑ 276 Clyde Drexler G	4.00	10.00
❑ 277 Brent Barry G	1.50	4.00
❑ 278 Tim Hardaway G	2.50	6.00
❑ 279 Glenn Robinson G	2.50	6.00
❑ 280 Allen Iverson G	6.00	15.00
❑ 281 Hakeem Olajuwon G	4.00	10.00
❑ 282 Marcus Camby G	4.00	10.00
❑ 283 John Stockton G	4.00	10.00
❑ 284 S.Abdur-Rahim G	6.00	15.00
❑ 285 Karl Malone G	4.00	10.00
❑ 286 Gary Payton G	4.00	10.00
❑ 287 Stephon Marbury G	4.00	10.00
❑ 288 Alonzo Mourning G	2.50	6.00
❑ 289 Shaquille O'Neal S	3.00	8.00
❑ 290 Charles Barkley G	5.00	12.00
❑ 291 Michael Jordan G	25.00	60.00

1997-98 Finest

❑ COMPLETE SET (326)	375.00	750.00
❑ COMPLETE SERIES 1 (173)	175.00	350.00
❑ COMPLETE SERIES 2 (153)	200.00	400.00
❑ COMP.BRONZE SET (220)	50.00	100.00
❑ COMP.BRONZE SER.1 (120)	30.00	60.00
❑ COMP.BRONZE SER.2 (100)	25.00	50.00
❑ COMMON BRONZE	.10	.30
❑ COMMON BRONZE RC	.25	.60
❑ COMP.SILVER SET (66)	75.00	150.00
❑ COMP.SILVER SER.1 (33)	40.00	80.00
❑ COMP.SILVER SER.2 (33)	30.00	60.00
❑ COMMON SILVER	.40	1.00
❑ COMP.GOLD SET (40)	250.00	500.00
❑ COMP.GOLD SER.1 (20)	100.00	200.00
❑ COMP.GOLD SER.2 (20)	150.00	300.00
❑ COMMON GOLD	1.50	4.00
❑ 1 Scottie Pippen B	.60	1.50
❑ 2 Tim Hardaway B	.25	.60
❑ 3 Bo Outlaw	.10	.30
❑ 4 Rik Smits B	.25	.60
❑ 5 Dale Ellis B	.10	.30
❑ 6 Clyde Drexler B	.40	1.00
❑ 7 Steve Smith B	.25	.60
❑ 8 Nick Anderson B	.10	.30
❑ 9 Juwan Howard B	.25	.60
❑ 10 Cedric Ceballos B	.10	.30
❑ 11 Shawn Bradley B	.10	.30
❑ 12 Loy Vaught B	.10	.30
❑ 13 Todd Day B	.10	.30
❑ 14 Glen Rice B	.25	.60
❑ 15 Bryant Stith B	.10	.30
❑ 16 Bob Sura B	.10	.30
❑ 17 Derrick McKey B	.10	.30
❑ 18 Ray Allen B	.40	1.00
❑ 19 Stephon Marbury B	.50	1.25
❑ 20 David Robinson B	.40	1.00

❑ 21 Anthony Peeler B	.10	.30
❑ 22 Isaiah Rider B	.25	.60
❑ 23 Mookie Blaylock B	.10	.30
❑ 24 Damon Stoudamire B	.25	.60
❑ 25 Rod Strickland B	.10	.30
❑ 26 Glenn Robinson B	.40	1.00
❑ 27 Chris Webber B	.40	1.00
❑ 28 Christian Laettner B	.25	.60
❑ 29 Joe Dumars B	.40	1.00
❑ 30 Mark Price B	.25	.60
❑ 31 Jamal Mashburn B	.25	.60
❑ 32 Danny Manning B	.25	.60
❑ 33 John Stockton B	.40	1.00
❑ 34 Detlef Schrempf B	.25	.60
❑ 35 Tyus Edney B	.10	.30
❑ 36 Chris Childs B	.10	.30
❑ 37 Dana Barros B	.10	.30
❑ 38 Bobby Phills B	.10	.30
❑ 39 Michael Jordan B	2.50	6.00
❑ 40 Grant Hill B	.40	1.00
❑ 41 Brent Barry B	.25	.60
❑ 42 Rony Seikaly B	.10	.30
❑ 43 Shareef Abdur-Rahim B	.60	1.50
❑ 44 Dominique Wilkins B	.40	1.00
❑ 45 Vin Baker B	.25	.60
❑ 46 Kendall Gill B	.10	.30
❑ 47 Muggsy Bogues B	.25	.60
❑ 48 Hakeem Olajuwon B	.40	1.00
❑ 49 Reggie Miller B	.40	1.00
❑ 50 Shaquille O'Neal B	1.00	2.50
❑ 51 Antonio McDyess B	.25	.60
❑ 52 Michael Finley B	.40	1.00
❑ 53 Jerry Stackhouse B	.40	1.00
❑ 54 Brian Grant B	.25	.60
❑ 55 Greg Anthony B	.10	.30
❑ 56 Patrick Ewing B	.40	1.00
❑ 57 Allen Iverson B	1.00	2.50
❑ 58 Rasheed Wallace B	.40	1.00
❑ 59 Shawn Kemp B	.25	.60
❑ 60 Bryant Reeves B	.10	.30
❑ 61 Kevin Garnett B	.75	2.00
❑ 62 Allan Houston B	.25	.60
❑ 63 Stacey Augmon B	.10	.30
❑ 64 Rick Fox B	.25	.60
❑ 65 Derek Harper B	.25	.60
❑ 66 Lindsey Hunter B	.10	.30
❑ 67 Eddie Jones B	.40	1.00
❑ 68 Joe Smith B	.25	.60
❑ 69 Alonzo Mourning B	.25	.60
❑ 70 LaPhonso Ellis B	.10	.30
❑ 71 Tyrone Hill B	.10	.30
❑ 72 Charles Barkley B	.50	1.25
❑ 73 Malik Sealy B	.10	.30
❑ 74 Shandon Anderson B	.10	.30
❑ 75 Arvydas Sabonis B	.25	.60
❑ 76 Tom Gugliotta B	.25	.60
❑ 77 Anfernee Hardaway B	.40	1.00
❑ 78 Sean Elliott B	.25	.60
❑ 79 Marcus Camby B	.40	1.00
❑ 80 Gary Payton B	.40	1.00
❑ 81 Kerry Kittles B	.40	1.00
❑ 82 Dikembe Mutombo B	.25	.60
❑ 83 Antoine Walker B	.50	1.25
❑ 84 Terrell Brandon B	.25	.60
❑ 85 Otis Thorpe B	.10	.30
❑ 86 Mark Jackson B	.25	.60
❑ 87 A.C. Green B	.25	.60
❑ 88 John Starks B	.25	.60
❑ 89 Kenny Anderson B	.25	.60
❑ 90 Karl Malone B	.40	1.00
❑ 91 Mitch Richmond B	.25	.60
❑ 92 Derrick Coleman B	.10	.30
❑ 93 Horace Grant B	.25	.60
❑ 94 John Williams B	.10	.30
❑ 95 Jason Kidd B	.60	1.50
❑ 96 Mahmoud Abdul-Rauf B	.10	.30
❑ 97 Walt Williams B	.10	.30
❑ 98 Anthony Mason B	.25	.60
❑ 99 Latrell Sprewell B	.40	1.00
❑ 100 Checklist	.10	.30
❑ 101 Tim Duncan B RC	3.00	8.00
❑ 102 Keith Van Horn B RC	1.00	2.50
❑ 103 Chauncey Billups B RC	3.00	8.00
❑ 104 Antonio Daniels B RC	.50	1.25
❑ 105 Tony Battie B RC	.50	1.25
❑ 106 Tim Thomas B RC	1.50	4.00
❑ 107 Tracy McGrady B RC	3.00	8.00
❑ 108 Adonal Foyle B RC	.30	.75
❑ 109 Maurice Taylor B RC	.75	2.00
❑ 110 Austin Croshere B RC	.75	2.00
❑ 111 Bobby Jackson B RC	.75	2.00
❑ 112 Olivier Saint-Jean B RC	.25	.60
❑ 113 John Thomas B RC	.25	.60
❑ 114 Derek Anderson B RC	1.00	2.50
❑ 115 Brevin Knight B RC	.60	1.50
❑ 116 Charles Smith B RC	.25	.60
❑ 117 Johnny Taylor B RC	.25	.60
❑ 118 Jacque Vaughn B RC	.30	.75
❑ 119 Anthony Parker B RC	.40	1.00
❑ 120 Paul Grant B RC	.25	.60
❑ 121 Stephon Marbury S	1.50	4.00
❑ 122 Terrell Brandon S	.75	2.00
❑ 123 Dikembe Mutombo S	.75	2.00
❑ 124 Patrick Ewing S	1.25	3.00
❑ 125 Scottie Pippen S	2.00	5.00
❑ 126 Antoine Walker S	1.50	4.00
❑ 127 Karl Malone S	1.25	3.00
❑ 128 Sean Elliott S	.75	2.00
❑ 129 Chris Webber S	1.25	3.00
❑ 130 Shawn Kemp S	.75	2.00
❑ 131 Hakeem Olajuwon S	1.25	3.00
❑ 132 Tim Hardaway S	.75	2.00
❑ 133 Glen Rice S	.75	2.00
❑ 134 Vin Baker S	.75	2.00
❑ 135 Jim Jackson S	.40	1.00
❑ 136 Kevin Garnett S	2.50	6.00
❑ 137 Kobe Bryant S	6.00	15.00
❑ 138 Damon Stoudamire S	.75	2.00
❑ 139 Larry Johnson S	.75	2.00
❑ 140 Latrell Sprewell S	1.25	3.00
❑ 141 Lorenzen Wright S	.40	1.00
❑ 142 Toni Kukoc S	.75	2.00
❑ 143 Allen Iverson S	3.00	8.00
❑ 144 Elden Campbell S	.40	1.00
❑ 145 Tom Gugliotta S	.75	2.00
❑ 146 David Robinson S	1.25	3.00
❑ 147 Jayson Williams S	.40	1.00
❑ 148 Shaquille O'Neal S	3.00	8.00
❑ 149 Grant Hill S	1.25	3.00
❑ 150 Reggie Miller S	1.25	3.00
❑ 151 Clyde Drexler S	1.25	3.00
❑ 152 Ray Allen S	.50	1.25
❑ 153 Eddie Jones S	1.25	3.00
❑ 154 Michael Jordan G	40.00	80.00
❑ 155 Dominique Wilkins G	5.00	12.00
❑ 156 Charles Barkley G	6.00	15.00
❑ 157 Jerry Stackhouse G	5.00	12.00
❑ 158 Juwan Howard G	3.00	8.00
❑ 159 Marcus Camby G	5.00	12.00
❑ 160 Christian Laettner G	3.00	8.00
❑ 161 Anthony Mason G	3.00	8.00
❑ 162 Joe Smith G	3.00	8.00
❑ 163 Kerry Kittles G	5.00	12.00
❑ 164 Mitch Richmond G	3.00	8.00
❑ 165 Shareef Abdur-Rahim G	10.00	20.00
❑ 166 Alonzo Mourning G	3.00	8.00
❑ 167 Dennis Rodman G	3.00	8.00
❑ 168 Antonio McDyess G	3.00	8.00
❑ 169 Shawn Bradley G	1.50	4.00
❑ 170 Anfernee Hardaway G	5.00	12.00
❑ 171 Jason Kidd G	10.00	20.00
❑ 172 Gary Payton G	5.00	12.00
❑ 173 John Stockton G	5.00	12.00
❑ 174 Allan Houston B	.25	.60
❑ 175 Bob Sura B	.10	.30
❑ 176 Clyde Drexler B	.40	1.00
❑ 177 Glenn Robinson B	.40	1.00
❑ 178 Joe Smith B	.25	.60
❑ 179 Larry Johnson B	.25	.60
❑ 180 Mitch Richmond B	.25	.60
❑ 181 Rony Seikaly B	.10	.30
❑ 182 Tyrone Hill B	.10	.30
❑ 183 Allen Iverson B	1.00	2.50
❑ 184 Brent Barry B	.25	.60
❑ 185 Damon Stoudamire B	.25	.60
❑ 186 Grant Hill B	.40	1.00
❑ 187 John Stockton B	.40	1.00
❑ 188 Latrell Sprewell B	.40	1.00
❑ 189 Mookie Blaylock B	.10	.30
❑ 190 Samaki Walker B	.10	.30
❑ 191 Vin Baker B	.25	.60
❑ 192 Alonzo Mourning B	.25	.60
❑ 193 Brevin Knight B	.25	.60
❑ 194 Danny Manning B	.25	.60
❑ 195 Hakeem Olajuwon B	.40	1.00
❑ 196 Johnny Taylor B	.10	.30
❑ 197 Lorenzen Wright B	.10	.30
❑ 198 Olden Polynice B	.10	.30
❑ 199 Scottie Pippen B	.60	1.50
❑ 200 Lindsey Hunter B	.10	.30
❑ 201 Anfernee Hardaway B	.40	1.00
❑ 202 Greg Anthony B	.10	.30
❑ 203 David Robinson B	.40	1.00
❑ 204 Horace Grant B	.25	.60
❑ 205 Calbert Cheaney B	.10	.30
❑ 206 Loy Vaught B	.10	.30
❑ 207 Tariq Abdul-Wahad B	.10	.30
❑ 208 Sean Elliott B	.25	.60
❑ 209 Rodney Rogers B	.10	.30
❑ 210 Anthony Mason B	.25	.60
❑ 211 Bryant Reeves B	.10	.30
❑ 212 David Wesley B	.10	.30
❑ 213 Isaiah Rider B	.25	.60
❑ 214 Karl Malone B	.40	1.00
❑ 215 Mahmoud Abdul-Rauf B	.10	.30
❑ 216 Patrick Ewing B	.40	1.00
❑ 217 Shaquille O'Neal B	1.00	2.50
❑ 218 Antoine Walker B	.50	1.25
❑ 219 Charles Barkley B	.50	1.25
❑ 220 Dennis Rodman B	.25	.60
❑ 221 Jamal Mashburn B	.25	.60
❑ 222 Kendall Gill B	.10	.30
❑ 223 Malik Sealy B	.10	.30
❑ 224 Rasheed Wallace B	.40	1.00
❑ 225 Shareef Abdur-Rahim B	.60	1.50
❑ 226 Antonio Daniels B	.25	.60
❑ 227 Charles Oakley B	.25	.60
❑ 228 Derek Anderson B	.25	.60
❑ 229 Jason Kidd B	.60	1.50
❑ 230 Kenny Anderson B	.25	.60
❑ 231 Marcus Camby B	.40	1.00
❑ 232 Ray Allen B	.40	1.00
❑ 233 Shawn Bradley B	.10	.30
❑ 234 Antonio McDyess B	.25	.60
❑ 235 Chauncey Billups B	.30	.75
❑ 236 Detlef Schrempf B	.25	.60
❑ 237 Jayson Williams B	.10	.30
❑ 238 Kerry Kittles B	.40	1.00
❑ 239 Jalen Rose B	.40	1.00
❑ 240 Reggie Miller B	.40	1.00
❑ 241 Shawn Kemp B	.25	.60
❑ 242 Arvydas Sabonis B	.25	.60
❑ 243 Tom Gugliotta B	.25	.60
❑ 244 Dikembe Mutombo B	.25	.60
❑ 245 Jeff Hornacek B	.25	.60
❑ 246 Kevin Garnett B	.75	2.00
❑ 247 Matt Maloney B	.10	.30
❑ 248 Rex Chapman B	.10	.30
❑ 249 Stephon Marbury B	.50	1.25
❑ 250 Austin Croshere B	.20	.50
❑ 251 Chris Childs B	.10	.30
❑ 252 Eddie Jones B	.40	1.00
❑ 253 Jerry Stackhouse B	.40	1.00
❑ 254 Kevin Johnson B	.25	.60
❑ 255 Maurice Taylor B	.30	.75
❑ 256 Chris Mullin B	.40	1.00
❑ 257 Terrell Brandon B	.25	.60
❑ 258 Avery Johnson B	.10	.30
❑ 259 Chris Webber B	.40	1.00
❑ 260 Gary Payton B	.40	1.00
❑ 261 Jim Jackson B	.10	.30
❑ 262 Kobe Bryant B	2.00	5.00
❑ 263 Michael Finley B	.40	1.00
❑ 264 Rod Strickland B	.10	.30
❑ 265 Tim Hardaway B	.25	.60
❑ 266 B.J. Armstrong B	.10	.30
❑ 267 Christian Laettner B	.25	.60
❑ 268 Glen Rice B	.25	.60
❑ 269 Joe Dumars B	.40	1.00
❑ 270 LaPhonso Ellis B	.10	.30
❑ 271 Michael Jordan B	2.50	6.00
❑ 272 Ron Mercer B RC	.75	2.00
❑ 273 Checklist B	.10	.30
❑ 274 Anfernee Hardaway S	1.25	3.00
❑ 275 Dennis Rodman S	.75	2.00
❑ 276 Gary Payton S	1.25	3.00
❑ 277 Jamal Mashburn S	.75	2.00
❑ 278 Shareef Abdur-Rahim S	2.00	5.00
❑ 279 Steve Smith S	.75	2.00
❑ 280 Tony Battie S	.75	2.00
❑ 281 Alonzo Mourning S	.75	2.00
❑ 282 Bobby Jackson S	.40	1.00
❑ 283 Christian Laettner S	.75	2.00
❑ 284 Jerry Stackhouse S	1.25	3.00
❑ 285 Terrell Brandon S	.75	2.00
❑ 286 Chauncey Billups S	1.00	2.50
❑ 287 Michael Jordan S	10.00	20.00

❑ 288 Glenn Robinson S	1.25	3.00
❑ 289 Jason Kidd S	2.00	5.00
❑ 290 Joe Smith S	.75	2.00
❑ 291 Michael Finley S	1.25	3.00
❑ 292 Rod Strickland S	.40	1.00
❑ 293 Ron Mercer S	.60	1.50
❑ 294 Tracy McGrady S	1.25	3.00
❑ 295 Adonal Foyle S	.40	1.00
❑ 296 Marcus Camby S	1.25	3.00
❑ 297 John Stockton S	1.25	3.00
❑ 298 Kerry Kittles S	1.25	3.00
❑ 299 Mitch Richmond S	.75	2.00
❑ 300 Shawn Bradley S	.40	1.00
❑ 301 Anthony Mason S	.75	2.00
❑ 302 Antonio Daniels S	.75	2.00
❑ 303 Antonio McDyess S	.75	2.00
❑ 304 Charles Barkley S	1.50	4.00
❑ 305 Keith Van Horn S	1.25	3.00
❑ 306 Tim Duncan S	1.25	3.00
❑ 307 Dikembe Mutombo G	3.00	8.00
❑ 308 Grant Hill G	5.00	12.00
❑ 309 Shaquille O'Neal G	12.50	30.00
❑ 310 Keith Van Horn G	5.00	12.00
❑ 311 Shawn Kemp G	3.00	8.00
❑ 312 Antoine Walker G	6.00	15.00
❑ 313 Hakeem Olajuwon G	5.00	12.00
❑ 314 Vin Baker G	3.00	8.00
❑ 315 Patrick Ewing G	5.00	12.00
❑ 316 Tracy McGrady G	4.00	10.00
❑ 317 Glen Rice G	3.00	8.00
❑ 318 Reggie Miller G	5.00	12.00
❑ 319 Kevin Garnett G	10.00	25.00
❑ 320 Allen Iverson G	12.50	30.00
❑ 321 Karl Malone G	5.00	12.00
❑ 322 Scottie Pippen G	10.00	20.00
❑ 323 Kobe Bryant G	20.00	50.00
❑ 324 Stephon Marbury G	6.00	15.00
❑ 325 Tim Duncan G	4.00	10.00
❑ 326 Chris Webber G	5.00	12.00
❑ P67 Eddie Jones	.75	2.00
❑ P68 Joe Smith	.75	2.00

1998-99 Finest

❑ COMPLETE SET (250)	50.00	100.00
❑ COMPLETE SERIES 1 (125)	15.00	30.00
❑ COMPLETE SERIES 2 (125)	25.00	60.00
❑ COMMON CARD (1-225)	.10	.30
❑ COMMON ROOKIE (226-250)	.25	.60
❑ 1 Chris Mills	.10	.30
❑ 2 Matt Maloney	.10	.30
❑ 3 Sam Mitchell	.10	.30
❑ 4 Corliss Williamson	.25	.60
❑ 5 Bryant Reeves	.10	.30
❑ 6 Juwan Howard	.25	.60
❑ 7 Eddie Jones	.40	1.00
❑ 8 Ray Allen	.40	1.00
❑ 9 Larry Johnson	.25	.60
❑ 10 Travis Best	.10	.30
❑ 11 Isaiah Rider	.10	.30
❑ 12 Hakeem Olajuwon	.40	1.00
❑ 13 Gary Trent	.10	.30
❑ 14 Kevin Garnett	.75	2.00
❑ 15 Dikembe Mutombo	.25	.60
❑ 16 Brevin Knight	.10	.30
❑ 17 Keith Van Horn	.40	1.00
❑ 18 Theo Ratliff	.25	.60
❑ 19 Tim Hardaway	.25	.60
❑ 20 Blue Edwards	.10	.30
❑ 21 David Wesley	.10	.30
❑ 22 Jaren Jackson	.10	.30
❑ 23 Nick Anderson	.10	.30
❑ 24 Rodney Rogers	.10	.30
❑ 25 Antonio Davis	.10	.30
❑ 26 Clarence Weatherspoon	.10	.30
❑ 27 Kelvin Cato	.10	.30
❑ 28 Tracy McGrady	1.00	2.50
❑ 29 Mookie Blaylock	.10	.30
❑ 30 Ron Harper	.25	.60
❑ 31 Allan Houston	.25	.60
❑ 32 Brian Williams	.10	.30
❑ 33 John Stockton	.40	1.00
❑ 34 Hersey Hawkins	.10	.30
❑ 35 Donyell Marshall	.25	.60
❑ 36 Mark Strickland	.10	.30
❑ 37 Rod Strickland	.10	.30
❑ 38 Cedric Ceballos	.10	.30
❑ 39 Danny Fortson	.10	.30
❑ 40 Shaquille O'Neal	1.00	2.50
❑ 41 Kendall Gill	.10	.30
❑ 42 Allen Iverson	.75	2.00
❑ 43 Travis Knight	.10	.30
❑ 44 Cedric Henderson	.10	.30
❑ 45 Steve Kerr	.25	.60
❑ 46 Antonio McDyess	.25	.60
❑ 47 Darrick Martin	.10	.30
❑ 48 Shandon Anderson	.10	.30
❑ 49 Shareef Abdur-Rahim	.40	1.00
❑ 50 Antoine Carr	.10	.30
❑ 51 Jason Kidd	.60	1.50
❑ 52 Calbert Cheaney	.10	.30
❑ 53 Antoine Walker	.40	1.00
❑ 54 Greg Anthony	.10	.30
❑ 55 Jeff Hornacek	.25	.60
❑ 56 Reggie Miller	.40	1.00
❑ 57 Lawrence Funderburke	.10	.30
❑ 58 Derek Strong	.10	.30
❑ 59 Robert Horry	.25	.60
❑ 60 Shawn Bradley	.10	.30
❑ 61 Matt Bullard	.10	.30
❑ 62 Terrell Brandon	.25	.60
❑ 63 Dan Majerle	.25	.60
❑ 64 Jim Jackson	.10	.30
❑ 65 Anthony Peeler	.10	.30
❑ 66 Bo Outlaw	.10	.30
❑ 67 Khalid Reeves	.10	.30
❑ 68 Toni Kukoc	.25	.60
❑ 69 Mario Elie	.10	.30
❑ 70 Derek Anderson	.30	.75
❑ 71 Jalen Rose	.40	1.00
❑ 72 Tyrone Corbin	.10	.30
❑ 73 Anthony Mason	.25	.60
❑ 74 Lamond Murray	.10	.30
❑ 75 Tom Gugliotta	.10	.30
❑ 76 Arvydas Sabonis	.25	.60
❑ 77 Brian Shaw	.10	.30
❑ 78 Rick Fox	.25	.60
❑ 79 Danny Manning	.10	.30
❑ 80 Lindsey Hunter	.10	.30
❑ 81 Michael Jordan	2.50	6.00
❑ 82 LaPhonso Ellis	.10	.30
❑ 83 David Robinson	.40	1.00
❑ 84 Christian Laettner	.25	.60
❑ 85 Armon Gilliam	.10	.30
❑ 86 Sherman Douglas	.10	.30
❑ 87 Charlie Ward	.10	.30
❑ 88 Shawn Kemp	.25	.60
❑ 89 Gary Payton	.40	1.00
❑ 90 Doug Christie	.25	.60
❑ 91 Voshon Lenard	.10	.30
❑ 92 Detlef Schrempf	.25	.60
❑ 93 Walter McCarty	.10	.30
❑ 94 Sam Cassell	.40	1.00
❑ 95 Jerry Stackhouse	.40	1.00
❑ 96 Billy Owens	.10	.30
❑ 97 Matt Geiger	.10	.30
❑ 98 Avery Johnson	.10	.30
❑ 99 Bobby Jackson	.25	.60
❑ 100 Rex Chapman	.10	.30
❑ 101 Andrew DeClercq	.10	.30
❑ 102 Vlade Divac	.25	.60
❑ 103 Erick Strickland	.10	.30
❑ 104 Dean Garrett	.10	.30
❑ 105 Grant Long	.10	.30
❑ 106 Adonal Foyle	.10	.30
❑ 107 Isaac Austin	.10	.30
❑ 108 Michael Curry	.10	.30
❑ 109 Darrell Armstrong	.10	.30
❑ 110 Aaron McKie	.25	.60
❑ 111 Stacey Augmon	.10	.30
❑ 112 Anthony Johnson	.10	.30
❑ 113 Vinny Del Negro	.10	.30
❑ 114 Reggie Slater	.10	.30
❑ 115 Lee Mayberry	.10	.30
❑ 116 Tracy Murray	.10	.30
❑ 117 Scottie Pippen	.60	1.50
❑ 118 Sam Perkins	.10	.30
❑ 119 Derek Fisher	.40	1.00
❑ 120 Mark Bryant	.10	.30
❑ 121 Dale Davis	.25	.60
❑ 122 B.J. Armstrong	.10	.30
❑ 123 Charles Barkley	.50	1.25
❑ 124 Horace Grant	.25	.60
❑ 125 Checklist	.10	.30
❑ 126 Alonzo Mourning	.25	.60
❑ 127 Kerry Kittles	.10	.30
❑ 128 Eldridge Recasner	.10	.30
❑ 129 Dell Curry	.10	.30
❑ 130 Jamal Mashburn	.25	.60
❑ 131 Eric Piatkowski	.25	.60
❑ 132 Othella Harrington	.10	.30
❑ 133 Pete Chilcutt	.10	.30
❑ 134 Dennis Rodman	.25	.60
❑ 135 Patrick Ewing	.40	1.00
❑ 136 Danny Schayes	.10	.30
❑ 137 John Williams	.10	.30
❑ 138 Joe Smith	.25	.60
❑ 139 Tariq Abdul-Wahad	.10	.30
❑ 140 Vin Baker	.25	.60
❑ 141 Elden Campbell	.10	.30
❑ 142 Chris Carr	.10	.30
❑ 143 John Starks	.25	.60
❑ 144 Felton Spencer	.10	.30
❑ 145 Mark Jackson	.25	.60
❑ 146 Dana Barros	.10	.30
❑ 147 Eric Williams	.10	.30
❑ 148 Wesley Person	.10	.30
❑ 149 Joe Dumars	.40	1.00
❑ 150 Steve Smith	.25	.60
❑ 151 Randy Brown	.10	.30
❑ 152 A.C. Green	.25	.60
❑ 153 Dee Brown	.10	.30
❑ 154 Brian Grant	.25	.60
❑ 155 Tim Thomas	.25	.60
❑ 156 Howard Eisley	.10	.30
❑ 157 Malik Sealy	.10	.30
❑ 158 Maurice Taylor	.20	.50
❑ 159 Tyrone Hill	.10	.30
❑ 160 Chris Gatling	.10	.30
❑ 161 Rodrick Rhodes	.10	.30
❑ 162 Muggsy Bogues	.25	.60
❑ 163 Kenny Anderson	.25	.60
❑ 164 Zydrunas Ilgauskas	.25	.60
❑ 165 Grant Hill	.40	1.00
❑ 166 Lorenzen Wright	.10	.30
❑ 167 Tony Battie	.10	.30
❑ 168 Bobby Phills	.10	.30
❑ 169 Michael Finley	.40	1.00
❑ 170 Anfernee Hardaway	.40	1.00
❑ 171 Terry Porter	.10	.30
❑ 172 P.J. Brown	.10	.30
❑ 173 Clifford Robinson	.10	.30
❑ 174 Olden Polynice	.10	.30
❑ 175 Kobe Bryant	1.50	4.00
❑ 176 Sean Elliott	.25	.60
❑ 177 Latrell Sprewell	.40	1.00
❑ 178 Rik Smits	.25	.60
❑ 179 Darrell Armstrong	.10	.30
❑ 180 Stephon Marbury	.40	1.00
❑ 181 Brent Price	.10	.30
❑ 182 Danny Fortson	.10	.30
❑ 183 Vitaly Potapenko	.10	.30
❑ 184 Anthony Parker	.10	.30
❑ 185 Glenn Robinson	.25	.60
❑ 186 Erick Dampier	.25	.60
❑ 187 George McCloud	.10	.30
❑ 188 Rasheed Wallace	.40	1.00
❑ 189 Aaron Williams	.10	.30
❑ 190 Tim Duncan	.60	1.50
❑ 191 Chauncey Billups	.25	.60
❑ 192 Jim McIlvaine	.10	.30
❑ 193 Chris Mullin	.40	1.00
❑ 194 George Lynch	.10	.30
❑ 195 Damon Stoudamire	.25	.60
❑ 196 Bryon Russell	.10	.30
❑ 197 Luc Longley	.10	.30
❑ 198 Ron Mercer	.20	.50
❑ 199 Alan Henderson	.10	.30
❑ 200 Jayson Williams	.10	.30
❑ 201 Ben Wallace	.40	1.00
❑ 202 Elliot Perry	.10	.30
❑ 203 Walt Williams	.10	.30
❑ 204 Cherokee Parks	.10	.30
❑ 205 Brent Barry	.25	.60
❑ 206 Hubert Davis	.10	.30

❑ 207 Terry Davis .10 .30
❑ 208 Loy Vaught .10 .30
❑ 209 Adam Keefe .10 .30
❑ 210 Karl Malone .40 1.00
❑ 211 Chuck Person .10 .30
❑ 212 Chris Childs .10 .30
❑ 213 Rony Seikaly .10 .30
❑ 214 Ervin Johnson .10 .30
❑ 215 Derrick McKey .10 .30
❑ 216 Jerome Williams .10 .30
❑ 217 Glen Rice .25 .60
❑ 218 Steve Nash .40 1.00
❑ 219 Nick Van Exel .40 1.00
❑ 220 Chris Webber .40 1.00
❑ 221 Marcus Camby .25 .60
❑ 222 Antonio Daniels .10 .30
❑ 223 Mitch Richmond .25 .60
❑ 224 Otis Thorpe .10 .30
❑ 225 Charles Oakley .10 .30
❑ 226 Michael Olowokandi RC .60 1.50
❑ 227 Mike Bibby RC 2.00 5.00
❑ 228 Raef LaFrentz RC .60 1.50
❑ 229 Antawn Jamison RC 2.00 5.00
❑ 230 Vince Carter RC 4.00 10.00
❑ 231 Robert Traylor RC .50 1.25
❑ 232 Jason Williams RC 1.50 4.00
❑ 233 Larry Hughes RC 1.25 3.00
❑ 234 Dirk Nowitzki RC 5.00 12.00
❑ 235 Paul Pierce RC 3.00 8.00
❑ 236 Bonzi Wells RC 1.50 4.00
❑ 237 Michael Doleac RC .50 1.25
❑ 238 Keon Clark RC .60 1.50
❑ 239 Michael Dickerson RC .75 2.00
❑ 240 Matt Harpring RC 1.00 2.50
❑ 241 Bryce Drew RC .50 1.25
❑ 242 Pat Garrity RC .30 .75
❑ 243 Roshown McLeod RC .30 .75
❑ 244 Ricky Davis RC 1.25 3.00
❑ 245 Brian Skinner RC .50 1.25
❑ 246 Tyronn Lue RC .50 1.25
❑ 247 Felipe Lopez RC .50 1.25
❑ 248 Sam Jacobson RC .25 .60
❑ 249 Corey Benjamin RC .50 1.25
❑ 250 Nazr Mohammed RC .30 .75
❑ PP5 Eddie Jones

1999-00 Finest

❑ COMPLETE SET (266) 140.00 280.00
❑ COMPLETE SERIES 1 (133) 40.00 80.00
❑ COMPLETE SERIES 2 (133) 100.00 200.00
❑ COMP.SERIES 2 w/o RC (118) 25.00 50.00
❑ COMMON CARD (1-266) .25 .60
❑ COMMON ROOKIE (110-124) .60 1.50
❑ COMMON ROOKIE (252-266) 2.50 6.00
❑ COMMON SUBSET .60 1.50
❑ 1 Shareef Abdur-Rahim .30 .75
❑ 2 Kevin Willis .25 .60
❑ 3 Sean Elliott .40 1.00
❑ 4 Vlade Divac .40 1.00
❑ 5 Tom Gugliotta .25 .60
❑ 6 Matt Harpring .30 .75
❑ 7 Kerry Kittles .25 .60
❑ 8 Joe Smith .30 .75
❑ 9 Jamal Mashburn .25 .60
❑ 10 Tyrone Nesby RC .40 1.00
❑ 11 Alan Henderson .25 .60
❑ 12 Vitaly Potapenko .25 .60
❑ 13 Dickey Simpkins .25 .60
❑ 14 Michael Finley .40 1.00
❑ 15 Lindsey Hunter .25 .60
❑ 16 Antawn Jamison .40 1.00
❑ 17 Reggie Miller .40 1.00
❑ 18 Maurice Taylor .30 .75
❑ 19 Clarence Weatherspoon .25 .60
❑ 20 Sam Mitchell .25 .60
❑ 21 Latrell Sprewell .30 .75
❑ 22 Michael Doleac .25 .60
❑ 23 Rex Chapman .25 .60
❑ 24 Peja Stojakovic .30 .75
❑ 25 Vladimir Stepania .25 .60
❑ 26 Tracy McGrady .75 2.00
❑ 27 Cherokee Parks .25 .60
❑ 28 LaPhonso Ellis .25 .60
❑ 29 Hakeem Olajuwon .40 1.00
❑ 30 Adonal Foyle .25 .60
❑ 31 Bryant Stith .25 .60
❑ 32 Andrew DeClercq .25 .60
❑ 33 Toni Kukoc .40 1.00
❑ 34 Kenny Anderson .30 .75
❑ 35 Mike Bibby .40 1.00
❑ 36 Glen Rice .40 1.00
❑ 37 Avery Johnson .30 .75
❑ 38 Arvydas Sabonis .30 .75
❑ 39 Kornel David RC .40 1.00
❑ 40 Hubert Davis .25 .60
❑ 41 Grant Hill .40 1.00
❑ 42 Donyell Marshall .30 .75
❑ 43 Jalen Rose .30 .75
❑ 44 Derrick Coleman .30 .75
❑ 45 P.J. Brown .25 .60
❑ 46 Vin Baker .40 1.00
❑ 47 Clifford Robinson .25 .60
❑ 48 Allan Houston .30 .75
❑ 49 Kendall Gill .25 .60
❑ 50 Matt Geiger .25 .60
❑ 51 Larry Hughes .30 .75
❑ 52 Corliss Williamson .25 .60
❑ 53 Darrell Armstrong .25 .60
❑ 54 Bobby Jackson .30 .75
❑ 55 Bryon Russell .25 .60
❑ 56 Juwan Howard .30 .75
❑ 57 Dikembe Mutombo .30 .75
❑ 58 Eddie Jones .40 1.00
❑ 59 Randy Brown .25 .60
❑ 60 Dirk Nowitzki .60 1.50
❑ 61 Jerome Williams .25 .60
❑ 62 Scottie Pippen .60 1.50
❑ 63 Dale Davis .25 .60
❑ 64 Kobe Bryant 2.00 5.00
❑ 65 Robert Traylor .25 .60
❑ 66 Tim Hardaway .40 1.00
❑ 67 Michael Olowokandi .25 .60
❑ 68 Walter McCarty .25 .60
❑ 69 Damon Stoudamire .40 1.00
❑ 70 Othella Harrington .25 .60
❑ 71 Chauncey Billups .40 1.00
❑ 72 John Starks .40 1.00
❑ 73 Ricky Davis .40 1.00
❑ 74 Glenn Robinson .30 .75
❑ 75 Dean Garrett .25 .60
❑ 76 Chris Childs .25 .60
❑ 77 Shawn Kemp .40 1.00
❑ 78 Allen Iverson .75 2.00
❑ 79 Brian Grant .25 .60
❑ 80 David Robinson .50 1.25
❑ 81 Tracy Murray .25 .60
❑ 82 Howard Eisley .25 .60
❑ 83 Doug Christie .30 .75
❑ 84 Gary Payton .40 1.00
❑ 85 John Stockton .50 1.25
❑ 86 Rod Strickland .25 .60
❑ 87 Tyrone Corbin .25 .60
❑ 88 Antonio Daniels .25 .60
❑ 89 Dee Brown .25 .60
❑ 90 Antoine Walker .40 1.00
❑ 91 Theo Ratliff .30 .75
❑ 92 Larry Johnson .40 1.00
❑ 93 Stephon Marbury .40 1.00
❑ 94 Brevin Knight .25 .60
❑ 95 Antonio McDyess .30 .75
❑ 96 Bison Dele .25 .60
❑ 97 Cuttino Mobley .30 .75
❑ 98 Haywoode Workman .25 .60
❑ 99 J.R. Reid .25 .60
❑ 100 Travis Best .25 .60
❑ 101 Chris Webber GEM .60 1.50
❑ 102 Grant Hill GEM .60 1.50
❑ 103 Kevin Garnett GEM 1.25 3.00
❑ 104 Jason Kidd GEM 1.00 2.50
❑ 105 Gary Payton GEM .60 1.50
❑ 106 Shaquille O'Neal GEM 1.50 4.00
❑ 107 Alonzo Mourning GEM .60 1.50
❑ 108 Karl Malone GEM .75 2.00
❑ 109 John Stockton GEM .75 2.00
❑ 110 Elton Brand RC 2.00 5.00
❑ 111 Baron Davis RC 2.50 6.00
❑ 112 A.Radojevic RC .60 1.50
❑ 113 Cal Bowdler RC .60 1.50
❑ 114 Jumaine Jones RC .60 1.50
❑ 115 Jason Terry RC 1.50 4.00
❑ 116 Trajan Langdon RC .60 1.50
❑ 117 Dion Glover RC .60 1.50
❑ 118 Jeff Foster RC .75 2.00
❑ 119 Lamar Odom RC 2.00 5.00
❑ 120 Wally Szczerbiak RC 2.00 5.00
❑ 121 Shawn Marion RC 2.00 5.00
❑ 122 Kenny Thomas RC .60 1.50
❑ 123 Devean George RC 1.00 2.50
❑ 124 Scott Padgett RC .60 1.50
❑ 125 Tim Duncan SEN 1.25 3.00
❑ 126 Jason Williams SEN .60 1.50
❑ 127 Paul Pierce SEN .60 1.50
❑ 128 Kobe Bryant SEN 3.00 8.00
❑ 129 Keith Van Horn SEN .50 1.25
❑ 130 Vince Carter SEN 1.25 3.00
❑ 131 Matt Harpring SEN .50 1.25
❑ 132 Antawn Jamison SEN .60 1.50
❑ 133 Tracy McGrady SEN 1.25 3.00
❑ 134 Tim Duncan .75 2.00
❑ 135 Tariq Abdul-Wahad .25 .60
❑ 136 Luc Longley .25 .60
❑ 137 Steve Smith .25 .60
❑ 138 Alonzo Mourning .40 1.00
❑ 139 Kevin Garnett .75 2.00
❑ 140 Christian Laettner .30 .75
❑ 141 Rik Smits .40 1.00
❑ 142 Cedric Henderson .25 .60
❑ 143 Jim Jackson .30 .75
❑ 144 Dan Majerle .40 1.00
❑ 145 Bryant Reeves .25 .60
❑ 146 Antonio Davis .25 .60
❑ 147 Michael Smith .25 .60
❑ 148 Charlie Ward .25 .60
❑ 149 Chris Mullin .40 1.00
❑ 150 Danny Manning .25 .60
❑ 151 Eric Williams .25 .60
❑ 152 Hersey Hawkins .25 .60
❑ 153 Isaiah Rider .25 .60
❑ 154 Shandon Anderson .25 .60
❑ 155 Jason Kidd .60 1.50
❑ 156 Chris Whitney .25 .60
❑ 157 Brent Barry .30 .75
❑ 158 Patrick Ewing .50 1.25
❑ 159 George Lynch .25 .60
❑ 160 Dickey Simpkins .25 .60
❑ 161 Derek Anderson .25 .60
❑ 162 Ron Mercer .25 .60
❑ 163 David Wesley .25 .60
❑ 164 Mookie Blaylock .25 .60
❑ 165 Terrell Brandon .25 .60
❑ 166 Detlef Schrempf .30 .75
❑ 167 Olden Polynice .25 .60
❑ 168 Jayson Williams .30 .75
❑ 169 Eric Piatkowski .30 .75
❑ 170 A.C. Green .40 1.00
❑ 171 Chris Mills .25 .60
❑ 172 Chris Webber .40 1.00
❑ 173 Jeff Hornacek .30 .75
❑ 174 Calbert Cheaney .25 .60
❑ 175 Wesley Person .25 .60
❑ 176 Corey Benjamin .25 .60
❑ 177 Loy Vaught .25 .60
❑ 178 Keith Closs .25 .60
❑ 179 Bo Outlaw .25 .60
❑ 180 Mitch Richmond .30 .75
❑ 181 Charles Oakley .30 .75
❑ 182 Felipe Lopez .25 .60
❑ 183 Eric Snow .30 .75
❑ 184 Paul Pierce .40 1.00
❑ 185 Elden Campbell .25 .60
❑ 186 Shaquille O'Neal 1.00 2.50
❑ 187 Charles Barkley .50 1.25
❑ 188 Mark Jackson .40 1.00
❑ 189 Scott Burrell .25 .60
❑ 190 Anfernee Hardaway .40 1.00
❑ 191 Samaki Walker .25 .60
❑ 192 Karl Malone .50 1.25
❑ 193 Jermaine O'Neal .40 1.00
❑ 194 Mario Elie .25 .60
❑ 195 Malik Sealy .25 .60
❑ 196 Voshon Lenard .25 .60
❑ 197 Chris Gatling .25 .60
❑ 198 Walt Williams .25 .60
❑ 199 Nick Van Exel .30 .75

❑ 200 Bimbo Coles	.25	.60
❑ 201 John Wallace	.25	.60
❑ 202 Anthony Mason	.25	.60
❑ 203 Steve Nash	.60	1.50
❑ 204 Erick Dampier	.30	.75
❑ 205 Cedric Ceballos	.25	.60
❑ 206 Derek Fisher	.40	1.00
❑ 207 Marcus Camby	.30	.75
❑ 208 Tyrone Hill	.25	.60
❑ 209 Nick Anderson	.25	.60
❑ 210 Sam Cassell	.30	.75
❑ 211 Raef LaFrentz	.30	.75
❑ 212 Ruben Patterson	.25	.60
❑ 213 Rick Fox	.25	.60
❑ 214 Jason Williams	.40	1.00
❑ 215 Vince Carter	.75	2.00
❑ 216 Michael Dickerson	.25	.60
❑ 217 Steve Kerr	.30	.75
❑ 218 Rasheed Wallace	.40	1.00
❑ 219 Keith Van Horn	.30	.75
❑ 220 Bob Sura	.25	.60
❑ 221 Ray Allen	.40	1.00
❑ 222 Jerry Stackhouse	.40	1.00
❑ 223 Shawn Bradley	.25	.60
❑ 224 Horace Grant	.30	.75
❑ 225 Tim Duncan USA	1.25	3.00
❑ 226 Kevin Garnett USA	1.25	3.00
❑ 227 Jason Kidd USA	1.00	2.50
❑ 228 Steve Smith USA	.40	1.00
❑ 229 Allan Houston USA	.50	1.25
❑ 230 Tom Gugliotta USA	.40	1.00
❑ 231 Gary Payton USA	.60	1.50
❑ 232 Tim Hardaway USA	.60	1.50
❑ 233 Vin Baker USA	.60	1.50
❑ 234 Karl Malone CAT	.75	2.00
❑ 235 Vince Carter CAT	1.25	3.00
❑ 236 Jason Williams CAT	.60	1.50
❑ 237 Alonzo Mourning CAT	.60	1.50
❑ 238 Anfernee Hardaway CAT	.60	1.50
❑ 239 Mitch Richmond CAT	.50	1.25
❑ 240 Steve Smith CAT	.40	1.00
❑ 241 Charles Barkley CAT	.75	2.00
❑ 242 Ron Mercer CAT	.40	1.00
❑ 243 Shaquille O'Neal EDGE	1.50	4.00
❑ 244 Jason Kidd EDGE	1.00	2.50
❑ 245 Kevin Garnett EDGE	1.25	3.00
❑ 246 Tim Duncan EDGE	1.25	3.00
❑ 247 Ray Allen EDGE	.60	1.50
❑ 248 Chris Webber EDGE	.60	1.50
❑ 249 Jerry Stackhouse EDGE	.60	1.50
❑ 250 Keith Van Horn EDGE	.50	1.25
❑ 251 Patrick Ewing EDGE	.75	2.00
❑ 252 Steve Francis RC	8.00	20.00
❑ 253 Jonathan Bender RC	2.50	6.00
❑ 254 Richard Hamilton RC	8.00	20.00
❑ 255 Andre Miller RC	8.00	20.00
❑ 256 Corey Maggette RC	8.00	20.00
❑ 257 William Avery RC	2.50	6.00
❑ 258 Ron Artest RC	10.00	25.00
❑ 259 James Posey RC	4.00	10.00
❑ 260 Quincy Lewis RC	2.50	6.00
❑ 261 Tim James RC	2.50	6.00
❑ 262 Vonteego Cummings RC	2.50	6.00
❑ 263 Anthony Carter RC	5.00	12.00
❑ 264 Mirsad Turkcan RC	2.50	6.00
❑ 265 Adrian Griffin RC	2.50	6.00
❑ 266 Ryan Robertson RC	2.50	6.00
❑ PP1 Reggie Miller Promo	.40	1.00

2000-01 Finest

❑ COMPLETE SET (173)	150.00	275.00
❑ COMPLETE SET w/o SP (125)	20.00	40.00
❑ COMMON CARD (1-173)	.25	.60
❑ COMMON ROOKIE (126-150)	2.50	6.00
❑ 1 Shaquille O'Neal	1.00	2.50
❑ 2 P.J. Brown	.25	.60
❑ 3 Joe Smith	.25	.60
❑ 4 Kendall Gill	.25	.60
❑ 5 Corey Maggette	.30	.75
❑ 6 Marcus Camby	.30	.75
❑ 7 Toni Kukoc	.30	.75
❑ 8 Kobe Bryant	2.00	5.00
❑ 9 David Robinson	.50	1.25
❑ 10 Ruben Patterson	.25	.60
❑ 11 Allen Iverson	.75	2.00
❑ 12 Glenn Robinson	.30	.75
❑ 13 Anthony Carter	.25	.60
❑ 14 Jonathan Bender	.25	.60
❑ 15 Vince Carter	.75	2.00
❑ 16 Jerry Stackhouse	.30	.75
❑ 17 Raef LaFrentz	.25	.60
❑ 18 Dikembe Mutombo	.30	.75
❑ 19 Baron Davis	.40	1.00
❑ 20 Kenny Anderson	.30	.75
❑ 21 Corey Benjamin	.25	.60
❑ 22 Andre Miller	.30	.75
❑ 23 Cedric Ceballos	.25	.60
❑ 24 Christian Laettner	.25	.60
❑ 25 Shandon Anderson	.25	.60
❑ 26 Rik Smits	.25	.60
❑ 27 Michael Olowokandi	.25	.60
❑ 28 Sam Cassell	.30	.75
❑ 29 Tom Gugliotta	.25	.60
❑ 30 Jason Williams	.30	.75
❑ 31 Avery Johnson	.30	.75
❑ 32 Karl Malone	.50	1.25
❑ 33 Grant Hill	.40	1.00
❑ 34 Paul Pierce	.40	1.00
❑ 35 Antonio Davis	.25	.60
❑ 36 Nick Anderson	.25	.60
❑ 37 Alan Henderson	.25	.60
❑ 38 Eddie Jones	.30	.75
❑ 39 Ron Artest	.40	1.00
❑ 40 Brevin Knight	.25	.60
❑ 41 Keon Clark	.25	.60
❑ 42 Elton Brand	.40	1.00
❑ 43 Reggie Miller	.40	1.00
❑ 44 Steve Francis	.40	1.00
❑ 45 Derek Anderson	.30	.75
❑ 46 Alonzo Mourning	.40	1.00
❑ 47 Terrell Brandon	.25	.60
❑ 48 Larry Johnson	.30	.75
❑ 49 Keith Van Horn	.30	.75
❑ 50 Jason Kidd	.60	1.50
❑ 51 Scottie Pippen	.60	1.50
❑ 52 Gary Payton	.40	1.00
❑ 53 Robert Pack	.25	.60
❑ 54 Adrian Griffin	.25	.60
❑ 55 Jim Jackson	.25	.60
❑ 56 Lamond Murray	.25	.60
❑ 57 Larry Hughes	.30	.75
❑ 58 Dirk Nowitzki	.60	1.50
❑ 59 Vonteego Cummings	.25	.60
❑ 60 Jalen Rose	.30	.75
❑ 61 Arvydas Sabonis	.30	.75
❑ 62 Kerry Kittles	.30	.75
❑ 63 Kevin Garnett	.75	2.00
❑ 64 Latrell Sprewell	.30	.75
❑ 65 Shawn Marion	.40	1.00
❑ 66 Darrell Armstrong	.25	.60
❑ 67 Ron Mercer	.25	.60
❑ 68 Damon Stoudamire	.30	.75
❑ 69 Tracy McGrady	.75	2.00
❑ 70 Theo Ratliff	.25	.60
❑ 71 Lamar Odom	.40	1.00
❑ 72 Charlie Ward	.25	.60
❑ 73 John Amaechi	.25	.60
❑ 74 Quincy Lewis	.25	.60
❑ 75 Othella Harrington	.25	.60
❑ 76 Doug Christie	.25	.60
❑ 77 Richard Hamilton	.30	.75
❑ 78 Donyell Marshall	.25	.60
❑ 79 Vlade Divac	.30	.75
❑ 80 Clifford Robinson	.25	.60
❑ 81 Sean Elliott	.30	.75
❑ 82 Rashard Lewis	.40	1.00
❑ 83 Wally Szczerbiak	.30	.75
❑ 84 Dale Davis	.25	.60
❑ 85 Kelvin Cato	.25	.60
❑ 86 Cuttino Mobley	.30	.75
❑ 87 Travis Best	.25	.60
❑ 88 Robert Horry	.30	.75
❑ 89 Maurice Taylor	.25	.60
❑ 90 Jamal Mashburn	.30	.75
❑ 91 Tim Thomas	.25	.60
❑ 92 Stephon Marbury	.40	1.00
❑ 93 Patrick Ewing	.50	1.25
❑ 94 Eric Snow	.25	.60
❑ 95 Anfernee Hardaway	.40	1.00
❑ 96 Steve Smith	.30	.75
❑ 97 Chris Webber	.40	1.00
❑ 98 Rodney Rogers	.25	.60
❑ 99 John Stockton	.50	1.25
❑ 100 Tim Duncan	.75	2.00
❑ 101 Ray Allen	.40	1.00
❑ 102 Glen Rice	.30	.75
❑ 103 Bryon Russell	.25	.60
❑ 104 Tim Hardaway	.30	.75
❑ 105 Allan Houston	.30	.75
❑ 106 Rasheed Wallace	.40	1.00
❑ 107 Vin Baker	.30	.75
❑ 108 Michael Dickerson	.25	.60
❑ 109 Juwan Howard	.30	.75
❑ 110 Hakeem Olajuwon	.50	1.25
❑ 111 Shareef Abdur-Rahim	.30	.75
❑ 112 Rod Strickland	.30	.75
❑ 113 Hersey Hawkins	.25	.60
❑ 114 Jason Terry	.40	1.00
❑ 115 Anthony Mason	.25	.60
❑ 116 Mike Bibby	.30	.75
❑ 117 Shawn Kemp	.40	1.00
❑ 118 Derrick Coleman	.30	.75
❑ 119 Antoine Walker	.30	.75
❑ 120 Antawn Jamison	.40	1.00
❑ 121 Michael Finley	.40	1.00
❑ 122 Antonio McDyess	.30	.75
❑ 123 Nick Van Exel	.30	.75
❑ 124 Mitch Richmond	.30	.75
❑ 125 Lindsey Hunter	.25	.60
❑ 126 Kenyon Martin RC	6.00	15.00
❑ 127 Stromile Swift RC	3.00	8.00
❑ 128 Darius Miles RC	3.00	8.00
❑ 129 Marcus Fizer RC	2.50	6.00
❑ 130 Mike Miller RC	4.00	10.00
❑ 131 DerMarr Johnson RC	2.50	6.00
❑ 132 Chris Mihm RC	2.50	6.00
❑ 133 Jamal Crawford RC	4.00	10.00
❑ 134 Joel Przybilla RC	2.50	6.00
❑ 135 Keyon Dooling RC	2.50	6.00
❑ 136 Jerome Moiso RC	2.50	6.00
❑ 137 Etan Thomas RC	2.50	6.00
❑ 138 Courtney Alexander RC	2.50	6.00
❑ 139 Mateen Cleaves RC	2.50	6.00
❑ 140 Jason Collier RC	2.50	6.00
❑ 141 Desmond Mason RC	3.00	8.00
❑ 142 Quentin Richardson RC	3.00	8.00
❑ 143 Jamaal Magloire RC	2.50	6.00
❑ 144 Speedy Claxton RC	2.50	6.00
❑ 145 Morris Peterson RC	4.00	10.00
❑ 146 Donnell Harvey RC	2.50	6.00
❑ 147 DeShawn Stevenson RC	2.50	6.00
❑ 148 Mamadou N'Diaye RC	2.50	6.00
❑ 149 Erick Barkley RC	2.50	6.00
❑ 150 Mark Madsen RC	2.50	6.00
❑ 151 A.Iverson/S.Marbury OTM	.60	1.50
❑ 152 V.Carter/K.Bryant OTM	1.25	3.00
❑ 153 K.Garnett/Abdur-Rahim OTM	1.00	2.50
❑ 154 T.McGrady/S.Pippen OTM	1.50	4.00
❑ 155 T.Duncan/E.Brand OTM	1.25	3.00
❑ 156 S.Francis/G.Payton OTM	1.00	2.50
❑ 157 C.Webber/K.Malone OTM	.40	1.00
❑ 158 A.Mourning/P.Ewing OTM	.40	1.00
❑ 159 L.Sprewell/E.Jones OTM	.40	1.00
❑ 160 J.Kidd/J.Stockton OTM	.60	1.50
❑ 161 R.Miller/A.Houston OTM	.40	1.00
❑ 162 R.Wallace/A.Walker OTM	.40	1.00
❑ 163 J.Stackhouse/J.Rose OTM	.40	1.00
❑ 164 Shaquille O'Neal GEM	2.50	6.00
❑ 165 Kobe Bryant GEM	5.00	12.00
❑ 166 Vince Carter GEM	2.00	5.00
❑ 167 Kevin Garnett GEM	2.00	5.00
❑ 168 Jason Williams GEM	.75	2.00
❑ 169 Tracy McGrady GEM	2.00	5.00
❑ 170 Steve Francis GEM	1.00	2.50
❑ 171 Tim Duncan GEM	2.00	5.00
❑ 172 Elton Brand GEM	1.00	2.50
❑ 173 Grant Hill GEM	1.00	2.50

2002-03 Finest

❑ COMP.DRAFT SET (10)	250.00	450.00
❑ COMMON CARD (1-100)	.25	.60
❑ COMMON AU RC (101-120)	4.00	10.00
❑ COMMON JSY (121-156)	2.50	6.00
❑ COMMON AU RC (157-177)	5.00	12.00
❑ 1 Dirk Nowitzki	.60	1.50

❑ 2 Jason Terry .40 1.00
❑ 3 Marcus Camby .30 .75
❑ 4 Joe Johnson .40 1.00
❑ 5 Shawn Marion .40 1.00
❑ 6 Andrei Kirilenko .40 1.00
❑ 7 Jamal Mashburn .30 .75
❑ 8 Andre Miller .30 .75
❑ 9 Jason Williams .30 .75
❑ 10 Tony Delk .25 .60
❑ 11 Tyson Chandler .30 .75
❑ 12 Jason Richardson .40 1.00
❑ 13 Derek Fisher .30 .75
❑ 14 Troy Hudson .25 .60
❑ 15 Kerry Kittles .30 .75
❑ 16 Peja Stojakovic .30 .75
❑ 17 Kurt Thomas .25 .60
❑ 18 Jamaal Tinsley .30 .75
❑ 19 Matt Harpring .30 .75
❑ 20 Kenny Thomas .25 .60
❑ 21 Kwame Brown .25 .60
❑ 22 Antonio Davis .25 .60
❑ 23 David Robinson .50 1.25
❑ 24 Keith Van Horn .30 .75
❑ 25 Howard Eisley .25 .60
❑ 26 Jalen Rose .30 .75
❑ 27 Chauncey Billups .40 1.00
❑ 28 Corey Maggette .30 .75
❑ 29 Pau Gasol .40 1.00
❑ 30 Desmond Mason .30 .75
❑ 31 Brian Grant .25 .60
❑ 32 Eddie Griffin .25 .60
❑ 33 Voshon Lenard .25 .60
❑ 34 Al Harrington .30 .75
❑ 35 Calbert Cheaney .25 .60
❑ 36 Malik Rose .25 .60
❑ 37 Bonzi Wells .30 .75
❑ 38 Pat Garrity .25 .60
❑ 39 P.J. Brown .25 .60
❑ 40 Ray Allen .40 1.00
❑ 41 Karl Malone .40 1.00
❑ 42 Steve Nash .60 1.50
❑ 43 Antawn Jamison .40 1.00
❑ 44 Ron Artest .30 .75
❑ 45 Shane Battier .30 .75
❑ 46 Gary Payton .40 1.00
❑ 47 Kobe Bryant 2.00 5.00
❑ 48 Lucious Harris .25 .60
❑ 49 Richard Hamilton .30 .75
❑ 50 Darius Miles .25 .60
❑ 51 Marcus Fizer .25 .60
❑ 52 Antoine Walker .30 .75
❑ 53 Juwan Howard .30 .75
❑ 54 Eddie Jones .30 .75
❑ 55 Kenyon Martin .40 1.00
❑ 56 Derek Anderson .30 .75
❑ 57 Stephen Jackson .30 .75
❑ 58 Vince Carter .75 2.00
❑ 59 Larry Hughes .30 .75
❑ 60 Doug Christie .25 .60
❑ 61 Derrick Coleman .30 .75
❑ 62 Michael Finley .40 1.00
❑ 63 Wally Szczerbiak .30 .75
❑ 64 David Wesley .25 .60
❑ 65 Brad Miller .30 .75
❑ 66 Clifford Robinson .25 .60
❑ 67 Shandon Anderson .25 .60
❑ 68 Stephon Marbury .40 1.00
❑ 69 Bobby Jackson .25 .60
❑ 70 Brent Barry .25 .60
❑ 71 Ruben Patterson .25 .60
❑ 72 Rashard Lewis .40 1.00
❑ 73 Tony Battie .25 .60
❑ 74 Ben Wallace .30 .75
❑ 75 Theo Ratliff .25 .60
❑ 76 Ricky Davis .30 .75
❑ 77 Nick Van Exel .30 .75
❑ 78 Mike Miller .30 .75
❑ 79 Sam Cassell .30 .75
❑ 80 Malik Allen .25 .60
❑ 81 Mike Bibby .30 .75
❑ 82 Scottie Pippen .60 1.50
❑ 83 Dikembe Mutombo .30 .75
❑ 84 Latrell Sprewell .30 .75
❑ 85 Predrag Drobnjak .25 .60
❑ 86 Joe Smith .25 .60
❑ 87 Aaron Mckie .25 .60
❑ 88 Jamaal Magloire .25 .60
❑ 89 Keon Clark .25 .60
❑ 90 Eric Williams .25 .60
❑ 91 Raef Lafrentz .25 .60
❑ 92 Troy Murphy .40 1.00
❑ 93 Rick Fox .30 .75
❑ 94 Michael Redd .40 1.00
❑ 95 Radoslav Nesterovic .25 .60
❑ 96 Donyell Marshall .25 .60
❑ 97 Elton Brand .40 1.00
❑ 98 Robert Horry .30 .75
❑ 99 Zydrunas Ilgauskas .30 .75
❑ 100 Michael Jordan 2.50 6.00
❑ 101 Juaquin Hawkins AU RC 4.00 10.00
❑ 102 Dan Dickau AU RC 4.00 10.00
❑ 104 John Salmons AU RC 6.00 15.00
❑ 105 Tamar Slay AU RC 4.00 10.00
❑ 106 Melvin Ely AU RC 4.00 10.00
❑ 107 Jared Jeffries AU RC 4.00 10.00
❑ 108 J.Harrington AU RC 4.00 10.00
❑ 110 Qyntel Woods AU RC 4.00 10.00
❑ 111 R.Humphrey AU RC 4.00 10.00
❑ 112 J.R. Bremer AU RC 4.00 10.00
❑ 113 A.Rigadeau AU RC 4.00 10.00
❑ 114 Jay Williams RC 5.00 12.00
❑ 115 Pat Burke AU RC 4.00 10.00
❑ 116 Smush Parker AU RC 4.00 10.00
❑ 117 Juan Dixon AU RC 6.00 15.00
❑ 118 V.Yarbrough AU RC 4.00 10.00
❑ 120 Rasual Butler AU RC 4.00 10.00
❑ 121 Baron Davis JSY 4.00 10.00
❑ 122 S.Abdur-Rahim JSY 3.00 8.00
❑ 123 Gilbert Arenas JSY 4.00 10.00
❑ 124 Travis Best JSY 2.50 6.00
❑ 125 Vlade Divac JSY 3.00 8.00
❑ 126 Tim Duncan JSY 8.00 20.00
❑ 127 Jason Kidd JSY 6.00 15.00
❑ 128 Kevin Garnett JSY 8.00 20.00
❑ 129 A.Hardaway JSY 4.00 10.00
❑ 130 Allen Iverson JSY 8.00 20.00
❑ 131 Cuttino Mobley JSY 3.00 8.00
❑ 132 Steve Francis JSY 4.00 10.00
❑ 133 Jermaine O'Neal JSY 4.00 10.00
❑ 134 Lamar Odom JSY 4.00 10.00
❑ 135 M.Olowokandi JSY 2.50 6.00
❑ 136 Paul Pierce JSY 4.00 10.00
❑ 137 Reggie Miller JSY 4.00 10.00
❑ 138 Chris Webber JSY 4.00 10.00
❑ 139 Richard Jefferson JSY 4.00 10.00
❑ 140 Allan Houston JSY 3.00 8.00
❑ 141 Glenn Robinson JSY 3.00 8.00
❑ 142 Jerome Williams JSY 2.50 6.00
❑ 143 John Stockton JSY 5.00 12.00
❑ 144 Rasheed Wallace JSY 4.00 10.00
❑ 145 Eric Snow JSY 2.50 6.00
❑ 146 Tracy McGrady JSY 8.00 20.00
❑ 147 S.O'Neal JSY 10.00 25.00
❑ 148 J.Stackhouse JSY 3.00 8.00
❑ 149 Morris Peterson JSY 3.00 8.00
❑ 150 D.Armstrong JSY 2.50 6.00
❑ 151 Tony Parker JSY 4.00 10.00
❑ 152 V.Radmanovic JSY 2.50 6.00
❑ 153 Anthony Mason JSY 2.50 6.00
❑ 154 Charles Oakley JSY 3.00 8.00
❑ 155 Grant Hill JSY 4.00 10.00
❑ 156 Vin Baker JSY 3.00 8.00
❑ 157 Chris Jefferies AU RC 5.00 12.00
❑ 158 Drew Gooden AU RC 8.00 20.00
❑ 159 C.Jacobsen AU RC 5.00 12.00
❑ 160 Kareem Rush AU RC 6.00 15.00
❑ 161 B.Nachbar AU RC 5.00 12.00
❑ 162 Tayshaun Prince AU RC 8.00 20.00
❑ 163 Manu Ginobili RC 12.00 30.00
❑ 164 Gordan Giricek AU RC 5.00 12.00
❑ 165 Raul Lopez AU RC 5.00 12.00
❑ 166 Dan Gadzuric AU RC 5.00 12.00
❑ 167 Marko Jaric AU 5.00 12.00
❑ 168 Lonny Baxter AU RC 5.00 12.00
❑ 169 Yao Ming AU RC 15.00 40.00
❑ 170 Mike Dunleavy AU RC 6.00 15.00
❑ 171 Caron Butler AU RC 10.00 25.00
❑ 172 Nene Hilario AU RC 6.00 15.00
❑ 173 A.Stoudemire AU RC 12.00 30.00
❑ 174 N.Tskitishvili AU RC 5.00 12.00
❑ 175 Fred Jones AU RC 6.00 15.00
❑ 176 D.Wagner AU RC 5.00 12.00
❑ 177 Carlos Boozer AU RC 10.00 25.00
❑ 178 LeBron James XRC 90.00 180.00
❑ 179 Darko Milicic XRC 10.00 25.00
❑ 180 Carmelo Anthony XRC 25.00 50.00
❑ 181 Chris Bosh XRC 10.00 25.00
❑ 182 Dwyane Wade XRC 20.00 40.00
❑ 183 Chris Kaman XRC 5.00 12.00
❑ 184 Kirk Hinrich XRC 8.00 20.00
❑ 185 T.J. Ford XRC 8.00 20.00
❑ 186 Mike Sweetney XRC 5.00 12.00
❑ 187 Jarvis Hayes XRC 5.00 12.00

2003-04 Finest

❑ COMP.SET w/o SP's (100) 15.00 40.00
❑ COMMON CARD (1-100) .25 .60
❑ COMMON JSY (101-130) 1.50 4.00
❑ COMMON ROOKIE (131-143) 2.50 6.00
❑ COMMON AU RC (144-172) 4.00 10.00
❑ COMMON XRC (173-185) 4.00 10.00
❑ 1 Zach Randolph .40 1.00
❑ 2 Keith Van Horn .30 .75
❑ 3 Steve Francis .40 1.00
❑ 4 Al Harrington .30 .75
❑ 5 Jason Kidd .60 1.50
❑ 6 Jamaal Tinsley .30 .75
❑ 7 Lamar Odom .40 1.00
❑ 8 Antoine Walker .40 1.00
❑ 9 Tony Parker .40 1.00
❑ 10 Jamal Mashburn .25 .60
❑ 11 Desmond Mason .30 .75
❑ 12 Carlos Arroyo .25 .60
❑ 13 Chris Andersen .50 1.25
❑ 14 Chris Wilcox .25 .60
❑ 15 Vince Carter .75 2.00
❑ 16 Peja Stojakovic .30 .75
❑ 17 Qyntel Woods .25 .60
❑ 18 Mike Dunleavy .30 .75
❑ 19 Sam Cassell .30 .75
❑ 20 Allan Houston .30 .75
❑ 21 Speedy Claxton .25 .60
❑ 22 Rafer Alston .25 .60
❑ 23 Michael Finley .40 1.00
❑ 24 Richard Jefferson .40 1.00
❑ 25 Larry Hughes .30 .75
❑ 26 Pau Gasol .40 1.00
❑ 27 Maurice Taylor .25 .60
❑ 28 Donyell Marshall .25 .60
❑ 29 Darrell Armstrong .25 .60
❑ 30 Latrell Sprewell .30 .75
❑ 31 Reggie Miller .40 1.00
❑ 32 Stephon Marbury .40 1.00
❑ 33 Antawn Jamison .40 1.00
❑ 34 DerMarr Johnson .25 .60
❑ 35 Shareef Abdur-Rahim .30 .75
❑ 36 Tony Battie .25 .60
❑ 37 Kwame Brown .25 .60
❑ 38 Fred Jones .30 .75
❑ 39 Jamal Crawford .30 .75
❑ 40 Kurt Thomas .25 .60
❑ 41 Eric Snow .25 .60
❑ 42 Andre Miller .30 .75
❑ 43 Ray Allen .25 .60
❑ 44 Caron Butler .30 .75
❑ 45 Corliss Williamson .25 .60
❑ 46 Kenny Thomas .25 .60
❑ 47 Jason Terry .30 .75
❑ 48 Ronald Murray .25 .60
❑ 49 Richard Hamilton .30 .75

❑ 50 Elton Brand	.40	1.00
❑ 51 Ron Artest	.30	.75
❑ 52 Jerome Williams	.25	.60
❑ 53 Ricky Davis	.30	.75
❑ 54 Brent Barry	.25	.60
❑ 55 Dikembe Mutombo	.30	.75
❑ 56 Earl Boykins	.25	.60
❑ 57 Brad Miller	.30	.75
❑ 58 Shane Battier	.30	.75
❑ 59 Tyson Chandler	.30	.75
❑ 60 Kelvin Cato	.25	.60
❑ 61 Shawn Marion	.40	1.00
❑ 62 Bobby Jackson	.25	.60
❑ 63 Corey Maggette	.25	.60
❑ 64 Antonio McDyess	.30	.75
❑ 65 Drew Gooden	.25	.60
❑ 66 Mike Miller	.30	.75
❑ 67 Darius Miles	.30	.75
❑ 68 Stephen Jackson	.30	.75
❑ 69 Cuttino Mobley	.30	.75
❑ 70 Gary Payton	.40	1.00
❑ 71 Toni Kukoc	.30	.75
❑ 72 Eddie Jones	.30	.75
❑ 73 Gilbert Arenas	.40	1.00
❑ 74 Matt Harpring	.30	.75
❑ 75 Marko Jaric	.25	.60
❑ 76 Bonzi Wells	.25	.60
❑ 77 Nick Van Exel	.30	.75
❑ 78 Quentin Richardson	.30	.75
❑ 79 Rasho Nesterovic	.25	.60
❑ 80 Steve Nash	.60	1.50
❑ 81 Morris Peterson	.30	.75
❑ 82 Nikoloz Tskitishvili	.25	.60
❑ 83 Damon Stoudamire	.30	.75
❑ 84 Bruce Bowen	.30	.75
❑ 85 Brian Grant	.25	.60
❑ 86 Jalen Rose	.30	.75
❑ 87 Jerry Stackhouse	.30	.75
❑ 88 Kobe Bryant	2.00	5.00
❑ 89 Eddy Curry	.30	.75
❑ 90 Tim Thomas	.25	.60
❑ 91 Erick Dampier	.25	.60
❑ 92 Jason Williams	.30	.75
❑ 93 Troy Murphy	.40	1.00
❑ 94 Kerry Kittles	.30	.75
❑ 95 Zydrunas Ilgauskas	.30	.75
❑ 96 Theo Ratliff	.25	.60
❑ 97 Samuel Dalembert	.30	.75
❑ 98 Jeff McInnis	.25	.60
❑ 99 Juwan Howard	.30	.75
❑ 100 Joe Johnson	.40	1.00
❑ 101 Paul Pierce JSY	2.50	6.00
❑ 102 Ben Wallace JSY	2.00	5.00
❑ 103 Yao Ming JSY	5.00	12.00
❑ 104 Jermaine O'Neal JSY	2.50	6.00
❑ 105 Rashard Lewis JSY	2.50	6.00
❑ 106 Karl Malone JSY	2.50	6.00
❑ 107 Allen Iverson JSY	5.00	12.00
❑ 108 Mike Bibby JSY	2.00	5.00
❑ 109 Rasheed Wallace JSY	2.50	6.00
❑ 110 Nene JSY	2.00	5.00
❑ 111 Tracy McGrady JSY	5.00	12.00
❑ 112 Andrei Kirilenko JSY	2.50	6.00
❑ 113 Manu Ginobili JSY	2.50	6.00
❑ 114 Kenyon Martin JSY	2.50	6.00
❑ 115 Amare Stoudemire JSY	5.00	12.00
❑ 116 Baron Davis JSY	2.50	6.00
❑ 117 Michael Olowokandi JSY	1.50	4.00
❑ 118 Carlos Boozer JSY	2.50	6.00
❑ 119 Jason Richardson JSY	2.50	6.00
❑ 120 Dirk Nowitzki JSY	4.00	10.00
❑ 121 Chauncey Billups JSY	2.50	6.00
❑ 122 Chris Webber JSY	2.50	6.00
❑ 123 Glenn Robinson JSY/807	2.00	5.00
❑ 124 Kevin Garnett JSY	5.00	12.00
❑ 125 Michael Redd JSY	2.50	6.00
❑ 126 David Wesley JSY	1.50	4.00
❑ 127 Tayshaun Prince JSY	2.00	5.00
❑ 128 Jamaal Magloire JSY	1.50	4.00
❑ 129 Tim Duncan JSY	5.00	12.00
❑ 130 Shaquille O'Neal JSY	6.00	15.00
❑ 131 Darko Milicic RC	3.00	8.00
❑ 132 Chris Kaman RC	3.00	8.00
❑ 133 LeBron James RC	80.00	160.00
❑ 134 Richie Frahm RC	2.50	6.00
❑ 135 Steve Blake RC	3.00	8.00
❑ 136 Zaza Pachulia RC	3.00	8.00
❑ 137 Keith Bogans RC	2.50	6.00
❑ 138 Kirk Hinrich AU RC	10.00	30.00
❑ 139 Jarvis Hayes RC	2.50	6.00
❑ 140 Zarko Cabarkapa AU RC	4.00	10.00
❑ 141 Zoran Planinic AU RC	4.00	10.00
❑ 142 Udonis Haslem RC	3.00	8.00
❑ 143 David West RC	3.00	8.00
❑ 144 Boris Diaw AU RC	6.00	15.00
❑ 146 Brian Cook AU RC	5.00	12.00
❑ 147 Ndudi Ebi AU RC	5.00	12.00
❑ 148 Josh Howard AU RC	8.00	20.00
❑ 149 Jason Kapono AU RC	4.00	10.00
❑ 150 Luke Walton AU RC	6.00	15.00
❑ 151 Travis Hansen AU RC	4.00	10.00
❑ 152 Willie Green AU RC	4.00	10.00
❑ 153 Maurice Williams AU RC	8.00	20.00
❑ 154 Francisco Elson AU RC	4.00	10.00
❑ 155 Kyle Korver AU RC	8.00	20.00
❑ 156 Marquis Daniels AU RC	6.00	15.00
❑ 157 Chris Bosh AU RC	25.00	40.00
❑ 158 Dwyane Wade AU RC	50.00	100.00
❑ 159 Aleksandar Pavlovic AU RC	5.00	12.00
❑ 160 Mike Sweetney AU RC	4.00	10.00
❑ 161 Marcus Banks AU RC	4.00	10.00
❑ 162 Luke Ridnour AU RC	8.00	20.00
❑ 163 Carmelo Anthony AU RC	40.00	80.00
❑ 164 Mickael Pietrus AU RC	4.00	10.00
❑ 165 Reece Gaines AU RC	4.00	10.00
❑ 166 Kendrick Perkins AU RC	6.00	15.00
❑ 167 Troy Bell AU RC	4.00	10.00
❑ 168 Leandro Barbosa AU RC	8.00	20.00
❑ 169 Dahntay Jones AU RC	4.00	10.00
❑ 170 T.J. Ford AU RC	8.00	20.00
❑ 171 Nick Collison AU RC	4.00	10.00
❑ 172 Theron Smith AU RC	4.00	10.00
❑ 173 Dwight Howard XRC	15.00	30.00
❑ 174 Emeka Okafor XRC	15.00	30.00
❑ 175 Ben Gordon XRC	20.00	50.00
❑ 176 Shaun Livingston XRC	6.00	15.00
❑ 177 Devin Harris XRC	6.00	15.00
❑ 178 Josh Childress XRC	4.00	10.00
❑ 179 Luol Deng XRC	8.00	20.00
❑ 180 Rafael Araujo XRC	4.00	10.00
❑ 181 Andre Iguodala XRC	8.00	20.00
❑ 182 Luke Jackson XRC	4.00	10.00
❑ 183 Andris Biedrins XRC	4.00	10.00
❑ 184 Robert Swift XRC	8.00	20.00
❑ 185 Sebastian Telfair XRC	4.00	10.00

2004-05 Finest

❑ COMP.SET w/o SP's (100)	15.00	40.00
❑ COMMON CARD (131-160)	2.00	5.00
❑ 1 Richard Hamilton	.30	.75
❑ 2 Mike Dunleavy	.30	.75
❑ 3 Jamaal Tinsley	.30	.75
❑ 4 Corey Maggette	.30	.75
❑ 5 Zach Randolph	.40	1.00
❑ 6 Desmond Mason	.30	.75
❑ 7 Marc Jackson	.25	.60
❑ 8 Kobe Bryant	2.00	5.00
❑ 9 Mike Bibby	.30	.75
❑ 10 Vince Carter	.75	2.00
❑ 11 Bonzi Wells	.25	.60
❑ 12 Ricky Davis	.30	.75
❑ 13 Steve Nash	.60	1.50
❑ 14 Rashard Lewis	.40	1.00
❑ 15 Eddy Curry	.30	.75
❑ 16 Carlos Boozer	.40	1.00
❑ 17 Brad Miller	.30	.75
❑ 18 Kurt Thomas	.25	.60
❑ 19 Shareef Abdur-Rahim	.30	.75
❑ 20 Grant Hill	.40	1.00
❑ 21 Jason Hart	.25	.60
❑ 22 Larry Hughes	.30	.75
❑ 23 Lebron James	2.50	6.00
❑ 24 Udonis Haslem	.30	.75
❑ 25 David Wesley	.25	.60
❑ 26 Kenny Thomas	.25	.60
❑ 27 Marcus Camby	.30	.75
❑ 28 Michael Redd	.40	1.00
❑ 29 Rasho Nesterovic	.25	.60
❑ 30 Keith Van Horn	.30	.75
❑ 31 Reggie Miller	.40	1.00
❑ 32 Stephon Marbury	.40	1.00
❑ 33 Donyell Marshall	.25	.60
❑ 34 Jermaine O'Neal	.40	1.00
❑ 35 Antoine Walker	.40	1.00
❑ 36 Rasheed Wallace	.40	1.00
❑ 37 Antonio Daniels	.25	.60
❑ 38 Damon Jones	.25	.60
❑ 39 Caron Butler	.30	.75
❑ 40 Shawn Marion	.40	1.00
❑ 41 Lee Nailon	.25	.60
❑ 42 Damon Stoudamire	.30	.75
❑ 43 Bob Sura	.25	.60
❑ 44 Mehmet Okur	.30	.75
❑ 45 Shane Battier	.30	.75
❑ 46 Michael Finley	.40	1.00
❑ 47 Doug Christie	.25	.60
❑ 48 Eddie Jones	.30	.75
❑ 49 Speedy Claxton	.25	.60
❑ 50 Wally Szczerbiak	.30	.75
❑ 51 Primoz Brezec	.25	.60
❑ 52 Marko Jaric	.25	.60
❑ 53 Antonio McDyess	.30	.75
❑ 54 Jeff Mcinnis	.25	.60
❑ 55 Tony Parker	.40	1.00
❑ 56 Rafer Alston	.25	.60
❑ 57 Troy Murphy	.40	1.00
❑ 58 Chris Mihm	.25	.60
❑ 59 Jarvis Hayes	.25	.60
❑ 60 Marquis Daniels	.25	.60
❑ 61 Jamal Crawford	.30	.75
❑ 62 Morris Peterson	.30	.75
❑ 63 Luke Ridnour	.25	.60
❑ 64 Mike Miller	.30	.75
❑ 65 Carlos Arroyo	.40	1.00
❑ 66 Gary Payton	.40	1.00
❑ 67 Joe Johnson	.40	1.00
❑ 68 Latrell Sprewell	.30	.75
❑ 69 Allan Houston	.30	.75
❑ 70 Earl Boykins	.25	.60
❑ 71 Brendan Haywood	.25	.60
❑ 72 Baron Davis	.40	1.00
❑ 73 Fred Jones	.25	.60
❑ 74 Joe Smith	.25	.60
❑ 75 Jalen Rose	.30	.75
❑ 76 Eddie Griffin	.25	.60
❑ 77 Lamar Odom	.40	1.00
❑ 78 Theo Ratliff	.25	.60
❑ 79 Gordan Giricek	.25	.60
❑ 80 Maurice Williams	.30	.75
❑ 81 Tayshaun Prince	.30	.75
❑ 82 Kyle Korver	.30	.75
❑ 83 Andre Miller	.30	.75
❑ 84 Chris Wilcox	.25	.60
❑ 85 Alonzo Mourning	.40	1.00
❑ 86 Gilbert Arenas	.40	1.00
❑ 87 Zydrunas Ilgauskas	.30	.75
❑ 88 Jamaal Magloire	.25	.60
❑ 89 Jason Williams	.30	.75
❑ 90 Chucky Atkins	.25	.60
❑ 91 Jeff Foster	.25	.60
❑ 92 Kareem Rush	.25	.60
❑ 93 Sam Cassell	.30	.75
❑ 94 Josh Howard	.40	1.00
❑ 95 Tyronn Lue	.25	.60
❑ 96 Vladimir Radmanovic	.25	.60
❑ 97 Chauncey Billups	.40	1.00
❑ 98 Brent Barry	.25	.60
❑ 99 Paul Pierce	.40	1.00
❑ 100 Dwyane Wade	1.25	3.00
❑ 101 Al Harrington JSY	3.00	8.00
❑ 102 Antawn Jamison JSY	3.00	8.00
❑ 103 Kirk Hinrich JSY	3.00	8.00
❑ 104 Tim Duncan JSY	5.00	12.00
❑ 105 Gerald Wallace JSY	3.00	8.00
❑ 106 Dirk Nowitzki JSY	4.00	10.00
❑ 107 Chris Webber JSY	3.00	8.00
❑ 108 Jason Kidd JSY	4.00	10.00
❑ 109 Carmelo Anthony JSY	5.00	12.00
❑ 110 Tracy McGrady JSY	6.00	15.00
❑ 111 Elton Brand JSY	3.00	8.00
❑ 112 Pau Gasol JSY	3.00	8.00
❑ 113 Jason Richardson JSY	3.00	8.00
❑ 114 Chris Bosh JSY	3.00	8.00
❑ 115 Kevin Garnett JSY	5.00	12.00

❑ 116 Steve Francis JSY	3.00	8.00
❑ 117 Richard Jefferson JSY	3.00	8.00
❑ 118 Baron Davis JSY	3.00	8.00
❑ 119 Manu Ginobili JSY	3.00	8.00
❑ 120 Shaquille O'Neal JSY	6.00	15.00
❑ 121 Amare Stoudemire JSY	5.00	12.00
❑ 122 Yao Ming JSY	6.00	15.00
❑ 123 Kenyon Martin JSY	3.00	8.00
❑ 124 Allen Iverson JSY	5.00	12.00
❑ 125 Peja Stojakovic JSY	3.00	8.00
❑ 126 Drew Gooden JSY	3.00	8.00
❑ 127 Ray Allen JSY	3.00	8.00
❑ 128 Ben Wallace JSY	3.00	8.00
❑ 129 Andrei Kirilenko JSY	3.00	8.00
❑ 130 Quentin Richardson JSY	3.00	8.00
❑ 131 Larry Bird	6.00	15.00
❑ 132 George Gervin	2.00	5.00
❑ 133 Walt Frazier	2.00	5.00
❑ 134 Oscar Robertson	2.50	6.00
❑ 135 Elgin Baylor	2.00	5.00
❑ 136 Moses Malone	2.50	6.00
❑ 137 Pete Maravich	10.00	25.00
❑ 138 Bob Cousy	2.50	6.00
❑ 139 Earl Monroe	2.00	5.00
❑ 140 Kareem Abdul-Jabbar	3.00	8.00
❑ 141 Isiah Thomas	2.00	5.00
❑ 142 Kevin McHale	2.50	6.00
❑ 143 Bill Walton	2.50	6.00
❑ 144 John Havlicek	2.50	6.00
❑ 145 Rick Barry	2.00	5.00
❑ 146 Wilt Chamberlain	4.00	10.00
❑ 147 Bill Russell	2.50	6.00
❑ 148 Willis Reed	2.00	5.00
❑ 149 Julius Erving	3.00	8.00
❑ 150 Drazen Petrovic	3.00	8.00
❑ 151 Andre Iguodala RC	5.00	12.00
❑ 152 Luke Jackson RC	2.00	5.00
❑ 153 Kirk Snyder RC	2.00	5.00
❑ 154 Kevin Martin RC	2.50	6.00
❑ 155 Antonio Burks RC	2.00	5.00
❑ 156 Robert Swift RC	2.00	5.00
❑ 157 Dorell Wright RC	2.50	6.00
❑ 158 David Harrison RC	2.00	5.00
❑ 159 Dwight Howard RC	6.00	15.00
❑ 160 Al Jefferson RC	4.00	10.00
❑ 161 Justin Reed AU RC	8.00	20.00
❑ 162 Shaun Livingston AU RC	12.50	30.00
❑ 163 Luol Deng AU RC	8.00	20.00
❑ 164 Josh Smith AU RC	12.50	30.00
❑ 165 Jameer Nelson AU RC	10.00	25.00
❑ 166 Pavel Podkolzin AU RC	8.00	20.00
❑ 167 Emeka Okafor AU RC	10.00	25.00
❑ 168 Kris Humphries AU RC	8.00	20.00
❑ 169 J.R. Smith AU RC	12.50	30.00
❑ 170 Sebastian Telfair AU RC	6.00	15.00
❑ 171 Sasha Vujacic AU RC	8.00	20.00
❑ 172 Tony Allen AU RC	10.00	25.00
❑ 173 Romain Sato AU RC	8.00	20.00
❑ 174 Ben Gordon AU RC	8.00	20.00
❑ 175 Devin Harris AU RC	12.50	30.00
❑ 176 Josh Childress AU RC	10.00	25.00
❑ 177 Andre Barrett AU RC	8.00	20.00
❑ 178 Jackson Vroman AU RC	8.00	20.00
❑ 179 Lionel Chalmers AU RC	8.00	20.00
❑ 180 Delonte West AU RC	15.00	40.00
❑ 181 Nenad Krstic AU RC	10.00	25.00
❑ 182 Donta Smith AU RC	8.00	20.00
❑ 183 Chris Duhon AU RC	12.50	30.00
❑ 184 Peter John Ramos AU RC	8.00	20.00
❑ 185 Bernard Robinson AU RC	8.00	20.00
❑ 186 Beno Udrih AU RC	10.00	25.00
❑ 187 Andris Biedrins AU RC	12.50	30.00
❑ 188 Trevor Ariza AU RC	10.00	25.00
❑ 189 Rafael Araujo AU RC	8.00	20.00
❑ 190 Andres Nocioni AU RC	10.00	25.00
❑ 191 Andrew Bogut XRC	12.50	30.00
❑ 192 Marvin Williams XRC	15.00	40.00
❑ 193 Deron Williams XRC	10.00	25.00
❑ 194 Chris Paul XRC	12.50	30.00
❑ 195 Raymond Felton XRC	8.00	20.00
❑ 196 Martell Webster XRC	6.00	15.00
❑ 197 Charlie Villanueva XRC	5.00	12.00
❑ 198 Channing Frye XRC	5.00	12.00
❑ 199 Ike Diogu XRC	4.00	10.00
❑ 200 Andrew Bynum XRC	5.00	12.00
❑ 201 Salim Stoudamire XRC	3.00	8.00
❑ 202 Yaroslav Korolev XRC	2.50	6.00
❑ 203 Sean May XRC	8.00	20.00
❑ 204 Rashad McCants XRC	8.00	20.00
❑ 205 Antoine Wright XRC	4.00	10.00
❑ 206 Joey Graham XRC	4.00	10.00
❑ 207 Danny Granger XRC	4.00	10.00
❑ 208 Gerald Green XRC	10.00	25.00
❑ 209 Hakim Warrick XRC	6.00	15.00
❑ 210 Julius Hodge XRC	5.00	12.00
❑ 211 Nate Robinson XRC	4.00	10.00
❑ 212 Jarrett Jack XRC	2.50	6.00
❑ 213 Francisco Garcia XRC	4.00	10.00
❑ 214 Luther Head XRC	4.00	10.00
❑ 215 Daniel Ewing XRC	2.50	6.00
❑ 216 Jason Maxiell XRC	2.50	6.00
❑ 217 Linas Kleiza XRC	2.50	6.00
❑ 218 Brandon Bass XRC	2.50	6.00
❑ 219 Wayne Simien XRC	3.00	8.00
❑ 220 David Lee XRC	2.50	6.00

2005-06 Finest

❑ COMP.SET w/o SP's (100)	15.00	40.00
❑ COMMON CARD (1-100)	.25	.60
❑ COMMON CELEB (101-105)	2.50	6.00
❑ COMMON ROOKIE (106-125)	1.50	4.00
❑ COMMON AU RC (126-139)	5.00	12.00
❑ COMMON XRC (140-169)	3.00	8.00
❑ XRC 140-169 ISSUED AS DRAFT EXCH		
❑ 1 Shaquille O'Neal	1.00	2.50
❑ 2 Eddy Curry	.30	.75
❑ 3 Ben Wallace	.40	1.00
❑ 4 Wally Szczerbiak	.30	.75
❑ 5 Richard Jefferson	.30	.75
❑ 6 Josh Howard	.40	1.00
❑ 7 Grant Hill	.40	1.00
❑ 8 Desmond Mason	.25	.60
❑ 9 Corey Maggette	.30	.75
❑ 10 Caron Butler	.40	1.00
❑ 11 Andrei Kirilenko	.40	1.00
❑ 12 Al Harrington	.25	.60
❑ 13 Tony Parker	.40	1.00
❑ 14 Stephon Marbury	.40	1.00
❑ 15 Rafer Alston	.25	.60
❑ 16 Marquis Daniels	.30	.75
❑ 17 Luke Ridnour	.30	.75
❑ 18 Kirk Hinrich	.40	1.00
❑ 19 Jason Kidd	.60	1.50
❑ 20 Morris Peterson	.30	.75
❑ 21 Yao Ming	1.00	2.50
❑ 22 Nenad Krstic	.30	.75
❑ 23 Mehmet Okur	.25	.60
❑ 24 Shareef Abdur-Rahim	.40	1.00
❑ 25 Rashard Lewis	.40	1.00
❑ 26 Luol Deng	.40	1.00
❑ 27 Elton Brand	.40	1.00
❑ 28 Dirk Nowitzki	.60	1.50
❑ 29 Bobby Simmons	.25	.60
❑ 30 Antawn Jamison	.40	1.00
❑ 31 Tracy McGrady	.75	2.00
❑ 32 Steve Francis	.40	1.00
❑ 33 Kobe Bryant	2.00	5.00
❑ 34 Jason Richardson	.40	1.00
❑ 35 J.R. Smith	.30	.75
❑ 36 Tayshaun Prince	.40	1.00
❑ 37 Chauncey Billups	.40	1.00
❑ 38 Allen Iverson	.75	2.00
❑ 39 Ricky Davis	.40	1.00
❑ 40 Josh Smith	.40	1.00
❑ 41 Brad Miller	.40	1.00
❑ 42 Zach Randolph	.40	1.00
❑ 43 Troy Murphy	.40	1.00
❑ 44 Shawn Marion	.40	1.00
❑ 45 Pau Gasol	.40	1.00
❑ 46 Lamar Odom	.40	1.00
❑ 47 Drew Gooden	.30	.75
❑ 48 Darius Miles	.40	1.00
❑ 49 Chris Bosh	.40	1.00
❑ 50 Antoine Walker	.30	.75
❑ 51 Amare Stoudemire	.75	2.00
❑ 52 Rasheed Wallace	.40	1.00
❑ 53 Emeka Okafor	.40	1.00
❑ 54 Steve Nash	.50	1.25
❑ 55 Sam Cassell	.40	1.00
❑ 56 Michael Finley	.40	1.00
❑ 57 Manu Ginobili	.40	1.00
❑ 58 Mike Dunleavy	.30	.75
❑ 59 Jason Terry	.40	1.00
❑ 60 Jalen Rose	.40	1.00
❑ 61 Ron Artest	.30	.75
❑ 62 Marcus Camby	.30	.75
❑ 63 Udonis Haslem	.40	1.00
❑ 64 Kenyon Martin	.40	1.00
❑ 65 Gerald Wallace	.40	1.00
❑ 66 David West	.40	1.00
❑ 67 Samuel Dalembert	.25	.60
❑ 68 Jermaine O'Neal	.40	1.00
❑ 69 Dwight Howard	.75	2.00
❑ 70 T.J. Ford	.30	.75
❑ 71 Smush Parker	.25	.60
❑ 72 Sebastian Telfair	.30	.75
❑ 73 Ray Allen	.40	1.00
❑ 74 Michael Redd	.40	1.00
❑ 75 Larry Hughes	.30	.75
❑ 76 Jamaal Tinsley	.30	.75
❑ 77 Chris Duhon	.30	.75
❑ 78 Baron Davis	.40	1.00
❑ 79 Andre Iguodala	.40	1.00
❑ 80 Paul Pierce	.40	1.00
❑ 81 Zydrunas Ilgauskas	.30	.75
❑ 82 Tim Duncan	.75	2.00
❑ 83 Shane Battier	.40	1.00
❑ 84 Peja Stojakovic	.40	1.00
❑ 85 LeBron James	2.00	5.00
❑ 86 Kevin Garnett	.75	2.00
❑ 87 Chris Webber	.40	1.00
❑ 88 Carmelo Anthony	.75	2.00
❑ 89 Vince Carter	.75	2.00
❑ 90 Stephen Jackson	.30	.75
❑ 91 Richard Hamilton	.30	.75
❑ 92 Mike Bibby	.40	1.00
❑ 93 Marko Jaric	.25	.60
❑ 94 Jamal Crawford	.30	.75
❑ 95 Gilbert Arenas	.40	1.00
❑ 96 Dwyane Wade	1.00	2.50
❑ 97 Delonte West	.30	.75
❑ 98 Ben Gordon	.50	1.25
❑ 99 Andre Miller	.30	.75
❑ 100 Joe Johnson	.40	1.00
❑ 101 Jay-Z	2.50	6.00
❑ 102 Shannon Elizabeth	2.50	6.00
❑ 103 Jenny McCarthy	2.50	6.00
❑ 104 Carmen Electra	2.50	6.00
❑ 105 Christie Brinkley	2.50	6.00
❑ 106 Chris Paul RC	5.00	12.00
❑ 107 Channing Frye RC	2.00	5.00
❑ 108 Ike Diogu RC	2.00	5.00
❑ 109 Marvin Williams RC	2.50	6.00
❑ 110 Rashad McCants RC	2.00	5.00
❑ 111 Luther Head RC	2.00	5.00
❑ 112 Gerald Green RC	1.50	4.00
❑ 113 Salim Stoudamire RC	2.00	5.00
❑ 114 Jose Calderon RC	1.50	4.00
❑ 115 Andrew Bynum RC	5.00	12.00
❑ 116 Wayne Simien RC	2.00	5.00
❑ 117 Chris Taft RC	1.50	4.00
❑ 118 Ryan Gomes RC	1.50	4.00
❑ 119 Martell Webster RC	1.50	4.00
❑ 120 Johan Petro RC	1.50	4.00
❑ 121 Antoine Wright RC	1.50	4.00
❑ 122 Jarrett Jack RC	1.50	4.00
❑ 123 Daniel Ewing RC	2.00	5.00
❑ 124 Joey Graham RC	1.50	4.00
❑ 125 Nate Robinson RC	2.50	6.00
❑ 126 Andrew Bogut AU RC	6.00	15.00
❑ 127 Raymond Felton AU RC	6.00	15.00
❑ 128 Francisco Garcia AU RC	6.00	15.00
❑ 129 Danny Granger AU RC	12.00	30.00
❑ 130 Orien Greene AU RC	5.00	12.00
❑ 131 Sarunas Jasikevicius AU RC	6.00	15.00
❑ 132 Linas Kleiza AU RC	6.00	15.00
❑ 133 David Lee AU RC	10.00	25.00
❑ 134 Sean May AU RC	6.00	15.00
❑ 135 Fabricio Oberto AU RC	5.00	12.00
❑ 136 Charlie Villanueva AU RC	8.00	20.00
❑ 137 Hakim Warrick AU RC	8.00	20.00
❑ 138 James Singleton AU RC	5.00	12.00
❑ 139 Deron Williams AU RC	12.00	30.00
❑ 140 Andrea Bargnani XRC	5.00	12.00

❑ 141 LaMarcus Aldridge XRC	6.00	15.00
❑ 142 Adam Morrison XRC	4.00	10.00
❑ 143 Tyrus Thomas XRC	4.00	10.00
❑ 144 Shelden Williams XRC	4.00	10.00
❑ 145 Brandon Roy XRC	10.00	25.00
❑ 146 Randy Foye XRC	3.00	8.00
❑ 147 Rudy Gay XRC	3.00	8.00
❑ 148 Patrick O'Bryant XRC	3.00	8.00
❑ 149 Saer Sene XRC	3.00	8.00
❑ 150 J.J. Redick XRC	3.00	8.00
❑ 151 Hilton Armstrong XRC	3.00	8.00
❑ 152 Thabo Sefolosha XRC	4.00	10.00
❑ 153 Ronnie Brewer XRC	4.00	10.00
❑ 154 Cedric Simmons XRC	3.00	8.00
❑ 155 Rodney Carney XRC	3.00	8.00
❑ 156 Shawne Williams XRC	3.00	8.00
❑ 157 Craig Smith XRC	3.00	8.00
❑ 158 Quincy Douby XRC	3.00	8.00
❑ 159 Renaldo Balkman XRC	3.00	8.00
❑ 160 Rajon Rondo XRC	10.00	25.00
❑ 161 Marcus Williams XRC	4.00	10.00
❑ 162 Josh Boone XRC	3.00	8.00
❑ 163 Kyle Lowry XRC	3.00	8.00
❑ 164 Shannon Brown XRC	3.00	8.00
❑ 165 Jordan Farmar XRC	4.00	10.00
❑ 166 Sergio Rodriguez XRC	3.00	8.00
❑ 167 Maurice Ager XRC	3.00	8.00
❑ 168 Mardy Collins XRC	3.00	8.00
❑ 169 Paul Millsap XRC	5.00	12.00

2006-07 Finest

❑ COMP.SET w/o SPs (100)	20.00	40.00
❑ 1 Carmelo Anthony	.60	1.50
❑ 2 Ben Wallace	.50	1.25
❑ 3 Baron Davis	.50	1.25
❑ 4 Jermaine O'Neal	.50	1.25
❑ 5 Dwyane Wade	1.25	3.00
❑ 6 Vince Carter	1.00	2.50
❑ 7 Dwight Howard	1.00	2.50
❑ 8 Steve Nash	.60	1.50
❑ 9 Tim Duncan	1.00	2.50
❑ 10 Gilbert Arenas	.50	1.25
❑ 11 Gerald Wallace	.50	1.25
❑ 12 Dirk Nowitzki	.75	2.00
❑ 13 Chauncey Billups	.50	1.25
❑ 14 Yao Ming	1.25	3.00
❑ 15 Pau Gasol	.50	1.25
❑ 16 Kevin Garnett	1.00	2.50
❑ 17 Chris Paul	1.00	2.50
❑ 18 Amare Stoudemire	1.00	2.50
❑ 19 Tony Parker	.50	1.25
❑ 20 Andrei Kirilenko	.50	1.25
❑ 21 Paul Pierce	.50	1.25
❑ 22 LeBron James	2.50	6.00
❑ 23 Richard Hamilton	.40	1.00
❑ 24 Tracy McGrady	1.00	2.50
❑ 25 Kobe Bryant	2.50	6.00
❑ 26 Michael Redd	.50	1.25
❑ 27 Stephon Marbury	.50	1.25
❑ 28 Andre Iguodala	.50	1.25
❑ 29 Mike Bibby	.50	1.25
❑ 30 Chris Bosh	.50	1.25
❑ 31 Joe Johnson	.40	1.00
❑ 32 Kirk Hinrich	.50	1.25
❑ 33 Josh Howard	.50	1.25
❑ 34 Jason Richardson	.50	1.25
❑ 35 Elton Brand	.50	1.25
❑ 36 Shaquille O'Neal	1.25	3.00
❑ 37 Jason Kidd	.75	2.00
❑ 38 Allen Iverson	1.00	2.50
❑ 39 Zach Randolph	.50	1.25
❑ 40 Ray Allen	.50	1.25
❑ 41 Larry Bird	3.00	8.00
❑ 42 Isiah Thomas	1.00	2.50
❑ 43 Dominique Wilkins	1.25	3.00
❑ 44 Willis Reed	1.00	2.50
❑ 45 Robert Parish	1.00	2.50
❑ 46 Chris Mullin	1.00	2.50
❑ 47 Karl Malone	1.25	3.00
❑ 48 Calvin Murphy	1.00	2.50
❑ 49 Xavier McDaniel	1.00	2.50
❑ 50 Nate Archibald	1.00	2.50
❑ 51 Steve Novak RC	1.25	3.00
❑ 52 Shannon Brown RC	1.25	3.00
❑ 53 Sergio Rodriguez RC	1.25	3.00
❑ 54 Saer Sene RC	1.25	3.00
❑ 55 Ryan Hollins RC	1.25	3.00
❑ 56 Ronnie Brewer RC	1.50	4.00
❑ 57 Mile Ilic RC	1.25	3.00
❑ 58 Kyle Lowry RC	1.25	3.00
❑ 59 Hilton Armstrong RC	1.25	3.00
❑ 60 Craig Smith RC	1.25	3.00
❑ 61 Will Blalock RC	1.25	3.00
❑ 62 Thabo Sefolosha RC	1.50	4.00
❑ 63 Rodney Carney RC	1.25	3.00
❑ 64 Quincy Douby RC	1.25	3.00
❑ 65 P.J. Tucker RC	1.25	3.00
❑ 66 Josh Boone RC	1.25	3.00
❑ 67 Jordan Farmar RC	1.50	4.00
❑ 68 Damir Markota RC	1.25	3.00
❑ 69 Cedric Simmons RC	1.25	3.00
❑ 70 Allan Ray RC	1.25	3.00
❑ 71 Rudy Gay RC	1.25	3.00
❑ 72 Rajon Rondo RC	5.00	12.00
❑ 73 Patrick O'Bryant RC	1.25	3.00
❑ 74 Marcus Williams RC	1.50	4.00
❑ 75 Marcus Vinicius RC	1.25	3.00
❑ 76 James White RC	1.25	3.00
❑ 77 Dee Brown RC	1.25	3.00
❑ 78 David Noel RC	1.25	3.00
❑ 79 Daniel Gibson RC	1.50	4.00
❑ 80 Bobby Jones RC	1.25	3.00
❑ 81 Tyrus Thomas RC	1.50	4.00
❑ 82 Shelden Williams RC	1.50	4.00
❑ 83 Pops Mensah-Bonsu RC	1.25	3.00
❑ 84 Paul Davis RC	1.25	3.00
❑ 85 Mardy Collins RC	1.25	3.00
❑ 86 James Augustine RC	1.25	3.00
❑ 87 Hassan Adams RC	1.50	4.00
❑ 88 Chris Quinn RC	1.25	3.00
❑ 89 Brandon Roy RC	3.00	8.00
❑ 90 Andrea Bargnani RC	2.00	5.00
❑ 91 Solomon Jones RC	1.25	3.00
❑ 92 Shawne Williams RC	1.25	3.00
❑ 93 Renaldo Balkman RC	1.25	3.00
❑ 94 Randy Foye RC	1.25	3.00
❑ 95 Maurice Ager RC	1.25	3.00
❑ 96 LaMarcus Aldridge RC	1.50	4.00
❑ 97 Jorge Garbajosa RC	2.50	6.00
❑ 98 J.J. Redick RC	1.25	3.00
❑ 99 Alexander Johnson RC	1.25	3.00
❑ 100 Adam Morrison RC	1.50	4.00
❑ 101 Greg Oden XRC	40.00	80.00
❑ 102 Kevin Durant XRC	40.00	80.00
❑ 103 Al Horford XRC	10.00	25.00
❑ 104 Mike Conley XRC	10.00	25.00
❑ 105 Jeff Green XRC	8.00	20.00
❑ 106 Yi Jianlian XRC	8.00	20.00
❑ 107 Corey Brewer XRC	8.00	20.00
❑ 108 Brandan Wright XRC	6.00	15.00
❑ 109 Joakim Noah XRC	8.00	20.00
❑ 110 Spencer Hawes XRC	4.00	10.00
❑ 111 Acie Law XRC	5.00	12.00
❑ 112 Thaddeus Young XRC	4.00	10.00
❑ 113 Julian Wright XRC	5.00	12.00
❑ 114 Al Thornton XRC	3.00	8.00
❑ 115 Rodney Stuckey XRC	4.00	10.00
❑ 116 Nick Young XRC	4.00	10.00
❑ 117 Sean Williams XRC	3.00	8.00
❑ 118 Marco Belinelli XRC	3.00	8.00
❑ 119 Javaris Crittenton XRC	3.00	8.00
❑ 120 Jason Smith XRC	3.00	8.00
❑ 121 Daequan Cook XRC	4.00	10.00
❑ 122 Jared Dudley XRC	3.00	8.00
❑ 123 Wilson Chandler XRC	3.00	8.00
❑ 124 Carl Landry XRC	3.00	8.00
❑ 125 Morris Almond XRC	3.00	8.00
❑ 126 Aaron Brooks XRC	4.00	10.00
❑ 127 Arron Afflalo XRC	3.00	8.00
❑ 128 Gabe Pruitt XRC	3.00	8.00
❑ 129 Alando Tucker XRC	3.00	8.00
❑ 130 Marcus Williams XRC	3.00	8.00

2007-08 Fines

❑ COMP.SET w/o DRAFT (100)	25.00	50.00
❑ 1 Gilbert Arenas	.50	1.25

❑ 2 Ray Allen	.50	1.25
❑ 3 Dwyane Wade	1.25	3.00
❑ 4 Dirk Nowitzki	.75	2.00
❑ 5 Manu Ginobili	.50	1.25
❑ 6 Eddy Curry	.30	.75
❑ 7 Jermaine O'Neal	.50	1.25
❑ 8 Carlos Boozer	.50	1.25
❑ 9 Tony Parker	.50	1.25
❑ 10 Jason Kidd	.75	2.00
❑ 11 Chris Bosh	.50	1.25
❑ 12 Al Jefferson	.50	1.25
❑ 13 Steve Nash	.60	1.50
❑ 14 Chris Paul	1.00	2.50
❑ 15 Carmelo Anthony	1.00	2.50
❑ 16 Pau Gasol	.50	1.25
❑ 17 Joe Johnson	.50	1.25
❑ 18 Chauncey Billups	.50	1.25
❑ 19 Andre Iguodala	.50	1.25
❑ 20 Yao Ming	1.25	3.00
❑ 21 Tim Duncan	1.00	2.50
❑ 22 Michael Redd	.50	1.25
❑ 23 Allen Iverson	1.00	2.50
❑ 24 Kobe Bryant	2.50	6.00
❑ 25 Kevin Garnett	1.25	3.00
❑ 26 Brandon Roy	.75	2.00
❑ 27 Luol Deng	.50	1.25
❑ 28 Deron Williams	.75	2.00
❑ 29 Amare Stoudemire	1.00	2.50
❑ 30 Vince Carter	1.00	2.50
❑ 31 Tracy McGrady	1.00	2.50
❑ 32 Shaquille O'Neal	1.25	3.00
❑ 33 Jason Richardson	.50	1.25
❑ 34 Paul Pierce	.50	1.25
❑ 35 Baron Davis	.50	1.25
❑ 36 Dwight Howard	1.00	2.50
❑ 37 Josh Howard	.50	1.25
❑ 38 Kevin Martin	.50	1.25
❑ 39 Ben Gordon	.60	1.50
❑ 40 LeBron James	2.50	6.00
❑ 41 Isiah Thomas	.50	1.25
❑ 42 Dominique Wilkins	.60	1.50
❑ 43 Magic Johnson	1.00	2.50
❑ 44 Bill Russell	.75	2.00
❑ 45 David Robinson	.75	2.00
❑ 46 John Stockton	.75	2.00
❑ 47 Jerry West	.60	1.50
❑ 48 Moses Malone	.50	1.25
❑ 49 Dennis Rodman	.50	1.25
❑ 50 Larry Bird	1.50	4.00
❑ 51 Al Horford RC	1.25	3.00
❑ 52 Ramon Sessions RC	1.25	3.00
❑ 53 JamesOn Curry RC	1.00	2.50
❑ 54 Arron Afflalo RC	1.00	2.50
❑ 55 Carl Landry RC	1.00	2.50
❑ 56 Glen Davis RC	2.00	5.00
❑ 57 Jermareo Davidson RC	1.00	2.50
❑ 58 Nick Fazekas RC	1.00	2.50
❑ 59 Taurean Green RC	1.00	2.50
❑ 60 Cheikh Samb RC	1.00	2.50
❑ 61 Mike Conley RC	1.25	3.00
❑ 62 Chris Richard RC	1.00	2.50
❑ 63 Josh McRoberts RC	1.25	3.00
❑ 64 Alando Tucker RC	1.00	2.50
❑ 65 Brandan Wright RC	1.25	3.00
❑ 66 Jamario Moon RC	2.00	5.00
❑ 67 Jared Dudley RC	1.00	2.50
❑ 68 Dominic McGuire RC	1.00	2.50
❑ 69 Sean Williams RC	1.00	2.50
❑ 70 Mario West RC	1.00	2.50
❑ 71 Kevin Durant RC	8.00	20.00
❑ 72 Julian Wright RC	1.25	3.00
❑ 73 Yi Jianlian RC	1.50	4.00
❑ 74 Coby Karl RC	1.00	2.50
❑ 75 Aaron Brooks RC	1.50	4.00
❑ 76 Kyrylo Fesenko RC	1.00	2.50

❑ 77 Greg Oden RC	1.50	4.00
❑ 78 Juan Carlos Navarro RC	1.25	3.00
❑ 79 Nick Young RC	1.00	2.50
❑ 80 Thaddeus Young RC	1.25	3.00
❑ 81 Joakim Noah RC	1.25	3.00
❑ 82 Luis Scola RC	1.50	4.00
❑ 83 Aaron Gray RC	1.00	2.50
❑ 84 Herbert Hill RC	1.00	2.50
❑ 85 Al Thornton RC	1.00	2.50
❑ 86 D.J. Strawberry RC	1.00	2.50
❑ 87 Javaris Crittenton RC	1.00	2.50
❑ 88 Morris Almond RC	1.00	2.50
❑ 89 Spencer Hawes RC	1.00	2.50
❑ 90 C.J. Watson RC	1.00	2.50
❑ 91 Corey Brewer RC	1.25	3.00
❑ 92 Jeff Green RC	1.25	3.00
❑ 93 Marco Belinelli RC	1.00	2.50
❑ 94 Marcin Gortat RC	1.50	4.00
❑ 95 Acie Law IV RC	1.25	3.00
❑ 96 Daequan Cook RC	1.25	3.00
❑ 97 Gabe Pruitt RC	1.00	2.50
❑ 98 Jason Smith RC	1.00	2.50
❑ 99 Rodney Stuckey RC	2.00	5.00
❑ 100 Wilson Chandler RC	1.00	2.50
❑ 101 1st Draft Pick EXCH	25.00	50.00
❑ 102 2nd Draft Pick EXCH	20.00	40.00
❑ 103 3rd Draft Pick EXCH	15.00	30.00
❑ 104 4th Draft Pick EXCH	6.00	15.00
❑ 105 5th Draft Pick EXCH	6.00	15.00
❑ 106 6th Draft Pick EXCH	5.00	12.00
❑ 107 7th Draft Pick EXCH	5.00	12.00
❑ 108 8th Draft Pick EXCH	5.00	12.00
❑ 109 9th Draft Pick EXCH	4.00	10.00
❑ 110 10th Draft Pick EXCH	4.00	10.00
❑ 111 11th Draft Pick EXCH	5.00	12.00
❑ 112 12th Draft Pick EXCH	4.00	10.00
❑ 113 13th Draft Pick EXCH	6.00	15.00
❑ 114 14th Draft Pick EXCH	4.00	10.00
❑ 115 15th Draft Pick EXCH	3.00	8.00
❑ 116 16th Draft Pick EXCH	3.00	8.00
❑ 117 17th Draft Pick EXCH	4.00	10.00
❑ 118 18th Draft Pick EXCH	2.50	6.00
❑ 119 19th Draft Pick EXCH	2.50	6.00
❑ 120 20th Draft Pick EXCH	2.50	6.00
❑ 121 21st Draft Pick EXCH	2.50	6.00
❑ 122 22nd Draft Pick EXCH	2.50	6.00
❑ 123 23rd Draft Pick EXCH	2.50	6.00
❑ 124 24th Draft Pick EXCH	2.50	6.00
❑ 125 25th Draft Pick EXCH	2.50	6.00
❑ 126 26th Draft Pick EXCH	2.50	6.00
❑ 127 27th Draft Pick EXCH	4.00	10.00
❑ 128 28th Draft Pick EXCH	2.50	6.00
❑ 129 29th Draft Pick EXCH	2.50	6.00
❑ 130 30th Draft Pick EXCH	2.50	6.00

1994-95 Flair

❑ COMPLETE SET (326)	25.00	50.00
❑ COMPLETE SERIES 1 (175)	7.50	15.00
❑ COMPLETE SERIES 2 (151)	15.00	30.00
❑ 1 Stacey Augmon	.05	.15
❑ 2 Mookie Blaylock	.05	.15
❑ 3 Craig Ehlo	.05	.15
❑ 4 Jon Koncak	.05	.15
❑ 5 Andrew Lang	.05	.15
❑ 6 Dee Brown	.05	.15
❑ 7 Sherman Douglas	.05	.15
❑ 8 Acie Earl	.05	.15
❑ 9 Rick Fox	.05	.15
❑ 10 Kevin Gamble	.05	.15
❑ 11 Xavier McDaniel	.05	.15
❑ 12 Dino Radja	.05	.15
❑ 13 Tony Bennett	.05	.15
❑ 14 Dell Curry	.05	.15
❑ 15 Kenny Gattison	.05	.15
❑ 16 Hersey Hawkins	.10	.30
❑ 17 Larry Johnson	.10	.30
❑ 18 Alonzo Mourning	.25	.60
❑ 19 David Wingate	.05	.15
❑ 20 B.J. Armstrong	.05	.15
❑ 21 Steve Kerr	.05	.15
❑ 22 Toni Kukoc	.30	.75
❑ 23 Pete Myers	.05	.15
❑ 24 Scottie Pippen	.60	1.50
❑ 25 Bill Wennington	.05	.15
❑ 26 Terrell Brandon	.10	.30
❑ 27 Brad Daugherty	.05	.15
❑ 28 Tyrone Hill	.05	.15
❑ 29 Bobby Phills	.05	.15
❑ 30 Mark Price	.05	.15
❑ 31 Gerald Wilkins	.05	.15
❑ 32 John Williams	.05	.15
❑ 33 Lucious Harris	.05	.15
❑ 34 Jim Jackson	.10	.30
❑ 35 Jamal Mashburn	.20	.50
❑ 36 Sean Rooks	.05	.15
❑ 37 Doug Smith	.05	.15
❑ 38 Mahmoud Abdul-Rauf	.05	.15
❑ 39 LaPhonso Ellis	.05	.15
❑ 40 Dikembe Mutombo	.10	.30
❑ 41 Robert Pack	.05	.15
❑ 42 Rodney Rogers	.05	.15
❑ 43 Brian Williams	.05	.15
❑ 44 Reggie Williams	.05	.15
❑ 45 Joe Dumars	.20	.50
❑ 46 Allan Houston	.30	.75
❑ 47 Lindsey Hunter	.10	.30
❑ 48 Terry Mills	.05	.15
❑ 49 Victor Alexander	.05	.15
❑ 50 Chris Gatling	.05	.15
❑ 51 Billy Owens	.05	.15
❑ 52 Latrell Sprewell	.20	.50
❑ 53 Chris Webber	.50	1.25
❑ 54 Sam Cassell	.20	.50
❑ 55 Carl Herrera	.05	.15
❑ 56 Robert Horry	.10	.30
❑ 57 Hakeem Olajuwon	.30	.75
❑ 58 Kenny Smith	.05	.15
❑ 59 Otis Thorpe	.05	.15
❑ 60 Antonio Davis	.05	.15
❑ 61 Dale Davis	.05	.15
❑ 62 Reggie Miller	.20	.50
❑ 63 Byron Scott	.10	.30
❑ 64 Rik Smits	.05	.15
❑ 65 Haywoode Workman	.05	.15
❑ 66 Terry Dehere	.05	.15
❑ 67 Harold Ellis	.05	.15
❑ 68 Gary Grant	.05	.15
❑ 69 Elmore Spencer	.05	.15
❑ 70 Loy Vaught	.05	.15
❑ 71 Elden Campbell	.05	.15
❑ 72 Doug Christie	.10	.30
❑ 73 Vlade Divac	.05	.15
❑ 74 George Lynch	.05	.15
❑ 75 Anthony Peeler	.05	.15
❑ 76 Nick Van Exel	.20	.50
❑ 77 James Worthy	.20	.50
❑ 78 Bimbo Coles	.05	.15
❑ 79 Harold Miner	.05	.15
❑ 80 John Salley	.05	.15
❑ 81 Rony Seikaly	.05	.15
❑ 82 Steve Smith	.10	.30
❑ 83 Vin Baker	.20	.50
❑ 84 Jon Barry	.05	.15
❑ 85 Todd Day	.05	.15
❑ 86 Lee Mayberry	.05	.15
❑ 87 Eric Murdock	.05	.15
❑ 88 Mike Brown	.05	.15
❑ 89 Christian Laettner	.10	.30
❑ 90 Isaiah Rider	.10	.30
❑ 91 Doug West	.05	.15
❑ 92 Micheal Williams	.05	.15
❑ 93 Kenny Anderson	.10	.30
❑ 94 Benoit Benjamin	.05	.15
❑ 95 P.J. Brown	.05	.15
❑ 96 Derrick Coleman	.10	.30
❑ 97 Kevin Edwards	.05	.15
❑ 98 Hubert Davis	.05	.15
❑ 99 Patrick Ewing	.20	.50
❑ 100 Derek Harper	.05	.15
❑ 101 Anthony Mason	.10	.30
❑ 102 Charles Oakley	.05	.15
❑ 103 Charles Smith	.05	.15
❑ 104 John Starks	.05	.15
❑ 105 Nick Anderson	.05	.15
❑ 106 Anfernee Hardaway	.50	1.25
❑ 107 Shaquille O'Neal	1.00	2.50
❑ 108 Dennis Scott	.05	.15
❑ 109 Jeff Turner	.05	.15
❑ 110 Dana Barros	.05	.15
❑ 111 Shawn Bradley	.05	.15
❑ 112 Jeff Malone	.05	.15
❑ 113 Tim Perry	.05	.15
❑ 114 Clarence Weatherspoon	.05	.15
❑ 115 Danny Ainge	.05	.15
❑ 116 Charles Barkley	.30	.75
❑ 117 A.C. Green	.10	.30
❑ 118 Kevin Johnson	.10	.30
❑ 119 Dan Majerle	.10	.30
❑ 120 Clyde Drexler	.20	.50
❑ 121 Harvey Grant	.05	.15
❑ 122 Jerome Kersey	.05	.15
❑ 123 Clifford Robinson	.10	.30
❑ 124 Rod Strickland	.10	.30
❑ 125 Buck Williams	.05	.15
❑ 126 Randy Brown	.05	.15
❑ 127 Olden Polynice	.05	.15
❑ 128 Mitch Richmond	.20	.50
❑ 129 Lionel Simmons	.05	.15
❑ 130 Spud Webb	.05	.15
❑ 131 Walt Williams	.05	.15
❑ 132 Willie Anderson	.05	.15
❑ 133 Vinny Del Negro	.05	.15
❑ 134 Sean Elliott	.10	.30
❑ 135 Avery Johnson	.05	.15
❑ 136 J.R. Reid	.05	.15
❑ 137 David Robinson	.30	.75
❑ 138 Dennis Rodman	.40	1.00
❑ 139 Kendall Gill	.10	.30
❑ 140 Ervin Johnson	.05	.15
❑ 141 Shawn Kemp	.30	.75
❑ 142 Nate McMillan	.05	.15
❑ 143 Gary Payton	.30	.75
❑ 144 Sam Perkins	.10	.30
❑ 145 David Benoit	.05	.15
❑ 146 Jeff Hornacek	.10	.30
❑ 147 Jay Humphries	.05	.15
❑ 148 Karl Malone	.30	.75
❑ 149 Bryon Russell	.05	.15
❑ 150 Felton Spencer	.05	.15
❑ 151 John Stockton	.20	.50
❑ 152 Rex Chapman	.05	.15
❑ 153 Calbert Cheaney	.05	.15
❑ 154 Tom Gugliotta	.10	.30
❑ 155 Don MacLean	.05	.15
❑ 156 Gheorghe Muresan	.05	.15
❑ 157 Doug Overton	.05	.15
❑ 158 Brent Price	.05	.15
❑ 159 Derrick Coleman USA	.05	.15
❑ 160 Joe Dumars USA	.10	.30
❑ 161 Tim Hardaway USA	.10	.30
❑ 162 Kevin Johnson USA	.05	.15
❑ 163 Larry Johnson USA	.05	.15
❑ 164 Shawn Kemp USA	.20	.50
❑ 165 Dan Majerle USA	.05	.15
❑ 166 Reggie Miller USA	.10	.30
❑ 167 Alonzo Mourning USA	.20	.50
❑ 168 Shaquille O'Neal USA	.40	1.00
❑ 169 Mark Price USA	.05	.15
❑ 170 Steve Smith USA	.05	.15
❑ 171 Isiah Thomas USA	.10	.30
❑ 172 Dominique Wilkins USA	.10	.30
❑ 173 Checklist	.05	.15
❑ 174 Checklist	.05	.15
❑ 175 Checklist	.05	.15
❑ 176 Tyrone Corbin	.05	.15
❑ 177 Grant Long	.05	.15
❑ 178 Ken Norman	.05	.15
❑ 179 Steve Smith	.10	.30
❑ 180 Blue Edwards	.05	.15
❑ 181 Pervis Ellison	.05	.15
❑ 182 Greg Minor RC	.05	.15
❑ 183 Eric Montross RC	.05	.15
❑ 184 Derek Strong	.05	.15
❑ 185 David Wesley	.05	.15
❑ 186 Dominique Wilkins	.20	.50
❑ 187 Michael Adams	.05	.15
❑ 188 Muggsy Bogues	.10	.30
❑ 189 Scott Burrell	.05	.15
❑ 190 Darrin Hancock	.05	.15
❑ 191 Robert Parish	.10	.30
❑ 192 Jud Buechler	.05	.15
❑ 193 Ron Harper	.10	.30
❑ 194 Larry Krystkowiak	.05	.15
❑ 195 Will Perdue	.05	.15

❑ 196 Dickey Simpkins RC	.05	.15
❑ 197 Michael Cage	.05	.15
❑ 198 Tony Campbell	.05	.15
❑ 199 Danny Ferry	.05	.15
❑ 200 Chris Mills	.10	.30
❑ 201 Popeye Jones	.05	.15
❑ 202 Jason Kidd RC	2.00	5.00
❑ 203 Roy Tarpley	.05	.15
❑ 204 Lorenzo Williams	.05	.15
❑ 205 Dale Ellis	.05	.15
❑ 206 Tom Hammonds	.05	.15
❑ 207 Jalen Rose RC	.75	2.00
❑ 208 Reggie Slater	.05	.15
❑ 209 Bryant Stith	.05	.15
❑ 210 Rafael Addison	.05	.15
❑ 211 Bill Curley RC	.05	.15
❑ 212 Johnny Dawkins	.05	.15
❑ 213 Grant Hill RC	1.25	3.00
❑ 214 Mark Macon	.05	.15
❑ 215 Oliver Miller	.05	.15
❑ 216 Ivano Newbill	.05	.15
❑ 217 Mark West	.05	.15
❑ 218 Tom Gugliotta	.10	.30
❑ 219 Tim Hardaway	.20	.50
❑ 220 Keith Jennings	.05	.15
❑ 221 Dwayne Morton	.05	.15
❑ 222 Chris Mullin	.20	.50
❑ 223 Ricky Pierce	.05	.15
❑ 224 Carlos Rogers RC	.05	.15
❑ 225 Clifford Rozier RC	.05	.15
❑ 226 Rony Seikaly	.05	.15
❑ 227 Tim Breaux	.05	.15
❑ 228 Scott Brooks	.05	.15
❑ 229 Mario Elie	.05	.15
❑ 230 Vernon Maxwell	.05	.15
❑ 231 Zan Tabak	.05	.15
❑ 232 Mark Jackson	.05	.15
❑ 233 Derrick McKey	.05	.15
❑ 234 Tony Massenburg	.05	.15
❑ 235 Lamond Murray RC	.10	.30
❑ 236 Bo Outlaw	.05	.15
❑ 237 Eric Piatkowski RC	.05	.15
❑ 238 Pooh Richardson	.05	.15
❑ 239 Malik Sealy	.05	.15
❑ 240 Cedric Ceballos	.05	.15
❑ 241 Eddie Jones RC	1.00	2.50
❑ 242 Anthony Miller	.05	.15
❑ 243 Tony Smith	.05	.15
❑ 244 Sedale Threatt	.05	.15
❑ 245 Ledell Eackles	.05	.15
❑ 246 Kevin Gamble	.05	.15
❑ 247 Matt Geiger	.05	.15
❑ 248 Brad Lohaus	.05	.15
❑ 249 Billy Owens	.05	.15
❑ 250 Khalid Reeves RC	.05	.15
❑ 251 Glen Rice	.10	.30
❑ 252 Kevin Willis	.05	.15
❑ 253 Marty Conlon	.05	.15
❑ 254 Eric Mobley RC	.05	.15
❑ 255 Johnny Newman	.05	.15
❑ 256 Ed Pinckney	.05	.15
❑ 257 Glenn Robinson RC	.60	1.50
❑ 258 Pat Durham	.05	.15
❑ 259 Howard Eisley	.05	.15
❑ 260 Winston Garland	.05	.15
❑ 261 Stacey King	.05	.15
❑ 262 Donyell Marshall RC	.20	.50
❑ 263 Sean Rooks	.05	.15
❑ 264 Chris Smith	.05	.15
❑ 265 Chris Childs RC	.20	.50
❑ 266 Sleepy Floyd	.05	.15
❑ 267 Armon Gilliam	.05	.15
❑ 268 Sean Higgins	.05	.15
❑ 269 Rex Walters	.05	.15
❑ 270 Greg Anthony	.05	.15
❑ 271 Charlie Ward RC	.20	.50
❑ 272 Herb Williams	.05	.15
❑ 273 Monty Williams RC	.05	.15
❑ 274 Anthony Avent	.05	.15
❑ 275 Anthony Bowie	.05	.15
❑ 276 Horace Grant	.10	.30
❑ 277 Donald Royal	.05	.15
❑ 278 Brian Shaw	.05	.15
❑ 279 Brooks Thompson	.05	.15
❑ 280 Derrick Alston	.05	.15
❑ 281 Willie Burton	.05	.15
❑ 282 Greg Graham	.05	.15
❑ 283 B.J.Tyler RC	.05	.15
❑ 284 Scott Williams	.05	.15
❑ 285 Sharone Wright RC	.05	.15
❑ 286 Joe Kleine	.05	.15
❑ 287 Danny Manning	.10	.30
❑ 288 Elliot Perry	.05	.15
❑ 289 Wesley Person RC	.20	.50
❑ 290 Trevor Ruffin RC	.05	.15
❑ 291 Wayman Tisdale	.05	.15
❑ 292 Mark Bryant	.05	.15
❑ 293 Chris Dudley	.05	.15
❑ 294 Aaron McKie RC	.40	1.00
❑ 295 Tracy Murray	.05	.15
❑ 296 Terry Porter	.05	.15
❑ 297 James Robinson	.05	.15
❑ 298 Alaa Abdelnaby	.05	.15
❑ 299 Duane Causwell	.05	.15
❑ 300 Brian Grant RC	.50	1.25
❑ 301 Bobby Hurley	.05	.15
❑ 302 Michael Smith RC	.05	.15
❑ 303 Terry Cummings	.05	.15
❑ 304 Moses Malone	.20	.50
❑ 305 Julius Nwosu	.05	.15
❑ 306 Chuck Person	.05	.15
❑ 307 Doc Rivers	.10	.30
❑ 308 Vincent Askew	.05	.15
❑ 309 Sarunas Marciulionis	.05	.15
❑ 310 Detlef Schrempf	.10	.30
❑ 311 Dontonio Wingfield	.05	.15
❑ 312 Antoine Carr	.05	.15
❑ 313 Tom Chambers	.05	.15
❑ 314 John Crotty	.05	.15
❑ 315 Adam Keefe	.05	.15
❑ 316 Jamie Watson RC	.05	.15
❑ 317 Mitchell Butler	.05	.15
❑ 318 Kevin Duckworth	.05	.15
❑ 319 Juwan Howard RC	.50	1.25
❑ 320 Jim McIlvaine	.05	.15
❑ 321 Scott Skiles	.05	.15
❑ 322 Anthony Tucker RC	.05	.15
❑ 323 Chris Webber	.50	1.25
❑ 324 Checklist	.05	.15
❑ 325 Checklist	.05	.15
❑ 326 Michael Jordan	4.00	10.00

1995-96 Flair

❑ COMPLETE SET (250)	40.00	80.00
❑ COMPLETE SERIES 1 (150)	20.00	40.00
❑ COMPLETE SERIES 2 (100)	20.00	40.00
❑ COMMON CARD (1-150)	.25	.60
❑ COMMON CARD (151-250)	.15	.40
❑ 1 Stacey Augmon	.25	.60
❑ 2 Mookie Blaylock	.25	.60
❑ 3 Grant Long	.25	.60
❑ 4 Steve Smith	.60	1.50
❑ 5 Dee Brown	.25	.60
❑ 6 Sherman Douglas	.25	.60
❑ 7 Eric Montross	.25	.60
❑ 8 Dino Radja	.25	.60
❑ 9 David Wesley	.25	.60
❑ 10 Muggsy Bogues	.60	1.50
❑ 11 Scott Burrell	.25	.60
❑ 12 Dell Curry	.25	.60
❑ 13 Larry Johnson	.60	1.50
❑ 14 Alonzo Mourning	.60	1.50
❑ 15 Michael Jordan	6.00	12.00
❑ 16 Steve Kerr	.60	1.50
❑ 17 Toni Kukoc	.60	1.50
❑ 18 Scottie Pippen	1.25	3.00
❑ 19 Terrell Brandon	.60	1.50
❑ 20 Tyrone Hill	.25	.60
❑ 21 Chris Mills	.25	.60
❑ 22 Bobby Phills	.25	.60
❑ 23 Mark Price	.60	1.50
❑ 24 John Williams	.25	.60
❑ 25 Jim Jackson	.25	.60
❑ 26 Popeye Jones	.25	.60
❑ 27 Jason Kidd	2.50	6.00
❑ 28 Jamal Mashburn	.60	1.50
❑ 29 Lorenzo Williams	.25	.60
❑ 30 Mahmoud Abdul-Rauf	.25	.60
❑ 31 Dikembe Mutombo	.60	1.50
❑ 32 Robert Pack	.25	.60
❑ 33 Jalen Rose	1.00	2.50
❑ 34 Bryant Stith	.25	.60
❑ 35 Reggie Williams	.25	.60
❑ 36 Joe Dumars	.75	2.00
❑ 37 Grant Hill	1.00	2.50
❑ 38 Allan Houston	.60	1.50
❑ 39 Lindsey Hunter	.25	.60
❑ 40 Terry Mills	.25	.60
❑ 41 Chris Gatling	.25	.60
❑ 42 Tim Hardaway	.60	1.50
❑ 43 Donyell Marshall	.60	1.50
❑ 44 Chris Mullin	.75	2.00
❑ 45 Carlos Rogers	.25	.60
❑ 46 Clifford Rozier	.25	.60
❑ 47 Latrell Sprewell	.75	2.00
❑ 48 Sam Cassell	.75	2.00
❑ 49 Clyde Drexler	.75	2.00
❑ 50 Mario Elie	.25	.60
❑ 51 Robert Horry	.60	1.50
❑ 52 Hakeem Olajuwon	.75	2.00
❑ 53 Kenny Smith	.25	.60
❑ 54 Antonio Davis	.25	.60
❑ 55 Dale Davis	.25	.60
❑ 56 Mark Jackson	.60	1.50
❑ 57 Derrick McKey	.25	.60
❑ 58 Reggie Miller	.75	2.00
❑ 59 Rik Smits	.60	1.50
❑ 60 Lamond Murray	.25	.60
❑ 61 Pooh Richardson	.25	.60
❑ 62 Malik Sealy	.25	.60
❑ 63 Loy Vaught	.25	.60
❑ 64 Elden Campbell	.25	.60
❑ 65 Cedric Ceballos	.25	.60
❑ 66 Vlade Divac	.60	1.50
❑ 67 Eddie Jones	1.00	2.50
❑ 68 Nick Van Exel	.75	2.00
❑ 69 Bimbo Coles	.25	.60
❑ 70 Billy Owens	.25	.60
❑ 71 Khalid Reeves	.25	.60
❑ 72 Glen Rice	.60	1.50
❑ 73 Kevin Willis	.60	1.50
❑ 74 Vin Baker	.60	1.50
❑ 75 Todd Day	.25	.60
❑ 76 Eric Murdock	.25	.60
❑ 77 Glenn Robinson	.75	2.00
❑ 78 Tom Gugliotta	.25	.60
❑ 79 Christian Laettner	.60	1.50
❑ 80 Isaiah Rider	.25	.60
❑ 81 Doug West	.25	.60
❑ 82 Kenny Anderson	.60	1.50
❑ 83 P.J. Brown	.25	.60
❑ 84 Derrick Coleman	.25	.60
❑ 85 Armon Gilliam	.25	.60
❑ 86 Chris Morris	.25	.60
❑ 87 Hubert Davis	.25	.60
❑ 88 Patrick Ewing	.75	2.00
❑ 89 Derek Harper	.60	1.50
❑ 90 Anthony Mason	.60	1.50
❑ 91 Charles Oakley	.25	.60
❑ 92 Charles Smith	.25	.60
❑ 93 John Starks	.60	1.50
❑ 94 Nick Anderson	.25	.60
❑ 95 Horace Grant	.60	1.50
❑ 96 Anfernee Hardaway	.75	2.00
❑ 97 Shaquille O'Neal	2.00	5.00
❑ 98 Dennis Scott	.25	.60
❑ 99 Brian Shaw	.25	.60
❑ 100 Dana Barros	.25	.60
❑ 101 Shawn Bradley	.25	.60
❑ 102 Clarence Weatherspoon	.25	.60
❑ 103 Sharone Wright	.25	.60
❑ 104 Charles Barkley	1.00	2.50
❑ 105 A.C. Green	.60	1.50
❑ 106 Kevin Johnson	.60	1.50
❑ 107 Dan Majerle	.60	1.50
❑ 108 Danny Manning	.60	1.50
❑ 109 Elliot Perry	.25	.60
❑ 110 Wesley Person	.25	.60
❑ 111 Terry Porter	.25	.60
❑ 112 Clifford Robinson	.25	.60
❑ 113 Rod Strickland	.25	.60
❑ 114 Otis Thorpe	.25	.60
❑ 115 Buck Williams	.25	.60
❑ 116 Brian Grant	.75	2.00

❑ 117 Bobby Hurley	.25	.60
❑ 118 Olden Polynice	.25	.60
❑ 119 Mitch Richmond	.60	1.50
❑ 120 Walt Williams	.25	.60
❑ 121 Vinny Del Negro	.25	.60
❑ 122 Sean Elliott	.60	1.50
❑ 123 Avery Johnson	.25	.60
❑ 124 David Robinson	.75	2.00
❑ 125 Dennis Rodman	.60	1.50
❑ 126 Shawn Kemp	.60	1.50
❑ 127 Nate McMillan	.25	.60
❑ 128 Gary Payton	.75	2.00
❑ 129 Sam Perkins	.60	1.50
❑ 130 Detlef Schrempf	.60	1.50
❑ 131 B.J. Armstrong	.25	.60
❑ 132 Jerome Kersey	.25	.60
❑ 133 Oliver Miller	.25	.60
❑ 134 John Salley	.25	.60
❑ 135 David Benoit	.25	.60
❑ 136 Antoine Carr	.25	.60
❑ 137 Jeff Hornacek	.60	1.50
❑ 138 Karl Malone	1.00	2.50
❑ 139 John Stockton	1.00	2.50
❑ 140 Greg Anthony	.25	.60
❑ 141 Benoit Benjamin	.25	.60
❑ 142 Blue Edwards	.25	.60
❑ 143 Byron Scott	.25	.60
❑ 144 Calbert Cheaney	.25	.60
❑ 145 Juwan Howard	.75	2.00
❑ 146 Gheorghe Muresan	.25	.60
❑ 147 Scott Skiles	.25	.60
❑ 148 Chris Webber	1.00	2.50
❑ 149 Checklist	.25	.60
❑ 150 Checklist	.25	.60
❑ 151 Stacey Augmon	.15	.40
❑ 152 Mookie Blaylock	.15	.40
❑ 153 Andrew Lang	.15	.40
❑ 154 Steve Smith	.30	.75
❑ 155 Dana Barros	.15	.40
❑ 156 Rick Fox	.30	.75
❑ 157 Kendall Gill	.15	.40
❑ 158 Khalid Reeves	.15	.40
❑ 159 Glen Rice	.30	.75
❑ 160 Dennis Rodman	.60	1.50
❑ 161 Dan Majerle	.30	.75
❑ 162 Tony Dumas	.15	.40
❑ 163 Dale Ellis	.15	.40
❑ 164 Otis Thorpe	.15	.40
❑ 165 Rony Seikaly	.15	.40
❑ 166 Sam Cassell	.50	1.25
❑ 167 Clyde Drexler	.50	1.25
❑ 168 Robert Horry	.30	.75
❑ 169 Hakeem Olajuwon	.75	2.00
❑ 170 Ricky Pierce	.15	.40
❑ 171 Rodney Rogers	.25	.60
❑ 172 Brian Williams	.15	.40
❑ 173 Magic Johnson	.75	2.00
❑ 174 Alonzo Mourning	.30	.75
❑ 175 Lee Mayberry	.15	.40
❑ 176 Terry Porter	.15	.40
❑ 177 Shawn Bradley	.15	.40
❑ 178 Jayson Williams	.15	.40
❑ 179 Gary Grant	.15	.40
❑ 180 Jon Koncak	.15	.40
❑ 181 Derrick Coleman	.25	.60
❑ 182 Vernon Maxwell	.15	.40
❑ 183 John Williams	.15	.40
❑ 184 Aaron McKie	.60	1.50
❑ 185 Michael Smith	.15	.40
❑ 186 Chuck Person	.15	.40
❑ 187 Hersey Hawkins	.15	.40
❑ 188 Shawn Kemp	.60	1.50
❑ 189 Gary Payton	.75	2.00
❑ 190 Detlef Schrempf	.30	.75
❑ 191 Chris Morris	.15	.40
❑ 192 Robert Pack	.15	.40
❑ 193 Willie Anderson EXP	.15	.40
❑ 194 Oliver Miller EXP	.15	.40
❑ 195 Alvin Robertson EXP	.15	.40
❑ 196 Greg Anthony EXP	.15	.40
❑ 197 Blue Edwards EXP	.15	.40
❑ 198 Byron Scott EXP	.15	.40
❑ 199 Cory Alexander RC	.15	.40
❑ 200 Brent Barry RC	.50	1.25
❑ 201 Travis Best RC	.25	.60
❑ 202 Jason Caffey RC	.30	.75
❑ 203 Sasha Danilovic RC	.15	.40
❑ 204 Tyus Edney RC	.15	.40
❑ 205 Michael Finley RC	1.25	3.00
❑ 206 Kevin Garnett RC	3.00	8.00
❑ 207 Alan Henderson RC	.50	1.25
❑ 208 Antonio McDyess RC	1.00	2.50
❑ 209 Loren Meyer RC	.15	.40
❑ 210 Lawrence Moten RC	.15	.40
❑ 211 Ed O'Bannon RC	.15	.40
❑ 212 Greg Ostertag RC	.15	.40
❑ 213 Cherokee Parks RC	.15	.40
❑ 214 Theo Ratliff RC	.60	1.50
❑ 215 Bryant Reeves RC	.50	1.25
❑ 216 Shawn Respert RC	.25	.60
❑ 217 Arvydas Sabonis RC	.60	1.50
❑ 218 Joe Smith RC	.75	2.00
❑ 219 Jerry Stackhouse RC	1.50	4.00
❑ 220 Damon Stoudamire RC	1.00	2.50
❑ 221 Bob Sura RC	.30	.75
❑ 222 Kurt Thomas RC	.30	.75
❑ 223 Gary Trent RC	.15	.40
❑ 224 David Vaughn RC	.15	.40
❑ 225 Rasheed Wallace RC	1.25	3.00
❑ 226 Eric Williams RC	.30	.75
❑ 227 Corliss Williamson RC	.50	1.25
❑ 228 George Zidek RC	.15	.40
❑ 229 Vin Baker STY	.15	.40
❑ 230 Charles Barkley STY	.50	1.25
❑ 231 Patrick Ewing STY	.30	.75
❑ 232 Anfernee Hardaway STY	.60	1.50
❑ 233 Grant Hill STY	.50	1.25
❑ 234 Larry Johnson STY	.15	.40
❑ 235 Michael Jordan STY	1.50	4.00
❑ 236 Jason Kidd STY	.75	2.00
❑ 237 Karl Malone STY	.50	1.25
❑ 238 Jamal Mashburn STY	.15	.40
❑ 239 Reggie Miller STY	.30	.75
❑ 240 Shaquille O'Neal STY	.60	1.50
❑ 241 Scottie Pippen STY	.50	1.25
❑ 242 Mitch Richmond STY	.15	.40
❑ 243 Clifford Robinson STY	.15	.40
❑ 244 David Robinson STY	.30	.75
❑ 245 Glenn Robinson STY	.30	.75
❑ 246 John Stockton STY	.50	1.25
❑ 247 Nick Van Exel STY	.15	.40
❑ 248 Chris Webber STY	.50	1.25
❑ 249 Checklist	.15	.40
❑ 250 Checklist	.15	.40

1996-97 Flair Showcase Row 2

❑ COMPLETE SET (90)	25.00	60.00
❑ 1 Anfernee Hardaway	.60	1.50
❑ 2 Mitch Richmond	.40	1.00
❑ 3 Allen Iverson RC	2.00	5.00
❑ 4 Charles Barkley	.75	2.00
❑ 5 Juwan Howard	.40	1.00
❑ 6 David Robinson	.60	1.50
❑ 7 Gary Payton	.60	1.50
❑ 8 Kerry Kittles RC	.60	1.50
❑ 9 Dennis Rodman	.40	1.00
❑ 10 Shaquille O'Neal	1.50	4.00
❑ 11 Stephon Marbury RC	1.25	3.00
❑ 12 John Stockton	.60	1.50
❑ 13 Glenn Robinson	.60	1.50
❑ 14 Hakeem Olajuwon	.60	1.50
❑ 15 Jason Kidd	1.00	2.50
❑ 16 Jerry Stackhouse	.75	2.00
❑ 17 Joe Smith	.40	1.00
❑ 18 Reggie Miller	.60	1.50
❑ 19 Grant Hill	.60	1.50
❑ 20 Damon Stoudamire	.60	1.50
❑ 21 Kevin Garnett	1.25	3.00
❑ 22 Clyde Drexler	.60	1.50
❑ 23 Michael Jordan	4.00	10.00
❑ 24 Antonio McDyess	.40	1.00
❑ 25 Chris Webber	.60	1.50
❑ 26 Antoine Walker RC	1.25	3.00
❑ 27 Scottie Pippen	1.00	2.50
❑ 28 Karl Malone	.60	1.50
❑ 29 Shareef Abdur-Rahim RC	1.50	4.00
❑ 30 Shawn Kemp	.40	1.00
❑ 31 Kobe Bryant RC	6.00	15.00
❑ 32 Derrick Coleman	.40	1.00
❑ 33 Alonzo Mourning	.40	1.00
❑ 34 Anthony Mason	.40	1.00
❑ 35 Ray Allen RC	1.25	3.00
❑ 36 Arvydas Sabonis	.40	1.00
❑ 37 Brian Grant	.60	1.50
❑ 38 Bryant Reeves	.20	.50
❑ 39 Christian Laettner	.40	1.00
❑ 40 Tom Gugliotta	.20	.50
❑ 41 Latrell Sprewell	.60	1.50
❑ 42 Erick Dampier RC	.60	1.50
❑ 43 Gheorghe Muresan	.20	.50
❑ 44 Glen Rice	.40	1.00
❑ 45 Patrick Ewing	.60	1.50
❑ 46 Jim Jackson	.20	.50
❑ 47 Michael Finley	.75	2.00
❑ 48 Toni Kukoc	.40	1.00
❑ 49 Marcus Camby RC	.75	2.00
❑ 50 Kenny Anderson	.20	.50
❑ 51 Mark Price	.40	1.00
❑ 52 Tim Hardaway	.40	1.00
❑ 53 Mookie Blaylock	.20	.50
❑ 54 Steve Smith	.40	1.00
❑ 55 Terrell Brandon	.40	1.00
❑ 56 Lorenzen Wright RC	.40	1.00
❑ 57 Sasha Danilovic	.20	.50
❑ 58 Jeff Hornacek	.40	1.00
❑ 59 Eddie Jones	.60	1.50
❑ 60 Vin Baker	.40	1.00
❑ 61 Chris Childs	.20	.50
❑ 62 Clifford Robinson	.20	.50
❑ 63 Anthony Peeler	.20	.50
❑ 64 Dino Radja	.20	.50
❑ 65 Joe Dumars	.60	1.50
❑ 66 Loy Vaught	.20	.50
❑ 67 Rony Seikaly	.20	.50
❑ 68 Vitaly Potapenko RC	.20	.50
❑ 69 Chris Gatling	.20	.50
❑ 70 Dale Ellis	.20	.50
❑ 71 Allan Houston	.40	1.00
❑ 72 Doug Christie	.40	1.00
❑ 73 LaPhonso Ellis	.20	.50
❑ 74 Kendall Gill	.20	.50
❑ 75 Rik Smits	.40	1.00
❑ 76 Bobby Phills	.20	.50
❑ 77 Malik Sealy	.20	.50
❑ 78 Sean Elliott	.40	1.00
❑ 79 Vlade Divac	.20	.50
❑ 80 David Wesley	.20	.50
❑ 81 Dominique Wilkins	.60	1.50
❑ 82 Danny Manning	.40	1.00
❑ 83 Detlef Schrempf	.40	1.00
❑ 84 Hersey Hawkins	.40	1.00
❑ 85 Lindsey Hunter	.20	.50
❑ 86 Mahmoud Abdul-Rauf	.20	.50
❑ 87 Shawn Bradley	.20	.50
❑ 88 Horace Grant	.40	1.00
❑ 89 Cedric Ceballos	.20	.50
❑ 90 Jamal Mashburn	.40	1.00
❑ NNO Jerry Stackhouse Promo 3-card strip	1.25	3.00

1997-98 Flair Showcase Row 3

❑ COMPLETE SET (80)	25.00	50.00
❑ 1 Michael Jordan	4.00	10.00
❑ 2 Grant Hill	.60	1.50
❑ 3 Allen Iverson	1.50	4.00
❑ 4 Kevin Garnett	1.25	3.00
❑ 5 Tim Duncan RC	1.50	4.00

❑ 6 Shawn Kemp	.40	1.00
❑ 7 Shaquille O'Neal	1.50	4.00
❑ 8 Antoine Walker	.75	2.00
❑ 9 Shareef Abdur-Rahim	1.00	2.50
❑ 10 Damon Stoudamire	.40	1.00
❑ 11 Anfernee Hardaway	.60	1.50
❑ 12 Keith Van Horn RC	.75	2.00
❑ 13 Dennis Rodman	.40	1.00
❑ 14 Ron Mercer RC	.60	1.50
❑ 15 Stephon Marbury	.75	2.00
❑ 16 Scottie Pippen	1.00	2.50
❑ 17 Kerry Kittles	.60	1.50
❑ 18 Kobe Bryant	2.50	6.00
❑ 19 Marcus Camby	.60	1.50
❑ 20 Chauncey Billups RC	2.50	6.00
❑ 21 Tracy McGrady RC	1.50	4.00
❑ 22 Joe Smith	.40	1.00
❑ 23 Brevin Knight RC	.40	1.00
❑ 24 Danny Fortson RC	.40	1.00
❑ 25 Tim Thomas RC	1.00	2.50
❑ 26 Gary Payton	.60	1.50
❑ 27 David Robinson	.60	1.50
❑ 28 Hakeem Olajuwon	.60	1.50
❑ 29 Antonio Daniels RC	.60	1.50
❑ 30 Antonio McDyess	.40	1.00
❑ 31 Eddie Jones	.60	1.50
❑ 32 Adonal Foyle RC	.40	1.00
❑ 33 Glenn Robinson	.60	1.50
❑ 34 Charles Barkley	.75	2.00
❑ 35 Vin Baker	.40	1.00
❑ 36 Jerry Stackhouse	.60	1.50
❑ 37 Ray Allen	.60	1.50
❑ 38 Derek Anderson RC	.40	1.00
❑ 39 Isaac Austin	.20	.50
❑ 40 Tony Battie RC	.60	1.50
❑ 41 Tariq Abdul-Wahad RC	.40	1.00
❑ 42 Dikembe Mutombo	.40	1.00
❑ 43 Clyde Drexler	.60	1.50
❑ 44 Chris Mullin	.60	1.50
❑ 45 Tim Hardaway	.40	1.00
❑ 46 Terrell Brandon	.40	1.00
❑ 47 John Stockton	.60	1.50
❑ 48 Patrick Ewing	.60	1.50
❑ 49 Horace Grant	.40	1.00
❑ 50 Tom Gugliotta	.40	1.00
❑ 51 Mookie Blaylock	.20	.50
❑ 52 Mitch Richmond	.40	1.00
❑ 53 Anthony Mason	.40	1.00
❑ 54 Michael Finley	.60	1.50
❑ 55 Jason Kidd	1.00	2.50
❑ 56 Karl Malone	.60	1.50
❑ 57 Reggie Miller	.60	1.50
❑ 58 Steve Smith	.40	1.00
❑ 59 Glen Rice	.40	1.00
❑ 60 Bryant Stith	.20	.50
❑ 61 Loy Vaught	.20	.50
❑ 62 Brian Grant	.40	1.00
❑ 63 Joe Dumars	.60	1.50
❑ 64 Juwan Howard	.40	1.00
❑ 65 Rik Smits	.40	1.00
❑ 66 Alonzo Mourning	.40	1.00
❑ 67 Allan Houston	.40	1.00
❑ 68 Chris Webber	.60	1.50
❑ 69 Kendall Gill	.20	.50
❑ 70 Rony Seikaly	.20	.50
❑ 71 Kenny Anderson	.40	1.00
❑ 72 John Wallace	.20	.50
❑ 73 Bryant Reeves	.20	.50
❑ 74 Brian Williams	.20	.50
❑ 75 Larry Johnson	.40	1.00
❑ 76 Shawn Bradley	.20	.50
❑ 77 Kevin Johnson	.40	1.00
❑ 78 Rod Strickland	.20	.50
❑ 79 Rodney Rogers	.20	.50
❑ 80 Rasheed Wallace	.60	1.50
❑ NNO Grant Hill Promo	.60	1.50

1998-99 Flair Showcase Row 3

❑ COMPLETE SET (90)	20.00	50.00
❑ COMMON CARD (1-90)	.08	.25
❑ COMMON ROOKIE	.20	.50
❑ 1 Keith Van Horn	.30	.75
❑ 1A K.Van Horn Promo	.40	1.00
❑ 2 Kobe Bryant	1.25	3.00
❑ 3 Tim Duncan	.50	1.25
❑ 4 Kevin Garnett	.60	1.50
❑ 5 Grant Hill	.30	.75
❑ 6 Allen Iverson	.60	1.50
❑ 7 Shaquille O'Neal	.75	2.00
❑ 8 Antoine Walker	.30	.75
❑ 9 Shareef Abdur-Rahim	.30	.75
❑ 10 Stephon Marbury	.30	.75
❑ 11 Ray Allen	.30	.75
❑ 12 Shawn Kemp	.20	.50
❑ 13 Tim Thomas	.20	.50
❑ 14 Scottie Pippen	.50	1.25
❑ 15 Latrell Sprewell	.30	.75
❑ 16 Dirk Nowitzki RC	3.00	8.00
❑ 17 Antawn Jamison RC	1.50	4.00
❑ 18 Anfernee Hardaway	.30	.75
❑ 19 Larry Hughes RC	1.00	2.50
❑ 20 Robert Traylor RC	.40	1.00
❑ 21 Kerry Kittles	.08	.25
❑ 22 Ron Mercer	.15	.40
❑ 23 Michael Olowokandi RC	.50	1.25
❑ 24 Jason Kidd	.40	1.00
❑ 25 Vince Carter RC	2.50	6.00
❑ 26 Charles Barkley	.30	.75
❑ 27 Antonio McDyess	.20	.50
❑ 28 Mike Bibby RC	1.00	2.50
❑ 29 Paul Pierce RC	2.50	6.00
❑ 30 Raef LaFrentz RC	.50	1.25
❑ 31 Reggie Miller	.30	.75
❑ 32 Michael Finley	.30	.75
❑ 33 Eddie Jones	.30	.75
❑ 34 Tim Hardaway	.20	.50
❑ 35 Glenn Robinson	.20	.50
❑ 36 Brevin Knight	.08	.25
❑ 37 Gary Payton	.30	.75
❑ 38 David Robinson	.30	.75
❑ 39 Karl Malone	.30	.75
❑ 40 Derek Anderson	.25	.60
❑ 41 Patrick Ewing	.30	.75
❑ 42 Juwan Howard	.20	.50
❑ 43 Jayson Williams	.08	.25
❑ 44 Terrell Brandon	.20	.50
❑ 45 Hakeem Olajuwon	.30	.75
❑ 46 Isaac Austin	.08	.25
❑ 47 Glen Rice	.20	.50
❑ 48 Maurice Taylor	.15	.40
❑ 49 Damon Stoudamire	.20	.50
❑ 50 Brian Skinner RC	.40	1.00
❑ 51 Nazr Mohammed RC	.20	.50
❑ 52 Tom Gugliotta	.08	.25
❑ 53 Al Harrington RC	.75	2.00
❑ 54 Pat Garrity RC	.25	.60
❑ 55 Jason Williams RC	1.25	3.00
❑ 56 Tracy McGrady	.60	1.50
❑ 57 Keon Clark RC	.50	1.25
❑ 58 Vin Baker	.20	.50
❑ 59 Bonzi Wells RC	1.25	3.00
❑ 60 John Stockton	.30	.75
❑ 61 Isaiah Rider	.08	.25
❑ 62 Alonzo Mourning	.20	.50
❑ 63 Allan Houston	.20	.50
❑ 64 Dennis Rodman	.20	.50
❑ 65 Felipe Lopez RC	.40	1.00
❑ 66 Joe Smith	.20	.50
❑ 67 Chris Webber	.30	.75
❑ 68 Mitch Richmond	.20	.50
❑ 69 Brent Barry	.20	.50
❑ 70 Mookie Blaylock	.08	.25
❑ 71 Donyell Marshall	.20	.50
❑ 72 Anthony Mason	.20	.50
❑ 73 Rod Strickland	.08	.25
❑ 74 Roshown McLeod RC	.25	.60
❑ 75 Matt Harpring RC	.75	2.00
❑ 76 Detlef Schrempf	.20	.50
❑ 77 Michael Dickerson RC	.60	1.50
❑ 78 Michael Doleac RC	.40	1.00
❑ 79 John Starks	.20	.50
❑ 80 Ricky Davis RC	.75	2.00
❑ 81 Steve Smith	.20	.50
❑ 82 Voshon Lenard	.08	.25
❑ 83 Toni Kukoc	.20	.50
❑ 84 Steve Nash	.30	.75
❑ 85 Vlade Divac	.20	.50
❑ 86 Rasheed Wallace	.30	.75
❑ 87 Bryon Russell	.08	.25
❑ 88 Antonio Daniels	.08	.25
❑ 89 Rik Smits	.20	.50
❑ 90 Joe Dumars	.30	.75

1999-00 Flair Showcase

❑ COMPLETE SET (130)	150.00	300.00
❑ COMPLETE SET w/o RC (100)	15.00	30.00
❑ COMMON CARD (1-100)	.25	.60
❑ COMMON ROOKIE (101-130)	1.25	3.00
❑ 1 Vince Carter	.75	2.00
❑ 2 Anfernee Hardaway	.40	1.00
❑ 3 Nick Van Exel	.30	.75
❑ 4 Kerry Kittles	.25	.60
❑ 5 Michael Doleac	.25	.60
❑ 6 Sean Elliott	.40	1.00
❑ 7 Shaquille O'Neal	1.00	2.50
❑ 8 Avery Johnson	.30	.75
❑ 9 Brian Grant	.25	.60
❑ 10 Jerome Williams	.25	.60
❑ 11 Larry Hughes	.30	.75
❑ 12 Jerry Stackhouse	.40	1.00
❑ 13 Alonzo Mourning	.40	1.00
❑ 14 Antonio McDyess	.30	.75
❑ 15 Jason Kidd	.60	1.50
❑ 16 Bryon Russell	.25	.60
❑ 17 Hakeem Olajuwon	.40	1.00
❑ 18 Juwan Howard	.30	.75
❑ 19 Paul Pierce	.40	1.00
❑ 20 Vin Baker	.40	1.00
❑ 21 Larry Johnson	.40	1.00
❑ 22 Gary Trent	.25	.60
❑ 23 Jayson Williams	.30	.75
❑ 24 Tim Hardaway	.40	1.00
❑ 25 Dirk Nowitzki	.60	1.50
❑ 26 Jamal Mashburn	.25	.60
❑ 27 Glenn Robinson	.30	.75
❑ 28 Shawn Bradley	.25	.60
❑ 29 Tom Gugliotta	.25	.60
❑ 30 Vlade Divac	.40	1.00
❑ 31 David Robinson	.50	1.25
❑ 32 Matt Geiger	.25	.60
❑ 33 Grant Hill	.40	1.00
❑ 34 Maurice Taylor	.30	.75
❑ 35 Toni Kukoc	.40	1.00
❑ 36 Cedric Ceballos	.25	.60
❑ 37 Patrick Ewing	.50	1.25
❑ 38 Ray Allen	.40	1.00
❑ 39 Michael Finley	.40	1.00
❑ 40 Robert Traylor	.25	.60
❑ 41 Brevin Knight	.25	.60
❑ 42 Marcus Camby	.30	.75
❑ 43 Sam Cassell	.30	.75
❑ 44 Antawn Jamison	.40	1.00
❑ 45 Steve Smith	.25	.60
❑ 46 Darrell Armstrong	.25	.60
❑ 47 Mookie Blaylock	.25	.60
❑ 48 Derek Anderson	.25	.60
❑ 49 Hersey Hawkins	.25	.60
❑ 50 Kobe Bryant	2.00	5.00
❑ 51 Shawn Kemp	.40	1.00
❑ 52 Scottie Pippen	.60	1.50
❑ 53 Chris Webber	.40	1.00
❑ 54 Damon Stoudamire	.40	1.00
❑ 55 Donyell Marshall	.30	.75
❑ 56 Isaiah Rider	.25	.60
❑ 57 Karl Malone	.50	1.25
❑ 58 Kevin Garnett	.75	2.00
❑ 59 Mario Elie	.25	.60
❑ 60 Michael Dickerson	.25	.60
❑ 61 Jahidi White	.25	.60

❑ 62 Joe Smith	.30	.75
❑ 63 Kenny Anderson	.30	.75
❑ 64 Reggie Miller	.40	1.00
❑ 65 Ruben Patterson	.25	.60
❑ 66 Shareef Abdur-Rahim	.30	.75
❑ 67 Allen Iverson	.75	2.00
❑ 68 Glen Rice	.40	1.00
❑ 69 Nick Anderson	.25	.60
❑ 70 Rex Chapman	.25	.60
❑ 71 Ron Mercer	.25	.60
❑ 72 Tim Duncan	.75	2.00
❑ 73 Al Harrington	.30	.75
❑ 74 Brent Barry	.30	.75
❑ 75 Eddie Jones	.40	1.00
❑ 76 Mike Bibby	.40	1.00
❑ 77 Anthony Mason	.25	.60
❑ 78 Michael Olowokandi	.25	.60
❑ 79 Matt Harpring	.30	.75
❑ 80 Stephon Marbury	.40	1.00
❑ 81 Tracy McGrady	.75	2.00
❑ 82 Allan Houston	.30	.75
❑ 83 Lindsey Hunter	.25	.60
❑ 84 Tariq Abdul-Wahad	.25	.60
❑ 85 Antoine Walker	.40	1.00
❑ 86 Charles Barkley	.50	1.25
❑ 87 Gary Payton	.40	1.00
❑ 88 John Stockton	.50	1.25
❑ 89 Mitch Richmond	.30	.75
❑ 90 Terrell Brandon	.25	.60
❑ 91 Charles Oakley	.30	.75
❑ 92 Bryant Reeves	.25	.60
❑ 93 Dikembe Mutombo	.30	.75
❑ 94 Elden Campbell	.25	.60
❑ 95 Jalen Rose	.30	.75
❑ 96 Jason Williams	.40	1.00
❑ 97 Keith Van Horn	.30	.75
❑ 98 Latrell Sprewell	.30	.75
❑ 99 Raef LaFrentz	.30	.75
❑ 100 Rasheed Wallace	.40	1.00
❑ 101 Cal Bowdler RC	1.25	3.00
❑ 102 Dion Glover RC	1.25	3.00
❑ 103 Jason Terry RC	3.00	8.00
❑ 104 Adrian Griffin RC	1.25	3.00
❑ 105 Baron Davis RC	5.00	12.00
❑ 106 Michael Ruffin RC	1.25	3.00
❑ 107 Elton Brand RC	4.00	10.00
❑ 108 Ron Artest RC	5.00	12.00
❑ 109 Andre Miller RC	4.00	10.00
❑ 110 Trajan Langdon RC	1.25	3.00
❑ 111 James Posey RC	2.00	5.00
❑ 112 Vonteego Cummings RC	1.25	3.00
❑ 113 Kenny Thomas RC	1.25	3.00
❑ 114 Steve Francis RC	4.00	10.00
❑ 115 Jonathan Bender RC	1.25	3.00
❑ 116 Lamar Odom RC	4.00	10.00
❑ 117 Devean George RC	2.00	5.00
❑ 118 Tim James RC	1.25	3.00
❑ 119 Anthony Carter RC	2.50	6.00
❑ 120 Wally Szczerbiak RC	4.00	10.00
❑ 121 William Avery RC	1.25	3.00
❑ 122 Evan Eschmeyer RC	1.25	3.00
❑ 123 Corey Maggette RC	4.00	10.00
❑ 124 Jumaine Jones RC	1.25	3.00
❑ 125 Shawn Marion RC	4.00	10.00
❑ 126 Ryan Robertson RC	1.25	3.00
❑ 127 A.Radojevic RC	1.25	3.00
❑ 128 Quincy Lewis RC	1.25	3.00
❑ 129 Scott Padgett RC	1.25	3.00
❑ 130 Richard Hamilton RC	4.00	10.00
❑ P1 Vince Carter PROMO	1.25	3.00

2001-02 Flair

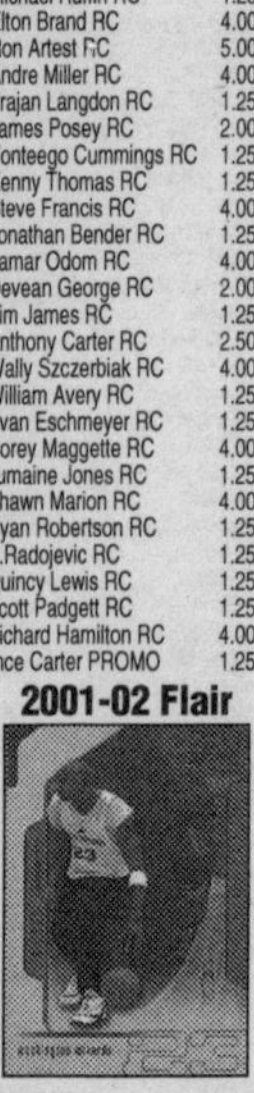

❑ COMP.SET w/o SP's (90)	25.00	50.00
❑ COMMON CARDS (1-121)	.25	.60
❑ COMMON ROOKIE (91-120)	1.25	3.00
❑ 1 Tracy McGrady	.75	2.00
❑ 2 Derek Fisher	.30	.75
❑ 3 Allen Iverson	.75	2.00
❑ 4 Chris Webber	.40	1.00
❑ 5 Jalen Rose	.30	.75
❑ 6 Kenyon Martin	.40	1.00
❑ 7 Jermaine O'Neal	.40	1.00
❑ 8 Kobe Bryant	2.00	5.00
❑ 9 Bryon Russell	.25	.60
❑ 10 Wally Szczerbiak	.30	.75
❑ 11 Damon Stoudamire	.30	.75
❑ 12 John Stockton	.50	1.25
❑ 13 Glenn Robinson	.30	.75
❑ 14 Steve Francis	.40	1.00
❑ 15 Vince Carter	.75	2.00
❑ 16 Peja Stojakovic	.30	.75
❑ 17 Rick Fox	.30	.75
❑ 18 Allan Houston	.30	.75
❑ 19 Danny Fortson	.25	.60
❑ 20 Gary Payton	.40	1.00
❑ 21 Darius Miles	.25	.60
❑ 22 Kevin Garnett	.75	2.00
❑ 23 Marcus Camby	.30	.75
❑ 24 Desmond Mason	.30	.75
❑ 25 Tim Duncan	.75	2.00
❑ 26 Jamal Mashburn	.30	.75
❑ 27 Andre Miller	.30	.75
❑ 28 Antonio McDyess	.30	.75
❑ 29 Morris Peterson	.30	.75
❑ 30 Rasheed Wallace	.40	1.00
❑ 31 Shawn Marion	.40	1.00
❑ 32 Karl Malone	.50	1.25
❑ 33 Grant Hill	.40	1.00
❑ 34 Shaquille O'Neal	1.00	2.50
❑ 35 Hakeem Olajuwon	.50	1.25
❑ 36 Corliss Williamson	.30	.75
❑ 37 Paul Pierce	.40	1.00
❑ 38 Antonio Davis	.25	.60
❑ 39 Antonio Daniels	.25	.60
❑ 40 Ray Allen	.40	1.00
❑ 41 Dirk Nowitzki	.60	1.50
❑ 42 Jerry Stackhouse	.30	.75
❑ 43 Donyell Marshall	.25	.60
❑ 44 Brian Grant	.25	.60
❑ 45 Raef LaFrentz	.25	.60
❑ 46 Corey Maggette	.30	.75
❑ 47 Mike Miller	.30	.75
❑ 48 Jason Williams	.30	.75
❑ 49 Jahidi White	.25	.60
❑ 50 David Robinson	.50	1.25
❑ 51 Shareef Abdur-Rahim	.30	.75
❑ 52 Anfernee Hardaway	.40	1.00
❑ 53 Baron Davis	.40	1.00
❑ 54 DerMarr Johnson	.25	.60
❑ 55 Dikembe Mutombo	.30	.75
❑ 56 David Wesley	.25	.60
❑ 57 Chris Mihm	.25	.60
❑ 58 Michael Finley	.40	1.00
❑ 59 Eddie House	.25	.60
❑ 60 Stromile Swift	.25	.60
❑ 61 Courtney Alexander	.25	.60
❑ 62 Ron Mercer	.25	.60
❑ 63 Cuttino Mobley	.30	.75
❑ 64 Tim Thomas	.25	.60
❑ 65 Eddie Jones	.30	.75
❑ 66 Lamar Odom	.40	1.00
❑ 67 Terrell Brandon	.25	.60
❑ 68 Rashard Lewis	.40	1.00
❑ 69 Antoine Walker	.30	.75
❑ 70 Latrell Sprewell	.30	.75
❑ 71 Sam Cassell	.30	.75
❑ 72 Mike Bibby	.30	.75
❑ 73 Speedy Claxton	.25	.60
❑ 74 Steve Nash	.60	1.50
❑ 75 Mark Jackson	.30	.75
❑ 76 Ron Artest	.30	.75
❑ 77 Matt Harpring	.30	.75
❑ 78 Wang Zhizhi	.30	.75
❑ 79 Nazr Mohammed	.25	.60
❑ 80 Jason Terry	.40	1.00
❑ 81 Nick Van Exel	.30	.75
❑ 82 Reggie Miller	.40	1.00
❑ 83 Joe Smith	.25	.60
❑ 84 Jason Kidd	.60	1.50
❑ 85 Richard Hamilton	.30	.75
❑ 86 Antawn Jamison	.40	1.00
❑ 87 Alonzo Mourning	.40	1.00
❑ 88 Stephon Marbury	.40	1.00
❑ 89 Scottie Pippen	.60	1.50
❑ 90 Elton Brand	.40	1.00
❑ 91 Kwame Brown RC	1.50	4.00
❑ 92 Eddie Griffin RC	1.25	3.00
❑ 93 Tyson Chandler RC	2.50	6.00
❑ 94 Omar Cook RC	1.25	3.00
❑ 95 Loren Woods RC	1.25	3.00
❑ 96 Alton Ford RC	1.25	3.00
❑ 97 Shane Battier RC	2.00	5.00
❑ 98 Joe Johnson RC	3.00	8.00
❑ 99 Rodney White RC	1.25	3.00
❑ 100 Pau Gasol RC	5.00	12.00
❑ 101 Zach Randolph RC	3.00	8.00
❑ 102 Vladimir Radmanovic RC	1.50	4.00
❑ 103 Brendan Haywood RC	1.50	4.00
❑ 104 Michael Bradley RC	1.25	3.00
❑ 105 Tony Parker RC	5.00	12.00
❑ 106 Jason Richardson RC	2.50	6.00
❑ 107 Gerald Wallace RC	3.00	8.00
❑ 108 Damone Brown RC	1.25	3.00
❑ 109 Richard Jefferson RC	3.00	8.00
❑ 111 DeSagana Diop RC	1.25	3.00
❑ 112 Brandon Armstrong RC	1.25	3.00
❑ 113 Troy Murphy RC	2.50	6.00
❑ 114 Kedrick Brown RC	1.25	3.00
❑ 115 Kirk Haston RC	1.25	3.00
❑ 116 Gilbert Arenas RC	2.00	5.00
❑ 117 Jeryl Sasser RC	1.25	3.00
❑ 118 Jamaal Tinsley RC	1.50	4.00
❑ 119 Terence Morris RC	1.25	3.00
❑ 120 Michael Wright RC	1.25	3.00
❑ 121 Michael Jordan	6.00	15.00

2002-03 Flair

❑ COMP.SET w/o SP's (90)	25.00	50.00
❑ COMMON CARD (1-90)	.25	.60
❑ COMMON ROOKIE (91-120)	2.00	5.00
❑ 1 Tracy McGrady	.75	2.00
❑ 2 Jamal Mashburn	.30	.75
❑ 3 Allen Iverson	.75	2.00
❑ 4 Alonzo Mourning	.40	1.00
❑ 5 Joe Smith	.25	.60
❑ 6 Wang Zhizhi	.25	.60
❑ 7 Karl Malone	.40	1.00
❑ 8 Keith Van Horn	.30	.75
❑ 9 Joseph Forte	.25	.60
❑ 10 Peja Stojakovic	.30	.75
❑ 11 Juwan Howard	.30	.75
❑ 12 Brian Grant	.25	.60
❑ 13 Glenn Robinson	.30	.75
❑ 14 Antonio McDyess	.30	.75
❑ 15 Vince Carter	.75	2.00
❑ 16 Pau Gasol	.40	1.00
❑ 17 Bonzi Wells	.30	.75
❑ 18 Chucky Atkins	.25	.60
❑ 19 Shane Battier	.30	.75
❑ 20 Steve Francis	.40	1.00
❑ 21 Kevin Garnett	.75	2.00
❑ 22 Antawn Jamison	.40	1.00
❑ 23 Hedo Turkoglu	.30	.75
❑ 24 Kenyon Martin	.40	1.00
❑ 25 Cuttino Mobley	.30	.75
❑ 26 Steve Nash	.60	1.50
❑ 27 Morris Peterson	.30	.75
❑ 28 Jason Richardson	.40	1.00
❑ 29 Antoine Walker	.30	.75
❑ 30 Rasheed Wallace	.40	1.00
❑ 31 Tim Duncan	.75	2.00
❑ 32 Paul Pierce	.40	1.00
❑ 33 Ben Wallace	.30	.75
❑ 34 Jason Kidd	.60	1.50
❑ 35 Gary Payton	.40	1.00
❑ 36 Mike Miller	.30	.75
❑ 37 Kobe Bryant	2.00	5.00
❑ 38 Baron Davis	.40	1.00
❑ 39 Steve Smith	.30	.75
❑ 40 Reggie Miller	.40	1.00
❑ 41 Dirk Nowitzki	.60	1.50

❑ 42 Rashard Lewis	.40	1.00
❑ 43 Andre Miller	.30	.75
❑ 44 David Wesley	.25	.60
❑ 45 Ray Allen	.40	1.00
❑ 46 Tyson Chandler	.30	.75
❑ 47 Jamaal Tinsley	.30	.75
❑ 48 Grant Hill	.40	1.00
❑ 49 Richard Jefferson	.40	1.00
❑ 50 Latrell Sprewell	.30	.75
❑ 51 Jason Terry	.40	1.00
❑ 52 Alvin Williams	.25	.60
❑ 53 Vin Baker	.30	.75
❑ 54 Robert Horry	.30	.75
❑ 55 Eddie Jones	.30	.75
❑ 56 Andrei Kirilenko	.40	1.00
❑ 57 Darius Miles	.25	.60
❑ 58 Kedrick Brown	.25	.60
❑ 59 Jermaine O'Neal	.40	1.00
❑ 60 David Robinson	.50	1.25
❑ 61 Jason Williams	.30	.75
❑ 62 Wally Szczerbiak	.30	.75
❑ 63 Mike Bibby	.30	.75
❑ 64 Shawn Marion	.40	1.00
❑ 65 Shaquille O'Neal	1.00	2.50
❑ 66 Michael Redd	.40	1.00
❑ 67 Chris Webber	.40	1.00
❑ 68 Quentin Richardson	.30	.75
❑ 69 Michael Jordan	2.50	6.00
❑ 70 Jamaal Magloire	.25	.60
❑ 71 Radoslav Nesterovic	.25	.60
❑ 72 Eddy Curry	.30	.75
❑ 73 Michael Finley	.40	1.00
❑ 74 Eddie Griffin	.25	.60
❑ 75 Aaron McKie	.25	.60
❑ 76 Tony Parker	.40	1.00
❑ 77 Shareef Abdur-Rahim	.30	.75
❑ 78 Jalen Rose	.30	.75
❑ 79 Jerry Stackhouse	.30	.75
❑ 80 Jumaine Jones	.25	.60
❑ 81 Toni Kukoc	.30	.75
❑ 82 Vladimir Radmanovic	.25	.60
❑ 83 Zach Randolph	.40	1.00
❑ 84 John Stockton	.50	1.25
❑ 85 Mengke Bateer	.25	.60
❑ 86 Dikembe Mutombo	.30	.75
❑ 87 Elton Brand	.40	1.00
❑ 88 Allan Houston	.30	.75
❑ 89 Joe Johnson	.40	1.00
❑ 90 Kwame Brown	.25	.60
❑ 91 Yao Ming RC	6.00	15.00
❑ 92 Jay Williams RC	2.50	6.00
❑ 93 Mike Dunleavy RC	2.50	6.00
❑ 94 Drew Gooden RC	3.00	8.00
❑ 95 DaJuan Wagner RC	2.00	5.00
❑ 96 Caron Butler RC	4.00	10.00
❑ 97 Jared Jeffries RC	2.00	5.00
❑ 98 Nene Hilario RC	2.50	6.00
❑ 99 Chris Wilcox RC	2.50	6.00
❑ 100 Nikoloz Tskitishvili RC	2.00	5.00
❑ 101 Kareem Rush RC	2.50	6.00
❑ 102 Curtis Borchardt RC	2.00	5.00
❑ 103 Qyntel Woods RC	2.00	5.00
❑ 104 Melvin Ely RC	2.00	5.00
❑ 105 Marcus Haislip RC	2.00	5.00
❑ 106 Carlos Boozer RC	4.00	10.00
❑ 107 Bostjan Nachbar RC	2.00	5.00
❑ 108 Amare Stoudemire RC	5.00	12.00
❑ 109 Frank Williams RC	2.00	5.00
❑ 110 Jiri Welsch RC	2.00	5.00
❑ 111 Fred Jones RC	2.50	6.00
❑ 112 Juan Dixon RC	3.00	8.00
❑ 113 Ryan Humphrey RC	2.00	5.00
❑ 114 Casey Jacobsen RC	2.00	5.00
❑ 115 Tayshaun Prince RC	3.00	8.00
❑ 116 Dan Dickau RC	2.00	5.00
❑ 117 Chris Jefferies RC	2.00	5.00
❑ 118 John Salmons RC	3.00	8.00
❑ 119 Manu Ginobili RC	5.00	12.00
❑ 120 Gordan Giricek RC	2.00	5.00

2003-04 Flair

❑ COMP.SET w/o SP's (90)	15.00	40.00
❑ COMMON CARD (1-90)	.20	.50
❑ COMMON ROOKIE (91-120)	1.50	4.00
❑ 1 Jerry Stackhouse	.25	.60
❑ 2 Eddie Griffin	.20	.50
❑ 3 Jermaine O'Neal	.30	.75
❑ 4 Kobe Bryant	1.50	4.00
❑ 5 Juwan Howard	.25	.60
❑ 6 Alonzo Mourning	.30	.75
❑ 7 Kenny Thomas	.20	.50
❑ 8 Chris Webber	.30	.75
❑ 9 Radoslav Nesterovic	.20	.50
❑ 10 Morris Peterson	.25	.60
❑ 11 DeShawn Stevenson	.20	.50
❑ 12 Steve Francis	.30	.75
❑ 13 Andrei Kirilenko	.30	.75
❑ 14 Kwame Brown	.20	.50
❑ 15 Tim Duncan	.60	1.50
❑ 16 Yao Ming	.60	1.50
❑ 17 Jamaal Tinsley	.25	.60
❑ 18 Shaquille O'Neal	.75	2.00
❑ 19 Tracy McGrady	.60	1.50
❑ 20 Dirk Nowitzki	.50	1.25
❑ 21 Marcus Camby	.25	.60
❑ 22 Elton Brand	.30	.75
❑ 23 Latrell Sprewell	.25	.60
❑ 24 Grant Hill	.30	.75
❑ 25 Shawn Marion	.30	.75
❑ 26 Rasheed Wallace	.30	.75
❑ 27 Ray Allen	.20	.50
❑ 28 Antonio Davis	.20	.50
❑ 29 Antoine Walker	.30	.75
❑ 30 Ricky Davis	.25	.60
❑ 31 Jason Kidd	.50	1.25
❑ 32 Tony Parker	.30	.75
❑ 33 Paul Pierce	.30	.75
❑ 34 Gary Payton	.30	.75
❑ 35 Kenyon Martin	.30	.75
❑ 36 Dale Davis	.20	.50
❑ 37 Vladimir Radmanovic	.20	.50
❑ 38 Matt Harpring	.25	.60
❑ 39 Shareef Abdur-Rahim	.25	.60
❑ 40 Antawn Jamison	.30	.75
❑ 41 Eddie Jones	.25	.60
❑ 42 Jamaal Magloire	.20	.50
❑ 43 Jason Richardson	.30	.75
❑ 44 Jonathan Bender	.20	.50
❑ 45 Chris Wilcox	.20	.50
❑ 46 Manu Ginobili	.30	.75
❑ 47 Chauncey Billups	.30	.75
❑ 48 Jamal Mashburn	.20	.50
❑ 49 Joe Smith	.20	.50
❑ 50 Aaron McKie	.20	.50
❑ 51 Theo Ratliff	.20	.50
❑ 52 Eddy Curry	.25	.60
❑ 53 Ron Artest	.25	.60
❑ 54 Quentin Richardson	.25	.60
❑ 55 Karl Malone	.30	.75
❑ 56 Pau Gasol	.30	.75
❑ 57 Dan Dickau	.20	.50
❑ 58 Darius Miles	.25	.60
❑ 59 Ben Wallace	.25	.60
❑ 60 Cuttino Mobley	.25	.60
❑ 61 Lamar Odom	.30	.75
❑ 62 Shane Battier	.25	.60
❑ 63 Allan Houston	.25	.60
❑ 64 Peja Stojakovic	.25	.60
❑ 65 Dajuan Wagner	.20	.50
❑ 66 Caron Butler	.25	.60
❑ 67 Keith Van Horn	.25	.60
❑ 68 Vincent Yarbrough	.20	.50
❑ 69 Tim Thomas	.20	.50
❑ 70 Troy Hudson	.20	.50
❑ 71 Amare Stoudemire	.60	1.50
❑ 72 Bobby Jackson	.20	.50
❑ 73 Bonzi Wells	.20	.50
❑ 74 Steve Nash	.50	1.25
❑ 75 Gilbert Arenas	.30	.75
❑ 76 Glenn Robinson	.25	.60
❑ 77 Jalen Rose	.25	.60
❑ 78 Michael Finley	.30	.75
❑ 79 Nene	.25	.60
❑ 80 Kevin Garnett	.60	1.50
❑ 81 Richard Jefferson	.30	.75
❑ 82 Baron Davis	.30	.75
❑ 83 Mike Bibby	.25	.60
❑ 84 Tyson Chandler	.25	.60
❑ 85 Michael Redd	.30	.75
❑ 86 Mike Dunleavy	.25	.60
❑ 87 Drew Gooden	.20	.50
❑ 88 Allen Iverson	.60	1.50
❑ 89 Vince Carter	.60	1.50
❑ 90 Larry Hughes	.25	.60
❑ 91 Josh Howard RC	2.00	5.00
❑ 92 Maciej Lampe RC	1.50	4.00
❑ 93 Zarko Cabarkapa RC	1.50	4.00
❑ 94 LeBron James RC	30.00	60.00
❑ 95 Reece Gaines RC	1.50	4.00
❑ 96 Jarvis Hayes RC	1.50	4.00
❑ 97 Mickael Pietrus RC	2.00	5.00
❑ 98 T.J. Ford RC	2.00	5.00
❑ 99 Zoran Planinic RC	1.50	4.00
❑ 100 Luke Ridnour RC	2.00	5.00
❑ 101 Boris Diaw RC	2.00	5.00
❑ 102 Nick Collison RC	1.50	4.00
❑ 103 Travis Outlaw RC	2.00	5.00
❑ 104 Carmelo Anthony RC	4.00	10.00
❑ 105 Chris Kaman RC	2.00	5.00
❑ 106 Mike Sweetney RC	1.50	4.00
❑ 107 Kendrick Perkins RC	2.50	6.00
❑ 108 Jason Kapono RC	2.00	5.00
❑ 109 Troy Bell RC	1.50	4.00
❑ 110 Chris Bosh RC	2.50	6.00
❑ 111 Jerome Beasley RC	1.50	4.00
❑ 112 Darko Milicic RC	2.00	5.00
❑ 113 Dwyane Wade RC	4.00	10.00
❑ 114 David West RC	2.00	5.00
❑ 115 Kirk Hinrich RC	2.00	5.00
❑ 116 Dahntay Jones RC	1.50	4.00
❑ 117 Leandro Barbosa RC	2.00	5.00
❑ 118 Marcus Banks RC	1.50	4.00
❑ 119 Luke Walton RC	2.00	5.00
❑ 120 Ndudi Ebi RC	1.50	4.00

2004-05 Flair

❑ COMP.SET w/o SP's (60)	30.00	70.00
❑ COMMON CARD (1-60)	.40	1.00
❑ COMMON ROOKIE (61-90)	1.50	4.00
❑ 1 Gilbert Arenas	.60	1.50
❑ 2 Richard Hamilton	.50	1.25
❑ 3 Stephon Marbury	.60	1.50
❑ 4 Tony Parker	.60	1.50
❑ 5 Michael Redd	.60	1.50
❑ 6 Latrell Sprewell	.50	1.25
❑ 7 Willie Green	.40	1.00
❑ 8 Joe Johnson	.60	1.50
❑ 9 Lamar Odom	.60	1.50
❑ 10 Tim Duncan	1.25	3.00
❑ 11 Ben Wallace	.50	1.25
❑ 12 Elton Brand	.60	1.50
❑ 13 Allen Iverson	1.25	3.00
❑ 14 Andrei Kirilenko	.60	1.50
❑ 15 Dirk Nowitzki	1.00	2.50
❑ 16 Paul Pierce	.60	1.50
❑ 17 Mike Dunleavy	.50	1.25
❑ 18 Zach Randolph	.60	1.50
❑ 19 David West	.60	1.50
❑ 20 Corey Maggette	.50	1.25
❑ 21 Dwyane Wade	2.00	5.00
❑ 22 Chris Bosh	.60	1.50
❑ 23 Michael Finley	.60	1.50
❑ 24 Kevin Garnett	1.25	3.00
❑ 25 Allan Houston	.50	1.25
❑ 26 Antawn Jamison	.60	1.50
❑ 27 Jermaine O'Neal	.60	1.50
❑ 28 Alonzo Mourning	.60	1.50
❑ 29 Gerald Wallace	.60	1.50
❑ 30 Jason Williams	.50	1.25
❑ 31 Tyronn Lue	.40	1.00
❑ 32 Pau Gasol	.60	1.50

❑ 33 Jason Kidd	1.00	2.50
❑ 34 Shareef Abdur-Rahim	.50	1.25
❑ 35 LeBron James	4.00	10.00
❑ 36 Shaquille O'Neal	1.50	4.00
❑ 37 Jason Richardson	.60	1.50
❑ 38 Rasheed Wallace	.60	1.50
❑ 39 Nene	.50	1.25
❑ 40 Tracy McGrady	1.25	3.00
❑ 41 Luke Ridnour	.40	1.00
❑ 42 Peja Stojakovic	.50	1.25
❑ 43 Amare Stoudemire	1.25	3.00
❑ 44 Carmelo Anthony	2.00	5.00
❑ 45 Steve Francis	.60	1.50
❑ 46 Antoine Walker	.60	1.50
❑ 47 Reggie Miller	.60	1.50
❑ 48 Mike Bibby	.50	1.25
❑ 49 Sam Cassell	.50	1.25
❑ 50 Richard Jefferson	.60	1.50
❑ 51 Jason Kapono	.40	1.00
❑ 52 Dajuan Wagner	.40	1.00
❑ 53 Kobe Bryant	3.00	8.00
❑ 54 Kenyon Martin	.60	1.50
❑ 55 T.J. Ford	.50	1.25
❑ 56 Ray Allen	.60	1.50
❑ 57 Vince Carter	1.25	3.00
❑ 58 Yao Ming	1.50	4.00
❑ 59 Baron Davis	.60	1.50
❑ 60 Joe Smith	.40	1.00
❑ 61 Luol Deng RC	2.00	5.00
❑ 62 J.R. Smith RC	3.00	8.00
❑ 63 Josh Childress RC	1.50	4.00
❑ 64 Shaun Livingston RC	1.50	4.00
❑ 65 Rafael Araujo RC	1.50	4.00
❑ 66 Devin Harris RC	3.00	8.00
❑ 67 Kevin Martin RC	2.00	5.00
❑ 68 Sasha Vujacic RC	1.50	4.00
❑ 69 Robert Swift RC	1.50	4.00
❑ 70 Andris Biedrins RC	2.50	6.00
❑ 71 Kirk Snyder RC	1.50	4.00
❑ 72 Jameer Nelson RC	2.00	5.00
❑ 73 Tony Allen RC	2.00	5.00
❑ 74 Chris Duhon RC	2.50	6.00
❑ 75 David Harrison RC	1.50	4.00
❑ 76 Andre Iguodala RC	4.00	10.00
❑ 77 Josh Smith RC	4.00	10.00
❑ 78 Andre Emmett RC	1.50	4.00
❑ 79 Luke Jackson RC	1.50	4.00
❑ 80 Dorell Wright RC	2.00	5.00
❑ 81 Ben Gordon RC	2.00	5.00
❑ 82 Dwight Howard RC	5.00	12.00
❑ 83 Kris Humphries RC	2.50	6.00
❑ 84 Al Jefferson RC	3.00	8.00
❑ 85 Jackson Vroman RC	1.50	4.00
❑ 86 Beno Udrih RC	2.00	5.00
❑ 87 Trevor Ariza RC	2.00	5.00
❑ 88 Sebastian Telfair RC	1.50	4.00
❑ 89 Emeka Okafor RC	3.00	8.00
❑ 90 Peter John Ramos RC	1.50	4.00

2003-04 Flair Final Edition

❑ COMP.SET w/o SP's (65)	12.50	30.00
❑ COMMON CARD (1-65)	.20	.50
❑ COMMON ROOKIE (66-90)	2.00	5.00
❑ 1 Allen Iverson	.60	1.50
❑ 2 Juwan Howard	.25	.60
❑ 3 Stephen Jackson	.25	.60
❑ 4 Manu Ginobili	.30	.75
❑ 5 Steve Nash	.50	1.25
❑ 6 Jason Terry	.25	.60
❑ 7 Tayshaun Prince	.25	.60
❑ 8 Stephon Marbury	.30	.75
❑ 9 Eddie Jones	.25	.60
❑ 10 Reggie Miller	.30	.75
❑ 11 Baron Davis	.30	.75
❑ 12 Donyell Marshall	.20	.50
❑ 13 Mike Bibby	.25	.60
❑ 14 Kobe Bryant	1.50	4.00
❑ 15 Jason Richardson	.30	.75
❑ 16 Cuttino Mobley	.25	.60
❑ 17 Andre Miller	.25	.60
❑ 18 Corey Maggette	.20	.50
❑ 19 Michael Finley	.30	.75
❑ 20 Jason Kidd	.50	1.25
❑ 21 Lamar Odom	.30	.75
❑ 22 Tracy McGrady	.60	1.50
❑ 23 Peja Stojakovic	.25	.60
❑ 24 Richard Jefferson	.30	.75
❑ 25 Rasheed Wallace	.30	.75
❑ 26 Eddy Curry	.25	.60
❑ 27 Ben Wallace	.25	.60
❑ 28 Rashard Lewis	.30	.75
❑ 29 Sam Cassell	.25	.60
❑ 30 Anfernee Hardaway	.30	.75
❑ 31 Carlos Boozer	.30	.75
❑ 32 Jamal Crawford	.25	.60
❑ 33 Dirk Nowitzki	.50	1.25
❑ 34 Steve Francis	.30	.75
❑ 35 Chris Webber	.30	.75
❑ 36 Elton Brand	.30	.75
❑ 37 Michael Redd	.30	.75
❑ 38 Jason Williams	.25	.60
❑ 39 Nene	.25	.60
❑ 40 Nick Van Exel	.25	.60
❑ 41 Amare Stoudemire	.60	1.50
❑ 42 Latrell Sprewell	.25	.60
❑ 43 Tony Parker	.30	.75
❑ 44 Keith Van Horn	.25	.60
❑ 45 Pau Gasol	.30	.75
❑ 46 Andrei Kirilenko	.30	.75
❑ 47 Shareef Abdur-Rahim	.25	.60
❑ 48 Tim Thomas	.20	.50
❑ 49 Jerry Stackhouse	.25	.60
❑ 50 Jermaine O'Neal	.30	.75
❑ 51 Jamal Mashburn	.20	.50
❑ 52 Matt Harpring	.25	.60
❑ 53 Damon Stoudamire	.25	.60
❑ 54 Zydrunas Ilgauskas	.25	.60
❑ 55 Kevin Garnett	.60	1.50
❑ 56 Tim Duncan	.60	1.50
❑ 57 Yao Ming	.60	1.50
❑ 58 Kenyon Martin	.30	.75
❑ 59 Paul Pierce	.30	.75
❑ 60 Ron Artest	.25	.60
❑ 61 Vince Carter	.60	1.50
❑ 62 Shaquille O'Neal	.75	2.00
❑ 63 Shawn Marion	.30	.75
❑ 64 Gilbert Arenas	.30	.75
❑ 65 Ray Allen	.20	.50
❑ 66 Chris Bosh RC	3.00	8.00
❑ 67 Brian Cook RC	2.00	5.00
❑ 68 Luke Ridnour RC	2.50	6.00
❑ 69 Willie Green RC	2.00	5.00
❑ 70 Zarko Cabarkapa RC	2.00	5.00
❑ 71 Maurice Williams RC	3.00	8.00
❑ 72 Luke Walton RC	2.50	6.00
❑ 73 David West RC	2.50	6.00
❑ 74 Mickael Pietrus RC	2.50	6.00
❑ 75 LeBron James RC	40.00	80.00
❑ 76 Marcus Banks RC	2.00	5.00
❑ 77 Keith Bogans RC	2.00	5.00
❑ 78 Darko Milicic RC	2.50	6.00
❑ 79 Jarvis Hayes RC	2.00	5.00
❑ 80 Josh Howard RC	2.50	6.00
❑ 81 Chris Kaman RC	2.50	6.00
❑ 82 Mike Sweetney RC	2.00	5.00
❑ 83 Carmelo Anthony RC	5.00	12.00
❑ 84 Travis Outlaw RC	2.50	6.00
❑ 85 Kyle Korver RC	2.50	6.00
❑ 86 Boris Diaw RC	2.50	6.00
❑ 87 Dwyane Wade RC	5.00	12.00
❑ 88 Troy Bell RC	2.00	5.00
❑ 89 T.J. Ford RC	2.50	6.00
❑ 90 Kirk Hinrich RC	2.50	6.00

1961-62 Fleer

❑ COMPLETE SET (66)	2800.00	4000.00
❑ 1 Al Attles RC	75.00	125.00
❑ 2 Paul Arizin	20.00	40.00
❑ 3 Elgin Baylor RC	150.00	250.00
❑ 4 Walt Bellamy RC	40.00	60.00
❑ 5 Arlen Bockhorn	10.00	15.00
❑ 6 Bob Boozer RC	15.00	25.00
❑ 7 Carl Braun	10.00	25.00
❑ 8 Wilt Chamberlain RC	400.00	800.00

❑ 9 Larry Costello	6.00	15.00
❑ 10 Bob Cousy !	80.00	160.00
❑ 11 Walter Dukes	6.00	15.00
❑ 12 Wayne Embry RC	15.00	30.00
❑ 13 Dave Gambee	10.00	15.00
❑ 14 Tom Gola	12.50	30.00
❑ 15 Sihugo Green RC	12.00	20.00
❑ 16 Hal Greer RC	50.00	80.00
❑ 17 Richie Guerin RC	25.00	40.00
❑ 18 Cliff Hagan	20.00	40.00
❑ 19 Tom Heinsohn	40.00	80.00
❑ 20 Bailey Howell RC	30.00	50.00
❑ 21 Rod Hundley	30.00	60.00
❑ 22 K.C.Jones RC	50.00	100.00
❑ 23 Sam Jones RC	50.00	100.00
❑ 24 Phil Jordan	10.00	15.00
❑ 25 John/Red Kerr	20.00	40.00
❑ 26 Rudy LaRusso RC	25.00	40.00
❑ 27 George Lee	10.00	15.00
❑ 28 Bob Leonard	6.00	15.00
❑ 29 Clyde Lovellette	20.00	40.00
❑ 30 John McCarthy	10.00	15.00
❑ 31 Tom Meschery RC	15.00	25.00
❑ 32 Willie Naulls	8.00	20.00
❑ 33 Don Ohl RC	15.00	25.00
❑ 34 Bob Pettit	40.00	80.00
❑ 35 Frank Ramsey	15.00	30.00
❑ 36 Oscar Robertson RC	250.00	400.00
❑ 37 Guy Rodgers RC	15.00	25.00
❑ 38 Bill Russell !	200.00	350.00
❑ 39 Dolph Schayes	25.00	50.00
❑ 40 Frank Selvy	6.00	15.00
❑ 41 Gene Shue	8.00	20.00
❑ 42 Jack Twyman	15.00	30.00
❑ 43 Jerry West RC	350.00	500.00
❑ 44 Len Wilkens UER RC	100.00	175.00
❑ 45 Paul Arizin IA	15.00	25.00
❑ 46 Elgin Baylor IA	65.00	100.00
❑ 47 Wilt Chamberlain IA !	250.00	400.00
❑ 48 Larry Costello IA	12.00	20.00
❑ 49 Bob Cousy IA UER	75.00	125.00
❑ 50 Walter Dukes IA	10.00	15.00
❑ 51 Tom Gola IA	15.00	25.00
❑ 52 Richie Guerin IA	12.00	20.00
❑ 53 Cliff Hagan IA	15.00	25.00
❑ 54 Tom Heinsohn IA	30.00	50.00
❑ 55 Bailey Howell IA	15.00	25.00
❑ 56 John/Red Kerr IA	18.00	30.00
❑ 57 Rudy LaRusso IA	12.00	20.00
❑ 58 Clyde Lovellette IA	18.00	30.00
❑ 59 Bob Pettit IA	30.00	50.00
❑ 60 Frank Ramsey IA	15.00	25.00
❑ 61 Oscar Robertson IA !	100.00	175.00
❑ 62 Bill Russell IA !	100.00	200.00
❑ 63 Dolph Schayes IA	15.00	40.00
❑ 64 Gene Shue IA	12.00	20.00
❑ 65 Jack Twyman IA	15.00	25.00
❑ 66 Jerry West IA !	175.00	300.00

1986-87 Fleer

❑ COMPLETE w/Stickers (143)	600.00	1000.00
❑ COMP.SET (132)	500.00	800.00
❑ 1 Kareem Abdul-Jabbar	6.00	15.00
❑ 2 Alvan Adams	.75	2.00
❑ 3 Mark Aguirre RC	1.25	3.00
❑ 4 Danny Ainge RC	3.00	8.00
❑ 5 John Bagley RC	.75	2.00
❑ 6 Thurl Bailey RC	.75	2.00
❑ 7 Charles Barkley RC	20.00	50.00
❑ 8 Benoit Benjamin RC	1.00	2.50
❑ 9 Larry Bird !	15.00	30.00
❑ 10 Otis Birdsong	.75	2.00
❑ 11 Rolando Blackman RC	1.00	2.50
❑ 12 Manute Bol RC	.75	2.00
❑ 14 Joe Barry Carroll	.75	2.00
❑ 15 Tom Chambers RC	1.50	4.00
❑ 16 Maurice Cheeks	.75	2.00
❑ 17 Michael Cooper	1.00	2.50
❑ 18 Wayne Cooper	.75	2.00
❑ 19 Pat Cummings	.75	2.00
❑ 20 Terry Cummings RC	1.25	3.00
❑ 21 Adrian Dantley	1.00	2.50
❑ 22 Brad Davis RC	.75	2.00
❑ 23 Walter Davis	.75	2.00
❑ 24 Darryl Dawkins	1.00	2.50
❑ 25 Larry Drew	.75	2.00
❑ 26 Clyde Drexler RC	10.00	25.00
❑ 27 Joe Dumars RC	6.00	15.00
❑ 28 Mark Eaton RC	.75	2.00
❑ 29 James Edwards	.75	2.00
❑ 30 Alex English	1.00	2.50
❑ 31 Julius Erving	6.00	15.00
❑ 32 Patrick Ewing RC	15.00	40.00
❑ 33 Vern Fleming RC	.75	2.00
❑ 34 Sleepy Floyd RC	.75	2.00
❑ 35 World B. Free	.75	2.00
❑ 36 George Gervin	1.50	4.00
❑ 37 Artis Gilmore	1.00	2.50
❑ 38 Mike Gminski	.75	2.00
❑ 39 Rickey Green	.75	2.00
❑ 40 Sidney Green	.75	2.00
❑ 41 David Greenwood	.75	2.00
❑ 42 Darrell Griffith	.75	2.00
❑ 43 Bill Hanzlik	.75	2.00
❑ 44 Derek Harper RC	2.50	6.00
❑ 45 Gerald Henderson	.75	2.00
❑ 46 Roy Hinson	.75	2.00
❑ 47 Craig Hodges RC	.75	2.00
❑ 48 Phil Hubbard	.75	2.00
❑ 49 Jay Humphries RC	.75	2.00
❑ 50 Dennis Johnson	.75	2.00
❑ 51 Eddie Johnson RC	1.25	3.00
❑ 52 Frank Johnson RC	.75	2.00
❑ 53 Magic Johnson	8.00	20.00
❑ 54 Marques Johnson	.75	2.00
❑ 55 Steve Johnson UER	.75	2.00
❑ 56 Vinnie Johnson	.75	2.00
❑ 57 Michael Jordan RC	300.00	600.00
❑ 58 Clark Kellogg RC	.75	2.00
❑ 59 Albert King	.75	2.00
❑ 60 Bernard King	1.00	2.50
❑ 61 Bill Laimbeer	1.00	2.50
❑ 62 Allen Leavell	.75	2.00
❑ 63 Fat Lever RC	.75	2.00
❑ 64 Alton Lister	.75	2.00
❑ 65 Lewis Lloyd	.75	2.00
❑ 66 Maurice Lucas	.75	2.00
❑ 67 Jeff Malone RC	.75	2.00
❑ 68 Karl Malone RC	15.00	40.00
❑ 69 Moses Malone	1.25	3.00
❑ 70 Cedric Maxwell	.75	2.00
❑ 71 Rodney McCray RC	.75	2.00
❑ 72 Xavier McDaniel RC	1.00	2.50
❑ 73 Kevin McHale	1.25	3.00
❑ 74 Mike Mitchell	.75	2.00
❑ 75 Sidney Moncrief	1.00	2.50
❑ 76 Johnny Moore	.75	2.00
❑ 77 Chris Mullin RC	10.00	25.00
❑ 78 Larry Nance RC	1.50	4.00
❑ 79 Calvin Natt	.75	2.00
❑ 80 Norm Nixon	.75	2.00
❑ 81 Charles Oakley RC	2.50	6.00
❑ 82 Hakeem Olajuwon RC	12.50	30.00
❑ 83 Louis Orr	.75	2.00
❑ 84 Robert Parish	1.25	3.00
❑ 85 Jim Paxson	.75	2.00
❑ 86 Sam Perkins RC	2.50	6.00
❑ 87 Ricky Pierce RC	1.00	2.50
❑ 88 Paul Pressey RC	.75	2.00
❑ 89 Kurt Rambis RC	.75	2.00
❑ 90 Robert Reid	.75	2.00
❑ 91 Doc Rivers RC	2.50	6.00
❑ 92 Alvin Robertson RC	.75	2.00
❑ 93 Cliff Robinson	.75	2.00
❑ 94 Tree Rollins	.75	2.00
❑ 95 Dan Roundfield	.75	2.00
❑ 96 Jeff Ruland	.75	2.00
❑ 97 Ralph Sampson RC	1.00	2.50
❑ 98 Danny Schayes RC	.75	2.00
❑ 99 Byron Scott RC	1.50	4.00
❑ 100 Purvis Short	.75	2.00
❑ 101 Jerry Sichting	.75	2.00
❑ 102 Jack Sikma	.75	2.00
❑ 103 Derek Smith	.75	2.00
❑ 104 Larry Smith	.75	2.00
❑ 105 Rory Sparrow	.75	2.00
❑ 106 Steve Stipanovich	.75	2.00
❑ 107 Terry Teagle	.75	2.00
❑ 108 Reggie Theus	1.00	2.50
❑ 109 Isiah Thomas RC	10.00	25.00
❑ 110 LaSalle Thompson RC	.75	2.00
❑ 111 Mychal Thompson	.75	2.00
❑ 112 Sedale Threatt RC	.75	2.00
❑ 113 Wayman Tisdale RC	1.00	2.50
❑ 114 Andrew Toney	.75	2.00
❑ 115 Kelly Tripucka RC	.75	2.00
❑ 116 Mel Turpin	.75	2.00
❑ 117 Kiki Vandeweghe RC	1.00	2.50
❑ 118 Jay Vincent	.75	2.00
❑ 119 Bill Walton	1.50	4.00
❑ 120 Spud Webb RC	2.50	6.00
❑ 121 Dominique Wilkins RC	12.50	30.00
❑ 122 Gerald Wilkins RC	1.00	2.50
❑ 123 Buck Williams RC	1.50	4.00
❑ 124 Gus Williams	.75	2.00
❑ 125 Herb Williams RC	.75	2.00
❑ 126 Kevin Willis RC	2.50	6.00
❑ 127 Randy Wittman	.75	2.00
❑ 128 Al Wood	.75	2.00
❑ 129 Mike Woodson	.75	2.00
❑ 130 Orlando Woolridge RC	.75	2.00
❑ 131 James Worthy RC	8.00	20.00
❑ 132 Checklist 1-132	8.00	20.00

1987-88 Fleer

❑ COMPLETE w/Stickers (143)	175.00	300.00
❑ COMPLETE SET (132)	100.00	200.00
❑ 1 Kareem Abdul-Jabbar !	3.00	8.00
❑ 2 Alvan Adams	.60	1.50
❑ 3 Mark Aguirre	.75	2.00
❑ 4 Danny Ainge	.75	2.00
❑ 5 John Bagley	.60	1.50
❑ 6 Thurl Bailey UER	.60	1.50
❑ 7 Greg Ballard	.60	1.50
❑ 8 Gene Banks	.60	1.50
❑ 9 Charles Barkley	6.00	15.00
❑ 10 Benoit Benjamin	.60	1.50
❑ 11 Larry Bird !	8.00	20.00
❑ 12 Rolando Blackman	.60	1.50
❑ 13 Manute Bol	.60	1.50
❑ 14 Tony Brown	.60	1.50
❑ 15 Michael Cage RC	.60	1.50
❑ 16 Joe Barry Carroll	.60	1.50
❑ 17 Bill Cartwright	.75	2.00
❑ 18 Terry Catledge RC	.60	1.50
❑ 19 Tom Chambers	.60	1.50
❑ 20 Maurice Cheeks	.60	1.50
❑ 21 Michael Cooper	.75	2.00
❑ 22 Dave Corzine	.60	1.50
❑ 23 Terry Cummings	.75	2.00
❑ 24 Adrian Dantley	.60	1.50
❑ 25 Brad Daugherty RC	1.00	2.50
❑ 26 Walter Davis	.60	1.50
❑ 27 Johnny Dawkins RC	.60	1.50
❑ 28 James Donaldson	.60	1.50
❑ 29 Larry Drew	.60	1.50
❑ 30 Clyde Drexler	5.00	12.00
❑ 31 Joe Dumars	1.50	4.00
❑ 32 Mark Eaton	.60	1.50
❑ 33 Dale Ellis RC	1.00	2.50
❑ 34 Alex English	.75	2.00
❑ 35 Julius Erving	5.00	12.00
❑ 36 Mike Evans	.60	1.50
❑ 37 Patrick Ewing	4.00	10.00
❑ 38 Vern Fleming	.60	1.50
❑ 39 Sleepy Floyd	.60	1.50
❑ 40 Artis Gilmore	.75	2.00
❑ 41 Mike Gminski UER	.60	1.50
❑ 42 A.C.Green RC	2.50	6.00
❑ 43 Rickey Green	.60	1.50
❑ 44 Sidney Green	.60	1.50
❑ 45 David Greenwood	.60	1.50
❑ 46 Darrell Griffith	.60	1.50
❑ 47 Bill Hanzlik	.60	1.50
❑ 48 Derek Harper	.75	2.00
❑ 49 Ron Harper RC	2.50	6.00
❑ 50 Gerald Henderson	.60	1.50
❑ 51 Roy Hinson	.60	1.50
❑ 52 Craig Hodges	.60	1.50
❑ 53 Phil Hubbard	.60	1.50
❑ 54 Dennis Johnson	.60	1.50
❑ 55 Eddie Johnson	.75	2.00
❑ 56 Magic Johnson	12.50	25.00
❑ 57 Steve Johnson	.60	1.50
❑ 58 Vinnie Johnson	.60	1.50
❑ 59 Michael Jordan !	25.00	60.00
❑ 60 Jerome Kersey RC	.60	1.50
❑ 61 Bill Laimbeer	.75	2.00
❑ 62 Lafayette Lever UER	.60	1.50
❑ 63 Cliff Levingston RC	.60	1.50
❑ 64 Alton Lister	.60	1.50
❑ 65 John Long	.60	1.50
❑ 66 John Lucas	.60	1.50
❑ 67 Jeff Malone	.60	1.50
❑ 68 Karl Malone	6.00	15.00
❑ 69 Moses Malone	1.00	2.50
❑ 70 Cedric Maxwell	.60	1.50
❑ 71 Tim McCormick	.60	1.50
❑ 72 Rodney McCray	.60	1.50
❑ 73 Xavier McDaniel	.60	1.50
❑ 74 Kevin McHale	1.00	2.50
❑ 75 Nate McMillan RC	1.00	2.50
❑ 76 Sidney Moncrief	.60	1.50
❑ 77 Chris Mullin	1.50	4.00
❑ 78 Larry Nance	.75	2.00
❑ 79 Charles Oakley	1.00	2.50
❑ 80 Hakeem Olajuwon	6.00	15.00
❑ 81 Robert Parish	1.00	2.50
❑ 82 Jim Paxson	.60	1.50
❑ 83 John Paxson RC	1.00	2.50
❑ 84 Sam Perkins	1.00	2.50
❑ 85 Chuck Person RC	1.00	2.50
❑ 86 Jim Petersen	.60	1.50
❑ 87 Ricky Pierce	.60	1.50
❑ 88 Ed Pinckney RC	.60	1.50
❑ 89 Terry Porter RC	1.00	2.50
❑ 90 Paul Pressey	.60	1.50
❑ 91 Robert Reid	.60	1.50
❑ 92 Doc Rivers	1.00	2.50
❑ 93 Alvin Robertson	.60	1.50
❑ 94 Tree Rollins	.60	1.50
❑ 95 Ralph Sampson	.60	1.50
❑ 96 Mike Sanders	.60	1.50
❑ 97 Detlef Schrempf RC	4.00	10.00
❑ 98 Byron Scott	.75	2.00
❑ 99 Jerry Sichting	.60	1.50
❑ 100 Jack Sikma	.60	1.50
❑ 101 Larry Smith	.60	1.50
❑ 102 Rory Sparrow	.60	1.50
❑ 103 Steve Stipanovich	.60	1.50
❑ 104 Jon Sundvold	.60	1.50
❑ 105 Reggie Theus	.75	2.00
❑ 106 Isiah Thomas	2.50	6.00
❑ 107 LaSalle Thompson	.60	1.50
❑ 108 Mychal Thompson	.60	1.50
❑ 109 Otis Thorpe RC	2.00	5.00
❑ 110 Sedale Threatt	.60	1.50
❑ 111 Wayman Tisdale	.60	1.50
❑ 112 Kelly Tripucka	.60	1.50
❑ 113 Trent Tucker RC	.60	1.50
❑ 114 Terry Tyler	.60	1.50
❑ 115 Darnell Valentine	.60	1.50
❑ 116 Kiki Vandeweghe	.60	1.50
❑ 117 Darrell Walker RC	.60	1.50

❑ 118 Dominique Wilkins	1.50	4.00
❑ 119 Gerald Wilkins	.60	1.50
❑ 120 Buck Williams	.75	2.00
❑ 121 Herb Williams	.60	1.50
❑ 122 John Williams RC	.60	1.50
❑ 123 Hot Rod Williams RC	.75	2.00
❑ 124 Kevin Willis	.75	2.00
❑ 125 David Wingate RC	.60	1.50
❑ 126 Randy Wittman	.60	1.50
❑ 127 Leon Wood	.60	1.50
❑ 128 Mike Woodson	.60	1.50
❑ 129 Orlando Woolridge	.60	1.50
❑ 130 James Worthy	1.50	4.00
❑ 131 Danny Young RC	.60	1.50
❑ 132 Checklist 1-132	4.00	10.00

1988-89 Fleer

❑ COMPLETE w/Stickers (143)	100.00	200.00
❑ COMPLETE SET (132)	75.00	150.00
❑ 1 Antoine Carr RC	.30	.75
❑ 2 Cliff Levingston	.20	.50
❑ 3 Doc Rivers	.30	.75
❑ 4 Spud Webb	.30	.75
❑ 5 Dominique Wilkins	.60	1.50
❑ 6 Kevin Willis	.30	.75
❑ 7 Randy Wittman	.20	.50
❑ 8 Danny Ainge	.30	.75
❑ 9 Larry Bird	4.00	10.00
❑ 10 Dennis Johnson	.20	.50
❑ 11 Kevin McHale	.60	1.50
❑ 12 Robert Parish	.60	1.50
❑ 13 Muggsy Bogues RC	.75	2.00
❑ 14 Dell Curry RC	.60	1.50
❑ 15 Dave Corzine	.20	.50
❑ 16 Horace Grant RC	2.00	5.00
❑ 17 Michael Jordan	12.50	30.00
❑ 18 Charles Oakley	.30	.75
❑ 19 John Paxson	.30	.75
❑ 20 Scottie Pippen UER RC	10.00	25.00
❑ 21 Brad Sellers RC	.20	.50
❑ 22 Brad Daugherty	.20	.50
❑ 23 Ron Harper	.30	.75
❑ 24 Larry Nance	.20	.50
❑ 25 Mark Price RC	.75	2.00
❑ 26 Hot Rod Williams	.20	.50
❑ 27 Mark Aguirre	.20	.50
❑ 28 Rolando Blackman	.20	.50
❑ 29 James Donaldson	.20	.50
❑ 30 Derek Harper	.30	.75
❑ 31 Sam Perkins	.30	.75
❑ 32 Roy Tarpley RC	.20	.50
❑ 33 Michael Adams RC	.20	.50
❑ 34 Alex English	.30	.75
❑ 35 Lafayette Lever	.20	.50
❑ 36 Blair Rasmussen RC	.20	.50
❑ 37 Danny Schayes	.20	.50
❑ 38 Jay Vincent	.20	.50
❑ 39 Adrian Dantley	.20	.50
❑ 40 Joe Dumars	.60	1.50
❑ 41 Vinnie Johnson	.20	.50
❑ 42 Bill Laimbeer	.30	.75
❑ 43 Dennis Rodman RC	5.00	12.00
❑ 44 John Salley RC	.30	.75
❑ 45 Isiah Thomas	.60	1.50
❑ 46 Winston Garland RC	.20	.50
❑ 47 Rod Higgins	.20	.50
❑ 48 Chris Mullin	.60	1.50
❑ 49 Ralph Sampson	.20	.50
❑ 50 Joe Barry Carroll	.20	.50
❑ 51 Sleepy Floyd	.20	.50
❑ 52 Rodney McCray	.20	.50
❑ 53 Hakeem Olajuwon	2.00	5.00
❑ 54 Purvis Short	.20	.50
❑ 55 Vern Fleming	.20	.50
❑ 56 John Long	.20	.50
❑ 57 Reggie Miller RC	8.00	20.00
❑ 58 Chuck Person	.30	.75
❑ 59 Steve Stipanovich	.20	.50
❑ 60 Wayman Tisdale	.20	.50
❑ 61 Benoit Benjamin	.20	.50
❑ 62 Michael Cage	.20	.50
❑ 63 Mike Woodson	.20	.50
❑ 64 Kareem Abdul-Jabbar	1.50	4.00
❑ 65 Michael Cooper	.20	.50
❑ 66 A.C.Green	.30	.75
❑ 67 Magic Johnson	4.00	10.00
❑ 68 Byron Scott	.30	.75
❑ 69 Mychal Thompson	.20	.50
❑ 70 James Worthy	.60	1.50
❑ 71 Duane Washington	.20	.50
❑ 72 Kevin Williams	.20	.50
❑ 73 Randy Breuer RC	.20	.50
❑ 74 Terry Cummings	.30	.75
❑ 75 Paul Pressey	.20	.50
❑ 76 Jack Sikma	.20	.50
❑ 77 John Bagley	.20	.50
❑ 78 Roy Hinson	.20	.50
❑ 79 Buck Williams	.30	.75
❑ 80 Patrick Ewing	1.25	3.00
❑ 81 Sidney Green	.20	.50
❑ 82 Mark Jackson RC	1.00	2.50
❑ 83 Kenny Walker RC	.20	.50
❑ 84 Gerald Wilkins	.20	.50
❑ 85 Charles Barkley	2.00	5.00
❑ 86 Maurice Cheeks	.20	.50
❑ 87 Mike Gminski	.20	.50
❑ 88 Cliff Robinson	.20	.50
❑ 89 Armon Gilliam RC	.60	1.50
❑ 90 Eddie Johnson	.20	.50
❑ 91 Mark West RC	.20	.50
❑ 92 Clyde Drexler	1.25	3.00
❑ 93 Kevin Duckworth RC	.20	.50
❑ 94 Steve Johnson	.20	.50
❑ 95 Jerome Kersey	.20	.50
❑ 96 Terry Porter	.20	.50
❑ 97 Joe Kleine RC	.20	.50
❑ 98 Reggie Theus	.30	.75
❑ 99 Otis Thorpe	.30	.75
❑ 100 Kenny Smith RC	.60	1.50
❑ 101 Greg Anderson RC	.20	.50
❑ 102 Walter Berry RC	.20	.50
❑ 103 Frank Brickowski RC	.20	.50
❑ 104 Johnny Dawkins	.20	.50
❑ 105 Alvin Robertson	.20	.50
❑ 106 Tom Chambers	.20	.50
❑ 107 Dale Ellis	.30	.75
❑ 108 Xavier McDaniel	.20	.50
❑ 109 Derrick McKey RC	.60	1.50
❑ 110 Nate McMillan UER	.20	.50
❑ 111 Thurl Bailey	.20	.50
❑ 112 Mark Eaton	.20	.50
❑ 113 Bobby Hansen RC	.20	.50
❑ 114 Karl Malone	2.00	5.00
❑ 115 John Stockton RC	8.00	20.00
❑ 116 Bernard King	.20	.50
❑ 117 Jeff Malone	.20	.50
❑ 118 Moses Malone	.60	1.50
❑ 119 John Williams	.20	.50
❑ 120 Michael Jordan AS	6.00	15.00
❑ 121 Mark Jackson AS	.60	1.50
❑ 122 Byron Scott AS	.20	.50
❑ 123 Magic Johnson AS	1.50	4.00
❑ 124 Larry Bird AS	2.00	5.00
❑ 125 Dominique Wilkins AS	.30	.75
❑ 126 Hakeem Olajuwon AS	.75	2.00
❑ 127 John Stockton AS	2.00	5.00
❑ 128 Alvin Robertson AS	.20	.50
❑ 129 Charles Barkley AS	.75	2.00
❑ 130 Patrick Ewing AS	.60	1.50
❑ 131 Mark Eaton AS	.20	.50
❑ 132 Checklist 1-132	.20	.50

1989-90 Fleer

❑ COMPLETE w/Stickers (179)	20.00	50.00
❑ COMPLETE SET (168)	15.00	30.00
❑ 1 John Battle RC	.05	.15
❑ 2 Jon Koncak RC	.05	.15
❑ 3 Cliff Levingston	.05	.15
❑ 4 Moses Malone	.20	.50
❑ 5 Doc Rivers	.08	.25
❑ 6 Spud Webb	.08	.25
❑ 7 Dominique Wilkins	.20	.50
❑ 8 Larry Bird	1.25	3.00
❑ 9 Dennis Johnson	.05	.15
❑ 10 Reggie Lewis RC	.30	.75
❑ 11 Kevin McHale	.20	.50

❑ 12 Robert Parish	.08	.25
❑ 13 Ed Pinckney	.05	.15
❑ 14 Brian Shaw RC	.20	.50
❑ 15 Rex Chapman RC	.30	.75
❑ 16 Kurt Rambis	.05	.15
❑ 17 Robert Reid	.05	.15
❑ 18 Kelly Tripucka	.05	.15
❑ 19 Bill Cartwright UER	.05	.15
❑ 20 Horace Grant	.08	.25
❑ 21 Michael Jordan	6.00	15.00
❑ 22 John Paxson	.05	.15
❑ 23 Scottie Pippen	2.00	5.00
❑ 24 Brad Sellers	.05	.15
❑ 25 Brad Daugherty	.05	.15
❑ 26 Craig Ehlo RC	.05	.15
❑ 27 Ron Harper	.08	.25
❑ 28 Larry Nance	.08	.25
❑ 29 Mark Price	.08	.25
❑ 30 Mike Sanders	.05	.15
❑ 31A Hot Rod Williams ERR		
❑ 31B Hot Rod Williams COR	.05	.15
❑ 32 Rolando Blackman	.05	.15
❑ 33 Adrian Dantley	.05	.15
❑ 34 James Donaldson	.05	.15
❑ 35 Derek Harper	.08	.25
❑ 36 Sam Perkins	.08	.25
❑ 37 Herb Williams	.05	.15
❑ 38 Michael Adams	.05	.15
❑ 39 Walter Davis	.05	.15
❑ 40 Alex English	.05	.15
❑ 41 Lafayette Lever	.05	.15
❑ 42 Blair Rasmussen	.05	.15
❑ 43 Danny Schayes	.05	.15
❑ 44 Mark Aguirre	.05	.15
❑ 45 Joe Dumars	.20	.50
❑ 46 James Edwards	.05	.15
❑ 47 Vinnie Johnson	.05	.15
❑ 48 Bill Laimbeer	.08	.25
❑ 49 Dennis Rodman	1.25	3.00
❑ 50 Isiah Thomas	.20	.50
❑ 51 John Salley	.05	.15
❑ 52 Manute Bol	.05	.15
❑ 53 Winston Garland	.05	.15
❑ 54 Rod Higgins	.05	.15
❑ 55 Chris Mullin	.20	.50
❑ 56 Mitch Richmond RC	1.50	4.00
❑ 57 Terry Teagle	.05	.15
❑ 58 Derrick Chievous UER	.05	.15
❑ 59 Sleepy Floyd	.05	.15
❑ 60 Tim McCormick	.05	.15
❑ 61 Hakeem Olajuwon	.50	1.25
❑ 62 Otis Thorpe	.08	.25
❑ 63 Mike Woodson	.05	.15
❑ 64 Vern Fleming	.05	.15
❑ 65 Reggie Miller	.75	2.00
❑ 66 Chuck Person	.08	.25
❑ 67 Detlef Schrempf	.08	.25
❑ 68 Rik Smits RC	.40	1.00
❑ 69 Benoit Benjamin	.05	.15
❑ 70 Gary Grant RC	.05	.15
❑ 71 Danny Manning RC	.40	1.00
❑ 72 Ken Norman RC	.05	.15
❑ 73 Charles Smith RC	.20	.50
❑ 74 Reggie Williams RC	.05	.15
❑ 75 Michael Cooper	.05	.15
❑ 76 A.C.Green	.08	.25
❑ 77 Magic Johnson	1.00	2.50
❑ 78 Byron Scott	.08	.25
❑ 79 Mychal Thompson	.05	.15
❑ 80 James Worthy	.20	.50
❑ 81 Kevin Edwards RC	.05	.15
❑ 82 Grant Long RC	.05	.15
❑ 83 Rony Seikaly RC	.20	.50
❑ 84 Rory Sparrow	.05	.15
❑ 85 Greg Anderson UER	.05	.15

❑ 86 Jay Humphries	.05	.15
❑ 87 Larry Krystkowiak RC	.05	.15
❑ 88 Ricky Pierce	.05	.15
❑ 89 Paul Pressey	.05	.15
❑ 90 Alvin Robertson	.05	.15
❑ 91 Jack Sikma	.05	.15
❑ 92 Steve Johnson	.05	.15
❑ 93 Rick Mahorn	.05	.15
❑ 94 David Rivers	.05	.15
❑ 95 Joe Barry Carroll	.05	.15
❑ 96 Lester Conner UER	.05	.15
❑ 97 Roy Hinson	.05	.15
❑ 98 Mike McGee	.05	.15
❑ 99 Chris Morris RC	.08	.25
❑ 100 Patrick Ewing	.30	.75
❑ 101 Mark Jackson	.08	.25
❑ 102 Johnny Newman RC	.05	.15
❑ 103 Charles Oakley	.08	.25
❑ 104 Rod Strickland RC	1.00	2.50
❑ 105 Trent Tucker	.05	.15
❑ 106 Kiki Vandeweghe	.05	.15
❑ 107A Gerald Wilkins	.05	.15
❑ 107B Gerald Wilkins	.05	.15
❑ 108 Terry Catledge	.05	.15
❑ 109 Dave Corzine	.05	.15
❑ 110 Scott Skiles RC	.08	.25
❑ 111 Reggie Theus	.08	.25
❑ 112 Ron Anderson RC	.05	.15
❑ 113 Charles Barkley	.50	1.25
❑ 114 Scott Brooks RC	.05	.15
❑ 115 Maurice Cheeks	.05	.15
❑ 116 Mike Gminski	.05	.15
❑ 117 Hersey Hawkins UER RC	.40	1.00
❑ 118 Christian Welp	.05	.15
❑ 119 Tom Chambers	.05	.15
❑ 120 Armon Gilliam	.05	.15
❑ 121 Jeff Hornacek RC	.40	1.00
❑ 122 Eddie Johnson	.08	.25
❑ 123 Kevin Johnson RC	.60	1.50
❑ 124 Dan Majerle RC	.40	1.00
❑ 125 Mark West	.05	.15
❑ 126 Richard Anderson	.05	.15
❑ 127 Mark Bryant RC	.05	.15
❑ 128 Clyde Drexler	.30	.75
❑ 129 Kevin Duckworth	.05	.15
❑ 130 Jerome Kersey	.05	.15
❑ 131 Terry Porter	.05	.15
❑ 132 Buck Williams	.08	.25
❑ 133 Danny Ainge	.08	.25
❑ 134 Ricky Berry	.05	.15
❑ 135 Rodney McCray	.05	.15
❑ 136 Jim Petersen	.05	.15
❑ 137 Harold Pressley	.05	.15
❑ 138 Kenny Smith	.05	.15
❑ 139 Wayman Tisdale	.05	.15
❑ 140 Willie Anderson RC	.05	.15
❑ 141 Frank Brickowski	.05	.15
❑ 142 Terry Cummings	.08	.25
❑ 143 Johnny Dawkins	.05	.15
❑ 144 Vernon Maxwell RC	.30	.75
❑ 145 Michael Cage	.05	.15
❑ 146 Dale Ellis	.08	.25
❑ 147 Alton Lister	.05	.15
❑ 148 Xavier McDaniel	.05	.15
❑ 149 Derrick McKey	.05	.15
❑ 150 Nate McMillan	.08	.25
❑ 151 Thurl Bailey	.05	.15
❑ 152 Mark Eaton	.05	.15
❑ 153 Darrell Griffith	.05	.15
❑ 154 Eric Leckner	.05	.15
❑ 155 Karl Malone	.50	1.25
❑ 156 John Stockton	.75	2.00
❑ 157 Mark Alarie	.05	.15
❑ 158 Ledell Eackles RC	.05	.15
❑ 159 Bernard King	.05	.15
❑ 160 Jeff Malone	.05	.15
❑ 161 Darrell Walker	.05	.15
❑ 162A John Williams ERR		
❑ 162B John Williams COR	.05	.15
❑ 163 Malone/Stockton/Eaton AS	.20	.50
❑ 164 H.Olajuwon/C.Drexler AS	.20	.50
❑ 165 ASG:Wilkins/M.Malone	.20	.50
❑ 166 ASG:Daugh/Price/Nance	.05	.15
❑ 167 ASG:Ewing/M.Jackson	.20	.50
❑ 168 Checklist 1-168	.05	.15

1990-91 Fleer

❑ COMPLETE SET (198)	3.00	6.00
❑ 1 John Battle UER	.02	.10
❑ 2 Cliff Levingston	.02	.10

❑ 3 Moses Malone	.05	.15
❑ 4 Kenny Smith	.02	.10
❑ 5 Spud Webb	.02	.10
❑ 6 Dominique Wilkins	.05	.15
❑ 7 Kevin Willis	.02	.10
❑ 8 Larry Bird	.25	.60
❑ 9 Dennis Johnson	.02	.10
❑ 10 Joe Kleine	.02	.10
❑ 11 Reggie Lewis	.02	.10
❑ 12 Kevin McHale	.02	.10
❑ 13 Robert Parish	.02	.10
❑ 14 Jim Paxson	.02	.10
❑ 15 Ed Pinckney	.02	.10
❑ 16 Muggsy Bogues	.02	.10
❑ 17 Rex Chapman	.05	.15
❑ 18 Dell Curry	.02	.10
❑ 19 Armon Gilliam	.02	.10
❑ 20 J.R.Reid RC	.02	.10
❑ 21 Kelly Tripucka	.02	.10
❑ 22 B.J.Armstrong RC	.02	.10
❑ 23A Bill Cartwright ERR		
❑ 23B Bill Cartwright COR	.02	.10
❑ 24 Horace Grant	.02	.10
❑ 25 Craig Hodges	.02	.10
❑ 26 Michael Jordan	1.50	4.00
❑ 27 Stacey King RC	.02	.10
❑ 28 John Paxson	.02	.10
❑ 29 Will Perdue	.02	.10
❑ 30 Scottie Pippen	.25	.60
❑ 31 Brad Daugherty	.02	.10
❑ 32 Craig Ehlo	.02	.10
❑ 33 Danny Ferry RC	.02	.10
❑ 34 Steve Kerr	.05	.15
❑ 35 Larry Nance	.02	.10
❑ 36 Mark Price	.02	.10
❑ 37 Hot Rod Williams	.02	.10
❑ 38 Rolando Blackman	.02	.10
❑ 39A Adrian Dantley ERR		
❑ 39B Adrian Dantley COR	.02	.10
❑ 40 Brad Davis	.02	.10
❑ 41 James Donaldson UER	.02	.10
❑ 42 Derek Harper	.02	.10
❑ 43 Sam Perkins UER	.02	.10
❑ 44 Bill Wennington	.02	.10
❑ 45 Herb Williams	.02	.10
❑ 46 Michael Adams	.02	.10
❑ 47 Walter Davis	.02	.10
❑ 48 Alex English UER	.02	.10
❑ 49 Bill Hanzlik	.02	.10
❑ 50 Lafayette Lever UER	.02	.10
❑ 51 Todd Lichti RC	.02	.10
❑ 52 Blair Rasmussen	.02	.10
❑ 53 Danny Schayes	.02	.10
❑ 54 Mark Aguirre	.02	.10
❑ 55 Joe Dumars	.05	.15
❑ 56 James Edwards	.02	.10
❑ 57 Vinnie Johnson	.02	.10
❑ 58 Bill Laimbeer	.02	.10
❑ 59 Dennis Rodman	.15	.40
❑ 60 John Salley	.02	.10
❑ 61 Isiah Thomas	.05	.15
❑ 62 Manute Bol	.02	.10
❑ 63 Tim Hardaway RC	.40	1.00
❑ 64 Rod Higgins	.02	.10
❑ 65 Sarun.Marciulionis RC	.02	.10
❑ 66 Chris Mullin	.05	.15
❑ 67 Mitch Richmond	.07	.20
❑ 68 Terry Teagle	.02	.10
❑ 69 Anthony Bowie RC	.02	.10
❑ 70 Sleepy Floyd	.02	.10
❑ 71 Buck Johnson	.02	.10
❑ 72 Vernon Maxwell	.02	.10
❑ 73 Hakeem Olajuwon	.08	.25
❑ 74 Otis Thorpe	.02	.10
❑ 75 Mitchell Wiggins	.02	.10
❑ 76 Vern Fleming	.02	.10
❑ 77 George McCloud RC	.05	.15
❑ 78 Reggie Miller	.07	.20
❑ 79 Chuck Person	.02	.10
❑ 80 Mike Sanders	.02	.10
❑ 81 Detlef Schrempf	.02	.10
❑ 82 Rik Smits	.05	.15
❑ 83 LaSalle Thompson	.02	.10
❑ 84 Benoit Benjamin	.02	.10
❑ 85 Winston Garland	.02	.10
❑ 86 Ron Harper	.02	.10
❑ 87 Danny Manning	.02	.10
❑ 88 Ken Norman	.02	.10
❑ 89 Charles Smith	.02	.10
❑ 90 Michael Cooper	.02	.10
❑ 91 Vlade Divac RC	.15	.40
❑ 92 A.C. Green	.02	.10
❑ 93 Magic Johnson	.20	.50
❑ 94 Byron Scott	.02	.10
❑ 95 Mychal Thompson UER	.02	.10
❑ 96 Orlando Woolridge	.02	.10
❑ 97 James Worthy	.05	.15
❑ 98 Sherman Douglas RC	.02	.10
❑ 99 Kevin Edwards	.02	.10
❑ 100 Grant Long	.02	.10
❑ 101 Glen Rice RC	.25	.60
❑ 102 Rony Seikaly Michael Jordan UER	.02	.10
❑ 103 Billy Thompson	.02	.10
❑ 104 Jeff Grayer RC	.02	.10
❑ 105 Jay Humphries	.02	.10
❑ 106 Ricky Pierce	.02	.10
❑ 107 Paul Pressey	.02	.10
❑ 108 Fred Roberts	.02	.10
❑ 109 Alvin Robertson	.02	.10
❑ 110 Jack Sikma	.02	.10
❑ 111 Randy Breuer	.02	.10
❑ 112 Tony Campbell	.02	.10
❑ 113 Tyrone Corbin	.02	.10
❑ 114 Sam Mitchell RC	.02	.10
❑ 115 Tod Murphy UER	.02	.10
❑ 116 Pooh Richardson RC	.02	.10
❑ 117 Mookie Blaylock RC	.08	.25
❑ 118 Sam Bowie	.02	.10
❑ 119 Lester Conner	.02	.10
❑ 120 Dennis Hopson	.02	.10
❑ 121 Chris Morris	.02	.10
❑ 122 Charles Shackleford	.02	.10
❑ 123 Purvis Short	.02	.10
❑ 124 Maurice Cheeks	.02	.10
❑ 125 Patrick Ewing	.05	.15
❑ 126 Mark Jackson	.02	.10
❑ 127A Johnny Newman ERR	.15	.40
❑ 127B Johnny Newman COR	.02	.10
❑ 128 Charles Oakley	.02	.10
❑ 129 Trent Tucker	.02	.10
❑ 130 Kenny Walker	.02	.10
❑ 131 Gerald Wilkins	.02	.10
❑ 132 Nick Anderson RC	.08	.25
❑ 133 Terry Catledge	.02	.10
❑ 134 Sidney Green	.02	.10
❑ 135 Otis Smith	.02	.10
❑ 136 Reggie Theus	.02	.10
❑ 137 Sam Vincent	.02	.10
❑ 138 Ron Anderson	.02	.10
❑ 139 Charles Barkley	.08	.25
❑ 140 Scott Brooks UER	.02	.10
❑ 141 Johnny Dawkins	.02	.10
❑ 142 Mike Gminski	.02	.10
❑ 143 Hersey Hawkins	.02	.10
❑ 144 Rick Mahorn	.02	.10
❑ 145 Derek Smith	.02	.10
❑ 146 Tom Chambers	.02	.10
❑ 147 Jeff Hornacek	.02	.10
❑ 148 Eddie Johnson	.02	.10
❑ 149 Kevin Johnson	.05	.15
❑ 150A Dan Majerle ERR 1988	.30	.75
❑ 150B Dan Majerle COR 1989	.05	.15
❑ 151 Tim Perry	.02	.10
❑ 152 Kurt Rambis	.02	.10
❑ 153 Mark West	.02	.10
❑ 154 Clyde Drexler	.05	.15
❑ 155 Kevin Duckworth	.02	.10
❑ 156 Byron Irvin	.02	.10
❑ 157 Jerome Kersey	.02	.10
❑ 158 Terry Porter	.02	.10
❑ 159 Clifford Robinson RC	.08	.25
❑ 160 Buck Williams	.02	.10
❑ 161 Danny Young	.02	.10

❑ 162 Danny Ainge	.02	.10
❑ 163 Antoine Carr	.02	.10
❑ 164 Pervis Ellison RC	.02	.10
❑ 165 Rodney McCray	.02	.10
❑ 166 Harold Pressley	.02	.10
❑ 167 Wayman Tisdale	.02	.10
❑ 168 Willie Anderson	.02	.10
❑ 169 Frank Brickowski	.02	.10
❑ 170 Terry Cummings	.02	.10
❑ 171 Sean Elliott RC	.10	.30
❑ 172 David Robinson	.20	.50
❑ 173 Rod Strickland	.05	.15
❑ 174 David Wingate	.02	.10
❑ 175 Dana Barros RC	.05	.15
❑ 176 Michael Cage UER	.02	.10
❑ 177 Dale Ellis	.02	.10
❑ 178 Shawn Kemp RC	.60	1.50
❑ 179 Xavier McDaniel	.02	.10
❑ 180 Derrick McKey	.02	.10
❑ 181 Nate McMillan	.02	.10
❑ 182 Thurl Bailey	.02	.10
❑ 183 Mike Brown	.02	.10
❑ 184 Mark Eaton	.02	.10
❑ 185 Blue Edwards RC	.02	.10
❑ 186 Bobby Hansen	.02	.10
❑ 187 Eric Leckner	.02	.10
❑ 188 Karl Malone	.08	.25
❑ 189 John Stockton	.07	.20
❑ 190 Mark Alarie	.02	.10
❑ 191 Ledell Eackles	.02	.10
❑ 192A Harvey Grant FFC Black	.30	.75
❑ 192B Harvey Grant FFC White	.02	.10
❑ 193 Tom Hammonds RC	.02	.10
❑ 194 Bernard King	.02	.10
❑ 195 Jeff Malone	.02	.10
❑ 196 Darrell Walker	.02	.10
❑ 197 Checklist 1-99	.02	.10
❑ 198 Checklist 100-198	.02	.10

1990-91 Fleer Update

❑ COMPLETE SET (100)	3.00	8.00
❑ U1 Jon Koncak	.01	.05
❑ U2 Tim McCormick	.01	.05
❑ U3 Doc Rivers	.05	.15
❑ U4 Rumeal Robinson RC	.01	.05
❑ U5 Trevor Wilson	.01	.05
❑ U6 Dee Brown RC	.10	.30
❑ U7 Dave Popson	.01	.05
❑ U8 Kevin Gamble FFC	.01	.05
❑ U9 Brian Shaw	.10	.30
❑ U10 Michael Smith	.01	.05
❑ U11 Kendall Gill RC	.25	.60
❑ U12 Johnny Newman	.01	.05
❑ U13 Steve Scheffler RC	.01	.05
❑ U14 Dennis Hopson	.01	.05
❑ U15 Cliff Levingston	.01	.05
❑ U16 Chucky Brown RC	.01	.05
❑ U17 John Morton	.01	.05
❑ U18 Gerald Paddio RC	.01	.05
❑ U19 Alex English	.01	.05
❑ U20 Fat Lever	.01	.05
❑ U21 Rodney McCray	.01	.05
❑ U22 Roy Tarpley	.01	.05
❑ U23 Randy White RC	.01	.05
❑ U24 Anthony Cook RC	.01	.05
❑ U25 Chris Jackson RC	.10	.30
❑ U26 Marcus Liberty RC	.01	.05
❑ U27 Orlando Woolridge	.01	.05
❑ U28 William Bedford RC	.01	.05
❑ U29 Lance Blanks RC	.01	.05
❑ U30 Scott Hastings	.01	.05
❑ U31 Tyrone Hill RC	.05	.15
❑ U32 Les Jepsen	.01	.05
❑ U33 Steve Johnson	.01	.05
❑ U34 Kevin Pritchard	.01	.05
❑ U35 Dave Jamerson RC	.01	.05
❑ U36 Kenny Smith	.01	.05
❑ U37 Greg Dreiling RC	.01	.05
❑ U38 Kenny Williams RC	.01	.05
❑ U39 Micheal Williams FFC UER	.05	.15
❑ U40 Gary Grant	.01	.05
❑ U41 Bo Kimble RC	.01	.05
❑ U42 Loy Vaught RC	.20	.50
❑ U43 Elden Campbell RC	.25	.60
❑ U44 Sam Perkins	.05	.15
❑ U45 Tony Smith RC	.01	.05
❑ U46 Terry Teagle	.01	.05
❑ U47 Willie Burton RC	.01	.05
❑ U48 Bimbo Coles RC	.10	.30
❑ U49 Terry Davis RC	.01	.05
❑ U50 Alec Kessler RC	.01	.05
❑ U51 Greg Anderson	.01	.05
❑ U52 Frank Brickowski	.01	.05
❑ U53 Steve Henson RC	.01	.05
❑ U54 Brad Lohaus	.01	.05
❑ U55 Danny Schayes	.01	.05
❑ U56 Gerald Glass RC	.01	.05
❑ U57 Felton Spencer RC	.05	.15
❑ U58 Doug West RC	.05	.15
❑ U59 Jud Buechler RC	.05	.15
❑ U60 Derrick Coleman RC	.25	.60
❑ U61 Tate George RC	.01	.05
❑ U62 Reggie Theus	.05	.15
❑ U63 Greg Grant RC	.01	.05
❑ U64 Jerrod Mustaf RC	.01	.05
❑ U65 Eddie Lee Wilkins RC	.01	.05
❑ U66 Michael Ansley	.01	.05
❑ U67 Jerry Reynolds	.01	.05
❑ U68 Dennis Scott RC	.15	.40
❑ U69 Manute Bol	.01	.05
❑ U70 Armon Gilliam	.01	.05
❑ U71 Brian Oliver	.01	.05
❑ U72 Kenny Payne RC	.01	.05
❑ U73 Jayson Williams RC	.40	1.00
❑ U74 Kenny Battle RC	.01	.05
❑ U75 Cedric Ceballos RC	.20	.50
❑ U76 Negele Knight RC	.01	.05
❑ U77 Xavier McDaniel	.01	.05
❑ U78 Alaa Abdelnaby RC	.01	.05
❑ U79 Danny Ainge	.05	.15
❑ U80 Mark Bryant	.01	.05
❑ U81 Drazen Petrovic RC	.05	.15
❑ U82 Anthony Bonner RC	.01	.05
❑ U83 Duane Causwell RC	.01	.05
❑ U84 Bobby Hansen	.01	.05
❑ U85 Eric Leckner	.01	.05
❑ U86 Travis Mays RC	.01	.05
❑ U87 Lionel Simmons RC	.05	.15
❑ U88 Sidney Green	.01	.05
❑ U89 Tony Massenburg	.01	.05
❑ U90 Paul Pressey	.01	.05
❑ U91 Dwayne Schintzius RC	.01	.05
❑ U92 Gary Payton RC	2.50	6.00
❑ U93 Olden Polynice	.01	.05
❑ U94 Jeff Malone	.01	.05
❑ U95 Walter Palmer	.01	.05
❑ U96 Delaney Rudd	.01	.05
❑ U97 Pervis Ellison	.05	.15
❑ U98 A.J.English RC	.01	.05
❑ U99 Greg Foster RC	.05	.15
❑ U100 Checklist 1-100	.01	.05

1991-92 Fleer

❑ COMPLETE SET (400)	5.00	10.00
❑ COMPLETE SERIES 1 (240)	2.50	5.00
❑ COMPLETE SERIES 2 (160)	2.50	5.00
❑ 1 John Battle	.02	.10
❑ 2 Jon Koncak	.02	.10
❑ 3 Rumeal Robinson	.02	.10
❑ 4 Spud Webb	.02	.10
❑ 5 Bob Weiss CO	.02	.10
❑ 6 Dominique Wilkins	.05	.15
❑ 7 Kevin Willis	.02	.10
❑ 8 Larry Bird	.25	.60
❑ 9 Dee Brown	.02	.10
❑ 10 Chris Ford CO	.02	.10
❑ 11 Kevin Gamble	.02	.10
❑ 12 Reggie Lewis	.02	.10
❑ 13 Kevin McHale	.02	.10
❑ 14 Robert Parish	.02	.10
❑ 15 Ed Pinckney	.02	.10
❑ 16 Brian Shaw	.02	.10
❑ 17 Muggsy Bogues	.02	.10
❑ 18 Rex Chapman	.02	.10
❑ 19 Dell Curry	.02	.10
❑ 20 Kendall Gill	.02	.10
❑ 21 Eric Leckner	.02	.10
❑ 22 Gene Littles CO	.02	.10
❑ 23 Johnny Newman	.02	.10
❑ 24 J.R. Reid	.02	.10
❑ 25 B.J.Armstrong	.02	.10
❑ 26 Bill Cartwright	.02	.10
❑ 27 Horace Grant	.02	.10
❑ 28 Phil Jackson CO	.02	.10
❑ 29 Michael Jordan	.75	2.00
❑ 30 Cliff Levingston	.02	.10
❑ 31 John Paxson	.02	.10
❑ 32 Will Perdue	.02	.10
❑ 33 Scottie Pippen	.20	.50
❑ 34 Brad Daugherty	.02	.10
❑ 35 Craig Ehlo	.02	.10
❑ 36 Danny Ferry	.02	.10
❑ 37 Larry Nance	.02	.10
❑ 38 Mark Price	.02	.10
❑ 39 Darnell Valentine	.02	.10
❑ 40 Hot Rod Williams	.02	.10
❑ 41 Lenny Wilkens CO	.02	.10
❑ 42 Richie Adubato CO	.02	.10
❑ 43 Rolando Blackman	.02	.10
❑ 44 James Donaldson	.02	.10
❑ 45 Derek Harper	.02	.10
❑ 46 Rodney McCray	.02	.10
❑ 47 Randy White	.02	.10
❑ 48 Herb Williams	.02	.10
❑ 49 Chris Jackson	.02	.10
❑ 50 Marcus Liberty	.02	.10
❑ 51 Todd Lichti	.02	.10
❑ 52 Blair Rasmussen	.02	.10
❑ 53 Paul Westhead CO	.02	.10
❑ 54 Reggie Williams	.02	.10
❑ 55 Joe Wolf	.02	.10
❑ 56 Orlando Woolridge	.02	.10
❑ 57 Mark Aguirre	.02	.10
❑ 58 Chuck Daly CO	.02	.10
❑ 59 Joe Dumars	.05	.15
❑ 60 James Edwards	.02	.10
❑ 61 Vinnie Johnson	.02	.10
❑ 62 Bill Laimbeer	.02	.10
❑ 63 Dennis Rodman	.10	.30
❑ 64 Isiah Thomas	.05	.15
❑ 65 Tim Hardaway	.08	.25
❑ 66 Rod Higgins	.02	.10
❑ 67 Tyrone Hill	.02	.10
❑ 68 Sarunas Marciulionis	.02	.10
❑ 69 Chris Mullin	.05	.15
❑ 70 Don Nelson CO	.02	.10
❑ 71 Mitch Richmond	.05	.15
❑ 72 Tom Tolbert	.02	.10
❑ 73 Don Chaney CO	.02	.10
❑ 74 Eric(Sleepy) Floyd	.02	.10
❑ 75 Buck Johnson	.02	.10
❑ 76 Vernon Maxwell	.02	.10
❑ 77 Hakeem Olajuwon	.08	.25
❑ 78 Kenny Smith	.02	.10
❑ 79 Larry Smith	.02	.10
❑ 80 Otis Thorpe	.02	.10
❑ 81 Vern Fleming	.02	.10
❑ 82 Bob Hill RC CO	.02	.10
❑ 83 Reggie Miller	.05	.15
❑ 84 Chuck Person	.02	.10
❑ 85 Detlef Schrempf	.02	.10
❑ 86 Rik Smits	.02	.10
❑ 87 LaSalle Thompson	.02	.10
❑ 88 Micheal Williams	.02	.10
❑ 89 Gary Grant	.02	.10
❑ 90 Ron Harper	.02	.10
❑ 91 Bo Kimble	.02	.10
❑ 92 Danny Manning	.02	.10
❑ 93 Ken Norman	.02	.10
❑ 94 Olden Polynice	.02	.10
❑ 95 Mike Schuler CO	.02	.10

❑ 96 Charles Smith	.02	.10
❑ 97 Vlade Divac	.02	.10
❑ 98 Mike Dunleavy CO	.02	.10
❑ 99 A.C. Green	.02	.10
❑ 100 Magic Johnson	.20	.50
❑ 101 Sam Perkins	.02	.10
❑ 102 Byron Scott	.02	.10
❑ 103 Terry Teagle	.02	.10
❑ 104 James Worthy	.05	.15
❑ 105 Willie Burton	.02	.10
❑ 106 Bimbo Coles	.02	.10
❑ 107 Sherman Douglas	.02	.10
❑ 108 Kevin Edwards	.02	.10
❑ 109 Grant Long	.02	.10
❑ 110 Kevin Loughery CO	.02	.10
❑ 111 Glen Rice	.05	.15
❑ 112 Rony Seikaly	.02	.10
❑ 113 Frank Brickowski	.02	.10
❑ 114 Dale Ellis	.02	.10
❑ 115 Del Harris CO	.02	.10
❑ 116 Jay Humphries	.02	.10
❑ 117 Fred Roberts	.02	.10
❑ 118 Alvin Robertson	.02	.10
❑ 119 Danny Schayes	.02	.10
❑ 120 Jack Sikma	.02	.10
❑ 121 Tony Campbell	.02	.10
❑ 122 Tyrone Corbin	.02	.10
❑ 123 Sam Mitchell	.02	.10
❑ 124 Tod Murphy	.02	.10
❑ 125 Pooh Richardson	.02	.10
❑ 126 Jimmy Rodgers CO	.02	.10
❑ 127 Felton Spencer	.02	.10
❑ 128 Mookie Blaylock	.02	.10
❑ 129 Sam Bowie	.02	.10
❑ 130 Derrick Coleman	.02	.10
❑ 131 Chris Dudley	.02	.10
❑ 132 Bill Fitch CO	.02	.10
❑ 133 Chris Morris	.02	.10
❑ 134 Drazen Petrovic	.02	.10
❑ 135 Maurice Cheeks	.02	.10
❑ 136 Patrick Ewing	.05	.15
❑ 137 Mark Jackson	.02	.10
❑ 138 Charles Oakley	.02	.10
❑ 139 Pat Riley CO	.02	.10
❑ 140 Trent Tucker	.02	.10
❑ 141 Kiki Vandeweghe	.02	.10
❑ 142 Gerald Wilkins	.02	.10
❑ 143 Nick Anderson	.02	.10
❑ 144 Terry Catledge	.02	.10
❑ 145 Matt Guokas CO	.02	.10
❑ 146 Jerry Reynolds	.02	.10
❑ 147 Dennis Scott	.02	.10
❑ 148 Scott Skiles	.02	.10
❑ 149 Otis Smith	.02	.10
❑ 150 Ron Anderson	.02	.10
❑ 151 Charles Barkley	.08	.25
❑ 152 Johnny Dawkins	.02	.10
❑ 153 Armon Gilliam	.02	.10
❑ 154 Hersey Hawkins	.02	.10
❑ 155 Jim Lynam CO	.02	.10
❑ 156 Rick Mahorn	.02	.10
❑ 157 Brian Oliver	.02	.10
❑ 158 Tom Chambers	.02	.10
❑ 159 Cotton Fitzsimmons CO	.02	.10
❑ 160 Jeff Hornacek	.02	.10
❑ 161 Kevin Johnson	.05	.15
❑ 162 Negele Knight	.02	.10
❑ 163 Dan Majerle	.02	.10
❑ 164 Xavier McDaniel	.02	.10
❑ 165 Mark West	.02	.10
❑ 166 Rick Adelman CO	.02	.10
❑ 167 Danny Ainge	.02	.10
❑ 168 Clyde Drexler	.05	.15
❑ 169 Kevin Duckworth	.02	.10
❑ 170 Jerome Kersey	.02	.10
❑ 171 Terry Porter	.02	.10
❑ 172 Clifford Robinson	.02	.10
❑ 173 Buck Williams	.02	.10
❑ 174 Antoine Carr	.02	.10
❑ 175 Duane Causwell	.02	.10
❑ 176 Jim Les RC	.02	.10
❑ 177 Travis Mays	.02	.10
❑ 178 Dick Motta CO	.02	.10
❑ 179 Lionel Simmons	.02	.10
❑ 180 Rory Sparrow	.02	.10
❑ 181 Wayman Tisdale	.02	.10
❑ 182 Willie Anderson	.02	.10
❑ 183 Larry Brown CO	.02	.10
❑ 184 Terry Cummings	.02	.10
❑ 185 Sean Elliott	.02	.10
❑ 186 Paul Pressey	.02	.10
❑ 187 David Robinson	.10	.30
❑ 188 Rod Strickland	.05	.15
❑ 189 Benoit Benjamin	.02	.10
❑ 190 Eddie Johnson	.02	.10
❑ 191 K.C. Jones CO	.02	.10
❑ 192 Shawn Kemp	.15	.40
❑ 193 Derrick McKey	.02	.10
❑ 194 Gary Payton	.15	.40
❑ 195 Ricky Pierce	.02	.10
❑ 196 Sedale Threatt	.02	.10
❑ 197 Thurl Bailey	.02	.10
❑ 198 Mark Eaton	.02	.10
❑ 199 Blue Edwards	.02	.10
❑ 200 Jeff Malone	.02	.10
❑ 201 Karl Malone	.08	.25
❑ 202 Jerry Sloan CO	.02	.10
❑ 203 John Stockton	.05	.15
❑ 204 Ledell Eackles	.02	.10
❑ 205 Pervis Ellison	.02	.10
❑ 206 A.J. English	.02	.10
❑ 207 Harvey Grant	.02	.10
❑ 208 Bernard King	.02	.10
❑ 209 Wes Unseld CO	.02	.10
❑ 210 Kevin Johnson AS	.02	.10
❑ 211 Michael Jordan AS	.40	1.00
❑ 212 Dominique Wilkins AS	.02	.10
❑ 213 Charles Barkley AS	.05	.15
❑ 214 Hakeem Olajuwon AS	.05	.15
❑ 215 Patrick Ewing AS	.02	.10
❑ 216 Tim Hardaway AS	.05	.15
❑ 217 John Stockton AS	.02	.10
❑ 218 Chris Mullin AS	.02	.10
❑ 219 Karl Malone AS	.05	.15
❑ 220 Michael Jordan LL	.40	1.00
❑ 221 John Stockton LL	.02	.10
❑ 222 Alvin Robertson LL	.02	.10
❑ 223 Hakeem Olajuwon LL	.05	.15
❑ 224 Buck Williams LL	.02	.10
❑ 225 David Robinson LL	.05	.15
❑ 226 Reggie Miller LL	.02	.10
❑ 227 Blue Edwards SD	.02	.10
❑ 228 Dee Brown SD	.02	.10
❑ 229 Rex Chapman SD	.02	.10
❑ 230 Kenny Smith SD	.02	.10
❑ 231 Shawn Kemp SD	.05	.15
❑ 232 Kendall Gill SD	.02	.10
❑ 233 M.Jordan/Group ASG	.20	.50
❑ 234 '91 All Star Game	.05	.15
❑ 235 '91 All Star Game	.02	.10
❑ 236 P.Ewing/K.Malone ASG	.02	.10
❑ 237 Superstars/Group ASG	.08	.25
❑ 238 M.Jordan/Group ASG	.20	.50
❑ 239 Checklist 1-120	.02	.10
❑ 240 Checklist 121-240	.02	.10
❑ 241 Stacey Augmon RC	.05	.15
❑ 242 Maurice Cheeks	.02	.10
❑ 243 Paul Graham RC	.02	.10
❑ 244 Rodney Monroe RC	.02	.10
❑ 245 Blair Rasmussen	.02	.10
❑ 246 Alexander Volkov	.02	.10
❑ 247 John Bagley	.02	.10
❑ 248 Rick Fox RC	.05	.15
❑ 249 Rickey Green	.02	.10
❑ 250 Joe Kleine	.02	.10
❑ 251 Stojko Vrankovic	.02	.10
❑ 252 Allan Bristow CO	.02	.10
❑ 253 Kenny Gattison	.02	.10
❑ 254 Mike Gminski	.02	.10
❑ 255 Larry Johnson RC	.25	.60
❑ 256 Bobby Hansen	.02	.10
❑ 257 Craig Hodges	.02	.10
❑ 258 Stacey King	.02	.10
❑ 259 Scott Williams RC	.02	.10
❑ 260 John Battle	.02	.10
❑ 261 Winston Bennett	.02	.10
❑ 262 Terrell Brandon RC	.20	.50
❑ 263 Henry James	.02	.10
❑ 264 Steve Kerr	.02	.10
❑ 265 Jimmy Oliver RC	.02	.10
❑ 266 Brad Davis	.02	.10
❑ 267 Terry Davis	.02	.10
❑ 268 Donald Hodge RC	.02	.10
❑ 269 Mike Iuzzolino RC	.02	.10
❑ 270 Fat Lever	.02	.10
❑ 271 Doug Smith RC	.02	.10
❑ 272 Greg Anderson	.02	.10
❑ 273 Kevin Brooks RC	.02	.10
❑ 274 Walter Davis	.02	.10
❑ 275 Winston Garland	.02	.10
❑ 276 Mark Macon RC	.02	.10
❑ 277 Dikembe Mutombo RC	.25	.60
❑ 277B D.Mutombo 91-92 RC	.25	.60
❑ 278 William Bedford	.02	.10
❑ 279 Lance Blanks	.02	.10
❑ 280 John Salley	.02	.10
❑ 281 Charles Thomas RC	.02	.10
❑ 282 Darrell Walker	.02	.10
❑ 283 Orlando Woolridge	.02	.10
❑ 284 Victor Alexander RC	.02	.10
❑ 285 Vincent Askew RC	.02	.10
❑ 286 Mario Elie RC	.05	.15
❑ 287 Alton Lister	.02	.10
❑ 288 Billy Owens RC	.05	.15
❑ 289 Matt Bullard RC	.02	.10
❑ 290 Carl Herrera RC	.02	.10
❑ 291 Tree Rollins	.02	.10
❑ 292 John Turner	.02	.10
❑ 293 Dale Davis RC	.05	.15
❑ 294 Sean Green RC	.02	.10
❑ 295 Kenny Williams	.02	.10
❑ 296 James Edwards	.02	.10
❑ 297 LeRon Ellis RC	.02	.10
❑ 298 Doc Rivers	.02	.10
❑ 299 Loy Vaught	.02	.10
❑ 300 Elden Campbell	.02	.10
❑ 301 Jack Haley	.02	.10
❑ 302 Keith Owens	.02	.10
❑ 303 Tony Smith	.02	.10
❑ 304 Sedale Threatt	.02	.10
❑ 305 Keith Askins RC	.02	.10
❑ 306 Alec Kessler	.02	.10
❑ 307 John Morton	.02	.10
❑ 308 Alan Ogg	.02	.10
❑ 309 Steve Smith RC	.25	.60
❑ 310 Lester Conner	.02	.10
❑ 311 Jeff Grayer	.02	.10
❑ 312 Frank Hamblen CO	.02	.10
❑ 313 Steve Henson	.02	.10
❑ 314 Larry Krystkowiak	.02	.10
❑ 315 Moses Malone	.05	.15
❑ 316 Thurl Bailey	.02	.10
❑ 317 Randy Breuer	.02	.10
❑ 318 Scott Brooks	.02	.10
❑ 319 Gerald Glass	.02	.10
❑ 320 Luc Longley RC	.05	.15
❑ 321 Doug West	.02	.10
❑ 322 Kenny Anderson RC	.10	.30
❑ 323 Tate George	.02	.10
❑ 324 Terry Mills RC	.05	.15
❑ 325 Greg Anthony RC	.05	.15
❑ 326 Anthony Mason RC	.10	.30
❑ 327 Tim McCormick	.02	.10
❑ 328 Xavier McDaniel	.02	.10
❑ 329 Brian Quinnett	.02	.10
❑ 330 John Starks RC	.05	.15
❑ 331 Stanley Roberts RC	.02	.10
❑ 332 Jeff Turner	.02	.10
❑ 333 Sam Vincent	.02	.10
❑ 334 Brian Williams RC	.05	.15
❑ 335 Manute Bol	.02	.10
❑ 336 Kenny Payne	.02	.10
❑ 337 Charles Shackleford	.02	.10
❑ 338 Jayson Williams	.05	.15
❑ 339 Cedric Ceballos	.02	.10
❑ 340 Andrew Lang	.02	.10
❑ 341 Jerrod Mustaf	.02	.10
❑ 342 Tim Perry	.02	.10
❑ 343 Kurt Rambis	.02	.10
❑ 344 Alaa Abdelnaby	.02	.10
❑ 345 Robert Pack RC	.02	.10
❑ 346 Danny Young	.02	.10
❑ 347 Anthony Bonner	.02	.10
❑ 348 Pete Chilcutt RC	.02	.10
❑ 349 Rex Hughes CO	.02	.10
❑ 350 Mitch Richmond	.05	.15
❑ 351 Dwayne Schintzius	.02	.10
❑ 352 Spud Webb	.02	.10
❑ 353 Antoine Carr	.02	.10
❑ 354 Sidney Green	.02	.10
❑ 355 Vinnie Johnson	.02	.10
❑ 356 Greg Sutton RC	.02	.10
❑ 357 Dana Barros	.02	.10
❑ 358 Michael Cage	.02	.10
❑ 359 Marty Conlon RC	.02	.10
❑ 360 Rich King RC	.02	.10
❑ 361 Nate McMillan	.02	.10

❑ 362 David Benoit RC	.02	.10
❑ 363 Mike Brown	.02	.10
❑ 364 Tyrone Corbin	.02	.10
❑ 365 Eric Murdock RC	.02	.10
❑ 366 Delaney Rudd	.02	.10
❑ 367 Michael Adams	.02	.10
❑ 368 Tom Hammonds	.02	.10
❑ 369 Larry Stewart RC	.02	.10
❑ 370 Andre Turner	.02	.10
❑ 371 David Wingate	.02	.10
❑ 372 Dominique Wilkins TL	.02	.10
❑ 373 Larry Bird TL	.10	.30
❑ 374 Rex Chapman TL	.02	.10
❑ 375 Michael Jordan TL	.40	1.00
❑ 376 Brad Daugherty TL	.02	.10
❑ 377 Derek Harper TL	.02	.10
❑ 378 Dikembe Mutombo TL	.05	.15
❑ 379 Joe Dumars TL	.02	.10
❑ 380 Chris Mullin TL	.02	.10
❑ 381 Hakeem Olajuwon TL	.05	.15
❑ 382 Chuck Person TL	.02	.10
❑ 383 Charles Smith TL	.02	.10
❑ 384 James Worthy TL	.02	.10
❑ 385 Glen Rice TL	.02	.10
❑ 386 Alvin Robertson TL	.02	.10
❑ 387 Tony Campbell TL	.02	.10
❑ 388 Derrick Coleman TL	.02	.10
❑ 389 Patrick Ewing TL	.02	.10
❑ 390 Scott Skiles TL	.02	.10
❑ 391 Charles Barkley TL	.05	.15
❑ 392 Kevin Johnson TL	.02	.10
❑ 393 Clyde Drexler TL	.02	.10
❑ 394 Lionel Simmons TL	.02	.10
❑ 395 David Robinson TL	.05	.15
❑ 396 Ricky Pierce TL	.02	.10
❑ 397 John Stockton TL	.02	.10
❑ 398 Michael Adams TL	.02	.10
❑ 399 Checklist	.02	.10
❑ 400 Checklist	.02	.10

1992-93 Fleer

❑ COMPLETE SET (444)	15.00	30.00
❑ COMPLETE SERIES 1 (264)	7.50	15.00
❑ COMPLETE SERIES 2 (180)	7.50	15.00
❑ 1 Stacey Augmon	.02	.10
❑ 2 Duane Ferrell	.02	.10
❑ 3 Paul Graham	.02	.10
❑ 4A Jon Koncak	.02	.10
❑ 4B Jon Koncak	.02	.10
❑ 5 Blair Rasmussen	.02	.10
❑ 6 Rumeal Robinson	.02	.10
❑ 7 Bob Weiss CO	.02	.10
❑ 8 Dominique Wilkins	.08	.25
❑ 9 Kevin Willis	.02	.10
❑ 10 John Bagley	.02	.10
❑ 11 Larry Bird	.40	1.00
❑ 12 Dee Brown	.02	.10
❑ 13 Chris Ford CO	.02	.10
❑ 14 Rick Fox	.02	.10
❑ 15 Kevin Gamble	.02	.10
❑ 16 Reggie Lewis	.02	.10
❑ 17 Kevin McHale	.08	.25
❑ 18 Robert Parish	.02	.10
❑ 19 Ed Pinckney	.02	.10
❑ 20 Muggsy Bogues	.02	.10
❑ 21 Allan Bristow CO	.02	.10
❑ 22 Dell Curry	.02	.10
❑ 23 Kenny Gattison	.02	.10
❑ 24 Kendall Gill	.02	.10
❑ 25 Larry Johnson	.10	.30
❑ 26 Johnny Newman	.02	.10
❑ 27 J.R. Reid	.02	.10
❑ 28 B.J. Armstrong	.02	.10
❑ 29 Bill Cartwright	.02	.10
❑ 30 Horace Grant	.02	.10
❑ 31 Phil Jackson CO	.02	.10
❑ 32 Michael Jordan	1.25	3.00
❑ 33 Stacey King	.02	.10
❑ 34 Cliff Levingston	.02	.10
❑ 35 John Paxson	.02	.10
❑ 36 Scottie Pippen	.30	.75
❑ 37 Scott Williams	.02	.10
❑ 38 John Battle	.02	.10
❑ 39 Terrell Brandon	.08	.25
❑ 40 Brad Daugherty	.02	.10
❑ 41 Craig Ehlo	.02	.10
❑ 42 Larry Nance	.02	.10
❑ 43 Mark Price	.02	.10
❑ 44 Mike Sanders	.02	.10
❑ 45 Lenny Wilkens CO	.02	.10
❑ 46 John Hot Rod Williams	.02	.10
❑ 47 Richie Adubato CO	.02	.10
❑ 48 Terry Davis	.02	.10
❑ 49 Derek Harper	.02	.10
❑ 50 Donald Hodge	.02	.10
❑ 51 Mike Iuzzolino	.02	.10
❑ 52 Rodney McCray	.02	.10
❑ 53 Doug Smith	.02	.10
❑ 54 Greg Anderson	.02	.10
❑ 55 Winston Garland	.02	.10
❑ 56 Dan Issel CO	.02	.10
❑ 57 Chris Jackson	.02	.10
❑ 58 Marcus Liberty	.02	.10
❑ 59 Mark Macon	.02	.10
❑ 60 Dikembe Mutombo	.10	.30
❑ 61 Reggie Williams	.02	.10
❑ 62 Mark Aguirre	.02	.10
❑ 63 Joe Dumars	.08	.25
❑ 64 Bill Laimbeer	.02	.10
❑ 65 Olden Polynice	.02	.10
❑ 66 Dennis Rodman	.20	.50
❑ 67 Ron Rothstein CO	.02	.10
❑ 68 John Salley	.02	.10
❑ 69 Isiah Thomas	.08	.25
❑ 70 Darrell Walker	.02	.10
❑ 71 Orlando Woolridge	.02	.10
❑ 72 Victor Alexander	.02	.10
❑ 73 Mario Elie	.02	.10
❑ 74 Tim Hardaway	.10	.30
❑ 75 Tyrone Hill	.02	.10
❑ 76 Sarunas Marciulionis	.02	.10
❑ 77 Chris Mullin	.08	.25
❑ 78 Don Nelson CO	.02	.10
❑ 79 Billy Owens	.02	.10
❑ 80 Sleepy Floyd UER	.02	.10
❑ 81 Avery Johnson	.02	.10
❑ 82 Buck Johnson	.02	.10
❑ 83 Vernon Maxwell	.02	.10
❑ 84 Hakeem Olajuwon	.15	.40
❑ 85 Kenny Smith	.02	.10
❑ 86 Otis Thorpe	.02	.10
❑ 87 Rudy Tomjanovich CO	.02	.10
❑ 88 Dale Davis	.02	.10
❑ 89 Vern Fleming	.02	.10
❑ 90 Bob Hill CO	.02	.10
❑ 91 Reggie Miller	.08	.25
❑ 92 Chuck Person	.02	.10
❑ 93 Detlef Schrempf	.02	.10
❑ 94 Rik Smits	.02	.10
❑ 95 LaSalle Thompson	.02	.10
❑ 96 Micheal Williams	.02	.10
❑ 97 Larry Brown CO	.02	.10
❑ 98 James Edwards	.02	.10
❑ 99 Gary Grant	.02	.10
❑ 100 Ron Harper	.02	.10
❑ 101 Danny Manning	.02	.10
❑ 102 Ken Norman	.02	.10
❑ 103 Doc Rivers	.02	.10
❑ 104 Charles Smith	.02	.10
❑ 105 Loy Vaught	.02	.10
❑ 106 Elden Campbell	.02	.10
❑ 107 Vlade Divac	.02	.10
❑ 108 A.C. Green	.02	.10
❑ 109 Sam Perkins	.02	.10
❑ 110 Randy Pfund RC CO	.02	.10
❑ 111 Byron Scott	.02	.10
❑ 112 Terry Teagle	.02	.10
❑ 113 Sedale Threatt	.02	.10
❑ 114 James Worthy	.08	.25
❑ 115 Willie Burton	.02	.10
❑ 116 Bimbo Coles	.02	.10
❑ 117 Kevin Edwards	.02	.10
❑ 118 Grant Long	.02	.10
❑ 119 Kevin Loughery CO	.02	.10
❑ 120 Glen Rice	.08	.25
❑ 121 Rony Seikaly	.02	.10
❑ 122 Brian Shaw	.02	.10
❑ 123 Steve Smith	.10	.30
❑ 124 Frank Brickowski	.02	.10
❑ 125 Mike Dunleavy CO	.02	.10
❑ 126 Blue Edwards	.02	.10
❑ 127 Moses Malone	.08	.25
❑ 128 Eric Murdock	.02	.10
❑ 129 Fred Roberts	.02	.10
❑ 130 Alvin Robertson	.02	.10
❑ 131 Thurl Bailey	.02	.10
❑ 132 Tony Campbell	.02	.10
❑ 133 Gerald Glass	.02	.10
❑ 134 Luc Longley	.02	.10
❑ 135 Sam Mitchell	.02	.10
❑ 136 Pooh Richardson	.02	.10
❑ 137 Jimmy Rodgers CO	.02	.10
❑ 138 Felton Spencer	.02	.10
❑ 139 Doug West	.02	.10
❑ 140 Kenny Anderson	.08	.25
❑ 141 Mookie Blaylock	.02	.10
❑ 142 Sam Bowie	.02	.10
❑ 143 Derrick Coleman	.02	.10
❑ 144 Chuck Daly CO	.02	.10
❑ 145 Terry Mills	.02	.10
❑ 146 Chris Morris	.02	.10
❑ 147 Drazen Petrovic	.02	.10
❑ 148 Greg Anthony	.02	.10
❑ 149 Rolando Blackman	.02	.10
❑ 150 Patrick Ewing	.08	.25
❑ 151 Mark Jackson	.02	.10
❑ 152 Anthony Mason	.08	.25
❑ 153 Xavier McDaniel	.02	.10
❑ 154 Charles Oakley	.02	.10
❑ 155 Pat Riley CO	.02	.10
❑ 156 John Starks	.02	.10
❑ 157 Gerald Wilkins	.02	.10
❑ 158 Nick Anderson	.02	.10
❑ 159 Anthony Bowie	.02	.10
❑ 160 Terry Catledge	.02	.10
❑ 161 Matt Guokas CO	.02	.10
❑ 162 Stanley Roberts	.02	.10
❑ 163 Dennis Scott	.02	.10
❑ 164 Scott Skiles	.02	.10
❑ 165 Brian Williams	.02	.10
❑ 166 Ron Anderson	.02	.10
❑ 167 Manute Bol	.02	.10
❑ 168 Johnny Dawkins	.02	.10
❑ 169 Armon Gilliam	.02	.10
❑ 170 Hersey Hawkins	.02	.10
❑ 171 Jeff Hornacek	.02	.10
❑ 172 Andrew Lang	.02	.10
❑ 173 Doug Moe CO	.02	.10
❑ 174 Tim Perry	.02	.10
❑ 175 Jeff Ruland	.02	.10
❑ 176 Charles Shackleford	.02	.10
❑ 177 Danny Ainge	.02	.10
❑ 178 Charles Barkley	.15	.40
❑ 179 Cedric Ceballos	.02	.10
❑ 180 Tom Chambers	.02	.10
❑ 181 Kevin Johnson	.08	.25
❑ 182 Dan Majerle	.02	.10
❑ 183 Mark West UER	.02	.10
❑ 184 Paul Westphal CO	.02	.10
❑ 185 Rick Adelman CO	.02	.10
❑ 186 Clyde Drexler	.08	.25
❑ 187 Kevin Duckworth	.02	.10
❑ 188 Jerome Kersey	.02	.10
❑ 189 Robert Pack	.02	.10
❑ 190 Terry Porter	.02	.10
❑ 191 Cliff Robinson	.02	.10
❑ 192 Rod Strickland	.08	.25
❑ 193 Buck Williams	.02	.10
❑ 194 Anthony Bonner	.02	.10
❑ 195 Duane Causwell	.02	.10
❑ 196 Mitch Richmond	.08	.25
❑ 197 Garry St.Jean RC CO	.02	.10
❑ 198 Lionel Simmons	.02	.10
❑ 199 Wayman Tisdale	.02	.10
❑ 200 Spud Webb	.02	.10
❑ 201 Willie Anderson	.02	.10
❑ 202 Antoine Carr	.02	.10
❑ 203 Terry Cummings	.02	.10
❑ 204 Sean Elliott	.02	.10
❑ 205 Dale Ellis	.02	.10
❑ 206 Vinnie Johnson	.02	.10
❑ 207 David Robinson	.15	.40
❑ 208 Jerry Tarkanian CO RC	.02	.10
❑ 209 Benoit Benjamin	.02	.10

❑ 210 Michael Cage	.02	.10
❑ 211 Eddie Johnson	.02	.10
❑ 212 George Karl CO	.02	.10
❑ 213 Shawn Kemp	.20	.50
❑ 214 Derrick McKey	.02	.10
❑ 215 Nate McMillan	.02	.10
❑ 216 Gary Payton	.20	.50
❑ 217 Ricky Pierce	.02	.10
❑ 218 David Benoit	.02	.10
❑ 219 Mike Brown	.02	.10
❑ 220 Tyrone Corbin	.02	.10
❑ 221 Mark Eaton	.02	.10
❑ 222 Jay Humphries	.02	.10
❑ 223 Larry Krystkowiak	.02	.10
❑ 224 Jeff Malone	.02	.10
❑ 225 Karl Malone	.15	.40
❑ 226 Jerry Sloan CO	.02	.10
❑ 227 John Stockton	.08	.25
❑ 228 Michael Adams	.02	.10
❑ 229 Rex Chapman	.02	.10
❑ 230 Ledell Eackles	.02	.10
❑ 231 Pervis Ellison	.02	.10
❑ 232 A.J. English	.02	.10
❑ 233 Harvey Grant	.02	.10
❑ 234 LaBradford Smith	.02	.10
❑ 235 Larry Stewart	.02	.10
❑ 236 Wes Unseld CO	.02	.10
❑ 237 David Wingate	.02	.10
❑ 238 Michael Jordan LL	.60	1.50
❑ 239 Dennis Rodman LL	.08	.25
❑ 240 John Stockton LL	.02	.10
❑ 241 Buck Williams LL	.02	.10
❑ 242 Mark Price LL	.02	.10
❑ 243 Dana Barros LL	.02	.10
❑ 244 David Robinson LL	.08	.25
❑ 245 Chris Mullin LL	.02	.10
❑ 246 Michael Jordan MVP	.60	1.50
❑ 247 Larry Johnson ROY	.08	.25
❑ 248 David Robinson POY	.08	.25
❑ 249 Detlef Schrempf	.02	.10
❑ 250 Clyde Drexler PV	.02	.10
❑ 251 Tim Hardaway PV	.08	.25
❑ 252 Kevin Johnson PV	.02	.10
❑ 253 Larry Johnson PV	.08	.25
❑ 254 Scottie Pippen PV	.15	.40
❑ 255 Isiah Thomas PV	.02	.10
❑ 256 Larry Bird SY	.20	.50
❑ 257 Brad Daugherty SY	.02	.10
❑ 258 Kevin Johnson SY	.02	.10
❑ 259 Larry Johnson SY	.08	.25
❑ 260 Scottie Pippen SY	.15	.40
❑ 261 Dennis Rodman SY	.08	.25
❑ 262 Checklist 1	.02	.10
❑ 263 Checklist 2	.02	.10
❑ 264 Checklist 3	.02	.10
❑ 265 Charles Barkley SD	.08	.25
❑ 266 Shawn Kemp SD	.08	.25
❑ 267 Dan Majerle SD	.02	.10
❑ 268 Karl Malone SD	.08	.25
❑ 269 Buck Williams SD	.02	.10
❑ 270 Clyde Drexler SD	.02	.10
❑ 271 Sean Elliott SD	.02	.10
❑ 272 Ron Harper SD	.02	.10
❑ 273 Michael Jordan SD	.60	1.50
❑ 274 James Worthy SD	.02	.10
❑ 275 Cedric Ceballos SD	.02	.10
❑ 276 Larry Nance SD	.02	.10
❑ 277 Kenny Walker SD	.02	.10
❑ 278 Spud Webb SD	.02	.10
❑ 279 Dominique Wilkins SD	.02	.10
❑ 280 Terrell Brandon SD	.02	.10
❑ 281 Dee Brown SD	.02	.10
❑ 282 Kevin Johnson SD	.02	.10
❑ 283 Doc Rivers SD	.02	.10
❑ 284 Byron Scott SD	.02	.10
❑ 285 Manute Bol SD	.02	.10
❑ 286 Dikembe Mutombo SD	.08	.25
❑ 287 Robert Parish SD	.02	.10
❑ 288 David Robinson SD	.08	.25
❑ 289 Dennis Rodman SD	.08	.25
❑ 290 Blue Edwards SD	.02	.10
❑ 291 Patrick Ewing SD	.02	.10
❑ 292 Larry Johnson SD	.08	.25
❑ 293 Jerome Kersey SD	.02	.10
❑ 294 Hakeem Olajuwon SD	.08	.25
❑ 295 Stacey Augmon SD	.02	.10
❑ 296 Derrick Coleman SD	.02	.10
❑ 297 Kendall Gill SD	.02	.10
❑ 298 Shaquille O'Neal SD	1.25	3.00
❑ 299 Scottie Pippen SD	.15	.40
❑ 300 Darryl Dawkins SD	.02	.10
❑ 301 Mookie Blaylock	.02	.10
❑ 302 Adam Keefe RC	.02	.10
❑ 303 Travis Mays	.02	.10
❑ 304 Morlon Wiley	.02	.10
❑ 305 Sherman Douglas	.02	.10
❑ 306 Joe Kleine	.02	.10
❑ 307 Xavier McDaniel	.02	.10
❑ 308 Tony Bennett RC	.02	.10
❑ 309 Tom Hammonds	.02	.10
❑ 310 Kevin Lynch	.02	.10
❑ 311 Alonzo Mourning RC	.60	1.50
❑ 312 David Wingate	.02	.10
❑ 313 Rodney McCray	.02	.10
❑ 314 Will Perdue	.02	.10
❑ 315 Trent Tucker	.02	.10
❑ 316 Corey Williams RC	.02	.10
❑ 317 Danny Ferry	.02	.10
❑ 318 Jay Guidinger RC	.02	.10
❑ 319 Jerome Lane	.02	.10
❑ 320 Gerald Wilkins	.02	.10
❑ 321 Steve Bardo RC	.02	.10
❑ 322 Walter Bond RC	.02	.10
❑ 323 Brian Howard RC	.02	.10
❑ 324 Tracy Moore RC	.02	.10
❑ 325 Sean Rooks RC	.02	.10
❑ 326 Randy White	.02	.10
❑ 327 Kevin Brooks	.02	.10
❑ 328 LaPhonso Ellis RC	.08	.25
❑ 329 Scott Hastings	.02	.10
❑ 330 Todd Lichti	.02	.10
❑ 331 Robert Pack	.02	.10
❑ 332 Bryant Stith RC	.02	.10
❑ 333 Gerald Glass	.02	.10
❑ 334 Terry Mills	.02	.10
❑ 335 Isaiah Morris RC	.02	.10
❑ 336 Mark Randall	.02	.10
❑ 337 Danny Young	.02	.10
❑ 338 Chris Gatling	.02	.10
❑ 339 Jeff Grayer	.02	.10
❑ 340 Byron Houston RC	.02	.10
❑ 341 Keith Jennings RC	.02	.10
❑ 342 Alton Lister	.02	.10
❑ 343 Latrell Sprewell RC	.75	2.00
❑ 344 Scott Brooks	.02	.10
❑ 345 Matt Bullard	.02	.10
❑ 346 Carl Herrera	.02	.10
❑ 347 Robert Horry RC	.08	.25
❑ 348 Tree Rollins	.02	.10
❑ 349 Greg Dreiling	.02	.10
❑ 350 George McCloud	.02	.10
❑ 351 Sam Mitchell	.02	.10
❑ 352 Pooh Richardson	.02	.10
❑ 353 Malik Sealy RC	.02	.10
❑ 354 Kenny Williams	.02	.10
❑ 355 Jaren Jackson RC	.02	.10
❑ 356 Mark Jackson	.02	.10
❑ 357 Stanley Roberts	.02	.10
❑ 358 Elmore Spencer RC	.02	.10
❑ 359 Kiki Vandeweghe	.02	.10
❑ 360 John S. Williams	.02	.10
❑ 361 Randy Woods RC	.02	.10
❑ 362 Duane Cooper RC	.02	.10
❑ 363 James Edwards	.02	.10
❑ 364 Anthony Peeler RC	.02	.10
❑ 365 Tony Smith	.02	.10
❑ 366 Keith Askins	.02	.10
❑ 367 Matt Geiger RC	.02	.10
❑ 368 Alec Kessler	.02	.10
❑ 369 Harold Miner RC	.02	.10
❑ 370 John Salley	.02	.10
❑ 371 Anthony Avent RC	.02	.10
❑ 372 Todd Day RC	.02	.10
❑ 373 Blue Edwards	.02	.10
❑ 374 Brad Lohaus	.02	.10
❑ 375 Lee Mayberry RC	.02	.10
❑ 376 Eric Murdock	.02	.10
❑ 377 Danny Schayes	.02	.10
❑ 378 Lance Blanks	.02	.10
❑ 379 Christian Laettner RC	.20	.50
❑ 380 Bob McCann RC	.02	.10
❑ 381 Chuck Person	.02	.10
❑ 382 Brad Sellers	.02	.10
❑ 383 Chris Smith RC	.02	.10
❑ 384 Micheal Williams	.02	.10
❑ 385 Rafael Addison	.02	.10
❑ 386 Chucky Brown	.02	.10
❑ 387 Chris Dudley	.02	.10
❑ 388 Tate George	.02	.10
❑ 389 Rick Mahorn	.02	.10
❑ 390 Rumeal Robinson	.02	.10
❑ 391 Jayson Williams	.02	.10
❑ 392 Eric Anderson RC	.02	.10
❑ 393 Rolando Blackman	.02	.10
❑ 394 Tony Campbell	.02	.10
❑ 395 Hubert Davis RC	.02	.10
❑ 396 Doc Rivers	.02	.10
❑ 397 Charles Smith	.02	.10
❑ 398 Herb Williams	.02	.10
❑ 399 Litterial Green RC	.02	.10
❑ 400 Greg Kite	.02	.10
❑ 401 Shaquille O'Neal RC	2.50	6.00
❑ 402 Jerry Reynolds	.02	.10
❑ 403 Jeff Turner	.02	.10
❑ 404 Greg Grant	.02	.10
❑ 405 Jeff Hornacek	.02	.10
❑ 406 Andrew Lang	.02	.10
❑ 407 Kenny Payne	.02	.10
❑ 408 Tim Perry	.02	.10
❑ 409 C.Weatherspoon RC	.08	.25
❑ 410 Danny Ainge	.02	.10
❑ 411 Charles Barkley	.15	.40
❑ 412 Negele Knight	.02	.10
❑ 413 Oliver Miller RC	.02	.10
❑ 414 Jerrod Mustaf	.02	.10
❑ 415 Mark Bryant	.02	.10
❑ 416 Mario Elie	.02	.10
❑ 417 Dave Johnson RC	.02	.10
❑ 418 Tracy Murray RC	.02	.10
❑ 419 Reggie Smith RC	.02	.10
❑ 420 Rod Strickland	.08	.25
❑ 421 Randy Brown	.02	.10
❑ 422 Pete Chilcutt	.02	.10
❑ 423 Jim Les	.02	.10
❑ 424 Walt Williams RC	.08	.25
❑ 425 Lloyd Daniels RC	.02	.10
❑ 426 Vinny Del Negro	.02	.10
❑ 427 Dale Ellis	.02	.10
❑ 428 Sidney Green	.02	.10
❑ 429 Avery Johnson	.02	.10
❑ 430 Dana Barros	.02	.10
❑ 431 Rich King	.02	.10
❑ 432 Isaac Austin RC	.02	.10
❑ 433 John Crotty RC	.02	.10
❑ 434 Stephen Howard RC	.02	.10
❑ 435 Jay Humphries	.02	.10
❑ 436 Larry Krystkowiak	.02	.10
❑ 437 Tom Gugliotta RC	.30	.75
❑ 438 Buck Johnson	.02	.10
❑ 439 Charles Jones	.02	.10
❑ 440 Don MacLean RC	.02	.10
❑ 441 Doug Overton	.02	.10
❑ 442 Brent Price RC	.02	.10
❑ 443 Checklist 1	.02	.10
❑ 444 Checklist 2	.02	.10
❑ SD266 Shawn Kemp AU	60.00	120.00
❑ SD277 Kenny Walker AU	12.50	30.00
❑ SD300 Darryl Dawkins AU	12.50	30.00
❑ NNO Slam Dunk Wrapper Exch.	1.25	3.00

1993-94 Fleer

❑ COMPLETE SET (400)	10.00	20.00
❑ COMPLETE SERIES 1 (240)	5.00	10.00
❑ COMPLETE SERIES 2 (160)	5.00	10.00
❑ 1 Stacey Augmon	.01	.05
❑ 2 Mookie Blaylock	.02	.10
❑ 3 Duane Ferrell	.01	.05
❑ 4 Paul Graham	.01	.05
❑ 5 Adam Keefe	.01	.05
❑ 6 Jon Koncak	.01	.05
❑ 7 Dominique Wilkins	.08	.25
❑ 8 Kevin Willis	.01	.05
❑ 9 Alaa Abdelnaby	.01	.05
❑ 10 Dee Brown	.01	.05

❑ 11 Sherman Douglas	.01	.05
❑ 12 Rick Fox	.01	.05
❑ 13 Kevin Gamble	.01	.05
❑ 14 Reggie Lewis	.02	.10
❑ 15 Xavier McDaniel	.01	.05
❑ 16 Robert Parish	.02	.10
❑ 17 Muggsy Bogues	.02	.10
❑ 18 Dell Curry	.01	.05
❑ 19 Kenny Gattison	.01	.05
❑ 20 Kendall Gill	.02	.10
❑ 21 Larry Johnson	.08	.25
❑ 22 Alonzo Mourning	.15	.40
❑ 23 Johnny Newman	.01	.05
❑ 24 David Wingate	.01	.05
❑ 25 B.J.Armstrong	.01	.05
❑ 26 Bill Cartwright	.01	.05
❑ 27 Horace Grant	.02	.10
❑ 28 Michael Jordan	1.25	3.00
❑ 29 Stacey King	.01	.05
❑ 30 John Paxson	.01	.05
❑ 31 Will Perdue	.01	.05
❑ 32 Scottie Pippen	.30	.75
❑ 33 Scott Williams	.01	.05
❑ 34 Terrell Brandon	.02	.10
❑ 35 Brad Daugherty	.01	.05
❑ 36 Craig Ehlo	.01	.05
❑ 37 Danny Ferry	.01	.05
❑ 38 Larry Nance	.01	.05
❑ 39 Mark Price	.01	.05
❑ 40 Mike Sanders	.01	.05
❑ 41 Gerald Wilkins	.01	.05
❑ 42 John Williams	.01	.05
❑ 43 Terry Davis	.01	.05
❑ 44 Derek Harper	.02	.10
❑ 45 Mike Iuzzolino	.01	.05
❑ 46 Jim Jackson	.02	.10
❑ 47 Sean Rooks	.01	.05
❑ 48 Doug Smith	.01	.05
❑ 49 Randy White	.01	.05
❑ 50 Mahmoud Abdul-Rauf	.01	.05
❑ 51 LaPhonso Ellis	.01	.05
❑ 52 Marcus Liberty	.01	.05
❑ 53 Mark Macon	.01	.05
❑ 54 Dikembe Mutombo	.08	.25
❑ 55 Robert Pack	.01	.05
❑ 56 Bryant Stith	.01	.05
❑ 57 Reggie Williams	.01	.05
❑ 58 Mark Aguirre	.01	.05
❑ 59 Joe Dumars	.08	.25
❑ 60 Bill Laimbeer	.01	.05
❑ 61 Terry Mills	.01	.05
❑ 62 Olden Polynice	.01	.05
❑ 63 Alvin Robertson	.01	.05
❑ 64 Dennis Rodman	.20	.50
❑ 65 Isiah Thomas	.08	.25
❑ 66 Victor Alexander	.01	.05
❑ 67 Tim Hardaway	.08	.25
❑ 68 Tyrone Hill	.01	.05
❑ 69 Byron Houston	.01	.05
❑ 70 Sarunas Marciulionis	.01	.05
❑ 71 Chris Mullin	.08	.25
❑ 72 Billy Owens	.01	.05
❑ 73 Latrell Sprewell	.25	.60
❑ 74 Scott Brooks	.01	.05
❑ 75 Matt Bullard	.01	.05
❑ 76 Carl Herrera	.01	.05
❑ 77 Robert Horry	.02	.10
❑ 78 Vernon Maxwell	.01	.05
❑ 79 Hakeem Olajuwon	.15	.40
❑ 80 Kenny Smith	.01	.05
❑ 81 Otis Thorpe	.02	.10
❑ 82 Dale Davis	.01	.05
❑ 83 Vern Fleming	.01	.05
❑ 84 George McCloud	.01	.05
❑ 85 Reggie Miller	.08	.25
❑ 86 Sam Mitchell	.01	.05
❑ 87 Pooh Richardson	.01	.05
❑ 88 Detlef Schrempf	.02	.10
❑ 89 Rik Smits	.02	.10
❑ 90 Gary Grant	.01	.05
❑ 91 Ron Harper	.02	.10
❑ 92 Mark Jackson	.02	.10
❑ 93 Danny Manning	.02	.10
❑ 94 Ken Norman	.01	.05
❑ 95 Stanley Roberts	.01	.05
❑ 96 Loy Vaught	.01	.05
❑ 97 John Williams	.01	.05
❑ 98 Elden Campbell	.01	.05
❑ 99 Doug Christie	.02	.10
❑ 100 Duane Cooper	.01	.05
❑ 101 Vlade Divac	.02	.10
❑ 102 A.C. Green	.02	.10
❑ 103 Anthony Peeler	.01	.05
❑ 104 Sedale Threatt	.01	.05
❑ 105 James Worthy	.08	.25
❑ 106 Bimbo Coles	.01	.05
❑ 107 Grant Long	.01	.05
❑ 108 Harold Miner	.01	.05
❑ 109 Glen Rice	.02	.10
❑ 110 John Salley	.01	.05
❑ 111 Rony Seikaly	.01	.05
❑ 112 Brian Shaw	.01	.05
❑ 113 Steve Smith	.08	.25
❑ 114 Anthony Avent	.01	.05
❑ 115 Jon Barry	.01	.05
❑ 116 Frank Brickowski	.01	.05
❑ 117 Todd Day	.01	.05
❑ 118 Blue Edwards	.01	.05
❑ 119 Brad Lohaus	.01	.05
❑ 120 Lee Mayberry	.01	.05
❑ 121 Eric Murdock	.01	.05
❑ 122 Thurl Bailey	.01	.05
❑ 123 Christian Laettner	.02	.10
❑ 124 Luc Longley	.02	.10
❑ 125 Chuck Person	.01	.05
❑ 126 Felton Spencer	.01	.05
❑ 127 Doug West	.01	.05
❑ 128 Micheal Williams	.01	.05
❑ 129 Rafael Addison	.01	.05
❑ 130 Kenny Anderson	.02	.10
❑ 131 Sam Bowie	.01	.05
❑ 132 Chucky Brown	.01	.05
❑ 133 Derrick Coleman	.02	.10
❑ 134 Chris Dudley	.01	.05
❑ 135 Chris Morris	.01	.05
❑ 136 Rumeal Robinson	.01	.05
❑ 137 Greg Anthony	.01	.05
❑ 138 Rolando Blackman	.01	.05
❑ 139 Tony Campbell	.01	.05
❑ 140 Hubert Davis	.01	.05
❑ 141 Patrick Ewing	.08	.25
❑ 142 Anthony Mason	.02	.10
❑ 143 Charles Oakley	.02	.10
❑ 144 Doc Rivers	.02	.10
❑ 145 Charles Smith	.01	.05
❑ 146 John Starks	.02	.10
❑ 147 Nick Anderson	.02	.10
❑ 148 Anthony Bowie	.01	.05
❑ 149 Shaquille O'Neal	.50	1.25
❑ 150 Donald Royal	.01	.05
❑ 151 Dennis Scott	.01	.05
❑ 152 Scott Skiles	.01	.05
❑ 153 Tom Tolbert	.01	.05
❑ 154 Jeff Turner	.01	.05
❑ 155 Ron Anderson	.01	.05
❑ 156 Johnny Dawkins	.01	.05
❑ 157 Hersey Hawkins	.02	.10
❑ 158 Jeff Hornacek	.02	.10
❑ 159 Andrew Lang	.01	.05
❑ 160 Tim Perry	.01	.05
❑ 161 Clarence Weatherspoon	.01	.05
❑ 162 Danny Ainge	.02	.10
❑ 163 Charles Barkley	.15	.40
❑ 164 Cedric Ceballos	.02	.10
❑ 165 Tom Chambers	.01	.05
❑ 166 Richard Dumas	.01	.05
❑ 167 Kevin Johnson	.02	.10
❑ 168 Negele Knight	.01	.05
❑ 169 Dan Majerle	.02	.10
❑ 170 Oliver Miller	.01	.05
❑ 171 Mark West	.01	.05
❑ 172 Mark Bryant	.01	.05
❑ 173 Clyde Drexler	.08	.25
❑ 174 Kevin Duckworth	.01	.05
❑ 175 Mario Elie	.01	.05
❑ 176 Jerome Kersey	.01	.05
❑ 177 Terry Porter	.01	.05
❑ 178 Cliff Robinson	.02	.10
❑ 179 Rod Strickland	.02	.10
❑ 180 Buck Williams	.01	.05
❑ 181 Anthony Bonner	.01	.05
❑ 182 Duane Causwell	.01	.05
❑ 183 Mitch Richmond	.08	.25
❑ 184 Lionel Simmons	.01	.05
❑ 185 Wayman Tisdale	.01	.05
❑ 186 Spud Webb	.02	.10
❑ 187 Walt Williams	.01	.05
❑ 188 Antoine Carr	.01	.05
❑ 189 Terry Cummings	.01	.05
❑ 190 Lloyd Daniels	.01	.05
❑ 191 Vinny Del Negro	.01	.05
❑ 192 Sean Elliott	.02	.10
❑ 193 Dale Ellis	.01	.05
❑ 194 Avery Johnson	.01	.05
❑ 195 J.R. Reid	.01	.05
❑ 196 David Robinson	.15	.40
❑ 197 Michael Cage	.01	.05
❑ 198 Eddie Johnson	.01	.05
❑ 199 Shawn Kemp	.15	.40
❑ 200 Derrick McKey	.01	.05
❑ 201 Nate McMillan	.01	.05
❑ 202 Gary Payton	.15	.40
❑ 203 Sam Perkins	.02	.10
❑ 204 Ricky Pierce	.01	.05
❑ 205 David Benoit	.01	.05
❑ 206 Tyrone Corbin	.01	.05
❑ 207 Mark Eaton	.01	.05
❑ 208 Jay Humphries	.01	.05
❑ 209 Larry Krystkowiak	.01	.05
❑ 210 Jeff Malone	.01	.05
❑ 211 Karl Malone	.15	.40
❑ 212 John Stockton	.08	.25
❑ 213 Michael Adams	.01	.05
❑ 214 Rex Chapman	.01	.05
❑ 215 Pervis Ellison	.01	.05
❑ 216 Harvey Grant	.01	.05
❑ 217 Tom Gugliotta	.08	.25
❑ 218 Buck Johnson	.01	.05
❑ 219 LaBradford Smith	.01	.05
❑ 220 Larry Stewart	.01	.05
❑ 221 B.J. Armstrong LL	.01	.05
❑ 222 Cedric Ceballos LL	.01	.05
❑ 223 Larry Johnson LL	.02	.10
❑ 224 Michael Jordan LL	.60	1.50
❑ 225 Hakeem Olajuwon LL	.08	.25
❑ 226 Mark Price LL	.01	.05
❑ 227 Dennis Rodman LL	.08	.25
❑ 228 John Stockton LL	.02	.10
❑ 229 Charles Barkley AW	.08	.25
❑ 230 Hakeem Olajuwon AW	.08	.25
❑ 231 Shaquille O'Neal AW	.20	.50
❑ 232 Clifford Robinson AW	.01	.05
❑ 233 Shawn Kemp PV	.08	.25
❑ 234 Alonzo Mourning PV	.08	.25
❑ 235 Hakeem Olajuwon PV	.08	.25
❑ 236 John Stockton PV	.02	.10
❑ 237 Dominique Wilkins PV	.02	.10
❑ 238 Checklist 1-85	.01	.05
❑ 239 Checklist 86-165	.01	.05
❑ 240 Checklist 166-240 UER	.01	.05
❑ 241 Doug Edwards RC	.01	.05
❑ 242 Craig Ehlo	.01	.05
❑ 243 Andrew Lang	.01	.05
❑ 244 Ennis Whatley	.01	.05
❑ 245 Chris Corchiani	.01	.05
❑ 246 Acie Earl RC	.01	.05
❑ 247 Jimmy Oliver	.01	.05
❑ 248 Ed Pinckney	.01	.05
❑ 249 Dino Radja RC	.01	.05
❑ 250 Matt Wenstrom RC	.01	.05
❑ 251 Tony Bennett	.01	.05
❑ 252 Scott Burrell RC	.08	.25
❑ 253 LeRon Ellis	.01	.05
❑ 254 Hersey Hawkins	.02	.10
❑ 255 Eddie Johnson	.01	.05
❑ 256 Corie Blount RC	.01	.05
❑ 257 Jo Jo English RC	.01	.05
❑ 258 Dave Johnson	.01	.05
❑ 259 Steve Kerr	.02	.10
❑ 260 Toni Kukoc RC	.40	1.00
❑ 261 Pete Myers	.01	.05
❑ 262 Bill Wennington	.01	.05
❑ 263 John Battle	.01	.05
❑ 264 Tyrone Hill	.01	.05
❑ 265 Gerald Madkins RC	.01	.05
❑ 266 Chris Mills RC	.08	.25
❑ 267 Bobby Phills	.01	.05
❑ 268 Greg Dreiling	.01	.05
❑ 269 Lucious Harris RC	.01	.05
❑ 270 Donald Hodge	.01	.05
❑ 271 Popeye Jones RC	.01	.05
❑ 272 Tim Legler RC	.01	.05
❑ 273 Fat Lever	.01	.05
❑ 274 Jamal Mashburn RC	.25	.60
❑ 275 Darren Morningstar RC	.01	.05
❑ 276 Tom Hammonds	.01	.05
❑ 277 Darnell Mee RC	.01	.05

278 Rodney Rogers RC	.08	.25
279 Brian Williams	.01	.05
280 Greg Anderson	.01	.05
281 Sean Elliott	.02	.10
282 Allan Houston RC	.40	1.00
283 Lindsey Hunter RC	.08	.25
284 Marcus Liberty	.01	.05
285 Mark Macon	.01	.05
286 David Wood	.01	.05
287 Jud Buechler	.01	.05
288 Chris Gatling	.01	.05
289 Josh Grant RC	.01	.05
290 Jeff Grayer	.01	.05
291 Avery Johnson	.01	.05
292 Chris Webber RC	1.00	2.50
293 Sam Cassell RC	.40	1.00
294 Mario Elie	.01	.05
295 Richard Petruska RC	.01	.05
296 Eric Riley RC	.01	.05
297 Antonio Davis RC	.10	.30
298 Scott Haskin RC	.01	.05
299 Derrick McKey	.01	.05
300 Byron Scott	.02	.10
301 Malik Sealy	.01	.05
302 LaSalle Thompson	.01	.05
303 Kenny Williams	.01	.05
304 Haywoode Workman	.01	.05
305 Mark Aguirre	.01	.05
306 Terry Dehere RC	.01	.05
307 Bob Martin RC	.01	.05
308 Elmore Spencer	.01	.05
309 Tom Tolbert	.01	.05
310 Randy Woods	.01	.05
311 Sam Bowie	.01	.05
312 James Edwards	.01	.05
313 Antonio Harvey RC	.01	.05
314 George Lynch RC	.01	.05
315 Tony Smith	.01	.05
316 Nick Van Exel RC	.30	.75
317 Manute Bol	.01	.05
318 Willie Burton	.01	.05
319 Matt Geiger	.01	.05
320 Alec Kessler	.01	.05
321 Vin Baker RC	.25	.60
322 Ken Norman	.01	.05
323 Danny Schayes	.01	.05
324 Derek Strong RC	.01	.05
325 Mike Brown	.01	.05
326 Brian Davis RC	.01	.05
327 Tellis Frank	.01	.05
328 Marlon Maxey	.01	.05
329 Isaiah Rider RC	.20	.50
330 Chris Smith	.01	.05
331 Benoit Benjamin	.01	.05
332 P.J.Brown RC	.08	.25
333 Kevin Edwards	.01	.05
334 Armon Gilliam	.01	.05
335 Rick Mahorn	.01	.05
336 Dwayne Schintzius	.01	.05
337 Rex Walters RC	.01	.05
338 David Wesley RC	.08	.25
339 Jayson Williams	.02	.10
340 Anthony Bonner	.01	.05
341 Herb Williams	.01	.05
342 Litterial Green	.01	.05
343 Anfernee Hardaway RC	.75	2.00
344 Greg Kite	.01	.05
345 Larry Krystkowiak	.01	.05
346 Todd Lichti	.01	.05
347 Keith Tower RC	.01	.05
348 Dana Barros	.01	.05
349 Shawn Bradley RC	.08	.25
350 Michael Curry RC	.01	.05
351 Greg Graham RC	.01	.05
352 Warren Kidd RC	.01	.05
353 Moses Malone	.08	.25
354 Orlando Woolridge	.01	.05
355 Duane Cooper	.01	.05
356 Joe Courtney RC	.01	.05
357 A.C. Green	.02	.10
358 Frank Johnson	.01	.05
359 Joe Kleine	.01	.05
360 Malcolm Mackey RC	.01	.05
361 Jerrod Mustaf	.01	.05
362 Chris Dudley	.01	.05
363 Harvey Grant	.01	.05
364 Tracy Murray	.01	.05
365 James Robinson RC	.01	.05
366 Reggie Smith	.01	.05
367 Kevin Thompson RC	.01	.05
368 Randy Breuer	.01	.05
369 Randy Brown	.01	.05
370 Evers Burns RC	.01	.05
371 Pete Chilcutt	.01	.05
372 Bobby Hurley RC	.02	.10
373 Jim Les	.01	.05
374 Mike Peplowski RC	.01	.05
375 Willie Anderson	.01	.05
376 Sleepy Floyd	.01	.05
377 Negele Knight	.01	.05
378 Dennis Rodman	.20	.50
379 Chris Whitney RC	.01	.05
380 Vincent Askew	.01	.05
381 Kendall Gill	.02	.10
382 Ervin Johnson RC	.02	.10
383 Chris King RC	.01	.05
384 Rich King	.01	.05
385 Steve Scheffler	.01	.05
386 Detlef Schrempf	.02	.10
387 Tom Chambers	.01	.05
388 John Crotty	.01	.05
389 Bryon Russell RC	.08	.25
390 Felton Spencer	.01	.05
391 Luther Wright RC	.01	.05
392 Mitchell Butler RC	.01	.05
393 Calbert Cheaney RC	.02	.10
394 Kevin Duckworth	.01	.05
395 Don MacLean	.01	.05
396 Gheorghe Muresan RC	.08	.25
397 Doug Overton	.01	.05
398 Brent Price	.01	.05
399 Checklist	.01	.05
400 Checklist	.01	.05

1994-95 Fleer

COMPLETE SET (390)	12.00	24.00
COMPLETE SERIES 1 (240)	6.00	12.00
COMPLETE SERIES 2 (150)	6.00	12.00
1 Stacey Augmon	.01	.05
2 Mookie Blaylock	.01	.05
3 Craig Ehlo	.01	.05
4 Duane Ferrell	.01	.05
5 Adam Keefe	.01	.05
6 Jon Koncak	.01	.05
7 Andrew Lang	.01	.05
8 Danny Manning	.02	.10
9 Kevin Willis	.01	.05
10 Dee Brown	.01	.05
11 Sherman Douglas	.01	.05
12 Acie Earl	.01	.05
13 Rick Fox	.01	.05
14 Kevin Gamble	.01	.05
15 Xavier McDaniel	.01	.05
16 Robert Parish	.02	.10
17 Ed Pinckney	.01	.05
18 Dino Radja	.01	.05
19 Muggsy Bogues	.02	.10
20 Frank Brickowski	.01	.05
21 Scott Burrell	.01	.05
22 Dell Curry	.01	.05
23 Kenny Gattison	.01	.05
24 Hersey Hawkins	.02	.10
25 Eddie Johnson	.01	.05
26 Larry Johnson	.02	.10
27 Alonzo Mourning	.10	.30
28 David Wingate	.01	.05
29 B.J. Armstrong	.01	.05
30 Horace Grant	.02	.10
31 Steve Kerr	.01	.05
32 Toni Kukoc	.15	.40
33 Luc Longley	.01	.05
34 Pete Myers	.01	.05
35 Scottie Pippen	.30	.75
36 Bill Wennington	.01	.05
37 Scott Williams	.01	.05
38 Terrell Brandon	.02	.10
39 Brad Daugherty	.01	.05
40 Tyrone Hill	.01	.05
41 Chris Mills	.02	.10
42 Larry Nance	.01	.05
43 Bobby Phills	.01	.05
44 Mark Price	.01	.05
45 Gerald Wilkins	.01	.05
46 John Williams	.01	.05
47 Lucious Harris	.01	.05
48 Donald Hodge	.01	.05
49 Jim Jackson	.02	.10
50 Popeye Jones	.01	.05
51 Tim Legler	.01	.05
52 Fat Lever	.01	.05
53 Jamal Mashburn	.08	.25
54 Sean Rooks	.01	.05
55 Doug Smith	.01	.05
56 Mahmoud Abdul-Rauf	.01	.05
57 LaPhonso Ellis	.01	.05
58 Dikembe Mutombo	.02	.10
59 Robert Pack	.01	.05
60 Rodney Rogers	.01	.05
61 Bryant Stith	.01	.05
62 Brian Williams	.01	.05
63 Reggie Williams	.01	.05
64 Greg Anderson	.01	.05
65 Joe Dumars	.08	.25
66 Sean Elliott	.02	.10
67 Allan Houston	.15	.40
68 Lindsey Hunter	.02	.10
69 Terry Mills	.01	.05
70 Victor Alexander	.01	.05
71 Chris Gatling	.01	.05
72 Tim Hardaway	.08	.25
73 Keith Jennings	.01	.05
74 Avery Johnson	.01	.05
75 Chris Mullin	.08	.25
76 Billy Owens	.01	.05
77 Latrell Sprewell	.08	.25
78 Chris Webber	.25	.60
79 Scott Brooks	.01	.05
80 Sam Cassell	.08	.25
81 Mario Elie	.01	.05
82 Carl Herrera	.01	.05
83 Robert Horry	.02	.10
84 Vernon Maxwell	.01	.05
85 Hakeem Olajuwon	.15	.40
86 Kenny Smith	.01	.05
87 Otis Thorpe	.01	.05
88 Antonio Davis	.01	.05
89 Dale Davis	.01	.05
90 Vern Fleming	.01	.05
91 Derrick McKey	.01	.05
92 Reggie Miller	.08	.25
93 Pooh Richardson	.01	.05
94 Byron Scott	.02	.10
95 Rik Smits	.01	.05
96 Haywoode Workman	.01	.05
97 Terry Dehere	.01	.05
98 Harold Ellis	.01	.05
99 Gary Grant	.01	.05
100 Ron Harper	.02	.10
101 Mark Jackson	.01	.05
102 Stanley Roberts	.01	.05
103 Elmore Spencer	.01	.05
104 Loy Vaught	.01	.05
105 Dominique Wilkins	.08	.25
106 Elden Campbell	.01	.05
107 Doug Christie	.02	.10
108 Vlade Divac	.01	.05
109 George Lynch	.01	.05
110 Anthony Peeler	.01	.05
111 Tony Smith	.01	.05
112 Sedale Threatt	.01	.05
113 Nick Van Exel	.08	.25
114 James Worthy	.08	.25
115 Bimbo Coles	.01	.05
116 Grant Long	.01	.05
117 Harold Miner	.01	.05
118 Glen Rice	.02	.10
119 John Salley	.01	.05
120 Rony Seikaly	.01	.05
121 Brian Shaw	.01	.05
122 Steve Smith	.02	.10
123 Vin Baker	.08	.25
124 Jon Barry	.01	.05
125 Todd Day	.01	.05
126 Blue Edwards	.01	.05

❑ 127 Lee Mayberry	.01	.05
❑ 128 Eric Murdock	.01	.05
❑ 129 Ken Norman	.01	.05
❑ 130 Derek Strong	.01	.05
❑ 131 Thurl Bailey	.01	.05
❑ 132 Stacey King	.01	.05
❑ 133 Christian Laettner	.02	.10
❑ 134 Chuck Person	.01	.05
❑ 135 Isaiah Rider	.02	.10
❑ 136 Chris Smith	.01	.05
❑ 137 Doug West	.01	.05
❑ 138 Micheal Williams	.01	.05
❑ 139 Kenny Anderson	.02	.10
❑ 140 Benoit Benjamin	.01	.05
❑ 141 P.J. Brown	.01	.05
❑ 142 Derrick Coleman	.02	.10
❑ 143 Kevin Edwards	.01	.05
❑ 144 Armon Gilliam	.01	.05
❑ 145 Chris Morris	.01	.05
❑ 146 Johnny Newman	.01	.05
❑ 147 Greg Anthony	.01	.05
❑ 148 Anthony Bonner	.01	.05
❑ 149 Hubert Davis	.01	.05
❑ 150 Patrick Ewing	.08	.25
❑ 151 Derek Harper	.01	.05
❑ 152 Anthony Mason	.02	.10
❑ 153 Charles Oakley	.01	.05
❑ 154 Doc Rivers	.02	.10
❑ 155 Charles Smith	.01	.05
❑ 156 John Starks	.01	.05
❑ 157 Nick Anderson	.01	.05
❑ 158 Anthony Avent	.01	.05
❑ 159 Anfernee Hardaway	.25	.60
❑ 160 Shaquille O'Neal	.50	1.25
❑ 161 Donald Royal	.01	.05
❑ 162 Dennis Scott	.01	.05
❑ 163 Scott Skiles	.01	.05
❑ 164 Jeff Turner	.01	.05
❑ 165 Dana Barros	.01	.05
❑ 166 Shawn Bradley	.01	.05
❑ 167 Greg Graham	.01	.05
❑ 168 Eric Leckner	.01	.05
❑ 169 Jeff Malone	.01	.05
❑ 170 Moses Malone	.08	.25
❑ 171 Tim Perry	.01	.05
❑ 172 Clarence Weatherspoon	.01	.05
❑ 173 Orlando Woolridge	.01	.05
❑ 174 Danny Ainge	.01	.05
❑ 175 Charles Barkley	.15	.40
❑ 176 Cedric Ceballos	.01	.05
❑ 177 A.C. Green	.02	.10
❑ 178 Kevin Johnson	.02	.10
❑ 179 Joe Kleine	.01	.05
❑ 180 Dan Majerle	.02	.10
❑ 181 Oliver Miller	.01	.05
❑ 182 Mark West	.01	.05
❑ 183 Clyde Drexler	.08	.25
❑ 184 Harvey Grant	.01	.05
❑ 185 Jerome Kersey	.01	.05
❑ 186 Tracy Murray	.01	.05
❑ 187 Terry Porter	.01	.05
❑ 188 Clifford Robinson	.02	.10
❑ 189 James Robinson	.01	.05
❑ 190 Rod Strickland	.02	.10
❑ 191 Buck Williams	.01	.05
❑ 192 Duane Causwell	.01	.05
❑ 193 Bobby Hurley	.01	.05
❑ 194 Olden Polynice	.01	.05
❑ 195 Mitch Richmond	.08	.25
❑ 196 Lionel Simmons	.01	.05
❑ 197 Wayman Tisdale	.01	.05
❑ 198 Spud Webb	.01	.05
❑ 199 Walt Williams	.01	.05
❑ 200 Trevor Wilson	.01	.05
❑ 201 Willie Anderson	.01	.05
❑ 202 Antoine Carr	.01	.05
❑ 203 Terry Cummings	.01	.05
❑ 204 Vinny Del Negro	.01	.05
❑ 205 Dale Ellis	.01	.05
❑ 206 Negele Knight	.01	.05
❑ 207 J.R. Reid	.01	.05
❑ 208 David Robinson	.15	.40
❑ 209 Dennis Rodman	.20	.50
❑ 210 Vincent Askew	.01	.05
❑ 211 Michael Cage	.01	.05
❑ 212 Kendall Gill	.02	.10
❑ 213 Shawn Kemp	.15	.40
❑ 214 Nate McMillan	.01	.05
❑ 215 Gary Payton	.15	.40
❑ 216 Sam Perkins	.02	.10
❑ 217 Ricky Pierce	.01	.05
❑ 218 Detlef Schrempf	.02	.10
❑ 219 David Benoit	.01	.05
❑ 220 Tom Chambers	.01	.05
❑ 221 Tyrone Corbin	.01	.05
❑ 222 Jeff Hornacek	.02	.10
❑ 223 Jay Humphries	.01	.05
❑ 224 Karl Malone	.15	.40
❑ 225 Bryon Russell	.01	.05
❑ 226 Felton Spencer	.01	.05
❑ 227 John Stockton	.08	.25
❑ 228 Michael Adams	.01	.05
❑ 229 Rex Chapman	.01	.05
❑ 230 Calbert Cheaney	.01	.05
❑ 231 Kevin Duckworth	.01	.05
❑ 232 Pervis Ellison	.01	.05
❑ 233 Tom Gugliotta	.02	.10
❑ 234 Don MacLean	.01	.05
❑ 235 Gheorghe Muresan	.01	.05
❑ 236 Brent Price	.01	.05
❑ 237 Toronto Raptors Logo	.01	.05
❑ 238 Checklist	.01	.05
❑ 239 Checklist	.01	.05
❑ 240 Checklist	.01	.05
❑ 241 Sergei Bazarevich RC	.01	.05
❑ 242 Tyrone Corbin	.01	.05
❑ 243 Grant Long	.01	.05
❑ 244 Ken Norman	.01	.05
❑ 245 Steve Smith	.02	.10
❑ 246 Fred Vinson	.01	.05
❑ 247 Blue Edwards	.01	.05
❑ 248 Greg Minor RC	.01	.05
❑ 249 Eric Montross RC	.01	.05
❑ 250 Derek Strong	.01	.05
❑ 251 David Wesley	.01	.05
❑ 252 Dominique Wilkins	.08	.25
❑ 253 Michael Adams	.01	.05
❑ 254 Tony Bennett	.01	.05
❑ 255 Darrin Hancock RC	.01	.05
❑ 256 Robert Parish	.02	.10
❑ 257 Corie Blount	.01	.05
❑ 258 Jud Buechler	.01	.05
❑ 259 Greg Foster	.01	.05
❑ 260 Ron Harper	.02	.10
❑ 261 Larry Krystkowiak	.01	.05
❑ 262 Will Perdue	.01	.05
❑ 263 Dickey Simpkins RC	.01	.05
❑ 264 Michael Cage	.01	.05
❑ 265 Tony Campbell	.01	.05
❑ 266 Terry Davis	.01	.05
❑ 267 Tony Dumas RC	.01	.05
❑ 268 Jason Kidd RC	1.00	2.50
❑ 269 Roy Tarpley	.01	.05
❑ 270 Morlon Wiley	.01	.05
❑ 271 Lorenzo Williams	.01	.05
❑ 272 Dale Ellis	.01	.05
❑ 273 Tom Hammonds	.01	.05
❑ 274 Cliff Levingston	.01	.05
❑ 275 Darnell Mee	.01	.05
❑ 276 Jalen Rose RC	.40	1.00
❑ 277 Reggie Slater	.01	.05
❑ 278 Bill Curley RC	.01	.05
❑ 279 Johnny Dawkins	.01	.05
❑ 280 Grant Hill RC	.50	1.25
❑ 281 Eric Leckner	.01	.05
❑ 282 Mark Macon	.01	.05
❑ 283 Oliver Miller	.01	.05
❑ 284 Mark West	.01	.05
❑ 285 Manute Bol	.01	.05
❑ 286 Tom Gugliotta	.02	.10
❑ 287 Ricky Pierce	.01	.05
❑ 288 Carlos Rogers RC	.01	.05
❑ 289 Clifford Rozier RC	.01	.05
❑ 290 Rony Seikaly	.01	.05
❑ 291 Tim Breaux	.01	.05
❑ 292 Chris Jent	.01	.05
❑ 293 Eric Riley	.01	.05
❑ 294 Zan Tabak	.01	.05
❑ 295 Duane Ferrell	.01	.05
❑ 296 Mark Jackson	.01	.05
❑ 297 John Williams	.01	.05
❑ 298 Matt Fish	.01	.05
❑ 299 Tony Massenburg	.01	.05
❑ 300 Lamond Murray RC	.02	.10
❑ 301 Bo Outlaw RC	.01	.05
❑ 302 Eric Piatkowski RC	.01	.05
❑ 303 Pooh Richardson	.01	.05
❑ 304 Randy Woods	.01	.05
❑ 305 Sam Bowie	.01	.05
❑ 306 Cedric Ceballos	.01	.05
❑ 307 Antonio Harvey	.01	.05
❑ 308 Eddie Jones RC	.50	1.25
❑ 309 Anthony Miller RC	.01	.05
❑ 310 Ledell Eackles	.01	.05
❑ 311 Kevin Gamble	.01	.05
❑ 312 Brad Lohaus	.01	.05
❑ 313 Billy Owens	.01	.05
❑ 314 Khalid Reeves RC	.01	.05
❑ 315 Kevin Willis	.01	.05
❑ 316 Marty Conlon	.01	.05
❑ 317 Eric Mobley RC	.01	.05
❑ 318 Johnny Newman	.01	.05
❑ 319 Ed Pinckney	.01	.05
❑ 320 Glenn Robinson RC	.30	.75
❑ 321 Mike Brown	.01	.05
❑ 322 Pat Durham	.01	.05
❑ 323 Howard Eisley RC	.01	.05
❑ 324 Andres Guibert	.01	.05
❑ 325 Donyell Marshall RC	.08	.25
❑ 326 Sean Rooks	.01	.05
❑ 327 Yinka Dare RC	.01	.05
❑ 328 Sleepy Floyd	.01	.05
❑ 329 Sean Higgins	.01	.05
❑ 330 Rick Mahorn	.01	.05
❑ 331 Rex Walters	.01	.05
❑ 332 Jayson Williams	.02	.10
❑ 333 Charlie Ward RC	.08	.25
❑ 334 Herb Williams	.01	.05
❑ 335 Monty Williams RC	.01	.05
❑ 336 Anthony Bowie	.01	.05
❑ 337 Horace Grant	.02	.10
❑ 338 Geert Hammink	.01	.05
❑ 339 Tree Rollins	.01	.05
❑ 340 Brian Shaw	.01	.05
❑ 341 Brooks Thompson RC	.01	.05
❑ 342 Derrick Alston RC	.01	.05
❑ 343 Willie Burton	.01	.05
❑ 344 Jaren Jackson	.01	.05
❑ 345 B.J.Tyler RC	.01	.05
❑ 346 Scott Williams	.01	.05
❑ 347 Sharone Wright RC	.01	.05
❑ 348 Antonio Lang RC	.01	.05
❑ 349 Danny Manning	.02	.10
❑ 350 Elliot Perry	.01	.05
❑ 351 Wesley Person RC	.08	.25
❑ 352 Trevor Ruffin	.01	.05
❑ 353 Danny Schayes	.01	.05
❑ 354 Aaron Swinson RC	.01	.05
❑ 355 Wayman Tisdale	.01	.05
❑ 356 Mark Bryant	.01	.05
❑ 357 Chris Dudley	.01	.05
❑ 358 James Edwards	.01	.05
❑ 359 Aaron McKie RC	.20	.50
❑ 360 Alaa Abdelnaby	.01	.05
❑ 361 Frank Brickowski	.01	.05
❑ 362 Randy Brown	.01	.05
❑ 363 Brian Grant RC	.25	.60
❑ 364 Michael Smith RC	.01	.05
❑ 365 Henry Turner	.01	.05
❑ 366 Sean Elliott	.02	.10
❑ 367 Avery Johnson	.01	.05
❑ 368 Moses Malone	.08	.25
❑ 369 Julius Nwosu	.01	.05
❑ 370 Chuck Person	.01	.05
❑ 371 Chris Whitney	.01	.05
❑ 372 Bill Cartwright	.01	.05
❑ 373 Byron Houston	.01	.05
❑ 374 Ervin Johnson	.01	.05
❑ 375 Sarunas Marciulionis	.01	.05
❑ 376 Antoine Carr	.01	.05
❑ 377 John Crotty	.01	.05
❑ 378 Adam Keefe	.01	.05
❑ 379 Jamie Watson RC	.01	.05
❑ 380 Mitchell Butler	.01	.05
❑ 381 Juwan Howard RC	.25	.60
❑ 382 Jim McIlvaine RC	.01	.05
❑ 383 Doug Overton	.01	.05
❑ 384 Scott Skiles	.01	.05
❑ 385 Larry Stewart	.01	.05
❑ 386 Kenny Walker	.01	.05
❑ 387 Chris Webber	.25	.60
❑ 388 Vancouver Grizzlies	.01	.05
❑ 389 Checklist	.01	.05
❑ 390 Checklist	.01	.05

1995-96 Fleer

❑ COMPLETE SET (350)	20.00	40.00
❑ COMPLETE SERIES 1 (200)	10.00	20.00

❑ COMPLETE SERIES 2 (150)	10.00	20.00
❑ 1 Stacey Augmon	.05	.15
❑ 2 Mookie Blaylock	.05	.15
❑ 3 Craig Ehlo	.05	.15
❑ 4 Andrew Lang	.05	.15
❑ 5 Grant Long	.05	.15
❑ 6 Ken Norman	.05	.15
❑ 7 Steve Smith	.10	.30
❑ 8 Dee Brown	.05	.15
❑ 9 Sherman Douglas	.05	.15
❑ 10 Eric Montross	.05	.15
❑ 11 Dino Radja	.05	.15
❑ 12 David Wesley	.05	.15
❑ 13 Dominique Wilkins	.20	.50
❑ 14 Muggsy Bogues	.10	.30
❑ 15 Scott Burrell	.05	.15
❑ 16 Dell Curry	.05	.15
❑ 17 Hersey Hawkins	.05	.15
❑ 18 Larry Johnson	.10	.30
❑ 19 Alonzo Mourning	.10	.30
❑ 20 Robert Parish	.10	.30
❑ 21 B.J. Armstrong	.05	.15
❑ 22 Michael Jordan	1.25	3.00
❑ 23 Steve Kerr	.10	.30
❑ 24 Toni Kukoc	.10	.30
❑ 25 Will Perdue	.05	.15
❑ 26 Scottie Pippen	.30	.75
❑ 27 Terrell Brandon	.10	.30
❑ 28 Tyrone Hill	.05	.15
❑ 29 Chris Mills	.05	.15
❑ 30 Bobby Phills	.05	.15
❑ 31 Mark Price	.10	.30
❑ 32 John Williams	.05	.15
❑ 33 Lucious Harris	.05	.15
❑ 34 Jim Jackson	.05	.15
❑ 35 Popeye Jones	.05	.15
❑ 36 Jason Kidd	.60	1.50
❑ 37 Jamal Mashburn	.10	.30
❑ 38 George McCloud	.05	.15
❑ 39 Roy Tarpley	.05	.15
❑ 40 Lorenzo Williams	.05	.15
❑ 41 Mahmoud Abdul-Rauf	.05	.15
❑ 42 Dale Ellis	.05	.15
❑ 43 LaPhonso Ellis	.05	.15
❑ 44 Dikembe Mutombo	.10	.30
❑ 45 Robert Pack	.05	.15
❑ 46 Rodney Rogers	.05	.15
❑ 47 Jalen Rose	.25	.60
❑ 48 Bryant Stith	.05	.15
❑ 49 Reggie Williams	.05	.15
❑ 50 Joe Dumars	.20	.50
❑ 51 Grant Hill	.25	.60
❑ 52 Allan Houston	.10	.30
❑ 53 Lindsey Hunter	.05	.15
❑ 54 Oliver Miller	.05	.15
❑ 55 Terry Mills	.05	.15
❑ 56 Mark West	.05	.15
❑ 57 Chris Gatling	.05	.15
❑ 58 Tim Hardaway	.10	.30
❑ 59 Donyell Marshall	.10	.30
❑ 60 Chris Mullin	.20	.50
❑ 61 Carlos Rogers	.05	.15
❑ 62 Clifford Rozier	.05	.15
❑ 63 Rony Seikaly	.05	.15
❑ 64 Latrell Sprewell	.20	.50
❑ 65 Sam Cassell	.20	.50
❑ 66 Clyde Drexler	.20	.50
❑ 67 Mario Elie	.05	.15
❑ 68 Carl Herrera	.05	.15
❑ 69 Robert Horry	.10	.30
❑ 70 Vernon Maxwell	.05	.15
❑ 71 Hakeem Olajuwon	.20	.50
❑ 72 Kenny Smith	.05	.15
❑ 73 Dale Davis	.05	.15
❑ 74 Mark Jackson	.10	.30
❑ 75 Derrick McKey	.05	.15
❑ 76 Reggie Miller	.20	.50
❑ 77 Sam Mitchell	.05	.15
❑ 78 Byron Scott	.05	.15
❑ 79 Rik Smits	.10	.30
❑ 80 Terry Dehere	.05	.15
❑ 81 Tony Massenburg	.05	.15
❑ 82 Lamond Murray	.05	.15
❑ 83 Pooh Richardson	.05	.15
❑ 84 Malik Sealy	.05	.15
❑ 85 Loy Vaught	.05	.15
❑ 86 Elden Campbell	.05	.15
❑ 87 Cedric Ceballos	.05	.15
❑ 88 Vlade Divac	.10	.30
❑ 89 Eddie Jones	.25	.60
❑ 90 Anthony Peeler	.05	.15
❑ 91 Sedale Threatt	.05	.15
❑ 92 Nick Van Exel	.20	.50
❑ 93 Bimbo Coles	.05	.15
❑ 94 Matt Geiger	.05	.15
❑ 95 Billy Owens	.05	.15
❑ 96 Khalid Reeves	.05	.15
❑ 97 Glen Rice	.10	.30
❑ 98 John Salley	.05	.15
❑ 99 Kevin Willis	.10	.30
❑ 100 Vin Baker	.10	.30
❑ 101 Marty Conlon	.05	.15
❑ 102 Todd Day	.05	.15
❑ 103 Lee Mayberry	.05	.15
❑ 104 Eric Murdock	.05	.15
❑ 105 Glenn Robinson	.20	.50
❑ 106 Winston Garland	.05	.15
❑ 107 Tom Gugliotta	.05	.15
❑ 108 Christian Laettner	.10	.30
❑ 109 Isaiah Rider	.05	.15
❑ 110 Sean Rooks	.05	.15
❑ 111 Doug West	.05	.15
❑ 112 Kenny Anderson	.10	.30
❑ 113 Benoit Benjamin	.05	.15
❑ 114 P.J. Brown	.05	.15
❑ 115 Derrick Coleman	.05	.15
❑ 116 Armon Gilliam	.05	.15
❑ 117 Chris Morris	.05	.15
❑ 118 Rex Walters	.05	.15
❑ 119 Hubert Davis	.05	.15
❑ 120 Patrick Ewing	.20	.50
❑ 121 Derek Harper	.10	.30
❑ 122 Anthony Mason	.10	.30
❑ 123 Charles Oakley	.05	.15
❑ 124 Charles Smith	.05	.15
❑ 125 John Starks	.10	.30
❑ 126 Nick Anderson	.05	.15
❑ 127 Anthony Bowie	.05	.15
❑ 128 Horace Grant	.10	.30
❑ 129 Anfernee Hardaway	.20	.50
❑ 130 Shaquille O'Neal	.50	1.25
❑ 131 Donald Royal	.05	.15
❑ 132 Dennis Scott	.05	.15
❑ 133 Brian Shaw	.05	.15
❑ 134 Derrick Alston	.05	.15
❑ 135 Dana Barros	.05	.15
❑ 136 Shawn Bradley	.05	.15
❑ 137 Willie Burton	.05	.15
❑ 138 Clarence Weatherspoon	.05	.15
❑ 139 Scott Williams	.05	.15
❑ 140 Sharone Wright	.05	.15
❑ 141 Danny Ainge	.05	.15
❑ 142 Charles Barkley	.25	.60
❑ 143 A.C. Green	.10	.30
❑ 144 Kevin Johnson	.10	.30
❑ 145 Dan Majerle	.10	.30
❑ 146 Danny Manning	.10	.30
❑ 147 Elliot Perry	.05	.15
❑ 148 Wesley Person	.05	.15
❑ 149 Wayman Tisdale	.05	.15
❑ 150 Chris Dudley	.05	.15
❑ 151 Jerome Kersey	.05	.15
❑ 152 Aaron McKie	.10	.30
❑ 153 Terry Porter	.05	.15
❑ 154 Clifford Robinson	.05	.15
❑ 155 James Robinson	.05	.15
❑ 156 Rod Strickland	.05	.15
❑ 157 Otis Thorpe	.05	.15
❑ 158 Buck Williams	.05	.15
❑ 159 Brian Grant	.20	.50
❑ 160 Bobby Hurley	.05	.15
❑ 161 Olden Polynice	.05	.15
❑ 162 Mitch Richmond	.10	.30
❑ 163 Michael Smith	.05	.15
❑ 164 Spud Webb	.10	.30
❑ 165 Walt Williams	.05	.15
❑ 166 Terry Cummings	.05	.15
❑ 167 Vinny Del Negro	.05	.15
❑ 168 Sean Elliott	.10	.30
❑ 169 Avery Johnson	.05	.15
❑ 170 Chuck Person	.05	.15
❑ 171 J.R. Reid	.05	.15
❑ 172 Doc Rivers	.10	.30
❑ 173 David Robinson	.20	.50
❑ 174 Dennis Rodman	.10	.30
❑ 175 Vincent Askew	.05	.15
❑ 176 Kendall Gill	.05	.15
❑ 177 Shawn Kemp	.10	.30
❑ 178 Sarunas Marciulionis	.05	.15
❑ 179 Nate McMillan	.05	.15
❑ 180 Gary Payton	.20	.50
❑ 181 Sam Perkins	.10	.30
❑ 182 Detlef Schrempf	.10	.30
❑ 183 David Benoit	.05	.15
❑ 184 Antoine Carr	.05	.15
❑ 185 Blue Edwards	.05	.15
❑ 186 Jeff Hornacek	.10	.30
❑ 187 Adam Keefe	.05	.15
❑ 188 Karl Malone	.25	.60
❑ 189 Felton Spencer	.05	.15
❑ 190 John Stockton	.25	.60
❑ 191 Rex Chapman	.05	.15
❑ 192 Calbert Cheaney	.05	.15
❑ 193 Juwan Howard	.20	.50
❑ 194 Don MacLean	.05	.15
❑ 195 Gheorghe Muresan	.05	.15
❑ 196 Scott Skiles	.05	.15
❑ 197 Chris Webber	.25	.60
❑ 198 Checklist	.05	.15
❑ 199 Checklist	.05	.15
❑ 200 Checklist	.05	.15
❑ 201 Stacey Augmon	.05	.15
❑ 202 Mookie Blaylock	.05	.15
❑ 203 Grant Long	.05	.15
❑ 204 Ken Norman	.05	.15
❑ 205 Steve Smith	.10	.30
❑ 206 Spud Webb	.10	.30
❑ 207 Dana Barros	.05	.15
❑ 208 Rick Fox	.10	.30
❑ 209 Kendall Gill	.05	.15
❑ 210 Khalid Reeves	.05	.15
❑ 211 Glen Rice	.10	.30
❑ 212 Luc Longley	.05	.15
❑ 213 Dennis Rodman	.10	.30
❑ 214 Dan Majerle	.10	.30
❑ 215 Tony Dumas	.05	.15
❑ 216 Tom Hammonds	.05	.15
❑ 217 Elmore Spencer	.05	.15
❑ 218 Otis Thorpe	.05	.15
❑ 219 B.J. Armstrong	.05	.15
❑ 220 Sam Cassell	.20	.50
❑ 221 Clyde Drexler	.20	.50
❑ 222 Mario Elie	.05	.15
❑ 223 Robert Horry	.10	.30
❑ 224 Hakeem Olajuwon	.20	.50
❑ 225 Kenny Smith	.05	.15
❑ 226 Antonio Davis	.05	.15
❑ 227 Eddie Johnson	.05	.15
❑ 228 Ricky Pierce	.05	.15
❑ 229 Eric Piatkowski	.02	.10
❑ 230 Rodney Rogers	.05	.15
❑ 231 Brian Williams	.05	.15
❑ 232 Corie Blount	.05	.15
❑ 233 George Lynch	.05	.15
❑ 234 Kevin Gamble	.05	.15
❑ 235 Alonzo Mourning	.10	.30
❑ 236 Eric Mobley	.05	.15
❑ 237 Terry Porter	.05	.15
❑ 238 Micheal Williams	.05	.15
❑ 239 Kevin Edwards	.05	.15
❑ 240 Vern Fleming	.05	.15
❑ 241 Charlie Ward	.05	.15
❑ 242 Jon Koncak	.05	.15
❑ 243 Richard Dumas	.05	.15
❑ 244 Jeff Malone	.05	.15
❑ 245 Vernon Maxwell	.05	.15
❑ 246 John Williams	.05	.15
❑ 247 Harvey Grant	.05	.15
❑ 248 Dontonio Wingfield	.05	.15
❑ 249 Tyrone Corbin	.05	.15
❑ 250 Sarunas Marciulionis	.05	.15
❑ 251 Will Perdue	.05	.15
❑ 252 Hersey Hawkins	.05	.15

❑ 253 Ervin Johnson	.05	.15
❑ 254 Shawn Kemp	.10	.30
❑ 255 Gary Payton	.20	.50
❑ 256 Sam Perkins	.10	.30
❑ 257 Detlef Schrempf	.10	.30
❑ 258 Chris Morris	.05	.15
❑ 259 Robert Pack	.05	.15
❑ 260 Willie Anderson ET	.05	.15
❑ 261 Jimmy King ET	.05	.15
❑ 262 Oliver Miller ET	.05	.15
❑ 263 Tracy Murray ET	.05	.15
❑ 264 Ed Pinckney ET	.05	.15
❑ 265 Alvin Robertson ET	.05	.15
❑ 266 Carlos Rogers ET	.05	.15
❑ 267 John Salley ET	.05	.15
❑ 268 Damon Stoudamire ET	.25	.60
❑ 269 Zan Tabak ET	.05	.15
❑ 270 Ashraf Amaya ET	.05	.15
❑ 271 Greg Anthony ET	.05	.15
❑ 272 Benoit Benjamin ET	.05	.15
❑ 273 Blue Edwards ET	.05	.15
❑ 274 Kenny Gattison ET	.05	.15
❑ 275 Antonio Harvey ET	.05	.15
❑ 276 Chris King ET	.05	.15
❑ 277 Lawrence Moten ET	.05	.15
❑ 278 Bryant Reeves ET	.10	.30
❑ 279 Byron Scott ET	.05	.15
❑ 280 Cory Alexander RC	.05	.15
❑ 281 Jerome Allen RC	.05	.15
❑ 282 Brent Barry RC	.20	.50
❑ 283 Mario Bennett RC	.05	.15
❑ 284 Travis Best RC	.05	.15
❑ 285 Junior Burrough RC	.05	.15
❑ 286 Jason Caffey RC	.10	.30
❑ 287 Randolph Childress RC	.05	.15
❑ 288 Sasha Danilovic RC	.05	.15
❑ 289 Mark Davis RC	.05	.15
❑ 290 Tyus Edney RC	.05	.15
❑ 291 Michael Finley RC	.50	1.25
❑ 292 Sherrell Ford RC	.05	.15
❑ 293 Kevin Garnett RC	1.25	3.00
❑ 294 Alan Henderson RC	.20	.50
❑ 295 Frankie King RC	.05	.15
❑ 296 Jimmy King RC	.05	.15
❑ 297 Donny Marshall RC	.10	.30
❑ 298 Antonio McDyess RC	.40	1.00
❑ 299 Loren Meyer RC	.05	.15
❑ 300 Lawrence Moten RC	.05	.15
❑ 301 Ed O'Bannon RC	.05	.15
❑ 302 Greg Ostertag RC	.05	.15
❑ 303 Cherokee Parks RC	.05	.15
❑ 304 Theo Ratliff RC	.25	.60
❑ 305 Bryant Reeves RC	.20	.50
❑ 306 Shawn Respert RC	.05	.15
❑ 307 Lou Roe RC	.05	.15
❑ 308 Arvydas Sabonis RC	.25	.60
❑ 309 Joe Smith RC	.30	.75
❑ 310 Jerry Stackhouse RC	.60	1.50
❑ 311 Damon Stoudamire RC	.40	1.00
❑ 312 Bob Sura RC	.10	.30
❑ 313 Kurt Thomas RC	.10	.30
❑ 314 Gary Trent RC	.05	.15
❑ 315 David Vaughn RC	.05	.15
❑ 316 Rasheed Wallace RC	.50	1.25
❑ 317 Eric Williams RC	.10	.30
❑ 318 Corliss Williamson RC	.20	.50
❑ 319 George Zidek RC	.05	.15
❑ 320 Mookie Blaylock FF	.05	.15
❑ 321 Dino Radja FF	.05	.15
❑ 322 Larry Johnson FF	.05	.15
❑ 323 Michael Jordan FF	.60	1.50
❑ 324 Tyrone Hill FF	.05	.15
❑ 325 Jason Kidd FF	.30	.75
❑ 326 Dikembe Mutombo FF	.05	.15
❑ 327 Grant Hill FF	.20	.50
❑ 328 Joe Smith FF	.10	.30
❑ 329 Hakeem Olajuwon FF	.10	.30
❑ 330 Reggie Miller FF	.10	.30
❑ 331 Loy Vaught FF	.05	.15
❑ 332 Nick Van Exel FF	.05	.15
❑ 333 Alonzo Mourning FF	.05	.15
❑ 334 Glenn Robinson FF	.10	.30
❑ 335 Kevin Garnett FF	.50	1.25
❑ 336 Kenny Anderson FF	.05	.15
❑ 337 Patrick Ewing FF	.10	.30
❑ 338 Shaquille O'Neal FF	.20	.50
❑ 339 Jerry Stackhouse FF	.30	.75
❑ 340 Charles Barkley FF	.20	.50
❑ 341 Clifford Robinson FF	.05	.15
❑ 342 Mitch Richmond FF	.05	.15
❑ 343 David Robinson FF	.10	.30
❑ 344 Shawn Kemp FF	.05	.15
❑ 345 Damon Stoudamire FF	.25	.60
❑ 346 Karl Malone FF	.20	.50
❑ 347 Bryant Reeves FF	.10	.30
❑ 348 Chris Webber FF	.10	.30
❑ 349 Checklist (201-319)	.05	.15
❑ 350 Checklist (320-350/ins.)	.05	.15

1996-97 Fleer

❑ COMPLETE SET (300)	17.50	35.00
❑ COMPLETE SERIES 1 (150)	7.50	15.00
❑ COMPLETE SERIES 2 (150)	10.00	20.00
❑ 1 Stacey Augmon	.05	.15
❑ 2 Mookie Blaylock	.05	.15
❑ 3 Christian Laettner	.10	.30
❑ 4 Grant Long	.05	.15
❑ 5 Steve Smith	.10	.30
❑ 6 Rick Fox	.05	.15
❑ 7 Dino Radja	.05	.15
❑ 8 Eric Williams	.05	.15
❑ 9 Kenny Anderson	.05	.15
❑ 10 Dell Curry	.05	.15
❑ 11 Larry Johnson	.10	.30
❑ 12 Glen Rice	.10	.30
❑ 13 Michael Jordan	1.25	3.00
❑ 14 Toni Kukoc	.10	.30
❑ 15 Scottie Pippen	.30	.75
❑ 16 Dennis Rodman	.10	.30
❑ 17 Terrell Brandon	.10	.30
❑ 18 Chris Mills	.05	.15
❑ 19 Bobby Phills	.05	.15
❑ 20 Bob Sura	.05	.15
❑ 21 Jim Jackson	.05	.15
❑ 22 Jason Kidd	.30	.75
❑ 23 Jamal Mashburn	.10	.30
❑ 24 George McCloud	.05	.15
❑ 25 Mahmoud Abdul-Rauf	.05	.15
❑ 26 Antonio McDyess	.10	.30
❑ 27 Dikembe Mutombo	.10	.30
❑ 28 Jalen Rose	.20	.50
❑ 29 Bryant Stith	.05	.15
❑ 30 Joe Dumars	.20	.50
❑ 31 Grant Hill	.20	.50
❑ 32 Allan Houston	.10	.30
❑ 33 Theo Ratliff	.10	.30
❑ 34 Otis Thorpe	.05	.15
❑ 35 Chris Mullin	.20	.50
❑ 36 Joe Smith	.10	.30
❑ 37 Latrell Sprewell	.20	.50
❑ 38 Kevin Willis	.05	.15
❑ 39 Sam Cassell	.20	.50
❑ 40 Clyde Drexler	.20	.50
❑ 41 Robert Horry	.10	.30
❑ 42 Hakeem Olajuwon	.20	.50
❑ 43 Dale Davis	.05	.15
❑ 44 Mark Jackson	.05	.15
❑ 45 Derrick McKey	.05	.15
❑ 46 Reggie Miller	.20	.50
❑ 47 Rik Smits	.10	.30
❑ 48 Brent Barry	.05	.15
❑ 49 Malik Sealy	.05	.15
❑ 50 Loy Vaught	.05	.15
❑ 51 Brian Williams	.05	.15
❑ 52 Elden Campbell	.05	.15
❑ 53 Cedric Ceballos	.05	.15
❑ 54 Vlade Divac	.05	.15
❑ 55 Eddie Jones	.20	.50
❑ 56 Nick Van Exel	.20	.50
❑ 57 Tim Hardaway	.10	.30
❑ 58 Alonzo Mourning	.10	.30
❑ 59 Kurt Thomas	.10	.30
❑ 60 Walt Williams	.05	.15
❑ 61 Vin Baker	.10	.30
❑ 62 Sherman Douglas	.05	.15
❑ 63 Glenn Robinson	.20	.50
❑ 64 Kevin Garnett	.40	1.00
❑ 65 Tom Gugliotta	.05	.15
❑ 66 Isaiah Rider	.10	.30
❑ 67 Shawn Bradley	.05	.15
❑ 68 Chris Childs	.05	.15
❑ 69 Armon Gilliam	.05	.15
❑ 70 Ed O'Bannon	.05	.15
❑ 71 Patrick Ewing	.20	.50
❑ 72 Derek Harper	.05	.15
❑ 73 Anthony Mason	.10	.30
❑ 74 Charles Oakley	.05	.15
❑ 75 John Starks	.10	.30
❑ 76 Nick Anderson	.05	.15
❑ 77 Horace Grant	.10	.30
❑ 78 Anfernee Hardaway	.20	.50
❑ 79 Shaquille O'Neal	.50	1.25
❑ 80 Dennis Scott	.05	.15
❑ 81 Derrick Coleman	.10	.30
❑ 82 Vernon Maxwell	.05	.15
❑ 83 Jerry Stackhouse	.25	.60
❑ 84 Clarence Weatherspoon	.05	.15
❑ 85 Charles Barkley	.25	.60
❑ 86 Michael Finley	.25	.60
❑ 87 Kevin Johnson	.10	.30
❑ 88 Wesley Person	.05	.15
❑ 89 Clifford Robinson	.05	.15
❑ 90 Arvydas Sabonis	.10	.30
❑ 91 Rod Strickland	.05	.15
❑ 92 Gary Trent	.05	.15
❑ 93 Tyus Edney	.05	.15
❑ 94 Brian Grant	.20	.50
❑ 95 Billy Owens	.05	.15
❑ 96 Mitch Richmond	.10	.30
❑ 97 Vinny Del Negro	.05	.15
❑ 98 Sean Elliott	.10	.30
❑ 99 Avery Johnson	.05	.15
❑ 100 David Robinson	.20	.50
❑ 101 Hersey Hawkins	.10	.30
❑ 102 Shawn Kemp	.10	.30
❑ 103 Gary Payton	.20	.50
❑ 104 Detlef Schrempf	.10	.30
❑ 105 Oliver Miller	.05	.15
❑ 106 Tracy Murray	.05	.15
❑ 107 Damon Stoudamire	.20	.50
❑ 108 Sharone Wright	.05	.15
❑ 109 Jeff Hornacek	.10	.30
❑ 110 Karl Malone	.20	.50
❑ 111 John Stockton	.20	.50
❑ 112 Greg Anthony	.05	.15
❑ 113 Bryant Reeves	.05	.15
❑ 114 Byron Scott	.05	.15
❑ 115 Calbert Cheaney	.05	.15
❑ 116 Juwan Howard	.10	.30
❑ 117 Gheorghe Muresan	.05	.15
❑ 118 Rasheed Wallace	.25	.60
❑ 119 Chris Webber	.20	.50
❑ 120 Mookie Blaylock HL	.05	.15
❑ 121 Dino Radja HL	.05	.15
❑ 122 Larry Johnson HL	.05	.15
❑ 123 Michael Jordan HL	.60	1.50
❑ 124 Terrell Brandon HL	.05	.15
❑ 125 Jason Kidd HL	.15	.40
❑ 126 Antonio McDyess HL	.10	.30
❑ 127 Grant Hill HL	.10	.30
❑ 128 Latrell Sprewell HL	.20	.50
❑ 129 Hakeem Olajuwon HL	.10	.30
❑ 130 Reggie Miller HL	.10	.30
❑ 131 Loy Vaught HL	.05	.15
❑ 132 Cedric Ceballos HL	.05	.15
❑ 133 Alonzo Mourning HL	.05	.15
❑ 134 Vin Baker HL	.05	.15
❑ 135 Isaiah Rider HL	.05	.15
❑ 136 Armon Gilliam HL	.05	.15
❑ 137 Patrick Ewing HL	.10	.30
❑ 138 Shaquille O'Neal HL	.20	.50
❑ 139 Jerry Stackhouse HL	.10	.30
❑ 140 Charles Barkley HL	.20	.50
❑ 141 Clifford Robinson HL	.05	.15
❑ 142 Mitch Richmond HL	.05	.15
❑ 143 David Robinson HL	.10	.30
❑ 144 Shawn Kemp HL	.05	.15
❑ 145 Damon Stoudamire HL	.10	.30
❑ 146 Karl Malone HL	.10	.30
❑ 147 Bryant Reeves HL	.05	.15
❑ 148 Juwan Howard HL	.05	.15
❑ 149 Checklist	.05	.15
❑ 150 Checklist	.05	.15
❑ 151 Alan Henderson	.05	.15

152 Priest Lauderdale RC	.05	.15
153 Dikembe Mutombo	.10	.30
154 Dana Barros	.05	.15
155 Todd Day	.05	.15
156 Brett Szabo RC	.05	.15
157 Antoine Walker RC	.30	.75
158 Scott Burrell	.05	.15
159 Tony Delk RC	.20	.50
160 Vlade Divac	.05	.15
161 Matt Geiger	.05	.15
162 Anthony Mason	.10	.30
163 Malik Rose RC	.10	.30
164 Ron Harper	.10	.30
165 Steve Kerr	.10	.30
166 Luc Longley	.05	.15
167 Danny Ferry	.05	.15
168 Tyrone Hill	.05	.15
169 Vitaly Potapenko RC	.05	.15
170 Tony Dumas	.05	.15
171 Chris Gatling	.05	.15
172 Oliver Miller	.05	.15
173 Eric Montross	.05	.15
174 Samaki Walker RC	.05	.15
175 Darvin Ham RC	.05	.15
176 Mark Jackson	.05	.15
177 Ervin Johnson	.05	.15
178 Stacey Augmon	.05	.15
179 Joe Dumars	.20	.50
180 Grant Hill	.20	.50
181 Grant Long	.05	.15
182 Terry Mills	.05	.15
183 Otis Thorpe	.05	.15
184 Jerome Williams RC	.20	.50
185 B.J. Armstrong	.05	.15
186 Todd Fuller RC	.05	.15
187 Ray Owes RC	.05	.15
188 Mark Price	.10	.30
189 Felton Spencer	.05	.15
190 Charles Barkley	.25	.60
191 Mario Elie	.05	.15
192 Othella Harrington RC	.20	.50
193 Matt Maloney RC	.10	.30
194 Brent Price	.05	.15
195 Kevin Willis	.05	.15
196 Travis Best	.05	.15
197 Erick Dampier RC	.20	.50
198 Antonio Davis	.05	.15
199 Jalen Rose	.20	.50
200 Pooh Richardson	.05	.15
201 Rodney Rogers	.05	.15
202 Lorenzen Wright RC	.10	.30
203 Kobe Bryant RC	3.00	8.00
204 Derek Fisher RC	.30	.75
205 Travis Knight RC	.05	.15
206 Shaquille O'Neal	.50	1.25
207 Byron Scott	.05	.15
208 P.J. Brown	.05	.15
209 Sasha Danilovic	.05	.15
210 Dan Majerle	.10	.30
211 Martin Muursepp RC	.05	.15
212 Ray Allen RC	.60	1.50
213 Armon Gilliam	.05	.15
214 Andrew Lang	.05	.15
215 Moochie Norris RC	.10	.30
216 Kevin Garnett	.40	1.00
217 Tom Gugliotta	.05	.15
218 Shane Heal RC	.05	.15
219 Stephon Marbury RC	.50	1.25
220 Stojko Vrankovic	.05	.15
221 Kerry Kittles RC	.20	.50
222 Robert Pack	.05	.15
223 Jayson Williams	.10	.30
224 Allan Houston	.10	.30
225 Larry Johnson	.10	.30
226 Dontae' Jones RC	.05	.15
227 Walter McCarty RC	.05	.15
228 John Wallace RC	.20	.50
229 Charlie Ward	.05	.15
230 Brian Evans RC	.05	.15
231 Amal McCaskill RC	.05	.15
232 Brian Shaw	.05	.15
233 Mark Davis	.05	.15
234 Lucious Harris	.05	.15
235 Allen Iverson RC	.60	1.50
236 Sam Cassell	.20	.50
237 Robert Horry	.10	.30
238 Danny Manning	.10	.30
239 Steve Nash RC	1.50	4.00
240 Kenny Anderson	.05	.15
241 Aleksandar Djordjevic RC	.05	.15
242 Jermaine O'Neal RC	.50	1.25
243 Isaiah Rider	.10	.30
244 Rasheed Wallace	.25	.60
245 Mahmoud Abdul-Rauf	.05	.15
246 Michael Smith	.05	.15
247 Corliss Williamson	.10	.30
248 Vernon Maxwell	.05	.15
249 Charles Smith	.05	.15
250 Dominique Wilkins	.20	.50
251 Craig Ehlo	.05	.15
252 Jim McIlvaine	.05	.15
253 Sam Perkins	.10	.30
254 Marcus Camby RC	.25	.60
255 Popeye Jones	.05	.15
256 Donald Whiteside RC	.05	.15
257 Walt Williams	.05	.15
258 Jeff Hornacek	.10	.30
259 Karl Malone	.20	.50
260 Bryon Russell	.05	.15
261 John Stockton	.20	.50
262 Shareef Abdur-Rahim RC	.60	1.50
263 Anthony Peeler	.05	.15
264 Roy Rogers RC	.05	.15
265 Tim Legler	.05	.15
266 Tracy Murray	.05	.15
267 Rod Strickland	.05	.15
268 Ben Wallace RC	1.25	3.00
269 Kevin Garnett CB	.20	.50
270 Allan Houston CB	.05	.15
271 Eddie Jones CB	.10	.30
272 Jamal Mashburn CB	.05	.15
273 Antonio McDyess CB	.10	.30
274 Glenn Robinson CB	.10	.30
275 Joe Smith CB	.05	.15
276 Steve Smith CB	.05	.15
277 Jerry Stackhouse CB	.20	.50
278 Damon Stoudamire CB	.10	.30
279 Hakeem Olajuwon AS	.10	.30
280 Charles Barkley AS	.10	.30
281 Patrick Ewing AS	.10	.30
282 Michael Jordan AS	.60	1.50
283 Clyde Drexler AS	.10	.30
284 Karl Malone AS	.10	.30
285 John Stockton AS	.10	.30
286 David Robinson AS	.10	.30
287 Scottie Pippen AS	.15	.40
288 Shawn Kemp AS	.05	.15
289 Shaquille O'Neal AS	.20	.50
290 Mitch Richmond AS	.05	.15
291 Reggie Miller AS	.10	.30
292 Alonzo Mourning AS	.05	.15
293 Gary Payton AS	.10	.30
294 Anfernee Hardaway AS	.10	.30
295 Grant Hill AS	.10	.30
296 Dennis Rodman AS	.05	.15
297 Juwan Howard AS	.05	.15
298 Jason Kidd AS	.15	.40
299 Checklist	.05	.15
300 Checklist	.05	.15

1997-98 Fleer

COMPLETE SET (350)	20.00	40.00
COMPLETE SERIES 1 (200)	10.00	20.00
COMPLETE SERIES 2 (150)	10.00	20.00
1 Anfernee Hardaway	.20	.50
2 Mitch Richmond	.10	.30
3 Allen Iverson	.50	1.25
4 Chris Webber	.20	.50
5 Sasha Danilovic	.05	.15
6 Avery Johnson	.05	.15
7 Kenny Anderson	.10	.30
8 Antoine Walker	.25	.60
9 Nick Van Exel	.20	.50
10 Mookie Blaylock	.05	.15
11 Wesley Person	.05	.15
12 Vlade Divac	.10	.30
13 Glenn Robinson	.20	.50
14 Chris Mills	.05	.15
15 Latrell Sprewell	.20	.50
16 Jayson Williams	.05	.15
17 Travis Best	.05	.15
18 Charlie Ward	.05	.15
19 Theo Ratliff	.05	.15
20 Gary Payton	.20	.50
21 Marcus Camby	.20	.50
22 Clyde Drexler	.20	.50
23 Michael Jordan	1.25	3.00
24 Antonio McDyess	.10	.30
25 Stephon Marbury	.25	.60
26 Isaac Austin	.05	.15
27 Shareef Abdur-Rahim	.30	.75
28 Malik Sealy	.05	.15
29 Arvydas Sabonis	.10	.30
30 Kerry Kittles	.20	.50
31 Reggie Miller	.20	.50
32 Karl Malone	.20	.50
33 Grant Hill	.20	.50
34 Hakeem Olajuwon	.20	.50
35 Danny Ferry	.05	.15
36 Dominique Wilkins	.20	.50
37 Armon Gilliam	.05	.15
38 Danny Manning	.10	.30
39 Larry Johnson	.10	.30
40 Dino Radja	.05	.15
41 Jason Caffey	.05	.15
42 Jerry Stackhouse	.20	.50
43 Alonzo Mourning	.10	.30
44 Shawn Bradley	.05	.15
45 Bo Outlaw	.05	.15
46 Bryon Russell	.05	.15
47 Doug West	.05	.15
48 Lawrence Moten	.05	.15
49 Dale Ellis	.05	.15
50 Kobe Bryant	.75	2.00
51 Carlos Rogers	.05	.15
52 Todd Fuller	.05	.15
53 Tyus Edney	.05	.15
54 Horace Grant	.10	.30
55 Dikembe Mutombo	.10	.30
56 Jim McIlvaine	.05	.15
57 Harvey Grant	.05	.15
58 Dean Garrett	.05	.15
59 Samaki Walker	.05	.15
60 Johnny Newman	.05	.15
61 Antonio Davis	.05	.15
62 Jamal Mashburn	.10	.30
63 Muggsy Bogues	.10	.30
64 Rod Strickland	.05	.15
65 Craig Ehlo	.05	.15
66 Rex Walters	.05	.15
67 Bob Sura	.05	.15
68 Travis Knight	.05	.15
69 Toni Kukoc	.10	.30
70 Antoine Carr	.05	.15
71 Mario Elie	.05	.15
72 Popeye Jones	.05	.15
73 David Wesley	.05	.15
74 John Wallace	.05	.15
75 Calbert Cheaney	.05	.15
76 Grant Long	.05	.15
77 Will Perdue	.05	.15
78 Rasheed Wallace	.20	.50
79 Chris Gatling	.05	.15
80 Corliss Williamson	.10	.30
81 B.J. Armstrong	.05	.15
82 Brian Shaw	.05	.15
83 Darrick Martin	.05	.15
84 Vinny Del Negro	.05	.15
85 Tony Delk	.05	.15
86 Greg Anthony	.05	.15
87 Mark Davis	.05	.15
88 Anthony Goldwire	.05	.15
89 Rex Chapman	.05	.15
90 Stojko Vrankovic	.05	.15
91 Dennis Rodman	.10	.30
92 Detlef Schrempf	.10	.30
93 Henry James	.05	.15
94 Tracy Murray	.05	.15
95 Voshon Lenard	.05	.15
96 Sharone Wright	.05	.15
97 Ed O'Bannon	.05	.15
98 Gerald Wilkins	.05	.15
99 Kevin Willis	.10	.30
100 Shaquille O'Neal	.50	1.25

☐ 101 Jim Jackson	.05	.15
☐ 102 Mark Price	.10	.30
☐ 103 Patrick Ewing	.20	.50
☐ 104 Lorenzen Wright	.05	.15
☐ 105 Tyrone Hill	.05	.15
☐ 106 Ray Allen	.20	.50
☐ 107 Jermaine O'Neal	.30	.75
☐ 108 Anthony Mason	.10	.30
☐ 109 Mahmoud Abdul-Rauf	.05	.15
☐ 110 Terry Mills	.05	.15
☐ 111 Gheorghe Muresan	.05	.15
☐ 112 Mark Jackson	.10	.30
☐ 113 Greg Ostertag	.05	.15
☐ 114 Kevin Johnson	.10	.30
☐ 115 Anthony Peeler	.05	.15
☐ 116 Rony Seikaly	.05	.15
☐ 117 Keith Askins	.05	.15
☐ 118 Todd Day	.05	.15
☐ 119 Chris Childs	.05	.15
☐ 120 Chris Carr	.05	.15
☐ 121 Erick Strickland RC	.10	.30
☐ 122 Elden Campbell	.05	.15
☐ 123 Elliot Perry	.05	.15
☐ 124 Pooh Richardson	.05	.15
☐ 125 Juwan Howard	.10	.30
☐ 126 Ervin Johnson	.05	.15
☐ 127 Eric Montross	.05	.15
☐ 128 Otis Thorpe	.05	.15
☐ 129 Hersey Hawkins	.05	.15
☐ 130 Bimbo Coles	.05	.15
☐ 131 Olden Polynice	.05	.15
☐ 132 Christian Laettner	.10	.30
☐ 133 Sean Elliott	.10	.30
☐ 134 Othella Harrington	.05	.15
☐ 135 Erick Dampier	.10	.30
☐ 136 Vitaly Potapenko	.05	.15
☐ 137 Doug Christie	.10	.30
☐ 138 Luc Longley	.05	.15
☐ 139 Clarence Weatherspoon	.05	.15
☐ 140 Gary Trent	.05	.15
☐ 141 Shandon Anderson	.05	.15
☐ 142 Sam Perkins	.10	.30
☐ 143 Derek Harper	.10	.30
☐ 144 Robert Horry	.10	.30
☐ 145 Roy Rogers	.05	.15
☐ 146 John Starks	.10	.30
☐ 147 Tyrone Corbin	.05	.15
☐ 148 Andrew Lang	.05	.15
☐ 149 Derek Strong	.05	.15
☐ 150 Joe Smith	.10	.30
☐ 151 Ron Harper	.10	.30
☐ 152 Sam Cassell	.20	.50
☐ 153 Brent Barry	.10	.30
☐ 154 LaPhonso Ellis	.05	.15
☐ 155 Matt Geiger	.05	.15
☐ 156 Steve Nash	.20	.50
☐ 157 Michael Smith	.05	.15
☐ 158 Eric Williams	.05	.15
☐ 159 Tom Gugliotta	.10	.30
☐ 160 Monty Williams	.05	.15
☐ 161 Lindsey Hunter	.05	.15
☐ 162 Oliver Miller	.05	.15
☐ 163 Brent Price	.05	.15
☐ 164 Derrick McKey	.05	.15
☐ 165 Robert Pack	.05	.15
☐ 166 Derrick Coleman	.05	.15
☐ 167 Isaiah Rider	.10	.30
☐ 168 Dan Majerle	.10	.30
☐ 169 Jeff Hornacek	.10	.30
☐ 170 Terrell Brandon	.10	.30
☐ 171 Nate McMillan	.05	.15
☐ 172 Cedric Ceballos	.05	.15
☐ 173 Derek Fisher	.20	.50
☐ 174 Rodney Rogers	.05	.15
☐ 175 Blue Edwards	.05	.15
☐ 176 Brooks Thompson	.05	.15
☐ 177 Sherman Douglas	.05	.15
☐ 178 Sam Mitchell	.05	.15
☐ 179 Charles Oakley	.10	.30
☐ 180 Greg Minor	.05	.15
☐ 181 Chris Mullin	.20	.50
☐ 182 P.J. Brown	.05	.15
☐ 183 Stacey Augmon	.05	.15
☐ 184 Don MacLean	.05	.15
☐ 185 Aaron McKie	.10	.30
☐ 186 Dale Davis	.05	.15
☐ 187 Vernon Maxwell	.05	.15
☐ 188 Dell Curry	.05	.15
☐ 189 Kendall Gill	.05	.15
☐ 190 Billy Owens	.05	.15
☐ 191 Steve Kerr	.10	.30
☐ 192 Matt Maloney	.05	.15
☐ 193 Dennis Scott	.05	.15
☐ 194 A.C. Green	.10	.30
☐ 195 George McCloud	.05	.15
☐ 196 Walt Williams	.05	.15
☐ 197 Eldridge Recasner	.05	.15
☐ 198 Checklist (Hawks/Bucks)	.05	.15
☐ 199 Checklist (T'wolves/Wizards)	.05	.15
☐ 200 Checklist (inserts)	.05	.15
☐ 201 Tim Duncan RC	.50	1.25
☐ 202 Tim Thomas RC	.30	.75
☐ 203 Clifford Rozier	.05	.15
☐ 204 Bryant Reeves	.05	.15
☐ 205 Glen Rice	.10	.30
☐ 206 Darrell Armstrong	.05	.15
☐ 207 Juwan Howard	.10	.30
☐ 208 John Stockton	.20	.50
☐ 209 Antonio McDyess	.10	.30
☐ 210 James Cotton RC	.05	.15
☐ 211 Brian Grant	.10	.30
☐ 212 Chris Whitney	.05	.15
☐ 213 Antonio Davis	.05	.15
☐ 214 Kendall Gill	.05	.15
☐ 215 Adonal Foyle RC	.10	.30
☐ 216 Dean Garrett	.05	.15
☐ 217 Dennis Scott	.05	.15
☐ 218 Zydrunas Ilgauskas	.10	.30
☐ 219 Antonio Daniels RC	.20	.50
☐ 220 Derek Harper	.10	.30
☐ 221 Travis Knight	.05	.15
☐ 222 Bobby Hurley	.05	.15
☐ 223 Greg Anderson	.05	.15
☐ 224 Rod Strickland	.05	.15
☐ 225 David Benoit	.05	.15
☐ 226 Tracy McGrady RC	.50	1.25
☐ 227 Brian Williams	.05	.15
☐ 228 James Robinson	.05	.15
☐ 229 Randy Brown	.05	.15
☐ 230 Greg Foster	.05	.15
☐ 231 Reggie Miller	.20	.50
☐ 232 Eric Montross	.05	.15
☐ 233 Malik Rose	.05	.15
☐ 234 Charles Barkley	.25	.60
☐ 235 Tony Battie RC	.20	.50
☐ 236 Terry Mills	.05	.15
☐ 237 Jerald Honeycutt RC	.05	.15
☐ 238 Bubba Wells RC	.05	.15
☐ 239 John Wallace	.05	.15
☐ 240 Jason Kidd	.30	.75
☐ 241 Mark Price	.10	.30
☐ 242 Ron Mercer RC	.20	.50
☐ 243 Derrick Coleman	.05	.15
☐ 244 Fred Hoiberg	.05	.15
☐ 245 Wesley Person	.05	.15
☐ 246 Eddie Jones	.20	.50
☐ 247 Allan Houston	.10	.30
☐ 248 Keith Van Horn RC	.25	.60
☐ 249 Johnny Newman	.05	.15
☐ 250 Kevin Garnett	.40	1.00
☐ 251 Latrell Sprewell	.20	.50
☐ 252 Tracy Murray	.05	.15
☐ 253 Charles O'Bannon RC	.05	.15
☐ 254 Lamond Murray	.05	.15
☐ 255 Jerry Stackhouse	.20	.50
☐ 256 Rik Smits	.10	.30
☐ 257 Alan Henderson	.05	.15
☐ 258 Tariq Abdul-Wahad RC	.10	.30
☐ 259 Nick Anderson	.05	.15
☐ 260 Calbert Cheaney	.05	.15
☐ 261 Scottie Pippen	.30	.75
☐ 262 Rodrick Rhodes RC	.05	.15
☐ 263 Derek Anderson RC	.20	.50
☐ 264 Dana Barros	.05	.15
☐ 265 Todd Day	.05	.15
☐ 266 Michael Finley	.20	.50
☐ 267 Kevin Edwards	.05	.15
☐ 268 Terrell Brandon	.10	.30
☐ 269 Bobby Phills	.05	.15
☐ 270 Kelvin Cato RC	.20	.50
☐ 271 Vin Baker	.10	.30
☐ 272 Eric Washington RC	.20	.50
☐ 273 Jim Jackson	.05	.15
☐ 274 Joe Dumars	.20	.50
☐ 275 David Robinson	.20	.50
☐ 276 Jayson Williams	.05	.15
☐ 277 Travis Best	.05	.15
☐ 278 Kurt Thomas	.10	.30
☐ 279 Otis Thorpe	.05	.15
☐ 280 Damon Stoudamire	.10	.30
☐ 281 John Williams	.05	.15
☐ 282 Loy Vaught	.05	.15
☐ 283 Bo Outlaw	.05	.15
☐ 284 Todd Fuller	.05	.15
☐ 285 Terry Dehere	.05	.15
☐ 286 Clarence Weatherspoon	.05	.15
☐ 287 Danny Fortson RC	.10	.30
☐ 288 Howard Eisley	.05	.15
☐ 289 Steve Smith	.10	.30
☐ 290 Chris Webber	.20	.50
☐ 291 Shawn Kemp	.10	.30
☐ 292 Sam Cassell	.20	.50
☐ 293 Rick Fox	.10	.30
☐ 294 Walter McCarty	.05	.15
☐ 295 Mark Jackson	.10	.30
☐ 296 Chris Mills	.05	.15
☐ 297 Jacque Vaughn RC	.10	.30
☐ 298 Shawn Respert	.05	.15
☐ 299 Scott Burrell	.05	.15
☐ 300 Allen Iverson	.50	1.25
☐ 301 Charles Smith RC	.05	.15
☐ 302 Ervin Johnson	.05	.15
☐ 303 Hubert Davis	.05	.15
☐ 304 Eddie Johnson	.05	.15
☐ 305 Erick Dampier	.10	.30
☐ 306 Eric Williams	.05	.15
☐ 307 Anthony Johnson RC	.05	.15
☐ 308 David Wesley	.05	.15
☐ 309 Eric Piatkowski	.10	.30
☐ 310 Austin Croshere RC	.15	.40
☐ 311 Malik Sealy	.05	.15
☐ 312 George McCloud	.05	.15
☐ 313 Anthony Parker RC	.15	.30
☐ 314 Cedric Henderson RC	.10	.30
☐ 315 John Thomas RC	.05	.15
☐ 316 Cory Alexander	.05	.15
☐ 317 Johnny Taylor RC	.05	.15
☐ 318 Chris Mullin	.20	.50
☐ 319 J.R. Reid	.05	.15
☐ 320 George Lynch	.05	.15
☐ 321 Lawrence Funderburke RC	.10	.30
☐ 322 God Shammgod RC	.05	.15
☐ 323 Bobby Jackson RC	.30	.75
☐ 324 Khalid Reeves	.05	.15
☐ 325 Zan Tabak	.05	.15
☐ 326 Chris Gatling	.05	.15
☐ 327 Alvin Williams RC	.05	.15
☐ 328 Scot Pollard RC	.10	.30
☐ 329 Kerry Kittles	.20	.50
☐ 330 Tim Hardaway	.10	.30
☐ 331 Maurice Taylor RC	.15	.40
☐ 332 Keith Booth RC	.05	.15
☐ 333 Chris Morris	.05	.15
☐ 334 Bryant Stith	.05	.15
☐ 335 Terry Cummings	.05	.15
☐ 336 Ed Gray RC	.05	.15
☐ 337 Eric Snow	.10	.30
☐ 338 Clifford Robinson	.05	.15
☐ 339 Chris Dudley	.05	.15
☐ 340 Chauncey Billups RC	.75	2.00
☐ 341 Paul Grant RC	.05	.15
☐ 342 Tyrone Hill	.05	.15
☐ 343 Joe Smith	.10	.30
☐ 344 Sean Rooks	.05	.15
☐ 345 Harvey Grant	.05	.15
☐ 346 Dale Davis	.05	.15
☐ 347 Brevin Knight RC	.10	.30
☐ 348 Serge Zwikker RC	.05	.15
☐ 349 Checklist (Hawks/Kings)	.05	.15
☐ 350 Checklist (Spurs/Wizards/Inserts)	.05	.15

1998-99 Fleer

☐ COMPLETE SET (150)	10.00	20.00
☐ 1 Kobe Bryant	.75	2.00

❏ 2 Corliss Williamson	.10	.30
❏ 3 Allen Iverson	.40	1.00
❏ 4 Michael Finley	.25	.60
❏ 5 Juwan Howard	.10	.30
❏ 6 Marcus Camby	.10	.30
❏ 7 Toni Kukoc	.10	.30
❏ 8 Antoine Walker	.25	.60
❏ 9 Stephon Marbury	.25	.60
❏ 10 Tim Hardaway	.10	.30
❏ 11 Zydrunas Ilgauskas	.10	.30
❏ 12 John Stockton	.25	.60
❏ 13 Glenn Robinson	.10	.30
❏ 14 Isaiah Rider	.05	.15
❏ 15 Danny Fortson	.05	.15
❏ 16 Donyell Marshall	.10	.30
❏ 17 Chris Mullin	.25	.60
❏ 18 Shareef Abdur-Rahim	.25	.60
❏ 19 Bobby Phills	.05	.15
❏ 20 Gary Payton	.25	.60
❏ 21 Derrick Coleman	.05	.15
❏ 22 Larry Johnson	.10	.30
❏ 23 Michael Jordan	1.25	3.00
❏ 24 Danny Manning	.05	.15
❏ 25 Nick Anderson	.05	.15
❏ 26 Chris Gatling	.05	.15
❏ 27 Steve Smith	.10	.30
❏ 28 Chris Whitney	.05	.15
❏ 29 Terrell Brandon	.10	.30
❏ 30 Rasheed Wallace	.25	.60
❏ 31 Reggie Miller	.25	.60
❏ 32 Karl Malone	.25	.60
❏ 33 Grant Hill	.25	.60
❏ 34 Hakeem Olajuwon	.25	.60
❏ 35 Erick Dampier	.10	.30
❏ 36 Vin Baker	.10	.30
❏ 37 Tim Thomas	.10	.30
❏ 38 Mark Price	.10	.30
❏ 39 Shawn Bradley	.05	.15
❏ 40 Calbert Cheaney	.05	.15
❏ 41 Glen Rice	.10	.30
❏ 42 Kevin Willis	.05	.15
❏ 43 Chris Carr	.05	.15
❏ 44 Keith Van Horn	.25	.60
❏ 45 Jamal Mashburn	.10	.30
❏ 46 Eddie Jones	.25	.60
❏ 47 Brevin Knight	.05	.15
❏ 48 Olden Polynice	.05	.15
❏ 49 Bobby Jackson	.10	.30
❏ 50 David Robinson	.25	.60
❏ 51 Patrick Ewing	.25	.60
❏ 52 Samaki Walker	.05	.15
❏ 53 Antonio Daniels	.05	.15
❏ 54 Rodney Rogers	.05	.15
❏ 55 Dikembe Mutombo	.10	.30
❏ 56 Tracy McGrady	.50	1.25
❏ 57 Walt Williams	.05	.15
❏ 58 Walter McCarty	.05	.15
❏ 59 Detlef Schrempf	.10	.30
❏ 60 Ervin Johnson	.05	.15
❏ 61 Michael Smith	.05	.15
❏ 62 Clifford Robinson	.05	.15
❏ 63 Brian Williams	.05	.15
❏ 64 Shandon Anderson	.05	.15
❏ 65 P.J. Brown	.05	.15
❏ 66 Scottie Pippen	.30	.75
❏ 67 Anthony Peeler	.05	.15
❏ 68 Tony Delk	.05	.15
❏ 69 David Wesley	.05	.15
❏ 70 John Starks	.10	.30
❏ 71 Nick Van Exel	.25	.60
❏ 72 Kerry Kittles	.05	.15
❏ 73 Tony Battie	.05	.15
❏ 74 Lamond Murray	.05	.15
❏ 75 Anfernee Hardaway	.25	.60
❏ 76 Jalen Rose	.25	.60
❏ 77 Derek Anderson	.20	.50
❏ 78 Avery Johnson	.05	.15
❏ 79 Michael Stewart	.05	.15
❏ 80 Brian Shaw	.05	.15
❏ 81 Chauncey Billups	.10	.30
❏ 82 Kenny Anderson	.10	.30
❏ 83 Bryon Russell	.05	.15
❏ 84 Jason Kidd	.30	.75
❏ 85 Tyrone Hill	.05	.15
❏ 86 Jim McIlvaine	.05	.15
❏ 87 Brian Grant	.10	.30
❏ 88 Bryant Stith	.05	.15
❏ 89 Brent Price	.05	.15
❏ 90 John Wallace	.05	.15
❏ 91 Dennis Rodman	.10	.30
❏ 92 Alonzo Mourning	.10	.30
❏ 93 Bimbo Coles	.05	.15
❏ 94 Chris Anstey	.05	.15
❏ 95 Lindsey Hunter	.05	.15
❏ 96 Ed Gray	.05	.15
❏ 97 Chris Mills	.05	.15
❏ 98 Rick Fox	.10	.30
❏ 99 Lorenzen Wright	.05	.15
❏ 100 Kevin Garnett	.40	1.00
❏ 101 Shawn Kemp	.10	.30
❏ 102 Mark Jackson	.10	.30
❏ 103 Sam Cassell	.25	.60
❏ 104 Monty Williams	.05	.15
❏ 105 Ron Mercer	.07	.20
❏ 106 Bryant Reeves	.05	.15
❏ 107 Tracy Murray	.05	.15
❏ 108 Ray Allen	.25	.60
❏ 109 Maurice Taylor	.08	.25
❏ 110 Jerome Williams	.05	.15
❏ 111 Horace Grant	.10	.30
❏ 112 Tariq Abdul-Wahad	.05	.15
❏ 113 Travis Knight	.05	.15
❏ 114 Kendall Gill	.05	.15
❏ 115 Aaron McKie	.10	.30
❏ 116 Dean Garrett	.05	.15
❏ 117 Jeff Hornacek	.10	.30
❏ 118 Todd Fuller	.05	.15
❏ 119 Arvydas Sabonis	.10	.30
❏ 120 Voshon Lenard	.05	.15
❏ 121 Steve Nash	.25	.60
❏ 122 Cedric Henderson	.05	.15
❏ 123 Rodrick Rhodes	.05	.15
❏ 124 Mookie Blaylock	.05	.15
❏ 125 Hersey Hawkins	.05	.15
❏ 126 Doug Christie	.10	.30
❏ 127 Eric Piatkowski	.10	.30
❏ 128 Sean Elliott	.10	.30
❏ 129 Anthony Mason	.10	.30
❏ 130 Allan Houston	.10	.30
❏ 131 Antonio Davis	.05	.15
❏ 132 Hubert Davis	.05	.15
❏ 133 Rod Strickland PF	.05	.15
❏ 134 Jason Kidd PF	.25	.60
❏ 135 Mark Jackson PF	.05	.15
❏ 136 Marcus Camby PF	.10	.30
❏ 137 Dikembe Mutombo PF	.05	.15
❏ 138 Shawn Bradley PF	.05	.15
❏ 139 Dennis Rodman PF	.05	.15
❏ 140 Jayson Williams PF	.05	.15
❏ 141 Tim Duncan PF	.20	.50
❏ 142 Michael Jordan PF	.60	1.50
❏ 143 Shaquille O'Neal PF	.30	.75
❏ 144 Karl Malone PF	.25	.60
❏ 145 Mookie Blaylock PF	.05	.15
❏ 146 Brevin Knight PF	.05	.15
❏ 147 Doug Christie PF	.10	.30
❏ 148 Checklist	.05	.15
❏ 149 Checklist	.05	.15
❏ 150 Checklist	.05	.15
❏ S44 Keith Van Horn SAMPLE	.40	1.00

1999-00 Fleer

❏ COMPLETE SET (220)	20.00	40.00
❏ COMMON CARD (1-200)	.25	.30
❏ COMMON ROOKIE (201-220)	.20	.50
❏ 1 Vince Carter	.40	1.00
❏ 2 Kobe Bryant	1.00	2.50
❏ 3 Keith Van Horn	.15	.40
❏ 4 Tim Duncan	.40	1.00
❏ 5 Grant Hill	.20	.50
❏ 6 Kevin Garnett	.40	1.00
❏ 7 Anfernee Hardaway	.20	.50
❏ 8 Jason Williams	.20	.50
❏ 9 Paul Pierce	.20	.50
❏ 10 Mookie Blaylock	.12	.30
❏ 11 Shawn Bradley	.12	.30
❏ 12 Kenny Anderson	.15	.40
❏ 13 Chauncey Billups	.20	.50
❏ 14 Elden Campbell	.12	.30
❏ 15 Jason Caffey	.12	.30
❏ 16 Brent Barry	.15	.40
❏ 17 Charles Barkley	.25	.60
❏ 18 Derek Anderson	.12	.30
❏ 19 Darrick Martin	.12	.30
❏ 20 Bison Dele	.12	.30
❏ 21 Rick Fox	.12	.30
❏ 22 Antonio Davis	.12	.30
❏ 23 Terrell Brandon	.12	.30
❏ 24 P.J. Brown	.12	.30
❏ 25 Toby Bailey	.12	.30
❏ 26 Ray Allen	.20	.50
❏ 27 Brian Grant	.12	.30
❏ 28 Scott Burrell	.12	.30
❏ 29 Tariq Abdul-Wahad	.12	.30
❏ 30 Marcus Camby	.15	.40
❏ 31 John Stockton	.25	.60
❏ 32 Nick Anderson	.12	.30
❏ 33 Antonio Daniels	.12	.30
❏ 34 Matt Geiger	.12	.30
❏ 35 Vin Baker	.20	.50
❏ 36 Dee Brown	.12	.30
❏ 37 Shandon Anderson	.12	.30
❏ 38 Calbert Cheaney	.12	.30
❏ 39 Shareef Abdur-Rahim	.15	.40
❏ 40 LaPhonso Ellis	.12	.30
❏ 41 Cedric Ceballos	.12	.30
❏ 42 Tony Battie	.15	.40
❏ 43 Keon Clark	.12	.30
❏ 44 Derrick Coleman	.15	.40
❏ 45 Erick Dampier	.15	.40
❏ 46 Corey Benjamin	.12	.30
❏ 47 Michael Dickerson	.12	.30
❏ 48 Cedric Henderson	.12	.30
❏ 49 Lamond Murray	.12	.30
❏ 50 Horace Grant	.15	.40
❏ 51 Shaquille O'Neal	.50	1.25
❏ 52 Dale Davis	.12	.30
❏ 53 Dean Garrett	.12	.30
❏ 54 Tim Hardaway	.20	.50
❏ 55 Gerald Brown RC	.20	.50
❏ 56 Sam Cassell	.15	.40
❏ 57 Jim Jackson	.15	.40
❏ 58 Kendall Gill	.12	.30
❏ 59 Eric Williams	.12	.30
❏ 60 Chris Childs	.12	.30
❏ 61 Vlade Divac	.20	.50
❏ 62 Darrell Armstrong	.12	.30
❏ 63 Mario Elie	.12	.30
❏ 64 Tyrone Hill	.12	.30
❏ 65 Dale Ellis	.12	.30
❏ 66 Doug Christie	.15	.40
❏ 67 Howard Eisley	.12	.30
❏ 68 Juwan Howard	.15	.40
❏ 69 Mike Bibby	.20	.50
❏ 70 Alan Henderson	.12	.30
❏ 71 Michael Finley	.20	.50
❏ 72 Dana Barros	.12	.30
❏ 73 Danny Fortson	.12	.30
❏ 74 Ricky Davis	.20	.50
❏ 75 Adonal Foyle	.12	.30
❏ 76 Cory Carr	.12	.30
❏ 77 Bryce Drew	.12	.30
❏ 78 Shawn Kemp	.20	.50
❏ 79 Tyrone Nesby RC	.20	.50
❏ 80 Lindsey Hunter	.12	.30
❏ 81 Ruben Patterson	.12	.30
❏ 82 Al Harrington	.15	.40
❏ 83 Bobby Jackson	.15	.40
❏ 84 Dan Majerle	.20	.50
❏ 85 Rex Chapman	.12	.30
❏ 86 Dell Curry	.12	.30
❏ 87 Walt Williams	.12	.30
❏ 88 Kerry Kittles	.12	.30
❏ 89 Isaiah Rider	.12	.30
❏ 90 Patrick Ewing	.25	.60
❏ 91 Lawrence Funderburke	.12	.30
❏ 92 Isaac Austin	.12	.30
❏ 93 Sean Elliott	.20	.50
❏ 94 Larry Hughes	.15	.40
❏ 95 Hersey Hawkins	.12	.30
❏ 96 Tracy McGrady	.40	1.00
❏ 97 Jeff Hornacek	.15	.40
❏ 98 Randell Jackson	.12	.30
❏ 99 J.R. Henderson	.12	.30

❑ 100 Roshown McLeod	.12	.30
❑ 101 Steve Nash	.30	.75
❑ 102 Ron Mercer	.12	.30
❑ 103 Raef LaFrentz	.15	.40
❑ 104 Eddie Jones	.20	.50
❑ 105 Antawn Jamison	.20	.50
❑ 106 Kornel David RC	.20	.50
❑ 107 Othella Harrington	.12	.30
❑ 108 Brevin Knight	.12	.30
❑ 109 Michael Olowokandi	.12	.30
❑ 110 Christian Laettner	.15	.40
❑ 111 J.R. Reid	.12	.30
❑ 112 Reggie Miller	.20	.50
❑ 113 Andrae Patterson	.12	.30
❑ 114 Jamal Mashburn	.12	.30
❑ 115 Glenn Robinson	.15	.40
❑ 116 Pat Garrity	.12	.30
❑ 117 Stephon Marbury	.20	.50
❑ 118 Arvydas Sabonis	.15	.40
❑ 119 Allan Houston	.15	.40
❑ 120 Peja Stojakovic	.15	.40
❑ 121 Michael Doleac	.12	.30
❑ 122 Avery Johnson	.15	.40
❑ 123 Allen Iverson	.40	1.00
❑ 124 Rashard Lewis	.20	.50
❑ 125 Charles Oakley	.15	.40
❑ 126 Karl Malone	.25	.60
❑ 127 Tracy Murray	.12	.30
❑ 128 Felipe Lopez	.12	.30
❑ 129 Dikembe Mutombo	.15	.40
❑ 130 Dirk Nowitzki	.30	.75
❑ 131 Vitaly Potapenko	.12	.30
❑ 132 Antonio McDyess	.15	.40
❑ 133 Anthony Mason	.12	.30
❑ 134 Donyell Marshall	.15	.40
❑ 135 Ron Harper	.12	.30
❑ 136 Cuttino Mobley	.15	.40
❑ 137 Wesley Person	.12	.30
❑ 138 Rodney Rogers	.12	.30
❑ 139 Jerry Stackhouse	.20	.50
❑ 140 Glen Rice	.20	.50
❑ 141 Chris Mullin	.20	.50
❑ 142 Anthony Peeler	.12	.30
❑ 143 Alonzo Mourning	.20	.50
❑ 144 Tom Gugliotta	.12	.30
❑ 145 Tim Thomas	.15	.40
❑ 146 Damon Stoudamire	.20	.50
❑ 147 Jayson Williams	.15	.40
❑ 148 Larry Johnson	.20	.50
❑ 149 Chris Webber	.20	.50
❑ 150 Matt Harpring	.15	.40
❑ 151 David Robinson	.25	.60
❑ 152 George Lynch	.12	.30
❑ 153 Gary Payton	.20	.50
❑ 154 John Wallace	.12	.30
❑ 155 Greg Ostertag	.12	.30
❑ 156 Mitch Richmond	.15	.40
❑ 157 Cherokee Parks	.12	.30
❑ 158 Steve Smith	.12	.30
❑ 159 Gary Trent	.12	.30
❑ 160 Antoine Walker	.20	.50
❑ 161 Johnny Taylor	.12	.30
❑ 162 Brad Miller	.15	.40
❑ 163 Chris Mills	.12	.30
❑ 164 Charles Jones	.12	.30
❑ 165 Hakeem Olajuwon	.20	.50
❑ 166 Bob Sura	.12	.30
❑ 167 Brian Skinner	.12	.30
❑ 168 Korleone Young	.12	.30
❑ 169 Tyronn Lue	.12	.30
❑ 170 Jalen Rose	.15	.40
❑ 171 Joe Smith	.15	.40
❑ 172 Clarence Weatherspoon	.12	.30
❑ 173 Jason Kidd	.30	.75
❑ 174 Robert Traylor	.12	.30
❑ 175 Rasheed Wallace	.20	.50
❑ 176 Latrell Sprewell	.15	.40
❑ 177 Corliss Williamson	.12	.30
❑ 178 Bo Outlaw	.12	.30
❑ 179 Malik Rose	.12	.30
❑ 180 Nazr Mohammed	.12	.30
❑ 181 Olden Polynice	.12	.30
❑ 182 Kevin Willis	.12	.30
❑ 183 Bryon Russell	.12	.30
❑ 184 Bryant Reeves	.12	.30
❑ 185 Rod Strickland	.12	.30
❑ 186 Samaki Walker	.12	.30
❑ 187 Nick Van Exel	.15	.40
❑ 188 David Wesley	.12	.30
❑ 189 John Starks	.20	.50
❑ 190 Toni Kukoc	.20	.50
❑ 191 Scottie Pippen	.30	.75
❑ 192 Zydrunas Ilgauskas	.15	.40
❑ 193 Maurice Taylor	.15	.40
❑ 194 Rik Smits	.20	.50
❑ 195 Clifford Robinson	.12	.30
❑ 196 Bonzi Wells	.12	.30
❑ 197 Charlie Ward	.12	.30
❑ 198 Detlef Schrempf	.15	.40
❑ 199 Theo Ratliff	.15	.40
❑ 200 Rodrick Rhodes	.12	.30
❑ 201 Ron Artest RC	.75	2.00
❑ 202 William Avery RC	.20	.50
❑ 203 Elton Brand RC	.60	1.50
❑ 204 Baron Davis RC	.75	2.00
❑ 205 Jumaine Jones RC	.20	.50
❑ 206 Andre Miller RC	.60	1.50
❑ 207 Lee Nailon RC	.20	.50
❑ 208 James Posey RC	.30	.75
❑ 209 Jason Terry RC	.50	1.25
❑ 210 Kenny Thomas RC	.20	.50
❑ 211 Steve Francis RC	.60	1.50
❑ 212 Wally Szczerbiak RC	.60	1.50
❑ 213 Richard Hamilton RC	.60	1.50
❑ 214 Jonathan Bender RC	.20	.50
❑ 215 Shawn Marion RC	.60	1.50
❑ 216 A.Radojevic RC	.20	.50
❑ 217 Tim James RC	.20	.50
❑ 218 Trajan Langdon RC	.20	.50
❑ 219 Lamar Odom RC	.60	1.50
❑ 220 Corey Maggette RC	.60	1.50
❑ NNO Checklist #3	.12	.30
❑ NNO Checklist #2	.12	.30
❑ NNO Checklist #1	.12	.30

2000-01 Fleer

❑ COMMON CARD (1-300)	.12	.30
❑ COMMON ROOKIE (227-271)	.25	.60
❑ 1 Lamar Odom	.20	.50
❑ 2 Christian Laettner	.12	.30
❑ 3 Michael Olowokandi	.12	.30
❑ 4 Anthony Carter	.12	.30
❑ 5 Steve Francis	.20	.50
❑ 6 Darvin Ham	.12	.30
❑ 7 Mitch Richmond	.15	.40
❑ 8 Corliss Williamson	.15	.40
❑ 9 Jason Terry	.20	.50
❑ 10 Brian Grant	.12	.30
❑ 11 Peja Stojakovic	.15	.40
❑ 12 Rick Fox	.15	.40
❑ 13 Tyrone Hill	.12	.30
❑ 14 Chauncey Billups	.20	.50
❑ 15 Otis Thorpe	.15	.40
❑ 16 Richard Hamilton	.15	.40
❑ 17 Ervin Johnson	.12	.30
❑ 18 Jim Jackson	.12	.30
❑ 19 Theo Ratliff	.12	.30
❑ 20 Doug Christie	.12	.30
❑ 21 Jalen Rose	.15	.40
❑ 22 John Wallace	.12	.30
❑ 23 Ruben Patterson	.12	.30
❑ 24 Steve Nash	.30	.75
❑ 25 Toni Kukoc	.15	.40
❑ 26 Anthony Peeler	.12	.30
❑ 27 Ray Allen	.20	.50
❑ 28 Adonal Foyle	.12	.30
❑ 29 Chris Whitney	.12	.30
❑ 30 Nick Van Exel	.15	.40
❑ 31 Sean Elliott	.15	.40
❑ 32 Erick Strickland	.12	.30
❑ 33 Jerry Stackhouse	.15	.40
❑ 34 Antawn Jamison	.20	.50
❑ 35 Grant Hill	.20	.50
❑ 36 Antonio Daniels	.12	.30
❑ 37 Karl Malone	.25	.60
❑ 38 Keith Van Horn	.15	.40
❑ 39 Ron Harper	.15	.40
❑ 40 Stephon Marbury	.20	.50
❑ 41 Bryon Russell	.12	.30
❑ 42 Corey Maggette	.15	.40
❑ 43 Hersey Hawkins	.12	.30
❑ 44 Vince Carter	.40	1.00
❑ 45 Paul Pierce	.20	.50
❑ 46 Mikki Moore	.12	.30
❑ 47 Othella Harrington	.12	.30
❑ 48 Erick Dampier	.12	.30
❑ 49 Jerome Williams	.12	.30
❑ 50 Nick Anderson	.12	.30
❑ 51 Tim Hardaway	.15	.40
❑ 52 Allan Houston	.15	.40
❑ 53 Tyrone Nesby	.12	.30
❑ 54 Brevin Knight	.12	.30
❑ 55 Chris Mills	.12	.30
❑ 56 Ron Artest	.20	.50
❑ 57 Walt Williams	.12	.30
❑ 58 Duane Causwell	.12	.30
❑ 59 Bonzi Wells	.12	.30
❑ 60 Rasheed Wallace	.20	.50
❑ 61 Dikembe Mutombo	.15	.40
❑ 62 Jahidi White	.12	.30
❑ 63 Chris Webber	.20	.50
❑ 64 Tony Battie	.12	.30
❑ 65 Mahmoud Abdul-Rauf	.12	.30
❑ 66 Monty Williams	.12	.30
❑ 67 Charlie Ward	.12	.30
❑ 68 David Robinson	.25	.60
❑ 69 Eric Snow	.12	.30
❑ 70 Jermaine O'Neal	.20	.50
❑ 71 Kurt Thomas	.12	.30
❑ 72 James Posey	.12	.30
❑ 73 Travis Best	.12	.30
❑ 74 Jonathan Bender	.12	.30
❑ 75 John Stockton	.25	.60
❑ 76 Jacque Vaughn	.12	.30
❑ 77 Ron Mercer	.12	.30
❑ 78 Shawn Marion	.20	.50
❑ 79 Larry Johnson	.15	.40
❑ 80 Maurice Taylor	.12	.30
❑ 81 Clifford Robinson	.12	.30
❑ 82 Scot Pollard	.12	.30
❑ 83 Patrick Ewing	.25	.60
❑ 84 Terrell Brandon	.12	.30
❑ 85 Horace Grant	.15	.40
❑ 86 Vin Baker	.15	.40
❑ 87 Al Harrington	.15	.40
❑ 88 Larry Hughes	.15	.40
❑ 89 David Wesley	.12	.30
❑ 90 Wally Szczerbiak	.15	.40
❑ 91 Charles Oakley	.15	.40
❑ 92 Tim Thomas	.12	.30
❑ 93 Mookie Blaylock	.15	.40
❑ 94 Jamal Mashburn	.15	.40
❑ 95 Roshown McLeod	.12	.30
❑ 96 John Starks	.12	.30
❑ 97 Rodney Rogers	.12	.30
❑ 98 Juwan Howard	.15	.40
❑ 99 Isaiah Rider	.15	.40
❑ 100 Rashard Lewis	.20	.50
❑ 101 Dion Glover	.12	.30
❑ 102 Johnny Newman	.12	.30
❑ 103 Avery Johnson	.15	.40
❑ 104 Darrell Armstrong	.12	.30
❑ 105 Eric Williams	.12	.30
❑ 106 Gary Payton	.20	.50
❑ 107 Antonio Davis	.12	.30
❑ 108 Dirk Nowitzki	.30	.75
❑ 109 Trajan Langdon	.12	.30
❑ 110 Michael Dickerson	.12	.30
❑ 111 Joe Smith	.12	.30
❑ 112 Rod Strickland	.15	.40
❑ 113 Shawn Kemp	.20	.50
❑ 114 Voshon Lenard	.12	.30
❑ 115 Marcus Camby	.15	.40
❑ 116 Matt Harpring	.15	.40
❑ 117 Isaac Austin	.12	.30
❑ 118 Malik Rose	.12	.30
❑ 119 Pat Garrity	.12	.30
❑ 120 Kenny Thomas	.12	.30
❑ 121 LaPhonso Ellis	.15	.40
❑ 122 Danny Fortson	.12	.30
❑ 123 Elton Brand	.20	.50
❑ 124 Jason Williams	.15	.40
❑ 125 Kobe Bryant	1.00	2.50
❑ 126 Tariq Abdul-Wahad	.12	.30

❑ 127 Tracy McGrady	.40	1.00
❑ 128 Matt Geiger	.12	.30
❑ 129 Antoine Walker	.15	.40
❑ 130 Michael Finley	.20	.50
❑ 131 Andre Miller	.15	.40
❑ 132 Robert Horry	.15	.40
❑ 133 Donyell Marshall	.12	.30
❑ 134 Shareef Abdur-Rahim	.15	.40
❑ 135 Vonteego Cummings	.12	.30
❑ 136 Anthony Mason	.12	.30
❑ 137 Mike Bibby	.15	.40
❑ 138 Raef LaFrentz	.12	.30
❑ 139 Glen Rice	.15	.40
❑ 140 Chris Gatling	.12	.30
❑ 141 Latrell Sprewell	.15	.40
❑ 142 Austin Croshere	.12	.30
❑ 143 Kenny Anderson	.15	.40
❑ 144 Elden Campbell	.12	.30
❑ 145 Jason Kidd	.30	.75
❑ 146 Michael Doleac	.12	.30
❑ 147 Muggsy Bogues	.15	.40
❑ 148 Tim Duncan	.40	1.00
❑ 149 Samaki Walker	.12	.30
❑ 150 Gary Trent	.12	.30
❑ 151 Kevin Garnett	.40	1.00
❑ 152 Allen Iverson	.40	1.00
❑ 153 Anfernee Hardaway	.20	.50
❑ 154 Robert Traylor	.12	.30
❑ 155 Scottie Pippen	.30	.75
❑ 156 Shaquille O'Neal	.50	1.25
❑ 157 Vlade Divac	.15	.40
❑ 158 Lucious Harris	.12	.30
❑ 159 Keon Clark	.12	.30
❑ 160 Bo Outlaw	.12	.30
❑ 161 P.J. Brown	.12	.30
❑ 162 Derrick Coleman	.15	.40
❑ 163 Mark Jackson	.15	.40
❑ 164 Lamond Murray	.12	.30
❑ 165 Dan Majerle	.15	.40
❑ 166 Eddie Jones	.15	.40
❑ 167 Cedric Ceballos	.12	.30
❑ 168 Kendall Gill	.12	.30
❑ 169 Tom Gugliotta	.12	.30
❑ 170 Jeff McInnis	.12	.30
❑ 171 Steve Smith	.15	.40
❑ 172 Kevin Willis	.12	.30
❑ 173 Lindsey Hunter	.12	.30
❑ 174 Derek Anderson	.15	.40
❑ 175 Shandon Anderson	.12	.30
❑ 176 Adrian Griffin	.12	.30
❑ 177 Baron Davis	.20	.50
❑ 178 Radoslav Nesterovic	.12	.30
❑ 179 Glenn Robinson	.15	.40
❑ 180 Sam Cassell	.15	.40
❑ 181 Chucky Atkins	.12	.30
❑ 182 Arvydas Sabonis	.15	.40
❑ 183 Damon Stoudamire	.15	.40
❑ 184 Antonio McDyess	.15	.40
❑ 185 Derek Fisher	.20	.50
❑ 186 Bryant Reeves	.12	.30
❑ 187 Hakeem Olajuwon	.25	.60
❑ 188 Kerry Kittles	.15	.40
❑ 189 Alan Henderson	.12	.30
❑ 190 Sam Perkins	.12	.30
❑ 191 Felipe Lopez	.12	.30
❑ 192 Tracy Murray	.12	.30
❑ 193 Shammond Williams	.12	.30
❑ 194 Vitaly Potapenko	.12	.30
❑ 195 John Amaechi	.12	.30
❑ 196 Quincy Lewis	.12	.30
❑ 197 Reggie Miller	.20	.50
❑ 198 Cuttino Mobley	.15	.40
❑ 199 Rex Chapman	.12	.30
❑ 200 Dale Davis	.12	.30
❑ 201 Andrew DeClercq	.12	.30
❑ 202 Kelvin Cato	.12	.30
❑ 203 Jon Barry	.12	.30
❑ 204 Greg Anthony	.12	.30
❑ 205 Brent Barry	.12	.30
❑ 206 Derrick McKey	.12	.30
❑ 207 Vince Carter UH	.20	.50
❑ 208 David Robinson UH	.20	.50
❑ 209 Eric Snow UH	.12	.30
❑ 210 Ray Allen UH	.20	.50
❑ 211 Lamar Odom UH	.20	.50
❑ 212 Dikembe Mutombo UH	.15	.40
❑ 213 Brevin Knight UH	.12	.30
❑ 214 Vin Baker UH	.15	.40
❑ 215 Antoine Walker UH	.15	.40

❑ 216 Mitch Richmond UH	.15	.40
❑ 217 Elton Brand UH	.20	.50
❑ 218 Jerome Williams UH	.12	.30
❑ 219 Keith Van Horn UH	.15	.40
❑ 220 Nick Van Exel UH	.15	.40
❑ 221 Shaquille O'Neal UH	.25	.60
❑ 222 Allan Houston UH	.15	.40
❑ 223 Shareef Abdur-Rahim UH	.15	.40
❑ 224 Karl Malone UH	.25	.60
❑ 225 Terrell Brandon UH	.12	.30
❑ 226 Eddie Jones UH	.15	.40
❑ 227 Stromile Swift RC	.30	.75
❑ 228 Dalibor Bagaric RC	.25	.60
❑ 229 Erick Barkley RC	.25	.60
❑ 230 Mike Miller RC	.40	1.00
❑ 231 Kenyon Martin RC	.60	1.50
❑ 232 Michael Redd RC	.60	1.50
❑ 233 Darius Miles RC	.30	.75
❑ 234 Chris Mihm RC	.25	.60
❑ 235 Brian Cardinal RC	.25	.60
❑ 236 Khalid El-Amin RC	.25	.60
❑ 237 Hanno Mottola RC	.25	.60
❑ 238 Jamaal Magloire RC	.25	.60
❑ 239 Courtney Alexander RC	.25	.60
❑ 240 Mamadou N'Diaye RC	.25	.60
❑ 241 Chris Porter RC	.25	.60
❑ 242 Quentin Richardson RC	.30	.75
❑ 243 Eddie House RC	.25	.60
❑ 244 Joel Przybilla RC	.25	.60
❑ 245 Soumaila Samake RC	.25	.60
❑ 246 Speedy Claxton RC	.25	.60
❑ 247 Desmond Mason RC	.30	.75
❑ 248 Mike Smith RC	.25	.60
❑ 249 Lavor Postell RC	.25	.60
❑ 250 Ruben Garces RC	.25	.60
❑ 251 DeShawn Stevenson RC	.25	.60
❑ 252 Hedo Turkoglu RC	.60	1.50
❑ 253 Keyon Dooling RC	.25	.60
❑ 254 Dan Langhi RC	.25	.60
❑ 255 Mateen Cleaves RC	.25	.60
❑ 256 Donnell Harvey RC	.25	.60
❑ 257 DerMarr Johnson RC	.25	.60
❑ 258 Jason Collier RC	.25	.60
❑ 259 Jake Voskuhl RC	.25	.60
❑ 260 Mark Madsen RC	.25	.60
❑ 261 Pepe Sanchez RC	.25	.60
❑ 262 Morris Peterson RC	.40	1.00
❑ 263 Daniel Santiago RC	.60	1.50
❑ 264 Etan Thomas RC	.25	.60
❑ 265 A.J. Guyton RC	.25	.60
❑ 266 Marcus Fizer RC	.25	.60
❑ 267 Jamal Crawford RC	.40	1.00
❑ 268 Jerome Moiso RC	.25	.60
❑ 269 Olumide Oyedeji RC	.25	.60
❑ 270 Paul McPherson RC	.25	.60
❑ 271 Eduardo Najera RC	.25	.60
❑ 272 Dallas Mavericks CL	.05	.15
❑ 273 Denver Nuggets CL	.05	.15
❑ 274 Houston Rockets CL	.10	.30
❑ 275 Minnesota Timberwolves CL	.10	.30
❑ 276 San Antonio Spurs CL	.10	.30
❑ 277 Utah Jazz CL	.10	.30
❑ 278 Vancouver Grizzlies CL	.20	.50
❑ 279 Golden State Warriors CL	.10	.30
❑ 280 Los Angeles Clippers CL	.20	.50
❑ 281 Los Angeles Lakers CL	.20	.50
❑ 282 Phoenix Suns CL	.10	.30
❑ 283 Portland Trail Blazers CL	.10	.30
❑ 284 Sacramento Kings CL	.10	.30
❑ 285 Seattle Supersonics CL	.10	.30
❑ 286 Boston Celtics CL	.05	.15
❑ 287 Miami Heat CL	.05	.15
❑ 288 New Jersey Nets CL	.10	.30
❑ 289 New York Knicks CL	.10	.30
❑ 290 Orlando Magic CL	.20	.50
❑ 291 Philadelphia 76ers CL	.10	.30
❑ 292 Washington Wizards CL	.05	.15
❑ 293 Atlanta Hawks CL	.05	.15
❑ 294 Charlotte Hornets CL	.05	.15
❑ 295 Chicago Bulls CL	.10	.30
❑ 296 Cleveland Cavaliers CL	.05	.15
❑ 297 Detroit Pistons CL	.05	.15
❑ 298 Indiana Pacers CL	.10	.30
❑ 299 Milwaukee Bucks CL	.05	.15
❑ 300 Toronto Raptors CL	.20	.50
❑ NNO V.Carter OSR Retail		
❑ NNO V.Carter OSR Sticker	2.00	5.00
❑ NNO V.Carter OSR/1986	8.00	20.00
❑ NNO V.Carter OSR AU/15		

2006-07 Fleer

❑ COMPLETE SET (250)	30.00	70.00
❑ 1 Josh Childress	.20	.50
❑ 2 Al Harrington	.15	.40
❑ 3 Joe Johnson	.20	.50
❑ 4 Tyronn Lue	.15	.40
❑ 5 Josh Smith	.25	.60
❑ 6 Salim Stoudamire	.20	.50
❑ 7 Marvin Williams	.25	.60
❑ 8 Tony Allen	.20	.50
❑ 9 Dan Dickau	.15	.40
❑ 10 Al Jefferson	.25	.60
❑ 11 Michael Olowokandi	.15	.40
❑ 12 Paul Pierce	.25	.60
❑ 13 Wally Szczerbiak	.20	.50
❑ 14 Gerald Green	.30	.75
❑ 15 Raymond Felton	.30	.75
❑ 16 Brevin Knight	.15	.40
❑ 17 Sean May	.20	.50
❑ 18 Emeka Okafor	.25	.60
❑ 19 Othella Harrington	.15	.40
❑ 20 Gerald Wallace	.25	.60
❑ 21 Tyson Chandler	.25	.60
❑ 22 Luol Deng	.25	.60
❑ 23 Chris Duhon	.15	.40
❑ 24 Ben Gordon	.30	.75
❑ 25 Kirk Hinrich	.25	.60
❑ 26 Mike Sweetney	.15	.40
❑ 27 Michael Jordan	1.50	4.00
❑ 28 Drew Gooden	.20	.50
❑ 29 Larry Hughes	.20	.50
❑ 30 Zydrunas Ilgauskas	.20	.50
❑ 31 Damon Jones	.20	.50
❑ 32 LeBron James	1.25	3.00
❑ 33 Donyell Marshall	.15	.40
❑ 34 Anderson Varejao	.20	.50
❑ 35 Erick Dampier	.15	.40
❑ 36 Marquis Daniels	.20	.50
❑ 37 Devin Harris	.25	.60
❑ 38 Josh Howard	.25	.60
❑ 39 Dirk Nowitzki	.40	1.00
❑ 40 Jerry Stackhouse	.25	.60
❑ 41 Jason Terry	.25	.60
❑ 42 Carmelo Anthony	.30	.75
❑ 43 Marcus Camby	.20	.50
❑ 44 Reggie Evans	.15	.40
❑ 45 Kenyon Martin	.25	.60
❑ 46 Andre Miller	.20	.50
❑ 47 Eduardo Najera	.15	.40
❑ 48 Nene	.15	.40
❑ 49 Chauncey Billups	.25	.60
❑ 50 Richard Hamilton	.20	.50
❑ 51 Jason Maxiell	.15	.40
❑ 52 Antonio McDyess	.15	.40
❑ 53 Tayshaun Prince	.25	.60
❑ 54 Ben Wallace	.25	.60
❑ 55 Rasheed Wallace	.25	.60
❑ 56 Baron Davis	.25	.60
❑ 57 Ike Diogu	.20	.50
❑ 58 Mike Dunleavy	.20	.50
❑ 59 Derek Fisher	.20	.50
❑ 60 Adonal Foyle	.15	.40
❑ 61 Troy Murphy	.25	.60
❑ 62 Jason Richardson	.25	.60
❑ 63 Rafer Alston	.15	.40
❑ 64 Chuck Hayes	.15	.40
❑ 65 Luther Head	.20	.50
❑ 66 Juwan Howard	.20	.50
❑ 67 Tracy McGrady	.50	1.25
❑ 68 Stromile Swift	.20	.50
❑ 69 Yao Ming	.60	1.50
❑ 70 Austin Croshere	.15	.40
❑ 71 Danny Granger	.20	.50
❑ 72 Sarunas Jasikevicius	.20	.50
❑ 73 Stephen Jackson	.20	.50

❑ 74 Jermaine O'Neal	.25	.60
❑ 75 Peja Stojakovic	.25	.60
❑ 76 Jamaal Tinsley	.20	.50
❑ 77 Elton Brand	.25	.60
❑ 78 Sam Cassell	.25	.60
❑ 79 Chris Kaman	.15	.40
❑ 80 Yaroslav Korolev	.15	.40
❑ 81 Shaun Livingston	.15	.40
❑ 82 Corey Maggette	.20	.50
❑ 83 Cuttino Mobley	.20	.50
❑ 84 Kwame Brown	.20	.50
❑ 85 Kobe Bryant	1.25	3.00
❑ 86 Andrew Bynum	.25	.60
❑ 87 Devean George	.20	.50
❑ 88 Lamar Odom	.25	.60
❑ 89 Ronny Turiaf	.20	.50
❑ 90 Luke Walton	.20	.50
❑ 91 Shane Battier	.25	.60
❑ 92 Pau Gasol	.25	.60
❑ 93 Bobby Jackson	.15	.40
❑ 94 Mike Miller	.25	.60
❑ 95 Lawrence Roberts	.15	.40
❑ 96 Damon Stoudamire	.20	.50
❑ 97 Hakim Warrick	.20	.50
❑ 98 Alonzo Mourning	.30	.75
❑ 99 Shaquille O'Neal	.60	1.50
❑ 100 Gary Payton	.25	.60
❑ 101 Wayne Simien	.20	.50
❑ 102 Dwyane Wade	.60	1.50
❑ 103 Antoine Walker	.20	.50
❑ 104 Jason Williams	.20	.50
❑ 105 Andrew Bogut	.25	.60
❑ 106 T.J. Ford	.20	.50
❑ 107 Jamaal Magloire	.15	.40
❑ 108 Michael Redd	.25	.60
❑ 109 Bobby Simmons	.15	.40
❑ 110 Maurice Williams	.20	.50
❑ 111 Mark Blount	.15	.40
❑ 112 Ricky Davis	.25	.60
❑ 113 Kevin Garnett	.50	1.25
❑ 114 Eddie Griffin	.15	.40
❑ 115 Troy Hudson	.15	.40
❑ 116 Rashad McCants	.20	.50
❑ 117 Vince Carter	.50	1.25
❑ 118 Jason Collins	.15	.40
❑ 119 Richard Jefferson	.20	.50
❑ 120 Jason Kidd	.40	1.00
❑ 121 Nenad Krstic	.20	.50
❑ 122 Jeff McInnis	.15	.40
❑ 123 Antoine Wright	.15	.40
❑ 124 Brandon Bass	.15	.40
❑ 125 David West	.25	.60
❑ 126 Desmond Mason	.15	.40
❑ 127 Chris Paul	.50	1.25
❑ 128 J.R. Smith	.20	.50
❑ 129 Kirk Snyder	.15	.40
❑ 130 Jamal Crawford	.15	.40
❑ 131 Steve Francis	.25	.60
❑ 132 Channing Frye	.20	.50
❑ 133 Stephon Marbury	.25	.60
❑ 134 Quentin Richardson	.20	.50
❑ 135 Nate Robinson	.25	.60
❑ 136 Jalen Rose	.20	.50
❑ 137 Carlos Arroyo	.25	.60
❑ 138 Keyon Dooling	.15	.40
❑ 139 Grant Hill	.25	.60
❑ 140 Dwight Howard	.50	1.25
❑ 141 Darko Milicic	.25	.60
❑ 142 Jameer Nelson	.20	.50
❑ 143 DeShawn Stevenson	.15	.40
❑ 144 Samuel Dalembert	.15	.40
❑ 145 Steven Hunter	.15	.40
❑ 146 Andre Iguodala	.25	.60
❑ 147 Allen Iverson	.50	1.25
❑ 148 Kyle Korver	.25	.60
❑ 149 Chris Webber	.25	.60
❑ 150 Leandro Barbosa	.25	.60
❑ 151 Raja Bell	.15	.40
❑ 152 Boris Diaw	.20	.50
❑ 153 Shawn Marion	.25	.60
❑ 154 Steve Nash	.30	.75
❑ 155 Amare Stoudemire	.50	1.25
❑ 156 Kurt Thomas	.15	.40
❑ 157 Steve Blake	.15	.40
❑ 158 Juan Dixon	.15	.40
❑ 159 Joel Przybilla	.15	.40
❑ 160 Zach Randolph	.25	.60
❑ 161 Travis Outlaw	.15	.40
❑ 162 Sebastian Telfair	.20	.50
❑ 163 Martell Webster	.20	.50
❑ 164 Shareef Abdur-Rahim	.25	.60
❑ 165 Ron Artest	.25	.60
❑ 166 Mike Bibby	.25	.60
❑ 167 Francisco Garcia	.15	.40
❑ 168 Brad Miller	.25	.60
❑ 169 Kenny Thomas	.15	.40
❑ 170 Bonzi Wells	.20	.50
❑ 171 Bruce Bowen	.15	.40
❑ 172 Tim Duncan	.50	1.25
❑ 173 Michael Finley	.25	.60
❑ 174 Manu Ginobili	.25	.60
❑ 175 Tony Parker	.25	.60
❑ 176 Ray Allen	.25	.60
❑ 177 Danny Fortson	.15	.40
❑ 178 Rashard Lewis	.25	.60
❑ 179 Luke Ridnour	.20	.50
❑ 180 Robert Swift	.15	.40
❑ 181 Chris Wilcox	.15	.40
❑ 182 Chris Bosh	.25	.60
❑ 183 Jose Calderon	.20	.50
❑ 184 Joey Graham	.20	.50
❑ 185 Pape Sow	.15	.40
❑ 186 Charlie Villanueva	.25	.60
❑ 187 Morris Peterson	.20	.50
❑ 188 Carlos Boozer	.25	.60
❑ 189 Gordan Giricek	.15	.40
❑ 190 Kris Humphries	.15	.40
❑ 191 Andrei Kirilenko	.25	.60
❑ 192 Mehmet Okur	.15	.40
❑ 193 Deron Williams	.40	1.00
❑ 194 Gilbert Arenas	.25	.60
❑ 195 Andray Blatche	.15	.40
❑ 196 Caron Butler	.25	.60
❑ 197 Brendan Haywood	.15	.40
❑ 198 Antawn Jamison	.25	.60
❑ 199 Etan Thomas	.15	.40
❑ 200 Antonio Daniels	.15	.40
❑ 201 Tyrus Thomas RC	.75	2.00
❑ 202 Adam Morrison RC	.75	2.00
❑ 203 LaMarcus Aldridge RC	.75	2.00
❑ 204 Rudy Gay RC	.60	1.50
❑ 205 Andrea Bargnani RC	1.00	2.50
❑ 206 Rodney Carney RC RC	.60	1.50
❑ 207 Alexander Johnson RC	.60	1.50
❑ 208 Brandon Roy RC	1.50	4.00
❑ 209 Patrick O'Bryant RC	.60	1.50
❑ 210 Randy Foye RC	.60	1.50
❑ 211 Ronnie Brewer RC	.75	2.00
❑ 212 Mardy Collins RC	.60	1.50
❑ 213 Shelden Williams RC	.75	2.00
❑ 214 J.J. Redick RC	.60	1.50
❑ 215 Hilton Armstrong RC	.60	1.50
❑ 216 Marcus Williams RC	.75	2.00
❑ 217 Rajon Rondo RC	2.50	6.00
❑ 218 Cedric Simmons RC	.60	1.50
❑ 219 Bobby Jones RC	.60	1.50
❑ 220 Jordan Farmar RC	.75	2.00
❑ 221 Maurice Ager RC	.60	1.50
❑ 222 David Noel RC	.60	1.50
❑ 223 James White RC	.60	1.50
❑ 224 Leon Powe RC	.60	1.50
❑ 225 Paul Millsap RC	1.00	2.50
❑ 226 Josh Boone RC	.60	1.50
❑ 227 Kevin Pittsnogle RC	.60	1.50
❑ 228 Daniel Gibson RC	.75	2.00
❑ 229 Hassan Adams RC	.75	2.00
❑ 230 Kyle Lowry RC	.60	1.50
❑ 231 Renaldo Balkman RC	.60	1.50
❑ 232 Dee Brown RC	.60	1.50
❑ 233 Shawne Williams RC	.60	1.50
❑ 234 P.J. Tucker RC	.60	1.50
❑ 235 Craig Smith RC	.60	1.50
❑ 236 Paul Davis RC	.60	1.50
❑ 237 Pops Mensah-Bonsu RC	.60	1.50
❑ 238 Denham Brown RC	.60	1.50
❑ 239 Ryan Hollins RC	.60	1.50
❑ 240 Allan Ray RC	.60	1.50
❑ 241 Saer Sene RC	.60	1.50
❑ 242 Shannon Brown RC	.60	1.50
❑ 243 Thabo Sefolosha RC	.75	2.00
❑ 244 Quincy Douby RC	.60	1.50
❑ 245 Solomon Jones RC	.60	1.50
❑ 246 Damir Markota RC	.60	1.50
❑ 247 Steve Novak RC	.60	1.50
❑ 248 Will Blalock RC	.60	1.50
❑ 249 Tarence Kinsey RC	.60	1.50
❑ 250 Vassilis Spanoulis RC	.60	1.50

2007-08 Fleer

❑ COMPLETE SET (235)	30.00	60.00
❑ 1 Chauncey Billups	.20	.50
❑ 2 Amir Johnson	.12	.30
❑ 3 Richard Hamilton	.15	.40
❑ 4 Jason Maxiell	.12	.30
❑ 5 Tayshaun Prince	.20	.50
❑ 6 Rasheed Wallace	.20	.50
❑ 7 Antonio McDyess	.12	.30
❑ 8 Daniel Gibson	.20	.50
❑ 9 Larry Hughes	.15	.40
❑ 10 Zydrunas Ilgauskas	.15	.40
❑ 11 Devin Brown	.12	.30
❑ 12 LeBron James	1.00	2.50
❑ 13 Donyell Marshall	.12	.30
❑ 14 Eric Snow	.12	.30
❑ 15 Andrea Bargnani	.25	.60
❑ 16 Chris Bosh	.20	.50
❑ 17 T.J. Ford	.15	.40
❑ 18 Jorge Garbajosa	.20	.50
❑ 19 Radoslav Nesterovic	.12	.30
❑ 20 Jose Calderon	.15	.40
❑ 21 James Posey	.12	.30
❑ 22 Alonzo Mourning	.25	.60
❑ 23 Shaquille O'Neal	.50	1.25
❑ 24 Dwyane Wade	.50	1.25
❑ 25 Antoine Walker	.15	.40
❑ 26 Jason Williams	.15	.40
❑ 27 Udonis Haslem	.20	.50
❑ 28 Luol Deng	.20	.50
❑ 29 Ben Gordon	.25	.60
❑ 30 Kirk Hinrich	.20	.50
❑ 31 Ben Wallace	.20	.50
❑ 32 Tyrus Thomas	.25	.60
❑ 33 Thabo Sefolosha	.20	.50
❑ 34 Chris Duhon	.15	.40
❑ 35 Vince Carter	.40	1.00
❑ 36 Jason Collins	.12	.30
❑ 37 Richard Jefferson	.20	.50
❑ 38 Jason Kidd	.30	.75
❑ 39 Nenad Krstic	.15	.40
❑ 40 Marcus Williams	.20	.50
❑ 41 Josh Boone	.12	.30
❑ 42 Gilbert Arenas	.20	.50
❑ 43 Caron Butler	.20	.50
❑ 44 Antawn Jamison	.20	.50
❑ 45 Brendan Haywood	.12	.30
❑ 46 Antonio Daniels	.12	.30
❑ 47 Etan Thomas	.12	.30
❑ 48 Trevor Ariza	.12	.30
❑ 49 Dwight Howard	.40	1.00
❑ 50 Rashard Lewis	.20	.50
❑ 51 Jameer Nelson	.15	.40
❑ 52 J.J. Redick	.20	.50
❑ 53 Hedo Turkoglu	.20	.50
❑ 54 Carlos Arroyo	.20	.50
❑ 55 Ike Diogu	.12	.30
❑ 56 Mike Dunleavy	.15	.40
❑ 57 Jeff Foster	.12	.30
❑ 58 Jermaine O'Neal	.20	.50
❑ 59 Jamaal Tinsley	.12	.30
❑ 60 Shawne Williams	.15	.40
❑ 61 Rodney Carney	.12	.30
❑ 62 Andre Iguodala	.20	.50
❑ 63 Kyle Korver	.20	.50
❑ 64 Andre Miller	.15	.40
❑ 65 Willie Green	.12	.30
❑ 66 Samuel Dalembert	.12	.30
❑ 67 Raymond Felton	.25	.60
❑ 68 Sean May	.15	.40
❑ 69 Adam Morrison	.20	.50
❑ 70 Emeka Okafor	.20	.50
❑ 71 Jason Richardson	.20	.50
❑ 72 Gerald Wallace	.20	.50
❑ 73 Ryan Hollins	.12	.30

❑ 74 David Lee	.15	.40
❑ 75 Jamal Crawford UER	.12	.30
❑ 76 Eddy Curry	.12	.30
❑ 77 Stephon Marbury	.20	.50
❑ 78 Zach Randolph	.20	.50
❑ 79 Nate Robinson	.20	.50
❑ 80 Quentin Richardson	.15	.40
❑ 81 Josh Childress	.15	.40
❑ 82 Joe Johnson	.20	.50
❑ 83 Tyronn Lue	.12	.30
❑ 84 Josh Smith	.20	.50
❑ 85 Marvin Williams	.20	.50
❑ 86 Shelden Williams	.20	.50
❑ 87 Salim Stoudamire	.12	.30
❑ 88 Andrew Bogut	.20	.50
❑ 89 Bobby Simmons	.12	.30
❑ 90 David Noel	.12	.30
❑ 91 Michael Redd	.20	.50
❑ 92 Charlie Villanueva	.20	.50
❑ 93 Desmond Mason	.12	.30
❑ 94 Ray Allen	.20	.50
❑ 95 Rajon Rondo	.20	.50
❑ 96 Al Jefferson	.20	.50
❑ 97 Paul Pierce	.20	.50
❑ 98 Leon Powe	.12	.30
❑ 99 Tony Allen	.12	.30
❑ 100 Pau Gasol	.20	.50
❑ 101 Rudy Gay	.15	.40
❑ 102 Darko Milicic	.20	.50
❑ 103 Damon Stoudamire	.15	.40
❑ 104 Hakim Warrick	.15	.40
❑ 105 Mike Miller	.20	.50
❑ 106 Johan Petro	.12	.30
❑ 107 Wally Szczerbiak	.15	.40
❑ 108 Delonte West	.15	.40
❑ 109 Luke Ridnour	.15	.40
❑ 110 Chris Wilcox	.15	.40
❑ 111 Nick Collison	.12	.30
❑ 112 LaMarcus Aldridge	.25	.60
❑ 113 Channing Frye	.15	.40
❑ 114 Jarrett Jack	.15	.40
❑ 115 Brandon Roy	.30	.75
❑ 116 Martell Webster	.15	.40
❑ 117 Sergio Rodriguez	.15	.40
❑ 118 James Jones	.12	.30
❑ 119 Shareef Abdur-Rahim	.20	.50
❑ 120 Ron Artest	.20	.50
❑ 121 Mike Bibby	.20	.50
❑ 122 Francisco Garcia	.15	.40
❑ 123 Kevin Martin	.20	.50
❑ 124 Brad Miller	.20	.50
❑ 125 Mikki Moore	.15	.40
❑ 126 Ricky Davis	.20	.50
❑ 127 Randy Foye	.20	.50
❑ 128 Kevin Garnett	.50	1.25
❑ 129 Juwan Howard	.12	.30
❑ 130 Marko Jaric	.15	.40
❑ 131 Rashad McCants	.15	.40
❑ 132 Craig Smith	.20	.50
❑ 133 Hilton Armstrong	.12	.30
❑ 134 Tyson Chandler	.20	.50
❑ 135 Bobby Jackson	.12	.30
❑ 136 Chris Paul	.40	1.00
❑ 137 Rasual Butler	.12	.30
❑ 138 Peja Stojakovic	.20	.50
❑ 139 Morris Peterson	.15	.40
❑ 140 Elton Brand	.20	.50
❑ 141 Sam Cassell	.20	.50
❑ 142 Paul Davis	.12	.30
❑ 143 Corey Maggette	.15	.40
❑ 144 Cuttino Mobley	.15	.40
❑ 145 Chris Kaman	.12	.30
❑ 146 Baron Davis	.20	.50
❑ 147 Monta Ellis	.15	.40
❑ 148 Al Harrington	.15	.40
❑ 149 Stephen Jackson	.15	.40
❑ 150 Matt Barnes	.12	.30
❑ 151 Andris Biedrins	.12	.30
❑ 152 Kwame Brown	.12	.30
❑ 153 Kobe Bryant	1.00	2.50
❑ 154 Andrew Bynum	.20	.50
❑ 155 Jordan Farmar	.15	.40
❑ 156 Lamar Odom	.20	.50
❑ 157 Luke Walton	.15	.40
❑ 158 Maurice Evans	.12	.30
❑ 159 Carmelo Anthony	.40	1.00
❑ 160 Marcus Camby	.12	.30
❑ 161 Allen Iverson	.40	1.00
❑ 162 Kenyon Martin	.20	.50
❑ 163 Nene	.12	.30
❑ 164 J.R. Smith	.15	.40
❑ 165 Yakhouba Diawara	.12	.30
❑ 166 Shane Battier	.20	.50
❑ 167 Luther Head	.15	.40
❑ 168 Tracy McGrady	.40	1.00
❑ 169 Yao Ming	.50	1.25
❑ 170 Rafer Alston	.12	.30
❑ 171 Bonzi Wells	.15	.40
❑ 172 Steve Novak	.12	.30
❑ 173 Carlos Boozer	.20	.50
❑ 174 Ronnie Brewer	.15	.40
❑ 175 Andrei Kirilenko	.20	.50
❑ 176 Paul Millsap	.15	.40
❑ 177 Mehmet Okur	.15	.40
❑ 178 Deron Williams	.30	.75
❑ 179 Jarron Collins	.12	.30
❑ 180 Tim Duncan	.40	1.00
❑ 181 Tony Parker	.20	.50
❑ 182 Manu Ginobili	.20	.50
❑ 183 Bruce Bowen	.12	.30
❑ 184 Brent Barry	.12	.30
❑ 185 Robert Horry	.15	.40
❑ 186 Michael Finley	.20	.50
❑ 187 Leandro Barbosa	.15	.40
❑ 188 Grant Hill	.20	.50
❑ 189 Shawn Marion	.20	.50
❑ 190 Steve Nash	.25	.60
❑ 191 Amare Stoudemire	.40	1.00
❑ 192 Boris Diaw	.15	.40
❑ 193 Raja Bell	.12	.30
❑ 194 Maurice Ager	.12	.30
❑ 195 Devean George	.12	.30
❑ 196 Devin Harris	.20	.50
❑ 197 Josh Howard	.20	.50
❑ 198 Dirk Nowitzki	.30	.75
❑ 199 Jerry Stackhouse	.15	.40
❑ 200 Jason Terry	.20	.50
❑ 201 Arron Afflalo RC	.50	1.25
❑ 202 Morris Almond RC	.50	1.25
❑ 203 Marco Belinelli RC	.50	1.25
❑ 204 Corey Brewer RC	.60	1.50
❑ 205 Wilson Chandler RC	.50	1.25
❑ 206 Mike Conley RC	.60	1.50
❑ 207 Daequan Cook RC	.60	1.50
❑ 208 Javaris Crittenton RC	.50	1.25
❑ 209 Jermareo Davidson RC	.50	1.25
❑ 210 Glen Davis RC	1.00	2.50
❑ 211 Jared Dudley RC	.50	1.25
❑ 212 Kevin Durant RC	4.00	10.00
❑ 213 Nick Fazekas RC	.50	1.25
❑ 214 Jeff Green RC	.60	1.50
❑ 215 Taurean Green RC	.50	1.25
❑ 216 Spencer Hawes RC	.50	1.25
❑ 217 Al Horford RC	.60	1.50
❑ 218 Aaron Brooks RC	.75	2.00
❑ 219 Carl Landry RC	.50	1.25
❑ 220 Acie Law RC	.60	1.50
❑ 221 Josh McRoberts RC	.60	1.50
❑ 222 Joakim Noah RC	.60	1.50
❑ 223 Greg Oden RC	.75	2.00
❑ 224 Gabe Pruitt RC	.50	1.25
❑ 225 Jason Smith RC	.50	1.25
❑ 226 Rodney Stuckey RC	1.00	2.50
❑ 227 Al Thornton RC	.50	1.25
❑ 228 Alando Tucker RC	.50	1.25
❑ 229 Sean Williams RC	.50	1.25
❑ 230 Yi Jianlian RC	.75	2.00
❑ 231 Brandan Wright RC	.60	1.50
❑ 232 Julian Wright RC	.60	1.50
❑ 233 Nick Young RC	.50	1.25
❑ 234 Thaddeus Young RC	.60	1.50
❑ 235 Chris Richard RC	.50	1.25
❑ RCF Michael Jordan Floor	15.00	30.00
❑ COAF Michael Jordan Floor AU/23		
❑ RCPJ Michael Jordan JSY White	30.00	60.00
❑ RCWU M.Jordan JSY Black/250	60.00	120.00

2008-09 Fleer

❑ COMPLETE SET (247)	25.00	50.00
❑ 1 Ray Allen	.20	.50
❑ 2 Kevin Garnett	.40	1.00
❑ 3 Paul Pierce	.25	.60
❑ 4 Glen Davis	.15	.40
❑ 5 Rajon Rondo	.20	.50
❑ 6 Leon Powe	.12	.30
❑ 7 James Posey	.15	.40
❑ 8 Chauncey Billups	.20	.50
❑ 9 Richard Hamilton	.15	.40
❑ 10 Jason Maxiell	.15	.40
❑ 11 Tayshaun Prince	.20	.50
❑ 12 Rasheed Wallace	.20	.50
❑ 13 Rodney Stuckey	.25	.60
❑ 14 Antonio McDyess	.12	.30
❑ 15 Keith Bogans	.12	.30
❑ 16 Maurice Evans	.12	.30
❑ 17 Dwight Howard	.40	1.00
❑ 18 Rashard Lewis	.20	.50
❑ 19 Jameer Nelson	.15	.40
❑ 20 Hedo Turkoglu	.20	.50
❑ 21 Anthony Johnson	.12	.30
❑ 22 Ben Wallace	.20	.50
❑ 23 LeBron James	1.00	2.50
❑ 24 Zydrunas Ilgauskas	.15	.40
❑ 25 Delonte West	.15	.40
❑ 26 Anderson Varejao	.15	.40
❑ 27 Daniel Gibson	.20	.50
❑ 28 Mo Williams	.15	.40
❑ 29 Gilbert Arenas	.20	.50
❑ 30 Caron Butler	.20	.50
❑ 31 Brendan Haywood	.12	.30
❑ 32 Antawn Jamison	.20	.50
❑ 33 DeShawn Stevenson	.12	.30
❑ 34 Nick Young	.12	.30
❑ 35 Antonio Daniels	.12	.30
❑ 36 Andrea Bargnani	.15	.40
❑ 37 Chris Bosh	.20	.50
❑ 38 Jose Calderon	.15	.40
❑ 39 Jermaine O'Neal	.20	.50
❑ 40 Anthony Parker	.15	.40
❑ 41 Jamario Moon	.20	.50
❑ 42 Elton Brand	.30	.75
❑ 43 Samuel Dalembert	.12	.30
❑ 44 Willie Green	.12	.30
❑ 45 Andre Iguodala	.20	.50
❑ 46 Andre Miller	.15	.40
❑ 47 Louis Williams	.12	.30
❑ 48 Thaddeus Young	.15	.40
❑ 49 Mike Bibby	.20	.50
❑ 50 Zaza Pachulia	.12	.30
❑ 51 Al Horford	.20	.50
❑ 52 Joe Johnson	.20	.50
❑ 53 Josh Smith	.20	.50
❑ 54 Marvin Williams	.20	.50
❑ 55 Acie Law IV	.15	.40
❑ 56 Danny Granger	.20	.50
❑ 57 T.J. Ford	.12	.30
❑ 58 Mike Dunleavy	.15	.40
❑ 59 Jamaal Tinsley	.12	.30
❑ 60 Troy Murphy	.20	.50
❑ 61 Jeff Foster	.12	.30
❑ 62 Vince Carter	.25	.60
❑ 63 Yi Jianlian	.20	.50
❑ 64 Sean Williams	.15	.40
❑ 65 Devin Harris	.20	.50
❑ 66 Keyon Dooling	.12	.30
❑ 67 Josh Boone	.12	.30
❑ 68 Michael Jordan	1.50	4.00
❑ 69 Luol Deng	.20	.50
❑ 70 Ben Gordon	.20	.50
❑ 71 Joakim Noah	.20	.50
❑ 72 Kirk Hinrich	.20	.50
❑ 73 Andres Nocioni	.15	.40
❑ 74 Larry Hughes	.15	.40
❑ 75 Gerald Wallace	.20	.50
❑ 76 Emeka Okafor	.20	.50
❑ 77 Jason Richardson	.20	.50
❑ 78 Raymond Felton	.15	.40
❑ 79 Adam Morrison	.20	.50
❑ 80 Jared Dudley	.20	.50
❑ 81 Nazr Mohammed	.12	.30
❑ 82 Andrew Bogut	.20	.50
❑ 83 Charlie Villanueva	.20	.50
❑ 84 Michael Redd	.20	.50
❑ 85 Ramon Sessions	.20	.50

❑ 86 Richard Jefferson	.20	.50
❑ 87 Charlie Bell	.12	.30
❑ 88 Jamal Crawford	.12	.30
❑ 89 Eddy Curry	.12	.30
❑ 90 Stephon Marbury	.20	.50
❑ 91 Zach Randolph	.20	.50
❑ 92 Quentin Richardson	.15	.40
❑ 93 Nate Robinson	.20	.50
❑ 94 David Lee	.15	.40
❑ 95 Dwyane Wade	.40	1.00
❑ 96 Daequan Cook	.15	.40
❑ 97 Shawn Marion	.20	.50
❑ 98 Alonzo Mourning	.20	.50
❑ 99 Udonis Haslem	.20	.50
❑ 100 Dorell Wright	.12	.30
❑ 101 Kobe Bryant	1.00	2.50
❑ 102 Andrew Bynum	.20	.50
❑ 103 Jordan Farmar	.15	.40
❑ 104 Pau Gasol	.20	.50
❑ 105 Lamar Odom	.20	.50
❑ 106 Luke Walton	.15	.40
❑ 107 Sasha Vujacic	.15	.40
❑ 108 Tyson Chandler	.15	.40
❑ 109 Chris Paul	.40	1.00
❑ 110 Hilton Armstrong	.12	.30
❑ 111 Peja Stojakovic	.20	.50
❑ 112 Rasual Butler	.15	.40
❑ 113 Julian Wright	.15	.40
❑ 114 Morris Peterson	.15	.40
❑ 115 Tony Parker	.20	.50
❑ 116 Tim Duncan	.30	.75
❑ 117 Manu Ginobili	.20	.50
❑ 118 Michael Finley	.20	.50
❑ 119 Kurt Thomas	.15	.40
❑ 120 Bruce Bowen	.12	.30
❑ 121 Fabricio Oberto	.12	.30
❑ 122 Mehmet Okur	.20	.50
❑ 123 Deron Williams	.25	.60
❑ 124 Carlos Boozer	.20	.50
❑ 125 Kyle Korver	.20	.50
❑ 126 Andrei Kirilenko	.20	.50
❑ 127 Paul Millsap	.15	.40
❑ 128 Ronnie Brewer	.15	.40
❑ 129 Shane Battier	.15	.40
❑ 130 Tracy McGrady	.25	.60
❑ 131 Yao Ming	.25	.60
❑ 132 Luis Scola	.15	.40
❑ 133 Luther Head	.15	.40
❑ 134 Carl Landry	.12	.30
❑ 135 Ron Artest	.20	.50
❑ 136 Grant Hill	.20	.50
❑ 137 Amare Stoudemire	.25	.60
❑ 138 Steve Nash	.20	.50
❑ 139 Shaquille O'Neal	.40	1.00
❑ 140 Leandro Barbosa	.15	.40
❑ 141 Boris Diaw	.15	.40
❑ 142 Raja Bell	.12	.30
❑ 143 Dirk Nowitzki	.25	.60
❑ 144 Jason Kidd	.20	.50
❑ 145 Josh Howard	.20	.50
❑ 146 Jerry Stackhouse	.15	.40
❑ 147 Jason Terry	.15	.40
❑ 148 Brandon Bass	.15	.40
❑ 149 Erick Dampier	.12	.30
❑ 150 Carmelo Anthony	.25	.60
❑ 151 Nene	.15	.40
❑ 152 Allen Iverson	.25	.60
❑ 153 Kenyon Martin	.20	.50
❑ 154 J.R. Smith	.15	.40
❑ 155 Linas Kleiza	.12	.30
❑ 156 Corey Maggette	.20	.50
❑ 157 Monta Ellis	.20	.50
❑ 158 Stephen Jackson	.15	.40
❑ 159 Al Harrington	.15	.40
❑ 160 Andris Biedrins	.12	.30
❑ 161 Kelenna Azubuike	.12	.30
❑ 162 C.J. Watson	.12	.30
❑ 163 LaMarcus Aldridge	.20	.50
❑ 164 Travis Outlaw	.20	.50
❑ 165 Greg Oden	.20	.50
❑ 166 Brandon Roy	.25	.60
❑ 167 Martell Webster	.15	.40
❑ 168 Steve Blake	.12	.30
❑ 169 Bobby Brown	.12	.30
❑ 170 Beno Udrih	.12	.30
❑ 171 Kevin Martin	.20	.50
❑ 172 Francisco Garcia	.15	.40
❑ 173 Brad Miller	.20	.50
❑ 174 John Salmons	.20	.50
❑ 175 Mikki Moore	.15	.40
❑ 176 Baron Davis	.20	.50
❑ 177 Chris Kaman	.12	.30
❑ 178 Shaun Livingston	.15	.40
❑ 179 Marcus Camby	.12	.30
❑ 180 Al Thornton	.20	.50
❑ 181 Cuttino Mobley	.15	.40
❑ 182 Ricky Davis	.20	.50
❑ 183 Corey Brewer	.15	.40
❑ 184 Randy Foye	.20	.50
❑ 185 Al Jefferson	.20	.50
❑ 186 Rashad McCants	.15	.40
❑ 187 Mike Miller	.20	.50
❑ 188 Sebastian Telfair	.15	.40
❑ 189 Mike Conley	.15	.40
❑ 190 Rudy Gay	.20	.50
❑ 191 Kyle Lowry	.12	.30
❑ 192 Hakim Warrick	.12	.30
❑ 193 Marko Jaric	.15	.40
❑ 194 Javaris Crittenton	.12	.30
❑ 195 Kevin Durant	.50	1.25
❑ 196 Jeff Green	.15	.40
❑ 197 Chris Wilcox	.15	.40
❑ 198 Damien Wilkins	.12	.30
❑ 199 Earl Watson	.12	.30
❑ 200 Desmond Mason	.12	.30
❑ 201 Derrick Rose RC	2.00	5.00
❑ 202 Michael Beasley RC	1.00	2.50
❑ 203 O.J. Mayo RC	.75	2.00
❑ 204 Russell Westbrook RC	1.25	3.00
❑ 205 Kevin Love RC	.60	1.50
❑ 206 Danilo Gallinari RC	.75	2.00
❑ 207 Eric Gordon RC	.60	1.50
❑ 208 Joe Alexander RC	.50	1.25
❑ 209 D.J. Augustin RC	.50	1.25
❑ 210 Brook Lopez RC	1.00	2.50
❑ 211 Jerryd Bayless RC	.50	1.25
❑ 212 Jason Thompson RC	.50	1.25
❑ 213 Brandon Rush RC	.50	1.25
❑ 214 Anthony Randolph RC	.75	2.00
❑ 215 Robin Lopez RC	.50	1.25
❑ 216 Marreese Speights RC	.50	1.25
❑ 217 Roy Hibbert RC	.60	1.50
❑ 218 Javale McGee RC	.50	1.25
❑ 219 J.J. Hickson RC	.75	2.00
❑ 220 Alexis Ajinca RC	.50	1.25
❑ 221 Ryan Anderson RC	.50	1.25
❑ 222 Courtney Lee RC	.75	2.00
❑ 223 Kosta Koufos RC	.50	1.25
❑ 224 George Hill RC	.75	2.00
❑ 225 Darrell Arthur RC	.50	1.25
❑ 226 Donte Greene RC	.50	1.25
❑ 227 D.J. White RC	.50	1.25
❑ 228 J.R. Giddens RC	.50	1.25
❑ 229 Walter Sharpe RC	.50	1.25
❑ 230 Joey Dorsey RC	.50	1.25
❑ 231 Mario Chalmers RC	.60	1.50
❑ 232 Kyle Weaver RC	.50	1.25
❑ 233 Sonny Weems RC	.50	1.25
❑ 234 Chris Douglas-Roberts RC	.60	1.50
❑ 235 Rudy Fernandez RC	1.00	2.50
❑ 236 Rose/Beasley/Mayo	3.00	8.00
❑ 237 Westbrook/Love/Gallinari	2.00	5.00
❑ 238 Gordon/Alexander/Augustin	2.50	6.00
❑ 239 Lopez/Bayless/Thompson	2.50	6.00
❑ 240 Rush/Randolph/Lopez	1.50	4.00
❑ 241 Speights/Hibbert/McGee	1.50	4.00
❑ 242 Hickson/Ajinca/Anderson	2.00	5.00
❑ 243 Lee/Koufos/Hill	2.00	5.00
❑ 244 Arthur/Greene/White	1.50	4.00
❑ 245 Giddens/Sharpe/Dorsey	1.50	4.00
❑ 246 Chalmers/Jordan/Weaver	2.00	5.00
❑ 247 Weems/Douglas-Roberts/Fernandez	1.50	4.00

2001-02 Fleer Authentix

❑ COMP.SET w/o SP'S	20.00	40.00
❑ COMMON CARD (1-100)	.20	.50
❑ COMMON ROOKIE (101-135)	1.25	3.00
❑ 1 Vince Carter	.60	1.50
❑ 2 Terrell Brandon	.20	.50
❑ 3 Raef LaFrentz	.20	.50
❑ 4 Iakovos Tsakalidis	.20	.50
❑ 5 Elton Brand	.30	.75
❑ 6 David Robinson	.40	1.00
❑ 7 Lamar Odom	.30	.75
❑ 8 Larry Hughes	.25	.60
❑ 9 Gary Payton	.30	.75
❑ 10 Rick Fox	.25	.60
❑ 11 Jamal Mashburn	.25	.60
❑ 12 Brian Grant	.20	.50
❑ 13 David Wesley	.20	.50
❑ 14 Steve Smith	.25	.60
❑ 15 Corey Maggette	.25	.60
❑ 16 Michael Jordan	5.00	12.00
❑ 17 Wally Szczerbiak	.25	.60
❑ 18 Antoine Walker	.25	.60
❑ 19 Marcus Camby	.25	.60
❑ 20 Rasheed Wallace	.30	.75
❑ 21 Travis Best	.20	.50
❑ 22 Theo Ratliff	.20	.50
❑ 23 LaPhonso Ellis	.25	.60
❑ 24 Dirk Nowitzki	.50	1.25
❑ 25 Kurt Thomas	.20	.50
❑ 26 Steve Francis	.30	.75
❑ 27 Tim Duncan	.60	1.50
❑ 28 Eddie House	.20	.50
❑ 29 Ron Mercer	.20	.50
❑ 30 Allan Houston	.25	.60
❑ 31 Trajan Langdon	.20	.50
❑ 32 Karl Malone	.40	1.00
❑ 33 Glenn Robinson	.25	.60
❑ 34 Wang Zhizhi	.25	.60
❑ 35 Jason Kidd	.50	1.25
❑ 36 Maurice Taylor	.20	.50
❑ 37 Chris Webber	.30	.75
❑ 38 Michael Dickerson	.20	.50
❑ 39 Paul Pierce	.30	.75
❑ 40 Bonzi Wells	.25	.60
❑ 41 Antawn Jamison	.30	.75
❑ 42 Rashard Lewis	.30	.75
❑ 43 Reggie Miller	.30	.75
❑ 44 Patrick Ewing	.40	1.00
❑ 45 Marcus Fizer	.20	.50
❑ 46 Aaron McKie	.20	.50
❑ 47 Marc Jackson	.20	.50
❑ 48 Desmond Mason	.25	.60
❑ 49 Jermaine O'Neal	.30	.75
❑ 50 DeShawn Stevenson	.20	.50
❑ 51 John Stockton	.40	1.00
❑ 52 Tim Thomas	.20	.50
❑ 53 Andre Miller	.25	.60
❑ 54 Jumaine Jones	.20	.50
❑ 55 Nick Van Exel	.25	.60
❑ 56 Damon Stoudamire	.25	.60
❑ 57 Stephon Marbury	.30	.75
❑ 58 Clifford Robinson	.20	.50
❑ 59 Hedo Turkoglu	.25	.60
❑ 60 Kobe Bryant	1.50	4.00
❑ 61 Richard Hamilton	.25	.60
❑ 62 Stromile Swift	.20	.50
❑ 63 Chris Mihm	.20	.50
❑ 64 Tracy McGrady	.60	1.50
❑ 65 Jalen Rose	.25	.60
❑ 66 Morris Peterson	.25	.60
❑ 67 Alonzo Mourning	.30	.75
❑ 68 Courtney Alexander	.20	.50
❑ 69 Michael Finley	.30	.75
❑ 70 Shawn Marion	.30	.75
❑ 71 Darius Miles	.20	.50
❑ 72 Antonio Davis	.20	.50
❑ 73 Ray Allen	.30	.75
❑ 74 Shareef Abdur-Rahim	.25	.60
❑ 75 Kevin Garnett	.60	1.50
❑ 76 Latrell Sprewell	.25	.60
❑ 77 Antonio McDyess	.25	.60
❑ 78 Derek Anderson	.25	.60
❑ 79 Derek Fisher	.25	.60
❑ 80 Jason Terry	.30	.75
❑ 81 Eddie Jones	.25	.60
❑ 82 Hakeem Olajuwon	.40	1.00
❑ 83 Toni Kukoc	.25	.60
❑ 84 Sam Cassell	.25	.60
❑ 85 Jamal Crawford	.25	.60
❑ 86 Allen Iverson	.60	1.50

❑ 87 Steve Nash	.50	1.25
❑ 88 Dikembe Mutombo	.25	.60
❑ 89 Shaquille O'Neal	.75	2.00
❑ 90 Jerome Moiso	.20	.50
❑ 91 Kenyon Martin	.30	.75
❑ 92 Chucky Atkins	.20	.50
❑ 93 Grant Hill	.30	.75
❑ 94 Jerry Stackhouse	.25	.60
❑ 95 Jason Williams	.25	.60
❑ 96 Baron Davis	.30	.75
❑ 97 Mike Miller	.25	.60
❑ 98 Joe Smith	.20	.50
❑ 99 Peja Stojakovic	.25	.60
❑ 100 Cuttino Mobley	.25	.60
❑ 101 Kwame Brown RC	1.50	4.00
❑ 102 Jason Collins RC	1.25	3.00
❑ 103 Willie Solomon RC	1.25	3.00
❑ 104 Brendan Haywood RC	1.50	4.00
❑ 105 Jeff Trepagnier RC	1.25	3.00
❑ 106 Eddie Griffin RC	1.25	3.00
❑ 107 Joseph Forte RC	1.25	3.00
❑ 108 Rodney White RC	1.25	3.00
❑ 109 Jeryl Sasser RC	1.25	3.00
❑ 110 Samuel Dalembert RC	1.50	4.00
❑ 111 Shane Battier RC	2.00	5.00
❑ 112 Tony Parker RC	5.00	12.00
❑ 113 DeSagana Diop RC	1.25	3.00
❑ 114 Steven Hunter RC	1.25	3.00
❑ 115 Trenton Hassell RC	1.50	4.00
❑ 116 Michael Bradley RC	1.25	3.00
❑ 117 Brian Scalabrine RC	1.25	3.00
❑ 118 Troy Murphy RC	2.50	6.00
❑ 119 Brandon Armstrong RC	1.25	3.00
❑ 120 Pau Gasol RC	5.00	12.00
❑ 121 Gerald Wallace RC	3.00	8.00
❑ 122 Jason Richardson RC	2.50	6.00
❑ 123 Joe Johnson RC	3.00	8.00
❑ 124 Loren Woods RC	1.25	3.00
❑ 125 Vladimir Radmanovic RC	1.50	4.00
❑ 126 Jamaal Tinsley RC	1.50	4.00
❑ 127 Omar Cook RC	1.25	3.00
❑ 128 Kedrick Brown RC	1.25	3.00
❑ 129 Terence Morris RC	1.25	3.00
❑ 130 Richard Jefferson RC	3.00	8.00
❑ 131 Gilbert Arenas RC	2.00	5.00
❑ 132 Tyson Chandler RC	2.50	6.00
❑ 133 Kirk Haston RC	1.25	3.00
❑ 134 Eddy Curry RC	2.00	5.00
❑ 135 Zach Randolph RC	3.00	8.00

2002-03 Fleer Authentix

❑ COMPLETE SET (135)	125.00	250.00
❑ COMP.SET w/o SP's (100)	15.00	40.00
❑ COMMON CARD (1-100)	.20	.50
❑ COMMON ROOKIE (101-135)	2.00	5.00
❑ 1 Vince Carter	.60	1.50
❑ 2 Bobby Jackson		
❑ 3 Cuttino Mobley	.25	.60
❑ 4 John Stockton	.40	1.00
❑ 5 Jamal Mashburn	.25	.60
❑ 6 Ben Wallace	.25	.60
❑ 7 Tim Duncan	.60	1.50
❑ 8 Richard Jefferson	.30	.75
❑ 9 Clifford Robinson	.20	.50
❑ 10 Gary Payton	.30	.75
❑ 11 Terrell Brandon	.20	.50
❑ 12 Michael Finley	.30	.75
❑ 13 Rasheed Wallace	.30	.75
❑ 14 Jason Williams	.25	.60
❑ 15 Andre Miller	.25	.60
❑ 16 Shawn Marion	.30	.75
❑ 17 Kobe Bryant	1.50	4.00
❑ 18 Jason Terry	.30	.75
❑ 19 Latrell Sprewell	.25	.60
❑ 20 Jerry Stackhouse	.25	.60
❑ 21 Tony Parker	.30	.75
❑ 22 Ray Allen	.30	.75
❑ 23 Dirk Nowitzki	.50	1.25
❑ 24 Chris Webber	.30	.75
❑ 25 Rick Fox	.25	.60
❑ 26 Jermaine O'Neal	.30	.75
❑ 27 Karl Malone	.30	.75
❑ 28 Allan Houston	.25	.60
❑ 29 Jason Richardson	.30	.75
❑ 30 Morris Peterson	.25	.60
❑ 31 Kevin Garnett	.60	1.50
❑ 32 Antawn Jamison	.30	.75
❑ 33 Rashard Lewis	.30	.75
❑ 34 Jason Kidd	.50	1.25
❑ 35 Joe Smith	.20	.50
❑ 36 David Robinson	.40	1.00
❑ 37 Brian Grant	.20	.50
❑ 38 Lamond Murray	.20	.50
❑ 39 Damon Stoudamire	.25	.60
❑ 40 Shane Battier	.25	.60
❑ 41 Eddy Curry	.25	.60
❑ 42 Dikembe Mutombo	.25	.60
❑ 43 Jamaal Tinsley	.25	.60
❑ 44 Courtney Alexander	.20	.50
❑ 45 Wally Szczerbiak	.25	.60
❑ 46 Antonio McDyess	.25	.60
❑ 47 Mike Bibby	.25	.60
❑ 48 Alonzo Mourning	.30	.75
❑ 49 Tyson Chandler	.25	.60
❑ 50 Stephon Marbury	.30	.75
❑ 51 Sam Cassell	.25	.60
❑ 52 Steve Nash	.50	1.25
❑ 53 Bonzi Wells	.25	.60
❑ 54 Pau Gasol	.30	.75
❑ 55 Rodney Rogers	.20	.50
❑ 56 Allen Iverson	.60	1.50
❑ 57 Derek Fisher	.25	.60
❑ 58 Travis Best	.20	.50
❑ 59 Aaron McKie	.20	.50
❑ 60 Darius Miles	.20	.50
❑ 61 Richard Hamilton	.25	.60
❑ 62 Marcus Camby	.25	.60
❑ 63 Eddie Griffin	.20	.50
❑ 64 Antonio Davis	.20	.50
❑ 65 David Wesley	.20	.50
❑ 66 Stromile Swift	.20	.50
❑ 67 Brent Barry	.20	.50
❑ 68 Glenn Robinson	.25	.60
❑ 69 Antoine Walker	.25	.60
❑ 70 Tracy McGrady	.60	1.50
❑ 71 Steve Smith	.25	.60
❑ 72 Michael Jordan	2.00	5.00
❑ 73 Mike Miller	.25	.60
❑ 74 DeShawn Stevenson	.20	.50
❑ 75 Raef LaFrentz	.20	.50
❑ 76 Al Harrington	.25	.60
❑ 77 Vlade Divac	.25	.60
❑ 78 Eddie Jones	.25	.60
❑ 79 Wesley Person	.20	.50
❑ 80 Kenny Anderson	.25	.60
❑ 81 Elton Brand	.30	.75
❑ 82 Jalen Rose	.25	.60
❑ 83 Joe Johnson	.30	.75
❑ 84 Shaquille O'Neal	.75	2.00
❑ 85 Paul Pierce	.30	.75
❑ 86 Grant Hill	.30	.75
❑ 87 Steve Francis	.30	.75
❑ 88 Keon Clark	.20	.50
❑ 89 Baron Davis	.30	.75
❑ 90 Tim Thomas	.20	.50
❑ 91 Shareef Abdur-Rahim	.25	.60
❑ 92 Kenyon Martin	.30	.75
❑ 93 Juwan Howard	.25	.60
❑ 94 Peja Stojakovic	.25	.60
❑ 95 Lamar Odom	.30	.75
❑ 96 Toni Kukoc	.25	.60
❑ 97 Darrell Armstrong	.20	.50
❑ 98 Reggie Miller	.30	.75
❑ 99 Andrei Kirilenko	.30	.75
❑ 100 Keith Van Horn	.25	.60
❑ 101 Yao Ming RC	6.00	15.00
❑ 102 Jay Williams RC	2.50	6.00
❑ 103 Mike Dunleavy RC	2.50	6.00
❑ 104 Drew Gooden RC	3.00	8.00
❑ 105 Nikoloz Tskitishvili RC	2.00	5.00
❑ 106 Caron Butler RC	4.00	10.00
❑ 107 Chris Wilcox RC	2.50	6.00
❑ 108 DaJuan Wagner RC	2.00	5.00
❑ 109 Nene Hilario RC	2.50	6.00
❑ 110 Qyntel Woods RC	2.00	5.00
❑ 111 Jared Jeffries RC	2.00	5.00
❑ 112 Tamar Slay RC	2.00	5.00
❑ 113 Marcus Haislip RC	2.00	5.00
❑ 114 Kareem Rush RC	2.50	6.00
❑ 115 Bostjan Nachbar RC	2.00	5.00
❑ 116 Melvin Ely RC	2.00	5.00
❑ 117 Jiri Welsch RC	2.00	5.00
❑ 118 Amare Stoudemire RC	5.00	12.00
❑ 119 Frank Williams RC	2.00	5.00
❑ 120 Rasual Butler RC	2.00	5.00
❑ 121 Dan Dickau RC	2.00	5.00
❑ 122 Carlos Boozer RC	4.00	10.00
❑ 123 Roger Mason RC	2.00	5.00
❑ 124 Corsley Edwards RC	2.00	5.00
❑ 125 Robert Archibald RC	2.00	5.00
❑ 126 John Salmons RC	3.00	8.00
❑ 127 Rod Grizzard RC	2.00	5.00
❑ 128 Dan Gadzuric RC	2.00	5.00
❑ 129 Sam Clancy RC	2.00	5.00
❑ 130 Fred Jones RC	2.50	6.00
❑ 131 Casey Jacobsen RC	2.00	5.00
❑ 132 Ryan Humphrey RC	2.00	5.00
❑ 133 Vincent Yarbrough RC	2.00	5.00
❑ 134 Juan Dixon RC	3.00	8.00
❑ 135 Tayshaun Prince RC	3.00	8.00

2003-04 Fleer Authentix

❑ COMP.SET w/o SP's (1-100)	15.00	40.00
❑ COMMON CARD (1-100)	.20	.50
❑ COMMON ROOKIE (101-130)	1.50	4.00
❑ 1 Vince Carter	.60	1.50
❑ 2 David Wesley	.20	.50
❑ 3 Eddie Griffin	.20	.50
❑ 4 Andrei Kirilenko	.30	.75
❑ 5 Kerry Kittles	.25	.60
❑ 6 Tayshaun Prince	.25	.60
❑ 7 Tim Duncan	.60	1.50
❑ 8 Troy Hudson	.20	.50
❑ 9 Ben Wallace	.25	.60
❑ 10 Manu Ginobili	.30	.75
❑ 11 Gary Payton	.30	.75
❑ 12 Dajuan Wagner	.20	.50
❑ 13 Stephon Marbury	.30	.75
❑ 14 Shane Battier	.25	.60
❑ 15 Zydrunas Ilgauskas	.25	.60
❑ 16 Eric Snow	.20	.50
❑ 17 Andre Miller	.25	.60
❑ 18 Shareef Abdur-Rahim	.25	.60
❑ 19 Kurt Thomas	.20	.50
❑ 20 Vincent Yarbrough	.20	.50
❑ 21 Mike Bibby	.25	.60
❑ 22 Desmond Mason	.25	.60
❑ 23 Steve Nash	.50	1.25
❑ 24 Rasheed Wallace	.30	.75
❑ 25 Kobe Bryant	1.50	4.00
❑ 26 Cuttino Mobley	.25	.60
❑ 27 Matt Harpring	.25	.60
❑ 28 Jamal Mashburn	.20	.50
❑ 29 Mike Dunleavy	.25	.60
❑ 30 Antonio Davis	.20	.50
❑ 31 Michael Redd	.30	.75
❑ 32 Richard Hamilton	.25	.60
❑ 33 Predrag Drobnjak	.20	.50
❑ 34 Kevin Garnett	.60	1.50
❑ 35 Nene	.25	.60
❑ 36 Bobby Jackson	.20	.50
❑ 37 Jason Williams	.25	.60
❑ 38 Ricky Davis	.25	.60
❑ 39 Shawn Marion	.30	.75
❑ 40 Kareem Rush	.20	.50
❑ 41 Eddy Curry	.25	.60
❑ 42 Gordan Giricek	.20	.50
❑ 43 Brad Miller	.25	.60
❑ 44 Kwame Brown	.20	.50
❑ 45 Sam Cassell	.25	.60
❑ 46 Juwan Howard	.25	.60

❑ 47 Peja Stojakovic .25 .60
❑ 48 Brian Grant .20 .50
❑ 49 Al Harrington .25 .60
❑ 50 Allen Iverson .60 1.50
❑ 51 Caron Butler .25 .60
❑ 52 Dirk Nowitzki .50 1.25
❑ 53 Zach Randolph .30 .75
❑ 54 Pau Gasol .30 .75
❑ 55 Tony Delk .20 .50
❑ 56 Grant Hill .30 .75
❑ 57 Shaquille O'Neal .75 2.00
❑ 58 Tyson Chandler .25 .60
❑ 59 Tracy McGrady .60 1.50
❑ 60 Ron Artest .25 .60
❑ 61 Jerry Stackhouse .25 .60
❑ 62 Jamaal Magloire .20 .50
❑ 63 Jason Richardson .30 .75
❑ 64 Morris Peterson .25 .60
❑ 65 Richard Jefferson .30 .75
❑ 66 Kenny Thomas .20 .50
❑ 67 Tony Parker .30 .75
❑ 68 Eddie Jones .25 .60
❑ 69 Paul Pierce .30 .75
❑ 70 Drew Gooden .20 .50
❑ 71 Jermaine O'Neal .30 .75
❑ 72 Juan Dixon .20 .50
❑ 73 Baron Davis .30 .75
❑ 74 Antawn Jamison .30 .75
❑ 75 Rashard Lewis .30 .75
❑ 76 Nick Van Exel .25 .60
❑ 77 Bonzi Wells .20 .50
❑ 78 Speedy Claxton .20 .50
❑ 79 Carlos Boozer .30 .75
❑ 80 Amare Stoudemire .60 1.50
❑ 81 Elton Brand .30 .75
❑ 82 Jalen Rose .25 .60
❑ 83 Keith Van Horn .25 .60
❑ 84 Corey Maggette .20 .50
❑ 85 Antoine Walker .30 .75
❑ 86 Latrell Sprewell .25 .60
❑ 87 Yao Ming .60 1.50
❑ 88 Glenn Robinson .25 .60
❑ 89 Jason Kidd .50 1.25
❑ 90 Gilbert Arenas .30 .75
❑ 91 Ray Allen .20 .50
❑ 92 Wally Szczerbiak .25 .60
❑ 93 Michael Finley .30 .75
❑ 94 Chris Webber .30 .75
❑ 95 Reggie Miller .30 .75
❑ 96 Jason Terry .25 .60
❑ 97 Allan Houston .25 .60
❑ 98 Steve Francis .30 .75
❑ 99 Karl Malone .30 .75
❑ 100 Kenyon Martin .30 .75
❑ 101 Carmelo Anthony RC 4.00 10.00
❑ 102 Troy Bell RC 1.50 4.00
❑ 103 T.J. Ford RC 2.00 5.00
❑ 104 LeBron James RC 30.00 60.00
❑ 105 Travis Outlaw RC 2.00 5.00
❑ 106 Mike Sweetney RC 1.50 4.00
❑ 107 Aleksandar Pavlovic RC 2.00 5.00
❑ 108 Dahntay Jones RC 1.50 4.00
❑ 109 Chris Bosh RC 2.50 6.00
❑ 110 Boris Diaw RC 2.00 5.00
❑ 111 Jarvis Hayes RC 1.50 4.00
❑ 112 Brian Cook RC 1.50 4.00
❑ 113 Luke Ridnour RC 2.00 5.00
❑ 114 David West RC 2.00 5.00
❑ 115 Zoran Planinic RC 1.50 4.00
❑ 116 Zarko Cabarkapa RC 1.50 4.00
❑ 117 Marcus Banks RC 1.50 4.00
❑ 118 Kirk Hinrich RC 2.00 5.00
❑ 119 Darko Milicic RC 2.00 5.00
❑ 120 Sofoklis Schortsanitis RC 1.50 4.00
❑ 121 Ndudi Ebi RC 1.50 4.00
❑ 122 Kendrick Perkins RC 2.50 6.00
❑ 123 Leandro Barbosa RC 2.00 5.00
❑ 124 Nick Collison RC 1.50 4.00
❑ 125 Reece Gaines RC 1.50 4.00
❑ 126 Chris Kaman RC 2.00 5.00
❑ 127 Mickael Pietrus RC 2.00 5.00
❑ 128 Dwyane Wade RC 4.00 10.00
❑ 129 Josh Howard RC 2.00 5.00
❑ 130 Carlos Delfino RC 2.00 5.00

2004-05 Fleer Authentix

❑ COMPLETE SET (137)
❑ COMP.SET w/o SP's (100) 15.00 40.00
❑ COMMON CARD (1-100) .20 .50
❑ COMMON ROOKIE (101-129) 1.50 4.00
❑ 101-129 RC PRINT RUN 750 SER.#'d SETS
❑ COMMON ROOKIE (130-140)
❑ 130-140 RC PRINT RUN 200 SER.#'d SETS
❑ 1 Allen Iverson .60 1.50
❑ 2 Allan Houston .25 .60
❑ 3 Jermaine O'Neal .30 .75
❑ 4 Andrei Kirilenko .30 .75
❑ 5 Baron Davis .30 .75
❑ 6 Rasheed Wallace .30 .75
❑ 7 Manu Ginobili .30 .75
❑ 8 Kenyon Martin .30 .75
❑ 9 Richard Hamilton .25 .60
❑ 10 Tony Parker .30 .75
❑ 11 Keith Van Horn .25 .60
❑ 12 Steve Nash .50 1.25
❑ 13 Darius Miles .25 .60
❑ 14 Jason Williams .25 .60
❑ 15 Carlos Boozer .30 .75
❑ 16 Amare Stoudemire .60 1.50
❑ 17 Kobe Bryant 1.50 4.00
❑ 18 Jason Terry .25 .60
❑ 19 Stephon Marbury .30 .75
❑ 20 Ben Wallace .25 .60
❑ 21 Tim Duncan .60 1.50
❑ 22 Michael Redd .30 .75
❑ 23 Antoine Walker .30 .75
❑ 24 Shareef Abdur-Rahim .25 .60
❑ 25 Luke Walton .25 .60
❑ 26 Reggie Miller .30 .75
❑ 27 Antawn Jamison .30 .75
❑ 28 Anfernee Hardaway .30 .75
❑ 29 Yao Ming .75 2.00
❑ 30 Chris Bosh .30 .75
❑ 31 Latrell Sprewell .25 .60
❑ 32 Mike Dunleavy .25 .60
❑ 33 Luke Ridnour .20 .50
❑ 34 Kevin Garnett .60 1.50
❑ 35 Darko Milicic .20 .50
❑ 36 Bobby Jackson .20 .50
❑ 37 Caron Butler .25 .60
❑ 38 Dirk Nowitzki .50 1.25
❑ 39 Joe Johnson .30 .75
❑ 40 Pau Gasol .30 .75
❑ 41 Kirk Hinrich .25 .60
❑ 42 Willie Green .20 .50
❑ 43 Jamaal Tinsley .25 .60
❑ 44 Jarvis Hayes .20 .50
❑ 45 Sam Cassell .25 .60
❑ 46 Nene .25 .60
❑ 47 Mike Bibby .25 .60
❑ 48 Lamar Odom .30 .75
❑ 49 LeBron James 2.00 5.00
❑ 50 Marquis Daniels .20 .50
❑ 51 T.J. Ford .25 .60
❑ 52 Michael Finley .30 .75
❑ 53 Zach Randolph .30 .75
❑ 54 Bonzi Wells .20 .50
❑ 56 Stephen Jackson .25 .60
❑ 57 Gary Payton .30 .75
❑ 58 Jason Kapono .20 .50
❑ 59 Glenn Robinson .25 .60
❑ 60 Elton Brand .30 .75
❑ 61 Jerry Stackhouse .25 .60
❑ 62 Jamaal Magloire .20 .50
❑ 63 Tracy McGrady .60 1.50
❑ 64 Jalen Rose .25 .60
❑ 65 Kerry Kittles .25 .60
❑ 66 Nick Van Exel .25 .60
❑ 67 Rashard Lewis .30 .75
❑ 68 Desmond Mason .25 .60
❑ 69 Gerald Wallace .30 .75
❑ 70 Drew Gooden .20 .50
❑ 71 Corey Maggette .25 .60
❑ 72 Gilbert Arenas .30 .75
❑ 73 Tim Thomas .20 .50
❑ 74 Jason Richardson .30 .75
❑ 75 Ray Allen .30 .75
❑ 76 Carmelo Anthony 1.00 2.50
❑ 77 Peja Stojakovic .25 .60
❑ 78 Dwyane Wade 1.00 2.50
❑ 79 Dajuan Wagner .20 .50
❑ 80 Shawn Marion .30 .75
❑ 81 Shaquille O'Neal .75 2.00
❑ 82 Eddy Curry .25 .60
❑ 83 Samuel Dalembert .20 .50
❑ 84 Karl Malone .30 .75
❑ 85 Ricky Davis .25 .60
❑ 86 Steve Francis .30 .75
❑ 87 Juwan Howard .25 .60
❑ 88 Carlos Arroyo .30 .75
❑ 89 Jamal Mashburn .25 .60
❑ 90 Mickael Pietrus .25 .60
❑ 91 Vince Carter .60 1.50
❑ 92 Jason Kidd .50 1.25
❑ 93 Andre Miller .25 .60
❑ 94 Chris Webber .30 .75
❑ 95 Chris Kaman .25 .60
❑ 96 Paul Pierce .30 .75
❑ 97 Cuttino Mobley .25 .60
❑ 98 Ron Artest .25 .60
❑ 99 Matt Harpring .25 .60
❑ 100 Richard Jefferson .30 .75
❑ 102 Albert Miralles RC 1.50 4.00
❑ 103 Chris Duhon RC 2.50 6.00
❑ 104 Ha Seung-Jin RC 1.50 4.00
❑ 105 Antonio Burks RC 1.50 4.00
❑ 106 Andre Emmett RC 1.50 4.00
❑ 107 Donta Smith RC 1.50 4.00
❑ 108 Lionel Chalmers RC 1.50 4.00
❑ 109 Rickey Paulding RC 1.50 4.00
❑ 110 Jackson Vroman RC 1.50 4.00
❑ 111 Anderson Varejao RC 2.00 5.00
❑ 112 Beno Udrih RC 2.00 5.00
❑ 113 Sasha Vujacic RC 1.50 4.00
❑ 114 Kevin Martin RC 2.00 5.00
❑ 115 Tony Allen RC 2.00 5.00
❑ 116 Delonte West RC 2.50 6.00
❑ 117 Sergei Monia RC 1.50 4.00
❑ 118 Romain Sato RC 1.50 4.00
❑ 119 Jameer Nelson RC 2.00 5.00
❑ 120 Josh Smith RC 4.00 10.00
❑ 121 Kirk Snyder RC 1.50 4.00
❑ 122 Robert Swift RC 1.50 4.00
❑ 123 Andre Iguodala RC 4.00 10.00
❑ 124 Rafael Araujo RC 1.50 4.00
❑ 125 Luol Deng RC 2.00 5.00
❑ 126 Josh Childress RC 1.50 4.00
❑ 127 Ben Gordon RC 2.00 5.00
❑ 128 Emeka Okafor RC 3.00 8.00
❑ 129 Dwight Howard RC 5.00 12.00
❑ 130 Harrison RC/Bird AU EXCH 30.00 75.00
❑ 131 Livingston RC/E.Baylor AU 10.00 25.00
❑ 132 D.Harris RC/D.Nelson AU 15.00 30.00
❑ 133 L.Jackson RC/P.Silas AU 6.00 15.00
❑ 134 A.Biedrins RC/C.Mullin AU 20.00 40.00
❑ 135 S.Telfair RC/M.Cheeks AU 5.00 12.00
❑ 136 K.Humphries RC/J.Sloan AU 20.00 40.00
❑ 137 A.Jefferson RC/D.Ainge AU 10.00 25.00
❑ 138 J.R.Smith RC/B.Scott AU 20.00 40.00
❑ 139 D.Wright RC/P.Riley AU 10.00 25.00
❑ 140 T.Ariza RC/I.Thomas AU 15.00 30.00

2000-01 Fleer Authority

❑ COMPLETE SET (141) 80.00 160.00
❑ COMP.SET w/o SP's (110) 10.00 25.00
❑ COMMON CARD (1-110) .05 .15
❑ COMMON ROOKIE (111-141) 1.50 4.00
❑ 1 Dikembe Mutombo .25 .60
❑ 2 Cuttino Mobley .25 .60
❑ 3 Brian Grant .20 .50
❑ 4 Grant Hill .30 .75

❑ 5 Jim Jackson	.20	.50
❑ 6 Derek Anderson	.25	.60
❑ 7 Jerry Stackhouse	.25	.60
❑ 8 Eddie Jones	.25	.60
❑ 9 Tracy McGrady	.60	1.50
❑ 10 Vin Baker	.25	.60
❑ 11 Jason Terry	.30	.75
❑ 12 Jerome Williams	.20	.50
❑ 13 Tim Hardaway	.25	.60
❑ 14 Darrell Armstrong	.20	.50
❑ 15 Rashard Lewis	.30	.75
❑ 16 Kenny Anderson	.25	.60
❑ 17 Larry Hughes	.25	.60
❑ 18 Anthony Mason	.20	.50
❑ 19 Allen Iverson	.60	1.50
❑ 20 Gary Payton	.30	.75
❑ 21 Antoine Walker	.25	.60
❑ 22 Antawn Jamison	.30	.75
❑ 23 Glenn Robinson	.25	.60
❑ 24 Toni Kukoc	.25	.60
❑ 25 Ruben Patterson	.20	.50
❑ 26 Paul Pierce	.30	.75
❑ 27 Mookie Blaylock	.25	.60
❑ 28 Ray Allen	.30	.75
❑ 29 Theo Ratliff	.20	.50
❑ 30 Vince Carter	.60	1.50
❑ 31 Jamal Mashburn	.25	.60
❑ 32 Steve Francis	.30	.75
❑ 33 Sam Cassell	.25	.60
❑ 34 Jason Kidd	.50	1.25
❑ 35 Mark Jackson	.25	.60
❑ 36 Baron Davis	.30	.75
❑ 37 Hakeem Olajuwon	.40	1.00
❑ 38 Darvin Ham	.20	.50
❑ 39 Anfernee Hardaway	.30	.75
❑ 40 Antonio Davis	.20	.50
❑ 41 Derrick Coleman	.25	.60
❑ 42 Maurice Taylor	.20	.50
❑ 43 Kevin Garnett	.60	1.50
❑ 44 Tom Gugliotta	.20	.50
❑ 45 Karl Malone	.40	1.00
❑ 46 Elton Brand	.30	.75
❑ 47 Jonathan Bender	.20	.50
❑ 48 Terrell Brandon	.20	.50
❑ 49 Clifford Robinson	.20	.50
❑ 50 John Stockton	.40	1.00
❑ 51 Ron Artest	.30	.75
❑ 52 Reggie Miller	.30	.75
❑ 53 Joe Smith	.20	.50
❑ 54 Shawn Kemp	.30	.75
❑ 55 Bryon Russell	.20	.50
❑ 56 Andre Miller	.25	.60
❑ 57 Austin Croshere	.20	.50
❑ 58 Wally Szczerbiak	.25	.60
❑ 59 Scottie Pippen	.50	1.25
❑ 60 Donyell Marshall	.20	.50
❑ 61 Brevin Knight	.20	.50
❑ 62 Travis Best	.20	.50
❑ 63 Chauncey Billups	.30	.75
❑ 64 Rasheed Wallace	.30	.75
❑ 65 Shareef Abdur-Rahim	.25	.60
❑ 66 Trajan Langdon	.20	.50
❑ 67 Jalen Rose	.25	.60
❑ 68 Stephon Marbury	.30	.75
❑ 69 Steve Smith	.25	.60
❑ 70 Mike Bibby	.25	.60
❑ 71 Lamond Murray	.20	.50
❑ 72 Lamar Odom	.30	.75
❑ 73 Keith Van Horn	.25	.60
❑ 74 Chris Webber	.30	.75
❑ 75 Michael Dickerson	.20	.50
❑ 76 Dirk Nowitzki	.50	1.25
❑ 77 Corey Maggette	.25	.60
❑ 78 Kerry Kittles	.25	.60
❑ 79 Jason Williams	.25	.60
❑ 80 Mitch Richmond	.25	.60
❑ 81 Michael Finley	.30	.75
❑ 82 Shaquille O'Neal	.75	2.00
❑ 83 Allan Houston	.25	.60
❑ 84 Peja Stojakovic	.25	.60
❑ 85 Juwan Howard	.25	.60
❑ 86 Nick Van Exel	.25	.60
❑ 87 Kobe Bryant	1.50	4.00
❑ 88 Latrell Sprewell	.25	.60
❑ 89 Tim Duncan	.60	1.50
❑ 90 Richard Hamilton	.25	.60
❑ 91 Antonio McDyess	.25	.60
❑ 92 Glen Rice	.25	.60
❑ 93 Larry Johnson	.25	.60
❑ 94 David Robinson	.40	1.00
❑ 95 Rod Strickland	.25	.60
❑ 96 Raef LaFrentz	.20	.50
❑ 97 Ron Harper	.25	.60
❑ 98 Patrick Ewing	.40	1.00
❑ 99 Sean Elliot	.25	.60
❑ 100 Tariq Abdul-Wahad	.20	.50
❑ 101 Chucky Atkins	.20	.50
❑ 102 Marcus Camby	.25	.60
❑ 103 Corliss Williamson	.25	.60
❑ 104 Rodney Rogers	.20	.50
❑ 105 Othella Harrington	.20	.50
❑ 106 Alan Henderson	.20	.50
❑ 107 David Wesley	.20	.50
❑ 108 Michael Doleac	.20	.50
❑ 109 Doug Christie	.20	.50
❑ 110 Vitaly Potapenko	.20	.50
❑ 111 DerMarr Johnson RC	1.50	4.00
❑ 112 Jamal Crawford RC	2.50	6.00
❑ 113 Morris Peterson RC	2.50	6.00
❑ 114 Erick Barkley RC	1.50	4.00
❑ 115 Kenyon Martin RC	4.00	10.00
❑ 116 Joel Przybilla RC	1.50	4.00
❑ 117 Speedy Claxton RC	1.50	4.00
❑ 118 Hedo Turkoglu RC	4.00	10.00
❑ 119 Etan Thomas RC	1.50	4.00
❑ 120 Eddie House RC	1.50	4.00
❑ 121 Marcus Fizer RC	1.50	4.00
❑ 122 Quentin Richardson RC	2.00	5.00
❑ 123 Donnell Harvey RC	1.50	4.00
❑ 124 DeShawn Stevenson RC	1.50	4.00
❑ 125 Chris Mihm RC	1.50	4.00
❑ 126 Courtney Alexander RC	1.50	4.00
❑ 127 Keyon Dooling RC	1.50	4.00
❑ 128 Jerome Moiso RC	1.50	4.00
❑ 129 Stephen Jackson RC	2.50	6.00
❑ 130 Chris Porter RC	1.50	4.00
❑ 131 Stromile Swift RC	2.00	5.00
❑ 132 Desmond Mason RC	2.00	5.00
❑ 133 Jason Collier RC	1.50	4.00
❑ 134 Mark Madsen RC	1.50	4.00
❑ 135 Mamadou N'Diaye RC	1.50	4.00
❑ 136 Darius Miles RC	2.00	5.00
❑ 137 Mateen Cleaves RC	1.50	4.00
❑ 138 Jamaal Magloire RC	1.50	4.00
❑ 139 Khalid El-Amin RC	1.50	4.00
❑ 140 Mike Miller RC	2.50	6.00
❑ 141 Marc Jackson RC	2.00	5.00
❑ NNO Fleer/BGS Redemption	3.00	8.00

2003-04 Fleer Avant

❑ COMP.SET w/o SP's	15.00	40.00
❑ COMMON USA (57-64)	1.00	2.50
❑ COMMON ROOKIE (65-90)	2.00	5.00
❑ 1 Ben Wallace	.50	1.25
❑ 2 Glenn Robinson	.50	1.25
❑ 3 Pau Gasol	.60	1.50
❑ 4 Keon Clark	.40	1.00
❑ 5 Kobe Bryant	3.00	8.00
❑ 6 Morris Peterson	.50	1.25
❑ 7 Steve Francis	.60	1.50
❑ 8 Amare Stoudemire	1.25	3.00
❑ 9 Mike Dunleavy Jr.	.50	1.25
❑ 10 Kevin Garnett	1.25	3.00
❑ 11 Yao Ming	1.25	3.00
❑ 12 Stephon Marbury	.60	1.50
❑ 13 Jason Richardson	.60	1.50
❑ 14 Rasheed Wallace	.60	1.50
❑ 15 Tayshaun Prince	.50	1.25
❑ 16 Steve Nash	1.00	2.50
❑ 17 Jamal Mashburn	.40	1.00
❑ 18 Reggie Miller	.60	1.50
❑ 19 Chris Webber	.60	1.50
❑ 20 Andre Miller	.50	1.25
❑ 21 Peja Stojakovic	.50	1.25
❑ 22 Nene	.50	1.25
❑ 23 Manu Ginobili	.60	1.50
❑ 24 Bonzi Wells	.40	1.00
❑ 25 Lamar Odom	.60	1.50
❑ 26 Kwame Brown	.40	1.00
❑ 27 Caron Butler	.50	1.25
❑ 28 Gilbert Arenas	.60	1.50
❑ 29 Dirk Nowitzki	1.00	2.50
❑ 30 Allan Houston	.50	1.25
❑ 31 Michael Finley	.60	1.50
❑ 32 Drew Gooden	.40	1.00
❑ 33 Shareef Abdur-Rahim	.50	1.25
❑ 34 Michael Redd	.60	1.50
❑ 35 Jerry Stackhouse	.50	1.25
❑ 36 Scottie Pippen	1.00	2.50
❑ 37 Latrell Sprewell	.50	1.25
❑ 38 Ron Artest	.50	1.25
❑ 39 Derrick Coleman	.50	1.25
❑ 40 Eddy Curry	.50	1.25
❑ 41 Wally Szczerbiak	.50	1.25
❑ 42 Dajuan Wagner	.40	1.00
❑ 43 Baron Davis	.60	1.50
❑ 44 Karl Malone	.60	1.50
❑ 45 Andrei Kirilenko	.60	1.50
❑ 46 Paul Pierce	.60	1.50
❑ 47 Desmond Mason	.50	1.25
❑ 48 Shaquille O'Neal	1.50	4.00
❑ 49 Rashard Lewis	.60	1.50
❑ 50 Ricky Davis	.50	1.25
❑ 51 Kerry Kittles	.50	1.25
❑ 52 Quentin Richardson	.50	1.25
❑ 53 Tony Parker	.60	1.50
❑ 54 Elton Brand	.60	1.50
❑ 55 Richard Jefferson	.60	1.50
❑ 56 Kenyon Martin	.60	1.50
❑ 57 Ray Allen	1.00	2.50
❑ 58 Mike Bibby	1.25	3.00
❑ 59 Tim Duncan	3.00	8.00
❑ 60 Allen Iverson	3.00	8.00
❑ 61 Jason Kidd	2.50	6.00
❑ 62 Tracy McGrady	3.00	8.00
❑ 63 Jermaine O'Neal	1.50	4.00
❑ 64 Larry Brown	3.00	8.00
❑ 65 LeBron James RC	50.00	100.00
❑ 66 Darko Milicic RC	2.50	6.00
❑ 67 Carmelo Anthony RC	5.00	12.00
❑ 68 Chris Bosh RC	3.00	8.00
❑ 69 Dwyane Wade RC	5.00	12.00
❑ 70 Chris Kaman RC	2.50	6.00
❑ 71 Kirk Hinrich RC	2.50	6.00
❑ 72 T.J. Ford RC	2.50	6.00
❑ 73 Mike Sweetney RC	2.00	5.00
❑ 74 Jarvis Hayes RC	2.00	5.00
❑ 75 Mickael Pietrus RC	2.50	6.00
❑ 76 Travis Hansen RC	2.00	5.00
❑ 77 Marcus Banks RC	2.00	5.00
❑ 78 Luke Ridnour RC	2.50	6.00
❑ 79 Reece Gaines RC	2.00	5.00
❑ 80 Troy Bell RC	2.00	5.00
❑ 81 Zarko Cabarkapa RC	2.00	5.00
❑ 82 David West RC	2.50	6.00
❑ 83 Aleksandar Pavlovic RC	2.50	6.00
❑ 84 Dahntay Jones RC	2.00	5.00
❑ 85 Boris Diaw RC	2.50	6.00
❑ 86 Zoran Planinic RC	2.00	5.00
❑ 87 Travis Outlaw RC	2.50	6.00
❑ 88 Brian Cook RC	2.00	5.00
❑ 89 Maciej Lampe RC	2.00	5.00
❑ 90 Nick Collison RC	2.00	5.00

2002-03 Fleer Box Score

❑ COMP.SET w/o SP's (135)	12.50	30.00
❑ COMMON CARD (1-135)	.25	.60
❑ COMMON RC (136-150)	1.00	2.50
❑ RS SEALED SET (151-180)	10.00	25.00
❑ COMMON RS (151-180)	1.00	2.50
❑ AS SEALED SET (181-210)	8.00	20.00

❑ AW SEALED SET (211-240)	8.00	20.00
❑ 1 Kwame Brown	.25	.60
❑ 2 Eddy Curry	.30	.75
❑ 3 Allen Iverson	.75	2.00
❑ 4 Elton Brand	.40	1.00
❑ 5 Jason Kidd	.60	1.50
❑ 6 Kedrick Brown	.25	.60
❑ 7 Elden Campbell	.25	.60
❑ 8 Jason Richardson	.40	1.00
❑ 9 Shawn Marion	.40	1.00
❑ 10 John Stockton	.50	1.25
❑ 11 Theo Ratliff	.25	.60
❑ 12 Marcus Fizer	.25	.60
❑ 13 Tony Parker	.40	1.00
❑ 14 Michael Redd	.40	1.00
❑ 15 Vince Carter	.75	2.00
❑ 16 Aaron McKie	.25	.60
❑ 17 Michael Finley	.40	1.00
❑ 18 Rashard Lewis	.40	1.00
❑ 19 Steve Nash	.60	1.50
❑ 20 Reggie Miller	.40	1.00
❑ 21 Tim Duncan	.75	2.00
❑ 22 Marcus Camby	.30	.75
❑ 23 Michael Jordan	2.50	6.00
❑ 24 Donnell Harvey	.25	.60
❑ 25 Michael Dickerson	.25	.60
❑ 26 James Posey	.25	.60
❑ 27 Vin Baker	.30	.75
❑ 28 Antonio McDyess	.30	.75
❑ 29 Mike Miller	.30	.75
❑ 30 Karl Malone	.40	1.00
❑ 31 Corliss Williamson	.30	.75
❑ 32 Derek Anderson	.30	.75
❑ 33 Scottie Pippen	.60	1.50
❑ 34 Paul Pierce	.40	1.00
❑ 35 Steve Francis	.40	1.00
❑ 36 Terrell Brandon	.25	.60
❑ 37 Cuttino Mobley	.30	.75
❑ 38 Ron Artest	.30	.75
❑ 39 Jonathan Bender	.25	.60
❑ 40 Ron Mercer	.25	.60
❑ 41 Dirk Nowitzki	.60	1.50
❑ 42 Jermaine O'Neal	.40	1.00
❑ 43 Ray Allen	.40	1.00
❑ 44 Jason Terry	.40	1.00
❑ 45 Pau Gasol	.40	1.00
❑ 46 Lamar Odom	.40	1.00
❑ 47 P.J. Brown	.25	.60
❑ 48 Kurt Thomas	.25	.60
❑ 49 Grant Hill	.40	1.00
❑ 50 David Robinson	.50	1.25
❑ 51 Rasheed Wallace	.40	1.00
❑ 52 Antawn Jamison	.40	1.00
❑ 53 Juwan Howard	.30	.75
❑ 54 Andre Miller	.30	.75
❑ 55 Kenyon Martin	.40	1.00
❑ 56 Jason Williams	.30	.75
❑ 57 Travis Best	.25	.60
❑ 58 Brian Grant	.25	.60
❑ 59 Keith Van Horn	.30	.75
❑ 60 Alonzo Mourning	.40	1.00
❑ 61 Rod Strickland	.30	.75
❑ 62 Jamaal Tinsley	.30	.75
❑ 63 Sam Cassell	.30	.75
❑ 64 Jalen Rose	.30	.75
❑ 65 Tim Thomas	.25	.60
❑ 66 Eddie Griffin	.25	.60
❑ 67 Kevin Garnett	.75	2.00
❑ 68 Darrell Armstrong	.25	.60
❑ 69 Joe Smith	.25	.60
❑ 70 Wally Szczerbiak	.30	.75
❑ 71 Richard Jefferson	.40	1.00
❑ 72 Chauncey Billups	.40	1.00
❑ 73 Kerry Kittles	.30	.75
❑ 74 Stromile Swift	.25	.60
❑ 75 Dikembe Mutombo	.30	.75
❑ 76 Courtney Alexander	.25	.60
❑ 77 Tony Delk	.25	.60
❑ 78 Baron Davis	.40	1.00
❑ 79 Ricky Davis	.30	.75
❑ 80 Vlade Divac	.30	.75
❑ 81 Allan Houston	.30	.75
❑ 82 Richard Hamilton	.30	.75
❑ 83 Moochie Norris	.25	.60
❑ 84 Quentin Richardson	.30	.75
❑ 85 Charlie Ward	.25	.60
❑ 86 Troy Hudson	.25	.60
❑ 87 Pat Garrity	.25	.60
❑ 88 Kobe Bryant	2.00	5.00
❑ 89 Tracy McGrady	.75	2.00
❑ 90 Clifford Robinson	.25	.60
❑ 91 Glenn Robinson	.30	.75
❑ 92 Todd MacCulloch	.25	.60
❑ 93 Lamond Murray	.25	.60
❑ 94 Eric Snow	.25	.60
❑ 95 Eddie Jones	.30	.75
❑ 96 Tom Gugliotta	.25	.60
❑ 97 Anfernee Hardaway	.40	1.00
❑ 98 Stephon Marbury	.40	1.00
❑ 99 Antoine Walker	.30	.75
❑ 100 Gilbert Arenas	.40	1.00
❑ 101 Ruben Patterson	.25	.60
❑ 102 Shane Battier	.30	.75
❑ 103 David Wesley	.25	.60
❑ 104 Damon Stoudamire	.30	.75
❑ 105 Shaquille O'Neal	1.00	2.50
❑ 106 Bonzi Wells	.30	.75
❑ 107 Mike Bibby	.30	.75
❑ 108 Jamal Mashburn	.30	.75
❑ 109 Peja Stojakovic	.30	.75
❑ 110 Latrell Sprewell	.30	.75
❑ 111 Chris Webber	.40	1.00
❑ 112 Alvin Williams	.25	.60
❑ 113 Trenton Hassell	.25	.60
❑ 114 Derek Fisher	.30	.75
❑ 115 Malik Rose	.25	.60
❑ 116 Kenny Anderson	.30	.75
❑ 117 Zydrunas Ilgauskas	.30	.75
❑ 118 Raef LaFrentz	.25	.60
❑ 119 Gary Payton	.40	1.00
❑ 120 Vladimir Radmanovic	.25	.60
❑ 121 Darius Miles	.25	.60
❑ 122 Antonio Davis	.25	.60
❑ 123 Larry Hughes	.30	.75
❑ 124 Maurice Taylor	.25	.60
❑ 125 Morris Peterson	.30	.75
❑ 126 Nick Van Exel	.30	.75
❑ 127 Ira Newble	.25	.60
❑ 128 Eric Williams	.25	.60
❑ 129 Andrei Kirilenko	.40	1.00
❑ 130 Ben Wallace	.30	.75
❑ 131 Tyson Chandler	.30	.75
❑ 132 Desmond Mason	.30	.75
❑ 133 Shareef Abdur-Rahim	.30	.75
❑ 134 Danny Fortson	.25	.60
❑ 135 Jerry Stackhouse	.30	.75
❑ 136 Yao Ming RC	3.00	8.00
❑ 137 Juan Dixon RC	1.50	4.00
❑ 138 Caron Butler RC	2.00	5.00
❑ 139 Drew Gooden RC	1.50	4.00
❑ 140 DaJuan Wagner RC	1.00	2.50
❑ 141 Jared Jeffries RC	1.00	2.50
❑ 142 Pat Burke RC	1.00	2.50
❑ 143 Kareem Rush RC	1.25	3.00
❑ 144 Ryan Humphrey RC	1.00	2.50
❑ 145 Manu Ginobili RC	2.50	6.00
❑ 146 Predrag Savovic RC	1.00	2.50
❑ 147 Marcus Haislip RC	1.00	2.50
❑ 148 John Salmons RC	1.50	4.00
❑ 149 Fred Jones RC	1.25	3.00
❑ 150 Roger Mason RC	1.00	2.50
❑ 151 Jay Williams RS RC	1.25	3.00
❑ 152 Mike Dunleavy RS RC	1.25	3.00
❑ 153 Carlos Boozer RS RC	2.00	5.00
❑ 154 Dan Dickau RS RC	1.00	2.50
❑ 155 Tayshaun Prince RS RC	1.50	4.00
❑ 156 Nene Hilario RS RC	1.25	3.00
❑ 157 Amare Stoudemire RS RC	2.50	6.00
❑ 158 Frank Williams RS RC	1.00	2.50
❑ 159 Chris Wilcox RS RC	1.25	3.00
❑ 160 Robert Archibald RS RC	1.00	2.50
❑ 161 Lonny Baxter RS RC	1.00	2.50
❑ 162 Curtis Borchardt RS RC	1.00	2.50
❑ 163 Sam Clancy RS RC	1.00	2.50
❑ 164 Melvin Ely RS RC	1.00	2.50
❑ 165 Dan Gadzuric RS RC	1.00	2.50
❑ 166 Smush Parker RS RC	1.00	2.50
❑ 167 Chris Jefferies RS RC	1.00	2.50
❑ 168 Nikoloz Tskitishvili RS RC	1.00	2.50
❑ 169 Casey Jacobsen RS RC	1.00	2.50
❑ 170 Ronald Murray RS RC	1.50	4.00
❑ 171 Gordan Giricek RS RC	1.00	2.50
❑ 172 Rasual Butler RS RC	1.00	2.50
❑ 173 Jannero Pargo RS RC	1.00	2.50
❑ 174 Bostjan Nachbar RS RC	1.00	2.50
❑ 175 Jiri Welsch RS RC	1.00	2.50
❑ 176 Qyntel Woods RS RC	1.00	2.50
❑ 177 Vincent Yarbrough RS RC	1.00	2.50
❑ 178 Raul Lopez RS RC	1.00	2.50
❑ 179 Mehmet Okur RS RC	1.25	3.00
❑ 180 Reggie Evans RS RC	1.00	2.50
❑ 181 Karl Malone AS	.40	1.00
❑ 182 Michael Jordan AS	2.50	6.00
❑ 183 Glen Rice AS	.30	.75
❑ 184 John Stockton AS	.50	1.25
❑ 185 David Robinson AS	.50	1.25
❑ 186 Shaquille O'Neal AS	1.00	2.50
❑ 187 Dikembe Mutombo AS	.30	.75
❑ 188 Gary Payton AS	.40	1.00
❑ 189 Alonzo Mourning AS	.40	1.00
❑ 190 Scottie Pippen AS	.60	1.50
❑ 191 Grant Hill AS	.40	1.00
❑ 192 Vin Baker AS	.30	.75
❑ 193 Kevin Garnett AS	.75	2.00
❑ 194 Jason Kidd AS	.60	1.50
❑ 195 Reggie Miller AS	.40	1.00
❑ 196 Ray Allen AS	.40	1.00
❑ 197 Kobe Bryant AS	2.00	5.00
❑ 198 Tim Duncan AS	.75	2.00
❑ 199 Chris Webber AS	.40	1.00
❑ 200 Anfernee Hardaway AS	.40	1.00
❑ 201 Latrell Sprewell AS	.30	.75
❑ 202 Vince Carter AS	.75	2.00
❑ 203 Allen Iverson AS	.75	2.00
❑ 204 Eddie Jones AS	.30	.75
❑ 205 Antoine Walker AS	.30	.75
❑ 206 Michael Finley AS	.40	1.00
❑ 207 Tracy McGrady AS	.75	2.00
❑ 208 Jerry Stackhouse AS	.30	.75
❑ 209 Glenn Robinson AS	.30	.75
❑ 210 Allan Houston AS	.30	.75
❑ 211 Baron Davis AW	.40	1.00
❑ 212 Tony Parker AW	.40	1.00
❑ 213 Rick Fox AW	.30	.75
❑ 214 Steve Nash AW	.60	1.50
❑ 215 Jamaal Magloire AW	.25	.60
❑ 216 Wang Zhizhi AW	.25	.60
❑ 217 Mengke Bateer AW	.25	.60
❑ 218 Dirk Nowitzki AW	.60	1.50
❑ 219 Jake Tsakalidis AW	.25	.60
❑ 220 Adonal Foyle AW	.25	.60
❑ 221 Marko Jaric AW	.40	1.00
❑ 222 Arvydas Sabonis AW	.30	.75
❑ 223 Eduardo Najera AW	.25	.60
❑ 224 Michael Olowokandi AW	.25	.60
❑ 225 Darius Miles AW	.25	.60
❑ 226 Andrei Kirilenko AW	.40	1.00
❑ 227 Mamadou N'Diaye AW	.25	.60
❑ 228 DeSagana Diop AW	.25	.60
❑ 229 Rasho Nesterovic AW	.25	.60
❑ 230 Pau Gasol AW	.40	1.00
❑ 231 Vladimir Radmanovic AW	.25	.60
❑ 232 Hedo Turkoglu AW	.30	.75
❑ 233 Tim Duncan AW	.75	2.00
❑ 234 Peja Stojakovic AW	.30	.75
❑ 235 Toni Kukoc AW	.30	.75
❑ 236 Zeljko Rebraca AW	.25	.60
❑ 237 Vlade Divac AW	.30	.75
❑ 238 Dikembe Mutombo AW	.30	.75
❑ 239 Shareef Abdur-Rahim AW	.30	.75
❑ 240 Jason Richardson AW	.40	1.00

1998-99 Fleer Brilliants

❑ COMPLETE SET (125)	25.00	60.00
❑ COMPLETE SET w/o SP (100)	15.00	30.00
❑ COMMON CARD (1-100)	.08	.25
❑ COMMON ROOKIE (101-125)	.40	1.00
❑ 1 Tim Duncan	.60	1.50
❑ 2 Dikembe Mutombo	.10	.30
❑ 3 Steve Nash	.20	.50
❑ 4 Charles Barkley	.50	1.25
❑ 5 Eddie Jones	.20	.50
❑ 6 Ray Allen	.20	.50
❑ 7 Stephon Marbury	.20	.50

❑ 8 Anfernee Hardaway	.20	.50
❑ 9 Gary Payton	.20	.50
❑ 10 Ron Mercer	.07	.20
❑ 11 Nick Van Exel	.20	.50
❑ 12 Brent Barry	.10	.30
❑ 13 Allan Houston	.10	.30
❑ 14 Avery Johnson	.08	.25
❑ 15 Shareef Abdur-Rahim	.20	.50
❑ 16 Rod Strickland	.08	.25
❑ 17 Vin Baker	.10	.30
❑ 18 Patrick Ewing	.20	.50
❑ 19 Maurice Taylor	.08	.25
❑ 20 Shawn Kemp	.10	.30
❑ 21 Michael Finley	.20	.50
❑ 22 Reggie Miller	.20	.50
❑ 23 Joe Smith	.10	.30
❑ 24 Toni Kukoc	.10	.30
❑ 25 Blue Edwards	.08	.25
❑ 26 Joe Dumars	.20	.50
❑ 27 Tom Gugliotta	.08	.25
❑ 28 Terrell Brandon	.10	.30
❑ 29 Erick Dampier	.10	.30
❑ 30 Antonio McDyess	.10	.30
❑ 31 Donyell Marshall	.10	.30
❑ 32 Jeff Hornacek	.10	.30
❑ 33 David Wesley	.08	.25
❑ 34 Derek Anderson	.15	.40
❑ 35 Ron Harper	.10	.30
❑ 36 John Starks	.10	.30
❑ 37 Kenny Anderson	.10	.30
❑ 38 Anthony Mason	.10	.30
❑ 39 Brevin Knight	.08	.25
❑ 40 Antoine Walker	.20	.50
❑ 41 Mookie Blaylock	.08	.25
❑ 42 LaPhonso Ellis	.08	.25
❑ 43 Tim Hardaway	.10	.30
❑ 44 Jim Jackson	.08	.25
❑ 45 Matt Maloney	.08	.25
❑ 46 Lamond Murray	.08	.25
❑ 47 Voshon Lenard	.08	.25
❑ 48 Isaiah Rider	.08	.25
❑ 49 Tracy Murray	.08	.25
❑ 50 Grant Hill	.20	.50
❑ 51 Vlade Divac	.10	.30
❑ 52 Glenn Robinson	.10	.30
❑ 53 Tony Battie	.08	.25
❑ 54 Bobby Jackson	.10	.30
❑ 55 Jayson Williams	.08	.25
❑ 56 Doug Christie	.10	.30
❑ 57 Glen Rice	.10	.30
❑ 58 Tim Thomas	.10	.30
❑ 59 Lindsey Hunter	.08	.25
❑ 60 Scottie Pippen	.60	1.50
❑ 61 Marcus Camby	.10	.30
❑ 61B K.Van Horn Promo	.20	.50
❑ 62 Clifford Robinson	.08	.25
❑ 63 John Wallace	.08	.25
❑ 64 Larry Johnson	.10	.30
❑ 65 Bryon Russell	.08	.25
❑ 66 Isaac Austin	.08	.25
❑ 67 Sam Cassell	.20	.50
❑ 68 Allen Iverson	.75	2.00
❑ 69 Chauncey Billups	.10	.30
❑ 70 Kobe Bryant	1.50	4.00
❑ 71 Kevin Willis	.08	.25
❑ 72 Jason Kidd	.60	1.50
❑ 73 Chris Webber	.20	.50
❑ 74 Rasheed Wallace	.20	.50
❑ 75 Karl Malone	.20	.50
❑ 76 Shawn Bradley	.08	.25
❑ 77 Kerry Kittles	.08	.25
❑ 78 Mitch Richmond	.10	.30
❑ 79 Antonio Daniels	.08	.25
❑ 80 Kevin Garnett	.75	2.00
❑ 81 Nick Anderson	.08	.25
❑ 82 David Robinson	.20	.50
❑ 83 Jamal Mashburn	.10	.30
❑ 84 Rodney Rogers	.08	.25
❑ 85 Michael Stewart	.08	.25
❑ 86 Rik Smits	.10	.30
❑ 87 Billy Owens	.08	.25
❑ 88 Damon Stoudamire	.10	.30
❑ 89 Theo Ratliff	.10	.30
❑ 90 Keith Van Horn	.20	.50
❑ 91 Hakeem Olajuwon	.20	.50
❑ 92 Alonzo Mourning	.10	.30
❑ 93 Steve Smith	.10	.30
❑ 94 Mark Jackson	.10	.30
❑ 95 Cedric Ceballos	.08	.25
❑ 96 Bryant Reeves	.08	.25
❑ 97 Juwan Howard	.10	.30
❑ 98 Detlef Schrempf	.10	.30
❑ 99 John Stockton	.20	.50
❑ 100 Shaquille O'Neal	1.00	2.50
❑ 101 Michael Olowokandi RC	.50	1.25
❑ 102 Mike Bibby RC	1.00	2.50
❑ 103 Raef LaFrentz RC	.50	1.25
❑ 104 Antawn Jamison RC	1.50	4.00
❑ 105 Vince Carter RC	2.00	5.00
❑ 106 Robert Traylor RC	.40	1.00
❑ 107 Jason Williams RC	1.25	3.00
❑ 108 Larry Hughes RC	1.00	2.50
❑ 109 Dirk Nowitzki RC	4.00	10.00
❑ 110 Paul Pierce RC	3.00	8.00
❑ 111 Bonzi Wells RC	1.25	3.00
❑ 112 Michael Doleac RC	.40	1.00
❑ 113 Keon Clark RC	.50	1.25
❑ 114 Michael Dickerson RC	.60	1.50
❑ 115 Matt Harpring RC	.50	1.25
❑ 116 Bryce Drew RC	.40	1.00
❑ 117 Pat Garrity RC	.40	1.00
❑ 118 Roshown McLeod RC	.40	1.00
❑ 119 Ricky Davis RC	1.00	2.50
❑ 120 Rashard Lewis RC	1.25	3.00
❑ 121 Tyronn Lue RC	.40	1.00
❑ 122 Al Harrington RC	.75	2.00
❑ 123 Corey Benjamin RC	.40	1.00
❑ 124 Felipe Lopez RC	.40	1.00
❑ 125 Korleone Young RC	.40	1.00

2001-02 Fleer Exclusive

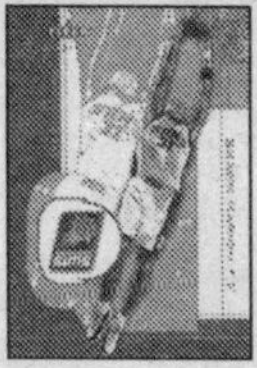

❑ COMPLETE SET (149)	350.00	700.00
❑ COMP.SET w/o SP's (120)	30.00	60.00
❑ COMMON CARD (1-100)	.25	.60
❑ 1 Vince Carter	.75	2.00
❑ 2 Tracy McGrady	.75	2.00
❑ 3 Dikembe Mutombo	.30	.75
❑ 4 Kobe Bryant	2.00	5.00
❑ 5 Baron Davis	.40	1.00
❑ 6 Alonzo Mourning	.40	1.00
❑ 7 Allan Houston	.30	.75
❑ 8 Paul Pierce	.40	1.00
❑ 9 Jason Williams	.30	.75
❑ 10 Marcus Camby	.30	.75
❑ 11 Jason Terry	.40	1.00
❑ 12 Anfernee Hardaway	.40	1.00
❑ 13 Cuttino Mobley	.30	.75
❑ 14 Kenyon Martin	.40	1.00
❑ 15 Rashard Lewis	.40	1.00
❑ 16 Darius Miles	.25	.60
❑ 17 Jamal Mashburn	.30	.75
❑ 18 Derek Fisher	.30	.75
❑ 19 Sam Cassell	.30	.75
❑ 20 Antonio McDyess	.30	.75
❑ 21 John Stockton	.50	1.25
❑ 22 Andre Miller	.30	.75
❑ 23 Shawn Marion	.40	1.00
❑ 24 Steve Nash	.60	1.50
❑ 25 Kevin Garnett	.75	2.00
❑ 26 Peja Stojakovic	.30	.75
❑ 27 Dirk Nowitzki	.60	1.50
❑ 28 Chris Webber	.40	1.00
❑ 29 Shaquille O'Neal	1.00	2.50
❑ 30 Stephon Marbury	.40	1.00
❑ 31 Eddie Jones	.30	.75
❑ 32 Raef LaFrentz	.25	.60
❑ 33 Wally Szczerbiak	.30	.75
❑ 34 Richard Hamilton	.30	.75
❑ 35 Michael Finley	.40	1.00
❑ 36 Jason Kidd	.60	1.50
❑ 37 Courtney Alexander	.25	.60
❑ 38 Glenn Robinson	.30	.75
❑ 39 Tim Duncan	.75	2.00
❑ 40 Steve Francis	.40	1.00
❑ 41 Stromile Swift	.25	.60
❑ 42 Desmond Mason	.30	.75
❑ 43 Shareef Abdur-Rahim	.30	.75
❑ 44 Terrell Brandon	.25	.60
❑ 45 Antawn Jamison	.40	1.00
❑ 46 Latrell Sprewell	.30	.75
❑ 47 Mateen Cleaves	.25	.60
❑ 48 Karl Malone	.50	1.25
❑ 49 Lamar Odom	.40	1.00
❑ 50 Grant Hill	.40	1.00
❑ 51 Reggie Miller	.40	1.00
❑ 52 Ray Allen	.40	1.00
❑ 53 David Robinson	.50	1.25
❑ 54 Elton Brand	.40	1.00
❑ 55 Jerry Stackhouse	.30	.75
❑ 56 Brian Grant	.25	.60
❑ 57 Hakeem Olajuwon	.50	1.25
❑ 58 Jalen Rose	.30	.75
❑ 59 Allen Iverson	.75	2.00
❑ 60 Darrell Armstrong	.25	.60
❑ 61 Joe Smith	.25	.60
❑ 62 Anthony Mason	.25	.60
❑ 63 Mike Bibby	.30	.75
❑ 64 Gary Payton	.40	1.00
❑ 65 Glen Rice	.30	.75
❑ 66 Shandon Anderson	.25	.60
❑ 67 Antoine Walker	.30	.75
❑ 68 Tim Thomas	.25	.60
❑ 69 Patrick Ewing	.50	1.25
❑ 70 Ben Wallace	.30	.75
❑ 71 Corey Maggette	.30	.75
❑ 72 Larry Hughes	.30	.75
❑ 73 Scottie Pippen	.60	1.50
❑ 74 Michael Doleac	.25	.60
❑ 75 Clifford Robinson	.25	.60
❑ 76 Aaron McKie	.25	.60
❑ 77 Marc Jackson	.25	.60
❑ 78 Tom Gugliotta	.25	.60
❑ 79 James Posey	.25	.60
❑ 80 Moochie Norris	.25	.60
❑ 81 Speedy Claxton	.25	.60
❑ 82 Michael Redd	.40	1.00
❑ 83 Rasheed Wallace	.40	1.00
❑ 84 Juwan Howard	.30	.75
❑ 85 Nick Van Exel	.30	.75
❑ 86 Toni Kukoc	.30	.75
❑ 87 Jamaal Magloire	.25	.60
❑ 88 Jermaine O'Neal	.40	1.00
❑ 89 Anthony Peeler	.25	.60
❑ 90 Marcus Fizer	.25	.60
❑ 91 Jumaine Jones	.25	.60
❑ 92 Kendall Gill	.25	.60
❑ 93 Antonio Daniels	.25	.60
❑ 94 DerMarr Johnson	.25	.60
❑ 95 Mitch Richmond	.30	.75
❑ 96 Antonio Davis	.25	.60
❑ 97 Ron Mercer	.25	.60
❑ 98 Keyon Dooling	.25	.60
❑ 99 Morris Peterson	.30	.75
❑ 100 Derek Anderson	.30	.75
❑ 101 Allen Iverson MO	.60	1.50
❑ 102 Glenn Robinson MO	.25	.60
❑ 103 Tim Duncan MO	.60	1.50
❑ 104 Shaquille O'Neal MO	.75	2.00
❑ 105 Vince Carter MO	.60	1.50
❑ 106 Tracy McGrady MO	.60	1.50
❑ 107 Jason Kidd MO	.50	1.25
❑ 108 Karl Malone MO	.40	1.00
❑ 109 Michael Jordan MO	6.00	15.00
❑ 110 Shareef Abdur-Rahim MO	.25	.60
❑ 111 Grant Hill MO	.30	.75
❑ 112 Stephon Marbury MO	.30	.75
❑ 113 Michael Finley MO	.30	.75
❑ 114 Antoine Walker MO	.25	.60
❑ 115 Kobe Bryant MO	1.50	4.00
❑ 116 Dirk Nowitzki MO	.50	1.25
❑ 117 Alonzo Mourning MO	.30	.75
❑ 118 John Stockton MO	.40	1.00
❑ 119 Kevin Garnett MO	.60	1.50
❑ 120 Eddie Jones MO	.25	.60
❑ 121 Steven Hunter/500 RC	2.50	6.00
❑ 122 Tony Parker/500 RC	10.00	25.00
❑ 123 Zach Randolph/478 RC	6.00	15.00
❑ 124 R.Jefferson/500 RC	6.00	15.00
❑ 125 Kedrick Brown/433 RC	2.50	6.00
❑ 126 Kwame Brown/472 RC	3.00	8.00
❑ 127 B.Armstrong/500 RC	2.50	6.00
❑ 128 Pau Gasol/474 RC	10.00	25.00
❑ 129 Troy Murphy/500 RC	5.00	12.00
❑ 130 Rodney White/500 RC	2.50	6.00

❑ 131 Jamaal Tinsley/500 RC	3.00	8.00
❑ 132 Jeryl Sasser/500 RC	2.50	6.00
❑ 133 Eddie Griffin/500 RC	2.50	6.00
❑ 134 Michael Bradley/476 RC	2.50	6.00
❑ 135 V.Radmanovic/500 RC	3.00	8.00
❑ 136 J.Richardson/388 RC	5.00	12.00
❑ 137 Shane Battier/500 RC	4.00	10.00
❑ 138 Joe Johnson/300 RC	6.00	15.00
❑ 139 Andrei Kirilenko/500 RC	6.00	15.00
❑ 140 Kirk Haston/500 RC	2.50	6.00
❑ 141 Jason Collins/500 RC	2.50	6.00
❑ 142 Tyson Chandler/500 RC	5.00	12.00
❑ 143 DeSagana Diop/499 RC	2.50	6.00
❑ 144 Gerald Wallace/467 RC	6.00	15.00
❑ 145 Joseph Forte/450 RC	2.50	6.00
❑ 146 B.Haywood/500 RC	3.00	8.00
❑ 147 S.Dalembert/360 RC	3.00	8.00
❑ 148 Eddy Curry/500 RC	4.00	10.00
❑ 149 Primoz Brezec/500 RC	3.00	8.00

1999-00 Fleer Focus

❑ COMPLETE SET (150)	75.00	150.00
❑ COMPLETE SET w/o RC (100)	10.00	20.00
❑ COMMON CARD (1-100)	.20	.50
❑ COMMON ROOKIE (101-150)	1.00	2.50
❑ 1 Anfernee Hardaway	.30	.75
❑ 2 Derek Anderson	.20	.50
❑ 3 Jayson Williams	.25	.60
❑ 4 Ron Mercer	.20	.50
❑ 5 Jerry Stackhouse	.30	.75
❑ 6 Tariq Abdul-Wahad	.20	.50
❑ 7 Sean Elliott	.30	.75
❑ 8 Lindsey Hunter	.20	.50
❑ 9 Larry Johnson	.30	.75
❑ 10 Steve Smith	.20	.50
❑ 11 Raef LaFrentz	.25	.60
❑ 12 Jalen Rose	.25	.60
❑ 13 Stephon Marbury	.30	.75
❑ 14 Detlef Schrempf	.25	.60
❑ 15 Rod Strickland	.20	.50
❑ 16 Paul Pierce	.30	.75
❑ 17 Maurice Taylor	.25	.60
❑ 18 Allen Iverson	.60	1.50
❑ 19 Mitch Richmond	.25	.60
❑ 20 Gary Trent	.20	.50
❑ 21 Reggie Miller	.30	.75
❑ 22 Kerry Kittles	.20	.50
❑ 23 Rasheed Wallace	.30	.75
❑ 24 Steve Nash	.50	1.25
❑ 25 Scottie Pippen	.50	1.25
❑ 26 Joe Smith	.25	.60
❑ 27 Jason Williams	.30	.75
❑ 28 Michael Finley	.30	.75
❑ 29 Hakeem Olajuwon	.30	.75
❑ 30 Kevin Garnett	.60	1.50
❑ 31 Darrell Armstrong	.20	.50
❑ 32 David Robinson	.40	1.00
❑ 33 Anthony Mason	.20	.50
❑ 34 Jamal Mashburn	.20	.50
❑ 35 Gary Payton	.30	.75
❑ 36 Bryon Russell	.20	.50
❑ 37 Cedric Ceballos	.20	.50
❑ 38 Michael Dickerson	.20	.50
❑ 39 Robert Traylor	.20	.50
❑ 40 Vin Baker	.30	.75
❑ 41 Shawn Kemp	.30	.75
❑ 42 Charles Barkley	.40	1.00
❑ 43 Glenn Robinson	.25	.60
❑ 44 Vince Carter	.60	1.50
❑ 45 Zydrunas Ilgauskas	.25	.60
❑ 46 Sam Cassell	.25	.60
❑ 47 Tracy McGrady	.60	1.50
❑ 48 Chris Mills	.20	.50
❑ 49 Antawn Jamison	.30	.75
❑ 50 Nick Anderson	.20	.50
❑ 51 Avery Johnson	.25	.60
❑ 52 Brent Barry	.25	.60
❑ 53 Alonzo Mourning	.30	.75
❑ 54 Karl Malone	.40	1.00
❑ 55 Toni Kukoc	.30	.75
❑ 56 Ray Allen	.30	.75
❑ 57 Charles Oakley	.25	.60
❑ 58 Cuttino Mobley	.25	.60
❑ 59 Kenny Anderson	.25	.60
❑ 60 Tom Gugliotta	.20	.50
❑ 61 Antoine Walker	.30	.75
❑ 62 Kobe Bryant	1.50	4.00
❑ 63 Larry Hughes	.25	.60
❑ 64 Vlade Divac	.30	.75
❑ 65 Juwan Howard	.25	.60
❑ 66 Isaiah Rider	.20	.50
❑ 67 Antonio McDyess	.25	.60
❑ 68 Rik Smits	.30	.75
❑ 69 Keith Van Horn	.25	.60
❑ 70 Doug Christie	.25	.60
❑ 71 Elden Campbell	.20	.50
❑ 72 Shaquille O'Neal	.75	2.00
❑ 73 Matt Geiger	.20	.50
❑ 74 Chris Webber	.30	.75
❑ 75 Troy Hudson	.30	.75
❑ 76 Eddie Jones	.30	.75
❑ 77 Tim Hardaway	.30	.75
❑ 78 Hersey Hawkins	.20	.50
❑ 79 Shareef Abdur-Rahim	.25	.60
❑ 80 Christian Laettner	.25	.60
❑ 81 Latrell Sprewell	.25	.60
❑ 82 Damon Stoudamire	.30	.75
❑ 83 Jason Caffey	.20	.50
❑ 84 Michael Olowokandi	.20	.50
❑ 85 Horace Grant	.25	.60
❑ 86 Grant Hill	.30	.75
❑ 87 Patrick Ewing	.40	1.00
❑ 88 Clifford Robinson	.20	.50
❑ 89 Ricky Davis	.30	.75
❑ 90 Glen Rice	.30	.75
❑ 91 Matt Harpring	.25	.60
❑ 92 Mike Bibby	.30	.75
❑ 93 Dikembe Mutombo	.25	.60
❑ 94 Chris Mullin	.30	.75
❑ 95 Marcus Camby	.25	.60
❑ 96 Jason Kidd	.50	1.25
❑ 97 John Starks	.30	.75
❑ 98 Terrell Brandon	.20	.50
❑ 99 Tim Duncan	.60	1.50
❑ 100 John Stockton	.40	1.00
❑ 101 Ron Artest RC	4.00	10.00
❑ 101A Ron Artest SP	6.00	15.00
❑ 102 William Avery RC	1.00	2.50
❑ 102A William Avery SP	1.50	4.00
❑ 103 Jonathan Bender RC	1.00	2.50
❑ 103A Jonathan Bender SP	1.50	4.00
❑ 104 Cal Bowdler RC	1.00	2.50
❑ 104A Cal Bowdler SP	1.50	4.00
❑ 105 Elton Brand RC	3.00	8.00
❑ 105A Elton Brand SP	5.00	12.00
❑ 106 Vonteego Cummings RC	1.00	2.50
❑ 106A Vonteego Cummings SP	1.50	4.00
❑ 107 Baron Davis RC	4.00	10.00
❑ 107A Baron Davis SP	6.00	15.00
❑ 108 Jeff Foster RC	1.25	3.00
❑ 108A Jeff Foster SP	2.00	5.00
❑ 109 Steve Francis RC	3.00	8.00
❑ 109A Steve Francis SP	5.00	12.00
❑ 110 Devean George RC	1.50	4.00
❑ 110A Devean George SP	2.50	6.00
❑ 111 Dion Glover RC	1.00	2.50
❑ 111A Dion Glover SP	1.50	4.00
❑ 112 Richard Hamilton RC	3.00	8.00
❑ 112A Richard Hamilton SP	5.00	12.00
❑ 113 Tim James RC	1.00	2.50
❑ 113A Tim James SP	1.50	4.00
❑ 114 Trajan Langdon RC	1.00	2.50
❑ 114A Trajan Langdon SP	1.50	4.00
❑ 115 Quincy Lewis RC	1.00	2.50
❑ 115A Quincy Lewis SP	1.50	4.00
❑ 116 Corey Maggette RC	3.00	8.00
❑ 116A Corey Maggette SP	5.00	12.00
❑ 117 Shawn Marion RC	3.00	8.00
❑ 117A Shawn Marion SP	5.00	12.00
❑ 118 Andre Miller RC	3.00	8.00
❑ 118A Andre Miller SP	5.00	12.00
❑ 119 Lamar Odom RC	3.00	8.00
❑ 119A Lamar Odom SP	5.00	12.00
❑ 120 Scott Padgett RC	1.00	2.50
❑ 120A Scott Padgett SP	1.50	4.00
❑ 121 James Posey RC	1.50	4.00
❑ 121A James Posey SP	2.50	6.00
❑ 122 A.Radojevic RC	1.00	2.50
❑ 122A Aleksandar Radojevic SP	1.50	4.00
❑ 123 Wally Szczerbiak RC	3.00	8.00
❑ 123A Wally Szczerbiak SP	5.00	12.00
❑ 124 Jason Terry RC	2.50	6.00
❑ 124A Jason Terry SP	4.00	10.00
❑ 125 Kenny Thomas RC	1.00	2.50
❑ 125A Kenny Thomas SP	1.50	4.00
❑ 126 Jumaine Jones RC	1.00	2.50
❑ 126A Jumaine Jones SP	1.50	4.00
❑ 127 Rick Hughes RC	1.00	2.50
❑ 127A Rick Hughes SP	1.50	4.00
❑ 128 John Celestand RC	1.00	2.50
❑ 128A John Celestand SP	1.50	4.00
❑ 129 Adrian Griffin RC	1.00	2.50
❑ 129A Adrian Griffin SP	1.50	4.00
❑ 130 Michael Ruffin RC	1.00	2.50
❑ 130A Michael Ruffin SP	1.50	4.00
❑ 131 Chris Herren RC	1.00	2.50
❑ 131A Chris Herren SP	1.50	4.00
❑ 132 Evan Eschmeyer RC	1.00	2.50
❑ 132A Evan Eschmeyer SP	1.50	4.00
❑ 133 Tim Young RC	1.00	2.50
❑ 133A Tim Young SP	1.50	4.00
❑ 134 Obinna Ekezie RC	1.00	2.50
❑ 134A Obinna Ekezie SP	1.50	4.00
❑ 135 Laron Profit RC	1.00	2.50
❑ 135A Laron Profit SP	1.50	4.00
❑ 136 A.J. Bramlett RC	1.00	2.50
❑ 136A A.J. Bramlett SP	1.50	4.00
❑ 137 Eddie Robinson RC	1.00	2.50
❑ 137A Eddie Robinson SP	1.50	4.00
❑ 138 Ryan Bowen RC	1.00	2.50
❑ 138A Ryan Bowen SP	1.50	4.00
❑ 139 Chucky Atkins RC	1.25	3.00
❑ 139A Chucky Atkins SP	2.00	5.00
❑ 140 Ryan Robertson RC	1.00	2.50
❑ 140A Ryan Robertson SP	1.50	4.00
❑ 141 Derrick Dial RC	1.00	2.50
❑ 141A Derrick Dial SP	1.50	4.00
❑ 142 Todd MacCulloch RC	1.00	2.50
❑ 142A Todd MacCulloch SP	1.50	4.00
❑ 143 DeMarco Johnson RC	1.00	2.50
❑ 143A DeMarco Johnson SP	1.50	4.00
❑ 144 Anthony Carter RC	2.00	5.00
❑ 144A Anthony Carter SP	3.00	8.00
❑ 145 Lazaro Borrell RC	1.00	2.50
❑ 145A Lazaro Borrell SP	1.50	4.00
❑ 146 Rafer Alston RC	2.00	5.00
❑ 146A Rafer Alston SP	3.00	8.00
❑ 147 Nikita Morgunov RC	1.00	2.50
❑ 147A Nikita Morgunov SP	1.50	4.00
❑ 148 Rodney Buford RC	1.00	2.50
❑ 148A Rodney Buford SP	1.50	4.00
❑ 149 Milt Palacio RC	1.00	2.50
❑ 149A Milt Palacio SP	1.50	4.00
❑ 150 Jermaine Jackson RC	1.00	2.50
❑ 150A Jermaine Jackson SP	1.50	4.00

2000-01 Fleer Focus

❑ COMPLETE SET w/o RC (200)	20.00	40.00
❑ COMMON CARD (1-180/217-236)	.20	.50
❑ COMMON ROOKIE (181-216)	.20	.50
❑ 1 Vince Carter	.60	1.50
❑ 2 Shawn Marion	.30	.75
❑ 3 Muggsy Bogues	.25	.60
❑ 4 Dikembe Mutombo	.25	.60
❑ 5 Stephon Marbury	.30	.75
❑ 6 Michael Dickerson	.20	.50
❑ 7 Andre Miller	.25	.60
❑ 8 Toni Kukoc	.25	.60
❑ 9 Nick Van Exel	.25	.60
❑ 10 Aaron Williams	.20	.50
❑ 11 Derrick Coleman	.25	.60

❑ 12 Wally Szczerbiak	.25	.60
❑ 13 Rodney Rogers	.20	.50
❑ 14 Tom Gugliotta	.20	.50
❑ 15 Vonteego Cummings	.20	.50
❑ 16 Cedric Ceballos	.20	.50
❑ 17 Malik Rose	.20	.50
❑ 18 Shawn Bradley	.20	.50
❑ 19 Shandon Anderson	.20	.50
❑ 20 Jacque Vaughn	.20	.50
❑ 21 Jamie Feick	.20	.50
❑ 22 Shawn Kemp	.30	.75
❑ 23 Monty Williams	.20	.50
❑ 24 Allan Houston	.25	.60
❑ 25 Chauncey Billups	.30	.75
❑ 26 Vlade Divac	.25	.60
❑ 27 Othella Harrington	.20	.50
❑ 28 Dale Davis	.20	.50
❑ 29 Charlie Ward	.20	.50
❑ 30 Hakeem Olajuwon	.40	1.00
❑ 31 Ray Allen	.30	.75
❑ 32 Lamar Odom	.30	.75
❑ 33 Shaquille O'Neal	.75	2.00
❑ 34 Chris Childs	.20	.50
❑ 35 Nick Anderson	.20	.50
❑ 36 Keon Clark	.20	.50
❑ 37 Danny Fortson	.20	.50
❑ 38 Sam Mitchell	.20	.50
❑ 39 Travis Best	.20	.50
❑ 40 Chris Webber	.30	.75
❑ 41 Brent Barry	.20	.50
❑ 42 Scottie Pippen	.50	1.25
❑ 43 Reggie Miller	.30	.75
❑ 44 Bryant Reeves	.20	.50
❑ 45 Bobby Jackson	.20	.50
❑ 46 Antonio McDyess	.25	.60
❑ 47 Elden Campbell	.20	.50
❑ 48 Kenny Anderson	.25	.60
❑ 49 Christian Laettner	.20	.50
❑ 50 Darrell Armstrong	.20	.50
❑ 51 Vinny Del Negro	.20	.50
❑ 52 Quincy Lewis	.20	.50
❑ 53 Peja Stojakovic	.25	.60
❑ 54 Matt Geiger	.20	.50
❑ 55 Larry Hughes	.25	.60
❑ 56 Tracy McGrady	.60	1.50
❑ 57 Tim Hardaway	.25	.60
❑ 58 Brevin Knight	.20	.50
❑ 59 Michael Finley	.30	.75
❑ 60 Jason Kidd	.50	1.25
❑ 61 Matt Harpring	.25	.60
❑ 62 Antawn Jamison	.30	.75
❑ 63 Wesley Person	.20	.50
❑ 64 Antonio Davis	.20	.50
❑ 65 Roshown McLeod	.20	.50
❑ 66 Anthony Peeler	.20	.50
❑ 67 Grant Hill	.30	.75
❑ 68 Michael Olowokandi	.20	.50
❑ 69 Kerry Kittles	.25	.60
❑ 70 Elton Brand	.30	.75
❑ 71 Tariq Abdul-Wahad	.20	.50
❑ 72 Aaron McKie	.20	.50
❑ 73 Andrew DeClercq	.20	.50
❑ 74 Anfernee Hardaway	.30	.75
❑ 75 Bimbo Coles	.20	.50
❑ 76 Terrell Brandon	.20	.50
❑ 77 Jalen Rose	.25	.60
❑ 78 Radoslav Nesterovic	.20	.50
❑ 79 Howard Eisley	.20	.50
❑ 80 Steve Smith	.25	.60
❑ 81 Arvydas Sabonis	.25	.60
❑ 82 Jim Jackson	.20	.50
❑ 83 Corey Maggette	.25	.60
❑ 84 James Posey	.20	.50
❑ 85 LaPhonso Ellis	.25	.60
❑ 86 Eric Snow	.20	.50
❑ 87 Mikki Moore	.20	.50
❑ 88 Baron Davis	.30	.75
❑ 89 Jason Williams	.25	.60
❑ 90 Mike Bibby	.25	.60
❑ 91 Marcus Camby	.25	.60
❑ 92 Bryon Russell	.20	.50
❑ 93 Steve Francis	.30	.75
❑ 94 Sam Cassell	.25	.60
❑ 95 Rasheed Wallace	.30	.75
❑ 96 Keith Van Horn	.25	.60
❑ 97 Eddie Jones	.25	.60
❑ 98 Corliss Williamson	.25	.60
❑ 99 Ron Mercer	.20	.50
❑ 100 Sean Elliott	.25	.60
❑ 101 Shareef Abdur-Rahim	.25	.60
❑ 102 Glen Rice	.25	.60
❑ 103 Patrick Ewing	.40	1.00
❑ 104 Adrian Griffin	.20	.50
❑ 105 David Robinson	.40	1.00
❑ 106 Isaac Austin	.20	.50
❑ 107 Anthony Mason	.20	.50
❑ 108 P.J. Brown	.20	.50
❑ 109 Kendall Gill	.20	.50
❑ 110 Tyrone Nesby	.20	.50
❑ 111 Damon Stoudamire	.25	.60
❑ 112 Latrell Sprewell	.25	.60
❑ 113 Tim Duncan	.60	1.50
❑ 114 Glenn Robinson	.25	.60
❑ 115 John Wallace	.20	.50
❑ 116 Erick Strickland	.20	.50
❑ 117 Doug Christie	.20	.50
❑ 118 Juwan Howard	.25	.60
❑ 119 Tim Thomas	.20	.50
❑ 120 Tyrone Hill	.20	.50
❑ 121 Avery Johnson	.25	.60
❑ 122 Jerome Williams	.20	.50
❑ 123 Mitch Richmond	.25	.60
❑ 124 Hersey Hawkins	.20	.50
❑ 125 Donyell Marshall	.20	.50
❑ 126 Derek Anderson	.25	.60
❑ 127 Jamal Mashburn	.25	.60
❑ 128 Richard Hamilton	.25	.60
❑ 129 Alonzo Mourning	.30	.75
❑ 130 Kelvin Cato	.20	.50
❑ 131 Lamond Murray	.20	.50
❑ 132 Bo Outlaw	.20	.50
❑ 133 Chris Carr	.20	.50
❑ 134 Jonathan Bender	.20	.50
❑ 135 Paul Pierce	.30	.75
❑ 136 Dan Majerle	.25	.60
❑ 137 Ron Artest	.30	.75
❑ 138 Jermaine O'Neal	.30	.75
❑ 139 Chris Whitney	.20	.50
❑ 140 Anthony Carter	.20	.50
❑ 141 Gary Payton	.30	.75
❑ 142 Kevin Garnett	.60	1.50
❑ 143 Kevin Willis	.20	.50
❑ 144 Charles Oakley	.25	.60
❑ 145 Larry Johnson	.25	.60
❑ 146 Bonzi Wells	.20	.50
❑ 147 Clifford Robinson	.20	.50
❑ 148 Chucky Atkins	.20	.50
❑ 149 Brian Grant	.20	.50
❑ 150 Voshon Lenard	.20	.50
❑ 151 Antoine Walker	.25	.60
❑ 152 Cuttino Mobley	.25	.60
❑ 153 Robert Horry	.25	.60
❑ 154 Tracy Murray	.20	.50
❑ 155 Kobe Bryant	1.50	4.00
❑ 156 Joe Smith	.20	.50
❑ 157 Jaren Jackson	.20	.50
❑ 158 Scott Williams	.20	.50
❑ 159 Allen Iverson	.60	1.50
❑ 160 Rashard Lewis	.30	.75
❑ 161 Chris Mills	.20	.50
❑ 162 Karl Malone	.40	1.00
❑ 163 John Amaechi	.20	.50
❑ 164 Jason Terry	.30	.75
❑ 165 Ruben Patterson	.20	.50
❑ 166 Austin Croshere	.20	.50
❑ 167 Maurice Taylor	.20	.50
❑ 168 Rod Strickland	.25	.60
❑ 169 Clarence Weatherspoon	.20	.50
❑ 170 Lindsey Hunter	.20	.50
❑ 171 David Wesley	.20	.50
❑ 172 Jerry Stackhouse	.25	.60
❑ 173 Scott Burrell	.20	.50
❑ 174 John Stockton	.40	1.00
❑ 175 Vitaly Potapenko	.20	.50
❑ 176 Dirk Nowitzki	.50	1.25
❑ 177 Vin Baker	.25	.60
❑ 178 Rick Fox	.25	.60
❑ 179 Mookie Blaylock	.25	.60
❑ 180 Felipe Lopez	.20	.50
❑ 181 Chris Mihm A RC	.40	1.00
❑ 182 Mamadou N'Diaye A RC	.40	1.00
❑ 183 Joel Przybilla A RC	.40	1.00
❑ 184 Jamaal Magloire A RC	.40	1.00
❑ 185 Iakovos Tsakalidis A RC	.40	1.00
❑ 186 Etan Thomas A RC	.40	1.00
❑ 187 Mark Madsen B RC	.40	1.00
❑ 188 Hanno Mottola B RC	.40	1.00
❑ 189 Donnell Harvey B RC	.40	1.00
❑ 190 Jason Collier B RC	.40	1.00
❑ 191 Eduardo Najera B RC	.40	1.00
❑ 192 Jerome Moiso B RC	.40	1.00
❑ 193 Mateen Cleaves C RC	.60	1.50
❑ 194 Keyon Dooling C RC	.60	1.50
❑ 195 Speedy Claxton C RC	.60	1.50
❑ 196 Erick Barkley C RC	.60	1.50
❑ 197 A.J. Guyton C RC	.60	1.50
❑ 198 Jamal Crawford C RC	1.00	2.50
❑ 199 Dan Langhi D RC	.40	1.00
❑ 200 Desmond Mason D RC	.50	1.25
❑ 201 Chris Porter D RC	.40	1.00
❑ 202 Corey Hightower D RC	.40	1.00
❑ 203 Morris Peterson D RC	.60	1.50
❑ 204 Hedo Turkoglu D RC	1.00	2.50
❑ 205 Courtney Alexander E RC	.75	2.00
❑ 206 Quentin Richardson E RC	1.00	2.50
❑ 207 DeShawn Stevenson E RC	.75	2.00
❑ 208 Michael Redd E RC	2.00	5.00
❑ 209 Chris Carrawell E RC	.75	2.00
❑ 210 Mark Karcher E RC	2.00	5.00
❑ 211 Kenyon Martin F RC	3.00	8.00
❑ 212 Marcus Fizer F RC	1.25	3.00
❑ 213 Darius Miles F RC	1.50	4.00
❑ 214 Mike Miller F RC	2.00	5.00
❑ 215 DerMarr Johnson F RC	1.25	3.00
❑ 216 Stromile Swift F RC	1.50	4.00
❑ 217 Shaquille O'Neal 20	.50	1.25
❑ 218 Allen Iverson 20	.40	1.00
❑ 219 Grant Hill 20	.20	.50
❑ 220 Vince Carter 20	.40	1.00
❑ 221 Karl Malone 20	.25	.60
❑ 222 Chris Webber 20	.20	.50
❑ 223 Gary Payton 20	.20	.50
❑ 224 Jerry Stackhouse 20	.15	.40
❑ 225 Tim Duncan 20	.40	1.00
❑ 226 Kevin Garnett 20	.40	1.00
❑ 227 Michael Finley 20	.20	.50
❑ 228 Kobe Bryant 20	1.00	2.50
❑ 229 Stephon Marbury 20	.20	.50
❑ 230 Ray Allen 20	.20	.50
❑ 231 Alonzo Mourning 20	.20	.50
❑ 232 Glenn Robinson 20	.15	.40
❑ 233 Antoine Walker 20	.15	.40
❑ 234 Shareef Abdur-Rahim 20	.15	.40
❑ 235 Elton Brand 20	.20	.50
❑ 236 Eddie Jones 20	.15	.40

2001-02 Fleer Focus

❑ COMP.SET w/o SP's (100)	20.00	40.00
❑ COMMON CARD 1-100	.20	.50
❑ COMMON ROOKIE (101-130)	.75	2.00
❑ 1 Vince Carter	.60	1.50
❑ 2 Steve Nash	.50	1.25
❑ 3 Anthony Mason	.20	.50
❑ 4 Avery Johnson	.25	.60
❑ 5 Peja Stojakovic	.25	.60
❑ 6 Shaquille O'Neal	.75	2.00
❑ 7 Jason Kidd	.50	1.25
❑ 8 Steve Smith	.25	.60
❑ 9 Kobe Bryant	1.50	4.00
❑ 10 Eddie Robinson	.20	.50
❑ 11 Allan Houston	.25	.60
❑ 12 Larry Hughes	.25	.60
❑ 13 Gary Payton	.30	.75
❑ 14 Alonzo Mourning	.30	.75
❑ 15 Baron Davis	.30	.75
❑ 16 Speedy Claxton	.20	.50
❑ 17 Hakeem Olajuwon	.40	1.00
❑ 18 Anthony Carter	.20	.50
❑ 19 Raef LaFrentz	.20	.50
❑ 20 Dikembe Mutombo	.25	.60
❑ 21 Moochie Norris	.20	.50
❑ 22 Karl Malone	.40	1.00
❑ 23 Darrell Armstrong	.20	.50
❑ 24 Allen Iverson	.60	1.50

❑ 25 Danny Fortson	.20	.50
❑ 26 Antonio Davis	.20	.50
❑ 27 Eddie Jones	.25	.60
❑ 28 Patrick Ewing	.40	1.00
❑ 29 Stephon Marbury	.30	.75
❑ 30 Cuttino Mobley	.25	.60
❑ 31 Morris Peterson	.25	.60
❑ 32 Glenn Robinson	.25	.60
❑ 33 Paul Pierce	.30	.75
❑ 34 Shawn Marion	.30	.75
❑ 35 Jermaine O'Neal	.30	.75
❑ 36 Donyell Marshall	.20	.50
❑ 37 Chauncey Billups	.25	.60
❑ 38 Tracy McGrady	.60	1.50
❑ 39 Vlade Divac	.25	.60
❑ 40 Lamar Odom	.30	.75
❑ 41 Chris Mihm	.20	.50
❑ 42 Kenyon Martin	.30	.75
❑ 43 Antonio McDyess	.25	.60
❑ 44 Mike Bibby	.25	.60
❑ 45 Darius Miles	.20	.50
❑ 46 Wesley Person	.20	.50
❑ 47 Mark Jackson	.25	.60
❑ 48 Nick Van Exel	.25	.60
❑ 49 Tim Duncan	.60	1.50
❑ 50 Sam Cassell	.25	.60
❑ 51 Jason Terry	.30	.75
❑ 52 Bonzi Wells	.25	.60
❑ 53 Al Harrington	.25	.60
❑ 54 Richard Hamilton	.25	.60
❑ 55 Wally Szczerbiak	.25	.60
❑ 56 Toni Kukoc	.25	.60
❑ 57 Rasheed Wallace	.30	.75
❑ 58 Reggie Miller	.30	.75
❑ 59 Courtney Alexander	.20	.50
❑ 60 Terrell Brandon	.20	.50
❑ 61 Dirk Nowitzki	.50	1.25
❑ 62 Chris Webber	.30	.75
❑ 63 Lindsey Hunter	.20	.50
❑ 64 Andre Miller	.25	.60
❑ 65 Clifford Robinson	.20	.50
❑ 66 David Robinson	.40	1.00
❑ 67 Stromile Swift	.20	.50
❑ 68 Nazr Mohammed	.20	.50
❑ 69 Kurt Thomas	.20	.50
❑ 70 Corliss Williamson	.25	.60
❑ 71 Rashard Lewis	.30	.75
❑ 72 Lorenzen Wright	.20	.50
❑ 73 David Wesley	.20	.50
❑ 74 Derrick Coleman	.25	.60
❑ 75 Jerry Stackhouse	.25	.60
❑ 76 Antonio Daniels	.20	.50
❑ 77 Mitch Richmond	.25	.60
❑ 78 Ron Mercer	.20	.50
❑ 79 Latrell Sprewell	.25	.60
❑ 80 Antawn Jamison	.30	.75
❑ 81 Desmond Mason	.25	.60
❑ 82 Jason Williams	.25	.60
❑ 83 Jamal Mashburn	.25	.60
❑ 84 Grant Hill	.30	.75
❑ 85 Elton Brand	.30	.75
❑ 86 Brian Grant	.20	.50
❑ 87 Antoine Walker	.25	.60
❑ 88 Anfernee Hardaway	.30	.75
❑ 89 Steve Francis	.30	.75
❑ 90 John Stockton	.40	1.00
❑ 91 Ray Allen	.30	.75
❑ 92 Tim Hardaway	.25	.60
❑ 93 Derek Anderson	.25	.60
❑ 94 Jalen Rose	.25	.60
❑ 95 Michael Jordan	6.00	15.00
❑ 96 Kevin Garnett	.60	1.50
❑ 97 Shareef Abdur-Rahim	.25	.60
❑ 98 Tony Delk	.20	.50
❑ 99 Quentin Richardson	.25	.60
❑ 100 Michael Finley	.30	.75
❑ 101 Jamaal Tinsley RC	1.00	2.50
❑ 102 Zach Randolph RC	2.00	5.00
❑ 103 Kedrick Brown RC	.75	2.00
❑ 104 Kirk Haston RC	.75	2.00
❑ 105 Tyson Chandler RC	1.50	4.00
❑ 106 Shane Battier RC	1.25	3.00
❑ 107 Richard Jefferson RC	2.00	5.00
❑ 108 Gerald Wallace RC	2.00	5.00
❑ 109 DeSagana Diop RC	.75	2.00
❑ 110 R.Boumtje-Boumtje RC	.75	2.00
❑ 111 Rodney White RC	.75	2.00
❑ 112 Eddie Griffin RC	.75	2.00
❑ 113 Pau Gasol RC	3.00	8.00
❑ 114 Tony Parker RC	3.00	8.00
❑ 115 Kwame Brown RC	1.00	2.50
❑ 116 Vladimir Radmanovic RC	1.00	2.50
❑ 117 Troy Murphy RC	1.50	4.00
❑ 118 Loren Woods RC	.75	2.00
❑ 119 Joe Johnson RC	2.00	5.00
❑ 120 Brandon Armstrong RC	.75	2.00
❑ 121 Trenton Hassell RC	1.00	2.50
❑ 122 Andrei Kirilenko RC	2.00	5.00
❑ 123 Jason Richardson RC	1.50	4.00
❑ 124 Jason Collins RC	.75	2.00
❑ 125 Jeryl Sasser RC	.75	2.00
❑ 126 Michael Bradley RC	.75	2.00
❑ 127 Eddy Curry RC	1.25	3.00
❑ 128 Joseph Forte RC	.75	2.00
❑ 129 Brendan Haywood RC	1.00	2.50
❑ 130 Zeljko Rebraca RC	.75	2.00

2003-04 Fleer Focus

❑ COMP.SET w/o SP's	12.50	30.00
❑ COMMON ROOKIE (121-160)	2.50	6.00
❑ 1 Allan Houston	.25	.60
❑ 2 Manu Ginobili	.30	.75
❑ 3 Allen Iverson	.60	1.50
❑ 4 Kenyon Martin	.30	.75
❑ 5 Rasho Nesterovic	.20	.50
❑ 6 Tracy McGrady	.60	1.50
❑ 7 Drew Gooden	.20	.50
❑ 8 Tony Parker	.30	.75
❑ 9 Troy Murphy	.30	.75
❑ 10 Alonzo Mourning	.30	.75
❑ 11 Rasual Butler	.20	.50
❑ 12 Alvin Williams	.20	.50
❑ 13 Troy Hudson	.20	.50
❑ 14 Gary Payton	.30	.75
❑ 15 Tyson Chandler	.25	.60
❑ 16 Ray Allen	.20	.50
❑ 17 Amare Stoudemire	.60	1.50
❑ 18 Chauncey Billups	.30	.75
❑ 19 Gilbert Arenas	.30	.75
❑ 20 Eddie Jones	.25	.60
❑ 21 Vince Carter	.60	1.50
❑ 22 Kobe Bryant	1.50	4.00
❑ 23 Reggie Miller	.30	.75
❑ 24 Vincent Yarbrough	.20	.50
❑ 25 Kevin Garnett	.60	1.50
❑ 26 Andre Miller	.25	.60
❑ 27 Glenn Robinson	.25	.60
❑ 28 Kurt Thomas	.20	.50
❑ 29 Vladimir Radmanovic	.20	.50
❑ 30 Richard Jefferson	.30	.75
❑ 31 Andrei Kirilenko	.30	.75
❑ 32 Wally Szczerbiak	.25	.60
❑ 33 Gordan Giricek	.20	.50
❑ 34 Kwame Brown	.20	.50
❑ 35 Yao Ming	.60	1.50
❑ 36 Devean George	.20	.50
❑ 37 Richard Hamilton	.25	.60
❑ 38 Anfernee Hardaway	.30	.75
❑ 39 Grant Hill	.30	.75
❑ 40 Zach Randolph	.30	.75
❑ 41 Dirk Nowitzki	.50	1.25
❑ 42 Zydrunas Ilgauskas	.25	.60
❑ 43 Antawn Jamison	.30	.75
❑ 44 J.R. Bremer	.20	.50
❑ 45 Latrell Sprewell	.25	.60
❑ 46 Ron Artest	.25	.60
❑ 47 Antoine Walker	.30	.75
❑ 48 Eddy Curry	.25	.60
❑ 49 Larry Hughes	.25	.60
❑ 50 Jalen Rose	.25	.60
❑ 51 Matt Harpring	.25	.60
❑ 52 Sam Cassell	.25	.60
❑ 53 Antonio McDyess	.25	.60
❑ 54 Jamaal Tinsley	.25	.60
❑ 55 Mehmet Okur	.25	.60
❑ 56 Scottie Pippen	.50	1.25
❑ 57 Antonio Davis	.20	.50
❑ 58 Jamaal Magloire	.20	.50
❑ 59 Michael Olowokandi	.20	.50
❑ 60 Shane Battier	.25	.60
❑ 61 Desmond Mason	.25	.60
❑ 62 Baron Davis	.30	.75
❑ 63 Jamal Mashburn	.20	.50
❑ 64 Michael Redd	.30	.75
❑ 65 Shaquille O'Neal	.75	2.00
❑ 66 Ben Wallace	.25	.60
❑ 67 Jason Terry	.25	.60
❑ 68 Michael Finley	.30	.75
❑ 69 Shareef Abdur-Rahim	.25	.60
❑ 70 Bobby Jackson	.20	.50
❑ 71 Jason Williams	.25	.60
❑ 72 Mike Bibby	.25	.60
❑ 73 Shawn Marion	.30	.75
❑ 74 Ricky Davis	.25	.60
❑ 75 Bonzi Wells	.20	.50
❑ 76 Jason Kidd	.50	1.25
❑ 77 Mike Miller	.25	.60
❑ 78 Stephen Jackson	.25	.60
❑ 79 Brad Miller	.25	.60
❑ 80 Jason Richardson	.30	.75
❑ 81 Mike Dunleavy Jr.	.25	.60
❑ 82 Stephon Marbury	.30	.75
❑ 83 Brian Grant	.20	.50
❑ 84 Jay Williams	.20	.50
❑ 85 Morris Peterson	.25	.60
❑ 86 Steve Nash	.50	1.25
❑ 87 Carlos Boozer	.30	.75
❑ 88 Jermaine O'Neal	.30	.75
❑ 89 Nene	.25	.60
❑ 90 Eric Snow	.20	.50
❑ 91 Steve Francis	.30	.75
❑ 92 Caron Butler	.25	.60
❑ 93 Jerry Stackhouse	.25	.60
❑ 94 Nick Van Exel	.25	.60
❑ 95 Tayshaun Prince	.25	.60
❑ 96 Calbert Cheaney	.20	.50
❑ 97 Pau Gasol	.30	.75
❑ 98 Theo Ratliff	.20	.50
❑ 99 Chris Webber	.30	.75
❑ 100 Juan Dixon	.20	.50
❑ 101 Paul Pierce	.30	.75
❑ 102 Tim Thomas	.20	.50
❑ 103 Eddie Griffin	.20	.50
❑ 104 Corey Maggette	.20	.50
❑ 105 Juwan Howard	.25	.60
❑ 106 Peja Stojakovic	.25	.60
❑ 107 Tim Duncan	.60	1.50
❑ 108 Keith Van Horn	.25	.60
❑ 109 Cuttino Mobley	.25	.60
❑ 110 Kareem Rush	.20	.50
❑ 111 Predrag Drobnjak	.20	.50
❑ 112 Tony Delk	.20	.50
❑ 113 Dajuan Wagner	.20	.50
❑ 114 Karl Malone	.30	.75
❑ 115 Rashard Lewis	.30	.75
❑ 116 David Wesley	.20	.50
❑ 117 Rasheed Wallace	.30	.75
❑ 118 Derrick Coleman	.25	.60
❑ 119 Donnell Harvey	.20	.50
❑ 120 Elton Brand	.30	.75
❑ 121 Carmelo Anthony RC	6.00	15.00
❑ 122 Keith Bogans RC	2.50	6.00
❑ 123 Leandro Barbosa RC	3.00	8.00
❑ 124 Troy Bell RC	2.50	6.00
❑ 125 Chris Bosh RC	4.00	10.00
❑ 126 Zarko Cabarkapa RC	2.50	6.00
❑ 127 Jason Kapono RC	3.00	8.00
❑ 128 Nick Collison RC	2.50	6.00
❑ 129 Boris Diaw-Riffiod RC	3.00	8.00
❑ 130 Marcus Banks RC	2.50	6.00
❑ 131 T.J. Ford RC	3.00	8.00
❑ 132 Reece Gaines RC	2.50	6.00
❑ 133 Travis Hansen RC	2.50	6.00
❑ 134 Jarvis Hayes RC	2.50	6.00
❑ 135 Kirk Hinrich RC	3.00	8.00
❑ 136 Josh Howard RC	3.00	8.00
❑ 137 LeBron James RC	40.00	80.00
❑ 138 Dahntay Jones RC	2.50	6.00
❑ 139 Chris Kaman RC	3.00	8.00
❑ 140 Maciej Lampe RC	2.50	6.00
❑ 141 Darko Milicic RC	3.00	8.00
❑ 142 Travis Outlaw RC	3.00	8.00
❑ 143 Mickael Pietrus RC	3.00	8.00
❑ 144 Rick Rickert RC	2.50	6.00

❑ 145 Luke Ridnour RC	3.00	8.00
❑ 146 Sofoklis Schortsanitis RC	2.50	6.00
❑ 147 Mike Sweetney RC	2.50	6.00
❑ 148 Dwyane Wade RC	6.00	15.00
❑ 149 Luke Walton RC	3.00	8.00
❑ 150 David West RC	3.00	8.00
❑ 151 Zoran Planinic RC	2.50	6.00
❑ 152 Ndudi Ebi RC	2.50	6.00
❑ 153 Aleksandar Pavlovic RC	3.00	8.00
❑ 154 Kendrick Perkins RC	4.00	10.00
❑ 155 Maurice Williams RC	4.00	10.00
❑ 156 Jerome Beasley RC	2.50	6.00
❑ 157 Slavko Vranes RC	2.50	6.00
❑ 158 Zaur Pachulia RC	3.00	8.00
❑ 159 Carlos Delfino RC	3.00	8.00
❑ 160 Brian Cook RC	2.50	6.00

1999-00 Fleer Force

❑ COMPLETE SET (235)	125.00	250.00
❑ COMPLETE SET w/o RC (200)	20.00	40.00
❑ COMMON CARD (1-200)	.20	.50
❑ COMMON ROOKIE (201-235)	2.00	5.00
❑ 1 Vince Carter	.60	1.50
❑ 2 Kobe Bryant	1.50	4.00
❑ 3 Keith Van Horn	.25	.60
❑ 4 Tim Duncan	.60	1.50
❑ 5 Grant Hill	.30	.75
❑ 6 Kevin Garnett	.60	1.50
❑ 7 Anfernee Hardaway	.30	.75
❑ 8 Jason Williams	.30	.75
❑ 9 Paul Pierce	.30	.75
❑ 10 Mookie Blaylock	.20	.50
❑ 11 Shawn Bradley	.20	.50
❑ 12 Kenny Anderson	.25	.60
❑ 13 Chauncey Billups	.30	.75
❑ 14 Elden Campbell	.20	.50
❑ 15 Jason Caffey	.20	.50
❑ 16 Brent Barry	.25	.60
❑ 17 Charles Barkley	.40	1.00
❑ 18 Derek Anderson	.20	.50
❑ 19 Darrick Martin	.20	.50
❑ 20 Michael Curry	.20	.50
❑ 21 Rick Fox	.20	.50
❑ 22 Antonio Davis	.20	.50
❑ 23 Terrell Brandon	.20	.50
❑ 24 P.J. Brown	.20	.50
❑ 25 Toby Bailey	.20	.50
❑ 26 Ray Allen	.30	.75
❑ 27 Brian Grant	.20	.50
❑ 28 Scott Burrell	.20	.50
❑ 29 Tariq Abdul-Wahad	.20	.50
❑ 30 Marcus Camby	.25	.60
❑ 31 John Stockton	.40	1.00
❑ 32 Nick Anderson	.20	.50
❑ 33 Jamie Feick RC	.30	.75
❑ 34 Matt Geiger	.20	.50
❑ 35 Vin Baker	.30	.75
❑ 36 Dee Brown	.20	.50
❑ 37 Shandon Anderson	.20	.50
❑ 38 Vernon Maxwell	.25	.60
❑ 39 Shareef Abdur-Rahim	.25	.60
❑ 40 LaPhonso Ellis	.20	.50
❑ 41 Cedric Ceballos	.20	.50
❑ 42 Tony Battie	.25	.60
❑ 43 Keon Clark	.20	.50
❑ 44 Derrick Coleman	.25	.60
❑ 45 Erick Dampier	.25	.60
❑ 46 Corey Benjamin	.20	.50
❑ 47 Michael Dickerson	.20	.50
❑ 48 Cedric Henderson	.20	.50
❑ 49 Lamond Murray	.20	.50
❑ 50 Jerome Williams	.20	.50
❑ 51 Shaquille O'Neal	.75	2.00
❑ 52 Dale Davis	.20	.50
❑ 53 Dean Garrett	.20	.50
❑ 54 Tim Hardaway	.30	.75
❑ 55 Dennis Rodman	.60	1.50
❑ 56 Sam Cassell	.25	.60
❑ 57 Jim Jackson	.25	.60
❑ 58 Kendall Gill	.20	.50
❑ 59 Eric Williams	.20	.50
❑ 60 Chris Childs	.20	.50
❑ 61 Vlade Divac	.30	.75
❑ 62 Darrell Armstrong	.20	.50
❑ 63 Mario Elie	.20	.50
❑ 64 Jaren Jackson	.20	.50
❑ 65 Dale Ellis	.20	.50
❑ 66 Doug Christie	.25	.60
❑ 67 Howard Eisley	.20	.50
❑ 68 Juwan Howard	.25	.60
❑ 69 Mike Bibby	.30	.75
❑ 70 Alan Henderson	.20	.50
❑ 71 Michael Finley	.30	.75
❑ 72 Dana Barros	.20	.50
❑ 73 Troy Hudson	.30	.75
❑ 74 Ricky Davis	.30	.75
❑ 75 John Amaechi RC	.30	.75
❑ 76 Erick Strickland	.20	.50
❑ 77 Bryce Drew	.20	.50
❑ 78 Shawn Kemp	.30	.75
❑ 79 Tyrone Nesby RC	.30	.75
❑ 80 Lindsey Hunter	.20	.50
❑ 81 Ruben Patterson	.20	.50
❑ 82 Al Harrington	.25	.60
❑ 83 Bobby Jackson	.25	.60
❑ 84 Dan Majerle	.30	.75
❑ 85 Rex Chapman	.20	.50
❑ 86 Dell Curry	.20	.50
❑ 87 Robert Pack	.20	.50
❑ 88 Kerry Kittles	.20	.50
❑ 89 Isaiah Rider	.20	.50
❑ 90 Patrick Ewing	.40	1.00
❑ 91 Lawrence Funderburke	.20	.50
❑ 92 Isaac Austin	.20	.50
❑ 93 Sean Elliott	.30	.75
❑ 94 Larry Hughes	.25	.60
❑ 95 Jelani McCoy	.20	.50
❑ 96 Tracy McGrady	.60	1.50
❑ 97 Jeff Hornacek	.25	.60
❑ 98 Jahidi White	.20	.50
❑ 99 Danny Manning	.20	.50
❑ 100 Roshown McLeod	.20	.50
❑ 101 Steve Nash	.50	1.25
❑ 102 Ron Mercer	.20	.50
❑ 103 Raef LaFrentz	.25	.60
❑ 104 Eddie Jones	.30	.75
❑ 105 Antawn Jamison	.30	.75
❑ 106 Chucky Atkins RC	.40	1.00
❑ 107 Othella Harrington	.20	.50
❑ 108 Brevin Knight	.20	.50
❑ 109 Michael Olowokandi	.20	.50
❑ 110 Christian Laettner	.25	.60
❑ 111 J.R. Reid	.20	.50
❑ 112 Reggie Miller	.30	.75
❑ 113 Lazaro Borrell RC	.30	.75
❑ 114 Jamal Mashburn	.20	.50
❑ 115 Glenn Robinson	.25	.60
❑ 116 Pat Garrity	.20	.50
❑ 117 Stephon Marbury	.30	.75
❑ 118 Arvydas Sabonis	.25	.60
❑ 119 Allan Houston	.25	.60
❑ 120 Peja Stojakovic	.25	.60
❑ 121 Michael Doleac	.20	.50
❑ 122 Avery Johnson	.25	.60
❑ 123 Allen Iverson	.60	1.50
❑ 124 Rashard Lewis	.30	.75
❑ 125 Charles Oakley	.25	.60
❑ 126 Karl Malone	.40	1.00
❑ 127 Tracy Murray	.20	.50
❑ 128 Felipe Lopez	.20	.50
❑ 129 Dikembe Mutombo	.25	.60
❑ 130 Dirk Nowitzki	.50	1.25
❑ 131 Vitaly Potapenko	.20	.50
❑ 132 Antonio McDyess	.25	.60
❑ 133 Anthony Mason	.20	.50
❑ 134 Donyell Marshall	.25	.60
❑ 135 Dickey Simpkins	.20	.50
❑ 136 Cuttino Mobley	.25	.60
❑ 137 Wesley Person	.20	.50
❑ 138 Rodney Rogers	.20	.50
❑ 139 Jerry Stackhouse	.30	.75
❑ 140 Glen Rice	.30	.75
❑ 141 Chris Mullin	.30	.75
❑ 142 Anthony Peeler	.20	.50
❑ 143 Alonzo Mourning	.30	.75
❑ 144 Tom Gugliotta	.20	.50
❑ 145 Tim Thomas	.25	.60
❑ 146 Damon Stoudamire	.30	.75
❑ 147 Jayson Williams	.25	.60
❑ 148 Larry Johnson	.30	.75
❑ 149 Chris Webber	.30	.75
❑ 150 Matt Harpring	.25	.60
❑ 151 David Robinson	.40	1.00
❑ 152 George Lynch	.20	.50
❑ 153 Gary Payton	.30	.75
❑ 154 John Wallace	.20	.50
❑ 155 Greg Ostertag	.20	.50
❑ 156 Mitch Richmond	.25	.60
❑ 157 Cherokee Parks	.20	.50
❑ 158 Steve Smith	.20	.50
❑ 159 Gary Trent	.20	.50
❑ 160 Antoine Walker	.30	.75
❑ 161 Chris Herren RC	.30	.75
❑ 162 Ron Harper	.20	.50
❑ 163 Chris Mills	.20	.50
❑ 164 Fred Hoiberg	.20	.50
❑ 165 Hakeem Olajuwon	.30	.75
❑ 166 Bob Sura	.20	.50
❑ 167 Brian Skinner	.20	.50
❑ 168 Loy Vaught	.20	.50
❑ 169 A.C. Green	.30	.75
❑ 170 Jalen Rose	.25	.60
❑ 171 Joe Smith	.25	.60
❑ 172 Clarence Weatherspoon	.20	.50
❑ 173 Jason Kidd	.50	1.25
❑ 174 Robert Traylor	.20	.50
❑ 175 Rasheed Wallace	.30	.75
❑ 176 Latrell Sprewell	.25	.60
❑ 177 Corliss Williamson	.20	.50
❑ 178 Bo Outlaw	.20	.50
❑ 179 Malik Rose	.20	.50
❑ 180 Nazr Mohammed	.20	.50
❑ 181 Eric Murdock	.20	.50
❑ 182 Kevin Willis	.20	.50
❑ 183 Bryon Russell	.20	.50
❑ 184 Bryant Reeves	.20	.50
❑ 185 Rod Strickland	.20	.50
❑ 186 Samaki Walker	.20	.50
❑ 187 Nick Van Exel	.25	.60
❑ 188 David Wesley	.20	.50
❑ 189 John Starks	.30	.75
❑ 190 Toni Kukoc	.30	.75
❑ 191 Scottie Pippen	.50	1.25
❑ 192 Johnny Newman	.20	.50
❑ 193 Maurice Taylor	.25	.60
❑ 194 Rik Smits	.30	.75
❑ 195 Clifford Robinson	.20	50
❑ 196 Bonzi Wells	.20	.50
❑ 197 Charlie Ward	.20	.50
❑ 198 Detlef Schrempf	.25	.60
❑ 199 Theo Ratliff	.25	.60
❑ 200 Kelvin Cato	.20	.50
❑ 201 Ron Artest RC	8.00	20.00
❑ 202 William Avery RC	2.00	5.00
❑ 203 Elton Brand RC	6.00	15.00
❑ 204 Baron Davis RC	8.00	20.00
❑ 205 Jumaine Jones RC	2.00	5.00
❑ 206 Andre Miller RC	6.00	15.00
❑ 207 Eddie Robinson RC	2.00	5.00
❑ 208 James Posey RC	3.00	8.00
❑ 209 Jason Terry RC	5.00	12.00
❑ 210 Kenny Thomas RC	2.00	5.00
❑ 211 Steve Francis RC	6.00	15.00
❑ 212 Wally Szczerbiak RC	6.00	15.00
❑ 213 Richard Hamilton RC	6.00	15.00
❑ 214 Jonathan Bender RC	2.00	5.00
❑ 215 Shawn Marion RC	6.00	15.00
❑ 216 A.Radojevic RC	2.00	5.00
❑ 217 Tim James RC	2.00	5.00
❑ 218 Trajan Langdon RC	2.00	5.00
❑ 219 Lamar Odom RC	6.00	15.00
❑ 220 Corey Maggette RC	6.00	15.00
❑ 221 Dion Glover RC	2.00	5.00
❑ 222 Cal Bowdler RC	2.00	5.00
❑ 223 Vonteego Cummings RC	2.00	5.00
❑ 224 Devean George RC	3.00	8.00
❑ 225 Anthony Carter RC	4.00	10.00
❑ 226 Laron Profit RC	2.00	5.00
❑ 227 Quincy Lewis RC	2.00	5.00
❑ 228 John Celestand RC	2.00	5.00
❑ 229 Obinna Ekezie RC	2.00	5.00
❑ 230 Scott Padgett RC	2.00	5.00
❑ 231 Michael Ruffin RC	2.00	5.00
❑ 232 Jeff Foster RC	2.50	6.00

❑ 233 Jermaine Jackson RC	2.00	5.00
❑ 234 Adrian Griffin RC	2.00	5.00
❑ 235 Todd MacCulloch RC	2.00	5.00
❑ NNO V.Carter Sgt.	8.00	20.00
❑ NNO V.Carter Sgt. AU	40.00	80.00

2001-02 Fleer Force

❑ COMPLETE SET (180)	100.00	250.00
❑ COMPLETE SET w/o SP's (150)	20.00	50.00
❑ COMMON CARD (1-180)	.08	.25
❑ COMMON ROOKIE (101-130)	1.00	2.50
❑ 1 Vince Carter	.60	1.50
❑ 2 Allan Houston	.25	.60
❑ 3 Steve Francis	.30	.75
❑ 4 Karl Malone	.40	1.00
❑ 5 Joe Smith	.20	.50
❑ 6 Raef LaFrentz	.20	.50
❑ 7 David Robinson	.40	1.00
❑ 8 Tim Thomas	.20	.50
❑ 9 Antonio McDyess	.25	.60
❑ 10 Steve Smith	.25	.60
❑ 11 Eddie Jones	.25	.60
❑ 12 Jumaine Jones	.20	.50
❑ 13 Derek Anderson	.25	.60
❑ 14 Shaquille O'Neal	.75	2.00
❑ 15 Eddie Robinson	.20	.50
❑ 16 Stephon Marbury	.30	.75
❑ 17 Darius Miles	.20	.50
❑ 18 Toni Kukoc	.25	.60
❑ 19 Latrell Sprewell	.25	.60
❑ 20 Wang Zhizhi	.25	.60
❑ 21 Tim Duncan	.60	1.50
❑ 22 Eddie House	.20	.50
❑ 23 Chris Mihm	.20	.50
❑ 24 Rasheed Wallace	.30	.75
❑ 25 Kobe Bryant	1.50	4.00
❑ 26 Kenny Thomas	.20	.50
❑ 27 John Stockton	.40	1.00
❑ 28 Mike Bibby	.25	.60
❑ 29 Larry Hughes	.25	.60
❑ 30 Antonio Davis	.20	.50
❑ 31 Ray Allen	.30	.75
❑ 32 Corliss Williamson	.25	.60
❑ 33 Desmond Mason	.25	.60
❑ 34 Sam Cassell	.25	.60
❑ 35 Dirk Nowitzki	.50	1.25
❑ 36 Chris Webber	.30	.75
❑ 37 Michael Dickerson	.20	.50
❑ 38 Ron Mercer	.20	.50
❑ 39 Iakovos Tsakalidis	.20	.50
❑ 40 Derek Fisher	.25	.60
❑ 41 Baron Davis	.30	.75
❑ 42 Allen Iverson	.60	1.50
❑ 43 Avery Johnson	.25	.60
❑ 44 Courtney Alexander	.20	.50
❑ 45 Alonzo Mourning	.30	.75
❑ 46 Steve Nash	.50	1.25
❑ 47 Hedo Turkoglu	.25	.60
❑ 48 Jason Williams	.25	.60
❑ 49 David Wesley	.20	.50
❑ 50 Dikembe Mutombo	.25	.60
❑ 51 LaPhonso Ellis	.25	.60
❑ 52 Trajan Langdon	.20	.50
❑ 53 Damon Stoudamire	.25	.60
❑ 54 Rick Fox	.25	.60
❑ 55 Paul Pierce	.30	.75
❑ 56 Tracy McGrady	.60	1.50
❑ 57 Lamar Odom	.30	.75
❑ 58 Antoine Walker	.25	.60
❑ 59 Mike Miller	.25	.60
❑ 60 Jermaine O'Neal	.30	.75
❑ 61 Michael Jordan	6.00	15.00
❑ 62 Jason Kidd	.50	1.25
❑ 63 Marc Jackson	.20	.50
❑ 64 Hakeem Olajuwon	.40	1.00
❑ 65 Kevin Garnett	.60	1.50
❑ 66 Nick Van Exel	.25	.60
❑ 67 Rashard Lewis	.30	.75
❑ 68 Brian Grant	.20	.50
❑ 69 Keith Van Horn	.25	.60
❑ 70 Grant Hill	.30	.75
❑ 71 Reggie Miller	.30	.75
❑ 72 Richard Hamilton	.25	.60
❑ 73 Marcus Camby	.25	.60
❑ 74 Clifford Robinson	.20	.50
❑ 75 Gary Payton	.30	.75
❑ 76 Andre Miller	.25	.60
❑ 77 Bonzi Wells	.25	.60
❑ 78 Stromile Swift	.20	.50
❑ 79 Marcus Fizer	.20	.50
❑ 80 Shawn Marion	.30	.75
❑ 81 Elton Brand	.30	.75
❑ 82 Jamal Mashburn	.25	.60
❑ 83 Aaron McKie	.20	.50
❑ 84 Corey Maggette	.25	.60
❑ 85 Jason Terry	.30	.75
❑ 86 Anfernee Hardaway	.30	.75
❑ 87 Antawn Jamison	.30	.75
❑ 88 Morris Peterson	.25	.60
❑ 89 Wally Szczerbiak	.25	.60
❑ 90 Jerry Stackhouse	.25	.60
❑ 91 Shareef Abdur-Rahim	.25	.60
❑ 92 Glenn Robinson	.25	.60
❑ 93 Michael Finley	.30	.75
❑ 94 Peja Stojakovic	.25	.60
❑ 95 Jalen Rose	.25	.60
❑ 96 Theo Ratliff	.20	.50
❑ 97 Kurt Thomas	.20	.50
❑ 98 Cuttino Mobley	.25	.60
❑ 99 DeShawn Stevenson	.20	.50
❑ 100 Terrell Brandon	.20	.50
❑ 101 Kwame Brown RC	1.25	3.00
❑ 102 Tyson Chandler RC	2.00	5.00
❑ 103 Pau Gasol RC	4.00	10.00
❑ 104 Eddy Curry RC	1.50	4.00
❑ 105 Jason Richardson RC	2.00	5.00
❑ 106 Shane Battier RC	1.50	4.00
❑ 107 Eddie Griffin RC	1.00	2.50
❑ 108 DeSagana Diop RC	1.00	2.50
❑ 109 Rodney White RC	1.00	2.50
❑ 110 Joe Johnson RC	2.50	6.00
❑ 111 Kedrick Brown RC	1.00	2.50
❑ 112 Vladimir Radmanovic RC	1.25	3.00
❑ 113 Richard Jefferson RC	2.50	6.00
❑ 114 Troy Murphy RC	2.00	5.00
❑ 115 Steven Hunter RC	1.00	2.50
❑ 116 Kirk Haston RC	1.00	2.50
❑ 117 Michael Bradley RC	1.00	2.50
❑ 118 Jason Collins RC	1.00	2.50
❑ 119 Zach Randolph RC	2.50	6.00
❑ 120 Brendan Haywood RC	1.25	3.00
❑ 121 Joseph Forte RC	1.00	2.50
❑ 122 Jeryl Sasser RC	1.00	2.50
❑ 123 Brandon Armstrong RC	1.00	2.50
❑ 124 Andrei Kirilenko RC	2.50	6.00
❑ 125 Gerald Wallace RC	2.50	6.00
❑ 126 Samuel Dalembert RC	1.25	3.00
❑ 127 Jamaal Tinsley RC	1.25	3.00
❑ 128 Tony Parker RC	4.00	10.00
❑ 129 Loren Woods RC	1.00	2.50
❑ 130 Primoz Brezec RC	1.25	3.00
❑ 131 Dion Glover	.20	.50
❑ 132 Moochie Norris	.20	.50
❑ 133 Mark Jackson	.25	.60
❑ 134 Bryon Russell	.20	.50
❑ 135 Danny Fortson	.20	.50
❑ 136 Kenyon Martin	.30	.75
❑ 137 Alvin Williams	.20	.50
❑ 138 Erick Dampier	.20	.50
❑ 139 Clarence Weatherspoon	.20	.50
❑ 140 Brent Barry	.20	.50
❑ 141 Lamond Murray	.20	.50
❑ 142 Lindsey Hunter	.20	.50
❑ 143 Speedy Claxton	.20	.50
❑ 144 James Posey	.20	.50
❑ 145 Anthony Mason	.20	.50
❑ 146 Mateen Cleaves	.20	.50
❑ 147 Kenny Anderson	.25	.60
❑ 148 Travis Best	.20	.50
❑ 149 Patrick Ewing	.40	1.00
❑ 150 Dana Barros	.20	.50
❑ 151 Lorenzen Wright	.20	.50
❑ 152 Rodney Rogers	.20	.50
❑ 153 Brad Miller	.25	.60
❑ 154 Anthony Peeler	.20	.50
❑ 155 Antonio Daniels	.20	.50
❑ 156 Tim Hardaway	.25	.60
❑ 157 Quentin Richardson	.25	.60
❑ 158 Darrell Armstrong	.20	.50
❑ 159 Nazr Mohammad	.20	.50
❑ 160 Todd MacCulloch	.20	.50
❑ 161 Ruben Patterson	.20	.50
❑ 162 Wesley Person	.20	.50
❑ 163 Jeff McInnis	.20	.50
❑ 164 Vin Baker	.25	.60
❑ 165 George McCloud	.20	.50
❑ 166 Chris Gatling	.20	.50
❑ 167 Derrick Coleman	.25	.60
❑ 168 Elden Campbell	.20	.50
❑ 169 Glen Rice	.25	.60
❑ 170 Donyell Marshall	.20	.50
❑ 171 Juwan Howard	.25	.60
❑ 172 Mitch Richmond	.25	.60
❑ 173 Tom Gugliotta	.20	.50
❑ 174 Chucky Atkins	.20	.50
❑ 175 Michael Redd	.30	.75
❑ 176 Malik Rose	.20	.50
❑ 177 Lee Nailon	.20	.50
❑ 178 Al Harrington	.25	.60
❑ 179 Matt Harpring	.25	.60
❑ 180 Tyronn Lue	.20	.50

2000-01 Fleer Futures

❑ COMPLETE SET (250)	40.00	80.00
❑ COMPLETE SET w/o RCs (200)	12.50	25.00
❑ COMMON CARD (1-200)	.07	.20
❑ COMMON EVEN RC (201-250)	.25	.60
❑ COMMON ODD RC (201-250)	.60	1.50
❑ 1 Vince Carter	.50	1.25
❑ 2 Dan Majerle	.20	.50
❑ 3 George McCloud	.15	.40
❑ 4 Radoslav Nesterovic	.15	.40
❑ 5 Corey Maggette	.20	.50
❑ 6 Derek Anderson	.20	.50
❑ 7 Ray Allen	.25	.60
❑ 8 Greg Ostertag	.15	.40
❑ 9 Cedric Ceballos	.15	.40
❑ 10 Danny Fortson	.15	.40
❑ 11 Roshown McLeod	.15	.40
❑ 12 Christian Laettner	.15	.40
❑ 13 Avery Johnson	.20	.50
❑ 14 Clarence Weatherspoon	.15	.40
❑ 15 Michael Curry	.15	.40
❑ 16 Chris Whitney	.15	.40
❑ 17 Anthony Mason	.15	.40
❑ 18 Antonio McDyess	.20	.50
❑ 19 Vitaly Potapenko	.15	.40
❑ 20 Shaquille O'Neal	.60	1.50
❑ 21 David Robinson	.30	.75
❑ 22 Tyrone Hill	.15	.40
❑ 23 Otis Thorpe	.20	.50
❑ 24 Reggie Miller	.25	.60
❑ 25 Kevin Garnett	.50	1.25
❑ 26 Michael Dickerson	.15	.40
❑ 27 John Amaechi	.15	.40
❑ 28 Jason Kidd	.40	1.00
❑ 29 Ron Artest	.25	.60
❑ 30 Muggsy Bogues	.20	.50
❑ 31 Antawn Jamison	.25	.60
❑ 32 Brian Grant	.15	.40
❑ 33 Stephon Marbury	.25	.60
❑ 34 William Avery	.15	.40
❑ 35 Paul Pierce	.25	.60
❑ 36 Marcus Camby	.20	.50
❑ 37 Kevin Willis	.15	.40
❑ 38 Dikembe Mutombo	.20	.50
❑ 39 Rashard Lewis	.25	.60
❑ 40 Allan Houston	.20	.50
❑ 41 Hakeem Olajuwon	.30	.75
❑ 42 Rod Strickland	.20	.50
❑ 43 Derrick Coleman	.20	.50

❑ 44 Tariq Abdul-Wahad	.15	.40
❑ 45 Terrell Brandon	.15	.40
❑ 46 Michael Olowokandi	.15	.40
❑ 47 Robert Horry	.20	.50
❑ 48 Kelvin Cato	.15	.40
❑ 49 Eric Williams	.15	.40
❑ 50 Glen Rice	.20	.50
❑ 51 Carlos Rogers	.15	.40
❑ 52 Allen Iverson	.50	1.25
❑ 53 P.J. Brown	.15	.40
❑ 54 Jalen Rose	.20	.50
❑ 55 Damon Stoudamire	.20	.50
❑ 56 Damon Jones RC	.15	.40
❑ 57 Darrell Armstrong	.15	.40
❑ 58 Samaki Walker	.15	.40
❑ 59 John Stockton	.30	.75
❑ 60 Chucky Atkins	.15	.40
❑ 61 Rasheed Wallace	.25	.60
❑ 62 Jason Terry	.25	.60
❑ 63 Aaron Williams	.15	.40
❑ 64 Steve Nash	.40	1.00
❑ 65 Antoine Walker	.20	.50
❑ 66 Patrick Ewing	.30	.75
❑ 67 Cuttino Mobley	.20	.50
❑ 68 Aaron McKie	.15	.40
❑ 69 Jamal Mashburn	.20	.50
❑ 70 Scottie Pippen	.40	1.00
❑ 71 Bryant Reeves	.15	.40
❑ 72 Isaiah Rider	.20	.50
❑ 73 Jaren Jackson	.15	.40
❑ 74 Lindsey Hunter	.15	.40
❑ 75 Jacque Vaughn	.15	.40
❑ 76 Travis Best	.15	.40
❑ 77 Vinny Del Negro	.15	.40
❑ 78 Othella Harrington	.15	.40
❑ 79 Michael Finley	.25	.60
❑ 80 Brent Barry	.15	.40
❑ 81 Brevin Knight	.15	.40
❑ 82 Kurt Thomas	.15	.40
❑ 83 Mark Jackson	.20	.50
❑ 84 Richard Hamilton	.20	.50
❑ 85 Anthony Carter	.15	.40
❑ 86 Matt Harpring	.20	.50
❑ 87 Bobby Jackson	.15	.40
❑ 88 Jerome Williams	.15	.40
❑ 89 Jahidi White	.15	.40
❑ 90 Lorenzen Wright	.15	.40
❑ 91 Kerry Kittles	.20	.50
❑ 92 Anthony Peeler	.15	.40
❑ 93 Kenny Anderson	.20	.50
❑ 94 Latrell Sprewell	.20	.50
❑ 95 Maurice Taylor	.15	.40
❑ 96 Toni Kukoc	.20	.50
❑ 97 Eddie Robinson	.15	.40
❑ 98 Voshon Lenard	.15	.40
❑ 99 Sam Mitchell	.15	.40
❑ 100 Isaac Austin	.15	.40
❑ 101 Michael Doleac	.15	.40
❑ 102 Andre Miller	.20	.50
❑ 103 Jason Williams	.20	.50
❑ 104 Charles Oakley	.20	.50
❑ 105 Mitch Richmond	.20	.50
❑ 106 Bruce Bowen	.15	.40
❑ 107 Keith Van Horn	.20	.50
❑ 108 Wally Szczerbiak	.20	.50
❑ 109 Tony Battie	.15	.40
❑ 110 Larry Johnson	.20	.50
❑ 111 Shandon Anderson	.15	.40
❑ 112 Sam Cassell	.20	.50
❑ 113 David Wesley	.15	.40
❑ 114 James Posey	.15	.40
❑ 115 Bonzi Wells	.15	.40
❑ 116 Mike Bibby	.20	.50
❑ 117 Andrew DeClercq	.15	.40
❑ 118 Clifford Robinson	.15	.40
❑ 119 Corliss Williamson	.20	.50
❑ 120 Antonio Davis	.15	.40
❑ 121 Eddie Jones	.20	.50
❑ 122 Jamie Feick	.15	.40
❑ 123 Anfernee Hardaway	.25	.60
❑ 124 Adrian Griffin	.15	.40
❑ 125 Erick Strickland	.15	.40
❑ 126 Doug Christie	.15	.40
❑ 127 Scot Pollard	.15	.40
❑ 128 Sam Perkins	.15	.40
❑ 129 Raef LaFrentz	.15	.40
❑ 130 Dale Davis	.15	.40
❑ 131 Tyrone Nesby	.15	.40
❑ 132 Rick Fox	.20	.50
❑ 133 Tom Gugliotta	.15	.40
❑ 134 Glenn Robinson	.20	.50
❑ 135 Quincy Lewis	.15	.40
❑ 136 Austin Croshere	.15	.40
❑ 137 Shawn Kemp	.25	.60
❑ 138 Lamar Odom	.25	.60
❑ 139 Tim Duncan	.50	1.25
❑ 140 Tim Thomas	.15	.40
❑ 141 Bryon Russell	.15	.40
❑ 142 Jermaine O'Neal	.25	.60
❑ 143 Erick Dampier	.15	.40
❑ 144 Shareef Abdur-Rahim	.20	.50
❑ 145 Bo Outlaw	.15	.40
❑ 146 Gary Payton	.25	.60
❑ 147 Chris Gatling	.15	.40
❑ 148 Vlade Divac	.20	.50
❑ 149 Ben Wallace	.20	.50
❑ 150 Larry Hughes	.20	.50
❑ 151 Ron Mercer	.15	.40
❑ 152 Karl Malone	.30	.75
❑ 153 Jonathan Bender	.15	.40
❑ 154 Mookie Blaylock	.20	.50
❑ 155 Jim Jackson	.15	.40
❑ 156 Chris Crawford	.15	.40
❑ 157 Vin Baker	.20	.50
❑ 158 Lamond Murray	.15	.40
❑ 159 Charlie Ward	.15	.40
❑ 160 Steve Francis	.25	.60
❑ 161 Cherokee Parks	.15	.40
❑ 162 Baron Davis	.25	.60
❑ 163 Keon Clark	.15	.40
❑ 164 Ruben Patterson	.15	.40
❑ 165 Tracy McGrady	.50	1.25
❑ 166 Antonio Daniels	.15	.40
❑ 167 Scott Williams	.15	.40
❑ 168 John Starks	.15	.40
❑ 169 Jerry Stackhouse	.20	.50
❑ 170 Vonteego Cummings	.15	.40
❑ 171 LaPhonso Ellis	.20	.50
❑ 172 Dirk Nowitzki	.40	1.00
❑ 173 Horace Grant	.20	.50
❑ 174 Wesley Person	.15	.40
❑ 175 Peja Stojakovic	.20	.50
❑ 176 Eric Snow	.15	.40
❑ 177 Juwan Howard	.20	.50
❑ 178 Tim Hardaway	.20	.50
❑ 179 Kendall Gill	.15	.40
❑ 180 Chauncey Billups	.25	.60
❑ 181 Kobe Bryant	1.25	3.00
❑ 182 Sean Elliott	.20	.50
❑ 183 Donyell Marshall	.15	.40
❑ 184 Al Harrington	.20	.50
❑ 185 Arvydas Sabonis	.20	.50
❑ 186 Grant Hill	.25	.60
❑ 187 Malik Rose	.15	.40
❑ 188 Nazr Mohammed	.15	.40
❑ 189 Elden Campbell	.15	.40
❑ 190 Nick Van Exel	.20	.50
❑ 191 Steve Smith	.20	.50
❑ 192 Sean Rooks	.15	.40
❑ 193 Monty Williams	.15	.40
❑ 194 Elton Brand	.25	.60
❑ 195 Chris Webber	.25	.60
❑ 196 Mikki Moore	.15	.40
❑ 197 Chris Mills	.15	.40
❑ 198 Alan Henderson	.15	.40
❑ 199 Shawn Bradley	.15	.40
❑ 200 Shawn Marion	.25	.60
❑ 201 Hedo Turkoglu RC	1.50	4.00
❑ 202 Iakovos Tsakalidis RC	.25	.60
❑ 203 Kenyon Martin RC	1.50	4.00
❑ 204 Mamadou N'Diaye RC	.25	.60
❑ 205 Stromile Swift RC	.75	2.00
❑ 206 Pepe Sanchez RC	.25	.60
❑ 207 Chris Mihm RC	.60	1.50
❑ 208 Lavor Postell RC	.25	.60
❑ 209 Marcus Fizer RC	.60	1.50
❑ 210 Ruben Garces RC	.25	.60
❑ 211 Courtney Alexander RC	.60	1.50
❑ 212 A.J. Guyton RC	.25	.60
❑ 213 Darius Miles RC	.75	2.00
❑ 214 Ademola Okulaja RC	.25	.60
❑ 215 Jerome Moiso RC	.60	1.50
❑ 216 Khalid El-Amin RC	.25	.60
❑ 217 Joel Przybilla RC	.60	1.50
❑ 218 Mike Smith RC	.25	.60
❑ 219 DerMarr Johnson RC	.60	1.50
❑ 220 Soumaila Samake RC	.25	.60
❑ 221 Mike Miller RC	1.00	2.50
❑ 222 Eddie House RC	.25	.60
❑ 223 Quentin Richardson RC	.75	2.00
❑ 224 Eduardo Najera RC	.25	.60
❑ 225 Morris Peterson RC	1.00	2.50
❑ 226 Hanno Mottola RC	.25	.60
❑ 227 Speedy Claxton RC	.60	1.50
❑ 228 Ruben Wolkowyski RC	.25	.60
❑ 229 Keyon Dooling RC	.60	1.50
❑ 230 Olumide Oyedeji RC	.25	.60
❑ 231 Mark Madsen RC	.60	1.50
❑ 232 Mike Penberthy RC	.25	.60
❑ 233 Mateen Cleaves RC	.60	1.50
❑ 234 Brian Cardinal RC	.25	.60
❑ 235 Etan Thomas RC	.60	1.50
❑ 236 Garth Joseph RC	.25	.60
❑ 237 Jason Collier RC	.60	1.50
❑ 238 Paul McPherson RC	.25	.60
❑ 239 Erick Barkley RC	.60	1.50
❑ 240 Stephen Jackson RC	.40	1.00
❑ 241 Desmond Mason RC	.75	2.00
❑ 242 Jason Hart RC	.25	.60
❑ 243 Jamal Crawford RC	1.00	2.50
❑ 244 Daniel Santiago RC	.60	1.50
❑ 245 DeShawn Stevenson RC	.60	1.50
❑ 246 Stanislav Medvedenko RC	.25	.60
❑ 247 Donnell Harvey RC	.60	1.50
❑ 248 Chris Porter RC	.25	.60
❑ 249 Jamaal Magloire RC	.60	1.50
❑ 250 Dalibor Bagaric RC	.25	.60

2000-01 Fleer Game Time

❑ COMPLETE SET w/o RC (90)	12.50	25.00
❑ COMMON CARD (1-90)	.08	.25
❑ COMMON ROOKIE (91-120)	.60	1.50
❑ 1 Vince Carter	.60	1.50
❑ 2 Raef LaFrentz	.20	.50
❑ 3 Kobe Bryant	1.50	4.00
❑ 4 Toni Kukoc	.25	.60
❑ 5 Bonzi Wells	.20	.50
❑ 6 Rashard Lewis	.30	.75
❑ 7 Karl Malone	.40	1.00
❑ 8 Juwan Howard	.25	.60
❑ 9 Lindsey Hunter	.20	.50
❑ 10 Alonzo Mourning	.30	.75
❑ 11 Larry Hughes	.25	.60
❑ 12 Austin Croshere	.20	.50
❑ 13 Charles Oakley	.25	.60
❑ 14 Patrick Ewing	.40	1.00
❑ 15 Vlade Divac	.25	.60
❑ 16 Michael Finley	.30	.75
❑ 17 Tim Hardaway	.25	.60
❑ 18 Jason Kidd	.50	1.25
❑ 19 Cal Bowdler	.20	.50
❑ 20 Dirk Nowitzki	.50	1.25
❑ 21 Terrell Brandon	.20	.50
❑ 22 Allan Houston	.25	.60
❑ 23 Theo Ratliff	.20	.50
❑ 24 Chris Webber	.30	.75
❑ 25 Shawn Kemp	.30	.75
❑ 26 Jalen Rose	.25	.60
❑ 27 Bryon Russell	.20	.50
❑ 28 Jahidi White	.20	.50
❑ 29 Trajan Langdon	.20	.50
❑ 30 Baron Davis	.30	.75
❑ 31 Cuttino Mobley	.25	.60
❑ 32 Wally Szczerbiak	.25	.60
❑ 33 Michael Dickerson	.20	.50
❑ 34 Andre Miller	.25	.60
❑ 35 Michael Olowokandi	.20	.50
❑ 36 Ray Allen	.30	.75
❑ 37 Latrell Sprewell	.25	.60
❑ 38 Jason Williams	.25	.60
❑ 39 Mikki Moore	.20	.50
❑ 40 Shawn Marion	.30	.75
❑ 41 Radoslav Nesterovic	.20	.50
❑ 42 Ron Artest	.30	.75

❑ 43 Vonteego Cummings	.20	.50
❑ 44 Anfernee Hardaway	.30	.75
❑ 45 Jerome Williams	.20	.50
❑ 46 John Stockton	.40	1.00
❑ 47 Antawn Jamison	.30	.75
❑ 48 Grant Hill	.30	.75
❑ 49 Elden Campbell	.20	.50
❑ 50 Steve Francis	.30	.75
❑ 51 Jamie Feick	.20	.50
❑ 52 Gary Payton	.30	.75
❑ 53 Elton Brand	.30	.75
❑ 54 Eddie Jones	.25	.60
❑ 55 Tom Gugliotta	.20	.50
❑ 56 Richard Hamilton	.25	.60
❑ 57 Dion Glover	.20	.50
❑ 58 Shaquille O'Neal	.75	2.00
❑ 59 Kevin Garnett	.60	1.50
❑ 60 Paul Pierce	.30	.75
❑ 61 Brian Grant	.20	.50
❑ 62 Tim Thomas	.20	.50
❑ 63 Tracy McGrady	.60	1.50
❑ 64 Jonathan Bender	.20	.50
❑ 65 Adrian Griffin	.20	.50
❑ 66 Lamar Odom	.30	.75
❑ 67 Rasheed Wallace	.30	.75
❑ 68 Mike Bibby	.25	.60
❑ 69 Glenn Robinson	.25	.60
❑ 70 Eddie Robinson	.20	.50
❑ 71 Robert Horry	.25	.60
❑ 72 Jerry Stackhouse	.25	.60
❑ 73 Stephon Marbury	.30	.75
❑ 74 Marcus Camby	.25	.60
❑ 75 Scottie Pippen	.50	1.25
❑ 76 David Robinson	.40	1.00
❑ 77 Jason Terry	.30	.75
❑ 78 Reggie Miller	.30	.75
❑ 79 Larry Johnson	.25	.60
❑ 80 Antonio Daniels	.20	.50
❑ 81 Shareef Abdur-Rahim	.25	.60
❑ 82 Ruben Patterson	.20	.50
❑ 83 Nick Van Exel	.25	.60
❑ 84 Keith Van Horn	.25	.60
❑ 85 Antonio Davis	.20	.50
❑ 86 Antoine Walker	.25	.60
❑ 87 Allen Iverson	.60	1.50
❑ 88 Antonio McDyess	.25	.60
❑ 89 Tim Duncan	.60	1.50
❑ 90 Hakeem Olajuwon	.40	1.00
❑ 91 Jamaal Magloire RC	.60	1.50
❑ 92 DerMarr Johnson RC	.60	1.50
❑ 93 Jerome Moiso RC	.60	1.50
❑ 94 Marcus Fizer RC	.60	1.50
❑ 95 Jamal Crawford RC	1.00	2.50
❑ 96 Chris Mihm RC	.60	1.50
❑ 97 Donnell Harvey RC	.60	1.50
❑ 98 Courtney Alexander RC	.60	1.50
❑ 99 Etan Thomas RC	.60	1.50
❑ 100 Mamadou N'Diaye RC	.60	1.50
❑ 101 Mateen Cleaves RC	.60	1.50
❑ 102 Chris Porter RC	.60	1.50
❑ 103 Jason Collier RC	.60	1.50
❑ 104 Keyon Dooling RC	.60	1.50
❑ 105 Darius Miles RC	.75	2.00
❑ 106 Mark Madsen RC	.60	1.50
❑ 107 Eddie House RC	.60	1.50
❑ 108 Joel Przybilla RC	.60	1.50
❑ 109 Kenyon Martin RC	1.50	4.00
❑ 110 Mike Miller RC	1.00	2.50
❑ 111 Speedy Claxton RC	.60	1.50
❑ 112 Iakovos Tsakalidis RC	.60	1.50
❑ 113 Erick Barkley RC	.60	1.50
❑ 114 Hedo Turkoglu RC	1.50	4.00
❑ 115 Eduardo Najera RC	.60	1.50
❑ 116 Desmond Mason RC	.75	2.00
❑ 117 Morris Peterson RC	1.00	2.50
❑ 118 DeShawn Stevenson RC	.60	1.50
❑ 119 Stromile Swift RC	.75	2.00
❑ 120 Mike Smith RC	.60	1.50

2000-01 Fleer Genuine

❑ COMPLETE SET w/o RC (100)	20.00	40.00
❑ COMMON CARD (1-100)	.25	.60
❑ COMMON ROOKIE (101-130)	1.50	4.00
❑ 1 Vince Carter	.75	2.00
❑ 2 Glenn Robinson	.30	.75
❑ 3 Rasheed Wallace	.40	1.00
❑ 4 Michael Dickerson	.25	.60
❑ 5 Mikki Moore	.25	.60
❑ 6 Wally Szczerbiak	.30	.75
❑ 7 Shawn Marion	.40	1.00
❑ 8 Dan Majerle	.30	.75
❑ 9 Trajan Langdon	.25	.60
❑ 10 Chauncey Billups	.40	1.00
❑ 11 Jason Kidd	.60	1.50
❑ 12 Derrick Coleman	.30	.75
❑ 13 Jason Terry	.40	1.00
❑ 14 Eddie Jones	.30	.75
❑ 15 Scottie Pippen	.60	1.50
❑ 16 Mike Bibby	.30	.75
❑ 17 Ron Mercer	.25	.60
❑ 18 Hakeem Olajuwon	.50	1.25
❑ 19 Patrick Ewing	.50	1.25
❑ 20 Ruben Patterson	.25	.60
❑ 21 Kenny Anderson	.30	.75
❑ 22 Alonzo Mourning	.40	1.00
❑ 23 Steve Smith	.30	.75
❑ 24 Juwan Howard	.30	.75
❑ 25 Antoine Walker	.30	.75
❑ 26 Kobe Bryant	2.00	5.00
❑ 27 Chris Webber	.40	1.00
❑ 28 Mitch Richmond	.30	.75
❑ 29 Paul Pierce	.40	1.00
❑ 30 Shaquille O'Neal	1.00	2.50
❑ 31 Jason Williams	.30	.75
❑ 32 Richard Hamilton	.30	.75
❑ 33 Michael Finley	.40	1.00
❑ 34 Jalen Rose	.30	.75
❑ 35 Grant Hill	.40	1.00
❑ 36 John Stockton	.50	1.25
❑ 37 Vitaly Potapenko	.25	.60
❑ 38 Glen Rice	.30	.75
❑ 39 Vlade Divac	.30	.75
❑ 40 Jahidi White	.25	.60
❑ 41 Baron Davis	.40	1.00
❑ 42 Michael Olowokandi	.25	.60
❑ 43 Tim Duncan	.75	2.00
❑ 44 Rod Strickland	.30	.75
❑ 45 Jamal Mashburn	.30	.75
❑ 46 Lamar Odom	.40	1.00
❑ 47 David Robinson	.50	1.25
❑ 48 Travis Best	.25	.60
❑ 49 Raef LaFrentz	.25	.60
❑ 50 Keith Van Horn	.30	.75
❑ 51 Vonteego Cummings	.25	.60
❑ 52 Jerome Williams	.25	.60
❑ 53 Kevin Garnett	.75	2.00
❑ 54 Anfernee Hardaway	.40	1.00
❑ 55 Antonio McDyess	.30	.75
❑ 56 Reggie Miller	.40	1.00
❑ 57 Tracy McGrady	.75	2.00
❑ 58 Bryon Russell	.25	.60
❑ 59 Nick Van Exel	.30	.75
❑ 60 Allen Iverson	.75	2.00
❑ 61 Karl Malone	.50	1.25
❑ 62 David Wesley	.25	.60
❑ 63 Bob Sura	.25	.60
❑ 64 Stephon Marbury	.40	1.00
❑ 65 Antonio Daniels	.25	.60
❑ 66 Shawn Kemp	.40	1.00
❑ 67 Cuttino Mobley	.30	.75
❑ 68 Marcus Camby	.30	.75
❑ 69 Gary Payton	.40	1.00
❑ 70 Dikembe Mutombo	.30	.75
❑ 71 Tim Hardaway	.30	.75
❑ 72 Bonzi Wells	.25	.60
❑ 73 Shareef Abdur-Rahim	.30	.75
❑ 74 Brevin Knight	.25	.60
❑ 75 Steve Francis	.40	1.00
❑ 76 Allan Houston	.30	.75
❑ 77 Dion Glover	.25	.60
❑ 78 Dirk Nowitzki	.60	1.50
❑ 79 Jonathan Bender	.25	.60
❑ 80 Darrell Armstrong	.25	.60
❑ 81 Antonio Davis	.25	.60
❑ 82 Jerry Stackhouse	.30	.75
❑ 83 Terrell Brandon	.25	.60
❑ 84 Tom Gugliotta	.25	.60
❑ 85 Sean Elliott	.30	.75
❑ 86 Elton Brand	.40	1.00
❑ 87 Larry Hughes	.30	.75
❑ 88 Kerry Kittles	.30	.75
❑ 89 Vin Baker	.30	.75
❑ 90 Donyell Marshall	.25	.60
❑ 91 Tim Thomas	.25	.60
❑ 92 Toni Kukoc	.30	.75
❑ 93 Charles Oakley	.30	.75
❑ 94 Andre Miller	.30	.75
❑ 95 Austin Croshere	.25	.60
❑ 96 Latrell Sprewell	.30	.75
❑ 97 Mark Jackson	.30	.75
❑ 98 Antawn Jamison	.40	1.00
❑ 99 Ray Allen	.40	1.00
❑ 100 Theo Ratliff	.25	.60
❑ 101 Chris Mihm RC	1.50	4.00
❑ 102 Mateen Cleaves RC	1.50	4.00
❑ 103 Etan Thomas RC	1.50	4.00
❑ 104 Morris Peterson RC	2.50	6.00
❑ 105 Jamal Crawford RC	2.50	6.00
❑ 106 Darius Miles RC	2.00	5.00
❑ 107 Desmond Mason RC	2.00	5.00
❑ 108 Joel Przybilla RC	1.50	4.00
❑ 109 Mike Miller RC	2.50	6.00
❑ 110 Quentin Richardson RC	2.00	5.00
❑ 111 Jason Collier RC	1.50	4.00
❑ 112 Keyon Dooling RC	1.50	4.00
❑ 113 Courtney Alexander RC	1.50	4.00
❑ 114 Eddie House RC	1.50	4.00
❑ 115 DerMarr Johnson RC	1.50	4.00
❑ 116 Michael Redd RC	4.00	10.00
❑ 117 Mark Madsen RC	1.50	4.00
❑ 118 Stromile Swift RC	2.00	5.00
❑ 119 Mamadou N'Diaye RC	1.50	4.00
❑ 120 DeShawn Stevenson RC	1.50	4.00
❑ 121 Hedo Turkoglu RC	4.00	10.00
❑ 122 Stephen Jackson RC	2.50	6.00
❑ 123 Marcus Fizer RC	1.50	4.00
❑ 124 Khalid El-Amin RC	1.50	4.00
❑ 125 Speedy Claxton RC	1.50	4.00
❑ 126 Hanno Mottola RC	1.50	4.00
❑ 127 Jerome Moiso RC	1.50	4.00
❑ 128 Jamaal Magloire RC	1.50	4.00
❑ 129 Donnell Harvey RC	1.50	4.00
❑ 130 Kenyon Martin RC	4.00	10.00
❑ NNO V.Carter Main Man	20.00	50.00
❑ NNO V.Carter Main Man AU	200.00	400.00

2001-02 Fleer Genuine

❑ COMMON CARD (1-120)	.25	.60
❑ COMMON ROOKIE (121-150)	1.25	3.00
❑ 1 Larry Hughes	.30	.75
❑ 2 Wally Szczerbiak	.30	.75
❑ 3 Jahidi White	.25	.60
❑ 4 Aaron McKie	.25	.60
❑ 5 Antonio McDyess	.30	.75
❑ 6 Tom Gugliotta	.25	.60
❑ 7 Elton Brand	.40	1.00
❑ 8 Lamar Odom	.40	1.00
❑ 9 Chris Webber	.40	1.00
❑ 10 Ron Artest	.30	.75
❑ 11 Gary Payton	.40	1.00
❑ 12 Brian Grant	.25	.60
❑ 13 Steve Nash	.60	1.50
❑ 14 DerMarr Johnson	.25	.60
❑ 15 Vince Carter	.75	2.00
❑ 16 Kurt Thomas	.25	.60
❑ 17 Cuttino Mobley	.30	.75
❑ 18 Marc Jackson	.25	.60
❑ 19 Stromile Swift	.25	.60
❑ 20 Grant Hill	.40	1.00
❑ 21 Raef LaFrentz	.25	.60
❑ 22 Marcus Fizer	.25	.60

❑ 23 Antonio Davis	.25	.60
❑ 24 John Starks	.25	.60
❑ 25 Trajan Langdon	.25	.60
❑ 26 Jason Williams	.30	.75
❑ 27 Toni Kukoc	.30	.75
❑ 28 Morris Peterson	.30	.75
❑ 29 Allen Iverson	.75	2.00
❑ 30 Andre Miller	.30	.75
❑ 31 Larry Johnson	.30	.75
❑ 32 Vitaly Potapenko	.25	.60
❑ 33 Tim Thomas	.25	.60
❑ 34 Eddie House	.25	.60
❑ 35 Juwan Howard	.30	.75
❑ 36 Joel Przybilla	.25	.60
❑ 37 John Stockton	.50	1.25
❑ 38 Michael Finley	.40	1.00
❑ 39 Hedo Turkoglu	.30	.75
❑ 40 Keith Van Horn	.30	.75
❑ 41 Shawn Marion	.40	1.00
❑ 42 Derek Fisher	.30	.75
❑ 43 Terrell Brandon	.25	.60
❑ 44 Jamal Mashburn	.30	.75
❑ 45 Shareef Abdur-Rahim	.30	.75
❑ 46 Brevin Knight	.25	.60
❑ 47 Antoine Walker	.30	.75
❑ 48 Mateen Cleaves	.25	.60
❑ 49 Alonzo Mourning	.40	1.00
❑ 50 Jermaine O'Neal	.40	1.00
❑ 51 Kenyon Martin	.40	1.00
❑ 52 Steve Smith	.30	.75
❑ 53 Jerry Stackhouse	.30	.75
❑ 54 Mike Bibby	.30	.75
❑ 55 Latrell Sprewell	.30	.75
❑ 56 Iakovos Tsakalidis	.25	.60
❑ 57 Sam Cassell	.30	.75
❑ 58 Michael Dickerson	.25	.60
❑ 59 Alan Henderson	.25	.60
❑ 60 Allan Houston	.30	.75
❑ 61 Patrick Ewing	.50	1.25
❑ 62 Joe Smith	.25	.60
❑ 63 Rick Fox	.30	.75
❑ 64 Tracy McGrady	.75	2.00
❑ 65 Scottie Pippen	.60	1.50
❑ 66 Chauncey Billups	.30	.75
❑ 67 Voshon Lenard	.25	.60
❑ 68 Jalen Rose	.30	.75
❑ 69 Derrick Coleman	.30	.75
❑ 70 Shaquille O'Neal	1.00	2.50
❑ 71 Anfernee Hardaway	.40	1.00
❑ 72 Derek Anderson	.30	.75
❑ 73 Travis Best	.25	.60
❑ 74 Darius Miles	.25	.60
❑ 75 Glenn Robinson	.30	.75
❑ 76 Darrell Armstrong	.25	.60
❑ 77 Dirk Nowitzki	.60	1.50
❑ 78 Stephon Marbury	.40	1.00
❑ 79 Tyronn Lue	.25	.60
❑ 80 Bonzi Wells	.30	.75
❑ 81 Mike Miller	.30	.75
❑ 82 Tim Duncan	.75	2.00
❑ 83 Tim Hardaway	.30	.75
❑ 84 Desmond Mason	.30	.75
❑ 85 Ray Allen	.40	1.00
❑ 86 Sean Elliott	.25	.60
❑ 87 David Wesley	.25	.60
❑ 88 Rasheed Wallace	.40	1.00
❑ 89 Kevin Garnett	.75	2.00
❑ 90 Dikembe Mutombo	.30	.75
❑ 91 Baron Davis	.40	1.00
❑ 92 Donyell Marshall	.25	.60
❑ 93 Eddie Jones	.30	.75
❑ 94 Vin Baker	.30	.75
❑ 95 Peja Stojakovic	.30	.75
❑ 96 Antawn Jamison	.40	1.00
❑ 97 Maurice Taylor	.25	.60
❑ 98 Courtney Alexander	.25	.60
❑ 99 Steve Francis	.40	1.00
❑ 100 Chris Mihm	.25	.60
❑ 101 Kobe Bryant	2.00	5.00
❑ 102 Hakeem Olajuwon	.50	1.25
❑ 103 Richard Hamilton	.30	.75
❑ 104 Karl Malone	.50	1.25
❑ 105 Chucky Atkins	.25	.60
❑ 106 Eric Snow	.25	.60
❑ 107 Ruben Patterson	.25	.60
❑ 108 David Robinson	.50	1.25
❑ 109 Bryon Russell	.25	.60
❑ 110 Jason Terry	.40	1.00
❑ 111 Jason Kidd	.60	1.50
❑ 112 Charles Oakley	.30	.75
❑ 113 Wang Zhizhi	.30	.75
❑ 114 Quentin Richardson	.30	.75
❑ 115 Clarence Weatherspoon	.25	.60
❑ 116 Nick Van Exel	.30	.75
❑ 117 Reggie Miller	.40	1.00
❑ 118 Marcus Camby	.30	.75
❑ 119 Corey Maggette	.30	.75
❑ 120 Paul Pierce	.40	1.00
❑ 121 Kwame Brown RC	1.50	4.00
❑ 122 Eddie Griffin RC	1.25	3.00
❑ 123 Eddy Curry RC	2.00	5.00
❑ 124 Jamaal Tinsley RC	1.50	4.00
❑ 125 Jason Richardson RC	2.50	6.00
❑ 126 Shane Battier RC	2.00	5.00
❑ 127 Troy Murphy RC	2.50	6.00
❑ 128 Richard Jefferson RC	3.00	8.00
❑ 129 DeSagana Diop RC	1.25	3.00
❑ 130 Tyson Chandler RC	2.50	6.00
❑ 131 Joe Johnson RC	3.00	8.00
❑ 132 Zach Randolph RC	3.00	8.00
❑ 133 Gerald Wallace RC	3.00	8.00
❑ 134 Loren Woods RC	1.25	3.00
❑ 135 Jason Collins RC	1.25	3.00
❑ 136 Rodney White RC	1.25	3.00
❑ 137 Jeryl Sasser RC	1.25	3.00
❑ 138 Kirk Haston RC	1.25	3.00
❑ 139 Pau Gasol RC	5.00	12.00
❑ 140 Kedrick Brown RC	1.25	3.00
❑ 141 Steven Hunter RC	1.25	3.00
❑ 142 Michael Bradley RC	1.25	3.00
❑ 143 Joseph Forte RC	1.25	3.00
❑ 144 Brandon Armstrong RC	1.25	3.00
❑ 145 Samuel Dalembert RC	1.50	4.00
❑ 146 Trenton Hassell RC	1.50	4.00
❑ 147 Gilbert Arenas RC	2.00	5.00
❑ 148 Omar Cook RC	1.25	3.00
❑ 149 Tony Parker RC	5.00	12.00
❑ 150 Terence Morris RC	1.25	3.00

2002-03 Fleer Genuine

❑ COMPLETE SET (135)	150.00	275.00
❑ COMP.SET w/o SP's (100)	20.00	40.00
❑ COMMON CARD (1-100)	.20	.50
❑ COMMON ROOKIE (101-135)	1.25	3.00
❑ 1 Shaquille O'Neal	.75	2.00
❑ 2 Allen Iverson	.60	1.50
❑ 3 Jerry Stackhouse	.25	.60
❑ 4 Kobe Bryant	1.50	4.00
❑ 5 Jason Kidd	.50	1.25
❑ 6 Andre Miller	.25	.60
❑ 7 David Robinson	.40	1.00
❑ 8 John Stockton	.40	1.00
❑ 9 Glenn Robinson	.25	.60
❑ 10 Chauncey Billups	.30	.75
❑ 11 Chris Webber	.30	.75
❑ 12 Antawn Jamison	.30	.75
❑ 13 Sam Cassell	.25	.60
❑ 14 Vlade Divac	.25	.60
❑ 15 P.J. Brown	.20	.50
❑ 16 Robert Horry	.25	.60
❑ 17 Eric Snow	.20	.50
❑ 18 Popeye Jones		
❑ 19 Paul Pierce	.30	.75
❑ 20 Eddie Griffin	.20	.50
❑ 21 Marcus Camby	.25	.60
❑ 22 Gary Payton	.30	.75
❑ 23 Michael Jordan	2.00	5.00
❑ 24 Shareef Abdur-Rahim	.25	.60
❑ 25 Anfernee Hardaway	.30	.75
❑ 26 Michael Finley	.30	.75
❑ 27 Steve Nash	.50	1.25
❑ 28 Shane Battier	.25	.60
❑ 29 Stephon Marbury	.30	.75
❑ 30 Dirk Nowitzki	.50	1.25
❑ 31 Pau Gasol	.30	.75
❑ 32 Shawn Marion	.30	.75
❑ 33 Rodney Rogers	.20	.50
❑ 34 Steve Smith	.25	.60
❑ 35 Darrell Armstrong	.20	.50
❑ 36 Alvin Williams	.20	.50
❑ 37 Nick Van Exel	.25	.60
❑ 38 Jason Williams	.25	.60
❑ 39 Ruben Patterson	.20	.50
❑ 40 Juwan Howard	.25	.60
❑ 41 Brian Grant	.20	.50
❑ 42 Damon Stoudamire	.25	.60
❑ 43 Antonio McDyess	.25	.60
❑ 44 Eddie Jones	.25	.60
❑ 45 Rasheed Wallace	.30	.75
❑ 46 Larry Hughes	.25	.60
❑ 47 Wally Szczerbiak	.25	.60
❑ 48 Tony Parker	.30	.75
❑ 49 Ron Artest	.25	.60
❑ 50 Kevin Garnett	.60	1.50
❑ 51 Tim Duncan	.60	1.50
❑ 52 Marcus Fizer	.20	.50
❑ 53 Darius Miles	.20	.50
❑ 54 Grant Hill	.30	.75
❑ 55 Andrei Kirilenko	.30	.75
❑ 56 Jalen Rose	.25	.60
❑ 57 Lamar Odom	.30	.75
❑ 58 Tracy McGrady	.60	1.50
❑ 59 Karl Malone	.30	.75
❑ 60 Jason Terry	.30	.75
❑ 61 Steve Francis	.30	.75
❑ 62 Kenyon Martin	.30	.75
❑ 63 Brent Barry	.20	.50
❑ 64 Antoine Walker	.25	.60
❑ 65 Reggie Miller	.30	.75
❑ 66 Allan Houston	.25	.60
❑ 67 Vince Carter	.60	1.50
❑ 68 Toni Kukoc	.25	.60
❑ 69 Lamond Murray	.20	.50
❑ 70 Jason Richardson	.30	.75
❑ 71 Rick Fox	.25	.60
❑ 72 Kerry Kittles	.25	.60
❑ 73 Dikembe Mutombo	.25	.60
❑ 74 Tyson Chandler	.25	.60
❑ 75 Richard Hamilton	.25	.60
❑ 76 Elden Campbell	.20	.50
❑ 77 Jermaine O'Neal	.30	.75
❑ 78 Mike Miller	.25	.60
❑ 79 Morris Peterson	.25	.60
❑ 80 Jamal Mashburn	.25	.60
❑ 81 Elton Brand	.30	.75
❑ 82 Kurt Thomas	.20	.50
❑ 83 Antonio Davis	.20	.50
❑ 84 Ben Wallace	.25	.60
❑ 85 Anthony Mason	.20	.50
❑ 86 Peja Stojakovic	.25	.60
❑ 87 Kenny Anderson	.25	.60
❑ 88 Cuttino Mobley	.25	.60
❑ 89 Keith Van Horn	.25	.60
❑ 90 Rashard Lewis	.30	.75
❑ 91 Clifford Robinson	.20	.50
❑ 92 Ray Allen	.30	.75
❑ 93 Mike Bibby	.25	.60
❑ 94 Baron Davis	.30	.75
❑ 95 Jamaal Tinsley	.25	.60
❑ 96 Latrell Sprewell	.25	.60
❑ 97 Jon Barry	.20	.50
❑ 98 Desmond Mason	.25	.60
❑ 99 Alonzo Mourning	.30	.75
❑ 100 Bonzi Wells	.25	.60
❑ 101 Jay Williams RC	1.50	4.00
❑ 102 Mike Dunleavy RC	1.50	4.00
❑ 103 Amare Stoudemire RC	3.00	8.00
❑ 104 Caron Butler RC	2.50	6.00
❑ 105 Jared Jeffries RC	1.25	3.00
❑ 106 Fred Jones RC	1.50	4.00
❑ 107 Bostjan Nachbar RC	1.25	3.00
❑ 108 Jiri Welsch RC	1.25	3.00
❑ 109 Juan Dixon RC	2.00	5.00
❑ 110 Curtis Borchardt RC	1.25	3.00
❑ 111 Kareem Rush RC	1.50	4.00
❑ 112 Qyntel Woods RC	1.25	3.00
❑ 113 Casey Jacobsen RC	1.25	3.00
❑ 114 Frank Williams RC	1.25	3.00
❑ 115 John Salmons RC	2.00	5.00
❑ 116 Dan Dickau RC	1.25	3.00
❑ 117 DaJuan Wagner RC	1.25	3.00
❑ 118 Drew Gooden RC	2.00	5.00
❑ 119 Nikoloz Tskitishvili RC	1.25	3.00
❑ 120 Yao Ming RC	4.00	10.00

❑ 121 Nene Hilario RC	1.50	4.00
❑ 122 Chris Wilcox RC	1.50	4.00
❑ 123 Melvin Ely RC	1.25	3.00
❑ 124 Marcus Haislip RC	1.25	3.00
❑ 125 Ryan Humphrey RC	1.25	3.00
❑ 126 Tayshaun Prince RC	2.00	5.00
❑ 127 Tito Maddox RC	1.25	3.00
❑ 128 Chris Jefferies RC	1.25	3.00
❑ 129 Manu Ginobili RC	3.00	8.00
❑ 130 Roger Mason RC	1.25	3.00
❑ 131 Robert Archibald RC	1.25	3.00
❑ 132 Vincent Yarbrough RC	1.25	3.00
❑ 133 Dan Gadzuric RC	1.25	3.00
❑ 134 Carlos Boozer RC	2.50	6.00
❑ 135 Rasual Butler RC	1.25	3.00

2003-04 Fleer Genuine Insider

❑ COMP.SET w/o SP's (100)	12.50	30.00
❑ COMMON ROOKIE (101-110)	2.00	5.00
❑ COMMON ROOKIE (111-140)	2.00	5.00
❑ COMMON ROOKIE (131-140)	2.00	5.00
❑ 1 Shareef Abdur-Rahim	.25	.60
❑ 2 Andre Miller	.25	.60
❑ 3 Reggie Miller	.30	.75
❑ 4 Michael Redd	.30	.75
❑ 5 Allan Houston	.25	.60
❑ 6 Mike Bibby	.25	.60
❑ 7 Kwame Brown	.20	.50
❑ 8 Earl Boykins	.20	.50
❑ 9 Ron Artest	.25	.60
❑ 10 Eddie Jones	.25	.60
❑ 11 Zach Randolph	.30	.75
❑ 12 Derek Anderson	.25	.60
❑ 13 Andrei Kirilenko	.30	.75
❑ 14 Carlos Boozer	.30	.75
❑ 15 Yao Ming	.60	1.50
❑ 16 Pau Gasol	.30	.75
❑ 17 Jamal Mashburn	.20	.50
❑ 18 Shawn Marion	.30	.75
❑ 19 Vince Carter	.60	1.50
❑ 20 Eddy Curry	.25	.60
❑ 21 Mike Dunleavy Jr.	.25	.60
❑ 22 Kobe Bryant	1.50	4.00
❑ 23 Tim Thomas	.20	.50
❑ 24 Drew Gooden	.20	.50
❑ 25 Tim Duncan	.60	1.50
❑ 26 Dajuan Wagner	.20	.50
❑ 27 Speedy Claxton	.20	.50
❑ 28 Karl Malone	.30	.75
❑ 29 Jason Kidd	.50	1.25
❑ 30 Kenny Thomas	.20	.50
❑ 31 Vladimir Radmanovic	.20	.50
❑ 32 Tyson Chandler	.25	.60
❑ 33 Jason Richardson	.30	.75
❑ 34 Quentin Richardson	.25	.60
❑ 35 Kerry Kittles	.25	.60
❑ 36 Derrick Coleman	.25	.60
❑ 37 Manu Ginobili	.30	.75
❑ 38 Paul Pierce	.30	.75
❑ 39 Ben Wallace	.25	.60
❑ 40 Corey Maggette	.20	.50
❑ 41 Sam Cassell	.25	.60
❑ 42 Hedo Turkoglu	.25	.60
❑ 43 Peja Stojakovic	.25	.60
❑ 44 Gilbert Arenas	.30	.75
❑ 45 Dirk Nowitzki	.50	1.25
❑ 46 Al Harrington	.25	.60
❑ 47 Caron Butler	.25	.60
❑ 48 Baron Davis	.30	.75
❑ 49 Rasheed Wallace	.30	.75
❑ 50 Morris Peterson	.25	.60
❑ 51 Steve Nash	.50	1.25
❑ 52 Steve Francis	.30	.75
❑ 53 Lamar Odom	.30	.75
❑ 54 Jamaal Magloire	.20	.50
❑ 55 Amare Stoudemire	.60	1.50
❑ 56 Antonio Davis	.20	.50
❑ 57 Dan Dickau	.20	.50
❑ 58 Cuttino Mobley	.25	.60
❑ 59 Jason Williams	.25	.60
❑ 60 David Wesley	.20	.50
❑ 61 Stephon Marbury	.30	.75
❑ 62 Ray Allen	.20	.50
❑ 63 Scottie Pippen	.50	1.25
❑ 64 Nick Van Exel	.25	.60
❑ 65 Shaquille O'Neal	.75	2.00
❑ 66 Richard Jefferson	.30	.75
❑ 67 Allen Iverson	.60	1.50
❑ 68 Tony Parker	.30	.75
❑ 69 Jason Terry	.25	.60
❑ 70 NenÃª	.25	.60
❑ 71 Marko Jaric	.20	.50
❑ 72 Troy Hudson	.20	.50
❑ 73 Malik Rose	.20	.50
❑ 74 Bobby Jackson	.20	.50
❑ 75 Jerry Stackhouse	.25	.60
❑ 76 Voshon Lenard	.20	.50
❑ 77 Richard Hamilton	.25	.60
❑ 78 Scot Pollard	.20	.50
❑ 79 Latrell Sprewell	.25	.60
❑ 80 Tracy McGrady	.60	1.50
❑ 81 Chris Webber	.30	.75
❑ 82 Raef LaFrentz	.20	.50
❑ 83 Tayshaun Prince	.25	.60
❑ 84 Elton Brand	.30	.75
❑ 85 Kevin Garnett	.60	1.50
❑ 86 Keon Clark	.20	.50
❑ 87 Brad Miller	.25	.60
❑ 88 Alvin Williams	.20	.50
❑ 89 Michael Finley	.30	.75
❑ 90 Jermaine O'Neal	.30	.75
❑ 91 Desmond Mason	.25	.60
❑ 92 Keith Van Horn	.25	.60
❑ 93 Bonzi Wells	.20	.50
❑ 94 Matt Harpring	.25	.60
❑ 95 Darius Miles	.25	.60
❑ 96 Eddie Griffin	.20	.50
❑ 97 Shane Battier	.25	.60
❑ 98 Kenyon Martin	.30	.75
❑ 99 Glenn Robinson	.25	.60
❑ 100 Rashard Lewis	.30	.75
❑ 101 Carmelo Anthony RC	5.00	12.00
❑ 102 Troy Bell RC	2.00	5.00
❑ 103 T.J. Ford RC	2.50	6.00
❑ 104 LeBron James RC	40.00	80.00
❑ 105 Mike Sweetney RC	2.00	5.00
❑ 106 Chris Bosh RC	3.00	8.00
❑ 107 Jarvis Hayes RC	2.00	5.00
❑ 108 Darko Milicic RC	2.50	6.00
❑ 109 Chris Kaman RC	2.50	6.00
❑ 110 Dwyane Wade RC	5.00	12.00
❑ 111 Udonis Haslem RC	2.50	6.00
❑ 112 Josh Howard RC	2.50	6.00
❑ 113 Mickael Pietrus RC	2.50	6.00
❑ 114 Reece Gaines RC	2.00	5.00
❑ 115 Nick Collison RC	2.00	5.00
❑ 116 Leandrinho Barbosa RC	2.50	6.00
❑ 117 Kendrick Perkins RC	3.00	8.00
❑ 118 Ndudi Ebi RC	2.00	5.00
❑ 119 Willie Green RC	2.00	5.00
❑ 120 Kirk Hinrich RC	2.50	6.00
❑ 121 Marcus Banks RC	2.00	5.00
❑ 122 Zarko Cabarkapa RC	2.00	5.00
❑ 123 Zoran Planinic RC	2.00	5.00
❑ 124 David West RC	2.50	6.00
❑ 125 Luke Ridnour RC	2.50	6.00
❑ 126 Brian Cook RC	2.00	5.00
❑ 127 Boris Diaw RC	2.50	6.00
❑ 128 Dahntay Jones RC	2.00	5.00
❑ 129 Maciej Lampe RC	2.00	5.00
❑ 130 Travis Outlaw RC	2.50	6.00
❑ 131 Ben Handlogten MM RC	2.00	5.00
❑ 132 Jerome Beasley MM RC	2.00	5.00
❑ 133 Marquis Daniels MM RC	2.50	6.00
❑ 134 Luke Walton MM RC	2.50	6.00
❑ 135 Aleksandar Pavlovic MM RC	2.50	6.00
❑ 136 Matt Carroll MM RC	2.00	5.00
❑ 137 Curtis Borchardt MM	2.00	5.00
❑ 138 Jason Kapono MM RC	2.50	6.00
❑ 139 Steve Blake MM RC	2.50	6.00
❑ 140 Keith Bogans MM RC	2.00	5.00

2004-05 Fleer Genuine

❑ COMP.SET w/o SP's (100)	15.00	40.00
❑ COMMON CARD (1-100)	.20	.50
❑ COMMON CARD (101-110)	2.00	5.00
❑ COMMON ROOKIE (111-135)	1.50	4.00
❑ 1 Rasheed Wallace	.30	.75
❑ 2 Larry Hughes	.25	.60
❑ 3 Allen Iverson	.60	1.50
❑ 4 Josh Howard	.30	.75
❑ 5 Bonzi Wells	.20	.50
❑ 6 Jamaal Magloire	.20	.50
❑ 7 Luke Ridnour	.20	.50
❑ 8 Chauncey Billups	.30	.75
❑ 9 Dwyane Wade	1.00	2.50
❑ 10 Amare Stoudemire	.60	1.50
❑ 11 Earl Boykins	.20	.50
❑ 12 Damon Jones	.20	.50
❑ 13 Marquis Daniels	.20	.50
❑ 14 Luke Walton	.25	.60
❑ 15 Jamal Crawford	.25	.60
❑ 16 Corliss Williamson	.20	.50
❑ 17 Vince Carter	.60	1.50
❑ 18 Antoine Walker	.30	.75
❑ 19 Jason Richardson	.30	.75
❑ 20 Jason Kidd	.50	1.25
❑ 21 Peja Stojakovic	.25	.60
❑ 22 Jeff McInnis	.20	.50
❑ 23 Lamar Odom	.30	.75
❑ 24 Allan Houston	.25	.60
❑ 25 Jalen Rose	.25	.60
❑ 26 LeBron James	2.00	5.00
❑ 27 Caron Butler	.25	.60
❑ 28 Stephon Marbury	.30	.75
❑ 29 Carlos Arroyo	.30	.75
❑ 30 Zydrunas Ilgauskas	.25	.60
❑ 31 Kobe Bryant	1.50	4.00
❑ 32 Steve Francis	.30	.75
❑ 33 Carlos Boozer	.30	.75
❑ 34 Primoz Brezec	.20	.50
❑ 35 Reggie Miller	.30	.75
❑ 36 Sam Cassell	.25	.60
❑ 37 Ray Allen	.30	.75
❑ 38 Drew Gooden	.20	.50
❑ 39 Chris Wilcox	.20	.50
❑ 40 Grant Hill	.30	.75
❑ 41 Andrei Kirilenko	.30	.75
❑ 42 Kirk Hinrich	.25	.60
❑ 43 Corey Maggette	.25	.60
❑ 44 Cuttino Mobley	.25	.60
❑ 45 Gilbert Arenas	.30	.75
❑ 46 Tyson Chandler	.25	.60
❑ 47 Elton Brand	.30	.75
❑ 48 Samuel Dalembert	.20	.50
❑ 49 Jarvis Hayes	.20	.50
❑ 50 Ben Wallace	.25	.60
❑ 51 Shawn Marion	.30	.75
❑ 52 Michael Redd	.30	.75
❑ 53 Richard Hamilton	.25	.60
❑ 54 Desmond Mason	.25	.60
❑ 55 Steve Nash	.50	1.25
❑ 56 Antawn Jamison	.30	.75
❑ 57 Kareem Rush	.20	.50
❑ 58 Jermaine O'Neal	.30	.75
❑ 59 Keith Van Horn	.25	.60
❑ 60 Rashard Lewis	.30	.75
❑ 61 Gerald Wallace	.30	.75
❑ 62 Jamaal Tinsley	.25	.60
❑ 63 Vladimir Radmanovic	.20	.50
❑ 64 Predrag Drobnjak	.20	.50
❑ 65 Mike Dunleavy	.25	.60
❑ 66 Baron Davis	.30	.75
❑ 67 Mike Bibby	.25	.60
❑ 68 Ricky Davis	.25	.60
❑ 69 Tracy McGrady	.60	1.50
❑ 70 Richard Jefferson	.30	.75

❑ 71 Chris Webber .30 .75
❑ 72 Michael Finley .30 .75
❑ 73 Pau Gasol .30 .75
❑ 74 David West .30 .75
❑ 75 Chris Bosh .30 .75
❑ 76 Gary Payton .30 .75
❑ 77 Yao Ming .75 2.00
❑ 78 Wally Szczerbiak .25 .60
❑ 79 Tim Duncan .60 1.50
❑ 80 Keith Bogans .20 .50
❑ 81 Stephen Jackson .25 .60
❑ 82 Kevin Garnett .60 1.50
❑ 83 Tony Parker .30 .75
❑ 84 Kenyon Martin .30 .75
❑ 85 Shaquille O'Neal .75 2.00
❑ 86 Shareef Abdur-Rahim .25 .60
❑ 87 Al Harrington .25 .60
❑ 88 Adonal Foyle .20 .50
❑ 89 Brian Scalabrine .20 .50
❑ 90 Brad Miller .25 .60
❑ 91 Carmelo Anthony 1.00 2.50
❑ 92 Udonis Haslem .25 .60
❑ 93 Zach Randolph .30 .75
❑ 94 Paul Pierce .30 .75
❑ 95 Maurice Taylor .20 .50
❑ 96 Latrell Sprewell .25 .60
❑ 97 Manu Ginobili .30 .75
❑ 98 Dirk Nowitzki .50 1.25
❑ 99 Jason Williams .25 .60
❑ 100 Nick Van Exel .25 .60
❑ 101 Charles Barkley 3.00 8.00
❑ 102 Jerry West 2.50 6.00
❑ 103 Magic Johnson 5.00 12.00
❑ 104 Kareem Abdul-Jabbar 3.00 8.00
❑ 105 Pete Maravich 10.00 25.00
❑ 106 Maurice Cheeks 2.50 6.00
❑ 107 Alex English 2.00 6.00
❑ 108 George Mikan 2.50 6.00
❑ 109 Wilt Chamberlain 3.00 8.00
❑ 110 Dominique Wilkins 2.50 6.00
❑ 111 Josh Childress RC 1.50 4.00
❑ 112 Josh Smith RC 4.00 10.00
❑ 113 Al Jefferson RC 3.00 8.00
❑ 114 Delonte West RC 2.50 6.00
❑ 115 Tony Allen RC 2.00 5.00
❑ 116 Emeka Okafor RC 3.00 8.00
❑ 117 Chris Duhon RC 2.50 6.00
❑ 118 Ben Gordon RC 2.00 5.00
❑ 119 Luol Deng RC 2.00 5.00
❑ 120 Andres Nocioni RC 2.00 5.00
❑ 121 David Harrison RC 1.50 4.00
❑ 122 Devin Harris RC 3.00 8.00
❑ 123 Shaun Livingston RC 1.50 4.00
❑ 124 Dorell Wright RC 2.00 5.00
❑ 125 J.R. Smith RC 3.00 8.00
❑ 126 Trevor Ariza RC 2.00 5.00
❑ 127 Dwight Howard RC 5.00 12.00
❑ 128 Jameer Nelson RC 2.00 5.00
❑ 129 Andre Iguodala RC 4.00 10.00
❑ 130 Sebastian Telfair RC 1.50 4.00
❑ 131 Kevin Martin RC 2.00 5.00
❑ 132 Ha Seung-Jin RC 1.50 4.00
❑ 133 Rafael Araujo RC 1.50 4.00
❑ 134 Kirk Snyder RC 1.50 4.00
❑ 135 Beno Udrih RC 2.00 5.00

2000-01 Fleer Glossy

❑ COMP.SET w/o SP's (200) 12.50 30.00
❑ COMMON CARD (1-200) .08 .25
❑ COMMON ROOKIE (201-210) 1.50 4.00
❑ COMMON ROOKIE (211-235) 1.25 3.00
❑ COMMON ROOKIE (236-245) 1.25 3.00
❑ 1 Lamar Odom .30 .75
❑ 2 Christian Laettner .20 .50
❑ 3 Michael Olowokandi .20 .50
❑ 4 Anthony Carter .20 .50
❑ 5 Steve Francis .30 .75
❑ 6 Darvin Ham .20 .50
❑ 7 Mitch Richmond .25 .60
❑ 8 Corliss Williamson .25 .60
❑ 9 Jason Terry .30 .75
❑ 10 Brian Grant .20 .50
❑ 11 Peja Stojakovic .25 .60
❑ 12 Rick Fox .25 .60
❑ 13 Tyrone Hill .20 .50
❑ 14 Chauncey Billups .30 .75
❑ 15 Otis Thorpe .25 .60
❑ 16 Richard Hamilton .25 .60
❑ 17 Ervin Johnson .20 .50
❑ 18 Jim Jackson .20 .50
❑ 19 Theo Ratliff .20 .50
❑ 20 Doug Christie .20 .50
❑ 21 Jalen Rose .25 .60
❑ 22 John Wallace .20 .50
❑ 23 Ruben Patterson .20 .50
❑ 24 Steve Nash .50 1.25
❑ 25 Toni Kukoc .25 .60
❑ 26 Anthony Peeler .20 .50
❑ 27 Ray Allen .30 .75
❑ 28 Adonal Foyle .20 .50
❑ 29 Chris Whitney .20 .50
❑ 30 Nick Van Exel .25 .60
❑ 31 Sean Elliott .25 .60
❑ 32 Erick Strickland .20 .50
❑ 33 Jerry Stackhouse .25 .60
❑ 34 Antawn Jamison .30 .75
❑ 35 Grant Hill .30 .75
❑ 36 Antonio Daniels .20 .50
❑ 37 Karl Malone .40 1.00
❑ 38 Keith Van Horn .25 .60
❑ 39 Ron Harper .25 .60
❑ 40 Stephon Marbury .30 .75
❑ 41 Bryon Russell .20 .50
❑ 42 Corey Maggette .25 .60
❑ 43 Hersey Hawkins .20 .50
❑ 44 Vince Carter .60 1.50
❑ 45 Paul Pierce .30 .75
❑ 46 Mikki Moore .20 .50
❑ 47 Othella Harrington .20 .50
❑ 48 Erick Dampier .20 .50
❑ 49 Jerome Williams .20 .50
❑ 50 Nick Anderson .20 .50
❑ 51 Tim Hardaway .25 .60
❑ 52 Allan Houston .25 .60
❑ 53 Tyrone Nesby .20 .50
❑ 54 Brevin Knight .20 .50
❑ 55 Chris Mills .20 .50
❑ 56 Ron Artest .30 .75
❑ 57 Walt Williams .20 .50
❑ 58 Duane Causwell .20 .50
❑ 59 Bonzi Wells .20 .50
❑ 60 Rasheed Wallace .30 .75
❑ 61 Dikembe Mutombo .25 .60
❑ 62 Jahidi White .20 .50
❑ 63 Chris Webber .30 .75
❑ 64 Tony Battie .20 .50
❑ 65 Mahmoud Abdul-Rauf .20 .50
❑ 66 Monty Williams .20 .50
❑ 67 Charlie Ward .20 .50
❑ 68 David Robinson .40 1.00
❑ 69 Eric Snow .20 .50
❑ 70 Jermaine O'Neal .30 .75
❑ 71 Kurt Thomas .20 .50
❑ 72 James Posey .20 .50
❑ 73 Travis Best .20 .50
❑ 74 Jonathan Bender .20 .50
❑ 75 John Stockton .40 1.00
❑ 76 Jacque Vaughn .20 .50
❑ 77 Ron Mercer .20 .50
❑ 78 Shawn Marion .30 .75
❑ 79 Larry Johnson .25 .60
❑ 80 Maurice Taylor .20 .50
❑ 81 Clifford Robinson .20 .50
❑ 82 Scot Pollard .20 .50
❑ 83 Patrick Ewing .40 1.00
❑ 84 Terrell Brandon .20 .50
❑ 85 Horace Grant .25 .60
❑ 86 Vin Baker .25 .60
❑ 87 Al Harrington .25 .60
❑ 88 Larry Hughes .25 .60
❑ 89 David Wesley .20 .50
❑ 90 Wally Szczerbiak .25 .60
❑ 91 Charles Oakley .25 .60
❑ 92 Tim Thomas .20 .50
❑ 93 Mookie Blaylock .25 .60
❑ 94 Jamal Mashburn .25 .60
❑ 95 Roshown McLeod .20 .50
❑ 96 John Starks .20 .50
❑ 97 Rodney Rogers .20 .50
❑ 98 Juwan Howard .25 .60
❑ 99 Isaiah Rider .25 .60
❑ 100 Rashard Lewis .30 .75
❑ 101 Dion Glover .20 .50
❑ 102 Johnny Newman .20 .50
❑ 103 Avery Johnson .25 .60
❑ 104 Darrell Armstrong .20 .50
❑ 105 Eric Williams .20 .50
❑ 106 Gary Payton .30 .75
❑ 107 Antonio Davis .20 .50
❑ 108 Dirk Nowitzki .50 1.25
❑ 109 Trajan Langdon .20 .50
❑ 110 Michael Dickerson .20 .50
❑ 111 Joe Smith .20 .50
❑ 112 Rod Strickland .25 .60
❑ 113 Shawn Kemp .30 .75
❑ 114 Voshon Lenard .20 .50
❑ 115 Marcus Camby .25 .60
❑ 116 Matt Harpring .25 .60
❑ 117 Isaac Austin .20 .50
❑ 118 Malik Rose .20 .50
❑ 119 Pat Garrity .20 .50
❑ 120 Kenny Thomas .20 .50
❑ 121 LaPhonso Ellis .25 .60
❑ 122 Danny Fortson .20 .50
❑ 123 Elton Brand .30 .75
❑ 124 Jason Williams .25 .60
❑ 125 Kobe Bryant 1.50 4.00
❑ 126 Tariq Abdul-Wahad .20 .50
❑ 127 Tracy McGrady .60 1.50
❑ 128 Matt Geiger .20 .50
❑ 129 Antoine Walker .25 .60
❑ 130 Michael Finley .30 .75
❑ 131 Andre Miller .25 .60
❑ 132 Robert Horry .25 .60
❑ 133 Donyell Marshall .20 .50
❑ 134 Shareef Abdur-Rahim .25 .60
❑ 135 Vonteego Cummings .20 .50
❑ 136 Anthony Mason .20 .50
❑ 137 Mike Bibby .25 .60
❑ 138 Raef LaFrentz .20 .50
❑ 139 Glen Rice .25 .60
❑ 140 Chris Gatling .20 .50
❑ 141 Latrell Sprewell .25 .60
❑ 142 Austin Croshere .20 .50
❑ 143 Kenny Anderson .25 .60
❑ 144 Elden Campbell .20 .50
❑ 145 Jason Kidd .50 1.25
❑ 146 Michael Doleac .20 .50
❑ 147 Muggsy Bogues .25 .60
❑ 148 Tim Duncan .60 1.50
❑ 149 Samaki Walker .20 .50
❑ 150 Gary Trent .20 .50
❑ 151 Kevin Garnett .60 1.50
❑ 152 Allen Iverson .60 1.50
❑ 153 Anfernee Hardaway .30 .75
❑ 154 Robert Traylor .20 .50
❑ 155 Scottie Pippen .50 1.25
❑ 156 Shaquille O'Neal .75 2.00
❑ 157 Vlade Divac .25 .60
❑ 158 Lucious Harris .20 .50
❑ 159 Keon Clark .20 .50
❑ 160 Bo Outlaw .20 .50
❑ 161 P.J. Brown .20 .50
❑ 162 Derrick Coleman .25 .60
❑ 163 Mark Jackson .25 .60
❑ 164 Lamond Murray .20 .50
❑ 165 Dan Majerle .25 .60
❑ 166 Eddie Jones .25 .60
❑ 167 Cedric Ceballos .20 .50
❑ 168 Kendall Gill .20 .50
❑ 169 Tom Gugliotta .20 .50
❑ 170 Jeff McInnis .20 .50
❑ 171 Steve Smith .25 .60
❑ 172 Kevin Willis .20 .50
❑ 173 Lindsey Hunter .20 .50
❑ 174 Derek Anderson .25 .60
❑ 175 Shandon Anderson .20 .50
❑ 176 Adrian Griffin .20 .50
❑ 177 Baron Davis .30 .75
❑ 178 Radoslav Nesterovic .20 .50
❑ 179 Glenn Robinson .25 .60
❑ 180 Sam Cassell .25 .60
❑ 181 Chucky Atkins .20 .50
❑ 182 Arvydas Sabonis .25 .60

❑ 183 Damon Stoudamire	.25	.60
❑ 184 Antonio McDyess	.25	.60
❑ 185 Derek Fisher	.30	.75
❑ 186 Bryant Reeves	.20	.50
❑ 187 Hakeem Olajuwon	.40	1.00
❑ 188 Kerry Kittles	.25	.60
❑ 189 Alan Henderson	.20	.50
❑ 190 Sam Perkins	.20	.50
❑ 191 Felipe Lopez	.20	.50
❑ 192 Tracy Murray	.20	.50
❑ 193 Shammond Williams	.20	.50
❑ 194 Vitaly Potapenko	.20	.50
❑ 195 John Amaechi	.20	.50
❑ 196 Quincy Lewis	.20	.50
❑ 197 Reggie Miller	.30	.75
❑ 198 Cuttino Mobley	.25	.60
❑ 199 Rex Chapman	.20	.50
❑ 200 Dale Davis	.20	.50
❑ 201 Stromile Swift RC	2.00	5.00
❑ 202 Stephen Jackson RC	2.50	6.00
❑ 203 Erick Barkley RC	1.50	4.00
❑ 204 Mike Miller RC	2.50	6.00
❑ 205 Kenyon Martin RC	4.00	10.00
❑ 206 Michael Redd RC	4.00	10.00
❑ 207 Darius Miles RC	2.00	5.00
❑ 208 Chris Mihm RC	1.50	4.00
❑ 209 Brian Cardinal RC	1.50	4.00
❑ 210 Khalid El-Amin RC	1.50	4.00
❑ 211 Hanno Mottola RC	1.25	3.00
❑ 212 Jamaal Magloire RC	1.25	3.00
❑ 213 Courtney Alexander RC	1.25	3.00
❑ 214 Mamadou N'Diaye RC	1.25	3.00
❑ 215 Chris Porter RC	1.25	3.00
❑ 216 Quentin Richardson RC	1.50	4.00
❑ 217 Eddie House RC	1.25	3.00
❑ 218 Joel Przybilla RC	1.25	3.00
❑ 219 Soumaila Samake RC	1.25	3.00
❑ 220 Speedy Claxton RC	1.25	3.00
❑ 221 Desmond Mason RC	1.50	4.00
❑ 222 Mike Smith RC	1.25	3.00
❑ 223 Lavor Postell RC	1.25	3.00
❑ 224 Pepe Sanchez RC	1.25	3.00
❑ 225 DeShawn Stevenson RC	1.25	3.00
❑ 226 Hedo Turkoglu RC	3.00	8.00
❑ 227 Keyon Dooling RC	1.25	3.00
❑ 228 Dan Langhi RC	1.25	3.00
❑ 229 Mateen Cleaves RC	1.25	3.00
❑ 230 Donnell Harvey RC	1.25	3.00
❑ 231 DerMarr Johnson RC	1.25	3.00
❑ 232 Jason Collier RC	1.25	3.00
❑ 233 Jake Voskuhl RC	1.25	3.00
❑ 234 Mark Madsen RC	1.25	3.00
❑ 235 Jabari Smith RC	1.25	3.00
❑ 236 Morris Peterson RC	2.00	5.00
❑ 237 Daniel Santiago RC	3.00	8.00
❑ 238 Etan Thomas RC	1.25	3.00
❑ 239 A.J. Guyton RC	1.25	3.00
❑ 240 Marcus Fizer RC	1.25	3.00
❑ 241 Jamal Crawford RC	2.00	5.00
❑ 242 Jerome Moiso RC	1.25	3.00
❑ 243 Olumide Oyedeji RC	1.25	3.00
❑ 244 Paul McPherson RC	1.25	3.00
❑ 245 Eduardo Najera RC	1.25	3.00
❑ 246 Marc Jackson AU	4.00	10.00
❑ 247 Mike Penberthy AU	3.00	8.00
❑ 248 Dragan Tarlac AU	3.00	8.00
❑ 249 Ruben Wolkowyski AU	3.00	8.00
❑ 250 Iakovos Tsakalidis AU	3.00	8.00
❑ 251 Ruben Garces AU	3.00	8.00

2006-07 Fleer Hot Prospects

❑ COMP.SET w/o SP's (60)	15.00	40.00
❑ 1 Joe Johnson	.30	.75
❑ 2 Marvin Williams	.40	1.00
❑ 3 Tony Allen	.30	.75
❑ 4 Paul Pierce	.40	1.00
❑ 5 Raymond Felton	.50	1.25
❑ 6 Emeka Okafor	.40	1.00
❑ 7 Ben Gordon	.50	1.25
❑ 8 Michael Jordan	2.50	6.00
❑ 9 Zydrunas Ilgauskas	.30	.75
❑ 10 LeBron James	2.00	5.00
❑ 11 Devin Harris	.40	1.00
❑ 12 Dirk Nowitzki	.60	1.50
❑ 13 Carmelo Anthony	.50	1.25
❑ 14 Nene	.25	.60
❑ 15 Chauncey Billups	.40	1.00
❑ 16 Ben Wallace	.40	1.00
❑ 17 Baron Davis	.40	1.00
❑ 18 Troy Murphy	.40	1.00
❑ 19 Tracy McGrady	.75	2.00
❑ 20 Yao Ming	1.00	2.50
❑ 21 Jermaine O'Neal	.40	1.00
❑ 22 Peja Stojakovic	.40	1.00
❑ 23 Corey Maggette	.30	.75
❑ 24 Sam Cassell	.40	1.00
❑ 25 Kobe Bryant	2.00	5.00
❑ 26 Lamar Odom	.40	1.00
❑ 27 Pau Gasol	.40	1.00
❑ 28 Hakim Warrick	.30	.75
❑ 29 Shaquille O'Neal	1.00	2.50
❑ 30 Dwyane Wade	1.00	2.50
❑ 31 T.J. Ford	.30	.75
❑ 32 Michael Redd	.40	1.00
❑ 33 Kevin Garnett	.75	2.00
❑ 34 Troy Hudson	.25	.60
❑ 35 Vince Carter	.75	2.00
❑ 36 Jason Kidd	.60	1.50
❑ 37 Desmond Mason	.25	.60
❑ 38 Chris Paul	.75	2.00
❑ 39 Stephon Marbury	.40	1.00
❑ 40 Nate Robinson	.40	1.00
❑ 41 Grant Hill	.40	1.00
❑ 42 Darko Milicic	.40	1.00
❑ 43 Andre Iguodala	.40	1.00
❑ 44 Allen Iverson	.75	2.00
❑ 45 Steve Nash	.50	1.25
❑ 46 Amare Stoudemire	.75	2.00
❑ 47 Zach Randolph	.40	1.00
❑ 48 Sebastian Telfair	.30	.75
❑ 49 Ron Artest	.40	1.00
❑ 50 Mike Bibby	.40	1.00
❑ 51 Tim Duncan	.75	2.00
❑ 52 Manu Ginobili	.40	1.00
❑ 53 Ray Allen	.40	1.00
❑ 54 Rashard Lewis	.40	1.00
❑ 55 Chris Bosh	.40	1.00
❑ 56 Charlie Villanueva	.40	1.00
❑ 57 Andrei Kirilenko	.40	1.00
❑ 58 Deron Williams	.60	1.50
❑ 59 Gilbert Arenas	.40	1.00
❑ 60 Antawn Jamison	.40	1.00
❑ 61 Ronnie Brewer JSY AU RC	15.00	40.00
❑ 62 LaMarcus Aldridge JSY AU RC	12.00	30.00
❑ 63 Tyrus Thomas JSY AU RC	20.00	40.00
❑ 64 Shelden Williams JSY AU RC	12.00	30.00
❑ 65 Cedric Simmons JSY AU RC	10.00	25.00
❑ 66 Randy Foye JSY AU RC	10.00	25.00
❑ 67 Rudy Gay JSY AU RC	10.00	25.00
❑ 68 Patrick O'Bryant JSY AU RC	10.00	25.00
❑ 69 Rodney Carney JSY AU RC	10.00	25.00
❑ 70 Hilton Armstrong JSY AU RC	10.00	25.00
❑ 71 Denham Brown JSY AU RC	6.00	15.00
❑ 72 Dee Brown JSY AU RC	6.00	15.00
❑ 73 Allan Ray JSY AU RC	8.00	20.00
❑ 74 Shawne Williams JSY AU RC	12.50	30.00
❑ 75 Quincy Douby JSY AU RC	6.00	15.00
❑ 76 Renaldo Balkman JSY AU RC	10.00	25.00
❑ 77 Rajon Rondo JSY AU RC	25.00	60.00
❑ 78 Marcus Williams JSY AU RC	8.00	20.00
❑ 79 Josh Boone JSY AU RC	6.00	15.00
❑ 80 Kyle Lowry JSY AU RC	6.00	15.00
❑ 81 Shannon Brown JSY AU RC	6.00	15.00
❑ 82 Jordan Farmar JSY AU RC	15.00	30.00
❑ 83 Maurice Ager JSY AU RC	6.00	15.00
❑ 84 Mardy Collins JSY AU RC	6.00	15.00
❑ 85 P.J. Tucker JSY AU RC	6.00	15.00
❑ 86 James White JSY AU RC	6.00	15.00
❑ 87 Steve Novak JSY AU RC	6.00	15.00
❑ 88 Solomon Jones JSY AU RC	6.00	15.00
❑ 89 Paul Davis JSY AU RC	6.00	15.00
❑ 90 Thabo Sefolosha AU RC	6.00	15.00
❑ 91 Craig Smith AU RC	5.00	12.00
❑ 92 Bobby Jones AU RC	5.00	12.00
❑ 93 David Noel AU RC	5.00	12.00
❑ 94 Andrea Bargnani AU/150 RC	15.00	30.00
❑ 95 James Augustine AU RC	5.00	12.00
❑ 96 Daniel Gibson AU RC	6.00	15.00
❑ 97 Brandon Roy AU/150 RC	30.00	60.00
❑ 98 Ryan Hollins AU RC	5.00	12.00
❑ 99 Hassan Adams AU RC	6.00	15.00
❑ 100 Pops Mensah-Bonsu AU RC	5.00	12.00
❑ 101 Will Blalock AU RC	5.00	12.00
❑ 102 Damir Markota AU RC	5.00	12.00
❑ 103 Saer Sene AU RC	5.00	12.00
❑ 104 Alexander Johnson RC	2.50	6.00
❑ 105 Leon Powe RC	2.50	6.00
❑ 106 J.J. Redick RC	2.50	6.00
❑ 107 Adam Morrison RC	3.00	8.00
❑ 108 Paul Millsap RC	4.00	10.00
❑ 109 J.R. Pinnock RC	2.50	6.00
❑ 110 Jorge Garbajosa RC	5.00	12.00
❑ 111 Vassilis Spanoulis RC	2.50	6.00
❑ 112 Yakhouba Diawara RC	2.50	6.00

2007-08 Fleer Hot Prospects

❑ COMP.SET w/o SP's (60)	10.00	25.00
❑ 1 Kobe Bryant	1.50	4.00
❑ 2 Carmelo Anthony	.60	1.50
❑ 3 Gilbert Arenas	.30	.75
❑ 4 Dwyane Wade	.75	2.00
❑ 5 LeBron James	1.50	4.00
❑ 6 Michael Redd	.30	.75
❑ 7 Ray Allen	.30	.75
❑ 8 Allen Iverson	.60	1.50
❑ 9 Vince Carter	.60	1.50
❑ 10 Yao Ming	.75	2.00
❑ 11 Joe Johnson	.30	.75
❑ 12 Paul Pierce	.30	.75
❑ 13 Tracy McGrady	.60	1.50
❑ 14 Dirk Nowitzki	.50	1.25
❑ 15 Zach Randolph	.30	.75
❑ 16 Chris Bosh	.30	.75
❑ 17 Kevin Garnett	.75	2.00
❑ 18 Rashard Lewis	.30	.75
❑ 19 Ben Gordon	.40	1.00
❑ 20 Carlos Boozer	.30	.75
❑ 21 Pau Gasol	.30	.75
❑ 22 Elton Brand	.30	.75
❑ 23 Michael Jordan	2.00	5.00
❑ 24 Amare Stoudemire	.60	1.50
❑ 25 Kevin Martin	.30	.75
❑ 26 Baron Davis	.30	.75
❑ 27 Tim Duncan	.60	1.50
❑ 28 Richard Hamilton	.25	.60
❑ 29 Eddy Curry	.20	.50
❑ 30 Jermaine O'Neal	.30	.75
❑ 31 Caron Butler	.30	.75
❑ 32 Josh Howard	.30	.75
❑ 33 Ron Artest	.30	.75
❑ 34 Luol Deng	.30	.75
❑ 35 Steve Nash	.40	1.00
❑ 36 Tony Parker	.30	.75
❑ 37 David West	.30	.75
❑ 38 Andre Iguodala	.30	.75
❑ 39 Gerald Wallace	.30	.75
❑ 40 Jamal Crawford	.20	.50
❑ 41 Dwight Howard	.60	1.50
❑ 42 Mehmet Okur	.25	.60
❑ 43 Shawn Marion	.30	.75
❑ 44 Maurice Williams	.25	.60
❑ 45 Shaquille O'Neal	.75	2.00
❑ 46 Chris Paul	.60	1.50
❑ 47 Chauncey Billups	.30	.75
❑ 48 Brandon Roy	.50	1.25
❑ 49 Josh Smith	.30	.75
❑ 50 Deron Williams	.50	1.25

❑ 51 Jason Richardson	.30	.75
❑ 52 Al Jefferson	.30	.75
❑ 53 Lamar Odom	.30	.75
❑ 54 Raymond Felton	.40	1.00
❑ 55 Andre Miller	.25	.60
❑ 56 Jason Kidd	.50	1.25
❑ 57 Zydrunas Ilgauskas	.25	.60
❑ 58 Andrea Bargnani	.40	1.00
❑ 59 Marcus Camby	.20	.50
❑ 60 Rudy Gay	.25	.60
❑ 61 LeBron James	3.00	8.00
❑ 62 Amare Stoudemire	1.25	3.00
❑ 63 Vince Carter	1.25	3.00
❑ 64 Tim Duncan	1.25	3.00
❑ 65 Allen Iverson	1.25	3.00
❑ 66 Shaquille O'Neal	1.50	4.00
❑ 67 David Robinson	1.50	4.00
❑ 68 Michael Jordan	6.00	15.00
❑ 69 Darrell Griffith	1.00	2.50
❑ 70 Larry Bird	3.00	8.00
❑ 71 Adrian Dantley	1.00	2.50
❑ 72 Bob McAdoo	1.00	2.50
❑ 73 Kareem Abdul-Jabbar	1.50	4.00
❑ 74 Wes Unseld	1.00	2.50
❑ 75 Dave Bing	1.00	2.50
❑ 76 Willis Reed	1.00	2.50
❑ 77 Oscar Robertson	1.00	2.50
❑ 78 Wilt Chamberlain	2.00	5.00
❑ 79 Greg Oden RC	8.00	20.00
❑ 80 Brandan Wright RC	6.00	15.00
❑ 81 Yi Jianlian RC	8.00	20.00
❑ 82 Nick Young RC	5.00	12.00
❑ 83 Thaddeus Young RC	6.00	15.00
❑ 84 Kyrylo Fesenko RC	5.00	12.00
❑ 85 Sun Yue AU RC		
❑ 86 Brad Newley AU RC		
❑ 87 Ramon Sessions AU RC	5.00	12.00
❑ 88 Sammy Mejia AU RC	4.00	10.00
❑ 89 JamesOn Curry AU RC	4.00	10.00
❑ 90 Renaldas Seibutis AU RC		
❑ 91 Milovan Rakovic AU RC		
❑ 92 Marco Belinelli AU RC	5.00	12.00
❑ 93 Darryl Watkins AU RC	4.00	10.00
❑ 94 Demetris Nichols JSY AU RC	6.00	15.00
❑ 95 Javaris Crittenton JSY AU RC	6.00	15.00
❑ 96 Jason Smith JSY AU RC	6.00	15.00
❑ 97 Daequan Cook JSY AU RC	8.00	20.00
❑ 98 Jared Dudley JSY AU RC	6.00	15.00
❑ 99 Wilson Chandler JSY AU RC	6.00	15.00
❑ 100 Morris Almond JSY AU RC	6.00	15.00
❑ 101 Aaron Brooks JSY AU RC	10.00	25.00
❑ 102 Arron Afflalo JSY AU RC	6.00	15.00
❑ 103 Alando Tucker JSY AU RC	6.00	15.00
❑ 104 Carl Landry JSY AU RC	6.00	15.00
❑ 105 Gabe Pruitt JSY AU RC	6.00	15.00
❑ 106 Marcus Williams JSY AU RC	6.00	15.00
❑ 107 Nick Fazekas JSY AU RC	6.00	15.00
❑ 108 Glen Davis JSY AU RC	12.00	30.00
❑ 109 Jermareo Davidson JSY AU RC	6.00	15.00
❑ 110 Josh McRoberts JSY AU RC	8.00	20.00
❑ 111 Herbert Hill JSY AU RC	6.00	15.00
❑ 112 Derrick Byars JSY AU RC	6.00	15.00
❑ 113 Adam Haluska JSY AU RC	6.00	15.00
❑ 114 Reyshawn Terry JSY AU RC	6.00	15.00
❑ 115 Jared Jordan JSY AU RC	6.00	15.00
❑ 116 Stephane Lasme JSY AU RC	6.00	15.00
❑ 117 Dominic McGuire JSY AU RC	6.00	15.00
❑ 118 Aaron Gray JSY AU RC	6.00	15.00
❑ 119 Taurean Green JSY AU RC	6.00	15.00
❑ 120 D.J. Strawberry JSY AU RC	6.00	15.00
❑ 121 Chris Richard JSY AU RC	6.00	15.00
❑ 122 Rodney Stuckey JSY AU RC	20.00	40.00
❑ 123 Kevin Durant JSY AU RC	125.00	250.00
❑ 124 Al Thornton JSY AU RC	8.00	20.00
❑ 125 Julian Wright JSY AU RC	20.00	40.00
❑ 126 Sean Williams JSY AU RC	15.00	30.00
❑ 127 Al Horford JSY AU RC	25.00	50.00
❑ 128 Michael Conley JSY AU RC	20.00	40.00
❑ 129 Jeff Green JSY AU RC	25.00	50.00
❑ 130 Corey Brewer JSY AU RC	20.00	40.00
❑ 131 Joakim Noah JSY AU RC	20.00	40.00
❑ 132 Spencer Hawes JSY AU RC	10.00	25.00
❑ 133 Acie Law JSY AU RC	15.00	30.00

2002-03 Fleer Hot Shots

❑ COMP.SET w/o SP's (168)	15.00	40.00
❑ COMMON CARD (1-168)	.20	.50
❑ COMMON ROOKIE (169-195)	4.00	10.00
❑ COMMON ROOKIE (196-201)	5.00	12.00
❑ COMMON ROOKIE (202-207)	2.00	5.00
❑ RC CARDS HAVE SHIRT UNLESS NOTED		
❑ 1 Shareef Abdur-Rahim	.25	.60
❑ 2 Kedrick Brown	.20	.50
❑ 3 Trenton Hassell	.20	.50
❑ 4 Raef LaFrentz	.20	.50
❑ 5 Donnell Harvey	.20	.50
❑ 6 Danny Fortson	.20	.50
❑ 7 Maurice Taylor	.20	.50
❑ 8 Wang Zhizhi	.20	.50
❑ 9 Malik Allen	.20	.50
❑ 10 Tim Thomas	.20	.50
❑ 11 Jason Kidd	.50	1.25
❑ 12 Jamaal Magloire	.20	.50
❑ 13 Grant Hill	.30	.75
❑ 14 Anfernee Hardaway	.30	.75
❑ 15 Bonzi Wells	.25	.60
❑ 16 Malik Rose	.20	.50
❑ 17 Antonio Davis	.20	.50
❑ 18 John Stockton	.40	1.00
❑ 19 Theo Ratliff	.20	.50
❑ 20 Paul Pierce	.30	.75
❑ 21 Jalen Rose	.25	.60
❑ 22 Eduardo Najera	.20	.50
❑ 23 Chauncey Billups	.30	.75
❑ 24 Antawn Jamison	.30	.75
❑ 25 Jonathan Bender	.20	.50
❑ 26 Rick Fox	.25	.60
❑ 27 Brian Grant	.20	.50
❑ 28 Kevin Garnett	.60	1.50
❑ 29 Kenyon Martin	.30	.75
❑ 30 Allan Houston	.25	.60
❑ 31 Tracy McGrady	.60	1.50
❑ 32 Stephon Marbury	.30	.75
❑ 33 Mike Bibby	.25	.60
❑ 34 Predrag Drobnjak	.20	.50
❑ 35 Lamond Murray	.20	.50
❑ 36 Kwame Brown	.20	.50
❑ 37 Glenn Robinson	.25	.60
❑ 38 Antoine Walker	.25	.60
❑ 39 Zydrunas Ilgauskas	.25	.60
❑ 40 Clifford Robinson	.20	.50
❑ 41 Dirk Nowitzki	.50	1.25
❑ 42 Troy Murphy	.30	.75
❑ 43 Al Harrington	.25	.60
❑ 44 Shaquille O'Neal	.75	2.00
❑ 45 Eddie House	.20	.50
❑ 46 Troy Hudson	.20	.50
❑ 47 Rodney Rogers	.20	.50
❑ 48 Latrell Sprewell	.25	.60
❑ 49 Allen Iverson	.60	1.50
❑ 50 Derek Anderson	.25	.60
❑ 51 Vlade Divac	.25	.60
❑ 52 Rashard Lewis	.30	.75
❑ 53 Morris Peterson	.25	.60
❑ 54 Jerry Stackhouse	.25	.60
❑ 55 Jason Terry	.30	.75
❑ 56 Tyson Chandler	.25	.60
❑ 57 Jumaine Jones	.20	.50
❑ 58 Nick Van Exel	.25	.60
❑ 59 Ben Wallace	.25	.60
❑ 60 Jason Richardson	.30	.75
❑ 61 Ron Mercer	.20	.50
❑ 62 Shane Battier	.25	.60
❑ 63 Eddie Jones	.25	.60
❑ 64 Joe Smith	.20	.50
❑ 65 Courtney Alexander	.20	.50
❑ 66 Kurt Thomas	.20	.50
❑ 67 Todd MacCulloch	.20	.50
❑ 68 Ruben Patterson	.20	.50
❑ 69 Tim Duncan	.60	1.50
❑ 70 Gary Payton	.30	.75
❑ 71 Jarron Collins	.20	.50
❑ 72 Vin Baker	.25	.60
❑ 73 Eddy Curry	.25	.60
❑ 74 Michael Finley	.30	.75
❑ 75 Marcus Camby	.25	.60
❑ 76 Corliss Williamson	.25	.60
❑ 77 Steve Francis	.30	.75
❑ 78 Jermaine O'Neal	.30	.75
❑ 79 Michael Dickerson	.20	.50
❑ 80 Alonzo Mourning	.30	.75
❑ 81 Rod Strickland	.25	.60
❑ 82 Elden Campbell	.20	.50
❑ 83 Charlie Ward	.20	.50
❑ 84 Aaron McKie	.20	.50
❑ 85 Scottie Pippen	.50	1.25
❑ 86 Tony Parker	.30	.75
❑ 87 Vladimir Radmanovic	.20	.50
❑ 88 Matt Harpring	.25	.60
❑ 89 Eddie Griffin	.20	.50
❑ 90 Michael Olowokandi	.20	.50
❑ 91 Stromile Swift	.20	.50
❑ 92 Michael Redd	.30	.75
❑ 93 Richard Jefferson	.30	.75
❑ 94 Baron Davis	.30	.75
❑ 95 Pat Garrity	.20	.50
❑ 96 Tom Gugliotta	.20	.50
❑ 97 Arvydas Sabonis	.25	.60
❑ 98 David Robinson	.40	1.00
❑ 99 Michael Bradley	.20	.50
❑ 100 Karl Malone	.30	.75
❑ 101 J.Terry/G.Robinson	.30	.75
❑ 102 T.Delk/P.Pierce	.20	.50
❑ 103 J.Rose/M. Fizer	.20	.50
❑ 104 D.Miles/R.Davis	.30	.75
❑ 105 S.Nash/D.Nowitzki	.40	1.00
❑ 106 K.Satterfield/J.Howard	.20	.50
❑ 107 R.Hamilton/B.Wallace	.30	.75
❑ 108 G.Arenas/A.Jamison	.30	.75
❑ 109 M.Norris/C.Mobley	.20	.50
❑ 110 J.Tinsley/R.Miller	.30	.75
❑ 111 A.Miller/L.Odom	.20	.50
❑ 112 D.Fisher/K.Bryant	.60	1.50
❑ 113 J.Williams/S.Battier	.30	.75
❑ 114 T.Best/E.Jones	.20	.50
❑ 115 S.Cassell/R.Allen	.30	.75
❑ 116 T.Brandon/W.Szczerbiak	.20	.50
❑ 117 K.Kittles/R.Jefferson	.20	.50
❑ 118 D.Wesley/J.Mashburn	.20	.50
❑ 119 L.Sprewell/A.McDyess	.20	.50
❑ 120 D.Armstrong/M.Miller	.20	.50
❑ 121 E.Snow/K.Van Horn	.20	.50
❑ 122 S.Marbury/S.Marion	.20	.50
❑ 123 D.Stoudamire/R.Wallace	.20	.50
❑ 124 M.Bibby/C.Webber	.30	.75
❑ 125 T.Parker/D.Robinson	.30	.75
❑ 126 K.Anderson/R.Lewis	.20	.50
❑ 127 A.Williams/V.Carter	.30	.75
❑ 128 J.Stockton/K.Malone	.30	.75
❑ 129 L.Hughes/M.Jordan	1.00	2.50
❑ 130 Joe Johnson AS	.30	.75
❑ 131 Andrei Kirilenko AS	.30	.75
❑ 132 Brendan Haywood AS	.20	.50
❑ 133 Zeljko Rebraca AS	.20	.50
❑ 134 Quentin Richardson AS	.25	.60
❑ 135 Chris Mihm AS	.20	.50
❑ 136 Darius Miles AS	.20	.50
❑ 137 Desmond Mason AS	.25	.60
❑ 138 Hedo Turkoglu AS	.25	.60
❑ 139 Jason Richardson AS	.30	.75
❑ 140 Gerald Wallace AS	.30	.75
❑ 141 Steve Francis AS	.30	.75
❑ 142 Steve Nash AS	.50	1.25
❑ 143 Peja Stojakovic AS	.25	.60
❑ 144 Ray Allen AS	.30	.75
❑ 145 Mike Miller AS	.25	.60
❑ 146 Pau Gasol AS	.30	.75
❑ 147 Steve Smith AS	.25	.60
❑ 148 Paul Pierce AS	.30	.75
❑ 149 Derek Fisher AS	.25	.60
❑ 150 Cuttino Mobley AS	.25	.60
❑ 151 Dikembe Mutombo AS	.25	.60
❑ 152 Vince Carter AS	.60	1.50
❑ 153 Antoine Walker AS	.25	.60
❑ 154 Allen Iverson AS	.60	1.50
❑ 155 Michael Jordan AS	2.00	5.00
❑ 156 Shaquille O'Neal AS	.75	2.00
❑ 157 Tim Duncan AS	.60	1.50
❑ 158 Kevin Garnett AS	.60	1.50
❑ 159 Kobe Bryant AS	1.50	4.00
❑ 160 Shareef Abdur-Rahim AS	.25	.60
❑ 161 Baron Davis AS	.30	.75
❑ 162 Jason Kidd AS	.50	1.25
❑ 163 Tracy McGrady AS	.60	1.50

❑ 164 Jermaine O'Neal AS	.30	.75
❑ 165 Elton Brand AS	.30	.75
❑ 166 Gary Payton AS	.30	.75
❑ 167 Wally Szczerbiak AS	.25	.60
❑ 168 Chris Webber AS	.30	.75
❑ 169 Yao Ming Jsy RC	12.00	30.00
❑ 170 Fred Jones RC	5.00	12.00
❑ 171 Ryan Humphrey RC	4.00	10.00
❑ 172 D.Gooden Hat/300 RC	6.00	15.00
❑ 173 Nikoloz Tskitishvili RC	4.00	10.00
❑ 174 C.Butler Shorts/350 RC	8.00	20.00
❑ 175 Vincent Yarbrough RC	4.00	10.00
❑ 176 DaJuan Wagner RC	4.00	10.00
❑ 177 Nene Hilario RC	5.00	12.00
❑ 178 Qyntel Woods/350 RC	4.00	10.00
❑ 179 Jared Jeffries RC	4.00	10.00
❑ 180 Casey Jacobsen RC	4.00	10.00
❑ 181 M.Haislip Hat/300 RC	4.00	10.00
❑ 182 Kareem Rush RC	5.00	12.00
❑ 183 Predrag Savovic RC	4.00	10.00
❑ 184 Melvin Ely RC	4.00	10.00
❑ 185 Amare Stoudmire RC	10.00	25.00
❑ 186 John Salmons RC	6.00	15.00
❑ 187 Chris Jefferies RC	4.00	10.00
❑ 188 Juan Dixon RC	6.00	15.00
❑ 189 Carlos Boozer RC	8.00	20.00
❑ 190 Roger Mason/350 RC	4.00	10.00
❑ 191 Ronald Murray/350 RC	6.00	15.00
❑ 192 Tayshaun Prince RC	6.00	15.00
❑ 193 Chris Wilcox/350 RC	5.00	12.00
❑ 194 Sam Clancy RC	4.00	10.00
❑ 195 Dan Gadzuric RC	4.00	10.00
❑ 196 D.Dickau RC/Carter Jsy	5.00	12.00
❑ 197 F.Williams RC/Carter Jsy	5.00	12.00
❑ 198 Dunleavy RC/VC Jsy/350	5.00	12.00
❑ 199 J.Will RC/Carter Jsy/350	5.00	12.00
❑ 200 Borchardt RC/VC Jsy/350	5.00	12.00
❑ 201 Giricek RC/Carter Jsy/350	5.00	12.00
❑ 202 Pat Burke RC	2.00	5.00
❑ 203 Reggie Evans RC	2.00	5.00
❑ 204 Rasual Butler RC	2.00	5.00
❑ 205 Jiri Welsch RC	2.00	5.00
❑ 206 Mehmet Okur RC	2.50	6.00
❑ 207 Jannero Pargo RC	2.00	5.00

2000-01 Fleer Legacy

❑ COMP.SET w/o SP's (90)	20.00	50.00
❑ COMMON CARD (1-90)	.25	.60
❑ COMMON ROOKIE (91-115)	2.00	5.00
❑ COMMON JSY RC (91-115)	3.00	8.00
❑ 1 Vince Carter	.75	2.00
❑ 2 Tim Duncan	.75	2.00
❑ 3 Darrell Armstrong	.25	.60
❑ 4 Chauncey Billups	.40	1.00
❑ 5 Shawn Kemp	.40	1.00
❑ 6 Stephon Marbury	.40	1.00
❑ 7 Dan Majerle	.30	.75
❑ 8 Antawn Jamison	.40	1.00
❑ 9 Hakeem Olajuwon	.50	1.25
❑ 10 Kobe Bryant	2.00	5.00
❑ 11 Paul Pierce	.40	1.00
❑ 12 Patrick Ewing	.50	1.25
❑ 13 Steve Francis	.40	1.00
❑ 14 Latrell Sprewell	.30	.75
❑ 15 Andre Miller	.30	.75
❑ 16 Gary Payton	.40	1.00
❑ 17 Michael Finley	.40	1.00
❑ 18 Brian Grant	.25	.60
❑ 19 Scottie Pippen	.60	1.50
❑ 20 Antonio Davis	.25	.60
❑ 21 Jason Williams	.30	.75
❑ 22 Chris Gatling	.25	.60
❑ 23 David Robinson	.50	1.25
❑ 24 John Stockton	.50	1.25
❑ 25 Matt Harpring	.30	.75
❑ 26 Rashard Lewis	.40	1.00
❑ 27 Dirk Nowitzki	.60	1.50
❑ 28 Alan Henderson	.25	.60
❑ 29 Rasheed Wallace	.40	1.00
❑ 30 Ben Wallace	.30	.75
❑ 31 Chris Webber	.40	1.00
❑ 32 Elton Brand	.40	1.00
❑ 33 Anfernee Hardaway	.40	1.00
❑ 34 Isaiah Rider	.30	.75
❑ 35 Baron Davis	.40	1.00
❑ 36 Eric Snow	.25	.60
❑ 37 Tom Gugliotta	.25	.60
❑ 38 Grant Hill	.40	1.00
❑ 39 Lamar Odom	.40	1.00
❑ 40 Kevin Garnett	.75	2.00
❑ 41 Reggie Miller	.40	1.00
❑ 42 Karl Malone	.50	1.25
❑ 43 Ray Allen	.40	1.00
❑ 44 Derek Anderson	.30	.75
❑ 45 Glen Rice	.30	.75
❑ 46 Antonio McDyess	.30	.75
❑ 47 Eddie Jones	.30	.75
❑ 48 Mitch Richmond	.30	.75
❑ 49 Mark Jackson	.30	.75
❑ 50 Larry Johnson	.30	.75
❑ 51 Ron Mercer	.25	.60
❑ 52 Jason Kidd	.60	1.50
❑ 53 Voshon Lenard	.25	.60
❑ 54 Rick Fox	.30	.75
❑ 55 Rod Strickland	.30	.75
❑ 56 Jalen Rose	.30	.75
❑ 57 Tracy McGrady	.75	2.00
❑ 58 Dikembe Mutombo	.30	.75
❑ 59 Richard Hamilton	.30	.75
❑ 60 Jerry Stackhouse	.30	.75
❑ 61 Peja Stojakovic	.30	.75
❑ 62 Sam Cassell	.30	.75
❑ 63 Sean Elliott	.30	.75
❑ 64 Keith Van Horn	.30	.75
❑ 65 Mike Bibby	.30	.75
❑ 66 Larry Hughes	.30	.75
❑ 67 Nick Van Exel	.30	.75
❑ 68 Michael Dickerson	.25	.60
❑ 69 Terrell Brandon	.25	.60
❑ 70 Chucky Atkins	.25	.60
❑ 71 John Starks	.25	.60
❑ 72 Glenn Robinson	.30	.75
❑ 73 Cuttino Mobley	.30	.75
❑ 74 Shaquille O'Neal	1.00	2.50
❑ 75 Shareef Abdur-Rahim	.30	.75
❑ 76 Danny Fortson	.25	.60
❑ 77 Austin Croshere	.25	.60
❑ 78 Jamal Mashburn	.30	.75
❑ 79 Kenny Anderson	.30	.75
❑ 80 Shawn Marion	.40	1.00
❑ 81 Travis Best	.25	.60
❑ 82 Derrick Coleman	.30	.75
❑ 83 Toni Kukoc	.30	.75
❑ 84 Allen Iverson	.75	2.00
❑ 85 Allan Houston	.30	.75
❑ 86 Antoine Walker	.30	.75
❑ 87 Wally Szczerbiak	.30	.75
❑ 88 Raef LaFrentz	.25	.60
❑ 89 Tim Hardaway	.30	.75
❑ 90 Juwan Howard	.30	.75
❑ 91 Kenyon Martin JSY RC	8.00	20.00
❑ 92 Stromile Swift RC	2.50	6.00
❑ 93 Darius Miles JSY RC	4.00	10.00
❑ 94 Mike Miller JSY RC	5.00	12.00
❑ 95 Marcus Fizer RC	2.00	5.00
❑ 96 Jerome Moiso JSY RC	3.00	8.00
❑ 97 DerMarr Johnson JSY RC	3.00	8.00
❑ 98 Quentin Richardson JSY RC	4.00	10.00
❑ 99 Morris Peterson JSY RC	5.00	12.00
❑ 100 Jamaal Magloire RC	2.00	5.00
❑ 101 Mateen Cleaves RC	2.00	5.00
❑ 102 Hedo Turkoglu RC	5.00	12.00
❑ 103 Chris Mihm JSY RC	3.00	8.00
❑ 104 Courtney Alexander RC	2.00	5.00
❑ 105 Joel Przybilla RC	2.00	5.00
❑ 106 Speedy Claxton JSY RC	3.00	8.00
❑ 107 Keyon Dooling JSY RC	3.00	8.00
❑ 108 Desmond Mason JSY RC	4.00	10.00
❑ 109 Jamal Crawford RC	3.00	8.00
❑ 110 DeShawn Stevenson RC	2.00	5.00
❑ 111 Stephen Jackson RC	3.00	8.00
❑ 112 Marc Jackson RC	2.50	6.00
❑ 113 Hanno Mottola JSY RC	3.00	8.00
❑ 114 Eduardo Najera RC	2.00	5.00
❑ 115 Wang Zhizhi RC	4.00	10.00
❑ WUSA1 Vince Carter/600	50.00	100.00

2001-02 Fleer Marquee

❑ COMPLETE SET w/o SPs	20.00	40.00
❑ COMMON ROOKIE (116-125)	1.25	3.00
❑ 1 DerMarr Johnson	.20	.50
❑ 2 Darius Miles	.20	.50
❑ 3 Michael Jordan	6.00	15.00
❑ 4 Speedy Claxton	.20	.50
❑ 5 Stromile Swift	.20	.50
❑ 6 Michael Finley	.30	.75
❑ 7 Kurt Thomas	.20	.50
❑ 8 Tim Duncan	.60	1.50
❑ 9 Kenyon Martin	.30	.75
❑ 10 Jermaine O'Neal	.30	.75
❑ 11 Elton Brand	.30	.75
❑ 12 Jamal Mashburn	.25	.60
❑ 13 Jumaine Jones	.20	.50
❑ 14 Stephon Marbury	.30	.75
❑ 15 Eddie Jones	.25	.60
❑ 16 Antonio McDyess	.25	.60
❑ 17 Tim Thomas	.20	.50
❑ 18 Gary Payton	.30	.75
❑ 19 Latrell Sprewell	.25	.60
❑ 20 Grant Hill	.30	.75
❑ 21 Jason Terry	.30	.75
❑ 22 Marcus Fizer	.20	.50
❑ 23 Anthony Mason	.20	.50
❑ 24 Bonzi Wells	.25	.60
❑ 25 Sam Cassell	.25	.60
❑ 26 Jerry Stackhouse	.25	.60
❑ 27 Hedo Turkoglu	.25	.60
❑ 28 Morris Peterson	.25	.60
❑ 29 John Stockton	.40	1.00
❑ 30 Dikembe Mutombo	.25	.60
❑ 31 Mitch Richmond	.25	.60
❑ 32 Andre Miller	.25	.60
❑ 33 Joe Smith	.20	.50
❑ 34 Mike Bibby	.25	.60
❑ 35 Wally Szczerbiak	.25	.60
❑ 36 Steve Francis	.30	.75
❑ 37 Nazr Mohammed	.20	.50
❑ 38 Antoine Walker	.25	.60
❑ 39 Courtney Alexander	.20	.50
❑ 40 Shawn Marion	.30	.75
❑ 41 Jason Williams	.25	.60
❑ 42 Steve Nash	.50	1.25
❑ 43 Antonio Davis	.20	.50
❑ 44 Steve Smith	.25	.60
❑ 45 Jason Kidd	.50	1.25
❑ 46 Reggie Miller	.30	.75
❑ 47 Quentin Richardson	.25	.60
❑ 48 Baron Davis	.30	.75
❑ 49 Juwan Howard	.25	.60
❑ 50 Rasheed Wallace	.30	.75
❑ 51 Brian Grant	.20	.50
❑ 52 Nick Van Exel	.25	.60
❑ 53 Donyell Marshall	.20	.50
❑ 54 Vin Baker	.25	.60
❑ 55 Allan Houston	.25	.60
❑ 56 Mike Miller	.25	.60
❑ 57 Shaquille O'Neal	.75	2.00
❑ 58 Ron Mercer	.20	.50
❑ 59 Lindsey Hunter	.20	.50
❑ 60 Peja Stojakovic	.25	.60
❑ 61 Ray Allen	.30	.75
❑ 62 Antawn Jamison	.30	.75
❑ 63 Theo Ratliff	.20	.50
❑ 64 Vince Carter	.60	1.50
❑ 65 DeShawn Stevenson	.20	.50
❑ 66 Allen Iverson	.60	1.50
❑ 67 Derek Fisher	.25	.60
❑ 68 Dirk Nowitzki	.50	1.25
❑ 69 Keith Van Horn	.25	.60
❑ 70 David Robinson	.40	1.00

❑ 71 Terrell Brandon	.20	.50
❑ 72 Cuttino Mobley	.25	.60
❑ 73 Shareef Abdur-Rahim	.25	.60
❑ 74 Paul Pierce	.30	.75
❑ 75 Elden Campbell	.20	.50
❑ 76 Anfernee Hardaway	.30	.75
❑ 77 Alonzo Mourning	.30	.75
❑ 78 Raef LaFrentz	.20	.50
❑ 79 Richard Hamilton	.25	.60
❑ 80 Rashard Lewis	.30	.75
❑ 81 Marcus Camby	.25	.60
❑ 82 Jalen Rose	.25	.60
❑ 83 Lamar Odom	.30	.75
❑ 84 David Wesley	.20	.50
❑ 85 James Posey	.20	.50
❑ 86 Derek Anderson	.25	.60
❑ 87 Glenn Robinson	.25	.60
❑ 88 Clifford Robinson	.20	.50
❑ 89 Kerry Kittles	.25	.60
❑ 90 Hakeem Olajuwon	.40	1.00
❑ 91 Patrick Ewing	.40	1.00
❑ 92 Tracy McGrady	.60	1.50
❑ 93 Kobe Bryant	1.50	4.00
❑ 94 Chris Mihm	.20	.50
❑ 95 Lorenzen Wright	.20	.50
❑ 96 Chris Webber	.30	.75
❑ 97 Kevin Garnett	.60	1.50
❑ 98 Larry Hughes	.25	.60
❑ 99 Keyon Dooling	.20	.50
❑ 100 Karl Malone	.40	1.00
❑ 101 Joe Johnson RC	2.00	5.00
❑ 102 Tyson Chandler RC	1.50	4.00
❑ 103 Eddy Curry RC	1.25	3.00
❑ 104 Jason Richardson RC	1.50	4.00
❑ 105 Troy Murphy RC	1.50	4.00
❑ 106 Eddie Griffin RC	.75	2.00
❑ 107 Jamaal Tinsley RC	1.00	2.50
❑ 108 Pau Gasol RC	3.00	8.00
❑ 109 Shane Battier RC	1.25	3.00
❑ 110 Richard Jefferson RC	2.00	5.00
❑ 111 Steven Hunter RC	.75	2.00
❑ 112 Tony Parker RC	3.00	8.00
❑ 113 Vladimir Radmanovic RC	1.00	2.50
❑ 114 Andrei Kirilenko RC	2.00	5.00
❑ 115 Kwame Brown RC	1.00	2.50
❑ 116 S.Dalembrt RC/D.Brown RC	1.25	3.00
❑ 117 J.Forte RC/Ke.Brown RC	1.25	3.00
❑ 118 Randolph RC/R.Boumtje RC	2.50	6.00
❑ 119 O.Torres RC/T.Morris RC	1.25	3.00
❑ 120 A.Ford RC/K.Satterfield RC	1.50	4.00
❑ 121 R.White RC/Z.Rebraca RC	1.25	3.00
❑ 122 T.Hassell RC/E.Watson RC	1.25	3.00
❑ 123 D.Diop RC/P.Brezec RC	1.50	4.00
❑ 124 E.Brown RC/G.Wallace RC	1.25	3.00
❑ 125 L.Woods RC/B.Haywood RC	1.25	3.00
❑ 126 Mengke Bateer RC	3.00	8.00
❑ NNO Vince Carter AU/113	25.00	50.00

2001-02 Fleer Maximum

❑ COMPLETE SET (220)	125.00	300.00
❑ COMP.SET w/o SP's (180)	15.00	40.00
❑ COMMON CARD (1-180)	.15	.40
❑ COMMON ROOKIE (181-220)	1.00	2.50
❑ CARTER AU NOT INCLUDED IN SET PRICE		
❑ 1 Ray Allen	.25	.60
❑ 2 Elton Brand	.25	.60
❑ 3 Grant Hill	.25	.60
❑ 4 Tracy McGrady	.50	1.25
❑ 5 Chris Webber	.25	.60
❑ 6 Latrell Sprewell	.20	.50
❑ 7 Paul Pierce	.25	.60
❑ 8 Jason Kidd	.40	1.00
❑ 9 Shaquille O'Neal	.60	1.50
❑ 10 Stephon Marbury	.25	.60
❑ 11 Steve Francis	.25	.60
❑ 12 Vince Carter	.50	1.25
❑ 13 Allen Iverson	.50	1.25
❑ 14 Kevin Garnett	.50	1.25
❑ 15 Eddie Jones	.20	.50
❑ 16 Antoine Walker	.20	.50
❑ 17 Kobe Bryant	1.25	3.00
❑ 18 Avery Johnson	.20	.50
❑ 19 Damon Stoudamire	.20	.50
❑ 20 Kurt Thomas	.15	.40
❑ 21 Aaron McKie	.15	.40
❑ 22 Chris Whitney	.15	.40
❑ 23 David Robinson	.30	.75
❑ 24 Erick Dampier	.15	.40
❑ 25 Jumaine Jones	.15	.40
❑ 26 Radoslav Nesterovic	.15	.40
❑ 27 Robert Horry	.20	.50
❑ 28 Ben Wallace	.20	.50
❑ 29 Christian Laettner	.15	.40
❑ 30 Eddie Robinson	.15	.40
❑ 31 Alvin Williams	.15	.40
❑ 32 Matt Harpring	.20	.50
❑ 33 Terrell Brandon	.15	.40
❑ 34 Tim Duncan	.50	1.25
❑ 35 Bonzi Wells	.20	.50
❑ 36 Clarence Weatherspoon	.15	.40
❑ 37 George McCloud	.15	.40
❑ 38 Jermaine O'Neal	.25	.60
❑ 39 Al Harrington	.20	.50
❑ 40 Antawn Jamison	.25	.60
❑ 41 John Amaechi	.15	.40
❑ 42 Rod Strickland	.20	.50
❑ 43 Stacey Augmon	.15	.40
❑ 44 Dion Glover	.15	.40
❑ 45 Michael Dickerson	.15	.40
❑ 46 Anfernee Hardaway	.25	.60
❑ 47 Rashard Lewis	.25	.60
❑ 48 Shawn Bradley	.15	.40
❑ 49 Todd MacCulloch	.15	.40
❑ 50 Antonio McDyess	.20	.50
❑ 51 Darrell Armstrong	.15	.40
❑ 52 Jalen Rose	.20	.50
❑ 53 Mike Bibby	.20	.50
❑ 54 P.J. Brown	.15	.40
❑ 55 Quincy Lewis	.15	.40
❑ 56 Doug Christie	.15	.40
❑ 57 Elden Campbell	.15	.40
❑ 58 James Posey	.15	.40
❑ 59 Karl Malone	.30	.75
❑ 60 Patrick Ewing	.30	.75
❑ 61 Sam Cassell	.20	.50
❑ 62 Baron Davis	.25	.60
❑ 63 Corey Maggette	.20	.50
❑ 64 Donyell Marshall	.15	.40
❑ 65 Ervin Johnson	.15	.40
❑ 66 Horace Grant	.20	.50
❑ 67 Nick Van Exel	.20	.50
❑ 68 Vlade Divac	.20	.50
❑ 69 Allan Houston	.20	.50
❑ 70 Antonio Davis	.15	.40
❑ 71 Dale Davis	.15	.40
❑ 72 Eduardo Najera	.15	.40
❑ 73 Kenny Anderson	.20	.50
❑ 74 Kevin Willis	.15	.40
❑ 75 LaPhonso Ellis	.20	.50
❑ 76 Anthony Mason	.15	.40
❑ 77 Greg Ostertag	.15	.40
❑ 78 Jamal Mashburn	.20	.50
❑ 79 Jeff McInnis	.15	.40
❑ 80 Peja Stojakovic	.20	.50
❑ 81 Scott Williams	.15	.40
❑ 82 Bryon Russell	.15	.40
❑ 83 Chucky Atkins	.15	.40
❑ 84 Darius Miles	.15	.40
❑ 85 David Wesley	.15	.40
❑ 86 Hedo Turkoglu	.20	.50
❑ 87 Mark Pope	.15	.40
❑ 88 Dana Barros	.15	.40
❑ 89 Glenn Robinson	.20	.50
❑ 90 John Stockton	.30	.75
❑ 91 Lamar Odom	.25	.60
❑ 92 Mike Miller	.20	.50
❑ 93 Ron Artest	.20	.50
❑ 94 Adonal Foyle	.15	.40
❑ 95 Andre Miller	.20	.50
❑ 96 Eric Snow	.15	.40
❑ 97 Stanislav Medvedenko	.15	.40
❑ 98 Steve Smith	.20	.50
❑ 99 Wally Szczerbiak	.20	.50
❑ 100 Chris Mihm	.15	.40
❑ 101 Danny Fortson	.15	.40
❑ 102 Dikembe Mutombo	.20	.50
❑ 103 Joe Smith	.15	.40
❑ 104 Lindsey Hunter	.15	.40
❑ 105 Malik Rose	.15	.40
❑ 106 Austin Croshere	.15	.40
❑ 107 Chris Gatling	.15	.40
❑ 108 Hakeem Olajuwon	.30	.75
❑ 109 Mark Jackson	.20	.50
❑ 110 Milt Palacio	.15	.40
❑ 111 Ruben Patterson	.15	.40
❑ 112 Steve Nash	.40	1.00
❑ 113 Brian Grant	.15	.40
❑ 114 Dirk Nowitzki	.40	1.00
❑ 115 Jeff Foster	.15	.40
❑ 116 Morris Peterson	.20	.50
❑ 117 Scottie Pippen	.40	1.00
❑ 118 Lamond Murray	.15	.40
❑ 119 Larry Hughes	.20	.50
❑ 120 Shareef Abdur-Rahim	.20	.50
❑ 121 Tony Delk	.15	.40
❑ 122 Vin Baker	.20	.50
❑ 123 Art Long	.15	.40
❑ 124 Kenyon Martin	.25	.60
❑ 125 Michael Finley	.25	.60
❑ 126 Stromile Swift	.15	.40
❑ 127 Toni Kukoc	.20	.50
❑ 128 Alonzo Mourning	.25	.60
❑ 129 Charlie Ward	.15	.40
❑ 130 Eric Williams	.15	.40
❑ 131 Jerome Williams	.15	.40
❑ 132 Raef LaFrentz	.15	.40
❑ 133 Rasheed Wallace	.25	.60
❑ 134 Reggie Miller	.25	.60
❑ 135 Cuttino Mobley	.20	.50
❑ 136 Desmond Mason	.20	.50
❑ 137 Jason Williams	.20	.50
❑ 138 Keith Van Horn	.20	.50
❑ 139 Nazr Mohammed	.15	.40
❑ 140 Shawn Marion	.25	.60
❑ 141 Tim Hardaway	.20	.50
❑ 142 Anthony Carter	.15	.40
❑ 143 Danny Manning	.15	.40
❑ 144 Derek Anderson	.20	.50
❑ 145 Jason Terry	.25	.60
❑ 146 Kenny Thomas	.15	.40
❑ 147 Othella Harrington	.15	.40
❑ 148 Corliss Williamson	.20	.50
❑ 149 Derek Fisher	.20	.50
❑ 150 Ricky Davis	.20	.50
❑ 151 Stephen Jackson	.20	.50
❑ 152 Tryone Nesby	.15	.40
❑ 153 Calvin Booth	.15	.40
❑ 154 Emanual Davis	.15	.40
❑ 155 Kerry Kittles	.20	.50
❑ 156 Marc Jackson	.15	.40
❑ 157 Samaki Walker	.15	.40
❑ 158 Tom Gugliotta	.15	.40
❑ 159 Wesley Person	.15	.40
❑ 160 Antonio Daniels	.15	.40
❑ 161 Charles Oakley	.20	.50
❑ 162 Chauncey Billups	.20	.50
❑ 163 Derrick Coleman	.20	.50
❑ 164 Jerry Stackhouse	.20	.50
❑ 165 Michael Jordan	4.00	10.00
❑ 166 Quentin Richardson	.20	.50
❑ 167 Gary Payton	.25	.60
❑ 168 Iakovos Tsakalidis	.15	.40
❑ 169 Juwan Howard	.20	.50
❑ 170 Lorenzen Wright	.15	.40
❑ 171 Marcus Camby	.20	.50
❑ 172 Maurice Taylor	.15	.40
❑ 173 Jacque Vaughn	.15	.40
❑ 174 Bruce Bowen	.15	.40
❑ 175 Clifford Robinson	.15	.40
❑ 176 Michael Olowokandi	.15	.40
❑ 177 Richard Hamilton	.20	.50
❑ 178 Ron Mercer	.15	.40
❑ 179 Speedy Claxton	.15	.40
❑ 180 Tim Thomas	.15	.40
❑ 181 Joe Johnson HW RC	2.50	6.00
❑ 182 Pau Gasol HW RC	4.00	10.00
❑ 183 Kwame Brown HW RC	1.25	3.00
❑ 184 Zach Randolph HW RC	2.50	6.00
❑ 185 Jason Richardson HW RC	2.00	5.00
❑ 186 Jamaal Tinsley HW RC	1.25	3.00
❑ 187 Oscar Torres HW RC	1.00	2.50
❑ 188 Rodney White HW RC	1.00	2.50
❑ 189 Kedrick Brown HW RC	1.00	2.50
❑ 190 Tony Parker HW RC	4.00	10.00

❑ 191 Samuel Dalembert HW RC	1.25	3.00
❑ 192 Shane Battier HW RC	1.50	4.00
❑ 193 Loren Woods HW RC	1.00	2.50
❑ 194 Richard Jefferson HW RC	2.50	6.00
❑ 195 Jeff Trepagnier HW RC	1.00	2.50
❑ 196 Terence Morris HW RC	1.00	2.50
❑ 197 Eddie Griffin TC RC	1.00	2.50
❑ 198 Primoz Brezec TC RC	1.25	3.00
❑ 199 V.Radmanovic TC RC	1.25	3.00
❑ 200 Gerald Wallace TC RC	2.50	6.00
❑ 201 Alton Ford TC RC	1.00	2.50
❑ 202 Steven Hunter TC RC	1.00	2.50
❑ 203 Michael Bradley TC RC	1.00	2.50
❑ 204 B.Armstrong TC RC	1.00	2.50
❑ 205 Jamaal Tinsley TC RC	1.25	3.00
❑ 206 Bobby Simmons TC RC	1.00	2.50
❑ 207 Zeljko Rebraca TC RC	1.00	2.50
❑ 208 Tony Parker TC RC	4.00	10.00
❑ 209 Troy Murphy TC RC	2.00	5.00
❑ 210 Kwame Brown TC RC	1.25	3.00
❑ 211 Andrei Kirilenko TC RC	2.50	6.00
❑ 212 Trenton Hassell TC RC	1.25	3.00
❑ 213 Pau Gasol TC RC	4.00	10.00
❑ 214 Tang Hamilton TC RC	1.00	2.50
❑ 215 Joseph Forte TC RC	1.00	2.50
❑ 216 Eddy Curry TC RC	1.50	4.00
❑ 217 DeSagana Diop TC RC	1.00	2.50
❑ 218 Joe Johnson TC RC	2.50	6.00
❑ 219 Tyson Chandler TC RC	2.00	5.00
❑ 220 Jason Collins TC RC	1.00	2.50
❑ NNO V.Carter AU/375	30.00	60.00

1999-00 Fleer Mystique

❑ COMPLETE SET (150)	75.00	150.00
❑ COMPLETE SET w/o SP (100)	15.00	30.00
❑ COMMON CARD (1-100)	.25	.60
❑ COMMON ROOKIE (101-140)	.75	2.00
❑ COMMON STAR (141-150)	.75	2.00
❑ 1 Allen Iverson	.75	2.00
❑ 2 Grant Hill	.40	1.00
❑ 3 Antawn Jamison	.40	1.00
❑ 4 Glenn Robinson	.30	.75
❑ 5 Kenny Anderson	.30	.75
❑ 6 Dikembe Mutombo	.30	.75
❑ 7 Gary Trent	.25	.60
❑ 8 Brevin Knight	.25	.60
❑ 9 Chucky Brown	.25	.60
❑ 10 Derek Anderson	.25	.60
❑ 11 Ricky Davis	.40	1.00
❑ 12 Chris Webber	.40	1.00
❑ 13 Jalen Rose	.30	.75
❑ 14 Antoine Walker	.40	1.00
❑ 15 Michael Dickerson	.25	.60
❑ 16 Tim Hardaway	.40	1.00
❑ 17 Toni Kukoc	.40	1.00
❑ 18 Raef LaFrentz	.30	.75
❑ 19 Anthony Mason	.25	.60
❑ 20 John Stockton	.50	1.25
❑ 21 Hakeem Olajuwon	.40	1.00
❑ 22 Shaquille O'Neal	1.00	2.50
❑ 23 Scottie Pippen	.60	1.50
❑ 24 Maurice Taylor	.30	.75
❑ 25 Tariq Abdul-Wahad	.25	.60
❑ 26 Tracy McGrady	.75	2.00
❑ 27 Joe Smith	.30	.75
❑ 28 Rod Strickland	.25	.60
❑ 29 Ruben Patterson	.25	.60
❑ 30 Tom Gugliotta	.25	.60
❑ 31 Ray Allen	.40	1.00
❑ 32 Elden Campbell	.25	.60
❑ 33 Lindsey Hunter	.25	.60
❑ 34 Larry Johnson	.40	1.00
❑ 35 Michael Olowokandi	.25	.60
❑ 36 Mario Elie	.25	.60
❑ 37 Anfernee Hardaway	.40	1.00
❑ 38 Juwan Howard	.30	.75
❑ 39 Karl Malone	.50	1.25
❑ 40 Alonzo Mourning	.40	1.00
❑ 41 Billy Owens	.25	.60
❑ 42 Mitch Richmond	.30	.75
❑ 43 Darrell Armstrong	.25	.60
❑ 44 Jason Williams	.40	1.00
❑ 45 Mookie Blaylock	.25	.60
❑ 46 Gary Payton	.40	1.00
❑ 47 Brian Grant	.25	.60
❑ 48 Paul Pierce	.40	1.00
❑ 49 Michael Finley	.40	1.00
❑ 50 Reggie Miller	.40	1.00
❑ 51 Corliss Williamson	.25	.60
❑ 52 Shandon Anderson	.25	.60
❑ 53 Stephon Marbury	.40	1.00
❑ 54 Sam Cassell	.30	.75
❑ 55 Bryon Russell	.25	.60
❑ 56 Rasheed Wallace	.40	1.00
❑ 57 Jayson Williams	.30	.75
❑ 58 Damon Stoudamire	.40	1.00
❑ 59 Terrell Brandon	.25	.60
❑ 60 Loy Vaught	.25	.60
❑ 61 Kobe Bryant	2.00	5.00
❑ 62 Vlade Divac	.40	1.00
❑ 63 Derek Fisher	.40	1.00
❑ 64 Isaiah Rider	.25	.60
❑ 65 Eddie Jones	.40	1.00
❑ 66 Kevin Garnett	.75	2.00
❑ 67 David Robinson	.50	1.25
❑ 68 Marcus Camby	.30	.75
❑ 69 Glen Rice	.40	1.00
❑ 70 Mike Bibby	.40	1.00
❑ 71 Patrick Ewing	.50	1.25
❑ 72 Robert Traylor	.25	.60
❑ 73 Tim Duncan	.75	2.00
❑ 74 Michael Doleac	.25	.60
❑ 75 Steve Smith	.25	.60
❑ 76 Allan Houston	.30	.75
❑ 77 Jamal Mashburn	.25	.60
❑ 78 Brent Barry	.30	.75
❑ 79 Charles Barkley	.50	1.25
❑ 80 Ron Mercer	.25	.60
❑ 81 Jerry Stackhouse	.40	1.00
❑ 82 Keith Van Horn	.30	.75
❑ 83 Hersey Hawkins	.25	.60
❑ 84 Avery Johnson	.30	.75
❑ 85 Cedric Ceballos	.25	.60
❑ 86 P.J. Brown	.25	.60
❑ 87 Doug Christie	.30	.75
❑ 88 Shawn Kemp	.40	1.00
❑ 89 Dirk Nowitzki	.60	1.50
❑ 90 Erick Dampier	.30	.75
❑ 91 Antonio McDyess	.30	.75
❑ 92 Mark Jackson	.40	1.00
❑ 93 Clifford Robinson	.25	.60
❑ 94 Vince Carter	.75	2.00
❑ 95 Shareef Abdur-Rahim	.30	.75
❑ 96 Vin Baker	.40	1.00
❑ 97 Larry Hughes	.30	.75
❑ 98 Jason Kidd	.60	1.50
❑ 99 Kerry Kittles	.25	.60
❑ 100 Latrell Sprewell	.30	.75
❑ 101 Lamar Odom RC	2.50	6.00
❑ 102 Elton Brand RC	2.50	6.00
❑ 103 Baron Davis RC	3.00	8.00
❑ 104 Jason Terry RC	2.00	5.00
❑ 105 Corey Maggette RC	2.50	6.00
❑ 106 Wally Szczerbiak RC	2.50	6.00
❑ 107 Richard Hamilton RC	2.50	6.00
❑ 108 Milt Palacio RC	.75	2.00
❑ 109 Ron Artest RC	3.00	8.00
❑ 110 Eddie Robinson RC	.75	2.00
❑ 111 Jumaine Jones RC	.75	2.00
❑ 112 Andre Miller RC	2.50	6.00
❑ 113 Chucky Atkins RC	1.00	2.50
❑ 114 Kenny Thomas RC	.75	2.00
❑ 115 Scott Padgett RC	.75	2.00
❑ 116 Devean George RC	1.25	3.00
❑ 117 Tim Young RC	.75	2.00
❑ 118 Tim James RC	.75	2.00
❑ 119 Quincy Lewis RC	.75	2.00
❑ 120 James Posey RC	1.25	3.00
❑ 121 Shawn Marion RC	2.50	6.00
❑ 122 A.Radojevic RC	.75	2.00
❑ 123 Trajan Langdon RC	.75	2.00
❑ 124 Laron Profit RC	.75	2.00
❑ 125 Jonathan Bender RC	.75	2.00
❑ 126 William Avery RC	.75	2.00
❑ 127 Cal Bowdler RC	.75	2.00
❑ 128 Dion Glover RC	.75	2.00
❑ 129 Jeff Foster RC	1.00	2.50
❑ 130 Steve Francis RC	2.50	6.00
❑ 131 Adrian Griffin RC	.75	2.00
❑ 132 Vonteego Cummings RC	.75	2.00
❑ 133 Rafer Alston RC	1.50	4.00
❑ 134 Michael Ruffin RC	.75	2.00
❑ 135 Chris Herren RC	.75	2.00
❑ 136 Jermaine Jackson RC	.75	2.00
❑ 137 Lazaro Borrell RC	.75	2.00
❑ 138 Obinna Ekezie RC	.75	2.00
❑ 139 Rick Hughes RC	.75	2.00
❑ 140 Todd MacCulloch RC	.75	2.00
❑ 141 Kobe Bryant STAR	6.00	15.00
❑ 142 Vince Carter STAR	2.50	6.00
❑ 143 Tim Duncan STAR	2.50	6.00
❑ 144 Kevin Garnett STAR	2.50	6.00
❑ 145 Allen Iverson STAR	2.50	6.00
❑ 146 Keith Van Horn STAR	1.00	2.50
❑ 147 Grant Hill STAR	1.25	3.00
❑ 148 Stephon Marbury STAR	1.25	3.00
❑ 149 Antoine Walker STAR	1.25	3.00
❑ 150 Shaquille O'Neal STAR	3.00	8.00

2000-01 Fleer Mystique

❑ COMPLETE SET w/o RC (100)	15.00	30.00
❑ COMMON CARD (1-100)	.08	.25
❑ COMMON ROOKIE (101-106)	2.50	6.00
❑ COMMON ROOKIE (107-112)	2.00	5.00
❑ COMMON ROOKIE (113-117)	1.50	4.00
❑ COMMON ROOKIE (118-124)	1.00	2.50
❑ COMMON ROOKIE (125-130)	.60	1.50
❑ COMMON ROOKIE (131-136)	.50	1.25
❑ 1 Shaquille O'Neal	.75	2.00
❑ 2 Gary Payton	.30	.75
❑ 3 Nick Van Exel	.25	.60
❑ 4 Alonzo Mourning	.30	.75
❑ 5 Shawn Marion	.30	.75
❑ 6 Rod Strickland	.25	.60
❑ 7 Mookie Blaylock	.25	.60
❑ 8 Terrell Brandon	.20	.50
❑ 9 Bryon Russell	.20	.50
❑ 10 Jerry Stackhouse	.25	.60
❑ 11 Glenn Robinson	.25	.60
❑ 12 Rasheed Wallace	.30	.75
❑ 13 Tracy McGrady	.60	1.50
❑ 14 Raef LaFrentz	.20	.50
❑ 15 P.J. Brown	.20	.50
❑ 16 Anfernee Hardaway	.30	.75
❑ 17 Mike Bibby	.25	.60
❑ 18 Elden Campbell	.20	.50
❑ 19 Steve Francis	.30	.75
❑ 20 Keith Van Horn	.25	.60
❑ 21 Karl Malone	.40	1.00
❑ 22 Dirk Nowitzki	.50	1.25
❑ 23 Glen Rice	.25	.60
❑ 24 Tom Gugliotta	.20	.50
❑ 25 Avery Johnson	.25	.60
❑ 26 Michael Finley	.30	.75
❑ 27 Theo Ratliff	.20	.50
❑ 28 Juwan Howard	.25	.60
❑ 29 Anthony Carter	.20	.50
❑ 30 Kobe Bryant	1.50	4.00
❑ 31 Toni Kukoc	.25	.60
❑ 32 Jason Terry	.30	.75
❑ 33 Elton Brand	.30	.75
❑ 34 Reggie Miller	.30	.75
❑ 35 Latrell Sprewell	.25	.60
❑ 36 Adrian Griffin	.20	.50
❑ 37 Cuttino Mobley	.25	.60
❑ 38 Maurice Taylor	.20	.50
❑ 39 Allen Iverson	.60	1.50
❑ 40 Tim Duncan	.60	1.50
❑ 41 Andre Miller	.25	.60
❑ 42 Antonio Davis	.20	.50
❑ 43 Howard Eisley	.20	.50

❑ 44 Vlade Divac	.25	.60
❑ 45 Brevin Knight	.20	.50
❑ 46 Lamar Odom	.30	.75
❑ 47 Ron Mercer	.20	.50
❑ 48 Jason Williams	.25	.60
❑ 49 Antawn Jamison	.30	.75
❑ 50 Wally Szczerbiak	.25	.60
❑ 51 Chris Webber	.30	.75
❑ 52 Larry Hughes	.25	.60
❑ 53 Kevin Garnett	.60	1.50
❑ 54 Michael Dickerson	.20	.50
❑ 55 Chucky Atkins	.20	.50
❑ 56 Jalen Rose	.25	.60
❑ 57 John Amaechi	.20	.50
❑ 58 Shareef Abdur-Rahim	.25	.60
❑ 59 Shawn Kemp	.30	.75
❑ 60 Derek Anderson	.25	.60
❑ 61 Darrell Armstrong	.20	.50
❑ 62 Vin Baker	.25	.60
❑ 63 Paul Pierce	.30	.75
❑ 64 Donyell Marshall	.20	.50
❑ 65 Jamie Feick	.20	.50
❑ 66 Travis Best	.20	.50
❑ 67 Baron Davis	.30	.75
❑ 68 Hakeem Olajuwon	.40	1.00
❑ 69 Joe Smith	.20	.50
❑ 70 Ruben Patterson	.20	.50
❑ 71 Antonio McDyess	.25	.60
❑ 72 Jamal Mashburn	.25	.60
❑ 73 Jason Kidd	.50	1.25
❑ 74 Eddie Jones	.25	.60
❑ 75 Kenny Thomas	.20	.50
❑ 76 Marcus Camby	.25	.60
❑ 77 Doug Christie	.20	.50
❑ 78 Ron Artest	.30	.75
❑ 79 Mark Jackson	.25	.60
❑ 80 Allan Houston	.25	.60
❑ 81 John Stockton	.40	1.00
❑ 82 Jerome Williams	.20	.50
❑ 83 Tim Thomas	.20	.50
❑ 84 Alan Henderson	.20	.50
❑ 85 Antoine Walker	.25	.60
❑ 86 Robert Horry	.25	.60
❑ 87 Stephon Marbury	.30	.75
❑ 88 David Robinson	.40	1.00
❑ 89 Lindsey Hunter	.20	.50
❑ 90 Richard Hamilton	.25	.60
❑ 91 Damon Stoudamire	.25	.60
❑ 92 Dikembe Mutombo	.25	.60
❑ 93 Anthony Mason	.20	.50
❑ 94 Austin Croshere	.20	.50
❑ 95 Patrick Ewing	.40	1.00
❑ 96 Mitch Richmond	.25	.60
❑ 97 Grant Hill	.30	.75
❑ 98 Ray Allen	.30	.75
❑ 99 Scottie Pippen	.50	1.25
❑ 100 Vince Carter	.60	1.50
❑ 101 Kenyon Martin A RC	6.00	15.00
❑ 102 Stromile Swift A RC	3.00	8.00
❑ 103 Darius Miles A RC	3.00	8.00
❑ 104 Marcus Fizer A RC	2.50	6.00
❑ 105 Mike Miller A RC	4.00	10.00
❑ 106 DerMarr Johnson A RC	2.50	6.00
❑ 107 Chris Mihm B RC	2.00	5.00
❑ 108 Jamal Crawford B RC	3.00	8.00
❑ 109 Joel Przybilla B RC	2.00	5.00
❑ 110 Keyon Dooling B RC	2.00	5.00
❑ 111 Jerome Moiso B RC	2.00	5.00
❑ 112 Etan Thomas B RC	2.00	5.00
❑ 113 Courtney Alexander C RC	1.50	4.00
❑ 114 Mateen Cleaves C RC	1.50	4.00
❑ 115 Jason Collier C RC	1.50	4.00
❑ 116 Hedo Turkoglu C RC	4.00	10.00
❑ 117 Desmond Mason C RC	2.00	5.00
❑ 118 Quentin Richardson C RC	2.00	5.00
❑ 119 Jamaal Magloire D RC	1.00	2.50
❑ 120 Speedy Claxton D RC	1.00	2.50
❑ 121 Morris Peterson D RC	1.50	4.00
❑ 122 Donnell Harvey D RC	1.00	2.50
❑ 123 DeShawn Stevenson D RC	1.00	2.50
❑ 124 Mark Karcher D RC	1.00	2.50
❑ 125 Mamadou N'Diaye E RC	.60	1.50
❑ 126 Erick Barkley E RC	.60	1.50
❑ 127 Mark Madsen E RC	.60	1.50
❑ 128 Corey Hightower E RC	.60	1.50
❑ 129 Dan McClintock E RC	.60	1.50
❑ 130 Soumaila Samake E RC	.60	1.50
❑ 131 Hanno Mottola F RC	.50	1.25
❑ 132 Chris Carrawell F RC	.50	1.25
❑ 133 Olumide Oyedeji F RC	.50	1.25
❑ 134 Michael Redd F RC	1.25	3.00
❑ 135 Chris Porter F RC	.50	1.25
❑ 136 Jabari Smith F RC	.50	1.25

2003-04 Fleer Mystique

❑ COMP.SET w/o SP's (80)	15.00	40.00
❑ COMMON CARD (1-80)	.20	.50
❑ COMMON ROOKIE (81-120)	2.00	5.00
❑ 1 Eric Williams	.20	.50
❑ 2 Dirk Nowitzki	.50	1.25
❑ 3 Jason Richardson	.30	.75
❑ 4 Corey Maggette	.20	.50
❑ 5 Troy Hudson	.20	.50
❑ 6 Tracy McGrady	.60	1.50
❑ 7 Zach Randolph	.30	.75
❑ 8 Bobby Jackson	.20	.50
❑ 9 Dan Gadzuric	.20	.50
❑ 10 Kevin Garnett	.60	1.50
❑ 11 Manu Ginobili	.30	.75
❑ 12 Andrei Kirilenko	.30	.75
❑ 13 Richard Hamilton	.25	.60
❑ 14 Mike Bibby	.25	.60
❑ 15 Vince Carter	.60	1.50
❑ 16 Jermaine O'Neal	.30	.75
❑ 17 Antoine Walker	.30	.75
❑ 18 Jalen Rose	.25	.60
❑ 19 Dajuan Wagner	.20	.50
❑ 20 Nene	.25	.60
❑ 21 Jamaal Tinsley	.25	.60
❑ 22 Kobe Bryant	1.50	4.00
❑ 23 Shane Battier	.25	.60
❑ 24 Allan Houston	.25	.60
❑ 25 Jerry Stackhouse	.25	.60
❑ 26 Eddie Jones	.25	.60
❑ 27 Morris Peterson	.25	.60
❑ 28 Richard Jefferson	.30	.75
❑ 29 Tony Parker	.30	.75
❑ 30 Glenn Robinson	.25	.60
❑ 31 Ron Artest	.25	.60
❑ 32 Marcus Haislip	.20	.50
❑ 33 Drew Gooden	.20	.50
❑ 34 Keith Van Horn	.25	.60
❑ 35 Shareef Abdur-Rahim	.25	.60
❑ 36 Michael Redd	.30	.75
❑ 37 Stephon Marbury	.30	.75
❑ 38 Tim Duncan	.60	1.50
❑ 39 Eddie Griffin	.20	.50
❑ 40 Kwame Brown	.20	.50
❑ 41 Steve Francis	.30	.75
❑ 42 Vladimir Radmanovic	.20	.50
❑ 43 Kenyon Martin	.30	.75
❑ 44 Eddy Curry	.25	.60
❑ 45 Nikoloz Tskitishvili	.20	.50
❑ 46 Shaquille O'Neal	.75	2.00
❑ 47 Allen Iverson	.60	1.50
❑ 48 Jason Kidd	.50	1.25
❑ 49 Ben Wallace	.25	.60
❑ 50 Caron Butler	.25	.60
❑ 51 Dan Dickau	.20	.50
❑ 52 Baron Davis	.30	.75
❑ 53 Bruce Bowen	.25	.60
❑ 54 Amare Stoudemire	.60	1.50
❑ 55 Michael Finley	.30	.75
❑ 56 Jamal Mashburn	.20	.50
❑ 57 Pau Gasol	.30	.75
❑ 58 Shawn Marion	.30	.75
❑ 59 Rasheed Wallace	.30	.75
❑ 60 Chris Webber	.30	.75
❑ 61 Rodney White	.20	.50
❑ 62 Tayshaun Prince	.25	.60
❑ 63 Yao Ming	.60	1.50
❑ 64 Latrell Sprewell	.25	.60
❑ 65 Aaron McKie	.20	.50
❑ 66 Bonzi Wells	.20	.50
❑ 67 HedoTurkoglu	.25	.60
❑ 68 Ray Allen	.20	.50
❑ 69 Matt Harpring	.25	.60
❑ 70 Paul Pierce	.30	.75
❑ 71 Darius Miles	.25	.60
❑ 72 Chris Wilcox	.20	.50
❑ 73 Steve Nash	.50	1.25
❑ 74 Antawn Jamison	.30	.75
❑ 75 Juan Dixon	.20	.50
❑ 76 Peja Stojakovic	.25	.60
❑ 77 Antonio Davis	.20	.50
❑ 78 Kenny Thomas	.20	.50
❑ 79 Elton Brand	.30	.75
❑ 80 Gilbert Arenas	.30	.75
❑ 81 Mickael Pietrus RC	2.50	6.00
❑ 82 Keith Bogans RC	2.00	5.00
❑ 83 Dahntay Jones RC	2.00	5.00
❑ 84 Darko Milicic RC	2.50	6.00
❑ 85 Torraye Braggs RC	2.00	5.00
❑ 86 Troy Bell RC	2.00	5.00
❑ 87 Maciej Lampe RC	2.00	5.00
❑ 88 Kendrick Perkins RC	3.00	8.00
❑ 89 Kirk Hinrich RC	2.50	6.00
❑ 90 Jason Kapono RC	2.50	6.00
❑ 91 Udonis Haslem RC	2.50	6.00
❑ 92 James Lang RC	2.00	5.00
❑ 93 Willie Green RC	2.00	5.00
❑ 94 Travis Outlaw RC	2.50	6.00
❑ 95 Nick Collison RC	2.00	5.00
❑ 96 Jarvis Hayes RC	2.00	5.00
❑ 97 Boris Diaw RC	2.50	6.00
❑ 98 Chris Bosh RC	3.00	8.00
❑ 99 LeBron James RC	40.00	80.00
❑ 100 Zarko Cabarkapa RC	2.00	5.00
❑ 101 Travis Hansen RC	2.00	5.00
❑ 102 James Jones RC	2.00	5.00
❑ 103 Aleksandar Pavlovic RC	2.50	6.00
❑ 104 Luke Walton RC	2.50	6.00
❑ 105 Maurice Williams RC	3.00	8.00
❑ 106 Linton Johnson RC	2.00	5.00
❑ 107 David West RC	2.50	6.00
❑ 108 Carmelo Anthony RC	5.00	12.00
❑ 109 T.J. Ford RC	2.50	6.00
❑ 110 Ndudi Ebi RC	2.00	5.00
❑ 111 Reece Gaines RC	2.00	5.00
❑ 112 Leandro Barbosa RC	2.50	6.00
❑ 113 Luke Ridnour RC	2.50	6.00
❑ 114 Brian Cook RC	2.00	5.00
❑ 115 Marcus Banks RC	2.00	5.00
❑ 116 Josh Howard RC	2.50	6.00
❑ 117 Chris Kaman RC	2.50	6.00
❑ 118 Zoran Planinic RC	2.00	5.00
❑ 119 Dwyane Wade RC	5.00	12.00
❑ 120 Mike Sweetney RC	2.00	5.00

2003-04 Fleer Patchworks

❑ COMP.SET w/o SP's (90)	12.50	30.00
❑ COMMON CARD (1-90)	.20	.50
❑ COMMON ROOKIE (91-120)	1.25	3.00
❑ 1 Shareef Abdur-Rahim	.25	.60
❑ 2 Theo Ratliff	.20	.50
❑ 3 Jason Terry	.25	.60
❑ 4 Carlos Boozer	.30	.75
❑ 5 Paul Pierce	.30	.75
❑ 6 Ricky Davis	.25	.60
❑ 7 Tyson Chandler	.25	.60
❑ 8 Jamal Crawford	.25	.60
❑ 9 Eddy Curry	.25	.60
❑ 10 Darius Miles	.25	.60
❑ 11 Dajuan Wagner	.20	.50
❑ 12 Michael Finley	.30	.75
❑ 13 Steve Nash	.50	1.25
❑ 14 Dirk Nowitzki	.50	1.25
❑ 15 Earl Boykins	.20	.50
❑ 16 Andre Miller	.25	.60

❑ 17 Nene	.25	.60
❑ 18 Richard Hamilton	.25	.60
❑ 19 Tayshaun Prince	.25	.60
❑ 20 Ben Wallace	.25	.60
❑ 21 Mike Dunleavy	.25	.60
❑ 22 Troy Murphy	.30	.75
❑ 23 Jason Richardson	.30	.75
❑ 24 Steve Francis	.30	.75
❑ 25 Yao Ming	.60	1.50
❑ 26 Cuttino Mobley	.25	.60
❑ 27 Maurice Taylor	.20	.50
❑ 28 Ron Artest	.25	.60
❑ 29 Reggie Miller	.30	.75
❑ 30 Jermaine O'Neal	.30	.75
❑ 31 Jamaal Tinsley	.25	.60
❑ 32 Elton Brand	.30	.75
❑ 33 Marko Jaric	.20	.50
❑ 34 Corey Maggette	.20	.50
❑ 35 Kobe Bryant	1.50	4.00
❑ 36 Karl Malone	.30	.75
❑ 37 Shaquille O'Neal	.75	2.00
❑ 38 Shane Battier	.25	.60
❑ 39 Pau Gasol	.30	.75
❑ 40 Jason Williams	.25	.60
❑ 41 Caron Butler	.25	.60
❑ 42 Lamar Odom	.30	.75
❑ 43 Desmond Mason	.25	.60
❑ 44 Michael Redd	.30	.75
❑ 45 Tim Thomas	.20	.50
❑ 46 Sam Cassell	.25	.60
❑ 47 Kevin Garnett	.60	1.50
❑ 48 Latrell Sprewell	.25	.60
❑ 49 Wally Szczerbiak	.25	.60
❑ 50 Richard Jefferson	.30	.75
❑ 51 Jason Kidd	.50	1.25
❑ 52 Kenyon Martin	.30	.75
❑ 53 Baron Davis	.30	.75
❑ 54 Jamal Mashburn	.20	.50
❑ 55 Jamaal Magloire	.20	.50
❑ 56 Allan Houston	.25	.60
❑ 57 Stephon Marbury	.30	.75
❑ 58 Kurt Thomas	.20	.50
❑ 59 Drew Gooden	.20	.50
❑ 60 Juwan Howard	.25	.60
❑ 61 Tracy McGrady	.60	1.50
❑ 62 Allen Iverson	.60	1.50
❑ 63 Aaron McKie	.20	.50
❑ 64 Glenn Robinson	.25	.60
❑ 65 Kenny Thomas	.20	.50
❑ 66 Shawn Marion	.30	.75
❑ 67 Antonio McDyess	.25	.60
❑ 68 Amare Stoudemire	.60	1.50
❑ 69 Zach Randolph	.30	.75
❑ 70 Damon Stoudamire	.25	.60
❑ 71 Rasheed Wallace	.30	.75
❑ 72 Qyntel Woods	.20	.50
❑ 73 Mike Bibby	.25	.60
❑ 74 Peja Stojakovic	.25	.60
❑ 75 Chris Webber	.30	.75
❑ 76 Tim Duncan	.60	1.50
❑ 77 Manu Ginobili	.30	.75
❑ 78 Tony Parker	.30	.75
❑ 79 Malik Rose	.20	.50
❑ 80 Ray Allen	.20	.50
❑ 81 Rashard Lewis	.30	.75
❑ 82 Vladimir Radmanovic	.20	.50
❑ 83 Vince Carter	.60	1.50
❑ 84 Donyell Marshall	.20	.50
❑ 85 Jalen Rose	.25	.60
❑ 86 Matt Harpring	.25	.60
❑ 87 Andrei Kirilenko	.30	.75
❑ 88 Gilbert Arenas	.30	.75
❑ 89 Larry Hughes	.25	.60
❑ 90 Jerry Stackhouse	.25	.60
❑ 91 Carmelo Anthony RC	3.00	8.00
❑ 92 Marcus Banks RC	1.25	3.00
❑ 93 Troy Bell RC	1.25	3.00
❑ 94 Chris Bosh RC	2.00	5.00
❑ 95 Zarko Cabarkapa RC	1.25	3.00
❑ 96 Nick Collison RC	1.25	3.00
❑ 97 Boris Diaw RC	1.50	4.00
❑ 98 Francisco Elson RC	1.25	3.00
❑ 99 T.J. Ford RC	1.50	4.00
❑ 100 Reece Gaines RC	1.25	3.00
❑ 101 Udonis Haslem RC	1.50	4.00
❑ 102 Jarvis Hayes RC	1.25	3.00
❑ 103 Kirk Hinrich RC	1.50	4.00
❑ 104 Josh Howard RC	1.50	4.00
❑ 105 LeBron James RC	25.00	50.00
❑ 106 Dahntay Jones RC	1.25	3.00
❑ 107 Chris Kaman RC	1.50	4.00
❑ 108 Jason Kapono RC	1.50	4.00
❑ 109 Raul Lopez	1.25	3.00
❑ 110 Darko Milicic RC	1.50	4.00
❑ 111 Zaur Pachulia RC	1.50	4.00
❑ 112 Mickael Pietrus RC	1.50	4.00
❑ 113 Zoran Planinic RC	1.25	3.00
❑ 114 Luke Ridnour RC	1.50	4.00
❑ 115 Darius Songaila	1.25	3.00
❑ 116 Mike Sweetney RC	1.25	3.00
❑ 117 Dwyane Wade RC	3.00	8.00
❑ 118 Luke Walton RC	1.50	4.00
❑ 119 David West RC	1.50	4.00
❑ 120 Maurice Williams RC	2.00	5.00

2001-02 Fleer Platinum

❑ COMPLETE SET (250)	150.00	300.00
❑ COMP.SET w/o SP's (200)	8.00	20.00
❑ COMMON CARD (1-200)	.07	.20
❑ COMMON HL (201-220)	1.00	2.50
❑ COMMON ROOKIE (221-250)	1.00	2.50
❑ 1 Tyrone Hill	.15	.40
❑ 2 Sam Cassell	.20	.50
❑ 3 Elton Brand	.25	.60
❑ 4 Andre Miller	.20	.50
❑ 5 Vitaly Potapenko	.15	.40
❑ 6 Lamar Odom	.25	.60
❑ 7 Mike Bibby	.20	.50
❑ 8 Alan Henderson	.15	.40
❑ 9 Dan Majerle	.20	.50
❑ 10 Donyell Marshall	.15	.40
❑ 11 Jason Williams	.20	.50
❑ 12 Glen Rice	.20	.50
❑ 13 Kobe Bryant	1.25	3.00
❑ 14 Pat Garrity	.15	.40
❑ 15 Shawn Bradley	.15	.40
❑ 16 Aaron Williams	.15	.40
❑ 17 Antonio McDyess	.20	.50
❑ 18 Jonathan Bender	.15	.40
❑ 19 Ben Wallace	.20	.50
❑ 20 Vince Carter	.50	1.25
❑ 21 Maurice Taylor	.15	.40
❑ 22 Antonio Daniels	.15	.40
❑ 23 Rodney Rogers	.15	.40
❑ 24 Patrick Ewing	.30	.75
❑ 25 Chauncey Billups	.20	.50
❑ 26 Steve Smith	.20	.50
❑ 27 Antawn Jamison	.25	.60
❑ 28 Mitch Richmond	.20	.50
❑ 29 Jumaine Jones	.15	.40
❑ 30 Glenn Robinson	.20	.50
❑ 31 Ron Mercer	.15	.40
❑ 32 Jelani McCoy	.15	.40
❑ 33 Paul Pierce	.25	.60
❑ 34 Jeff McInnis	.15	.40
❑ 35 Michael Dickerson	.15	.40
❑ 36 Toni Kukoc	.20	.50
❑ 37 Anthony Mason	.15	.40
❑ 38 Jamal Mashburn	.20	.50
❑ 39 John Stockton	.30	.75
❑ 40 Peja Stojakovic	.20	.50
❑ 41 Charlie Ward	.15	.40
❑ 42 Donnell Harvey	.15	.40
❑ 43 Darrell Armstrong	.15	.40
❑ 44 Michael Finley	.25	.60
❑ 45 Kerry Kittles	.20	.50
❑ 46 Voshon Lenard	.15	.40
❑ 47 Reggie Miller	.25	.60
❑ 48 Joe Smith	.15	.40
❑ 49 Antonio Davis	.15	.40
❑ 50 Hakeem Olajuwon	.30	.75
❑ 51 David Robinson	.30	.75
❑ 52 Tony Delk	.15	.40
❑ 53 Gary Payton	.25	.60
❑ 54 Kevin Garnett	.50	1.25
❑ 55 Arvydas Sabonis	.20	.50
❑ 56 Larry Hughes	.20	.50
❑ 57 Richard Hamilton	.20	.50
❑ 58 Aaron McKie	.15	.40
❑ 59 Tim Thomas	.15	.40
❑ 60 Ron Artest	.20	.50
❑ 61 Matt Harpring	.20	.50
❑ 62 Kenny Anderson	.20	.50
❑ 63 Quentin Richardson	.20	.50
❑ 64 Damon Jones	.15	.40
❑ 65 Theo Ratliff	.15	.40
❑ 66 Brian Grant	.15	.40
❑ 67 Eddie Robinson	.15	.40
❑ 68 Karl Malone	.30	.75
❑ 69 Bobby Jackson	.15	.40
❑ 70 Larry Johnson	.20	.50
❑ 71 Shareef Abdur-Rahim	.20	.50
❑ 72 Grant Hill	.25	.60
❑ 73 Eduardo Najera	.15	.40
❑ 74 Keith Van Horn	.20	.50
❑ 75 Nick Van Exel	.20	.50
❑ 76 Jalen Rose	.20	.50
❑ 77 Jerry Stackhouse	.20	.50
❑ 78 Jerome Williams	.15	.40
❑ 79 Cuttino Mobley	.20	.50
❑ 80 Derek Anderson	.20	.50
❑ 81 Anfernee Hardaway	.25	.60
❑ 82 Rashard Lewis	.25	.60
❑ 83 Terrell Brandon	.15	.40
❑ 84 Scottie Pippen	.40	1.00
❑ 85 Danny Fortson	.15	.40
❑ 86 Jahidi White	.15	.40
❑ 87 Eric Snow	.15	.40
❑ 88 Ervin Johnson	.15	.40
❑ 89 Marcus Fizer	.15	.40
❑ 90 Lamond Murray	.15	.40
❑ 91 Antoine Walker	.20	.50
❑ 92 Keyon Dooling	.15	.40
❑ 93 Bryant Reeves	.15	.40
❑ 94 Hanno Mottola	.15	.40
❑ 95 Tim Hardaway	.20	.50
❑ 96 David Wesley	.15	.40
❑ 97 John Starks	.15	.40
❑ 98 Hedo Turkoglu	.20	.50
❑ 99 Allan Houston	.20	.50
❑ 100 Rick Fox	.20	.50
❑ 101 Bo Outlaw	.15	.40
❑ 102 Juwan Howard	.20	.50
❑ 103 Kendall Gill	.15	.40
❑ 104 Raef LaFrentz	.15	.40
❑ 105 Austin Croshere	.15	.40
❑ 106 Chucky Atkins	.15	.40
❑ 107 Morris Peterson	.20	.50
❑ 108 Shandon Anderson	.15	.40
❑ 109 Sean Elliott	.15	.40
❑ 110 Tom Gugliotta	.15	.40
❑ 111 Vin Baker	.20	.50
❑ 112 Wally Szczerbiak	.20	.50
❑ 113 Rasheed Wallace	.25	.60
❑ 114 Vonteego Cummings	.15	.40
❑ 115 Christian Laettner	.15	.40
❑ 116 Dikembe Mutombo	.20	.50
❑ 117 Lindsey Hunter	.15	.40
❑ 118 Jamal Crawford	.20	.50
❑ 119 Jim Jackson	.15	.40
❑ 120 Bryant Stith	.15	.40
❑ 121 Corey Maggette	.20	.50
❑ 122 Mahmoud Abdul-Rauf	.15	.40
❑ 123 Lorenzen Wright	.15	.40
❑ 124 Alonzo Mourning	.25	.60
❑ 125 Jamaal Magloire	.15	.40
❑ 126 Bryon Russell	.15	.40
❑ 127 Vlade Divac	.20	.50
❑ 128 Marcus Camby	.20	.50
❑ 129 Derek Fisher	.20	.50
❑ 130 Mike Miller	.20	.50
❑ 131 Steve Nash	.40	1.00
❑ 132 Kenyon Martin	.25	.60
❑ 133 James Posey	.15	.40
❑ 134 Travis Best	.15	.40
❑ 135 Corliss Williamson	.20	.50
❑ 136 Alvin Williams	.15	.40
❑ 137 Walt Williams	.15	.40
❑ 138 Malik Rose	.15	.40
❑ 139 Clifford Robinson	.15	.40
❑ 140 Ruben Patterson	.15	.40
❑ 141 LaPhonso Ellis	.20	.50
❑ 142 Rod Strickland	.20	.50
❑ 143 Marc Jackson	.15	.40

❑ 144 Hubert Davis	.15	.40
❑ 145 Speedy Claxton	.15	.40
❑ 146 Scott Williams	.15	.40
❑ 147 Tyronn Lue	.15	.40
❑ 148 Chris Mihm	.15	.40
❑ 149 George Lynch	.15	.40
❑ 150 Michael Olowokandi	.15	.40
❑ 151 Nazr Mohammed	.15	.40
❑ 152 Eddie House	.15	.40
❑ 153 Elden Campbell	.15	.40
❑ 154 DeShawn Stevenson	.15	.40
❑ 155 Doug Christie	.15	.40
❑ 156 Kurt Thomas	.15	.40
❑ 157 Robert Horry	.20	.50
❑ 158 Radoslav Nesterovic	.15	.40
❑ 159 Wang Zhizhi	.20	.50
❑ 160 Stephen Jackson	.20	.50
❑ 161 George McCloud	.15	.40
❑ 162 Jermaine O'Neal	.25	.60
❑ 163 Mateen Cleaves	.15	.40
❑ 164 Charles Oakley	.20	.50
❑ 165 Kenny Thomas	.15	.40
❑ 166 Terry Porter	.15	.40
❑ 167 Iakovos Tsakalidis	.15	.40
❑ 168 Shammond Williams	.15	.40
❑ 169 Anthony Peeler	.15	.40
❑ 170 Damon Stoudamire	.20	.50
❑ 171 Chris Porter	.15	.40
❑ 172 Chris Whitney	.15	.40
❑ 173 Raja Bell RC	.30	.75
❑ 174 Darvin Ham	.15	.40
❑ 175 A.J. Guyton	.15	.40
❑ 176 Trajan Langdon	.15	.40
❑ 177 Jerome Moiso	.15	.40
❑ 178 Anthony Carter	.15	.40
❑ 179 P.J. Brown	.15	.40
❑ 180 Danny Manning	.15	.40
❑ 181 Scot Pollard	.15	.40
❑ 182 Mark Jackson	.20	.50
❑ 183 Mark Madsen	.15	.40
❑ 184 Michael Doleac	.15	.40
❑ 185 Calvin Booth	.15	.40
❑ 186 Kevin Willis	.15	.40
❑ 187 Al Harrington	.20	.50
❑ 188 Mikki Moore	.15	.40
❑ 189 Keon Clark	.15	.40
❑ 190 Moochie Norris	.15	.40
❑ 191 Ron Harper	.20	.50
❑ 192 Danny Ferry	.15	.40
❑ 193 Jacque Vaughn	.15	.40
❑ 194 Derrick Coleman	.20	.50
❑ 195 Brent Barry	.15	.40
❑ 196 Dion Glover	.15	.40
❑ 197 Felipe Lopez	.15	.40
❑ 198 Shawn Kemp	.20	.50
❑ 199 Mookie Blaylock	.20	.50
❑ 200 Bonzi Wells	.20	.50
❑ 201 Vince Carter HL	2.00	5.00
❑ 202 Ray Allen HL	1.00	2.50
❑ 203 Darius Miles HL	.60	1.50
❑ 204 Shaquille O'Neal HL	2.50	6.00
❑ 205 Stromile Swift HL	.60	1.50
❑ 206 DerMarr Johnson HL	.60	1.50
❑ 207 Eddie Jones HL	.75	2.00
❑ 208 Chris Webber HL	1.00	2.50
❑ 209 Latrell Sprewell HL	.75	2.00
❑ 210 Tracy McGrady HL	2.00	5.00
❑ 211 Dirk Nowitzki HL	1.50	4.00
❑ 212 Stephon Marbury HL	1.00	2.50
❑ 213 Steve Francis HL	1.00	2.50
❑ 214 Tim Duncan HL	2.00	5.00
❑ 215 Jason Kidd HL	1.50	4.00
❑ 216 Shawn Marion HL	1.00	2.50
❑ 217 Desmond Mason HL	.75	2.00
❑ 218 Courtney Alexander HL	.60	1.50
❑ 219 Baron Davis HL	1.00	2.50
❑ 220 Allen Iverson HL	2.00	5.00
❑ 221 Joe Johnson RC	2.50	6.00
❑ 222 Kedrick Brown RC	1.00	2.50
❑ 223 Joseph Forte RC	1.00	2.50
❑ 224 Kirk Haston RC	1.00	2.50
❑ 225 Tyson Chandler RC	2.00	5.00
❑ 226 Eddy Curry RC	1.50	4.00
❑ 227 DeSagana Diop RC	1.00	2.50
❑ 228 Jeff Trepagnier RC	1.00	2.50
❑ 229 Oscar Torres RC	1.00	2.50
❑ 230 Rodney White RC	1.00	2.50
❑ 231 Jason Richardson RC	2.00	5.00
❑ 232 Troy Murphy RC	2.00	5.00
❑ 233 Eddie Griffin RC	1.00	2.50
❑ 234 Jamaal Tinsley RC	1.25	3.00
❑ 235 Pau Gasol RC	4.00	10.00
❑ 236 Shane Battier RC	1.50	4.00
❑ 237 Richard Jefferson RC	2.50	6.00
❑ 238 Jason Collins RC	1.00	2.50
❑ 239 Brendan Haywood RC	1.25	3.00
❑ 240 Steven Hunter RC	1.00	2.50
❑ 241 Zach Randolph RC	2.50	6.00
❑ 242 Gerald Wallace RC	2.50	6.00
❑ 243 Tony Parker RC	4.00	10.00
❑ 244 Vladimir Radmanovic RC	1.25	3.00
❑ 245 Michael Bradley RC	1.00	2.50
❑ 246 Andrei Kirilenko RC	2.50	6.00
❑ 247 Kwame Brown RC	1.25	3.00
❑ 248 Alton Ford RC	1.00	2.50
❑ 249 Zeljko Rebraca RC	1.00	2.50
❑ 250 Trenton Hassell RC	1.25	3.00

2002-03 Fleer Platinum

❑ COMP.SET w/o SP's (160)	15.00	40.00
❑ COMMON CARD (1-160)	.08	.20
❑ COMMON ROOKIE (161-170)	1.25	3.00
❑ COMMON ROOKIE (171-180)	2.50	6.00
❑ COMMON ROOKIE (181-190)	2.50	6.00
❑ COMMON ROOKIE (191-200)	3.00	8.00
❑ 1 Vince Carter	.60	1.50
❑ 2 Lamar Odom	.30	.75
❑ 3 Darrell Armstrong	.20	.50
❑ 4 Kwame Brown	.20	.50
❑ 5 Ron Artest	.25	.60
❑ 6 Kurt Thomas	.20	.50
❑ 7 Jerry Stackhouse	.25	.60
❑ 8 Eddie Griffin	.20	.50
❑ 9 David Wesley	.20	.50
❑ 10 Morris Peterson	.25	.60
❑ 11 Jon Barry	.20	.50
❑ 12 Troy Hudson	.20	.50
❑ 13 Kenny Anderson	.25	.60
❑ 14 Corliss Williamson	.25	.60
❑ 15 Kevin Garnett	.60	1.50
❑ 16 Desmond Mason	.25	.60
❑ 17 Lucious Harris	.20	.50
❑ 18 Steve Smith	.25	.60
❑ 19 Nick Van Exel	.25	.60
❑ 20 Tyson Chandler	.25	.60
❑ 21 Shane Battier	.25	.60
❑ 22 Rasheed Wallace	.30	.75
❑ 23 Donyell Marshall	.20	.50
❑ 24 Anfernee Hardaway	.30	.75
❑ 25 Antoine Walker	.25	.60
❑ 26 Kobe Bryant	1.50	4.00
❑ 27 Keith Van Horn	.25	.60
❑ 28 Elton Brand	.30	.75
❑ 29 Grant Hill	.30	.75
❑ 30 Elden Campbell	.20	.50
❑ 31 John Stockton	.40	1.00
❑ 32 Wally Szczerbiak	.25	.60
❑ 33 Speedy Claxton	.20	.50
❑ 34 Voshon Lenard	.20	.50
❑ 35 Eddie Jones	.25	.60
❑ 36 Bonzi Wells	.25	.60
❑ 37 Jalen Rose	.25	.60
❑ 38 Jason Williams	.25	.60
❑ 39 Tom Gugliotta	.20	.50
❑ 40 Juwan Howard	.25	.60
❑ 41 Michael Redd	.30	.75
❑ 42 David Robinson	.40	1.00
❑ 43 Steve Nash	.50	1.25
❑ 44 Vlade Divac	.25	.60
❑ 45 Avery Johnson	.25	.60
❑ 46 Scottie Pippen	.50	1.25
❑ 47 Eric Williams	.20	.50
❑ 48 Derek Fisher	.25	.60
❑ 49 Tony Battie	.20	.50
❑ 50 Rick Fox	.25	.60
❑ 51 Theo Ratliff	.20	.50
❑ 52 Corey Maggette	.25	.60
❑ 53 Jermaine O'Neal	.30	.75
❑ 54 Bryon Russell	.20	.50
❑ 55 Steve Francis	.30	.75
❑ 56 Jamal Mashburn	.25	.60
❑ 57 Jerome Williams	.20	.50
❑ 58 Gilbert Arenas	.30	.75
❑ 59 Joe Smith	.20	.50
❑ 60 Brent Barry	.20	.50
❑ 61 Marcus Camby	.25	.60
❑ 62 Toni Kukoc	.25	.60
❑ 63 Tim Duncan	.60	1.50
❑ 64 Ira Newble	.20	.50
❑ 65 Brian Grant	.20	.50
❑ 66 Jason Terry	.30	.75
❑ 67 Andre Miller	.25	.60
❑ 68 Mike Miller	.25	.60
❑ 69 Troy Murphy	.30	.75
❑ 70 P.J. Brown	.20	.50
❑ 71 Jason Richardson	.30	.75
❑ 72 Glenn Robinson	.25	.60
❑ 73 Richard Jefferson	.30	.75
❑ 74 Richard Hamilton	.25	.60
❑ 75 Jason Kidd	.50	1.25
❑ 76 Rashard Lewis	.30	.75
❑ 77 Kenny Satterfield	.20	.50
❑ 78 Terrell Brandon	.20	.50
❑ 79 Dirk Nowitzki	.50	1.25
❑ 80 Chris Webber	.30	.75
❑ 81 Michael Finley	.30	.75
❑ 82 Malik Allen	.20	.50
❑ 83 Bobby Jackson	.20	.50
❑ 84 Darius Miles	.20	.50
❑ 85 Kendall Gill	.20	.50
❑ 86 Damon Stoudamire	.25	.60
❑ 87 Shammond Williams	.20	.50
❑ 88 Stephon Marbury	.30	.75
❑ 89 Shareef Abdur-Rahim	.25	.60
❑ 90 Charlie Ward	.20	.50
❑ 91 Michael Jordan	2.00	5.00
❑ 92 Jamaal Magloire	.20	.50
❑ 93 Karl Malone	.30	.75
❑ 94 Kerry Kittles	.25	.60
❑ 95 Lindsey Hunter	.20	.50
❑ 96 Gary Payton	.30	.75
❑ 97 Travis Best	.20	.50
❑ 98 Derek Anderson	.25	.60
❑ 99 Stromile Swift	.20	.50
❑ 100 Shaquille O'Neal	.75	2.00
❑ 101 Derrick Coleman	.25	.60
❑ 102 DeShawn Stevenson	.20	.50
❑ 103 Jamaal Tinsley	.25	.60
❑ 104 Latrell Sprewell	.25	.60
❑ 105 Larry Hughes	.25	.60
❑ 106 Eddy Curry	.25	.60
❑ 107 Shawn Marion	.30	.75
❑ 108 Paul Pierce	.30	.75
❑ 109 Samaki Walker	.20	.50
❑ 110 Allen Iverson	.60	1.50
❑ 111 Michael Olowokandi	.20	.50
❑ 112 Tracy McGrady	.60	1.50
❑ 113 Shawn Bradley	.20	.50
❑ 114 Reggie Miller	.30	.75
❑ 115 Antonio McDyess	.25	.60
❑ 116 Calbert Cheaney	.20	.50
❑ 117 Al Harrington	.25	.60
❑ 118 Allan Houston	.25	.60
❑ 119 Andrei Kirilenko	.30	.75
❑ 120 Courtney Alexander	.20	.50
❑ 121 Alvin Williams	.20	.50
❑ 122 Antawn Jamison	.30	.75
❑ 123 Dikembe Mutombo	.25	.60
❑ 124 Tony Parker	.30	.75
❑ 125 Raef LaFrentz	.20	.50
❑ 126 Ray Allen	.30	.75
❑ 127 Peja Stojakovic	.25	.60
❑ 128 Zydrunas Ilgauskas	.25	.60
❑ 129 Gerald Wallace	.30	.75
❑ 130 Ruben Patterson	.20	.50
❑ 131 Pau Gasol	.30	.75
❑ 132 Joe Johnson	.30	.75
❑ 133 Aaron McKie	.20	.50
❑ 134 Walter McCarty	.20	.50
❑ 135 Baron Davis	.30	.75
❑ 136 Kenyon Martin	.30	.75
❑ 137 Antonio Davis	.20	.50
❑ 138 Ben Wallace	.25	.60
❑ 139 Sam Cassell	.25	.60

❑ 140 Mike Bibby	.25	.60
❑ 141 Cuttino Mobley	.25	.60
❑ 142 LaPhonso Ellis	.25	.60
❑ 143 Shandon Anderson	.20	.50
❑ 144 Hedo Turkoglu	.25	.60
❑ 145 Matt Harpring	.25	.60
❑ 146 Dion Glover	.20	.50
❑ 147 Tony Delk	.20	.50
❑ 148 Ricky Davis	.25	.60
❑ 149 James Posey	.20	.50
❑ 150 Chucky Atkins	.20	.50
❑ 151 Danny Fortson	.20	.50
❑ 152 Robert Horry	.25	.60
❑ 153 Radoslav Nesterovic	.20	.50
❑ 154 Pat Garrity	.20	.50
❑ 155 Todd MacCulloch	.20	.50
❑ 156 Eric Snow	.20	.50
❑ 157 Malik Rose	.20	.50
❑ 158 Vladimir Radmanovic	.20	.50
❑ 159 Trenton Hassell	.20	.50
❑ 160 Brad Miller	.25	.60
❑ 161 Kareem Rush RC	1.50	4.00
❑ 162 Nikoloz Tskitishvili RC	1.25	3.00
❑ 163 Nene Hilario RC	1.50	4.00
❑ 164 Marcus Haislip RC	1.25	3.00
❑ 165 Jiri Welsch RC	1.25	3.00
❑ 166 Dan Dickau RC	1.25	3.00
❑ 167 Vincent Yarbrough RC	1.25	3.00
❑ 168 Tito Maddox RC	1.25	3.00
❑ 169 Mike Dunleavy RC	1.50	4.00
❑ 170 Chris Wilcox RC	1.50	4.00
❑ 171 Jared Jeffries RC	2.00	5.00
❑ 172 Bostjan Nachbar RC	2.00	5.00
❑ 173 Frank Williams RC	2.00	5.00
❑ 174 Reggie Evans RC	2.00	5.00
❑ 175 Casey Jacobsen RC	2.00	5.00
❑ 176 Tayshaun Prince RC	3.00	8.00
❑ 177 Mike Batiste RC	2.00	5.00
❑ 178 Drew Gooden RC	3.00	8.00
❑ 179 DaJuan Wagner RC	2.00	5.00
❑ 180 Tamar Slay RC	2.00	5.00
❑ 181 Melvin Ely RC	2.50	6.00
❑ 182 Rasual Butler RC	2.50	6.00
❑ 183 Dan Gadzuric RC	2.50	6.00
❑ 184 Ryan Humphrey RC	2.50	6.00
❑ 185 Gordan Giricek RC	2.50	6.00
❑ 186 Mehmet Okur RC	3.00	8.00
❑ 187 Jay Williams RC	3.00	8.00
❑ 188 Caron Butler RC	5.00	12.00
❑ 189 Qyntel Woods RC	2.50	6.00
❑ 190 Amare Stoudemire RC	6.00	15.00
❑ 191 Yao Ming RC	10.00	25.00
❑ 192 Carlos Boozer RC	6.00	15.00
❑ 193 John Salmons RC	5.00	12.00
❑ 194 Fred Jones RC	4.00	10.00
❑ 195 Juan Dixon RC	5.00	12.00
❑ 196 Manu Ginobili RC	8.00	20.00
❑ 197 Pat Burke RC	3.00	8.00
❑ 198 Smush Parker RC	3.00	8.00
❑ 199 Lonny Baxter RC	3.00	8.00
❑ 200 Ronald Murray RC	5.00	12.00

2003-04 Fleer Platinum

❑ COMMON CARD (1-170)	.15	.40
❑ COMMON ROOKIE (171-180)	1.00	2.50
❑ COMMON ROOKIE (181-190)	1.50	4.00
❑ COMMON ROOKIE (191-200)	2.00	5.00
❑ 1 Shane Battier	.20	.50
❑ 2 Brad Miller	.20	.50
❑ 3 Jason Kidd	.40	1.00
❑ 4 Nick Van Exel	.20	.50
❑ 5 David Wesley	.15	.40
❑ 6 Corey Maggette	.15	.40
❑ 7 Juan Dixon	.15	.40
❑ 8 Jamaal Tinsley	.20	.50
❑ 9 Stromile Swift	.15	.40
❑ 10 Dajuan Wagner	.15	.40
❑ 11 Joe Smith	.15	.40
❑ 12 Jermaine O'Neal	.25	.60
❑ 13 Steve Nash	.40	1.00
❑ 14 Karl Malone	.25	.60
❑ 15 Vince Carter	.50	1.25
❑ 16 Antonio McDyess	.20	.50
❑ 17 Tim Thomas	.15	.40
❑ 18 Vladimir Radmanovic	.15	.40
❑ 19 Scottie Pippen	.40	1.00
❑ 20 Tracy McGrady	.50	1.25
❑ 21 Darius Miles	.20	.50
❑ 22 Toni Kukoc	.20	.50
❑ 23 Antonio Davis	.15	.40
❑ 24 Jamal Crawford	.20	.50
❑ 25 Rasho Nesterovic	.15	.40
❑ 26 Carlos Boozer	.25	.60
❑ 27 Cuttino Mobley	.20	.50
❑ 28 Larry Hughes	.20	.50
❑ 29 Alvin Williams	.15	.40
❑ 30 Andre Miller	.20	.50
❑ 31 Amare Stoudemire	.50	1.25
❑ 32 Eric Williams	.15	.40
❑ 33 Pau Gasol	.25	.60
❑ 34 Kenyon Martin	.25	.60
❑ 35 Elton Brand	.25	.60
❑ 36 Charlie Ward	.15	.40
❑ 37 Andrei Kirilenko	.25	.60
❑ 38 Aaron McKie	.15	.40
❑ 39 Maurice Taylor	.15	.40
❑ 40 Baron Davis	.25	.60
❑ 41 Dirk Nowitzki	.40	1.00
❑ 42 Gary Payton	.25	.60
❑ 43 Grant Hill	.25	.60
❑ 44 Jalen Rose	.20	.50
❑ 45 Allan Houston	.20	.50
❑ 46 Erick Dampier	.15	.40
❑ 47 Brian Grant	.15	.40
❑ 48 Wally Szczerbiak	.20	.50
❑ 49 Greg Ostertag	.15	.40
❑ 50 Gilbert Arenas	.25	.60
❑ 51 Kenny Anderson	.20	.50
❑ 52 Juwan Howard	.20	.50
❑ 53 Jason Terry	.20	.50
❑ 54 Raef LaFrentz	.15	.40
❑ 55 Ricky Davis	.20	.50
❑ 56 Kobe Bryant	1.25	3.00
❑ 57 Chris Webber	.25	.60
❑ 58 P.J. Brown	.15	.40
❑ 59 Nene	.20	.50
❑ 60 Kenny Thomas	.15	.40
❑ 61 Mike Bibby	.20	.50
❑ 62 Chris Wilcox	.15	.40
❑ 63 Anfernee Hardaway	.25	.60
❑ 64 Drew Gooden	.15	.40
❑ 65 Rodney White	.15	.40
❑ 66 Shareef Abdur-Rahim	.20	.50
❑ 67 Quentin Richardson	.20	.50
❑ 68 Ben Wallace	.20	.50
❑ 69 Latrell Sprewell	.20	.50
❑ 70 Shaquille O'Neal	.60	1.50
❑ 71 Vin Baker	.15	.40
❑ 72 Tony Parker	.25	.60
❑ 73 Stephen Jackson	.20	.50
❑ 74 Ray Allen	.15	.40
❑ 75 Eric Snow	.15	.40
❑ 76 Jason Richardson	.25	.60
❑ 77 Shammond Williams	.15	.40
❑ 78 Tayshaun Prince	.20	.50
❑ 79 Antawn Jamison	.25	.60
❑ 80 Derek Fisher	.20	.50
❑ 81 Jeff Foster	.15	.40
❑ 82 Kwame Brown	.15	.40
❑ 83 Yao Ming	.50	1.25
❑ 84 Rasheed Wallace	.25	.60
❑ 85 Tyson Chandler	.20	.50
❑ 86 Mike Dunleavy	.20	.50
❑ 87 Alan Henderson	.15	.40
❑ 88 Rashard Lewis	.25	.60
❑ 89 Jamaal Magloire	.15	.40
❑ 90 Stephon Marbury	.25	.60
❑ 91 DeShawn Stevenson	.15	.40
❑ 92 Damon Stoudamire	.20	.50
❑ 93 Eddy Curry	.20	.50
❑ 94 Peja Stojakovic	.20	.50
❑ 95 Glenn Robinson	.20	.50
❑ 96 Mike Miller	.20	.50
❑ 97 Richard Hamilton	.20	.50
❑ 98 Kevin Garnett	.50	1.25
❑ 99 Zach Randolph	.25	.60
❑ 100 Tony Delk	.15	.40
❑ 101 Clifford Robinson	.15	.40
❑ 102 Steve Francis	.25	.60
❑ 103 Curtis Borchardt	.25	.60
❑ 104 Jerry Stackhouse	.20	.50
❑ 105 Desmond Mason	.20	.50
❑ 106 Chauncey Billups	.25	.60
❑ 107 Sam Cassell	.20	.50
❑ 108 Michael Finley	.25	.60
❑ 109 Hedo Turkoglu	.20	.50
❑ 110 Ronald Murray	.15	.40
❑ 111 Allen Iverson	.50	1.25
❑ 112 Richard Jefferson	.25	.60
❑ 113 Theo Ratliff	.15	.40
❑ 114 Ron Artest	.20	.50
❑ 115 Doug Christie	.15	.40
❑ 116 Lamar Odom	.25	.60
❑ 117 Lamond Murray	.15	.40
❑ 118 Bonzi Wells	.15	.40
❑ 119 Caron Butler	.20	.50
❑ 120 Marcus Camby	.20	.50
❑ 121 Manu Ginobili	.25	.60
❑ 122 Paul Pierce	.25	.60
❑ 123 Troy Hudson	.15	.40
❑ 124 Jim Jackson	.15	.40
❑ 125 Keith Van Horn	.20	.50
❑ 126 Reggie Miller	.25	.60
❑ 127 Tim Duncan	.50	1.25
❑ 128 Shawn Marion	.25	.60
❑ 129 Eddie Jones	.20	.50
❑ 130 Matt Harpring	.20	.50
❑ 131 Elden Campbell	.15	.40
❑ 132 Marko Jaric	.15	.40
❑ 133 John Wallace	.15	.40
❑ 134 Erick Strickland	.15	.40
❑ 135 Voshon Lenard	.15	.40
❑ 136 Aaron Williams	.15	.40
❑ 137 Qyntel Woods	.15	.40
❑ 138 Kelvin Cato	.15	.40
❑ 139 Michael Curry	.15	.40
❑ 140 Vlade Divac	.20	.50
❑ 141 Jason Hart	.15	.40
❑ 142 Nazr Mohammed UH	.15	.40
❑ 143 Mike James UH	.15	.40
❑ 144 Jerome Williams UH	.15	.40
❑ 145 Zydrunas Ilgauskas UH	.20	.50
❑ 146 Antoine Walker UH	.25	.60
❑ 147 Earl Boykins UH	.15	.40
❑ 148 Mehmet Okur UH	.20	.50
❑ 149 Brian Cardinal UH	.15	.40
❑ 150 Bostjan Nachbar UH	.15	.40
❑ 151 Al Harrington UH	.20	.50
❑ 152 Eddie House UH	.15	.40
❑ 153 Devean George UH	.15	.40
❑ 154 Jason Williams UH	.20	.50
❑ 155 Rafer Alston UH	.15	.40
❑ 156 Michael Redd UH	.25	.60
❑ 157 Gary Trent UH	.15	.40
❑ 158 Kerry Kittles UH	.20	.50
❑ 159 Jamal Mashburn UH	.15	.40
❑ 160 Kurt Thomas UH	.15	.40
❑ 161 Tyronn Lue UH	.15	.40
❑ 162 Derrick Coleman UH	.20	.50
❑ 163 Joe Johnson UH	.25	.60
❑ 164 Dale Davis UH	.15	.40
❑ 165 Bobby Jackson UH	.15	.40
❑ 166 Malik Rose UH	.15	.40
❑ 167 Brent Barry UH	.15	.40
❑ 168 Donyell Marshall UH	.15	.40
❑ 169 Carlos Arroyo UH	.15	.40
❑ 170 Etan Thomas UH	.15	.40
❑ 171 Zoran Planinic RC	1.00	2.50
❑ 172 Jason Kapono RC	1.25	3.00
❑ 173 Zarko Cabarkapa RC	1.00	2.50
❑ 174 Darko Milicic RC	1.25	3.00
❑ 175 Aleksandar Pavlovic RC	1.25	3.00
❑ 176 Marcus Banks RC	1.00	2.50
❑ 177 Willie Green RC	1.00	2.50
❑ 178 Udonis Haslem RC	1.25	3.00
❑ 179 Nick Collison RC	1.00	2.50
❑ 180 Chris Kaman RC	1.25	3.00
❑ 181 T.J. Ford RC	2.00	5.00
❑ 182 Travis Outlaw RC	2.00	5.00
❑ 183 LeBron James RC	20.00	50.00
❑ 184 Troy Bell RC	1.50	4.00
❑ 185 Reece Gaines RC	1.50	4.00
❑ 186 David West RC	2.00	5.00
❑ 187 Kirk Hinrich RC	2.00	5.00

❑ 188 Chris Bosh RC	2.50	6.00
❑ 189 Leandro Barbosa RC	2.00	5.00
❑ 190 Dwyane Wade RC	4.00	10.00
❑ 191 Mike Sweetney RC	2.00	5.00
❑ 192 Darius Songaila	2.00	5.00
❑ 193 Luke Ridnour RC	2.50	6.00
❑ 194 Carmelo Anthony RC	5.00	12.00
❑ 195 Jarvis Hayes RC	2.00	5.00
❑ 196 Mickael Pietrus RC	2.50	6.00
❑ 197 Dahntay Jones RC	2.00	5.00
❑ 198 Josh Howard RC	2.50	6.00
❑ 199 Maciej Lampe RC	2.00	5.00
❑ 200 Luke Walton RC	2.50	6.00

2000-01 Fleer Premium

❑ COMPLETE SET w/o RC (200)	20.00	40.00
❑ COMMON CARD (1-200)	.20	.50
❑ COMMON ROOKIE (201-241)	1.25	3.00
❑ 1 Vince Carter	.60	1.50
❑ 2 Kobe Bryant	1.50	4.00
❑ 3 Jermaine Jackson	.20	.50
❑ 4 Lamar Odom	.30	.75
❑ 5 Robert Traylor	.20	.50
❑ 6 Jason Kidd	.50	1.25
❑ 7 Rashard Lewis	.30	.75
❑ 8 Ron Artest	.30	.75
❑ 9 Grant Hill	.30	.75
❑ 10 Kenny Thomas	.20	.50
❑ 11 Anthony Carter	.20	.50
❑ 12 Kerry Kittles	.25	.60
❑ 13 Pat Garrity	.20	.50
❑ 14 David Robinson	.40	1.00
❑ 15 Bryant Reeves	.20	.50
❑ 16 Fred Hoiberg	.20	.50
❑ 17 Jerry Stackhouse	.25	.60
❑ 18 Donyell Marshall	.20	.50
❑ 19 Ron Harper	.25	.60
❑ 20 Scott Burrell	.20	.50
❑ 21 Ron Mercer	.20	.50
❑ 22 Avery Johnson	.25	.60
❑ 23 Jacque Vaughn	.20	.50
❑ 24 Adrian Griffin	.20	.50
❑ 25 Antonio McDyess	.25	.60
❑ 26 Adonal Foyle	.20	.50
❑ 27 Derek Fisher	.30	.75
❑ 28 Terrell Brandon	.20	.50
❑ 29 Matt Harpring	.25	.60
❑ 30 Nazr Mohammed	.20	.50
❑ 31 Tom Gugliotta	.20	.50
❑ 32 Scott Padgett	.20	.50
❑ 33 Detlef Schrempf	.25	.60
❑ 34 Dirk Nowitzki	.50	1.25
❑ 35 Mookie Blaylock	.25	.60
❑ 36 James Posey	.20	.50
❑ 37 Latrell Sprewell	.25	.60
❑ 38 Michael Doleac	.20	.50
❑ 39 Damon Stoudamire	.25	.60
❑ 40 Tim Duncan	.60	1.50
❑ 41 John Stockton	.40	1.00
❑ 42 Danny Fortson	.20	.50
❑ 43 Raef LaFrentz	.20	.50
❑ 44 Steve Francis	.30	.75
❑ 45 Travis Knight	.20	.50
❑ 46 Kevin Garnett	.60	1.50
❑ 47 Mitch Richmond	.25	.60
❑ 48 Olden Polynice	.20	.50
❑ 49 Derrick Coleman	.25	.60
❑ 50 Ervin Johnson	.20	.50
❑ 51 Shandon Anderson	.20	.50
❑ 52 Jamal Mashburn	.25	.60
❑ 53 Joe Smith	.20	.50
❑ 54 Bo Outlaw	.20	.50
❑ 55 Clifford Robinson	.20	.50
❑ 56 Scottie Pippen	.50	1.25
❑ 57 Chris Webber	.30	.75
❑ 58 Doug Christie	.20	.50
❑ 59 Michael Dickerson	.20	.50
❑ 60 Anthony Mason	.20	.50
❑ 61 Shawn Bradley	.20	.50
❑ 62 Reggie Miller	.30	.75
❑ 63 P.J. Brown	.20	.50
❑ 64 Wally Szczerbiak	.25	.60
❑ 65 Keon Clark	.20	.50
❑ 66 Anthony Peeler	.20	.50
❑ 67 Doug West	.20	.50
❑ 68 Antoine Walker	.25	.60
❑ 69 Trajan Langdon	.20	.50
❑ 70 Mark Jackson	.25	.60
❑ 71 Sam Cassell	.25	.60
❑ 72 Kurt Thomas	.20	.50
❑ 73 Ruben Patterson	.20	.50
❑ 74 Alvin Williams	.20	.50
❑ 75 Juwan Howard	.25	.60
❑ 76 Baron Davis	.30	.75
❑ 77 Otis Thorpe	.25	.60
❑ 78 Austin Croshere	.20	.50
❑ 79 Tony Delk	.20	.50
❑ 80 William Avery	.20	.50
❑ 81 Matt Geiger	.20	.50
❑ 82 Richard Hamilton	.25	.60
❑ 83 Ricky Davis	.25	.60
❑ 84 Hubert Davis	.20	.50
❑ 85 Jalen Rose	.25	.60
❑ 86 Theo Ratliff	.20	.50
❑ 87 Bobby Jackson	.20	.50
❑ 88 Glenn Robinson	.25	.60
❑ 89 Kendall Gill	.20	.50
❑ 90 Laron Profit	.20	.50
❑ 91 Brad Miller	.25	.60
❑ 92 Cedric Ceballos	.20	.50
❑ 93 Arvydas Sabonis	.25	.60
❑ 94 Vitaly Potapenko	.20	.50
❑ 95 Rod Strickland	.25	.60
❑ 96 Erick Dampier	.20	.50
❑ 97 Ryan Bowen	.20	.50
❑ 98 Dale Davis	.20	.50
❑ 99 Larry Johnson	.25	.60
❑ 100 John Thomas	.20	.50
❑ 101 Rodney Rogers	.20	.50
❑ 102 Ray Allen	.30	.75
❑ 103 Isaac Austin	.20	.50
❑ 104 Radoslav Nesterovic	.20	.50
❑ 105 Tariq Abdul-Wahad	.20	.50
❑ 106 Jonathan Bender	.20	.50
❑ 107 Tim Hardaway	.25	.60
❑ 108 Jamie Feick	.20	.50
❑ 109 Toni Kukoc	.25	.60
❑ 110 Tyrone Corbin	.20	.50
❑ 111 Aleksandar Radojevic	.20	.50
❑ 112 Tony Battie	.20	.50
❑ 113 Andre Miller	.25	.60
❑ 114 Derek Anderson	.25	.60
❑ 115 Tim Thomas	.20	.50
❑ 116 Corey Maggette	.25	.60
❑ 117 Rasheed Wallace	.30	.75
❑ 118 Shammond Williams	.20	.50
❑ 119 Charlie Ward	.20	.50
❑ 120 Paul Pierce	.30	.75
❑ 121 Shawn Kemp	.30	.75
❑ 122 Darrell Armstrong	.20	.50
❑ 123 Fred Vinson	.20	.50
❑ 124 Jim Jackson	.20	.50
❑ 125 Steve Nash	.50	1.25
❑ 126 Michael Stewart	.20	.50
❑ 127 Maurice Taylor	.20	.50
❑ 128 Michael Ruffin	.20	.50
❑ 129 Vlade Divac	.25	.60
❑ 130 LaPhonso Ellis	.25	.60
❑ 131 Eddie Jones	.25	.60
❑ 132 Hakeem Olajuwon	.40	1.00
❑ 133 Rick Fox	.25	.60
❑ 134 Patrick Ewing	.40	1.00
❑ 135 Brian Grant	.20	.50
❑ 136 Jaren Jackson	.20	.50
❑ 137 Christian Laettner	.20	.50
❑ 138 Greg Ostertag	.20	.50
❑ 139 Anfernee Hardaway	.30	.75
❑ 140 Nick Van Exel	.25	.60
❑ 141 Jason Caffey	.20	.50
❑ 142 Michael Olowokandi	.20	.50
❑ 143 Darvin Ham	.20	.50
❑ 144 Calbert Cheaney	.20	.50
❑ 145 Steve Smith	.25	.60
❑ 146 Jason Williams	.25	.60
❑ 147 Jelani McCoy	.20	.50
❑ 148 Karl Malone	.40	1.00
❑ 149 Dikembe Mutombo	.25	.60
❑ 150 Wesley Person	.20	.50
❑ 151 Kelvin Cato	.20	.50
❑ 152 Alonzo Mourning	.30	.75
❑ 153 Terry Mills	.20	.50
❑ 154 Allen Iverson	.60	1.50
❑ 155 Bonzi Wells	.20	.50
❑ 156 Antonio Daniels	.20	.50
❑ 157 Shareef Abdur-Rahim	.25	.60
❑ 158 Randy Brown	.20	.50
❑ 159 Mike Bibby	.25	.60
❑ 160 Travis Best	.20	.50
❑ 161 Dan Majerle	.25	.60
❑ 162 Aaron McKie	.20	.50
❑ 163 Jason Terry	.30	.75
❑ 164 Michael Finley	.30	.75
❑ 165 Antonio Davis	.20	.50
❑ 166 Lindsey Hunter	.20	.50
❑ 167 Cuttino Mobley	.25	.60
❑ 168 Glen Rice	.25	.60
❑ 169 Stephon Marbury	.30	.75
❑ 170 Sean Elliott	.25	.60
❑ 171 Cedric Henderson	.20	.50
❑ 172 Eric Snow	.20	.50
❑ 173 Othella Harrington	.20	.50
❑ 174 Vonteego Cummings	.20	.50
❑ 175 John Amaechi	.20	.50
❑ 176 Allan Houston	.25	.60
❑ 177 Shawn Marion	.30	.75
❑ 178 Scot Pollard	.20	.50
❑ 179 Elton Brand	.30	.75
❑ 180 Loy Vaught	.20	.50
❑ 181 Larry Hughes	.25	.60
❑ 182 Shaquille O'Neal	.75	2.00
❑ 183 Keith Van Horn	.25	.60
❑ 184 Terry Porter	.25	.60
❑ 185 Quincy Lewis	.20	.50
❑ 186 Alan Henderson	.20	.50
❑ 187 Brevin Knight	.20	.50
❑ 188 Walt Williams	.20	.50
❑ 189 Clarence Weatherspoon	.20	.50
❑ 190 Marcus Camby	.25	.60
❑ 191 Corliss Williamson	.25	.60
❑ 192 Gary Payton	.30	.75
❑ 193 Felipe Lopez	.20	.50
❑ 194 Elden Campbell	.20	.50
❑ 195 Jerome Williams	.20	.50
❑ 196 Antawn Jamison	.30	.75
❑ 197 Gerard King	.20	.50
❑ 198 Andrae Patterson	.20	.50
❑ 199 Vin Baker	.25	.60
❑ 200 Tracy McGrady	.60	1.50
❑ 201 Chris Carrawell RC	1.25	3.00
❑ 202 Eduardo Najera RC	1.25	3.00
❑ 203 Olumide Oyedeji RC	1.25	3.00
❑ 204 Hanno Mottola RC	1.25	3.00
❑ 205 Dan McClintock RC	1.25	3.00
❑ 206 Jacquay Walls RC	1.25	3.00
❑ 207 Corey Hightower RC	1.25	3.00
❑ 208 Jamal Crawford RC	2.00	5.00
❑ 209 Soumaila Samake RC	1.25	3.00
❑ 210 Michael Redd RC	3.00	8.00
❑ 211 Jason Hart RC	1.25	3.00
❑ 212 Mark Karcher RC	1.25	3.00
❑ 213 Chris Porter RC	1.25	3.00
❑ 214 Eddie House RC	1.25	3.00
❑ 215 Jabari Smith RC	1.25	3.00
❑ 216 Dan Langhi RC	1.25	3.00
❑ 217 Desmond Mason RC	1.50	4.00
❑ 218 Darius Miles RC	1.50	4.00
❑ 219 Donnell Harvey RC	1.25	3.00
❑ 220 DeShawn Stevenson RC	1.25	3.00
❑ 221 Kenyon Martin RC	3.00	8.00
❑ 222 Joel Przybilla RC	1.25	3.00
❑ 223 Keyon Dooling RC	1.25	3.00
❑ 224 Speedy Claxton RC	1.25	3.00
❑ 225 Jerome Moiso RC	1.25	3.00
❑ 226 Hedo Turkoglu RC	3.00	8.00
❑ 227 Mark Madsen RC	1.25	3.00
❑ 228 Morris Peterson RC	2.00	5.00
❑ 229 Courtney Alexander RC	1.25	3.00
❑ 230 Etan Thomas RC	1.25	3.00
❑ 231 Mateen Cleaves RC	1.25	3.00
❑ 232 Stromile Swift RC	1.50	4.00
❑ 233 Marcus Fizer RC	1.25	3.00
❑ 234 Quentin Richardson RC	1.50	4.00
❑ 235 Jason Collier RC	1.25	3.00
❑ 236 Jamaal Magloire RC	1.25	3.00

❑ 237 Erick Barkley RC	1.25	3.00
❑ 238 DerMarr Johnson RC	1.25	3.00
❑ 239 Chris Mihm RC	1.25	3.00
❑ 240 Mamadou N'Diaye RC	1.25	3.00
❑ 241 Mike Miller RC	2.00	5.00

2001-02 Fleer Premium

❑ COMPLETE SET (185)	175.00	350.00
❑ COMP.SET w/o SP's (1-150)	20.00	40.00
❑ COMMON CARD (1-150)	.08	.25
❑ COMMON ROOKIE (151-185)	1.25	3.00
❑ 1 Shareef Abdur-Rahim	.25	.60
❑ 2 Charlie Ward	.20	.50
❑ 3 Anfernee Hardaway	.30	.75
❑ 4 Robert Horry	.25	.60
❑ 5 Michael Jordan	6.00	15.00
❑ 6 Trajan Langdon	.20	.50
❑ 7 Dan Majerle	.25	.60
❑ 8 Tracy McGrady	.60	1.50
❑ 9 Alonzo Mourning	.30	.75
❑ 10 Gary Payton	.30	.75
❑ 11 Erick Barkley	.20	.50
❑ 12 Jerry Stackhouse	.25	.60
❑ 13 Vince Carter	.60	1.50
❑ 14 Speedy Claxton	.20	.50
❑ 15 DerMarr Johnson	.20	.50
❑ 16 Bryon Russell	.20	.50
❑ 17 Derrick Coleman	.25	.60
❑ 18 Kevin Willis	.20	.50
❑ 19 Dirk Nowitzki	.50	1.25
❑ 20 Derek Anderson	.25	.60
❑ 21 Tim Hardaway	.25	.60
❑ 22 Avery Johnson	.25	.60
❑ 23 Quincy Lewis	.20	.50
❑ 24 Shawn Marion	.30	.75
❑ 25 Joe Smith	.20	.50
❑ 26 Tim Thomas	.20	.50
❑ 27 Bonzi Wells	.25	.60
❑ 28 Ron Artest	.25	.60
❑ 29 Elton Brand	.30	.75
❑ 30 Mateen Cleaves	.20	.50
❑ 31 Marcus Fizer	.20	.50
❑ 32 Ervin Johnson	.20	.50
❑ 33 Mark Madsen	.20	.50
❑ 34 Andre Miller	.25	.60
❑ 35 Nazr Mohammed	.20	.50
❑ 36 Dikembe Mutombo	.25	.60
❑ 37 Ben Wallace	.25	.60
❑ 38 Scottie Pippen	.50	1.25
❑ 39 Theo Ratliff	.20	.50
❑ 40 Hedo Turkoglu	.25	.60
❑ 41 Alvin Williams	.20	.50
❑ 42 Corey Maggette	.25	.60
❑ 43 Steve Francis	.30	.75
❑ 44 Dean Garrett	.20	.50
❑ 45 Wally Szczerbiak	.25	.60
❑ 46 Brent Barry	.20	.50
❑ 47 Vlade Divac	.25	.60
❑ 48 LaPhonso Ellis	.25	.60
❑ 49 Tyrone Hill	.20	.50
❑ 50 Toni Kukoc	.25	.60
❑ 51 George Lynch	.20	.50
❑ 52 Antonio McDyess	.25	.60
❑ 53 Paul Pierce	.30	.75
❑ 54 Mitch Richmond	.25	.60
❑ 55 Latrell Sprewell	.25	.60
❑ 56 Otis Thorpe		
❑ 57 Ray Allen	.30	.75
❑ 58 Mike Bibby	.25	.60
❑ 59 P.J. Brown	.20	.50
❑ 60 Allan Houston	.25	.60
❑ 61 Stephon Marbury	.30	.75
❑ 62 Aaron McKie	.20	.50
❑ 63 Reggie Miller	.30	.75
❑ 64 Eduardo Najera	.20	.50
❑ 65 Eddie Robinson	.20	.50
❑ 66 John Stockton	.40	1.00
❑ 67 Chris Webber	.30	.75
❑ 68 Kenny Anderson	.25	.60
❑ 69 Alan Henderson	.20	.50
❑ 70 Dan Langhi	.20	.50
❑ 71 Rashard Lewis	.30	.75
❑ 72 Donyell Marshall	.20	.50
❑ 73 Charles Oakley	.25	.60
❑ 74 Stephen Jackson	.25	.60
❑ 75 Clarence Weatherspoon	.20	.50
❑ 76 David Wesley	.20	.50
❑ 77 Kobe Bryant	1.50	4.00
❑ 78 Tom Gugliotta	.20	.50
❑ 79 Darius Miles	.20	.50
❑ 80 Cuttino Mobley	.25	.60
❑ 81 Jason Terry	.30	.75
❑ 82 Shandon Anderson	.20	.50
❑ 83 Antonio Daniels	.20	.50
❑ 84 Larry Hughes	.25	.60
❑ 85 Raef LaFrentz	.20	.50
❑ 86 Kenyon Martin	.30	.75
❑ 87 Lamar Odom	.30	.75
❑ 88 Jermaine O'Neal	.30	.75
❑ 89 Glenn Robinson	.25	.60
❑ 90 Damon Stoudamire	.25	.60
❑ 91 Eddie House	.20	.50
❑ 92 Antonio Davis	.20	.50
❑ 93 Rick Fox	.25	.60
❑ 94 Allen Iverson	.60	1.50
❑ 95 Chris Mihm	.20	.50
❑ 96 Hakeem Olajuwon	.40	1.00
❑ 97 Clifford Robinson	.20	.50
❑ 98 Derek Fisher	.25	.60
❑ 99 Joel Przybilla	.20	.50
❑ 100 Sean Rooks	.20	.50
❑ 101 Jason Kidd	.50	1.25
❑ 102 Antoine Walker	.25	.60
❑ 103 Jason Williams	.25	.60
❑ 104 Jamal Mashburn	.25	.60
❑ 105 Courtney Alexander	.20	.50
❑ 106 Vin Baker	.25	.60
❑ 107 Chauncey Billups	.25	.60
❑ 108 Marcus Camby	.25	.60
❑ 109 Kevin Garnett	.60	1.50
❑ 110 Juwan Howard	.25	.60
❑ 111 Marc Jackson	.20	.50
❑ 112 Karl Malone	.40	1.00
❑ 113 Ricky Davis	.25	.60
❑ 114 Desmond Mason	.25	.60
❑ 115 Jerome Moiso	.20	.50
❑ 116 Steve Nash	.50	1.25
❑ 117 Quentin Richardson	.25	.60
❑ 118 Peja Stojakovic	.25	.60
❑ 119 Rasheed Wallace	.30	.75
❑ 120 Travis Best	.20	.50
❑ 121 Terrell Brandon	.20	.50
❑ 122 Austin Croshere	.20	.50
❑ 123 Tony Delk	.20	.50
❑ 124 Anthony Mason	.20	.50
❑ 125 Patrick Ewing	.40	1.00
❑ 126 Brian Grant	.20	.50
❑ 127 Bobby Jackson	.20	.50
❑ 128 Eddie Jones	.25	.60
❑ 129 Popeye Jones	.20	.50
❑ 130 Brevin Knight	.20	.50
❑ 131 Mike Miller	.25	.60
❑ 132 Shaquille O'Neal	.75	2.00
❑ 133 Morris Peterson	.25	.60
❑ 134 Mookie Blaylock	.25	.60
❑ 135 David Robinson	.40	1.00
❑ 136 John Starks	.20	.50
❑ 137 Stromile Swift	.20	.50
❑ 138 Nick Van Exel	.25	.60
❑ 139 Keith Van Horn	.25	.60
❑ 140 Antawn Jamison	.30	.75
❑ 141 Kurt Thomas	.20	.50
❑ 142 Sam Cassell	.25	.60
❑ 143 Tim Duncan	.60	1.50
❑ 144 Baron Davis	.30	.75
❑ 145 Jerome Williams	.20	.50
❑ 146 Michael Finley	.30	.75
❑ 147 Richard Hamilton	.25	.60
❑ 148 Grant Hill	.30	.75
❑ 149 Jalen Rose	.25	.60
❑ 150 Steve Smith	.25	.60
❑ 151 Kwame Brown RC	1.50	4.00
❑ 152 Jeryl Sasser RC	1.25	3.00
❑ 153 Shane Battier RC	2.00	5.00
❑ 154 Gilbert Arenas RC	2.00	5.00
❑ 155 Jarron Collins RC	1.25	3.00
❑ 156 Jamaal Tinsley RC	1.50	4.00
❑ 157 Brandon Armstrong RC	1.25	3.00
❑ 158 Michael Bradley RC	1.25	3.00
❑ 159 Tyson Chandler RC	2.50	6.00
❑ 160 Joseph Forte RC	1.25	3.00
❑ 161 Brendan Haywood RC	1.50	4.00
❑ 162 Joe Johnson RC	3.00	8.00
❑ 163 Vladimir Radmanovic RC	1.50	4.00
❑ 164 Gerald Wallace RC	3.00	8.00
❑ 165 Steven Hunter RC	1.25	3.00
❑ 166 Richard Jefferson RC	3.00	8.00
❑ 167 DeSagana Diop RC	1.25	3.00
❑ 168 Terence Morris RC	1.25	3.00
❑ 169 Jason Richardson RC	2.50	6.00
❑ 170 Jeff Trepagnier RC	1.25	3.00
❑ 171 Kirk Haston RC	1.25	3.00
❑ 172 Eddy Curry RC	2.00	5.00
❑ 173 Eddie Griffin RC	1.25	3.00
❑ 174 Omar Cook RC	1.25	3.00
❑ 175 Pau Gasol RC	5.00	12.00
❑ 176 Troy Murphy RC	2.50	6.00
❑ 177 Trenton Hassell RC	1.50	4.00
❑ 178 Kedrick Brown RC	1.25	3.00
❑ 179 Zeljko Rebraca RC	1.25	3.00
❑ 180 Tony Parker RC	5.00	12.00
❑ 181 Rodney White RC	1.25	3.00
❑ 182 Jason Collins RC	1.25	3.00
❑ 183 Samuel Dalembert RC	1.50	4.00
❑ 184 Zach Randolph RC	3.00	8.00
❑ 185 Will Solomon RC	1.25	3.00

2002-03 Fleer Premium

❑ COMP.SET w/o SP's (110)	15.00	40.00
❑ COMMON ROOKIE (111-140)	1.50	4.00
❑ 1 Tracy McGrady	.60	1.50
❑ 2 Tim Duncan	.60	1.50
❑ 3 Shaquille O'Neal	.75	2.00
❑ 4 Jason Kidd	.50	1.25
❑ 5 Kobe Bryant	1.50	4.00
❑ 6 Kevin Garnett	.60	1.50
❑ 7 Chris Webber	.30	.75
❑ 8 Dirk Nowitzki	.50	1.25
❑ 9 Gary Payton	.30	.75
❑ 10 Allen Iverson	.60	1.50
❑ 11 Ben Wallace	.25	.60
❑ 12 Jermaine O'Neal	.30	.75
❑ 13 Dikembe Mutombo	.25	.60
❑ 14 Paul Pierce	.30	.75
❑ 15 Steve Nash	.50	1.25
❑ 16 Pau Gasol	.30	.75
❑ 17 Jason Richardson	.30	.75
❑ 18 Tony Parker	.30	.75
❑ 19 Andrei Kirilenko	.30	.75
❑ 20 Shane Battier	.25	.60
❑ 21 Jamaal Tinsley	.25	.60
❑ 22 Richard Jefferson	.30	.75
❑ 23 Joe Johnson	.30	.75
❑ 24 Eddie Griffin	.20	.50
❑ 25 Zeljko Rebraca	.20	.50
❑ 26 Vladimir Radmanovic	.20	.50
❑ 27 Damon Stoudamire	.25	.60
❑ 28 Eddie Jones	.25	.60
❑ 29 Tyson Chandler	.25	.60
❑ 30 Karl Malone	.30	.75
❑ 31 David Wesley	.20	.50
❑ 32 Steve Francis	.30	.75
❑ 33 Hakeem Olajuwon	.40	1.00
❑ 34 Baron Davis	.30	.75
❑ 35 Antonio McDyess	.25	.60
❑ 36 Mike Bibby	.25	.60
❑ 37 Bonzi Wells	.25	.60
❑ 38 Ray Allen	.30	.75
❑ 39 Doug Christie	.20	.50
❑ 40 Richard Hamilton	.25	.60
❑ 41 Grant Hill	.30	.75

❑ 42 Elton Brand	.30	.75
❑ 43 Gilbert Arenas	.30	.75
❑ 44 Vlade Divac	.25	.60
❑ 45 Sam Cassell	.25	.60
❑ 46 Jalen Rose	.25	.60
❑ 47 Peja Stojakovic	.25	.60
❑ 48 Glenn Robinson	.25	.60
❑ 49 Ricky Davis	.25	.60
❑ 50 Antonio Daniels	.20	.50
❑ 51 Tim Thomas	.20	.50
❑ 52 Andre Miller	.25	.60
❑ 53 Stephon Marbury	.30	.75
❑ 54 Robert Horry	.25	.60
❑ 55 Tony Delk	.20	.50
❑ 56 David Robinson	.40	1.00
❑ 57 Radoslav Nesterovic	.20	.50
❑ 58 Lamond Murray	.20	.50
❑ 59 Brent Barry	.20	.50
❑ 60 Wally Szczerbiak	.25	.60
❑ 61 Lee Nailon	.20	.50
❑ 62 Rashard Lewis	.30	.75
❑ 63 Kenyon Martin	.30	.75
❑ 64 Michael Finley	.30	.75
❑ 65 John Stockton	.40	1.00
❑ 66 Allan Houston	.25	.60
❑ 67 Terrell Brandon	.20	.50
❑ 68 Donyell Marshall	.20	.50
❑ 69 Marcus Camby	.25	.60
❑ 70 Cuttino Mobley	.25	.60
❑ 71 Shawn Marion	.30	.75
❑ 72 Jason Williams	.25	.60
❑ 73 Rodney Rogers	.20	.50
❑ 74 Scottie Pippen	.50	1.25
❑ 75 Brian Grant	.20	.50
❑ 76 Clifford Robinson	.20	.50
❑ 77 Antoine Walker	.25	.60
❑ 78 Michael Dickerson	.20	.50
❑ 79 Latrell Sprewell	.25	.60
❑ 80 Ron Artest	.25	.60
❑ 81 Shareef Abdur-Rahim	.25	.60
❑ 82 Michael Jordan	2.00	5.00
❑ 83 Mike Miller	.25	.60
❑ 84 Corey Maggette	.25	.60
❑ 85 Antawn Jamison	.30	.75
❑ 86 Rasheed Wallace	.30	.75
❑ 87 Alonzo Mourning	.30	.75
❑ 88 Eddy Curry	.25	.60
❑ 89 Derrick Coleman	.25	.60
❑ 90 Joe Smith	.20	.50
❑ 91 Darius Miles	.20	.50
❑ 92 Nick Van Exel	.25	.60
❑ 93 Derek Fisher	.25	.60
❑ 94 Nazr Mohammed	.20	.50
❑ 95 Morris Peterson	.25	.60
❑ 96 Jamal Mashburn	.25	.60
❑ 97 Jerry Stackhouse	.25	.60
❑ 98 Kwame Brown	.20	.50
❑ 99 Darrell Armstrong	.20	.50
❑ 100 Reggie Miller	.30	.75
❑ 101 Desmond Mason	.25	.60
❑ 102 Antonio Davis	.20	.50
❑ 103 Elden Campbell	.20	.50
❑ 104 Voshon Lenard	.20	.50
❑ 105 Eric Snow	.20	.50
❑ 106 Lamar Odom	.30	.75
❑ 107 Toni Kukoc	.25	.60
❑ 108 Vince Carter	.60	1.50
❑ 109 Keith Van Horn	.25	.60
❑ 110 Juwan Howard	.25	.60
❑ 111 Jay Williams RC	2.00	5.00
❑ 112 Yao Ming RC	5.00	12.00
❑ 113 Mike Dunleavy RC	2.00	5.00
❑ 114 Drew Gooden RC	2.50	6.00
❑ 115 Nikoloz Tskitishvili RC	1.50	4.00
❑ 116 DaJuan Wagner RC	1.50	4.00
❑ 117 Nene Hilario RC	2.00	5.00
❑ 118 Chris Wilcox RC	2.00	5.00
❑ 119 Amare Stoudemire RC	4.00	10.00
❑ 120 Caron Butler RC	3.00	8.00
❑ 121 Melvin Ely RC	1.50	4.00
❑ 122 Marcus Haislip RC	1.50	4.00
❑ 123 Jared Jeffries RC	1.50	4.00
❑ 124 Fred Jones RC	2.00	5.00
❑ 125 Bostjan Nachbar RC	1.50	4.00
❑ 126 Jiri Welsch RC	1.50	4.00
❑ 127 Juan Dixon RC	2.50	6.00
❑ 128 Curtis Borchardt RC	1.50	4.00
❑ 129 Ryan Humphrey RC	1.50	4.00
❑ 130 Kareem Rush RC	2.00	5.00
❑ 131 Qyntel Woods RC	1.50	4.00
❑ 132 Casey Jacobsen RC	1.50	4.00
❑ 133 Tayshaun Prince RC	2.50	6.00
❑ 134 Carlos Boozer RC	3.00	8.00
❑ 135 Frank Williams RC	1.50	4.00
❑ 136 John Salmons RC	2.50	6.00
❑ 137 Chris Jefferies RC	1.50	4.00
❑ 138 Dan Dickau RC	1.50	4.00
❑ 139 Manu Ginobili RC	4.00	10.00
❑ 140 Roger Mason RC	1.50	4.00

2001-02 Fleer Shoebox

❑ COMP.SET w/o SP's (150)	20.00	40.00
❑ COMMON CARD (1-150)	.20	.50
❑ COMMON ROOKIE (151-180)	.75	2.00
❑ 1 Tariq Abdul-Wahad	.20	.50
❑ 2 Glen Rice	.25	.60
❑ 3 Derek Anderson	.25	.60
❑ 4 Desmond Mason	.25	.60
❑ 5 Al Harrington	.25	.60
❑ 6 Mitch Richmond	.25	.60
❑ 7 Felipe Lopez	.20	.50
❑ 8 Andre Miller	.25	.60
❑ 9 Jerry Stackhouse	.25	.60
❑ 10 Jalen Rose	.25	.60
❑ 11 Lindsey Hunter	.20	.50
❑ 12 Tim Thomas	.20	.50
❑ 13 Wally Szczerbiak	.25	.60
❑ 14 Vince Carter	.60	1.50
❑ 15 Nick Van Exel	.25	.60
❑ 16 Jon Barry	.20	.50
❑ 17 Aaron McKie	.20	.50
❑ 18 Iakovos Tsakalidis	.20	.50
❑ 19 Chris Webber	.30	.75
❑ 20 Karl Malone	.40	1.00
❑ 21 Shareef Abdur-Rahim	.25	.60
❑ 22 Baron Davis	.30	.75
❑ 23 Michael Doleac	.20	.50
❑ 24 Jermaine O'Neal	.30	.75
❑ 25 Elton Brand	.30	.75
❑ 26 Glenn Robinson	.25	.60
❑ 27 Tracy McGrady	.60	1.50
❑ 28 Allen Iverson	.60	1.50
❑ 29 Anfernee Hardaway	.30	.75
❑ 30 Scot Pollard	.20	.50
❑ 31 David Robinson	.40	1.00
❑ 32 John Stockton	.40	1.00
❑ 33 Jason Williams	.25	.60
❑ 34 Voshon Lenard	.20	.50
❑ 35 Shaquille O'Neal	.75	2.00
❑ 36 Grant Hill	.30	.75
❑ 37 Shawn Marion	.30	.75
❑ 38 Vin Baker	.25	.60
❑ 39 Raef LaFrentz	.20	.50
❑ 40 Steve Francis	.30	.75
❑ 41 Michael Dickerson	.20	.50
❑ 42 Hedo Turkoglu	.25	.60
❑ 43 Patrick Ewing	.40	1.00
❑ 44 Dirk Nowitzki	.50	1.25
❑ 45 Keyon Dooling	.20	.50
❑ 46 Marcus Camby	.25	.60
❑ 47 Bonzi Wells	.25	.60
❑ 48 Tim Duncan	.60	1.50
❑ 49 Jamaal Magloire	.20	.50
❑ 50 Rick Fox	.25	.60
❑ 51 Kendall Gill	.20	.50
❑ 52 Michael Redd	.30	.75
❑ 53 Keith Van Horn	.25	.60
❑ 54 Eric Snow	.20	.50
❑ 55 Theo Ratliff	.20	.50
❑ 56 Clifford Robinson	.20	.50
❑ 57 Moochie Norris	.20	.50
❑ 58 Alonzo Mourning	.30	.75
❑ 59 Joe Smith	.20	.50
❑ 60 Brent Barry	.20	.50
❑ 61 Alvin Williams	.20	.50
❑ 62 Antoine Walker	.25	.60
❑ 63 Antonio McDyess	.25	.60
❑ 64 Derek Fisher	.25	.60
❑ 65 Ron Mercer	.20	.50
❑ 66 Hakeem Olajuwon	.40	1.00
❑ 67 Jamal Crawford	.25	.60
❑ 68 Chris Mihm	.20	.50
❑ 69 Ben Wallace	.25	.60
❑ 70 Brian Grant	.20	.50
❑ 71 Kevin Garnett	.60	1.50
❑ 72 Shandon Anderson	.20	.50
❑ 73 Shawn Bradley	.20	.50
❑ 74 Danny Fortson	.20	.50
❑ 75 Jeff McInnis	.20	.50
❑ 76 LaPhonso Ellis	.25	.60
❑ 77 Sam Cassell	.25	.60
❑ 78 Rasheed Wallace	.30	.75
❑ 79 Malik Rose	.20	.50
❑ 80 Jahidi White	.20	.50
❑ 81 Milt Palacio	.20	.50
❑ 82 Tim Hardaway	.25	.60
❑ 83 Antonio Daniels	.20	.50
❑ 84 Tyronn Lue	.20	.50
❑ 85 Cuttino Mobley	.25	.60
❑ 86 DerMarr Johnson	.20	.50
❑ 87 Lamond Murray	.20	.50
❑ 88 Larry Hughes	.25	.60
❑ 89 Reggie Miller	.30	.75
❑ 90 Lorenzen Wright	.20	.50
❑ 91 Eddie Jones	.25	.60
❑ 92 Anthony Mason	.20	.50
❑ 93 Todd MacCulloch	.20	.50
❑ 94 Speedy Claxton	.20	.50
❑ 95 Mateen Cleaves	.20	.50
❑ 96 Gary Payton	.30	.75
❑ 97 Morris Peterson	.25	.60
❑ 98 Mike Miller	.25	.60
❑ 99 Hanno Mottola	.20	.50
❑ 100 Steve Nash	.50	1.25
❑ 101 Stromile Swift	.20	.50
❑ 102 Ray Allen	.30	.75
❑ 103 Mark Jackson	.25	.60
❑ 104 Stephon Marbury	.30	.75
❑ 105 Mike Bibby	.25	.60
❑ 106 Rashard Lewis	.30	.75
❑ 107 Jason Kidd	.50	1.25
❑ 108 P.J. Brown	.20	.50
❑ 109 Kobe Bryant	1.50	4.00
❑ 110 Tom Gugliotta	.20	.50
❑ 111 Richard Hamilton	.25	.60
❑ 112 Antawn Jamison	.30	.75
❑ 113 Lamar Odom	.30	.75
❑ 114 Kurt Thomas	.20	.50
❑ 115 Robert Horry	.25	.60
❑ 116 Dikembe Mutombo	.25	.60
❑ 117 Tony Delk	.20	.50
❑ 118 Peja Stojakovic	.25	.60
❑ 119 Donyell Marshall	.20	.50
❑ 120 Paul Pierce	.30	.75
❑ 121 Michael Finley	.30	.75
❑ 122 Quentin Richardson	.25	.60
❑ 123 Kenyon Martin	.30	.75
❑ 124 Allan Houston	.25	.60
❑ 125 Scottie Pippen	.50	1.25
❑ 126 Steve Smith	.25	.60
❑ 127 Bryon Russell	.20	.50
❑ 128 James Posey	.20	.50
❑ 129 Terrell Brandon	.20	.50
❑ 130 Toni Kukoc	.25	.60
❑ 131 Stephen Jackson	.25	.60
❑ 132 Marc Jackson	.20	.50
❑ 133 Kelvin Cato	.20	.50
❑ 134 Travis Best	.20	.50
❑ 135 David Wesley	.20	.50
❑ 136 Anthony Carter	.20	.50
❑ 137 Michael Jordan	5.00	12.00
❑ 138 Darrell Armstrong	.20	.50
❑ 139 Matt Harpring	.25	.60
❑ 140 Antonio Davis	.20	.50
❑ 141 Courtney Alexander	.20	.50
❑ 142 Jamal Mashburn	.25	.60
❑ 143 Jason Terry	.30	.75
❑ 144 Marcus Fizer	.20	.50
❑ 145 Juwan Howard	.25	.60
❑ 146 Darius Miles	.20	.50
❑ 147 Latrell Sprewell	.25	.60
❑ 148 Damon Stoudamire	.25	.60
❑ 149 John Starks	.20	.50
❑ 150 Jumaine Jones	.20	.50

❑ 151 Kedrick Brown RC .75 2.00
❑ 152 Trenton Hassell RC 1.00 2.50
❑ 153 Kwame Brown RC 1.00 2.50
❑ 154 Terence Morris RC .75 2.00
❑ 155 Richard Jefferson RC 2.00 5.00
❑ 156 Vladimir Radmanovic RC 1.00 2.50
❑ 157 Brandon Armstrong RC .75 2.00
❑ 158 Kirk Haston RC .75 2.00
❑ 159 Eddie Griffin RC .75 2.00
❑ 160 Steven Hunter RC .75 2.00
❑ 161 Troy Murphy RC 1.50 4.00
❑ 162 Andrei Kirilenko RC 2.00 5.00
❑ 163 Jeryl Sasser RC .75 2.00
❑ 164 Michael Bradley RC .75 2.00
❑ 165 Rodney White RC .75 2.00
❑ 166 Loren Woods RC .75 2.00
❑ 167 Zach Randolph RC 2.00 5.00
❑ 168 Joe Johnson RC 2.00 5.00
❑ 169 Eddy Curry RC 1.25 3.00
❑ 170 Jason Richardson RC 1.50 4.00
❑ 171 DeSagana Diop RC .75 2.00
❑ 172 Jamaal Tinsley RC 1.00 2.50
❑ 173 Pau Gasol RC 3.00 8.00
❑ 174 Jason Collins RC .75 2.00
❑ 175 Zeljko Rebraca RC .75 2.00
❑ 176 Shane Battier RC 1.25 3.00
❑ 177 Gerald Wallace RC 2.00 5.00
❑ 178 Joseph Forte RC .75 2.00
❑ 179 Tyson Chandler RC 1.50 4.00
❑ 180 Tony Parker RC 3.00 8.00

2000-01 Fleer Showcase

❑ COMPLETE SET w/o RCs (90) 15.00 30.00
❑ COMMON CARD (1-90) .25 .60
❑ COMMON ROOKIE (91-100) 3.00 8.00
❑ COMMON ROOKIE (101-110) 2.00 5.00
❑ COMMON ROOKIE (111-121) 1.50 4.00
❑ 1 Vince Carter .75 2.00
❑ 2 Lamar Odom .40 1.00
❑ 3 Larry Hughes .30 .75
❑ 4 Brian Grant .25 .60
❑ 5 Bryon Russell .25 .60
❑ 6 Allan Houston .30 .75
❑ 7 Juwan Howard .30 .75
❑ 8 Cuttino Mobley .30 .75
❑ 9 Keith Van Horn .30 .75
❑ 10 Mike Bibby .30 .75
❑ 11 Jerome Williams .25 .60
❑ 12 Ray Allen .40 1.00
❑ 13 Antonio Davis .25 .60
❑ 14 Adrian Griffin .25 .60
❑ 15 Dan Majerle .30 .75
❑ 16 Rasheed Wallace .40 1.00
❑ 17 Antonio McDyess .30 .75
❑ 18 Tim Thomas .25 .60
❑ 19 Theo Ratliff .25 .60
❑ 20 Charles Oakley .30 .75
❑ 21 Nick Van Exel .30 .75
❑ 22 Glenn Robinson .30 .75
❑ 23 Cal Bowdler .25 .60
❑ 24 Raef LaFrentz .25 .60
❑ 25 Terrell Brandon .25 .60
❑ 26 Allen Iverson .75 2.00
❑ 27 Patrick Ewing .50 1.25
❑ 28 Ron Artest .40 1.00
❑ 29 Michael Olowokandi .25 .60
❑ 30 Derek Anderson .30 .75
❑ 31 Dirk Nowitzki .60 1.50
❑ 32 Wally Szczerbiak .30 .75
❑ 33 Gary Payton .40 1.00
❑ 34 Michael Finley .40 1.00
❑ 35 Chauncey Billups .40 1.00
❑ 36 Jason Kidd .60 1.50
❑ 37 Rashard Lewis .40 1.00
❑ 38 Andre Miller .30 .75
❑ 39 Kevin Garnett .75 2.00
❑ 40 Tim Duncan .75 2.00
❑ 41 Jalen Rose .30 .75
❑ 42 Marcus Camby .30 .75
❑ 43 Richard Hamilton .30 .75
❑ 44 Austin Croshere .25 .60
❑ 45 Latrell Sprewell .30 .75
❑ 46 Shawn Marion .40 1.00
❑ 47 Jahidi White .25 .60
❑ 48 Elton Brand .40 1.00
❑ 49 Reggie Miller .40 1.00
❑ 50 David Robinson .50 1.25
❑ 51 Trajan Langdon .25 .60
❑ 52 Jonathan Bender .25 .60
❑ 53 Antonio Daniels .25 .60
❑ 54 Jason Terry .40 1.00
❑ 55 Eddie Jones .30 .75
❑ 56 Mitch Richmond .30 .75
❑ 57 Antoine Walker .30 .75
❑ 58 Robert Horry .30 .75
❑ 59 Tracy McGrady .75 2.00
❑ 60 Scottie Pippen .60 1.50
❑ 61 Jerry Stackhouse .30 .75
❑ 62 Zydrunas Ilgauskas .30 .75
❑ 63 Toni Kukoc .30 .75
❑ 64 Karl Malone .50 1.25
❑ 65 Baron Davis .40 1.00
❑ 66 Shaquille O'Neal 1.00 2.50
❑ 67 Vlade Divac .30 .75
❑ 68 Eddie Robinson .25 .60
❑ 69 Dion Glover .25 .60
❑ 70 Jason Williams .30 .75
❑ 71 Steve Francis .40 1.00
❑ 72 Glen Rice .30 .75
❑ 73 Clifford Robinson .25 .60
❑ 74 Shareef Abdur-Rahim .30 .75
❑ 75 Hakeem Olajuwon .50 1.25
❑ 76 Paul Pierce .40 1.00
❑ 77 Tim Hardaway .30 .75
❑ 78 Darrell Armstrong .25 .60
❑ 79 Bonzi Wells .25 .60
❑ 80 Antawn Jamison .40 1.00
❑ 81 Stephon Marbury .40 1.00
❑ 82 Tony Delk .25 .60
❑ 83 Michael Dickerson .25 .60
❑ 84 Jamal Mashburn .30 .75
❑ 85 Kobe Bryant 2.00 5.00
❑ 86 Grant Hill .40 1.00
❑ 87 Chris Webber .40 1.00
❑ 88 Vonteego Cummings .25 .60
❑ 89 Jamie Feick .25 .60
❑ 90 John Stockton .50 1.25
❑ 91 Kenyon Martin RC 8.00 20.00
❑ 92 Stromile Swift RC 4.00 10.00
❑ 93 Darius Miles RC 4.00 10.00
❑ 94 Marcus Fizer RC 3.00 8.00
❑ 95 Mike Miller RC 5.00 12.00
❑ 96 DerMarr Johnson RC 3.00 8.00
❑ 97 Chris Mihm RC 3.00 8.00
❑ 98 Jamal Crawford RC 5.00 12.00
❑ 99 Joel Przybilla RC 3.00 8.00
❑ 100 Keyon Dooling RC 3.00 8.00
❑ 101 Jerome Moiso RC 2.00 5.00
❑ 102 Etan Thomas RC 2.00 5.00
❑ 103 Courtney Alexander RC 2.00 5.00
❑ 104 Mateen Cleaves RC 2.00 5.00
❑ 105 Jason Collier RC 2.00 5.00
❑ 106 Hedo Turkoglu RC 5.00 12.00
❑ 107 Desmond Mason RC 2.50 6.00
❑ 108 Quentin Richardson RC 2.50 6.00
❑ 109 Jamaal Magloire RC 2.00 5.00
❑ 110 Speedy Claxton RC 2.00 5.00
❑ 111 Morris Peterson RC 2.50 6.00
❑ 112 Donnell Harvey RC 1.50 4.00
❑ 113 DeShawn Stevenson RC 1.50 4.00
❑ 114 Dalibor Bagaric RC 1.50 4.00
❑ 115 Mamadou N'Diaye RC 1.50 4.00
❑ 116 Erick Barkley RC 1.50 4.00
❑ 117 Mark Madsen RC 1.50 4.00
❑ 118 Chris Porter RC 1.50 4.00
❑ 119 Brian Cardinal RC 1.50 4.00
❑ 120 Iakovos Tsakalidis RC 1.50 4.00
❑ 121 Marc Jackson RC 4.00 10.00

2001-02 Fleer Showcase

❑ COMPLETE SET (123) 200.00 400.00
❑ COMP.SET w/o SP's (86) 20.00 50.00
❑ COMMON AVANT(87-91/123) 6.00 15.00
❑ COMMON AVANT RC (92-97) 8.00 20.00
❑ COMMON ROOKIE (98-112) 1.25 3.00
❑ COMMON ROOKIE (113-122) 1.25 3.00

❑ CARTER AU/150 NOT INCL.IN SET PRICE
❑ 1 Grant Hill .40 1.00
❑ 2 Elton Brand .40 1.00
❑ 3 Sam Cassell .30 .75
❑ 4 John Stockton .50 1.25
❑ 5 James Posey .25 .60
❑ 6 Eddie Jones .30 .75
❑ 7 Damon Stoudamire .30 .75
❑ 8 Nick Van Exel .30 .75
❑ 9 Brian Grant .25 .60
❑ 10 Mike Miller .30 .75
❑ 11 Steve Smith .30 .75
❑ 12 Michael Finley .40 1.00
❑ 13 Peja Stojakovic .30 .75
❑ 14 DerMarr Johnson .25 .60
❑ 15 Reggie Miller .40 1.00
❑ 16 Quentin Richardson .30 .75
❑ 17 Latrell Sprewell .30 .75
❑ 18 Richard Hamilton .30 .75
❑ 19 Michael Doleac .25 .60
❑ 20 Derek Fisher .30 .75
❑ 21 Marcus Camby .30 .75
❑ 22 Stephon Marbury .40 1.00
❑ 23 Bryon Russell .25 .60
❑ 24 Jumaine Jones .25 .60
❑ 25 Anfernee Hardaway .40 1.00
❑ 26 P.J. Brown .25 .60
❑ 27 Marc Jackson .25 .60
❑ 28 Dikembe Mutombo .30 .75
❑ 29 Andre Miller .30 .75
❑ 30 Robert Horry .30 .75
❑ 31 Tom Gugliotta .25 .60
❑ 32 David Robinson .50 1.25
❑ 33 Ron Mercer .25 .60
❑ 34 Shawn Marion .40 1.00
❑ 35 Ron Artest .30 .75
❑ 36 Jason Williams .30 .75
❑ 37 Scottie Pippen .60 1.50
❑ 38 Jerry Stackhouse .30 .75
❑ 39 Stromile Swift .25 .60
❑ 40 Rasheed Wallace .40 1.00
❑ 41 Alonzo Mourning .40 1.00
❑ 42 Eddie Robinson .25 .60
❑ 43 Shareef Abdur-Rahim .30 .75
❑ 44 Wally Szczerbiak .30 .75
❑ 45 Antonio Davis .25 .60
❑ 46 Glen Rice .30 .75
❑ 47 Jason Kidd .60 1.50
❑ 48 Gary Payton .40 1.00
❑ 49 Steve Nash .60 1.50
❑ 50 Lamar Odom .40 1.00
❑ 51 Glenn Robinson .30 .75
❑ 52 Mike Bibby .30 .75
❑ 53 Hakeem Olajuwon .50 1.25
❑ 54 Theo Ratliff .25 .60
❑ 55 Kenyon Martin .40 1.00
❑ 56 Jamal Mashburn .30 .75
❑ 57 Larry Hughes .30 .75
❑ 58 Speedy Claxton .25 .60
❑ 59 Rashard Lewis .40 1.00
❑ 60 Raef LaFrentz .25 .60
❑ 61 Antonio Daniels .25 .60
❑ 62 Jason Terry .40 1.00
❑ 63 Jalen Rose .30 .75
❑ 64 Terrell Brandon .25 .60
❑ 65 Karl Malone .50 1.25
❑ 66 Antonio McDyess .30 .75
❑ 67 Anthony Carter .25 .60
❑ 68 Tim Hardaway .30 .75
❑ 69 Antoine Walker .30 .75
❑ 70 Cuttino Mobley .30 .75
❑ 71 Allan Houston .30 .75
❑ 72 Desmond Mason .30 .75
❑ 73 Kurt Thomas .25 .60
❑ 74 Juwan Howard .30 .75

❑ 75 Tim Thomas .25 .60
❑ 76 Tracy McGrady .75 2.00
❑ 77 Dirk Nowitzki .60 1.50
❑ 78 Tim Duncan .75 2.00
❑ 79 Chris Webber .40 1.00
❑ 80 Steve Francis .40 1.00
❑ 81 Paul Pierce .40 1.00
❑ 82 Darius Miles .25 .60
❑ 83 Ray Allen .40 1.00
❑ 84 Baron Davis .40 1.00
❑ 85 Antawn Jamison .40 1.00
❑ 86 Michael Jordan 6.00 15.00
❑ 87 Vince Carter AVANT 6.00 15.00
❑ 87A V.Carter AU/150 60.00 120.00
❑ 88 Kobe Bryant AVANT 15.00 40.00
❑ 89 Allen Iverson AVANT 6.00 15.00
❑ 90 Kevin Garnett AVANT 6.00 15.00
❑ 91 S.O'Neal AVANT 8.00 20.00
❑ 92 K.Brown AVANT RC 6.00 15.00
❑ 93 E.Griffin AVANT RC 5.00 12.00
❑ 94 E.Curry AVANT RC 8.00 20.00
❑ 95 S.Battier AVANT RC 8.00 20.00
❑ 96 J.Johnson AVANT RC 12.00 30.00
❑ 97 T.Chandler AVANT RC 10.00 25.00
❑ 98 Jason Richardson RC 2.50 6.00
❑ 99 Zach Randolph RC 3.00 8.00
❑ 100 Rodney White RC 1.25 3.00
❑ 101 Pau Gasol RC 5.00 12.00
❑ 102 Jamaal Tinsley RC 1.50 4.00
❑ 103 Troy Murphy RC 2.50 6.00
❑ 104 Richard Jefferson RC 3.00 8.00
❑ 105 DeSagana Diop RC 1.25 3.00
❑ 106 Joseph Forte RC 1.25 3.00
❑ 107 Gerald Wallace RC 3.00 8.00
❑ 108 Loren Woods RC 1.25 3.00
❑ 109 Jason Collins RC 1.25 3.00
❑ 110 Jeryl Sasser RC 1.25 3.00
❑ 111 Zeljko Rebraca RC 1.25 3.00
❑ 112 Kirk Haston RC 1.25 3.00
❑ 113 Kedrick Brown RC 1.25 3.00
❑ 114 Steven Hunter RC 1.25 3.00
❑ 115 Michael Bradley RC 1.25 3.00
❑ 116 Brandon Armstrong RC 1.25 3.00
❑ 117 Samuel Dalembert RC 1.50 4.00
❑ 118 Primoz Brezec RC 1.50 4.00
❑ 119 Andrei Kirilenko RC 3.00 8.00
❑ 120 Vladimir Radmanovic RC 1.50 4.00
❑ 121 Ratko Varda RC 1.25 3.00
❑ 122 Brendan Haywood RC 1.50 4.00
❑ 123 Wang Zhizhi AVANT 6.00 15.00

2002-03 Fleer Showcase

❑ COMP.SET w/o SP's (100) 12.50 30.00
❑ COMMON CARD (1-100) .25 .60
❑ COMM.AVANT.ROW 2 (101-112) .75 2.00
❑ COMM.AVANT.ROW 0 (113-118)
❑ COMM.RC AVANT (119-124) 2.50 6.00
❑ COMMON ROOKIE (125-148) 2.50 6.00
❑ 1 Michael Jordan 2.50 6.00
❑ 2 Shareef Abdur-Rahim .30 .75
❑ 3 Jalen Rose .30 .75
❑ 4 Antonio McDyess .30 .75
❑ 5 Malik Rose .25 .60
❑ 6 Juwan Howard .30 .75
❑ 7 Jason Williams .30 .75
❑ 8 Darrell Armstrong .25 .60
❑ 9 Karl Malone .40 1.00
❑ 10 Jason Terry .40 1.00
❑ 11 David Wesley .25 .60
❑ 12 David Robinson .50 1.25
❑ 13 Gary Payton .40 1.00
❑ 14 Quentin Richardson .30 .75
❑ 15 Allan Houston .30 .75
❑ 16 Alvin Williams .25 .60
❑ 17 Jamal Mashburn .30 .75
❑ 18 Theo Ratliff .25 .60
❑ 19 Tyson Chandler .30 .75
❑ 20 Gilbert Arenas .40 1.00
❑ 21 Dikembe Mutombo .30 .75
❑ 22 Calbert Cheaney .25 .60
❑ 23 Rodney Rogers .25 .60
❑ 24 Shane Battier .30 .75
❑ 25 Mike Miller .30 .75
❑ 26 John Stockton .50 1.25
❑ 27 Mengke Bateer .25 .60
❑ 28 Andre Miller .30 .75
❑ 29 Sam Cassell .30 .75
❑ 30 Anfernee Hardaway .40 1.00
❑ 31 Keith Van Horn .30 .75
❑ 32 Tony Battie .25 .60
❑ 33 Derek Fisher .30 .75
❑ 34 Grant Hill .40 1.00
❑ 35 Andrei Kirilenko .40 1.00
❑ 36 Toni Kukoc .30 .75
❑ 37 Jerry Stackhouse .30 .75
❑ 38 Latrell Sprewell .30 .75
❑ 39 Morris Peterson .30 .75
❑ 40 Darius Miles .25 .60
❑ 41 Eddie Jones .30 .75
❑ 42 Stephon Marbury .40 1.00
❑ 43 Brent Barry .25 .60
❑ 44 DeShawn Stevenson .25 .60
❑ 45 Brian Grant .25 .60
❑ 46 Derrick Coleman .30 .75
❑ 47 Richard Hamilton .30 .75
❑ 48 Jason Richardson .40 1.00
❑ 49 Kerry Kittles .30 .75
❑ 50 Desmond Mason .30 .75
❑ 51 Stromile Swift .25 .60
❑ 52 Richard Jefferson .40 1.00
❑ 53 Vladimir Radmanovic .25 .60
❑ 54 Lamond Murray .25 .60
❑ 55 Troy Murphy .40 1.00
❑ 56 Kenyon Martin .40 1.00
❑ 57 Vlade Divac .30 .75
❑ 58 Chris Mihm .25 .60
❑ 59 Eddie Griffin .25 .60
❑ 60 Marc Jackson .25 .60
❑ 61 Peja Stojakovic .30 .75
❑ 62 Vin Baker .30 .75
❑ 63 Cuttino Mobley .30 .75
❑ 64 Joe Smith .25 .60
❑ 65 Damon Stoudamire .30 .75
❑ 66 Eddy Curry .30 .75
❑ 67 Alonzo Mourning .40 1.00
❑ 68 Aaron McKie .25 .60
❑ 69 Kwame Brown .25 .60
❑ 70 Raef LaFrentz .25 .60
❑ 71 Jermaine O'Neal .40 1.00
❑ 72 Terrell Brandon .25 .60
❑ 73 Bonzi Wells .30 .75
❑ 74 Steve Nash .60 1.50
❑ 75 Jamaal Tinsley .30 .75
❑ 76 Wally Szczerbiak .30 .75
❑ 77 Scottie Pippen .60 1.50
❑ 78 Michael Finley .40 1.00
❑ 79 Reggie Miller .40 1.00
❑ 80 Glenn Robinson .30 .75
❑ 81 Rasheed Wallace .40 1.00
❑ 82 Antoine Walker .30 .75
❑ 83 Robert Horry .30 .75
❑ 84 Kurt Thomas .25 .60
❑ 85 Antonio Davis .25 .60
❑ 86 Nick Van Exel .30 .75
❑ 87 Al Harrington .30 .75
❑ 88 Tony Delk .25 .60
❑ 89 Joe Johnson .40 1.00
❑ 90 Chauncey Billups .40 1.00
❑ 91 P.J. Brown .25 .60
❑ 92 Tony Parker .40 1.00
❑ 93 Antawn Jamison .40 1.00
❑ 94 Courtney Alexander .25 .60
❑ 95 Kenny Anderson .30 .75
❑ 96 Clifford Robinson .25 .60
❑ 97 Lamar Odom .40 1.00
❑ 98 Anthony Carter .25 .60
❑ 99 Shawn Marion .40 1.00
❑ 100 Hedo Turkoglu .30 .75
❑ 101 Paul Pierce AVANT 1.00 2.50
❑ 102 Dirk Nowitzki AVANT 1.50 4.00
❑ 103 Ben Wallace AVANT .75 2.00
❑ 104 Steve Francis AVANT 1.00 2.50
❑ 105 Pau Gasol AVANT 1.00 2.50
❑ 106 Ray Allen AVANT 1.00 2.50
❑ 107 Kevin Garnett AVANT 2.00 5.00
❑ 108 Jason Kidd AVANT 1.50 4.00
❑ 109 Baron Davis AVANT 1.00 2.50
❑ 110 Mike Bibby AVANT .75 2.00
❑ 111 Chris Webber AVANT 1.00 2.50
❑ 112 Tim Duncan AVANT 2.00 5.00
❑ 113 Kobe Bryant AVANT 8.00 20.00
❑ 114 Shaquille O'Neal AVANT 4.00 10.00
❑ 115 Tracy McGrady AVANT 3.00 8.00
❑ 116 Allen Iverson AVANT 3.00 8.00
❑ 117 Vince Carter AVANT 3.00 8.00
❑ 118 Elton Brand AVANT 1.50 4.00
❑ 119 J.Williams AVANT RC 3.00 8.00
❑ 120 Yao Ming AVANT RC 8.00 20.00
❑ 121 M.Dunleavy AVANT RC 3.00 8.00
❑ 122 D.Wagner AVANT RC 2.50 6.00
❑ 123 C.Butler AVANT RC 5.00 12.00
❑ 124 D.Gooden AVANT RC 4.00 10.00
❑ 125 Manu Ginobili RC 6.00 15.00
❑ 126 Mehmet Okur RC 3.00 8.00
❑ 127 Nene Hilario RC 3.00 8.00
❑ 128 Nikoloz Tskitishvili RC 2.50 6.00
❑ 129 Tayshaun Prince RC 4.00 10.00
❑ 130 Bostjan Nachbar RC 2.50 6.00
❑ 131 Fred Jones RC 3.00 8.00
❑ 132 Melvin Ely RC 2.50 6.00
❑ 133 Chris Wilcox RC 3.00 8.00
❑ 134 Kareem Rush RC 3.00 8.00
❑ 135 Marcus Haislip RC 2.50 6.00
❑ 136 Frank Williams RC 2.50 6.00
❑ 137 Ryan Humphrey RC 2.50 6.00
❑ 138 John Salmons RC 4.00 10.00
❑ 139 Casey Jacobsen RC 2.50 6.00
❑ 140 Amare Stoudemire RC 6.00 15.00
❑ 141 Qyntel Woods RC 2.50 6.00
❑ 142 Chris Jefferies RC 2.50 6.00
❑ 143 Juan Dixon RC 4.00 10.00
❑ 144 Jared Jeffries RC 2.50 6.00
❑ 145 Lonny Baxter RC 2.50 6.00
❑ 146 Dan Dickau RC 2.50 6.00
❑ 147 Carlos Boozer RC 5.00 12.00
❑ 148 Vincent Yarbrough RC 2.50 6.00

2003-04 Fleer Showcase

❑ COMP.SET w/o SP's (100) 15.00 40.00
❑ COMMON SP (91-100) .75 2.00
❑ COMMON ROOKIE (101-130) 2.00 5.00
❑ 1 Jason Richardson .50 1.25
❑ 2 Andrei Kirilenko .50 1.25
❑ 3 Steve Francis .50 1.25
❑ 4 Shareef Abdur-Rahim .40 1.00
❑ 5 Ben Wallace .40 1.00
❑ 6 Predrag Drobnjak .30 .75
❑ 7 Jalen Rose .40 1.00
❑ 8 Rashard Lewis .50 1.25
❑ 9 Darius Miles .40 1.00
❑ 10 Bobby Jackson .30 .75
❑ 11 Steve Nash .75 2.00
❑ 12 Gilbert Arenas .50 1.25
❑ 13 Aaron McKie .30 .75
❑ 14 Reggie Miller .50 1.25
❑ 15 Elton Brand .50 1.25
❑ 16 Allan Houston .40 1.00
❑ 17 Pau Gasol .50 1.25
❑ 18 Jamaal Magloire .30 .75
❑ 19 Eddie Jones .40 1.00
❑ 20 Richard Jefferson .50 1.25
❑ 21 Wally Szczerbiak .40 1.00
❑ 22 Antonio McDyess .40 1.00
❑ 23 Michael Redd .50 1.25
❑ 24 Grant Hill .50 1.25
❑ 25 Jason Williams .40 1.00
❑ 26 Rasheed Wallace .50 1.25
❑ 27 Andre Miller .40 1.00
❑ 28 Peja Stojakovic .40 1.00
❑ 29 Cuttino Mobley .40 1.00
❑ 30 David Robinson .75 2.00

❑ 31 Richard Hamilton	.40	1.00
❑ 32 Morris Peterson	.40	1.00
❑ 33 Karl Malone	.50	1.25
❑ 34 Zydrunas Ilgauskas	.40	1.00
❑ 35 Jerry Stackhouse	.40	1.00
❑ 36 Eddy Curry	.40	1.00
❑ 37 Sam Cassell	.40	1.00
❑ 38 Troy Hudson	.30	.75
❑ 39 Jason Terry	.40	1.00
❑ 40 Kenyon Martin	.50	1.25
❑ 41 Bonzi Wells	.30	.75
❑ 42 Donnell Harvey	.30	.75
❑ 43 Tracy McGrady	1.00	2.50
❑ 44 Allen Iverson	1.00	2.50
❑ 45 Jermaine O'Neal	.50	1.25
❑ 46 Larry Hughes	.40	1.00
❑ 47 Scottie Pippen	.75	2.00
❑ 48 Antonio Davis	.30	.75
❑ 49 Chris Webber	.50	1.25
❑ 50 Vladimir Radmanovic	.30	.75
❑ 51 Glenn Robinson	.40	1.00
❑ 52 Antoine Walker	.50	1.25
❑ 53 Ricky Davis	.40	1.00
❑ 54 Michael Finley	.50	1.25
❑ 55 Nick Van Exel	.40	1.00
❑ 56 Tayshaun Prince	.40	1.00
❑ 57 Antawn Jamison	.50	1.25
❑ 58 Jamal Mashburn	.30	.75
❑ 59 Jamaal Tinsley	.40	1.00
❑ 60 Kerry Kittles	.40	1.00
❑ 61 Derek Fisher	.40	1.00
❑ 62 Radoslav Nesterovic	.30	.75
❑ 63 Mike Miller	.40	1.00
❑ 64 Gary Payton	.50	1.25
❑ 65 Brian Grant	.30	.75
❑ 66 Baron Davis	.50	1.25
❑ 67 Shane Battier	.40	1.00
❑ 68 Latrell Sprewell	.40	1.00
❑ 69 Keith Van Horn	.40	1.00
❑ 70 Eddie Griffin	.30	.75
❑ 71 Stephon Marbury	.50	1.25
❑ 72 Chauncey Billups	.50	1.25
❑ 73 Shawn Marion	.50	1.25
❑ 74 Juwan Howard	.40	1.00
❑ 75 Mike Bibby	.40	1.00
❑ 76 DaJuan Wagner	.30	.75
❑ 77 Tony Parker	.50	1.25
❑ 78 Tyson Chandler	.40	1.00
❑ 79 Ray Allen	.30	.75
❑ 80 Matt Harpring	.40	1.00
❑ 81 Kwame Brown	.30	.75
❑ 82 Troy Murphy	.50	1.25
❑ 83 Ron Artest	.40	1.00
❑ 84 Corey Maggette	.30	.75
❑ 85 Tony Delk	.30	.75
❑ 86 Jamal Crawford	.40	1.00
❑ 87 Vince Carter	1.00	2.50
❑ 88 Kevin Garnett	1.00	2.50
❑ 89 Jason Kidd	.75	2.00
❑ 90 Paul Pierce	.50	1.25
❑ 91 Nene SP	1.00	2.50
❑ 92 Drew Gooden SP	.75	2.00
❑ 93 Caron Butler SP	1.00	2.50
❑ 94 Manu Ginobili SP	1.25	3.00
❑ 95 Dirk Nowitzki SP	2.00	5.00
❑ 96 Yao Ming SP	2.50	6.00
❑ 97 Amare Stoudemire SP	2.50	6.00
❑ 98 Kobe Bryant SP	6.00	15.00
❑ 99 Tim Duncan SP	2.50	6.00
❑ 100 Shaquille O'Neal SP	3.00	8.00
❑ 101 T.J. Ford RC	2.50	6.00
❑ 102 Chris Bosh RC	3.00	8.00
❑ 103 Boris Diaw RC	2.50	6.00
❑ 104 Luke Ridnour RC	2.50	6.00
❑ 105 Zoran Planinic RC	2.00	5.00
❑ 106 Josh Howard RC	2.50	6.00
❑ 107 Darko Milicic RC	2.50	6.00
❑ 108 Dahntay Jones RC	2.00	5.00
❑ 109 Mike Sweetney RC	2.00	5.00
❑ 110 Kirk Hinrich RC	2.50	6.00
❑ 111 Marcus Banks RC	2.00	5.00
❑ 112 Travis Outlaw RC	2.50	6.00
❑ 113 Brian Cook RC	2.00	5.00
❑ 114 Mario Austin RC	2.00	5.00
❑ 115 Dwyane Wade RC	5.00	12.00
❑ 116 Chris Kaman RC	2.50	6.00
❑ 117 Zarko Cabarkapa RC	2.00	5.00
❑ 118 Ndudi Ebi RC	2.00	5.00
❑ 119 Mickael Pietrus RC	2.50	6.00
❑ 120 Carmelo Anthony RC	5.00	12.00
❑ 121 Kendrick Perkins RC	3.00	8.00
❑ 122 Troy Bell RC	2.00	5.00
❑ 123 Maciej Lampe RC	2.00	5.00
❑ 124 Carlos Delfino RC	2.50	6.00
❑ 125 Leandro Barbosa RC	2.50	6.00
❑ 126 Sofoklis Schortsanitis RC	2.00	5.00
❑ 127 Reece Gaines RC	2.00	5.00
❑ 128 Nick Collison RC	2.00	5.00
❑ 129 David West RC	2.50	6.00
❑ 130 LeBron James RC	40.00	80.00

2004-05 Fleer Showcase

❑ COMP.SET w/o SP's (90)	15.00	40.00
❑ COMMON CARD (1-90)	.20	.50
❑ COMMON ROOKIE/199	5.00	12.00
❑ COMMON ROOKIE/499	2.50	6.00
❑ COMMON ROOKIE/699	2.00	5.00
❑ 1 Kirk Hinrich	.25	.60
❑ 2 Shaquille O'Neal	.75	2.00
❑ 3 Allen Iverson	.60	1.50
❑ 4 Carlos Arroyo	.30	.75
❑ 5 Darko Milicic	.20	.50
❑ 6 Sam Cassell	.25	.60
❑ 7 Peja Stojakovic	.25	.60
❑ 8 Ben Wallace	.25	.60
❑ 9 T.J. Ford	.25	.60
❑ 10 Chris Webber	.30	.75
❑ 11 LeBron James	2.00	5.00
❑ 12 Karl Malone	.30	.75
❑ 13 Glenn Robinson	.25	.60
❑ 14 Jarvis Hayes	.20	.50
❑ 15 Bob Sura	.20	.50
❑ 16 Yao Ming	.75	2.00
❑ 17 Baron Davis	.30	.75
❑ 18 Rashard Lewis	.30	.75
❑ 19 Carlos Boozer	.30	.75
❑ 20 Pau Gasol	.30	.75
❑ 21 Tim Duncan	.60	1.50
❑ 22 Gilbert Arenas	.30	.75
❑ 23 Dajuan Wagner	.20	.50
❑ 24 Bonzi Wells	.20	.50
❑ 25 Dirk Nowitzki	.50	1.25
❑ 26 Jason Williams	.25	.60
❑ 27 Amare Stoudemire	.60	1.50
❑ 28 Gerald Wallace	.30	.75
❑ 29 Corey Maggette	.25	.60
❑ 30 Tim Thomas	.20	.50
❑ 31 Andrei Kirilenko	.30	.75
❑ 32 Steve Nash	.50	1.25
❑ 33 Caron Butler	.25	.60
❑ 34 Shawn Marion	.30	.75
❑ 35 Michael Finley	.30	.75
❑ 36 Dwyane Wade	1.00	2.50
❑ 37 Joe Johnson	.30	.75
❑ 38 Carmelo Anthony	1.00	2.50
❑ 39 Lamar Odom	.30	.75
❑ 40 Darius Miles	.25	.60
❑ 41 Mike Dunleavy	.25	.60
❑ 42 Jason Kidd	.50	1.25
❑ 43 Manu Ginobili	.30	.75
❑ 44 Jason Richardson	.30	.75
❑ 45 Latrell Sprewell	.25	.60
❑ 46 Willie Green	.20	.50
❑ 47 Theron Smith	.20	.50
❑ 48 Elton Brand	.30	.75
❑ 49 Tracy McGrady	.60	1.50
❑ 50 Matt Harpring	.25	.60
❑ 51 Eddy Curry	.25	.60
❑ 52 Chris Kaman	.25	.60
❑ 53 Drew Gooden	.20	.50
❑ 54 Stephen Jackson	.25	.60
❑ 55 Mickael Pietrus	.25	.60
❑ 56 Kenyon Martin	.30	.75
❑ 57 Tony Parker	.30	.75
❑ 58 Paul Pierce	.30	.75
❑ 59 Cuttino Mobley	.25	.60
❑ 60 Jamal Mashburn	.25	.60
❑ 61 Luke Ridnour	.20	.50
❑ 62 Jamal Crawford	.25	.60
❑ 63 Kobe Bryant	1.50	4.00
❑ 64 Keith Bogans	.20	.50
❑ 65 Jerry Stackhouse	.25	.60
❑ 66 Ricky Davis	.25	.60
❑ 67 Jermaine O'Neal	.30	.75
❑ 68 Jamaal Magloire	.20	.50
❑ 69 Vince Carter	.60	1.50
❑ 70 Jason Kapono	.20	.50
❑ 71 Ron Artest	.25	.60
❑ 72 Allan Houston	.25	.60
❑ 73 Chris Bosh	.30	.75
❑ 74 Rasheed Wallace	.30	.75
❑ 75 Kevin Garnett	.60	1.50
❑ 76 Mike Bibby	.25	.60
❑ 77 Jason Terry	.25	.60
❑ 78 Steve Francis	.30	.75
❑ 79 Richard Jefferson	.30	.75
❑ 80 Ray Allen	.30	.75
❑ 81 Andre Miller	.25	.60
❑ 82 Desmond Mason	.25	.60
❑ 83 Zach Randolph	.30	.75
❑ 84 Marcus Banks	.20	.50
❑ 85 Reggie Miller	.30	.75
❑ 86 Stephon Marbury	.30	.75
❑ 87 Jalen Rose	.25	.60
❑ 88 Nene	.25	.60
❑ 89 Michael Redd	.30	.75
❑ 90 Shareef Abdur-Rahim	.25	.60
❑ 91 Emeka Okafor/199 RC	10.00	25.00
❑ 92 Jameer Nelson/199 RC	6.00	15.00
❑ 93 Dwight Howard/199 RC	15.00	40.00
❑ 94 Josh Smith/199 RC	12.00	30.00
❑ 95 Pavel Podkolzine/699 RC	2.00	5.00
❑ 96 Shaun Livingston/199 RC	5.00	12.00
❑ 97 Andre Iguodala/199 RC	12.00	30.00
❑ 98 Luol Deng/199 RC	6.00	15.00
❑ 99 Delonte West/699 RC	3.00	8.00
❑ 100 Andris Biedrins/699 RC	3.00	8.00
❑ 101 Sasha Vujacic/499 RC	2.50	6.00
❑ 102 Kris Humphries/499 RC	4.00	10.00
❑ 103 Ben Gordon/199 RC	6.00	15.00
❑ 104 Robert Swift/499 RC	2.50	6.00
❑ 105 Al Jefferson/499 RC	5.00	12.00
❑ 106 Sergei Monia/499 RC	2.50	6.00
❑ 107 Devin Harris/499 RC	5.00	12.00
❑ 108 Luke Jackson/499 RC	2.50	6.00
❑ 109 Anderson Varejao/499 RC	3.00	8.00
❑ 110 Sebastian Telfair/199 RC	5.00	12.00
❑ 111 Josh Childress/199 RC	5.00	12.00
❑ 112 J.R. Smith/499 RC	5.00	12.00
❑ 113 Viktor Khryapa/699 RC	2.00	5.00
❑ 114 Rafael Araujo/499 RC	2.50	6.00
❑ 115 Dorell Wright/499 RC	3.00	8.00
❑ 116 Ha Seung-Jin/699 RC	2.00	5.00
❑ 117 Tony Allen/699 RC	2.50	6.00
❑ 118 Kirk Snyder/699 RC	2.00	5.00
❑ 119 Chris Duhon/699 RC	3.00	8.00
❑ 120 Beno Udrih/699 RC	2.50	6.00

2004-05 Fleer Sweet Sigs

❑ COMP.SET w/o SP's (75)	15.00	40.00
❑ COMMON CARD (1-75)	.20	.50
❑ COMMON ROOKIE (76-100)	1.50	4.00
❑ 1 Kirk Hinrich	.25	.60
❑ 2 Ron Artest	.25	.60
❑ 3 T.J. Ford	.25	.60
❑ 4 Stephon Marbury	.30	.75
❑ 5 Antawn Jamison	.30	.75
❑ 6 Jason Richardson	.30	.75
❑ 7 Dwyane Wade	1.00	2.50
❑ 8 Shawn Marion	.30	.75
❑ 9 Jermaine O'Neal	.30	.75

❑ 10 Ricky Davis .25 .60
❑ 11 Richard Hamilton .25 .60
❑ 12 Karl Malone .30 .75
❑ 13 Jason Williams .25 .60
❑ 14 Lamar Odom .30 .75
❑ 15 Allan Houston .25 .60
❑ 16 Allen Iverson .60 1.50
❑ 17 Peja Stojakovic .25 .60
❑ 18 Jarvis Hayes .20 .50
❑ 19 Stephen Jackson .25 .60
❑ 20 Richard Jefferson .30 .75
❑ 21 Jahidi White .20 .50
❑ 22 Carmelo Anthony 1.00 2.50
❑ 23 Baron Davis .30 .75
❑ 24 Dajuan Wagner .20 .50
❑ 25 Nene .25 .60
❑ 26 Ben Wallace .25 .60
❑ 27 Latrell Sprewell .25 .60
❑ 28 Ray Allen .30 .75
❑ 29 Andrei Kirilenko .30 .75
❑ 30 Antoine Walker .30 .75
❑ 31 Marcus Banks .20 .50
❑ 32 Pau Gasol .30 .75
❑ 33 Tony Parker .30 .75
❑ 34 Vince Carter .60 1.50
❑ 35 Mike Bibby .25 .60
❑ 36 Jim Jackson .20 .50
❑ 37 Shaquille O'Neal .75 2.00
❑ 38 Bonzi Wells .20 .50
❑ 39 Paul Pierce .30 .75
❑ 40 Jason Kapono .20 .50
❑ 41 Reggie Miller .30 .75
❑ 42 Drew Gooden .20 .50
❑ 43 Shareef Abdur-Rahim .25 .60
❑ 44 Chris Bosh .30 .75
❑ 45 Steve Nash .50 1.25
❑ 46 Elton Brand .30 .75
❑ 47 Kevin Garnett .60 1.50
❑ 48 Kenyon Martin .30 .75
❑ 49 Jamal Crawford .25 .60
❑ 50 Dirk Nowitzki .50 1.25
❑ 51 Yao Ming .75 2.00
❑ 52 Jamaal Magloire .20 .50
❑ 53 Tim Duncan .60 1.50
❑ 54 Gilbert Arenas .30 .75
❑ 55 Steve Francis .30 .75
❑ 56 Corey Maggette .25 .60
❑ 57 Caron Butler .25 .60
❑ 58 Michael Redd .30 .75
❑ 59 Kyle Korver .25 .60
❑ 60 Amare Stoudemire .60 1.50
❑ 61 Carlos Boozer .30 .75
❑ 62 Darko Milicic .20 .50
❑ 63 Kobe Bryant 1.50 4.00
❑ 64 Tracy McGrady .60 1.50
❑ 65 Zach Randolph .30 .75
❑ 66 Luke Ridnour .20 .50
❑ 67 Carlos Arroyo .30 .75
❑ 68 Michael Finley .30 .75
❑ 69 Mickael Pietrus .25 .60
❑ 70 Darius Miles .25 .60
❑ 71 Chris Webber .30 .75
❑ 72 Eddy Curry .25 .60
❑ 73 Jason Kidd .50 1.25
❑ 74 Manu Ginobili .30 .75
❑ 75 LeBron James 2.00 5.00
❑ 76 Emeka Okafor RC 3.00 8.00
❑ 77 Rafael Araujo RC 1.50 4.00
❑ 78 Andre Iguodala RC 4.00 10.00
❑ 79 Kris Humphries RC 2.50 6.00
❑ 80 Kevin Martin RC 2.00 5.00
❑ 81 Delonte West RC 2.50 6.00
❑ 82 Pavel Podkolzine RC 1.50 4.00
❑ 83 Al Jefferson RC 3.00 8.00
❑ 84 Shaun Livingston RC 1.50 4.00
❑ 85 Luke Jackson RC 1.50 4.00
❑ 86 Dorell Wright RC 2.00 5.00
❑ 87 Andris Biedrins RC 2.50 6.00
❑ 88 Sasha Vujacic RC 1.50 4.00
❑ 89 Jameer Nelson RC 2.00 5.00
❑ 90 Dwight Howard RC 5.00 12.00
❑ 91 Robert Swift RC 1.50 4.00
❑ 92 Josh Childress RC 1.50 4.00
❑ 93 Luol Deng RC 2.00 5.00
❑ 94 J.R. Smith RC 3.00 8.00
❑ 95 Kirk Snyder RC 1.50 4.00
❑ 96 Josh Smith RC 4.00 10.00
❑ 97 Devin Harris RC 3.00 8.00
❑ 98 Viktor Khryapa RC 1.50 4.00
❑ 99 Ben Gordon RC 2.00 5.00
❑ 100 Sebastian Telfair RC 1.50 4.00

2004-05 Fleer Throwbacks

❑ COMP.SET w/o RC's (65) 15.00 40.00
❑ COMMON CARD (1-65) .20 .50
❑ SEMISTARS 1-65 .25 .60
❑ UNLISTED STARS 1-65 .30 .75
❑ COMMON ROOKIE (66-76) 3.00 8.00
❑ 66-76 RC PRINT RUN 50 SER.#'d SETS
❑ COMMON JSY RC (77-100) 4.00 10.00
❑ 77-100 JSY RC PRINT RUN 499 #'d SETS
❑ 1 Baron Davis .30 .75
❑ 2 Willie Green .20 .50
❑ 3 Allen Iverson .60 1.50
❑ 4 Jason Williams .25 .60
❑ 5 Kevin Garnett .60 1.50
❑ 6 Jason Richardson .30 .75
❑ 7 Lamar Odom .30 .75
❑ 8 Ben Wallace .25 .60
❑ 9 Steve Nash .50 1.25
❑ 10 Kobe Bryant 1.50 4.00
❑ 11 Kenyon Martin .30 .75
❑ 12 Jermaine O'Neal .30 .75
❑ 13 Tracy McGrady .60 1.50
❑ 14 Darko Milicic .20 .50
❑ 15 Pau Gasol .30 .75
❑ 16 Darius Miles .25 .60
❑ 17 Ray Allen .30 .75
❑ 18 Michael Redd .30 .75
❑ 19 Chris Bosh .30 .75
❑ 20 Peja Stojakovic .25 .60
❑ 21 Tim Duncan .60 1.50
❑ 22 Corey Maggette .25 .60
❑ 23 LeBron James 2.00 5.00
❑ 24 Antoine Walker .30 .75
❑ 25 Stephon Marbury .30 .75
❑ 26 Carlos Boozer .30 .75
❑ 27 Jason Kapono .20 .50
❑ 28 Grant Hill .30 .75
❑ 29 Mike Bibby .25 .60
❑ 30 Jamaal Magloire .20 .50
❑ 31 Rashard Lewis .30 .75
❑ 32 Jason Kidd .50 1.25
❑ 33 Al Harrington .25 .60
❑ 34 Steve Francis .30 .75
❑ 35 Kirk Hinrich .25 .60
❑ 36 Amare Stoudemire .60 1.50
❑ 37 Gilbert Arenas .30 .75
❑ 38 Allan Houston .25 .60
❑ 39 Eddy Curry .25 .60
❑ 40 Latrell Sprewell .25 .60
❑ 41 Mickael Pietrus .25 .60
❑ 42 Zach Randolph .30 .75
❑ 43 Shaquille O'Neal .75 2.00
❑ 44 Jason Terry .25 .60
❑ 45 Richard Hamilton .25 .60
❑ 46 Karl Malone .30 .75
❑ 47 Elton Brand .30 .75
❑ 48 Richard Jefferson .30 .75
❑ 49 Andrei Kirilenko .30 .75
❑ 50 Reggie Miller .30 .75
❑ 51 Yao Ming .75 2.00
❑ 52 Gary Payton .30 .75
❑ 53 Dirk Nowitzki .50 1.25
❑ 54 Dwyane Wade 1.00 2.50
❑ 55 Carmelo Anthony 1.00 2.50
❑ 56 Tony Parker .30 .75
❑ 57 T.J. Ford .25 .60
❑ 58 Vince Carter .60 1.50
❑ 59 Paul Pierce .30 .75
❑ 60 Drew Gooden .20 .50
❑ 61 Antawn Jamison .30 .75
❑ 62 Manu Ginobili .30 .75
❑ 63 Chris Webber .30 .75
❑ 64 Shawn Marion .30 .75
❑ 65 Jerry Stackhouse .25 .60
❑ 66 Andris Biedrins RC 5.00 12.00
❑ 67 Robert Swift RC 3.00 8.00
❑ 68 Pavel Podkolzin RC 3.00 8.00
❑ 69 Kevin Martin RC 4.00 10.00
❑ 70 Beno Udrih RC 4.00 10.00
❑ 71 David Harrison RC 3.00 8.00
❑ 72 Victor Khryapa RC 3.00 8.00
❑ 73 Jackson Vroman RC 3.00 8.00
❑ 74 Emeka Okafor RC 6.00 15.00
❑ 75 Andre Emmett RC 3.00 8.00
❑ 76 Andres Nocioni RC 4.00 10.00
❑ 77 Dwight Howard JSY RC 8.00 20.00
❑ 78 Ben Gordon JSY RC 3.00 8.00
❑ 79 Shaun Livingston JSY RC 2.50 6.00
❑ 80 Devin Harris JSY RC 5.00 12.00
❑ 81 Josh Childress JSY RC 2.50 6.00
❑ 82 Luol Deng JSY RC 3.00 8.00
❑ 83 Rafael Araujo JSY RC 2.50 6.00
❑ 84 Andre Iguodala JSY RC 6.00 15.00
❑ 85 Luke Jackson JSY RC 2.50 6.00
❑ 86 Sebastian Telfair JSY RC 2.50 6.00
❑ 87 Kris Humphries JSY RC 4.00 10.00
❑ 88 Al Jefferson JSY RC 5.00 12.00
❑ 89 Kirk Snyder JSY RC 2.50 6.00
❑ 90 Josh Smith JSY RC 6.00 15.00
❑ 91 JR Smith JSY RC 5.00 12.00
❑ 92 Dorell Wright JSY RC 3.00 8.00
❑ 93 Jameer Nelson JSY RC 3.00 8.00
❑ 94 Chris Duhon JSY RC 4.00 10.00
❑ 95 Delonte West JSY RC 4.00 10.00
❑ 96 Tony Allen JSY RC 3.00 8.00
❑ 97 Anderson Varejao JSY RC 3.00 8.00
❑ 98 Lionel Chalmers JSY RC 2.50 6.00
❑ 99 Bernard Robinson JSY RC 2.50 6.00
❑ 100 Trevor Ariza JSY RC 3.00 8.00

2002-03 Fleer Tradition

❑ COMPLETE SET (300) 30.00 80.00
❑ COMMON CARD (1-270) .15 .40
❑ COMMON ROOKIE (271-300) 1.00 2.50
❑ 1 Shareef Abdur-Rahim .20 .50
❑ 2 Dion Glover .15 .40
❑ 3 Theo Ratliff .15 .40
❑ 4 Nazr Mohammed .15 .40
❑ 5 Ira Newble .15 .40
❑ 6 Alan Henderson .15 .40
❑ 7 Vin Baker .20 .50
❑ 8 Tony Battie .15 .40
❑ 9 Eric Williams .15 .40
❑ 10 Shammond Williams .15 .40
❑ 11 Walter McCarty .15 .40
❑ 12 Bruno Sundov .15 .40
❑ 13 Donyell Marshall .15 .40
❑ 14 Marcus Fizer .15 .40
❑ 15 Eddie Robinson .15 .40
❑ 16 Trenton Hassell .15 .40
❑ 17 Ricky Davis .20 .50
❑ 18 Jumaine Jones .15 .40
❑ 19 Chris Mihm .15 .40
❑ 20 Zydrunas Ilgauskas .20 .50
❑ 21 Tyrone Hill .15 .40
❑ 22 Adrian Griffin .15 .40
❑ 23 Nick Van Exel .20 .50
❑ 24 Raef LaFrentz .15 .40
❑ 25 Eduardo Najera .15 .40
❑ 26 Shawn Bradley .15 .40
❑ 27 Evan Eschmeyer .15 .40
❑ 28 Walt Williams .15 .40
❑ 29 Raja Bell .20 .50
❑ 30 Marcus Camby .20 .50
❑ 31 Donnell Harvey .15 .40
❑ 32 Kenny Satterfield .15 .40
❑ 33 Rodney White .15 .40

34 Chris Whitney	.15	.40
35 Clifford Robinson	.15	.40
36 Zeljko Rebraca	.15	.40
37 Corliss Williamson	.20	.50
38 Chucky Atkins	.15	.40
39 Jon Barry	.15	.40
40 Michael Curry	.15	.40
41 Erick Dampier	.15	.40
42 Danny Fortson	.15	.40
43 Adonal Foyle	.15	.40
44 Troy Murphy	.25	.60
45 Bob Sura	.15	.40
46 Moochie Norris	.15	.40
47 Kenny Thomas	.15	.40
48 Terence Morris	.15	.40
49 Glen Rice	.20	.50
50 Maurice Taylor	.15	.40
51 Erick Strickland	.15	.40
52 Al Harrington	.20	.50
53 Ron Artest	.20	.50
54 Austin Croshere	.15	.40
55 Ron Mercer	.15	.40
56 Brad Miller	.20	.50
57 Lamar Odom	.25	.60
58 Keyon Dooling	.15	.40
59 Corey Maggette	.20	.50
60 Michael Olowokandi	.15	.40
61 Stanislav Medvedenko	.15	.40
62 Rick Fox	.20	.50
63 Derek Fisher	.20	.50
64 Samaki Walker	.15	.40
65 Robert Horry	.20	.50
66 Mark Madsen	.15	.40
67 Wesley Person	.15	.40
68 Michael Dickerson	.15	.40
69 Lorenzen Wright	.15	.40
70 Brevin Knight	.15	.40
71 Travis Best	.15	.40
72 Brian Grant	.15	.40
73 Eddie Jones	.20	.50
74 LaPhonso Ellis	.20	.50
75 Anthony Carter	.15	.40
76 Tim Thomas	.15	.40
77 Toni Kukoc	.20	.50
78 Anthony Mason	.15	.40
79 Ervin Johnson	.15	.40
80 Joel Przybilla	.15	.40
81 Rod Strickland	.20	.50
82 Terrell Brandon	.15	.40
83 Anthony Peeler	.15	.40
84 Joe Smith	.15	.40
85 Gary Trent	.15	.40
86 Rasho Nesterovic	.15	.40
87 Loren Woods	.15	.40
88 Felipe Lopez	.15	.40
89 Dikembe Mutombo	.20	.50
90 Rodney Rogers	.15	.40
91 Jason Collins	.15	.40
92 Kerry Kittles	.20	.50
93 Lucious Harris	.15	.40
94 Aaron Williams	.15	.40
95 Jamal Mashburn	.20	.50
96 David Wesley	.15	.40
97 Elden Campbell	.15	.40
98 Jerome Moiso		
99 P.J. Brown	.15	.40
100 George Lynch	.15	.40
101 Robert Traylor	.15	.40
102 Antonio McDyess	.20	.50
103 Kurt Thomas	.15	.40
104 Clarence Weatherspoon	.15	.40
105 Charlie Ward	.15	.40
106 Lavor Postell	.15	.40
107 Shandon Anderson	.15	.40
108 Michael Doleac	.15	.40
109 Othella Harrington	.15	.40
110 Darrell Armstrong	.15	.40
111 Steven Hunter	.15	.40
112 Pat Garrity	.15	.40
113 Horace Grant	.20	.50
114 Jacque Vaughn	.15	.40
115 Jeryl Sasser	.15	.40
116 Todd MacCulloch	.15	.40
117 Greg Buckner	.15	.40
118 Eric Snow	.15	.40
119 Samuel Dalembert	.15	.40
120 Monty Williams	.15	.40
121 Stephon Marbury	.25	.60
122 Anfernee Hardaway	.25	.60
123 Tom Gugliotta	.15	.40
124 Iakovos Tsakalidis	.15	.40
125 Bo Outlaw	.15	.40
126 Damon Stoudamire	.20	.50
127 Jeff McInnis	.15	.40
128 Derek Anderson	.20	.50
129 Antonio Daniels	.15	.40
130 Dale Davis	.15	.40
131 Zach Randolph	.25	.60
132 Bobby Jackson	.15	.40
133 Chris Webber	.25	.60
134 Vlade Divac	.20	.50
135 Keon Clark	.15	.40
136 Doug Christie	.15	.40
137 Scot Pollard	.15	.40
138 Mengke Bateer	.15	.40
139 David Robinson	.30	.75
140 Steve Smith	.20	.50
141 Malik Rose	.15	.40
142 Speedy Claxton	.15	.40
143 Danny Ferry	.15	.40
144 Brent Barry	.15	.40
145 Joseph Forte	.15	.40
146 Vladimir Radmanovic	.15	.40
147 Kenny Anderson	.20	.50
148 Predrag Drobnjak	.15	.40
149 Calvin Booth	.15	.40
150 Ansu Sesay	.15	.40
151 Voshon Lenard	.15	.40
152 Lamond Murray	.15	.40
153 Antonio Davis	.15	.40
154 Lindsey Hunter	.15	.40
155 Michael Bradley	.15	.40
156 Jerome Williams	.15	.40
157 Alvin Williams	.15	.40
158 Mamadou N'Diaye	.15	.40
159 Raul Lopez	.25	.60
160 John Stockton	.30	.75
161 Mark Jackson	.20	.50
162 DeShawn Stevenson	.15	.40
163 Calbert Cheaney	.15	.40
164 Matt Harpring	.20	.50
165 Jarron Collins	.15	.40
166 Tyronn Lue	.15	.40
167 Bryon Russell	.15	.40
168 Larry Hughes	.20	.50
169 Brendan Haywood	.15	.40
170 Christian Laettner	.15	.40
171 Glenn Robinson	.20	.50
172 Tony Delk	.15	.40
173 Antoine Walker	.20	.50
174 Jalen Rose	.20	.50
175 Jamal Crawford	.20	.50
176 DeSagana Diop	.15	.40
177 Michael Finley	.25	.60
178 Dirk Nowitzki	.40	1.00
179 Juwan Howard	.20	.50
180 Chauncey Billups	.25	.60
181 Richard Hamilton	.20	.50
182 Antawn Jamison	.25	.60
183 Steve Francis	.25	.60
184 Eddie Griffin	.15	.40
185 Jonathan Bender	.15	.40
186 Reggie Miller	.25	.60
187 Elton Brand	.25	.60
188 Marco Jaric	.25	.60
189 Kobe Bryant	1.25	3.00
190 Shaquille O'Neal	.60	1.50
191 Jason Williams	.20	.50
192 Stromile Swift	.15	.40
193 Alonzo Mourning	.25	.60
194 Malik Allen	.15	.40
195 Sam Cassell	.20	.50
196 Ray Allen	.25	.60
197 Wally Szczerbiak	.20	.50
197B Vince Carter Promo	1.00	2.50
198 Jason Kidd	.40	1.00
199 Kenyon Martin	.25	.60
200 Courtney Alexander	.15	.40
201 Baron Davis	.25	.60
202 Allan Houston	.20	.50
203 Grant Hill	.25	.60
204 Aaron McKie	.15	.40
205 Keith Van Horn	.20	.50
206 Shawn Marion	.25	.60
207 Joe Johnson	.25	.60
208 Scottie Pippen	.40	1.00
209 Rasheed Wallace	.25	.60
210 Peja Stojakovic	.20	.50
211 Hedo Turkoglu	.20	.50
212 Tony Parker	.25	.60
213 Tim Duncan	.50	1.25
214 Gary Payton	.25	.60
215 Desmond Mason	.20	.50
216 Vince Carter	.50	1.25
217 Karl Malone	.25	.60
218 Andrei Kirilenko	.25	.60
219 Jerry Stackhouse	.20	.50
220 Michael Jordan	1.50	4.00
221 DerMarr Johnson	.15	.40
222 Kedrick Brown	.15	.40
223 Eddy Curry	.20	.50
224 Tyson Chandler	.20	.50
225 Darius Miles	.15	.40
226 Wang ZhiZhi	.15	.40
227 James Posey	.15	.40
228 Ben Wallace	.20	.50
229 Jason Richardson	.25	.60
230 Gilbert Arenas	.25	.60
231 Eddie Griffin	.15	.40
232 Jermaine O'Neal	.25	.60
233 Quentin Richardson	.20	.50
234 Devean George	.15	.40
235 Shane Battier	.20	.50
236 Pau Gasol	.25	.60
237 Eddie House	.15	.40
238 Michael Redd	.25	.60
239 Troy Hudson	.15	.40
240 Richard Jefferson	.25	.60
241 Jamal Magloire	.15	.40
242 Mike Miller	.20	.50
243 Joe Johnson	.25	.60
244 Ruben Patterson	.15	.40
245 Gerald Wallace	.25	.60
246 Tony Parker	.25	.60
247 Rashard Lewis	.25	.60
248 Morris Peterson	.20	.50
249 Andrei Kirilenko	.25	.60
250 Kwame Brown	.15	.40
251 Jason Terry	.25	.60
252 Paul Pierce	.25	.60
253 Darius Miles	.15	.40
254 Steve Nash	.40	1.00
255 Cuttino Mobley	.20	.50
256 Jamaal Tinsley	.20	.50
257 Andre Miller	.20	.50
258 Shaquille O'Neal	.60	1.50
259 Kobe Bryant	1.25	3.00
260 Kevin Garnett	.50	1.25
261 Kenyon Martin	.25	.60
262 Latrell Sprewell	.20	.50
263 Tracy McGrady	.50	1.25
264 Allen Iverson	.50	1.25
265 Shawn Marion	.25	.60
266 Bonzi Wells	.20	.50
267 Mike Bibby	.20	.50
268 Tim Duncan	.50	1.25
269 Vince Carter	.50	1.25
270 Michael Jordan	1.50	4.00
271 Ming/Williams/Dunlvy RC	1.00	2.50
272 Ginobili/Prince/Giricek RC	1.50	4.00
273 Jeffries/Williams/Pargo RC	1.00	2.50
274 Wilcox/Dixon/Baxter RC	1.00	2.50
275 Wagnr/Dickau/Ginbili RC	.75	2.00
276 Ely/Jefferies/Maddox RC	1.00	2.50
277 Evans/Brmer/Williams RC	1.50	4.00
278 Butler/Haislip/Hmphry RC	1.00	2.50
279 Archbld/Burke/Huffmn RC	1.00	2.50
280 Goodn/Amare/Woods RC	1.50	4.00
281 Nachbr/Welsch/Savovic RC	1.00	2.50
282 Borchrdt/Jacobsn/Gadzu RC	1.00	2.50
283 Clancy/Okur/Sampson RC	1.00	2.50
284 Prince/Rush/Salmons RC	2.50	6.00
285 Ming/Tskitishvili/Hilario RC	1.50	4.00
286 Wagner/Woods/Slay RC	1.00	1.25
287 Ely/Haislip/Jones RC	1.00	2.50
288 Butler/Ginobili/Haislip RC	1.00	2.50
289 Mason/Yrbrogh/Dickau RC	1.00	2.50
290 Murray/Owens/Parker RC	1.50	4.00
291 Butler/Pargo/Giricek RC	1.00	2.50
292 Goodn/Tskitish/Wagnr RC	1.00	1.00
293 Hilario/Wilcox/Amare RC	2.00	5.00
294 Jay Will/Hmphry/Woods RC	1.00	2.00
295 Ming/Stoudemire/Rush RC	4.00	10.00
296 Tskitishvili/Butler/Dixon RC	1.00	2.50
297 Wilcox/Jones/Nachbar RC	1.25	3.00
298 Dunlvy/Hilario/Jacobsn RC	1.00	2.00
299 Jeffries/Dixon/Gooden RC	1.00	2.00

❑ 300 Boozer/Jay Will/Dunlvy RC 1.00 2.00
❑ PROMO Caron Butler

2003-04 Fleer Tradition

❑ COMP.SET w/o RC's (260) 20.00 50.00
❑ COMMON CARD (1-260) .15 .40
❑ COMMON ROOKIE (261-290) .60 1.50
❑ COMMON TRIPLE (291-300) 1.00 2.50
❑ 1 Shareef Abdur-Rahim .20 .50
❑ 2 Vince Carter .50 1.25
❑ 3 Kevin Garnett .50 1.25
❑ 4 Bobby Jackson .15 .40
❑ 5 Courtney Alexander .15 .40
❑ 6 Tracy McGrady .50 1.25
❑ 7 Paul Pierce .25 .60
❑ 8 Sam Cassell .20 .50
❑ 9 Maurice Taylor .15 .40
❑ 10 Pat Garrity .15 .40
❑ 11 Casey Jacobsen .15 .40
❑ 12 Malik Allen .15 .40
❑ 13 Aaron McKie .15 .40
❑ 14 Tyson Chandler .20 .50
❑ 15 Scottie Pippen .40 1.00
❑ 16 Jason Terry .20 .50
❑ 17 Pau Gasol .25 .60
❑ 18 Antawn Jamison .25 .60
❑ 19 Stanislav Medvedenko .15 .40
❑ 20 Ray Allen .15 .40
❑ 21 James Posey .15 .40
❑ 22 Calbert Cheaney .15 .40
❑ 23 Devean George .15 .40
❑ 24 Tim Thomas .15 .40
❑ 25 Marko Jaric .15 .40
❑ 26 Ron Mercer .15 .40
❑ 27 Rafer Alston .15 .40
❑ 28 Tayshaun Prince .20 .50
❑ 29 Doug Christie .15 .40
❑ 30 Kendall Gill .15 .40
❑ 31 Kurt Thomas .15 .40
❑ 32 Richard Jefferson .25 .60
❑ 33 Darius Miles .20 .50
❑ 34 Kenny Anderson .20 .50
❑ 35 Keon Clark .15 .40
❑ 36 Vladimir Radmanovic .15 .40
❑ 37 Kenny Thomas .15 .40
❑ 38 Manu Ginobili .25 .60
❑ 39 Jared Jeffries .15 .40
❑ 40 Brad Miller .20 .50
❑ 41 Derek Anderson .20 .50
❑ 42 Zach Randolph .25 .60
❑ 43 Speedy Claxton .15 .40
❑ 44 Jamaal Tinsley .20 .50
❑ 45 Gordan Giricek .15 .40
❑ 46 Joe Johnson .25 .60
❑ 47 Mike Miller .20 .50
❑ 48 Shandon Anderson .15 .40
❑ 49 Theo Ratliff .15 .40
❑ 50 Derrick Coleman .20 .50
❑ 51 Dion Glover .15 .40
❑ 52 Nikoloz Tskitishvili .15 .40
❑ 53 Jumaine Jones .15 .40
❑ 54 Gilbert Arenas .25 .60
❑ 55 Reggie Miller .25 .60
❑ 56 Michael Redd .25 .60
❑ 57 Jason Collins .15 .40
❑ 58 Drew Gooden .15 .40
❑ 59 Hedo Turkoglu .20 .50
❑ 60 Eddie Jones .20 .50
❑ 61 Andre Miller .20 .50
❑ 62 Darrell Armstrong .15 .40
❑ 63 Glen Rice .15 .40
❑ 64 Jarron Collins .15 .40
❑ 65 Nick Van Exel .20 .50
❑ 66 Brian Grant .15 .40
❑ 67 Shawn Kemp .25 .60
❑ 68 Yao Ming .50 1.25
❑ 69 Ron Artest .20 .50
❑ 70 Jamal Crawford .20 .50
❑ 71 Jason Richardson .25 .60
❑ 72 Eddie Griffin .15 .40
❑ 73 Keith Van Horn .20 .50
❑ 74 Jason Kidd .40 1.00
❑ 75 Cuttino Mobley .20 .50
❑ 76 Brent Barry .15 .40
❑ 77 Eddy Curry .20 .50
❑ 78 Quentin Richardson .20 .50
❑ 79 Dajuan Wagner .15 .40
❑ 80 Tom Gugliotta .15 .40
❑ 81 Andrei Kirilenko .25 .60
❑ 82 Shane Battier .20 .50
❑ 83 Alonzo Mourning .25 .60
❑ 84 Clifford Robinson .15 .40
❑ 85 Erick Dampier .15 .40
❑ 86 Antoine Walker .25 .60
❑ 87 Marcus Haislip .15 .40
❑ 88 Kerry Kittles .20 .50
❑ 89 Lonny Baxter .15 .40
❑ 90 Troy Murphy .25 .60
❑ 91 Glenn Robinson .20 .50
❑ 92 Ricky Davis .20 .50
❑ 93 Richard Hamilton .20 .50
❑ 94 Ben Wallace .20 .50
❑ 95 Toni Kukoc .20 .50
❑ 96 Raja Bell .20 .50
❑ 97 Dikembe Mutombo .20 .50
❑ 98 Eddie Robinson .15 .40
❑ 99 Antonio Davis .15 .40
❑ 100 Anfernee Hardaway .25 .60
❑ 101 Rasheed Wallace .25 .60
❑ 102 Christian Laettner .15 .40
❑ 103 Eduardo Najera .15 .40
❑ 104 Jonathan Bender .15 .40
❑ 105 Rodney Rogers .15 .40
❑ 106 Baron Davis .25 .60
❑ 107 Chris Webber .25 .60
❑ 108 Matt Harpring .20 .50
❑ 109 Raef LaFrentz .15 .40
❑ 110 Steve Nash .40 1.00
❑ 111 Travis Best .15 .40
❑ 112 Tony Delk .15 .40
❑ 113 Malik Rose .15 .40
❑ 114 Al Harrington .20 .50
❑ 115 Bonzi Wells .15 .40
❑ 116 Voshon Lenard .15 .40
❑ 117 Radoslav Nesterovic .15 .40
❑ 118 Mike Bibby .20 .50
❑ 119 Dan Dickau .15 .40
❑ 120 Jalen Rose .20 .50
❑ 121 Lucious Harris .15 .40
❑ 122 David Wesley .15 .40
❑ 123 Rashard Lewis .25 .60
❑ 124 Ira Newble .15 .40
❑ 125 Chauncey Billups .25 .60
❑ 126 Kareem Rush .15 .40
❑ 127 Michael Dickerson .15 .40
❑ 128 Walt Williams .15 .40
❑ 129 Donnell Harvey .15 .40
❑ 130 Tyronn Lue .15 .40
❑ 131 Carlos Boozer .25 .60
❑ 132 Moochie Norris .15 .40
❑ 133 John Salmons .20 .50
❑ 134 Vlade Divac .20 .50
❑ 135 Shammond Williams .15 .40
❑ 136 Brendan Haywood .15 .40
❑ 137 George Lynch .15 .40
❑ 138 Dirk Nowitzki .40 1.00
❑ 139 Bruce Bowen .20 .50
❑ 140 Brian Skinner .15 .40
❑ 141 Juan Dixon .15 .40
❑ 142 Eric Williams .15 .40
❑ 143 Grant Hill .25 .60
❑ 144 Corey Maggette .15 .40
❑ 145 Earl Boykins .15 .40
❑ 146 Lamar Odom .25 .60
❑ 147 Keyon Dooling .15 .40
❑ 148 Joe Smith .15 .40
❑ 149 Corliss Williamson .15 .40
❑ 150 Robert Horry .20 .50
❑ 151 Jamaal Magloire .15 .40
❑ 152 Mehmet Okur .20 .50
❑ 153 Elton Brand .25 .60
❑ 154 Steve Smith .15 .40
❑ 155 Predrag Drobnjak .15 .40
❑ 156 Allan Houston .20 .50
❑ 157 Jerome Williams .15 .40
❑ 158 Karl Malone .25 .60
❑ 159 Michael Olowokandi .15 .40
❑ 160 Terrell Brandon .15 .40
❑ 161 Eric Snow .15 .40
❑ 162 Tim Duncan .50 1.25
❑ 163 Juwan Howard .20 .50
❑ 164 Jason Williams .20 .50
❑ 165 Stephon Marbury .25 .60
❑ 166 J.R. Bremer .15 .40
❑ 167 Shaquille O'Neal .60 1.50
❑ 168 Mike Dunleavy .20 .50
❑ 169 Latrell Sprewell .20 .50
❑ 170 Troy Hudson .15 .40
❑ 171 Alvin Williams .15 .40
❑ 172 Shawn Marion .25 .60
❑ 173 Jermaine O'Neal .25 .60
❑ 174 P.J. Brown .15 .40
❑ 175 Howard Eisley .15 .40
❑ 176 Jerry Stackhouse .20 .50
❑ 177 Qyntel Woods .15 .40
❑ 178 Larry Hughes .20 .50
❑ 179 Donyell Marshall .15 .40
❑ 180 Greg Ostertag .15 .40
❑ 181 Kwame Brown .15 .40
❑ 182 Reggie Evans .15 .40
❑ 183 DeShawn Stevenson .15 .40
❑ 184 Lorenzen Wright .15 .40
❑ 185 Lindsey Hunter .15 .40
❑ 186 Kenyon Martin .25 .60
❑ 187 Kobe Bryant 1.25 3.00
❑ 188 Scott Padgett .15 .40
❑ 189 Michael Finley .25 .60
❑ 190 Peja Stojakovic .20 .50
❑ 191 Zydrunas Ilgauskas .20 .50
❑ 192 Vincent Yarbrough .15 .40
❑ 193 Jamal Mashburn .15 .40
❑ 194 Smush Parker .15 .40
❑ 195 Caron Butler .20 .50
❑ 196 Derek Fisher .20 .50
❑ 197 Damon Stoudamire .20 .50
❑ 198 Nene Hilario .20 .50
❑ 199 Allen Iverson .50 1.25
❑ 200 Anthony Mason .15 .40
❑ 201 Rasual Butler .15 .40
❑ 202 Tony Parker .25 .60
❑ 203 Marcus Fizer .15 .40
❑ 204 Amare Stoudemire .50 1.25
❑ 205 Marc Jackson .20 .50
❑ 206 Desmond Mason .20 .50
❑ 207 Marcus Camby .20 .50
❑ 208 Ruben Patterson .15 .40
❑ 209 Bob Sura .15 .40
❑ 210 Rick Fox .15 .40
❑ 211 Jim Jackson .15 .40
❑ 212 Walter McCarty .15 .40
❑ 213 Gary Payton .25 .60
❑ 214 Elden Campbell .15 .40
❑ 215 Steve Francis .25 .60
❑ 216 Stromile Swift .15 .40
❑ 217 Stephen Jackson .20 .50
❑ 218 Antonio McDyess .20 .50
❑ 219 Morris Peterson .20 .50
❑ 220 Wally Szczerbiak .20 .50
❑ 221 Tim Duncan AW .50 1.25
❑ 222 Amare Stoudemire AW .50 1.25
❑ 223 Bobby Jackson AW .15 .40
❑ 224 Ben Wallace AW .20 .50
❑ 225 Gilbert Arenas AW .25 .60
❑ 226 Tracy McGrady AW .50 1.25
❑ 227 Kobe Bryant AW 1.25 3.00
❑ 228 Kevin Garnett AW .50 1.25
❑ 229 Shaquille O'Neal AW .60 1.50
❑ 230 Yao Ming AW .50 1.25
❑ 231 Stephon Marbury BS .25 .60
❑ 232 Ron Artest BS .20 .50
❑ 233 Troy Hudson BS .15 .40
❑ 234 Ray Allen BS .15 .40
❑ 235 Matt Harpring BS .20 .50
❑ 236 Jermaine O'Neal BS .25 .60
❑ 237 Jason Kidd BS .40 1.00
❑ 238 Jason Williams BS .20 .50
❑ 239 Zydrunas Ilgauskas BS .20 .50
❑ 240 Jamal Mashburn BS .15 .40
❑ 241 Yao Ming BS .50 1.25
❑ 242 Peja Stojakovic BS .20 .50
❑ 243 Tony Parker BS .25 .60
❑ 244 Caron Butler BS .20 .50
❑ 245 Amare Stoudemire BS .50 1.25
❑ 246 Troy Murphy BS .25 .60

❑ 247 Nene Hilario BS	.20	.50
❑ 248 Allen Iverson BS	.50	1.25
❑ 249 Kobe Bryant BS	1.25	3.00
❑ 250 Tim Duncan BS	.50	1.25
❑ 251 Tracy McGrady BS	.50	1.25
❑ 252 Kevin Garnett BS	.50	1.25
❑ 253 Drew Gooden BS	.15	.40
❑ 254 Kenyon Martin BS	.25	.60
❑ 255 Dirk Nowitzki BS	.40	1.00
❑ 256 Paul Pierce BS	.25	.60
❑ 257 Steve Francis BS	.25	.60
❑ 258 Steve Nash BS	.40	1.00
❑ 259 Gary Payton BS	.25	.60
❑ 260 Chris Webber BS	.25	.60
❑ 261 LeBron James RC	8.00	20.00
❑ 262 Darko Milicic RC	.75	2.00
❑ 263 Carmelo Anthony RC	1.50	4.00
❑ 264 Chris Bosh RC	1.00	2.50
❑ 265 Dwyane Wade RC	1.50	4.00
❑ 266 Chris Kaman RC	.75	2.00
❑ 267 Kirk Hinrich RC	.75	2.00
❑ 268 T.J. Ford RC	.75	2.00
❑ 269 Mike Sweetney RC	.60	1.50
❑ 270 Mickael Pietrus RC	.75	2.00
❑ 271 Jarvis Hayes RC	.60	1.50
❑ 272 Nick Collison RC	.60	1.50
❑ 273 Marcus Banks RC	.60	1.50
❑ 274 Luke Ridnour RC	.75	2.00
❑ 275 Reece Gaines RC	.60	1.50
❑ 276 Troy Bell RC	.60	1.50
❑ 277 Zarko Cabarkapa RC	.60	1.50
❑ 278 David West RC	.75	2.00
❑ 279 Luke Walton RC	.75	2.00
❑ 280 Dahntay Jones RC	.60	1.50
❑ 281 Boris Diaw RC	.75	2.00
❑ 282 Zoran Planinic RC	.60	1.50
❑ 283 Travis Outlaw RC	.75	2.00
❑ 284 Brian Cook RC	.60	1.50
❑ 285 Jason Kapono RC	.75	2.00
❑ 286 Ndudi Ebi RC	.60	1.50
❑ 287 Kendrick Perkins RC	1.00	2.50
❑ 288 Leandro Barbosa RC	.75	2.00
❑ 289 Josh Howard RC	.75	2.00
❑ 290 Maciej Lampe RC	.60	1.50
❑ 291 James/Darko/Melo	10.00	25.00
❑ 292 Sweetney/Bosh/Hayes	1.50	4.00
❑ 293 Hinrich/Collison/Kaman	1.50	3.00
❑ 294 Sweetney/West/Cook	2.00	5.00
❑ 295 Kaman/Bosh/Darko	1.50	2.50
❑ 296 Ford/Wade/Hinrich	2.50	6.00
❑ 297 Pietrus/Jones/Gaines	1.50	4.00
❑ 298 Ford/Banks/Ridnour	2.00	5.00
❑ 299 Pietrus/Zarko/Hayes	1.50	4.00
❑ 300 LeBron/Melo/Wade	20.00	40.00

2004-05 Fleer Tradition

❑ COMPLETE SET (268)		
❑ COMP.SET w/o RC's (220)	20.00	50.00
❑ COMMON CARD (1-208)	.15	.40
❑ SEMISTARS 1-208	.20	.50
❑ UNLISTED STARS 1-208	.25	.60
❑ COMMON AW (209-220)	.25	.60
❑ COMMON ROOKIE (221-250)	.75	2.00
❑ RC STATED ODDS 1:4		
❑ COMMON RC TRIO (251-268)	1.25	3.00
❑ TRIO STATED ODDS 1:18		
❑ 1 Jonathan Bender	.15	.40
❑ 2 Boris Diaw	.20	.50
❑ 3 Eddie Robinson	.15	.40
❑ 4 Jason Richardson	.25	.60
❑ 5 Bonzi Wells	.15	.40
❑ 6 Elden Campbell	.15	.40
❑ 7 P.J. Brown	.15	.40
❑ 8 Ray Allen	.25	.60
❑ 9 Theron Smith	.15	.40
❑ 10 Darko Milicic	.15	.40
❑ 11 Bob Sura	.15	.40
❑ 12 Sam Cassell	.20	.50
❑ 13 Cuttino Mobley	.20	.50
❑ 14 Andrei Kirilenko	.25	.60
❑ 15 Raef LaFrentz	.15	.40
❑ 16 Aleksandar Pavlovic	.15	.40
❑ 17 Carmelo Anthony	.75	2.00
❑ 18 Mickael Pietrus	.20	.50
❑ 19 James Posey	.15	.40
❑ 20 Nazr Mohammed	.15	.40
❑ 21 Jalen Rose	.20	.50
❑ 22 Jiri Welsch	.15	.40
❑ 23 Drew Gooden	.15	.40
❑ 24 Nene	.20	.50
❑ 25 Troy Murphy	.25	.60
❑ 26 Mike Miller	.20	.50
❑ 27 T.J. Ford	.20	.50
❑ 28 Allan Houston	.20	.50
❑ 29 Donyell Marshall	.15	.40
❑ 30 Chris Crawford	.15	.40
❑ 31 Eric Snow	.15	.40
❑ 32 Marcus Camby	.20	.50
❑ 33 Devean George	.15	.40
❑ 34 Eric Williams	.15	.40
❑ 35 Kurt Thomas	.15	.40
❑ 36 Rashard Lewis	.25	.60
❑ 37 Alvin Williams	.15	.40
❑ 38 David West	.25	.60
❑ 39 Shawn Marion	.25	.60
❑ 40 Mark Blount	.15	.40
❑ 41 Dikembe Mutombo	.20	.50
❑ 42 Stephen Jackson	.20	.50
❑ 43 Rasual Butler	.15	.40
❑ 44 Michael Redd	.25	.60
❑ 45 Jason Kidd	.40	1.00
❑ 46 Malik Rose	.15	.40
❑ 47 Chris Bosh	.25	.60
❑ 48 Antonio Daniels	.15	.40
❑ 49 Doug Christie	.15	.40
❑ 50 Stephon Marbury	.25	.60
❑ 51 Gary Payton	.25	.60
❑ 52 Michael Finley	.25	.60
❑ 53 Ben Wallace	.20	.50
❑ 54 Jason Williams	.20	.50
❑ 55 Michael Olowokandi	.15	.40
❑ 56 Steve Francis	.25	.60
❑ 57 Chris Webber	.25	.60
❑ 58 Tim Duncan	.50	1.25
❑ 59 Carlos Arroyo	.25	.60
❑ 60 Eddie House	.15	.40
❑ 61 Mike Bibby	.20	.50
❑ 62 Tony Parker	.25	.60
❑ 63 Matt Harpring	.20	.50
❑ 64 Richard Hamilton	.20	.50
❑ 65 Corey Maggette	.20	.50
❑ 66 Damon Jones	.15	.40
❑ 67 Keith Bogans	.15	.40
❑ 68 Willie Green	.15	.40
❑ 69 Kirk Hinrich	.20	.50
❑ 70 Jerry Stackhouse	.20	.50
❑ 71 Chris Kaman	.20	.50
❑ 72 Lamar Odom	.25	.60
❑ 73 Dwyane Wade	.75	2.00
❑ 74 Kevin Garnett	.50	1.25
❑ 75 Allen Iverson	.50	1.25
❑ 76 Theo Ratliff	.15	.40
❑ 77 Shareef Abdur-Rahim	.20	.50
❑ 78 Gilbert Arenas	.25	.60
❑ 79 Jamal Sampson	.15	.40
❑ 80 Josh Howard	.25	.60
❑ 81 Latrell Sprewell	.20	.50
❑ 82 Kyle Korver	.20	.50
❑ 83 Brad Miller	.20	.50
❑ 84 Rasho Nesterovic	.15	.40
❑ 85 Larry Hughes	.20	.50
❑ 86 Eddy Curry	.20	.50
❑ 87 Rasheed Wallace	.25	.60
❑ 88 Chris Wilcox	.15	.40
❑ 89 Mark Madsen	.15	.40
❑ 90 Kenny Thomas	.15	.40
❑ 91 Zach Randolph	.25	.60
❑ 92 Juan Dixon	.15	.40
❑ 93 Tyson Chandler	.20	.50
❑ 94 Stromile Swift	.15	.40
❑ 95 Udonis Haslem	.20	.50
❑ 96 Jason Collins	.15	.40
❑ 97 Glenn Robinson	.20	.50
❑ 98 Darius Miles	.20	.50
❑ 99 Jared Jeffries	.15	.40
❑ 100 Bobby Jackson	.15	.40
❑ 101 Jahidi White	.15	.40
❑ 102 Dirk Nowitzki	.40	1.00
❑ 103 Wally Szczerbiak	.20	.50
❑ 104 John Salmons	.25	.60
❑ 105 Kwame Brown	.15	.40
❑ 106 Jason Kapono	.15	.40
❑ 107 Chauncey Billups	.25	.60
❑ 108 Shane Battier	.20	.50
❑ 109 Samuel Dalembert	.15	.40
❑ 110 Manu Ginobili	.25	.60
❑ 111 Anfernee Hardaway	.25	.60
❑ 112 Yao Ming	.60	1.50
❑ 113 Eric Piatkowski	.15	.40
❑ 114 Vlade Divac	.20	.50
❑ 115 Ron Mercer	.15	.40
❑ 116 Quentin Richardson	.20	.50
❑ 117 Derek Anderson	.20	.50
❑ 118 Jarvis Hayes	.15	.40
❑ 119 Antonio Davis	.15	.40
❑ 120 Erick Dampier	.15	.40
❑ 121 Antonio McDyess	.20	.50
❑ 122 Fred Jones	.15	.40
❑ 123 Damon Stoudamire	.20	.50
❑ 124 Jason Collier	.15	.40
❑ 125 Frank Williams	.15	.40
❑ 126 Kobe Bryant	1.25	3.00
❑ 127 Keith Van Horn	.20	.50
❑ 128 Darrell Armstrong	.15	.40
❑ 129 Steve Nash	.40	1.00
❑ 130 Nick Collison	.15	.40
❑ 131 Ricky Davis	.20	.50
❑ 132 Tracy McGrady	.50	1.25
❑ 133 Shaquille O'Neal	.60	1.50
❑ 134 Desmond Mason	.20	.50
❑ 135 Richard Jefferson	.25	.60
❑ 136 Casey Jacobsen	.15	.40
❑ 137 Ronald Murray	.15	.40
❑ 138 Rafer Alston	.15	.40
❑ 139 Tony Delk	.15	.40
❑ 140 LeBron James	1.50	4.00
❑ 141 Earl Boykins	.15	.40
❑ 142 Speedy Claxton	.15	.40
❑ 143 Jamaal Tinsley	.20	.50
❑ 144 Elton Brand	.25	.60
❑ 145 Jamaal Magloire	.15	.40
❑ 146 Jamal Crawford	.20	.50
❑ 147 Peja Stojakovic	.20	.50
❑ 148 Bruce Bowen	.15	.40
❑ 149 Paul Pierce	.25	.60
❑ 150 Jason Terry	.20	.50
❑ 151 Kenyon Martin	.25	.60
❑ 152 Maurice Taylor	.15	.40
❑ 153 Toni Kukoc	.20	.50
❑ 154 Aaron Williams	.15	.40
❑ 155 Tony Battie	.15	.40
❑ 156 Leandro Barbosa	.25	.60
❑ 157 Carlos Boozer	.25	.60
❑ 158 Brevin Knight	.15	.40
❑ 159 Marquis Daniels	.15	.40
❑ 160 Jim Jackson	.15	.40
❑ 161 Caron Butler	.20	.50
❑ 162 Troy Hudson	.15	.40
❑ 163 DeShawn Stevenson	.15	.40
❑ 164 Nick Van Exel	.20	.50
❑ 165 Antawn Jamison	.25	.60
❑ 166 Marcus Banks	.15	.40
❑ 167 Derek Fisher	.20	.50
❑ 168 Juwan Howard	.20	.50
❑ 169 Reggie Miller	.25	.60
❑ 170 Joe Smith	.15	.40
❑ 171 Alonzo Mourning	.25	.60
❑ 172 Mike Sweetney	.15	.40
❑ 173 Mehmet Okur	.20	.50
❑ 174 Brent Barry	.15	.40
❑ 175 Al Harrington	.20	.50
❑ 176 Dajuan Wagner	.15	.40
❑ 177 Voshon Lenard	.15	.40
❑ 178 Jermaine O'Neal	.25	.60
❑ 179 Bobby Simmons	.15	.40
❑ 180 Karl Malone	.25	.60
❑ 181 Dan Gadzuric	.15	.40
❑ 182 David Wesley	.15	.40
❑ 183 Tim Thomas	.15	.40
❑ 184 Amare Stoudemire	.50	1.25
❑ 185 Morris Peterson	.20	.50
❑ 186 Fred Hoiberg	.15	.40
❑ 187 Jeff McInnis	.15	.40
❑ 188 Andre Miller	.20	.50

❑ 189 Mike Dunleavy	.20	.50
❑ 190 Ron Artest	.20	.50
❑ 191 Kerry Kittles	.20	.50
❑ 192 Baron Davis	.25	.60
❑ 193 Vince Carter	.50	1.25
❑ 194 Gerald Wallace	.25	.60
❑ 195 Tayshaun Prince	.20	.50
❑ 196 Marko Jaric	.15	.40
❑ 197 Luke Walton	.20	.50
❑ 198 Eddie Jones	.20	.50
❑ 199 Hedo Turkoglu	.20	.50
❑ 200 Joe Johnson	.25	.60
❑ 201 Vladimir Radmanovic	.15	.40
❑ 202 Gordan Giricek	.15	.40
❑ 203 Antoine Walker	.25	.60
❑ 204 Zydrunas Ilgauskas	.20	.50
❑ 205 Clifford Robinson	.15	.40
❑ 206 Pau Gasol	.25	.60
❑ 207 Jamal Mashburn	.20	.50
❑ 208 Luke Ridnour	.15	.40
❑ 209 Kevin Garnett AW	.60	1.50
❑ 210 LeBron James AW	2.00	5.00
❑ 211 Jason Kidd AW	.50	1.25
❑ 212 Kobe Bryant AW	1.50	4.00
❑ 213 Shaquille O'Neal AW	.75	2.00
❑ 214 Tim Duncan AW	.60	1.50
❑ 215 Ron Artest AW	.25	.60
❑ 216 Dwyane Wade AW	1.00	2.50
❑ 217 Kirk Hinrich AW	.25	.60
❑ 218 Chris Bosh AW	.30	.75
❑ 219 Carmelo Anthony AW	1.00	2.50
❑ 220 Antawn Jamison AW	.30	.75
❑ 221 Dwight Howard RC	2.50	6.00
❑ 222 Emeka Okafor RC	1.50	4.00
❑ 223 Ben Gordon RC	1.00	2.50
❑ 224 Shaun Livingston RC	.75	2.00
❑ 225 Devin Harris RC	1.50	4.00
❑ 226 Josh Childress RC	.75	2.00
❑ 227 Luol Deng RC	1.00	2.50
❑ 228 Rafael Araujo RC	.75	2.00
❑ 229 Andre Iguodala RC	2.00	5.00
❑ 230 Luke Jackson RC	.75	2.00
❑ 231 Andris Biedrins RC	1.25	3.00
❑ 232 Robert Swift RC	.75	2.00
❑ 233 Sebastian Telfair RC	.75	2.00
❑ 234 Kris Humphries RC	1.25	3.00
❑ 235 Al Jefferson RC	1.50	4.00
❑ 236 Kirk Snyder RC	.75	2.00
❑ 237 Josh Smith RC	2.00	5.00
❑ 238 J.R. Smith RC	1.50	4.00
❑ 239 Dorell Wright RC	1.00	2.50
❑ 240 Jameer Nelson RC	1.00	2.50
❑ 241 Pavel Podkolzine RC	.75	2.00
❑ 242 Nenad Krstic RC	1.00	2.50
❑ 243 Andres Nocioni RC	1.00	2.50
❑ 244 Delonte West RC	1.25	3.00
❑ 245 Tony Allen RC	1.00	2.50
❑ 246 Kevin Martin RC	1.00	2.50
❑ 247 Sasha Vujacic RC	.75	2.00
❑ 248 Beno Udrih RC	1.00	2.50
❑ 249 David Harrison RC	.75	2.00
❑ 250 Anderson Varejao RC	1.00	2.50
❑ 251 Okafor/Gordon/Howard	2.50	6.00
❑ 252 Howard/Kasun RC/Nelson	1.25	4.00
❑ 253 Allen/Jefferson/West	3.00	8.00
❑ 254 Deng/Duhon/Gordon	2.50	6.00
❑ 255 Nocioni/Martin/Telfair	1.50	4.00
❑ 256 Childress/Ivey RC/Smith	1.50	4.00
❑ 257 Harris/Nelson/Telfair	1.25	4.00
❑ 258 Chalmers RC/Burks RC/Emmett RC	1.50	4.00
❑ 259 Deng/Duhon RC/Pickett RC	1.25	3.00
❑ 260 Childress/Jackson/Iguodala	1.50	4.00
❑ 261 Livingston/Howard/Swift	1.25	3.00
❑ 262 Smith/Jefferson/Telfair	1.50	4.00
❑ 263 Livingston/Wright/Smith	1.25	3.00
❑ 264 Reed RC/Vroman RC/Ramos RC	1.50	4.00
❑ 265 Podkolzine/Biedrins/Krstic	1.50	4.00
❑ 266 Vujacic/Tabuse RC/Udrih	3.00	8.00
❑ 267 Araujo/Humphries/Snyder	1.50	4.00
❑ 268 Robinson RC/Sow RC/Ariza RC	2.00	5.00

2000-01 Fleer Triple Crown

❑ COMPLETE SET w/o RC (200)	12.50	25.00
❑ COMMON CARD (41-240)	.07	.20
❑ COMMON ROOKIE (1-40/241)	.40	1.00
❑ 1 Quentin Richardson RC	.50	1.25
❑ 2 Khalid El-Amin RC	.40	1.00
❑ 3 Courtney Alexander RC	.40	1.00
❑ 4 Mike Penberthy RC	.40	1.00
❑ 5 DerMarr Johnson RC	.40	1.00
❑ 6 A.J. Guyton RC	.40	1.00
❑ 7 Erick Barkley RC	.40	1.00
❑ 8 Jamal Crawford RC	.60	1.50
❑ 9 Hedo Turkoglu RC	1.00	2.50
❑ 10 Michael Redd RC	1.00	2.50
❑ 11 Stromile Swift RC	.50	1.25
❑ 12 Eddie House RC	.40	1.00
❑ 13 Keyon Dooling RC	.40	1.00
❑ 14 Lavor Postell RC	.40	1.00
❑ 15 Mateen Cleaves RC	.40	1.00
❑ 16 Morris Peterson RC	.60	1.50
❑ 17 DeShawn Stevenson RC	.40	1.00
❑ 18 Darius Miles RC	.50	1.25
❑ 19 Hanno Mottola RC	.40	1.00
❑ 20 Jerome Moiso RC	.40	1.00
❑ 21 Desmond Mason RC	.50	1.25
❑ 22 Jason Collier RC	.40	1.00
❑ 23 Ruben Wolkowyski RC	.40	1.00
❑ 24 Eduardo Najera RC	.40	1.00
❑ 25 Kenyon Martin RC	1.00	2.50
❑ 26 Marcus Fizer RC	.40	1.00
❑ 27 Etan Thomas RC	.40	1.00
❑ 28 Mark Madsen RC	.40	1.00
❑ 29 Pepe Sanchez RC	.40	1.00
❑ 30 Brian Cardinal RC	.40	1.00
❑ 31 Chris Porter RC	.40	1.00
❑ 32 Dan Langhi RC	.40	1.00
❑ 33 Mike Miller RC	.60	1.50
❑ 34 Chris Mihm RC	.40	1.00
❑ 35 Mamadou N'Diaye RC	.40	1.00
❑ 36 Dragan Tarlac RC	.40	1.00
❑ 37 Iakovos Tsakalidis RC	.40	1.00
❑ 38 Stephen Jackson RC	.60	1.50
❑ 39 Jamaal Magloire RC	.40	1.00
❑ 40 Joel Przybilla RC	.40	1.00
❑ 41 Adrian Griffin	.15	.40
❑ 42 Allan Houston	.20	.50
❑ 43 Mahmoud Abdul-Rauf	.15	.40
❑ 44 Avery Johnson	.20	.50
❑ 45 Damon Stoudamire	.20	.50
❑ 46 Jim Jackson	.15	.40
❑ 47 Jason Williams	.20	.50
❑ 48 Jason Kidd	.40	1.00
❑ 49 Ray Allen	.25	.60
❑ 50 Baron Davis	.25	.60
❑ 51 Mark Jackson	.20	.50
❑ 52 Darrick Martin	.15	.40
❑ 53 Derek Fisher	.25	.60
❑ 54 Anthony Peeler	.15	.40
❑ 55 Vince Carter	.50	1.25
❑ 56 Tim Hardaway	.20	.50
❑ 57 Richard Hamilton	.20	.50
❑ 58 Malik Rose	.15	.40
❑ 59 Antonio Daniels	.15	.40
❑ 60 Lindsey Hunter	.15	.40
❑ 61 William Avery	.15	.40
❑ 62 Reggie Miller	.25	.60
❑ 63 Shareef Abdur-Rahim	.20	.50
❑ 64 Travis Best	.15	.40
❑ 65 John Stockton	.30	.75
❑ 66 Kenny Anderson	.20	.50
❑ 67 Trajan Langdon	.15	.40
❑ 68 Sam Cassell	.20	.50
❑ 69 Chucky Atkins	.15	.40
❑ 70 Laron Profit	.15	.40
❑ 71 Andre Miller	.20	.50
❑ 72 Erick Strickland	.15	.40
❑ 73 Ron Artest	.25	.60
❑ 74 Kobe Bryant	1.25	3.00
❑ 75 Ricky Davis	.20	.50
❑ 76 Allen Iverson	.50	1.25
❑ 77 Steve Smith	.20	.50
❑ 78 Alvin Williams	.15	.40
❑ 79 Randy Brown	.15	.40
❑ 80 Michael Dickerson	.15	.40
❑ 81 Tyronn Lue	.15	.40
❑ 82 Bonzi Wells	.15	.40
❑ 83 Felipe Lopez	.15	.40
❑ 84 Steve Francis	.25	.60
❑ 85 Jaren Jackson	.15	.40
❑ 86 Anthony Carter	.15	.40
❑ 87 Mitch Richmond	.20	.50
❑ 88 Sherman Douglas	.15	.40
❑ 89 Cuttino Mobley	.20	.50
❑ 90 Mario Elie	.15	.40
❑ 91 Tariq Abdul-Wahad	.15	.40
❑ 92 Ron Mercer	.15	.40
❑ 93 Jalen Rose	.20	.50
❑ 94 Mike Bibby	.20	.50
❑ 95 Voshon Lenard	.15	.40
❑ 96 Derek Anderson	.20	.50
❑ 97 Kendall Gill	.15	.40
❑ 98 Muggsy Bogues	.20	.50
❑ 99 Eddie Jones	.20	.50
❑ 100 Larry Hughes	.20	.50
❑ 101 Latrell Sprewell	.20	.50
❑ 102 Stephon Marbury	.25	.60
❑ 103 Eric Piatkowski	.15	.40
❑ 104 Brevin Knight	.15	.40
❑ 105 Isaiah Rider	.20	.50
❑ 106 Wesley Person	.15	.40
❑ 107 Nick Van Exel	.20	.50
❑ 108 Dell Curry	.15	.40
❑ 109 Tony Delk	.15	.40
❑ 110 Glen Rice	.20	.50
❑ 111 Bobby Jackson	.15	.40
❑ 112 Kerry Kittles	.20	.50
❑ 113 John Starks	.15	.40
❑ 114 Gary Payton	.25	.60
❑ 115 Mookie Blaylock	.20	.50
❑ 116 David Wesley	.15	.40
❑ 117 Rod Strickland	.20	.50
❑ 118 Terrell Brandon	.15	.40
❑ 119 Steve Nash	.40	1.00
❑ 120 Moochie Norris	.15	.40
❑ 121 Eric Snow	.15	.40
❑ 122 Chauncey Billups	.25	.60
❑ 123 Darrell Armstrong	.15	.40
❑ 124 Ron Harper	.20	.50
❑ 125 Dion Glover	.15	.40
❑ 126 Vin Baker	.20	.50
❑ 127 Terry Mills	.15	.40
❑ 128 Joe Smith	.15	.40
❑ 129 Kurt Thomas	.15	.40
❑ 130 Dirk Nowitzki	.40	1.00
❑ 131 Sean Elliott	.20	.50
❑ 132 Jerome Williams	.15	.40
❑ 133 Larry Johnson	.20	.50
❑ 134 LaPhonso Ellis	.20	.50
❑ 135 Pat Garrity	.15	.40
❑ 136 Lawrence Funderburke	.15	.40
❑ 137 Elton Brand	.25	.60
❑ 138 Rashard Lewis	.25	.60
❑ 139 Shawn Kemp	.25	.60
❑ 140 Elden Campbell	.15	.40
❑ 141 Christian Laettner	.15	.40
❑ 142 Al Harrington	.20	.50
❑ 143 Billy Owens	.15	.40
❑ 144 Wally Szczerbiak	.20	.50
❑ 145 Jonathan Bender	.15	.40
❑ 146 Karl Malone	.30	.75
❑ 147 Andrew DeClercq	.15	.40
❑ 148 Danny Manning	.15	.40
❑ 149 Antoine Walker	.20	.50
❑ 150 Jason Caffey	.15	.40
❑ 151 P.J. Brown	.15	.40
❑ 152 Matt Harpring	.20	.50
❑ 153 Mark Strickland	.15	.40
❑ 154 Theo Ratliff	.15	.40
❑ 155 Ruben Patterson	.15	.40
❑ 156 Tom Gugliotta	.15	.40
❑ 157 Derrick Coleman	.20	.50
❑ 158 Lorenzen Wright	.15	.40
❑ 159 Tracy McGrady	.50	1.25
❑ 160 Quincy Lewis	.15	.40
❑ 161 Tony Battie	.15	.40
❑ 162 Keith Van Horn	.20	.50
❑ 163 Paul Pierce	.25	.60
❑ 164 Glenn Robinson	.20	.50

❑ 165 John Wallace	.15	.40
❑ 166 Popeye Jones	.15	.40
❑ 167 Kevin Garnett	.50	1.25
❑ 168 Donyell Marshall	.15	.40
❑ 169 Michael Finley	.25	.60
❑ 170 Nick Anderson	.15	.40
❑ 171 Danny Fortson	.15	.40
❑ 172 Keon Clark	.15	.40
❑ 173 Juwan Howard	.20	.50
❑ 174 Brian Grant	.15	.40
❑ 175 Marcus Camby	.20	.50
❑ 176 Scottie Pippen	.40	1.00
❑ 177 Shawn Marion	.25	.60
❑ 178 Lamar Odom	.25	.60
❑ 179 Charles Oakley	.20	.50
❑ 180 Tim James	.15	.40
❑ 181 Eric Williams	.15	.40
❑ 182 Tim Duncan	.50	1.25
❑ 183 Andrae Patterson	.15	.40
❑ 184 Toni Kukoc	.20	.50
❑ 185 Chris Mullin	.25	.60
❑ 186 Alan Henderson	.15	.40
❑ 187 Maurice Taylor	.15	.40
❑ 188 Chris Webber	.25	.60
❑ 189 Jamal Mashburn	.20	.50
❑ 190 Rodney Rogers	.15	.40
❑ 191 Loy Vaught	.15	.40
❑ 192 Carlos Rogers	.15	.40
❑ 193 Grant Hill	.25	.60
❑ 194 George Lynch	.15	.40
❑ 195 Antonio McDyess	.20	.50
❑ 196 Tim Thomas	.15	.40
❑ 197 Roshown McLeod	.15	.40
❑ 198 Antawn Jamison	.25	.60
❑ 199 Clifford Robinson	.15	.40
❑ 200 Corey Maggette	.20	.50
❑ 201 Horace Grant	.20	.50
❑ 202 David Benoit	.15	.40
❑ 203 Cedric Ceballos	.15	.40
❑ 204 Antonio Davis	.15	.40
❑ 205 Lamond Murray	.15	.40
❑ 206 Jerry Stackhouse	.20	.50
❑ 207 Jermaine O'Neal	.25	.60
❑ 208 Anthony Mason	.15	.40
❑ 209 Cedric Henderson	.15	.40
❑ 210 Corliss Williamson	.20	.50
❑ 211 Austin Croshere	.15	.40
❑ 212 Radoslav Nesterovic	.15	.40
❑ 213 Hakeem Olajuwon	.30	.75
❑ 214 Nazr Mohammed	.15	.40
❑ 215 David Robinson	.30	.75
❑ 216 Jeff McInnis	.15	.40
❑ 217 Brad Miller	.20	.50
❑ 218 Evan Eschmeyer	.15	.40
❑ 219 Jelani McCoy	.15	.40
❑ 220 Sean Rooks	.15	.40
❑ 221 Dikembe Mutombo	.20	.50
❑ 222 Othella Harrington	.15	.40
❑ 223 John Amaechi	.15	.40
❑ 224 Erick Dampier	.15	.40
❑ 225 Calvin Booth	.15	.40
❑ 226 Adonal Foyle	.15	.40
❑ 227 Michael Doleac	.15	.40
❑ 228 Michael Olowokandi	.15	.40
❑ 229 Matt Geiger	.15	.40
❑ 230 Vlade Divac	.20	.50
❑ 231 Bryant Reeves	.15	.40
❑ 232 Shaquille O'Neal	.60	1.50
❑ 233 Todd Fuller	.15	.40
❑ 234 Arvydas Sabonis	.20	.50
❑ 235 Jim McIlvaine	.15	.40
❑ 236 Isaac Austin	.15	.40
❑ 237 Raef LaFrentz	.15	.40
❑ 238 Rasheed Wallace	.25	.60
❑ 239 Kelvin Cato	.15	.40
❑ 240 Patrick Ewing	.30	.75
❑ 241 Marc Jackson RC	.50	1.25

2001 Greats of the Game

❑ COMPLETE SET (84)	20.00	50.00
❑ COMMON CARD (1-84)	.30	.75
❑ COMMON QC (76-83)	1.25	3.00
❑ 1 Adolph Rupp	.30	.75
❑ 2 Alonzo Mourning	.30	.75
❑ 3 Antawn Jamison	.60	1.50
❑ 4 Antoine Walker	.60	1.50
❑ 5 Bill Walton	.60	1.50
❑ 6 Bob Cousy	.60	1.50
❑ 7 Bob Lanier	.60	1.50
❑ 8 Bobby Cremins	.30	.75

❑ 9 Bobby Hurley	.60	1.50
❑ 10 Bobby Knight	.75	2.00
❑ 11 Cazzie Russell	.30	.75
❑ 12 Charlie Ward	.30	.75
❑ 13 Christian Laettner	.75	2.00
❑ 14 Clyde Drexler	.30	.75
❑ 15 Danny Ainge	.30	.75
❑ 16 Danny Ferry	.75	2.00
❑ 17 Danny Manning	.75	2.00
❑ 18 Darrell Griffith	.30	.75
❑ 19 Dave Cowens	.30	.75
❑ 20 David Robinson	.60	1.50
❑ 21 David Thompson	.75	2.00
❑ 22 Dean Smith	.30	.75
❑ 23 Don Haskins	.30	.75
❑ 24 Eddie Jones	.30	.75
❑ 25 Elvin Hayes	.30	.75
❑ 26 Gene Keady	.30	.75
❑ 27 George Mikan	.60	1.50
❑ 28 Glen Rice	.30	.75
❑ 29 Hakeem Olajuwon	.60	1.50
❑ 30 Isiah Thomas	.60	1.50
❑ 31 Jalen Rose	.30	.75
❑ 32 Jamal Mashburn	.30	.75
❑ 33 James Worthy	.60	1.50
❑ 34 Jerry Stackhouse	.60	1.50
❑ 35 Jerry Lucas	.30	.75
❑ 36 Jerry Tarkanian	.30	.75
❑ 37 Jerry West	.30	.75
❑ 38 Jim Valvano	.60	1.50
❑ 39 Joe Smith	.30	.75
❑ 40 John Thompson	.30	.75
❑ 41 John Havlicek	.60	1.50
❑ 42 John Wooden	.60	1.50
❑ 43 John Lucas	.30	.75
❑ 44 Kareem Abdul-Jabbar	1.00	2.50
❑ 45 Keith Van Horn	.60	1.50
❑ 46 Kent Benson	.30	.75
❑ 47 Kerry Kittles	.30	.75
❑ 48 Lamar Odom	.60	1.50
❑ 49 Larry Bird	2.00	5.00
❑ 50 Larry Johnson	.30	.75
❑ 51 Lefty Driesell	.75	2.00
❑ 52 Lenny Wilkens	.60	1.50
❑ 53 Lou Carnesecca	.30	.75
❑ 54 Marques Johnson	.30	.75
❑ 55 Mateen Cleaves	.60	1.50
❑ 56 Mike Bibby	.60	1.50
❑ 57 Mike Krzyzewski	.75	2.00
❑ 58 Mychal Thompson	.30	.75
❑ 59 Nate Archibald	.30	.75
❑ 60 Pat Riley	.60	1.50
❑ 61 Paul Arizin	.60	1.50
❑ 62 Pete Maravich	.75	2.00
❑ 63 Phil Ford	.60	1.50
❑ 64 Ralph Sampson	.30	.75
❑ 65 Ray Meyer	.30	.75
❑ 66 Rick Pitino	.75	2.00
❑ 67 Rick Barry	.30	.75
❑ 68 Rollie Massimino	.30	.75
❑ 69 Sam Jones	.30	.75
❑ 70 Sidney Moncrief	.30	.75
❑ 71 Spud Webb	.30	.75
❑ 72 Steve Alford	.60	1.50
❑ 73 Vince Carter	.75	2.00
❑ 74 Walt Frazier	.75	2.00
❑ 75 Wilt Chamberlain	.75	2.00
❑ 76 Carol Blazejowski QC	1.25	3.00
❑ 77 Cynthia Cooper QC	1.25	3.00
❑ 78 Chamique Holdsclaw QC	1.25	3.00
❑ 79 Lisa Leslie QC	1.25	3.00
❑ 80 Nancy Lieberman QC	1.25	3.00
❑ 81 Rebecca Lobo QC	1.25	3.00
❑ 82 Cheryl Miller QC	1.25	3.00
❑ 83 Sheryl Swoopes QC	1.50	4.00
❑ 84 Marcus Camby	.30	.75

2005-06 Greats of the Game

❑ COMP.SET w/o SP's (100)	35.00	75.00
❑ COMMON CARD (1-100)	.75	2.00
❑ SEMISTARS	.75	2.00
❑ UNLISTED STARS	.75	2.00
❑ COMMON AU RC (101-152)	8.00	20.00
❑ COMMON ROOKIE (153-169)	3.00	8.00
❑ 101-169 PRINT RUN 99 SER.#'d SETS		
❑ 1 Earl Monroe	.75	2.00
❑ 2 World Free	.75	2.00
❑ 3 James Worthy	.75	2.00
❑ 4 Bob McAdoo	.75	2.00
❑ 5 Connie Hawkins	.75	2.00
❑ 6 John Starks	.75	2.00
❑ 7 Byron Scott	.75	2.00
❑ 8 Brad Daugherty	.75	2.00
❑ 9 Chris Ford	.75	2.00
❑ 10 Jamaal Wilkes	.75	2.00
❑ 11 Julius Erving	1.50	4.00
❑ 12 Joe Carroll	.75	2.00
❑ 13 Bill Laimbeer	.75	2.00
❑ 14 Bill Walton	.75	2.00
❑ 15 Brian Winters	.75	2.00
❑ 16 David Robinson	1.00	2.50
❑ 17 Horace Grant	.75	2.00
❑ 18 Bob Pettit	.75	2.00
❑ 19 Dan Roundfield	.75	2.00
❑ 20 Kenny Walker	.75	2.00
❑ 21 Kenny Smith	.75	2.00
❑ 22 Thurl Bailey	.75	2.00
❑ 23 Cedric Maxwell	.75	2.00
❑ 24 Joe Dumars	.75	2.00
❑ 25 Adrian Dantley	.75	2.00
❑ 26 Dale Ellis	.75	2.00
❑ 27 John Stockton	1.50	4.00
❑ 28 Bob Lanier	.75	2.00
❑ 29 Bernard King	.75	2.00
❑ 30 Jerry Lucas	.75	2.00
❑ 31 Bill Russell	1.50	4.00
❑ 32 Hal Greer	.75	2.00
❑ 33 Billy Cunningham	.75	2.00
❑ 34 Jack Sikma	.75	2.00
❑ 35 Michael Cooper	.75	2.00
❑ 36 David Thompson	.75	2.00
❑ 37 Kareem Abdul-Jabbar	1.25	3.00
❑ 38 Bill Sharman	.75	2.00
❑ 39 George Gervin	.75	2.00
❑ 40 Kiki Vandeweghe	.75	2.00
❑ 41 Calvin Murphy	.75	2.00
❑ 42 Darryl Dawkins	.75	2.00
❑ 43 Vern Mikkelsen	.75	2.00
❑ 44 Dee Brown	.75	2.00
❑ 45 Dennis Rodman	1.25	3.00
❑ 46 Bobby Jones	.75	2.00
❑ 47 Hakeem Olajuwon	1.00	2.50
❑ 48 Alvin Robertson	.75	2.00
❑ 49 Dennis Johnson	1.00	2.50
❑ 50 Clyde Drexler	1.00	2.50
❑ 51 Anthony Mason	.75	2.00
❑ 52 Larry Bird	2.50	6.00
❑ 53 LeBron James	4.00	10.00
❑ 54 Magic Johnson	1.50	4.00
❑ 55 Manute Bol	.75	2.00
❑ 56 Mookie Blaylock	.75	2.00
❑ 57 Mark Eaton	.75	2.00
❑ 58 Kevin McHale	1.00	2.50
❑ 59 Maurice Cheeks	.75	2.00
❑ 60 Maurice Lucas	.75	2.00
❑ 61 Michael Jordan	5.00	12.00
❑ 62 Michael Ray Richardson	.75	2.00
❑ 63 B.J. Armstrong	.75	2.00
❑ 64 ML Carr	.75	2.00
❑ 65 Muggsy Bogues	.75	2.00

❑ 66 Nate Archibald	.75	2.00
❑ 67 Glen Rice	.75	2.00
❑ 68 Nate Thurmond	.75	2.00
❑ 69 Norm Nixon	.75	2.00
❑ 70 Bob Love	.75	2.00
❑ 71 Paul Arizin	.75	2.00
❑ 72 Ralph Sampson	.75	2.00
❑ 73 Rolando Blackman	.75	2.00
❑ 74 Reggie Theus	.75	2.00
❑ 75 Mitch Richmond	.75	2.00
❑ 76 Robert Parish	.75	2.00
❑ 77 Paul Westphal	.75	2.00
❑ 78 Sam Perkins	.75	2.00
❑ 79 Scottie Pippen	.75	2.00
❑ 80 Sean Elliott	.75	2.00
❑ 81 Spud Webb	.75	2.00
❑ 82 Steve Kerr	.75	2.00
❑ 83 Tom Chambers	.75	2.00
❑ 84 Walt Bellamy	.75	2.00
❑ 85 Walt Frazier	.75	2.00
❑ 86 Jeff Hornacek	.75	2.00
❑ 87 Danny Manning	.75	2.00
❑ 88 Wes Unseld	.75	2.00
❑ 89 Geoff Petrie	.75	2.00
❑ 90 Xavier McDaniel	.75	2.00
❑ 91 Chris Mullin	.75	2.00
❑ 92 Buck Williams CC	.75	2.00
❑ 93 Dave Bing CC	.75	2.00
❑ 94 John Havlicek CC	.75	2.00
❑ 95 Karl Malone CC	1.00	2.50
❑ 96 Artis Gilmore CC	.75	2.00
❑ 97 Doug Moe CC	.75	2.00
❑ 98 Doug Collins CC	.75	2.00
❑ 99 Chuck Daly CC	.75	2.00
❑ 100 Bob Knight CC	1.00	2.50
❑ 101 Alex Acker AU RC	8.00	20.00
❑ 102 Amir Johnson AU RC	40.00	80.00
❑ 103 Andray Blatche AU RC	20.00	40.00
❑ 104 Andrew Bogut AU RC	30.00	60.00
❑ 105 Andrew Bynum AU RC	100.00	200.00
❑ 106 Antoine Wright AU RC	8.00	20.00
❑ 107 Yaroslav Korolev AU RC	10.00	25.00
❑ 108 Bracey Wright AU RC	8.00	20.00
❑ 109 Brandon Bass AU RC	8.00	20.00
❑ 110 C.J. Miles AU RC	10.00	25.00
❑ 111 Channing Frye AU RC	25.00	50.00
❑ 112 Charlie Villanueva AU RC	25.00	50.00
❑ 113 Chris Paul AU RC	150.00	250.00
❑ 114 Chris Taft AU RC	8.00	20.00
❑ 115 Chuck Hayes AU RC	8.00	20.00
❑ 116 Daniel Ewing AU RC	10.00	25.00
❑ 117 Danny Granger AU RC	40.00	80.00
❑ 118 David Lee AU RC	30.00	60.00
❑ 119 Deron Williams AU	125.00	225.00
❑ 120 Dijon Thompson AU RC	8.00	20.00
❑ 121 Ersan Ilyasova AU RC	10.00	25.00
❑ 122 Francisco Garcia RC	8.00	20.00
❑ 123 Gerald Green AU RC	50.00	100.00
❑ 124 Hakim Warrick AU RC	25.00	50.00
❑ 125 Ike Diogu AU RC	15.00	30.00
❑ 126 Jarrett Jack AU RC	15.00	30.00
❑ 127 Jason Maxiell AU RC	15.00	30.00
❑ 128 Joey Graham AU RC	10.00	25.00
❑ 129 Johan Petro AU RC	8.00	20.00
❑ 130 Julius Hodge AU RC	8.00	20.00
❑ 131 Lawrence Roberts AU RC	8.00	20.00
❑ 132 Linas Kleiza AU RC	10.00	25.00
❑ 133 Louis Williams AU RC	30.00	60.00
❑ 134 Luther Head AU RC	15.00	30.00
❑ 135 Martell Webster AU RC	15.00	30.00
❑ 136 M.Andriuskevicius AU RC	8.00	20.00
❑ 137 Marvin Williams AU RC	50.00	100.00
❑ 138 Monta Ellis AU RC	75.00	150.00
❑ 139 Nate Robinson AU RC	20.00	40.00
❑ 140 Orien Greene AU RC	8.00	20.00
❑ 141 Rashad McCants AU EXCH	25.00	50.00
❑ 142 Raymond Felton AU RC	40.00	80.00
❑ 143 Robert Whaley AU RC	8.00	20.00
❑ 144 Ronny Turiaf AU RC	30.00	60.00
❑ 145 Ryan Gomes AU RC	10.00	25.00
❑ 146 Salim Stoudamire AU RC	25.00	50.00
❑ 147 Sarunas Jasikevicius AU	8.00	20.00
❑ 148 Sean May AU RC	30.00	60.00
❑ 149 Stephen Graham AU RC	8.00	20.00
❑ 150 Travis Diener AU RC	8.00	20.00
❑ 151 Von Wafer AU RC	8.00	20.00
❑ 152 Wayne Simien AU RC	15.00	30.00
❑ 153 Shavlik Randolph RC	3.00	8.00
❑ 154 Alan Anderson RC	3.00	8.00
❑ 155 Andre Owens RC	3.00	8.00
❑ 156 Anthony Roberson RC	3.00	8.00
❑ 157 Arvydas Macijauskas RC	3.00	8.00
❑ 158 Boniface N'Dong RC	3.00	8.00
❑ 159 Devin Green RC	3.00	8.00
❑ 160 Donell Taylor RC	3.00	8.00
❑ 161 Earl Barron RC	3.00	8.00
❑ 162 Esteban Batista RC	3.00	8.00
❑ 163 Fabricio Oberto RC	3.00	8.00
❑ 164 Rawle Marshall RC	3.00	8.00
❑ 165 James Singleton RC	3.00	8.00
❑ 166 Jose Calderon RC	3.00	8.00
❑ 167 Josh Powell RC	3.00	8.00
❑ 168 Kevin Burleson RC	3.00	8.00
❑ 169 Ronnie Price RC	3.00	8.00

2009-10 Greats of the Game

❑ 1 Mark Jackson	.40	1.00
❑ 2 Freddie Lewis	.40	1.00
❑ 3 Brad Daugherty	.40	1.00
❑ 4 John Stockton	.60	1.50
❑ 5 Shareef Abdur-Rahim	.25	.60
❑ 6 Michael Jordan	3.00	8.00
❑ 7 Larry Johnson	.40	1.00
❑ 8 B.J. Armstrong	.40	1.00
❑ 9 Hakeem Olajuwon	.50	1.25
❑ 10 Sam Perkins	.40	1.00
❑ 11 Steve Kerr	.40	1.00
❑ 12 Julius Erving	.75	2.00
❑ 13 John Havlicek	.40	1.00
❑ 14 Clyde Lovellette	.40	1.00
❑ 15 Danny Manning	.40	1.00
❑ 16 Isiah Thomas	.40	1.00
❑ 17 Kevin Pittsnogle	.25	.60
❑ 18 Clyde Drexler	.50	1.25
❑ 19 Bill Cartwright	.40	1.00
❑ 20 Jerry West	.50	1.25
❑ 21 Darrell Walker	.40	1.00
❑ 22 Pat Riley	.40	1.00
❑ 23 Cazzie Russell	.40	1.00
❑ 24 Lionel Hollins	.40	1.00
❑ 25 George Karl	.40	1.00
❑ 26 Terry Porter	.40	1.00
❑ 27 Jack Sikma	.40	1.00
❑ 28 Adrian Dantley	.40	1.00
❑ 29 Billy Donovan	.50	1.25
❑ 30 Micheal Ray Richardson	.40	1.00
❑ 31 Hal Greer	.40	1.00
❑ 32 Terry Cummings	.40	1.00
❑ 33 Rick Mahorn	.40	1.00
❑ 34 Larry Nance	.40	1.00
❑ 35 Oscar Robertson	.40	1.00
❑ 36 James Harden	.75	2.00
❑ 37 Horace Grant	.40	1.00
❑ 38 Steve Alford	.40	1.00
❑ 39 Magic Johnson	.75	2.00
❑ 40 LeBron James	2.00	5.00
❑ 41 Yao Ming	.50	1.25
❑ 42 Larry Bird	1.25	3.00
❑ 43 Tito Horford	.40	1.00
❑ 44 Ricky Rubio	.60	1.50
❑ 45 George Gervin	.40	1.00
❑ 46 Gail Goodrich	.40	1.00
❑ 47 Chet Walker	.40	1.00
❑ 48 Vlade Divac	.40	1.00
❑ 49 Thurl Bailey	.40	1.00
❑ 50 Dominique Wilkins	.50	1.25
❑ 51 Bob Lanier	.40	1.00
❑ 52 Bill Sharman	.40	1.00
❑ 53 Don Nelson	.40	1.00
❑ 54 Ron Harper	.40	1.00
❑ 55 Bernard King	.40	1.00
❑ 56 Robert Parish	.40	1.00
❑ 57 Elgin Baylor	.40	1.00
❑ 58 Dave Cowens	.40	1.00
❑ 59 Dennis Rodman	.60	1.50
❑ 60 Rod Hundley	.40	1.00
❑ 61 Bill Walton	.40	1.00
❑ 62 David Thompson	.50	1.25
❑ 63 Bill Laimbeer	.40	1.00
❑ 64 Bob McAdoo	.40	1.00
❑ 65 Kareem Abdul-Jabbar	.60	1.50
❑ 66 Bill Russell	.60	1.50
❑ 67 Alonzo Mourning	.50	1.25
❑ 68 Jerry Sloan	.40	1.00
❑ 69 Avery Johnson	.40	1.00
❑ 70 Bobby Hurley	.50	1.25
❑ 71 Moses Malone	.40	1.00
❑ 72 Chris Mullin	.40	1.00
❑ 73 Derrick Rose	.75	2.00
❑ 74 Stacey Augmon	.40	1.00
❑ 75 Darrell Griffith	.40	1.00
❑ 76 Danny Ferry	.60	1.50
❑ 77 Michael Cooper	.40	1.00
❑ 78 Brandon Roy	.50	1.25
❑ 79 Bob Pettit	.40	1.00
❑ 80 David Robinson	.60	1.50
❑ 81 Sam Cassell	.40	1.00
❑ 82 Glen Rice	.40	1.00
❑ 83 Calbert Cheaney	.40	1.00
❑ 84 Christian Laettner	.60	1.50
❑ 85 Mateen Cleaves	.25	.60
❑ 86 Derrick Rose GD	1.25	3.00
❑ 87 Yao Ming GD	.75	2.00
❑ 88 Brandon Roy GD	.75	2.00
❑ 89 LeBron James GD	3.00	8.00
❑ 90 James Harden GD	1.25	3.00
❑ 91 Michael Jordan GD	4.00	10.00
❑ 92 Michael Cooper GD	.60	1.50
❑ 93 Moses Malone GD	.60	1.50
❑ 94 Kevin Pittsnogle GD	.40	1.00
❑ 95 Chris Mullin GD	.60	1.50
❑ 96 Alonzo Mourning GD	.75	2.00
❑ 97 Horace Grant GD	.60	1.50
❑ 98 Larry Nance GD	.60	1.50
❑ 99 Larry Bird GD	2.00	5.00
❑ 100 Julius Erving GD	1.25	3.00
❑ 101 Tito Horford GD	.60	1.50
❑ 102 George Gervin GD	.60	1.50
❑ 103 Red Hundley GD	.60	1.50
❑ 104 Mateen Cleaves GD	.40	1.00
❑ 105 Calbert Cheaney GD	.60	1.50
❑ 106 Brandon Roy BMC	1.00	2.50
❑ 107 Calbert Cheaney BMC	.75	2.00
❑ 108 Bill Cartwright BMC	.75	2.00
❑ 109 Danny Ferry BMC	1.25	3.00
❑ 110 Danny Manning BMC	.75	2.00
❑ 111 Darrell Walker BMC	.75	2.00
❑ 112 Bill Laimbeer BMC	.75	2.00
❑ 113 LeBron James BMC	4.00	10.00
❑ 114 Derrick Rose BMC	1.50	4.00
❑ 115 Hakeem Olajuwon BMC	1.00	2.50
❑ 116 Horace Grant BMC	.75	2.00
❑ 117 James Harden BMC	1.50	4.00
❑ 118 Bill Russell BMC	1.25	3.00
❑ 119 Larry Bird BMC	2.50	6.00
❑ 120 Larry Johnson BMC	.75	2.00
❑ 121 Michael Jordan BMC	6.00	15.00
❑ 122 Bill Walton BMC	.75	2.00
❑ 123 Shareef Abdur-Rahim BMC	.50	1.25
❑ 124 Sam Perkins BMC	.75	2.00
❑ 125 J.West/K.Pittsnogle	1.25	3.00
❑ 126 B.Walton/K.Abdul-Jabbar	1.50	4.00
❑ 127 L.Johnson/S.Augmon	1.00	2.50
❑ 128 D.Cowens/S.Cassell	1.00	2.50
❑ 129 D.Thompson/T.Bailey	1.25	3.00
❑ 130 M.Johnson/M.Cleaves	2.00	5.00
❑ 131 B.Cartwright/B.Russell	1.50	4.00
❑ 132 B.Hurley/D.Ferry	1.50	4.00
❑ 133 H.Grant/L.Nance	1.00	2.50
❑ 134 C.Laettner/D.Ferry	1.50	4.00
❑ 135 F.Lewis/L.Hollins	1.00	2.50
❑ 136 C.Russell/G.Rice	1.00	2.50
❑ 137 B.Armstrong/D.Nelson	1.00	2.50
❑ 138 A.Dantley/B.Laimbeer	1.00	2.50
❑ 139 C.Mullin/M.Jackson	1.00	2.50
❑ 140 B.McAdoo/G.Karl	1.00	2.50
❑ 141 C.Lovellette/D.Manning	1.00	2.50
❑ 142 C.Drexler/H.Olajuwon	1.25	3.00
❑ 143 Dave Cowens OS	.75	2.00
❑ 144 Bernard King OS	.75	2.00
❑ 145 Mark Jackson OS	.75	2.00
❑ 146 Danny Ferry OS	1.25	3.00

❑ 147 Darrell Griffith OS	.75	2.00
❑ 148 Cazzie Russell OS	.75	2.00
❑ 149 George Karl OS	.75	2.00
❑ 150 Sam Perkins OS	.75	2.00
❑ 151 Julius Erving OS	1.50	4.00
❑ 152 Larry Bird OS	2.50	6.00
❑ 153 Isiah Thomas OS	.75	2.00
❑ 154 Michael Jordan OS	6.00	15.00
❑ 155 Freddie Lewis OS	.75	2.00
❑ 156 John Stockton OS	1.25	3.00
❑ 157 Pat Riley OS	.75	2.00
❑ 158 Jack Sikma OS	.75	2.00
❑ 159 Oscar Robertson OS	.75	2.00
❑ 160 Chris Mullin OS	.75	2.00
❑ 161 George Gervin OS	.75	2.00
❑ 162 Bill Walton OS	.75	2.00
❑ 163 Kareem Abdul-Jabbar OS	1.25	3.00

1989-90 Hoops

❑ COMPLETE SET (352)	12.50	25.00
❑ COMPLETE SERIES 1 (300)	10.00	20.00
❑ COMPLETE SERIES 2 (52)	2.50	5.00
❑ COMMON CARD (1-352)	.04	.10
❑ COMMON SP	.05	.15
❑ 1 Joe Dumars	.08	.25
❑ 2 Tree Rollins	.02	.10
❑ 3 Kenny Walker	.02	.10
❑ 4 Mychal Thompson	.02	.10
❑ 5 Alvin Robertson SP	.05	.15
❑ 6 Vinny Del Negro RC	.08	.25
❑ 7 Greg Anderson SP	.05	.15
❑ 8 Rod Strickland RC	.30	.75
❑ 9 Ed Pinckney	.02	.10
❑ 10 Dale Ellis	.02	.10
❑ 11 Chuck Daly CO RC	.08	.25
❑ 12 Eric Leckner	.02	.10
❑ 13 Charles Davis	.02	.10
❑ 14 Cotton Fitzsimmons CO	.02	.10
❑ 15 Byron Scott	.02	.10
❑ 16 Derrick Chievous	.02	.10
❑ 17 Reggie Lewis RC	.08	.25
❑ 18 Jim Paxson	.02	.10
❑ 19 Tony Campbell RC	.02	.10
❑ 20 Rolando Blackman	.02	.10
❑ 21 Michael Jordan AS	.60	1.50
❑ 22 Cliff Levingston	.02	.10
❑ 23 Roy Tarpley	.02	.10
❑ 24 Harold Pressley UER	.02	.10
❑ 25 Larry Nance	.02	.10
❑ 26 Chris Morris RC	.02	.10
❑ 27 Bob Hansen UER	.02	.10
❑ 28 Mark Price AS	.02	.10
❑ 29 Reggie Miller	.25	.60
❑ 30 Karl Malone	.15	.40
❑ 31 Sidney Lowe SP	.05	.15
❑ 32 Ron Anderson	.02	.10
❑ 33 Mike Gminski	.02	.10
❑ 34 Scott Brooks RC	.02	.10
❑ 35 Kevin Johnson RC	.20	.50
❑ 36 Mark Bryant RC	.02	.10
❑ 37 Rik Smits RC	.10	.30
❑ 38 Tim Perry RC	.02	.10
❑ 39 Ralph Sampson	.02	.10
❑ 40 Danny Manning RC	.10	.30
❑ 41 Kevin Edwards RC	.02	.10
❑ 42 Paul Mokeski	.02	.10
❑ 43 Dale Ellis AS	.02	.10
❑ 44 Walter Berry	.02	.10
❑ 45 Chuck Person	.02	.10
❑ 46 Rick Mahorn SP	.05	.15
❑ 47 Joe Kleine	.02	.10
❑ 48 Brad Daugherty AS	.02	.10
❑ 49 Mike Woodson	.02	.10
❑ 50 Brad Daugherty	.02	.10
❑ 51 Shelton Jones SP	.05	.15
❑ 52 Michael Adams	.02	.10
❑ 53 Wes Unseld CO	.02	.10
❑ 54 Rex Chapman RC	.08	.25
❑ 55 Kelly Tripucka	.02	.10
❑ 56 Rickey Green	.02	.10
❑ 57 Frank Johnson SP	.05	.15
❑ 58 Johnny Newman RC	.02	.10
❑ 59 Billy Thompson	.02	.10
❑ 60 Stu Jackson CO	.02	.10
❑ 61 Walter Davis	.02	.10
❑ 62 Brian Shaw SP UER RC	.08	.25
❑ 63 Gerald Wilkins	.02	.10
❑ 64 Armon Gilliam	.02	.10
❑ 65 Maurice Cheeks SP	.08	.25
❑ 66 Jack Sikma	.02	.10
❑ 67 Harvey Grant RC	.02	.10
❑ 68 Jim Lynam CO	.02	.10
❑ 69 Clyde Drexler AS	.02	.10
❑ 70 Xavier McDaniel	.02	.10
❑ 71 Danny Young	.02	.10
❑ 72 Fennis Dembo	.02	.10
❑ 73 Mark Acres SP	.05	.15
❑ 74 Brad Lohaus RC SP	.05	.15
❑ 75 Manute Bol	.02	.10
❑ 76 Purvis Short	.02	.10
❑ 77 Allen Leavell	.02	.10
❑ 78 Johnny Dawkins SP	.05	.15
❑ 79 Paul Pressey	.02	.10
❑ 80 Patrick Ewing	.08	.25
❑ 81 Bill Wennington RC	.08	.25
❑ 82 Danny Schayes	.02	.10
❑ 83 Derek Smith	.02	.10
❑ 84 Moses Malone AS	.02	.10
❑ 85 Jeff Malone	.02	.10
❑ 86 Otis Smith SP RC	.05	.15
❑ 87 Trent Tucker	.02	.10
❑ 88 Robert Reid	.02	.10
❑ 89 John Paxson	.02	.10
❑ 90 Chris Mullin	.08	.25
❑ 91 Tom Garrick	.02	.10
❑ 92 Willis Reed CO SP	.08	.25
❑ 93 Dave Corzine SP	.05	.15
❑ 94 Mark Alarie	.02	.10
❑ 95 Mark Aguirre	.02	.10
❑ 96 Charles Barkley AS	.07	.20
❑ 97 Sidney Green SP	.05	.15
❑ 98 Kevin Willis	.02	.10
❑ 99 Dave Hoppen	.02	.10
❑ 100 Terry Cummings SP	.08	.25
❑ 101 Dwayne Washington SP	.05	.15
❑ 102 Larry Brown CO	.02	.10
❑ 103 Kevin Duckworth	.02	.10
❑ 104 Uwe Blab SP	.05	.15
❑ 105 Terry Porter	.02	.10
❑ 106 Craig Ehlo RC	.02	.10
❑ 107 Don Casey CO	.02	.10
❑ 108 Pat Riley CO	.08	.25
❑ 109 John Salley	.02	.10
❑ 110 Charles Barkley	.15	.40
❑ 111 Sam Bowie SP	.05	.15
❑ 112 Earl Cureton	.02	.10
❑ 113 Craig Hodges UER	.02	.10
❑ 114 Benoit Benjamin	.02	.10
❑ 115A Spud Webb 9/27/89	.08	.25
❑ 115B Spud Webb 9/26/85	.02	.10
❑ 116 Karl Malone AS	.08	.25
❑ 117 Sleepy Floyd	.02	.10
❑ 118 Hot Rod Williams	.02	.10
❑ 119 Michael Holton	.02	.10
❑ 120 Alex English	.02	.10
❑ 121 Dennis Johnson	.02	.10
❑ 122 Wayne Cooper SP	.05	.15
❑ 123A Don Chaney CO	.02	.10
❑ 123B Don Chaney CO	.02	.10
❑ 124 A.C.Green	.02	.10
❑ 125 Adrian Dantley	.02	.10
❑ 126 Del Harris CO	.02	.10
❑ 127 Dick Harter CO	.02	.10
❑ 128 Reggie Williams RC	.02	.10
❑ 129 Bill Hanzlik	.02	.10
❑ 130 Dominique Wilkins	.08	.25
❑ 131 Herb Williams	.02	.10
❑ 132 Steve Johnson SP	.05	.15
❑ 133 Alex English AS	.02	.10
❑ 134 Darrell Walker	.02	.10
❑ 135 Bill Laimbeer	.02	.10
❑ 136 Fred Roberts RC	.02	.10
❑ 137 Hersey Hawkins RC	.10	.30
❑ 138 David Robinson SP RC	4.00	10.00
❑ 139 Brad Sellers SP	.05	.15
❑ 140 John Stockton	.25	.60
❑ 141 Grant Long RC	.02	.10
❑ 142 Marc Iavaroni SP	.05	.15
❑ 143 Steve Alford SP RC	.08	.25
❑ 144 Jeff Lamp SP	.05	.15
❑ 145 Buck Williams SP	.08	.25
❑ 146 Mark Jackson AS	.02	.10
❑ 147 Jim Petersen	.02	.10
❑ 148 Steve Stipanovich SP	.05	.15
❑ 149 Sam Vincent SP RC	.05	.15
❑ 150 Larry Bird	.40	1.00
❑ 151 Jon Koncak RC	.02	.10
❑ 152 Olden Polynice RC	.02	.10
❑ 153 Randy Breuer	.02	.10
❑ 154 John Battle RC	.02	.10
❑ 155 Mark Eaton	.02	.10
❑ 156 Kevin McHale AS UER	.02	.10
❑ 157 Jerry Sichting SP	.05	.15
❑ 158 Pat Cummings SP	.05	.15
❑ 159 Patrick Ewing AS	.02	.10
❑ 160 Mark Price	.02	.10
❑ 161 Jerry Reynolds CO	.02	.10
❑ 162 Ken Norman RC	.02	.10
❑ 163 John Bagley SP UER	.05	.15
❑ 164 Christian Welp SP	.05	.15
❑ 165 Reggie Theus SP	.08	.25
❑ 166 Magic Johnson AS	.15	.40
❑ 167 John Long UER	.02	.10
❑ 168 Larry Smith SP	.05	.15
❑ 169 Charles Shackleford RC	.02	.10
❑ 170 Tom Chambers	.02	.10
❑ 171A John MacLeod CO SP	.05	.15
❑ 171B John MacLeod CO	.02	.10
❑ 172 Ron Rothstein CO	.02	.10
❑ 173 Joe Wolf	.02	.10
❑ 174 Mark Eaton AS	.02	.10
❑ 175 Jon Sundvold	.02	.10
❑ 176 Scott Hastings SP	.05	.15
❑ 177 Isiah Thomas AS	.02	.10
❑ 178 Hakeem Olajuwon AS	.08	.25
❑ 179 Mike Fratello CO	.02	.10
❑ 180 Hakeem Olajuwon	.15	.40
❑ 181 Randolph Keys	.02	.10
❑ 182 Richard Anderson UER	.02	.10
❑ 183 Dan Majerle RC	.10	.30
❑ 184 Derek Harper	.02	.10
❑ 185 Robert Parish	.02	.10
❑ 186 Ricky Berry SP	.05	.15
❑ 187 Michael Cooper	.02	.10
❑ 188 Vinnie Johnson	.02	.10
❑ 189 James Donaldson	.02	.10
❑ 190 Clyde Drexler	.08	.25
❑ 191 Jay Vincent SP	.05	.15
❑ 192 Nate McMillan	.02	.10
❑ 193 Kevin Duckworth AS	.02	.10
❑ 194 Ledell Eackles RC	.02	.10
❑ 195 Eddie Johnson	.02	.10
❑ 196 Terry Teagle	.02	.10
❑ 197 Tom Chambers AS	.02	.10
❑ 198 Joe Barry Carroll	.02	.10
❑ 199 Dennis Hopson RC	.02	.10
❑ 200 Michael Jordan	1.25	3.00
❑ 201 Jerome Lane RC	.02	.10
❑ 202 Greg Kite RC	.02	.10
❑ 203 David Rivers SP	.05	.15
❑ 204 Sylvester Gray	.02	.10
❑ 205 Ron Harper	.02	.10
❑ 206 Frank Brickowski	.02	.10
❑ 207 Rory Sparrow	.02	.10
❑ 208 Gerald Henderson	.02	.10
❑ 209 Rod Higgins UER	.02	.10
❑ 210 James Worthy	.08	.25
❑ 211 Dennis Rodman	.40	1.00
❑ 212 Ricky Pierce	.02	.10
❑ 213 Charles Oakley	.02	.10
❑ 214 Steve Colter	.02	.10
❑ 215 Danny Ainge	.02	.10
❑ 216 Lenny Wilkens CO UER	.02	.10
❑ 217 Larry Nance AS	.02	.10
❑ 218 Muggsy Bogues	.02	.10
❑ 219 James Worthy AS	.02	.10
❑ 220 Lafayette Lever	.02	.10
❑ 221 Quintin Dailey SP	.05	.15
❑ 222 Lester Conner	.02	.10
❑ 223 Jose Ortiz	.02	.10
❑ 224 Micheal Williams SP UER RC	.08	.25
❑ 225 Wayman Tisdale	.02	.10
❑ 226 Mike Sanders SP	.05	.15
❑ 227 Jim Farmer SP	.05	.15

❑ 228 Mark West	.02	.10
❑ 229 Jeff Hornacek RC	.10	.30
❑ 230 Chris Mullin AS	.02	.10
❑ 231 Vern Fleming	.02	.10
❑ 232 Kenny Smith	.02	.10
❑ 233 Derrick McKey	.02	.10
❑ 234 Dominique Wilkins AS	.02	.10
❑ 235 Willie Anderson RC	.02	.10
❑ 236 Keith Lee SP	.05	.15
❑ 237 Buck Johnson RC	.02	.10
❑ 238 Randy Wittman	.02	.10
❑ 239 Terry Catledge SP	.05	.15
❑ 240 Bernard King	.02	.10
❑ 241 Darrell Griffith	.02	.10
❑ 242 Horace Grant	.02	.10
❑ 243 Rony Seikaly RC	.08	.25
❑ 244 Scottie Pippen	.60	1.50
❑ 245 Michael Cage UER	.02	.10
❑ 246 Kurt Rambis	.02	.10
❑ 247 Morlon Wiley SP RC	.05	.15
❑ 248 Ronnie Grandison	.02	.10
❑ 249 Scott Skiles SP RC	.08	.25
❑ 250 Isiah Thomas	.08	.25
❑ 251 Thurl Bailey	.02	.10
❑ 252 Doc Rivers	.02	.10
❑ 253 Stuart Gray SP	.05	.15
❑ 254 John Williams	.02	.10
❑ 255 Bill Cartwright	.02	.10
❑ 256 Terry Cummings AS	.02	.10
❑ 257 Rodney McCray	.02	.10
❑ 258 Larry Krystkowiak RC	.02	.10
❑ 259 Will Perdue RC	.02	.10
❑ 260 Mitch Richmond RC	.50	1.25
❑ 261 Blair Rasmussen	.02	.10
❑ 262 Charles Smith RC	.08	.25
❑ 263 Tyrone Corbin SP RC	.05	.15
❑ 264 Kelvin Upshaw	.02	.10
❑ 265 Otis Thorpe	.02	.10
❑ 266 Phil Jackson CO	.08	.25
❑ 267 Jerry Sloan CO	.02	.10
❑ 268 John Shasky	.02	.10
❑ 269A B. Bickerstaff CO SP	.05	.15
❑ 269B B. Bickerstaff CO	.02	.10
❑ 270 Magic Johnson	.30	.75
❑ 271 Vernon Maxwell RC	.08	.25
❑ 272 Tim McCormick	.02	.10
❑ 273 Don Nelson CO	.02	.10
❑ 274 Gary Grant RC	.02	.10
❑ 275 Sidney Moncrief SP	.05	.15
❑ 276 Roy Hinson	.02	.10
❑ 277 Jimmy Rodgers CO	.02	.10
❑ 278 Antoine Carr	.02	.10
❑ 279A Orlando Woolridge SP	.05	.15
❑ 279B Orlando Woolridge	.02	.10
❑ 280 Kevin McHale	.08	.25
❑ 281 LaSalle Thompson	.02	.10
❑ 282 Detlef Schrempf	.02	.10
❑ 283 Doug Moe CO	.02	.10
❑ 284A James Edwards	.02	.10
❑ 284B James Edwards	.02	.10
❑ 285 Jerome Kersey	.02	.10
❑ 286 Sam Perkins	.02	.10
❑ 287 Sedale Threatt	.02	.10
❑ 288 Tim Kempton SP	.05	.15
❑ 289 Mark McNamara	.02	.10
❑ 290 Moses Malone	.08	.25
❑ 291 Rick Adelman CO UER	.02	.10
❑ 292 Dick Versace CO	.02	.10
❑ 293 Alton Lister SP	.05	.15
❑ 294 Winston Garland	.02	.10
❑ 295 Kiki Vandeweghe	.02	.10
❑ 296 Brad Davis	.02	.10
❑ 297 John Stockton AS	.08	.25
❑ 298 Jay Humphries	.02	.10
❑ 299 Dell Curry	.02	.10
❑ 300 Mark Jackson	.02	.10
❑ 301 Morlon Wiley	.02	.10
❑ 302 Reggie Theus	.02	.10
❑ 303 Otis Smith	.02	.10
❑ 304 Tod Murphy RC	.02	.10
❑ 305 Sidney Green	.02	.10
❑ 306 Shelton Jones	.02	.10
❑ 307 Mark Acres	.02	.10
❑ 308 Terry Catledge	.02	.10
❑ 309 Larry Smith	.02	.10
❑ 310 David Robinson IA	.75	2.00
❑ 311 Johnny Dawkins	.02	.10
❑ 312 Terry Cummings	.02	.10
❑ 313 Sidney Lowe	.02	.10

❑ 314 Bill Musselman CO	.02	.10
❑ 315 Buck Williams	.02	.10
❑ 316 Mel Turpin	.02	.10
❑ 317 Scott Hastings	.02	.10
❑ 318 Scott Skiles	.02	.10
❑ 319 Tyrone Corbin	.02	.10
❑ 320 Maurice Cheeks	.02	.10
❑ 321 Matt Guokas CO	.02	.10
❑ 322 Jeff Turner	.02	.10
❑ 323 David Wingate	.02	.10
❑ 324 Steve Johnson	.02	.10
❑ 325 Alton Lister	.02	.10
❑ 326 Ken Bannister	.02	.10
❑ 327 Bill Fitch CO UER	.02	.10
❑ 328 Sam Vincent	.02	.10
❑ 329 Larry Drew	.02	.10
❑ 330 Rick Mahorn	.02	.10
❑ 331 Christian Welp	.02	.10
❑ 332 Brad Lohaus	.02	.10
❑ 333 Frank Johnson	.02	.10
❑ 334 Jim Farmer	.02	.10
❑ 335 Wayne Cooper	.02	.10
❑ 336 Mike Brown RC	.02	.10
❑ 337 Sam Bowie	.02	.10
❑ 338 Kevin Gamble RC	.02	.10
❑ 339 Jerry Ice Reynolds RC	.02	.10
❑ 340 Mike Sanders	.02	.10
❑ 341 Bill Jones UER	.02	.10
❑ 342 Greg Anderson	.02	.10
❑ 343 Dave Corzine	.02	.10
❑ 344 Micheal Williams UER	.02	.10
❑ 345 Jay Vincent	.02	.10
❑ 346 David Rivers	.02	.10
❑ 347 Caldwell Jones UER	.02	.10
❑ 348 Brad Sellers	.02	.10
❑ 349 Scott Roth	.02	.10
❑ 350 Alvin Robertson	.02	.10
❑ 351 Steve Kerr RC	.20	.50
❑ 352 Stuart Gray	.02	.10
❑ 353A Pistons Champions SP	1.50	4.00
❑ 353B Pistons Champions	.20	.50

1990-91 Hoops

❑ COMPLETE SET (440)	7.50	15.00
❑ COMPLETE SERIES 1 (336)	5.00	10.00
❑ COMPLETE SERIES 2 (104)	2.50	5.00
❑ COMMON CARD (1-440)	.04	.10
❑ COMMON SP	.02	.10
❑ 1 Charles Barkley AS SP	.08	.25
❑ 2 Larry Bird AS SP	.25	.60
❑ 3 Joe Dumars AS SP	.05	.15
❑ 4 Patrick Ewing AS SP	.05	.15
❑ 5 Michael Jordan AS SP	.75	2.00
❑ 6 Kevin McHale AS SP	.02	.10
❑ 7 Reggie Miller AS SP	.05	.15
❑ 8 Robert Parish AS SP	.02	.10
❑ 9 Scottie Pippen AS SP	.25	.60
❑ 10 Dennis Rodman AS SP	.15	.40
❑ 11 Isiah Thomas AS SP	.05	.15
❑ 12 Dominique Wilkins AS SP	.05	.15
❑ 13A AS CL: ERR NNO SP	.08	.25
❑ 13B AS CL: COR SP	.02	.10
❑ 14 Rolando Blackman AS SP	.02	.10
❑ 15 Tom Chambers AS SP	.02	.10
❑ 16 Clyde Drexler AS SP	.02	.10
❑ 17 A.C. Green AS SP	.02	.10
❑ 18 Magic Johnson AS SP	.20	.50
❑ 19 Kevin Johnson AS SP	.05	.15
❑ 20 Lafayette Lever AS SP	.02	.10
❑ 21 Karl Malone AS SP	.08	.25
❑ 22 Chris Mullin AS SP	.05	.15
❑ 23 Hakeem Olajuwon AS SP	.08	.25
❑ 24 David Robinson AS SP	.20	.50
❑ 25 John Stockton AS SP	.07	.20
❑ 26 James Worthy AS SP	.05	.15
❑ 27 John Battle	.02	.10

❑ 28 Jon Koncak	.02	.10
❑ 29 Cliff Levingston SP	.02	.10
❑ 30 John Long SP	.02	.10
❑ 31 Moses Malone	.05	.15
❑ 32 Doc Rivers	.02	.10
❑ 33 Kenny Smith SP	.02	.10
❑ 34 Alexander Volkov	.02	.10
❑ 35 Spud Webb	.02	.10
❑ 36 Dominique Wilkins	.05	.15
❑ 37 Kevin Willis	.02	.10
❑ 38 John Bagley	.02	.10
❑ 39 Larry Bird	.25	.60
❑ 40 Kevin Gamble	.02	.10
❑ 41 Dennis Johnson SP	.02	.10
❑ 42 Joe Kleine	.02	.10
❑ 43 Reggie Lewis	.02	.10
❑ 44 Kevin McHale	.02	.10
❑ 45 Robert Parish	.02	.10
❑ 46 Jim Paxson SP	.02	.10
❑ 47 Ed Pinckney	.02	.10
❑ 48 Brian Shaw	.05	.15
❑ 49 Richard Anderson SP	.02	.10
❑ 50 Muggsy Bogues	.02	.10
❑ 51 Rex Chapman	.05	.15
❑ 52 Dell Curry	.02	.10
❑ 53 Kenny Gattison RC	.02	.10
❑ 54 Armon Gilliam	.02	.10
❑ 55 Dave Hoppen	.02	.10
❑ 56 Randolph Keys	.02	.10
❑ 57 J.R.Reid RC	.02	.10
❑ 58 Robert Reid SP	.02	.10
❑ 59 Kelly Tripucka	.02	.10
❑ 60 B.J.Armstrong RC	.02	.10
❑ 61 Bill Cartwright	.02	.10
❑ 62 Charles Davis SP	.02	.10
❑ 63 Horace Grant	.02	.10
❑ 64 Craig Hodges	.02	.10
❑ 65 Michael Jordan	.75	2.00
❑ 66 Stacey King RC	.02	.10
❑ 67 John Paxson	.02	.10
❑ 68 Will Perdue	.02	.10
❑ 69 Scottie Pippen	.25	.60
❑ 70 Winston Bennett	.02	.10
❑ 71 Chucky Brown RC	.02	.10
❑ 72 Derrick Chievous	.02	.10
❑ 73 Brad Daugherty	.02	.10
❑ 74 Craig Ehlo	.02	.10
❑ 75 Steve Kerr	.05	.15
❑ 76 Paul Mokeski SP	.02	.10
❑ 77 John Morton	.02	.10
❑ 78 Larry Nance	.02	.10
❑ 79 Mark Price	.02	.10
❑ 80 Hot Rod Williams	.02	.10
❑ 81 Steve Alford	.02	.10
❑ 82 Rolando Blackman	.02	.10
❑ 83 Adrian Dantley SP	.02	.10
❑ 84 Brad Davis	.02	.10
❑ 85 James Donaldson	.02	.10
❑ 86 Derek Harper	.02	.10
❑ 87 Sam Perkins SP	.02	.10
❑ 88 Roy Tarpley	.02	.10
❑ 89 Bill Wennington SP	.02	.10
❑ 90 Herb Williams	.02	.10
❑ 91 Michael Adams	.02	.10
❑ 92 Joe Barry Carroll SP	.02	.10
❑ 93 Walter Davis UER	.02	.10
❑ 94 Alex English SP	.02	.10
❑ 95 Bill Hanzlik	.02	.10
❑ 96 Jerome Lane	.02	.10
❑ 97 Lafayette Lever SP	.02	.10
❑ 98 Todd Lichti RC	.02	.10
❑ 99 Blair Rasmussen	.02	.10
❑ 100 Danny Schayes SP	.02	.10
❑ 101 Mark Aguirre	.02	.10
❑ 102 William Bedford RC	.02	.10
❑ 103 Joe Dumars	.05	.15
❑ 104 James Edwards	.02	.10
❑ 105 Scott Hastings	.02	.10
❑ 106 Gerald Henderson SP	.02	.10
❑ 107 Vinnie Johnson	.02	.10
❑ 108 Bill Laimbeer	.02	.10
❑ 109 Dennis Rodman	.15	.40
❑ 110 John Salley	.02	.10
❑ 111 Isiah Thomas	.05	.15
❑ 112 Manute Bol SP	.02	.10
❑ 113 Tim Hardaway RC	.40	1.00
❑ 114 Rod Higgins	.02	.10
❑ 115 Sarun.Marciulionis RC	.02	.10
❑ 116 Chris Mullin	.05	.15

❑ 117 Jim Petersen	.02	.10
❑ 118 Mitch Richmond	.07	.20
❑ 119 Mike Smrek	.02	.10
❑ 120 Terry Teagle SP	.02	.10
❑ 121 Tom Tolbert RC	.02	.10
❑ 122 Christian Welp SP	.02	.10
❑ 123 Byron Dinkins SP	.02	.10
❑ 124 Eric(Sleepy) Floyd	.02	.10
❑ 125 Buck Johnson	.02	.10
❑ 126 Vernon Maxwell	.02	.10
❑ 127 Hakeem Olajuwon	.08	.25
❑ 128 Larry Smith	.02	.10
❑ 129 Otis Thorpe	.02	.10
❑ 130 Mitchell Wiggins SP	.02	.10
❑ 131 Mike Woodson	.02	.10
❑ 132 Greg Dreiling RC	.02	.10
❑ 133 Vern Fleming	.02	.10
❑ 134 Rickey Green SP	.02	.10
❑ 135 Reggie Miller	.07	.20
❑ 136 Chuck Person	.02	.10
❑ 137 Mike Sanders	.02	.10
❑ 138 Detlef Schrempf	.02	.10
❑ 139 Rik Smits	.05	.15
❑ 140 LaSalle Thompson	.02	.10
❑ 141 Randy Wittman	.02	.10
❑ 142 Benoit Benjamin	.02	.10
❑ 143 Winston Garland	.02	.10
❑ 144 Tom Garrick	.02	.10
❑ 145 Gary Grant	.02	.10
❑ 146 Ron Harper	.02	.10
❑ 147 Danny Manning	.02	.10
❑ 148 Jeff Martin	.02	.10
❑ 149 Ken Norman	.02	.10
❑ 150 David Rivers SP	.02	.10
❑ 151 Charles Smith	.02	.10
❑ 152 Joe Wolf SP	.02	.10
❑ 153 Michael Cooper SP	.02	.10
❑ 154 Vlade Divac RC	.15	.40
❑ 155 Larry Drew	.02	.10
❑ 156 A.C. Green	.02	.10
❑ 157 Magic Johnson	.20	.50
❑ 158 Mark McNamara SP	.02	.10
❑ 159 Byron Scott	.02	.10
❑ 160 Mychal Thompson	.02	.10
❑ 161 Jay Vincent SP	.02	.10
❑ 162 Orlando Woolridge SP	.02	.10
❑ 163 James Worthy	.05	.15
❑ 164 Sherman Douglas RC	.02	.10
❑ 165 Kevin Edwards	.02	.10
❑ 166 Tellis Frank SP	.02	.10
❑ 167 Grant Long	.02	.10
❑ 168 Glen Rice RC	.25	.60
❑ 169A Rony Seikaly Athens	.02	.10
❑ 169B Rony Seikaly Beirut	.02	.10
❑ 170 Rory Sparrow SP	.02	.10
❑ 171A Jon Sundvold	.02	.10
❑ 171B Billy Thompson	.02	.10
❑ 172A Billy Thompson	.02	.10
❑ 172B Jon Sundvold	.02	.10
❑ 173 Greg Anderson	.02	.10
❑ 174 Jeff Grayer RC	.02	.10
❑ 175 Jay Humphries	.02	.10
❑ 176 Frank Kornet	.02	.10
❑ 177 Larry Krystkowiak	.02	.10
❑ 178 Brad Lohaus	.02	.10
❑ 179 Ricky Pierce	.02	.10
❑ 180 Paul Pressey SP	.02	.10
❑ 181 Fred Roberts	.02	.10
❑ 182 Alvin Robertson	.02	.10
❑ 183 Jack Sikma	.02	.10
❑ 184 Randy Breuer	.02	.10
❑ 185 Tony Campbell	.02	.10
❑ 186 Tyrone Corbin	.02	.10
❑ 187 Sidney Lowe SP	.02	.10
❑ 188 Sam Mitchell RC	.02	.10
❑ 189 Tod Murphy	.02	.10
❑ 190 Pooh Richardson RC	.02	.10
❑ 191 Scott Roth SP	.02	.10
❑ 192 Brad Sellers SP	.02	.10
❑ 193 Mookie Blaylock RC	.08	.25
❑ 194 Sam Bowie	.02	.10
❑ 195 Lester Conner	.02	.10
❑ 196 Derrick Gervin	.02	.10
❑ 197 Jack Haley RC	.02	.10
❑ 198 Roy Hinson	.02	.10
❑ 199 Dennis Hopson SP	.02	.10
❑ 200 Chris Morris	.02	.10
❑ 201 Purvis Short SP	.02	.10
❑ 202 Maurice Cheeks	.02	.10
❑ 203 Patrick Ewing	.05	.15
❑ 204 Stuart Gray	.02	.10
❑ 205 Mark Jackson	.02	.10
❑ 206 Johnny Newman SP	.02	.10
❑ 207 Charles Oakley	.02	.10
❑ 208 Trent Tucker	.02	.10
❑ 209 Kiki Vandeweghe	.02	.10
❑ 210 Kenny Walker	.02	.10
❑ 211 Eddie Lee Wilkins	.02	.10
❑ 212 Gerald Wilkins	.02	.10
❑ 213 Mark Acres	.02	.10
❑ 214 Nick Anderson RC	.08	.25
❑ 215 Michael Ansley UER	.02	.10
❑ 216 Terry Catledge	.02	.10
❑ 217 Dave Corzine SP	.02	.10
❑ 218 Sidney Green SP	.02	.10
❑ 219 Jerry Reynolds	.02	.10
❑ 220 Scott Skiles	.02	.10
❑ 221 Otis Smith	.02	.10
❑ 222 Reggie Theus SP	.02	.10
❑ 223A S.Vincent w/M.Jordan	1.50	4.00
❑ 223B Sam Vincent	.02	.10
❑ 224 Ron Anderson	.02	.10
❑ 225 Charles Barkley	.08	.25
❑ 226 Scott Brooks SP UER	.02	.10
❑ 227 Johnny Dawkins	.02	.10
❑ 228 Mike Gminski	.02	.10
❑ 229 Hersey Hawkins	.02	.10
❑ 230 Rick Mahorn	.02	.10
❑ 231 Derek Smith SP	.02	.10
❑ 232 Bob Thornton	.02	.10
❑ 233 Kenny Battle RC	.02	.10
❑ 234A Tom Chambers Forward	.02	.10
❑ 234B Tom Chambers Guard	.02	.10
❑ 235 Greg Grant RC SP	.02	.10
❑ 236 Jeff Hornacek	.02	.10
❑ 237 Eddie Johnson	.02	.10
❑ 238A Kevin Johnson Guard	.05	.15
❑ 238B Kevin Johnson Forward	.05	.15
❑ 239 Dan Majerle	.05	.15
❑ 240 Tim Perry	.02	.10
❑ 241 Kurt Rambis	.02	.10
❑ 242 Mark West	.02	.10
❑ 243 Mark Bryant	.02	.10
❑ 244 Wayne Cooper	.02	.10
❑ 245 Clyde Drexler	.05	.15
❑ 246 Kevin Duckworth	.02	.10
❑ 247 Jerome Kersey	.02	.10
❑ 248 Drazen Petrovic RC	.02	.10
❑ 249A Terry Porter ERR	.20	.50
❑ 249B Terry Porter COR	.02	.10
❑ 250 Clifford Robinson RC	.08	.25
❑ 251 Buck Williams	.02	.10
❑ 252 Danny Young	.02	.10
❑ 253 Danny Ainge SP UER	.02	.10
❑ 254 Randy Allen SP	.02	.10
❑ 255 Antoine Carr	.02	.10
❑ 256 Vinny Del Negro SP	.02	.10
❑ 257 Pervis Ellison RC SP	.02	.10
❑ 258 Greg Kite SP	.02	.10
❑ 259 Rodney McCray SP	.02	.10
❑ 260 Harold Pressley SP	.02	.10
❑ 261 Ralph Sampson	.02	.10
❑ 262 Wayman Tisdale	.02	.10
❑ 263 Willie Anderson	.02	.10
❑ 264 Uwe Blab SP	.02	.10
❑ 265 Frank Brickowski SP	.02	.10
❑ 266 Terry Cummings	.02	.10
❑ 267 Sean Elliott RC	.10	.30
❑ 268 Caldwell Jones SP	.02	.10
❑ 269 Johnny Moore SP	.02	.10
❑ 270 David Robinson	.20	.50
❑ 271 Rod Strickland	.05	.15
❑ 272 Reggie Williams	.02	.10
❑ 273 David Wingate SP	.02	.10
❑ 274 Dana Barros RC	.05	.15
❑ 275 Michael Cage UER	.02	.10
❑ 276 Quintin Dailey	.02	.10
❑ 277 Dale Ellis	.02	.10
❑ 278 Steve Johnson SP	.02	.10
❑ 279 Shawn Kemp RC	.60	1.50
❑ 280 Xavier McDaniel	.02	.10
❑ 281 Derrick McKey	.02	.10
❑ 282 Nate McMillan	.02	.10
❑ 283 Olden Polynice	.02	.10
❑ 284 Sedale Threatt	.02	.10
❑ 285 Thurl Bailey	.02	.10
❑ 286 Mike Brown	.02	.10
❑ 287 Mark Eaton UER	.02	.10
❑ 288 Blue Edwards RC	.02	.10
❑ 289 Darrell Griffith	.02	.10
❑ 290 Bobby Hansen SP	.02	.10
❑ 291 Eric Leckner SP	.02	.10
❑ 292 Karl Malone	.08	.25
❑ 293 Delaney Rudd	.02	.10
❑ 294 John Stockton	.07	.20
❑ 295 Mark Alarie	.02	.10
❑ 296 Ledell Eackles SP	.02	.10
❑ 297 Harvey Grant	.02	.10
❑ 298A Tom Hammonds No Star RC	.02	.10
❑ 298B Tom Hammonds Star RC	.02	.10
❑ 299 Charles Jones	.02	.10
❑ 300 Bernard King	.02	.10
❑ 301 Jeff Malone SP	.02	.10
❑ 302 Mel Turpin SP	.02	.10
❑ 303 Darrell Walker	.02	.10
❑ 304 John Williams	.02	.10
❑ 305 Bob Weiss CO	.02	.10
❑ 306 Chris Ford CO	.02	.10
❑ 307 Gene Littles CO	.02	.10
❑ 308 Phil Jackson CO	.05	.15
❑ 309 Lenny Wilkens CO	.02	.10
❑ 310 Richie Adubato CO	.02	.10
❑ 311 Doug Moe CO SP	.02	.10
❑ 312 Chuck Daly CO	.02	.10
❑ 313 Don Nelson CO	.02	.10
❑ 314 Don Chaney CO	.02	.10
❑ 315 Dick Versace CO	.02	.10
❑ 316 Mike Schuler CO	.02	.10
❑ 317 Pat Riley CO SP	.05	.15
❑ 318 Ron Rothstein CO	.02	.10
❑ 319 Del Harris CO	.02	.10
❑ 320 Bill Musselman CO	.02	.10
❑ 321 Bill Fitch CO	.02	.10
❑ 322 Stu Jackson CO	.02	.10
❑ 323 Matt Guokas CO	.02	.10
❑ 324 Jim Lynam CO	.02	.10
❑ 325 Cotton Fitzsimmons CO	.02	.10
❑ 326 Rick Adelman CO	.02	.10
❑ 327 Dick Motta CO	.02	.10
❑ 328 Larry Brown CO	.02	.10
❑ 329 K.C. Jones CO	.02	.10
❑ 330 Jerry Sloan CO	.02	.10
❑ 331 Wes Unseld CO	.02	.10
❑ 332 Checklist 1 SP	.02	.10
❑ 333 Checklist 2 SP	.02	.10
❑ 334 Checklist 3 SP	.02	.10
❑ 335 Checklist 4 SP	.02	.10
❑ 336 Danny Ferry SP RC	.08	.25
❑ 337 NBA Final Game 1	.05	.15
❑ 338 NBA Final Game 2	.05	.15
❑ 339 NBA Final Game 3	.05	.15
❑ 340 NBA Final Game 4	.02	.10
❑ 341A Pistons Win ERR w/o	.02	.10
❑ 341B Pistons Win COR Sports	.02	.10
❑ 342 Pistons Back to Back UER	.02	.10
❑ 343 K.C. Jones CO	.02	.10
❑ 344 Wes Unseld CO	.02	.10
❑ 345 Don Nelson CO	.02	.10
❑ 346 Bob Weiss CO	.02	.10
❑ 347 Chris Ford CO	.02	.10
❑ 348 Phil Jackson CO	.05	.15
❑ 349 Lenny Wilkens CO	.02	.10
❑ 350 Don Chaney CO	.02	.10
❑ 351 Mike Dunleavy CO	.02	.10
❑ 352 Matt Guokas CO	.02	.10
❑ 353 Rick Adelman CO	.02	.10
❑ 354 Jerry Sloan CO	.02	.10
❑ 355 Dominique Wilkins TC	.02	.10
❑ 356 Larry Bird TC	.10	.30
❑ 357 Rex Chapman TC	.02	.10
❑ 358 Michael Jordan TC	.40	1.00
❑ 359 Mark Price TC	.02	.10
❑ 360 Rolando Blackman TC	.02	.10
❑ 361 Michael Adams TC UER	.02	.10
❑ 362 Joe Dumars TC	.02	.10
❑ 363 Chris Mullin TC	.02	.10
❑ 364 Hakeem Olajuwon TC	.05	.15
❑ 365 Reggie Miller TC	.05	.15
❑ 366 Danny Manning TC	.02	.10
❑ 367 Magic Johnson TC	.08	.25
❑ 368 Rony Seikaly TC	.02	.10
❑ 369 Alvin Robertson TC	.02	.10
❑ 370 Pooh Richardson TC	.02	.10
❑ 371 Chris Morris TC	.02	.10
❑ 372 Patrick Ewing TC	.02	.10
❑ 373 Nick Anderson TC	.05	.15
❑ 374 Charles Barkley TC	.05	.15

❑ 375 Kevin Johnson TC	.02	.10
❑ 376 Clyde Drexler TC	.02	.10
❑ 377 Wayman Tisdale TC	.02	.10
❑ 378 David Robinson TC	.08	.25
❑ 378B David Robinson TC half	.10	.30
❑ 379 Xavier McDaniel TC	.02	.10
❑ 380 Karl Malone TC	.05	.15
❑ 381 Bernard King TC	.02	.10
❑ 382 M.Jordan Playground	.40	1.00
❑ 383 Karl Malone Lights	.05	.15
❑ 384 V.Divac/Marciulionis	.02	.10
❑ 385 M.Johnson/M.Jordan	.40	1.00
❑ 386 Johnny Newman	.02	.10
❑ 387 Dell Curry	.02	.10
❑ 388 Patrick Ewing DFO	.02	.10
❑ 389 Isiah Thomas DFO	.02	.10
❑ 390 Derrick Coleman LS RC	.10	.30
❑ 391 Gary Payton LS RC	.60	1.50
❑ 392 Chris Jackson LS RC	.02	.10
❑ 393 Dennis Scott LS RC	.07	.20
❑ 394 Kendall Gill LS RC	.10	.30
❑ 395 Felton Spencer LS RC	.02	.10
❑ 396 Lionel Simmons LS RC	.02	.10
❑ 397 Bo Kimble LS RC	.02	.10
❑ 398 Willie Burton LS RC	.02	.10
❑ 399 Rumeal Robinson LS RC	.02	.10
❑ 400 Tyrone Hill LS RC	.02	.10
❑ 401 Tim McCormick U	.02	.10
❑ 402 Sidney Moncrief U	.02	.10
❑ 403 Johnny Newman U	.02	.10
❑ 404 Dennis Hopson U	.02	.10
❑ 405 Cliff Levingston U	.02	.10
❑ 406A Danny Ferry U ERR	.10	.30
❑ 406B Danny Ferry U COR	.05	.15
❑ 407 Alex English U	.02	.10
❑ 408 Lafayette Lever U	.02	.10
❑ 409 Rodney McCray U	.02	.10
❑ 410 Mike Dunleavy U CO	.02	.10
❑ 411 Orlando Woolridge U	.02	.10
❑ 412 Joe Wolf U	.02	.10
❑ 413 Tree Rollins U	.02	.10
❑ 414 Kenny Smith U	.02	.10
❑ 415 Sam Perkins U	.02	.10
❑ 416 Terry Teagle U	.02	.10
❑ 417 Frank Brickowski U	.02	.10
❑ 418 Danny Schayes U	.02	.10
❑ 419 Scott Brooks U	.02	.10
❑ 420 Reggie Theus U	.02	.10
❑ 421 Greg Grant U	.02	.10
❑ 422 Paul Westhead U CO	.02	.10
❑ 423 Greg Kite U	.02	.10
❑ 424 Manute Bol U	.02	.10
❑ 425 Rickey Green U	.02	.10
❑ 426 Ed Nealy U	.02	.10
❑ 427 Danny Ainge U	.02	.10
❑ 428 Bobby Hansen U	.02	.10
❑ 429 Eric Leckner U	.02	.10
❑ 430 Rory Sparrow U	.02	.10
❑ 431 Bill Wennington U	.02	.10
❑ 432 Paul Pressey U	.02	.10
❑ 433 David Greenwood U	.02	.10
❑ 434 Mark McNamara U	.02	.10
❑ 435 Sidney Green U	.02	.10
❑ 436 Dave Corzine U	.02	.10
❑ 437 Jeff Malone U	.02	.10
❑ 438 Pervis Ellison U	.02	.10
❑ 439 Checklist 5	.02	.10
❑ 440 Checklist 6	.02	.10
❑ NNO D.Robinson/ART NoStats	.50	1.25
❑ NNO D.Robinson/ART Stats	2.00	5.00

1991-92 Hoops

❑ COMPLETE SET (590)	12.50	25.00
❑ COMPLETE SERIES 1 (330)	5.00	10.00
❑ COMPLETE SERIES 2 (260)	7.50	15.00
❑ 1 John Battle	.02	.10
❑ 2 Moses Malone	.08	.25
❑ 3 Sidney Moncrief	.02	.10
❑ 4 Doc Rivers	.02	.10
❑ 5 Rumeal Robinson UER	.02	.10
❑ 6 Spud Webb	.02	.10
❑ 7 Dominique Wilkins	.08	.25
❑ 8 Kevin Willis	.02	.10
❑ 9 Larry Bird	.40	1.00
❑ 10 Dee Brown FHC	.02	.10
❑ 11 Kevin Gamble	.02	.10
❑ 12 Joe Kleine	.02	.10
❑ 13 Reggie Lewis	.02	.10
❑ 14 Kevin McHale	.02	.10
❑ 15 Robert Parish	.02	.10
❑ 16 Ed Pinckney	.02	.10
❑ 17 Brian Shaw	.02	.10
❑ 18 Muggsy Bogues	.02	.10
❑ 19 Rex Chapman	.02	.10
❑ 20 Dell Curry	.02	.10
❑ 21 Kendall Gill	.02	.10
❑ 22 Mike Gminski	.02	.10
❑ 23 Johnny Newman	.02	.10
❑ 24 J.R. Reid	.02	.10
❑ 25 Kelly Tripucka	.02	.10
❑ 26 B.J.Armstrong	.02	.10
❑ 27 Bill Cartwright	.02	.10
❑ 28 Horace Grant	.02	.10
❑ 29 Craig Hodges	.02	.10
❑ 30 Michael Jordan	1.25	3.00
❑ 31 Stacey King	.02	.10
❑ 32 Cliff Levingston	.02	.10
❑ 33 John Paxson	.02	.10
❑ 34 Scottie Pippen	.30	.75
❑ 35 Chucky Brown	.02	.10
❑ 36 Brad Daugherty	.02	.10
❑ 37 Craig Ehlo	.02	.10
❑ 38 Danny Ferry	.02	.10
❑ 39 Larry Nance	.02	.10
❑ 40 Mark Price	.02	.10
❑ 41 Darnell Valentine	.02	.10
❑ 42 Hot Rod Williams	.02	.10
❑ 43 Rolando Blackman	.02	.10
❑ 44 Brad Davis	.02	.10
❑ 45 James Donaldson	.02	.10
❑ 46 Derek Harper	.02	.10
❑ 47 Fat Lever	.02	.10
❑ 48 Rodney McCray	.02	.10
❑ 49 Roy Tarpley	.02	.10
❑ 50 Herb Williams	.02	.10
❑ 51 Michael Adams	.02	.10
❑ 52 Chris Jackson	.02	.10
❑ 53 Jerome Lane	.02	.10
❑ 54 Todd Lichti	.02	.10
❑ 55 Blair Rasmussen	.02	.10
❑ 56 Reggie Williams	.02	.10
❑ 57 Joe Wolf	.02	.10
❑ 58 Orlando Woolridge	.02	.10
❑ 59 Mark Aguirre	.02	.10
❑ 60 Joe Dumars	.08	.25
❑ 61 James Edwards	.02	.10
❑ 62 Vinnie Johnson	.02	.10
❑ 63 Bill Laimbeer	.02	.10
❑ 64 Dennis Rodman	.20	.50
❑ 65 John Salley	.02	.10
❑ 66 Isiah Thomas	.08	.25
❑ 67 Tim Hardaway	.15	.40
❑ 68 Rod Higgins	.02	.10
❑ 69 Tyrone Hill	.02	.10
❑ 70 Alton Lister	.02	.10
❑ 71 Sarunas Marciulionis	.02	.10
❑ 72 Chris Mullin	.08	.25
❑ 73 Mitch Richmond	.08	.25
❑ 74 Tom Tolbert	.02	.10
❑ 75 Eric(Sleepy) Floyd	.02	.10
❑ 76 Buck Johnson	.02	.10
❑ 77 Vernon Maxwell	.02	.10
❑ 78 Hakeem Olajuwon	.15	.40
❑ 79 Kenny Smith	.02	.10
❑ 80 Larry Smith	.02	.10
❑ 81 Otis Thorpe	.02	.10
❑ 82 David Wood RC	.02	.10
❑ 83 Vern Fleming	.02	.10
❑ 84 Reggie Miller	.08	.25
❑ 85 Chuck Person	.02	.10
❑ 86 Mike Sanders	.02	.10
❑ 87 Detlef Schrempf	.02	.10
❑ 88 Rik Smits	.02	.10
❑ 89 LaSalle Thompson	.02	.10
❑ 90 Micheal Williams	.02	.10
❑ 91 Winston Garland	.02	.10
❑ 92 Gary Grant	.02	.10
❑ 93 Ron Harper	.02	.10
❑ 94 Danny Manning	.02	.10
❑ 95 Jeff Martin	.02	.10
❑ 96 Ken Norman	.02	.10
❑ 97 Olden Polynice	.02	.10
❑ 98 Charles Smith	.02	.10
❑ 99 Vlade Divac	.02	.10
❑ 100 A.C. Green	.02	.10
❑ 101 Magic Johnson	.30	.75
❑ 102 Sam Perkins	.02	.10
❑ 103 Byron Scott	.02	.10
❑ 104 Terry Teagle	.02	.10
❑ 105 Mychal Thompson	.02	.10
❑ 106 James Worthy	.08	.25
❑ 107 Willie Burton	.02	.10
❑ 108 Bimbo Coles FHC	.02	.10
❑ 109 Terry Davis	.02	.10
❑ 110 Sherman Douglas	.02	.10
❑ 111 Kevin Edwards	.02	.10
❑ 112 Alec Kessler	.02	.10
❑ 113 Glen Rice	.08	.25
❑ 114 Rony Seikaly	.02	.10
❑ 115 Frank Brickowski	.02	.10
❑ 116 Dale Ellis	.02	.10
❑ 117 Jay Humphries	.02	.10
❑ 118 Brad Lohaus	.02	.10
❑ 119 Fred Roberts	.02	.10
❑ 120 Alvin Robertson	.02	.10
❑ 121 Danny Schayes	.02	.10
❑ 122 Jack Sikma	.02	.10
❑ 123 Randy Breuer	.02	.10
❑ 124 Tony Campbell	.02	.10
❑ 125 Tyrone Corbin	.02	.10
❑ 126 Gerald Glass	.02	.10
❑ 127 Sam Mitchell	.02	.10
❑ 128 Tod Murphy	.02	.10
❑ 129 Pooh Richardson	.02	.10
❑ 130 Felton Spencer	.02	.10
❑ 131 Mookie Blaylock	.02	.10
❑ 132 Sam Bowie	.02	.10
❑ 133 Jud Buechler	.02	.10
❑ 134 Derrick Coleman	.02	.10
❑ 135 Chris Dudley	.02	.10
❑ 136 Chris Morris	.02	.10
❑ 137 Drazen Petrovic	.02	.10
❑ 138 Reggie Theus	.02	.10
❑ 139 Maurice Cheeks	.02	.10
❑ 140 Patrick Ewing	.08	.25
❑ 141 Mark Jackson	.02	.10
❑ 142 Charles Oakley	.02	.10
❑ 143 Trent Tucker	.02	.10
❑ 144 Kiki Vandeweghe	.02	.10
❑ 145 Kenny Walker	.02	.10
❑ 146 Gerald Wilkins	.02	.10
❑ 147 Nick Anderson	.02	.10
❑ 148 Michael Ansley	.02	.10
❑ 149 Terry Catledge	.02	.10
❑ 150 Jerry Reynolds	.02	.10
❑ 151 Dennis Scott	.02	.10
❑ 152 Scott Skiles	.02	.10
❑ 153 Otis Smith	.02	.10
❑ 154 Sam Vincent	.02	.10
❑ 155 Ron Anderson	.02	.10
❑ 156 Charles Barkley	.15	.40
❑ 157 Manute Bol	.02	.10
❑ 158 Johnny Dawkins	.02	.10
❑ 159 Armon Gilliam	.02	.10
❑ 160 Rickey Green	.02	.10
❑ 161 Hersey Hawkins	.02	.10
❑ 162 Rick Mahorn	.02	.10
❑ 163 Tom Chambers	.02	.10
❑ 164 Jeff Hornacek	.02	.10
❑ 165 Kevin Johnson	.08	.25
❑ 166 Andrew Lang	.02	.10
❑ 167 Dan Majerle	.02	.10
❑ 168 Xavier McDaniel	.02	.10
❑ 169 Kurt Rambis	.02	.10
❑ 170 Mark West	.02	.10
❑ 171 Danny Ainge	.02	.10
❑ 172 Mark Bryant	.02	.10
❑ 173 Walter Davis	.02	.10
❑ 174 Clyde Drexler	.08	.25
❑ 175 Kevin Duckworth	.02	.10
❑ 176 Jerome Kersey	.02	.10
❑ 177 Terry Porter	.02	.10
❑ 178 Clifford Robinson	.02	.10
❑ 179 Buck Williams	.02	.10

❑ 180 Anthony Bonner	.02	.10
❑ 181 Antoine Carr	.02	.10
❑ 182 Duane Causwell	.02	.10
❑ 183 Bobby Hansen	.02	.10
❑ 184 Travis Mays	.02	.10
❑ 185 Lionel Simmons	.02	.10
❑ 186 Rory Sparrow	.02	.10
❑ 187 Wayman Tisdale	.02	.10
❑ 188 Willie Anderson	.02	.10
❑ 189 Terry Cummings	.02	.10
❑ 190 Sean Elliott	.02	.10
❑ 191 Sidney Green	.02	.10
❑ 192 David Greenwood	.02	.10
❑ 193 Paul Pressey	.02	.10
❑ 194 David Robinson	.20	.50
❑ 195 Dwayne Schintzius	.02	.10
❑ 196 Rod Strickland	.08	.25
❑ 197 Benoit Benjamin	.02	.10
❑ 198 Michael Cage	.02	.10
❑ 199 Eddie Johnson	.02	.10
❑ 200 Shawn Kemp	.25	.60
❑ 201 Derrick McKey	.02	.10
❑ 202 Gary Payton	.25	.60
❑ 203 Ricky Pierce	.02	.10
❑ 204 Sedale Threatt	.02	.10
❑ 205 Thurl Bailey	.02	.10
❑ 206 Mike Brown	.02	.10
❑ 207 Mark Eaton	.02	.10
❑ 208 Blue Edwards UER	.02	.10
❑ 209 Darrell Griffith	.02	.10
❑ 210 Jeff Malone	.02	.10
❑ 211 Karl Malone	.15	.40
❑ 212 John Stockton	.08	.25
❑ 213 Ledell Eackles	.02	.10
❑ 214 Pervis Ellison	.02	.10
❑ 215 A.J. English	.02	.10
❑ 216 Harvey Grant	.02	.10
❑ 217 Charles Jones	.02	.10
❑ 218 Bernard King	.02	.10
❑ 219 Darrell Walker	.02	.10
❑ 220 John Williams	.02	.10
❑ 221 Bob Weiss CO	.02	.10
❑ 222 Chris Ford CO	.02	.10
❑ 223 Gene Littles CO	.02	.10
❑ 224 Phil Jackson CO	.02	.10
❑ 225 Lenny Wilkens CO	.02	.10
❑ 226 Richie Adubato CO	.02	.10
❑ 227 Paul Westhead CO	.02	.10
❑ 228 Chuck Daly CO	.02	.10
❑ 229 Don Nelson CO	.02	.10
❑ 230 Don Chaney CO	.02	.10
❑ 231 Bob Hill RC CO	.02	.10
❑ 232 Mike Schuler CO	.02	.10
❑ 233 Mike Dunleavy CO	.02	.10
❑ 234 Kevin Loughery CO	.02	.10
❑ 235 Del Harris CO	.02	.10
❑ 236 Jimmy Rodgers CO	.02	.10
❑ 237 Bill Fitch CO	.02	.10
❑ 238 Pat Riley CO	.02	.10
❑ 239 Matt Guokas CO	.02	.10
❑ 240 Jim Lynam CO	.02	.10
❑ 241 Cotton Fitzsimmons CO	.02	.10
❑ 242 Rick Adelman CO	.02	.10
❑ 243 Dick Motta CO	.02	.10
❑ 244 Larry Brown CO	.02	.10
❑ 245 K.C. Jones CO	.02	.10
❑ 246 Jerry Sloan CO	.02	.10
❑ 247 Wes Unseld CO	.02	.10
❑ 248 Charles Barkley AS	.08	.25
❑ 249 Brad Daugherty AS	.02	.10
❑ 250 Joe Dumars AS	.02	.10
❑ 251 Patrick Ewing AS	.02	.10
❑ 252 Hersey Hawkins AS	.02	.10
❑ 253 Michael Jordan AS	.60	1.50
❑ 254 Bernard King AS	.02	.10
❑ 255 Kevin McHale AS	.02	.10
❑ 256 Robert Parish AS	.02	.10
❑ 257 Ricky Pierce AS	.02	.10
❑ 258 Alvin Robertson AS	.02	.10
❑ 259 Dominique Wilkins AS	.02	.10
❑ 260 Chris Ford CO AS	.02	.10
❑ 261 Tom Chambers AS	.02	.10
❑ 262 Clyde Drexler AS	.02	.10
❑ 263 Kevin Duckworth AS	.02	.10
❑ 264 Tim Hardaway AS	.08	.25
❑ 265 Kevin Johnson AS	.02	.10
❑ 266 Magic Johnson AS	.15	.40
❑ 267 Karl Malone AS	.08	.25
❑ 268 Chris Mullin AS	.02	.10
❑ 269 Terry Porter AS	.02	.10
❑ 270 David Robinson AS	.08	.25
❑ 271 John Stockton AS	.02	.10
❑ 272 James Worthy AS	.02	.10
❑ 273 Rick Adelman CO AS	.02	.10
❑ 274 Atlanta Hawks	.02	.10
❑ 275 Boston Celtics	.02	.10
❑ 276 Charlotte Hornets	.02	.10
❑ 277 Chicago Bulls	.02	.10
❑ 278 Cleveland Cavaliers	.02	.10
❑ 279 Dallas Mavericks	.02	.10
❑ 280 Denver Nuggets	.02	.10
❑ 281 Detroit Pistons	.02	.10
❑ 282 Golden State Warriors	.02	.10
❑ 283 Houston Rockets	.02	.10
❑ 284 Indiana Pacers	.02	.10
❑ 285 Los Angeles Clippers	.02	.10
❑ 286 Los Angeles Lakers	.02	.10
❑ 287 Miami Heat	.02	.10
❑ 288 Milwaukee Bucks	.02	.10
❑ 289 Minnesota Timberwolves	.02	.10
❑ 290 New Jersey Nets	.02	.10
❑ 291 New York Knicks	.02	.10
❑ 292 Orlando Magic	.02	.10
❑ 293 Philadelphia 76ers	.02	.10
❑ 294 Phoenix Suns	.02	.10
❑ 295 Portland Trail Blazers	.02	.10
❑ 296 Sacramento Kings	.02	.10
❑ 297 San Antonio Spurs	.02	.10
❑ 298 Seattle Supersonics	.02	.10
❑ 299 Utah Jazz	.02	.10
❑ 300 Washington Bullets	.02	.10
❑ 301 Centennial Card	.02	.10
❑ 302 Kevin Johnson IS	.02	.10
❑ 303 Reggie Miller IS	.02	.10
❑ 304 Hakeem Olajuwon IS	.08	.25
❑ 305 Robert Parish IS	.02	.10
❑ 306 M.Jordan/K.Malone LL	.40	1.00
❑ 307 3-Point FG Percent	.02	.10
❑ 308 R.Miller/J.Malone LL	.02	.10
❑ 309 Olajuwon/D.Robinson LL	.08	.25
❑ 310 Steals League Leaders	.02	.10
❑ 311 D.Robinson/Rodman LL	.20	.50
❑ 312 J.Stockton/M.Johnson LL	.02	.10
❑ 313 Field Goal Percent	.02	.10
❑ 314 Larry Bird MS	.20	.50
❑ 315 A.English/M.Malone	.02	.10
❑ 316 Magic Johnson MS	.15	.40
❑ 317 Michael Jordan MS	.60	1.50
❑ 318 Moses Malone	.02	.10
❑ 319 Larry Bird YB	.20	.50
❑ 320 Maurice Cheeks	.02	.10
❑ 321 Magic Johnson YB	.15	.40
❑ 322 Bernard King	.02	.10
❑ 323 Moses Malone	.02	.10
❑ 324 Robert Parish	.02	.10
❑ 325 All-Star Jam	.02	.10
❑ 326 All-Star Jam	.02	.10
❑ 327 David Robinson DON'T	.08	.25
❑ 328 Checklist 1	.02	.10
❑ 329 Checklist 2 UER	.02	.10
❑ 330 Checklist 3 UER	.02	.10
❑ 331 Maurice Cheeks	.02	.10
❑ 332 Duane Ferrell	.02	.10
❑ 333 Jon Koncak	.02	.10
❑ 334 Gary Leonard	.02	.10
❑ 335 Travis Mays	.02	.10
❑ 336 Blair Rasmussen	.02	.10
❑ 337 Alexander Volkov	.02	.10
❑ 338 John Bagley	.02	.10
❑ 339 Rickey Green UER	.02	.10
❑ 340 Derek Smith	.02	.10
❑ 341 Stojko Vrankovic	.02	.10
❑ 342 Anthony Frederick RC	.02	.10
❑ 343 Kenny Gattison	.02	.10
❑ 344 Eric Leckner	.02	.10
❑ 345 Will Perdue	.02	.10
❑ 346 Scott Williams RC	.02	.10
❑ 347 John Battle	.02	.10
❑ 348 Winston Bennett	.02	.10
❑ 349 Henry James	.02	.10
❑ 350 Steve Kerr	.02	.10
❑ 351 John Morton	.02	.10
❑ 352 Terry Davis	.02	.10
❑ 353 Randy White	.02	.10
❑ 354 Greg Anderson	.02	.10
❑ 355 Anthony Cook	.02	.10
❑ 356 Walter Davis	.02	.10
❑ 357 Winston Garland	.02	.10
❑ 358 Scott Hastings	.02	.10
❑ 359 Marcus Liberty	.02	.10
❑ 360 William Bedford	.02	.10
❑ 361 Lance Blanks	.02	.10
❑ 362 Brad Sellers	.02	.10
❑ 363 Darrell Walker	.02	.10
❑ 364 Orlando Woolridge	.02	.10
❑ 365 Vincent Askew RC	.02	.10
❑ 366 Mario Elie RC	.08	.25
❑ 367 Jim Petersen	.02	.10
❑ 368 Matt Bullard RC	.02	.10
❑ 369 Gerald Henderson	.02	.10
❑ 370 Dave Jamerson	.02	.10
❑ 371 Tree Rollins	.02	.10
❑ 372 Greg Dreiling	.02	.10
❑ 373 George McCloud	.02	.10
❑ 374 Kenny Williams	.02	.10
❑ 375 Randy Wittman	.02	.10
❑ 376 Tony Brown	.02	.10
❑ 377 Lanard Copeland	.02	.10
❑ 378 James Edwards	.02	.10
❑ 379 Bo Kimble	.02	.10
❑ 380 Doc Rivers	.02	.10
❑ 381 Loy Vaught	.02	.10
❑ 382 Elden Campbell FHC	.08	.25
❑ 383 Jack Haley	.02	.10
❑ 384 Tony Smith	.02	.10
❑ 385 Sedale Threatt	.02	.10
❑ 386 Keith Askins RC	.02	.10
❑ 387 Grant Long	.02	.10
❑ 388 Alan Ogg	.02	.10
❑ 389 Jon Sundvold	.02	.10
❑ 390 Lester Conner	.02	.10
❑ 391 Jeff Grayer	.02	.10
❑ 392 Steve Henson	.02	.10
❑ 393 Larry Krystkowiak	.02	.10
❑ 394 Moses Malone	.08	.25
❑ 395 Scott Brooks	.02	.10
❑ 396 Tellis Frank	.02	.10
❑ 397 Doug West	.02	.10
❑ 398 Rafael Addison RC	.02	.10
❑ 399 Dave Feitl RC	.02	.10
❑ 400 Tate George	.02	.10
❑ 401 Terry Mills RC	.08	.25
❑ 402 Tim McCormick	.02	.10
❑ 403 Xavier McDaniel	.02	.10
❑ 404 Anthony Mason RC	.20	.50
❑ 405 Brian Quinnett	.02	.10
❑ 406 John Starks RC	.08	.25
❑ 407 Mark Acres	.02	.10
❑ 408 Greg Kite	.02	.10
❑ 409 Jeff Turner	.02	.10
❑ 410 Morlon Wiley	.02	.10
❑ 411 Dave Hoppen	.02	.10
❑ 412 Brian Oliver	.02	.10
❑ 413 Kenny Payne	.02	.10
❑ 414 Charles Shackleford	.02	.10
❑ 415 Mitchell Wiggins	.02	.10
❑ 416 Jayson Williams	.08	.25
❑ 417 Cedric Ceballos	.02	.10
❑ 418 Negele Knight FHC	.02	.10
❑ 419 Andrew Lang	.02	.10
❑ 420 Jerrod Mustaf	.02	.10
❑ 421 Ed Nealy	.02	.10
❑ 422 Tim Perry	.02	.10
❑ 423 Alaa Abdelnaby	.02	.10
❑ 424 Wayne Cooper	.02	.10
❑ 425 Danny Young	.02	.10
❑ 426 Dennis Hopson	.02	.10
❑ 427 Les Jepsen	.02	.10
❑ 428 Jim Les RC	.02	.10
❑ 429 Mitch Richmond	.08	.25
❑ 430 Dwayne Schintzius	.02	.10
❑ 431 Spud Webb	.02	.10
❑ 432 Jud Buechler	.02	.10
❑ 433 Antoine Carr	.02	.10
❑ 434 Tom Garrick	.02	.10
❑ 435 Sean Higgins RC	.02	.10
❑ 436 Avery Johnson	.02	.10
❑ 437 Tony Massenburg	.02	.10
❑ 438 Dana Barros	.02	.10
❑ 439 Quintin Dailey	.02	.10
❑ 440 Bart Kofoed RC	.02	.10
❑ 441 Nate McMillan	.02	.10
❑ 442 Delaney Rudd	.02	.10
❑ 443 Michael Adams	.02	.10
❑ 444 Mark Alarie	.02	.10
❑ 445 Greg Foster	.02	.10
❑ 446 Tom Hammonds	.02	.10

❑ 447 Andre Turner	.02	.10
❑ 448 David Wingate	.02	.10
❑ 449 Dominique Wilkins SC	.02	.10
❑ 450 Kevin Willis SC	.02	.10
❑ 451 Larry Bird SC	.20	.50
❑ 452 Robert Parish SC	.02	.10
❑ 453 Rex Chapman SC	.02	.10
❑ 454 Kendall Gill SC	.02	.10
❑ 455 Michael Jordan SC	.60	1.50
❑ 456 Scottie Pippen SC	.15	.40
❑ 457 Brad Daugherty SC	.02	.10
❑ 458 Larry Nance SC	.02	.10
❑ 459 Rolando Blackman SC	.02	.10
❑ 460 Derek Harper SC	.02	.10
❑ 461 Chris Jackson SC	.02	.10
❑ 462 Todd Lichti SC	.02	.10
❑ 463 Joe Dumars SC	.02	.10
❑ 464 Isiah Thomas SC	.02	.10
❑ 465 Tim Hardaway SC	.08	.25
❑ 466 Chris Mullin SC	.02	.10
❑ 467 Hakeem Olajuwon SC	.08	.25
❑ 468 Otis Thorpe SC	.02	.10
❑ 469 Reggie Miller SC	.02	.10
❑ 470 Detlef Schrempf SC	.02	.10
❑ 471 Ron Harper SC	.02	.10
❑ 472 Charles Smith SC	.02	.10
❑ 473 Magic Johnson SC	.15	.40
❑ 474 James Worthy SC	.02	.10
❑ 475 Sherman Douglas SC	.02	.10
❑ 476 Rony Seikaly SC	.02	.10
❑ 477 Jay Humphries SC	.02	.10
❑ 478 Alvin Robertson SC	.02	.10
❑ 479 Tyrone Corbin SC	.02	.10
❑ 480 Pooh Richardson SC	.02	.10
❑ 481 Sam Bowie SC	.02	.10
❑ 482 Derrick Coleman SC	.02	.10
❑ 483 Patrick Ewing SC	.02	.10
❑ 484 Charles Oakley SC	.02	.10
❑ 485 Dennis Scott SC	.02	.10
❑ 486 Scott Skiles SC	.02	.10
❑ 487 Charles Barkley SC	.08	.25
❑ 488 Hersey Hawkins SC	.02	.10
❑ 489 Tom Chambers SC	.02	.10
❑ 490 Kevin Johnson SC	.02	.10
❑ 491 Clyde Drexler SC	.02	.10
❑ 492 Terry Porter SC	.02	.10
❑ 493 Lionel Simmons SC	.02	.10
❑ 494 Wayman Tisdale SC	.02	.10
❑ 495 Terry Cummings SC	.02	.10
❑ 496 David Robinson SC	.08	.25
❑ 497 Shawn Kemp SC	.08	.25
❑ 498 Ricky Pierce SC	.02	.10
❑ 499 Karl Malone SC	.08	.25
❑ 500 John Stockton SC	.02	.10
❑ 501 Harvey Grant SC	.02	.10
❑ 502 Bernard King SC	.02	.10
❑ 503 Travis Mays Art	.02	.10
❑ 504 Kevin McHale Art	.02	.10
❑ 505 Muggsy Bogues Art	.02	.10
❑ 506 Scottie Pippen TC	.15	.40
❑ 507 Brad Daugherty TC	.02	.10
❑ 508 Derek Harper Art	.02	.10
❑ 509 Chris Jackson Art	.02	.10
❑ 510 Isiah Thomas TC	.02	.10
❑ 511 Tim Hardaway TC	.08	.25
❑ 512 Otis Thorpe Art	.02	.10
❑ 513 Chuck Person Art	.02	.10
❑ 514 Ron Harper Art	.02	.10
❑ 515 James Worthy Art	.02	.10
❑ 516 Sherman Douglas Art	.02	.10
❑ 517 Dale Ellis Art	.02	.10
❑ 518 Tony Campbell Art	.02	.10
❑ 519 Derrick Coleman TC	.02	.10
❑ 520 Gerald Wilkins Art	.02	.10
❑ 521 Scott Skiles Art	.02	.10
❑ 522 Manute Bol Art	.02	.10
❑ 523 Tom Chambers Art	.02	.10
❑ 524 Terry Porter Art	.02	.10
❑ 525 Lionel Simmons TC	.02	.10
❑ 526 Sean Elliott TC	.02	.10
❑ 527 Shawn Kemp TC	.08	.25
❑ 528 John Stockton TC	.02	.10
❑ 529 Harvey Grant Art	.02	.10
❑ 530 Michael Adams	.02	.10
❑ 531 Charles Barkley AL	.08	.25
❑ 532 Larry Bird AL	.20	.50
❑ 533 Maurice Cheeks	.02	.10
❑ 534 Mark Eaton	.02	.10
❑ 535 Magic Johnson AL	.15	.40

❑ 536 Michael Jordan AL	.60	1.50
❑ 537 Moses Malone	.02	.10
❑ 538 NBA Finals Game 1	.02	.10
❑ 539 S.Pippen/J.Worthy FIN	.08	.25
❑ 540 NBA Finals Game 3	.02	.10
❑ 541 NBA Finals Game 4	.02	.10
❑ 542 Michael Jordan FIN	.60	1.50
❑ 543 Michael Jordan FIN	.60	1.50
❑ 544 Otis Smith	.02	.10
❑ 545 Jeff Turner	.02	.10
❑ 546 Larry Johnson RC	.40	1.00
❑ 547 Kenny Anderson RC	.20	.50
❑ 548 Billy Owens RC	.08	.25
❑ 549 Dikembe Mutombo RC	.40	1.00
❑ 550 Steve Smith RC	.40	1.00
❑ 551 Doug Smith RC	.02	.10
❑ 552 Luc Longley RC	.08	.25
❑ 553 Mark Macon RC	.02	.10
❑ 554 Stacey Augmon RC	.08	.25
❑ 555 Brian Williams RC	.08	.25
❑ 556 Terrell Brandon RC	.30	.75
❑ 557 Walter Davis	.02	.10
❑ 558 Vern Fleming	.02	.10
❑ 559 Joe Kleine	.02	.10
❑ 560 Jon Koncak	.02	.10
❑ 561 Sam Perkins	.02	.10
❑ 562 Alvin Robertson	.02	.10
❑ 563 Wayman Tisdale	.02	.10
❑ 564 Jeff Turner	.02	.10
❑ 565 Willie Anderson	.02	.10
❑ 566 Stacey Augmon USA	.08	.25
❑ 567 Bimbo Coles	.02	.10
❑ 568 Jeff Grayer	.02	.10
❑ 569 Hersey Hawkins	.02	.10
❑ 570 Dan Majerle USA	.02	.10
❑ 571 Danny Manning USA	.02	.10
❑ 572 J.R. Reid	.02	.10
❑ 573 Mitch Richmond USA	.20	.50
❑ 574 Charles Smith	.02	.10
❑ 575 Charles Barkley USA	.30	.75
❑ 576 Larry Bird USA	.75	2.00
❑ 577 Patrick Ewing USA	.20	.50
❑ 578 Magic Johnson USA	.60	1.50
❑ 579 Michael Jordan USA	2.50	6.00
❑ 580 Karl Malone USA	.30	.75
❑ 581 Chris Mullin USA	.08	.25
❑ 582 Scottie Pippen USA	.60	1.50
❑ 583 David Robinson USA	.40	1.00
❑ 584 John Stockton USA	.20	.50
❑ 585 Chuck Daly CO	.02	.10
❑ 586 Lenny Wilkens CO	.02	.10
❑ 587 P.J.Carlesimo USA CO RC	.02	.10
❑ 588 Mike Krzyzewski USA RC	.15	.40
❑ 589 Checklist Card 1	.02	.10
❑ 590 Checklist Card 2	.02	.10
❑ CC1 Naismith Special	.40	1.00
❑ XX Head of the Class	10.00	20.00
❑ NNO Centennial Sendaway Card	.20	.50
❑ NNO Team USA Title Card	.40	1.00

1992-93 Hoops

❑ COMPLETE SET (490)	17.50	35.00
❑ COMPLETE SERIES 1 (350)	7.50	15.00
❑ COMPLETE SERIES 2 (140)	10.00	20.00
❑ COMMON CARD (1-350)	.04	.10
❑ COMMON CARD (351-490)	.02	.10
❑ BAR.PLASTIC PRICED UNDER SKYBOX USA		
❑ 1 Stacey Augmon	.02	.10
❑ 2 Maurice Cheeks	.02	.10
❑ 3 Duane Ferrell	.02	.10
❑ 4 Paul Graham	.02	.10
❑ 5 Jon Koncak	.02	.10
❑ 6 Blair Rasmussen	.02	.10
❑ 7 Rumeal Robinson	.02	.10
❑ 8 Dominique Wilkins	.08	.25
❑ 9 Kevin Willis	.02	.10
❑ 10 Larry Bird	.40	1.00
❑ 11 Dee Brown	.02	.10
❑ 12 Sherman Douglas	.02	.10
❑ 13 Rick Fox	.02	.10
❑ 14 Kevin Gamble	.02	.10
❑ 15 Reggie Lewis	.02	.10
❑ 16 Kevin McHale	.08	.25
❑ 17 Robert Parish	.02	.10
❑ 18 Ed Pinckney UER	.02	.10
❑ 19 Muggsy Bogues	.02	.10
❑ 20 Dell Curry	.02	.10
❑ 21 Kenny Gattison	.02	.10
❑ 22 Kendall Gill	.02	.10
❑ 23 Mike Gminski	.02	.10
❑ 24 Larry Johnson	.10	.30
❑ 25 Johnny Newman	.02	.10
❑ 26 J.R. Reid	.02	.10
❑ 27 B.J. Armstrong	.02	.10
❑ 28 Bill Cartwright	.02	.10
❑ 29 Horace Grant	.02	.10
❑ 30 Michael Jordan	1.25	3.00
❑ 31 Stacey King	.02	.10
❑ 32 John Paxson	.02	.10
❑ 33 Will Perdue	.02	.10
❑ 34 Scottie Pippen	.30	.75
❑ 35 Scott Williams	.02	.10
❑ 36 John Battle	.02	.10
❑ 37 Terrell Brandon	.08	.25
❑ 38 Brad Daugherty	.02	.10
❑ 39 Craig Ehlo	.02	.10
❑ 40 Danny Ferry	.02	.10
❑ 41 Henry James	.02	.10
❑ 42 Larry Nance	.02	.10
❑ 43 Mark Price	.02	.10
❑ 44 Hot Rod Williams	.02	.10
❑ 45 Rolando Blackman	.02	.10
❑ 46 Terry Davis	.02	.10
❑ 47 Derek Harper	.02	.10
❑ 48 Mike Iuzzolino	.02	.10
❑ 49 Fat Lever	.02	.10
❑ 50 Rodney McCray	.02	.10
❑ 51 Doug Smith	.02	.10
❑ 52 Randy White	.02	.10
❑ 53 Herb Williams	.02	.10
❑ 54 Greg Anderson	.02	.10
❑ 55 Winston Garland	.02	.10
❑ 56 Chris Jackson	.02	.10
❑ 57 Marcus Liberty	.02	.10
❑ 58 Todd Lichti	.02	.10
❑ 59 Mark Macon	.02	.10
❑ 60 Dikembe Mutombo	.10	.30
❑ 61 Reggie Williams	.02	.10
❑ 62 Mark Aguirre	.02	.10
❑ 63 William Bedford	.02	.10
❑ 64 Joe Dumars	.08	.25
❑ 65 Bill Laimbeer	.02	.10
❑ 66 Dennis Rodman	.20	.50
❑ 67 John Salley	.02	.10
❑ 68 Isiah Thomas	.08	.25
❑ 69 Darrell Walker	.02	.10
❑ 70 Orlando Woolridge	.02	.10
❑ 71 Victor Alexander	.02	.10
❑ 72 Mario Elie	.02	.10
❑ 73 Chris Gatling	.02	.10
❑ 74 Tim Hardaway	.10	.30
❑ 75 Tyrone Hill	.02	.10
❑ 76 Alton Lister	.02	.10
❑ 77 Sarunas Marciulionis	.02	.10
❑ 78 Chris Mullin	.08	.25
❑ 79 Billy Owens	.02	.10
❑ 80 Matt Bullard	.02	.10
❑ 81 Sleepy Floyd	.02	.10
❑ 82 Avery Johnson	.02	.10
❑ 83 Buck Johnson	.02	.10
❑ 84 Vernon Maxwell	.02	.10
❑ 85 Hakeem Olajuwon	.15	.40
❑ 86 Kenny Smith	.02	.10
❑ 87 Larry Smith	.02	.10
❑ 88 Otis Thorpe	.02	.10
❑ 89 Dale Davis	.02	.10
❑ 90 Vern Fleming	.02	.10
❑ 91 George McCloud	.02	.10
❑ 92 Reggie Miller	.08	.25
❑ 93 Chuck Person	.02	.10
❑ 94 Detlef Schrempf	.02	.10
❑ 95 Rik Smits	.02	.10
❑ 96 LaSalle Thompson	.02	.10
❑ 97 Micheal Williams	.02	.10
❑ 98 James Edwards	.02	.10

❑ 99 Gary Grant	.02	.10
❑ 100 Ron Harper	.02	.10
❑ 101 Danny Manning	.02	.10
❑ 102 Ken Norman	.02	.10
❑ 103 Olden Polynice	.02	.10
❑ 104 Doc Rivers	.02	.10
❑ 105 Charles Smith	.02	.10
❑ 106 Loy Vaught	.02	.10
❑ 107 Elden Campbell	.02	.10
❑ 108 Vlade Divac	.02	.10
❑ 109 A.C. Green	.02	.10
❑ 110 Sam Perkins	.02	.10
❑ 111 Byron Scott	.02	.10
❑ 112 Tony Smith	.02	.10
❑ 113 Terry Teagle	.02	.10
❑ 114 Sedale Threatt	.02	.10
❑ 115 James Worthy	.08	.25
❑ 116 Willie Burton	.02	.10
❑ 117 Bimbo Coles	.02	.10
❑ 118 Kevin Edwards	.02	.10
❑ 119 Alec Kessler	.02	.10
❑ 120 Grant Long	.02	.10
❑ 121 Glen Rice	.08	.25
❑ 122 Rony Seikaly	.02	.10
❑ 123 Brian Shaw	.02	.10
❑ 124 Steve Smith	.10	.30
❑ 125 Frank Brickowski	.02	.10
❑ 126 Dale Ellis	.02	.10
❑ 127 Jeff Grayer	.02	.10
❑ 128 Jay Humphries	.02	.10
❑ 129 Larry Krystkowiak	.02	.10
❑ 130 Moses Malone	.08	.25
❑ 131 Fred Roberts	.02	.10
❑ 132 Alvin Robertson	.02	.10
❑ 133 Danny Schayes	.02	.10
❑ 134 Thurl Bailey	.02	.10
❑ 135 Scott Brooks	.02	.10
❑ 136 Tony Campbell	.02	.10
❑ 137 Gerald Glass	.02	.10
❑ 138 Luc Longley	.02	.10
❑ 139 Sam Mitchell	.02	.10
❑ 140 Pooh Richardson	.02	.10
❑ 141 Felton Spencer	.02	.10
❑ 142 Doug West	.02	.10
❑ 143 Rafael Addison	.02	.10
❑ 144 Kenny Anderson	.08	.25
❑ 145 Mookie Blaylock	.02	.10
❑ 146 Sam Bowie	.02	.10
❑ 147 Derrick Coleman	.02	.10
❑ 148 Chris Dudley	.02	.10
❑ 149 Terry Mills	.02	.10
❑ 150 Chris Morris	.02	.10
❑ 151 Drazen Petrovic	.02	.10
❑ 152 Greg Anthony	.02	.10
❑ 153 Patrick Ewing	.08	.25
❑ 154 Mark Jackson	.02	.10
❑ 155 Anthony Mason	.08	.25
❑ 156 Xavier McDaniel	.02	.10
❑ 157 Charles Oakley	.02	.10
❑ 158 John Starks	.02	.10
❑ 159 Gerald Wilkins	.02	.10
❑ 160 Nick Anderson	.02	.10
❑ 161 Terry Catledge	.02	.10
❑ 162 Jerry Reynolds	.02	.10
❑ 163 Stanley Roberts	.02	.10
❑ 164 Dennis Scott	.02	.10
❑ 165 Scott Skiles	.02	.10
❑ 166 Jeff Turner	.02	.10
❑ 167 Sam Vincent	.02	.10
❑ 168 Brian Williams	.02	.10
❑ 169 Ron Anderson	.02	.10
❑ 170 Charles Barkley	.15	.40
❑ 171 Manute Bol	.02	.10
❑ 172 Johnny Dawkins	.02	.10
❑ 173 Armon Gilliam	.02	.10
❑ 174 Hersey Hawkins	.02	.10
❑ 175 Brian Oliver	.02	.10
❑ 176 Charles Shackleford	.02	.10
❑ 177 Jayson Williams	.02	.10
❑ 178 Cedric Ceballos	.02	.10
❑ 179 Tom Chambers	.02	.10
❑ 180 Jeff Hornacek	.02	.10
❑ 181 Kevin Johnson	.08	.25
❑ 182 Negele Knight	.02	.10
❑ 183 Andrew Lang	.02	.10
❑ 184 Dan Majerle	.02	.10
❑ 185 Tim Perry	.02	.10
❑ 186 Mark West	.02	.10
❑ 187 Alaa Abdelnaby	.02	.10

❑ 188 Danny Ainge	.02	.10
❑ 189 Clyde Drexler	.08	.25
❑ 190 Kevin Duckworth	.02	.10
❑ 191 Jerome Kersey	.02	.10
❑ 192 Robert Pack	.02	.10
❑ 193 Terry Porter	.02	.10
❑ 194 Cliff Robinson	.02	.10
❑ 195 Buck Williams	.02	.10
❑ 196 Anthony Bonner	.02	.10
❑ 197 Duane Causwell	.02	.10
❑ 198 Pete Chilcutt	.02	.10
❑ 199 Dennis Hopson	.02	.10
❑ 200 Mitch Richmond	.08	.25
❑ 201 Lionel Simmons	.02	.10
❑ 202 Wayman Tisdale	.02	.10
❑ 203 Spud Webb	.02	.10
❑ 204 Willie Anderson	.02	.10
❑ 205 Antoine Carr	.02	.10
❑ 206 Terry Cummings	.02	.10
❑ 207 Sean Elliott	.02	.10
❑ 208 Sidney Green	.02	.10
❑ 209 David Robinson	.15	.40
❑ 210 Rod Strickland	.08	.25
❑ 211 Greg Sutton	.02	.10
❑ 212 Dana Barros	.02	.10
❑ 213 Benoit Benjamin	.02	.10
❑ 214 Michael Cage	.02	.10
❑ 215 Eddie Johnson	.02	.10
❑ 216 Shawn Kemp	.20	.50
❑ 217 Derrick McKey	.02	.10
❑ 218 Nate McMillan	.02	.10
❑ 219 Gary Payton	.20	.50
❑ 220 Ricky Pierce	.02	.10
❑ 221 David Benoit	.02	.10
❑ 222 Mike Brown	.02	.10
❑ 223 Tyrone Corbin	.02	.10
❑ 224 Mark Eaton	.02	.10
❑ 225 Blue Edwards	.02	.10
❑ 226 Jeff Malone	.02	.10
❑ 227 Karl Malone	.15	.40
❑ 228 Eric Murdock	.02	.10
❑ 229 John Stockton	.08	.25
❑ 230 Michael Adams	.02	.10
❑ 231 Rex Chapman	.02	.10
❑ 232 Ledell Eackles	.02	.10
❑ 233 Pervis Ellison	.02	.10
❑ 234 A.J. English	.02	.10
❑ 235 Harvey Grant	.02	.10
❑ 236 Charles Jones	.02	.10
❑ 237 LaBradford Smith	.02	.10
❑ 238 Larry Stewart	.02	.10
❑ 239 Bob Weiss CO	.02	.10
❑ 240 Chris Ford CO	.02	.10
❑ 241 Allan Bristow CO	.02	.10
❑ 242 Phil Jackson CO	.02	.10
❑ 243 Lenny Wilkens CO	.02	.10
❑ 244 Richie Adubato CO	.02	.10
❑ 245 Dan Issel CO	.02	.10
❑ 246 Ron Rothstein CO	.02	.10
❑ 247 Don Nelson CO	.02	.10
❑ 248 Rudy Tomjanovich CO	.02	.10
❑ 249 Bob Hill CO	.02	.10
❑ 250 Larry Brown CO	.02	.10
❑ 251 Randy Pfund RC CO	.02	.10
❑ 252 Kevin Loughery CO	.02	.10
❑ 253 Mike Dunleavy CO	.02	.10
❑ 254 Jimmy Rodgers CO	.02	.10
❑ 255 Chuck Daly CO	.02	.10
❑ 256 Pat Riley CO	.02	.10
❑ 257 Matt Guokas CO	.02	.10
❑ 258 Doug Moe CO	.02	.10
❑ 259 Paul Westphal CO	.02	.10
❑ 260 Rick Adelman CO	.02	.10
❑ 261 Garry St.Jean RC CO	.02	.10
❑ 262 Jerry Tarkanian RC	.02	.10
❑ 263 George Karl CO	.02	.10
❑ 264 Jerry Sloan CO	.02	.10
❑ 265 Wes Unseld CO	.02	.10
❑ 266 Atlanta Hawks	.02	.10
❑ 267 Boston Celtics	.02	.10
❑ 268 Charlotte Hornets	.02	.10
❑ 269 Chicago Bulls	.02	.10
❑ 270 Cleveland Cavaliers	.02	.10
❑ 271 Dallas Mavericks	.02	.10
❑ 272 Denver Nuggets	.02	.10
❑ 273 Detroit Pistons	.02	.10
❑ 274 Golden State Warriors	.02	.10
❑ 275 Houston Rockets	.02	.10
❑ 276 Indiana Pacers	.02	.10

❑ 277 Los Angeles Clippers	.02	.10
❑ 278 Los Angeles Lakers	.02	.10
❑ 279 Miami Heat	.02	.10
❑ 280 Milwaukee Bucks	.02	.10
❑ 281 Minnesota Timberwolves	.02	.10
❑ 282 New Jersey Nets	.02	.10
❑ 283 New York Knicks	.02	.10
❑ 284 Orlando Magic	.02	.10
❑ 285 Philadelphia 76ers	.02	.10
❑ 286 Phoenix Suns	.02	.10
❑ 287 Portland Trail Blazers	.02	.10
❑ 288 Sacramento Kings	.02	.10
❑ 289 San Antonio Spurs	.02	.10
❑ 290 Seattle Supersonics	.02	.10
❑ 291 Utah Jazz	.02	.10
❑ 292 Washington Bullets	.02	.10
❑ 293 Michael Adams AS	.02	.10
❑ 294 Charles Barkley AS	.08	.25
❑ 295 Brad Daugherty AS	.02	.10
❑ 296 Joe Dumars AS	.02	.10
❑ 297 Patrick Ewing AS	.02	.10
❑ 298 Michael Jordan AS	.60	1.50
❑ 299 Reggie Lewis AS	.02	.10
❑ 300 Scottie Pippen AS	.15	.40
❑ 301 Mark Price AS	.02	.10
❑ 302 Dennis Rodman AS	.08	.25
❑ 303 Isiah Thomas AS	.02	.10
❑ 304 Kevin Willis AS	.02	.10
❑ 305 Phil Jackson CO AS	.02	.10
❑ 306 Clyde Drexler AS	.02	.10
❑ 307 Tim Hardaway AS	.08	.25
❑ 308 Jeff Hornacek AS	.02	.10
❑ 309 Magic Johnson AS	.15	.40
❑ 310 Dan Majerle AS	.02	.10
❑ 311 Karl Malone AS	.08	.25
❑ 312 Chris Mullin AS	.02	.10
❑ 313 Dikembe Mutombo AS	.08	.25
❑ 314 Hakeem Olajuwon AS	.08	.25
❑ 315 David Robinson AS	.08	.25
❑ 316 John Stockton AS	.02	.10
❑ 317 Otis Thorpe AS	.02	.10
❑ 318 James Worthy AS	.02	.10
❑ 319 Don Nelson CO AS	.02	.10
❑ 320 M.Jordan/K.Malone LL	.40	1.00
❑ 321 Three-Point Field	.02	.10
❑ 322 M.Price/L.Bird LL	.10	.30
❑ 323 D.Robinson/H.Olajuwon LL	.08	.25
❑ 324 J.Stockton/M.Williams LL	.08	.25
❑ 325 D.Rodman/K.Willis LL	.08	.25
❑ 326 J.Stockton/K.Johnson LL	.08	.25
❑ 327 Field Goal Percent	.02	.10
❑ 328 Magic Moments 1980	.08	.25
❑ 329 Magic Moments 1985	.08	.25
❑ 330 Magic Moments 1987&1988	.08	.25
❑ 331 Magic Numbers	.08	.25
❑ 332 Drazen Petrovic	.02	.10
❑ 333 Patrick Ewing IS	.02	.10
❑ 334 David Robinson STAY	.08	.25
❑ 335 Kevin Johnson STAY	.02	.10
❑ 336 Charles Barkley USA	.08	.25
❑ 337 Larry Bird USA	.20	.50
❑ 338 Clyde Drexler USA	.02	.10
❑ 339 Patrick Ewing USA	.02	.10
❑ 340 Magic Johnson USA	.15	.40
❑ 341 Michael Jordan USA	.60	1.50
❑ 342 Christian Laettner USA RC	.20	.50
❑ 343 Karl Malone USA	.08	.25
❑ 344 Chris Mullin USA	.02	.10
❑ 345 Scottie Pippen USA	.15	.40
❑ 346 David Robinson USA	.08	.25
❑ 347 John Stockton USA	.02	.10
❑ 348 Checklist 1	.02	.10
❑ 349 Checklist 2	.02	.10
❑ 350 Checklist 3	.02	.10
❑ 351 Mookie Blaylock	.07	.20
❑ 352 Adam Keefe RC	.02	.10
❑ 353 Travis Mays	.02	.10
❑ 354 Morlon Wiley	.02	.10
❑ 355 Joe Kleine	.02	.10
❑ 356 Bart Kofoed	.02	.10
❑ 357 Xavier McDaniel	.02	.10
❑ 358 Tony Bennett RC	.02	.10
❑ 359 Tom Hammonds	.02	.10
❑ 360 Kevin Lynch	.02	.10
❑ 361 Alonzo Mourning RC	1.00	2.50
❑ 362 Rodney McCray	.02	.10
❑ 363 Trent Tucker	.02	.10
❑ 364 Corey Williams RC	.02	.10
❑ 365 Steve Kerr	.07	.20

❑ 366 Jerome Lane	.02	.10
❑ 367 Bobby Phills RC	.15	.40
❑ 368 Mike Sanders	.02	.10
❑ 369 Gerald Wilkins	.02	.10
❑ 370 Donald Hodge	.02	.10
❑ 371 Brian Howard RC	.02	.10
❑ 372 Tracy Moore RC	.02	.10
❑ 373 Sean Rooks RC	.02	.10
❑ 374 Kevin Brooks	.02	.10
❑ 375 LaPhonso Ellis RC	.15	.40
❑ 376 Scott Hastings	.02	.10
❑ 377 Robert Pack	.02	.10
❑ 378 Bryant Stith RC	.07	.20
❑ 379 Robert Werdann RC	.02	.10
❑ 380 Lance Blanks	.02	.10
❑ 381 Terry Mills	.02	.10
❑ 382 Isaiah Morris RC	.02	.10
❑ 383 Olden Polynice	.02	.10
❑ 384 Brad Sellers	.02	.10
❑ 385 Jud Buechler	.02	.10
❑ 386 Jeff Grayer	.02	.10
❑ 387 Byron Houston RC	.02	.10
❑ 388 Keith Jennings RC	.02	.10
❑ 389 Latrell Sprewell RC	1.25	3.00
❑ 390 Scott Brooks	.02	.10
❑ 391 Carl Herrera	.02	.10
❑ 392 Robert Horry RC	.15	.40
❑ 393 Tree Rollins	.02	.10
❑ 394 Kennard Winchester	.02	.10
❑ 395 Greg Dreiling	.02	.10
❑ 396 Sean Green	.02	.10
❑ 397 Sam Mitchell	.02	.10
❑ 398 Pooh Richardson	.02	.10
❑ 399 Malik Sealy RC	.07	.20
❑ 400 Kenny Williams	.02	.10
❑ 401 Jaren Jackson RC	.07	.20
❑ 402 Mark Jackson	.07	.20
❑ 403 Stanley Roberts	.02	.10
❑ 404 Elmore Spencer RC	.02	.10
❑ 405 Kiki Vandeweghe	.02	.10
❑ 406 John Williams	.02	.10
❑ 407 Randy Woods RC	.02	.10
❑ 408 Alex Blackwell RC	.02	.10
❑ 409 Duane Cooper RC	.02	.10
❑ 410 Anthony Peeler RC	.07	.20
❑ 411 Keith Askins	.02	.10
❑ 412 Matt Geiger RC	.07	.20
❑ 413 Harold Miner RC	.07	.20
❑ 414 John Salley	.02	.10
❑ 415 Alaa Abdelnaby	.02	.10
❑ 416 Todd Day RC	.07	.20
❑ 417 Blue Edwards	.02	.10
❑ 418 Brad Lohaus	.02	.10
❑ 419 Lee Mayberry RC	.02	.10
❑ 420 Eric Murdock	.02	.10
❑ 421 Christian Laettner	.30	.75
❑ 422 Bob McCann RC	.02	.10
❑ 423 Chuck Person	.02	.10
❑ 424 Chris Smith RC	.02	.10
❑ 425 Gundars Vetra RC	.02	.10
❑ 426 Micheal Williams	.02	.10
❑ 427 Chucky Brown	.02	.10
❑ 428 Tate George	.02	.10
❑ 429 Rick Mahorn	.02	.10
❑ 430 Rumeal Robinson	.02	.10
❑ 431 Jayson Williams	.07	.20
❑ 432 Eric Anderson RC	.02	.10
❑ 433 Rolando Blackman	.02	.10
❑ 434 Tony Campbell	.02	.10
❑ 435 Hubert Davis RC	.07	.20
❑ 436 Bo Kimble	.02	.10
❑ 437 Doc Rivers	.07	.20
❑ 438 Charles Smith	.02	.10
❑ 439 Anthony Bowie	.02	.10
❑ 440 Litterial Green RC	.02	.10
❑ 441 Greg Kite	.02	.10
❑ 442 Shaquille O'Neal RC	4.00	10.00
❑ 443 Donald Royal	.02	.10
❑ 444 Greg Grant	.02	.10
❑ 445 Jeff Hornacek	.07	.20
❑ 446 Andrew Lang	.02	.10
❑ 447 Kenny Payne	.02	.10
❑ 448 Tim Perry	.02	.10
❑ 449 C.Weatherspoon RC	.15	.40
❑ 450 Danny Ainge	.07	.20
❑ 451 Charles Barkley	.25	.60
❑ 452 Tim Kempton	.02	.10
❑ 453 Oliver Miller RC	.07	.20
❑ 454 Mark Bryant	.02	.10
❑ 455 Mario Elie	.07	.20
❑ 456 Dave Johnson RC	.02	.10
❑ 457 Tracy Murray RC	.07	.20
❑ 458 Rod Strickland	.15	.40
❑ 459 Vincent Askew	.02	.10
❑ 460 Randy Brown	.02	.10
❑ 461 Marty Conlon	.02	.10
❑ 462 Jim Les	.02	.10
❑ 463 Walt Williams RC	.15	.40
❑ 464 William Bedford	.02	.10
❑ 465 Lloyd Daniels RC	.02	.10
❑ 466 Vinny Del Negro	.02	.10
❑ 467 Dale Ellis	.02	.10
❑ 468 Larry Smith	.02	.10
❑ 469 David Wood	.02	.10
❑ 470 Rich King	.02	.10
❑ 471 Isaac Austin RC	.07	.20
❑ 472 John Crotty RC	.02	.10
❑ 473 Stephen Howard RC	.02	.10
❑ 474 Jay Humphries	.02	.10
❑ 475 Larry Krystkowiak	.02	.10
❑ 476 Tom Gugliotta RC	.50	1.25
❑ 477 Buck Johnson	.02	.10
❑ 478 Don MacLean RC	.02	.10
❑ 479 Doug Overton	.02	.10
❑ 480 Brent Price RC w/Mark	.07	.20
❑ 481 David Robinson TRV	.15	.40
❑ 482 Magic Johnson TRV	.25	.60
❑ 483 John Stockton TRV	.07	.20
❑ 484 Patrick Ewing TRV	.07	.20
❑ 485 D.Rob/Ew/Stock/Mag TRV	.15	.40
❑ 486 John Stockton STAY	.07	.20
❑ 487 Ahmad Rashad	.07	.20
❑ 488 Rookie Checklist	.02	.10
❑ 489 Checklist 1	.02	.10
❑ 490 Checklist 2	.02	.10
❑ AC1 P.Ewing Art Card	.20	.50
❑ SU1 J.Stockton Game AU	100.00	200.00
❑ SU1 J.Stockton Game	.60	1.50
❑ TR1 M.Jordan/C.Drexler FIN	1.25	3.00
❑ NNO M.Johnson Comm	.40	1.00
❑ NNO M.Johnson Comm AU	75.00	150.00
❑ NNO P.Ewing Game	.20	.50
❑ NNO P.Ewing Game AU	80.00	160.00

1993-94 Hoops

❑ COMPLETE SET (421)	10.00	20.00
❑ COMPLETE SERIES 1 (300)	6.00	12.00
❑ COMPLETE SERIES 2 (121)	4.00	8.00
❑ BEWARE COUNTERFEIT BIRD/MAGIC AU		
❑ 1 Stacey Augmon	.01	.05
❑ 2 Mookie Blaylock	.02	.10
❑ 3 Duane Ferrell	.01	.05
❑ 4 Paul Graham	.01	.05
❑ 5 Adam Keefe	.01	.05
❑ 6 Blair Rasmussen	.01	.05
❑ 7 Dominique Wilkins	.08	.25
❑ 8 Kevin Willis	.01	.05
❑ 9 Alaa Abdelnaby	.01	.05
❑ 10 Dee Brown	.01	.05
❑ 11 Sherman Douglas	.01	.05
❑ 12 Rick Fox	.01	.05
❑ 13 Kevin Gamble	.01	.05
❑ 14 Joe Kleine	.01	.05
❑ 15 Xavier McDaniel	.01	.05
❑ 16 Robert Parish	.02	.10
❑ 17 Tony Bennett	.01	.05
❑ 18 Muggsy Bogues	.02	.10
❑ 19 Dell Curry	.01	.05
❑ 20 Kenny Gattison	.01	.05
❑ 21 Kendall Gill	.02	.10
❑ 22 Larry Johnson	.08	.25
❑ 23 Alonzo Mourning	.15	.40
❑ 24 Johnny Newman	.01	.05
❑ 25 B.J. Armstrong	.01	.05
❑ 26 Bill Cartwright	.01	.05
❑ 27 Horace Grant	.02	.10
❑ 28 Michael Jordan	1.25	3.00
❑ 29 Stacey King	.01	.05
❑ 30 John Paxson	.01	.05
❑ 31 Will Perdue	.01	.05
❑ 32 Scottie Pippen	.30	.75
❑ 33 Scott Williams	.01	.05
❑ 34 Moses Malone	.08	.25
❑ 35 John Battle	.01	.05
❑ 36 Terrell Brandon	.02	.10
❑ 37 Brad Daugherty	.01	.05
❑ 38 Craig Ehlo	.01	.05
❑ 39 Danny Ferry	.01	.05
❑ 40 Larry Nance	.01	.05
❑ 41 Mark Price	.01	.05
❑ 42 Gerald Wilkins	.01	.05
❑ 43 John Williams	.01	.05
❑ 44 Terry Davis	.01	.05
❑ 45 Derek Harper	.02	.10
❑ 46 Donald Hodge	.01	.05
❑ 47 Mike Iuzzolino	.01	.05
❑ 48 Jim Jackson	.02	.10
❑ 49 Sean Rooks	.01	.05
❑ 50 Doug Smith	.01	.05
❑ 51 Randy White	.01	.05
❑ 52 Mahmoud Abdul-Rauf	.01	.05
❑ 53 LaPhonso Ellis	.01	.05
❑ 54 Marcus Liberty	.01	.05
❑ 55 Mark Macon	.01	.05
❑ 56 Dikembe Mutombo	.08	.25
❑ 57 Robert Pack	.01	.05
❑ 58 Bryant Stith	.01	.05
❑ 59 Reggie Williams	.01	.05
❑ 60 Mark Aguirre	.01	.05
❑ 61 Joe Dumars	.08	.25
❑ 62 Bill Laimbeer	.01	.05
❑ 63 Terry Mills	.01	.05
❑ 64 Olden Polynice	.01	.05
❑ 65 Alvin Robertson	.01	.05
❑ 66 Dennis Rodman	.20	.50
❑ 67 Isiah Thomas	.08	.25
❑ 68 Victor Alexander	.01	.05
❑ 69 Tim Hardaway	.08	.25
❑ 70 Tyrone Hill	.01	.05
❑ 71 Byron Houston	.01	.05
❑ 72 Sarunas Marciulionis	.01	.05
❑ 73 Chris Mullin	.08	.25
❑ 74 Billy Owens	.01	.05
❑ 75 Latrell Sprewell	.25	.60
❑ 76 Scott Brooks	.01	.05
❑ 77 Matt Bullard	.01	.05
❑ 78 Carl Herrera	.01	.05
❑ 79 Robert Horry	.02	.10
❑ 80 Vernon Maxwell	.01	.05
❑ 81 Hakeem Olajuwon	.15	.40
❑ 82 Kenny Smith	.01	.05
❑ 83 Otis Thorpe	.02	.10
❑ 84 Dale Davis	.01	.05
❑ 85 Vern Fleming	.01	.05
❑ 86 George McCloud	.01	.05
❑ 87 Reggie Miller	.08	.25
❑ 88 Sam Mitchell	.01	.05
❑ 89 Pooh Richardson	.01	.05
❑ 90 Detlef Schrempf	.02	.10
❑ 91 Malik Sealy	.01	.05
❑ 92 Rik Smits	.02	.10
❑ 93 Gary Grant	.01	.05
❑ 94 Ron Harper	.02	.10
❑ 95 Mark Jackson	.02	.10
❑ 96 Danny Manning	.02	.10
❑ 97 Ken Norman	.01	.05
❑ 98 Stanley Roberts	.01	.05
❑ 99 Elmore Spencer	.01	.05
❑ 100 Loy Vaught	.01	.05
❑ 101 John Williams	.01	.05
❑ 102 Randy Woods	.01	.05
❑ 103 Benoit Benjamin	.01	.05
❑ 104 Elden Campbell	.01	.05
❑ 105 Doug Christie	.02	.10
❑ 106 Vlade Divac	.02	.10
❑ 107 Anthony Peeler	.01	.05
❑ 108 Tony Smith	.01	.05
❑ 109 Sedale Threatt	.01	.05
❑ 110 James Worthy	.08	.25
❑ 111 Bimbo Coles	.01	.05
❑ 112 Grant Long	.01	.05
❑ 113 Harold Miner	.01	.05
❑ 114 Glen Rice	.02	.10
❑ 115 John Salley	.01	.05

116 Rony Seikaly	.01	.05
117 Brian Shaw	.01	.05
118 Steve Smith	.08	.25
119 Anthony Avent	.01	.05
120 Jon Barry	.01	.05
121 Frank Brickowski	.01	.05
122 Todd Day	.01	.05
123 Blue Edwards	.01	.05
124 Brad Lohaus	.01	.05
125 Lee Mayberry	.01	.05
126 Eric Murdock	.01	.05
127 Derek Strong RC	.01	.05
128 Thurl Bailey	.01	.05
129 Christian Laettner	.02	.10
130 Luc Longley	.02	.10
131 Marlon Maxey	.01	.05
132 Chuck Person	.01	.05
133 Chris Smith	.01	.05
134 Doug West	.01	.05
135 Micheal Williams	.01	.05
136 Rafael Addison	.01	.05
137 Kenny Anderson	.02	.10
138 Sam Bowie	.01	.05
139 Chucky Brown	.01	.05
140 Derrick Coleman	.02	.10
141 Chris Morris	.01	.05
142 Rumeal Robinson	.01	.05
143 Greg Anthony	.01	.05
144 Rolando Blackman	.01	.05
145 Hubert Davis	.01	.05
146 Patrick Ewing	.08	.25
147 Anthony Mason	.02	.10
148 Charles Oakley	.02	.10
149 Doc Rivers	.02	.10
150 Charles Smith	.01	.05
151 John Starks	.02	.10
152 Nick Anderson	.02	.10
153 Anthony Bowie	.01	.05
154 Litterial Green	.01	.05
155 Shaquille O'Neal	.50	1.25
156 Donald Royal	.01	.05
157 Dennis Scott	.01	.05
158 Scott Skiles	.01	.05
159 Tom Tolbert	.01	.05
160 Jeff Turner	.01	.05
161 Ron Anderson	.01	.05
162 Johnny Dawkins	.01	.05
163 Hersey Hawkins	.02	.10
164 Jeff Hornacek	.02	.10
165 Andrew Lang	.01	.05
166 Tim Perry	.01	.05
167 Clarence Weatherspoon	.01	.05
168 Danny Ainge	.02	.10
169 Charles Barkley	.15	.40
170 Cedric Ceballos	.02	.10
171 Richard Dumas	.01	.05
172 Kevin Johnson	.02	.10
173 Dan Majerle	.02	.10
174 Oliver Miller	.01	.05
175 Mark West	.01	.05
176 Clyde Drexler	.08	.25
177 Kevin Duckworth	.01	.05
178 Mario Elie	.01	.05
179 Dave Johnson	.01	.05
180 Jerome Kersey	.01	.05
181 Tracy Murray	.01	.05
182 Terry Porter	.01	.05
183 Cliff Robinson	.02	.10
184 Rod Strickland	.02	.10
185 Buck Williams	.01	.05
186 Anthony Bonner	.01	.05
187 Randy Brown	.01	.05
188 Duane Causwell	.01	.05
189 Pete Chilcutt	.01	.05
190 Mitch Richmond	.08	.25
191 Lionel Simmons	.01	.05
192 Wayman Tisdale	.01	.05
193 Spud Webb	.02	.10
194 Walt Williams	.01	.05
195 Willie Anderson	.01	.05
196 Antoine Carr	.01	.05
197 Terry Cummings	.01	.05
198 Lloyd Daniels	.01	.05
199 Sean Elliott	.02	.10
200 Dale Ellis	.01	.05
201 Avery Johnson	.01	.05
202 J.R. Reid	.01	.05
203 David Robinson	.15	.40
204 Dana Barros	.01	.05
205 Michael Cage	.01	.05
206 Eddie Johnson	.01	.05
207 Shawn Kemp	.15	.40
208 Derrick McKey	.01	.05
209 Nate McMillan	.01	.05
210 Gary Payton	.15	.40
211 Sam Perkins	.02	.10
212 Ricky Pierce	.01	.05
213 David Benoit	.01	.05
214 Tyrone Corbin	.01	.05
215 Mark Eaton	.01	.05
216 Jay Humphries	.01	.05
217 Jeff Malone	.01	.05
218 Karl Malone	.15	.40
219 John Stockton	.08	.25
220 Michael Adams	.01	.05
221 Rex Chapman	.01	.05
222 Pervis Ellison	.01	.05
223 Harvey Grant	.01	.05
224 Tom Gugliotta	.08	.25
225 Don MacLean	.01	.05
226 Doug Overton	.01	.05
227 Brent Price	.01	.05
228 LaBradford Smith	.01	.05
229 Larry Stewart	.01	.05
230 Lenny Wilkens CO	.02	.10
231 Chris Ford CO	.01	.05
232 Allan Bristow CO	.01	.05
233 Phil Jackson CO	.02	.10
234 Mike Fratello CO	.02	.10
235 Quinn Buckner CO	.01	.05
236 Dan Issel CO	.01	.05
237 Don Chaney CO	.01	.05
238 Don Nelson CO	.02	.10
239 Rudy Tomjanovich CO	.02	.10
240 Larry Brown CO	.02	.10
241 Bob Weiss CO	.01	.05
242 Randy Pfund CO	.01	.05
243 Kevin Loughery CO	.01	.05
244 Mike Dunleavy CO	.01	.05
245 Sidney Lowe CO	.01	.05
246 Chuck Daly CO	.02	.10
247 Pat Riley CO	.02	.10
248 Brian Hill CO	.01	.05
249 Fred Carter CO	.01	.05
250 Paul Westphal CO	.01	.05
251 Rick Adelman CO	.01	.05
252 Garry St. Jean CO	.01	.05
253 John Lucas CO	.01	.05
254 George Karl CO	.02	.10
255 Jerry Sloan CO	.02	.10
256 Wes Unseld CO	.02	.10
257 Michael Jordan AS	.60	1.50
258 Isiah Thomas AS	.02	.10
259 Scottie Pippen AS	.15	.40
260 Larry Johnson AS	.02	.10
261 Dominique Wilkins AS	.02	.10
262 Joe Dumars AS	.02	.10
263 Mark Price AS	.01	.05
264 Shaquille O'Neal AS	.20	.50
265 Patrick Ewing AS	.02	.10
266 Larry Nance AS	.01	.05
267 Detlef Schrempf AS	.01	.05
268 Brad Daugherty AS	.01	.05
269 Charles Barkley AS	.08	.25
270 Clyde Drexler AS	.02	.10
271 Sean Elliott AS	.01	.05
272 Tim Hardaway AS	.02	.10
273 Shawn Kemp AS	.08	.25
274 Dan Majerle AS	.01	.05
275 Karl Malone AS	.08	.25
276 Danny Manning AS	.01	.05
277 Hakeem Olajuwon AS	.08	.25
278 Terry Porter AS	.01	.05
279 David Robinson AS	.08	.25
280 John Stockton AS	.02	.10
281 East Team Photo	.01	.05
282 West Team Photo	.01	.05
283 Jordan/Wilkins/Malone LL	.30	.75
284 Rodman/O'Neal/Mut. LL	.20	.50
285 Field Goal Percentage	.01	.05
286 Stock./Hardaway/Skiles L	.02	.10
287 Price/A-Rauf/L.Johnson L	.01	.05
288 3-point FG Percentage	.01	.05
289 Jordan/Blaylock/Stock. LL	.30	.75
290 Olajuwon/O'Neal/Mut. LL	.15	.40
291 D.Robinson BOYS/GIRLS	.02	.10
292 Tribune 1	.01	.05
293 Scottie Pippen TRIB	.15	.40
294 Tribune 3	.01	.05
295 Charles Barkley TRIB	.08	.25
296 Richard Dumas TRIB	.01	.05
297 Tribune 6	.01	.05
298 Checklist 1	.01	.05
299 Checklist 2	.01	.05
300 Checklist 3	.01	.05
301 Craig Ehlo	.01	.05
302 Jon Koncak	.01	.05
303 Andrew Lang	.01	.05
304 Chris Corchiani	.01	.05
305 Acie Earl RC	.01	.05
306 Dino Radja RC	.01	.05
307 Scott Burrell RC	.08	.25
308 Hersey Hawkins	.02	.10
309 Eddie Johnson	.01	.05
310 David Wingate	.01	.05
311 Corie Blount RC	.01	.05
312 Steve Kerr	.02	.10
313 Toni Kukoc RC	.40	1.00
314 Pete Myers	.01	.05
315 Jay Guidinger	.01	.05
316 Tyrone Hill	.01	.05
317 Gerald Madkins RC	.01	.05
318 Chris Mills RC	.08	.25
319 Bobby Phills	.01	.05
320 Lucious Harris RC	.01	.05
321 Popeye Jones RC	.01	.05
322 Fat Lever	.01	.05
323 Jamal Mashburn RC	.25	.60
324 Darren Morningstar RC	.01	.05
325 Kevin Brooks	.01	.05
326 Tom Hammonds	.01	.05
327 Darnell Mee RC	.01	.05
328 Rodney Rogers RC	.08	.25
329 Brian Williams	.01	.05
330 Greg Anderson	.01	.05
331 Sean Elliott	.02	.10
332 Allan Houston RC	.40	1.00
333 Lindsey Hunter RC	.08	.25
334 David Wood UER	.01	.05
335 Jud Buechler	.01	.05
336 Chris Gatling	.01	.05
337 Josh Grant RC	.01	.05
338 Jeff Grayer	.01	.05
339 Keith Jennings	.01	.05
340 Avery Johnson	.01	.05
341 Chris Webber RC	1.00	2.50
342 Sam Cassell RC	.40	1.00
343 Mario Elie	.01	.05
344 Eric Riley RC	.01	.05
345 Antonio Davis RC	.10	.30
346 Scott Haskin RC	.01	.05
347 Gerald Paddio	.01	.05
348 LaSalle Thompson	.01	.05
349 Ken Williams	.01	.05
350 Mark Aguirre	.01	.05
351 Terry Dehere RC	.01	.05
352 Henry James	.01	.05
353 Sam Bowie	.01	.05
354 George Lynch RC	.01	.05
355 Kurt Rambis	.01	.05
356 Nick Van Exel RC	.30	.75
357 Trevor Wilson	.01	.05
358 Keith Askins	.01	.05
359 Manute Bol	.01	.05
360 Willie Burton	.01	.05
361 Matt Geiger	.01	.05
362 Alec Kessler	.01	.05
363 Vin Baker RC	.25	.60
364 Ken Norman	.01	.05
365 Danny Schayes	.01	.05
366 Mike Brown	.01	.05
367 Isaiah Rider RC	.20	.50
368 Benoit Benjamin	.01	.05
369 P.J.Brown RC	.08	.25
370 Kevin Edwards	.01	.05
371 Armon Gilliam	.01	.05
372 Rick Mahorn	.01	.05
373 Dwayne Schintzius	.01	.05
374 Rex Walters RC	.01	.05
375 Jayson Williams	.02	.10
376 Eric Anderson	.01	.05
377 Anthony Bonner	.01	.05
378 Tony Campbell	.01	.05
379 Herb Williams	.01	.05
380 Anfernee Hardaway RC	.75	2.00
381 Greg Kite	.01	.05
382 Larry Krystkowiak	.01	.05

❑ 383 Todd Lichti	.01	.05
❑ 384 Dana Barros	.01	.05
❑ 385 Shawn Bradley RC	.08	.25
❑ 386 Greg Graham RC	.01	.05
❑ 387 Warren Kidd RC	.01	.05
❑ 388 Eric Leckner	.01	.05
❑ 389 Moses Malone	.08	.25
❑ 390 A.C. Green	.02	.10
❑ 391 Frank Johnson	.01	.05
❑ 392 Joe Kleine	.01	.05
❑ 393 Malcolm Mackey RC	.01	.05
❑ 394 Jerrod Mustaf	.01	.05
❑ 395 Mark Bryant	.01	.05
❑ 396 Chris Dudley	.01	.05
❑ 397 Harvey Grant	.01	.05
❑ 398 James Robinson RC	.01	.05
❑ 399 Reggie Smith	.01	.05
❑ 400 Randy Brown	.01	.05
❑ 401 Bobby Hurley RC	.02	.10
❑ 402 Jim Les	.01	.05
❑ 403 Vinny Del Negro	.01	.05
❑ 404 Sleepy Floyd	.01	.05
❑ 405 Dennis Rodman	.20	.50
❑ 406 Chris Whitney RC	.01	.05
❑ 407 Vincent Askew	.01	.05
❑ 408 Kendall Gill	.02	.10
❑ 409 Ervin Johnson RC	.02	.10
❑ 410 Rich King	.01	.05
❑ 411 Detlef Schrempf	.02	.10
❑ 412 Tom Chambers	.01	.05
❑ 413 John Crotty	.01	.05
❑ 414 Felton Spencer	.01	.05
❑ 415 Luther Wright RC	.01	.05
❑ 416 Calbert Cheaney RC	.02	.10
❑ 417 Kevin Duckworth	.01	.05
❑ 418 Gheorghe Muresan RC	.08	.25
❑ 419 Checklist 1	.01	.05
❑ 420 Checklist 2	.01	.05
❑ 421 Rookie Checklist	.01	.05
❑ DR1 D.Robinson Comm	.15	.40
❑ MB1 Magic/Bird Comm	.20	.50
❑ MB1A Magic/Bird Comm AU	75.00	150.00
❑ NNO D.Robinson Comm AU	40.00	80.00
❑ NNO D.Robinson Exp.Vouch.	4.00	10.00
❑ NNO Magic/Bird Exp.Vouch.	15.00	30.00

1994-95 Hoops

❑ COMPLETE SET (450)	12.00	24.00
❑ COMPLETE SERIES 1 (300)	6.00	12.00
❑ COMPLETE SERIES 2 (150)	6.00	12.00
❑ 1 Stacey Augmon	.01	.05
❑ 2 Mookie Blaylock	.01	.05
❑ 3 Doug Edwards	.01	.05
❑ 4 Craig Ehlo	.01	.05
❑ 5 Jon Koncak	.01	.05
❑ 6 Danny Manning	.02	.10
❑ 7 Kevin Willis	.01	.05
❑ 8 Dee Brown	.01	.05
❑ 9 Sherman Douglas	.01	.05
❑ 10 Acie Earl	.01	.05
❑ 11 Kevin Gamble	.01	.05
❑ 12 Xavier McDaniel	.01	.05
❑ 13 Robert Parish	.02	.10
❑ 14 Dino Radja	.01	.05
❑ 15 Tony Bennett	.01	.05
❑ 16 Muggsy Bogues	.02	.10
❑ 17 Scott Burrell	.01	.05
❑ 18 Dell Curry	.01	.05
❑ 19 Hersey Hawkins	.02	.10
❑ 20 Eddie Johnson	.01	.05
❑ 21 Larry Johnson	.02	.10
❑ 22 Alonzo Mourning	.10	.30
❑ 23 B.J. Armstrong	.01	.05
❑ 24 Corie Blount	.01	.05
❑ 25 Bill Cartwright	.01	.05
❑ 26 Horace Grant	.02	.10
❑ 27 Toni Kukoc	.15	.40
❑ 28 Luc Longley	.01	.05
❑ 29 Pete Myers	.01	.05
❑ 30 Scottie Pippen	.30	.75
❑ 31 Scott Williams	.01	.05
❑ 32 Terrell Brandon	.02	.10
❑ 33 Brad Daugherty	.01	.05
❑ 34 Tyrone Hill	.01	.05
❑ 35 Chris Mills	.02	.10
❑ 36 Larry Nance	.01	.05
❑ 37 Bobby Phills	.01	.05
❑ 38 Mark Price	.01	.05
❑ 39 Gerald Wilkins	.01	.05
❑ 40 John Williams	.01	.05
❑ 41 Terry Davis	.01	.05
❑ 42 Lucious Harris	.01	.05
❑ 43 Jim Jackson	.02	.10
❑ 44 Popeye Jones	.01	.05
❑ 45 Tim Legler	.01	.05
❑ 46 Jamal Mashburn	.08	.25
❑ 47 Sean Rooks	.01	.05
❑ 48 Mahmoud Abdul-Rauf	.01	.05
❑ 49 LaPhonso Ellis	.01	.05
❑ 50 Dikembe Mutombo	.02	.10
❑ 51 Robert Pack	.01	.05
❑ 52 Rodney Rogers	.01	.05
❑ 53 Bryant Stith	.01	.05
❑ 54 Brian Williams	.01	.05
❑ 55 Reggie Williams	.01	.05
❑ 56 Greg Anderson	.01	.05
❑ 57 Joe Dumars	.08	.25
❑ 58 Sean Elliott	.02	.10
❑ 59 Allan Houston	.15	.40
❑ 60 Lindsey Hunter	.02	.10
❑ 61 Mark Macon	.01	.05
❑ 62 Terry Mills	.01	.05
❑ 63 Victor Alexander	.01	.05
❑ 64 Chris Gatling	.01	.05
❑ 65 Tim Hardaway	.08	.25
❑ 66 Avery Johnson	.01	.05
❑ 67 Sarunas Marciulionis	.01	.05
❑ 68 Chris Mullin	.08	.25
❑ 69 Billy Owens	.01	.05
❑ 70 Latrell Sprewell	.08	.25
❑ 71 Chris Webber	.25	.60
❑ 72 Matt Bullard	.01	.05
❑ 73 Sam Cassell	.08	.25
❑ 74 Mario Elie	.01	.05
❑ 75 Carl Herrera	.01	.05
❑ 76 Robert Horry	.02	.10
❑ 77 Vernon Maxwell	.01	.05
❑ 78 Hakeem Olajuwon	.15	.40
❑ 79 Kenny Smith	.01	.05
❑ 80 Otis Thorpe	.01	.05
❑ 81 Antonio Davis	.01	.05
❑ 82 Dale Davis	.01	.05
❑ 83 Vern Fleming	.01	.05
❑ 84 Scott Haskin	.01	.05
❑ 85 Derrick McKey	.01	.05
❑ 86 Reggie Miller	.08	.25
❑ 87 Byron Scott	.02	.10
❑ 88 Rik Smits	.01	.05
❑ 89 Haywoode Workman	.01	.05
❑ 90 Terry Dehere	.01	.05
❑ 91 Harold Ellis	.01	.05
❑ 92 Gary Grant	.01	.05
❑ 93 Ron Harper	.02	.10
❑ 94 Mark Jackson	.01	.05
❑ 95 Stanley Roberts	.01	.05
❑ 96 Loy Vaught	.01	.05
❑ 97 Dominique Wilkins	.08	.25
❑ 98 Elden Campbell	.01	.05
❑ 99 Doug Christie	.02	.10
❑ 100 Vlade Divac	.01	.05
❑ 101 Reggie Jordan	.01	.05
❑ 102 George Lynch	.01	.05
❑ 103 Anthony Peeler	.01	.05
❑ 104 Sedale Threatt	.01	.05
❑ 105 Nick Van Exel	.08	.25
❑ 106 James Worthy	.08	.25
❑ 107 Bimbo Coles	.01	.05
❑ 108 Matt Geiger	.01	.05
❑ 109 Grant Long	.01	.05
❑ 110 Harold Miner	.01	.05
❑ 111 Glen Rice	.02	.10
❑ 112 John Salley	.01	.05
❑ 113 Rony Seikaly	.01	.05
❑ 114 Brian Shaw	.01	.05
❑ 115 Steve Smith	.02	.10
❑ 116 Vin Baker	.08	.25
❑ 117 Jon Barry	.01	.05
❑ 118 Todd Day	.01	.05
❑ 119 Lee Mayberry	.01	.05
❑ 120 Eric Murdock	.01	.05
❑ 121 Ken Norman	.01	.05
❑ 122 Mike Brown	.01	.05
❑ 123 Stacey King	.01	.05
❑ 124 Christian Laettner	.02	.10
❑ 125 Chuck Person	.01	.05
❑ 126 Isaiah Rider	.02	.10
❑ 127 Chris Smith	.01	.05
❑ 128 Doug West	.01	.05
❑ 129 Micheal Williams	.01	.05
❑ 130 Kenny Anderson	.02	.10
❑ 131 Benoit Benjamin	.01	.05
❑ 132 P.J. Brown	.01	.05
❑ 133 Derrick Coleman	.02	.10
❑ 134 Kevin Edwards	.01	.05
❑ 135 Armon Gilliam	.01	.05
❑ 136 Chris Morris	.01	.05
❑ 137 Rex Walters	.01	.05
❑ 138 David Wesley	.01	.05
❑ 139 Greg Anthony	.01	.05
❑ 140 Anthony Bonner	.01	.05
❑ 141 Hubert Davis	.01	.05
❑ 142 Patrick Ewing	.08	.25
❑ 143 Derek Harper	.01	.05
❑ 144 Anthony Mason	.02	.10
❑ 145 Charles Oakley	.01	.05
❑ 146 Charles Smith	.01	.05
❑ 147 John Starks	.01	.05
❑ 148 Nick Anderson	.01	.05
❑ 149 Anthony Avent	.01	.05
❑ 150 Anthony Bowie	.01	.05
❑ 151 Anfernee Hardaway	.25	.60
❑ 152 Shaquille O'Neal	.50	1.25
❑ 153 Donald Royal	.01	.05
❑ 154 Dennis Scott	.01	.05
❑ 155 Scott Skiles	.01	.05
❑ 156 Jeff Turner	.01	.05
❑ 157 Dana Barros	.01	.05
❑ 158 Shawn Bradley	.01	.05
❑ 159 Greg Graham	.01	.05
❑ 160 Warren Kidd	.01	.05
❑ 161 Eric Leckner	.01	.05
❑ 162 Jeff Malone	.01	.05
❑ 163 Tim Perry	.01	.05
❑ 164 Clarence Weatherspoon	.01	.05
❑ 165 Danny Ainge	.01	.05
❑ 166 Charles Barkley	.15	.40
❑ 167 Cedric Ceballos	.01	.05
❑ 168 A.C. Green	.02	.10
❑ 169 Kevin Johnson	.02	.10
❑ 170 Malcolm Mackey	.01	.05
❑ 171 Dan Majerle	.02	.10
❑ 172 Oliver Miller	.01	.05
❑ 173 Mark West	.01	.05
❑ 174 Clyde Drexler	.08	.25
❑ 175 Chris Dudley	.01	.05
❑ 176 Harvey Grant	.01	.05
❑ 177 Tracy Murray	.01	.05
❑ 178 Terry Porter	.01	.05
❑ 179 Clifford Robinson	.02	.10
❑ 180 James Robinson	.01	.05
❑ 181 Rod Strickland	.02	.10
❑ 182 Buck Williams	.01	.05
❑ 183 Duane Causwell	.01	.05
❑ 184 Bobby Hurley	.01	.05
❑ 185 Olden Polynice	.01	.05
❑ 186 Mitch Richmond	.08	.25
❑ 187 Lionel Simmons	.01	.05
❑ 188 Wayman Tisdale	.01	.05
❑ 189 Spud Webb	.01	.05
❑ 190 Walt Williams	.01	.05
❑ 191 Willie Anderson	.01	.05
❑ 192 Lloyd Daniels	.01	.05
❑ 193 Vinny Del Negro	.01	.05
❑ 194 Dale Ellis	.01	.05
❑ 195 J.R. Reid	.01	.05
❑ 196 David Robinson	.15	.40
❑ 197 Dennis Rodman	.20	.50
❑ 198 Kendall Gill	.02	.10
❑ 199 Ervin Johnson	.01	.05
❑ 200 Shawn Kemp	.15	.40
❑ 201 Chris King	.01	.05
❑ 202 Nate McMillan	.01	.05
❑ 203 Gary Payton	.15	.40
❑ 204 Sam Perkins	.02	.10

205 Ricky Pierce	.01	.05
206 Detlef Schrempf	.02	.10
207 David Benoit	.01	.05
208 Tom Chambers	.01	.05
209 Tyrone Corbin	.01	.05
210 Jeff Hornacek	.02	.10
211 Karl Malone	.15	.40
212 Bryon Russell	.01	.05
213 Felton Spencer	.01	.05
214 John Stockton	.08	.25
215 Luther Wright	.01	.05
216 Michael Adams	.01	.05
217 Mitchell Butler	.01	.05
218 Rex Chapman	.01	.05
219 Calbert Cheaney	.01	.05
220 Pervis Ellison	.01	.05
221 Tom Gugliotta	.02	.10
222 Don MacLean	.01	.05
223 Gheorghe Muresan	.01	.05
224 Kenny Anderson AS	.01	.05
225 B.J. Armstrong AS	.01	.05
226 Mookie Blaylock AS	.01	.05
227 Derrick Coleman AS	.01	.05
228 Patrick Ewing AS	.02	.10
229 Horace Grant AS	.01	.05
230 Alonzo Mourning AS	.08	.25
231 Shaquille O'Neal AS	.20	.50
232 Charles Oakley AS	.01	.05
233 Scottie Pippen AS	.15	.40
234 Mark Price AS	.01	.05
235 John Starks AS	.01	.05
236 Dominique Wilkins AS	.02	.10
237 East Team	.01	.05
238 Charles Barkley AS	.08	.25
239 Clyde Drexler AS	.02	.10
240 Kevin Johnson AS	.01	.05
241 Shawn Kemp AS	.08	.25
242 Karl Malone AS	.08	.25
243 Danny Manning AS	.01	.05
244 Hakeem Olajuwon AS	.08	.25
245 Gary Payton AS	.08	.25
246 Mitch Richmond AS	.02	.10
247 Clifford Robinson AS	.01	.05
248 David Robinson AS	.08	.25
249 Latrell Sprewell AS	.08	.25
250 John Stockton AS	.02	.10
251 West Team	.01	.05
252 Tracy Murray LL	.01	.05
253 John Stockton LL	.02	.10
254 Mutombo/Olaj/D.Rob LL	.08	.25
255 Mahmoud Abdul-Rauf LL	.01	.05
256 Rodman/O'Neal/Willis LL	.15	.40
257 D.Rob/O'Neal/Olaj LL	.15	.40
258 Nate McMillan LL	.08	.25
259 Chris Webber AW	.10	.30
260 Hakeem Olajuwon AW	.08	.25
261 Hakeem Olajuwon AW	.08	.25
262 Dell Curry AW	.01	.05
263 Scottie Pippen AW	.15	.40
264 Anfernee Hardaway AW	.10	.30
265 Don MacLean AW	.01	.05
266 Hakeem Olajuwon FIN	.08	.25
267 Derek Harper FINALS	.01	.05
268 Sam Cassell TRIB	.08	.25
269 Hakeem Olajuwon TRIB	.08	.25
270 Patrick Ewing TRIB	.02	.10
271 Carl Herrera FINALS	.01	.05
272 Vernon Maxwell FINALS	.01	.05
273 Hakeem Olajuwon FIN	.08	.25
274 Lenny Wilkens CO	.02	.10
275 Chris Ford CO	.01	.05
276 Allan Bristow CO	.01	.05
277 Phil Jackson CO	.02	.10
278 Mike Fratello CO	.02	.10
279 Dick Motta CO	.01	.05
280 Dan Issel CO	.02	.10
281 Don Chaney CO	.01	.05
282 Don Nelson CO	.02	.10
283 Rudy Tomjanovich CO	.02	.10
284 Larry Brown CO	.02	.10
285 Del Harris CO UER	.01	.05
286 Kevin Loughery CO	.01	.05
287 Mike Dunleavy CO	.01	.05
288 Sidney Lowe CO	.01	.05
289 Pat Riley CO	.02	.10
290 Brian Hill CO	.01	.05
291 John Lucas CO	.02	.10
292 Paul Westphal CO	.01	.05
293 Garry St. Jean CO	.01	.05
294 George Karl CO	.02	.10
295 Jerry Sloan CO	.02	.10
296 Magic Johnson COMM	.30	.75
297 Denzel Washington SPEC	.02	.10
298 Checklist	.01	.05
299 Checklist	.01	.05
300 Checklist	.01	.05
301 Sergei Bazarevich RC	.01	.05
302 Tyrone Corbin	.01	.05
303 Grant Long	.01	.05
304 Ken Norman	.01	.05
305 Steve Smith	.02	.10
306 Blue Edwards	.01	.05
307 Greg Minor RC	.01	.05
308 Eric Montross RC	.01	.05
309 Dominique Wilkins	.08	.25
310 Michael Adams	.01	.05
311 Darrin Hancock RC	.01	.05
312 Robert Parish	.02	.10
313 Ron Harper	.02	.10
314 Dickey Simpkins RC	.01	.05
315 Michael Cage	.01	.05
316 Tony Dumas RC	.01	.05
317 Jason Kidd RC	1.25	3.00
318 Roy Tarpley	.01	.05
319 Dale Ellis	.01	.05
320 Jalen Rose RC	.40	1.00
321 Bill Curley RC	.01	.05
322 Grant Hill RC	.50	1.25
323 Oliver Miller	.01	.05
324 Mark West	.01	.05
325 Tom Gugliotta	.02	.10
326 Ricky Pierce	.01	.05
327 Carlos Rogers RC	.01	.05
328 Clifford Rozier RC	.01	.05
329 Rony Seikaly	.01	.05
330 Tim Breaux	.01	.05
331 Duane Ferrell	.01	.05
332 Mark Jackson	.01	.05
333 Lamond Murray RC	.02	.10
334 Bo Outlaw RC	.01	.05
335 Eric Piatkowski RC	.01	.05
336 Pooh Richardson	.01	.05
337 Malik Sealy	.01	.05
338 Cedric Ceballos	.01	.05
339 Eddie Jones RC	.50	1.25
340 Anthony Miller RC	.01	.05
341 Kevin Gamble	.01	.05
342 Brad Lohaus	.01	.05
343 Billy Owens	.01	.05
344 Khalid Reeves RC	.01	.05
345 Kevin Willis	.01	.05
346 Eric Mobley RC	.01	.05
347 Johnny Newman	.01	.05
348 Ed Pinckney	.01	.05
349 Glenn Robinson RC	.30	.75
350 Howard Eisley RC	.01	.05
351 Donyell Marshall RC	.08	.25
352 Yinka Dare RC	.01	.05
353 Charlie Ward RC	.08	.25
354 Monty Williams RC	.01	.05
355 Horace Grant	.02	.10
356 Brian Shaw	.01	.05
357 Brooks Thompson RC	.01	.05
358 Derrick Alston RC	.01	.05
359 B.J.Tyler RC	.01	.05
360 Scott Williams	.01	.05
361 Sharone Wright RC	.01	.05
362 Antonio Lang RC	.01	.05
363 Danny Manning	.02	.10
364 Wesley Person RC	.08	.25
365 Wayman Tisdale	.01	.05
366 Trevor Ruffin RC	.01	.05
367 Aaron McKie RC	.20	.50
368 Brian Grant RC	.25	.60
369 Michael Smith RC	.01	.05
370 Sean Elliott	.02	.10
371 Avery Johnson	.01	.05
372 Chuck Person	.01	.05
373 Bill Cartwright	.01	.05
374 Sarunas Marciulionis	.01	.05
375 Dontonio Wingfield RC	.01	.05
376 Antoine Carr	.01	.05
377 Jamie Watson RC	.01	.05
378 Juwan Howard RC	.25	.60
379 Jim McIlvaine RC	.01	.05
380 Scott Skiles	.01	.05
381 Anthony Tucker RC	.01	.05
382 Chris Webber	.25	.60
383 Bill Fitch CO	.01	.05
384 Bill Blair CO	.01	.05
385 Butch Beard CO	.01	.05
386 P.J. Carlesimo CO	.01	.05
387 Bob Hill CO	.01	.05
388 Jim Lynam CO	.01	.05
389 Checklist 4	.01	.05
390 Checklist 5	.01	.05
391 Atlanta Hawks TC	.01	.05
392 Boston Celtics TC	.01	.05
393 Charlotte Hornets TC	.01	.05
394 Chicago Bulls TC	.01	.05
395 Cleveland Cavaliers TC	.01	.05
396 Dallas Mavericks TC	.01	.05
397 Denver Nuggets TC	.01	.05
398 Detroit Pistons TC	.01	.05
399 Golden State	.01	.05
400 Houston Rockets TC	.01	.05
401 Indiana Pacers TC	.01	.05
402 Los Angeles Clippers TC	.01	.05
403 Los Angeles Lakers TC	.01	.05
404 Miami Heat TC	.01	.05
405 Milwaukee Bucks TC	.01	.05
406 Minnesota	.01	.05
407 New Jersey Nets TC	.01	.05
408 New York Knicks TC	.01	.05
409 Orlando Magic TC	.01	.05
410 Philadelphia 76ers TC	.01	.05
411 Phoenix Suns TC	.01	.05
412 Portland Trail	.01	.05
413 Sacramento Kings TC	.01	.05
414 San Antonio Spurs TC	.01	.05
415 Seattle Supersonics TC	.01	.05
416 Utah Jazz TC	.01	.05
417 Washington Bullets TC	.01	.05
418 Toronto Raptors TC	.01	.05
419 Vancouver Grizzlies TC	.01	.05
420 NBA Logo Card	.01	.05
421 G.Rob/C.Webber TOP	.08	.25
422 J.Kidd/S.Bradley TOP	.20	.50
423 G.Hill/A.Hardaway TOP	.20	.50
424 D.Marshall/J.Mashburn TO	.08	.25
425 J.Howard/I.Rider TOP	.08	.25
426 S.Wright/C.Cheaney TOP	.01	.05
427 L.Murray/B.Hurley TOP	.01	.05
428 B.Grant/V.Baker TOP	.08	.25
429 E.Montross/R.Rogers TOP	.01	.05
430 E.Jones/L.Hunter TOP	.10	.30
431 Craig Ehlo GM	.01	.05
432 Dino Radja GM	.01	.05
433 Toni Kukoc GM	.08	.25
434 Mark Price GM	.01	.05
435 Latrell Sprewell GM	.08	.25
436 Sam Cassell GM	.08	.25
437 Vernon Maxwell GM	.01	.05
438 Haywoode Workman GM	.01	.05
439 Harold Ellis GM	.01	.05
440 Cedric Ceballos GM	.01	.05
441 Vlade Divac GM	.01	.05
442 Nick Van Exel GM	.02	.10
443 John Starks GM	.01	.05
444 Scott Williams GM	.01	.05
445 Clifford Robinson GM	.01	.05
446 Spud Webb GM	.01	.05
447 Avery Johnson GM	.01	.05
448 Dennis Rodman GM	.08	.25
449 Sarunas Marciulionis GM	.01	.05
450 Nate McMillan GM	.01	.05
NNO Shaq Sheet Wrap.Exch. AU	200.00	400.00
NNO G.Hill Wrapper Exch.	1.50	4.00
NNO Shaq Sheet Wrap.Exch.	15.00	30.00

1995-96 Hoops

COMPLETE SET (400)	17.50	35.00
COMPLETE SERIES 1 (250)	10.00	20.00

❑ COMPLETE SERIES 2 (150)	7.50	15.00
❑ 1 Stacey Augmon	.05	.15
❑ 2 Mookie Blaylock	.05	.15
❑ 3 Craig Ehlo	.05	.15
❑ 4 Andrew Lang	.05	.15
❑ 5 Grant Long	.05	.15
❑ 6 Ken Norman	.05	.15
❑ 7 Steve Smith	.10	.30
❑ 8 Dee Brown	.05	.15
❑ 9 Sherman Douglas	.05	.15
❑ 10 Pervis Ellison	.05	.15
❑ 11 Eric Montross	.05	.15
❑ 12 Dino Radja	.05	.15
❑ 13 Dominique Wilkins	.20	.50
❑ 14 Muggsy Bogues	.10	.30
❑ 15 Scott Burrell	.05	.15
❑ 16 Dell Curry	.05	.15
❑ 17 Hersey Hawkins	.05	.15
❑ 18 Larry Johnson	.10	.30
❑ 19 Alonzo Mourning	.10	.30
❑ 20 B.J. Armstrong	.05	.15
❑ 21 Michael Jordan	1.25	3.00
❑ 22 Toni Kukoc	.10	.30
❑ 23 Will Perdue	.05	.15
❑ 24 Scottie Pippen	.30	.75
❑ 25 Dickey Simpkins	.05	.15
❑ 26 Terrell Brandon	.10	.30
❑ 27 Tyrone Hill	.05	.15
❑ 28 Chris Mills	.05	.15
❑ 29 Bobby Phills	.05	.15
❑ 30 Mark Price	.10	.30
❑ 31 John Williams	.05	.15
❑ 32 Tony Dumas	.05	.15
❑ 33 Jim Jackson	.05	.15
❑ 34 Popeye Jones	.05	.15
❑ 35 Jason Kidd	.60	1.50
❑ 36 Jamal Mashburn	.10	.30
❑ 37 Roy Tarpley	.05	.15
❑ 38 Mahmoud Abdul-Rauf	.05	.15
❑ 39 LaPhonso Ellis	.05	.15
❑ 40 Dikembe Mutombo	.10	.30
❑ 41 Robert Pack	.05	.15
❑ 42 Rodney Rogers	.05	.15
❑ 43 Jalen Rose	.25	.60
❑ 44 Bryant Stith	.05	.15
❑ 45 Joe Dumars	.20	.50
❑ 46 Grant Hill	.25	.60
❑ 47 Allan Houston	.10	.30
❑ 48 Lindsey Hunter	.05	.15
❑ 49 Oliver Miller	.05	.15
❑ 50 Terry Mills	.05	.15
❑ 51 Chris Gatling	.05	.15
❑ 52 Tim Hardaway	.10	.30
❑ 53 Donyell Marshall	.10	.30
❑ 54 Chris Mullin	.20	.50
❑ 55 Carlos Rogers	.05	.15
❑ 56 Clifford Rozier	.05	.15
❑ 57 Rony Seikaly	.05	.15
❑ 58 Latrell Sprewell	.20	.50
❑ 59 Sam Cassell	.20	.50
❑ 60 Clyde Drexler	.20	.50
❑ 61 Robert Horry	.10	.30
❑ 62 Vernon Maxwell	.05	.15
❑ 63 Hakeem Olajuwon	.20	.50
❑ 64 Kenny Smith	.05	.15
❑ 65 Dale Davis	.05	.15
❑ 66 Mark Jackson	.10	.30
❑ 67 Derrick McKey	.05	.15
❑ 68 Reggie Miller	.20	.50
❑ 69 Byron Scott	.05	.15
❑ 70 Rik Smits	.10	.30
❑ 71 Terry Dehere	.05	.15
❑ 72 Lamond Murray	.05	.15
❑ 73 Eric Piatkowski	.10	.30
❑ 74 Pooh Richardson	.05	.15
❑ 75 Malik Sealy	.05	.15
❑ 76 Loy Vaught	.05	.15
❑ 77 Elden Campbell	.05	.15
❑ 78 Cedric Ceballos	.05	.15
❑ 79 Vlade Divac	.10	.30
❑ 80 Eddie Jones	.25	.60
❑ 81 Sedale Threatt	.05	.15
❑ 82 Nick Van Exel	.20	.50
❑ 83 Bimbo Coles	.05	.15
❑ 84 Harold Miner	.05	.15
❑ 85 Billy Owens	.05	.15
❑ 86 Khalid Reeves	.05	.15
❑ 87 Glen Rice	.10	.30
❑ 88 Kevin Willis	.10	.30
❑ 89 Vin Baker	.10	.30
❑ 90 Marty Conlon	.05	.15
❑ 91 Todd Day	.05	.15
❑ 92 Eric Mobley	.05	.15
❑ 93 Eric Murdock	.05	.15
❑ 94 Glenn Robinson	.20	.50
❑ 95 Winston Garland	.05	.15
❑ 96 Tom Gugliotta	.05	.15
❑ 97 Christian Laettner	.10	.30
❑ 98 Isaiah Rider	.05	.15
❑ 99 Sean Rooks	.05	.15
❑ 100 Doug West	.05	.15
❑ 101 Kenny Anderson	.10	.30
❑ 102 Benoit Benjamin	.05	.15
❑ 103 Derrick Coleman	.05	.15
❑ 104 Kevin Edwards	.05	.15
❑ 105 Armon Gilliam	.05	.15
❑ 106 Chris Morris	.05	.15
❑ 107 Patrick Ewing	.20	.50
❑ 108 Derek Harper	.10	.30
❑ 109 Anthony Mason	.10	.30
❑ 110 Charles Oakley	.05	.15
❑ 111 Charles Smith	.05	.15
❑ 112 John Starks	.10	.30
❑ 113 Monty Williams	.05	.15
❑ 114 Nick Anderson	.05	.15
❑ 115 Horace Grant	.10	.30
❑ 116 Anfernee Hardaway	.20	.50
❑ 117 Shaquille O'Neal	.50	1.25
❑ 118 Dennis Scott	.05	.15
❑ 119 Brian Shaw	.05	.15
❑ 120 Dana Barros	.05	.15
❑ 121 Shawn Bradley	.05	.15
❑ 122 Willie Burton	.05	.15
❑ 123 Jeff Malone	.05	.15
❑ 124 Clarence Weatherspoon	.05	.15
❑ 125 Sharone Wright	.05	.15
❑ 126 Charles Barkley	.25	.60
❑ 127 A.C. Green	.10	.30
❑ 128 Kevin Johnson	.10	.30
❑ 129 Dan Majerle	.10	.30
❑ 130 Danny Manning	.10	.30
❑ 131 Elliot Perry	.05	.15
❑ 132 Wesley Person	.05	.15
❑ 133 Chris Dudley	.05	.15
❑ 134 Clifford Robinson	.05	.15
❑ 135 James Robinson	.05	.15
❑ 136 Rod Strickland	.05	.15
❑ 137 Otis Thorpe	.05	.15
❑ 138 Buck Williams	.05	.15
❑ 139 Brian Grant	.20	.50
❑ 140 Olden Polynice	.05	.15
❑ 141 Mitch Richmond	.10	.30
❑ 142 Michael Smith	.05	.15
❑ 143 Spud Webb	.10	.30
❑ 144 Walt Williams	.05	.15
❑ 145 Vinny Del Negro	.05	.15
❑ 146 Sean Elliott	.10	.30
❑ 147 Avery Johnson	.05	.15
❑ 148 Chuck Person	.05	.15
❑ 149 David Robinson	.20	.50
❑ 150 Dennis Rodman	.10	.30
❑ 151 Kendall Gill	.05	.15
❑ 152 Ervin Johnson	.05	.15
❑ 153 Shawn Kemp	.10	.30
❑ 154 Nate McMillan	.05	.15
❑ 155 Gary Payton	.20	.50
❑ 156 Detlef Schrempf	.10	.30
❑ 157 Dontonio Wingfield	.05	.15
❑ 158 David Benoit	.05	.15
❑ 159 Jeff Hornacek	.10	.30
❑ 160 Karl Malone	.25	.60
❑ 161 Felton Spencer	.05	.15
❑ 162 John Stockton	.25	.60
❑ 163 Jamie Watson	.05	.15
❑ 164 Rex Chapman	.05	.15
❑ 165 Calbert Cheaney	.05	.15
❑ 166 Juwan Howard	.20	.50
❑ 167 Don MacLean	.05	.15
❑ 168 Gheorghe Muresan	.05	.15
❑ 169 Scott Skiles	.05	.15
❑ 170 Chris Webber	.25	.60
❑ 171 Lenny Wilkens CO	.10	.30
❑ 172 Allan Bristow CO	.05	.15
❑ 173 Phil Jackson CO	.10	.30
❑ 174 Mike Fratello CO	.10	.30
❑ 175 Dick Motta CO	.05	.15
❑ 176 Bernie Bickerstaff CO	.05	.15
❑ 177 Doug Collins CO	.05	.15
❑ 178 Rick Adelman CO	.05	.15
❑ 179 Rudy Tomjanovich CO	.10	.30
❑ 180 Larry Brown CO	.10	.30
❑ 181 Bill Fitch CO	.05	.15
❑ 182 Del Harris CO	.05	.15
❑ 183 Mike Dunleavy CO	.05	.15
❑ 184 Bill Blair CO	.05	.15
❑ 185 Butch Beard CO	.05	.15
❑ 186 Pat Riley CO	.10	.30
❑ 187 Brian Hill CO	.05	.15
❑ 188 John Lucas CO	.10	.30
❑ 189 Paul Westphal CO	.05	.15
❑ 190 P.J. Carlesimo CO	.05	.15
❑ 191 Garry St. Jean CO	.05	.15
❑ 192 Bob Hill CO	.05	.15
❑ 193 George Karl CO	.10	.30
❑ 194 Brendan Malone CO	.05	.15
❑ 195 Jerry Sloan CO	.10	.30
❑ 196 Kevin Pritchard	.05	.15
❑ 197 Jim Lynam CO	.05	.15
❑ 198 Brian Grant SS	.10	.30
❑ 199 Grant Hill SS	.10	.30
❑ 200 Juwan Howard SS	.10	.30
❑ 201 Eddie Jones SS	.20	.50
❑ 202 Jason Kidd SS	.30	.75
❑ 203 Donyell Marshall SS	.10	.30
❑ 204 Eric Montross SS	.05	.15
❑ 205 Glenn Robinson SS	.10	.30
❑ 206 Jalen Rose SS	.20	.50
❑ 207 Sharone Wright SS	.05	.15
❑ 208 Dana Barros MS	.05	.15
❑ 209 Joe Dumars MS	.10	.30
❑ 210 A.C. Green MS	.05	.15
❑ 211 Grant Hill MS	.20	.50
❑ 212 Karl Malone MS	.20	.50
❑ 213 Reggie Miller MS	.10	.30
❑ 214 Glen Rice MS	.05	.15
❑ 215 John Stockton MS	.20	.50
❑ 216 Lenny Wilkens MS	.10	.30
❑ 217 Dominique Wilkins MS	.10	.30
❑ 218 Kenny Anderson BB	.05	.15
❑ 219 Mookie Blaylock BB	.05	.15
❑ 220 Larry Johnson BB	.05	.15
❑ 221 Shawn Kemp BB	.05	.15
❑ 222 Toni Kukoc BB	.05	.15
❑ 223 Jamal Mashburn BB	.05	.15
❑ 224 Glen Rice BB	.05	.15
❑ 225 Mitch Richmond BB	.05	.15
❑ 226 Latrell Sprewell BB	.20	.50
❑ 227 Rod Strickland BB	.05	.15
❑ 228 Michael Adams PL	.05	.15
❑ 229 Craig Ehlo PL	.05	.15
❑ 230 Mario Elie PL	.05	.15
❑ 231 Anthony Mason PL	.05	.15
❑ 232 John Starks PL	.05	.15
❑ 233 Muggsy Bogues CA	.05	.15
❑ 234 Joe Dumars CA	.10	.30
❑ 235 LaPhonso Ellis CA	.05	.15
❑ 236 Patrick Ewing CA	.10	.30
❑ 237 Grant Hill CA	.20	.50
❑ 238 Kevin Johnson CA	.05	.15
❑ 239 Dan Majerle CA	.05	.15
❑ 240 Karl Malone CA	.20	.50
❑ 241 Hakeem Olajuwon CA	.10	.30
❑ 242 David Robinson CA	.10	.30
❑ 243 Dana Barros TT	.05	.15
❑ 244 Scott Burrell TT	.05	.15
❑ 245 Reggie Miller TT	.10	.30
❑ 246 Glen Rice TT	.05	.15
❑ 247 John Stockton TT	.20	.50
❑ 248 Checklist #1	.05	.15
❑ 249 Checklist #2	.05	.15
❑ 250 Checklist #3	.05	.15
❑ 251 Alan Henderson RC	.20	.50
❑ 252 Junior Burrough RC	.05	.15
❑ 253 Eric Williams RC	.10	.30
❑ 254 George Zidek RC	.05	.15
❑ 255 Jason Caffey RC	.10	.30
❑ 256 Donny Marshall RC	.05	.15
❑ 257 Bob Sura RC	.10	.30
❑ 258 Loren Meyer RC	.05	.15
❑ 259 Cherokee Parks RC	.05	.15
❑ 260 Antonio McDyess RC	.40	1.00
❑ 261 Theo Ratliff RC	.25	.60
❑ 262 Lou Roe RC	.05	.15
❑ 263 Andrew DeClercq RC	.05	.15
❑ 264 Joe Smith RC	.30	.75
❑ 265 Travis Best RC	.05	.15
❑ 266 Brent Barry RC	.20	.50

❑ 267 Frankie King RC	.05	.15
❑ 268 Sasha Danilovic RC	.05	.15
❑ 269 Kurt Thomas RC	.10	.30
❑ 270 Shawn Respert RC	.05	.15
❑ 271 Jerome Allen RC	.05	.15
❑ 272 Kevin Garnett RC	1.25	3.00
❑ 273 Ed O'Bannon RC	.05	.15
❑ 274 David Vaughn RC	.05	.15
❑ 275 Jerry Stackhouse RC	.60	1.50
❑ 276 Mario Bennett RC	.05	.15
❑ 277 Michael Finley RC	.50	1.25
❑ 278 Randolph Childress RC	.05	.15
❑ 279 Arvydas Sabonis RC	.25	.60
❑ 280 Gary Trent RC	.05	.15
❑ 281 Tyus Edney RC	.05	.15
❑ 282 Corliss Williamson RC	.20	.50
❑ 283 Cory Alexander RC	.05	.15
❑ 284 Sherrell Ford RC	.05	.15
❑ 285 Jimmy King RC	.05	.15
❑ 286 Damon Stoudamire RC	.40	1.00
❑ 287 Greg Ostertag RC	.05	.15
❑ 288 Lawrence Moten RC	.05	.15
❑ 289 Bryant Reeves RC	.20	.50
❑ 290 Rasheed Wallace RC	.50	1.25
❑ 291 Spud Webb	.10	.30
❑ 292 Dana Barros	.05	.15
❑ 293 Rick Fox	.10	.30
❑ 294 Kendall Gill	.05	.15
❑ 295 Khalid Reeves	.05	.15
❑ 296 Glen Rice	.10	.30
❑ 297 Luc Longley	.05	.15
❑ 298 Dennis Rodman	.10	.30
❑ 299 Dan Majerle	.10	.30
❑ 300 Lorenzo Williams	.05	.15
❑ 301 Dale Ellis	.05	.15
❑ 302 Reggie Williams	.05	.15
❑ 303 Otis Thorpe	.05	.15
❑ 304 B.J. Armstrong	.05	.15
❑ 305 Pete Chilcutt	.05	.15
❑ 306 Mario Elie	.05	.15
❑ 307 Antonio Davis	.05	.15
❑ 308 Ricky Pierce	.05	.15
❑ 309 Rodney Rogers	.05	.15
❑ 310 Brian Williams	.05	.15
❑ 311 Corie Blount	.05	.15
❑ 312 George Lynch	.05	.15
❑ 313 Alonzo Mourning	.10	.30
❑ 314 Lee Mayberry	.05	.15
❑ 315 Terry Porter	.05	.15
❑ 316 P.J. Brown	.05	.15
❑ 317 Hubert Davis	.05	.15
❑ 318 Charlie Ward	.05	.15
❑ 319 Jon Koncak	.05	.15
❑ 320 Derrick Coleman	.05	.15
❑ 321 Richard Dumas	.05	.15
❑ 322 Vernon Maxwell	.05	.15
❑ 323 Wayman Tisdale	.05	.15
❑ 324 Dontonio Wingfield	.05	.15
❑ 325 Tyrone Corbin	.05	.15
❑ 326 Bobby Hurley	.05	.15
❑ 327 Will Perdue	.05	.15
❑ 328 J.R. Reid	.05	.15
❑ 329 Hersey Hawkins	.05	.15
❑ 330 Sam Perkins	.10	.30
❑ 331 Adam Keefe	.05	.15
❑ 332 Chris Morris	.05	.15
❑ 333 Robert Pack	.05	.15
❑ 334 M.L. Carr CO	.05	.15
❑ 335 Pat Riley CO	.10	.30
❑ 336 Don Nelson CO	.10	.30
❑ 337 Brian Winters CO	.05	.15
❑ 338 Willie Anderson ET	.05	.15
❑ 339 Acie Earl ET	.05	.15
❑ 340 Jimmy King ET	.05	.15
❑ 341 Oliver Miller ET	.05	.15
❑ 342 Tracy Murray ET	.05	.15
❑ 343 Ed Pinckney ET	.05	.15
❑ 344 Alvin Robertson ET	.05	.15
❑ 345 Carlos Rogers ET	.05	.15
❑ 346 John Salley ET	.05	.15
❑ 347 Damon Stoudamire ET	.25	.60
❑ 348 Zan Tabak ET	.05	.15
❑ 349 Greg Anthony ET	.05	.15
❑ 350 Blue Edwards ET	.05	.15
❑ 351 Kenny Gattison ET	.05	.15
❑ 352 Antonio Harvey ET	.05	.15
❑ 353 Chris King ET	.05	.15
❑ 354 Darrick Martin ET	.05	.15
❑ 355 Lawrence Moten ET	.05	.15
❑ 356 Bryant Reeves ET	.10	.30
❑ 357 Byron Scott ET	.05	.15
❑ 358 Michael Jordan ES	.60	1.50
❑ 359 Dikembe Mutombo ES	.05	.15
❑ 360 Grant Hill ES	.10	.30
❑ 361 Robert Horry ES	.05	.15
❑ 362 Alonzo Mourning ES	.05	.15
❑ 363 Vin Baker ES	.05	.15
❑ 364 Isaiah Rider ES	.05	.15
❑ 365 Charles Oakley ES	.05	.15
❑ 366 Shaquille O'Neal ES	.20	.50
❑ 367 Jerry Stackhouse ES	.30	.75
❑ 368 Clarence Weatherspoon ES	.05	.15
❑ 369 Charles Barkley ES	.20	.50
❑ 370 Sean Elliott ES	.05	.15
❑ 371 Shawn Kemp ES	.05	.15
❑ 372 Chris Webber ES	.10	.30
❑ 373 Spud Webb RH	.05	.15
❑ 374 Muggsy Bogues RH	.05	.15
❑ 375 Toni Kukoc RH	.05	.15
❑ 376 Dennis Rodman RH	.05	.15
❑ 377 Jamal Mashburn RH	.05	.15
❑ 378 Jalen Rose RH	.20	.50
❑ 379 Clyde Drexler RH	.10	.30
❑ 380 Mark Jackson RH	.05	.15
❑ 381 Cedric Ceballos RH	.05	.15
❑ 382 Nick Van Exel RH	.05	.15
❑ 383 John Starks RH	.05	.15
❑ 384 Vernon Maxwell RH	.05	.15
❑ 385 Shawn Kemp RH	.05	.15
❑ 386 Gary Payton RH	.10	.30
❑ 387 Karl Malone RH	.20	.50
❑ 388 Mookie Blaylock WD	.05	.15
❑ 389 Muggsy Bogues WD	.05	.15
❑ 390 Jason Kidd WD	.30	.75
❑ 391 Tim Hardaway WD	.05	.15
❑ 392 Nick Van Exel WD	.05	.15
❑ 393 Kenny Anderson WD	.05	.15
❑ 394 Anfernee Hardaway WD	.10	.30
❑ 395 Rod Strickland WD	.05	.15
❑ 396 Avery Johnson WD	.05	.15
❑ 397 John Stockton WD	.20	.50
❑ 398 Grant Hill SPEC	.20	.50
❑ 399 Checklist (251-367)	.05	.15
❑ 400 Checklist (368-400/Ins.)	.05	.15
❑ NNO G.Hill Co-ROY Exch.	5.00	12.00
❑ NNO G.Hill Sweepstakes	.25	.60
❑ NNO G.Hill Tribute	10.00	25.00

1996-97 Hoops

❑ COMPLETE SET (350)	15.00	30.00
❑ COMPLETE SERIES 1 (200)	7.50	15.00
❑ COMPLETE SERIES 2 (150)	7.50	15.00
❑ 1 Stacey Augmon	.05	.15
❑ 2 Mookie Blaylock	.05	.15
❑ 3 Alan Henderson	.05	.15
❑ 4 Christian Laettner	.10	.30
❑ 5 Grant Long	.05	.15
❑ 6 Steve Smith	.10	.30
❑ 7 Dana Barros	.05	.15
❑ 8 Todd Day	.05	.15
❑ 9 Rick Fox	.05	.15
❑ 10 Eric Montross	.05	.15
❑ 11 Dino Radja	.05	.15
❑ 12 Eric Williams	.05	.15
❑ 13 Kenny Anderson	.05	.15
❑ 14 Scott Burrell	.05	.15
❑ 15 Dell Curry	.05	.15
❑ 16 Matt Geiger	.05	.15
❑ 17 Larry Johnson	.10	.30
❑ 18 Glen Rice	.10	.30
❑ 19 Ron Harper	.10	.30
❑ 20 Michael Jordan	1.25	3.00
❑ 21 Steve Kerr	.10	.30
❑ 22 Toni Kukoc	.10	.30
❑ 23 Luc Longley	.05	.15
❑ 24 Scottie Pippen	.30	.75
❑ 25 Dennis Rodman	.10	.30
❑ 26 Terrell Brandon	.10	.30
❑ 27 Danny Ferry	.05	.15
❑ 28 Tyrone Hill	.05	.15
❑ 29 Chris Mills	.05	.15
❑ 30 Bobby Phills	.05	.15
❑ 31 Bob Sura	.05	.15
❑ 32 Tony Dumas	.05	.15
❑ 33 Jim Jackson	.05	.15
❑ 34 Popeye Jones	.05	.15
❑ 35 Jason Kidd	.30	.75
❑ 36 Jamal Mashburn	.10	.30
❑ 37 George McCloud	.05	.15
❑ 38 Cherokee Parks	.05	.15
❑ 39 Mahmoud Abdul-Rauf	.05	.15
❑ 40 LaPhonso Ellis	.05	.15
❑ 41 Antonio McDyess	.10	.30
❑ 42 Dikembe Mutombo	.10	.30
❑ 43 Jalen Rose	.20	.50
❑ 44 Bryant Stith	.05	.15
❑ 45 Joe Dumars	.20	.50
❑ 46 Grant Hill	.20	.50
❑ 47 Allan Houston	.10	.30
❑ 48 Lindsey Hunter	.05	.15
❑ 49 Terry Mills	.05	.15
❑ 50 Theo Ratliff	.10	.30
❑ 51 Otis Thorpe	.05	.15
❑ 52 B.J. Armstrong	.05	.15
❑ 53 Donyell Marshall	.10	.30
❑ 54 Chris Mullin	.20	.50
❑ 55 Joe Smith	.10	.30
❑ 56 Rony Seikaly	.05	.15
❑ 57 Latrell Sprewell	.20	.50
❑ 58 Mark Bryant	.05	.15
❑ 59 Sam Cassell	.20	.50
❑ 60 Clyde Drexler	.20	.50
❑ 61 Mario Elie	.05	.15
❑ 62 Robert Horry	.10	.30
❑ 63 Hakeem Olajuwon	.20	.50
❑ 64 Travis Best	.05	.15
❑ 65 Antonio Davis	.05	.15
❑ 66 Mark Jackson	.05	.15
❑ 67 Derrick McKey	.05	.15
❑ 68 Reggie Miller	.20	.50
❑ 69 Rik Smits	.10	.30
❑ 70 Brent Barry	.05	.15
❑ 71 Terry Dehere	.05	.15
❑ 72 Pooh Richardson	.05	.15
❑ 73 Rodney Rogers	.05	.15
❑ 74 Loy Vaught	.05	.15
❑ 75 Brian Williams	.05	.15
❑ 76 Elden Campbell	.05	.15
❑ 77 Cedric Ceballos	.05	.15
❑ 78 Vlade Divac	.05	.15
❑ 79 Eddie Jones	.20	.50
❑ 80 Anthony Peeler	.05	.15
❑ 81 Nick Van Exel	.20	.50
❑ 82 Sasha Danilovic	.05	.15
❑ 83 Tim Hardaway	.10	.30
❑ 84 Alonzo Mourning	.10	.30
❑ 85 Kurt Thomas	.10	.30
❑ 86 Walt Williams	.05	.15
❑ 87 Vin Baker	.10	.30
❑ 88 Sherman Douglas	.05	.15
❑ 89 Johnny Newman	.05	.15
❑ 90 Shawn Respert	.05	.15
❑ 91 Glenn Robinson	.20	.50
❑ 92 Kevin Garnett	.40	1.00
❑ 93 Tom Gugliotta	.05	.15
❑ 94 Andrew Lang	.05	.15
❑ 95 Sam Mitchell	.05	.15
❑ 96 Isaiah Rider	.10	.30
❑ 97 Shawn Bradley	.05	.15
❑ 98 P.J. Brown	.05	.15
❑ 99 Chris Childs	.05	.15
❑ 100 Armon Gilliam	.05	.15
❑ 101 Ed O'Bannon	.05	.15
❑ 102 Jayson Williams	.10	.30
❑ 103 Hubert Davis	.05	.15
❑ 104 Patrick Ewing	.20	.50
❑ 105 Anthony Mason	.10	.30
❑ 106 Charles Oakley	.05	.15
❑ 107 John Starks	.10	.30
❑ 108 Charlie Ward	.05	.15
❑ 109 Nick Anderson	.05	.15
❑ 110 Horace Grant	.10	.30
❑ 111 Anfernee Hardaway	.20	.50
❑ 112 Shaquille O'Neal	.50	1.25

❑ 113 Dennis Scott	.05	.15
❑ 114 Brian Shaw	.05	.15
❑ 115 Derrick Coleman	.10	.30
❑ 116 Vernon Maxwell	.05	.15
❑ 117 Trevor Ruffin	.05	.15
❑ 118 Jerry Stackhouse	.25	.60
❑ 119 Clarence Weatherspoon	.05	.15
❑ 120 Charles Barkley	.25	.60
❑ 121 Michael Finley	.25	.60
❑ 122 A.C. Green	.10	.30
❑ 123 Kevin Johnson	.10	.30
❑ 124 Danny Manning	.10	.30
❑ 125 Wesley Person	.05	.15
❑ 126 John Williams	.05	.15
❑ 127 Harvey Grant	.05	.15
❑ 128 Aaron McKie	.10	.30
❑ 129 Clifford Robinson	.05	.15
❑ 130 Arvydas Sabonis	.10	.30
❑ 131 Rod Strickland	.05	.15
❑ 132 Gary Trent	.05	.15
❑ 133 Tyus Edney	.05	.15
❑ 134 Brian Grant	.20	.50
❑ 135 Billy Owens	.05	.15
❑ 136 Olden Polynice	.05	.15
❑ 137 Mitch Richmond	.10	.30
❑ 138 Corliss Williamson	.10	.30
❑ 139 Vinny Del Negro	.05	.15
❑ 140 Sean Elliott	.10	.30
❑ 141 Avery Johnson	.05	.15
❑ 142 Chuck Person	.05	.15
❑ 143 David Robinson	.20	.50
❑ 144 Charles Smith	.05	.15
❑ 145 Sherrell Ford	.05	.15
❑ 146 Hersey Hawkins	.10	.30
❑ 147 Shawn Kemp	.10	.30
❑ 148 Nate McMillan	.05	.15
❑ 149 Gary Payton	.20	.50
❑ 150 Detlef Schrempf	.10	.30
❑ 151 Oliver Miller	.05	.15
❑ 152 Tracy Murray	.05	.15
❑ 153 Carlos Rogers	.05	.15
❑ 154 Damon Stoudamire	.20	.50
❑ 155 Zan Tabak	.05	.15
❑ 156 Sharone Wright	.05	.15
❑ 157 Antoine Carr	.05	.15
❑ 158 Jeff Hornacek	.10	.30
❑ 159 Adam Keefe	.05	.15
❑ 160 Karl Malone	.20	.50
❑ 161 Chris Morris	.05	.15
❑ 162 John Stockton	.20	.50
❑ 163 Greg Anthony	.05	.15
❑ 164 Blue Edwards	.05	.15
❑ 165 Chris King	.05	.15
❑ 166 Lawrence Moten	.05	.15
❑ 167 Bryant Reeves	.05	.15
❑ 168 Byron Scott	.05	.15
❑ 169 Calbert Cheaney	.05	.15
❑ 170 Juwan Howard	.10	.30
❑ 171 Tim Legler	.05	.15
❑ 172 Gheorghe Muresan	.05	.15
❑ 173 Rasheed Wallace	.25	.60
❑ 174 Chris Webber	.20	.50
❑ 175 Steve Smith BF	.05	.15
❑ 176 Michael Jordan BF	.60	1.50
❑ 177 Scottie Pippen BF	.10	.30
❑ 178 Dennis Rodman BF	.05	.15
❑ 179 Allan Houston BF	.05	.15
❑ 180 Hakeem Olajuwon BF	.10	.30
❑ 181 Patrick Ewing BF	.10	.30
❑ 182 Anfernee Hardaway BF	.10	.30
❑ 183 Shaquille O'Neal BF	.20	.50
❑ 184 Charles Barkley BF	.20	.50
❑ 185 Arvydas Sabonis BF	.05	.15
❑ 186 David Robinson BF	.10	.30
❑ 187 Shawn Kemp BF	.05	.15
❑ 188 Gary Payton BF	.10	.30
❑ 189 Karl Malone BF	.20	.50
❑ 190 Kenny Anderson PLA	.05	.15
❑ 191 Toni Kukoc PLA	.05	.15
❑ 192 Brent Barry PLA	.05	.15
❑ 193 Cedric Ceballos PLA	.05	.15
❑ 194 Shawn Bradley PLA	.05	.15
❑ 195 Charles Oakley PLA	.05	.15
❑ 196 Dennis Scott PLA	.05	.15
❑ 197 Clifford Robinson PLA	.05	.15
❑ 198 Mitch Richmond PLA	.05	.15
❑ 199 Checklist	.05	.15
❑ 200 Checklist	.05	.15
❑ 201 Dikembe Mutombo	.10	.30
❑ 202 Dee Brown	.05	.15
❑ 203 David Wesley	.05	.15
❑ 204 Vlade Divac	.05	.15
❑ 205 Anthony Mason	.10	.30
❑ 206 Chris Gatling	.05	.15
❑ 207 Eric Montross	.05	.15
❑ 208 Ervin Johnson	.05	.15
❑ 209 Stacey Augmon	.05	.15
❑ 210 Joe Dumars	.20	.50
❑ 211 Grant Hill	.20	.50
❑ 212 Charles Barkley	.25	.60
❑ 213 Jalen Rose	.20	.50
❑ 214 Lamond Murray	.05	.15
❑ 215 Shaquille O'Neal	.50	1.25
❑ 216 P.J. Brown	.05	.15
❑ 217 Dan Majerle	.10	.30
❑ 218 Armon Gilliam	.05	.15
❑ 219 Andrew Lang	.05	.15
❑ 220 Kevin Garnett	.40	1.00
❑ 221 Tom Gugliotta	.05	.15
❑ 222 Cherokee Parks	.05	.15
❑ 223 Doug West	.05	.15
❑ 224 Kendall Gill	.05	.15
❑ 225 Robert Pack	.05	.15
❑ 226 Allan Houston	.10	.30
❑ 227 Larry Johnson	.10	.30
❑ 228 Rony Seikaly	.05	.15
❑ 229 Gerald Wilkins	.05	.15
❑ 230 Michael Cage	.05	.15
❑ 231 Lucious Harris	.05	.15
❑ 232 Sam Cassell	.20	.50
❑ 233 Robert Horry	.10	.30
❑ 234 Kenny Anderson	.05	.15
❑ 235 Isaiah Rider	.10	.30
❑ 236 Rasheed Wallace	.25	.60
❑ 237 Mahmoud Abdul-Rauf	.05	.15
❑ 238 Vernon Maxwell	.05	.15
❑ 239 Dominique Wilkins	.20	.50
❑ 240 Jim McIlvaine	.05	.15
❑ 241 Hubert Davis	.05	.15
❑ 242 Popeye Jones	.05	.15
❑ 243 Walt Williams	.05	.15
❑ 244 Karl Malone	.20	.50
❑ 245 John Stockton	.20	.50
❑ 246 Anthony Peeler	.05	.15
❑ 247 Tracy Murray	.05	.15
❑ 248 Rod Strickland	.05	.15
❑ 249 Lenny Wilkens CO	.10	.30
❑ 250 M.L. Carr CO	.05	.15
❑ 251 Dave Cowens CO	.05	.15
❑ 252 Phil Jackson CO	.10	.30
❑ 253 Mike Fratello CO	.10	.30
❑ 254 Jim Cleamons CO	.05	.15
❑ 255 Dick Motta CO	.05	.15
❑ 256 Doug Collins CO	.05	.15
❑ 257 Rick Adelman CO	.05	.15
❑ 258 Rudy Tomjanovich CO	.10	.30
❑ 259 Larry Brown CO	.10	.30
❑ 260 Bill Fitch CO	.05	.15
❑ 261 Del Harris CO	.05	.15
❑ 262 Pat Riley CO	.10	.30
❑ 263 Chris Ford CO	.05	.15
❑ 264 Flip Saunders CO	.05	.15
❑ 265 John Calipari CO	.10	.30
❑ 266 Jeff Van Gundy CO	.05	.15
❑ 267 Brian Hill CO	.05	.15
❑ 268 Johnny Davis CO	.05	.15
❑ 269 Danny Ainge CO	.10	.30
❑ 270 P.J. Carlesimo CO	.05	.15
❑ 271 Garry St. Jean CO	.05	.15
❑ 272 Bob Hill CO	.05	.15
❑ 273 George Karl CO	.10	.30
❑ 274 Darrell Walker CO	.05	.15
❑ 275 Jerry Sloan CO	.10	.30
❑ 276 Brian Winters CO	.05	.15
❑ 277 Jim Lynam CO	.05	.15
❑ 278 Shareef Abdur-Rahim RC	.60	1.50
❑ 279 Ray Allen RC	.60	1.50
❑ 280 Shandon Anderson RC	.10	.30
❑ 281 Kobe Bryant RC	4.00	10.00
❑ 282 Marcus Camby RC	.25	.60
❑ 283 Erick Dampier RC	.20	.50
❑ 284 Emanual Davis RC	.05	.15
❑ 285 Tony Delk RC	.20	.50
❑ 286 Brian Evans RC	.05	.15
❑ 287 Derek Fisher RC	.30	.75
❑ 288 Todd Fuller RC	.05	.15
❑ 289 Dean Garrett RC	.05	.15
❑ 290 Reggie Geary RC	.05	.15
❑ 291 Darvin Ham RC	.05	.15
❑ 292 Othella Harrington RC	.20	.50
❑ 293 Shane Heal RC	.05	.15
❑ 294 Mark Hendrickson RC	.05	.15
❑ 295 Allen Iverson RC	.60	1.50
❑ 296 Dontae' Jones RC	.05	.15
❑ 297 Kerry Kittles RC	.20	.50
❑ 298 Priest Lauderdale RC	.05	.15
❑ 299 Matt Maloney RC	.10	.30
❑ 300 Stephon Marbury RC	.50	1.25
❑ 301 Walter McCarty RC	.05	.15
❑ 302 Jeff McInnis RC	.05	.15
❑ 303 Martin Muursepp RC	.05	.15
❑ 304 Steve Nash RC	1.50	4.00
❑ 305 Moochie Norris RC	.10	.30
❑ 306 Jermaine O'Neal RC	.50	1.25
❑ 307 Vitaly Potapenko RC	.05	.15
❑ 308 Virginius Praskevicius RC	.05	.15
❑ 309 Roy Rogers RC	.05	.15
❑ 310 Malik Rose RC	.10	.30
❑ 311 James Scott RC	.05	.15
❑ 312 Antoine Walker RC	.50	1.25
❑ 313 Samaki Walker RC	.05	.15
❑ 314 Ben Wallace RC	1.25	3.00
❑ 315 John Wallace RC	.20	.50
❑ 316 Jerome Williams RC	.20	.50
❑ 317 Lorenzen Wright RC	.10	.30
❑ 318 Charles Barkley ST	.20	.50
❑ 319 Derrick Coleman ST	.05	.15
❑ 320 Michael Finley ST	.20	.50
❑ 321 Stephon Marbury ST	.30	.75
❑ 322 Reggie Miller ST	.10	.30
❑ 323 Alonzo Mourning ST	.05	.15
❑ 324 Shaquille O'Neal ST	.20	.50
❑ 325 Gary Payton ST	.10	.30
❑ 326 Dennis Rodman ST	.05	.15
❑ 327 Damon Stoudamire ST	.10	.30
❑ 328 Vin Baker CBG	.05	.15
❑ 329 Clyde Drexler CBG	.10	.30
❑ 330 Patrick Ewing CBG	.10	.30
❑ 331 Anfernee Hardaway CBG	.10	.30
❑ 332 Grant Hill CBG	.10	.30
❑ 333 Juwan Howard CBG	.05	.15
❑ 334 Larry Johnson CBG	.05	.15
❑ 335 Michael Jordan CBG	.60	1.50
❑ 336 Shawn Kemp CBG	.05	.15
❑ 337 Jason Kidd CBG	.10	.30
❑ 338 Karl Malone CBG	.20	.50
❑ 339 Reggie Miller CBG	.10	.30
❑ 340 Hakeem Olajuwon CBG	.10	.30
❑ 341 Scottie Pippen CBG	.10	.30
❑ 342 Mitch Richmond CBG	.05	.15
❑ 343 David Robinson CBG	.10	.30
❑ 344 Dennis Rodman CBG	.05	.15
❑ 345 Joe Smith CBG	.05	.15
❑ 346 Jerry Stackhouse CBG	.20	.50
❑ 347 John Stockton CBG	.20	.50
❑ 348 Jerry Stackhouse BG	.20	.50
❑ 349 Checklist (201-350/inserts)	.05	.15
❑ 350 Checklist (inserts)	.05	.15
❑ NNO G.Hill/J.Stackhouse Promo	.75	2.00
❑ NNO G.Hill Z-Force Preview	4.00	10.00

1997-98 Hoops

❑ COMPLETE SET (330)	15.00	30.00
❑ COMPLETE SERIES 1 (165)	6.00	12.00
❑ COMPLETE SERIES 2 (165)	9.00	18.00
❑ 1 Michael Jordan LL	.60	1.50
❑ 2 Dennis Rodman LL	.05	.15
❑ 3 Mark Jackson LL	.10	.30
❑ 4 Shawn Bradley LL	.05	.15
❑ 5 Glen Rice LL	.05	.15
❑ 6 Mookie Blaylock LL	.05	.15
❑ 7 Gheorghe Muresan LL	.05	.15
❑ 8 Mark Price LL	.10	.30
❑ 9 Tyrone Corbin	.05	.15

❑ 10 Christian Laettner	.10	.30
❑ 11 Priest Lauderdale	.05	.15
❑ 12 Dikembe Mutombo	.10	.30
❑ 13 Steve Smith	.10	.30
❑ 14 Todd Day	.05	.15
❑ 15 Rick Fox	.10	.30
❑ 16 Brett Szabo	.05	.15
❑ 17 Antoine Walker	.25	.60
❑ 18 David Wesley	.05	.15
❑ 19 Muggsy Bogues	.10	.30
❑ 20 Dell Curry	.05	.15
❑ 21 Tony Delk	.05	.15
❑ 22 Anthony Mason	.10	.30
❑ 23 Glen Rice	.10	.30
❑ 24 Malik Rose	.05	.15
❑ 25 Steve Kerr	.10	.30
❑ 26 Toni Kukoc	.10	.30
❑ 27 Luc Longley	.05	.15
❑ 28 Robert Parish	.10	.30
❑ 29 Scottie Pippen	.30	.75
❑ 30 Dennis Rodman	.10	.30
❑ 31 Terrell Brandon	.10	.30
❑ 32 Danny Ferry	.05	.15
❑ 33 Tyrone Hill	.05	.15
❑ 34 Bobby Phills	.05	.15
❑ 35 Vitaly Potapenko	.05	.15
❑ 36 Shawn Bradley	.05	.15
❑ 37 Sasha Danilovic	.05	.15
❑ 38 Derek Harper	.10	.30
❑ 39 Martin Muursepp	.05	.15
❑ 40 Robert Pack	.05	.15
❑ 41 Khalid Reeves	.05	.15
❑ 42 Vincent Askew	.05	.15
❑ 43 Dale Ellis	.05	.15
❑ 44 LaPhonso Ellis	.05	.15
❑ 45 Antonio McDyess	.10	.30
❑ 46 Bryant Stith	.05	.15
❑ 47 Joe Dumars	.20	.50
❑ 48 Grant Hill	.20	.50
❑ 49 Lindsey Hunter	.05	.15
❑ 50 Aaron McKie	.10	.30
❑ 51 Theo Ratliff	.05	.15
❑ 52 Scott Burrell	.05	.15
❑ 53 Todd Fuller	.05	.15
❑ 54 Chris Mullin	.20	.50
❑ 55 Mark Price	.10	.30
❑ 56 Joe Smith	.10	.30
❑ 57 Latrell Sprewell	.20	.50
❑ 58 Clyde Drexler	.20	.50
❑ 59 Mario Elie	.05	.15
❑ 60 Othella Harrington	.05	.15
❑ 61 Matt Maloney	.05	.15
❑ 62 Hakeem Olajuwon	.20	.50
❑ 63 Kevin Willis	.10	.30
❑ 64 Travis Best	.05	.15
❑ 65 Erick Dampier	.10	.30
❑ 66 Antonio Davis	.05	.15
❑ 67 Dale Davis	.05	.15
❑ 68 Mark Jackson	.10	.30
❑ 69 Reggie Miller	.20	.50
❑ 70 Brent Barry	.10	.30
❑ 71 Darrick Martin	.05	.15
❑ 72 Bo Outlaw	.05	.15
❑ 73 Loy Vaught	.05	.15
❑ 74 Lorenzen Wright	.05	.15
❑ 75 Kobe Bryant	.75	2.00
❑ 76 Derek Fisher	.20	.50
❑ 77 Robert Horry	.10	.30
❑ 78 Eddie Jones	.20	.50
❑ 79 Travis Knight	.05	.15
❑ 80 George McCloud	.05	.15
❑ 81 Shaquille O'Neal	.50	1.25
❑ 82 P.J. Brown	.05	.15
❑ 83 Tim Hardaway	.10	.30
❑ 84 Voshon Lenard	.05	.15
❑ 85 Jamal Mashburn	.10	.30
❑ 86 Alonzo Mourning	.10	.30
❑ 87 Ray Allen	.20	.50
❑ 88 Vin Baker	.10	.30
❑ 89 Sherman Douglas	.05	.15
❑ 90 Armon Gilliam	.05	.15
❑ 91 Glenn Robinson	.20	.50
❑ 92 Kevin Garnett	.40	1.00
❑ 93 Dean Garrett	.05	.15
❑ 94 Tom Gugliotta	.10	.30
❑ 95 Stephon Marbury	.25	.60
❑ 96 Doug West	.05	.15
❑ 97 Chris Gatling	.05	.15
❑ 98 Kendall Gill	.05	.15
❑ 99 Kerry Kittles	.20	.50
❑ 100 Jayson Williams	.05	.15
❑ 101 Chris Childs	.05	.15
❑ 102 Patrick Ewing	.20	.50
❑ 103 Allan Houston	.10	.30
❑ 104 Larry Johnson	.10	.30
❑ 105 Charles Oakley	.10	.30
❑ 106 John Starks	.10	.30
❑ 107 John Wallace	.05	.15
❑ 108 Nick Anderson	.05	.15
❑ 109 Horace Grant	.10	.30
❑ 110 Anfernee Hardaway	.20	.50
❑ 111 Rony Seikaly	.05	.15
❑ 112 Derek Strong	.05	.15
❑ 113 Derrick Coleman	.05	.15
❑ 114 Allen Iverson	.50	1.25
❑ 115 Doug Overton	.05	.15
❑ 116 Jerry Stackhouse	.20	.50
❑ 117 Rex Walters	.05	.15
❑ 118 Cedric Ceballos	.05	.15
❑ 119 Kevin Johnson	.10	.30
❑ 120 Jason Kidd	.30	.75
❑ 121 Steve Nash	.20	.50
❑ 122 Wesley Person	.05	.15
❑ 123 Kenny Anderson	.10	.30
❑ 124 Jermaine O'Neal	.30	.75
❑ 125 Isaiah Rider	.10	.30
❑ 126 Arvydas Sabonis	.10	.30
❑ 127 Gary Trent	.05	.15
❑ 128 Tyus Edney	.05	.15
❑ 129 Brian Grant	.10	.30
❑ 130 Olden Polynice	.05	.15
❑ 131 Mitch Richmond	.10	.30
❑ 132 Corliss Williamson	.10	.30
❑ 133 Vinny Del Negro	.05	.15
❑ 134 Sean Elliott	.10	.30
❑ 135 Avery Johnson	.05	.15
❑ 136 Will Perdue	.05	.15
❑ 137 Dominique Wilkins	.20	.50
❑ 138 Craig Ehlo	.05	.15
❑ 139 Hersey Hawkins	.05	.15
❑ 140 Shawn Kemp	.10	.30
❑ 141 Jim McIlvaine	.05	.15
❑ 142 Sam Perkins	.10	.30
❑ 143 Detlef Schrempf	.10	.30
❑ 144 Marcus Camby	.20	.50
❑ 145 Doug Christie	.10	.30
❑ 146 Popeye Jones	.05	.15
❑ 147 Damon Stoudamire	.10	.30
❑ 148 Walt Williams	.05	.15
❑ 149 Jeff Hornacek	.10	.30
❑ 150 Karl Malone	.20	.50
❑ 151 Greg Ostertag	.05	.15
❑ 152 Bryon Russell	.05	.15
❑ 153 John Stockton	.20	.50
❑ 154 Shareef Abdur-Rahim	.30	.75
❑ 155 Greg Anthony	.05	.15
❑ 156 Anthony Peeler	.05	.15
❑ 157 Bryant Reeves	.05	.15
❑ 158 Roy Rogers	.05	.15
❑ 159 Calbert Cheaney	.05	.15
❑ 160 Juwan Howard	.10	.30
❑ 161 Gheorghe Muresan	.05	.15
❑ 162 Rod Strickland	.05	.15
❑ 163 Chris Webber	.20	.50
❑ 164 Checklist	.05	.15
❑ 165 Checklist	.05	.15
❑ 166 Tim Duncan RC	.40	1.00
❑ 167 Chauncey Billups RC	.75	2.00
❑ 168 Keith Van Horn RC	.25	.60
❑ 169 Tracy McGrady RC	.50	1.25
❑ 170 John Thomas RC	.05	.15
❑ 171 Tim Thomas RC	.30	.75
❑ 172 Ron Mercer RC	.20	.50
❑ 173 Scot Pollard RC	.10	.30
❑ 174 Jason Lawson RC	.05	.15
❑ 175 Keith Booth RC	.05	.15
❑ 176 Adonal Foyle RC	.10	.30
❑ 177 Bubba Wells RC	.05	.15
❑ 178 Derek Anderson RC	.20	.50
❑ 179 Rodrick Rhodes RC	.05	.15
❑ 180 Kelvin Cato RC	.20	.50
❑ 181 Serge Zwikker RC	.05	.15
❑ 182 Ed Gray RC	.05	.15
❑ 183 Brevin Knight RC	.10	.30
❑ 184 Alvin Williams RC	.05	.15
❑ 185 Paul Grant RC	.05	.15
❑ 186 Austin Croshere RC	.15	.40
❑ 187 Chris Crawford RC	.05	.15
❑ 188 Anthony Johnson RC	.05	.15
❑ 189 James Cotton RC	.05	.15
❑ 190 James Collins RC	.05	.15
❑ 191 Tony Battie RC	.20	.50
❑ 192 Tariq Abdul-Wahad RC	.10	.30
❑ 193 Danny Fortson RC	.10	.30
❑ 194 Maurice Taylor RC	.15	.40
❑ 195 Bobby Jackson RC	.30	.75
❑ 196 Charles Smith RC	.05	.15
❑ 197 Johnny Taylor RC	.05	.15
❑ 198 Jerald Honeycutt RC	.05	.15
❑ 199 Marko Milic RC	.05	.15
❑ 200 Anthony Parker RC	.15	.30
❑ 201 Jacque Vaughn RC	.10	.30
❑ 202 Antonio Daniels RC	.20	.50
❑ 203 Charles O'Bannon RC	.05	.15
❑ 204 God Shammgod RC	.05	.15
❑ 205 Kebu Stewart RC	.05	.15
❑ 206 Mookie Blaylock	.05	.15
❑ 207 Chucky Brown	.05	.15
❑ 208 Alan Henderson	.05	.15
❑ 209 Dana Barros	.05	.15
❑ 210 Tyus Edney	.05	.15
❑ 211 Travis Knight	.05	.15
❑ 212 Walter McCarty	.05	.15
❑ 213 Vlade Divac	.10	.30
❑ 214 Matt Geiger	.05	.15
❑ 215 Bobby Phills	.05	.15
❑ 216 J.R. Reid	.05	.15
❑ 217 David Wesley	.05	.15
❑ 218 Scott Burrell	.05	.15
❑ 219 Ron Harper	.10	.30
❑ 220 Michael Jordan	1.25	3.00
❑ 221 Bill Wennington	.05	.15
❑ 222 Mitchell Butler	.05	.15
❑ 223 Zydrunas Ilgauskas	.10	.30
❑ 224 Shawn Kemp	.10	.30
❑ 225 Wesley Person	.05	.15
❑ 226 Shawnelle Scott RC	.05	.15
❑ 227 Bob Sura	.05	.15
❑ 228 Hubert Davis	.05	.15
❑ 229 Michael Finley	.20	.50
❑ 230 Dennis Scott	.05	.15
❑ 231 Erick Strickland RC	.10	.30
❑ 232 Samaki Walker	.05	.15
❑ 233 Dean Garrett	.05	.15
❑ 234 Priest Lauderdale	.05	.15
❑ 235 Eric Williams	.05	.15
❑ 236 Grant Long	.05	.15
❑ 237 Malik Sealy	.05	.15
❑ 238 Brian Williams	.05	.15
❑ 239 Muggsy Bogues	.10	.30
❑ 240 Bimbo Coles	.05	.15
❑ 241 Brian Shaw	.05	.15
❑ 242 Joe Smith	.10	.30
❑ 243 Latrell Sprewell	.20	.50
❑ 244 Charles Barkley	.25	.60
❑ 245 Emanual Davis	.05	.15
❑ 246 Brent Price	.05	.15
❑ 247 Reggie Miller	.20	.50
❑ 248 Chris Mullin	.20	.50
❑ 249 Jalen Rose	.20	.50
❑ 250 Rik Smits	.10	.30
❑ 251 Mark West	.05	.15
❑ 252 Lamond Murray	.05	.15
❑ 253 Pooh Richardson	.05	.15
❑ 254 Rodney Rogers	.05	.15
❑ 255 Stojko Vrankovic	.05	.15
❑ 256 Jon Barry	.05	.15
❑ 257 Corie Blount	.05	.15
❑ 258 Elden Campbell	.05	.15
❑ 259 Rick Fox	.10	.30
❑ 260 Nick Van Exel	.20	.50
❑ 261 Isaac Austin	.05	.15
❑ 262 Dan Majerle	.10	.30
❑ 263 Terry Mills	.05	.15
❑ 264 Mark Strickland RC	.05	.15
❑ 265 Terrell Brandon	.10	.30
❑ 266 Tyrone Hill	.05	.15
❑ 267 Ervin Johnson	.05	.15
❑ 268 Andrew Lang	.05	.15
❑ 269 Elliot Perry	.05	.15
❑ 270 Chris Carr	.05	.15
❑ 271 Reggie Jordan	.05	.15
❑ 272 Sam Mitchell	.05	.15
❑ 273 Stanley Roberts	.05	.15
❑ 274 Michael Cage	.05	.15
❑ 275 Sam Cassell	.20	.50
❑ 276 Lucious Harris	.05	.15

❑ 277 Kerry Kittles	.20	.50
❑ 278 Don MacLean	.05	.15
❑ 279 Chris Dudley	.05	.15
❑ 280 Chris Mills	.05	.15
❑ 281 Charlie Ward	.05	.15
❑ 282 Buck Williams	.05	.15
❑ 283 Herb Williams	.05	.15
❑ 284 Derek Harper	.10	.30
❑ 285 Mark Price	.10	.30
❑ 286 Gerald Wilkins	.05	.15
❑ 287 Allen Iverson	.50	1.25
❑ 288 Jim Jackson	.05	.15
❑ 289 Eric Montross	.05	.15
❑ 290 Jerry Stackhouse	.20	.50
❑ 291 Clarence Weatherspoon	.05	.15
❑ 292 Tom Chambers	.05	.15
❑ 293 Rex Chapman	.05	.15
❑ 294 Danny Manning	.10	.30
❑ 295 Antonio McDyess	.10	.30
❑ 296 Clifford Robinson	.05	.15
❑ 297 Stacey Augmon	.05	.15
❑ 298 Brian Grant	.10	.30
❑ 299 Rasheed Wallace	.20	.50
❑ 300 Mahmoud Abdul-Rauf	.05	.15
❑ 301 Terry Dehere	.05	.15
❑ 302 Billy Owens	.05	.15
❑ 303 Michael Smith	.05	.15
❑ 304 Cory Alexander	.05	.15
❑ 305 Chuck Person	.05	.15
❑ 306 David Robinson	.20	.50
❑ 307 Charles Smith	.05	.15
❑ 308 Monty Williams	.05	.15
❑ 309 Vin Baker	.10	.30
❑ 310 Jerome Kersey	.05	.15
❑ 311 Nate McMillan	.05	.15
❑ 312 Gary Payton	.20	.50
❑ 313 Eric Snow	.10	.30
❑ 314 Carlos Rogers	.05	.15
❑ 315 Zan Tabak	.05	.15
❑ 316 John Wallace	.05	.15
❑ 317 Sharone Wright	.05	.15
❑ 318 Shandon Anderson	.05	.15
❑ 319 Antoine Carr	.05	.15
❑ 320 Howard Eisley	.05	.15
❑ 321 Chris Morris	.05	.15
❑ 322 Pete Chilcutt	.05	.15
❑ 323 George Lynch	.05	.15
❑ 324 Chris Robinson	.05	.15
❑ 325 Otis Thorpe	.05	.15
❑ 326 Harvey Grant	.05	.15
❑ 327 Darvin Ham	.05	.15
❑ 328 Juwan Howard	.10	.30
❑ 329 Ben Wallace	.20	.50
❑ 330 Chris Webber	.20	.50
❑ NNO Grant Hill Promo	.20	.50

1998-99 Hoops

❑ COMPLETE SET (167)	10.00	20.00
❑ 1 Kobe Bryant	.75	2.00
❑ 2 Glenn Robinson	.10	.30
❑ 3 Derek Anderson	.15	.40
❑ 4 Terry Dehere	.05	.15
❑ 5 Jalen Rose	.20	.50
❑ 6 Zydrunas Ilgauskas	.10	.30
❑ 7 Scott Williams	.05	.15
❑ 8 Toni Kukoc	.10	.30
❑ 9 John Stockton	.20	.50
❑ 10 Kevin Garnett	.40	1.00
❑ 11 Jerome Williams	.05	.15
❑ 12 Anthony Mason	.10	.30
❑ 13 Harvey Grant	.05	.15
❑ 14 Mookie Blaylock	.05	.15
❑ 15 Tyrone Hill	.05	.15
❑ 16 Dale Davis	.10	.30
❑ 17 Eric Washington	.05	.15
❑ 18 Aaron McKie	.10	.30
❑ 19 Jermaine O'Neal	.20	.50
❑ 20 Anfernee Hardaway	.20	.50
❑ 21 Derrick Coleman	.05	.15
❑ 22 Allan Houston	.10	.30
❑ 23 Michael Jordan	1.25	3.00
❑ 24 Jason Kidd	.30	.75
❑ 25 Tyrone Corbin	.05	.15
❑ 26 Jacque Vaughn	.05	.15
❑ 27 Bobby Jackson	.10	.30
❑ 28 Chris Anstey	.05	.15
❑ 29 Brent Barry	.10	.30
❑ 30 Shareef Abdur-Rahim	.20	.50
❑ 31 Jeff Hornacek	.10	.30
❑ 32 Ed Gray	.05	.15
❑ 33 Grant Hill	.20	.50
❑ 34 Steve Smith	.10	.30
❑ 35 Rony Seikaly	.05	.15
❑ 36 Mark Jackson	.10	.30
❑ 37 Shawn Bradley	.05	.15
❑ 38 Corie Blount	.05	.15
❑ 39 Erick Dampier	.10	.30
❑ 40 Kerry Kittles	.05	.15
❑ 41 David Wesley	.05	.15
❑ 42 Horace Grant	.10	.30
❑ 43 Bobby Hurley	.05	.15
❑ 44 Tariq Abdul-Wahad	.05	.15
❑ 45 Brian Williams	.05	.15
❑ 46 Ray Allen	.20	.50
❑ 47 Kenny Anderson	.10	.30
❑ 48 Rodrick Rhodes	.05	.15
❑ 49 Greg Foster	.05	.15
❑ 50 Tim Duncan	.30	.75
❑ 51 Steve Nash	.20	.50
❑ 52 Kelvin Cato	.05	.15
❑ 53 Donyell Marshall	.10	.30
❑ 54 Marcus Camby	.10	.30
❑ 55 Kevin Willis	.05	.15
❑ 56 Michael Finley	.20	.50
❑ 57 Muggsy Bogues	.10	.30
❑ 58 Mark Price	.10	.30
❑ 59 Larry Johnson	.10	.30
❑ 60 Karl Malone	.20	.50
❑ 61 Greg Ostertag	.05	.15
❑ 62 Sean Elliott	.10	.30
❑ 63 Johnny Taylor	.05	.15
❑ 64 Howard Eisley	.05	.15
❑ 65 Chris Childs	.05	.15
❑ 66 Walt Williams	.05	.15
❑ 67 Tracy Murray	.05	.15
❑ 68 Patrick Ewing	.20	.50
❑ 69 Olden Polynice	.05	.15
❑ 70 Allen Iverson	.40	1.00
❑ 71 David Robinson	.20	.50
❑ 72 Colbert Cheaney	.05	.15
❑ 73 Lamond Murray	.05	.15
❑ 74 Scot Pollard	.05	.15
❑ 75 Alonzo Mourning	.10	.30
❑ 76 Tracy McGrady	.50	1.25
❑ 77 Jim McIlvaine	.05	.15
❑ 78 Bob Sura	.05	.15
❑ 79 Anthony Peeler	.05	.15
❑ 80 Keith Van Horn	.20	.50
❑ 81 Maurice Taylor	.07	.20
❑ 82 Charles Smith	.05	.15
❑ 83 Dikembe Mutombo	.10	.30
❑ 84 Nick Anderson	.05	.15
❑ 85 Austin Croshere	.15	.40
❑ 86 Armon Gilliam	.05	.15
❑ 87 Eddie Jones	.20	.50
❑ 88 Glen Rice	.10	.30
❑ 89 Sam Cassell	.20	.50
❑ 90 Stephon Marbury	.20	.50
❑ 91 Elliot Perry UER	.05	.15
❑ 92 Jamal Mashburn	.10	.30
❑ 93 Adonal Foyle	.05	.15
❑ 94 Avery Johnson	.05	.15
❑ 95 Micheal Williams	.05	.15
❑ 96 Danny Fortson	.05	.15
❑ 97 Brevin Knight	.05	.15
❑ 98 Ron Harper	.10	.30
❑ 99 Chauncey Billups	.10	.30
❑ 100 Shaquille O'Neal	.50	1.25
❑ 101 Brent Price	.05	.15
❑ 102 Tim Thomas	.10	.30
❑ 103 Khalid Reeves	.05	.15
❑ 104 Chris Gatling	.05	.15
❑ 105 Terry Cummings	.05	.15
❑ 106 Vin Baker	.10	.30
❑ 107 Bryant Reeves	.05	.15
❑ 108 John Starks	.10	.30
❑ 109 Juwan Howard	.10	.30
❑ 110 Antoine Walker	.20	.50
❑ 111 Rodney Rogers	.05	.15
❑ 112 Nick Van Exel	.20	.50
❑ 113 Chris Whitney	.05	.15
❑ 114 Bobby Phills	.05	.15
❑ 115 Travis Knight	.05	.15
❑ 116 Robert Horry	.10	.30
❑ 117 Erick Strickland	.05	.15
❑ 118 Dontae Jones	.05	.15
❑ 119 Tony Battie	.05	.15
❑ 120 Lindsey Hunter	.05	.15
❑ 121 Reggie Miller	.20	.50
❑ 122 John Wallace	.05	.15
❑ 123 Ron Mercer	.08	.25
❑ 124 Antonio Daniels	.05	.15
❑ 125 Paul Grant	.05	.15
❑ 126 Voshon Lenard	.05	.15
❑ 127 Shawn Kemp	.10	.30
❑ 128 Antonio Davis	.05	.15
❑ 129 Hakeem Olajuwon	.20	.50
❑ 130 Danny Manning	.05	.15
❑ 131 Bimbo Coles	.05	.15
❑ 132 Tim Hardaway	.10	.30
❑ 133 Lorenzo Williams	.05	.15
❑ 134 Dan Majerle	.10	.30
❑ 135 Bryant Stith	.05	.15
❑ 136 Randy Brown	.05	.15
❑ 137 Hubert Davis	.05	.15
❑ 138 Gary Payton	.20	.50
❑ 139 Rasheed Wallace	.20	.50
❑ 140 Chris Robinson	.05	.15
❑ 141 Doug Christie	.10	.30
❑ 142 Brian Grant	.10	.30
❑ 143 Isaiah Rider	.05	.15
❑ 144 Kendall Gill	.05	.15
❑ 145 Lorenzen Wright	.05	.15
❑ 146 Ervin Johnson	.05	.15
❑ 147 Monty Williams	.05	.15
❑ 148 Keith Closs	.05	.15
❑ 149 Tony Delk	.05	.15
❑ 150 Hersey Hawkins	.05	.15
❑ 151 Dean Garrett	.05	.15
❑ 152 Cedric Henderson	.05	.15
❑ 153 Detlef Schrempf	.10	.30
❑ 154 Dana Barros	.05	.15
❑ 155 Dee Brown	.05	.15
❑ 156 Jayson Williams SO	.05	.15
❑ 157 Charles Barkley SO	.20	.50
❑ 158 Damon Stoudamire SO	.05	.15
❑ 159 Scottie Pippen SO	.20	.50
❑ 160 Joe Smith SO	.05	.15
❑ 161 Antonio McDyess SO	.10	.30
❑ 162 Jerry Stackhouse SO	.10	.30
❑ 163 Dennis Rodman SO	.05	.15
❑ 164 Shaquille O'Neal SO	.20	.50
❑ 165 Grant Hill SO	.10	.30
❑ 166 Checklist	.05	.15
❑ 167 Checklist	.05	.15

1999-00 Hoops

❑ COMPLETE SET (185)	15.00	30.00
❑ COMMON CARD (1-165)	.05	.15
❑ COMMON ROOKIE (166-185)	.20	.50
❑ 1 Paul Pierce	.20	.50
❑ 2 Ray Allen	.20	.50
❑ 3 Jason Williams	.20	.50
❑ 4 Sean Elliott	.20	.50
❑ 5 Al Harrington	.15	.40
❑ 6 Bobby Phills	.12	.30
❑ 7 Tyronn Lue	.12	.30
❑ 8 James Cotton	.12	.30
❑ 9 Anthony Peeler	.12	.30
❑ 10 LaPhonso Ellis	.12	.30
❑ 11 Voshon Lenard	.12	.30

❑ 12 Kornel David RC	.20	.50
❑ 13 Michael Finley	.20	.50
❑ 14 Danny Fortson	.12	.30
❑ 15 Antawn Jamison	.20	.50
❑ 16 Reggie Miller	.20	.50
❑ 17 Shaquille O'Neal	.50	1.25
❑ 18 P.J. Brown	.12	.30
❑ 19 Roshown McLeod	.12	.30
❑ 20 Larry Johnson	.20	.50
❑ 21 Rashard Lewis	.20	.50
❑ 22 Tracy McGrady	.40	1.00
❑ 23 Peja Stojakovic	.15	.40
❑ 24 Tracy Murray	.12	.30
❑ 25 Gary Payton	.20	.50
❑ 26 Ricky Davis	.20	.50
❑ 27 Kobe Bryant	1.00	2.50
❑ 28 Avery Johnson	.15	.40
❑ 29 Kevin Garnett	.40	1.00
❑ 30 Charles Jones	.12	.30
❑ 31 Brevin Knight	.12	.30
❑ 32 Lindsey Hunter	.12	.30
❑ 33 Felipe Lopez	.12	.30
❑ 34 Rik Smits	.20	.50
❑ 35 Maurice Taylor	.15	.40
❑ 36 Corey Benjamin	.12	.30
❑ 37 Ervin Johnson	.12	.30
❑ 38 Steve Smith	.12	.30
❑ 39 Austin Croshere	.12	.30
❑ 40 Matt Geiger	.12	.30
❑ 41 Tom Gugliotta	.12	.30
❑ 42 Radoslav Nesterovic RC	.25	.60
❑ 43 Juwan Howard	.15	.40
❑ 44 Keon Clark	.12	.30
❑ 45 Latrell Sprewell	.15	.40
❑ 46 George Lynch	.12	.30
❑ 47 Greg Ostertag	.12	.30
❑ 48 J.R. Henderson	.12	.30
❑ 49 Kerry Kittles	.12	.30
❑ 50 Matt Harpring	.15	.40
❑ 51 Duane Causwell	.12	.30
❑ 52 Andrae Patterson	.12	.30
❑ 53 Jerry Stackhouse	.20	.50
❑ 54 Adonal Foyle	.12	.30
❑ 55 Bryce Drew	.12	.30
❑ 56 Chris Childs	.12	.30
❑ 57 Charles Smith	.12	.30
❑ 58 Rony Seikaly	.20	.50
❑ 59 Chauncey Billups	.20	.50
❑ 60 Grant Hill	.20	.50
❑ 61 Marlon Garnett RC	.20	.50
❑ 62 Tim Hardaway	.20	.50
❑ 63 Vlade Divac	.20	.50
❑ 64 Chris Gatling	.12	.30
❑ 65 Glenn Robinson	.15	.40
❑ 66 Michael Olowokandi	.12	.30
❑ 67 Elliot Perry	.12	.30
❑ 68 Howard Eisley	.12	.30
❑ 69 Glen Rice	.20	.50
❑ 70 Marcus Camby	.15	.40
❑ 71 Theo Ratliff	.15	.40
❑ 72 Brian Skinner	.12	.30
❑ 73 Kenny Anderson	.15	.40
❑ 74 Jamal Mashburn	.12	.30
❑ 75 Vladimir Stepania	.12	.30
❑ 76 Jayson Williams	.15	.40
❑ 77 Brian Grant	.12	.30
❑ 78 Raef LaFrentz	.15	.40
❑ 79 John Starks	.20	.50
❑ 80 Mike Bibby	.20	.50
❑ 81 Stephon Marbury	.20	.50
❑ 82 Armon Gilliam	.12	.30
❑ 83 Sam Jacobson	.12	.30
❑ 84 Derrick Coleman	.15	.40
❑ 85 Allan Houston	.15	.40
❑ 86 Miles Simon	.12	.30
❑ 87 Allen Iverson	.40	1.00
❑ 88 Derek Anderson	.12	.30
❑ 89 Chris Anstey	.12	.30
❑ 90 Larry Hughes	.15	.40
❑ 91 Vitaly Potapenko	.12	.30
❑ 92 Cherokee Parks	.12	.30
❑ 93 Donyell Marshall	.15	.40
❑ 94 Danny Manning	.12	.30
❑ 95 Bryon Russell	.12	.30
❑ 96 Randell Jackson	.12	.30
❑ 97 Antoine Walker	.20	.50
❑ 98 Dirk Nowitzki	.30	.75
❑ 99 Karl Malone	.25	.60
❑ 100 Vince Carter	.40	1.00
❑ 101 Eddie Jones	.20	.50
❑ 102 Bryant Stith	.12	.30
❑ 103 Korleone Young	.12	.30
❑ 104 Tim Duncan	.40	1.00
❑ 105 Jerome Kersey	.12	.30
❑ 106 Bonzi Wells	.12	.30
❑ 107 Wesley Person	.12	.30
❑ 108 Steve Nash	.30	.75
❑ 109 Tyrone Nesby RC	.20	.50
❑ 110 Doug Christie	.15	.40
❑ 111 David Robinson	.25	.60
❑ 112 Ruben Patterson	.12	.30
❑ 113 Dikembe Mutombo	.15	.40
❑ 114 Ron Mercer	.12	.30
❑ 115 Elden Campbell	.12	.30
❑ 116 Kevin Willis	.12	.30
❑ 117 Hakeem Olajuwon	.20	.50
❑ 118 Shawn Kemp	.20	.50
❑ 119 Eric Montross	.12	.30
❑ 120 Shareef Abdur-Rahim	.15	.40
❑ 121 Bob Sura	.12	.30
❑ 122 James Robinson	.12	.30
❑ 123 Shawn Bradley	.12	.30
❑ 124 Robert Traylor	.12	.30
❑ 125 Dean Garrett	.12	.30
❑ 126 Keith Van Horn	.15	.40
❑ 127 Patrick Ewing	.25	.60
❑ 128 Isaac Austin	.12	.30
❑ 129 Jason Kidd	.30	.75
❑ 130 Isaiah Rider	.12	.30
❑ 131 Jerome James RC	.20	.50
❑ 132 John Stockton	.25	.60
❑ 133 Jason Caffey	.12	.30
❑ 134 Bryant Reeves	.12	.30
❑ 135 Michael Dickerson	.12	.30
❑ 136 Chris Mullin	.20	.50
❑ 137 Rasheed Wallace	.20	.50
❑ 138 Cuttino Mobley	.15	.40
❑ 139 Antonio McDyess	.15	.40
❑ 140 Chris Webber	.20	.50
❑ 141 Jelani McCoy	.12	.30
❑ 142 Damon Stoudamire	.20	.50
❑ 143 Gerald Brown	.20	.50
❑ 144 Cory Carr	.12	.30
❑ 145 Brent Barry	.15	.40
❑ 146 Alan Henderson	.12	.30
❑ 147 Nazr Mohammed	.12	.30
❑ 148 Bison Dele	.12	.30
❑ 149 Scottie Pippen	.30	.75
❑ 150 Michael Doleac	.12	.30
❑ 151 Nick Anderson	.12	.30
❑ 152 Alonzo Mourning	.20	.50
❑ 153 Jahidi White	.12	.30
❑ 154 Jalen Rose	.15	.40
❑ 155 Brad Miller	.15	.40
❑ 156 Andrew DeClercq	.12	.30
❑ 157 Erick Strickland	.12	.30
❑ 158 Toni Kukoc	.20	.50
❑ 159 Pat Garrity	.12	.30
❑ 160 Bobby Jackson	.15	.40
❑ 161 Steve Kerr	.15	.40
❑ 162 Toby Bailey	.12	.30
❑ 163 Charles Oakley	.15	.40
❑ 164 Rod Strickland	.12	.30
❑ 165 Rodrick Rhodes	.12	.30
❑ 166 Ron Artest RC	.75	2.00
❑ 167 William Avery RC	.20	.50
❑ 168 Elton Brand RC	.60	1.50
❑ 169 Baron Davis RC	.75	2.00
❑ 170 John Celestand RC	.20	.50
❑ 171 Jumaine Jones RC	.20	.50
❑ 172 Andre Miller RC	.60	1.50
❑ 173 Lee Nailon RC	.20	.50
❑ 174 James Posey RC	.30	.75
❑ 175 Jason Terry RC	.50	1.25
❑ 176 Kenny Thomas RC	.20	.50
❑ 177 Steve Francis RC	.60	1.50
❑ 178 Wally Szczerbiak RC	.60	1.50
❑ 179 Richard Hamilton RC	.60	1.50
❑ 180 Jonathan Bender RC	.20	.50
❑ 181 Shawn Marion RC	.60	1.50
❑ 182 A.Radojevic RC	.20	.50
❑ 183 Tim James RC	.20	.50
❑ 184 Trajan Langdon RC	.20	.50
❑ 185 Corey Maggette RC	.60	1.50

2004-05 Hoops

❑ COMP.SET w/o SP's (165)	15.00	40.00
❑ COMMON CARD (1-165)	.15	.40
❑ COMMON HH (166-175)	3.00	8.00

❑ COMMON ROOKIE (176-200)	1.25	3.00
❑ CARDS 168-170 NOT RELEASED		
❑ 1 Dwyane Wade	.75	2.00
❑ 2 Vince Carter	.50	1.25
❑ 3 Luke Walton	.20	.50
❑ 4 Alonzo Mourning	.25	.60
❑ 5 Antoine Walker	.25	.60
❑ 6 Jerry Stackhouse	.20	.50
❑ 7 Chris Wilcox	.15	.40
❑ 8 Udonis Haslem	.20	.50
❑ 9 Michael Redd	.25	.60
❑ 10 Darius Miles	.20	.50
❑ 11 Jarvis Hayes	.15	.40
❑ 12 Kirk Hinrich	.20	.50
❑ 13 Tayshaun Prince	.20	.50
❑ 14 Caron Butler	.20	.50
❑ 15 Sam Cassell	.20	.50
❑ 16 Kurt Thomas	.15	.40
❑ 17 Bruce Bowen	.15	.40
❑ 18 Jared Jeffries	.15	.40
❑ 19 Keith Bogans	.15	.40
❑ 20 Chauncey Billups	.25	.60
❑ 21 Lamar Odom	.25	.60
❑ 22 Fred Hoiberg	.15	.40
❑ 23 Cuttino Mobley	.20	.50
❑ 24 Manu Ginobili	.25	.60
❑ 25 Juan Dixon	.15	.40
❑ 26 Predrag Drobnjak	.15	.40
❑ 27 Nene	.20	.50
❑ 28 Elton Brand	.25	.60
❑ 29 Rasual Butler	.15	.40
❑ 30 Nick Van Exel	.20	.50
❑ 31 Carlos Arroyo	.25	.60
❑ 32 Zydrunas Ilgauskas	.20	.50
❑ 33 Troy Murphy	.25	.60
❑ 34 Jason Williams	.20	.50
❑ 35 Jason Kidd	.40	1.00
❑ 36 Samuel Dalembert	.15	.40
❑ 37 Vladimir Radmanovic	.15	.40
❑ 38 Kenny Anderson	.20	.50
❑ 39 Kenyon Martin	.25	.60
❑ 40 Jamaal Tinsley	.20	.50
❑ 41 Damon Jones	.15	.40
❑ 42 Shareef Abdur-Rahim	.20	.50
❑ 43 Ricky Davis	.20	.50
❑ 44 Earl Boykins	.15	.40
❑ 45 Austin Croshere	.15	.40
❑ 46 Keith Van Horn	.20	.50
❑ 47 Theo Ratliff	.15	.40
❑ 48 Mehmet Okur	.20	.50
❑ 49 Paul Pierce	.25	.60
❑ 50 Marcus Camby	.20	.50
❑ 51 Stephen Jackson	.20	.50
❑ 52 Maurice Williams	.20	.50
❑ 53 Brad Miller	.20	.50
❑ 54 Carlos Boozer	.25	.60
❑ 55 Dirk Nowitzki	.40	1.00
❑ 56 Dikembe Mutombo	.20	.50
❑ 57 James Posey	.15	.40
❑ 58 Baron Davis	.25	.60
❑ 59 Shawn Marion	.25	.60
❑ 60 Ronald Murray	.15	.40
❑ 61 Gary Payton	.25	.60
❑ 62 Andre Miller	.20	.50
❑ 63 Reggie Miller	.25	.60
❑ 64 Zaza Pachulia	.15	.40
❑ 65 Bobby Jackson	.15	.40
❑ 66 Peja Stojakovic	.20	.50
❑ 67 Jiri Welsch	.15	.40
❑ 68 Darko Milicic	.15	.40
❑ 69 Ron Artest	.20	.50
❑ 70 T.J. Ford	.20	.50
❑ 71 Andrei Kirilenko	.25	.60
❑ 72 Jason Kapono	.15	.40
❑ 73 Jermaine O'Neal	.25	.60

❑ 74 Desmond Mason .20 .50
❑ 75 Chris Webber .25 .60
❑ 76 Morris Peterson .20 .50
❑ 77 Ben Wallace .20 .50
❑ 78 Antonio Davis .15 .40
❑ 79 Slava Medvedenko .15 .40
❑ 80 Brian Scalabrine .15 .40
❑ 81 Jamal Crawford .20 .50
❑ 82 Josh Howard .25 .60
❑ 83 Tyson Chandler .20 .50
❑ 84 Rasheed Wallace .25 .60
❑ 85 Chris Mihm .15 .40
❑ 86 Latrell Sprewell .20 .50
❑ 87 Mike Sweetney .15 .40
❑ 88 Robert Horry .20 .50
❑ 89 Michael Finley .25 .60
❑ 90 Bostjan Nachbar .15 .40
❑ 91 Allan Houston .20 .50
❑ 92 Joe Johnson .25 .60
❑ 93 Jalen Rose .20 .50
❑ 94 Marquis Daniels .15 .40
❑ 95 Tyronn Lue .15 .40
❑ 96 Stephon Marbury .25 .60
❑ 97 Quentin Richardson .20 .50
❑ 98 Chris Bosh .25 .60
❑ 99 Dajuan Wagner .15 .40
❑ 100 Derek Fisher .20 .50
❑ 101 Devean George .15 .40
❑ 102 Zoran Planinic .15 .40
❑ 103 Corliss Williamson .15 .40
❑ 104 Brent Barry .15 .40
❑ 105 Drew Gooden .15 .40
❑ 106 Clifford Robinson .15 .40
❑ 107 Shane Battier .20 .50
❑ 108 P.J. Brown .15 .40
❑ 109 Willie Green .15 .40
❑ 110 Nick Collison .15 .40
❑ 111 Al Harrington .20 .50
❑ 112 Carmelo Anthony .75 2.00
❑ 113 Corey Maggette .20 .50
❑ 114 Eddie Jones .20 .50
❑ 115 Zach Randolph .25 .60
❑ 116 Raja Bell .20 .50
❑ 117 Jeff McInnis .15 .40
❑ 118 Yao Ming .60 1.50
❑ 119 Brian Cardinal .15 .40
❑ 120 Jamaal Magloire .15 .40
❑ 121 Kyle Korver .20 .50
❑ 122 Luke Ridnour .15 .40
❑ 123 Jason Terry .20 .50
❑ 124 Maurice Taylor .15 .40
❑ 125 Bonzi Wells .15 .40
❑ 126 David West .25 .60
❑ 127 Amare Stoudemire .50 1.25
❑ 128 Ray Allen .25 .60
❑ 129 Eddy Curry .20 .50
❑ 130 Richard Hamilton .20 .50
❑ 131 Kobe Bryant 1.25 3.00
❑ 132 Kevin Garnett .50 1.25
❑ 133 Steve Francis .25 .60
❑ 134 Tim Duncan .50 1.25
❑ 135 Larry Hughes .20 .50
❑ 136 LeBron James 1.50 4.00
❑ 137 Adonal Foyle .15 .40
❑ 138 Pau Gasol .25 .60
❑ 139 Richard Jefferson .25 .60
❑ 140 Allen Iverson .50 1.25
❑ 141 Antonio Daniels .15 .40
❑ 142 Eric Williams .15 .40
❑ 143 Primoz Brezec .15 .40
❑ 144 Jason Richardson .25 .60
❑ 145 Chris Kaman .20 .50
❑ 146 Troy Hudson .15 .40
❑ 147 Hedo Turkoglu .20 .50
❑ 148 Tony Parker .25 .60
❑ 149 Gilbert Arenas .25 .60
❑ 150 Eric Snow .15 .40
❑ 151 Tracy McGrady .50 1.25
❑ 152 Stromile Swift .15 .40
❑ 153 Dan Dickau .15 .40
❑ 154 Steve Nash .40 1.00
❑ 155 Rashard Lewis .25 .60
❑ 156 Gerald Wallace .25 .60
❑ 157 Mike Dunleavy .20 .50
❑ 158 Bobby Simmons .15 .40
❑ 159 Wally Szczerbiak .20 .50
❑ 160 Grant Hill .25 .60
❑ 161 Mike Bibby .20 .50
❑ 162 Antawn Jamison .25 .60
❑ 163 Antonio McDyess .20 .50
❑ 164 Shaquille O'Neal .60 1.50
❑ 165 Rafer Alston .15 .40
❑ 166 Charles Barkley HH 3.00 8.00
❑ 167 David Robinson HH 5.00 12.00
❑ 171 Larry Bird HH 8.00 20.00
❑ 172 Scottie Pippen HH 5.00 12.00
❑ 173 Isiah Thomas HH 5.00 12.00
❑ 174 Kevin McHale HH 3.00 8.00
❑ 175 Dominique Wilkins HH 3.00 8.00
❑ 176 Josh Childress RC 1.25 3.00
❑ 177 Josh Smith RC 3.00 8.00
❑ 178 Al Jefferson RC 2.50 6.00
❑ 179 Delonte West RC 2.00 5.00
❑ 180 Tony Allen RC 1.50 4.00
❑ 181 Emeka Okafor RC 2.50 6.00
❑ 182 Bernard Robinson RC 1.25 3.00
❑ 183 Ben Gordon RC 1.50 4.00
❑ 184 Luol Deng RC 1.50 4.00
❑ 185 Andres Nocioni RC 1.50 4.00
❑ 186 Luke Jackson RC 1.25 3.00
❑ 187 Devin Harris RC 2.50 6.00
❑ 188 Andris Biedrins RC 2.00 5.00
❑ 189 Shaun Livingston RC 1.25 3.00
❑ 190 Dorell Wright RC 1.50 4.00
❑ 191 J.R. Smith RC 2.50 6.00
❑ 192 Trevor Ariza RC 1.50 4.00
❑ 193 Dwight Howard RC 4.00 10.00
❑ 194 Jameer Nelson RC 1.50 4.00
❑ 195 Andre Iguodala RC 3.00 8.00
❑ 196 Sebastian Telfair RC 1.25 3.00
❑ 197 Kevin Martin RC 1.50 4.00
❑ 198 David Harrison RC 1.25 3.00
❑ 199 Rafael Araujo RC 1.25 3.00
❑ 200 Kirk Snyder RC 1.25 3.00

2005-06 Hoops

❑ COMPLETE SET (184) 20.00 50.00
❑ COMMON CARD (1-142) .15 .40
❑ COMMON ROOKIE (143-184) .75 2.00
❑ 1 Josh Childress .20 .50
❑ 2 Al Harrington .15 .40
❑ 3 Josh Smith .25 .60
❑ 4 Tony Delk .15 .40
❑ 5 Joe Johnson .25 .60
❑ 6 Al Jefferson .25 .60
❑ 7 Paul Pierce .25 .60
❑ 8 Ricky Davis .25 .60
❑ 9 Tony Allen .15 .40
❑ 10 Dan Dickau .15 .40
❑ 11 Keith Bogans .15 .40
❑ 12 Emeka Okafor .25 .60
❑ 13 Kareem Rush .15 .40
❑ 14 Gerald Wallace .25 .60
❑ 15 Primoz Brezec .15 .40
❑ 16 Ben Gordon .30 .75
❑ 17 Luol Deng .25 .60
❑ 18 Kirk Hinrich .25 .60
❑ 19 Chris Duhon .20 .50
❑ 20 Michael Jordan 1.50 4.00
❑ 21 LeBron James 1.25 3.00
❑ 22 Larry Hughes .20 .50
❑ 23 Donyell Marshall .15 .40
❑ 24 Drew Gooden .20 .50
❑ 25 Zydrunas Ilgauskas .20 .50
❑ 26 Erick Dampier .15 .40
❑ 27 Jason Terry .25 .60
❑ 28 Josh Howard .25 .60
❑ 29 Dirk Nowitzki .40 1.00
❑ 30 Jerry Stackhouse .25 .60
❑ 31 Carmelo Anthony .50 1.25
❑ 32 Marcus Camby .20 .50
❑ 33 Nene .15 .40
❑ 34 Kenyon Martin .25 .60
❑ 35 Chauncey Billups .25 .60
❑ 36 Richard Hamilton .20 .50
❑ 37 Ben Wallace .25 .60
❑ 38 Rasheed Wallace .25 .60
❑ 39 Tayshaun Prince .25 .60
❑ 40 Baron Davis .25 .60
❑ 41 Mike Dunleavy .20 .50
❑ 42 Mickael Pietrus .20 .50
❑ 43 Jason Richardson .25 .60
❑ 44 Tracy McGrady .50 1.25
❑ 45 Yao Ming .60 1.50
❑ 46 Stromile Swift .20 .50
❑ 47 Bob Sura .15 .40
❑ 48 Jermaine O'Neal .25 .60
❑ 49 Ron Artest .20 .50
❑ 50 Fred Jones .20 .50
❑ 51 Stephen Jackson .20 .50
❑ 52 Corey Maggette .20 .50
❑ 53 Elton Brand .25 .60
❑ 54 Shaun Livingston .15 .40
❑ 55 Chris Wilcox .15 .40
❑ 56 Chris Kaman .15 .40
❑ 57 Kobe Bryant 1.25 3.00
❑ 58 Lamar Odom .25 .60
❑ 59 Kwame Brown .20 .50
❑ 60 Luke Walton .20 .50
❑ 61 Devean George .20 .50
❑ 62 Pau Gasol .25 .60
❑ 63 Shane Battier .25 .60
❑ 64 Bobby Jackson .15 .40
❑ 65 Eddie Jones .15 .40
❑ 66 Lorenzen Wright .15 .40
❑ 67 Shaquille O'Neal .60 1.50
❑ 68 Dwyane Wade .60 1.50
❑ 69 Antoine Walker .20 .50
❑ 70 Jason Williams .20 .50
❑ 71 James Posey .15 .40
❑ 72 T.J. Ford .20 .50
❑ 73 Dan Gadzuric .15 .40
❑ 74 Desmond Mason .15 .40
❑ 75 Michael Redd .25 .60
❑ 76 Kevin Garnett .50 1.25
❑ 77 Sam Cassell .25 .60
❑ 78 Eddie Griffin .15 .40
❑ 79 Wally Szczerbiak .20 .50
❑ 80 Michael Olowokandi .15 .40
❑ 81 Jeff McInnis .15 .40
❑ 82 Vince Carter .50 1.25
❑ 83 Jason Kidd .40 1.00
❑ 84 Richard Jefferson .20 .50
❑ 85 Clifford Robinson .15 .40
❑ 86 P.J. Brown .15 .40
❑ 87 Jamaal Magloire .15 .40
❑ 88 J.R. Smith .20 .50
❑ 89 Speedy Claxton .15 .40
❑ 90 Jamal Crawford .20 .50
❑ 91 Stephon Marbury .25 .60
❑ 92 Quentin Richardson .20 .50
❑ 93 Mike Sweetney .20 .50
❑ 94 Malik Rose .15 .40
❑ 95 Steve Francis .25 .60
❑ 96 Dwight Howard .50 1.25
❑ 97 Keyon Dooling .15 .40
❑ 98 Grant Hill .25 .60
❑ 99 Jameer Nelson .20 .50
❑ 100 Allen Iverson .50 1.25
❑ 101 Samuel Dalembert .15 .40
❑ 102 Chris Webber .25 .60
❑ 103 Andre Iguodala .25 .60
❑ 104 Kyle Korver .25 .60
❑ 105 Steve Nash .30 .75
❑ 106 Shawn Marion .25 .60
❑ 107 Amare Stoudemire .50 1.25
❑ 108 Kurt Thomas .15 .40
❑ 109 Darius Miles .25 .60
❑ 110 Zach Randolph .25 .60
❑ 111 Sebastian Telfair .20 .50
❑ 112 Ruben Patterson .15 .40
❑ 113 Joel Przybilla .15 .40
❑ 114 Mike Bibby .25 .60
❑ 115 Peja Stojakovic .25 .60
❑ 116 Brad Miller .25 .60
❑ 117 Bonzi Wells .20 .50
❑ 118 Tim Duncan .50 1.25
❑ 119 Manu Ginobili .25 .60
❑ 120 Tony Parker .25 .60
❑ 121 Robert Horry .20 .50
❑ 122 Bruce Bowen .15 .40
❑ 123 Ray Allen .25 .60
❑ 124 Rashard Lewis .25 .60
❑ 125 Vladimir Radmanovic .15 .40

❑ 126 Luke Ridnour	.20	.50
❑ 127 Reggie Evans	.15	.40
❑ 128 Chris Bosh	.25	.60
❑ 129 Morris Peterson	.20	.50
❑ 130 Rafer Alston	.15	.40
❑ 131 Rafael Araujo	.15	.40
❑ 132 Jalen Rose	.25	.60
❑ 133 Carlos Boozer	.25	.60
❑ 134 Gordan Giricek	.15	.40
❑ 135 Matt Harpring	.20	.50
❑ 136 Andrei Kirilenko	.25	.60
❑ 137 Mehmet Okur	.15	.40
❑ 138 Gilbert Arenas	.25	.60
❑ 139 Antawn Jamison	.25	.60
❑ 140 Caron Butler	.25	.60
❑ 141 Antonio Daniels	.15	.40
❑ 142 Brendan Haywood	.15	.40
❑ 143 Sarunas Jasikevicius RC	1.00	2.50
❑ 144 Ryan Gomes RC	.75	2.00
❑ 145 Andray Blatche RC	1.00	2.50
❑ 146 Bracey Wright RC	.75	2.00
❑ 147 Louis Williams RC	1.25	3.00
❑ 148 Martynas Andriuskevicius RC	.75	2.00
❑ 149 Chris Taft RC	.75	2.00
❑ 150 Monta Ellis RC	2.00	5.00
❑ 151 Travis Diener RC	.75	2.00
❑ 152 Ersan Ilyasova RC	.75	2.00
❑ 153 Yaroslav Korolev RC	.75	2.00
❑ 154 C.J. Miles RC	.75	2.00
❑ 155 Brandon Bass RC	.75	2.00
❑ 156 Daniel Ewing RC	1.00	2.50
❑ 157 Salim Stoudamire RC	1.00	2.50
❑ 158 David Lee RC	1.50	4.00
❑ 159 Wayne Simien RC	1.00	2.50
❑ 160 Linas Kleiza RC	1.00	2.50
❑ 161 Jason Maxiell RC	1.00	2.50
❑ 162 Johan Petro RC	.75	2.00
❑ 163 Luther Head RC	1.00	2.50
❑ 164 Francisco Garcia RC	1.00	2.50
❑ 165 Jarrett Jack RC	.75	2.00
❑ 166 Nate Robinson RC	1.25	3.00
❑ 167 Julius Hodge RC	1.00	2.50
❑ 168 Hakim Warrick RC	1.25	3.00
❑ 169 Gerald Green RC	.75	2.00
❑ 170 Danny Granger RC	2.00	5.00
❑ 171 Joey Graham RC	.75	2.00
❑ 172 Antoine Wright RC	.75	2.00
❑ 173 Rashad McCants RC	1.00	2.50
❑ 174 Sean May RC	1.00	2.50
❑ 175 Andrew Bynum RC	2.50	6.00
❑ 176 Ike Diogu RC	1.00	2.50
❑ 177 Channing Frye RC	1.00	2.50
❑ 178 Charlie Villanueva RC	1.25	3.00
❑ 179 Martell Webster RC	.75	2.00
❑ 180 Raymond Felton RC	1.00	2.50
❑ 181 Chris Paul RC	2.50	6.00
❑ 182 Deron Williams RC	2.00	5.00
❑ 183 Marvin Williams RC	1.25	3.00
❑ 184 Andrew Bogut RC	1.00	2.50

1999-00 Hoops Decade

❑ COMPLETE SET (180)	20.00	40.00
❑ COMMON CARD (1-180)	.12	.30
❑ COMMON ROOKIE	.20	.50
❑ 1 David Robinson	.25	.60
❑ 2 Mookie Blaylock	.12	.30
❑ 3 Jaren Jackson	.12	.30
❑ 4 Andre Miller RC	.60	1.50
❑ 5 Michael Olowokandi	.12	.30
❑ 6 Glenn Robinson	.15	.40
❑ 7 Steve Smith	.12	.30
❑ 8 Eric Snow	.15	.40
❑ 9 Antoine Walker	.20	.50
❑ 10 Nick Anderson	.12	.30
❑ 11 Jonathan Bender RC	.20	.50
❑ 12 Sean Elliott	.20	.50
❑ 13 Danny Fortson	.12	.30
❑ 14 Adonal Foyle	.12	.30
❑ 15 Richard Hamilton RC	.60	1.50
❑ 16 Shawn Kemp	.20	.50
❑ 17 Christian Laettner	.15	.40
❑ 18 Rashard Lewis	.20	.50
❑ 19 Danny Manning	.12	.30
❑ 20 Mitch Richmond	.15	.40
❑ 21 Shawn Bradley	.12	.30
❑ 22 Tim Duncan	.40	1.00
❑ 23 Tim Hardaway	.20	.50
❑ 24 Antawn Jamison	.20	.50
❑ 25 Jeff Hornacek	.15	.40
❑ 26 Jumaine Jones RC	.20	.50
❑ 27 Corey Maggette RC	.60	1.50
❑ 28 Vitaly Potapenko	.12	.30
❑ 29 Jerry Stackhouse	.20	.50
❑ 30 Jason Terry RC	.50	1.25
❑ 31 Baron Davis RC	.75	2.00
❑ 32 Matt Harpring	.15	.40
❑ 33 Glen Rice	.20	.50
❑ 34 Vladimir Stepania	.12	.30
❑ 35 Jayson Williams	.15	.40
❑ 36 Wally Szczerbiak RC	.60	1.50
❑ 37 Michael Doleac	.12	.30
❑ 38 Hersey Hawkins	.12	.30
❑ 39 Allan Houston	.15	.40
❑ 40 Hakeem Olajuwon	.20	.50
❑ 41 Damon Stoudamire	.20	.50
❑ 42 Jelani McCoy	.12	.30
❑ 43 A.Radojevic RC	.20	.50
❑ 44 Cal Bowdler RC	.20	.50
❑ 45 Tyronn Lue	.12	.30
❑ 46 Andrae Patterson	.12	.30
❑ 47 Karl Malone	.25	.60
❑ 48 Alonzo Mourning	.20	.50
❑ 49 Vince Carter	.40	1.00
❑ 50 Darrell Armstrong	.12	.30
❑ 51 Terrell Brandon	.12	.30
❑ 52 John Celestand RC	.20	.50
❑ 53 Grant Hill	.20	.50
❑ 54 Stephon Marbury	.20	.50
❑ 55 Tracy McGrady	.40	1.00
❑ 56 Reggie Miller	.20	.50
❑ 57 Clifford Robinson	.12	.30
❑ 58 Arvydas Sabonis	.15	.40
❑ 59 William Avery RC	.20	.50
❑ 60 Calbert Cheaney	.12	.30
❑ 61 Jermaine Jackson RC	.20	.50
❑ 62 Allen Iverson	.40	1.00
❑ 63 Larry Johnson	.20	.50
❑ 64 Toni Kukoc	.20	.50
❑ 65 Raef LaFrentz	.15	.40
❑ 66 Isaiah Rider	.12	.30
❑ 67 Jeff Foster RC	.25	.60
❑ 68 Juwan Howard	.15	.40
❑ 69 Kerry Kittles	.12	.30
❑ 70 Brevin Knight	.12	.30
❑ 71 Voshon Lenard	.12	.30
❑ 72 Latrell Sprewell	.15	.40
❑ 73 Maurice Taylor	.15	.40
❑ 74 Chris Webber	.20	.50
❑ 75 Jerome Williams	.12	.30
❑ 76 Scott Padgett RC	.20	.50
❑ 77 Vin Baker	.20	.50
❑ 78 Chris Childs	.12	.30
❑ 79 Erick Dampier	.15	.40
❑ 80 Anfernee Hardaway	.20	.50
❑ 81 Jamal Mashburn	.12	.30
❑ 82 Todd Fuller	.12	.30
❑ 83 Eric Piatkowski	.15	.40
❑ 84 Gary Trent	.12	.30
❑ 85 Kevin Garnett	.40	1.00
❑ 86 Chris Mullin	.20	.50
❑ 87 Charles Oakley	.15	.40
❑ 88 Detlef Schrempf	.15	.40
❑ 89 Elton Brand RC	.60	1.50
❑ 90 Patrick Ewing	.25	.60
❑ 91 Devean George RC	.30	.75
❑ 92 Brian Grant	.12	.30
❑ 93 Larry Hughes	.15	.40
❑ 94 Dan Majerle	.20	.50
❑ 95 Shawn Marion RC	.60	1.50
❑ 96 Cuttino Mobley	.15	.40
❑ 97 Paul Pierce	.20	.50
❑ 98 Bryant Reeves	.12	.30
❑ 99 Keith Van Horn	.15	.40
❑ 100 Corliss Williamson	.12	.30
❑ 101 Tariq Abdul-Wahad	.12	.30
❑ 102 Brent Barry	.15	.40
❑ 103 Elden Campbell	.12	.30
❑ 104 Mark Jackson	.20	.50
❑ 105 Lamond Murray	.12	.30
❑ 106 Bryon Russell	.12	.30
❑ 107 Jason Williams	.20	.50
❑ 108 Ray Allen	.20	.50
❑ 109 Ron Artest RC	.75	2.00
❑ 110 Charles Barkley	.25	.60
❑ 111 Cedric Ceballos	.12	.30
❑ 112 Jason Kidd	.30	.75
❑ 113 Donyell Marshall	.15	.40
❑ 114 John Stockton	.25	.60
❑ 115 Mike Bibby	.20	.50
❑ 116 Ricky Davis	.20	.50
❑ 117 Steve Francis RC	.60	1.50
❑ 118 Tom Gugliotta	.12	.30
❑ 119 Laron Profit RC	.20	.50
❑ 120 Joe Smith	.15	.40
❑ 121 Doug Christie	.15	.40
❑ 122 Kenny Anderson	.15	.40
❑ 123 Michael Dickerson	.12	.30
❑ 124 Zydrunas Ilgauskas	.15	.40
❑ 125 Bobby Jackson	.15	.40
❑ 126 Quincy Lewis RC	.20	.50
❑ 127 Shandon Anderson	.12	.30
❑ 128 Bo Outlaw	.12	.30
❑ 129 Scottie Pippen	.30	.75
❑ 130 Rodney Rogers	.12	.30
❑ 131 Rik Smits	.20	.50
❑ 132 Chauncey Billups	.20	.50
❑ 133 Chris Crawford	.12	.30
❑ 134 Kornel David RC	.20	.50
❑ 135 Tony Delk	.12	.30
❑ 136 Kendall Gill	.12	.30
❑ 137 Trajan Langdon RC	.20	.50
❑ 138 Ron Mercer	.12	.30
❑ 139 Othella Harrington	.12	.30
❑ 140 Gheorghe Muresan	.12	.30
❑ 141 Isaac Austin	.12	.30
❑ 142 Dion Glover RC	.20	.50
❑ 143 Avery Johnson	.15	.40
❑ 144 Antonio McDyess	.15	.40
❑ 145 Steve Nash	.30	.75
❑ 146 Tyrone Nesby RC	.20	.50
❑ 147 Shaquille O'Neal	.50	1.25
❑ 148 James Posey RC	.30	.75
❑ 149 Rod Strickland	.12	.30
❑ 150 Kobe Bryant	1.00	2.50
❑ 151 Michael Finley	.20	.50
❑ 152 Anthony Mason	.12	.30
❑ 153 Dikembe Mutombo	.15	.40
❑ 154 John Starks	.20	.50
❑ 155 Kenny Thomas RC	.20	.50
❑ 156 Matt Geiger	.12	.30
❑ 157 Tim James RC	.20	.50
❑ 158 Eddie Jones	.20	.50
❑ 159 Lamar Odom RC	.60	1.50
❑ 160 Nick Van Exel	.15	.40
❑ 161 Sam Cassell	.15	.40
❑ 162 Vonteego Cummings RC	.20	.50
❑ 163 Lindsey Hunter	.12	.30
❑ 164 Dirk Nowitzki	.30	.75
❑ 165 Gary Payton	.20	.50
❑ 166 Shareef Abdur-Rahim	.15	.40
❑ 167 Jalen Rose	.15	.40
❑ 168 Robert Traylor	.12	.30
❑ 169 Derek Anderson	.12	.30
❑ 170 Corey Benjamin	.12	.30
❑ 171 Marcus Camby	.15	.40
❑ 172 Vlade Divac	.20	.50
❑ 173 Mario Elie	.12	.30
❑ 174 Felipe Lopez	.12	.30
❑ 175 Rafer Alston RC	.40	1.00
❑ 176 Antonio Davis	.12	.30
❑ 177 Howard Eisley	.12	.30
❑ 178 Theo Ratliff	.15	.40
❑ 179 Tim Thomas	.15	.40
❑ 180 Rasheed Wallace	.20	.50

2000-01 Hoops Hot Prospects

❑ COMPLETE SET w/o RC (120)	20.00	40.00
❑ COMMON CARD (1-120)	.25	.60
❑ COMMON ROOKIE (121-145)	2.00	5.00
❑ 1 Vince Carter	.75	2.00
❑ 2 Wesley Person	.25	.60
❑ 3 Juwan Howard	.30	.75
❑ 4 Rodney Rogers	.25	.60

❑ 5 Tim Duncan	.75	2.00
❑ 6 Rasheed Wallace	.40	1.00
❑ 7 Anthony Peeler	.25	.60
❑ 8 John Amaechi	.25	.60
❑ 9 Tim Hardaway	.30	.75
❑ 10 Mark Jackson	.30	.75
❑ 11 Latrell Sprewell	.30	.75
❑ 12 Kevin Garnett	.75	2.00
❑ 13 Alonzo Mourning	.40	1.00
❑ 14 Jerome Williams	.25	.60
❑ 15 Anfernee Hardaway	.40	1.00
❑ 16 Clifford Robinson	.25	.60
❑ 17 Mike Bibby	.30	.75
❑ 18 Allen Iverson	.75	2.00
❑ 19 Terrell Brandon	.25	.60
❑ 20 Jerry Stackhouse	.30	.75
❑ 21 Brian Grant	.25	.60
❑ 22 Lamond Murray	.25	.60
❑ 23 Nick Anderson	.25	.60
❑ 24 Alan Henderson	.25	.60
❑ 25 Bryon Russell	.25	.60
❑ 26 Elton Brand	.40	1.00
❑ 27 Antawn Jamison	.40	1.00
❑ 28 Mitch Richmond	.30	.75
❑ 29 Marcus Camby	.30	.75
❑ 30 Raef LaFrentz	.25	.60
❑ 31 Damon Stoudamire	.30	.75
❑ 32 Vin Baker	.30	.75
❑ 33 Allan Houston	.30	.75
❑ 34 Doug Christie	.25	.60
❑ 35 Stephon Marbury	.40	1.00
❑ 36 Tim Thomas	.25	.60
❑ 37 Tracy McGrady	.75	2.00
❑ 38 Shareef Abdur-Rahim	.30	.75
❑ 39 Eddie Jones	.30	.75
❑ 40 Glenn Robinson	.30	.75
❑ 41 Sam Cassell	.30	.75
❑ 42 Dan Majerle	.30	.75
❑ 43 Maurice Taylor	.25	.60
❑ 44 Anthony Mason	.25	.60
❑ 45 Dirk Nowitzki	.60	1.50
❑ 46 Kobe Bryant	2.00	5.00
❑ 47 Kerry Kittles	.30	.75
❑ 48 Derrick Coleman	.30	.75
❑ 49 Cuttino Mobley	.30	.75
❑ 50 Nick Van Exel	.30	.75
❑ 51 LaPhonso Ellis	.30	.75
❑ 52 Kendall Gill	.25	.60
❑ 53 Hakeem Olajuwon	.50	1.25
❑ 54 Rashard Lewis	.40	1.00
❑ 55 Dale Davis	.25	.60
❑ 56 Keith Van Horn	.30	.75
❑ 57 Michael Finley	.40	1.00
❑ 58 Othella Harrington	.25	.60
❑ 59 Gary Payton	.40	1.00
❑ 60 Michael Dickerson	.25	.60
❑ 61 Voshon Lenard	.25	.60
❑ 62 Patrick Ewing	.50	1.25
❑ 63 Ron Mercer	.25	.60
❑ 64 Kenny Anderson	.30	.75
❑ 65 Shaquille O'Neal	1.00	2.50
❑ 66 Tariq Abdul-Wahad	.25	.60
❑ 67 Antonio Davis	.25	.60
❑ 68 Rick Fox	.30	.75
❑ 69 Lamar Odom	.40	1.00
❑ 70 Derek Anderson	.30	.75
❑ 71 Vitaly Potapenko	.25	.60
❑ 72 Karl Malone	.50	1.25
❑ 73 Wally Szczerbiak	.30	.75
❑ 74 Jason Williams	.30	.75
❑ 75 Steve Francis	.40	1.00
❑ 76 John Starks	.25	.60
❑ 77 Ron Artest	.40	1.00
❑ 78 Grant Hill	.40	1.00
❑ 79 Theo Ratliff	.25	.60
❑ 80 Antonio McDyess	.30	.75
❑ 81 Antoine Walker	.30	.75
❑ 82 Sean Elliott	.30	.75
❑ 83 Ruben Patterson	.25	.60
❑ 84 Ray Allen	.40	1.00
❑ 85 Tom Gugliotta	.25	.60
❑ 86 Scottie Pippen	.60	1.50
❑ 87 Jim Jackson	.25	.60
❑ 88 Joe Smith	.25	.60
❑ 89 Reggie Miller	.40	1.00
❑ 90 Richard Hamilton	.30	.75
❑ 91 Paul Pierce	.40	1.00
❑ 92 Mookie Blaylock	.30	.75
❑ 93 Glen Rice	.30	.75
❑ 94 P.J. Brown	.25	.60
❑ 95 Avery Johnson	.30	.75
❑ 96 John Stockton	.50	1.25
❑ 97 Tyrone Hill	.25	.60
❑ 98 Tracy Murray	.25	.60
❑ 99 Darrell Armstrong	.25	.60
❑ 100 Steve Smith	.30	.75
❑ 101 Shawn Kemp	.40	1.00
❑ 102 Jalen Rose	.30	.75
❑ 103 Vonteego Cummings	.25	.60
❑ 104 Larry Hughes	.30	.75
❑ 105 Charles Oakley	.30	.75
❑ 106 Rod Strickland	.30	.75
❑ 107 Christian Laettner	.25	.60
❑ 108 Baron Davis	.40	1.00
❑ 109 Jamal Mashburn	.30	.75
❑ 110 Lindsey Hunter	.25	.60
❑ 111 Toni Kukoc	.30	.75
❑ 112 Austin Croshere	.25	.60
❑ 113 Chris Webber	.40	1.00
❑ 114 Vlade Divac	.30	.75
❑ 115 Andre Miller	.30	.75
❑ 116 Larry Johnson	.30	.75
❑ 117 Jason Kidd	.60	1.50
❑ 118 David Robinson	.50	1.25
❑ 119 Donyell Marshall	.25	.60
❑ 120 Jason Terry	.40	1.00
❑ 121 Kenyon Martin RC	5.00	12.00
❑ 122 Stromile Swift RC	2.50	6.00
❑ 123 Chris Mihm RC	2.00	5.00
❑ 124 Marcus Fizer RC	2.00	5.00
❑ 125 Courtney Alexander RC	2.00	5.00
❑ 126 Darius Miles RC	2.50	6.00
❑ 127 Jerome Moiso RC	2.00	5.00
❑ 128 Joel Przybilla RC	2.00	5.00
❑ 129 DerMarr Johnson RC	2.00	5.00
❑ 130 Mike Miller RC	3.00	8.00
❑ 131 Quentin Richardson RC	2.50	6.00
❑ 132 Morris Peterson RC	3.00	8.00
❑ 133 Speedy Claxton RC	2.00	5.00
❑ 134 Keyon Dooling RC	2.00	5.00
❑ 135 Mark Madsen RC	2.00	5.00
❑ 136 Mateen Cleaves RC	2.00	5.00
❑ 137 Etan Thomas RC	2.00	5.00
❑ 138 Jason Collier RC	2.00	5.00
❑ 139 Erick Barkley RC	2.00	5.00
❑ 140 Desmond Mason RC	2.50	6.00
❑ 141 Mamadou N'Diaye RC	2.00	5.00
❑ 142 DeShawn Stevenson RC	2.00	5.00
❑ 143 Donnell Harvey RC	2.00	5.00
❑ 144 Jamaal Magloire RC	2.00	5.00
❑ 145 Hedo Turkoglu RC	5.00	12.00

2001-02 Hoops Hot Prospects

❑ COMP.SET w/o SP's (80)	20.00	40.00
❑ COMMON CARD (1-80)	.25	.60
❑ COMMON ROOKIE (81-108)	2.50	6.00
❑ 1 Vince Carter	.75	2.00
❑ 2 John Stockton	.50	1.25
❑ 3 Steve Smith	.30	.75
❑ 4 Kevin Garnett	.75	2.00
❑ 5 Larry Hughes	.30	.75
❑ 6 Ron Mercer	.25	.60
❑ 7 Marcus Fizer	.25	.60
❑ 8 Rashard Lewis	.40	1.00
❑ 9 Mike Miller	.30	.75
❑ 10 Darius Miles	.25	.60
❑ 11 Michael Finley	.40	1.00
❑ 12 Marcus Camby	.30	.75
❑ 13 Morris Peterson	.30	.75
❑ 14 Shawn Marion	.40	1.00
❑ 15 Alonzo Mourning	.40	1.00
❑ 16 Jamal Mashburn	.30	.75
❑ 17 Michael Jordan	6.00	15.00
❑ 18 Jason Williams	.30	.75
❑ 19 Latrell Sprewell	.30	.75
❑ 20 Reggie Miller	.40	1.00
❑ 21 Glenn Robinson	.30	.75
❑ 22 Steve Francis	.40	1.00
❑ 23 Antoine Walker	.30	.75
❑ 24 Stromile Swift	.25	.60
❑ 25 Damon Stoudamire	.30	.75
❑ 26 Allan Houston	.30	.75
❑ 27 Kobe Bryant	2.00	5.00
❑ 28 Dirk Nowitzki	.60	1.50
❑ 29 Iakovos Tsakalidis	.25	.60
❑ 30 Gary Payton	.40	1.00
❑ 31 Allen Iverson	.75	2.00
❑ 32 Eddie Jones	.30	.75
❑ 33 Mateen Cleaves	.25	.60
❑ 34 Nick Van Exel	.30	.75
❑ 35 Terrell Brandon	.25	.60
❑ 36 Wally Szczerbiak	.30	.75
❑ 37 Jalen Rose	.30	.75
❑ 38 Elton Brand	.40	1.00
❑ 39 DerMarr Johnson	.25	.60
❑ 40 Peja Stojakovic	.30	.75
❑ 41 Jason Kidd	.60	1.50
❑ 42 Sam Cassell	.30	.75
❑ 43 Cuttino Mobley	.30	.75
❑ 44 Toni Kukoc	.30	.75
❑ 45 DeShawn Stevenson	.25	.60
❑ 46 David Robinson	.50	1.25
❑ 47 Grant Hill	.40	1.00
❑ 48 Shaquille O'Neal	1.00	2.50
❑ 49 Andre Miller	.30	.75
❑ 50 Corey Maggette	.30	.75
❑ 51 Jason Terry	.40	1.00
❑ 52 Aaron McKie	.25	.60
❑ 53 Eddie House	.25	.60
❑ 54 Steve Nash	.60	1.50
❑ 55 Clifford Robinson	.25	.60
❑ 56 Chris Webber	.40	1.00
❑ 57 Kenyon Martin	.40	1.00
❑ 58 Jermaine O'Neal	.40	1.00
❑ 59 Baron Davis	.40	1.00
❑ 60 Mitch Richmond	.30	.75
❑ 61 Antawn Jamison	.40	1.00
❑ 62 Paul Pierce	.40	1.00
❑ 63 Shareef Abdur-Rahim	.30	.75
❑ 64 Rasheed Wallace	.40	1.00
❑ 65 Ray Allen	.40	1.00
❑ 66 Lamar Odom	.40	1.00
❑ 67 Chris Mihm	.25	.60
❑ 68 Raef LaFrentz	.25	.60
❑ 69 Patrick Ewing	.50	1.25
❑ 70 Tracy McGrady	.75	2.00
❑ 71 Derek Fisher	.30	.75
❑ 72 Jerry Stackhouse	.30	.75
❑ 73 Antonio McDyess	.30	.75
❑ 74 Karl Malone	.50	1.25
❑ 75 Dikembe Mutombo	.30	.75
❑ 76 Hakeem Olajuwon	.50	1.25
❑ 77 David Wesley	.25	.60
❑ 78 Courtney Alexander	.25	.60
❑ 79 Tim Duncan	.75	2.00
❑ 80 Stephon Marbury	.40	1.00
❑ 81 Kwame Brown JSY RC	3.00	8.00
❑ 82 Tyson Chandler JSY RC	5.00	12.00
❑ 83 Pau Gasol JSY RC	10.00	25.00
❑ 84 Eddy Curry JSY RC	4.00	10.00
❑ 85 J.Richardson JSY/300 RC	10.00	25.00
❑ 86 Shane Battier JSY RC	4.00	10.00
❑ 87 E.Griffin JSY/300 RC	5.00	12.00
❑ 88 DeSagana Diop JSY RC	2.50	6.00
❑ 89 Rodney White JSY RC	2.50	6.00
❑ 90 J.Johnson JSY/300 RC	12.00	30.00
❑ 91 Ke.Brown JSY/300 RC	5.00	12.00
❑ 92 V.Radmanovic JSY RC	3.00	8.00

❑ 93 Richard Jefferson JSY RC 6.00 15.00
❑ 94 Troy Murphy JSY RC 5.00 12.00
❑ 95 Steven Hunter JSY RC 2.50 6.00
❑ 96 Kirk Haston JSY RC 2.50 6.00
❑ 97 Michael Bradley JSY RC 2.50 6.00
❑ 98 Jason Collins JSY RC 2.50 6.00
❑ 99 Zach Randolph JSY RC 6.00 15.00
❑ 100 Brendan Haywood JSY RC 3.00 8.00
❑ 101 Joseph Forte JSY RC 2.50 6.00
❑ 102 Jeryl Sasser JSY RC 2.50 6.00
❑ 103 B.Armstrong JSY/300 RC 5.00 12.00
❑ 104 Andrei Kirilenko JSY RC 6.00 15.00
❑ 105 Primos Brezec JSY RC 3.00 8.00
❑ 106 S.Dalembert JSY/300 RC 6.00 15.00
❑ 107 Jamaal Tinsley JSY RC 3.00 8.00
❑ 108 Tony Parker JSY RC 10.00 25.00

2002-03 Hoops Hot Prospects

❑ COMP.SET w/o SP's (80) 20.00 50.00
❑ COMMON JSY RC (81-108) 4.00 10.00
❑ COMMON ROOKIE (109-120) 3.00 8.00
❑ 1 Vince Carter .75 2.00
❑ 2 Chris Webber .40 1.00
❑ 3 Latrell Sprewell .30 .75
❑ 4 Brian Grant .25 .60
❑ 5 Jerry Stackhouse .30 .75
❑ 6 Joe Smith .25 .60
❑ 7 Jason Terry .40 1.00
❑ 8 Shawn Marion .40 1.00
❑ 9 Wally Szczerbiak .30 .75
❑ 10 Reggie Miller .40 1.00
❑ 11 Steve Nash .60 1.50
❑ 12 Karl Malone .40 1.00
❑ 13 Damon Stoudamire .30 .75
❑ 14 Jamal Mashburn .30 .75
❑ 15 Kobe Bryant 2.00 5.00
❑ 16 Paul Pierce .40 1.00
❑ 17 Tony Parker .40 1.00
❑ 18 Mike Miller .30 .75
❑ 19 Sam Cassell .30 .75
❑ 20 Eddie Griffin .25 .60
❑ 21 Jason Williams .30 .75
❑ 22 Jason Richardson .40 1.00
❑ 23 Antoine Walker .30 .75
❑ 24 Tim Duncan .75 2.00
❑ 25 Baron Davis .40 1.00
❑ 26 Glenn Robinson .30 .75
❑ 27 Darius Miles .25 .60
❑ 28 Dirk Nowitzki .60 1.50
❑ 29 John Stockton .50 1.25
❑ 30 Allen Iverson .75 2.00
❑ 31 Richard Jefferson .40 1.00
❑ 32 Rick Fox .30 .75
❑ 33 Ben Wallace .30 .75
❑ 34 Michael Jordan 2.50 6.00
❑ 35 Rasheed Wallace .40 1.00
❑ 36 Alonzo Mourning .40 1.00
❑ 37 Steve Francis .40 1.00
❑ 38 Jalen Rose .30 .75
❑ 39 Rashard Lewis .40 1.00
❑ 40 Tracy McGrady .75 2.00
❑ 41 David Wesley .25 .60
❑ 42 Pau Gasol .40 1.00
❑ 43 Antawn Jamison .40 1.00
❑ 44 Shareef Abdur-Rahim .30 .75
❑ 45 Mike Bibby .30 .75
❑ 46 Dikembe Mutombo .30 .75
❑ 47 Kevin Garnett .75 2.00
❑ 48 Elton Brand .40 1.00
❑ 49 Lamond Murray .25 .60
❑ 50 Morris Peterson .30 .75
❑ 51 Joe Johnson .40 1.00
❑ 52 Kenyon Martin .40 1.00
❑ 53 Shaquille O'Neal 1.00 2.50
❑ 54 Antonio McDyess .30 .75
❑ 55 Vin Baker .30 .75
❑ 56 Marcus Camby .30 .75
❑ 57 Ray Allen .40 1.00
❑ 58 Jermain O'Neal 1.00 2.50
❑ 59 Eddy Curry .30 .75
❑ 60 David Robinson .50 1.25
❑ 61 Clifford Robinson .25 .60
❑ 62 Rodney Rogers .25 .60
❑ 63 Peja Stojakovic .30 .75
❑ 64 Allan Houston .30 .75
❑ 65 Shane Battier .30 .75
❑ 66 Jamaal Tinsley .30 .75
❑ 67 Michael Finley .40 1.00
❑ 68 Kenny Anderson .30 .75
❑ 69 Stephon Marbury .40 1.00
❑ 70 Terrell Brandon .25 .60
❑ 71 Lamar Odom .40 1.00
❑ 72 Raef LaFrentz .25 .60
❑ 73 Jamaal Magloire .25 .60
❑ 74 Bonzi Wells .30 .75
❑ 75 Jason Kidd .60 1.50
❑ 76 Cuttino Mobley .30 .75
❑ 77 Tyson Chandler .30 .75
❑ 78 Gary Payton .40 1.00
❑ 79 Grant Hill .40 1.00
❑ 80 Eddie Jones .30 .75
❑ 81 Yao Ming JSY RC 12.00 30.00
❑ 82 Fred Jones JSY RC 5.00 12.00
❑ 83 R.Humphrey JSY RC 4.00 10.00
❑ 84 Drew Gooden JSY RC 6.00 15.00
❑ 85 N.Tskitishvili JSY RC 4.00 10.00
❑ 86 Caron Butler JSY RC 8.00 20.00
❑ 87 V.Yarbrough JSY RC 4.00 10.00
❑ 88 DaJ.Wagner JSY RC 4.00 10.00
❑ 89 Nene Hilario JSY RC 5.00 12.00
❑ 90 Qyntel Woods JSY RC 4.00 10.00
❑ 91 Jared Jeffries JSY RC 4.00 10.00
❑ 92 C.Jacobsen JSY RC 4.00 10.00
❑ 93 Marcus Haislip JSY RC 4.00 10.00
❑ 94 Kareem Rush JSY RC 5.00 12.00
❑ 95 P.Savovic JSY RC 4.00 10.00
❑ 96 Melvin Ely JSY RC 4.00 10.00
❑ 97 Steve Logan JSY RC 4.00 10.00
❑ 98 A.Stoudemire JSY RC 10.00 25.00
❑ 99 John Salmons JSY RC 6.00 15.00
❑ 100 Chris Jefferies JSY RC 4.00 10.00
❑ 101 Juan Dixon JSY RC 6.00 15.00
❑ 102 Carlos Boozer JSY RC 8.00 20.00
❑ 103 Roger Mason JSY RC 4.00 10.00
❑ 104 Rod Grizzard JSY RC 4.00 10.00
❑ 105 T.Prince JSY RC 6.00 15.00
❑ 106 Chris Wilcox JSY RC 5.00 12.00
❑ 107 Sam Clancy JSY RC 4.00 10.00
❑ 108 Dan Gadzuric JSY RC 4.00 10.00
❑ 109 Dan Dickau/900 RC 4.00 10.00
❑ 110 Jay Williams/900 RC 5.00 12.00
❑ 111 Mike Dunleavy/900 RC 5.00 12.00
❑ 112 Robert Archibald/900 RC 4.00 10.00
❑ 113 Curtis Borchardt/900 RC 4.00 10.00
❑ 114 Bostjan Nachbar/900 RC 4.00 10.00
❑ 115 Jiri Welsch/1500 RC 4.00 10.00
❑ 116 Frank Williams/1500 RC 4.00 10.00
❑ 117 Rasual Butler/1500 RC 4.00 10.00
❑ 118 Tamar Slay/1500 RC 4.00 10.00
❑ 119 Ronald Murray/1500 RC 6.00 15.00
❑ 120 Corsley Edwards/1500 RC 4.00 10.00

2003-04 Hoops Hot Prospects

❑ COMP.SET w/o SP's 15.00 40.00
❑ COMMON CARD (1-80) .25 .60
❑ COMMON AU RC (81-87) 5.00 12.00
❑ COMMON JSY RC (88-94) 5.00 12.00
❑ COMMON JSY AU RC (95-111) 10.00 25.00
❑ COMMON ROOKIE (112-117) 2.00 5.00
❑ WHITE HOT ONE OF ONE's EXIST
❑ WHITE HOT UNPRICED DUE TO SCARCITY
❑ 1 Shareef Abdur-Rahim .30 .75
❑ 2 Mike Bibby .30 .75
❑ 3 Allan Houston .30 .75
❑ 4 Pau Gasol .40 1.00
❑ 5 Tayshaun Prince .30 .75
❑ 6 Darius Miles .30 .75
❑ 7 Ray Allen .25 .60
❑ 8 Amare Stoudemire .75 2.00
❑ 9 Latrell Sprewell .30 .75
❑ 10 Jamaal Tinsley .30 .75
❑ 11 Nene .30 .75
❑ 12 Matt Harpring .30 .75
❑ 13 Bonzi Wells .25 .60
❑ 14 Alonzo Mourning .40 1.00
❑ 15 Elton Brand .40 1.00
❑ 16 Paul Pierce .40 1.00
❑ 17 Tony Parker .40 1.00
❑ 18 Glenn Robinson .30 .75
❑ 19 Marcus Haislip .25 .60
❑ 20 Eddie Griffin .25 .60
❑ 21 Jamaal Magloire .25 .60
❑ 22 Gilbert Arenas .40 1.00
❑ 23 Antoine Walker .40 1.00
❑ 24 Manu Ginobili .40 1.00
❑ 25 Jamal Mashburn .25 .60
❑ 26 Michael Redd .40 1.00
❑ 27 Ron Artest .30 .75
❑ 28 Steve Nash .60 1.50
❑ 29 Andrei Kirilenko .40 1.00
❑ 30 Stephon Marbury .40 1.00
❑ 31 Richard Jefferson .40 1.00
❑ 32 Kobe Bryant 2.00 5.00
❑ 33 Cuttino Mobley .30 .75
❑ 34 Juan Dixon .25 .60
❑ 35 Rasheed Wallace .40 1.00
❑ 36 Eddie Jones .30 .75
❑ 37 Steve Francis .40 1.00
❑ 38 Dajuan Wagner .25 .60
❑ 39 Vladimir Radmanovic .25 .60
❑ 40 Drew Gooden .25 .60
❑ 41 Baron Davis .40 1.00
❑ 42 Mike Miller .30 .75
❑ 43 Jason Richardson .40 1.00
❑ 44 Dan Dickau .25 .60
❑ 45 Chris Webber .40 1.00
❑ 46 Kenny Thomas .25 .60
❑ 47 Kevin Garnett .75 2.00
❑ 48 Reggie Miller .40 1.00
❑ 49 Dirk Nowitzki .60 1.50
❑ 50 Vince Carter .75 2.00
❑ 51 Zach Randolph .40 1.00
❑ 52 Jason Kidd .60 1.50
❑ 53 Shaquille O'Neal 1.00 2.50
❑ 54 Nikoloz Tskitishvili .25 .60
❑ 55 Jerry Stackhouse .30 .75
❑ 56 Tracy McGrady .75 2.00
❑ 57 Desmond Mason .30 .75
❑ 58 Yao Ming .75 2.00
❑ 59 Jalen Rose .30 .75
❑ 60 Tim Duncan .75 2.00
❑ 61 Ben Wallace .30 .75
❑ 62 Mike Dunleavy .30 .75
❑ 63 Peja Stojakovic .30 .75
❑ 64 Keith Van Horn .30 .75
❑ 65 Karl Malone .40 1.00
❑ 66 Jermaine O'Neal .40 1.00
❑ 67 Michael Finley .40 1.00
❑ 68 Morris Peterson .30 .75
❑ 69 Shawn Marion .40 1.00
❑ 70 John Salmons .30 .75
❑ 71 Chris Wilcox .25 .60
❑ 72 Rodney White .25 .60
❑ 73 Kwame Brown .25 .60
❑ 74 Bobby Jackson .25 .60
❑ 75 Kenyon Martin .40 1.00
❑ 76 Antawn Jamison .40 1.00
❑ 77 Eddy Curry .30 .75
❑ 78 Bruce Bowen .30 .75
❑ 79 Allen Iverson .75 2.00
❑ 80 Caron Butler .30 .75
❑ 81 Boris Diaw AU RC 6.00 15.00
❑ 82 Quinton Ross AU RC 5.00 12.00
❑ 83 Matt Carroll AU RC 5.00 12.00
❑ 84 Travis Hansen AU RC 5.00 12.00
❑ 85 Zaur Pachulia AU RC 5.00 12.00
❑ 86 Zarko Cabarkapa AU RC 5.00 12.00

87 Maciej Lampe AU RC	5.00	12.00
88 Ndudi Ebi JSY RC	6.00	15.00
89 Jarvis Hayes JSY RC	8.00	20.00
90 Steve Blake JSY RC	5.00	12.00
91 Keith Bogans JSY RC	5.00	12.00
92 Reece Gaines JSY RC	5.00	12.00
93 Chris Kaman JSY RC	10.00	25.00
94 Slavko Vranes JSY RC	5.00	12.00
95 C.Anthony JSY AU RC	75.00	150.00
96 Troy Bell JSY AU RC	10.00	25.00
97 Travis Outlaw JSY AU RC	15.00	30.00
98 M.Sweetney JSY AU RC	10.00	25.00
99 Dahntay Jones JSY AU RC	10.00	25.00
100 Chris Bosh JSY AU RC	50.00	100.00
101 Brian Cook JSY AU RC	10.00	25.00
102 Luke Ridnour JSY AU RC	12.50	30.00
103 David West JSY AU RC	20.00	40.00
104 Banks JSY AU RC EXCH	10.00	25.00
105 Ken.Perkins JSY AU RC	12.50	30.00
106 Barbosa JSY AU RC EXCH	15.00	40.00
107 M.Pietrus JSY AU RC	10.00	25.00
108 D.Wade JSY AU RC	100.00	200.00
109 Josh Howard JSY AU RC	10.00	25.00
110 J.Kapono JSY AU RC	10.00	20.00
111 Luke Walton JSY AU RC	10.00	20.00
112 LeBron James RC	25.00	60.00
113 T.J. Ford RC	2.50	6.00
114 Zoran Planinic RC	2.00	5.00
115 Darko Milicic RC	2.50	6.00
116 Kirk Hinrich RC	2.50	6.00
117 Nick Collison RC	2.00	5.00

2004-05 Hoops Hot Prospects

COMP.SET w/o SP's (70)	15.00	40.00
COMMON CARD (1-70)	.25	.60
COMMON JSY AU RC (71-90)	6.00	15.00
COMMON JSY RC (91-100)	5.00	12.00
COMMON ROOKIE (100-110)	2.00	5.00
1 Dwyane Wade	1.25	3.00
2 Chris Bosh	.40	1.00
3 Peja Stojakovic	.30	.75
4 Darius Miles	.30	.75
5 Drew Gooden	.25	.60
6 Latrell Sprewell	.30	.75
7 Caron Butler	.30	.75
8 Shaquille O'Neal	1.00	2.50
9 Reggie Miller	.40	1.00
10 Corey Maggette	.30	.75
11 Tracy McGrady	.75	2.00
12 Ben Wallace	.30	.75
13 Steve Nash	.60	1.50
14 Paul Pierce	.40	1.00
15 Jarvis Hayes	.25	.60
16 Ray Allen	.40	1.00
17 Chris Webber	.40	1.00
18 Amare Stoudemire	.75	2.00
19 Pau Gasol	.40	1.00
20 Jermaine O'Neal	.40	1.00
21 Yao Ming	1.00	2.50
22 Richard Hamilton	.30	.75
23 Kirk Hinrich	.30	.75
24 Antoine Walker	.40	1.00
25 Carlos Arroyo	.40	1.00
26 Luke Ridnour	.25	.60
27 Mike Bibby	.30	.75
28 Tim Duncan	.75	2.00
29 Shareef Abdur-Rahim	.30	.75
30 Willie Green	.25	.60
31 Jamaal Magloire	.25	.60
32 Stephen Jackson	.30	.75
33 Karl Malone	.40	1.00
34 Elton Brand	.40	1.00
35 Jason Richardson	.40	1.00
36 Steve Francis	.40	1.00
37 Jason Kidd	.60	1.50
38 Kevin Garnett	.75	2.00
39 Jason Williams	.30	.75
40 Ron Artest	.30	.75
41 Darko Milicic	.25	.60
42 Carmelo Anthony	1.25	3.00
43 Carlos Boozer	.40	1.00
44 Michael Finley	.40	1.00
45 Marcus Fizer	.25	.60
46 Ricky Davis	.30	.75
47 Andrei Kirilenko	.40	1.00
48 Tony Parker	.40	1.00
49 Shawn Marion	.40	1.00
50 Allan Houston	.30	.75
51 Kenyon Martin	.40	1.00
52 T.J. Ford	.30	.75
53 Nene	.30	.75
54 LeBron James	2.50	6.00
55 Eddy Curry	.30	.75
56 Jason Terry	.30	.75
57 Vince Carter	.75	2.00
58 Zach Randolph	.40	1.00
59 Allen Iverson	.75	2.00
60 Stephon Marbury	.40	1.00
61 Richard Jefferson	.40	1.00
62 Baron Davis	.40	1.00
63 Michael Redd	.40	1.00
64 Lamar Odom	.40	1.00
65 Kobe Bryant	2.00	5.00
66 Mickael Pietrus	.30	.75
67 Dirk Nowitzki	.60	1.50
68 Dajuan Wagner	.25	.60
69 Jason Kapono	.25	.60
70 Antawn Jamison	.40	1.00
71 B.Gordon JSY AU/350 RC	15.00	30.00
72 Livingston JSY AU/350 RC	20.00	40.00
73 Devin Harris JSY AU/150 RC	30.00	60.00
74 J.Childress JSY AU/150 RC	20.00	40.00
75 Luol Deng JSY AU/150 RC	20.00	40.00
76 R.Araujo JSY AU/350 RC	6.00	15.00
77 L.Jackson JSY AU/150 RC	8.00	20.00
78 Andris Biedrins JSY AU RC		
79 Y.Tabuse JSY AU/350 RC	8.00	20.00
80 S.Telfair JSY AU/350 RC	5.00	12.00
81 Humphries JSY AU/350 RC	6.00	15.00
82 Kirk Snyder JSY AU/150 RC	8.00	20.00
83 Josh Smith JSY AU/150 RC	20.00	50.00
84 J.R. Smith JSY AU/350 RC	15.00	30.00
85 D.Wright JSY AU/350 RC	8.00	20.00
86 J.Nelson JSY AU/350 RC	10.00	25.00
87 D.West JSY AU/350 RC	6.00	15.00
88 Tony Allen JSY AU/350 RC	6.00	15.00
89 Seung-Jin JSY AU/350 RC	6.00	15.00
90 A.Jefferson JSY AU/150 RC	25.00	50.00
91 Dwight Howard JSY RC	15.00	30.00
92 Andre Iguodala JSY RC	15.00	30.00
93 Jackson Vroman JSY RC	5.00	12.00
94 Lionel Chalmers JSY RC	5.00	12.00
95 Kevin Martin JSY RC	8.00	20.00
96 Sasha Vujacic JSY RC	5.00	12.00
97 Andre Emmett JSY RC	5.00	12.00
98 David Harrison JSY RC	5.00	12.00
99 A.Varejao JSY RC	5.00	12.00
100 Chris Duhon JSY RC	10.00	25.00
101 Emeka Okafor RC	4.00	10.00
102 Viktor Khryapa RC	2.00	5.00
103 Peter John Ramos RC	2.00	5.00
104 Sergei Monia RC	2.00	5.00
105 Beno Udrih RC	2.50	6.00
106 Pavel Podkolzine RC	2.00	5.00
107 Trevor Ariza RC	2.50	6.00
108 Royal Ivey RC	2.00	5.00
109 Bernard Robinson RC	2.00	5.00
110 Robert Swift RC	2.00	5.00

2002-03 Hoops Stars

COMP.SET w/o RC's (170)	12.50	30.00
COMMON CARD (1-170)	.20	.50
COMMON ROOKIE (171-200)	1.00	2.50
1 Tracy McGrady	.60	1.50
2 Kevin Garnett	.60	1.50
3 Allen Iverson	.60	1.50
4 Keith Van Horn	.25	.60
5 Kwame Brown	.20	.50
6 Alan Henderson	.20	.50
7 Kenny Anderson	.25	.60
8 Antoine Walker	.25	.60
9 Tony Delk	.20	.50
10 Tony Battie	.20	.50
11 Wally Szczerbiak	.25	.60
12 Paul Pierce	.30	.75
13 Glenn Robinson	.25	.60
14 Tim Thomas	.20	.50
15 Vince Carter	.60	1.50
16 Pau Gasol	.30	.75
17 Eddy Curry	.25	.60
18 Darrell Armstrong	.20	.50
19 Sam Cassell	.25	.60
20 Darius Miles	.20	.50
21 Jason Richardson	.30	.75
22 Elton Brand	.30	.75
23 Michael Jordan	2.00	5.00
24 Andre Miller	.25	.60
25 Anfernee Hardaway	.30	.75
26 Steve Nash	.50	1.25
27 Ron Artest	.25	.60
28 Raef LaFrentz	.20	.50
29 Troy Hudson	.20	.50
30 Rasheed Wallace	.30	.75
31 Ricky Davis	.25	.60
32 Juwan Howard	.25	.60
33 Steve Francis	.30	.75
34 Shaquille O'Neal	.75	2.00
35 James Posey	.20	.50
36 DeShawn Stevenson	.20	.50
37 Clifford Robinson	.20	.50
38 Jerry Stackhouse	.25	.60
39 Chauncey Billups	.30	.75
40 Mike Bibby	.25	.60
41 Dirk Nowitzki	.50	1.25
42 Corliss Williamson	.25	.60
43 Antawn Jamison	.30	.75
44 Jamal Mashburn	.25	.60
45 Danny Fortson	.20	.50
46 Reggie Miller	.30	.75
47 Scottie Pippen	.50	1.25
48 Donnell Harvey	.20	.50
49 Moochie Norris	.20	.50
50 Corey Maggette	.25	.60
51 Eddie Griffin	.20	.50
52 Karl Malone	.30	.75
53 Maurice Taylor	.20	.50
54 Al Harrington	.25	.60
55 Kenyon Martin	.30	.75
56 Nick Van Exel	.25	.60
57 Jermaine O'Neal	.30	.75
58 Anthony Mason	.20	.50
59 Jamaal Tinsley	.25	.60
60 Chris Mihm	.20	.50
61 Lamar Odom	.30	.75
62 Cuttino Mobley	.25	.60
63 Michael Olowokandi	.20	.50
64 Michael Finley	.30	.75
65 Anthony Peeler	.20	.50
66 Mengke Bateer	.20	.50
67 Rick Fox	.25	.60
68 Steve Smith	.25	.60
69 Robert Horry	.25	.60
70 Devean George	.20	.50
71 Jason Williams	.25	.60
72 Stromile Swift	.20	.50
73 Marcus Fizer	.20	.50
74 Michael Dickerson	.20	.50
75 Shane Battier	.25	.60
76 Larry Hughes	.25	.60
77 Brian Skinner	.20	.50
78 Eddie Jones	.25	.60
79 Malik Allen	.20	.50
80 Ray Allen	.30	.75
81 Jumaine Jones	.20	.50
82 Donyell Marshall	.20	.50
83 Toni Kukoc	.25	.60
84 Michael Redd	.30	.75
85 Ron Mercer	.20	.50
86 Terrell Brandon	.20	.50

❑ 87 Latrell Sprewell	.25	.60
❑ 88 Kobe Bryant	1.50	4.00
❑ 89 Kurt Thomas	.20	.50
❑ 90 Rasho Nesterovic	.20	.50
❑ 91 Shareef Abdur-Rahim	.25	.60
❑ 92 Eduardo Najera	.20	.50
❑ 93 Jamaal Magloire	.20	.50
❑ 94 Antonio Davis	.20	.50
❑ 95 Rodney Rogers	.20	.50
❑ 96 Jason Collins	.20	.50
❑ 97 Marcus Camby	.25	.60
❑ 98 Joe Smith	.20	.50
❑ 99 Richard Jefferson	.30	.75
❑ 100 Gilbert Arenas	.30	.75
❑ 101 Courtney Alexander	.20	.50
❑ 102 David Wesley	.20	.50
❑ 103 Baron Davis	.30	.75
❑ 104 Elden Campbell	.20	.50
❑ 105 Jason Kidd	.50	1.25
❑ 106 P.J. Brown	.20	.50
❑ 107 Rashard Lewis	.30	.75
❑ 108 Alvin Williams	.20	.50
❑ 109 Kerry Kittles	.25	.60
❑ 110 Charlie Ward	.20	.50
❑ 111 Kedrick Brown	.20	.50
❑ 112 Shandon Anderson	.20	.50
❑ 113 Grant Hill	.30	.75
❑ 114 Tyson Chandler	.25	.60
❑ 115 Brent Barry	.20	.50
❑ 116 Travis Best	.20	.50
❑ 117 Mike Miller	.25	.60
❑ 118 Aaron McKie	.20	.50
❑ 119 Theo Ratliff	.20	.50
❑ 120 Todd MacCulloch	.20	.50
❑ 121 Trenton Hassell	.20	.50
❑ 122 Vin Baker	.25	.60
❑ 123 Dion Glover	.20	.50
❑ 124 Stephon Marbury	.30	.75
❑ 125 Ben Wallace	.25	.60
❑ 126 Glen Rice	.25	.60
❑ 127 Joe Johnson	.30	.75
❑ 128 Chris Webber	.30	.75
❑ 129 Damon Stoudamire	.25	.60
❑ 130 Voshon Lenard	.20	.50
❑ 131 Troy Murphy	.30	.75
❑ 132 Desmond Mason	.25	.60
❑ 133 Ruben Patterson	.20	.50
❑ 134 John Stockton	.40	1.00
❑ 135 Bobby Jackson	.20	.50
❑ 136 Shawn Marion	.30	.75
❑ 137 Jarron Collins	.20	.50
❑ 138 Tom Gugliotta	.20	.50
❑ 139 Doug Christie	.20	.50
❑ 140 Zeljko Rebraca	.20	.50
❑ 141 Tim Duncan	.60	1.50
❑ 142 David Robinson	.40	1.00
❑ 143 Tony Parker	.30	.75
❑ 144 Derek Fisher	.25	.60
❑ 145 Speedy Claxton	.20	.50
❑ 146 Eric Snow	.20	.50
❑ 147 Gary Payton	.30	.75
❑ 148 Pat Garrity	.20	.50
❑ 149 Joseph Forte	.20	.50
❑ 150 Derek Anderson	.25	.60
❑ 151 Vladimir Radmanovic	.20	.50
❑ 152 Samuel Dalembert	.20	.50
❑ 153 Allan Houston	.25	.60
❑ 154 Jalen Rose	.25	.60
❑ 155 Dikembe Mutombo	.25	.60
❑ 156 Jerome Williams	.20	.50
❑ 157 Antonio McDyess	.25	.60
❑ 158 Morris Peterson	.25	.60
❑ 159 Bonzi Wells	.25	.60
❑ 160 Hedo Turkoglu	.25	.60
❑ 161 Gerald Wallace	.30	.75
❑ 162 Andrei Kirilenko	.30	.75
❑ 163 Matt Harpring	.25	.60
❑ 164 Peja Stojakovic	.25	.60
❑ 165 Zydrunas Ilgauskas	.25	.60
❑ 166 Richard Hamilton	.25	.60
❑ 167 Brian Grant	.20	.50
❑ 168 Christian Laettner	.20	.50
❑ 169 Jason Terry	.30	.75
❑ 170 Alonzo Mourning	.30	.75
❑ 171 Yao Ming RC	3.00	8.00
❑ 172 Jay Williams RC	1.25	3.00
❑ 173 Mike Dunleavy RC	1.25	3.00
❑ 174 Chris Wilcox RC	1.25	3.00
❑ 175 Amare Stoudemire RC	2.50	6.00
❑ 176 Fred Jones RC	1.25	3.00
❑ 177 Caron Butler RC	2.00	5.00
❑ 178 Melvin Ely RC	1.00	2.50
❑ 179 Drew Gooden RC	1.50	4.00
❑ 180 DaJuan Wagner RC	1.00	2.50
❑ 181 Jared Jeffries RC	1.00	2.50
❑ 182 Nikoloz Tskitishvili RC	1.00	2.50
❑ 183 Nene Hilario RC	1.25	3.00
❑ 184 Dan Dickau RC	1.00	2.50
❑ 185 Marcus Haislip RC	1.00	2.50
❑ 186 Gordan Giricek RC	1.00	2.50
❑ 187 Jiri Welsch RC	1.00	2.50
❑ 188 Juan Dixon RC	1.50	4.00
❑ 189 Curtis Borchardt RC	1.00	2.50
❑ 190 Ryan Humphrey RC	1.00	2.50
❑ 191 Kareem Rush RC	1.25	3.00
❑ 192 Qyntel Woods RC	1.00	2.50
❑ 193 Casey Jacobsen RC	1.00	2.50
❑ 194 Tayshaun Prince RC	1.50	4.00
❑ 195 Frank Williams RC	1.00	2.50
❑ 196 Pat Burke RC	1.00	2.50
❑ 197 Chris Jefferies RC	1.00	2.50
❑ 198 Carlos Boozer RC	2.00	5.00
❑ 199 Manu Ginobili RC	2.50	6.00
❑ 200 Vincent Yarbrough RC	1.00	2.50

2008-09 Hot Prospects

❑ COMP.SET w/o SPs (90)	10.00	25.00
❑ 1 LaMarcus Aldridge	.40	1.00
❑ 2 Ray Allen	.40	1.00
❑ 3 Carmelo Anthony	.50	1.25
❑ 4 Gilbert Arenas	.40	1.00
❑ 5 Ron Artest	.40	1.00
❑ 6 Mike Bibby	.40	1.00
❑ 7 Chauncey Billups	.40	1.00
❑ 8 Andrew Bogut	.40	1.00
❑ 9 Carlos Boozer	.40	1.00
❑ 10 Chris Bosh	.40	1.00
❑ 11 Elton Brand	.60	1.50
❑ 12 Corey Brewer	.30	.75
❑ 13 Kobe Bryant	2.00	5.00
❑ 14 Caron Butler	.40	1.00
❑ 15 Jose Calderon	.30	.75
❑ 16 Marcus Camby	.25	.60
❑ 17 Vince Carter	.50	1.25
❑ 18 Mike Conley	.30	.75
❑ 19 Daequan Cook	.30	.75
❑ 20 Jamal Crawford	.25	.60
❑ 21 Baron Davis	.40	1.00
❑ 22 Luol Deng	.40	1.00
❑ 23 Tim Duncan	.60	1.50
❑ 24 Mike Dunleavy	.30	.75
❑ 25 Kevin Durant	1.00	2.50
❑ 26 Francisco Garcia	.30	.75
❑ 27 Kevin Garnett	.75	2.00
❑ 28 Pau Gasol	.40	1.00
❑ 29 Rudy Gay	.40	1.00
❑ 30 Daniel Gibson	.40	1.00
❑ 31 Manu Ginobili	.40	1.00
❑ 32 Ben Gordon	.40	1.00
❑ 33 Danny Granger	.40	1.00
❑ 34 Jeff Green	.30	.75
❑ 35 Richard Hamilton	.30	.75
❑ 36 Al Harrington	.30	.75
❑ 37 Al Horford	.40	1.00
❑ 38 Dwight Howard	.75	2.00
❑ 39 Josh Howard	.40	1.00
❑ 40 Andre Iguodala	.40	1.00
❑ 41 Allen Iverson	.50	1.25
❑ 42 Stephen Jackson	.30	.75
❑ 43 LeBron James	2.00	5.00
❑ 44 Antawn Jamison	.40	1.00
❑ 45 Al Jefferson	.40	1.00
❑ 46 Richard Jefferson	.40	1.00
❑ 47 Yi Jianlian	.40	1.00
❑ 48 Joe Johnson	.40	1.00
❑ 49 Chris Kaman	.25	.60
❑ 50 Jason Kidd	.40	1.00
❑ 51 Kyle Korver	.40	1.00
❑ 52 Rashard Lewis	.40	1.00
❑ 53 Corey Maggette	.40	1.00
❑ 54 Stephon Marbury	.40	1.00
❑ 55 Shawn Marion	.40	1.00
❑ 56 Kevin Martin	.40	1.00
❑ 57 Rashad McCants	.30	.75
❑ 58 Tracy McGrady	.50	1.25
❑ 59 Andre Miller	.30	.75
❑ 60 Yao Ming	.50	1.25
❑ 61 Jamario Moon	.40	1.00
❑ 62 Steve Nash	.40	1.00
❑ 63 Joakim Noah	.40	1.00
❑ 64 Andres Nocioni	.30	.75
❑ 65 Dirk Nowitzki	.50	1.25
❑ 66 Jermaine O'Neal	.40	1.00
❑ 67 Shaquille O'Neal	.75	2.00
❑ 68 Greg Oden	.40	1.00
❑ 69 Emeka Okafor	.40	1.00
❑ 70 Tony Parker	.40	1.00
❑ 71 Chris Paul	.75	2.00
❑ 72 Paul Pierce	.50	1.25
❑ 73 Zach Randolph	.40	1.00
❑ 74 Michael Redd	.40	1.00
❑ 75 Jason Richardson	.40	1.00
❑ 76 Brandon Roy	.50	1.25
❑ 77 Luis Scola	.30	.75
❑ 78 Peja Stojakovic	.40	1.00
❑ 79 Amare Stoudemire	.50	1.25
❑ 80 Hedo Turkoglu	.40	1.00
❑ 81 Dwyane Wade	.75	2.00
❑ 82 Ben Wallace	.40	1.00
❑ 83 Gerald Wallace	.40	1.00
❑ 84 Rasheed Wallace	.40	1.00
❑ 85 Luke Walton	.30	.75
❑ 86 David West	.40	1.00
❑ 87 Chris Wilcox	.30	.75
❑ 88 Deron Williams	.50	1.25
❑ 89 Sean Williams	.30	.75
❑ 90 Thaddeus Young	.30	.75
❑ 91 Ray Allen	.75	2.00
❑ 92 Carmelo Anthony	1.00	2.50
❑ 93 Chauncey Billups	.75	2.00
❑ 94 Kobe Bryant	4.00	10.00
❑ 95 Vince Carter	1.00	2.50
❑ 96 Baron Davis	.75	2.00
❑ 97 Tim Duncan	1.25	3.00
❑ 98 Kevin Garnett	1.50	4.00
❑ 99 Pau Gasol	.75	2.00
❑ 100 Dwight Howard	1.50	4.00
❑ 101 Allen Iverson	1.00	2.50
❑ 102 LeBron James	4.00	10.00
❑ 103 Michael Jordan	6.00	15.00
❑ 104 Tracy McGrady	1.00	2.50
❑ 105 Yao Ming	1.00	2.50
❑ 106 Steve Nash	.75	2.00
❑ 107 Joakim Noah	.75	2.00
❑ 108 Dirk Nowitzki	1.00	2.50
❑ 109 Shaquille O'Neal	1.50	4.00
❑ 110 Dwyane Wade	1.50	4.00
❑ 111 Kyle Weaver JSY AU RC	5.00	12.00
❑ 112 Joe Alexander JSY AU RC	10.00	25.00
❑ 113 D.J. Augustin JSY AU RC	8.00	20.00
❑ 114 Brook Lopez JSY AU RC	8.00	20.00
❑ 115 Jerryd Bayless JSY AU RC	10.00	25.00
❑ 116 Jason Thompson JSY AU RC	10.00	25.00
❑ 117 Brandon Rush JSY AU RC	10.00	25.00
❑ 118 Anthony Randolph JSY AU RC	15.00	30.00
❑ 119 Robin Lopez JSY AU RC	8.00	20.00
❑ 120 Marreese Speights JSY AU RC	8.00	20.00
❑ 121 Roy Hibbert JSY AU RC	8.00	20.00
❑ 122 Javale McGee JSY AU RC	8.00	20.00
❑ 123 J.J. Hickson JSY AU RC	8.00	20.00
❑ 124 Ryan Anderson JSY AU RC	5.00	12.00
❑ 125 Courtney Lee JSY AU RC	8.00	20.00
❑ 126 Kosta Koufos JSY AU RC	5.00	12.00
❑ 127 George Hill JSY AU RC	10.00	25.00
❑ 128 Darrell Arthur JSY AU RC	8.00	20.00
❑ 129 Donte Greene JSY AU RC	8.00	20.00
❑ 130 Sonny Weems JSY AU RC	5.00	12.00
❑ 131 J.R. Giddens JSY AU RC	6.00	15.00
❑ 132 Walter Sharpe JSY AU RC	5.00	12.00
❑ 133 Joey Dorsey JSY AU RC	5.00	12.00
❑ 134 Mario Chalmers JSY AU RC	8.00	20.00

❑ 135 DeAndre Jordan JSY AU RC 5.00 12.00
❑ 136 Patrick Ewing Jr JSY AU RC 5.00 12.00
❑ 137 Derrick Rose JSY AU/199 RC 100.00 200.00
❑ 138 M.Beasley JSY AU/199 RC 40.00 80.00
❑ 139 O.J. Mayo JSY AU/199 RC 25.00 50.00
❑ 140 R.Westbrook JSY AU/199 RC 20.00 40.00
❑ 141 Kevin Love JSY AU/199 RC 25.00 50.00
❑ 142 Eric Gordon JSY AU/199 RC 20.00 40.00
❑ 146 Chris Douglas-Roberts AU RC 15.00 30.00
❑ 149 Bill Walker AU RC 15.00 30.00
❑ 150 Malik Hairston AU RC 6.00 15.00
❑ 151 Richard Hendrix AU RC 6.00 15.00
❑ 152 DeVon Hardin AU RC 6.00 15.00
❑ 153 Darnell Jackson AU RC 6.00 15.00
❑ 155 Mike Taylor AU RC 6.00 15.00
❑ 156 James Gist AU RC 6.00 15.00
❑ 157 Sean Singletary RC 8.00 20.00

2009-10 Limited

❑ 1 Andre Iguodala 1.50 4.00
❑ 2 Elton Brand 1.50 4.00
❑ 3 Samuel Dalembert 1.00 2.50
❑ 4 Chris Duhon 1.00 2.50
❑ 5 David Lee 1.25 3.00
❑ 6 Wilson Chandler 1.00 2.50
❑ 7 Kevin Garnett 3.00 8.00
❑ 8 Paul Pierce 2.00 5.00
❑ 9 Rasheed Wallace 1.50 4.00
❑ 10 Ray Allen 1.50 4.00
❑ 11 Brook Lopez 1.00 2.50
❑ 12 Courtney Lee 1.25 3.00
❑ 13 Devin Harris 1.50 4.00
❑ 14 Andrea Bargnani 1.25 3.00
❑ 15 Chris Bosh 1.50 4.00
❑ 16 Hedo Turkoglu 1.50 4.00
❑ 17 Ben Wallace 1.50 4.00
❑ 18 Richard Hamilton 1.25 3.00
❑ 19 Rodney Stuckey 1.50 4.00
❑ 20 Tayshaun Prince 1.50 4.00
❑ 21 Derrick Rose 3.00 8.00
❑ 22 Luol Deng 1.50 4.00
❑ 23 Tyrus Thomas 1.25 3.00
❑ 24 Daniel Gibson 1.50 4.00
❑ 25 LeBron James 8.00 20.00
❑ 26 Mo Williams 1.25 3.00
❑ 27 Shaquille O'Neal 3.00 8.00
❑ 28 Danny Granger 1.50 4.00
❑ 29 Jeff Foster 1.00 2.50
❑ 30 T.J. Ford 1.00 2.50
❑ 31 Andrew Bogut 1.50 4.00
❑ 32 Kurt Thomas 1.00 2.50
❑ 33 Michael Redd 1.50 4.00
❑ 34 Dwight Howard 3.00 8.00
❑ 35 Jameer Nelson 1.25 3.00
❑ 36 Rashard Lewis 1.50 4.00
❑ 37 Vince Carter 2.00 5.00
❑ 38 Joe Johnson 1.50 4.00
❑ 39 Marvin Williams 1.25 3.00
❑ 40 Mike Bibby 1.00 2.50
❑ 41 Antawn Jamison 1.50 4.00
❑ 42 Caron Butler 1.50 4.00
❑ 43 Gilbert Arenas 1.50 4.00
❑ 44 Gerald Wallace 1.50 4.00
❑ 45 Raymond Felton 1.25 3.00
❑ 46 Tyson Chandler 1.25 3.00
❑ 47 Dwyane Wade 3.00 8.00
❑ 48 Jermaine O'Neal 1.50 4.00
❑ 49 Mario Chalmers 1.50 4.00
❑ 50 Michael Beasley 2.00 5.00
❑ 51 Aaron Brooks 1.25 3.00
❑ 52 Shane Battier 1.25 3.00
❑ 53 Trevor Ariza 1.50 4.00
❑ 54 O.J. Mayo 2.00 5.00
❑ 55 Rudy Gay 1.50 4.00
❑ 56 Zach Randolph 1.00 2.50
❑ 57 Chris Paul 3.00 8.00
❑ 58 David West 1.50 4.00
❑ 59 Emeka Okafor 1.50 4.00
❑ 60 James Posey 1.25 3.00
❑ 61 Dirk Nowitzki 2.00 5.00
❑ 62 Jason Kidd 1.50 4.00
❑ 63 Jason Terry 1.25 3.00
❑ 64 Josh Howard 1.50 4.00
❑ 65 Antonio McDyess 1.00 2.50
❑ 66 Tim Duncan 2.50 6.00
❑ 67 Tony Parker 1.50 4.00
❑ 68 Brandon Roy 2.00 5.00
❑ 69 Greg Oden 1.25 3.00
❑ 70 LaMarcus Aldridge 1.50 4.00
❑ 71 Rudy Fernandez 1.50 4.00
❑ 72 Corey Brewer 1.00 2.50
❑ 73 Kevin Love 1.25 3.00
❑ 74 Ramon Sessions 1.00 2.50
❑ 75 Andrei Kirilenko 1.25 3.00
❑ 76 Carlos Boozer 1.50 4.00
❑ 77 Deron Williams 2.00 5.00
❑ 78 Jeff Green 1.25 3.00
❑ 79 Kevin Durant 4.00 10.00
❑ 80 Russell Westbrook 1.50 4.00
❑ 81 Carmelo Anthony 2.00 5.00
❑ 82 Chauncey Billups 1.50 4.00
❑ 83 Kenyon Martin 1.50 4.00
❑ 84 Derek Fisher 1.25 3.00
❑ 85 Kobe Bryant 8.00 20.00
❑ 86 Lamar Odom 1.50 4.00
❑ 87 Pau Gasol 1.50 4.00
❑ 88 Ron Artest 1.50 4.00
❑ 89 Andris Biedrins 1.00 2.50
❑ 90 Anthony Randolph 1.50 4.00
❑ 91 Stephen Jackson 1.25 3.00
❑ 92 Amare Stoudemire 2.00 5.00
❑ 93 Channing Frye 1.25 3.00
❑ 94 Steve Nash 1.50 4.00
❑ 95 Baron Davis 1.50 4.00
❑ 96 Eric Gordon 1.50 4.00
❑ 97 Marcus Camby 1.00 2.50
❑ 98 Andres Nocioni 1.25 3.00
❑ 99 Kevin Martin 1.50 4.00
❑ 100 Spencer Hawes 1.25 3.00
❑ 101 Magic Johnson 4.00 10.00
❑ 102 Glen Rice 2.00 5.00
❑ 103 Wilt Chamberlain 4.00 10.00
❑ 104 World B. Free 2.00 5.00
❑ 105 Julius Erving 4.00 10.00
❑ 106 Alex English 2.00 5.00
❑ 107 Al Cervi 2.00 5.00
❑ 108 John Salley 2.00 5.00
❑ 109 Al Attles 2.00 5.00
❑ 110 Maurice Cheeks 2.00 5.00
❑ 111 Bob Cousy 3.00 8.00
❑ 112 Cazzie Russell 2.00 5.00
❑ 113 Dave Bing 2.00 5.00
❑ 114 Bob McAdoo 2.00 5.00
❑ 115 Albert King 2.00 5.00
❑ 116 Alonzo Mourning 2.50 6.00
❑ 117 Sleepy Floyd 2.00 5.00
❑ 118 John Havlicek 2.00 5.00
❑ 119 Gheorghe Muresan 2.00 5.00
❑ 120 Sidney Moncrief 2.00 5.00
❑ 121 Jamal Mashburn 2.00 5.00
❑ 122 Kevin McHale 2.00 5.00
❑ 123 Larry Bird 6.00 15.00
❑ 124 Vlade Divac 2.00 5.00
❑ 125 Sean Elliott 2.00 5.00
❑ 126 Chris Ford 2.00 5.00
❑ 127 Campy Russell 2.00 5.00
❑ 128 Muggsy Bogues 2.00 5.00
❑ 129 Elgin Baylor 2.00 5.00
❑ 130 Bill Walton 2.00 5.00
❑ 131 Rickey Green 2.00 5.00
❑ 132 Hal Greer 2.00 5.00
❑ 133 Norm Nixon 2.00 5.00
❑ 134 Jerry Sloan 2.00 5.00
❑ 135 David Robinson 3.00 8.00
❑ 136 Darryl Dawkins 2.00 5.00
❑ 137 Cliff Hagan 2.00 5.00
❑ 138 Clyde Drexler 2.50 6.00
❑ 139 Dikembe Mutombo 2.00 5.00
❑ 140 Jo Jo White 2.00 5.00
❑ 141 LaSalle Thompson 2.00 5.00
❑ 142 Michael Cooper 2.00 5.00
❑ 143 Shawn Bradley 2.00 5.00
❑ 144 Walt Frazier 2.00 5.00
❑ 145 Harry Gallatin 2.00 5.00
❑ 146 Connie Hawkins 2.00 5.00
❑ 147 Moses Malone 2.00 5.00
❑ 148 Walt Bellamy 2.00 5.00
❑ 149 Pete Maravich 15.00 30.00
❑ 150 Bill Russell 3.00 8.00
❑ 151 Blake Griffin JSY AU RC 25.00 50.00
❑ 152 Hasheem Thabeet JSY AU RC 6.00 15.00
❑ 153 James Harden JSY AU RC 10.00 25.00
❑ 154 Tyreke Evans JSY AU RC 50.00 100.00
❑ 155 Jonny Flynn JSY AU RC 10.00 25.00
❑ 156 Stephen Curry JSY AU RC 20.00 40.00
❑ 157 Jordan Hill JSY AU RC 3.00 15.00
❑ 158 Brandon Jennings JSY AU RC 30.00 60.00
❑ 159 Terrence Williams JSY AU RC 8.00 20.00
❑ 160 Gerald Henderson JSY AU RC 6.00 15.00
❑ 161 Tyler Hansbrough JSY AU RC 15.00 30.00
❑ 162 Earl Clark JSY AU RC 6.00 15.00
❑ 163 Austin Daye JSY AU RC 6.00 15.00
❑ 164 James Johnson JSY AU RC 6.00 15.00
❑ 165 Jrue Holiday JSY AU RC 6.00 15.00
❑ 166 Ty Lawson JSY AU RC 10.00 25.00
❑ 167 Jeff Teague JSY AU RC 6.00 15.00
❑ 168 Eric Maynor JSY AU RC 6.00 15.00
❑ 169 Darren Collison JSY AU RC 8.00 20.00
❑ 170 Omri Casspi JSY AU RC 10.00 25.00
❑ 171 B.J. Mullens JSY AU RC 6.00 15.00
❑ 172 Rodrigue Beaubois JSY AU RC 8.00 20.00
❑ 173 Taj Gibson JSY AU RC 8.00 20.00
❑ 174 DeMarre Carroll JSY AU RC 6.00 15.00
❑ 175 Wayne Ellington JSY AU RC 6.00 15.00
❑ 176 Toney Douglas JSY AU RC 6.00 15.00
❑ 177 DeJuan Blair JSY AU RC 10.00 25.00
❑ 178 Chase Budinger JSY AU RC 6.00 15.00
❑ 179 Sam Young JSY AU RC 6.00 15.00
❑ 180 Jodie Meeks JSY AU RC 8.00 20.00

1995-96 Metal

❑ COMPLETE SET (220) 20.00 40.00
❑ COMPLETE SERIES 1 (120) 10.00 20.00
❑ COMPLETE SERIES 2 (100) 10.00 20.00
❑ 1 Stacey Augmon .08 .25
❑ 2 Mookie Blaylock .08 .25
❑ 3 Grant Long .08 .25
❑ 4 Steve Smith .20 .50
❑ 5 Dee Brown .08 .25
❑ 6 Sherman Douglas .08 .25
❑ 7 Eric Montross .08 .25
❑ 8 Dino Radja .08 .25
❑ 9 Muggsy Bogues .20 .50
❑ 10 Scott Burrell .08 .25
❑ 11 Larry Johnson .20 .50
❑ 12 Alonzo Mourning .20 .50
❑ 13 Michael Jordan 2.00 5.00
❑ 14 Toni Kukoc .20 .50
❑ 15 Scottie Pippen .50 1.25
❑ 16 Terrell Brandon .20 .50
❑ 17 Tyrone Hill .08 .25
❑ 18 Mark Price .20 .50
❑ 19 John Williams .08 .25
❑ 20 Jim Jackson .08 .25
❑ 21 Popeye Jones .08 .25
❑ 22 Jason Kidd 1.00 2.50
❑ 23 Jamal Mashburn .20 .50
❑ 24 Mahmoud Abdul-Rauf .08 .25
❑ 25 Dikembe Mutombo .20 .50
❑ 26 Robert Pack .08 .25
❑ 27 Jalen Rose .50 1.25

❑ 28 Joe Dumars	.30	.75
❑ 29 Grant Hill	.40	1.00
❑ 30 Lindsey Hunter	.08	.25
❑ 31 Terry Mills	.08	.25
❑ 32 Tim Hardaway	.20	.50
❑ 33 Donyell Marshall	.20	.50
❑ 34 Chris Mullin	.30	.75
❑ 35 Clifford Rozier	.08	.25
❑ 36 Latrell Sprewell	.30	.75
❑ 37 Sam Cassell	.30	.75
❑ 38 Clyde Drexler	.30	.75
❑ 39 Robert Horry	.20	.50
❑ 40 Hakeem Olajuwon	.30	.75
❑ 41 Kenny Smith	.08	.25
❑ 42 Dale Davis	.08	.25
❑ 43 Mark Jackson	.20	.50
❑ 44 Derrick McKey	.08	.25
❑ 45 Reggie Miller	.30	.75
❑ 46 Rik Smits	.20	.50
❑ 47 Lamond Murray	.08	.25
❑ 48 Pooh Richardson	.08	.25
❑ 49 Malik Sealy	.08	.25
❑ 50 Loy Vaught	.08	.25
❑ 51 Elden Campbell	.08	.25
❑ 52 Cedric Ceballos	.08	.25
❑ 53 Vlade Divac	.20	.50
❑ 54 Eddie Jones	.40	1.00
❑ 55 Nick Van Exel	.30	.75
❑ 56 Bimbo Coles	.08	.25
❑ 57 Billy Owens	.08	.25
❑ 58 Khalid Reeves	.08	.25
❑ 59 Glen Rice	.20	.50
❑ 60 Kevin Willis	.20	.50
❑ 61 Vin Baker	.20	.50
❑ 62 Todd Day	.08	.25
❑ 63 Eric Murdock	.08	.25
❑ 64 Glenn Robinson	.30	.75
❑ 65 Tom Gugliotta	.08	.25
❑ 66 Christian Laettner	.20	.50
❑ 67 Isaiah Rider	.08	.25
❑ 68 Kenny Anderson	.20	.50
❑ 69 P.J. Brown	.08	.25
❑ 70 Derrick Coleman	.08	.25
❑ 71 Patrick Ewing	.30	.75
❑ 72 Anthony Mason	.20	.50
❑ 73 Charles Oakley	.08	.25
❑ 74 John Starks	.20	.50
❑ 75 Nick Anderson	.08	.25
❑ 76 Horace Grant	.20	.50
❑ 77 Anfernee Hardaway	.30	.75
❑ 78 Shaquille O'Neal	.75	2.00
❑ 79 Dennis Scott	.08	.25
❑ 80 Dana Barros	.08	.25
❑ 81 Shawn Bradley	.08	.25
❑ 82 Clarence Weatherspoon	.08	.25
❑ 83 Sharone Wright	.08	.25
❑ 84 Charles Barkley	.40	1.00
❑ 85 Kevin Johnson	.20	.50
❑ 86 Dan Majerle	.20	.50
❑ 87 Danny Manning	.20	.50
❑ 88 Wesley Person	.08	.25
❑ 89 Clifford Robinson	.08	.25
❑ 90 Rod Strickland	.08	.25
❑ 91 Otis Thorpe	.08	.25
❑ 92 Buck Williams	.08	.25
❑ 93 Brian Grant	.30	.75
❑ 94 Olden Polynice	.08	.25
❑ 95 Mitch Richmond	.20	.50
❑ 96 Walt Williams	.08	.25
❑ 97 Sean Elliott	.20	.50
❑ 98 Avery Johnson	.08	.25
❑ 99 David Robinson	.30	.75
❑ 100 Dennis Rodman	.20	.50
❑ 101 Shawn Kemp	.20	.50
❑ 102 Nate McMillan	.08	.25
❑ 103 Gary Payton	.30	.75
❑ 104 Detlef Schrempf	.20	.50
❑ 105 B.J. Armstrong	.08	.25
❑ 106 Oliver Miller	.08	.25
❑ 107 John Salley	.08	.25
❑ 108 David Benoit	.08	.25
❑ 109 Jeff Hornacek	.20	.50
❑ 110 Karl Malone	.40	1.00
❑ 111 John Stockton	.40	1.00
❑ 112 Greg Anthony	.08	.25
❑ 113 Benoit Benjamin	.08	.25
❑ 114 Byron Scott	.08	.25
❑ 115 Calbert Cheaney	.08	.25
❑ 116 Juwan Howard	.30	.75
❑ 117 Gheorghe Muresan	.08	.25
❑ 118 Chris Webber	.40	1.00
❑ 119 Checklist	.08	.25
❑ 120 Checklist	.08	.25
❑ 121 Stacey Augmon	.08	.25
❑ 122 Mookie Blaylock	.08	.25
❑ 123 Alan Henderson RC	.30	.75
❑ 124 Andrew Lang	.08	.25
❑ 125 Ken Norman	.08	.25
❑ 126 Steve Smith	.20	.50
❑ 127 Dana Barros	.08	.25
❑ 128 Rick Fox	.20	.50
❑ 129 Eric Williams RC	.20	.50
❑ 130 Kendall Gill	.08	.25
❑ 131 Khalid Reeves	.08	.25
❑ 132 Glen Rice	.20	.50
❑ 133 George Zidek RC	.08	.25
❑ 134 Dennis Rodman	.20	.50
❑ 135 Danny Ferry	.08	.25
❑ 136 Dan Majerle	.20	.50
❑ 137 Chris Mills	.08	.25
❑ 138 Bobby Phills	.08	.25
❑ 139 Bob Sura RC	.20	.50
❑ 140 Tony Dumas	.08	.25
❑ 141 Dale Ellis	.08	.25
❑ 142 Don MacLean	.08	.25
❑ 143 Antonio McDyess RC	.60	1.50
❑ 144 Bryant Stith	.08	.25
❑ 145 Allan Houston	.20	.50
❑ 146 Theo Ratliff RC	.40	1.00
❑ 147 Otis Thorpe	.08	.25
❑ 148 B.J. Armstrong	.08	.25
❑ 149 Rony Seikaly	.08	.25
❑ 150 Joe Smith RC	.50	1.25
❑ 151 Sam Cassell	.30	.75
❑ 152 Clyde Drexler	.30	.75
❑ 153 Robert Horry	.20	.50
❑ 154 Hakeem Olajuwon	.30	.75
❑ 155 Antonio Davis	.08	.25
❑ 156 Ricky Pierce	.08	.25
❑ 157 Brent Barry RC	.30	.75
❑ 158 Terry Dehere	.08	.25
❑ 159 Rodney Rogers	.08	.25
❑ 160 Brian Williams	.08	.25
❑ 161 Magic Johnson	.50	1.25
❑ 162 Sasha Danilovic RC	.08	.25
❑ 163 Alonzo Mourning	.20	.50
❑ 164 Kurt Thomas RC	.20	.50
❑ 165 Sherman Douglas	.08	.25
❑ 166 Shawn Respert RC	.08	.25
❑ 167 Kevin Garnett RC	2.00	5.00
❑ 168 Terry Porter	.08	.25
❑ 169 Shawn Bradley	.08	.25
❑ 170 Kevin Edwards	.08	.25
❑ 171 Ed O'Bannon RC	.08	.25
❑ 172 Jayson Williams	.08	.25
❑ 173 Derek Harper	.20	.50
❑ 174 Charles Smith	.08	.25
❑ 175 Brian Shaw	.08	.25
❑ 176 Derrick Coleman	.08	.25
❑ 177 Vernon Maxwell	.08	.25
❑ 178 Trevor Ruffin	.08	.25
❑ 179 Jerry Stackhouse RC	1.00	2.50
❑ 180 Michael Finley RC	.75	2.00
❑ 181 A.C. Green	.20	.50
❑ 182 John Williams	.08	.25
❑ 183 Aaron McKie	.20	.50
❑ 184 Arvydas Sabonis RC	.40	1.00
❑ 185 Gary Trent RC	.08	.25
❑ 186 Tyus Edney RC	.08	.25
❑ 187 Sarunas Marciulionis	.08	.25
❑ 188 Michael Smith	.08	.25
❑ 189 Corliss Williamson RC	.30	.75
❑ 190 Vinny Del Negro	.08	.25
❑ 191 Hersey Hawkins	.08	.25
❑ 192 Shawn Kemp	.20	.50
❑ 193 Gary Payton	.30	.75
❑ 194 Sam Perkins	.20	.50
❑ 195 Detlef Schrempf	.20	.50
❑ 196 Willie Anderson	.08	.25
❑ 197 Oliver Miller	.08	.25
❑ 198 Tracy Murray	.08	.25
❑ 199 Alvin Robertson	.08	.25
❑ 200 Damon Stoudamire RC	.60	1.50
❑ 201 Chris Morris	.08	.25
❑ 202 Greg Anthony	.08	.25
❑ 203 Blue Edwards	.08	.25
❑ 204 Eric Murdock	.08	.25
❑ 205 Bryant Reeves RC	.30	.75
❑ 206 Byron Scott	.08	.25
❑ 207 Robert Pack	.08	.25
❑ 208 Rasheed Wallace RC	.75	2.00
❑ 209 Anfernee Hardaway NB	.20	.50
❑ 210 Grant Hill NB	.30	.75
❑ 211 Larry Johnson NB	.08	.25
❑ 212 Michael Jordan NB	1.00	2.50
❑ 213 Jason Kidd NB	.50	1.25
❑ 214 Karl Malone NB	.30	.75
❑ 215 Shaquille O'Neal NB	.30	.75
❑ 216 Scottie Pippen NB	.30	.75
❑ 217 David Robinson NB	.20	.50
❑ 218 Glenn Robinson NB	.20	.50
❑ 219 Checklist	.08	.25
❑ 220 Checklist	.08	.25

1996-97 Metal

❑ COMPLETE SET (250)	25.00	45.00
❑ COMPLETE SERIES 1 (150)	15.00	25.00
❑ COMPLETE SERIES 2 (100)	10.00	20.00
❑ 1 Mookie Blaylock	.08	.25
❑ 2 Christian Laettner	.20	.50
❑ 3 Steve Smith	.20	.50
❑ 4 Dana Barros	.08	.25
❑ 5 Rick Fox	.08	.25
❑ 6 Dino Radja	.08	.25
❑ 7 Eric Williams	.08	.25
❑ 8 Dell Curry	.08	.25
❑ 9 Matt Geiger	.08	.25
❑ 10 Glen Rice	.20	.50
❑ 11 Michael Jordan	2.00	5.00
❑ 12 Toni Kukoc	.20	.50
❑ 13 Luc Longley	.08	.25
❑ 14 Scottie Pippen	.50	1.25
❑ 15 Dennis Rodman	.20	.50
❑ 16 Terrell Brandon	.20	.50
❑ 17 Danny Ferry	.08	.25
❑ 18 Chris Mills	.08	.25
❑ 19 Bobby Phills	.08	.25
❑ 20 Bob Sura	.08	.25
❑ 21 Jim Jackson	.08	.25
❑ 22 Jason Kidd	.50	1.25
❑ 23 Jamal Mashburn	.20	.50
❑ 24 George McCloud	.08	.25
❑ 25 LaPhonso Ellis	.08	.25
❑ 26 Antonio McDyess	.20	.50
❑ 27 Bryant Stith	.08	.25
❑ 28 Joe Dumars	.30	.75
❑ 29 Grant Hill	.30	.75
❑ 30 Theo Ratliff	.20	.50
❑ 31 Otis Thorpe	.08	.25
❑ 32 Chris Mullin	.30	.75
❑ 33 Joe Smith	.20	.50
❑ 34 Latrell Sprewell	.30	.75
❑ 35 Sam Cassell	.30	.75
❑ 36 Clyde Drexler	.30	.75
❑ 37 Robert Horry	.20	.50
❑ 38 Hakeem Olajuwon	.30	.75
❑ 39 Antonio Davis	.08	.25
❑ 40 Dale Davis	.08	.25
❑ 41 Derrick McKey	.08	.25
❑ 42 Reggie Miller	.30	.75
❑ 43 Rik Smits	.20	.50
❑ 44 Brent Barry	.08	.25
❑ 45 Malik Sealy	.08	.25
❑ 46 Loy Vaught	.08	.25
❑ 47 Elden Campbell	.08	.25
❑ 48 Cedric Ceballos	.08	.25
❑ 49 Eddie Jones	.30	.75
❑ 50 Nick Van Exel	.30	.75
❑ 51 Sasha Danilovic	.08	.25
❑ 52 Tim Hardaway	.20	.50
❑ 53 Alonzo Mourning	.20	.50
❑ 54 Kurt Thomas	.20	.50
❑ 55 Vin Baker	.20	.50
❑ 56 Sherman Douglas	.08	.25

❑ 57 Glenn Robinson	.30	.75
❑ 58 Kevin Garnett	.60	1.50
❑ 59 Tom Gugliotta	.08	.25
❑ 60 Doug West	.08	.25
❑ 61 Shawn Bradley	.08	.25
❑ 62 Ed O'Bannon	.08	.25
❑ 63 Jayson Williams	.20	.50
❑ 64 Patrick Ewing	.30	.75
❑ 65 Charles Oakley	.08	.25
❑ 66 John Starks	.20	.50
❑ 67 Nick Anderson	.08	.25
❑ 68 Horace Grant	.20	.50
❑ 69 Anfernee Hardaway	.30	.75
❑ 70 Dennis Scott	.08	.25
❑ 71 Brian Shaw	.08	.25
❑ 72 Derrick Coleman	.20	.50
❑ 73 Jerry Stackhouse	.25	.60
❑ 74 Clarence Weatherspoon	.08	.25
❑ 75 Charles Barkley	.40	1.00
❑ 76 Michael Finley	.40	1.00
❑ 77 Kevin Johnson	.20	.50
❑ 78 Wesley Person	.08	.25
❑ 79 Aaron McKie	.20	.50
❑ 80 Clifford Robinson	.08	.25
❑ 81 Arvydas Sabonis	.20	.50
❑ 82 Gary Trent	.08	.25
❑ 83 Tyus Edney	.08	.25
❑ 84 Brian Grant	.30	.75
❑ 85 Billy Owens	.08	.25
❑ 86 Olden Polynice	.08	.25
❑ 87 Mitch Richmond	.20	.50
❑ 88 Vinny Del Negro	.08	.25
❑ 89 Sean Elliott	.20	.50
❑ 90 Avery Johnson	.08	.25
❑ 91 David Robinson	.30	.75
❑ 92 Hersey Hawkins	.20	.50
❑ 93 Shawn Kemp	.20	.50
❑ 94 Gary Payton	.30	.75
❑ 95 Sam Perkins	.20	.50
❑ 96 Detlef Schrempf	.20	.50
❑ 97 Doug Christie	.20	.50
❑ 98 Damon Stoudamire	.30	.75
❑ 99 Sharone Wright	.08	.25
❑ 100 Jeff Hornacek	.20	.50
❑ 101 Karl Malone	.30	.75
❑ 102 John Stockton	.30	.75
❑ 103 Greg Anthony	.08	.25
❑ 104 Blue Edwards	.08	.25
❑ 105 Bryant Reeves	.08	.25
❑ 106 Juwan Howard	.20	.50
❑ 107 Gheorghe Muresan	.08	.25
❑ 108 Chris Webber	.30	.75
❑ 109 Kenny Anderson OTM	.08	.25
❑ 110 Stacey Augmon OTM	.08	.25
❑ 111 Chris Childs OTM	.08	.25
❑ 112 Vlade Divac OTM	.08	.25
❑ 113 Allan Houston OTM	.08	.25
❑ 114 Mark Jackson OTM	.08	.25
❑ 115 Larry Johnson OTM	.08	.25
❑ 116 Grant Long OTM	.08	.25
❑ 117 Anthony Mason OTM	.08	.25
❑ 118 Dikembe Mutombo OTM	.08	.25
❑ 119 Shaquille O'Neal OTM	.30	.75
❑ 120 Isaiah Rider OTM	.08	.25
❑ 121 Rod Strickland OTM	.08	.25
❑ 122 Rasheed Wallace OTM	.30	.75
❑ 123 Jalen Rose OTM	.20	.50
❑ 124 Anfernee Hardaway MET	.20	.50
❑ 125 Tim Hardaway MET	.08	.25
❑ 126 Allan Houston MET	.08	.25
❑ 127 Eddie Jones MET	.20	.50
❑ 128 Michael Jordan MET	1.00	2.50
❑ 129 Reggie Miller MET	.20	.50
❑ 130 Glen Rice MET	.08	.25
❑ 131 Mitch Richmond MET	.08	.25
❑ 132 Steve Smith MET	.08	.25
❑ 133 John Stockton MET	.30	.75
❑ 134 Stephon Marbury FF RC	.60	1.50
❑ 135 S.Abdur-Rahim FF RC	1.00	2.50
❑ 136 Ray Allen FF RC	1.00	2.50
❑ 137 Kobe Bryant FF RC	5.00	12.00
❑ 138 Steve Nash FF RC	2.00	5.00
❑ 139 Grant Hill MS	.20	.50
❑ 140 Jason Kidd MS	.25	.60
❑ 141 Karl Malone MS	.30	.75
❑ 142 Hakeem Olajuwon MS	.20	.50
❑ 143 Shaquille O'Neal MS	.30	.75
❑ 144 Gary Payton MS	.20	.50
❑ 145 Scottie Pippen MS	.25	.60
❑ 146 Jerry Stackhouse MS	.30	.75
❑ 147 Damon Stoudamire MS	.20	.50
❑ 148 Rod Strickland MS	.08	.25
❑ 149 Checklist (1-102)	.08	.25
❑ 150 Checklist (103-150/inserts)	.08	.25
❑ 151 Tyrone Corbin	.08	.25
❑ 152 Dikembe Mutombo	.20	.50
❑ 153 Antoine Walker RC	.60	1.50
❑ 154 David Wesley	.08	.25
❑ 155 Vlade Divac	.08	.25
❑ 156 Anthony Mason	.20	.50
❑ 157 Ron Harper	.20	.50
❑ 158 Steve Kerr	.20	.50
❑ 159 Robert Parish	.20	.50
❑ 160 Tyrone Hill	.08	.25
❑ 161 Vitaly Potapenko RC	.08	.25
❑ 162 Sam Cassell	.30	.75
❑ 163 Chris Gatling	.08	.25
❑ 164 Samaki Walker RC	.08	.25
❑ 165 Dale Ellis	.08	.25
❑ 166 Mark Jackson	.08	.25
❑ 167 Ervin Johnson	.08	.25
❑ 168 Grant Hill	.30	.75
❑ 169 Lindsey Hunter	.08	.25
❑ 170 Todd Fuller RC	.08	.25
❑ 171 Mark Price	.20	.50
❑ 172 Charles Barkley	.40	1.00
❑ 173 Othella Harrington RC	.30	.75
❑ 174 Matt Maloney RC	.20	.50
❑ 175 Kevin Willis	.08	.25
❑ 176 Travis Best	.08	.25
❑ 177 Erick Dampier RC	.30	.75
❑ 178 Jalen Rose	.30	.75
❑ 179 Rodney Rogers	.08	.25
❑ 180 Lorenzen Wright RC	.20	.50
❑ 181 Kobe Bryant	2.50	6.00
❑ 182 Robert Horry	.20	.50
❑ 183 Shaquille O'Neal	.75	2.00
❑ 184 P.J. Brown	.08	.25
❑ 185 Dan Majerle	.20	.50
❑ 186 Ray Allen	.50	1.25
❑ 187 Armon Gilliam	.08	.25
❑ 188 Andrew Lang	.08	.25
❑ 189 Stephon Marbury	.30	.75
❑ 190 Stojko Vrankovic	.08	.25
❑ 191 Kendall Gill	.08	.25
❑ 192 Kerry Kittles RC	.30	.75
❑ 193 Robert Pack	.08	.25
❑ 194 Chris Childs	.08	.25
❑ 195 Allan Houston	.20	.50
❑ 196 Larry Johnson	.20	.50
❑ 197 John Wallace RC	.30	.75
❑ 198 Rony Seikaly	.08	.25
❑ 199 Gerald Wilkins	.08	.25
❑ 200 Lucious Harris	.08	.25
❑ 201 Allen Iverson RC	1.25	3.00
❑ 202 Cedric Ceballos	.08	.25
❑ 203 Jason Kidd	.50	1.25
❑ 204 Danny Manning	.20	.50
❑ 205 Steve Nash	.40	1.00
❑ 206 Kenny Anderson	.08	.25
❑ 207 Isaiah Rider	.20	.50
❑ 208 Rasheed Wallace	.40	1.00
❑ 209 Mahmoud Abdul-Rauf	.08	.25
❑ 210 Corliss Williamson	.20	.50
❑ 211 Vernon Maxwell	.08	.25
❑ 212 Dominique Wilkins	.30	.75
❑ 213 Craig Ehlo	.08	.25
❑ 214 Jim McIlvaine	.08	.25
❑ 215 Marcus Camby RC	.40	1.00
❑ 216 Hubert Davis	.08	.25
❑ 217 Walt Williams	.08	.25
❑ 218 Shandon Anderson RC	.20	.50
❑ 219 Bryon Russell	.08	.25
❑ 220 Shareef Abdur-Rahim	.50	1.25
❑ 221 Roy Rogers RC	.08	.25
❑ 222 Tracy Murray	.08	.25
❑ 223 Rod Strickland	.08	.25
❑ 224 Kevin Garnett MET	.30	.75
❑ 225 Karl Malone MET	.30	.75
❑ 226 Alonzo Mourning MET	.08	.25
❑ 227 Hakeem Olajuwon MET	.20	.50
❑ 228 Gary Payton MET	.20	.50
❑ 229 Scottie Pippen MET	.25	.60
❑ 230 David Robinson MET	.20	.50
❑ 231 Dennis Rodman MET	.08	.25
❑ 232 Latrell Sprewell MET	.30	.75
❑ 233 Jerry Stackhouse MET	.30	.75
❑ 234 Marcus Camby FF	.30	.75
❑ 235 Todd Fuller FF	.08	.25
❑ 236 Allen Iverson FF	.50	1.25
❑ 237 Kerry Kittles FF	.30	.75
❑ 238 Roy Rogers FF	.08	.25
❑ 239 Anfernee Hardaway MS	.20	.50
❑ 240 Juwan Howard MS	.08	.25
❑ 241 Michael Jordan MS	1.00	2.50
❑ 242 Shawn Kemp MS	.08	.25
❑ 243 Gary Payton MS	.20	.50
❑ 244 Mitch Richmond MS	.08	.25
❑ 245 Glenn Robinson MS	.20	.50
❑ 246 John Stockton MS	.30	.75
❑ 247 Damon Stoudamire MS	.20	.50
❑ 248 Chris Webber MS	.20	.50
❑ 249 Checklist	.08	.25
❑ 250 Checklist	.08	.25

1999-00 Metal

❑ COMPLETE SET (180)	25.00	50.00
❑ COMMON CARD (1-150)	.12	.30
❑ COMMON ROOKIE (151-180)	.30	.75
❑ 1 Vince Carter	.40	1.00
❑ 2 Stephon Marbury	.20	.50
❑ 3 David Robinson	.25	.60
❑ 4 Ray Allen	.20	.50
❑ 5 P.J. Brown	.12	.30
❑ 6 Shawn Kemp	.20	.50
❑ 7 Cedric Ceballos	.12	.30
❑ 8 Dale Davis	.12	.30
❑ 9 Rodney Rogers	.12	.30
❑ 10 Chris Gatling	.12	.30
❑ 11 Bryant Reeves	.12	.30
❑ 12 Al Harrington	.15	.40
❑ 13 Brent Barry	.15	.40
❑ 14 Brevin Knight	.12	.30
❑ 15 Radoslav Nesterovic RC	.25	.60
❑ 16 Tom Gugliotta	.12	.30
❑ 17 Charles Barkley	.25	.60
❑ 18 Cuttino Mobley	.15	.40
❑ 19 Corliss Williamson	.12	.30
❑ 20 Hersey Hawkins	.12	.30
❑ 21 Mike Bibby	.20	.50
❑ 22 Pat Garrity	.12	.30
❑ 23 Kelvin Cato	.12	.30
❑ 24 Alan Henderson	.12	.30
❑ 25 Alvin Williams	.12	.30
❑ 26 Antonio McDyess	.15	.40
❑ 27 Damon Stoudamire	.20	.50
❑ 28 Kerry Kittles	.12	.30
❑ 29 Michael Olowokandi	.12	.30
❑ 30 Brent Price	.12	.30
❑ 31 Fred Hoiberg	.12	.30
❑ 32 Glenn Robinson	.15	.40
❑ 33 Hakeem Olajuwon	.20	.50
❑ 34 Monty Williams	.12	.30
❑ 35 Terry Porter	.12	.30
❑ 36 Allen Iverson	.40	1.00
❑ 37 Juwan Howard	.15	.40
❑ 38 Mario Elie	.12	.30
❑ 39 Mookie Blaylock	.12	.30
❑ 40 Sam Cassell	.15	.40
❑ 41 Toni Kukoc	.20	.50
❑ 42 Anthony Mason	.12	.30
❑ 43 George Lynch	.12	.30
❑ 44 John Starks	.20	.50
❑ 45 Malik Rose	.12	.30
❑ 46 Rod Strickland	.12	.30
❑ 47 Tim Thomas	.15	.40
❑ 48 Howard Eisley	.12	.30
❑ 49 Kenny Anderson	.15	.40
❑ 50 Kurt Thomas	.15	.40
❑ 51 Lindsey Hunter	.12	.30
❑ 52 Rick Fox	.12	.30
❑ 53 Vlade Divac	.20	.50
❑ 54 Avery Johnson	.15	.40
❑ 55 Dale Ellis	.12	.30

❑ 56 Donyell Marshall	.15	.40
❑ 57 Elden Campbell	.12	.30
❑ 58 Larry Hughes	.15	.40
❑ 59 Mitch Richmond	.15	.40
❑ 60 Chris Mills	.12	.30
❑ 61 David Wesley	.12	.30
❑ 62 Gary Payton	.20	.50
❑ 63 Isaac Austin	.12	.30
❑ 64 Robert Traylor	.12	.30
❑ 65 Theo Ratliff	.15	.40
❑ 66 Antawn Jamison	.20	.50
❑ 67 Eddie Jones	.20	.50
❑ 68 Kevin Garnett	.40	1.00
❑ 69 Matt Geiger	.12	.30
❑ 70 Vernon Maxwell	.15	.40
❑ 71 Antonio Davis	.12	.30
❑ 72 Dirk Nowitzki	.30	.75
❑ 73 Johnny Newman	.12	.30
❑ 74 Maurice Taylor	.15	.40
❑ 75 Steve Smith	.12	.30
❑ 76 Derek Anderson	.12	.30
❑ 77 Doug Christie	.15	.40
❑ 78 Erick Strickland	.12	.30
❑ 79 Keith Van Horn	.15	.40
❑ 80 Luc Longley	.12	.30
❑ 81 Alonzo Mourning	.20	.50
❑ 82 Christian Laettner	.15	.40
❑ 83 Jamal Mashburn	.12	.30
❑ 84 Jon Barry	.15	.40
❑ 85 Patrick Ewing	.25	.60
❑ 86 Shareef Abdur-Rahim	.15	.40
❑ 87 Vitaly Potapenko	.12	.30
❑ 88 Darrell Armstrong	.12	.30
❑ 89 Eric Williams	.12	.30
❑ 90 Jerome Williams	.12	.30
❑ 91 Nick Anderson	.12	.30
❑ 92 Othella Harrington	.12	.30
❑ 93 Tim Hardaway	.20	.50
❑ 94 Eric Piatkowski	.15	.40
❑ 95 Isaiah Rider	.12	.30
❑ 96 Kendall Gill	.12	.30
❑ 97 Rasheed Wallace	.20	.50
❑ 98 Robert Pack	.12	.30
❑ 99 Tracy McGrady	.40	1.00
❑ 100 Allan Houston	.15	.40
❑ 101 Brian Grant	.12	.30
❑ 102 Dikembe Mutombo	.15	.40
❑ 103 Karl Malone	.25	.60
❑ 104 Nick Van Exel	.15	.40
❑ 105 Shaquille O'Neal	.50	1.25
❑ 106 Chris Anstey	.12	.30
❑ 107 Michael Dickerson	.12	.30
❑ 108 Shandon Anderson	.12	.30
❑ 109 Tariq Adbul-Wahad	.12	.30
❑ 110 Tim Duncan	.40	1.00
❑ 111 Voshon Lenard	.12	.30
❑ 112 Bimbo Coles	.12	.30
❑ 113 Detlef Schrempf	.15	.40
❑ 114 John Stockton	.25	.60
❑ 115 Kobe Bryant	1.00	2.50
❑ 116 Latrell Sprewell	.15	.40
❑ 117 Raef LaFrentz	.15	.40
❑ 118 Antoine Walker	.20	.50
❑ 119 Bryon Russell	.12	.30
❑ 120 Derek Fisher	.20	.50
❑ 121 Jason Williams	.20	.50
❑ 122 Jerry Stackhouse	.20	.50
❑ 123 Larry Johnson	.20	.50
❑ 124 Clifford Robinson	.12	.30
❑ 125 Horace Grant	.15	.40
❑ 126 Malik Sealy	.12	.30
❑ 127 Michael Finley	.20	.50
❑ 128 Rik Smits	.20	.50
❑ 129 Dell Curry	.12	.30
❑ 130 Jim Jackson	.15	.40
❑ 131 Ron Mercer	.12	.30
❑ 132 Scott Burrell	.12	.30
❑ 133 Scottie Pippen	.30	.75
❑ 134 Troy Hudson	.20	.50
❑ 135 Anfernee Hardaway	.20	.50
❑ 136 Anthony Peeler	.12	.30
❑ 137 Jalen Rose	.15	.40
❑ 138 Lamond Murray	.12	.30
❑ 139 Ruben Patterson	.12	.30
❑ 140 Chris Webber	.20	.50
❑ 141 Glen Rice	.20	.50
❑ 142 Grant Hill	.20	.50
❑ 143 Jeff Hornacek	.15	.40
❑ 144 Marcus Camby	.15	.40
❑ 145 Paul Pierce	.20	.50
❑ 146 Bob Sura	.12	.30
❑ 147 Jason Kidd	.30	.75
❑ 148 Reggie Miller	.20	.50
❑ 149 Terrell Brandon	.12	.30
❑ 150 Vin Baker	.20	.50
❑ 151 Lamar Odom RC	1.00	2.50
❑ 152 Steve Francis RC	1.00	2.50
❑ 153 Elton Brand RC	1.00	2.50
❑ 154 Wally Szczerbiak RC	1.00	2.50
❑ 155 Adrian Griffin RC	.30	.75
❑ 156 Andre Miller RC	1.00	2.50
❑ 157 Jason Terry RC	.75	2.00
❑ 158 Richard Hamilton RC	1.00	2.50
❑ 159 Ron Artest RC	1.25	3.00
❑ 160 Shawn Marion RC	1.00	2.50
❑ 161 James Posey RC	.50	1.25
❑ 162 Greg Buckner RC	.30	.75
❑ 163 Chucky Atkins RC	.40	1.00
❑ 164 Corey Maggette RC	1.00	2.50
❑ 165 Todd MacCulloch RC	.30	.75
❑ 166 Baron Davis RC	1.25	3.00
❑ 167 Trajan Langdon RC	.30	.75
❑ 168 Bruno Sundov RC	.30	.75
❑ 169 Scott Padgett RC	.30	.75
❑ 170 Vonteego Cummings RC	.30	.75
❑ 171 Ryan Bowen RC	.30	.75
❑ 172 Jonathan Bender RC	.30	.75
❑ 173 Jermaine Jackson RC	.30	.75
❑ 174 Devean George RC	.50	1.25
❑ 175 Chris Herren RC	.30	.75
❑ 176 Rodney Buford RC	.30	.75
❑ 177 Laron Profit RC	.30	.75
❑ 178 Mirsad Turkcan RC	.30	.75
❑ 179 Eddie Robinson RC	.30	.75
❑ 180 Anthony Carter RC	.60	1.50

1997-98 Metal Universe

❑ COMPLETE SET (125)	12.50	25.00
❑ 1 Charles Barkley	.40	1.00
❑ 2 Dell Curry	.08	.25
❑ 3 Derek Fisher	.30	.75
❑ 4 Derek Harper	.20	.50
❑ 5 Avery Johnson	.08	.25
❑ 6 Steve Smith	.20	.50
❑ 7 Alonzo Mourning	.20	.50
❑ 8 Rod Strickland	.08	.25
❑ 9 Chris Mullin	.30	.75
❑ 10 Rony Seikaly	.08	.25
❑ 11 Vin Baker	.20	.50
❑ 12 Austin Croshere RC	.25	.60
❑ 13 Vinny Del Negro	.08	.25
❑ 14 Sherman Douglas	.08	.25
❑ 15 Priest Lauderdale	.08	.25
❑ 16 Cedric Ceballos	.08	.25
❑ 17 LaPhonso Ellis	.08	.25
❑ 18 Luc Longley	.08	.25
❑ 19 Brian Grant	.20	.50
❑ 20 Allen Iverson	.75	2.00
❑ 21 Anthony Mason	.20	.50
❑ 22 Bryant Reeves	.08	.25
❑ 23 Michael Jordan	2.00	5.00
❑ 24 Dale Ellis	.08	.25
❑ 25 Terrell Brandon	.20	.50
❑ 26 Patrick Ewing	.30	.75
❑ 27 Allan Houston	.20	.50
❑ 28 Damon Stoudamire	.20	.50
❑ 29 Loy Vaught	.08	.25
❑ 30 Walt Williams	.08	.25
❑ 31 Shareef Abdur-Rahim	.50	1.25
❑ 32 Mario Elie	.08	.25
❑ 33 Juwan Howard	.20	.50
❑ 34 Tom Gugliotta	.20	.50
❑ 35 Glen Rice	.20	.50
❑ 36 Isaiah Rider	.20	.50
❑ 37 Arvydas Sabonis	.20	.50
❑ 38 Derrick Coleman	.08	.25
❑ 39 Kevin Willis	.20	.50
❑ 40 Kendall Gill	.08	.25
❑ 41 John Wallace	.08	.25
❑ 42 Tracy McGrady RC	.75	2.00
❑ 43 Travis Best	.08	.25
❑ 44 Malik Rose	.08	.25
❑ 45 Anfernee Hardaway	.30	.75
❑ 46 Roy Rogers	.08	.25
❑ 47 Kerry Kittles	.30	.75
❑ 48 Matt Maloney	.08	.25
❑ 49 Antonio McDyess	.20	.50
❑ 50 Shaquille O'Neal	.75	2.00
❑ 51 George McCloud	.08	.25
❑ 52 Wesley Person	.08	.25
❑ 53 Shawn Bradley	.08	.25
❑ 54 Antonio Davis	.08	.25
❑ 55 P.J. Brown	.08	.25
❑ 56 Joe Dumars	.30	.75
❑ 57 Horace Grant	.20	.50
❑ 58 Steve Kerr	.20	.50
❑ 59 Hakeem Olajuwon	.30	.75
❑ 60 Tim Hardaway	.20	.50
❑ 61 Toni Kukoc	.20	.50
❑ 62 Ron Mercer RC	.30	.75
❑ 63 Gary Payton	.30	.75
❑ 64 Grant Hill	.30	.75
❑ 65 Detlef Schrempf	.20	.50
❑ 66 Tim Duncan RC	.75	2.00
❑ 67 Shawn Kemp	.20	.50
❑ 68 Voshon Lenard	.08	.25
❑ 69 Othella Harrington	.08	.25
❑ 70 Hersey Hawkins	.08	.25
❑ 71 Lindsey Hunter	.08	.25
❑ 72 Antoine Walker	.40	1.00
❑ 73 Jamal Mashburn	.20	.50
❑ 74 Kenny Anderson	.20	.50
❑ 75 Todd Day	.08	.25
❑ 76 Todd Fuller	.08	.25
❑ 77 Jermaine O'Neal	.50	1.25
❑ 78 David Robinson	.30	.75
❑ 79 Erick Dampier	.20	.50
❑ 80 Keith Van Horn RC	.40	1.00
❑ 81 Kobe Bryant	1.25	3.00
❑ 82 Chris Childs	.08	.25
❑ 83 Scottie Pippen	.50	1.25
❑ 84 Marcus Camby	.30	.75
❑ 85 Danny Ferry	.08	.25
❑ 86 Jeff Hornacek	.20	.50
❑ 87 Bo Outlaw	.08	.25
❑ 88 Larry Johnson	.20	.50
❑ 89 Tony Delk	.08	.25
❑ 90 Stephon Marbury	.40	1.00
❑ 91 Robert Pack	.08	.25
❑ 92 Chris Webber	.30	.75
❑ 93 Clyde Drexler	.30	.75
❑ 94 Eddie Jones	.30	.75
❑ 95 Jerry Stackhouse	.30	.75
❑ 96 Tyrone Hill	.08	.25
❑ 97 Karl Malone	.30	.75
❑ 98 Reggie Miller	.30	.75
❑ 99 Bryon Russell	.08	.25
❑ 100 Dale Davis	.08	.25
❑ 101 Steve Nash	.30	.75
❑ 102 Vitaly Potapenko	.08	.25
❑ 103 Nick Anderson	.08	.25
❑ 104 Ray Allen	.30	.75
❑ 105 Sean Elliott	.20	.50
❑ 106 Dikembe Mutombo	.20	.50
❑ 107 Dennis Rodman	.20	.50
❑ 108 Lorenzen Wright	.08	.25
❑ 109 Kevin Garnett	.60	1.50
❑ 110 Christian Laettner	.20	.50
❑ 111 Mitch Richmond	.20	.50
❑ 112 Joe Smith	.20	.50
❑ 113 Jason Kidd	.50	1.25
❑ 114 Glenn Robinson	.30	.75
❑ 115 Mark Price	.20	.50
❑ 116 Mark Jackson	.20	.50
❑ 117 Bobby Phills	.08	.25
❑ 118 John Starks	.20	.50
❑ 119 John Stockton	.30	.75
❑ 120 Mookie Blaylock	.08	.25
❑ 121 Dean Garrett	.08	.25
❑ 122 Olden Polynice	.08	.25
❑ 123 Latrell Sprewell	.30	.75
❑ 124 Checklist	.08	.25
❑ 125 Checklist	.08	.25

1998-99 Metal Universe

❑ COMPLETE SET (125)	12.50	25.00
❑ 1 Michael Jordan	2.00	5.00
❑ 2 Mario Elie	.08	.25
❑ 3 Voshon Lenard	.08	.25
❑ 4 John Starks	.20	.50
❑ 5 Juwan Howard	.20	.50
❑ 6 Michael Finley	.30	.75
❑ 7 Bobby Jackson	.20	.50
❑ 8 Glenn Robinson	.20	.50
❑ 9 Antonio McDyess	.20	.50
❑ 10 Marcus Camby	.20	.50
❑ 11 Zydrunas Ilgauskas	.20	.50
❑ 12 LaPhonso Ellis	.08	.25
❑ 13 Terrell Brandon	.20	.50
❑ 14 Rex Chapman	.08	.25
❑ 15 Rod Strickland	.08	.25
❑ 16 Dennis Rodman	.20	.50
❑ 17 Clarence Weatherspoon	.08	.25
❑ 18 P.J. Brown	.08	.25
❑ 19 Anfernee Hardaway	.30	.75
❑ 20 Dikembe Mutombo	.20	.50
❑ 21 Gary Trent	.08	.25
❑ 22 Patrick Ewing	.30	.75
❑ 23 Sam Mack	.08	.25
❑ 24 Scottie Pippen	.50	1.25
❑ 25 Shaquille O'Neal	.75	2.00
❑ 26 Donyell Marshall	.20	.50
❑ 27 Bo Outlaw	.08	.25
❑ 28 Isaiah Rider	.08	.25
❑ 29 Detlef Schrempf	.20	.50
❑ 30 Mark Price	.20	.50
❑ 31 Jim Jackson	.08	.25
❑ 32 Eddie Jones	.30	.75
❑ 33 Allen Iverson	.60	1.50
❑ 34 Corliss Williamson	.20	.50
❑ 35 Tim Duncan	.50	1.25
❑ 36 Ron Harper	.20	.50
❑ 37 Tony Delk	.08	.25
❑ 38 Derek Fisher	.30	.75
❑ 39 Kendall Gill	.08	.25
❑ 40 Theo Ratliff	.20	.50
❑ 41 Kelvin Cato	.08	.25
❑ 42 Antoine Walker	.30	.75
❑ 43 Lamond Murray	.08	.25
❑ 44 Avery Johnson	.08	.25
❑ 45 John Stockton	.30	.75
❑ 46 David Wesley	.08	.25
❑ 47 Brian Williams	.08	.25
❑ 48 Elden Campbell	.08	.25
❑ 49 Sam Cassell	.30	.75
❑ 50 Grant Hill	.30	.75
❑ 51 Tracy McGrady	.75	2.00
❑ 52 Glen Rice	.20	.50
❑ 53 Kobe Bryant	1.25	3.00
❑ 54 Cherokee Parks	.08	.25
❑ 55 John Wallace	.08	.25
❑ 56 Bobby Phills	.08	.25
❑ 57 Jerry Stackhouse	.30	.75
❑ 58 Lorenzen Wright	.08	.25
❑ 59 Stephon Marbury	.30	.75
❑ 60 Shandon Anderson	.08	.25
❑ 61 Jeff Hornacek	.20	.50
❑ 62 Joe Dumars	.30	.75
❑ 63 Tom Gugliotta	.08	.25
❑ 64 Johnny Newman	.08	.25
❑ 65 Kevin Garnett	.60	1.50
❑ 66 Clifford Robinson	.08	.25
❑ 67 Dennis Scott	.08	.25
❑ 68 Anthony Mason	.20	.50
❑ 69 Rodney Rogers	.08	.25
❑ 70 Bryon Russell	.08	.25
❑ 71 Maurice Taylor	.15	.40
❑ 72 Mookie Blaylock	.08	.25
❑ 73 Shawn Bradley	.08	.25
❑ 74 Matt Maloney	.08	.25
❑ 75 Karl Malone	.30	.75
❑ 76 Larry Johnson	.20	.50
❑ 77 Calbert Cheaney	.08	.25
❑ 78 Steve Smith	.20	.50
❑ 79 Toni Kukoc	.20	.50
❑ 80 Reggie Miller	.30	.75
❑ 81 Jayson Williams	.08	.25
❑ 82 Gary Payton	.30	.75
❑ 83 George Lynch	.08	.25
❑ 84 Wesley Person	.08	.25
❑ 85 Charles Barkley	.40	1.00
❑ 86 Tim Hardaway	.20	.50
❑ 87 Darrell Armstrong	.08	.25
❑ 88 Rasheed Wallace	.30	.75
❑ 89 Tariq Abdul-Wahad	.08	.25
❑ 90 Kenny Anderson	.20	.50
❑ 91 Chris Mullin	.30	.75
❑ 92 Keith Van Horn	.30	.75
❑ 93 Hersey Hawkins	.08	.25
❑ 94 Billy Owens	.08	.25
❑ 95 Ron Mercer	.15	.40
❑ 96 Rik Smits	.20	.50
❑ 97 David Robinson	.30	.75
❑ 98 Derek Anderson	.25	.60
❑ 99 Danny Fortson	.08	.25
❑ 100 Jason Kidd	.50	1.25
❑ 101 Sean Elliott	.20	.50
❑ 102 Chauncey Billups	.20	.50
❑ 103 Tyrone Hill	.08	.25
❑ 104 Alan Henderson	.08	.25
❑ 105 Chris Anstey	.08	.25
❑ 106 Hakeem Olajuwon	.30	.75
❑ 107 Allan Houston	.20	.50
❑ 108 Bryant Reeves	.08	.25
❑ 109 Anthony Johnson	.08	.25
❑ 110 Shawn Kemp	.20	.50
❑ 111 Brevin Knight	.08	.25
❑ 112 A.C. Green	.20	.50
❑ 113 Ray Allen	.30	.75
❑ 114 Tim Thomas	.20	.50
❑ 115 Walter McCarty	.08	.25
❑ 116 Jalen Rose	.30	.75
❑ 117 Kerry Kittles	.08	.25
❑ 118 Vin Baker	.20	.50
❑ 119 Shareef Abdur-Rahim	.30	.75
❑ 120 Alonzo Mourning	.20	.50
❑ 121 Joe Smith	.20	.50
❑ 122 Tracy Murray	.08	.25
❑ 123 Damon Stoudamire	.20	.50
❑ 124 Checklist	.08	.25
❑ 125 Checklist	.08	.25
❑ NNO Grant Hill SAMPLE	.60	1.50

1997-98 Metal Universe Championship

❑ COMPLETE SET (100)	12.50	25.00
❑ 1 Shaquille O'Neal	.75	2.00
❑ 2 Chris Mills	.08	.25
❑ 3 Tariq Abdul-Wahad RC	.20	.50
❑ 4 Adonal Foyle RC	.20	.50
❑ 5 Kendall Gill	.08	.25
❑ 6 Vin Baker	.20	.50
❑ 7 Chauncey Billups RC	1.00	2.50
❑ 8 Bobby Jackson RC	.40	1.00
❑ 9 Keith Van Horn RC	.40	1.00
❑ 10 Avery Johnson	.08	.25
❑ 11 Juwan Howard	.20	.50
❑ 12 Steve Smith	.20	.50
❑ 13 Alonzo Mourning	.20	.50
❑ 14 Anfernee Hardaway	.30	.75
❑ 15 Sean Elliott	.20	.50
❑ 16 Danny Fortson RC	.20	.50
❑ 17 John Stockton	.30	.75
❑ 18 John Thomas RC	.08	.25
❑ 19 Lorenzen Wright	.08	.25
❑ 20 Mark Price	.20	.50
❑ 21 Rasheed Wallace	.30	.75
❑ 22 Ray Allen	.30	.75
❑ 23 Michael Jordan	2.00	5.00
❑ 24 John Wallace	.08	.25
❑ 25 Bryant Reeves	.08	.25
❑ 26 Allen Iverson	.75	2.00
❑ 27 Antoine Walker	.40	1.00
❑ 28 Terrell Brandon	.20	.50
❑ 29 Damon Stoudamire	.20	.50
❑ 30 Antonio Daniels RC	.30	.75
❑ 31 Corey Beck	.08	.25
❑ 32 Tyrone Hill	.08	.25
❑ 33 Grant Hill	.30	.75
❑ 34 Tim Thomas RC	.50	1.25
❑ 35 Clifford Robinson	.08	.25
❑ 36 Tracy McGrady RC	.75	2.00
❑ 37 Chris Webber	.30	.75
❑ 38 Austin Croshere RC	.25	.60
❑ 39 Reggie Miller	.30	.75
❑ 40 Derek Anderson RC	.30	.75
❑ 41 Kevin Garnett	.60	1.50
❑ 42 Kevin Johnson	.20	.50
❑ 43 Antonio McDyess	.20	.50
❑ 44 Brevin Knight RC	.20	.50
❑ 45 Charles Barkley	.40	1.00
❑ 46 Tom Gugliotta	.20	.50
❑ 47 Jason Kidd	.50	1.25
❑ 48 Marcus Camby	.30	.75
❑ 49 God Shammgod RC	.08	.25
❑ 50 Wesley Person	.08	.25
❑ 51 Clyde Drexler	.30	.75
❑ 52 Paul Grant RC	.08	.25
❑ 53 Rod Strickland	.08	.25
❑ 54 Tony Delk	.08	.25
❑ 55 Stephon Marbury	.40	1.00
❑ 56 Detlef Schrempf	.20	.50
❑ 57 Joe Smith	.20	.50
❑ 58 Sam Cassell	.30	.75
❑ 59 Gary Payton	.30	.75
❑ 60 Chris Crawford RC	.08	.25
❑ 61 Hakeem Olajuwon	.30	.75
❑ 62 Dennis Rodman	.20	.50
❑ 63 Eddie Jones	.30	.75
❑ 64 Mitch Richmond	.20	.50
❑ 65 David Wesley	.08	.25
❑ 66 Tony Battie RC	.30	.75
❑ 67 Isaac Austin	.08	.25
❑ 68 Isaiah Rider	.20	.50
❑ 69 Jacque Vaughn RC	.20	.50
❑ 70 Tim Hardaway	.20	.50
❑ 71 Darrell Armstrong	.08	.25
❑ 72 Tim Duncan RC	.75	2.00
❑ 73 Glen Rice	.20	.50
❑ 74 Bubba Wells RC	.08	.25
❑ 75 Maurice Taylor RC	.25	.60
❑ 76 Kelvin Cato RC	.30	.75
❑ 77 Shareef Abdur-Rahim	.50	1.25
❑ 78 Shawn Kemp	.20	.50
❑ 79 Michael Finley	.30	.75
❑ 80 Chris Mullin	.30	.75
❑ 81 Ron Mercer RC	.30	.75
❑ 82 Brian Williams	.08	.25
❑ 83 Kerry Kittles	.30	.75
❑ 84 David Robinson	.30	.75
❑ 85 Scottie Pippen	.50	1.25
❑ 86 Kobe Bryant	1.25	3.00
❑ 87 Anthony Johnson RC	.08	.25
❑ 88 Karl Malone	.30	.75
❑ 89 Mookie Blaylock	.08	.25
❑ 90 Joe Dumars	.30	.75
❑ 91 Patrick Ewing	.30	.75
❑ 92 Bobby Phills	.08	.25
❑ 93 Dennis Scott	.08	.25
❑ 94 Rodney Rogers	.08	.25
❑ 95 Jim Jackson	.08	.25
❑ 96 Kenny Anderson	.20	.50
❑ 97 Jerry Stackhouse	.30	.75
❑ 98 Larry Johnson	.20	.50
❑ 99 Checklist	.08	.25
❑ 100 Checklist	.08	.25

2009-10 Panini

❑ 1 Eddie House	.10	.25
❑ 2 Glen Davis	.12	.30
❑ 3 Kendrick Perkins	.10	.25
❑ 4 Kevin Garnett	.30	.75
❑ 5 Leon Powe	.10	.25
❑ 6 Paul Pierce	.20	.50

❑ 7 Rajon Rondo	.15	.40
❑ 8 Rasheed Wallace	.15	.40
❑ 9 Ray Allen	.15	.40
❑ 10 Stephon Marbury	.12	.30
❑ 11 Tony Allen	.10	.25
❑ 12 Bobby Simmons	.12	.30
❑ 13 Brook Lopez	.10	.25
❑ 14 Chris Douglas-Roberts	.10	.25
❑ 15 Courtney Lee	.12	.30
❑ 16 Devin Harris	.15	.40
❑ 17 Jarvis Hayes	.10	.25
❑ 18 Josh Boone	.10	.25
❑ 19 Keyon Dooling	.10	.25
❑ 20 Rafer Alston	.12	.30
❑ 21 Tony Battie	.10	.25
❑ 22 Yi Jianlian	.15	.40
❑ 23 Al Harrington	.12	.30
❑ 24 Chris Duhon	.10	.25
❑ 25 Danilo Gallinari	.15	.40
❑ 26 Darko Milicic	.10	.25
❑ 27 David Lee	.12	.30
❑ 28 Jared Jeffries	.10	.25
❑ 29 Larry Hughes	.10	.25
❑ 30 Nate Robinson	.15	.40
❑ 31 Wilson Chandler	.10	.25
❑ 32 Andre Iguodala	.15	.40
❑ 33 Donyell Marshall	.10	.25
❑ 34 Elton Brand	.15	.40
❑ 35 Jason Kapono	.12	.30
❑ 36 Louis Williams	.10	.25
❑ 37 Marreese Speights	.12	.30
❑ 38 Samuel Dalembert	.10	.25
❑ 39 Thaddeus Young	.10	.25
❑ 40 Willie Green	.10	.25
❑ 41 Andrea Bargnani	.12	.30
❑ 42 Chris Bosh	.15	.40
❑ 43 Hedo Turkoglu	.15	.40
❑ 44 Joey Graham	.10	.25
❑ 45 Jose Calderon	.12	.30
❑ 46 Pops Mensah-Bonsu	.10	.25
❑ 47 Quincy Douby	.10	.25
❑ 48 Reggie Evans	.10	.25
❑ 49 Devean George	.12	.30
❑ 50 Antoine Wright	.10	.25
❑ 51 Jarrett Jack	.12	.30
❑ 52 Aaron Gray	.10	.25
❑ 53 Brad Miller	.15	.40
❑ 54 Derrick Rose	.30	.75
❑ 55 Joakim Noah	.15	.40
❑ 56 John Salmons	.15	.40
❑ 57 Kirk Hinrich	.15	.40
❑ 58 Luol Deng	.15	.40
❑ 59 Tyrus Thomas	.12	.30
❑ 60 Anderson Varejao	.12	.30
❑ 61 Daniel Gibson	.15	.40
❑ 62 Delonte West	.10	.25
❑ 63 Joe Smith	.10	.25
❑ 64 LeBron James	.75	2.00
❑ 65 Mo Williams	.12	.30
❑ 66 Shaquille O'Neal	.30	.75
❑ 67 Wally Szczerbiak	.12	.30
❑ 68 Zydrunas Ilgauskas	.10	.25
❑ 69 Anthony Parker	.12	.30
❑ 70 Jamario Moon	.15	.40
❑ 71 Allen Iverson	.20	.50
❑ 72 Ben Gordon	.15	.40
❑ 73 Charlie Villanueva	.12	.30
❑ 74 Fabricio Oberto		
❑ 75 Jason Maxiell	.10	.25
❑ 76 Kwame Brown	.10	.25
❑ 77 Chris Wilcox	.10	.25
❑ 78 Richard Hamilton	.12	.30
❑ 79 Rodney Stuckey	.15	.40
❑ 80 Tayshaun Prince	.15	.40
❑ 81 Will Bynum	.10	.25
❑ 82 Brandon Rush	.10	.25
❑ 83 Danny Granger	.15	.40
❑ 84 Jeff Foster	.10	.25
❑ 85 Marquis Daniels	.10	.25
❑ 86 Mike Dunleavy	.10	.25
❑ 87 Rasho Nesterovic	.10	.25
❑ 88 Roy Hibbert	.10	.25
❑ 89 Stephen Graham	.10	.25
❑ 90 T.J. Ford	.10	.25
❑ 91 Travis Diener	.10	.25
❑ 92 Troy Murphy	.10	.25
❑ 93 Dahntay Jones	.10	.25
❑ 94 Earl Watson	.10	.25
❑ 95 Andrew Bogut	.15	.40
❑ 96 Bruce Bowen	.10	.25
❑ 97 Joe Alexander	.15	.40
❑ 98 Keith Bogans	.10	.25
❑ 99 Kurt Thomas	.10	.25
❑ 100 Luc Mbah a Moute	.10	.25
❑ 101 Luke Ridnour	.10	.25
❑ 102 Michael Redd	.15	.40
❑ 103 Ramon Sessions	.10	.25
❑ 104 Al Horford	.15	.40
❑ 105 Joe Johnson	.15	.40
❑ 106 Josh Smith	.15	.40
❑ 107 Marvin Williams	.12	.30
❑ 108 Maurice Evans	.10	.25
❑ 109 Mike Bibby	.10	.25
❑ 110 Ronald Murray	.10	.25
❑ 111 Solomon Jones	.10	.25
❑ 112 Jamal Crawford	.10	.25
❑ 113 Zaza Pachulia	.10	.25
❑ 114 Boris Diaw	.12	.30
❑ 115 D.J. Augustin	.12	.30
❑ 116 DeSagana Diop	.10	.25
❑ 117 Dontell Jefferson RC	.15	.40
❑ 118 Gerald Wallace	.15	.40
❑ 119 Juwan Howard	.10	.25
❑ 120 Nazr Mohammed	.10	.25
❑ 121 Raja Bell	.12	.30
❑ 122 Raymond Felton	.12	.30
❑ 123 Vladimir Radmanovic	.10	.25
❑ 124 Tyson Chandler	.12	.30
❑ 125 Chris Quinn	.10	.25
❑ 126 Daequan Cook	.12	.30
❑ 127 Dwyane Wade	.30	.75
❑ 128 James Jones RC	.15	.40
❑ 129 Jermaine O'Neal	.15	.40
❑ 130 Luther Head	.15	.40
❑ 131 Mario Chalmers	.15	.40
❑ 132 Michael Beasley	.20	.50
❑ 133 Udonis Haslem	.12	.30
❑ 134 Anthony Johnson	.10	.25
❑ 135 Dwight Howard	.30	.75
❑ 136 J.J. Redick	.15	.40
❑ 137 Jameer Nelson	.12	.30
❑ 138 Mickael Pietrus	.10	.25
❑ 139 Rashard Lewis	.15	.40
❑ 140 Vince Carter	.20	.50
❑ 141 Brandon Bass	.10	.25
❑ 142 Matt Barnes	.10	.25
❑ 143 Andray Blatche	.10	.25
❑ 144 Antawn Jamison	.15	.40
❑ 145 Brendan Haywood	.10	.25
❑ 146 Caron Butler	.15	.40
❑ 147 DeShawn Stevenson	.10	.25
❑ 148 Gilbert Arenas	.15	.40
❑ 149 Mike James	.10	.25
❑ 150 Mike Miller	.15	.40
❑ 151 Nick Young	.10	.25
❑ 152 Randy Foye	.10	.25
❑ 153 Tim Thomas	.10	.25
❑ 154 Dirk Nowitzki	.20	.50
❑ 155 Erick Dampier	.10	.25
❑ 156 Gerald Green	.10	.25
❑ 157 James Singleton	.10	.25
❑ 158 Jason Kidd	.15	.40
❑ 159 Jason Terry	.12	.30
❑ 160 Greg Buckner	.10	.25
❑ 161 Shawn Marion	.15	.40
❑ 162 Jose Barea	.15	.40
❑ 163 Josh Howard	.15	.40
❑ 164 Aaron Brooks	.12	.30
❑ 165 Brent Barry	.12	.30
❑ 166 Carl Landry	.10	.25
❑ 167 Dikembe Mutombo	.15	.40
❑ 168 Luis Scola	.10	.25
❑ 169 Shane Battier	.12	.30
❑ 170 Tracy McGrady	.20	.50
❑ 171 Trevor Ariza	.15	.40
❑ 172 Von Wafer	.10	.25
❑ 173 Yao Ming	.20	.50
❑ 174 Darius Miles	.12	.30
❑ 175 Darrell Arthur	.12	.30
❑ 176 Hakim Warrick	.12	.30
❑ 177 Marc Gasol	.15	.40
❑ 178 Mike Conley	.10	.25
❑ 179 O.J. Mayo	.20	.50
❑ 180 Jerry Stackhouse	.10	.25
❑ 181 Zach Randolph	.10	.25
❑ 182 Rudy Gay	.15	.40
❑ 183 Chris Paul	.30	.75
❑ 184 Emeka Okafor	.15	.40
❑ 185 David West	.15	.40
❑ 186 Devin Brown	.10	.25
❑ 187 James Posey	.12	.30
❑ 188 Julian Wright	.10	.25
❑ 189 Morris Peterson	.10	.25
❑ 190 Peja Stojakovic	.10	.25
❑ 191 Rasual Butler	.10	.25
❑ 192 Drew Gooden	.12	.30
❑ 193 Manu Ginobili	.15	.40
❑ 194 Matt Bonner	.10	.25
❑ 195 Michael Finley	.10	.25
❑ 196 Richard Jefferson	.15	.40
❑ 197 Roger Mason	.10	.25
❑ 198 Tim Duncan	.25	.60
❑ 199 Antonio McDyess	.10	.25
❑ 200 Tony Parker	.15	.40
❑ 201 Anthony Carter	.10	.25
❑ 202 Carmelo Anthony	.20	.50
❑ 203 Chauncey Billups	.15	.40
❑ 204 Chris Andersen	.15	.40
❑ 205 J.R. Smith	.12	.30
❑ 206 Kenyon Martin	.15	.40
❑ 207 Linas Kleiza	.10	.25
❑ 208 Arron Afflalo	.10	.25
❑ 209 Nene	.12	.30
❑ 210 Al Jefferson	.15	.40
❑ 211 Bobby Brown	.10	.25
❑ 212 Corey Brewer	.10	.25
❑ 213 Darius Songaila	.10	.25
❑ 214 Kevin Love	.12	.30
❑ 215 Rodney Carney	.10	.25
❑ 216 Quentin Richardson	.10	.25
❑ 217 Ryan Gomes	.10	.25
❑ 218 Brandon Roy	.20	.50
❑ 219 Greg Oden	.12	.30
❑ 220 Jerryd Bayless	.12	.30
❑ 221 Joel Przybilla	.10	.25
❑ 222 LaMarcus Aldridge	.15	.40
❑ 223 Nicolas Batum	.10	.25
❑ 224 Rudy Fernandez	.15	.40
❑ 225 Steve Blake	.10	.25
❑ 226 Travis Outlaw	.15	.40
❑ 227 Andre Miller	.12	.30
❑ 228 D.J. White	.10	.25
❑ 229 Desmond Mason	.10	.25
❑ 230 Jeff Green	.12	.30
❑ 231 Kevin Durant	.40	1.00
❑ 232 Nenad Krstic	.12	.30
❑ 233 Nick Collison	.10	.25
❑ 234 Russell Westbrook	.15	.40
❑ 235 Thabo Sefolosha	.10	.25
❑ 236 Andrei Kirilenko	.12	.30
❑ 237 C.J. Miles	.10	.25
❑ 238 Carlos Boozer	.15	.40
❑ 239 Deron Williams	.20	.50
❑ 240 Kosta Koufos	.10	.25
❑ 241 Kyle Korver	.12	.30
❑ 242 Matt Harpring	.10	.25
❑ 243 Mehmet Okur	.10	.25
❑ 244 Paul Millsap	.12	.30
❑ 245 Ronnie Brewer	.10	.25
❑ 246 Andris Biedrins	.10	.25
❑ 247 Anthony Morrow	.10	.25
❑ 248 Anthony Randolph	.15	.40
❑ 249 Brandan Wright	.10	.25
❑ 250 C.J. Watson	.10	.25
❑ 251 Corey Maggette	.12	.30
❑ 252 Kelenna Azubuike	.10	.25
❑ 253 Marco Belinelli	.10	.25
❑ 254 Monta Ellis	.15	.40
❑ 255 Acie Law	.10	.25
❑ 256 Ronny Turiaf	.10	.25
❑ 257 Stephen Jackson	.12	.30
❑ 258 Al Thornton	.15	.40
❑ 259 Baron Davis	.15	.40

❑ 260 Chris Kaman	.15	.40
❑ 261 Eric Gordon	.15	.40
❑ 262 Fred Jones	.10	.25
❑ 263 Marcus Camby	.10	.25
❑ 264 Ricky Davis	.10	.25
❑ 265 Steve Novak	.10	.25
❑ 266 Sebastian Telfair	.10	.25
❑ 267 Craig Smith	.10	.25
❑ 268 Adam Morrison	.12	.30
❑ 269 Andrew Bynum	.15	.40
❑ 270 Derek Fisher	.12	.30
❑ 271 Jordan Farmar	.12	.30
❑ 272 Josh Powell	.10	.25
❑ 273 Kobe Bryant	.75	2.00
❑ 274 Lamar Odom	.15	.40
❑ 275 Luke Walton	.10	.25
❑ 276 Pau Gasol	.15	.40
❑ 277 Ron Artest	.15	.40
❑ 278 Sasha Vujacic	.10	.25
❑ 279 Alando Tucker	.10	.25
❑ 280 Sasha Pavlovic	.10	.25
❑ 281 Amare Stoudemire	.20	.50
❑ 282 Ben Wallace	.15	.40
❑ 283 Goran Dragic	.10	.25
❑ 284 Grant Hill	.15	.40
❑ 285 Jared Dudley	.10	.25
❑ 286 Jason Richardson	.15	.40
❑ 287 Leandro Barbosa	.12	.30
❑ 288 Channing Frye	.12	.30
❑ 289 Steve Nash	.15	.40
❑ 290 Andres Nocioni	.12	.30
❑ 291 Beno Udrih	.10	.25
❑ 292 Bobby Jackson	.10	.25
❑ 293 Francisco Garcia	.12	.30
❑ 294 Ike Diogu	.10	.25
❑ 295 Jason Thompson	.10	.25
❑ 296 Kevin Martin	.15	.40
❑ 297 Rashad McCants	.10	.25
❑ 298 Sergio Rodriguez	.10	.25
❑ 299 Sean May	.10	.25
❑ 300 Spencer Hawes	.12	.30
❑ 301 Blake Griffin RC	2.00	5.00
❑ 302 Hasheem Thabeet RC	.75	2.00
❑ 303 James Harden RC	1.50	4.00
❑ 304 Tyreke Evans RC	3.00	8.00
❑ 305 Hasheem Thabeet RC	.75	2.00
❑ 306 Jonny Flynn RC	1.25	3.00
❑ 307 Stephen Curry RC	2.00	5.00
❑ 308 Jordan Hill RC	1.00	2.50
❑ 309 DeMar DeRozan RC	1.25	3.00
❑ 310 Brandon Jennings RC	2.00	5.00
❑ 311 Terrence Williams RC	1.50	4.00
❑ 312 Gerald Henderson RC	1.25	3.00
❑ 313 Tyler Hansbrough RC	1.25	3.00
❑ 314 Earl Clark RC	1.25	3.00
❑ 315 Austin Daye RC	1.00	2.50
❑ 316 James Johnson RC	1.25	3.00
❑ 317 Jrue Holiday RC	1.25	3.00
❑ 318 Ty Lawson RC	1.00	2.50
❑ 319 Jeff Teague RC	1.00	2.50
❑ 320 Eric Maynor RC	1.25	3.00
❑ 321 Darren Collison RC	1.25	3.00
❑ 322 Blake Griffin RC	2.00	5.00
❑ 323 Omri Casspi RC	1.25	3.00
❑ 324 B.J. Mullens RC	.75	2.00
❑ 325 Rodrigue Beaubois RC	1.50	4.00
❑ 326 Taj Gibson RC	1.25	3.00
❑ 327 DeMarre Carroll RC	1.00	2.50
❑ 328 Wayne Ellington RC	1.25	3.00
❑ 329 Toney Douglas RC	.75	2.00
❑ 330 Tyreke Evans RC	3.00	8.00
❑ 331 Jeff Pendergraph RC	1.00	2.50
❑ 332 Jermaine Taylor RC	1.00	2.50
❑ 333 Dante Cunningham RC	.75	2.00
❑ 334 DaJuan Summers RC	.75	2.00
❑ 335 Sam Young RC	1.25	3.00
❑ 336 DeJuan Blair RC	1.25	3.00
❑ 337 Jon Brockman RC	.75	2.00
❑ 338 Derrick Brown RC	.75	2.00
❑ 339 Jodie Meeks RC	.75	2.00
❑ 340 Patrick Beverley RC	.75	2.00
❑ 341 Marcus Thornton RC	.75	2.00
❑ 342 Chase Budinger RC	1.25	3.00
❑ 343 Jack McClinton RC	.75	2.00
❑ 344 Daniel Green RC	1.00	2.50
❑ 345 Taylor Griffin RC	.75	2.00
❑ 346 A.J. Price RC	.75	2.00
❑ 347 Jonas Jerebko RC	.75	2.00
❑ 348 Lester Hudson RC	.75	2.00
❑ 349 Goran Suton RC	.75	2.00
❑ 350 Ty Lawson RC	1.00	2.50
❑ 351 Blake Griffin RC	2.00	5.00
❑ 352 Hasheem Thabeet RC	.75	2.00
❑ 353 James Harden RC	1.50	4.00
❑ 354 Tyreke Evans RC	3.00	8.00
❑ 355 Jordan Hill RC	1.00	2.50
❑ 356 Jonny Flynn RC	1.25	3.00
❑ 357 Stephen Curry RC	2.00	5.00
❑ 358 Jordan Hill RC	1.00	2.50
❑ 359 DeMar DeRozan RC	1.25	3.00
❑ 360 Brandon Jennings RC	2.00	5.00
❑ 361 Terrence Williams RC	1.50	4.00
❑ 362 Gerald Henderson RC	1.25	3.00
❑ 363 Tyler Hansbrough RC	1.25	3.00
❑ 364 Earl Clark RC	1.25	3.00
❑ 365 Austin Daye RC	1.00	2.50
❑ 366 James Johnson RC	1.25	3.00
❑ 367 Jrue Holiday RC	1.25	3.00
❑ 368 Ty Lawson RC	1.00	2.50
❑ 369 Jeff Teague RC	1.00	2.50
❑ 370 Eric Maynor RC	1.25	3.00
❑ 371 Darren Collison RC	1.25	3.00
❑ 372 Stephen Curry RC	2.00	5.00
❑ 373 Omri Casspi RC	1.25	3.00
❑ 374 B.J. Mullens RC	.75	2.00
❑ 375 Rodrigue Beaubois RC	1.50	4.00
❑ 376 Taj Gibson RC	1.25	3.00
❑ 377 DeMarre Carroll RC	1.00	2.50
❑ 378 Wayne Ellington RC	1.25	3.00
❑ 379 Toney Douglas RC	.75	2.00
❑ 380 Tyler Hansbrough RC	1.25	3.00
❑ 381 Jeff Pendergraph RC	1.00	2.50
❑ 382 Jermaine Taylor RC	1.00	2.50
❑ 383 Dante Cunningham RC	.75	2.00
❑ 384 DaJuan Summers RC	.75	2.00
❑ 385 Sam Young RC	1.25	3.00
❑ 386 DeJuan Blair RC	1.25	3.00
❑ 387 Jon Brockman RC	.75	2.00
❑ 388 Derrick Brown RC	.75	2.00
❑ 389 Jodie Meeks RC	.75	2.00
❑ 390 Patrick Beverley RC	.75	2.00
❑ 391 Marcus Thornton RC	.75	2.00
❑ 392 Chase Budinger RC	1.25	3.00
❑ 393 Jack McClinton RC	.75	2.00
❑ 394 Daniel Green RC	1.00	2.50
❑ 395 Taylor Griffin RC	.75	2.00
❑ 396 A.J. Price RC	.75	2.00
❑ 397 Jonas Jerebko RC	.75	2.00
❑ 398 Lester Hudson RC	.75	2.00
❑ 399 Goran Suton RC	.75	2.00
❑ 400 James Harden RC	1.50	4.00

2009-10 Playoff Contenders

❑ 1 Kevin Garnett	1.00	2.50
❑ 2 Paul Pierce	.60	1.50
❑ 3 Rajon Rondo	.50	1.25
❑ 4 Dirk Nowitzki	.60	1.50
❑ 5 Jason Terry	.40	1.00
❑ 6 Josh Howard	.50	1.25
❑ 7 Shawn Marion	.50	1.25
❑ 8 Brook Lopez	.30	.75
❑ 9 Devin Harris	.50	1.25
❑ 10 Yi Jianlian	.50	1.25
❑ 11 Luis Scola	.30	.75
❑ 12 Tracy McGrady	.60	1.50
❑ 13 Trevor Ariza	.50	1.25
❑ 14 Danilo Gallinari	.50	1.25
❑ 15 Darko Milicic	.30	.75
❑ 16 David Lee	.40	1.00
❑ 17 Nate Robinson	.50	1.25
❑ 18 Allen Iverson	.60	1.50
❑ 19 Marc Gasol	.50	1.25
❑ 20 O.J. Mayo	.60	1.50
❑ 21 Zach Randolph	.30	.75
❑ 22 Andre Iguodala	.50	1.25
❑ 23 Elton Brand	.50	1.25
❑ 24 Thaddeus Young	.30	.75
❑ 25 Chris Paul	1.00	2.50
❑ 26 David West	.50	1.25
❑ 27 Peja Stojakovic	.30	.75
❑ 28 Andrea Bargnani	.40	1.00
❑ 29 Chris Bosh	.50	1.25
❑ 30 Jarrett Jack	.40	1.00
❑ 31 Jose Calderon	.40	1.00
❑ 32 Michael Finley	.30	.75
❑ 33 Richard Jefferson	.50	1.25
❑ 34 Tim Duncan	.75	2.00
❑ 35 Tony Parker	.50	1.25
❑ 36 Derrick Rose	1.00	2.50
❑ 37 Joakim Noah	.50	1.25
❑ 38 Tyrus Thomas	.40	1.00
❑ 39 Carmelo Anthony	.60	1.50
❑ 40 Chauncey Billups	.50	1.25
❑ 41 J.R. Smith	.40	1.00
❑ 42 Nene	.40	1.00
❑ 43 LeBron James	2.50	6.00
❑ 44 Shaquille O'Neal	1.00	2.50
❑ 45 Zydrunas Ilgauskas	.30	.75
❑ 46 Al Jefferson	.50	1.25
❑ 47 Kevin Love	.40	1.00
❑ 48 Ryan Gomes	.30	.75
❑ 49 Ben Gordon	.50	1.25
❑ 50 Richard Hamilton	.40	1.00
❑ 51 Tayshaun Prince	.50	1.25
❑ 52 Andre Miller	.40	1.00
❑ 53 Brandon Roy	.60	1.50
❑ 54 LaMarcus Aldridge	.50	1.25
❑ 55 Rudy Fernandez	.50	1.25
❑ 56 Danny Granger	.50	1.25
❑ 57 T.J. Ford	.30	.75
❑ 58 Troy Murphy	.30	.75
❑ 59 Jeff Green	.40	1.00
❑ 60 Kevin Durant	1.25	3.00
❑ 61 Russell Westbrook	.50	1.25
❑ 62 Andrew Bogut	.50	1.25
❑ 63 Kurt Thomas	.30	.75
❑ 64 Michael Redd	.50	1.25
❑ 65 Andrei Kirilenko	.40	1.00
❑ 66 Deron Williams	.60	1.50
❑ 67 Mehmet Okur	.30	.75
❑ 68 Joe Johnson	.50	1.25
❑ 69 Josh Smith	.50	1.25
❑ 70 Mike Bibby	.30	.75
❑ 71 Anthony Randolph	.50	1.25
❑ 72 Corey Maggette	.40	1.00
❑ 73 Stephen Jackson	.40	1.00
❑ 74 Boris Diaw	.40	1.00
❑ 75 D.J. Augustin	.40	1.00
❑ 76 Gerald Wallace	.50	1.25
❑ 77 Raja Bell	.40	1.00
❑ 78 Al Thornton	.50	1.25
❑ 79 Baron Davis	.50	1.25
❑ 80 Chris Kaman	.50	1.25
❑ 81 Eric Gordon	.50	1.25
❑ 82 Daequan Cook	.40	1.00
❑ 83 Dwyane Wade	1.00	2.50
❑ 84 Jermaine O'Neal	.50	1.25
❑ 85 Andrew Bynum	.50	1.25
❑ 86 Kobe Bryant	2.50	6.00
❑ 87 Pau Gasol	.50	1.25
❑ 88 Ron Artest	.50	1.25
❑ 89 Dwight Howard	1.00	2.50
❑ 90 Jameer Nelson	.40	1.00
❑ 91 Vince Carter	.60	1.50
❑ 92 Amare Stoudemire	.60	1.50
❑ 93 Grant Hill	.50	1.25
❑ 94 Steve Nash	.50	1.25
❑ 95 Antawn Jamison	.50	1.25
❑ 96 Caron Butler	.50	1.25
❑ 97 Gilbert Arenas	.50	1.25
❑ 98 Andres Nocioni	.40	1.00
❑ 99 Kevin Martin	.50	1.25
❑ 100 Sean May	.30	.75
❑ 101 Blake Griffin SP AU RC	30.00	60.00
❑ 102 Hasheem Thabeet SP AU RC	6.00	15.00
❑ 103 James Harden SP AU RC	20.00	40.00
❑ 104 T.Evans SP AU RC EXCH	100.00	200.00
❑ 105 Jonny Flynn SP AU RC	10.00	25.00
❑ 106 Stephen Curry SP AU RC	30.00	60.00
❑ 107 Jordan Hill SP AU RC	8.00	20.00
❑ 108 Brandon Jennings SP AU RC	30.00	60.00
❑ 109 T.Williams SP AU RC EXCH	10.00	25.00

❑ 110 G.Henderson AU RC EXCH	6.00	15.00
❑ 111 Tyler Hansbrough SP AU RC	15.00	30.00
❑ 112 Earl Clark SP AU RC	8.00	20.00
❑ 113 Austin Daye AU RC	6.00	15.00
❑ 114 James Johnson AU RC	6.00	15.00
❑ 115 Jrue Holiday AU RC	8.00	20.00
❑ 116 Ty Lawson AU RC	15.00	30.00
❑ 117 Jeff Teague AU RC	6.00	15.00
❑ 118 Eric Maynor AU RC	6.00	15.00
❑ 119 D.Collison AU RC EXCH	15.00	30.00
❑ 120 Omri Casspi AU RC	10.00	25.00
❑ 121 B.J. Mullens AU RC	6.00	15.00
❑ 122 Rodrigue Beaubois AU RC	10.00	25.00
❑ 123 Taj Gibson AU RC	8.00	20.00
❑ 124 DeMarre Carroll AU RC	6.00	15.00
❑ 125 Wayne Ellington AU RC	6.00	15.00
❑ 126 Toney Douglas AU RC	6.00	15.00
❑ 127 J.Pendergraph AU RC EXCH	6.00	15.00
❑ 128 Jermaine Taylor AU RC	6.00	15.00
❑ 129 D.Cunningham SP AU RC EXCH	8.00	20.00
❑ 130 DaJuan Summers AU RC	6.00	15.00
❑ 131 Sam Young AU RC	6.00	15.00
❑ 132 DeJuan Blair AU RC	10.00	25.00
❑ 133 Jodie Meeks AU RC	6.00	15.00
❑ 134 Chase Budinger AU RC	6.00	15.00
❑ 135 Taylor Griffin AU RC	6.00	15.00
❑ 136 Kareem Abdul-Jabbar	2.00	5.00
❑ 137 Isiah Thomas	1.25	3.00
❑ 138 Bernard King	1.25	3.00
❑ 139 Danny Manning	1.25	3.00
❑ 140 Larry Bird	4.00	10.00
❑ 141 Artis Gilmore	1.25	3.00
❑ 142 Jalen Rose	1.25	3.00
❑ 143 John Havlicek	1.25	3.00
❑ 144 A.C. Green	1.25	3.00
❑ 145 Spencer Haywood	1.25	3.00
❑ 146 Hal Greer	1.25	3.00
❑ 147 Oscar Robertson	1.25	3.00
❑ 148 World B. Free	1.25	3.00
❑ 149 Sidney Moncrief	1.25	3.00
❑ 150 Maurice Cheeks	1.25	3.00

2006-07 Press Pass Legends

❑ COMPLETE SET (70)	20.00	50.00
❑ 1 Ronnie Brewer	.75	2.00
❑ 2 J.J. Redick	.60	1.50
❑ 3 Shelden Williams	.75	2.00
❑ 4 Adam Morrison	.75	2.00
❑ 5 Rajon Rondo	2.50	6.00
❑ 6 Tyrus Thomas	.75	2.00
❑ 7 Rodney Carney	.60	1.50
❑ 8 Shawne Williams	.60	1.50
❑ 9 Maurice Ager	.60	1.50
❑ 10 Shannon Brown	.60	1.50
❑ 11 Cedric Simmons	.60	1.50
❑ 12 Mardy Collins	.60	1.50
❑ 13 LaMarcus Aldridge	.75	2.00
❑ 14 Hilton Armstrong	.60	1.50
❑ 15 Rudy Gay	.60	1.50
❑ 16 Marcus Williams	.75	2.00
❑ 17 Randy Foye	.60	1.50
❑ 18 Brandon Roy	1.50	4.00
❑ 19 Sidney Moncrief	.60	1.50
❑ 20 Nate Thurmond	.60	1.50
❑ 21 Larry Nance	.60	1.50
❑ 22 Sue Bird	2.00	5.00
❑ 23 Diana Taurasi	2.00	5.00
❑ 24 Jay Bilas	.60	1.50
❑ 25 Sleepy Floyd	.60	1.50
❑ 26 Dominique Wilkins	.75	2.00
❑ 27 Clyde Drexler	.75	2.00
❑ 28 Elvin Hayes	.60	1.50
❑ 29 Hakeem Olajuwon	.75	2.00
❑ 30 Steve Alford	.60	1.50
❑ 31 Calbert Cheaney	.60	1.50
❑ 32 Scott May	.60	1.50
❑ 33 Isiah Thomas	.60	1.50
❑ 34 Larry Bird	2.00	5.00
❑ 35 Connie Hawkins	.60	1.50
❑ 36 Danny Manning	.60	1.50
❑ 37 Jo Jo White	.60	1.50
❑ 38 Rex Chapman	.60	1.50
❑ 39 Dan Issel	.60	1.50
❑ 40 Pat Riley	.75	2.00
❑ 41 Pete Maravich	4.00	10.00
❑ 42 Wes Unseld	.60	1.50
❑ 43 Rick Barry	.60	1.50
❑ 44 Lou Hudson	.60	1.50
❑ 45 David Robinson	.75	2.00
❑ 46 Spud Webb	.60	1.50
❑ 47 David Thompson	.60	1.50
❑ 48 Brad Daugherty	.60	1.50
❑ 49 Bob McAdoo	.60	1.50
❑ 50 Sam Perkins	.60	1.50
❑ 51 Kenny Smith	.60	1.50
❑ 52 Bill Laimbeer	.60	1.50
❑ 53 Adrian Dantley	.60	1.50
❑ 54 John Havlicek	.60	1.50
❑ 55 A.C. Green	.60	1.50
❑ 56 Bill Russell	1.25	3.00
❑ 57 Walt Frazier	.60	1.50
❑ 58 Mark Jackson	.60	1.50
❑ 59 Bernard King	.60	1.50
❑ 60 Henry Bibby	.60	1.50
❑ 61 Bill Walton	.60	1.50
❑ 62 Stacey Augmon	.60	1.50
❑ 63 Reggie Theus	.60	1.50
❑ 64 Ralph Sampson	.60	1.50
❑ 65 Jerry West	.75	2.00
❑ 66 Dean Smith	.60	1.50
❑ 67 Digger Phelps	.60	1.50
❑ 68 John Wooden	.60	1.50
❑ 69 Jerry Tarkanian	.60	1.50
❑ 70 Larry Bird CL	1.25	3.00

2007-08 Press Pass Legends

❑ COMPLETE SET (70)	20.00	40.00
❑ 1 Jared Dudley	.75	2.00
❑ 2 Jason Smith	.75	2.00
❑ 3 Josh McRoberts	1.00	2.50
❑ 4 Taurean Green	.75	2.00
❑ 5 Javaris Crittenton	.75	2.00
❑ 6 Glen Davis	1.50	4.00
❑ 7 Nick Fazekas	.75	2.00
❑ 8 Aaron Gray	.75	2.00
❑ 9 Morris Almond	.75	2.00
❑ 10 Acie Law	1.00	2.50
❑ 11 Aaron Afflalo	.75	2.00
❑ 12 Brandan Wright	1.00	2.50
❑ 13 Nick Young	.75	2.00
❑ 14 Gabe Pruitt	.75	2.00
❑ 15 Spencer Hawes	.75	2.00
❑ 16 Sean Elliott	.75	2.00
❑ 17 Lafette Lever	.75	2.00
❑ 18 Byron Scott	.75	2.00
❑ 19 Robert Parish	.75	2.00
❑ 20 Scottie Pippen	1.00	2.50
❑ 21 Dan Majerle	1.00	2.50
❑ 22 Tree Rollins	.75	2.00
❑ 23 Sue Bird	2.00	5.00
❑ 24 Jay Bilas	.75	2.00
❑ 25 Bobby Hurley	.75	2.00
❑ 26 George Gervin	.75	2.00
❑ 27 Dominique Wilkins	1.00	2.50
❑ 28 Kenny Anderson	.75	2.00
❑ 29 Willis Reed	.75	2.00
❑ 30 Larry Bird	2.50	6.00
❑ 31 Artis Gilmore	.75	2.00
❑ 32 JoJo White	.75	2.00
❑ 33 Rolando Blackman	.75	2.00
❑ 34 Dan Issel	.75	2.00
❑ 35 Pete Maravich	2.50	6.00
❑ 36 Joe Dumars	.75	2.00
❑ 37 Hal Greer	.75	2.00
❑ 38 Rick Barry	.75	2.00
❑ 39 Glen Rice	.75	2.00
❑ 40 David Robinson	1.25	3.00
❑ 41 Michael Cooper	.75	2.00
❑ 42 Calvin Murphy	.75	2.00
❑ 43 John Paxson	.75	2.00
❑ 44 John Havlicek	.75	2.00
❑ 45 Jerry Lucas	.75	2.00
❑ 46 A.C. Green	.75	2.00
❑ 47 Lenny Wilkens	.75	2.00
❑ 48 Bill Russell	1.25	3.00
❑ 49 Elgin Baylor	.75	2.00
❑ 50 Alex English	.75	2.00
❑ 51 Dick McGuire	.75	2.00
❑ 52 Sherman Douglas	.75	2.00
❑ 53 Henry Bibby	.75	2.00
❑ 54 Bill Walton	.75	2.00
❑ 55 Kiki Vandeweghe	.75	2.00
❑ 56 Phil Ford	.75	2.00
❑ 57 George Karl	.75	2.00
❑ 58 Sam Perkins	.75	2.00
❑ 59 Kenny Smith	.75	2.00
❑ 60 James Worthy	1.00	2.50
❑ 61 Stacey Augmon	.75	2.00
❑ 62 Larry Johnson	.75	2.00
❑ 63 Jerry Tarkanian	.75	2.00
❑ 64 Gus Williams	.75	2.00
❑ 65 Nate Archibald	.75	2.00
❑ 66 Muggsy Bogues	.75	2.00
❑ 67 Detlef Schrempf	.75	2.00
❑ 68 Earl Monroe	.75	2.00
❑ 69 Jerry West	1.00	2.50
❑ 70 Tarkanian/L.Johnson/S.Augmon	.75	2.00

2008-09 Press Pass Legends

❑ COMPLETE SET (70)	20.00	40.00
❑ 1 Jerryd Bayless	.75	2.00
❑ 2 Sonny Weems	.75	2.00
❑ 3 Trent Plaisted	.75	2.00
❑ 4 DeVon Hardin	.75	2.00
❑ 5 Marreese Speights	.75	2.00
❑ 6 Patrick Ewing Jr.	.75	2.00
❑ 7 Roy Hibbert	1.00	2.50
❑ 8 Eric Gordon	1.00	2.50
❑ 9 D.J. White	.75	2.00
❑ 10 Danilo Gallinari	1.25	3.00
❑ 11 Mario Chalmers	1.00	2.50
❑ 12 Darnell Jackson	.75	2.00
❑ 13 Brandon Rush	.75	2.00
❑ 14 Michael Beasley	1.50	4.00
❑ 15 Anthony Randolph	1.25	3.00
❑ 16 Joey Dorsey	.75	2.00
❑ 17 Chris Douglas-Roberts	1.00	2.50
❑ 18 Derrick Rose	3.00	8.00
❑ 19 J.J. Hickson	1.25	3.00
❑ 20 J.R. Giddens	.75	2.00
❑ 21 Kosta Koufos	.75	2.00
❑ 22 Malik Hairston	.75	2.00
❑ 23 Bryce Taylor	.75	2.00
❑ 24 Brook Lopez	1.50	4.00
❑ 25 Robin Lopez	.75	2.00
❑ 26 Chris Lofton	.75	2.00
❑ 27 Candace Parker	6.00	15.00
❑ 28 D.J. Augustin	.75	2.00
❑ 29 DeAndre Jordan	.75	2.00
❑ 30 Kevin Love	1.00	2.50
❑ 31 Russell Westbrook	2.00	5.00
❑ 32 O.J. Mayo	1.25	3.00
❑ 33 Shan Foster	.75	2.00
❑ 34 Courtney Lee	1.25	3.00
❑ 35 Sean Elliott	.75	2.00
❑ 36 Sidney Moncrief	.75	2.00
❑ 37 Corliss Williamson	.75	2.00
❑ 38 Larry Nance	.75	2.00
❑ 39 Bobby Hurley	.75	2.00
❑ 40 Sleepy Floyd	.75	2.00
❑ 41 Clyde Drexler	1.00	2.50
❑ 42 Calbert Cheaney	.75	2.00
❑ 43 Larry Bird	2.50	6.00
❑ 44 Danny Manning	.75	2.00

❑ 45 Rolando Blackman .75 2.00
❑ 46 Cliff Hagan .75 2.00
❑ 47 Darrell Griffith .75 2.00
❑ 48 Bailey Howell .75 2.00
❑ 49 David Robinson 1.25 3.00
❑ 50 Sidney Lowe .75 2.00
❑ 51 Michael Cooper .75 2.00
❑ 52 Calvin Murphy .75 2.00
❑ 53 Willis Reed .75 2.00
❑ 54 Brad Daugherty .75 2.00
❑ 55 Nate Archibald .75 2.00
❑ 56 James Worthy .75 2.00
❑ 57 Jerry Lucas .75 2.00
❑ 58 Elgin Baylor .75 2.00
❑ 59 Mark Jackson .75 2.00
❑ 60 Ernie Grunfeld .75 2.00
❑ 61 Bernard King .75 2.00
❑ 62 Henry Bibby .75 2.00
❑ 63 Gail Goodrich .75 2.00
❑ 64 Bill Walton .75 2.00
❑ 65 John Wooden 1.00 2.50
❑ 66 Stacey Augmon .75 2.00
❑ 67 Jerry Tarkanian .75 2.00
❑ 68 Gus Williams .75 2.00
❑ 69 Jerry West 1.00 2.50
❑ 70 UCLA CL .75 2.00

2009-10 Prestige

❑ 1 Joe Johnson .40 1.00
❑ 2 Josh Smith .40 1.00
❑ 3 Mike Bibby .25 .60
❑ 4 Jamal Crawford .25 .60
❑ 5 Kevin Garnett .75 2.00
❑ 6 Paul Pierce .50 1.25
❑ 7 Ray Allen .40 1.00
❑ 8 Rajon Rondo .40 1.00
❑ 9 Gerald Wallace .40 1.00
❑ 10 Boris Diaw .30 .75
❑ 11 Emeka Okafor .40 1.00
❑ 12 Ben Gordon .40 1.00
❑ 13 John Salmons .40 1.00
❑ 14 Derrick Rose .75 2.00
❑ 15 Luol Deng .40 1.00
❑ 16 LeBron James 2.00 5.00
❑ 17 Mo Williams .30 .75
❑ 18 Zydrunas Ilgauskas .25 .60
❑ 19 Delonte West .25 .60
❑ 20 Shaquille O'Neal .75 2.00
❑ 21 Dirk Nowitzki .50 1.25
❑ 22 Jason Terry .30 .75
❑ 23 Josh Howard .40 1.00
❑ 24 Jason Kidd .40 1.00
❑ 25 Carmelo Anthony .50 1.25
❑ 26 Chauncey Billups .40 1.00
❑ 27 Nene .30 .75
❑ 28 Richard Hamilton .30 .75
❑ 29 Allen Iverson .50 1.25
❑ 30 Tayshaun Prince .40 1.00
❑ 31 Rasheed Wallace .40 1.00
❑ 32 Stephen Jackson .30 .75
❑ 33 Corey Maggette .30 .75
❑ 34 Yao Ming .50 1.25
❑ 35 Tracy McGrady .50 1.25
❑ 36 Ron Artest .40 1.00
❑ 37 Luis Scola .25 .60
❑ 38 Danny Granger .40 1.00
❑ 39 T.J. Ford .25 .60
❑ 40 Mike Dunleavy .25 .60
❑ 41 Marquis Daniels .25 .60
❑ 42 Zach Randolph .25 .60
❑ 43 Al Thornton .40 1.00
❑ 44 Eric Gordon .40 1.00
❑ 45 Baron Davis .40 1.00
❑ 46 Kobe Bryant 2.00 5.00
❑ 47 Pau Gasol .40 1.00
❑ 48 Lamar Odom .40 1.00
❑ 49 Derek Fisher .30 .75
❑ 50 O.J. Mayo .50 1.25
❑ 51 Rudy Gay .40 1.00
❑ 52 Marc Gasol .40 1.00
❑ 53 Dwyane Wade .75 2.00
❑ 54 Jermaine O'Neal .40 1.00
❑ 55 Michael Beasley .50 1.25
❑ 56 Udonis Haslem .30 .75
❑ 57 Michael Redd .40 1.00
❑ 58 Charlie Villanueva .30 .75
❑ 59 Al Jefferson .40 1.00
❑ 60 Ryan Gomes .25 .60
❑ 61 Kevin Love .30 .75
❑ 62 Devin Harris .40 1.00
❑ 63 Brook Lopez .25 .60
❑ 64 Yi Jianlian .40 1.00
❑ 65 Chris Paul .75 2.00
❑ 66 David West .40 1.00
❑ 67 Peja Stojakovic .25 .60
❑ 68 Rasual Butler .25 .60
❑ 69 Al Harrington .30 .75
❑ 70 Nate Robinson .40 1.00
❑ 71 David Lee .30 .75
❑ 72 Larry Hughes .25 .60
❑ 73 Kevin Durant 1.00 2.50
❑ 74 Jeff Green .30 .75
❑ 75 Russell Westbrook .40 1.00
❑ 76 Dwight Howard .75 2.00
❑ 77 Rashard Lewis .40 1.00
❑ 78 Hedo Turkoglu .40 1.00
❑ 79 Jameer Nelson .30 .75
❑ 80 Vince Carter .50 1.25
❑ 81 Andre Iguodala .40 1.00
❑ 82 Andre Miller .30 .75
❑ 83 Thaddeus Young .25 .60
❑ 84 Elton Brand .40 1.00
❑ 85 Amare Stoudemire .50 1.25
❑ 86 Steve Nash .40 1.00
❑ 87 Jason Richardson .40 1.00
❑ 88 Brandon Roy .50 1.25
❑ 89 LaMarcus Aldridge .40 1.00
❑ 90 Greg Oden .30 .75
❑ 91 Kevin Martin .40 1.00
❑ 92 Andres Nocioni .30 .75
❑ 93 Jason Thompson .25 .60
❑ 94 Tony Parker .40 1.00
❑ 95 Tim Duncan .60 1.50
❑ 96 Manu Ginobili .40 1.00
❑ 97 Michael Finley .25 .60
❑ 98 Richard Jefferson .40 1.00
❑ 99 Chris Bosh .40 1.00
❑ 100 Andrea Bargnani .30 .75
❑ 101 Shawn Marion .40 1.00
❑ 102 Deron Williams .50 1.25
❑ 103 Mehmet Okur .25 .60
❑ 104 Carlos Boozer .40 1.00
❑ 105 Ronnie Brewer .25 .60
❑ 106 Antawn Jamison .40 1.00
❑ 107 Caron Butler .40 1.00
❑ 108 Nick Young .25 .60
❑ 109 Andray Blatche .25 .60
❑ 110 Randy Foye .25 .60
❑ 111 Kareem Abdul-Jabbar 1.00 2.50
❑ 112 Bob Dandridge .60 1.50
❑ 113 Alvan Adams .60 1.50
❑ 114 A.C. Green .60 1.50
❑ 115 Dave Bing .60 1.50
❑ 116 Larry Bird 2.00 5.00
❑ 117 Nate Thurmond .60 1.50
❑ 118 Michael Cooper .60 1.50
❑ 119 Bob Cousy 1.00 2.50
❑ 120 Adrian Dantley .60 1.50
❑ 121 Darryl Dawkins .60 1.50
❑ 122 Clyde Drexler .75 2.00
❑ 123 Elvin Hayes .60 1.50
❑ 124 Walt Frazier .60 1.50
❑ 125 World B. Free .60 1.50
❑ 126 George Gervin .60 1.50
❑ 127 Gail Goodrich .60 1.50
❑ 128 Tim Hardaway .60 1.50
❑ 129 Connie Hawkins .60 1.50
❑ 130 K.C. Jones .60 1.50
❑ 131 Bernard King .60 1.50
❑ 132 Bob Lanier .60 1.50
❑ 133 Dan Majerle .60 1.50
❑ 134 Karl Malone .75 2.00
❑ 135 Sam Perkins .60 1.50
❑ 136 Slick Watts .60 1.50
❑ 137 Bob McAdoo .60 1.50
❑ 138 Xavier McDaniel .60 1.50
❑ 139 Sidney Moncrief .60 1.50
❑ 140 Robert Parish .60 1.50
❑ 141 Oscar Robertson .60 1.50
❑ 142 Paul Silas .60 1.50
❑ 143 Moses Malone .60 1.50
❑ 144 Dennis Rodman 1.00 2.50
❑ 145 Bill Russell 1.00 2.50
❑ 146 Bill Bradley .60 1.50
❑ 147 Bill Walton .60 1.50
❑ 148 Spud Webb .60 1.50
❑ 149 Cedric Ceballos .60 1.50
❑ 150 Jerry West .75 2.00
❑ 151 Blake Griffin RC 3.00 8.00
❑ 152 Hasheem Thabeet RC 1.25 3.00
❑ 153 James Harden RC 2.50 6.00
❑ 154 Tyreke Evans RC 5.00 12.00
❑ 155 Blake Griffin College RC 3.00 8.00
❑ 156 Jonny Flynn RC 2.00 5.00
❑ 157 Stephen Curry RC 3.00 8.00
❑ 158 Jordan Hill RC 1.50 4.00
❑ 159 DeMar DeRozan RC 2.00 5.00
❑ 160 Brandon Jennings SP 15.00 30.00
❑ 161 Terrence Williams RC 2.50 6.00
❑ 162 Gerald Henderson RC 2.00 5.00
❑ 163 Tyler Hansbrough SP 10.00 25.00
❑ 164 Earl Clark RC 2.00 5.00
❑ 165 Austin Daye RC 1.50 4.00
❑ 166 James Johnson RC 2.00 5.00
❑ 167 Jrue Holiday RC 2.00 5.00
❑ 168 Ty Lawson RC 1.50 4.00
❑ 169 Jeff Teague RC 1.50 4.00
❑ 170 Eric Maynor RC 2.00 5.00
❑ 171 Darren Collison RC 2.00 5.00
❑ 172 Hasheem Thabeet UConn RC 1.25 3.00
❑ 173 Omri Casspi RC 2.00 5.00
❑ 174 B.J. Mullens RC 1.25 3.00
❑ 175 Rodrigue Beaubois RC 2.50 6.00
❑ 176 Taj Gibson SP 8.00 20.00
❑ 177 DeMarre Carroll SP 6.00 15.00
❑ 178 Wayne Ellington RC 2.00 5.00
❑ 179 Toney Douglas RC 1.25 3.00
❑ 180 Tyreke Evans Memphis RC 5.00 12.00
❑ 181 Jeff Pendergraph RC 1.50 4.00
❑ 182 Jermaine Taylor RC 1.50 4.00
❑ 183 Dante Cunningham RC 1.25 3.00
❑ 184 DaJuan Summers RC 1.25 3.00
❑ 185 Sam Young RC 2.00 5.00
❑ 186 DeJuan Blair RC 2.00 5.00
❑ 187 Jon Brockman RC 1.25 3.00
❑ 188 Derrick Brown RC 1.25 3.00
❑ 189 Jodie Meeks RC 1.25 3.00
❑ 190 Jonas Jerebko SP 5.00 12.00
❑ 191 Marcus Thornton RC 1.25 3.00
❑ 192 Chase Budinger RC 2.00 5.00
❑ 193 Goran Suton RC 1.25 3.00
❑ 194 Danny Green RC 1.50 4.00
❑ 195 Taylor Griffin RC 1.25 3.00
❑ 196 A.J. Price RC 1.25 3.00
❑ 197 Jrue Holiday UCLA RC 2.00 5.00
❑ 198 Lester Hudson RC 1.25 3.00
❑ 199 Jack McClinton RC 1.25 3.00
❑ 200 Patrick Beverley RC 1.25 3.00
❑ 201 Blake Griffin RC 3.00 8.00
❑ 202 Hasheem Thabeet RC 1.25 3.00
❑ 203 James Harden RC 2.50 6.00
❑ 204 Tyreke Evans RC 5.00 12.00
❑ 205 Jordan Hill Arizona SP 8.00 20.00
❑ 206 Jonny Flynn RC 2.00 5.00
❑ 207 Stephen Curry RC 3.00 8.00
❑ 208 Jordan Hill RC 1.50 4.00
❑ 209 DeMar DeRozan RC 2.00 5.00
❑ 210 Brandon Jennings RC 3.00 8.00
❑ 211 Terrence Williams RC 2.50 6.00
❑ 212 Gerald Henderson RC 2.00 5.00
❑ 213 Tyler Hansbrough RC 2.00 5.00
❑ 214 Earl Clark RC 2.00 5.00
❑ 215 Austin Daye RC 1.50 4.00
❑ 216 James Johnson RC 2.00 5.00
❑ 217 Jrue Holiday RC 2.00 5.00
❑ 218 Ty Lawson SP 6.00 15.00
❑ 219 Jeff Teague RC 1.50 4.00
❑ 220 Eric Maynor SP 6.00 15.00
❑ 221 Darren Collison RC 2.00 5.00
❑ 222 Tyler Hansbrough RC 2.00 5.00
❑ 223 Omri Casspi RC 2.00 5.00
❑ 224 B.J. Mullens RC 1.25 3.00
❑ 225 Rodrigue Beaubois RC 2.50 6.00
❑ 226 Taj Gibson RC 2.00 5.00

❑ 227 DeMarre Carroll RC 1.50 4.00
❑ 228 Wayne Ellington RC 2.00 5.00
❑ 229 Toney Douglas RC 1.25 3.00
❑ 230 Stephen Curry Davidson RC 3.00 8.00
❑ 231 Jeff Pendergraph RC 1.50 4.00
❑ 232 Jermaine Taylor RC 1.50 4.00
❑ 233 Dante Cunningham SP 5.00 12.00
❑ 234 DaJuan Summers RC 1.25 3.00
❑ 235 Sam Young RC 2.00 5.00
❑ 236 DeJuan Blair RC 2.00 5.00
❑ 237 Jon Brockman RC 1.25 3.00
❑ 238 Derrick Brown RC 1.25 3.00
❑ 239 Jodie Meeks RC 1.25 3.00
❑ 240 Jonas Jerebko RC 1.25 3.00
❑ 241 Marcus Thornton RC 1.25 3.00
❑ 242 Chase Budinger RC 2.00 5.00
❑ 243 Goran Suton RC 1.25 3.00
❑ 244 Danny Green RC 1.50 4.00
❑ 245 Taylor Griffin RC 1.25 3.00
❑ 246 A.J. Price RC 1.25 3.00
❑ 247 James Johnson Wake SP 6.00 15.00
❑ 248 Lester Hudson RC 1.25 3.00
❑ 249 Jack McClinton RC 1.25 3.00
❑ 250 Patrick Beverley RC 1.25 3.00

2005-06 Reflections

❑ COMP.SET w/o RC's (100) 20.00 50.00
❑ COMMON CARD (1-100) .40 1.00
❑ COMMON ROOKIE (101-150) 1.50 4.00
❑ 1 Al Harrington .40 1.00
❑ 2 Josh Smith .60 1.50
❑ 3 Josh Childress .50 1.25
❑ 4 Joe Johnson .60 1.50
❑ 5 Paul Pierce .60 1.50
❑ 6 Antoine Walker .50 1.25
❑ 7 Gary Payton .60 1.50
❑ 8 Al Jefferson .60 1.50
❑ 9 Emeka Okafor .60 1.50
❑ 10 Primoz Brezec 40 1.00
❑ 11 Gerald Wallace .60 1.50
❑ 12 Michael Jordan 4.00 10.00
❑ 13 Ben Gordon .75 2.00
❑ 14 Luol Deng .60 1.50
❑ 15 Kirk Hinrich .60 1.50
❑ 16 LeBron James 3.00 8.00
❑ 17 Dajuan Wagner .40 1.00
❑ 18 Drew Gooden .50 1.25
❑ 19 Larry Hughes .50 1.25
❑ 20 Dirk Nowitzki 1.00 2.50
❑ 21 Jason Terry .60 1.50
❑ 22 Michael Finley .60 1.50
❑ 23 Jerry Stackhouse .60 1.50
❑ 24 Andre Miller .50 1.25
❑ 25 Carmelo Anthony 1.25 3.00
❑ 26 Kenyon Martin .60 1.50
❑ 27 Earl Boykins .40 1.00
❑ 28 Rasheed Wallace .60 1.50
❑ 29 Ben Wallace .60 1.50
❑ 30 Richard Hamilton .50 1.25
❑ 31 Chauncey Billups .60 1.50
❑ 32 Baron Davis .60 1.50
❑ 33 Derek Fisher .40 1.00
❑ 34 Jason Richardson .60 1.50
❑ 35 Tracy McGrady 1.25 3.00
❑ 36 Yao Ming 1.50 4.00
❑ 37 Juwan Howard .50 1.25
❑ 38 Jermaine O'Neal .60 1.50
❑ 39 Ron Artest .50 1.25
❑ 40 Jamaal Tinsley .50 1.25
❑ 41 Corey Maggette .50 1.25
❑ 42 Elton Brand .60 1.50
❑ 43 Shaun Livingston .40 1.00
❑ 44 Kobe Bryant 3.00 8.00
❑ 45 Brian Cook .40 1.00
❑ 46 Lamar Odom .60 1.50
❑ 47 Mike Miller .60 1.50
❑ 48 Pau Gasol .60 1.50
❑ 49 Shane Battier .60 1.50
❑ 50 Shaquille O'Neal 1.50 4.00
❑ 51 Dwyane Wade 1.50 4.00
❑ 52 Udonis Haslem .60 1.50
❑ 53 Joe Smith .50 1.25
❑ 54 Michael Redd .60 1.50
❑ 55 Desmond Mason .40 1.00
❑ 56 Kevin Garnett 1.25 3.00
❑ 57 Wally Szczerbiak .50 1.25
❑ 58 Sam Cassell .60 1.50
❑ 59 Vince Carter 1.25 3.00
❑ 60 Jason Kidd 1.00 2.50
❑ 61 Richard Jefferson .50 1.25
❑ 62 Jamaal Magloire .40 1.00
❑ 63 J.R. Smith .50 1.25
❑ 64 Bostjan Nachbar .40 1.00
❑ 65 Allan Houston .40 1.00
❑ 66 Stephon Marbury .60 1.50
❑ 67 Jamal Crawford .50 1.25
❑ 68 Dwight Howard 1.25 3.00
❑ 69 Grant Hill .60 1.50
❑ 70 Jameer Nelson .50 1.25
❑ 71 Steve Francis .60 1.50
❑ 72 Allen Iverson 1.25 3.00
❑ 73 Andre Iguodala .60 1.50
❑ 74 Chris Webber .60 1.50
❑ 75 Samuel Dalembert .40 1.00
❑ 76 Amare Stoudemire 1.25 3.00
❑ 77 Steve Nash .75 2.00
❑ 78 Quentin Richardson .50 1.25
❑ 79 Shawn Marion .60 1.50
❑ 80 Damon Stoudamire .50 1.25
❑ 81 Zach Randolph .60 1.50
❑ 82 Sebastian Telfair .50 1.25
❑ 83 Peja Stojakovic .60 1.50
❑ 84 Mike Bibby .60 1.50
❑ 85 Cuttino Mobley .50 1.25
❑ 86 Manu Ginobili .60 1.50
❑ 87 Tim Duncan 1.25 3.00
❑ 88 Tony Parker .60 1.50
❑ 89 Ray Allen .60 1.50
❑ 90 Rashard Lewis .60 1.50
❑ 91 Luke Ridnour .50 1.25
❑ 92 Ronald Murray .40 1.00
❑ 93 Chris Bosh .60 1.50
❑ 94 Morris Peterson .50 1.25
❑ 95 Rafael Araujo .40 1.00
❑ 96 Andrei Kirilenko .60 1.50
❑ 97 Raul Lopez .40 1.00
❑ 98 Carlos Boozer .60 1.50
❑ 99 Antawn Jamison .60 1.50
❑ 100 Gilbert Arenas .60 1.50
❑ 101 Travis Diener RC 1.50 4.00
❑ 102 Julius Hodge RC 2.00 5.00
❑ 103 David Lee RC 3.00 8.00
❑ 104 Sarunas Jasikevicius RC 2.00 5.00
❑ 105 Jason Maxiell RC 2.00 5.00
❑ 106 Luther Head RC 2.00 5.00
❑ 107 Amir Johnson RC 1.50 4.00
❑ 108 Linas Kleiza RC 2.00 5.00
❑ 109 Uros Slokar RC 1.50 4.00
❑ 110 Andray Blatche RC 2.00 5.00
❑ 111 Sean May RC 2.00 5.00
❑ 112 Alex Acker RC 1.50 4.00
❑ 113 Nate Robinson RC 2.50 6.00
❑ 114 Brandon Bass RC 1.50 4.00
❑ 115 Ike Diogu RC 2.00 5.00
❑ 116 Daniel Ewing RC 2.00 5.00
❑ 117 Salim Stoudamire RC 2.00 5.00
❑ 118 Dijon Thompson RC 1.50 4.00
❑ 119 Danny Granger RC 4.00 10.00
❑ 120 Chris Taft RC 1.50 4.00
❑ 121 Louis Williams RC 2.50 6.00
❑ 122 Channing Frye RC 2.00 5.00
❑ 123 Francisco Garcia RC 2.00 5.00
❑ 124 Ryan Gomes RC 1.50 4.00
❑ 125 Von Wafer RC 1.50 4.00
❑ 126 Jarrett Jack RC 1.50 4.00
❑ 127 Lawrence Roberts RC 1.50 4.00
❑ 128 Ricky Sanchez RC 1.50 4.00
❑ 129 C.J. Miles RC 1.50 4.00
❑ 130 Ersan Ilyasova RC 1.50 4.00
❑ 131 Robert Whaley RC 1.50 4.00
❑ 132 Monta Ellis RC 4.00 10.00
❑ 133 Bracey Wright RC 1.50 4.00
❑ 134 Johan Petro RC 1.50 4.00
❑ 135 Will Bynum RC 1.50 4.00
❑ 136 Andrew Bynum RC 5.00 12.00
❑ 137 Martynas Andriuskevicius RC 1.50 4.00
❑ 138 Charlie Villanueva RC 2.50 6.00
❑ 139 Antoine Wright RC 1.50 4.00
❑ 140 Joey Graham RC 1.50 4.00
❑ 141 Wayne Simien RC 2.00 5.00
❑ 142 Hakim Warrick RC 2.50 6.00
❑ 143 Gerald Green RC 1.50 4.00
❑ 144 Marvin Williams RC 2.50 6.00
❑ 145 Deron Williams RC 4.00 10.00
❑ 146 Rashad McCants RC 2.00 5.00
❑ 147 Martell Webster RC 1.50 4.00
❑ 148 Raymond Felton RC 2.00 5.00
❑ 149 Chris Paul RC 5.00 12.00
❑ 150 Andrew Bogut RC 2.00 5.00

2006-07 Reflections

❑ COMP.SET w/o SP's 25.00 60.00
❑ 1 Josh Childress .50 1.25
❑ 2 Joe Johnson .50 1.25
❑ 3 Marvin Williams .60 1.50
❑ 4 Dan Dickau .40 1.00
❑ 5 Paul Pierce .60 1.50
❑ 6 Wally Szczerbiak .50 1.25
❑ 7 Raymond Felton .75 2.00
❑ 8 Emeka Okafor .60 1.50
❑ 9 Kareem Rush .40 1.00
❑ 10 Gerald Wallace .60 1.50
❑ 11 Tyson Chandler .60 1.50
❑ 12 Luol Deng .60 1.50
❑ 13 Ben Gordon .75 2.00
❑ 14 Michael Jordan 4.00 10.00
❑ 15 Larry Hughes .50 1.25
❑ 16 Zydrunas Ilgauskas .50 1.25
❑ 17 LeBron James 3.00 8.00
❑ 18 Donyell Marshall .40 1.00
❑ 19 Marquis Daniels .50 1.25
❑ 20 Josh Howard .60 1.50
❑ 21 Dirk Nowitzki 1.00 2.50
❑ 22 Jason Terry .60 1.50
❑ 23 Carmelo Anthony .75 2.00
❑ 24 Earl Boykins .40 1.00
❑ 25 Marcus Camby .50 1.25
❑ 26 Kenyon Martin .60 1.50
❑ 27 Chauncey Billups .60 1.50
❑ 28 Richard Hamilton .50 1.25
❑ 29 Rasheed Wallace .60 1.50
❑ 30 Baron Davis .60 1.50
❑ 31 Ike Diogu .50 1.25
❑ 32 Mike Dunleavy .50 1.25
❑ 33 Troy Murphy .60 1.50
❑ 34 Luther Head .50 1.25
❑ 35 Tracy McGrady 1.25 3.00
❑ 36 Yao Ming 1.50 4.00
❑ 37 Jermaine O'Neal .60 1.50
❑ 38 Peja Stojakovic .60 1.50
❑ 39 Jamaal Tinsley .50 1.25
❑ 40 Chris Kaman .40 1.00
❑ 41 Sam Cassell .60 1.50
❑ 42 Shaun Livingston .40 1.00
❑ 43 Cuttino Mobley .50 1.25
❑ 44 Kobe Bryant 3.00 8.00
❑ 45 Devean George .50 1.25
❑ 46 Lamar Odom .60 1.50
❑ 47 Pau Gasol .60 1.50
❑ 48 Bobby Jackson .40 1.00
❑ 49 Mike Miller .60 1.50
❑ 50 Shaquille O'Neal 1.50 4.00
❑ 51 Dwyane Wade 1.50 4.00
❑ 52 Jason Williams .50 1.25
❑ 53 Andrew Bogut .60 1.50
❑ 54 T.J. Ford .50 1.25
❑ 55 Michael Redd .60 1.50
❑ 56 Ricky Davis .60 1.50
❑ 57 Kevin Garnett 1.25 3.00
❑ 58 Troy Hudson .40 1.00
❑ 59 Vince Carter 1.25 3.00

❑ 60 Jason Collins	.40	1.00
❑ 61 Richard Jefferson	.50	1.25
❑ 62 Jason Kidd	1.00	2.50
❑ 63 Desmond Mason	.40	1.00
❑ 64 Chris Paul	1.25	3.00
❑ 65 J.R. Smith	.50	1.25
❑ 66 Steve Francis	.60	1.50
❑ 67 Channing Frye	.50	1.25
❑ 68 Stephon Marbury	.60	1.50
❑ 69 Dwight Howard	1.25	3.00
❑ 70 Darko Milicic	.60	1.50
❑ 71 Jameer Nelson	.50	1.25
❑ 72 Andre Iguodala	.60	1.50
❑ 73 Allen Iverson	1.25	3.00
❑ 74 Chris Webber	.60	1.50
❑ 75 Boris Diaw	.50	1.25
❑ 76 Shawn Marion	.60	1.50
❑ 77 Steve Nash	.75	2.00
❑ 78 Amare Stoudemire	1.25	3.00
❑ 79 Juan Dixon	.40	1.00
❑ 80 Darius Miles	.40	1.00
❑ 81 Sebastian Telfair	.50	1.25
❑ 82 Ron Artest	.60	1.50
❑ 83 Mike Bibby	.60	1.50
❑ 84 Brad Miller	.60	1.50
❑ 85 Tim Duncan	1.25	3.00
❑ 86 Manu Ginobili	.60	1.50
❑ 87 Robert Horry	.50	1.25
❑ 88 Tony Parker	.60	1.50
❑ 89 Ray Allen	.60	1.50
❑ 90 Rashard Lewis	.60	1.50
❑ 91 Luke Ridnour	.50	1.25
❑ 92 Chris Bosh	.60	1.50
❑ 93 Joey Graham	.50	1.25
❑ 94 Charlie Villanueva	.60	1.50
❑ 95 Carlos Boozer	.60	1.50
❑ 96 Andrei Kirilenko	.60	1.50
❑ 97 Deron Williams	1.00	2.50
❑ 98 Gilbert Arenas	.60	1.50
❑ 99 Caron Butler	.60	1.50
❑ 100 Antawn Jamison	.60	1.50
❑ 101 Adam Morrison RC	3.00	8.00
❑ 102 Tyrus Thomas RC	3.00	8.00
❑ 103 Rudy Gay RC	2.50	6.00
❑ 104 Andrea Bargnani RC	4.00	10.00
❑ 105 LaMarcus Aldridge RC	3.00	8.00
❑ 106 Brandon Roy RC	6.00	15.00
❑ 107 Randy Foye RC	2.50	6.00
❑ 108 Marcus Williams RC	3.00	8.00
❑ 109 Rodney Carney RC	2.50	6.00
❑ 110 Shelden Williams RC	3.00	8.00
❑ 111 Patrick O'Bryant RC	1.50	4.00
❑ 112 Cedric Simmons RC	1.50	4.00
❑ 113 Jordan Farmar RC	2.00	5.00
❑ 114 J.J. Redick RC	1.50	4.00
❑ 115 Tarence Kinsey RC	1.50	4.00
❑ 116 Kevin Pittsnogle RC	1.50	4.00
❑ 117 Ronnie Brewer RC	2.00	5.00
❑ 118 Shawne Williams RC	1.50	4.00
❑ 119 Allan Ray RC	1.50	4.00
❑ 120 Shannon Brown RC	1.50	4.00
❑ 121 Kyle Lowry RC	1.50	4.00
❑ 122 Mardy Collins RC	1.50	4.00
❑ 123 Hilton Armstrong RC	1.50	4.00
❑ 124 Maurice Ager RC	1.50	4.00
❑ 125 Quincy Douby RC	1.50	4.00
❑ 126 Rajon Rondo RC	8.00	20.00
❑ 127 Mike Gansey RC	2.00	5.00
❑ 128 Joel Freeland RC	2.00	5.00
❑ 129 Josh Boone RC	2.00	5.00
❑ 130 Saer Sene RC	2.00	5.00
❑ 131 Denham Brown RC	2.00	5.00
❑ 132 Renaldo Balkman RC	2.00	5.00
❑ 133 Will Blalock RC	2.00	5.00
❑ 134 David Noel RC	2.00	5.00
❑ 135 Steve Novak RC	2.00	5.00
❑ 136 Solomon Jones RC	2.00	5.00
❑ 137 Dee Brown RC	2.00	5.00
❑ 138 Hassan Adams RC	2.50	6.00
❑ 139 Bobby Jones RC	2.00	5.00
❑ 140 Thabo Sefolosha RC	2.50	6.00
❑ 141 James White RC	2.00	5.00
❑ 142 Paul Davis RC	2.00	5.00
❑ 143 P.J. Tucker RC	2.00	5.00
❑ 144 Ryan Hollins RC	2.00	5.00
❑ 145 Damir Markota RC	2.00	5.00
❑ 146 Leon Powe RC	2.00	5.00
❑ 147 James Augustine RC	2.00	5.00
❑ 148 Alexander Johnson RC	2.00	5.00
❑ 149 Daniel Gibson RC	2.50	6.00

2009-10 Rookies and Stars

❑ 1 Josh Smith	.50	1.25
❑ 2 Joe Johnson	.50	1.25
❑ 3 Mike Bibby	.30	.75
❑ 4 Paul Pierce	.60	1.50
❑ 5 Ray Allen	.50	1.25
❑ 6 Rajon Rondo	.50	1.25
❑ 7 Kevin Garnett	1.00	2.50
❑ 8 Gerald Wallace	.50	1.25
❑ 9 Boris Diaw	.40	1.00
❑ 10 Raja Bell	.40	1.00
❑ 11 Derrick Rose	1.00	2.50
❑ 12 John Salmons	.50	1.25
❑ 13 Kirk Hinrich	.50	1.25
❑ 14 LeBron James	2.50	6.00
❑ 15 Shaquille O'Neal	1.00	2.50
❑ 16 Mo Williams	.40	1.00
❑ 17 Dirk Nowitzki	.60	1.50
❑ 18 Josh Howard	.50	1.25
❑ 19 Jason Kidd	.50	1.25
❑ 20 Jason Terry	.40	1.00
❑ 21 Shawn Marion	.50	1.25
❑ 22 Carmelo Anthony	.60	1.50
❑ 23 Chauncey Billups	.50	1.25
❑ 24 J.R. Smith	.40	1.00
❑ 25 Richard Hamilton	.40	1.00
❑ 26 Tayshaun Prince	.50	1.25
❑ 27 Allen Iverson	.60	1.50
❑ 28 Stephen Jackson	.40	1.00
❑ 29 Corey Maggette	.40	1.00
❑ 30 Monta Ellis	.50	1.25
❑ 31 Yao Ming	.60	1.50
❑ 32 Tracy McGrady	.60	1.50
❑ 33 Trevor Ariza	.50	1.25
❑ 34 Danny Granger	.50	1.25
❑ 35 Mike Dunleavy	.30	.75
❑ 36 T.J. Ford	.30	.75
❑ 37 Al Thornton	.50	1.25
❑ 38 Eric Gordon	.50	1.25
❑ 39 Kobe Bryant	2.50	6.00
❑ 40 Pau Gasol	.50	1.25
❑ 41 Ron Artest	.50	1.25
❑ 42 Andrew Bynum	.50	1.25
❑ 43 Rudy Gay	.50	1.25
❑ 44 O.J. Mayo	.60	1.50
❑ 45 Mike Conley	.30	.75
❑ 46 Zach Randolph	.30	.75
❑ 47 Dwyane Wade	1.00	2.50
❑ 48 Michael Beasley	.60	1.50
❑ 49 Jermaine O'Neal	.50	1.25
❑ 50 Udonis Haslem	.40	1.00
❑ 51 Michael Redd	.50	1.25
❑ 52 Ramon Sessions	.30	.75
❑ 53 Andrew Bogut	.50	1.25
❑ 54 Al Jefferson	.50	1.25
❑ 55 Ryan Gomes	.30	.75
❑ 56 Kevin Love	.40	1.00
❑ 57 Devin Harris	.50	1.25
❑ 58 Brook Lopez	.30	.75
❑ 59 Rafer Alston	.40	1.00
❑ 60 Chris Paul	1.00	2.50
❑ 61 David West	.50	1.25
❑ 62 Peja Stojakovic	.30	.75
❑ 63 Al Harrington	.40	1.00
❑ 64 Nate Robinson	.50	1.25
❑ 65 Wilson Chandler	.30	.75
❑ 66 Kevin Durant	1.25	3.00
❑ 67 Jeff Green	.40	1.00
❑ 68 Russell Westbrook	.50	1.25
❑ 69 Dwight Howard	1.00	2.50
❑ 70 Rashard Lewis	.50	1.25
❑ 71 Jameer Nelson	.40	1.00
❑ 72 Vince Carter	.60	1.50
❑ 73 Andre Iguodala	.50	1.25
❑ 74 Elton Brand	.50	1.25
❑ 75 Thaddeus Young	.30	.75
❑ 76 Amare Stoudemire	.60	1.50
❑ 77 Steve Nash	.50	1.25
❑ 78 Leandro Barbosa	.40	1.00
❑ 79 Channing Frye	.40	1.00
❑ 80 Brandon Roy	.60	1.50
❑ 81 LaMarcus Aldridge	.50	1.25
❑ 82 Greg Oden	.40	1.00
❑ 83 Kevin Martin	.50	1.25
❑ 84 Andres Nocioni	.40	1.00
❑ 85 Spencer Hawes	.40	1.00
❑ 86 Tony Parker	.50	1.25
❑ 87 Tim Duncan	.75	2.00
❑ 88 Manu Ginobili	.50	1.25
❑ 89 Richard Jefferson	.50	1.25
❑ 90 Chris Bosh	.50	1.25
❑ 91 Hedo Turkoglu	.50	1.25
❑ 92 Andrea Bargnani	.40	1.00
❑ 93 Deron Williams	.60	1.50
❑ 94 Carlos Boozer	.50	1.25
❑ 95 Andrei Kirilenko	.40	1.00
❑ 96 Ronnie Brewer	.30	.75
❑ 97 Antawn Jamison	.50	1.25
❑ 98 Gilbert Arenas	.50	1.25
❑ 99 Caron Butler	.50	1.25
❑ 100 Randy Foye	.30	.75
❑ 101 Kareem Abdul-Jabbar	.75	2.00
❑ 102 Elvin Hayes	.50	1.25
❑ 103 Karl Malone	.60	1.50
❑ 104 Arnie Risen	.50	1.25
❑ 105 Jalen Rose	.50	1.25
❑ 106 Dave DeBusschere	.50	1.25
❑ 107 Artis Gilmore	.50	1.25
❑ 108 Nate Archibald	.50	1.25
❑ 109 Mark Eaton	.50	1.25
❑ 110 Darryl Dawkins	.50	1.25
❑ 111 Spencer Haywood	.50	1.25
❑ 112 Bill Cartwright	.50	1.25
❑ 113 Moses Malone	.50	1.25
❑ 114 Magic Johnson	1.00	2.50
❑ 115 Sleepy Floyd	.50	1.25
❑ 116 Dante Cunningham RC	.50	1.25
❑ 117 Jon Brockman RC	.50	1.25
❑ 118 Jonas Jerebko RC	.50	1.25
❑ 119 Derrick Brown RC	.50	1.25
❑ 120 Dionte Christmas RC	.50	1.25
❑ 121 Marcus Thornton RC	.50	1.25
❑ 122 Daniel Green RC	1.00	2.50
❑ 123 Goran Suton RC	.75	2.00
❑ 124 Jack McClinton RC	.75	2.00
❑ 125 A.J. Price RC	.75	2.00
❑ 126 Serge Ibaka RC	1.00	2.50
❑ 127 DeMar DeRozan RC	1.25	3.00
❑ 128 Chris Hunter RC	.75	2.00
❑ 129 Lester Hudson RC	.75	2.00
❑ 130 David Andersen RC	.75	2.00
❑ 131 Blake Griffin AU/449 RC	30.00	60.00
❑ 132 Hasheem Thabeet AU/449 RC	8.00	20.00
❑ 133 James Harden AU/449 RC	10.00	25.00
❑ 134 Tyreke Evans AU/379 RC	50.00	100.00
❑ 135 Jonny Flynn AU/449 RC	10.00	25.00
❑ 136 Stephen Curry AU/449 RC	20.00	40.00
❑ 137 Jordan Hill AU/449 RC	8.00	20.00
❑ 138 Dante Cunningham AU/437 RC	6.00	15.00
❑ 139 Brandon Jennings AU/379 RC	30.00	60.00
❑ 140 Terrence Williams AU/356 RC	10.00	25.00
❑ 141 Gerald Henderson AU/449 RC	6.00	15.00
❑ 142 Tyler Hansbrough AU/449 RC	15.00	30.00
❑ 143 Earl Clark AU/449 RC	8.00	20.00
❑ 144 Austin Daye AU/369 RC	6.00	15.00
❑ 145 James Johnson AU/449 RC	8.00	20.00
❑ 146 Jrue Holiday AU/449 RC	8.00	20.00
❑ 147 Ty Lawson AU/369 EXCH	15.00	30.00
❑ 148 Jeff Teague AU/449 RC	6.00	15.00
❑ 149 Eric Maynor AU/369 EXCH	6.00	15.00
❑ 150 Darren Collison AU/347 RC	8.00	20.00
❑ 151 Omri Casspi AU/449 RC	10.00	25.00
❑ 152 B.J. Mullens AU/379 RC	6.00	15.00
❑ 153 Rodrigue Beaubois AU/390 RC	10.00	25.00

❑ 154 Taj Gibson AU/369 EXCH	8.00	20.00
❑ 155 DeMarre Carroll AU/449 RC	6.00	15.00
❑ 156 Wayne Ellington AU/416 RC	8.00	20.00
❑ 157 Toney Douglas AU/379 EXCH	6.00	15.00
❑ 158 Jermaine Taylor AU/449 RC	6.00	15.00
❑ 159 Jeff Pendergraph AU/449 RC	6.00	15.00
❑ 160 DaJuan Summers AU/378 RC	6.00	15.00
❑ 161 Sam Young AU/369 EXCH	10.00	25.00
❑ 162 DeJuan Blair AU/449 RC	10.00	25.00
❑ 163 Chase Budinger AU/369 EXCH	8.00	20.00
❑ 164 Jodie Meeks AU/449 RC	8.00	20.00
❑ 165 Taylor Griffin AU/380 RC	6.00	15.00

1990-91 SkyBox

❑ COMPLETE SET (423)	10.00	20.00
❑ COMPLETE SERIES 1 (300)	6.00	12.00
❑ COMPLETE SERIES 2 (123)	4.00	8.00
❑ COMMON CARD (1-300)	.04	.10
❑ COMMON CARD (301-423)	.02	.10
❑ COMMON SP	.02	.10
❑ 1 John Battle	.02	.10
❑ 2 Duane Ferrell SP RC	.02	.10
❑ 3 Jon Koncak	.02	.10
❑ 4 Cliff Levingston SP	.02	.10
❑ 5 John Long SP	.02	.10
❑ 6 Moses Malone	.08	.25
❑ 7 Doc Rivers	.02	.10
❑ 8 Kenny Smith SP	.02	.10
❑ 9 Alexander Volkov	.02	.10
❑ 10 Spud Webb	.02	.10
❑ 11 Dominique Wilkins	.08	.25
❑ 12 Kevin Willis	.02	.10
❑ 13 John Bagley	.02	.10
❑ 14 Larry Bird	.40	1.00
❑ 15 Kevin Gamble	.02	.10
❑ 16 Dennis Johnson SP	.02	.10
❑ 17 Joe Kleine	.02	.10
❑ 18 Reggie Lewis	.02	.10
❑ 19 Kevin McHale	.02	.10
❑ 20 Robert Parish	.02	.10
❑ 21 Jim Paxson SP	.02	.10
❑ 22 Ed Pinckney	.02	.10
❑ 23 Brian Shaw	.08	.25
❑ 24 Michael Smith	.02	.10
❑ 25 Richard Anderson SP	.02	.10
❑ 26 Muggsy Bogues	.02	.10
❑ 27 Rex Chapman	.08	.25
❑ 28 Dell Curry	.02	.10
❑ 29 Armon Gilliam	.02	.10
❑ 30 Michael Holton SP	.02	.10
❑ 31 Dave Hoppen	.02	.10
❑ 32 J.R.Reid RC	.02	.10
❑ 33 Robert Reid SP	.02	.10
❑ 34 Brian Rowsom SP	.02	.10
❑ 35 Kelly Tripucka	.02	.10
❑ 36 Micheal Williams SP UER	.02	.10
❑ 37 B.J.Armstrong RC	.02	.10
❑ 38 Bill Cartwright	.02	.10
❑ 39 Horace Grant	.02	.10
❑ 40 Craig Hodges	.02	.10
❑ 41 Michael Jordan	1.25	3.00
❑ 42 Stacey King RC	.02	.10
❑ 43 Ed Nealy SP	.02	.10
❑ 44 John Paxson	.02	.10
❑ 45 Will Perdue	.02	.10
❑ 46 Scottie Pippen	.40	1.00
❑ 47 Jeff Sanders SP RC	.02	.10
❑ 48 Winston Bennett	.02	.10
❑ 49 Chucky Brown RC	.02	.10
❑ 50 Brad Daugherty	.02	.10
❑ 51 Craig Ehlo	.02	.10
❑ 52 Steve Kerr	.08	.25
❑ 53 Paul Mokeski SP	.02	.10
❑ 54 John Morton	.02	.10
❑ 55 Larry Nance	.02	.10
❑ 56 Mark Price	.02	.10
❑ 57 Tree Rollins SP	.02	.10
❑ 58 Hot Rod Williams	.02	.10
❑ 59 Steve Alford	.02	.10
❑ 60 Rolando Blackman	.02	.10
❑ 61 Adrian Dantley SP	.02	.10
❑ 62 Brad Davis	.02	.10
❑ 63 James Donaldson	.02	.10
❑ 64 Derek Harper	.02	.10
❑ 65 Anthony Jones SP	.02	.10
❑ 66 Sam Perkins SP	.02	.10
❑ 67 Roy Tarpley	.02	.10
❑ 68 Bill Wennington SP	.02	.10
❑ 69 Randy White RC	.02	.10
❑ 70 Herb Williams	.02	.10
❑ 71 Michael Adams	.02	.10
❑ 72 Joe Barry Carroll SP	.02	.10
❑ 73 Walter Davis	.02	.10
❑ 74 Alex English SP	.02	.10
❑ 75 Bill Hanzlik	.02	.10
❑ 76 Tim Kempton SP	.02	.10
❑ 77 Jerome Lane	.02	.10
❑ 78 Lafayette Lever SP	.02	.10
❑ 79 Todd Lichti RC	.02	.10
❑ 80 Blair Rasmussen	.02	.10
❑ 81 Danny Schayes SP	.02	.10
❑ 82 Mark Aguirre	.02	.10
❑ 83 William Bedford RC	.02	.10
❑ 84 Joe Dumars	.08	.25
❑ 85 James Edwards	.02	.10
❑ 86 David Greenwood SP	.02	.10
❑ 87 Scott Hastings	.02	.10
❑ 88 Gerald Henderson SP	.02	.10
❑ 89 Vinnie Johnson	.02	.10
❑ 90 Bill Laimbeer	.02	.10
❑ 91 Dennis Rodman	.25	.60
❑ 91B Dennis Rodman Left	.40	1.00
❑ 92 John Salley	.02	.10
❑ 93 Isiah Thomas	.08	.25
❑ 94 Manute Bol SP	.02	.10
❑ 95 Tim Hardaway RC	.60	1.50
❑ 96 Rod Higgins	.02	.10
❑ 97 Sarun.Marciulionis RC	.02	.10
❑ 98 Chris Mullin	.08	.25
❑ 99 Jim Petersen	.02	.10
❑ 100 Mitch Richmond	.10	.30
❑ 101 Mike Smrek	.02	.10
❑ 102 Terry Teagle SP	.02	.10
❑ 103 Tom Tolbert RC	.02	.10
❑ 104 Kelvin Upshaw SP	.02	.10
❑ 105 Anthony Bowie SP RC	.02	.10
❑ 106 Adrian Caldwell	.02	.10
❑ 107 Eric(Sleepy) Floyd	.02	.10
❑ 108 Buck Johnson	.02	.10
❑ 109 Vernon Maxwell	.02	.10
❑ 110 Hakeem Olajuwon	.15	.40
❑ 111 Larry Smith	.02	.10
❑ 112A Otis Thorpe ERR	.60	1.50
❑ 112B Otis Thorpe COR	.02	.10
❑ 113A M. Wiggins SP ERR	.60	1.50
❑ 113B M. Wiggins SP COR	.02	.10
❑ 114 Vern Fleming	.02	.10
❑ 115 Rickey Green SP	.02	.10
❑ 116 George McCloud RC	.08	.25
❑ 117 Reggie Miller	.10	.30
❑ 118A Dyron Nix SP ERR	.60	1.50
❑ 118B Dyron Nix SP COR	.02	.10
❑ 119 Chuck Person	.02	.10
❑ 120 Mike Sanders	.02	.10
❑ 121 Detlef Schrempf	.02	.10
❑ 122 Rik Smits	.08	.25
❑ 123 LaSalle Thompson	.02	.10
❑ 124 Benoit Benjamin	.02	.10
❑ 125 Winston Garland	.02	.10
❑ 126 Tom Garrick	.02	.10
❑ 127 Gary Grant	.02	.10
❑ 128 Ron Harper	.02	.10
❑ 129 Danny Manning	.02	.10
❑ 130 Jeff Martin	.02	.10
❑ 131 Ken Norman	.02	.10
❑ 132 Charles Smith	.02	.10
❑ 133 Joe Wolf SP	.02	.10
❑ 134 Michael Cooper SP	.02	.10
❑ 135 Vlade Divac RC	.25	.60
❑ 136 Larry Drew	.02	.10
❑ 137 A.C. Green	.02	.10
❑ 138 Magic Johnson	.30	.75
❑ 139 Mark McNamara SP	.02	.10
❑ 140 Byron Scott	.02	.10
❑ 141 Mychal Thompson	.02	.10
❑ 142 Orlando Woolridge SP	.02	.10
❑ 143 James Worthy	.08	.25
❑ 144 Terry Davis RC	.02	.10
❑ 145 Sherman Douglas RC	.02	.10
❑ 146 Kevin Edwards	.02	.10
❑ 147 Tellis Frank SP	.02	.10
❑ 148 Scott Haffner SP	.02	.10
❑ 149 Grant Long	.02	.10
❑ 150 Glen Rice RC	.40	1.00
❑ 151 Rony Seikaly	.02	.10
❑ 152 Rory Sparrow SP	.02	.10
❑ 153 Jon Sundvold	.02	.10
❑ 154 Billy Thompson	.02	.10
❑ 155 Greg Anderson	.02	.10
❑ 156 Ben Coleman SP	.02	.10
❑ 157 Jeff Grayer RC	.02	.10
❑ 158 Jay Humphries	.02	.10
❑ 159 Frank Kornet	.02	.10
❑ 160 Larry Krystkowiak	.02	.10
❑ 161 Brad Lohaus	.02	.10
❑ 162 Ricky Pierce	.02	.10
❑ 163 Paul Pressey SP	.02	.10
❑ 164 Fred Roberts	.02	.10
❑ 165 Alvin Robertson	.02	.10
❑ 166 Jack Sikma	.02	.10
❑ 167 Randy Breuer	.02	.10
❑ 168 Tony Campbell	.02	.10
❑ 169 Tyrone Corbin	.02	.10
❑ 170 Sidney Lowe SP	.02	.10
❑ 171 Sam Mitchell RC	.02	.10
❑ 172 Tod Murphy	.02	.10
❑ 173 Pooh Richardson RC	.02	.10
❑ 174 Donald Royal SP RC	.02	.10
❑ 175 Brad Sellers SP	.02	.10
❑ 176 Mookie Blaylock RC	.15	.40
❑ 177 Sam Bowie	.02	.10
❑ 178 Lester Conner	.02	.10
❑ 179 Derrick Gervin	.02	.10
❑ 180 Jack Haley RC	.02	.10
❑ 181 Roy Hinson	.02	.10
❑ 182 Dennis Hopson SP	.02	.10
❑ 183 Chris Morris	.02	.10
❑ 184 Pete Myers RC SP	.02	.10
❑ 185 Purvis Short SP	.02	.10
❑ 186 Maurice Cheeks	.02	.10
❑ 187 Patrick Ewing	.08	.25
❑ 188 Stuart Gray	.02	.10
❑ 189 Mark Jackson	.02	.10
❑ 190 Johnny Newman SP	.02	.10
❑ 191 Charles Oakley	.02	.10
❑ 192 Brian Quinnett	.02	.10
❑ 193 Trent Tucker	.02	.10
❑ 194 Kiki Vandeweghe	.02	.10
❑ 195 Kenny Walker	.02	.10
❑ 196 Eddie Lee Wilkins	.02	.10
❑ 197 Gerald Wilkins	.02	.10
❑ 198 Mark Acres	.02	.10
❑ 199 Nick Anderson RC	.15	.40
❑ 200 Michael Ansley	.02	.10
❑ 201 Terry Catledge	.02	.10
❑ 202 Dave Corzine SP	.02	.10
❑ 203 Sidney Green SP	.02	.10
❑ 204 Jerry Reynolds	.02	.10
❑ 205 Scott Skiles	.02	.10
❑ 206 Otis Smith	.02	.10
❑ 207 Reggie Theus SP	.02	.10
❑ 208 Jeff Turner	.02	.10
❑ 209 Sam Vincent	.02	.10
❑ 210 Ron Anderson	.02	.10
❑ 211 Charles Barkley	.15	.40
❑ 212 Scott Brooks SP	.02	.10
❑ 213 Lanard Copeland SP	.02	.10
❑ 214 Johnny Dawkins	.02	.10
❑ 215 Mike Gminski	.02	.10
❑ 216 Hersey Hawkins	.02	.10
❑ 217 Rick Mahorn	.02	.10
❑ 218 Derek Smith SP	.02	.10
❑ 219 Bob Thornton	.02	.10
❑ 220 Tom Chambers	.02	.10
❑ 221 Greg Grant RC SP	.02	.10
❑ 222 Jeff Hornacek	.02	.10
❑ 223 Eddie Johnson	.02	.10
❑ 224A Kevin Johnson Lower	.08	.25
❑ 224B Kevin Johnson Upper	.08	.25
❑ 225 Andrew Lang RC	.08	.25
❑ 226 Dan Majerle	.08	.25

❑ 227 Mike McGee SP	.02	.10
❑ 228 Tim Perry	.02	.10
❑ 229 Kurt Rambis	.02	.10
❑ 230 Mark West	.02	.10
❑ 231 Mark Bryant	.02	.10
❑ 232 Wayne Cooper	.02	.10
❑ 233 Clyde Drexler	.08	.25
❑ 234 Kevin Duckworth	.02	.10
❑ 235 Byron Irvin SP	.02	.10
❑ 236 Jerome Kersey	.02	.10
❑ 237 Drazen Petrovic RC	.10	.30
❑ 238 Terry Porter	.02	.10
❑ 239 Clifford Robinson RC	.15	.40
❑ 240 Buck Williams	.02	.10
❑ 241 Danny Young	.02	.10
❑ 242 Danny Ainge SP	.02	.10
❑ 243 Randy Allen SP	.02	.10
❑ 244A Antoine Carr SP	.05	.15
❑ 244B Antoine Carr	.02	.10
❑ 245 Vinny Del Negro SP	.02	.10
❑ 246 Pervis Ellison RC SP	.02	.10
❑ 247 Greg Kite SP	.02	.10
❑ 248 Rodney McCray SP	.02	.10
❑ 249 Harold Pressley SP	.02	.10
❑ 250 Ralph Sampson	.02	.10
❑ 251 Wayman Tisdale	.02	.10
❑ 252 Willie Anderson	.02	.10
❑ 253 Uwe Blab SP	.02	.10
❑ 254 Frank Brickowski SP	.02	.10
❑ 255 Terry Cummings	.02	.10
❑ 256 Sean Elliott RC	.20	.50
❑ 257 Caldwell Jones SP	.02	.10
❑ 258 Johnny Moore SP	.02	.10
❑ 259 Zarko Paspalj SP	.02	.10
❑ 260 David Robinson	.30	.75
❑ 261 Rod Strickland	.08	.25
❑ 262 David Wingate SP	.02	.10
❑ 263 Dana Barros RC	.08	.25
❑ 264 Michael Cage	.02	.10
❑ 265 Quintin Dailey	.02	.10
❑ 266 Dale Ellis	.02	.10
❑ 267 Steve Johnson SP	.02	.10
❑ 268 Shawn Kemp RC	1.00	2.50
❑ 269 Xavier McDaniel	.02	.10
❑ 270 Derrick McKey	.02	.10
❑ 271A Nate McMillan SP ERR	.07	.20
❑ 271B Nate McMillan COR	.02	.10
❑ 272 Olden Polynice	.02	.10
❑ 273 Sedale Threatt	.02	.10
❑ 274 Thurl Bailey	.02	.10
❑ 275 Mike Brown	.02	.10
❑ 276 Mark Eaton	.02	.10
❑ 277 Blue Edwards RC	.02	.10
❑ 278 Darrell Griffith	.02	.10
❑ 279 Bobby Hansen SP	.02	.10
❑ 280 Eric Johnson	.02	.10
❑ 281 Eric Leckner SP	.02	.10
❑ 282 Karl Malone	.15	.40
❑ 283 Delaney Rudd	.02	.10
❑ 284 John Stockton	.10	.30
❑ 285 Mark Alarie	.02	.10
❑ 286 Steve Colter SP	.02	.10
❑ 287 Ledell Eackles SP	.02	.10
❑ 288 Harvey Grant	.02	.10
❑ 289 Tom Hammonds RC	.02	.10
❑ 290 Charles Jones	.02	.10
❑ 291 Bernard King	.02	.10
❑ 292 Jeff Malone SP	.02	.10
❑ 293 Darrell Walker	.02	.10
❑ 294 John Williams	.02	.10
❑ 295 Checklist 1 SP	.02	.10
❑ 296 Checklist 2 SP	.02	.10
❑ 297 Checklist 3 SP	.02	.10
❑ 298 Checklist 4 SP	.02	.10
❑ 299 Checklist 5 SP	.02	.10
❑ 300 Danny Ferry SP RC	.20	.50
❑ 301 Bob Weiss CO	.02	.10
❑ 302 Chris Ford CO	.02	.10
❑ 303 Gene Littles CO	.02	.10
❑ 304 Phil Jackson CO	.10	.30
❑ 305 Lenny Wilkens CO	.10	.30
❑ 306 Richie Adubato CO	.02	.10
❑ 307 Paul Westhead CO	.02	.10
❑ 308 Chuck Daly CO	.10	.30
❑ 309 Don Nelson CO	.10	.30
❑ 310 Don Chaney CO	.02	.10
❑ 311 Dick Versace CO	.02	.10
❑ 312 Mike Schuler CO	.02	.10
❑ 313 Mike Dunleavy CO	.02	.10

❑ 314 Ron Rothstein CO	.02	.10
❑ 315 Del Harris CO	.02	.10
❑ 316 Bill Musselman CO	.02	.10
❑ 317 Bill Fitch CO	.02	.10
❑ 318 Stu Jackson CO	.02	.10
❑ 319 Matt Guokas CO	.02	.10
❑ 320 Jim Lynam CO	.02	.10
❑ 321 Cotton Fitzsimmons CO	.02	.10
❑ 322 Rick Adelman CO	.02	.10
❑ 323 Dick Motta CO	.02	.10
❑ 324 Larry Brown CO	.02	.10
❑ 325 K.C. Jones CO	.10	.30
❑ 326 Jerry Sloan CO	.10	.30
❑ 327 Wes Unseld CO	.02	.10
❑ 328 Atlanta Hawks TC	.02	.10
❑ 329 Boston Celtics TC	.02	.10
❑ 330 Charlotte Hornets TC	.02	.10
❑ 331 Chicago Bulls TC	.10	.30
❑ 332 Cleveland Cavaliers TC	.02	.10
❑ 333 Dallas Mavericks TC	.02	.10
❑ 334 Denver Nuggets TC	.02	.10
❑ 335 Detroit Pistons TC	.02	.10
❑ 336 Golden State Warriors TC	.02	.10
❑ 337 Houston Rockets TC	.02	.10
❑ 338 Indiana Pacers TC	.02	.10
❑ 339 Los Angeles Clippers TC	.02	.10
❑ 340 Los Angeles Lakers TC	.02	.10
❑ 341 Miami Heat TC	.02	.10
❑ 342 Milwaukee Bucks TC	.02	.10
❑ 343 Minnesota Timberwolves TC	.02	.10
❑ 344 New Jersey Nets TC	.02	.10
❑ 345 New York Knicks TC	.02	.10
❑ 346 Orlando Magic TC	.02	.10
❑ 347 Philadelphia 76ers TC	.02	.10
❑ 348 Phoenix Suns TC	.02	.10
❑ 349 Portland Trail Blazers TC	.02	.10
❑ 350 Sacramento Kings TC	.02	.10
❑ 351 San Antonio Spurs TC	.02	.10
❑ 352 Seattle SuperSonics TC	.02	.10
❑ 353 Utah Jazz TC	.02	.10
❑ 354 Washington Bullets TC	.02	.10
❑ 355 Rumeal Robinson RC	.02	.10
❑ 356 Kendall Gill RC	.50	1.25
❑ 357 Chris Jackson RC	.25	.60
❑ 358 Tyrone Hill RC	.20	.50
❑ 359 Bo Kimble RC	.02	.10
❑ 360 Willie Burton RC	.02	.10
❑ 361 Felton Spencer RC	.10	.30
❑ 362 Derrick Coleman RC	.50	1.25
❑ 363 Dennis Scott RC	.30	.75
❑ 364 Lionel Simmons RC	.10	.30
❑ 365 Gary Payton RC	2.00	5.00
❑ 366 Tim McCormick	.02	.10
❑ 367 Sidney Moncrief	.02	.10
❑ 368 Kenny Gattison RC	.02	.10
❑ 369 Randolph Keys	.02	.10
❑ 370 Johnny Newman	.02	.10
❑ 371 Dennis Hopson	.02	.10
❑ 372 Cliff Levingston	.02	.10
❑ 373 Derrick Chievous	.02	.10
❑ 374 Danny Ferry	.10	.30
❑ 375 Alex English	.02	.10
❑ 376 Lafayette Lever	.02	.10
❑ 377 Rodney McCray	.02	.10
❑ 378 T.R. Dunn	.02	.10
❑ 379 Corey Gaines	.02	.10
❑ 380 Avery Johnson RC	.30	.75
❑ 381 Joe Wolf	.02	.10
❑ 382 Orlando Woolridge	.02	.10
❑ 383 Tree Rollins	.02	.10
❑ 384 Steve Johnson	.02	.10
❑ 385 Kenny Smith	.02	.10
❑ 386 Mike Woodson	.02	.10
❑ 387 Greg Dreiling RC	.02	.10
❑ 388 Micheal Williams	.10	.30
❑ 389 Randy Wittman	.02	.10
❑ 390 Ken Bannister	.02	.10
❑ 391 Sam Perkins	.10	.30
❑ 392 Terry Teagle	.02	.10
❑ 393 Milt Wagner	.02	.10
❑ 394 Frank Brickowski	.02	.10
❑ 395 Danny Schayes	.02	.10
❑ 396 Scott Brooks	.02	.10
❑ 397 Doug West RC	.10	.30
❑ 398 Chris Dudley RC	.02	.10
❑ 399 Reggie Theus	.10	.30
❑ 400 Greg Grant	.02	.10
❑ 401 Greg Kite	.02	.10
❑ 402 Mark McNamara	.02	.10

❑ 403 Manute Bol	.02	.10
❑ 404 Rickey Green	.02	.10
❑ 405 Kenny Battle RC	.02	.10
❑ 406 Ed Nealy	.02	.10
❑ 407 Danny Ainge	.10	.30
❑ 408 Steve Colter	.02	.10
❑ 409 Bobby Hansen	.02	.10
❑ 410 Eric Leckner	.02	.10
❑ 411 Rory Sparrow	.02	.10
❑ 412 Bill Wennington	.02	.10
❑ 413 Sidney Green	.02	.10
❑ 414 David Greenwood	.02	.10
❑ 415 Paul Pressey	.02	.10
❑ 416 Reggie Williams	.02	.10
❑ 417 Dave Corzine	.02	.10
❑ 418 Jeff Malone	.02	.10
❑ 419 Pervis Ellison	.02	.10
❑ 420 Byron Irvin	.02	.10
❑ 421 Checklist 1	.02	.10
❑ 422 Checklist 2	.02	.10
❑ 423 Checklist 3	.02	.10
❑ NNO SkyBox Salutes the NBA	2.00	5.00

1991-92 SkyBox

❑ COMPLETE SET (659)	30.00	60.00
❑ COMPLETE SERIES 1 (350)	10.00	20.00
❑ COMPLETE SERIES 2 (309)	20.00	40.00
❑ 1 John Battle	.02	.10
❑ 2 Duane Ferrell	.02	.10
❑ 3 Jon Koncak	.02	.10
❑ 4 Moses Malone	.15	.40
❑ 5 Tim McCormick	.02	.10
❑ 6 Sidney Moncrief	.02	.10
❑ 7 Doc Rivers	.07	.20
❑ 8 Rumeal Robinson UER	.02	.10
❑ 9 Spud Webb	.07	.20
❑ 10 Dominique Wilkins	.15	.40
❑ 11 Kevin Willis	.02	.10
❑ 12 Larry Bird	.60	1.50
❑ 13 Dee Brown FSBC	.02	.10
❑ 14 Kevin Gamble	.02	.10
❑ 15 Joe Kleine	.02	.10
❑ 16 Reggie Lewis	.07	.20
❑ 17 Kevin McHale	.07	.20
❑ 18 Robert Parish	.07	.20
❑ 19 Ed Pinckney	.02	.10
❑ 20 Brian Shaw	.02	.10
❑ 21 Michael Smith	.02	.10
❑ 22 Stojko Vrankovic	.02	.10
❑ 23 Muggsy Bogues	.07	.20
❑ 24 Rex Chapman	.07	.20
❑ 25 Dell Curry	.02	.10
❑ 26 Kenny Gattison	.02	.10
❑ 27 Kendall Gill	.07	.20
❑ 28 Mike Gminski	.02	.10
❑ 29 Randolph Keys	.02	.10
❑ 30 Eric Leckner	.02	.10
❑ 31 Johnny Newman	.02	.10
❑ 32 J.R. Reid	.02	.10
❑ 33 Kelly Tripucka	.02	.10
❑ 34 B.J.Armstrong	.02	.10
❑ 35 Bill Cartwright	.02	.10
❑ 36 Horace Grant	.07	.20
❑ 37 Craig Hodges	.02	.10
❑ 38 Dennis Hopson	.02	.10
❑ 39 Michael Jordan	2.00	5.00
❑ 40 Stacey King	.02	.10
❑ 41 Cliff Levingston	.02	.10
❑ 42 John Paxson	.02	.10
❑ 43 Will Perdue	.02	.10
❑ 44 Scottie Pippen	.50	1.25
❑ 45 Winston Bennett	.02	.10
❑ 46 Chucky Brown	.02	.10
❑ 47 Brad Daugherty	.02	.10
❑ 48 Craig Ehlo	.02	.10
❑ 49 Danny Ferry	.02	.10

❑ 50 Steve Kerr	.07	.20
❑ 51 John Morton	.02	.10
❑ 52 Larry Nance	.07	.20
❑ 53 Mark Price	.02	.10
❑ 54 Darnell Valentine	.02	.10
❑ 55 John Williams	.02	.10
❑ 56 Steve Alford	.02	.10
❑ 57 Rolando Blackman	.02	.10
❑ 58 Brad Davis	.02	.10
❑ 59 James Donaldson	.02	.10
❑ 60 Derek Harper	.07	.20
❑ 61 Fat Lever	.02	.10
❑ 62 Rodney McCray	.02	.10
❑ 63 Roy Tarpley	.02	.10
❑ 64 Kelvin Upshaw	.02	.10
❑ 65 Randy White	.02	.10
❑ 66 Herb Williams	.02	.10
❑ 67 Michael Adams	.02	.10
❑ 68 Greg Anderson	.02	.10
❑ 69 Anthony Cook	.02	.10
❑ 70 Chris Jackson	.02	.10
❑ 71 Jerome Lane	.02	.10
❑ 72 Marcus Liberty	.02	.10
❑ 73 Todd Lichti	.02	.10
❑ 74 Blair Rasmussen	.02	.10
❑ 75 Reggie Williams	.02	.10
❑ 76 Joe Wolf	.02	.10
❑ 77 Orlando Woolridge	.02	.10
❑ 78 Mark Aguirre	.02	.10
❑ 79 William Bedford	.02	.10
❑ 80 Lance Blanks	.02	.10
❑ 81 Joe Dumars	.15	.40
❑ 82 James Edwards	.02	.10
❑ 83 Scott Hastings	.02	.10
❑ 84 Vinnie Johnson	.02	.10
❑ 85 Bill Laimbeer	.07	.20
❑ 86 Dennis Rodman	.30	.75
❑ 87 John Salley	.02	.10
❑ 88 Isiah Thomas	.15	.40
❑ 89 Mario Elie RC	.15	.40
❑ 90 Tim Hardaway	.25	.60
❑ 91 Rod Higgins	.02	.10
❑ 92 Tyrone Hill	.07	.20
❑ 93 Les Jepsen	.02	.10
❑ 94 Alton Lister	.02	.10
❑ 95 Sarunas Marciulionis	.02	.10
❑ 96 Chris Mullin	.15	.40
❑ 97 Jim Petersen	.02	.10
❑ 98 Mitch Richmond	.15	.40
❑ 99 Tom Tolbert	.02	.10
❑ 100 Adrian Caldwell	.02	.10
❑ 101 Eric(Sleepy) Floyd	.02	.10
❑ 102 Dave Jamerson	.02	.10
❑ 103 Buck Johnson	.02	.10
❑ 104 Vernon Maxwell	.02	.10
❑ 105 Hakeem Olajuwon	.25	.60
❑ 106 Kenny Smith	.02	.10
❑ 107 Larry Smith	.02	.10
❑ 108 Otis Thorpe	.07	.20
❑ 109 Kennard Winchester RC	.02	.10
❑ 110 David Wood RC	.02	.10
❑ 111 Greg Dreiling	.02	.10
❑ 112 Vern Fleming	.02	.10
❑ 113 George McCloud	.02	.10
❑ 114 Reggie Miller	.15	.40
❑ 115 Chuck Person	.02	.10
❑ 116 Mike Sanders	.02	.10
❑ 117 Detlef Schrempf	.07	.20
❑ 118 Rik Smits	.07	.20
❑ 119 LaSalle Thompson	.02	.10
❑ 120 Kenny Williams	.02	.10
❑ 121 Micheal Williams	.02	.10
❑ 122 Ken Bannister	.02	.10
❑ 123 Winston Garland	.02	.10
❑ 124 Gary Grant	.02	.10
❑ 125 Ron Harper	.07	.20
❑ 126 Bo Kimble	.02	.10
❑ 127 Danny Manning	.07	.20
❑ 128 Jeff Martin	.02	.10
❑ 129 Ken Norman	.02	.10
❑ 130 Olden Polynice	.02	.10
❑ 131 Charles Smith	.02	.10
❑ 132 Loy Vaught	.02	.10
❑ 133 Elden Campbell	.07	.20
❑ 134 Vlade Divac	.07	.20
❑ 135 Larry Drew	.02	.10
❑ 136 A.C. Green	.07	.20
❑ 137 Magic Johnson	.50	1.25
❑ 138 Sam Perkins	.07	.20
❑ 139 Byron Scott	.07	.20
❑ 140 Tony Smith	.02	.10
❑ 141 Terry Teagle	.02	.10
❑ 142 Mychal Thompson	.02	.10
❑ 143 James Worthy	.15	.40
❑ 144 Willie Burton	.02	.10
❑ 145 Bimbo Coles FSBC	.02	.10
❑ 146 Terry Davis	.02	.10
❑ 147 Sherman Douglas	.02	.10
❑ 148 Kevin Edwards	.02	.10
❑ 149 Alec Kessler	.02	.10
❑ 150 Grant Long	.02	.10
❑ 151 Glen Rice	.15	.40
❑ 152 Rony Seikaly	.02	.10
❑ 153 Jon Sundvold	.02	.10
❑ 154 Billy Thompson	.02	.10
❑ 155 Frank Brickowski	.02	.10
❑ 156 Lester Conner	.02	.10
❑ 157 Jeff Grayer	.02	.10
❑ 158 Jay Humphries	.02	.10
❑ 159 Larry Krystkowiak	.02	.10
❑ 160 Brad Lohaus	.02	.10
❑ 161 Dale Ellis	.07	.20
❑ 162 Fred Roberts	.02	.10
❑ 163 Alvin Robertson	.02	.10
❑ 164 Danny Schayes	.02	.10
❑ 165 Jack Sikma	.02	.10
❑ 166 Randy Breuer	.02	.10
❑ 167 Scott Brooks	.02	.10
❑ 168 Tony Campbell	.02	.10
❑ 169 Tyrone Corbin	.02	.10
❑ 170 Gerald Glass	.02	.10
❑ 171 Sam Mitchell	.02	.10
❑ 172 Tod Murphy	.02	.10
❑ 173 Pooh Richardson	.02	.10
❑ 174 Felton Spencer	.02	.10
❑ 175 Bob Thornton	.02	.10
❑ 176 Doug West	.02	.10
❑ 177 Mookie Blaylock	.07	.20
❑ 178 Sam Bowie	.02	.10
❑ 179 Jud Buechler	.02	.10
❑ 180 Derrick Coleman	.07	.20
❑ 181 Chris Dudley	.02	.10
❑ 182 Tate George	.02	.10
❑ 183 Jack Haley	.02	.10
❑ 184 Terry Mills RC	.15	.40
❑ 185 Chris Morris	.02	.10
❑ 186 Drazen Petrovic	.07	.20
❑ 187 Reggie Theus	.07	.20
❑ 188 Maurice Cheeks	.02	.10
❑ 189 Patrick Ewing	.15	.40
❑ 190 Mark Jackson	.07	.20
❑ 191 Jerrod Mustaf FSBC	.02	.10
❑ 192 Charles Oakley	.07	.20
❑ 193 Brian Quinnett	.02	.10
❑ 194 John Starks RC	.15	.40
❑ 195 Trent Tucker	.02	.10
❑ 196 Kiki Vandeweghe	.02	.10
❑ 197 Kenny Walker	.02	.10
❑ 198 Gerald Wilkins	.02	.10
❑ 199 Mark Acres	.02	.10
❑ 200 Nick Anderson	.07	.20
❑ 201 Michael Ansley	.02	.10
❑ 202 Terry Catledge	.02	.10
❑ 203 Greg Kite	.02	.10
❑ 204 Jerry Reynolds	.02	.10
❑ 205 Dennis Scott	.07	.20
❑ 206 Scott Skiles	.02	.10
❑ 207 Otis Smith	.02	.10
❑ 208 Jeff Turner	.02	.10
❑ 209 Sam Vincent	.02	.10
❑ 210 Ron Anderson	.02	.10
❑ 211 Charles Barkley	.25	.60
❑ 212 Manute Bol	.02	.10
❑ 213 Johnny Dawkins	.02	.10
❑ 214 Armon Gilliam	.02	.10
❑ 215 Rickey Green	.02	.10
❑ 216 Hersey Hawkins	.07	.20
❑ 217 Rick Mahorn	.02	.10
❑ 218 Brian Oliver	.02	.10
❑ 219 Andre Turner	.02	.10
❑ 220 Jayson Williams	.15	.40
❑ 221 Joe Barry Carroll	.02	.10
❑ 222 Cedric Ceballos	.07	.20
❑ 223 Tom Chambers	.02	.10
❑ 224 Jeff Hornacek	.07	.20
❑ 225 Kevin Johnson	.15	.40
❑ 226 Negele Knight FSBC	.02	.10
❑ 227 Andrew Lang	.02	.10
❑ 228 Dan Majerle	.07	.20
❑ 229 Xavier McDaniel	.02	.10
❑ 230 Kurt Rambis	.02	.10
❑ 231 Mark West	.02	.10
❑ 232 Alaa Abdelnaby	.02	.10
❑ 233 Danny Ainge	.07	.20
❑ 234 Mark Bryant	.02	.10
❑ 235 Wayne Cooper	.02	.10
❑ 236 Walter Davis	.02	.10
❑ 237 Clyde Drexler	.15	.40
❑ 238 Kevin Duckworth	.02	.10
❑ 239 Jerome Kersey	.02	.10
❑ 240 Terry Porter	.02	.10
❑ 241 Clifford Robinson	.07	.20
❑ 242 Buck Williams	.02	.10
❑ 243 Anthony Bonner	.02	.10
❑ 244 Antoine Carr	.02	.10
❑ 245 Duane Causwell	.02	.10
❑ 246 Bobby Hansen	.02	.10
❑ 247 Jim Les RC	.02	.10
❑ 248 Travis Mays	.02	.10
❑ 249 Ralph Sampson	.02	.10
❑ 250 Lionel Simmons	.02	.10
❑ 251 Rory Sparrow	.02	.10
❑ 252 Wayman Tisdale	.02	.10
❑ 253 Bill Wennington	.02	.10
❑ 254 Willie Anderson	.02	.10
❑ 255 Terry Cummings	.02	.10
❑ 256 Sean Elliott	.07	.20
❑ 257 Sidney Green	.02	.10
❑ 258 David Greenwood	.02	.10
❑ 259 Avery Johnson	.07	.20
❑ 260 Paul Pressey	.02	.10
❑ 261 David Robinson	.30	.75
❑ 262 Dwayne Schintzius	.02	.10
❑ 263 Rod Strickland	.15	.40
❑ 264 David Wingate	.02	.10
❑ 265 Dana Barros	.02	.10
❑ 266 Benoit Benjamin	.02	.10
❑ 267 Michael Cage	.02	.10
❑ 268 Quintin Dailey	.02	.10
❑ 269 Ricky Pierce	.02	.10
❑ 270 Eddie Johnson	.07	.20
❑ 271 Shawn Kemp	.40	1.00
❑ 272 Derrick McKey	.02	.10
❑ 273 Nate McMillan	.02	.10
❑ 274 Gary Payton	.40	1.00
❑ 275 Sedale Threatt	.02	.10
❑ 276 Thurl Bailey	.02	.10
❑ 277 Mike Brown	.02	.10
❑ 278 Tony Brown	.02	.10
❑ 279 Mark Eaton	.02	.10
❑ 280 Blue Edwards	.02	.10
❑ 281 Darrell Griffith	.02	.10
❑ 282 Jeff Malone	.02	.10
❑ 283 Karl Malone	.25	.60
❑ 284 Delaney Rudd	.02	.10
❑ 285 John Stockton	.15	.40
❑ 286 Andy Toolson	.02	.10
❑ 287 Mark Alarie	.02	.10
❑ 288 Ledell Eackles	.02	.10
❑ 289 Pervis Ellison	.02	.10
❑ 290 A.J. English	.02	.10
❑ 291 Harvey Grant	.02	.10
❑ 292 Tom Hammonds	.02	.10
❑ 293 Charles Jones	.02	.10
❑ 294 Bernard King	.02	.10
❑ 295 Darrell Walker	.02	.10
❑ 296 John Williams	.02	.10
❑ 297 Haywoode Workman RC	.07	.20
❑ 298 Muggsy Bogues	.02	.10
❑ 299 Lester Conner	.02	.10
❑ 300 Michael Adams	.02	.10
❑ 301 Chris Mullin Minutes	.07	.20
❑ 302 Otis Thorpe	.02	.10
❑ 303 Rich/Hard/Mullin TRIO	.15	.40
❑ 304 Darrell Walker	.02	.10
❑ 305 Jerome Lane	.02	.10
❑ 306 John Stockton Assists	.07	.20
❑ 307 Michael Jordan Points	1.00	2.50
❑ 308 Michael Adams	.02	.10
❑ 309 Larry Smith	.02	.10
❑ 310 Scott Skiles	.02	.10
❑ 311 H.Olajuwon/D.Robinson	.15	.40
❑ 312 Alvin Robertson	.02	.10
❑ 313 Stay In School Jam	.02	.10
❑ 314 Craig Hodges	.02	.10
❑ 315 Dee Brown SD	.02	.10
❑ 316 Charles Barkley AS-MVP	.15	.40

❑ 317 Behind the Scenes	.15	.40
❑ 318 Derrick Coleman ART	.02	.10
❑ 319 Lionel Simmons ART	.02	.10
❑ 320 Dennis Scott ART	.02	.10
❑ 321 Kendall Gill ART	.02	.10
❑ 322 Dee Brown ART	.02	.10
❑ 323 Magic Johnson GQ	.25	.60
❑ 324 Hakeem Olajuwon GQ	.15	.40
❑ 325 K.Willis/D.Wilkins GQ	.07	.20
❑ 326 K.Willis/D.Wilkins GQ	.07	.20
❑ 327 Gerald Wilkins	.02	.10
❑ 328 Centennial Logo Card	.02	.10
❑ 329 Old-Fashioned Ball	.02	.10
❑ 330 Women Take the Court	.02	.10
❑ 331 The Peach Basket	.02	.10
❑ 332 Dr.James Naismith	.07	.20
❑ 333 M.Johnson/M.Jordan IA	.75	2.00
❑ 334 Michael Jordan IA	1.00	2.50
❑ 335 Vlade Divac	.02	.10
❑ 336 John Paxson	.02	.10
❑ 337 Bulls Team/M.Jordan	.50	1.25
❑ 338 Language Arts	.02	.10
❑ 339 Mathematics	.02	.10
❑ 340 Vocational Education	.02	.10
❑ 341 Social Studies	.02	.10
❑ 342 Physical Education	.02	.10
❑ 343 Art	.02	.10
❑ 344 Science	.02	.10
❑ 345 Checklist 1 (1-60)	.02	.10
❑ 346 Checklist 2 (61-120)	.02	.10
❑ 347 Checklist 3 (121-180)	.02	.10
❑ 348 Checklist 4 (181-244)	.02	.10
❑ 349 Checklist 5 (245-305)	.02	.10
❑ 350 Checklist 6 (306-350)	.02	.10
❑ 351 Atlanta Hawks	.02	.10
❑ 352 Boston Celtics	.02	.10
❑ 353 Charlotte Hornets	.02	.10
❑ 354 Chicago Bulls	.02	.10
❑ 355 Cleveland Cavaliers	.02	.10
❑ 356 Dallas Mavericks	.02	.10
❑ 357 Denver Nuggets	.02	.10
❑ 358 Detroit Pistons	.02	.10
❑ 359 Golden State Warriors	.02	.10
❑ 360 Houston Rockets	.02	.10
❑ 361 Indiana Pacers	.02	.10
❑ 362 Los Angeles Clippers	.02	.10
❑ 363 Los Angeles Lakers	.02	.10
❑ 364 Miami Heat	.02	.10
❑ 365 Milwaukee Bucks	.02	.10
❑ 366 Minnesota Timberwolves	.02	.10
❑ 367 New Jersey Nets	.02	.10
❑ 368 New York Knicks	.02	.10
❑ 369 Orlando Magic	.02	.10
❑ 370 Philadelphia 76ers	.02	.10
❑ 371 Phoenix Suns	.02	.10
❑ 372 Portland Trail Blazers	.02	.10
❑ 373 Sacramento Kings	.02	.10
❑ 374 San Antonio Spurs	.02	.10
❑ 375 Seattle Supersonics	.02	.10
❑ 376 Utah Jazz	.02	.10
❑ 377 Washington Bullets	.02	.10
❑ 378 Bob Weiss CO	.02	.10
❑ 379 Chris Ford CO	.02	.10
❑ 380 Allan Bristow CO	.02	.10
❑ 381 Phil Jackson CO	.07	.20
❑ 382 Lenny Wilkens CO	.07	.20
❑ 383 Richie Adubato CO	.02	.10
❑ 384 Paul Westhead CO	.02	.10
❑ 385 Chuck Daly CO	.07	.20
❑ 386 Don Nelson CO	.07	.20
❑ 387 Don Chaney CO	.02	.10
❑ 388 Bob Hill RC CO	.02	.10
❑ 389 Mike Schuler CO	.02	.10
❑ 390 Mike Dunleavy CO	.02	.10
❑ 391 Kevin Loughery CO	.02	.10
❑ 392 Del Harris CO	.02	.10
❑ 393 Jimmy Rodgers CO	.02	.10
❑ 394 Bill Fitch CO	.02	.10
❑ 395 Pat Riley CO	.07	.20
❑ 396 Matt Guokas CO	.02	.10
❑ 397 Jim Lynam CO	.02	.10
❑ 398 Cotton Fitzsimmons CO	.02	.10
❑ 399 Rick Adelman CO	.02	.10
❑ 400 Dick Motta CO	.02	.10
❑ 401 Larry Brown CO	.02	.10
❑ 402 K.C. Jones CO	.07	.20
❑ 403 Jerry Sloan CO	.07	.20
❑ 404 Wes Unseld CO	.07	.20
❑ 405 Mo Cheeks GF	.02	.10
❑ 406 Celtics/Dee Brown GF	.02	.10
❑ 407 Rex Chapman GF	.02	.10
❑ 408 Michael Jordan GF	1.00	2.50
❑ 409 John Williams GF	.02	.10
❑ 410 James Donaldson GF	.02	.10
❑ 411 Dikembe Mutombo GF	.15	.40
❑ 412 Pistons/Isiah GF	.07	.20
❑ 413 Warriors/Hardaway GF	.15	.40
❑ 414 Hakeem Olajuwon GF	.15	.40
❑ 415 Pacers/Schrempf GF	.02	.10
❑ 416 Danny Manning GF	.02	.10
❑ 417 Magic Johnson GF	.25	.60
❑ 418 Bimbo Coles GF	.02	.10
❑ 419 Alvin Robertson GF	.02	.10
❑ 420 Sam Mitchell GF	.02	.10
❑ 421 Sam Bowie GF	.02	.10
❑ 422 Mark Jackson GF	.02	.10
❑ 423 Orlando Magic	.02	.10
❑ 424 Charles Barkley GF	.15	.40
❑ 425 Suns/Majerle GF	.02	.10
❑ 426 Robert Pack GF	.02	.10
❑ 427 Wayman Tisdale GF	.02	.10
❑ 428 David Robinson GF	.15	.40
❑ 429 Nate McMillan GF	.02	.10
❑ 430 Jazz/Karl Malone GF	.15	.40
❑ 431 Michael Adams GF	.02	.10
❑ 432 Duane Ferrell SM	.02	.10
❑ 433 Kevin McHale SM	.02	.10
❑ 434 Dell Curry SM	.02	.10
❑ 435 B.J.Armstrong SM	.02	.10
❑ 436 John Williams SM	.02	.10
❑ 437 Brad Davis SM	.02	.10
❑ 438 Marcus Liberty SM	.02	.10
❑ 439 Mark Aguirre SM	.02	.10
❑ 440 Rod Higgins SM	.02	.10
❑ 441 Eric(Sleepy) Floyd SM	.02	.10
❑ 442 Detlef Schrempf SM	.02	.10
❑ 443 Loy Vaught SM	.02	.10
❑ 444 Terry Teagle SM	.02	.10
❑ 445 Kevin Edwards SM	.02	.10
❑ 446 Dale Ellis SM	.02	.10
❑ 447 Tod Murphy SM	.02	.10
❑ 448 Chris Dudley SM	.02	.10
❑ 449 Mark Jackson SM	.02	.10
❑ 450 Jerry Reynolds SM	.02	.10
❑ 451 Ron Anderson SM	.02	.10
❑ 452 Dan Majerle SM	.02	.10
❑ 453 Danny Ainge SM	.02	.10
❑ 454 Jim Les SM	.02	.10
❑ 455 Paul Pressey SM	.02	.10
❑ 456 Ricky Pierce SM	.02	.10
❑ 457 Mike Brown SM	.02	.10
❑ 458 Ledell Eackles SM	.02	.10
❑ 459 D.Wilkins/Willis TW	.07	.20
❑ 460 L.Bird/R.Parish TW	.15	.40
❑ 461 R.Chapman/Gill TW	.02	.10
❑ 462 M.Jordan/S.Pippen TW	.60	1.50
❑ 463 Cleveland Cavaliers	.02	.10
❑ 464 Dallas Mavericks	.02	.10
❑ 465 Denver Nuggets	.02	.10
❑ 466 I.Thomas/Laimbeer TW	.07	.20
❑ 467 T.Hardaway/C.Mullin TW	.07	.20
❑ 468 Houston Rockets	.02	.10
❑ 469 R.Miller/D.Schrempf TW	.07	.20
❑ 470 Los Angeles Clippers	.02	.10
❑ 471 M.Johnson/J.Worthy TW	.15	.40
❑ 472 G.Rice/Seikaly TW	.15	.40
❑ 473 Milwaukee Bucks	.02	.10
❑ 474 Minnesota Timberwolves	.02	.10
❑ 475 D.Coleman/Bowie TW	.02	.10
❑ 476 P.Ewing/Oakley TW	.07	.20
❑ 477 Orlando Magic	.02	.10
❑ 478 C.Barkley/Hawkins TW	.15	.40
❑ 479 K.Johnson/Chambers TW	.07	.20
❑ 480 C.Drexler/Porter TW	.15	.40
❑ 481 L.Simmons/Tisdale TW	.02	.10
❑ 482 T.Cummings/Elliott TW	.02	.10
❑ 483 Seattle Supersonics	.02	.10
❑ 484 K.Malone/J.Stockton TW	.15	.40
❑ 485 Washington Bullets	.02	.10
❑ 486 Rumeal Robinson RS	.02	.10
❑ 487 Dee Brown RIS	.02	.10
❑ 488 Kendall Gill RIS	.02	.10
❑ 489 B.J.Armstrong RIS	.02	.10
❑ 490 Danny Ferry RS	.02	.10
❑ 491 Randy White RS	.02	.10
❑ 492 Chris Jackson RS	.02	.10
❑ 493 Lance Blanks RS	.02	.10
❑ 494 Tim Hardaway RIS	.15	.40
❑ 495 Vernon Maxwell RS	.02	.10
❑ 496 Micheal Williams RS	.02	.10
❑ 497 Charles Smith RS	.02	.10
❑ 498 Vlade Divac RS	.02	.10
❑ 499 Willie Burton RS	.02	.10
❑ 500 Jeff Grayer RS	.02	.10
❑ 501 Pooh Richardson RS	.02	.10
❑ 502 Derrick Coleman RIS	.02	.10
❑ 503 John Starks RIS	.07	.20
❑ 504 Dennis Scott RIS	.02	.10
❑ 505 Hersey Hawkins RS	.02	.10
❑ 506 Negele Knight RS	.02	.10
❑ 507 Cliff Robinson RIS	.02	.10
❑ 508 Lionel Simmons RIS	.02	.10
❑ 509 David Robinson RIS	.15	.40
❑ 510 Gary Payton RIS	.20	.50
❑ 511 Blue Edwards RS	.02	.10
❑ 512 Harvey Grant RS	.02	.10
❑ 513 Larry Johnson RC	.60	1.50
❑ 514 Kenny Anderson RC	.30	.75
❑ 515 Billy Owens RC	.15	.40
❑ 516 Dikembe Mutombo RC	.60	1.50
❑ 517 Steve Smith RC	.60	1.50
❑ 518 Doug Smith RC	.02	.10
❑ 519 Luc Longley RC	.15	.40
❑ 520 Mark Macon RC	.02	.10
❑ 521 Stacey Augmon RC	.15	.40
❑ 522 Brian Williams RC	.15	.40
❑ 523 Terrell Brandon RC	.50	1.25
❑ 524 The Ball	.02	.10
❑ 525 The Basket	.02	.10
❑ 526 The 24-second Shot	.02	.10
❑ 527 The Game Program	.02	.10
❑ 528 The Championship Gift	.02	.10
❑ 529 Championship Trophy	.02	.10
❑ 530 Charles Barkley USA	.50	1.25
❑ 531 Larry Bird USA	1.25	3.00
❑ 532 Patrick Ewing USA	.30	.75
❑ 533 Magic Johnson USA	1.00	2.50
❑ 534 Michael Jordan USA	3.00	8.00
❑ 535 Karl Malone USA	.50	1.25
❑ 536 Chris Mullin USA	.15	.40
❑ 537 Scottie Pippen USA	1.00	2.50
❑ 538 David Robinson USA	.60	1.50
❑ 539 John Stockton USA	.30	.75
❑ 540 Chuck Daly CO USA	.07	.20
❑ 541 P.J.Carlesimo USA CO RC	.02	.10
❑ 542 M.Krzyzewski CO USA RC	.25	.60
❑ 543 Lenny Wilkens CO USA	.07	.20
❑ 544 Team USA 1	1.00	2.50
❑ 545 Team USA 2	1.00	2.50
❑ 546 Team USA 3	1.00	2.50
❑ 547 Willie Anderson USA	.02	.10
❑ 548 Stacey Augmon USA	.15	.40
❑ 549 Bimbo Coles USA	.02	.10
❑ 550 Jeff Grayer USA	.02	.10
❑ 551 Hersey Hawkins USA	.02	.10
❑ 552 Dan Majerle USA	.02	.10
❑ 553 Danny Manning USA	.02	.10
❑ 554 J.R. Reid USA	.02	.10
❑ 555 Mitch Richmond USA	.30	.75
❑ 556 Charles Smith USA	.02	.10
❑ 557 Vern Fleming USA	.02	.10
❑ 558 Joe Kleine USA	.02	.10
❑ 559 Jon Koncak USA	.02	.10
❑ 560 Sam Perkins USA	.02	.10
❑ 561 Alvin Robertson USA	.02	.10
❑ 562 Wayman Tisdale USA	.02	.10
❑ 563 Jeff Turner USA	.02	.10
❑ 564 Tony Campbell	.02	.10
❑ 565 Joe Dumars	.07	.20
❑ 566 Horace Grant	.02	.10
❑ 567 Reggie Lewis MAG	.02	.10
❑ 568 Hakeem Olajuwon MAG	.15	.40
❑ 569 Sam Perkins	.02	.10
❑ 570 Chuck Person	.02	.10
❑ 571 Buck Williams	.02	.10
❑ 572 Michael Jordan SAL	1.00	2.50
❑ 573 Bernard King	.02	.10
❑ 574 Moses Malone	.07	.20
❑ 575 Robert Parish	.02	.10
❑ 576 Pat Riley CO	.07	.20
❑ 577 Dee Brown SM	.02	.10
❑ 578 Rex Chapman	.02	.10
❑ 579 Clyde Drexler SKM	.07	.20
❑ 580 Blue Edwards	.02	.10
❑ 581 Ron Harper	.02	.10
❑ 582 Kevin Johnson SKM	.07	.20
❑ 583 Michael Jordan SKM	1.00	2.50

❑ 584 Shawn Kemp SKM	.30	.75
❑ 585 Xavier McDaniel	.02	.10
❑ 586 Scottie Pippen SKM	.25	.60
❑ 587 Kenny Smith	.02	.10
❑ 588 Dominique Wilkins SKM	.07	.20
❑ 589 Michael Adams	.02	.10
❑ 590 Danny Ainge	.02	.10
❑ 591 Larry Bird SS	.30	.75
❑ 592 Dale Ellis	.02	.10
❑ 593 Hersey Hawkins	.02	.10
❑ 594 Jeff Hornacek	.02	.10
❑ 595 Jeff Malone	.02	.10
❑ 596 Reggie Miller SS	.07	.20
❑ 597 Chris Mullin SS	.07	.20
❑ 598 John Paxson	.02	.10
❑ 599 Drazen Petrovic SS	.02	.10
❑ 600 Ricky Pierce	.02	.10
❑ 601 Mark Price SS	.02	.10
❑ 602 Dennis Scott SS	.02	.10
❑ 603 Manute Bol	.02	.10
❑ 604 Jerome Kersey	.02	.10
❑ 605 Charles Oakley	.02	.10
❑ 606 Scottie Pippen SMALL	.25	.60
❑ 607 Terry Porter	.02	.10
❑ 608 Dennis Rodman SMALL	.15	.40
❑ 609 Sedale Threatt	.02	.10
❑ 610 Business	.02	.10
❑ 611 Engineering	.02	.10
❑ 612 Law	.02	.10
❑ 613 Liberal Arts	.02	.10
❑ 614 Medicine	.02	.10
❑ 615 Maurice Cheeks	.02	.10
❑ 616 Travis Mays	.02	.10
❑ 617 Blair Rasmussen	.02	.10
❑ 618 Alexander Volkov	.02	.10
❑ 619 Rickey Green	.02	.10
❑ 620 Bobby Hansen	.02	.10
❑ 621 John Battle	.02	.10
❑ 622 Terry Davis	.02	.10
❑ 623 Walter Davis	.02	.10
❑ 624 Winston Garland	.02	.10
❑ 625 Scott Hastings	.02	.10
❑ 626 Brad Sellers	.02	.10
❑ 627 Darrell Walker	.02	.10
❑ 628 Orlando Woolridge	.02	.10
❑ 629 Tony Brown	.02	.10
❑ 630 James Edwards	.02	.10
❑ 631 Doc Rivers	.07	.20
❑ 632 Jack Haley	.02	.10
❑ 633 Sedale Threatt	.02	.10
❑ 634 Moses Malone	.15	.40
❑ 635 Thurl Bailey	.02	.10
❑ 636 Rafael Addison RC	.02	.10
❑ 637 Tim McCormick	.02	.10
❑ 638 Xavier McDaniel	.02	.10
❑ 639 Charles Shackleford	.02	.10
❑ 640 Mitchell Wiggins	.02	.10
❑ 641 Jerrod Mustaf	.02	.10
❑ 642 Dennis Hopson	.02	.10
❑ 643 Les Jepsen	.02	.10
❑ 644 Mitch Richmond	.15	.40
❑ 645 Dwayne Schintzius	.02	.10
❑ 646 Spud Webb	.07	.20
❑ 647 Jud Buechler	.02	.10
❑ 648 Antoine Carr	.02	.10
❑ 649 Tyrone Corbin	.02	.10
❑ 650 Michael Adams	.02	.10
❑ 651 Ralph Sampson	.02	.10
❑ 652 Andre Turner	.02	.10
❑ 653 David Wingate	.02	.10
❑ 654 Checklist %%S~	.02	.10
❑ 655 Checklist %%K~	.02	.10
❑ 656 Checklist %%Y~	.02	.10
❑ 657 Checklist %%B~	.02	.10
❑ 658 Checklist %%O~	.02	.10
❑ 659 Checklist %%X~	.02	.10
❑ NNO Clyde Drexler USA	40.00	75.00
❑ NNO Team USA Card	6.00	12.00

1992-93 SkyBox

❑ COMPLETE SET (413)	25.00	50.00
❑ COMPLETE SERIES 1 (327)	15.00	30.00
❑ COMPLETE SERIES 2 (86)	10.00	20.00
❑ COMMON SP RC	.20	.50
❑ 1 Stacey Augmon	.08	.25
❑ 2 Maurice Cheeks	.02	.10
❑ 3 Duane Ferrell	.02	.10
❑ 4 Paul Graham	.02	.10
❑ 5 Jon Koncak	.02	.10
❑ 6 Blair Rasmussen	.02	.10

❑ 7 Rumeal Robinson	.02	.10
❑ 8 Dominique Wilkins	.20	.50
❑ 9 Kevin Willis	.02	.10
❑ 10 Larry Bird	.75	2.00
❑ 11 Dee Brown	.02	.10
❑ 12 Sherman Douglas	.02	.10
❑ 13 Rick Fox	.08	.25
❑ 14 Kevin Gamble	.02	.10
❑ 15 Reggie Lewis	.08	.25
❑ 16 Kevin McHale	.20	.50
❑ 17 Robert Parish	.08	.25
❑ 18 Ed Pinckney	.02	.10
❑ 19 Muggsy Bogues	.08	.25
❑ 20 Dell Curry	.02	.10
❑ 21 Kenny Gattison	.02	.10
❑ 22 Kendall Gill	.08	.25
❑ 23 Mike Gminski	.02	.10
❑ 24 Tom Hammonds	.02	.10
❑ 25 Larry Johnson	.25	.60
❑ 26 Johnny Newman	.02	.10
❑ 27 J.R. Reid	.02	.10
❑ 28 B.J. Armstrong	.02	.10
❑ 29 Bill Cartwright	.02	.10
❑ 30 Horace Grant	.08	.25
❑ 31 Michael Jordan	2.50	6.00
❑ 32 Stacey King	.02	.10
❑ 33 John Paxson	.02	.10
❑ 34 Will Perdue	.02	.10
❑ 35 Scottie Pippen	.60	1.50
❑ 36 Scott Williams	.02	.10
❑ 37 John Battle	.02	.10
❑ 38 Terrell Brandon	.20	.50
❑ 39 Brad Daugherty	.02	.10
❑ 40 Craig Ehlo	.02	.10
❑ 41 Danny Ferry	.02	.10
❑ 42 Henry James	.02	.10
❑ 43 Larry Nance	.02	.10
❑ 44 Mark Price	.02	.10
❑ 45 Mike Sanders	.02	.10
❑ 46 Hot Rod Williams	.02	.10
❑ 47 Rolando Blackman	.02	.10
❑ 48 Terry Davis	.02	.10
❑ 49 Derek Harper	.08	.25
❑ 50 Donald Hodge	.02	.10
❑ 51 Mike Iuzzolino	.02	.10
❑ 52 Fat Lever	.02	.10
❑ 53 Rodney McCray	.02	.10
❑ 54 Doug Smith	.02	.10
❑ 55 Randy White	.02	.10
❑ 56 Herb Williams	.02	.10
❑ 57 Greg Anderson	.02	.10
❑ 58 Walter Davis	.02	.10
❑ 59 Winston Garland	.02	.10
❑ 60 Chris Jackson	.02	.10
❑ 61 Marcus Liberty	.02	.10
❑ 62 Todd Lichti	.02	.10
❑ 63 Mark Macon	.02	.10
❑ 64 Dikembe Mutombo	.25	.60
❑ 65 Reggie Williams	.02	.10
❑ 66 Mark Aguirre	.02	.10
❑ 67 William Bedford	.02	.10
❑ 68 Lance Blanks	.02	.10
❑ 69 Joe Dumars	.20	.50
❑ 70 Bill Laimbeer	.08	.25
❑ 71 Dennis Rodman	.40	1.00
❑ 72 John Salley	.02	.10
❑ 73 Isiah Thomas	.20	.50
❑ 74 Darrell Walker	.02	.10
❑ 75 Orlando Woolridge	.02	.10
❑ 76 Victor Alexander	.02	.10
❑ 77 Mario Elie	.08	.25
❑ 78 Chris Gatling	.02	.10
❑ 79 Tim Hardaway	.25	.60
❑ 80 Tyrone Hill	.02	.10
❑ 81 Alton Lister	.02	.10

❑ 82 Sarunas Marciulionis	.02	.10
❑ 83 Chris Mullin	.20	.50
❑ 84 Billy Owens	.08	.25
❑ 85 Matt Bullard	.02	.10
❑ 86 Sleepy Floyd	.02	.10
❑ 87 Avery Johnson	.02	.10
❑ 88 Buck Johnson	.02	.10
❑ 89 Vernon Maxwell	.02	.10
❑ 90 Hakeem Olajuwon	.30	.75
❑ 91 Kenny Smith	.02	.10
❑ 92 Larry Smith	.02	.10
❑ 93 Otis Thorpe	.08	.25
❑ 94 Dale Davis	.02	.10
❑ 95 Vern Fleming	.02	.10
❑ 96 George McCloud	.02	.10
❑ 97 Reggie Miller	.20	.50
❑ 98 Chuck Person	.02	.10
❑ 99 Detlef Schrempf	.08	.25
❑ 100 Rik Smits	.08	.25
❑ 101 LaSalle Thompson	.02	.10
❑ 102 Micheal Williams	.02	.10
❑ 103 James Edwards	.02	.10
❑ 104 Gary Grant	.02	.10
❑ 105 Ron Harper	.08	.25
❑ 106 Bo Kimble	.02	.10
❑ 107 Danny Manning	.08	.25
❑ 108 Ken Norman	.02	.10
❑ 109 Olden Polynice	.02	.10
❑ 110 Doc Rivers	.08	.25
❑ 111 Charles Smith	.02	.10
❑ 112 Loy Vaught	.02	.10
❑ 113 Elden Campbell	.08	.25
❑ 114 Vlade Divac	.08	.25
❑ 115 A.C. Green	.08	.25
❑ 116 Jack Haley	.02	.10
❑ 117 Sam Perkins	.08	.25
❑ 118 Byron Scott	.08	.25
❑ 119 Tony Smith	.02	.10
❑ 120 Sedale Threatt	.02	.10
❑ 121 James Worthy	.20	.50
❑ 122 Keith Askins	.02	.10
❑ 123 Willie Burton	.02	.10
❑ 124 Bimbo Coles	.02	.10
❑ 125 Kevin Edwards	.02	.10
❑ 126 Alec Kessler	.02	.10
❑ 127 Grant Long	.02	.10
❑ 128 Glen Rice	.20	.50
❑ 129 Rony Seikaly	.02	.10
❑ 130 Brian Shaw	.02	.10
❑ 131 Steve Smith	.25	.60
❑ 132 Frank Brickowski	.02	.10
❑ 133 Dale Ellis	.02	.10
❑ 104 Jeff Grayer	.02	.10
❑ 135 Jay Humphries	.02	.10
❑ 136 Larry Krystkowiak	.02	.10
❑ 137 Moses Malone	.20	.50
❑ 138 Fred Roberts	.02	.10
❑ 139 Alvin Robertson	.02	.10
❑ 140 Danny Schayes	.02	.10
❑ 141 Thurl Bailey	.02	.10
❑ 142 Scott Brooks	.02	.10
❑ 143 Tony Campbell	.02	.10
❑ 144 Gerald Glass	.02	.10
❑ 145 Luc Longley	.08	.25
❑ 146 Sam Mitchell	.02	.10
❑ 147 Pooh Richardson	.02	.10
❑ 148 Felton Spencer	.02	.10
❑ 149 Doug West	.02	.10
❑ 150 Rafael Addison	.02	.10
❑ 151 Kenny Anderson	.20	.50
❑ 152 Mookie Blaylock	.08	.25
❑ 153 Sam Bowie	.02	.10
❑ 154 Derrick Coleman	.08	.25
❑ 155 Chris Dudley	.02	.10
❑ 156 Tate George	.02	.10
❑ 157 Terry Mills	.02	.10
❑ 158 Chris Morris	.02	.10
❑ 159 Drazen Petrovic	.02	.10
❑ 160 Greg Anthony	.02	.10
❑ 161 Patrick Ewing	.20	.50
❑ 162 Mark Jackson	.08	.25
❑ 163 Anthony Mason	.20	.50
❑ 164 Tim McCormick	.02	.10
❑ 165 Xavier McDaniel	.02	.10
❑ 166 Charles Oakley	.08	.25
❑ 167 John Starks	.08	.25
❑ 168 Gerald Wilkins	.02	.10
❑ 169 Nick Anderson	.08	.25
❑ 170 Terry Catledge	.02	.10

❑ 171 Jerry Reynolds	.02	.10
❑ 172 Stanley Roberts	.02	.10
❑ 173 Dennis Scott	.08	.25
❑ 174 Scott Skiles	.02	.10
❑ 175 Jeff Turner	.02	.10
❑ 176 Sam Vincent	.02	.10
❑ 177 Brian Williams	.02	.10
❑ 178 Ron Anderson	.02	.10
❑ 179 Charles Barkley	.30	.75
❑ 180 Manute Bol	.02	.10
❑ 181 Johnny Dawkins	.02	.10
❑ 182 Armon Gilliam	.02	.10
❑ 183 Greg Grant	.02	.10
❑ 184 Hersey Hawkins	.08	.25
❑ 185 Brian Oliver	.02	.10
❑ 186 Charles Shackleford	.02	.10
❑ 187 Jayson Williams	.08	.25
❑ 188 Cedric Ceballos	.08	.25
❑ 189 Tom Chambers	.02	.10
❑ 190 Jeff Hornacek	.08	.25
❑ 191 Kevin Johnson	.20	.50
❑ 192 Negele Knight	.02	.10
❑ 193 Andrew Lang	.02	.10
❑ 194 Dan Majerle	.08	.25
❑ 195 Jerrod Mustaf	.02	.10
❑ 196 Tim Perry	.02	.10
❑ 197 Mark West	.02	.10
❑ 198 Alaa Abdelnaby	.02	.10
❑ 199 Danny Ainge	.08	.25
❑ 200 Mark Bryant	.02	.10
❑ 201 Clyde Drexler	.20	.50
❑ 202 Kevin Duckworth	.02	.10
❑ 203 Jerome Kersey	.02	.10
❑ 204 Robert Pack	.02	.10
❑ 205 Terry Porter	.02	.10
❑ 206 Cliff Robinson	.08	.25
❑ 207 Buck Williams	.08	.25
❑ 208 Anthony Bonner	.02	.10
❑ 209 Randy Brown	.02	.10
❑ 210 Duane Causwell	.02	.10
❑ 211 Pete Chilcutt	.02	.10
❑ 212 Dennis Hopson	.02	.10
❑ 213 Jim Les	.02	.10
❑ 214 Mitch Richmond	.20	.50
❑ 215 Lionel Simmons	.02	.10
❑ 216 Wayman Tisdale	.02	.10
❑ 217 Spud Webb	.08	.25
❑ 218 Willie Anderson	.02	.10
❑ 219 Antoine Carr	.02	.10
❑ 220 Terry Cummings	.08	.25
❑ 221 Sean Elliott	.08	.25
❑ 222 Sidney Green	.02	.10
❑ 223 Vinnie Johnson	.02	.10
❑ 224 David Robinson	.30	.75
❑ 225 Rod Strickland	.20	.50
❑ 226 Greg Sutton	.02	.10
❑ 227 Dana Barros	.02	.10
❑ 228 Benoit Benjamin	.02	.10
❑ 229 Michael Cage	.02	.10
❑ 230 Eddie Johnson	.02	.10
❑ 231 Shawn Kemp	.40	1.00
❑ 232 Derrick McKey	.02	.10
❑ 233 Nate McMillan	.02	.10
❑ 234 Gary Payton	.40	1.00
❑ 235 Ricky Pierce	.02	.10
❑ 236 David Benoit	.02	.10
❑ 237 Mike Brown	.02	.10
❑ 238 Tyrone Corbin	.02	.10
❑ 239 Mark Eaton	.02	.10
❑ 240 Blue Edwards	.02	.10
❑ 241 Jeff Malone	.02	.10
❑ 242 Karl Malone	.30	.75
❑ 243 Eric Murdock	.02	.10
❑ 244 John Stockton	.20	.50
❑ 245 Michael Adams	.02	.10
❑ 246 Rex Chapman	.02	.10
❑ 247 Ledell Eackles	.02	.10
❑ 248 Pervis Ellison	.02	.10
❑ 249 A.J. English	.02	.10
❑ 250 Harvey Grant	.02	.10
❑ 251 Charles Jones	.02	.10
❑ 252 Bernard King	.02	.10
❑ 253 LaBradford Smith	.02	.10
❑ 254 Larry Stewart	.02	.10
❑ 255 Bob Weiss CO	.02	.10
❑ 256 Chris Ford CO	.02	.10
❑ 257 Allan Bristow CO	.02	.10
❑ 258 Phil Jackson CO	.08	.25
❑ 259 Lenny Wilkens CO	.08	.25
❑ 260 Richie Adubato CO	.02	.10
❑ 261 Dan Issel CO	.02	.10
❑ 262 Ron Rothstein CO	.02	.10
❑ 263 Don Nelson CO	.08	.25
❑ 264 Rudy Tomjanovich CO	.08	.25
❑ 265 Bob Hill CO	.02	.10
❑ 266 Larry Brown CO	.08	.25
❑ 267 Randy Pfund RC CO	.02	.10
❑ 268 Kevin Loughery CO	.02	.10
❑ 269 Mike Dunleavy CO	.02	.10
❑ 270 Jimmy Rodgers CO	.02	.10
❑ 271 Chuck Daly CO	.08	.25
❑ 272 Pat Riley CO	.08	.25
❑ 273 Matt Guokas CO	.02	.10
❑ 274 Doug Moe CO	.02	.10
❑ 275 Paul Westphal CO	.02	.10
❑ 276 Rick Adelman CO	.02	.10
❑ 277 Garry St.Jean RC CO	.02	.10
❑ 278 Jerry Tarkanian RC	.02	.10
❑ 279 George Karl CO	.08	.25
❑ 280 Jerry Sloan CO	.08	.25
❑ 281 Wes Unseld CO	.08	.25
❑ 282 Dominique Wilkins TT	.08	.25
❑ 283 Reggie Lewis TT	.02	.10
❑ 284 Kendall Gill TT	.02	.10
❑ 285 Horace Grant TT	.02	.10
❑ 286 Brad Daugherty TT	.02	.10
❑ 287 Derek Harper TT	.02	.10
❑ 288 Chris Jackson TT	.02	.10
❑ 289 Isiah Thomas TT	.08	.25
❑ 290 Chris Mullin TT	.08	.25
❑ 291 Kenny Smith TT	.02	.10
❑ 292 Reggie Miller TT	.08	.25
❑ 293 Ron Harper TT	.02	.10
❑ 294 Vlade Divac TT	.02	.10
❑ 295 Glen Rice TT	.08	.25
❑ 296 Moses Malone TT	.08	.25
❑ 297 Doug West TT	.02	.10
❑ 298 Derrick Coleman TT	.02	.10
❑ 299 Patrick Ewing TT	.08	.25
❑ 300 Scott Skiles TT	.02	.10
❑ 301 Hersey Hawkins TT	.02	.10
❑ 302 Kevin Johnson TT	.08	.25
❑ 303 Cliff Robinson TT	.02	.10
❑ 304 Spud Webb TT	.02	.10
❑ 305 David Robinson TT	.20	.50
❑ 305A Dav.Robinson TT ERR 299	.20	.50
❑ 306 Shawn Kemp TT	.20	.50
❑ 307 John Stockton TT	.08	.25
❑ 308 Pervis Ellison TT	.02	.10
❑ 309 Craig Hodges AS	.02	.10
❑ 310 Magic Johnson AS MVP	.30	.75
❑ 311 Cedric Ceballos AS	.02	.10
❑ 312 D.Rodman/Group AS	.20	.50
❑ 313 K.Malone/Group AS	.20	.50
❑ 314 Michael Jordan MVP	1.25	3.00
❑ 315 Clyde Drexler FINALS	.08	.25
❑ 316 Western Conference	.08	.25
❑ 317 Scottie Pippen FINALS	.30	.75
❑ 318 NBA Champs	.02	.10
❑ 319 L.Johnson/D.Mut. ART	.20	.50
❑ 320 NBA Stay in School	.02	.10
❑ 321 Boys and Girls	.02	.10
❑ 322 Checklist 1	.02	.10
❑ 323 Checklist 2	.02	.10
❑ 324 Checklist 3	.02	.10
❑ 325 Checklist 4	.02	.10
❑ 326 Checklist 5	.02	.10
❑ 327 Checklist 6	.02	.10
❑ 328 Adam Keefe SP RC	.02	.10
❑ 329 Sean Rooks SP RC	.02	.10
❑ 330 Xavier McDaniel	.02	.10
❑ 331 Kiki Vandeweghe	.02	.10
❑ 332 Alonzo Mourning SP RC	1.25	3.00
❑ 333 Rodney McCray	.02	.10
❑ 334 Gerald Wilkins	.02	.10
❑ 335 Tony Bennett SP RC	.02	.10
❑ 336 LaPhonso Ellis SP RC	.20	.50
❑ 337 Bryant Stith SP RC	.20	.50
❑ 338 Isaiah Morris SP RC	.02	.10
❑ 339 Olden Polynice	.02	.10
❑ 340 Jeff Grayer	.02	.10
❑ 341 Byron Houston SP RC	.02	.10
❑ 342 Latrell Sprewell SP RC	1.50	4.00
❑ 343 Scott Brooks	.02	.10
❑ 344 Frank Johnson	.02	.10
❑ 345 Robert Horry SP RC	.20	.50
❑ 346 David Wood	.02	.10
❑ 347 Sam Mitchell	.02	.10
❑ 348 Pooh Richardson	.02	.10
❑ 349 Malik Sealy SP RC	.20	.50
❑ 350 Morlon Wiley	.02	.10
❑ 351 Mark Jackson	.08	.25
❑ 352 Stanley Roberts	.02	.10
❑ 353 Elmore Spencer SP RC	.02	.10
❑ 354 John Williams	.02	.10
❑ 355 Randy Woods SP RC	.02	.10
❑ 356 James Edwards	.02	.10
❑ 357 Jeff Sanders	.02	.10
❑ 358 Magic Johnson	.60	1.50
❑ 359 Anthony Peeler SP RC	.20	.50
❑ 360 Harold Miner SP RC	.20	.50
❑ 361 John Salley	.02	.10
❑ 362 Alaa Abdelnaby	.02	.10
❑ 363 Todd Day SP RC	.20	.50
❑ 364 Blue Edwards	.02	.10
❑ 365 Lee Mayberry SP RC	.02	.10
❑ 366 Eric Murdock	.02	.10
❑ 367 Mookie Blaylock	.08	.25
❑ 368 Anthony Avent RC	.02	.10
❑ 369 Christian Laettner SP RC	.40	1.00
❑ 370 Chuck Person	.02	.10
❑ 371 Chris Smith SP RC	.20	.50
❑ 372 Micheal Williams	.02	.10
❑ 373 Rolando Blackman	.02	.10
❑ 374 Tony Campbell UER	.02	.10
❑ 375 Hubert Davis SP RC	.20	.50
❑ 376 Travis Mays	.02	.10
❑ 377 Doc Rivers	.08	.25
❑ 378 Charles Smith	.02	.10
❑ 379 Rumeal Robinson	.02	.10
❑ 380 Vinny Del Negro	.02	.10
❑ 381 Steve Kerr	.08	.25
❑ 382 Shaquille O'Neal SP RC	5.00	12.00
❑ 383 Donald Royal	.02	.10
❑ 384 Jeff Hornacek	.08	.25
❑ 385 Andrew Lang	.02	.10
❑ 386 Tim Perry UER	.02	.10
❑ 387 C.Weatherspoon SP RC	.20	.50
❑ 388 Danny Ainge	.08	.25
❑ 389 Charles Barkley	.30	.75
❑ 390 Tim Kempton	.02	.10
❑ 391 Oliver Miller SP RC	.20	.50
❑ 392 Dave Johnson SP RC	.20	.50
❑ 393 Tracy Murray SP RC	.20	.50
❑ 394 Rod Strickland	.20	.50
❑ 395 Marty Conlon	.02	.10
❑ 396 Walt Williams SP RC	.20	.50
❑ 397 Lloyd Daniels RC	.02	.10
❑ 398 Dale Ellis	.02	.10
❑ 399 Dave Hoppen	.02	.10
❑ 400 Larry Smith	.02	.10
❑ 401 Doug Overton	.02	.10
❑ 402 Isaac Austin RC	.08	.25
❑ 403 Jay Humphries	.02	.10
❑ 404 Larry Krystkowiak	.02	.10
❑ 405 Tom Gugliotta SP RC	.60	1.50
❑ 406 Buck Johnson	.02	.10
❑ 407 Don MacLean SP RC	.20	.50
❑ 408 Marlon Maxey SP RC	.20	.50
❑ 409 Corey Williams SP RC	.20	.50
❑ 410 Special Olympics	.08	.25
❑ 411 Checklist 1	.02	.10
❑ 412 Checklist 2	.02	.10
❑ 413 Checklist 3	.02	.10
❑ NNO David Robinson AU	50.00	100.00
❑ NNO Admiral Comes Prepared	1.50	4.00
❑ NNO Magic Johnson AU	100.00	200.00
❑ NNO Head of the Class	15.00	30.00
❑ NNO Magic Never Ends	2.50	6.00

2008-09 SkyBox

❑ COMPLETE SET (230)	40.00	80.00
❑ 1 Mike Bibby	.30	.75
❑ 2 Acie Law IV	.25	.60

❑ 3 Al Horford	.30	.75
❑ 4 Joe Johnson	.30	.75
❑ 5 Josh Smith	.30	.75
❑ 6 Marvin Williams	.30	.75
❑ 7 Ray Allen	.30	.75
❑ 8 Glen Davis	.25	.60
❑ 9 Kevin Garnett	.60	1.50
❑ 10 Paul Pierce	.40	1.00
❑ 11 Leon Powe	.20	.50
❑ 12 Rajon Rondo	.30	.75
❑ 13 Raymond Felton	.25	.60
❑ 14 Adam Morrison	.30	.75
❑ 15 Emeka Okafor	.30	.75
❑ 16 Boris Diaw	.25	.60
❑ 17 Gerald Wallace	.30	.75
❑ 18 Luol Deng	.30	.75
❑ 19 Ben Gordon	.30	.75
❑ 20 Kirk Hinrich	.30	.75
❑ 21 Joakim Noah	.30	.75
❑ 22 Andres Nocioni	.25	.60
❑ 23 Tyrus Thomas	.25	.60
❑ 24 Daniel Gibson	.30	.75
❑ 25 Zydrunas Ilgauskas	.25	.60
❑ 26 LeBron James	1.50	4.00
❑ 27 Anderson Varejao	.25	.60
❑ 28 Ben Wallace	.30	.75
❑ 29 Jose Barea	.25	.60
❑ 30 Josh Howard	.30	.75
❑ 31 Jason Kidd	.30	.75
❑ 32 Dirk Nowitzki	.40	1.00
❑ 33 Jason Terry	.25	.60
❑ 34 Carmelo Anthony	.40	1.00
❑ 35 Shaun Livingston	.25	.60
❑ 36 Chauncey Billups	.30	.75
❑ 37 Kenyon Martin	.30	.75
❑ 38 J.R. Smith	.25	.60
❑ 39 Allen Iverson	.40	1.00
❑ 40 Richard Hamilton	.25	.60
❑ 41 Jason Maxiell	.25	.60
❑ 42 Tayshaun Prince	.30	.75
❑ 43 Rodney Stuckey	.40	1.00
❑ 44 Rasheed Wallace	.30	.75
❑ 45 Kelenna Azubuike	.20	.50
❑ 46 Matt Barnes	.20	.50
❑ 47 Corey Maggette	.30	.75
❑ 48 Monta Ellis	.30	.75
❑ 49 Jamal Crawford	.20	.50
❑ 50 Stephen Jackson	.25	.60
❑ 51 Shane Battier	.25	.60
❑ 52 Luther Head	.25	.60
❑ 53 Carl Landry	.20	.50
❑ 54 Tracy McGrady	.40	1.00
❑ 55 Yao Ming	.40	1.00
❑ 56 Luis Scola	.25	.60
❑ 57 Mike Dunleavy	.25	.60
❑ 58 Danny Granger	.30	.75
❑ 59 Troy Murphy	.30	.75
❑ 60 T.J. Ford	.20	.50
❑ 61 Jamaal Tinsley	.20	.50
❑ 62 Elton Brand	.50	1.25
❑ 63 Chris Kaman	.20	.50
❑ 64 Ricky Davis	.30	.75
❑ 65 Baron Davis	.30	.75
❑ 66 Zach Randolph	.30	.75
❑ 67 Al Thornton	.30	.75
❑ 68 Kobe Bryant	1.50	4.00
❑ 69 Andrew Bynum	.30	.75
❑ 70 Jordan Farmar	.25	.60
❑ 71 Pau Gasol	.30	.75
❑ 72 Lamar Odom	.30	.75
❑ 73 Sasha Vujacic	.25	.60
❑ 74 Mike Conley	.25	.60
❑ 75 Rudy Gay	.30	.75
❑ 76 Kyle Lowry	.20	.50
❑ 77 Mike Miller	.30	.75
❑ 78 Hakim Warrick	.20	.50
❑ 79 Daequan Cook	.25	.60
❑ 80 Marcus Camby	.20	.50
❑ 81 Udonis Haslem	.30	.75
❑ 82 Shawn Marion	.30	.75
❑ 83 Alonzo Mourning	.30	.75
❑ 84 Dwyane Wade	.60	1.50
❑ 85 Andrew Bogut	.30	.75
❑ 86 Richard Jefferson	.30	.75
❑ 87 Desmond Mason	.20	.50
❑ 88 Michael Redd	.30	.75
❑ 89 Ramon Sessions	.30	.75
❑ 90 Mo Williams	.25	.60
❑ 91 Corey Brewer	.25	.60
❑ 92 Randy Foye	.30	.75
❑ 93 Al Jefferson	.30	.75
❑ 94 Rashad McCants	.25	.60
❑ 95 Sebastian Telfair	.25	.60
❑ 96 Josh Boone	.20	.50
❑ 97 Vince Carter	.40	1.00
❑ 98 Devin Harris	.30	.75
❑ 99 Yi Jianlian	.30	.75
❑ 100 Keyon Dooling	.20	.50
❑ 101 Sean Williams	.25	.60
❑ 102 Tyson Chandler	.25	.60
❑ 103 Chris Paul	.60	1.50
❑ 104 Morris Peterson	.25	.60
❑ 105 Peja Stojakovic	.30	.75
❑ 106 David West	.30	.75
❑ 107 Julian Wright	.25	.60
❑ 108 Al Harrington	.25	.60
❑ 109 Eddy Curry	.20	.50
❑ 110 David Lee	.25	.60
❑ 111 Stephon Marbury	.30	.75
❑ 112 Cuttino Mobley	.25	.60
❑ 113 Quentin Richardson	.25	.60
❑ 114 Keith Bogans	.20	.50
❑ 115 Maurice Evans	.20	.50
❑ 116 Dwight Howard	.60	1.50
❑ 117 Rashard Lewis	.30	.75
❑ 118 Jameer Nelson	.25	.60
❑ 119 Hedo Turkoglu	.30	.75
❑ 120 Samuel Dalembert	.20	.50
❑ 121 Reggie Evans	.20	.50
❑ 122 Willie Green	.20	.50
❑ 123 Andre Iguodala	.30	.75
❑ 124 Andre Miller	.25	.60
❑ 125 Thaddeus Young	.25	.60
❑ 126 Leandro Barbosa	.25	.60
❑ 127 Jason Richardson	.30	.75
❑ 128 Grant Hill	.30	.75
❑ 129 Steve Nash	.30	.75
❑ 130 Shaquille O'Neal	.60	1.50
❑ 131 Amare Stoudemire	.40	1.00
❑ 132 LaMarcus Aldridge	.30	.75
❑ 133 Steve Blake	.20	.50
❑ 134 Greg Oden	.30	.75
❑ 135 Brandon Roy	.40	1.00
❑ 136 Martell Webster	.25	.60
❑ 137 Beno Udrih	.20	.50
❑ 138 Ron Artest	.30	.75
❑ 139 Francisco Garcia	.25	.60
❑ 140 Kevin Martin	.30	.75
❑ 141 Brad Miller	.30	.75
❑ 142 Brent Barry	.20	.50
❑ 143 Bruce Bowen	.20	.50
❑ 144 Tim Duncan	.50	1.25
❑ 145 Michael Finley	.30	.75
❑ 146 Manu Ginobili	.30	.75
❑ 147 Tony Parker	.30	.75
❑ 148 Nick Collison	.20	.50
❑ 149 Kevin Durant	.75	2.00
❑ 150 Jeff Green	.25	.60
❑ 151 Earl Watson	.20	.50
❑ 152 Chris Wilcox	.25	.60
❑ 153 Damien Wilkins	.20	.50
❑ 154 Andrea Bargnani	.25	.60
❑ 155 Chris Bosh	.30	.75
❑ 156 Jose Calderon	.25	.60
❑ 157 Jermaine O'Neal	.30	.75
❑ 158 Jamario Moon	.30	.75
❑ 159 Anthony Parker	.25	.60
❑ 160 Carlos Boozer	.30	.75
❑ 161 Ronnie Brewer	.25	.60
❑ 162 Andrei Kirilenko	.30	.75
❑ 163 Kyle Korver	.30	.75
❑ 164 Mehmet Okur	.30	.75
❑ 165 Deron Williams	.40	1.00
❑ 166 Gilbert Arenas	.30	.75
❑ 167 Caron Butler	.30	.75
❑ 168 Antawn Jamison	.30	.75
❑ 169 DeShawn Stevenson	.20	.50
❑ 170 Nick Young	.20	.50
❑ 171 Al Horford CU	.40	1.00
❑ 172 Joe Johnson CU	.40	1.00
❑ 173 Kevin Garnett CU	.75	2.00
❑ 174 Paul Pierce CU	.50	1.25
❑ 175 Larry Johnson CU	.40	1.00
❑ 176 Michael Jordan CU	3.00	8.00
❑ 177 LeBron James CU	2.00	5.00
❑ 178 Ben Wallace CU	.40	1.00
❑ 179 Dirk Nowitzki CU	.50	1.25
❑ 180 Carmelo Anthony CU	.50	1.25
❑ 181 Allen Iverson CU	.50	1.25
❑ 182 Isiah Thomas CU	.40	1.00
❑ 183 Monta Ellis CU	.40	1.00
❑ 184 Magic Johnson CU	.75	2.00
❑ 185 Kobe Bryant CU	2.00	5.00
❑ 186 Dwyane Wade CU	.75	2.00
❑ 187 Oscar Robertson CU	.40	1.00
❑ 188 Vince Carter CU	.50	1.25
❑ 189 Chris Paul CU	.75	2.00
❑ 190 Patrick Ewing CU	.50	1.25
❑ 191 Dwight Howard CU	.75	2.00
❑ 192 Julius Erving CU	.75	2.00
❑ 193 Steve Nash CU	.40	1.00
❑ 194 Shaquille O'Neal CU	.75	2.00
❑ 195 Brandon Roy CU	.50	1.25
❑ 196 Tim Duncan CU	.60	1.50
❑ 197 Kevin Durant CU	1.00	2.50
❑ 198 Chris Bosh CU	.40	1.00
❑ 199 Deron Williams CU	.50	1.25
❑ 200 Gilbert Arenas CU	.40	1.00
❑ 201 Derrick Rose RC	4.00	10.00
❑ 202 Michael Beasley RC	2.00	5.00
❑ 203 O.J. Mayo RC	1.50	4.00
❑ 204 Russell Westbrook RC	2.50	6.00
❑ 205 Kevin Love RC	1.25	3.00
❑ 206 Danilo Gallinari RC	1.50	4.00
❑ 207 Eric Gordon RC	1.25	3.00
❑ 208 Joe Alexander RC	1.00	2.50
❑ 209 D.J. Augustin RC	1.00	2.50
❑ 210 Brook Lopez RC	2.00	5.00
❑ 211 Jerryd Bayless RC	1.00	2.50
❑ 212 Jason Thompson RC	1.00	2.50
❑ 213 Brandon Rush RC	1.00	2.50
❑ 214 Robin Lopez RC	1.00	2.50
❑ 215 Roy Hibbert RC	1.25	3.00
❑ 216 Alexis Ajinca RC	1.00	2.50
❑ 217 George Hill RC	1.50	4.00
❑ 218 Donte Greene RC	1.00	2.50
❑ 219 J.J. Hickson RC	1.50	4.00
❑ 220 D.J. White RC	1.00	2.50
❑ 221 Mario Chalmers RC	1.25	3.00
❑ 222 Mike Taylor RC	1.00	2.50
❑ 223 Kosta Koufos RC	1.00	2.50
❑ 224 Kyle Weaver RC	1.00	2.50
❑ 225 Rudy Fernandez RC	2.00	5.00
❑ 226 Nicolas Batum RC	1.25	3.00
❑ 227 Luc Richard Mbah A Moute RC	1.00	2.50
❑ 228 Marc Gasol RC	1.50	4.00
❑ 229 Darnell Jackson RC	1.00	2.50
❑ 230 Richard Hendrix RC	1.00	2.50

1993-94 SkyBox Premium

❑ COMPLETE SET (341)	15.00	30.00
❑ COMPLETE SERIES 1 (191)	7.50	15.00
❑ COMPLETE SERIES 2 (150)	7.50	15.00
❑ 1 Checklist	.01	.05
❑ 2 Checklist	.01	.05
❑ 3 Checklist	.01	.05
❑ 4 Larry Johnson PO	.05	.15
❑ 5 Alonzo Mourning PO	.10	.30
❑ 6 Hakeem Olajuwon PO	.10	.30
❑ 7 Brad Daugherty PO	.01	.05
❑ 8 Oliver Miller PO	.01	.05
❑ 9 David Robinson PO	.10	.30
❑ 10 Patrick Ewing PO	.05	.15
❑ 11 Ricky Pierce PO	.01	.05
❑ 12 Sam Perkins PO	.01	.05
❑ 13 John Starks PO	.01	.05
❑ 14 Michael Jordan PO	.75	2.00
❑ 15 Dan Majerle PO	.01	.05
❑ 16 Scottie Pippen PO	.20	.50
❑ 17 Shawn Kemp PO	.10	.30
❑ 18 Charles Barkley PO	.10	.30
❑ 19 Horace Grant PO	.01	.05
❑ 20 Kevin Johnson PO	.01	.05
❑ 21 John Paxson PO	.01	.05

❑ 22 Inside Stuff	.10	.30
❑ 23 NBA On NBC	.01	.05
❑ 24 Stacey Augmon	.01	.05
❑ 25 Mookie Blaylock	.05	.15
❑ 26 Craig Ehlo	.01	.05
❑ 27 Adam Keefe	.01	.05
❑ 28 Dominique Wilkins	.10	.30
❑ 29 Kevin Willis	.01	.05
❑ 30 Dee Brown	.01	.05
❑ 31 Sherman Douglas	.01	.05
❑ 32 Rick Fox	.01	.05
❑ 33 Kevin Gamble	.01	.05
❑ 34 Xavier McDaniel	.01	.05
❑ 35 Robert Parish	.05	.15
❑ 36 Muggsy Bogues	.05	.15
❑ 37 Dell Curry	.01	.05
❑ 38 Kendall Gill	.05	.15
❑ 39 Larry Johnson	.10	.30
❑ 40 Alonzo Mourning	.20	.50
❑ 41 Johnny Newman	.01	.05
❑ 42 B.J. Armstrong	.01	.05
❑ 43 Bill Cartwright	.01	.05
❑ 44 Horace Grant	.05	.15
❑ 45 Michael Jordan	1.50	4.00
❑ 46 John Paxson	.01	.05
❑ 47 Scottie Pippen	.40	1.00
❑ 48 Scott Williams	.01	.05
❑ 49 Terrell Brandon	.05	.15
❑ 50 Brad Daugherty	.01	.05
❑ 51 Larry Nance	.01	.05
❑ 52 Mark Price	.01	.05
❑ 53 Gerald Wilkins	.01	.05
❑ 54 John Williams	.01	.05
❑ 55 Terry Davis	.01	.05
❑ 56 Derek Harper	.05	.15
❑ 57 Jim Jackson	.05	.15
❑ 58 Sean Rooks	.01	.05
❑ 59 Doug Smith	.01	.05
❑ 60 Mahmoud Abdul-Rauf	.01	.05
❑ 61 LaPhonso Ellis	.01	.05
❑ 62 Mark Macon	.01	.05
❑ 63 Dikembe Mutombo	.10	.30
❑ 64 Bryant Stith	.01	.05
❑ 65 Reggie Williams	.01	.05
❑ 66 Joe Dumars	.10	.30
❑ 67 Bill Laimbeer	.01	.05
❑ 68 Terry Mills	.01	.05
❑ 69 Alvin Robertson	.01	.05
❑ 70 Dennis Rodman	.25	.60
❑ 71 Isiah Thomas	.10	.30
❑ 72 Victor Alexander	.01	.05
❑ 73 Tim Hardaway	.10	.30
❑ 74 Tyrone Hill	.01	.05
❑ 75 Sarunas Marciulionis	.01	.05
❑ 76 Chris Mullin	.10	.30
❑ 77 Billy Owens	.01	.05
❑ 78 Latrell Sprewell	.30	.75
❑ 79 Robert Horry	.05	.15
❑ 80 Vernon Maxwell	.01	.05
❑ 81 Hakeem Olajuwon	.20	.50
❑ 82 Kenny Smith	.01	.05
❑ 83 Otis Thorpe	.05	.15
❑ 84 Dale Davis	.01	.05
❑ 85 Reggie Miller	.10	.30
❑ 86 Pooh Richardson	.01	.05
❑ 87 Detlef Schrempf	.05	.15
❑ 88 Malik Sealy	.01	.05
❑ 89 Rik Smits	.05	.15
❑ 90 Ron Harper	.05	.15
❑ 91 Mark Jackson	.05	.15
❑ 92 Danny Manning	.05	.15
❑ 93 Stanley Roberts	.01	.05
❑ 94 Loy Vaught	.01	.05
❑ 95 Randy Woods	.01	.05
❑ 96 Sam Bowie	.01	.05
❑ 97 Doug Christie	.05	.15
❑ 98 Vlade Divac	.05	.15
❑ 99 Anthony Peeler	.01	.05
❑ 100 Sedale Threatt	.01	.05
❑ 101 James Worthy	.10	.30
❑ 102 Grant Long	.01	.05
❑ 103 Harold Miner	.01	.05
❑ 104 Glen Rice	.05	.15
❑ 105 John Salley	.01	.05
❑ 106 Rony Seikaly	.01	.05
❑ 107 Steve Smith	.10	.30
❑ 108 Anthony Avent	.01	.05
❑ 109 Jon Barry	.01	.05
❑ 110 Frank Brickowski	.01	.05
❑ 111 Blue Edwards	.01	.05
❑ 112 Todd Day	.01	.05
❑ 113 Lee Mayberry	.01	.05
❑ 114 Eric Murdock	.01	.05
❑ 115 Thurl Bailey	.01	.05
❑ 116 Christian Laettner	.05	.15
❑ 117 Chuck Person	.01	.05
❑ 118 Doug West	.01	.05
❑ 119 Micheal Williams	.01	.05
❑ 120 Kenny Anderson	.05	.15
❑ 121 Benoit Benjamin	.01	.05
❑ 122 Derrick Coleman	.05	.15
❑ 123 Chris Morris	.01	.05
❑ 124 Rumeal Robinson	.01	.05
❑ 125 Rolando Blackman	.01	.05
❑ 126 Patrick Ewing	.10	.30
❑ 127 Anthony Mason	.05	.15
❑ 128 Charles Oakley	.05	.15
❑ 129 Doc Rivers	.05	.15
❑ 130 Charles Smith	.01	.05
❑ 131 John Starks	.05	.15
❑ 132 Nick Anderson	.05	.15
❑ 133 Shaquille O'Neal	.60	1.50
❑ 134 Donald Royal	.01	.05
❑ 135 Dennis Scott	.01	.05
❑ 136 Scott Skiles	.01	.05
❑ 137 Brian Williams	.01	.05
❑ 138 Johnny Dawkins	.01	.05
❑ 139 Hersey Hawkins	.05	.15
❑ 140 Jeff Hornacek	.05	.15
❑ 141 Andrew Lang	.01	.05
❑ 142 Tim Perry	.01	.05
❑ 143 Clarence Weatherspoon	.01	.05
❑ 144 Danny Ainge	.05	.15
❑ 145 Charles Barkley	.20	.50
❑ 146 Cedric Ceballos	.05	.15
❑ 147 Kevin Johnson	.05	.15
❑ 148 Oliver Miller	.01	.05
❑ 149 Dan Majerle	.05	.15
❑ 150 Clyde Drexler	.10	.30
❑ 151 Harvey Grant	.01	.05
❑ 152 Jerome Kersey	.01	.05
❑ 153 Terry Porter	.01	.05
❑ 154 Clifford Robinson	.05	.15
❑ 155 Rod Strickland	.05	.15
❑ 156 Buck Williams	.01	.05
❑ 157 Mitch Richmond	.10	.30
❑ 158 Lionel Simmons	.01	.05
❑ 159 Wayman Tisdale	.01	.05
❑ 160 Spud Webb	.05	.15
❑ 161 Walt Williams	.01	.05
❑ 162 Antoine Carr	.01	.05
❑ 163 Lloyd Daniels	.01	.05
❑ 164 Sean Elliott	.05	.15
❑ 165 Dale Ellis	.01	.05
❑ 166 Avery Johnson	.01	.05
❑ 167 J.R. Reid	.01	.05
❑ 168 David Robinson	.20	.50
❑ 169 Shawn Kemp	.20	.50
❑ 170 Derrick McKey	.01	.05
❑ 171 Nate McMillan	.01	.05
❑ 172 Gary Payton	.20	.50
❑ 173 Sam Perkins	.05	.15
❑ 174 Ricky Pierce	.01	.05
❑ 175 Tyrone Corbin	.01	.05
❑ 176 Jay Humphries	.01	.05
❑ 177 Jeff Malone	.01	.05
❑ 178 Karl Malone	.20	.50
❑ 179 John Stockton	.10	.30
❑ 180 Michael Adams	.01	.05
❑ 181 Kevin Duckworth	.01	.05
❑ 182 Pervis Ellison	.01	.05
❑ 183 Tom Gugliotta	.10	.30
❑ 184 Don MacLean	.01	.05
❑ 185 Brent Price	.01	.05
❑ 186 George Lynch RC	.01	.05
❑ 187 Rex Walters RC	.01	.05
❑ 188 Shawn Bradley RC	.10	.30
❑ 189 Ervin Johnson RC	.05	.15
❑ 190 Luther Wright RC	.01	.05
❑ 191 Calbert Cheaney RC	.05	.15
❑ 192 Craig Ehlo	.01	.05
❑ 193 Duane Ferrell	.01	.05
❑ 194 Paul Graham	.01	.05
❑ 195 Andrew Lang	.01	.05
❑ 196 Chris Corchiani	.01	.05
❑ 197 Acie Earl RC	.01	.05
❑ 198 Dino Radja RC	.01	.05
❑ 199 Ed Pinckney	.01	.05
❑ 200 Tony Bennett	.01	.05
❑ 201 Scott Burrell RC	.10	.30
❑ 202 Kenny Gattison	.01	.05
❑ 203 Hersey Hawkins	.05	.15
❑ 204 Eddie Johnson	.01	.05
❑ 205 Corie Blount RC	.01	.05
❑ 206 Steve Kerr	.05	.15
❑ 207 Toni Kukoc RC	.50	1.25
❑ 208 Pete Myers	.01	.05
❑ 209 Danny Ferry	.01	.05
❑ 210 Tyrone Hill	.01	.05
❑ 211 Gerald Madkins RC	.01	.05
❑ 212 Chris Mills RC	.10	.30
❑ 213 Lucious Harris RC	.01	.05
❑ 214 Popeye Jones RC	.01	.05
❑ 215 Jamal Mashburn RC	.30	.75
❑ 216 Darnell Mee RC	.01	.05
❑ 217 Rodney Rogers RC	.10	.30
❑ 218 Brian Williams	.01	.05
❑ 219 Greg Anderson	.01	.05
❑ 220 Sean Elliott	.05	.15
❑ 221 Allan Houston RC	.50	1.25
❑ 222 Lindsey Hunter RC	.10	.30
❑ 223 Chris Gatling	.01	.05
❑ 224 Josh Grant RC	.01	.05
❑ 225 Keith Jennings	.01	.05
❑ 226 Avery Johnson	.01	.05
❑ 227 Chris Webber RC	1.25	3.00
❑ 228 Sam Cassell RC	.50	1.25
❑ 229 Mario Elie	.01	.05
❑ 230 Richard Petruska RC	.01	.05
❑ 231 Eric Riley RC	.01	.05
❑ 232 Antonio Davis RC	.15	.40
❑ 233 Scott Haskin RC	.01	.05
❑ 234 Derrick McKey	.01	.05
❑ 235 Mark Aguirre	.01	.05
❑ 236 Terry Dehere RC	.01	.05
❑ 237 Gary Grant	.01	.05
❑ 238 Randy Woods	.01	.05
❑ 239 Sam Bowie	.01	.05
❑ 240 Elden Campbell	.01	.05
❑ 241 Nick Van Exel RC	.40	1.00
❑ 242 Manute Bol	.01	.05
❑ 243 Brian Shaw	.01	.05
❑ 244 Vin Baker RC	.30	.75
❑ 245 Brad Lohaus	.01	.05
❑ 246 Ken Norman	.01	.05
❑ 247 Derek Strong RC	.01	.05
❑ 248 Danny Schayes	.01	.05
❑ 249 Mike Brown	.01	.05
❑ 250 Luc Longley	.05	.15
❑ 251 Isaiah Rider RC	.25	.60
❑ 252 Kevin Edwards	.01	.05
❑ 253 Armon Gilliam	.01	.05
❑ 254 Greg Anthony	.01	.05
❑ 255 Anthony Bonner	.01	.05
❑ 256 Tony Campbell	.01	.05
❑ 257 Hubert Davis	.01	.05
❑ 258 Litterial Green	.01	.05
❑ 259 Anfernee Hardaway RC	1.00	2.50
❑ 260 Larry Krystkowiak	.01	.05
❑ 261 Todd Lichti	.01	.05
❑ 262 Dana Barros	.01	.05
❑ 263 Greg Graham RC	.01	.05
❑ 264 Warren Kidd RC	.01	.05
❑ 265 Moses Malone	.10	.30
❑ 266 A.C. Green	.05	.15
❑ 267 Joe Kleine	.01	.05
❑ 268 Malcolm Mackey RC	.01	.05
❑ 269 Mark Bryant	.01	.05
❑ 270 Chris Dudley	.01	.05
❑ 271 Harvey Grant	.01	.05
❑ 272 James Robinson RC	.01	.05
❑ 273 Duane Causwell	.01	.05
❑ 274 Bobby Hurley RC	.05	.15
❑ 275 Jim Les	.01	.05
❑ 276 Willie Anderson	.01	.05
❑ 277 Terry Cummings	.01	.05
❑ 278 Vinny Del Negro	.01	.05
❑ 279 Sleepy Floyd	.01	.05
❑ 280 Dennis Rodman	.25	.60
❑ 281 Vincent Askew	.01	.05
❑ 282 Kendall Gill	.05	.15
❑ 283 Steve Scheffler	.01	.05
❑ 284 Detlef Schrempf	.05	.15
❑ 285 David Benoit	.01	.05
❑ 286 Tom Chambers	.01	.05
❑ 287 Felton Spencer	.01	.05
❑ 288 Rex Chapman	.01	.05

289 Kevin Duckworth	.01	.05
290 Gheorghe Muresan RC	.10	.30
291 Kenny Walker	.01	.05
292 Andrew Lang CF	.01	.05
293 D.Radja/A.Earl CF	.01	.05
294 Eddie Johnson CF	.01	.05
295 T.Kukoc/C.Blount CF	.10	.30
296 Tyrone Hill CF	.01	.05
297 J.Mashburn/P.Jones CF	.10	.30
298 Darnell Mee CF	.01	.05
299 L.Hunter/A.Houston CF	.05	.15
300 C.Webber/A.Johnson CF	.25	.60
301 Sam Cassell CF	.10	.30
302 Derrick McKey CF	.01	.05
303 Terry Dehere CF	.01	.05
304 N.Van Exel/G.Lynch CF	.10	.30
305 Harold Miner CF	.01	.05
306 K.Norman/V.Baker CF	.05	.15
307 M.Brown/I.Rider CF	.05	.15
308 Kevin Edwards CF	.01	.05
309 Hubert Davis CF	.01	.05
310 A.Hardaway/L.Kryst. CF	.40	1.00
311 M.Malone/S.Bradley CF	.10	.30
312 Joe Kleine CF	.01	.05
313 Harvey Grant CF	.01	.05
314 B.Hurley/M.Richmond CF	.10	.30
315 S.Floyd/D.Rodman CF	.10	.30
316 Kendall Gill CF	.01	.05
317 Felton Spencer CF	.01	.05
318 C.Cheaney/Duckworth CF	.01	.05
319 Karl Malone PC	.10	.30
320 Alonzo Mourning PC	.10	.30
321 Scottie Pippen PC	.20	.50
322 Mark Price PC	.01	.05
323 LaPhonso Ellis PC	.01	.05
324 Joe Dumars PC	.05	.15
325 Chris Mullin PC	.05	.15
326 Ron Harper PC	.01	.05
327 Glen Rice PC	.01	.05
328 Christian Laettner PC	.01	.05
329 Kenny Anderson PC	.01	.05
330 John Starks PC	.01	.05
331 Shaquille O'Neal PC	.25	.60
332 Charles Barkley PC	.10	.30
333 Clifford Robinson PC	.01	.05
334 Clyde Drexler PC	.05	.15
335 Mitch Richmond PC	.05	.15
336 David Robinson PC	.10	.30
337 Shawn Kemp PC	.10	.30
338 John Stockton PC	.05	.15
339 Checklist 4	.01	.05
340 Checklist 5	.01	.05
341 Checklist 6	.01	.05
DP4 Jim Jackson 1992	.60	1.50
DP17 Doug Christie 1992	.15	.40
NNO Expired HOC Exchange	.60	1.50
NNO Head of Class Card	15.00	30.00

1994-95 SkyBox Premium

COMPLETE SET (350)	15.00	30.00
COMPLETE SERIES 1 (200)	7.50	15.00
COMPLETE SERIES 2 (150)	7.50	15.00
COMMON CARD (1-200)	.02	.10
COMMON CARD (201-350)	.01	.05
1 Stacey Augmon	.02	.10
2 Mookie Blaylock	.02	.10
3 Doug Edwards	.02	.10
4 Craig Ehlo	.02	.10
5 Adam Keefe	.02	.10
6 Danny Manning	.07	.20
7 Kevin Willis	.02	.10
8 Dee Brown	.02	.10
9 Sherman Douglas	.02	.10
10 Acie Earl	.02	.10
11 Kevin Gamble	.02	.10
12 Xavier McDaniel	.02	.10
13 Dino Radja	.02	.10
14 Muggsy Bogues	.07	.20
15 Scott Burrell	.02	.10
16 Dell Curry	.02	.10
17 LeRon Ellis	.02	.10
18 Hersey Hawkins	.07	.20
19 Larry Johnson	.07	.20
20 Alonzo Mourning	.20	.50
21 B.J. Armstrong	.02	.10
22 Corie Blount	.02	.10
23 Horace Grant	.07	.20
24 Toni Kukoc	.25	.60
25 Luc Longley	.02	.10
26 Scottie Pippen	.50	1.25
27 Scott Williams	.02	.10
28 Terrell Brandon	.07	.20
29 Brad Daugherty	.02	.10
30 Tyrone Hill	.02	.10
31 Chris Mills	.07	.20
32 Bobby Phills	.02	.10
33 Mark Price	.02	.10
34 Gerald Wilkins	.02	.10
35 Lucious Harris	.02	.10
36 Jim Jackson	.07	.20
37 Popeye Jones	.02	.10
38 Jamal Mashburn	.15	.40
39 Sean Rooks	.02	.10
40 Mahmoud Abdul-Rauf	.02	.10
41 LaPhonso Ellis	.02	.10
42 Dikembe Mutombo	.07	.20
43 Robert Pack	.02	.10
44 Rodney Rogers	.02	.10
45 Bryant Stith	.02	.10
46 Reggie Williams	.02	.10
47 Joe Dumars	.15	.40
48 Sean Elliott	.07	.20
49 Allan Houston	.25	.60
50 Lindsey Hunter	.07	.20
51 Terry Mills	.02	.10
52 Victor Alexander	.02	.10
53 Tim Hardaway	.15	.40
54 Chris Mullin	.15	.40
55 Billy Owens	.02	.10
56 Latrell Sprewell	.15	.40
57 Chris Webber	.40	1.00
58 Sam Cassell	.15	.40
59 Carl Herrera	.02	.10
60 Robert Horry	.07	.20
61 Vernon Maxwell	.02	.10
62 Hakeem Olajuwon	.25	.60
63 Kenny Smith	.02	.10
64 Otis Thorpe	.02	.10
65 Antonio Davis	.02	.10
66 Dale Davis	.02	.10
67 Derrick McKey	.02	.10
68 Reggie Miller	.15	.40
69 Pooh Richardson	.02	.10
70 Rik Smits	.02	.10
71 Haywoode Workman	.02	.10
72 Terry Dehere	.02	.10
73 Harold Ellis	.02	.10
74 Ron Harper	.07	.20
75 Mark Jackson	.02	.10
76 Loy Vaught	.02	.10
77 Dominique Wilkins	.15	.40
78 Elden Campbell	.02	.10
79 Doug Christie	.07	.20
80 Vlade Divac	.02	.10
81 George Lynch	.02	.10
82 Anthony Peeler	.02	.10
83 Sedale Threatt	.02	.10
84 Nick Van Exel	.15	.40
85 Harold Miner	.02	.10
86 Glen Rice	.07	.20
87 John Salley	.02	.10
88 Rony Seikaly	.02	.10
89 Brian Shaw	.02	.10
90 Steve Smith	.07	.20
91 Vin Baker	.15	.40
92 Jon Barry	.02	.10
93 Todd Day	.02	.10
94 Blue Edwards	.02	.10
95 Lee Mayberry	.02	.10
96 Eric Murdock	.02	.10
97 Mike Brown	.02	.10
98 Stacey King	.02	.10
99 Christian Laettner	.07	.20
100 Isaiah Rider	.07	.20
101 Doug West	.02	.10
102 Micheal Williams	.02	.10
103 Kenny Anderson	.07	.20
104 P.J. Brown	.02	.10
105 Derrick Coleman	.07	.20
106 Kevin Edwards	.02	.10
107 Chris Morris	.02	.10
108 Rex Walters	.02	.10
109 Hubert Davis	.02	.10
110 Patrick Ewing	.15	.40
111 Derek Harper	.02	.10
112 Anthony Mason	.07	.20
113 Charles Oakley	.02	.10
114 Charles Smith	.02	.10
115 John Starks	.02	.10
116 Nick Anderson	.02	.10
117 Anfernee Hardaway	.40	1.00
118 Shaquille O'Neal	.75	2.00
119 Donald Royal	.02	.10
120 Dennis Scott	.02	.10
121 Scott Skiles	.02	.10
122 Dana Barros	.02	.10
123 Shawn Bradley	.02	.10
124 Johnny Dawkins	.02	.10
125 Greg Graham	.02	.10
126 Clarence Weatherspoon	.02	.10
127 Danny Ainge	.02	.10
128 Charles Barkley	.25	.60
129 Cedric Ceballos	.02	.10
130 A.C. Green	.07	.20
131 Kevin Johnson	.07	.20
132 Dan Majerle	.07	.20
133 Oliver Miller	.02	.10
134 Clyde Drexler	.15	.40
135 Harvey Grant	.02	.10
136 Tracy Murray	.02	.10
137 Terry Porter	.02	.10
138 Clifford Robinson	.07	.20
139 James Robinson	.02	.10
140 Rod Strickland	.07	.20
141 Bobby Hurley	.02	.10
142 Olden Polynice	.02	.10
143 Mitch Richmond	.15	.40
144 Lionel Simmons	.02	.10
145 Wayman Tisdale	.02	.10
146 Spud Webb	.02	.10
147 Walt Williams	.02	.10
148 Willie Anderson	.02	.10
149 Vinny Del Negro	.02	.10
150 Dale Ellis	.02	.10
151 J.R. Reid	.02	.10
152 David Robinson	.25	.60
153 Dennis Rodman	.30	.75
154 Kendall Gill	.07	.20
155 Shawn Kemp	.25	.60
156 Nate McMillan	.02	.10
157 Gary Payton	.25	.60
158 Sam Perkins	.07	.20
159 Ricky Pierce	.02	.10
160 Detlef Schrempf	.07	.20
161 David Benoit	.02	.10
162 Tyrone Corbin	.02	.10
163 Jeff Hornacek	.07	.20
164 Jay Humphries	.02	.10
165 Karl Malone	.25	.60
166 Bryon Russell	.02	.10
167 Felton Spencer	.02	.10
168 John Stockton	.15	.40
169 Michael Adams	.02	.10
170 Rex Chapman	.02	.10
171 Calbert Cheaney	.02	.10
172 Pervis Ellison	.02	.10
173 Tom Gugliotta	.07	.20
174 Don MacLean	.02	.10
175 Gheorghe Muresan	.02	.10
176 Charles Barkley PO	.15	.40
177 Charles Oakley NBC	.02	.10
178 Hakeem Olajuwon PO	.15	.40
179 Dikembe Mutombo NBC	.02	.10
180 Scottie Pippen PO	.25	.60
181 Sam Cassell NBC	.15	.40
182 Karl Malone NBC	.15	.40
183 Reggie Miller PO	.07	.20
184 Patrick Ewing PO	.07	.20
185 Vernon Maxwell NBC	.02	.10
186 A.Hardaway/S.Smith DD	.15	.40
187 S.O'Neal/C.Webber DD	.15	.40
188 R.Rogers/J.Mashburn DD	.02	.10
189 Toni Kukoc DD	.07	.20
190 Lindsey Hunter DD	.02	.10

❑ 191 L.Sprewell/J.Jackson DD .07 .20
❑ 192 C.Weatherspoon/V.Baker DD .07 .20
❑ 193 Calbert Cheaney DD .02 .10
❑ 194 Isaiah Rider DD .07 .20
❑ 195 Sam Cassell DD .02 .10
❑ 196 Gheorghe Muresan DD .02 .10
❑ 197 LaPhonso Ellis DD .02 .10
❑ 198 USA Basketball Card .02 .10
❑ 199 Checklist .02 .10
❑ 200 Checklist .02 .10
❑ 201 Sergei Bazarevich RC .01 .05
❑ 202 Tyrone Corbin .01 .05
❑ 203 Grant Long .01 .05
❑ 204 Ken Norman .01 .05
❑ 205 Steve Smith .02 .10
❑ 206 Blue Edwards .01 .05
❑ 207 Greg Minor RC .01 .05
❑ 208 Eric Montross RC .01 .05
❑ 209 Dominique Wilkins .08 .25
❑ 210 Michael Adams .01 .05
❑ 211 Kenny Gattison .01 .05
❑ 212 Darrin Hancock .01 .05
❑ 213 Robert Parish .02 .10
❑ 214 Ron Harper .02 .10
❑ 215 Steve Kerr .01 .05
❑ 216 Will Perdue .01 .05
❑ 217 Dickey Simpkins RC .01 .05
❑ 218 John Battle .01 .05
❑ 219 Michael Cage .01 .05
❑ 220 Tony Dumas RC .01 .05
❑ 221 Jason Kidd RC 1.00 2.50
❑ 222 Roy Tarpley .01 .05
❑ 223 Dale Ellis .01 .05
❑ 224 Jalen Rose RC .40 1.00
❑ 225 Bill Curley RC .01 .05
❑ 226 Grant Hill RC .50 1.25
❑ 227 Oliver Miller .01 .05
❑ 228 Mark West .01 .05
❑ 229 Tom Gugliotta .02 .10
❑ 230 Ricky Pierce .01 .05
❑ 231 Carlos Rogers RC .01 .05
❑ 232 Clifford Rozier RC .01 .05
❑ 233 Rony Seikaly .01 .05
❑ 234 Tim Breaux .01 .05
❑ 235 Duane Ferrell .01 .05
❑ 236 Mark Jackson .01 .05
❑ 237 Byron Scott .02 .10
❑ 238 John Williams .01 .05
❑ 239 Lamond Murray RC .02 .10
❑ 240 Eric Piatkowski RC .01 .05
❑ 241 Pooh Richardson .01 .05
❑ 242 Malik Sealy .01 .05
❑ 243 Cedric Ceballos .01 .05
❑ 244 Eddie Jones RC .50 1.25
❑ 245 Anthony Miller RC .01 .05
❑ 246 Tony Smith .01 .05
❑ 247 Kevin Gamble .01 .05
❑ 248 Brad Lohaus .01 .05
❑ 249 Billy Owens .01 .05
❑ 250 Khalid Reeves RC .01 .05
❑ 251 Kevin Willis .01 .05
❑ 252 Eric Mobley RC .01 .05
❑ 253 Johnny Newman .01 .05
❑ 254 Ed Pinckney .01 .05
❑ 255 Glenn Robinson RC .30 .75
❑ 256 Howard Eisley .01 .05
❑ 257 Donyell Marshall RC .08 .25
❑ 258 Yinka Dare RC .01 .05
❑ 259 Sean Higgins .01 .05
❑ 260 Jayson Williams .02 .10
❑ 261 Charlie Ward RC .08 .25
❑ 262 Monty Williams RC .01 .05
❑ 263 Horace Grant .02 .10
❑ 264 Brian Shaw .01 .05
❑ 265 Brooks Thompson RC .01 .05
❑ 266 Derrick Alston RC .01 .05
❑ 267 B.J.Tyler RC .01 .05
❑ 268 Scott Williams .01 .05
❑ 269 Sharone Wright RC .01 .05
❑ 270 Antonio Lang RC .01 .05
❑ 271 Danny Manning .02 .10
❑ 272 Wesley Person RC .08 .25
❑ 273 Trevor Ruffin RC .01 .05
❑ 274 Wayman Tisdale .01 .05
❑ 275 Jerome Kersey .01 .05
❑ 276 Aaron McKie RC .20 .50
❑ 277 Frank Brickowski .01 .05
❑ 278 Brian Grant RC .25 .60
❑ 279 Michael Smith RC .01 .05
❑ 280 Terry Cummings .01 .05
❑ 281 Sean Elliott .02 .10
❑ 282 Avery Johnson .01 .05
❑ 283 Moses Malone .08 .25
❑ 284 Chuck Person .01 .05
❑ 285 Vincent Askew .01 .05
❑ 286 Bill Cartwright .01 .05
❑ 287 Sarunas Marciulionis .01 .05
❑ 288 Dontonio Wingfield RC .01 .05
❑ 289 Jay Humphries .01 .05
❑ 290 Adam Keefe .01 .05
❑ 291 Jamie Watson RC .01 .05
❑ 292 Kevin Duckworth .01 .05
❑ 293 Juwan Howard RC .25 .60
❑ 294 Jim McIlvaine .01 .05
❑ 295 Scott Skiles .01 .05
❑ 296 Anthony Tucker RC .01 .05
❑ 297 Chris Webber .25 .60
❑ 298 Checklist 201-265 .01 .05
❑ 299 Checklist 266-345 .01 .05
❑ 300 Checklist 346-350/Inserts .01 .05
❑ 301 Vin Baker SSL .02 .10
❑ 302 Charles Barkley SSL .08 .25
❑ 303 Derrick Coleman SSL .01 .05
❑ 304 Clyde Drexler SSL .02 .10
❑ 305 LaPhonso Ellis SSL .01 .05
❑ 306 Larry Johnson SSL .01 .05
❑ 307 Shawn Kemp SSL .08 .25
❑ 308 Karl Malone SSL .08 .25
❑ 309 Jamal Mashburn SSL .02 .10
❑ 310 Scottie Pippen SSL .15 .40
❑ 311 Dominique Wilkins SSL .02 .10
❑ 312 Walt Williams SSL .01 .05
❑ 313 Sharone Wright SSL .01 .05
❑ 314 B.J. Armstrong SSH .01 .05
❑ 315 Joe Dumars SSH .02 .10
❑ 316 Tony Dumas SSH .01 .05
❑ 317 Tim Hardaway SSH .02 .10
❑ 318 Toni Kukoc SSH .08 .25
❑ 319 Danny Manning SSH .01 .05
❑ 320 Reggie Miller SSH .02 .10
❑ 321 Chris Mullin SSH .02 .10
❑ 322 Wesley Person SSH .02 .10
❑ 323 John Starks SSH .01 .05
❑ 324 John Stockton SSH .02 .10
❑ 325 Clarence Weatherspoon SSH .01 .05
❑ 326 Shawn Bradley SSW .01 .05
❑ 327 Vlade Divac SSW .01 .05
❑ 328 Patrick Ewing SSW .02 .10
❑ 329 Christian Laettner SSW .01 .05
❑ 330 Eric Montross SSW .01 .05
❑ 331 Gheorghe Muresan SSW .01 .05
❑ 332 Dikembe Mutombo SSW .01 .05
❑ 333 Hakeem Olajuwon SSW .08 .25
❑ 334 Robert Parish SSW .01 .05
❑ 335 David Robinson SSW .08 .25
❑ 336 Dennis Rodman SSW .08 .25
❑ 337 Rony Seikaly SSW .01 .05
❑ 338 Rik Smits SSW .02 .10
❑ 339 Kenny Anderson SPI .01 .05
❑ 340 Dee Brown SPI .01 .05
❑ 341 Bobby Hurley SPI .01 .05
❑ 342 Kevin Johnson SPI .01 .05
❑ 343 Jason Kidd SPI .40 1.00
❑ 344 Gary Payton SPI .08 .25
❑ 345 Mark Price SPI .01 .05
❑ 346 Khalid Reeves SPI .01 .05
❑ 347 Jalen Rose SPI .02 .10
❑ 348 Latrell Sprewell SPI .08 .25
❑ 349 B.J. Tyler SPI .01 .05
❑ 350 Charlie Ward SPI .02 .10
❑ GHO Grant Hill Gold 5.00 12.00
❑ NNO Grant Hill Hoops JUMBO 2.50 6.00
❑ NNO Grant Hill SkyBox JUMBO 2.50 6.00
❑ NNO H.Olajuwon Gold 4.00 10.00
❑ NNO G.Hill Slammin' Univ. JUMBO 2.50 6.00
❑ NNO Emotion Sheet A 15.00 30.00
❑ NNO Emotion Sheet B 15.00 30.00
❑ NNO Exp.Emotion Exch.A .40 1.00
❑ NNO Exp.Emotion Exch.B .40 1.00
❑ NNO Exp.Emotion Exch.C .40 1.00
❑ NNO Exp.3rd Prize Game Card .08 .25
❑ NNO Olajuwon/D.Rob AU 150.00 300.00
❑ NNO M.Johnson Exch.Card 2.00 5.00
❑ NNO Three-Card Panel Exch. 1.50 4.00

1995-96 SkyBox Premium

❑ COMPLETE SET (301) 17.50 35.00
❑ COMPLETE SERIES 1 (150) 7.50 15.00
❑ COMPLETE SERIES 2 (151) 10.00 20.00
❑ 1 Stacey Augmon .07 .20
❑ 2 Mookie Blaylock .07 .20
❑ 3 Grant Long .07 .20
❑ 4 Steve Smith .15 .40
❑ 5 Dee Brown .07 .20
❑ 6 Sherman Douglas .07 .20
❑ 7 Eric Montross .07 .20
❑ 8 Dino Radja .07 .20
❑ 9 Dominique Wilkins .25 .60
❑ 10 Muggsy Bogues .15 .40
❑ 11 Scott Burrell .07 .20
❑ 12 Dell Curry .07 .20
❑ 13 Larry Johnson .15 .40
❑ 14 Alonzo Mourning .15 .40
❑ 15 Michael Jordan 1.50 4.00
❑ 16 Steve Kerr .15 .40
❑ 17 Toni Kukoc .15 .40
❑ 18 Scottie Pippen .40 1.00
❑ 19 Terrell Brandon .15 .40
❑ 20 Tyrone Hill .07 .20
❑ 21 Chris Mills .07 .20
❑ 22 Mark Price .15 .40
❑ 23 John Williams .07 .20
❑ 24 Tony Dumas .07 .20
❑ 25 Jim Jackson .07 .20
❑ 26 Popeye Jones .07 .20
❑ 27 Jason Kidd .75 2.00
❑ 28 Jamal Mashburn .15 .40
❑ 29 LaPhonso Ellis .07 .20
❑ 30 Dikembe Mutombo .15 .40
❑ 31 Robert Pack .07 .20
❑ 32 Jalen Rose .30 .75
❑ 33 Bryant Stith .07 .20
❑ 34 Joe Dumars .25 .60
❑ 35 Grant Hill .30 .75
❑ 36 Allan Houston .15 .40
❑ 37 Lindsey Hunter .07 .20
❑ 38 Chris Gatling .07 .20
❑ 39 Tim Hardaway .15 .40
❑ 40 Donyell Marshall .15 .40
❑ 41 Chris Mullin .25 .60
❑ 42 Carlos Rogers .07 .20
❑ 43 Latrell Sprewell .25 .60
❑ 44 Sam Cassell .25 .60
❑ 45 Clyde Drexler .25 .60
❑ 46 Robert Horry .15 .40
❑ 47 Hakeem Olajuwon .25 .60
❑ 48 Kenny Smith .07 .20
❑ 49 Dale Davis .07 .20
❑ 50 Mark Jackson .15 .40
❑ 51 Reggie Miller .25 .60
❑ 52 Rik Smits .15 .40
❑ 53 Lamond Murray .07 .20
❑ 54 Eric Piatkowski .15 .40
❑ 55 Pooh Richardson .07 .20
❑ 56 Rodney Rogers .07 .20
❑ 57 Loy Vaught .07 .20
❑ 58 Elden Campbell .07 .20
❑ 59 Cedric Ceballos .07 .20
❑ 60 Vlade Divac .15 .40
❑ 61 Eddie Jones .30 .75
❑ 62 Anthony Peeler .07 .20
❑ 63 Nick Van Exel .25 .60
❑ 64 Bimbo Coles .07 .20
❑ 65 Billy Owens .07 .20
❑ 66 Khalid Reeves .07 .20
❑ 67 Glen Rice .15 .40
❑ 68 Kevin Willis .15 .40
❑ 69 Vin Baker .15 .40
❑ 70 Todd Day .07 .20
❑ 71 Eric Murdock .07 .20

❑ 72 Glenn Robinson	.25	.60
❑ 73 Tom Gugliotta	.07	.20
❑ 74 Christian Laettner	.15	.40
❑ 75 Isaiah Rider	.07	.20
❑ 76 Doug West	.07	.20
❑ 77 Kenny Anderson	.15	.40
❑ 78 P.J. Brown	.07	.20
❑ 79 Derrick Coleman	.07	.20
❑ 80 Armon Gilliam	.07	.20
❑ 81 Patrick Ewing	.25	.60
❑ 82 Derek Harper	.15	.40
❑ 83 Anthony Mason	.15	.40
❑ 84 Charles Oakley	.07	.20
❑ 85 John Starks	.15	.40
❑ 86 Nick Anderson	.07	.20
❑ 87 Horace Grant	.15	.40
❑ 88 Anfernee Hardaway	.25	.60
❑ 89 Shaquille O'Neal	.60	1.50
❑ 90 Dana Barros	.07	.20
❑ 91 Shawn Bradley	.07	.20
❑ 92 Clarence Weatherspoon	.07	.20
❑ 93 Sharone Wright	.07	.20
❑ 94 Charles Barkley	.30	.75
❑ 95 Kevin Johnson	.15	.40
❑ 96 Dan Majerle	.15	.40
❑ 97 Danny Manning	.15	.40
❑ 98 Wesley Person	.07	.20
❑ 99 Clifford Robinson	.07	.20
❑ 100 Rod Strickland	.07	.20
❑ 101 Otis Thorpe	.07	.20
❑ 102 Buck Williams	.07	.20
❑ 103 Brian Grant	.25	.60
❑ 104 Olden Polynice	.07	.20
❑ 105 Mitch Richmond	.15	.40
❑ 106 Walt Williams	.07	.20
❑ 107 Vinny Del Negro	.07	.20
❑ 108 Sean Elliott	.15	.40
❑ 109 Avery Johnson	.07	.20
❑ 110 David Robinson	.25	.60
❑ 111 Dennis Rodman	.15	.40
❑ 112 Shawn Kemp	.15	.40
❑ 113 Gary Payton	.25	.60
❑ 114 Sam Perkins	.15	.40
❑ 115 Detlef Schrempf	.15	.40
❑ 116 David Benoit	.07	.20
❑ 117 Jeff Hornacek	.15	.40
❑ 118 Karl Malone	.30	.75
❑ 119 John Stockton	.30	.75
❑ 120 Calbert Cheaney	.07	.20
❑ 121 Juwan Howard	.25	.60
❑ 122 Don MacLean	.07	.20
❑ 123 Gheorghe Muresan	.07	.20
❑ 124 Chris Webber	.30	.75
❑ 125 Robert Horry FC	.07	.20
❑ 126 Mark Jackson FC	.07	.20
❑ 127 Steve Smith FC	.07	.20
❑ 128 Lamond Murray FC	.07	.20
❑ 129 Christian Laettner FC	.07	.20
❑ 130 Kenny Anderson FC	.07	.20
❑ 131 Anthony Mason FC	.07	.20
❑ 132 Kevin Johnson FC	.07	.20
❑ 133 Jeff Hornacek FC	.07	.20
❑ 134 Larry Johnson TP	.07	.20
❑ 135 Popeye Jones TP	.07	.20
❑ 136 Allan Houston TP	.07	.20
❑ 137 Chris Gatling TP	.07	.20
❑ 138 Sam Cassell TP	.07	.20
❑ 139 Anthony Peeler TP	.07	.20
❑ 140 Vin Baker TP	.07	.20
❑ 141 Dana Barros TP	.07	.20
❑ 142 Gheorghe Muresan TP	.07	.20
❑ 143 Toronto Raptors	.07	.20
❑ 144 Vancouver Grizzlies	.07	.20
❑ 145 G.Rice/M.Bogues EXP	.15	.40
❑ 146 N.Anderson/C.Laettner EXP	.07	.20
❑ 147 John Salley TF	.07	.20
❑ 148 Greg Anthony TF	.07	.20
❑ 149 Checklist #1	.07	.20
❑ 150 Checklist #2	.07	.20
❑ 151 Craig Ehlo	.07	.20
❑ 152 Spud Webb	.15	.40
❑ 153 Dana Barros	.07	.20
❑ 155 Kendall Gill	.07	.20
❑ 156 Khalid Reeves	.07	.20
❑ 157 Glen Rice	.15	.40
❑ 158 Luc Longley	.07	.20
❑ 159 Dennis Rodman	.15	.40
❑ 160 Dickey Simpkins	.07	.20
❑ 161 Danny Ferry	.07	.20
❑ 162 Dan Majerle	.15	.40
❑ 163 Bobby Phills	.07	.20
❑ 164 Lucious Harris	.07	.20
❑ 165 George McCloud	.07	.20
❑ 166 Mahmoud Abdul-Rauf	.07	.20
❑ 167 Don MacLean	.07	.20
❑ 168 Reggie Williams	.07	.20
❑ 169 Terry Mills	.07	.20
❑ 170 Otis Thorpe	.07	.20
❑ 171 B.J. Armstrong	.07	.20
❑ 172 Rony Seikaly	.07	.20
❑ 173 Chucky Brown	.07	.20
❑ 174 Mario Elie	.07	.20
❑ 175 Antonio Davis	.07	.20
❑ 176 Ricky Pierce	.07	.20
❑ 177 Terry Dehere	.07	.20
❑ 178 Rodney Rogers	.07	.20
❑ 179 Malik Sealy	.07	.20
❑ 180 Brian Williams	.07	.20
❑ 181 Sedale Threatt	.07	.20
❑ 182 Alonzo Mourning	.15	.40
❑ 183 Lee Mayberry	.07	.20
❑ 184 Sean Rooks	.07	.20
❑ 185 Shawn Bradley	.07	.20
❑ 186 Kevin Edwards	.07	.20
❑ 187 Hubert Davis	.07	.20
❑ 188 Charles Smith	.07	.20
❑ 189 Charlie Ward	.07	.20
❑ 190 Dennis Scott	.07	.20
❑ 191 Brian Shaw	.07	.20
❑ 192 Derrick Coleman	.07	.20
❑ 193 Richard Dumas	.07	.20
❑ 194 Vernon Maxwell	.07	.20
❑ 195 A.C. Green	.15	.40
❑ 196 Elliot Perry	.07	.20
❑ 197 John Williams	.07	.20
❑ 198 Aaron McKie	.15	.40
❑ 199 Bobby Hurley	.07	.20
❑ 200 Michael Smith UER front Mike Smith	.07	.20
❑ 201 J.R. Reid	.07	.20
❑ 202 Hersey Hawkins	.07	.20
❑ 203 Willie Anderson	.07	.20
❑ 204 Oliver Miller	.07	.20
❑ 205 Tracy Murray	.07	.20
❑ 206 Alvin Robertson	.07	.20
❑ 207 Carlos Rogers UER	.07	.20
❑ 208 John Salley	.07	.20
❑ 209 Zan Tabak	.07	.20
❑ 210 Adam Keefe	.07	.20
❑ 211 Chris Morris	.07	.20
❑ 212 Greg Anthony	.07	.20
❑ 213 Blue Edwards	.07	.20
❑ 214 Kenny Gattison	.07	.20
❑ 215 Antonio Harvey	.07	.20
❑ 216 Chris King	.07	.20
❑ 217 Byron Scott	.07	.20
❑ 218 Robert Pack	.07	.20
❑ 219 Alan Henderson RC	.25	.60
❑ 220 Eric Williams RC	.15	.40
❑ 221 George Zidek RC	.07	.20
❑ 222 Jason Caffey RC	.15	.40
❑ 223 Bob Sura RC	.15	.40
❑ 224 Cherokee Parks RC	.07	.20
❑ 225 Antonio McDyess RC	.50	1.25
❑ 226 Theo Ratliff RC	.30	.75
❑ 227 Joe Smith RC	.40	1.00
❑ 228 Travis Best RC	.07	.20
❑ 229 Brent Barry RC	.25	.60
❑ 230 Sasha Danilovic RC	.07	.20
❑ 231 Kurt Thomas RC	.15	.40
❑ 232 Shawn Respert RC	.07	.20
❑ 233 Kevin Garnett RC	1.50	4.00
❑ 234 Ed O'Bannon RC	.07	.20
❑ 235 Jerry Stackhouse RC	.75	2.00
❑ 236 Michael Finley RC	.60	1.50
❑ 237 Mario Bennett RC	.07	.20
❑ 238 Randolph Childress RC	.07	.20
❑ 239 Arvydas Sabonis RC	.30	.75
❑ 240 Gary Trent RC	.07	.20
❑ 241 Tyus Edney RC	.07	.20
❑ 242 Corliss Williamson RC	.25	.60
❑ 243 Cory Alexander RC	.07	.20
❑ 244 Damon Stoudamire RC	.50	1.25
❑ 245 Greg Ostertag RC	.07	.20
❑ 246 Lawrence Moten RC	.07	.20
❑ 247 Bryant Reeves RC	.25	.60
❑ 248 Rasheed Wallace RC	.60	1.50
❑ 249 Muggsy Bogues HR	.07	.20
❑ 250 Dell Curry HR	.07	.20
❑ 251 Scottie Pippen HR	.15	.40
❑ 252 Danny Ferry HR	.07	.20
❑ 253 Mahmoud Abdul-Rauf HR	.07	.20
❑ 254 Joe Dumars HR	.15	.40
❑ 255 Tim Hardaway HR	.07	.20
❑ 256 Chris Mullin HR	.15	.40
❑ 257 Hakeem Olajuwon HR	.15	.40
❑ 258 Kenny Smith HR	.07	.20
❑ 259 Reggie Miller HR	.15	.40
❑ 260 Rik Smits HR	.07	.20
❑ 261 Vlade Divac HR	.07	.20
❑ 262 Doug West HR	.07	.20
❑ 263 Patrick Ewing HR	.15	.40
❑ 264 Charles Oakley HR	.07	.20
❑ 265 Nick Anderson HR	.07	.20
❑ 266 Dennis Scott HR	.07	.20
❑ 267 Jeff Turner HR	.07	.20
❑ 268 Charles Barkley HR	.25	.60
❑ 269 Kevin Johnson HR	.07	.20
❑ 270 Clifford Robinson HR	.07	.20
❑ 271 Buck Williams HR	.07	.20
❑ 272 Lionel Simmons HR	.07	.20
❑ 273 David Robinson HR	.15	.40
❑ 274 Gary Payton HR	.15	.40
❑ 275 Karl Malone HR	.25	.60
❑ 276 John Stockton HR	.25	.60
❑ 277 Steve Smith ELE	.07	.20
❑ 278 Michael Jordan ELE	.75	2.00
❑ 279 Jim Jackson ELE	.07	.20
❑ 280 Jason Kidd ELE	.40	1.00
❑ 281 Jamal Mashburn ELE	.07	.20
❑ 282 Dikembe Mutombo ELE	.07	.20
❑ 283 Grant Hill ELE	.25	.60
❑ 284 Tim Hardaway ELE	.07	.20
❑ 285 Clyde Drexler ELE	.15	.40
❑ 286 Cedric Ceballos ELE	.07	.20
❑ 287 Gary Payton ELE	.15	.40
❑ 288 Billy Owens ELE	.07	.20
❑ 289 Vin Baker ELE	.07	.20
❑ 290 Glenn Robinson ELE	.15	.40
❑ 291 Kenny Anderson ELE	.07	.20
❑ 292 Anfernee Hardaway ELE	.15	.40
❑ 293 Shaquille O'Neal ELE	.25	.60
❑ 294 Charles Barkley ELE	.25	.60
❑ 295 Rod Strickland ELE	.07	.20
❑ 296 Mitch Richmond ELE	.07	.20
❑ 297 Juwan Howard ELE	.15	.40
❑ 298 Chris Webber ELE	.25	.60
❑ 299 Checklist #1	.07	.20
❑ 300 Checklist #2	.07	.20
❑ 301 Magic Johnson	.40	1.00
❑ PR Grant Hill JUMBO	2.50	6.00
❑ NNO G.Hill Melt.Exch	10.00	25.00
❑ NNO J.Stackhouse Melt.Exch	12.50	30.00

1996-97 SkyBox Premium

❑ COMPLETE SET (281)	20.00	35.00
❑ COMPLETE SERIES 1 (131)	12.50	25.00
❑ COMPLETE SERIES 2 (150)	7.50	15.00
❑ 1 Mookie Blaylock	.07	.20
❑ 2 Alan Henderson	.07	.20
❑ 3 Christian Laettner	.15	.40
❑ 4 Dikembe Mutombo	.15	.40
❑ 5 Steve Smith	.15	.40
❑ 6 Dana Barros	.07	.20
❑ 7 Rick Fox	.07	.20
❑ 8 Dino Radja	.07	.20
❑ 9 Antoine Walker RC	.60	1.50
❑ 10 Eric Williams	.07	.20
❑ 11 Dell Curry	.07	.20
❑ 12 Tony Delk RC	.25	.60
❑ 13 Matt Geiger	.07	.20
❑ 14 Glen Rice	.15	.40
❑ 15 Ron Harper	.15	.40
❑ 16 Michael Jordan	1.50	4.00

❑ 17 Toni Kukoc	.15	.40
❑ 18 Scottie Pippen	.40	1.00
❑ 19 Dennis Rodman	.15	.40
❑ 20 Terrell Brandon	.15	.40
❑ 21 Danny Ferry	.07	.20
❑ 22 Chris Mills	.07	.20
❑ 23 Bobby Phills	.07	.20
❑ 24 Vitaly Potapenko RC	.07	.20
❑ 25 Jim Jackson	.07	.20
❑ 26 Jason Kidd	.40	1.00
❑ 27 Jamal Mashburn	.15	.40
❑ 28 George McCloud	.07	.20
❑ 29 Samaki Walker RC	.07	.20
❑ 30 LaPhonso Ellis	.07	.20
❑ 31 Antonio McDyess	.15	.40
❑ 32 Bryant Stith	.07	.20
❑ 33 Joe Dumars	.25	.60
❑ 34 Grant Hill	.25	.60
❑ 35 Lindsey Hunter	.07	.20
❑ 36 Theo Ratliff	.15	.40
❑ 37 Otis Thorpe	.07	.20
❑ 38 Todd Fuller RC	.07	.20
❑ 39 Chris Mullin	.25	.60
❑ 40 Joe Smith	.15	.40
❑ 41 Latrell Sprewell	.25	.60
❑ 42 Charles Barkley	.30	.75
❑ 43 Clyde Drexler	.25	.60
❑ 44 Mario Elie	.07	.20
❑ 45 Hakeem Olajuwon	.25	.60
❑ 46 Erick Dampier RC	.25	.60
❑ 47 Dale Davis	.07	.20
❑ 48 Derrick McKey	.07	.20
❑ 49 Reggie Miller	.25	.60
❑ 50 Rik Smits	.15	.40
❑ 51 Brent Barry	.07	.20
❑ 52 Rodney Rogers	.07	.20
❑ 53 Loy Vaught	.07	.20
❑ 54 Lorenzen Wright RC	.15	.40
❑ 55 Kobe Bryant RC	8.00	20.00
❑ 56 Cedric Ceballos	.07	.20
❑ 57 Eddie Jones	.25	.60
❑ 58 Shaquille O'Neal	.60	1.50
❑ 59 Nick Van Exel	.25	.60
❑ 60 Tim Hardaway	.15	.40
❑ 61 Alonzo Mourning	.15	.40
❑ 62 Kurt Thomas	.15	.40
❑ 63 Ray Allen RC	1.00	2.50
❑ 64 Vin Baker	.15	.40
❑ 65 Shawn Respert	.07	.20
❑ 66 Glenn Robinson	.25	.60
❑ 67 Kevin Garnett	.50	1.25
❑ 68 Tom Gugliotta	.07	.20
❑ 69 Stephon Marbury RC	.60	1.50
❑ 70 Sam Mitchell	.07	.20
❑ 71 Shawn Bradley	.07	.20
❑ 72 Kendall Gill	.07	.20
❑ 73 Kerry Kittles RC	.25	.60
❑ 74 Ed O'Bannon	.07	.20
❑ 75 Patrick Ewing	.25	.60
❑ 76 Larry Johnson	.15	.40
❑ 77 Charles Oakley	.07	.20
❑ 78 John Starks	.15	.40
❑ 79 John Wallace RC	.25	.60
❑ 80 Nick Anderson	.07	.20
❑ 81 Horace Grant	.15	.40
❑ 82 Anfernee Hardaway	.25	.60
❑ 83 Dennis Scott	.07	.20
❑ 84 Derrick Coleman	.15	.40
❑ 85 Allen Iverson RC	1.00	2.50
❑ 86 Jerry Stackhouse	.30	.75
❑ 87 Clarence Weatherspoon	.07	.20
❑ 88 Michael Finley	.30	.75
❑ 89 Robert Horry	.15	.40
❑ 90 Kevin Johnson	.15	.40
❑ 91 Steve Nash RC	2.00	5.00
❑ 92 Wesley Person	.07	.20
❑ 93 Aaron McKie	.15	.40
❑ 94 Jermaine O'Neal RC	.60	1.50
❑ 95 Clifford Robinson	.07	.20
❑ 96 Arvydas Sabonis	.15	.40
❑ 97 Gary Trent	.07	.20
❑ 98 Tyus Edney	.07	.20
❑ 99 Brian Grant	.25	.60
❑ 100 Mitch Richmond	.15	.40
❑ 101 Billy Owens	.07	.20
❑ 102 Corliss Williamson	.15	.40
❑ 103 Vinny Del Negro	.07	.20
❑ 104 Sean Elliott	.15	.40
❑ 105 Avery Johnson	.07	.20
❑ 106 Chuck Person	.07	.20
❑ 107 David Robinson	.25	.60
❑ 108 Hersey Hawkins	.15	.40
❑ 109 Shawn Kemp	.15	.40
❑ 110 Gary Payton	.25	.60
❑ 111 Sam Perkins	.15	.40
❑ 112 Detlef Schrempf	.15	.40
❑ 113 Marcus Camby RC	.30	.75
❑ 114 Carlos Rogers	.07	.20
❑ 115 Damon Stoudamire	.25	.60
❑ 116 Zan Tabak	.07	.20
❑ 117 Antoine Carr	.07	.20
❑ 118 Jeff Hornacek	.15	.40
❑ 119 Karl Malone	.25	.60
❑ 120 Chris Morris	.07	.20
❑ 121 John Stockton	.25	.60
❑ 122 Shareef Abdur-Rahim RC	.75	2.00
❑ 123 Greg Anthony	.07	.20
❑ 124 Bryant Reeves	.07	.20
❑ 125 Roy Rogers RC	.07	.20
❑ 126 Calbert Cheaney	.07	.20
❑ 127 Juwan Howard	.15	.40
❑ 128 Gheorghe Muresan	.07	.20
❑ 129 Chris Webber	.25	.60
❑ 130 Checklist	.07	.20
❑ 131 Checklist	.07	.20
❑ 132 Jon Barry	.07	.20
❑ 133 Christian Laettner	.15	.40
❑ 134 Dikembe Mutombo	.15	.40
❑ 135 Dee Brown	.07	.20
❑ 136 Todd Day	.07	.20
❑ 137 David Wesley	.07	.20
❑ 138 Vlade Divac	.07	.20
❑ 139 Anthony Goldwire	.07	.20
❑ 140 Anthony Mason	.15	.40
❑ 141 Jason Caffey	.07	.20
❑ 142 Luc Longley	.07	.20
❑ 143 Tyrone Hill	.07	.20
❑ 144 Antonio Lang	.07	.20
❑ 145 Sam Cassell	.25	.60
❑ 146 Chris Gatling	.07	.20
❑ 147 Eric Montross	.07	.20
❑ 148 Ervin Johnson	.07	.20
❑ 149 Sarunas Marciulionis	.07	.20
❑ 150 Stacey Augmon	.07	.20
❑ 151 Grant Long	.07	.20
❑ 152 Terry Mills	.07	.20
❑ 153 Kenny Smith	.07	.20
❑ 154 B.J. Armstrong	.07	.20
❑ 155 Bimbo Coles	.07	.20
❑ 156 Charles Barkley	.30	.75
❑ 157 Brent Price	.07	.20
❑ 158 Duane Ferrell	.07	.20
❑ 159 Jalen Rose	.25	.60
❑ 160 Terry Dehere	.07	.20
❑ 161 Bo Outlaw	.07	.20
❑ 162 Corie Blount	.07	.20
❑ 163 Shaquille O'Neal	.60	1.50
❑ 164 Rumeal Robinson	.07	.20
❑ 165 P.J. Brown	.07	.20
❑ 166 Ronnie Grandison	.07	.20
❑ 167 Sherman Douglas	.07	.20
❑ 168 Johnny Newman	.07	.20
❑ 169 James Robinson	.07	.20
❑ 170 Doug West	.07	.20
❑ 171 Robert Pack	.07	.20
❑ 172 Khalid Reeves	.07	.20
❑ 173 Chris Childs	.07	.20
❑ 174 Allan Houston	.15	.40
❑ 175 Charlie Ward	.07	.20
❑ 176 Darrell Armstrong RC	.75	2.00
❑ 177 Gerald Wilkins	.07	.20
❑ 178 Lucious Harris	.07	.20
❑ 179 Robert Horry	.15	.40
❑ 180 Danny Manning	.15	.40
❑ 181 Kenny Anderson	.07	.20
❑ 182 Isaiah Rider	.15	.40
❑ 183 Rasheed Wallace	.30	.75
❑ 184 Mahmoud Abdul-Rauf	.07	.20
❑ 185 Cory Alexander	.07	.20
❑ 186 Vernon Maxwell	.07	.20
❑ 187 Dominique Wilkins	.25	.60
❑ 188 Nate McMillan	.07	.20
❑ 189 Larry Stewart	.07	.20
❑ 190 Doug Christie	.15	.40
❑ 191 Hubert Davis	.07	.20
❑ 192 Walt Williams	.07	.20
❑ 193 Adam Keefe	.07	.20
❑ 194 Greg Ostertag	.07	.20
❑ 195 John Stockton	.25	.60
❑ 196 George Lynch	.07	.20
❑ 197 Lee Mayberry	.07	.20
❑ 198 Tracy Murray	.07	.20
❑ 199 Rod Strickland	.07	.20
❑ 200 Shareef Abdur-Rahim ROO	.40	1.00
❑ 201 Ray Allen ROO	.40	1.00
❑ 202 Shandon Anderson ROO RC	.15	.40
❑ 203 Kobe Bryant ROO	1.25	3.00
❑ 204 Marcus Camby ROO	.15	.40
❑ 205 Erick Dampier ROO	.07	.20
❑ 206 Emanual Davis ROO RC	.07	.20
❑ 207 Tony Delk ROO	.15	.40
❑ 208 Brian Evans ROO RC	.07	.20
❑ 209 Derek Fisher ROO RC	.40	1.00
❑ 210 Todd Fuller ROO	.07	.20
❑ 211 Dean Garrett ROO RC	.07	.20
❑ 212 Reggie Geary ROO RC	.07	.20
❑ 213 Darvin Ham ROO RC	.07	.20
❑ 214 Othella Harrington ROO RC	.15	.40
❑ 215 Shane Heal ROO RC	.07	.20
❑ 216 Allen Iverson ROO	.40	1.00
❑ 217 Dontae' Jones ROO RC	.07	.20
❑ 218 Kerry Kittles ROO	.25	.60
❑ 219 Priest Lauderdale ROO RC	.07	.20
❑ 220 Randy Livingston ROO RC	.07	.20
❑ 221 Matt Maloney ROO RC	.07	.20
❑ 222 Stephon Marbury ROO	.40	1.00
❑ 223 Walter McCarty ROO RC	.07	.20
❑ 224 Amal McCaskill ROO RC	.07	.20
❑ 225 Jeff McInnis ROO RC	.07	.20
❑ 226 Martin Muursepp ROO RC	.07	.20
❑ 227 Steve Nash ROO	.30	.75
❑ 228 Ruben Nembhard ROO RC	.07	.20
❑ 229 Jermaine O'Neal ROO	.25	.60
❑ 230 Vitaly Potapenko ROO	.07	.20
❑ 231 Virginius Praskevicius ROO RC	.07	.20
❑ 232 Roy Rogers ROO	.07	.20
❑ 233 Malik Rose ROO RC	.15	.40
❑ 234 Antoine Walker ROO	.50	1.25
❑ 235 Samaki Walker ROO	.07	.20
❑ 236 Ben Wallace ROO RC	1.50	4.00
❑ 237 John Wallace ROO	.15	.40
❑ 238 Jerome Williams ROO RC	.25	.60
❑ 239 Lorenzen Wright ROO	.07	.20
❑ 240 Sam Cassell PM	.07	.20
❑ 241 Anfernee Hardaway PM	.15	.40
❑ 242 Tim Hardaway PM	.07	.20
❑ 243 Grant Hill PM	.15	.40
❑ 244 Allan Houston PM	.07	.20
❑ 245 Juwan Howard PM	.07	.20
❑ 246 Kevin Johnson PM	.15	.40
❑ 247 Michael Jordan PM	.75	2.00
❑ 248 Jason Kidd PM	.20	.50
❑ 249 Karl Malone PM	.25	.60
❑ 250 Reggie Miller PM	.15	.40
❑ 251 Gary Payton PM	.15	.40
❑ 252 Wesley Person PM	.07	.20
❑ 253 Glen Rice PM	.07	.20
❑ 254 David Robinson PM	.15	.40
❑ 255 Steve Smith PM	.07	.20
❑ 256 Latrell Sprewell PM	.25	.60
❑ 257 Jerry Stackhouse PM	.25	.60
❑ 258 Rod Strickland PM	.07	.20
❑ 259 Nick Van Exel PM	.07	.20
❑ 260 Charles Barkley DT	.25	.60
❑ 261 Dale Davis DT	.07	.20
❑ 262 Patrick Ewing DT	.15	.40
❑ 263 Michael Finley DT	.25	.60
❑ 264 Chris Gatling DT	.07	.20
❑ 265 Armon Gilliam DT	.07	.20
❑ 266 Tyrone Hill DT	.07	.20
❑ 267 Robert Horry DT	.07	.20
❑ 268 Mark Jackson DT	.07	.20
❑ 269 Shawn Kemp DT	.07	.20
❑ 270 Jamal Mashburn DT	.07	.20
❑ 271 Anthony Mason DT	.07	.20
❑ 272 Alonzo Mourning DT	.07	.20
❑ 273 Dikembe Mutombo DT	.07	.20
❑ 274 Shaquille O'Neal DT	.25	.60
❑ 275 Isaiah Rider DT	.07	.20
❑ 276 Dennis Rodman DT	.07	.20
❑ 277 Damon Stoudamire DT	.15	.40
❑ 278 Chris Webber DT	.15	.40
❑ 279 Jayson Williams DT	.07	.20
❑ 280 Checklist	.07	.20
❑ 281 Checklist	.07	.20
❑ NNO Jerry Stackhouse Promo	.75	2.00

1997-98 SkyBox Premium

❑ COMPLETE SET (250)	50.00	90.00
❑ COMPLETE SERIES 1 (125)	12.50	25.00
❑ COMPLETE SERIES 2 (125)	40.00	70.00
❑ 1 Grant Hill	.30	.75
❑ 2 Matt Maloney	.08	.25
❑ 3 Vinny Del Negro	.08	.25
❑ 4 Kevin Willis	.20	.50
❑ 5 Mark Jackson	.20	.50
❑ 6 Ray Allen	.30	.75
❑ 7 Derrick Coleman	.08	.25
❑ 8 Isaiah Rider	.20	.50
❑ 9 Rod Strickland	.08	.25
❑ 10 Danny Ferry	.08	.25
❑ 11 Antonio Davis	.08	.25
❑ 12 Glenn Robinson	.30	.75
❑ 13 Cedric Ceballos	.08	.25
❑ 14 Sean Elliott	.20	.50
❑ 15 Walt Williams	.08	.25
❑ 16 Glen Rice	.20	.50
❑ 17 Clyde Drexler	.30	.75
❑ 18 Sherman Douglas	.08	.25
❑ 19 Othella Harrington	.08	.25
❑ 20 John Stockton	.30	.75
❑ 21 Priest Lauderdale	.08	.25
❑ 22 Khalid Reeves	.08	.25
❑ 23 Kobe Bryant	1.25	3.00
❑ 24 Vin Baker UER	.20	.50
❑ 25 Steve Nash	.30	.75
❑ 26 Jeff Hornacek	.20	.50
❑ 27 Tyrone Corbin	.08	.25
❑ 28 Charles Barkley	.40	1.00
❑ 29 Michael Jordan	2.00	5.00
❑ 30 Latrell Sprewell	.30	.75
❑ 31 Anfernee Hardaway	.30	.75
❑ 32 Steve Kerr	.20	.50
❑ 33 Joe Smith	.20	.50
❑ 34 Jermaine O'Neal	.50	1.25
❑ 35 Ron Mercer RC	.25	.60
❑ 36 Antonio McDyess	.20	.50
❑ 37 Patrick Ewing	.30	.75
❑ 38 Avery Johnson	.08	.25
❑ 39 Toni Kukoc	.20	.50
❑ 40 Sam Perkins	.20	.50
❑ 41 Voshon Lenard	.08	.25
❑ 42 Detlef Schrempf	.20	.50
❑ 43 Horace Grant	.20	.50
❑ 44 Luc Longley	.08	.25
❑ 45 Todd Fuller	.08	.25
❑ 46 Tim Hardaway	.20	.50
❑ 47 Nick Anderson	.08	.25
❑ 48 Scottie Pippen	.50	1.25
❑ 49 Lindsey Hunter	.08	.25
❑ 50 Shawn Kemp	.20	.50
❑ 51 Larry Johnson	.20	.50
❑ 52 Shawn Bradley	.08	.25
❑ 53 Martin Muursepp	.08	.25
❑ 54 Jamal Mashburn	.20	.50
❑ 55 John Starks	.20	.50
❑ 56 Rony Seikaly	.08	.25
❑ 57 Gary Payton	.30	.75
❑ 58 Juwan Howard	.20	.50
❑ 59 Vitaly Potapenko	.08	.25
❑ 60 Reggie Miller	.30	.75
❑ 61 Alonzo Mourning	.20	.50
❑ 62 Roy Rogers	.08	.25
❑ 63 Antoine Walker	.40	1.00
❑ 64 Joe Dumars	.30	.75
❑ 65 Allan Houston	.20	.50
❑ 66 Hersey Hawkins	.08	.25
❑ 67 Dell Curry	.08	.25
❑ 68 Tony Delk	.08	.25
❑ 69 Mookie Blaylock	.08	.25
❑ 70 Derek Harper	.20	.50
❑ 71 Loy Vaught	.08	.25
❑ 72 Tom Gugliotta	.20	.50
❑ 73 Mitch Richmond	.20	.50
❑ 74 Dikembe Mutombo	.20	.50
❑ 75 Tony Battie RC	.30	.75
❑ 76 Derek Fisher	.30	.75
❑ 77 Jason Kidd	.50	1.25
❑ 78 Shareef Abdur-Rahim	.50	1.25
❑ 79 Tracy McGrady RC	1.00	2.50
❑ 80 Anthony Mason	.20	.50
❑ 81 Mario Elie	.08	.25
❑ 82 Karl Malone	.30	.75
❑ 83 Mark Price	.20	.50
❑ 84 Steve Smith	.20	.50
❑ 85 LaPhonso Ellis	.08	.25
❑ 86 Robert Horry	.20	.50
❑ 87 Wesley Person	.08	.25
❑ 88 Marcus Camby	.30	.75
❑ 89 Antonio Daniels RC	.30	.75
❑ 90 Eddie Jones	.30	.75
❑ 91 Gary Trent	.08	.25
❑ 92 Danny Fortson RC	.30	.75
❑ 93 Chris Childs	.08	.25
❑ 94 David Robinson	.30	.75
❑ 95 Bryant Reeves	.08	.25
❑ 96 Chris Webber	.30	.75
❑ 97 P.J. Brown	.08	.25
❑ 98 Tyrone Hill	.08	.25
❑ 99 Dale Davis	.08	.25
❑ 100 Allen Iverson	.75	2.00
❑ 101 Jerry Stackhouse	.30	.75
❑ 102 Arvydas Sabonis	.20	.50
❑ 103 Damon Stoudamire	.20	.50
❑ 104 Tim Thomas RC	.60	1.50
❑ 105 Christian Laettner	.20	.50
❑ 106 Robert Pack	.08	.25
❑ 107 Lorenzen Wright	.08	.25
❑ 108 Olden Polynice	.08	.25
❑ 109 Terrell Brandon	.20	.50
❑ 110 Theo Ratliff	.08	.25
❑ 111 Kevin Garnett	.60	1.50
❑ 112 Tim Duncan RC	1.50	4.00
❑ 113 Bryon Russell	.08	.25
❑ 114 Chauncey Billups RC	1.50	4.00
❑ 115 Dale Ellis	.08	.25
❑ 116 Shaquille O'Neal	.75	2.00
❑ 117 Keith Van Horn RC	.50	1.25
❑ 118 Kenny Anderson	.20	.50
❑ 119 Dennis Rodman	.20	.50
❑ 120 Hakeem Olajuwon	.30	.75
❑ 121 Stephon Marbury	.40	1.00
❑ 122 Kendall Gill	.08	.25
❑ 123 Kerry Kittles	.30	.75
❑ 124 Checklist	.08	.25
❑ 125 Checklist	.08	.25
❑ 126 Anthony Johnson RC	.08	.25
❑ 127 Chris Anstey RC	.08	.25
❑ 128 Dean Garrett	.08	.25
❑ 129 Rik Smits	.20	.50
❑ 130 Tracy Murray	.08	.25
❑ 131 Charles O'Bannon RC	.08	.25
❑ 132 Eldridge Recasner	.08	.25
❑ 133 Johnny Taylor RC	.08	.25
❑ 134 Priest Lauderdale	.08	.25
❑ 135 Rod Strickland	.08	.25
❑ 136 Alan Henderson	.08	.25
❑ 137 Austin Croshere RC	.25	.60
❑ 138 Buck Williams	.08	.25
❑ 139 Clifford Robinson	.08	.25
❑ 140 Darrell Armstrong	.08	.25
❑ 141 Dennis Scott	.08	.25
❑ 142 Carl Herrera	.08	.25
❑ 143 Maurice Taylor RC	.25	.60
❑ 144 Chris Gatling	.08	.25
❑ 145 Alvin Williams RC	.08	.25
❑ 146 Antonio McDyess	.20	.50
❑ 147 Chauncey Billups	.25	.60
❑ 148 George McCloud	.08	.25
❑ 149 George Lynch	.08	.25
❑ 150 John Thomas RC	.08	.25
❑ 151 Jayson Williams	.08	.25
❑ 152 Otis Thorpe	.08	.25
❑ 153 Serge Zwikker RC	.08	.25
❑ 154 Chris Crawford RC	.08	.25
❑ 155 Muggsy Bogues	.20	.50
❑ 156 Mark Jackson	.20	.50
❑ 157 Dontonio Wingfield	.08	.25
❑ 158 Rodrick Rhodes RC	.08	.25
❑ 159 Sam Cassell	.30	.75
❑ 160 Hubert Davis	.08	.25
❑ 161 Clarence Weatherspoon	.08	.25
❑ 162 Eddie Johnson	.08	.25
❑ 163 Jacque Vaughn RC	.20	.50
❑ 164 Mark Price	.20	.50
❑ 165 Terry Dehere	.08	.25
❑ 166 Travis Knight	.08	.25
❑ 167 Charles Smith RC	.08	.25
❑ 168 David Wesley	.08	.25
❑ 169 David Wingate	.08	.25
❑ 170 Todd Day	.08	.25
❑ 171 Adonal Foyle RC	.20	.50
❑ 172 Chris Mills	.08	.25
❑ 173 Paul Grant RC	.08	.25
❑ 174 Adam Keefe	.08	.25
❑ 175 Erick Dampier	.20	.50
❑ 176 Ervin Johnson	.08	.25
❑ 177 Lamond Murray	.08	.25
❑ 178 Vlade Divac	.20	.50
❑ 179 Bobby Phills	.08	.25
❑ 180 Brian Williams	.08	.25
❑ 181 Chris Dudley	.08	.25
❑ 182 Tyrone Hill	.08	.25
❑ 183 Donyell Marshall	.20	.50
❑ 184 Kevin Gamble	.08	.25
❑ 185 Scot Pollard RC	.20	.50
❑ 186 Cherokee Parks	.08	.25
❑ 187 Terry Mills	.08	.25
❑ 188 Glen Rice	.20	.50
❑ 189 Shawn Respert	.08	.25
❑ 190 Terrell Brandon	.20	.50
❑ 191 Keith Closs RC	.08	.25
❑ 192 Tariq Abdul-Wahad RC	.20	.50
❑ 193 Wesley Person	.08	.25
❑ 194 Chuck Person	.08	.25
❑ 195 Derek Anderson RC	.30	.75
❑ 196 Jon Barry	.08	.25
❑ 197 Chris Mullin	.30	.75
❑ 198 Ed Gray RC	.08	.25
❑ 199 Charlie Ward	.08	.25
❑ 200 Kelvin Cato RC	.30	.75
❑ 201 Michael Finley	.30	.75
❑ 202 Rick Fox	.20	.50
❑ 203 Scott Burrell	.08	.25
❑ 204 Vin Baker	.20	.50
❑ 205 Eric Snow	.20	.50
❑ 206 Isaac Austin	.08	.25
❑ 207 Keith Booth RC	.08	.25
❑ 208 Brian Grant	.20	.50
❑ 209 Chris Webber	.30	.75
❑ 210 Eric Williams	.08	.25
❑ 211 Jim Jackson	.08	.25
❑ 212 Anthony Parker RC	.20	.50
❑ 213 Brevin Knight RC	.30	.75
❑ 214 Cory Alexander	.08	.25
❑ 215 James Robinson	.08	.25
❑ 216 Bobby Jackson RC	.50	1.25
❑ 217 Bo Outlaw	.08	.25
❑ 218 God Shammgod RC	.08	.25
❑ 219 James Cotton RC	.08	.25
❑ 220 Jud Buechler	.08	.25
❑ 221 Shandon Anderson	.08	.25
❑ 222 Kevin Johnson	.20	.50
❑ 223 Chris Morris	.08	.25
❑ 224 Shareef Abdur-Rahim TS	1.00	2.50
❑ 225 Ray Allen TS	.30	.75
❑ 226 Kobe Bryant TS	2.50	6.00
❑ 227 Marcus Camby TS	.30	.75
❑ 228 Antonio Daniels TS	.40	1.00
❑ 229 Tim Duncan TS	.75	2.00
❑ 230 Kevin Garnett TS	1.25	3.00
❑ 231 Anfernee Hardaway TS	.75	2.00
❑ 232 Grant Hill TS	.60	1.50
❑ 233 Allen Iverson TS	1.50	4.00
❑ 234 Bobby Jackson TS	.30	.75
❑ 235 Michael Jordan TS	4.00	10.00
❑ 236 Shawn Kemp TS	.60	1.50
❑ 237 Karl Malone TS	.30	.75
❑ 238 Stephon Marbury TS	1.00	2.50
❑ 239 Hakeem Olajuwon TS	.60	1.50
❑ 240 Shaquille O'Neal TS	1.50	4.00
❑ 241 Gary Payton TS	.50	1.25
❑ 242 Scottie Pippen TS	1.00	2.50
❑ 243 David Robinson TS	.60	1.50
❑ 244 Dennis Rodman TS	1.00	2.50
❑ 245 Jerry Stackhouse TS	.40	1.00
❑ 246 Damon Stoudamire TS	.40	1.00
❑ 247 Keith Van Horn TS	1.00	2.50
❑ 248 Antoine Walker TS	1.50	4.00
❑ 249 Grant Hill CL	.20	.50

❑ 250 Hakeem Olajuwon CL .20 .50
❑ NNO A.Iverson Shoe Bronze .50 1.25
❑ NNO A.Iverson Shoe Ruby 5.00 12.00
❑ NNO A.Iverson Shoe Gold 1.50 4.00
❑ NNO A.Iverson Shoe Silver .75 2.00
❑ NNO A.Iverson Shoe Emerald 12.50 30.00

1998-99 SkyBox Premium

❑ COMPLETE SET (265) 60.00 120.00
❑ COMPLETE SET w/o SP (225) 20.00 40.00
❑ COMPLETE SERIES 1 (125) 12.50 25.00
❑ COMPLETE SERIES 2 (140) 50.00 100.00
❑ COMMON CARD (1-225) .08 .25
❑ COMMON ROOKIE (226-265) .30 .75
❑ 1 Tim Duncan .50 1.25
❑ 2 Voshon Lenard .08 .25
❑ 3 John Starks .20 .50
❑ 4 Juwan Howard .20 .50
❑ 5 Michael Finley .30 .75
❑ 6 Bobby Jackson .20 .50
❑ 7 Glenn Robinson .20 .50
❑ 8 Antonio McDyess .20 .50
❑ 9 Eric Williams .08 .25
❑ 10 Zydrunas Ilgauskas .20 .50
❑ 11 Terrell Brandon .20 .50
❑ 12 Shandon Anderson .08 .25
❑ 13 Rod Strickland .08 .25
❑ 14 Dennis Rodman .20 .50
❑ 15 Clarence Weatherspoon .08 .25
❑ 16 P.J. Brown .08 .25
❑ 17 Anfernee Hardaway .30 .75
❑ 18 Dikembe Mutombo .20 .50
❑ 19 Patrick Ewing .30 .75
❑ 20 Scottie Pippen .50 1.25
❑ 21 Shaquille O'Neal .75 2.00
❑ 22 Donyell Marshall .20 .50
❑ 23 Michael Jordan 2.00 5.00
❑ 24 Mark Price .20 .50
❑ 25 Jim Jackson .08 .25
❑ 26 Isaiah Rider .08 .25
❑ 27 Eddie Jones .30 .75
❑ 28 Detlef Schrempf .20 .50
❑ 29 Corliss Williamson .20 .50
❑ 30 Bo Outlaw .08 .25
❑ 31 Allen Iverson .60 1.50
❑ 32 Luc Longley .08 .25
❑ 33 Theo Ratliff .20 .50
❑ 34 Antoine Walker .30 .75
❑ 35 Lamond Murray .08 .25
❑ 36 Avery Johnson .08 .25
❑ 37 John Stockton .30 .75
❑ 38 David Wesley .08 .25
❑ 39 Elden Campbell .08 .25
❑ 40 Grant Hill .30 .75
❑ 41 Sam Cassell .30 .75
❑ 42 Tracy McGrady .75 2.00
❑ 43 Glen Rice .20 .50
❑ 44 Kobe Bryant 1.25 3.00
❑ 45 John Wallace .08 .25
❑ 46 Bobby Phills .08 .25
❑ 47 Jerry Stackhouse .30 .75
❑ 48 Stephon Marbury .30 .75
❑ 49 Jeff Hornacek .20 .50
❑ 50 Tom Gugliotta .08 .25
❑ 51 Joe Dumars .30 .75
❑ 52 Johnny Newman .08 .25
❑ 53 Kevin Garnett .60 1.50
❑ 54 Dennis Scott .08 .25
❑ 55 Anthony Mason .20 .50
❑ 56 Rodney Rogers .08 .25
❑ 57 Bryon Russell .08 .25
❑ 58 Maurice Taylor .15 .40
❑ 59 Mookie Blaylock .08 .25
❑ 60 Shawn Bradley .08 .25
❑ 61 Matt Maloney .08 .25
❑ 62 Karl Malone .30 .75
❑ 63 Larry Johnson .20 .50
❑ 64 Calbert Cheaney .08 .25
❑ 65 Steve Smith .20 .50
❑ 66 Toni Kukoc .20 .50
❑ 67 Reggie Miller .30 .75
❑ 68 Jayson Williams .08 .25
❑ 69 Gary Payton .30 .75
❑ 70 Sean Elliott .20 .50
❑ 71 Charles Barkley .40 1.00
❑ 72 Tim Hardaway .20 .50
❑ 73 Rasheed Wallace .30 .75
❑ 74 Tariq Abdul-Wahad .08 .25
❑ 75 Kenny Anderson .20 .50
❑ 76 Chris Mullin .30 .75
❑ 77 Keith Van Horn .30 .75
❑ 78 Hersey Hawkins .08 .25
❑ 79 Ron Mercer .15 .40
❑ 80 Rik Smits .20 .50
❑ 81 David Robinson .30 .75
❑ 82 Derek Anderson .25 .60
❑ 83 Danny Fortson .08 .25
❑ 84 Jason Kidd .50 1.25
❑ 85 Chauncey Billups .20 .50
❑ 86 Chris Anstey .08 .25
❑ 87 Hakeem Olajuwon .30 .75
❑ 88 Bryant Reeves .08 .25
❑ 89 Anthony Johnson .08 .25
❑ 90 Shawn Kemp .20 .50
❑ 91 Brevin Knight .08 .25
❑ 92 Ray Allen .30 .75
❑ 93 Tim Thomas .20 .50
❑ 94 Jalen Rose .30 .75
❑ 95 Kerry Kittles .08 .25
❑ 96 Vin Baker .20 .50
❑ 97 Shareef Abdur-Rahim .30 .75
❑ 98 Alonzo Mourning .20 .50
❑ 99 Joe Smith .20 .50
❑ 100 Damon Stoudamire .20 .50
❑ 101 Alan Henderson .08 .25
❑ 102 Walter McCarty .08 .25
❑ 103 Vlade Divac .20 .50
❑ 104 Wesley Person .08 .25
❑ 105 A.C. Green .20 .50
❑ 106 Malik Sealy .08 .25
❑ 107 Carl Thomas .08 .25
❑ 108 Brent Price .08 .25
❑ 109 Mark Jackson .20 .50
❑ 110 Lorenzen Wright .08 .25
❑ 111 Derek Fisher .30 .75
❑ 112 Michael Smith .08 .25
❑ 113 Tyrone Hill .08 .25
❑ 114 Cherokee Parks .08 .25
❑ 115 Kendall Gill .08 .25
❑ 116 Darrell Armstrong .08 .25
❑ 117 Derrick Coleman .08 .25
❑ 118 Rex Chapman .08 .25
❑ 119 Arvydas Sabonis .20 .50
❑ 120 Billy Owens .08 .25
❑ 121 Sam Perkins .08 .25
❑ 122 Gary Trent .08 .25
❑ 123 Sam Mack .08 .25
❑ 124 Tracy Murray .08 .25
❑ 125 Allan Houston .20 .50
❑ 126 Mitch Richmond .20 .50
❑ 127 Carl Herrera .08 .25
❑ 128 Ron Harper .20 .50
❑ 129 Gary Trent .08 .25
❑ 130 Chris Webber .30 .75
❑ 131 Antonio Daniels .08 .25
❑ 132 Charles Oakley .08 .25
❑ 133 Marcus Camby .20 .50
❑ 134 Tony Battie .08 .25
❑ 135 Otis Thorpe .08 .25
❑ 136 Dale Davis .20 .50
❑ 137 Chuck Person .08 .25
❑ 138 Ervin Johnson .08 .25
❑ 139 Jamal Mashburn .20 .50
❑ 140 Brian Grant .20 .50
❑ 141 Chris Mills .08 .25
❑ 142 Doug Christie .20 .50
❑ 143 George McCloud .08 .25
❑ 144 Todd Fuller .08 .25
❑ 145 Jerome Williams .08 .25
❑ 146 Chauncey Billups .20 .50
❑ 147 Dean Garrett .08 .25
❑ 148 Robert Pack .08 .25
❑ 149 Clarence Weatherspoon .08 .25
❑ 150 Tim Legler .08 .25
❑ 151 Bob Sura .08 .25
❑ 152 B.J. Armstrong .08 .25
❑ 153 Charlie Ward .08 .25
❑ 154 Rony Seikaly .08 .25
❑ 155 Chris Carr .08 .25
❑ 156 Eldridge Recasner .08 .25
❑ 157 Michael Stewart .08 .25
❑ 158 Jim McIlvaine .08 .25
❑ 159 Adam Keefe .08 .25
❑ 160 Antonio Davis .08 .25
❑ 161 Lawrence Funderburke .08 .25
❑ 162 Greg Ostertag .08 .25
❑ 163 Dan Majerle .20 .50
❑ 164 Dale Ellis .08 .25
❑ 165 Greg Anthony .08 .25
❑ 166 Chris Whitney .08 .25
❑ 167 Eric Piatkowski .20 .50
❑ 168 Tom Gugliotta .08 .25
❑ 169 Luc Longley .08 .25
❑ 170 Antonio McDyess .20 .50
❑ 171 George Lynch .08 .25
❑ 172 Dell Curry .08 .25
❑ 173 Johnny Newman .08 .25
❑ 174 Christian Laettner .20 .50
❑ 175 Steve Kerr .20 .50
❑ 176 Popeye Jones .08 .25
❑ 177 Brent Barry .20 .50
❑ 178 Billy Owens .08 .25
❑ 179 Cherokee Parks .08 .25
❑ 180 Derek Harper .08 .25
❑ 181 Howard Eisley .08 .25
❑ 182 Matt Geiger .08 .25
❑ 183 Darrick Martin .08 .25
❑ 184 Isaac Austin .08 .25
❑ 185 Dennis Scott .08 .25
❑ 186 Derrick Coleman .08 .25
❑ 187 Sam Perkins .08 .25
❑ 188 Latrell Sprewell .30 .75
❑ 189 Jud Buechler .08 .25
❑ 190 Jason Caffey .08 .25
❑ 191 Vlade Divac .20 .50
❑ 192 Travis Best .08 .25
❑ 193 Loy Vaught .08 .25
❑ 194 Mario Elie .08 .25
❑ 195 Ed Gray .08 .25
❑ 196 Joe Smith .20 .50
❑ 197 John Starks .20 .50
❑ 198 Anthony Johnson .08 .25
❑ 199 Kurt Thomas .20 .50
❑ 200 Chris Dudley .08 .25
❑ 201 Shareef Abdur-Rahim NF .08 .25
❑ 202 Ray Allen NF .08 .25
❑ 203 Vin Baker NF .08 .25
❑ 204 Charles Barkley NF .08 .25
❑ 205 Kobe Bryant NF .60 1.50
❑ 206 Tim Duncan NF .30 .75
❑ 207 Anfernee Hardaway NF .08 .25
❑ 208 Grant Hill NF .30 .75
❑ 209 Allen Iverson NF .50 1.25
❑ 210 Jason Kidd NF .30 .75
❑ 211 Shawn Kemp NF .08 .25
❑ 212 Shaquille O'Neal NF .40 1.00
❑ 213 Kerry Kittles NF .08 .25
❑ 214 Karl Malone NF .08 .25
❑ 215 Stephon Marbury NF .08 .25
❑ 216 Ron Mercer NF .07 .20
❑ 217 Reggie Miller NF .08 .25
❑ 218 Kevin Garnett NF .30 .75
❑ 219 Gary Payton NF .08 .25
❑ 220 Scottie Pippen NF .30 .75
❑ 221 David Robinson NF .08 .25
❑ 222 Hakeem Olajuwon NF .08 .25
❑ 223 Damon Stoudamire NF .08 .25
❑ 224 Keith Van Horn NF .08 .25
❑ 225 Antoine Walker NF .08 .25
❑ 226 Cory Carr RC .30 .75
❑ 227 Cuttino Mobley RC 2.50 6.00
❑ 228 Miles Simon RC .30 .75
❑ 229 J.R. Henderson RC .30 .75
❑ 230 Jason Williams RC 2.00 5.00
❑ 231 Felipe Lopez RC .60 1.50
❑ 232 Shammond Williams RC 1.25 3.00
❑ 233 Ricky Davis RC 2.00 5.00
❑ 234 Vince Carter RC 4.00 10.00
❑ 235 Antawn Jamison RC 2.50 6.00
❑ 236 Ryan Stack RC .30 .75
❑ 237 Nazr Mohammed RC .40 1.00
❑ 238 Sam Jacobson RC .30 .75
❑ 239 Larry Hughes RC 1.50 4.00
❑ 240 Ruben Patterson RC 1.00 2.50

❑ 241 Al Harrington RC	1.25	3.00
❑ 242 Ansu Sesay RC	.30	.75
❑ 243 Vladimir Stepania RC	.30	.75
❑ 244 Matt Harpring RC	.75	2.00
❑ 245 Andrae Patterson RC	.30	.75
❑ 246 Pat Garrity RC	.40	1.00
❑ 247 Bonzi Wells RC	2.00	5.00
❑ 248 Bryce Drew RC	.60	1.50
❑ 249 Toby Bailey RC	.30	.75
❑ 250 Michael Doleac RC	.60	1.50
❑ 251 Michael Dickerson RC	1.00	2.50
❑ 252 Peja Stojakovic RC	2.00	5.00
❑ 253 Robert Traylor RC	.60	1.50
❑ 254 Tyronn Lue RC	.75	2.00
❑ 255 Dirk Nowitzki RC	6.00	12.00
❑ 256 Raef LaFrentz RC	.75	2.00
❑ 257 Jelani McCoy RC	.30	.75
❑ 258 Michael Olowokandi RC	.75	2.00
❑ 259 Brian Skinner RC	.60	1.50
❑ 260 Keon Clark RC	.75	2.00
❑ 261 Roshown McLeod RC	.40	1.00
❑ 262 Mike Bibby RC	1.50	4.00
❑ 263 Paul Pierce RC	4.00	10.00
❑ 264 Tyson Wheeler RC	.30	.75
❑ 265 Corey Benjamin RC	.60	1.50

1999-00 SkyBox Premium

❑ COMPLETE SET (150)	60.00	120.00
❑ COMPLETE SET w/o SP (125)	15.00	40.00
❑ COMMON CARD (1-100)	.20	.50
❑ COMMON ROOKIE (101-125)	.20	.50
❑ COMMON SP (101-125)	.75	2.00
❑ 1 Vince Carter	.60	1.50
❑ 2 Nick Anderson	.20	.50
❑ 3 Isaiah Rider	.20	.50
❑ 4 Mitch Richmond	.25	.60
❑ 5 Danny Fortson	.20	.50
❑ 6 Kenny Anderson	.25	.60
❑ 7 Reggie Miller	.30	.75
❑ 8 Tracy McGrady	.60	1.50
❑ 9 Steve Nash	.50	1.25
❑ 10 Robert Traylor	.20	.50
❑ 11 Tom Gugliotta	.20	.50
❑ 12 Steve Smith	.20	.50
❑ 13 Jalen Rose	.25	.60
❑ 14 Kerry Kittles	.20	.50
❑ 15 Nick Van Exel	.25	.60
❑ 16 Raef LaFrentz	.25	.60
❑ 17 Damon Stoudamire	.30	.75
❑ 18 Gary Trent	.20	.50
❑ 19 Jayson Williams	.25	.60
❑ 20 Brian Grant	.20	.50
❑ 21 Rod Strickland	.20	.50
❑ 22 Larry Hughes	.25	.60
❑ 23 Derek Anderson	.20	.50
❑ 24 Hakeem Olajuwon	.30	.75
❑ 25 Ray Allen	.30	.75
❑ 26 Gary Payton	.30	.75
❑ 27 Michael Finley	.30	.75
❑ 28 Keith Van Horn	.25	.60
❑ 29 Clifford Robinson	.20	.50
❑ 30 Shawn Kemp	.30	.75
❑ 31 Glenn Robinson	.25	.60
❑ 32 Theo Ratliff	.25	.60
❑ 33 Lindsey Hunter	.20	.50
❑ 34 Chris Webber	.30	.75
❑ 35 Grant Hill	.30	.75
❑ 36 Vlade Divac	.30	.75
❑ 37 Paul Pierce	.30	.75
❑ 38 Tyrone Nesby RC	.30	.75
❑ 39 Larry Johnson	.30	.75
❑ 40 Bryon Russell	.20	.50
❑ 41 Antoine Walker	.30	.75
❑ 42 Michael Olowokandi	.20	.50
❑ 43 John Stockton	.40	1.00
❑ 44 Elden Campbell	.20	.50
❑ 45 Christian Laettner	.25	.60
❑ 46 Maurice Taylor	.25	.60
❑ 47 Shareef Abdur-Rahim	.25	.60
❑ 48 Ricky Davis	.30	.75
❑ 49 Jerry Stackhouse	.30	.75
❑ 50 Kobe Bryant	1.50	4.00
❑ 51 Jason Williams	.30	.75
❑ 52 Mike Bibby	.30	.75
❑ 53 Eddie Jones	.30	.75
❑ 54 Antawn Jamison	.30	.75
❑ 55 Shaquille O'Neal	.75	2.00
❑ 56 Tim Duncan	.60	1.50
❑ 57 Cherokee Parks	.20	.50
❑ 58 Antonio McDyess	.25	.60
❑ 59 Rasheed Wallace	.30	.75
❑ 60 Anthony Mason	.20	.50
❑ 61 Chris Mills	.20	.50
❑ 62 Glen Rice	.30	.75
❑ 63 Latrell Sprewell	.25	.60
❑ 64 Darrell Armstrong	.20	.50
❑ 65 Sean Elliott	.30	.75
❑ 66 Juwan Howard	.25	.60
❑ 67 Brent Barry	.25	.60
❑ 68 John Starks	.30	.75
❑ 69 Tim Hardaway	.30	.75
❑ 70 Marcus Camby	.25	.60
❑ 71 Anfernee Hardaway	.30	.75
❑ 72 Avery Johnson	.25	.60
❑ 73 Tariq Abdul-Wahad	.20	.50
❑ 74 Charles Barkley	.40	1.00
❑ 75 Stephon Marbury	.30	.75
❑ 76 Jamal Mashburn	.20	.50
❑ 77 Matt Harpring	.25	.60
❑ 78 David Robinson	.40	1.00
❑ 79 Cedric Ceballos	.20	.50
❑ 80 Terrell Brandon	.20	.50
❑ 81 Jason Kidd	.50	1.25
❑ 82 Toni Kukoc	.30	.75
❑ 83 Michael Dickerson	.20	.50
❑ 84 Alonzo Mourning	.30	.75
❑ 85 Kevin Garnett	.60	1.50
❑ 86 Matt Geiger	.20	.50
❑ 87 Vin Baker	.30	.75
❑ 88 Dikembe Mutombo	.25	.60
❑ 89 Hersey Hawkins	.20	.50
❑ 90 Joe Smith	.25	.60
❑ 91 Charles Oakley	.25	.60
❑ 92 Ron Mercer	.20	.50
❑ 93 Rik Smits	.30	.75
❑ 94 Patrick Ewing	.40	1.00
❑ 95 Karl Malone	.40	1.00
❑ 96 Scottie Pippen	.50	1.25
❑ 97 Zydrunas Ilgauskas	.25	.60
❑ 98 Sam Cassell	.25	.60
❑ 99 Detlef Schrempf	.25	.60
❑ 100 Allen Iverson	.60	1.50
❑ 101 Elton Brand RC	.60	1.50
❑ 101A Elton Brand SP	2.50	6.00
❑ 102 Steve Francis RC	.60	1.50
❑ 102A Steve Francis SP	2.50	6.00
❑ 103 Baron Davis RC	.75	2.00
❑ 103A Baron Davis SP	3.00	8.00
❑ 104 Lamar Odom RC	.60	1.50
❑ 104A Lamar Odom SP	2.50	6.00
❑ 105 Jonathan Bender RC	.20	.50
❑ 105A Jonathan Bender SP	.75	2.00
❑ 106 Wally Szczerbiak RC	.60	1.50
❑ 106A Wally Szczerbiak SP	2.50	6.00
❑ 107 Richard Hamilton RC	.60	1.50
❑ 107A Richard Hamilton SP	2.50	6.00
❑ 108 Andre Miller RC	.60	1.50
❑ 108A Andre Miller SP	2.50	6.00
❑ 109 Shawn Marion RC	.60	1.50
❑ 109A Shawn Marion SP	2.50	6.00
❑ 110 Jason Terry RC	.50	1.25
❑ 110A Jason Terry SP	2.00	5.00
❑ 111 Trajan Langdon RC	.20	.50
❑ 111A Trajan Langdon SP	.75	2.00
❑ 112 A.Radojevic RC	.20	.50
❑ 112A A.Radojevic SP	.75	2.00
❑ 113 Corey Maggette RC	.60	1.50
❑ 113A Corey Maggette SP	2.50	6.00
❑ 114 William Avery RC	.20	.50
❑ 114A William Avery SP	.75	2.00
❑ 115 Vonteego Cummings RC	.20	.50
❑ 115A Vonteego Cummings SP	.75	2.00
❑ 116 Ron Artest RC	.75	2.00
❑ 116A Ron Artest SP	3.00	8.00
❑ 117 Cal Bowdler RC	.20	.50
❑ 117A Cal Bowdler SP	.75	2.00
❑ 118 James Posey RC	.30	.75
❑ 118A James Posey SP	1.25	3.00
❑ 119 Quincy Lewis RC	.20	.50
❑ 119A Quincy Lewis SP	.75	2.00
❑ 120 Dion Glover RC	.20	.50
❑ 120A Dion Glover SP	.75	2.00
❑ 121 Jeff Foster RC	.25	.60
❑ 121A Jeff Foster SP	1.00	2.50
❑ 122 Kenny Thomas RC	.20	.50
❑ 122A Kenny Thomas SP	.75	2.00
❑ 123 Devean George RC	.30	.75
❑ 123A Devean George SP	1.25	3.00
❑ 124 Scott Padgett RC	.20	.50
❑ 124A Scott Padgett SP	.75	2.00
❑ 125 Tim James RC	.20	.50
❑ 125A Tim James SP	.75	2.00

2004-05 SkyBox Premium

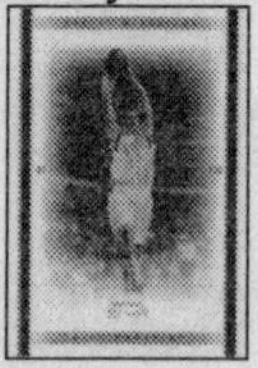

❑ COMP.SET w/) SP's (75)	15.00	40.00
❑ COMMON CARD (1-75)	.25	.60
❑ COMMON ROOKIE (76-100)	1.50	4.00
❑ 1 Dwyane Wade	1.25	3.00
❑ 2 Rashard Lewis	.40	1.00
❑ 3 Jermaine O'Neal	.40	1.00
❑ 4 Ben Wallace	.30	.75
❑ 5 Steve Francis	.40	1.00
❑ 6 Lamar Odom	.40	1.00
❑ 7 Jason Richardson	.40	1.00
❑ 8 Jarvis Hayes	.25	.60
❑ 9 Carmelo Anthony	1.25	3.00
❑ 10 Tony Parker	.40	1.00
❑ 11 Eddy Curry	.30	.75
❑ 12 Nene	.30	.75
❑ 13 Kevin Garnett	.75	2.00
❑ 14 Darius Miles	.30	.75
❑ 15 Elton Brand	.40	1.00
❑ 16 Zach Randolph	.40	1.00
❑ 17 Mike Dunleavy	.30	.75
❑ 18 Dajuan Wagner	.25	.60
❑ 19 Steve Nash	.00	1.60
❑ 20 Ron Artest	.30	.75
❑ 21 Ricky Davis	.30	.75
❑ 22 Antawn Jamison	.40	1.00
❑ 23 Jamal Mashburn	.30	.75
❑ 24 T.J. Ford	.30	.75
❑ 25 Amare Stoudemire	.75	2.00
❑ 26 Jason Kapono	.25	.60
❑ 27 Shawn Marion	.40	1.00
❑ 28 Corliss Williamson	.25	.60
❑ 29 Reggie Miller	.40	1.00
❑ 30 Desmond Mason	.30	.75
❑ 31 Pau Gasol	.40	1.00
❑ 32 Baron Davis	.40	1.00
❑ 33 Allen Iverson	.75	2.00
❑ 34 Darko Milicic	.25	.60
❑ 35 Ray Allen	.40	1.00
❑ 36 Jason Williams	.30	.75
❑ 37 Michael Redd	.40	1.00
❑ 38 Yao Ming	1.00	2.50
❑ 39 Antoine Walker	.40	1.00
❑ 40 Jason Terry	.30	.75
❑ 41 Sam Cassell	.30	.75
❑ 42 Richard Jefferson	.40	1.00
❑ 43 Manu Ginobili	.40	1.00
❑ 44 Dirk Nowitzki	.60	1.50
❑ 45 Peja Stojakovic	.30	.75
❑ 46 Samuel Dalembert	.25	.60
❑ 47 Latrell Sprewell	.30	.75
❑ 48 Gerald Wallace	.40	1.00
❑ 49 Andrei Kirilenko	.40	1.00
❑ 50 Nick Van Exel	.30	.75
❑ 51 Jalen Rose	.30	.75
❑ 52 Shaquille O'Neal	1.00	2.50
❑ 53 Shareef Abdur-Rahim	.30	.75
❑ 54 Tracy McGrady	.75	2.00

❑ 55 Rasheed Wallace	.40	1.00
❑ 56 Cuttino Mobley	.30	.75
❑ 57 Jason Kidd	.60	1.50
❑ 58 Chris Webber	.40	1.00
❑ 59 Paul Pierce	.40	1.00
❑ 60 Mike Bibby	.30	.75
❑ 61 Allan Houston	.30	.75
❑ 62 Kobe Bryant	2.00	5.00
❑ 63 Kenyon Martin	.40	1.00
❑ 64 LeBron James	2.50	6.00
❑ 65 Tim Duncan	.75	2.00
❑ 66 Stephon Marbury	.40	1.00
❑ 67 Kirk Hinrich	.30	.75
❑ 68 Chris Bosh	.40	1.00
❑ 69 Corey Maggette	.30	.75
❑ 70 Vince Carter	.75	2.00
❑ 71 Caron Butler	.30	.75
❑ 72 Stephen Jackson	.30	.75
❑ 73 Carlos Boozer	.40	1.00
❑ 74 Michael Finley	.40	1.00
❑ 75 Jamal Crawford	.30	.75
❑ 76 Dwight Howard RC	5.00	12.00
❑ 77 Emeka Okafor RC	3.00	8.00
❑ 78 Ben Gordon RC	2.00	5.00
❑ 79 Shaun Livingston RC	1.50	4.00
❑ 80 Devin Harris RC	3.00	8.00
❑ 81 Josh Childress RC	1.50	4.00
❑ 82 Luol Deng RC	2.00	5.00
❑ 83 Rafael Araujo RC	1.50	4.00
❑ 84 Andre Iguodala RC	4.00	10.00
❑ 85 Luke Jackson RC	1.50	4.00
❑ 86 Andris Biedrins RC	2.50	6.00
❑ 87 Robert Swift RC	1.50	4.00
❑ 88 Sebastian Telfair RC	1.50	4.00
❑ 89 Kris Humphries RC	2.50	6.00
❑ 90 Al Jefferson RC	3.00	8.00
❑ 91 Kirk Snyder RC	1.50	4.00
❑ 92 Josh Smith RC	4.00	10.00
❑ 93 J.R. Smith RC	3.00	8.00
❑ 94 Dorell Wright RC	2.00	5.00
❑ 95 Jameer Nelson RC	2.00	5.00
❑ 96 Bernard Robinson RC	1.50	4.00
❑ 97 Andre Emmett RC	1.50	4.00
❑ 98 Delonte West RC	2.50	6.00
❑ 99 Tony Allen RC	2.00	5.00
❑ 100 Kevin Martin RC	2.00	5.00

1999-00 SkyBox APEX

❑ COMPLETE SET (163)	60.00	120.00
❑ COMPLETE SET w/o RC (150)	12.50	25.00
❑ COMMON CARD (1-150)	.20	.50
❑ COMMON ROOKIE (151-163)	.50	1.25
❑ 1 Paul Pierce	.30	.75
❑ 2 Stephon Marbury	.30	.75
❑ 3 Chris Webber	.30	.75
❑ 4 Kobe Bryant	1.50	4.00
❑ 5 David Robinson	.40	1.00
❑ 6 Gary Payton	.30	.75
❑ 7 Kornel David RC	.30	.75
❑ 8 Glenn Robinson	.25	.60
❑ 9 Nick Van Exel	.25	.60
❑ 10 Jelani McCoy	.20	.50
❑ 11 Charles Oakley	.25	.60
❑ 12 Michael Finley	.30	.75
❑ 13 Steve Smith	.20	.50
❑ 14 Arvydas Sabonis	.25	.60
❑ 15 Cuttino Mobley	.25	.60
❑ 16 Eric Piatkowski	.25	.60
❑ 17 Bobby Jackson	.25	.60
❑ 18 Keith Van Horn	.25	.60
❑ 19 Shaquille O'Neal	.75	2.00
❑ 20 Karl Malone	.40	1.00
❑ 21 Allan Houston	.25	.60
❑ 22 Ron Mercer	.20	.50
❑ 23 Vince Carter	.60	1.50
❑ 24 Lindsey Hunter	.20	.50
❑ 25 Scottie Pippen	.50	1.25
❑ 26 Wesley Person	.20	.50
❑ 27 Vitaly Potapenko	.20	.50
❑ 28 Glen Rice	.30	.75
❑ 29 Tyrone Nesby RC	.30	.75
❑ 30 Detlef Schrempf	.25	.60
❑ 31 Clifford Robinson	.20	.50
❑ 32 Joe Smith	.25	.60
❑ 33 P.J. Brown	.20	.50
❑ 34 Christian Laettner	.25	.60
❑ 35 Avery Johnson	.25	.60
❑ 36 Kevin Garnett	.60	1.50
❑ 37 Jason Kidd	.50	1.25
❑ 38 Kenny Anderson	.25	.60
❑ 39 Shawn Kemp	.30	.75
❑ 40 Bison Dele	.20	.50
❑ 41 Rodney Rogers	.20	.50
❑ 42 Jamal Mashburn	.20	.50
❑ 43 Grant Hill	.30	.75
❑ 44 Larry Johnson	.30	.75
❑ 45 Darrell Armstrong	.20	.50
❑ 46 Shandon Anderson	.20	.50
❑ 47 Kendall Gill	.20	.50
❑ 48 Jason Williams	.30	.75
❑ 49 Tom Gugliotta	.20	.50
❑ 50 Ray Allen	.30	.75
❑ 51 Sam Mitchell	.20	.50
❑ 52 Brent Barry	.25	.60
❑ 53 Antawn Jamison	.30	.75
❑ 54 Chris Mullin	.30	.75
❑ 55 Alan Henderson	.20	.50
❑ 56 Derek Anderson	.20	.50
❑ 57 Tim Thomas	.25	.60
❑ 58 Anfernee Hardaway	.30	.75
❑ 59 Pat Garrity	.20	.50
❑ 60 Corliss Williamson	.20	.50
❑ 61 Gary Trent	.20	.50
❑ 62 Greg Ostertag	.20	.50
❑ 63 Vin Baker	.30	.75
❑ 64 LaPhonso Ellis	.20	.50
❑ 65 Brevin Knight	.20	.50
❑ 66 Rick Fox	.20	.50
❑ 67 Bryant Reeves	.20	.50
❑ 68 Mark Jackson	.30	.75
❑ 69 John Starks	.30	.75
❑ 70 Robert Traylor	.20	.50
❑ 71 Maurice Taylor	.25	.60
❑ 72 Hersey Hawkins	.20	.50
❑ 73 Zydrunas Ilgauskas	.25	.60
❑ 74 Charles Barkley	.40	1.00
❑ 75 Isaac Austin	.20	.50
❑ 76 Mike Bibby	.30	.75
❑ 77 Michael Olowokandi	.20	.50
❑ 78 Brian Grant	.20	.50
❑ 79 Felipe Lopez	.20	.50
❑ 80 Chris Crawford	.20	.50
❑ 81 Dee Brown	.20	.50
❑ 82 Antoine Walker	.30	.75
❑ 83 Vlade Divac	.30	.75
❑ 84 Rod Strickland	.20	.50
❑ 85 Dickey Simpkins	.20	.50
❑ 86 Donyell Marshall	.25	.60
❑ 87 Larry Hughes	.25	.60
❑ 88 Rasheed Wallace	.30	.75
❑ 89 Erick Dampier	.25	.60
❑ 90 Kerry Kittles	.20	.50
❑ 91 Mitch Richmond	.25	.60
❑ 92 Isaiah Rider	.20	.50
❑ 93 Bobby Phills	.20	.50
❑ 94 Dirk Nowitzki	.50	1.25
❑ 95 Cedric Henderson	.20	.50
❑ 96 Howard Eisley	.20	.50
❑ 97 Toni Kukoc	.30	.75
❑ 98 Jalen Rose	.25	.60
❑ 99 Michael Doleac	.20	.50
❑ 100 Matt Geiger	.20	.50
❑ 101 Bryon Russell	.20	.50
❑ 102 Alvin Williams	.20	.50
❑ 103 Shawn Bradley	.20	.50
❑ 104 Latrell Sprewell	.25	.60
❑ 105 Vernon Maxwell	.25	.60
❑ 106 Tim Hardaway	.30	.75
❑ 107 Peja Stojakovic	.25	.60
❑ 108 Tracy Murray	.20	.50
❑ 109 Theo Ratliff	.25	.60
❑ 110 Dikembe Mutombo	.25	.60
❑ 111 Alonzo Mourning	.30	.75
❑ 112 Raef LaFrentz	.25	.60
❑ 113 Marcus Camby	.25	.60
❑ 114 Eddie Jones	.30	.75
❑ 115 Chauncey Billups	.30	.75
❑ 116 Jayson Williams	.25	.60
❑ 117 Anthony Mason	.20	.50
❑ 118 Tracy McGrady	.60	1.50
❑ 119 John Stockton	.40	1.00
❑ 120 Matt Harpring	.25	.60
❑ 121 Mario Elie	.20	.50
❑ 122 Juwan Howard	.25	.60
❑ 123 Antonio McDyess	.25	.60
❑ 124 Ricky Davis	.30	.75
❑ 125 Reggie Miller	.30	.75
❑ 126 Allen Iverson	.60	1.50
❑ 127 Terrell Brandon	.20	.50
❑ 128 Hakeem Olajuwon	.30	.75
❑ 129 Damon Stoudamire	.30	.75
❑ 130 Randy Brown	.20	.50
❑ 131 Cedric Ceballos	.20	.50
❑ 132 Jerry Stackhouse	.30	.75
❑ 133 Michael Dickerson	.20	.50
❑ 134 Rik Smits	.30	.75
❑ 135 Cherokee Parks	.20	.50
❑ 136 Tim Duncan	.60	1.50
❑ 137 Shareef Abdur-Rahim	.25	.60
❑ 138 Derek Fisher	.30	.75
❑ 139 Bo Outlaw	.20	.50
❑ 140 Eric Snow	.25	.60
❑ 141 Jaren Jackson	.20	.50
❑ 142 Tony Battie	.25	.60
❑ 143 Derrick Coleman	.25	.60
❑ 144 Corey Benjamin	.20	.50
❑ 145 Steve Nash	.50	1.25
❑ 146 Mookie Blaylock	.20	.50
❑ 147 Voshon Lenard	.20	.50
❑ 148 Vinny Del Negro	.20	.50
❑ 149 Jeff Hornacek	.25	.60
❑ 150 Patrick Ewing	.40	1.00
❑ 151 Elton Brand RC	1.50	4.00
❑ 152 Steve Francis RC	1.50	4.00
❑ 153 Baron Davis RC	2.00	5.00
❑ 154 Lamar Odom RC	1.50	4.00
❑ 155 Jonathan Bender RC	.50	1.25
❑ 156 Wally Szczerbiak RC	1.50	4.00
❑ 157 Richard Hamilton RC	1.50	4.00
❑ 158 Andre Miller RC	1.50	4.00
❑ 159 Shawn Marion RC	1.50	4.00
❑ 160 Jason Terry RC	1.25	3.00
❑ 161 Trajan Langdon RC	.50	1.25
❑ 162 A.Radojevic RC	.50	1.25
❑ 163 Corey Maggette RC	1.50	4.00
❑ P2 Stephon Marbury PROMO	.50	1.25
❑ NNO K.Van Horn AU JSY/50	30.00	80.00

2003-04 SkyBox Autographics

❑ COMP.SET w/o SP's (45)	12.50	30.00
❑ COMMON CARD (1-45)	.25	.60
❑ COMMON ROOKIE (46-90)	1.50	4.00
❑ 1 Vince Carter	.75	2.00
❑ 2 Kobe Bryant	2.00	5.00
❑ 3 Tony Parker	.40	1.00
❑ 4 Richard Hamilton	.30	.75
❑ 5 Jamal Mashburn	.25	.60
❑ 6 Paul Pierce	.40	1.00
❑ 7 Allan Houston	.30	.75
❑ 8 Carlos Boozer	.40	1.00
❑ 9 Michael Redd	.40	1.00
❑ 10 Chris Webber	.40	1.00
❑ 11 Yao Ming	.75	2.00
❑ 12 Tracy McGrady	.75	2.00
❑ 13 Zach Randolph	.40	1.00
❑ 14 Ben Wallace	.30	.75
❑ 15 Kenyon Martin	.40	1.00
❑ 16 Ray Allen	.25	.60
❑ 17 Jermaine O'Neal	.40	1.00

❑ 18 Bonzi Wells	.25	.60
❑ 19 Ron Artest	.30	.75
❑ 20 Peja Stojakovic	.30	.75
❑ 21 Dirk Nowitzki	.60	1.50
❑ 22 Desmond Mason	.30	.75
❑ 23 Morris Peterson	.30	.75
❑ 24 Eddy Curry	.30	.75
❑ 25 Kevin Garnett	.75	2.00
❑ 26 Rashard Lewis	.40	1.00
❑ 27 Jason Richardson	.40	1.00
❑ 28 Amare Stoudemire	.75	2.00
❑ 29 Steve Francis	.40	1.00
❑ 30 Allen Iverson	.75	2.00
❑ 31 Jason Terry	.30	.75
❑ 32 Pau Gasol	.40	1.00
❑ 33 Manu Ginobili	.40	1.00
❑ 34 Reggie Miller	.40	1.00
❑ 35 Cuttino Mobley	.30	.75
❑ 36 Mike Bibby	.30	.75
❑ 37 Mike Dunleavy	.30	.75
❑ 38 Jason Kidd	.60	1.50
❑ 39 Shareef Abdur-Rahim	.30	.75
❑ 40 Elton Brand	.40	1.00
❑ 41 Kwame Brown	.25	.60
❑ 42 Shaquille O'Neal	1.00	2.50
❑ 43 Tim Duncan	.75	2.00
❑ 44 Nene	.30	.75
❑ 45 Baron Davis	.40	1.00
❑ 46 Boris Diaw RC	2.00	5.00
❑ 47 Luke Walton RC	2.00	5.00
❑ 48 Willie Green RC	1.50	4.00
❑ 49 Marcus Banks RC	1.50	4.00
❑ 50 Dahntay Jones RC	1.50	4.00
❑ 51 Leandro Barbosa RC	2.00	5.00
❑ 52 Josh Howard RC	2.00	5.00
❑ 53 Ndudi Ebi RC	1.50	4.00
❑ 54 Chris Bosh RC	2.50	6.00
❑ 55 Carmelo Anthony RC	4.00	10.00
❑ 56 Zoran Planinic RC	1.50	4.00
❑ 57 Aleksandar Pavlovic RC	2.00	5.00
❑ 58 Marquis Daniels RC	2.00	5.00
❑ 59 Keith McLeod RC	1.50	4.00
❑ 60 Ben Handlogten RC	1.50	4.00
❑ 61 Francisco Elson RC	1.50	4.00
❑ 62 David West RC	2.00	5.00
❑ 63 Maurice Williams RC	2.50	6.00
❑ 64 Brian Cook RC	1.50	4.00
❑ 65 Keith Bogans RC	1.50	4.00
❑ 66 Kendrick Perkins RC	2.50	6.00
❑ 67 Troy Bell RC	1.50	4.00
❑ 68 Kyle Korver RC	2.00	5.00
❑ 69 Mickael Pietrus RC	2.00	5.00
❑ 70 Maciej Lampe RC	1.50	4.00
❑ 71 Steve Blake RC	2.00	5.00
❑ 72 Chris Kaman RC	2.00	5.00
❑ 73 Curtis Borchardt	1.50	4.00
❑ 74 Kirk Hinrich RC	2.00	5.00
❑ 75 Dwyane Wade RC	4.00	10.00
❑ 76 Zarko Cabarkapa RC	1.50	4.00
❑ 77 LeBron James RC	20.00	50.00
❑ 78 Jerome Beasley RC	1.50	4.00
❑ 79 Nick Collison RC	1.50	4.00
❑ 80 Linton Johnson RC	1.50	4.00
❑ 81 Udonis Haslem RC	2.00	5.00
❑ 82 Travis Outlaw RC	2.00	5.00
❑ 83 Jason Kapono RC	2.00	5.00
❑ 84 T.J. Ford RC	2.00	5.00
❑ 85 Luke Ridnour RC	2.00	5.00
❑ 86 Darko Milicic RC	2.00	5.00
❑ 87 Mike Sweetney RC	1.50	4.00
❑ 88 Jarvis Hayes RC	1.50	4.00
❑ 89 Josh Moore RC	1.50	4.00
❑ 90 Reece Gaines RC	1.50	4.00

2004-05 SkyBox Autographics

❑ COMP.SET w/o SP's (60)	15.00	40.00
❑ COMMON CARD (1-60)	.25	.60
❑ COMMON ROOKIE (61-105)	1.50	4.00
❑ 1 Dwyane Wade	1.25	3.00
❑ 2 Derek Fisher	.30	.75
❑ 3 Latrell Sprewell	.30	.75
❑ 4 Peja Stojakovic	.30	.75
❑ 5 LeBron James	2.50	6.00
❑ 6 Elton Brand	.40	1.00
❑ 7 Allan Houston	.30	.75
❑ 8 Chris Bosh	.40	1.00
❑ 9 Carmelo Anthony	1.25	3.00
❑ 10 Shaquille O'Neal	1.00	2.50

❑ 11 Steve Nash	.60	1.50
❑ 12 Antawn Jamison	.40	1.00
❑ 13 Darko Milicic	.25	.60
❑ 14 Michael Redd	.40	1.00
❑ 15 Shawn Marion	.40	1.00
❑ 16 Dirk Nowitzki	.60	1.50
❑ 17 Kobe Bryant	2.00	5.00
❑ 18 Steve Francis	.40	1.00
❑ 19 Carlos Boozer	.40	1.00
❑ 20 Karl Malone	.40	1.00
❑ 21 T.J. Ford	.30	.75
❑ 22 Darius Miles	.30	.75
❑ 23 Paul Pierce	.40	1.00
❑ 24 Jermaine O'Neal	.40	1.00
❑ 25 Baron Davis	.40	1.00
❑ 26 Tony Parker	.40	1.00
❑ 27 Kirk Hinrich	.30	.75
❑ 28 Chris Kaman	.30	.75
❑ 29 Stephon Marbury	.40	1.00
❑ 30 Rashard Lewis	.40	1.00
❑ 31 Ben Wallace	.30	.75
❑ 32 Antoine Walker	.40	1.00
❑ 33 Amare Stoudemire	.75	2.00
❑ 34 Gary Payton	.40	1.00
❑ 35 Yao Ming	1.00	2.50
❑ 36 Richard Jefferson	.40	1.00
❑ 37 Tim Duncan	.75	2.00
❑ 38 Drew Gooden	.25	.60
❑ 39 Lamar Odom	.40	1.00
❑ 40 Grant Hill	.40	1.00
❑ 41 Vince Carter	.75	2.00
❑ 42 Michael Finley	.40	1.00
❑ 43 Jason Williams	.30	.75
❑ 44 Samuel Dalembert	.25	.60
❑ 45 Andrei Kirilenko	.40	1.00
❑ 46 Jason Kapono	.25	.60
❑ 47 Reggie Miller	.40	1.00
❑ 48 Jamaal Magloire	.25	.60
❑ 49 Ray Allen	.40	1.00
❑ 50 Kenyon Martin	.40	1.00
❑ 51 Pau Gasol	.40	1.00
❑ 52 Allen Iverson	.75	2.00
❑ 53 Gilbert Arenas	.40	1.00
❑ 54 Jason Richardson	.40	1.00
❑ 55 Kevin Garnett	.75	2.00
❑ 56 Zach Randolph	.40	1.00
❑ 57 Al Harrington	.30	.75
❑ 58 Tracy McGrady	.75	2.00
❑ 59 Jason Kidd	.60	1.50
❑ 60 Chris Webber	.40	1.00
❑ 61 Andris Biedrins RC	2.50	6.00
❑ 62 Robert Swift RC	1.50	4.00
❑ 63 Pavel Podkolzine RC	1.50	4.00
❑ 64 Kevin Martin RC	2.00	5.00
❑ 65 Beno Udrih RC	2.00	5.00
❑ 66 David Harrison RC	1.50	4.00
❑ 67 Andre Emmett RC	1.50	4.00
❑ 68 Emeka Okafor RC	3.00	8.00
❑ 69 Dwight Howard RC	5.00	12.00
❑ 70 Ben Gordon RC	2.00	5.00
❑ 71 Shaun Livingston RC	1.50	4.00
❑ 72 Devin Harris RC	3.00	8.00
❑ 73 Josh Childress RC	1.50	4.00
❑ 74 Luol Deng RC	2.00	5.00
❑ 75 Rafael Araujo RC	1.50	4.00
❑ 76 Andre Iguodala RC	4.00	10.00
❑ 77 Luke Jackson RC	1.50	4.00
❑ 78 Sebastian Telfair RC	1.50	4.00
❑ 79 Kris Humphries RC	2.50	6.00
❑ 80 Al Jefferson RC	3.00	8.00
❑ 81 Kirk Snyder RC	1.50	4.00
❑ 82 Josh Smith RC	4.00	10.00
❑ 83 J.R. Smith RC	3.00	8.00
❑ 84 Dorell Wright RC	2.00	5.00
❑ 85 Jameer Nelson RC	2.00	5.00
❑ 86 Delonte West RC	2.50	6.00
❑ 87 Tony Allen RC	2.00	5.00
❑ 88 Sasha Vujacic RC	1.50	4.00
❑ 89 Andres Nocioni RC	2.00	5.00
❑ 90 Royal Ivey RC	1.50	4.00
❑ 91 Trevor Ariza RC	2.00	5.00
❑ 92 Chris Duhon RC	2.50	6.00
❑ 93 John Edwards RC	1.50	4.00
❑ 94 Jackson Vroman RC	1.50	4.00
❑ 95 Quinton Ross	1.50	4.00
❑ 96 Erik Daniels RC	1.50	4.00
❑ 97 Anderson Varejao RC	2.00	5.00
❑ 98 Lionel Chalmers RC	1.50	4.00
❑ 99 Carlos Delfino	1.50	4.00
❑ 100 Jared Reiner RC	1.50	4.00
❑ 101 Bernard Robinson RC	1.50	4.00
❑ 102 Peter John Ramos RC	1.50	4.00
❑ 103 D.J. Mbenga RC	1.50	4.00
❑ 104 Mario Kasun RC	1.50	4.00
❑ 105 Nenad Krstic RC	2.00	5.00

1999-00 SkyBox Dominion

❑ COMPLETE SET (220)	25.00	50.00
❑ COMMON CARD (1-200)	.12	.30
❑ COMMON ROOKIE (201-220)	.20	.50
❑ 1 Jason Williams	.20	.50
❑ 2 Isaiah Rider	.12	.30
❑ 3 Tim Hardaway	.20	.50
❑ 4 Isaac Austin	.12	.30
❑ 5 Joe Smith	.15	.40
❑ 6 Mitch Richmond	.15	.40
❑ 7 Sam Mitchell	.12	.30
❑ 8 Terrell Brandon	.12	.30
❑ 9 Grant Long	.12	.30
❑ 10 Shaquille O'Neal	.50	1.25
❑ 11 Derrick Coleman	.15	.40
❑ 12 Rod Strickland	.12	.30
❑ 13 J.R. Reid	.12	.30
❑ 14 Tyrone Corbin	.12	.30
❑ 15 Jeff Hornacek	.15	.40
❑ 16 Malik Rose	.12	.30
❑ 17 Terry Davis	.12	.30
❑ 18 Theo Ratliff	.15	.40
❑ 19 Kevin Willis	.12	.30
❑ 20 Raef LaFrentz	.15	.40
❑ 21 Othella Harrington	.12	.30
❑ 22 Marcus Camby	.15	.40
❑ 23 Keon Clark	.12	.30
❑ 24 Robert Pack	.12	.30
❑ 25 Sam Mack	.12	.30
❑ 26 Shawn Kemp	.20	.50
❑ 27 Nick Anderson	.12	.30
❑ 28 Bill Wennington	.12	.30
❑ 29 Steve Smith	.12	.30
❑ 30 Kobe Bryant	1.00	2.50
❑ 31 Bobby Phills	.12	.30
❑ 32 Cedric Ceballos	.12	.30
❑ 33 Derek Fisher	.20	.50
❑ 34 Doug Christie	.15	.40
❑ 35 Danny Manning	.12	.30
❑ 36 Eric Murdock	.12	.30
❑ 37 Glen Rice	.20	.50
❑ 38 Dikembe Mutombo	.15	.40
❑ 39 Jason Kidd	.30	.75
❑ 40 Cedric Henderson	.12	.30
❑ 41 Rasheed Wallace	.20	.50
❑ 42 Tim Duncan	.40	1.00
❑ 43 John Stockton	.25	.60
❑ 44 Dell Curry	.12	.30
❑ 45 Muggsy Bogues	.15	.40
❑ 46 Danny Fortson	.12	.30
❑ 47 Charles Oakley	.15	.40
❑ 48 Elden Campbell	.12	.30
❑ 49 Tony Massenburg	.12	.30
❑ 50 Kevin Garnett	.40	1.00
❑ 51 Cherokee Parks	.12	.30

❑ 52 LaPhonso Ellis	.12	.30
❑ 53 Sam Cassell	.15	.40
❑ 54 Shawn Bradley	.12	.30
❑ 55 David Robinson	.25	.60
❑ 56 Juwan Howard	.15	.40
❑ 57 Lindsey Hunter	.12	.30
❑ 58 Mark Jackson	.20	.50
❑ 59 Olden Polynice	.12	.30
❑ 60 Tracy McGrady	.40	1.00
❑ 61 Michael Finley	.20	.50
❑ 62 Matt Geiger	.12	.30
❑ 63 Maurice Taylor	.15	.40
❑ 64 Rex Chapman	.12	.30
❑ 65 Chris Mullin	.20	.50
❑ 66 Ray Allen	.20	.50
❑ 67 Bison Dele	.12	.30
❑ 68 Dickey Simpkins	.12	.30
❑ 69 Alvin Williams	.12	.30
❑ 70 Grant Hill	.20	.50
❑ 71 Mark Bryant	.12	.30
❑ 72 Adam Keefe	.12	.30
❑ 73 Alan Henderson	.12	.30
❑ 74 Eric Snow	.15	.40
❑ 75 Matt Harpring	.15	.40
❑ 76 Jalen Rose	.15	.40
❑ 77 Derek Harper	.15	.40
❑ 78 Kerry Kittles	.12	.30
❑ 79 Tony Battie	.15	.40
❑ 80 Larry Hughes	.15	.40
❑ 81 Arvydas Sabonis	.15	.40
❑ 82 Allan Houston	.15	.40
❑ 83 Tom Gugliotta	.12	.30
❑ 84 Reggie Miller	.20	.50
❑ 85 Dejuan Wheat	.12	.30
❑ 86 Pat Garrity	.12	.30
❑ 87 Karl Malone	.25	.60
❑ 88 Sam Perkins	.12	.30
❑ 89 Michael Olowokandi	.12	.30
❑ 90 Anfernee Hardaway	.20	.50
❑ 91 Bryant Reeves	.12	.30
❑ 92 Gary Trent	.12	.30
❑ 93 George Lynch	.12	.30
❑ 94 Scottie Pippen	.30	.75
❑ 95 Jerry Stackhouse	.20	.50
❑ 96 Kendall Gill	.12	.30
❑ 97 Vin Baker	.20	.50
❑ 98 Dale Davis	.12	.30
❑ 99 Charles Barkley	.25	.60
❑ 100 Allen Iverson	.40	1.00
❑ 101 Keith Van Horn	.15	.40
❑ 102 Andrew DeClercq	.12	.30
❑ 103 Michael Doleac	.12	.30
❑ 104 Chauncey Billups	.20	.50
❑ 105 Chris Mills	.12	.30
❑ 106 Lamond Murray	.12	.30
❑ 107 Glenn Robinson	.15	.40
❑ 108 Brian Grant	.12	.30
❑ 109 Christian Laettner	.15	.40
❑ 110 Antawn Jamison	.20	.50
❑ 111 Erick Dampier	.15	.40
❑ 112 Vernon Maxwell	.15	.40
❑ 113 Kenny Anderson	.15	.40
❑ 114 Clarence Weatherspoon	.12	.30
❑ 115 Corliss Williamson	.12	.30
❑ 116 Paul Pierce	.20	.50
❑ 117 Clifford Robinson	.12	.30
❑ 118 Damon Stoudamire	.20	.50
❑ 119 Dana Barros	.12	.30
❑ 120 Stephon Marbury	.20	.50
❑ 120B Stephon Marbury Promo	.20	.50
❑ 121 Latrell Sprewell	.15	.40
❑ 122 Tyronn Lue	.12	.30
❑ 123 Walt Williams	.12	.30
❑ 124 P.J. Brown	.12	.30
❑ 125 Gary Payton	.20	.50
❑ 126 Nick Van Exel	.15	.40
❑ 127 Bryant Stith	.12	.30
❑ 128 Eric Piatkowski	.15	.40
❑ 129 Tyrone Nesby RC	.20	.50
❑ 130 Ron Mercer	.12	.30
❑ 131 Hersey Hawkins	.12	.30
❑ 132 Vlade Divac	.20	.50
❑ 133 Darrick Martin	.12	.30
❑ 134 Avery Johnson	.15	.40
❑ 135 Jaren Jackson	.12	.30
❑ 136 Brevin Knight	.12	.30
❑ 137 Wesley Person	.12	.30
❑ 138 Derek Anderson	.12	.30
❑ 139 Tim Thomas	.15	.40
❑ 140 Antonio McDyess	.15	.40
❑ 141 A.C. Green	.20	.50
❑ 142 Chris Webber	.20	.50
❑ 143 Scott Burrell	.12	.30
❑ 144 John Starks	.20	.50
❑ 145 Howard Eisley	.12	.30
❑ 146 Mike Bibby	.20	.50
❑ 147 Toni Kukoc	.20	.50
❑ 148 Eddie Jones	.20	.50
❑ 149 Otis Thorpe	.12	.30
❑ 150 Shareef Abdur-Rahim	.15	.40
❑ 151 Calbert Cheaney	.12	.30
❑ 152 Cuttino Mobley	.15	.40
❑ 153 Michael Dickerson	.12	.30
❑ 154 Sean Elliott	.20	.50
❑ 155 Terry Porter	.12	.30
❑ 156 Dean Garrett	.12	.30
❑ 157 Charlie Ward	.12	.30
❑ 158 Larry Johnson	.20	.50
❑ 159 Dan Majerle	.20	.50
❑ 160 Jayson Williams	.15	.40
❑ 161 Anthony Peeler	.12	.30
❑ 162 Ron Harper	.12	.30
❑ 163 Darrell Armstrong	.12	.30
❑ 164 Kurt Thomas	.15	.40
❑ 165 Brent Barry	.15	.40
❑ 166 Lawrence Funderburke	.12	.30
❑ 167 Terry Cummings	.12	.30
❑ 168 Jamal Mashburn	.12	.30
❑ 169 Robert Traylor	.12	.30
❑ 170 Greg Ostertag	.12	.30
❑ 171 Brad Miller	.15	.40
❑ 172 Mario Elie	.12	.30
❑ 173 Antoine Walker	.20	.50
❑ 174 Ricky Davis	.20	.50
❑ 175 Vince Carter	.40	1.00
❑ 176 Hakeem Olajuwon WT	.20	.50
❑ 177 Luc Longley WT	.12	.30
❑ 178 Tim Duncan WT	.40	1.00
❑ 179 Rick Fox WT	.12	.30
❑ 180 Zydrunas Ilgauskas WT	.15	.40
❑ 181 Toni Kukoc WT	.20	.50
❑ 182 Felipe Lopez WT	.12	.30
❑ 183 Dikembe Mutombo WT	.15	.40
❑ 184 Steve Nash WT	.30	.75
❑ 185 Dirk Nowitzki WT	.30	.75
❑ 186 Vitaly Potapenko WT	.12	.30
❑ 187 Detlef Schrempf WT	.15	.40
❑ 188 Rik Smits WT	.20	.50
❑ 189 Vladimir Stepania WT	.12	.30
❑ 190 Peja Stojakovic WT	.15	.40
❑ 191 Donyell Marshall 3FA	.15	.40
❑ 192 Shareef Abdur-Rahim 3FA	.15	.40
❑ 193 Michael Dickerson 3FA	.12	.30
❑ 194 Damon Stoudamire 3FA	.20	.50
❑ 195 Allen Iverson 3FA	.40	1.00
❑ 196 Grant Hill 3FA	.20	.50
❑ 197 Scottie Pippen 3FA	.30	.75
❑ 198 Bryon Russell 3FA	.12	.30
❑ 199 Alonzo Mourning 3FA	.20	.50
❑ 200 Patrick Ewing 3FA	.25	.60
❑ 201 Ron Artest RC	.75	2.00
❑ 202 William Avery RC	.20	.50
❑ 203 Lamar Odom RC	.60	1.50
❑ 204 Baron Davis RC	.75	2.00
❑ 205 John Celestand RC	.20	.50
❑ 206 Jumaine Jones RC	.20	.50
❑ 207 Andre Miller RC	.60	1.50
❑ 208 Elton Brand RC	.60	1.50
❑ 209 James Posey RC	.30	.75
❑ 210 Jason Terry RC	.50	1.25
❑ 211 Kenny Thomas RC	.20	.50
❑ 212 Steve Francis RC	.60	1.50
❑ 213 Wally Szczerbiak RC	.60	1.50
❑ 214 Richard Hamilton RC	.60	1.50
❑ 215 Jonathan Bender RC	.20	.50
❑ 216 Shawn Marion RC	.60	1.50
❑ 217 A.Radojevic RC	.20	.50
❑ 218 Tim James RC	.20	.50
❑ 219 Trajan Langdon RC	.20	.50
❑ 220 Corey Maggette RC	.60	1.50

2004-05 SkyBox Fresh Ink

❑ COMP.SET w/o SP's (90)	15.00	40.00
❑ COMMON CARD (1-90)	.20	.50
❑ COMMON ROOKIE (91-120)	1.50	4.00
❑ 1 T.J. Ford	.25	.60
❑ 2 Pau Gasol	.30	.75
❑ 3 Kirk Hinrich	.25	.60
❑ 4 Shawn Marion	.30	.75

❑ 5 Darius Miles	.25	.60
❑ 6 Dirk Nowitzki	.50	1.25
❑ 7 Paul Pierce	.30	.75
❑ 8 Theron Smith	.20	.50
❑ 9 Rasheed Wallace	.30	.75
❑ 10 Kobe Bryant	1.50	4.00
❑ 11 Kevin Garnett	.60	1.50
❑ 12 Steve Nash	.50	1.25
❑ 13 Gilbert Arenas	.30	.75
❑ 14 Udonis Haslem	.25	.60
❑ 15 Ben Wallace	.25	.60
❑ 16 Ray Allen	.30	.75
❑ 17 Elton Brand	.30	.75
❑ 18 Caron Butler	.25	.60
❑ 19 Drew Gooden	.20	.50
❑ 20 Richard Hamilton	.25	.60
❑ 21 Grant Hill	.30	.75
❑ 22 Jason Kapono	.20	.50
❑ 23 Tony Parker	.30	.75
❑ 24 Jalen Rose	.25	.60
❑ 25 Amare Stoudemire	.60	1.50
❑ 26 Gerald Wallace	.30	.75
❑ 27 Jason Williams	.25	.60
❑ 28 LeBron James	2.00	5.00
❑ 29 Jamal Crawford	.25	.60
❑ 30 Earl Boykins	.20	.50
❑ 31 Michael Finley	.30	.75
❑ 32 Chris Kaman	.25	.60
❑ 33 Stephon Marbury	.30	.75
❑ 34 Shaquille O'Neal	.75	2.00
❑ 35 Antoine Walker	.30	.75
❑ 36 Ron Artest	.25	.60
❑ 37 Samuel Dalembert	.20	.50
❑ 38 Reece Gaines	.20	.50
❑ 39 Rashard Lewis	.30	.75
❑ 40 Desmond Mason	.25	.60
❑ 41 Jason Richardson	.30	.75
❑ 42 Wally Szczerbiak	.25	.60
❑ 43 Bonzi Wells	.20	.50
❑ 44 Tim Duncan	.60	1.50
❑ 45 Lamar Odom	.30	.75
❑ 46 Jermaine O'Neal	.30	.75
❑ 47 Mickael Pietrus	.25	.60
❑ 48 Zach Randolph	.30	.75
❑ 49 Joe Smith	.20	.50
❑ 50 Allan Houston	.25	.60
❑ 51 Carmelo Anthony	1.00	2.50
❑ 52 Manu Ginobili	.30	.75
❑ 53 Tyronn Lue	.20	.50
❑ 54 Tayshaun Prince	.25	.60
❑ 55 Luke Ridnour	.20	.50
❑ 56 Peja Stojakovic	.25	.60
❑ 57 Dwyane Wade	1.00	2.50
❑ 58 David West	.30	.75
❑ 59 Allen Iverson	.60	1.50
❑ 60 Richard Jefferson	.30	.75
❑ 61 Andrei Kirilenko	.30	.75
❑ 62 Latrell Sprewell	.25	.60
❑ 63 Jason Kidd	.50	1.25
❑ 64 Baron Davis	.30	.75
❑ 65 Al Harrington	.25	.60
❑ 66 Jarvis Hayes	.20	.50
❑ 67 Gary Payton	.30	.75
❑ 68 Chris Webber	.30	.75
❑ 69 Vince Carter	.60	1.50
❑ 70 Eric Williams	.20	.50
❑ 71 Nene	.25	.60
❑ 72 Chris Bosh	.30	.75
❑ 73 Sam Cassell	.25	.60
❑ 74 Mike Dunleavy	.25	.60
❑ 75 Steve Francis	.30	.75
❑ 76 Antawn Jamison	.30	.75
❑ 77 Joe Johnson	.30	.75
❑ 78 Corey Maggette	.25	.60
❑ 79 Jamaal Magloire	.20	.50

❑ 80 Kenyon Martin	.30	.75
❑ 81 Reggie Miller	.30	.75
❑ 82 Yao Ming	.75	2.00
❑ 83 Dajuan Wagner	.20	.50
❑ 84 Willie Green	.20	.50
❑ 85 Shareef Abdur-Rahim	.25	.60
❑ 86 Tracy McGrady	.60	1.50
❑ 87 Carlos Arroyo	.30	.75
❑ 88 Michael Redd	.30	.75
❑ 89 Alonzo Mourning	.30	.75
❑ 90 Mike Bibby	.25	.60
❑ 91 Luke Jackson RC	1.50	4.00
❑ 92 Matt Freije RC	1.50	4.00
❑ 93 Kevin Martin RC	2.00	5.00
❑ 94 Josh Smith RC	4.00	10.00
❑ 95 Kris Humphries RC	2.50	6.00
❑ 96 Trevor Ariza RC	2.00	5.00
❑ 97 Shaun Livingston RC	1.50	4.00
❑ 98 Pavel Podkolzin RC	1.50	4.00
❑ 99 Kirk Snyder RC	1.50	4.00
❑ 100 Beno Udrih RC	2.00	5.00
❑ 101 Tony Allen RC	2.00	5.00
❑ 102 Chris Duhon RC	2.50	6.00
❑ 103 Josh Childress RC	1.50	4.00
❑ 104 David Harrison RC	1.50	4.00
❑ 105 Al Jefferson RC	3.00	8.00
❑ 106 Rafael Araujo RC	1.50	4.00
❑ 107 Andre Emmett RC	1.50	4.00
❑ 108 Devin Harris RC	3.00	8.00
❑ 109 Andre Iguodala RC	4.00	10.00
❑ 110 Emeka Okafor RC	3.00	8.00
❑ 111 Dorell Wright RC	2.00	5.00
❑ 112 Luol Deng RC	2.00	5.00
❑ 113 Dwight Howard RC	5.00	12.00
❑ 114 J.R. Smith RC	3.00	8.00
❑ 115 Sasha Vujacic RC	1.50	4.00
❑ 116 Jameer Nelson RC	2.00	5.00
❑ 117 Robert Swift RC	1.50	4.00
❑ 118 Sebastian Telfair RC	1.50	4.00
❑ 119 Andris Biedrins RC	2.50	6.00
❑ 120 Ben Gordon RC	2.00	5.00

2003-04 SkyBox LE

❑ COMP.SET w/o SP's (110)	12.50	30.00
❑ COMMON CARD (1-110)	.20	.50
❑ COMMON ROOKIE (111-160)	2.50	6.00
❑ 1 Jason Terry	.25	.60
❑ 2 Antoine Walker	.30	.75
❑ 3 Paul Pierce	.30	.75
❑ 4 Eddy Curry	.25	.60
❑ 5 Ricky Davis	.25	.60
❑ 6 Jamal Crawford	.25	.60
❑ 7 Raef LaFrentz	.20	.50
❑ 8 Darius Miles	.25	.60
❑ 9 Ray Allen	.20	.50
❑ 10 Sam Cassell	.25	.60
❑ 11 Andre Miller	.25	.60
❑ 12 Dirk Nowitzki	.50	1.25
❑ 13 Zach Randolph	.30	.75
❑ 14 Tim Duncan	.60	1.50
❑ 15 Gary Payton	.30	.75
❑ 16 Ben Wallace	.25	.60
❑ 17 Michael Finley	.30	.75
❑ 18 David Wesley	.20	.50
❑ 19 Nick Van Exel	.25	.60
❑ 20 Marcus Camby	.25	.60
❑ 21 Gilbert Arenas	.30	.75
❑ 22 Marcus Haislip	.20	.50
❑ 23 Cuttino Mobley	.25	.60
❑ 24 Tayshaun Prince	.25	.60
❑ 25 Chris Webber	.30	.75
❑ 26 Reggie Miller	.30	.75
❑ 27 Chauncey Billups	.30	.75
❑ 28 Quentin Richardson	.25	.60
❑ 29 Mike Dunleavy	.25	.60
❑ 30 Karl Malone	.30	.75
❑ 31 Yao Ming	.60	1.50
❑ 32 Tyson Chandler	.25	.60
❑ 33 Jason Williams	.25	.60
❑ 34 Eddie Griffin	.20	.50
❑ 35 Eddie Jones	.25	.60
❑ 36 Jamaal Tinsley	.25	.60
❑ 37 Michael Redd	.30	.75
❑ 38 Elton Brand	.30	.75
❑ 39 Rashard Lewis	.30	.75
❑ 40 Vince Carter	.60	1.50
❑ 41 Wally Szczerbiak	.25	.60
❑ 42 Chris Wilcox	.20	.50
❑ 43 Kenyon Martin	.30	.75
❑ 44 Shaquille O'Neal	.75	2.00
❑ 45 Baron Davis	.30	.75
❑ 46 Pau Gasol	.30	.75
❑ 47 Dikembe Mutombo	.25	.60
❑ 48 Shane Battier	.25	.60
❑ 49 Drew Gooden	.20	.50
❑ 50 Lamar Odom	.30	.75
❑ 51 Glenn Robinson	.25	.60
❑ 52 Tim Thomas	.20	.50
❑ 53 Shawn Marion	.30	.75
❑ 54 Kevin Garnett	.60	1.50
❑ 55 Stephon Marbury	.30	.75
❑ 56 Rasheed Wallace	.30	.75
❑ 57 Troy Hudson	.20	.50
❑ 58 Mike Bibby	.25	.60
❑ 59 Jason Kidd	.50	1.25
❑ 60 Tony Parker	.30	.75
❑ 61 Andrei Kirilenko	.30	.75
❑ 62 Manu Ginobili	.30	.75
❑ 63 Kerry Kittles	.25	.60
❑ 64 Brent Barry	.20	.50
❑ 65 Allan Houston	.25	.60
❑ 66 Morris Peterson	.25	.60
❑ 67 Tracy McGrady	.60	1.50
❑ 68 Matt Harpring	.25	.60
❑ 69 Erick Dampier	.20	.50
❑ 70 Jerry Stackhouse	.25	.60
❑ 71 John Salmons	.25	.60
❑ 72 Stephen Jackson	.25	.60
❑ 73 Scottie Pippen	.50	1.25
❑ 74 Dajuan Wagner	.20	.50
❑ 75 Keon Clark	.20	.50
❑ 76 Carlos Boozer	.30	.75
❑ 77 Steve Nash	.50	1.25
❑ 78 Nene	.25	.60
❑ 79 Keith Van Horn	.25	.60
❑ 80 Earl Boykins	.20	.50
❑ 81 Richard Hamilton	.25	.60
❑ 82 Jason Richardson	.30	.75
❑ 83 Steve Francis	.30	.75
❑ 84 Jermaine O'Neal	.30	.75
❑ 85 Ron Artest	.25	.60
❑ 86 Corey Maggette	.20	.50
❑ 87 Kwame Brown	.20	.50
❑ 88 Kobe Bryant	1.50	4.00
❑ 89 Mike Miller	.25	.60
❑ 90 Caron Butler	.25	.60
❑ 91 Desmond Mason	.25	.60
❑ 92 Latrell Sprewell	.25	.60
❑ 93 Richard Jefferson	.30	.75
❑ 94 Jamal Mashburn	.20	.50
❑ 95 Troy Murphy	.30	.75
❑ 96 Peja Stojakovic	.25	.60
❑ 97 Allen Iverson	.60	1.50
❑ 98 Amare Stoudemire	.60	1.50
❑ 99 Rasho Nesterovic	.20	.50
❑ 100 Bonzi Wells	.20	.50
❑ 101 Bobby Jackson	.20	.50
❑ 102 Anfernee Hardaway	.30	.75
❑ 103 Larry Hughes	.25	.60
❑ 104 Shareef Abdur-Rahim	.25	.60
❑ 105 Hedo Turkoglu	.25	.60
❑ 106 Alvin Williams	.20	.50
❑ 107 Qyntel Woods	.20	.50
❑ 108 Brad Miller	.25	.60
❑ 109 Jalen Rose	.25	.60
❑ 110 Antonio Davis	.20	.50
❑ 111 David West RC	3.00	8.00
❑ 112 Boris Diaw RC	3.00	8.00
❑ 113 Travis Hansen RC	2.50	6.00
❑ 114 Marcus Banks RC	2.50	6.00
❑ 115 Kendrick Perkins RC	4.00	10.00
❑ 116 Darius Songaila	2.50	6.00
❑ 117 Kirk Hinrich/99 RC	10.00	25.00
❑ 118 LeBron James/99 RC	450.00	750.00
❑ 119 Jason Kapono RC	3.00	8.00
❑ 120 Josh Howard RC	3.00	8.00
❑ 121 Marquis Daniels RC	3.00	8.00
❑ 122 Carmelo Anthony/99 RC	60.00	120.00
❑ 123 Darko Milicic/99 RC	10.00	25.00
❑ 124 Zaur Pachulia RC	3.00	8.00
❑ 125 Mickael Pietrus RC	3.00	8.00
❑ 126 Ben Handlogten RC	2.50	6.00
❑ 127 James Jones RC	2.50	6.00
❑ 128 Chris Kaman RC	3.00	8.00
❑ 129 Josh Moore RC	2.50	6.00
❑ 130 Brian Cook RC	2.50	6.00
❑ 131 Luke Walton RC	3.00	8.00
❑ 132 Troy Bell RC	2.50	6.00
❑ 133 Dahntay Jones RC	2.50	6.00
❑ 134 Dwyane Wade/99 RC	75.00	150.00
❑ 135 Udonis Haslem RC	3.00	8.00
❑ 136 T.J. Ford/99 RC	10.00	25.00
❑ 137 Ndudi Ebi RC	2.50	6.00
❑ 138 Zoran Planinic RC	2.50	6.00
❑ 139 Raul Lopez	2.50	6.00
❑ 140 Francisco Elson RC	2.50	6.00
❑ 141 Mike Sweetney RC	2.50	6.00
❑ 142 Maciej Lampe RC	2.50	6.00
❑ 143 Slavko Vranes RC	2.50	6.00
❑ 144 Keith Bogans/99 RC	8.00	20.00
❑ 145 Reece Gaines RC	2.50	6.00
❑ 146 Willie Green RC	2.50	6.00
❑ 147 Kyle Korver RC	3.00	8.00
❑ 148 Zarko Cabarkapa RC	2.50	6.00
❑ 149 Leandro Barbosa RC	3.00	8.00
❑ 150 Travis Outlaw RC	3.00	8.00
❑ 151 Curtis Borchardt	2.50	6.00
❑ 152 Alex Garcia RC	2.50	6.00
❑ 153 Richie Frahm RC	2.50	6.00
❑ 154 Nick Collison RC	2.50	6.00
❑ 155 Luke Ridnour/99 RC	10.00	25.00
❑ 156 Chris Bosh/99 RC	12.00	30.00
❑ 157 Aleksandar Pavlovic RC	3.00	8.00
❑ 158 Maurice Williams RC	4.00	10.00
❑ 159 Jarvis Hayes/99 RC	8.00	20.00
❑ 160 Steve Blake RC	3.00	8.00

2004-05 SkyBox LE

❑ COMMON CARD (1-75)	.20	.50
❑ COMMON ROOKIE/99	3.00	8.00
❑ COMMON ROOKIE/499	2.00	5.00
❑ 1 Tony Parker	.30	.75
❑ 2 Vince Carter	.60	1.50
❑ 3 Al Harrington	.25	.60
❑ 4 Dwyane Wade	1.00	2.50
❑ 5 Latrell Sprewell	.25	.60
❑ 6 Michael Finley	.30	.75
❑ 7 Caron Butler	.25	.60
❑ 8 Zach Randolph	.30	.75
❑ 9 Peja Stojakovic	.25	.60
❑ 10 Eddy Curry	.25	.60
❑ 11 Allen Iverson	.60	1.50
❑ 12 Kirk Hinrich	.25	.60
❑ 13 Jason Williams	.25	.60
❑ 14 Hedo Turkoglu	.25	.60
❑ 15 Manu Ginobili	.30	.75
❑ 16 Eddie House	.20	.50
❑ 17 Reggie Miller	.30	.75
❑ 18 Steve Francis	.30	.75
❑ 19 LeBron James	2.00	5.00
❑ 20 Dirk Nowitzki	.50	1.25
❑ 21 Stephon Marbury	.30	.75
❑ 22 Ray Allen	.30	.75
❑ 23 Carmelo Anthony	1.00	2.50
❑ 24 Lamar Odom	.30	.75
❑ 25 Jamaal Magloire	.20	.50
❑ 26 Shareef Abdur-Rahim	.25	.60
❑ 27 Chris Webber	.30	.75
❑ 28 Jason Richardson	.30	.75
❑ 29 Richard Jefferson	.30	.75
❑ 30 Richard Hamilton	.25	.60

❑ 31 Alonzo Mourning	.30	.75
❑ 32 Chris Bosh	.30	.75
❑ 33 Mike Dunleavy	.25	.60
❑ 34 Andrei Kirilenko	.30	.75
❑ 35 Tracy McGrady	.60	1.50
❑ 36 T.J. Ford	.25	.60
❑ 37 Jason Kidd	.50	1.25
❑ 38 Carlos Arroyo	.30	.75
❑ 39 Rasheed Wallace	.30	.75
❑ 40 Gilbert Arenas	.30	.75
❑ 41 Kenyon Martin	.30	.75
❑ 42 Tim Duncan	.60	1.50
❑ 43 Yao Ming	.75	2.00
❑ 44 Carlos Boozer	.30	.75
❑ 45 Michael Redd	.30	.75
❑ 46 Larry Hughes	.25	.60
❑ 47 Antoine Walker	.30	.75
❑ 48 Kevin Garnett	.60	1.50
❑ 49 Willie Green	.20	.50
❑ 50 Tyson Chandler	.25	.60
❑ 51 Elton Brand	.30	.75
❑ 52 Allan Houston	.25	.60
❑ 53 Shawn Marion	.30	.75
❑ 54 Ricky Davis	.25	.60
❑ 55 Shaquille O'Neal	.75	2.00
❑ 56 Steve Nash	.50	1.25
❑ 57 Jarvis Hayes	.20	.50
❑ 58 Zydrunas Ilgauskas	.25	.60
❑ 59 Corey Maggette	.25	.60
❑ 60 Ben Wallace	.25	.60
❑ 61 Darius Miles	.25	.60
❑ 62 Drew Gooden	.20	.50
❑ 63 Pau Gasol	.30	.75
❑ 64 Jamal Crawford	.25	.60
❑ 65 Gary Payton	.30	.75
❑ 66 Jermaine O'Neal	.30	.75
❑ 67 Jason Kapono	.20	.50
❑ 68 Marquis Daniels	.20	.50
❑ 69 Kobe Bryant	1.50	4.00
❑ 70 Baron Davis	.30	.75
❑ 71 Mike Bibby	.25	.60
❑ 72 Rashard Lewis	.30	.75
❑ 73 Paul Pierce	.30	.75
❑ 74 Sam Cassell	.25	.60
❑ 75 Amare Stoudemire	.60	1.50
❑ 76 Dwight Howard/99 RC	10.00	25.00
❑ 77 Emeka Okafor/99 RC	6.00	15.00
❑ 78 Ben Gordon/99 RC	4.00	10.00
❑ 79 Shaun Livingston/99 RC	3.00	8.00
❑ 80 Devin Harris/99 RC	6.00	15.00
❑ 81 Josh Childress/99 RC	3.00	8.00
❑ 82 Luol Deng/99 RC	4.00	10.00
❑ 83 Rafael Araujo/99 RC	3.00	8.00
❑ 84 Andre Iguodala/99 RC	8.00	20.00
❑ 85 Luke Jackson/99 RC	3.00	8.00
❑ 86 Andris Biedrins/99 RC	5.00	12.00
❑ 87 Robert Swift RC	2.00	5.00
❑ 88 Sebastian Telfair/99 RC	3.00	8.00
❑ 89 Kris Humphries RC	3.00	8.00
❑ 90 Al Jefferson RC	4.00	10.00
❑ 91 Kirk Snyder RC	2.00	5.00
❑ 92 Josh Smith/99 RC	8.00	20.00
❑ 93 J.R. Smith/99 RC	6.00	15.00
❑ 94 Dorell Wright RC	2.50	6.00
❑ 95 Jameer Nelson/99 RC	4.00	10.00
❑ 96 Pavel Podkolzine RC	2.00	5.00
❑ 97 Nenad Krstic RC	2.50	6.00
❑ 98 Andres Nocioni/99 RC	4.00	10.00
❑ 99 Delonte West RC	3.00	8.00
❑ 100 Tony Allen RC	2.50	6.00
❑ 101 Kevin Martin RC	2.50	6.00
❑ 102 Sasha Vujacic/99 RC	3.00	8.00
❑ 103 Beno Udrih RC	2.50	6.00
❑ 104 David Harrison RC	2.00	5.00
❑ 105 Anderson Varejao/99 RC	4.00	10.00
❑ 106 Jackson Vroman RC	2.00	5.00
❑ 107 Peter John Ramos RC	2.00	5.00
❑ 108 Lionel Chalmers RC	2.00	5.00
❑ 109 Donta Smith RC	2.00	5.00
❑ 110 Andre Emmett RC	2.00	5.00
❑ 111 Antonio Burks RC	2.00	5.00
❑ 112 Royal Ivey RC	2.00	5.00
❑ 113 Chris Duhon/99 RC	5.00	12.00
❑ 114 Erik Daniels RC	2.00	5.00
❑ 115 Justin Reed RC	2.00	5.00
❑ 116 Horace Jenkins RC	2.00	5.00
❑ 117 D.J. Mbenga RC	2.00	5.00
❑ 118 Trevor Ariza RC	2.50	6.00
❑ 119 Tim Pickett RC	2.00	5.00
❑ 120 Bernard Robinson RC	2.00	5.00
❑ 121 Ibrahim Kutluay RC	2.00	5.00
❑ 122 Romain Sato RC	2.00	5.00
❑ 123 Luis Flores RC	2.00	5.00
❑ 124 Damien Wilkins RC	2.00	5.00
❑ 125 Yuta Tabuse/99 RC		

1998-99 SkyBox Molten Metal

❑ COMPLETE SET (150)	40.00	80.00
❑ COMMON CARD (1-100)	.02	.10
❑ COMMON ROOKIE	.25	.60
❑ COMMON CARD (101-130)	.05	.15
❑ COMMON CARD (131-150)	.20	.50
❑ 1 Maurice Taylor	.05	.15
❑ 2 Bison Dele	.02	.10
❑ 3 Anthony Mason	.05	.15
❑ 4 John Starks	.05	.15
❑ 5 Anthony Johnson	.02	.10
❑ 6 Calbert Cheaney	.02	.10
❑ 7 Roshown McLeod RC	.25	.60
❑ 8 Jalen Rose	.08	.25
❑ 9 Kelvin Cato	.02	.10
❑ 10 Walter McCarty	.02	.10
❑ 11 Isaac Austin	.02	.10
❑ 12 Arvydas Sabonis	.05	.15
❑ 13 David Wesley	.02	.10
❑ 14 Jim Jackson	.02	.10
❑ 15 Elden Campbell	.02	.10
❑ 16 Michael Doleac RC	.50	1.25
❑ 17 Chris Webber	.08	.25
❑ 18 Mitch Richmond	.05	.15
❑ 19 Johnny Newman	.02	.10
❑ 20 Jayson Williams	.02	.10
❑ 21 George Lynch	.02	.10
❑ 22 Ron Harper	.05	.15
❑ 23 Donyell Marshall	.05	.15
❑ 24 Derek Fisher	.08	.25
❑ 25 Matt Harpring RC	.75	2.00
❑ 26 Jason Williams RC	2.00	5.00
❑ 27 Toni Kukoc	.05	.15
❑ 28 Clarence Weatherspoon	.02	.10
❑ 29 Eddie Jones	.08	.25
❑ 30 Bo Outlaw	.02	.10
❑ 31 Zydrunas Ilgauskas	.05	.15
❑ 32 Michael Dickerson RC	1.00	2.50
❑ 33 Tyronn Lue RC	.60	1.50
❑ 34 Theo Ratliff	.05	.15
❑ 35 Dirk Nowitzki RC	6.00	12.00
❑ 36 Robert Traylor RC	.50	1.25
❑ 37 Gary Trent	.02	.10
❑ 38 Wesley Person	.02	.10
❑ 39 Bryce Drew RC	.50	1.25
❑ 40 P.J. Brown	.02	.10
❑ 41 Joe Smith	.05	.15
❑ 42 Avery Johnson	.02	.10
❑ 43 Chris Anstey	.02	.10
❑ 44 Mario Elie	.02	.10
❑ 45 Voshon Lenard	.02	.10
❑ 46 Rex Chapman	.02	.10
❑ 47 Hersey Hawkins	.02	.10
❑ 48 Shawn Bradley	.02	.10
❑ 49 Matt Maloney	.02	.10
❑ 50 Dan Majerle	.05	.15
❑ 51 Pat Garrity RC	.30	.75
❑ 52 Sam Perkins	.02	.10
❑ 53 Mookie Blaylock	.02	.10
❑ 54 Al Harrington RC	1.25	3.00
❑ 55 Clifford Robinson	.02	.10
❑ 56 Alan Henderson	.02	.10
❑ 57 Chris Mullin	.08	.25
❑ 58 Dennis Scott	.02	.10
❑ 59 A.C. Green	.05	.15
❑ 60 Tyrone Hill	.02	.10
❑ 61 Chauncey Billups	.05	.15
❑ 62 Michael Finley	.08	.25
❑ 63 Terrell Brandon	.05	.15
❑ 64 Detlef Schrempf	.05	.15
❑ 65 Bonzi Wells RC	2.00	5.00
❑ 66 Larry Johnson	.05	.15
❑ 67 Bryant Reeves	.02	.10
❑ 68 Raef LaFrentz RC	.75	2.00
❑ 69 Kendall Gill	.02	.10
❑ 70 Bryon Russell	.02	.10
❑ 71 Bobby Phills	.02	.10
❑ 72 Tony Delk	.02	.10
❑ 73 Lorenzen Wright	.02	.10
❑ 74 Keon Clark RC	.75	2.00
❑ 75 Billy Owens	.02	.10
❑ 76 Tracy Murray	.02	.10
❑ 77 Bobby Jackson	.05	.15
❑ 78 Sam Cassell	.08	.25
❑ 79 Corliss Williamson	.05	.15
❑ 80 Jeff Hornacek	.05	.15
❑ 81 LaPhonso Ellis	.02	.10
❑ 82 Sam Mitchell	.02	.10
❑ 83 Sean Elliott	.05	.15
❑ 84 John Wallace	.02	.10
❑ 85 Dikembe Mutombo	.05	.15
❑ 86 Rik Smits	.05	.15
❑ 87 Isaiah Rider	.02	.10
❑ 88 Joe Dumars	.08	.25
❑ 89 Allan Houston	.05	.15
❑ 90 Sam Mack	.02	.10
❑ 91 Paul Pierce RC	4.00	10.00
❑ 92 Lamond Murray	.02	.10
❑ 93 Rasheed Wallace	.08	.25
❑ 94 Danny Fortson	.02	.10
❑ 95 Cherokee Parks	.02	.10
❑ 96 Antonio Daniels	.02	.10
❑ 97 Shandon Anderson	.02	.10
❑ 98 Ricky Davis RC	1.50	4.00
❑ 99 Rodney Rogers	.02	.10
❑ 100 Tariq Abdul-Wahad	.05	.15
❑ 101 Glenn Robinson	.07	.20
❑ 102 Ron Mercer	.05	.15
❑ 103 Alonzo Mourning	.07	.20
❑ 104 Marcus Camby	.07	.20
❑ 105 Steve Smith	.07	.20
❑ 106 Tim Hardaway	.07	.20
❑ 107 Rod Strickland	.05	.15
❑ 108 Reggie Miller	.15	.40
❑ 109 Juwan Howard	.07	.20
❑ 110 Hakeem Olajuwon	.15	.40
❑ 111 John Stockton	.08	.25
❑ 112 Antonio McDyess	.07	.20
❑ 113 Charles Barkley	.40	1.00
❑ 114 Karl Malone	.08	.25
❑ 115 Jerry Stackhouse	.15	.40
❑ 116 Tracy McGrady	.75	2.00
❑ 117 Brevin Knight	.05	.15
❑ 118 Gary Payton	.15	.40
❑ 119 Derek Anderson	.10	.30
❑ 120 Glen Rice	.07	.20
❑ 121 David Robinson	.15	.40
❑ 122 Vin Baker	.07	.20
❑ 123 Tom Gugliotta	.05	.15
❑ 124 Patrick Ewing	.15	.40
❑ 125 Ray Allen	.15	.40
❑ 126 Anfernee Hardaway	.15	.40
❑ 127 Jason Kidd	.50	1.25
❑ 128 Kenny Anderson	.07	.20
❑ 129 Kerry Kittles	.05	.15
❑ 130 Tim Thomas	.07	.20
❑ 131 Shareef Abdur-Rahim	.60	1.50
❑ 132 Mike Bibby RC	2.00	5.00
❑ 133 Kobe Bryant	2.50	6.00
❑ 134 Vince Carter RC	4.00	10.00
❑ 135 Tim Duncan	1.00	2.50
❑ 136 Kevin Garnett	1.25	3.00
❑ 137 Grant Hill	.08	.25
❑ 138 Larry Hughes RC	2.00	5.00
❑ 139 Allen Iverson	1.25	3.00
❑ 140 Antawn Jamison RC	3.00	8.00
❑ 141 Michael Jordan	4.00	10.00
❑ 142 Shawn Kemp	.40	1.00
❑ 143 Stephon Marbury	.60	1.50
❑ 144 Michael Olowokandi RC	1.00	2.50
❑ 145 Shaquille O'Neal	1.50	4.00
❑ 146 Scottie Pippen	1.00	2.50
❑ 147 Dennis Rodman	.40	1.00
❑ 148 Damon Stoudamire	.40	1.00
❑ 149 Keith Van Horn	.60	1.50
❑ 150 Antoine Walker	.60	1.50

1998-99 SkyBox Thunder

❑ COMPLETE SET (127)	10.00	25.00
❑ 1 Kerry Kittles	.05	.15
❑ 2 Larry Johnson	.10	.30
❑ 3 Hakeem Olajuwon	.20	.50
❑ 4 Glenn Robinson	.10	.30
❑ 5 Alonzo Mourning	.10	.30
❑ 6 Reggie Miller	.20	.50
❑ 7 Toni Kukoc	.10	.30
❑ 8 Corliss Williamson	.10	.30
❑ 9 Nick Van Exel	.20	.50
❑ 10 Mookie Blaylock	.05	.15
❑ 11 Michael Smith	.05	.15
❑ 12 Avery Johnson	.05	.15
❑ 13 Brian Williams	.05	.15
❑ 14 Doug Christie	.10	.30
❑ 15 Danny Fortson	.05	.15
❑ 16 Michael Stewart	.05	.15
❑ 17 Anthony Peeler	.05	.15
❑ 18 Cedric Henderson	.05	.15
❑ 19 Lamond Murray	.05	.15
❑ 20 Walt Williams	.05	.15
❑ 21 Samaki Walker	.05	.15
❑ 22 David Wesley	.05	.15
❑ 23 Maurice Taylor	.08	.25
❑ 24 Todd Fuller	.05	.15
❑ 25 Jeff Hornacek	.10	.30
❑ 26 Danny Manning	.05	.15
❑ 27 Detlef Schrempf	.10	.30
❑ 28 Nick Anderson	.05	.15
❑ 29 Ron Harper	.10	.30
❑ 30 Brian Shaw	.05	.15
❑ 31 Bryant Stith	.05	.15
❑ 32 Chris Whitney	.05	.15
❑ 33 Patrick Ewing	.20	.50
❑ 34 Travis Knight	.05	.15
❑ 35 Tracy McGrady	.50	1.25
❑ 36 Dan Majerle	.10	.30
❑ 37 Dale Davis	.10	.30
❑ 38 Kelvin Cato	.05	.15
❑ 39 Zydrunas Ilgauskas	.10	.30
❑ 40 Sean Elliott	.10	.30
❑ 41 Tony Delk	.05	.15
❑ 42 Bobby Phills	.05	.15
❑ 43 Clifford Robinson	.05	.15
❑ 44 Shawn Bradley	.05	.15
❑ 45 Aaron McKie	.10	.30
❑ 46 Mark Jackson	.10	.30
❑ 47 P.J. Brown	.05	.15
❑ 48 Armon Gilliam	.05	.15
❑ 49 Ed Gray	.05	.15
❑ 50 Olden Polynice	.05	.15
❑ 51 Kendall Gill	.05	.15
❑ 52 Bryon Russell	.05	.15
❑ 53 Dale Ellis	.05	.15
❑ 54 Mark Price	.10	.30
❑ 55 Donyell Marshall	.10	.30
❑ 56 John Starks	.10	.30
❑ 57 Jerome Williams	.05	.15
❑ 58 Rodney Rogers	.05	.15
❑ 59 Michael Finley	.20	.50
❑ 60 Marcus Camby	.10	.30
❑ 61 Chris Anstey	.05	.15
❑ 62 Rodrick Rhodes	.05	.15
❑ 63 Derek Anderson	.15	.40
❑ 64 Jermaine O'Neal	.20	.50
❑ 65 Glen Rice	.10	.30
❑ 66 Bryant Reeves	.05	.15
❑ 67 Jalen Rose	.20	.50
❑ 68 Calbert Cheaney	.05	.15
❑ 69 Steve Smith	.10	.30
❑ 70 Shandon Anderson	.05	.15
❑ 71 Tony Battie	.05	.15
❑ 72 Kenny Anderson	.10	.30
❑ 73 Tim Hardaway	.10	.30
❑ 74 Antonio Daniels	.05	.15
❑ 75 Charles Barkley	.25	.60
❑ 76 Chauncey Billups	.10	.30
❑ 77 Lindsey Hunter	.05	.15
❑ 78 Terrell Brandon	.10	.30
❑ 79 Anthony Mason	.10	.30
❑ 80 Elden Campbell	.05	.15
❑ 81 Rasheed Wallace	.20	.50
❑ 82 Erick Dampier	.10	.30
❑ 83 Tracy Murray	.05	.15
❑ 84 Sam Cassell	.20	.50
❑ 85 Bobby Jackson	.10	.30
❑ 86 Horace Grant	.10	.30
❑ 87 Brent Price	.05	.15
❑ 88 Allan Houston	.10	.30
❑ 89 Brevin Knight	.05	.15
❑ 90 Steve Nash	.20	.50
❑ 91 Lorenzen Wright	.05	.15
❑ 92 Hubert Davis	.05	.15
❑ 93 Walter McCarty	.05	.15
❑ 94 Jamal Mashburn	.10	.30
❑ 95 Dikembe Mutombo	.10	.30
❑ 96 Chris Carr	.05	.15
❑ 97 Tariq Abdul-Wahad	.05	.15
❑ 98 Chris Mullin	.20	.50
❑ 99 Charlie Ward	.05	.15
❑ 100 Tim Thomas	.10	.30
❑ 101 Tim Duncan	.40	1.00
❑ 102 Antoine Walker	.25	.60
❑ 103 Stephon Marbury	.25	.60
❑ 104 Ray Allen	.25	.60
❑ 105 Shawn Kemp	.15	.40
❑ 106 Michael Jordan	1.50	4.00
❑ 107 Gary Payton	.25	.60
❑ 108 Kobe Bryant	1.00	2.50
❑ 109 Karl Malone	.20	.50
❑ 110 Kevin Garnett	.40	1.00
❑ 111 Jason Kidd	.40	1.00
❑ 112 Dennis Rodman	.15	.40
❑ 113 Grant Hill	.20	.50
❑ 114 Keith Van Horn	.25	.60
❑ 115 Shareef Abdur-Rahim	.25	.60
❑ 116 Ron Mercer	.10	.30
❑ 117 Allen Iverson	.50	1.25
❑ 118 Shaquille O'Neal	.60	1.50
❑ 119 Anfernee Hardaway	.25	.60
❑ 120 Scottie Pippen	.40	1.00
❑ 121 David Robinson	.25	.60
❑ 122 Vin Baker	.15	.40
❑ 123 John Stockton	.20	.50
❑ 124 Eddie Jones	.25	.60
❑ 125 Juwan Howard	.15	.40
❑ 126 Checklist	.05	.15
❑ 127 Checklist	.05	.15
❑ NNO Grant Hill SAMPLE	.40	1.00

1994-95 SP

❑ COMPLETE SET (165)	15.00	30.00
❑ COMMON FOIL RC (1-30)	.20	.50
❑ COMMON CARD (31-165)	.05	.15
❑ 1 Glenn Robinson FOIL RC	1.00	2.50
❑ 2 Jason Kidd FOIL RC	3.00	8.00
❑ 3 Grant Hill FOIL RC	2.00	5.00
❑ 4 Donyell Marshall FOIL RC	.30	.75
❑ 5 Juwan Howard FOIL RC	.60	1.50
❑ 6 Sharone Wright FOIL RC	.20	.50
❑ 7 Lamond Murray FOIL RC	.20	.50
❑ 8 Brian Grant FOIL RC	.75	2.00
❑ 9 Eric Montross FOIL RC	.20	.50
❑ 10 Eddie Jones FOIL RC	1.25	3.00
❑ 11 Carlos Rogers FOIL RC	.20	.50
❑ 12 Khalid Reeves FOIL RC	.20	.50
❑ 13 Jalen Rose FOIL RC	1.25	3.00
❑ 14 Eric Piatkowski FOIL RC	.20	.50
❑ 15 Clifford Rozier FOIL RC	.20	.50
❑ 16 Aaron McKie FOIL RC	.60	1.50
❑ 17 Eric Mobley FOIL RC	.20	.50
❑ 18 Tony Dumas FOIL RC	.20	.50
❑ 19 B.J.Tyler FOIL RC	.20	.50
❑ 20 Dickey Simpkins FOIL RC	.20	.50
❑ 21 Bill Curley FOIL RC	.20	.50
❑ 22 Wesley Person FOIL RC	.30	.75
❑ 23 Monty Williams FOIL RC	.20	.50
❑ 24 Greg Minor FOIL RC	.20	.50
❑ 25 Charlie Ward FOIL RC	.20	.50
❑ 26 Brooks Thompson FOIL RC	.20	.50
❑ 27 Trevor Ruffin FOIL RC	.20	.50
❑ 28 Derrick Alston FOIL RC	.20	.50
❑ 29 Michael Smith FOIL RC	.20	.50
❑ 30 Dontonio Wingfield FOIL RC	.20	.50
❑ 31 Stacey Augmon	.05	.15
❑ 32 Steve Smith	.08	.25
❑ 33 Mookie Blaylock	.05	.15
❑ 34 Grant Long	.05	.15
❑ 35 Ken Norman	.05	.15
❑ 36 Dominique Wilkins	.20	.50
❑ 37 Dino Radja	.05	.15
❑ 38 Dee Brown	.05	.15
❑ 39 David Wesley	.05	.15
❑ 40 Rick Fox	.05	.15
❑ 41 Alonzo Mourning	.25	.60
❑ 42 Larry Johnson	.08	.25
❑ 43 Hersey Hawkins	.08	.25
❑ 44 Scott Burrell	.05	.15
❑ 45 Muggsy Bogues	.08	.25
❑ 46 Scottie Pippen	.60	1.50
❑ 47 Toni Kukoc	.30	.75
❑ 48 B.J. Armstrong	.05	.15
❑ 49 Will Perdue	.05	.15
❑ 50 Ron Harper	.08	.25
❑ 51 Mark Price	.05	.15
❑ 52 Tyrone Hill	.05	.15
❑ 53 Chris Mills	.08	.25
❑ 54 John Williams	.05	.15
❑ 55 Bobby Phills	.05	.15
❑ 56 Jim Jackson	.08	.25
❑ 57 Jamal Mashburn	.20	.50
❑ 58 Popeye Jones	.05	.15
❑ 59 Roy Tarpley	.05	.15
❑ 60 Lorenzo Williams	.05	.15
❑ 61 Mahmoud Abdul-Rauf	.05	.15
❑ 62 Rodney Rogers	.05	.15
❑ 63 Bryant Stith	.05	.15
❑ 64 Dikembe Mutombo	.08	.25
❑ 65 Robert Pack	.05	.15
❑ 66 Joe Dumars	.20	.50
❑ 67 Terry Mills	.05	.15
❑ 68 Oliver Miller	.05	.15
❑ 69 Lindsey Hunter	.08	.25
❑ 70 Mark West	.05	.15
❑ 71 Latrell Sprewell	.20	.50
❑ 72 Tim Hardaway	.20	.50
❑ 73 Ricky Pierce	.05	.15
❑ 74 Rony Seikaly	.05	.15
❑ 75 Tom Gugliotta	.08	.25
❑ 76 Hakeem Olajuwon	.30	.75
❑ 77 Clyde Drexler	.20	.50
❑ 78 Vernon Maxwell	.05	.15
❑ 79 Robert Horry	.08	.25
❑ 80 Sam Cassell	.20	.50
❑ 81 Reggie Miller	.20	.50
❑ 82 Rik Smits	.05	.15
❑ 83 Derrick McKey	.05	.15
❑ 84 Mark Jackson	.05	.15
❑ 85 Dale Davis	.05	.15
❑ 86 Loy Vaught	.05	.15
❑ 87 Terry Dehere	.05	.15
❑ 88 Malik Sealy	.05	.15
❑ 89 Pooh Richardson	.05	.15
❑ 90 Tony Massenburg	.05	.15
❑ 91 Cedric Ceballos	.05	.15
❑ 92 Nick Van Exel	.20	.50
❑ 93 George Lynch	.05	.15
❑ 94 Vlade Divac	.05	.15
❑ 95 Elden Campbell	.05	.15
❑ 96 Glen Rice	.08	.25
❑ 97 Kevin Willis	.05	.15
❑ 98 Billy Owens	.05	.15
❑ 99 Bimbo Coles	.05	.15
❑ 100 Harold Miner	.05	.15
❑ 101 Vin Baker	.20	.50
❑ 102 Todd Day	.05	.15
❑ 103 Marty Conlon	.05	.15
❑ 104 Lee Mayberry	.05	.15
❑ 105 Eric Murdock	.05	.15

❑ 106 Isaiah Rider	.08	.25
❑ 107 Doug West	.05	.15
❑ 108 Christian Laettner	.08	.25
❑ 109 Sean Rooks	.05	.15
❑ 110 Stacey King	.05	.15
❑ 111 Derrick Coleman	.08	.25
❑ 112 Kenny Anderson	.08	.25
❑ 113 Chris Morris	.05	.15
❑ 114 Armon Gilliam	.05	.15
❑ 115 Benoit Benjamin	.05	.15
❑ 116 Patrick Ewing	.20	.50
❑ 117 Charles Oakley	.05	.15
❑ 118 John Starks	.05	.15
❑ 119 Derek Harper	.05	.15
❑ 120 Charles Smith	.05	.15
❑ 121 Shaquille O'Neal	1.00	2.50
❑ 122 Anfernee Hardaway	.50	1.25
❑ 123 Nick Anderson	.05	.15
❑ 124 Horace Grant	.08	.25
❑ 125 Donald Royal	.05	.15
❑ 126 Clarence Weatherspoon	.05	.15
❑ 127 Dana Barros	.05	.15
❑ 128 Jeff Malone	.05	.15
❑ 129 Willie Burton	.05	.15
❑ 130 Shawn Bradley	.05	.15
❑ 131 Charles Barkley	.30	.75
❑ 132 Kevin Johnson	.08	.25
❑ 133 Danny Manning	.08	.25
❑ 134 Dan Majerle	.08	.25
❑ 135 A.C. Green	.08	.25
❑ 136 Otis Thorpe	.05	.15
❑ 137 Clifford Robinson	.08	.25
❑ 138 Rod Strickland	.08	.25
❑ 139 Buck Williams	.05	.15
❑ 140 James Robinson	.05	.15
❑ 141 Mitch Richmond	.20	.50
❑ 142 Walt Williams	.05	.15
❑ 143 Olden Polynice	.05	.15
❑ 144 Spud Webb	.05	.15
❑ 145 Duane Causwell	.05	.15
❑ 146 David Robinson	.30	.75
❑ 147 Dennis Rodman	.40	1.00
❑ 148 Sean Elliott	.08	.25
❑ 149 Avery Johnson	.05	.15
❑ 150 J.R. Reid	.05	.15
❑ 151 Shawn Kemp	.30	.75
❑ 152 Gary Payton	.30	.75
❑ 153 Detlef Schrempf	.08	.25
❑ 154 Nate McMillan	.05	.15
❑ 155 Kendall Gill	.08	.25
❑ 156 Karl Malone	.30	.75
❑ 157 John Stockton	.20	.50
❑ 158 Jeff Hornacek	.08	.25
❑ 159 Felton Spencer	.05	.15
❑ 160 David Benoit	.05	.15
❑ 161 Chris Webber	.50	1.25
❑ 162 Rex Chapman	.05	.15
❑ 163 Don MacLean	.05	.15
❑ 164 Calbert Cheaney	.05	.15
❑ 165 Scott Skiles	.05	.15
❑ P23 M.Jordan Promo	4.00	10.00
❑ MJ1R M.Jordan Red	2.00	5.00
❑ MJ1S M.Jordan Silver	6.00	15.00

1995-96 SP

❑ COMPLETE SET (167)	15.00	30.00
❑ 1 Stacey Augmon	.08	.25
❑ 2 Mookie Blaylock	.08	.25
❑ 3 Andrew Lang	.08	.25
❑ 4 Steve Smith	.20	.50
❑ 5 Spud Webb	.20	.50
❑ 6 Dana Barros	.08	.25
❑ 7 Dee Brown	.08	.25
❑ 8 Todd Day	.08	.25
❑ 9 Rick Fox	.20	.50
❑ 10 Eric Montross	.08	.25
❑ 11 Dino Radja	.08	.25
❑ 12 Kenny Anderson	.20	.50
❑ 13 Scott Burrell	.08	.25
❑ 14 Dell Curry	.08	.25
❑ 15 Matt Geiger	.08	.25
❑ 16 Larry Johnson	.20	.50
❑ 17 Glen Rice	.20	.50
❑ 18 Steve Kerr	.20	.50
❑ 19 Toni Kukoc	.20	.50
❑ 20 Luc Longley	.08	.25
❑ 21 Scottie Pippen	.50	1.25
❑ 22 Dennis Rodman	.20	.50
❑ 23 Michael Jordan	2.00	5.00
❑ 24 Terrell Brandon	.20	.50
❑ 25 Michael Cage	.08	.25
❑ 26 Danny Ferry	.08	.25
❑ 27 Chris Mills	.08	.25
❑ 28 Bobby Phills	.08	.25
❑ 29 Tony Dumas	.08	.25
❑ 30 Jim Jackson	.08	.25
❑ 31 Popeye Jones	.08	.25
❑ 32 Jason Kidd	1.00	2.50
❑ 33 Jamal Mashburn	.20	.50
❑ 34 Mahmoud Abdul-Rauf	.08	.25
❑ 35 LaPhonso Ellis	.08	.25
❑ 36 Dikembe Mutombo	.20	.50
❑ 37 Jalen Rose	.40	1.00
❑ 38 Bryant Stith	.08	.25
❑ 39 Joe Dumars	.30	.75
❑ 40 Grant Hill	.40	1.00
❑ 41 Lindsey Hunter	.08	.25
❑ 42 Allan Houston	.20	.50
❑ 43 Otis Thorpe	.08	.25
❑ 44 B.J. Armstrong	.08	.25
❑ 45 Tim Hardaway	.20	.50
❑ 46 Chris Mullin	.30	.75
❑ 47 Latrell Sprewell	.30	.75
❑ 48 Rony Seikaly	.08	.25
❑ 49 Sam Cassell	.30	.75
❑ 50 Clyde Drexler	.30	.75
❑ 51 Robert Horry	.20	.50
❑ 52 Hakeem Olajuwon	.30	.75
❑ 53 Kenny Smith	.08	.25
❑ 54 Dale Davis	.08	.25
❑ 55 Derrick McKey	.08	.25
❑ 56 Reggie Miller	.30	.75
❑ 57 Ricky Pierce	.08	.25
❑ 58 Rik Smits	.20	.50
❑ 59 Lamond Murray	.08	.25
❑ 60 Rodney Rogers	.08	.25
❑ 61 Malik Sealy	.08	.25
❑ 62 Loy Vaught	.08	.25
❑ 63 Brian Williams	.08	.25
❑ 64 Elden Campbell	.08	.25
❑ 65 Cedric Ceballos	.08	.25
❑ 66 Magic Johnson	.50	1.25
❑ 67 Eddie Jones	.40	1.00
❑ 68 Nick Van Exel	.30	.75
❑ 69 Bimbo Coles	.08	.25
❑ 70 Alonzo Mourning	.20	.50
❑ 71 Billy Owens	.08	.25
❑ 72 Kevin Willis	.20	.50
❑ 73 Vin Baker	.20	.50
❑ 74 Benoit Benjamin	.08	.25
❑ 75 Sherman Douglas	.08	.25
❑ 76 Lee Mayberry	.08	.25
❑ 77 Glenn Robinson	.30	.75
❑ 78 Tom Gugliotta	.08	.25
❑ 79 Christian Laettner	.20	.50
❑ 80 Sam Mitchell	.08	.25
❑ 81 Terry Porter	.08	.25
❑ 82 Isaiah Rider	.08	.25
❑ 83 Shawn Bradley	.08	.25
❑ 84 P.J. Brown	.08	.25
❑ 85 Kendall Gill	.08	.25
❑ 86 Armon Gilliam	.08	.25
❑ 87 Jayson Williams	.08	.25
❑ 88 Patrick Ewing	.30	.75
❑ 89 Derek Harper	.20	.50
❑ 90 Anthony Mason	.20	.50
❑ 91 Charles Oakley	.08	.25
❑ 92 John Starks	.20	.50
❑ 93 Nick Anderson	.08	.25
❑ 94 Horace Grant	.20	.50
❑ 95 Anfernee Hardaway	.30	.75
❑ 96 Shaquille O'Neal	.75	2.00
❑ 97 Dennis Scott	.08	.25
❑ 98 Derrick Coleman	.08	.25
❑ 99 Vernon Maxwell	.08	.25
❑ 100 Trevor Ruffin	.08	.25
❑ 101 Clarence Weatherspoon	.08	.25
❑ 102 Sharone Wright	.08	.25
❑ 103 Charles Barkley	.40	1.00
❑ 104 A.C. Green	.20	.50
❑ 105 Kevin Johnson	.20	.50
❑ 106 Wesley Person	.08	.25
❑ 107 John Williams	.08	.25
❑ 108 Chris Dudley	.08	.25
❑ 109 Harvey Grant	.08	.25
❑ 110 Aaron McKie	.20	.50
❑ 111 Clifford Robinson	.08	.25
❑ 112 Rod Strickland	.08	.25
❑ 113 Brian Grant	.30	.75
❑ 114 Sarunas Marciulionis	.08	.25
❑ 115 Olden Polynice	.08	.25
❑ 116 Mitch Richmond	.20	.50
❑ 117 Walt Williams	.08	.25
❑ 118 Vinny Del Negro	.08	.25
❑ 119 Sean Elliott	.20	.50
❑ 120 Avery Johnson	.08	.25
❑ 121 Chuck Person	.08	.25
❑ 122 David Robinson	.30	.75
❑ 123 Hersey Hawkins	.08	.25
❑ 124 Shawn Kemp	.20	.50
❑ 125 Gary Payton	.30	.75
❑ 126 Sam Perkins	.20	.50
❑ 127 Detlef Schrempf	.20	.50
❑ 128 Oliver Miller	.08	.25
❑ 129 Tracy Murray	.08	.25
❑ 130 Ed Pinckney	.08	.25
❑ 131 Alvin Robertson	.08	.25
❑ 132 Zan Tabak	.08	.25
❑ 133 Jeff Hornacek	.20	.50
❑ 134 Adam Keefe	.08	.25
❑ 135 Karl Malone	.40	1.00
❑ 136 Chris Morris	.08	.25
❑ 137 John Stockton	.40	1.00
❑ 138 Greg Anthony	.08	.25
❑ 139 Blue Edwards	.08	.25
❑ 140 Kenny Gattison	.08	.25
❑ 141 Chris King	.08	.25
❑ 142 Byron Scott	.08	.25
❑ 143 Calbert Cheaney	.08	.25
❑ 144 Juwan Howard	.30	.75
❑ 145 Gheorghe Muresan	.08	.25
❑ 146 Robert Pack	.08	.25
❑ 147 Chris Webber	.40	1.00
❑ 148 Alan Henderson RC	.30	.75
❑ 149 Eric Williams RC	.20	.50
❑ 150 George Zidek RC	.08	.25
❑ 151 Bob Sura RC	.20	.50
❑ 152 Antonio McDyess RC	.60	1.50
❑ 153 Theo Ratliff RC	.40	1.00
❑ 154 Joe Smith RC	.50	1.25
❑ 155 Brent Barry RC	.30	.75
❑ 156 Sasha Danilovic RC	.08	.25
❑ 157 Kurt Thomas RC	.20	.50
❑ 158 Shawn Respert RC	.08	.25
❑ 159 Kevin Garnett RC	6.00	15.00
❑ 160 Ed O'Bannon RC	.08	.25
❑ 161 Jerry Stackhouse RC	2.00	5.00
❑ 162 Michael Finley RC	1.00	2.50
❑ 163 Arvydas Sabonis RC	.40	1.00
❑ 164 Cory Alexander RC	.08	.25
❑ 165 Damon Stoudamire RC	.60	1.50
❑ 166 Bryant Reeves RC	.30	.75
❑ 167 Rasheed Wallace RC	1.00	2.50
❑ C1 H.Olajuwon Comm.	5.00	12.00
❑ P23 Michael Jordan Promo	4.00	10.00

1996-97 SP

❑ COMPLETE SET (146)	17.50	35.00
❑ COMMON CARD (1-126)	.08	.25
❑ COMMON ROOKIE (127-146)	.30	.75
❑ 1 Mookie Blaylock	.08	.25

❑ 2 Christian Laettner	.20	.50
❑ 3 Dikembe Mutombo	.20	.50
❑ 4 Steve Smith	.20	.50
❑ 5 Dana Barros	.08	.25
❑ 6 Rick Fox	.08	.25
❑ 7 Dino Radja	.08	.25
❑ 8 Eric Williams	.08	.25
❑ 9 Dell Curry	.08	.25
❑ 10 Vlade Divac	.08	.25
❑ 11 Anthony Mason	.20	.50
❑ 12 Glen Rice	.20	.50
❑ 13 Scottie Pippen	.50	1.25
❑ 14 Toni Kukoc	.20	.50
❑ 15 Luc Longley	.08	.25
❑ 16 Michael Jordan	2.00	5.00
❑ 17 Dennis Rodman	.20	.50
❑ 18 Terrell Brandon	.20	.50
❑ 19 Tyrone Hill	.08	.25
❑ 20 Bobby Phills	.08	.25
❑ 21 Bob Sura	.08	.25
❑ 22 Chris Gatling	.08	.25
❑ 23 Jim Jackson	.08	.25
❑ 24 Sam Cassell	.30	.75
❑ 25 Jamal Mashburn	.20	.50
❑ 26 Dale Ellis	.08	.25
❑ 27 LaPhonso Ellis	.08	.25
❑ 28 Mark Jackson	.08	.25
❑ 29 Antonio McDyess	.20	.50
❑ 30 Bryant Stith	.08	.25
❑ 31 Joe Dumars	.30	.75
❑ 32 Grant Hill	.30	.75
❑ 33 Lindsey Hunter	.08	.25
❑ 34 Otis Thorpe	.08	.25
❑ 35 Chris Mullin	.30	.75
❑ 36 Mark Price	.20	.50
❑ 37 Joe Smith	.20	.50
❑ 38 Latrell Sprewell	.30	.75
❑ 39 Charles Barkley	.40	1.00
❑ 40 Clyde Drexler	.30	.75
❑ 41 Mario Elie	.08	.25
❑ 42 Hakeem Olajuwon	.30	.75
❑ 43 Travis Best	.08	.25
❑ 44 Dale Davis	.08	.25
❑ 45 Reggie Miller	.30	.75
❑ 46 Rik Smits	.20	.50
❑ 47 Pooh Richardson	.08	.25
❑ 48 Rodney Rogers	.08	.25
❑ 49 Malik Sealy	.08	.25
❑ 50 Loy Vaught	.08	.25
❑ 51 Elden Campbell	.08	.25
❑ 52 Robert Horry	.20	.50
❑ 53 Eddie Jones	.30	.75
❑ 54 Shaquille O'Neal	.75	2.00
❑ 55 Nick Van Exel	.30	.75
❑ 56 Sasha Danilovic	.08	.25
❑ 57 Tim Hardaway	.20	.50
❑ 58 Dan Majerle	.20	.50
❑ 59 Alonzo Mourning	.20	.50
❑ 60 Vin Baker	.20	.50
❑ 61 Sherman Douglas	.08	.25
❑ 62 Armon Gilliam	.08	.25
❑ 63 Glenn Robinson	.30	.75
❑ 64 Kevin Garnett	.60	1.50
❑ 65 Tom Gugliotta	.08	.25
❑ 66 Terry Porter	.08	.25
❑ 67 Doug West	.08	.25
❑ 68 Shawn Bradley	.08	.25
❑ 69 Kendall Gill	.08	.25
❑ 70 Robert Pack	.08	.25
❑ 71 Jayson Williams	.20	.50
❑ 72 Chris Childs	.08	.25
❑ 73 Patrick Ewing	.30	.75
❑ 74 Allan Houston	.20	.50
❑ 75 Larry Johnson	.20	.50
❑ 76 John Starks	.20	.50
❑ 77 Nick Anderson	.08	.25
❑ 78 Horace Grant	.20	.50
❑ 79 Anfernee Hardaway	.30	.75
❑ 80 Dennis Scott	.08	.25
❑ 81 Derrick Coleman	.20	.50
❑ 82 Mark Davis	.08	.25
❑ 83 Jerry Stackhouse	.40	1.00
❑ 84 Clarence Weatherspoon	.08	.25
❑ 85 Cedric Ceballos	.08	.25
❑ 86 Kevin Johnson	.20	.50
❑ 87 Jason Kidd	.50	1.25
❑ 88 Danny Manning	.20	.50
❑ 89 Wesley Person	.08	.25
❑ 90 Kenny Anderson	.08	.25
❑ 91 Isaiah Rider	.20	.50
❑ 92 Clifford Robinson	.08	.25
❑ 93 Arvydas Sabonis	.20	.50
❑ 94 Rasheed Wallace	.40	1.00
❑ 95 Mahmoud Abdul-Rauf	.08	.25
❑ 96 Brian Grant	.30	.75
❑ 97 Olden Polynice	.08	.25
❑ 98 Mitch Richmond	.20	.50
❑ 99 Corliss Williamson	.20	.50
❑ 100 Sean Elliott	.20	.50
❑ 101 Avery Johnson	.08	.25
❑ 102 David Robinson	.30	.75
❑ 103 Dominique Wilkins	.30	.75
❑ 104 Hersey Hawkins	.20	.50
❑ 105 Jim McIlvaine	.08	.25
❑ 106 Shawn Kemp	.20	.50
❑ 107 Gary Payton	.30	.75
❑ 108 Detlef Schrempf	.20	.50
❑ 109 Doug Christie	.20	.50
❑ 110 Popeye Jones	.08	.25
❑ 111 Damon Stoudamire	.30	.75
❑ 112 Walt Williams	.08	.25
❑ 113 Jeff Hornacek	.20	.50
❑ 114 Karl Malone	.30	.75
❑ 115 Greg Ostertag	.08	.25
❑ 116 Bryon Russell	.08	.25
❑ 117 John Stockton	.30	.75
❑ 118 Greg Anthony	.08	.25
❑ 119 Blue Edwards	.08	.25
❑ 120 Anthony Peeler	.08	.25
❑ 121 Bryant Reeves	.08	.25
❑ 122 Calbert Cheaney	.08	.25
❑ 123 Juwan Howard	.20	.50
❑ 124 Gheorghe Muresan	.08	.25
❑ 125 Rod Strickland	.08	.25
❑ 126 Chris Webber	.30	.75
❑ 127 Antoine Walker RC	.75	2.00
❑ 128 Tony Delk RC	.30	.75
❑ 129 Vitaly Potapenko RC	.30	.75
❑ 130 Samaki Walker RC	.30	.75
❑ 131 Todd Fuller RC	.30	.75
❑ 132 Erick Dampier RC	.30	.75
❑ 133 Lorenzen Wright RC	.30	.75
❑ 134 Kobe Bryant RC	10.00	25.00
❑ 135 Derek Fisher RC	.60	1.50
❑ 136 Ray Allen RC	1.50	4.00
❑ 137 Stephon Marbury RC	.75	2.00
❑ 138 Kerry Kittles RC	.30	.75
❑ 139 Walter McCarty RC	.30	.75
❑ 140 John Wallace RC	.30	.75
❑ 141 Allen Iverson RC	2.00	5.00
❑ 142 Steve Nash RC	4.00	10.00
❑ 143 Jermaine O'Neal RC	1.25	3.00
❑ 144 Marcus Camby RC	.60	1.50
❑ 145 Shareef Abdur-Rahim RC	1.25	3.00
❑ 146 Roy Rogers RC	.30	.75
❑ S16 M.Jordan Sample	2.00	5.00

1997-98 SP Authentic

❑ COMPLETE SET (176)	60.00	120.00
❑ COMMON CARD (1-176)	.15	.40
❑ COMMON ROOKIE	.30	.75
❑ 1 Steve Smith	.30	.75
❑ 2 Dikembe Mutombo	.30	.75
❑ 3 Christian Laettner	.30	.75
❑ 4 Mookie Blaylock	.15	.40
❑ 5 Alan Henderson	.15	.40
❑ 6 Antoine Walker	.60	1.50
❑ 7 Ron Mercer RC	1.25	3.00
❑ 8 Walter McCarty	.15	.40
❑ 9 Kenny Anderson	.30	.75
❑ 10 Travis Knight	.15	.40
❑ 11 Dana Barros	.15	.40
❑ 12 Glen Rice	.30	.75
❑ 13 Vlade Divac	.30	.75
❑ 14 Dell Curry	.15	.40
❑ 15 David Wesley	.15	.40
❑ 16 Bobby Phills	.15	.40
❑ 17 Anthony Mason	.30	.75
❑ 18 Toni Kukoc	.30	.75
❑ 19 Dennis Rodman	.30	.75
❑ 20 Ron Harper	.30	.75
❑ 21 Steve Kerr	.30	.75
❑ 22 Scottie Pippen	.75	2.00
❑ 23 Michael Jordan	3.00	8.00
❑ 24 Shawn Kemp	.30	.75
❑ 25 Wesley Person	.15	.40
❑ 26 Derek Anderson RC	1.50	4.00
❑ 27 Zydrunas Ilgauskas	.30	.75
❑ 28 Brevin Knight RC	.60	1.50
❑ 29 Michael Finley	.50	1.25
❑ 30 Shawn Bradley	.15	.40
❑ 31 A.C. Green	.30	.75
❑ 32 Hubert Davis	.15	.40
❑ 33 Dennis Scott	.15	.40
❑ 34 Tony Battie RC	.60	1.50
❑ 35 Bobby Jackson RC	3.00	8.00
❑ 36 LaPhonso Ellis	.15	.40
❑ 37 Bryant Stith	.15	.40
❑ 38 Dean Garrett	.15	.40
❑ 39 Danny Fortson RC	1.50	4.00
❑ 40 Grant Hill	.50	1.25
❑ 41 Brian Williams	.15	.40
❑ 42 Lindsey Hunter	.15	.40
❑ 43 Malik Sealy	.15	.40
❑ 44 Jerry Stackhouse	.50	1.25
❑ 45 Muggsy Bogues	.30	.75
❑ 46 Joe Smith	.30	.75
❑ 47 Donyell Marshall	.30	.75
❑ 48 Erick Dampier	.30	.75
❑ 49 Bimbo Coles	.15	.40
❑ 50 Charles Barkley	.60	1.50
❑ 51 Hakeem Olajuwon	.50	1.25
❑ 52 Clyde Drexler	.50	1.25
❑ 53 Kevin Willis	.30	.75
❑ 54 Mario Elie	.15	.40
❑ 55 Reggie Miller	.50	1.25
❑ 56 Rik Smits	.30	.75
❑ 57 Chris Mullin	.50	1.25
❑ 58 Antonio Davis	.15	.40
❑ 59 Dale Davis	.15	.40
❑ 60 Mark Jackson	.30	.75
❑ 61 Brent Barry	.30	.75
❑ 62 Loy Vaught	.15	.40
❑ 63 Rodney Rogers	.15	.40
❑ 64 Lamond Murray	.15	.40
❑ 65 Maurice Taylor RC	1.25	3.00
❑ 66 Shaquille O'Neal	1.25	3.00
❑ 67 Eddie Jones	.50	1.25
❑ 68 Kobe Bryant	2.00	5.00
❑ 69 Nick Van Exel	.50	1.25
❑ 70 Robert Horry	.30	.75
❑ 71 Tim Hardaway	.30	.75
❑ 72 Jamal Mashburn	.30	.75
❑ 73 Alonzo Mourning	.30	.75
❑ 74 Isaac Austin	.15	.40
❑ 75 P.J. Brown	.15	.40
❑ 76 Ray Allen	.50	1.25
❑ 77 Glenn Robinson	.50	1.25
❑ 78 Ervin Johnson	.15	.40
❑ 79 Terrell Brandon	.30	.75
❑ 80 Tyrone Hill	.15	.40
❑ 81 Stephon Marbury	.60	1.50
❑ 82 Kevin Garnett	1.00	2.50
❑ 83 Tom Gugliotta	.30	.75
❑ 84 Chris Carr	.15	.40
❑ 85 Cherokee Parks	.15	.40
❑ 86 Sam Cassell	.50	1.25
❑ 87 Chris Gatling	.15	.40
❑ 88 Kendall Gill	.15	.40
❑ 89 Keith Van Horn RC	1.50	4.00
❑ 90 Jayson Williams	.15	.40
❑ 91 Kerry Kittles	.50	1.25
❑ 92 Patrick Ewing	.50	1.25
❑ 93 Larry Johnson	.30	.75
❑ 94 Chris Childs	.15	.40
❑ 95 John Starks	.30	.75
❑ 96 Charles Oakley	.30	.75
❑ 97 Allan Houston	.30	.75
❑ 98 Mark Price	.30	.75
❑ 99 Anfernee Hardaway	.50	1.25
❑ 100 Rony Seikaly	.15	.40
❑ 101 Horace Grant	.30	.75
❑ 102 Bo Outlaw	.15	.40
❑ 103 Clarence Weatherspoon	.15	.40

❑ 104 Allen Iverson	1.25	3.00
❑ 105 Jim Jackson	.15	.40
❑ 106 Theo Ratliff	.15	.40
❑ 107 Tim Thomas RC	3.00	8.00
❑ 108 Danny Manning	.30	.75
❑ 109 Jason Kidd	.75	2.00
❑ 110 Kevin Johnson	.30	.75
❑ 111 Rex Chapman	.15	.40
❑ 112 Clifford Robinson	.15	.40
❑ 113 Antonio McDyess	.30	.75
❑ 114 Damon Stoudamire	.30	.75
❑ 115 Isaiah Rider	.30	.75
❑ 116 Arvydas Sabonis	.30	.75
❑ 117 Rasheed Wallace	.50	1.25
❑ 118 Brian Grant	.30	.75
❑ 119 Gary Trent	.15	.40
❑ 120 Mitch Richmond	.30	.75
❑ 121 Corliss Williamson	.30	.75
❑ 122 Lawrence Funderburke RC	.40	1.00
❑ 123 Olden Polynice	.15	.40
❑ 124 Billy Owens	.15	.40
❑ 125 Avery Johnson	.15	.40
❑ 126 Sean Elliott	.30	.75
❑ 127 David Robinson	.50	1.25
❑ 128 Tim Duncan RC !	6.00	15.00
❑ 129 Jaren Jackson	.15	.40
❑ 130 Detlef Schrempf	.30	.75
❑ 131 Gary Payton	.50	1.25
❑ 132 Vin Baker	.30	.75
❑ 133 Hersey Hawkins	.15	.40
❑ 134 Dale Ellis	.15	.40
❑ 135 Sam Perkins	.30	.75
❑ 136 Marcus Camby	.50	1.25
❑ 137 John Wallace	.15	.40
❑ 138 Doug Christie	.30	.75
❑ 139 Chauncey Billups RC	6.00	15.00
❑ 140 Walt Williams	.15	.40
❑ 141 Karl Malone	.50	1.25
❑ 142 Bryon Russell	.15	.40
❑ 143 Jeff Hornacek	.30	.75
❑ 144 Greg Ostertag	.15	.40
❑ 145 John Stockton	.50	1.25
❑ 146 Shandon Anderson	.15	.40
❑ 147 Shareef Abdur-Rahim	.75	2.00
❑ 148 Bryant Reeves	.15	.40
❑ 149 Antonio Daniels RC	.60	1.50
❑ 150 Otis Thorpe	.15	.40
❑ 151 Blue Edwards	.15	.40
❑ 152 Chris Webber	.50	1.25
❑ 153 Juwan Howard	.30	.75
❑ 154 Rod Strickland	.15	.40
❑ 155 Calbert Cheaney	.15	.40
❑ 156 Tracy Murray	.15	.40
❑ 157 Chauncey Billups FW	.40	1.00
❑ 158 Ed Gray FW RC	.30	.75
❑ 159 Tony Battie FW	.40	1.00
❑ 160 Keith Van Horn FW	.75	2.00
❑ 161 Cedric Henderson FW RC	.40	1.00
❑ 162 Kelvin Cato FW RC	.60	1.50
❑ 163 Tariq Abdul-Wahad FW RC	.40	1.00
❑ 164 Derek Anderson FW	.50	1.25
❑ 165 Tim Duncan FW	1.25	3.00
❑ 166 Tracy McGrady FW RC	10.00	25.00
❑ 167 Ron Mercer FW	.50	1.25
❑ 168 Bobby Jackson FW	.30	.75
❑ 169 Antonio Daniels FW	.40	1.00
❑ 170 Zydrunas Ilgauskas FW	.30	.75
❑ 171 Maurice Taylor FW	.40	1.00
❑ 172 Tim Thomas FW	.75	2.00
❑ 173 Brevin Knight FW	.30	.75
❑ 174 Lawrence Funderburke FW	.30	.75
❑ 175 Jacque Vaughn FW RC	.40	1.00
❑ 176 Danny Fortson FW	.40	1.00
❑ SPA23 M.Jordan Promo	2.50	6.00

1998-99 SP Authentic

❑ COMPLETE SET w/o RC (90)	20.00	40.00
❑ COMMON MJ (1-10)	1.25	3.00
❑ COMMON CARD (11-90)	.10	.30
❑ COMMON ROOKIE (91-120)	2.00	5.00
❑ 1 Michael Jordan	1.25	3.00
❑ 2 Michael Jordan	1.25	3.00
❑ 3 Michael Jordan	1.25	3.00
❑ 4 Michael Jordan	1.25	3.00
❑ 5 Michael Jordan	1.25	3.00
❑ 6 Michael Jordan	1.25	3.00
❑ 7 Michael Jordan	1.25	3.00
❑ 8 Michael Jordan	1.25	3.00
❑ 9 Michael Jordan	1.25	3.00
❑ 10 Michael Jordan	1.25	3.00
❑ 11 Steve Smith	.25	.60
❑ 12 Dikembe Mutombo	.25	.60
❑ 13 Alan Henderson	.10	.30
❑ 14 Antoine Walker	.40	1.00
❑ 15 Ron Mercer	.20	.50
❑ 16 Kenny Anderson	.25	.60
❑ 17 Derrick Coleman	.10	.30
❑ 18 David Wesley	.10	.30
❑ 19 Glen Rice	.25	.60
❑ 20 Toni Kukoc	.25	.60
❑ 21 Ron Harper	.25	.60
❑ 22 Brent Barry	.25	.60
❑ 23 Shawn Kemp	.25	.60
❑ 24 Zydrunas Ilgauskas	.25	.60
❑ 25 Brevin Knight	.10	.30
❑ 26 Michael Finley	.40	1.00
❑ 27 Steve Nash	.40	1.00
❑ 28 Cedric Ceballos	.10	.30
❑ 29 Antonio McDyess	.25	.60
❑ 30 Nick Van Exel	.40	1.00
❑ 31 Grant Hill	.40	1.00
❑ 32 Jerry Stackhouse	.40	1.00
❑ 33 Bison Dele	.10	.30
❑ 34 John Starks	.25	.60
❑ 35 Chris Mills	.10	.30
❑ 36 Hakeem Olajuwon	.40	1.00
❑ 37 Charles Barkley	.50	1.25
❑ 38 Scottie Pippen	.60	1.50
❑ 39 Reggie Miller	.40	1.00
❑ 40 Chris Mullin	.40	1.00
❑ 41 Rik Smits	.25	.60
❑ 42 Lamond Murray	.10	.30
❑ 43 Maurice Taylor	.20	.50
❑ 44 Kobe Bryant	1.50	4.00
❑ 45 Dennis Rodman	.25	.60
❑ 46 Shaquille O'Neal	1.00	2.50
❑ 47 Alonzo Mourning	.25	.60
❑ 48 Tim Hardaway	.25	.60
❑ 49 Jamal Mashburn	.25	.60
❑ 50 Ray Allen	.40	1.00
❑ 51 Glenn Robinson	.25	.60
❑ 52 Terrell Brandon	.25	.60
❑ 53 Kevin Garnett	.75	2.00
❑ 54 Stephon Marbury	.40	1.00
❑ 55 Joe Smith	.25	.60
❑ 56 Keith Van Horn	.40	1.00
❑ 57 Kendall Gill	.10	.30
❑ 58 Jayson Williams	.10	.30
❑ 59 Patrick Ewing	.40	1.00
❑ 60 Allan Houston	.25	.60
❑ 61 Larry Johnson	.25	.60
❑ 62 Anfernee Hardaway	.40	1.00
❑ 63 Horace Grant	.25	.60
❑ 64 Allen Iverson	.75	2.00
❑ 65 Tim Thomas	.25	.60
❑ 66 Jason Kidd	.60	1.50
❑ 67 Tom Gugliotta	.10	.30
❑ 68 Rex Chapman	.10	.30
❑ 69 Damon Stoudamire	.25	.60
❑ 70 Isaiah Rider	.10	.30
❑ 71 Rasheed Wallace	.40	1.00
❑ 72 Chris Webber	.40	1.00
❑ 73 Vlade Divac	.25	.60
❑ 74 Corliss Williamson	.25	.60
❑ 75 Tim Duncan	.60	1.50
❑ 76 David Robinson	.40	1.00
❑ 77 Sean Elliott	.25	.60
❑ 78 Detlef Schrempf	.25	.60
❑ 79 Vin Baker	.25	.60
❑ 80 Gary Payton	.40	1.00
❑ 81 Doug Christie	.25	.60
❑ 82 Tracy McGrady	1.00	2.50
❑ 83 Karl Malone	.40	1.00
❑ 84 John Stockton	.40	1.00
❑ 85 Jeff Hornacek	.25	.60
❑ 86 Shareef Abdur-Rahim	.40	1.00
❑ 87 Bryant Reeves	.10	.30
❑ 88 Juwan Howard	.25	.60
❑ 89 Mitch Richmond	.25	.60
❑ 90 Rod Strickland	.10	.30
❑ 91 Michael Olowokandi RC	2.00	5.00
❑ 92 Mike Bibby RC	6.00	15.00
❑ 93 Raef LaFrentz RC	4.00	10.00
❑ 94 Antawn Jamison RC	15.00	30.00
❑ 95 Vince Carter RC	30.00	60.00
❑ 96 Robert Traylor RC	2.00	5.00
❑ 97 Jason Williams RC	10.00	25.00
❑ 98 Larry Hughes RC	8.00	20.00
❑ 99 Dirk Nowitzki RC	25.00	50.00
❑ 100 Paul Pierce RC	20.00	40.00
❑ 101 Bonzi Wells RC	10.00	25.00
❑ 102 Michael Doleac RC	2.00	5.00
❑ 103 Keon Clark RC	5.00	12.00
❑ 104 Michael Dickerson RC	6.00	10.00
❑ 105 Matt Harpring RC	2.00	5.00
❑ 106 Bryce Drew RC	2.00	5.00
❑ 107 Pat Garrity RC	2.00	5.00
❑ 108 Roshown McLeod RC	2.00	5.00
❑ 109 Ricky Davis RC	6.00	15.00
❑ 110 Brian Skinner RC	2.00	5.00
❑ 111 Tyronn Lue RC	2.00	5.00
❑ 112 Felipe Lopez RC	2.00	5.00
❑ 113 Al Harrington RC	8.00	20.00
❑ 114 Sam Jacobson RC	2.00	5.00
❑ 115 Cory Carr RC	2.00	5.00
❑ 116 Corey Benjamin RC	2.00	5.00
❑ 117 Nazr Mohammed RC	2.00	5.00
❑ 118 Rashard Lewis RC	15.00	30.00
❑ 119 Peja Stojakovic RC	15.00	30.00
❑ 120 Andrae Patterson RC	2.00	5.00
❑ 23P Michael Jordan PROMO	2.00	5.00

1999-00 SP Authentic

❑ COMPLETE SET w/o RC (90)	20.00	40.00
❑ COMMON CARD (1-90)	.25	.60
❑ COMMON ROOKIE (91-135)	3.00	8.00
❑ 1 Dikembe Mutombo	.30	.75
❑ 2 Jim Jackson	.30	.75
❑ 3 Alan Henderson	.25	.60
❑ 4 Antoine Walker	.40	1.00
❑ 5 Paul Pierce	.40	1.00
❑ 6 Kenny Anderson	.30	.75
❑ 7 Eddie Jones	.40	1.00
❑ 8 Derrick Coleman	.30	.75
❑ 9 Anthony Mason	.25	.60
❑ 10 Chris Carr	.25	.60
❑ 11 Hersey Hawkins	.25	.60
❑ 12 B.J. Armstrong	.25	.60
❑ 13 Shawn Kemp	.40	1.00
❑ 14 Bob Sura	.25	.60
❑ 15 Lamond Murray	.25	.60
❑ 16 Michael Finley	.40	1.00
❑ 17 Cedric Ceballos	.25	.60
❑ 18 Dirk Nowitzki	.60	1.50
❑ 19 Erick Strickland	.25	.60
❑ 20 Antonio McDyess	.30	.75
❑ 21 Nick Van Exel	.30	.75
❑ 22 Grant Hill	.40	1.00
❑ 23 Jerry Stackhouse	.40	1.00
❑ 24 Lindsey Hunter	.25	.60
❑ 25 Christian Laettner	.30	.75
❑ 26 Antawn Jamison	.40	1.00
❑ 27 Chris Mills	.25	.60
❑ 28 Larry Hughes	.30	.75
❑ 29 Charles Barkley	.50	1.25
❑ 30 Hakeem Olajuwon	.40	1.00
❑ 31 Cuttino Mobley	.30	.75
❑ 32 Reggie Miller	.40	1.00
❑ 33 Jalen Rose	.30	.75
❑ 34 Rik Smits	.40	1.00
❑ 35 Maurice Taylor	.30	.75

❑ 36 Derek Anderson	.25	.60
❑ 37 Tyrone Nesby RC	.40	1.00
❑ 38 Kobe Bryant	2.00	5.00
❑ 39 Shaquille O'Neal	1.00	2.50
❑ 40 Glen Rice	.40	1.00
❑ 41 Tim Hardaway	.40	1.00
❑ 42 Alonzo Mourning	.40	1.00
❑ 43 Jamal Mashburn	.25	.60
❑ 44 Ray Allen	.40	1.00
❑ 45 Sam Cassell	.30	.75
❑ 46 Glenn Robinson	.30	.75
❑ 47 Kevin Garnett	.75	2.00
❑ 48 Terrell Brandon	.25	.60
❑ 49 Joe Smith	.30	.75
❑ 50 Stephon Marbury	.40	1.00
❑ 51 Keith Van Horn	.30	.75
❑ 52 Jamie Feick RC	.40	1.00
❑ 53 Kerry Kittles	.25	.60
❑ 54 Allan Houston	.30	.75
❑ 55 Latrell Sprewell	.30	.75
❑ 56 Patrick Ewing	.50	1.25
❑ 57 Darrell Armstrong	.25	.60
❑ 58 Ron Mercer	.25	.60
❑ 59 Michael Doleac	.25	.60
❑ 60 Allen Iverson	.75	2.00
❑ 61 Toni Kukoc	.40	1.00
❑ 62 Eric Snow	.30	.75
❑ 63 Anfernee Hardaway	.40	1.00
❑ 64 Jason Kidd	.60	1.50
❑ 65 Tom Gugliotta	.25	.60
❑ 66 Scottie Pippen	.60	1.50
❑ 67 Steve Smith	.25	.60
❑ 68 Damon Stoudamire	.40	1.00
❑ 69 Jason Williams	.40	1.00
❑ 70 Peja Stojakovic	.30	.75
❑ 71 Chris Webber	.40	1.00
❑ 72 Vlade Divac	.40	1.00
❑ 73 Tim Duncan	.75	2.00
❑ 74 David Robinson	.50	1.25
❑ 75 Avery Johnson	.30	.75
❑ 76 Gary Payton	.40	1.00
❑ 77 Vin Baker	.40	1.00
❑ 78 Vernon Maxwell	.30	.75
❑ 79 Vince Carter	.75	2.00
❑ 80 Tracy McGrady	.75	2.00
❑ 81 Doug Christie	.30	.75
❑ 82 Karl Malone	.50	1.25
❑ 83 John Stockton	.50	1.25
❑ 84 Jeff Hornacek	.30	.75
❑ 85 Mike Bibby	.40	1.00
❑ 86 Shareef Abdur-Rahim	.30	.75
❑ 87 Othella Harrington	.25	.60
❑ 88 Mitch Richmond	.30	.75
❑ 89 Juwan Howard	.30	.75
❑ 90 Rod Strickland	.25	.60
❑ 91 Elton Brand RC	10.00	25.00
❑ 92 Steve Francis RC	10.00	25.00
❑ 93 Baron Davis RC	12.00	30.00
❑ 94 Lamar Odom RC	10.00	25.00
❑ 95 Jonathan Bender RC	3.00	8.00
❑ 96 Wally Szczerbiak RC	10.00	25.00
❑ 97 Richard Hamilton RC	10.00	25.00
❑ 98 Andre Miller RC	10.00	25.00
❑ 99 Shawn Marion RC	10.00	25.00
❑ 100 Jason Terry RC	8.00	20.00
❑ 101 Trajan Langdon RC	3.00	8.00
❑ 102 A.Radojevic RC	3.00	8.00
❑ 103 Corey Maggette RC	10.00	25.00
❑ 104 William Avery RC	3.00	8.00
❑ 105 Ron Artest RC	12.00	30.00
❑ 106 James Posey RC	5.00	12.00
❑ 107 Quincy Lewis RC	3.00	8.00
❑ 108 Dion Glover RC	3.00	8.00
❑ 109 Kenny Thomas RC	3.00	8.00
❑ 110 Devean George RC	5.00	12.00
❑ 111 Tim James RC	3.00	8.00
❑ 112 Vonteego Cummings RC	3.00	8.00
❑ 113 Jumaine Jones RC	3.00	8.00
❑ 114 Scott Padgett RC	3.00	8.00
❑ 115 Adrian Griffin RC	3.00	8.00
❑ 116 Anthony Carter RC	6.00	15.00
❑ 117 Todd MacCulloch RC	3.00	8.00
❑ 118 Chucky Atkins RC	4.00	10.00
❑ 119 Obinna Ekezie RC	3.00	8.00
❑ 120 Eddie Robinson RC	3.00	8.00
❑ 121 Michael Ruffin RC	3.00	8.00
❑ 122 Laron Profit RC	3.00	8.00
❑ 123 Cal Bowdler RC	3.00	8.00
❑ 124 Chris Herren RC	3.00	8.00
❑ 125 Milt Palacio RC	3.00	8.00
❑ 126 Jeff Foster RC	4.00	10.00
❑ 127 Ryan Bowen RC	3.00	8.00
❑ 128 Tim Young RC	3.00	8.00
❑ 129 Derrick Dial RC	3.00	8.00
❑ 130 Greg Buckner RC	3.00	8.00
❑ 131 Rodney Buford RC	3.00	8.00
❑ 132 Evan Eschmeyer RC	3.00	8.00
❑ 133 Jermaine Jackson RC	3.00	8.00
❑ 134 John Celestand RC	3.00	8.00
❑ 135 Ryan Robertson RC	3.00	8.00
❑ KG Kevin Garnett PROMO	.75	2.00

2000-01 SP Authentic

❑ COMP.SET w/o SP's (90)	10.00	25.00
❑ COMMON CARD (1-90)	.25	.60
❑ COMMON RC/500 (91-136)	5.00	12.00
❑ COMMON RC/1250 (91-136)	2.50	6.00
❑ COMMON RC/2000 (91-136)	2.00	5.00
❑ 1 Jason Terry	.40	1.00
❑ 2 Alan Henderson	.25	.60
❑ 3 Lorenzen Wright	.25	.60
❑ 4 Paul Pierce	.40	1.00
❑ 5 Antoine Walker	.30	.75
❑ 6 Bryant Stith	.25	.60
❑ 7 Jamal Mashburn	.30	.75
❑ 8 Baron Davis	.40	1.00
❑ 9 David Wesley	.25	.60
❑ 10 Elton Brand	.40	1.00
❑ 11 Ron Artest	.40	1.00
❑ 12 Ron Mercer	.25	.60
❑ 13 Andre Miller	.30	.75
❑ 14 Lamond Murray	.25	.60
❑ 15 Jim Jackson	.25	.60
❑ 16 Michael Finley	.40	1.00
❑ 17 Dirk Nowitzki	.60	1.50
❑ 18 Steve Nash	.60	1.50
❑ 19 Antonio McDyess	.30	.75
❑ 20 Nick Van Exel	.30	.75
❑ 21 Raef LaFrentz	.25	.60
❑ 22 Jerry Stackhouse	.30	.75
❑ 23 Chucky Atkins	.25	.60
❑ 24 Joe Smith	.25	.60
❑ 25 Antawn Jamison	.40	1.00
❑ 26 Larry Hughes	.30	.75
❑ 27 Mookie Blaylock	.30	.75
❑ 28 Steve Francis	.40	1.00
❑ 29 Hakeem Olajuwon	.50	1.25
❑ 30 Cuttino Mobley	.30	.75
❑ 31 Reggie Miller	.40	1.00
❑ 32 Jermaine O'Neal	.40	1.00
❑ 33 Jalen Rose	.30	.75
❑ 34 Travis Best	.25	.60
❑ 35 Lamar Odom	.40	1.00
❑ 36 Corey Maggette	.30	.75
❑ 37 Eric Piatkowski	.25	.60
❑ 38 Shaquille O'Neal	1.00	2.50
❑ 39 Kobe Bryant	2.00	5.00
❑ 40 Isaiah Rider	.30	.75
❑ 41 Horace Grant	.30	.75
❑ 42 Eddie Jones	.30	.75
❑ 43 Brian Grant	.25	.60
❑ 44 Tim Hardaway	.30	.75
❑ 45 Ray Allen	.40	1.00
❑ 46 Glenn Robinson	.30	.75
❑ 47 Sam Cassell	.30	.75
❑ 48 Kevin Garnett	.75	2.00
❑ 49 Terrell Brandon	.25	.60
❑ 50 Chauncey Billups	.40	1.00
❑ 51 Wally Szczerbiak	.30	.75
❑ 52 Stephon Marbury	.40	1.00
❑ 53 Keith Van Horn	.30	.75
❑ 54 Aaron Williams	.25	.60
❑ 55 Latrell Sprewell	.30	.75
❑ 56 Allan Houston	.30	.75
❑ 57 Glen Rice	.30	.75
❑ 58 Tracy McGrady	.75	2.00
❑ 59 Grant Hill	.40	1.00
❑ 60 Darrell Armstrong	.25	.60
❑ 61 Allen Iverson	.75	2.00
❑ 62 Dikembe Mutombo	.30	.75
❑ 63 Aaron McKie	.25	.60
❑ 64 Jason Kidd	.60	1.50
❑ 65 Clifford Robinson	.25	.60
❑ 66 Shawn Marion	.40	1.00
❑ 67 Damon Stoudamire	.30	.75
❑ 68 Steve Smith	.30	.75
❑ 69 Rasheed Wallace	.40	1.00
❑ 70 Chris Webber	.40	1.00
❑ 71 Jason Williams	.30	.75
❑ 72 Peja Stojakovic	.30	.75
❑ 73 Tim Duncan	.75	2.00
❑ 74 David Robinson	.50	1.25
❑ 75 Derek Anderson	.30	.75
❑ 76 Gary Payton	.40	1.00
❑ 77 Rashard Lewis	.40	1.00
❑ 78 Patrick Ewing	.50	1.25
❑ 79 Vince Carter	.75	2.00
❑ 80 Charles Oakley	.30	.75
❑ 81 Antonio Davis	.25	.60
❑ 82 Karl Malone	.50	1.25
❑ 83 John Stockton	.50	1.25
❑ 84 John Starks	.25	.60
❑ 85 Shareef Abdur-Rahim	.30	.75
❑ 86 Mike Bibby	.30	.75
❑ 87 Michael Dickerson	.25	.60
❑ 88 Richard Hamilton	.30	.75
❑ 89 Mitch Richmond	.30	.75
❑ 90 Christian Laettner	.25	.60
❑ 91 K.Martin AU/500 RC	12.00	30.00
❑ 92 S.Swift AU/500 RC	6.00	15.00
❑ 93 Darius Miles AU/500 RC	6.00	15.00
❑ 94 Marcus Fizer/1250 RC	2.50	6.00
❑ 95 Mike Miller AU/500 RC	8.00	20.00
❑ 96 D.Johnson AU/500 RC	5.00	12.00
❑ 97 Chris Mihm/1250 RC	2.50	6.00
❑ 98 Jamal Crawford/1250 RC	4.00	10.00
❑ 99 Joel Przybilla/2000 RC	2.00	5.00
❑ 100 Keyon Dooling/1250 RC	2.50	6.00
❑ 101 Jerome Moiso/1250 RC	2.50	6.00
❑ 102 Etan Thomas/2000 RC	2.00	5.00
❑ 103 C.Alexander/1250 RC	2.50	6.00
❑ 104 Mateen Cleaves/1250 RC	2.50	6.00
❑ 105 Jason Collier/2000 RC	2.00	5.00
❑ 106 Hedo Turkoglu/1250 RC	6.00	15.00
❑ 107 Desmond Mason/1250 RC	3.00	8.00
❑ 108 Q.Richardson/1250 RC	3.00	8.00
❑ 109 Jamaal Magloire/1250 RC	2.50	6.00
❑ 110 Speedy Claxton/2000 RC	2.00	5.00
❑ 111 Morris Peterson AU/500 RC	8.00	20.00
❑ 112 Donnell Harvey/2000 RC	2.00	5.00
❑ 113 D.Stevenson/1250 RC	2.50	6.00
❑ 114 I.Tsakalidis/2000 RC	2.00	5.00
❑ 115 Soumaila Samake/2000 RC	2.00	5.00
❑ 116 Erick Barkley/2000 RC	2.00	5.00
❑ 117 Mark Madsen/2000 RC	2.00	5.00
❑ 118 A.J. Guyton/1250 RC	2.50	6.00
❑ 119 Olumide Oyedeji/2000 RC	2.00	5.00
❑ 120 Eddie House/1250 RC	2.50	6.00
❑ 121 Eduardo Najera/2000 RC	2.00	5.00
❑ 122 Lavor Postell/2000 RC	2.00	5.00
❑ 123 Hanno Mottola/1250 RC	2.50	6.00
❑ 124 Ira Newble/2000 RC	2.00	5.00
❑ 125 Chris Porter/1250 RC	2.50	6.00
❑ 126 R.Wolkowyski/2000 RC	2.00	5.00
❑ 127 Pepe Sanchez/2000 RC	2.00	5.00
❑ 128 Stephen Jackson/1250 RC	4.00	10.00
❑ 129 Marc Jackson/1250 RC	3.00	8.00
❑ 130 Dragan Tarlac/2000 RC	2.00	5.00
❑ 131 Lee Nailon/2000 RC	2.00	5.00
❑ 132 Mike Penberthy/1250 RC	2.50	6.00
❑ 133 Mark Blount/2000 RC	2.00	5.00
❑ 134 Dan Langhi/2000 RC	2.00	5.00
❑ 135 Daniel Santiago/2000 RC	5.00	12.00
❑ 136 Wang Zhizhi AU/500 RC	10.00	25.00

2001-02 SP Authentic

❑ COMP.SET w/o SP's (90)	20.00	40.00
❑ COMMON CARD (1-165)	.25	.60
❑ COMMON ROOKIE (91-106)	2.00	5.00
❑ COMMON ROOKIE (107-115)	3.00	8.00
❑ COMMON ROOKIE (116-131)	4.00	10.00
❑ COMMON ROOKIE (132-140)	5.00	12.00
❑ 1 Shareef Abdur-Rahim	.30	.75
❑ 2 Jason Terry	.40	1.00
❑ 3 Dion Glover	.25	.60

❑ 4 Paul Pierce	.40	1.00
❑ 5 Antoine Walker	.30	.75
❑ 6 Kenny Anderson	.30	.75
❑ 7 Baron Davis	.40	1.00
❑ 8 David Wesley	.25	.60
❑ 9 Jamal Mashburn	.30	.75
❑ 10 Jalen Rose	.30	.75
❑ 11 Fred Hoiberg	.25	.60
❑ 12 Marcus Fizer	.25	.60
❑ 13 Andre Miller	.30	.75
❑ 14 Lamond Murray	.25	.60
❑ 15 Chris Mihm	.25	.60
❑ 16 Dirk Nowitzki	.60	1.50
❑ 17 Steve Nash	.60	1.50
❑ 18 Michael Finley	.40	1.00
❑ 19 Nick Van Exel	.30	.75
❑ 20 Antonio McDyess	.30	.75
❑ 21 Juwan Howard	.30	.75
❑ 22 James Posey	.25	.60
❑ 23 Jerry Stackhouse	.30	.75
❑ 24 Clifford Robinson	.25	.60
❑ 25 Ben Wallace	.30	.75
❑ 26 Antawn Jamison	.40	1.00
❑ 27 Larry Hughes	.30	.75
❑ 28 Danny Fortson	.25	.60
❑ 29 Steve Francis	.40	1.00
❑ 30 Cuttino Mobley	.30	.75
❑ 31 Reggie Miller	.40	1.00
❑ 32 Al Harrington	.30	.75
❑ 33 Jermaine Oâ•™Neal	.40	1.00
❑ 34 Darius Miles	.25	.60
❑ 35 Elton Brand	.40	1.00
❑ 36 Lamar Odom	.40	1.00
❑ 37 Corey Maggette	.30	.75
❑ 38 Kobe Bryant	2.00	5.00
❑ 39 Shaquille O'Neal	1.00	2.50
❑ 40 Rick Fox	.30	.75
❑ 41 Lindsey Hunter	.25	.60
❑ 42 Stromile Swift	.25	.60
❑ 43 Michael Dickerson	.25	.60
❑ 44 Jason Williams	.30	.75
❑ 45 Alonzo Mourning	.40	1.00
❑ 46 Eddie Jones	.30	.75
❑ 47 Anthony Carter	.25	.60
❑ 48 Ray Allen	.40	1.00
❑ 49 Glenn Robinson	.30	.75
❑ 50 Sam Cassell	.30	.75
❑ 51 Kevin Garnett	.75	2.00
❑ 52 Terrell Brandon	.25	.60
❑ 53 Wally Szczerbiak	.30	.75
❑ 54 Joe Smith	.25	.60
❑ 55 Jason Kidd	.60	1.50
❑ 56 Kenyon Martin	.40	1.00
❑ 57 Mark Jackson	.30	.75
❑ 58 Allan Houston	.30	.75
❑ 59 Latrell Sprewell	.30	.75
❑ 60 Marcus Camby	.30	.75
❑ 61 Tracy McGrady	.75	2.00
❑ 62 Grant Hill	.40	1.00
❑ 63 Mike Miller	.30	.75
❑ 64 Allen Iverson	.75	2.00
❑ 65 Dikembe Mutombo	.30	.75
❑ 66 Aaron McKie	.25	.60
❑ 67 Stephon Marbury	.40	1.00
❑ 68 Shawn Marion	.40	1.00
❑ 69 Anfernee Hardaway	.40	1.00
❑ 70 Rasheed Wallace	.40	1.00
❑ 71 Bonzi Wells	.30	.75
❑ 72 Derek Anderson	.30	.75
❑ 73 Chris Webber	.40	1.00
❑ 74 Mike Bibby	.30	.75
❑ 75 Peja Stojakovic	.30	.75
❑ 76 Tim Duncan	.75	2.00
❑ 77 David Robinson	.50	1.25
❑ 78 Antonio Daniels	.25	.60
❑ 79 Gary Payton	.40	1.00
❑ 80 Rashard Lewis	.40	1.00
❑ 81 Desmond Mason	.30	.75
❑ 82 Vince Carter	.75	2.00
❑ 83 Morris Peterson	.30	.75
❑ 84 Antonio Davis	.25	.60
❑ 85 Karl Malone	.50	1.25
❑ 86 John Stockton	.50	1.25
❑ 87 Donyell Marshall	.25	.60
❑ 88 Richard Hamilton	.30	.75
❑ 89 Courtney Alexander	.25	.60
❑ 90 Michael Jordan	6.00	15.00
❑ 91 Tierre Brown RC	2.00	5.00
❑ 92 Damone Brown RC	2.00	5.00
❑ 93 Michael Bradley RC	2.00	5.00
❑ 94 Kedrick Brown RC	2.00	5.00
❑ 95 Alton Ford RC	2.00	5.00
❑ 96 Jason Collins RC	2.00	5.00
❑ 97 Antonis Fotsis RC	2.00	5.00
❑ 98 Mengke Bateer RC	2.00	5.00
❑ 99 Trenton Hassell RC	2.50	6.00
❑ 100 Jamison Brewer RC	2.00	5.00
❑ 101 Bobby Simmons RC	2.00	5.00
❑ 102 Mike James RC	2.00	5.00
❑ 103 Oscar Torres RC	2.00	5.00
❑ 104 Brandon Armstrong RC	2.00	5.00
❑ 105 Will Solomon RC	2.00	5.00
❑ 106 Vladimir Radmanovic RC	2.50	6.00
❑ 107 Kirk Haston RC	3.00	8.00
❑ 108 Gerald Wallace RC	8.00	20.00
❑ 109 Andrei Kirilenko RC	8.00	20.00
❑ 110 Joseph Forte RC	3.00	8.00
❑ 111 Brendan Haywood RC	4.00	10.00
❑ 112 Zach Randolph RC	8.00	20.00
❑ 113 DeSagana Diop RC	3.00	8.00
❑ 114 Shane Battier RC	5.00	12.00
❑ 115 Pau Gasol RC	12.00	30.00
❑ 116 Alvin Jones AU RC	4.00	10.00
❑ 117 Zeljko Rebraca AU RC	4.00	10.00
❑ 118 Kenny Satterfield AU RC	4.00	10.00
❑ 119 Jarron Collins AU RC	4.00	10.00
❑ 120 R.Boumtje-Boumtje AU RC	4.00	10.00
❑ 121 Loren Woods AU RC	4.00	10.00
❑ 122 Earl Watson AU RC	4.00	10.00
❑ 123 Jeff Trepagnier AU RC	4.00	10.00
❑ 124 Brian Scalabrine AU RC	4.00	10.00
❑ 125 Terence Morris AU RC	4.00	10.00
❑ 126 Gilbert Arenas AU RC	20.00	40.00
❑ 127 Samuel Dalembert AU RC	4.00	10.00
❑ 128 Jeryl Sasser AU RC	4.00	10.00
❑ 129 Rodney White AU RC	4.00	10.00
❑ 130 Eddie Griffin AU RC	5.00	12.00
❑ 131 Tyson Chandler AU RC	15.00	30.00
❑ 132 Steven Hunter AU RC	5.00	12.00
❑ 133 Troy Murphy AU RC	5.00	12.00
❑ 134 R.Jefferson AU RC	12.50	30.00
❑ 135 Joe Johnson AU RC	15.00	40.00
❑ 136 Eddy Curry AU RC	10.00	25.00
❑ 137 Jason Richardson AU RC	20.00	40.00
❑ 138 Tony Parker AU RC	25.00	50.00
❑ 139 Jamaal Tinsley AU RC	8.00	20.00
❑ 140 Kwame Brown AU RC	8.00	20.00
❑ 141 Paul Pierce SPEC	2.00	5.00
❑ 142 Tim Duncan SPEC	4.00	10.00
❑ 143 Stephon Marbury SPEC	2.00	5.00
❑ 144 S.Abdur-Rahim SPEC	1.50	4.00
❑ 145 Ray Allen SPEC	2.00	5.00
❑ 146 Bonzi Wells SPEC	1.50	4.00
❑ 147 Kenyon Martin SPEC	2.00	5.00
❑ 148 Darius Miles SPEC	1.25	3.00
❑ 149 Baron Davis SPEC	2.00	5.00
❑ 150 Dirk Nowitzki SPEC	3.00	8.00
❑ 151 Antoine Walker SPEC	1.50	4.00
❑ 152 Mike Miller SPEC	1.50	4.00
❑ 153 Shawn Marion SPEC	2.00	5.00
❑ 154 Jason Kidd SPEC	3.00	8.00
❑ 155 Elton Brand SPEC	2.00	5.00
❑ 156 Antawn Jamison SPEC	2.00	5.00
❑ 157 Rashard Lewis SPEC	2.00	5.00
❑ 158 Steve Francis SPEC	2.00	5.00
❑ 159 Tracy McGrady SPEC	4.00	10.00
❑ 160 Kobe Bryant SPECT	12.00	30.00
❑ 161 Allen Iverson SPECT	5.00	12.00
❑ 162 Vince Carter SPECT	5.00	12.00
❑ 163 Shaquille O'Neal SPECT	6.00	15.00
❑ 164 Kevin Garnett SPECT	5.00	12.00
❑ 165 Michael Jordan SPECT	15.00	40.00
❑ PROMO Michael Jordan	4.00	10.00

2002-03 SP Authentic

❑ COMP.SET w/o SP's (100)	15.00	40.00
❑ COMMON CARD (1-100)	.10	.25
❑ COMMON SPEC (101-142)	2.00	5.00
❑ COMMON AU RC (143-174)	2.50	6.00
❑ COMMON ROOKIE (175-203)	1.50	4.00
❑ 1 Glenn Robinson	.30	.75
❑ 2 Shareef Abdur-Rahim	.30	.75
❑ 3 Jason Terry	.40	1.00
❑ 4 Theo Ratliff	.25	.60
❑ 5 Paul Pierce	.40	1.00
❑ 5A Paul Pierce AU	12.50	30.00
❑ 6 Antoine Walker	.30	.75
❑ 6A Antoine Walker AU	10.00	25.00
❑ 7 Tony Delk	.25	.60
❑ 8 Vin Baker	.30	.75
❑ 9 Jalen Rose	.30	.75
❑ 10 Eddy Curry	.30	.75
❑ 11 Tyson Chandler	.30	.75
❑ 11A Tyson Chandler AU	8.00	20.00
❑ 12 Marcus Fizer	.25	.60
❑ 12A Marcus Fizer AU	6.00	15.00
❑ 13 Darius Miles	.25	.60
❑ 14 Zydrunas Ilgauskas	.30	.75
❑ 15 Dirk Nowitzki	.60	1.50
❑ 16 Michael Finley	.40	1.00
❑ 17 Steve Nash	.60	1.50
❑ 18 Raef LaFrentz	.25	.60
❑ 19 Juwan Howard	.30	.75
❑ 20 Rodney White	.25	.60
❑ 21 Ben Wallace	.30	.75
❑ 22 Richard Hamilton	.30	.75
❑ 23 Chauncey Billups	.40	1.00
❑ 24 Chucky Atkins	.25	.60
❑ 25 Jason Richardson	.40	1.00
❑ 26 Antawn Jamison	.40	1.00
❑ 27 Gilbert Arenas	.40	1.00
❑ 28 Steve Francis	.40	1.00
❑ 29 Cuttino Mobley	.30	.75
❑ 30 Jermaine O'Neal	.40	1.00
❑ 30A Jermaine O'Neal AU	10.00	25.00
❑ 31 Jamaal Tinsley	.30	.75
❑ 32 Reggie Miller	.40	1.00
❑ 33 Ron Artest	.30	.75
❑ 34 Elton Brand	.40	1.00
❑ 35 Andre Miller	.30	.75
❑ 36 Michael Olowokandi	.25	.60
❑ 37 Kobe Bryant	2.00	5.00
❑ 38 Shaquille O'Neal	1.00	2.50
❑ 39 Robert Horry	.30	.75
❑ 40 Derek Fisher	.30	.75
❑ 41 Pau Gasol	.40	1.00
❑ 42 Shane Battier	.30	.75
❑ 43 Eddie Jones	.30	.75
❑ 44 Brian Grant	.25	.60
❑ 45 Malik Allen	.25	.60
❑ 46 Gary Payton	.40	1.00
❑ 47 Sam Cassell	.30	.75
❑ 48 Kevin Garnett	.75	2.00
❑ 49 Wally Szczerbiak	.30	.75
❑ 50 Troy Hudson	.25	.60
❑ 51 Radoslav Nesterovic	.25	.60
❑ 52 Jason Kidd	.60	1.50
❑ 53 Richard Jefferson	.40	1.00
❑ 54 Kenyon Martin	.40	1.00
❑ 54A Kenyon Martin AU	8.00	20.00
❑ 55 Kerry Kittles	.30	.75
❑ 56 Baron Davis	.40	1.00
❑ 57 Jamal Mashburn	.30	.75
❑ 58 David Wesley	.25	.60
❑ 59 P.J. Brown	.25	.60
❑ 60 Jamaal Magloire	.25	.60
❑ 60A Jamaal Magloire AU	5.00	12.00
❑ 61 Allan Houston	.30	.75
❑ 62 Kurt Thomas	.25	.60

❑ 63 Latrell Sprewell	.30	.75
❑ 64 Clarence Weatherspoon	.25	.60
❑ 65 Tracy McGrady	.75	2.00
❑ 66 Grant Hill	.40	1.00
❑ 67 Mike Miller	.30	.75
❑ 67A Mike Miller AU	8.00	20.00
❑ 68 Allen Iverson	.75	2.00
❑ 69 Keith Van Horn	.30	.75
❑ 70 Stephon Marbury	.40	1.00
❑ 71 Shawn Marion	.40	1.00
❑ 72 Anfernee Hardaway	.40	1.00
❑ 73 Rasheed Wallace	.40	1.00
❑ 74 Derek Anderson	.30	.75
❑ 75 Scottie Pippen	.60	1.50
❑ 76 Bonzi Wells	.30	.75
❑ 77 Chris Webber	.40	1.00
❑ 78 Mike Bibby	.30	.75
❑ 78A Mike Bibby AU	10.00	25.00
❑ 79 Peja Stojakovic	.30	.75
❑ 80 Hedo Turkoglu	.30	.75
❑ 81 Vlade Divac	.30	.75
❑ 82 Tim Duncan	.75	2.00
❑ 83 David Robinson	.50	1.25
❑ 84 Tony Parker	.40	1.00
❑ 85 Steve Smith	.30	.75
❑ 86 Ray Allen	.40	1.00
❑ 87 Rashard Lewis	.40	1.00
❑ 88 Brent Barry	.25	.60
❑ 89 Elden Campbell	.25	.60
❑ 90 Vince Carter	.75	2.00
❑ 91 Morris Peterson	.30	.75
❑ 92 Antonio Davis	.25	.60
❑ 93 Alvin Williams	.25	.60
❑ 94 Karl Malone	.40	1.00
❑ 95 John Stockton	.50	1.25
❑ 96 Andrei Kirilenko	.40	1.00
❑ 97 DeShawn Stevenson	.25	.60
❑ 97A DeShawn Stevenson AU	5.00	12.00
❑ 98 Jerry Stackhouse	.30	.75
❑ 99 Michael Jordan	2.50	6.00
❑ 100 Kwame Brown	.25	.60
❑ 101 Kobe Bryant SPEC	3.00	8.00
❑ 102 Allen Iverson SPEC	2.50	6.00
❑ 103 Pau Gasol SPEC	2.00	5.00
❑ 104 Antoine Walker SPEC	2.00	5.00
❑ 105 J.O'Neal SPEC	2.00	5.00
❑ 106 Ray Allen SPEC	2.00	5.00
❑ 107 Baron Davis SPEC	2.00	5.00
❑ 108 Tim Duncan SPEC	2.50	6.00
❑ 109 Rashard Lewis SPEC	2.00	5.00
❑ 110 Michael Jordan SPEC	8.00	20.00
❑ 111 S.Marbury SPEC	2.00	5.00
❑ 112 S.Abdur-Rahim SPEC	2.00	5.00
❑ 113 Vince Carter SPEC	3.00	8.00
❑ 114 Allan Houston SPEC	2.00	5.00
❑ 115 Dirk Nowitzki SPEC	2.50	6.00
❑ 116 Grant Hill SPEC	2.00	5.00
❑ 117 Mike Bibby SPEC	2.00	5.00
❑ 118 Der.Anderson SPEC	2.00	5.00
❑ 119 S.O'Neal SPEC	3.00	8.00
❑ 120 Steve Francis SPEC	2.00	5.00
❑ 121 R.Jefferson SPEC	2.00	5.00
❑ 122 Ben Wallace SPEC	2.00	5.00
❑ 123 Jason Kidd SPEC	2.50	6.00
❑ 124 Jalen Rose SPEC	2.00	5.00
❑ 125 Paul Pierce SPEC	2.00	5.00
❑ 126 Michael Finley SPEC	2.00	5.00
❑ 127 J.Mashburn SPEC	2.00	5.00
❑ 128 Elton Brand SPEC	2.00	5.00
❑ 129 R.Wallace SPEC	2.00	5.00
❑ 130 Gary Payton SPEC	2.00	5.00
❑ 131 Tracy McGrady SPEC	3.00	8.00
❑ 132 Rich.Hamilton SPEC	2.00	5.00
❑ 133 Chris Webber SPEC	2.00	5.00
❑ 134 Karl Malone SPEC	2.00	5.00
❑ 135 Darius Miles SPEC	2.00	5.00
❑ 136 Shawn Marion SPEC	2.00	5.00
❑ 137 Kevin Garnett SPEC	2.50	6.00
❑ 138 Eddie Jones SPEC	2.00	5.00
❑ 139 J.Richardson SPEC	2.00	5.00
❑ 140 Glenn Robinson SPEC	2.00	5.00
❑ 141 J.Stackhouse SPEC	2.00	5.00
❑ 142 Shane Battier SPEC	2.00	5.00
❑ 143 Yao Ming AU RC	30.00	60.00
❑ 144 Jay Williams AU RC	5.00	12.00
❑ 145 Drew Gooden AU RC	6.00	15.00
❑ 146 N.Tskitishvili AU RC	3.00	8.00
❑ 147 D.Wagner AU RC	4.00	10.00
❑ 148 Nene Hilario AU RC	4.00	10.00
❑ 149 Chris Wilcox AU RC	4.00	10.00
❑ 150 A.Stoudemire AU RC	20.00	40.00
❑ 151 Caron Butler AU RC	6.00	15.00
❑ 152 Jared Jeffries AU RC	3.00	8.00
❑ 153 Melvin Ely AU RC	2.50	6.00
❑ 154 Marcus Haislip AU RC	2.50	6.00
❑ 155 Fred Jones AU RC	2.50	6.00
❑ 156 B.Nachbar AU RC	2.50	6.00
❑ 157 Jiri Welsch AU RC	2.50	6.00
❑ 158 Juan Dixon AU RC	5.00	12.00
❑ 159 C.Borchardt AU RC	2.50	6.00
❑ 160 R.Humphrey AU RC	2.50	6.00
❑ 161 Kareem Rush AU RC	4.00	10.00
❑ 162 Qyntel Woods AU RC	3.00	8.00
❑ 163 C.Jacobsen AU RC	2.50	6.00
❑ 164 Tayshaun Prince AU RC	8.00	20.00
❑ 165 Frank Williams AU RC	2.50	6.00
❑ 166 John Salmons AU RC	6.00	15.00
❑ 167 Chris Jefferies AU RC	2.50	6.00
❑ 168 Dan Dickau AU RC	2.50	6.00
❑ 169 Carlos Boozer AU RC	10.00	25.00
❑ 170 Marko Jaric AU	2.50	6.00
❑ 171 Sam Clancy AU RC	2.50	6.00
❑ 172 M.Ginobili AU RC	15.00	30.00
❑ 173 V.Yarbrough AU RC	2.50	6.00
❑ 174 Gordan Giricek AU RC	4.00	10.00
❑ 175 Predrag Savovic RC	1.50	4.00
❑ 176 Mike Dunleavy RC	2.00	5.00
❑ 177 Tamar Slay RC	1.50	4.00
❑ 178 Rasual Butler RC	1.50	4.00
❑ 179 Reggie Evans RC	1.50	4.00
❑ 180 Igor Rakocevic RC	1.50	4.00
❑ 181 Juaquin Hawkins RC	1.50	4.00
❑ 182 J.R. Bremer RC	1.50	4.00
❑ 183 Cezary Trybanski RC	1.50	4.00
❑ 184 Junior Harrington RC	1.50	4.00
❑ 185 Efthimios Rentzias RC	1.50	4.00
❑ 186 Smush Parker RC	1.50	4.00
❑ 187 Jamal Sampson RC	1.50	4.00
❑ 188 Roger Mason RC	1.50	4.00
❑ 189 Robert Archibald RC	1.50	4.00
❑ 190 Mehmet Okur RC	2.00	5.00
❑ 191 Dan Gadzuric RC	1.50	4.00
❑ 192 Pat Burke RC	1.50	4.00
❑ 193 Lonny Baxter RC	1.50	4.00
❑ 194 Tito Maddox RC	1.50	4.00
❑ 195 Jannero Pargo RC	1.50	4.00
❑ 196 Ronald Murray RC	2.50	6.00
❑ 197 Mike Wilks RC	1.50	4.00
❑ 198 Mike Batiste RC	1.50	4.00
❑ 199 Chris Owens RC	1.50	4.00
❑ 200 Raul Lopez RC	1.50	4.00
❑ 201 Antoine Rigaudeau RC	1.50	4.00
❑ 202 Ken Johnson RC	1.50	4.00
❑ 203 Maceo Baston RC	1.50	4.00
❑ NNO Michael Jordan PROMO	2.00	5.00

2003-04 SP Authentic

❑ COMP.SET w/o SP's (90)	15.00	40.00
❑ COMMON CARD (1-90)	.25	.60
❑ COMMON SPEC (91-132 & 144)	.60	1.50
❑ COMMON ROOKIE (133-147)	2.50	6.00
❑ COMMON AU RC (148-153)	6.00	15.00
❑ COMMON AU RC (154-189)	4.00	10.00
❑ 1 Shareef Abdur-Rahim	.30	.75
❑ 2 Theo Ratliff	.25	.60
❑ 3 Jason Terry	.30	.75
❑ 4 Raef LaFrentz	.25	.60
❑ 5 Vin Baker	.25	.60
❑ 6 Paul Pierce	.40	1.00
❑ 7 Antonio Davis	.25	.60
❑ 8 Scottie Pippen	.60	1.50
❑ 9 Tyson Chandler	.30	.75
❑ 10 Dajuan Wagner	.25	.60
❑ 11 Carlos Boozer	.40	1.00
❑ 12 Zydrunas Ilgauskas	.30	.75
❑ 13 Dirk Nowitzki	.60	1.50
❑ 14 Antoine Walker	.40	1.00
❑ 15 Steve Nash	.60	1.50
❑ 16 Michael Finley	.40	1.00
❑ 17 Earl Boykins	.25	.60
❑ 18 Andre Miller	.30	.75
❑ 19 Nene	.30	.75
❑ 20 Chauncey Billups	.40	1.00
❑ 21 Richard Hamilton	.30	.75
❑ 22 Ben Wallace	.30	.75
❑ 23 Clifford Robinson	.25	.60
❑ 24 Jason Richardson	.40	1.00
❑ 25 Nick Van Exel	.30	.75
❑ 26 Yao Ming	.75	2.00
❑ 27 Cuttino Mobley	.30	.75
❑ 28 Steve Francis	.40	1.00
❑ 29 Jermaine O'Neal	.40	1.00
❑ 30 Reggie Miller	.40	1.00
❑ 31 Ron Artest	.30	.75
❑ 32 Elton Brand	.40	1.00
❑ 33 Corey Maggette	.25	.60
❑ 34 Quentin Richardson	.30	.75
❑ 35 Kobe Bryant	2.00	5.00
❑ 36 Karl Malone	.40	1.00
❑ 37 Gary Payton	.40	1.00
❑ 38 Shaquille O'Neal	1.00	2.50
❑ 39 Pau Gasol	.40	1.00
❑ 40 Bonzi Wells	.25	.60
❑ 41 Mike Miller	.30	.75
❑ 42 Lamar Odom	.40	1.00
❑ 43 Eddie Jones	.30	.75
❑ 44 Caron Butler	.30	.75
❑ 45 Toni Kukoc	.30	.75
❑ 46 Desmond Mason	.30	.75
❑ 47 Michael Redd	.40	1.00
❑ 48 Latrell Sprewell	.30	.75
❑ 49 Kevin Garnett	.75	2.00
❑ 50 Sam Cassell	.30	.75
❑ 51 Richard Jefferson	.40	1.00
❑ 52 Kenyon Martin	.40	1.00
❑ 53 Jason Kidd	.60	1.50
❑ 54 Jamal Mashburn	.25	.60
❑ 55 Baron Davis	.40	1.00
❑ 56 David Wesley	.25	.60
❑ 57 Allan Houston	.30	.75
❑ 58 Stephon Marbury	.40	1.00
❑ 59 Keith Van Horn	.30	.75
❑ 60 Gordan Giricek	.25	.60
❑ 61 Drew Gooden	.25	.60
❑ 62 Tracy McGrady	.75	2.00
❑ 63 Glenn Robinson	.30	.75
❑ 64 Allen Iverson	.75	2.00
❑ 65 Eric Snow	.25	.60
❑ 66 Amare Stoudemire	.75	2.00
❑ 67 Antonio McDyess	.30	.75
❑ 68 Shawn Marion	.40	1.00
❑ 69 Zach Randolph	.40	1.00
❑ 70 Damon Stoudamire	.30	.75
❑ 71 Rasheed Wallace	.40	1.00
❑ 72 Peja Stojakovic	.30	.75
❑ 73 Chris Webber	.40	1.00
❑ 74 Mike Bibby	.30	.75
❑ 75 Brad Miller	.30	.75
❑ 76 Tony Parker	.40	1.00
❑ 77 Tim Duncan	.75	2.00
❑ 78 Manu Ginobili	.40	1.00
❑ 79 Vladimir Radmanovic	.25	.60
❑ 80 Ray Allen	.25	.60
❑ 81 Rashard Lewis	.40	1.00
❑ 82 Morris Peterson	.30	.75
❑ 83 Vince Carter	.75	2.00
❑ 84 Jalen Rose	.30	.75
❑ 85 Andrei Kirilenko	.40	1.00
❑ 86 Matt Harpring	.30	.75
❑ 87 Carlos Arroyo	.25	.60
❑ 88 Gilbert Arenas	.40	1.00
❑ 89 Larry Hughes	.30	.75
❑ 90 Jerry Stackhouse	.30	.75
❑ 91 Kobe Bryant SPEC	5.00	12.00
❑ 92 Jason Kidd SPEC	1.50	4.00
❑ 93 Rasheed Wallace SPEC	1.00	2.50
❑ 94 Jalen Rose SPEC	.75	2.00
❑ 95 Tim Duncan SPEC	2.00	5.00
❑ 96 S.Abdur-Rahim SPEC	.75	2.00
❑ 97 Baron Davis SPEC	1.00	2.50
❑ 98 Pau Gasol SPEC	1.00	2.50
❑ 99 Allen Iverson SPEC	2.00	5.00
❑ 100 Yao Ming SPEC	2.00	5.00
❑ 101 Gary Payton SPEC	1.00	2.50

102 Ray Allen SPEC	.60	1.50
103 Tracy McGrady SPEC	2.00	5.00
104 Amare Stoudemire SPEC	2.00	5.00
105 Tony Parker SPEC	1.00	2.50
106 Stephon Marbury SPEC	1.00	2.50
107 Richard Hamilton SPEC	.75	2.00
108 Chris Webber SPEC	1.00	2.50
109 Elton Brand SPEC	1.00	2.50
110 Jerry Stackhouse SPEC	.75	2.00
111 Andre Miller SPEC	.75	2.00
112 Kevin Garnett SPEC	2.00	5.00
113 Jason Richardson SPEC	1.00	2.50
114 Allan Houston SPEC	.75	2.00
115 Dajuan Wagner SPEC	.60	1.50
116 Richard Jefferson SPEC	1.00	2.50
117 Shaquille O'Neal SPEC	2.50	6.00
118 Latrell Sprewell SPEC	.75	2.00
119 Rashard Lewis SPEC	1.00	2.50
120 Steve Nash SPEC	1.50	4.00
121 Desmond Mason SPEC	.75	2.00
122 Mike Bibby SPEC	.75	2.00
123 Shawn Marion SPEC	1.00	2.50
124 Vince Carter SPEC	2.00	5.00
125 Caron Butler SPEC	.75	2.00
126 Gilbert Arenas SPEC	1.00	2.50
127 Dirk Nowitzki SPEC	1.50	4.00
128 Paul Pierce SPEC	1.00	2.50
129 Jermaine O'Neal SPEC	1.00	2.50
130 Andrei Kirilenko SPEC	1.00	2.50
131 Michael Jordan SPEC	8.00	20.00
132 Steve Francis SPEC	1.00	2.50
133 T.J. Ford RC	3.00	8.00
134 Kirk Hinrich RC	3.00	8.00
135 Nick Collison RC	2.50	6.00
136 Maurice Carter RC	2.50	6.00
137 Francisco Elson RC	2.50	6.00
138 Udonis Haslem RC	3.00	8.00
139 Jon Stefansson RC	2.50	6.00
140 Richie Frahm RC	2.50	6.00
141 Ronald Dupree RC	2.50	6.00
142 Josh Moore RC	2.50	6.00
143 Alex Garcia RC	2.50	6.00
144 Zach Randolph SPEC	1.00	2.50
145 Ben Handlogten RC	2.50	6.00
146 Devin Brown RC	2.50	6.00
147 Marquis Daniels RC	3.00	8.00
148 LeBron James AU RC	750.00	925.00
149 Darko Milicic AU RC	15.00	30.00
150 Carmelo Anthony AU RC	80.00	160.00
151 Chris Bosh AU RC	40.00	100.00
152 Dwyane Wade AU RC	150.00	300.00
153 Jarvis Hayes AU RC	6.00	15.00
154 Mickael Pietrus AU RC	6.00	15.00
155 Chris Kaman AU RC	6.00	15.00
156 Dahntay Jones AU RC	4.00	10.00
157 Marcus Banks AU RC	4.00	10.00
158 Luke Ridnour AU RC	6.00	15.00
159 Reece Gaines AU RC	4.00	10.00
160 Troy Bell AU RC	4.00	10.00
161 Mike Sweetney AU RC	4.00	10.00
162 David West AU RC	10.00	25.00
163 Aleksandar Pavlovic AU RC	5.00	12.00
164 Steve Blake AU RC	5.00	12.00
165 Boris Diaw AU RC	5.00	12.00
166 Zoran Planinic AU RC	4.00	10.00
167 Travis Outlaw AU RC	5.00	12.00
168 Brian Cook AU RC	4.00	10.00
169 Jerome Beasley AU RC	4.00	10.00
170 Ndudi Ebi AU RC	4.00	10.00
171 Kendrick Perkins AU RC	6.00	15.00
172 Leandro Barbosa AU RC	10.00	25.00
173 Josh Howard AU RC	8.00	20.00
174 Maciej Lampe AU RC	4.00	10.00
175 Jason Kapono AU RC	5.00	12.00
176 Luke Walton AU RC	8.00	20.00
177 Slavko Vranes AU RC	4.00	10.00
178 Zarko Cabarkapa AU RC	4.00	10.00
179 Zaur Pachulia AU RC	5.00	12.00
180 Maurice Williams AU RC	15.00	30.00
181 Brandon Hunter AU RC	4.00	10.00
182 Keith Bogans AU RC	4.00	10.00
183 Travis Hansen AU RC	4.00	10.00
184 Theron Smith AU RC	4.00	10.00
185 Willie Green AU RC	4.00	10.00
186 James Jones AU RC	4.00	10.00
187 Kyle Korver AU RC	5.00	12.00
188 Udonis Haslem AU RC	5.00	12.00
189 James Lang AU RC	4.00	10.00

2004-05 SP Authentic

COMP.SET w/o SP's (90)		
COMMON CARD (1-90)	.25	.60
COMMON ESS (91-130)	2.00	5.00
COMMON RC (131-140)	2.00	5.00
COMMON AU RC (141-180)	3.00	8.00
SIX AU VERSIONS FOR CARD 146		
1 Al Harrington	.30	.75
2 Antoine Walker	.40	1.00
3 Tony Delk	.25	.60
4 Gary Payton	.40	1.00
5 Mark Blount	.25	.60
6 Paul Pierce	.40	1.00
7 Kareem Rush	.25	.60
8 Gerald Wallace	.40	1.00
9 Jason Kapono	.25	.60
10 Eddy Curry	.30	.75
11 Kirk Hinrich	.30	.75
12 Tyson Chandler	.30	.75
13 Drew Gooden	.25	.60
14 LeBron James	2.50	6.00
15 Zydrunas Ilgauskas	.30	.75
16 Dirk Nowitzki	.60	1.50
17 Jason Terry	.30	.75
18 Michael Finley	.40	1.00
19 Carmelo Anthony	1.25	3.00
20 Kenyon Martin	.40	1.00
21 Andre Miller	.30	.75
22 Ben Wallace	.30	.75
23 Chauncey Billups	.40	1.00
24 Rasheed Wallace	.40	1.00
25 Derek Fisher	.30	.75
26 Jason Richardson	.40	1.00
27 Speedy Claxton	.25	.60
28 Juwan Howard	.30	.75
29 Tracy McGrady	.75	2.00
30 Yao Ming	1.00	2.50
31 Jermaine O'Neal	.40	1.00
32 Reggie Miller	.40	1.00
33 Fred Jones	.25	.60
34 Corey Maggette	.30	.75
35 Elton Brand	.40	1.00
36 Kerry Kittles	.30	.75
37 Caron Butler	.30	.75
38 Kobe Bryant	2.00	5.00
39 Lamar Odom	.40	1.00
40 Bonzi Wells	.25	.60
41 Jason Williams	.30	.75
42 Pau Gasol	.40	1.00
43 Dwyane Wade	1.25	3.00
44 Eddie Jones	.30	.75
45 Shaquille O'Neal	1.00	2.50
46 Desmond Mason	.30	.75
47 Keith Van Horn	.30	.75
48 Michael Redd	.40	1.00
49 Kevin Garnett	.75	2.00
50 Latrell Sprewell	.30	.75
51 Sam Cassell	.30	.75
52 Vince Carter	.75	2.00
53 Jason Kidd	.60	1.50
54 Richard Jefferson	.40	1.00
55 Baron Davis	.40	1.00
56 Jamaal Magloire	.25	.60
57 P.J. Brown	.25	.60
58 Allan Houston	.30	.75
59 Jamal Crawford	.30	.75
60 Stephon Marbury	.40	1.00
61 Hedo Turkoglu	.30	.75
62 Grant Hill	.40	1.00
63 Steve Francis	.40	1.00
64 Allen Iverson	.75	2.00
65 Glenn Robinson	.30	.75
66 Kyle Korver	.30	.75
67 Amare Stoudemire	.75	2.00
68 Shawn Marion	.40	1.00
69 Steve Nash	.60	1.50
70 Darius Miles	.30	.75
71 Shareef Abdur-Rahim	.30	.75
72 Zach Randolph	.40	1.00
73 Chris Webber	.40	1.00
74 Mike Bibby	.30	.75
75 Peja Stojakovic	.30	.75
76 Manu Ginobili	.40	1.00
77 Tim Duncan	.75	2.00
78 Tony Parker	.40	1.00
79 Rashard Lewis	.40	1.00
80 Ray Allen	.40	1.00
81 Ronald Murray	.25	.60
82 Donyell Marshall	.25	.60
83 Jalen Rose	.30	.75
84 Chris Bosh	.40	1.00
85 Andrei Kirilenko	.40	1.00
86 Carlos Boozer	.40	1.00
87 Matt Harpring	.30	.75
88 Antawn Jamison	.40	1.00
89 Gilbert Arenas	.40	1.00
90 Larry Hughes	.30	.75
91 Bill Russell ESS	2.50	6.00
92 Larry Bird ESS	5.00	12.00
93 Paul Pierce ESS	2.00	5.00
94 Michael Jordan ESS	6.00	15.00
95 LeBron James ESS	6.00	15.00
96 Dirk Nowitzki ESS	2.00	5.00
97 Carmelo Anthony ESS	2.00	5.00
98 Ben Wallace ESS	2.00	5.00
99 Isiah Thomas ESS	2.50	6.00
100 Tracy McGrady ESS	2.50	6.00
101 Yao Ming ESS	2.50	6.00
102 Jermaine O'Neal ESS	2.00	5.00
103 Reggie Miller ESS	2.00	5.00
104 Elton Brand ESS	2.00	5.00
105 Kareem Abdul-Jabbar ESS	3.00	8.00
106 Kobe Bryant ESS	3.00	8.00
107 Magic Johnson ESS	4.00	10.00
108 Wilt Chamberlain ESS	4.00	10.00
109 Pau Gasol ESS	2.00	5.00
110 Dwyane Wade ESS	3.00	8.00
111 Shaquille O'Neal ESS	2.50	6.00
112 Michael Redd ESS	2.00	5.00
113 Oscar Robertson ESS	3.00	8.00
114 Kevin Garnett ESS	2.00	5.00
115 Sam Cassell ESS	2.00	5.00
116 Jason Kidd ESS	2.00	5.00
117 Baron Davis ESS	2.00	5.00
118 Stephon Marbury ESS	2.00	5.00
119 Steve Francis ESS	2.00	5.00
120 Allen Iverson ESS	2.00	5.00
121 Julius Erving ESS	2.50	6.00
122 Amare Stoudemire ESS	2.00	5.00
123 Shawn Marion ESS	2.00	5.00
124 Chris Webber ESS	2.00	5.00
125 Peja Stojakovic ESS	2.00	5.00
126 Tim Duncan ESS	2.00	5.00
127 Ray Allen ESS	2.00	5.00
128 Vince Carter ESS	2.50	6.00
129 Andrei Kirilenko ESS	2.00	5.00
130 John Stockton ESS	2.50	6.00
131 Emeka Okafor RC	4.00	10.00
132 Mario Kasun RC	2.00	5.00
133 Andre Barrett RC	2.00	5.00
134 Ha Seung-Jin RC	2.00	5.00
135 Horace Jenkins RC	2.00	5.00
136 Tony Bobbitt RC	2.00	5.00
137 Luis Flores RC	2.00	5.00
138 John Edwards RC	2.00	5.00
139 Beno Udrih RC	2.50	6.00
140 Erik Daniels RC	2.00	5.00
141 Nenad Krstic AU RC	5.00	12.00
142 Yuta Tabuse AU RC	15.00	30.00
143 Pape Sow AU RC	4.00	10.00
144 Andres Nocioni AU RC	8.00	20.00
145 B.Robinson AU RC EXCH	4.00	10.00
146A Michael Jordan AU		
146B Dwight Howard AU		
146C LeBron James AU		
146D Steve Nash AU		
146E Scottie Pippen AU		
146F Larry Brown AU		
147 Trevor Ariza AU RC	8.00	20.00
148 Damien Wilkins AU RC	3.00	8.00
149 Justin Reed AU RC EXCH	3.00	8.00
150 Chris Duhon AU RC	5.00	12.00
151 Royal Ivey AU RC	3.00	8.00
152 Antonio Burks AU RC	3.00	8.00

❑ 153 Andre Emmett AU RC	3.00	8.00
❑ 154 Donta Smith AU RC	3.00	8.00
❑ 155 Lionel Chalmers AU RC	3.00	8.00
❑ 156 P.J. Ramos AU RC EXCH	3.00	8.00
❑ 157 Jackson Vroman AU RC	3.00	8.00
❑ 158 Anderson Varejao AU RC	5.00	12.00
❑ 159 David Harrison AU RC	3.00	8.00
❑ 160 D.J. Mbenga AU RC	3.00	8.00
❑ 161 Sasha Vujacic AU RC	4.00	10.00
❑ 162 Kevin Martin AU RC	8.00	20.00
❑ 163 Tony Allen AU RC	5.00	12.00
❑ 164 Delonte West AU RC EXCH	6.00	15.00
❑ 165 Romain Sato AU RC	3.00	8.00
❑ 166 Viktor Khryapa AU RC	3.00	8.00
❑ 167 Pavel Podkolzine AU RC	3.00	8.00
❑ 168 Jameer Nelson AU RC EXCH	5.00	12.00
❑ 169 Dorell Wright AU RC	5.00	12.00
❑ 170 J.R. Smith AU RC	15.00	30.00
❑ 171 Josh Smith AU RC EXCH	15.00	30.00
❑ 172 Kirk Snyder AU RC EXCH	3.00	8.00
❑ 173 Al Jefferson AU RC	20.00	40.00
❑ 174 Kris Humphries AU RC	3.00	8.00
❑ 175 Sebastian Telfair AU RC	5.00	12.00
❑ 176 Robert Swift AU RC	3.00	8.00
❑ 177 Andris Biedrins AU RC	5.00	12.00
❑ 178 Luke Jackson AU RC	3.00	8.00
❑ 179 Andre Iguodala AU RC	20.00	40.00
❑ 180 Rafael Araujo AU RC	3.00	8.00
❑ 181 Luol Deng AU RC	10.00	25.00
❑ 182 Josh Childress AU RC	8.00	20.00
❑ 183 Devin Harris AU RC EXCH	8.00	20.00
❑ 184 Shaun Livingston AU RC	8.00	20.00
❑ 185 Ben Gordon AU RC	15.00	30.00
❑ 186 Dwight Howard AU RC	100.00	200.00

2005-06 SP Authentic

❑ COMP.SET w/o SP's (90)	15.00	40.00
❑ COMMON CARD (1-90)	.25	.60
❑ SEMISTARS	.30	.75
❑ UNLISTED STARS	.40	1.00
❑ COMMON AU RC (91-125)	5.00	12.00
❑ 91-125 PRINT RUN 1299 SER.#'d SETS		
❑ 91-125 #'d 1-100 ARE PATCH PARALLEL		
❑ COMMON AU RC (126-132)	6.00	15.00
❑ 126-132 PRINT RUN 1299 SER.#'d SETS		
❑ COMMON ROOKIE (133-157)	2.00	5.00
❑ 133-157 PRINT RUN 999 SER.#'d SETS		
❑ 1 Boris Diaw	.30	.75
❑ 2 Josh Childress	.30	.75
❑ 3 Josh Smith	.40	1.00
❑ 4 Antoine Walker	.30	.75
❑ 5 Al Jefferson	.40	1.00
❑ 6 Paul Pierce	.40	1.00
❑ 7 Kareem Rush	.25	.60
❑ 8 Emeka Okafor	.40	1.00
❑ 9 Gerald Wallace	.40	1.00
❑ 10 Ben Gordon	.50	1.25
❑ 11 Kirk Hinrich	.40	1.00
❑ 12 Michael Jordan	2.50	6.00
❑ 13 Drew Gooden	.30	.75
❑ 14 LeBron James	2.00	5.00
❑ 15 Luke Jackson	.25	.60
❑ 16 Dirk Nowitzki	.60	1.50
❑ 17 Jason Terry	.40	1.00
❑ 18 Josh Howard	.40	1.00
❑ 19 Nene Hilario	.25	.60
❑ 20 Carmelo Anthony	.75	2.00
❑ 21 Kenyon Martin	.40	1.00
❑ 22 Ben Wallace	.40	1.00
❑ 23 Chauncey Billups	.40	1.00
❑ 24 Rasheed Wallace	.40	1.00
❑ 25 Baron Davis	.40	1.00
❑ 26 Jason Richardson	.40	1.00
❑ 27 Mike Dunleavy	.30	.75
❑ 28 David Wesley	.25	.60
❑ 29 Tracy McGrady	.75	2.00
❑ 30 Yao Ming	1.00	2.50
❑ 31 Jamaal Tinsley	.30	.75
❑ 32 Jermaine O'Neal	.40	1.00
❑ 33 Fred Jones	.30	.75
❑ 34 Corey Maggette	.30	.75
❑ 35 Elton Brand	.40	1.00
❑ 36 Shaun Livingston	.25	.60
❑ 37 Caron Butler	.40	1.00
❑ 38 Kobe Bryant	2.00	5.00
❑ 39 Wilt Chamberlain	.75	2.00
❑ 40 Jason Williams	.30	.75
❑ 41 Pau Gasol	.40	1.00
❑ 42 Shane Battier	.40	1.00
❑ 43 Udonis Haslem	.40	1.00
❑ 44 Dwyane Wade	1.00	2.50
❑ 45 Shaquille O'Neal	1.00	2.50
❑ 46 Desmond Mason	.25	.60
❑ 47 T.J. Ford	.30	.75
❑ 48 Michael Redd	.40	1.00
❑ 49 Kevin Garnett	.75	2.00
❑ 50 Wally Szczerbiak	.30	.75
❑ 51 Ndudi Ebi	.25	.60
❑ 52 Jason Kidd	.60	1.50
❑ 53 Richard Jefferson	.30	.75
❑ 54 Vince Carter	.75	2.00
❑ 55 Lee Nailon	.25	.60
❑ 56 J.R. Smith	.30	.75
❑ 57 Jamaal Magloire	.25	.60
❑ 58 Jamal Crawford	.30	.75
❑ 59 Stephon Marbury	.40	1.00
❑ 60 Quentin Richardson	.30	.75
❑ 61 Dwight Howard	.75	2.00
❑ 62 Grant Hill	.40	1.00
❑ 63 Steve Francis	.40	1.00
❑ 64 Allen Iverson	.75	2.00
❑ 65 Andre Iguodala	.40	1.00
❑ 66 Chris Webber	.40	1.00
❑ 67 Amare Stoudemire	.75	2.00
❑ 68 Shawn Marion	.40	1.00
❑ 69 Steve Nash	.50	1.25
❑ 70 Sebastian Telfair	.30	.75
❑ 71 Darius Miles	.40	1.00
❑ 72 Zach Randolph	.40	1.00
❑ 73 Brad Miller	.40	1.00
❑ 74 Mike Bibby	.40	1.00
❑ 75 Peja Stojakovic	.40	1.00
❑ 76 Manu Ginobili	.40	1.00
❑ 77 Tim Duncan	.75	2.00
❑ 78 Tony Parker	.40	1.00
❑ 79 Luke Ridnour	.30	.75
❑ 80 Rashard Lewis	.40	1.00
❑ 81 Ray Allen	.40	1.00
❑ 82 Chris Bosh	.40	1.00
❑ 83 Morris Peterson	.30	.75
❑ 84 Jalen Rose	.40	1.00
❑ 85 Andrei Kirilenko	.40	1.00
❑ 86 Carlos Boozer	.40	1.00
❑ 87 John Stockton	.75	2.00
❑ 88 Antawn Jamison	.40	1.00
❑ 89 Gilbert Arenas	.40	1.00
❑ 90 Brendan Haywood	.25	.60
❑ 91 Andrew Bogut AU RC	8.00	20.00
❑ 92 Marvin Williams AU RC	15.00	30.00
❑ 93 Deron Williams AU RC	40.00	75.00
❑ 94 Chris Paul AU RC	75.00	150.00
❑ 95 Raymond Felton AU RC	8.00	20.00
❑ 96 Martell Webster AU RC	5.00	12.00
❑ 97 Charlie Villanueva AU RC	10.00	25.00
❑ 98 Channing Frye AU RC	8.00	20.00
❑ 99 Brandon Bass AU RC	6.00	15.00
❑ 100 Travis Diener AU RC	5.00	12.00
❑ 101 Andray Blatche AU RC	6.00	15.00
❑ 102 Monta Ellis AU RC	25.00	40.00
❑ 103 Sean May AU RC	6.00	15.00
❑ 104 Rashad McCants AU RC	10.00	25.00
❑ 105 Antoine Wright AU RC	5.00	12.00
❑ 106 Joey Graham AU RC	5.00	12.00
❑ 107 Danny Granger AU RC	20.00	40.00
❑ 108 Gerald Green AU RC	10.00	25.00
❑ 109 Hakim Warrick AU RC	10.00	25.00
❑ 110 Julius Hodge AU RC	5.00	12.00
❑ 111 Sarunas Jasikevicius AU RC	6.00	15.00
❑ 112 M.Andriuskevicius AU RC	5.00	12.00
❑ 113 Francisco Garcia AU RC	6.00	15.00
❑ 114 Luther Head AU RC	6.00	15.00
❑ 115 Nate Robinson AU RC	15.00	30.00
❑ 116 Jason Maxiell AU RC	6.00	15.00
❑ 117 Wayne Simien AU RC	8.00	20.00
❑ 118 David Lee AU RC	10.00	25.00
❑ 119 Daniel Ewing AU RC	5.00	12.00
❑ 120 Louis Williams AU RC	10.00	25.00
❑ 121 Salim Stoudamire AU RC	6.00	15.00
❑ 122 Jarrett Jack AU RC	5.00	12.00
❑ 123 Andrew Bynum AU RC	50.00	100.00
❑ 124 C.J. Miles AU RC	5.00	12.00
❑ 125 Irsan Ilyasova AU RC	5.00	12.00
❑ 126 Will Bynum AU RC	5.00	12.00
❑ 127 Lawrence Roberts AU RC	5.00	12.00
❑ 128 Dijon Thompson AU RC	5.00	12.00
❑ 129 Johan Petro AU RC	5.00	12.00
❑ 130 Bracey Wright AU RC	5.00	12.00
❑ 131 Ike Diogu AU RC	6.00	15.00
❑ 132 Ryan Gomes AU RC	5.00	12.00
❑ 133 Ronnie Price RC	2.00	5.00
❑ 134 Alan Anderson RC	2.00	5.00
❑ 135 Esteban Batista RC	2.00	5.00
❑ 136 Linas Kleiza RC	2.50	6.00
❑ 137 Eddie Basden RC	2.00	5.00
❑ 138 Josh Powell RC	2.00	5.00
❑ 139 Kevin Burleson RC	2.00	5.00
❑ 140 Von Wafer RC	2.00	5.00
❑ 141 Rawle Marshall RC	2.00	5.00
❑ 142 Gerald Fitch RC	2.00	5.00
❑ 143 Robert Whaley RC	2.00	5.00
❑ 144 Orien Greene RC	2.00	5.00
❑ 145 Fabricio Oberto RC	2.00	5.00
❑ 146 Amir Johnson RC	2.00	5.00
❑ 147 Shavlik Randolph RC	2.00	5.00
❑ 148 Arvydas Macijauskas RC	2.00	5.00
❑ 149 Alex Acker RC	2.00	5.00
❑ 150 James Singleton RC	2.00	5.00
❑ 151 Anthony Roberson RC	2.00	5.00
❑ 152 Earl Barron RC	2.00	5.00
❑ 153 Dwayne Jones RC	2.00	5.00
❑ 154 Sean Banks RC	2.00	5.00
❑ 155 Sharrod Ford RC	2.00	5.00
❑ 156 Andre Owens RC	2.00	5.00
❑ 157 Donell Taylor RC	2.00	5.00

2006-07 SP Authentic

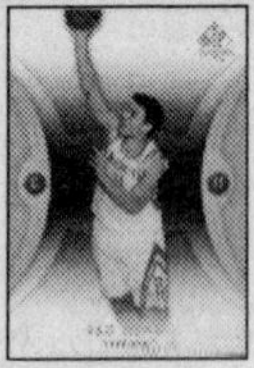

❑ COMP.SET w/o SP's (100)	15.00	35.00
❑ 1 Joe Johnson	.30	.75
❑ 2 Marvin Williams	.40	1.00
❑ 3 Josh Childress	.30	.75
❑ 4 Paul Pierce	.40	1.00
❑ 5 Sebastian Telfair	.30	.75
❑ 6 Gerald Green	.50	1.25
❑ 7 Emeka Okafor	.40	1.00
❑ 8 Raymond Felton	.50	1.25
❑ 9 Gerald Wallace	.40	1.00
❑ 10 Ben Wallace	.40	1.00
❑ 11 Ben Gordon	.50	1.25
❑ 12 Kirk Hinrich	.40	1.00
❑ 13 LeBron James	2.00	5.00
❑ 14 Zydrunas Ilgauskas	.30	.75
❑ 15 Drew Gooden	.30	.75
❑ 16 Jason Terry	.40	1.00
❑ 17 Dirk Nowitzki	.60	1.50
❑ 18 Devin Harris	.40	1.00
❑ 19 Carmelo Anthony	.50	1.25
❑ 20 Kenyon Martin	.40	1.00
❑ 21 Andre Miller	.30	.75
❑ 22 Chauncey Billups	.40	1.00
❑ 23 Richard Hamilton	.30	.75
❑ 24 Rasheed Wallace	.40	1.00
❑ 25 Jason Richardson	.40	1.00
❑ 26 Baron Davis	.40	1.00
❑ 27 Troy Murphy	.40	1.00
❑ 28 Tracy McGrady	.75	2.00
❑ 29 Yao Ming	1.00	2.50
❑ 30 Shane Battier	.40	1.00
❑ 31 Jermaine O'Neal	.40	1.00
❑ 32 Sarunas Jasikevicius	.30	.75
❑ 33 Al Harrington	.25	.60
❑ 34 Elton Brand	.40	1.00

❑ 35 Sam Cassell .40 1.00
❑ 36 Chris Kaman .25 .60
❑ 37 Kobe Bryant 2.00 5.00
❑ 38 Lamar Odom .40 1.00
❑ 39 Vladimir Radmanovic .25 .60
❑ 40 Pau Gasol .40 1.00
❑ 41 Hakim Warrick .30 .75
❑ 42 Damon Stoudamire .30 .75
❑ 43 Shaquille O'Neal 1.00 2.50
❑ 44 Dwyane Wade 1.00 2.50
❑ 45 Alonzo Mourning .50 1.25
❑ 46 Andrew Bogut .40 1.00
❑ 47 Charlie Villanueva .40 1.00
❑ 48 Michael Redd .40 1.00
❑ 49 Kevin Garnett .75 2.00
❑ 50 Ricky Davis .40 1.00
❑ 51 Rashad McCants .30 .75
❑ 52 Vince Carter .75 2.00
❑ 53 Jason Kidd .60 1.50
❑ 54 Richard Jefferson .30 .75
❑ 55 Chris Paul .75 2.00
❑ 56 Peja Stojakovic .40 1.00
❑ 57 Tyson Chandler .40 1.00
❑ 58 Stephon Marbury .40 1.00
❑ 59 Channing Frye .30 .75
❑ 60 Nate Robinson .40 1.00
❑ 61 Grant Hill .40 1.00
❑ 62 Dwight Howard .75 2.00
❑ 63 Jameer Nelson .30 .75
❑ 64 Allen Iverson .75 2.00
❑ 65 Andre Iguodala .40 1.00
❑ 66 Kyle Korver .40 1.00
❑ 67 Steve Nash .50 1.25
❑ 68 Amare Stoudemire .75 2.00
❑ 69 Shawn Marion .40 1.00
❑ 70 Jamaal Magloire .25 .60
❑ 71 Martell Webster .30 .75
❑ 72 Jarrett Jack .30 .75
❑ 73 Mike Bibby .40 1.00
❑ 74 Ron Artest .40 1.00
❑ 75 Brad Miller .40 1.00
❑ 76 Tony Parker .40 1.00
❑ 77 Tim Duncan .75 2.00
❑ 78 Manu Ginobili .40 1.00
❑ 79 Ray Allen .40 1.00
❑ 80 Rashard Lewis .40 1.00
❑ 81 Luke Ridnour .30 .75
❑ 82 Chris Bosh .40 1.00
❑ 83 T.J. Ford .30 .75
❑ 84 Joey Graham .30 .75
❑ 85 Carlos Boozer .40 1.00
❑ 86 Andrei Kirilenko .40 1.00
❑ 87 Deron Williams .60 1.50
❑ 88 Gilbert Arenas .40 1.00
❑ 89 Antawn Jamison .40 1.00
❑ 90 Andray Blatche .25 .60
❑ 91 Adam Morrison RC 2.50 6.00
❑ 92 Alexander Johnson RC 2.00 5.00
❑ 93 J.J. Redick RC 2.00 5.00
❑ 94 Vassilis Spanoulis RC 2.00 5.00
❑ 95 Jorge Garbajosa RC 4.00 10.00
❑ 96 Leon Powe RC 2.00 5.00
❑ 97 Chris Quinn RC 2.00 5.00
❑ 98 Tarence Kinsey RC 2.00 5.00
❑ 99 Yakhouba Diawara RC 2.00 5.00
❑ 100 Robert Hite RC 2.00 5.00
❑ 101 Thabo Sefolosha AU RC 8.00 20.00
❑ 102 Ronnie Brewer AU RC 8.00 20.00
❑ 103 Cedric Simmons AU RC 6.00 15.00
❑ 104 Dee Brown AU RC EXCH 6.00 15.00
❑ 105 Craig Smith AU RC 6.00 15.00
❑ 106 Rodney Carney AU RC 6.00 15.00
❑ 107 Pops Mensah-Bonsu AU RC 6.00 15.00
❑ 108 Shawne Williams AU RC 6.00 15.00
❑ 109 Quincy Douby AU RC 6.00 15.00
❑ 110 Renaldo Balkman AU RC 6.00 15.00
❑ 111 Rajon Rondo AU RC 25.00 60.00
❑ 112 Marcus Williams AU RC 8.00 20.00
❑ 113 Josh Boone AU RC 6.00 15.00
❑ 114 Kyle Lowry AU RC 6.00 15.00
❑ 115 Shannon Brown AU RC 6.00 15.00
❑ 116 Jordan Farmar AU RC 8.00 20.00
❑ 117 Sergio Rodriguez AU RC 6.00 15.00
❑ 118 Maurice Ager AU RC 6.00 15.00
❑ 119 Mardy Collins AU RC 6.00 15.00
❑ 120 James White AU RC 6.00 15.00
❑ 121 Steve Novak AU RC 6.00 15.00
❑ 122 Solomon Jones AU RC 6.00 15.00
❑ 123 Andrea Bargnani
AU RC EXCH 12.00 30.00
❑ 124 LaMarcus Aldridge AU RC 15.00 30.00
❑ 125 Tyrus Thomas AU RC 20.00 40.00
❑ 126 Shelden Williams AU RC 10.00 25.00
❑ 127 Brandon Roy AU RC 40.00 80.00
❑ 128 Randy Foye AU RC 8.00 20.00
❑ 129 Rudy Gay AU RC 8.00 20.00
❑ 130 Patrick O'Bryant AU RC 8.00 20.00
❑ 131 Saer Sene AU RC 8.00 20.00
❑ 132 Hilton Armstrong AU RC 8.00 20.00

2007-08 SP Authentic

❑ COMP.SET w/o SP's (100) 25.00 50.00
❑ 1 Brandon Roy .75 2.00
❑ 2 Channing Frye .40 1.00
❑ 3 Jarrett Jack .40 1.00
❑ 4 LaMarcus Aldridge .60 1.50
❑ 5 Delonte West .40 1.00
❑ 6 Johan Petro .30 .75
❑ 7 Nick Collison .30 .75
❑ 8 Joe Johnson .50 1.25
❑ 9 Josh Smith .50 1.25
❑ 10 Marvin Williams .50 1.25
❑ 11 Hakim Warrick .40 1.00
❑ 12 Pau Gasol .50 1.25
❑ 13 Rudy Gay .40 1.00
❑ 14 Al Jefferson .50 1.25
❑ 15 Paul Pierce .50 1.25
❑ 16 Ray Allen .50 1.25
❑ 17 Andrew Bogut .50 1.25
❑ 18 Charlie Villanueva .50 1.25
❑ 19 Maurice Williams .40 1.00
❑ 20 Michael Redd .50 1.25
❑ 21 Kevin Garnett 1.25 3.00
❑ 22 Randy Foye .50 1.25
❑ 23 Ricky Davis .50 1.25
❑ 24 Emeka Okafor .50 1.25
❑ 25 Gerald Wallace .50 1.25
❑ 26 Jason Richardson .50 1.25
❑ 27 David Lee .40 1.00
❑ 28 Eddy Curry .30 .75
❑ 29 Stephon Marbury .50 1.25
❑ 30 Zach Randolph .50 1.25
❑ 31 Brad Miller .50 1.25
❑ 32 Kevin Martin .50 1.25
❑ 33 Mike Bibby .50 1.25
❑ 34 Ron Artest .50 1.25
❑ 35 Jamaal Tinsley .30 .75
❑ 36 Jermaine O'Neal .50 1.25
❑ 37 Mike Dunleavy .40 1.00
❑ 38 Andre Iguodala .50 1.25
❑ 39 Andre Miller .40 1.00
❑ 40 Rodney Carney .30 .75
❑ 41 Chris Paul 1.00 2.50
❑ 42 David West .50 1.25
❑ 43 Tyson Chandler .50 1.25
❑ 44 Corey Maggette .40 1.00
❑ 45 Cuttino Mobley .40 1.00
❑ 46 Elton Brand .50 1.25
❑ 47 Darko Milicic .50 1.25
❑ 48 Dwight Howard 1.00 2.50
❑ 49 Hedo Turkoglu .50 1.25
❑ 50 Rashard Lewis .50 1.25
❑ 51 Antawn Jamison .50 1.25
❑ 52 Caron Butler .50 1.25
❑ 53 Gilbert Arenas .50 1.25
❑ 54 Jason Kidd .75 2.00
❑ 55 Richard Jefferson .50 1.25
❑ 56 Vince Carter 1.00 2.50
❑ 57 Baron Davis .50 1.25
❑ 58 Monta Ellis .40 1.00
❑ 59 Stephen Jackson .40 1.00
❑ 60 Jordan Farmar .40 1.00
❑ 61 Kobe Bryant 2.50 6.00
❑ 62 Lamar Odom .50 1.25
❑ 63 Alonzo Mourning .60 1.50
❑ 64 Dwyane Wade 1.25 3.00
❑ 65 Shaquille O'Neal 1.25 3.00
❑ 66 Allen Iverson 1.00 2.50
❑ 67 Carmelo Anthony 1.00 2.50
❑ 68 Marcus Camby .30 .75
❑ 69 Andrea Bargnani .60 1.50
❑ 70 Chris Bosh .50 1.25
❑ 71 Jose Calderon .40 1.00
❑ 72 T.J. Ford .40 1.00
❑ 73 Ben Gordon .60 1.50
❑ 74 Ben Wallace .50 1.25
❑ 75 Kirk Hinrich .50 1.25
❑ 76 Luol Deng .50 1.25
❑ 77 Larry Hughes .40 1.00
❑ 78 LeBron James 2.50 6.00
❑ 79 Zydrunas Ilgauskas .40 1.00
❑ 80 Andrei Kirilenko .50 1.25
❑ 81 Carlos Boozer .50 1.25
❑ 82 Deron Williams .75 2.00
❑ 83 Mehmet Okur .40 1.00
❑ 84 Luther Head .40 1.00
❑ 85 Tracy McGrady 1.00 2.50
❑ 86 Yao Ming 1.25 3.00
❑ 87 Chauncey Billups .50 1.25
❑ 88 Rasheed Wallace .50 1.25
❑ 89 Richard Hamilton .40 1.00
❑ 90 Tayshaun Prince .50 1.25
❑ 91 Manu Ginobili .50 1.25
❑ 92 Tim Duncan 1.00 2.50
❑ 93 Tony Parker .50 1.25
❑ 94 Amare Stoudemire 1.00 2.50
❑ 95 Grant Hill .50 1.25
❑ 96 Shawn Marion .50 1.25
❑ 97 Steve Nash .60 1.50
❑ 98 Dirk Nowitzki .75 2.00
❑ 99 Jason Terry .50 1.25
❑ 100 Josh Howard .50 1.25
❑ 101 Greg Oden/299 RC 20.00 40.00
❑ 102 Yi Jianlian/299 RC 6.00 15.00
❑ 103 Brandan Wright/299 RC 5.00 12.00
❑ 104 Thaddeus Young/299 RC 5.00 12.00
❑ 105 Nick Young/299 RC 4.00 10.00
❑ 106 Jamario Moon/299 RC 20.00 40.00
❑ 106B Guillermo Diaz/299 4.00 10.00
❑ 107 Marco Belinelli AU/999 RC 5.00 12.00
❑ 108 Darryl Watkins AU/999 RC 5.00 12.00
❑ 109 Oleksiy Pecherov AU/999 RC 5.00 12.00
❑ 110 Juan Carlos Navarro
AU/999 RC 5.00 12.00
❑ 111 JamesOn Curry AU/999 RC
❑ 112 Demetris Nichols AU/999 RC
❑ 113 Herbert Hill AU/999 RC 5.00 12.00
❑ 114 Coby Karl/299 RC 4.00 10.00
❑ 115 Darius Washington/299 RC 4.00 10.00
❑ 116 Louis Amundson/299 RC 4.00 10.00
❑ 117 Cheikh Samb/299 RC 4.00 10.00
❑ 118 Ramon Sessions AU/999 RC 6.00 15.00
❑ 119 Luis Scola AU/999 RC 6.00 15.00
❑ 122 Spencer Hawes JSY
AU/599 RC 8.00 20.00
❑ 123 Acie Law IV JSY AU/599 RC 6.00 15.00
❑ 124 Julian Wright JSY
AU/599 RC 10.00 25.00
❑ 125 Al Thornton JSY AU/599 RC 25.00 50.00
❑ 126 R.Stuckey JSY AU/599 RC 20.00 40.00
❑ 127 Sean Williams JSY
AU/599 RC 10.00 25.00
❑ 128 J.Crittenton JSY AU/599 RC 8.00 20.00
❑ 129 Jason Smith JSY AU/599 RC 6.00 15.00
❑ 130 Daequan Cook JSY
AU/599 RC 6.00 15.00
❑ 131 Jared Dudley JSY
AU/599 RC 6.00 15.00
❑ 132 W.Chandler JSY AU/599 RC 6.00 15.00
❑ 133 Morris Almond JSY
AU/599 RC 6.00 15.00
❑ 134 Arron Afflalo JSY AU/599 RC 8.00 20.00
❑ 135 Alando Tucker JSY
AU/599 RC 6.00 15.00
❑ 136 Carl Landry JSY AU/599 RC 8.00 20.00
❑ 137 Gabe Pruitt JSY AU/599 RC 6.00 15.00
❑ 138 Aaron Brooks/299 RC 6.00 15.00
❑ 139 Nick Fazekas JSY
AU/599 RC 6.00 15.00
❑ 140 J.Davidson JSY AU/599 RC 6.00 15.00
❑ 141 J.McRoberts JSY AU/599 RC 6.00 15.00
❑ 142 Glen Davis/299 RC 15.00 30.00

❑ 143 Adam Haluska JSY AU/599 RC 6.00 15.00
❑ 147 Dominic McGuire JSY AU/599 RC
❑ 148 Aaron Gray JSY AU/599 RC 6.00 15.00
❑ 149 Taurean Green JSY AU/599 RC 6.00 15.00
❑ 150 D.J. Strawberry JSY AU/599 RC 8.00 20.00
❑ 151 Chris Richard JSY AU/399 RC 6.00 15.00
❑ 152 Kevin Durant JSY AU/299 RC 300.00 550.00
❑ 153 Al Horford JSY AU/299 RC 25.00 50.00
❑ 154 Mike Conley JSY AU/299 RC 20.00 40.00
❑ 155 Jeff Green JSY AU/299 RC 25.00 50.00
❑ 156 Corey Brewer JSY AU/299 RC 20.00 40.00
❑ 157 Joakim Noah JSY AU/299 RC 20.00 40.00

2008-09 SP Authentic

❑ COMP.SET w/o SP's (100) 25.00 50.00
❑ 1 Dwyane Wade 1.00 2.50
❑ 2 Alonzo Mourning .50 1.25
❑ 3 Daequan Cook .40 1.00
❑ 4 Kevin Durant 1.25 3.00
❑ 5 Jeff Green .40 1.00
❑ 6 Chris Wilcox .40 1.00
❑ 7 Al Jefferson .50 1.25
❑ 8 Corey Brewer .40 1.00
❑ 9 Randy Foye .50 1.25
❑ 10 Rudy Gay .50 1.25
❑ 11 Mike Conley .40 1.00
❑ 12 Mike Miller .50 1.25
❑ 13 Jamal Crawford .30 .75
❑ 14 Eddy Curry .30 .75
❑ 15 Quentin Richardson .40 1.00
❑ 16 Stephon Marbury .50 1.25
❑ 17 Chris Kaman .30 .75
❑ 18 Marcus Camby .30 .75
❑ 19 Baron Davis .50 1.25
❑ 20 Michael Redd .50 1.25
❑ 21 Richard Jefferson .50 1.25
❑ 22 Mo Williams .40 1.00
❑ 23 Emeka Okafor .50 1.25
❑ 24 Gerald Wallace .50 1.25
❑ 25 Jason Richardson .50 1.25
❑ 26 Joakim Noah .50 1.25
❑ 27 Luol Deng .50 1.25
❑ 28 Ben Gordon .50 1.25
❑ 29 Michael Jordan 4.00 10.00
❑ 30 Vince Carter .60 1.50
❑ 31 Yi Jianlian .50 1.25
❑ 32 Devin Harris .50 1.25
❑ 33 T.J. Ford .30 .75
❑ 34 Danny Granger .50 1.25
❑ 35 Mike Dunleavy .40 1.00
❑ 36 Ron Artest .50 1.25
❑ 37 Kevin Martin .50 1.25
❑ 38 Brad Miller .50 1.25
❑ 39 Brandon Roy .60 1.50
❑ 40 LaMarcus Aldridge .50 1.25
❑ 41 Greg Oden .50 1.25
❑ 42 Corey Maggette .50 1.25
❑ 43 Al Harrington .40 1.00
❑ 44 Monta Ellis .50 1.25
❑ 45 Al Horford .50 1.25
❑ 46 Joe Johnson .50 1.25
❑ 47 Josh Smith .50 1.25
❑ 48 Mike Bibby .50 1.25
❑ 49 Andre Iguodala .50 1.25
❑ 50 Andre Miller .40 1.00
❑ 51 Thaddeus Young .40 1.00
❑ 52 Chris Bosh .50 1.25
❑ 53 Jermaine O'Neal .50 1.25
❑ 54 Jose Calderon .40 1.00
❑ 55 Antawn Jamison .50 1.25
❑ 56 Caron Butler .50 1.25
❑ 57 Gilbert Arenas .50 1.25
❑ 58 LeBron James 2.50 6.00
❑ 59 Daniel Gibson .50 1.25
❑ 60 Anderson Varejao .40 1.00
❑ 61 Allen Iverson .60 1.50
❑ 62 Carmelo Anthony .60 1.50
❑ 63 Elton Brand .75 2.00
❑ 64 Jason Kidd .50 1.25
❑ 65 Dirk Nowitzki .60 1.50
❑ 66 Josh Howard .50 1.25
❑ 67 Dwight Howard 1.00 2.50
❑ 68 Hedo Turkoglu .50 1.25
❑ 69 Rashard Lewis .50 1.25
❑ 70 Deron Williams .60 1.50
❑ 71 Carlos Boozer .50 1.25
❑ 72 Andrei Kirilenko .50 1.25
❑ 73 Ronnie Brewer .40 1.00
❑ 74 Shaquille O'Neal 1.00 2.50
❑ 75 Steve Nash .50 1.25
❑ 76 Amare Stoudemire .60 1.50
❑ 77 Leandro Barbosa .40 1.00
❑ 78 Yao Ming .60 1.50
❑ 79 Tracy McGrady .60 1.50
❑ 80 Shane Battier .40 1.00
❑ 81 Luis Scola .40 1.00
❑ 82 Tim Duncan .75 2.00
❑ 83 Tony Parker .50 1.25
❑ 84 Manu Ginobili .50 1.25
❑ 85 Chris Paul 1.00 2.50
❑ 86 David West .50 1.25
❑ 87 Tyson Chandler .40 1.00
❑ 88 Peja Stojakovic .50 1.25
❑ 89 Kobe Bryant 2.50 6.00
❑ 90 Pau Gasol .50 1.25
❑ 91 Lamar Odom .50 1.25
❑ 92 Andrew Bynum .50 1.25
❑ 93 Chauncey Billups .50 1.25
❑ 94 Richard Hamilton .40 1.00
❑ 95 Rasheed Wallace .50 1.25
❑ 96 Tayshaun Prince .50 1.25
❑ 97 Kevin Garnett 1.00 2.50
❑ 98 Paul Pierce .60 1.50
❑ 99 Ray Allen .50 1.25
❑ 100 Rajon Rondo .50 1.25
❑ 101 Alexis Ajinca AU/199 RC 15.00 30.00
❑ 102 Joe Alexander JSY AU/499 RC 10.00 25.00
❑ 103 Ryan Anderson JSY AU/499 RC 10.00 25.00
❑ 104 Darrell Arthur JSY AU/499 RC 15.00 30.00
❑ 105 D.J. Augustin JSY AU/299 RC 25.00 50.00
❑ 106 Jerryd Bayless JSY AU/299 RC 35.00 75.00
❑ 107 M.Beasley JSY AU/299 RC 40.00 80.00
❑ 108 Mario Chalmers JSY AU/499 RC 20.00 40.00
❑ 109 Joe Crawford AU/199 RC 8.00 20.00
❑ 110 Joey Dorsey JSY AU/499 RC 10.00 25.00
❑ 111 C.D-Roberts JSY AU/499 RC 10.00 25.00
❑ 112 Patrick Ewing Jr. JSY AU/499 RC 8.00 20.00
❑ 113 Danilo Gallinari AU/199 RC 20.00 40.00
❑ 114 J.R. Giddens JSY AU/499 RC 8.00 20.00
❑ 115 Eric Gordon JSY AU/299 RC 30.00 60.00
❑ 116 Donte Greene JSY AU/499 RC 8.00 20.00
❑ 117 Malik Hairston AU/199 RC 8.00 20.00
❑ 118 Roy Hibbert JSY AU/499 RC 10.00 25.00
❑ 119 J.J. Hickson JSY AU/499 RC 15.00 30.00
❑ 120 George Hill JSY AU/499 RC 25.00 50.00
❑ 121 DeAndre Jordan JSY AU/499 RC 10.00 25.00
❑ 122 Kosta Koufos JSY AU/499 RC 8.00 20.00
❑ 123 Courtney Lee JSY AU/499 RC 25.00 50.00
❑ 124 Brook Lopez JSY AU/299 RC 40.00 80.00
❑ 125 Robin Lopez JSY AU/499 RC 8.00 20.00
❑ 126 Kevin Love JSY AU/299 RC 25.00 50.00
❑ 127 O.J. Mayo JSY AU/299 RC 60.00 120.00
❑ 128 Javale McGee JSY AU/499 RC 10.00 25.00
❑ 129 A.Randolph JSY AU/499 RC 35.00 75.00
❑ 130 Derrick Rose JSY AU/299 RC 175.00 275.00
❑ 131 Brandon Rush JSY AU/299 RC 10.00 25.00
❑ 132 Walter Sharpe JSY AU/499 RC 8.00 20.00
❑ 133 Sean Singletary AU/199 RC 8.00 20.00
❑ 134 M.Speights JSY AU/499 RC 10.00 25.00
❑ 135 Mike Taylor AU/199 RC 8.00 20.00
❑ 136 J.Thompson JSY AU/499 RC 15.00 30.00
❑ 137 Kyle Weaver JSY AU/499 RC 8.00 20.00
❑ 138 Sonny Weems JSY AU/499 RC 8.00 20.00
❑ 139 R.Westbrook JSY AU/299 RC 50.00 100.00
❑ 140 D.J. White JSY AU/499 RC 8.00 20.00
❑ 147 Rudy Fernandez JSY AU/499 RC 40.00 80.00

1994-95 SP Championship

❑ COMPLETE SET (135) 15.00 30.00
❑ 1 Mookie Blaylock RF .02 .10
❑ 2 Dominique Wilkins RF .07 .20
❑ 3 Alonzo Mourning RF .15 .40
❑ 4 Michael Jordan RF 1.50 4.00
❑ 5 Mark Price RF .02 .10
❑ 6 Jamal Mashburn RF .07 .20
❑ 7 Dikembe Mutombo RF .02 .10
❑ 8 Grant Hill RF .40 1.00
❑ 9 Latrell Sprewell RF .15 .40
❑ 10 Hakeem Olajuwon RF .15 .40
❑ 11 Reggie Miller RF .07 .20
❑ 12 Loy Vaught RF .02 .10
❑ 13 Nick Van Exel RF .07 .20
❑ 14 Glen Rice RF .02 .10
❑ 15 Glenn Robinson RF .25 .60
❑ 16 Isaiah Rider RF .02 .10
❑ 17 Kenny Anderson RF .02 .10
❑ 18 Patrick Ewing RF .07 .20
❑ 19 Shaquille O'Neal RF .30 .75
❑ 20 Dana Barros RF .02 .10
❑ 21 Charles Barkley RF .15 .40
❑ 22 Clifford Robinson RF .02 .10
❑ 23 Mitch Richmond RF .07 .20
❑ 24 David Robinson RF .15 .40
❑ 25 Shawn Kemp RF .15 .40
❑ 26 Karl Malone RF .15 .40
❑ 27 Chris Webber RF .20 .50
❑ 28 Stacey Augmon .02 .10
❑ 29 Mookie Blaylock .02 .10
❑ 30 Grant Long .02 .10
❑ 31 Steve Smith .07 .20
❑ 32 Dee Brown .02 .10
❑ 33 Eric Montross RC .02 .10
❑ 34 Dino Radja .02 .10
❑ 35 Dominique Wilkins .15 .40
❑ 36 Muggsy Bogues .07 .20
❑ 37 Scott Burrell .02 .10
❑ 38 Larry Johnson .07 .20
❑ 39 Alonzo Mourning .20 .50
❑ 40 B.J. Armstrong .02 .10
❑ 41 Michael Jordan 3.00 8.00
❑ 42 Toni Kukoc .25 .60
❑ 43 Scottie Pippen .50 1.25
❑ 44 Tyrone Hill .02 .10
❑ 45 Chris Mills .07 .20
❑ 46 Mark Price .02 .10
❑ 47 John Williams .02 .10
❑ 48 Jim Jackson .07 .20
❑ 49 Jason Kidd RC 1.50 4.00
❑ 50 Jamal Mashburn .15 .40

❑ 51 Roy Tarpley	.02	.10
❑ 52 Mahmoud Abdul-Rauf	.02	.10
❑ 53 Dikembe Mutombo	.07	.20
❑ 54 Rodney Rogers	.02	.10
❑ 55 Bryant Stith	.02	.10
❑ 56 Joe Dumars	.15	.40
❑ 57 Grant Hill RC	.75	2.00
❑ 58 Lindsey Hunter	.07	.20
❑ 59 Terry Mills	.02	.10
❑ 60 Tim Hardaway	.15	.40
❑ 61 Donyell Marshall RC	.15	.40
❑ 62 Chris Mullin	.15	.40
❑ 63 Latrell Sprewell	.15	.40
❑ 64 Sam Cassell	.15	.40
❑ 65 Clyde Drexler	.15	.40
❑ 66 Vernon Maxwell	.02	.10
❑ 67 Hakeem Olajuwon	.25	.60
❑ 68 Dale Davis	.02	.10
❑ 69 Mark Jackson	.02	.10
❑ 70 Reggie Miller	.15	.40
❑ 71 Rik Smits	.02	.10
❑ 72 Terry Dehere	.02	.10
❑ 73 Lamond Murray RC	.07	.20
❑ 74 Pooh Richardson	.02	.10
❑ 75 Loy Vaught	.02	.10
❑ 76 Cedric Ceballos	.02	.10
❑ 77 Vlade Divac	.02	.10
❑ 78 Eddie Jones RC	.75	2.00
❑ 79 Nick Van Exel	.15	.40
❑ 80 Bimbo Coles	.02	.10
❑ 81 Billy Owens	.02	.10
❑ 82 Glen Rice	.07	.20
❑ 83 Kevin Willis	.02	.10
❑ 84 Vin Baker	.15	.40
❑ 85 Marty Conlon	.02	.10
❑ 86 Eric Murdock	.02	.10
❑ 87 Glenn Robinson RC	.50	1.25
❑ 88 Tom Gugliotta	.07	.20
❑ 89 Christian Laettner	.07	.20
❑ 90 Isaiah Rider	.07	.20
❑ 91 Doug West	.02	.10
❑ 92 Kenny Anderson	.07	.20
❑ 93 Benoit Benjamin	.02	.10
❑ 94 Derrick Coleman	.07	.20
❑ 95 Armon Gilliam	.02	.10
❑ 96 Patrick Ewing	.15	.40
❑ 97 Derek Harper	.02	.10
❑ 98 Charles Oakley	.02	.10
❑ 99 John Starks	.02	.10
❑ 100 Nick Anderson	.02	.10
❑ 101 Horace Grant	.07	.20
❑ 102 Anfernee Hardaway	.40	1.00
❑ 103 Shaquille O'Neal	.75	2.00
❑ 104 Dana Barros	.02	.10
❑ 105 Shawn Bradley	.02	.10
❑ 106 Clarence Weatherspoon	.02	.10
❑ 107 Sharone Wright RC	.02	.10
❑ 108 Charles Barkley	.25	.60
❑ 109 Kevin Johnson	.07	.20
❑ 110 Dan Majerle	.07	.20
❑ 111 Wesley Person RC	.15	.40
❑ 112 Terry Porter	.02	.10
❑ 113 Clifford Robinson	.07	.20
❑ 114 Rod Strickland	.07	.20
❑ 115 Buck Williams	.02	.10
❑ 116 Brian Grant RC	.40	1.00
❑ 117 Mitch Richmond	.15	.40
❑ 118 Spud Webb	.02	.10
❑ 119 Walt Williams	.02	.10
❑ 120 Vinny Del Negro	.02	.10
❑ 121 Sean Elliott	.07	.20
❑ 122 David Robinson	.25	.60
❑ 123 Dennis Rodman	.30	.75
❑ 124 Kendall Gill	.07	.20
❑ 125 Shawn Kemp	.25	.60
❑ 126 Gary Payton	.25	.60
❑ 127 Detlef Schrempf	.07	.20
❑ 128 David Benoit	.02	.10
❑ 129 Jeff Hornacek	.07	.20
❑ 130 Karl Malone	.25	.60
❑ 131 John Stockton	.15	.40
❑ 132 Rex Chapman	.02	.10
❑ 133 Calbert Cheaney	.02	.10
❑ 134 Juwan Howard RC	.40	1.00
❑ 135 Chris Webber	.40	1.00

1995-96 SP Championship

❑ COMPLETE SET (146)	20.00	40.00
❑ 1 Stacey Augmon	.08	.25
❑ 2 Mookie Blaylock	.08	.25
❑ 3 Alan Henderson RC	.30	.75
❑ 4 Steve Smith	.20	.50
❑ 5 Dana Barros	.08	.25
❑ 6 Dee Brown	.08	.25
❑ 7 Eric Montross	.08	.25
❑ 8 Dino Radja	.08	.25
❑ 9 Eric Williams RC	.20	.50
❑ 10 Kenny Anderson	.20	.50
❑ 11 Larry Johnson	.20	.50
❑ 12 Glen Rice	.20	.50
❑ 13 George Zidek RC	.08	.25
❑ 14 Toni Kukoc	.20	.50
❑ 15 Scottie Pippen	.50	1.25
❑ 16 Dennis Rodman	.20	.50
❑ 17 Michael Jordan	2.00	5.00
❑ 18 Terrell Brandon	.20	.50
❑ 19 Danny Ferry	.08	.25
❑ 20 Chris Mills	.08	.25
❑ 21 Bobby Phills	.08	.25
❑ 22 Jim Jackson	.08	.25
❑ 23 Popeye Jones	.08	.25
❑ 24 Jason Kidd	1.00	2.50
❑ 25 Jamal Mashburn	.20	.50
❑ 26 Mahmoud Abdul-Rauf	.08	.25
❑ 27 Dale Ellis	.08	.25
❑ 28 Antonio McDyess RC	.60	1.50
❑ 29 Dikembe Mutombo	.20	.50
❑ 30 Joe Dumars	.30	.75
❑ 31 Grant Hill	.40	1.00
❑ 32 Allan Houston	.20	.50
❑ 33 Otis Thorpe	.08	.25
❑ 34 Tim Hardaway	.20	.50
❑ 35 Chris Mullin	.30	.75
❑ 36 Latrell Sprewell	.30	.75
❑ 37 Joe Smith RC	.50	1.25
❑ 38 Sam Cassell	.30	.75
❑ 39 Clyde Drexler	.30	.75
❑ 40 Robert Horry	.20	.50
❑ 41 Hakeem Olajuwon	.30	.75
❑ 42 Dale Davis	.08	.25
❑ 43 Derrick McKey	.08	.25
❑ 44 Reggie Miller	.30	.75
❑ 45 Rik Smits	.20	.50
❑ 46 Brent Barry RC	.30	.75
❑ 47 Lamond Murray	.08	.25
❑ 48 Loy Vaught	.08	.25
❑ 49 Brian Williams	.08	.25
❑ 50 Cedric Ceballos	.08	.25
❑ 51 Magic Johnson	.50	1.25
❑ 52 Eddie Jones	.40	1.00
❑ 53 Nick Van Exel	.30	.75
❑ 54 Sasha Danilovic RC	.08	.25
❑ 55 Alonzo Mourning	.20	.50
❑ 56 Billy Owens	.08	.25
❑ 57 Kevin Willis	.20	.50
❑ 58 Vin Baker	.20	.50
❑ 59 Sherman Douglas	.08	.25
❑ 60 Lee Mayberry	.08	.25
❑ 61 Glenn Robinson	.30	.75
❑ 62 Kevin Garnett RC	3.00	8.00
❑ 63 Tom Gugliotta	.08	.25
❑ 64 Christian Laettner	.20	.50
❑ 65 Isaiah Rider	.08	.25
❑ 66 Chris Childs	.08	.25
❑ 67 Kendall Gill	.08	.25
❑ 68 Armon Gilliam	.08	.25
❑ 69 Ed O'Bannon RC	.08	.25
❑ 70 Patrick Ewing	.30	.75
❑ 71 Derek Harper	.20	.50
❑ 72 Charles Oakley	.08	.25
❑ 73 John Starks	.20	.50
❑ 74 Horace Grant	.20	.50
❑ 75 Anfernee Hardaway	.30	.75
❑ 76 Shaquille O'Neal	.75	2.00
❑ 77 Dennis Scott	.08	.25
❑ 78 Derrick Coleman	.08	.25
❑ 79 Trevor Ruffin	.08	.25
❑ 80 Jerry Stackhouse RC	1.00	2.50
❑ 81 Clarence Weatherspoon	.08	.25
❑ 82 Charles Barkley	.40	1.00
❑ 83 Michael Finley RC	.75	2.00
❑ 84 Kevin Johnson	.20	.50
❑ 85 Danny Manning	.20	.50
❑ 86 Randolph Childress RC	.08	.25
❑ 87 Clifford Robinson	.08	.25
❑ 88 Arvydas Sabonis RC	.40	1.00
❑ 89 Rod Strickland	.08	.25
❑ 90 Tyus Edney RC	.08	.25
❑ 91 Brian Grant	.30	.75
❑ 92 Mitch Richmond	.20	.50
❑ 93 Walt Williams	.08	.25
❑ 94 Sean Elliott	.20	.50
❑ 95 Avery Johnson	.08	.25
❑ 96 Chuck Person	.08	.25
❑ 97 David Robinson	.30	.75
❑ 98 Shawn Kemp	.20	.50
❑ 99 Gary Payton	.30	.75
❑ 100 Sam Perkins	.20	.50
❑ 101 Detlef Schrempf	.20	.50
❑ 102 Ed Pinckney	.08	.25
❑ 103 Tracy Murray	.08	.25
❑ 104 Alvin Robertson	.08	.25
❑ 105 Damon Stoudamire RC	.60	1.50
❑ 106 Jeff Hornacek	.20	.50
❑ 107 Karl Malone	.40	1.00
❑ 108 Chris Morris	.08	.25
❑ 109 John Stockton	.40	1.00
❑ 110 Greg Anthony	.08	.25
❑ 111 Blue Edwards	.08	.25
❑ 112 Bryant Reeves RC	.30	.75
❑ 113 Byron Scott	.08	.25
❑ 114 Juwan Howard	.30	.75
❑ 115 Gheorghe Muresan	.08	.25
❑ 116 Rasheed Wallace RC	.75	2.00
❑ 117 Chris Webber	.40	1.00
❑ 118 Mookie Blaylock RP	.08	.25
❑ 119 Dana Barros RP	.08	.25
❑ 120 Larry Johnson RP	.08	.25
❑ 121 Michael Jordan RP	1.00	2.50
❑ 122 Terrell Brandon RP	.08	.25
❑ 123 Jason Kidd RP	.50	1.25
❑ 124 Mahmoud Abdul-Rauf RP	.08	.25
❑ 125 Grant Hill RP	.30	.75
❑ 126 Latrell Sprewell RP	.30	.75
❑ 127 Hakeem Olajuwon RP	.20	.50
❑ 128 Reggie Miller RP	.20	.50
❑ 129 Loy Vaught RP	.08	.25
❑ 130 Magic Johnson RP	.30	.75
❑ 131 Alonzo Mourning RP	.08	.25
❑ 132 Vin Baker RP	.08	.25
❑ 133 Tom Gugliotta RP	.08	.25
❑ 134 Ed O'Bannon RP	.08	.25
❑ 135 Patrick Ewing RP	.20	.50
❑ 136 Anfernee Hardaway RP	.20	.50
❑ 137 Jerry Stackhouse RP	.50	1.25
❑ 138 Charles Barkley RP	.30	.75
❑ 139 Clifford Robinson RP	.08	.25
❑ 140 Mitch Richmond RP	.08	.25
❑ 141 David Robinson RP	.20	.50
❑ 142 Shawn Kemp RP	.08	.25
❑ 143 Damon Stoudamire RP	.40	1.00
❑ 144 John Stockton RP	.30	.75
❑ 145 Bryant Reeves RP	.20	.50
❑ 146 Juwan Howard RP	.20	.50

2000-01 SP Game Floor

❑ COMMON CARD (1-60)	.60	1.50
❑ COMMON ROOKIE (61-100)	2.50	6.00
❑ 1 Jason Terry	1.00	2.50
❑ 2 Toni Kukoc	.75	2.00
❑ 3 Antoine Walker	.75	2.00

❑ 4 Paul Pierce	1.00	2.50
❑ 5 Jamal Mashburn	.75	2.00
❑ 6 Baron Davis	1.00	2.50
❑ 7 Elton Brand	1.00	2.50
❑ 8 Ron Mercer	.60	1.50
❑ 9 Andre Miller	.75	2.00
❑ 10 Lamond Murray	.60	1.50
❑ 11 Michael Finley	1.00	2.50
❑ 12 Dirk Nowitzki	1.50	4.00
❑ 13 Antonio McDyess	.75	2.00
❑ 14 Nick Van Exel	.75	2.00
❑ 15 Jerry Stackhouse	.75	2.00
❑ 16 Joe Smith	.60	1.50
❑ 17 Antawn Jamison	1.00	2.50
❑ 18 Larry Hughes	.75	2.00
❑ 19 Steve Francis	1.00	2.50
❑ 20 Maurice Taylor	.60	1.50
❑ 21 Jalen Rose	.75	2.00
❑ 22 Reggie Miller	1.00	2.50
❑ 23 Lamar Odom	1.00	2.50
❑ 24 Corey Maggette	.75	2.00
❑ 25 Kobe Bryant	5.00	12.00
❑ 26 Shaquille O'Neal	2.50	6.00
❑ 27 Horace Grant	.75	2.00
❑ 28 Eddie Jones	.75	2.00
❑ 29 Tim Hardaway	.75	2.00
❑ 30 Glenn Robinson	.75	2.00
❑ 31 Ray Allen	1.00	2.50
❑ 32 Kevin Garnett	2.00	5.00
❑ 33 Terrell Brandon	.60	1.50
❑ 34 Wally Szczerbiak	.75	2.00
❑ 35 Stephon Marbury	1.00	2.50
❑ 36 Keith Van Horn	.75	2.00
❑ 37 Latrell Sprewell	.75	2.00
❑ 38 Allan Houston	.75	2.00
❑ 39 Tracy McGrady	2.00	5.00
❑ 40 Darrell Armstrong	.60	1.50
❑ 41 Allen Iverson	2.00	5.00
❑ 42 Dikembe Mutombo	.75	2.00
❑ 43 Jason Kidd	1.50	4.00
❑ 44 Shawn Marion	1.00	2.50
❑ 45 Rasheed Wallace	1.00	2.50
❑ 46 Damon Stoudamire	.75	2.00
❑ 47 Chris Webber	1.00	2.50
❑ 48 Jason Williams	.75	2.00
❑ 49 Tim Duncan	2.00	5.00
❑ 50 David Robinson	1.25	3.00
❑ 51 Gary Payton	1.00	2.50
❑ 52 Rashard Lewis	1.00	2.50
❑ 53 Vince Carter	2.00	5.00
❑ 54 Charles Oakley	.75	2.00
❑ 55 Karl Malone	1.25	3.00
❑ 56 John Stockton	1.25	3.00
❑ 57 Shareef Abdur-Rahim	.75	2.00
❑ 58 Mike Bibby	.75	2.00
❑ 59 Richard Hamilton	.75	2.00
❑ 60 Mitch Richmond	.75	2.00
❑ 61 Kenyon Martin RC	6.00	15.00
❑ 62 Marc Jackson RC	3.00	8.00
❑ 63 Darius Miles RC	3.00	8.00
❑ 64 Morris Peterson RC	4.00	10.00
❑ 65 Mike Miller RC	4.00	10.00
❑ 66 Quentin Richardson RC	3.00	8.00
❑ 67 DerMarr Johnson RC	2.50	6.00
❑ 68 Chris Mihm RC	2.50	6.00
❑ 69 Jamal Crawford RC	4.00	10.00
❑ 70 Joel Przybilla RC	2.50	6.00
❑ 71 Keyon Dooling RC	2.50	6.00
❑ 72 Jerome Moiso RC	2.50	6.00
❑ 73 Mike Penberthy RC	2.50	6.00
❑ 74 Courtney Alexander RC	2.50	6.00
❑ 75 Mateen Cleaves RC	2.50	6.00
❑ 76 Wang Zhizhi RC	5.00	12.00
❑ 77 Hedo Turkoglu RC	6.00	15.00
❑ 78 Desmond Mason RC	3.00	8.00
❑ 79 Marcus Fizer RC	2.50	6.00
❑ 80 Jamaal Magloire RC	2.50	6.00
❑ 81 Stromile Swift RC	3.00	8.00
❑ 82 DeShawn Stevenson RC	2.50	6.00
❑ 83 Stephen Jackson RC	4.00	10.00
❑ 84 Erick Barkley RC	2.50	6.00
❑ 85 Mark Madsen RC	2.50	6.00
❑ 86 Dan Langhi RC	2.50	6.00
❑ 87 Hanno Mottola RC	2.50	6.00
❑ 88 Paul McPherson RC	2.50	6.00
❑ 89 Eddie House RC	2.50	6.00
❑ 90 Chris Porter RC	2.50	6.00
❑ 91 Jason Collier RC	2.50	6.00
❑ 92 Speedy Claxton RC	2.50	6.00
❑ 93 Ruben Wolkowyski RC	2.50	6.00
❑ 94 A.J. Guyton RC	2.50	6.00
❑ 95 Donnell Harvey RC	2.50	6.00
❑ 96 Ira Newble RC	2.50	6.00
❑ 97 Lee Nailon RC	2.50	6.00
❑ 98 Pepe Sanchez RC	2.50	6.00
❑ 99 Eduardo Najera RC	2.50	6.00
❑ 100 David Vanterpool RC	2.50	6.00

2002-03 SP Game Used

❑ COMMON CARD (1-102)	1.25	3.00
❑ COMMON JSY	5.00	12.00
❑ COMMON ROOKIE (103-144)	4.00	10.00
❑ 1 S.Abdur-Rahim JSY	6.00	15.00
❑ 2 DerMarr Johnson JSY	5.00	12.00
❑ 3 Jason Terry JSY	6.00	15.00
❑ 4 Antoine Walker JSY	6.00	15.00
❑ 5 Paul Pierce SP JSY	15.00	40.00
❑ 6 Kedrick Brown JSY	5.00	12.00
❑ 7 Tony Battie	1.25	3.00
❑ 8 Jamal Mashburn JSY	5.00	12.00
❑ 9 Baron Davis	2.00	5.00
❑ 10 David Wesley	1.25	3.00
❑ 11 Jalen Rose	1.50	4.00
❑ 12 Eddy Curry JSY	6.00	15.00
❑ 13 Tyson Chandler JSY	6.00	15.00
❑ 14 Marcus Fizer JSY	5.00	12.00
❑ 15 Lamond Murray	1.25	3.00
❑ 16 Andre Miller JSY	5.00	12.00
❑ 17 Chris Mihm JSY	5.00	12.00
❑ 18 Ricky Davis	1.50	4.00
❑ 19 Dirk Nowitzki	3.00	8.00
❑ 20 Michael Finley	2.00	5.00
❑ 21 Steve Nash	3.00	8.00
❑ 22 Nick Van Exel	1.50	4.00
❑ 23 Antonio McDyess JSY	5.00	12.00
❑ 24 Juwan Howard	1.50	4.00
❑ 25 James Posey	1.25	3.00
❑ 26 Jerry Stackhouse	1.50	4.00
❑ 27 Clifford Robinson	1.25	3.00
❑ 28 Ben Wallace	1.50	4.00
❑ 29 Antawn Jamison	2.00	5.00
❑ 30 J.Richardson SP JSY	6.00	15.00
❑ 31 Gilbert Arenas	2.00	5.00
❑ 32 Steve Francis	2.00	5.00
❑ 33 Cuttino Mobley	1.50	4.00
❑ 34 Eddie Griffin JSY	5.00	12.00
❑ 35 Reggie Miller JSY	6.00	15.00
❑ 36 Jermaine O'Neal	2.00	5.00
❑ 37 Jamaal Tinsley JSY	6.00	15.00
❑ 38 Elton Brand	2.00	5.00
❑ 39 Darius Miles JSY	6.00	15.00
❑ 40 Lamar Odom JSY	6.00	15.00
❑ 41 Corey Maggette JSY	6.00	15.00
❑ 42 Kobe Bryant SP JSY	30.00	80.00
❑ 43 Shaquille O'Neal	5.00	12.00
❑ 44 Derek Fisher	1.50	4.00
❑ 45 Devean George	1.25	3.00
❑ 46 Pau Gasol	2.00	5.00
❑ 47 Jason Williams	1.50	4.00
❑ 48 Shane Battier	1.50	4.00
❑ 49 Stromile Swift	1.25	3.00
❑ 50 Alonzo Mourning	2.00	5.00
❑ 51 Eddie Jones	1.50	4.00
❑ 52 Brian Grant	1.25	3.00
❑ 53 Ray Allen	2.00	5.00
❑ 54 Glenn Robinson	1.50	4.00
❑ 55 Sam Cassell	1.50	4.00
❑ 56 Kevin Garnett SP JSY	15.00	40.00
❑ 57 Wally Szczerbiak JSY	6.00	15.00
❑ 58 Terrell Brandon JSY	5.00	12.00
❑ 59 Chauncey Billups JSY	5.00	12.00
❑ 60 Jason Kidd SP JSY	15.00	40.00
❑ 61 Richard Jefferson	2.00	5.00
❑ 62 Kenyon Martin JSY	5.00	12.00
❑ 63 B.Armstrong JSY	5.00	12.00
❑ 64 Keith Van Horn	1.50	4.00
❑ 65 Allan Houston	1.50	4.00
❑ 66 Latrell Sprewell	1.50	4.00
❑ 67 Kurt Thomas	1.25	3.00
❑ 68 Tracy McGrady	4.00	10.00
❑ 69 Mike Miller JSY	6.00	15.00
❑ 70 Darrell Armstrong JSY	5.00	12.00
❑ 71 Allen Iverson JSY	10.00	25.00
❑ 72 D.Mutombo JSY	6.00	15.00
❑ 73 Aaron McKie	1.25	3.00
❑ 74 Stephon Marbury	2.00	5.00
❑ 75 Shawn Marion	2.00	5.00
❑ 76 Joe Johnson JSY	5.00	12.00
❑ 77 Anfernee Hardaway	2.00	5.00
❑ 78 Rasheed Wallace	2.00	5.00
❑ 79 Damon Stoudamire	1.50	4.00
❑ 80 Scottie Pippen	3.00	8.00
❑ 81 Chris Webber	2.00	5.00
❑ 82 Peja Stojakovic	1.50	4.00
❑ 83 Mike Bibby JSY	6.00	15.00
❑ 84 Gerald Wallace JSY	5.00	12.00
❑ 85 Tim Duncan	4.00	10.00
❑ 86 David Robinson	2.50	6.00
❑ 87 Tony Parker JSY	8.00	20.00
❑ 88 Gary Payton	2.00	5.00
❑ 89 Rashard Lewis	2.00	5.00
❑ 90 Desmond Mason	1.50	4.00
❑ 91 V.Radmanovic JSY	5.00	12.00
❑ 92 Morris Peterson	1.50	4.00
❑ 93 Antonio Davis	1.25	3.00
❑ 94 Vince Carter	4.00	10.00
❑ 95 Karl Malone	2.00	5.00
❑ 96 John Stockton JSY	8.00	20.00
❑ 97 Donyell Marshall	1.25	3.00
❑ 98 Andrei Kirilenko	2.00	5.00
❑ 99 Richard Hamilton	1.50	4.00
❑ 100 Michael Jordan SP JSY	150.00	300.00
❑ 101 C.Alexander JSY	5.00	12.00
❑ 102 Kwame Brown JSY	5.00	12.00
❑ 103 Jay Williams RC	5.00	12.00
❑ 104 Yao Ming RC	12.00	30.00
❑ 105 Drew Gooden RC	6.00	15.00
❑ 106 DaJuan Wagner RC	4.00	10.00
❑ 107 Curtis Borchardt RC	4.00	10.00
❑ 108 Amare Stoudemire RC	10.00	25.00
❑ 109 Caron Butler RC	8.00	20.00
❑ 110 Jared Jeffries RC	4.00	10.00
❑ 111 Chris Wilcox RC	5.00	12.00
❑ 112 Qyntel Woods RC	4.00	10.00
❑ 113 Casey Jacobsen RC	4.00	10.00
❑ 114 Melvin Ely RC	4.00	10.00
❑ 115 Kareem Rush RC	5.00	12.00
❑ 116 Mike Dunleavy RC	5.00	12.00
❑ 117 Dan Dickau RC	4.00	10.00
❑ 118 Juan Dixon RC	6.00	15.00
❑ 119 Sam Clancy RC	4.00	10.00
❑ 120 Tayshaun Prince RC	6.00	15.00
❑ 121 Dan Gadzuric RC	4.00	10.00
❑ 122 Chris Jefferies RC	4.00	10.00
❑ 123 Steve Logan RC	4.00	10.00
❑ 124 Vincent Yarbrough RC	4.00	10.00
❑ 125 Fred Jones RC	5.00	12.00
❑ 126 Efthimios Rentzias RC	4.00	10.00
❑ 127 Nene Hilario RC	5.00	12.00
❑ 128 Rod Grizzard RC	4.00	10.00
❑ 129 Matt Barnes RC	5.00	12.00
❑ 130 Nikoloz Tskitishvili RC	4.00	10.00
❑ 131 Bostjan Nachbar RC	4.00	10.00
❑ 132 Marcus Haislip RC	4.00	10.00
❑ 133 Jamal Sampson RC	4.00	10.00
❑ 134 Frank Williams RC	4.00	10.00
❑ 135 Tito Maddox RC	4.00	10.00
❑ 136 Carlos Boozer RC	8.00	20.00
❑ 137 Jiri Welsch RC	4.00	10.00
❑ 138 John Salmons RC	6.00	15.00
❑ 139 Predrag Savovic RC	4.00	10.00
❑ 140 Marko Jaric	4.00	10.00
❑ 141 Robert Archibald RC	4.00	10.00
❑ 142 Manu Ginobili RC	10.00	25.00
❑ 143 Chris Owens RC	4.00	10.00
❑ 144 Ryan Humphrey RC	4.00	10.00

2003-04 SP Game Used

❑ COMMON CARD (1-94)	1.00	2.50
❑ COMMON JSY (1-94)	2.00	5.00
❑ COMMON MJ TRIB (95-106)	10.00	25.00
❑ COMMON ROOKIE (107-148)	3.00	8.00
❑ 1 Shareef Abdur-Rahim	1.25	3.00
❑ 2 Glenn Robinson	1.25	3.00
❑ 3 Jason Terry JSY	2.50	6.00

❑ 4 Paul Pierce	1.50	4.00
❑ 5 Antoine Walker	1.50	4.00
❑ 6 Eddy Curry	1.25	3.00
❑ 7 Tyson Chandler JSY	2.50	6.00
❑ 8 Jalen Rose JSY	2.50	6.00
❑ 9 Jay Williams JSY	2.00	5.00
❑ 10 DaJuan Wagner JSY	2.00	5.00
❑ 11 Darius Miles JSY	2.50	6.00
❑ 12 Carlos Boozer JSY	3.00	8.00
❑ 13 Steve Nash	2.50	6.00
❑ 14 Michael Finley	1.50	4.00
❑ 15 Nick Van Exel	1.25	3.00
❑ 16 Dirk Nowitzki JSY	5.00	12.00
❑ 17 Rodney White	1.00	2.50
❑ 18 Marcus Camby	1.25	3.00
❑ 19 Nikoloz Tskitishvili	1.00	2.50
❑ 20 Nene Hilario JSY	2.50	6.00
❑ 21 Richard Hamilton	1.25	3.00
❑ 22 Chauncey Billups	1.50	4.00
❑ 23 Ben Wallace	1.25	3.00
❑ 24 Gilbert Arenas	1.50	4.00
❑ 25 Troy Murphy	1.50	4.00
❑ 26 Jason Richardson JSY	3.00	8.00
❑ 27 Antawn Jamison JSY	3.00	8.00
❑ 28 Cuttino Mobley	1.25	3.00
❑ 29 Steve Francis	1.50	4.00
❑ 30 Eddie Griffin	1.00	2.50
❑ 31 Jermaine O'Neal	1.50	4.00
❑ 32 Reggie Miller	1.50	4.00
❑ 33 Jamaal Tinsley JSY	2.50	6.00
❑ 34 Lamar Odom	1.50	4.00
❑ 35 Chris Wilcox	1.00	2.50
❑ 36 Marko Jaric	1.00	2.50
❑ 37 Elton Brand JSY	3.00	8.00
❑ 38 Andre Miller JSY	2.50	6.00
❑ 39 Kobe Bryant	8.00	20.00
❑ 40 Shaquille O'Neal	4.00	10.00
❑ 41 Gary Payton	1.50	4.00
❑ 42 Kareem Rush JSY	2.00	5.00
❑ 43 Mike Miller	1.25	3.00
❑ 44 Shane Battier JSY	2.50	6.00
❑ 45 Pau Gasol JSY	3.00	8.00
❑ 46 Eddie Jones	1.25	3.00
❑ 47 Brian Grant	1.00	2.50
❑ 48 Caron Butler JSY	2.50	6.00
❑ 49 Joe Smith	1.00	2.50
❑ 50 Desmond Mason	1.25	3.00
❑ 51 Toni Kukoc	1.25	3.00
❑ 52 Wally Szczerbiak	1.25	3.00
❑ 53 Kevin Garnett JSY	6.00	15.00
❑ 54 Alonzo Mourning	1.50	4.00
❑ 55 Kenyon Martin	1.50	4.00
❑ 56 Jason Kidd JSY	5.00	12.00
❑ 57 Richard Jefferson JSY	3.00	8.00
❑ 58 Baron Davis	1.50	4.00
❑ 59 Jamal Mashburn JSY	2.00	5.00
❑ 60 Latrell Sprewell	1.25	3.00
❑ 61 Allan Houston	1.25	3.00
❑ 62 Antonio McDyess	1.25	3.00
❑ 63 Juwan Howard	1.25	3.00
❑ 64 Drew Gooden JSY	2.00	5.00
❑ 65 Tracy McGrady JSY	6.00	15.00
❑ 66 Keith Van Horn	1.25	3.00
❑ 67 Aaron McKie	1.00	2.50
❑ 68 Allen Iverson JSY	6.00	15.00
❑ 69 Stephon Marbury	1.50	4.00
❑ 70 Shawn Marion	1.50	4.00
❑ 71 Anfernee Hardaway	1.50	4.00
❑ 72 Joe Johnson	1.50	4.00
❑ 73 Amare Stoudemire JSY	6.00	15.00
❑ 74 Rasheed Wallace	1.50	4.00
❑ 75 Scottie Pippen	2.50	6.00
❑ 76 Mike Bibby	1.25	3.00
❑ 77 Peja Stojakovic	1.25	3.00
❑ 78 Gerald Wallace	1.50	4.00
❑ 79 Chris Webber JSY	3.00	8.00
❑ 80 Tim Duncan	3.00	8.00
❑ 81 Manu Ginobili	1.50	4.00
❑ 82 Tony Parker JSY	3.00	8.00
❑ 83 Ray Allen	1.00	2.50
❑ 84 Rashard Lewis JSY	3.00	8.00
❑ 85 Morris Peterson	1.25	3.00
❑ 86 Antonio Davis	1.00	2.50
❑ 87 Vince Carter	3.00	8.00
❑ 88 John Stockton JSY	4.00	10.00
❑ 89 Karl Malone JSY	3.00	8.00
❑ 90 Jerry Stackhouse	1.25	3.00
❑ 91 Michael Jordan	10.00	25.00
❑ 92 Michael Jordan JSY	50.00	100.00
❑ 93 Kobe Bryant JSY	15.00	40.00
❑ 94 Yao Ming JSY	6.00	15.00
❑ 95 M.Jordan Tribute	10.00	25.00
❑ 96 M.Jordan Tribute	10.00	25.00
❑ 97 M.Jordan Tribute	10.00	25.00
❑ 98 M.Jordan Tribute	10.00	25.00
❑ 99 M.Jordan Tribute	10.00	25.00
❑ 100 M.Jordan Tribute	10.00	25.00
❑ 101 M.Jordan Tribute	10.00	25.00
❑ 102 M.Jordan Tribute	10.00	25.00
❑ 103 M.Jordan Tribute	10.00	25.00
❑ 104 M.Jordan Tribute	10.00	25.00
❑ 105 M.Jordan Tribute	10.00	25.00
❑ 106 M.Jordan Tribute	10.00	25.00
❑ 107 Lebron James RC	75.00	150.00
❑ 108 Darko Milicic RC	4.00	10.00
❑ 109 Carmelo Anthony RC	8.00	20.00
❑ 110 Chris Bosh RC	5.00	12.00
❑ 111 Dwyane Wade RC	8.00	20.00
❑ 112 Chris Kaman RC	4.00	10.00
❑ 113 Kirk Hinrich RC	4.00	10.00
❑ 114 T.J. Ford RC	4.00	10.00
❑ 115 Mike Sweetney RC	3.00	8.00
❑ 116 Jarvis Hayes RC	3.00	8.00
❑ 117 Mickael Pietrus RC	4.00	10.00
❑ 118 Nick Collison RC	3.00	8.00
❑ 119 Marcus Banks RC	3.00	8.00
❑ 120 Luke Ridnour RC	4.00	10.00
❑ 121 Reece Gaines RC	3.00	8.00
❑ 122 Troy Bell RC	3.00	8.00
❑ 123 Zarko Cabarkapa RC	3.00	8.00
❑ 124 David West RC	4.00	10.00
❑ 125 Aleksandar Pavlovic RC	4.00	10.00
❑ 126 Dahntay Jones RC	3.00	8.00
❑ 127 Boris Diaw RC	4.00	10.00
❑ 128 Zoran Planinic RC	3.00	8.00
❑ 129 Travis Outlaw RC	4.00	10.00
❑ 130 Brian Cook RC	3.00	8.00
❑ 131 Carlos Delfino RC	4.00	10.00
❑ 132 Ndudi Ebi RC	3.00	8.00
❑ 133 Kendrick Perkins RC	5.00	12.00
❑ 134 Leandro Barbosa RC	4.00	10.00
❑ 135 Josh Howard RC	4.00	10.00
❑ 136 Maciej Lampe RC	3.00	8.00
❑ 137 Jason Kapono RC	4.00	10.00
❑ 138 Luke Walton RC	4.00	10.00
❑ 139 Jerome Beasley RC	3.00	8.00
❑ 140 Sofoklis Schortsanitis RC	3.00	8.00
❑ 141 Mario Austin RC	3.00	8.00
❑ 142 Travis Hansen RC	3.00	8.00
❑ 143 Steve Blake RC	4.00	10.00
❑ 144 Slavko Vranes RC	3.00	8.00
❑ 145 Zaur Pachulia RC	4.00	10.00
❑ 146 Keith Bogans RC	3.00	8.00
❑ 147 Matt Bonner RC	4.00	10.00
❑ 148 Maurice Williams RC	5.00	12.00

2004-05 SP Game Used

❑ COMMON CARD (1-60)	.50	1.25
❑ COMMON JSY (61-90)	2.50	6.00
❑ COMMON ROOKIE (91-132)	3.00	8.00
❑ COMMON LEBRON SIR (133-162)	4.00	10.00
❑ 1 Tony Delk	.50	1.25
❑ 2 Boris Diaw	.50	1.25
❑ 3 Ricky Davis	1.50	4.00
❑ 4 Gary Payton	1.50	4.00
❑ 5 Gerald Wallace	1.00	2.50
❑ 6 Jason Kapono	1.00	2.50
❑ 7 Tyson Chandler	1.50	4.00
❑ 8 Kirk Hinrich	1.50	4.00
❑ 9 Dajuan Wagner	1.00	2.50
❑ 10 Zydrunas Ilgauskas	1.00	2.50
❑ 11 Jerry Stackhouse	1.50	4.00
❑ 12 Michael Finley	1.50	4.00
❑ 13 Andre Miller	1.00	2.50
❑ 14 Nene	1.00	2.50
❑ 15 Richard Hamilton	1.00	2.50
❑ 16 Rasheed Wallace	1.50	4.00
❑ 17 Derek Fisher	1.50	4.00
❑ 18 Mike Dunleavy	1.00	2.50
❑ 19 Tracy McGrady	4.00	10.00
❑ 20 Jim Jackson	.50	1.25
❑ 21 Reggie Miller	1.50	4.00
❑ 22 Jermaine O'Neal	1.50	4.00
❑ 23 Elton Brand	1.50	4.00
❑ 24 Corey Maggette	1.00	2.50
❑ 25 Lamar Odom	1.50	4.00
❑ 26 Caron Butler	1.50	4.00
❑ 27 Pau Gasol	1.50	4.00
❑ 28 Bonzi Wells	1.00	2.50
❑ 29 Dwyane Wade	5.00	12.00
❑ 30 Shaquille O'Neal	4.00	10.00
❑ 31 Michael Redd	1.00	2.50
❑ 32 T.J. Ford	1.00	2.50
❑ 33 Latrell Sprewell	1.50	4.00
❑ 34 Sam Cassell	1.50	4.00
❑ 35 Jason Kidd	2.50	6.00
❑ 36 Richard Jefferson	1.00	2.50
❑ 37 Baron Davis	1.50	4.00
❑ 38 Jamaal Magloire	.50	1.25
❑ 39 Allan Houston	1.00	2.50
❑ 40 Stephon Marbury	1.50	4.00
❑ 41 Steve Francis	1.50	4.00
❑ 42 Cuttino Mobley	1.00	2.50
❑ 43 Glenn Robinson	1.50	4.00
❑ 44 Kenny Thomas	.50	1.25
❑ 45 Shawn Marion	1.50	4.00
❑ 46 Amare Stoudemire	3.00	8.00
❑ 47 Zach Randolph	1.50	4.00
❑ 48 Damon Stoudamire	1.00	2.50
❑ 49 Chris Webber	1.50	4.00
❑ 50 Peja Stojakovic	1.50	4.00
❑ 51 Manu Ginobili	1.50	4.00
❑ 52 Tim Duncan	3.00	8.00
❑ 53 Rashard Lewis	1.50	4.00
❑ 54 Ray Allen	1.50	4.00
❑ 55 Jalen Rose	1.50	4.00
❑ 56 Vince Carter	4.00	10.00
❑ 57 Carlos Boozer	1.50	4.00
❑ 58 Andrei Kirilenko	1.50	4.00
❑ 59 Larry Hughes	1.00	2.50
❑ 60 Gilbert Arenas	1.50	4.00
❑ 61 Paul Pierce JSY	2.50	6.00
❑ 62 Eddy Curry JSY	2.50	6.00
❑ 63 LeBron James JSY	20.00	40.00
❑ 64 Antawn Jamison JSY	2.50	6.00
❑ 65 Dirk Nowitzki JSY	4.00	10.00
❑ 66 Antoine Walker JSY	2.50	6.00
❑ 67 Carmelo Anthony JSY	6.00	15.00
❑ 68 Ben Wallace JSY	2.50	6.00
❑ 69 Jason Richardson JSY	2.50	6.00
❑ 70 Yao Ming JSY	5.00	12.00
❑ 71 Michael Jordan JSY	50.00	100.00
❑ 72 Kobe Bryant JSY	15.00	30.00
❑ 73 Quentin Richardson JSY	2.50	6.00
❑ 74 Jason Williams JSY	2.50	6.00
❑ 75 Eddie Jones JSY	2.50	6.00
❑ 76 Keith Van Horn JSY	2.50	6.00
❑ 77 Kevin Garnett JSY	4.00	10.00
❑ 78 Kenyon Martin JSY	2.50	6.00
❑ 79 Jamal Mashburn JSY	2.50	6.00
❑ 80 Kurt Thomas JSY	2.50	6.00
❑ 81 Juwan Howard JSY	2.50	6.00
❑ 82 Allen Iverson JSY	4.00	10.00
❑ 83 Joe Johnson JSY	2.50	6.00
❑ 84 Shareef Abdur-Rahim JSY	2.50	6.00
❑ 85 Mike Bibby JSY	2.50	6.00
❑ 86 Tony Parker JSY	2.50	6.00
❑ 87 Luke Ridnour JSY	2.50	6.00
❑ 88 Jalen Rose JSY	2.50	6.00
❑ 89 Gordan Giricek JSY	2.50	6.00

❑ 90 Juan Dixon JSY	2.50	6.00
❑ 91 Emeka Okafor RC	6.00	15.00
❑ 92 Dwight Howard RC	10.00	25.00
❑ 93 Shaun Livingston RC	3.00	8.00
❑ 94 Luol Deng RC	4.00	10.00
❑ 95 Ben Gordon RC	4.00	10.00
❑ 96 Devin Harris RC	6.00	15.00
❑ 97 Andre Iguodala RC	8.00	20.00
❑ 98 Andris Biedrins RC	5.00	12.00
❑ 99 Josh Childress RC	3.00	8.00
❑ 100 Josh Smith RC	8.00	20.00
❑ 101 Jameer Nelson RC	4.00	10.00
❑ 102 J.R. Smith RC	6.00	15.00
❑ 103 Sergei Monia RC	3.00	8.00
❑ 104 Sebastian Telfair RC	3.00	8.00
❑ 105 Pavel Podkolzine RC	3.00	8.00
❑ 106 Luke Jackson RC	3.00	8.00
❑ 107 Dorell Wright RC	4.00	10.00
❑ 108 Robert Swift RC	3.00	8.00
❑ 109 Anderson Varejao RC	4.00	10.00
❑ 110 Sasha Vujacic RC	3.00	8.00
❑ 111 Rafael Araujo RC	3.00	8.00
❑ 112 Al Jefferson RC	6.00	15.00
❑ 113 Kris Humphries RC	5.00	12.00
❑ 114 Kirk Snyder RC	3.00	8.00
❑ 115 Peter John Ramos RC	3.00	8.00
❑ 116 Beno Udrih RC	4.00	10.00
❑ 117 Viktor Khryapa RC	3.00	8.00
❑ 118 David Harrison RC	3.00	8.00
❑ 119 Trevor Ariza RC	4.00	10.00
❑ 120 Ha Seung-Jin RC	3.00	8.00
❑ 121 Kevin Martin RC	4.00	10.00
❑ 122 Delonte West RC	5.00	12.00
❑ 123 Blake Stepp RC	3.00	8.00
❑ 124 Chris Duhon RC	5.00	12.00
❑ 125 Tony Allen RC	4.00	10.00
❑ 126 Donta Smith RC	3.00	8.00
❑ 127 Andre Emmett RC	3.00	8.00
❑ 128 Royal Ivey RC	3.00	8.00
❑ 129 Nenad Krstic RC	4.00	10.00
❑ 130 Romain Sato RC	3.00	8.00
❑ 131 Antonio Burks RC	3.00	8.00
❑ 132 Lionel Chalmers RC	3.00	8.00
❑ 133 LeBron James SIR	4.00	10.00
❑ 134 LeBron James SIR	4.00	10.00
❑ 135 LeBron James SIR	4.00	10.00
❑ 136 LeBron James SIR	4.00	10.00
❑ 137 LeBron James SIR	4.00	10.00
❑ 138 LeBron James SIR	4.00	10.00
❑ 139 LeBron James SIR	4.00	10.00
❑ 140 LeBron James SIR	4.00	10.00
❑ 141 LeBron James SIR	4.00	10.00
❑ 142 LeBron James SIR	4.00	10.00
❑ 143 LeBron James SIR	4.00	10.00
❑ 144 LeBron James SIR	4.00	10.00
❑ 145 LeBron James SIR	4.00	10.00
❑ 146 LeBron James SIR	4.00	10.00
❑ 147 LeBron James SIR	4.00	10.00
❑ 148 LeBron James SIR	4.00	10.00
❑ 149 LeBron James SIR	4.00	10.00
❑ 150 LeBron James SIR	4.00	10.00
❑ 151 LeBron James SIR	4.00	10.00
❑ 152 LeBron James SIR	4.00	10.00
❑ 153 LeBron James SIR	4.00	10.00
❑ 154 LeBron James SIR	4.00	10.00
❑ 155 LeBron James SIR	4.00	10.00
❑ 156 LeBron James SIR	4.00	10.00
❑ 157 LeBron James SIR	4.00	10.00
❑ 158 LeBron James SIR	4.00	10.00
❑ 159 LeBron James SIR	4.00	10.00
❑ 160 LeBron James SIR	4.00	10.00
❑ 161 LeBron James SIR	4.00	10.00
❑ 162 LeBron James SIR	4.00	10.00

2005-06 SP Game Used

❑ COMMON CARD (1-100)	.60	1.50
❑ COMMON ROOKIE (101-150)	3.00	8.00
❑ 1 Al Harrington	.60	1.50
❑ 2 Josh Smith	1.00	2.50
❑ 3 Josh Childress	.75	2.00
❑ 4 Joe Johnson	1.00	2.50
❑ 5 Paul Pierce	1.00	2.50
❑ 6 Antoine Walker	.75	2.00
❑ 7 Gary Payton	1.00	2.50
❑ 8 Al Jefferson	1.00	2.50
❑ 9 Emeka Okafor	1.00	2.50
❑ 10 Primoz Brezec	.60	1.50
❑ 11 Gerald Wallace	1.00	2.50
❑ 12 Michael Jordan	6.00	15.00
❑ 13 Ben Gordon	1.25	3.00
❑ 14 Luol Deng	1.00	2.50
❑ 15 Eddy Curry	.75	2.00
❑ 16 LeBron James	5.00	12.00
❑ 17 Dajuan Wagner	.60	1.50
❑ 18 Drew Gooden	.75	2.00
❑ 19 Larry Hughes	.75	2.00
❑ 20 Dirk Nowitzki	1.50	4.00
❑ 21 Marquis Daniels	.75	2.00
❑ 22 Michael Finley	1.00	2.50
❑ 23 Jerry Stackhouse	1.00	2.50
❑ 24 Andre Miller	.75	2.00
❑ 25 Carmelo Anthony	2.00	5.00
❑ 26 Kenyon Martin	1.00	2.50
❑ 27 Nene	.60	1.50
❑ 28 Rasheed Wallace	1.00	2.50
❑ 29 Ben Wallace	1.00	2.50
❑ 30 Richard Hamilton	.75	2.00
❑ 31 Chauncey Billups	1.00	2.50
❑ 32 Baron Davis	1.00	2.50
❑ 33 Derek Fisher	.60	1.50
❑ 34 Jason Richardson	1.00	2.50
❑ 35 Tracy McGrady	2.00	5.00
❑ 36 Yao Ming	2.50	6.00
❑ 37 Juwan Howard	.75	2.00
❑ 38 Jermaine O'Neal	1.00	2.50
❑ 39 Ron Artest	.75	2.00
❑ 40 Jamaal Tinsley	.75	2.00
❑ 41 Corey Maggette	.75	2.00
❑ 42 Elton Brand	1.00	2.50
❑ 43 Shaun Livingston	.60	1.50
❑ 44 Kobe Bryant	5.00	12.00
❑ 45 Brian Cook	.60	1.50
❑ 46 Lamar Odom	1.00	2.50
❑ 47 Bonzi Wells	.75	2.00
❑ 48 Pau Gasol	1.00	2.50
❑ 49 Shane Battier	1.00	2.50
❑ 50 Shaquille O'Neal	2.50	6.00
❑ 51 Dwyane Wade	2.50	6.00
❑ 52 Dorell Wright	.60	1.50
❑ 53 Eddie Jones	.60	1.50
❑ 54 Joe Smith	.75	2.00
❑ 55 Michael Redd	1.00	2.50
❑ 56 Desmond Mason	.60	1.50
❑ 57 Kevin Garnett	2.00	5.00
❑ 58 Wally Szczerbiak	.75	2.00
❑ 59 Sam Cassell	1.00	2.50
❑ 60 Vince Carter	2.00	5.00
❑ 61 Jason Kidd	1.50	4.00
❑ 62 Richard Jefferson	.75	2.00
❑ 63 Jamaal Magloire	.60	1.50
❑ 64 J.R. Smith	.75	2.00
❑ 65 Bostjan Nachbar	.60	1.50
❑ 66 Allan Houston	.60	1.50
❑ 67 Stephon Marbury	1.00	2.50
❑ 68 Jamal Crawford	.75	2.00
❑ 69 Dwight Howard	2.00	5.00
❑ 70 Grant Hill	1.00	2.50
❑ 71 Jameer Nelson	.75	2.00
❑ 72 Steve Francis	1.00	2.50
❑ 73 Allen Iverson	2.00	5.00
❑ 74 Andre Iguodala	1.00	2.50
❑ 75 Chris Webber	1.00	2.50
❑ 76 Samuel Dalembert	.60	1.50
❑ 77 Amare Stoudemire	2.00	5.00
❑ 78 Steve Nash	1.25	3.00
❑ 79 Quentin Richardson	.75	2.00
❑ 80 Shawn Marion	1.00	2.50
❑ 81 Darius Miles	1.00	2.50
❑ 82 Zach Randolph	1.00	2.50
❑ 83 Shareef Abdur-Rahim	1.00	2.50
❑ 84 Peja Stojakovic	1.00	2.50
❑ 85 Mike Bibby	1.00	2.50
❑ 86 Manu Ginobili	1.00	2.50
❑ 87 Tim Duncan	2.00	5.00
❑ 88 Tony Parker	1.00	2.50
❑ 89 Ray Allen	1.00	2.50
❑ 90 Rashard Lewis	1.00	2.50
❑ 91 Robert Swift	.60	1.50
❑ 92 Ronald Murray	.60	1.50
❑ 93 Chris Bosh	1.00	2.50
❑ 94 Morris Peterson	.75	2.00
❑ 95 Rafael Araujo	.60	1.50
❑ 96 Andrei Kirilenko	1.00	2.50
❑ 97 Raul Lopez	.60	1.50
❑ 98 Carlos Boozer	1.00	2.50
❑ 99 Antawn Jamison	1.00	2.50
❑ 100 Gilbert Arenas	1.00	2.50
❑ 101 Andrew Bynum RC	10.00	25.00
❑ 102 Julius Hodge RC	4.00	10.00
❑ 103 David Lee RC	6.00	15.00
❑ 104 Sarunas Jasikevicius RC	4.00	10.00
❑ 105 Ike Diogu RC	4.00	10.00
❑ 106 Luther Head RC	4.00	10.00
❑ 107 Jason Maxiell RC	4.00	10.00
❑ 108 Linas Kleiza RC	4.00	10.00
❑ 109 Amir Johnson RC	3.00	8.00
❑ 110 Andray Blatche RC	4.00	10.00
❑ 111 Sean May RC	4.00	10.00
❑ 112 Alex Acker RC	3.00	8.00
❑ 113 Nate Robinson RC	5.00	12.00
❑ 114 Brandon Bass RC	3.00	8.00
❑ 115 Ricky Sanchez RC	3.00	8.00
❑ 116 Daniel Ewing RC	4.00	10.00
❑ 117 Salim Stoudamire RC	4.00	10.00
❑ 118 Dijon Thompson RC	3.00	8.00
❑ 119 Danny Granger RC	8.00	20.00
❑ 120 Raymond Felton RC	4.00	10.00
❑ 121 Louis Williams RC	5.00	12.00
❑ 122 Channing Frye RC	4.00	10.00
❑ 123 Francisco Garcia RC	4.00	10.00
❑ 124 Ryan Gomes RC	3.00	8.00
❑ 125 Ersan Ilyasova RC	3.00	8.00
❑ 126 Jarrett Jack RC	3.00	8.00
❑ 127 Lawrence Roberts RC	3.00	8.00
❑ 128 Bracey Wright RC	3.00	8.00
❑ 129 C.J. Miles RC	3.00	8.00
❑ 130 Will Bynum RC	3.00	8.00
❑ 131 Travis Diener RC	3.00	8.00
❑ 132 Monta Ellis RC	8.00	20.00
❑ 133 Martell Webster RC	3.00	8.00
❑ 134 Johan Petro RC	3.00	8.00
❑ 135 Uros Slokar RC	3.00	8.00
❑ 136 Von Wafer RC	3.00	8.00
❑ 137 Martynas Andriuskevicius RC	3.00	8.00
❑ 138 Charlie Villanueva RC	5.00	12.00
❑ 139 Antoine Wright RC	3.00	8.00
❑ 140 Joey Graham RC	3.00	8.00
❑ 141 Wayne Simien RC	4.00	10.00
❑ 142 Hakim Warrick RC	5.00	12.00
❑ 143 Gerald Green RC	3.00	8.00
❑ 144 Marvin Williams RC	5.00	12.00
❑ 145 Deron Williams RC	8.00	20.00
❑ 146 Rashad McCants RC	4.00	10.00
❑ 147 Robert Whaley RC	3.00	8.00
❑ 148 Chris Taft RC	3.00	8.00
❑ 149 Chris Paul RC	10.00	25.00
❑ 150 Andrew Bogut RC	4.00	10.00

2006-07 SP Game Used

❑ COMP.SET w/o SP's (100)	25.00	60.00
❑ 1 Al Harrington	.50	1.25
❑ 2 Joe Johnson	.60	1.50
❑ 3 Salim Stoudamire	.60	1.50
❑ 4 Tony Allen	.60	1.50
❑ 5 Dan Dickau	.50	1.25
❑ 6 Gerald Green	1.00	2.50
❑ 7 Michael Olowokandi	.50	1.25
❑ 8 Brevin Knight	.50	1.25
❑ 9 Peja Stojakovic	.75	2.00
❑ 10 Gerald Wallace	.75	2.00

❑ 11 Luol Deng	.75	2.00
❑ 12 Chris Duhon	.50	1.25
❑ 13 Mike Sweetney	.50	1.25
❑ 14 Drew Gooden	.60	1.50
❑ 15 Luke Jackson	.50	1.25
❑ 16 Damon Jones	.60	1.50
❑ 17 Eric Snow	.50	1.25
❑ 18 Erick Dampier	.50	1.25
❑ 19 Marquis Daniels	.60	1.50
❑ 20 Jerry Stackhouse	.75	2.00
❑ 21 Jason Terry	.75	2.00
❑ 22 Earl Boykins	.50	1.25
❑ 23 Marcus Camby	.60	1.50
❑ 24 Kenyon Martin	.75	2.00
❑ 25 Andre Miller	.60	1.50
❑ 26 Kelvin Cato	.50	1.25
❑ 27 Lindsey Hunter	.50	1.25
❑ 28 Antonio McDyess	.50	1.25
❑ 29 Mike Dunleavy	.60	1.50
❑ 30 Derek Fisher	.60	1.50
❑ 31 Troy Murphy	.75	2.00
❑ 32 Rafer Alston	.50	1.25
❑ 33 Juwan Howard	.60	1.50
❑ 34 Stromile Swift	.60	1.50
❑ 35 Austin Croshere	.50	1.25
❑ 36 Stephen Jackson	.60	1.50
❑ 37 Jamaal Tinsley	.60	1.50
❑ 38 Sam Cassell	.75	2.00
❑ 39 Chris Kaman	.50	1.25
❑ 40 Yaroslav Korolev	.50	1.25
❑ 41 Cuttino Mobley	.60	1.50
❑ 42 Devean George	.60	1.50
❑ 43 Smush Parker	.50	1.25
❑ 44 Ronny Turiaf	.60	1.50
❑ 45 Shane Battier	.75	2.00
❑ 46 Bobby Jackson	.50	1.25
❑ 47 Mike Miller	.75	2.00
❑ 48 Damon Stoudamire	.60	1.50
❑ 49 Alonzo Mourning	1.00	2.50
❑ 50 Gary Payton	.75	2.00
❑ 51 Dwyane Wade	2.00	5.00
❑ 52 Jason Williams	.60	1.50
❑ 53 T.J. Ford	.60	1.50
❑ 54 Jamaal Magloire	.50	1.25
❑ 55 Maurice Williams	.60	1.50
❑ 56 Marcus Banks	.50	1.25
❑ 57 Eddie Griffin	.50	1.25
❑ 58 Troy Hudson	.50	1.25
❑ 59 Jason Collins	.50	1.25
❑ 60 Nenad Krstic	.60	1.50
❑ 61 Antoine Wright	.50	1.25
❑ 62 P.J. Brown	.50	1.25
❑ 63 Speedy Claxton	.50	1.25
❑ 64 Marc Jackson	.50	1.25
❑ 65 Jamal Crawford	.50	1.25
❑ 66 Eddy Curry	.60	1.50
❑ 67 Quentin Richardson	.60	1.50
❑ 68 Carlos Arroyo	.75	2.00
❑ 69 Keyon Dooling	.50	1.25
❑ 70 Darko Milicic	.75	2.00
❑ 71 Steven Hunter	.50	1.25
❑ 72 Allen Iverson	1.50	4.00
❑ 73 Kyle Korver	.75	2.00
❑ 74 Raja Bell	.50	1.25
❑ 75 Boris Diaw	.60	1.50
❑ 76 Kurt Thomas	.50	1.25
❑ 77 Steve Blake	.50	1.25
❑ 78 Darius Miles	.50	1.25
❑ 79 Joel Przybilla	.50	1.25
❑ 80 Ha Seung-Jin	.50	1.25
❑ 81 Shareef Abdur-Rahim	.75	2.00
❑ 82 Brad Miller	.75	2.00
❑ 83 Kenny Thomas	.50	1.25
❑ 84 Bonzi Wells	.60	1.50
❑ 85 Brent Barry	.50	1.25
❑ 86 Bruce Bowen	.50	1.25
❑ 87 Michael Finley	.75	2.00
❑ 88 Robert Horry	.60	1.50
❑ 89 Luke Ridnour	.60	1.50
❑ 90 Robert Swift	.50	1.25
❑ 91 Chris Wilcox	.50	1.25
❑ 92 Rafael Araujo	.50	1.25
❑ 93 Jose Calderon	.60	1.50
❑ 94 Mike James	.50	1.25
❑ 95 Matt Harpring	.60	1.50
❑ 96 Kris Humphries	.50	1.25
❑ 97 Jason Richardson	.75	2.00
❑ 98 Gilbert Arenas	.75	2.00
❑ 99 Antonio Daniels	.50	1.25
❑ 100 Brendan Haywood	.50	1.25
❑ 101 Josh Childress JSY	3.00	8.00
❑ 102 Josh Smith JSY	3.00	8.00
❑ 103 Marvin Williams JSY	3.00	8.00
❑ 104 Al Jefferson JSY	3.00	8.00
❑ 105 Paul Pierce JSY	3.00	8.00
❑ 106 Wally Szczerbiak JSY	3.00	8.00
❑ 107 Raymond Felton JSY	4.00	10.00
❑ 108 Sean May JSY	3.00	8.00
❑ 109 Emeka Okafor JSY	3.00	8.00
❑ 110 Tyson Chandler JSY	3.00	8.00
❑ 111 Ben Gordon JSY	4.00	10.00
❑ 112 Kirk Hinrich JSY	3.00	8.00
❑ 113 Michael Jordan SP JSY	30.00	75.00
❑ 114 Larry Hughes JSY	3.00	8.00
❑ 115 Zydrunas Ilgauskas JSY	3.00	8.00
❑ 116 LeBron James JSY	15.00	40.00
❑ 117 Devin Harris JSY	3.00	8.00
❑ 118 Josh Howard JSY	3.00	8.00
❑ 119 Dirk Nowitzki JSY	4.00	10.00
❑ 120 Carmelo Anthony JSY	4.00	10.00
❑ 121 Julius Hodge JSY	3.00	8.00
❑ 122 Linas Kleiza JSY	3.00	8.00
❑ 123 Chauncey Billups JSY	3.00	8.00
❑ 124 Tayshaun Prince JSY	3.00	8.00
❑ 125 Ben Wallace JSY	3.00	8.00
❑ 126 Rasheed Wallace JSY	3.00	8.00
❑ 127 Baron Davis JSY	3.00	8.00
❑ 128 Ike Diogu JSY	3.00	8.00
❑ 129 Jason Richardson JSY	3.00	8.00
❑ 130 Chris Taft JSY	3.00	8.00
❑ 131 Luther Head JSY	3.00	8.00
❑ 132 Tracy McGrady JSY	4.00	10.00
❑ 133 Yao Ming JSY	4.00	10.00
❑ 134 Danny Granger JSY	3.00	8.00
❑ 135 Sarunas Jasikevicius JSY	3.00	8.00
❑ 136 Jermaine O'Neal JSY	3.00	8.00
❑ 137 Peja Stojakovic SP JSY	3.00	8.00
❑ 138 Elton Brand JSY	3.00	8.00
❑ 139 Shaun Livingston JSY	3.00	8.00
❑ 140 Corey Maggette JSY	3.00	8.00
❑ 141 Kwame Brown JSY	3.00	8.00
❑ 142 Kobe Bryant JSY	10.00	25.00
❑ 143 Andrew Bynum JSY	3.00	8.00
❑ 144 Lamar Odom JSY	3.00	8.00
❑ 145 Pau Gasol JSY	3.00	8.00
❑ 146 Eddie Jones JSY	3.00	8.00
❑ 147 Hakim Warrick JSY	3.00	8.00
❑ 148 Shaquille O'Neal JSY	5.00	12.00
❑ 149 Wayne Simien JSY	3.00	8.00
❑ 150 Antoine Walker JSY	3.00	8.00
❑ 151 Andrew Bogut JSY	3.00	8.00
❑ 152 Ersan Ilyasova JSY	3.00	8.00
❑ 153 Michael Redd JSY	3.00	8.00
❑ 154 Ricky Davis JSY	3.00	8.00
❑ 155 Kevin Garnett JSY	4.00	10.00
❑ 156 Rashad McCants JSY	3.00	8.00
❑ 157 Bracey Wright JSY	3.00	8.00
❑ 158 Vince Carter JSY	5.00	12.00
❑ 159 Richard Jefferson JSY	3.00	8.00
❑ 160 Jason Kidd JSY	4.00	10.00
❑ 161 Jeff McInnis JSY	3.00	8.00
❑ 163 Chris Paul JSY	5.00	12.00
❑ 164 J.R. Smith JSY	3.00	8.00
❑ 165 David West JSY	3.00	8.00
❑ 166 Steve Francis JSY	3.00	8.00
❑ 167 Channing Frye JSY	3.00	8.00
❑ 168 Stephon Marbury JSY	3.00	8.00
❑ 169 Nate Robinson JSY	3.00	8.00
❑ 170 Grant Hill JSY	3.00	8.00
❑ 171 Dwight Howard JSY	4.00	10.00
❑ 172 Jameer Nelson JSY	3.00	8.00
❑ 173 Samuel Dalembert JSY	3.00	8.00
❑ 174 Andre Iguodala JSY	3.00	8.00
❑ 175 Chris Webber JSY	3.00	8.00
❑ 176 Shawn Marion JSY	3.00	8.00
❑ 177 Steve Nash JSY	3.00	8.00
❑ 178 Amare Stoudemire JSY	4.00	10.00
❑ 179 Zach Randolph JSY	3.00	8.00
❑ 180 Sebastian Telfair JSY	3.00	8.00
❑ 181 Martell Webster JSY	3.00	8.00
❑ 182 Ron Artest JSY	3.00	8.00
❑ 183 Mike Bibby JSY	3.00	8.00
❑ 184 Francisco Garcia JSY	3.00	8.00
❑ 185 Tim Duncan JSY	4.00	10.00
❑ 186 Manu Ginobili JSY	3.00	8.00
❑ 187 Tony Parker JSY	3.00	8.00
❑ 188 Ray Allen JSY	3.00	8.00
❑ 189 Rashard Lewis JSY	3.00	8.00
❑ 190 Johan Petro JSY	3.00	8.00
❑ 191 Chris Bosh JSY	3.00	8.00
❑ 192 Joey Graham JSY	3.00	8.00
❑ 193 Charlie Villanueva JSY	3.00	8.00
❑ 194 Carlos Boozer JSY	3.00	8.00
❑ 195 Andrei Kirilenko JSY	3.00	8.00
❑ 196 C.J. Miles JSY	3.00	8.00
❑ 197 Deron Williams JSY	4.00	10.00
❑ 198 Andray Blatche JSY	3.00	8.00
❑ 199 Caron Butler JSY	3.00	8.00
❑ 200 Antawn Jamison JSY	3.00	8.00
❑ 201 Andrea Bargnani RC	4.00	10.00
❑ 202 LaMarcus Aldridge RC	3.00	8.00
❑ 203 Adam Morrison RC	3.00	8.00
❑ 204 Tyrus Thomas RC	3.00	8.00
❑ 205 Shelden Williams RC	3.00	8.00
❑ 206 Brandon Roy RC	6.00	15.00
❑ 207 Randy Foye RC	2.50	6.00
❑ 208 Rudy Gay RC	2.50	6.00
❑ 209 Patrick O'Bryant RC	2.50	6.00
❑ 210 Saer Sene RC	2.50	6.00
❑ 211 J.J. Redick RC	2.50	6.00
❑ 212 Hilton Armstrong RC	2.50	6.00
❑ 213 Thabo Sefolosha RC	3.00	8.00
❑ 214 Ronnie Brewer RC	3.00	8.00
❑ 215 Cedric Simmons RC	2.50	6.00
❑ 216 Rodney Carney RC	2.50	6.00
❑ 217 Shawne Williams RC	2.50	6.00
❑ 218 Hassan Adams RC	3.00	8.00
❑ 219 Quincy Douby RC	2.50	6.00
❑ 220 Renaldo Balkman RC	2.50	6.00
❑ 221 Rajon Rondo RC	10.00	25.00
❑ 222 Marcus Williams RC	3.00	8.00
❑ 223 Josh Boone RC	2.50	6.00
❑ 224 Kyle Lowry RC	2.50	6.00
❑ 225 Shannon Brown RC	2.50	6.00
❑ 226 Jordan Farmar RC	3.00	8.00
❑ 227 Maurice Ager RC	2.50	6.00
❑ 228 Mardy Collins RC	2.50	6.00
❑ 229 Will Blalock RC	2.50	6.00
❑ 230 James White RC	2.50	6.00
❑ 231 Steve Novak RC	2.50	6.00
❑ 232 Solomon Jones RC	2.50	6.00
❑ 233 Paul Davis RC	2.50	6.00
❑ 234 P.J. Tucker RC	2.50	6.00
❑ 235 Craig Smith RC	2.50	6.00
❑ 236 Bobby Jones RC	2.50	6.00
❑ 237 David Noel RC	2.50	6.00
❑ 238 Denham Brown RC	2.50	6.00
❑ 239 James Augustine RC	2.50	6.00
❑ 240 Daniel Gibson RC	3.00	8.00
❑ 241 Ryan Hollins RC	2.50	6.00
❑ 242 Alexander Johnson RC	2.50	6.00
❑ 243 Dee Brown RC	2.50	6.00
❑ 244 Paul Millsap RC	4.00	10.00
❑ 245 Leon Powe RC	2.50	6.00
❑ 246 Mike Gansey RC	2.50	6.00
❑ 247 Tarence Kinsey RC	2.50	6.00
❑ 248 Damir Markota RC	2.50	6.00
❑ 249 J.R. Pinnock RC	2.50	6.00
❑ 250 Kevin Pittsnogle RC	2.50	6.00

2007-08 SP Game Used

❑ COMP.SET w/o SP's (100)	35.00	70.00
❑ 1 Joe Johnson	1.00	2.50
❑ 2 Marvin Williams	1.00	2.50
❑ 3 Josh Smith	1.00	2.50
❑ 4 Al Jefferson	1.00	2.50
❑ 5 Paul Pierce	1.00	2.50
❑ 6 Delonte West	.75	2.00
❑ 7 Raymond Felton	1.25	3.00
❑ 8 Gerald Wallace	1.00	2.50
❑ 9 Emeka Okafor	1.00	2.50
❑ 10 Michael Jordan	6.00	15.00
❑ 11 Ben Gordon	1.25	3.00
❑ 12 Luol Deng	1.00	2.50

13 Kirk Hinrich	1.00	2.50
14 LeBron James	5.00	12.00
15 Larry Hughes	.75	2.00
16 Zydrunas Ilgauskas	.75	2.00
17 Dirk Nowitzki	1.50	4.00
18 Josh Howard	1.00	2.50
19 Jason Terry	1.00	2.50
20 Allen Iverson	2.00	5.00
21 Carmelo Anthony	2.00	5.00
22 Marcus Camby	.60	1.50
23 J.R. Smith	.75	2.00
24 Chauncey Billups	1.00	2.50
25 Rasheed Wallace	1.00	2.50
26 Richard Hamilton	.75	2.00
27 Tayshaun Prince	1.00	2.50
28 Jason Richardson	1.00	2.50
29 Baron Davis	1.00	2.50
30 Monta Ellis	.75	2.00
31 Tracy McGrady	2.00	5.00
32 Yao Ming	2.50	6.00
33 Rafer Alston	.60	1.50
34 Jermaine O'Neal	1.00	2.50
35 Danny Granger	.75	2.00
36 Jamaal Tinsley	.60	1.50
37 Elton Brand	1.00	2.50
38 Corey Maggette	.75	2.00
39 Cuttino Mobley	.75	2.00
40 Kobe Bryant	5.00	12.00
41 Lamar Odom	1.00	2.50
42 Luke Walton	.75	2.00
43 Kwame Brown	.60	1.50
44 Pau Gasol	1.00	2.50
45 Mike Miller	1.00	2.50
46 Hakim Warrick	.75	2.00
47 Dwyane Wade	2.50	6.00
48 Shaquille O'Neal	2.50	6.00
49 Jason Williams	.75	2.00
50 Michael Redd	1.00	2.50
51 Mo Williams	.75	2.00
52 Andrew Bogut	1.00	2.50
53 Kevin Garnett	2.50	6.00
54 Ricky Davis	1.00	2.50
55 Mike James	.60	1.50
56 Vince Carter	2.00	5.00
57 Jason Kidd	1.50	4.00
58 Nenad Krstic	.75	2.00
59 Richard Jefferson	1.00	2.50
60 Stephon Marbury	1.00	2.50
61 Eddy Curry	.60	1.50
62 Jamal Crawford	.60	1.50
63 David Lee	.75	2.00
64 Chris Paul	2.00	5.00
65 Tyson Chandler	1.00	2.50
66 David West	1.00	2.50
67 Peja Stojakovic	1.00	2.50
68 Dwight Howard	2.00	5.00
69 Grant Hill	1.00	2.50
70 Jameer Nelson	.75	2.00
71 Andre Miller	.75	2.00
72 Andre Iguodala	1.00	2.50
73 Kyle Korver	1.00	2.50
74 Steve Nash	1.25	3.00
75 Amare Stoudemire	2.00	5.00
76 Shawn Marion	1.00	2.50
77 Leandro Barbosa	.75	2.00
78 Brandon Roy	1.50	4.00
79 Zach Randolph	1.00	2.50
80 LaMarcus Aldridge	1.25	3.00
81 Mike Bibby	1.00	2.50
82 Kevin Martin	1.00	2.50
83 Ron Artest	1.00	2.50
84 Tony Parker	1.00	2.50
85 Manu Ginobili	1.00	2.50
86 Tim Duncan	2.00	5.00
87 Rashard Lewis	1.00	2.50
88 Ray Allen	1.00	2.50
89 Chris Wilcox	.75	2.00
90 T.J. Ford	.75	2.00
91 Chris Bosh	1.00	2.50
92 Juan Dixon	.60	1.50
93 Andrea Bargnani	1.25	3.00
94 Carlos Boozer	1.00	2.50
95 Mehmet Okur	.75	2.00
96 Deron Williams	1.50	4.00
97 Gilbert Arenas	1.00	2.50
98 Antawn Jamison	1.00	2.50
99 Caron Butler	1.00	2.50
100 DeShawn Stevenson	.60	1.50
101 Al Jefferson JSY	3.00	8.00
102 Allen Iverson JSY	5.00	12.00
103 Amare Stoudemire JSY	5.00	12.00
104 Andre Iguodala JSY	3.00	8.00
105 Andre Miller JSY	3.00	8.00
106 Ben Gordon JSY	4.00	10.00
107 Bruce Bowen JSY	3.00	8.00
108 Carmelo Anthony JSY	5.00	12.00
109 Charlie Villanueva JSY	3.00	8.00
110 Corey Maggette JSY	3.00	8.00
111 Danny Granger JSY	3.00	8.00
112 Darko Milicic JSY	3.00	8.00
113 Devin Harris JSY	3.00	8.00
114 Dirk Nowitzki JSY	4.00	10.00
115 Donyell Marshall JSY	3.00	8.00
116 Drew Gooden JSY	3.00	8.00
117 Dwight Howard JSY	4.00	10.00
118 Elton Brand JSY	3.00	8.00
119 Gilbert Arenas JSY	3.00	8.00
120 Grant Hill JSY	5.00	12.00
121 Jason Kidd JSY	4.00	10.00
122 Jason Richardson JSY	3.00	8.00
123 Jermaine O'Neal JSY	3.00	8.00
124 Kevin Garnett JSY	5.00	12.00
125 Kobe Bryant JSY	8.00	20.00
126 LeBron James JSY	10.00	25.00
127 Luol Deng JSY	3.00	8.00
128 Manu Ginobili JSY	3.00	8.00
129 Mike Bibby JSY	3.00	8.00
130 Nenad Krstic JSY	3.00	8.00
131 Pau Gasol JSY	3.00	8.00
132 Paul Pierce JSY	3.00	8.00
133 Rashard Lewis JSY	3.00	8.00
134 Ray Allen JSY	3.00	8.00
135 Richard Jefferson JSY	3.00	8.00
136 Shaquille O'Neal JSY	6.00	15.00
137 Shaun Livingston JSY	3.00	8.00
138 Shawn Marion JSY	3.00	8.00
139 Tayshaun Prince JSY	3.00	8.00
140 Tim Duncan JSY	5.00	12.00
141 Greg Oden RC	5.00	12.00
142 Kevin Durant RC	25.00	60.00
143 Al Horford RC	4.00	10.00
144 Mike Conley Jr. RC	4.00	10.00
145 Jeff Green RC	4.00	10.00
146 Dominic McGuire RC	3.00	8.00
147 Corey Brewer RC	4.00	10.00
148 Brandan Wright RC	4.00	10.00
149 Joakim Noah RC	4.00	10.00
150 Spencer Hawes RC	3.00	8.00
151 Acie Law RC	4.00	10.00
152 Thaddeus Young RC	4.00	10.00
153 Julian Wright RC	4.00	10.00
154 Al Thornton RC	3.00	8.00
155 Rodney Stuckey RC	6.00	15.00
156 Nick Young RC	3.00	8.00
157 Sean Williams RC	3.00	8.00
158 Marco Belinelli RC	3.00	8.00
159 Javaris Crittenton RC	3.00	8.00
160 Jason Smith RC	3.00	8.00
161 Daequan Cook RC	4.00	10.00
162 Jared Dudley RC	3.00	8.00
163 Wilson Chandler RC	3.00	8.00
164 Morris Almond RC	3.00	8.00
165 Aaron Brooks RC	5.00	12.00
166 Arron Afflalo RC	3.00	8.00
167 Alando Tucker RC	3.00	8.00
168 Petteri Koponen RC	3.00	8.00
169 Carl Landry RC	3.00	8.00
170 Gabe Pruitt RC	3.00	8.00
171 Marcus Williams RC	3.00	8.00
172 Nick Fazekas RC	3.00	8.00
173 Glen Davis RC	6.00	15.00
174 Jermareo Davidson RC	3.00	8.00
175 Josh McRoberts RC	4.00	10.00
176 Chris Richard RC	3.00	8.00
177 Derrick Byars RC	3.00	8.00
178 Adam Haluska RC	3.00	8.00
179 Reyshawn Terry RC	3.00	8.00
180 Jared Jordan RC	3.00	8.00
181 Aaron Gray RC	3.00	8.00
182 JamesOn Curry RC	3.00	8.00
183 Taurean Green RC	3.00	8.00
184 Demetris Nichols RC	3.00	8.00
185 Herbert Hill RC	3.00	8.00
186 Brad Newley RC	3.00	8.00
187 Ramon Sessions RC	4.00	10.00
188 Sammy Mejia RC	3.00	8.00
189 D.J. Strawberry RC	3.00	8.00
190 Stephane Lasme RC	3.00	8.00

2009-10 SP Game Used

1 Al Harrington	.75	2.00
2 Al Horford	1.00	2.50
3 Al Jefferson	1.00	2.50
4 Al Thornton	1.00	2.50
5 Allen Iverson	1.25	3.00
6 Andre Iguodala	1.00	2.50
7 Andre Miller	.75	2.00
8 Andrea Bargnani	.75	2.00
9 Antawn Jamison	1.00	2.50
10 Baron Davis	1.00	2.50
11 Ben Gordon	1.00	2.50
12 Ben Wallace	1.00	2.50
13 Beno Udrih	.60	1.50
14 Brad Miller	1.00	2.50
15 Brandon Roy	1.25	3.00
16 Carlos Boozer	1.00	2.50
17 Carmelo Anthony	1.25	3.00
18 Chauncey Billups	1.00	2.50
19 Chris Bosh	1.00	2.50
20 Chris Duhon	.60	1.50
21 Chris Paul	2.00	5.00
22 Courtney Lee	.75	2.00
23 D.J. Augustin	.75	2.00
24 Danny Granger	1.00	2.50
25 David Lee	.75	2.00
26 David West	1.00	2.50
27 Derek Fisher	.75	2.00
28 Deron Williams	1.25	3.00
29 Derrick Rose	2.00	5.00
30 DeShawn Stevenson	.60	1.50
31 Devin Harris	1.00	2.50
32 Dirk Nowitzki	1.25	3.00
33 Dwight Howard	2.00	5.00
34 Dwyane Wade	2.00	5.00
35 Elton Brand	1.00	2.50
36 Eric Gordon	1.00	2.50
37 Gilbert Arenas	1.00	2.50
38 Hedo Turkoglu	1.00	2.50
39 Jamal Crawford	.60	1.50
40 Jason Kidd	1.00	2.50
41 Jason Richardson	1.00	2.50
42 Jeff Green	.75	2.00
43 Jermaine O'Neal	1.00	2.50
44 Jerryd Bayless	.75	2.00
45 Joe Johnson	1.00	2.50
46 Jose Calderon	.75	2.00
47 Josh Howard	1.00	2.50
48 Josh Smith	1.00	2.50
49 Kenyon Martin	1.00	2.50
50 Kevin Durant	2.50	6.00
51 Kevin Garnett	2.00	5.00
52 Kevin Love	.75	2.00
53 Kevin Martin	1.00	2.50
54 Kobe Bryant	5.00	12.00
55 Lamar Odom	1.00	2.50
56 LaMarcus Aldridge	1.00	2.50
57 LeBron James	5.00	12.00
58 Luis Scola	.60	1.50
59 Luke Ridnour	.60	1.50
60 Luol Deng	1.00	2.50
61 Manu Ginobili	1.00	2.50
62 Marc Gasol	1.00	2.50
63 Mario Chalmers	1.00	2.50
64 Michael Beasley	1.25	3.00
65 Michael Redd	1.00	2.50
66 Mike Bibby	.60	1.50
67 Mike Dunleavy	.60	1.50
68 Mo Williams	.75	2.00
69 Monta Ellis	1.00	2.50
70 O.J. Mayo	1.25	3.00
71 Pau Gasol	1.00	2.50
72 Paul Pierce	1.25	3.00
73 Peja Stojakovic	.60	1.50
74 Quentin Richardson	.60	1.50

❑ 75 Raja Bell	.75	2.00
❑ 76 Ray Allen	1.00	2.50
❑ 77 Raymond Felton	.75	2.00
❑ 78 Richard Hamilton	.75	2.00
❑ 79 Richard Jefferson	1.00	2.50
❑ 80 Rodney Stuckey	1.00	2.50
❑ 81 Ron Artest	1.00	2.50
❑ 82 Ronnie Brewer	.60	1.50
❑ 83 Rudy Fernandez	1.00	2.50
❑ 84 Rudy Gay	1.00	2.50
❑ 85 Russell Westbrook	1.00	2.50
❑ 86 Sebastian Telfair	.60	1.50
❑ 87 Shaquille O'Neal	2.00	5.00
❑ 88 Shawn Marion	1.00	2.50
❑ 89 Stephen Jackson	.75	2.00
❑ 90 Steve Nash	1.00	2.50
❑ 91 T.J. Ford	.60	1.50
❑ 92 Tayshaun Prince	1.00	2.50
❑ 93 Thaddeus Young	.60	1.50
❑ 94 Tim Duncan	1.50	4.00
❑ 95 Tony Parker	1.00	2.50
❑ 96 Tracy McGrady	1.25	3.00
❑ 97 Tyson Chandler	.75	2.00
❑ 98 Vince Carter	1.25	3.00
❑ 99 Yao Ming	1.25	3.00
❑ 100 Yi Jianlian	1.00	2.50
❑ 101 A.J. Price RC	3.00	8.00
❑ 102 B.J. Mullens RC	3.00	8.00
❑ 103 Blake Griffin RC	8.00	20.00
❑ 104 Brandon Jennings RC	8.00	20.00
❑ 105 Chase Budinger RC	5.00	12.00
❑ 106 DaJuan Summers RC	3.00	8.00
❑ 107 Rodrigue Beaubois RC	6.00	15.00
❑ 108 Danny Green RC	4.00	10.00
❑ 109 Dante Cunningham RC	3.00	8.00
❑ 110 Darren Collison RC	5.00	12.00
❑ 111 DeJuan Blair RC	5.00	12.00
❑ 112 DeMar DeRozan RC	5.00	12.00
❑ 113 Derrick Brown RC	3.00	8.00
❑ 114 Earl Clark RC	5.00	12.00
❑ 115 Eric Maynor RC	5.00	12.00
❑ 116 Gerald Henderson RC	5.00	12.00
❑ 117 Hasheem Thabeet RC	3.00	8.00
❑ 118 James Harden RC	6.00	15.00
❑ 119 James Johnson RC	5.00	12.00
❑ 120 Jeff Pendergraph RC	4.00	10.00
❑ 121 Jeff Teague RC	4.00	10.00
❑ 122 Jonny Flynn RC	5.00	12.00
❑ 123 Jordan Hill RC	4.00	10.00
❑ 124 Austin Daye RC	4.00	10.00
❑ 125 Jrue Holiday RC	5.00	12.00
❑ 126 Marcus Thornton RC	3.00	8.00
❑ 127 Nick Calathes RC	3.00	8.00
❑ 128 Omri Casspi RC	5.00	12.00
❑ 129 Patrick Mills RC	4.00	10.00
❑ 130 Ricky Rubio RC	5.00	12.00
❑ 131 Sam Young RC	5.00	12.00
❑ 132 Sergio Llull RC	3.00	8.00
❑ 133 Stephen Curry RC	8.00	20.00
❑ 134 Taj Gibson RC	5.00	12.00
❑ 135 Terrence Williams RC	6.00	15.00
❑ 136 Toney Douglas RC	3.00	8.00
❑ 137 Ty Lawson RC	4.00	10.00
❑ 138 Tyler Hansbrough RC	5.00	12.00
❑ 139 Jermaine Taylor RC	4.00	10.00
❑ 140 Tyreke Evans RC	12.00	30.00
❑ 141 DeMarre Carroll RC	4.00	10.00
❑ 142 Wayne Ellington RC	5.00	12.00

2007-08 SP Rookie Edition

❑ 1 Andre Iguodala	.50	1.25
❑ 2 Andre Miller	.40	1.00
❑ 3 Gerald Wallace	.50	1.25
❑ 4 Jason Richardson	.50	1.25
❑ 5 Andrew Bogut	.50	1.25
❑ 6 Michael Redd	.50	1.25
❑ 7 Ben Gordon	.60	1.50
❑ 8 Ben Wallace	.50	1.25
❑ 9 LeBron James	2.50	6.00
❑ 10 Larry Hughes	.40	1.00
❑ 11 Paul Pierce	.50	1.25
❑ 12 Ray Allen	.50	1.25
❑ 13 Elton Brand	.50	1.25
❑ 14 Pau Gasol	.50	1.25
❑ 15 Kyle Lowry	.30	.75
❑ 16 Joe Johnson	.50	1.25
❑ 17 Josh Smith	.50	1.25
❑ 18 Dwyane Wade	1.25	3.00
❑ 19 Shaquille O'Neal	1.25	3.00
❑ 20 Chris Paul	1.00	2.50
❑ 21 Morris Peterson	.40	1.00
❑ 22 Carlos Boozer	.50	1.25
❑ 23 Michael Jordan	3.00	8.00
❑ 24 Deron Williams	.75	2.00
❑ 25 Mehmet Okur	.40	1.00
❑ 26 Ron Artest	.50	1.25
❑ 27 Mike Bibby	.50	1.25
❑ 28 Eddy Curry	.30	.75
❑ 29 Zach Randolph	.50	1.25
❑ 30 Kobe Bryant	2.50	6.00
❑ 31 Lamar Odom	.50	1.25
❑ 32 Dwight Howard	1.00	2.50
❑ 33 Rashard Lewis	.50	1.25
❑ 34 Dirk Nowitzki	.75	2.00
❑ 35 Josh Howard	.50	1.25
❑ 36 Jason Kidd	.75	2.00
❑ 37 Vince Carter	1.00	2.50
❑ 38 Allen Iverson	1.00	2.50
❑ 39 Carmelo Anthony	1.00	2.50
❑ 40 Jermaine O'Neal	.50	1.25
❑ 41 Tayshaun Prince	.50	1.25
❑ 42 Chauncey Billups	.50	1.25
❑ 43 Richard Hamilton	.40	1.00
❑ 44 T.J. Ford	.40	1.00
❑ 45 Chris Bosh	.50	1.25
❑ 46 Tracy McGrady	1.00	2.50
❑ 47 Yao Ming	1.25	3.00
❑ 48 Tim Duncan	1.00	2.50
❑ 49 Tony Parker	.50	1.25
❑ 50 Amare Stoudemire	1.00	2.50
❑ 51 Shawn Marion	.50	1.25
❑ 52 Steve Nash	.60	1.50
❑ 53 Chris Wilcox	.40	1.00
❑ 54 Kevin Garnett	1.25	3.00
❑ 55 Brandon Roy	.75	2.00
❑ 56 LaMarcus Aldridge	.60	1.50
❑ 57 Baron Davis	.50	1.25
❑ 58 Caron Butler	.50	1.25
❑ 59 Gilbert Arenas	.50	1.25
❑ 60 Antawn Jamison	.50	1.25
❑ 61 Kevin Durant RC	6.00	15.00
❑ 62 Al Horford RC	1.00	2.50
❑ 63 Mike Conley RC	1.00	2.50
❑ 64 Jeff Green RC	1.00	2.50
❑ 65 Corey Brewer RC	1.00	2.50
❑ 66 Joakim Noah RC	1.00	2.50
❑ 67 Spencer Hawes RC	.75	2.00
❑ 68 Acie Law IV RC	1.00	2.50
❑ 69 Julian Wright RC	1.00	2.50
❑ 70 Al Thornton RC	.75	2.00
❑ 71 Rodney Stuckey RC	1.50	4.00
❑ 72 Sean Williams RC	.75	2.00
❑ 73 Marco Belinelli RC	.75	2.00
❑ 74 Javaris Crittenton RC	.75	2.00
❑ 75 Jason Smith RC	.75	2.00
❑ 76 Daequan Cook RC	1.00	2.50
❑ 77 Jared Dudley RC	.75	2.00
❑ 78 Wilson Chandler RC	.75	2.00
❑ 79 Morris Almond RC	.75	2.00
❑ 80 Aaron Brooks RC	1.25	3.00
❑ 81 Arron Afflalo RC	.75	2.00
❑ 82 Alando Tucker RC	.75	2.00
❑ 83 Carl Landry RC	.75	2.00
❑ 84 Gabe Pruitt RC	.75	2.00
❑ 85 Juan Carlos Navarro RC	1.00	2.50
❑ 86 Yi Jianlian RC	1.25	3.00
❑ 87 Glen Davis RC	1.50	4.00
❑ 88 Jermareo Davidson RC	.75	2.00
❑ 89 Thaddeus Young RC	1.00	2.50
❑ 90 Brandan Wright RC	1.00	2.50
❑ 91 Luis Scola RC	1.25	3.00
❑ 92 Chris Richard RC	.75	2.00
❑ 93 Adam Haluska RC	.75	2.00
❑ 94 D.J. Strawberry RC	.75	2.00
❑ 95 Darryl Watkins RC	.75	2.00
❑ 96 Cheikh Samb RC	.75	2.00
❑ 97 Greg Oden RC	1.25	3.00
❑ 98 Aaron Gray RC	.75	2.00
❑ 99 JamesOn Curry RC	.75	2.00
❑ 100 Taurean Green RC	.75	2.00
❑ 101 Demetris Nichols RC	.75	2.00
❑ 102 Nick Young RC	.75	2.00
❑ 103 Ramon Sessions RC	1.00	2.50
❑ 104 Coby Karl RC	.75	2.00
❑ 105 Jason Smith 96-97	1.00	2.50
❑ 106 Kevin Durant 96-97	8.00	20.00
❑ 107 Al Horford 96-97	1.25	3.00
❑ 108 Mike Conley 96-97	1.25	3.00
❑ 109 Jeff Green 96-97	1.25	3.00
❑ 110 Corey Brewer 96-97	1.25	3.00
❑ 111 Joakim Noah 96-97	1.25	3.00
❑ 112 Spencer Hawes 96-97	1.00	2.50
❑ 113 Acie Law IV 96-97	1.25	3.00
❑ 114 Julian Wright 96-97	1.25	3.00
❑ 115 Al Thornton 96-97	1.00	2.50
❑ 116 Rodney Stuckey 96-97	2.00	5.00
❑ 117 Sean Williams 96-97	1.00	2.50
❑ 118 Marco Belinelli 96-97	1.00	2.50
❑ 119 Javaris Crittenton 96-97	1.00	2.50
❑ 120 Jason Smith 96-97	1.00	2.50
❑ 121 Kevin Durant 97-98	12.00	30.00
❑ 122 Al Horford 97-98	2.00	5.00
❑ 123 Mike Conley 97-98	2.00	5.00
❑ 124 Jeff Green 97-98	2.00	5.00
❑ 125 Corey Brewer 97-98	2.00	5.00
❑ 126 Joakim Noah 97-98	2.00	5.00
❑ 127 Spencer Hawes 97-98	1.50	4.00
❑ 128 Acie Law IV 97-98	2.00	5.00
❑ 129 Julian Wright 97-98	2.00	5.00
❑ 130 Al Thornton 97-98	1.50	4.00
❑ 131 Rodney Stuckey 97-98	3.00	8.00
❑ 132 Sean Williams 97-98	1.50	4.00
❑ 133 Marco Belinelli 97-98	1.50	4.00
❑ 134 Javaris Crittenton 97-98	1.50	4.00
❑ 135 Jason Smith 97-98	1.50	4.00
❑ 136 Daequan Cook 97-98	2.00	5.00
❑ 137 Jared Dudley 97-98	1.50	4.00
❑ 138 Wilson Chandler 97-98	1.50	4.00
❑ 139 Brandan Wright 97-98	2.00	5.00
❑ 140 Aaron Brooks 97-98	2.50	6.00
❑ 141 Alando Tucker 97-98	1.50	4.00
❑ 142 Carl Landry 97-98	1.50	4.00
❑ 143 Gabe Pruitt 97-98	1.50	4.00
❑ 144 D.J. Strawberry 97-98	1.50	4.00
❑ 145 Yi Jianlian 97-98	2.50	6.00
❑ 146 Glen Davis 97-98	3.00	8.00
❑ 147 Greg Oden 97-98	2.50	6.00
❑ 148 Aaron Gray 97-98	1.50	4.00
❑ 149 Taurean Green 97-98	1.50	4.00
❑ 150 D.J. Strawberry 97-98	1.50	4.00
❑ 151 Kevin Durant 94-95	12.00	30.00
❑ 152 Al Horford 94-95	2.00	5.00
❑ 153 Mike Conley 94-95	2.00	5.00
❑ 154 Jeff Green 94-95	2.00	5.00
❑ 155 Corey Brewer 94-95	2.00	5.00
❑ 156 Joakim Noah 94-95	2.00	5.00
❑ 157 Spencer Hawes 94-95	1.50	4.00
❑ 158 Acie Law IV 94-95	2.00	5.00
❑ 159 Julian Wright 94-95	2.00	5.00
❑ 160 Al Thornton 94-95	1.50	4.00
❑ 161 Rodney Stuckey 94-95	3.00	8.00
❑ 162 Sean Williams 94-95	1.50	4.00
❑ 163 Marco Belinelli 94-95	1.50	4.00
❑ 164 Javaris Crittenton 94-95	1.50	4.00
❑ 165 Jason Smith 94-95	1.50	4.00
❑ 166 Daequan Cook 94-95	2.00	5.00
❑ 167 Jared Dudley 94-95	1.50	4.00
❑ 168 Wilson Chandler 94-95	1.50	4.00
❑ 169 Morris Almond 94-95	1.50	4.00
❑ 170 Aaron Brooks 94-95	2.50	6.00
❑ 171 Arron Afflalo 94-95	1.50	4.00
❑ 172 Alando Tucker 94-95	1.50	4.00
❑ 173 Carl Landry 94-95	1.50	4.00
❑ 174 Gabe Pruitt 94-95	1.50	4.00
❑ 175 Darius Washington 94-95	1.50	4.00
❑ 176 Oleksiy Pecherov 94-95	1.50	4.00
❑ 177 Luis Scola 94-95	2.50	6.00
❑ 178 Greg Oden 94-95	2.50	6.00
❑ 179 Dominique Wilkins 94-95	2.00	5.00
❑ 180 Yi Jianlian 94-95	2.50	6.00
❑ 181 Carmelo Anthony 98-99	2.00	5.00
❑ 182 B.J. Armstrong 98-99	1.50	4.00

❑ 183 Larry Bird 98-99	5.00	12.00
❑ 184 Steve Novak 98-99	1.50	4.00
❑ 185 Kobe Bryant 98-99	5.00	12.00
❑ 186 Vince Carter 98-99	2.00	5.00
❑ 187 Tom Chambers 98-99	1.50	4.00
❑ 188 Baron Davis 98-99	1.50	4.00
❑ 189 Boris Diaw 98-99	1.50	4.00
❑ 190 Hilton Armstrong 98-99	1.50	4.00
❑ 191 Hal Greer 98-99	1.50	4.00
❑ 192 Keyon Dooling 98-99	1.50	4.00
❑ 193 LeBron James 98-99	8.00	20.00
❑ 194 Antawn Jamison 98-99	1.50	4.00
❑ 195 Magic Johnson 98-99	3.00	8.00
❑ 196 Michael Jordan 98-99	10.00	25.00
❑ 197 Danny Manning 98-99	1.50	4.00
❑ 198 Tracy McGrady 98-99	3.00	8.00
❑ 199 Chris Mihm 98-99	1.50	4.00
❑ 200 Yao Ming 98-99	4.00	10.00
❑ 201 Steve Nash 98-99	1.50	4.00
❑ 202 Hakeem Olajuwon 98-99	2.00	5.00
❑ 203 Tony Parker 98-99	1.50	4.00
❑ 204 Paul Pierce 98-99	1.50	4.00
❑ 205 Quentin Richardson 98-99	1.50	4.00
❑ 206 Dennis Rodman 98-99	1.50	4.00
❑ 207 DeShawn Stevenson 98-99	1.50	4.00
❑ 208 John Stockton 98-99	2.50	6.00
❑ 209 Shelden Williams 98-99	1.50	4.00
❑ 210 Dominique Wilkins 98-99	2.00	5.00

2007-08 SP Rookie Threads

❑ COMP.SET w/o SP's (42)	20.00	40.00
❑ 1 Allen Iverson	1.00	2.50
❑ 2 Amare Stoudemire	1.00	2.50
❑ 3 Andre Iguodala	.50	1.25
❑ 4 Andrea Bargnani	.60	1.50
❑ 5 Baron Davis	.50	1.25
❑ 6 Ben Gordon	.60	1.50
❑ 7 Brandon Roy	.75	2.00
❑ 8 Carmelo Anthony	1.00	2.50
❑ 9 Chauncey Billups	.50	1.25
❑ 10 Chris Bosh	.50	1.25
❑ 11 Chris Paul	1.00	2.50
❑ 12 David Lee	.40	1.00
❑ 13 Deron Williams	.75	2.00
❑ 14 Dirk Nowitzki	.75	2.00
❑ 15 Dwight Howard	1.00	2.50
❑ 16 Dwyane Wade	1.25	3.00
❑ 17 Elton Brand	.50	1.25
❑ 18 Emeka Okafor	.50	1.25
❑ 19 Gilbert Arenas	.50	1.25
❑ 20 Jason Kidd	.75	2.00
❑ 21 Jermaine O'Neal	.50	1.25
❑ 22 Kevin Garnett	1.25	3.00
❑ 23 Kirk Hinrich	.50	1.25
❑ 24 Kobe Bryant	2.50	6.00
❑ 25 LaMarcus Aldridge	.60	1.50
❑ 26 LeBron James	2.50	6.00
❑ 27 Luke Ridnour	.40	1.00
❑ 28 Marvin Williams	.50	1.25
❑ 29 Michael Jordan	3.00	8.00
❑ 30 Michael Redd	.50	1.25
❑ 31 Mike Bibby	.50	1.25
❑ 32 Paul Pierce	.50	1.25
❑ 33 Randy Foye	.50	1.25
❑ 34 Rudy Gay	.40	1.00
❑ 35 Shaquille O'Neal	1.25	3.00
❑ 36 Stephon Marbury	.50	1.25
❑ 37 Steve Nash	.60	1.50
❑ 38 Tim Duncan	1.00	2.50
❑ 39 Tony Parker	.50	1.25
❑ 40 Tracy McGrady	1.00	2.50
❑ 41 Vince Carter	1.00	2.50
❑ 42 Yao Ming	1.25	3.00
❑ 43 Greg Oden RC	4.00	10.00
❑ 44 Yi Jianlian RC	4.00	10.00
❑ 45 Brandan Wright RC	3.00	8.00
❑ 46 Thaddeus Young RC	3.00	8.00
❑ 47 Nick Young RC	2.50	6.00
❑ 48 Juan Carlos Navarro RC	3.00	8.00
❑ 49 Kevin Durant AU RC	125.00	250.00
❑ 50 Al Horford AU RC	25.00	50.00
❑ 51 Mike Conley AU RC	15.00	30.00
❑ 52 Jeff Green AU RC	15.00	30.00
❑ 53 Corey Brewer AU RC	10.00	25.00
❑ 54 Joakim Noah AU RC	15.00	30.00
❑ 55 Spencer Hawes AU RC	8.00	20.00
❑ 56 Acie Law IV AU RC	10.00	25.00
❑ 57 Julian Wright AU RC	10.00	25.00
❑ 59 Rodney Stuckey AU RC	20.00	40.00
❑ 60 Jason Smith AU RC	8.00	20.00
❑ 61 Taurean Green AU RC	4.00	10.00
❑ 62 Javaris Crittenton AU RC	4.00	10.00
❑ 63 Sean Williams AU RC	6.00	15.00
❑ 64 Daequan Cook AU RC	4.00	10.00
❑ 65 Jared Dudley AU RC	4.00	10.00
❑ 66 Wilson Chandler AU RC	4.00	10.00
❑ 67 Morris Almond AU RC	4.00	10.00
❑ 68 Aaron Brooks AU RC	8.00	20.00
❑ 69 Arron Afflalo AU RC	5.00	12.00
❑ 70 Alando Tucker AU RC	4.00	10.00
❑ 71 Aaron Gray AU RC	4.00	10.00
❑ 72 Carl Landry AU RC	6.00	15.00
❑ 73 Gabe Pruitt AU RC	4.00	10.00
❑ 74 Nick Fazekas AU RC	4.00	10.00
❑ 75 Adam Haluska AU RC	4.00	10.00
❑ 76 Glen Davis AU RC	6.00	15.00
❑ 84 D.J. Strawberry AU RC	6.00	15.00

2008-09 SP Rookie Threads

❑ COMP.SET w/o SPs (60)	20.00	50.00
❑ 1 Antawn Jamison	.60	1.50
❑ 2 Gilbert Arenas	.60	1.50
❑ 3 Carlos Boozer	.60	1.50
❑ 4 Deron Williams	.75	2.00
❑ 5 Jermaine O'Neal	.60	1.50
❑ 6 Chris Bosh	.60	1.50
❑ 7 Jeff Green	.50	1.25
❑ 8 Kevin Durant	1.50	4.00
❑ 9 Tim Duncan	1.00	2.50
❑ 10 Tony Parker	.60	1.50
❑ 11 Beno Udrih	.40	1.00
❑ 12 Kevin Martin	.60	1.50
❑ 13 Brandon Roy	.75	2.00
❑ 14 Greg Oden	.60	1.50
❑ 15 Amare Stoudemire	.75	2.00
❑ 16 Steve Nash	.60	1.50
❑ 17 Thaddeus Young	.50	1.25
❑ 18 Andre Iguodala	.60	1.50
❑ 19 Hedo Turkoglu	.60	1.50
❑ 20 Dwight Howard	1.25	3.00
❑ 21 Jamal Crawford	.40	1.00
❑ 22 Stephon Marbury	.60	1.50
❑ 23 David West	.60	1.50
❑ 24 Chris Paul	1.25	3.00
❑ 25 Yi Jianlian	.60	1.50
❑ 26 Vince Carter	.75	2.00
❑ 27 Al Jefferson	.60	1.50
❑ 28 Corey Brewer	.50	1.25
❑ 29 Richard Jefferson	.60	1.50
❑ 30 Michael Redd	.60	1.50
❑ 31 Dwyane Wade	1.25	3.00
❑ 32 Shawn Marion	.60	1.50
❑ 33 Mike Conley	.50	1.25
❑ 34 Rudy Gay	.60	1.50
❑ 35 Pau Gasol	.60	1.50
❑ 36 Kobe Bryant	3.00	8.00
❑ 37 Al Thornton	.60	1.50
❑ 38 Baron Davis	.60	1.50
❑ 39 Danny Granger	.60	1.50
❑ 40 T.J. Ford	.40	1.00
❑ 41 Tracy McGrady	.75	2.00
❑ 42 Yao Ming	.75	2.00
❑ 43 Stephen Jackson	.50	1.25
❑ 44 Monta Ellis	.60	1.50
❑ 45 Richard Hamilton	.50	1.25
❑ 46 Chauncey Billups	.60	1.50
❑ 47 Allen Iverson	.75	2.00
❑ 48 Carmelo Anthony	.75	2.00
❑ 49 Jason Kidd	.60	1.50
❑ 50 Dirk Nowitzki	.75	2.00
❑ 51 LeBron James	3.00	8.00
❑ 52 Ben Wallace	.60	1.50
❑ 53 Ben Gordon	.60	1.50
❑ 54 Joakim Noah	.60	1.50
❑ 55 Gerald Wallace	.60	1.50
❑ 56 Jason Richardson	.60	1.50
❑ 57 Kevin Garnett	1.25	3.00
❑ 58 Paul Pierce	.75	2.00
❑ 59 Al Horford	.60	1.50
❑ 60 Joe Johnson	.60	1.50
❑ 61 James Gist RC	2.00	5.00
❑ 62 Danilo Gallinari RC	3.00	8.00
❑ 63 Malik Hairston RC	2.00	5.00
❑ 64 Mike Taylor RC	2.00	5.00
❑ 65 Joe Crawford RC	3.00	8.00
❑ 66 Trent Plaisted RC	2.00	5.00
❑ 67 Russell Westbrook JSY AU RC	20.00	40.00
❑ 68 Sonny Weems JSY AU RC	4.00	10.00
❑ 69 Joe Alexander JSY AU RC	5.00	12.00
❑ 70 D.J. Augustin RC EXCH	8.00	20.00
❑ 71 Brook Lopez JSY AU RC	8.00	20.00
❑ 72 Jason Thompson JSY AU RC	6.00	15.00
❑ 73 Brandon Rush RC EXCH	5.00	12.00
❑ 74 Anthony Randolph RC EXCH	8.00	20.00
❑ 75 Robin Lopez RC EXCH	5.00	12.00
❑ 76 Marreese Speights JSY AU RC	4.00	10.00
❑ 77 Roy Hibbert JSY AU RC	6.00	15.00
❑ 78 Javale McGee JSY AU RC	4.00	10.00
❑ 79 J.J. Hickson JSY AU RC	8.00	20.00
❑ 80 Kyle Weaver JSY AU RC	4.00	10.00
❑ 81 Ryan Anderson JSY AU RC	4.00	10.00
❑ 82 Courtney Lee RC EXCH	10.00	25.00
❑ 83 Kosta Koufos RC EXCH	6.00	15.00
❑ 84 George Hill JSY AU RC	8.00	20.00
❑ 85 Darrell Arthur JSY AU RC	8.00	20.00
❑ 86 Donte Greene JSY AU RC	6.00	15.00
❑ 87 D.J. White JSY AU RC	5.00	12.00
❑ 88 J.R. Giddens JSY AU RC	5.00	12.00
❑ 89 Walter Sharpe JSY AU RC	4.00	10.00
❑ 90 Joey Dorsey JSY AU RC	4.00	10.00
❑ 91 Mario Chalmers JSY AU RC	8.00	20.00
❑ 92 DeAndre Jordan JSY AU RC	4.00	10.00
❑ 93 C.Douglas-Roberts JSY AU RC	6.00	15.00
❑ 94 Patrick Ewing Jr. JSY AU RC	5.00	12.00
❑ 95 Derrick Rose JSY AU RC	60.00	120.00
❑ 96 Michael Beasley RC EXCH	20.00	40.00
❑ 97 O.J. Mayo JSY AU RC	25.00	50.00
❑ 98 Kevin Love JSY AU RC	20.00	40.00
❑ 99 Eric Gordon JSY AU RC	6.00	15.00
❑ 100 Jerryd Bayless JSY AU RC	8.00	20.00

2003-04 SP Signature Edition

❑ COMP.SET w/o SP's (100)	30.00	80.00
❑ COMMON CARD (1-100)	.40	1.00
❑ COMMON ROOKIE (101-142)	4.00	10.00
❑ MOST UNPRICED DUE TO SCARCITY		
❑ 1 Shareef Abdur-Rahim	.50	1.25
❑ 2 Jason Terry	.50	1.25
❑ 3 Theo Ratliff	.40	1.00

❑ 4 Raef LaFrentz .40 1.00
❑ 5 Paul Pierce .60 1.50
❑ 6 Larry Bird 2.00 5.00
❑ 7 Jalen Rose .50 1.25
❑ 8 Scottie Pippen 1.00 2.50
❑ 9 Michael Jordan 4.00 10.00
❑ 10 Dennis Rodman .75 2.00
❑ 11 Dajuan Wagner .40 1.00
❑ 12 Darius Miles .50 1.25
❑ 13 Carlos Boozer .60 1.50
❑ 14 Zydrunas Ilgauskas .50 1.25
❑ 15 Dirk Nowitzki 1.00 2.50
❑ 16 Steve Nash 1.00 2.50
❑ 17 Antoine Walker .60 1.50
❑ 18 Antawn Jamison .60 1.50
❑ 19 Andre Miller .50 1.25
❑ 20 Nene .50 1.25
❑ 21 Nikoloz Tskitishvili .40 1.00
❑ 22 Ben Wallace .50 1.25
❑ 23 Richard Hamilton .50 1.25
❑ 24 Chauncey Billups .60 1.50
❑ 25 Nick Van Exel .50 1.25
❑ 26 Jason Richardson .60 1.50
❑ 27 Mike Dunleavy .50 1.25
❑ 28 Yao Ming 1.25 3.00
❑ 29 Steve Francis .60 1.50
❑ 30 Cuttino Mobley .50 1.25
❑ 31 Reggie Miller .60 1.50
❑ 32 Jermaine O'Neal .60 1.50
❑ 33 Jamaal Tinsley .50 1.25
❑ 34 Chris Wilcox .40 1.00
❑ 35 Elton Brand .60 1.50
❑ 36 Wang Zhizhi .50 1.25
❑ 37 Corey Maggette .40 1.00
❑ 38 Kobe Bryant 3.00 8.00
❑ 39 Shaquille O'Neal 1.50 4.00
❑ 40 Gary Payton .60 1.50
❑ 41 Karl Malone .60 1.50
❑ 42 Pau Gasol .60 1.50
❑ 43 Shane Battier .50 1.25
❑ 44 Mike Miller .50 1.25
❑ 45 Caron Butler .50 1.25
❑ 46 Eddie Jones .50 1.25
❑ 47 Lamar Odom .60 1.50
❑ 48 Brian Grant .40 1.00
❑ 49 Desmond Mason .50 1.25
❑ 50 Michael Redd .60 1.50
❑ 51 Tim Thomas .40 1.00
❑ 52 Wally Szczerbiak .50 1.25
❑ 53 Kevin Garnett 1.25 3.00
❑ 54 Latrell Sprewell .50 1.25
❑ 55 Sam Cassell .50 1.25
❑ 56 Richard Jefferson .60 1.50
❑ 57 Kenyon Martin .60 1.50
❑ 58 Jason Kidd 1.00 2.50
❑ 59 Alonzo Mourning .60 1.50
❑ 60 Jamal Mashburn .40 1.00
❑ 61 Baron Davis .60 1.50
❑ 62 David Wesley .40 1.00
❑ 63 Allan Houston .50 1.25
❑ 64 Keith Van Horn .50 1.25
❑ 65 Antonio McDyess .50 1.25
❑ 66 Gordan Giricek .40 1.00
❑ 67 Tracy McGrady 1.25 3.00
❑ 68 Drew Gooden .40 1.00
❑ 69 Grant Hill .60 1.50
❑ 70 Glenn Robinson .50 1.25
❑ 71 Allen Iverson 1.25 3.00
❑ 72 Julius Erving 1.25 3.00
❑ 73 Eric Snow .40 1.00
❑ 74 Shawn Marion .60 1.50
❑ 75 Amare Stoudemire 1.25 3.00
❑ 76 Stephon Marbury .60 1.50
❑ 77 Damon Stoudamire .50 1.25
❑ 78 Rasheed Wallace .60 1.50
❑ 79 Derek Anderson .50 1.25
❑ 80 Zach Randolph .60 1.50
❑ 81 Mike Bibby .50 1.25
❑ 82 Chris Webber .60 1.50
❑ 83 Peja Stojakovic .50 1.25
❑ 84 Brad Miller .50 1.25
❑ 85 Tony Parker .60 1.50
❑ 86 Tim Duncan 1.25 3.00
❑ 87 Manu Ginobili .60 1.50
❑ 88 David Robinson 1.00 2.50
❑ 89 Rashard Lewis .60 1.50
❑ 90 Ray Allen .40 1.00
❑ 91 Vladimir Radmanovic .40 1.00
❑ 92 Morris Peterson .50 1.25
❑ 93 Vince Carter 1.25 3.00
❑ 94 Antonio Davis .40 1.00
❑ 95 Andrei Kirilenko .60 1.50
❑ 96 Matt Harpring .50 1.25
❑ 97 Jarron Collins .40 1.00
❑ 98 Gilbert Arenas .60 1.50
❑ 99 Jerry Stackhouse .50 1.25
❑ 100 Kwame Brown .40 1.00
❑ 101 LeBron James RC 100.00 200.00
❑ 102 Darko Milicic RC 5.00 12.00
❑ 103 Carmelo Anthony RC 10.00 25.00
❑ 104 Chris Bosh RC 6.00 15.00
❑ 105 Dwyane Wade RC 10.00 25.00
❑ 106 Chris Kaman RC 5.00 12.00
❑ 107 Kirk Hinrich RC 5.00 12.00
❑ 108 T.J. Ford RC 5.00 12.00
❑ 109 Mike Sweetney RC 4.00 10.00
❑ 110 Jarvis Hayes RC 4.00 10.00
❑ 111 Mickael Pietrus RC 5.00 12.00
❑ 112 Nick Collison RC 4.00 10.00
❑ 113 Marcus Banks RC 4.00 10.00
❑ 114 Luke Ridnour RC 5.00 12.00
❑ 115 Reece Gaines RC 4.00 10.00
❑ 116 Troy Bell RC 4.00 10.00
❑ 117 Zarko Cabarkapa RC 4.00 10.00
❑ 118 David West RC 5.00 12.00
❑ 119 Aleksandar Pavlovic RC 5.00 12.00
❑ 120 Dahntay Jones RC 4.00 10.00
❑ 121 Boris Diaw RC 5.00 12.00
❑ 122 Zoran Planinic RC 4.00 10.00
❑ 123 Travis Outlaw RC 5.00 12.00
❑ 124 Brian Cook RC 4.00 10.00
❑ 125 James Lang RC 4.00 10.00
❑ 126 Ndudi Ebi RC 4.00 10.00
❑ 127 Kendrick Perkins RC 6.00 15.00
❑ 128 Leandro Barbosa RC 5.00 12.00
❑ 129 Josh Howard RC 5.00 12.00
❑ 130 Maciej Lampe RC 4.00 10.00
❑ 131 Jason Kapono RC 5.00 12.00
❑ 132 Luke Walton RC 5.00 12.00
❑ 133 Jerome Beasley RC 4.00 10.00
❑ 134 Willie Green RC 4.00 10.00
❑ 135 James Jones RC 4.00 10.00
❑ 136 Travis Hansen RC 4.00 10.00
❑ 137 Steve Blake RC 5.00 12.00
❑ 138 Slavko Vranes RC 4.00 10.00
❑ 139 Zaur Pachulia RC 5.00 12.00
❑ 140 Keith Bogans RC 4.00 10.00
❑ 141 Kyle Korver RC 5.00 12.00
❑ 142 Brandon Hunter RC 4.00 10.00
❑ 152 Ray Allen/34 20.00 50.00
❑ 153 Paul Pierce/34 20.00 50.00
❑ 160 Andrei Kirilenko/47 10.00 25.00
❑ 162 Nene/31 10.00 20.00
❑ 163 Elton Brand/42 10.00 25.00
❑ 168 Jerry Stackhouse/42 10.00 25.00
❑ 171 Darko Milicic/31 20.00 40.00
❑ 174 Glenn Robinson/31 10.00 20.00
❑ 177 Scottie Pippen/33 50.00 100.00
❑ 178 Richard Hamilton/32 10.00 25.00
❑ 179 Corey Maggette/50 8.00 20.00
❑ 182 Amare Stoudemire/32 15.00 40.00
❑ 185 Dirk Nowitzki/41 12.50 30.00
❑ 187 Magic Johnson/32 25.00 60.00
❑ 190 Rasheed Wallace/30 12.50 30.00
❑ 192 Jason Terry/31 10.00 25.00
❑ 203 Mike Miller/33 8.00 20.00
❑ 210 Shaquille O'Neal/34 25.00 60.00
❑ 213 Shawn Marion/31 10.00 25.00
❑ 215 Larry Bird/33 75.00 150.00
❑ 216 Antawn Jamison/33 10.00 25.00
❑ 217 Reggie Miller/31 15.00 40.00
❑ 223 Spike Lee 1.50 4.00
❑ 224 Summer Sanders 1.25 3.00
❑ 225 Cheryl Miller .75 2.00

2004-05 SP Signature Edition

❑ COMMON CARD (1-100) .40 1.00
❑ COMMON JSY RC (101-142) 3.00 8.00
❑ COMMON ROOKIE (101-142) 2.00 5.00
❑ SOME NOT PRICED DUE TO SCARCITY
❑ 1 Antoine Walker .60 1.50
❑ 2 Al Harrington .50 1.25
❑ 3 Boris Diaw .50 1.25
❑ 4 Paul Pierce .60 1.50
❑ 5 Ricky Davis .50 1.25
❑ 6 Gary Payton .60 1.50
❑ 7 Gerald Wallace .60 1.50

❑ 8 Emeka Okafor RC 2.50 6.00
❑ 9 Jahidi White .40 1.00
❑ 10 Eddy Curry .50 1.25
❑ 11 Kirk Hinrich .50 1.25
❑ 12 Michael Jordan 4.00 10.00
❑ 13 LeBron James 4.00 10.00
❑ 14 Dajuan Wagner .40 1.00
❑ 15 Jeff McInnis .40 1.00
❑ 16 Drew Gooden .40 1.00
❑ 17 Dirk Nowitzki 1.00 2.50
❑ 18 Michael Finley .60 1.50
❑ 19 Jerry Stackhouse .50 1.25
❑ 20 Jason Terry .50 1.25
❑ 21 Kenyon Martin .60 1.50
❑ 22 Andre Miller .50 1.25
❑ 23 Carmelo Anthony 2.00 5.00
❑ 24 Nene .50 1.25
❑ 25 Chauncey Billups .60 1.50
❑ 26 Rasheed Wallace .60 1.50
❑ 27 Ben Wallace .50 1.25
❑ 28 Richard Hamilton .50 1.25
❑ 29 Derek Fisher .50 1.25
❑ 30 Jason Richardson .60 1.50
❑ 31 Mike Dunleavy .50 1.25
❑ 32 Yao Ming 1.50 4.00
❑ 33 Tracy McGrady 1.25 3.00
❑ 34 Juwan Howard .50 1.25
❑ 35 Jermaine O'Neal .60 1.50
❑ 36 Reggie Miller .60 1.50
❑ 37 Ron Artest .50 1.25
❑ 38 Jamaal Tinsley .50 1.25
❑ 39 Elton Brand .60 1.50
❑ 40 Corey Maggette .50 1.25
❑ 41 Marko Jaric .40 1.00
❑ 42 Kerry Kittles .50 1.25
❑ 43 Kobe Bryant 3.00 8.00
❑ 44 Karl Malone .60 1.50
❑ 45 Lamar Odom .60 1.50
❑ 46 Caron Butler .50 1.25
❑ 47 Pau Gasol .60 1.50
❑ 48 Jason Williams .50 1.25
❑ 49 Bonzi Wells .40 1.00
❑ 50 Shaquille O'Neal 1.50 4.00
❑ 51 Dwyane Wade 2.00 5.00
❑ 52 Eddie Jones .50 1.25
❑ 53 Michael Redd .60 1.50
❑ 54 Desmond Mason .50 1.25
❑ 55 T.J. Ford .50 1.25
❑ 56 Latrell Sprewell .50 1.25
❑ 57 Kevin Garnett 1.25 3.00
❑ 58 Sam Cassell .50 1.25
❑ 59 Troy Hudson .40 1.00
❑ 60 Vince Carter 1.25 3.00
❑ 61 Richard Jefferson .60 1.50
❑ 62 Jason Kidd 1.00 2.50
❑ 63 Jamal Mashburn .50 1.25
❑ 64 Baron Davis .60 1.50
❑ 65 Jamaal Magloire .40 1.00
❑ 66 Allan Houston .50 1.25
❑ 67 Jamal Crawford .50 1.25
❑ 68 Stephon Marbury .60 1.50
❑ 69 Grant Hill .60 1.50
❑ 70 Cuttino Mobley .50 1.25
❑ 71 Steve Francis .60 1.50
❑ 72 Glenn Robinson .50 1.25
❑ 73 Allen Iverson 1.25 3.00
❑ 74 Kyle Korver .50 1.25
❑ 75 Amare Stoudemire 1.25 3.00
❑ 76 Steve Nash 1.00 2.50
❑ 77 Quentin Richardson .50 1.25
❑ 78 Shawn Marion .60 1.50
❑ 79 Shareef Abdur-Rahim .50 1.25
❑ 80 Damon Stoudamire .50 1.25
❑ 81 Zach Randolph .60 1.50
❑ 82 Darius Miles .50 1.25

❑ 83 Peja Stojakovic	.50	1.25
❑ 84 Chris Webber	.60	1.50
❑ 85 Mike Bibby	.50	1.25
❑ 86 Tony Parker	.60	1.50
❑ 87 Tim Duncan	1.25	3.00
❑ 88 Manu Ginobili	.60	1.50
❑ 89 Ronald Murray	.40	1.00
❑ 90 Ray Allen	.60	1.50
❑ 91 Rashard Lewis	.60	1.50
❑ 92 Chris Bosh	.60	1.50
❑ 93 Jalen Rose	.50	1.25
❑ 94 Rafer Alston	.40	1.00
❑ 95 Andrei Kirilenko	.60	1.50
❑ 96 Matt Harpring	.50	1.25
❑ 97 Carlos Boozer	.60	1.50
❑ 98 Gilbert Arenas	.60	1.50
❑ 99 Jarvis Hayes	.40	1.00
❑ 100 Antawn Jamison	.60	1.50
❑ 101 Dwight Howard JSY RC	10.00	25.00
❑ 102 Ben Gordon JSY RC	4.00	10.00
❑ 103 Shaun Livingston JSY RC	5.00	12.00
❑ 104 Devin Harris JSY RC	5.00	12.00
❑ 105 Josh Childress JSY RC	4.00	10.00
❑ 106 Luol Deng JSY RC	4.00	10.00
❑ 107 Rafael Araujo JSY RC	3.00	8.00
❑ 108 Andre Iguodala JSY RC	8.00	20.00
❑ 109 Luke Jackson JSY RC	3.00	8.00
❑ 110 Sebastian Telfair JSY RC	3.00	8.00
❑ 111 Kris Humphries JSY RC	3.00	8.00
❑ 112 Al Jefferson JSY RC	6.00	15.00
❑ 113 Kirk Snyder JSY RC	3.00	8.00
❑ 114 Josh Smith JSY RC	6.00	15.00
❑ 115 J.R. Smith JSY RC	3.00	15.00
❑ 116 Dorell Wright JSY RC	5.00	12.00
❑ 117 Jameer Nelson JSY RC	4.00	10.00
❑ 118 Delonte West JSY RC	6.00	15.00
❑ 119 Tony Allen JSY RC	4.00	10.00
❑ 120 Kevin Martin JSY RC	5.00	12.00
❑ 121 David Harrison JSY RC	3.00	8.00
❑ 122 Anderson Varejao JSY RC	4.00	10.00
❑ 123 Jackson Vroman JSY RC	3.00	8.00
❑ 124 Lionel Chalmers JSY RC	3.00	8.00
❑ 125 Andre Emmett JSY RC	3.00	8.00
❑ 126 Chris Duhon JSY RC	5.00	12.00
❑ 127 Bernard Robinson JSY RC	3.00	8.00
❑ 128 Tim Pickett RC	2.00	5.00
❑ 129 Nenad Krstic JSY RC	4.00	10.00
❑ 130 Andris Biedrins JSY RC	5.00	12.00
❑ 131 Robert Swift RC	2.00	5.00
❑ 132 Andres Nocioni RC	3.00	8.00
❑ 133 Justin Reed RC	2.00	5.00
❑ 134 Romain Sato RC	2.00	5.00
❑ 135 Sasha Vujacic JSY RC	2.50	6.00
❑ 136 Beno Udrih RC	3.00	8.00
❑ 137 Peter John Ramos JSY RC	3.00	8.00
❑ 138 Donta Smith JSY RC	3.00	8.00
❑ 139 Antonio Burks RC	2.00	5.00
❑ 140 Yuta Tabuse JSY RC	6.00	15.00
❑ 141 Trevor Ariza JSY RC	5.00	12.00

2005-06 SP Signature Edition

❑ COMPLETE SET (142)		
❑ COMP.SET w/o SP's (100)	50.00	100.00
❑ COMMON CARD (1-100)	.40	1.00
❑ SEMISTARS (1-100)	.50	1.25
❑ UNLISTED STARS	.60	1.50
❑ COMMON ROOKIE (101-142)	3.00	8.00
❑ 101-142 RC PRINT RUN 499 SER.#'d SETS		
❑ 1 Josh Smith	.60	1.50
❑ 2 Josh Childress	.50	1.25
❑ 3 Joe Johnson	.60	1.50
❑ 4 Paul Pierce	.60	1.50
❑ 5 Ricky Davis	.60	1.50
❑ 6 Al Jefferson	.60	1.50
❑ 7 Emeka Okafor	.60	1.50
❑ 8 Kareem Rush	.40	1.00
❑ 9 Gerald Wallace	.60	1.50
❑ 10 Michael Jordan	4.00	10.00
❑ 11 Ben Gordon	.75	2.00
❑ 12 Luol Deng	.60	1.50
❑ 13 Kirk Hinrich	.60	1.50
❑ 14 LeBron James	3.00	8.00
❑ 15 Larry Hughes	.50	1.25
❑ 16 Zydrunas Ilgauskas	.50	1.25
❑ 17 Donyell Marshall	.40	1.00
❑ 18 Dirk Nowitzki	1.00	2.50
❑ 19 Jason Terry	.60	1.50
❑ 20 Josh Howard	.60	1.50
❑ 21 Devin Harris	.60	1.50
❑ 22 Carmelo Anthony	1.25	3.00
❑ 23 Marcus Camby	.50	1.25
❑ 24 Andre Miller	.50	1.25
❑ 25 Kenyon Martin	.60	1.50
❑ 26 Chauncey Billups	.60	1.50
❑ 27 Ben Wallace	.60	1.50
❑ 28 Richard Hamilton	.50	1.25
❑ 29 Jason Richardson	.60	1.50
❑ 30 Troy Murphy	.60	1.50
❑ 31 Baron Davis	.60	1.50
❑ 32 Tracy McGrady	1.25	3.00
❑ 33 Yao Ming	1.50	4.00
❑ 34 Stromile Swift	.50	1.25
❑ 35 Jermaine O'Neal	.60	1.50
❑ 36 Ron Artest	.50	1.25
❑ 37 Stephen Jackson	.50	1.25
❑ 38 Corey Maggette	.50	1.25
❑ 39 Shaun Livingston	.40	1.00
❑ 40 Chris Wilcox	.40	1.00
❑ 41 Elton Brand	.60	1.50
❑ 42 Kobe Bryant	3.00	8.00
❑ 43 Kwame Brown	.50	1.25
❑ 44 Lamar Odom	.60	1.50
❑ 45 Pau Gasol	.60	1.50
❑ 46 Damon Stoudamire	.50	1.25
❑ 47 Lorenzen Wright	.40	1.00
❑ 48 Shaquille O'Neal	1.50	4.00
❑ 49 Dwyane Wade	1.50	4.00
❑ 50 Antoine Walker	.50	1.25
❑ 51 Jason Williams	.50	1.25
❑ 52 Desmond Mason	.40	1.00
❑ 53 Michael Redd	.60	1.50
❑ 54 Maurice Williams	.50	1.25
❑ 55 Kevin Garnett	1.25	3.00
❑ 56 Marko Jaric	.40	1.00
❑ 57 Wally Szczerbiak	.50	1.25
❑ 58 Jason Kidd	1.00	2.50
❑ 59 Richard Jefferson	.50	1.25
❑ 60 Vince Carter	1.25	3.00
❑ 61 Jamaal Magloire	.40	1.00
❑ 62 J.R. Smith	.50	1.25
❑ 63 Speedy Claxton	.40	1.00
❑ 64 Stephon Marbury	.60	1.50
❑ 65 Quentin Richardson	.50	1.25
❑ 66 Mike Sweetney	.50	1.25
❑ 67 Grant Hill	.60	1.50
❑ 68 Dwight Howard	1.25	3.00
❑ 69 Steve Francis	.60	1.50
❑ 70 Allen Iverson	1.25	3.00
❑ 71 Samuel Dalembert	.40	1.00
❑ 72 Kyle Korver	.60	1.50
❑ 73 Chris Webber	.60	1.50
❑ 74 Steve Nash	.75	2.00
❑ 75 Amare Stoudemire	1.25	3.00
❑ 76 Shawn Marion	.60	1.50
❑ 77 Sebastian Telfair	.50	1.25
❑ 78 Zach Randolph	.60	1.50
❑ 79 Juan Dixon	.40	1.00
❑ 80 Mike Bibby	.60	1.50
❑ 81 Peja Stojakovic	.60	1.50
❑ 82 Brad Miller	.60	1.50
❑ 83 Tim Duncan	1.25	3.00
❑ 84 Manu Ginobili	.60	1.50
❑ 85 Robert Horry	.50	1.25
❑ 86 Tony Parker	.60	1.50
❑ 87 Ray Allen	.60	1.50
❑ 88 Rashard Lewis	.60	1.50
❑ 89 Vladimir Radmanovic	.40	1.00
❑ 90 Chris Bosh	.60	1.50
❑ 91 Rafer Alston	.40	1.00
❑ 92 Jalen Rose	.60	1.50
❑ 93 Andrei Kirilenko	.60	1.50
❑ 94 Matt Harpring	.50	1.25
❑ 95 Carlos Boozer	.60	1.50
❑ 96 Mehmet Okur	.40	1.00
❑ 97 Gilbert Arenas	.60	1.50
❑ 98 Antawn Jamison	.60	1.50
❑ 99 Caron Butler	.60	1.50
❑ 100 Antonio Daniels	.40	1.00
❑ 101 Andrew Bogut RC	4.00	10.00
❑ 102 Marvin Williams RC	5.00	12.00
❑ 103 Deron Williams RC	8.00	20.00
❑ 104 Chris Paul RC	10.00	25.00
❑ 105 Raymond Felton RC	4.00	10.00
❑ 106 Martell Webster RC	3.00	8.00
❑ 107 Charlie Villanueva RC	5.00	12.00
❑ 108 Channing Frye RC	5.00	12.00
❑ 109 Ike Diogu RC	4.00	10.00
❑ 110 Andrew Bynum RC	10.00	25.00
❑ 111 Sean May RC	4.00	10.00
❑ 112 Rashad McCants RC	4.00	10.00
❑ 113 Antoine Wright RC	3.00	8.00
❑ 114 Joey Graham RC	3.00	8.00
❑ 115 Danny Granger RC	8.00	20.00
❑ 116 Gerald Green RC	3.00	8.00
❑ 117 Hakim Warrick RC	5.00	12.00
❑ 118 Julius Hodge RC	4.00	10.00
❑ 119 Nate Robinson RC	5.00	12.00
❑ 120 Jarrett Jack RC	3.00	8.00
❑ 121 Francisco Garcia RC	4.00	10.00
❑ 122 Luther Head RC	4.00	10.00
❑ 123 Johan Petro RC	3.00	8.00
❑ 124 Jason Maxiell RC	4.00	10.00
❑ 125 Linas Kleiza RC	4.00	10.00
❑ 126 Wayne Simien RC	4.00	10.00
❑ 127 David Lee RC	6.00	15.00
❑ 128 Salim Stoudamire RC	4.00	10.00
❑ 129 Daniel Ewing RC	4.00	10.00
❑ 130 Brandon Bass RC	3.00	8.00
❑ 131 C.J. Miles RC	3.00	8.00
❑ 132 Ersan Ilyasova RC	3.00	8.00
❑ 133 Travis Diener RC	3.00	8.00
❑ 134 Monta Ellis RC	8.00	20.00
❑ 135 Chris Taft RC	3.00	8.00
❑ 136 Martynas Andriuskevicius RC	3.00	8.00
❑ 137 Louis Williams RC	6.00	15.00
❑ 138 Bracey Wright RC	3.00	8.00
❑ 139 Robert Whaley RC	3.00	8.00
❑ 140 Andray Blatche RC	5.00	12.00
❑ 141 Ryan Gomes RC	3.00	8.00
❑ 142 Sarunas Jasikevicius RC	4.00	10.00

2006-07 SP Signature Edition

❑ 1 Josh Childress	.75	2.00
❑ 2 Joe Johnson	.75	2.00
❑ 3 Marvin Williams	1.00	2.50
❑ 4 Al Jefferson	1.00	2.50
❑ 5 Paul Pierce	1.00	2.50
❑ 6 Sebastian Telfair	.75	2.00
❑ 7 Raymond Felton	1.25	3.00
❑ 8 Emeka Okafor	1.00	2.50
❑ 9 Gerald Wallace	1.00	2.50
❑ 10 Ben Gordon	1.25	3.00
❑ 11 Kirk Hinrich	1.00	2.50
❑ 12 Ben Wallace	1.00	2.50
❑ 13 Drew Gooden	.75	2.00
❑ 14 LeBron James	5.00	12.00
❑ 15 Donyell Marshall	.60	1.50
❑ 16 Devin Harris	1.00	2.50
❑ 17 Josh Howard	1.00	2.50
❑ 18 Dirk Nowitzki	1.50	4.00
❑ 19 Jason Terry	1.00	2.50
❑ 20 Carmelo Anthony	1.25	3.00
❑ 21 Kenyon Martin	1.00	2.50
❑ 22 J.R. Smith	.75	2.00
❑ 23 Chauncey Billups	1.00	2.50
❑ 24 Richard Hamilton	.75	2.00
❑ 25 Rasheed Wallace	1.00	2.50

❑ 26 Baron Davis	1.00	2.50
❑ 27 Troy Murphy	1.00	2.50
❑ 28 Jason Richardson	1.00	2.50
❑ 29 Rafer Alston	.60	1.50
❑ 30 Shane Battier	1.00	2.50
❑ 31 Tracy McGrady	2.00	5.00
❑ 32 Yao Ming	2.50	6.00
❑ 33 Marquis Daniels	.75	2.00
❑ 34 Al Harrington	.60	1.50
❑ 35 Jermaine O'Neal	1.00	2.50
❑ 36 Elton Brand	1.00	2.50
❑ 37 Sam Cassell	1.00	2.50
❑ 38 Chris Kaman	.60	1.50
❑ 39 Corey Maggette	.75	2.00
❑ 40 Kobe Bryant	5.00	12.00
❑ 41 Lamar Odom	1.00	2.50
❑ 42 Kwame Brown	.75	2.00
❑ 43 Eddie Jones	.60	1.50
❑ 44 Mike Miller	1.00	2.50
❑ 45 Hakim Warrick	.75	2.00
❑ 46 Pau Gasol	1.00	2.50
❑ 47 Alonzo Mourning	1.25	3.00
❑ 48 Shaquille O'Neal	2.50	6.00
❑ 49 Dwyane Wade	2.50	6.00
❑ 50 Jason Williams	.75	2.00
❑ 51 Andrew Bogut	1.00	2.50
❑ 52 Michael Redd	1.00	2.50
❑ 53 Charlie Villanueva	1.00	2.50
❑ 54 Kevin Garnett	2.00	5.00
❑ 55 Mike James	.60	1.50
❑ 56 Rashad McCants	.75	2.00
❑ 57 Vince Carter	2.00	5.00
❑ 58 Richard Jefferson	.75	2.00
❑ 59 Jason Kidd	1.50	4.00
❑ 60 Tyson Chandler	1.00	2.50
❑ 61 Desmond Mason	.60	1.50
❑ 62 Chris Paul	2.00	5.00
❑ 63 Peja Stojakovic	1.00	2.50
❑ 64 Steve Francis	1.00	2.50
❑ 65 Stephon Marbury	1.00	2.50
❑ 66 Quentin Richardson	.75	2.00
❑ 67 Nate Robinson	1.00	2.50
❑ 68 Carlos Arroyo	1.00	2.50
❑ 69 Dwight Howard	2.00	5.00
❑ 70 Darko Milicic	1.00	2.50
❑ 71 Andre Iguodala	1.00	2.50
❑ 72 Allen Iverson	2.00	5.00
❑ 73 Kyle Korver	1.00	2.50
❑ 74 Chris Webber	1.00	2.50
❑ 75 Boris Diaw	.75	2.00
❑ 76 Shawn Marion	1.00	2.50
❑ 77 Steve Nash	1.25	3.00
❑ 78 Amare Stoudemire	2.00	5.00
❑ 79 Jamaal Magloire	.60	1.50
❑ 80 Zach Randolph	1.00	2.50
❑ 81 Martell Webster	.75	2.00
❑ 82 Ron Artest	1.00	2.50
❑ 83 Brad Miller	1.00	2.50
❑ 84 Mike Bibby	1.00	2.50
❑ 85 Tim Duncan	2.00	5.00
❑ 86 Michael Finley	1.00	2.50
❑ 87 Manu Ginobili	1.00	2.50
❑ 88 Tony Parker	1.00	2.50
❑ 89 Ray Allen	1.00	2.50
❑ 90 Rashard Lewis	1.00	2.50
❑ 91 Luke Ridnour	.75	2.00
❑ 92 Chris Bosh	1.00	2.50
❑ 93 T.J. Ford	.75	2.00
❑ 94 Joey Graham	.75	2.00
❑ 95 Carlos Boozer	1.00	2.50
❑ 96 Andrei Kirilenko	1.00	2.50
❑ 97 Deron Williams	1.50	4.00
❑ 98 Gilbert Arenas	1.00	2.50
❑ 99 Caron Butler	1.00	2.50
❑ 100 Antawn Jamison	1.00	2.50
❑ 101 Andrea Bargnani RC	4.00	10.00
❑ 102 LaMarcus Aldridge RC	3.00	8.00
❑ 103 Adam Morrison RC	3.00	8.00
❑ 104 Tyrus Thomas RC	3.00	8.00
❑ 105 Shelden Williams RC	3.00	8.00
❑ 106 Brandon Roy RC	6.00	15.00
❑ 107 Randy Foye RC	2.50	6.00
❑ 108 Rudy Gay RC	2.50	6.00
❑ 109 Patrick O'Bryant RC	2.50	6.00
❑ 110 Saer Sene RC	2.50	6.00
❑ 111 J.J. Redick RC	2.50	6.00
❑ 112 Hilton Armstrong RC	2.50	6.00
❑ 113 Thabo Sefolosha RC	3.00	8.00
❑ 114 Ronnie Brewer RC	3.00	8.00
❑ 115 Cedric Simmons RC	2.50	6.00
❑ 116 Rodney Carney RC	2.50	6.00
❑ 117 Shawne Williams RC	2.50	6.00
❑ 118 Quincy Douby RC	2.50	6.00
❑ 119 Renaldo Balkman RC	2.50	6.00
❑ 120 Rajon Rondo RC	10.00	25.00
❑ 121 Marcus Williams RC	3.00	8.00
❑ 122 Josh Boone RC	2.50	6.00
❑ 123 Kyle Lowry RC	2.50	6.00
❑ 124 Shannon Brown RC	2.50	6.00
❑ 125 Jordan Farmar RC	3.00	8.00
❑ 126 Sergio Rodriguez RC	2.50	6.00
❑ 127 Maurice Ager RC	2.50	6.00
❑ 128 Mardy Collins RC	2.50	6.00
❑ 129 James White RC	2.50	6.00
❑ 130 Steve Novak RC	2.50	6.00
❑ 131 Solomon Jones RC	2.50	6.00
❑ 132 Paul Davis RC	2.50	6.00
❑ 133 P.J. Tucker RC	2.50	6.00
❑ 134 Craig Smith RC	2.50	6.00
❑ 135 Bobby Jones RC	2.50	6.00
❑ 136 David Noel RC	2.50	6.00
❑ 137 James Augustine RC	2.50	6.00
❑ 138 Daniel Gibson RC	3.00	8.00
❑ 139 Marcus Vinicius RC	2.50	6.00
❑ 140 Dee Brown RC	2.50	6.00
❑ 141 Ryan Hollins RC	2.50	6.00
❑ 142 Hassan Adams RC	3.00	8.00

2009-10 SP Signature Edition

❑ 1 Al Harrington	.75	2.00
❑ 2 Al Horford	1.00	2.50
❑ 3 Al Jefferson	1.00	2.50
❑ 4 Al Thornton	1.00	2.50
❑ 5 Allen Iverson	1.25	3.00
❑ 6 Andre Iguodala	1.00	2.50
❑ 7 Andre Miller	.75	2.00
❑ 8 Andrea Bargnani	.75	2.00
❑ 9 Antawn Jamison	1.00	2.50
❑ 10 Baron Davis	1.00	2.50
❑ 11 Ben Gordon	1.00	2.50
❑ 12 Ben Wallace	1.00	2.50
❑ 13 Beno Udrih	.60	1.50
❑ 14 Brad Miller	1.00	2.50
❑ 15 Brandon Roy	1.25	3.00
❑ 16 Carlos Boozer	1.00	2.50
❑ 17 Carmelo Anthony	1.25	3.00
❑ 18 Chauncey Billups	1.00	2.50
❑ 19 Chris Bosh	1.00	2.50
❑ 20 Chris Duhon	.60	1.50
❑ 21 Chris Paul	2.00	5.00
❑ 22 Courtney Lee	.75	2.00
❑ 23 D.J. Augustin	.75	2.00
❑ 24 Danny Granger	1.00	2.50
❑ 25 David Lee	.75	2.00
❑ 26 David West	1.00	2.50
❑ 27 Derek Fisher	.75	2.00
❑ 28 Deron Williams	1.25	3.00
❑ 29 Derrick Rose	2.00	5.00
❑ 30 DeShawn Stevenson	.60	1.50
❑ 31 Devin Harris	1.00	2.50
❑ 32 Dirk Nowitzki	1.25	3.00
❑ 33 Dwight Howard	2.00	5.00
❑ 34 Dwyane Wade	2.00	5.00
❑ 35 Elton Brand	1.00	2.50
❑ 36 Eric Gordon	1.00	2.50
❑ 37 Gilbert Arenas	1.00	2.50
❑ 38 Hedo Turkoglu	1.00	2.50
❑ 39 Jamal Crawford	.60	1.50
❑ 40 Jason Kidd	1.00	2.50
❑ 41 Jason Richardson	1.00	2.50
❑ 42 Jeff Green	.75	2.00
❑ 43 Jermaine O'Neal	1.00	2.50
❑ 44 Jerryd Bayless	.75	2.00
❑ 45 Joe Johnson	1.00	2.50
❑ 46 Jose Calderon	.75	2.00
❑ 47 Josh Howard	1.00	2.50
❑ 48 Josh Smith	1.00	2.50
❑ 49 Kenyon Martin	1.00	2.50
❑ 50 Kevin Durant	2.50	6.00
❑ 51 Kevin Garnett	2.00	5.00
❑ 52 Kevin Love	.75	2.00
❑ 53 Kevin Martin	1.00	2.50
❑ 54 Kobe Bryant	5.00	12.00
❑ 55 Lamar Odom	1.00	2.50
❑ 56 LaMarcus Aldridge	1.00	2.50
❑ 57 LeBron James	5.00	12.00
❑ 58 Luis Scola	.60	1.50
❑ 59 Luke Ridnour	.60	1.50
❑ 60 Luol Deng	1.00	2.50
❑ 61 Manu Ginobili	1.00	2.50
❑ 62 Marc Gasol	1.00	2.50
❑ 63 Mario Chalmers	1.00	2.50
❑ 64 Michael Beasley	1.25	3.00
❑ 65 Michael Redd	1.00	2.50
❑ 66 Mike Bibby	.60	1.50
❑ 67 Mike Dunleavy	.60	1.50
❑ 68 Mo Williams	.75	2.00
❑ 69 Monta Ellis	1.00	2.50
❑ 70 O.J. Mayo	1.25	3.00
❑ 71 Pau Gasol	1.00	2.50
❑ 72 Paul Pierce	1.25	3.00
❑ 73 Peja Stojakovic	.60	1.50
❑ 74 Quentin Richardson	.60	1.50
❑ 75 Raja Bell	.75	2.00
❑ 76 Ray Allen	1.00	2.50
❑ 77 Raymond Felton	.75	2.00
❑ 78 Richard Hamilton	.75	2.00
❑ 79 Richard Jefferson	1.00	2.50
❑ 80 Rodney Stuckey	1.00	2.50
❑ 81 Ron Artest	1.00	2.50
❑ 82 Ronnie Brewer	.60	1.50
❑ 83 Rudy Fernandez	1.00	2.50
❑ 84 Rudy Gay	1.00	2.50
❑ 85 Russell Westbrook	1.00	2.50
❑ 86 Sebastian Telfair	.60	1.50
❑ 87 Shaquille O'Neal	2.00	5.00
❑ 88 Shawn Marion	1.00	2.50
❑ 89 Stephen Jackson	.75	2.00
❑ 90 Steve Nash	1.00	2.50
❑ 91 T.J. Ford	.60	1.50
❑ 92 Tayshaun Prince	1.00	2.50
❑ 93 Thaddeus Young	.60	1.50
❑ 94 Tim Duncan	1.50	4.00
❑ 95 Tony Parker	1.00	2.50
❑ 96 Tracy McGrady	1.25	3.00
❑ 97 Tyson Chandler	.75	2.00
❑ 98 Vince Carter	1.25	3.00
❑ 99 Yao Ming	1.25	3.00
❑ 100 Yi Jianlian	1.00	2.50

1996 SPx

❑ COMPLETE SET (50)	30.00	60.00
❑ 1 Stacey Augmon	.40	1.00
❑ 2 Mookie Blaylock	.40	1.00
❑ 3 Eric Montross	.40	1.00
❑ 4 Eric Williams	.40	1.00
❑ 5 Larry Johnson	.75	2.00
❑ 6 George Zidek	.40	1.00
❑ 7 Jason Caffey	.40	1.00
❑ 8 Michael Jordan	10.00	20.00
❑ 9 Chris Mills	.40	1.00
❑ 10 Bob Sura	.40	1.00
❑ 11 Jason Kidd	2.00	5.00
❑ 12 Jamal Mashburn	.75	2.00
❑ 13 Antonio McDyess	1.25	3.00
❑ 14 Jalen Rose	1.25	3.00
❑ 15 Grant Hill	1.25	3.00
❑ 16 Theo Ratliff	.75	2.00
❑ 17 Joe Smith	.75	2.00

❑ 18 Latrell Sprewell	1.25	3.00
❑ 19 Hakeem Olajuwon	1.25	3.00
❑ 20 Reggie Miller	1.25	3.00
❑ 21 Rik Smits	.75	2.00
❑ 22 Brent Barry	.40	1.00
❑ 23 Lamond Murray	.40	1.00
❑ 24 Magic Johnson	2.00	5.00
❑ 25 Eddie Jones	1.25	3.00
❑ 26 Nick Van Exel	1.25	3.00
❑ 27 Alonzo Mourning	.75	2.00
❑ 28 Kurt Thomas	.75	2.00
❑ 29 Vin Baker	.75	2.00
❑ 30 Glenn Robinson	1.25	3.00
❑ 31 Kevin Garnett	2.50	6.00
❑ 32 Ed O'Bannon	.40	1.00
❑ 33 Patrick Ewing	1.25	3.00
❑ 34 Anfernee Hardaway	1.25	3.00
❑ 35 Shaquille O'Neal	3.00	8.00
❑ 36 Jerry Stackhouse	1.50	4.00
❑ 37 Charles Barkley	1.50	4.00
❑ 38 Michael Finley	1.50	4.00
❑ 39 Randolph Childress	.40	1.00
❑ 40 Gary Trent	.40	1.00
❑ 41 Brian Grant	1.25	3.00
❑ 42 Mitch Richmond	.75	2.00
❑ 43 David Robinson	1.25	3.00
❑ 44 Shawn Kemp	.75	2.00
❑ 45 Gary Payton	1.25	3.00
❑ 46 Damon Stoudamire	1.25	3.00
❑ 47 Karl Malone	1.25	3.00
❑ 48 John Stockton	1.25	3.00
❑ 49 Bryant Reeves	.40	1.00
❑ 50 Rasheed Wallace	1.50	4.00
❑ R1 Michael Jordan RB	5.00	12.00
❑ T1 Anfernee Hardaway TRIB	1.25	3.00
❑ NNO Anfernee Hardaway AU	40.00	80.00
❑ NNO A.Hardaway Expired	15.00	30.00
❑ NNO Michael Jordan AU	800.00	1400.00
❑ NNO M.Jordan Expired	750.00	1000.00

1997 SPx

❑ COMPLETE SET (50)	50.00	100.00
❑ 1 Mookie Blaylock	.40	1.00
❑ 2 Antoine Walker	1.50	4.00
❑ 3 Eric Williams	.40	1.00
❑ 4 Tony Delk	.40	1.00
❑ 5 Michael Jordan	8.00	20.00
❑ 6 Dennis Rodman	.75	2.00
❑ 7 Vitaly Potapenko	.40	1.00
❑ 8 Bob Sura	.40	1.00
❑ 9 Jamal Mashburn	.75	2.00
❑ 10 Samaki Walker	.40	1.00
❑ 11 Antonio McDyess	.75	2.00
❑ 12 Joe Dumars	1.25	3.00
❑ 13 Grant Hill	1.25	3.00
❑ 14 Joe Smith	.75	2.00
❑ 15 Latrell Sprewell	1.25	3.00
❑ 16 Charles Barkley	1.50	4.00
❑ 17 Hakeem Olajuwon	1.25	3.00
❑ 18 Erick Dampier	.75	2.00
❑ 19 Reggie Miller	1.25	3.00
❑ 20 Brent Barry	.75	2.00
❑ 21 Lorenzen Wright	.40	1.00
❑ 22 Kobe Bryant	8.00	20.00
❑ 23 Eddie Jones	1.25	3.00
❑ 24 Shaquille O'Neal	3.00	8.00
❑ 25 Alonzo Mourning	.75	2.00
❑ 26 Kurt Thomas	.75	2.00
❑ 27 Vin Baker	.75	2.00
❑ 28 Glenn Robinson	1.25	3.00
❑ 29 Kevin Garnett	2.50	6.00
❑ 30 Stephon Marbury	1.50	4.00
❑ 31 Kerry Kittles	1.25	3.00
❑ 32 Patrick Ewing	1.25	3.00
❑ 33 Larry Johnson	.75	2.00
❑ 34 Anfernee Hardaway	1.25	3.00
❑ 35 Allen Iverson	4.00	10.00
❑ 36 Jerry Stackhouse	1.25	3.00
❑ 37 Kevin Johnson	.75	2.00
❑ 38 Steve Nash	1.25	3.00
❑ 39 Jermaine O'Neal	1.50	4.00
❑ 40 Mitch Richmond	.75	2.00
❑ 41 David Robinson	1.25	3.00
❑ 42 Shawn Kemp	.75	2.00
❑ 43 Gary Payton	1.25	3.00
❑ 44 Marcus Camby	1.25	3.00
❑ 45 Damon Stoudamire	.75	2.00
❑ 46 Karl Malone	1.25	3.00
❑ 47 John Stockton	1.25	3.00
❑ 48 Shareef Abdur-Rahim	2.00	5.00
❑ 49 Bryant Reeves	.40	1.00
❑ 50 Juwan Howard	.75	2.00
❑ SPX5 Michael Jordan Promo	6.00	15.00

1997-98 SPx

❑ COMPLETE SET (50)	40.00	75.00
❑ 1 Mookie Blaylock	.25	.60
❑ 2 Dikembe Mutombo	.60	1.50
❑ 3 Chauncey Billups RC	3.00	8.00
❑ 4 Antoine Walker	1.00	2.50
❑ 5 Glen Rice	.60	1.50
❑ 6 Michael Jordan	6.00	12.00
❑ 7 Scottie Pippen	1.25	3.00
❑ 8 Dennis Rodman	.60	1.50
❑ 9 Shawn Kemp	.60	1.50
❑ 10 Michael Finley	.75	2.00
❑ 11 Tony Battie RC	.75	2.00
❑ 12 LaPhonso Ellis	.25	.60
❑ 13 Grant Hill	.75	2.00
❑ 14 Joe Dumars	.75	2.00
❑ 15 Joe Smith	.60	1.50
❑ 16 Clyde Drexler	.75	2.00
❑ 17 Charles Barkley	1.00	2.50
❑ 18 Hakeem Olajuwon	.75	2.00
❑ 19 Reggie Miller	.75	2.00
❑ 20 Brent Barry	.60	1.50
❑ 21 Kobe Bryant	3.00	8.00
❑ 22 Shaquille O'Neal	2.00	5.00
❑ 23 Alonzo Mourning	.60	1.50
❑ 24 Glenn Robinson	.75	2.00
❑ 25 Kevin Garnett	1.50	4.00
❑ 26 Stephon Marbury	1.00	2.50
❑ 27 Keith Van Horn RC	1.25	3.00
❑ 28 Patrick Ewing	.75	2.00
❑ 29 Anfernee Hardaway	.75	2.00
❑ 30 Allen Iverson	2.00	5.00
❑ 31 Kevin Johnson	.60	1.50
❑ 32 Antonio McDyess	.60	1.50
❑ 33 Jason Kidd	1.25	3.00
❑ 34 Kenny Anderson	.60	1.50
❑ 35 Rasheed Wallace	.75	2.00
❑ 36 Mitch Richmond	.60	1.50
❑ 37 Tim Duncan RC	4.00	10.00
❑ 38 David Robinson	.75	2.00
❑ 39 Vin Baker	.60	1.50
❑ 40 Gary Payton	.75	2.00
❑ 41 Marcus Camby	.75	2.00
❑ 42 Tracy McGrady RC	4.00	10.00
❑ 43 Damon Stoudamire	.60	1.50
❑ 44 Karl Malone	.75	2.00
❑ 45 John Stockton	.75	2.00
❑ 46 Shareef Abdur-Rahim	1.25	3.00
❑ 47 Antonio Daniels RC	.75	2.00
❑ 48 Bryant Reeves	.25	.60
❑ 49 Juwan Howard	.60	1.50
❑ 50 Chris Webber	.75	2.00
❑ T1 Piece of History Trade	125.00	200.00

1998-99 SPx Finite

❑ COMPLETE SET w/o RC (90)	60.00	100.00
❑ COMP.ST.POWER SET (60)	75.00	125.00
❑ COMMON ST.POWER (91-150)	.50	1.25

❑ COMP.SPx 2000 SET (30)	75.00	125.00
❑ COMMON SPx 2000 (151-180)	.75	2.00
❑ COMP.TP.FLIGHT SET (20)	60.00	100.00
❑ COMMON TP.FLIGHT (181-200)	1.00	2.50
❑ COMP.FIN.EXC.SET (10)	75.00	125.00
❑ COMMON FIN.EXC. (201-210)	1.50	4.00
❑ COMP.ROOKIE SET (28)	150.00	300.00
❑ COMMON ROOKIE (211-240)	2.00	5.00
❑ 1 Michael Jordan	7.50	15.00
❑ 2 Hakeem Olajuwon	1.00	2.50
❑ 3 Keith Van Horn	1.00	2.50
❑ 4 Rasheed Wallace	1.00	2.50
❑ 5 Mookie Blaylock	.30	.75
❑ 6 Bobby Jackson	.60	1.50
❑ 7 Detlef Schrempf	.60	1.50
❑ 8 Antonio McDyess	.60	1.50
❑ 9 Lamond Murray	.30	.75
❑ 10 Chris Mullin	1.00	2.50
❑ 11 Zydrunas Ilgauskas	.60	1.50
❑ 12 Tracy Murray	.30	.75
❑ 13 Jerry Stackhouse	1.00	2.50
❑ 14 Avery Johnson	.30	.75
❑ 15 Larry Johnson	.60	1.50
❑ 16 Alan Henderson	.30	.75
❑ 17 David Wesley	.30	.75
❑ 18 Kevin Willis	.30	.75
❑ 19 Eddie Jones	1.00	2.50
❑ 20 Horace Grant	.60	1.50
❑ 21 Ray Allen	1.00	2.50
❑ 22 Derrick Coleman	.30	.75
❑ 23 Derek Anderson	.75	2.00
❑ 24 Tim Hardaway	.60	1.50
❑ 25 Danny Fortson	.30	.75
❑ 26 Tariq Abdul-Wahad	.30	.75
❑ 27 Charles Barkley	1.25	3.00
❑ 28 Sam Cassell	1.00	2.50
❑ 29 Kevin Garnett	2.00	5.00
❑ 30 Jeff Hornacek	.60	1.50
❑ 31 Isaac Austin	.30	.75
❑ 32 Allan Houston	1.00	2.50
❑ 33 David Robinson	1.00	2.50
❑ 34 Tracy McGrady	2.50	6.00
❑ 35 LaPhonso Ellis	.30	.75
❑ 36 Shawn Kemp	.60	1.50
❑ 37 Glenn Robinson	.60	1.50
❑ 38 Shareef Abdur-Rahim	1.00	2.50
❑ 39 Vin Baker	.60	1.50
❑ 40 Rik Smits	.60	1.50
❑ 41 Jason Kidd	1.50	4.00
❑ 42 Erick Dampier	.60	1.50
❑ 43 Shawn Bradley	.30	.75
❑ 44 Anfernee Hardaway	1.00	2.50
❑ 45 John Stockton	1.00	2.50
❑ 46 Calbert Cheaney	.30	.75
❑ 47 Terrell Brandon	.60	1.50
❑ 48 Hubert Davis	.30	.75
❑ 49 Patrick Ewing	1.00	2.50
❑ 50 Kobe Bryant	4.00	10.00
❑ 51 Gary Payton	1.00	2.50
❑ 52 Marcus Camby	.60	1.50
❑ 53 Bryant Reeves	.30	.75
❑ 54 Reggie Miller	1.00	2.50
❑ 55 Antoine Walker	1.00	2.50
❑ 56 Scottie Pippen	1.50	4.00
❑ 57 Hersey Hawkins	.30	.75
❑ 58 John Starks	.60	1.50
❑ 59 Dikembe Mutombo	.60	1.50
❑ 60 Damon Stoudamire	.60	1.50
❑ 61 Rodney Rogers	.30	.75
❑ 62 Nick Anderson	.30	.75
❑ 63 Brian Williams	.30	.75
❑ 64 Ron Mercer	.50	1.25
❑ 65 Donyell Marshall	.60	1.50
❑ 66 Glen Rice	.60	1.50
❑ 67 Michael Finley	1.00	2.50

❑ 68 Tim Duncan	1.50	4.00
❑ 69 Stephon Marbury	1.00	2.50
❑ 70 Antonio Daniels	.30	.75
❑ 71 Chauncey Billups	.60	1.50
❑ 72 Kerry Kittles	.30	.75
❑ 73 Brian Grant	.60	1.50
❑ 74 Anthony Mason	.60	1.50
❑ 75 Allen Iverson	2.00	5.00
❑ 76 Juwan Howard	.60	1.50
❑ 77 Grant Hill	1.00	2.50
❑ 78 Tony Delk	.30	.75
❑ 79 Olden Polynice	.30	.75
❑ 80 Alonzo Mourning	.60	1.50
❑ 81 Karl Malone	1.00	2.50
❑ 82 Isaiah Rider	.30	.75
❑ 83 Shaquille O'Neal	2.50	6.00
❑ 84 Steve Smith	.60	1.50
❑ 85 Kenny Anderson	.60	1.50
❑ 86 Toni Kukoc	.60	1.50
❑ 87 Anthony Peeler	.30	.75
❑ 88 Tim Thomas	.60	1.50
❑ 89 Nick Van Exel	1.00	2.50
❑ 90 Jamal Mashburn	.60	1.50
❑ 91 Reggie Miller SP	1.50	4.00
❑ 92 Juwan Howard SP	1.00	2.50
❑ 93 Glen Rice SP	1.00	2.50
❑ 94 Grant Hill SP	1.50	4.00
❑ 95 Maurice Taylor SP	.75	2.00
❑ 96 Vin Baker SP	1.00	2.50
❑ 97 Tim Thomas SP	1.00	2.50
❑ 98 Bobby Jackson SP	.50	1.25
❑ 99 Damon Stoudamire SP	1.00	2.50
❑ 100 Michael Jordan SP	12.50	30.00
❑ 101 Eddie Jones SP	1.50	4.00
❑ 102 Keith Van Horn SP	1.50	4.00
❑ 103 Dikembe Mutombo SP	1.00	2.50
❑ 104 Brevin Knight SP	.50	1.25
❑ 105 Shawn Bradley SP	.50	1.25
❑ 106 Lamond Murray SP	.50	1.25
❑ 107 Tim Duncan SP	2.50	6.00
❑ 108 Bryant Reeves SP	.50	1.25
❑ 109 Antoine Walker SP	1.50	4.00
❑ 110 John Stockton SP	1.50	4.00
❑ 111 Nick Anderson SP	.50	1.25
❑ 112 Chris Mullin SP	1.50	4.00
❑ 113 Glenn Robinson SP	1.00	2.50
❑ 114 Kevin Garnett SP	3.00	8.00
❑ 115 Michael Stewart SP	.50	1.25
❑ 116 Antonio McDyess SP	1.00	2.50
❑ 117 Jim Jackson SP	.50	1.25
❑ 118 Chauncey Billups SP	.50	1.25
❑ 119 Sam Cassell SP	1.50	4.00
❑ 120 Dennis Rodman SP	1.00	2.50
❑ 121 Rasheed Wallace SP	1.50	4.00
❑ 122 Brian Williams SP	.50	1.25
❑ 123 Anfernee Hardaway SP	1.50	4.00
❑ 124 Scottie Pippen SP	2.50	6.00
❑ 125 Terrell Brandon SP	1.00	2.50
❑ 126 Michael Finley SP	1.50	4.00
❑ 127 Kerry Kittles SP	.50	1.25
❑ 128 Toni Kukoc SP	1.00	2.50
❑ 129 Hakeem Olajuwon SP	1.50	4.00
❑ 130 Tim Hardaway SP	1.00	2.50
❑ 131 Shareef Abdur-Rahim SP	1.50	4.00
❑ 132 Donyell Marshall SP	.50	1.25
❑ 133 David Robinson SP	1.50	4.00
❑ 134 LaPhonso Ellis SP	.50	1.25
❑ 135 Ray Allen SP	1.50	4.00
❑ 136 Nick Van Exel SP	1.50	4.00
❑ 137 Patrick Ewing SP	1.50	4.00
❑ 138 Anthony Mason SP	1.00	2.50
❑ 139 Shaquille O'Neal SP	4.00	10.00
❑ 140 Shawn Kemp SP	1.00	2.50
❑ 141 Stephon Marbury SP	1.50	4.00
❑ 142 Karl Malone SP	1.50	4.00
❑ 143 Allen Iverson SP	3.00	8.00
❑ 144 Kenny Anderson SP	1.00	2.50
❑ 145 Marcus Camby SP	1.50	4.00
❑ 146 Steve Smith SP	1.00	2.50
❑ 147 Gary Payton SP	1.50	4.00
❑ 148 Jason Kidd SP	2.50	6.00
❑ 149 Alonzo Mourning SP	1.50	4.00
❑ 150 Charles Barkley SP	2.00	5.00
❑ 151 Kobe Bryant SPx	10.00	25.00
❑ 152 Ron Mercer SPx	2.00	5.00
❑ 153 Maurice Taylor SPx	1.25	3.00
❑ 154 Tim Duncan SPx	2.50	6.00
❑ 155 Shareef Abdur-Rahim SPx	2.50	6.00
❑ 156 Eddie Jones SPx	2.50	6.00
❑ 157 Chauncey Billups SPx	.75	2.00
❑ 158 Derek Anderson SPx	2.00	5.00
❑ 159 Bobby Jackson SPx	.75	2.00
❑ 160 Stephon Marbury SPx	2.50	6.00
❑ 161 Anfernee Hardaway SPx	2.50	6.00
❑ 162 Zydrunas Ilgauskas SPx	1.50	4.00
❑ 163 Allen Iverson SPx	5.00	12.00
❑ 164 Antoine Walker SPx	2.50	6.00
❑ 165 Tracy McGrady SPx	6.00	15.00
❑ 166 Rasheed Wallace SPx	2.50	6.00
❑ 167 Jason Kidd SPx	4.00	10.00
❑ 168 Kevin Garnett SPx	5.00	12.00
❑ 169 Damon Stoudamire SPx	1.50	4.00
❑ 170 Brevin Knight SPx	.75	2.00
❑ 171 Tim Thomas SPx	1.50	4.00
❑ 172 Danny Fortson SPx	.75	2.00
❑ 173 Jermaine O'Neal SPx	2.50	6.00
❑ 174 Keith Van Horn SPx	2.50	6.00
❑ 175 Ray Allen SPx	2.50	6.00
❑ 176 Kerry Kittles SPx	.75	2.00
❑ 177 Vin Baker SPx	1.50	4.00
❑ 178 Allan Houston SPx	2.50	6.00
❑ 179 Alan Henderson SPx	.75	2.00
❑ 180 Bryon Russell SPx	.75	2.00
❑ 181 Michael Jordan TF	20.00	50.00
❑ 182 Maurice Taylor TF	1.50	4.00
❑ 183 Isaiah Rider TF	1.00	2.50
❑ 184 Antonio McDyess TF	2.00	5.00
❑ 185 Anfernee Hardaway TF	3.00	8.00
❑ 186 Glenn Robinson TF	2.00	5.00
❑ 187 Dikembe Mutombo TF	2.00	5.00
❑ 188 Shawn Kemp TF	2.00	5.00
❑ 189 Tracy McGrady TF	8.00	20.00
❑ 190 Reggie Miller TF	3.00	8.00
❑ 191 Derek Anderson TF	2.50	6.00
❑ 192 Allan Houston TF	3.00	8.00
❑ 193 Michael Finley TF	3.00	8.00
❑ 194 Nick Van Exel TF	3.00	8.00
❑ 195 Juwan Howard TF	2.00	5.00
❑ 196 LaPhonso Ellis TF	1.00	2.50
❑ 197 Ron Mercer TF	1.50	4.00
❑ 198 Glen Rice TF	2.00	5.00
❑ 199 Joe Smith TF	2.00	5.00
❑ 200 Kobe Bryant TF	12.50	30.00
❑ 201 Michael Jordan FE	40.00	80.00
❑ 202 Karl Malone FE	1.50	4.00
❑ 203 Hakeem Olajuwon FE	5.00	12.00
❑ 204 David Robinson FE	5.00	12.00
❑ 205 Shaquille O'Neal FE	12.50	30.00
❑ 206 John Stockton FE	5.00	12.00
❑ 207 Grant Hill FE	5.00	12.00
❑ 208 Tim Hardaway FE	3.00	8.00
❑ 209 Scottie Pippen FE	8.00	20.00
❑ 210 Gary Payton FE	5.00	12.00
❑ 211 Michael Olowokandi RC	2.00	5.00
❑ 212 Mike Bibby RC	4.00	10.00
❑ 213 Raef LaFrentz RC	2.50	6.00
❑ 214 Antawn Jamison RC	6.00	15.00
❑ 215 Vince Carter RC	20.00	40.00
❑ 216 Robert Traylor RC	2.00	5.00
❑ 217 Jason Williams RC	5.00	12.00
❑ 218 Larry Hughes RC	4.00	10.00
❑ 219 Dirk Nowitzki RC	10.00	25.00
❑ 220 Paul Pierce RC	10.00	25.00
❑ 221 Bonzi Wells RC	5.00	12.00
❑ 222 Michael Doleac RC	2.00	5.00
❑ 223 Keon Clark RC	2.50	6.00
❑ 224 Michael Dickerson RC	4.00	10.00
❑ 225 Matt Harpring RC	2.50	6.00
❑ 226 Bryce Drew RC	2.00	5.00
❑ 227 Does not exist		
❑ 228 Does not exist		
❑ 229 Pat Garrity RC	2.00	5.00
❑ 230 Roshown McLeod RC	2.00	5.00
❑ 231 Ricky Davis RC	3.00	8.00
❑ 232 Brian Skinner RC	2.00	5.00
❑ 233 Tyronn Lue RC	2.50	6.00
❑ 234 Felipe Lopez RC	2.00	5.00
❑ 235 Al Harrington RC	4.00	10.00
❑ 236 Ruben Patterson RC	2.50	6.00
❑ 237 Jelani McCoy RC	2.00	5.00
❑ 238 Corey Benjamin RC	2.00	5.00
❑ 239 Nazr Mohammed RC	2.00	5.00
❑ 240 Rashard Lewis RC	6.00	15.00

1999-00 SPx

❑ COMPLETE SET w/o RC (90)	18.00	30.00
❑ COMMON CARD (1-90)	.15	.40
❑ COMMON ROOKIE (91-120)	2.50	6.00
❑ 1 Dikembe Mutombo	.40	1.00

❑ 2 Alan Henderson	.30	.75
❑ 3 Antoine Walker	.50	1.25
❑ 4 Paul Pierce	.50	1.25
❑ 5 Kenny Anderson	.40	1.00
❑ 6 Eddie Jones	.50	1.25
❑ 7 David Wesley	.30	.75
❑ 8 Elden Campbell	.30	.75
❑ 9 Toni Kukoc	.50	1.25
❑ 10 Dickey Simpkins	.30	.75
❑ 11 Shawn Kemp	.50	1.25
❑ 12 Brevin Knight	.30	.75
❑ 13 Michael Finley	.50	1.25
❑ 14 Cedric Ceballos	.30	.75
❑ 15 Dirk Nowitzki	.75	2.00
❑ 16 Antonio McDyess	.40	1.00
❑ 17 Nick Van Exel	.40	1.00
❑ 18 Chauncey Billups	.50	1.25
❑ 19 Grant Hill	.50	1.25
❑ 20 Jerry Stackhouse	.50	1.25
❑ 21 Bison Dele	.30	.75
❑ 22 Lindsey Hunter	.30	.75
❑ 23 Antawn Jamison	.50	1.25
❑ 24 Donyell Marshall	.40	1.00
❑ 25 John Starks	.50	1.25
❑ 26 Chris Mills	.30	.75
❑ 27 Hakeem Olajuwon	.50	1.25
❑ 28 Scottie Pippen	.75	2.00
❑ 29 Charles Barkley	.60	1.50
❑ 30 Reggie Miller	.50	1.25
❑ 31 Rik Smits	.50	1.25
❑ 32 Jalen Rose	.40	1.00
❑ 33 Chris Mullin	.50	1.25
❑ 34 Maurice Taylor	.40	1.00
❑ 35 Michael Olowokandi	.30	.75
❑ 36 Shaquille O'Neal	1.25	3.00
❑ 37 Kobe Bryant	2.50	6.00
❑ 38 Glen Rice	.50	1.25
❑ 39 Tim Hardaway	.50	1.25
❑ 40 Alonzo Mourning	.50	1.25
❑ 41 Dan Majerle	.50	1.25
❑ 42 P.J. Brown	.30	.75
❑ 43 Glenn Robinson	.40	1.00
❑ 44 Ray Allen	.50	1.25
❑ 45 Sam Cassell	.40	1.00
❑ 46 Tim Thomas	.40	1.00
❑ 47 Kevin Garnett	1.00	2.50
❑ 48 Bobby Jackson	.40	1.00
❑ 49 Joe Smith	.40	1.00
❑ 50 Stephon Marbury	.50	1.25
❑ 51 Keith Van Horn	.40	1.00
❑ 52 Jayson Williams	.40	1.00
❑ 53 Patrick Ewing	.60	1.50
❑ 54 Latrell Sprewell	.40	1.00
❑ 55 Allan Houston	.40	1.00
❑ 56 Marcus Camby	.40	1.00
❑ 57 Bo Outlaw	.30	.75
❑ 58 Darrell Armstrong	.30	.75
❑ 59 Allen Iverson	1.00	2.50
❑ 60 Theo Ratliff	.40	1.00
❑ 61 Larry Hughes	.40	1.00
❑ 62 Jason Kidd	.75	2.00
❑ 63 Tom Gugliotta	.30	.75
❑ 64 Clifford Robinson	.30	.75
❑ 65 Brian Grant	.30	.75
❑ 66 Jermaine O'Neal	.50	1.25
❑ 67 Rasheed Wallace	.50	1.25
❑ 68 Damon Stoudamire	.50	1.25
❑ 69 Jason Williams	.50	1.25
❑ 70 Chris Webber	.50	1.25
❑ 71 Vlade Divac	.50	1.25
❑ 72 Avery Johnson	.40	1.00
❑ 73 Tim Duncan	1.00	2.50
❑ 74 David Robinson	.60	1.50
❑ 75 Sean Elliott	.50	1.25
❑ 76 Gary Payton	.50	1.25

❑ 77 Vin Baker	.50	1.25
❑ 78 Jelani McCoy	.30	.75
❑ 79 Charles Oakley	.40	1.00
❑ 80 Vince Carter	1.00	2.50
❑ 81 Tracy McGrady	1.00	2.50
❑ 82 Doug Christie	.40	1.00
❑ 83 Karl Malone	.60	1.50
❑ 84 John Stockton	.60	1.50
❑ 85 Shareef Abdur-Rahim	.40	1.00
❑ 86 Bryant Reeves	.30	.75
❑ 87 Mike Bibby	.50	1.25
❑ 88 Juwan Howard	.40	1.00
❑ 89 Mitch Richmond	.40	1.00
❑ 90 Rod Strickland	.30	.75
❑ 91 Elton Brand RC	8.00	20.00
❑ 92 Steve Francis AU/500 RC	15.00	30.00
❑ 93 Baron Davis AU/500 RC	30.00	60.00
❑ 94 Lamar Odom RC	8.00	20.00
❑ 95 Jonathan Bender RC	2.50	6.00
❑ 96 W.Szczerbiak AU/500 RC	10.00	25.00
❑ 97 Richard Hamilton AU RC	10.00	25.00
❑ 98 Andre Miller AU/500 RC	15.00	30.00
❑ 99 Shawn Marion AU RC	8.00	20.00
❑ 100 Jason Terry AU RC	5.00	12.00
❑ 101 Trajan Langdon AU RC	2.50	6.00
❑ 102 Venson Hamilton RC	2.50	6.00
❑ 103 C.Maggette AU/500 RC	10.00	25.00
❑ 104 William Avery AU RC	2.50	6.00
❑ 105 Dion Glover RC	2.50	6.00
❑ 106 Ron Artest AU RC	15.00	30.00
❑ 107 Cal Bowdler RC	1.25	3.00
❑ 108 James Posey AU RC	4.00	10.00
❑ 109 Quincy Lewis AU RC	2.50	6.00
❑ 110 Devean George AU RC	5.00	12.00
❑ 111 Tim James AU RC	2.50	6.00
❑ 112 Vonteego Cummings RC	2.50	6.00
❑ 113 Jumaine Jones AU RC	3.00	8.00
❑ 114 Scott Padgett AU RC	2.50	6.00
❑ 115 Kenny Thomas RC	2.50	6.00
❑ 116 Jeff Foster RC	3.00	8.00
❑ 117 Ryan Robertson RC	2.50	6.00
❑ 118 Chris Herren AU RC	2.50	6.00
❑ 119 Evan Eschmeyer AU RC	2.50	6.00
❑ 120 A.J. Bramlett AU RC	2.50	6.00
❑ P32 Karl Malone	.50	1.25

2000-01 SPx

❑ COMPLETE SET w/o RC (90)	20.00	40.00
❑ COMMON CARD (1-90)	.15	.40
❑ COMM.RC (91/93-98/138)	1.00	2.50
❑ COMMON RC (99-104)	1.50	4.00
❑ COMMON RC (105-110)	2.50	6.00
❑ COMM.RC (92/111-130/136-137)	3.00	8.00
❑ COMMON RC (131-135)	4.00	10.00
❑ 1 Dikembe Mutombo	.40	1.00
❑ 2 Jim Jackson	.30	.75
❑ 3 Jason Terry	.50	1.25
❑ 4 Paul Pierce	.50	1.25
❑ 5 Kenny Anderson	.40	1.00
❑ 6 Antoine Walker	.40	1.00
❑ 7 Derrick Coleman	.40	1.00
❑ 8 Baron Davis	.50	1.25
❑ 9 David Wesley	.30	.75
❑ 10 Elton Brand	.50	1.25
❑ 11 Ron Artest	.50	1.25
❑ 12 Corey Benjamin	.30	.75
❑ 13 Trajan Langdon	.30	.75
❑ 14 Lamond Murray	.30	.75
❑ 15 Andre Miller	.40	1.00
❑ 16 Michael Finley	.50	1.25
❑ 17 Gary Trent	.30	.75
❑ 18 Dirk Nowitzki	.75	2.00
❑ 19 Antonio McDyess	.40	1.00
❑ 20 Nick Van Exel	.40	1.00
❑ 21 Raef LaFrentz	.30	.75
❑ 22 Jerry Stackhouse	.40	1.00
❑ 23 Michael Curry	.30	.75
❑ 24 Jerome Williams	.30	.75
❑ 25 Larry Hughes	.40	1.00
❑ 26 Antawn Jamison	.50	1.25
❑ 27 Mookie Blaylock	.40	1.00
❑ 28 Hakeem Olajuwon	.60	1.50
❑ 29 Steve Francis	.50	1.25
❑ 30 Shandon Anderson	.30	.75
❑ 31 Reggie Miller	.50	1.25
❑ 32 Jalen Rose	.40	1.00
❑ 33 Austin Croshere	.30	.75
❑ 34 Lamar Odom	.50	1.25
❑ 35 Michael Olowokandi	.30	.75
❑ 36 Tyrone Nesby	.30	.75
❑ 37 Shaquille O'Neal	1.25	3.00
❑ 38 Kobe Bryant	2.50	6.00
❑ 39 Robert Horry	.40	1.00
❑ 40 Ron Harper	.40	1.00
❑ 41 Alonzo Mourning	.50	1.25
❑ 42 Eddie Jones	.40	1.00
❑ 43 Tim Hardaway	.40	1.00
❑ 44 Glenn Robinson	.40	1.00
❑ 45 Sam Cassell	.40	1.00
❑ 46 Ray Allen	.50	1.25
❑ 47 Tim Thomas	.30	.75
❑ 48 Kevin Garnett	1.00	2.50
❑ 49 Terrell Brandon	.30	.75
❑ 50 Wally Szczerbiak	.40	1.00
❑ 51 Keith Van Horn	.40	1.00
❑ 52 Stephon Marbury	.50	1.25
❑ 53 Jamie Feick	.30	.75
❑ 54 Latrell Sprewell	.40	1.00
❑ 55 Marcus Camby	.40	1.00
❑ 56 Allan Houston	.40	1.00
❑ 57 Grant Hill	.50	1.25
❑ 58 Tracy McGrady	1.00	2.50
❑ 59 Darrell Armstrong	.30	.75
❑ 60 Allen Iverson	1.00	2.50
❑ 61 Toni Kukoc	.40	1.00
❑ 62 Theo Ratliff	.30	.75
❑ 63 Anfernee Hardaway	.50	1.25
❑ 64 Jason Kidd	.75	2.00
❑ 65 Shawn Marion	.50	1.25
❑ 66 Steve Smith	.40	1.00
❑ 67 Rasheed Wallace	.50	1.25
❑ 68 Scottie Pippen	.75	2.00
❑ 69 Bonzi Wells	.30	.75
❑ 70 Jason Williams	.40	1.00
❑ 71 Vlade Divac	.40	1.00
❑ 72 Chris Webber	.50	1.25
❑ 73 David Robinson	.60	1.50
❑ 74 Sean Elliott	.40	1.00
❑ 75 Tim Duncan	1.00	2.50
❑ 76 Gary Payton	.50	1.25
❑ 77 Rashard Lewis	.50	1.25
❑ 78 Vin Baker	.40	1.00
❑ 79 Vince Carter	1.00	2.50
❑ 80 Muggsy Bogues	.40	1.00
❑ 81 Antonio Davis	.30	.75
❑ 82 Karl Malone	.60	1.50
❑ 83 John Stockton	.60	1.50
❑ 84 Bryon Russell	.30	.75
❑ 85 Shareef Abdur-Rahim	.40	1.00
❑ 86 Michael Dickerson	.30	.75
❑ 87 Mike Bibby	.40	1.00
❑ 88 Mitch Richmond	.40	1.00
❑ 89 Richard Hamilton	.40	1.00
❑ 90 Juwan Howard	.40	1.00
❑ 91 Lavor Postell RC	1.00	2.50
❑ 92 Mark Madsen JSY AU RC	3.00	8.00
❑ 93 Soumaila Samake RC	1.00	2.50
❑ 94 Michael Redd RC	2.50	6.00
❑ 95 Paul McPherson RC	1.00	2.50
❑ 96 Ruben Wolkowyski RC	1.00	2.50
❑ 97 Daniel Santiago RC	2.50	6.00
❑ 98 Pepe Sanchez RC	1.00	2.50
❑ 99 Marc Jackson RC	2.00	5.00
❑ 100 Khalid El-Amin RC	1.50	4.00
❑ 101 Iakovos Tsakalidis RC	1.50	4.00
❑ 102 Jabari Smith RC	1.50	4.00
❑ 103 Jason Hart RC	1.50	4.00
❑ 104 Stephen Jackson RC	2.50	6.00
❑ 105 Eduardo Najera RC	2.50	6.00
❑ 106 Hanno Mottola RC	2.50	6.00
❑ 107 Eddie House RC	2.50	6.00
❑ 108 Dan Langhi RC	2.50	6.00
❑ 109 A.J. Guyton RC	2.50	6.00
❑ 110 Chris Porter RC	2.50	6.00
❑ 111 Mike Miller JSY AU RC	5.00	12.00
❑ 112 Keyon Dooling JSY AU RC	3.00	8.00
❑ 113 C.Alexander JSY AU RC	3.00	8.00
❑ 114 Desmond Mason JSY AU RC	4.00	10.00
❑ 115 Jamaal Magloire JSY AU RC	3.00	8.00
❑ 116 DeShawn Stevenson JSY AU RC	3.00	8.00
❑ 117 Dermarr Johnson JSY AU RC	3.00	8.00
❑ 118 Mateen Cleaves JSY AU RC	3.00	8.00
❑ 119 Morris Peterson JSY AU RC	5.00	12.00
❑ 120 Jerome Moiso JSY AU RC	3.00	8.00
❑ 121 Donnell Harvey JSY AU RC	3.00	8.00
❑ 122 Quentin Richardson JSY AU RC	4.00	10.00
❑ 123 Jamal Crawford JSY AU RC	5.00	12.00
❑ 124 Erick Barkley JSY AU RC	3.00	8.00
❑ 125 Hedo Turkoglu JSY AU RC	8.00	20.00
❑ 126 Etan Thomas JSY AU RC	3.00	8.00
❑ 127 Mamadou N'Diaye JSY AU RC	3.00	8.00
❑ 128 Joel Przybilla JSY AU RC	3.00	8.00
❑ 129 Jason Collier JSY AU RC	3.00	8.00
❑ 130 Speedy Claxton JSY AU RC	3.00	8.00
❑ 131 Kenyon Martin JSY AU RC	10.00	25.00
❑ 132 Stromile Swift JSY AU RC	5.00	12.00
❑ 133 Darius Miles JSY AU RC	20.00	40.00
❑ 134 Marcus Fizer JSY AU RC	4.00	10.00
❑ 135 Chris Mihm JSY AU RC	4.00	10.00
❑ 136 Jake Voskuhl JSY AU RC	3.00	8.00
❑ 137 Pete Mickeal JSY AU RC	3.00	8.00
❑ 138 Dalibor Bagaric RC	1.00	2.50

2001-02 SPx

❑ COMPLETE SET (173)	1250.00	3500.00
❑ COMP.SET w/o SP's (90)	30.00	60.00
❑ COMMON CARD (1-90)	.30	.75
❑ COMMON ROOKIE (91-105)	3.00	8.00
❑ COMMON ROOKIE (106-111)	4.00	10.00
❑ COMMON ROOKIE (121-140)	2.50	6.00
❑ 1 Jason Terry	.50	1.25
❑ 2 Shareef Abdur-Rahim	.40	1.00
❑ 3 DerMarr Johnson	.30	.75
❑ 4 Paul Pierce	.50	1.25
❑ 5 Antoine Walker	.40	1.00
❑ 6 Kenny Anderson	.40	1.00
❑ 7 Baron Davis	.50	1.25
❑ 8 Jamal Mashburn	.40	1.00
❑ 9 David Wesley	.30	.75
❑ 10 Ron Mercer	.30	.75
❑ 11 Ron Artest	.40	1.00
❑ 12 Marcus Fizer	.30	.75
❑ 13 Andre Miller	.40	1.00
❑ 14 Lamond Murray	.30	.75
❑ 15 Chris Mihm	.30	.75
❑ 16 Michael Finley	.50	1.25
❑ 17 Dirk Nowitzki	.75	2.00
❑ 18 Steve Nash	.75	2.00
❑ 19 Antonio McDyess	.40	1.00
❑ 20 Nick Van Exel	.40	1.00
❑ 21 Raef LaFrentz	.30	.75
❑ 22 Jerry Stackhouse	.40	1.00
❑ 23 Chucky Atkins	.30	.75
❑ 24 Corliss Williamson	.40	1.00
❑ 25 Antawn Jamison	.50	1.25
❑ 26 Larry Hughes	.40	1.00
❑ 27 Chris Porter	.30	.75
❑ 28 Steve Francis	.50	1.25
❑ 29 Cuttino Mobley	.40	1.00
❑ 30 Maurice Taylor	.30	.75
❑ 31 Reggie Miller	.50	1.25
❑ 32 Jalen Rose	.40	1.00
❑ 33 Jermaine Oâ•™Neal	.50	1.25
❑ 34 Darius Miles	.30	.75
❑ 35 Elton Brand	.50	1.25
❑ 36 Lamar Odom	.50	1.25
❑ 37 Quentin Richardson	.40	1.00
❑ 38 Kobe Bryant	2.50	6.00
❑ 39 Shaquille O'Neal	1.25	3.00

❑ 40 Rick Fox	.40	1.00
❑ 41 Derek Fisher	.40	1.00
❑ 42 Stromile Swift	.30	.75
❑ 43 Jason Williams	.40	1.00
❑ 44 Michael Dickerson	.30	.75
❑ 45 Alonzo Mourning	.50	1.25
❑ 46 Eddie Jones	.40	1.00
❑ 47 Anthony Carter	.30	.75
❑ 48 Glenn Robinson	.40	1.00
❑ 49 Ray Allen	.50	1.25
❑ 50 Sam Cassell	.40	1.00
❑ 51 Kevin Garnett	1.00	2.50
❑ 52 Wally Szczerbiak	.40	1.00
❑ 53 Terrell Brandon	.30	.75
❑ 54 Chauncey Billups	.40	1.00
❑ 55 Kenyon Martin	.50	1.25
❑ 56 Keith Van Horn	.40	1.00
❑ 57 Jason Kidd	.75	2.00
❑ 58 Latrell Sprewell	.40	1.00
❑ 59 Allan Houston	.40	1.00
❑ 60 Marcus Camby	.40	1.00
❑ 61 Tracy McGrady	1.00	2.50
❑ 62 Mike Miller	.40	1.00
❑ 63 Grant Hill	.50	1.25
❑ 64 Allen Iverson	1.00	2.50
❑ 65 Dikembe Mutombo	.40	1.00
❑ 66 Aaron McKie	.30	.75
❑ 67 Stephon Marbury	.50	1.25
❑ 68 Shawn Marion	.50	1.25
❑ 69 Tom Gugliotta	.30	.75
❑ 70 Rasheed Wallace	.50	1.25
❑ 71 Damon Stoudamire	.40	1.00
❑ 72 Bonzi Wells	.40	1.00
❑ 73 Chris Webber	.50	1.25
❑ 74 Peja Stojakovic	.40	1.00
❑ 75 Mike Bibby	.40	1.00
❑ 76 Tim Duncan	1.00	2.50
❑ 77 David Robinson	.60	1.50
❑ 78 Antonio Daniels	.30	.75
❑ 79 Gary Payton	.50	1.25
❑ 80 Rashard Lewis	.50	1.25
❑ 81 Desmond Mason	.40	1.00
❑ 82 Vince Carter	1.00	2.50
❑ 83 Morris Peterson	.40	1.00
❑ 84 Antonio Davis	.30	.75
❑ 85 Karl Malone	.60	1.50
❑ 86 John Stockton	.60	1.50
❑ 87 Donyell Marshall	.30	.75
❑ 88 Richard Hamilton	.40	1.00
❑ 89 Courtney Alexander	.30	.75
❑ 90 Michael Jordan	10.00	25.00
❑ 91A Tony Parker JSY AU RC	20.00	40.00
❑ 91B Tony Parker JSY AU RC	20.00	40.00
❑ 91C Tony Parker JSY AU RC	20.00	40.00
❑ 92A J.Tinsley JSY AU RC	6.00	15.00
❑ 92B J.Tinsley JSY AU HC	6.00	15.00
❑ 92C J.Tinsley JSY AU RC	6.00	15.00
❑ 93A S.Dalembert JSY AU RC	3.00	8.00
❑ 93B S.Dalembert JSY AU RC	3.00	8.00
❑ 93C S.Dalembert JSY AU RC	3.00	8.00
❑ 94A G.Wallace JSY AU RC	8.00	20.00
❑ 94B G.Wallace JSY AU RC	8.00	20.00
❑ 94C G.Wallace JSY AU RC	8.00	20.00
❑ 95A B.Armstrong JSY AU RC	4.00	10.00
❑ 95B B.Armstrong JSY AU RC	4.00	10.00
❑ 95C B.Armstrong JSY AU RC	4.00	10.00
❑ 96A Jeryl Sasser JSY AU RC	3.00	8.00
❑ 96B Jeryl Sasser JSY AU RC	3.00	8.00
❑ 96C Jeryl Sasser JSY AU RC	3.00	8.00
❑ 97A Jas.Collins JSY AU RC	3.00	8.00
❑ 97B Jas.Collins JSY AU RC	3.00	8.00
❑ 97C Jas.Collins JSY AU RC	3.00	8.00
❑ 98A M.Bradley JSY AU RC	3.00	8.00
❑ 98B M.Bradley JSY AU RC	3.00	8.00
❑ 98C M.Bradley JSY AU RC	3.00	8.00
❑ 99A S.Hunter JSY AU RC	3.00	8.00
❑ 99B S.Hunter JSY AU RC	3.00	8.00
❑ 99C S.Hunter JSY AU RC	3.00	8.00
❑ 100A T.Murphy JSY AU RC	5.00	12.00
❑ 100B T.Murphy JSY AU RC	5.00	12.00
❑ 100C T.Murphy JSY AU RC	5.00	12.00
❑ 101A R.Jefferson JSY AU RC	10.00	25.00
❑ 101B R.Jefferson JSY AU RC	10.00	25.00
❑ 101C R.Jefferson JSY AU RC	10.00	25.00
❑ 102A V.Radmanov JSY AU RC	4.00	10.00
❑ 102B V.Radmanov JSY AU RC	4.00	10.00
❑ 102C V.Radmanov JSY AU RC	4.00	10.00
❑ 103A Ke.Brown JSY AU RC	3.00	8.00
❑ 103B Ke.Brown JSY AU RC	3.00	8.00
❑ 103C Ke.Brown JSY AU RC	3.00	8.00
❑ 104A J.Johnson JSY AU ERR RC	15.00	30.00
❑ 104B J.Johnson JSY AU ERR RC	15.00	30.00
❑ 104C J.Johnson JSY AU ERR RC	15.00	30.00
❑ 104D J.Johnson JSY AU COR RC		
❑ 104E J.Johnson JSY AU COR RC		
❑ 104F J.Johnson JSY AU COR RC		
❑ 105A Kirk Haston JSY AU RC	3.00	8.00
❑ 105B Kirk Haston JSY AU RC	3.00	8.00
❑ 105C Kirk Haston JSY AU RC	3.00	8.00
❑ 106A R.White JSY AU RC	4.00	10.00
❑ 106B R.White JSY AU RC	4.00	10.00
❑ 106C R.White JSY AU RC	4.00	10.00
❑ 107A Eddie Griffin JSY AU RC	8.00	20.00
❑ 107B Eddie Griffin JSY AU RC	8.00	20.00
❑ 107C Eddie Griffin JSY AU RC	8.00	20.00
❑ 108A J.Richardson JSY AU RC	10.00	25.00
❑ 108B J.Richardson JSY AU RC	10.00	25.00
❑ 108C J.Richardson JSY AU RC	10.00	25.00
❑ 109A Eddy Curry JSY AU RC	10.00	25.00
❑ 109B Eddy Curry JSY AU RC	10.00	25.00
❑ 109C Eddy Curry JSY AU RC	10.00	25.00
❑ 110A T.Chandler JSY AU RC	10.00	25.00
❑ 110B T.Chandler JSY AU RC	10.00	25.00
❑ 110C T.Chandler JSY AU RC	10.00	25.00
❑ 111A Kw.Brown JSY AU RC	8.00	20.00
❑ 111B Kw.Brown JSY AU RC	8.00	20.00
❑ 111C Kw.Brown JSY AU RC	8.00	20.00
❑ 121 Shane Battier RC	4.00	10.00
❑ 122 Brendan Haywood RC	3.00	8.00
❑ 123 Joseph Forte RC	2.50	6.00
❑ 124 Zach Randolph RC	6.00	15.00
❑ 125 DeSagana Diop RC	2.50	6.00
❑ 126 Damone Brown RC	2.50	6.00
❑ 127 Andrei Kirilenko RC	6.00	15.00
❑ 128 Trenton Hassell RC	3.00	8.00
❑ 129 Gilbert Arenas RC	4.00	10.00
❑ 130 Earl Watson RC	3.00	8.00
❑ 131 Kenny Satterfield RC	2.50	6.00
❑ 132 Will Solomon RC	2.50	6.00
❑ 133 Bobby Simmons RC	2.50	6.00
❑ 134 Brian Scalabrine RC	2.50	6.00
❑ 135 Charlie Bell RC	2.50	6.00
❑ 136 Zeljko Rebraca RC	2.50	6.00
❑ 137 Loren Woods RC	2.50	6.00
❑ 138 Terence Morris RC	2.50	6.00
❑ 139 Jamison Brewer RC	2.50	6.00
❑ 140 Pau Gasol RC	10.00	25.00
❑ NNO Kobe Bryant Promo	2.00	5.00

2002-03 SPx

❑ COMP.SET w/o SP's (90)	25.00	60.00
❑ COMMON CARD (1-90)	.15	.40
❑ COMMON JSY AU (91-110)	5.00	12.00
❑ COM. JSY AU RC (111-132)	4.00	10.00
❑ COMMON ROOKIE (133-138)	2.00	5.00
❑ COMMON ROOKIE (139-147)	2.00	5.00
❑ COMMON ROOKIE (148-162)	2.00	5.00
❑ 1 Shareef Abdur-Rahim	.40	1.00
❑ 2 Jason Terry	.50	1.25
❑ 3 Glenn Robinson	.40	1.00
❑ 4 Paul Pierce	.50	1.25
❑ 5 Antoine Walker	.40	1.00
❑ 6 Kedrick Brown	.30	.75
❑ 7 Vin Baker	.40	1.00
❑ 8 Jalen Rose	.40	1.00
❑ 9 Tyson Chandler	.40	1.00
❑ 10 Eddy Curry	.40	1.00
❑ 11 Ricky Davis	.40	1.00
❑ 12 Chris Mihm	.30	.75
❑ 13 Darius Miles	.30	.75
❑ 14 Dirk Nowitzki	.75	2.00
❑ 15 Michael Finley	.50	1.25
❑ 16 Steve Nash	.75	2.00
❑ 17 Raef LaFrentz	.30	.75
❑ 18 James Posey	.30	.75
❑ 19 Juwan Howard	.40	1.00
❑ 20 Richard Hamilton	.40	1.00
❑ 21 Ben Wallace	.40	1.00
❑ 22 Chauncey Billups	.50	1.25
❑ 23 Antawn Jamison	.50	1.25
❑ 24 Jason Richardson	.50	1.25
❑ 25 Steve Francis	.50	1.25
❑ 26 Eddie Griffin	.30	.75
❑ 27 Cuttino Mobley	.40	1.00
❑ 28 Reggie Miller	.50	1.25
❑ 29 Jamaal Tinsley	.40	1.00
❑ 30 Jermaine O'Neal	.50	1.25
❑ 31 Elton Brand	.50	1.25
❑ 32 Andre Miller	.40	1.00
❑ 33 Lamar Odom	.50	1.25
❑ 34 Kobe Bryant	2.50	6.00
❑ 35 Shaquille O'Neal	1.25	3.00
❑ 36 Robert Horry	.40	1.00
❑ 37 Devean George	.30	.75
❑ 38 Pau Gasol	.50	1.25
❑ 39 Shane Battier	.40	1.00
❑ 40 Jason Williams	.40	1.00
❑ 41 Alonzo Mourning	.50	1.25
❑ 42 Eddie Jones	.40	1.00
❑ 43 Brian Grant	.30	.75
❑ 44 Ray Allen	.50	1.25
❑ 45 Tim Thomas	.30	.75
❑ 46 Kevin Garnett	1.00	2.50
❑ 47 Terrell Brandon	.30	.75
❑ 48 Wally Szczerbiak	.40	1.00
❑ 49 Jason Kidd	.75	2.00
❑ 50 Richard Jefferson	.50	1.25
❑ 51 Kenyon Martin	.50	1.25
❑ 52 Baron Davis	.50	1.25
❑ 53 Jamal Mashburn	.40	1.00
❑ 54 David Wesley	.30	.75
❑ 55 P.J. Brown	.30	.75
❑ 56 Allan Houston	.40	1.00
❑ 57 Antonio McDyess	.40	1.00
❑ 58 Latrell Sprewell	.40	1.00
❑ 59 Tracy McGrady	1.00	2.50
❑ 60 Mike Miller	.40	1.00
❑ 61 Darrell Armstrong	.30	.75
❑ 62 Allen Iverson	1.00	2.50
❑ 63 Keith Van Horn	.40	1.00
❑ 64 Stephon Marbury	.50	1.25
❑ 65 Shawn Marion	.50	1.25
❑ 66 Anfernee Hardaway	.50	1.25
❑ 67 Rasheed Wallace	.50	1.25
❑ 68 Damon Stoudamire	.40	1.00
❑ 69 Scottie Pippen	.75	2.00
❑ 70 Chris Webber	.50	1.25
❑ 71 Mike Bibby	.40	1.00
❑ 72 Peja Stojakovic	.40	1.00
❑ 73 Hedo Turkoglu	.40	1.00
❑ 74 Tim Duncan	1.00	2.50
❑ 75 David Robinson	.60	1.50
❑ 76 Tony Parker	.50	1.25
❑ 77 Steve Smith	.40	1.00
❑ 78 Gary Payton	.50	1.25
❑ 79 Rashard Lewis	.50	1.25
❑ 80 Brent Barry	.30	.75
❑ 81 Desmond Mason	.40	1.00
❑ 82 Vince Carter	1.00	2.50
❑ 83 Morris Peterson	.40	1.00
❑ 84 Antonio Davis	.30	.75
❑ 85 Karl Malone	.50	1.25
❑ 86 John Stockton	.60	1.50
❑ 87 Andrei Kirilenko	.50	1.25
❑ 88 Jerry Stackhouse	.40	1.00
❑ 89 Michael Jordan	3.00	8.00
❑ 90 Kwame Brown	.30	.75
❑ 91 J.Richardson JSY AU	.50	1.25
❑ 92 Tyson Chandler JSY AU	6.00	15.00
❑ 93 Kenyon Martin JSY AU	15.00	30.00
❑ 94 G.Wallace JSY AU SP	6.00	15.00
❑ 95 K.Abdul-Jbbr JSY AU SP	60.00	120.00
❑ 96 Mo.Peterson JSY AU SP	6.00	15.00
❑ 97 Andre Miller JSY AU	6.00	15.00
❑ 98 Q.Richardson JSY AU	6.00	15.00
❑ 99 Mike Miller JSY AU	6.00	15.00
❑ 100 J.O'Neal JSY AU SP	10.00	25.00
❑ 101 Marcus Fizer JSY AU	6.00	15.00
❑ 102 Mike Bibby JSY AU	20.00	40.00
❑ 103 C.Billups JSY AU SP		
❑ 104 Lamar Odom JSY AU SP	15.00	30.00
❑ 105 Antoine Walker JSY AU	10.00	25.00
❑ 106 Paul Pierce JSY AU	15.00	30.00
❑ 107 Jason Kidd JSY AU SP	20.00	40.00

❑ 108 K.Garnett JSY AU SP		
❑ 109 K.Bryant JSY AU SP		
❑ 110 M.Jordan JSY AU SP		
❑ 111 Chris Jefferies JSY AU RC	4.00	10.00
❑ 112 John Salmons JSY AU RC	6.00	15.00
❑ 113 T.Prince JSY AU RC	8.00	20.00
❑ 114 C.Jacobsen JSY AU RC	4.00	10.00
❑ 115 Qyntel Woods JSY AU RC	5.00	12.00
❑ 116 Kareem Rush JSY AU RC	6.00	15.00
❑ 117 R.Humphrey JSY AU RC	4.00	10.00
❑ 118 Carlos Boozer JSY AU RC	10.00	25.00
❑ 119 Sam Clancy JSY AU RC	4.00	10.00
❑ 120 Fred Jones JSY AU RC	5.00	12.00
❑ 121 Marcus Haislip JSY AU RC	4.00	10.00
❑ 122 Melvin Ely JSY AU RC	4.00	10.00
❑ 123 Jared Jeffries JSY AU RC	5.00	12.00
❑ 124 Dan Gadzuric JSY AU RC	4.00	10.00
❑ 125 A.Stoudemire JSY AU RC	25.00	50.00
❑ 126 Caron Butler JSY AU RC	10.00	25.00
❑ 127 Nene Hilario JSY AU RC	8.00	20.00
❑ 128 D.Wagner JSY AU RC	6.00	15.00
❑ 129 N.Tskitishvili JSY AU RC	5.00	12.00
❑ 130 Drew Gooden JSY AU RC	10.00	25.00
❑ 131 Jay Williams JSY AU RC	6.00	15.00
❑ 132 Yao Ming JSY AU RC	40.00	80.00
❑ 133 Mike Dunleavy RC	2.50	6.00
❑ 134 Frank Williams RC	2.00	5.00
❑ 135 Jiri Welsch RC	2.00	5.00
❑ 136 Dan Dickau RC	2.00	5.00
❑ 137 Efthimios Rentzias RC	2.00	5.00
❑ 138 Chris Wilcox RC	2.50	6.00
❑ 139 Curtis Borchardt RC	2.00	5.00
❑ 140 Predrag Savovic RC	2.00	5.00
❑ 141 Tito Maddox RC	2.00	5.00
❑ 142 Roger Mason RC	2.00	5.00
❑ 143 Juan Dixon RC	3.00	8.00
❑ 144 Pat Burke RC	2.00	5.00
❑ 145 Marko Jaric	2.00	5.00
❑ 146 Gordan Giricek RC	2.00	5.00
❑ 147 Juaquin Hawkins RC	2.00	5.00
❑ 148 Vincent Yarbrough RC	2.00	5.00
❑ 149 Robert Archibald RC	2.00	5.00
❑ 150 Bostjan Nachbar RC	2.00	5.00
❑ 151 Jamal Sampson RC	2.00	5.00
❑ 152 Lonny Baxter RC	2.00	5.00
❑ 153 J.R. Bremer RC	2.00	5.00
❑ 154 Cezary Trybanski RC	2.00	5.00
❑ 155 Manu Ginobili RC	5.00	12.00
❑ 156 Raul Lopez RC	2.00	5.00
❑ 157 Rasual Butler RC	2.00	5.00
❑ 158 Tamar Slay RC	2.00	5.00
❑ 159 Ronald Murray RC	3.00	8.00
❑ 160 Igor Rakocevic RC	2.00	5.00
❑ 161 Reggie Evans RC	2.00	5.00
❑ 162 Jannero Pargo RC	2.00	5.00

2003-04 SPx

❑ COMP.SET w/o SP's (90)	25.00	60.00
❑ COMMON SPXCCL (91-132)	1.25	3.00
❑ COMMON ROOKIE (133-150)	3.00	8.00
❑ COMMON JSY AU RC (151-156)	12.50	30.00
❑ COMMON JSY AU RC (163-185)	5.00	12.00
❑ COMMON JSY AU (186-206)	12.50	30.00
❑ SOME UNPRICED DUE TO SCARCITY		
❑ 1 Shafreef Abdur-Rahim	.40	1.00
❑ 2 Jason Terry	.40	1.00
❑ 3 Theo Ratliff	.30	.75
❑ 4 Paul Pierce	.50	1.25
❑ 5 Raef LaFrentz	.30	.75
❑ 6 Vin Baker	.30	.75
❑ 7 Jalen Rose	.40	1.00
❑ 8 Tyson Chandler	.40	1.00
❑ 9 Michael Jordan	4.00	10.00
❑ 10 Dajuan Wagner	.30	.75
❑ 11 Darius Miles	.40	1.00
❑ 12 Carlos Boozer	.50	1.25
❑ 13 Dirk Nowitzki	.75	2.00
❑ 14 Antoine Walker	.50	1.25
❑ 15 Steve Nash	.75	2.00
❑ 16 Nene	.40	1.00
❑ 17 Marcus Camby	.40	1.00
❑ 18 Andre Miller	.40	1.00
❑ 19 Richard Hamilton	.40	1.00
❑ 20 Ben Wallace	.40	1.00
❑ 21 Chauncey Billups	.50	1.25
❑ 22 Nick Van Exel	.40	1.00
❑ 23 Jason Richardson	.50	1.25
❑ 24 Speedy Claxton	.30	.75
❑ 25 Steve Francis	.50	1.25
❑ 26 Yao Ming	1.00	2.50
❑ 27 Cuttino Mobley	.40	1.00
❑ 28 Reggie Miller	.50	1.25
❑ 29 Jamaal Tinsley	.40	1.00
❑ 30 Jermaine O'Neal	.50	1.25
❑ 31 Elton Brand	.50	1.25
❑ 32 Corey Maggette	.30	.75
❑ 33 Quentin Richardson	.40	1.00
❑ 34 Kobe Bryant	2.50	6.00
❑ 35 Karl Malone	.50	1.25
❑ 36 Shaquille Oâ•™Neal	1.25	3.00
❑ 37 Gary Payton	.50	1.25
❑ 38 Pau Gasol	.50	1.25
❑ 39 Shane Battier	.40	1.00
❑ 40 Mike Miller	.40	1.00
❑ 41 Eddie Jones	.40	1.00
❑ 42 Lamar Odom	.50	1.25
❑ 43 Caron Butler	.40	1.00
❑ 44 Michael Redd	.50	1.25
❑ 45 Joe Smith	.30	.75
❑ 46 Desmond Mason	.40	1.00
❑ 47 Kevin Garnett	1.00	2.50
❑ 48 Latrell Sprewell	.40	1.00
❑ 49 Michael Olowokandi	.30	.75
❑ 50 Jason Kidd	.75	2.00
❑ 51 Richard Jefferson	.50	1.25
❑ 52 Kenyon Martin	.50	1.25
❑ 53 Baron Davis	.50	1.25
❑ 54 Jamal Mashburn	.30	.75
❑ 55 David Wesley	.30	.75
❑ 56 Allan Houston	.40	1.00
❑ 57 Antonio McDyess	.40	1.00
❑ 58 Keith Van Horn	.40	1.00
❑ 59 Tracy McGrady	1.00	2.50
❑ 60 Grant Hill	.50	1.25
❑ 61 Drew Gooden	.30	.75
❑ 62 Juwan Howard	.40	1.00
❑ 63 Allen Iverson	1.00	2.50
❑ 64 Glenn Robinson	.40	1.00
❑ 65 Eric Snow	.30	.75
❑ 66 Stephon Marbury	.50	1.25
❑ 67 Shawn Marion	.50	1.25
❑ 68 Amare Stoudemire	1.00	2.50
❑ 69 Rasheed Wallace	.50	1.25
❑ 70 Bonzi Wells	.30	.75
❑ 71 Damon Stoudamire	.40	1.00
❑ 72 Chris Webber	.50	1.25
❑ 73 Mike Bibby	.40	1.00
❑ 74 Peja Stojakovic	.40	1.00
❑ 75 Brad Miller	.40	1.00
❑ 76 Tim Duncan	1.00	2.50
❑ 77 Tony Parker	.50	1.25
❑ 78 Manu Ginobili	.50	1.25
❑ 79 Ray Allen	.30	.75
❑ 80 Rashard Lewis	.50	1.25
❑ 81 Vladimir Radmanovic	.30	.75
❑ 82 Vince Carter	1.00	2.50
❑ 83 Morris Peterson	.40	1.00
❑ 84 Antonio Davis	.30	.75
❑ 85 Raul Lopez	.50	1.25
❑ 86 Matt Harpring	.40	1.00
❑ 87 Andrei Kirilenko	.50	1.25
❑ 88 Jerry Stackhouse	.40	1.00
❑ 89 Gilbert Arenas	.50	1.25
❑ 90 Larry Hughes	.40	1.00
❑ 91 Allen Iverson	2.00	5.00
❑ 92 Dirk Nowitzki	1.50	4.00
❑ 93 Kobe Bryant	5.00	12.00
❑ 94 Michael Jordan	8.00	20.00
❑ 95 Vince Carter	2.00	5.00
❑ 96 Shaquille O'Neal	2.50	6.00
❑ 97 Yao Ming	2.00	5.00
❑ 98 Amare Stoudemire	2.00	5.00
❑ 99 Paul Pierce	1.00	2.50
❑ 100 Jason Richardson	1.00	2.50
❑ 101 Steve Francis	1.00	2.50
❑ 102 Jermaine O'Neal	1.00	2.50
❑ 103 Karl Malone	1.00	2.50
❑ 104 Tracy McGrady	2.00	5.00
❑ 105 Stephon Marbury	1.00	2.50
❑ 106 Chris Webber	1.00	2.50
❑ 107 Tim Duncan	2.00	5.00
❑ 108 Ray Allen	.60	1.50
❑ 109 Antoine Walker	1.00	2.50
❑ 110 Steve Nash	1.50	4.00
❑ 111 Elton Brand	1.00	2.50
❑ 112 Rashard Lewis	1.00	2.50
❑ 113 Jerry Stackhouse	.75	2.00
❑ 114 Shawn Marion	1.00	2.50
❑ 115 Mike Bibby	.75	2.00
❑ 116 Tony Parker	1.00	2.50
❑ 117 Michael Finley	1.00	2.50
❑ 118 Allan Houston	.75	2.00
❑ 119 Richard Hamilton	.75	2.00
❑ 120 Ben Wallace	.75	2.00
❑ 121 Reggie Miller	1.00	2.50
❑ 122 Richard Jefferson	1.00	2.50
❑ 123 Glenn Robinson	.75	2.00
❑ 124 Rasheed Wallace	1.00	2.50
❑ 125 Gilbert Arenas	1.00	2.50
❑ 126 Jason Kidd	1.50	4.00
❑ 127 Latrell Sprewell	.75	2.00
❑ 128 Kevin Garnett	2.00	5.00
❑ 129 Caron Butler	.75	2.00
❑ 130 Pau Gasol	1.00	2.50
❑ 131 Alonzo Mourning	1.00	2.50
❑ 132 Gary Payton	1.00	2.50
❑ 133 Kirk Hinrich RC	4.00	10.00
❑ 134 T.J. Ford RC	4.00	10.00
❑ 135 Nick Collison RC	3.00	8.00
❑ 136 Keith McLeod RC	3.00	8.00
❑ 137 Jon Stefansson RC	3.00	8.00
❑ 138 Britton Johnsen RC	3.00	8.00
❑ 139 Matt Carroll RC	3.00	8.00
❑ 140 Linton Johnson RC	3.00	8.00
❑ 141 Francisco Elson RC	3.00	8.00
❑ 142 Willie Green RC	3.00	8.00
❑ 143 Kyle Korver RC	4.00	10.00
❑ 144 Theron Smith RC	3.00	8.00
❑ 145 Brandon Hunter RC	3.00	8.00
❑ 146 Josh Moore RC	3.00	8.00
❑ 147 Marquis Daniels RC	4.00	10.00
❑ 148 James Lang RC	3.00	8.00
❑ 149 Udonis Haslem RC	4.00	10.00
❑ 150 Alex Garcia RC	3.00	8.00
❑ 151 LeBron James JSY AU RC	800.00	1200.00
❑ 152 Darko Milicic JSY AU RC	10.00	25.00
❑ 153 Carmelo Anthony JSY AU RC	125.00	225.00
❑ 154 Chris Bosh JSY AU RC	50.00	100.00
❑ 155 Dwyane Wade JSY AU RC	150.00	300.00
❑ 156 Chris Kaman JSY AU RC	12.50	30.00
❑ 157 Jarvis Hayes JSY AU RC	12.50	30.00
❑ 158 M.Pietrus JSY AU RC	6.00	15.00
❑ 159 Dahntay Jones JSY AU RC	6.00	15.00
❑ 160 Marcus Banks JSY AU RC	6.00	15.00
❑ 161 Luke Ridnour JSY AU RC	12.50	30.00
❑ 162 Reece Gaines JSY AU RC	5.00	12.00
❑ 163 Troy Bell JSY AU RC	5.00	12.00
❑ 164 Mike Sweetney JSY AU RC	5.00	12.00
❑ 165 David West JSY AU RC	15.00	30.00
❑ 166 A.Pavlovic JSY AU RC	6.00	15.00
❑ 167 Mo Williams JSY AU RC	15.00	30.00
❑ 168 Boris Diaw JSY AU RC	8.00	20.00
❑ 169 Zoran Planinic JSY AU RC	5.00	12.00
❑ 170 Travis Outlaw JSY AU RC	8.00	20.00
❑ 171 Brian Cook JSY AU RC	5.00	12.00
❑ 172 Jarome Beasley JSY AU RC	5.00	12.00
❑ 173 Ndudi Ebi JSY AU RC	5.00	12.00
❑ 174 Kendrick Perkins JSY AU RC	8.00	20.00
❑ 175 Leandro Barbosa JSY AU RC	12.50	30.00
❑ 176 Josh Howard JSY AU RC	8.00	20.00
❑ 177 Maciej Lampe JSY AU RC	5.00	12.00
❑ 178 Jason Kapono JSY AU RC	6.00	15.00
❑ 179 Luke Walton JSY AU RC	8.00	20.00
❑ 180 Slavko Vranes JSY AU RC	5.00	12.00
❑ 181 Z.Cabarkapa JSY AU RC	5.00	12.00
❑ 182 Travis Hansen JSY AU RC	5.00	12.00
❑ 183 Steve Blake JSY AU RC	5.00	12.00
❑ 184 Zaur Pachulia JSY AU RC	5.00	12.00
❑ 185 Keith Bogans JSY AU RC	5.00	12.00
❑ 186 M.Jordan JSY AU/23		

❑ 187 Kobe Bryant JSY AU/25
❑ 188 K.Garnett JSY AU/150 60.00 120.00
❑ 189 R.Jefferson JSY AU/215 12.50 30.00
❑ 190 G.Arenas JSY AU/215 15.00 40.00
❑ 191 A.Jamison JSY AU/215 12.50 30.00
❑ 192 T.McGrady JSY AU/50 60.00 120.00
❑ 193 S.Francis JSY AU/100 20.00 50.00
❑ 194 Ming JSY AU/100 EXCH 30.00 80.00
❑ 195 A.Stoudemire JSY AU/215 30.00 60.00
❑ 196 Abdur-Rahim JSY AU/342 12.50 30.00
❑ 197 Shane Battier JSY AU/280 12.50 30.00
❑ 198 Tony Parker JSY AU/200 12.50 30.00
❑ 199 Andre Miller JSY AU/215 12.50 30.00
❑ 200 Shawn Marion JSY AU/265 12.50 30.00
❑ 201 R.Hamilton JSY AU/215 15.00 40.00
❑ 202 Lamar Odom JSY AU/215 12.50 30.00
❑ 203 J.Stackhouse JSY AU/215 12.50 30.00
❑ 204 A.McDyess JSY AU/230
❑ 205 Manu Ginobili JSY AU/215 15.00 40.00
❑ 206 Drew Gooden JSY AU/215 12.50 30.00

2004-05 SPx

❑ COMP.SET w/o SP's (90) 25.00 60.00
❑ COMMON CARD (1-90) .30 .75
❑ COMMON ROOKIE (91-111) 3.00 8.00
❑ COMMON ROOKIE (112-117) 15.00 40.00
❑ COM.JSY AU RC (108, 118-139) 4.00 10.00
❑ COMMON JSY AU RC (140-147) 10.00 25.00
❑ COMMON FLASH AU (148-168) 12.50 30.00
❑ 1 Antoine Walker .50 1.25
❑ 2 Al Harrington .40 1.00
❑ 3 Boris Diaw .40 1.00
❑ 4 Paul Pierce .50 1.25
❑ 5 Ricky Davis .40 1.00
❑ 6 Gary Payton .50 1.25
❑ 7 Jahidi White .30 .75
❑ 8 Jason Kapono .30 .75
❑ 9 Gerald Wallace .50 1.25
❑ 10 Eddy Curry .40 1.00
❑ 11 Kirk Hinrich .40 1.00
❑ 12 Tyson Chandler .40 1.00
❑ 13 LeBron James 3.00 8.00
❑ 14 Drew Gooden .30 .75
❑ 15 Dajuan Wagner .30 .75
❑ 16 Dirk Nowitzki .75 2.00
❑ 17 Michael Finley .50 1.25
❑ 18 Jerry Stackhouse .40 1.00
❑ 19 Carmelo Anthony 1.50 4.00
❑ 20 Kenyon Martin .50 1.25
❑ 21 Nene .40 1.00
❑ 22 Chauncey Billups .50 1.25
❑ 23 Richard Hamilton .40 1.00
❑ 24 Ben Wallace .40 1.00
❑ 25 Mike Dunleavy .40 1.00
❑ 26 Jason Richardson .50 1.25
❑ 27 Derek Fisher .40 1.00
❑ 28 Yao Ming 1.25 3.00
❑ 29 Jim Jackson .30 .75
❑ 30 Tracy McGrady 1.00 2.50
❑ 31 Jermaine O'Neal .50 1.25
❑ 32 Reggie Miller .50 1.25
❑ 33 Stephen Jackson .40 1.00
❑ 34 Elton Brand .50 1.25
❑ 35 Corey Maggette .40 1.00
❑ 36 Chris Kaman .40 1.00
❑ 37 Kobe Bryant 2.50 6.00
❑ 38 Chris Mihm .30 .75
❑ 39 Lamar Odom .50 1.25
❑ 40 Pau Gasol .50 1.25
❑ 41 Jason Williams .40 1.00
❑ 42 Bonzi Wells .30 .75
❑ 43 Shaquille O'Neal 1.25 3.00
❑ 44 Dwyane Wade 1.50 4.00
❑ 45 Eddie Jones .40 1.00
❑ 46 Michael Redd .50 1.25
❑ 47 Desmond Mason .40 1.00
❑ 48 T.J. Ford .40 1.00
❑ 49 Latrell Sprewell .40 1.00
❑ 50 Kevin Garnett 1.00 2.50
❑ 51 Sam Cassell .40 1.00
❑ 52 Richard Jefferson .50 1.25
❑ 53 Alonzo Mourning .50 1.25
❑ 54 Jason Kidd .75 2.00
❑ 55 Jamal Mashburn .40 1.00
❑ 56 Baron Davis .50 1.25
❑ 57 Jamaal Magloire .30 .75
❑ 58 Allan Houston .40 1.00
❑ 59 Jamal Crawford .40 1.00
❑ 60 Stephon Marbury .50 1.25
❑ 61 Cuttino Mobley .40 1.00
❑ 62 Hedo Turkoglu .40 1.00
❑ 63 Steve Francis .50 1.25
❑ 64 Glenn Robinson .40 1.00
❑ 65 Allen Iverson 1.00 2.50
❑ 66 Aaron McKie .30 .75
❑ 67 Amare Stoudemire 1.00 2.50
❑ 68 Steve Nash .75 2.00
❑ 69 Shawn Marion .50 1.25
❑ 70 Shareef Abdur-Rahim .40 1.00
❑ 71 Damon Stoudamire .40 1.00
❑ 72 Zach Randolph .50 1.25
❑ 73 Peja Stojakovic .40 1.00
❑ 74 Chris Webber .50 1.25
❑ 75 Mike Bibby .40 1.00
❑ 76 Tony Parker .50 1.25
❑ 77 Tim Duncan 1.00 2.50
❑ 78 Manu Ginobili .50 1.25
❑ 79 Ronald Murray .30 .75
❑ 80 Ray Allen .50 1.25
❑ 81 Rashard Lewis .50 1.25
❑ 82 Chris Bosh .50 1.25
❑ 83 Vince Carter 1.00 2.50
❑ 84 Jalen Rose .40 1.00
❑ 85 Andrei Kirilenko .50 1.25
❑ 86 Carlos Boozer .50 1.25
❑ 87 Carlos Arroyo .50 1.25
❑ 88 Gilbert Arenas .50 1.25
❑ 89 Jarvis Hayes .30 .75
❑ 90 Antawn Jamison .50 1.25
❑ 91 Matt Freije RC 3.00 8.00
❑ 92 Horace Jenkins RC 3.00 8.00
❑ 93 Luis Flores RC 3.00 8.00
❑ 94 Jared Reiner RC 3.00 8.00
❑ 95 D.J. Mbenga RC 3.00 8.00
❑ 96 Pape Sow RC 3.00 8.00
❑ 97 Erik Daniels RC 3.00 8.00
❑ 98 Arthur Johnson RC 3.00 8.00
❑ 99 John Edwards RC 3.00 8.00
❑ 100 Andre Barrett RC 3.00 8.00
❑ 101 Romain Sato RC 3.00 8.00
❑ 102 Tim Pickett RC 3.00 8.00
❑ 103 Bernard Robinson RC 3.00 8.00
❑ 104 Justin Reed RC 3.00 8.00
❑ 105 Andres Nocioni RC 4.00 10.00
❑ 106 Awvee Storey RC 3.00 8.00
❑ 107 Damien Wilkins RC 3.00 8.00
❑ 108 Nenad Krstic JSY AU RC 6.00 15.00
❑ 109 Viktor Khryapa RC 3.00 8.00
❑ 110 Royal Ivey RC 3.00 8.00
❑ 111 Antonio Burks RC 3.00 8.00
❑ 112 Robert Swift RC 15.00 40.00
❑ 113 Trevor Ariza RC 20.00 50.00
❑ 114 Chris Duhon RC 25.00 60.00
❑ 115 Beno Udrih RC 25.00 60.00
❑ 116 Pavel Podkolzine RC 15.00 40.00
❑ 117 Emeka Okafor RC 20.00 40.00
❑ 118 Yuta Tabuse JSY AU RC 10.00 25.00
❑ 119 Andre Emmett JSY AU RC 4.00 10.00
❑ 120 Sasha Vujacic JSY AU RC 6.00 15.00
❑ 121 Lionel Chalmers JSY AU RC 4.00 10.00
❑ 122 J.R. Smith JSY AU RC 10.00 25.00
❑ 123 Dorell Wright JSY AU RC 5.00 12.00
❑ 124 Jameer Nelson JSY AU RC 8.00 20.00
❑ 125 Andris Biedrins JSY AU RC 8.00 20.00
❑ 126 Jackson Vroman JSY AU RC 4.00 10.00
❑ 127 A.Varejao JSY AU RC 8.00 20.00
❑ 128 Delonte West JSY AU RC 10.00 25.00
❑ 129 Tony Allen JSY AU RC 10.00 25.00
❑ 130 Kevin Martin JSY AU RC 10.00 25.00
❑ 131 Rafael Araujo JSY AU RC 4.00 10.00
❑ 132 David Harrison JSY AU RC 4.00 10.00
❑ 133 Kris Humphries JSY AU RC 4.00 10.00
❑ 134 Al Jefferson JSY AU RC 20.00 40.00
❑ 135 Kirk Snyder JSY AU RC 4.00 10.00
❑ 136 Peter J.Ramos JSY AU RC 4.00 10.00
❑ 137 Luke Jackson JSY AU RC 4.00 10.00
❑ 138 Donta Smith JSY AU RC 4.00 10.00
❑ 139 Josh Smith JSY AU RC 15.00 30.00
❑ 140 Sebastian Telfair JSY AU RC 8.0020.00
❑ 141 Andre Iguodala JSY AU RC 25.0050.00
❑ 142 Luol Deng JSY AU RC 20.00 40.00
❑ 143 Josh Childress JSY AU RC 10.00 25.00
❑ 144 Devin Harris JSY AU RC 25.00 50.00
❑ 145 S.Livingston JSY AU RC 12.50 30.00
❑ 146 Ben Gordon JSY AU RC 8.00 20.00
❑ 147 Dwight Howard JSY AU RC 100.00 200.00
❑ 148 Kobe Bryant AU SP
❑ 149 Pau Gasol AU 12.50 30.00
❑ 150 Jason Kidd AU 25.00 60.00
❑ 151 Richard Hamilton AU 20.00 50.00
❑ 152 Amare Stoudemire AU 25.00 60.00
❑ 153 Chauncey Billups AU 15.00 40.00
❑ 154 Mike Bibby AU 12.50 30.00
❑ 155 Jason Richardson AU 12.50 30.00
❑ 156 LeBron James AU SP
❑ 157 Larry Bird AU SP
❑ 158 Reggie Miller AU 40.00 80.00
❑ 159 Kevin Garnett AU
❑ 160 Baron Davis AU 15.00 40.00
❑ 161 Carmelo Anthony AU
❑ 162 Magic Johnson AU SP
❑ 163 Tracy McGrady AU 40.00 80.00
❑ 164 Yao Ming AU 25.00 60.00
❑ 165 Michael Jordan AU SP
❑ 166 Andrei Kirilenko AU 15.00 40.00
❑ 167 Stephon Marbury AU 15.00 40.00
❑ 168 Shawn Marion AU 12.50 30.00

2005-06 SPx

❑ COMP.SET w/o SP's (90) 20.00 50.00
❑ COMMON CARD (1-90) .30 .75
❑ COMMON ROOKIE (91-120) 2.00 5.00
❑ COMMON JSY AU RC (121-146) 4.0010.00
❑ ASTERISK* INDICATES EXCHANGE CARDS
❑ 1 Josh Childress .40 1.00
❑ 2 Josh Smith .50 1.25
❑ 3 Al Harrington .30 .75
❑ 4 Antoine Walker .40 1.00
❑ 5 Gary Payton .50 1.25
❑ 6 Paul Pierce .50 1.25
❑ 7 Kareem Rush .30 .75
❑ 8 Emeka Okafor .50 1.25
❑ 9 Gerald Wallace .50 1.25
❑ 10 Michael Jordan 3.00 8.00
❑ 11 Kirk Hinrich .50 1.25
❑ 12 Ben Gordon .60 1.50
❑ 13 Drew Gooden .40 1.00
❑ 14 Larry Hughes .40 1.00
❑ 15 LeBron James 2.50 6.00
❑ 16 Zydrunas Ilgauskas .40 1.00
❑ 17 Dirk Nowitzki .75 2.00
❑ 18 Jason Terry .50 1.25
❑ 19 Michael Finley .50 1.25
❑ 20 Carmelo Anthony 1.00 2.50
❑ 21 Kenyon Martin .50 1.25
❑ 22 Andre Miller .40 1.00
❑ 23 Ben Wallace .50 1.25
❑ 24 Chauncey Billups .50 1.25
❑ 25 Richard Hamilton .40 1.00
❑ 26 Troy Murphy .50 1.25
❑ 27 Jason Richardson .50 1.25
❑ 28 Baron Davis .50 1.25
❑ 29 Tracy McGrady 1.00 2.50
❑ 30 Yao Ming 1.25 3.00
❑ 31 David Wesley .30 .75
❑ 32 Jermaine O'Neal .50 1.25
❑ 33 Jamaal Tinsley .40 1.00
❑ 34 Ron Artest .40 1.00
❑ 35 Corey Maggette .40 1.00
❑ 36 Elton Brand .50 1.25

❑ 37 Bobby Simmons	.30	.75
❑ 38 Caron Butler	.50	1.25
❑ 39 Kobe Bryant	2.50	6.00
❑ 40 Lamar Odom	.50	1.25
❑ 41 Mike Miller	.50	1.25
❑ 42 Jason Williams	.40	1.00
❑ 43 Pau Gasol	.50	1.25
❑ 44 Dwyane Wade	1.25	3.00
❑ 45 Eddie Jones	.30	.75
❑ 46 Shaquille O'Neal	1.25	3.00
❑ 47 Desmond Mason	.30	.75
❑ 48 Keith Van Horn	.40	1.00
❑ 49 Michael Redd	.50	1.25
❑ 50 Kevin Garnett	1.00	2.50
❑ 51 Latrell Sprewell	.30	.75
❑ 52 Sam Cassell	.50	1.25
❑ 53 Vince Carter	1.00	2.50
❑ 54 Jason Kidd	.75	2.00
❑ 55 Richard Jefferson	.40	1.00
❑ 56 Dan Dickau	.30	.75
❑ 57 Jamaal Magloire	.30	.75
❑ 58 J.R. Smith	.40	1.00
❑ 59 Jamal Crawford	.40	1.00
❑ 60 Stephon Marbury	.50	1.25
❑ 61 Quentin Richardson	.40	1.00
❑ 62 Dwight Howard	1.00	2.50
❑ 63 Grant Hill	.50	1.25
❑ 64 Steve Francis	.50	1.25
❑ 65 Allen Iverson	1.00	2.50
❑ 66 Andre Iguodala	.50	1.25
❑ 67 Chris Webber	.50	1.25
❑ 68 Amare Stoudemire	1.00	2.50
❑ 69 Shawn Marion	.50	1.25
❑ 70 Steve Nash	.60	1.50
❑ 71 Damon Stoudamire	.40	1.00
❑ 72 Shareef Abdur-Rahim	.50	1.25
❑ 73 Zach Randolph	.50	1.25
❑ 74 Brad Miller	.50	1.25
❑ 75 Mike Bibby	.50	1.25
❑ 76 Peja Stojakovic	.50	1.25
❑ 77 Manu Ginobili	.50	1.25
❑ 78 Tim Duncan	1.00	2.50
❑ 79 Tony Parker	.50	1.25
❑ 80 Rashard Lewis	.50	1.25
❑ 81 Ray Allen	.50	1.25
❑ 82 Luke Ridnour	.40	1.00
❑ 83 Rafer Alston	.30	.75
❑ 84 Jalen Rose	.50	1.25
❑ 85 Chris Bosh	.50	1.25
❑ 86 Andrei Kirilenko	.50	1.25
❑ 87 Carlos Boozer	.50	1.25
❑ 88 Matt Harpring	.40	1.00
❑ 89 Antawn Jamison	.50	1.25
❑ 90 Gilbert Arenas	.50	1.25
❑ 91 Bracey Wright RC	2.00	5.00
❑ 92 Chris Taft RC	2.00	5.00
❑ 93 Jose Calderon RC	2.00	5.00
❑ 94 Dijon Thompson RC	2.00	5.00
❑ 95 Esteban Batista RC	2.00	5.00
❑ 96 Linas Kleiza RC	2.50	6.00
❑ 97 Earl Barron RC	2.00	5.00
❑ 98 Ike Diogu RC	2.50	6.00
❑ 99 Alan Anderson RC	2.00	5.00
❑ 100 Shavlik Randolph RC	2.00	5.00
❑ 101 Eddie Basden RC	2.00	5.00
❑ 102 Johan Petro RC	2.00	5.00
❑ 103 Ersan Ilyasova RC	2.00	5.00
❑ 104 Dwayne Jones RC	2.00	5.00
❑ 105 Aaron Miles RC	2.00	5.00
❑ 106 James Singleton RC	2.00	5.00
❑ 107 Von Wafer RC	2.00	5.00
❑ 108 Josh Powell RC	2.00	5.00
❑ 109 Yaroslav Korolev RC	2.00	5.00
❑ 110 Ronnie Price RC	2.00	5.00
❑ 111 Andray Blatche RC	2.50	6.00
❑ 112 Robert Whaley RC	2.00	5.00
❑ 113 Donell Taylor RC	2.00	5.00
❑ 114 Orien Greene RC	2.00	5.00
❑ 115 Lawrence Roberts RC	2.00	5.00
❑ 116 Amir Johnson RC	2.00	5.00
❑ 117 Matt Walsh RC	2.00	5.00
❑ 118 Fabricio Oberto RC	2.00	5.00
❑ 119 Arvydas Macijauskas RC	2.00	5.00
❑ 120 Alex Acker RC	2.00	5.00
❑ 121 Salim Stoudamire JSY AU RC	4.00	10.00
❑ 122 Francisco Garcia JSY AU RC	4.00	10.00
❑ 123 Daniel Ewing JSY AU RC	4.00	10.00
❑ 124 N.Robinson JSY AU/199 RC	40.00	75.00
❑ 125 Luther Head JSY AU RC	4.00	10.00
❑ 126 Louis Williams JSY AU RC	6.00	15.00
❑ 127 Jarrett Jack JSY AU RC	4.00	10.00
❑ 128 J.Maxiell JSY AU/1453 RC	5.00	12.00
❑ 129 Wayne Simien JSY AU RC	4.00	10.00
❑ 130 Julius Hodge JSY AU RC	4.00	10.00
❑ 131 C.J. Miles JSY AU RC	4.00	10.00
❑ 132 Andrew Bynum JSY AU RC	25.00	50.00
❑ 133 Monta Ellis JSY AU/99 RC	150.00	300.00
❑ 134 Joey Graham JSY AU RC	4.00	10.00
❑ 135 Antoine Wright JSY AU RC	4.00	10.00
❑ 136 Sean May JSY AU/1458 RC	4.00	10.00
❑ 137 Channing Frye JSY AU RC	6.00	15.00
❑ 138 Gerald Green JSY AU RC	8.00	20.00
❑ 139 S.Jasikevicius JSY AU RC	5.00	12.00
❑ 140 Danny Granger JSY AU RC	15.00	30.00
❑ 141 H.Warrick JSY AU/99 RC	20.00	40.00
❑ 142 David Lee JSY AU RC	8.00	20.00
❑ 143 Brandon Bass JSY AU RC	5.00	12.00
❑ 144 Ryan Gomes JSY AU RC	4.00	10.00
❑ 145 M.Andriuskevicius JSY AU RC	4.00	10.00
❑ 146 Travis Diener JSY AU RC	4.00	10.00
❑ 147 Martell Webster JSY AU RC	6.00	15.00
❑ 148 Rashad McCants JSY AU RC	10.00	25.00
❑ 149 Deron Williams JSY AU RC	25.00	50.00
❑ 150 Charlie Villanueva JSY AU RC	10.00	25.00
❑ 151 Raymond Felton JSY AU RC	6.00	15.00
❑ 152 Andrew Bogut JSY AU RC	10.00	25.00
❑ 153 Chris Paul JSY AU RC	75.00	150.00
❑ 154 Marvin Williams JSY AU RC	15.00	30.00

2006-07 SPx

❑ COMP.SET w/o RC's (100)	25.00	60.00
❑ 1 Joe Johnson	.40	1.00
❑ 2 Salim Stoudamire	.40	1.00
❑ 3 Marvin Williams	.50	1.25
❑ 4 Tony Allen	.40	1.00
❑ 5 Al Jefferson	.50	1.25
❑ 6 Paul Pierce	.50	1.25
❑ 7 Raymond Felton	.60	1.50
❑ 8 Emeka Okafor	.50	1.25
❑ 9 Gerald Wallace	.50	1.25
❑ 10 Tyson Chandler	.50	1.25
❑ 11 Ben Gordon	.60	1.50
❑ 12 Michael Jordan	3.00	8.00
❑ 13 Drew Gooden	.40	1.00
❑ 14 Zydrunas Ilgauskas	.40	1.00
❑ 15 LeBron James	2.50	6.00
❑ 16 Devin Harris	.50	1.25
❑ 17 Dirk Nowitzki	.75	2.00
❑ 18 Jason Terry	.50	1.25
❑ 19 Carmelo Anthony	.60	1.50
❑ 20 Andre Miller	.40	1.00
❑ 21 Eduardo Najera	.30	.75
❑ 22 Chauncey Billups	.50	1.25
❑ 23 Richard Hamilton	.40	1.00
❑ 24 Ben Wallace	.50	1.25
❑ 25 Rasheed Wallace	.50	1.25
❑ 26 Baron Davis	.50	1.25
❑ 27 Troy Murphy	.50	1.25
❑ 28 Jason Richardson	.50	1.25
❑ 29 Rafer Alston	.30	.75
❑ 30 Tracy McGrady	1.00	2.50
❑ 31 Yao Ming	1.25	3.00
❑ 32 Sarunas Jasikevicius	.40	1.00
❑ 33 Jermaine O'Neal	.50	1.25
❑ 34 Peja Stojakovic	.50	1.25
❑ 35 Elton Brand	.50	1.25
❑ 36 Sam Cassell	.50	1.25
❑ 37 Chris Kaman	.30	.75
❑ 38 Shaun Livingston	.30	.75
❑ 39 Kobe Bryant	2.50	6.00
❑ 40 Lamar Odom	.50	1.25
❑ 41 Ronny Turiaf	.40	1.00
❑ 42 Pau Gasol	.50	1.25
❑ 43 Mike Miller	.50	1.25
❑ 44 Damon Stoudamire	.40	1.00
❑ 45 Shaquille O'Neal	1.25	3.00
❑ 46 Wayne Simien	.40	1.00
❑ 47 Dwyane Wade	1.25	3.00
❑ 48 Jason Williams	.40	1.00
❑ 49 Andrew Bogut	.50	1.25
❑ 50 T.J. Ford	.40	1.00
❑ 51 Jamaal Magloire	.30	.75
❑ 52 Michael Redd	.50	1.25
❑ 53 Ricky Davis	.50	1.25
❑ 54 Kevin Garnett	1.00	2.50
❑ 55 Rashad McCants	.40	1.00
❑ 56 Vince Carter	1.00	2.50
❑ 57 Richard Jefferson	.40	1.00
❑ 58 Jason Kidd	.75	2.00
❑ 59 Speedy Claxton	.30	.75
❑ 60 Desmond Mason	.30	.75
❑ 61 Chris Paul	1.00	2.50
❑ 62 Steve Francis	.50	1.25
❑ 63 Channing Frye	.40	1.00
❑ 64 Stephon Marbury	.50	1.25
❑ 65 Nate Robinson	.50	1.25
❑ 66 Carlos Arroyo	.50	1.25
❑ 67 Grant Hill	.50	1.25
❑ 68 Dwight Howard	1.00	2.50
❑ 69 Jameer Nelson	.40	1.00
❑ 70 Andre Iguodala	.50	1.25
❑ 71 Allen Iverson	1.00	2.50
❑ 72 Chris Webber	.50	1.25
❑ 73 Boris Diaw	.40	1.00
❑ 74 Shawn Marion	.50	1.25
❑ 75 Steve Nash	.60	1.50
❑ 76 Amare Stoudemire	1.00	2.50
❑ 77 Zach Randolph	.50	1.25
❑ 78 Sebastian Telfair	.40	1.00
❑ 79 Martell Webster	.40	1.00
❑ 80 Shareef Abdur-Rahim	.50	1.25
❑ 81 Ron Artest	.50	1.25
❑ 82 Mike Bibby	.50	1.25
❑ 83 Brad Miller	.50	1.25
❑ 84 Tim Duncan	1.00	2.50
❑ 85 Michael Finley	.50	1.25
❑ 86 Manu Ginobili	.50	1.25
❑ 87 Tony Parker	.50	1.25
❑ 88 Ray Allen	.50	1.25
❑ 89 Rashard Lewis	.50	1.25
❑ 90 Chris Wilcox	.30	.75
❑ 91 Chris Bosh	.50	1.25
❑ 92 Joey Graham	.40	1.00
❑ 93 Charlie Villanueva	.50	1.25
❑ 94 Carlos Boozer	.50	1.25
❑ 95 Andrei Kirilenko	.50	1.25
❑ 96 C.J. Miles	.30	.75
❑ 97 Deron Williams	.75	2.00
❑ 98 Gilbert Arenas	.50	1.25
❑ 99 Caron Butler	.50	1.25
❑ 100 Antawn Jamison	.50	1.25
❑ 101 Adam Morrison RC	2.50	6.00
❑ 102 Alexander Johnson RC	2.00	5.00
❑ 103 Damir Markota RC	2.00	5.00
❑ 104 J.J. Redick RC	2.00	5.00
❑ 105 Will Blalock RC	2.00	5.00
❑ 106 Leon Powe RC	2.00	5.00
❑ 107 Thabo Sefolosha RC	2.50	6.00
❑ 108 Pops Mensah-Bonsu RC	2.00	5.00
❑ 109 Robert Hite RC	2.00	5.00
❑ 110 Tarence Kinsey RC	2.00	5.00
❑ 111 Vassilis Spanoulis RC	2.00	5.00
❑ 112 Yakhouba Diawara RC	2.00	5.00
❑ 113 Daniel Gibson RC	2.50	6.00
❑ 114 Hassan Adams RC	2.50	6.00
❑ 115 James Augustine RC	2.00	5.00
❑ 116 Chris Quinn RC	2.00	5.00
❑ 117 Mardy Collins RC	2.00	5.00
❑ 118 Paul Millsap RC	3.00	8.00
❑ 119 P.J. Tucker RC	2.00	5.00
❑ 120 Ryan Hollins RC	2.00	5.00
❑ 121 Saer Sene RC	2.00	5.00
❑ 122 Andrea Bargnani JSY AU RC	25.00	50.00
❑ 123 LaMarcus Aldridge JSY AU RC	25.00	50.00
❑ 124 Tyrus Thomas JSY AU RC	25.00	50.00
❑ 125 Shelden Williams JSY AU RC	30.00	60.00

❑ 126 Brandon Roy JSY AU RC 60.00 120.00
❑ 127 Randy Foye JSY AU RC 30.00 60.00
❑ 128 Paul Davis JSY AU RC 6.00 15.00
❑ 129 Solomon Jones JSY AU RC 6.00 15.00
❑ 130 David Noel JSY AU RC 6.00 15.00
❑ 131 Allan Ray JSY AU RC 6.00 15.00
❑ 132 Bobby Jones JSY AU RC 6.00 15.00
❑ 133 Cedric Simmons JSY AU RC 6.00 15.00
❑ 134 Dee Brown JSY AU RC 6.00 15.00
❑ 135 Shawne Williams JSY AU RC 6.00 15.00
❑ 136 Hilton Armstrong JSY AU RC 6.00 15.00
❑ 137 James White JSY AU RC 6.00 15.00
❑ 138 Jordan Farmar JSY AU RC 10.00 25.00
❑ 139 Josh Boone JSY AU RC 6.00 15.00
❑ 140 Kyle Lowry JSY AU RC 6.00 15.00
❑ 141 Marcus Williams JSY AU RC 8.00 20.00
❑ 142 Maurice Ager JSY AU RC 6.00 15.00
❑ 143 Patrick O'Bryant JSY AU RC 6.00 15.00
❑ 144 Quincy Douby JSY AU RC 6.00 15.00
❑ 145 Rajon Rondo JSY AU RC 40.00 80.00
❑ 146 Renaldo Balkman JSY AU RC 6.00 15.00
❑ 147 Rodney Carney JSY AU RC 6.00 15.00
❑ 148 Ronnie Brewer JSY AU RC 8.00 20.00
❑ 149 Rudy Gay JSY AU RC 15.00 30.00
❑ 150 Shannon Brown JSY AU RC 6.00 15.00
❑ 151 Steve Novak JSY AU RC 6.00 15.00
❑ 152 Craig Smith JSY AU RC 6.00 15.00

2007-08 SPx

❑ COMPLETE SET (140) 25.00 50.00
❑ 91-100 PRINT RUN 299 SER.#'d SETS
❑ 101-110 PRINT RUN 299 SER.#'d SETS
❑ 111-140 PRINT RUN 825 SER.#'d SETS
❑ 1 Chauncey Billups .50 1.25
❑ 2 Tayshaun Prince .50 1.25
❑ 3 Richard Hamilton .40 1.00
❑ 4 Rasheed Wallace .50 1.25
❑ 5 Zydrunas Ilgauskas .40 1.00
❑ 6 Larry Hughes .40 1.00
❑ 7 LeBron James 2.50 6.00
❑ 8 T.J. Ford .40 1.00
❑ 9 Andrea Bargnani .60 1.50
❑ 10 Chris Bosh .50 1.25
❑ 11 Shaquille O'Neal 1.25 3.00
❑ 12 Dwyane Wade 1.25 3.00
❑ 13 Udonis Haslem .50 1.25
❑ 14 Ben Wallace .50 1.25
❑ 15 Ben Gordon .60 1.50
❑ 16 Luol Deng .50 1.25
❑ 17 Kirk Hinrich .50 1.25
❑ 18 Vince Carter 1.00 2.50
❑ 19 Richard Jefferson .50 1.25
❑ 20 Jason Kidd .75 2.00
❑ 21 Gilbert Arenas .50 1.25
❑ 22 Caron Butler .50 1.25
❑ 23 Antawn Jamison .50 1.25
❑ 24 Dwight Howard 1.00 2.50
❑ 25 Jameer Nelson .40 1.00
❑ 26 Jermaine O'Neal .50 1.25
❑ 27 Danny Granger .40 1.00
❑ 28 Mike Dunleavy .40 1.00
❑ 29 Andre Iguodala .50 1.25
❑ 30 Kyle Korver .50 1.25
❑ 31 Gerald Wallace .50 1.25
❑ 32 Emeka Okafor .50 1.25
❑ 33 Jason Richardson .50 1.25
❑ 34 Eddy Curry .30 .75
❑ 35 Stephon Marbury .50 1.25
❑ 36 Quentin Richardson .40 1.00
❑ 37 David Lee .40 1.00
❑ 38 Marvin Williams .50 1.25
❑ 39 Josh Smith .50 1.25
❑ 40 Joe Johnson .50 1.25
❑ 41 Michael Redd .50 1.25
❑ 42 Andrew Bogut .50 1.25
❑ 43 Paul Pierce .50 1.25
❑ 44 Al Jefferson .50 1.25
❑ 45 Ray Allen .50 1.25
❑ 46 Dirk Nowitzki .75 2.00
❑ 47 Jerry Stackhouse .40 1.00
❑ 48 Jason Terry .50 1.25
❑ 49 Josh Howard .50 1.25
❑ 50 Amare Stoudemire 1.00 2.50
❑ 51 Steve Nash .60 1.50
❑ 52 Leandro Barbosa .40 1.00
❑ 53 Shawn Marion .50 1.25
❑ 54 Tony Parker .50 1.25
❑ 55 Tim Duncan 1.00 2.50
❑ 56 Manu Ginobili .50 1.25
❑ 57 Michael Finley .50 1.25
❑ 58 Andrei Kirilenko .50 1.25
❑ 59 Carlos Boozer .50 1.25
❑ 60 Deron Williams .75 2.00
❑ 61 Mehmet Okur .40 1.00
❑ 62 Tracy McGrady 1.00 2.50
❑ 63 Yao Ming 1.25 3.00
❑ 64 Carmelo Anthony 1.00 2.50
❑ 65 Allen Iverson 1.00 2.50
❑ 66 Marcus Camby .30 .75
❑ 67 Kobe Bryant 2.50 6.00
❑ 68 Lamar Odom .50 1.25
❑ 69 Baron Davis .50 1.25
❑ 70 Al Harrington .40 1.00
❑ 71 Stephen Jackson .40 1.00
❑ 72 Elton Brand .50 1.25
❑ 73 Corey Maggette .40 1.00
❑ 74 Shaun Livingston .30 .75
❑ 75 David West .50 1.25
❑ 76 Chris Paul 1.00 2.50
❑ 77 Tyson Chandler .50 1.25
❑ 78 Kevin Garnett 1.25 3.00
❑ 79 Ricky Davis .50 1.25
❑ 80 Randy Foye .50 1.25
❑ 81 Kevin Martin .50 1.25
❑ 82 Ron Artest .50 1.25
❑ 83 Mike Bibby .50 1.25
❑ 84 Steve Francis .40 1.00
❑ 85 Brandon Roy .75 2.00
❑ 86 Jarrett Jack .40 1.00
❑ 87 Delonte West .40 1.00
❑ 88 Rashard Lewis .50 1.25
❑ 89 Pau Gasol .50 1.25
❑ 90 Mike Miller .50 1.25
❑ 91 Greg Oden RC 15.00 30.00
❑ 92 Thaddeus Young RC 4.00 10.00
❑ 93 Brandan Wright RC 4.00 10.00
❑ 94 Yi Jianlian RC 5.00 12.00
❑ 95 Nick Young RC 3.00 8.00
❑ 96 Chris Richard RC 3.00 8.00
❑ 97 Marco Belinelli RC 3.00 8.00
❑ 98 Juan Carlos Navarro RC 4.00 10.00
❑ 99 Sammy Mejia RC 3.00 8.00
❑ 100 Kyrylo Fesenko RC 3.00 8.00
❑ 101 Kevin Durant AU JSY RC 150.00 300.00
❑ 102 Al Horford AU JSY RC 12.00 30.00
❑ 103 Michael Conley AU JSY RC 12.00 30.00
❑ 104 Jeff Green AU JSY RC 12.00 30.00
❑ 105 Corey Brewer AU JSY RC 12.00 30.00
❑ 106 Joakim Noah AU JSY RC 12.00 30.00
❑ 107 Spencer Hawes AU JSY RC 10.00 25.00
❑ 108 Acie Law IV AU JSY RC 12.00 30.00
❑ 109 Julian Wright AU JSY RC 12.00 30.00
❑ 110 Al Thornton AU JSY RC 10.00 25.00
❑ 111 Javaris Crittenton AU JSY RC 5.00 12.00
❑ 112 Daequan Cook AU JSY RC 6.00 15.00
❑ 113 Jared Dudley AU JSY RC 5.00 12.00
❑ 114 Wilson Chandler AU JSY RC 5.00 12.00
❑ 115 Morris Almond AU JSY RC 5.00 12.00
❑ 116 Arron Afflalo AU JSY RC 5.00 12.00
❑ 117 Alando Tucker AU JSY RC 5.00 12.00
❑ 118 Carl Landry AU JSY RC 5.00 12.00
❑ 119 Gabe Pruitt AU JSY RC 5.00 12.00
❑ 120 Marcus Williams AU JSY RC
❑ 121 Nick Fazekas AU JSY RC 5.00 12.00
❑ 122 Jermareo Davidson AU JSY RC 5.00 12.00
❑ 123 Josh McRoberts AU JSY RC 6.00 15.00
❑ 124 Glen Davis AU JSY RC 10.00 25.00
❑ 125 Adam Haluska AU JSY RC 5.00 12.00
❑ 126 Reyshawn Terry AU JSY RC
❑ 127 Jared Jordan AU JSY RC
❑ 128 Stephane Lasme AU JSY RC 5.00 12.00
❑ 129 Aaron Gray AU JSY RC 5.00 12.00
❑ 130 Taurean Green AU JSY RC 5.00 12.00
❑ 131 Demetris Nichols AU JSY RC 5.00 12.00
❑ 132 Herbert Hill AU JSY RC 5.00 12.00
❑ 133 Aaron Brooks AU JSY RC 8.00 20.00
❑ 134 D.J. Strawberry AU JSY RC 5.00 12.00
❑ 135 Dominic McGuire AU JSY RC 5.00 12.00
❑ 136 Jason Smith AU JSY RC 5.00 12.00
❑ 137 Sean Williams AU JSY RC 5.00 12.00
❑ 138 Derrick Byars AU JSY RC
❑ 139 Ramon Sessions AU JSY RC
❑ 140 Rodney Stuckey AU JSY RC 20.00 40.00

2008-09 SPx

❑ COMP.SET w/o SP's (90) 30.00 60.00
❑ 1 Kevin Garnett 1.25 3.00
❑ 2 Ray Allen .60 1.50
❑ 3 Paul Pierce .75 2.00
❑ 4 Chauncey Billups .60 1.50
❑ 5 Rasheed Wallace .60 1.50
❑ 6 Richard Hamilton .50 1.25
❑ 7 Tayshaun Prince .60 1.50
❑ 8 Dwight Howard 1.25 3.00
❑ 9 Hedo Turkoglu .60 1.50
❑ 10 Rashard Lewis .60 1.50
❑ 11 Daniel Gibson .60 1.50
❑ 12 Ben Wallace .60 1.50
❑ 13 LeBron James 3.00 8.00
❑ 14 Antawn Jamison .60 1.50
❑ 15 Caron Butler .60 1.50
❑ 16 Gilbert Arenas .60 1.50
❑ 17 Chris Bosh .60 1.50
❑ 18 Jamario Moon .60 1.50
❑ 19 Jermaine O'Neal .60 1.50
❑ 20 Andre Iguodala .60 1.50
❑ 21 Andre Miller .50 1.25
❑ 22 Thaddeus Young .50 1.25
❑ 23 Al Horford .60 1.50
❑ 24 Joe Johnson .60 1.50
❑ 25 Josh Smith .60 1.50
❑ 26 Danny Granger .60 1.50
❑ 27 T.J. Ford .40 1.00
❑ 28 Devin Harris .60 1.50
❑ 29 Yi Jianlian .60 1.50
❑ 30 Vince Carter .75 2.00
❑ 31 Ben Gordon .60 1.50
❑ 32 Joakim Noah .60 1.50
❑ 33 Luol Deng .60 1.50
❑ 34 Emeka Okafor .60 1.50
❑ 35 Gerald Wallace .60 1.50
❑ 36 Jason Richardson .60 1.50
❑ 37 Andrew Bogut .60 1.50
❑ 38 Michael Redd .60 1.50
❑ 39 Richard Jefferson .60 1.50
❑ 40 Eddy Curry .40 1.00
❑ 41 Jamal Crawford .40 1.00
❑ 42 Stephon Marbury .60 1.50
❑ 43 Zach Randolph .60 1.50
❑ 44 Daequan Cook .50 1.25
❑ 45 Dwyane Wade 1.25 3.00
❑ 46 Shawn Marion .60 1.50
❑ 47 Jordan Farmar .50 1.25
❑ 48 Kobe Bryant 3.00 8.00
❑ 49 Pau Gasol .60 1.50
❑ 50 Lamar Odom .60 1.50
❑ 51 Chris Paul 1.25 3.00
❑ 52 David West .60 1.50
❑ 53 Peja Stojakovic .60 1.50
❑ 54 Manu Ginobili .60 1.50
❑ 55 Tim Duncan 1.00 2.50
❑ 56 Tony Parker .60 1.50
❑ 57 Carlos Boozer .60 1.50
❑ 58 Deron Williams .75 2.00
❑ 59 Mehmet Okur .60 1.50
❑ 60 Luis Scola .50 1.25
❑ 61 Tracy McGrady .75 2.00
❑ 62 Yao Ming .75 2.00

❑ 63 Amare Stoudemire	.75	2.00
❑ 64 Shaquille O'Neal	1.25	3.00
❑ 65 Steve Nash	.60	1.50
❑ 66 Jason Kidd	.60	1.50
❑ 67 Dirk Nowitzki	.75	2.00
❑ 68 Josh Howard	.60	1.50
❑ 69 Allen Iverson	.75	2.00
❑ 70 Carmelo Anthony	.75	2.00
❑ 71 Kenyon Martin	.60	1.50
❑ 72 Elton Brand	1.00	2.50
❑ 73 Monta Ellis	.60	1.50
❑ 74 Stephen Jackson	.50	1.25
❑ 75 Brandon Roy	.75	2.00
❑ 76 Greg Oden	.60	1.50
❑ 77 LaMarcus Aldridge	.60	1.50
❑ 78 Francisco Garcia	.50	1.25
❑ 79 Kevin Martin	.60	1.50
❑ 80 Ron Artest	.60	1.50
❑ 81 Al Thornton	.60	1.50
❑ 82 Chris Kaman	.40	1.00
❑ 83 Baron Davis	.60	1.50
❑ 84 Al Jefferson	.60	1.50
❑ 85 Corey Brewer	.50	1.25
❑ 86 Mike Conley	.50	1.25
❑ 87 Rudy Gay	.60	1.50
❑ 88 Damien Wilkins	.40	1.00
❑ 89 Jeff Green	.50	1.25
❑ 90 Kevin Durant	1.50	4.00
❑ 91 Danilo Gallinari RC	5.00	12.00
❑ 92 Rudy Fernandez RC	15.00	30.00
❑ 93 Sean Singletary RC	3.00	8.00
❑ 94 Othello Hunter RC	3.00	8.00
❑ 95 Shan Foster RC	3.00	8.00
❑ 96 Mike Taylor RC	3.00	8.00
❑ 97 Joe Crawford RC	5.00	12.00
❑ 98 Thomas Gardner RC	3.00	8.00
❑ 99 Nicolas Batum RC	4.00	10.00
❑ 100 Malik Hairston RC	3.00	8.00
❑ 101 Danilo Gallinari RC	5.00	12.00
❑ 102 Rudy Fernandez RC	15.00	30.00
❑ 103 Sean Singletary RC	3.00	8.00
❑ 104 Othello Hunter RC	3.00	8.00
❑ 105 Shan Foster RC	3.00	8.00
❑ 106 Mike Taylor RC	3.00	8.00
❑ 107 Joe Crawford RC	5.00	12.00
❑ 108 Thomas Gardner RC	3.00	8.00
❑ 109 Nicolas Batum RC	4.00	10.00
❑ 110 Malik Hairston RC	3.00	8.00
❑ 111 Derrick Rose JSY AU RC	100.00	200.00
❑ 112 Michael Beasley JSY AU RC	60.00	120.00
❑ 113 O.J. Mayo JSY AU RC	50.00	100.00
❑ 114 Russell Westbrook JSY AU RC	20.00	40.00
❑ 115 Kevin Love JSY AU RC	10.00	25.00
❑ 116 Eric Gordon JSY AU RC		
❑ 117 D.J. Augustin JSY AU RC	15.00	30.00
❑ 118 Jerryd Bayless JSY AU RC	15.00	30.00
❑ 119 Brook Lopez JSY AU RC	15.00	30.00
❑ 120 Brandon Rush JSY AU RC	10.00	25.00
❑ 121 Derrick Rose JSY AU RC	100.00	200.00
❑ 122 Michael Beasley JSY AU RC	60.00	120.00
❑ 123 O.J. Mayo JSY AU RC	50.00	100.00
❑ 124 Russell Westbrook JSY AU RC	25.00	50.00
❑ 125 Kevin Love JSY AU RC	10.00	25.00
❑ 126 Eric Gordon JSY AU RC	15.00	30.00
❑ 127 D.J. Augustin JSY AU RC	15.00	30.00
❑ 128 Jerryd Bayless JSY AU RC	15.00	30.00
❑ 129 Brook Lopez JSY AU RC	15.00	30.00
❑ 130 Brandon Rush JSY AU RC	10.00	25.00
❑ 131 Joe Alexander JSY AU RC	5.00	12.00
❑ 132 Jason Thompson JSY AU RC	5.00	12.00
❑ 133 Anthony Randolph JSY AU RC	8.00	20.00
❑ 134 Robin Lopez JSY AU RC	5.00	12.00
❑ 135 Marreese Speights JSY AU RC	5.00	12.00
❑ 136 Roy Hibbert JSY AU RC	6.00	15.00
❑ 137 Javale McGee JSY AU RC	5.00	12.00
❑ 138 J.J. Hickson JSY AU RC	8.00	20.00
❑ 139 Ryan Anderson JSY AU RC	5.00	12.00
❑ 140 Courtney Lee JSY AU RC	8.00	20.00
❑ 141 Kosta Koufos JSY AU RC	5.00	12.00
❑ 142 George Hill JSY AU RC	8.00	20.00
❑ 143 Darrell Arthur JSY AU RC	5.00	12.00
❑ 144 Donte Greene JSY AU RC	5.00	12.00
❑ 145 D.J. White JSY AU RC	5.00	12.00
❑ 146 J.R. Giddens JSY AU RC	5.00	12.00
❑ 147 Walter Sharpe JSY AU RC	5.00	12.00
❑ 148 Joey Dorsey JSY AU RC	5.00	12.00
❑ 149 Mario Chalmers JSY AU RC	6.00	15.00
❑ 150 DeAndre Jordan JSY AU RC	5.00	12.00
❑ 151 Kyle Weaver JSY AU RC	5.00	12.00
❑ 152 Sonny Weems JSY AU RC	5.00	12.00
❑ 153 Chris Douglas-Roberts JSY AU RC	6.00	15.00
❑ 154 Patrick Ewing Jr. JSY AU RC	5.00	12.00
❑ 155 Joe Alexander JSY AU RC	5.00	12.00
❑ 156 Jason Thompson JSY AU RC	5.00	12.00
❑ 157 Anthony Randolph JSY AU RC	8.00	20.00
❑ 158 Robin Lopez JSY AU RC	5.00	12.00
❑ 159 Marreese Speights JSY AU RC	5.00	12.00
❑ 160 Roy Hibbert JSY AU RC	6.00	15.00
❑ 161 Javale McGee JSY AU RC	5.00	12.00
❑ 162 J.J. Hickson JSY AU RC	8.00	20.00
❑ 163 Ryan Anderson JSY AU RC	5.00	12.00
❑ 164 Courtney Lee JSY AU RC	8.00	20.00
❑ 165 Kosta Koufos JSY AU RC	5.00	12.00
❑ 166 George Hill JSY AU RC	8.00	20.00
❑ 167 Darrell Arthur JSY AU RC	5.00	12.00
❑ 168 Donte Greene JSY AU RC	5.00	12.00
❑ 169 D.J. White JSY AU RC	5.00	12.00
❑ 170 J.R. Giddens JSY AU RC	5.00	12.00
❑ 171 Walter Sharpe JSY AU RC	5.00	12.00
❑ 172 Joey Dorsey JSY AU RC	5.00	12.00
❑ 173 Mario Chalmers JSY AU RC	6.00	15.00
❑ 174 DeAndre Jordan JSY AU RC	5.00	12.00
❑ 175 Kyle Weaver JSY AU RC	5.00	12.00
❑ 176 Sonny Weems JSY AU RC	5.00	12.00
❑ 177 Chris Douglas-Roberts JSY AU RC	6.00	15.00
❑ 178 Patrick Ewing Jr. JSY AU RC	5.00	12.00

1992-93 Stadium Club

❑ COMPLETE SET (400)	25.00	50.00
❑ COMPLETE SERIES 1 (200)	10.00	20.00
❑ COMPLETE SERIES 2 (200)	15.00	30.00
❑ 1 Michael Jordan	3.00	8.00
❑ 2 Greg Anthony	.02	.10
❑ 3 Otis Thorpe	.10	.30
❑ 4 Jim Les	.02	.10
❑ 5 Kevin Willis	.02	.10
❑ 6 Derek Harper	.10	.30
❑ 7 Elden Campbell	.10	.30
❑ 8 A.J. English	.02	.10
❑ 9 Kenny Gattison	.02	.10
❑ 10 Drazen Petrovic	.02	.10
❑ 11 Chris Mullin	.25	.60
❑ 12 Mark Price	.02	.10
❑ 13 Karl Malone	.40	1.00
❑ 14 Gerald Glass	.02	.10
❑ 15 Negele Knight	.02	.10
❑ 16 Mark Macon	.02	.10
❑ 17 Michael Cage	.02	.10
❑ 18 Kevin Edwards	.02	.10
❑ 19 Sherman Douglas	.02	.10
❑ 20 Ron Harper	.10	.30
❑ 21 Cliff Robinson	.10	.30
❑ 22 Byron Scott	.10	.30
❑ 23 Antoine Carr	.02	.10
❑ 24 Greg Drelling	.02	.10
❑ 25 Bill Laimbeer	.10	.30
❑ 26 Hersey Hawkins	.10	.30
❑ 27 Will Perdue	.02	.10
❑ 28 Todd Lichti	.02	.10
❑ 29 Gary Grant	.02	.10
❑ 30 Sam Perkins	.10	.30
❑ 31 Jayson Williams	.10	.30
❑ 32 Magic Johnson	.75	2.00
❑ 33 Larry Bird	1.00	2.50
❑ 34 Chris Morris	.02	.10
❑ 35 Nick Anderson	.10	.30
❑ 36 Scott Hastings	.02	.10
❑ 37 Ledell Eackles	.02	.10
❑ 38 Robert Pack	.02	.10
❑ 39 Dana Barros	.02	.10
❑ 40 Anthony Bonner	.02	.10
❑ 41 J.R. Reid	.02	.10
❑ 42 Tyrone Hill	.02	.10
❑ 43 Rik Smits	.10	.30
❑ 44 Kevin Duckworth	.02	.10
❑ 45 LaSalle Thompson	.02	.10
❑ 46 Brian Williams	.02	.10
❑ 47 Willie Anderson	.02	.10
❑ 48 Ken Norman	.02	.10
❑ 49 Mike Iuzzolino	.02	.10
❑ 50 Isiah Thomas	.25	.60
❑ 51 Alec Kessler	.02	.10
❑ 52 Johnny Dawkins	.02	.10
❑ 53 Avery Johnson	.02	.10
❑ 54 Stacey Augmon	.10	.30
❑ 55 Charles Oakley	.10	.30
❑ 56 Rex Chapman	.02	.10
❑ 57 Charles Shackleford	.02	.10
❑ 58 Jeff Ruland	.02	.10
❑ 59 Craig Ehlo	.02	.10
❑ 60 Jon Koncak	.02	.10
❑ 61 Danny Schayes	.02	.10
❑ 62 David Benoit	.02	.10
❑ 63 Robert Parish	.10	.30
❑ 64 Mookie Blaylock	.10	.30
❑ 65 Sean Elliott	.10	.30
❑ 66 Mark Aguirre	.02	.10
❑ 67 Scott Williams	.02	.10
❑ 68 Doug West	.02	.10
❑ 69 Kenny Anderson	.25	.60
❑ 70 Randy Brown	.02	.10
❑ 71 Muggsy Bogues	.10	.30
❑ 72 Spud Webb	.10	.30
❑ 73 Sedale Threatt	.02	.10
❑ 74 Chris Gatling	.02	.10
❑ 75 Derrick McKey	.02	.10
❑ 76 Sleepy Floyd	.02	.10
❑ 77 Chris Jackson	.02	.10
❑ 78 Thurl Bailey	.02	.10
❑ 79 Steve Smith	.30	.75
❑ 80 Cedric Ceballos	.02	.10
❑ 81 Anthony Bowie	.02	.10
❑ 82 John Williams	.02	.10
❑ 83 Paul Graham	.02	.10
❑ 84 Willie Burton	.02	.10
❑ 85 Vernon Maxwell	.02	.10
❑ 86 Stacey King	.02	.10
❑ 87 B.J.Armstrong	.02	.10
❑ 88 Kevin Gamble	.02	.10
❑ 89 Terry Catledge	.02	.10
❑ 90 Jeff Malone	.02	.10
❑ 91 Sam Bowie	.02	.10
❑ 92 Orlando Woolridge	.02	.10
❑ 93 Steve Kerr	.10	.30
❑ 94 Eric Leckner	.02	.10
❑ 95 Loy Vaught	.02	.10
❑ 96 Jud Buechler	.02	.10
❑ 97 Doug Smith	.02	.10
❑ 98 Sidney Green	.02	.10
❑ 99 Jerome Kersey	.02	.10
❑ 100 Patrick Ewing	.25	.60
❑ 101 Ed Nealy	.02	.10
❑ 102 Shawn Kemp	.50	1.25
❑ 103 Luc Longley	.10	.30
❑ 104 George McCloud	.02	.10
❑ 105 Ron Anderson	.02	.10
❑ 106 Moses Malone	.25	.60
❑ 107 Tony Smith	.02	.10
❑ 108 Terry Porter	.02	.10
❑ 109 Blair Rasmussen	.02	.10
❑ 110 Bimbo Coles	.02	.10
❑ 111 Grant Long	.02	.10
❑ 112 John Battle	.02	.10
❑ 113 Brian Oliver	.02	.10
❑ 114 Tyrone Corbin	.02	.10
❑ 115 Benoit Benjamin	.02	.10
❑ 116 Rick Fox	.10	.30
❑ 117 Rafael Addison	.02	.10
❑ 118 Danny Young	.02	.10
❑ 119 Fat Lever	.02	.10
❑ 120 Terry Cummings	.10	.30
❑ 121 Felton Spencer	.02	.10
❑ 122 Joe Kleine	.02	.10
❑ 123 Johnny Newman	.02	.10

124 Gary Payton	.50	1.25
125 Kurt Rambis	.02	.10
126 Vlade Divac	.10	.30
127 John Paxson	.02	.10
128 Lionel Simmons	.02	.10
129 Randy Wittman	.02	.10
130 Winston Garland	.02	.10
131 Jerry Reynolds	.02	.10
132 Dell Curry	.02	.10
133 Fred Roberts	.02	.10
134 Michael Adams	.02	.10
135 Charles Jones	.02	.10
136 Frank Brickowski	.02	.10
137 Alton Lister	.02	.10
138 Horace Grant	.10	.30
139 Greg Sutton	.02	.10
140 John Starks	.10	.30
141 Detlef Schrempf	.10	.30
142 Rodney Monroe	.02	.10
143 Pete Chilcutt	.02	.10
144 Mike Brown	.02	.10
145 Rony Seikaly	.02	.10
146 Donald Hodge	.02	.10
147 Kevin McHale	.25	.60
148 Ricky Pierce	.02	.10
149 Brian Shaw	.02	.10
150 Reggie Williams	.02	.10
151 Kendall Gill	.10	.30
152 Tom Chambers	.02	.10
153 Jack Haley	.02	.10
154 Terrell Brandon	.25	.60
155 Dennis Scott	.10	.30
156 Mark Randall	.02	.10
157 Kenny Payne	.02	.10
158 Bernard King	.02	.10
159 Tate George	.02	.10
160 Scott Skiles	.02	.10
161 Pervis Ellison	.02	.10
162 Marcus Liberty	.02	.10
163 Rumeal Robinson	.02	.10
164 Anthony Mason	.25	.60
165 Les Jepsen	.02	.10
166 Kenny Smith	.02	.10
167 Randy White	.02	.10
168 Dee Brown	.02	.10
169 Chris Dudley	.02	.10
170 Armon Gilliam	.02	.10
171 Eddie Johnson	.02	.10
172 A.C. Green	.10	.30
173 Darrell Walker	.02	.10
174 Bill Cartwright	.02	.10
175 Mike Gminski	.02	.10
176 Tom Tolbert	.02	.10
177 Buck Williams	.10	.30
178 Mark Eaton	.02	.10
179 Danny Manning	.10	.30
180 Glen Rice	.25	.60
181 Sarunas Marciulionis	.02	.10
182 Danny Ferry	.02	.10
183 Chris Corchiani	.02	.10
184 Dan Majerle	.10	.30
185 Alvin Robertson	.02	.10
186 Vern Fleming	.02	.10
187 Kevin Lynch	.02	.10
188 John Williams	.02	.10
189 Checklist 1-100	.02	.10
190 Checklist 101-200	.02	.10
191 David Robinson MC	.25	.60
192 Larry Johnson MC	.25	.60
193 Derrick Coleman MC	.02	.10
194 Larry Bird MC	.50	1.25
195 Billy Owens MC	.02	.10
196 Dikembe Mutombo MC	.25	.60
197 Charles Barkley MC	.25	.60
198 Scottie Pippen MC	.40	1.00
199 Clyde Drexler MC	.10	.30
200 John Stockton MC	.10	.30
201 Shaquille O'Neal MC	3.00	8.00
202 Chris Mullin MC	.10	.30
203 Glen Rice MC	.10	.30
204 Isiah Thomas MC	.10	.30
205 Karl Malone MC	.25	.60
206 Christian Laettner MC	.25	.60
207 Patrick Ewing MC	.10	.30
208 Dominique Wilkins MC	.10	.30
209 Alonzo Mourning MC	.50	1.25
210 Michael Jordan MC	1.50	4.00
211 Tim Hardaway	.30	.75
212 Rodney McCray	.02	.10
213 Larry Johnson	.30	.75
214 Charles Smith	.02	.10
215 Kevin Brooks	.02	.10
216 Kevin Johnson	.25	.60
217 Duane Cooper RC	.02	.10
218 Christian Laettner RC	.50	1.25
219 Tim Perry	.02	.10
220 Hakeem Olajuwon	.40	1.00
221 Lee Mayberry RC	.02	.10
222 Mark Bryant	.02	.10
223 Robert Horry RC	.25	.60
224 Tracy Murray RC	.10	.30
225 Greg Grant	.02	.10
226 Rolando Blackman	.02	.10
227 James Edwards UER	.02	.10
228 Sean Green	.02	.10
229 Buck Johnson	.02	.10
230 Andrew Lang	.02	.10
231 Tracy Moore RC	.02	.10
232 Adam Keefe RC	.02	.10
233 Tony Campbell	.02	.10
234 Rod Strickland	.25	.60
235 Terry Mills	.02	.10
236 Billy Owens	.10	.30
237 Bryant Stith RC	.10	.30
238 Tony Bennett RC	.02	.10
239 David Wood	.02	.10
240 Jay Humphries	.02	.10
241 Doc Rivers	.10	.30
242 Wayman Tisdale	.02	.10
243 Litterial Green RC	.02	.10
244 Jon Barry	.10	.30
245 Brad Daugherty	.02	.10
246 Nate McMillan	.02	.10
247 Shaquille O'Neal RC	6.00	15.00
248 Chris Smith RC	.02	.10
249 Duane Ferrell	.02	.10
250 Anthony Peeler RC	.10	.30
251 Gundars Vetra RC	.02	.10
252 Danny Ainge	.10	.30
253 Mitch Richmond	.25	.60
254 Malik Sealy RC	.10	.30
255 Brent Price RC	.10	.30
256 Xavier McDaniel	.02	.10
257 Bobby Phills RC	.25	.60
258 Donald Royal	.02	.10
259 Olden Polynice	.02	.10
260 Dominique Wilkins	.25	.60
261 Larry Krystkowiak	.02	.10
262 Duane Causwell	.02	.10
263 Todd Day RC	.10	.30
264 Sam Mack RC	.10	.30
265 John Stockton	.25	.60
266 Eddie Lee Wilkins	.02	.10
267 Gerald Glass	.02	.10
268 Robert Pack	.02	.10
269 Gerald Wilkins	.02	.10
270 Reggie Lewis	.10	.30
271 Scott Brooks	.02	.10
272 Randy Woods RC	.02	.10
273 Dikembe Mutombo	.30	.75
274 Kiki Vandeweghe	.02	.10
275 Rich King	.02	.10
276 Jeff Turner	.02	.10
277 Vinny Del Negro	.02	.10
278 Marlon Maxey RC	.02	.10
279 Elmore Spencer RC	.02	.10
280 Cedric Ceballos	.10	.30
281 Alex Blackwell RC	.02	.10
282 Terry Davis	.02	.10
283 Morlon Wiley	.02	.10
284 Trent Tucker	.02	.10
285 Carl Herrera	.02	.10
286 Eric Anderson RC	.02	.10
287 Clyde Drexler	.25	.60
288 Tom Gugliotta RC	.75	2.00
289 Dale Ellis	.02	.10
290 Lance Blanks	.02	.10
291 Tom Hammonds	.02	.10
292 Eric Murdock	.02	.10
293 Walt Williams RC	.25	.60
294 Gerald Paddio	.02	.10
295 Brian Howard RC	.02	.10
296 Ken Williams	.02	.10
297 Alonzo Mourning RC	1.50	4.00
298 Larry Nance	.02	.10
299 Jeff Grayer	.02	.10
300 Dave Johnson RC	.02	.10
301 Bob McCann RC	.02	.10
302 Bart Kofoed	.02	.10
303 Anthony Cook	.02	.10
304 Radisav Curcic RC	.02	.10
305 John Crotty RC	.02	.10
306 Brad Sellers	.02	.10
307 Marcus Webb RC	.02	.10
308 Winston Garland	.02	.10
309 Walter Palmer	.02	.10
310 Rod Higgins	.02	.10
311 Travis Mays	.02	.10
312 Alex Stivrins RC	.02	.10
313 Greg Kite	.02	.10
314 Dennis Rodman	.50	1.25
315 Mike Sanders	.02	.10
316 Ed Pinckney	.02	.10
317 Harold Miner RC	.10	.30
318 Pooh Richardson	.02	.10
319 Oliver Miller RC	.10	.30
320 Latrell Sprewell RC	2.00	5.00
321 Anthony Pullard RC	.02	.10
322 Mark Randall	.02	.10
323 Jeff Hornacek	.10	.30
324 Rick Mahorn UER	.02	.10
325 Sean Rooks RC	.02	.10
326 Paul Pressey	.02	.10
327 James Worthy	.25	.60
328 Matt Bullard	.02	.10
329 Reggie Smith RC	.02	.10
330 Don MacLean RC	.02	.10
331 John Williams UER	.02	.10
332 Frank Johnson	.02	.10
333 Hubert Davis RC	.10	.30
334 Lloyd Daniels RC	.02	.10
335 Steve Bardo RC	.02	.10
336 Jeff Sanders	.02	.10
337 Tree Rollins	.02	.10
338 Micheal Williams	.02	.10
339 Lorenzo Williams RC	.02	.10
340 Harvey Grant	.02	.10
341 Avery Johnson	.02	.10
342 Bo Kimble	.02	.10
343 LaPhonso Ellis RC	.25	.60
344 Mookie Blaylock	.10	.30
345 Isaiah Morris RC	.02	.10
346 C.Weatherspoon RC	.25	.60
347 Manute Bol	.02	.10
348 Victor Alexander	.02	.10
349 Corey Williams RC	.02	.10
350 Byron Houston RC	.02	.10
351 Stanley Roberts	.02	.10
352 Anthony Avent RC	.02	.10
353 Vincent Askew	.02	.10
354 Herb Williams	.02	.10
355 J.R. Reid	.02	.10
356 Brad Lohaus	.02	.10
357 Reggie Miller	.25	.60
358 Blue Edwards	.02	.10
359 Tom Tolbert	.02	.10
360 Charles Barkley	.40	1.00
361 David Robinson	.40	1.00
362 Dale Davis	.02	.10
363 Robert Werdann RC	.02	.10
364 Chuck Person	.02	.10
365 Alaa Abdelnaby	.02	.10
366 Dave Jamerson	.02	.10
367 Scottie Pippen	.75	2.00
368 Mark Jackson	.10	.30
369 Keith Askins	.02	.10
370 Marty Conlon	.02	.10
371 Chucky Brown	.02	.10
372 LaBradford Smith	.02	.10
373 Tim Kempton	.02	.10
374 Sam Mitchell	.02	.10
375 John Salley	.02	.10
376 Mario Elie	.10	.30
377 Mark West	.02	.10
378 David Wingate	.02	.10
379 Jaren Jackson RC	.10	.30
380 Rumeal Robinson	.02	.10
381 Kennard Winchester	.02	.10
382 Walter Bond RC	.02	.10
383 Isaac Austin RC	.10	.30
384 Derrick Coleman	.10	.30
385 Larry Smith	.02	.10
386 Joe Dumars	.25	.60
387 Matt Geiger RC	.10	.30
388 Stephen Howard RC	.02	.10
389 William Bedford	.02	.10
390 Jayson Williams	.10	.30

❑ 391 Kurt Rambis	.02	.10
❑ 392 Keith Jennings RC	.02	.10
❑ 393 Steve Kerr UER	.10	.30
❑ 394 Larry Stewart	.02	.10
❑ 395 Danny Young	.02	.10
❑ 396 Doug Overton	.02	.10
❑ 397 Mark Acres	.02	.10
❑ 398 John Bagley	.02	.10
❑ 399 Checklist 201-300	.02	.10
❑ 400 Checklist 301-400	.02	.10

1993-94 Stadium Club

❑ COMPLETE SET (360)	20.00	40.00
❑ COMPLETE SERIES 1 (180)	10.00	20.00
❑ COMPLETE SERIES 2 (180)	10.00	20.00
❑ COMMON CARD (1-180)	.02	.10
❑ COMMON CARD (181-360)	.01	.05
❑ 1 Michael Jordan TD	1.00	2.50
❑ 2 Kenny Anderson TD	.02	.10
❑ 3 Steve Smith TD	.07	.20
❑ 4 Kevin Gamble TD	.02	.10
❑ 5 Detlef Schrempf TD	.02	.10
❑ 6 Larry Johnson TD	.07	.20
❑ 7 Brad Daugherty TD	.02	.10
❑ 8 Rumeal Robinson TD	.02	.10
❑ 9 Micheal Williams TD	.02	.10
❑ 10 David Robinson TD	.15	.40
❑ 11 Sam Perkins TD	.02	.10
❑ 12 Thurl Bailey	.02	.10
❑ 13 Sherman Douglas	.02	.10
❑ 14 Larry Stewart	.02	.10
❑ 15 Kevin Johnson	.07	.20
❑ 16 Bill Cartwright	.02	.10
❑ 17 Larry Nance	.02	.10
❑ 18 P.J.Brown RC	.15	.40
❑ 19 Tony Bennett	.02	.10
❑ 20 Robert Parish	.07	.20
❑ 21 David Benoit	.02	.10
❑ 22 Detlef Schrempf	.07	.20
❑ 23 Hubert Davis	.02	.10
❑ 24 Donald Hodge	.02	.10
❑ 25 Hersey Hawkins	.07	.20
❑ 26 Mark Jackson	.07	.20
❑ 27 Reggie Williams	.02	.10
❑ 28 Lionel Simmons	.02	.10
❑ 29 Ron Harper	.07	.20
❑ 30 Chris Mills RC	.15	.40
❑ 31 Danny Schayes	.02	.10
❑ 32 J.R. Reid	.02	.10
❑ 33 Willie Burton	.02	.10
❑ 34 Greg Anthony	.02	.10
❑ 35 Elden Campbell	.02	.10
❑ 36 Ervin Johnson RC	.07	.20
❑ 37 Scott Brooks	.02	.10
❑ 38 Johnny Newman	.02	.10
❑ 39 Rex Chapman	.02	.10
❑ 40 Chuck Person	.02	.10
❑ 41 John Williams	.02	.10
❑ 42 Anthony Bowie	.02	.10
❑ 43 Negele Knight	.02	.10
❑ 44 Tyrone Corbin	.02	.10
❑ 45 Jud Buechler	.02	.10
❑ 46 Adam Keefe	.02	.10
❑ 47 Glen Rice	.07	.20
❑ 48 Tracy Murray	.02	.10
❑ 49 Rick Mahorn	.02	.10
❑ 50 Vlade Divac	.07	.20
❑ 51 Eric Murdock	.02	.10
❑ 52 Isaiah Morris	.02	.10
❑ 53 Bobby Hurley RC	.07	.20
❑ 54 Mitch Richmond	.15	.40
❑ 55 Danny Ainge	.07	.20
❑ 56 Dikembe Mutombo	.15	.40
❑ 57 Jeff Hornacek	.07	.20
❑ 58 Tony Campbell	.02	.10
❑ 59 Vinny Del Negro	.02	.10
❑ 60 Xavier McDaniel HC	.02	.10
❑ 61 Scottie Pippen HC	.25	.60
❑ 62 Larry Nance HC	.02	.10
❑ 63 Dikembe Mutombo HC	.07	.20
❑ 64 Hakeem Olajuwon HC	.15	.40
❑ 65 Dominique Wilkins HC	.07	.20
❑ 66 Clarence Weatherspoon HC	.02	.10
❑ 67 Chris Morris HC	.02	.10
❑ 68 Patrick Ewing HC	.07	.20
❑ 69 Kevin Willis HC	.02	.10
❑ 70 Jon Barry	.02	.10
❑ 71 Jerry Reynolds	.02	.10
❑ 72 Sarunas Marciulionis	.02	.10
❑ 73 Mark West	.02	.10
❑ 74 B.J. Armstrong	.02	.10
❑ 75 Greg Kite	.02	.10
❑ 76 LaSalle Thompson	.02	.10
❑ 77 Randy White	.02	.10
❑ 78 Alaa Abdelnaby	.02	.10
❑ 79 Kevin Brooks	.02	.10
❑ 80 Vern Fleming	.02	.10
❑ 81 Doc Rivers	.07	.20
❑ 82 Shawn Bradley RC	.15	.40
❑ 83 Wayman Tisdale	.02	.10
❑ 84 Olden Polynice	.02	.10
❑ 85 Michael Cage	.02	.10
❑ 86 Harold Miner	.02	.10
❑ 87 Doug Smith	.02	.10
❑ 88 Tom Gugliotta	.15	.40
❑ 89 Hakeem Olajuwon	.25	.60
❑ 90 Loy Vaught	.02	.10
❑ 91 James Worthy	.15	.40
❑ 92 John Paxson	.02	.10
❑ 93 Jon Koncak	.02	.10
❑ 94 Lee Mayberry	.02	.10
❑ 95 Clarence Weatherspoon	.02	.10
❑ 96 Mark Eaton	.02	.10
❑ 97 Rex Walters RC	.02	.10
❑ 98 Alvin Robertson	.02	.10
❑ 99 Dan Majerle	.07	.20
❑ 100 Shaquille O'Neal	.75	2.00
❑ 101 Derrick Coleman TD	.02	.10
❑ 102 Hersey Hawkins TD	.02	.10
❑ 103 Scottie Pippen TD	.25	.60
❑ 104 Scott Skiles TD	.02	.10
❑ 105 Rod Strickland TD	.02	.10
❑ 106 Pooh Richardson TD	.02	.10
❑ 107 Tom Gugliotta TD	.07	.20
❑ 108 Mark Jackson TD	.02	.10
❑ 109 Dikembe Mutombo TD	.07	.20
❑ 110 Charles Barkley TD	.15	.40
❑ 111 Otis Thorpe TD	.02	.10
❑ 112 Malik Sealy	.02	.10
❑ 113 Mark Macon	.02	.10
❑ 114 Dee Brown	.02	.10
❑ 115 Nate McMillan	.02	.10
❑ 116 John Starks	.07	.20
❑ 117 Clyde Drexler	.15	.40
❑ 118 Antoine Carr	.02	.10
❑ 119 Doug West	.02	.10
❑ 120 Victor Alexander	.02	.10
❑ 121 Kenny Gattison	.02	.10
❑ 122 Spud Webb	.07	.20
❑ 123 Rumeal Robinson	.02	.10
❑ 124 Tim Kempton	.02	.10
❑ 125 Karl Malone	.25	.60
❑ 126 Randy Woods	.02	.10
❑ 127 Calbert Cheaney RC	.07	.20
❑ 128 Johnny Dawkins	.02	.10
❑ 129 Dominique Wilkins	.15	.40
❑ 130 Horace Grant	.07	.20
❑ 131 Bill Laimbeer	.02	.10
❑ 132 Kenny Smith	.02	.10
❑ 133 Sedale Threatt	.02	.10
❑ 134 Brian Shaw	.02	.10
❑ 135 Dennis Scott	.02	.10
❑ 136 Mark Bryant	.02	.10
❑ 137 Xavier McDaniel	.02	.10
❑ 138 David Wood	.02	.10
❑ 139 Luther Wright RC	.02	.10
❑ 140 Lloyd Daniels	.02	.10
❑ 141 Marlon Maxey UER	.02	.10
❑ 142 Pooh Richardson	.02	.10
❑ 143 Jeff Grayer	.02	.10
❑ 144 LaPhonso Ellis	.02	.10
❑ 145 Gerald Wilkins	.02	.10
❑ 146 Dell Curry	.02	.10
❑ 147 Duane Causwell	.02	.10
❑ 148 Tim Hardaway	.15	.40
❑ 149 Isiah Thomas	.15	.40
❑ 150 Doug Edwards RC	.02	.10
❑ 151 Anthony Peeler	.02	.10
❑ 152 Tate George	.02	.10
❑ 153 Terry Davis	.02	.10
❑ 154 Sam Perkins	.07	.20
❑ 155 John Salley	.02	.10
❑ 156 Vernon Maxwell	.02	.10
❑ 157 Anthony Avent	.02	.10
❑ 158 Clifford Robinson	.07	.20
❑ 159 Corie Blount RC	.02	.10
❑ 160 Gerald Paddio	.02	.10
❑ 161 Blair Rasmussen	.02	.10
❑ 162 Carl Herrera	.02	.10
❑ 163 Chris Smith	.02	.10
❑ 164 Pervis Ellison	.02	.10
❑ 165 Rod Strickland	.07	.20
❑ 166 Jeff Malone	.02	.10
❑ 167 Danny Ferry	.02	.10
❑ 168 Kevin Lynch	.02	.10
❑ 169 Michael Jordan	2.00	5.00
❑ 170 Derrick Coleman HC	.02	.10
❑ 171 Jerome Kersey HC	.02	.10
❑ 172 David Robinson HC	.15	.40
❑ 173 Shawn Kemp HC	.15	.40
❑ 174 Karl Malone HC	.15	.40
❑ 175 Shaquille O'Neal HC	.30	.75
❑ 176 Alonzo Mourning HC	.15	.40
❑ 177 Charles Barkley HC	.15	.40
❑ 178 Larry Johnson HC	.07	.20
❑ 179 Checklist 1-90	.02	.10
❑ 180 Checklist 91-180	.02	.10
❑ 181 Michael Jordan FF	.75	2.00
❑ 182 Dominique Wilkins FF	.05	.15
❑ 183 Dennis Rodman FF	.10	.30
❑ 184 Scottie Pippen FF	.20	.50
❑ 185 Larry Johnson FF	.07	.20
❑ 186 Karl Malone FF	.10	.30
❑ 187 Clarence Weatherspoon FF	.01	.05
❑ 188 Charles Barkley FF	.10	.30
❑ 189 Patrick Ewing FF	.07	.20
❑ 190 Derrick Coleman FF	.01	.05
❑ 191 LaBradford Smith	.01	.05
❑ 192 Derek Harper	.05	.15
❑ 193 Ken Norman	.01	.05
❑ 194 Rodney Rogers RC	.10	.30
❑ 195 Chris Dudley	.01	.05
❑ 196 Gary Payton	.20	.50
❑ 197 Andrew Lang	.01	.05
❑ 198 Billy Owens	.01	.05
❑ 199 Bryon Russell RC	.10	.30
❑ 200 Patrick Ewing	.10	.30
❑ 201 Stacey King	.01	.05
❑ 202 Grant Long	.01	.05
❑ 203 Sean Elliott	.05	.15
❑ 204 Muggsy Bogues	.05	.15
❑ 205 Kevin Edwards	.01	.05
❑ 206 Dale Davis	.01	.05
❑ 207 Dale Ellis	.01	.05
❑ 208 Terrell Brandon	.05	.15
❑ 209 Kevin Gamble	.01	.05
❑ 210 Robert Horry	.05	.15
❑ 211 Moses Malone	.15	.40
❑ 212 Gary Grant	.01	.05
❑ 213 Bobby Hurley	.05	.15
❑ 214 Larry Krystkowiak	.01	.05
❑ 215 A.C. Green	.05	.15
❑ 216 Christian Laettner	.05	.15
❑ 217 Orlando Woolridge	.01	.05
❑ 218 Craig Ehlo	.01	.05
❑ 219 Terry Porter	.01	.05
❑ 220 Jamal Mashburn RC	.40	1.00
❑ 221 Kevin Duckworth	.01	.05
❑ 222 Shawn Kemp	.20	.50
❑ 223 Frank Brickowski	.01	.05
❑ 224 Chris Webber RC	1.25	3.00
❑ 225 Charles Oakley	.05	.15
❑ 226 Jay Humphries	.01	.05
❑ 227 Steve Kerr	.05	.15
❑ 228 Tim Perry	.01	.05
❑ 229 Sleepy Floyd	.01	.05
❑ 230 Bimbo Coles	.01	.05
❑ 231 Eddie Johnson	.01	.05
❑ 232 Terry Mills	.01	.05
❑ 233 Danny Manning	.05	.15
❑ 234 Isaiah Rider RC	.30	.75
❑ 235 Darnell Mee RC	.01	.05
❑ 236 Haywoode Workman	.01	.05
❑ 237 Scott Skiles	.01	.05

❑ 238 Otis Thorpe	.05	.15
❑ 239 Mike Peplowski RC	.01	.05
❑ 240 Eric Leckner	.01	.05
❑ 241 Johnny Newman	.01	.05
❑ 242 Benoit Benjamin	.01	.05
❑ 243 Doug Christie	.05	.15
❑ 244 Acie Earl RC	.01	.05
❑ 245 Luc Longley	.05	.15
❑ 246 Tyrone Hill	.01	.05
❑ 247 Allan Houston RC	.50	1.25
❑ 248 Joe Kleine	.01	.05
❑ 249 Mookie Blaylock	.05	.15
❑ 250 Anthony Bonner	.01	.05
❑ 251 Luther Wright	.01	.05
❑ 252 Todd Day	.01	.05
❑ 253 Kendall Gill	.05	.15
❑ 254 Mario Elie	.01	.05
❑ 255 Pete Myers	.01	.05
❑ 256 Jim Les	.01	.05
❑ 257 Stanley Roberts	.01	.05
❑ 258 Michael Adams	.01	.05
❑ 259 Hersey Hawkins	.05	.15
❑ 260 Shawn Bradley	.07	.20
❑ 261 Scott Haskin RC	.01	.05
❑ 262 Corie Blount	.01	.05
❑ 263 Charles Smith	.01	.05
❑ 264 Armon Gilliam	.01	.05
❑ 265 Jamal Mashburn NW	.10	.30
❑ 266 Anfernee Hardaway NW	.50	1.25
❑ 267 Shawn Bradley NW	.07	.20
❑ 268 Chris Webber NW	.60	1.50
❑ 269 Bobby Hurley NW	.01	.05
❑ 270 Isaiah Rider NW	.10	.30
❑ 271 Dino Radja NW	.01	.05
❑ 272 Chris Mills NW	.05	.15
❑ 273 Nick Van Exel NW	.10	.30
❑ 274 Lindsey Hunter NW UER	.07	.20
❑ 275 Toni Kukoc NW	.10	.30
❑ 276 Popeye Jones NW	.01	.05
❑ 277 Chris Mills	.15	.40
❑ 278 Ricky Pierce	.01	.05
❑ 279 Negele Knight	.01	.05
❑ 280 Kenny Walker	.01	.05
❑ 281 Nick Van Exel RC	.40	1.00
❑ 282 Derrick Coleman	.05	.15
❑ 283 Popeye Jones RC	.01	.05
❑ 284 Derrick McKey	.01	.05
❑ 285 Rick Fox	.01	.05
❑ 286 Jerome Kersey	.01	.05
❑ 287 Steve Smith	.10	.30
❑ 288 Brian Williams	.01	.05
❑ 289 Chris Mullin	.10	.30
❑ 290 Terry Cummings	.01	.05
❑ 291 Donald Royal	.01	.05
❑ 292 Alonzo Mourning	.20	.50
❑ 293 Mike Brown	.01	.05
❑ 294 Latrell Sprewell	.30	.75
❑ 295 Oliver Miller	.01	.05
❑ 296 Terry Dehere RC	.01	.05
❑ 297 Detlef Schrempf	.05	.15
❑ 298 Sam Bowie UER	.01	.05
❑ 299 Chris Morris	.01	.05
❑ 300 Scottie Pippen	.40	1.00
❑ 301 Warren Kidd RC	.01	.05
❑ 302 Don MacLean	.01	.05
❑ 303 Sean Rooks	.01	.05
❑ 304 Matt Geiger	.01	.05
❑ 305 Dennis Rodman	.25	.60
❑ 306 Reggie Miller	.10	.30
❑ 307 Vin Baker RC	.30	.75
❑ 308 Anfernee Hardaway RC	1.00	2.50
❑ 309 Lindsey Hunter RC	.10	.30
❑ 310 Stacey Augmon	.01	.05
❑ 311 Randy Brown	.01	.05
❑ 312 Anthony Mason	.05	.15
❑ 313 John Stockton	.10	.30
❑ 314 Sam Cassell RC	.50	1.25
❑ 315 Buck Williams	.01	.05
❑ 316 Bryant Stith	.01	.05
❑ 317 Brad Daugherty	.01	.05
❑ 318 Dino Radja RC	.01	.05
❑ 319 Rony Seikaly	.01	.05
❑ 320 Charles Barkley	.25	.60
❑ 321 Avery Johnson	.01	.05
❑ 322 Mahmoud Abdul-Rauf	.01	.05
❑ 323 Larry Johnson	.10	.30
❑ 324 Micheal Williams	.01	.05
❑ 325 Mark Aguirre	.01	.05
❑ 326 Jim Jackson	.05	.15
❑ 327 Antonio Harvey RC	.01	.05
❑ 328 David Robinson	.20	.50
❑ 329 Calbert Cheaney	.02	.10
❑ 330 Kenny Anderson	.07	.20
❑ 331 Walt Williams	.02	.10
❑ 332 Kevin Willis	.01	.05
❑ 333 Nick Anderson	.05	.15
❑ 334 Rik Smits	.05	.15
❑ 335 Joe Dumars	.15	.40
❑ 336 Toni Kukoc RC	.50	1.25
❑ 337 Harvey Grant	.01	.05
❑ 338 Tom Chambers	.01	.05
❑ 339 Blue Edwards	.01	.05
❑ 340 Mark Price	.01	.05
❑ 341 Ervin Johnson	.05	.15
❑ 342 Rolando Blackman	.01	.05
❑ 343 Scott Burrell RC	.10	.30
❑ 344 Gheorghe Muresan RC	.10	.30
❑ 345 Chris Corchiani UER 336	.01	.05
❑ 346 Richard Petruska RC	.01	.05
❑ 347 Dana Barros	.01	.05
❑ 348 Hakeem Olajuwon FF	.10	.30
❑ 349 Dee Brown FF	.01	.05
❑ 350 John Starks FF	.01	.05
❑ 351 Ron Harper FF	.01	.05
❑ 352 Chris Webber FF	.60	1.50
❑ 353 Dan Majerle FF	.01	.05
❑ 354 Clyde Drexler FF	.05	.15
❑ 355 Shawn Kemp FF	.10	.30
❑ 356 David Robinson FF	.10	.30
❑ 357 Chris Morris FF	.01	.05
❑ 358 Shaquille O'Neal FF	.25	.60
❑ 359 Checklist	.01	.05
❑ 360 Checklist	.01	.05

1994-95 Stadium Club

❑ COMPLETE SET (362)	20.00	40.00
❑ COMPLETE SERIES 1 (182)	10.00	20.00
❑ COMPLETE SERIES 2 (180)	10.00	20.00
❑ 1 Patrick Ewing	.15	.40
❑ 2 Patrick Ewing TG	.05	.15
❑ 3 Bimbo Coles	.02	.10
❑ 4 Elden Campbell	.02	.10
❑ 5 Brent Price	.02	.10
❑ 6 Hubert Davis	.02	.10
❑ 7 Donald Royal	.02	.10
❑ 8 Tim Perry	.02	.10
❑ 9 Chris Webber	.40	1.00
❑ 10 Chris Webber TG	.20	.50
❑ 11 Brad Daugherty	.02	.10
❑ 12 P.J. Brown	.02	.10
❑ 13 Charles Barkley	.25	.60
❑ 14 Mario Elie	.02	.10
❑ 15 Tyrone Hill	.02	.10
❑ 16 Anfernee Hardaway	.40	1.00
❑ 17 Anfernee Hardaway TG	.20	.50
❑ 18 Toni Kukoc	.25	.60
❑ 19 Chris Morris	.02	.10
❑ 20 Gerald Wilkins	.02	.10
❑ 21 David Benoit	.02	.10
❑ 22 Kevin Duckworth	.02	.10
❑ 23 Derrick Coleman	.05	.15
❑ 24 Adam Keefe	.02	.10
❑ 25 Marlon Maxey	.02	.10
❑ 26 Vern Fleming	.02	.10
❑ 27 Jeff Malone	.02	.10
❑ 28 Rodney Rogers	.02	.10
❑ 29 Terry Mills	.02	.10
❑ 30 Doug West	.02	.10
❑ 31 Doug West TTG	.02	.10
❑ 32 Shaquille O'Neal	.75	2.00
❑ 33 Scottie Pippen	.50	1.25
❑ 34 Lee Mayberry	.02	.10
❑ 35 Dale Ellis	.02	.10
❑ 36 Cedric Ceballos	.02	.10
❑ 37 Lionel Simmons	.02	.10
❑ 38 Kenny Gattison	.02	.10
❑ 39 Popeye Jones	.02	.10
❑ 40 Jerome Kersey	.02	.10
❑ 41 Jerome Kersey TTG	.02	.10
❑ 42 Larry Stewart	.02	.10
❑ 43 Rod Strickland	.05	.15
❑ 44 Chris Mills	.05	.15
❑ 45 Latrell Sprewell	.15	.40
❑ 46 Haywoode Workman	.02	.10
❑ 47 Charles Smith	.02	.10
❑ 48 Detlef Schrempf	.05	.15
❑ 49 Gary Grant	.02	.10
❑ 50 Gary Grant TTG	.02	.10
❑ 51 Tom Chambers	.02	.10
❑ 52 J.R. Reid	.02	.10
❑ 53 Mookie Blaylock	.02	.10
❑ 54 Mookie Blaylock TTG	.02	.10
❑ 55 Rony Seikaly	.02	.10
❑ 56 Isaiah Rider	.05	.15
❑ 57 Isaiah Rider TTG	.02	.10
❑ 58 Nick Anderson	.02	.10
❑ 59 Victor Alexander	.02	.10
❑ 60 Lucious Harris	.02	.10
❑ 61 Mark Macon	.02	.10
❑ 62 Otis Thorpe	.02	.10
❑ 63 Randy Woods	.02	.10
❑ 64 Clyde Drexler	.15	.40
❑ 65 Dikembe Mutombo	.05	.15
❑ 66 Todd Day	.02	.10
❑ 67 Greg Anthony	.02	.10
❑ 68 Sherman Douglas	.02	.10
❑ 69 Chris Mullin	.15	.40
❑ 70 Kevin Johnson	.05	.15
❑ 71 Kendall Gill	.05	.15
❑ 72 Dennis Rodman	.30	.75
❑ 73 Dennis Rodman TG	.15	.40
❑ 74 Jeff Turner	.02	.10
❑ 75 John Stockton	.15	.40
❑ 76 John Stockton TTG	.05	.15
❑ 77 Doug Edwards	.02	.10
❑ 78 Jim Jackson	.05	.15
❑ 79 Hakeem Olajuwon	.25	.60
❑ 80 Glen Rice	.05	.15
❑ 81 Christian Laettner	.05	.15
❑ 82 Terry Porter	.02	.10
❑ 83 Joe Dumars	.15	.40
❑ 84 David Wingate	.02	.10
❑ 85 B.J. Armstrong	.02	.10
❑ 86 Derrick McKey	.02	.10
❑ 87 Elmore Spencer	.02	.10
❑ 88 Walt Williams	.02	.10
❑ 89 Shawn Bradley	.02	.10
❑ 90 Acie Earl	.02	.10
❑ 91 Acie Earl TTG	.02	.10
❑ 92 Randy Brown	.02	.10
❑ 93 Grant Long	.02	.10
❑ 94 Terry Dehere	.02	.10
❑ 95 Spud Webb	.02	.10
❑ 96 Lindsey Hunter	.05	.15
❑ 97 Blair Rasmussen	.02	.10
❑ 98 Tim Hardaway	.15	.40
❑ 99 Kevin Edwards	.02	.10
❑ 100 Patrick Ewing CT	.05	.15
❑ 101 Chuck Person CT	.15	.40
❑ 102 S.O'Neal/Abdul-Rauf CT	.15	.40
❑ 103 Rony Seikaly CT	.02	.10
❑ 104 H.Olajuwon/C.Drexler CT	.15	.40
❑ 105 Chris Mullin CT	.05	.15
❑ 106 R.Horry/L.Sprewell CT	.15	.40
❑ 107 Pooh Richardson CT	.05	.15
❑ 108 Dennis Scott CT	.02	.10
❑ 109 Kendall Gill CT	.02	.10
❑ 110 Scott Skiles CT	.02	.10
❑ 111 Terry Mills CT	.05	.15
❑ 112 Christian Laettner CT	.02	.10
❑ 113 Stacey Augmon CT	.02	.10
❑ 114 Sam Perkins CT	.05	.15
❑ 115 Carl Herrera	.02	.10
❑ 116 Sam Bowie	.02	.10
❑ 117 Gary Payton	.25	.60
❑ 118 Danny Ainge	.02	.10
❑ 119 Danny Ainge TTG	.02	.10
❑ 120 Luc Longley	.02	.10
❑ 121 Antonio Davis	.02	.10
❑ 122 Terry Cummings	.02	.10
❑ 123 Terry Cummings TTG	.02	.10
❑ 124 Mark Price	.02	.10
❑ 125 Jamal Mashburn	.15	.40
❑ 126 Mahmoud Abdul-Rauf	.02	.10

❑ 127 Charles Oakley	.02	.10
❑ 128 Steve Smith	.05	.15
❑ 129 Vin Baker	.15	.40
❑ 130 Robert Horry	.05	.15
❑ 131 Doug Christie	.05	.15
❑ 132 Wayman Tisdale	.02	.10
❑ 133 Wayman Tisdale TTG	.02	.10
❑ 134 Muggsy Bogues	.05	.15
❑ 135 Dino Radja	.02	.10
❑ 136 Jeff Hornacek	.05	.15
❑ 137 Gheorghe Muresan	.02	.10
❑ 138 Loy Vaught	.02	.10
❑ 139 Loy Vaught TTG	.02	.10
❑ 140 Benoit Benjamin	.02	.10
❑ 141 Johnny Dawkins	.02	.10
❑ 142 Allan Houston	.25	.60
❑ 143 Jon Barry	.02	.10
❑ 144 Reggie Miller	.15	.40
❑ 145 Kevin Willis	.02	.10
❑ 146 James Worthy	.15	.40
❑ 147 James Worthy TTG	.05	.15
❑ 148 Scott Burrell	.02	.10
❑ 149 Tom Gugliotta	.05	.15
❑ 150 LaPhonso Ellis	.02	.10
❑ 151 Doug Smith	.02	.10
❑ 152 A.C. Green	.05	.15
❑ 153 A.C. Green TTG	.02	.10
❑ 154 George Lynch	.02	.10
❑ 155 Sam Perkins	.05	.15
❑ 156 Corie Blount	.02	.10
❑ 157 Xavier McDaniel	.02	.10
❑ 158 Xavier McDaniel TTG	.02	.10
❑ 159 Eric Murdock	.02	.10
❑ 160 David Robinson	.25	.60
❑ 161 Karl Malone	.25	.60
❑ 162 Karl Malone TTG	.15	.40
❑ 163 Clarence Weatherspoon	.02	.10
❑ 164 Calbert Cheaney	.02	.10
❑ 165 Tom Hammonds	.02	.10
❑ 166 Tom Hammonds TTG	.02	.10
❑ 167 Alonzo Mourning	.20	.50
❑ 168 Clifford Robinson	.05	.15
❑ 169 Micheal Williams	.02	.10
❑ 170 Ervin Johnson	.02	.10
❑ 171 Mike Gminski	.02	.10
❑ 172 Jason Kidd RC	1.50	4.00
❑ 173 Anthony Bonner	.02	.10
❑ 174 Stacey King	.02	.10
❑ 175 Rex Chapman	.02	.10
❑ 176 Greg Graham	.02	.10
❑ 177 Stanley Roberts	.02	.10
❑ 178 Mitch Richmond	.15	.40
❑ 179 Eric Montross RC	.02	.10
❑ 180 Eddie Jones RC	.75	2.00
❑ 181 Grant Hill RC	.75	2.00
❑ 182 Donyell Marshall RC	.15	.40
❑ 183 Glenn Robinson RC	.50	1.25
❑ 184 Dominique Wilkins	.15	.40
❑ 185 Mark Price	.02	.10
❑ 186 Anthony Mason	.05	.15
❑ 187 Tyrone Corbin	.02	.10
❑ 188 Dale Davis	.02	.10
❑ 189 Nate McMillan	.02	.10
❑ 190 Jason Kidd	.75	2.00
❑ 191 John Salley	.02	.10
❑ 192 Keith Jennings	.02	.10
❑ 193 Mark Bryant	.02	.10
❑ 194 Sleepy Floyd	.02	.10
❑ 195 Grant Hill	.40	1.00
❑ 196 Joe Kleine	.02	.10
❑ 197 Anthony Peeler	.02	.10
❑ 198 Malik Sealy	.02	.10
❑ 199 Kenny Walker	.02	.10
❑ 200 Donyell Marshall	.15	.40
❑ 201 Vlade Divac AI	.02	.10
❑ 202 Dino Radja AI	.02	.10
❑ 203 Carl Herrera AI	.02	.10
❑ 204 Olden Polynice AI	.02	.10
❑ 205 Patrick Ewing AI	.05	.15
❑ 206 Willie Anderson	.02	.10
❑ 207 Mitch Richmond	.15	.40
❑ 208 John Crotty	.02	.10
❑ 209 Tracy Murray	.02	.10
❑ 210 Juwan Howard RC	.40	1.00
❑ 211 Robert Parish	.05	.15
❑ 212 Steve Kerr	.02	.10
❑ 213 Anthony Bowie	.02	.10
❑ 214 Tim Breaux	.02	.10
❑ 215 Sharone Wright RC	.02	.10

❑ 216 Brian Williams	.02	.10
❑ 217 Rick Fox	.02	.10
❑ 218 Harold Miner	.02	.10
❑ 219 Duane Ferrell	.02	.10
❑ 220 Lamond Murray RC	.05	.15
❑ 221 Blue Edwards	.02	.10
❑ 222 Bill Cartwright	.02	.10
❑ 223 Sergei Bazarevich RC	.02	.10
❑ 224 Herb Williams	.02	.10
❑ 225 Brian Grant RC	.40	1.00
❑ 226 Derek Harper BCT	.02	.10
❑ 227 Rod Strickland BCT	.15	.40
❑ 228 Kevin Johnson BCT	.02	.10
❑ 229 Lindsey Hunter BCT	.02	.10
❑ 230 T.Hardaway/Sprewell BCT	.05	.15
❑ 231 Bill Wennington	.02	.10
❑ 232 Brian Shaw	.02	.10
❑ 233 Jamie Watson RC	.02	.10
❑ 234 Chris Whitney	.02	.10
❑ 235 Eric Montross	.02	.10
❑ 236 Kenny Smith	.02	.10
❑ 237 Andrew Lang	.02	.10
❑ 238 Lorenzo Williams	.02	.10
❑ 239 Dana Barros	.02	.10
❑ 240 Eddie Jones	.40	1.00
❑ 241 Harold Ellis	.02	.10
❑ 242 James Edwards	.02	.10
❑ 243 Don MacLean	.02	.10
❑ 244 Ed Pinckney	.02	.10
❑ 245 Carlos Rogers RC	.02	.10
❑ 246 Michael Adams	.02	.10
❑ 247 Rex Walters	.02	.10
❑ 248 John Starks	.02	.10
❑ 249 Terrell Brandon	.05	.15
❑ 250 Khalid Reeves RC	.02	.10
❑ 251 Dominique Wilkins AI	.05	.15
❑ 252 Toni Kukoc AI	.15	.40
❑ 253 Rick Fox AI	.02	.10
❑ 254 Detlef Schrempf AI	.02	.10
❑ 255 Rik Smits AI	.02	.10
❑ 256 Johnny Dawkins	.02	.10
❑ 257 Dan Majerle	.05	.15
❑ 258 Mike Brown	.02	.10
❑ 259 Byron Scott	.05	.15
❑ 260 Jalen Rose RC	.60	1.50
❑ 261 Byron Houston	.02	.10
❑ 262 Frank Brickowski	.02	.10
❑ 263 Vernon Maxwell	.02	.10
❑ 264 Craig Ehlo	.02	.10
❑ 265 Yinka Dare RC	.02	.10
❑ 266 Dee Brown	.02	.10
❑ 267 Felton Spencer	.02	.10
❑ 268 Harvey Grant	.02	.10
❑ 269 Nick Van Exel	.15	.40
❑ 270 Bob Martin	.02	.10
❑ 271 Hersey Hawkins	.05	.15
❑ 272 Scott Williams	.02	.10
❑ 273 Sarunas Marciulionis	.02	.10
❑ 274 Kevin Gamble	.02	.10
❑ 275 Clifford Rozier RC	.02	.10
❑ 276 B.J. Armstrong BCT	.02	.10
❑ 277 John Stockton BCT	.05	.15
❑ 278 Bobby Hurley BCT	.05	.15
❑ 279 A.Hardaway/D.Scott BCT	.10	.30
❑ 280 J.Kidd/J.Jackson BCT	.15	.40
❑ 281 Ron Harper	.05	.15
❑ 282 Chuck Person	.02	.10
❑ 283 John Williams	.02	.10
❑ 284 Robert Pack	.02	.10
❑ 285 Aaron McKie RC	.30	.75
❑ 286 Chris Smith	.02	.10
❑ 287 Horace Grant	.05	.15
❑ 288 Oliver Miller	.02	.10
❑ 289 Derek Harper	.02	.10
❑ 290 Eric Mobley RC	.02	.10
❑ 291 Scott Skiles	.02	.10
❑ 292 Olden Polynice	.02	.10
❑ 293 Mark Jackson	.02	.10
❑ 294 Wayman Tisdale	.02	.10
❑ 295 Tony Dumas RC	.02	.10
❑ 296 Bryon Russell	.02	.10
❑ 297 Vlade Divac	.02	.10
❑ 298 David Wesley	.02	.10
❑ 299 Askia Jones RC	.02	.10
❑ 300 B.J.Tyler RC	.02	.10
❑ 301 Hakeem Olajuwon AI	.15	.40
❑ 302 Luc Longley AI	.02	.10
❑ 303 Rony Seikaly AI	.02	.10
❑ 304 Sarunas Marciulionis AI	.02	.10

❑ 305 Dikembe Mutombo AI	.02	.10
❑ 306 Ken Norman	.02	.10
❑ 307 Dell Curry	.02	.10
❑ 308 Danny Ferry	.02	.10
❑ 309 Shawn Kemp	.25	.60
❑ 310 Dickey Simpkins RC	.02	.10
❑ 311 Johnny Newman	.02	.10
❑ 312 Dwayne Schintzius	.02	.10
❑ 313 Sean Elliott	.05	.15
❑ 314 Sean Rooks	.02	.10
❑ 315 Bill Curley RC	.02	.10
❑ 316 Bryant Stith	.02	.10
❑ 317 Pooh Richardson	.02	.10
❑ 318 Jim McIlvaine	.02	.10
❑ 319 Dennis Scott	.02	.10
❑ 320 Wesley Person RC	.15	.40
❑ 321 Bobby Hurley	.02	.10
❑ 322 Armon Gilliam	.02	.10
❑ 323 Rik Smits	.02	.10
❑ 324 Tony Smith	.02	.10
❑ 325 Monty Williams RC	.02	.10
❑ 326 G.Payton/K.Gill BCT	.15	.40
❑ 327 Mookie Blaylock BCT	.02	.10
❑ 328 Mark Jackson BCT	.05	.15
❑ 329 Sam Cassell BCT	.15	.40
❑ 330 Harold Miner BCT	.02	.10
❑ 331 Vinny Del Negro	.02	.10
❑ 332 Billy Owens	.02	.10
❑ 333 Mark West	.02	.10
❑ 334 Matt Geiger	.02	.10
❑ 335 Greg Minor RC	.02	.10
❑ 336 Larry Johnson	.05	.15
❑ 337 Donald Hodge	.02	.10
❑ 338 Aaron Williams RC	.02	.10
❑ 339 Jay Humphries	.02	.10
❑ 340 Charlie Ward RC	.15	.40
❑ 341 Scott Brooks	.02	.10
❑ 342 Stacey Augmon	.02	.10
❑ 343 Will Perdue	.02	.10
❑ 344 Dale Ellis	.02	.10
❑ 345 Brooks Thompson RC	.02	.10
❑ 346 Manute Bol	.02	.10
❑ 347 Kenny Anderson	.05	.15
❑ 348 Willie Burton	.02	.10
❑ 349 Michael Cage	.02	.10
❑ 350 Danny Manning	.05	.15
❑ 351 Ricky Pierce	.02	.10
❑ 352 Sam Cassell	.15	.40
❑ 353 Reggie Miller FG	.05	.15
❑ 354 David Robinson FG	.15	.40
❑ 355 Shaquille O'Neal FG	.30	.75
❑ 356 Scottie Pippen FG	.25	.60
❑ 357 Alonzo Mourning FG	.15	.40
❑ 358 Clarence Weatherspoon FG	.02	.10
❑ 359 Derrick Coleman FG	.02	.10
❑ 360 Charles Barkley FG	.15	.40
❑ 361 Karl Malone FG	.15	.40
❑ 362 Chris Webber FG	.20	.50

1995-96 Stadium Club

❑ COMPLETE SET (361)	25.00	50.00
❑ COMPLETE SERIES 1 (180)	15.00	25.00
❑ COMPLETE SERIES 2 (181)	10.00	25.00
❑ 1 Michael Jordan	2.00	5.00
❑ 2 Glenn Robinson	.30	.75
❑ 3 Jason Kidd	1.00	2.50
❑ 4 Clyde Drexler	.30	.75
❑ 5 Horace Grant	.20	.50
❑ 6 Allan Houston	.20	.50
❑ 7 Xavier McDaniel	.08	.25
❑ 8 Jeff Hornacek	.20	.50
❑ 9 Vlade Divac	.20	.50
❑ 10 Juwan Howard	.30	.75
❑ 11 Keith Jennings EXP	.08	.25
❑ 12 Grant Long	.08	.25
❑ 13 Jalen Rose	.40	1.00

❑ 14 Malik Sealy	.08	.25
❑ 15 Gary Payton	.30	.75
❑ 16 Danny Ferry	.08	.25
❑ 17 Glen Rice	.20	.50
❑ 18 Randy Brown	.08	.25
❑ 19 Greg Graham	.08	.25
❑ 20 Kenny Anderson	.20	.50
❑ 21 Aaron McKie	.20	.50
❑ 22 John Salley EXP	.08	.25
❑ 23 Darrin Hancock	.08	.25
❑ 24 Carlos Rogers	.08	.25
❑ 25 Vin Baker	.20	.50
❑ 26 Bill Wennington	.08	.25
❑ 27 Kenny Smith	.08	.25
❑ 28 Sherman Douglas	.08	.25
❑ 29 Terry Davis	.08	.25
❑ 30 Grant Hill	.40	1.00
❑ 31 Reggie Miller	.30	.75
❑ 32 Anfernee Hardaway	.30	.75
❑ 33 Patrick Ewing	.30	.75
❑ 34 Charles Barkley	.40	1.00
❑ 35 Eddie Jones	.40	1.00
❑ 36 Kevin Duckworth	.08	.25
❑ 37 Tom Hammonds	.08	.25
❑ 38 Craig Ehlo	.08	.25
❑ 39 Micheal Williams	.08	.25
❑ 40 Alonzo Mourning	.20	.50
❑ 41 John Williams	.08	.25
❑ 42 Felton Spencer	.08	.25
❑ 43 Lamond Murray	.08	.25
❑ 44 Dontonio Wingfield EXP	.08	.25
❑ 45 Rik Smits	.20	.50
❑ 46 Donyell Marshall	.20	.50
❑ 47 Clarence Weatherspoon	.08	.25
❑ 48 Kevin Edwards	.08	.25
❑ 49 Charlie Ward	.08	.25
❑ 50 David Robinson	.30	.75
❑ 51 James Robinson	.08	.25
❑ 52 Bill Cartwright	.08	.25
❑ 53 Bobby Hurley	.08	.25
❑ 54 Kevin Gamble	.08	.25
❑ 55 B.J. Tyler EXP	.08	.25
❑ 56 Chris Smith	.08	.25
❑ 57 Wesley Person	.08	.25
❑ 58 Tim Breaux	.08	.25
❑ 59 Mitchell Butler	.08	.25
❑ 60 Toni Kukoc	.20	.50
❑ 61 Roy Tarpley	.08	.25
❑ 62 Todd Day	.08	.25
❑ 63 Anthony Peeler	.08	.25
❑ 64 Brian Williams	.08	.25
❑ 65 Muggsy Bogues	.20	.50
❑ 66 Jerome Kersey EXP	.08	.25
❑ 67 Eric Piatkowski	.20	.50
❑ 68 Tim Perry	.08	.25
❑ 69 Chris Gatling	.08	.25
❑ 70 Mark Price	.20	.50
❑ 71 Terry Mills	.08	.25
❑ 72 Anthony Avent	.08	.25
❑ 73 Matt Geiger	.08	.25
❑ 74 Walt Williams	.08	.25
❑ 75 Sean Elliott	.20	.50
❑ 76 Ken Norman	.08	.25
❑ 77 Kendall Gill TA	.08	.25
❑ 78 Byron Houston	.08	.25
❑ 79 Rick Fox	.20	.50
❑ 80 Derek Harper	.20	.50
❑ 81 Rod Strickland	.08	.25
❑ 82 Bryon Russell	.08	.25
❑ 83 Antonio Davis	.08	.25
❑ 84 Isaiah Rider	.08	.25
❑ 85 Kevin Johnson	.20	.50
❑ 86 Derrick Coleman	.08	.25
❑ 87 Doug Overton	.08	.25
❑ 88 Hersey Hawkins TA	.08	.25
❑ 89 Popeye Jones	.08	.25
❑ 90 Dickey Simpkins	.08	.25
❑ 91 Rodney Rogers TA	.08	.25
❑ 92 Rex Chapman TA	.08	.25
❑ 93 Spud Webb TA	.08	.25
❑ 94 Lee Mayberry	.08	.25
❑ 95 Cedric Ceballos	.08	.25
❑ 96 Tyrone Hill	.08	.25
❑ 97 Bill Curley	.08	.25
❑ 98 Jeff Turner	.08	.25
❑ 99 Tyrone Corbin TA	.08	.25
❑ 100 John Stockton	.40	1.00
❑ 101 Mookie Blaylock EC	.08	.25
❑ 102 Dino Radja EC	.08	.25
❑ 103 Alonzo Mourning EC	.20	.50
❑ 104 Scottie Pippen EC	.50	1.25
❑ 105 Terrell Brandon EC	.20	.50
❑ 106 Jim Jackson EC	.08	.25
❑ 107 Mahmoud Abdul-Rauf EC	.08	.25
❑ 108 Grant Hill EC	.40	1.00
❑ 109 Tim Hardaway EC	.08	.25
❑ 110 Hakeem Olajuwon EC	.20	.50
❑ 111 Rik Smits EC	.08	.25
❑ 112 Loy Vaught EC	.08	.25
❑ 113 Vlade Divac EC	.08	.25
❑ 114 Kevin Willis EC	.08	.25
❑ 115 Glenn Robinson EC	.30	.75
❑ 116 Christian Laettner EC	.20	.50
❑ 117 Derrick Coleman EC	.08	.25
❑ 118 Patrick Ewing EC	.30	.75
❑ 119 Shaquille O'Neal EC	.75	2.00
❑ 120 Dana Barros EC	.08	.25
❑ 121 Charles Barkley EC	.30	.75
❑ 122 Rod Strickland EC	.08	.25
❑ 123 Brian Grant EC	.30	.75
❑ 124 David Robinson EC	.20	.50
❑ 125 Shawn Kemp EC	.08	.25
❑ 126 Oliver Miller EC	.08	.25
❑ 127 Karl Malone EC	.30	.75
❑ 128 Benoit Benjamin EC	.08	.25
❑ 129 Chris Webber EC	.30	.75
❑ 130 Dan Majerle	.20	.50
❑ 131 Calbert Cheaney	.08	.25
❑ 132 Mark Jackson	.20	.50
❑ 133 Greg Anthony EXP	.08	.25
❑ 134 Scott Burrell	.08	.25
❑ 135 Detlef Schrempf	.20	.50
❑ 136 Marty Conlon	.08	.25
❑ 137 Rony Seikaly	.08	.25
❑ 138 Olden Polynice	.08	.25
❑ 139 Terry Cummings	.08	.25
❑ 140 Stacey Augmon	.08	.25
❑ 141 Bryant Stith	.08	.25
❑ 142 Sean Higgins	.08	.25
❑ 143 Antoine Carr	.08	.25
❑ 144 Blue Edwards EXP	.08	.25
❑ 145 A.C. Green	.20	.50
❑ 146 Bobby Phills	.08	.25
❑ 147 Terry Dehere	.08	.25
❑ 148 Sharone Wright	.08	.25
❑ 149 Nick Anderson	.08	.25
❑ 150 Jim Jackson	.08	.25
❑ 151 Eric Montross	.08	.25
❑ 152 Doug West	.08	.25
❑ 153 Charles Smith	.08	.25
❑ 154 Will Perdue	.08	.25
❑ 155 Gerald Wilkins EXP	.08	.25
❑ 156 Robert Horry	.20	.50
❑ 157 Robert Parish	.20	.50
❑ 158 Lindsey Hunter	.08	.25
❑ 159 Harvey Grant	.08	.25
❑ 160 Tim Hardaway	.20	.50
❑ 161 Sarunas Marciulionis	.08	.25
❑ 162 Khalid Reeves	.08	.25
❑ 163 Bo Outlaw	.08	.25
❑ 164 Dale Davis	.08	.25
❑ 165 Nick Van Exel	.30	.75
❑ 166 Byron Scott EXP	.08	.25
❑ 167 Steve Smith	.20	.50
❑ 168 Brian Grant	.30	.75
❑ 169 Avery Johnson	.08	.25
❑ 170 Dikembe Mutombo	.20	.50
❑ 171 Tom Gugliotta	.08	.25
❑ 172 Armon Gilliam	.08	.25
❑ 173 Shawn Bradley	.08	.25
❑ 174 Herb Williams	.08	.25
❑ 175 Dino Radja	.08	.25
❑ 176 Billy Owens	.08	.25
❑ 177 Kenny Gattison EXP	.08	.25
❑ 178 J.R. Reid	.08	.25
❑ 179 Otis Thorpe	.08	.25
❑ 180 Sam Cassell	.30	.75
❑ 181 Sam Cassell	.30	.75
❑ 182 Pooh Richardson	.08	.25
❑ 183 Johnny Newman	.08	.25
❑ 184 Dennis Scott	.08	.25
❑ 185 Will Perdue	.08	.25
❑ 186 Andrew Lang	.08	.25
❑ 187 Karl Malone	.40	1.00
❑ 188 Buck Williams	.08	.25
❑ 189 P.J. Brown	.08	.25
❑ 190 Khalid Reeves	.08	.25
❑ 191 Kevin Willis	.20	.50
❑ 192 Robert Pack	.08	.25
❑ 193 Joe Dumars	.30	.75
❑ 194 Sam Perkins	.20	.50
❑ 195 Dan Majerle	.20	.50
❑ 196 John Williams	.08	.25
❑ 197 Reggie Williams	.08	.25
❑ 198 Greg Anthony	.08	.25
❑ 199 Steve Kerr	.20	.50
❑ 200 Richard Dumas	.08	.25
❑ 201 Dee Brown	.08	.25
❑ 202 Zan Tabak	.08	.25
❑ 203 David Wood	.08	.25
❑ 204 Duane Causwell	.08	.25
❑ 205 Sedale Threatt	.08	.25
❑ 206 Hubert Davis	.08	.25
❑ 207 Donald Hodge	.08	.25
❑ 208 Duane Ferrell	.08	.25
❑ 209 Sam Mitchell	.08	.25
❑ 210 Adam Keefe	.08	.25
❑ 211 Clifford Robinson	.08	.25
❑ 212 Rodney Rogers	.08	.25
❑ 213 Jayson Williams	.08	.25
❑ 214 Brian Shaw	.08	.25
❑ 215 Luc Longley	.08	.25
❑ 216 Don MacLean	.08	.25
❑ 217 Rex Chapman	.08	.25
❑ 218 Wayman Tisdale	.08	.25
❑ 219 Shawn Kemp	.20	.50
❑ 220 Chris Webber	.40	1.00
❑ 221 Antonio Harvey	.08	.25
❑ 222 Sarunas Marciulionis	.08	.25
❑ 223 Jeff Malone	.08	.25
❑ 224 Chucky Brown	.08	.25
❑ 225 Greg Minor	.08	.25
❑ 226 Clifford Rozier	.08	.25
❑ 227 Derrick McKey	.08	.25
❑ 228 Tony Dumas	.08	.25
❑ 229 Oliver Miller	.08	.25
❑ 230 Charles Oakley	.08	.25
❑ 231 Fred Roberts	.08	.25
❑ 232 Glen Rice	.20	.50
❑ 233 Terry Porter	.08	.25
❑ 234 Mark Macon	.08	.25
❑ 235 Michael Cage	.08	.25
❑ 236 Eric Murdock	.08	.25
❑ 237 Vinny Del Negro	.08	.25
❑ 238 Spud Webb	.20	.50
❑ 239 Mario Elie	.08	.25
❑ 240 Blue Edwards	.08	.25
❑ 241 Dontonio Wingfield	.08	.25
❑ 242 Brooks Thompson	.08	.25
❑ 243 Alonzo Mourning	.20	.50
❑ 244 Dennis Rodman	.20	.50
❑ 245 Lorenzo Williams	.08	.25
❑ 246 Haywoode Workman	.08	.25
❑ 247 Loy Vaught	.08	.25
❑ 248 Vernon Maxwell	.08	.25
❑ 249 Lionel Simmons	.08	.25
❑ 250 Chris Childs	.08	.25
❑ 251 Mahmoud Abdul-Rauf	.08	.25
❑ 252 Vincent Askew	.08	.25
❑ 253 Chris Morris	.08	.25
❑ 254 Elliot Perry	.08	.25
❑ 255 Dell Curry	.08	.25
❑ 256 Dana Barros	.08	.25
❑ 257 Terrell Brandon	.20	.50
❑ 258 Monty Williams	.08	.25
❑ 259 Corie Blount	.08	.25
❑ 260 B.J. Armstrong	.08	.25
❑ 261 Jim McIlvaine	.08	.25
❑ 262 Otis Thorpe	.08	.25
❑ 263 Sean Rooks	.08	.25
❑ 264 Tony Massenburg	.08	.25
❑ 265 Steve Smith	.20	.50
❑ 266 Ron Harper	.20	.50
❑ 267 Dale Ellis	.08	.25
❑ 268 Clyde Drexler	.30	.75
❑ 269 Jamie Watson	.08	.25
❑ 270 Doc Rivers	.20	.50
❑ 271 Derrick Alston	.08	.25
❑ 272 Eric Mobley	.08	.25
❑ 273 Ricky Pierce	.08	.25
❑ 274 David Wesley	.08	.25
❑ 275 John Starks	.20	.50
❑ 276 Chris Mullin	.30	.75
❑ 277 Ervin Johnson	.08	.25
❑ 278 Jamal Mashburn	.20	.50
❑ 279 Joe Kleine	.08	.25
❑ 280 Mitch Richmond	.20	.50

❑ 281 Chris Mills	.08	.25
❑ 282 Bimbo Coles	.08	.25
❑ 283 Larry Johnson	.20	.50
❑ 284 Stanley Roberts	.08	.25
❑ 285 Rex Walters	.08	.25
❑ 286 Donald Royal	.08	.25
❑ 287 Benoit Benjamin	.08	.25
❑ 288 Chris Dudley	.08	.25
❑ 289 Elden Campbell	.08	.25
❑ 290 Mookie Blaylock	.08	.25
❑ 291 Hersey Hawkins	.08	.25
❑ 292 Anthony Mason	.20	.50
❑ 293 Latrell Sprewell	.30	.75
❑ 294 Harold Miner	.08	.25
❑ 295 Scott Williams	.08	.25
❑ 296 David Benoit	.08	.25
❑ 297 Christian Laettner	.20	.50
❑ 298 LaPhonso Ellis	.08	.25
❑ 299 Gheorghe Muresan	.08	.25
❑ 300 Kendall Gill	.08	.25
❑ 301 Eddie Johnson	.08	.25
❑ 302 Terry Cummings	.08	.25
❑ 303 Chuck Person	.08	.25
❑ 304 Michael Smith	.08	.25
❑ 305 Mark West	.08	.25
❑ 306 Willie Anderson	.08	.25
❑ 307 Pervis Ellison	.08	.25
❑ 308 Brian Williams	.08	.25
❑ 309 Danny Manning	.20	.50
❑ 310 Hakeem Olajuwon	.30	.75
❑ 311 Scottie Pippen	.50	1.25
❑ 312 Jon Koncak	.08	.25
❑ 313 Sasha Danilovic RC	.08	.25
❑ 314 Lucious Harris	.08	.25
❑ 315 Yinka Dare	.08	.25
❑ 316 Eric Williams RC	.20	.50
❑ 317 Gary Trent RC	.08	.25
❑ 318 Theo Ratliff RC	.40	1.00
❑ 319 Lawrence Moten RC	.08	.25
❑ 320 Jerome Allen RC	.08	.25
❑ 321 Tyus Edney RC	.08	.25
❑ 322 Loren Meyer RC	.08	.25
❑ 323 Michael Finley RC	.75	2.00
❑ 324 Alan Henderson RC	.30	.75
❑ 325 Bob Sura RC	.20	.50
❑ 326 Joe Smith RC	.50	1.25
❑ 327 Damon Stoudamire RC	.60	1.50
❑ 328 Sherrell Ford RC	.08	.25
❑ 329 Jerry Stackhouse RC	1.00	2.50
❑ 330 George Zidek RC	.08	.25
❑ 331 Brent Barry RC	.30	.75
❑ 332 Shawn Respert RC	.08	.25
❑ 333 Rasheed Wallace RC	.75	2.00
❑ 334 Antonio McDyess RC	.60	1.50
❑ 335 David Vaughn RC	.08	.25
❑ 336 Cory Alexander RC	.08	.25
❑ 337 Jason Caffey RC	.20	.50
❑ 338 Frankie King RC	.08	.25
❑ 339 Travis Best RC	.08	.25
❑ 340 Greg Ostertag RC	.08	.25
❑ 341 Ed O'Bannon RC	.08	.25
❑ 342 Kurt Thomas RC	.20	.50
❑ 343 Kevin Garnett RC	2.00	5.00
❑ 344 Bryant Reeves RC	.30	.75
❑ 345 Corliss Williamson RC	.30	.75
❑ 346 Cherokee Parks RC	.08	.25
❑ 347 Junior Burrough RC	.08	.25
❑ 348 Randolph Childress RC	.08	.25
❑ 349 Lou Roe RC	.08	.25
❑ 350 Mario Bennett RC	.08	.25
❑ 351 Dikembe Mutombo XP	.08	.25
❑ 352 Larry Johnson XP	.20	.50
❑ 353 Vlade Divac XP	.08	.25
❑ 354 Karl Malone XP	.30	.75
❑ 355 John Stockton XP	.30	.75
❑ 356 Alonzo Mourning TA	.08	.25
❑ 357 Glen Rice TA	.08	.25
❑ 358 Dan Majerle TA	.08	.25
❑ 359 John Williams TA	.08	.25
❑ 360 Mark Price TA	.08	.25
❑ 361 Magic Johnson	.50	1.25

1996-97 Stadium Club

❑ COMPLETE SET (180)	12.50	25.00
❑ COMPLETE SERIES 1 (90)	5.00	10.00
❑ COMPLETE SERIES 2 (90)	7.50	15.00
❑ 1 Scottie Pippen	.50	1.25
❑ 2 Dale Davis	.08	.25
❑ 3 Horace Grant	.20	.50
❑ 4 Gheorghe Muresan	.08	.25

❑ 5 Elliot Perry	.08	.25
❑ 6 Carlos Rogers	.08	.25
❑ 7 Glenn Robinson	.30	.75
❑ 8 Avery Johnson	.08	.25
❑ 9 Dee Brown	.08	.25
❑ 10 Grant Hill	.30	.75
❑ 11 Tyus Edney	.08	.25
❑ 12 Patrick Ewing	.30	.75
❑ 13 Jason Kidd	.50	1.25
❑ 14 Clifford Robinson	.08	.25
❑ 15 Robert Horry	.20	.50
❑ 16 Dell Curry	.08	.25
❑ 17 Terry Porter	.08	.25
❑ 18 Shaquille O'Neal	.75	2.00
❑ 19 Bryant Stith	.08	.25
❑ 20 Shawn Kemp	.20	.50
❑ 21 Kurt Thomas	.20	.50
❑ 22 Pooh Richardson	.08	.25
❑ 23 Bob Sura	.08	.25
❑ 24 Olden Polynice	.08	.25
❑ 25 Lawrence Moten	.08	.25
❑ 26 Kendall Gill	.08	.25
❑ 27 Cedric Ceballos	.08	.25
❑ 28 Latrell Sprewell	.30	.75
❑ 29 Christian Laettner	.20	.50
❑ 30 Jamal Mashburn	.20	.50
❑ 31 Jerry Stackhouse	.40	1.00
❑ 32 John Stockton	.30	.75
❑ 33 Arvydas Sabonis	.20	.50
❑ 34 Detlef Schrempf	.20	.50
❑ 35 Toni Kukoc	.20	.50
❑ 36 Sasha Danilovic	.08	.25
❑ 37 Dana Barros	.08	.25
❑ 38 Loy Vaught	.08	.25
❑ 39 John Starks	.20	.50
❑ 40 Marty Conlon	.08	.25
❑ 41 Antonio McDyess	.20	.50
❑ 42 Michael Finley	.40	1.00
❑ 43 Tom Gugliotta	.08	.25
❑ 44 Terrell Brandon	.20	.50
❑ 45 Derrick McKey	.08	.25
❑ 46 Damon Stoudamire	.30	.75
❑ 47 Elden Campbell	.08	.25
❑ 48 Luc Longley	.08	.25
❑ 49 B.J. Armstrong	.08	.25
❑ 50 Lindsey Hunter	.08	.25
❑ 51 Glen Rice	.20	.50
❑ 52 Shawn Respert	.08	.25
❑ 53 Cory Alexander	.08	.25
❑ 54 Tim Legler	.08	.25
❑ 55 Bryant Reeves	.08	.25
❑ 56 Anfernee Hardaway	.30	.75
❑ 57 Charles Barkley	.40	1.00
❑ 58 Mookie Blaylock	.08	.25
❑ 59 Kevin Garnett	.60	1.50
❑ 60 Hersey Hawkins	.20	.50
❑ 61 Ed O'Bannon	.08	.25
❑ 62 George Zidek	.08	.25
❑ 63 Mitch Richmond	.20	.50
❑ 64 Derrick Coleman	.20	.50
❑ 65 Chris Webber	.30	.75
❑ 66 Bobby Phills	.08	.25
❑ 67 Rik Smits	.20	.50
❑ 68 Jeff Hornacek	.20	.50
❑ 69 Sam Cassell	.30	.75
❑ 70 Gary Trent	.08	.25
❑ 71 LaPhonso Ellis	.08	.25
❑ 72 Oliver Miller	.08	.25
❑ 73 Rex Chapman	.08	.25
❑ 74 Jim Jackson	.08	.25
❑ 75 Eric Williams	.08	.25
❑ 76 Brent Barry	.08	.25
❑ 77 Nick Anderson	.08	.25
❑ 78 David Robinson	.30	.75
❑ 79 Calbert Cheaney	.08	.25
❑ 80 Joe Smith	.20	.50
❑ 81 Steve Kerr	.20	.50
❑ 82 Wayman Tisdale	.08	.25
❑ 83 Steve Smith	.20	.50
❑ 84 Clyde Drexler	.30	.75
❑ 85 Theo Ratliff	.20	.50
❑ 86 Charlie Ward	.08	.25
❑ 87 Karl Malone	.30	.75
❑ 88 Clarence Weatherspoon	.08	.25
❑ 89 Greg Anthony	.08	.25
❑ 90 Shawn Bradley	.08	.25
❑ 91 Otis Thorpe	.08	.25
❑ 92 Larry Johnson	.20	.50
❑ 93 Sharone Wright	.08	.25
❑ 94 Charles Barkley	.40	1.00
❑ 95 Wesley Person	.08	.25
❑ 96 Dikembe Mutombo	.20	.50
❑ 97 Eddie Jones	.30	.75
❑ 98 Juwan Howard	.20	.50
❑ 99 Grant Hill	.30	.75
❑ 100 Chris Carr RC	.08	.25
❑ 101 Michael Jordan	2.00	5.00
❑ 102 Vincent Askew	.08	.25
❑ 103 Gary Payton	.30	.75
❑ 104 Chris Mills	.08	.25
❑ 105 Reggie Miller	.30	.75
❑ 106 Don MacLean	.08	.25
❑ 107 John Stockton	.30	.75
❑ 108 Mahmoud Abdul-Rauf	.08	.25
❑ 109 P.J. Brown	.08	.25
❑ 110 Kenny Anderson	.08	.25
❑ 111 Mark Price	.20	.50
❑ 112 Derek Harper	.08	.25
❑ 113 Dino Radja	.08	.25
❑ 114 Terry Dehere	.08	.25
❑ 115 Mark Jackson	.08	.25
❑ 116 Vin Baker	.20	.50
❑ 117 Dennis Scott	.08	.25
❑ 118 Sean Elliott	.20	.50
❑ 119 Lee Mayberry	.08	.25
❑ 120 Vlade Divac	.08	.25
❑ 121 Joe Dumars	.30	.75
❑ 122 Isaiah Rider	.20	.50
❑ 123 Hakeem Olajuwon	.30	.75
❑ 124 Robert Pack	.08	.25
❑ 125 Jalen Rose	.30	.75
❑ 126 Allan Houston	.20	.50
❑ 127 Nate McMillan	.08	.25
❑ 128 Rod Strickland	.08	.25
❑ 129 Sean Rooks	.08	.25
❑ 130 Dennis Rodman	.20	.50
❑ 131 Alonzo Mourning	.20	.50
❑ 132 Danny Ferry	.08	.25
❑ 133 Sam Cassell	.30	.75
❑ 134 Brian Grant	.30	.75
❑ 135 Karl Malone	.30	.75
❑ 136 Chris Gatling	.08	.25
❑ 137 Tom Gugliotta	.08	.25
❑ 138 Hubert Davis	.08	.25
❑ 139 Lucious Harris	.08	.25
❑ 140 Rony Seikaly	.08	.25
❑ 141 Alan Henderson	.08	.25
❑ 142 Mario Elie	.08	.25
❑ 143 Vinny Del Negro	.08	.25
❑ 144 Harvey Grant	.08	.25
❑ 145 Muggsy Bogues	.08	.25
❑ 146 Rodney Rogers	.08	.25
❑ 147 Kevin Johnson	.20	.50
❑ 148 Anthony Peeler	.08	.25
❑ 149 Jon Koncak	.08	.25
❑ 150 Ricky Pierce	.08	.25
❑ 151 Todd Day	.08	.25
❑ 152 Tyrone Hill	.08	.25
❑ 153 Nick Van Exel	.30	.75
❑ 154 Rasheed Wallace	.40	1.00
❑ 155 Jayson Williams	.20	.50
❑ 156 Sherman Douglas	.08	.25
❑ 157 Bryon Russell	.08	.25
❑ 158 Ron Harper	.20	.50
❑ 159 Stacey Augmon	.08	.25
❑ 160 Antonio Davis	.08	.25
❑ 161 Tim Hardaway	.20	.50
❑ 162 Charles Oakley	.08	.25
❑ 163 Billy Owens	.08	.25
❑ 164 Sam Perkins	.20	.50
❑ 165 Chris Whitney	.08	.25
❑ 166 Matt Geiger	.08	.25
❑ 167 Andrew Lang	.08	.25
❑ 168 Danny Manning	.20	.50

❑ 169 Doug Christie	.20	.50
❑ 170 George Lynch	.08	.25
❑ 171 Malik Sealy	.08	.25
❑ 172 Eric Montross	.08	.25
❑ 173 Rick Fox	.08	.25
❑ 174 Chris Mullin	.30	.75
❑ 175 Ken Norman	.08	.25
❑ 176 Sarunas Marciulionis	.08	.25
❑ 177 Kevin Garnett	.60	1.50
❑ 178 Brian Shaw	.08	.25
❑ 179 Will Perdue	.08	.25
❑ 180 Scott Williams	.08	.25
❑ NNO Checklist	.08	.25

1997-98 Stadium Club

❑ COMPLETE SET (240)	22.50	45.00
❑ COMPLETE SERIES 1 (120)	12.50	25.00
❑ COMPLETE SERIES 2 (120)	10.00	20.00
❑ 1 Scottie Pippen	.50	1.25
❑ 2 Bryon Russell	.08	.25
❑ 3 Muggsy Bogues	.20	.50
❑ 4 Gary Payton	.30	.75
❑ 5 Bulls - Team of the 90s	2.00	5.00
❑ 6 Corliss Williamson	.20	.50
❑ 7 Samaki Walker	.08	.25
❑ 8 Allan Houston	.20	.50
❑ 9 Ray Allen	.30	.75
❑ 10 Nick Van Exel	.30	.75
❑ 11 Chris Mullin	.30	.75
❑ 12 Popeye Jones	.08	.25
❑ 13 Horace Grant	.20	.50
❑ 14 Rik Smits	.20	.50
❑ 15 Wayman Tisdale	.08	.25
❑ 16 Donny Marshall	.08	.25
❑ 17 Rod Strickland	.08	.25
❑ 18 Rod Strickland	.08	.25
❑ 19 Greg Anthony	.08	.25
❑ 20 Lindsey Hunter	.08	.25
❑ 21 Glen Rice	.20	.50
❑ 22 Anthony Goldwire	.08	.25
❑ 23 Mahmoud Abdul-Rauf	.08	.25
❑ 24 Sean Elliott	.20	.50
❑ 25 Cory Alexander	.08	.25
❑ 26 Tyrone Corbin	.08	.25
❑ 27 Sam Perkins	.20	.50
❑ 28 Brian Shaw	.08	.25
❑ 29 Doug Christie	.20	.50
❑ 30 Mark Jackson	.20	.50
❑ 31 Christian Laettner	.20	.50
❑ 32 Damon Stoudamire	.20	.50
❑ 33 Eric Williams	.08	.25
❑ 34 Glenn Robinson	.30	.75
❑ 35 Brooks Thompson	.08	.25
❑ 36 Derrick Coleman	.08	.25
❑ 37 Theo Ratliff	.08	.25
❑ 38 Ron Harper	.20	.50
❑ 39 Hakeem Olajuwon	.30	.75
❑ 40 Mitch Richmond	.20	.50
❑ 41 Reggie Miller	.30	.75
❑ 42 Reggie Miller	.30	.75
❑ 43 Shaquille O'Neal	.75	2.00
❑ 44 Zydrunas Ilgauskas	.20	.50
❑ 45 Jamal Mashburn	.20	.50
❑ 46 Isaiah Rider	.20	.50
❑ 47 Tom Gugliotta	.20	.50
❑ 48 Rex Chapman	.08	.25
❑ 49 Lorenzen Wright	.08	.25
❑ 50 Pooh Richardson	.08	.25
❑ 51 Armon Gilliam	.08	.25
❑ 52 Kevin Johnson	.20	.50
❑ 53 Kerry Kittles	.30	.75
❑ 54 Kerry Kittles	.30	.75
❑ 55 Charles Oakley	.20	.50
❑ 56 Dennis Rodman	.20	.50
❑ 57 Greg Ostertag	.08	.25
❑ 58 Todd Fuller	.08	.25
❑ 59 Mark Davis	.08	.25
❑ 60 Erick Strickland RC	.20	.50
❑ 61 Clifford Robinson	.08	.25
❑ 62 Nate McMillan	.08	.25
❑ 63 Steve Kerr	.20	.50
❑ 64 Bob Sura	.08	.25
❑ 65 Danny Ferry	.08	.25
❑ 66 Loy Vaught	.08	.25
❑ 67 A.C. Green	.20	.50
❑ 68 John Stockton	.30	.75
❑ 69 Terry Mills	.08	.25
❑ 70 Voshon Lenard	.08	.25
❑ 71 Matt Maloney	.08	.25
❑ 72 Charlie Ward	.08	.25
❑ 73 Brent Barry	.20	.50
❑ 74 Chris Webber	.30	.75
❑ 75 Stephon Marbury	.40	1.00
❑ 76 Bryant Stith	.08	.25
❑ 77 Shareef Abdur-Rahim	.50	1.25
❑ 78 Sean Rooks	.08	.25
❑ 79 Rony Seikaly	.08	.25
❑ 80 Brent Price	.08	.25
❑ 81 Wesley Person	.08	.25
❑ 82 Michael Smith	.08	.25
❑ 83 Gary Trent	.08	.25
❑ 84 Dan Majerle	.20	.50
❑ 85 Rex Walters	.08	.25
❑ 86 Clarence Weatherspoon	.08	.25
❑ 87 Patrick Ewing	.30	.75
❑ 88 B.J. Armstrong	.08	.25
❑ 89 Travis Best	.08	.25
❑ 90 Steve Smith	.20	.50
❑ 91 Vitaly Potapenko	.08	.25
❑ 92 Derek Strong	.08	.25
❑ 93 Michael Finley	.30	.75
❑ 94 Will Perdue	.08	.25
❑ 95 Antoine Walker	.40	1.00
❑ 96 Chuck Person	.08	.25
❑ 97 Mookie Blaylock	.08	.25
❑ 98 Eric Snow	.20	.50
❑ 99 Tony Delk	.08	.25
❑ 100 Mario Elie	.08	.25
❑ 101 Terrell Brandon	.20	.50
❑ 102 Shawn Bradley	.08	.25
❑ 103 Latrell Sprewell	.30	.75
❑ 104 Latrell Sprewell	.30	.75
❑ 105 Tim Hardaway	.20	.50
❑ 106 Terry Porter	.08	.25
❑ 107 Darrell Armstrong	.08	.25
❑ 108 Rasheed Wallace	.30	.75
❑ 109 Vinny Del Negro	.08	.25
❑ 110 Tracy Murray	.08	.25
❑ 111 Lawrence Moten	.08	.25
❑ 112 Lamond Murray	.08	.25
❑ 113 Juwan Howard	.20	.50
❑ 114 Juwan Howard	.20	.50
❑ 115 Karl Malone	.30	.75
❑ 116 Aaron McKie	.20	.50
❑ 117 Shawn Respert	.08	.25
❑ 118 Michael Jordan	2.00	5.00
❑ 119 Shawn Kemp	.20	.50
❑ 120 Arvydas Sabonis	.20	.50
❑ 121 Tyus Edney	.08	.25
❑ 122 Bryant Reeves	.08	.25
❑ 123 Jason Kidd	.50	1.25
❑ 124 Dikembe Mutombo	.20	.50
❑ 125 Allen Iverson	.75	2.00
❑ 126 Allen Iverson	.75	2.00
❑ 127 Larry Johnson	.20	.50
❑ 128 Jerry Stackhouse	.30	.75
❑ 129 Kendall Gill	.08	.25
❑ 130 Kendall Gill	.08	.25
❑ 131 Vin Baker	.20	.50
❑ 132 Joe Dumars	.30	.75
❑ 133 Calbert Cheaney	.08	.25
❑ 134 Alonzo Mourning	.20	.50
❑ 135 Isaac Austin	.08	.25
❑ 136 Joe Smith	.20	.50
❑ 137 Elden Campbell	.08	.25
❑ 138 Kevin Garnett	.60	1.50
❑ 139 Malik Sealy	.08	.25
❑ 140 John Starks	.20	.50
❑ 141 Clyde Drexler	.30	.75
❑ 142 Matt Geiger	.08	.25
❑ 143 Mark Price	.20	.50
❑ 144 Buck Williams	.08	.25
❑ 145 Grant Hill	.30	.75
❑ 146 Kobe Bryant	1.25	3.00
❑ 147 Dale Ellis	.08	.25
❑ 148 Jason Caffey	.08	.25
❑ 149 Toni Kukoc	.20	.50
❑ 150 Avery Johnson	.08	.25
❑ 151 Alan Henderson	.08	.25
❑ 152 Walt Williams	.08	.25
❑ 153 Greg Minor	.08	.25
❑ 154 Calbert Cheaney	.08	.25
❑ 155 Vlade Divac	.20	.50
❑ 156 Greg Foster	.08	.25
❑ 157 LaPhonso Ellis	.08	.25
❑ 158 Charles Barkley	.40	1.00
❑ 159 Antonio Davis	.08	.25
❑ 160 Roy Rogers	.08	.25
❑ 161 Robert Horry	.20	.50
❑ 162 Sam Cassell	.30	.75
❑ 163 Chris Carr	.08	.25
❑ 164 Robert Pack	.08	.25
❑ 165 Sam Cassell	.30	.75
❑ 166 Rodney Rogers	.08	.25
❑ 167 Chris Childs	.08	.25
❑ 168 Shandon Anderson	.08	.25
❑ 169 Kenny Anderson	.20	.50
❑ 170 Anthony Mason	.20	.50
❑ 171 Olden Polynice	.08	.25
❑ 172 David Wingate	.08	.25
❑ 173 David Robinson	.30	.75
❑ 174 Billy Owens	.08	.25
❑ 175 Detlef Schrempf	.20	.50
❑ 176 Carlos Rogers	.08	.25
❑ 177 Marcus Camby	.30	.75
❑ 178 Dana Barros	.08	.25
❑ 179 Shandon Anderson	.08	.25
❑ 180 Jayson Williams	.08	.25
❑ 181 Eldridge Recasner	.08	.25
❑ 182 Doug West	.08	.25
❑ 183 Kevin Willis	.20	.50
❑ 184 Eddie Johnson	.08	.25
❑ 185 Derek Fisher	.30	.75
❑ 186 Eddie Jones	.30	.75
❑ 187 Sherman Douglas	.08	.25
❑ 188 Anthony Peeler	.08	.25
❑ 189 Danny Manning	.20	.50
❑ 190 Stacey Augmon	.08	.25
❑ 191 Hersey Hawkins	.08	.25
❑ 192 Micheal Williams	.08	.25
❑ 193 Jeff Hornacek	.20	.50
❑ 194 Anfernee Hardaway	.30	.75
❑ 195 Harvey Grant	.08	.25
❑ 196 Nick Anderson	.08	.25
❑ 197 Luc Longley	.08	.25
❑ 198 Andrew Lang	.08	.25
❑ 199 P.J. Brown	.08	.25
❑ 200 Cedric Ceballos	.08	.25
❑ 201 Tim Duncan RC	.75	2.00
❑ 202 Ervin Johnson TRAN	.08	.25
❑ 203 Keith Van Horn RC	.40	1.00
❑ 204 David Wesley TRAN	.08	.25
❑ 205 Chauncey Billups RC	1.25	3.00
❑ 206 Jim Jackson TRAN	.08	.25
❑ 207 Antonio Daniels RC	.30	.75
❑ 208 Travis Knight TRAN	.08	.25
❑ 209 Tony Battie RC	.30	.75
❑ 210 Bobby Phills TRAN	.08	.25
❑ 211 Bobby Jackson RC	.40	1.00
❑ 212 Otis Thorpe TRAN	.08	.25
❑ 213 Tim Thomas RC	.50	1.25
❑ 214 Chris Mullin TRAN	.20	.50
❑ 215 Adonal Foyle RC	.20	.50
❑ 216 Brian Williams TRAN	.08	.25
❑ 217 Tracy McGrady RC	.75	2.00
❑ 218 Tyus Edney TRAN	.08	.25
❑ 219 Danny Fortson RC	.20	.50
❑ 220 Clifford Robinson TRAN	.08	.25
❑ 221 Olivier Saint-Jean RC	.08	.25

❑ 222 Vin Baker TRAN	.08	.25
❑ 223 Austin Croshere RC	.25	.60
❑ 224 John Wallace TRAN	.08	.25
❑ 225 Derek Anderson RC	.30	.75
❑ 226 Kelvin Cato RC	.30	.75
❑ 227 Maurice Taylor RC	.25	.60
❑ 228 Scot Pollard RC	.20	.50
❑ 229 John Thomas RC	.08	.25
❑ 230 Dean Garrett TRAN	.08	.25
❑ 231 Brevin Knight RC	.20	.50
❑ 232 Ron Mercer RC	.30	.75
❑ 233 Johnny Taylor RC	.08	.25
❑ 234 Antonio McDyess TRAN	.20	.50
❑ 235 Ed Gray RC	.08	.25
❑ 236 Terrell Brandon TRAN	.08	.25
❑ 237 Anthony Parker RC	.20	.50
❑ 238 Shawn Kemp TRAN	.08	.25
❑ 239 Paul Grant RC	.08	.25
❑ 240 Dennis Scott TRAN	.08	.25

1998-99 Stadium Club

❑ COMPLETE SET (240)	125.00	250.00
❑ COMPLETE SERIES 1 (120)	75.00	200.00
❑ COMP.SERIES 1 w/o RC (100)	7.50	15.00
❑ COMPLETE SERIES 2 (120)	15.00	30.00
❑ COMMON CARD (1-240)	.08	.25
❑ COMMON CARD (101-120)	1.00	2.50
❑ 1 Eddie Jones	.30	.75
❑ 2 Matt Geiger	.08	.25
❑ 3 Ray Allen	.30	.75
❑ 4 Billy Owens	.08	.25
❑ 5 Larry Johnson	.20	.50
❑ 6 Jerry Stackhouse	.30	.75
❑ 7 Travis Best	.08	.25
❑ 8 Sam Cassell	.30	.75
❑ 9 Isaiah Rider	.08	.25
❑ 10 Walter McCarty	.08	.25
❑ 11 Hakeem Olajuwon	.30	.75
❑ 12 Detlef Schrempf	.20	.50
❑ 13 Chris Garner	.08	.25
❑ 14 Voshon Lenard	.08	.25
❑ 15 Kevin Garnett	.60	1.50
❑ 16 Doug Christie	.20	.50
❑ 17 Dikembe Mutombo	.20	.50
❑ 18 Terrell Brandon	.20	.50
❑ 19 Brevin Knight	.08	.25
❑ 20 Dan Majerle	.20	.50
❑ 21 Keith Van Horn	.30	.75
❑ 22 Jim Jackson	.08	.25
❑ 23 Theo Ratliff	.20	.50
❑ 24 Anthony Peeler	.08	.25
❑ 25 Tim Hardaway	.20	.50
❑ 26 Bo Outlaw	.08	.25
❑ 27 Blue Edwards	.08	.25
❑ 28 Khalid Reeves	.08	.25
❑ 29 David Wesley	.08	.25
❑ 30 Toni Kukoc	.20	.50
❑ 31 Jaren Jackson	.08	.25
❑ 32 Mario Elie	.08	.25
❑ 33 Nick Anderson	.08	.25
❑ 34 Derek Anderson	.25	.60
❑ 35 Rodney Rogers	.08	.25
❑ 36 Jalen Rose	.30	.75
❑ 37 Corliss Williamson	.20	.50
❑ 38 Tyrone Corbin	.08	.25
❑ 39 Antonio Davis	.08	.25
❑ 40 Chris Mills	.08	.25
❑ 41 Clarence Weatherspoon	.08	.25
❑ 42 George Lynch	.08	.25
❑ 43 Kelvin Cato	.08	.25
❑ 44 Anthony Mason	.20	.50
❑ 45 Tracy McGrady	.75	2.00
❑ 46 Lamond Murray	.08	.25
❑ 47 Mookie Blaylock	.08	.25
❑ 48 Tracy Murray	.08	.25
❑ 49 Ron Harper	.20	.50
❑ 50 Tom Gugliotta	.08	.25
❑ 51 Allan Houston	.20	.50
❑ 52 Arvydas Sabonis	.20	.50
❑ 53 Brian Williams	.08	.25
❑ 54 Brian Shaw	.08	.25
❑ 55 John Stockton	.30	.75
❑ 56 Rick Fox	.20	.50
❑ 57 Hersey Hawkins	.08	.25
❑ 58 Danny Manning	.08	.25
❑ 59 Chris Carr	.08	.25
❑ 60 Lindsey Hunter	.08	.25
❑ 61 Donyell Marshall	.20	.50
❑ 62 Michael Jordan	2.00	5.00
❑ 63 Mark Strickland	.08	.25
❑ 64 LaPhonso Ellis	.08	.25
❑ 65 Rod Strickland	.08	.25
❑ 66 David Robinson	.30	.75
❑ 67 Cedric Ceballos	.08	.25
❑ 68 Christian Laettner	.20	.50
❑ 69 Anthony Goldwire	.08	.25
❑ 70 Armon Gilliam	.08	.25
❑ 71 Shaquille O'Neal	.75	2.00
❑ 72 Sherman Douglas	.08	.25
❑ 73 Kendall Gill	.08	.25
❑ 74 Charlie Ward	.08	.25
❑ 75 Allen Iverson	.60	1.50
❑ 76 Shawn Kemp	.20	.50
❑ 77 Travis Knight	.08	.25
❑ 78 Gary Payton	.30	.75
❑ 79 Cedric Henderson	.08	.25
❑ 80 Matt Bullard	.08	.25
❑ 81 Steve Kerr	.20	.50
❑ 82 Shawn Bradley	.08	.25
❑ 83 Antonio McDyess	.20	.50
❑ 84 Robert Horry	.20	.50
❑ 85 Darrick Martin	.08	.25
❑ 86 Derek Strong	.08	.25
❑ 87 Shandon Anderson	.08	.25
❑ 88 Lawrence Funderburke	.08	.25
❑ 89 Brent Price	.08	.25
❑ 90 Reggie Miller	.30	.75
❑ 91 Shareef Abdur-Rahim	.30	.75
❑ 92 Jeff Hornacek	.20	.50
❑ 93 Antoine Carr	.08	.25
❑ 94 Greg Anthony	.08	.25
❑ 95 Rex Chapman	.08	.25
❑ 96 Antoine Walker	.30	.75
❑ 97 Bobby Jackson	.20	.50
❑ 98 Calbert Cheaney	.08	.25
❑ 99 Avery Johnson	.08	.25
❑ 100 Jason Kidd	.50	1.25
❑ 101 Michael Olowokandi RC	1.50	4.00
❑ 102 Mike Bibby RC	2.50	6.00
❑ 103 Raef LaFrentz RC	1.50	4.00
❑ 104 Antawn Jamison RC	10.00	25.00
❑ 105 Vince Carter RC	20.00	30.00
❑ 106 Robert Traylor RC	1.50	4.00
❑ 107 Jason Williams RC	4.00	10.00
❑ 108 Larry Hughes RC	2.00	5.00
❑ 109 Dirk Nowitzki RC	15.00	40.00
❑ 110 Paul Pierce RC	8.00	20.00
❑ 111 Bonzi Wells RC	3.00	8.00
❑ 112 Michael Doleac RC	1.50	4.00
❑ 113 Keon Clark RC	1.50	4.00
❑ 114 Michael Dickerson RC	2.00	5.00
❑ 115 Matt Harpring RC	1.50	4.00
❑ 116 Bryce Drew RC	1.50	4.00
❑ 117 Pat Garrity RC	1.00	2.50
❑ 118 Roshown McLeod RC	1.00	2.50
❑ 119 Ricky Davis RC	3.00	8.00
❑ 120 Brian Skinner RC	1.50	4.00
❑ 121 Dee Brown	.08	.25
❑ 122 Hubert Davis	.08	.25
❑ 123 Vitaly Potapenko	.08	.25
❑ 124 Ervin Johnson	.08	.25
❑ 125 Chris Gatling	.08	.25
❑ 126 Darrell Armstrong	.08	.25
❑ 127 Glen Rice	.20	.50
❑ 128 Ben Wallace	.30	.75
❑ 129 Sam Mitchell	.08	.25
❑ 130 Joe Dumars	.30	.75
❑ 131 Terry Davis	.08	.25
❑ 132 A.C. Green	.20	.50
❑ 133 Alan Henderson	.08	.25
❑ 134 Ron Mercer	.15	.40
❑ 135 Brian Grant	.20	.50
❑ 136 Chris Childs	.08	.25
❑ 137 Rony Seikaly	.08	.25
❑ 138 Pete Chilcutt	.08	.25
❑ 139 Anfernee Hardaway	.30	.75
❑ 140 Bryon Russell	.08	.25
❑ 141 Tim Thomas	.20	.50
❑ 142 Erick Dampier	.20	.50
❑ 143 Charles Barkley	.40	1.00
❑ 144 Mark Jackson	.20	.50
❑ 145 Bryant Reeves	.08	.25
❑ 146 Tyrone Hill	.08	.25
❑ 147 Rasheed Wallace	.30	.75
❑ 148 Tim Duncan	.50	1.25
❑ 149 Steve Smith	.20	.50
❑ 150 Alonzo Mourning	.20	.50
❑ 151 Danny Fortson	.08	.25
❑ 152 Aaron Williams	.08	.25
❑ 153 Andrew DeClercq	.08	.25
❑ 154 Elden Campbell	.08	.25
❑ 155 Don Reid	.08	.25
❑ 156 Rik Smits	.20	.50
❑ 157 Adonal Foyle	.08	.25
❑ 158 Muggsy Bogues	.20	.50
❑ 159 Chris Mullin	.30	.75
❑ 160 Randy Brown	.08	.25
❑ 161 Kenny Anderson	.20	.50
❑ 162 Tariq Abdul-Wahad	.08	.25
❑ 163 P.J. Brown	.08	.25
❑ 164 Jayson Williams	.08	.25
❑ 165 Grant Hill	.30	.75
❑ 166 Clifford Robinson	.08	.25
❑ 167 Damon Stoudamire	.20	.50
❑ 168 Aaron McKie	.20	.50
❑ 169 Erick Strickland	.08	.25
❑ 170 Kobe Bryant	1.25	3.00
❑ 171 Karl Malone	.30	.75
❑ 172 Eric Piatkowski	.20	.50
❑ 173 Rodrick Rhodes	.08	.25
❑ 174 Sean Elliott	.20	.50
❑ 175 John Wallace	.08	.25
❑ 176 Derek Fisher	.30	.75
❑ 177 Maurice Taylor	.15	.40
❑ 178 Wesley Person	.08	.25
❑ 179 Jamal Mashburn	.20	.50
❑ 180 Patrick Ewing	.30	.75
❑ 181 Howard Eisley	.08	.25
❑ 182 Michael Finley	.30	.75
❑ 183 Juwan Howard	.20	.50
❑ 184 Matt Maloney	.08	.25
❑ 185 Glenn Robinson	.20	.50
❑ 186 Zydrunas Ilgauskas	.20	.50
❑ 187 Dana Barros	.08	.25
❑ 188 Stacey Augmon	.08	.25
❑ 189 Bobby Phills	.08	.25
❑ 190 Kerry Kittles	.08	.25
❑ 191 Vin Baker	.20	.50
❑ 192 Stephon Marbury	.30	.75
❑ 193 Peja Stojakovic RC	.60	1.50
❑ 194 Michael Olowokandi	.25	.60
❑ 195 Mike Bibby	.75	2.00
❑ 196 Raef LaFrentz	.25	.60
❑ 197 Antawn Jamison	.75	2.00
❑ 198 Vince Carter	1.50	4.00
❑ 199 Robert Traylor	.08	.25
❑ 200 Jason Williams	.60	1.50
❑ 201 Larry Hughes	.50	1.25
❑ 202 Dirk Nowitzki	1.50	4.00
❑ 203 Paul Pierce	.75	2.00
❑ 204 Bonzi Wells	.60	1.50
❑ 205 Michael Doleac	.20	.50
❑ 206 Keon Clark	.30	.75
❑ 207 Michael Dickerson	.30	.75
❑ 208 Matt Harpring	.30	.75
❑ 209 Bryce Drew	.20	.50
❑ 210 Pat Garrity	.08	.25
❑ 211 Roshown McLeod	.20	.50
❑ 212 Ricky Davis	.30	.75
❑ 213 Brian Skinner	.20	.50
❑ 214 Tyronn Lue RC	.20	.50
❑ 215 Felipe Lopez RC	.20	.50
❑ 216 Al Harrington RC	.40	1.00
❑ 217 Sam Jacobson RC	.08	.25
❑ 218 Vladimir Stepania RC	.08	.25
❑ 219 Corey Benjamin RC	.30	.75
❑ 220 Nazr Mohammed RC	.20	.50
❑ 221 Tom Gugliotta TRAN	.08	.25
❑ 222 Derrick Coleman TRAN	.08	.25
❑ 223 Mitch Richmond TRAN	.20	.50
❑ 224 John Starks TRAN	.08	.25
❑ 225 Antonio McDyess TRAN	.20	.50
❑ 226 Joe Smith TRAN	.08	.25
❑ 227 Bobby Jackson TRAN	.08	.25

228 Luc Longley TRAN	.08	.25
229 Isaac Austin TRAN	.08	.25
230 Chris Webber TRAN	.20	.50
231 Chauncey Billups TRAN	.20	.50
232 Sam Perkins TRAN	.08	.25
233 Loy Vaught TRAN	.08	.25
234 Antonio Daniels TRAN	.08	.25
235 Brent Barry TRAN	.08	.25
236 Latrell Sprewell TRAN	.30	.75
237 Vlade Divac TRAN	.08	.25
238 Marcus Camby TRAN	.20	.50
239 Charles Oakley TRAN	.08	.25
240 Scottie Pippen TRAN	.25	.60

1999-00 Stadium Club

COMPLETE SET (201)	40.00	80.00
COMPLETE SET w/o RC (175)	20.00	40.00
COMMON CARD (1-175)	.15	.40
COMMON ROOKIE (176-201)	.40	1.00
1 Allen Iverson	.50	1.25
2 Chris Crawford	.15	.40
3 Chris Webber	.25	.60
4 Antawn Jamison	.25	.60
5 Karl Malone	.30	.75
6 Sam Cassell	.20	.50
7 Kerry Kittles	.15	.40
8 Tim Thomas	.20	.50
9 Chauncey Billups	.25	.60
10 Shawn Bradley	.15	.40
11 Alan Henderson	.15	.40
12 David Wesley	.15	.40
13 Glenn Robinson	.20	.50
14 Mitch Richmond	.20	.50
15 Luc Longley	.15	.40
16 Shareef Abdur-Rahim	.20	.50
17 Christian Laettner	.20	.50
18 Anthony Mason	.15	.40
19 Randy Brown	.15	.40
20 Charles Barkley	.30	.75
21 Bob Sura	.15	.40
22 Bobby Jackson	.20	.50
23 Arvydas Sabonis	.20	.50
24 Tracy Murray	.15	.40
25 Matt Harpring	.20	.50
26 Shawn Kemp	.25	.60
27 Travis Best	.15	.40
28 Ruben Patterson	.15	.40
29 Mike Bibby	.25	.60
30 Vlade Divac	.25	.60
31 Tyrone Hill	.15	.40
32 David Robinson	.30	.75
33 Keith Van Horn	.20	.50
34 Alvin Williams	.15	.40
35 Juwan Howard	.20	.50
36 Shaquille O'Neal	.60	1.50
37 Dale Davis	.15	.40
38 Alonzo Mourning	.25	.60
39 Michael Olowokandi	.15	.40
40 Jason Caffey	.15	.40
41 Andrew DeClercq	.15	.40
42 Jud Buechler	.15	.40
43 Toni Kukoc	.25	.60
44 Dikembe Mutombo	.20	.50
45 Steve Nash	.40	1.00
46 Eddie Jones	.25	.60
47 Reggie Miller	.25	.60
48 Rick Fox	.15	.40
49 Larry Hughes	.20	.50
50 Tim Duncan	.50	1.25
51 Jerome Williams	.15	.40
52 Rod Strickland	.15	.40
53 Anthony Peeler	.15	.40
54 Greg Ostertag	.15	.40
55 Patrick Ewing	.30	.75
56 Grant Hill	.25	.60
57 Derrick Coleman	.20	.50
58 Raef LaFrentz	.20	.50
59 Mark Bryant	.15	.40
60 Rik Smits	.25	.60
61 Latrell Sprewell	.20	.50
62 John Starks	.25	.60
63 Brevin Knight	.15	.40
64 Cuttino Mobley	.20	.50
65 Clarence Weatherspoon	.15	.40
66 Marcus Camby	.20	.50
67 Stephon Marbury	.25	.60
68 Tom Gugliotta	.15	.40
69 Vince Carter	.50	1.25
70 Vladimir Stepania	.15	.40
71 Chris Mullin	.25	.60
72 Tyrone Nesby RC	.25	.60
73 Kornel David RC	.25	.60
74 Elden Campbell	.15	.40
75 Lindsey Hunter	.15	.40
76 Chris Childs	.15	.40
77 Ervin Johnson	.15	.40
78 Rasheed Wallace	.25	.60
79 Jeff Hornacek	.20	.50
80 Matt Geiger	.15	.40
81 Antoine Walker	.25	.60
82 Jason Williams	.25	.60
83 Robert Horry	.25	.60
84 Jaren Jackson	.15	.40
85 Kendall Gill	.15	.40
86 Dan Majerle	.25	.60
87 Bobby Phills	.15	.40
88 Eric Piatkowski	.20	.50
89 Robert Traylor	.15	.40
90 Cory Carr	.15	.40
91 P.J. Brown	.15	.40
92 Terrell Brandon	.15	.40
93 Corliss Williamson	.15	.40
94 Bryant Reeves	.15	.40
95 Larry Johnson	.25	.60
96 Keith Closs	.15	.40
97 Gary Trent	.15	.40
98 Walter McCarty	.15	.40
99 Wesley Person	.15	.40
100 Chris Mills	.15	.40
101 Glen Rice	.25	.60
102 Peja Stojakovic	.20	.50
103 Jason Kidd	.40	1.00
104 Dirk Nowitzki	.40	1.00
105 Bryon Russell	.15	.40
106 Vin Baker	.25	.60
107 Darrell Armstrong	.15	.40
108 Eric Snow	.20	.50
109 Hakeem Olajuwon	.25	.60
110 Tracy McGrady	.50	1.25
111 Kenny Anderson	.20	.50
112 Jalen Rose	.20	.50
113 Greg Anthony	.15	.40
114 Tim Hardaway	.25	.60
115 Doug Christie	.20	.50
116 Allan Houston	.20	.50
117 Kobe Bryant	1.25	3.00
118 Kevin Garnett	.50	1.25
119 Vitaly Potapenko	.15	.40
120 Steve Kerr	.20	.50
121 Nick Van Exel	.20	.50
122 Jerry Stackhouse	.25	.60
123 Derek Fisher	.25	.60
124 Donyell Marshall	.20	.50
125 Mark Jackson	.25	.60
126 Ray Allen	.25	.60
127 Avery Johnson	.20	.50
128 Michael Doleac	.15	.40
129 Charles Oakley	.20	.50
130 Gary Payton	.25	.60
131 Theo Ratliff	.20	.50
132 Cedric Ceballos	.15	.40
133 Paul Pierce	.25	.60
134 Michael Finley	.25	.60
135 Malik Sealy	.15	.40
136 Brian Grant	.15	.40
137 John Stockton	.30	.75
138 Chris Whitney	.15	.40
139 Maurice Taylor	.20	.50
140 Antonio McDyess	.20	.50
141 Adrian Griffin RC	.25	.60
142 Vernon Maxwell	.20	.50
143 Jamal Mashburn	.15	.40
144 Jayson Williams	.20	.50
145 Joe Smith	.20	.50
146 Clifford Robinson	.15	.40
147 Mario Elie	.15	.40
148 Damon Stoudamire	.25	.60
149 Felipe Lopez	.15	.40
150 Rex Chapman	.15	.40
151 Antonio Davis TRAN	.15	.40
152 Mookie Blaylock TRAN	.15	.40
153 Ron Mercer TRAN	.15	.40
154 Horace Grant TRAN	.20	.50
155 Steve Smith TRAN	.15	.40
156 Isaiah Rider TRAN	.15	.40
157 Tariq Abdul-Wahad TRAN	.15	.40
158 Michael Dickerson TRAN	.15	.40
159 Nick Anderson TRAN	.15	.40
160 Jim Jackson TRAN	.20	.50
161 Hersey Hawkins TRAN	.15	.40
162 Brent Barry TRAN	.20	.50
163 Shandon Anderson TRAN	.15	.40
164 Scottie Pippen TRAN	.40	1.00
165 Isaac Austin TRAN	.15	.40
166 Anfernee Hardaway TRAN	.25	.60
167 Natalie Williams USA	.30	.75
168 Teresa Edwards USA	.30	.75
169 Yolanda Griffith USA	.40	1.00
170 Nikki McCray USA	.30	.75
171 Katie Smith USA	.50	1.25
172 Chamique Holdsclaw USA	.60	1.50
173 Dawn Staley USA	.30	.75
174 Ruthie Bolton-Holifield USA	.30	.75
175 Lisa Leslie USA	.75	2.00
176 Elton Brand RC	1.25	3.00
177 Steve Francis RC	1.25	3.00
178 Baron Davis RC	1.50	4.00
179 Lamar Odom RC	1.25	3.00
180 Jonathan Bender RC	.40	1.00
181 Wally Szczerbiak RC	1.25	3.00
182 Richard Hamilton RC	1.25	3.00
183 Andre Miller RC	1.25	3.00
184 Shawn Marion RC	1.25	3.00
185 Jason Terry RC	1.00	2.50
186 Trajan Langdon RC	.40	1.00
187 A.Radojevic RC	.40	1.00
188 Corey Maggette RC	1.25	3.00
189 William Avery RC	.40	1.00
190 DeMarco Johnson RC	.40	1.00
191 Ron Artest RC	1.50	4.00
192 Cal Bowdler RC	.40	1.00
193 James Posey RC	.60	1.50
194 Quincy Lewis RC	.40	1.00
195 Scott Padgett RC	.40	1.00
196 Jeff Foster RC	.50	1.25
197 Kenny Thomas RC	.40	1.00
198 Devean George RC	.60	1.50
199 Tim James RC	.40	1.00
200 Vonteego Cummings RC	.40	1.00
201 Jumaine Jones RC	.40	1.00

2000-01 Stadium Club

COMPLETE SET (175)	30.00	60.00
COMPLETE SET w/o RC (150)	12.50	25.00
COMMON CARD (1-150)	.15	.40
COMMON ROOKIE (151-175)	.40	1.00
1 Baron Davis	.25	.60
2 Adrian Griffin	.15	.40
3 Dikembe Mutombo	.20	.50
4 Andre Miller	.20	.50
5 Kenny Anderson	.20	.50
6 Keon Clark	.15	.40
7 Larry Hughes	.20	.50
8 Ruben Patterson	.15	.40
9 Shandon Anderson	.15	.40
10 Reggie Miller	.25	.60
11 Lamar Odom	.25	.60
12 John Stockton	.30	.75
13 Rod Strickland	.20	.50
14 Michael Dickerson	.15	.40
15 Quincy Lewis	.15	.40

❑ 16 Vin Baker	.20	.50
❑ 17 Vince Carter	.50	1.25
❑ 18 Avery Johnson	.20	.50
❑ 19 Michael Finley	.25	.60
❑ 20 Eric Snow	.15	.40
❑ 21 Kevin Garnett	.50	1.25
❑ 22 Rodney Rogers	.15	.40
❑ 23 Bonzi Wells	.15	.40
❑ 24 Jason Kidd	.40	1.00
❑ 25 Toni Kukoc	.20	.50
❑ 26 Darrell Armstrong	.15	.40
❑ 27 Larry Johnson	.20	.50
❑ 28 Kendall Gill	.15	.40
❑ 29 Wally Szczerbiak	.20	.50
❑ 30 Tim Thomas	.15	.40
❑ 31 Dan Majerle	.20	.50
❑ 32 Karl Malone	.30	.75
❑ 33 Juwan Howard	.20	.50
❑ 34 Kobe Bryant	1.25	3.00
❑ 35 Bryant Reeves	.15	.40
❑ 36 Cuttino Mobley	.20	.50
❑ 37 Mookie Blaylock	.20	.50
❑ 38 Jerome Williams	.15	.40
❑ 39 James Posey	.15	.40
❑ 40 Shawn Bradley	.15	.40
❑ 41 Tim Hardaway	.20	.50
❑ 42 Theo Ratliff	.15	.40
❑ 43 Damon Stoudamire	.20	.50
❑ 44 Derrick Coleman	.20	.50
❑ 45 Ron Artest	.25	.60
❑ 46 Antoine Walker	.20	.50
❑ 47 Jason Terry	.25	.60
❑ 48 Antonio McDyess	.20	.50
❑ 49 Jonathan Bender	.15	.40
❑ 50 Shaquille O'Neal	.60	1.50
❑ 51 Anthony Carter	.15	.40
❑ 52 Ray Allen	.25	.60
❑ 53 Joe Smith	.15	.40
❑ 54 Marcus Camby	.20	.50
❑ 55 Keith Van Horn	.20	.50
❑ 56 Charlie Ward	.15	.40
❑ 57 John Amaechi	.15	.40
❑ 58 Tom Gugliotta	.15	.40
❑ 59 Allan Houston	.20	.50
❑ 60 Anfernee Hardaway	.25	.60
❑ 61 Scottie Pippen	.40	1.00
❑ 62 Jason Williams	.20	.50
❑ 63 Steve Smith	.20	.50
❑ 64 David Robinson	.30	.75
❑ 65 Gary Payton	.25	.60
❑ 66 Robert Horry	.20	.50
❑ 67 Greg Ostertag	.15	.40
❑ 68 Mike Bibby	.20	.50
❑ 69 Tim Duncan	.50	1.25
❑ 70 Richard Hamilton	.20	.50
❑ 71 Bryon Russell	.15	.40
❑ 72 Charles Oakley	.20	.50
❑ 73 Rashard Lewis	.25	.60
❑ 74 Chris Webber	.25	.60
❑ 75 Arvydas Sabonis	.20	.50
❑ 76 Allen Iverson	.50	1.25
❑ 77 Bo Outlaw	.15	.40
❑ 78 Elden Campbell	.15	.40
❑ 79 Dirk Nowitzki	.40	1.00
❑ 80 Elton Brand	.25	.60
❑ 81 Brevin Knight	.15	.40
❑ 82 David Wesley	.15	.40
❑ 83 Raef LaFrentz	.15	.40
❑ 84 Antawn Jamison	.25	.60
❑ 85 Hakeem Olajuwon	.30	.75
❑ 86 Jamie Feick	.15	.40
❑ 87 Jalen Rose	.20	.50
❑ 88 Michael Olowokandi	.15	.40
❑ 89 Rick Fox	.20	.50
❑ 90 Austin Croshere	.15	.40
❑ 91 Glenn Robinson	.20	.50
❑ 92 Stephon Marbury	.25	.60
❑ 93 Clifford Robinson	.15	.40
❑ 94 Derek Fisher	.25	.60
❑ 95 Vlade Divac	.20	.50
❑ 96 Jim Jackson	.15	.40
❑ 97 Paul Pierce	.25	.60
❑ 98 Corey Benjamin	.15	.40
❑ 99 Lamond Murray	.15	.40
❑ 100 Steve Francis	.25	.60
❑ 101 Mitch Richmond	.20	.50
❑ 102 Othella Harrington	.15	.40
❑ 103 Nick Anderson	.15	.40
❑ 104 Antonio Davis	.15	.40
❑ 105 Ervin Johnson	.15	.40
❑ 106 Rasheed Wallace	.25	.60
❑ 107 Shawn Marion	.25	.60
❑ 108 Latrell Sprewell	.20	.50
❑ 109 Terrell Brandon	.15	.40
❑ 110 Sam Cassell	.20	.50
❑ 111 Shareef Abdur-Rahim	.20	.50
❑ 112 Travis Best	.15	.40
❑ 113 Tyrone Nesby	.15	.40
❑ 114 Alan Henderson	.15	.40
❑ 115 Vonteego Cummings	.15	.40
❑ 116 Kelvin Cato	.15	.40
❑ 117 Jerry Stackhouse	.20	.50
❑ 118 Nick Van Exel	.20	.50
❑ 119 Corliss Williamson TRAN	.20	.50
❑ 120 Doug Christie TRAN	.15	.40
❑ 121 Horace Grant TRAN	.20	.50
❑ 122 Glen Rice TRAN	.20	.50
❑ 123 Patrick Ewing TRAN	.30	.75
❑ 124 Dale Davis TRAN	.15	.40
❑ 125 Brian Grant TRAN	.15	.40
❑ 126 Shawn Kemp TRAN	.25	.60
❑ 127 Cedric Ceballos TRAN	.15	.40
❑ 128 Christian Laettner TRAN	.15	.40
❑ 129 Lindsey Hunter TRAN	.15	.40
❑ 130 Donyell Marshall TRAN	.15	.40
❑ 131 Robert Pack TRAN	.15	.40
❑ 132 Danny Fortson TRAN	.15	.40
❑ 133 Howard Eisley TRAN	.15	.40
❑ 134 Andrew DeClercq TRAN	.15	.40
❑ 135 Mark Jackson TRAN	.20	.50
❑ 136 Grant Hill TRAN	.25	.60
❑ 137 Tracy McGrady TRAN	.50	1.25
❑ 138 Maurice Taylor TRAN	.15	.40
❑ 139 Derek Anderson TRAN	.20	.50
❑ 140 Corey Maggette TRAN	.20	.50
❑ 141 Jermaine O'Neal TRAN	.25	.60
❑ 142 Ben Wallace TRAN	.20	.50
❑ 143 Ron Mercer TRAN	.15	.40
❑ 144 John Starks TRAN	.15	.40
❑ 145 Erick Strickland TRAN	.15	.40
❑ 146 Isaiah Rider TRAN	.20	.50
❑ 147 Eddie Jones TRAN	.20	.50
❑ 148 Anthony Mason TRAN	.15	.40
❑ 149 P.J. Brown TRAN	.15	.40
❑ 150 Jamal Mashburn TRAN	.20	.50
❑ 151 Kenyon Martin RC	1.00	2.50
❑ 152 Stromile Swift RC	.50	1.25
❑ 153 Darius Miles RC	.50	1.25
❑ 154 Marcus Fizer RC	.40	1.00
❑ 155 Mike Miller RC	.60	1.50
❑ 156 DerMarr Johnson RC	.40	1.00
❑ 157 Chris Mihm RC	.40	1.00
❑ 158 Jamal Crawford RC	.00	1.50
❑ 159 Joel Przybilla RC	.40	1.00
❑ 160 Keyon Dooling RC	.40	1.00
❑ 161 Jerome Moiso RC	.40	1.00
❑ 162 Etan Thomas RC	.40	1.00
❑ 163 Courtney Alexander RC	.40	1.00
❑ 164 Mateen Cleaves RC	.40	1.00
❑ 165 Jason Collier RC	.40	1.00
❑ 166 Desmond Mason RC	.50	1.25
❑ 167 Quentin Richardson RC	.50	1.25
❑ 168 Jamaal Magloire RC	.40	1.00
❑ 169 Speedy Claxton RC	.40	1.00
❑ 170 Morris Peterson RC	.60	1.50
❑ 171 Donnell Harvey RC	.40	1.00
❑ 172 DeShawn Stevenson RC	.40	1.00
❑ 173 Mamadou N'Diaye RC	.40	1.00
❑ 174 Erick Barkley RC	.40	1.00
❑ 175 Mark Madsen RC	.40	1.00

2001-02 Stadium Club

❑ COMP.SET w/o SP's (101)	12.50	25.00
❑ COMMON CARD (1-134)	.15	.40
❑ COMMON ROOKIE (101-133)	.75	2.00
❑ 1 Dikembe Mutombo	.20	.50
❑ 2 Clifford Robinson	.15	.40
❑ 3 Bonzi Wells	.20	.50
❑ 4 Peja Stojakovic	.20	.50
❑ 5 Gary Payton	.25	.60
❑ 6 Morris Peterson	.20	.50
❑ 7 Patrick Ewing	.30	.75
❑ 8 Terrell Brandon	.15	.40
❑ 9 Tim Thomas	.15	.40
❑ 10 Kobe Bryant	1.25	3.00
❑ 11 Hakeem Olajuwon	.30	.75
❑ 12 Marc Jackson	.15	.40
❑ 13 Wang Zhizhi	.20	.50
❑ 14 Andre Miller	.20	.50
❑ 15 Elton Brand	.25	.60
❑ 16 Eddie Robinson	.15	.40
❑ 17 Jason Terry	.25	.60
❑ 18 Allan Houston	.20	.50
❑ 19 Grant Hill	.25	.60
❑ 20 Tim Duncan	.50	1.25
❑ 21 Kevin Garnett	.50	1.25
❑ 22 Jahidi White	.15	.40
❑ 23 Michael Dickerson	.15	.40
❑ 24 Karl Malone	.30	.75
❑ 25 Chris Webber	.25	.60
❑ 26 Scottie Pippen	.40	1.00
❑ 27 Latrell Sprewell	.20	.50
❑ 28 Keith Van Horn	.20	.50
❑ 29 Ray Allen	.25	.60
❑ 30 Alonzo Mourning	.25	.60
❑ 31 Lamar Odom	.25	.60
❑ 32 Jalen Rose	.20	.50
❑ 33 Ben Wallace	.20	.50
❑ 34 Shaquille O'Neal	.60	1.50
❑ 35 Antonio McDyess	.20	.50
❑ 36 Dirk Nowitzki	.40	1.00
❑ 37 Marcus Fizer	.15	.40
❑ 38 Jamal Mashburn	.20	.50
❑ 39 Paul Pierce	.25	.60
❑ 40 DerMarr Johnson	.15	.40
❑ 41 Steve Nash	.40	1.00
❑ 42 Jerry Stackhouse	.20	.50
❑ 43 Larry Hughes	.20	.50
❑ 44 Cuttino Mobley	.20	.50
❑ 45 Horace Grant	.20	.50
❑ 46 Eddie Jones	.20	.50
❑ 47 Wally Szczerbiak	.20	.50
❑ 48 Marcus Camby	.20	.50
❑ 49 Jamal Crawford	.20	.50
❑ 50 Vince Carter	.50	1.25
❑ 51 Donyell Marshall	.15	.40
❑ 52 Shareef Abdur-Rahim	.20	.50
❑ 53 Courtney Alexander	.15	.40
❑ 54 Kenny Anderson	.20	.50
❑ 55 Ron Mercer	.15	.40
❑ 56 Lamond Murray	.15	.40
❑ 57 Michael Finley	.25	.60
❑ 58 Raef LaFrentz	.15	.40
❑ 59 Reggie Miller	.25	.60
❑ 60 Steve Francis	.25	.60
❑ 61 Rick Fox	.20	.50
❑ 62 Tim Hardaway	.20	.50
❑ 63 Glenn Robinson	.20	.50
❑ 64 LaPhonso Ellis	.20	.50
❑ 65 Kenyon Martin	.25	.60
❑ 66 Jason Williams	.20	.50
❑ 67 Derek Anderson	.20	.50
❑ 68 Eric Snow	.15	.40
❑ 69 Darius Miles	.15	.40
❑ 70 Antawn Jamison	.25	.60
❑ 71 Mateen Cleaves	.15	.40
❑ 72 Jason Kidd	.40	1.00
❑ 73 Rasheed Wallace	.25	.60
❑ 74 Chris Porter	.15	.40
❑ 75 Tracy McGrady	.50	1.25
❑ 76 Aaron McKie	.15	.40
❑ 77 Baron Davis	.25	.60
❑ 78 Toni Kukoc	.20	.50
❑ 79 Antoine Walker	.20	.50
❑ 80 Shawn Marion	.25	.60
❑ 81 Mike Miller	.20	.50
❑ 82 Stephon Marbury	.25	.60
❑ 83 Glen Rice	.20	.50
❑ 84 David Robinson	.30	.75
❑ 85 Rashard Lewis	.25	.60
❑ 86 John Stockton	.30	.75
❑ 87 Stromile Swift	.15	.40
❑ 88 Richard Hamilton	.20	.50
❑ 89 Desmond Mason	.20	.50

❑ 90 Brian Grant	.15	.40
❑ 91 Keyon Dooling	.15	.40
❑ 92 Jermaine O'Neal	.25	.60
❑ 93 Nick Van Exel	.20	.50
❑ 94 Tom Gugliotta	.15	.40
❑ 95 Darrell Armstrong	.15	.40
❑ 96 Sam Cassell	.20	.50
❑ 97 Mike Bibby	.20	.50
❑ 98 DeShawn Stevenson	.15	.40
❑ 99 Antonio Davis	.15	.40
❑ 100 Allen Iverson	.50	1.25
❑ 101 Kwame Brown RC	1.00	2.50
❑ 102 Tyson Chandler RC	1.50	4.00
❑ 103 Pau Gasol RC	3.00	8.00
❑ 104 Eddy Curry RC	1.25	3.00
❑ 105 Jason Richardson RC	1.50	4.00
❑ 106 Shane Battier RC	1.25	3.00
❑ 107 Eddie Griffin RC	.75	2.00
❑ 108 DeSagana Diop RC	.75	2.00
❑ 109 Rodney White RC	.75	2.00
❑ 110 Joe Johnson RC	2.00	5.00
❑ 111 Kedrick Brown RC	.75	2.00
❑ 112 Vladimir Radmanovic RC	1.00	2.50
❑ 113 Richard Jefferson RC	2.00	5.00
❑ 114 Troy Murphy RC	1.50	4.00
❑ 115 Steven Hunter RC	.75	2.00
❑ 116 Kirk Haston RC	.75	2.00
❑ 117 Michael Bradley RC	.75	2.00
❑ 118 Jason Collins RC	.75	2.00
❑ 119 Zach Randolph RC	2.00	5.00
❑ 120 Brendan Haywood RC	1.00	2.50
❑ 121 Joseph Forte RC	.75	2.00
❑ 122 Jeryl Sasser RC	.75	2.00
❑ 123 Brandon Armstrong RC	.75	2.00
❑ 124 Gerald Wallace RC	2.00	5.00
❑ 125 Samuel Dalembert RC	1.00	2.50
❑ 126 Jamaal Tinsley RC	1.00	2.50
❑ 127 Tony Parker RC	3.00	8.00
❑ 128 Trenton Hassell RC	1.00	2.50
❑ 129 Gilbert Arenas RC	1.25	3.00
❑ 130 Omar Cook RC	.75	2.00
❑ 131 Jeff Trepagnier RC	.75	2.00
❑ 132 Loren Woods RC	.75	2.00
❑ 133 Terence Morris RC	.75	2.00
❑ 134 Michael Jordan	6.00	15.00

2002-03 Stadium Club

❑ COMPLETE SET (133)	50.00	100.00
❑ COMP.SET w/o SP's (100)	10.00	25.00
❑ COMMON CARD (1-100)	.15	.40
❑ COMMON ROOKIE (101-133)	.75	2.00
❑ 1 Shaquille O'Neal	.60	1.50
❑ 2 Pau Gasol	.25	.60
❑ 3 Allen Iverson	.50	1.25
❑ 4 Bonzi Wells	.20	.50
❑ 5 Mike Bibby	.20	.50
❑ 6 Rashard Lewis	.25	.60
❑ 7 Aaron McKie	.15	.40
❑ 8 Shane Battier	.20	.50
❑ 9 Kenyon Martin	.25	.60
❑ 10 Tim Duncan	.50	1.25
❑ 11 Richard Jefferson	.25	.60
❑ 12 Jalen Rose	.20	.50
❑ 13 Antoine Walker	.20	.50
❑ 14 Michael Finley	.25	.60
❑ 15 Clifford Robinson	.15	.40
❑ 16 Antawn Jamison	.25	.60
❑ 17 Reggie Miller	.25	.60
❑ 18 Elton Brand	.25	.60
❑ 19 Robert Horry	.20	.50
❑ 20 Kevin Garnett	.50	1.25
❑ 21 Baron Davis	.25	.60
❑ 22 Latrell Sprewell	.20	.50
❑ 23 Glenn Robinson	.20	.50
❑ 24 Wally Szczerbiak	.20	.50
❑ 25 Tracy McGrady	.50	1.25
❑ 26 Stephon Marbury	.25	.60
❑ 27 Rasheed Wallace	.25	.60
❑ 28 Doug Christie	.15	.40
❑ 29 Desmond Mason	.20	.50
❑ 30 Vince Carter	.50	1.25
❑ 31 Andrei Kirilenko	.25	.60
❑ 32 Richard Hamilton	.20	.50
❑ 33 Jamaal Tinsley	.20	.50
❑ 34 Steve Francis	.25	.60
❑ 35 Ben Wallace	.20	.50
❑ 36 Juwan Howard	.20	.50
❑ 37 Dirk Nowitzki	.40	1.00
❑ 38 Andre Miller	.20	.50
❑ 39 Elden Campbell	.15	.40
❑ 40 Paul Pierce	.25	.60
❑ 41 Shareef Abdur-Rahim	.20	.50
❑ 42 John Stockton	.30	.75
❑ 43 Gary Payton	.25	.60
❑ 44 David Robinson	.30	.75
❑ 45 Scottie Pippen	.40	1.00
❑ 46 Morris Peterson	.20	.50
❑ 47 Mike Miller	.20	.50
❑ 48 Marcus Camby	.20	.50
❑ 49 Joe Smith	.15	.40
❑ 50 Kobe Bryant	1.25	3.00
❑ 51 Alonzo Mourning	.25	.60
❑ 52 Ray Allen	.25	.60
❑ 53 Keith Van Horn	.20	.50
❑ 54 Grant Hill	.25	.60
❑ 55 Dikembe Mutombo	.20	.50
❑ 56 Shawn Marion	.25	.60
❑ 57 Peja Stojakovic	.20	.50
❑ 58 Tony Parker	.25	.60
❑ 59 Keon Clark	.15	.40
❑ 60 Brendan Haywood	.15	.40
❑ 61 Derek Anderson	.20	.50
❑ 62 Allan Houston	.20	.50
❑ 63 Brian Grant	.15	.40
❑ 64 Lamar Odom	.25	.60
❑ 65 Jermaine O'Neal	.25	.60
❑ 66 Kenny Anderson	.20	.50
❑ 67 Desmond Johnson	.15	.40
❑ 68 Lamond Murray	.15	.40
❑ 69 Jason Richardson	.25	.60
❑ 70 Rodney Rogers	.15	.40
❑ 71 Rick Fox	.20	.50
❑ 72 Tim Thomas	.15	.40
❑ 73 Darrell Armstrong	.15	.40
❑ 74 Anfernee Hardaway	.25	.60
❑ 75 Chris Webber	.25	.60
❑ 76 Derrick Coleman	.20	.50
❑ 77 Karl Malone	.25	.60
❑ 78 Antonio Davis	.15	.40
❑ 79 Jason Terry	.25	.60
❑ 80 Wang Zhizhi	.15	.40
❑ 81 Steve Nash	.40	1.00
❑ 82 Eddy Curry UER	.20	.50
❑ 83 Tim Hardaway	.20	.50
❑ 84 Corliss Williamson	.20	.50
❑ 85 Eddie Griffin	.15	.40
❑ 86 Darius Miles	.15	.40
❑ 87 Jason Williams	.20	.50
❑ 88 Sam Cassell	.20	.50
❑ 89 Kwame Brown	.15	.40
❑ 90 Jason Kidd	.40	1.00
❑ 91 Jamal Mashburn	.20	.50
❑ 92 Jamaal Magloire	.15	.40
❑ 93 Tyson Chandler	.20	.50
❑ 94 Jumaine Jones	.15	.40
❑ 95 Antonio McDyess	.20	.50
❑ 96 Jerry Stackhouse	.20	.50
❑ 97 Gilbert Arenas	.25	.60
❑ 98 Cuttino Mobley	.20	.50
❑ 99 Eddie Jones	.20	.50
❑ 100 Michael Jordan	1.50	4.00
❑ 101 Yao Ming RC	2.50	6.00
❑ 102 Jay Williams RC	1.00	2.50
❑ 103 Mike Dunleavy RC	1.00	2.50
❑ 104 Drew Gooden RC	1.25	3.00
❑ 105 Nikoloz Tskitishvili RC	.75	2.00
❑ 106 DaJuan Wagner RC	.75	2.00
❑ 107 Nene Hilario RC	1.00	2.50
❑ 108 Chris Wilcox RC	1.00	2.50
❑ 109 Amare Stoudemire RC	2.00	5.00
❑ 110 Caron Butler RC	1.50	4.00
❑ 111 Jared Jeffries RC	.75	2.00
❑ 112 Melvin Ely RC	.75	2.00
❑ 113 Marcus Haislip RC	.75	2.00
❑ 114 Fred Jones RC	1.00	2.50
❑ 115 Bostjan Nachbar RC	.75	2.00
❑ 116 Dan Dickau RC	.75	2.00
❑ 117 Juan Dixon RC	1.25	3.00
❑ 118 Dan Gadzuric RC	.75	2.00
❑ 119 Ryan Humphrey RC	.75	2.00
❑ 120 Kareem Rush RC	1.00	2.50
❑ 121 Qyntel Woods RC	.75	2.00
❑ 122 Casey Jacobsen RC	.75	2.00
❑ 123 Tayshaun Prince RC	1.25	3.00
❑ 124 Frank Williams RC	.75	2.00
❑ 125 John Salmons RC	1.25	3.00
❑ 126 Chris Jefferies RC	.75	2.00
❑ 127 Sam Clancy RC	.75	2.00
❑ 128 Ronald Murray RC	1.25	3.00
❑ 129 Roger Mason RC	.75	2.00
❑ 130 Robert Archibald RC	.75	2.00
❑ 131 Vincent Yarbrough RC	.75	2.00
❑ 132 Darius Songaila RC	.75	2.00
❑ 133 Carlos Boozer RC	1.50	4.00

2007-08 Stadium Club

❑ COMP.SET w/o SP's (100)	20.00	50.00
❑ 1 Amare Stoudemire	.75	2.00
❑ 2 Baron Davis	.40	1.00
❑ 3 Dwyane Wade	1.00	2.50
❑ 4 Chris Bosh	.40	1.00
❑ 5 Josh Smith	.40	1.00
❑ 6 Tyson Chandler	.40	1.00
❑ 7 Al Jefferson	.40	1.00
❑ 8 Deron Williams	.60	1.50
❑ 9 Andre Iguodala	.40	1.00
❑ 10 Jermaine O'Neal	.40	1.00
❑ 11 Yao Ming	1.00	2.50
❑ 12 Kirk Hinrich	.40	1.00
❑ 13 Steve Nash	.50	1.25
❑ 14 Jameer Nelson	.30	.75
❑ 15 Carmelo Anthony	.75	2.00
❑ 16 Pau Gasol	.40	1.00
❑ 17 Andrew Bynum	.40	1.00
❑ 18 Gerald Wallace	.40	1.00
❑ 19 Carlos Boozer	.40	1.00
❑ 20 Rasheed Wallace	.40	1.00
❑ 21 Tim Duncan	.75	2.00
❑ 22 Michael Redd	.40	1.00
❑ 23 LeBron James	2.00	5.00
❑ 24 Kobe Bryant	2.00	5.00
❑ 25 Richard Jefferson	.40	1.00
❑ 26 Mike Bibby	.40	1.00
❑ 27 Ben Gordon	.50	1.25
❑ 28 Caron Butler	.40	1.00
❑ 29 Corey Maggette	.30	.75
❑ 30 Kevin Garnett	1.00	2.50
❑ 31 Shawn Marion	.40	1.00
❑ 32 Shaquille O'Neal	1.00	2.50
❑ 33 Allen Iverson	.75	2.00
❑ 34 Eddy Curry	.25	.60
❑ 35 Chris Wilcox	.30	.75
❑ 36 T.J. Ford	.30	.75
❑ 37 LaMarcus Aldridge	.50	1.25
❑ 38 Drew Gooden	.30	.75
❑ 39 Antawn Jamison	.40	1.00
❑ 40 Richard Hamilton	.30	.75
❑ 41 Dirk Nowitzki	.60	1.50
❑ 42 Elton Brand	.40	1.00
❑ 43 Jason Richardson	.40	1.00
❑ 44 Paul Pierce	.40	1.00
❑ 45 Manu Ginobili	.40	1.00
❑ 46 Danny Granger	.30	.75
❑ 47 Andrei Kirilenko	.40	1.00
❑ 48 Jarrett Jack	.30	.75
❑ 49 Andre Miller	.30	.75
❑ 50 Gilbert Arenas	.40	1.00
❑ 51 Mehmet Okur	.30	.75
❑ 52 Rudy Gay	.30	.75
❑ 53 Ben Wallace	.40	1.00
❑ 54 Tayshaun Prince	.40	1.00

❑ 55 Jason Kidd	.60	1.50
❑ 56 Josh Howard	.40	1.00
❑ 57 Daniel Gibson	.40	1.00
❑ 58 Rafer Alston	.25	.60
❑ 59 Monta Ellis	.30	.75
❑ 60 Dwight Howard	.75	2.00
❑ 61 Chauncey Billups	.40	1.00
❑ 62 Joe Johnson	.40	1.00
❑ 63 Kevin Martin	.40	1.00
❑ 64 Ray Allen	.40	1.00
❑ 65 Luol Deng	.40	1.00
❑ 66 Raymond Felton	.50	1.25
❑ 67 Lamar Odom	.40	1.00
❑ 68 Mo Williams	.30	.75
❑ 69 Tony Parker	.40	1.00
❑ 70 Brandon Roy	.60	1.50
❑ 71 Tracy McGrady	.75	2.00
❑ 72 Marcus Camby	.25	.60
❑ 73 Stephon Marbury	.40	1.00
❑ 74 Jason Terry	.40	1.00
❑ 75 Randy Foye	.40	1.00
❑ 76 Vince Carter	.75	2.00
❑ 77 Andrea Bargnani	.50	1.25
❑ 78 Chris Paul	.75	2.00
❑ 79 Rashard Lewis	.40	1.00
❑ 80 Leandro Barbosa	.30	.75
❑ 81 Larry Johnson	1.00	2.50
❑ 82 Patrick Ewing	1.25	3.00
❑ 83 Hakeem Olajuwon	1.25	3.00
❑ 84 Clyde Drexler	1.25	3.00
❑ 85 David Robinson	1.50	4.00
❑ 86 Bill Walton	1.00	2.50
❑ 87 Wilt Chamberlain	2.00	5.00
❑ 88 Bill Russell	1.50	4.00
❑ 89 Bob Lanier	1.00	2.50
❑ 90 Dennis Rodman	1.00	2.50
❑ 91 John Stockton	1.50	4.00
❑ 92 Isiah Thomas	1.00	2.50
❑ 93 Magic Johnson	2.00	5.00
❑ 94 Larry Bird	3.00	8.00
❑ 95 Elgin Baylor	1.00	2.50
❑ 96 Oscar Robertson	1.00	2.50
❑ 97 Joe Barry Carroll	1.00	2.50
❑ 98 James Worthy	1.25	3.00
❑ 99 Pete Maravich	3.00	8.00
❑ 100 Kenny Smith	1.00	2.50
❑ 101 Greg Oden RC	2.50	6.00
❑ 102 Kevin Durant RC	12.00	30.00
❑ 103 Al Horford RC	2.00	5.00
❑ 104 Michael Conley RC	2.00	5.00
❑ 105 Jeff Green RC	2.00	5.00
❑ 106 Yi Jianlian RC	2.50	6.00
❑ 107 Corey Brewer RC	2.00	5.00
❑ 108 Brandan Wright RC	2.00	5.00
❑ 109 Joakim Noah RC	2.00	5.00
❑ 110 Spencer Hawes RC	1.50	4.00
❑ 111 Acie Law IV RC	2.00	5.00
❑ 112 Thaddeus Young RC	2.00	5.00
❑ 113 Julian Wright RC	2.00	5.00
❑ 114 Al Thornton RC	1.50	4.00
❑ 115 Rodney Stuckey RC	3.00	8.00
❑ 116 Nick Young RC	1.50	4.00
❑ 117 Sean Williams RC	1.50	4.00
❑ 118 Marco Belinelli RC	1.50	4.00
❑ 119 Javaris Crittenton RC	1.50	4.00
❑ 120 Jason Smith RC	1.50	4.00
❑ 121 Daequan Cook RC	2.00	5.00
❑ 122 Jared Dudley RC	1.50	4.00
❑ 123 Wilson Chandler RC	1.50	4.00
❑ 124 D.J. Strawberry RC	1.50	4.00
❑ 125 Morris Almond RC	1.50	4.00
❑ 126 Aaron Brooks RC	2.50	6.00
❑ 127 Arron Afflalo RC	1.50	4.00
❑ 128 Luis Scola RC	2.50	6.00
❑ 129 Alando Tucker RC	1.50	4.00
❑ 130 Carl Landry RC	1.50	4.00
❑ 131 Gabe Pruitt RC	1.50	4.00
❑ 132 Marcus Williams RC	1.50	4.00
❑ 133 Nick Fazekas RC	1.50	4.00
❑ 134 Glen Davis RC	3.00	8.00
❑ 135 Jermareo Davidson RC	1.50	4.00
❑ 136 Josh McRoberts RC	2.00	5.00
❑ 137 Oleksiy Pecherov RC	1.50	4.00
❑ 138 Derrick Byars RC	1.50	4.00
❑ 139 Adam Haluska RC	1.50	4.00
❑ 140 Reyshawn Terry RC	1.50	4.00
❑ 141 Jared Jordan RC	1.50	4.00
❑ 142 Stephane Lasme RC	1.50	4.00
❑ 143 Dominic McGuire RC	1.50	4.00
❑ 144 Aaron Gray RC	1.50	4.00
❑ 145 JamesOn Curry RC	1.50	4.00
❑ 146 Taurean Green RC	1.50	4.00
❑ 147 Demetris Nichols RC	1.50	4.00
❑ 148 Herbert Hill RC	1.50	4.00
❑ 149 Ramon Sessions RC	2.00	5.00
❑ 150 Sammy Mejia RC	1.50	4.00
❑ NNO G.Oden AU 8x10 EXCH	125.00	225.00

1999-00 Stadium Club Chrome

❑ COMPLETE SET (150)	30.00	80.00
❑ COMMON CARD (1-150)	.20	.50
❑ COMMON ROOKIE	.40	1.00
❑ 1 Allen Iverson	.60	1.50
❑ 2 Chris Webber	.30	.75
❑ 3 Antawn Jamison	.30	.75
❑ 4 Karl Malone	.40	1.00
❑ 5 Sam Cassell	.25	.60
❑ 6 Kerry Kittles	.20	.50
❑ 7 Tim Thomas	.25	.60
❑ 8 Shawn Bradley	.20	.50
❑ 9 David Wesley	.20	.50
❑ 10 Glenn Robinson	.25	.60
❑ 11 Mitch Richmond	.25	.60
❑ 12 Shareef Abdur-Rahim	.25	.60
❑ 13 Christian Laettner	.25	.60
❑ 14 Anthony Mason	.20	.50
❑ 15 Randy Brown	.20	.50
❑ 16 Charles Barkley	.40	1.00
❑ 17 Bobby Jackson	.25	.60
❑ 18 Matt Harpring	.25	.60
❑ 19 Shawn Kemp	.30	.75
❑ 20 Ruben Patterson	.20	.50
❑ 21 Mike Bibby	.30	.75
❑ 22 Vlade Divac	.30	.75
❑ 23 David Robinson	.40	1.00
❑ 24 Keith Van Horn	.25	.60
❑ 25 Juwan Howard	.25	.60
❑ 26 Shaquille O'Neal	.75	2.00
❑ 27 Alonzo Mourning	.30	.75
❑ 28 Michael Olowokandi	.20	.50
❑ 29 Andrew DeClercq	.20	.50
❑ 30 Toni Kukoc	.30	.75
❑ 31 Dikembe Mutombo	.25	.60
❑ 32 Steve Nash	.50	1.25
❑ 33 Eddie Jones	.30	.75
❑ 34 Reggie Miller	.30	.75
❑ 35 Larry Hughes	.25	.60
❑ 36 Tim Duncan	.60	1.50
❑ 37 Jerome Williams	.20	.50
❑ 38 Rod Strickland	.20	.50
❑ 39 Patrick Ewing	.40	1.00
❑ 40 Grant Hill	.30	.75
❑ 41 Derrick Coleman	.25	.60
❑ 42 Raef LaFrentz	.25	.60
❑ 43 Rik Smits	.30	.75
❑ 44 Latrell Sprewell	.25	.60
❑ 45 John Starks	.30	.75
❑ 46 Cuttino Mobley	.25	.60
❑ 47 Marcus Camby	.25	.60
❑ 48 Stephon Marbury	.30	.75
❑ 49 Tom Gugliotta	.20	.50
❑ 50 Vince Carter	.60	1.50
❑ 51 Chris Mullin	.30	.75
❑ 52 Tyrone Nesby RC	.30	.75
❑ 53 Elden Campbell	.20	.50
❑ 54 Lindsey Hunter	.20	.50
❑ 55 Rasheed Wallace	.30	.75
❑ 56 Jeff Hornacek	.25	.60
❑ 57 Matt Geiger	.20	.50
❑ 58 Antoine Walker	.30	.75
❑ 59 Jason Williams	.30	.75
❑ 60 Robert Horry	.30	.75
❑ 61 Kendall Gill	.20	.50
❑ 62 Dan Majerle	.30	.75
❑ 63 Robert Traylor	.20	.50
❑ 64 P.J. Brown	.20	.50
❑ 65 Terrell Brandon	.20	.50
❑ 66 Corliss Williamson	.20	.50
❑ 67 Bryant Reeves	.20	.50
❑ 68 Larry Johnson	.30	.75
❑ 69 Keith Closs	.20	.50
❑ 70 Walter McCarty	.20	.50
❑ 71 Wesley Person	.20	.50
❑ 72 Chris Mills	.20	.50
❑ 73 Glen Rice	.30	.75
❑ 74 Jason Kidd	.50	1.25
❑ 75 Dirk Nowitzki	.50	1.25
❑ 76 Bryon Russell	.20	.50
❑ 77 Vin Baker	.30	.75
❑ 78 Darrell Armstrong	.20	.50
❑ 79 Eric Snow	.25	.60
❑ 80 Hakeem Olajuwon	.30	.75
❑ 81 Tracy McGrady	.60	1.50
❑ 82 Kenny Anderson	.25	.60
❑ 83 Jalen Rose	.25	.60
❑ 84 Tim Hardaway	.30	.75
❑ 85 Doug Christie	.25	.60
❑ 86 Allan Houston	.25	.60
❑ 87 Kobe Bryant	1.50	4.00
❑ 88 Kevin Garnett	.60	1.50
❑ 89 Steve Kerr	.25	.60
❑ 90 Nick Van Exel	.25	.60
❑ 91 Jerry Stackhouse	.30	.75
❑ 92 Derek Fisher	.30	.75
❑ 93 Donyell Marshall	.25	.60
❑ 94 Mark Jackson	.30	.75
❑ 95 Ray Allen	.30	.75
❑ 96 Avery Johnson	.25	.60
❑ 97 Michael Doleac	.20	.50
❑ 98 Charles Oakley	.25	.60
❑ 99 Gary Payton	.30	.75
❑ 100 Theo Ratliff	.25	.60
❑ 101 Cedric Ceballos	.20	.50
❑ 102 Paul Pierce	.30	.75
❑ 103 Michael Finley	.30	.75
❑ 104 Brian Grant	.20	.50
❑ 105 John Stockton	.40	1.00
❑ 106 Maurice Taylor	.25	.60
❑ 107 Antonio McDyess	.25	.60
❑ 108 Adrian Griffin RC	.30	.75
❑ 109 Jamal Mashburn	.20	.50
❑ 110 Jayson Williams	.25	.60
❑ 111 Joe Smith	.25	.60
❑ 112 Clifford Robinson	.20	.50
❑ 113 Mario Elie	.20	.50
❑ 114 Damon Stoudamire	.30	.75
❑ 115 Felipe Lopez	.20	.50
❑ 116 Antonio Davis TRAN	.20	.50
❑ 117 Mookie Blaylock TRAN	.20	.50
❑ 118 Ron Mercer TRAN	.20	.50
❑ 119 Horace Grant TRAN	.25	.60
❑ 120 Steve Smith TRAN	.20	.50
❑ 121 Isaiah Rider TRAN	.20	.50
❑ 122 Tariq Abdul-Wahad TRAN	.20	.50
❑ 123 Michael Dickerson TRAN	.20	.50
❑ 124 Nick Anderson TRAN	.20	.50
❑ 125 Jim Jackson TRAN	.25	.60
❑ 126 Hersey Hawkins TRAN	.20	.50
❑ 127 Brent Barry TRAN	.25	.60
❑ 128 Shandon Anderson TRAN	.20	.50
❑ 129 Scottie Pippen TRAN	.50	1.25
❑ 130 Isaac Austin TRAN	.20	.50
❑ 131 Anfernee Hardaway TRAN	.30	.75
❑ 132 Elton Brand RC	1.50	4.00
❑ 133 Steve Francis RC	1.50	4.00
❑ 134 Baron Davis RC	2.00	5.00
❑ 135 Lamar Odom RC	1.50	4.00
❑ 136 Jonathan Bender RC	.50	1.25
❑ 137 Wally Szczerbiak RC	1.50	4.00
❑ 138 Richard Hamilton RC	1.50	4.00
❑ 139 Andre Miller RC	1.50	4.00
❑ 140 Shawn Marion RC	1.50	4.00
❑ 141 Jason Terry RC	1.25	3.00
❑ 142 Trajan Langdon RC	.50	1.25
❑ 143 A.Radojevic RC	.50	1.25
❑ 144 Corey Maggette RC	1.50	4.00
❑ 145 William Avery RC	.50	1.25
❑ 146 Ron Artest RC	2.00	5.00
❑ 147 Cal Bowdler RC	.50	1.25
❑ 148 James Posey RC	.75	2.00
❑ 149 Quincy Lewis RC	.50	1.25
❑ 150 Scott Padgett RC	.50	1.25

2009-10 Studio

1 Andrew Bynum	.50	1.25
2 Derek Fisher	.40	1.00
3 Kobe Bryant	2.50	6.00
4 Lamar Odom	.50	1.25
5 Carmelo Anthony	.60	1.50
6 Chauncey Billups	.50	1.25
7 Chris Andersen	.50	1.25
8 Brandon Roy	.60	1.50
9 LaMarcus Aldridge	.50	1.25
10 Rudy Fernandez	.50	1.25
11 Manu Ginobili	.50	1.25
12 Tim Duncan	.75	2.00
13 Tony Parker	.50	1.25
14 Luis Scola	.30	.75
15 Shane Battier	.40	1.00
16 Tracy McGrady	.60	1.50
17 Dirk Nowitzki	.60	1.50
18 Jason Kidd	.50	1.25
19 Jason Terry	.40	1.00
20 Josh Howard	.50	1.25
21 Chris Paul	1.00	2.50
22 David West	.50	1.25
23 Peja Stojakovic	.30	.75
24 Rasual Butler	.30	.75
25 Andrei Kirilenko	.40	1.00
26 Carlos Boozer	.50	1.25
27 Deron Williams	.60	1.50
28 Amare Stoudemire	.60	1.50
29 Grant Hill	.50	1.25
30 Jason Richardson	.50	1.25
31 Steve Nash	.50	1.25
32 Anthony Randolph	.50	1.25
33 Corey Maggette	.40	1.00
34 Monta Ellis	.50	1.25
35 Raja Bell	.40	1.00
36 Marc Gasol	.50	1.25
37 Mike Conley	.30	.75
38 O.J. Mayo	.60	1.50
39 Rudy Gay	.50	1.25
40 Al Jefferson	.50	1.25
41 Kevin Love	.40	1.00
42 Ryan Gomes	.30	.75
43 Jeff Green	.40	1.00
44 Kevin Durant	1.25	3.00
45 Russell Westbrook	.50	1.25
46 Al Thornton	.50	1.25
47 Chris Kaman	.50	1.25
48 Eric Gordon	.50	1.25
49 Andres Nocioni	.40	1.00
50 Francisco Garcia	.40	1.00
51 Kevin Martin	.50	1.25
52 LeBron James	2.50	6.00
53 Mo Williams	.40	1.00
54 Shaquille O'Neal	1.00	2.50
55 Kevin Garnett	1.00	2.50
56 Paul Pierce	.60	1.50
57 Rajon Rondo	.50	1.25
58 Ray Allen	.50	1.25
59 Dwight Howard	1.00	2.50
60 Jameer Nelson	.40	1.00
61 Rashard Lewis	.50	1.25
62 Al Horford	.50	1.25
63 Joe Johnson	.50	1.25
64 Josh Smith	.50	1.25
65 Mike Bibby	.30	.75
66 Dwyane Wade	1.00	2.50
67 Jermaine O'Neal	.50	1.25
68 Michael Beasley	.60	1.50
69 Derrick Rose	1.00	2.50
70 Joakim Noah	.50	1.25
71 John Salmons	.50	1.25
72 Andre Iguodala	.50	1.25
73 Elton Brand	.50	1.25
74 Thaddeus Young	.30	.75
75 Ben Gordon	.50	1.25
76 Richard Hamilton	.40	1.00
77 Tayshaun Prince	.50	1.25
78 Danny Granger	.50	1.25
79 Mike Dunleavy	.30	.75
80 T.J. Ford	.30	.75
81 Troy Murphy	.30	.75
82 Boris Diaw	.40	1.00
83 Gerald Wallace	.50	1.25
84 Stephen Jackson	.40	1.00
85 Raymond Felton	.40	1.00
86 Andrew Bogut	.50	1.25
87 Luke Ridnour	.30	.75
88 Michael Redd	.50	1.25
89 Brook Lopez	.30	.75
90 Devin Harris	.50	1.25
91 Yi Jianlian	.50	1.25
92 Andrea Bargnani	.40	1.00
93 Chris Bosh	.50	1.25
94 Jose Calderon	.40	1.00
95 Al Harrington	.40	1.00
96 David Lee	.40	1.00
97 Wilson Chandler	.30	.75
98 Antawn Jamison	.50	1.25
99 Caron Butler	.50	1.25
100 Mike Miller	.50	1.25
101 Wes Unseld	.50	1.25
102 Arnie Risen	.50	1.25
103 Bailey Howell	.50	1.25
104 Bill Cartwright	.50	1.25
105 Byron Scott	.50	1.25
106 Darryl Dawkins	.50	1.25
107 Jeff Hornacek	.50	1.25
108 Jerry Lucas	.50	1.25
109 Kelly Tripucka	.50	1.25
110 Manute Bol	.50	1.25
111 Mark Eaton	.50	1.25
112 Michael Cage	.50	1.25
113 Mitch Richmond	.50	1.25
114 Norm Nixon	.50	1.25
115 Paul Westphal	.50	1.25
116 Rick Barry	.50	1.25
117 Ron Harper	.50	1.25
118 Spencer Haywood	.50	1.25
119 Dennis Rodman	.75	2.00
120 Anfernee Hardaway	1.25	3.00
121 Ty Lawson RC	1.25	3.00
122 Jeff Pendergraph RC	1.25	3.00
123 DeJuan Blair RC	1.50	4.00
124 Jermaine Taylor RC	1.25	3.00
125 Rodrigue Beaubois RC	2.00	5.00
126 Darren Collison RC	1.50	4.00
127 Eric Maynor RC	1.50	4.00
128 Earl Clark RC	1.50	4.00
129 Stephen Curry RC	2.50	6.00
130 DeMarre Carroll RC	1.25	3.00
131 Hasheem Thabeet RC	1.00	2.50
132 Jonny Flynn RC	1.50	4.00
133 Wayne Ellington RC	1.50	4.00
134 B.J. Mullens RC	1.00	2.50
135 James Harden RC	2.00	5.00
136 Blake Griffin RC	2.50	6.00
137 Omri Casspi RC	1.50	4.00
138 Tyreke Evans RC	4.00	10.00
139 Jeff Teague RC	1.25	3.00
140 James Johnson RC	1.50	4.00
141 Taj Gibson RC	1.50	4.00
142 Jrue Holiday RC	1.50	4.00
143 Austin Daye RC	1.25	3.00
144 Tyler Hansbrough RC	1.50	4.00
145 Gerald Henderson RC	1.50	4.00
146 Brandon Jennings RC	2.50	6.00
147 Terrence Williams RC	2.00	5.00
148 DeMar DeRozan RC	1.50	4.00
149 Jordan Hill RC	1.25	3.00
150 Toney Douglas RC	1.00	2.50

2001-02 Sweet Shot

COMP.SET w/o SP's	20.00	40.00
COMMON CARD (1-90)	.20	.50
COMMON ROOKIE (91-110)	2.00	5.00
COMMON ROOKIE (110-120)	2.50	6.00
1 Jason Terry	.30	.75
2 Shareef Abdur-Rahim	.25	.60
3 Toni Kukoc	.25	.60
4 Paul Pierce	.30	.75
5 Antoine Walker	.25	.60
6 Kenny Anderson	.25	.60
7 Baron Davis	.30	.75
8 Jamal Mashburn	.25	.60
9 David Wesley	.20	.50
10 Ron Mercer	.20	.50
11 Ron Artest	.25	.60
12 A.J. Guyton	.20	.50
13 Andre Miller	.25	.60
14 Lamond Murray	.20	.50
15 Chris Mihm	.20	.50
16 Michael Finley	.30	.75
17 Dirk Nowitzki	.50	1.25
18 Steve Nash	.50	1.25
19 Antonio McDyess	.25	.60
20 Nick Van Exel	.25	.60
21 Raef LaFrentz	.20	.50
22 Jerry Stackhouse	.25	.60
23 Chucky Atkins	.20	.50
24 Corliss Williamson	.25	.60
25 Antawn Jamison	.30	.75
26 Marc Jackson	.20	.50
27 Larry Hughes	.25	.60
28 Steve Francis	.30	.75
29 Cuttino Mobley	.25	.60
30 Maurice Taylor	.20	.50
31 Reggie Miller	.30	.75
32 Jalen Rose	.25	.60
33 Jermaine O'Neal	.30	.75
34 Darius Miles	.20	.50
35 Elton Brand	.30	.75
36 Corey Maggette	.25	.60
37 Quentin Richardson	.25	.60
38 Kobe Bryant	1.50	4.00
39 Shaquille O'Neal	.75	2.00
40 Rick Fox	.25	.60
41 Derek Fisher	.25	.60
42 Stromile Swift	.20	.50
43 Jason Williams	.25	.60
44 Michael Dickerson	.20	.50
45 Alonzo Mourning	.30	.75
46 Eddie Jones	.25	.60
47 Anthony Carter	.20	.50
48 Glenn Robinson	.25	.60
49 Ray Allen	.30	.75
50 Sam Cassell	.25	.60
51 Kevin Garnett	.60	1.50
52 Chauncey Billups	.25	.60
53 Terrell Brandon	.20	.50
54 Joe Smith	.20	.50
55 Kenyon Martin	.30	.75
56 Keith Van Horn	.25	.60
57 Jason Kidd	.50	1.25
58 Latrell Sprewell	.25	.60
59 Allan Houston	.25	.60
60 Marcus Camby	.25	.60
61 Tracy McGrady	.60	1.50
62 Mike Miller	.25	.60
63 Grant Hill	.30	.75
64 Allen Iverson	.60	1.50
65 Dikembe Mutombo	.25	.60
66 Aaron McKie	.20	.50
67 Stephon Marbury	.30	.75
68 Shawn Marion	.30	.75
69 Tom Gugliotta	.20	.50
70 Rasheed Wallace	.30	.75

❑ 71 Damon Stoudamire	.25	.60
❑ 72 Bonzi Wells	.25	.60
❑ 73 Chris Webber	.30	.75
❑ 74 Peja Stojakovic	.25	.60
❑ 75 Mike Bibby	.25	.60
❑ 76 Tim Duncan	.60	1.50
❑ 77 David Robinson	.40	1.00
❑ 78 Antonio Daniels	.20	.50
❑ 79 Gary Payton	.30	.75
❑ 80 Rashard Lewis	.30	.75
❑ 81 Desmond Mason	.25	.60
❑ 82 Vince Carter	.60	1.50
❑ 83 Morris Peterson	.25	.60
❑ 84 Antonio Davis	.20	.50
❑ 85 Karl Malone	.40	1.00
❑ 86 John Stockton	.40	1.00
❑ 87 Donyell Marshall	.20	.50
❑ 88 Richard Hamilton	.25	.60
❑ 89 Courtney Alexander	.20	.50
❑ 90 Michael Jordan	6.00	15.00
❑ 91 Zach Randolph RC	5.00	12.00
❑ 92 Troy Murphy RC	4.00	10.00
❑ 93 Michael Bradley RC	2.00	5.00
❑ 94 Vladimir Radmanovic RC	2.50	6.00
❑ 95 Kirk Haston RC	2.00	5.00
❑ 96 Joseph Forte RC	2.00	5.00
❑ 97 Jamaal Tinsley RC	2.50	6.00
❑ 98 Jason Collins RC	2.00	5.00
❑ 99 Brendan Haywood RC	2.50	6.00
❑ 100 Richard Jefferson RC	5.00	12.00
❑ 101 Gerald Wallace RC	5.00	12.00
❑ 102 Jeryl Sasser RC	2.00	5.00
❑ 103 Samuel Dalembert RC	2.50	6.00
❑ 104 Tony Parker RC	8.00	20.00
❑ 105 Kedrick Brown RC	2.00	5.00
❑ 106 Brandon Armstrong RC	2.00	5.00
❑ 107 Steven Hunter RC	2.00	5.00
❑ 108 Andrei Kirilenko RC	5.00	12.00
❑ 109 Primoz Brezec RC	2.50	6.00
❑ 110 Terence Morris RC	2.00	5.00
❑ 111 Eddie Griffin RC	2.50	6.00
❑ 112 DeSagana Diop RC	2.50	6.00
❑ 113 Tyson Chandler RC	5.00	12.00
❑ 114 Joe Johnson RC	6.00	15.00
❑ 115 Rodney White RC	2.50	6.00
❑ 116 Eddy Curry RC	4.00	10.00
❑ 117 Shane Battier RC	4.00	10.00
❑ 118 Jason Richardson RC	5.00	12.00
❑ 119 Kwame Brown RC	3.00	8.00
❑ 120 Pau Gasol RC	10.00	25.00

2002-03 Sweet Shot

❑ COMP.SET w/o SP's (90)	15.00	40.00
❑ COMMON ROOKIE (91-123)	3.00	8.00
❑ COMMON ROOKIE (124-132)	6.00	15.00
❑ 1 Shareef Abdur-Rahim	.25	.60
❑ 2 Jason Terry	.30	.75
❑ 3 Glenn Robinson	.25	.60
❑ 4 Paul Pierce	.30	.75
❑ 5 Antoine Walker	.25	.60
❑ 6 Kedrick Brown	.20	.50
❑ 7 Vin Baker	.25	.60
❑ 8 Jalen Rose	.25	.60
❑ 9 Eddy Curry	.25	.60
❑ 10 Tyson Chandler	.25	.60
❑ 11 Zydrunas Ilgauskas	.25	.60
❑ 12 Chris Mihm	.20	.50
❑ 13 Darius Miles	.20	.50
❑ 14 Dirk Nowitzki	.50	1.25
❑ 15 Michael Finley	.30	.75
❑ 16 Steve Nash	.50	1.25
❑ 17 Raef LaFrentz	.20	.50
❑ 18 James Posey	.20	.50
❑ 19 Juwan Howard	.25	.60
❑ 20 Richard Hamilton	.25	.60
❑ 21 Ben Wallace	.25	.60
❑ 22 Chauncey Billups	.30	.75
❑ 23 Jason Richardson	.30	.75
❑ 24 Antawn Jamison	.30	.75
❑ 25 Steve Francis	.30	.75
❑ 26 Eddie Griffin	.20	.50
❑ 27 Cuttino Mobley	.25	.60
❑ 28 Reggie Miller	.30	.75
❑ 29 Jamaal Tinsley	.25	.60
❑ 30 Jermaine O'Neal	.30	.75
❑ 31 Elton Brand	.30	.75
❑ 32 Lamar Odom	.30	.75
❑ 33 Andre Miller	.25	.60
❑ 34 Kobe Bryant	1.50	4.00
❑ 35 Shaquille O'Neal	.75	2.00
❑ 36 Devean George	.20	.50
❑ 37 Pau Gasol	.30	.75
❑ 38 Shane Battier	.25	.60
❑ 39 Jason Williams	.25	.60
❑ 40 Eddie House	.20	.50
❑ 41 Eddie Jones	.25	.60
❑ 42 Brian Grant	.20	.50
❑ 43 Ray Allen	.30	.75
❑ 44 Tim Thomas	.20	.50
❑ 45 Kevin Garnett	.60	1.50
❑ 46 Terrell Brandon	.20	.50
❑ 47 Wally Szczerbiak	.25	.60
❑ 48 Joe Smith	.20	.50
❑ 49 Jason Kidd	.50	1.25
❑ 50 Richard Jefferson	.30	.75
❑ 51 Kenyon Martin	.30	.75
❑ 52 Dikembe Mutombo	.25	.60
❑ 53 Jamal Mashburn	.25	.60
❑ 54 Baron Davis	.30	.75
❑ 55 David Wesley	.20	.50
❑ 56 Allan Houston	.25	.60
❑ 57 Antonio McDyess	.25	.60
❑ 58 Latrell Sprewell	.25	.60
❑ 59 Tracy McGrady	.60	1.50
❑ 60 Mike Miller	.25	.60
❑ 61 Darrell Armstrong	.20	.50
❑ 62 Allen Iverson	.60	1.50
❑ 63 Keith Van Horn	.25	.60
❑ 64 Stephon Marbury	.30	.75
❑ 65 Shawn Marion	.30	.75
❑ 66 Anfernee Hardaway	.30	.75
❑ 67 Rasheed Wallace	.30	.75
❑ 68 Bonzi Wells	.25	.60
❑ 69 Scottie Pippen	.50	1.25
❑ 70 Chris Webber	.30	.75
❑ 71 Mike Bibby	.25	.60
❑ 72 Peja Stojakovic	.25	.60
❑ 73 Hedo Turkoglu	.25	.60
❑ 74 Tim Duncan	.60	1.50
❑ 75 David Robinson	.40	1.00
❑ 76 Tony Parker	.30	.75
❑ 77 Steve Smith	.25	.60
❑ 78 Gary Payton	.30	.75
❑ 79 Rashard Lewis	.30	.75
❑ 80 Desmond Mason	.25	.60
❑ 81 Brent Barry	.20	.50
❑ 82 Vince Carter	.60	1.50
❑ 83 Morris Peterson	.25	.60
❑ 84 Antonio Davis	.20	.50
❑ 85 Karl Malone	.30	.75
❑ 86 John Stockton	.40	1.00
❑ 87 Andrei Kirilenko	.30	.75
❑ 88 Jerry Stackhouse	.25	.60
❑ 89 Michael Jordan	2.00	5.00
❑ 90 Kwame Brown	.20	.50
❑ 91 Efthimios Rentzias RC	3.00	8.00
❑ 92 Marko Jaric	3.00	8.00
❑ 93 Rasual Butler RC	3.00	8.00
❑ 94 Predrag Savovic RC	4.00	10.00
❑ 95 Sam Clancy RC	3.00	8.00
❑ 96 Lonny Baxter RC	3.00	8.00
❑ 97 Raul Lopez RC	3.00	8.00
❑ 98 Rod Grizzard RC	3.00	8.00
❑ 99 Tito Maddox RC	3.00	8.00
❑ 100 Carlos Boozer RC	8.00	20.00
❑ 101 Dan Gadzuric RC	3.00	8.00
❑ 102 Vincent Yarbrough RC	3.00	8.00
❑ 103 Robert Archibald RC	3.00	8.00
❑ 104 Roger Mason RC	3.00	8.00
❑ 105 Ronald Murray RC	5.00	12.00
❑ 106 Dan Dickau RC	3.00	8.00
❑ 107 Chris Jefferies RC	4.00	10.00
❑ 108 John Salmons RC	5.00	12.00
❑ 109 Frank Williams RC	4.00	10.00
❑ 110 Tayshaun Prince RC	6.00	15.00
❑ 111 Casey Jacobsen RC	3.00	8.00
❑ 112 Qyntel Woods RC	5.00	12.00
❑ 113 Kareem Rush RC	6.00	15.00
❑ 114 Ryan Humphrey RC	3.00	8.00
❑ 115 Curtis Borchardt RC	3.00	8.00
❑ 116 Juan Dixon RC	8.00	20.00
❑ 117 Jiri Welsch RC	3.00	8.00
❑ 118 Bostjan Nachbar RC	4.00	10.00
❑ 119 Fred Jones RC	5.00	12.00
❑ 120 Marcus Haislip RC	3.00	8.00
❑ 121 Melvin Ely RC	4.00	10.00
❑ 122 Jared Jeffries RC	4.00	10.00
❑ 123 Caron Butler RC	12.50	30.00
❑ 124 Amare Stoudemire RC	15.00	40.00
❑ 125 Chris Wilcox RC	8.00	20.00
❑ 126 Nene Hilario RC	8.00	20.00
❑ 127 DaJuan Wagner RC	6.00	15.00
❑ 128 Nikoloz Tskitishvili RC	6.00	15.00
❑ 129 Drew Gooden RC	10.00	25.00
❑ 130 Mike Dunleavy RC	8.00	20.00
❑ 131 Jay Williams RC	8.00	20.00
❑ 132 Yao Ming RC	20.00	50.00

2003-04 Sweet Shot

❑ COMP.SET w/o SP's (90)	15.00	40.00
❑ COMMON CARD (1-90)	.20	.50
❑ COMMON ROOKIE (91-96)	8.00	20.00
❑ COMMON ROOKIE (97-132)	4.00	10.00
❑ COMMON JORDAN (133-144)	10.00	25.00
❑ 1 Shareef Abdur-Rahim	.25	.60
❑ 2 Jason Terry	.25	.60
❑ 3 Theo Ratliff	.20	.50
❑ 4 Paul Pierce	.30	.75
❑ 5 Antoine Walker	.30	.75
❑ 6 Vin Baker	.20	.50
❑ 7 Jalen Rose	.25	.60
❑ 8 Tyson Chandler	.25	.60
❑ 9 Jay Williams	.20	.50
❑ 10 Dajuan Wagner	.20	.50
❑ 11 Zydrunas Ilgauskas	.25	.60
❑ 12 Darius Miles	.25	.60
❑ 13 Dirk Nowitzki	.50	1.25
❑ 14 Antawn Jamison	.30	.75
❑ 15 Steve Nash	.50	1.25
❑ 16 Nene Hilario	.25	.60
❑ 17 Marcus Camby	.25	.60
❑ 18 Andre Miller	.25	.60
❑ 19 Richard Hamilton	.25	.60
❑ 20 Ben Wallace	.25	.60
❑ 21 Chauncey Billups	.30	.75
❑ 22 Nick Van Exel	.25	.60
❑ 23 Jason Richardson	.30	.75
❑ 24 Erick Dampier	.20	.50
❑ 25 Steve Francis	.30	.75
❑ 26 Yao Ming	.60	1.50
❑ 27 Cuttino Mobley	.25	.60
❑ 28 Reggie Miller	.30	.75
❑ 29 Jamaal Tinsley	.25	.60
❑ 30 Jermaine O'Neal	.30	.75
❑ 31 Elton Brand	.30	.75
❑ 32 Corey Maggette	.20	.50
❑ 33 Marko Jaric	.20	.50
❑ 34 Kobe Bryant	1.50	4.00
❑ 35 Gary Payton	.30	.75
❑ 36 Shaquille O'Neal	.75	2.00
❑ 37 Karl Malone	.30	.75
❑ 38 Pau Gasol	.30	.75
❑ 39 Shane Battier	.25	.60
❑ 40 Mike Miller	.25	.60
❑ 41 Eddie Jones	.25	.60
❑ 42 Lamar Odom	.30	.75
❑ 43 Caron Butler	.25	.60
❑ 44 Michael Redd	.30	.75
❑ 45 Joe Smith	.20	.50
❑ 46 Desmond Mason	.25	.60
❑ 47 Kevin Garnett	.60	1.50

❑ 48 Wally Szczerbiak	.25	.60
❑ 49 Latrell Sprewell	.25	.60
❑ 50 Jason Kidd	.50	1.25
❑ 51 Richard Jefferson	.30	.75
❑ 52 Kenyon Martin	.30	.75
❑ 53 Baron Davis	.30	.75
❑ 54 Jamal Mashburn	.20	.50
❑ 55 David Wesley	.20	.50
❑ 56 Allan Houston	.25	.60
❑ 57 Antonio McDyess	.25	.60
❑ 58 Keith Van Horn	.25	.60
❑ 59 Tracy McGrady	.60	1.50
❑ 60 Grant Hill	.30	.75
❑ 61 Drew Gooden	.20	.50
❑ 62 Allen Iverson	.60	1.50
❑ 63 Does Not Exist		
❑ 64 Eric Snow	.20	.50
❑ 64A Glenn Robinson	.25	.60
❑ 65 Stephon Marbury	.30	.75
❑ 66 Shawn Marion	.30	.75
❑ 67 Amare Stoudemire	.60	1.50
❑ 68 Rasheed Wallace	.30	.75
❑ 69 Bonzi Wells	.20	.50
❑ 70 Damon Stoudamire	.25	.60
❑ 71 Chris Webber	.30	.75
❑ 72 Mike Bibby	.25	.60
❑ 73 Peja Stojakovic	.25	.60
❑ 74 Vlade Divac	.25	.60
❑ 75 Tim Duncan	.60	1.50
❑ 76 David Robinson	.50	1.25
❑ 77 Tony Parker	.30	.75
❑ 78 Manu Ginobili	.30	.75
❑ 79 Ray Allen	.20	.50
❑ 80 Rashard Lewis	.30	.75
❑ 81 Vladimir Radmanovic	.20	.50
❑ 82 Vince Carter	.60	1.50
❑ 83 Morris Peterson	.25	.60
❑ 84 Antonio Davis	.20	.50
❑ 85 Keon Clark	.20	.50
❑ 86 John Stockton	.40	1.00
❑ 87 Andrei Kirilenko	.30	.75
❑ 88 Jerry Stackhouse	.25	.60
❑ 89 Kwame Brown	.20	.50
❑ 90 Larry Hughes	.25	.60
❑ 91 LeBron James RC	60.00	150.00
❑ 92 Darko Milicic RC	6.00	15.00
❑ 93 Carmelo Anthony RC	12.00	30.00
❑ 94 Chris Bosh RC	8.00	20.00
❑ 95 Dwyane Wade RC	12.00	30.00
❑ 96 Chris Kaman RC	6.00	15.00
❑ 97 Kirk Hinrich RC	5.00	12.00
❑ 98 T.J. Ford RC	5.00	12.00
❑ 99 Mike Sweetney RC	4.00	10.00
❑ 100 Jarvis Hayes RC	4.00	10.00
❑ 101 Mickael Pietrus RC	5.00	12.00
❑ 102 Nick Collison RC	4.00	10.00
❑ 103 Marcus Banks RC	4.00	10.00
❑ 104 Luke Ridnour RC	5.00	12.00
❑ 105 Reece Gaines RC	4.00	10.00
❑ 106 Troy Bell RC	4.00	10.00
❑ 107 Zarko Cabarkapa RC	4.00	10.00
❑ 108 David West RC	5.00	12.00
❑ 109 Aleksandar Pavlovic RC	5.00	12.00
❑ 110 Dahntay Jones RC	4.00	10.00
❑ 111 Boris Diaw RC	5.00	12.00
❑ 112 Zoran Planinic RC	4.00	10.00
❑ 113 Travis Outlaw RC	5.00	12.00
❑ 114 Brian Cook RC	4.00	10.00
❑ 115 Carlos Delfino RC	5.00	12.00
❑ 116 Ndudi Ebi RC	4.00	10.00
❑ 117 Kendrick Perkins RC	6.00	15.00
❑ 118 Leandro Barbosa RC	5.00	12.00
❑ 119 Josh Howard RC	5.00	12.00
❑ 120 Jason Kapono RC	5.00	12.00
❑ 121 Luke Walton RC	5.00	12.00
❑ 122 Jerome Beasley RC	4.00	10.00
❑ 123 Kyle Korver RC	5.00	12.00
❑ 124 Maciej Lampe RC	4.00	10.00
❑ 125 Travis Hansen RC	4.00	10.00
❑ 126 Steve Blake RC	5.00	12.00
❑ 127 Willie Green RC	4.00	10.00
❑ 128 Slavko Vranes RC	4.00	10.00
❑ 129 Keith Bogans RC	4.00	10.00
❑ 130 Maurice Williams RC	6.00	15.00
❑ 131 Matt Bonner RC	5.00	12.00
❑ 132 Zaur Pachulia RC	5.00	12.00
❑ 133 Michael Jordan	10.00	25.00
❑ 134 Michael Jordan	10.00	25.00
❑ 135 Michael Jordan	10.00	25.00
❑ 136 Michael Jordan	10.00	25.00
❑ 137 Michael Jordan	10.00	25.00
❑ 138 Michael Jordan	10.00	25.00
❑ 139 Michael Jordan	10.00	25.00
❑ 140 Michael Jordan	10.00	25.00
❑ 141 Michael Jordan	10.00	25.00
❑ 142 Michael Jordan	10.00	25.00
❑ 143 Michael Jordan	10.00	25.00
❑ 144 Michael Jordan	10.00	25.00

2004-05 Sweet Shot

❑ COMP.SET w/o SP's (90)	15.00	40.00
❑ COMMON CARD (1-90)	.20	.50
❑ COMMON ROOKIE (91-130)	2.00	5.00
❑ COMMON ROOKIE (131-136)	3.00	8.00
❑ 1 Antoine Walker	.30	.75
❑ 2 Al Harrington	.25	.60
❑ 3 Boris Diaw	.25	.60
❑ 4 Paul Pierce	.30	.75
❑ 5 Ricky Davis	.25	.60
❑ 6 Gary Payton	.30	.75
❑ 7 Gerald Wallace	.30	.75
❑ 8 Jason Kapono	.20	.50
❑ 9 Jahidi White	.20	.50
❑ 10 Eddy Curry	.25	.60
❑ 11 Kirk Hinrich	.25	.60
❑ 12 Antonio Davis	.20	.50
❑ 13 LeBron James	2.00	5.00
❑ 14 Dajuan Wagner	.20	.50
❑ 15 Jeff McInnis	.20	.50
❑ 16 Dirk Nowitzki	.50	1.25
❑ 17 Michael Finley	.30	.75
❑ 18 Jerry Stackhouse	.25	.60
❑ 19 Kenyon Martin	.30	.75
❑ 20 Andre Miller	.25	.60
❑ 21 Carmelo Anthony	1.00	2.50
❑ 22 Chauncey Billups	.30	.75
❑ 23 Rasheed Wallace	.30	.75
❑ 24 Ben Wallace	.25	.60
❑ 25 Derek Fisher	.25	.60
❑ 26 Jason Richardson	.30	.75
❑ 27 Mike Dunleavy	.25	.60
❑ 28 Yao Ming	.75	2.00
❑ 29 Tracy McGrady	.60	1.50
❑ 30 Juwan Howard	.25	.60
❑ 31 Jermaine O'Neal	.30	.75
❑ 32 Reggie Miller	.30	.75
❑ 33 Ron Artest	.25	.60
❑ 34 Elton Brand	.30	.75
❑ 35 Corey Maggette	.25	.60
❑ 36 Marko Jaric	.20	.50
❑ 37 Kobe Bryant	1.50	4.00
❑ 38 Karl Malone	.30	.75
❑ 39 Lamar Odom	.30	.75
❑ 40 Pau Gasol	.30	.75
❑ 41 Jason Williams	.25	.60
❑ 42 Bonzi Wells	.20	.50
❑ 43 Shaquille O'Neal	.75	2.00
❑ 44 Dwyane Wade	1.00	2.50
❑ 45 Eddie Jones	.25	.60
❑ 46 Michael Redd	.30	.75
❑ 47 Desmond Mason	.25	.60
❑ 48 T.J. Ford	.25	.60
❑ 49 Latrell Sprewell	.25	.60
❑ 50 Kevin Garnett	.60	1.50
❑ 51 Sam Cassell	.25	.60
❑ 52 Aaron Williams	.20	.50
❑ 53 Richard Jefferson	.30	.75
❑ 54 Jason Kidd	.50	1.25
❑ 55 Jamal Mashburn	.25	.60
❑ 56 Baron Davis	.30	.75
❑ 57 Jamaal Magloire	.20	.50
❑ 58 Allan Houston	.25	.60
❑ 59 Jamal Crawford	.25	.60
❑ 60 Stephon Marbury	.30	.75
❑ 61 Keith Bogans	.20	.50
❑ 62 Cuttino Mobley	.25	.60
❑ 63 Steve Francis	.30	.75
❑ 64 Glenn Robinson	.25	.60
❑ 65 Allen Iverson	.60	1.50
❑ 66 Kenny Thomas	.20	.50
❑ 67 Amare Stoudemire	.60	1.50
❑ 68 Steve Nash	.50	1.25
❑ 69 Quentin Richardson	.25	.60
❑ 70 Shareef Abdur-Rahim	.25	.60
❑ 71 Damon Stoudamire	.25	.60
❑ 72 Zach Randolph	.30	.75
❑ 73 Peja Stojakovic	.25	.60
❑ 74 Chris Webber	.30	.75
❑ 75 Mike Bibby	.25	.60
❑ 76 Tony Parker	.30	.75
❑ 77 Tim Duncan	.60	1.50
❑ 78 Manu Ginobili	.30	.75
❑ 79 Ronald Murray	.20	.50
❑ 80 Ray Allen	.30	.75
❑ 81 Rashard Lewis	.30	.75
❑ 82 Chris Bosh	.30	.75
❑ 83 Vince Carter	.60	1.50
❑ 84 Jalen Rose	.25	.60
❑ 85 Andrei Kirilenko	.30	.75
❑ 86 Matt Harpring	.25	.60
❑ 87 Carlos Boozer	.30	.75
❑ 88 Gilbert Arenas	.30	.75
❑ 89 Jarvis Hayes	.20	.50
❑ 90 Antawn Jamison	.30	.75
❑ 91 Anderson Varejao RC	2.50	6.00
❑ 92 Jackson Vroman RC	2.00	5.00
❑ 93 Peter John Ramos RC	2.00	5.00
❑ 94 Lionel Chalmers RC	2.00	5.00
❑ 95 Donta Smith RC	2.00	5.00
❑ 96 Andre Emmett RC	2.00	5.00
❑ 97 Antonio Burks RC	2.00	5.00
❑ 98 Royal Ivey RC	2.00	5.00
❑ 99 Chris Duhon RC	3.00	8.00
❑ 100 Albert Miralles RC	2.00	5.00
❑ 101 Justin Reed RC	2.00	5.00
❑ 102 David Young RC	2.00	5.00
❑ 103 Trevor Ariza RC	2.50	6.00
❑ 104 Luol Deng RC	2.50	6.00
❑ 105 Rafael Araujo RC	2.00	5.00
❑ 106 Andre Iguodala RC	5.00	12.00
❑ 107 Luke Jackson RC	2.00	5.00
❑ 108 Andris Biedrins RC	3.00	8.00
❑ 109 Robert Swift RC	2.00	5.00
❑ 110 Sebastian Telfair RC	2.00	5.00
❑ 111 Kris Humphries RC	3.00	8.00
❑ 112 Al Jefferson RC	4.00	10.00
❑ 113 Kirk Snyder RC	2.00	5.00
❑ 114 Josh Smith RC	5.00	12.00
❑ 115 J.R. Smith RC	4.00	10.00
❑ 116 Dorell Wright RC	2.50	6.00
❑ 117 Jameer Nelson RC	2.50	6.00
❑ 118 Pavel Podkolzine RC	2.00	5.00
❑ 119 Viktor Khryapa RC	2.00	5.00
❑ 120 Sergei Monia RC	2.00	5.00
❑ 121 Nenad Krstic RC	2.50	6.00
❑ 122 Tim Pickett RC	2.00	5.00
❑ 123 Bernard Robinson RC	2.00	5.00
❑ 124 Yuta Tabuse RC	4.00	10.00
❑ 125 Delonte West RC	3.00	8.00
❑ 126 Tony Allen RC	2.50	6.00
❑ 127 Kevin Martin RC	2.50	6.00
❑ 128 Sasha Vujacic RC	2.00	5.00
❑ 129 Beno Udrih RC	2.50	6.00
❑ 130 David Harrison RC	2.00	5.00
❑ 131 Dwight Howard RC	10.00	25.00
❑ 132 Emeka Okafor RC	6.00	15.00
❑ 133 Ben Gordon RC	4.00	10.00
❑ 134 Shaun Livingston RC	3.00	8.00
❑ 135 Devin Harris RC	6.00	15.00
❑ 136 Josh Childress RC	3.00	8.00

2005-06 Sweet Shot

❑ COMP.SET w/o SP's (100)	15.00	40.00
❑ COMMON CARD (1-100)	.25	.60
❑ COMMON ROOKIE (101-142)	2.00	5.00
❑ COMMON ROOKIE (143-150)	3.00	8.00
❑ 1 Al Harrington	.25	.60
❑ 2 Josh Smith	.40	1.00
❑ 3 Josh Childress	.30	.75
❑ 4 Tyronn Lue	.25	.60
❑ 5 Paul Pierce	.40	1.00
❑ 6 Antoine Walker	.30	.75
❑ 7 Gary Payton	.40	1.00
❑ 8 Al Jefferson	.40	1.00
❑ 9 Emeka Okafor	.40	1.00
❑ 10 Primoz Brezec	.25	.60
❑ 11 Gerald Wallace	.40	1.00
❑ 12 Michael Jordan	2.50	6.00
❑ 13 Ben Gordon	.50	1.25
❑ 14 Luol Deng	.40	1.00
❑ 15 Kirk Hinrich	.40	1.00
❑ 16 LeBron James	2.00	5.00
❑ 17 Luke Jackson	.25	.60
❑ 18 Drew Gooden	.30	.75
❑ 19 Larry Hughes	.30	.75
❑ 20 Dirk Nowitzki	.60	1.50
❑ 21 Jason Terry	.40	1.00
❑ 22 Michael Finley	.40	1.00
❑ 23 Jerry Stackhouse	.40	1.00
❑ 24 Andre Miller	.30	.75
❑ 25 Carmelo Anthony	.75	2.00
❑ 26 Kenyon Martin	.40	1.00
❑ 27 Earl Boykins	.25	.60
❑ 28 Rasheed Wallace	.40	1.00
❑ 29 Ben Wallace	.40	1.00
❑ 30 Richard Hamilton	.30	.75
❑ 31 Chauncey Billups	.40	1.00
❑ 32 Baron Davis	.40	1.00
❑ 33 Derek Fisher	.25	.60
❑ 34 Jason Richardson	.40	1.00
❑ 35 Tracy McGrady	.75	2.00
❑ 36 Yao Ming	1.00	2.50
❑ 37 Juwan Howard	.30	.75
❑ 38 Jermaine O'Neal	.40	1.00
❑ 39 Ron Artest	.30	.75
❑ 40 Jamaal Tinsley	.30	.75
❑ 41 Corey Maggette	.30	.75
❑ 42 Elton Brand	.40	1.00
❑ 43 Shaun Livingston	.25	.60
❑ 44 Kobe Bryant	2.00	5.00
❑ 45 Brian Cook	.25	.60
❑ 46 Lamar Odom	.40	1.00
❑ 47 Mike Miller	.40	1.00
❑ 48 Pau Gasol	.40	1.00
❑ 49 Shane Battier	.40	1.00
❑ 50 Shaquille O'Neal	1.00	2.50
❑ 51 Dwyane Wade	1.00	2.50
❑ 52 Udonis Haslem	.40	1.00
❑ 53 Joe Smith	.30	.75
❑ 54 Michael Redd	.40	1.00
❑ 55 Desmond Mason	.25	.60
❑ 56 Kevin Garnett	.75	2.00
❑ 57 Wally Szczerbiak	.30	.75
❑ 58 Sam Cassell	.40	1.00
❑ 59 Vince Carter	.75	2.00
❑ 60 Jason Kidd	.60	1.50
❑ 61 Richard Jefferson	.30	.75
❑ 62 Jamaal Magloire	.25	.60
❑ 63 J.R. Smith	.30	.75
❑ 64 Speedy Claxton	.25	.60
❑ 65 Allan Houston	.25	.60
❑ 66 Stephon Marbury	.40	1.00
❑ 67 Jamal Crawford	.30	.75
❑ 68 Dwight Howard	.75	2.00
❑ 69 Grant Hill	.40	1.00
❑ 70 Jameer Nelson	.30	.75
❑ 71 Steve Francis	.40	1.00
❑ 72 Allen Iverson	.75	2.00
❑ 73 Andre Iguodala	.40	1.00
❑ 74 Chris Webber	.40	1.00
❑ 75 Kyle Korver	.40	1.00
❑ 76 Amare Stoudemire	.75	2.00
❑ 77 Steve Nash	.50	1.25
❑ 78 Quentin Richardson	.30	.75
❑ 79 Shawn Marion	.40	1.00
❑ 80 Damon Stoudamire	.30	.75
❑ 81 Zach Randolph	.40	1.00
❑ 82 Sebastian Telfair	.30	.75
❑ 83 Peja Stojakovic	.40	1.00
❑ 84 Mike Bibby	.40	1.00
❑ 85 Cuttino Mobley	.30	.75
❑ 86 Manu Ginobili	.40	1.00
❑ 87 Tim Duncan	.75	2.00
❑ 88 Tony Parker	.40	1.00
❑ 89 Ray Allen	.40	1.00
❑ 90 Rashard Lewis	.40	1.00
❑ 91 Luke Ridnour	.30	.75
❑ 92 Ronald Murray	.25	.60
❑ 93 Chris Bosh	.40	1.00
❑ 94 Morris Peterson	.30	.75
❑ 95 Jalen Rose	.40	1.00
❑ 96 Andrei Kirilenko	.40	1.00
❑ 97 Raul Lopez	.25	.60
❑ 98 Carlos Boozer	.40	1.00
❑ 99 Antawn Jamison	.40	1.00
❑ 100 Gilbert Arenas	.40	1.00
❑ 101 Ike Diogu RC	2.50	6.00
❑ 102 Julius Hodge RC	2.50	6.00
❑ 103 David Lee RC	4.00	10.00
❑ 104 Linas Kleiza RC	2.50	6.00
❑ 105 Jason Maxiell RC	2.50	6.00
❑ 106 Luther Head RC	2.50	6.00
❑ 107 Jose Calderon RC	2.00	5.00
❑ 108 Brandon Bass RC	2.00	5.00
❑ 109 Ricky Sanchez RC	2.00	5.00
❑ 110 Andray Blatche RC	2.50	6.00
❑ 111 Sean May RC	2.50	6.00
❑ 112 Travis Diener RC	2.00	5.00
❑ 113 Nate Robinson RC	3.00	8.00
❑ 114 Von Wafer RC	2.00	5.00
❑ 115 James Singleton RC	2.00	5.00
❑ 116 Daniel Ewing RC	2.50	6.00
❑ 117 Salim Stoudamire RC	2.50	6.00
❑ 118 Dijon Thompson RC	2.00	5.00
❑ 119 Danny Granger RC	5.00	12.00
❑ 120 Will Bynum RC	2.00	5.00
❑ 121 Louis Williams RC	3.00	8.00
❑ 122 Channing Frye RC	2.50	6.00
❑ 123 Francisco Garcia RC	2.50	6.00
❑ 124 Ryan Gomes RC	2.00	5.00
❑ 125 Ronnie Price RC	2.00	5.00
❑ 126 Jarrett Jack RC	2.00	5.00
❑ 127 Alan Anderson RC	2.00	5.00
❑ 128 Ersan Ilyasova RC	2.00	5.00
❑ 129 C.J. Miles RC	2.00	5.00
❑ 130 Arvydas Macijauskas RC	2.00	5.00
❑ 131 Bracey Wright RC	2.00	5.00
❑ 132 Monta Ellis RC	5.00	12.00
❑ 133 Chris Taft RC	2.00	5.00
❑ 134 Johan Petro RC	2.00	5.00
❑ 135 Yaroslav Korolev RC	2.00	5.00
❑ 136 Andrew Bynum RC	6.00	15.00
❑ 137 Martynas Andriuskevicius RC	2.00	5.00
❑ 138 Charlie Villanueva RC	3.00	8.00
❑ 139 Antoine Wright RC	2.00	5.00
❑ 140 Joey Graham RC	2.00	5.00
❑ 141 Wayne Simien RC	2.50	6.00
❑ 142 Hakim Warrick RC	3.00	8.00
❑ 143 Gerald Green RC	3.00	8.00
❑ 144 Marvin Williams RC	5.00	12.00
❑ 145 Deron Williams RC	8.00	20.00
❑ 146 Rashad McCants RC	4.00	10.00
❑ 147 Raymond Felton RC	4.00	10.00
❑ 148 Martell Webster RC	3.00	8.00
❑ 149 Chris Paul RC	10.00	25.00
❑ 150 Andrew Bogut RC	4.00	10.00

2006-07 Sweet Shot

❑ COMP.SET w/o SP's (90)	15.00	40.00
❑ 1 Josh Childress	.30	.75
❑ 2 Joe Johnson	.30	.75
❑ 3 Marvin Williams	.40	1.00
❑ 4 Al Jefferson	.40	1.00
❑ 5 Paul Pierce	.40	1.00
❑ 6 Wally Szczerbiak	.30	.75
❑ 7 Raymond Felton	.50	1.25
❑ 8 Emeka Okafor	.40	1.00
❑ 9 Gerald Wallace	.40	1.00
❑ 10 Ben Gordon	.50	1.25
❑ 11 Kirk Hinrich	.40	1.00
❑ 12 Michael Jordan	2.50	6.00
❑ 13 Larry Hughes	.30	.75
❑ 14 Zydrunas Ilgauskas	.30	.75
❑ 15 LeBron James	2.00	5.00
❑ 16 Marquis Daniels	.30	.75
❑ 17 Dirk Nowitzki	.60	1.50
❑ 18 Jason Terry	.40	1.00
❑ 19 Carmelo Anthony	.50	1.25
❑ 20 Marcus Camby	.30	.75
❑ 21 Kenyon Martin	.40	1.00
❑ 22 Chauncey Billups	.40	1.00
❑ 23 Richard Hamilton	.30	.75
❑ 24 Ben Wallace	.40	1.00
❑ 25 Baron Davis	.40	1.00
❑ 26 Mike Dunleavy	.30	.75
❑ 27 Jason Richardson	.40	1.00
❑ 28 Rafer Alston	.25	.60
❑ 29 Tracy McGrady	.75	2.00
❑ 30 Yao Ming	1.00	2.50
❑ 31 Austin Croshere	.25	.60
❑ 32 Jermaine O'Neal	.40	1.00
❑ 33 Peja Stojakovic	.40	1.00
❑ 34 Elton Brand	.40	1.00
❑ 35 Sam Cassell	.40	1.00
❑ 36 Shaun Livingston	.25	.60
❑ 37 Kwame Brown	.30	.75
❑ 38 Kobe Bryant	2.00	5.00
❑ 39 Lamar Odom	.40	1.00
❑ 40 Pau Gasol	.40	1.00
❑ 41 Bobby Jackson	.25	.60
❑ 42 Hakim Warrick	.30	.75
❑ 43 Shaquille O'Neal	1.00	2.50
❑ 44 Dwyane Wade	1.00	2.50
❑ 45 Jason Williams	.30	.75
❑ 46 Andrew Bogut	.40	1.00
❑ 47 T.J. Ford	.30	.75
❑ 48 Jamaal Magloire	.25	.60
❑ 49 Ricky Davis	.40	1.00
❑ 50 Kevin Garnett	.75	2.00
❑ 51 Rashad McCants	.30	.75
❑ 52 Vince Carter	.75	2.00
❑ 53 Richard Jefferson	.30	.75
❑ 54 Jason Kidd	.60	1.50
❑ 55 Desmond Mason	.25	.60
❑ 56 Chris Paul	.75	2.00
❑ 57 J.R. Smith	.30	.75
❑ 58 Channing Frye	.30	.75
❑ 59 Stephon Marbury	.40	1.00
❑ 60 Quentin Richardson	.30	.75
❑ 61 Carlos Arroyo	.40	1.00
❑ 62 Dwight Howard	.75	2.00
❑ 63 Darko Milicic	.40	1.00
❑ 64 Andre Iguodala	.40	1.00
❑ 65 Allen Iverson	.75	2.00
❑ 66 Chris Webber	.40	1.00
❑ 67 Boris Diaw	.30	.75
❑ 68 Shawn Marion	.40	1.00
❑ 69 Steve Nash	.50	1.25
❑ 70 Juan Dixon	.25	.60
❑ 71 Zach Randolph	.40	1.00
❑ 72 Sebastian Telfair	.30	.75
❑ 73 Ron Artest	.40	1.00

❑ 74 Mike Bibby	.40	1.00
❑ 75 Brad Miller	.40	1.00
❑ 76 Tim Duncan	.75	2.00
❑ 77 Manu Ginobili	.40	1.00
❑ 78 Tony Parker	.40	1.00
❑ 79 Ray Allen	.40	1.00
❑ 80 Rashard Lewis	.40	1.00
❑ 81 Luke Ridnour	.30	.75
❑ 82 Chris Bosh	.40	1.00
❑ 83 Joey Graham	.30	.75
❑ 84 Charlie Villanueva	.40	1.00
❑ 85 Carlos Boozer	.40	1.00
❑ 86 Andrei Kirilenko	.40	1.00
❑ 87 Deron Williams	.60	1.50
❑ 88 Gilbert Arenas	.40	1.00
❑ 89 Caron Butler	.40	1.00
❑ 90 Antawn Jamison	.40	1.00
❑ 91 David Noel AU RC	5.00	12.00
❑ 92 James Augustine AU RC	5.00	12.00
❑ 93 Kyle Lowry AU RC	5.00	12.00
❑ 94 Bobby Jones AU RC	5.00	12.00
❑ 95 Solomon Jones AU RC	5.00	12.00
❑ 96 Craig Smith AU RC	5.00	12.00
❑ 97 Josh Boone AU RC	5.00	12.00
❑ 98 Jordan Farmar AU RC	10.00	25.00
❑ 99 Marcus Williams AU RC	6.00	15.00
❑ 100 Hassan Adams AU RC	6.00	15.00
❑ 101 Dee Brown AU RC	5.00	12.00
❑ 102 Denham Brown AU RC	5.00	12.00
❑ 103 Steve Novak AU RC	5.00	12.00
❑ 104 James White AU RC	5.00	12.00
❑ 105 Daniel Gibson AU RC	6.00	15.00
❑ 106 Renaldo Balkman AU RC	5.00	12.00
❑ 107 P.J. Tucker AU RC	5.00	12.00
❑ 108 Saer Sene AU RC	5.00	12.00
❑ 109 Thabo Sefolosha AU RC	6.00	15.00
❑ 110 Maurice Ager AU RC	5.00	12.00
❑ 111 Rajon Rondo AU RC	20.00	50.00
❑ 112 Shawne Williams AU RC	5.00	12.00
❑ 113 Mardy Collins AU RC	5.00	12.00
❑ 114 Paul Davis AU RC	5.00	12.00
❑ 115 Quincy Douby AU RC	5.00	12.00
❑ 121 Rodney Carney AU RC	6.00	15.00
❑ 122 Randy Foye AU RC	6.00	15.00
❑ 123 Ronnie Brewer AU RC	8.00	20.00
❑ 124 Cedric Simmons AU RC	6.00	15.00
❑ 125 Andrea Bargnani AU RC	10.00	25.00
❑ 126 LaMarcus Aldridge AU RC	8.00	20.00
❑ 127 Tyrus Thomas AU RC	8.00	20.00
❑ 128 Rudy Gay AU RC	6.00	15.00
❑ 129 Shelden Williams AU RC	8.00	20.00
❑ 130 Patrick O'Bryant AU RC	6.00	15.00
❑ 131 Hilton Armstrong AU RC	6.00	15.00
❑ 132 Brandon Roy AU RC	20.00	40.00
❑ 133 Adam Morrison RC	6.00	15.00
❑ 134 J.J. Redick RC	5.00	12.00
❑ 135 Alexander Johnson RC	5.00	12.00
❑ 136 Damir Markota RC	5.00	12.00
❑ 137 Leon Powe RC	5.00	12.00
❑ 138 Ryan Hollins RC	5.00	12.00
❑ 139 Tarence Kinsey RC	5.00	12.00
❑ 140 Jorge Garbajosa RC	10.00	25.00

2007-08 Sweet Shot

❑ 1 Joe Johnson	1.00	2.50
❑ 2 Marvin Williams	1.00	2.50
❑ 3 Josh Smith	1.00	2.50
❑ 4 Al Jefferson	1.00	2.50
❑ 5 Paul Pierce	1.00	2.50
❑ 6 Ray Allen	1.00	2.50
❑ 7 Adam Morrison	1.00	2.50
❑ 8 Raymond Felton	1.25	3.00
❑ 9 Gerald Wallace	1.00	2.50
❑ 10 Jason Richardson	1.00	2.50
❑ 11 Ben Gordon	1.25	3.00
❑ 12 Luol Deng	1.00	2.50
❑ 13 Ben Wallace	1.00	2.50
❑ 14 Michael Jordan	6.00	15.00
❑ 15 Larry Hughes	.75	2.00
❑ 16 LeBron James	5.00	12.00
❑ 17 Zydrunas Ilgauskas	.75	2.00
❑ 18 Dirk Nowitzki	1.50	4.00
❑ 19 Josh Howard	1.00	2.50
❑ 20 Jason Terry	1.00	2.50
❑ 21 Allen Iverson	2.00	5.00
❑ 22 Nene	.60	1.50
❑ 23 Carmelo Anthony	2.00	5.00
❑ 24 Chauncey Billups	1.00	2.50
❑ 25 Richard Hamilton	.75	2.00
❑ 26 Tayshaun Prince	1.00	2.50
❑ 27 Baron Davis	1.00	2.50
❑ 28 Stephen Jackson	.75	2.00
❑ 29 Brandan Wright RC	2.00	5.00
❑ 30 Tracy McGrady	2.00	5.00
❑ 31 Yao Ming	2.50	6.00
❑ 32 Shane Battier	1.00	2.50
❑ 33 Jermaine O'Neal	1.00	2.50
❑ 34 Danny Granger	.75	2.00
❑ 35 Elton Brand	1.00	2.50
❑ 36 Corey Maggette	.75	2.00
❑ 37 Kobe Bryant	5.00	12.00
❑ 38 Lamar Odom	1.00	2.50
❑ 39 Luke Walton	.75	2.00
❑ 40 Rudy Gay	.75	2.00
❑ 41 Pau Gasol	1.00	2.50
❑ 42 Dwyane Wade	2.50	6.00
❑ 43 Antoine Walker	.75	2.00
❑ 44 Shaquille O'Neal	2.50	6.00
❑ 45 Michael Redd	1.00	2.50
❑ 46 Maurice Williams	.75	2.00
❑ 47 Andrew Bogut	1.00	2.50
❑ 48 Yi Jianlian RC	2.50	6.00
❑ 49 Kevin Garnett	2.50	6.00
❑ 50 Ricky Davis	1.00	2.50
❑ 51 Randy Foye	1.00	2.50
❑ 52 Vince Carter	2.00	5.00
❑ 53 Jason Kidd	1.50	4.00
❑ 54 Richard Jefferson	1.00	2.50
❑ 55 Tyson Chandler	1.00	2.50
❑ 56 David West	1.00	2.50
❑ 57 Chris Paul	2.00	5.00
❑ 58 Eddy Curry	.60	1.50
❑ 59 Jamal Crawford	.60	1.50
❑ 60 Stephon Marbury	1.00	2.50
❑ 61 Zach Randolph	1.00	2.50
❑ 62 Dwight Howard	2.00	5.00
❑ 63 Grant Hill	1.00	2.50
❑ 64 Andre Miller	.75	2.00
❑ 65 Thaddeus Young RC	2.00	5.00
❑ 66 Andre Iguodala	1.00	2.50
❑ 67 Steve Nash	1.25	3.00
❑ 68 Amare Stoudemire	2.00	5.00
❑ 69 Shawn Marion	1.00	2.50
❑ 70 Brandon Roy	1.50	4.00
❑ 71 Greg Oden RC	6.00	15.00
❑ 72 Ron Artest	1.00	2.50
❑ 73 Mike Bibby	1.00	2.50
❑ 74 Kevin Martin	1.00	2.50
❑ 75 Tim Duncan	2.00	5.00
❑ 76 Manu Ginobili	1.00	2.50
❑ 77 Tony Parker	1.00	2.50
❑ 78 Wally Szczerbiak	.75	2.00
❑ 79 Delonte West	.75	2.00
❑ 80 Rashard Lewis	1.00	2.50
❑ 81 T.J. Ford	.75	2.00
❑ 82 Chris Bosh	1.00	2.50
❑ 83 Andrea Bargnani	1.25	3.00
❑ 84 Carlos Boozer	1.00	2.50
❑ 85 Mehmet Okur	.75	2.00
❑ 86 Deron Williams	1.50	4.00
❑ 87 Gilbert Arenas	1.00	2.50
❑ 88 Antawn Jamison	1.00	2.50
❑ 89 Caron Butler	1.00	2.50
❑ 90 Nick Young RC	1.50	4.00
❑ 91 Al Horford AU RC	8.00	20.00
❑ 92 Acie Law IV AU RC	8.00	20.00
❑ 93 Joakim Noah AU RC	8.00	20.00
❑ 94 Marco Belinelli AU RC	6.00	15.00
❑ 95 Al Thornton AU RC	6.00	15.00
❑ 96 Javaris Crittenton AU RC	6.00	15.00
❑ 97 Michael Conley AU RC	8.00	20.00
❑ 98 Corey Brewer AU RC	8.00	20.00
❑ 99 Julian Wright AU RC	8.00	20.00
❑ 100 Spencer Hawes AU RC	6.00	15.00
❑ 101 Kevin Durant AU RC	60.00	120.00
❑ 102 Jeff Green AU RC	8.00	20.00
❑ 103 Daequan Cook AU RC	6.00	15.00
❑ 104 Jared Dudley AU RC	5.00	12.00
❑ 105 Wilson Chandler AU RC	5.00	12.00
❑ 106 Rodney Stuckey AU RC	10.00	25.00
❑ 107 Morris Almond AU RC	5.00	12.00
❑ 108 Arron Afflalo AU RC	5.00	12.00
❑ 109 Alando Tucker AU RC	5.00	12.00
❑ 110 Sean Williams AU RC	5.00	12.00
❑ 111 Carl Landry AU RC	5.00	12.00
❑ 112 Gabe Pruitt AU RC	5.00	12.00
❑ 113 Marcus Williams AU RC	5.00	12.00
❑ 114 Nick Fazekas AU RC	5.00	12.00
❑ 115 Jermareo Davidson AU RC	5.00	12.00
❑ 116 Josh McRoberts AU RC	6.00	15.00
❑ 117 Aaron Brooks AU RC	8.00	20.00
❑ 118 Derrick Byars AU RC	5.00	12.00
❑ 119 Adam Haluska AU RC	5.00	12.00
❑ 120 Reyshawn Terry AU RC	5.00	12.00
❑ 121 Jared Jordan AU RC	5.00	12.00
❑ 122 Stephane Lasme AU RC	5.00	12.00
❑ 123 Aaron Gray AU RC	5.00	12.00
❑ 124 Renaldas Seibutis AU RC	5.00	12.00
❑ 125 Taurean Green AU RC	5.00	12.00
❑ 126 Demetris Nichols AU RC	5.00	12.00
❑ 127 Herbert Hill AU RC	5.00	12.00
❑ 128 Sammy Mejia AU RC	5.00	12.00
❑ 129 D.J. Strawberry AU RC	5.00	12.00
❑ 130 Chris Richard AU RC	5.00	12.00
❑ 131 Glen Davis AU RC	10.00	25.00
❑ 132 Jason Smith AU RC	5.00	12.00

2009-10 Threads

❑ 1 LeBron James	2.00	5.00
❑ 2 Dwyane Wade	.75	2.00
❑ 3 Chris Paul	.75	2.00
❑ 4 Kobe Bryant	2.00	5.00
❑ 5 Dirk Nowitzki	.50	1.25
❑ 6 Dwight Howard	.75	2.00
❑ 7 Al Jefferson	.40	1.00
❑ 8 Chris Bosh	.40	1.00
❑ 9 Kevin Durant	1.00	2.50
❑ 10 Danny Granger	.40	1.00
❑ 11 Tim Duncan	.60	1.50
❑ 12 Antawn Jamison	.40	1.00
❑ 13 Deron Williams	.50	1.25
❑ 14 Carmelo Anthony	.50	1.25
❑ 15 Zach Randolph	.25	.60
❑ 16 Brandon Roy	.50	1.25
❑ 17 Stephen Jackson	.30	.75
❑ 18 Pau Gasol	.40	1.00
❑ 19 Tony Parker	.40	1.00
❑ 20 David West	.40	1.00
❑ 21 Devin Harris	.40	1.00
❑ 22 Joe Johnson	.40	1.00
❑ 23 Amare Stoudemire	.50	1.25
❑ 24 Yao Ming	.50	1.25
❑ 25 Caron Butler	.40	1.00
❑ 26 Kevin Martin	.40	1.00
❑ 27 Vince Carter	.50	1.25
❑ 28 David Lee	.30	.75
❑ 29 Andre Iguodala	.40	1.00
❑ 30 Paul Pierce	.50	1.25
❑ 31 Carlos Boozer	.40	1.00
❑ 32 Troy Murphy	.25	.60
❑ 33 Steve Nash	.40	1.00
❑ 34 Shaquille O'Neal	.75	2.00
❑ 35 Al Harrington	.30	.75
❑ 36 Ben Gordon	.40	1.00
❑ 37 LaMarcus Aldridge	.40	1.00
❑ 38 Gilbert Arenas	.40	1.00
❑ 39 Andre Miller	.30	.75
❑ 40 Chauncey Billups	.40	1.00
❑ 41 Gerald Wallace	.40	1.00
❑ 42 Jamal Crawford	.25	.60
❑ 43 Michael Redd	.40	1.00

❑ 44 Derrick Rose .75 2.00
❑ 45 Monta Ellis .40 1.00
❑ 46 Hedo Turkoglu .40 1.00
❑ 47 Kevin Garnett .75 2.00
❑ 48 Richard Jefferson .40 1.00
❑ 49 Mehmet Okur .25 .60
❑ 50 Baron Davis .40 1.00
❑ 51 Rudy Gay .40 1.00
❑ 52 Rashard Lewis .40 1.00
❑ 53 Corey Maggette .30 .75
❑ 54 Richard Hamilton .30 .75
❑ 55 John Salmons .40 1.00
❑ 56 Ron Artest .40 1.00
❑ 57 Jameer Nelson .30 .75
❑ 58 Russell Westbrook .40 1.00
❑ 59 Allen Iverson .50 1.25
❑ 60 O.J. Mayo .50 1.25
❑ 61 Rajon Rondo .40 1.00
❑ 62 Jason Terry .30 .75
❑ 63 Mo Williams .30 .75
❑ 64 Josh Smith .40 1.00
❑ 65 Jeff Green .30 .75
❑ 66 Nate Robinson .40 1.00
❑ 67 Andris Biedrins .25 .60
❑ 68 Tracy McGrady .50 1.25
❑ 69 Raymond Felton .30 .75
❑ 70 Josh Howard .40 1.00
❑ 71 Charlie Villanueva .30 .75
❑ 72 Jose Calderon .30 .75
❑ 73 Ray Allen .40 1.00
❑ 74 Andrew Bogut .40 1.00
❑ 75 Emeka Okafor .40 1.00
❑ 76 Paul Millsap .30 .75
❑ 77 Jason Kidd .40 1.00
❑ 78 Elton Brand .40 1.00
❑ 79 Nene .30 .75
❑ 80 T.J. Ford .25 .60
❑ 81 Andrew Bynum .40 1.00
❑ 82 Randy Foye .25 .60
❑ 83 Manu Ginobili .40 1.00
❑ 84 Marcus Camby .25 .60
❑ 85 Shawn Marion .40 1.00
❑ 86 Al Thornton .40 1.00
❑ 87 Mike Bibby .25 .60
❑ 88 Jason Richardson .40 1.00
❑ 89 Al Horford .40 1.00
❑ 90 Tayshaun Prince .40 1.00
❑ 91 Luis Scola .25 .60
❑ 92 Brad Miller .40 1.00
❑ 93 Boris Diaw .30 .75
❑ 94 Brook Lopez .25 .60
❑ 95 Lamar Odom .40 1.00
❑ 96 Luol Deng .40 1.00
❑ 97 Andrea Bargnani .30 .75
❑ 98 Jermaine O'Neal .40 1.00
❑ 99 Rasheed Wallace .40 1.00
❑ 100 Michael Beasley .50 1.25
❑ 101 Blake Griffin/640 AU RC 25.00 50.00
❑ 102 Hasheem Thabeet/315 AU RC 6.00 15.00
❑ 103 James Harden/660 AU RC 10.00 25.00
❑ 104 Tyreke Evans/150 EXCH 50.00 100.00
❑ 105 Rodrigue Beaubois/640 AU RC 10.00 25.00
❑ 106 Jonny Flynn/625 AU RC 15.00 30.00
❑ 107 Stephen Curry/625 AU RC 20.00 40.00
❑ 108 Jordan Hill/700 AU RC 5.00 12.00
❑ 109 Derrick Brown/150 EXCH 6.00 15.00
❑ 110 Brandon Jennings/640 AU RC 30.00 60.00
❑ 112 Gerald Henderson/630 AU RC 6.00 15.00
❑ 113 Tyler Hansbrough/650 AU RC 15.00 30.00
❑ 114 Earl Clark/625 AU RC 8.00 20.00
❑ 115 Austin Daye/700 AU RC 5.00 12.00
❑ 116 James Johnson/630 AU RC 6.00 15.00
❑ 117 Jrue Holiday/630 AU RC 8.00 20.00
❑ 118 Ty Lawson/330 AU RC 15.00 30.00
❑ 119 Jeff Teague/660 AU RC 5.00 12.00
❑ 120 Eric Maynor/126 AU RC 8.00 20.00
❑ 121 Darren Collison/160 EXCH 8.00 20.00
❑ 122 Dante Cunningham/650 AU RC 5.00 12.00
❑ 123 Omri Casspi/660 AU RC 10.00 25.00
❑ 124 B.J. Mullens/630 AU RC 5.00 12.00
❑ 125 Taj Gibson/330 AU RC 10.00 25.00
❑ 126 DeMarre Carroll/630 AU RC 5.00 12.00
❑ 127 Wayne Ellington/630 AU RC 6.00 15.00
❑ 128 Toney Douglas/630 AU RC 5.00 12.00
❑ 129 Jeff Pendergraph/660 AU RC 5.00 12.00
❑ 130 DaJuan Summers/630 AU RC 5.00 12.00
❑ 131 Sam Young/365 AU RC 6.00 15.00
❑ 132 DeJuan Blair/625 AU RC 15.00 30.00
❑ 133 Jodie Meeks/625 AU RC 8.00 20.00
❑ 134 Chase Budinger/640 AU RC 6.00 15.00
❑ 135 Taylor Griffin/640 AU RC 5.00 12.00

2009-10 Timeless Treasures

❑ 1 Kobe Bryant 5.00 12.00
❑ 2 LeBron James 5.00 12.00
❑ 3 Chris Paul 2.00 5.00
❑ 4 Dwight Howard 2.00 5.00
❑ 5 Dwyane Wade 2.00 5.00
❑ 6 Dirk Nowitzki 1.25 3.00
❑ 7 Danny Granger 1.00 2.50
❑ 8 Kevin Durant 2.50 6.00
❑ 9 Pau Gasol 1.00 2.50
❑ 10 Amare Stoudemire 1.25 3.00
❑ 11 Chris Bosh 1.00 2.50
❑ 12 Brandon Roy 1.25 3.00
❑ 13 Kevin Garnett 2.00 5.00
❑ 14 Al Jefferson 1.00 2.50
❑ 15 Deron Williams 1.25 3.00
❑ 16 Chauncey Billups 1.00 2.50
❑ 17 Steve Nash 1.00 2.50
❑ 18 Tim Duncan 1.50 4.00
❑ 19 Andre Iguodala 1.00 2.50
❑ 20 Jason Kidd 1.00 2.50
❑ 21 Devin Harris 1.00 2.50
❑ 22 Joe Johnson 1.00 2.50
❑ 23 Gerald Wallace 1.00 2.50
❑ 24 Vince Carter 1.25 3.00
❑ 25 Paul Pierce 1.25 3.00
❑ 26 Brook Lopez .60 1.50
❑ 27 Kevin Martin 1.00 2.50
❑ 28 Antawn Jamison 1.00 2.50
❑ 29 David West 1.00 2.50
❑ 30 Carmelo Anthony 1.25 3.00
❑ 31 Troy Murphy .60 1.50
❑ 32 Rashard Lewis 1.00 2.50
❑ 33 Elton Brand 1.00 2.50
❑ 34 Josh Smith 1.00 2.50
❑ 35 Baron Davis 1.00 2.50
❑ 36 Ray Allen 1.00 2.50
❑ 37 Carlos Boozer 1.00 2.50
❑ 38 David Lee .75 2.00
❑ 39 Derrick Rose 2.00 5.00
❑ 40 Rajon Rondo 1.00 2.50
❑ 41 O.J. Mayo 1.25 3.00
❑ 42 Nene .75 2.00
❑ 43 Andrea Bargnani .75 2.00
❑ 44 Charlie Villanueva .75 2.00
❑ 45 Ben Gordon 1.00 2.50
❑ 46 Mike Bibby .60 1.50
❑ 47 Tony Parker 1.00 2.50
❑ 48 Andrew Bynum 1.00 2.50
❑ 49 Russell Westbrook 1.00 2.50
❑ 50 Anthony Randolph 1.00 2.50
❑ 51 Eric Gordon 1.00 2.50
❑ 52 Jeff Green .75 2.00
❑ 53 Shaquille O'Neal 2.00 5.00
❑ 54 Aaron Brooks .75 2.00
❑ 55 Chris Kaman 1.00 2.50
❑ 56 D.J. Augustin .75 2.00
❑ 57 Emeka Okafor 1.00 2.50
❑ 58 Derek Fisher .75 2.00
❑ 59 Jermaine O'Neal 1.00 2.50
❑ 60 Josh Howard 1.00 2.50
❑ 61 Kevin Love .75 2.00
❑ 62 Lamar Odom 1.00 2.50
❑ 63 Michael Beasley 1.25 3.00
❑ 64 Richard Hamilton .75 2.00
❑ 65 Ron Artest 1.00 2.50
❑ 66 Ronnie Brewer .60 1.50
❑ 67 Rudy Fernandez 1.00 2.50
❑ 68 Ryan Gomes .60 1.50
❑ 69 Shane Battier .75 2.00
❑ 70 T.J. Ford .60 1.50
❑ 71 Tracy McGrady 1.25 3.00
❑ 72 Trevor Ariza 1.00 2.50
❑ 73 Greg Oden .75 2.00
❑ 74 Nate Archibald 1.00 2.50
❑ 75 Al Cervi 1.00 2.50
❑ 76 Bob Cousy 1.50 4.00
❑ 77 Harry Gallatin 1.00 2.50
❑ 78 Gail Goodrich 1.00 2.50
❑ 79 Hal Greer 1.00 2.50
❑ 80 John Havlicek 1.00 2.50
❑ 81 Connie Hawkins 1.00 2.50
❑ 82 Elvin Hayes 1.00 2.50
❑ 83 Bob McAdoo 1.00 2.50
❑ 84 Pete Maravich 3.00 8.00
❑ 85 Bill Russell 1.50 4.00
❑ 86 Dolph Schayes 1.00 2.50
❑ 87 Bill Sharman 1.00 2.50
❑ 88 David Thompson 1.25 3.00
❑ 89 Nate Thurmond 1.00 2.50
❑ 90 Jack Twyman 1.00 2.50
❑ 91 Wes Unseld 1.00 2.50
❑ 92 Bill Walton 1.00 2.50
❑ 93 Bobby Wanzer 1.00 2.50
❑ 94 Frank Ramsey 1.00 2.50
❑ 95 Willis Reed 1.00 2.50
❑ 96 Pat Riley 1.00 2.50
❑ 97 Xavier McDaniel 1.00 2.50
❑ 98 Oscar Robertson 1.00 2.50
❑ 99 Lenny Wilkens 1.00 2.50
❑ 100 James Worthy 1.25 3.00
❑ 101 Blake Griffin AU/299 RC 25.00 50.00
❑ 102 Hasheem Thabeet AU/299 RC 8.00 20.00
❑ 103 James Harden AU/299 RC 10.00 25.00
❑ 104 Tyreke Evans AU/299 RC 40.00 80.00
❑ 105 Jonny Flynn AU/299 RC 10.00 25.00
❑ 106 Stephen Curry AU/299 RC 30.00 60.00
❑ 107 Jordan Hill AU/99 RC 5.00 12.00
❑ 108 Ricky Rubio AU/99 RC 30.00 60.00
❑ 109 Brandon Jennings AU/299 RC 30.00 60.00
❑ 110 Terrence Williams AU/299 RC 8.00 20.00
❑ 111 Gerald Henderson AU/299 RC 5.00 12.00
❑ 112 Tyler Hansbrough AU/299 RC 10.00 25.00
❑ 113 Earl Clark AU/299 RC 5.00 12.00
❑ 114 Austin Daye AU/299 RC 5.00 12.00
❑ 115 James Johnson AU/280 RC 5.00 12.00
❑ 116 Jrue Holiday AU/286 RC 6.00 15.00
❑ 117 Ty Lawson AU/299 RC 10.00 25.00
❑ 118 Jeff Teague AU/299 RC 5.00 12.00
❑ 119 Eric Maynor AU/299 RC 5.00 12.00
❑ 120 Darren Collison AU/299 RC 15.00 30.00
❑ 121 Omri Casspi AU/299 RC 8.00 20.00
❑ 122 B.J. Mullens AU/99 RC 5.00 12.00
❑ 123 Rodrigue Beaubois AU/299 RC 8.00 20.00
❑ 124 Taj Gibson AU/299 RC 6.00 15.00
❑ 125 DeMarre Carroll AU/299 RC 5.00 12.00
❑ 126 Wayne Ellington AU/249 RC 5.00 12.00
❑ 127 Toney Douglas AU/299 RC 5.00 12.00
❑ 128 Jeff Pendergraph AU/299 RC 5.00 12.00
❑ 129 Jermaine Taylor AU/99 RC 5.00 12.00
❑ 130 DaJuan Summers AU/299 RC 5.00 12.00
❑ 131 Sam Young AU/99 RC 5.00 12.00
❑ 132 DeJuan Blair AU/299 RC 6.00 15.00
❑ 133 Jodie Meeks AU/99 RC 5.00 12.00
❑ 134 Chase Budinger AU/299 RC 5.00 12.00
❑ 135 Taylor Griffin AU/299 RC 5.00 12.00
❑ 136 Marcus Thornton AU/299 RC 8.00 20.00
❑ 137 Daniel Green AU/299 RC 5.00 12.00
❑ 138 Derrick Brown AU/99 RC 5.00 12.00
❑ 139 Jonas Jerebko AU/299 RC 6.00 15.00
❑ 140 Serge Ibaka AU/293 RC 10.00 25.00
❑ 141 Jon Brockman AU/299 RC 5.00 12.00
❑ 142 Dante Cunningham AU/299 RC 5.00 12.00
❑ 143 Wes Matthews AU/265 RC 10.00 25.00
❑ 144 A.J. Price AU/299 RC 5.00 12.00
❑ 145 Lester Hudson AU/99 RC 6.00 15.00
❑ 146 Marcus Landry AU/299 RC 5.00 12.00
❑ 147 Sundiata Gaines AU/299 RC 5.00 12.00
❑ 148 David Andersen AU/99 RC 5.00 12.00
❑ 149 Patrick Mills AU/99 RC 10.00 25.00
❑ 150 DeMar DeRozan AU/99 RC 15.00 30.00

1957-58 Topps

❑ COMPLETE SET (80)	4000.00	5500.00
❑ COMMON NON-DP (1-80)	25.00	40.00
❑ COMMON DP	12.50	25.00
❑ 1 Nat Clifton RC DP	150.00	250.00
❑ 2 George Yardley DP RC	45.00	70.00
❑ 3 Neil Johnston DP RC	35.00	55.00
❑ 4 Carl Braun DP	30.00	50.00
❑ 5 Bill Sharman DP RC	75.00	125.00
❑ 6 George King DP RC	15.00	40.00
❑ 7 Kenny Sears DP RC	15.00	40.00
❑ 8 Dick Ricketts DP RC	15.00	40.00
❑ 9 Jack Nichols DP	15.00	25.00
❑ 10 Paul Arizin DP RC	40.00	80.00
❑ 11 Chuck Noble DP	15.00	25.00
❑ 12 Slater Martin DP RC	30.00	60.00
❑ 13 Dolph Schayes DP RC	30.00	60.00
❑ 14 Dick Atha DP	15.00	25.00
❑ 15 Frank Ramsey DP RC	40.00	80.00
❑ 16 Dick McGuire DP RC	25.00	50.00
❑ 17 Bob Cousy DP RC	200.00	350.00
❑ 18 Larry Foust DP RC	15.00	40.00
❑ 19 Tom Heinsohn RC	125.00	225.00
❑ 20 Bill Thieben DP	15.00	25.00
❑ 21 Don Meineke DP RC	15.00	40.00
❑ 22 Tom Marshall	25.00	40.00
❑ 23 Dick Garmaker	25.00	40.00
❑ 24 Bob Pettit QP RC	60.00	120.00
❑ 25 Jim Krebs DP RC	15.00	40.00
❑ 26 Gene Shue DP RC	40.00	60.00
❑ 27 Ed Macauley DP RC	45.00	70.00
❑ 28 Vern Mikkelsen RC	60.00	100.00
❑ 29 Willie Naulls RC	40.00	60.00
❑ 30 Walter Dukes DP RC	30.00	45.00
❑ 31 Dave Piontek DP	15.00	25.00
❑ 32 Johnny Red Kerr RC	60.00	100.00
❑ 33 Larry Costello DP RC	30.00	50.00
❑ 34 Woody Sauldsberry DP RC	15.00	40.00
❑ 35 Ray Felix RC	30.00	45.00
❑ 36 Ernie Beck	25.00	40.00
❑ 37 Cliff Hagan RC	60.00	100.00
❑ 38 Guy Sparrow DP	15.00	25.00
❑ 39 Jim Loscutoff RC	40.00	60.00
❑ 40 Arnie Hisen DP	30.00	45.00
❑ 41 Joe Graboski	25.00	40.00
❑ 42 Maurice Stokes DP RC	60.00	100.00
❑ 43 Rod Hundley DP RC	60.00	100.00
❑ 44 Tom Gola DP RC	50.00	80.00
❑ 45 Med Park RC	30.00	45.00
❑ 46 Mel Hutchins DP	15.00	25.00
❑ 47 Larry Friend DP	15.00	25.00
❑ 48 Lennie Rosenbluth DP RC	30.00	50.00
❑ 49 Walt Davis	25.00	40.00
❑ 50 Richie Regan RC	30.00	45.00
❑ 51 Frank Selvy DP RC	30.00	50.00
❑ 52 Art Spoelstra DP	15.00	25.00
❑ 53 Bob Hopkins RC	30.00	45.00
❑ 54 Earl Lloyd RC	30.00	50.00
❑ 55 Phil Jordan DP	15.00	25.00
❑ 56 Bob Houbregs DP RC	25.00	40.00
❑ 57 Lou Tsioropoulos DP	15.00	25.00
❑ 58 Ed Conlin RC	30.00	45.00
❑ 59 Al Bianchi RC	50.00	80.00
❑ 60 George Dempsey RC	30.00	45.00
❑ 61 Chuck Share	25.00	40.00
❑ 62 Harry Gallatin DP RC	30.00	50.00
❑ 63 Bob Harrison	25.00	40.00
❑ 64 Bob Burrow DP	15.00	25.00
❑ 65 Win Wilfong DP	15.00	25.00
❑ 66 Jack McMahon DP RC	15.00	40.00
❑ 67 Jack George	25.00	40.00
❑ 68 Charlie Tyra DP	15.00	25.00
❑ 69 Ron Sobie	25.00	40.00
❑ 70 Jack Coleman	25.00	40.00
❑ 71 Jack Twyman DP RC	65.00	110.00
❑ 72 Paul Seymour RC	30.00	45.00
❑ 73 Jim Paxson DP UER RC	35.00	55.00
❑ 74 Bob Leonard RC	30.00	50.00
❑ 75 Andy Phillip	40.00	60.00
❑ 76 Joe Holup	25.00	40.00
❑ 77 Bill Russell RC	700.00	1100.00
❑ 78 Clyde Lovellette DP RC	60.00	100.00
❑ 79 Ed Fleming DP	15.00	25.00
❑ 80 Dick Schnittker RC	60.00	120.00

1969-70 Topps

❑ COMPLETE SET (99)	1200.00	1800.00
❑ 1 Wilt Chamberlain !	75.00	150.00
❑ 2 Gail Goodrich RC	15.00	30.00
❑ 3 Cazzie Russell RC	8.00	15.00
❑ 4 Darrall Imhoff RC	2.50	6.00
❑ 5 Bailey Howell	3.00	8.00
❑ 6 Lucius Allen RC	5.00	10.00
❑ 7 Tom Boerwinkle RC	2.50	6.00
❑ 8 Jimmy Walker RC	3.00	8.00
❑ 9 John Block RC	2.50	6.00
❑ 10 Nate Thurmond RC	15.00	30.00
❑ 11 Gary Gregor	1.50	4.00
❑ 12 Gus Johnson RC	6.00	15.00
❑ 13 Luther Rackley	1.50	4.00
❑ 14 Jon McGlocklin RC	15.00	30.00
❑ 15 Connie Hawkins RC	20.00	40.00
❑ 16 Johnny Egan	1.50	4.00
❑ 17 Jim Washington	1.50	4.00
❑ 18 Dick Barnett RC	3.00	8.00
❑ 19 Tom Meschery	3.00	8.00
❑ 20 John Havlicek RC	40.00	80.00
❑ 21 Eddie Miles	1.50	4.00
❑ 22 Walt Wesley	2.50	6.00
❑ 23 Rick Adelman RC	3.00	8.00
❑ 24 Al Attles	3.00	8.00
❑ 25 Lew Alcindor RC	150.00	275.00
❑ 26 Jack Marin RC	3.00	8.00
❑ 27 Walt Hazzard RC	4.00	10.00
❑ 28 Connie Dierking	1.50	4.00
❑ 29 Keith Erickson RC	4.00	10.00
❑ 30 Bob Rule RC	5.00	10.00
❑ 31 Dick Van Arsdale RC	4.00	10.00
❑ 32 Archie Clark RC	4.00	10.00
❑ 33 Terry Dischinger RC	1.50	4.00
❑ 34 Henry Finkel RC	1.50	4.00
❑ 35 Elgin Baylor	15.00	30.00
❑ 36 Ron Williams	1.50	4.00
❑ 37 Loy Petersen	1.50	4.00
❑ 38 Guy Rodgers	3.00	8.00
❑ 39 Toby Kimball	1.50	4.00
❑ 40 Billy Cunningham RC	15.00	30.00
❑ 41 Joe Caldwell RC	3.00	8.00
❑ 42 Leroy Ellis RC	2.50	6.00
❑ 43 Bill Bradley RC	40.00	80.00
❑ 44 Len Wilkens UER	12.50	25.00
❑ 45 Jerry Lucas RC	15.00	30.00
❑ 46 Neal Walk RC	2.50	6.00
❑ 47 Emmette Bryant RC	2.50	6.00
❑ 48 Bob Kauffman RC	1.50	4.00
❑ 49 Mel Counts RC	2.50	6.00
❑ 50 Oscar Robertson	15.00	30.00
❑ 51 Jim Barnett RC	3.00	8.00
❑ 52 Don Smith	1.50	4.00
❑ 53 Jim Davis	1.50	4.00
❑ 54 Wali Jones RC	2.50	6.00
❑ 55 Dave Bing RC	15.00	30.00
❑ 56 Wes Unseld RC	20.00	40.00
❑ 57 Joe Ellis	1.50	4.00
❑ 58 John Tresvant	1.50	4.00
❑ 59 Larry Siegfried RC	2.50	6.00
❑ 60 Willis Reed RC	15.00	30.00
❑ 61 Paul Silas RC	6.00	15.00
❑ 62 Bob Weiss RC	3.00	8.00
❑ 63 Willie McCarter	1.50	4.00
❑ 64 Don Kojis RC	1.50	4.00
❑ 65 Lou Hudson RC	6.00	15.00
❑ 66 Jim King	1.50	4.00
❑ 67 Luke Jackson RC	2.50	6.00
❑ 68 Len Chappell RC	1.50	4.00
❑ 69 Ray Scott	1.50	4.00
❑ 70 Jeff Mullins RC	3.00	8.00
❑ 71 Howie Komives	1.50	4.00
❑ 72 Tom Sanders RC	5.00	10.00
❑ 73 Dick Snyder	1.50	4.00
❑ 74 Dave Stallworth RC	2.50	6.00
❑ 75 Elvin Hayes RC	30.00	60.00
❑ 76 Art Harris	1.50	4.00
❑ 77 Don Ohl	2.50	6.00
❑ 78 Bob Love RC	15.00	30.00
❑ 79 Tom Van Arsdale RC	5.00	10.00
❑ 80 Earl Monroe RC	15.00	30.00
❑ 81 Greg Smith	1.50	4.00
❑ 82 Don Nelson RC	15.00	30.00
❑ 83 Happy Hairston RC	3.00	8.00
❑ 84 Hal Greer	6.00	12.00
❑ 85 Dave DeBusschere RC	15.00	30.00
❑ 86 Bill Bridges RC	3.00	8.00
❑ 87 Herm Gilliam RC	2.50	6.00
❑ 88 Jim Fox	1.50	4.00
❑ 89 Bob Boozer	2.50	6.00
❑ 90 Jerry West	30.00	60.00
❑ 91 Chet Walker RC	5.00	12.00
❑ 92 Flynn Robinson RC	2.50	6.00
❑ 93 Clyde Lee	1.50	4.00
❑ 94 Kevin Loughery RC	5.00	10.00
❑ 95 Walt Bellamy	5.00	10.00
❑ 96 Art Williams	1.50	4.00
❑ 97 Adrian Smith RC	2.50	6.00
❑ 98 Walt Frazier RC	25.00	50.00
❑ 99 Checklist 1-99	125.00	250.00

1970-71 Topps

❑ COMPLETE SET (175)	700.00	1200.00
❑ COMMON CARD (1-110)	1.00	2.50
❑ COMMON CARD (111-175)	1.25	3.00
❑ 1 Alcind/West/Hayes LL !	15.00	40.00
❑ 2 West/Alcin/Hayes LL SP	15.00	40.00
❑ 3 Green/Imhoff/Hudson LL	2.00	5.00
❑ 4 Rob/Walker/Mull LL SP !	5.00	10.00
❑ 5 Hayes/Uns/Alcindor LL	15.00	25.00
❑ 6 Wilkens/Fraz/Hask LL SP	6.00	12.00
❑ 7 Bill Bradley	30.00	50.00
❑ 8 Ron Williams	1.00	2.50
❑ 9 Otto Moore	1.00	2.50
❑ 10 John Havlicek SP !	40.00	75.00
❑ 11 George Wilson RC	1.00	2.50
❑ 12 John Trapp	1.00	2.50
❑ 13 Pat Riley RC	35.00	60.00
❑ 14 Jim Washington	1.00	2.50
❑ 15 Bob Rule	1.50	4.00
❑ 16 Bob Weiss	1.50	4.00
❑ 17 Neil Johnson	1.00	2.50
❑ 18 Walt Bellamy	2.50	6.00
❑ 19 McCoy McLemore	1.00	2.50
❑ 20 Earl Monroe	7.50	15.00
❑ 21 Wally Anderzunas	1.00	2.50
❑ 22 Guy Rodgers	1.50	4.00
❑ 23 Rick Roberson	1.00	2.50
❑ 24 Checklist 1-110	20.00	40.00
❑ 25 Jimmy Walker	1.50	4.00
❑ 26 Mike Riordan RC	2.50	6.00
❑ 27 Henry Finkel	1.00	2.50
❑ 28 Joe Ellis	1.00	2.50
❑ 29 Mike Davis	1.00	2.50
❑ 30 Lou Hudson	2.50	6.00
❑ 31 Lucius Allen SP	4.00	10.00
❑ 32 Toby Kimball SP	3.00	8.00
❑ 33 Luke Jackson SP	3.00	8.00
❑ 34 Johnny Egan	3.00	8.00
❑ 35 Leroy Ellis SP	3.00	8.00
❑ 36 Jack Marin SP	4.00	10.00

❑ 37 Joe Caldwell SP	4.00	10.00
❑ 38 Keith Erickson	2.50	6.00
❑ 39 Don Smith	1.00	2.50
❑ 40 Flynn Robinson	1.50	4.00
❑ 41 Bob Boozer	1.00	2.50
❑ 42 Howie Komives	1.00	2.50
❑ 43 Dick Barnett	1.50	4.00
❑ 44 Stu Lantz RC	1.25	3.00
❑ 45 Dick Van Arsdale	2.50	6.00
❑ 46 Jerry Lucas	5.00	10.00
❑ 47 Don Chaney RC	5.00	10.00
❑ 48 Ray Scott	1.00	2.50
❑ 49 Dick Cunningham SP	4.00	10.00
❑ 50 Wilt Chamberlain	50.00	80.00
❑ 51 Kevin Loughery	1.50	4.00
❑ 52 Stan McKenzie	1.00	2.50
❑ 53 Fred Foster	1.00	2.50
❑ 54 Jim Davis	1.00	2.50
❑ 55 Walt Wesley	1.00	2.50
❑ 56 Bill Hewitt	1.00	2.50
❑ 57 Darrall Imhoff	1.00	2.50
❑ 58 John Block	1.00	2.50
❑ 59 Al Attles SP	4.00	10.00
❑ 60 Chet Walker	2.50	6.00
❑ 61 Luther Rackley	1.00	2.50
❑ 62 Jerry Chambers SP RC	4.00	10.00
❑ 63 Bob Dandridge RC	3.00	8.00
❑ 64 Dick Snyder	1.00	2.50
❑ 65 Elgin Baylor	18.00	30.00
❑ 66 Connie Dierking	1.00	2.50
❑ 67 Steve Kuberski RC	1.00	2.50
❑ 68 Tom Boerwinkle	1.00	2.50
❑ 69 Paul Silas	2.50	6.00
❑ 70 Elvin Hayes	18.00	30.00
❑ 71 Bill Bridges	1.50	4.00
❑ 72 Wes Unseld	7.50	15.00
❑ 73 Herm Gilliam	1.00	2.50
❑ 74 Bobby Smith SP RC	4.00	10.00
❑ 75 Lew Alcindor	50.00	80.00
❑ 76 Jeff Mullins	1.50	4.00
❑ 77 Happy Hairston	1.50	4.00
❑ 78 Dave Stallworth SP	3.00	8.00
❑ 79 Fred Hetzel	1.00	2.50
❑ 80 Len Wilkens SP	12.00	25.00
❑ 81 Johnny Green RC	2.50	6.00
❑ 82 Erwin Mueller	1.00	2.50
❑ 83 Wally Jones	1.50	4.00
❑ 84 Bob Love	3.00	8.00
❑ 85 Dick Garrett RC	1.00	2.50
❑ 86 Don Nelson SP	12.00	25.00
❑ 87 Neal Walk SP	3.00	8.00
❑ 88 Larry Siegfried	1.00	2.50
❑ 89 Gary Gregor	1.00	2.50
❑ 90 Nate Thurmond	3.00	8.00
❑ 91 John Warren	1.00	2.50
❑ 92 Gus Johnson	2.50	6.00
❑ 93 Gail Goodrich	7.50	15.00
❑ 94 Dorrie Murrey	1.00	2.50
❑ 95 Cazzie Russell SP	5.00	12.00
❑ 96 Terry Dischinger	1.00	2.50
❑ 97 Norm Van Lier SP RC	7.50	15.00
❑ 98 Jim Fox	1.00	2.50
❑ 99 Tom Meschery	1.00	2.50
❑ 100 Oscar Robertson	15.00	40.00
❑ 101A Checklist 111-175	15.00	30.00
❑ 101B Checklist 111-175	15.00	30.00
❑ 102 Rich Johnson	1.00	2.50
❑ 103 Mel Counts	1.50	4.00
❑ 104 Bill Hosket SP RC	3.00	8.00
❑ 105 Archie Clark	1.50	4.00
❑ 106 Walt Frazier AS	5.00	10.00
❑ 107 Jerry West AS	12.50	25.00
❑ 108 Billy Cunningham AS SP	5.00	10.00
❑ 109 Connie Hawkins AS	3.00	8.00
❑ 110 Willis Reed AS	3.00	8.00
❑ 111 Nate Thurmond AS	2.00	5.00
❑ 112 John Havlicek AS	18.00	30.00
❑ 113 Elgin Baylor AS	8.00	20.00
❑ 114 Oscar Robertson AS	12.00	20.00
❑ 115 Lou Hudson AS	1.50	4.00
❑ 116 Emmette Bryant	1.25	3.00
❑ 117 Greg Howard	1.25	3.00
❑ 118 Rick Adelman	2.00	5.00
❑ 119 Barry Clemens	1.25	3.00
❑ 120 Walt Frazier	18.00	30.00
❑ 121 Jim Barnes RC	1.25	3.00
❑ 122 Bernie Williams	1.25	3.00
❑ 123 Pete Maravich RC	175.00	300.00
❑ 124 Matt Guokas RC	3.00	8.00
❑ 125 Dave Bing	6.00	12.00
❑ 126 John Tresvant	1.25	3.00
❑ 127 Shaler Halimon	1.25	3.00
❑ 128 Don Ohl	1.25	3.00
❑ 129 Fred Carter RC	2.50	6.00
❑ 130 Connie Hawkins	8.00	20.00
❑ 131 Jim King	1.25	3.00
❑ 132 Ed Manning RC	2.50	6.00
❑ 133 Adrian Smith	1.25	3.00
❑ 134 Walt Hazzard	2.50	6.00
❑ 135 Dave DeBusschere	7.50	15.00
❑ 136 Don Kojis	1.25	3.00
❑ 137 Calvin Murphy RC	15.00	40.00
❑ 138 Nate Bowman	1.25	3.00
❑ 139 Jon McGlocklin	2.00	5.00
❑ 140 Billy Cunningham	8.00	20.00
❑ 141 Willie McCarter	1.25	3.00
❑ 142 Jim Barnett	1.25	3.00
❑ 143 Jo Jo White RC	10.00	20.00
❑ 144 Clyde Lee	1.25	3.00
❑ 145 Tom Van Arsdale	2.50	6.00
❑ 146 Len Chappell	1.25	3.00
❑ 147 Lee Winfield	1.25	3.00
❑ 148 Jerry Sloan RC	10.00	25.00
❑ 149 Art Harris	1.25	3.00
❑ 150 Willis Reed	10.00	20.00
❑ 151 Art Williams	1.25	3.00
❑ 152 Don May	1.25	3.00
❑ 153 Loy Petersen	1.25	3.00
❑ 154 Dave Gambee	1.25	3.00
❑ 155 Hal Greer	2.50	6.00
❑ 156 Dave Newmark	1.25	3.00
❑ 157 Jimmy Collins	1.25	3.00
❑ 158 Bill Turner	1.25	3.00
❑ 159 Eddie Miles	1.25	3.00
❑ 160 Jerry West	30.00	50.00
❑ 161 Bob Quick	1.25	3.00
❑ 162 Fred Crawford	1.25	3.00
❑ 163 Tom Sanders	2.50	6.00
❑ 164 Dale Schlueter	1.25	3.00
❑ 165 Clem Haskins RC	4.00	10.00
❑ 166 Greg Smith	1.25	3.00
❑ 167 Rod Thorn RC	3.00	8.00
❑ 168 Playoff G1/W.Reed	5.00	10.00
❑ 169 Playoff G2/D.Garnett	2.00	5.00
❑ 170 Playoff G3/DeBussch	5.00	10.00
❑ 171 Playoff G4/J.West	8.00	20.00
❑ 172 Playoff G5/Bradley	8.00	20.00
❑ 173 Playoff G6/Wilt	8.00	20.00
❑ 174 Playoff G7/Frazier	6.00	12.00
❑ 175 Knicks Celebrate	10.00	20.00

1971-72 Topps

❑ COMPLETE SET (233)	500.00	750.00
❑ COM. NBA CARD (1-144)	.60	1.50
❑ COM. ABA CARD (145-233)	.75	2.00
❑ 1 Oscar Robertson !	8.00	20.00
❑ 2 Bill Bradley	6.00	15.00
❑ 3 Jim Fox	.60	1.50
❑ 4 John Johnson RC	.75	2.00
❑ 5 Luke Jackson	.75	2.00
❑ 6 Don May DP	.60	1.50
❑ 7 Kevin Loughery	.75	2.00
❑ 8 Terry Dischinger	.60	1.50
❑ 9 Neal Walk	.75	2.00
❑ 10 Elgin Baylor	5.00	12.00
❑ 11 Rick Adelman	.75	2.00
❑ 12 Clyde Lee	.60	1.50
❑ 13 Jerry Chambers	.60	1.50
❑ 14 Fred Carter	.75	2.00
❑ 15 Tom Boerwinkle DP	.60	1.50
❑ 16 John Block	.60	1.50
❑ 17 Dick Barnett	.75	2.00
❑ 18 Henry Finkel	.60	1.50
❑ 19 Norm Van Lier	1.50	4.00
❑ 20 Spencer Haywood RC	4.00	10.00
❑ 21 George Johnson	.60	1.50
❑ 22 Bobby Lewis	.60	1.50
❑ 23 Bill Hewitt	.60	1.50
❑ 24 Walt Hazzard	1.50	4.00
❑ 25 Happy Hairston	.75	2.00
❑ 26 George Wilson	.60	1.50
❑ 27 Lucius Allen	.75	2.00
❑ 28 Jim Washington	.60	1.50
❑ 29 Nate Archibald RC	6.00	15.00
❑ 30 Willis Reed	3.00	8.00
❑ 31 Erwin Mueller	.60	1.50
❑ 32 Art Harris	.60	1.50
❑ 33 Pete Cross	.60	1.50
❑ 34 Geoff Petrie RC	1.50	4.00
❑ 35 John Havlicek	6.00	15.00
❑ 36 Larry Siegfried	.60	1.50
❑ 37 John Tresvant DP	.60	1.50
❑ 38 Ron Williams	.60	1.50
❑ 39 Lamar Green DP	.60	1.50
❑ 40 Bob Rule DP	.75	2.00
❑ 41 Jim McMillian RC	.75	2.00
❑ 42 Wally Jones	.75	2.00
❑ 43 Bob Boozer	.60	1.50
❑ 44 Eddie Miles	.60	1.50
❑ 45 Bob Love DP	2.00	5.00
❑ 46 Claude English	.60	1.50
❑ 47 Dave Cowens RC	10.00	25.00
❑ 48 Emmette Bryant	.60	1.50
❑ 49 Dave Stallworth	.75	2.00
❑ 50 Jerry West	8.00	20.00
❑ 51 Joe Ellis	.60	1.50
❑ 52 Walt Wesley DP	.60	1.50
❑ 53 Howie Komives	.60	1.50
❑ 54 Paul Silas	1.50	4.00
❑ 55 Pete Maravich DP	10.00	25.00
❑ 56 Gary Gregor	.60	1.50
❑ 57 Sam Lacey RC	1.50	4.00
❑ 58 Calvin Murphy DP	2.50	6.00
❑ 59 Bob Dandridge	.75	2.00
❑ 60 Hal Greer	1.50	4.00
❑ 61 Keith Erickson	1.50	4.00
❑ 62 Joe Cooke	.60	1.50
❑ 63 Bob Lanier RC	10.00	25.00
❑ 64 Don Kojis	.60	1.50
❑ 65 Walt Frazier	4.00	10.00
❑ 66 Chet Walker DP	1.50	4.00
❑ 67 Dick Garrett	.60	1.50
❑ 68 John Trapp	.75	2.00
❑ 69 Jo Jo White	2.50	6.00
❑ 70 Wilt Chamberlain	10.00	25.00
❑ 71 Dave Sorenson	.60	1.50
❑ 72 Jim King	.60	1.50
❑ 73 Cazzie Russell	1.50	4.00
❑ 74 Jon McGlocklin	.75	2.00
❑ 75 Tom Van Arsdale	.75	2.00
❑ 76 Dale Schlueter	.60	1.50
❑ 77 Gus Johnson DP	1.50	4.00
❑ 78 Dave Bing	2.50	6.00
❑ 79 Billy Cunningham	3.00	8.00
❑ 80 Len Wilkens	3.00	8.00
❑ 81 Jerry Lucas DP	2.00	5.00
❑ 82 Don Chaney	1.50	4.00
❑ 83 McCoy McLemore	.60	1.50
❑ 84 Bob Kauffman DP	.60	1.50
❑ 85 Dick Van Arsdale	1.50	4.00
❑ 86 Johnny Green	.75	2.00
❑ 87 Jerry Sloan	2.00	5.00
❑ 88 Luther Rackley DP	.60	1.50
❑ 89 Shaler Halimon	.60	1.50
❑ 90 Jimmy Walker	.75	2.00
❑ 91 Rudy Tomjanovich RC	6.00	15.00
❑ 92 Levi Fontaine	.60	1.50
❑ 93 Bobby Smith	.75	2.00
❑ 94 Bob Arnzen	.60	1.50
❑ 95 Wes Unseld DP	2.50	6.00
❑ 96 Clem Haskins DP	1.50	4.00
❑ 97 Jim Davis	.60	1.50
❑ 98 Steve Kuberski	.60	1.50
❑ 99 Mike Davis DP	.60	1.50
❑ 100 Lew Alcindor	10.00	25.00
❑ 101 Willie McCarter	.60	1.50
❑ 102 Charlie Paulk	.60	1.50
❑ 103 Lee Winfield	.60	1.50
❑ 104 Jim Barnett	.60	1.50
❑ 105 Connie Hawkins DP	2.50	6.00
❑ 106 Archie Clark DP	.75	2.00
❑ 107 Dave DeBusschere	2.50	6.00
❑ 108 Stu Lantz DP	.75	2.00
❑ 109 Don Smith	.60	1.50

❑ 110 Lou Hudson	1.50	4.00
❑ 111 Leroy Ellis	.60	1.50
❑ 112 Jack Marin	.75	2.00
❑ 113 Matt Guokas	.75	2.00
❑ 114 Don Nelson	2.50	6.00
❑ 115 Jeff Mullins DP	.75	2.00
❑ 116 Walt Bellamy	2.50	6.00
❑ 117 Bob Quick	.60	1.50
❑ 118 John Warren	.60	1.50
❑ 119 Barry Clemens	.60	1.50
❑ 120 Elvin Hayes DP	3.00	8.00
❑ 121 Gail Goodrich	2.50	6.00
❑ 122 Ed Manning	.75	2.00
❑ 123 Herm Gilliam DP	.60	1.50
❑ 124 Dennis Awtrey RC	.75	2.00
❑ 125 John Hummer DP	.60	1.50
❑ 126 Mike Riordan	.75	2.00
❑ 127 Mel Counts	.60	1.50
❑ 128 Bob Weiss DP	.60	1.50
❑ 129 Greg Smith DP	.60	1.50
❑ 130 Earl Monroe	3.00	8.00
❑ 131 Nate Thurmond DP	1.50	4.00
❑ 132 Bill Bridges DP	.75	2.00
❑ 133 Playoffs G1/Alcindor	3.00	8.00
❑ 134 NBA Playoffs G2	1.25	3.00
❑ 135 NBA Playoffs G3	1.25	3.00
❑ 136 Playoffs G4/Oscar	2.50	6.00
❑ 137 NBA Champs/Oscar	4.00	10.00
❑ 138 Alcind/Hayes/Havl LL	5.00	12.00
❑ 139 Alcind/Havl/Hayes LL	5.00	12.00
❑ 140 Green/Alcind/Wilt LL	4.00	10.00
❑ 141 Walker/Oscar/Williams LL	2.00	5.00
❑ 142 Wilt/Hayes/Alcind LL	6.00	15.00
❑ 143 Van Lier/Oscar/West LL	3.00	8.00
❑ 144A NBA Checklist 1-144	6.00	15.00
❑ 144B NBA Checklist 1-144	6.00	15.00
❑ 145 ABA Checklist 145-233	6.00	15.00
❑ 146 Issel/Brisker/Scott LL	2.50	6.00
❑ 147 Issel/Barry/Brisker LL	3.00	8.00
❑ 148 ABA 2pt FG Pct Leaders	1.50	4.00
❑ 149 Barry/Carrier/Keller LL	3.00	8.00
❑ 150 ABA Rebound Leaders	1.50	4.00
❑ 151 ABA Assist Leaders	1.50	4.00
❑ 152 Larry Brown RC	5.00	12.00
❑ 153 Bob Bedell	.75	2.00
❑ 154 Merv Jackson	.75	2.00
❑ 155 Joe Caldwell	1.00	2.50
❑ 156 Billy Paultz RC	2.00	5.00
❑ 157 Les Hunter	1.00	2.50
❑ 158 Charlie Williams	.75	2.00
❑ 159 Stew Johnson	.75	2.00
❑ 160 Mack Calvin RC	2.00	5.00
❑ 161 Don Sidle	.75	2.00
❑ 162 Mike Barrett	.75	2.00
❑ 163 Tom Workman	.75	2.00
❑ 164 Joe Hamilton	1.00	2.50
❑ 165 Zelmo Beaty RC	2.50	6.00
❑ 166 Dan Hester	.75	2.00
❑ 167 Bob Verga	.75	2.00
❑ 168 Wilbert Jones	.75	2.00
❑ 169 Skeeter Swift	.75	2.00
❑ 170 Rick Barry RC	15.00	30.00
❑ 171 Billy Keller RC	1.50	4.00
❑ 172 Ron Franz	.75	2.00
❑ 173 Roland Taylor RC	1.00	2.50
❑ 174 Julian Hammond	.75	2.00
❑ 175 Steve Jones RC	2.50	6.00
❑ 176 Gerald Govan	1.00	2.50
❑ 177 Darrell Carrier RC	1.00	2.50
❑ 178 Ron Boone RC	2.00	5.00
❑ 179 George Peeples	.75	2.00
❑ 180 John Brisker	1.00	2.50
❑ 181 Doug Moe RC	2.50	6.00
❑ 182 Ollie Taylor	.75	2.00
❑ 183 Bob Netolicky RC	1.00	2.50
❑ 184 Sam Robinson	.75	2.00
❑ 185 James Jones	1.00	2.50
❑ 186 Julius Keye	1.00	2.50
❑ 187 Wayne Hightower	.75	2.00
❑ 188 Warren Armstrong RC	1.00	2.50
❑ 189 Mike Lewis	.75	2.00
❑ 190 Charlie Scott RC	2.50	6.00
❑ 191 Jim Ard	.75	2.00
❑ 192 George Lehmann	.75	2.00
❑ 193 Ira Harge	.75	2.00
❑ 194 Willie Wise RC	2.00	5.00
❑ 195 Mel Daniels RC	2.50	6.00
❑ 196 Larry Cannon	.75	2.00
❑ 197 Jim Eakins	1.00	2.50
❑ 198 Rich Jones	1.00	2.50
❑ 199 Bill Melchionni RC	1.50	4.00
❑ 200 Dan Issel RC	8.00	20.00
❑ 201 George Stone	.75	2.00
❑ 202 George Thompson	.75	2.00
❑ 203 Craig Raymond	.75	2.00
❑ 204 Freddie Lewis RC	1.00	2.50
❑ 205 George Carter	1.00	2.50
❑ 206 Lonnie Wright	.75	2.00
❑ 207 Cincy Powell	1.00	2.50
❑ 208 Larry Miller	1.00	2.50
❑ 209 Sonny Dove	.75	2.00
❑ 210 Byron Beck RC	1.00	2.50
❑ 211 John Beasley	.75	2.00
❑ 212 Lee Davis	.75	2.00
❑ 213 Rick Mount RC	2.50	6.00
❑ 214 Walt Simon	.75	2.00
❑ 215 Glen Combs	.75	2.00
❑ 216 Neil Johnson	.75	2.00
❑ 217 Manny Leaks	.75	2.00
❑ 218 Chuck Williams	1.00	2.50
❑ 219 Warren Davis	.75	2.00
❑ 220 Donnie Freeman RC	1.00	2.50
❑ 221 Randy Mahaffey	.75	2.00
❑ 222 John Barnhill	.75	2.00
❑ 223 Al Cueto	.75	2.00
❑ 224 Louie Dampier RC	2.50	6.00
❑ 225 Roger Brown RC	2.00	5.00
❑ 226 Joe DePre	.75	2.00
❑ 227 Ray Scott	.75	2.00
❑ 228 Arvesta Kelly	.75	2.00
❑ 229 Vann Williford	.75	2.00
❑ 230 Larry Jones	1.00	2.50
❑ 231 Gene Moore	.75	2.00
❑ 232 Ralph Simpson RC	1.00	2.50
❑ 233 Red Robbins RC	2.00	5.00

1972-73 Topps

❑ COMPLETE SET (264)	500.00	800.00
❑ COM. NBA CARD (1-176)	.40	1.00
❑ COM. ABA CARD (177-264)	.60	1.50
❑ 1 Wilt Chamberlain !	40.00	60.00
❑ 2 Stan Love	.40	1.00
❑ 3 Geoff Petrie	.60	1.50
❑ 4 Curtis Perry RC	.40	1.00
❑ 5 Pete Maravich	15.00	40.00
❑ 6 Gus Johnson	1.25	3.00
❑ 7 Dave Cowens	7.50	15.00
❑ 8 Randy Smith RC	1.50	4.00
❑ 9 Matt Guokas	.60	1.50
❑ 10 Spencer Haywood	1.50	4.00
❑ 11 Jerry Sloan	1.25	3.00
❑ 12 Dave Sorenson	.40	1.00
❑ 13 Howie Komives	.40	1.00
❑ 14 Joe Ellis	.40	1.00
❑ 15 Jerry Lucas	2.00	5.00
❑ 16 Stu Lantz	.60	1.50
❑ 17 Bill Bridges	.60	1.50
❑ 18 Leroy Ellis	.40	1.00
❑ 19 Art Williams	.40	1.00
❑ 20 Sidney Wicks RC	3.00	8.00
❑ 21 Wes Unseld	2.50	6.00
❑ 22 Jim Washington	.40	1.00
❑ 23 Fred Hilton	.40	1.00
❑ 24 Curtis Rowe RC	.60	1.50
❑ 25 Oscar Robertson	10.00	20.00
❑ 26 Larry Steele RC	.60	1.50
❑ 27 Charlie Davis	.40	1.00
❑ 28 Nate Thurmond	2.00	5.00
❑ 29 Fred Carter	.60	1.50
❑ 30 Connie Hawkins	3.00	8.00
❑ 31 Calvin Murphy	2.00	5.00
❑ 32 Phil Jackson RC	25.00	40.00
❑ 33 Lee Winfield	.40	1.00
❑ 34 Jim Fox	.40	1.00
❑ 35 Dave Bing	2.50	6.00
❑ 36 Gary Gregor	.40	1.00
❑ 37 Mike Riordan	.60	1.50
❑ 38 George Trapp	.40	1.00
❑ 39 Mike Davis	.40	1.00
❑ 40 Bob Rule	.60	1.50
❑ 41 John Block	.40	1.00
❑ 42 Bob Dandridge	.60	1.50
❑ 43 John Johnson	.60	1.50
❑ 44 Rick Barry	8.00	20.00
❑ 45 Jo Jo White	1.50	4.00
❑ 46 Cliff Meely	.40	1.00
❑ 47 Charlie Scott	1.25	3.00
❑ 48 Johnny Green	.60	1.50
❑ 49 Pete Cross	.40	1.00
❑ 50 Gail Goodrich	2.50	6.00
❑ 51 Jim Davis	.40	1.00
❑ 52 Dick Barnett	.60	1.50
❑ 53 Bob Christian	.40	1.00
❑ 54 Jon McGlocklin	.60	1.50
❑ 55 Paul Silas	1.25	3.00
❑ 56 Hal Greer	1.25	3.00
❑ 57 Barry Clemens	.40	1.00
❑ 58 Nick Jones	.40	1.00
❑ 59 Cornell Warner	.40	1.00
❑ 60 Walt Frazier	5.00	10.00
❑ 61 Dorie Murrey	.40	1.00
❑ 62 Dick Cunningham	.40	1.00
❑ 63 Sam Lacey	.60	1.50
❑ 64 John Warren	.40	1.00
❑ 65 Tom Boerwinkle	.40	1.00
❑ 66 Fred Foster	.40	1.00
❑ 67 Mel Counts	.40	1.00
❑ 68 Toby Kimball	.40	1.00
❑ 69 Dale Schlueter	.40	1.00
❑ 70 Jack Marin	.60	1.50
❑ 71 Jim Barnett	.40	1.00
❑ 72 Clem Haskins	1.25	3.00
❑ 73 Earl Monroe	2.50	6.00
❑ 74 Tom Sanders	.60	1.50
❑ 75 Jerry West	12.50	25.00
❑ 76 Elmore Smith RC	.60	1.50
❑ 77 Don Adams	.40	1.00
❑ 78 Wally Jones	.60	1.50
❑ 79 Tom Van Arsdale	.60	1.50
❑ 80 Bob Lanier	10.00	20.00
❑ 81 Len Wilkens	3.00	8.00
❑ 82 Neal Walk	.60	1.50
❑ 83 Kevin Loughery	.60	1.50
❑ 84 Stan McKenzie	.40	1.00
❑ 85 Jeff Mullins	.60	1.50
❑ 86 Otto Moore	.40	1.00
❑ 87 John Tresvant	.40	1.00
❑ 88 Dean Meminger RC	.40	1.00
❑ 89 Jim McMillian	.60	1.50
❑ 90 Austin Carr RC	3.00	8.00
❑ 91 Clifford Ray RC	.60	1.50
❑ 92 Don Nelson	1.50	4.00
❑ 93 Mahdi Abdul-Rahman	.60	1.50
❑ 94 Willie Norwood	.40	1.00
❑ 95 Dick Van Arsdale	.60	1.50
❑ 96 Don May	.40	1.00
❑ 97 Walt Bellamy	1.50	4.00
❑ 98 Garfield Heard RC	1.50	4.00
❑ 99 Dave Wohl	.40	1.00
❑ 100 Kareem Abdul-Jabbar	15.00	30.00
❑ 101 Ron Knight	.40	1.00
❑ 102 Phil Chenier RC	1.50	4.00
❑ 103 Rudy Tomjanovich	3.00	8.00
❑ 104 Flynn Robinson	.40	1.00
❑ 105 Dave DeBusschere	2.50	6.00
❑ 106 Dennis Layton	.40	1.00
❑ 107 Bill Hewitt	.40	1.00
❑ 108 Dick Garrett	.40	1.00
❑ 109 Walt Wesley	.40	1.00
❑ 110 John Havlicek	12.50	25.00
❑ 111 Norm Van Lier	.60	1.50
❑ 112 Cazzie Russell	1.25	3.00
❑ 113 Herm Gilliam	.40	1.00
❑ 114 Greg Smith	.40	1.00
❑ 115 Nate Archibald	2.50	6.00
❑ 116 Don Kojis	.40	1.00
❑ 117 Rick Adelman	.60	1.50
❑ 118 Luke Jackson	.60	1.50
❑ 119 Lamar Green	.40	1.00
❑ 120 Archie Clark	.60	1.50
❑ 121 Happy Hairston	.60	1.50
❑ 122 Bill Bradley	10.00	20.00
❑ 123 Ron Williams	.40	1.00
❑ 124 Jimmy Walker	.60	1.50

❑ 125 Bob Kauffman	.40	1.00
❑ 126 Rick Roberson	.40	1.00
❑ 127 Howard Porter RC	.60	1.50
❑ 128 Mike Newlin RC	.60	1.50
❑ 129 Willis Reed	3.00	8.00
❑ 130 Lou Hudson	1.25	3.00
❑ 131 Don Chaney	1.25	3.00
❑ 132 Dave Stallworth	.40	1.00
❑ 133 Charlie Yelverton	.40	1.00
❑ 134 Ken Durrett	.40	1.00
❑ 135 John Brisker	.60	1.50
❑ 136 Dick Snyder	.40	1.00
❑ 137 Jim McDaniels	.40	1.00
❑ 138 Clyde Lee	.40	1.00
❑ 139 Dennis Awtrey UER	.60	1.50
❑ 140 Keith Erickson	.60	1.50
❑ 141 Bob Weiss	.60	1.50
❑ 142 Butch Beard RC	1.25	3.00
❑ 143 Terry Dischinger	.40	1.00
❑ 144 Pat Riley	8.00	20.00
❑ 145 Lucius Allen	.60	1.50
❑ 146 John Mengelt RC	.40	1.00
❑ 147 John Hummer	.40	1.00
❑ 148 Bob Love	2.00	5.00
❑ 149 Bobby Smith	.60	1.50
❑ 150 Elvin Hayes	5.00	10.00
❑ 151 Nate Williams	.40	1.00
❑ 152 Chet Walker	1.25	3.00
❑ 153 Steve Kuberski	.40	1.00
❑ 154 Playoffs G1/Monroe	1.25	3.00
❑ 155 NBA Playoffs G2	1.00	2.50
❑ 156 NBA Playoffs G3	1.00	2.50
❑ 157 NBA Playoffs G4	1.00	2.50
❑ 158 Playoffs G5/J.West	3.00	8.00
❑ 159 Champs Lakers/Wilt	5.00	10.00
❑ 160 NBA Checklist 1-176	6.00	15.00
❑ 161 John Havlicek AS	5.00	10.00
❑ 162 Spencer Haywood AS	.75	2.00
❑ 163 Kareem Abdul-Jabbar AS	12.50	25.00
❑ 164 Jerry West AS	8.00	20.00
❑ 165 Walt Frazier AS	2.00	5.00
❑ 166 Bob Love AS	.75	2.00
❑ 167 Billy Cunningham AS	1.50	4.00
❑ 168 Wilt Chamberlain AS	10.00	20.00
❑ 169 Nate Archibald AS	1.50	4.00
❑ 170 Archie Clark AS	.75	2.00
❑ 171 Jabbar/Havl/Arch LL	6.00	15.00
❑ 172 Jabbar/Arch/Havl LL	6.00	15.00
❑ 173 Wilt/Jabbar/Bell LL	6.00	15.00
❑ 174 Marin/Murphy/Goodr LL	1.25	3.00
❑ 175 Wilt/Jabbar/Unseld LL	6.00	15.00
❑ 176 Wilkens/West/Arch LL	6.00	12.00
❑ 177 Roland Taylor	.60	1.50
❑ 178 Art Becker	.60	1.50
❑ 179 Mack Calvin	.75	2.00
❑ 180 Artis Gilmore RC	10.00	20.00
❑ 181 Collis Jones	.60	1.50
❑ 182 John Roche RC	.75	2.00
❑ 183 George McGinnis RC	6.00	15.00
❑ 184 Johnny Neumann	.75	2.00
❑ 185 Willie Wise	.75	2.00
❑ 186 Bernie Williams	.60	1.50
❑ 187 Byron Beck	.75	2.00
❑ 188 Larry Miller	.75	2.00
❑ 189 Cincy Powell	.60	1.50
❑ 190 Donnie Freeman	.75	2.00
❑ 191 John Baum	.60	1.50
❑ 192 Billy Keller	.75	2.00
❑ 193 Wilbert Jones	.60	1.50
❑ 194 Glen Combs	.60	1.50
❑ 195 Julius Erving RC	125.00	200.00
❑ 196 Al Smith	.60	1.50
❑ 197 George Carter	.60	1.50
❑ 198 Louie Dampier	1.25	3.00
❑ 199 Rich Jones	.60	1.50
❑ 200 Mel Daniels	1.25	3.00
❑ 201 Gene Moore	.60	1.50
❑ 202 Randy Denton	.60	1.50
❑ 203 Larry Jones	.60	1.50
❑ 204 Jim Ligon	.60	1.50
❑ 205 Warren Jabali	.75	2.00
❑ 206 Joe Caldwell	.75	2.00
❑ 207 Darrell Carrier	.75	2.00
❑ 208 Gene Kennedy	.60	1.50
❑ 209 Ollie Taylor	.60	1.50
❑ 210 Roger Brown	.75	2.00
❑ 211 George Lehmann	.60	1.50
❑ 212 Red Robbins	.75	2.00
❑ 213 Jim Eakins	.75	2.00
❑ 214 Willie Long	.60	1.50
❑ 215 Billy Cunningham	3.00	8.00
❑ 216 Steve Jones	.75	2.00
❑ 217 Les Hunter	.60	1.50
❑ 218 Billy Paultz	.75	2.00
❑ 219 Freddie Lewis	.75	2.00
❑ 220 Zelmo Beaty	.75	2.00
❑ 221 George Thompson	.60	1.50
❑ 222 Neil Johnson	.60	1.50
❑ 223 Dave Robisch RC	.75	2.00
❑ 224 Walt Simon	.60	1.50
❑ 225 Bill Melchionni	.75	2.00
❑ 226 Wendell Ladner RC	.75	2.00
❑ 227 Joe Hamilton	.60	1.50
❑ 228 Bob Netolicky	.75	2.00
❑ 229 James Jones	.75	2.00
❑ 230 Dan Issel	5.00	10.00
❑ 231 Charlie Williams	.60	1.50
❑ 232 Willie Sojourner	.60	1.50
❑ 233 Merv Jackson	.60	1.50
❑ 234 Mike Lewis	.60	1.50
❑ 235 Ralph Simpson	.75	2.00
❑ 236 Darnell Hillman	.75	2.00
❑ 237 Rick Mount	1.25	3.00
❑ 238 Gerald Govan	.60	1.50
❑ 239 Ron Boone	.75	2.00
❑ 240 Tom Washington	.60	1.50
❑ 241 ABA Playoffs G1	1.00	2.50
❑ 242 Playoffs G2/Barry	2.00	5.00
❑ 243 Playoffs G3/McGinnis	1.50	4.00
❑ 244 Playoffs G4/Barry	2.00	5.00
❑ 245 ABA Playoffs G5	1.00	2.50
❑ 246 ABA Playoffs G6	1.00	2.50
❑ 247 ABA Champs: Pacers	1.25	3.00
❑ 248 ABA Checklist 177-264	6.00	15.00
❑ 249 Dan Issel AS	2.50	6.00
❑ 250 Rick Barry AS	3.00	8.00
❑ 251 Artis Gilmore AS	2.50	6.00
❑ 252 Donnie Freeman AS	1.00	2.50
❑ 253 Bill Melchionni AS	1.00	2.50
❑ 254 Willie Wise AS	1.00	2.50
❑ 255 Julius Erving AS	25.00	50.00
❑ 256 Zelmo Beaty AS	1.00	2.50
❑ 257 Ralph Simpson AS	1.00	2.50
❑ 258 Charlie Scott AS	1.00	2.50
❑ 259 Scott/Barry/Issel LL	3.00	8.00
❑ 260 Gilmore/Wash/Jones LL	1.50	4.00
❑ 261 ABA 3pt FG Pct.	1.00	2.50
❑ 262 Barry/Calvin/Jones LL	1.50	4.00
❑ 263 Gilmore/Erving/Dan LL	10.00	20.00
❑ 264 Melch/Brown/Damp LL!	2.50	6.00

1973-74 Topps

❑ COMPLETE SET (264)	225.00	325.00
❑ COM. NBA CARD (1-176)	.20	.50
❑ COM. ABA CARD (177-264)	.40	1.00
❑ 1 Nate Archibald !	5.00	10.00
❑ 2 Steve Kuberski	.20	.50
❑ 3 John Mengelt	.20	.50
❑ 4 Jim McMillian	.40	1.00
❑ 5 Nate Thurmond	1.50	4.00
❑ 6 Dave Wohl	.20	.50
❑ 7 John Brisker	.20	.50
❑ 8 Charlie Davis	.20	.50
❑ 9 Lamar Green	.20	.50
❑ 10 Walt Frazier	2.50	6.00
❑ 11 Bob Christian	.20	.50
❑ 12 Cornell Warner	.20	.50
❑ 13 Calvin Murphy	1.50	4.00
❑ 14 Dave Sorenson	.20	.50
❑ 15 Archie Clark	.40	1.00
❑ 16 Clifford Ray	.40	1.00
❑ 17 Terry Driscoll	.20	.50
❑ 18 Matt Guokas	.40	1.00
❑ 19 Elmore Smith	.40	1.00
❑ 20 John Havlicek	7.50	15.00
❑ 21 Pat Riley	3.00	8.00
❑ 22 George Trapp	.20	.50
❑ 23 Ron Williams	.20	.50
❑ 24 Jim Fox	.20	.50
❑ 25 Dick Van Arsdale	.40	1.00
❑ 26 John Tresvant	.20	.50
❑ 27 Rick Adelman	.40	1.00
❑ 28 Eddie Mast	.20	.50
❑ 29 Jim Cleamons	.40	1.00
❑ 30 Dave DeBusschere	2.00	5.00
❑ 31 Norm Van Lier	.40	1.00
❑ 32 Stan McKenzie	.20	.50
❑ 33 Bob Dandridge	.40	1.00
❑ 34 Leroy Ellis	.40	1.00
❑ 35 Mike Riordan	.40	1.00
❑ 36 Fred Hilton	.20	.50
❑ 37 Toby Kimball	.20	.50
❑ 38 Jim Price	.20	.50
❑ 39 Willie Norwood	.20	.50
❑ 40 Dave Cowens	5.00	10.00
❑ 41 Cazzie Russell	.40	1.00
❑ 42 Lee Winfield	.20	.50
❑ 43 Connie Hawkins	2.00	5.00
❑ 44 Mike Newlin	.40	1.00
❑ 45 Chet Walker	.40	1.00
❑ 46 Walt Bellamy	1.50	4.00
❑ 47 John Johnson	.40	1.00
❑ 48 Henry Bibby RC	2.00	5.00
❑ 49 Bobby Smith	.40	1.00
❑ 50 Kareem Abdul-Jabbar	15.00	25.00
❑ 51 Mike Price	.20	.50
❑ 52 John Hummer	.20	.50
❑ 53 Kevin Porter RC	2.00	5.00
❑ 54 Nate Williams	.20	.50
❑ 55 Gail Goodrich	1.50	4.00
❑ 56 Fred Foster	.20	.50
❑ 57 Don Chaney	.40	1.00
❑ 58 Bud Stallworth	.20	.50
❑ 59 Clem Haskins	.40	1.00
❑ 60 Bob Love	1.25	3.00
❑ 61 Jimmy Walker	.40	1.00
❑ 62 NBA Eastern Semis	.40	1.00
❑ 63 NBA Eastern Semis	.40	1.00
❑ 64 Western Semis/Wilt	3.00	8.00
❑ 65 NBA Western Semis	.40	1.00
❑ 66 Eastern Finals/Reed	1.25	3.00
❑ 67 NBA Western Finals	.40	1.00
❑ 68 Knicks Champs/Frazier	1.50	4.00
❑ 69 Larry Steele	.40	1.00
❑ 70 Oscar Robertson	7.50	15.00
❑ 71 Phil Jackson	7.50	15.00
❑ 72 John Wetzel	.20	.50
❑ 73 Steve Patterson RC	.40	1.00
❑ 74 Manny Leaks	.20	.50
❑ 75 Jeff Mullins	.40	1.00
❑ 76 Stan Love	.20	.50
❑ 77 Dick Garrett	.20	.50
❑ 78 Don Nelson	1.50	4.00
❑ 79 Chris Ford RC	1.25	3.00
❑ 80 Wilt Chamberlain	15.00	25.00
❑ 81 Dennis Layton	.20	.50
❑ 82 Bill Bradley	7.50	15.00
❑ 83 Jerry Sloan	.40	1.00
❑ 84 Cliff Meely	.20	.50
❑ 85 Sam Lacey	.20	.50
❑ 86 Dick Snyder	.20	.50
❑ 87 Jim Washington	.20	.50
❑ 88 Lucius Allen	.40	1.00
❑ 89 LaRue Martin	.20	.50
❑ 90 Rick Barry	3.00	8.00
❑ 91 Fred Boyd	.20	.50
❑ 92 Barry Clemens	.20	.50
❑ 93 Dean Meminger	.20	.50
❑ 94 Henry Finkel	.20	.50
❑ 95 Elvin Hayes	2.50	6.00
❑ 96 Stu Lantz	.40	1.00
❑ 97 Bill Hewitt	.20	.50
❑ 98 Neal Walk	.20	.50
❑ 99 Garfield Heard	.40	1.00
❑ 100 Jerry West	10.00	20.00
❑ 101 Otto Moore	.20	.50
❑ 102 Don Kojis	.20	.50
❑ 103 Fred Brown RC	2.50	6.00
❑ 104 Dwight Davis	.20	.50
❑ 105 Willis Reed	2.50	6.00
❑ 106 Herm Gilliam	.20	.50
❑ 107 Mickey Davis	.20	.50
❑ 108 Jim Barnett	.20	.50
❑ 109 Ollie Johnson	.20	.50

❑ 110 Bob Lanier	2.50	6.00
❑ 111 Fred Carter	.40	1.00
❑ 112 Paul Silas	1.25	3.00
❑ 113 Phil Chenier	.40	1.00
❑ 114 Dennis Awtrey	.20	.50
❑ 115 Austin Carr	.40	1.00
❑ 116 Bob Kauffman	.20	.50
❑ 117 Keith Erickson	.40	1.00
❑ 118 Walt Wesley	.20	.50
❑ 119 Steve Bracey	.20	.50
❑ 120 Spencer Haywood	1.25	3.00
❑ 121 NBA Checklist 1-176	6.00	12.00
❑ 122 Jack Marin	.40	1.00
❑ 123 Jon McGlocklin	.20	.50
❑ 124 Johnny Green	.40	1.00
❑ 125 Jerry Lucas	1.25	3.00
❑ 126 Paul Westphal RC	10.00	20.00
❑ 127 Curtis Rowe	.40	1.00
❑ 128 Mahdi Abdul-Rahman	.40	1.00
❑ 129 Lloyd Neal RC	.20	.50
❑ 130 Pete Maravich	18.00	30.00
❑ 131 Don May	.20	.50
❑ 132 Bob Weiss	.40	1.00
❑ 133 Dave Stallworth	.20	.50
❑ 134 Dick Cunningham	.20	.50
❑ 135 Bob McAdoo RC	10.00	20.00
❑ 136 Butch Beard	.40	1.00
❑ 137 Happy Hairston	.40	1.00
❑ 138 Bob Rule	.40	1.00
❑ 139 Don Adams	.20	.50
❑ 140 Charlie Scott	.40	1.00
❑ 141 Ron Riley	.20	.50
❑ 142 Earl Monroe	1.50	4.00
❑ 143 Clyde Lee	.20	.50
❑ 144 Rick Roberson	.20	.50
❑ 145 Rudy Tomjanovich	2.50	6.00
❑ 146 Tom Van Arsdale	.40	1.00
❑ 147 Art Williams	.20	.50
❑ 148 Curtis Perry	.20	.50
❑ 149 Rich Rinaldi	.20	.50
❑ 150 Lou Hudson	.40	1.00
❑ 151 Mel Counts	.20	.50
❑ 152 Jim McDaniels	.20	.50
❑ 153 Arch/Jabbar/Hayw LL	3.00	8.00
❑ 154 Arch/Jabbar/Hayw LL	3.00	8.00
❑ 155 Wilt/Guokas/Jabbar LL	6.00	12.00
❑ 156 Barry/Murphy/Newlin LL	1.50	4.00
❑ 157 Wilt/Thurm/Cowens LL	3.00	8.00
❑ 158 Arch/Wilkens/Bing LL	1.50	4.00
❑ 159 Don Smith	.20	.50
❑ 160 Sidney Wicks	1.25	3.00
❑ 161 Howie Komives	.20	.50
❑ 162 John Gianelli	.20	.50
❑ 163 Jeff Halliburton	.20	.50
❑ 164 Kennedy McIntosh	.20	.50
❑ 165 Len Wilkens	2.50	6.00
❑ 166 Corky Calhoun	.20	.50
❑ 167 Howard Porter	.40	1.00
❑ 168 Jo Jo White	1.25	3.00
❑ 169 John Block	.20	.50
❑ 170 Dave Bing	1.50	4.00
❑ 171 Joe Ellis	.20	.50
❑ 172 Chuck Terry	.20	.50
❑ 173 Randy Smith	.40	1.00
❑ 174 Bill Bridges	.40	1.00
❑ 175 Geoff Petrie	.40	1.00
❑ 176 Wes Unseld	1.50	4.00
❑ 177 Skeeter Swift	.40	1.00
❑ 178 Jim Eakins	.60	1.50
❑ 179 Steve Jones	.60	1.50
❑ 180 George McGinnis	1.25	3.00
❑ 181 Al Smith	.40	1.00
❑ 182 Tom Washington	.40	1.00
❑ 183 Louie Dampier	.60	1.50
❑ 184 Simmie Hill	.40	1.00
❑ 185 George Thompson	.40	1.00
❑ 186 Cincy Powell	.60	1.50
❑ 187 Larry Jones	.40	1.00
❑ 188 Neil Johnson	.40	1.00
❑ 189 Tom Owens	.40	1.00
❑ 190 Ralph Simpson AS2	.60	1.50
❑ 191 George Carter	.60	1.50
❑ 192 Rick Mount	.60	1.50
❑ 193 Red Robbins	.60	1.50
❑ 194 George Lehmann	.40	1.00
❑ 195 Mel Daniels	.60	1.50
❑ 196 Bob Warren	.40	1.00
❑ 197 Gene Kennedy	.40	1.00
❑ 198 Mike Barr	.40	1.00
❑ 199 Dave Robisch	.40	1.00
❑ 200 Billy Cunningham	2.00	5.00
❑ 201 John Roche	.60	1.50
❑ 202 ABA Western Semis	.75	2.00
❑ 203 ABA Western Semis	.75	2.00
❑ 204 ABA Eastern Semis	.75	2.00
❑ 205 ABA Eastern Semis	.75	2.00
❑ 206 ABA Western Finals	.75	2.00
❑ 207 Eastern Finals/Gilmore	1.25	3.00
❑ 208 ABA Championship	.75	2.00
❑ 209 Glen Combs	.40	1.00
❑ 210 Dan Issel	2.50	6.00
❑ 211 Randy Denton	.40	1.00
❑ 212 Freddie Lewis	.60	1.50
❑ 213 Stew Johnson	.40	1.00
❑ 214 Roland Taylor	.40	1.00
❑ 215 Rich Jones	.40	1.00
❑ 216 Billy Paultz	.60	1.50
❑ 217 Ron Boone	.60	1.50
❑ 218 Walt Simon	.40	1.00
❑ 219 Mike Lewis	.40	1.00
❑ 220 Warren Jabali AS1	.60	1.50
❑ 221 Wilbert Jones	.40	1.00
❑ 222 Don Buse RC	.60	1.50
❑ 223 Gene Moore	.40	1.00
❑ 224 Joe Hamilton	.60	1.50
❑ 225 Zelmo Beaty	.60	1.50
❑ 226 Brian Taylor RC	.60	1.50
❑ 227 Julius Keye	.40	1.00
❑ 228 Mike Gale RC	.60	1.50
❑ 229 Warren Davis	.40	1.00
❑ 230 Mack Calvin	.60	1.50
❑ 231 Roger Brown	.60	1.50
❑ 232 Chuck Williams	.60	1.50
❑ 233 Gerald Govan	.60	1.50
❑ 234 Erving/McG/Issel LL	5.00	10.00
❑ 235 ABA 2 Pt. Pct.	.75	2.00
❑ 236 ABA 3 Pt. Pct.	.75	2.00
❑ 237 ABA F.T. Pct. Leaders	.75	2.00
❑ 238 Gilmore/Daniels/Paultz LL	1.25	3.00
❑ 239 ABA Assist Leaders	.75	2.00
❑ 240 Julius Erving	30.00	50.00
❑ 241 Jimmy O'Brien	.40	1.00
❑ 242 ABA Checklist 177-264	6.00	12.00
❑ 243 Johnny Neumann	.40	1.00
❑ 244 Darnell Hillman	.60	1.50
❑ 245 Willie Wise	.60	1.50
❑ 246 Collis Jones	.40	1.00
❑ 247 Ted McClain	.40	1.00
❑ 248 George Irvine RC	.40	1.00
❑ 249 Bill Melchionni	.60	1.50
❑ 250 Artis Gilmore	2.50	6.00
❑ 251 Willie Long	.40	1.00
❑ 252 Larry Miller	.40	1.00
❑ 253 Lee Davis	.40	1.00
❑ 254 Donnie Freeman	.60	1.50
❑ 255 Joe Caldwell	.60	1.50
❑ 256 Bob Netolicky	.60	1.50
❑ 257 Bernie Williams	.40	1.00
❑ 258 Byron Beck	.60	1.50
❑ 259 Jim Chones RC	1.25	3.00
❑ 260 James Jones AS1	.60	1.50
❑ 261 Wendell Ladner	.40	1.00
❑ 262 Ollie Taylor	.40	1.00
❑ 263 Les Hunter	.40	1.00
❑ 264 Billy Keller !	1.25	3.00

1974-75 Topps

❑ COMPLETE SET (264)	200.00	325.00
❑ COM. NBA CARD (1-176)	.20	.50
❑ COM. ABA CARD (177-264)	.40	1.00
❑ 1 Kareem Abdul-Jabbar !	15.00	30.00
❑ 2 Don May	.20	.50
❑ 3 Bernie Fryer RC	.40	1.00
❑ 4 Don Adams	.20	.50
❑ 5 Herm Gilliam	.20	.50
❑ 6 Jim Chones	.40	1.00
❑ 7 Rick Adelman	.40	1.00
❑ 8 Randy Smith	.40	1.00
❑ 9 Paul Silas	1.25	3.00
❑ 10 Pete Maravich	12.50	25.00
❑ 11 Ron Behagen	.20	.50
❑ 12 Kevin Porter	.40	1.00
❑ 13 Bill Bridges	.40	1.00
❑ 14 Charles Johnson RC	.20	.50
❑ 15 Bob Love	.40	1.00
❑ 16 Henry Bibby	.40	1.00
❑ 17 Neal Walk	.20	.50
❑ 18 John Brisker	.20	.50
❑ 19 Lucius Allen	.20	.50
❑ 20 Tom Van Arsdale	.40	1.00
❑ 21 Larry Steele	.20	.50
❑ 22 Curtis Rowe	.40	1.00
❑ 23 Dean Meminger	.20	.50
❑ 24 Steve Patterson	.20	.50
❑ 25 Earl Monroe	1.25	3.00
❑ 26 Jack Marin	.20	.50
❑ 27 Jo Jo White	1.25	3.00
❑ 28 Rudy Tomjanovich	2.50	6.00
❑ 29 Otto Moore	.20	.50
❑ 30 Elvin Hayes	2.00	5.00
❑ 31 Pat Riley	3.00	8.00
❑ 32 Clyde Lee	.20	.50
❑ 33 Bob Weiss	.20	.50
❑ 34 Jim Fox	.20	.50
❑ 35 Charlie Scott	.40	1.00
❑ 36 Cliff Meely	.20	.50
❑ 37 Jon McGlocklin	.20	.50
❑ 38 Jim McMillian	.40	1.00
❑ 39 Bill Walton RC	30.00	50.00
❑ 40 Dave Bing	1.25	3.00
❑ 41 Jim Washington	.20	.50
❑ 42 Jim Cleamons	.40	1.00
❑ 43 Mel Davis	.20	.50
❑ 44 Garfield Heard	.40	1.00
❑ 45 Jimmy Walker	.40	1.00
❑ 46 Don Nelson	.40	1.00
❑ 47 Jim Barnett	.20	.50
❑ 48 Manny Leaks	.20	.50
❑ 49 Elmore Smith	.40	1.00
❑ 50 Rick Barry	2.50	6.00
❑ 51 Jerry Sloan	.40	1.00
❑ 52 John Hummer	.20	.50
❑ 53 Keith Erickson	.40	1.00
❑ 54 George E. Johnson	.20	.50
❑ 55 Oscar Robertson	6.00	12.00
❑ 56 Steve Mix RC	.40	1.00
❑ 57 Rick Roberson	.20	.50
❑ 58 John Mengelt	.20	.50
❑ 59 Dwight Jones RC	.40	1.00
❑ 60 Austin Carr	.40	1.00
❑ 61 Nick Weatherspoon RC	.40	1.00
❑ 62 Clem Haskins	.40	1.00
❑ 63 Don Kojis	.20	.50
❑ 64 Paul Westphal	1.25	3.00
❑ 65 Walt Bellamy	1.50	4.00
❑ 66 John Johnson	.40	1.00
❑ 67 Butch Beard	.40	1.00
❑ 68 Happy Hairston	.40	1.00
❑ 69 Tom Boerwinkle	.20	.50
❑ 70 Spencer Haywood	1.25	3.00
❑ 71 Gary Melchionni	.20	.50
❑ 72 Ed Ratleff RC	.40	1.00
❑ 73 Mickey Davis	.20	.50
❑ 74 Dennis Awtrey	.20	.50
❑ 75 Fred Carter	.40	1.00
❑ 76 George Trapp	.20	.50
❑ 77 John Wetzel	.20	.50
❑ 78 Bobby Smith	.40	1.00
❑ 79 John Gianelli	.20	.50
❑ 80 Bob McAdoo	2.50	6.00
❑ 81 Hawks TL/Maravich/Bell	2.50	6.00
❑ 82 Celtics TL/Havlicek	2.00	5.00
❑ 83 Buffalo Braves TL	.40	1.00
❑ 84 Bulls TL/Love/Walker	1.25	3.00
❑ 85 Cleveland Cavs TL	.40	1.00
❑ 86 Detroit Pistons TL	.40	1.00
❑ 87 Warriors TL/Barry	1.25	3.00
❑ 88 Houston Rockets TL	.40	1.00
❑ 89 Kansas City Omaha TL	.40	1.00
❑ 90 Lakers TL/Goodrich	.40	1.00
❑ 91 Bucks TL/Jabbar/Oscar	6.00	12.00
❑ 92 New Orleans Jazz	.40	1.00
❑ 93 Knicks TL/Fraz/Brad/DeB	2.00	5.00
❑ 94 Philadelphia 76ers TL	.40	1.00

❑ 95 Phoenix Suns TL	.40	1.00
❑ 96 Trail Blazers TL	.40	1.00
❑ 97 Seattle Supersonics TL	.40	1.00
❑ 98 Capitol Bullets TL	.40	1.00
❑ 99 Sam Lacey	.20	.50
❑ 100 John Havlicek	5.00	10.00
❑ 101 Stu Lantz	.40	1.00
❑ 102 Mike Riordan	.20	.50
❑ 103 Larry Jones	.20	.50
❑ 104 Connie Hawkins	1.50	4.00
❑ 105 Nate Thurmond	1.25	3.00
❑ 106 Dick Gibbs	.20	.50
❑ 107 Corky Calhoun	.20	.50
❑ 108 Dave Wohl	.20	.50
❑ 109 Cornell Warner	.20	.50
❑ 110 Geoff Petrie	.40	1.00
❑ 111 Leroy Ellis	.40	1.00
❑ 112 Chris Ford	.40	1.00
❑ 113 Bill Bradley	5.00	10.00
❑ 114 Clifford Ray	.40	1.00
❑ 115 Dick Snyder	.20	.50
❑ 116 Nate Williams	.20	.50
❑ 117 Matt Guokas	.40	1.00
❑ 118 Henry Finkel	.20	.50
❑ 119 Curtis Perry	.20	.50
❑ 120 Gail Goodrich	1.25	3.00
❑ 121 Wes Unseld	1.25	3.00
❑ 122 Howard Porter	.40	1.00
❑ 123 Jeff Mullins	.20	.50
❑ 124 Mike Bantom RC	.40	1.00
❑ 125 Fred Brown	.40	1.00
❑ 126 Bob Dandridge	.40	1.00
❑ 127 Mike Newlin	.40	1.00
❑ 128 Greg Smith	.20	.50
❑ 129 Doug Collins RC	6.00	15.00
❑ 130 Lou Hudson	.40	1.00
❑ 131 Bob Lanier	2.00	5.00
❑ 132 Phil Jackson	5.00	10.00
❑ 133 Don Chaney	.40	1.00
❑ 134 Jim Brewer RC	.40	1.00
❑ 135 Ernie DiGregorio RC	1.25	3.00
❑ 136 Steve Kuberski	.20	.50
❑ 137 Jim Price	.20	.50
❑ 138 Mike D'Antoni	.20	.50
❑ 139 John Brown	.20	.50
❑ 140 Norm Van Lier	.40	1.00
❑ 141 NBA Checklist 1-176	5.00	10.00
❑ 142 Slick Watts RC	.40	1.00
❑ 143 Walt Wesley	.20	.50
❑ 144 McAd/Jabbar/Marav LL	6.00	12.00
❑ 145 McAd/Marav/Jabbar LL	6.00	12.00
❑ 146 McAd/Jabbar/Tomjan LL	5.00	10.00
❑ 147 NBA F.T. Pct. Leaders	.40	1.00
❑ 148 Hayes/Cowens/McAd LL	1.50	4.00
❑ 149 NBA Assist Leaders	.40	1.00
❑ 150 Walt Frazier	2.00	5.00
❑ 151 Cazzie Russell	.40	1.00
❑ 152 Calvin Murphy	1.25	3.00
❑ 153 Bob Kauffman	.20	.50
❑ 154 Fred Boyd	.20	.50
❑ 155 Dave Cowens	2.50	6.00
❑ 156 Willie Norwood	.20	.50
❑ 157 Lee Winfield	.20	.50
❑ 158 Dwight Davis	.20	.50
❑ 159 George T. Johnson	.20	.50
❑ 160 Dick Van Arsdale	.40	1.00
❑ 161 NBA Eastern Semis	.40	1.00
❑ 162 NBA Western Semis	.40	1.00
❑ 163 NBA Div. Finals	.40	1.00
❑ 164 NBA Championship	.60	1.50
❑ 165 Phil Chenier	.40	1.00
❑ 166 Kermit Washington RC	.40	1.00
❑ 167 Dale Schlueter	.20	.50
❑ 168 John Block	.20	.50
❑ 169 Don Smith	.20	.50
❑ 170 Nate Archibald	1.50	4.00
❑ 171 Chet Walker	.40	1.00
❑ 172 Archie Clark	.40	1.00
❑ 173 Kennedy McIntosh	.20	.50
❑ 174 George Thompson	.20	.50
❑ 175 Sidney Wicks	1.25	3.00
❑ 176 Jerry West	10.00	20.00
❑ 177 Dwight Lamar	.40	1.00
❑ 178 George Carter	.60	1.50
❑ 179 Wil Robinson	.40	1.00
❑ 180 Artis Gilmore	1.50	4.00
❑ 181 Brian Taylor	.60	1.50
❑ 182 Darnell Hillman	.60	1.50
❑ 183 Dave Robisch	.60	1.50
❑ 184 Gene Littles RC	.60	1.50
❑ 185 Willie Wise AS2	.60	1.50
❑ 186 James Silas RC	1.25	3.00
❑ 187 Caldwell Jones RC	1.25	3.00
❑ 188 Roland Taylor	.40	1.00
❑ 189 Randy Denton	.40	1.00
❑ 190 Dan Issel	2.00	5.00
❑ 191 Mike Gale	.40	1.00
❑ 192 Mel Daniels	.60	1.50
❑ 193 Steve Jones	.60	1.50
❑ 194 Marv Roberts	.40	1.00
❑ 195 Ron Boone AS2	.60	1.50
❑ 196 George Gervin RC	25.00	40.00
❑ 197 Flynn Robinson	.40	1.00
❑ 198 Cincy Powell	.60	1.50
❑ 199 Glen Combs	.40	1.00
❑ 200 Julius Erving UER	25.00	40.00
❑ 201 Billy Keller	.60	1.50
❑ 202 Willie Long	.40	1.00
❑ 203 ABA Checklist 177-264	5.00	10.00
❑ 204 Joe Caldwell	.60	1.50
❑ 205 Swen Nater RC	.60	1.50
❑ 206 Rick Mount	.60	1.50
❑ 207 Erving/McG/Issel LL	5.00	10.00
❑ 208 ABA Two-Point Field	.75	2.00
❑ 209 ABA Three-Point Field	.75	2.00
❑ 210 ABA Free Throw	.75	2.00
❑ 211 Gil/McGinn/Jones LL	.75	2.00
❑ 212 ABA Assist Leaders	.75	2.00
❑ 213 Larry Miller	.40	1.00
❑ 214 Stew Johnson	.40	1.00
❑ 215 Larry Finch RC	.60	1.50
❑ 216 Larry Kenon RC	1.25	3.00
❑ 217 Joe Hamilton	.60	1.50
❑ 218 Gerald Govan	.60	1.50
❑ 219 Ralph Simpson	.60	1.50
❑ 220 George McGinnis	1.25	3.00
❑ 221 Carolina Cougars TL	.75	2.00
❑ 222 Denver Nuggets TL	.75	2.00
❑ 223 Indiana Pacers TL	.75	2.00
❑ 224 Colonels TL/Issel	1.25	3.00
❑ 225 Memphis Sounds TL	.75	2.00
❑ 226 Nets TL/Erving	5.00	10.00
❑ 227 Spurs TL/Gervin	2.50	6.00
❑ 228 San Diego Conq. TL	.75	2.00
❑ 229 Utah Stars TL	.75	2.00
❑ 230 Virginia Squires TL	.75	2.00
❑ 231 Bird Averitt	.40	1.00
❑ 232 John Roche	.40	1.00
❑ 233 George Irvine	.40	1.00
❑ 234 John Williamson RC	.60	1.50
❑ 235 Billy Cunningham	1.50	4.00
❑ 236 Jimmy O'Brien	.40	1.00
❑ 237 Wilbert Jones	.40	1.00
❑ 238 Johnny Neumann	.40	1.00
❑ 239 Al Smith	.40	1.00
❑ 240 Roger Brown	.60	1.50
❑ 241 Chuck Williams	.60	1.50
❑ 242 Rich Jones	.40	1.00
❑ 243 Dave Twardzik RC	.60	1.50
❑ 244 Wendell Ladner	.60	1.50
❑ 245 Mack Calvin	.60	1.50
❑ 246 ABA Eastern Semis	.75	2.00
❑ 247 ABA Western Semis	.75	2.00
❑ 248 ABA Div. Finals	.75	2.00
❑ 249 ABA Championships/Dr.J.	6.00	12.00
❑ 250 Wilt Chamberlain CO	15.00	40.00
❑ 251 Ron Robinson	.40	1.00
❑ 252 Zelmo Beaty	.60	1.50
❑ 253 Donnie Freeman	.60	1.50
❑ 254 Mike Green	.40	1.00
❑ 255 Louie Dampier AS2	.60	1.50
❑ 256 Tom Owens	.40	1.00
❑ 257 George Karl RC	5.00	10.00
❑ 258 Jim Eakins	.60	1.50
❑ 259 Travis Grant	.60	1.50
❑ 260 James Jones AS1	.60	1.50
❑ 261 Mike Jackson	.40	1.00
❑ 262 Billy Paultz	.60	1.50
❑ 263 Freddie Lewis	.60	1.50
❑ 264 Byron Beck !	1.25	3.00

1975-76 Topps

❑ COMPLETE SET (330)	275.00	450.00
❑ COM. NBA CARD (1-220)	.30	.75
❑ COM. ABA CARD (221-330)	.60	1.50
❑ 1 McAd/Barry/Jabbar LL !	6.00	12.00
❑ 2 Nelson/Beard/Tomj LL	1.50	4.00
❑ 3 Barry/Murphy/Bradley LL	2.00	5.00
❑ 4 Unseld/Cowens/Lacey LL	.60	1.50
❑ 5 Porter/Bing/Arch LL	.60	1.50
❑ 6 Barry/Frazier/Steele LL	1.50	4.00
❑ 7 Tom Van Arsdale	.50	1.25
❑ 8 Paul Silas	.50	1.25
❑ 9 Jerry Sloan	.50	1.25
❑ 10 Bob McAdoo	2.50	6.00
❑ 11 Dwight Davis	.30	.75
❑ 12 John Mengelt	.30	.75
❑ 13 George Johnson	.30	.75
❑ 14 Ed Ratleff	.30	.75
❑ 15 Nate Archibald	1.50	4.00
❑ 16 Elmore Smith	.30	.75
❑ 17 Bob Dandridge	.50	1.25
❑ 18 Louie Nelson RC	.30	.75
❑ 19 Neal Walk	.30	.75
❑ 20 Billy Cunningham	1.50	4.00
❑ 21 Gary Melchionni	.30	.75
❑ 22 Barry Clemens	.30	.75
❑ 23 Jimmy Jones	.30	.75
❑ 24 Tom Burleson RC	.50	1.25
❑ 25 Lou Hudson	.50	1.25
❑ 26 Henry Finkel	.30	.75
❑ 27 Jim McMillian	.50	1.25
❑ 28 Matt Guokas	.50	1.25
❑ 29 Fred Foster DP	.30	.75
❑ 30 Bob Lanier	2.00	5.00
❑ 31 Jimmy Walker	.50	1.25
❑ 32 Cliff Meely	.30	.75
❑ 33 Butch Beard	.50	1.25
❑ 34 Cazzie Russell	.50	1.25
❑ 35 Jon McGlocklin	.30	.75
❑ 36 Bernie Fryer	.30	.75
❑ 37 Bill Bradley	5.00	10.00
❑ 38 Fred Carter	.50	1.25
❑ 39 Dennis Awtrey DP	.30	.75
❑ 40 Sidney Wicks	.50	1.25
❑ 41 Fred Brown	.50	1.25
❑ 42 Rowland Garrett	.30	.75
❑ 43 Herm Gilliam	.30	.75
❑ 44 Don Nelson	.50	1.25
❑ 45 Ernie DiGregorio	.50	1.25
❑ 46 Jim Brewer	.30	.75
❑ 47 Chris Ford	.50	1.25
❑ 48 Nick Weatherspoon	.30	.75
❑ 49 Zaid Abdul-Aziz	.30	.75
❑ 50 Keith/Jamaal Wilkes RC	5.00	10.00
❑ 51 Ollie Johnson DP	.30	.75
❑ 52 Lucius Allen	.50	1.25
❑ 53 Mickey Davis	.30	.75
❑ 54 Otto Moore	.30	.75
❑ 55 Walt Frazier	2.00	5.00
❑ 56 Steve Mix	.50	1.25
❑ 57 Nate Hawthorne	.30	.75
❑ 58 Lloyd Neal	.30	.75
❑ 59 Don Watts	.50	1.25
❑ 60 Elvin Hayes	2.00	5.00
❑ 61 Checklist 1-110	3.00	8.00
❑ 62 Mike Sojourner	.30	.75
❑ 63 Randy Smith	.50	1.25
❑ 64 John Block DP	.30	.75
❑ 65 Charlie Scott	.50	1.25
❑ 66 Jim Chones	.50	1.25
❑ 67 Rick Adelman	.50	1.25
❑ 68 Curtis Rowe	.30	.75
❑ 69 Derrek Dickey RC	.50	1.25
❑ 70 Rudy Tomjanovich	2.00	5.00
❑ 71 Pat Riley	2.50	6.00

❑ 72 Cornell Warner	.30	.75
❑ 73 Earl Monroe	1.25	3.00
❑ 74 Allan Bristow RC	1.25	3.00
❑ 75 Pete Maravich DP	12.00	20.00
❑ 76 Curtis Perry	.30	.75
❑ 77 Bill Walton	12.00	20.00
❑ 78 Leonard Gray	.30	.75
❑ 79 Kevin Porter	.50	1.25
❑ 80 John Havlicek	5.00	10.00
❑ 81 Dwight Jones	.30	.75
❑ 82 Jack Marin	.30	.75
❑ 83 Dick Snyder	.30	.75
❑ 84 George Trapp	.30	.75
❑ 85 Nate Thurmond	1.25	3.00
❑ 86 Charles Johnson	.30	.75
❑ 87 Ron Riley	.30	.75
❑ 88 Stu Lantz	.50	1.25
❑ 89 Scott Wedman RC	.50	1.25
❑ 90 Kareem Abdul-Jabbar	12.00	20.00
❑ 91 Aaron James	.30	.75
❑ 92 Jim Barnett	.30	.75
❑ 93 Clyde Lee	.30	.75
❑ 94 Larry Steele	.50	1.25
❑ 95 Mike Riordan	.30	.75
❑ 96 Archie Clark	.50	1.25
❑ 97 Mike Bantom	.30	.75
❑ 98 Bob Kauffman	.30	.75
❑ 99 Kevin Stacom RC	.30	.75
❑ 100 Rick Barry	2.50	6.00
❑ 101 Ken Charles	.30	.75
❑ 102 Tom Boerwinkle	.30	.75
❑ 103 Mike Newlin	.50	1.25
❑ 104 Leroy Ellis	.50	1.25
❑ 105 Austin Carr	.50	1.25
❑ 106 Ron Behagen	.30	.75
❑ 107 Jim Price	.30	.75
❑ 108 Bud Stallworth	.30	.75
❑ 109 Earl Williams	.30	.75
❑ 110 Gail Goodrich	1.25	3.00
❑ 111 Phil Jackson	2.50	6.00
❑ 112 Rod Derline	.30	.75
❑ 113 Keith Erickson	.30	.75
❑ 114 Phil Lumpkin	.30	.75
❑ 115 Wes Unseld	1.25	3.00
❑ 116 Atlanta Hawks TL	.60	1.50
❑ 117 Cowens/White TL	1.25	3.00
❑ 118 Buffalo Braves TL	1.25	3.00
❑ 119 Love/Walk/Thur TL	1.25	3.00
❑ 120 Cleveland Cavs TL	.60	1.50
❑ 121 Lanier/Bing TL	1.25	3.00
❑ 122 Rick Barry TL	1.25	3.00
❑ 123 Houston Rockets TL	.75	2.00
❑ 124 Kansas City Kings TL	.75	2.00
❑ 125 Los Angeles Lakers TL	.60	1.50
❑ 126 Kareem A.-Jabbar TL	3.00	8.00
❑ 127 Pete Maravich TL	5.00	10.00
❑ 128 Frazier/Bradley TL DP	1.25	3.00
❑ 129 Car/Coll/Cunn TL DP	.75	2.00
❑ 130 Phoenix Suns TL DP	.60	1.50
❑ 131 Portland Blazers TL DP	.60	1.50
❑ 132 Seattle Sonics TL	.75	2.00
❑ 133 Hayes/Unseld TL	1.25	3.00
❑ 134 John Drew RC	.50	1.25
❑ 135 Jo Jo White	.75	2.00
❑ 136 Garfield Heard	.50	1.25
❑ 137 Jim Cleamons	.30	.75
❑ 138 Howard Porter	.50	1.25
❑ 139 Phil Smith RC	.50	1.25
❑ 140 Bob Love	.50	1.25
❑ 141 John Gianelli DP	.30	.75
❑ 142 Larry McNeill RC	.30	.75
❑ 143 Brian Winters RC	1.25	3.00
❑ 144 George Thompson	.30	.75
❑ 145 Kevin Kunnert	.30	.75
❑ 146 Henry Bibby	.50	1.25
❑ 147 John Johnson	.30	.75
❑ 148 Doug Collins	1.50	4.00
❑ 149 John Brisker	.30	.75
❑ 150 Dick Van Arsdale	.50	1.25
❑ 151 Leonard Robinson RC	1.25	3.00
❑ 152 Dean Meminger	.30	.75
❑ 153 Phil Hankinson	.30	.75
❑ 154 Dale Schlueter	.30	.75
❑ 155 Norm Van Lier	.50	1.25
❑ 156 Campy Russell RC	1.25	3.00
❑ 157 Jeff Mullins	.50	1.25
❑ 158 Sam Lacey	.30	.75
❑ 159 Happy Hairston	.50	1.25
❑ 160 Dave Bing DP	1.25	3.00
❑ 161 Kevin Restani RC	.30	.75
❑ 162 Dave Wohl	.30	.75
❑ 163 E.C. Coleman	.30	.75
❑ 164 Jim Fox	.30	.75
❑ 165 Geoff Petrie	.50	1.25
❑ 166 Hawthorne Wingo DP UER	.30	.75
❑ 167 Fred Boyd	.30	.75
❑ 168 Willie Norwood	.30	.75
❑ 169 Bob Wilson	.30	.75
❑ 170 Dave Cowens	2.50	6.00
❑ 171 Tom Henderson RC	.30	.75
❑ 172 Jim Washington	.30	.75
❑ 173 Clem Haskins	.50	1.25
❑ 174 Jim Davis	.30	.75
❑ 175 Bobby Smith DP	.30	.75
❑ 176 Mike D'Antoni	.30	.75
❑ 177 Zelmo Beaty	.50	1.25
❑ 178 Gary Brokaw RC	.30	.75
❑ 179 Mel Davis	.30	.75
❑ 180 Calvin Murphy	1.25	3.00
❑ 181 Checklist 111-220 DP	3.00	8.00
❑ 182 Nate Williams	.30	.75
❑ 183 LaRue Martin	.30	.75
❑ 184 George McGinnis	1.25	3.00
❑ 185 Clifford Ray	.30	.75
❑ 186 Paul Westphal	1.50	4.00
❑ 187 Talvin Skinner	.30	.75
❑ 188 NBA Playoff Semis DP	.60	1.50
❑ 189 NBA Playoff Finals	.60	1.50
❑ 190 Phil Chenier AS2 DP	.50	1.25
❑ 191 John Brown	.30	.75
❑ 192 Lee Winfield	.30	.75
❑ 193 Steve Patterson	.30	.75
❑ 194 Charles Dudley	.30	.75
❑ 195 Connie Hawkins DP	1.25	3.00
❑ 196 Leon Benbow	.30	.75
❑ 197 Don Kojis	.30	.75
❑ 198 Ron Williams	.30	.75
❑ 199 Mel Counts	.30	.75
❑ 200 Spencer Haywood	1.25	3.00
❑ 201 Greg Jackson	.30	.75
❑ 202 Tom Kozelko DP	.30	.75
❑ 203 Atlanta Hawks	.60	1.50
❑ 204 Celtics Team CL	1.25	3.00
❑ 205 Buffalo Braves CL	.60	1.50
❑ 206 Bulls Team CL	1.25	3.00
❑ 207 Cleveland Cavs	.60	1.50
❑ 208 Detroit Pistons	.60	1.50
❑ 209 Golden State	.60	1.50
❑ 210 Houston Rockets	.60	1.50
❑ 211 Kansas City Kings DP	.60	1.50
❑ 212 Los Angeles Lakers DP	.60	1.50
❑ 213 Milwaukee Bucks	.60	1.50
❑ 214 New Orleans Jazz	.60	1.50
❑ 215 New York Knicks	.60	1.50
❑ 216 Philadelphia 76ers	.60	1.50
❑ 217 Phoenix Suns DP	.60	1.50
❑ 218 Portland Blazers	.60	1.50
❑ 219 Sonics Team/B.Russell	5.00	10.00
❑ 220 Washington Bullets	.60	1.50
❑ 221 McGin/Erving/Boone LL	3.00	8.00
❑ 222 Jones/Gilmore/Malone LL	3.00	8.00
❑ 223 ABA 3 Pt. Field Goal	.75	2.00
❑ 224 ABA Free Throw	.75	2.00
❑ 225 ABA Rebounds Leaders	.75	2.00
❑ 226 ABA Assists Leaders	.75	2.00
❑ 227 Mack Calvin	.75	2.00
❑ 228 Billy Knight RC	1.25	3.00
❑ 229 Bird Averitt	.60	1.50
❑ 230 George Carter	.60	1.50
❑ 231 Swen Nater	.75	2.00
❑ 232 Steve Jones	.75	2.00
❑ 233 George Gervin	10.00	20.00
❑ 234 Lee Davis	.60	1.50
❑ 235 Ron Boone AS1	.75	2.00
❑ 236 Mike Jackson	.60	1.50
❑ 237 Kevin Joyce RC	.60	1.50
❑ 238 Marv Roberts	.60	1.50
❑ 239 Tom Owens	.60	1.50
❑ 240 Ralph Simpson	.75	2.00
❑ 241 Gus Gerard	.60	1.50
❑ 242 Brian Taylor AS2	.75	2.00
❑ 243 Rich Jones	.60	1.50
❑ 244 John Roche	.60	1.50
❑ 245 Travis Grant	.75	2.00
❑ 246 Dave Twardzik	.75	2.00
❑ 247 Mike Green	.60	1.50
❑ 248 Billy Keller	.75	2.00
❑ 249 Stew Johnson	.60	1.50
❑ 250 Artis Gilmore	1.50	4.00
❑ 251 John Williamson	.75	2.00
❑ 252 Marvin Barnes RC	1.50	4.00
❑ 253 James Silas	.75	2.00
❑ 254 Moses Malone RC	15.00	40.00
❑ 255 Willie Wise	.75	2.00
❑ 256 Dwight Lamar	.60	1.50
❑ 257 Checklist 221-330	3.00	8.00
❑ 258 Byron Beck	.75	2.00
❑ 259 Len Elmore RC	1.25	3.00
❑ 260 Dan Issel	2.00	5.00
❑ 261 Rick Mount	.60	1.50
❑ 262 Billy Paultz	.75	2.00
❑ 263 Donnie Freeman	.60	1.50
❑ 264 George Adams	.60	1.50
❑ 265 Don Chaney	.75	2.00
❑ 266 Randy Denton	.60	1.50
❑ 267 Don Washington	.60	1.50
❑ 268 Roland Taylor	.60	1.50
❑ 269 Charlie Edge	.60	1.50
❑ 270 Louie Dampier	.75	2.00
❑ 271 Collis Jones	.60	1.50
❑ 272 Al Skinner RC	.60	1.50
❑ 273 Coby Dietrick	.60	1.50
❑ 274 Tim Bassett	.60	1.50
❑ 275 Freddie Lewis	.75	2.00
❑ 276 Gerald Govan	.60	1.50
❑ 277 Ron Thomas	.60	1.50
❑ 278 Denver Nuggets TL	.75	2.00
❑ 279 McGinnis/Keller TL	1.00	2.50
❑ 280 Gilmore/Dampier TL	1.00	2.50
❑ 281 Memphis Sounds TL	.75	2.00
❑ 282 Julius Erving TL	6.00	15.00
❑ 283 Barnes/Lewis TL	1.00	2.50
❑ 284 George Gervin TL	2.00	5.00
❑ 285 San Diego Sails TL	.75	2.00
❑ 286 Malone/Boone TL	3.00	8.00
❑ 287 Virginia Squires TL	.75	2.00
❑ 288 Claude Terry	.60	1.50
❑ 289 Wilbert Jones	.60	1.50
❑ 290 Darnell Hillman	.75	2.00
❑ 291 Bill Melchionni	.75	2.00
❑ 292 Mel Daniels	.75	2.00
❑ 293 Fly Williams RC	.75	2.00
❑ 294 Larry Kenon	.75	2.00
❑ 295 Red Robbins	.75	2.00
❑ 296 Warren Jabali	.75	2.00
❑ 297 Jim Eakins	.75	2.00
❑ 298 Bobby Jones RC	6.00	12.00
❑ 299 Don Buse	.75	2.00
❑ 300 Julius Erving	15.00	40.00
❑ 301 Billy Shepherd	.60	1.50
❑ 302 Maurice Lucas RC	2.50	6.00
❑ 303 George Karl	2.00	5.00
❑ 304 Jim Bradley	.60	1.50
❑ 305 Caldwell Jones	.75	2.00
❑ 306 Al Smith	.60	1.50
❑ 307 Jan VanBredaKolff RC	.75	2.00
❑ 308 Darrell Elston	.60	1.50
❑ 309 ABA Playoff Semifinals	.75	2.00
❑ 310 Artis Gilmore PO	1.00	2.50
❑ 311 Ted McClain	.60	1.50
❑ 312 Willie Sojourner	.60	1.50
❑ 313 Bob Warren	.60	1.50
❑ 314 Bob Netolicky	.75	2.00
❑ 315 Chuck Williams	.60	1.50
❑ 316 Gene Kennedy	.60	1.50
❑ 317 Jimmy O'Brien	.60	1.50
❑ 318 Dave Robisch	.60	1.50
❑ 319 Wali Jones	.60	1.50
❑ 320 George Irvine	.60	1.50
❑ 321 Denver Nuggets	.75	2.00
❑ 322 Indiana Pacers	.75	2.00
❑ 323 Kentucky Colonels	.75	2.00
❑ 324 Memphis Sounds	.75	2.00
❑ 325 New York Nets	.75	2.00
❑ 326 St. Louis Spirits	.75	2.00
❑ 327 San Antonio Spurs	.75	2.00
❑ 328 San Diego Sails	.75	2.00
❑ 329 Utah Stars	.75	2.00
❑ 330 Squires Checklist !	1.50	4.00

1976-77 Topps

❑ COMPLETE SET (144)	200.00	375.00
❑ 1 Julius Erving !	30.00	60.00
❑ 2 Dick Snyder	.75	2.00
❑ 3 Paul Silas	1.00	2.50
❑ 4 Keith Erickson	.75	2.00
❑ 5 Wes Unseld	2.00	5.00
❑ 6 Butch Beard	1.00	2.50
❑ 7 Lloyd Neal	.75	2.00
❑ 8 Tom Henderson	.75	2.00
❑ 9 Jim McMillian	1.00	2.50
❑ 10 Bob Lanier	2.50	6.00
❑ 11 Junior Bridgeman RC	1.00	2.50
❑ 12 Corky Calhoun	.75	2.00
❑ 13 Billy Keller	1.00	2.50
❑ 14 Mickey Johnson RC	.75	2.00
❑ 15 Fred Brown	1.00	2.50
❑ 16 Keith Wilkes	1.00	2.50
❑ 17 Louie Nelson	.75	2.00
❑ 18 Ed Ratleff	.75	2.00
❑ 19 Billy Paultz	1.00	2.50
❑ 20 Nate Archibald	2.00	5.00
❑ 21 Steve Mix	1.00	2.50
❑ 22 Ralph Simpson	.75	2.00
❑ 23 Campy Russell	1.00	2.50
❑ 24 Charlie Scott	1.00	2.50
❑ 25 Artis Gilmore	2.00	5.00
❑ 26 Dick Van Arsdale	1.00	2.50
❑ 27 Phil Chenier	1.00	2.50
❑ 28 Spencer Haywood	2.00	5.00
❑ 29 Chris Ford	1.00	2.50
❑ 30 Dave Cowens	5.00	10.00
❑ 31 Sidney Wicks	1.00	2.50
❑ 32 Jim Price	.75	2.00
❑ 33 Dwight Jones	.75	2.00
❑ 34 Lucius Allen	.75	2.00
❑ 35 Marvin Barnes	1.00	2.50
❑ 36 Henry Bibby	1.00	2.50
❑ 37 Joe C.Meriweather RC	.75	2.00
❑ 38 Doug Collins	2.50	6.00
❑ 39 Garfield Heard	1.00	2.50
❑ 40 Randy Smith	1.00	2.50
❑ 41 Tom Burleson	1.00	2.50
❑ 42 Dave Twardzik	1.00	2.50
❑ 43 Bill Bradley	6.00	12.00
❑ 44 Calvin Murphy	2.00	5.00
❑ 45 Bob Love	1.00	2.50
❑ 46 Brian Winters	1.00	2.50
❑ 47 Glenn McDonald	.75	2.00
❑ 48 Checklist 1-144	15.00	30.00
❑ 49 Bird Averitt	.75	2.00
❑ 50 Rick Barry	5.00	10.00
❑ 51 Ticky Burden	.75	2.00
❑ 52 Rich Jones	.75	2.00
❑ 53 Austin Carr	1.00	2.50
❑ 54 Steve Kuberski	.75	2.00
❑ 55 Paul Westphal	1.00	2.50
❑ 56 Mike Riordan	.75	2.00
❑ 57 Bill Walton	15.00	25.00
❑ 58 Eric Money RC	.75	2.00
❑ 59 John Drew	1.00	2.50
❑ 60 Pete Maravich	25.00	45.00
❑ 61 John Shumate RC	1.00	2.50
❑ 62 Mack Calvin	1.00	2.50
❑ 63 Bruce Seals	.75	2.00
❑ 64 Walt Frazier	2.50	6.00
❑ 65 Elmore Smith	.75	2.00
❑ 66 Rudy Tomjanovich	2.50	6.00
❑ 67 Sam Lacey	.75	2.00
❑ 68 George Gervin	15.00	25.00
❑ 69 Gus Williams RC	2.00	5.00
❑ 70 George McGinnis	1.00	2.50
❑ 71 Len Elmore	.75	2.00
❑ 72 Jack Marin	.75	2.00
❑ 73 Brian Taylor	.75	2.00
❑ 74 Jim Brewer	.75	2.00
❑ 75 Alvan Adams RC	2.50	6.00
❑ 76 Dave Bing	2.00	5.00
❑ 77 Phil Jackson	5.00	10.00
❑ 78 Geoff Petrie	1.00	2.50
❑ 79 Mike Sojourner	.75	2.00
❑ 80 James Silas	1.00	2.50
❑ 81 Bob Dandridge	1.00	2.50
❑ 82 Ernie DiGregorio	1.00	2.50
❑ 83 Cazzie Russell	1.00	2.50
❑ 84 Kevin Porter	1.00	2.50
❑ 85 Tom Boerwinkle	.75	2.00
❑ 86 Darnell Hillman	1.00	2.50
❑ 87 Herm Gilliam	.75	2.00
❑ 88 Nate Williams	.75	2.00
❑ 89 Phil Smith	1.00	2.50
❑ 90 John Havlicek	7.50	15.00
❑ 91 Kevin Kunnert	.75	2.00
❑ 92 Jimmy Walker	1.00	2.50
❑ 93 Billy Cunningham	2.00	5.00
❑ 94 Dan Issel	2.50	6.00
❑ 95 Ron Boone	1.00	2.50
❑ 96 Lou Hudson	1.00	2.50
❑ 97 Jim Chones	1.00	2.50
❑ 98 Earl Monroe	2.00	5.00
❑ 99 Tom Van Arsdale	1.00	2.50
❑ 100 Kareem Abdul-Jabbar	20.00	40.00
❑ 101 Moses Malone	12.50	25.00
❑ 102 Ricky Sobers RC	.75	2.00
❑ 103 Swen Nater	1.00	2.50
❑ 104 Leonard Robinson	1.00	2.50
❑ 105 Don Watts	1.00	2.50
❑ 106 Otto Moore	.75	2.00
❑ 107 Maurice Lucas	1.00	2.50
❑ 108 Norm Van Lier	1.00	2.50
❑ 109 Clifford Ray	.75	2.00
❑ 110 David Thompson RC	20.00	40.00
❑ 111 Fred Carter	1.00	2.50
❑ 112 Caldwell Jones	1.00	2.50
❑ 113 John Williamson	1.00	2.50
❑ 114 Bobby Smith	1.00	2.50
❑ 115 Jo Jo White	1.00	2.50
❑ 116 Curtis Perry	.75	2.00
❑ 117 John Gianelli	.75	2.00
❑ 118 Curtis Rowe	.75	2.00
❑ 119 Lionel Hollins RC	1.00	2.50
❑ 120 Elvin Hayes	2.50	6.00
❑ 121 Ken Charles	.75	2.00
❑ 122 Dave Meyers RC	1.00	2.50
❑ 123 Jerry Sloan	1.00	2.50
❑ 124 Billy Knight	1.00	2.50
❑ 125 Gail Goodrich	1.00	2.50
❑ 126 K. Abdul-Jabbar AS	12.00	20.00
❑ 127 Julius Erving AS	15.00	25.00
❑ 128 George McGinnis AS	1.00	2.50
❑ 129 Nate Archibald AS	1.00	2.50
❑ 130 Pete Maravich AS	15.00	25.00
❑ 131 Dave Cowens AS	2.00	5.00
❑ 132 Rick Barry AS	2.00	5.00
❑ 133 Elvin Hayes AS	2.00	5.00
❑ 134 James Silas AS	.75	2.00
❑ 135 Randy Smith AS	.75	2.00
❑ 136 Leonard Gray	.75	2.00
❑ 137 Charles Johnson	.75	2.00
❑ 138 Ron Behagen	.75	2.00
❑ 139 Mike Newlin	1.00	2.50
❑ 140 Bob McAdoo	2.50	6.00
❑ 141 Mike Gale	.75	2.00
❑ 142 Scott Wedman	1.00	2.50
❑ 143 Lloyd Free RC	2.50	6.00
❑ 144 Bobby Jones !	3.00	8.00

1977-78 Topps

❑ COMPLETE SET (132)	50.00	100.00
❑ 1 Kareem Abdul-Jabbar !	7.50	15.00
❑ 2 Henry Bibby	.15	.40
❑ 3 Curtis Rowe	.10	.30
❑ 4 Norm Van Lier	.15	.40
❑ 5 Darnell Hillman	.15	.40
❑ 6 Earl Monroe	.60	1.50
❑ 7 Leonard Gray	.10	.30
❑ 8 Bird Averitt	.10	.30
❑ 9 Jim Brewer	.10	.30
❑ 10 Paul Westphal	.40	1.00
❑ 11 Bob Gross RC	.15	.40
❑ 12 Phil Smith	.10	.30
❑ 13 Dan Roundfield RC	.25	.60
❑ 14 Brian Taylor	.10	.30
❑ 15 Rudy Tomjanovich	.75	2.00
❑ 16 Kevin Porter	.15	.40
❑ 17 Scott Wedman	.15	.40
❑ 18 Lloyd Free	.25	.60
❑ 19 Tom Boswell RC	.10	.30
❑ 20 Pete Maravich	7.50	15.00
❑ 21 Cliff Poindexter	.10	.30
❑ 22 Bubbles Hawkins	.15	.40
❑ 23 Kevin Grevey RC	.50	1.25
❑ 24 Ken Charles	.10	.30
❑ 25 Bob Dandridge	.15	.40
❑ 26 Lonnie Shelton RC	.15	.40
❑ 27 Don Chaney	.15	.40
❑ 28 Larry Kenon	.15	.40
❑ 29 Checklist 1-132		
❑ 30 Fred Brown	.15	.40
❑ 31 John Gianelli UER	.10	.30
❑ 32 Austin Carr	.15	.40
❑ 33 Keith/Jamaal Wilkes	.25	.60
❑ 34 Caldwell Jones	.15	.40
❑ 35 Jo Jo White	.25	.60
❑ 36 Scott May RC	.50	1.25
❑ 37 Mike Newlin	.10	.30
❑ 38 Mel Davis	.10	.30
❑ 39 Lionel Hollins	.25	.60
❑ 40 Elvin Hayes	1.00	2.50
❑ 41 Dan Issel	.75	2.00
❑ 42 Ricky Sobers	.10	.30
❑ 43 Don Ford	.10	.30
❑ 44 John Williamson	.10	.30
❑ 45 Bob McAdoo	.75	2.00
❑ 46 Geoff Petrie	.15	.40
❑ 47 M.L.Carr RC	.75	2.00
❑ 48 Brian Winters	.20	.60
❑ 49 Sam Lacey	.10	.30
❑ 50 George McGinnis	.25	.60
❑ 51 Don Watts	.15	.40
❑ 52 Sidney Wicks	.25	.60
❑ 53 Wilbur Holland	.10	.30
❑ 54 Tim Bassett	.10	.30
❑ 55 Phil Chenier	.15	.40
❑ 56 Adrian Dantley RC	3.00	8.00
❑ 57 Jim Chones	.15	.40
❑ 58 John Lucas RC	1.00	2.50
❑ 59 Cazzie Russell	.15	.40
❑ 60 David Thompson	2.00	5.00
❑ 61 Bob Lanier	.75	2.00
❑ 62 Dave Twardzik	.15	.40
❑ 63 Wilbert Jones	.10	.30
❑ 64 Clifford Ray	.10	.30
❑ 65 Doug Collins	.60	1.50
❑ 66 Tom McMillen RC	1.00	2.50
❑ 67 Rich Kelley RC	.10	.30
❑ 68 Mike Bantom	.10	.30
❑ 69 Tom Boerwinkle	.10	.30
❑ 70 John Havlicek	2.50	6.00
❑ 71 Marvin Webster RC	.15	.40
❑ 72 Curtis Perry	.10	.30
❑ 73 George Gervin	3.00	8.00
❑ 74 Leonard Robinson	.25	.60
❑ 75 Wes Unseld	.60	1.50
❑ 76 Dave Meyers	.15	.40
❑ 77 Gail Goodrich	.25	.60
❑ 78 Richard Washington RC	.25	.60
❑ 79 Mike Gale	.10	.30
❑ 80 Maurice Lucas	.25	.60
❑ 81 Harvey Catchings RC	.15	.40
❑ 82 Randy Smith	.10	.30
❑ 83 Campy Russell	.15	.40
❑ 84 Kevin Kunnert	.10	.30
❑ 85 Lou Hudson	.15	.40
❑ 86 Mickey Johnson	.10	.30
❑ 87 Lucius Allen	.10	.30
❑ 88 Spencer Haywood	.40	1.00
❑ 89 Gus Williams	.25	.60
❑ 90 Dave Cowens	1.25	3.00
❑ 91 Al Skinner	.10	.30

❑ 92 Swen Nater	.10	.30
❑ 93 Tom Henderson	.10	.30
❑ 94 Don Buse	.15	.40
❑ 95 Alvan Adams	.25	.60
❑ 96 Mack Calvin	.15	.40
❑ 97 Tom Burleson	.10	.30
❑ 98 John Drew	.15	.40
❑ 99 Mike Green	.10	.30
❑ 100 Julius Erving	7.50	15.00
❑ 101 John Mengelt	.10	.30
❑ 102 Howard Porter	.15	.40
❑ 103 Billy Paultz	.15	.40
❑ 104 John Shumate	.15	.40
❑ 105 Calvin Murphy	.60	1.50
❑ 106 Elmore Smith	.10	.30
❑ 107 Jim McMillian	.10	.30
❑ 108 Kevin Stacom	.10	.30
❑ 109 Jan Van Breda Kolff	.10	.30
❑ 110 Billy Knight	.15	.40
❑ 111 Robert Parish RC	10.00	25.00
❑ 112 Larry Wright	.10	.30
❑ 113 Bruce Seals	.10	.30
❑ 114 Junior Bridgeman	.15	.40
❑ 115 Artis Gilmore	.60	1.50
❑ 116 Steve Mix	.15	.40
❑ 117 Ron Lee	.10	.30
❑ 118 Bobby Jones	.25	.60
❑ 119 Ron Boone	.15	.40
❑ 120 Bill Walton	3.00	8.00
❑ 121 Chris Ford	.15	.40
❑ 122 Earl Tatum	.10	.30
❑ 123 E.C. Coleman	.10	.30
❑ 124 Moses Malone	2.50	6.00
❑ 125 Charlie Scott	.15	.40
❑ 126 Bobby Smith	.10	.30
❑ 127 Nate Archibald	.60	1.50
❑ 128 Mitch Kupchak RC	.50	1.25
❑ 129 Walt Frazier	1.00	2.50
❑ 130 Rick Barry	1.25	3.00
❑ 131 Ernie DiGregorio	.15	.40
❑ 132 Darryl Dawkins RC	5.00	10.00

1978-79 Topps

❑ 1 Bill Walton !	5.00	10.00
❑ 2 Doug Collins	.60	1.50
❑ 3 Jamaal Wilkes	.30	.75
❑ 4 Wilbur Holland	.10	.30
❑ 5 Bob McAdoo	.50	1.25
❑ 6 Lucius Allen	.10	.30
❑ 7 Wes Unseld	.50	1.25
❑ 8 Dave Meyers	.20	.50
❑ 9 Austin Carr	.20	.50
❑ 10 Walter Davis RC	3.00	8.00
❑ 11 John Williamson	.10	.30
❑ 12 E.C. Coleman	.10	.30
❑ 13 Calvin Murphy	.40	1.00
❑ 14 Bobby Jones	.30	.75
❑ 15 Chris Ford	.20	.50
❑ 16 Kermit Washington	.20	.50
❑ 17 Butch Beard	.20	.50
❑ 18 Steve Mix	.10	.30
❑ 19 Marvin Webster	.20	.50
❑ 20 George Gervin	2.50	6.00
❑ 21 Steve Hawes	.10	.30
❑ 22 Johnny Davis RC	.20	.50
❑ 23 Swen Nater	.10	.30
❑ 24 Lou Hudson	.20	.50
❑ 25 Elvin Hayes	.60	1.50
❑ 26 Nate Archibald	.40	1.00
❑ 27 James Edwards RC	1.25	3.00
❑ 28 Howard Porter	.20	.50
❑ 29 Quinn Buckner RC	.50	1.25
❑ 30 Leonard Robinson	.20	.50
❑ 31 Jim Cleamons	.10	.30
❑ 32 Campy Russell	.20	.50
❑ 33 Phil Smith	.10	.30
❑ 34 Darryl Dawkins	.75	2.00
❑ 35 Don Buse	.20	.50
❑ 36 Mickey Johnson	.10	.30
❑ 37 Mike Gale	.10	.30
❑ 38 Moses Malone	1.50	4.00
❑ 39 Gus Williams	.30	.75
❑ 40 Dave Cowens	.75	2.00
❑ 41 Bobby Wilkerson RC	.20	.50
❑ 42 Wilbert Jones	.10	.30
❑ 43 Charlie Scott	.20	.50
❑ 44 John Drew	.20	.50
❑ 45 Earl Monroe	.50	1.25
❑ 46 John Shumate	.20	.50
❑ 47 Earl Tatum	.10	.30
❑ 48 Mitch Kupchak	.20	.50
❑ 49 Ron Boone	.20	.50
❑ 50 Maurice Lucas	.30	.75
❑ 51 Louie Dampier	.20	.50
❑ 52 Aaron James	.10	.30
❑ 53 John Mengelt	.10	.30
❑ 54 Garfield Heard	.20	.50
❑ 55 George Johnson	.10	.30
❑ 56 Junior Bridgeman	.10	.30
❑ 57 Elmore Smith	.10	.30
❑ 58 Rudy Tomjanovich	.60	1.50
❑ 59 Fred Brown	.20	.50
❑ 60 Rick Barry	.75	2.00
❑ 61 Dave Bing	.50	1.25
❑ 62 Anthony Roberts	.10	.30
❑ 63 Norm Nixon RC	.75	2.00
❑ 64 Leon Douglas RC	.20	.50
❑ 65 Henry Bibby	.20	.50
❑ 66 Lonnie Shelton	.10	.30
❑ 67 Checklist 1-132	.75	2.00
❑ 68 Tom Henderson	.10	.30
❑ 69 Dan Roundfield	.20	.50
❑ 70 Armond Hill RC	.20	.50
❑ 71 Larry Kenon	.20	.50
❑ 72 Billy Knight	.20	.50
❑ 73 Artis Gilmore	.40	1.00
❑ 74 Lionel Hollins	.20	.50
❑ 75 Bernard King RC	3.00	8.00
❑ 76 Brian Winters	.30	.75
❑ 77 Alvan Adams	.30	.75
❑ 78 Dennis Johnson RC	3.00	8.00
❑ 79 Scott Wedman	.10	.30
❑ 80 Pete Maravich	5.00	10.00
❑ 81 Dan Issel	.60	1.50
❑ 82 M.L. Carr	.30	.75
❑ 83 Walt Frazier	.60	1.50
❑ 84 Dwight Jones	.10	.30
❑ 85 Jo Jo White	.30	.75
❑ 86 Robert Parish	2.00	5.00
❑ 87 Charlie Criss RC	.20	.50
❑ 88 Jim McMillian	.10	.30
❑ 89 Chuck Williams	.10	.30
❑ 90 George McGinnis	.30	.75
❑ 91 Billy Paultz	.20	.50
❑ 92 Bob Dandridge	.20	.50
❑ 93 Ricky Sobers	.10	.30
❑ 94 Paul Silas	.20	.50
❑ 95 Gail Goodrich	.30	.75
❑ 96 Tim Bassett	.10	.30
❑ 97 Ron Lee	.10	.30
❑ 98 Bob Gross	.20	.50
❑ 99 Sam Lacey	.10	.30
❑ 100 David Thompson	1.25	3.00
❑ 101 John Gianelli	.10	.30
❑ 102 Norm Van Lier	.20	.50
❑ 103 Caldwell Jones	.20	.50
❑ 104 Eric Money	.10	.30
❑ 105 Jim Chones	.20	.50
❑ 106 John Lucas	.40	1.00
❑ 107 Spencer Haywood	.30	.75
❑ 108 Fast Eddie Johnson RC	.10	.30
❑ 109 Sidney Wicks	.30	.75
❑ 110 Kareem Abdul-Jabbar	3.00	8.00
❑ 111 Sonny Parker RC	.20	.50
❑ 112 Randy Smith	.10	.30
❑ 113 Kevin Grevey	.20	.50
❑ 114 Rich Kelley	.10	.30
❑ 115 Scott May	.20	.50
❑ 116 Lloyd Free	.30	.75
❑ 117 Jack Sikma RC	.75	2.00
❑ 118 Kevin Porter	.20	.50
❑ 119 Darnell Hillman	.20	.50
❑ 120 Paul Westphal	.40	1.00
❑ 121 Richard Washington	.10	.30
❑ 122 Dave Twardzik	.20	.50
❑ 123 Mike Bantom	.10	.30
❑ 124 Mike Newlin	.10	.30
❑ 125 Bob Lanier	.60	1.50
❑ 126 Marques Johnson RC	1.50	4.00
❑ 127 Foots Walker RC	.20	.50
❑ 128 Cedric Maxwell RC	.50	1.25
❑ 129 Ray Williams RC	.20	.50
❑ 130 Julius Erving	5.00	10.00
❑ 131 Clifford Ray	.10	.30
❑ 132 Adrian Dantley !	1.25	3.00

1979-80 Topps

❑ COMPLETE SET (132)	40.00	80.00
❑ 1 George Gervin !	2.50	6.00
❑ 2 Mitch Kupchak	.15	.40
❑ 3 Henry Bibby	.15	.40
❑ 4 Bob Gross	.15	.40
❑ 5 Dave Cowens	.75	2.00
❑ 6 Dennis Johnson	.60	1.50
❑ 7 Scott Wedman	.10	.30
❑ 8 Earl Monroe	.50	1.25
❑ 9 Mike Bantom	.10	.30
❑ 10 Kareem Abdul-Jabbar	3.00	8.00
❑ 11 Jo Jo White	.25	.60
❑ 12 Spencer Haywood	.25	.60
❑ 13 Kevin Porter	.15	.40
❑ 14 Bernard King	.60	1.50
❑ 15 Mike Newlin	.10	.30
❑ 16 Sidney Wicks	.25	.60
❑ 17 Dan Issel	.50	1.25
❑ 18 Tom Henderson	.10	.30
❑ 19 Jim Chones	.15	.40
❑ 20 Julius Erving	5.00	10.00
❑ 21 Brian Winters	.25	.60
❑ 22 Billy Paultz	.15	.40
❑ 23 Cedric Maxwell	.15	.40
❑ 24 Eddie Johnson	.10	.30
❑ 25 Artis Gilmore	.30	.75
❑ 26 Maurice Lucas	.25	.60
❑ 27 Gus Williams	.25	.60
❑ 28 Sam Lacey	.10	.30
❑ 29 Toby Knight	.10	.30
❑ 30 Paul Westphal	.25	.60
❑ 31 Alex English RC	3.00	8.00
❑ 32 Gail Goodrich	.25	.60
❑ 33 Caldwell Jones	.15	.40
❑ 34 Kevin Grevey	.15	.40
❑ 35 Jamaal Wilkes	.25	.60
❑ 36 Sonny Parker	.10	.30
❑ 37 John Gianelli	.10	.30
❑ 38 John Long RC	.15	.40
❑ 39 George Johnson	.10	.30
❑ 40 Lloyd Free AS2	.25	.60
❑ 41 Rudy Tomjanovich	.50	1.25
❑ 42 Foots Walker	.15	.40
❑ 43 Dan Roundfield	.15	.40
❑ 44 Reggie Theus RC	1.25	3.00
❑ 45 Bill Walton	1.25	3.00
❑ 46 Fred Brown	.15	.40
❑ 47 Darnell Hillman	.15	.40
❑ 48 Ray Williams	.10	.30
❑ 49 Larry Kenon	.15	.40
❑ 50 David Thompson	.75	2.00
❑ 51 Billy Knight	.15	.40
❑ 52 Alvan Adams	.25	.60
❑ 53 Phil Smith	.10	.30
❑ 54 Adrian Dantley	.50	1.25
❑ 55 John Williamson	.10	.30
❑ 56 Campy Russell	.15	.40
❑ 57 Armond Hill	.15	.40
❑ 58 Bob Lanier	.50	1.25
❑ 59 Mickey Johnson	.10	.30
❑ 60 Pete Maravich	5.00	10.00
❑ 61 Nick Weatherspoon	.10	.30
❑ 62 Robert Reid RC	.25	.60
❑ 63 Mychal Thompson RC	.60	1.50

❑ 64 Doug Collins	.40	1.00
❑ 65 Wes Unseld	.50	1.25
❑ 66 Jack Sikma	.25	.60
❑ 67 Bobby Wilkerson	.10	.30
❑ 68 Bill Robinzine	.10	.30
❑ 69 Joe Meriweather	.10	.30
❑ 70 Marques Johnson	.15	.40
❑ 71 Ricky Sobers	.10	.30
❑ 72 Clifford Ray	.10	.30
❑ 73 Tim Bassett	.10	.30
❑ 74 James Silas	.15	.40
❑ 75 Bob McAdoo	.30	.75
❑ 76 Austin Carr	.15	.40
❑ 77 Don Ford	.10	.30
❑ 78 Steve Hawes	.10	.30
❑ 79 Ron Brewer RC	.10	.30
❑ 80 Walter Davis	.40	1.00
❑ 81 Calvin Murphy	.30	.75
❑ 82 Tom Boswell	.10	.30
❑ 83 Lonnie Shelton	.10	.30
❑ 84 Terry Tyler RC	.15	.40
❑ 85 Randy Smith	.10	.30
❑ 86 Rich Kelley	.10	.30
❑ 87 Otis Birdsong RC	.25	.60
❑ 88 Marvin Webster	.10	.30
❑ 89 Eric Money	.10	.30
❑ 90 Elvin Hayes	.60	1.50
❑ 91 Junior Bridgeman	.10	.30
❑ 92 Johnny Davis	.10	.30
❑ 93 Robert Parish	1.25	3.00
❑ 94 Eddie Jordan	.15	.40
❑ 95 Leonard Robinson	.15	.40
❑ 96 Rick Robey RC	.15	.40
❑ 97 Norm Nixon	.25	.60
❑ 98 Mark Olberding	.10	.30
❑ 99 Wilbur Holland	.10	.30
❑ 100 Moses Malone	1.25	3.00
❑ 101 Checklist 1-132	.75	2.00
❑ 102 Tom Owens	.10	.30
❑ 103 Phil Chenier	.15	.40
❑ 104 John Johnson	.10	.30
❑ 105 Darryl Dawkins	.40	1.00
❑ 106 Charlie Scott	.15	.40
❑ 107 M.L. Carr	.25	.60
❑ 108 Phil Ford RC	1.00	2.50
❑ 109 Swen Nater	.10	.30
❑ 110 Nate Archibald	.50	1.25
❑ 111 Aaron James	.10	.30
❑ 112 Jim Cleamons	.10	.30
❑ 113 James Edwards	.25	.60
❑ 114 Don Buse	.15	.40
❑ 115 Steve Mix	.10	.30
❑ 116 Charles Johnson	.10	.30
❑ 117 Elmore Smith	.10	.30
❑ 118 John Drew	.10	.30
❑ 119 Lou Hudson	.15	.40
❑ 120 Rick Barry	.75	2.00
❑ 121 Kent Benson RC	.15	.40
❑ 122 Mike Gale	.10	.30
❑ 123 Jan Van Breda Kolff	.10	.30
❑ 124 Chris Ford	.15	.40
❑ 125 George McGinnis	.25	.60
❑ 126 Leon Douglas	.10	.30
❑ 127 John Lucas	.25	.60
❑ 128 Kermit Washington	.15	.40
❑ 129 Lionel Hollins	.15	.40
❑ 130 Bob Dandridge AS2	.15	.40
❑ 131 James McElroy	.10	.30
❑ 132 Bobby Jones !	.60	1.50

1980-81 Topps

❑ COMPLETE SET (176)	300.00	500.00
❑ 1 3/Erving/258 Brewer	2.00	5.00
❑ 2 7 Malone AS/185/Parish T	.60	1.50
❑ 3 12 Gus Williams AS	.25	.60
❑ 4 24/32/248 Elvin Hayes	.40	1.00
❑ 5 29 Dan Roundfield	.25	.60
❑ 6 34 Bird RC/Erving/Magic RC	125.00	250.00
❑ 7 36 Cowens/186/Wilkes	.40	1.00
❑ 8 38 Maravich/264/194 DJ	2.50	6.00
❑ 9 40 Rick Robey	.25	.60
❑ 10 47 Scott May	.10	.30
❑ 11 55 Don Ford	.10	.30
❑ 12 58 Campy Russell	.10	.30
❑ 13 60 Foots Walker	.10	.30
❑ 14 61/Jabbar AS/200 Natt	1.25	3.00
❑ 15 63 Jim Cleamons	.10	.30
❑ 16 69 Tom LaGarde	.10	.30
❑ 17 71 Jerome Whitehead	.25	.60
❑ 18 74 John Roche TL	.10	.30
❑ 19 75 English/2/68	.50	1.25
❑ 20 82 Terry Tyler TL	.10	.30
❑ 21 84 Kent Benson	.25	.60
❑ 22 86/Parish TL/126	.60	1.50
❑ 23 88/Erving AS/Sobers	1.25	3.00
❑ 24 90 Eric Money	.10	.30
❑ 25 95 Wayne Cooper	.10	.30
❑ 26 97 Parish/187/46	.75	2.00
❑ 27 98 Sonny Parker	.10	.30
❑ 28 105 Barry/122/48	.40	1.00
❑ 29 106 Allen Leavell	.10	.30
❑ 30 108/176 Cheeks TL/87	.25	.60
❑ 31 110 Robert Reid	.25	.60
❑ 32 111 Rudy Tomjanovich	.25	.60
❑ 33 112/28 Tree Rollins/15	.10	.30
❑ 34 115 Mike Bantom	.25	.60
❑ 35 116 Dudley Bradley	.10	.30
❑ 36 118 James Edwards	.10	.30
❑ 37 119 Mickey Johnson	.10	.30
❑ 38 120 Billy Knight	.25	.60
❑ 39 121 George McGinnis	.25	.60
❑ 40 124 Phil Ford TL	.10	.30
❑ 41 127 Phil Ford	.10	.30
❑ 42 131 Scott Wedman	.25	.60
❑ 43 132 Jabbar TL/Mitch/81	1.25	3.00
❑ 44 135 Jabbar/79/216	2.00	5.00
❑ 45 137 Coop/Malone TL/148	.60	1.50
❑ 46 140/Lanier AS/Walton	.60	1.50
❑ 47 141 Norm Nixon	.25	.60
❑ 48 143/30 Bird TL/Sikma	8.00	20.00
❑ 49 146/31 Bird TL/Brewer	7.50	15.00
❑ 50 147/133 Jabbar TL/207	1.25	3.00
❑ 51 149/262 Erving SD/62	1.25	3.00
❑ 52 151 Moncrief/260/220	1.25	3.00
❑ 53 156 George Johnson	.25	.60
❑ 54 158 Maurice Lucas	.25	.60
❑ 55 159 Mike Newlin	.10	.30
❑ 56 160 Roger Phegley	.10	.30
❑ 57 161 Cliff Robinson	.10	.30
❑ 58 162 Jan V.Breda Kolff	.25	.60
❑ 59 165/214/Gilmore	.10	.30
❑ 60 166 Cartwright/244/25	.60	1.50
❑ 61 168/14/Dantley	.10	.30
❑ 62 169 Joe Meriweather	.25	.60
❑ 63 170 Monroe/27/85	.25	.60
❑ 64 172 Marvin Webster	.25	.60
❑ 65 173 Ray Williams	.10	.30
❑ 66 178 Cheeks/Magic AS/237	6.00	12.00
❑ 67 183 Bobby Jones	.40	1.00
❑ 68 189/163/Issel	.40	1.00
❑ 69 190 Don Buse	.25	.60
❑ 70 191 Davis/Gervin AS/136	.40	1.00
❑ 71 192/Malone TL/64	.40	1.00
❑ 72 201 Tom Owens	.10	.30
❑ 73 208 Gervin/Issel TL/249	.60	1.50
❑ 74 217/263/107 Malone	.60	1.50
❑ 75 219 Swen Nater	.25	.60
❑ 76 221 Brian Taylor	.10	.30
❑ 77 228 Fred Brown	.10	.30
❑ 78 230/W.Davis AS/Archibald	.40	1.00
❑ 79 231 Lonnie Shelton	.25	.60
❑ 80 233 Gus Williams	.10	.30
❑ 81 236 Allan Bristow TL	.10	.30
❑ 82 238/109/Lanier	.40	1.00
❑ 83 241 Ben Poquette	.40	1.00
❑ 84 245 Greg Ballard	.10	.30
❑ 85 246 Bob Dandridge	.25	.60
❑ 86 250 Kevin Porter	.10	.30
❑ 87 251 Unseld/195/78	.25	.60
❑ 88 257 Hayes SD/144/McAdoo	.25	.60
❑ 89 3 Dan Roundfield	.25	.60
❑ 90 7 Malone AS/247/52	.40	1.00
❑ 91 12 Gus Williams	.10	.30
❑ 92 24 Steve Hawes	.10	.30
❑ 93 29 Dan Roundfield	.10	.30
❑ 94 34 Bird/Cartwright/23	20.00	40.00
❑ 95 36 Cowens/16/59	.40	1.00
❑ 96 38 Maravich/187/46	2.00	5.00
❑ 97 40 Rick Robey	.25	.60
❑ 98 47/30 Bird TL/Sikma	7.50	15.00
❑ 99 55 Don Ford	.40	1.00
❑ 100 58 Campy Russell	.25	.60
❑ 101 60 Foots Walker	.10	.30
❑ 102 61 Austin Carr	.10	.30
❑ 103 63 Jim Cleamons	.10	.30
❑ 104 69/109/Bob Lanier	.40	1.00
❑ 105 71 Jerome Whitehead	.25	.60
❑ 106 74/28 Tree Rollins/15	.10	.30
❑ 107 75 English/Malone TL/64	.60	1.50
❑ 108 82 Terry Tyler TL	.10	.30
❑ 109 84 Kent Benson	.25	.60
❑ 110 86 Phil Hubbard	.10	.30
❑ 111 88/18 Magic AS/237	4.00	10.00
❑ 112 90 Eric Money	.10	.30
❑ 113 95 Wayne Cooper	.10	.30
❑ 114 97 Parish/Malone TL/148	.75	2.00
❑ 115 98 Sonny Parker	.25	.60
❑ 116 105 Barry/123/54	.40	1.00
❑ 117 106 Allen Leavell	.10	.30
❑ 118 108 Calvin Murphy	.25	.60
❑ 119 110 Robert Reid	.25	.60
❑ 120 111 Rudy Tomjanovich	.40	1.00
❑ 121 112/264/D.Johnson	.40	1.00
❑ 122 115 Mike Bantom	.25	.60
❑ 123 116 Dudley Bradley	.40	1.00
❑ 124 118/Archibald TL/Hayes	.50	1.25
❑ 125 119 Mickey Johnson	.40	1.00
❑ 126 120 Billy Knight	.10	.30
❑ 127 121/Lanier AS/Walton	.60	1.50
❑ 128 124 Phil Ford TL	.25	.60
❑ 129 127 Phil Ford	.25	.60
❑ 130 131 Scott Wedman	.10	.30
❑ 131 132 Jabbar TL/Par.TL/126	1.50	4.00
❑ 132 135 Jabbar/253/167	2.00	5.00
❑ 133 137 M.Cooper/212/229	.40	1.00
❑ 134 140/214/Gilmore	.25	.60
❑ 135 141 Norm Nixon	.25	.60
❑ 136 143 Marq.Johnson TL	.10	.30
❑ 137 146/Erving AS/Sobers	1.25	3.00
❑ 138 147 Quinn Buckner	.25	.60
❑ 139 149 Marques Johnson	.10	.30
❑ 140 151 Moncrief/Jabb.TL/207	1.50	4.00
❑ 141 156 George Johnson	.10	.30
❑ 142 158/262 Erving SD/62	1.25	3.00
❑ 143 159 Mike Newlin	.25	.60
❑ 144 160 Roger Phegley	.10	.30
❑ 145 161 Cliff Robinson	.10	.30
❑ 146 162/Erving SD/139 Magic	15.00	40.00
❑ 147 165/185/Parish TL	.40	1.00
❑ 148 166 Cartwright/13/179	.40	1.00
❑ 149 168 Toby Knight	.25	.60
❑ 150 169 Joe Meriweather	.10	.30
❑ 151 170 Monroe/206/91	.10	.30
❑ 152 172 Marvin Webster	.25	.60
❑ 153 173 Ray Williams	.10	.30
❑ 154 178 Cheeks/Gervin AS/136	1.50	4.00
❑ 155 183 Bobby Jones	.25	.60
❑ 156 189/14/Dantley	.25	.60
❑ 157 190 Don Buse	.25	.60
❑ 158 191 Walter Davis	.25	.60
❑ 159 192/263/107 Malone	.60	1.50
❑ 160 201 Tom Owens	.25	.60
❑ 161 208 Gervin/53/223	.60	1.50
❑ 162 217/8 Jabbar AS/Natt	1.25	3.00
❑ 163 219 Swen Nater	.10	.30
❑ 164 221 Brian Taylor	.10	.30
❑ 165 228/31 Bird TL/Brewer	7.50	15.00
❑ 166 230/163/Issel	.40	1.00
❑ 167 231 Lonnie Shelton	.10	.30
❑ 168 233 Gus Williams	.25	.60
❑ 169 236 Allan Bristow TL	.10	.30
❑ 170 238 Tom Boswell	.10	.30
❑ 171 241/Cheeks TL/87	.40	1.00
❑ 172 245/W.Davis AS/Archibald	.40	1.00
❑ 173 246 Bob Dandridge	.10	.30
❑ 174 250 Kevin Porter	.10	.30
❑ 175 251 Unseld/67/5	.40	1.00
❑ 176 257 Hayes SD/Erving/258	2.00	5.00

1981-82 Topps

❑ COMPLETE SET (198)	40.00	80.00
❑ COMMON CARD (1-66)	.02	.10
❑ COMMON CARD (E67-E110)	.05	.15
❑ COMMON CARD (MW67-MW110)	.05	.15
❑ COMMON CARD (W67-W110)	.05	.15
❑ TL (44-66)	.05	.15
❑ 1 John Drew	.07	.20
❑ 2 Dan Roundfield	.07	.20
❑ 3 Nate Archibald	.25	.60
❑ 4 Larry Bird !	6.00	15.00
❑ 5 Cedric Maxwell	.07	.20
❑ 6 Robert Parish	.60	1.50
❑ 7 Artis Gilmore	.25	.60
❑ 8 Ricky Sobers	.02	.10
❑ 9 Mike Mitchell	.07	.20
❑ 10 Tom LaGarde	.02	.10
❑ 11 Dan Issel	.30	.75
❑ 12 David Thompson	.30	.75
❑ 13 Lloyd Free	.08	.25
❑ 14 Moses Malone	.60	1.50
❑ 15 Calvin Murphy	.08	.25
❑ 16 Johnny Davis	.02	.10
❑ 17 Otis Birdsong	.08	.25
❑ 18 Phil Ford	.07	.20
❑ 19 Scott Wedman	.02	.10
❑ 20 Kareem Abdul-Jabbar	1.50	4.00
❑ 21 Magic Johnson !	4.00	10.00
❑ 22 Norm Nixon	.08	.25
❑ 23 Jamaal Wilkes	.08	.25
❑ 24 Marques Johnson	.08	.25
❑ 25 Bob Lanier	.30	.75
❑ 26 Bill Cartwright	.20	.50
❑ 27 Michael Ray Richardson	.07	.20
❑ 28 Ray Williams	.07	.20
❑ 29 Darryl Dawkins	.08	.25
❑ 30 Julius Erving	1.50	4.00
❑ 31 Lionel Hollins	.02	.10
❑ 32 Bobby Jones	.08	.25
❑ 33 Walter Davis	.20	.50
❑ 34 Dennis Johnson	.20	.50
❑ 35 Leonard Robinson	.08	.25
❑ 36 Mychal Thompson	.08	.25
❑ 37 George Gervin	.75	2.00
❑ 38 Swen Nater	.02	.10
❑ 39 Jack Sikma	.08	.25
❑ 40 Adrian Dantley	.25	.60
❑ 41 Darrell Griffith RC	.40	1.00
❑ 42 Elvin Hayes	.30	.75
❑ 43 Fred Brown	.08	.25
❑ 44 Atlanta Hawks TL	.05	.15
❑ 45 Celtics TL/Bird/Arch	.75	2.00
❑ 46 Chicago Bulls TL	.08	.25
❑ 47 Cleveland Cavs TL	.05	.15
❑ 48 Dallas Mavericks TL	.05	.15
❑ 49 Denver Nuggets TL	.08	.25
❑ 50 Detroit Pistons TL	.05	.15
❑ 51 Golden State TL	.08	.25
❑ 52 Rockets TL/Malone	.15	.40
❑ 53 Indiana Pacers TL	.08	.25
❑ 54 Kansas City Kings TL	.05	.15
❑ 55 Lakers TL/Jabbar	.50	1.25
❑ 56 Milwaukee Bucks TL	.08	.25
❑ 57 New Jersey Nets TL	.05	.15
❑ 58 New York Knicks TL	.08	.25
❑ 59 76ers TL/Erving	.50	1.25
❑ 60 Phoenix Suns TL	.08	.25
❑ 61 Trail Blazers TL	.05	.15
❑ 62 San Antonio Spurs TL	.08	.25
❑ 63 San Diego Clippers TL	.05	.15
❑ 64 Seattle Sonics TL	.08	.25
❑ 65 Utah Jazz TL	.08	.25
❑ 66 Washington Bullets TL	.08	.25
❑ E67 Charlie Criss	.08	.25
❑ E68 Eddie Johnson	.05	.15
❑ E69 Wes Matthews	.05	.15
❑ E70 Tom McMillen	.15	.40
❑ E71 Tree Rollins	.15	.40
❑ E72 M.L. Carr	.08	.25
❑ E73 Chris Ford	.08	.25
❑ E74 Gerald Henderson RC	.15	.40
❑ E75 Kevin McHale RC	8.00	20.00
❑ E76 Rick Robey	.08	.25
❑ E77 Darwin Cook RC	.05	.15
❑ E78 Mike Gminski RC	.30	.75
❑ E79 Maurice Lucas	.08	.25
❑ E80 Mike Newlin	.08	.25
❑ E81 Mike O'Koren RC	.08	.25
❑ E82 Steve Hawes	.05	.15
❑ E83 Foots Walker	.08	.25
❑ E84 Campy Russell	.08	.25
❑ E85 DeWayne Scales	.05	.15
❑ E86 Randy Smith	.08	.25
❑ E87 Marvin Webster	.08	.25
❑ E88 Sly Williams	.05	.15
❑ E89 Mike Woodson RC	.08	.25
❑ E90 Maurice Cheeks	.60	1.50
❑ E91 Caldwell Jones	.08	.25
❑ E92 Steve Mix	.08	.25
❑ E93A Checklist 1-110 ERR	.75	2.00
❑ E93B Checklist 1-110 COR		
❑ E94 Greg Ballard	.05	.15
❑ E95 Don Collins	.05	.15
❑ E96 Kevin Grevey	.08	.25
❑ E97 Mitch Kupchak	.08	.25
❑ E98 Rick Mahorn RC	.30	.75
❑ E99 Kevin Porter	.08	.25
❑ E100 Nate Archibald SA	.08	.25
❑ E101 Larry Bird SA	5.00	12.00
❑ E102 Bill Cartwright SA	.05	.15
❑ E103 Darryl Dawkins SA	.08	.25
❑ E104 Julius Erving SA	.75	2.00
❑ E105 Kevin Porter SA	.08	.25
❑ E106 Bobby Jones SA	.08	.25
❑ E107 Cedric Maxwell SA	.08	.25
❑ E108 Robert Parish SA	.40	1.00
❑ E109 M.R.Richardson SA	.08	.25
❑ E110 Dan Roundfield SA	.08	.25
❑ W67 T.R.Dunn RC	.05	.15
❑ W68 Alex English	.60	1.50
❑ W69 Billy McKinney RC	.08	.25
❑ W70 Dave Robisch	.08	.25
❑ W71 Joe Barry Carroll RC	.15	.40
❑ W72 Bernard King	.40	1.00
❑ W73 Sonny Parker	.05	.15
❑ W74 Purvis Short	.08	.25
❑ W75 Larry Smith RC	.15	.40
❑ W76 Jim Chones	.08	.25
❑ W77 Michael Cooper	.30	.75
❑ W78 Mark Landsberger	.05	.15
❑ W79 Alvan Adams	.08	.25
❑ W80 Jeff Cook	.05	.15
❑ W81 Rich Kelley	.05	.15
❑ W82 Kyle Macy RC	.15	.40
❑ W83 Billy Ray Bates RC	.15	.40
❑ W84 Bob Gross	.08	.25
❑ W85 Calvin Natt	.08	.25
❑ W86 Lonnie Shelton	.08	.25
❑ W87 Jim Paxson RC	.30	.75
❑ W88 Kelvin Ransey	.05	.15
❑ W89 Kermit Washington	.08	.25
❑ W90 Henry Bibby	.08	.25
❑ W91 Michael Brooks RC	.05	.15
❑ W92 Joe Bryant	.05	.15
❑ W93 Phil Smith	.05	.15
❑ W94 Brian Taylor	.05	.15
❑ W95 Freeman Williams	.08	.25
❑ W96 James Bailey	.05	.15
❑ W97 Checklist 1-110		
❑ W98 John Johnson	.05	.15
❑ W99 Vinnie Johnson RC	.60	1.50
❑ W100 Wally Walker RC	.08	.25
❑ W101 Paul Westphal	.08	.25
❑ W102 Allan Bristow	.08	.25
❑ W103 Wayne Cooper	.05	.15
❑ W104 Carl Nicks	.05	.15
❑ W105 Ben Poquette	.05	.15
❑ W106 Kar.Abdul-Jabbar SA	.75	2.00
❑ W107 Dan Issel SA	.20	.50
❑ W108 Dennis Johnson SA	.08	.25
❑ W109 Magic Johnson SA !	3.00	8.00
❑ W110 Jack Sikma SA	.08	.25
❑ MW67 David Greenwood	.08	.25
❑ MW68 Dwight Jones	.05	.15
❑ MW69 Reggie Theus	.08	.25
❑ MW70 Bobby Wilkerson	.05	.15
❑ MW71 Mike Bratz	.05	.15
❑ MW72 Kenny Carr	.05	.15
❑ MW73 Geoff Huston	.05	.15
❑ MW74 Bill Laimbeer RC	1.25	3.00
❑ MW75 Roger Phegley	.05	.15
❑ MW76 Checklist 1-110		
❑ MW77 Abdul Jeelani	.05	.15
❑ MW78 Bill Robinzine	.05	.15
❑ MW79 Jim Spanarkel	.05	.15
❑ MW80 Kent Benson	.08	.25
❑ MW81 Keith Herron	.05	.15
❑ MW82 Phil Hubbard	.05	.15
❑ MW83 John Long	.05	.15
❑ MW84 Terry Tyler	.05	.15
❑ MW85 Mike Dunleavy RC	.30	.75
❑ MW86 Tom Henderson	.05	.15
❑ MW87 Billy Paultz	.08	.25
❑ MW88 Robert Reid	.05	.15
❑ MW89 Mike Bantom	.05	.15
❑ MW90 James Edwards	.08	.25
❑ MW91 Billy Knight	.08	.25
❑ MW92 George McGinnis	.08	.25
❑ MW93 Louis Orr	.05	.15
❑ MW94 Ernie Grunfeld RC	.15	.40
❑ MW95 Reggie King	.05	.15
❑ MW96 Sam Lacey	.05	.15
❑ MW97 Junior Bridgeman	.08	.25
❑ MW98 Mickey Johnson	.08	.25
❑ MW99 Sidney Moncrief	.30	.75
❑ MW100 Brian Winters	.08	.25
❑ MW101 Dave Corzine RC	.05	.15
❑ MW102 Paul Griffin	.05	.15
❑ MW103 Johnny Moore RC	.08	.25
❑ MW104 Mark Olberding	.05	.15
❑ MW105 James Silas	.08	.25
❑ MW106 George Gervin SA	.30	.75
❑ MW107 Artis Gilmore SA	.08	.25
❑ MW108 Marques Johnson SA	.08	.25
❑ MW109 Bob Lanier SA	.20	.50
❑ MW110 Moses Malone SA	.40	1.00

1992-93 Topps

❑ COMPLETE SET (396)	6.00	15.00
❑ COMPLETE FACT. SET (408)	8.00	20.00
❑ COMPLETE SERIES 1 (198)	2.00	4.00
❑ COMPLETE SERIES 2 (198)	5.00	12.00
❑ 1 Larry Bird	.25	.60
❑ 2 Magic Johnson HL	.08	.25
❑ 3 Michael Jordan HL	.40	1.00
❑ 4 David Robinson HL	.05	.15
❑ 5 Johnny Newman	.02	.10
❑ 6 Mike Iuzzolino	.02	.10
❑ 7 Ken Norman	.02	.10
❑ 8 Chris Jackson	.02	.10
❑ 9 Duane Ferrell	.02	.10
❑ 10 Sean Elliott	.02	.10
❑ 11 Bernard King	.02	.10
❑ 12 Armon Gilliam	.02	.10
❑ 13 Reggie Williams	.02	.10
❑ 14 Steve Kerr	.02	.10
❑ 15 Anthony Bowie	.02	.10
❑ 16 Alton Lister	.02	.10
❑ 17 Dee Brown	.02	.10
❑ 18 Tom Chambers	.02	.10
❑ 19 Otis Thorpe	.02	.10
❑ 20 Karl Malone	.08	.25
❑ 21 Kenny Gattison	.02	.10
❑ 22 Lionel Simmons UER	.02	.10
❑ 23 Vern Fleming	.02	.10
❑ 24 John Paxson	.02	.10
❑ 25 Mitch Richmond	.05	.15
❑ 26 Danny Schayes	.02	.10
❑ 27 Derrick McKey	.02	.10
❑ 28 Mark Randall	.02	.10

❑ 29 Bill Laimbeer	.02	.10
❑ 30 Chris Morris	.02	.10
❑ 31 Alec Kessler	.02	.10
❑ 32 Vlade Divac	.02	.10
❑ 33 Rick Fox	.02	.10
❑ 34 Charles Shackleford	.02	.10
❑ 35 Dominique Wilkins	.05	.15
❑ 36 Sleepy Floyd	.02	.10
❑ 37 Doug West	.02	.10
❑ 38 Pete Chilcutt	.02	.10
❑ 39 Orlando Woolridge	.02	.10
❑ 40 Eric Leckner	.02	.10
❑ 41 Joe Kleine	.02	.10
❑ 42 Scott Skiles	.02	.10
❑ 43 Jerrod Mustaf	.02	.10
❑ 44 John Starks	.02	.10
❑ 45 Sedale Threatt	.02	.10
❑ 46 Doug Smith	.02	.10
❑ 47 Byron Scott	.02	.10
❑ 48 Willie Anderson	.02	.10
❑ 49 David Benoit	.02	.10
❑ 50 Scott Hastings	.02	.10
❑ 51 Terry Porter	.02	.10
❑ 52 Sidney Green	.02	.10
❑ 53 Danny Young	.02	.10
❑ 54 Magic Johnson	.20	.50
❑ 55 Brian Williams	.02	.10
❑ 56 Randy Wittman	.02	.10
❑ 57 Kevin McHale	.05	.15
❑ 58 Dana Barros	.02	.10
❑ 59 Thurl Bailey	.02	.10
❑ 60 Kevin Duckworth	.02	.10
❑ 61 John Williams	.02	.10
❑ 62 Willie Burton	.02	.10
❑ 63 Spud Webb	.02	.10
❑ 64 Detlef Schrempf	.02	.10
❑ 65 Sherman Douglas	.02	.10
❑ 66 Patrick Ewing	.05	.15
❑ 67 Michael Adams	.02	.10
❑ 68 Vernon Maxwell	.02	.10
❑ 69 Terrell Brandon	.05	.15
❑ 70 Terry Catledge	.02	.10
❑ 71 Mark Eaton	.02	.10
❑ 72 Tony Smith	.02	.10
❑ 73 B.J. Armstrong	.02	.10
❑ 74 Moses Malone	.05	.15
❑ 75 Anthony Bonner	.02	.10
❑ 76 George McCloud	.02	.10
❑ 77 Glen Rice	.05	.15
❑ 78 Jon Koncak	.02	.10
❑ 79 Michael Cage	.02	.10
❑ 80 Ron Harper	.02	.10
❑ 81 Tom Tolbert	.02	.10
❑ 82 Brad Sellers	.02	.10
❑ 83 Winston Garland	.02	.10
❑ 84 Negele Knight	.02	.10
❑ 85 Ricky Pierce	.02	.10
❑ 86 Mark Aguirre	.02	.10
❑ 87 Ron Anderson	.02	.10
❑ 88 Loy Vaught	.02	.10
❑ 89 Luc Longley	.02	.10
❑ 90 Jerry Reynolds	.02	.10
❑ 91 Terry Cummings	.02	.10
❑ 92 Rony Seikaly	.02	.10
❑ 93 Derek Harper	.02	.10
❑ 94 Cliff Robinson	.02	.10
❑ 95 Kenny Anderson	.05	.15
❑ 96 Chris Gatling	.02	.10
❑ 97 Stacey Augmon	.02	.10
❑ 98 Chris Corchiani	.02	.10
❑ 99 Pervis Ellison	.02	.10
❑ 100 Larry Bird AS	.10	.30
❑ 101 John Stockton AS	.02	.10
❑ 102 Clyde Drexler AS	.02	.10
❑ 103 Scottie Pippen AS	.08	.25
❑ 104 Reggie Lewis AS	.02	.10
❑ 105 Hakeem Olajuwon AS	.05	.15
❑ 106 David Robinson AS	.05	.15
❑ 107 Charles Barkley AS	.05	.15
❑ 108 James Worthy AS	.02	.10
❑ 109 Kevin Willis AS	.02	.10
❑ 110 Dikembe Mutombo AS	.05	.15
❑ 111 Joe Dumars AS	.02	.10
❑ 112 Jeff Hornacek AS UER	.02	.10
❑ 113 Mark Price AS	.02	.10
❑ 114 Michael Adams AS	.02	.10
❑ 115 Michael Jordan AS	.40	1.00
❑ 116 Brad Daugherty AS	.02	.10
❑ 117 Dennis Rodman AS	.05	.15
❑ 118 Isiah Thomas AS	.02	.10
❑ 119 Tim Hardaway AS	.05	.15
❑ 120 Chris Mullin AS	.02	.10
❑ 121 Patrick Ewing AS	.02	.10
❑ 122 Dan Majerle AS	.02	.10
❑ 123 Karl Malone AS	.05	.15
❑ 124 Otis Thorpe AS	.02	.10
❑ 125 Dominique Wilkins AS	.02	.10
❑ 126 Magic Johnson AS	.08	.25
❑ 127 Charles Oakley	.02	.10
❑ 128 Robert Pack	.02	.10
❑ 129 Billy Owens	.02	.10
❑ 130 Jeff Malone	.02	.10
❑ 131 Danny Ferry	.02	.10
❑ 132 Sam Bowie	.02	.10
❑ 133 Avery Johnson	.02	.10
❑ 134 Jayson Williams	.02	.10
❑ 135 Fred Roberts	.02	.10
❑ 136 Greg Sutton	.02	.10
❑ 137 Dennis Rodman	.10	.30
❑ 138 John Williams	.02	.10
❑ 139 Greg Dreiling	.02	.10
❑ 140 Rik Smits	.02	.10
❑ 141 Michael Jordan	.75	2.00
❑ 142 Nick Anderson	.02	.10
❑ 143 Jerome Kersey	.02	.10
❑ 144 Fat Lever	.02	.10
❑ 145 Tyrone Corbin	.02	.10
❑ 146 Robert Parish	.02	.10
❑ 147 Steve Smith	.07	.20
❑ 148 Chris Dudley	.02	.10
❑ 149 Antoine Carr	.02	.10
❑ 150 Elden Campbell	.02	.10
❑ 151 Randy White	.02	.10
❑ 152 Felton Spencer	.02	.10
❑ 153 Cedric Ceballos	.02	.10
❑ 154 Mark Macon	.02	.10
❑ 155 Jack Haley	.02	.10
❑ 156 Bimbo Coles	.02	.10
❑ 157 A.J. English	.02	.10
❑ 158 Kendall Gill	.02	.10
❑ 159 A.C. Green	.02	.10
❑ 160 Mark West	.02	.10
❑ 161 Benoit Benjamin	.02	.10
❑ 162 Tyrone Hill	.02	.10
❑ 163 Larry Nance	.02	.10
❑ 164 Gary Grant	.02	.10
❑ 165 Bill Cartwright	.02	.10
❑ 166 Greg Anthony	.02	.10
❑ 167 Jim Les	.02	.10
❑ 168 Johnny Dawkins	.02	.10
❑ 169 Alvin Robertson	.02	.10
❑ 170 Kenny Smith	.02	.10
❑ 171 Gerald Glass	.02	.10
❑ 172 Harvey Grant	.02	.10
❑ 173 Paul Graham	.02	.10
❑ 174 Sam Perkins	.02	.10
❑ 175 Manute Bol	.02	.10
❑ 176 Muggsy Bogues	.02	.10
❑ 177 Mike Brown	.02	.10
❑ 178 Donald Hodge	.02	.10
❑ 179 Dave Jamerson	.02	.10
❑ 180 Mookie Blaylock	.02	.10
❑ 181 Randy Brown	.02	.10
❑ 182 Todd Lichti	.02	.10
❑ 183 Kevin Gamble	.02	.10
❑ 184 Gary Payton	.10	.30
❑ 185 Brian Shaw	.02	.10
❑ 186 Grant Long	.02	.10
❑ 187 Frank Brickowski	.02	.10
❑ 188 Tim Hardaway	.07	.20
❑ 189 Danny Manning	.02	.10
❑ 190 Kevin Johnson	.05	.15
❑ 191 Craig Ehlo	.02	.10
❑ 192 Dennis Scott	.02	.10
❑ 193 Reggie Miller	.05	.15
❑ 194 Darrell Walker	.02	.10
❑ 195 Anthony Mason	.05	.15
❑ 196 Buck Williams	.02	.10
❑ 197 Checklist 1-99	.02	.10
❑ 198 Checklist 100-198	.02	.10
❑ 199 Karl Malone 50P	.05	.15
❑ 200 Dominique Wilkins 50P	.02	.10
❑ 201 Tom Chambers 50P	.02	.10
❑ 202 Bernard King 50P	.02	.10
❑ 203 Kiki Vandeweghe 50P	.02	.10
❑ 204 Dale Ellis 50P	.02	.10
❑ 205 Michael Jordan 50P	.40	1.00
❑ 206 Michael Adams 50P	.02	.10
❑ 207 Charles Smith 50P	.02	.10
❑ 208 Moses Malone 50P	.02	.10
❑ 209 Terry Cummings 50P	.02	.10
❑ 210 Vernon Maxwell 50P	.02	.10
❑ 211 Patrick Ewing 50P	.02	.10
❑ 212 Clyde Drexler 50P	.02	.10
❑ 213 Kevin McHale 50P	.02	.10
❑ 214 Hakeem Olajuwon 50P	.05	.15
❑ 215 Reggie Miller 50P	.02	.10
❑ 216 Gary Grant 20A	.02	.10
❑ 217 Doc Rivers 20A	.02	.10
❑ 218 Mark Price 20A	.02	.10
❑ 219 Isiah Thomas 20A	.02	.10
❑ 220 Nate McMillan 20A	.02	.10
❑ 221 Fat Lever 20A	.02	.10
❑ 222 Kevin Johnson 20A	.02	.10
❑ 223 John Stockton 20A	.02	.10
❑ 224 Scott Skiles 20A	.02	.10
❑ 225 Kevin Brooks	.02	.10
❑ 226 Bobby Phills RC	.05	.15
❑ 227 Oliver Miller RC	.02	.10
❑ 228 John Williams	.02	.10
❑ 229 Brad Lohaus	.02	.10
❑ 230 Derrick Coleman	.02	.10
❑ 231 Ed Pinckney	.02	.10
❑ 232 Trent Tucker	.02	.10
❑ 233 Lance Blanks	.02	.10
❑ 234 Drazen Petrovic	.02	.10
❑ 235 Mark Bryant	.02	.10
❑ 236 Lloyd Daniels RC	.02	.10
❑ 237 Dale Davis	.02	.10
❑ 238 Jayson Williams	.02	.10
❑ 239 Mike Sanders	.02	.10
❑ 240 Mike Gminski	.02	.10
❑ 241 William Bedford	.02	.10
❑ 242 Dell Curry	.02	.10
❑ 243 Gerald Paddio	.02	.10
❑ 244 Chris Smith RC	.02	.10
❑ 245 Jud Buechler	.02	.10
❑ 246 Walter Palmer	.02	.10
❑ 247 Larry Krystkowiak	.02	.10
❑ 248 Marcus Liberty	.02	.10
❑ 249 Sam Mitchell	.02	.10
❑ 250 Kiki Vandeweghe	.02	.10
❑ 251 Vincent Askew	.02	.10
❑ 252 Travis Mays	.02	.10
❑ 253 Charles Smith	.02	.10
❑ 254 John Bagley	.02	.10
❑ 255 James Worthy	.05	.15
❑ 256 Paul Pressey P/CO	.02	.10
❑ 257 Rumeal Robinson	.02	.10
❑ 258 Tom Gugliotta RC	.20	.50
❑ 259 Eric Anderson RC	.02	.10
❑ 260 Hersey Hawkins	.02	.10
❑ 261 Terry Davis	.02	.10
❑ 262 Rex Chapman	.02	.10
❑ 263 Chucky Brown	.02	.10
❑ 264 Danny Young	.02	.10
❑ 265 Olden Polynice	.02	.10
❑ 266 Kevin Willis	.02	.10
❑ 267 Shawn Kemp	.10	.30
❑ 268 Mookie Blaylock	.02	.10
❑ 269 Malik Sealy RC	.02	.10
❑ 270 Charles Barkley	.08	.25
❑ 271 Corey Williams RC	.02	.10
❑ 272 Stephen Howard RC	.02	.10
❑ 273 Keith Askins	.02	.10
❑ 274 Matt Bullard	.02	.10
❑ 275 John Battle	.02	.10
❑ 276 Andrew Lang	.02	.10
❑ 277 David Robinson	.08	.25
❑ 278 Harold Miner RC	.02	.10
❑ 279 Tracy Murray RC	.02	.10
❑ 280 Pooh Richardson	.02	.10
❑ 281 Dikembe Mutombo	.07	.20
❑ 282 Wayman Tisdale	.02	.10
❑ 283 Larry Johnson	.07	.20
❑ 284 Todd Day RC	.02	.10
❑ 285 Stanley Roberts	.02	.10
❑ 286 Randy Woods UER RC	.02	.10
❑ 287 Avery Johnson	.02	.10
❑ 288 Anthony Peeler RC	.02	.10
❑ 289 Mario Elie	.02	.10
❑ 290 Doc Rivers	.02	.10
❑ 291 Blue Edwards	.02	.10
❑ 292 Sean Rooks RC	.02	.10
❑ 293 Xavier McDaniel	.02	.10
❑ 294 C.Weatherspoon RC	.05	.15
❑ 295 Morlon Wiley	.02	.10

❑ 296 LaBradford Smith	.02	.10
❑ 297 Reggie Lewis	.02	.10
❑ 298 Chris Mullin	.05	.15
❑ 299 Litterial Green RC	.02	.10
❑ 300 Elmore Spencer RC	.02	.10
❑ 301 John Stockton	.05	.15
❑ 302 Walt Williams RC	.05	.15
❑ 303 Anthony Pullard RC	.02	.10
❑ 304 Gundars Vetra RC	.02	.10
❑ 305 LaSalle Thompson	.02	.10
❑ 306 Nate McMillan	.02	.10
❑ 307 Steve Bardo RC	.02	.10
❑ 308 Robert Horry RC	.05	.15
❑ 309 Scott Williams	.02	.10
❑ 310 Bo Kimble	.02	.10
❑ 311 Tree Rollins	.02	.10
❑ 312 Tim Perry	.02	.10
❑ 313 Isaac Austin RC	.02	.10
❑ 314 Tate George	.02	.10
❑ 315 Kevin Lynch	.02	.10
❑ 316 Victor Alexander	.02	.10
❑ 317 Doug Overton	.02	.10
❑ 318 Tom Hammonds	.02	.10
❑ 319 LaPhonso Ellis RC	.05	.15
❑ 320 Scott Brooks	.02	.10
❑ 321 Anthony Avent RC	.02	.10
❑ 322 Matt Geiger RC	.02	.10
❑ 323 Duane Causwell	.02	.10
❑ 324 Horace Grant	.02	.10
❑ 325 Mark Jackson	.02	.10
❑ 326 Dan Majerle	.02	.10
❑ 327 Chuck Person	.02	.10
❑ 328 Buck Johnson	.02	.10
❑ 329 Duane Cooper RC	.02	.10
❑ 330 Rod Strickland	.05	.15
❑ 331 Isiah Thomas	.05	.15
❑ 332 Greg Kite	.02	.10
❑ 333 Don MacLean RC	.02	.10
❑ 334 Christian Laettner RC	.10	.30
❑ 335 John Crotty RC	.02	.10
❑ 336 Tracy Moore RC	.02	.10
❑ 337 Hakeem Olajuwon	.08	.25
❑ 338 Byron Houston RC	.02	.10
❑ 339 Walter Bond RC	.02	.10
❑ 340 Brent Price RC	.02	.10
❑ 341 Bryant Stith RC	.02	.10
❑ 342 Will Perdue	.02	.10
❑ 343 Jeff Hornacek	.02	.10
❑ 344 Adam Keefe RC	.02	.10
❑ 345 Rafael Addison	.02	.10
❑ 346 Marlon Maxey RC	.02	.10
❑ 347 Joe Dumars	.05	.15
❑ 348 Jon Barry RC	.02	.10
❑ 349 Marty Conlon	.02	.10
❑ 350 Alaa Abdelnaby	.02	.10
❑ 351 Micheal Williams	.02	.10
❑ 352 Brad Daugherty	.02	.10
❑ 353 Tony Bennett RC	.02	.10
❑ 354 Clyde Drexler	.05	.15
❑ 355 Rolando Blackman	.02	.10
❑ 356 Tom Tolbert	.02	.10
❑ 357 Sarunas Marciulionis	.02	.10
❑ 358 Jaren Jackson RC	.02	.10
❑ 359 Stacey King	.02	.10
❑ 360 Danny Ainge	.02	.10
❑ 361 Dale Ellis	.02	.10
❑ 362 Shaquille O'Neal RC	4.00	10.00
❑ 363 Bob McCann RC	.02	.10
❑ 364 Reggie Smith RC	.02	.10
❑ 365 Vinny Del Negro	.02	.10
❑ 366 Robert Pack	.02	.10
❑ 367 David Wood	.02	.10
❑ 368 Rodney McCray	.02	.10
❑ 369 Terry Mills	.02	.10
❑ 370 Eric Murdock	.02	.10
❑ 371 Alex Blackwell RC	.02	.10
❑ 372 Jay Humphries	.02	.10
❑ 373 Eddie Lee Wilkins	.02	.10
❑ 374 James Edwards	.02	.10
❑ 375 Tim Kempton	.02	.10
❑ 376 J.R. Reid	.02	.10
❑ 377 Sam Mack RC	.02	.10
❑ 378 Donald Royal	.02	.10
❑ 379 Mark Price	.02	.10
❑ 380 Mark Acres	.02	.10
❑ 381 Hubert Davis RC	.02	.10
❑ 382 Dave Johnson RC	.02	.10
❑ 383 John Salley	.02	.10
❑ 384 Eddie Johnson	.02	.10
❑ 385 Brian Howard RC	.02	.10
❑ 386 Isaiah Morris RC	.02	.10
❑ 387 Frank Johnson	.02	.10
❑ 388 Rick Mahorn	.02	.10
❑ 389 Scottie Pippen	.20	.50
❑ 390 Lee Mayberry RC	.02	.10
❑ 391 Tony Campbell	.02	.10
❑ 392 Latrell Sprewell RC	.50	1.25
❑ 393 Alonzo Mourning RC	.40	1.00
❑ 394 Robert Werdann RC	.02	.10
❑ 395 Checklist 199-297 UER	.02	.10
❑ 396 Checklist 298-396	.04	.10

1993-94 Topps

❑ COMPLETE SET (396)	10.00	20.00
❑ COMPLETE FACT.SET (410)	12.50	25.00
❑ COMPLETE SERIES 1 (198)	5.00	10.00
❑ COMPLETE SERIES 2 (198)	5.00	10.00
❑ 1 Charles Barkley HL	.08	.25
❑ 2 Hakeem Olajuwon HL	.08	.25
❑ 3 Shaquille O'Neal HL	.20	.50
❑ 4 Chris Jackson HL	.01	.05
❑ 5 Cliff Robinson HL	.01	.05
❑ 6 Donald Hodge	.01	.05
❑ 7 Victor Alexander	.01	.05
❑ 8 Chris Morris	.01	.05
❑ 9 Muggsy Bogues	.02	.10
❑ 10 Steve Smith UER	.08	.25
❑ 11 Dave Johnson	.01	.05
❑ 12 Tom Gugliotta	.08	.25
❑ 13 Doug Edwards RC	.01	.05
❑ 14 Vlade Divac	.02	.10
❑ 15 Corie Blount RC	.01	.05
❑ 16 Derek Harper	.02	.10
❑ 17 Matt Bullard	.01	.05
❑ 18 Terry Catledge	.01	.05
❑ 19 Mark Eaton	.01	.05
❑ 20 Mark Jackson	.02	.10
❑ 21 Terry Mills	.01	.05
❑ 22 Johnny Dawkins	.01	.05
❑ 23 Michael Jordan	1.25	3.00
❑ 24 Rick Fox UER	.01	.05
❑ 25 Charles Oakley	.02	.10
❑ 26 Derrick McKey	.01	.05
❑ 27 Christian Laettner	.02	.10
❑ 28 Todd Day	.01	.05
❑ 29 Danny Ferry	.01	.05
❑ 30 Kevin Johnson	.02	.10
❑ 31 Vinny Del Negro	.01	.05
❑ 32 Kevin Brooks	.01	.05
❑ 33 Pete Chilcutt	.01	.05
❑ 34 Larry Stewart	.01	.05
❑ 35 Dave Jamerson	.01	.05
❑ 36 Sidney Green	.01	.05
❑ 37 J.R. Reid	.01	.05
❑ 38 Jim Jackson	.02	.10
❑ 39 Micheal Williams UER	.01	.05
❑ 40 Rex Walters RC	.01	.05
❑ 41 Shawn Bradley RC	.08	.25
❑ 42 Jon Koncak	.01	.05
❑ 43 Byron Houston	.01	.05
❑ 44 Brian Shaw	.01	.05
❑ 45 Bill Cartwright	.01	.05
❑ 46 Jerome Kersey	.01	.05
❑ 47 Danny Schayes	.01	.05
❑ 48 Olden Polynice	.01	.05
❑ 49 Anthony Peeler	.01	.05
❑ 50 Nick Anderson 50	.01	.05
❑ 51 David Benoit	.01	.05
❑ 52 David Robinson 50P	.08	.25
❑ 53 Greg Kite	.01	.05
❑ 54 Gerald Paddio	.01	.05
❑ 55 Don MacLean	.01	.05
❑ 56 Randy Woods	.01	.05
❑ 57 Reggie Miller 50P	.02	.10
❑ 58 Kevin Gamble	.01	.05
❑ 59 Sean Green	.01	.05
❑ 60 Jeff Hornacek	.02	.10
❑ 61 John Starks	.02	.10
❑ 62 Gerald Wilkins	.01	.05
❑ 63 Jim Les	.01	.05
❑ 64 Michael Jordan 50P	.60	1.50
❑ 65 Alvin Robertson	.01	.05
❑ 66 Tim Kempton	.01	.05
❑ 67 Bryant Stith	.01	.05
❑ 68 Jeff Turner	.01	.05
❑ 69 Malik Sealy	.01	.05
❑ 70 Dell Curry	.01	.05
❑ 71 Brent Price	.01	.05
❑ 72 Kevin Lynch	.01	.05
❑ 73 Bimbo Coles	.01	.05
❑ 74 Larry Nance	.01	.05
❑ 75 Luther Wright RC	.01	.05
❑ 76 Willie Anderson	.01	.05
❑ 77 Dennis Rodman	.20	.50
❑ 78 Anthony Mason	.02	.10
❑ 79 Chris Gatling	.01	.05
❑ 80 Antoine Carr	.01	.05
❑ 81 Kevin Willis	.01	.05
❑ 82 Thurl Bailey	.01	.05
❑ 83 Reggie Williams	.01	.05
❑ 84 Rod Strickland	.02	.10
❑ 85 Rolando Blackman	.01	.05
❑ 86 Bobby Hurley RC	.02	.10
❑ 87 Jeff Malone	.01	.05
❑ 88 James Worthy	.08	.25
❑ 89 Alaa Abdelnaby	.01	.05
❑ 90 Duane Ferrell	.01	.05
❑ 91 Anthony Avent	.01	.05
❑ 92 Scottie Pippen	.30	.75
❑ 93 Ricky Pierce	.01	.05
❑ 94 P.J.Brown RC	.08	.25
❑ 95 Jeff Grayer	.01	.05
❑ 96 Jerrod Mustaf	.01	.05
❑ 97 Elmore Spencer	.01	.05
❑ 98 Walt Williams	.01	.05
❑ 99 Otis Thorpe	.02	.10
❑ 100 Patrick Ewing AS	.02	.10
❑ 101 Michael Jordan AS	.60	1.50
❑ 102 John Stockton AS	.02	.10
❑ 103 Dominique Wilkins AS	.02	.10
❑ 104 Charles Barkley AS	.08	.25
❑ 105 Lee Mayberry	.01	.05
❑ 106 James Edwards	.01	.05
❑ 107 Scott Brooks	.01	.05
❑ 108 John Battle	.01	.05
❑ 109 Kenny Gattison	.01	.05
❑ 110 Pooh Richardson	.01	.05
❑ 111 Rony Seikaly	.01	.05
❑ 112 Mahmoud Abdul-Rauf	.01	.05
❑ 113 Nick Anderson	.02	.10
❑ 114 Gundars Vetra	.01	.05
❑ 115 Joe Dumars AS	.02	.10
❑ 116 Hakeem Olajuwon AS	.08	.25
❑ 117 Scottie Pippen AS	.15	.40
❑ 118 Mark Price AS	.01	.05
❑ 119 Karl Malone AS	.08	.25
❑ 120 Michael Cage	.01	.05
❑ 121 Ed Pinckney	.01	.05
❑ 122 Jay Humphries	.01	.05
❑ 123 Dale Davis	.01	.05
❑ 124 Sean Rooks	.01	.05
❑ 125 Mookie Blaylock	.02	.10
❑ 126 Buck Williams	.01	.05
❑ 127 John Williams	.01	.05
❑ 128 Stacey King	.01	.05
❑ 129 Tim Perry	.01	.05
❑ 130 Tim Hardaway AS	.02	.10
❑ 131 Larry Johnson AS	.02	.10
❑ 132 Detlef Schrempf AS	.01	.05
❑ 133 Reggie Miller AS	.02	.10
❑ 134 Shaquille O'Neal AS	.20	.50
❑ 135 Dale Ellis	.01	.05
❑ 136 Duane Causwell	.01	.05
❑ 137 Rumeal Robinson	.01	.05
❑ 138 Billy Owens	.01	.05
❑ 139 Malcolm Mackey RC	.01	.05
❑ 140 Vernon Maxwell	.01	.05
❑ 141 LaPhonso Ellis	.01	.05
❑ 142 Robert Parish	.02	.10
❑ 143 LaBradford Smith	.01	.05
❑ 144 Charles Smith	.01	.05
❑ 145 Terry Porter	.01	.05
❑ 146 Elden Campbell	.01	.05
❑ 147 Bill Laimbeer	.01	.05

❑ 148 Chris Mills RC	.08	.25
❑ 149 Brad Lohaus	.01	.05
❑ 150 Jim Jackson ART	.01	.05
❑ 151 Tom Gugliotta ART	.02	.10
❑ 152 Shaquille O'Neal ART	.20	.50
❑ 153 Latrell Sprewell ART	.08	.25
❑ 154 Walt Williams ART	.01	.05
❑ 155 Gary Payton	.15	.40
❑ 156 Orlando Woolridge	.01	.05
❑ 157 Adam Keefe	.01	.05
❑ 158 Calbert Cheaney RC	.02	.10
❑ 159 Rick Mahorn	.01	.05
❑ 160 Robert Horry	.02	.10
❑ 161 John Salley	.01	.05
❑ 162 Sam Mitchell	.01	.05
❑ 163 Stanley Roberts	.01	.05
❑ 164 Clarence Weatherspoon	.01	.05
❑ 165 Anthony Bowie	.01	.05
❑ 166 Derrick Coleman	.02	.10
❑ 167 Negele Knight	.01	.05
❑ 168 Marlon Maxey	.01	.05
❑ 169 Spud Webb UER	.02	.10
❑ 170 Alonzo Mourning	.15	.40
❑ 171 Ervin Johnson RC	.02	.10
❑ 172 Sedale Threatt	.01	.05
❑ 173 Mark Macon	.01	.05
❑ 174 B.J. Armstrong	.01	.05
❑ 175 Harold Miner ART	.01	.05
❑ 176 Anthony Peeler ART	.01	.05
❑ 177 Alonzo Mourning ART	.08	.25
❑ 178 Christian Laettner ART	.01	.05
❑ 179 Clarence Weatherspoon ART	.01	.05
❑ 180 Dee Brown	.01	.05
❑ 181 Shaquille O'Neal	.50	1.25
❑ 182 Loy Vaught	.01	.05
❑ 183 Terrell Brandon	.02	.10
❑ 184 Lionel Simmons	.01	.05
❑ 185 Mark Aguirre	.01	.05
❑ 186 Danny Ainge	.02	.10
❑ 187 Reggie Miller	.08	.25
❑ 188 Terry Davis	.01	.05
❑ 189 Mark Bryant	.01	.05
❑ 190 Tyrone Corbin	.01	.05
❑ 191 Chris Mullin	.08	.25
❑ 192 Johnny Newman	.01	.05
❑ 193 Doug West	.01	.05
❑ 194 Keith Askins	.01	.05
❑ 195 Bo Kimble	.01	.05
❑ 196 Sean Elliott	.02	.10
❑ 197 Checklist 1-99 UER	.01	.05
❑ 198 Checklist 100-198	.01	.05
❑ 199 Michael Jordan FPM	.60	1.50
❑ 200 Patrick Ewing FPM	.02	.10
❑ 201 John Stockton FPM	.02	.10
❑ 202 Shawn Kemp FPM	.08	.25
❑ 203 Mark Price FPM	.01	.05
❑ 204 Charles Barkley FPM	.08	.25
❑ 205 Hakeem Olajuwon FPM	.08	.25
❑ 206 Clyde Drexler FPM	.02	.10
❑ 207 Kevin Johnson FPM	.01	.05
❑ 208 John Starks FPM	.01	.05
❑ 209 Chris Mullin FPM	.02	.10
❑ 210 Doc Rivers	.02	.10
❑ 211 Kenny Walker	.01	.05
❑ 212 Doug Christie	.02	.10
❑ 213 James Robinson RC	.01	.05
❑ 214 Larry Krystkowiak	.01	.05
❑ 215 Manute Bol	.01	.05
❑ 216 Carl Herrera	.01	.05
❑ 217 Paul Graham	.01	.05
❑ 218 Jud Buechler	.01	.05
❑ 219 Mike Brown	.01	.05
❑ 220 Tom Chambers	.01	.05
❑ 221 Kendall Gill	.02	.10
❑ 222 Kenny Anderson	.02	.10
❑ 223 Larry Johnson	.08	.25
❑ 224 Chris Webber RC	1.00	2.50
❑ 225 Randy White	.01	.05
❑ 226 Rik Smits	.02	.10
❑ 227 A.C. Green	.02	.10
❑ 228 David Robinson	.15	.40
❑ 229 Sean Elliott	.02	.10
❑ 230 Gary Grant	.01	.05
❑ 231 Dana Barros	.01	.05
❑ 232 Bobby Hurley	.02	.10
❑ 233 Blue Edwards	.01	.05
❑ 234 Tom Hammonds	.01	.05
❑ 235 Pete Myers	.01	.05
❑ 236 Acie Earl RC	.01	.05
❑ 237 Tony Smith	.01	.05
❑ 238 Bill Wennington	.01	.05
❑ 239 Andrew Lang	.01	.05
❑ 240 Ervin Johnson	.02	.10
❑ 241 Byron Scott	.02	.10
❑ 242 Eddie Johnson	.01	.05
❑ 243 Anthony Bonner	.01	.05
❑ 244 Luther Wright	.01	.05
❑ 245 LaSalle Thompson	.01	.05
❑ 246 Harold Miner	.01	.05
❑ 247 Chris Smith	.01	.05
❑ 248 John Williams	.01	.05
❑ 249 Clyde Drexler	.08	.25
❑ 250 Calbert Cheaney	.02	.10
❑ 251 Avery Johnson	.01	.05
❑ 252 Steve Kerr	.02	.10
❑ 253 Warren Kidd RC	.01	.05
❑ 254 Wayman Tisdale	.01	.05
❑ 255 Bob Martin RC	.01	.05
❑ 256 Popeye Jones RC	.01	.05
❑ 257 Jimmy Oliver	.01	.05
❑ 258 Kevin Edwards	.01	.05
❑ 259 Dan Majerle	.02	.10
❑ 260 Jon Barry	.01	.05
❑ 261 Allan Houston RC	.40	1.00
❑ 262 Dikembe Mutombo	.08	.25
❑ 263 Sleepy Floyd	.01	.05
❑ 264 George Lynch RC	.01	.05
❑ 265 Stacey Augmon UER	.01	.05
❑ 266 Hakeem Olajuwon	.15	.40
❑ 267 Scott Skiles	.01	.05
❑ 268 Detlef Schrempf	.02	.10
❑ 269 Brian Davis RC	.01	.05
❑ 270 Tracy Murray	.01	.05
❑ 271 Gheorghe Muresan RC	.08	.25
❑ 272 Terry Dehere RC	.01	.05
❑ 273 Terry Cummings	.01	.05
❑ 274 Keith Jennings	.01	.05
❑ 275 Tyrone Hill	.01	.05
❑ 276 Hersey Hawkins	.02	.10
❑ 277 Grant Long	.01	.05
❑ 278 Herb Williams	.01	.05
❑ 279 Karl Malone	.15	.40
❑ 280 Mitch Richmond	.08	.25
❑ 281 Derek Strong RC	.01	.05
❑ 282 Dino Radja RC	.01	.05
❑ 283 Jack Haley	.01	.05
❑ 284 Derek Harper	.02	.10
❑ 285 Dwayne Schintzius	.01	.05
❑ 286 Michael Curry RC	.01	.05
❑ 287 Rodney Rogers RC	.08	.25
❑ 288 Horace Grant	.02	.10
❑ 289 Oliver Miller	.01	.05
❑ 290 Luc Longley	.02	.10
❑ 291 Walter Bond	.01	.05
❑ 292 Dominique Wilkins	.08	.25
❑ 293 Vern Fleming	.01	.05
❑ 294 Mark Price	.01	.05
❑ 295 Mark Aguirre	.01	.05
❑ 296 Shawn Kemp	.15	.40
❑ 297 Pervis Ellison	.01	.05
❑ 298 Josh Grant RC	.01	.05
❑ 299 Scott Burrell RC	.08	.25
❑ 300 Patrick Ewing	.08	.25
❑ 301 Sam Cassell RC	.40	1.00
❑ 302 Nick Van Exel RC	.30	.75
❑ 303 Clifford Robinson	.02	.10
❑ 304 Frank Johnson	.01	.05
❑ 305 Matt Geiger	.01	.05
❑ 306 Vin Baker RC	.25	.60
❑ 307 Benoit Benjamin	.01	.05
❑ 308 Shawn Bradley	.08	.25
❑ 309 Chris Whitney RC	.01	.05
❑ 310 Eric Riley RC	.01	.05
❑ 311 Isiah Thomas	.08	.25
❑ 312 Jamal Mashburn RC	.25	.60
❑ 313 Xavier McDaniel	.01	.05
❑ 314 Mike Peplowski RC	.01	.05
❑ 315 Darnell Mee RC	.01	.05
❑ 316 Toni Kukoc RC	.40	1.00
❑ 317 Felton Spencer	.01	.05
❑ 318 Sam Bowie	.01	.05
❑ 319 Mario Elie	.01	.05
❑ 320 Tim Hardaway	.08	.25
❑ 321 Ken Norman	.01	.05
❑ 322 Isaiah Rider RC	.20	.50
❑ 323 Rex Chapman	.01	.05
❑ 324 Dennis Rodman	.20	.50
❑ 325 Derrick McKey	.01	.05
❑ 326 Corie Blount	.01	.05
❑ 327 Fat Lever	.01	.05
❑ 328 Ron Harper	.02	.10
❑ 329 Eric Anderson	.01	.05
❑ 330 Armon Gilliam	.01	.05
❑ 331 Lindsey Hunter RC	.08	.25
❑ 332 Eric Leckner	.01	.05
❑ 333 Chris Corchiani	.01	.05
❑ 334 Anfernee Hardaway RC	.75	2.00
❑ 335 Randy Brown	.01	.05
❑ 336 Sam Perkins	.02	.10
❑ 337 Glen Rice	.02	.10
❑ 338 Orlando Woolridge	.01	.05
❑ 339 Mike Gminski	.01	.05
❑ 340 Latrell Sprewell	.25	.60
❑ 341 Harvey Grant	.01	.05
❑ 342 Doug Smith	.01	.05
❑ 343 Kevin Duckworth	.01	.05
❑ 344 Cedric Ceballos	.02	.10
❑ 345 Chuck Person	.01	.05
❑ 346 Scott Haskin RC	.01	.05
❑ 347 Frank Brickowski	.01	.05
❑ 348 Scott Williams	.01	.05
❑ 349 Brad Daugherty	.01	.05
❑ 350 Willie Burton	.01	.05
❑ 351 Joe Dumars	.08	.25
❑ 352 Craig Ehlo	.01	.05
❑ 353 Lucious Harris RC	.01	.05
❑ 354 Danny Manning	.02	.10
❑ 355 Litterial Green	.01	.05
❑ 356 John Stockton	.08	.25
❑ 357 Nate McMillan	.01	.05
❑ 358 Greg Graham RC	.01	.05
❑ 359 Rex Walters	.01	.05
❑ 360 Lloyd Daniels	.01	.05
❑ 361 Antonio Harvey RC	.01	.05
❑ 362 Brian Williams	.01	.05
❑ 363 LeRon Ellis	.01	.05
❑ 364 Chris Dudley	.01	.05
❑ 365 Hubert Davis	.01	.05
❑ 366 Evers Burns RC	.01	.05
❑ 367 Sherman Douglas	.01	.05
❑ 368 Sarunas Marciulionis	.01	.05
❑ 369 Tom Tolbert	.01	.05
❑ 370 Robert Pack	.01	.05
❑ 371 Michael Adams	.01	.05
❑ 372 Negele Knight	.01	.05
❑ 373 Charles Barkley	.15	.40
❑ 374 Bryon Russell RC	.08	.25
❑ 375 Greg Anthony	.01	.05
❑ 376 Ken Williams	.01	.05
❑ 377 John Paxson	.01	.05
❑ 378 Corey Gaines	.01	.05
❑ 379 Eric Murdock	.01	.05
❑ 380 Kevin Thompson RC	.01	.05
❑ 381 Moses Malone	.08	.25
❑ 382 Kenny Smith	.01	.05
❑ 383 Dennis Scott	.01	.05
❑ 384 Michael Jordan FSL	.60	1.50
❑ 385 Hakeem Olajuwon FSL	.08	.25
❑ 386 Shaquille O'Neal FSL	.20	.50
❑ 387 David Robinson FSL	.08	.25
❑ 388 Derrick Coleman FSL	.01	.05
❑ 389 Karl Malone FSL	.08	.25
❑ 390 Patrick Ewing FSL	.02	.10
❑ 391 Scottie Pippen FSL	.15	.40
❑ 392 Dominique Wilkins FSL	.02	.10
❑ 393 Charles Barkley FSL	.08	.25
❑ 394 Larry Johnson FSL	.02	.10
❑ 395 Checklist	.01	.05
❑ 396 Checklist	.01	.05
❑ NNO Expired Finest Redempt.	.40	1.00

1994-95 Topps

❑ COMPLETE SET (396)	12.50	25.00
❑ COMPLETE SERIES 1 (198)	5.00	10.00

❑ COMPLETE SERIES 2 (198)	7.50	15.00
❑ 1 Patrick Ewing AS	.02	.10
❑ 2 Mookie Blaylock AS	.01	.05
❑ 3 Charles Oakley AS	.01	.05
❑ 4 Mark Price AS	.01	.05
❑ 5 John Starks AS	.01	.05
❑ 6 Dominique Wilkins AS	.02	.10
❑ 7 Horace Grant AS	.01	.05
❑ 8 Alonzo Mourning AS	.08	.25
❑ 9 B.J. Armstrong AS	.01	.05
❑ 10 Kenny Anderson AS	.01	.05
❑ 11 Scottie Pippen AS	.15	.40
❑ 12 Derrick Coleman AS	.01	.05
❑ 13 Shaquille O'Neal AS	.20	.50
❑ 14 Anfernee Hardaway AS	.15	.40
❑ 15 Isaiah Rider SPEC	.01	.05
❑ 16 John Williams	.01	.05
❑ 17 Todd Day	.01	.05
❑ 18 Dale Davis	.01	.05
❑ 19 Sean Rooks	.01	.05
❑ 20 George Lynch	.01	.05
❑ 21 Mitchell Butler	.01	.05
❑ 22 Stacey King	.01	.05
❑ 23 Sherman Douglas	.01	.05
❑ 24 Derrick McKey	.01	.05
❑ 25 Joe Dumars	.08	.25
❑ 26 Scott Brooks	.01	.05
❑ 27 Clarence Weatherspoon	.01	.05
❑ 28 Jayson Williams	.02	.10
❑ 29 Scottie Pippen	.30	.75
❑ 30 John Starks	.01	.05
❑ 31 Robert Pack	.01	.05
❑ 32 Donald Royal	.01	.05
❑ 33 Haywoode Workman	.01	.05
❑ 34 Greg Graham	.01	.05
❑ 35 Terry Cummings	.01	.05
❑ 36 Andrew Lang	.01	.05
❑ 37 Jason Kidd RC	1.00	2.50
❑ 38 Terry Mills	.01	.05
❑ 39 Alonzo Mourning	.10	.30
❑ 40 Shawn Kemp	.15	.40
❑ 41 Kevin Willis FTR	.01	.05
❑ 42 Kevin Willis	.01	.05
❑ 43 Armon Gilliam	.01	.05
❑ 44 Bobby Hurley	.01	.05
❑ 45 Jerome Kersey	.01	.05
❑ 46 Xavier McDaniel	.01	.05
❑ 47 Chris Webber	.25	.60
❑ 48 Chris Webber FR	.10	.30
❑ 49 Jeff Malone	.01	.05
❑ 50 Dikembe Mutombo SPEC	.01	.05
❑ 51 Dan Majerle SPEC	.01	.05
❑ 52 Dee Brown SPEC	.01	.05
❑ 53 John Stockton SPEC	.02	.10
❑ 54 Dennis Rodman SPEC	.08	.25
❑ 55 Eric Murdock SPEC	.01	.05
❑ 56 Glen Rice	.02	.10
❑ 57 Glen Rice FTR	.01	.05
❑ 58 Dino Radja	.01	.05
❑ 59 Billy Owens	.01	.05
❑ 60 Doc Rivers	.02	.10
❑ 61 Don MacLean	.01	.05
❑ 62 Lindsey Hunter	.02	.10
❑ 63 Sam Cassell	.08	.25
❑ 64 James Worthy	.08	.25
❑ 65 Christian Laettner	.02	.10
❑ 66 Wesley Person RC	.08	.25
❑ 67 Rich King	.01	.05
❑ 68 Jon Koncak	.01	.05
❑ 69 Muggsy Bogues	.02	.10
❑ 70 Jamal Mashburn	.08	.25
❑ 71 Gary Grant	.01	.05
❑ 72 Eric Murdock	.01	.05
❑ 73 Scott Burrell	.01	.05
❑ 74 Scott Burrell FTR	.01	.05
❑ 75 Anfernee Hardaway	.25	.60
❑ 76 Anfernee Hardaway FR	.10	.30
❑ 77 Yinka Dare RC	.01	.05
❑ 78 Anthony Avent	.01	.05
❑ 79 Jon Barry	.01	.05
❑ 80 Rodney Rogers	.01	.05
❑ 81 Chris Mills	.02	.10
❑ 82 Antonio Davis	.01	.05
❑ 83 Steve Smith	.02	.10
❑ 84 Buck Williams	.01	.05
❑ 85 Spud Webb	.01	.05
❑ 86 Stacey Augmon	.01	.05
❑ 87 Allan Houston	.15	.40
❑ 88 Will Perdue	.01	.05
❑ 89 Chris Gatling	.01	.05
❑ 90 Danny Ainge	.01	.05
❑ 91 Rick Mahorn	.01	.05
❑ 92 Elmore Spencer	.01	.05
❑ 93 Vin Baker	.08	.25
❑ 94 Rex Chapman	.01	.05
❑ 95 Dale Ellis	.01	.05
❑ 96 Doug Smith	.01	.05
❑ 97 Tim Perry	.01	.05
❑ 98 Toni Kukoc	.15	.40
❑ 99 Terry Dehere	.01	.05
❑ 100 Shaquille O'Neal PP	.20	.50
❑ 101 Shawn Kemp PP	.08	.25
❑ 102 Hakeem Olajuwon PP	.08	.25
❑ 103 Derrick Coleman PP	.01	.05
❑ 104 Alonzo Mourning PP	.08	.25
❑ 105 Dikembe Mutombo PP	.01	.05
❑ 106 Chris Webber PP	.10	.30
❑ 107 Dennis Rodman PP	.08	.25
❑ 108 David Robinson PP	.08	.25
❑ 109 Charles Barkley PP	.08	.25
❑ 110 Brad Daugherty	.01	.05
❑ 111 Derek Harper	.01	.05
❑ 112 Detlef Schrempf	.02	.10
❑ 113 Harvey Grant	.01	.05
❑ 114 Vlade Divac	.01	.05
❑ 115 Isaiah Rider	.02	.10
❑ 116 Mitch Richmond	.08	.25
❑ 117 Tom Chambers	.01	.05
❑ 118 Kenny Gattison	.01	.05
❑ 119 Kenny Gattison FTR	.01	.05
❑ 120 Vernon Maxwell	.01	.05
❑ 121 Reggie Williams	.01	.05
❑ 122 Chris Mullin	.08	.25
❑ 123 Harold Miner	.01	.05
❑ 124 Harold Miner FTR	.01	.05
❑ 125 Calbert Cheaney	.01	.05
❑ 126 Randy Woods	.01	.05
❑ 127 Mike Gminski	.01	.05
❑ 128 Willie Anderson	.01	.05
❑ 129 Mark Macon	.01	.05
❑ 130 Avery Johnson	.01	.05
❑ 131 Bimbo Coles	.01	.05
❑ 132 Kenny Smith	.01	.05
❑ 133 Dennis Scott	.01	.05
❑ 134 Lionel Simmons	.01	.05
❑ 135 Nate McMillan	.01	.05
❑ 136 Eric Montross RC	.01	.05
❑ 137 Sedale Threatt	.01	.05
❑ 138 Kenny Anderson	.02	.10
❑ 139 Micheal Williams	.01	.05
❑ 140 Grant Long	.01	.05
❑ 141 Grant Long FTR	.01	.05
❑ 142 Tyrone Corbin	.01	.05
❑ 143 Craig Ehlo	.01	.05
❑ 144 Gerald Wilkins	.01	.05
❑ 145 LaPhonso Ellis	.01	.05
❑ 146 Reggie Miller	.08	.25
❑ 147 Tracy Murray	.01	.05
❑ 148 Victor Alexander	.01	.05
❑ 149 Victor Alexander FTR	.01	.05
❑ 150 Clifford Robinson	.02	.10
❑ 151 Anthony Mason FTR	.01	.05
❑ 152 Anthony Mason	.02	.10
❑ 153 Jim Jackson	.02	.10
❑ 154 Jeff Hornacek	.02	.10
❑ 155 Nick Anderson	.01	.05
❑ 156 Mike Brown	.01	.05
❑ 157 Kevin Johnson	.02	.10
❑ 158 John Paxson	.01	.05
❑ 159 Loy Vaught	.01	.05
❑ 160 Carl Herrera	.01	.05
❑ 161 Shawn Bradley	.01	.05
❑ 162 Hubert Davis	.01	.05
❑ 163 David Benoit	.01	.05
❑ 164 Dell Curry	.01	.05
❑ 165 Dee Brown	.01	.05
❑ 166 LaSalle Thompson	.01	.05
❑ 167 Eddie Jones RC	.50	1.25
❑ 168 Walt Williams	.01	.05
❑ 169 A.C. Green	.02	.10
❑ 170 Kendall Gill	.02	.10
❑ 171 Kendall Gill FTR	.01	.05
❑ 172 Danny Ferry	.01	.05
❑ 173 Bryant Stith	.01	.05
❑ 174 John Salley	.01	.05
❑ 175 Cedric Ceballos	.01	.05
❑ 176 Derrick Coleman	.02	.10
❑ 177 Tony Bennett	.01	.05
❑ 178 Kevin Duckworth	.01	.05
❑ 179 Jay Humphries	.01	.05
❑ 180 Sean Elliott	.02	.10
❑ 181 Sam Perkins	.02	.10
❑ 182 Luc Longley	.01	.05
❑ 183 Mitch Richmond AS	.02	.10
❑ 184 Clyde Drexler AS	.02	.10
❑ 185 Karl Malone AS	.08	.25
❑ 186 Shawn Kemp AS	.08	.25
❑ 187 Hakeem Olajuwon AS	.08	.25
❑ 188 Danny Manning AS	.01	.05
❑ 189 Kevin Johnson AS	.01	.05
❑ 190 John Stockton AS	.02	.10
❑ 191 Latrell Sprewell AS	.08	.25
❑ 192 Gary Payton AS	.08	.25
❑ 193 Clifford Robinson AS	.01	.05
❑ 194 David Robinson AS	.08	.25
❑ 195 Charles Barkley AS	.08	.25
❑ 196 Mark Price SPEC	.01	.05
❑ 197 Checklist 1-99	.01	.05
❑ 198 Checklist 100-198	.01	.05
❑ 199 Patrick Ewing	.08	.25
❑ 200 Patrick Ewing FR	.02	.10
❑ 201 Tracy Murray PP	.01	.05
❑ 202 Craig Ehlo PP	.01	.05
❑ 203 Nick Anderson PP	.01	.05
❑ 204 John Starks PP	.01	.05
❑ 205 Rex Chapman PP	.01	.05
❑ 206 Hersey Hawkins PP	.01	.05
❑ 207 Glen Rice PP	.01	.05
❑ 208 Jeff Malone PP	.01	.05
❑ 209 Dan Majerle PP	.01	.05
❑ 210 Chris Mullin PP	.02	.10
❑ 211 Grant Hill RC	.50	1.25
❑ 212 Bobby Phills	.01	.05
❑ 213 Dennis Rodman	.20	.50
❑ 214 Doug West	.01	.05
❑ 215 Harold Ellis	.01	.05
❑ 216 Kevin Edwards	.01	.05
❑ 217 Lorenzo Williams	.01	.05
❑ 218 Rick Fox	.01	.05
❑ 219 Mookie Blaylock	.01	.05
❑ 220 Mookie Blaylock FR	.01	.05
❑ 221 John Williams	.01	.05
❑ 222 Keith Jennings	.01	.05
❑ 223 Nick Van Exel	.08	.25
❑ 224 Gary Payton	.15	.40
❑ 225 John Stockton	.08	.25
❑ 226 Ron Harper	.02	.10
❑ 227 Monty Williams RC	.01	.05
❑ 228 Marty Conlon	.01	.05
❑ 229 Hersey Hawkins	.02	.10
❑ 230 Rik Smits	.01	.05
❑ 231 James Robinson	.01	.05
❑ 232 Malik Sealy	.01	.05
❑ 233 Sergei Bazarevich RC	.01	.05
❑ 234 Brad Lohaus	.01	.05
❑ 235 Olden Polynice	.01	.05
❑ 236 Brian Williams	.01	.05
❑ 237 Tyrone Hill	.01	.05
❑ 238 Jim McIlvaine RC	.01	.05
❑ 239 Latrell Sprewell	.08	.25
❑ 240 Latrell Sprewell FR	.08	.25
❑ 241 Popeye Jones	.01	.05
❑ 242 Scott Williams	.01	.05
❑ 243 Eddie Jones	.25	.60
❑ 244 Moses Malone	.08	.25
❑ 245 B.J. Armstrong	.01	.05
❑ 246 Jim Les	.01	.05
❑ 247 Greg Grant	.01	.05
❑ 248 Lee Mayberry	.01	.05
❑ 249 Mark Jackson	.01	.05
❑ 250 Larry Johnson	.02	.10
❑ 251 Terrell Brandon	.02	.10
❑ 252 Ledell Eackles	.01	.05
❑ 253 Yinka Dare	.01	.05
❑ 254 Dontonio Wingfield RC	.01	.05
❑ 255 Clyde Drexler	.08	.25
❑ 256 Andres Guibert	.01	.05
❑ 257 Gheorghe Muresan	.01	.05
❑ 258 Tom Hammonds	.01	.05
❑ 259 Charles Barkley	.15	.40
❑ 260 Charles Barkley FR	.08	.25
❑ 261 Acie Earl	.01	.05
❑ 262 Lamond Murray RC	.02	.10
❑ 263 Dana Barros	.01	.05
❑ 264 Greg Anthony	.01	.05
❑ 265 Dan Majerle	.02	.10
❑ 266 Zan Tabak	.01	.05

❑ 267 Ricky Pierce	.01	.05
❑ 268 Eric Leckner	.01	.05
❑ 269 Duane Ferrell	.01	.05
❑ 270 Mark Price	.01	.05
❑ 271 Anthony Peeler	.01	.05
❑ 272 Adam Keefe	.01	.05
❑ 273 Rex Walters	.01	.05
❑ 274 Scott Skiles	.01	.05
❑ 275 Glenn Robinson RC	.30	.75
❑ 276 Tony Dumas RC	.01	.05
❑ 277 Elliot Perry	.01	.05
❑ 278 Bo Outlaw RC	.01	.05
❑ 279 Karl Malone	.15	.40
❑ 280 Karl Malone FR	.08	.25
❑ 281 Herb Williams	.01	.05
❑ 282 Vincent Askew	.01	.05
❑ 283 Askia Jones RC	.01	.05
❑ 284 Shawn Bradley	.01	.05
❑ 285 Tim Hardaway	.08	.25
❑ 286 Mark West	.01	.05
❑ 287 Chuck Person	.01	.05
❑ 288 James Edwards	.01	.05
❑ 289 Antonio Lang RC	.01	.05
❑ 290 Dominique Wilkins	.08	.25
❑ 291 Khalid Reeves RC	.01	.05
❑ 292 Jamie Watson RC	.01	.05
❑ 293 Darnell Mee	.01	.05
❑ 294 Brian Grant RC	.25	.60
❑ 295 Hakeem Olajuwon	.15	.40
❑ 296 Dickey Simpkins RC	.01	.05
❑ 297 Tyrone Corbin	.01	.05
❑ 298 David Wingate	.01	.05
❑ 299 Shaquille O'Neal	.50	1.25
❑ 300 Shaquille O'Neal FR	.20	.50
❑ 301 B.J. Armstrong PP	.01	.05
❑ 302 Mitch Richmond PP	.02	.10
❑ 303 Jim Jackson PP	.01	.05
❑ 304 Jeff Hornacek PP	.01	.05
❑ 305 Mark Price PP	.01	.05
❑ 306 Kendall Gill PP	.01	.05
❑ 307 Dale Ellis PP	.01	.05
❑ 308 Vernon Maxwell PP	.01	.05
❑ 309 Joe Dumars PP	.02	.10
❑ 310 Reggie Miller PP	.02	.10
❑ 311 Geert Hammink	.01	.05
❑ 312 Charles Smith	.01	.05
❑ 313 Bill Cartwright	.01	.05
❑ 314 Aaron McKie RC	.30	.75
❑ 315 Tom Gugliotta	.02	.10
❑ 316 P.J. Brown	.01	.05
❑ 317 David Wesley	.01	.05
❑ 318 Felton Spencer	.01	.05
❑ 319 Robert Horry	.02	.10
❑ 320 Robert Horry FR	.01	.05
❑ 321 Larry Krystkowiak	.01	.05
❑ 322 Eric Piatkowski RC	.01	.05
❑ 323 Anthony Bonner	.01	.05
❑ 324 Keith Askins	.01	.05
❑ 325 Mahmoud Abdul-Rauf	.01	.05
❑ 326 Darrin Hancock RC	.01	.05
❑ 327 Vern Fleming	.01	.05
❑ 328 Wayman Tisdale	.01	.05
❑ 329 Sam Bowie	.01	.05
❑ 330 Billy Owens	.01	.05
❑ 331 Donald Hodge	.01	.05
❑ 332 Derrick Alston RC	.01	.05
❑ 333 Doug Edwards	.01	.05
❑ 334 Johnny Newman	.01	.05
❑ 335 Otis Thorpe	.01	.05
❑ 336 Bill Curley RC	.01	.05
❑ 337 Michael Cage	.01	.05
❑ 338 Chris Smith	.01	.05
❑ 339 Dikembe Mutombo	.02	.10
❑ 340 Dikembe Mutombo FR	.01	.05
❑ 341 Duane Causwell	.01	.05
❑ 342 Sean Higgins	.01	.05
❑ 343 Steve Kerr	.01	.05
❑ 344 Eric Montross	.01	.05
❑ 345 Charles Oakley	.01	.05
❑ 346 Brooks Thompson RC	.01	.05
❑ 347 Rony Seikaly	.01	.05
❑ 348 Chris Dudley	.01	.05
❑ 349 Sharone Wright RC	.01	.05
❑ 350 Sarunas Marciulionis	.01	.05
❑ 351 Anthony Miller RC	.01	.05
❑ 352 Pooh Richardson	.01	.05
❑ 353 Byron Scott	.02	.10
❑ 354 Michael Adams	.01	.05
❑ 355 Ken Norman	.01	.05
❑ 356 Clifford Rozier RC	.01	.05
❑ 357 Tim Breaux	.01	.05
❑ 358 Derek Strong	.01	.05
❑ 359 David Robinson	.15	.40
❑ 360 David Robinson FR	.08	.25
❑ 361 Benoit Benjamin	.01	.05
❑ 362 Terry Porter	.01	.05
❑ 363 Ervin Johnson	.01	.05
❑ 364 Alaa Abdelnaby	.01	.05
❑ 365 Robert Parish	.02	.10
❑ 366 Mario Elie	.01	.05
❑ 367 Antonio Harvey	.01	.05
❑ 368 Charlie Ward RC	.08	.25
❑ 369 Kevin Gamble	.01	.05
❑ 370 Rod Strickland	.02	.10
❑ 371 Jason Kidd	.50	1.25
❑ 372 Oliver Miller	.01	.05
❑ 373 Eric Mobley RC	.01	.05
❑ 374 Brian Shaw	.01	.05
❑ 375 Horace Grant	.02	.10
❑ 376 Corie Blount	.01	.05
❑ 377 Sam Mitchell	.01	.05
❑ 378 Jalen Rose RC	.40	1.00
❑ 379 Elden Campbell	.01	.05
❑ 380 Elden Campbell FR	.01	.05
❑ 381 Donyell Marshall RC	.08	.25
❑ 382 Frank Brickowski	.01	.05
❑ 383 B.J.Tyler RC	.01	.05
❑ 384 Bryon Russell	.01	.05
❑ 385 Danny Manning	.02	.10
❑ 386 Manute Bol	.01	.05
❑ 387 Brent Price	.01	.05
❑ 388 J.R. Reid	.01	.05
❑ 389 Byron Houston	.01	.05
❑ 390 Blue Edwards	.01	.05
❑ 391 Adrian Caldwell	.01	.05
❑ 392 Wesley Person	.02	.10
❑ 393 Juwan Howard RC	.25	.60
❑ 394 Chris Morris	.01	.05
❑ 395 Checklist 199-296	.01	.05
❑ 396 Checklist 297-396	.01	.05

1995-96 Topps

❑ COMPLETE SET (291)	15.00	30.00
❑ COMPLETE SERIES 1 (181)	7.50	15.00
❑ COMPLETE SERIES 2 (110)	7.50	15.00
❑ 1 Michael Jordan AL	.60	1.50
❑ 2 Dennis Rodman AL	.05	.15
❑ 3 John Stockton AL	.20	.50
❑ 4 Michael Jordan AL	.60	1.50
❑ 5 David Robinson AL	.10	.30
❑ 6 Shaquille O'Neal LL	.20	.50
❑ 7 Hakeem Olajuwon LL	.10	.30
❑ 8 David Robinson LL	.10	.30
❑ 9 Karl Malone LL	.20	.50
❑ 10 Jamal Mashburn LL	.05	.15
❑ 11 Dennis Rodman LL	.05	.15
❑ 12 Dikembe Mutombo LL	.05	.15
❑ 13 Shaquille O'Neal LL	.20	.50
❑ 14 Patrick Ewing LL	.10	.30
❑ 15 Tyrone Hill LL	.05	.15
❑ 16 John Stockton LL	.20	.50
❑ 17 Kenny Anderson LL	.05	.15
❑ 18 Tim Hardaway LL	.05	.15
❑ 19 Rod Strickland LL	.05	.15
❑ 20 Muggsy Bogues LL	.05	.15
❑ 21 Scottie Pippen LL	.10	.30
❑ 22 Mookie Blaylock LL	.05	.15
❑ 23 Gary Payton LL	.10	.30
❑ 24 John Stockton LL	.20	.50
❑ 25 Nate McMillan LL	.05	.15
❑ 26 Dikembe Mutombo LL	.05	.15
❑ 27 Hakeem Olajuwon LL	.10	.30
❑ 28 Shawn Bradley LL	.05	.15
❑ 29 David Robinson LL	.10	.30
❑ 30 Alonzo Mourning LL	.05	.15
❑ 31 Reggie Miller	.20	.50
❑ 32 Karl Malone	.25	.60
❑ 33 Grant Hill	.25	.60
❑ 34 Charles Barkley	.25	.60
❑ 35 Cedric Ceballos	.05	.15
❑ 36 Gheorghe Muresan	.05	.15
❑ 37 Doug West	.05	.15
❑ 38 Tony Dumas	.05	.15
❑ 39 Kenny Gattison	.05	.15
❑ 40 Chris Mullin	.20	.50
❑ 41 Pervis Ellison	.05	.15
❑ 42 Vinny Del Negro	.05	.15
❑ 43 Mario Elie	.05	.15
❑ 44 Todd Day	.05	.15
❑ 45 Scottie Pippen	.30	.75
❑ 46 Buck Williams	.05	.15
❑ 47 P.J. Brown	.05	.15
❑ 48 Bimbo Coles	.05	.15
❑ 49 Terrell Brandon	.10	.30
❑ 50 Charles Oakley	.05	.15
❑ 51 Sam Perkins	.10	.30
❑ 52 Dale Ellis	.05	.15
❑ 53 Andrew Lang	.05	.15
❑ 54 Harold Ellis	.05	.15
❑ 55 Clarence Weatherspoon	.05	.15
❑ 56 Bill Curley	.05	.15
❑ 57 Robert Parish	.10	.30
❑ 58 David Benoit	.05	.15
❑ 59 Anthony Avent	.05	.15
❑ 60 Jamal Mashburn	.10	.30
❑ 61 Duane Ferrell	.05	.15
❑ 62 Elden Campbell	.05	.15
❑ 63 Rex Chapman	.05	.15
❑ 64 Wesley Person	.05	.15
❑ 65 Mitch Richmond	.10	.30
❑ 66 Micheal Williams	.05	.15
❑ 67 Clifford Rozier	.05	.15
❑ 68 Eric Montross	.05	.15
❑ 69 Dennis Rodman	.10	.30
❑ 70 Vin Baker	.10	.30
❑ 71 Tyrone Hill	.05	.15
❑ 72 Tyrone Corbin	.05	.15
❑ 73 Chris Dudley	.05	.15
❑ 74 Nate McMillan	.05	.15
❑ 75 Kenny Anderson	.10	.30
❑ 76 Monty Williams	.05	.15
❑ 77 Kenny Smith	.05	.15
❑ 78 Rodney Rogers	.05	.15
❑ 79 Corie Blount	.05	.15
❑ 80 Glen Rice	.10	.30
❑ 81 Walt Williams	.05	.15
❑ 82 Scott Williams	.05	.15
❑ 83 Michael Adams	.05	.15
❑ 84 Terry Mills	.05	.15
❑ 85 Horace Grant	.10	.30
❑ 86 Chuck Person	.05	.15
❑ 87 Adam Keefe	.05	.15
❑ 88 Scott Brooks	.05	.15
❑ 89 George Lynch	.05	.15
❑ 90 Kevin Johnson	.10	.30
❑ 91 Armon Gilliam	.05	.15
❑ 92 Greg Minor	.05	.15
❑ 93 Derrick McKey	.05	.15
❑ 94 Victor Alexander	.05	.15
❑ 95 B.J. Armstrong	.05	.15
❑ 96 Terry Dehere	.05	.15
❑ 97 Christian Laettner	.10	.30
❑ 98 Hubert Davis	.05	.15
❑ 99 Aaron McKie	.10	.30
❑ 100 Hakeem Olajuwon	.20	.50
❑ 101 Michael Cage	.05	.15
❑ 102 Grant Long	.05	.15
❑ 103 Calbert Cheaney	.05	.15
❑ 104 Olden Polynice	.05	.15
❑ 105 Sharone Wright	.05	.15
❑ 106 Lee Mayberry	.05	.15
❑ 107 Robert Pack	.05	.15
❑ 108 Loy Vaught	.05	.15
❑ 109 Khalid Reeves	.05	.15
❑ 110 Shawn Kemp	.10	.30
❑ 111 Lindsey Hunter	.05	.15
❑ 112 Dell Curry	.05	.15
❑ 113 Dan Majerle	.10	.30
❑ 114 Bryon Russell	.05	.15
❑ 115 John Starks	.10	.30
❑ 116 Roy Tarpley	.05	.15
❑ 117 Dale Davis	.05	.15
❑ 118 Nick Anderson	.05	.15
❑ 119 Rex Walters	.05	.15

❑ 120 Dominique Wilkins	.20	.50
❑ 121 Sam Cassell	.20	.50
❑ 122 Sean Elliott	.10	.30
❑ 123 B.J. Tyler	.05	.15
❑ 124 Eric Mobley	.05	.15
❑ 125 Toni Kukoc	.10	.30
❑ 126 Pooh Richardson	.05	.15
❑ 127 Isaiah Rider	.05	.15
❑ 128 Steve Smith	.10	.30
❑ 129 Chris Mills	.05	.15
❑ 130 Detlef Schrempf	.10	.30
❑ 131 Donyell Marshall	.10	.30
❑ 132 Eddie Jones	.25	.60
❑ 133 Otis Thorpe	.05	.15
❑ 134 Lionel Simmons	.05	.15
❑ 135 Jeff Hornacek	.10	.30
❑ 136 Jalen Rose	.25	.60
❑ 137 Kevin Willis	.10	.30
❑ 138 Don MacLean	.05	.15
❑ 139 Dee Brown	.05	.15
❑ 140 Glenn Robinson	.20	.50
❑ 141 Joe Kleine	.05	.15
❑ 142 Ron Harper	.10	.30
❑ 143 Antonio Davis	.05	.15
❑ 144 Jeff Malone	.05	.15
❑ 145 Joe Dumars	.20	.50
❑ 146 Jason Kidd	.60	1.50
❑ 147 J.R. Reid	.05	.15
❑ 148 Lamond Murray	.05	.15
❑ 149 Derrick Coleman	.05	.15
❑ 150 Alonzo Mourning	.10	.30
❑ 151 Clifford Robinson	.05	.15
❑ 152 Kendall Gill	.05	.15
❑ 153 Doug Christie	.10	.30
❑ 154 Stacey Augmon	.05	.15
❑ 155 Anfernee Hardaway	.20	.50
❑ 156 Mahmoud Abdul-Rauf	.05	.15
❑ 157 Latrell Sprewell	.20	.50
❑ 158 Mark Price	.10	.30
❑ 159 Brian Grant	.20	.50
❑ 160 Clyde Drexler	.20	.50
❑ 161 Juwan Howard	.20	.50
❑ 162 Tom Gugliotta	.05	.15
❑ 163 Nick Van Exel	.20	.50
❑ 164 Billy Owens	.05	.15
❑ 165 Brooks Thompson	.05	.15
❑ 166 Acie Earl	.05	.15
❑ 167 Ed Pinckney	.05	.15
❑ 168 Oliver Miller	.05	.15
❑ 169 John Salley	.05	.15
❑ 170 Jerome Kersey	.05	.15
❑ 171 Willie Anderson	.05	.15
❑ 172 Keith Jennings	.05	.15
❑ 173 Doug Smith	.05	.15
❑ 174 Gerald Wilkins	.05	.15
❑ 175 Byron Scott	.05	.15
❑ 176 Benoit Benjamin	.05	.15
❑ 177 Blue Edwards	.05	.15
❑ 178 Greg Anthony	.05	.15
❑ 179 Trevor Ruffin	.05	.15
❑ 180 Kenny Gattison	.05	.15
❑ 181 Checklist 1-181	.05	.15
❑ 182 Cherokee Parks RC	.05	.15
❑ 183 Kurt Thomas RC	.10	.30
❑ 184 Ervin Johnson	.05	.15
❑ 185 Chucky Brown	.05	.15
❑ 186 Luc Longley	.05	.15
❑ 187 Anthony Miller	.05	.15
❑ 188 Ed O'Bannon RC	.05	.15
❑ 189 Bobby Hurley	.05	.15
❑ 190 Dikembe Mutombo	.10	.30
❑ 191 Robert Horry	.10	.30
❑ 192 George Zidek RC	.05	.15
❑ 193 Rasheed Wallace RC	.50	1.25
❑ 194 Marty Conlon	.05	.15
❑ 195 A.C. Green	.10	.30
❑ 196 Mike Brown	.05	.15
❑ 197 Oliver Miller	.05	.15
❑ 198 Charles Smith	.05	.15
❑ 199 Eric Williams RC	.10	.30
❑ 200 Rik Smits	.10	.30
❑ 201 Donald Royal	.05	.15
❑ 202 Bryant Reeves RC	.20	.50
❑ 203 Danny Ferry	.05	.15
❑ 204 Brian Williams	.05	.15
❑ 205 Joe Smith RC	.30	.75
❑ 206 Gary Trent RC	.05	.15
❑ 207 Greg Ostertag RC	.05	.15
❑ 208 Ken Norman	.05	.15

❑ 209 Avery Johnson	.05	.15
❑ 210 Theo Ratliff RC	.25	.60
❑ 211 Corie Blount	.05	.15
❑ 212 Hersey Hawkins	.05	.15
❑ 213 Loren Meyer RC	.05	.15
❑ 214 Mario Bennett RC	.05	.15
❑ 215 Randolph Childress RC	.05	.15
❑ 216 Spud Webb	.10	.30
❑ 217 Popeye Jones	.05	.15
❑ 218 Shawn Respert RC	.05	.15
❑ 219 Malik Sealy	.05	.15
❑ 220 Dino Radja	.05	.15
❑ 221 James Robinson	.05	.15
❑ 222 David Vaughn	.05	.15
❑ 223 Michael Smith	.05	.15
❑ 224 Jamie Watson	.05	.15
❑ 225 LaPhonso Ellis	.05	.15
❑ 226 Kevin Gamble	.05	.15
❑ 227 Dennis Rodman	.10	.30
❑ 228 B.J. Armstrong	.05	.15
❑ 229 Jerry Stackhouse RC	.60	1.50
❑ 230 Muggsy Bogues	.10	.30
❑ 231 Lawrence Moten RC	.05	.15
❑ 232 Cory Alexander RC	.05	.15
❑ 233 Carlos Rogers	.05	.15
❑ 234 Tyus Edney RC	.05	.15
❑ 235 Doc Rivers	.10	.30
❑ 236 Antonio Harvey	.05	.15
❑ 237 Kevin Garnett RC	1.25	3.00
❑ 238 Derek Harper	.10	.30
❑ 239 Kevin Edwards	.05	.15
❑ 240 Chris Smith	.05	.15
❑ 241 Haywoode Workman	.05	.15
❑ 242 Bobby Phills	.05	.15
❑ 243 Sherrell Ford RC	.05	.15
❑ 244 Corliss Williamson RC	.20	.50
❑ 245 Shawn Bradley	.05	.15
❑ 246 Jason Caffey RC	.10	.30
❑ 247 Bryant Stith	.05	.15
❑ 248 Mark West	.05	.15
❑ 249 Dennis Scott	.05	.15
❑ 250 Jim Jackson	.05	.15
❑ 251 Travis Best RC	.05	.15
❑ 252 Sean Rooks	.05	.15
❑ 253 Yinka Dare	.05	.15
❑ 254 Felton Spencer	.05	.15
❑ 255 Vlade Divac	.10	.30
❑ 256 Michael Finley RC	.50	1.25
❑ 257 Damon Stoudamire RC	.40	1.00
❑ 258 Mark Bryant	.05	.15
❑ 259 Brent Barry RC	.20	.50
❑ 260 Rony Seikaly	.05	.15
❑ 261 Alan Henderson RC	.20	.50
❑ 262 Kendall Gill	.05	.15
❑ 263 Rex Chapman	.05	.15
❑ 264 Eric Murdock	.05	.15
❑ 265 Rodney Rogers	.05	.15
❑ 266 Greg Graham	.05	.15
❑ 267 Jayson Williams	.05	.15
❑ 268 Antonio McDyess RC	.40	1.00
❑ 269 Sedale Threatt	.05	.15
❑ 270 Danny Manning	.10	.30
❑ 271 Pete Chilcutt	.05	.15
❑ 272 Bob Sura RC	.10	.30
❑ 273 Dana Barros	.05	.15
❑ 274 Allan Houston	.10	.30
❑ 275 Tracy Murray	.05	.15
❑ 276 Anthony Mason	.10	.30
❑ 277 Michael Jordan	1.25	3.00
❑ 278 Patrick Ewing	.20	.50
❑ 279 Shaquille O'Neal	.50	1.25
❑ 280 Larry Johnson	.10	.30
❑ 281 Mark Jackson	.10	.30
❑ 282 Chris Webber	.25	.60
❑ 283 David Robinson	.20	.50
❑ 284 John Stockton	.25	.60
❑ 285 Mookie Blaylock	.05	.15
❑ 286 Mark Price	.10	.30
❑ 287 Tim Hardaway	.10	.30
❑ 288 Rod Strickland	.05	.15
❑ 289 Sherman Douglas	.05	.15
❑ 290 Gary Payton	.20	.50
❑ 291 Checklist (182-291)	.05	.15

1996-97 Topps

❑ COMPLETE SET (221)	15.00	30.00
❑ COMP.FACT.HOB.SET (227)	15.00	35.00
❑ COMPLETE SERIES 1 (110)	6.00	12.00
❑ COMPLETE SERIES 2 (111)	10.00	20.00
❑ 1 Patrick Ewing	.20	.50
❑ 2 Christian Laettner	.10	.30
❑ 3 Mahmoud Abdul-Rauf	.05	.15
❑ 4 Chris Webber	.20	.50
❑ 5 Jason Kidd	.30	.75
❑ 6 Clifford Rozier	.05	.15
❑ 7 Elden Campbell	.05	.15
❑ 8 Chuck Person	.05	.15
❑ 9 Jeff Hornacek	.10	.30
❑ 10 Rik Smits	.10	.30
❑ 11 Kurt Thomas	.10	.30
❑ 12 Rod Strickland	.05	.15
❑ 13 Kendall Gill	.05	.15
❑ 14 Brian Williams	.05	.15
❑ 15 Tom Gugliotta	.05	.15
❑ 16 Ron Harper	.10	.30
❑ 17 Eric Williams	.05	.15
❑ 18 A.C. Green	.10	.30
❑ 19 Scott Williams	.05	.15
❑ 20 Damon Stoudamire	.20	.50
❑ 21 Bryant Reeves	.05	.15
❑ 22 Bob Sura	.05	.15
❑ 23 Mitch Richmond	.10	.30
❑ 24 Larry Johnson	.10	.30
❑ 25 Vin Baker	.10	.30
❑ 26 Mark Bryant	.05	.15
❑ 27 Horace Grant	.10	.30
❑ 28 Allan Houston	.10	.30
❑ 29 Sam Perkins	.10	.30
❑ 30 Antonio McDyess	.10	.30
❑ 31 Rasheed Wallace	.25	.60
❑ 32 Malik Sealy	.05	.15
❑ 33 Scottie Pippen	.30	.75
❑ 34 Charles Barkley	.25	.60
❑ 35 Hakeem Olajuwon	.20	.50
❑ 36 John Starks	.10	.30
❑ 37 Byron Scott	.05	.15
❑ 38 Arvydas Sabonis	.10	.30
❑ 39 Vlade Divac	.05	.15
❑ 40 Joe Dumars	.20	.50
❑ 41 Danny Ferry	.05	.15
❑ 42 Jerry Stackhouse	.25	.60
❑ 43 B.J. Armstrong	.05	.15
❑ 44 Shawn Bradley	.05	.15
❑ 45 Kevin Garnett	.40	1.00
❑ 46 Dee Brown	.05	.15
❑ 47 Michael Smith	.05	.15
❑ 48 Doug Christie	.10	.30
❑ 49 Mark Jackson	.05	.15
❑ 50 Shawn Kemp	.10	.30
❑ 51 Sasha Danilovic	.05	.15
❑ 52 Nick Anderson	.05	.15
❑ 53 Matt Geiger	.05	.15
❑ 54 Charles Smith	.05	.15
❑ 55 Mookie Blaylock	.05	.15
❑ 56 Johnny Newman	.05	.15
❑ 57 George McCloud	.05	.15
❑ 58 Greg Ostertag	.05	.15
❑ 59 Reggie Williams	.05	.15
❑ 60 Brent Barry	.05	.15
❑ 61 Doug West	.05	.15
❑ 62 Donald Royal	.05	.15
❑ 63 Randy Brown	.05	.15
❑ 64 Vincent Askew	.05	.15
❑ 65 John Stockton	.20	.50
❑ 66 Joe Kleine	.05	.15
❑ 67 Keith Askins	.05	.15
❑ 68 Bobby Phills	.05	.15
❑ 69 Chris Mullin	.20	.50
❑ 70 Nick Van Exel	.20	.50

❑ 71 Rick Fox	.05	.15
❑ 72 Chicago Bulls - 72 Wins	.60	1.50
❑ 73 Shawn Respert	.05	.15
❑ 74 Hubert Davis	.05	.15
❑ 75 Jim Jackson	.05	.15
❑ 76 Olden Polynice	.05	.15
❑ 77 Gheorghe Muresan	.05	.15
❑ 78 Theo Ratliff	.10	.30
❑ 79 Khalid Reeves	.05	.15
❑ 80 David Robinson	.20	.50
❑ 81 Lawrence Moten	.05	.15
❑ 82 Sam Cassell	.20	.50
❑ 83 George Zidek	.05	.15
❑ 84 Sharone Wright	.05	.15
❑ 85 Clarence Weatherspoon	.05	.15
❑ 86 Alan Henderson	.05	.15
❑ 87 Chris Dudley	.05	.15
❑ 88 Ed O'Bannon	.05	.15
❑ 89 Calbert Cheaney	.05	.15
❑ 90 Cedric Ceballos	.05	.15
❑ 91 Michael Cage	.05	.15
❑ 92 Ervin Johnson	.05	.15
❑ 93 Gary Trent	.05	.15
❑ 94 Sherman Douglas	.05	.15
❑ 95 Joe Smith	.10	.30
❑ 96 Dale Davis	.05	.15
❑ 97 Tony Dumas	.05	.15
❑ 98 Muggsy Bogues	.05	.15
❑ 99 Toni Kukoc	.10	.30
❑ 100 Grant Hill	.20	.50
❑ 101 Michael Finley	.25	.60
❑ 102 Isaiah Rider	.10	.30
❑ 103 Bryant Stith	.05	.15
❑ 104 Pooh Richardson	.05	.15
❑ 105 Karl Malone	.20	.50
❑ 106 Brian Grant	.20	.50
❑ 107 Sean Elliott	.10	.30
❑ 108 Charles Oakley	.05	.15
❑ 109 Pervis Ellison	.05	.15
❑ 110 Anfernee Hardaway	.20	.50
❑ 111 Checklist SP	.20	.50
❑ 112 Dikembe Mutombo	.10	.30
❑ 113 Alonzo Mourning	.10	.30
❑ 114 Hubert Davis	.05	.15
❑ 115 Rony Seikaly	.05	.15
❑ 116 Danny Manning	.10	.30
❑ 117 Donyell Marshall	.10	.30
❑ 118 Gerald Wilkins	.05	.15
❑ 119 Ervin Johnson	.05	.15
❑ 120 Jalen Rose	.20	.50
❑ 121 Dino Radja	.05	.15
❑ 122 Glenn Robinson	.20	.50
❑ 123 John Stockton	.20	.50
❑ 124 Matt Maloney RC	.10	.30
❑ 125 Clifford Robinson	.05	.15
❑ 126 Steve Kerr	.10	.30
❑ 127 Nate McMillan	.05	.15
❑ 128 Shareef Abdur-Rahim RC	.60	1.50
❑ 129 Loy Vaught	.05	.15
❑ 130 Anthony Mason	.10	.30
❑ 131 Kevin Garnett	.40	1.00
❑ 132 Roy Rogers RC	.05	.15
❑ 133 Erick Dampier RC	.20	.50
❑ 134 Tyus Edney	.05	.15
❑ 135 Chris Mills	.05	.15
❑ 136 Cory Alexander	.05	.15
❑ 137 Juwan Howard	.10	.30
❑ 138 Kobe Bryant RC	6.00	15.00
❑ 139 Michael Jordan	1.25	3.00
❑ 140 Jayson Williams	.10	.30
❑ 141 Rod Strickland	.05	.15
❑ 142 Lorenzen Wright RC	.10	.30
❑ 143 Will Perdue	.05	.15
❑ 144 Derek Harper	.05	.15
❑ 145 Billy Owens	.05	.15
❑ 146 Antoine Walker RC	.50	1.25
❑ 147 P.J. Brown	.05	.15
❑ 148 Terrell Brandon	.10	.30
❑ 149 Larry Johnson	.10	.30
❑ 150 Steve Smith	.10	.30
❑ 151 Eddie Jones	.20	.50
❑ 152 Detlef Schrempf	.10	.30
❑ 153 Dale Ellis	.05	.15
❑ 154 Isaiah Rider	.10	.30
❑ 155 Tony Delk RC	.20	.50
❑ 156 Adrian Caldwell	.05	.15
❑ 157 Jamal Mashburn	.10	.30
❑ 158 Dennis Scott	.05	.15
❑ 159 Dana Barros	.05	.15
❑ 160 Martin Muursepp RC	.05	.15
❑ 161 Marcus Camby RC	.25	.60
❑ 162 Jerome Williams RC	.20	.50
❑ 163 Wesley Person	.05	.15
❑ 164 Luc Longley	.05	.15
❑ 165 Charlie Ward	.05	.15
❑ 166 Mark Jackson	.05	.15
❑ 167 Derrick Coleman	.10	.30
❑ 168 Dell Curry	.05	.15
❑ 169 Armon Gilliam	.05	.15
❑ 170 Vlade Divac	.05	.15
❑ 171 Allen Iverson RC	1.00	2.50
❑ 172 Vitaly Potapenko RC	.05	.15
❑ 173 Jon Koncak	.05	.15
❑ 174 Lindsey Hunter	.05	.15
❑ 175 Kevin Johnson	.10	.30
❑ 176 Dennis Rodman	.10	.30
❑ 177 Stephon Marbury RC	.40	1.00
❑ 178 Karl Malone	.20	.50
❑ 179 Charles Barkley	.25	.60
❑ 180 Popeye Jones	.05	.15
❑ 181 Samaki Walker RC	.05	.15
❑ 182 Steve Nash RC	1.50	4.00
❑ 183 Latrell Sprewell	.20	.50
❑ 184 Kenny Anderson	.05	.15
❑ 185 Tyrone Hill	.05	.15
❑ 186 Robert Pack	.05	.15
❑ 187 Greg Anthony	.05	.15
❑ 188 Derrick McKey	.05	.15
❑ 189 John Wallace RC	.20	.50
❑ 190 Bryon Russell	.05	.15
❑ 191 Jermaine O'Neal RC	.50	1.25
❑ 192 Clyde Drexler	.20	.50
❑ 193 Mahmoud Abdul-Rauf	.05	.15
❑ 194 Eric Montross	.05	.15
❑ 195 Allan Houston	.10	.30
❑ 196 Harvey Grant	.05	.15
❑ 197 Rodney Rogers	.05	.15
❑ 198 Kerry Kittles RC	.20	.50
❑ 199 Grant Hill	.20	.50
❑ 200 Lionel Simmons	.05	.15
❑ 201 Reggie Miller	.20	.50
❑ 202 Avery Johnson	.05	.15
❑ 203 LaPhonso Ellis	.05	.15
❑ 204 Brian Shaw	.05	.15
❑ 205 Priest Lauderdale RC	.05	.15
❑ 206 Derek Fisher RC	.50	1.25
❑ 207 Terry Porter	.05	.15
❑ 208 Todd Fuller RC	.05	.15
❑ 209 Hersey Hawkins	.10	.30
❑ 210 Tim Legler	.05	.15
❑ 211 Terry Dehere	.05	.15
❑ 212 Gary Payton	.20	.50
❑ 213 Joe Dumars	.20	.50
❑ 214 Don MacLean	.05	.15
❑ 215 Greg Minor	.05	.15
❑ 216 Tim Hardaway	.10	.30
❑ 217 Ray Allen RC	.50	1.25
❑ 218 Mario Elie	.05	.15
❑ 219 Brooks Thompson	.05	.15
❑ 220 Shaquille O'Neal	.50	1.25

1997-98 Topps

❑ COMPLETE SET (220)	15.00	30.00
❑ COMPLETE SERIES 1 (110)	5.00	10.00
❑ COMPLETE SERIES 2 (110)	10.00	20.00
❑ 1 Scottie Pippen	.30	.75
❑ 2 Nate McMillan	.05	.15
❑ 3 Byron Scott	.05	.15
❑ 4 Mark Davis	.05	.15
❑ 5 Rod Strickland	.05	.15
❑ 6 Brian Grant	.10	.30
❑ 7 Damon Stoudamire	.10	.30
❑ 8 John Stockton	.20	.50
❑ 9 Grant Long	.05	.15
❑ 10 Darrell Armstrong	.05	.15
❑ 11 Anthony Mason	.10	.30
❑ 12 Travis Best	.05	.15
❑ 13 Stephon Marbury	.25	.60
❑ 14 Jamal Mashburn	.10	.30
❑ 15 Detlef Schrempf	.10	.30
❑ 16 Terrell Brandon	.10	.30
❑ 17 Charles Barkley	.25	.60
❑ 18 Vin Baker	.10	.30
❑ 19 Gary Trent	.05	.15
❑ 20 Vinny Del Negro	.05	.15
❑ 21 Todd Day	.05	.15
❑ 22 Malik Sealy	.05	.15
❑ 23 Wesley Person	.05	.15
❑ 24 Reggie Miller	.20	.50
❑ 25 Dan Majerle	.10	.30
❑ 26 Todd Fuller	.05	.15
❑ 27 Juwan Howard	.10	.30
❑ 28 Clarence Weatherspoon	.05	.15
❑ 29 Grant Hill	.20	.50
❑ 30 John Williams	.10	.30
❑ 31 Ken Norman	.05	.15
❑ 32 Patrick Ewing	.20	.50
❑ 33 Bryon Russell	.05	.15
❑ 34 Tony Smith	.05	.15
❑ 35 Andrew Lang	.05	.15
❑ 36 Rony Seikaly	.05	.15
❑ 37 Billy Owens	.05	.15
❑ 38 Dino Radja	.05	.15
❑ 39 Chris Gatling	.05	.15
❑ 40 Dale Davis	.05	.15
❑ 41 Arvydas Sabonis	.10	.30
❑ 42 Chris Mills	.05	.15
❑ 43 A.C. Green	.10	.30
❑ 44 Tyrone Hill	.05	.15
❑ 45 Tracy Murray	.05	.15
❑ 46 David Robinson	.20	.50
❑ 47 Lee Mayberry	.05	.15
❑ 48 Jayson Williams	.05	.15
❑ 49 Jason Kidd	.30	.75
❑ 50 Bryant Stith	.05	.15
❑ 51 Latrell Sprewell	.20	.50
❑ 52 Brent Barry	.10	.30
❑ 53 Henry James	.05	.15
❑ 54 Allen Iverson	.50	1.25
❑ 55 Shandon Anderson	.05	.15
❑ 56 Mitch Richmond	.10	.30
❑ 57 Allan Houston	.10	.30
❑ 58 Ron Harper	.10	.30
❑ 59 Gheorghe Muresan	.05	.15
❑ 60 Vincent Askew	.05	.15
❑ 61 Ray Allen	.20	.50
❑ 62 Kenny Anderson	.10	.30
❑ 63 Dikembe Mutombo	.10	.30
❑ 64 Sam Perkins	.10	.30
❑ 65 Walt Williams	.05	.15
❑ 66 Chris Carr	.05	.15
❑ 67 Vlade Divac	.10	.30
❑ 68 LaPhonso Ellis	.05	.15
❑ 69 B.J. Armstrong	.05	.15
❑ 70 Jim Jackson	.05	.15
❑ 71 Clyde Drexler	.20	.50
❑ 72 Lindsey Hunter	.05	.15
❑ 73 Sasha Danilovic	.05	.15
❑ 74 Elden Campbell	.05	.15
❑ 75 Robert Pack	.05	.15
❑ 76 Dennis Scott	.05	.15
❑ 77 Will Perdue	.05	.15
❑ 78 Anthony Peeler	.05	.15
❑ 79 Steve Smith	.10	.30
❑ 80 Steve Kerr	.10	.30
❑ 81 Buck Williams	.05	.15
❑ 82 Terry Mills	.05	.15
❑ 83 Michael Smith	.05	.15
❑ 84 Adam Keefe	.05	.15
❑ 85 Kevin Willis	.10	.30
❑ 86 David Wesley	.05	.15
❑ 87 Muggsy Bogues	.10	.30
❑ 88 Bimbo Coles	.05	.15
❑ 89 Tom Gugliotta	.10	.30
❑ 90 Jermaine O'Neal	.30	.75
❑ 91 Cedric Ceballos	.05	.15
❑ 92 Shawn Kemp	.10	.30
❑ 93 Horace Grant	.10	.30
❑ 94 Shareef Abdur-Rahim	.30	.75
❑ 95 Robert Horry	.10	.30
❑ 96 Vitaly Potapenko	.05	.15
❑ 97 Pooh Richardson	.05	.15
❑ 98 Doug Christie	.10	.30
❑ 99 Voshon Lenard	.05	.15

❑ 100 Dominique Wilkins	.20	.50
❑ 101 Alonzo Mourning	.10	.30
❑ 102 Sam Cassell	.20	.50
❑ 103 Sherman Douglas	.05	.15
❑ 104 Shawn Bradley	.05	.15
❑ 105 Mark Jackson	.10	.30
❑ 106 Dennis Rodman	.10	.30
❑ 107 Charles Oakley	.10	.30
❑ 108 Matt Maloney	.05	.15
❑ 109 Shaquille O'Neal	.50	1.25
❑ 110 Checklist	.05	.15
❑ 111 Antonio McDyess	.10	.30
❑ 112 Bob Sura	.05	.15
❑ 113 Terrell Brandon	.10	.30
❑ 114 Tim Thomas RC	.30	.75
❑ 115 Tim Duncan RC	.40	1.00
❑ 116 Antonio Daniels RC	.20	.50
❑ 117 Bryant Reeves	.05	.15
❑ 118 Keith Van Horn RC	.25	.60
❑ 119 Loy Vaught	.05	.15
❑ 120 Rasheed Wallace	.20	.50
❑ 121 Bobby Jackson RC	.30	.75
❑ 122 Kevin Johnson	.10	.30
❑ 123 Michael Jordan	1.25	3.00
❑ 124 Ron Mercer RC	.20	.50
❑ 125 Tracy McGrady RC	.60	1.50
❑ 126 Antoine Walker	.25	.60
❑ 127 Carlos Rogers	.05	.15
❑ 128 Isaac Austin	.05	.15
❑ 129 Mookie Blaylock	.05	.15
❑ 130 Rodrick Rhodes RC	.05	.15
❑ 131 Dennis Scott	.05	.15
❑ 132 Chris Mullin	.20	.50
❑ 133 P.J. Brown	.05	.15
❑ 134 Rex Chapman	.05	.15
❑ 135 Sean Elliott	.10	.30
❑ 136 Alan Henderson	.05	.15
❑ 137 Austin Croshere RC	.15	.40
❑ 138 Nick Van Exel	.20	.50
❑ 139 Derek Strong	.05	.15
❑ 140 Glenn Robinson	.20	.50
❑ 141 Avery Johnson	.05	.15
❑ 142 Calbert Cheaney	.05	.15
❑ 143 Mahmoud Abdul-Rauf	.05	.15
❑ 144 Stojko Vrankovic	.05	.15
❑ 145 Chris Childs	.05	.15
❑ 146 Danny Manning	.10	.30
❑ 147 Jeff Hornacek	.10	.30
❑ 148 Kevin Garnett	.40	1.00
❑ 149 Joe Dumars	.20	.50
❑ 150 Johnny Taylor RC	.05	.15
❑ 151 Mark Price	.10	.30
❑ 152 Toni Kukoc	.10	.30
❑ 153 Erick Dampier	.10	.30
❑ 154 Lorenzen Wright	.05	.15
❑ 155 Matt Geiger	.05	.15
❑ 156 Tim Hardaway	.10	.30
❑ 157 Charles Smith RC	.05	.15
❑ 158 Hersey Hawkins	.05	.15
❑ 159 Michael Finley	.20	.50
❑ 160 Tyus Edney	.05	.15
❑ 161 Christian Laettner	.10	.30
❑ 162 Doug West	.05	.15
❑ 163 Jim Jackson	.05	.15
❑ 164 Larry Johnson	.10	.30
❑ 165 Vin Baker	.10	.30
❑ 166 Karl Malone	.20	.50
❑ 167 Kelvin Cato RC	.20	.50
❑ 168 Luc Longley	.05	.15
❑ 169 Dale Davis	.05	.15
❑ 170 Joe Smith	.10	.30
❑ 171 Kobe Bryant	.75	2.00
❑ 172 Scot Pollard RC	.10	.30
❑ 173 Derek Anderson RC	.20	.50
❑ 174 Erick Strickland RC	.10	.30
❑ 175 Olden Polynice	.05	.15
❑ 176 Chris Whitney	.05	.15
❑ 177 Anthony Parker RC	.15	.30
❑ 178 Armon Gilliam	.05	.15
❑ 179 Gary Payton	.20	.50
❑ 180 Glen Rice	.10	.30
❑ 181 Chauncey Billups RC	.75	2.00
❑ 182 Derek Fisher	.20	.50
❑ 183 John Starks	.10	.30
❑ 184 Mario Elie	.05	.15
❑ 185 Chris Webber	.20	.50
❑ 186 Shawn Kemp	.10	.30
❑ 187 Greg Ostertag	.05	.15
❑ 188 Olivier Saint-Jean RC	.05	.15
❑ 189 Eric Snow	.10	.30
❑ 190 Isaiah Rider	.10	.30
❑ 191 Paul Grant RC	.05	.15
❑ 192 Samaki Walker	.05	.15
❑ 193 Cory Alexander	.05	.15
❑ 194 Eddie Jones	.20	.50
❑ 195 John Thomas RC	.05	.15
❑ 196 Otis Thorpe	.05	.15
❑ 197 Rod Strickland	.05	.15
❑ 198 David Wesley	.05	.15
❑ 199 Jacque Vaughn RC	.10	.30
❑ 200 Rik Smits	.10	.30
❑ 201 Brevin Knight RC	.10	.30
❑ 202 Clifford Robinson	.05	.15
❑ 203 Hakeem Olajuwon	.20	.50
❑ 204 Jerry Stackhouse	.20	.50
❑ 205 Tyrone Hill	.05	.15
❑ 206 Kendall Gill	.05	.15
❑ 207 Marcus Camby	.20	.50
❑ 208 Tony Battie RC	.20	.50
❑ 209 Brent Price	.05	.15
❑ 210 Danny Fortson RC	.10	.30
❑ 211 Jerome Williams	.10	.30
❑ 212 Maurice Taylor RC	.15	.40
❑ 213 Brian Williams	.05	.15
❑ 214 Keith Booth RC	.05	.15
❑ 215 Nick Anderson	.05	.15
❑ 216 Travis Knight	.05	.15
❑ 217 Adonal Foyle RC	.10	.30
❑ 218 Anfernee Hardaway	.20	.50
❑ 219 Kerry Kittles	.20	.50
❑ 220 Checklist	.05	.15

1998-99 Topps

❑ COMPLETE SET (220)	15.00	30.00
❑ COMPLETE SERIES 1 (110)	5.00	10.00
❑ COMPLETE SERIES 2 (110)	10.00	20.00
❑ 1 Scottie Pippen	.30	.75
❑ 2 Shareef Abdur-Rahim	.20	.50
❑ 3 Rod Strickland	.05	.15
❑ 4 Keith Van Horn	.20	.50
❑ 5 Ray Allen	.20	.50
❑ 6 Chris Mullin	.20	.50
❑ 7 Anthony Parker	.05	.15
❑ 8 Lindsey Hunter	.05	.15
❑ 9 Mario Elie	.05	.15
❑ 10 Jerry Stackhouse	.20	.50
❑ 11 Eldridge Recasner	.05	.15
❑ 12 Jeff Hornacek	.10	.30
❑ 13 Chris Webber	.20	.50
❑ 14 Lee Mayberry	.05	.15
❑ 15 Erick Strickland	.05	.15
❑ 16 Arvydas Sabonis	.10	.30
❑ 17 Tim Thomas	.10	.30
❑ 18 Luc Longley	.05	.15
❑ 19 Detlef Schrempf	.10	.30
❑ 20 Alonzo Mourning	.10	.30
❑ 21 Adonal Foyle	.05	.15
❑ 22 Tony Battie	.05	.15
❑ 23 Robert Horry	.10	.30
❑ 24 Derek Harper	.05	.15
❑ 25 Jamal Mashburn	.10	.30
❑ 26 Elliot Perry	.05	.15
❑ 27 Jalen Rose	.20	.50
❑ 28 Joe Smith	.10	.30
❑ 29 Henry James	.05	.15
❑ 30 Travis Knight	.05	.15
❑ 31 Tom Gugliotta	.05	.15
❑ 32 Chris Anstey	.05	.15
❑ 33 Antonio Daniels	.05	.15
❑ 34 Elden Campbell	.05	.15
❑ 35 Charlie Ward	.05	.15
❑ 36 Eddie Johnson	.05	.15
❑ 37 John Wallace	.05	.15
❑ 38 Antonio Davis	.05	.15
❑ 39 Antoine Walker	.20	.50
❑ 40 Patrick Ewing	.20	.50
❑ 41 Doug Christie	.10	.30
❑ 42 Andrew Lang	.05	.15
❑ 43 Joe Dumars	.20	.50
❑ 44 Jaren Jackson	.05	.15
❑ 45 Loy Vaught	.05	.15
❑ 46 Allan Houston	.10	.30
❑ 47 Mark Jackson	.10	.30
❑ 48 Tracy Murray	.05	.15
❑ 49 Tim Duncan	.30	.75
❑ 50 Micheal Williams	.05	.15
❑ 51 Steve Nash	.20	.50
❑ 52 Matt Maloney	.05	.15
❑ 53 Sam Cassell	.20	.50
❑ 54 Voshon Lenard	.05	.15
❑ 55 Dikembe Mutombo	.10	.30
❑ 56 Malik Sealy	.05	.15
❑ 57 Dell Curry	.05	.15
❑ 58 Stephon Marbury	.20	.50
❑ 59 Tariq Abdul-Wahad	.05	.15
❑ 60 Isaiah Rider	.05	.15
❑ 61 Kelvin Cato	.05	.15
❑ 62 LaPhonso Ellis	.05	.15
❑ 63 Jim Jackson	.05	.15
❑ 64 Greg Ostertag	.05	.15
❑ 65 Glenn Robinson	.10	.30
❑ 66 Chris Carr	.05	.15
❑ 67 Marcus Camby	.10	.30
❑ 68 Kobe Bryant	.75	2.00
❑ 69 Bobby Jackson	.10	.30
❑ 70 B.J. Armstrong	.05	.15
❑ 71 Alan Henderson	.05	.15
❑ 72 Terry Davis	.05	.15
❑ 73 John Stockton	.20	.50
❑ 74 Lamond Murray	.05	.15
❑ 75 Mark Price	.10	.30
❑ 76 Rex Chapman	.05	.15
❑ 77 Michael Jordan	1.25	3.00
❑ 78 Terry Cummings	.05	.15
❑ 79 Dan Majerle	.10	.30
❑ 80 Bo Outlaw	.05	.15
❑ 81 Michael Finley	.20	.50
❑ 82 Vin Baker	.10	.30
❑ 83 Clifford Robinson	.05	.15
❑ 84 Greg Anthony	.05	.15
❑ 85 Brevin Knight	.05	.15
❑ 86 Jacque Vaughn	.05	.15
❑ 87 Bobby Phills	.05	.15
❑ 88 Sherman Douglas	.05	.15
❑ 89 Kevin Johnson	.10	.30
❑ 90 Mahmoud Abdul-Rauf	.05	.15
❑ 91 Lorenzen Wright	.05	.15
❑ 92 Eric Williams	.05	.15
❑ 93 Will Perdue	.05	.15
❑ 94 Charles Barkley	.25	.60
❑ 95 Kendall Gill	.05	.15
❑ 96 Wesley Person	.05	.15
❑ 97 Buck Williams	.05	.15
❑ 98 Erick Dampier	.10	.30
❑ 99 Nate McMillan	.05	.15
❑ 100 Sean Elliott	.10	.30
❑ 101 Rasheed Wallace	.20	.50
❑ 102 Zydrunas Ilgauskas	.10	.30
❑ 103 Eddie Jones	.20	.50
❑ 104 Ron Mercer	.08	.25
❑ 105 Horace Grant	.10	.30
❑ 106 Corliss Williamson	.10	.30
❑ 107 Anthony Mason	.10	.30
❑ 108 Mookie Blaylock	.05	.15
❑ 109 Dennis Rodman	.10	.30
❑ 110 Checklist	.05	.15
❑ 111 Steve Smith	.10	.30
❑ 112 Cedric Henderson	.05	.15
❑ 113 Raef LaFrentz RC	.20	.50
❑ 114 Calbert Cheaney	.05	.15
❑ 115 Rik Smits	.10	.30
❑ 116 Rony Seikaly	.05	.15
❑ 117 Lawrence Funderburke	.05	.15
❑ 118 Ricky Davis RC	.60	1.50
❑ 119 Howard Eisley	.05	.15
❑ 120 Kenny Anderson	.10	.30
❑ 121 Corey Benjamin RC	.10	.30
❑ 122 Maurice Taylor	.08	.25
❑ 123 Eric Murdock	.05	.15
❑ 124 Derek Fisher	.20	.50
❑ 125 Kevin Garnett	.40	1.00
❑ 126 Walt Williams	.05	.15
❑ 127 Bryce Drew RC	.10	.30
❑ 128 A.C. Green	.10	.30

❑ 129 Ervin Johnson	.05	.15
❑ 130 Christian Laettner	.10	.30
❑ 131 Chauncey Billups	.10	.30
❑ 132 Hakeem Olajuwon	.20	.50
❑ 133 Al Harrington RC	.30	.75
❑ 134 Danny Manning	.05	.15
❑ 135 Paul Pierce RC	1.50	4.00
❑ 136 Terrell Brandon	.10	.30
❑ 137 Bob Sura	.05	.15
❑ 138 Chris Gatling	.05	.15
❑ 139 Donyell Marshall	.10	.30
❑ 140 Marcus Camby	.10	.30
❑ 141 Brian Skinner RC	.10	.30
❑ 142 Charles Oakley	.05	.15
❑ 143 Antawn Jamison RC	.60	1.50
❑ 144 Nazr Mohammed RC	.07	.20
❑ 145 Karl Malone	.20	.50
❑ 146 Chris Mills	.05	.15
❑ 147 Bison Dele	.05	.15
❑ 148 Gary Payton	.20	.50
❑ 149 Terry Porter	.05	.15
❑ 150 Tim Hardaway	.10	.30
❑ 151 Larry Hughes RC	.40	1.00
❑ 152 Derek Anderson	.15	.40
❑ 153 Jason Williams RC	.50	1.25
❑ 154 Dirk Nowitzki RC	2.00	5.00
❑ 155 Juwan Howard	.10	.30
❑ 156 Avery Johnson	.05	.15
❑ 157 Matt Harpring RC	.25	.60
❑ 158 Reggie Miller	.20	.50
❑ 159 Walter McCarty	.05	.15
❑ 160 Allen Iverson	.40	1.00
❑ 161 Felipe Lopez RC	.15	.40
❑ 162 Tracy McGrady	.50	1.25
❑ 163 Damon Stoudamire	.10	.30
❑ 164 Antonio McDyess	.10	.30
❑ 165 Grant Hill	.20	.50
❑ 166 Tyronn Lue RC	.15	.40
❑ 167 P.J. Brown	.05	.15
❑ 168 Antonio Daniels	.05	.15
❑ 169 Mitch Richmond	.10	.30
❑ 170 David Robinson	.20	.50
❑ 171 Shawn Bradley	.05	.15
❑ 172 Shandon Anderson	.05	.15
❑ 173 Chris Childs	.05	.15
❑ 174 Shawn Kemp	.10	.30
❑ 175 Shaquille O'Neal	.50	1.25
❑ 176 John Starks	.10	.30
❑ 177 Tyrone Hill	.05	.15
❑ 178 Jayson Williams	.05	.15
❑ 179 Anfernee Hardaway	.20	.50
❑ 180 Chris Webber	.20	.50
❑ 181 Don Reid	.05	.15
❑ 182 Stacey Augmon	.05	.15
❑ 183 Hersey Hawkins	.05	.15
❑ 184 Sam Mitchell	.05	.15
❑ 185 Jason Kidd	.30	.75
❑ 186 Nick Van Exel	.20	.50
❑ 187 Larry Johnson	.10	.30
❑ 188 Bryant Reeves	.05	.15
❑ 189 Glen Rice	.10	.30
❑ 190 Kerry Kittles	.05	.15
❑ 191 Toni Kukoc	.10	.30
❑ 192 Ron Harper	.10	.30
❑ 193 Bryon Russell	.05	.15
❑ 194 Vladimir Stepania RC	.05	.15
❑ 195 Michael Olowokandi RC	.20	.50
❑ 196 Mike Bibby RC	.50	1.25
❑ 197 Dale Ellis	.05	.15
❑ 198 Muggsy Bogues	.10	.30
❑ 199 Vince Carter RC	1.50	4.00
❑ 200 Robert Traylor RC	.10	.30
❑ 201 Peja Stojakovic RC	1.25	3.00
❑ 202 Aaron McKie	.10	.30
❑ 203 Hubert Davis	.05	.15
❑ 204 Dana Barros	.05	.15
❑ 205 Bonzi Wells RC	.50	1.25
❑ 206 Michael Doleac RC	.10	.30
❑ 207 Keon Clark RC	.20	.50
❑ 208 Michael Dickerson RC	.25	.60
❑ 209 Nick Anderson	.05	.15
❑ 210 Brent Price	.05	.15
❑ 211 Cherokee Parks	.05	.15
❑ 212 Sam Jacobson RC	.05	.15
❑ 213 Pat Garrity RC	.07	.20
❑ 214 Tyrone Corbin	.05	.15
❑ 215 David Wesley	.05	.15
❑ 216 Rodney Rogers	.05	.15
❑ 217 Dean Garrett	.05	.15
❑ 218 Roshown McLeod RC	.07	.20
❑ 219 Dale Davis	.10	.30
❑ 220 Checklist	.05	.15

1999-00 Topps

❑ COMPLETE SET (257)	30.00	60.00
❑ COMPLETE SERIES 1 (120)	12.50	25.00
❑ COMPLETE SERIES 2 (137)	17.50	35.00
❑ COMP.SERIES 1 w/o SP (110)	6.00	12.00
❑ COMP.SERIES 2 w/o SP (110)	5.00	10.00
❑ COMMON CARD (1-257)	.12	.30
❑ COMMON RC(111-120/231-248)	.30	.75
❑ COMMON USA (249-257)	.10	.30
❑ 1 Steve Smith	.12	.30
❑ 2 Ron Harper	.12	.30
❑ 3 Michael Dickerson	.12	.30
❑ 4 LaPhonso Ellis	.12	.30
❑ 5 Chris Webber	.20	.50
❑ 6 Jason Caffey	.12	.30
❑ 7 Bryon Russell	.12	.30
❑ 8 Bison Dele	.12	.30
❑ 9 Isaiah Rider	.12	.30
❑ 10 Dean Garrett	.12	.30
❑ 11 Eric Murdock	.12	.30
❑ 12 Juwan Howard	.15	.40
❑ 13 Latrell Sprewell	.15	.40
❑ 14 Jalen Rose	.15	.40
❑ 15 Larry Johnson	.20	.50
❑ 16 Eric Williams	.12	.30
❑ 17 Bryant Reeves	.12	.30
❑ 18 Tony Battie	.15	.40
❑ 19 Luc Longley	.12	.30
❑ 20 Gary Payton	.20	.50
❑ 21 Tariq Abdul-Wahad	.12	.30
❑ 22 Armen Gilliam UER	.12	.30
❑ 23 Shaquille O'Neal	.50	1.25
❑ 24 Gary Trent	.12	.30
❑ 25 John Stockton	.25	.60
❑ 26 Mark Jackson	.20	.50
❑ 27 Cherokee Parks	.12	.30
❑ 28 Michael Olowokandi	.12	.30
❑ 29 Raef LaFrentz	.15	.40
❑ 30 Dell Curry	.12	.30
❑ 31 Travis Best	.12	.30
❑ 32 Shawn Kemp	.20	.50
❑ 33 Voshon Lenard	.12	.30
❑ 34 Brian Grant	.12	.30
❑ 35 Alvin Williams	.12	.30
❑ 36 Derek Fisher	.20	.50
❑ 37 Allan Houston	.15	.40
❑ 38 Arvydas Sabonis	.15	.40
❑ 39 Terry Cummings	.12	.30
❑ 40 Dale Ellis	.12	.30
❑ 41 Maurice Taylor	.15	.40
❑ 42 Grant Hill	.20	.50
❑ 43 Anthony Mason	.12	.30
❑ 44 John Wallace	.12	.30
❑ 45 David Wesley	.12	.30
❑ 46 Nick Van Exel	.15	.40
❑ 47 Cuttino Mobley	.15	.40
❑ 48 Anfernee Hardaway	.20	.50
❑ 49 Terry Porter	.12	.30
❑ 50 Brent Barry	.15	.40
❑ 51 Derek Harper	.15	.40
❑ 52 Antoine Walker	.20	.50
❑ 53 Karl Malone	.25	.60
❑ 54 Ben Wallace	.15	.40
❑ 55 Vlade Divac	.20	.50
❑ 56 Sam Mitchell	.12	.30
❑ 57 Joe Smith	.15	.40
❑ 58 Shawn Bradley	.12	.30
❑ 59 Darrell Armstrong	.12	.30
❑ 60 Kenny Anderson	.15	.40
❑ 61 Jason Williams	.20	.50
❑ 62 Alonzo Mourning	.20	.50
❑ 63 Matt Harpring	.15	.40
❑ 64 Antonio Davis	.12	.30
❑ 65 Lindsey Hunter	.12	.30
❑ 66 Allen Iverson	.40	1.00
❑ 67 Mookie Blaylock	.12	.30
❑ 68 Wesley Person	.12	.30
❑ 69 Bobby Phills	.12	.30
❑ 70 Theo Ratliff	.15	.40
❑ 71 Antonio Daniels	.12	.30
❑ 72 P.J. Brown	.12	.30
❑ 73 David Robinson	.25	.60
❑ 74 Sean Elliott	.20	.50
❑ 75 Zydrunas Ilgauskas	.15	.40
❑ 76 Kerry Kittles	.12	.30
❑ 77 Otis Thorpe	.12	.30
❑ 78 John Starks	.20	.50
❑ 79 Jaren Jackson	.12	.30
❑ 80 Hersey Hawkins	.12	.30
❑ 81 Glenn Robinson	.15	.40
❑ 82 Paul Pierce	.20	.50
❑ 83 Glen Rice	.20	.50
❑ 84 Charlie Ward	.12	.30
❑ 85 Dee Brown	.12	.30
❑ 86 Danny Fortson	.12	.30
❑ 87 Billy Owens	.12	.30
❑ 88 Jason Kidd	.30	.75
❑ 89 Brent Price	.12	.30
❑ 90 Don Reid	.12	.30
❑ 91 Mark Bryant	.12	.30
❑ 92 Vinny Del Negro	.12	.30
❑ 93 Stephon Marbury	.20	.50
❑ 94 Donyell Marshall	.15	.40
❑ 95 Jim Jackson	.15	.40
❑ 96 Horace Grant	.15	.40
❑ 97 Calbert Cheaney	.12	.30
❑ 98 Vince Carter	.40	1.00
❑ 99 Bobby Jackson	.15	.40
❑ 100 Alan Henderson	.12	.30
❑ 101 Mike Bibby	.20	.50
❑ 102 Cedric Henderson	.12	.30
❑ 103 Lamond Murray	.12	.30
❑ 104 A.C. Green	.20	.50
❑ 105 Hakeem Olajuwon	.20	.50
❑ 106 George Lynch	.12	.30
❑ 107 Kendall Gill	.12	.30
❑ 108 Rex Chapman	.12	.30
❑ 109 Eddie Jones	.20	.50
❑ 110 Kornel David RC	.30	.75
❑ 111 Jason Terry RC	.75	2.00
❑ 112 Corey Maggette RC	1.00	2.50
❑ 113 Ron Artest RC	1.25	3.00
❑ 114 Richard Hamilton RC	1.00	2.50
❑ 115 Elton Brand RC	1.00	2.50
❑ 116 Baron Davis RC	1.25	3.00
❑ 117 Wally Szczerbiak RC	1.00	2.50
❑ 118 Steve Francis RC	1.00	2.50
❑ 119 James Posey RC	.50	1.25
❑ 120 Shawn Marion RC	1.00	2.50
❑ 121 Tim Duncan	.40	1.00
❑ 122 Danny Manning	.12	.30
❑ 123 Chris Mullin	.20	.50
❑ 124 Antawn Jamison	.20	.50
❑ 125 Kobe Bryant	1.00	2.50
❑ 126 Matt Geiger	.12	.30
❑ 127 Rod Strickland	.12	.30
❑ 128 Howard Eisley	.12	.30
❑ 129 Steve Nash	.30	.75
❑ 130 Felipe Lopez	.12	.30
❑ 131 Ron Mercer	.12	.30
❑ 132 Ruben Patterson	.12	.30
❑ 133 Dana Barros	.12	.30
❑ 134 Dale Davis	.12	.30
❑ 135 Bo Outlaw	.12	.30
❑ 136 Shandon Anderson	.12	.30
❑ 137 Mitch Richmond	.15	.40
❑ 138 Doug Christie	.15	.40
❑ 139 Rasheed Wallace	.20	.50
❑ 140 Chris Childs	.12	.30
❑ 141 Jamal Mashburn	.12	.30
❑ 142 Terrell Brandon	.12	.30
❑ 143 Jamie Feick RC	.20	.50
❑ 144 Robert Traylor	.12	.30
❑ 145 Rick Fox	.12	.30
❑ 146 Charles Barkley	.25	.60
❑ 147 Tyrone Nesby RC	.20	.50
❑ 148 Jerry Stackhouse	.20	.50
❑ 149 Cedric Ceballos	.12	.30
❑ 150 Dikembe Mutombo	.15	.40
❑ 151 Anthony Peeler	.12	.30
❑ 152 Larry Hughes	.15	.40

❑ 153 Clifford Robinson .12 .30
❑ 154 Corliss Williamson .12 .30
❑ 155 Olden Polynice .12 .30
❑ 156 Avery Johnson .15 .40
❑ 157 Tracy Murray .12 .30
❑ 158 Tom Gugliotta .12 .30
❑ 159 Tim Thomas .15 .40
❑ 160 Reggie Miller .20 .50
❑ 161 Tim Hardaway .20 .50
❑ 162 Dan Majerle .20 .50
❑ 163 Will Perdue .12 .30
❑ 164 Brevin Knight .12 .30
❑ 165 Elden Campbell .12 .30
❑ 166 Chris Gatling .12 .30
❑ 167 Walter McCarty .12 .30
❑ 168 Chauncey Billups .20 .50
❑ 169 Chris Mills .12 .30
❑ 170 Christian Laettner .15 .40
❑ 171 Robert Pack .12 .30
❑ 172 Rik Smits .20 .50
❑ 173 Tyrone Hill .12 .30
❑ 174 Damon Stoudamire .20 .50
❑ 175 Nick Anderson .12 .30
❑ 176 Peja Stojakovic .15 .40
❑ 177 Vladimir Stepania .12 .30
❑ 178 Tracy McGrady .40 1.00
❑ 179 Adam Keefe .12 .30
❑ 180 Shareef Abdur-Rahim .15 .40
❑ 181 Isaac Austin .12 .30
❑ 182 Mario Elie .12 .30
❑ 183 Rashard Lewis .20 .50
❑ 184 Scott Burrell .12 .30
❑ 185 Othella Harrington .12 .30
❑ 186 Eric Piatkowski .15 .40
❑ 187 Bryant Stith .12 .30
❑ 188 Michael Finley .20 .50
❑ 189 Chris Crawford .12 .30
❑ 190 Toni Kukoc .20 .50
❑ 191 Danny Ferry .12 .30
❑ 192 Erick Dampier .15 .40
❑ 193 Clarence Weatherspoon .12 .30
❑ 194 Bob Sura .12 .30
❑ 195 Jayson Williams .15 .40
❑ 196 Kurt Thomas .15 .40
❑ 197 Greg Anthony .12 .30
❑ 198 Rodney Rogers .12 .30
❑ 199 Detlef Schrempf .15 .40
❑ 200 Keith Van Horn .15 .40
❑ 201 Robert Horry .20 .50
❑ 202 Sam Cassell .15 .40
❑ 203 Malik Sealy .12 .30
❑ 204 Kelvin Cato .12 .30
❑ 205 Antonio McDyess .15 .40
❑ 206 Andrew DeClercq .12 .30
❑ 207 Ricky Davis .20 .50
❑ 208 Vitaly Potapenko .12 .30
❑ 209 Loy Vaught .12 .30
❑ 210 Kevin Garnett .40 1.00
❑ 211 Eric Snow .15 .40
❑ 212 Anfernee Hardaway .20 .50
❑ 213 Vin Baker .20 .50
❑ 214 Lawrence Funderburke .12 .30
❑ 215 Jeff Hornacek .15 .40
❑ 216 Doug West .12 .30
❑ 217 Michael Doleac .12 .30
❑ 218 Ray Allen .20 .50
❑ 219 Derek Anderson .12 .30
❑ 220 Jerome Williams .12 .30
❑ 221 Derrick Coleman .15 .40
❑ 222 Randy Brown .12 .30
❑ 223 Patrick Ewing .25 .60
❑ 224 Walt Williams .12 .30
❑ 225 Charles Oakley .15 .40
❑ 226 Steve Kerr .15 .40
❑ 227 Muggsy Bogues .15 .40
❑ 228 Kevin Willis .12 .30
❑ 229 Marcus Camby .15 .40
❑ 230 Scottie Pippen .30 .75
❑ 231 Lamar Odom RC 1.00 2.50
❑ 232 Jonathan Bender RC .30 .75
❑ 233 Andre Miller RC 1.00 2.50
❑ 234 Trajan Langdon RC .30 .75
❑ 235 A.Radojevic RC .30 .75
❑ 236 William Avery RC .30 .75
❑ 237 Cal Bowdler RC .30 .75
❑ 238 Quincy Lewis RC .30 .75
❑ 239 Dion Glover RC .30 .75
❑ 240 Jeff Foster RC .40 1.00
❑ 241 Kenny Thomas RC .30 .75
❑ 242 Devean George RC .50 1.25
❑ 243 Tim James RC .30 .75
❑ 244 Vonteego Cummings RC .30 .75
❑ 245 Jumaine Jones RC .30 .75
❑ 246 Scott Padgett RC .30 .75
❑ 247 Adrian Griffin RC .30 .75
❑ 248 Chris Herren RC .30 .75
❑ 249 Allan Houston USA .15 .40
❑ 250 Kevin Garnett USA .40 1.00
❑ 251 Gary Payton USA .20 .50
❑ 252 Steve Smith USA .12 .30
❑ 253 Tim Hardaway USA .20 .50
❑ 254 Tim Duncan USA .40 1.00
❑ 255 Jason Kidd USA .30 .75
❑ 256 Tom Gugliotta USA .12 .30
❑ 257 Vin Baker USA .20 .50

2000-01 Topps

❑ COMPLETE SET (295) 40.00 80.00
❑ COMPLETE SERIES 1 (155) 30.00 60.00
❑ COMP.SERIES 1 w/o RC (130) 7.50 15.00
❑ COMPLETE SERIES 2 (140) 12.50 25.00
❑ COMP.SERIES 2 w/o RC (120) 7.50 15.00
❑ COMMON CARD (1-295) .12 .30
❑ COMMON RC (125-149/266-285) .40 1.00
❑ 1 Elton Brand .20 .50
❑ 2 Marcus Camby .15 .40
❑ 3 Jalen Rose .15 .40
❑ 4 Jamie Feick .12 .30
❑ 5 Toni Kukoc .15 .40
❑ 6 Todd MacCulloch .12 .30
❑ 7 Mario Elie .12 .30
❑ 8 Doug Christie .12 .30
❑ 9 Sam Cassell .15 .40
❑ 10 Shaquille O'Neal .50 1.25
❑ 11 Larry Hughes .15 .40
❑ 12 Jerry Stackhouse .15 .40
❑ 13 Rick Fox .15 .40
❑ 14 Clifford Robinson .12 .30
❑ 15 Felipe Lopez .12 .30
❑ 16 Dirk Nowitzki .30 .75
❑ 17 Cuttino Mobley .15 .40
❑ 18 Latrell Sprewell .15 .40
❑ 19 Nick Anderson .12 .30
❑ 20 Kevin Garnett .40 1.00
❑ 21 Rik Smits .12 .30
❑ 22 Jerome Williams .12 .30
❑ 23 Chris Webber .20 .50
❑ 24 Jason Terry .20 .50
❑ 25 Elden Campbell .12 .30
❑ 26 Kelvin Cato .12 .30
❑ 27 Tyrone Nesby .12 .30
❑ 28 Jonathan Bender .12 .30
❑ 29 Otis Thorpe .15 .40
❑ 30 Scottie Pippen .30 .75
❑ 31 Radoslav Nesterovic .12 .30
❑ 32 P.J. Brown .12 .30
❑ 33 Reggie Miller .20 .50
❑ 34 Andre Miller .15 .40
❑ 35 Tariq Abdul-Wahad .12 .30
❑ 36 Michael Doleac .12 .30
❑ 37 Rashard Lewis .20 .50
❑ 38 Jacque Vaughn .12 .30
❑ 39 Larry Johnson .15 .40
❑ 40 Steve Francis .20 .50
❑ 41 Arvydas Sabonis .15 .40
❑ 42 Jaren Jackson .12 .30
❑ 43 Howard Eisley .12 .30
❑ 44 Rod Strickland .15 .40
❑ 45 Tim Thomas .12 .30
❑ 46 Robert Horry .15 .40
❑ 47 Kenny Thomas .12 .30
❑ 48 Anthony Peeler .12 .30
❑ 49 Darrell Armstrong .12 .30
❑ 50 Vince Carter .40 1.00
❑ 51 Othella Harrington .12 .30
❑ 52 Derek Anderson .15 .40
❑ 53 Anthony Carter .12 .30
❑ 54 Scott Burrell .12 .30
❑ 55 Ray Allen .20 .50
❑ 56 Jason Kidd .30 .75
❑ 57 Sean Elliott .15 .40
❑ 58 Muggsy Bogues .15 .40
❑ 59 LaPhonso Ellis .15 .40
❑ 60 Tim Duncan .40 1.00
❑ 61 Adrian Griffin .12 .30
❑ 62 Wally Szczerbiak .15 .40
❑ 63 Austin Croshere .12 .30
❑ 64 Wesley Person .12 .30
❑ 65 James Posey .12 .30
❑ 66 Alan Henderson .12 .30
❑ 67 Ruben Patterson .12 .30
❑ 68 Jahidi White .12 .30
❑ 69 Shawn Marion .20 .50
❑ 70 Lamar Odom .20 .50
❑ 71 Lindsey Hunter .12 .30
❑ 72 Keon Clark .12 .30
❑ 73 Gary Trent .12 .30
❑ 74 Lamond Murray .12 .30
❑ 75 Paul Pierce .20 .50
❑ 76 Charlie Ward .12 .30
❑ 77 Matt Geiger .12 .30
❑ 78 Greg Anthony .12 .30
❑ 79 Horace Grant .15 .40
❑ 80 John Stockton .25 .60
❑ 81 Peja Stojakovic .15 .40
❑ 82 William Avery .12 .30
❑ 83 Dan Majerle .15 .40
❑ 84 Christian Laettner .12 .30
❑ 85 Dana Barros .12 .30
❑ 86 Corey Benjamin .12 .30
❑ 87 Keith Van Horn .15 .40
❑ 88 Patrick Ewing .25 .60
❑ 89 Steve Smith .15 .40
❑ 90 Antonio Davis .12 .30
❑ 91 Samaki Walker .12 .30
❑ 92 Mitch Richmond .15 .40
❑ 93 Michael Olowokandi .12 .30
❑ 94 Baron Davis .20 .50
❑ 95 Dikembe Mutombo .15 .40
❑ 96 Andrew DeClercq .12 .30
❑ 97 Raef LaFrentz .12 .30
❑ 98 Trajan Langdon .12 .30
❑ 99 Ervin Johnson .12 .30
❑ 100 Alonzo Mourning .20 .50
❑ 101 Kendall Gill .12 .30
❑ 102 George Lynch .12 .30
❑ 103 Detlef Schrempf .15 .40
❑ 104 Donyell Marshall .12 .30
❑ 105 Bo Outlaw .12 .30
❑ 106 Kenny Anderson .15 .40
❑ 107 Eddie Robinson .12 .30
❑ 108 Jermaine O'Neal .20 .50
❑ 109 John Amaechi .12 .30
❑ 110 Glen Rice .15 .40
❑ 111 Vlade Divac .15 .40
❑ 112 Vin Baker .15 .40
❑ 113 Mike Bibby .15 .40
❑ 114 Richard Hamilton .15 .40
❑ 115 Mookie Blaylock .15 .40
❑ 116 Vitaly Potapenko .12 .30
❑ 117 Anthony Mason .12 .30
❑ 118 Robert Pack .12 .30
❑ 119 Vonteego Cummings .12 .30
❑ 120 Michael Finley .20 .50
❑ 121 Ron Artest .20 .50
❑ 122 Tyrone Hill .12 .30
❑ 123 Rodney Rogers .12 .30
❑ 124 Quincy Lewis .12 .30
❑ 125 Kenyon Martin RC 1.00 2.50
❑ 126 Stromile Swift RC .50 1.25
❑ 127 Darius Miles RC .50 1.25
❑ 128 Marcus Fizer RC .40 1.00
❑ 129 Mike Miller RC .60 1.50
❑ 130 DerMarr Johnson RC .40 1.00
❑ 131 Chris Mihm RC .40 1.00
❑ 132 Jamal Crawford RC .60 1.50
❑ 133 Joel Przybilla RC .40 1.00
❑ 134 Keyon Dooling RC .40 1.00
❑ 135 Jerome Moiso RC .40 1.00
❑ 136 Etan Thomas RC .40 1.00
❑ 137 Courtney Alexander RC .40 1.00
❑ 138 Mateen Cleaves RC .40 1.00
❑ 139 Jason Collier RC .40 1.00
❑ 140 Desmond Mason RC .50 1.25

❑ 141 Quentin Richardson RC .50 1.25
❑ 142 Jamaal Magloire RC .40 1.00
❑ 143 Speedy Claxton RC .40 1.00
❑ 144 Morris Peterson RC .60 1.50
❑ 145 Donnell Harvey RC .40 1.00
❑ 146 DeShawn Stevenson RC .40 1.00
❑ 147 Mamadou N'Diaye RC .40 1.00
❑ 148 Erick Barkley RC .40 1.00
❑ 149 Mark Madsen RC .40 1.00
❑ 150 Shaq/Iverson/G.Hill SL .15 .40
❑ 151 Kidd/Cassell/Van Exel SL .20 .50
❑ 152 Mutombo/Shaq/Duncan SL .25 .60
❑ 153 E.Jones/Pierce/Armstrong SL .10 .30
❑ 154 Mourning/Mutombo/Shaq SL .20 .50
❑ 155 Team Championship SL .30 .75
❑ 156 Jason Williams .15 .40
❑ 157 David Robinson .25 .60
❑ 158 Shammond Williams .12 .30
❑ 159 Charles Oakley .15 .40
❑ 160 Greg Ostertag .12 .30
❑ 161 Juwan Howard .15 .40
❑ 162 Antoine Walker .15 .40
❑ 163 Alan Henderson .12 .30
❑ 164 Eddie Jones .15 .40
❑ 165 Allen Iverson .40 1.00
❑ 166 Grant Hill .20 .50
❑ 167 Terrell Brandon .12 .30
❑ 168 Stephon Marbury .20 .50
❑ 169 Jason Caffey .12 .30
❑ 170 Sam Mitchell .12 .30
❑ 171 Jamal Mashburn .15 .40
❑ 172 Ron Harper .15 .40
❑ 173 Eric Piatkowski .12 .30
❑ 174 Sam Perkins .12 .30
❑ 175 Walt Williams .12 .30
❑ 176 Bob Sura .12 .30
❑ 177 Michael Curry .12 .30
❑ 178 Nick Van Exel .15 .40
❑ 179 Danny Ferry .12 .30
❑ 180 Randy Brown .12 .30
❑ 181 Danny Fortson .12 .30
❑ 182 Jim Jackson .12 .30
❑ 183 Brad Miller .15 .40
❑ 184 Shawn Bradley .12 .30
❑ 185 Voshon Lenard .12 .30
❑ 186 Erick Dampier .12 .30
❑ 187 Mark Jackson .15 .40
❑ 188 Maurice Taylor .12 .30
❑ 189 Kobe Bryant 1.00 2.50
❑ 190 Clarence Weatherspoon .12 .30
❑ 191 Bobby Jackson .12 .30
❑ 192 Eric Snow .12 .30
❑ 193 Allan Houston .15 .40
❑ 194 Kurt Thomas .12 .30
❑ 195 Chauncey Billups .20 .50
❑ 196 Tom Gugliotta .12 .30
❑ 197 Theo Ratliff .12 .30
❑ 198 Rasheed Wallace .20 .50
❑ 199 Jon Barry .12 .30
❑ 200 Malik Rose .12 .30
❑ 201 Vernon Maxwell .12 .30
❑ 202 Dee Brown .12 .30
❑ 203 Bryon Russell .12 .30
❑ 204 Brent Barry .12 .30
❑ 205 Tracy McGrady .40 1.00
❑ 206 Bryant Reeves .12 .30
❑ 207 Isaac Austin .12 .30
❑ 208 Damon Stoudamire .15 .40
❑ 209 Anfernee Hardaway .20 .50
❑ 210 Aaron McKie .12 .30
❑ 211 Johnny Newman .12 .30
❑ 212 Scott Williams .12 .30
❑ 213 Brian Shaw .12 .30
❑ 214 Corey Maggette .15 .40
❑ 215 Travis Best .12 .30
❑ 216 Hakeem Olajuwon .25 .60
❑ 217 Antawn Jamison .20 .50
❑ 218 John Starks .12 .30
❑ 219 Antonio McDyess .15 .40
❑ 220 Cedric Ceballos .12 .30
❑ 221 Chris Carr .12 .30
❑ 222 Roshown McLeod .12 .30
❑ 223 Calbert Cheaney .12 .30
❑ 224 Gary Payton .20 .50
❑ 225 Karl Malone .25 .60
❑ 226 Michael Dickerson .12 .30
❑ 227 Tracy Murray .12 .30
❑ 228 Chris Childs .12 .30
❑ 229 Pat Garrity .12 .30
❑ 230 Rex Chapman .12 .30
❑ 231 Jumaine Jones .12 .30
❑ 232 Fred Hoiberg .12 .30
❑ 233 Bimbo Coles .12 .30
❑ 234 Shawn Kemp .20 .50
❑ 235 David Wesley .12 .30
❑ 236 Tony Battie .12 .30
❑ 237 Ron Mercer .12 .30
❑ 238 John Wallace .12 .30
❑ 239 Robert Traylor .12 .30
❑ 240 Derrick Coleman .15 .40
❑ 241 Steve Nash .30 .75
❑ 242 Ben Wallace .15 .40
❑ 243 Brian Skinner .12 .30
❑ 244 Chris Gatling .12 .30
❑ 245 Dale Davis .12 .30
❑ 246 Joe Smith .12 .30
❑ 247 Glenn Robinson .15 .40
❑ 248 Kerry Kittles .15 .40
❑ 249 Erick Strickland .12 .30
❑ 250 Sam Cassell .15 .40
❑ 251 Chucky Atkins .12 .30
❑ 252 Brian Grant .12 .30
❑ 253 Bonzi Wells .12 .30
❑ 254 Corliss Williamson .15 .40
❑ 255 Shareef Abdur-Rahim .15 .40
❑ 256 Kevin Willis .12 .30
❑ 257 Scott Padgett .12 .30
❑ 258 Terry Porter .15 .40
❑ 259 Tony Delk .12 .30
❑ 260 Avery Johnson .15 .40
❑ 261 Tim Hardaway .15 .40
❑ 262 Derek Fisher .20 .50
❑ 263 Isaiah Rider .15 .40
❑ 264 Shandon Anderson .12 .30
❑ 265 Adonal Foyle .12 .30
❑ 266 Hedo Turkoglu RC 1.00 2.50
❑ 267 Brian Cardinal RC .40 1.00
❑ 268 Iakovos Tsakalidis RC .40 1.00
❑ 269 Dalibor Bagaric RC .40 1.00
❑ 270 Marko Jaric RC .40 1.00
❑ 271 Dan Langhi RC .40 1.00
❑ 272 A.J. Guyton RC .40 1.00
❑ 273 Jake Voskuhl RC .40 1.00
❑ 274 Khalid El-Amin RC .40 1.00
❑ 275 Mike Smith RC .40 1.00
❑ 276 Soumaila Samake RC .40 1.00
❑ 277 Eddie House RC .40 1.00
❑ 278 Eduardo Najera RC .40 1.00
❑ 279 Lavor Postell RC .40 1.00
❑ 280 Hanno Mottola RC .40 1.00
❑ 281 Chris Carrawell RC .40 1.00
❑ 282 Olumide Oyedeji RC .40 1.00
❑ 283 Michael Redd RC 1.00 2.50
❑ 284 Chris Porter RC .40 1.00
❑ 285 Mark Karcher RC .40 1.00
❑ 286 S.Francis/G.Payton SC .20 .50
❑ 287 D.Miles/K.Garnett SC .12 .30
❑ 288 L.Odom/Abdur-Rahim SC .20 .50
❑ 289 T.Duncan/A.Mourning SC .25 .60
❑ 290 E.Brand/K.Malone SC .20 .50
❑ 291 L.Hughes/A.Iverson SC .20 .50
❑ 292 K.Bryant/R.Miller SC .50 1.25
❑ 293 V.Carter/G.Hill SC .25 .60
❑ 294 T.McGrady/S.Pippen SC .40 1.00
❑ 295 K.Martin/M.Camby SC .75 2.00

2001-02 Topps

❑ COMPLETE SET (257) 40.00 80.00
❑ COMP.SET w/o RC (220) 15.00 30.00
❑ COMMON CARD (1-220) .05 .15
❑ COMMON ROOKIE (221-256) .60 1.50
❑ 1 Shaquille O'Neal .50 1.25
❑ 2 Travis Best .12 .30
❑ 3 Allen Iverson .40 1.00
❑ 4 Shawn Marion .20 .50
❑ 5 Rasheed Wallace .20 .50
❑ 6 Antonio Daniels .12 .30
❑ 7 Rashard Lewis .20 .50
❑ 8 John Starks .12 .30
❑ 9 Stromile Swift .12 .30
❑ 10 Vince Carter .40 1.00
❑ 11 George Lynch .12 .30
❑ 12 Kendall Gill .12 .30
❑ 13 Glen Rice .15 .40
❑ 14 Glenn Robinson .15 .40
❑ 15 Wally Szczerbiak .15 .40
❑ 16 Rick Fox .15 .40
❑ 17 Darius Miles .12 .30
❑ 18 Jermaine O'Neal .20 .50
❑ 19 Erick Dampier .12 .30
❑ 20 Tracy McGrady .40 1.00
❑ 21 Kevin Garnett .40 1.00
❑ 22 Tim Thomas .12 .30
❑ 23 Larry Hughes .15 .40
❑ 24 Jerry Stackhouse .15 .40
❑ 25 Voshon Lenard .12 .30
❑ 26 Howard Eisley .12 .30
❑ 27 Clarence Weatherspoon .12 .30
❑ 28 Marcus Fizer .12 .30
❑ 29 Elden Campbell .12 .30
❑ 30 Tim Duncan .40 1.00
❑ 31 Doug Christie .12 .30
❑ 32 Keon Clark .12 .30
❑ 33 Patrick Ewing .25 .60
❑ 34 Hakeem Olajuwon .25 .60
❑ 35 Stephen Jackson .15 .40
❑ 36 Larry Johnson .15 .40
❑ 37 Eric Snow .12 .30
❑ 38 Tom Gugliotta .12 .30
❑ 39 Scottie Pippen .30 .75
❑ 40 Chris Webber .20 .50
❑ 41 David Robinson .25 .60
❑ 42 Elton Brand .20 .50
❑ 43 Theo Ratliff .12 .30
❑ 44 Paul Pierce .20 .50
❑ 45 Jamal Mashburn .15 .40
❑ 46 Eric Williams .12 .30
❑ 47 DerMarr Johnson .12 .30
❑ 48 Andre Miller .15 .40
❑ 49 Dirk Nowitzki .30 .75
❑ 50 Kobe Bryant 1.00 2.50
❑ 51 Keyon Dooling .12 .30
❑ 52 Brian Grant .12 .30
❑ 53 Ervin Johnson .12 .30
❑ 54 Anthony Peeler .12 .30
❑ 55 Dikembe Mutombo .15 .40
❑ 56 Steve Smith .15 .40
❑ 57 Hedo Turkoglu .15 .40
❑ 58 Terry Porter .12 .30
❑ 59 Lorenzen Wright .12 .30
❑ 60 Jason Terry .20 .50
❑ 61 Vitaly Potapenko .12 .30
❑ 62 Derrick Coleman .15 .40
❑ 63 Ron Artest .15 .40
❑ 64 Chris Gatling .12 .30
❑ 65 Chris Mihm .12 .30
❑ 66 Reggie Miller .20 .50
❑ 67 Lamar Odom .20 .50
❑ 68 Ron Harper .15 .40
❑ 69 Baron Davis .20 .50
❑ 70 Brad Miller .15 .40
❑ 71 Shawn Bradley .12 .30
❑ 72 James Posey .12 .30
❑ 73 Ben Wallace .15 .40
❑ 74 Marc Jackson .12 .30
❑ 75 Maurice Taylor .12 .30
❑ 76 Aaron McKie .12 .30
❑ 77 Grant Hill .20 .50
❑ 78 Arvydas Sabonis .15 .40
❑ 79 Peja Stojakovic .15 .40
❑ 80 Jason Kidd .30 .75
❑ 81 Vin Baker .15 .40
❑ 82 Morris Peterson .15 .40
❑ 83 Bryon Russell .12 .30
❑ 84 Michael Dickerson .12 .30
❑ 85 Christian Laettner .12 .30
❑ 86 Jerome Williams .12 .30
❑ 87 Desmond Mason .15 .40
❑ 88 Sean Elliott .12 .30
❑ 89 Marcus Camby .15 .40
❑ 90 Stephon Marbury .20 .50
❑ 91 Joel Przybilla .12 .30
❑ 92 Alonzo Mourning .20 .50
❑ 93 Brian Shaw .12 .30

❏ 94 Austin Croshere .12 .30
❏ 95 Mookie Blaylock .15 .40
❏ 96 Mateen Cleaves .12 .30
❏ 97 Nick Van Exel .15 .40
❏ 98 Michael Finley .20 .50
❏ 99 Jamal Crawford .15 .40
❏ 100 Steve Francis .20 .50
❏ 101 Tim Hardaway .15 .40
❏ 102 Sam Cassell .15 .40
❏ 103 Shammond Williams .12 .30
❏ 104 DeShawn Stevenson .12 .30
❏ 105 Bryant Reeves .12 .30
❏ 106 Richard Hamilton .15 .40
❏ 107 Antonio Davis .12 .30
❏ 108 Brent Barry .12 .30
❏ 109 Derek Anderson .15 .40
❏ 110 Kenny Anderson .15 .40
❏ 111 Brevin Knight .12 .30
❏ 112 Tyrone Nesby .12 .30
❏ 113 Erick Strickland .12 .30
❏ 114 Jacque Vaughn .12 .30
❏ 115 John Stockton .25 .60
❏ 116 Alvin Williams .12 .30
❏ 117 Speedy Claxton .12 .30
❏ 118 Bo Outlaw .12 .30
❏ 119 Jahidi White .12 .30
❏ 120 Karl Malone .25 .60
❏ 121 Charles Oakley .15 .40
❏ 122 Malik Rose .12 .30
❏ 123 Avery Johnson .15 .40
❏ 124 Toni Kukoc .15 .40
❏ 125 Bryant Stith .12 .30
❏ 126 P.J. Brown .12 .30
❏ 127 Ron Mercer .12 .30
❏ 128 Lamond Murray .12 .30
❏ 129 Steve Nash .30 .75
❏ 130 Raef LaFrentz .12 .30
❏ 131 Corliss Williamson .15 .40
❏ 132 Danny Fortson .12 .30
❏ 133 Chris Porter .12 .30
❏ 134 Shandon Anderson .12 .30
❏ 135 Jalen Rose .15 .40
❏ 136 Corey Maggette .15 .40
❏ 137 Horace Grant .15 .40
❏ 138 Eddie Jones .15 .40
❏ 139 Chauncey Billups .15 .40
❏ 140 Ray Allen .20 .50
❏ 141 Terrell Brandon .12 .30
❏ 142 Keith Van Horn .15 .40
❏ 143 Allan Houston .15 .40
❏ 144 Mark Jackson .15 .40
❏ 145 Pat Garrity .12 .30
❏ 146 Anfernee Hardaway .20 .50
❏ 147 Iakovos Tsakalidis .12 .30
❏ 148 Damon Stoudamire .15 .40
❏ 149 Bobby Jackson .12 .30
❏ 150 Antawn Jamison .20 .50
❏ 151 Kenny Thomas .12 .30
❏ 152 Jonathan Bender .12 .30
❏ 153 Jeff McInnis .12 .30
❏ 154 Robert Horry .15 .40
❏ 155 Anthony Mason .12 .30
❏ 156 Lindsey Hunter .12 .30
❏ 157 LaPhonso Ellis .15 .40
❏ 158 Jamie Feick .12 .30
❏ 159 Kurt Thomas .12 .30
❏ 160 Gary Payton .20 .50
❏ 161 Rod Strickland .15 .40
❏ 162 Bonzi Wells .15 .40
❏ 163 Scot Pollard .12 .30
❏ 164 Raja Bell RC .50 1.25
❏ 165 Rodney Rogers .12 .30
❏ 166 John Amaechi .12 .30
❏ 167 Darrell Armstrong .12 .30
❏ 168 Aaron Williams .12 .30
❏ 169 Latrell Sprewell .15 .40
❏ 170 Radoslav Nesterovic .12 .30
❏ 171 Anthony Carter .12 .30
❏ 172 Quentin Richardson .15 .40
❏ 173 Primoz Brezec RC .60 1.50
❏ 174 Michael Olowokandi .12 .30
❏ 175 Jason Williams .15 .40
❏ 176 Ruben Patterson .12 .30
❏ 177 Chris Childs .12 .30
❏ 178 Greg Ostertag .12 .30
❏ 179 Mike Bibby .15 .40
❏ 180 Mitch Richmond .15 .40
❏ 181 Donyell Marshall .12 .30
❏ 182 Dale Davis .12 .30
❏ 183 Tony Delk .12 .30
❏ 184 Mike Miller .15 .40
❏ 185 Charlie Ward .12 .30
❏ 186 Kenyon Martin .20 .50
❏ 187 Walt Williams .12 .30
❏ 188 Al Harrington .15 .40
❏ 189 Chucky Atkins .12 .30
❏ 190 Kevin Willis .12 .30
❏ 191 Juwan Howard .15 .40
❏ 192 Jim Jackson .12 .30
❏ 193 Antonio McDyess .15 .40
❏ 194 Jamaal Magloire .12 .30
❏ 195 Mark Blount .12 .30
❏ 196 Fred Hoiberg .12 .30
❏ 197 Nazr Mohammed .12 .30
❏ 198 Antoine Walker .15 .40
❏ 199 Wang Zhizhi .15 .40
❏ 200 Shareef Abdur-Rahim .15 .40
❏ 201 Chris Whitney .12 .30
❏ 202 David Wesley .12 .30
❏ 203 Matt Harpring .15 .40
❏ 204 George McCloud .12 .30
❏ 205 Joe Smith .12 .30
❏ 206 Cuttino Mobley .15 .40
❏ 207 Tyrone Hill .12 .30
❏ 208 Clifford Robinson .12 .30
❏ 209 Vlade Divac .15 .40
❏ 210 Eddie Robinson .12 .30
❏ 211 Michael Curry .12 .30
❏ 212 Courtney Alexander .12 .30
❏ 213 Grant Long .12 .30
❏ 214 Dan Majerle .15 .40
❏ 215 Points Leaders .30 .75
❏ 216 Rebounds Leaders .10 .30
❏ 217 Assists Leaders .20 .50
❏ 218 Steals Leaders .10 .30
❏ 219 Blocks Leaders .10 .30
❏ 220 Team Championship .40 1.00
❏ 221 Kwame Brown RC .75 2.00
❏ 222 Tyson Chandler RC 1.25 3.00
❏ 223 Pau Gasol RC 2.50 6.00
❏ 224 Eddy Curry RC 1.00 2.50
❏ 225 Jason Richardson RC 1.25 3.00
❏ 226 Shane Battier RC 1.00 2.50
❏ 227 Eddie Griffin RC .60 1.50
❏ 228 DeSagana Diop RC .60 1.50
❏ 229 Rodney White RC .60 1.50
❏ 230 Joe Johnson RC 1.50 4.00
❏ 231 Kedrick Brown RC .60 1.50
❏ 232 Vladimir Radmanovic RC .75 2.00
❏ 233 Richard Jefferson RC 1.50 4.00
❏ 234 Troy Murphy RC 1.25 3.00
❏ 235 Steven Hunter RC .60 1.50
❏ 236 Kirk Haston RC .60 1.50
❏ 237 Michael Bradley RC .60 1.50
❏ 238 Jason Collins RC .60 1.50
❏ 239 Zach Randolph RC 1.50 4.00
❏ 240 Brendan Haywood RC .75 2.00
❏ 241 Joseph Forte RC .60 1.50
❏ 242 Jeryl Sasser RC .60 1.50
❏ 243 Brandon Armstrong RC .60 1.50
❏ 244 Gerald Wallace RC 1.50 4.00
❏ 245 Samuel Dalembert RC .75 2.00
❏ 246 Jamaal Tinsley RC .75 2.00
❏ 247 Tony Parker RC 2.50 6.00
❏ 248 Trenton Hassell RC .75 2.00
❏ 249 Gilbert Arenas RC 1.00 2.50
❏ 250 Jeff Trepagnier RC .60 1.50
❏ 251 Damone Brown RC .60 1.50
❏ 252 Loren Woods RC .60 1.50
❏ 253 Ousmane Cisse RC .60 1.50
❏ 254 Ken Johnson RC .60 1.50
❏ 255 Kenny Satterfield RC .60 1.50
❏ 256 Alvin Jones RC .60 1.50
❏ 257 Pau Gasol Preseason 5.00 12.00
❏ TRSC S.O'Neal/K.Abdul-Jabbar 125.00 250.00
❏ NNO G.Arenas SPEC AU 25.00 50.00

2002-03 Topps

❏ COMPLETE SET (220) 40.00 80.00
❏ COMMON CARD (1-184) .12 .30
❏ COMMON ROOKIE (185-220) .75 2.00
❏ 1 Shaquille O'Neal .50 1.25
❏ 2 Pau Gasol .20 .50
❏ 3 Allen Iverson .40 1.00
❏ 4 Tom Gugliotta .12 .30
❏ 5 Rasheed Wallace .20 .50
❏ 6 Peja Stojakovic .15 .40
❏ 7 Jason Richardson .20 .50
❏ 8 Rashard Lewis .20 .50
❏ 9 Morris Peterson .15 .40
❏ 10 Michael Jordan 1.25 3.00
❏ 11 Matt Harpring .15 .40
❏ 12 Shareef Abdur-Rahim .15 .40
❏ 13 Antoine Walker .15 .40
❏ 14 Stephon Marbury .20 .50
❏ 15 Jamal Mashburn .15 .40
❏ 16 Eddy Curry .15 .40
❏ 17 Jumaine Jones .12 .30
❏ 18 Wang Zhizhi .12 .30
❏ 19 James Posey .12 .30
❏ 20 Jason Kidd .30 .75
❏ 21 Jerry Stackhouse .15 .40
❏ 22 Kenny Thomas .12 .30
❏ 23 Ron Mercer .12 .30
❏ 24 Jeff Mcinnis .12 .30
❏ 25 Kobe Bryant 1.00 2.50
❏ 26 Jason Williams .15 .40
❏ 27 Eddie Jones .15 .40
❏ 28 Anthony Mason .12 .30
❏ 29 Kenyon Martin .20 .50
❏ 30 Kevin Garnett .40 1.00
❏ 31 Kurt Thomas .12 .30
❏ 32 Karl Malone .20 .50
❏ 33 Patrick Ewing .25 .60
❏ 34 Antonio McDyess .15 .40
❏ 35 Dirk Nowitzki .30 .75
❏ 36 Wesley Person .12 .30
❏ 37 Theo Ratliff .12 .30
❏ 38 Jarron Collins .12 .30
❏ 39 Horace Grant .15 .40
❏ 40 Vince Carter .40 1.00
❏ 41 Desmond Mason .15 .40
❏ 42 Todd MacCulloch .12 .30
❏ 43 Bobby Jackson .12 .30
❏ 44 Vlade Divac .15 .40
❏ 45 Keith Van Horn .15 .40
❏ 46 Bo Outlaw .12 .30
❏ 47 Eric Snow .12 .30
❏ 48 Grant Hill .20 .50
❏ 49 Terrell Brandon .12 .30
❏ 50 Tracy Mcgrady .40 1.00
❏ 51 Tim Thomas .12 .30
❏ 52 Loren Woods .12 .30
❏ 53 Michael Redd .20 .50
❏ 54 Stromile Swift .12 .30
❏ 55 Dikembe Mutombo .15 .40
❏ 56 Richard Jefferson .20 .50
❏ 57 Glenn Robinson .15 .40
❏ 58 Samaki Walker .12 .30
❏ 59 Quentin Richardson .15 .40
❏ 60 Elton Brand .20 .50
❏ 61 Reggie Miller .20 .50
❏ 62 Eddie Griffin .12 .30
❏ 63 Gilbert Arenas .20 .50
❏ 64 Zeljko Rebraca .12 .30
❏ 65 Donnell Harvey .12 .30
❏ 66 Juwan Howard .15 .40
❏ 67 Nick Van Exel .15 .40
❏ 68 Donyell Marshall .12 .30
❏ 69 Tyson Chandler .15 .40
❏ 70 Baron Davis .20 .50
❏ 71 Nazr Mohammed .12 .30

❑ 72 Marcus Camby	.15	.40
❑ 73 Jamaal Magloire	.12	.30
❑ 74 Marcus Fizer	.12	.30
❑ 75 Steve Francis	.20	.50
❑ 76 Aaron Mckie	.12	.30
❑ 77 Anfernee Hardaway	.20	.50
❑ 78 Scottie Pippen	.30	.75
❑ 79 Mike Bibby	.15	.40
❑ 80 Paul Pierce	.20	.50
❑ 81 Tony Delk	.12	.30
❑ 82 Kwame Brown	.12	.30
❑ 83 Andrei Kirilenko	.20	.50
❑ 84 Keon Clark	.12	.30
❑ 85 Alvin Williams	.12	.30
❑ 86 Brent Barry	.12	.30
❑ 87 David Robinson	.25	.60
❑ 88 Doug Christie	.12	.30
❑ 89 Derek Anderson	.15	.40
❑ 90 Chris Webber	.20	.50
❑ 91 Speedy Claxton	.12	.30
❑ 92 Robert Horry	.15	.40
❑ 93 Allan Houston	.15	.40
❑ 94 Kerry Kittles	.15	.40
❑ 95 Wally Szczerbiak	.15	.40
❑ 96 Jonathan Bender	.12	.30
❑ 97 Sam Cassell	.15	.40
❑ 98 Rod Strickland	.15	.40
❑ 99 Shane Battier	.15	.40
❑ 100 Tim Duncan	.40	1.00
❑ 101 Jermaine O'Neal	.20	.50
❑ 102 Cuttino Mobley	.15	.40
❑ 103 Danny Fortson	.12	.30
❑ 104 Clifford Robinson	.12	.30
❑ 105 Tim Hardaway	.15	.40
❑ 106 Steve Nash	.30	.75
❑ 107 Zydrunas Ilgauskas	.15	.40
❑ 108 Travis Best	.12	.30
❑ 109 Eddie Robinson	.12	.30
❑ 110 David Wesley	.12	.30
❑ 111 Kenny Anderson	.15	.40
❑ 112 DerMarr Johnson	.12	.30
❑ 113 Courtney Alexander	.12	.30
❑ 114 Brian Grant	.12	.30
❑ 115 Lorenzen Wright	.12	.30
❑ 116 Corliss Williamson	.15	.40
❑ 117 Malik Rose	.12	.30
❑ 118 Tony Parker	.20	.50
❑ 119 Vladimir Radmanovic	.12	.30
❑ 120 Hedo Turkoglu	.15	.40
❑ 121 Damon Stoudamire	.15	.40
❑ 122 Brendan Haywood	.12	.30
❑ 123 Jalen Rose	.15	.40
❑ 124 Mike Miller	.15	.40
❑ 125 Derrick Coleman	.15	.40
❑ 126 Mark Jackson	.15	.40
❑ 127 Raef Lafrentz	.12	.30
❑ 128 Ben Wallace	.15	.40
❑ 129 Larry Hughes	.15	.40
❑ 130 Ray Allen	.20	.50
❑ 131 Gary Payton	.20	.50
❑ 132 P.J. Brown	.12	.30
❑ 133 Derek Fisher	.15	.40
❑ 134 Michael Olowokandi	.12	.30
❑ 135 Jamaal Tinsley	.15	.40
❑ 136 Moochie Norris	.12	.30
❑ 137 Chris Mihm	.12	.30
❑ 138 Antawn Jamison	.20	.50
❑ 139 Chucky Atkins	.12	.30
❑ 140 Mengke Bateer	.12	.30
❑ 141 Brad Miller	.15	.40
❑ 142 Michael Finley	.20	.50
❑ 143 Andre Miller	.15	.40
❑ 144 Michael Dickerson	.12	.30
❑ 145 Elden Campbell	.12	.30
❑ 146 Kedrick Brown	.12	.30
❑ 147 Jason Terry	.20	.50
❑ 148 Chris Whitney	.12	.30
❑ 149 Bryon Russell	.12	.30
❑ 150 Darius Miles	.12	.30
❑ 151 Latrell Sprewell	.15	.40
❑ 152 Darrell Armstrong	.12	.30
❑ 153 Joe Johnson	.20	.50
❑ 154 Bonzi Wells	.15	.40
❑ 155 Jim Jackson	.12	.30
❑ 156 Steve Smith	.15	.40
❑ 157 Vin Baker	.15	.40
❑ 158 Antonio Davis	.12	.30
❑ 159 John Stockton	.25	.60
❑ 160 Shawn Marion	.20	.50
❑ 161 Devean George	.12	.30
❑ 162 Clarence Weatherspoon	.12	.30
❑ 163 Rick Fox	.15	.40
❑ 164 Chauncey Billups	.20	.50
❑ 165 Joe Smith	.12	.30
❑ 166 Laphonso Ellis	.15	.40
❑ 167 Maurice Taylor	.12	.30
❑ 168 Lamond Murray	.12	.30
❑ 169 Lamar Odom	.20	.50
❑ 170 Toni Kukoc	.15	.40
❑ 171 Alonzo Mourning	.20	.50
❑ 172 Antonio Daniels	.12	.30
❑ 173 Troy Murphy	.20	.50
❑ 174 Hakeem Olajuwon	.25	.60
❑ 175 Richard Hamilton	.15	.40
❑ 176 Rodney Rogers	.12	.30
❑ 177 Ruben Patterson	.12	.30
❑ 178 Dale Davis	.12	.30
❑ 179 League Leaders	.50	1.25
❑ 180 League Leaders	.20	.50
❑ 181 League Leaders	.20	.50
❑ 182 League Leaders	.20	.50
❑ 183 League Leaders	.20	.50
❑ 184 Team Championship Card	.60	1.50
❑ 185 Yao Ming RC	2.50	6.00
❑ 186 Jay Williams RC	1.00	2.50
❑ 187 Mike Dunleavy RC	1.00	2.50
❑ 188 Drew Gooden RC	1.25	3.00
❑ 189 Nikoloz Tskitishvili RC	.75	2.00
❑ 190 DaJuan Wagner RC	.75	2.00
❑ 191 Nene Hilario RC	1.00	2.50
❑ 192 Chris Wilcox RC	1.00	2.50
❑ 193 Amare Stoudemire RC	2.00	5.00
❑ 194 Caron Butler RC	1.50	4.00
❑ 195 Jared Jeffries RC	.75	2.00
❑ 196 Melvin Ely RC	.75	2.00
❑ 197 Marcus Haislip RC	.75	2.00
❑ 198 Fred Jones RC	1.00	2.50
❑ 199 Bostjan Nachbar RC	.75	2.00
❑ 200 Jiri Welsch RC	.75	2.00
❑ 201 Juan Dixon RC	1.25	3.00
❑ 202 Curtis Borchardt RC	.75	2.00
❑ 203 Ryan Humphrey RC	.75	2.00
❑ 204 Kareem Rush RC	1.00	2.50
❑ 205 Qyntel Woods RC	.75	2.00
❑ 206 Casey Jacobsen RC	.75	2.00
❑ 207 Tayshaun Prince RC	1.25	3.00
❑ 208 Frank Williams RC	.75	2.00
❑ 209 John Salmons RC	1.25	3.00
❑ 210 Chris Jefferies ERR RC	.75	2.00
❑ 211 Sam Clancy RC	.75	2.00
❑ 212 Dan Gadzuric RC	.75	2.00
❑ 213 Matt Barnes RC	1.00	2.50
❑ 214 Robert Archibald RC	.75	2.00
❑ 215 Vincent Yarbrough RC	.75	2.00
❑ 216 Dan Dickau RC	.75	2.00
❑ 217 Carlos Boozer RC	1.50	4.00
❑ 218 Tito Maddox RC	.75	2.00
❑ 219 Chris Owens RC	.75	2.00
❑ 220 Ronald Murray RC	1.25	3.00

2003-04 Topps

❑ COMPLETE SET (249)	25.00	60.00
❑ COMMON CARD (1-220)	.12	.30
❑ COMMON ROOKIE (221-249)	1.00	2.50
❑ 1 Tracy McGrady	.40	1.00
❑ 2 DaJuan Wagner	.12	.30
❑ 3 Allen Iverson	.40	1.00
❑ 4 Chris Webber	.20	.50
❑ 5 Jason Kidd	.30	.75
❑ 6 Stephon Marbury	.20	.50
❑ 7 Jermaine O'Neal	.20	.50
❑ 8 Antoine Walker	.20	.50
❑ 9 Tony Parker	.20	.50
❑ 10 Mike Bibby	.15	.40
❑ 11 Yao Ming	.40	1.00
❑ 12 Walter McCarty	.12	.30
❑ 13 Steve Nash	.30	.75
❑ 14 Paul Pierce	.20	.50
❑ 15 Vince Carter	.40	1.00
❑ 16 Peja Stojakovic	.15	.40
❑ 17 Kenny Anderson	.15	.40
❑ 18 Kenyon Martin	.20	.50
❑ 19 Pau Gasol	.20	.50
❑ 20 Gary Payton	.20	.50
❑ 21 Tim Duncan	.40	1.00
❑ 22 Jay Williams	.12	.30
❑ 23 Jason Richardson	.20	.50
❑ 24 Andre Miller	.15	.40
❑ 25 Latrell Sprewell	.15	.40
❑ 26 Darius Miles	.15	.40
❑ 27 Richard Jefferson	.20	.50
❑ 28 Shawn Marion	.20	.50
❑ 29 Baron Davis	.20	.50
❑ 30 Ben Wallace	.15	.40
❑ 31 Reggie Miller	.20	.50
❑ 32 Karl Malone	.20	.50
❑ 33 Grant Hill	.20	.50
❑ 34 Shaquille O'Neal	.50	1.25
❑ 35 Steve Francis	.20	.50
❑ 36 Kobe Bryant	1.00	2.50
❑ 37 Mike Dunleavy	.15	.40
❑ 38 Glenn Robinson	.15	.40
❑ 39 Allan Houston	.15	.40
❑ 40 Kevin Ollie	.12	.30
❑ 41 Dirk Nowitzki	.30	.75
❑ 42 Elton Brand	.20	.50
❑ 43 Juan Dixon	.12	.30
❑ 44 Brian Grant	.12	.30
❑ 45 Jason Terry	.15	.40
❑ 46 Richard Hamilton	.15	.40
❑ 47 Morris Peterson	.15	.40
❑ 48 Ray Allen	.12	.30
❑ 49 Scottie Pippen	.30	.75
❑ 50 David Robinson	.30	.75
❑ 51 Cuttino Mobley	.15	.40
❑ 52 Jerry Stackhouse	.15	.40
❑ 53 Marcus Camby	.15	.40
❑ 54 Jalen Rose	.15	.40
❑ 55 Dikembe Mutombo	.15	.40
❑ 56 P.J. Brown	.12	.30
❑ 57 Jumaine Jones	.12	.30
❑ 58 Shawn Bradley	.12	.30
❑ 59 Juwan Howard	.15	.40
❑ 60 Clifford Robinson	.12	.30
❑ 61 Antawn Jamison	.20	.50
❑ 62 Raef LaFrentz	.12	.30
❑ 63 Kareem Rush	.12	.30
❑ 64 LaPhonso Ellis	.12	.30
❑ 65 Toni Kukoc	.15	.40
❑ 66 Mike Miller	.15	.40
❑ 67 Aaron McKie	.12	.30
❑ 68 Tom Gugliotta	.12	.30
❑ 69 Dale Davis	.12	.30
❑ 70 Jared Jeffries	.12	.30
❑ 71 Alvin Williams	.12	.30
❑ 72 DeShawn Stevenson	.12	.30
❑ 73 Doug Christie	.12	.30
❑ 74 Troy Hudson	.12	.30
❑ 75 Jason Collins	.12	.30
❑ 76 Eddie Griffin	.12	.30
❑ 77 Vladimir Radmanovic	.12	.30
❑ 78 Michael Olowokandi	.12	.30
❑ 79 Michael Redd	.20	.50
❑ 80 Tim Thomas	.12	.30
❑ 81 Ron Mercer	.12	.30
❑ 82 Shareef Abdur-Rahim	.15	.40
❑ 83 Eduardo Najera	.12	.30
❑ 84 Jon Barry	.12	.30
❑ 85 Erick Dampier	.12	.30
❑ 86 Derek Fisher	.15	.40
❑ 87 Drew Gooden	.12	.30
❑ 88 Dan Gadzuric	.12	.30
❑ 89 Antonio McDyess	.15	.40
❑ 90 Derrick Coleman	.15	.40
❑ 91 Carlos Boozer	.20	.50
❑ 92 Rasheed Wallace	.20	.50
❑ 93 Antonio Davis	.12	.30
❑ 94 Kwame Brown	.12	.30
❑ 95 Manu Ginobili	.20	.50
❑ 96 Eric Williams	.12	.30
❑ 97 Trenton Hassell	.12	.30
❑ 98 Chris Whitney	.12	.30
❑ 99 Chauncey Billups	.20	.50
❑ 100 Kevin Garnett	.40	1.00

❑ 101 Marko Jaric	.12	.30
❑ 102 Rasual Butler	.12	.30
❑ 103 Gilbert Arenas	.20	.50
❑ 104 Keith Van Horn	.15	.40
❑ 105 Iakovos Tsakalidis	.12	.30
❑ 106 Ruben Patterson	.12	.30
❑ 107 Jarron Collins	.12	.30
❑ 108 Rodney White	.12	.30
❑ 109 Rashard Lewis	.20	.50
❑ 110 Malik Rose	.12	.30
❑ 111 Bobby Jackson	.12	.30
❑ 112 Brendan Haywood	.12	.30
❑ 113 Charlie Ward	.12	.30
❑ 114 Courtney Alexander	.12	.30
❑ 115 Kerry Kittles	.15	.40
❑ 116 Wally Szczerbiak	.15	.40
❑ 117 Darrell Armstrong	.12	.30
❑ 118 Anfernee Hardaway	.20	.50
❑ 119 Qyntel Woods	.12	.30
❑ 120 Quentin Richardson	.15	.40
❑ 121 Jonathan Bender	.12	.30
❑ 122 Robert Horry	.15	.40
❑ 123 Lorenzen Wright	.12	.30
❑ 124 Malik Allen	.12	.30
❑ 125 Sam Cassell	.15	.40
❑ 126 Joe Smith	.12	.30
❑ 127 Dion Glover	.12	.30
❑ 128 Jamal Crawford	.15	.40
❑ 129 Ricky Davis	.15	.40
❑ 130 Nikoloz Tskitishvili	.12	.30
❑ 131 Tyronn Lue	.12	.30
❑ 132 Scott Padgett	.12	.30
❑ 133 Jerome James	.12	.30
❑ 134 Hedo Turkoglu	.15	.40
❑ 135 Jamal Mashburn	.12	.30
❑ 136 Pat Burke	.12	.30
❑ 137 Joe Johnson	.20	.50
❑ 138 Anthony Peeler	.12	.30
❑ 139 Ron Artest	.15	.40
❑ 140 Theo Ratliff	.12	.30
❑ 141 Caron Butler	.15	.40
❑ 142 Anthony Mason	.12	.30
❑ 143 Vin Baker	.12	.30
❑ 144 Donyell Marshall	.12	.30
❑ 145 Nene	.15	.40
❑ 146 Chucky Atkins	.12	.30
❑ 147 Tyson Chandler	.15	.40
❑ 148 Jason Williams	.15	.40
❑ 149 Larry Hughes	.15	.40
❑ 150 Stephen Jackson	.15	.40
❑ 151 Kurt Thomas	.12	.30
❑ 152 Mehmet Okur	.15	.40
❑ 153 Amare Stoudemire	.40	1.00
❑ 154 Elden Campbell	.12	.30
❑ 155 Jamaal Tinsley	.15	.40
❑ 156 Chris Wilcox	.12	.30
❑ 157 Rick Fox	.12	.30
❑ 158 Gordan Giricek	.12	.30
❑ 159 Voshon Lenard	.12	.30
❑ 160 Brent Barry	.12	.30
❑ 161 Dan Dickau	.12	.30
❑ 162 Junior Harrington	.12	.30
❑ 163 Jiri Welsch	.12	.30
❑ 164 Vladimir Stepania	.12	.30
❑ 165 Brad Miller	.15	.40
❑ 166 Moochie Norris	.12	.30
❑ 167 Wesley Person	.12	.30
❑ 168 Greg Buckner	.12	.30
❑ 169 Bonzi Wells	.12	.30
❑ 170 Predrag Drobnjak	.12	.30
❑ 171 Andrei Kirilenko	.20	.50
❑ 172 Vlade Divac	.15	.40
❑ 173 Rodney Rogers	.12	.30
❑ 174 Kendall Gill	.12	.30
❑ 175 Kenny Thomas	.12	.30
❑ 176 Derek Anderson	.15	.40
❑ 177 Steve Smith	.12	.30
❑ 178 Christian Laettner	.12	.30
❑ 179 Tony Delk	.12	.30
❑ 180 Zydrunas Ilgauskas	.15	.40
❑ 181 James Posey	.12	.30
❑ 182 Tayshaun Prince	.15	.40
❑ 183 Devean George	.12	.30
❑ 184 Eddie Jones	.15	.40
❑ 185 Corey Maggette	.12	.30
❑ 186 Ira Newble	.12	.30
❑ 187 Shane Battier	.15	.40
❑ 188 Clarence Weatherspoon	.12	.30
❑ 189 Eric Snow	.12	.30
❑ 190 Damon Stoudamire	.15	.40
❑ 191 Keon Clark	.12	.30
❑ 192 Desmond Mason	.15	.40
❑ 193 Matt Harpring	.15	.40
❑ 194 Radoslav Nesterovic	.12	.30
❑ 195 Jamaal Magloire	.12	.30
❑ 196 Pat Garrity	.12	.30
❑ 197 Fred Jones	.15	.40
❑ 198 Tony Battie	.12	.30
❑ 199 Tyrone Hill	.12	.30
❑ 200 Adrian Griffin	.12	.30
❑ 201 Nick Van Exel	.15	.40
❑ 202 Shammond Williams	.12	.30
❑ 203 Corliss Williamson	.12	.30
❑ 204 Lamar Odom	.20	.50
❑ 205 Travis Best	.12	.30
❑ 206 Howard Eisley	.12	.30
❑ 207 Jerome Williams	.12	.30
❑ 208 David Wesley	.12	.30
❑ 209 Bostjan Nachbar	.12	.30
❑ 210 Marcus Fizer	.12	.30
❑ 211 Michael Finley	.20	.50
❑ 212 Troy Murphy	.20	.50
❑ 213 Adonal Foyle	.12	.30
❑ 214 Samaki Walker	.12	.30
❑ 215 Lucious Harris	.12	.30
❑ 216 Lindsey Hunter	.12	.30
❑ 217 Stromile Swift	.12	.30
❑ 218 Eddy Curry	.15	.40
❑ 219 Kelvin Cato	.12	.30
❑ 220 Chris Anderson	.25	.60
❑ 221 LeBron James RC	12.00	30.00
❑ 222 Darko Milicic RC	1.25	3.00
❑ 223 Carmelo Anthony RC	2.50	6.00
❑ 224 Chris Bosh RC	1.50	4.00
❑ 225 Dwyane Wade RC	2.50	6.00
❑ 226 Chris Kaman RC	1.25	3.00
❑ 227 Kirk Hinrich RC	1.25	3.00
❑ 228 T.J. Ford RC	1.25	3.00
❑ 229 Mike Sweetney RC	1.00	2.50
❑ 230 Jarvis Hayes RC	1.00	2.50
❑ 231 Mickael Pietrus RC	1.25	3.00
❑ 232 Nick Collison RC	1.00	2.50
❑ 233 Marcus Banks RC	1.00	2.50
❑ 234 Luke Ridnour RC	1.25	3.00
❑ 235 Reece Gaines RC	1.00	2.50
❑ 236 Troy Bell RC	1.00	2.50
❑ 237 Zarko Cabarkapa RC	1.00	2.50
❑ 238 David West RC	1.25	3.00
❑ 239 Aleksandar Pavlovic RC	1.25	3.00
❑ 240 Dahntay Jones RC	1.00	2.50
❑ 241 Boris Diaw RC	1.25	3.00
❑ 242 Zoran Planinic RC	1.00	2.50
❑ 243 Travis Outlaw RC	1.25	3.00
❑ 244 Brian Cook RC	1.00	2.50
❑ 245 Carlos Delfino RC	1.25	3.00
❑ 246 Ndudi Ebi RC	1.00	2.50
❑ 247 Kendrick Perkins RC	1.50	4.00
❑ 248 Leandro Barbosa RC	1.25	3.00
❑ 249 Josh Howard RC	1.25	3.00

2004-05 Topps

❑ COMPLETE SET (249)	20.00	50.00
❑ COMMON CARD (1-220)	.06	.15
❑ COMMON ROOKIE (221-249)	.75	2.00
❑ 1 Allen Iverson	.40	1.00
❑ 2 Eddy Curry	.15	.40
❑ 3 Stephon Marbury	.20	.50
❑ 4 Chris Bosh	.20	.50
❑ 5 Jason Kidd	.30	.75
❑ 6 Bonzi Wells	.12	.30
❑ 7 Fred Jones	.12	.30
❑ 8 Kobe Bryant	1.00	2.50
❑ 9 Ben Wallace	.15	.40
❑ 10 Darrell Armstrong	.12	.30
❑ 11 Yao Ming	.50	1.25
❑ 12 Udonis Haslem	.15	.40
❑ 13 Nene	.15	.40
❑ 14 Michael Redd	.20	.50
❑ 15 Carmelo Anthony	.60	1.50
❑ 16 Gary Trent	.12	.30
❑ 17 Larry Hughes	.15	.40
❑ 18 Kareem Rush	.12	.30
❑ 19 Antonio McDyess	.15	.40
❑ 20 Drew Gooden	.12	.30
❑ 21 Kevin Garnett	.40	1.00
❑ 22 DeShawn Stevenson	.12	.30
❑ 23 LeBron James	1.25	3.00
❑ 24 Robert Horry	.15	.40
❑ 25 Shareef Abdur-Rahim	.15	.40
❑ 26 Antonio Daniels	.12	.30
❑ 27 Scottie Pippen	.30	.75
❑ 28 Mike Dunleavy	.15	.40
❑ 29 Joe Smith	.12	.30
❑ 30 Vince Carter	.40	1.00
❑ 31 Reggie Miller	.20	.50
❑ 32 Chris Wilcox	.12	.30
❑ 33 Rasheed Wallace	.20	.50
❑ 34 Paul Pierce	.20	.50
❑ 35 Tayshaun Prince	.15	.40
❑ 36 Raja Bell	.15	.40
❑ 37 Stephen Jackson	.15	.40
❑ 38 Eric Snow	.12	.30
❑ 39 Zydrunas Ilgauskas	.15	.40
❑ 40 Andre Miller	.15	.40
❑ 41 Dirk Nowitzki	.30	.75
❑ 42 Steve Francis	.20	.50
❑ 43 Ray Allen	.20	.50
❑ 44 Donyell Marshall	.12	.30
❑ 45 Pau Gasol	.20	.50
❑ 46 T.J. Ford	.15	.40
❑ 47 Andrei Kirilenko	.20	.50
❑ 48 Jamaal Tinsley	.15	.40
❑ 49 Earl Boykins	.12	.30
❑ 50 Tim Duncan	.40	1.00
❑ 51 Erick Dampier	.12	.30
❑ 52 Nazr Mohammed	.12	.30
❑ 53 Tim Thomas	.12	.30
❑ 54 Keyon Dooling	.12	.30
❑ 55 Jason Kapono	.12	.30
❑ 56 Kirk Hinrich	.15	.40
❑ 57 Aaron McKie	.12	.30
❑ 58 Brad Miller	.15	.40
❑ 59 Al Harrington	.15	.40
❑ 60 Gary Payton	.20	.50
❑ 61 Nick Van Exel	.15	.40
❑ 62 Cuttino Mobley	.15	.40
❑ 63 Marcus Camby	.15	.40
❑ 64 Desmond Mason	.15	.40
❑ 65 Boris Diaw	.15	.40
❑ 66 Kenyon Martin	.20	.50
❑ 67 Mike Miller	.15	.40
❑ 68 Dwyane Wade	.60	1.50
❑ 69 Allan Houston	.15	.40
❑ 70 Jermaine O'Neal	.20	.50
❑ 71 Travis Hansen	.12	.30
❑ 72 Qyntel Woods	.12	.30
❑ 73 Jamal Crawford	.15	.40
❑ 74 Bobby Jackson	.12	.30
❑ 75 Derrick Coleman	.15	.40
❑ 76 Brian Skinner	.12	.30
❑ 77 Elton Brand	.20	.50
❑ 78 Rodney Rogers	.12	.30
❑ 79 Zarko Cabarkapa	.12	.30
❑ 80 Mike Bibby	.15	.40
❑ 81 Jim Jackson	.12	.30
❑ 82 Kurt Thomas	.12	.30
❑ 83 Vin Baker	.12	.30
❑ 84 Rodney White	.12	.30
❑ 85 Gordan Giricek	.12	.30
❑ 86 Jamal Mashburn	.15	.40
❑ 87 Kenny Thomas	.12	.30
❑ 88 Antoine Walker	.20	.50
❑ 89 Rasho Nesterovic	.12	.30
❑ 90 Shawn Marion	.20	.50
❑ 91 Shane Battier	.15	.40
❑ 92 Marquis Daniels	.12	.30
❑ 93 Ruben Patterson	.12	.30
❑ 94 Michael Olowokandi	.12	.30
❑ 95 Bruce Bowen	.12	.30
❑ 96 Caron Butler	.15	.40
❑ 97 Corliss Williamson	.12	.30
❑ 98 Jeff Foster	.12	.30
❑ 99 Carlos Boozer	.20	.50
❑ 100 Tracy McGrady	.40	1.00

❑ 101 Stromile Swift	.12	.30
❑ 102 Keith Van Horn	.15	.40
❑ 103 Derek Fisher	.15	.40
❑ 104 Juwan Howard	.15	.40
❑ 105 Tony Parker	.20	.50
❑ 106 Jason Terry	.15	.40
❑ 107 Vlade Divac	.15	.40
❑ 108 Marcus Banks	.12	.30
❑ 109 Derek Anderson	.15	.40
❑ 110 Karl Malone	.20	.50
❑ 111 Baron Davis	.20	.50
❑ 112 Chris Crawford	.12	.30
❑ 113 Kwame Brown	.12	.30
❑ 114 Jiri Welsch	.12	.30
❑ 115 Maciej Lampe	.12	.30
❑ 116 Josh Howard	.20	.50
❑ 117 Luke Walton	.15	.40
❑ 118 John Salmons	.20	.50
❑ 119 David West	.20	.50
❑ 120 Amare Stoudemire	.40	1.00
❑ 121 Antawn Jamison	.20	.50
❑ 122 Clarence Weatherspoon	.12	.30
❑ 123 Aleksandar Pavlovic	.12	.30
❑ 124 Kerry Kittles	.15	.40
❑ 125 Rafer Alston	.12	.30
❑ 126 Jarvis Hayes	.12	.30
❑ 127 Toni Kukoc	.15	.40
❑ 128 Latrell Sprewell	.15	.40
❑ 129 Keith Bogans	.12	.30
❑ 130 Jason Richardson	.20	.50
❑ 131 Brent Barry	.12	.30
❑ 132 Darko Milicic	.12	.30
❑ 133 Peja Stojakovic	.15	.40
❑ 134 Jerome Williams	.12	.30
❑ 135 Malik Rose	.12	.30
❑ 136 Quentin Richardson	.15	.40
❑ 137 Wally Szczerbiak	.15	.40
❑ 138 Theo Ratliff	.12	.30
❑ 139 Gilbert Arenas	.20	.50
❑ 140 Richard Hamilton	.15	.40
❑ 141 Rashard Lewis	.20	.50
❑ 142 Joe Johnson	.20	.50
❑ 143 P.J. Brown	.12	.30
❑ 144 Jason Collins	.12	.30
❑ 145 Chauncey Billups	.20	.50
❑ 146 Raef LaFrentz	.12	.30
❑ 147 Mickael Pietrus	.15	.40
❑ 148 Lamar Odom	.20	.50
❑ 149 Vladimir Radmanovic	.12	.30
❑ 150 Chris Webber	.20	.50
❑ 151 Tony Delk	.12	.30
❑ 152 Troy Hudson	.12	.30
❑ 153 David Wesley	.12	.30
❑ 154 Juan Dixon	.12	.30
❑ 155 Darius Miles	.15	.40
❑ 156 Gerald Wallace	.20	.50
❑ 157 Jalen Rose	.15	.40
❑ 158 Charlie Ward	.12	.30
❑ 159 Michael Finley	.20	.50
❑ 160 Jonathan Bender	.12	.30
❑ 161 Lorenzen Wright	.12	.30
❑ 162 George Lynch	.12	.30
❑ 163 Leandro Barbosa	.20	.50
❑ 164 Dajuan Wagner	.12	.30
❑ 165 Francisco Elson	.12	.30
❑ 166 Jerry Stackhouse	.15	.40
❑ 167 Manu Ginobili	.20	.50
❑ 168 Chris Kaman	.15	.40
❑ 169 James Posey	.12	.30
❑ 170 Doug Christie	.12	.30
❑ 171 Zoran Planinic	.12	.30
❑ 172 Maurice Taylor	.12	.30
❑ 173 Carlos Arroyo	.20	.50
❑ 174 Damon Stoudamire	.15	.40
❑ 175 Brian Cardinal	.12	.30
❑ 176 Devean George	.12	.30
❑ 177 Hedo Turkoglu	.15	.40
❑ 178 Anfernee Hardaway	.20	.50
❑ 179 Tony Battie	.12	.30
❑ 180 Steve Nash	.30	.75
❑ 181 Glenn Robinson	.15	.40
❑ 182 Morris Peterson	.15	.40
❑ 183 Luke Ridnour	.12	.30
❑ 184 Mehmet Okur	.15	.40
❑ 185 Eddie Jones	.15	.40
❑ 186 Tyronn Lue	.12	.30
❑ 187 Raul Lopez	.12	.30
❑ 188 Lucious Harris	.12	.30
❑ 189 Alvin Williams	.12	.30
❑ 190 Zach Randolph	.20	.50
❑ 191 Steve Blake	.12	.30
❑ 192 Marko Jaric	.12	.30
❑ 193 Anthony Peeler	.12	.30
❑ 194 Troy Murphy	.20	.50
❑ 195 Jamaal Magloire	.12	.30
❑ 196 Brandon Hunter	.12	.30
❑ 197 Jason Williams	.15	.40
❑ 198 Corey Maggette	.15	.40
❑ 199 Ron Artest	.15	.40
❑ 200 Shaquille O'Neal	.50	1.25
❑ 201 Richard Jefferson	.20	.50
❑ 202 Kelvin Cato	.12	.30
❑ 203 Mark Blount	.12	.30
❑ 204 Eric Williams	.12	.30
❑ 205 Sam Cassell	.15	.40
❑ 206 Voshon Lenard	.12	.30
❑ 207 Bob Sura	.12	.30
❑ 208 Speedy Claxton	.12	.30
❑ 209 Samuel Dalembert	.12	.30
❑ 210 Tyson Chandler	.15	.40
❑ 211 Brian Grant	.12	.30
❑ 212 Stanislav Medvedenko	.12	.30
❑ 213 Danny Fortson	.12	.30
❑ 214 Chucky Atkins	.12	.30
❑ 215 Matt Harpring	.15	.40
❑ 216 Trenton Hassell	.12	.30
❑ 217 Ronald Murray	.12	.30
❑ 218 Jeff McInnis	.12	.30
❑ 219 Primoz Brezec	.12	.30
❑ 220 Ricky Davis	.15	.40
❑ 221 Dwight Howard RC	2.50	6.00
❑ 222 Emeka Okafor RC	1.50	4.00
❑ 223 Ben Gordon RC	1.00	2.50
❑ 224 Shaun Livingston RC	.75	2.00
❑ 225 Devin Harris RC	1.50	4.00
❑ 226 Josh Childress RC	.75	2.00
❑ 227 Luol Deng RC	1.00	2.50
❑ 228 Rafael Araujo RC	.75	2.00
❑ 229 Andre Iguodala RC	2.00	5.00
❑ 230 Luke Jackson RC	.75	2.00
❑ 231 Andris Biedrins RC	1.25	3.00
❑ 232 Robert Swift RC	.75	2.00
❑ 233 Sebastian Telfair RC	.75	2.00
❑ 234 Kris Humphries RC	1.25	3.00
❑ 235 Al Jefferson RC	1.50	4.00
❑ 236 Kirk Snyder RC	.75	2.00
❑ 237 Josh Smith RC	2.00	5.00
❑ 238 J.R. Smith RC	1.50	4.00
❑ 239 Dorell Wright RC	1.00	2.50
❑ 240 Jameer Nelson RC	1.00	2.50
❑ 241 Pavel Podkolzine RC	.75	2.00
❑ 242 Viktor Khryapa RC	.75	2.00
❑ 243 Sergei Monia RC	.75	2.00
❑ 244 Delonte West RC	1.25	3.00
❑ 245 Tony Allen RC	1.00	2.50
❑ 246 Kevin Martin RC	1.00	2.50
❑ 247 Sasha Vujacic RC	.75	2.00
❑ 248 Beno Udrih RC	1.00	2.50
❑ 249 David Harrison RC	.75	2.00

2005-06 Topps

❑ COMPLETE SET (255)	20.00	50.00
❑ COMMON CARD (1-220)	.12	.30
❑ SEMISTARS	.15	.40
❑ UNLISTED STARS	.20	.50
❑ COMMON ROOKIE (221-250)	.75	2.00
❑ COMMON CELEBRITY (251-255)	1.50	4.00
❑ 1 Grant Hill	.20	.50
❑ 2 Keith Van Horn	.15	.40
❑ 3 Quentin Richardson	.15	.40
❑ 4 Damon Jones	.15	.40
❑ 5 Lamar Odom	.20	.50
❑ 6 Jamal Crawford	.15	.40
❑ 7 Ben Gordon	.25	.60
❑ 8 Zach Randolph	.20	.50
❑ 9 Rafer Alston	.12	.30
❑ 10 Gilbert Arenas	.20	.50
❑ 11 Yao Ming	.50	1.25
❑ 12 Cuttino Mobley	.15	.40
❑ 13 Josh Smith	.20	.50
❑ 14 Ray Allen	.20	.50
❑ 15 Vince Carter	.40	1.00
❑ 16 Kenyon Martin	.20	.50
❑ 17 Mark Blount	.12	.30
❑ 18 Carlos Arroyo	.20	.50
❑ 19 Lee Nailon	.12	.30
❑ 20 Bobby Simmons	.12	.30
❑ 21 Tim Duncan	.40	1.00
❑ 22 Michael Redd	.20	.50
❑ 23 Antawn Jamison	.20	.50
❑ 24 Matt Bonner	.12	.30
❑ 25 Shane Battier	.20	.50
❑ 26 Nick Van Exel	.20	.50
❑ 27 Jason Hart	.12	.30
❑ 28 Nene	.12	.30
❑ 29 Fred Jones	.15	.40
❑ 30 Baron Davis	.20	.50
❑ 31 Danny Fortson	.12	.30
❑ 32 Caron Butler	.20	.50
❑ 33 Allen Iverson	.40	1.00
❑ 34 Eddie Griffin	.12	.30
❑ 35 Jameer Nelson	.15	.40
❑ 36 Brent Barry	.12	.30
❑ 37 Zydrunas Ilgauskas	.15	.40
❑ 38 Jason Terry	.20	.50
❑ 39 Mike Dunleavy	.15	.40
❑ 40 Paul Pierce	.20	.50
❑ 41 Reggie Miller	.20	.50
❑ 42 Lorenzen Wright	.12	.30
❑ 43 Peja Stojakovic	.20	.50
❑ 44 Zaza Pachulia	.12	.30
❑ 45 Dan Dickau	.12	.30
❑ 46 Andre Iguodala	.20	.50
❑ 47 Andrei Kirilenko	.20	.50
❑ 48 Nenad Krstic	.15	.40
❑ 49 Damon Stoudamire	.15	.40
❑ 50 Emeka Okafor	.20	.50
❑ 51 Jalen Rose	.20	.50
❑ 52 Beno Udrih	.12	.30
❑ 53 Jared Jeffries	.12	.30
❑ 54 Ricky Davis	.20	.50
❑ 55 Jason Kidd	.30	.75
❑ 56 Eddy Curry	.15	.40
❑ 57 Chauncey Billups	.20	.50
❑ 58 Eric Snow	.12	.30
❑ 59 Derek Fisher	.12	.30
❑ 60 Amare Stoudemire	.40	1.00
❑ 61 Josh Childress	.15	.40
❑ 62 Juwan Howard	.15	.40
❑ 63 Mehmet Okur	.12	.30
❑ 64 Jerome Williams	.12	.30
❑ 65 Shaun Livingston	.12	.30
❑ 66 Stephen Jackson	.15	.40
❑ 67 Alonzo Mourning	.25	.60
❑ 68 J.R. Smith	.15	.40
❑ 69 Kobe Bryant	1.00	2.50
❑ 70 Dwight Howard	.40	1.00
❑ 71 Manu Ginobili	.20	.50
❑ 72 Kyle Korver	.20	.50
❑ 73 Reggie Evans	.12	.30
❑ 74 Shareef Abdur-Rahim	.20	.50
❑ 75 Rafael Araujo	.12	.30
❑ 76 Kirk Snyder	.12	.30
❑ 77 Jermaine O'Neal	.20	.50
❑ 78 Melvin Ely	.12	.30
❑ 79 Chris Kaman	.12	.30
❑ 80 Stephon Marbury	.20	.50
❑ 81 Joe Smith	.15	.40
❑ 82 Samuel Dalembert	.12	.30
❑ 83 Luke Ridnour	.15	.40
❑ 84 Sebastian Telfair	.15	.40
❑ 85 Larry Hughes	.15	.40
❑ 86 Tyson Chandler	.20	.50
❑ 87 Michael Finley	.20	.50
❑ 88 Drew Gooden	.15	.40
❑ 89 Marcus Camby	.15	.40
❑ 90 Dwyane Wade	.50	1.25
❑ 91 Troy Murphy	.20	.50
❑ 92 David Wesley	.12	.30
❑ 93 Stromile Swift	.15	.40
❑ 94 Clifford Robinson	.12	.30
❑ 95 Sam Cassell	.20	.50
❑ 96 Joe Johnson	.20	.50
❑ 97 Bobby Jackson	.12	.30

❑ 98 Derek Anderson	.15	.40
❑ 99 Rashard Lewis	.20	.50
❑ 100 Shaquille O'Neal	.50	1.25
❑ 101 Keith McLeod	.12	.30
❑ 102 Keith Bogans	.12	.30
❑ 103 Al Harrington	.12	.30
❑ 104 Anderson Varejao	.15	.40
❑ 105 Al Jefferson	.20	.50
❑ 106 Jerry Stackhouse	.20	.50
❑ 107 Chris Duhon	.15	.40
❑ 108 Earl Boykins	.12	.30
❑ 109 Tayshaun Prince	.20	.50
❑ 110 Carlos Boozer	.20	.50
❑ 111 Rasual Butler	.12	.30
❑ 112 Bonzi Wells	.15	.40
❑ 113 Chris Wilcox	.12	.30
❑ 114 Latrell Sprewell	.12	.30
❑ 115 Richard Jefferson	.15	.40
❑ 116 Toni Kukoc	.12	.30
❑ 117 Doug Christie	.12	.30
❑ 118 Brad Miller	.20	.50
❑ 119 Antonio Daniels	.12	.30
❑ 120 Richard Hamilton	.15	.40
❑ 121 Kevin Garnett	.40	1.00
❑ 122 Tony Parker	.20	.50
❑ 123 Mike Sweetney	.15	.40
❑ 124 Speedy Claxton	.12	.30
❑ 125 Udonis Haslem	.20	.50
❑ 126 Chucky Atkins	.12	.30
❑ 127 David Harrison	.12	.30
❑ 128 Jason Collier	.12	.30
❑ 129 Pau Gasol	.20	.50
❑ 130 Chris Webber	.20	.50
❑ 131 Kelvin Cato	.12	.30
❑ 132 Michael Olowokandi	.12	.30
❑ 133 Ben Wallace	.20	.50
❑ 134 Antoine Walker	.15	.40
❑ 135 Marquis Daniels	.15	.40
❑ 136 Ira Newble	.12	.30
❑ 137 Austin Croshere	.12	.30
❑ 138 Mike James	.12	.30
❑ 139 Michael Doleac	.12	.30
❑ 140 Carmelo Anthony	.40	1.00
❑ 141 Sasha Vujacic	.15	.40
❑ 142 Brian Cardinal	.12	.30
❑ 143 Ron Mercer	.12	.30
❑ 144 Tim Thomas	.12	.30
❑ 145 Juan Dixon	.12	.30
❑ 146 Rodney Rogers	.12	.30
❑ 147 Hedo Turkoglu	.15	.40
❑ 148 Nazr Mohammed	.12	.30
❑ 149 Gerald Wallace	.20	.50
❑ 150 Dirk Nowitzki	.30	.75
❑ 151 Tony Allen	.12	.30
❑ 152 Adonal Foyle	.12	.30
❑ 153 Corey Maggette	.15	.40
❑ 154 Rasheed Wallace	.20	.50
❑ 155 Andre Miller	.15	.40
❑ 156 Luol Deng	.20	.50
❑ 157 Mike Miller	.20	.50
❑ 158 Wally Szczerbiak	.15	.40
❑ 159 Maurice Williams	.15	.40
❑ 160 Chris Bosh	.20	.50
❑ 161 Jamaal Magloire	.12	.30
❑ 162 Leandro Barbosa	.20	.50
❑ 163 Kevin Martin	.20	.50
❑ 164 Jeff Foster	.12	.30
❑ 165 Nick Collison	.12	.30
❑ 166 Matt Harpring	.15	.40
❑ 167 Kirk Hinrich	.20	.50
❑ 168 Antonio McDyess	.12	.30
❑ 169 Josh Howard	.20	.50
❑ 170 Elton Brand	.20	.50
❑ 171 Kurt Thomas	.12	.30
❑ 172 Tyronn Lue	.12	.30
❑ 173 Bob Sura	.12	.30
❑ 174 Chris Mihm	.12	.30
❑ 175 Jason Williams	.15	.40
❑ 176 Jim Jackson	.12	.30
❑ 177 Brevin Knight	.12	.30
❑ 178 Eduardo Najera	.20	.50
❑ 179 Jeff McInnis	.12	.30
❑ 180 Jason Richardson	.20	.50
❑ 181 Vladimir Radmanovic	.12	.30
❑ 182 Jamaal Tinsley	.15	.40
❑ 183 Eddie Jones	.12	.30
❑ 184 P.J. Brown	.12	.30
❑ 185 Troy Hudson	.12	.30
❑ 186 Steve Francis	.20	.50
❑ 187 Marc Jackson	.12	.30
❑ 188 Kenny Thomas	.12	.30
❑ 189 Joel Przybilla	.12	.30
❑ 190 Steve Nash	.25	.60
❑ 191 Devin Brown	.12	.30
❑ 192 Donyell Marshall	.12	.30
❑ 193 Raja Bell	.12	.30
❑ 194 Brendan Haywood	.12	.30
❑ 195 Primoz Brezec	.12	.30
❑ 196 Gary Payton	.20	.50
❑ 197 Devin Harris	.20	.50
❑ 198 Predrag Drobnjak	.12	.30
❑ 199 Dikembe Mutombo	.15	.40
❑ 200 LeBron James	1.00	2.50
❑ 201 Marko Jaric	.12	.30
❑ 202 Mike Bibby	.20	.50
❑ 203 Desmond Mason	.12	.30
❑ 204 Morris Peterson	.15	.40
❑ 205 Jarvis Hayes	.12	.30
❑ 206 Bruce Bowen	.12	.30
❑ 207 Trevor Ariza	.15	.40
❑ 208 Raef LaFrentz	.12	.30
❑ 209 Brian Grant	.12	.30
❑ 210 Shawn Marion	.20	.50
❑ 211 Dan Gadzuric	.12	.30
❑ 212 Andres Nocioni	.12	.30
❑ 213 Tony Delk	.12	.30
❑ 214 Darius Miles	.20	.50
❑ 215 Gordan Giricek	.12	.30
❑ 216 Rasho Nesterovic	.12	.30
❑ 217 Jason Collins	.12	.30
❑ 218 Mickael Pietrus	.15	.40
❑ 219 Erick Dampier	.12	.30
❑ 220 Tracy McGrady	.40	1.00
❑ 221 Andrew Bogut RC	1.00	2.50
❑ 222 Marvin Williams RC	1.25	3.00
❑ 223 Deron Williams RC	2.00	5.00
❑ 224 Chris Paul RC	2.50	6.00
❑ 225 Raymond Felton RC	1.00	2.50
❑ 226 Martell Webster RC	.75	2.00
❑ 227 Charlie Villanueva RC	1.25	3.00
❑ 228 Channing Frye RC	1.00	2.50
❑ 229 Ike Diogu RC	1.00	2.50
❑ 230 Andrew Bynum RC	2.50	6.00
❑ 231 Fran Vazquez RC	.75	2.00
❑ 232 Daniel Ewing RC	1.00	2.50
❑ 233 Sean May RC	1.00	2.50
❑ 234 Rashad McCants RC	1.00	2.50
❑ 235 Antoine Wright RC	.75	2.00
❑ 236 Joey Graham RC	.75	2.00
❑ 237 Danny Granger RC	2.00	5.00
❑ 238 Gerald Green RC	.75	2.00
❑ 239 Hakim Warrick RC	1.25	3.00
❑ 240 Julius Hodge RC	1.00	2.50
❑ 241 Nate Robinson RC	1.25	3.00
❑ 242 Jarrett Jack RC	.75	2.00
❑ 243 Francisco Garcia RC	1.00	2.50
❑ 244 Luther Head RC	1.00	2.50
❑ 245 Johan Petro RC	.75	2.00
❑ 246 Jason Maxiell RC	1.00	2.50
❑ 247 Linas Kleiza RC	1.00	2.50
❑ 248 Ryan Gomes RC	.75	2.00
❑ 249 Wayne Simien RC	1.00	2.50
❑ 250 David Lee RC	1.50	4.00
❑ 251 Shannon Elizabeth	1.50	4.00
❑ 252 Carmen Electra	1.50	4.00
❑ 253 Jenny McCarthy	1.50	4.00
❑ 254 Christie Brinkley	1.50	4.00
❑ 255 Jay-Z	1.50	4.00

2006-07 Topps

❑ COMPLETE SET (275)	25.00	60.00
❑ 1 Elton Brand	.20	.50
❑ 2 Tim Duncan	.40	1.00
❑ 3 Chris Paul	.40	1.00
❑ 4 Joe Johnson	.15	.40
❑ 5 Chauncey Billups	.20	.50
❑ 6 Al Harrington	.12	.30
❑ 7 Andres Nocioni	.12	.30
❑ 8 Kobe Bryant	1.00	2.50
❑ 9 Al Jefferson	.20	.50
❑ 10 Gerald Wallace	.20	.50
❑ 11 Jason Terry	.20	.50
❑ 12 Dwight Howard	.40	1.00
❑ 13 Larry Hughes	.15	.40
❑ 14 Sebastian Telfair	.15	.40
❑ 15 Vince Carter	.40	1.00
❑ 16 Mike Bibby	.20	.50
❑ 17 Ben Gordon	.25	.60
❑ 18 Desmond Mason	.12	.30
❑ 19 Eddie Jones	.12	.30
❑ 20 Raymond Felton	.25	.60
❑ 21 Paul Pierce	.20	.50
❑ 22 Eddy Curry	.15	.40
❑ 23 Jason Richardson	.20	.50
❑ 24 Rasheed Wallace	.20	.50
❑ 25 Andrew Bogut	.20	.50
❑ 26 Stromile Swift	.15	.40
❑ 27 Peja Stojakovic	.20	.50
❑ 28 Deron Williams	.30	.75
❑ 29 Kwame Brown	.15	.40
❑ 30 Michael Redd	.20	.50
❑ 31 Shawn Marion	.20	.50
❑ 32 Shaquille O'Neal	.50	1.25
❑ 33 Larry Bird	3.00	8.00
❑ 34 Ray Allen	.20	.50
❑ 35 Marko Jaric	.12	.30
❑ 36 Luther Head	.15	.40
❑ 37 Robert Horry	.15	.40
❑ 38 Jason Collins	.12	.30
❑ 39 Cuttino Mobley	.15	.40
❑ 40 Donyell Marshall	.12	.30
❑ 41 Dirk Nowitzki	.30	.75
❑ 42 Jermaine O'Neal	.20	.50
❑ 43 Kurt Thomas	.12	.30
❑ 44 Gerald Green	.25	.60
❑ 45 Marvin Williams	.20	.50
❑ 46 Bonzi Wells	.15	.40
❑ 47 Andrei Kirilenko	.20	.50
❑ 48 J.R. Smith	.15	.40
❑ 49 Baron Davis	.20	.50
❑ 50 Tracy McGrady	.40	1.00
❑ 51 Chris Kaman	.12	.30
❑ 52 Luol Deng	.20	.50
❑ 53 Emeka Okafor	.20	.50
❑ 54 Grant Hill	.20	.50
❑ 55 Amare Stoudemire	.40	1.00
❑ 56 Lamar Odom	.20	.50
❑ 57 Eric Snow	.12	.30
❑ 58 Ike Diogu	.15	.40
❑ 50 Alonzo Mourning	.25	.60
❑ 60 Maurice Evans	.12	.30
❑ 61 Marcus Camby	.15	.40
❑ 62 Bobby Simmons	.12	.30
❑ 63 Vladimir Radmanovic	.12	.30
❑ 64 Ryan Gomes	.12	.30
❑ 65 Fred Jones	.15	.40
❑ 66 Kirk Snyder	.12	.30
❑ 67 Flip Murray	.07	.20
❑ 68 T.J. Ford	.15	.40
❑ 69 DeSagana Diop	.12	.30
❑ 70 Josh Smith	.20	.50
❑ 71 Lorenzen Wright	.12	.30
❑ 72 Nate Robinson	.20	.50
❑ 73 Brendan Haywood	.12	.30
❑ 74 Darius Miles	.12	.30
❑ 75 Keith Van Horn	.12	.30
❑ 76 Johan Petro	.12	.30
❑ 77 Yao Ming	.50	1.25
❑ 78 Darko Milicic	.20	.50
❑ 79 Smush Parker	.12	.30
❑ 80 Sarunas Jasikevicius	.15	.40
❑ 81 Mike Dunleavy	.15	.40
❑ 82 Joey Graham	.15	.40
❑ 83 Jason Williams	.15	.40
❑ 84 Melvin Ely	.12	.30
❑ 85 Ricky Davis	.20	.50
❑ 86 Michael Finley	.20	.50
❑ 87 Steve Blake	.12	.30
❑ 88 Nenad Krstic	.15	.40
❑ 89 Earl Boykins	.12	.30
❑ 90 Richard Hamilton	.15	.40
❑ 91 Chris Duhon	.12	.30
❑ 92 Hakim Warrick	.15	.40
❑ 93 Wally Szczerbiak	.15	.40

94 Corey Maggette	.15	.40
95 Leandro Barbosa	.20	.50
96 Jamaal Tinsley	.15	.40
97 Kenyon Martin	.20	.50
98 Kyle Korver	.20	.50
99 Jason Kidd	.30	.75
100 Dwyane Wade	.50	1.25
101 Ben Wallace	.20	.50
102 Mike James	.12	.30
103 Josh Howard	.20	.50
104 Joe Smith	.15	.40
105 Josh Childress	.15	.40
106 Eddie Griffin	.12	.30
107 Richard Jefferson	.15	.40
108 Jalen Rose	.15	.40
109 Mickael Pietrus	.15	.40
110 Steve Nash	.25	.60
111 Juwan Howard	.15	.40
112 Drew Gooden	.15	.40
113 Eduardo Najera	.12	.30
114 Chris Mihm	.12	.30
115 Jose Calderon	.15	.40
116 Kevin Garnett	.40	1.00
117 Rafer Alston	.12	.30
118 Delonte West	.15	.40
119 Jamaal Magloire	.12	.30
120 Channing Frye	.15	.40
121 Andre Iguodala	.20	.50
122 Pau Gasol	.20	.50
123 LeBron James	1.00	2.50
124 Antonio Daniels	.12	.30
125 James Posey	.12	.30
126 Devean George	.15	.40
127 Linas Kleiza	.12	.30
128 Brian Cook	.12	.30
129 Sean May	.15	.40
130 Sam Cassell	.20	.50
131 Mehmet Okur	.12	.30
132 Bruce Bowen	.12	.30
133 Kirk Hinrich	.20	.50
134 Chris Wilcox	.12	.30
135 Brad Miller	.20	.50
136 Erick Dampier	.12	.30
137 Primoz Brezec	.12	.30
138 Derek Fisher	.15	.40
139 Antonio McDyess	.12	.30
140 Chris Bosh	.20	.50
141 Jamal Crawford	.12	.30
142 Mike Miller	.20	.50
143 Danny Granger	.15	.40
144 Quinton Ross	.12	.30
145 Manu Ginobili	.20	.50
146 Udonis Haslem	.20	.50
147 Marquis Daniels	.15	.40
148 Maurice Williams	.15	.40
149 Viktor Khryapa	.12	.30
150 Gilbert Arenas	.20	.50
151 Tony Parker	.20	.50
152 Carlos Boozer	.20	.50
153 Quentin Richardson	.15	.40
154 Clifford Robinson	.12	.30
155 Speedy Claxton	.12	.30
156 Charlie Villanueva	.20	.50
157 Rashard Lewis	.20	.50
158 DeShawn Stevenson	.12	.30
159 Boris Diaw	.15	.40
160 Francisco Garcia	.12	.30
161 Zaza Pachulia	.12	.30
162 Raja Bell	.12	.30
163 Juan Dixon	.12	.30
164 Shaun Livingston	.12	.30
165 Shareef Abdur-Rahim	.20	.50
166 Devin Harris	.20	.50
167 Brevin Knight	.12	.30
168 Troy Murphy	.20	.50
169 Antawn Jamison	.20	.50
170 Tyson Chandler	.20	.50
171 Stephen Jackson	.15	.40
172 Shane Battier	.20	.50
173 Chris Webber	.20	.50
174 Trenton Hassell	.12	.30
175 Devin Brown	.12	.30
176 Luke Ridnour	.15	.40
177 Joel Przybilla	.12	.30
178 David West	.20	.50
179 John Salmons	.20	.50
180 Nazr Mohammed	.12	.30
181 Caron Butler	.20	.50
182 Troy Hudson	.12	.30
183 Zydrunas Ilgauskas	.15	.40
184 David Wesley	.12	.30
185 Andre Miller	.15	.40
186 Nick Collison	.12	.30
187 Ron Artest	.20	.50
188 Samuel Dalembert	.12	.30
189 Tayshaun Prince	.20	.50
190 Jameer Nelson	.15	.40
191 Zach Randolph	.20	.50
192 Stephon Marbury	.20	.50
193 Steve Francis	.20	.50
194 Matt Harpring	.15	.40
195 Kevin Martin	.20	.50
196 Rashad McCants	.15	.40
197 Carmelo Anthony	.25	.60
198 Morris Peterson	.15	.40
199 Etan Thomas	.12	.30
200 Allen Iverson	.40	1.00
201 Antoine Walker	.15	.40
202 Eddie House	.12	.30
203 Adrian Griffin	.12	.30
204 Salim Stoudamire	.15	.40
205 Raef LaFrentz	.12	.30
206 Jared Jeffries	.12	.30
207 Rasual Butler	.12	.30
208 Damon Jones	.15	.40
209 Chuck Hayes	.12	.30
210 James Singleton	.12	.30
211 Marcus Banks	.12	.30
212 P.J. Brown	.12	.30
213 Hedo Turkoglu	.15	.40
214 Jarrett Jack	.15	.40
215 Kendrick Perkins	.12	.30
217 Leon Powe RC	.75	2.00
219 Alexander Johnson RC	.75	2.00
220 Will Blalock RC	.75	2.00
221 Steve Novak RC	.75	2.00
222 Shawne Williams RC	.75	2.00
223 Guillermo Diaz RC	.75	2.00
224 Mardy Collins RC	.75	2.00
225 Ryan Hollins RC	.75	2.00
226 Kyle Lowry RC	.75	2.00
227 Craig Smith RC	.75	2.00
228 Denham Brown RC	.75	2.00
229 Dee Brown RC	.75	2.00
230 Daniel Gibson RC	1.00	2.50
233 Cedric Simmons RC	.75	2.00
234 P.J. Tucker RC	.75	2.00
235 Hassan Adams RC	1.00	2.50
236 Hilton Armstrong RC	.75	2.00
237 James Augustine RC	.75	2.00
238 Josh Boone RC	.75	2.00
239 James White RC	.75	2.00
242 Maurice Ager RC	.75	2.00
244 Paul Davis RC	.75	2.00
245 Jordan Farmar RC	1.00	2.50
247 Quincy Douby RC	.75	2.00
248 Ronnie Brewer RC	1.00	2.50
249 Rodney Carney RC	.75	2.00
251 Rajon Rondo RC	3.00	8.00
252 Rudy Gay RC	.75	2.00
253 Paul Millsap RC	1.25	3.00
254 Saer Sene RC	.75	2.00
256 Allan Ray RC	.75	2.00
257 Thabo Sefolosha RC	1.00	2.50
258 Darius Washington RC	.75	2.00
259 Renaldo Balkman RC	.75	2.00
260 Mike Gansey RC	.75	2.00
261 Solomon Jones RC	.75	2.00
262 Bobby Jones RC	.75	2.00
263 David Noel RC	.75	2.00
264 Kevin Pittsnogle RC	.75	2.00
265 Shannon Brown RC	.75	2.00
216A Adam Morrison RC	1.00	2.50
216B Adam Morrison Draft RC	1.00	2.50
218A Shelden Williams RC	1.00	2.50
218B Shelden Williams Draft RC	1.00	2.50
231A Tyrus Thomas RC	1.00	2.50
231B Tyrus Thomas Draft RC	1.00	2.50
232A Patrick O'Bryant RC	.75	2.00
232B Patrick O'Bryant Draft RC	.75	2.00
240A J.J. Redick RC	.75	2.00
240B J.J. Redick Draft RC	.75	2.00
241A LaMarcus Aldridge RC	1.00	2.50
241B LaMarcus Aldridge Draft RC	1.00	2.50
243A Marcus Williams RC	1.00	2.50
243B Marcus Williams Draft RC	1.00	2.50
246A Brandon Roy RC	2.00	5.00
246B Brandon Roy Draft RC	2.00	5.00
250A Randy Foye RC	.75	2.00
250B Randy Foye Draft RC	.75	2.00
255A Andrea Bargnani RC	1.25	3.00
255B Andrea Bargnani Draft RC	1.25	3.00

2007-08 Topps

COMPLETE SET (135)	20.00	50.00
1 Amare Stoudemire	.40	1.00
2 Joe Johnson	.20	.50
3 Dwyane Wade	.50	1.25
4 Chris Bosh	.20	.50
5 Jason Kidd	.30	.75
6 Bill Russell	.30	.75
7 Jermaine O'Neal	.20	.50
8 Mike Miller	.20	.50
9 Ray Allen	.20	.50
10 Elton Brand	.20	.50
11 Yao Ming	.50	1.25
12 Al Harrington	.15	.40
13 Steve Nash	.25	.60
14 Dwight Howard	.40	1.00
15 Carmelo Anthony	.40	1.00
16 Pau Gasol	.20	.50
17 Chauncey Billups	.20	.50
18 Antawn Jamison	.20	.50
19 Shane Battier	.20	.50
20 Kevin Garnett	.50	1.25
21 Tim Duncan	.40	1.00
22 Michael Redd	.20	.50
23 LeBron James	1.00	2.50
24 Kobe Bryant	1.00	2.50
25 Eddy Curry	.12	.30
26 Peja Stojakovic	.20	.50
27 Andrew Bogut	.20	.50
28 Vince Carter	.40	1.00
29 Corey Maggette	.15	.40
30 Rasheed Wallace	.20	.50
31 Shawn Marion	.20	.50
32 Shaquille O'Neal	.50	1.25
33 Allen Iverson	.40	1.00
34 Paul Pierce	.20	.50
35 Adam Morrison	.20	.50
36 Tony Parker	.20	.50
37 Mike Bibby	.20	.50
38 Andrea Bargnani	.25	.60
39 Luol Deng	.20	.50
40 Chris Paul	.40	1.00
41 Dirk Nowitzki	.30	.75
42 David Lee	.15	.40
43 Paul Millsap	.15	.40
44 Danny Granger	.15	.40
45 Al Jefferson	.20	.50
46 Rafer Alston	.12	.30
47 Andrei Kirilenko	.20	.50
48 Shaun Livingston	.12	.30
49 Chris Wilcox	.15	.40
50 Emeka Okafor	.20	.50
51 Zach Randolph	.20	.50
52 Devin Harris	.20	.50
53 Mo Williams	.15	.40
54 Leandro Barbosa	.15	.40
55 Smush Parker	.12	.30
56 Andre Miller	.15	.40
57 Manu Ginobili	.20	.50
58 Jason Richardson	.20	.50
59 Jason Terry	.20	.50
60 Gerald Wallace	.20	.50
61 Richard Hamilton	.15	.40
62 Ricky Davis	.20	.50
63 Boris Diaw	.15	.40
64 Carlos Boozer	.20	.50
65 Rashard Lewis	.20	.50
66 Josh Childress	.15	.40
67 Lamar Odom	.20	.50
68 Kyle Korver	.20	.50
69 Stephon Marbury	.20	.50

❑ 70 Luke Walton .15 .40
❑ 71 Baron Davis .20 .50
❑ 72 Larry Hughes .15 .40
❑ 73 Jameer Nelson .15 .40
❑ 74 Caron Butler .20 .50
❑ 75 Udonis Haslem .20 .50
❑ 76 Mike Dunleavy .15 .40
❑ 77 Ben Gordon .25 .60
❑ 78 Andrew Bynum .20 .50
❑ 79 Hakim Warrick .15 .40
❑ 80 Josh Smith .20 .50
❑ 81 Mehmet Okur .15 .40
❑ 82 J.R. Smith .15 .40
❑ 83 Raymond Felton .25 .60
❑ 84 Chris Webber .20 .50
❑ 85 Jamal Crawford .12 .30
❑ 86 Jarrett Jack .15 .40
❑ 87 Anderson Varejao .15 .40
❑ 88 Ryan Gomes .12 .30
❑ 89 Charlie Villanueva .20 .50
❑ 90 Marcus Camby .12 .30
❑ 91 Kirk Hinrich .20 .50
❑ 92 Tayshaun Prince .20 .50
❑ 93 Ron Artest .20 .50
❑ 94 T.J. Ford .15 .40
❑ 95 Richard Jefferson .20 .50
❑ 96 Zydrunas Ilgauskas .15 .40
❑ 97 Josh Howard .20 .50
❑ 98 Monta Ellis .15 .40
❑ 99 Deron Williams .30 .75
❑ 100 Gilbert Arenas .20 .50
❑ 101 Tracy McGrady .40 1.00
❑ 102 Steve Blake .12 .30
❑ 103 Ben Wallace .20 .50
❑ 104 Kevin Martin .20 .50
❑ 105 Marcus Williams .20 .50
❑ 106 J.J. Redick .20 .50
❑ 107 Brandon Roy .30 .75
❑ 108 Desmond Mason .12 .30
❑ 109 Randy Foye .20 .50
❑ 110 Andre Iguodala .20 .50
❑ 111 Greg Oden RC 1.25 3.00
❑ 112 Kevin Durant RC 6.00 15.00
❑ 113 Al Horford RC 1.00 2.50
❑ 114 Mike Conley RC 1.00 2.50
❑ 115 Jeff Green RC 1.00 2.50
❑ 116 Yi Jianlian RC 1.25 3.00
❑ 117 Corey Brewer RC 1.00 2.50
❑ 118 Brandan Wright RC 1.00 2.50
❑ 119 Joakim Noah RC 1.00 2.50
❑ 120 Spencer Hawes RC .75 2.00
❑ 121 Acie Law RC 1.00 2.50
❑ 122 Thaddeus Young RC 1.00 2.50
❑ 123 Julian Wright RC 1.00 2.50
❑ 124 Al Thornton RC .75 2.00
❑ 125 Rodney Stuckey RC 1.50 4.00
❑ 126 Nick Young RC .75 2.00
❑ 127 Sean Williams RC .75 2.00
❑ 128 Marco Belinelli RC .75 2.00
❑ 129 Javaris Crittenton RC .75 2.00
❑ 130 Jason Smith RC .75 2.00
❑ 131 Daequan Cook RC 1.00 2.50
❑ 132 Jared Dudley RC .75 2.00
❑ 133 Wilson Chandler RC .75 2.00
❑ 134 Morris Almond RC .75 2.00
❑ 135 Aaron Brooks RC 1.25 3.00

2008-09 Topps

❑ COMPLETE SET (220) 25.00 50.00
❑ 1 Chris Paul .40 1.00
❑ 2 Joe Johnson .20 .50
❑ 3 Allen Iverson .25 .60
❑ 4 Luis Scola .15 .40
❑ 5 Kevin Garnett .40 1.00
❑ 6 Andrew Bogut .20 .50
❑ 7 Ben Gordon .20 .50
❑ 8 Carlos Boozer .20 .50
❑ 9 Tony Parker .20 .50
❑ 10 Gilbert Arenas .20 .50
❑ 11 Yao Ming .25 .60
❑ 12 Dwight Howard .40 1.00
❑ 13 Steve Nash .20 .50
❑ 14 Daequan Cook .15 .40
❑ 15 Carmelo Anthony .25 .60
❑ 16 Pau Gasol .20 .50
❑ 17 Mike Dunleavy .15 .40
❑ 18 Jason Maxiell .15 .40
❑ 19 Al Thornton .20 .50
❑ 20 Ray Allen .20 .50
❑ 21 Tim Duncan .30 .75
❑ 22 Michael Redd .20 .50
❑ 23 LeBron James 1.00 2.50
❑ 24 Kobe Bryant 1.00 2.50
❑ 25 Al Jefferson .20 .50
❑ 26 Raymond Felton .15 .40
❑ 27 LaMarcus Aldridge .20 .50
❑ 28 Jose Calderon .15 .40
❑ 29 Andris Biedrins .12 .30
❑ 30 Rasheed Wallace .20 .50
❑ 31 Shawn Marion .20 .50
❑ 32 Shaquille O'Neal .40 1.00
❑ 33 Mike Miller .20 .50
❑ 34 Paul Pierce .25 .60
❑ 35 Brad Miller .20 .50
❑ 36 Richard Jefferson .20 .50
❑ 37 DeShawn Stevenson .12 .30
❑ 38 Zach Randolph .20 .50
❑ 39 Daniel Gibson .20 .50
❑ 40 Nazr Mohammed .12 .30
❑ 41 Dirk Nowitzki .25 .60
❑ 42 Elton Brand .30 .75
❑ 43 Linas Kleiza .12 .30
❑ 44 Andrea Bargnani .15 .40
❑ 45 Josh Smith .20 .50
❑ 46 Luol Deng .20 .50
❑ 47 Andrei Kirilenko .20 .50
❑ 48 Danny Granger .20 .50
❑ 49 Rashad McCants .15 .40
❑ 50 Emeka Okafor .20 .50
❑ 51 Kyle Korver .20 .50
❑ 52 Jamario Moon .20 .50
❑ 53 Nick Young .12 .30
❑ 54 Rashard Lewis .20 .50
❑ 55 Jason Kidd .20 .50
❑ 56 Josh Howard .20 .50
❑ 57 Desmond Mason .12 .30
❑ 58 Andre Miller .15 .40
❑ 59 Rafer Alston .12 .30
❑ 60 Baron Davis .20 .50
❑ 61 Zydrunas Ilgauskas .15 .40
❑ 62 Marvin Williams .20 .50
❑ 63 Manu Ginobili .20 .50
❑ 64 David West .20 .50
❑ 65 Rajon Rondo .20 .50
❑ 66 Kenyon Martin .20 .50
❑ 67 Josh Boone .12 .30
❑ 68 Travis Outlaw .20 .50
❑ 69 Andre Iguodala .20 .50
❑ 70 Yi Jianlian .20 .50
❑ 71 Jordan Farmar .15 .40
❑ 72 Udonis Haslem .20 .50
❑ 73 Caron Butler .20 .50
❑ 74 Craig Smith .20 .50
❑ 75 Tayshaun Prince .20 .50
❑ 76 Rudy Gay .20 .50
❑ 77 Jermaine O'Neal .20 .50
❑ 78 Devin Harris .20 .50
❑ 79 Fabricio Oberto .12 .30
❑ 80 Hedo Turkoglu .20 .50
❑ 81 Jannero Pargo .12 .30
❑ 82 Corey Maggette .20 .50
❑ 83 Ricky Davis .20 .50
❑ 84 Grant Hill .20 .50
❑ 85 Josh Childress .20 .50
❑ 86 Jeff Green .15 .40
❑ 87 Lamar Odom .20 .50
❑ 88 Brandan Wright .15 .40
❑ 89 Sean Williams .15 .40
❑ 90 Drew Gooden .15 .40
❑ 91 Amare Stoudemire .25 .60
❑ 92 Charlie Villanueva .20 .50
❑ 93 Ron Artest .20 .50
❑ 94 Derek Fisher .20 .50
❑ 95 Willie Green .12 .30
❑ 96 Kirk Hinrich .20 .50
❑ 97 Jameer Nelson .15 .40
❑ 98 Al Harrington .15 .40
❑ 99 Ronnie Brewer .15 .40
❑ 100 Dwyane Wade .40 1.00
❑ 101 Jamal Crawford .12 .30
❑ 102 Ryan Gomes .15 .40
❑ 103 Marcus Camby .12 .30
❑ 104 Antawn Jamison .20 .50
❑ 105 Cuttino Mobley .15 .40
❑ 106 Tyson Chandler .15 .40
❑ 107 Al Horford .20 .50
❑ 108 Chris Wilcox .15 .40
❑ 109 Gerald Wallace .20 .50
❑ 110 Andrew Bynum .20 .50
❑ 111 Tracy McGrady .25 .60
❑ 112 Mo Williams .15 .40
❑ 113 Nate Robinson .20 .50
❑ 114 Wally Szczerbiak .15 .40
❑ 115 Vince Carter .25 .60
❑ 116 T.J. Ford .12 .30
❑ 117 Kevin Martin .20 .50
❑ 118 Steve Blake .12 .30
❑ 119 Anderson Varejao .15 .40
❑ 120 Mike Conley .15 .40
❑ 121 Chris Kaman .12 .30
❑ 122 Louis Williams .12 .30
❑ 123 Jason Richardson .20 .50
❑ 124 John Salmons .20 .50
❑ 125 Martell Webster .15 .40
❑ 126 Juan Carlos Navarro .15 .40
❑ 127 Raja Bell .12 .30
❑ 128 Jason Terry .15 .40
❑ 129 Corey Brewer .15 .40
❑ 130 Bruce Bowen .12 .30
❑ 131 Glen Davis .15 .40
❑ 132 Richard Hamilton .15 .40
❑ 133 Ben Wallace .20 .50
❑ 134 Chris Bosh .20 .50
❑ 135 Beno Udrih .12 .30
❑ 136 Jarrett Jack .15 .40
❑ 137 Stephen Jackson .15 .40
❑ 138 Damien Wilkins .12 .30
❑ 139 Jamaal Tinsley .12 .30
❑ 140 Deron Williams .25 .60
❑ 141 Andres Nocioni .15 .40
❑ 142 David Lee .15 .40
❑ 143 Rodney Stuckey .25 .60
❑ 144 Luke Walton .15 .40
❑ 145 Jerry Stackhouse .15 .40
❑ 146 Samuel Dalembert .12 .30
❑ 147 Brandon Roy .25 .60
❑ 148 Chauncey Billups .20 .50
❑ 149 Michael Finley .20 .50
❑ 150 Leandro Barbosa .15 .40
❑ 151 Keith Bogans .12 .30
❑ 152 Mike Bibby .20 .50
❑ 153 Troy Murphy .20 .50
❑ 154 Eddy Curry .12 .30
❑ 155 Anthony Parker .15 .40
❑ 156 Kevin Durant .50 1.25
❑ 157 Larry Hughes .15 .40
❑ 158 Peja Stojakovic .20 .50
❑ 159 Shane Battier .15 .40
❑ 160 Kendrick Perkins .15 .40
❑ 161 Mehmet Okur .20 .50
❑ 162 Brendan Haywood .12 .30
❑ 163 Monta Ellis .20 .50
❑ 164 J.R. Smith .15 .40
❑ 165 Greg Oden .20 .50
❑ 166 John Stockton .30 .75
❑ 167 Tim Hardaway .20 .50
❑ 168 Dennis Rodman .20 .50
❑ 169 Dominique Wilkins .25 .60
❑ 170 David Thompson .25 .60
❑ 171 Spencer Haywood .20 .50
❑ 172 Larry Bird .60 1.50
❑ 173 Isiah Thomas .20 .50
❑ 174 Magic Johnson .40 1.00
❑ 175 Bill Russell .30 .75
❑ 176 Moses Malone .20 .50
❑ 177 Sidney Moncrief .20 .50
❑ 178 George Gervin .25 .60
❑ 179 David Robinson .30 .75
❑ 180 Jerry West .25 .60
❑ 181 Rick Barry .20 .50
❑ 182 Sam Perkins .20 .50
❑ 183 Lenny Wilkens .20 .50
❑ 184 Jo Jo White .20 .50
❑ 185 Elgin Baylor .20 .50

❑ 186 Micheal Ray Richardson	.20	.50
❑ 187 Otis Birdsong	.20	.50
❑ 188 Derrick Coleman	.20	.50
❑ 189 Mark Eaton	.20	.50
❑ 190 Pete Maravich	.60	1.50
❑ 191 Wilt Chamberlain	.40	1.00
❑ 192 Alex English	.20	.50
❑ 193 Patrick Ewing	.25	.60
❑ 194 Julius Erving	.40	1.00
❑ 195 Hakeem Olajuwon	.25	.60
❑ 196 Derrick Rose RC	2.50	6.00
❑ 197 Michael Beasley RC	1.25	3.00
❑ 198 O.J. Mayo RC	1.00	2.50
❑ 199 Russell Westbrook RC	1.50	4.00
❑ 200 Kevin Love RC	.75	2.00
❑ 201 Danilo Gallinari RC	1.00	2.50
❑ 202 Eric Gordon RC	.75	2.00
❑ 203 Joe Alexander RC	.60	1.50
❑ 204 D.J. Augustin RC	.60	1.50
❑ 205 Brook Lopez RC	1.25	3.00
❑ 206 Jerryd Bayless RC	.60	1.50
❑ 207 Jason Thompson RC	.60	1.50
❑ 208 Brandon Rush RC	.60	1.50
❑ 209 Anthony Randolph RC	1.00	2.50
❑ 210 Robin Lopez RC	.60	1.50
❑ 211 Marreese Speights RC	.60	1.50
❑ 212 Roy Hibbert RC	.75	2.00
❑ 213 George Hill RC	1.00	2.50
❑ 214 J.J. Hickson RC	1.00	2.50
❑ 215 Alexis Ajinca RC	.60	1.50
❑ 216 Ryan Anderson RC	.60	1.50
❑ 217 Courtney Lee RC	1.00	2.50
❑ 218 Kosta Koufos RC	.60	1.50
❑ 219 Darrell Arthur RC	.60	1.50
❑ 220 Donte Greene RC	.60	1.50
❑ BO Barack Obama	30.00	60.00

2009-10 Topps

❑ 1 Joe Johnson	.20	.50
❑ 2 Josh Smith	.20	.50
❑ 3 Mike Bibby	.12	.30
❑ 4 Marvin Williams	.15	.40
❑ 5 Al Horford	.20	.50
❑ 6 Ronald Murray	.12	.30
❑ 7 Zaza Pachulia	.12	.30
❑ 8 Acie Law IV	.12	.30
❑ 9 Solomon Jones	.12	.30
❑ 10 Maurice Evans	.12	.30
❑ 11 Mario West	.12	.30
❑ 12 Paul Pierce	.25	.60
❑ 13 Ray Allen	.20	.50
❑ 14 Kevin Garnett	.40	1.00
❑ 15 Rajon Rondo	.20	.50
❑ 16 Eddie House	.12	.30
❑ 17 Kendrick Perkins	.12	.30
❑ 18 Tony Allen	.12	.30
❑ 19 Leon Powe	.12	.30
❑ 20 Glen Davis	.15	.40
❑ 21 Brian Scalabrine	.12	.30
❑ 22 Stephon Marbury	.15	.40
❑ 23 Gerald Wallace	.20	.50
❑ 24 Boris Diaw	.15	.40
❑ 25 Emeka Okafor	.20	.50
❑ 26 Raymond Felton	.15	.40
❑ 27 Raja Bell	.15	.40
❑ 28 D.J. Augustin	.15	.40
❑ 29 Vladimir Radmanovic	.12	.30
❑ 30 Sean Singletary	.12	.30
❑ 31 DeSagana Diop	.12	.30
❑ 32 Ben Gordon	.20	.50
❑ 33 Derrick Rose	.40	1.00
❑ 34 Luol Deng	.20	.50
❑ 35 John Salmons	.20	.50
❑ 36 Tim Thomas	.12	.30
❑ 37 Brad Miller	.20	.50
❑ 38 Kirk Hinrich	.20	.50
❑ 39 Tyrus Thomas	.15	.40
❑ 40 Joakim Noah	.20	.50
❑ 41 Aaron Gray	.12	.30
❑ 42 LeBron James	1.00	2.50
❑ 43 Mo Williams	.15	.40
❑ 44 Zydrunas Ilgauskas	.12	.30
❑ 45 Delonte West	.12	.30
❑ 46 Anderson Varejao	.15	.40
❑ 47 Daniel Gibson	.20	.50
❑ 48 Ben Wallace	.20	.50
❑ 49 J.J. Hickson	.12	.30
❑ 50 Wally Szczerbiak	.15	.40
❑ 51 Aleksandar Pavlovic	.12	.30
❑ 52 Dirk Nowitzki	.25	.60
❑ 53 Jason Terry	.15	.40
❑ 54 Josh Howard	.20	.50
❑ 55 Jason Kidd	.20	.50
❑ 56 Brandon Bass	.12	.30
❑ 57 Jose Barea	.20	.50
❑ 58 Antoine Wright	.12	.30
❑ 59 Gerald Green	.12	.30
❑ 60 Erick Dampier	.12	.30
❑ 61 Devean George	.15	.40
❑ 62 Carmelo Anthony	.25	.60
❑ 63 Chauncey Billups	.20	.50
❑ 64 Nene	.15	.40
❑ 65 J.R. Smith	.15	.40
❑ 66 Kenyon Martin	.20	.50
❑ 67 Linas Kleiza	.12	.30
❑ 68 Dahntay Jones	.12	.30
❑ 69 Chris Andersen	.20	.50
❑ 70 Renaldo Balkman	.12	.30
❑ 71 Anthony Carter	.12	.30
❑ 72 Allen Iverson	.25	.60
❑ 73 Richard Hamilton	.15	.40
❑ 74 Tayshaun Prince	.20	.50
❑ 75 Rodney Stuckey	.20	.50
❑ 76 Rasheed Wallace	.20	.50
❑ 77 Antonio McDyess	.12	.30
❑ 78 Jason Maxiell	.12	.30
❑ 79 Arron Afflalo	.12	.30
❑ 80 Amir Johnson	.12	.30
❑ 81 Walter Herrmann	.12	.30
❑ 82 Stephen Jackson	.15	.40
❑ 83 Corey Maggette	.15	.40
❑ 84 Jamal Crawford	.12	.30
❑ 85 Kelenna Azubuike	.12	.30
❑ 86 Monta Ellis	.20	.50
❑ 87 Andris Biedrins	.12	.30
❑ 88 Marco Belinelli	.12	.30
❑ 89 C.J. Watson	.12	.30
❑ 90 Anthony Morrow	.12	.30
❑ 91 Brandan Wright	.12	.30
❑ 92 Anthony Randolph	.20	.50
❑ 93 Yao Ming	.25	.60
❑ 94 Ron Artest	.20	.50
❑ 95 Tracy McGrady	.25	.60
❑ 96 Luis Scola	.12	.30
❑ 97 Von Wafer	.12	.30
❑ 98 Aaron Brooks	.15	.40
❑ 99 Carl Landry	.12	.30
❑ 100 Shane Battier	.15	.40
❑ 101 Kyle Lowry	.12	.30
❑ 102 Chuck Hayes	.12	.30
❑ 103 Danny Granger	.20	.50
❑ 104 Mike Dunleavy	.12	.30
❑ 105 T.J. Ford	.12	.30
❑ 106 Marquis Daniels	.12	.30
❑ 107 Troy Murphy	.12	.30
❑ 108 Jarrett Jack	.15	.40
❑ 109 Rasho Nesterovic	.12	.30
❑ 110 Brandon Rush	.12	.30
❑ 111 Roy Hibbert	.12	.30
❑ 112 Jeff Foster	.12	.30
❑ 113 Zach Randolph	.12	.30
❑ 114 Al Thornton	.20	.50
❑ 115 Baron Davis	.20	.50
❑ 116 Eric Gordon	.20	.50
❑ 117 Chris Kaman	.20	.50
❑ 118 Marcus Camby	.12	.30
❑ 119 Mardy Collins	.12	.30
❑ 120 Ricky Davis	.12	.30
❑ 121 DeAndre Jordan	.12	.30
❑ 122 Steve Novak	.12	.30
❑ 123 Kobe Bryant	1.00	2.50
❑ 124 Pau Gasol	.20	.50
❑ 125 Andrew Bynum	.20	.50
❑ 126 Derek Fisher	.15	.40
❑ 127 Lamar Odom	.20	.50
❑ 128 Trevor Ariza	.20	.50
❑ 129 Jordan Farmar	.15	.40
❑ 130 Adam Morrison	.15	.40
❑ 131 Sasha Vujacic	.12	.30
❑ 132 Luke Walton	.12	.30
❑ 133 D.J. Mbenga	.12	.30
❑ 134 O.J. Mayo	.25	.60
❑ 135 Rudy Gay	.20	.50
❑ 136 Hakim Warrick	.15	.40
❑ 137 Marc Gasol	.20	.50
❑ 138 Mike Conley	.12	.30
❑ 139 Darko Milicic	.12	.30
❑ 140 Darrell Arthur	.15	.40
❑ 141 Hamed Haddadi	.20	.50
❑ 142 Quinton Ross	.12	.30
❑ 143 Dwyane Wade	.40	1.00
❑ 144 Michael Beasley	.25	.60
❑ 145 Jermaine O'Neal	.20	.50
❑ 146 Udonis Haslem	.15	.40
❑ 147 Daequan Cook	.15	.40
❑ 148 Mario Chalmers	.20	.50
❑ 149 Chris Quinn	.12	.30
❑ 150 Jamario Moon	.20	.50
❑ 151 Joel Anthony RC	.20	.50
❑ 152 Luther Head	.20	.50
❑ 153 Michael Redd	.20	.50
❑ 154 Richard Jefferson	.20	.50
❑ 155 Charlie Villanueva	.15	.40
❑ 156 Andrew Bogut	.20	.50
❑ 157 Luke Ridnour	.12	.30
❑ 158 Ramon Sessions	.12	.30
❑ 159 Luc Mbah a Moute	.12	.30
❑ 160 Joe Alexander	.20	.50
❑ 161 Charlie Bell	.12	.30
❑ 162 Keith Bogans	.12	.30
❑ 163 Shelden Williams	.12	.30
❑ 164 Al Jefferson	.20	.50
❑ 165 Randy Foye	.12	.30
❑ 166 Ryan Gomes	.12	.30
❑ 167 Kevin Love	.15	.40
❑ 168 Craig Smith	.12	.30
❑ 169 Mike Miller	.20	.50
❑ 170 Sebastian Telfair	.12	.30
❑ 171 Corey Brewer	.12	.30
❑ 172 Brian Cardinal	.12	.30
❑ 173 Rodney Carney	.12	.30
❑ 174 Devin Harris	.20	.50
❑ 175 Vince Carter	.25	.60
❑ 176 Brook Lopez	.12	.30
❑ 177 Yi Jianlian	.20	.50
❑ 178 Keyon Dooling	.12	.30
❑ 179 Jarvis Hayes	.12	.30
❑ 180 Bobby Simmons	.15	.40
❑ 181 Ryan Anderson	.12	.30
❑ 182 Josh Boone	.12	.30
❑ 183 Chris Douglas-Roberts	.12	.30
❑ 184 Sean Williams	.12	.30
❑ 185 Chris Paul	.40	1.00
❑ 186 David West	.20	.50
❑ 187 Peja Stojakovic	.12	.30
❑ 188 Rasual Butler	.12	.30
❑ 189 James Posey	.15	.40
❑ 190 Tyson Chandler	.15	.40
❑ 191 Devin Brown	.12	.30
❑ 192 Morris Peterson	.12	.30
❑ 193 Hilton Armstrong	.12	.30
❑ 194 Julian Wright	.12	.30
❑ 195 Antonio Daniels	.12	.30
❑ 196 Chris Wilcox	.12	.30
❑ 197 Al Harrington	.15	.40
❑ 198 David Lee	.15	.40
❑ 199 Nate Robinson	.20	.50
❑ 200 Wilson Chandler	.12	.30
❑ 201 Chris Duhon	.12	.30
❑ 202 Quentin Richardson	.12	.30
❑ 203 Larry Hughes	.12	.30
❑ 204 Danilo Gallinari	.20	.50
❑ 205 Jared Jeffries	.12	.30
❑ 206 Russell Westbrook	.20	.50
❑ 207 Earl Watson	.12	.30
❑ 208 Robert Swift	.12	.30
❑ 209 Joe Smith	.12	.30
❑ 210 Desmond Mason	.12	.30
❑ 211 Kevin Durant	.50	1.25
❑ 212 Jeff Green	.15	.40
❑ 213 Nick Collison	.12	.30
❑ 214 Thabo Sefolosha	.12	.30
❑ 215 Damien Wilkins	.12	.30
❑ 216 Rafer Alston	.15	.40

❑ 217 Dwight Howard	.40	1.00
❑ 218 Rashard Lewis	.20	.50
❑ 219 Hedo Turkoglu	.20	.50
❑ 220 Jameer Nelson	.15	.40
❑ 221 Mickael Pietrus	.12	.30
❑ 222 Courtney Lee	.15	.40
❑ 223 J.J. Redick	.20	.50
❑ 224 Tyronn Lue	.12	.30
❑ 225 Anthony Johnson	.12	.30
❑ 226 Tony Battie	.12	.30
❑ 227 Andre Iguodala	.20	.50
❑ 228 Andre Miller	.15	.40
❑ 229 Elton Brand	.20	.50
❑ 230 Thaddeus Young	.12	.30
❑ 231 Louis Williams	.12	.30
❑ 232 Willie Green	.12	.30
❑ 233 Marreese Speights	.15	.40
❑ 234 Samuel Dalembert	.12	.30
❑ 235 Reggie Evans	.12	.30
❑ 236 Donyell Marshall	.12	.30
❑ 237 Amare Stoudemire	.25	.60
❑ 238 Shaquille O'Neal	.40	1.00
❑ 239 Jason Richardson	.20	.50
❑ 240 Steve Nash	.20	.50
❑ 241 Leandro Barbosa	.15	.40
❑ 242 Grant Hill	.20	.50
❑ 243 Matt Barnes	.12	.30
❑ 244 Alando Tucker	.12	.30
❑ 245 Louis Amundson	.12	.30
❑ 246 Robin Lopez	.12	.30
❑ 247 Goran Dragic	.12	.30
❑ 248 Jared Dudley	.12	.30
❑ 249 Brandon Roy	.25	.60
❑ 250 LaMarcus Aldridge	.20	.50
❑ 251 Travis Outlaw	.20	.50
❑ 252 Steve Blake	.12	.30
❑ 253 Rudy Fernandez	.20	.50
❑ 254 Greg Oden	.15	.40
❑ 255 Jerryd Bayless	.15	.40
❑ 256 Joel Przybilla	.12	.30
❑ 257 Nicolas Batum	.12	.30
❑ 258 Sergio Rodriguez	.12	.30
❑ 259 Martell Webster	.15	.40
❑ 260 Channing Frye	.15	.40
❑ 261 Kevin Martin	.20	.50
❑ 262 Andres Nocioni	.15	.40
❑ 263 Francisco Garcia	.15	.40
❑ 264 Beno Udrih	.12	.30
❑ 265 Jason Thompson	.12	.30
❑ 266 Spencer Hawes	.15	.40
❑ 267 Bobby Jackson	.12	.30
❑ 268 Rashad McCants	.12	.30
❑ 269 Donte Greene	.12	.30
❑ 270 Quincy Douby	.12	.30
❑ 271 Tony Parker	.20	.50
❑ 272 Tim Duncan	.30	.75
❑ 273 Manu Ginobili	.20	.50
❑ 274 Roger Mason	.12	.30
❑ 275 Michael Finley	.12	.30
❑ 276 Matt Bonner	.12	.30
❑ 277 George Hill	.15	.40
❑ 278 Kurt Thomas	.12	.30
❑ 279 Bruce Bowen	.12	.30
❑ 280 Ime Udoka	.15	.40
❑ 281 Drew Gooden	.15	.40
❑ 282 Chris Bosh	.20	.50
❑ 283 Andrea Bargnani	.15	.40
❑ 284 Shawn Marion	.20	.50
❑ 285 Jose Calderon	.15	.40
❑ 286 Anthony Parker	.15	.40
❑ 287 Jason Kapono	.15	.40
❑ 288 Marcus Banks	.12	.30
❑ 289 Joey Graham	.12	.30
❑ 290 Roko Ukic	.12	.30
❑ 291 Pops Mensah-Bonsu	.12	.30
❑ 292 Kris Humphries	.12	.30
❑ 293 Carlos Boozer	.20	.50
❑ 294 Deron Williams	.25	.60
❑ 295 Mehmet Okur	.12	.30
❑ 296 Paul Millsap	.15	.40
❑ 297 Ronnie Brewer	.12	.30
❑ 298 Andrei Kirilenko	.15	.40
❑ 299 C.J. Miles	.12	.30
❑ 300 Ronnie Price	.12	.30
❑ 301 Kyle Korver	.15	.40
❑ 302 Kosta Koufos	.12	.30
❑ 303 Matt Harpring	.12	.30
❑ 304 Brevin Knight	.12	.30
❑ 305 Antawn Jamison	.20	.50
❑ 306 Caron Butler	.20	.50
❑ 307 Nick Young	.12	.30
❑ 308 Andray Blatche	.12	.30
❑ 309 DeShawn Stevenson	.12	.30
❑ 310 JaVale McGee	.12	.30
❑ 311 Mike James	.12	.30
❑ 312 Gilbert Arenas	.20	.50
❑ 313 Juan Dixon	.12	.30
❑ 314 Dominic McGuire	.12	.30
❑ 315 Darius Songaila	.12	.30
❑ 316 Blake Griffin RC	2.00	5.00
❑ 317 Ricky Rubio RC	1.25	3.00
❑ 318 Hasheem Thabeet RC	.75	2.00
❑ 319 James Harden RC	1.50	4.00
❑ 320 DeMar DeRozan RC	1.25	3.00
❑ 321 Stephen Curry RC	2.00	5.00
❑ 322 Brandon Jennings RC	2.00	5.00
❑ 323 Jordan Hill RC	1.00	2.50
❑ 324 Earl Clark RC	1.25	3.00
❑ 325 Gerald Henderson RC	1.25	3.00
❑ 326 Jonny Flynn RC	1.25	3.00
❑ 327 Tyreke Evans RC	3.00	8.00
❑ 328 Tyler Hansbrough RC	1.25	3.00
❑ 329 Terrence Williams RCÂ•	1.50	4.00
❑ 330 Jrue Holiday RC	1.25	3.00

2005-06 Topps Big Game

❑ COMMON CARD (1-110)	.60	1.50
❑ COMMON ROOKIE (111-141)	2.00	5.00
❑ COMMON CELEBRITY (142-146)	2.50	6.00
❑ 1 Vince Carter	2.00	5.00
❑ 2 Mehmet Okur	.60	1.50
❑ 3 Andre Iguodala	1.00	2.50
❑ 4 Baron Davis	1.00	2.50
❑ 5 Drew Gooden	.75	2.00
❑ 6 Yao Ming	2.50	6.00
❑ 7 Gary Payton	1.00	2.50
❑ 8 Shaun Livingston	.60	1.50
❑ 9 Marcus Camby	.75	2.00
❑ 10 Ben Wallace	1.00	2.50
❑ 11 Mike Miller	1.00	2.50
❑ 12 Steve Francis	1.00	2.50
❑ 13 Sam Cassell	1.00	2.50
❑ 14 Gilbert Arenas	1.00	2.50
❑ 15 Chris Bosh	1.00	2.50
❑ 16 Jamaal Magloire	.60	1.50
❑ 17 Zach Randolph	1.00	2.50
❑ 18 Josh Childress	.75	2.00
❑ 19 Kirk Hinrich	1.00	2.50
❑ 20 Dirk Nowitzki	1.50	4.00
❑ 21 Trevor Ariza	.75	2.00
❑ 22 Primoz Brezec	.60	1.50
❑ 23 LeBron James	5.00	12.00
❑ 24 Vladimir Radmanovic	.60	1.50
❑ 25 Tim Duncan	2.00	5.00
❑ 26 Damon Jones	.75	2.00
❑ 27 Rasheed Wallace	1.00	2.50
❑ 28 Corey Maggette	.75	2.00
❑ 29 Stephen Jackson	.75	2.00
❑ 30 Amare Stoudemire	2.00	5.00
❑ 31 Jason Richardson	1.00	2.50
❑ 32 Brad Miller	1.00	2.50
❑ 33 Kenyon Martin	1.00	2.50
❑ 34 Paul Pierce	1.00	2.50
❑ 35 Lamar Odom	1.00	2.50
❑ 36 Marquis Daniels	.75	2.00
❑ 37 Shane Battier	1.00	2.50
❑ 38 Eddy Curry	.75	2.00
❑ 39 Michael Redd	1.00	2.50
❑ 40 Ray Allen	1.00	2.50
❑ 41 Latrell Sprewell	.60	1.50
❑ 42 Rafer Alston	.60	1.50
❑ 43 Brendan Haywood	.60	1.50
❑ 44 Al Harrington	.60	1.50
❑ 45 Udonis Haslem	1.00	2.50
❑ 46 Chauncey Billups	1.00	2.50
❑ 47 Andrei Kirilenko	1.00	2.50
❑ 48 Chris Webber	1.00	2.50
❑ 49 Stephon Marbury	1.00	2.50
❑ 50 Emeka Okafor	1.00	2.50
❑ 51 Cuttino Mobley	.75	2.00
❑ 52 Shawn Marion	1.00	2.50
❑ 53 Jamaal Tinsley	.75	2.00
❑ 54 Nenad Krstic	.75	2.00
❑ 55 Bob Sura	.60	1.50
❑ 56 Manu Ginobili	1.00	2.50
❑ 57 Dan Dickau	.60	1.50
❑ 58 Wally Szczerbiak	.75	2.00
❑ 59 Mike Dunleavy	.75	2.00
❑ 60 Carmelo Anthony	2.00	5.00
❑ 61 Zydrunas Ilgauskas	.75	2.00
❑ 62 Elton Brand	1.00	2.50
❑ 63 Jamal Crawford	.75	2.00
❑ 64 Grant Hill	1.00	2.50
❑ 65 Ben Gordon	1.25	3.00
❑ 66 Rashard Lewis	1.00	2.50
❑ 67 Josh Howard	1.00	2.50
❑ 68 Jalen Rose	1.00	2.50
❑ 69 Pau Gasol	1.00	2.50
❑ 70 Steve Nash	1.25	3.00
❑ 71 Larry Hughes	.75	2.00
❑ 72 J.R. Smith	.75	2.00
❑ 73 Jason Kidd	1.50	4.00
❑ 74 Mike Bibby	1.00	2.50
❑ 75 Josh Smith	1.00	2.50
❑ 76 Richard Hamilton	.75	2.00
❑ 77 Caron Butler	1.00	2.50
❑ 78 Richard Jefferson	.75	2.00
❑ 79 Mike Sweetney	.75	2.00
❑ 80 Shaquille O'Neal	2.50	6.00
❑ 81 Dwight Howard	2.00	5.00
❑ 82 Allen Iverson	2.00	5.00
❑ 83 Luol Deng	1.00	2.50
❑ 84 Luke Ridnour	.75	2.00
❑ 85 Desmond Mason	.60	1.50
❑ 86 Gerald Wallace	1.00	2.50
❑ 87 Carlos Boozer	1.00	2.50
❑ 88 Antoine Walker	.75	2.00
❑ 89 Tony Parker	1.00	2.50
❑ 90 Tracy McGrady	2.00	5.00
❑ 91 Jermaine O'Neal	1.00	2.50
❑ 92 Andre Miller	.75	2.00
❑ 93 Quentin Richardson	.75	2.00
❑ 94 Dwyane Wade	2.50	6.00
❑ 95 Kevin Garnett	2.00	5.00
❑ 96 Peja Stojakovic	1.00	2.50
❑ 97 Antawn Jamison	1.00	2.50
❑ 98 Devin Harris	1.00	2.50
❑ 99 Kobe Bryant	5.00	12.00
❑ 100 Sebastian Telfair	.75	2.00
❑ 101 Samuel Dalembert	.60	1.50
❑ 102 Darius Miles	1.00	2.50
❑ 103 Al Jefferson	1.00	2.50
❑ 104 Brevin Knight	.60	1.50
❑ 105 Anderson Varejao	.75	2.00
❑ 106 Troy Murphy	1.00	2.50
❑ 107 Mike James	.60	1.50
❑ 108 Maurice Williams	.75	2.00
❑ 109 Robert Horry	.75	2.00
❑ 110 Bobby Simmons	.60	1.50
❑ 111 Andrew Bogut RC	2.50	6.00
❑ 112 Gerald Green RC	2.00	5.00
❑ 113 Raymond Felton RC	2.50	6.00
❑ 114 Francisco Garcia RC	2.50	6.00
❑ 115 Hakim Warrick RC	3.00	8.00
❑ 116 Jarrett Jack RC	2.00	5.00
❑ 117 Wayne Simien RC	2.50	6.00
❑ 118 Nate Robinson RC	3.00	8.00
❑ 119 Julius Hodge RC	2.50	6.00
❑ 120 Chris Paul RC	6.00	15.00
❑ 121 Rashad McCants RC	2.50	6.00
❑ 122 Ike Diogu RC	2.50	6.00
❑ 123 Antoine Wright RC	2.00	5.00
❑ 124 Luther Head RC	2.50	6.00
❑ 125 Ryan Gomes RC	2.00	5.00
❑ 126 David Lee RC	4.00	10.00
❑ 127 Andrew Bynum RC	6.00	15.00
❑ 128 Salim Stoudamire RC	2.50	6.00
❑ 129 Sean May RC	2.50	6.00
❑ 130 Deron Williams RC	5.00	12.00
❑ 131 Joey Graham RC	2.00	5.00
❑ 132 Fran Vazquez RC	2.00	5.00
❑ 133 Brandon Bass RC	2.00	5.00
❑ 134 Jason Maxiell RC	2.50	6.00
❑ 135 Charlie Villanueva RC	3.00	8.00

❑ 136 Daniel Ewing RC 2.50 6.00
❑ 137 Channing Frye RC 2.50 6.00
❑ 138 Chris Taft RC 2.00 5.00
❑ 139 Marvin Williams RC 3.00 8.00
❑ 140 Danny Granger RC 5.00 12.00
❑ 141 Travis Diener RC 2.00 5.00
❑ 142 Shannon Elizabeth 2.50 6.00
❑ 143 Jenny McCarthy 2.50 6.00
❑ 144 Christie Brinkley 2.50 6.00
❑ 145 Jay-Z 4.00 10.00
❑ 146 Carmen Electra 2.50 6.00

2006-07 Topps Big Game

❑ 1 Dirk Nowitzki 1.25 3.00
❑ 2 Tracy McGrady 1.50 4.00
❑ 3 Elton Brand .75 2.00
❑ 4 Ricky Davis .75 2.00
❑ 5 Marcus Camby .60 1.50
❑ 6 Gilbert Arenas .75 2.00
❑ 7 Channing Frye .60 1.50
❑ 8 Chauncey Billups .75 2.00
❑ 9 Shaquille O'Neal 2.00 5.00
❑ 10 Lamar Odom .75 2.00
❑ 11 Pau Gasol .75 2.00
❑ 12 Charlie Villanueva .75 2.00
❑ 13 Larry Hughes .60 1.50
❑ 14 Peja Stojakovic .75 2.00
❑ 15 Andre Iguodala .75 2.00
❑ 16 Vince Carter 1.50 4.00
❑ 17 Jason Terry .75 2.00
❑ 18 Ron Artest .75 2.00
❑ 19 Luke Ridnour .60 1.50
❑ 20 Paul Pierce .75 2.00
❑ 21 Michael Redd .75 2.00
❑ 22 Rasheed Wallace .75 2.00
❑ 23 Baron Davis .75 2.00
❑ 24 Amare Stoudemire 1.50 4.00
❑ 25 Zach Randolph .75 2.00
❑ 26 Yao Ming 2.00 5.00
❑ 27 Raymond Felton 1.00 2.50
❑ 28 Stephon Marbury .75 2.00
❑ 29 Kirk Hinrich .75 2.00
❑ 30 Andre Miller .60 1.50
❑ 31 Jason Kidd 1.25 3.00
❑ 32 Tayshaun Prince .75 2.00
❑ 33 Antoine Walker .60 1.50
❑ 34 LeBron James 4.00 10.00
❑ 35 Brad Miller .75 2.00
❑ 36 Tim Duncan 1.50 4.00
❑ 37 Jermaine O'Neal .75 2.00
❑ 38 Josh Smith .75 2.00
❑ 39 Gerald Wallace .75 2.00
❑ 40 Delonte West .60 1.50
❑ 41 Darius Miles .50 1.25
❑ 42 Chris Paul 1.50 4.00
❑ 43 Mike Bibby .75 2.00
❑ 44 Sam Cassell .75 2.00
❑ 45 Josh Howard .75 2.00
❑ 46 Allen Iverson 1.50 4.00
❑ 47 Jameer Nelson .60 1.50
❑ 48 Mehmet Okur .50 1.25
❑ 49 Shawn Marion .75 2.00
❑ 50 Ray Allen .75 2.00
❑ 51 Joe Johnson .60 1.50
❑ 52 Richard Hamilton .60 1.50
❑ 53 Richard Jefferson .60 1.50
❑ 54 Kobe Bryant 4.00 10.00
❑ 55 Manu Ginobili .75 2.00
❑ 56 Carmelo Anthony 1.00 2.50
❑ 57 Ben Gordon 1.00 2.50
❑ 58 Andrew Bogut .75 2.00
❑ 59 Antawn Jamison .75 2.00
❑ 60 Chris Bosh .75 2.00
❑ 61 David West .75 2.00
❑ 62 Steve Nash 1.00 2.50
❑ 63 Ben Wallace .75 2.00
❑ 64 Chris Webber .75 2.00
❑ 65 Caron Butler .75 2.00
❑ 66 Danny Granger .60 1.50
❑ 67 Andrei Kirilenko .75 2.00
❑ 68 Kevin Garnett 1.50 4.00
❑ 69 Dwyane Wade 2.00 5.00
❑ 70 Tony Parker .75 2.00
❑ 71 Dwight Howard 1.50 4.00
❑ 72 Rashard Lewis .75 2.00
❑ 73 Mike Miller .75 2.00
❑ 74 Jason Richardson .75 2.00
❑ 75 T.J. Ford .60 1.50
❑ 76 J.J. Redick RC 1.50 4.00
❑ 77 Marcus Williams RC 2.00 5.00
❑ 78 Shelden Williams RC 2.00 5.00
❑ 79 Tyrus Thomas RC 2.00 5.00
❑ 80 LaMarcus Aldridge RC 2.00 5.00
❑ 81 Cedric Simmons RC 1.50 4.00
❑ 82 Saer Sene RC 1.50 4.00
❑ 83 Randy Foye RC 1.50 4.00
❑ 84 Patrick O'Bryant RC 1.50 4.00
❑ 85 Adam Morrison RC 2.00 5.00
❑ 86 Rudy Gay RC 1.50 4.00
❑ 87 Ronnie Brewer RC 2.00 5.00
❑ 88 Josh Boone RC 1.50 4.00
❑ 89 Maurice Ager RC 1.50 4.00
❑ 90 Shannon Brown RC 1.50 4.00
❑ 91 Renaldo Balkman RC 1.50 4.00
❑ 92 Thabo Sefolosha RC 2.00 5.00
❑ 93 Shawne Williams RC 1.50 4.00
❑ 94 Hilton Armstrong RC 1.50 4.00
❑ 95 Brandon Roy RC 4.00 10.00
❑ 96 Kyle Lowry RC 1.50 4.00
❑ 97 Steve Novak RC 1.50 4.00
❑ 98 Paul Davis RC 1.50 4.00
❑ 99 Solomon Jones RC 1.50 4.00
❑ 100 P.J. Tucker RC 1.50 4.00
❑ 101 Rajon Rondo RC 6.00 15.00
❑ 102 Dee Brown RC 1.50 4.00
❑ 103 Craig Smith RC 1.50 4.00
❑ 104 Bobby Jones RC 1.50 4.00
❑ 105 James White RC 1.50 4.00
❑ 106 Jordan Farmar RC 2.00 5.00
❑ 107 Mardy Collins RC 1.50 4.00
❑ 108 Quincy Douby RC 1.50 4.00
❑ 109 Rodney Carney RC 1.50 4.00
❑ 110 Andrea Bargnani RC 2.50 6.00

1996-97 Topps Chrome

❑ COMPLETE SET (220) 500.00 700.00
❑ COMMON CARD (1-220) .20 .50
❑ COMMON RC 1.00 2.50
❑ 1 Patrick Ewing .60 1.50
❑ 2 Christian Laettner .40 1.00
❑ 3 Mahmoud Abdul-Rauf .20 .50
❑ 4 Chris Webber .60 1.50
❑ 5 Jason Kidd 1.00 2.50
❑ 6 Clifford Rozier .20 .50
❑ 7 Elden Campbell .20 .50
❑ 8 Chuck Person .20 .50
❑ 9 Jeff Hornacek .40 1.00
❑ 10 Rik Smits .40 1.00
❑ 11 Kurt Thomas .40 1.00
❑ 12 Rod Strickland .20 .50
❑ 13 Kendall Gill .20 .50
❑ 14 Brian Williams .20 .50
❑ 15 Tom Gugliotta .20 .50
❑ 16 Ron Harper .40 1.00
❑ 17 Eric Williams .20 .50
❑ 18 A.C. Green .40 1.00
❑ 19 Scott Williams .20 .50
❑ 20 Damon Stoudamire .60 1.50
❑ 21 Bryant Reeves .20 .50
❑ 22 Bob Sura .20 .50
❑ 23 Mitch Richmond .40 1.00
❑ 24 Larry Johnson .40 1.00
❑ 25 Vin Baker .40 1.00
❑ 26 Mark Bryant .20 .50
❑ 27 Horace Grant .40 1.00
❑ 28 Allan Houston .40 1.00
❑ 29 Sam Perkins .40 1.00
❑ 30 Antonio McDyess .40 1.00
❑ 31 Rasheed Wallace .75 2.00
❑ 32 Malik Sealy .20 .50
❑ 33 Scottie Pippen 1.00 2.50
❑ 34 Charles Barkley .75 2.00
❑ 35 Hakeem Olajuwon .60 1.50
❑ 36 John Starks .40 1.00
❑ 37 Byron Scott .20 .50
❑ 38 Arvydas Sabonis .40 1.00
❑ 39 Vlade Divac .20 .50
❑ 40 Joe Dumars .60 1.50
❑ 41 Danny Ferry .20 .50
❑ 42 Jerry Stackhouse .75 2.00
❑ 43 B.J. Armstrong .20 .50
❑ 44 Shawn Bradley .20 .50
❑ 45 Kevin Garnett 1.50 4.00
❑ 46 Dee Brown .20 .50
❑ 47 Michael Smith .20 .50
❑ 48 Doug Christie .40 1.00
❑ 49 Mark Jackson .20 .50
❑ 50 Shawn Kemp .40 1.00
❑ 51 Sasha Danilovic .20 .50
❑ 52 Nick Anderson .20 .50
❑ 53 Matt Geiger .20 .50
❑ 54 Charles Smith .20 .50
❑ 55 Mookie Blaylock .20 .50
❑ 56 Johnny Newman .20 .50
❑ 57 George McCloud .20 .50
❑ 58 Greg Ostertag .20 .50
❑ 59 Reggie Williams .20 .50
❑ 60 Brent Barry .20 .50
❑ 61 Doug West .20 .50
❑ 62 Donald Royal .20 .50
❑ 63 Randy Brown .20 .50
❑ 64 Vincent Askew .20 .50
❑ 65 John Stockton .60 1.50
❑ 66 Joe Kleine .20 .50
❑ 67 Keith Askins .20 .50
❑ 68 Bobby Phills .20 .50
❑ 69 Chris Mullin .60 1.50
❑ 70 Nick Van Exel .60 1.50
❑ 71 Rick Fox .20 .50
❑ 72 Chicago Bulls - 72 Wins 1.50 4.00
❑ 73 Shawn Respert .20 .50
❑ 74 Hubert Davis .20 .50
❑ 75 Jim Jackson .20 .50
❑ 76 Olden Polynice .20 .50
❑ 77 Ghoorgho Murocan .20 .50
❑ 78 Theo Ratliff .40 1.00
❑ 79 Khalid Reeves .20 .50
❑ 80 David Robinson .60 1.50
❑ 81 Lawrence Moten .20 .50
❑ 82 Sam Cassell .60 1.50
❑ 83 George Zidek .20 .50
❑ 84 Sharone Wright .20 .50
❑ 85 Clarence Weatherspoon .20 .50
❑ 86 Alan Henderson .20 .50
❑ 87 Chris Dudley .20 .50
❑ 88 Ed O'Bannon .20 .50
❑ 89 Calbert Cheaney .20 .50
❑ 90 Cedric Ceballos .20 .50
❑ 91 Michael Cage .20 .50
❑ 92 Ervin Johnson .20 .50
❑ 93 Gary Trent .20 .50
❑ 94 Sherman Douglas .20 .50
❑ 95 Joe Smith .40 1.00
❑ 96 Dale Davis .20 .50
❑ 97 Tony Dumas .20 .50
❑ 98 Muggsy Bogues .20 .50
❑ 99 Toni Kukoc .40 1.00
❑ 100 Grant Hill .60 1.50
❑ 101 Michael Finley .75 2.00
❑ 102 Isaiah Rider .40 1.00
❑ 103 Bryant Stith .20 .50
❑ 104 Pooh Richardson .20 .50
❑ 105 Karl Malone .60 1.50
❑ 106 Brian Grant .60 1.50
❑ 107 Sean Elliott .40 1.00
❑ 108 Charles Oakley .20 .50
❑ 109 Pervis Ellison .20 .50
❑ 110 Anfernee Hardaway .60 1.50
❑ 111 Checklist (1-220) .20 .50
❑ 112 Dikembe Mutombo .40 1.00
❑ 113 Alonzo Mourning .40 1.00

❑ 114 Hubert Davis	.20	.50
❑ 115 Rony Seikaly	.20	.50
❑ 116 Danny Manning	.40	1.00
❑ 117 Donyell Marshall	.40	1.00
❑ 118 Gerald Wilkins	.20	.50
❑ 119 Ervin Johnson	.20	.50
❑ 120 Jalen Rose	.60	1.50
❑ 121 Dino Radja	.20	.50
❑ 122 Glenn Robinson	.60	1.50
❑ 123 John Stockton	.60	1.50
❑ 124 Matt Maloney RC	1.00	2.50
❑ 125 Clifford Robinson	.20	.50
❑ 126 Steve Kerr	.40	1.00
❑ 127 Nate McMillan	.20	.50
❑ 128 Shareef Abdur-Rahim RC	12.50	30.00
❑ 129 Loy Vaught	.20	.50
❑ 130 Anthony Mason	.40	1.00
❑ 131 Kevin Garnett	1.50	4.00
❑ 132 Roy Rogers RC	1.00	2.50
❑ 133 Erick Dampier RC	2.00	5.00
❑ 134 Tyus Edney	.20	.50
❑ 135 Chris Mills	.20	.50
❑ 136 Cory Alexander	.20	.50
❑ 137 Juwan Howard	.40	1.00
❑ 138 Kobe Bryant RC	175.00	275.00
❑ 139 Michael Jordan	8.00	20.00
❑ 140 Jayson Williams	.40	1.00
❑ 141 Rod Strickland	.20	.50
❑ 142 Lorenzen Wright RC	1.25	3.00
❑ 143 Will Perdue	.20	.50
❑ 144 Derek Harper	.20	.50
❑ 145 Billy Owens	.20	.50
❑ 146 Antoine Walker RC	10.00	25.00
❑ 147 P.J. Brown	.20	.50
❑ 148 Terrell Brandon	.40	1.00
❑ 149 Larry Johnson	.40	1.00
❑ 150 Steve Smith	.40	1.00
❑ 151 Eddie Jones	.60	1.50
❑ 152 Detlef Schrempf	.40	1.00
❑ 153 Dale Ellis	.20	.50
❑ 154 Isaiah Rider	.40	1.00
❑ 155 Tony Delk RC	2.50	6.00
❑ 156 Adrian Caldwell	.20	.50
❑ 157 Jamal Mashburn	.40	1.00
❑ 158 Dennis Scott	.20	.50
❑ 159 Dana Barros	.20	.50
❑ 160 Martin Muursepp RC	1.00	2.50
❑ 161 Marcus Camby RC	5.00	12.00
❑ 162 Jerome Williams RC	3.00	8.00
❑ 163 Wesley Person	.20	.50
❑ 164 Luc Longley	.20	.50
❑ 165 Charlie Ward	.20	.50
❑ 166 Mark Jackson	.20	.50
❑ 167 Derrick Coleman	.40	1.00
❑ 168 Dell Curry	.20	.50
❑ 169 Armon Gilliam	.20	.50
❑ 170 Vlade Divac	.20	.50
❑ 171 Allen Iverson RC	15.00	30.00
❑ 172 Vitaly Potapenko RC	1.00	2.50
❑ 173 Jon Koncak	.20	.50
❑ 174 Lindsey Hunter	.20	.50
❑ 175 Kevin Johnson	.40	1.00
❑ 176 Dennis Rodman	.40	1.00
❑ 177 Stephon Marbury RC	10.00	25.00
❑ 178 Karl Malone	.60	1.50
❑ 179 Charles Barkley	.75	2.00
❑ 180 Popeye Jones	.20	.50
❑ 181 Samaki Walker RC	1.00	2.50
❑ 182 Steve Nash RC	25.00	50.00
❑ 183 Latrell Sprewell	.60	1.50
❑ 184 Kenny Anderson	.20	.50
❑ 185 Tyrone Hill	.20	.50
❑ 186 Robert Pack	.20	.50
❑ 187 Greg Anthony	.20	.50
❑ 188 Derrick McKey	.20	.50
❑ 189 John Wallace RC	2.00	5.00
❑ 190 Bryon Russell	.20	.50
❑ 191 Jermaine O'Neal RC	12.50	30.00
❑ 192 Clyde Drexler	.60	1.50
❑ 193 Mahmoud Abdul-Rauf	.20	.50
❑ 194 Eric Montross	.20	.50
❑ 195 Allan Houston	.40	1.00
❑ 196 Harvey Grant	.20	.50
❑ 197 Rodney Rogers	.20	.50
❑ 198 Kerry Kittles RC	2.00	5.00
❑ 199 Grant Hill	.60	1.50
❑ 200 Lionel Simmons	.20	.50
❑ 201 Reggie Miller	.60	1.50
❑ 202 Avery Johnson	.20	.50
❑ 203 LaPhonso Ellis	.20	.50
❑ 204 Brian Shaw	.20	.50
❑ 205 Priest Lauderdale RC	1.00	2.50
❑ 206 Derek Fisher RC	8.00	20.00
❑ 207 Terry Porter	.20	.50
❑ 208 Todd Fuller RC	1.00	2.50
❑ 209 Hersey Hawkins	.40	1.00
❑ 210 Tim Legler	.20	.50
❑ 211 Terry Dehere	.20	.50
❑ 212 Gary Payton	.60	1.50
❑ 213 Joe Dumars	.60	1.50
❑ 214 Don MacLean	.20	.50
❑ 215 Greg Minor	.20	.50
❑ 216 Tim Hardaway	.40	1.00
❑ 217 Ray Allen RC	15.00	40.00
❑ 218 Mario Elie	.20	.50
❑ 219 Brooks Thompson	.20	.50
❑ 220 Shaquille O'Neal	1.50	4.00

1997-98 Topps Chrome

❑ COMPLETE SET (220)	60.00	120.00
❑ COMMON CARD (1-220)	.20	.50
❑ COMMON ROOKIE	.60	1.50
❑ 1 Scottie Pippen	1.00	2.50
❑ 2 Nate McMillan	.20	.50
❑ 3 Byron Scott	.20	.50
❑ 4 Mark Davis	.20	.50
❑ 5 Rod Strickland	.20	.50
❑ 6 Brian Grant	.40	1.00
❑ 7 Damon Stoudamire	.40	1.00
❑ 8 John Stockton	.60	1.50
❑ 9 Grant Long	.20	.50
❑ 10 Darrell Armstrong	.20	.50
❑ 11 Anthony Mason	.40	1.00
❑ 12 Travis Best	.20	.50
❑ 13 Stephon Marbury	.75	2.00
❑ 14 Jamal Mashburn	.40	1.00
❑ 15 Detlef Schrempf	.40	1.00
❑ 16 Terrell Brandon	.40	1.00
❑ 17 Charles Barkley	.75	2.00
❑ 18 Vin Baker	.40	1.00
❑ 19 Gary Trent	.20	.50
❑ 20 Vinny Del Negro	.20	.50
❑ 21 Todd Day	.20	.50
❑ 22 Malik Sealy	.20	.50
❑ 23 Wesley Person	.20	.50
❑ 24 Reggie Miller	.60	1.50
❑ 25 Dan Majerle	.40	1.00
❑ 26 Todd Fuller	.20	.50
❑ 27 Juwan Howard	.40	1.00
❑ 28 Clarence Weatherspoon	.20	.50
❑ 29 Grant Hill	.60	1.50
❑ 30 John Williams	.20	.50
❑ 31 Ken Norman	.20	.50
❑ 32 Patrick Ewing	.60	1.50
❑ 33 Bryon Russell	.20	.50
❑ 34 Tony Smith	.20	.50
❑ 35 Andrew Lang	.20	.50
❑ 36 Rony Seikaly	.20	.50
❑ 37 Billy Owens	.20	.50
❑ 38 Dino Radja	.20	.50
❑ 39 Chris Gatling	.20	.50
❑ 40 Dale Davis	.20	.50
❑ 41 Arvydas Sabonis	.40	1.00
❑ 42 Chris Mills	.20	.50
❑ 43 A.C. Green	.40	1.00
❑ 44 Tyrone Hill	.20	.50
❑ 45 Tracy Murray	.20	.50
❑ 46 David Robinson	.60	1.50
❑ 47 Lee Mayberry	.20	.50
❑ 48 Jayson Williams	.20	.50
❑ 49 Jason Kidd	1.00	2.50
❑ 50 Bryant Stith	.20	.50
❑ 51 CL/Bulls - Team of the 90s	1.50	4.00
❑ 52 Brent Barry	.40	1.00
❑ 53 Henry James	.20	.50
❑ 54 Allen Iverson	1.50	4.00
❑ 55 Shandon Anderson	.20	.50
❑ 56 Mitch Richmond	.40	1.00
❑ 57 Allan Houston	.40	1.00
❑ 58 Ron Harper	.40	1.00
❑ 59 Gheorghe Muresan	.20	.50
❑ 60 Vincent Askew	.20	.50
❑ 61 Ray Allen	.60	1.50
❑ 62 Kenny Anderson	.40	1.00
❑ 63 Dikembe Mutombo	.40	1.00
❑ 64 Sam Perkins	.40	1.00
❑ 65 Walt Williams	.20	.50
❑ 66 Chris Carr	.20	.50
❑ 67 Vlade Divac	.40	1.00
❑ 68 LaPhonso Ellis	.20	.50
❑ 69 B.J. Armstrong	.20	.50
❑ 70 Jim Jackson	.20	.50
❑ 71 Clyde Drexler	.60	1.50
❑ 72 Lindsey Hunter	.20	.50
❑ 73 Sasha Danilovic	.20	.50
❑ 74 Elden Campbell	.20	.50
❑ 75 Robert Pack	.20	.50
❑ 76 Dennis Scott	.20	.50
❑ 77 Will Perdue	.20	.50
❑ 78 Anthony Peeler	.20	.50
❑ 79 Steve Smith	.40	1.00
❑ 80 Steve Kerr	.40	1.00
❑ 81 Buck Williams	.20	.50
❑ 82 Terry Mills	.20	.50
❑ 83 Michael Smith	.20	.50
❑ 84 Adam Keefe	.20	.50
❑ 85 Kevin Willis	.40	1.00
❑ 86 David Wesley	.20	.50
❑ 87 Muggsy Bogues	.40	1.00
❑ 88 Bimbo Coles	.20	.50
❑ 89 Tom Gugliotta	.40	1.00
❑ 90 Jermaine O'Neal	1.00	2.50
❑ 91 Cedric Ceballos	.20	.50
❑ 92 Shawn Kemp	.40	1.00
❑ 93 Horace Grant	.40	1.00
❑ 94 Shareef Abdur-Rahim	1.00	2.50
❑ 95 Robert Horry	.40	1.00
❑ 96 Vitaly Potapenko	.20	.50
❑ 97 Pooh Richardson	.20	.50
❑ 98 Doug Christie	.40	1.00
❑ 99 Voshon Lenard	.20	.50
❑ 100 Dominique Wilkins	.60	1.50
❑ 101 Alonzo Mourning	.40	1.00
❑ 102 Sam Cassell	.60	1.50
❑ 103 Sherman Douglas	.20	.50
❑ 104 Shawn Bradley	.20	.50
❑ 105 Mark Jackson	.40	1.00
❑ 106 Dennis Rodman	.40	1.00
❑ 107 Charles Oakley	.40	1.00
❑ 108 Matt Maloney	.20	.50
❑ 109 Shaquille O'Neal	1.50	4.00
❑ 110 CL/K.Malone MVP	.60	1.50
❑ 111 Antonio McDyess	.40	1.00
❑ 112 Bob Sura	.20	.50
❑ 113 Terrell Brandon	.40	1.00
❑ 114 Tim Thomas RC	3.00	8.00
❑ 115 Tim Duncan RC	8.00	20.00
❑ 116 Antonio Daniels RC	.75	2.00
❑ 117 Bryant Reeves	.20	.50
❑ 118 Keith Van Horn RC	2.50	6.00
❑ 119 Loy Vaught	.20	.50
❑ 120 Rasheed Wallace	.60	1.50
❑ 121 Bobby Jackson RC	2.00	5.00
❑ 122 Kevin Johnson	.40	1.00
❑ 123 Michael Jordan	5.00	12.00
❑ 124 Ron Mercer RC	1.50	4.00
❑ 125 Tracy McGrady RC	6.00	15.00
❑ 126 Antoine Walker	.75	2.00
❑ 127 Carlos Rogers	.20	.50
❑ 128 Isaac Austin	.20	.50
❑ 129 Mookie Blaylock	.20	.50
❑ 130 Rodrick Rhodes RC	.60	1.50
❑ 131 Dennis Scott	.20	.50
❑ 132 Chris Mullin	.60	1.50
❑ 133 P.J. Brown	.20	.50
❑ 134 Rex Chapman	.20	.50
❑ 135 Sean Elliott	.40	1.00
❑ 136 Alan Henderson	.20	.50
❑ 137 Austin Croshere RC	1.50	4.00
❑ 138 Nick Van Exel	.60	1.50
❑ 139 Derek Strong	.20	.50
❑ 140 Glenn Robinson	.60	1.50
❑ 141 Avery Johnson	.20	.50
❑ 142 Calbert Cheaney	.20	.50

❑ 143 Mahmoud Abdul-Rauf	.20	.50
❑ 144 Stojko Vrankovic	.20	.50
❑ 145 Chris Childs	.20	.50
❑ 146 Danny Manning	.40	1.00
❑ 147 Jeff Hornacek	.40	1.00
❑ 148 Kevin Garnett	1.25	3.00
❑ 149 Joe Dumars	.60	1.50
❑ 150 Johnny Taylor RC	.60	1.50
❑ 151 Mark Price	.40	1.00
❑ 152 Toni Kukoc	.40	1.00
❑ 153 Erick Dampier	.40	1.00
❑ 154 Lorenzen Wright	.20	.50
❑ 155 Matt Geiger	.20	.50
❑ 156 Tim Hardaway	.40	1.00
❑ 157 Charles Smith RC	.60	1.50
❑ 158 Hersey Hawkins	.20	.50
❑ 159 Michael Finley	.60	1.50
❑ 160 Tyus Edney	.20	.50
❑ 161 Christian Laettner	.40	1.00
❑ 162 Doug West	.20	.50
❑ 163 Jim Jackson	.20	.50
❑ 164 Larry Johnson	.40	1.00
❑ 165 Vin Baker	.40	1.00
❑ 166 Karl Malone	.60	1.50
❑ 167 Kelvin Cato RC	.75	2.00
❑ 168 Luc Longley	.20	.50
❑ 169 Dale Davis	.20	.50
❑ 170 Joe Smith	.40	1.00
❑ 171 Kobe Bryant	3.00	8.00
❑ 172 Scot Pollard RC	.75	2.00
❑ 173 Derek Anderson RC	1.50	4.00
❑ 174 Erick Strickland RC	.75	2.00
❑ 175 Olden Polynice	.20	.50
❑ 176 Chris Whitney	.20	.50
❑ 177 Anthony Parker RC	1.50	4.00
❑ 178 Armon Gilliam	.20	.50
❑ 179 Gary Payton	.60	1.50
❑ 180 Glen Rice	.40	1.00
❑ 181 Chauncey Billups RC	5.00	12.00
❑ 182 Derek Fisher	.60	1.50
❑ 183 John Starks	.40	1.00
❑ 184 Mario Elie	.20	.50
❑ 185 Chris Webber	.60	1.50
❑ 186 Shawn Kemp	.40	1.00
❑ 187 Greg Ostertag	.20	.50
❑ 188 Olivier Saint-Jean RC	.60	1.50
❑ 189 Eric Snow	.40	1.00
❑ 190 Isaiah Rider	.40	1.00
❑ 191 Paul Grant RC	.60	1.50
❑ 192 Samaki Walker	.20	.50
❑ 193 Cory Alexander	.20	.50
❑ 194 Eddie Jones	.60	1.50
❑ 195 John Thomas RC	.60	1.50
❑ 196 Otis Thorpe	.20	.50
❑ 197 Rod Strickland	.20	.50
❑ 198 David Wesley	.20	.50
❑ 199 Jacque Vaughn RC	.75	2.00
❑ 200 Rik Smits	.40	1.00
❑ 201 Brevin Knight RC	1.00	2.50
❑ 202 Clifford Robinson	.20	.50
❑ 203 Hakeem Olajuwon	.60	1.50
❑ 204 Jerry Stackhouse	.60	1.50
❑ 205 Tyrone Hill	.20	.50
❑ 206 Kendall Gill	.20	.50
❑ 207 Marcus Camby	.60	1.50
❑ 208 Tony Battie RC	.75	2.00
❑ 209 Brent Price	.20	.50
❑ 210 Danny Fortson RC	2.00	5.00
❑ 211 Jerome Williams	.40	1.00
❑ 212 Maurice Taylor RC	2.00	5.00
❑ 213 Brian Williams	.20	.50
❑ 214 Keith Booth RC	.60	1.50
❑ 215 Nick Anderson	.20	.50
❑ 216 Travis Knight	.20	.50
❑ 217 Adonal Foyle RC	.75	2.00
❑ 218 Anfernee Hardaway	.60	1.50
❑ 219 Kerry Kittles	.60	1.50
❑ 220 CL/D.Mutombo Def POY	.20	.50

1998-99 Topps Chrome

❑ COMPLETE SET (220)	75.00	150.00
❑ COMP.SET W/PREV (230)	100.00	200.00
❑ COMMON CARD (1-235)	.15	.40
❑ COMMON ROOKIE	.40	1.00
❑ 1 Scottie Pippen	.75	2.00
❑ 2 Shareef Abdur-Rahim	.50	1.25
❑ 3 Rod Strickland	.15	.40
❑ 4 Keith Van Horn	.50	1.25
❑ 5 Ray Allen	.50	1.25
❑ 6 Does not exist		
❑ 7 Anthony Parker	.15	.40
❑ 8 Lindsey Hunter	.15	.40
❑ 9 Mario Elie	.15	.40
❑ 10 Does not exist		
❑ 11 Eldridge Recasner	.15	.40
❑ 12 Jeff Hornacek	.30	.75
❑ 13 Chris Webber	.50	1.25
❑ 14 Lee Mayberry	.15	.40
❑ 15 Erick Strickland	.15	.40
❑ 16 Arvydas Sabonis	.30	.75
❑ 17 Tim Thomas	.30	.75
❑ 18 Luc Longley	.15	.40
❑ 19 Does not exist		
❑ 20 Alonzo Mourning	.30	.75
❑ 21 Adonal Foyle	.15	.40
❑ 22 Tony Battie	.15	.40
❑ 23 Robert Horry	.30	.75
❑ 24 Derek Harper	.15	.40
❑ 25 Jamal Mashburn	.30	.75
❑ 26 Elliott Perry	.15	.40
❑ 27 Jalen Rose	.50	1.25
❑ 28 Joe Smith	.30	.75
❑ 29 Henry James	.15	.40
❑ 30 Travis Knight	.15	.40
❑ 31 Tom Gugliotta	.15	.40
❑ 32 Chris Anstey	.15	.40
❑ 33 Antonio Daniels	.15	.40
❑ 34 Eldon Campbell	.15	.40
❑ 35 Charlie Ward	.15	.40
❑ 36 Eddie Johnson	.15	.40
❑ 37 John Wallace	.15	.40
❑ 38 Antonio Davis	.15	.40
❑ 39 Antoine Walker	.50	1.25
❑ 40 Does not exist		
❑ 41 Doug Christie	.30	.75
❑ 42 Andrew Lang	.15	.40
❑ 43 Does not exist		
❑ 44 Jaren Jackson	.15	.40
❑ 45 Loy Vaught	.15	.40
❑ 46 Allan Houston	.30	.75
❑ 47 Mark Jackson	.30	.75
❑ 48 Tracy Murray	.15	.40
❑ 49 Tim Duncan	.75	2.00
❑ 50 Micheal Williams	.15	.40
❑ 51 Steve Nash	.50	1.25
❑ 52 Matt Maloney	.15	.40
❑ 53 Sam Cassell	.50	1.25
❑ 54 Voshon Lenard	.15	.40
❑ 55 Dikembe Mutombo	.30	.75
❑ 56 Malik Sealy	.15	.40
❑ 57 Dell Curry	.15	.40
❑ 58 Stephon Marbury	.50	1.25
❑ 59 Tariq Abdul-Wahad	.15	.40
❑ 60 Does not exist		
❑ 61 Kelvin Cato	.15	.40
❑ 62 LaPhonso Ellis	.15	.40
❑ 63 Jim Jackson	.15	.40
❑ 64 Greg Ostertag	.15	.40
❑ 65 Glenn Robinson	.30	.75
❑ 66 Chris Carr	.15	.40
❑ 67 Marcus Camby	.30	.75
❑ 68 Kobe Bryant	2.00	5.00
❑ 69 Bobby Jackson	.30	.75
❑ 70 B.J. Armstrong	.15	.40
❑ 71 Alan Henderson	.15	.40
❑ 72 Terry Davis	.15	.40
❑ 73 Does not exist		
❑ 74 Lamond Murray	.15	.40
❑ 75 Does not exist		
❑ 76 Rex Chapman	.15	.40
❑ 77 Does not exist		
❑ 78 Terry Cummings	.15	.40
❑ 79 Dan Majerle	.30	.75
❑ 80 Bo Outlaw	.15	.40
❑ 81 Does not exist		
❑ 82 Vin Baker	.30	.75
❑ 83 Clifford Robinson	.15	.40
❑ 84 Greg Anthony	.15	.40
❑ 85 Brevin Knight	.15	.40
❑ 86 Jacque Vaughn	.15	.40
❑ 87 Bobby Phills	.15	.40
❑ 88 Sherman Douglas	.15	.40
❑ 89 Does not exist		
❑ 90 Does not exist		
❑ 91 Lorenzen Wright	.15	.40
❑ 92 Eric Williams	.15	.40
❑ 93 Will Perdue	.15	.40
❑ 94 Charles Barkley	.60	1.50
❑ 95 Kendall Gill	.15	.40
❑ 96 Wesley Person	.15	.40
❑ 97 Does not exist		
❑ 98 Erick Dampier	.30	.75
❑ 99 Does not exist		
❑ 100 Does not exist		
❑ 101 Rasheed Wallace	.50	1.25
❑ 102 Zydrunas Ilgauskas	.30	.75
❑ 103 Eddie Jones	.50	1.25
❑ 104 Ron Mercer	.25	.60
❑ 105 Horace Grant	.30	.75
❑ 106 Corliss Williamson	.30	.75
❑ 107 Anthony Mason	.30	.75
❑ 108 Mookie Blaylock	.15	.40
❑ 109 Dennis Rodman	.30	.75
❑ 110 Checklist	.15	.40
❑ 111 Steve Smith	.30	.75
❑ 112 Cedric Henderson	.15	.40
❑ 113 Raef LaFrentz RC	1.25	3.00
❑ 114 Calbert Cheaney	.15	.40
❑ 115 Rik Smits	.30	.75
❑ 116 Rony Seikaly	.15	.40
❑ 117 Lawrence Funderburke	.15	.40
❑ 118 Ricky Davis RC	2.00	5.00
❑ 119 Howard Eisley	.15	.40
❑ 120 Kenny Anderson	.30	.75
❑ 121 Corey Benjamin RC	.75	2.00
❑ 122 Maurice Taylor	.25	.60
❑ 123 Eric Murdock	.15	.40
❑ 124 Derek Fisher	.50	1.25
❑ 125 Kevin Garnett	1.00	2.50
❑ 126 Walt Williams	.15	.40
❑ 127 Bryce Drew RC	.75	2.00
❑ 128 A.C. Green	.30	.75
❑ 129 Ervin Johnson	.15	.40
❑ 130 Christian Laettner	.30	.75
❑ 131 Chauncey Billups	.30	.75
❑ 132 Hakeem Olajuwon	.50	1.25
❑ 133 Al Harrington RC	1.50	4.00
❑ 134 Danny Manning	.15	.40
❑ 135 Paul Pierce RC	6.00	15.00
❑ 136 Terrell Brandon	.30	.75
❑ 137 Bob Sura	.15	.40
❑ 138 Chris Gatling	.15	.40
❑ 139 Donyell Marshall	.30	.75
❑ 140 Marcus Camby	.30	.75
❑ 141 Brian Skinner RC	.75	2.00
❑ 142 Charles Oakley	.15	.40
❑ 143 Antawn Jamison RC	2.00	5.00
❑ 144 Nazr Mohammed RC	.40	1.00
❑ 145 Karl Malone	.50	1.25
❑ 146 Chris Mills	.15	.40
❑ 147 Bison Dele	.15	.40
❑ 148 Gary Payton	.50	1.25
❑ 149 Terry Porter	.15	.40
❑ 150 Tim Hardaway	.30	.75
❑ 151 Larry Hughes RC	1.50	4.00
❑ 152 Derek Anderson	.40	1.00
❑ 153 Jason Williams RC	2.00	5.00
❑ 154 Dirk Nowitzki RC	6.00	15.00
❑ 155 Juwan Howard	.30	.75
❑ 156 Avery Johnson	.15	.40
❑ 157 Matt Harpring RC	1.00	2.50
❑ 158 Reggie Miller	.50	1.25
❑ 159 Walter McCarty	.15	.40

❑ 160 Allen Iverson	1.00	2.50
❑ 161 Felipe Lopez RC	.75	2.00
❑ 162 Tracy McGrady	1.25	3.00
❑ 163 Damon Stoudamire	.30	.75
❑ 164 Antonio McDyess	.30	.75
❑ 165 Grant Hill	.50	1.25
❑ 166 Tyronn Lue RC	.75	2.00
❑ 167 P.J. Brown	.15	.40
❑ 168 Antonio Daniels	.15	.40
❑ 169 Mitch Richmond	.30	.75
❑ 170 David Robinson	.50	1.25
❑ 171 Shawn Bradley	.15	.40
❑ 172 Shandon Anderson	.15	.40
❑ 173 Chris Childs	.15	.40
❑ 174 Shawn Kemp	.30	.75
❑ 175 Shaquille O'Neal	1.25	3.00
❑ 176 John Starks	.30	.75
❑ 177 Tyrone Hill	.15	.40
❑ 178 Jayson Williams	.15	.40
❑ 179 Anfernee Hardaway	.50	1.25
❑ 180 Chris Webber	.50	1.25
❑ 181 Don Reid	.15	.40
❑ 182 Stacey Augmon	.15	.40
❑ 183 Hersey Hawkins	.15	.40
❑ 184 Sam Mitchell	.15	.40
❑ 185 Jason Kidd	.75	2.00
❑ 186 Nick Van Exel	.50	1.25
❑ 187 Larry Johnson	.30	.75
❑ 188 Bryant Reeves	.15	.40
❑ 189 Glen Rice	.30	.75
❑ 190 Kerry Kittles	.15	.40
❑ 191 Toni Kukoc	.30	.75
❑ 192 Ron Harper	.30	.75
❑ 193 Bryon Russell	.15	.40
❑ 194 Vladimir Stepania RC	.40	1.00
❑ 195 Michael Olowokandi RC	.75	2.00
❑ 196 Mike Bibby RC	2.50	6.00
❑ 197 Dale Ellis	.15	.40
❑ 198 Muggsy Bogues	.30	.75
❑ 199 Vince Carter RC	6.00	15.00
❑ 200 Robert Traylor RC	.75	2.00
❑ 201 Peja Stojakovic RC	2.00	5.00
❑ 202 Aaron McKie	.30	.75
❑ 203 Hubert Davis	.15	.40
❑ 204 Dana Barros	.15	.40
❑ 205 Bonzi Wells RC	2.00	5.00
❑ 206 Michael Doleac RC	.75	2.00
❑ 207 Keon Clark RC	1.00	2.50
❑ 208 Michael Dickerson RC	1.25	3.00
❑ 209 Nick Anderson	.15	.40
❑ 210 Brent Price	.15	.40
❑ 211 Cherokee Parks	.15	.40
❑ 212 Sam Jacobson RC	.40	1.00
❑ 213 Pat Garrity RC	.50	1.25
❑ 214 Tyrone Corbin	.15	.40
❑ 215 David Wesley	.15	.40
❑ 216 Rodney Rogers	.15	.40
❑ 217 Dean Garrett	.15	.40
❑ 218 Roshown McLeod RC	.50	1.25
❑ 219 Dale Davis	.30	.75
❑ 220 Checklist	.15	.40
❑ 221 Scottie Pippen MO	.50	1.25
❑ 222 Antonio McDyess MO	.30	.75
❑ 223 Stephon Marbury MO	.50	1.25
❑ 224 Tom Gugliotta MO	.15	.40
❑ 225 Chris Webber MO	.30	.75
❑ 226 Latrell Sprewell MO	.50	1.25
❑ 227 Mitch Richmond MO	.30	.75
❑ 228 Joe Smith MO	.15	.40
❑ 229 John Starks MO	.15	.40
❑ 230 Charles Oakley MO	.15	.40
❑ 231 Dennis Rodman MO	.15	.40
❑ 232 Eddie Jones MO	.50	1.25
❑ 233 Nick Van Exel MO	.15	.40
❑ 234 Bobby Jackson MO	.30	.75
❑ 235 Glen Rice MO	.15	.40

1999-00 Topps Chrome

❑ COMMON CARD (1-257)	.25	.60
❑ COMMON USA (249-257)	.50	1.25
❑ COMMON ROOKIE	.75	2.00
❑ 1 Steve Smith	.25	.60
❑ 2 Ron Harper	.25	.60
❑ 3 Michael Dickerson	.25	.60
❑ 4 LaPhonso Ellis	.25	.60
❑ 5 Chris Webber	.40	1.00
❑ 6 Jason Caffey	.25	.60
❑ 7 Bryon Russell	.25	.60
❑ 8 Bison Dele	.25	.60
❑ 9 Isaiah Rider	.25	.60
❑ 10 Dean Garrett	.25	.60
❑ 11 Eric Murdock	.25	.60
❑ 12 Juwan Howard	.30	.75
❑ 13 Latrell Sprewell	.30	.75
❑ 14 Jalen Rose	.30	.75
❑ 15 Larry Johnson	.40	1.00
❑ 16 Eric Williams	.25	.60
❑ 17 Bryant Reeves	.25	.60
❑ 18 Tony Battie	.30	.75
❑ 19 Luc Longley	.25	.60
❑ 20 Gary Payton	.40	1.00
❑ 21 Tariq Abdul-Wahad	.25	.60
❑ 22 Armon Gilliam UER	.25	.60
❑ 23 Shaquille O'Neal	1.00	2.50
❑ 24 Gary Trent	.25	.60
❑ 25 John Stockton	.50	1.25
❑ 26 Mark Jackson	.40	1.00
❑ 27 Cherokee Parks	.25	.60
❑ 28 Michael Olowokandi	.25	.60
❑ 29 Raef LaFrentz	.30	.75
❑ 30 Dell Curry	.25	.60
❑ 31 Travis Best	.25	.60
❑ 32 Shawn Kemp	.40	1.00
❑ 33 Voshon Lenard	.25	.60
❑ 34 Brian Grant	.25	.60
❑ 35 Alvin Williams	.25	.60
❑ 36 Derek Fisher	.40	1.00
❑ 37 Allan Houston	.30	.75
❑ 38 Arvydas Sabonis	.30	.75
❑ 39 Terry Cummings	.25	.60
❑ 40 Dale Ellis	.25	.60
❑ 41 Maurice Taylor	.30	.75
❑ 42 Grant Hill	.40	1.00
❑ 43 Anthony Mason	.25	.60
❑ 44 John Wallace	.25	.60
❑ 45 David Wesley	.25	.60
❑ 46 Nick Van Exel	.30	.75
❑ 47 Cuttino Mobley	.30	.75
❑ 48 Anfernee Hardaway	.40	1.00
❑ 49 Terry Porter	.25	.60
❑ 50 Brent Barry	.30	.75
❑ 51 Derek Harper	.30	.75
❑ 52 Antoine Walker	.40	1.00
❑ 53 Karl Malone	.50	1.25
❑ 54 Ben Wallace	.30	.75
❑ 55 Vlade Divac	.40	1.00
❑ 56 Sam Mitchell	.25	.60
❑ 57 Joe Smith	.30	.75
❑ 58 Shawn Bradley	.25	.60
❑ 59 Darrell Armstrong	.25	.60
❑ 60 Kenny Anderson	.30	.75
❑ 61 Jason Williams	.40	1.00
❑ 62 Alonzo Mourning	.40	1.00
❑ 63 Matt Harpring	.30	.75
❑ 64 Antonio Davis	.25	.60
❑ 65 Lindsey Hunter	.25	.60
❑ 66 Allen Iverson	.75	2.00
❑ 67 Mookie Blaylock	.25	.60
❑ 68 Wesley Person	.25	.60
❑ 69 Bobby Phills	.25	.60
❑ 70 Theo Ratliff	.30	.75
❑ 71 Antonio Daniels	.25	.60

❑ 72 P.J. Brown	.25	.60
❑ 73 David Robinson	.50	1.25
❑ 74 Sean Elliott	.40	1.00
❑ 75 Zydrunas Ilgauskas	.30	.75
❑ 76 Kerry Kittles	.25	.60
❑ 77 Otis Thorpe	.25	.60
❑ 78 John Starks	.40	1.00
❑ 79 Jaren Jackson	.25	.60
❑ 80 Hersey Hawkins	.25	.60
❑ 81 Glenn Robinson	.30	.75
❑ 82 Paul Pierce	.40	1.00
❑ 83 Glen Rice	.40	1.00
❑ 84 Charlie Ward	.25	.60
❑ 85 Dee Brown	.25	.60
❑ 86 Danny Fortson	.25	.60
❑ 87 Billy Owens	.25	.60
❑ 88 Jason Kidd	.60	1.50
❑ 89 Brent Price	.25	.60
❑ 90 Don Reid	.25	.60
❑ 91 Mark Bryant	.25	.60
❑ 92 Vinny Del Negro	.25	.60
❑ 93 Stephon Marbury	.40	1.00
❑ 94 Donyell Marshall	.30	.75
❑ 95 Jim Jackson	.30	.75
❑ 96 Horace Grant	.30	.75
❑ 97 Calbert Cheaney	.25	.60
❑ 98 Vince Carter	.75	2.00
❑ 99 Bobby Jackson	.30	.75
❑ 100 Alan Henderson	.25	.60
❑ 101 Mike Bibby	.40	1.00
❑ 102 Cedric Henderson	.25	.60
❑ 103 Lamond Murray	.25	.60
❑ 104 A.C. Green	.40	1.00
❑ 105 Hakeem Olajuwon	.40	1.00
❑ 106 George Lynch	.25	.60
❑ 107 Kendall Gill	.25	.60
❑ 108 Rex Chapman	.25	.60
❑ 109 Eddie Jones	.40	1.00
❑ 110 Kornel David RC	.75	2.00
❑ 111 Jason Terry RC	2.00	5.00
❑ 112 Corey Maggette RC	2.50	6.00
❑ 113 Ron Artest RC	3.00	8.00
❑ 114 Richard Hamilton RC	2.50	6.00
❑ 115 Elton Brand RC	2.50	6.00
❑ 116 Baron Davis RC	3.00	8.00
❑ 117 Wally Szczerbiak RC	2.50	6.00
❑ 118 Steve Francis RC	2.50	6.00
❑ 119 James Posey RC	1.25	3.00
❑ 120 Shawn Marion RC	2.50	6.00
❑ 121 Tim Duncan	.75	2.00
❑ 122 Danny Manning	.25	.60
❑ 123 Chris Mullin	.40	1.00
❑ 124 Antawn Jamison	.40	1.00
❑ 125 Kobe Bryant	2.00	5.00
❑ 126 Matt Geiger	.25	.60
❑ 127 Rod Strickland	.25	.60
❑ 128 Howard Eisley	.25	.60
❑ 129 Steve Nash	.60	1.50
❑ 130 Felipe Lopez	.25	.60
❑ 131 Ron Mercer	.25	.60
❑ 132 Ruben Patterson	.25	.60
❑ 133 Dana Barros	.25	.60
❑ 134 Dale Davis	.25	.60
❑ 135 Bo Outlaw	.25	.60
❑ 136 Shandon Anderson	.25	.60
❑ 137 Mitch Richmond	.30	.75
❑ 138 Doug Christie	.30	.75
❑ 139 Rasheed Wallace	.40	1.00
❑ 140 Chris Childs	.25	.60
❑ 141 Jamal Mashburn	.25	.60
❑ 142 Terrell Brandon	.25	.60
❑ 143 Jamie Feick RC	.40	1.00
❑ 144 Robert Traylor	.25	.60
❑ 145 Rick Fox	.25	.60
❑ 146 Charles Barkley	.50	1.25
❑ 147 Tyrone Nesby RC	.40	1.00
❑ 148 Jerry Stackhouse	.40	1.00
❑ 149 Cedric Ceballos	.25	.60
❑ 150 Dikembe Mutombo	.30	.75
❑ 151 Anthony Peeler	.25	.60
❑ 152 Larry Hughes	.30	.75
❑ 153 Clifford Robinson	.25	.60
❑ 154 Corliss Williamson	.25	.60
❑ 155 Olden Polynice	.25	.60
❑ 156 Avery Johnson	.30	.75
❑ 157 Tracy Murray	.25	.60
❑ 158 Tom Gugliotta	.25	.60
❑ 159 Tim Thomas	.30	.75
❑ 160 Reggie Miller	.40	1.00

❑ 161 Tim Hardaway	.40	1.00
❑ 162 Dan Majerle	.40	1.00
❑ 163 Will Perdue	.25	.60
❑ 164 Brevin Knight	.25	.60
❑ 165 Elden Campbell	.25	.60
❑ 166 Chris Gatling	.25	.60
❑ 167 Walter McCarty	.25	.60
❑ 168 Chauncey Billups	.40	1.00
❑ 169 Chris Mills	.25	.60
❑ 170 Christian Laettner	.30	.75
❑ 171 Robert Pack	.25	.60
❑ 172 Rik Smits	.40	1.00
❑ 173 Tyrone Hill	.25	.60
❑ 174 Damon Stoudamire	.40	1.00
❑ 175 Nick Anderson	.25	.60
❑ 176 Peja Stojakovic	.30	.75
❑ 177 Vladimir Stepania	.25	.60
❑ 178 Tracy McGrady	.75	2.00
❑ 179 Adam Keefe	.25	.60
❑ 180 Shareef Abdur-Rahim	.30	.75
❑ 181 Isaac Austin	.25	.60
❑ 182 Mario Elie	.25	.60
❑ 183 Rashard Lewis	.40	1.00
❑ 184 Scott Burrell	.25	.60
❑ 185 Othella Harrington	.25	.60
❑ 186 Eric Piatkowski	.30	.75
❑ 187 Bryant Stith	.25	.60
❑ 188 Michael Finley	.40	1.00
❑ 189 Chris Crawford	.25	.60
❑ 190 Toni Kukoc	.40	1.00
❑ 191 Danny Ferry	.25	.60
❑ 192 Erick Dampier	.30	.75
❑ 193 Clarence Weatherspoon	.25	.60
❑ 194 Bob Sura	.25	.60
❑ 195 Jayson Williams	.30	.75
❑ 196 Kurt Thomas	.30	.75
❑ 197 Greg Anthony	.25	.60
❑ 198 Rodney Rogers	.25	.60
❑ 199 Detlef Schrempf	.30	.75
❑ 200 Keith Van Horn	.30	.75
❑ 201 Robert Horry	.40	1.00
❑ 202 Sam Cassell	.30	.75
❑ 203 Malik Sealy	.25	.60
❑ 204 Kelvin Cato	.25	.60
❑ 205 Antonio McDyess	.30	.75
❑ 206 Andrew DeClercq	.25	.60
❑ 207 Ricky Davis	.40	1.00
❑ 208 Vitaly Potapenko	.25	.60
❑ 209 Loy Vaught	.25	.60
❑ 210 Kevin Garnett	.75	2.00
❑ 211 Eric Snow	.30	.75
❑ 212 Anfernee Hardaway	.40	1.00
❑ 213 Vin Baker	.40	1.00
❑ 214 Lawrence Funderburke	.25	.60
❑ 215 Jeff Hornacek	.30	.75
❑ 216 Doug West	.25	.60
❑ 217 Michael Doleac	.25	.60
❑ 218 Ray Allen	.40	1.00
❑ 219 Derek Anderson	.25	.60
❑ 220 Jerome Williams	.25	.60
❑ 221 Derrick Coleman	.30	.75
❑ 222 Randy Brown	.25	.60
❑ 223 Patrick Ewing	.50	1.25
❑ 224 Walt Williams	.25	.60
❑ 225 Charles Oakley	.30	.75
❑ 226 Steve Kerr	.30	.75
❑ 227 Muggsy Bogues	.30	.75
❑ 228 Kevin Willis	.25	.60
❑ 229 Marcus Camby	.30	.75
❑ 230 Scottie Pippen	.60	1.50
❑ 231 Lamar Odom RC	2.50	6.00
❑ 232 Jonathan Bender RC	.75	2.00
❑ 233 Andre Miller RC	2.50	6.00
❑ 234 Trajan Langdon RC	.75	2.00
❑ 235 A.Radojevic RC	.75	2.00
❑ 236 William Avery RC	.75	2.00
❑ 237 Cal Bowdler RC	.75	2.00
❑ 238 Quincy Lewis RC	.75	2.00
❑ 239 Dion Glover RC	.75	2.00
❑ 240 Jeff Foster RC	1.00	2.50
❑ 241 Kenny Thomas RC	.75	2.00
❑ 242 Devean George RC	1.25	3.00
❑ 243 Tim James RC	.75	2.00
❑ 244 Vonteego Cummings RC	.75	2.00
❑ 245 Jumaine Jones RC	.75	2.00
❑ 246 Scott Padgett RC	.75	2.00
❑ 247 Adrian Griffin RC	.75	2.00
❑ 248 Chris Herren RC	.75	2.00
❑ 249 Allan Houston USA	.60	1.50
❑ 250 Kevin Garnett USA	1.50	4.00
❑ 251 Gary Payton USA	.75	2.00
❑ 252 Steve Smith USA	.50	1.25
❑ 253 Tim Hardaway USA	.75	2.00
❑ 254 Tim Duncan USA	1.50	4.00
❑ 255 Jason Kidd USA	1.25	3.00
❑ 256 Tom Gugliotta USA	.50	1.25
❑ 257 Vin Baker USA	.75	2.00

2000-01 Topps Chrome

❑ COMPLETE SET (200)	150.00	300.00
❑ COMPLETE SET w/o SP's (150)	15.00	40.00
❑ COMMON CARD (1-150)	.25	.60
❑ COMMON ROOKIE (151-200)	1.50	4.00
❑ 1 Elton Brand	.40	1.00
❑ 2 Marcus Camby	.30	.75
❑ 3 Jalen Rose	.30	.75
❑ 4 Jamie Feick	.25	.60
❑ 5 Toni Kukoc	.30	.75
❑ 6 Doug Christie	.25	.60
❑ 7 Sam Cassell	.30	.75
❑ 8 Shaquille O'Neal	1.00	2.50
❑ 9 Larry Hughes	.30	.75
❑ 10 Jerry Stackhouse	.30	.75
❑ 11 Rick Fox	.30	.75
❑ 12 Clifford Robinson	.25	.60
❑ 13 Dirk Nowitzki	.60	1.50
❑ 14 Cuttino Mobley	.30	.75
❑ 15 Latrell Sprewell	.30	.75
❑ 16 Kevin Garnett	.75	2.00
❑ 17 Jerome Williams	.25	.60
❑ 18 Chris Webber	.40	1.00
❑ 19 Jason Terry	.40	1.00
❑ 20 Elden Campbell	.25	.60
❑ 21 Jonathan Bender	.25	.60
❑ 22 Scottie Pippen	.60	1.50
❑ 23 Radoslav Nesterovic	.25	.60
❑ 24 Reggie Miller	.40	1.00
❑ 25 Andre Miller	.30	.75
❑ 26 Rashard Lewis	.40	1.00
❑ 27 Larry Johnson	.30	.75
❑ 28 Steve Francis	.40	1.00
❑ 29 Rod Strickland	.30	.75
❑ 30 Tim Thomas	.25	.60
❑ 31 Robert Horry	.30	.75
❑ 32 Darrell Armstrong	.25	.60
❑ 33 Vince Carter	.75	2.00
❑ 34 Othella Harrington	.25	.60
❑ 35 Derek Anderson	.30	.75
❑ 36 Anthony Carter	.25	.60
❑ 37 Ray Allen	.40	1.00
❑ 38 Jason Kidd	.60	1.50
❑ 39 Sean Elliott	.30	.75
❑ 40 Tim Duncan	.75	2.00
❑ 41 Adrian Griffin	.25	.60
❑ 42 Wally Szczerbiak	.30	.75
❑ 43 Austin Croshere	.25	.60
❑ 44 James Posey	.25	.60
❑ 45 Alan Henderson	.25	.60
❑ 46 Jahidi White	.25	.60
❑ 47 Shawn Marion	.40	1.00
❑ 48 Lamar Odom	.40	1.00
❑ 49 Keon Clark	.25	.60
❑ 50 Lamond Murray	.25	.60
❑ 51 Paul Pierce	.40	1.00
❑ 52 Charlie Ward	.25	.60
❑ 53 Horace Grant	.30	.75
❑ 54 John Stockton	.50	1.25
❑ 55 Peja Stojakovic	.30	.75
❑ 56 Christian Laettner	.25	.60
❑ 57 Keith Van Horn	.30	.75
❑ 58 Patrick Ewing	.50	1.25
❑ 59 Steve Smith	.30	.75
❑ 60 Antonio Davis	.25	.60
❑ 61 Mitch Richmond	.30	.75
❑ 62 Michael Olowokandi	.25	.60
❑ 63 Baron Davis	.40	1.00
❑ 64 Dikembe Mutombo	.30	.75
❑ 65 Raef LaFrentz	.25	.60
❑ 66 Ervin Johnson	.25	.60
❑ 67 Alonzo Mourning	.40	1.00
❑ 68 Kendall Gill	.25	.60
❑ 69 George Lynch	.25	.60
❑ 70 Donyell Marshall	.25	.60
❑ 71 Bo Outlaw	.25	.60
❑ 72 Kenny Anderson	.30	.75
❑ 73 John Amaechi	.25	.60
❑ 74 Vlade Divac	.30	.75
❑ 75 Vin Baker	.30	.75
❑ 76 Mike Bibby	.30	.75
❑ 77 Richard Hamilton	.30	.75
❑ 78 Mookie Blaylock	.30	.75
❑ 79 Vitaly Potapenko	.25	.60
❑ 80 Anthony Mason	.25	.60
❑ 81 Vonteego Cummings	.25	.60
❑ 82 Michael Finley	.40	1.00
❑ 83 Ron Artest	.40	1.00
❑ 84 Rodney Rogers	.25	.60
❑ 85 Team Championship	.75	2.00
❑ 86 Jason Williams	.30	.75
❑ 87 David Robinson	.50	1.25
❑ 88 Charles Oakley	.30	.75
❑ 89 Juwan Howard	.30	.75
❑ 90 Antoine Walker	.30	.75
❑ 91 Roshown McLeod	.25	.60
❑ 92 Eddie Jones	.30	.75
❑ 93 Allen Iverson	.75	2.00
❑ 94 Grant Hill	.40	1.00
❑ 95 Terrell Brandon	.25	.60
❑ 96 Stephon Marbury	.40	1.00
❑ 97 Jamal Mashburn	.30	.75
❑ 98 Ron Harper	.30	.75
❑ 99 Jermaine O'Neal	.40	1.00
❑ 100 Nick Van Exel	.30	.75
❑ 101 Danny Fortson	.25	.60
❑ 102 Jim Jackson	.25	.60
❑ 103 Brad Miller	.30	.75
❑ 104 Shawn Bradley	.25	.60
❑ 105 Mark Jackson	.30	.75
❑ 106 Maurice Taylor	.25	.60
❑ 107 Kobe Bryant	2.00	5.00
❑ 108 Clarence Weatherspoon	.25	.60
❑ 109 Eric Snow	.25	.60
❑ 110 Allan Houston	.30	.75
❑ 111 Chauncey Billups	.40	1.00
❑ 112 Tom Gugliotta	.25	.60
❑ 113 Theo Ratliff	.25	.60
❑ 114 Rasheed Wallace	.40	1.00
❑ 115 Glen Rice	.30	.75
❑ 116 Bryon Russell	.25	.60
❑ 117 Tracy McGrady	.75	2.00
❑ 118 Bryant Reeves	.25	.60
❑ 119 Damon Stoudamire	.30	.75
❑ 120 Anfernee Hardaway	.40	1.00
❑ 121 Johnny Newman	.25	.60
❑ 122 Corey Maggette	.30	.75
❑ 123 Travis Best	.25	.60
❑ 124 Hakeem Olajuwon	.50	1.25
❑ 125 Antawn Jamison	.40	1.00
❑ 126 John Starks	.25	.60
❑ 127 Antonio McDyess	.30	.75
❑ 128 Gary Payton	.40	1.00
❑ 129 Karl Malone	.50	1.25
❑ 130 Michael Dickerson	.25	.60
❑ 131 Shawn Kemp	.40	1.00
❑ 132 David Wesley	.25	.60
❑ 133 P.J. Brown	.25	.60
❑ 134 Ron Mercer	.25	.60
❑ 135 Robert Traylor	.25	.60
❑ 136 Derrick Coleman	.30	.75
❑ 137 Steve Nash	.60	1.50
❑ 138 Ben Wallace	.30	.75
❑ 139 Brian Skinner	.25	.60
❑ 140 Chris Gatling	.25	.60
❑ 141 Dale Davis	.25	.60
❑ 142 Glenn Robinson	.30	.75
❑ 143 Chucky Atkins	.25	.60
❑ 144 Brian Grant	.25	.60
❑ 145 Corliss Williamson	.30	.75
❑ 146 Shareef Abdur-Rahim	.30	.75
❑ 147 Avery Johnson	.30	.75
❑ 148 Tim Hardaway	.30	.75
❑ 149 Isaiah Rider	.30	.75
❑ 150 Shandon Anderson	.25	.60
❑ 151 Kenyon Martin RC	4.00	10.00

❑ 152 Stromile Swift RC	2.00	5.00
❑ 153 Darius Miles RC	2.00	5.00
❑ 154 Marcus Fizer RC	1.50	4.00
❑ 155 Mike Miller RC	2.50	6.00
❑ 156 DerMarr Johnson RC	1.50	4.00
❑ 157 Chris Mihm RC	1.50	4.00
❑ 158 Jamal Crawford RC	2.50	6.00
❑ 159 Joel Przybilla RC	1.50	4.00
❑ 160 Keyon Dooling RC	1.50	4.00
❑ 161 Jerome Moiso RC	1.50	4.00
❑ 162 Etan Thomas RC	1.50	4.00
❑ 163 Courtney Alexander RC	1.50	4.00
❑ 164 Mateen Cleaves RC	1.50	4.00
❑ 165 Jason Collier RC	1.50	4.00
❑ 166 Desmond Mason RC	2.00	5.00
❑ 167 Quentin Richardson RC	2.00	5.00
❑ 168 Jamaal Magloire RC	1.50	4.00
❑ 169 Speedy Claxton RC	1.50	4.00
❑ 170 Morris Peterson RC	2.50	6.00
❑ 171 Donnell Harvey RC	1.50	4.00
❑ 172 DeShawn Stevenson RC	1.50	4.00
❑ 173 Mamadou N'Diaye RC	1.50	4.00
❑ 174 Erick Barkley RC	1.50	4.00
❑ 175 Mark Madsen RC	1.50	4.00
❑ 176 Hedo Turkoglu RC	4.00	10.00
❑ 177 Brian Cardinal RC	1.50	4.00
❑ 178 Iakovos Tsakalidis RC	1.50	4.00
❑ 179 Dalibor Bagaric RC	1.50	4.00
❑ 180 Dragan Tarlac RC	1.50	4.00
❑ 181 Dan Langhi RC	1.50	4.00
❑ 182 A.J. Guyton RC	1.50	4.00
❑ 183 Jake Voskuhl RC	1.50	4.00
❑ 184 Khalid El-Amin RC	1.50	4.00
❑ 185 Mike Smith RC	1.50	4.00
❑ 186 Soumaila Samake RC	1.50	4.00
❑ 187 Eddie House RC	1.50	4.00
❑ 188 Eduardo Najera RC	1.50	4.00
❑ 189 Lavor Postell RC	1.50	4.00
❑ 190 Hanno Mottola RC	1.50	4.00
❑ 191 Olumide Oyedeji RC	1.50	4.00
❑ 192 Michael Redd RC	4.00	10.00
❑ 193 Chris Porter RC	1.50	4.00
❑ 194 Jabari Smith RC	1.50	4.00
❑ 195 Marc Jackson RC	2.00	5.00
❑ 196 Stephen Jackson RC	2.50	6.00
❑ 197 Pepe Sanchez RC	1.50	4.00
❑ 198 Daniel Santiago RC	4.00	10.00
❑ 199 Paul McPherson RC	1.50	4.00
❑ 200 Mike Penberthy RC	1.50	4.00

2001-02 Topps Chrome

❑ COMP.SET w/o RC's (129)	30.00	60.00
❑ COMMON CARD (1-129)	.25	.60
❑ COMMON ROOKIE (130-165)	1.00	2.50
❑ 1 Shaquille O'Neal	1.00	2.50
❑ 2 Steve Nash	.60	1.50
❑ 3 Allen Iverson	.75	2.00
❑ 4 Shawn Marion	.40	1.00
❑ 5 Rasheed Wallace	.40	1.00
❑ 6 Antonio Daniels	.25	.60
❑ 7 Rashard Lewis	.40	1.00
❑ 8 Raef LaFrentz	.25	.60
❑ 9 Stromile Swift	.25	.60
❑ 10 Vince Carter	.75	2.00
❑ 11 Danny Fortson	.25	.60
❑ 12 Jalen Rose	.30	.75
❑ 13 Glen Rice	.30	.75
❑ 14 Glenn Robinson	.30	.75
❑ 15 Wally Szczerbiak	.30	.75
❑ 16 Rick Fox	.30	.75
❑ 17 Darius Miles	.25	.60
❑ 18 Jermaine O'Neal	.40	1.00
❑ 19 Eddie Jones	.30	.75
❑ 20 Tracy McGrady	.75	2.00
❑ 21 Kevin Garnett	.75	2.00
❑ 22 Tim Thomas	.25	.60
❑ 23 Larry Hughes	.30	.75
❑ 24 Jerry Stackhouse	.30	.75
❑ 25 Ray Allen	.40	1.00
❑ 26 Terrell Brandon	.25	.60
❑ 27 Keith Van Horn	.30	.75
❑ 28 Marcus Fizer	.25	.60
❑ 29 Elden Campbell	.25	.60
❑ 30 Tim Duncan	.75	2.00
❑ 31 Doug Christie	.25	.60
❑ 32 Allan Houston	.30	.75
❑ 33 Patrick Ewing	.50	1.25
❑ 34 Hakeem Olajuwon	.50	1.25
❑ 35 Anfernee Hardaway	.40	1.00
❑ 36 Larry Johnson	.30	.75
❑ 37 Eric Snow	.25	.60
❑ 38 Tom Gugliotta	.25	.60
❑ 39 Scottie Pippen	.60	1.50
❑ 40 Chris Webber	.40	1.00
❑ 41 David Robinson	.50	1.25
❑ 42 Elton Brand	.40	1.00
❑ 43 Theo Ratliff	.25	.60
❑ 44 Paul Pierce	.40	1.00
❑ 45 Jamal Mashburn	.30	.75
❑ 46 Damon Stoudamire	.30	.75
❑ 47 DerMarr Johnson	.25	.60
❑ 48 Andre Miller	.30	.75
❑ 49 Dirk Nowitzki	.60	1.50
❑ 50 Kobe Bryant	2.00	5.00
❑ 51 Keyon Dooling	.25	.60
❑ 52 Brian Grant	.25	.60
❑ 53 Antawn Jamison	.40	1.00
❑ 54 Jonathan Bender	.25	.60
❑ 55 Dikembe Mutombo	.30	.75
❑ 56 Steve Smith	.30	.75
❑ 57 Hedo Turkoglu	.30	.75
❑ 58 Robert Horry	.30	.75
❑ 59 Kurt Thomas	.25	.60
❑ 60 Jason Terry	.40	1.00
❑ 61 Vitaly Potapenko	.25	.60
❑ 62 Gary Payton	.40	1.00
❑ 63 Bonzi Wells	.30	.75
❑ 64 Raja Bell RC	2.00	5.00
❑ 65 Chris Mihm	.25	.60
❑ 66 Reggie Miller	.40	1.00
❑ 67 Lamar Odom	.40	1.00
❑ 68 Darrell Armstrong	.25	.60
❑ 69 Baron Davis	.40	1.00
❑ 70 Aaron Williams	.25	.60
❑ 71 Latrell Sprewell	.30	.75
❑ 72 James Posey	.25	.60
❑ 73 Ben Wallace	.30	.75
❑ 74 Marc Jackson	.25	.60
❑ 75 Maurice Taylor	.25	.60
❑ 76 Aaron McKie	.25	.60
❑ 77 Grant Hill	.40	1.00
❑ 78 Anthony Carter	.25	.60
❑ 79 Peja Stojakovic	.30	.75
❑ 80 Jason Kidd	.60	1.50
❑ 81 Vin Baker	.30	.75
❑ 82 Morris Peterson	.30	.75
❑ 83 Bryon Russell	.25	.60
❑ 84 Michael Dickerson	.25	.60
❑ 85 Quentin Richardson	.30	.75
❑ 86 Primoz Brezec RC	1.25	3.00
❑ 87 Desmond Mason	.30	.75
❑ 88 Jason Williams	.30	.75
❑ 89 Marcus Camby	.30	.75
❑ 90 Stephon Marbury	.40	1.00
❑ 91 Mike Bibby	.30	.75
❑ 92 Alonzo Mourning	.40	1.00
❑ 93 Mitch Richmond	.30	.75
❑ 94 Donyell Marshall	.25	.60
❑ 95 Michael Jordan	8.00	20.00
❑ 96 Mike Miller	.30	.75
❑ 97 Nick Van Exel	.30	.75
❑ 98 Michael Finley	.40	1.00
❑ 99 Jamal Crawford	.30	.75
❑ 100 Steve Francis	.40	1.00
❑ 101 Kenyon Martin	.40	1.00
❑ 102 Sam Cassell	.30	.75
❑ 103 Chucky Atkins	.25	.60
❑ 104 Juwan Howard	.30	.75
❑ 105 Bryant Reeves	.25	.60
❑ 106 Richard Hamilton	.30	.75
❑ 107 Antonio Davis	.25	.60
❑ 108 Antonio McDyess	.30	.75
❑ 109 Derek Anderson	.30	.75
❑ 110 Kenny Anderson	.30	.75
❑ 111 Antoine Walker	.30	.75
❑ 112 Wang ZhiZhi	.30	.75
❑ 113 Shareef Abdur-Rahim	.30	.75
❑ 114 Chris Whitney	.25	.60
❑ 115 John Stockton	.50	1.25
❑ 116 Alvin Williams	.25	.60
❑ 117 David Wesley	.25	.60
❑ 118 Joe Smith	.25	.60
❑ 119 Jahidi White	.25	.60
❑ 120 Karl Malone	.50	1.25
❑ 121 Cuttino Mobley	.30	.75
❑ 122 Tyrone Hill	.25	.60
❑ 123 Clifford Robinson	.25	.60
❑ 124 Toni Kukoc	.30	.75
❑ 125 Eddie Robinson	.25	.60
❑ 126 Courtney Alexander	.25	.60
❑ 127 Ron Mercer	.25	.60
❑ 128 Lamond Murray	.25	.60
❑ 129 Rodney Rogers	.25	.60
❑ 130 Tyson Chandler RC	2.00	5.00
❑ 131 Pau Gasol RC	4.00	10.00
❑ 132 Eddy Curry RC	1.50	4.00
❑ 133 Jason Richardson RC	2.00	5.00
❑ 134 Shane Battier RC	1.50	4.00
❑ 135 Eddie Griffin RC	1.00	2.50
❑ 136 DeSagana Diop RC	1.00	2.50
❑ 137 Rodney White RC	1.00	2.50
❑ 138 Joe Johnson RC	2.50	6.00
❑ 139 Kedrick Brown RC	1.00	2.50
❑ 140 Vladimir Radmanovic RC	1.25	3.00
❑ 141 Richard Jefferson RC	2.50	6.00
❑ 142 Troy Murphy RC	2.00	5.00
❑ 143 Steven Hunter RC	1.00	2.50
❑ 144 Kirk Haston RC	1.00	2.50
❑ 145 Michael Bradley RC	1.00	2.50
❑ 146 Jason Collins RC	1.00	2.50
❑ 147 Zach Randolph RC	2.50	6.00
❑ 148 Brendan Haywood RC	1.25	3.00
❑ 149 Joseph Forte RC	1.00	2.50
❑ 150 Jeryl Sasser RC	1.00	2.50
❑ 151 Brandon Armstrong RC	1.00	2.50
❑ 152 Gerald Wallace RC	2.50	6.00
❑ 153 Samuel Dalembert RC	1.25	3.00
❑ 154 Jamaal Tinsley RC	1.25	3.00
❑ 155 Tony Parker RC	4.00	10.00
❑ 156 Trenton Hassell RC	1.25	3.00
❑ 157 Gilbert Arenas RC	1.50	4.00
❑ 158 Jeff Trepagnier RC	1.00	2.50
❑ 159 Damone Brown RC	1.00	2.50
❑ 160 Loren Woods RC	1.00	2.50
❑ 161 Andrei Kirilenko RC	2.50	6.00
❑ 162 Zeljko Rebraca RC	1.00	2.50
❑ 163 Kenny Satterfield RC	1.00	2.50
❑ 164 Alvin Jones RC	1.00	2.50
❑ 165 Kwame Brown RC	1.25	3.00

2002-03 Topps Chrome

❑ COMPLETE SET (175)	75.00	180.00
❑ COMMON CARD (1-165)	.25	.60
❑ COMMON ROOKIE	1.50	4.00
❑ 1 Shaquille O'Neal	1.00	2.50
❑ 2 Pau Gasol	.40	1.00
❑ 3 Allen Iverson	.75	2.00
❑ 4 Tom Gugliotta	.25	.60
❑ 5 Rasheed Wallace	.40	1.00
❑ 6 Peja Stojakovic	.30	.75
❑ 7 Jason Richardson	.40	1.00
❑ 8 Rashard Lewis	.40	1.00
❑ 9 Morris Peterson	.30	.75
❑ 10 Michael Jordan	2.50	6.00
❑ 11 Matt Harpring	.30	.75
❑ 12 Shareef Abdur-Rahim	.30	.75
❑ 13 Antoine Walker	.30	.75
❑ 14 Stephon Marbury	.40	1.00
❑ 15 Jamal Mashburn	.30	.75
❑ 16 Eddy Curry	.30	.75
❑ 17 Jumaine Jones	.25	.60

❑ 18 Jason Kidd .60 1.50
❑ 19 Jerry Stackhouse .30 .75
❑ 20 Kenny Thomas .25 .60
❑ 21 Kobe Bryant 2.00 5.00
❑ 22 Jason Williams .30 .75
❑ 23 Eddie Jones .30 .75
❑ 24 Kenyon Martin .40 1.00
❑ 25 Kevin Garnett .75 2.00
❑ 26 Kurt Thomas .25 .60
❑ 27 Karl Malone .40 1.00
❑ 28 Reggie Evans RC 1.50 4.00
❑ 29 Dirk Nowitzki .60 1.50
❑ 30 Vince Carter .75 2.00
❑ 31 Desmond Mason .30 .75
❑ 32 Todd MacCulloch .25 .60
❑ 33 Grant Hill .40 1.00
❑ 34 Terrell Brandon .25 .60
❑ 35 Tracy McGrady .75 2.00
❑ 36 Tim Thomas .25 .60
❑ 37 Loren Woods .25 .60
❑ 38 Michael Redd .40 1.00
❑ 39 Stromile Swift .25 .60
❑ 40 Dikembe Mutombo .30 .75
❑ 41 Richard Jefferson .40 1.00
❑ 42 Glenn Robinson .30 .75
❑ 43 Quentin Richardson .30 .75
❑ 44 Elton Brand .40 1.00
❑ 45 Reggie Miller .40 1.00
❑ 46 Eddie Griffin .25 .60
❑ 47 Gilbert Arenas .40 1.00
❑ 48 Zeljko Rebraca .25 .60
❑ 49 Mark Jackson .30 .75
❑ 50 Juwan Howard .30 .75
❑ 51 Nick Van Exel .30 .75
❑ 52 Donyell Marshall .25 .60
❑ 53 Tyson Chandler .30 .75
❑ 54 Baron Davis .40 1.00
❑ 55 Nate Huffman RC .40 1.00
❑ 56 Jamaal Magloire .25 .60
❑ 57 Marcus Fizer .25 .60
❑ 58 Steve Francis .40 1.00
❑ 59 Aaron McKie .25 .60
❑ 60 Scottie Pippen .60 1.50
❑ 61 Mike Bibby .30 .75
❑ 62 Paul Pierce .40 1.00
❑ 63 Kwame Brown .25 .60
❑ 64 Andrei Kirilenko .40 1.00
❑ 65 Keon Clark .25 .60
❑ 66 Alvin Williams .25 .60
❑ 67 Brent Barry .25 .60
❑ 68 Doug Christie .25 .60
❑ 69 Chris Webber .40 1.00
❑ 70 Robert Horry .30 .75
❑ 71 Allan Houston .30 .75
❑ 72 Kerry Kittles .30 .75
❑ 73 Wally Szczerbiak .30 .75
❑ 74 Jonathan Bender .25 .60
❑ 75 Sam Cassell .30 .75
❑ 76 Rod Strickland .30 .75
❑ 77 Shane Battier .30 .75
❑ 78 Tim Duncan .75 2.00
❑ 79 Jermaine O'Neal .40 1.00
❑ 80 Cuttino Mobley .30 .75
❑ 81 Clifford Robinson .25 .60
❑ 82 Steve Nash .60 1.50
❑ 83 Dermarr Johnson .25 .60
❑ 84 Courtney Alexander .25 .60
❑ 85 Corliss Williamson .30 .75
❑ 86 Tony Parker .40 1.00
❑ 87 Damon Stoudamire .30 .75
❑ 88 Jalen Rose .30 .75
❑ 89 Mike Miller .30 .75
❑ 90 Raef Lafrentz .25 .60
❑ 91 Ben Wallace .30 .75
❑ 92 Ray Allen .40 1.00
❑ 93 Gary Payton .40 1.00
❑ 94 Derek Fisher .30 .75
❑ 95 Michael Olowokandi .25 .60
❑ 96 Jamaal Tinsley .30 .75
❑ 97 Chris Mihm .25 .60
❑ 98 Antawn Jamison .40 1.00
❑ 99 Mengke Bateer .25 .60
❑ 100 Michael Finley .40 1.00
❑ 101 Andre Miller .30 .75
❑ 102 Elden Campbell .25 .60
❑ 103 Kedrick Brown .25 .60
❑ 104 Jason Terry .40 1.00
❑ 105 Kenny Anderson .30 .75
❑ 106 Darius Miles .25 .60
❑ 107 Latrell Sprewell .30 .75
❑ 108 Darrell Armstrong .25 .60
❑ 109 Joe Johnson .40 1.00
❑ 110 Bonzi Wells .30 .75
❑ 111 LaPhonso Ellis .30 .75
❑ 112 Steve Smith .30 .75
❑ 113 Vin Baker .30 .75
❑ 114 Antonio Davis .25 .60
❑ 115 John Stockton .50 1.25
❑ 116 Shawn Marion .40 1.00
❑ 117 Devean George .25 .60
❑ 118 Joe Smith .25 .60
❑ 119 Sean Lampley .25 .60
❑ 120 Lamar Odom .40 1.00
❑ 121 Alonzo Mourning .40 1.00
❑ 122 Antonio Daniels .25 .60
❑ 123 Troy Murphy .40 1.00
❑ 124A Manu Ginobili RC 4.00 10.00
❑ 124B Manu Ginobili RC 4.00 10.00
❑ 125 Richard Hamilton .30 .75
❑ 126 Amare Stoudemire RC 4.00 10.00
❑ 127 Carlos Boozer RC 3.00 8.00
❑ 128 Casey Jacobsen RC 1.50 4.00
❑ 129 Juaquin Hawkins RC 1.50 4.00
❑ 130 Pat Burke RC 1.50 4.00
❑ 131 Dan Dickau RC 1.50 4.00
❑ 132 Drew Gooden RC 2.50 6.00
❑ 133 Fred Jones RC 2.00 5.00
❑ 134 Jared Jeffries RC 1.50 4.00
❑ 135A Jiri Welsch RC 1.50 4.00
❑ 135B Jiri Welsch RC 1.50 4.00
❑ 136 Juan Dixon RC 2.50 6.00
❑ 137 Marcus Haislip RC 1.50 4.00
❑ 138 Melvin Ely RC 1.50 4.00
❑ 139A Nene Hilario RC 2.00 5.00
❑ 139B Nene Hilario RC 2.00 5.00
❑ 140 Qyntel Woods RC 1.50 4.00
❑ 141 Lonny Baxter RC 1.50 4.00
❑ 142 Ryan Humphrey RC 1.50 4.00
❑ 143 Smush Parker RC 1.50 4.00
❑ 144 Tayshaun Prince RC 2.50 6.00
❑ 145 Vincent Yarbrough RC 1.50 4.00
❑ 146A Yao Ming RC 5.00 12.00
❑ 146B Yao Ming RC 5.00 12.00
❑ 147 Pete Mickeal .25 .60
❑ 148 Tamar Slay RC 1.50 4.00
❑ 149A Efthimios Rentzias RC 1.50 4.00
❑ 149B Efthimios Rentzias RC 1.50 4.00
❑ 150A Igor Rakocevic RC 1.50 4.00
❑ 150B Igor Rakocevic RC 1.50 4.00
❑ 151A Gordan Giricek RC 1.50 4.00
❑ 151B Gordan Giricek RC 1.50 4.00
❑ 152A Nikoloz Tskitishvili RC 1.50 4.00
❑ 152B Nikoloz Tskitishvili RC 1.50 4.00
❑ 153 Mike Dunleavy RC 2.00 5.00
❑ 154A Marko Jaric 1.50 4.00
❑ 154B Marko Jaric 1.50 4.00
❑ 155 Kareem Rush RC 2.00 5.00
❑ 156 John Salmons RC 2.50 6.00
❑ 157 Jay Williams RC 2.00 5.00
❑ 158 J.R. Bremer RC 1.50 4.00
❑ 159 Frank Williams RC 1.50 4.00
❑ 160 Adam Harrington RC 1.50 4.00
❑ 161 DaJuan Wagner RC 1.50 4.00
❑ 162 Chris Wilcox RC 2.00 5.00
❑ 163 Chris Jefferies RC 1.50 4.00
❑ 164 Caron Butler RC 3.00 8.00
❑ 165A Bostjan Nachbar RC 1.50 4.00
❑ 165B Bostjan Nachbar RC 1.50 4.00

2003-04 Topps Chrome

❑ COMP.SET w/o RC's (110) 20.00 50.00
❑ COMMON CARD (1-110) .25 .60
❑ COMMON ROOKIE (111-165) 2.50 6.00
❑ B VERSION FOR CARDS 112, 121, 127
❑ 129, 131, 132, 138, 140, 146, 147, 149, 154
❑ CARD B VERSION NOT IN ENGLISH
❑ 1 Tracy McGrady .75 2.00
❑ 2 Dajuan Wagner .25 .60
❑ 3 Allen Iverson .75 2.00
❑ 4 Chris Webber .40 1.00
❑ 5 Jason Kidd .60 1.50
❑ 6 Stephon Marbury .40 1.00
❑ 7 Jermaine O'Neal .40 1.00
❑ 8 Antoine Walker .40 1.00
❑ 9 Tony Parker .40 1.00
❑ 10 Mike Bibby .30 .75
❑ 11 Yao Ming .75 2.00
❑ 12 Bobby Jackson .25 .60
❑ 13 Steve Nash .60 1.50
❑ 14 Paul Pierce .40 1.00
❑ 15 Vince Carter .75 2.00
❑ 16 Peja Stojakovic .30 .75
❑ 17 Wally Szczerbiak .30 .75
❑ 18 Kenyon Martin .40 1.00
❑ 19 Pau Gasol .40 1.00
❑ 20 Gary Payton .40 1.00
❑ 21 Tim Duncan .75 2.00
❑ 22 Anfernee Hardaway .40 1.00
❑ 23 Jason Richardson .40 1.00
❑ 24 Andre Miller .30 .75
❑ 25 Latrell Sprewell .30 .75
❑ 26 Darius Miles .30 .75
❑ 27 Richard Jefferson .40 1.00
❑ 28 Shawn Marion .40 1.00
❑ 29 Baron Davis .40 1.00
❑ 30 Ben Wallace .30 .75
❑ 31 Reggie Miller .40 1.00
❑ 32 Karl Malone .40 1.00
❑ 33 Jonathan Bender .25 .60
❑ 34 Shaquille O'Neal 1.00 2.50
❑ 35 Steve Francis .40 1.00
❑ 36 Kobe Bryant 2.00 5.00
❑ 37 Mike Dunleavy .30 .75
❑ 38 Glenn Robinson .30 .75
❑ 39 Allan Houston .30 .75
❑ 40 Sam Cassell .30 .75
❑ 41 Dirk Nowitzki .60 1.50
❑ 42 Elton Brand .40 1.00
❑ 43 Joe Smith .25 .60
❑ 44 Brian Grant .25 .60
❑ 45 Jason Terry .30 .75
❑ 46 Richard Hamilton .30 .75
❑ 47 Morris Peterson .30 .75
❑ 48 Ray Allen .25 .60
❑ 49 Scottie Pippen .60 1.50
❑ 50 Jamal Crawford .30 .75
❑ 51 Cuttino Mobley .30 .75
❑ 52 Jerry Stackhouse .30 .75
❑ 53 Marcus Camby .30 .75
❑ 54 Jalen Rose .30 .75
❑ 55 Ricky Davis .30 .75
❑ 56 Jamal Mashburn .25 .60
❑ 57 Ron Artest .30 .75
❑ 58 Theo Ratliff .25 .60
❑ 59 Juwan Howard .30 .75
❑ 60 Caron Butler .30 .75
❑ 61 Antawn Jamison .40 1.00
❑ 62 Nene .30 .75
❑ 63 Tyson Chandler .30 .75
❑ 64 Jason Williams .30 .75
❑ 65 Kurt Thomas .25 .60
❑ 66 Mike Miller .30 .75
❑ 67 Amare Stoudemire .75 2.00
❑ 68 Jamaal Tinsley .30 .75
❑ 69 Brent Barry .25 .60
❑ 70 Brad Miller .30 .75
❑ 71 Bonzi Wells .25 .60
❑ 72 Andrei Kirilenko .40 1.00
❑ 73 Kenny Thomas .25 .60
❑ 74 Derek Anderson .30 .75
❑ 75 Zydrunas Ilgauskas .30 .75
❑ 76 Eddie Griffin .25 .60
❑ 77 Tayshaun Prince .30 .75
❑ 78 Michael Olowokandi .25 .60
❑ 79 Michael Redd .40 1.00
❑ 80 Tim Thomas .25 .60
❑ 81 Eddie Jones .30 .75
❑ 82 Shareef Abdur-Rahim .30 .75
❑ 83 Corey Maggette .25 .60
❑ 84 Eric Snow .25 .60
❑ 85 Keon Clark .25 .60
❑ 86 Desmond Mason .30 .75
❑ 87 Drew Gooden .25 .60
❑ 88 Matt Harpring .30 .75

❑ 89 Antonio McDyess	.30	.75
❑ 90 Radoslav Nesterovic	.25	.60
❑ 91 Jamaal Magloire	.25	.60
❑ 92 Rasheed Wallace	.40	1.00
❑ 93 Antonio Davis	.25	.60
❑ 94 Kwame Brown	.25	.60
❑ 95 Manu Ginobili	.40	1.00
❑ 96 Eric Williams	.25	.60
❑ 97 Nick Van Exel	.30	.75
❑ 98 Lamar Odom	.40	1.00
❑ 99 Chauncey Billups	.40	1.00
❑ 100 Kevin Garnett	.75	2.00
❑ 101 Marko Jaric	.25	.60
❑ 102 David Wesley	.25	.60
❑ 103 Gilbert Arenas	.40	1.00
❑ 104 Keith Van Horn	.30	.75
❑ 105 Bostjan Nachbar	.25	.60
❑ 106 Michael Finley	.40	1.00
❑ 107 Troy Murphy	.40	1.00
❑ 108 Eddy Curry	.30	.75
❑ 109 Rashard Lewis	.40	1.00
❑ 110 Tony Battie	.25	.60
❑ 111 Lebron James RC	50.00	100.00
❑ 112A Darko Milicic RC	3.00	8.00
❑ 112B Darko Milicic	3.00	8.00
❑ 113 Carmelo Anthony RC	6.00	15.00
❑ 114 Chris Bosh RC	4.00	10.00
❑ 115 Dwyane Wade RC	6.00	15.00
❑ 116 Chris Kaman RC	3.00	8.00
❑ 117 Kirk Hinrich RC	3.00	8.00
❑ 118 T.J. Ford RC	3.00	8.00
❑ 119 Mike Sweetney RC	2.50	6.00
❑ 120 Jarvis Hayes RC	2.50	6.00
❑ 121A Mickael Pietrus RC	3.00	8.00
❑ 121B Mickael Pietrus	3.00	8.00
❑ 122 Nick Collison RC	2.50	6.00
❑ 123 Marcus Banks RC	2.50	6.00
❑ 124 Luke Ridnour RC	3.00	8.00
❑ 125 Reece Gaines RC	2.50	6.00
❑ 126 Troy Bell RC	2.50	6.00
❑ 127A Zarko Cabarkapa RC	2.50	6.00
❑ 127B Zarko Cabarkapa	2.50	6.00
❑ 128 David West RC	3.00	8.00
❑ 129A Aleksandar Pavlovic RC	3.00	8.00
❑ 129B Aleksandar Pavlovic	3.00	8.00
❑ 130 Dahntay Jones RC	2.50	6.00
❑ 131A Boris Diaw RC	3.00	8.00
❑ 131B Boris Diaw RC	3.00	8.00
❑ 132A Zoran Planinic RC	2.50	6.00
❑ 132B Zoran Planinic	2.50	6.00
❑ 133 Travis Outlaw RC	3.00	8.00
❑ 134 Brian Cook RC	2.50	6.00
❑ 135 Matt Carroll RC	2.50	6.00
❑ 136 Ndudi Ebi RC	2.50	6.00
❑ 137 Kendrick Perkins RC	4.00	10.00
❑ 138A Leandro Barbosa RC	3.00	8.00
❑ 138B Leandro Barbosa	3.00	8.00
❑ 139 Josh Howard RC	3.00	8.00
❑ 140A Maciej Lampe RC	2.50	6.00
❑ 140B Maciej Lampe	2.50	6.00
❑ 141 Jason Kapono RC	3.00	8.00
❑ 142 Luke Walton RC	3.00	8.00
❑ 143 Jerome Beasley RC	2.50	6.00
❑ 144 Travis Hansen RC	2.50	6.00
❑ 145 Steve Blake RC	3.00	8.00
❑ 146A Slavko Vranes RC	2.50	6.00
❑ 146B Slavko Vranes	2.50	6.00
❑ 147A Francisco Elson RC	2.50	6.00
❑ 147B Francisco Elson RC	2.50	6.00
❑ 148 Willie Green RC	2.50	6.00
❑ 149A Zaur Pachulia RC	3.00	8.00
❑ 149B Zaur Pachulia	3.00	8.00
❑ 150 Keith Bogans RC	2.50	6.00
❑ 151 Maurice Williams RC	4.00	10.00
❑ 152 James Jones RC	2.50	6.00
❑ 153 Kyle Korver RC	3.00	8.00
❑ 154A Jon Stefansson RC	2.50	6.00
❑ 154B Jon Stefansson	2.50	6.00
❑ 155 Brandon Hunter RC	2.50	6.00
❑ 156 Josh Moore RC	2.50	6.00
❑ 157 Torraye Braggs RC	2.50	6.00
❑ 158 Devin Brown RC	2.50	6.00
❑ 159 James Lang RC	2.50	6.00
❑ 160 Theron Smith RC	2.50	6.00
❑ 161 Linton Johnson RC	2.50	6.00
❑ 162 Marquis Daniels RC	3.00	8.00
❑ 163 Keith Mcleod RC	2.50	6.00
❑ 164 Udonis Haslem RC	3.00	8.00
❑ 165 Ben Handlogten RC	2.50	6.00

2004-05 Topps Chrome

❑ COMP.SET w/o RC's (165)	15.00	40.00
❑ COMMON CARD (1-165)	.25	.60
❑ COMMON ROOKIE (166-220)	1.50	4.00
❑ 1 Allen Iverson	.75	2.00
❑ 2 Eddy Curry	.30	.75
❑ 3 Stephon Marbury	.40	1.00
❑ 4 Chris Bosh	.40	1.00
❑ 5 Jason Kidd	.60	1.50
❑ 6 Baron Davis	.40	1.00
❑ 7 Kwame Brown	.25	.60
❑ 8 Kobe Bryant	2.00	5.00
❑ 9 Ben Wallace	.30	.75
❑ 10 Josh Howard	.40	1.00
❑ 11 Yao Ming	1.00	2.50
❑ 12 Luke Walton	.30	.75
❑ 13 Nene	.30	.75
❑ 14 Michael Redd	.40	1.00
❑ 15 Carmelo Anthony	1.25	3.00
❑ 16 Amare Stoudemire	.75	2.00
❑ 17 Jarvis Hayes	.25	.60
❑ 18 Toni Kukoc	.30	.75
❑ 19 Latrell Sprewell	.30	.75
❑ 20 Jason Richardson	.40	1.00
❑ 21 Kevin Garnett	.75	2.00
❑ 22 Darko Milicic	.25	.60
❑ 23 LeBron James	2.50	6.00
❑ 24 Peja Stojakovic	.30	.75
❑ 25 Wally Szczerbiak	.30	.75
❑ 26 Theo Ratliff	.25	.60
❑ 27 Gilbert Arenas	.40	1.00
❑ 28 Mike Dunleavy	.30	.75
❑ 29 Joe Smith	.25	.60
❑ 30 Vince Carter	.75	2.00
❑ 31 Reggie Miller	.40	1.00
❑ 32 Chris Wilcox	.25	.60
❑ 33 Rasheed Wallace	.40	1.00
❑ 34 Paul Pierce	.40	1.00
❑ 35 Tayshaun Prince	.30	.75
❑ 36 Richard Hamilton	.30	.75
❑ 37 Rashard Lewis	.40	1.00
❑ 38 Joe Johnson	.40	1.00
❑ 39 Zydrunas Ilgauskas	.30	.75
❑ 40 Andre Miller	.30	.75
❑ 41 Dirk Nowitzki	.60	1.50
❑ 42 Chauncey Billups	.40	1.00
❑ 43 Ray Allen	.40	1.00
❑ 44 Raef LaFrentz	.25	.60
❑ 45 Mickael Pietrus	.30	.75
❑ 46 T.J. Ford	.30	.75
❑ 47 Chris Webber	.40	1.00
❑ 48 Jamaal Tinsley	.30	.75
❑ 49 Earl Boykins	.25	.60
❑ 50 Tim Duncan	.75	2.00
❑ 51 Troy Hudson	.25	.60
❑ 52 Juan Dixon	.25	.60
❑ 53 Tim Thomas	.25	.60
❑ 54 Darius Miles	.30	.75
❑ 55 Jalen Rose	.30	.75
❑ 56 Kirk Hinrich	.30	.75
❑ 57 Michael Finley	.40	1.00
❑ 58 Brad Miller	.30	.75
❑ 59 Jonathan Bender	.25	.60
❑ 60 Manu Ginobili	.40	1.00
❑ 61 Chris Kaman	.30	.75
❑ 62 Doug Christie	.25	.60
❑ 63 Marcus Camby	.30	.75
❑ 64 Desmond Mason	.30	.75
❑ 65 Boris Diaw	.30	.75
❑ 66 Maurice Taylor	.25	.60
❑ 67 Damon Stoudamire	.30	.75
❑ 68 Dwyane Wade	1.25	3.00
❑ 69 Allan Houston	.30	.75
❑ 70 Jermaine O'Neal	.40	1.00
❑ 71 Glenn Robinson	.30	.75
❑ 72 Morris Peterson	.30	.75
❑ 73 Luke Ridnour	.25	.60
❑ 74 Bobby Jackson	.25	.60
❑ 75 Eddie Jones	.30	.75
❑ 76 Alvin Williams	.25	.60
❑ 77 Elton Brand	.40	1.00
❑ 78 Zach Randolph	.40	1.00
❑ 79 Marko Jaric	.25	.60
❑ 80 Mike Bibby	.30	.75
❑ 81 Jim Jackson	.25	.60
❑ 82 Kurt Thomas	.25	.60
❑ 83 Troy Murphy	.40	1.00
❑ 84 Rodney White	.25	.60
❑ 85 Jamaal Magloire	.25	.60
❑ 86 Jamal Mashburn	.30	.75
❑ 87 Kenny Thomas	.25	.60
❑ 88 Corey Maggette	.30	.75
❑ 89 Rasho Nesterovic	.25	.60
❑ 90 Shawn Marion	.40	1.00
❑ 91 Antonio Daniels	.25	.60
❑ 92 Marquis Daniels	.25	.60
❑ 93 Richard Jefferson	.40	1.00
❑ 94 Michael Olowokandi	.25	.60
❑ 95 Bruce Bowen	.25	.60
❑ 96 Mark Blount	.25	.60
❑ 97 Sam Cassell	.30	.75
❑ 98 Voshon Lenard	.25	.60
❑ 99 Speedy Claxton	.25	.60
❑ 100 Samuel Dalembert	.25	.60
❑ 101 Tyson Chandler	.30	.75
❑ 102 Keith Van Horn	.30	.75
❑ 103 Udonis Haslem	.30	.75
❑ 104 Trenton Hassell	.25	.60
❑ 105 Tony Parker	.40	1.00
❑ 106 Ronald Murray	.25	.60
❑ 107 Jeff McInnis	.25	.60
❑ 108 Marcus Banks	.25	.60
❑ 109 Ricky Davis	.30	.75
❑ 110 Karl Malone	.40	1.00
❑ 111 Bonzi Wells	.25	.60
❑ 112 Antonio McDyess	.30	.75
❑ 113 Drew Gooden	.25	.60
❑ 114 Stephen Jackson	.30	.75
❑ 115 Eric Snow	.25	.60
❑ 116 Steve Francis	.40	1.00
❑ 117 Pau Gasol	.40	1.00
❑ 118 Andrei Kirilenko	.40	1.00
❑ 119 Erick Dampier	.25	.60
❑ 120 Jason Kapono	.25	.60
❑ 121 Al Harrington	.30	.75
❑ 122 Gary Payton	.40	1.00
❑ 123 Nick Van Exel	.30	.75
❑ 124 Cuttino Mobley	.30	.75
❑ 125 Kenyon Martin	.40	1.00
❑ 126 Mike Miller	.30	.75
❑ 127 Jamal Crawford	.30	.75
❑ 128 Kerry Kittles	.30	.75
❑ 129 Derrick Coleman	.30	.75
❑ 130 Gordan Giricek	.25	.60
❑ 131 Antoine Walker	.40	1.00
❑ 132 Shane Battier	.30	.75
❑ 133 Caron Butler	.30	.75
❑ 134 Corliss Williamson	.25	.60
❑ 135 Carlos Boozer	.40	1.00
❑ 136 Tracy McGrady	.75	2.00
❑ 137 Stromile Swift	.25	.60
❑ 138 Derek Fisher	.30	.75
❑ 139 Juwan Howard	.30	.75
❑ 140 Jason Terry	.30	.75
❑ 141 Vlade Divac	.30	.75
❑ 142 Antawn Jamison	.40	1.00
❑ 143 Aleksandar Pavlovic	.25	.60
❑ 144 Rafer Alston	.25	.60
❑ 145 Brent Barry	.25	.60
❑ 146 Quentin Richardson	.30	.75
❑ 147 Lamar Odom	.40	1.00
❑ 148 Gerald Wallace	.40	1.00
❑ 149 Charlie Ward	.25	.60
❑ 150 Jerry Stackhouse	.30	.75
❑ 151 Carlos Arroyo	.40	1.00
❑ 152 Hedo Turkoglu	.30	.75
❑ 153 Steve Nash	.60	1.50
❑ 154 Mehmet Okur	.30	.75
❑ 155 Tyronn Lue	.25	.60
❑ 156 Bob Sura	.25	.60
❑ 157 Jason Williams	.30	.75
❑ 158 Shaquille O'Neal	1.00	2.50
❑ 159 Kelvin Cato	.25	.60
❑ 160 Eric Williams	.25	.60

❑ 161 Brian Grant	.25	.60
❑ 162 Danny Fortson	.25	.60
❑ 163 Chucky Atkins	.25	.60
❑ 164 Matt Harpring	.30	.75
❑ 165 Primoz Brezec	.25	.60
❑ 166 Dwight Howard RC	5.00	12.00
❑ 167 Emeka Okafor RC	3.00	8.00
❑ 168 Ben Gordon RC	2.00	5.00
❑ 169 Shaun Livingston RC	1.50	4.00
❑ 170 Devin Harris RC	3.00	8.00
❑ 171 Josh Childress RC	1.50	4.00
❑ 172 Luol Deng RC	2.00	5.00
❑ 173 Rafael Araujo RC	1.50	4.00
❑ 174 Andre Iguodala RC	4.00	10.00
❑ 175 Luke Jackson RC	1.50	4.00
❑ 176 Andris Biedrins RC	2.50	6.00
❑ 177 Robert Swift RC	1.50	4.00
❑ 178 Sebastian Telfair RC	1.50	4.00
❑ 179 Kris Humphries RC	2.50	6.00
❑ 180 Al Jefferson RC	3.00	8.00
❑ 181 Kirk Snyder RC	1.50	4.00
❑ 182 Josh Smith RC	4.00	10.00
❑ 183 J.R. Smith RC	3.00	8.00
❑ 184 Dorell Wright RC	2.00	5.00
❑ 185 Jameer Nelson RC	2.00	5.00
❑ 186 Pavel Podkolzine RC	1.50	4.00
❑ 187 Horace Jenkins RC	1.50	4.00
❑ 188 Luis Flores RC	1.50	4.00
❑ 189 Delonte West RC	2.50	6.00
❑ 190 Tony Allen RC	2.00	5.00
❑ 191 Kevin Martin RC	2.00	5.00
❑ 192 Sasha Vujacic RC	1.50	4.00
❑ 193 Beno Udrih RC	2.00	5.00
❑ 194 David Harrison RC	1.50	4.00
❑ 195 Yuta Tabuse RC	3.00	8.00
❑ 196 Peter John Ramos RC	1.50	4.00
❑ 197 Chris Duhon RC	2.50	6.00
❑ 198 Trevor Ariza RC	2.00	5.00
❑ 199 Bernard Robinson RC	1.50	4.00
❑ 200 Andre Emmett RC	1.50	4.00
❑ 201 Mario Kasun RC	1.50	4.00
❑ 202 Matt Freije RC	1.50	4.00
❑ 203 Maurice Evans RC	1.50	4.00
❑ 204 Erik Daniels RC	1.50	4.00
❑ 205 Lionel Chalmers RC	1.50	4.00
❑ 206 Jared Reiner RC	1.50	4.00
❑ 207 D.J. Mbenga RC	1.50	4.00
❑ 208 Antonio Burks RC	1.50	4.00
❑ 209 Justin Reed RC	1.50	4.00
❑ 210 Pape Sow RC	1.50	4.00
❑ 211 Jackson Vroman RC	1.50	4.00
❑ 212 Romain Sato RC	1.50	4.00
❑ 213 Nenad Kristic RC	2.00	5.00
❑ 214 Damien Wilkins RC	1.50	4.00
❑ 215 Arthur Johnson RC	1.50	4.00
❑ 216 Ibrahim Kutluay RC	1.50	4.00
❑ 217 Andres Nocioni RC	2.00	5.00
❑ 218 Josh Davis RC	1.50	4.00
❑ 219 Donta Smith RC	1.50	4.00
❑ 220 Anderson Varejao RC	2.00	5.00

2005-06 Topps Chrome

❑ COMPLETE SET (274)	60.00	120.00
❑ COMMON CARD (1-165)	.25	.60
❑ SEMISTARS	.30	.75
❑ UNLISTED STARS	.40	1.00
❑ COMMON ROOKIE (166-215)	2.00	5.00
❑ COMMON CELEBRITY (216-220)	1.50	4.00
❑ COMMON NBDL (221-274)	1.00	2.50
❑ 1 Grant Hill	.40	1.00
❑ 2 Lamar Odom	.40	1.00
❑ 3 Jamal Crawford	.30	.75
❑ 4 Ben Gordon	.50	1.25
❑ 5 Zach Randolph	.40	1.00
❑ 6 Chris Duhon	.30	.75
❑ 7 Gilbert Arenas	.40	1.00
❑ 8 Yao Ming	1.00	2.50
❑ 9 Josh Smith	.40	1.00
❑ 10 Ray Allen	.40	1.00
❑ 11 Vince Carter	.75	2.00
❑ 12 Kenyon Martin	.40	1.00
❑ 13 Tim Duncan	.75	2.00
❑ 14 Michael Redd	.40	1.00
❑ 15 Antawn Jamison	.40	1.00
❑ 16 Shane Battier	.40	1.00
❑ 17 Baron Davis	.40	1.00
❑ 18 Allen Iverson	.75	2.00
❑ 19 Jameer Nelson	.30	.75
❑ 20 Brent Barry	.25	.60
❑ 21 Zydrunas Ilgauskas	.30	.75
❑ 22 Jason Terry	.40	1.00
❑ 23 Mike Dunleavy	.30	.75
❑ 24 Paul Pierce	.40	1.00
❑ 25 Peja Stojakovic	.40	1.00
❑ 26 Andre Iguodala	.40	1.00
❑ 27 Andrei Kirilenko	.40	1.00
❑ 28 Nenad Krstic	.30	.75
❑ 29 Emeka Okafor	.40	1.00
❑ 30 Jalen Rose	.40	1.00
❑ 31 Ricky Davis	.40	1.00
❑ 32 Jason Kidd	.60	1.50
❑ 33 Chauncey Billups	.40	1.00
❑ 34 Amare Stoudemire	.75	2.00
❑ 35 Josh Childress	.30	.75
❑ 36 Mehmet Okur	.25	.60
❑ 37 Shaun Livingston	.25	.60
❑ 38 Bruce Bowen	.25	.60
❑ 39 J.R. Smith	.30	.75
❑ 40 Kobe Bryant	2.00	5.00
❑ 41 Dwight Howard	.75	2.00
❑ 42 Manu Ginobili	.40	1.00
❑ 43 Keith Van Horn	.30	.75
❑ 44 Stephon Marbury	.40	1.00
❑ 45 Samuel Dalembert	.25	.60
❑ 46 Luke Ridnour	.30	.75
❑ 47 Sebastian Telfair	.30	.75
❑ 48 Tyson Chandler	.40	1.00
❑ 49 Drew Gooden	.30	.75
❑ 50 Marcus Camby	.30	.75
❑ 51 Dwyane Wade	1.00	2.50
❑ 52 Troy Murphy	.40	1.00
❑ 53 Rashard Lewis	.40	1.00
❑ 54 Shaquille O'Neal	1.00	2.50
❑ 55 Al Harrington	.25	.60
❑ 56 Al Jefferson	.40	1.00
❑ 57 Earl Boykins	.25	.60
❑ 58 Tayshaun Prince	.40	1.00
❑ 59 Carlos Boozer	.40	1.00
❑ 60 Richard Jefferson	.30	.75
❑ 61 Toni Kukoc	.25	.60
❑ 62 Brad Miller	.40	1.00
❑ 63 Richard Hamilton	.30	.75
❑ 64 Kevin Garnett	.75	2.00
❑ 65 Tony Parker	.40	1.00
❑ 66 Udonis Haslem	.40	1.00
❑ 67 Dikembe Mutombo	.30	.75
❑ 68 Pau Gasol	.40	1.00
❑ 69 Chris Webber	.40	1.00
❑ 70 Ben Wallace	.40	1.00
❑ 71 Carmelo Anthony	.75	2.00
❑ 72 Dirk Nowitzki	.60	1.50
❑ 73 Tony Allen	.25	.60
❑ 74 Corey Maggette	.30	.75
❑ 75 Rasheed Wallace	.40	1.00
❑ 76 Andre Miller	.30	.75
❑ 77 Luol Deng	.40	1.00
❑ 78 Mike Miller	.40	1.00
❑ 79 Wally Szczerbiak	.30	.75
❑ 80 Chris Bosh	.40	1.00
❑ 81 Marquis Daniels	.30	.75
❑ 82 Nick Collison	.25	.60
❑ 83 Matt Harpring	.30	.75
❑ 84 Kirk Hinrich	.40	1.00
❑ 85 Josh Howard	.40	1.00
❑ 86 Elton Brand	.40	1.00
❑ 87 Tyronn Lue	.25	.60
❑ 88 Bob Sura	.25	.60
❑ 89 Chris Mihm	.25	.60
❑ 90 Brevin Knight	.25	.60
❑ 91 Jason Richardson	.40	1.00
❑ 92 Vladimir Radmanovic	.25	.60
❑ 93 Eddie Griffin	.25	.60
❑ 94 P.J. Brown	.25	.60
❑ 95 Troy Hudson	.25	.60
❑ 96 Steve Francis	.40	1.00
❑ 97 Joel Przybilla	.25	.60
❑ 98 Steve Nash	.50	1.25
❑ 99 Brendan Haywood	.25	.60
❑ 100 Primoz Brezec	.25	.60
❑ 101 Devin Harris	.40	1.00
❑ 102 Lebron James	2.00	5.00
❑ 103 Mike Bibby	.40	1.00
❑ 104 Jared Jeffries	.25	.60
❑ 105 Morris Peterson	.30	.75
❑ 106 Trevor Ariza	.30	.75
❑ 107 Shawn Marion	.40	1.00
❑ 108 Andres Nocioni	.25	.60
❑ 109 Darius Miles	.40	1.00
❑ 110 Tracy Mcgrady	.75	2.00
❑ 111 Stephen Jackson	.30	.75
❑ 112 Joe Johnson	.40	1.00
❑ 113 Bonzi Wells	.30	.75
❑ 114 Damon Jones	.30	.75
❑ 115 Rafer Alston	.25	.60
❑ 116 Cuttino Mobley	.30	.75
❑ 117 Nick Van Exel	.40	1.00
❑ 118 Jason Hart	.25	.60
❑ 119 Fred Jones	.30	.75
❑ 120 Dan Dickau	.25	.60
❑ 121 Damon Stoudamire	.30	.75
❑ 122 Kirk Snyder	.25	.60
❑ 123 Larry Hughes	.30	.75
❑ 124 Michael Finley	.40	1.00
❑ 125 Sam Cassell	.40	1.00
❑ 126 Bobby Jackson	.25	.60
❑ 127 Austin Croshere	.25	.60
❑ 128 Kwame Brown	.30	.75
❑ 129 Doug Christie	.25	.60
❑ 130 Antonio Daniels	.25	.60
❑ 131 Eddy Curry	.30	.75
❑ 132 Mike James	.25	.60
❑ 133 Juan Dixon	.25	.60
❑ 134 Jason Williams	.30	.75
❑ 135 Jeff Mcinnis	.25	.60
❑ 136 Jamaal Tinsley	.30	.75
❑ 137 Derek Anderson	.30	.75
❑ 138 Devin Brown	.25	.60
❑ 139 Raja Bell	.25	.60
❑ 140 Gary Payton	.40	1.00
❑ 141 Marko Jaric	.25	.60
❑ 142 Ron Artest	.30	.75
❑ 143 Zaza Pachulia	.25	.60
❑ 144 Jermaine O'Neal	.40	1.00
❑ 145 Quentin Richardson	.30	.75
❑ 146 Lee Nailon	.25	.60
❑ 147 Bobby Simmons	.25	.60
❑ 148 Caron Butler	.40	1.00
❑ 149 Shareef Abdur-Rahim	.40	1.00
❑ 150 Stromile Swift	.30	.75
❑ 151 Rasual Butler	.25	.60
❑ 152 Mike Sweetney	.30	.75
❑ 153 Antoine Walker	.30	.75
❑ 154 Eddie Jones	.25	.60
❑ 155 David Harrison	.25	.60
❑ 156 Kurt Thomas	.25	.60
❑ 157 Donyell Marshall	.25	.60
❑ 158 Brian Grant	.25	.60
❑ 159 Desmond Mason	.25	.60
❑ 160 Tim Thomas	.25	.60
❑ 161 Marc Jackson	.25	.60
❑ 162 Chucky Atkins	.25	.60
❑ 163 Jeff Foster	.25	.60
❑ 164 Jamaal Magloire	.25	.60
❑ 165 Desagana Diop	.25	.60
❑ 166 Danny Granger RC	5.00	12.00
❑ 167 Hakim Warrick RC	3.00	8.00
❑ 168 Chris Paul RC	6.00	15.00
❑ 169 Marvin Williams RC	3.00	8.00
❑ 170 Ike Diogu RC	2.50	6.00
❑ 171 Wayne Simien RC	2.50	6.00
❑ 172 James Singleton RC	2.00	5.00
❑ 173 Robert Whaley RC	2.00	5.00
❑ 174 Arvydas Macijauskas RC	2.00	5.00
❑ 175 Linas Kleiza RC	2.50	6.00
❑ 176 Raymond Felton RC	2.50	6.00
❑ 177 Ersan Ilyasova RC	2.00	5.00
❑ 178 Jarrett Jack RC	2.00	5.00
❑ 179 Antoine Wright RC	2.00	5.00
❑ 180 David Lee RC	4.00	10.00
❑ 181 Esteban Batista RC	2.00	5.00
❑ 182 Sarunas Jasikevicius RC	2.50	6.00
❑ 183 Francisco Garcia RC	2.50	6.00
❑ 184 C.J. Miles RC	2.00	5.00
❑ 185 Ryan Gomes RC	2.00	5.00

❑ 186 Andrew Bynum RC	6.00	15.00
❑ 187 Sean May RC	2.50	6.00
❑ 188 Jose Calderon RC	2.00	5.00
❑ 189 Rashad Mccants RC	2.50	6.00
❑ 190 Johan Petro RC	2.00	5.00
❑ 191 Jason Maxiell RC	2.50	6.00
❑ 192 Martell Webster RC	2.00	5.00
❑ 193 Nate Robinson RC	3.00	8.00
❑ 194 Daniel Ewing RC	2.50	6.00
❑ 195 Fabricio Oberto RC	2.00	5.00
❑ 196 Travis Diener RC	2.00	5.00
❑ 197 Salim Stoudamire RC	2.50	6.00
❑ 198 Charlie Villanueva RC	3.00	8.00
❑ 199 Orien Greene RC	2.00	5.00
❑ 200 Deron Williams RC	5.00	12.00
❑ 201 Bracey Wright RC	2.00	5.00
❑ 202 Lawrence Roberts RC	2.00	5.00
❑ 203 Eddie Basden RC	2.00	5.00
❑ 204 Brandon Bass RC	2.00	5.00
❑ 205 Martynas Andriuskevicius RC	2.00	5.00
❑ 206 Channing Frye RC	2.50	6.00
❑ 207 Julius Hodge RC	2.50	6.00
❑ 208 Luther Head RC	2.50	6.00
❑ 209 Chris Taft RC	2.00	5.00
❑ 210 Andrew Bogut RC	2.50	6.00
❑ 211 Gerald Green RC	2.00	5.00
❑ 212 Joey Graham RC	2.00	5.00
❑ 213 Louis Williams RC	3.00	8.00
❑ 214 Yaroslav Korolev RC	2.00	5.00
❑ 215 Monta Ellis RC	5.00	12.00
❑ 216 Christie Brinkley	1.50	4.00
❑ 217 Jay-Z	1.50	4.00
❑ 218 Shannon Elizabeth	1.50	4.00
❑ 219 Carmen Electra	1.50	4.00
❑ 220 Jenny McCarthy Cut Out	25.00	60.00
❑ 221 Joe Shipp DL RC	1.00	2.50
❑ 222 Dwayne Jones DL RC	1.00	2.50
❑ 223 Will Conroy DL RC	1.00	2.50
❑ 224 Darnell Miller DL RC	1.00	2.50
❑ 225 Will Bynum DL RC	1.00	2.50
❑ 226 Jamar Smith DL RC	1.00	2.50
❑ 227 Daryl Dorsey DL RC	1.00	2.50
❑ 228 Tony Bland DL RC	1.00	2.50
❑ 229 Hiram Fuller DL RC	1.00	2.50
❑ 230 Tyrone Sally DL RC	1.00	2.50
❑ 231 Clay Tucker DL RC	1.00	2.50
❑ 232 George Leach DL RC	1.00	2.50
❑ 233 Marcus Douthit DL RC	1.00	2.50
❑ 234 Carlos Hurt DL RC	1.00	2.50
❑ 235 Seamus Boxley DL RC	1.00	2.50
❑ 236 Ramel Curry DL RC	1.00	2.50
❑ 237 Andreas Glyniadakis DL RC	1.00	2.50
❑ 238 Kareem Reid DL RC	1.00	2.50
❑ 239 Austin Nichols DL RC	1.00	2.50
❑ 240 Chris Shumate DL RC	1.00	2.50
❑ 241 Brandon Robinson DL RC	1.00	2.50
❑ 242 Harvey Thomas DL RC	1.00	2.50
❑ 243 Desmon Farmer DL RC	1.00	2.50
❑ 244 Marcus Hill DL RC	1.00	2.50
❑ 245 Robb Dryden DL RC	1.00	2.50
❑ 246 Nate Daniels DL RC	1.00	2.50
❑ 247 James Lang DL RC	1.00	2.50
❑ 248 Anthony Terrell DL RC	1.00	2.50
❑ 249 Jeff Hagen DL RC	1.00	2.50
❑ 250 Kevin Owens DL RC	1.00	2.50
❑ 251 Myron Allen DL RC	1.00	2.50
❑ 252 Ayudeji Akindele DL RC	1.00	2.50
❑ 253 T.J. Cummings DL RC	1.00	2.50
❑ 254 Mike King DL RC	1.00	2.50
❑ 255 Otis George DL RC	1.00	2.50
❑ 256 Ezra Williams DL RC	1.00	2.50
❑ 257 Anthony Wilkins DL RC	1.00	2.50
❑ 258 Scott Merritt DL RC	1.00	2.50
❑ 259 Seth Doliboa DL RC	1.00	2.50
❑ 260 Anthony Fuqua DL RC	1.00	2.50
❑ 261 Malik Moore DL RC	1.00	2.50
❑ 262 Randall Orr DL RC	1.00	2.50
❑ 263 Ricky Shields DL RC	1.00	2.50
❑ 264 John Lucas DL RC	1.00	2.50
❑ 265 Butter Johnson DL RC	1.00	2.50
❑ 266 Isiah Victor DL RC	1.00	2.50
❑ 267 Roderick Riley DL RC	1.00	2.50
❑ 268 Bernard King DL RC	1.00	2.50
❑ 269 E.J. Rowland DL RC	1.00	2.50
❑ 270 Anthony Grundy DL RC	1.00	2.50
❑ 271 Brian Jackson DL RC	1.00	2.50
❑ 272 Keith Langford DL RC	1.00	2.50
❑ 273 Chuck Hayes DL RC	1.00	2.50
❑ 274 Jonathan Moore DL RC	1.00	2.50

2006-07 Topps Chrome

❑ COMPLETE SET (210)	60.00	120.00
❑ 1 Elton Brand	.40	1.00
❑ 2 Tim Duncan	.75	2.00
❑ 3 Chris Paul	.75	2.00
❑ 4 Joe Johnson	.30	.75
❑ 5 Chauncey Billups	.40	1.00
❑ 6 Andres Nocioni	.25	.60
❑ 7 Al Jefferson	.40	1.00
❑ 8 Gerald Wallace	.40	1.00
❑ 9 Jason Terry	.40	1.00
❑ 10 Dwight Howard	.75	2.00
❑ 11 Larry Hughes	.30	.75
❑ 12 Vince Carter	.75	2.00
❑ 13 Mike Bibby	.40	1.00
❑ 14 Ben Gordon	.50	1.25
❑ 15 Desmond Mason	.25	.60
❑ 16 Raymond Felton	.50	1.25
❑ 17 Paul Pierce	.40	1.00
❑ 18 Jason Richardson	.40	1.00
❑ 19 Rasheed Wallace	.40	1.00
❑ 20 Leandro Barbosa	.40	1.00
❑ 21 Deron Williams	.60	1.50
❑ 22 Kwame Brown	.30	.75
❑ 23 Josh Childress	.30	.75
❑ 24 Shawn Marion	.40	1.00
❑ 25 Shaquille O'Neal	1.00	2.50
❑ 26 Ray Allen	.40	1.00
❑ 27 Cuttino Mobley	.30	.75
❑ 28 Dirk Nowitzki	.60	1.50
❑ 29 Jermaine O'Neal	.40	1.00
❑ 30 Marvin Williams	.40	1.00
❑ 31 Eddy Curry	.30	.75
❑ 32 Andrei Kirilenko	.40	1.00
❑ 33 Baron Davis	.40	1.00
❑ 34 Tracy McGrady	.75	2.00
❑ 35 Chris Kaman	.25	.60
❑ 36 Luol Deng	.40	1.00
❑ 37 Emeka Okafor	.40	1.00
❑ 38 Lamar Odom	.40	1.00
❑ 39 Alonzo Mourning	.50	1.25
❑ 40 Marcus Camby	.30	.75
❑ 41 Ike Diogu	.30	.75
❑ 42 Josh Smith	.40	1.00
❑ 43 Nate Robinson	.40	1.00
❑ 44 Yao Ming	1.00	2.50
❑ 45 Darko Milicic	.40	1.00
❑ 46 Smush Parker	.25	.60
❑ 47 Mike Dunleavy	.30	.75
❑ 48 Ricky Davis	.40	1.00
❑ 49 Michael Finley	.40	1.00
❑ 50 Nenad Krstic	.30	.75
❑ 51 Earl Boykins	.25	.60
❑ 52 Richard Hamilton	.30	.75
❑ 53 Hakim Warrick	.30	.75
❑ 54 Corey Maggette	.30	.75
❑ 55 Kenyon Martin	.40	1.00
❑ 56 Jason Kidd	.60	1.50
❑ 57 Dwyane Wade	1.00	2.50
❑ 58 Josh Howard	.40	1.00
❑ 59 Richard Jefferson	.30	.75
❑ 60 Steve Nash	.50	1.25
❑ 61 Drew Gooden	.30	.75
❑ 62 Kevin Garnett	.75	2.00
❑ 63 Delonte West	.30	.75
❑ 64 Channing Frye	.30	.75
❑ 65 Andre Iguodala	.40	1.00
❑ 66 Pau Gasol	.40	1.00
❑ 67 LeBron James	2.00	5.00
❑ 68 Sam Cassell	.40	1.00
❑ 69 Mehmet Okur	.25	.60
❑ 70 Bruce Bowen	.25	.60
❑ 71 Kirk Hinrich	.40	1.00
❑ 72 Chris Wilcox	.25	.60
❑ 73 Brad Miller	.40	1.00

❑ 74 Chris Bosh	.40	1.00
❑ 75 Jamal Crawford	.25	.60
❑ 76 Mike Miller	.40	1.00
❑ 77 Danny Granger	.30	.75
❑ 78 Manu Ginobili	.40	1.00
❑ 79 Udonis Haslem	.40	1.00
❑ 80 Gilbert Arenas	.40	1.00
❑ 81 Tony Parker	.40	1.00
❑ 82 Carlos Boozer	.40	1.00
❑ 83 Rashard Lewis	.40	1.00
❑ 84 Boris Diaw	.30	.75
❑ 85 Shaun Livingston	.25	.60
❑ 86 Shareef Abdur-Rahim	.40	1.00
❑ 87 Devin Harris	.40	1.00
❑ 88 Brevin Knight	.25	.60
❑ 89 Troy Murphy	.40	1.00
❑ 90 Antawn Jamison	.40	1.00
❑ 91 Stephen Jackson	.30	.75
❑ 92 Chris Webber	.40	1.00
❑ 93 Luke Ridnour	.30	.75
❑ 94 Joel Przybilla	.25	.60
❑ 95 David West	.40	1.00
❑ 96 Caron Butler	.40	1.00
❑ 97 Andre Miller	.30	.75
❑ 98 Ron Artest	.40	1.00
❑ 99 Samuel Dalembert	.25	.60
❑ 100 Tayshaun Prince	.40	1.00
❑ 101 Jameer Nelson	.30	.75
❑ 102 Zach Randolph	.40	1.00
❑ 103 Stephon Marbury	.40	1.00
❑ 104 Steve Francis	.40	1.00
❑ 105 Kevin Martin	.40	1.00
❑ 106 Carmelo Anthony	.50	1.25
❑ 107 Morris Peterson	.30	.75
❑ 108 Allen Iverson	.75	2.00
❑ 109 Antoine Walker	.30	.75
❑ 110 Jarrett Jack	.30	.75
❑ 111 Ben Wallace	.40	1.00
❑ 112 Vladimir Radmanovic	.25	.60
❑ 113 Andrew Bogut	.40	1.00
❑ 114 Nazr Mohammed	.25	.60
❑ 115 Kirk Snyder	.25	.60
❑ 116 Marquis Daniels	.30	.75
❑ 117 T.J. Ford	.30	.75
❑ 118 Stromile Swift	.30	.75
❑ 119 Lorenzen Wright	.25	.60
❑ 120 Mike James	.25	.60
❑ 121 Amare Stoudemire	.75	2.00
❑ 122 Raef LaFrentz	.25	.60
❑ 123 Adrian Griffin	.25	.60
❑ 124 Maurice Evans	.25	.60
❑ 125 David Wesley	.25	.60
❑ 126 J.R. Smith	.30	.75
❑ 127 Ronald Murray	.15	.40
❑ 128 Shane Battier	.40	1.00
❑ 129 Kobe Bryant	2.00	5.00
❑ 130 Jamaal Magloire	.25	.60
❑ 131 Charlie Villanueva	.40	1.00
❑ 132 Tyson Chandler	.40	1.00
❑ 133 Eddie House	.25	.60
❑ 134 Marcus Banks	.25	.60
❑ 135 Derek Fisher	.30	.75
❑ 136 Bobby Simmons	.25	.60
❑ 137 Al Harrington	.25	.60
❑ 138 Speedy Claxton	.25	.60
❑ 139 Viktor Khryapa	.25	.60
❑ 140 Sean May	.30	.75
❑ 141 Devean George	.30	.75
❑ 142 Joe Smith	.30	.75
❑ 143 Peja Stojakovic	.40	1.00
❑ 144 DeShawn Stevenson	.25	.60
❑ 145 Fred Jones	.30	.75
❑ 146 P.J. Brown	.25	.60
❑ 147 Sebastian Telfair	.30	.75
❑ 148 Bonzi Wells	.30	.75
❑ 149 Michael Redd	.40	1.00
❑ 150 Jared Jeffries	.25	.60
❑ 151 Larry Bird	1.25	3.00
❑ 152 Dominique Wilkins	.50	1.25
❑ 153 Isiah Thomas	.40	1.00
❑ 154 Wilt Chamberlain	.75	2.00
❑ 155 Bill Walton	.40	1.00
❑ 156 Oscar Robertson	.40	1.00
❑ 157 Walt Frazier	.40	1.00
❑ 158 Elgin Baylor	.40	1.00
❑ 159 George Gervin	.40	1.00
❑ 160 Moses Malone	.40	1.00
❑ 161 Solomon Jones RC	1.25	3.00
❑ 162 Kyle Lowry RC	1.25	3.00

163 Maurice Ager RC	1.25	3.00
164 Patrick O'Bryant RC	1.25	3.00
165 Marcus Vinicius RC	1.25	3.00
166 Jorge Garbajosa RC	2.50	6.00
167 Josh Boone RC	1.25	3.00
168 Mardy Collins RC	1.25	3.00
169 Rodney Carney RC	1.25	3.00
170 P.J. Tucker RC	1.25	3.00
171 Shelden Williams RC	1.50	4.00
172 Ryan Hollins RC	1.25	3.00
173 Pops Mensah-Bonsu RC	1.25	3.00
174 Steve Novak RC	1.25	3.00
175 Paul Davis RC	1.25	3.00
176 David Noel RC	1.25	3.00
177 Marcus Williams RC	1.50	4.00
178 Renaldo Balkman RC	1.25	3.00
179 Quincy Douby RC	1.25	3.00
180 Andrea Bargnani RC	2.00	5.00
181 Chris Quinn RC	1.25	3.00
182 Thabo Sefolosha RC	1.50	4.00
183 LaMarcus Aldridge RC	1.50	4.00
184 Rudy Gay RC	1.25	3.00
185 Jordan Farmar RC	1.50	4.00
186 Damir Markota RC	1.25	3.00
187 Mile Ilic RC	1.25	3.00
188 James Augustine RC	1.25	3.00
189 Tyrus Thomas RC	1.50	4.00
190 Brandon Roy RC	3.00	8.00
191 Allan Ray RC	1.25	3.00
192 Shannon Brown RC	1.25	3.00
193 Will Blalock RC	1.25	3.00
194 James White RC	1.25	3.00
195 Adam Morrison RC	1.50	4.00
196 Craig Smith RC	1.25	3.00
197 Cedric Simmons RC	1.25	3.00
198 J.J. Redick RC	1.25	3.00
199 Sergio Rodriguez RC	1.25	3.00
200 Ronnie Brewer RC	1.50	4.00
201 Rajon Rondo RC	5.00	12.00
202 Daniel Gibson RC	1.50	4.00
203 Hassan Adams RC	1.50	4.00
204 Shawne Williams RC	1.25	3.00
205 Alexander Johnson RC	1.25	3.00
206 Randy Foye RC	1.25	3.00
207 Hilton Armstrong RC	1.25	3.00
208 Bobby Jones RC	1.25	3.00
209 Saer Sene RC	1.25	3.00
210 Dee Brown RC	1.25	3.00

2007-08 Topps Chrome

COMPLETE SET (160)	50.00	100.00
1 Amare Stoudemire	1.00	2.50
2 Joe Johnson	.50	1.25
3 Dwyane Wade	1.25	3.00
4 Chris Bosh	.50	1.25
5 Jason Kidd	.75	2.00
6 Bill Russell	.75	2.00
7 Jermaine O'Neal	.50	1.25
8 Mike Miller	.50	1.25
9 Ray Allen	.50	1.25
10 Elton Brand	.50	1.25
11 Yao Ming	1.25	3.00
12 Al Harrington	.40	1.00
13 Steve Nash	.60	1.50
14 Dwight Howard	1.00	2.50
15 Carmelo Anthony	1.00	2.50
16 Pau Gasol	.50	1.25
17 Chauncey Billups	.50	1.25
18 Bob Pettit	.60	1.50
19 Jason Kapono	.30	.75
20 Kevin Garnett	1.25	3.00
21 Tim Duncan	1.00	2.50
22 Michael Redd	.50	1.25
23 LeBron James	2.50	6.00
24 Kobe Bryant	2.50	6.00
25 Eddy Curry	.30	.75
26 Gerald Green	.50	1.25
27 Andrew Bogut	.50	1.25
28 Vince Carter	1.00	2.50
29 Corey Maggette	.40	1.00
30 Morris Peterson	.40	1.00
31 Shawn Marion	.50	1.25
32 Shaquille O'Neal	1.25	3.00
33 Allen Iverson	1.00	2.50
34 Paul Pierce	.50	1.25
35 Bill Sharman	.50	1.25
36 Tony Parker	.50	1.25
37 Mike Bibby	.50	1.25
38 Andrea Bargnani	.60	1.50
39 Luol Deng	.50	1.25
40 Chris Paul	1.00	2.50
41 Dirk Nowitzki	.75	2.00
42 David Lee	.40	1.00
43 Vern Mikkelsen	.50	1.25
44 Darko Milicic	.50	1.25
45 Al Jefferson	.50	1.25
46 Bob Cousy	.75	2.00
47 Andrei Kirilenko	.50	1.25
48 Penny Hardaway	1.25	3.00
49 Chris Wilcox	.40	1.00
50 Dolph Schayes	.50	1.25
51 Zach Randolph	.50	1.25
52 Grant Hill	.50	1.25
53 Jim Loscutoff	.50	1.25
54 Leandro Barbosa	.40	1.00
55 Smush Parker	.30	.75
56 Sam Jones	.60	1.50
57 Manu Ginobili	.50	1.25
58 Jason Richardson	.50	1.25
59 Jason Terry	.50	1.25
60 Gerald Wallace	.50	1.25
61 Richard Hamilton	.40	1.00
62 Cliff Hagan	.50	1.25
63 Tom Heinsohn	.50	1.25
64 Carlos Boozer	.50	1.25
65 Rashard Lewis	.50	1.25
66 Josh Childress	.40	1.00
67 Channing Frye	.40	1.00
68 Mike James	.30	.75
69 Kurt Thomas	.40	1.00
70 Mikki Moore	.40	1.00
71 Baron Davis	.50	1.25
72 Reggie Theus	.50	1.25
73 Jameer Nelson	.40	1.00
74 Caron Butler	.50	1.25
75 Jamaal Magloire	.30	.75
76 Darryl Dawkins	.50	1.25
77 Ben Gordon	.60	1.50
78 Andrew Bynum	.50	1.25
79 Oscar Robertson	.50	1.25
80 Josh Smith	.50	1.25
81 Spud Webb	.50	1.25
82 Chris Mullin	.50	1.25
83 Raymond Felton	.60	1.50
84 Sebastian Telfair	.40	1.00
85 Clyde Drexler	.60	1.50
86 Jarrett Jack	.40	1.00
87 Anderson Varejao	.40	1.00
88 Ryan Gomes	.30	.75
89 Bill Walton	.50	1.25
90 Marcus Camby	.30	.75
91 Kirk Hinrich	.50	1.25
92 David Robinson	.75	2.00
93 Dennis Rodman	.50	1.25
94 Dominique Wilkins	.60	1.50
95 Richard Jefferson	.50	1.25
96 Isiah Thomas	.50	1.25
97 Josh Howard	.50	1.25
98 John Stockton	.75	2.00
99 Deron Williams	.75	2.00
100 Gilbert Arenas	.50	1.25
101 Tracy McGrady	1.00	2.50
102 Steve Blake	.30	.75
103 Ben Wallace	.50	1.25
104 Kevin Martin	.50	1.25
105 Larry Bird	1.50	4.00
106 Magic Johnson	1.00	2.50
107 Brandon Roy	.75	2.00
108 Desmond Mason	.30	.75
109 Rick Barry	.50	1.25
110 Andre Iguodala	.50	1.25
111 Mike Conley Jr. RC	1.50	4.00
112 Glen Davis RC	2.50	6.00
113 Julian Wright RC	1.50	4.00
114 Rodney Stuckey RC	2.50	6.00
115 Chris Richard RC	1.25	3.00
116 Coby Karl RC	1.25	3.00
117 Thaddeus Young RC	1.50	4.00
118 Spencer Hawes RC	1.25	3.00
119 Jermareo Davidson RC	1.25	3.00
120 Daequan Cook RC	1.50	4.00
121 Josh McRoberts RC	1.50	4.00
122 Aaron Gray RC	1.25	3.00
123 Wilson Chandler RC	1.25	3.00
124 Herbert Hill RC	1.25	3.00
125 Stephane Lasme RC	1.25	3.00
126 Cheikh Samb RC	1.25	3.00
127 Adam Haluska RC	1.25	3.00
128 Al Thornton RC	1.25	3.00
129 Corey Brewer RC	1.50	4.00
130 Ramon Sessions RC	1.50	4.00
131 Kevin Durant RC	10.00	25.00
132 Alando Tucker RC	1.25	3.00
133 Marco Belinelli RC	1.25	3.00
134 Nick Fazekas RC	1.25	3.00
135 Yi Jianlian RC	2.00	5.00
136 Luis Scola RC	2.00	5.00
137 Jared Dudley RC	1.25	3.00
138 Taurean Green RC	1.25	3.00
139 Kosta Perovic RC	1.25	3.00
140 Kyrylo Fesenko RC	1.25	3.00
141 JamesOn Curry RC	1.25	3.00
142 D.J. Strawberry RC	1.25	3.00
143 Javaris Crittenton RC	1.25	3.00
144 Acie Law IV RC	1.50	4.00
145 Nick Young RC	1.25	3.00
146 Joakim Noah RC	1.50	4.00
147 Dominic McGuire RC	1.25	3.00
148 Arron Afflalo RC	1.25	3.00
149 Gabe Pruitt RC	1.25	3.00
150 Carl Landry RC	1.25	3.00
151 Jeff Green RC	1.50	4.00
152 Greg Oden RC	2.00	5.00
153 Jason Smith RC	1.25	3.00
154 Morris Almond RC	1.25	3.00
155 Juan Carlos Navarro RC	1.50	4.00
156 Brandon Wallace RC	1.25	3.00
157 Aaron Brooks RC	2.00	5.00
158 Brandan Wright RC	1.50	4.00
159 Sean Williams RC	1.25	3.00
160 Al Horford RC	1.50	4.00

2008-09 Topps Chrome

COMPLETE SET (255)	40.00	80.00
1 Chris Paul	1.00	2.50
2 Joe Johnson	.50	1.25
3 Allen Iverson	.60	1.50
4 Luis Scola	.40	1.00
5 Kevin Garnett	1.00	2.50
6 Andrew Bogut	.50	1.25
7 Ben Gordon	.50	1.25
8 Carlos Boozer	.50	1.25
9 Tony Parker	.50	1.25
10 Gilbert Arenas	.50	1.25
11 Yao Ming	.60	1.50
12 Dwight Howard	1.00	2.50
13 Steve Nash	.50	1.25
14 Daequan Cook	.40	1.00
15 Carmelo Anthony	.60	1.50
16 Pau Gasol	.50	1.25
17 Mike Dunleavy	.40	1.00
18 Jason Maxiell	.40	1.00
19 Al Thornton	.50	1.25
20 Ray Allen	.50	1.25
21 Tim Duncan	.75	2.00
22 Michael Redd	.50	1.25
23 LeBron James	2.50	6.00
24 Kobe Bryant	2.50	6.00
25 Al Jefferson	.50	1.25
26 Raymond Felton	.40	1.00
27 LaMarcus Aldridge	.50	1.25

❑ 28 Jose Calderon	.40	1.00
❑ 29 Andris Biedrins	.30	.75
❑ 30 Rasheed Wallace	.50	1.25
❑ 31 Shawn Marion	.50	1.25
❑ 32 Shaquille O'Neal	1.00	2.50
❑ 33 Mike Miller	.50	1.25
❑ 34 Paul Pierce	.60	1.50
❑ 35 Brad Miller	.50	1.25
❑ 36 Richard Jefferson	.50	1.25
❑ 37 DeShawn Stevenson	.30	.75
❑ 38 Zach Randolph	.50	1.25
❑ 39 Daniel Gibson	.50	1.25
❑ 40 Nazr Mohammed	.30	.75
❑ 41 Dirk Nowitzki	.60	1.50
❑ 42 Elton Brand	.75	2.00
❑ 43 Linas Kleiza	.30	.75
❑ 44 Andrea Bargnani	.40	1.00
❑ 45 Josh Smith	.50	1.25
❑ 46 Luol Deng	.50	1.25
❑ 47 Andrei Kirilenko	.50	1.25
❑ 48 Danny Granger	.50	1.25
❑ 49 Rashad McCants	.40	1.00
❑ 50 Emeka Okafor	.50	1.25
❑ 51 Kyle Korver	.50	1.25
❑ 52 Jamario Moon	.50	1.25
❑ 53 Nick Young	.30	.75
❑ 54 Rashard Lewis	.50	1.25
❑ 55 Jason Kidd	.50	1.25
❑ 56 Josh Howard	.50	1.25
❑ 57 Desmond Mason	.30	.75
❑ 58 Andre Miller	.40	1.00
❑ 59 Rafer Alston	.30	.75
❑ 60 Baron Davis	.50	1.25
❑ 61 Zydrunas Ilgauskas	.40	1.00
❑ 62 Marvin Williams	.50	1.25
❑ 63 Manu Ginobili	.50	1.25
❑ 64 David West	.50	1.25
❑ 65 Rajon Rondo	.50	1.25
❑ 66 Kenyon Martin	.50	1.25
❑ 67 Josh Boone	.30	.75
❑ 68 Travis Outlaw	.50	1.25
❑ 69 Andre Iguodala	.50	1.25
❑ 70 Yi Jianlian	.50	1.25
❑ 71 Jordan Farmar	.40	1.00
❑ 72 Udonis Haslem	.50	1.25
❑ 73 Caron Butler	.50	1.25
❑ 74 Craig Smith	.50	1.25
❑ 75 Tayshaun Prince	.50	1.25
❑ 76 Rudy Gay	.50	1.25
❑ 77 Jermaine O'Neal	.50	1.25
❑ 78 Devin Harris	.50	1.25
❑ 79 Fabricio Oberto	.30	.75
❑ 80 Hedo Turkoglu	.50	1.25
❑ 81 James Posey	.40	1.00
❑ 82 Corey Maggette	.50	1.25
❑ 83 Ricky Davis	.50	1.25
❑ 84 Grant Hill	.50	1.25
❑ 85 Eddie House	.30	.75
❑ 86 Jeff Green	.40	1.00
❑ 87 Lamar Odom	.50	1.25
❑ 88 Brandan Wright	.40	1.00
❑ 89 Sean Williams	.40	1.00
❑ 90 Drew Gooden	.40	1.00
❑ 91 Amare Stoudemire	.60	1.50
❑ 92 Charlie Villanueva	.50	1.25
❑ 93 Ron Artest	.50	1.25
❑ 94 Derek Fisher	.50	1.25
❑ 95 Willie Green	.30	.75
❑ 96 Kirk Hinrich	.50	1.25
❑ 97 Jameer Nelson	.40	1.00
❑ 98 Al Harrington	.40	1.00
❑ 99 Ronnie Brewer	.40	1.00
❑ 100 Dwyane Wade	1.00	2.50
❑ 101 Jamal Crawford	.30	.75
❑ 102 Ryan Gomes	.40	1.00
❑ 103 Marcus Camby	.30	.75
❑ 104 Antawn Jamison	.50	1.25
❑ 105 Cuttino Mobley	.40	1.00
❑ 106 Tyson Chandler	.40	1.00
❑ 107 Al Horford	.50	1.25
❑ 108 Chris Wilcox	.40	1.00
❑ 109 Gerald Wallace	.50	1.25
❑ 110 Andrew Bynum	.50	1.25
❑ 111 Tracy McGrady	.60	1.50
❑ 112 Mo Williams	.40	1.00
❑ 113 Nate Robinson	.50	1.25
❑ 114 Wally Szczerbiak	.40	1.00
❑ 115 Vince Carter	.60	1.50
❑ 116 T.J. Ford	.30	.75

❑ 117 Kevin Martin	.50	1.25
❑ 118 Steve Blake	.30	.75
❑ 119 Anderson Varejao	.40	1.00
❑ 120 Mike Conley	.40	1.00
❑ 121 Chris Kaman	.30	.75
❑ 122 Louis Williams	.30	.75
❑ 123 Jason Richardson	.50	1.25
❑ 124 John Salmons	.50	1.25
❑ 125 Martell Webster	.40	1.00
❑ 126 Kurt Thomas	.40	1.00
❑ 127 Raja Bell	.30	.75
❑ 128 Jason Terry	.40	1.00
❑ 129 Corey Brewer	.40	1.00
❑ 130 Bruce Bowen	.30	.75
❑ 131 Glen Davis	.40	1.00
❑ 132 Richard Hamilton	.40	1.00
❑ 133 Ben Wallace	.50	1.25
❑ 134 Chris Bosh	.50	1.25
❑ 135 Beno Udrih	.30	.75
❑ 136 Jarrett Jack	.40	1.00
❑ 137 Stephen Jackson	.40	1.00
❑ 138 Damien Wilkins	.30	.75
❑ 139 Jamaal Tinsley	.30	.75
❑ 140 Deron Williams	.60	1.50
❑ 141 Andres Nocioni	.40	1.00
❑ 142 David Lee	.40	1.00
❑ 143 Rodney Stuckey	.60	1.50
❑ 144 Luke Walton	.40	1.00
❑ 145 Jerry Stackhouse	.40	1.00
❑ 146 Samuel Dalembert	.30	.75
❑ 147 Brandon Roy	.60	1.50
❑ 148 Chauncey Billups	.50	1.25
❑ 149 Michael Finley	.50	1.25
❑ 150 Leandro Barbosa	.40	1.00
❑ 151 Keith Bogans	.30	.75
❑ 152 Mike Bibby	.50	1.25
❑ 153 Troy Murphy	.50	1.25
❑ 154 Eddy Curry	.30	.75
❑ 155 Anthony Parker	.40	1.00
❑ 156 Kevin Durant	1.25	3.00
❑ 157 Larry Hughes	.40	1.00
❑ 158 Peja Stojakovic	.50	1.25
❑ 159 Shane Battier	.40	1.00
❑ 160 Kendrick Perkins	.40	1.00
❑ 161 Mehmet Okur	.50	1.25
❑ 162 Brendan Haywood	.30	.75
❑ 163 Monta Ellis	.50	1.25
❑ 164 J.R. Smith	.40	1.00
❑ 165 Greg Oden	.50	1.25
❑ 166 John Stockton	.75	2.00
❑ 167 Dennis Rodman	.50	1.25
❑ 168 Dominique Wilkins	.60	1.50
❑ 169 Larry Bird	1.50	4.00
❑ 170 Isiah Thomas	.50	1.25
❑ 171 Magic Johnson	1.00	2.50
❑ 172 Bill Russell	.75	2.00
❑ 173 David Robinson	.75	2.00
❑ 174 Jerry West	.60	1.50
❑ 175 Micheal Ray Richardson	.50	1.25
❑ 176 Jo Jo White	.50	1.25
❑ 177 Pete Maravich	1.50	4.00
❑ 178 Wilt Chamberlain	1.00	2.50
❑ 179 Patrick Ewing	.60	1.50
❑ 180 Julius Erving	1.00	2.50
❑ 181 Derrick Rose RC	5.00	12.00
❑ 182 Michael Beasley RC	2.50	6.00
❑ 183 O.J. Mayo RC	2.00	5.00
❑ 184 Russell Westbrook RC	3.00	8.00
❑ 185 Kevin Love RC	1.50	4.00
❑ 186 Danilo Gallinari RC	2.00	5.00
❑ 187 Eric Gordon RC	1.50	4.00
❑ 188 Joe Alexander RC	1.25	3.00
❑ 189 D.J. Augustin RC	1.25	3.00
❑ 190 Brook Lopez RC	2.50	6.00
❑ 191 Jerryd Bayless RC	1.25	3.00
❑ 192 Jason Thompson RC	1.25	3.00
❑ 193 Anthony Randolph RC	2.00	5.00
❑ 194 Robin Lopez RC	1.25	3.00
❑ 195 Marreese Speights RC	1.25	3.00
❑ 196 Roy Hibbert RC	1.50	4.00
❑ 197 JaVale McGee RC	1.25	3.00
❑ 198 J.J. Hickson RC	2.00	5.00
❑ 199 Alexis Ajinca RC	1.25	3.00
❑ 200 Ryan Anderson RC	1.25	3.00
❑ 201 Courtney Lee RC	2.00	5.00
❑ 202 Kosta Koufos RC	1.25	3.00
❑ 203 Donte Greene RC	1.25	3.00
❑ 204 George Hill RC	2.00	5.00
❑ 205 D.J. White RC	1.25	3.00

❑ 206 J.R. Giddens RC	1.25	3.00
❑ 207 Joey Dorsey RC	1.25	3.00
❑ 208 Mario Chalmers RC	1.50	4.00
❑ 209 DeAndre Jordan RC	1.25	3.00
❑ 210 Chris Douglas-Roberts RC	1.50	4.00
❑ 211 Malik Hairston RC	1.25	3.00
❑ 212 Marc Gasol RC	2.00	5.00
❑ 213 Kyle Weaver RC	1.25	3.00
❑ 214 Patrick Ewing Jr. RC	1.25	3.00
❑ 215 Walter Sharpe RC	1.25	3.00
❑ 216 Sonny Weems RC	1.25	3.00
❑ 217 Trent Plaisted RC	1.25	3.00
❑ 218 Nicolas Batum RC	1.50	4.00
❑ 219 Brandon Rush RC	1.25	3.00
❑ 220 Darrell Arthur RC	1.25	3.00

2009-10 Topps Chrome

❑ 1 Joe Johnson	.50	1.25
❑ 2 Josh Smith	.50	1.25
❑ 3 Mike Bibby	.30	.75
❑ 4 Marvin Williams	.40	1.00
❑ 5 Al Horford	.50	1.25
❑ 6 Paul Pierce	.60	1.50
❑ 7 Ray Allen	.50	1.25
❑ 8 Kevin Garnett	1.00	2.50
❑ 9 Rajon Rondo	.50	1.25
❑ 10 Glen Davis	.40	1.00
❑ 11 Gerald Wallace	.50	1.25
❑ 12 Raymond Felton	.40	1.00
❑ 13 Ben Gordon	.50	1.25
❑ 14 Derrick Rose	1.00	2.50
❑ 15 Luol Deng	.50	1.25
❑ 16 LeBron James	2.50	6.00
❑ 17 Mo Williams	.40	1.00
❑ 18 Anderson Varejao	.40	1.00
❑ 19 Daniel Gibson	.50	1.25
❑ 20 Ben Wallace	.50	1.25
❑ 21 Dirk Nowitzki	.60	1.50
❑ 22 Jason Terry	.40	1.00
❑ 23 Josh Howard	.50	1.25
❑ 24 Jason Kidd	.50	1.25
❑ 25 Carmelo Anthony	.60	1.50
❑ 26 Chauncey Billups	.50	1.25
❑ 27 J.R. Smith	.40	1.00
❑ 28 Allen Iverson	.60	1.50
❑ 29 Richard Hamilton	.40	1.00
❑ 30 Tayshaun Prince	.50	1.25
❑ 31 Corey Maggette	.40	1.00
❑ 32 Monta Ellis	.50	1.25
❑ 33 Anthony Randolph	.50	1.25
❑ 34 Yao Ming	.60	1.50
❑ 35 Ron Artest	.50	1.25
❑ 36 Tracy McGrady	.60	1.50
❑ 37 Shane Battier	.40	1.00
❑ 38 Danny Granger	.50	1.25
❑ 39 T.J. Ford	.30	.75
❑ 40 Troy Murphy	.30	.75
❑ 41 Al Thornton	.50	1.25
❑ 42 Baron Davis	.50	1.25
❑ 43 Eric Gordon	.50	1.25
❑ 44 Kobe Bryant	2.50	6.00
❑ 45 Pau Gasol	.50	1.25
❑ 46 Andrew Bynum	.50	1.25
❑ 47 Lamar Odom	.50	1.25
❑ 48 O.J. Mayo	.60	1.50
❑ 49 Rudy Gay	.50	1.25
❑ 50 Marc Gasol	.50	1.25
❑ 51 Dwyane Wade	1.00	2.50
❑ 52 Michael Beasley	.60	1.50
❑ 53 Michael Redd	.50	1.25
❑ 54 Richard Jefferson	.50	1.25
❑ 55 Andrew Bogut	.50	1.25
❑ 56 Al Jefferson	.50	1.25
❑ 57 Kevin Love	.40	1.00
❑ 58 Mike Miller	.50	1.25
❑ 59 Devin Harris	.50	1.25

❑ 60 Vince Carter	.60	1.50
❑ 61 Brook Lopez	.30	.75
❑ 62 Yi Jianlian	.50	1.25
❑ 63 Chris Paul	1.00	2.50
❑ 64 David West	.50	1.25
❑ 65 David Lee	.40	1.00
❑ 66 Nate Robinson	.50	1.25
❑ 67 Russell Westbrook	.50	1.25
❑ 68 Kevin Durant	1.25	3.00
❑ 69 Dwight Howard	1.00	2.50
❑ 70 Rashard Lewis	.50	1.25
❑ 71 Hedo Turkoglu	.50	1.25
❑ 72 Jameer Nelson	.40	1.00
❑ 73 Andre Iguodala	.50	1.25
❑ 74 Elton Brand	.50	1.25
❑ 75 Thaddeus Young	.30	.75
❑ 76 Amare Stoudemire	.60	1.50
❑ 77 Shaquille O'Neal	1.00	2.50
❑ 78 Jason Richardson	.50	1.25
❑ 79 Steve Nash	.50	1.25
❑ 80 Brandon Roy	.60	1.50
❑ 81 LaMarcus Aldridge	.50	1.25
❑ 82 Rudy Fernandez	.50	1.25
❑ 83 Greg Oden	.40	1.00
❑ 84 Kevin Martin	.50	1.25
❑ 85 Tony Parker	.50	1.25
❑ 86 Tim Duncan	.75	2.00
❑ 87 Manu Ginobili	.50	1.25
❑ 88 Chris Bosh	.50	1.25
❑ 89 Andrea Bargnani	.40	1.00
❑ 90 Shawn Marion	.50	1.25
❑ 91 Jose Calderon	.40	1.00
❑ 92 Carlos Boozer	.50	1.25
❑ 93 Deron Williams	.60	1.50
❑ 94 Antawn Jamison	.50	1.25
❑ 95 Gilbert Arenas	.50	1.25
❑ 96 Blake Griffin RC	8.00	20.00
❑ 97 Ricky Rubio RC	5.00	12.00
❑ 98 Hasheem Thabeet RC	3.00	8.00
❑ 99 James Harden RC	6.00	15.00
❑ 100 DeMar DeRozan RC	5.00	12.00
❑ 101 Stephen Curry RC	8.00	20.00
❑ 102 Brandon Jennings RC	10.00	25.00
❑ 103 Jordan Hill RC	4.00	10.00
❑ 104 Earl Clark RC	5.00	12.00
❑ 105 Gerald Henderson RC	5.00	12.00
❑ 106 Jonny Flynn RC	5.00	12.00
❑ 107 Tyreke Evans RC	12.00	30.00
❑ 108 Tyler Hansbrough RC	5.00	12.00
❑ 109 Terrence Williams RC	6.00	15.00
❑ 110 Jrue Holiday RC	5.00	12.00

2003-04 Topps Contemporary Collection

❑ COMMON ROOKIE (1-20)	3.00	8.00
❑ COMMON AU RC (21-30)	6.00	15.00
❑ COMMON CARD (31-130)	.60	1.50
❑ COMMON AU (131-140)	6.00	15.00
❑ 1 LeBron James RC	30.00	80.00
❑ 2 Darko Milicic RC	3.00	8.00
❑ 3 Chris Bosh RC	4.00	10.00
❑ 4 Dwyane Wade RC	6.00	15.00
❑ 5 Chris Kaman RC	3.00	8.00
❑ 6 Kirk Hinrich RC	3.00	8.00
❑ 7 Jarvis Hayes RC	2.50	6.00
❑ 8 Mickael Pietrus RC	3.00	8.00
❑ 9 Luke Ridnour RC	3.00	8.00
❑ 10 David West RC	3.00	8.00
❑ 11 Aleksandar Pavlovic RC	3.00	8.00
❑ 12 Boris Diaw RC	3.00	8.00
❑ 13 Zoran Planinic RC	2.50	6.00
❑ 14 Francisco Elson RC	2.50	6.00
❑ 15 Leandro Barbosa RC	3.00	8.00
❑ 16 Josh Howard RC	3.00	8.00
❑ 17 Luke Walton RC	3.00	8.00
❑ 18 Willie Green RC	2.50	6.00
❑ 19 Maurice Williams RC	4.00	10.00
❑ 20 Udonis Haslem RC	3.00	8.00
❑ 21 Reece Gaines AU RC	6.00	15.00
❑ 22 Carmelo Anthony AU RC	40.00	80.00
❑ 23 Zarko Cabarkapa AU RC	6.00	15.00
❑ 24 Troy Bell AU RC	6.00	15.00
❑ 25 Travis Outlaw AU RC	8.00	20.00
❑ 26 Marcus Banks AU RC	6.00	15.00
❑ 27 Kendrick Perkins AU RC	10.00	25.00
❑ 28 Dahntay Jones AU RC	6.00	15.00
❑ 29 T.J. Ford AU RC	10.00	25.00
❑ 30 Mike Sweetney AU RC	6.00	15.00
❑ 31 Jason Terry	.75	2.00
❑ 32 Theo Ratliff	.60	1.50
❑ 33 Raef LaFrentz	.60	1.50
❑ 34 Eddy Curry	.75	2.00
❑ 35 Ricky Davis	.75	2.00
❑ 36 Zydrunas Ilgauskas	.75	2.00
❑ 37 Darius Miles	.75	2.00
❑ 38 Dirk Nowitzki	1.50	4.00
❑ 39 Steve Nash	1.50	4.00
❑ 40 Antawn Jamison	1.00	2.50
❑ 41 Antoine Walker	1.00	2.50
❑ 42 Andre Miller	.75	2.00
❑ 43 Nene	.75	2.00
❑ 44 Richard Hamilton	.75	2.00
❑ 45 Ben Wallace	.75	2.00
❑ 46 Jason Richardson	1.00	2.50
❑ 47 Nick Van Exel	.75	2.00
❑ 48 Troy Murphy	1.00	2.50
❑ 49 Yao Ming	2.00	5.00
❑ 50 Steve Francis	1.00	2.50
❑ 51 Ron Artest	.75	2.00
❑ 52 Jermaine O'Neal	1.00	2.50
❑ 53 Al Harrington	.75	2.00
❑ 54 Marko Jaric	.60	1.50
❑ 55 Corey Maggette	.60	1.50
❑ 56 Kobe Bryant	5.00	12.00
❑ 57 Shaquille O'Neal	2.50	6.00
❑ 58 Devean George	.60	1.50
❑ 59 Gary Payton	1.00	2.50
❑ 60 Pau Gasol	1.00	2.50
❑ 61 Stromile Swift	.60	1.50
❑ 62 Mike Miller	.75	2.00
❑ 63 Lamar Odom	1.00	2.50
❑ 64 Caron Butler	.75	2.00
❑ 65 Eddie Jones	.75	2.00
❑ 66 Brian Grant	.60	1.50
❑ 67 Desmond Mason	.75	2.00
❑ 68 Tim Thomas	.60	1.50
❑ 69 Michael Redd	1.00	2.50
❑ 70 Sam Cassell	.75	2.00
❑ 71 Kevin Garnett	2.00	5.00
❑ 72 Latrell Sprewell	.75	2.00
❑ 73 Michael Olowokandi	.60	1.50
❑ 74 Wally Szczerbiak	.75	2.00
❑ 75 Richard Jefferson	1.00	2.50
❑ 76 Kenyon Martin	1.00	2.50
❑ 77 Alonzo Mourning	1.00	2.50
❑ 78 Baron Davis	1.00	2.50
❑ 79 Jamal Mashburn	.60	1.50
❑ 80 Allan Houston	.75	2.00
❑ 81 Keith Van Horn	.75	2.00
❑ 82 Kurt Thomas	.60	1.50
❑ 83 Tracy McGrady	2.00	5.00
❑ 84 Juwan Howard	.75	2.00
❑ 85 Drew Gooden	.60	1.50
❑ 86 Allen Iverson	2.00	5.00
❑ 87 Glenn Robinson	.75	2.00
❑ 88 Derrick Coleman	.75	2.00
❑ 89 Stephon Marbury	1.00	2.50
❑ 90 Shawn Marion	1.00	2.50
❑ 91 Amare Stoudemire	2.00	5.00
❑ 92 Zach Randolph	1.00	2.50
❑ 93 Rasheed Wallace	1.00	2.50
❑ 94 Bonzi Wells	.60	1.50
❑ 95 Mike Bibby	.75	2.00
❑ 96 Chris Webber	1.00	2.50
❑ 97 Brad Miller	.75	2.00
❑ 98 Tim Duncan	2.00	5.00
❑ 99 Rasho Nesterovic	.60	1.50
❑ 100 Tony Parker	1.00	2.50
❑ 101 Manu Ginobili	1.00	2.50
❑ 102 Brent Barry	.60	1.50
❑ 103 Rashard Lewis	1.00	2.50
❑ 104 Ray Allen	.60	1.50
❑ 105 Vince Carter	2.00	5.00
❑ 106 Jerome Williams	.60	1.50
❑ 107 Carlos Arroyo	.60	1.50
❑ 108 Matt Harpring	.75	2.00
❑ 109 Andrei Kirilenko	1.00	2.50
❑ 110 Gilbert Arenas	1.00	2.50
❑ 111 Kwame Brown	.60	1.50
❑ 112 Jerry Stackhouse	.75	2.00
❑ 113 Darrell Armstrong	.60	1.50
❑ 114 Alvin Williams	.60	1.50
❑ 115 Kelvin Cato	.60	1.50
❑ 116 Stephen Jackson	.75	2.00
❑ 117 Shareef Abdur-Rahim	.75	2.00
❑ 118 Eric Williams	.60	1.50
❑ 119 Tony Battie	.60	1.50
❑ 120 Tyson Chandler	.75	2.00
❑ 121 Scottie Pippen	1.50	4.00
❑ 122 Nikoloz Tskitishvili	.60	1.50
❑ 123 Chauncey Billups	1.00	2.50
❑ 124 Quentin Richardson	.75	2.00
❑ 125 Dikembe Mutombo	.75	2.00
❑ 126 Joe Smith	.60	1.50
❑ 127 Qyntel Woods	.60	1.50
❑ 128 Dajuan Wagner	.60	1.50
❑ 129 Robert Horry	.75	2.00
❑ 130 Cuttino Mobley	.75	2.00
❑ 131 Bobby Jackson AU	6.00	15.00
❑ 132 Elton Brand AU	6.00	15.00
❑ 133 Peja Stojakovic AU	6.00	15.00
❑ 134 Jamal Crawford AU	6.00	15.00
❑ 135 Jalen Rose AU	6.00	15.00
❑ 136 Paul Pierce AU	12.50	30.00
❑ 137 Jason Kidd AU	12.50	30.00
❑ 138 Tayshaun Prince AU	8.00	20.00
❑ 139 Morris Peterson AU	6.00	15.00
❑ 140 Speedy Claxton AU	6.00	15.00

2007-08 Topps Co-Signers

❑ COMP.SET w/o SP's (50)	20.00	40.00
❑ COMMON CARD (1-50)	.40	1.00
❑ COMMON ROOKIE (51-100)	2.00	5.00
❑ ROOKIE PRINT RUN 499 SER.#'d SETS		
❑ 1 Dwyane Wade	1.00	2.50
❑ 2 Chauncey Billups	.40	1.00
❑ 3 Allen Iverson	.75	2.00
❑ 4 Amare Stoudemire	.75	2.00
❑ 5 Jason Kidd	.60	1.50
❑ 6 Dirk Nowitzki	.60	1.50
❑ 7 Jermaine O'Neal	.40	1.00
❑ 8 Elton Brand	.40	1.00
❑ 9 Carlos Boozer	.40	1.00
❑ 10 Ray Allen	.40	1.00
❑ 11 Yao Ming	1.00	2.50
❑ 12 Dwight Howard	.75	2.00
❑ 13 Steve Nash	.50	1.25
❑ 14 Chris Paul	.75	2.00
❑ 15 Carmelo Anthony	.75	2.00
❑ 16 Pau Gasol	.40	1.00
❑ 17 Ben Gordon	.50	1.25
❑ 18 Andre Iguodala	.40	1.00
❑ 19 Paul Pierce	.40	1.00
❑ 20 Tracy McGrady	.75	2.00
❑ 21 Tim Duncan	.75	2.00
❑ 22 Josh Smith	.40	1.00
❑ 23 LeBron James	2.00	5.00
❑ 24 Kobe Bryant	2.00	5.00
❑ 25 Vince Carter	.75	2.00
❑ 26 Shaquille O'Neal	1.00	2.50
❑ 27 Kevin Garnett	1.00	2.50
❑ 28 Chris Bosh	.40	1.00
❑ 29 Baron Davis	.40	1.00
❑ 30 Gilbert Arenas	.40	1.00
❑ 31 John Stockton	1.00	2.50
❑ 32 Magic Johnson	1.25	3.00
❑ 33 Larry Bird	2.00	5.00
❑ 34 Rick Barry	.60	1.50

❑ 35 Isiah Thomas	.60	1.50
❑ 36 Dominique Wilkins	.75	2.00
❑ 37 Dennis Rodman	.60	1.50
❑ 38 Wilt Chamberlain	1.25	3.00
❑ 39 Pete Maravich	2.00	5.00
❑ 40 Bill Russell	1.00	2.50
❑ 41 Byron Scott	.60	1.50
❑ 42 Karl Malone	.75	2.00
❑ 43 Chris Mullin	.60	1.50
❑ 44 Kevin McHale	.75	2.00
❑ 45 Clyde Drexler	.75	2.00
❑ 46 James Worthy	.75	2.00
❑ 47 Bill Walton	.60	1.50
❑ 48 Earl Monroe	.60	1.50
❑ 49 Elgin Baylor	.60	1.50
❑ 50 David Robinson	1.00	2.50
❑ 51 Nick Young RC	2.00	5.00
❑ 52 Greg Oden RC	3.00	8.00
❑ 53 Morris Almond RC	2.00	5.00
❑ 54 Alando Tucker RC	2.00	5.00
❑ 55 Arron Afflalo RC	2.00	5.00
❑ 56 Derrick Byars RC	2.00	5.00
❑ 57 Adam Haluska RC	2.00	5.00
❑ 58 Corey Brewer RC	2.50	6.00
❑ 59 Ramon Sessions RC	2.50	6.00
❑ 60 Daequan Cook RC	2.50	6.00
❑ 61 Michael Conley RC	2.50	6.00
❑ 62 Javaris Crittenton RC	2.00	5.00
❑ 63 Jared Jordan RC	2.00	5.00
❑ 64 Aaron Brooks RC	3.00	8.00
❑ 65 Marco Belinelli RC	2.00	5.00
❑ 66 Sammy Mejia RC	2.00	5.00
❑ 67 Jared Dudley RC	2.00	5.00
❑ 68 Rodney Stuckey RC	4.00	10.00
❑ 69 JamesOn Curry RC	2.00	5.00
❑ 70 Gabe Pruitt RC	2.00	5.00
❑ 71 Acie Law IV RC	2.50	6.00
❑ 72 Dominic McGuire RC	2.00	5.00
❑ 73 Herbert Hill RC	2.00	5.00
❑ 74 Jeff Green RC	2.50	6.00
❑ 75 Wilson Chandler RC	2.00	5.00
❑ 76 Marcus Williams RC	2.00	5.00
❑ 77 Josh McRoberts RC	2.50	6.00
❑ 78 Thaddeus Young RC	2.50	6.00
❑ 79 Jared Newson RC	2.00	5.00
❑ 80 Stephane Lasme RC	2.00	5.00
❑ 81 Demetris Nichols RC	2.00	5.00
❑ 82 Julian Wright RC	2.50	6.00
❑ 83 Sean Williams RC	2.00	5.00
❑ 84 Chris Richard RC	2.00	5.00
❑ 85 Yi Jianlian RC	3.00	8.00
❑ 86 Al Thornton RC	2.00	5.00
❑ 87 Carl Landry RC	2.00	5.00
❑ 88 Kevin Durant RC	15.00	40.00
❑ 89 Brandan Wright RC	2.50	6.00
❑ 90 Nick Fazekas RC	2.00	5.00
❑ 91 Joakim Noah RC	2.50	6.00
❑ 92 Jermareo Davidson RC	2.00	5.00
❑ 93 D.J. Strawberry RC	2.00	5.00
❑ 94 Glen Davis RC	4.00	10.00
❑ 95 Al Horford RC	2.50	6.00
❑ 96 Spencer Hawes RC	2.00	5.00
❑ 97 Taurean Green RC	2.00	5.00
❑ 98 Jason Smith RC	2.00	5.00
❑ 99 Luis Scola RC	3.00	8.00
❑ 100 Aaron Gray RC	2.00	5.00

2008-09 Topps Co-Signers

❑ COMP.SET w/o RC's (100)	25.00	50.00
❑ 1 Tracy McGrady	.60	1.50
❑ 2 Jason Kidd	.50	1.25
❑ 3 Allen Iverson	.60	1.50
❑ 4 Chris Bosh	.50	1.25
❑ 5 Baron Davis	.50	1.25
❑ 6 Chauncey Billups	.50	1.25
❑ 7 Ben Gordon	.50	1.25
❑ 8 Jermaine O'Neal	.50	1.25
❑ 9 Jason Richardson	.50	1.25
❑ 10 Gilbert Arenas	.50	1.25
❑ 11 Jamal Crawford	.30	.75
❑ 12 Dwight Howard	1.00	2.50
❑ 13 Steve Nash	.50	1.25
❑ 14 Vince Carter	.60	1.50
❑ 15 Carmelo Anthony	.60	1.50
❑ 16 Pau Gasol	.50	1.25
❑ 17 Josh Smith	.50	1.25
❑ 18 Yi Jianlian	.50	1.25
❑ 19 Andre Iguodala	.50	1.25
❑ 20 Ray Allen	.50	1.25
❑ 21 Tim Duncan	.75	2.00
❑ 22 Tayshaun Prince	.50	1.25
❑ 23 LeBron James	2.50	6.00
❑ 24 Kobe Bryant	2.50	6.00
❑ 25 Rudy Gay	.50	1.25
❑ 26 Caron Butler	.50	1.25
❑ 27 Al Jefferson	.50	1.25
❑ 28 Deron Williams	.60	1.50
❑ 29 Luol Deng	.50	1.25
❑ 30 Chris Paul	1.00	2.50
❑ 31 Brad Miller	.50	1.25
❑ 32 Shaquille O'Neal	1.00	2.50
❑ 33 Dwyane Wade	1.00	2.50
❑ 34 Paul Pierce	.60	1.50
❑ 35 Kevin Durant	1.25	3.00
❑ 36 Anderson Varejao	.40	1.00
❑ 37 Rashard Lewis	.50	1.25
❑ 38 Jamario Moon	.50	1.25
❑ 39 Manu Ginobili	.50	1.25
❑ 40 Mo Williams	.40	1.00
❑ 41 Dirk Nowitzki	.60	1.50
❑ 42 David Lee	.40	1.00
❑ 43 Stephen Jackson	.40	1.00
❑ 44 Antawn Jamison	.50	1.25
❑ 45 Mike Dunleavy	.40	1.00
❑ 46 Devin Harris	.50	1.25
❑ 47 Andrei Kirilenko	.50	1.25
❑ 48 Gerald Wallace	.50	1.25
❑ 49 Mike Miller	.50	1.25
❑ 50 Corey Maggette	.50	1.25
❑ 51 Yao Ming	.60	1.50
❑ 52 Greg Oden	.50	1.25
❑ 53 Kevin Martin	.50	1.25
❑ 54 Joe Johnson	.50	1.25
❑ 55 Kevin Garnett	1.00	2.50
❑ 56 Ricky Davis	.50	1.25
❑ 57 Chris Wilcox	.40	1.00
❑ 58 Rashad McCants	.40	1.00
❑ 59 T.J. Ford	.30	.75
❑ 60 David West	.50	1.25
❑ 61 Amare Stoudemire	.60	1.50
❑ 62 Al Thornton	.50	1.25
❑ 63 Kirk Hinrich	.50	1.25
❑ 64 Samuel Dalembert	.30	.75
❑ 65 Tony Parker	.50	1.25
❑ 66 Ben Wallace	.50	1.25
❑ 67 Shawn Marion	.50	1.25
❑ 68 LaMarcus Aldridge	.50	1.25
❑ 69 Eddy Curry	.30	.75
❑ 70 Richard Hamilton	.40	1.00
❑ 71 Danny Granger	.50	1.25
❑ 72 Elton Brand	.75	2.00
❑ 73 Raymond Felton	.40	1.00
❑ 74 Richard Jefferson	.50	1.25
❑ 75 Hedo Turkoglu	.50	1.25
❑ 76 Peja Stojakovic	.50	1.25
❑ 77 Brandon Roy	.60	1.50
❑ 78 Ryan Gomes	.40	1.00
❑ 79 Jeff Green	.40	1.00
❑ 80 Michael Redd	.50	1.25
❑ 81 Andre Miller	.40	1.00
❑ 82 Carlos Boozer	.50	1.25
❑ 83 Marcus Camby	.30	.75
❑ 84 Hakim Warrick	.30	.75
❑ 85 Mike Bibby	.50	1.25
❑ 86 Josh Howard	.50	1.25
❑ 87 Andrew Bynum	.50	1.25
❑ 88 Monta Ellis	.50	1.25
❑ 89 Shane Battier	.40	1.00
❑ 90 Ron Artest	.50	1.25
❑ 91 Dennis Rodman	.50	1.25
❑ 92 Dominique Wilkins	.60	1.50
❑ 93 Larry Bird	1.50	4.00
❑ 94 John Stockton	.75	2.00
❑ 95 Moses Malone	.50	1.25
❑ 96 David Robinson	.75	2.00
❑ 97 Jerry West	.60	1.50
❑ 98 Bill Russell	.75	2.00
❑ 99 George Gervin	.60	1.50
❑ 100 Magic Johnson	1.00	2.50
❑ 101 Derrick Rose RC	4.00	10.00
❑ 102 Michael Beasley RC	2.00	5.00
❑ 103 O.J. Mayo RC	1.50	4.00
❑ 104 Russell Westbrook RC	2.50	6.00
❑ 105 Kevin Love RC	1.25	3.00
❑ 106 Danilo Gallinari RC	1.50	4.00
❑ 107 Eric Gordon RC	1.25	3.00
❑ 108 Joe Alexander RC	1.00	2.50
❑ 109 D.J. Augustin RC	1.00	2.50
❑ 110 Brook Lopez RC	2.00	5.00
❑ 111 Jerryd Bayless RC	1.00	2.50
❑ 112 Jason Thompson RC	1.00	2.50
❑ 113 Anthony Randolph RC	1.50	4.00
❑ 114 Robin Lopez RC	1.00	2.50
❑ 115 Marreese Speights RC	1.00	2.50
❑ 116 Roy Hibbert RC	1.25	3.00
❑ 117 JaVale McGee RC	1.00	2.50
❑ 118 J.J. Hickson RC	1.50	4.00
❑ 119 Alexis Ajinca RC	1.00	2.50
❑ 120 Ryan Anderson RC	1.00	2.50
❑ 121 Courtney Lee RC	1.50	4.00
❑ 122 Kosta Koufos RC	1.00	2.50
❑ 123 Donte Greene RC	1.00	2.50
❑ 124 George Hill RC	1.50	4.00
❑ 125 D.J. White RC	1.00	2.50
❑ 126 J.R. Giddens RC	1.00	2.50
❑ 127 Joey Dorsey RC	1.00	2.50
❑ 128 Mario Chalmers RC	1.25	3.00
❑ 129 DeAndre Jordan RC	1.00	2.50
❑ 130 Chris Douglas-Roberts RC	1.25	3.00
❑ 131 Malik Hairston RC	1.00	2.50
❑ 132 Sonny Weems RC	1.00	2.50
❑ 133 Kyle Weaver RC	1.00	2.50
❑ 134 Patrick Ewing Jr. RC	1.00	2.50
❑ 135 Mike Taylor RC	1.00	2.50
❑ 136 Walter Sharpe RC	1.00	2.50
❑ 137 Rudy Fernandez RC	2.00	5.00
❑ 138 Nicolas Batum RC	1.25	3.00
❑ 139 Brandon Rush RC	1.00	2.50
❑ 140 Darrell Arthur RC	1.00	2.50

2007-08 Topps Echelon

❑ 1 Tracy McGrady	2.50	6.00
❑ 2 Chris Paul	2.50	6.00
❑ 3 Dwyane Wade	3.00	8.00
❑ 4 Elton Brand	1.25	3.00
❑ 5 Josh Smith	1.25	3.00
❑ 6 Brandon Roy	2.00	5.00
❑ 7 Andrea Bargnani	1.50	4.00
❑ 8 Deron Williams	2.00	5.00
❑ 9 Andre Iguodala	1.25	3.00
❑ 10 Mike Bibby	1.25	3.00
❑ 11 Yao Ming	3.00	8.00
❑ 12 Dwight Howard	2.50	6.00
❑ 13 Steve Nash	1.50	4.00
❑ 14 Randy Foye	1.25	3.00
❑ 15 Carmelo Anthony	2.50	6.00
❑ 16 Pau Gasol	1.25	3.00
❑ 17 Jermaine O'Neal	1.25	3.00
❑ 18 Ben Gordon	1.50	4.00
❑ 19 Vince Carter	2.50	6.00
❑ 20 Tim Duncan	2.50	6.00
❑ 21 Kevin Garnett	3.00	8.00
❑ 22 Michael Redd	1.25	3.00
❑ 23 LeBron James	6.00	15.00
❑ 24 Kobe Bryant	6.00	15.00
❑ 25 Chris Webber	1.25	3.00
❑ 26 Allen Iverson	2.50	6.00
❑ 27 Chauncey Billups	1.25	3.00
❑ 28 Paul Pierce	1.25	3.00

❑ 29 Amare Stoudemire	2.50	6.00
❑ 30 Emeka Okafor	1.25	3.00
❑ 31 Jason Kidd	2.00	5.00
❑ 32 Shaquille O'Neal	3.00	8.00
❑ 33 Grant Hill	1.25	3.00
❑ 34 Ray Allen	1.25	3.00
❑ 35 Adam Morrison	1.25	3.00
❑ 36 Gilbert Arenas	1.25	3.00
❑ 37 Baron Davis	1.25	3.00
❑ 38 Mike Miller	1.25	3.00
❑ 39 Chris Bosh	1.25	3.00
❑ 40 Dirk Nowitzki	2.00	5.00
❑ 41 Bob Pettit	2.00	5.00
❑ 42 Bill Russell	2.50	6.00
❑ 43 Rick Barry	1.50	4.00
❑ 44 Oscar Robertson	1.50	4.00
❑ 45 Jerry Lucas	1.50	4.00
❑ 46 Magic Johnson	3.00	8.00
❑ 47 Larry Bird	5.00	12.00
❑ 48 Wes Unseld	1.50	4.00
❑ 49 James Worthy	2.00	5.00
❑ 50 Bob McAdoo	1.50	4.00
❑ 51 Greg Oden RC	8.00	20.00
❑ 52 Yi Jianlian RC	8.00	20.00
❑ 53 Brandan Wright RC	6.00	15.00
❑ 54 Nick Young RC	5.00	12.00
❑ 55 Spencer Hawes RC	4.00	10.00
❑ 56 Acie Law RC	5.00	12.00
❑ 57 Rodney Stuckey RC	8.00	20.00
❑ 58 Al Thornton RC	4.00	10.00
❑ 59 Arron Afflalo RC	4.00	10.00
❑ 60 Marco Belinelli RC	4.00	10.00
❑ 61 Gabe Pruitt RC	4.00	10.00
❑ 62 Wilson Chandler RC	4.00	10.00
❑ 63 Jared Dudley RC	4.00	10.00
❑ 64 Marcus Williams RC	4.00	10.00
❑ 65 Aaron Brooks RC	6.00	15.00
❑ 66 Daequan Cook RC	5.00	12.00
❑ 67 Thaddeus Young RC	5.00	12.00
❑ 68 Josh McRoberts RC	5.00	12.00
❑ 69 Nick Fazekas RC	4.00	10.00
❑ 70 Javaris Crittenton RC	4.00	10.00
❑ 71 Alando Tucker RC	4.00	10.00
❑ 72 Carl Landry RC	4.00	10.00
❑ 73 Al Horford RC	4.00	10.00
❑ 74 Kevin Durant RC	25.00	60.00
❑ 75 Corey Brewer RC	4.00	10.00
❑ 76 Jeff Green RC	4.00	10.00
❑ 77 Mike Conley RC	4.00	10.00
❑ 78 Joakim Noah RC	4.00	10.00
❑ 79 Sean Williams RC	3.00	8.00
❑ 80 Julian Wright RC	4.00	10.00
❑ 81 Reyshawn Terry RC	3.00	8.00
❑ 82 Aaron Gray RC	3.00	8.00
❑ 83 Glen Davis RC	6.00	15.00
❑ 84 Jermareo Davidson RC	3.00	8.00
❑ 85 Taurean Green RC	3.00	8.00

2005-06 Topps First Row

❑ COMP.SET (100)		
❑ COMMON CARD (1-100)	.30	.75
❑ COMMON ROOKIE (101-145)	2.50	6.00
❑ COMMON CELEBRITY (146-150)	4.00	10.00
❑ 1 Shaquille O'Neal	1.25	3.00
❑ 2 Marcus Camby	.40	1.00
❑ 3 Caron Butler	.50	1.25
❑ 4 Carlos Boozer	.50	1.25
❑ 5 Peja Stojakovic	.50	1.25
❑ 6 Chris Webber	.50	1.25
❑ 7 Vince Carter	1.00	2.50
❑ 8 Bobby Simmons	.30	.75
❑ 9 Pau Gasol	.50	1.25
❑ 10 Stromile Swift	.40	1.00
❑ 11 Carmelo Anthony	1.00	2.50
❑ 12 Drew Gooden	.40	1.00
❑ 13 Al Harrington	.30	.75
❑ 14 Emeka Okafor	.50	1.25
❑ 15 Gilbert Arenas	.50	1.25
❑ 16 Tony Parker	.50	1.25
❑ 17 Steve Nash	.60	1.50
❑ 18 Jamal Crawford	.40	1.00
❑ 19 Troy Hudson	.30	.75
❑ 20 Kobe Bryant	2.50	6.00
❑ 21 Tracy McGrady	1.00	2.50
❑ 22 Chauncey Billups	.50	1.25
❑ 23 Devin Harris	.50	1.25
❑ 24 Brevin Knight	.30	.75
❑ 25 Joe Johnson	.50	1.25
❑ 26 Nenad Krstic	.40	1.00
❑ 27 Primoz Brezec	.30	.75
❑ 28 Mehmet Okur	.30	.75
❑ 29 Shareef Abdur-Rahim	.50	1.25
❑ 30 Amare Stoudemire	1.00	2.50
❑ 31 Quentin Richardson	.40	1.00
❑ 32 Kevin Garnett	1.00	2.50
❑ 33 Shane Battier	.50	1.25
❑ 34 Elton Brand	.50	1.25
❑ 35 Kenyon Martin	.50	1.25
❑ 36 LeBron James	2.50	6.00
❑ 37 Al Jefferson	.50	1.25
❑ 38 Jermaine O'Neal	.50	1.25
❑ 39 Ron Artest	.40	1.00
❑ 40 Luke Ridnour	.40	1.00
❑ 41 Sebastian Telfair	.40	1.00
❑ 42 Steve Francis	.50	1.25
❑ 43 Jason Kidd	.75	2.00
❑ 44 Ben Wallace	.50	1.25
❑ 45 Mike Miller	.50	1.25
❑ 46 Jamaal Tinsley	.40	1.00
❑ 47 Richard Hamilton	.40	1.00
❑ 48 Jerry Stackhouse	.50	1.25
❑ 49 Kirk Hinrich	.50	1.25
❑ 50 Josh Childress	.40	1.00
❑ 51 Jamaal Magloire	.30	.75
❑ 52 Yao Ming	1.25	3.00
❑ 53 Tyson Chandler	.50	1.25
❑ 54 Andrei Kirilenko	.50	1.25
❑ 55 Rashard Lewis	.50	1.25
❑ 56 Shawn Marion	.50	1.25
❑ 57 Grant Hill	.50	1.25
❑ 58 Wally Szczerbiak	.40	1.00
❑ 59 Antoine Walker	.40	1.00
❑ 60 Corey Maggette	.40	1.00
❑ 61 Rasheed Wallace	.50	1.25
❑ 62 Dirk Nowitzki	.75	2.00
❑ 63 Paul Pierce	.50	1.25
❑ 64 Tim Duncan	1.00	2.50
❑ 65 Desmond Mason	.30	.75
❑ 66 Ray Allen	.50	1.25
❑ 67 Mike Bibby	.50	1.25
❑ 68 Andre Iguodala	.50	1.25
❑ 69 J.R. Smith	.40	1.00
❑ 70 Dwyane Wade	1.25	3.00
❑ 71 Shaun Livingston	.30	.75
❑ 72 Jason Richardson	.50	1.25
❑ 73 Earl Boykins	.30	.75
❑ 74 Ben Gordon	.60	1.50
❑ 75 Stephen Jackson	.40	1.00
❑ 76 Samuel Dalembert	.30	.75
❑ 77 Kwame Brown	.40	1.00
❑ 78 Zydrunas Ilgauskas	.40	1.00
❑ 79 Antawn Jamison	.50	1.25
❑ 80 Chris Bosh	.50	1.25
❑ 81 Zach Randolph	.50	1.25
❑ 82 Dwight Howard	1.00	2.50
❑ 83 Richard Jefferson	.40	1.00
❑ 84 Udonis Haslem	.50	1.25
❑ 85 Lamar Odom	.50	1.25
❑ 86 Mike Dunleavy	.40	1.00
❑ 87 Josh Howard	.50	1.25
❑ 88 Luol Deng	.50	1.25
❑ 89 Josh Smith	.50	1.25
❑ 90 Jalen Rose	.50	1.25
❑ 91 Rafer Alston	.30	.75
❑ 92 Manu Ginobili	.50	1.25
❑ 93 Allen Iverson	1.00	2.50
❑ 94 Stephon Marbury	.50	1.25
❑ 95 Michael Redd	.50	1.25
❑ 96 Sam Cassell	.50	1.25
❑ 97 Baron Davis	.50	1.25
❑ 98 Andre Miller	.40	1.00
❑ 99 Larry Hughes	.40	1.00
❑ 100 Ricky Davis	.50	1.25
❑ 101 Nate Robinson RC	3.00	8.00
❑ 102 Danny Granger RC	5.00	12.00
❑ 103 Marvin Williams RC	3.00	8.00
❑ 104 Rashad McCants RC	3.00	8.00
❑ 105 Jarrett Jack RC	2.00	5.00
❑ 106 Andrew Bogut RC	2.50	6.00
❑ 107 Ike Diogu RC	2.50	6.00
❑ 108 Chris Paul RC	6.00	15.00
❑ 109 Julius Hodge RC	2.50	6.00
❑ 110 C.J. Miles RC	2.00	5.00
❑ 111 Francisco Garcia RC	2.50	6.00
❑ 112 Channing Frye RC	2.50	6.00
❑ 113 Deron Williams RC	5.00	12.00
❑ 114 Hakim Warrick RC	3.00	8.00
❑ 115 Salim Stoudamire RC	2.50	6.00
❑ 116 Raymond Felton RC	2.50	6.00
❑ 117 Joey Graham RC	2.00	5.00
❑ 118 Wayne Simien RC	2.50	6.00
❑ 119 David Lee RC	4.00	10.00
❑ 120 Luther Head RC	2.50	6.00
❑ 121 Andrew Bynum RC	6.00	15.00
❑ 122 Monta Ellis RC	5.00	12.00
❑ 123 Brandon Bass RC	2.00	5.00
❑ 124 Antoine Wright RC	2.00	5.00
❑ 125 Gerald Green RC	2.00	5.00
❑ 126 Charlie Villanueva RC	3.00	8.00
❑ 127 Chris Taft RC	2.00	5.00
❑ 128 Sarunas Jasikevicius RC	2.50	6.00
❑ 129 Sean May RC	2.50	6.00
❑ 130 Martell Webster RC	2.00	5.00
❑ 131 Yaroslav Korolev RC	2.00	5.00
❑ 132 Eddie Basden RC	2.00	5.00
❑ 133 Ersan Ilyasova RC	2.00	5.00
❑ 134 Martynas Andriuskevicius RC	2.00	5.00
❑ 135 Orien Greene RC	2.00	5.00
❑ 136 Johan Petro RC	2.00	5.00
❑ 137 Linas Kleiza RC	2.50	6.00
❑ 138 Daniel Ewing RC	2.50	6.00
❑ 139 Fabricio Oberto RC	2.00	5.00
❑ 140 Travis Diener RC	2.00	5.00
❑ 141 Ryan Gomes RC	2.00	5.00
❑ 142 Andray Blatche RC	2.50	6.00
❑ 143 Louis Williams RC	3.00	8.00
❑ 144 Jose Calderon RC	2.00	5.00
❑ 145 Robert Whaley RC	2.00	5.00
❑ 146 Jay-Z	4.00	10.00
❑ 147 Carmen Electra	4.00	10.00
❑ 148 Christie Brinkley	4.00	10.00
❑ 149 Shannon Elizabeth	4.00	10.00
❑ 150 Jenny McCarthy	4.00	10.00

2006-07 Topps Full Court

❑ COMP.SET w/o RC's (100)	12.50	30.00
❑ 1 Vince Carter	.60	1.50
❑ 2 Josh Smith	.30	.75
❑ 3 Dwyane Wade	.75	2.00
❑ 4 Lamar Odom	.30	.75
❑ 5 Jermaine O'Neal	.30	.75
❑ 6 Andrei Kirilenko	.30	.75
❑ 7 Rasheed Wallace	.30	.75
❑ 8 Manu Ginobili	.30	.75
❑ 9 Richard Hamilton	.25	.60
❑ 10 Tim Duncan	.60	1.50
❑ 11 Ricky Davis	.30	.75
❑ 12 Antoine Walker	.25	.60
❑ 13 Troy Murphy	.30	.75
❑ 14 Ray Allen	.30	.75
❑ 15 Ben Wallace	.30	.75
❑ 16 Dwight Howard	.60	1.50
❑ 17 Joe Johnson	.25	.60
❑ 18 Jason Kidd	.50	1.25
❑ 19 Michael Redd	.30	.75
❑ 20 Kobe Bryant	1.50	4.00
❑ 21 Al Harrington	.20	.50
❑ 22 Mehmet Okur	.20	.50
❑ 23 Danny Granger	.25	.60
❑ 24 Caron Butler	.30	.75
❑ 25 Elton Brand	.30	.75

❑ 26 Gilbert Arenas	.30	.75
❑ 27 Sam Cassell	.30	.75
❑ 28 Antawn Jamison	.30	.75
❑ 29 Carmelo Anthony	.40	1.00
❑ 30 Zach Randolph	.30	.75
❑ 31 Ben Gordon	.40	1.00
❑ 32 Andre Iguodala	.30	.75
❑ 33 Paul Pierce	.30	.75
❑ 34 Peja Stojakovic	.30	.75
❑ 35 Andrew Bogut	.30	.75
❑ 36 Mike Miller	.30	.75
❑ 37 Mike James	.20	.50
❑ 38 Shaquille O'Neal	.75	2.00
❑ 39 Baron Davis	.30	.75
❑ 40 Jason Richardson	.30	.75
❑ 41 Rashard Lewis	.30	.75
❑ 42 Marcus Camby	.25	.60
❑ 43 Ron Artest	.30	.75
❑ 44 Larry Hughes	.25	.60
❑ 45 Allen Iverson	.60	1.50
❑ 46 Al Jefferson	.30	.75
❑ 47 Chris Paul	.60	1.50
❑ 48 Tony Parker	.30	.75
❑ 49 Pau Gasol	.30	.75
❑ 50 Kevin Garnett	.60	1.50
❑ 51 Richard Jefferson	.25	.60
❑ 52 Corey Maggette	.25	.60
❑ 53 Yao Ming	.75	2.00
❑ 54 T.J. Ford	.25	.60
❑ 55 Andre Miller	.25	.60
❑ 56 Mike Bibby	.30	.75
❑ 57 LeBron James	1.50	4.00
❑ 58 Chris Webber	.30	.75
❑ 59 Emeka Okafor	.30	.75
❑ 60 Tyson Chandler	.30	.75
❑ 61 Raymond Felton	.40	1.00
❑ 62 Channing Frye	.25	.60
❑ 63 Gerald Wallace	.30	.75
❑ 64 Stephon Marbury	.30	.75
❑ 65 Kirk Hinrich	.30	.75
❑ 66 Jameer Nelson	.25	.60
❑ 67 Charlie Villanueva	.30	.75
❑ 68 Smush Parker	.20	.50
❑ 69 Tracy McGrady	.60	1.50
❑ 70 Chris Bosh	.30	.75
❑ 71 Chauncey Billups	.30	.75
❑ 72 Brad Miller	.30	.75
❑ 73 Drew Gooden	.25	.60
❑ 74 Amare Stoudemire	.60	1.50
❑ 75 Dirk Nowitzki	.50	1.25
❑ 76 Shawn Marion	.30	.75
❑ 77 Jason Terry	.30	.75
❑ 78 Steve Nash	.40	1.00
❑ 79 Josh Howard	.30	.75
❑ 80 Darius Miles	.20	.50
❑ 81 John Stockton	2.00	5.00
❑ 82 Wilt Chamberlain	2.00	5.00
❑ 83 Dennis Rodman	1.00	2.50
❑ 84 Karl Malone	1.25	3.00
❑ 85 Dominique Wilkins	1.25	3.00
❑ 86 Isiah Thomas	1.00	2.50
❑ 87 Earl Monroe	1.00	2.50
❑ 88 Hakeem Olajuwon	1.25	3.00
❑ 89 Clyde Drexler	1.25	3.00
❑ 90 George Gervin	1.00	2.50
❑ 91 Oscar Robertson	1.00	2.50
❑ 92 Rick Barry	1.00	2.50
❑ 93 Walt Frazier	1.00	2.50
❑ 94 Drazen Petrovic	1.25	3.00
❑ 95 Dan Majerle	1.25	3.00
❑ 96 Jerry West	1.25	3.00
❑ 97 Larry Bird	3.00	8.00
❑ 98 Moses Malone	1.00	2.50
❑ 99 Kareem Abdul-Jabbar	1.50	4.00
❑ 100 Bill Russell	2.00	5.00
❑ 101 Shelden Williams RC	2.00	5.00
❑ 102 Adam Morrison RC	2.00	5.00
❑ 103 Daniel Gibson RC	2.00	5.00
❑ 104 Mile Ilic RC	1.50	4.00
❑ 105 Jorge Garbajosa RC	3.00	8.00
❑ 106 David Noel RC	1.50	4.00
❑ 107 Hassan Adams RC	2.00	5.00
❑ 108 J.J. Redick RC	1.50	4.00
❑ 109 Brandon Roy RC	4.00	10.00
❑ 110 Damir Markota RC	1.50	4.00
❑ 111 Solomon Jones RC	1.50	4.00
❑ 112 Yakhouba Diawara RC	1.50	4.00
❑ 113 Maurice Ager RC	1.50	4.00
❑ 114 Steve Novak RC	1.50	4.00
❑ 115 Jordan Farmar RC	2.00	5.00
❑ 116 Randy Foye RC	1.50	4.00
❑ 117 Cedric Simmons RC	1.50	4.00
❑ 118 James Augustine RC	1.50	4.00
❑ 119 Sergio Rodriguez RC	1.50	4.00
❑ 120 P.J. Tucker RC	1.50	4.00
❑ 121 Rajon Rondo RC	6.00	15.00
❑ 122 Tyrus Thomas RC	2.00	5.00
❑ 123 Will Blalock RC	1.50	4.00
❑ 124 Shawne Williams RC	1.50	4.00
❑ 125 Rudy Gay RC	1.50	4.00
❑ 126 Craig Smith RC	1.50	4.00
❑ 127 Hilton Armstrong RC	1.50	4.00
❑ 128 Bobby Jones RC	1.50	4.00
❑ 129 Quincy Douby RC	1.50	4.00
❑ 130 Andrea Bargnani RC	2.50	6.00
❑ 131 Vassilis Spanoulis RC	1.50	4.00
❑ 132 Thabo Sefolosha RC	2.00	5.00
❑ 133 Pops Mensah-Bonsu RC	1.50	4.00
❑ 134 Paul Milsap RC	2.50	6.00
❑ 135 Kyle Lowry RC	1.50	4.00
❑ 136 Marcus Williams RC	2.00	5.00
❑ 137 Renaldo Balkman RC	1.50	4.00
❑ 138 Rodney Carney RC	1.50	4.00
❑ 139 Marcus Vinicius RC	1.50	4.00
❑ 140 Ronnie Brewer RC	2.00	5.00
❑ 141 Leon Powe RC	1.50	4.00
❑ 142 Shannon Brown RC	1.50	4.00
❑ 143 Patrick O'Bryant RC	1.50	4.00
❑ 144 Paul Davis RC	1.50	4.00
❑ 145 Alexander Johnson RC	1.50	4.00
❑ 146 Josh Boone RC	1.50	4.00
❑ 147 Mardy Collins RC	1.50	4.00
❑ 148 LaMarcus Aldridge RC	2.00	5.00
❑ 149 Saer Sene RC	1.50	4.00
❑ 150 Dee Brown RC	1.50	4.00

1995-96 Topps Gallery

❑ COMPLETE SET (144)	15.00	30.00
❑ 1 Shaquille O'Neal	.75	2.00
❑ 2 Shawn Kemp	.20	.50
❑ 3 Reggie Miller	.30	.75
❑ 4 Mitch Richmond	.20	.50
❑ 5 Grant Hill	.40	1.00
❑ 6 Magic Johnson	.50	1.25
❑ 7 Vin Baker	.20	.50
❑ 8 Charles Barkley	.40	1.00
❑ 9 Hakeem Olajuwon	.30	.75
❑ 10 Michael Jordan	2.50	6.00
❑ 11 Patrick Ewing	.30	.75
❑ 12 David Robinson	.30	.75
❑ 13 Alonzo Mourning	.20	.50
❑ 14 Karl Malone	.40	1.00
❑ 15 Chris Webber	.40	1.00
❑ 16 Dikembe Mutombo	.20	.50
❑ 17 Larry Johnson	.20	.50
❑ 18 Jamal Mashburn	.20	.50
❑ 19 Anfernee Hardaway	.30	.75
❑ 20 Bryant Stith	.08	.25
❑ 21 Juwan Howard	.30	.75
❑ 22 Jason Kidd	1.00	2.50
❑ 23 Sharone Wright	.08	.25
❑ 24 Tom Gugliotta	.08	.25
❑ 25 Eric Montross	.08	.25
❑ 26 Allan Houston	.20	.50
❑ 27 Antonio Davis	.08	.25
❑ 28 Brian Grant	.30	.75
❑ 29 Terrell Brandon	.20	.50
❑ 30 Eddie Jones	.40	1.00
❑ 31 James Robinson	.08	.25
❑ 32 Wesley Person	.08	.25
❑ 33 Glenn Robinson	.30	.75
❑ 34 Donyell Marshall	.20	.50
❑ 35 Sam Cassell	.30	.75
❑ 36 Lamond Murray	.08	.25
❑ 37 Damon Stoudamire RC	.60	1.50
❑ 38 Tyus Edney RC	.08	.25
❑ 39 Jerry Stackhouse RC	1.00	2.50
❑ 40 Arvydas Sabonis RC	.40	1.00
❑ 41 Kevin Garnett RC	2.00	5.00
❑ 42 Brent Barry RC	.30	.75
❑ 43 Alan Henderson RC	.30	.75
❑ 44 Bryant Reeves RC	.30	.75
❑ 45 Shawn Respert RC	.08	.25
❑ 46 Michael Finley RC	.75	2.00
❑ 47 Gary Trent RC	.08	.25
❑ 48 Antonio McDyess RC	.60	1.50
❑ 49 George Zidek RC	.08	.25
❑ 50 Joe Smith RC	.50	1.25
❑ 51 Ed O'Bannon RC	.08	.25
❑ 52 Rasheed Wallace RC	.75	2.00
❑ 53 Eric Williams RC	.20	.50
❑ 54 Kurt Thomas RC	.20	.50
❑ 55 Mookie Blaylock	.08	.25
❑ 56 Robert Pack	.08	.25
❑ 57 Dana Barros	.08	.25
❑ 58 Eric Murdock	.08	.25
❑ 59 Glen Rice	.20	.50
❑ 60 John Stockton	.40	1.00
❑ 61 Scottie Pippen	.50	1.25
❑ 62 Oliver Miller	.08	.25
❑ 63 Tyrone Hill	.08	.25
❑ 64 Gary Payton	.30	.75
❑ 65 Jim Jackson	.08	.25
❑ 66 Avery Johnson	.08	.25
❑ 67 Mahmoud Abdul-Rauf	.08	.25
❑ 68 Olden Polynice	.08	.25
❑ 69 Joe Dumars	.30	.75
❑ 70 Rod Strickland	.08	.25
❑ 71 Chris Mullin	.30	.75
❑ 72 Kevin Johnson	.20	.50
❑ 73 Derrick Coleman	.08	.25
❑ 74 Clyde Drexler	.30	.75
❑ 75 Dale Davis	.08	.25
❑ 76 Horace Grant	.20	.50
❑ 77 Loy Vaught	.08	.25
❑ 78 Armon Gilliam	.08	.25
❑ 79 Nick Van Exel	.30	.75
❑ 80 Charles Oakley	.08	.25
❑ 81 Kevin Willis	.20	.50
❑ 82 Sherman Douglas	.08	.25
❑ 83 Isaiah Rider	.08	.25
❑ 84 Steve Smith	.20	.50
❑ 85 Dee Brown	.08	.25
❑ 86 Dell Curry	.08	.25
❑ 87 Calbert Cheaney	.08	.25
❑ 88 Greg Anthony	.08	.25
❑ 89 Jeff Hornacek	.20	.50
❑ 90 Dennis Rodman	.20	.50
❑ 91 Willie Anderson	.08	.25
❑ 92 Chris Mills	.08	.25
❑ 93 Hersey Hawkins	.08	.25
❑ 94 Popeye Jones	.08	.25
❑ 95 Chuck Person	.08	.25
❑ 96 Reggie Williams	.08	.25
❑ 97 A.C. Green	.20	.50
❑ 98 Otis Thorpe	.08	.25
❑ 99 Walt Williams	.08	.25
❑ 100 Latrell Sprewell	.30	.75
❑ 101 Buck Williams	.08	.25
❑ 102 Robert Horry	.20	.50
❑ 103 Clarence Weatherspoon	.08	.25
❑ 104 Dennis Scott	.08	.25
❑ 105 Rik Smits	.20	.50
❑ 106 Jayson Williams	.08	.25
❑ 107 Pooh Richardson	.08	.25
❑ 108 Anthony Mason	.20	.50
❑ 109 Cedric Ceballos	.08	.25
❑ 110 Billy Owens	.08	.25
❑ 111 Johnny Newman	.08	.25
❑ 112 Christian Laettner	.20	.50
❑ 113 Stacey Augmon	.08	.25
❑ 114 Chris Morris	.08	.25
❑ 115 Detlef Schrempf	.20	.50
❑ 116 Dino Radja	.08	.25
❑ 117 Sean Elliott	.20	.50
❑ 118 Muggsy Bogues	.20	.50
❑ 119 Toni Kukoc	.20	.50
❑ 120 Clifford Robinson	.08	.25
❑ 121 Bobby Hurley	.08	.25
❑ 122 Lorenzo Williams	.08	.25
❑ 123 Wayman Tisdale	.08	.25
❑ 124 Bobby Phills	.08	.25
❑ 125 Nick Anderson	.08	.25
❑ 126 LaPhonso Ellis	.08	.25

❑ 127 Scott Williams	.08	.25
❑ 128 Mark West	.08	.25
❑ 129 P.J. Brown	.08	.25
❑ 130 Tim Hardaway	.20	.50
❑ 131 Derek Harper	.20	.50
❑ 132 Mario Elie	.08	.25
❑ 133 Benoit Benjamin	.08	.25
❑ 134 Terry Porter	.08	.25
❑ 135 Derrick McKey	.08	.25
❑ 136 Bimbo Coles	.08	.25
❑ 137 John Salley	.08	.25
❑ 138 Malik Sealy	.08	.25
❑ 139 Byron Scott	.08	.25
❑ 140 Vlade Divac	.20	.50
❑ 141 Mark Price	.20	.50
❑ 142 Rony Seikaly	.08	.25
❑ 143 Mark Jackson	.20	.50
❑ 144 John Starks	.20	.50

1999-00 Topps Gallery

❑ COMPLETE SET (150)	30.00	60.00
❑ COMMON CARD (1-124)	.20	.50
❑ COMMON ROOKIE (125-150)	.30	.75
❑ 1 Gary Payton	.30	.75
❑ 2 Derek Anderson	.20	.50
❑ 3 Jalen Rose	.25	.60
❑ 4 Tim Hardaway	.30	.75
❑ 5 Jerry Stackhouse	.30	.75
❑ 6 Antonio McDyess	.25	.60
❑ 7 Paul Pierce	.30	.75
❑ 8 Reggie Miller	.30	.75
❑ 9 Maurice Taylor	.25	.60
❑ 10 Stephon Marbury	.30	.75
❑ 11 Terrell Brandon	.20	.50
❑ 12 Marcus Camby	.25	.60
❑ 13 Michael Doleac	.20	.50
❑ 14 Doug Christie	.25	.60
❑ 15 Brent Barry	.25	.60
❑ 16 John Stockton	.40	1.00
❑ 17 Rod Strickland	.20	.50
❑ 18 Shareef Abdur-Rahim	.25	.60
❑ 19 Vin Baker	.30	.75
❑ 20 Jason Kidd	.50	1.25
❑ 21 Nick Anderson	.20	.50
❑ 22 Brian Grant	.20	.50
❑ 23 Chris Webber	.30	.75
❑ 24 Tariq Abdul-Wahad	.20	.50
❑ 25 Jason Williams	.30	.75
❑ 26 Joe Smith	.25	.60
❑ 27 Ray Allen	.30	.75
❑ 28 Glenn Robinson	.25	.60
❑ 29 Alonzo Mourning	.30	.75
❑ 30 Scottie Pippen	.50	1.25
❑ 31 Mookie Blaylock	.20	.50
❑ 32 Christian Laettner	.25	.60
❑ 33 Mark Jackson	.30	.75
❑ 34 Shawn Kemp	.30	.75
❑ 35 Anfernee Hardaway	.30	.75
❑ 36 Chris Mullin	.30	.75
❑ 37 Dennis Rodman	.60	1.50
❑ 38 Lamond Murray	.20	.50
❑ 39 Jim Jackson	.25	.60
❑ 40 Shaquille O'Neal	.75	2.00
❑ 41 Randy Brown	.20	.50
❑ 42 Nick Van Exel	.25	.60
❑ 43 Robert Traylor	.20	.50
❑ 44 Vlade Divac	.30	.75
❑ 45 Karl Malone	.40	1.00
❑ 46 Avery Johnson	.25	.60
❑ 47 Jayson Williams	.25	.60
❑ 48 Darrell Armstrong	.20	.50
❑ 49 Michael Olowokandi	.20	.50
❑ 50 Kevin Garnett	.60	1.50
❑ 51 Dirk Nowitzki	.50	1.25
❑ 52 Antawn Jamison	.30	.75
❑ 53 Latrell Sprewell	.25	.60
❑ 54 Ruben Patterson	.20	.50
❑ 55 Vince Carter	.60	1.50
❑ 56 Michael Dickerson	.20	.50
❑ 57 Raef LaFrentz	.25	.60
❑ 58 Keith Van Horn	.25	.60
❑ 59 Tom Gugliotta	.20	.50
❑ 60 Allen Iverson	.60	1.50
❑ 61 Eric Snow	.25	.60
❑ 62 Kerry Kittles	.20	.50
❑ 63 Sam Cassell	.25	.60
❑ 64 Rik Smits	.30	.75
❑ 65 Isaiah Rider	.20	.50
❑ 66 Anthony Mason	.20	.50
❑ 67 Hersey Hawkins	.20	.50
❑ 68 Cuttino Mobley	.25	.60
❑ 69 Allan Houston	.25	.60
❑ 70 Kobe Bryant	1.50	4.00
❑ 71 Damon Stoudamire	.30	.75
❑ 72 Charles Oakley	.25	.60
❑ 73 Mike Bibby	.30	.75
❑ 74 David Robinson	.40	1.00
❑ 75 Eddie Jones	.30	.75
❑ 76 Juwan Howard	.25	.60
❑ 77 Antoine Walker	.30	.75
❑ 78 Michael Finley	.30	.75
❑ 79 Larry Hughes	.25	.60
❑ 80 Charles Barkley	.40	1.00
❑ 81 Tracy McGrady	.60	1.50
❑ 82 Dikembe Mutombo	.25	.60
❑ 83 Rasheed Wallace	.30	.75
❑ 84 Jeff Hornacek	.25	.60
❑ 85 Patrick Ewing	.40	1.00
❑ 86 P.J. Brown	.20	.50
❑ 87 Brevin Knight	.20	.50
❑ 88 Elden Campbell	.20	.50
❑ 89 Kenny Anderson	.25	.60
❑ 90 Grant Hill	.30	.75
❑ 91 Mitch Richmond	.25	.60
❑ 92 Steve Smith	.20	.50
❑ 93 Jamal Mashburn	.20	.50
❑ 94 Toni Kukoc	.30	.75
❑ 95 Hakeem Olajuwon	.30	.75
❑ 96 Ron Mercer	.20	.50
❑ 97 John Starks	.30	.75
❑ 98 Glen Rice	.30	.75
❑ 99 Cedric Ceballos	.20	.50
❑ 100 Tim Duncan	.60	1.50
❑ 101 Karl Malone MAS	.40	1.00
❑ 102 Alonzo Mourning MAS	.30	.75
❑ 103 Gary Payton MAS	.30	.75
❑ 104 Scottie Pippen MAS	.50	1.25
❑ 105 Shaquille O'Neal MAS	.75	2.00
❑ 106 Charles Barkley MAS	.40	1.00
❑ 107 Grant Hill MAS	.30	.75
❑ 108 John Stockton MAS	.40	1.00
❑ 109 Jason Kidd MAS	.50	1.25
❑ 110 Reggie Miller MAS	.30	.75
❑ 111 Shawn Kemp MAS	.30	.75
❑ 112 Patrick Ewing MAS	.40	1.00
❑ 113 Kevin Garnett ART	.60	1.50
❑ 114 Vince Carter ART	.60	1.50
❑ 115 Kobe Bryant ART	1.50	4.00
❑ 116 Chris Webber ART	.30	.75
❑ 117 Tracy McGrady ART	.60	1.50
❑ 118 Shareef Abdur-Rahim ART	.25	.60
❑ 119 Paul Pierce ART	.30	.75
❑ 120 Jason Williams ART	.30	.75
❑ 121 Tim Duncan ART	.60	1.50
❑ 122 Eddie Jones ART	.30	.75
❑ 123 Allen Iverson ART	.60	1.50
❑ 124 Stephon Marbury ART	.30	.75
❑ 125 Elton Brand RC	1.00	2.50
❑ 126 Lamar Odom RC	1.00	2.50
❑ 127 Steve Francis RC	1.00	2.50
❑ 128 Adrian Griffin RC	.30	.75
❑ 129 Wally Szczerbiak RC	1.00	2.50
❑ 130 Baron Davis RC	1.25	3.00
❑ 131 Richard Hamilton RC	1.00	2.50
❑ 132 Jonathan Bender RC	.30	.75
❑ 133 Andre Miller RC	1.00	2.50
❑ 134 Shawn Marion RC	1.00	2.50
❑ 135 Jason Terry RC	.75	2.00
❑ 136 Trajan Langdon RC	.30	.75
❑ 137 Corey Maggette RC	1.00	2.50
❑ 138 William Avery RC	.30	.75
❑ 139 Ron Artest RC	1.25	3.00
❑ 140 Cal Bowdler RC	.30	.75
❑ 141 James Posey RC	.50	1.25
❑ 142 Quincy Lewis RC	.30	.75
❑ 143 Kenny Thomas RC	.30	.75
❑ 144 Vonteego Cummings RC	.30	.75
❑ 145 Todd MacCulloch RC	.30	.75
❑ 146 Anthony Carter RC	.60	1.50
❑ 147 A.Radojevic RC	.30	.75
❑ 148 Devean George RC	.50	1.25
❑ 149 Scott Padgett RC	.30	.75
❑ 150 Jumaine Jones RC	.30	.75

2000-01 Topps Gallery

❑ COMP.SET w/o RC's (125)	15.00	40.00
❑ COMMON CARD (1-125)	.15	.40
❑ COMMON ROOKIE (126-150)	1.25	3.00
❑ 1 Allen Iverson	.50	1.25
❑ 2 Terrell Brandon	.15	.40
❑ 3 Tracy McGrady	.50	1.25
❑ 4 Shawn Marion	.25	.60
❑ 5 Steve Smith	.20	.50
❑ 6 Avery Johnson	.20	.50
❑ 7 Gary Payton	.25	.60
❑ 8 Mark Jackson	.20	.50
❑ 9 Mike Bibby	.20	.50
❑ 10 Karl Malone	.30	.75
❑ 11 Kevin Garnett	.50	1.25
❑ 12 Tim Hardaway	.20	.50
❑ 13 Isaiah Rider	.20	.50
❑ 14 Corey Maggette	.20	.50
❑ 15 Vince Carter	.50	1.25
❑ 16 Vin Baker	.20	.50
❑ 17 Paul Pierce	.25	.60
❑ 18 Matt Harpring	.20	.50
❑ 19 Ron Artest	.25	.60
❑ 20 Kenny Anderson	.20	.50
❑ 21 Larry Hughes	.20	.50
❑ 22 Antonio McDyess	.20	.50
❑ 23 Shandon Anderson	.15	.40
❑ 24 Joe Smith	.15	.40
❑ 25 Jermaine O'Neal	.25	.60
❑ 26 Horace Grant	.20	.50
❑ 27 Ray Allen	.25	.60
❑ 28 Keith Van Horn	.20	.50
❑ 29 Darrell Armstrong	.15	.40
❑ 30 Shaquille O'Neal	.60	1.50
❑ 31 Reggie Miller	.25	.60
❑ 32 Allan Houston	.20	.50
❑ 33 Grant Hill	.25	.60
❑ 34 David Robinson	.30	.75
❑ 35 Clifford Robinson	.15	.40
❑ 36 Theo Ratliff	.15	.40
❑ 37 Rashard Lewis	.25	.60
❑ 38 Peja Stojakovic	.20	.50
❑ 39 Jason Kidd	.40	1.00
❑ 40 Latrell Sprewell	.20	.50
❑ 41 Stephon Marbury	.25	.60
❑ 42 Sam Cassell	.20	.50
❑ 43 Brian Grant	.15	.40
❑ 44 Jalen Rose	.20	.50
❑ 45 Antawn Jamison	.25	.60
❑ 46 Raef LaFrentz	.15	.40
❑ 47 Dirk Nowitzki	.40	1.00
❑ 48 Lamond Murray	.15	.40
❑ 49 Derrick Coleman	.20	.50
❑ 50 Steve Francis	.25	.60
❑ 51 Dikembe Mutombo	.20	.50
❑ 52 Elton Brand	.25	.60
❑ 53 Christian Laettner	.15	.40
❑ 54 Ben Wallace	.20	.50
❑ 55 Jim Jackson	.15	.40
❑ 56 Cuttino Mobley	.20	.50
❑ 57 Jonathan Bender	.15	.40
❑ 58 Anthony Mason	.15	.40
❑ 59 Tim Thomas	.15	.40
❑ 60 Lamar Odom	.25	.60
❑ 61 Glenn Robinson	.20	.50
❑ 62 Kendall Gill	.15	.40
❑ 63 Glen Rice	.20	.50

❑ 64 Anfernee Hardaway	.25	.60
❑ 65 Jason Williams	.20	.50
❑ 66 Shawn Kemp	.25	.60
❑ 67 Derek Anderson	.20	.50
❑ 68 Patrick Ewing	.30	.75
❑ 69 Shareef Abdur-Rahim	.20	.50
❑ 70 Tim Duncan	.50	1.25
❑ 71 Rod Strickland	.20	.50
❑ 72 Bryon Russell	.15	.40
❑ 73 Antonio Davis	.15	.40
❑ 74 Rasheed Wallace	.25	.60
❑ 75 Wally Szczerbiak	.20	.50
❑ 76 Eric Snow	.15	.40
❑ 77 Toni Kukoc	.20	.50
❑ 78 Michael Olowokandi	.15	.40
❑ 79 Hakeem Olajuwon	.30	.75
❑ 80 Kobe Bryant	1.25	3.00
❑ 81 Mookie Blaylock	.20	.50
❑ 82 Michael Finley	.25	.60
❑ 83 Jerry Stackhouse	.20	.50
❑ 84 Baron Davis	.25	.60
❑ 85 Jason Terry	.25	.60
❑ 86 Andre Miller	.20	.50
❑ 87 Antoine Walker	.20	.50
❑ 88 Jamal Mashburn	.20	.50
❑ 89 Nick Van Exel	.20	.50
❑ 90 Eddie Jones	.20	.50
❑ 91 Marcus Camby	.20	.50
❑ 92 Scottie Pippen	.40	1.00
❑ 93 John Stockton	.30	.75
❑ 94 Richard Hamilton	.20	.50
❑ 95 John Starks	.15	.40
❑ 96 Juwan Howard	.20	.50
❑ 97 Michael Dickerson	.15	.40
❑ 98 Ron Mercer	.15	.40
❑ 99 Chris Webber	.25	.60
❑ 100 Magic Johnson	1.25	3.00
❑ 101 Shaquille O'Neal MAS	.60	1.50
❑ 102 Tim Duncan MAS	.50	1.25
❑ 103 Chris Webber MAS	.25	.60
❑ 104 Grant Hill MAS	.25	.60
❑ 105 Kevin Garnett MAS	.50	1.25
❑ 106 Vince Carter MAS	.50	1.25
❑ 107 Gary Payton MAS	.25	.60
❑ 108 Jason Kidd MAS	.40	1.00
❑ 109 Kobe Bryant MAS	1.25	3.00
❑ 110 Karl Malone MAS	.30	.75
❑ 111 Scottie Pippen MAS	.40	1.00
❑ 112 Reggie Miller MAS	.25	.60
❑ 113 John Stockton MAS	.30	.75
❑ 114 Elton Brand ART	.25	.60
❑ 115 Tracy McGrady ART	.50	1.25
❑ 116 Steve Francis ART	.25	.60
❑ 117 Lamar Odom ART	.25	.60
❑ 118 Baron Davis ART	.25	.60
❑ 119 Andre Miller ART	.20	.50
❑ 120 Jonathan Bender ART	.15	.40
❑ 121 Paul Pierce ART	.25	.60
❑ 122 Jason Williams ART	.20	.50
❑ 123 Rashard Lewis ART	.25	.60
❑ 124 Larry Hughes ART	.20	.50
❑ 125 Shawn Marion ART	.25	.60
❑ 126 Kenyon Martin RC	3.00	8.00
❑ 127 Stromile Swift RC	1.50	4.00
❑ 128 Darius Miles RC	1.50	4.00
❑ 129 Marcus Fizer RC	1.25	3.00
❑ 130 Mike Miller RC	2.00	5.00
❑ 131 DerMarr Johnson RC	1.25	3.00
❑ 132 Chris Mihm RC	1.25	3.00
❑ 133 Jamal Crawford RC	2.00	5.00
❑ 134 Joel Przybilla RC	1.25	3.00
❑ 135 Keyon Dooling RC	1.25	3.00
❑ 136 Jerome Moiso RC	1.25	3.00
❑ 137 Etan Thomas RC	1.25	3.00
❑ 138 Courtney Alexander RC	1.25	3.00
❑ 139 Mateen Cleaves RC	1.25	3.00
❑ 140 Jason Collier RC	1.25	3.00
❑ 141 Hedo Turkoglu RC	3.00	8.00
❑ 142 Desmond Mason RC	1.50	4.00
❑ 143 Quentin Richardson RC	1.50	4.00
❑ 144 Jamaal Magloire RC	1.25	3.00
❑ 145 Speedy Claxton RC	1.25	3.00
❑ 146 Morris Peterson RC	2.00	5.00
❑ 147 Donnell Harvey RC	1.25	3.00
❑ 148 DeShawn Stevenson RC	1.25	3.00
❑ 149 Stephen Jackson RC	2.00	5.00
❑ 150 Marc Jackson RC	1.50	4.00

1999-00 Topps Gold Label Class 1

❑ COMPLETE SET (100)	30.00	60.00
❑ COMMON CARD (1-85)	.25	.60
❑ COMMON ROOKIE (86-100)	.40	1.00
❑ 1 Tim Duncan	.75	2.00
❑ 2 Steve Smith	.25	.60
❑ 3 Jeff Hornacek	.30	.75
❑ 4 Kevin Garnett	.75	2.00
❑ 5 Paul Pierce	.40	1.00
❑ 6 Doug Christie	.30	.75
❑ 7 Charles Barkley	.50	1.25
❑ 8 Nick Van Exel	.30	.75
❑ 9 Shareef Abdur-Rahim	.30	.75
❑ 10 Rod Strickland	.25	.60
❑ 11 Keith Van Horn	.30	.75
❑ 12 Matt Harpring	.30	.75
❑ 13 Randy Brown	.25	.60
❑ 14 Vin Baker	.40	1.00
❑ 15 Mark Jackson	.40	1.00
❑ 16 Latrell Sprewell	.30	.75
❑ 17 Anthony Mason	.25	.60
❑ 18 Brian Grant	.25	.60
❑ 19 Brevin Knight	.25	.60
❑ 20 Elden Campbell	.25	.60
❑ 21 Allen Iverson	.75	2.00
❑ 22 Kobe Bryant	2.00	5.00
❑ 23 Antawn Jamison	.40	1.00
❑ 24 Lindsey Hunter	.25	.60
❑ 25 Eddie Jones	.40	1.00
❑ 26 Michael Finley	.40	1.00
❑ 27 Juwan Howard	.30	.75
❑ 28 Antonio McDyess	.30	.75
❑ 29 David Robinson	.50	1.25
❑ 30 Karl Malone	.50	1.25
❑ 31 Jason Kidd	.60	1.50
❑ 32 Zydrunas Ilgauskas	.30	.75
❑ 33 Vince Carter	.75	2.00
❑ 34 Maurice Taylor	.30	.75
❑ 35 Alonzo Mourning	.40	1.00
❑ 36 Tim Thomas	.30	.75
❑ 37 Dikembe Mutombo	.30	.75
❑ 38 Grant Hill	.40	1.00
❑ 39 Jason Williams	.40	1.00
❑ 40 Scottie Pippen	.60	1.50
❑ 41 Stephon Marbury	.40	1.00
❑ 42 Reggie Miller	.40	1.00
❑ 43 Tyrone Nesby RC	.40	1.00
❑ 44 Ron Mercer	.25	.60
❑ 45 Terrell Brandon	.25	.60
❑ 46 Darrell Armstrong	.25	.60
❑ 47 Larry Hughes	.30	.75
❑ 48 Alan Henderson	.25	.60
❑ 49 Ray Allen	.40	1.00
❑ 50 Rasheed Wallace	.40	1.00
❑ 51 Toni Kukoc	.40	1.00
❑ 52 Patrick Ewing	.50	1.25
❑ 53 Tom Gugliotta	.25	.60
❑ 54 Chris Mills	.25	.60
❑ 55 Gary Payton	.40	1.00
❑ 56 Michael Olowokandi	.25	.60
❑ 57 Chris Mullin	.40	1.00
❑ 58 Shawn Kemp	.40	1.00
❑ 59 Joe Smith	.30	.75
❑ 60 Steve Nash	.60	1.50
❑ 61 Gary Trent	.25	.60
❑ 62 Shaquille O'Neal	1.00	2.50
❑ 63 Kerry Kittles	.25	.60
❑ 64 Tim Hardaway	.40	1.00
❑ 65 Glenn Robinson	.30	.75
❑ 66 Damon Stoudamire	.40	1.00
❑ 67 Anfernee Hardaway	.40	1.00
❑ 68 Vlade Divac	.40	1.00
❑ 69 John Starks	.40	1.00
❑ 70 Allan Houston	.30	.75
❑ 71 Jerry Stackhouse	.40	1.00
❑ 72 Avery Johnson	.30	.75
❑ 73 Glen Rice	.40	1.00
❑ 74 Felipe Lopez	.25	.60
❑ 75 Clifford Robinson	.25	.60
❑ 76 Jamal Mashburn	.25	.60
❑ 77 Hakeem Olajuwon	.40	1.00
❑ 78 Matt Geiger	.25	.60
❑ 79 John Stockton	.50	1.25
❑ 80 Chauncey Billups	.40	1.00
❑ 81 Chris Webber	.40	1.00
❑ 82 Antoine Walker	.40	1.00
❑ 83 Mike Bibby	.40	1.00
❑ 84 Tracy McGrady	.75	2.00
❑ 85 Mitch Richmond	.30	.75
❑ 86 Elton Brand RC	1.25	3.00
❑ 87 Steve Francis RC	1.25	3.00
❑ 88 Baron Davis RC	1.50	4.00
❑ 89 Lamar Odom RC	1.25	3.00
❑ 90 Jonathan Bender RC	.40	1.00
❑ 91 Wally Szczerbiak RC	1.25	3.00
❑ 92 Richard Hamilton RC	1.25	3.00
❑ 93 Andre Miller RC	1.25	3.00
❑ 94 Shawn Marion RC	1.25	3.00
❑ 95 Jason Terry RC	1.00	2.50
❑ 96 Trajan Langdon RC	.40	1.00
❑ 97 A.Radojevic RC	.40	1.00
❑ 98 Corey Maggette RC	1.25	3.00
❑ 99 William Avery RC	.40	1.00
❑ 100 Cal Bowdler RC	.40	1.00

2000-01 Topps Gold Label Class 1

❑ COMPLETE SET w/o RC (80)	15.00	30.00
❑ COMMON CARD (1-80)	.10	.30
❑ COMMON ROOKIE (81-100)	1.50	4.00
❑ 1 Steve Francis	.40	1.00
❑ 2 Jalen Rose	.30	.75
❑ 3 Allen Iverson	.75	2.00
❑ 4 Damon Stoudamire	.30	.75
❑ 5 David Robinson	.50	1.25
❑ 6 Bryon Russell	.25	.60
❑ 7 Toni Kukoc	.30	.75
❑ 8 Tracy McGrady	.75	2.00
❑ 9 John Stockton	.50	1.25
❑ 10 Tim Duncan	.75	2.00
❑ 11 Hakeem Olajuwon	.50	1.25
❑ 12 Antoine Walker	.30	.75
❑ 13 Dikembe Mutombo	.30	.75
❑ 14 Shawn Kemp	.40	1.00
❑ 15 Ron Artest	.40	1.00
❑ 16 Eddie Jones	.30	.75
❑ 17 Dirk Nowitzki	.60	1.50
❑ 18 Nick Van Exel	.30	.75
❑ 19 Grant Hill	.40	1.00
❑ 20 Antawn Jamison	.40	1.00
❑ 21 Cuttino Mobley	.30	.75
❑ 22 Jonathan Bender	.25	.60
❑ 23 Maurice Taylor	.25	.60
❑ 24 Kobe Bryant	2.00	5.00
❑ 25 Tim Hardaway	.30	.75
❑ 26 Tim Thomas	.25	.60
❑ 27 Terrell Brandon	.25	.60
❑ 28 Marcus Camby	.30	.75
❑ 29 Keith Van Horn	.30	.75
❑ 30 Shawn Marion	.40	1.00
❑ 31 Rasheed Wallace	.40	1.00
❑ 32 Corey Maggette	.30	.75
❑ 33 Jason Kidd	.60	1.50
❑ 34 Shaquille O'Neal	1.00	2.50
❑ 35 Rashard Lewis	.40	1.00
❑ 36 Karl Malone	.50	1.25
❑ 37 Michael Dickerson	.25	.60
❑ 38 Richard Hamilton	.30	.75

❑ 39 Darrell Armstrong	.25	.60
❑ 40 Wally Szczerbiak	.30	.75
❑ 41 Glen Rice	.30	.75
❑ 42 Glenn Robinson	.30	.75
❑ 43 Reggie Miller	.40	1.00
❑ 44 Alonzo Mourning	.40	1.00
❑ 45 Larry Hughes	.30	.75
❑ 46 Antonio McDyess	.30	.75
❑ 47 Derrick Coleman	.30	.75
❑ 48 Brevin Knight	.25	.60
❑ 49 Jason Terry	.40	1.00
❑ 50 Elton Brand	.40	1.00
❑ 51 Latrell Sprewell	.30	.75
❑ 52 Theo Ratliff	.25	.60
❑ 53 Scottie Pippen	.60	1.50
❑ 54 Jason Williams	.30	.75
❑ 55 Gary Payton	.40	1.00
❑ 56 Mitch Richmond	.30	.75
❑ 57 Vin Baker	.30	.75
❑ 58 Raef LaFrentz	.25	.60
❑ 59 Anfernee Hardaway	.40	1.00
❑ 60 Steve Smith	.30	.75
❑ 61 Stephon Marbury	.40	1.00
❑ 62 Vlade Divac	.30	.75
❑ 63 Jamal Mashburn	.30	.75
❑ 64 Jerome Williams	.25	.60
❑ 65 Patrick Ewing	.50	1.25
❑ 66 Lamar Odom	.40	1.00
❑ 67 Jerry Stackhouse	.30	.75
❑ 68 Michael Finley	.40	1.00
❑ 69 Vince Carter	.75	2.00
❑ 70 Andre Miller	.30	.75
❑ 71 Paul Pierce	.40	1.00
❑ 72 Baron Davis	.40	1.00
❑ 73 Derek Anderson	.30	.75
❑ 74 Chris Webber	.40	1.00
❑ 75 Ray Allen	.40	1.00
❑ 76 Kevin Garnett	.75	2.00
❑ 77 Allan Houston	.30	.75
❑ 78 Mike Bibby	.30	.75
❑ 79 Shareef Abdur-Rahim	.30	.75
❑ 80 Juwan Howard	.30	.75
❑ 81 Kenyon Martin RC	4.00	10.00
❑ 82 Stromile Swift RC	2.00	5.00
❑ 83 Darius Miles RC	2.00	5.00
❑ 84 Marcus Fizer RC	1.50	4.00
❑ 85 Mike Miller RC	2.50	6.00
❑ 86 DerMarr Johnson RC	1.50	4.00
❑ 87 Chris Mihm RC	1.50	4.00
❑ 88 Jamal Crawford RC	2.50	6.00
❑ 89 Joel Przybilla RC	1.50	4.00
❑ 90 Keyon Dooling RC	1.50	4.00
❑ 91 Jerome Moiso RC	1.50	4.00
❑ 92 Etan Thomas RC	1.50	4.00
❑ 93 Courtney Alexander RC	1.50	4.00
❑ 94 Mateen Cleaves RC	1.50	4.00
❑ 95 Jason Collier RC	1.50	4.00
❑ 96 Desmond Mason RC	2.00	5.00
❑ 97 Quentin Richardson RC	2.00	5.00
❑ 98 Jamaal Magloire RC	1.50	4.00
❑ 99 Speedy Claxton RC	1.50	4.00
❑ 100 Morris Peterson RC	2.50	6.00

2008-09 Topps Hardwood

❑ COMP.SET w/o SPs (100)	20.00	40.00
❑ 1 Paul Pierce	.50	1.25
❑ 2 Andrew Bogut	.40	1.00
❑ 3 Greg Oden	.40	1.00
❑ 4 Monta Ellis	.40	1.00
❑ 5 Shaquille O'Neal	.75	2.00
❑ 6 Al Horford	.40	1.00
❑ 7 Al Thornton	.40	1.00
❑ 8 Anderson Varejao	.30	.75
❑ 9 Andre Iguodala	.40	1.00
❑ 10 Carlos Boozer	.40	1.00
❑ 11 Chris Bosh	.40	1.00
❑ 12 Corey Maggette	.40	1.00
❑ 13 Craig Smith	.40	1.00
❑ 14 Danny Granger	.40	1.00
❑ 15 David West	.40	1.00
❑ 16 Josh Howard	.40	1.00
❑ 17 Kevin Durant	1.00	2.50
❑ 18 Kevin Garnett	.75	2.00
❑ 19 Luis Scola	.30	.75
❑ 20 Luol Deng	.40	1.00
❑ 21 Yi Jianlian	.40	1.00
❑ 22 Pau Gasol	.40	1.00
❑ 23 Rasheed Wallace	.40	1.00
❑ 24 Ben Gordon	.40	1.00
❑ 25 Dwyane Wade	.75	2.00
❑ 26 Gilbert Arenas	.40	1.00
❑ 27 Jamal Crawford	.25	.60
❑ 28 Gerald Wallace	.40	1.00
❑ 29 Jason Richardson	.40	1.00
❑ 30 Kevin Martin	.40	1.00
❑ 31 Mike Conley	.30	.75
❑ 32 Richard Hamilton	.30	.75
❑ 33 Tony Parker	.40	1.00
❑ 34 Vince Carter	.50	1.25
❑ 35 Brad Miller	.40	1.00
❑ 36 Al Jefferson	.40	1.00
❑ 37 Antawn Jamison	.40	1.00
❑ 38 Carmelo Anthony	.50	1.25
❑ 39 David Lee	.30	.75
❑ 40 Dirk Nowitzki	.50	1.25
❑ 41 Elton Brand	.60	1.50
❑ 42 Jose Calderon	.30	.75
❑ 43 Josh Smith	.40	1.00
❑ 44 LaMarcus Aldridge	.40	1.00
❑ 45 LeBron James	2.00	5.00
❑ 46 Peja Stojakovic	.40	1.00
❑ 47 Rashard Lewis	.40	1.00
❑ 48 Richard Jefferson	.40	1.00
❑ 49 Devin Harris	.40	1.00
❑ 50 Joe Johnson	.40	1.00
❑ 51 Shawn Marion	.40	1.00
❑ 52 Stephen Jackson	.30	.75
❑ 53 Tayshaun Prince	.40	1.00
❑ 54 Baron Davis	.40	1.00
❑ 55 Chris Paul	.75	2.00
❑ 56 Mike Dunleavy	.30	.75
❑ 57 Deron Williams	.50	1.25
❑ 58 Kobe Bryant	2.00	5.00
❑ 59 Jason Kidd	.40	1.00
❑ 60 Ray Allen	.40	1.00
❑ 61 Manu Ginobili	.40	1.00
❑ 62 Michael Redd	.40	1.00
❑ 63 Rajon Rondo	.40	1.00
❑ 64 Raymond Felton	.30	.75
❑ 65 Steve Nash	.40	1.00
❑ 66 T.J. Ford	.25	.60
❑ 67 Tracy McGrady	.50	1.25
❑ 68 Amare Stoudemire	.50	1.25
❑ 69 Andrew Bynum	.40	1.00
❑ 70 Ben Wallace	.40	1.00
❑ 71 Eddy Curry	.25	.60
❑ 72 Marcus Camby	.25	.60
❑ 73 Tyson Chandler	.30	.75
❑ 74 Yao Ming	.50	1.25
❑ 75 Andrei Kirilenko	.40	1.00
❑ 76 Andres Nocioni	.30	.75
❑ 77 Caron Butler	.40	1.00
❑ 78 Hedo Turkoglu	.40	1.00
❑ 79 Jeff Green	.30	.75
❑ 80 Mike Miller	.40	1.00
❑ 81 Ron Artest	.40	1.00
❑ 82 Rudy Gay	.40	1.00
❑ 83 Tim Duncan	.60	1.50
❑ 84 Udonis Haslem	.40	1.00
❑ 85 Dwight Howard	.75	2.00
❑ 86 Jermaine O'Neal	.40	1.00
❑ 87 Allen Iverson	.50	1.25
❑ 88 Andre Miller	.30	.75
❑ 89 Brandon Roy	.50	1.25
❑ 90 Chauncey Billups	.40	1.00
❑ 91 Dominique Wilkins	.50	1.25
❑ 92 Isiah Thomas	.40	1.00
❑ 93 John Stockton	.60	1.50
❑ 94 Magic Johnson	.75	2.00
❑ 95 George Gervin	.50	1.25
❑ 96 Bill Russell	.60	1.50
❑ 97 David Robinson	.60	1.50
❑ 98 Larry Bird	1.25	3.00
❑ 99 Jerry West	.50	1.25
❑ 100 Dennis Rodman	.40	1.00
❑ 101 Derrick Rose 1 Ball RC	5.00	12.00
❑ 101B Derrick Rose 2 Balls RC	5.00	12.00
❑ 102 M.Beasley Shooting RC	2.50	6.00
❑ 102B M.Beasley Pointing RC	2.50	6.00
❑ 103 O.J. Mayo Shooting RC	2.00	5.00
❑ 103B O.J. Mayo Standing RC	2.00	5.00
❑ 104 R.Westbrook Shooting RC	3.00	8.00
❑ 104B R.Westbrook Standing RC	3.00	8.00
❑ 105 Kevin Love Shooting RC	1.50	4.00
❑ 105B Kevin Love Posing RC	1.50	4.00
❑ 106 D.Gallinari Dribbling RC	2.00	5.00
❑ 106B D.Gallinari Standing RC	2.00	5.00
❑ 107 Eric Gordon Shooting RC	1.50	4.00
❑ 107B Eric Gordon Standing RC	1.50	4.00
❑ 108 Joe Alexander Shooting RC	1.25	3.00
❑ 108B Joe Alexander Passing RC	1.25	3.00
❑ 109 D.J. Augustin Shooting RC	1.25	3.00
❑ 109B D.J. Augustin Posing RC	1.25	3.00
❑ 110 Brook Lopez Shooting RC	2.50	6.00
❑ 110B Brook Lopez Posing RC	2.50	6.00
❑ 111 Jerryd Bayless Passing RC	1.25	3.00
❑ 111B Jerryd Bayless Posing RC	1.25	3.00
❑ 112 J.Thompson Shooting RC	1.25	3.00
❑ 112B Jason Thompson Posing RC	1.25	3.00
❑ 113 Brandon Rush Action RC	1.25	3.00
❑ 113B Brandon Rush Posing RC	1.25	3.00
❑ 114 A.Randolph Finger RC	2.00	5.00
❑ 114B A.Randolph Posing RC	2.00	5.00
❑ 115 Robin Lopez Shooting RC	1.25	3.00
❑ 115B Robin Lopez Posing RC	1.25	3.00
❑ 116 M.Speights Action RC	1.25	3.00
❑ 116B M.Speights Posing RC	1.25	3.00
❑ 117 Roy Hibbert Shooting RC	1.50	4.00
❑ 117B Roy Hibbert Posing RC	1.50	4.00
❑ 118 J.J.Hickson Ball in Front RC	2.00	5.00
❑ 118B J.J.Hickson Ball on Side RC	2.00	5.00
❑ 119 Ryan Anderson Ball RC	1.25	3.00
❑ 119B Ryan Anderson Posing RC	1.25	3.00
❑ 120 Courtney Lee Face Right RC	2.00	5.00
❑ 120B Courtney Lee Face Left RC	2.00	5.00
❑ 121 Kosta Koufos Shooting RC	1.25	3.00
❑ 121B Kosta Koufos Posing RC	1.25	3.00
❑ 122 Darrell Arthur Forward RC	1.25	3.00
❑ 122B Darrell Arthur Face Left RC	1.25	3.00
❑ 123 Donte Greene Ball Up RC	1.25	3.00
❑ 123B Donte Greene Ball Down RC	1.25	3.00
❑ 124 Mario Chalmers 2 Balls RC	1.50	4.00
❑ 124B Mario Chalmers 1 Ball RC	1.50	4.00
❑ 125 Rudy Fernandez 2 Balls RC	2.50	6.00
❑ 125B Rudy Fernandez 1 Ball RC	2.50	6.00

2000-01 Topps Heritage

❑ COMPLETE SET w/o RC (197)	30.00	60.00
❑ COMMON CARD (1-233)	.25	.60
❑ COMMON ROOKIE (25-60)	1.50	4.00
❑ 1 Jason Kidd	.60	1.50
❑ 2 Allen Iverson	.75	2.00
❑ 3 Tracy McGrady	.75	2.00
❑ 4 Tim Duncan	.75	2.00
❑ 5 Michael Finley	.40	1.00
❑ 6 Jason Williams	.30	.75
❑ 7 Kobe Bryant	2.00	5.00
❑ 8 Gary Payton	.40	1.00
❑ 9 Latrell Sprewell	.30	.75
❑ 10 Antonio McDyess	.30	.75
❑ 11 Antoine Walker	.30	.75
❑ 12 Steve Francis	.40	1.00
❑ 13 Elton Brand	.40	1.00
❑ 14 Larry Hughes	.30	.75
❑ 15 Shaquille O'Neal	1.00	2.50
❑ 16 Lamar Odom	.40	1.00
❑ 17 Kevin Garnett	.75	2.00
❑ 18 Vince Carter	.75	2.00
❑ 19 Ray Allen	.40	1.00
❑ 20 Grant Hill	.40	1.00
❑ 21 Chris Webber	.40	1.00

❑ 22 Paul Pierce	.40	1.00
❑ 23 Shareef Abdur-Rahim	.30	.75
❑ 24 Eddie Jones	.30	.75
❑ 25 Kenyon Martin RC	4.00	10.00
❑ 26 Stromile Swift RC	2.00	5.00
❑ 27 Darius Miles RC	2.00	5.00
❑ 28 Marcus Fizer RC	1.50	4.00
❑ 29 Mike Miller RC	2.50	6.00
❑ 30 DerMarr Johnson RC	1.50	4.00
❑ 31 Chris Mihm RC	1.50	4.00
❑ 32 Jamal Crawford RC	2.50	6.00
❑ 33 Joel Przybilla RC	1.50	4.00
❑ 34 Keyon Dooling RC	1.50	4.00
❑ 35 Jerome Moiso RC	1.50	4.00
❑ 36 Etan Thomas RC	1.50	4.00
❑ 37 Courtney Alexander RC	1.50	4.00
❑ 38 Mateen Cleaves RC	1.50	4.00
❑ 39 Jason Collier RC	1.50	4.00
❑ 40 Hedo Turkoglu RC	4.00	10.00
❑ 41 Desmond Mason RC	2.00	5.00
❑ 42 Quentin Richardson RC	2.00	5.00
❑ 43 Jamaal Magloire RC	1.50	4.00
❑ 44 Speedy Claxton RC	1.50	4.00
❑ 45 Morris Peterson RC	2.50	6.00
❑ 46 Donnell Harvey RC	1.50	4.00
❑ 47 DeShawn Stevenson RC	1.50	4.00
❑ 48 Dalibor Bagaric RC	1.50	4.00
❑ 49 Iakovos Tsakalidis RC	1.50	4.00
❑ 50 Mamadou N'Diaye RC	1.50	4.00
❑ 51 Erick Barkley RC	1.50	4.00
❑ 52 Mark Madsen RC	1.50	4.00
❑ 53 Dan Langhi RC	1.50	4.00
❑ 54 A.J. Guyton RC	1.50	4.00
❑ 55 Jake Voskuhl RC	1.50	4.00
❑ 56 Khalid El-Amin RC	1.50	4.00
❑ 57 Lavor Postell RC	1.50	4.00
❑ 58 Eduardo Najera RC	1.50	4.00
❑ 59 Michael Redd RC	4.00	10.00
❑ 60 Stephen Jackson RC	2.50	6.00
❑ 61 Andrew DeClercq	.25	.60
❑ 62 Darrell Armstrong	.25	.60
❑ 63 Al Harrington	.30	.75
❑ 64 Johnny Newman	.25	.60
❑ 65 Baron Davis	.40	1.00
❑ 66 Adrian Griffin	.25	.60
❑ 67 Anthony Mason	.25	.60
❑ 68 Ron Harper	.30	.75
❑ 69 Michael Olowokandi	.25	.60
❑ 70 Maurice Taylor	.25	.60
❑ 71 Travis Best	.25	.60
❑ 72 Chucky Atkins	.25	.60
❑ 73 Bob Sura	.25	.60
❑ 74 Jason Terry	.40	1.00
❑ 75 Ervin Johnson	.25	.60
❑ 76 Eric Snow	.25	.60
❑ 77 Shawn Bradley	.25	.60
❑ 78 Christian Laettner	.25	.60
❑ 79 Keith Van Horn	.30	.75
❑ 80 Damon Stoudamire	.30	.75
❑ 81 Peja Stojakovic	.30	.75
❑ 82 Clifford Robinson	.25	.60
❑ 83 Elden Campbell	.25	.60
❑ 84 Kenny Anderson	.30	.75
❑ 85 Patrick Ewing	.50	1.25
❑ 86 Mookie Blaylock	.30	.75
❑ 87 Brian Skinner	.25	.60
❑ 88 Rick Fox	.30	.75
❑ 89 Tim Hardaway	.30	.75
❑ 90 Brian Grant	.25	.60
❑ 91 Joe Smith	.25	.60
❑ 92 Kerry Kittles	.30	.75
❑ 93 Scottie Pippen	.60	1.50
❑ 94 Steve Smith	.30	.75
❑ 95 Sean Elliott	.30	.75
❑ 96 Rashard Lewis	.40	1.00
❑ 97 Michael Dickerson	.25	.60
❑ 98 Rod Strickland	.30	.75
❑ 99 Sam Cassell	.30	.75
❑ 100 Kareem Abdul-Jabbar	1.25	3.00
❑ 101 John Amaechi	.25	.60
❑ 102 Kendall Gill	.25	.60
❑ 103 Terrell Brandon	.25	.60
❑ 104 Dan Majerle	.30	.75
❑ 105 Mark Jackson	.30	.75
❑ 106 Hakeem Olajuwon	.50	1.25
❑ 107 Antawn Jamison	.40	1.00
❑ 108 Cedric Ceballos	.25	.60
❑ 109 Shandon Anderson	.25	.60
❑ 110 Gary Trent	.25	.60
❑ 111 Wesley Person	.25	.60
❑ 112 James Posey	.25	.60
❑ 113 David Wesley	.25	.60
❑ 114 Vitaly Potapenko	.25	.60
❑ 115 P.J. Brown	.25	.60
❑ 116 Alan Henderson	.25	.60
❑ 117 Terry Porter	.30	.75
❑ 118 Lindsey Hunter	.25	.60
❑ 119 Chauncey Billups	.40	1.00
❑ 120 Doug Christie	.25	.60
❑ 121 Glen Rice	.30	.75
❑ 122 Jamie Feick	.25	.60
❑ 123 Tom Gugliotta	.25	.60
❑ 124 Arvydas Sabonis	.30	.75
❑ 125 Toni Kukoc	.30	.75
❑ 126 Shawn Marion	.40	1.00
❑ 127 Dale Davis	.25	.60
❑ 128 Corliss Williamson	.30	.75
❑ 129 Brent Barry	.25	.60
❑ 130 Shammond Williams	.25	.60
❑ 131 Nick Anderson	.25	.60
❑ 132 Charles Oakley	.30	.75
❑ 133 Shaquille O'Neal CHAMP	.50	1.25
❑ 134 Ron Harper CHAMP	.30	.75
❑ 135 Kobe Bryant CHAMP	1.00	2.50
❑ 136 Shaquille O'Neal CHAMP	.50	1.25
❑ 137 L.A. Lakers CHAMP	.40	1.00
❑ 138 V.Carter/Iverson/J.Stack	.50	1.25
❑ 139 Iverson/G.Hill/V.Carter	.40	1.00
❑ 140 Mutombo/Mourning/D.Davis	.40	1.00
❑ 141 R.Miller/D.Arm/R.Allen	.40	1.00
❑ 142 Mutombo/Brand/Je.Williams	.40	1.00
❑ 143 S.Cassell/M.Jackson/E.Snow	.40	1.00
❑ 144 Checklist	.10	.30
❑ 145 Checklist	.10	.30
❑ 146 Shaq/K.Malone/Payton	.75	2.00
❑ 147 Shaq/K.Malone/Webber	.60	1.50
❑ 148 Shaq/Patterson/R.Wallace	.60	1.50
❑ 149 Hornacek/Brandon/Stojakovic	.10	.30
❑ 150 Shaq/Garnett/Duncan	.60	1.50
❑ 151 Payton/Van Exel/Stockton	.40	1.00
❑ 152 Chris Whitney	.25	.60
❑ 153 Isaac Austin	.25	.60
❑ 154 Kevin Willis	.25	.60
❑ 155 Vin Baker	.30	.75
❑ 156 Avery Johnson	.30	.75
❑ 157 Rodney Rogers	.25	.60
❑ 158 Allan Houston	.30	.75
❑ 159 Austin Croshere	.25	.60
❑ 160 George Lynch	.25	.60
❑ 161 Howard Eisley	.25	.60
❑ 162 Jerome Williams	.25	.60
❑ 163 LaPhonso Ellis	.30	.75
❑ 164 Ron Mercer	.25	.60
❑ 165 Andre Miller	.30	.75
❑ 166 Tariq Abdul-Wahad	.25	.60
❑ 167 Donyell Marshall	.25	.60
❑ 168 Quincy Lewis	.25	.60
❑ 169 Mitch Richmond	.30	.75
❑ 170 Richard Hamilton	.30	.75
❑ 171 Bryant Reeves	.25	.60
❑ 172 Jim Jackson	.25	.60
❑ 173 David Robinson	.50	1.25
❑ 174 Derrick Coleman	.30	.75
❑ 175 Anthony Peeler	.25	.60
❑ 176 Theo Ratliff	.25	.60
❑ 177 Roshown McLeod	.25	.60
❑ 178 Ron Artest	.40	1.00
❑ 179 Bryon Russell	.25	.60
❑ 180 Othella Harrington	.25	.60
❑ 181 Juwan Howard	.30	.75
❑ 182 Antonio Davis	.25	.60
❑ 183 Ruben Patterson	.25	.60
❑ 184 Shawn Kemp	.40	1.00
❑ 185 Larry Johnson	.30	.75
❑ 186 Marcus Camby	.30	.75
❑ 187 Eric Piatkowski	.25	.60
❑ 188 Reggie Miller	.40	1.00
❑ 189 Anfernee Hardaway	.40	1.00
❑ 190 Kelvin Cato	.25	.60
❑ 191 Erick Dampier	.25	.60
❑ 192 Keon Clark	.25	.60
❑ 193 Dirk Nowitzki	.60	1.50
❑ 194 Robert Traylor	.25	.60
❑ 195 Lamond Murray	.25	.60
❑ 196 John Wallace	.25	.60
❑ 197 Robert Horry	.30	.75
❑ 198 Robert Pack	.25	.60
❑ 199 Jamal Mashburn	.30	.75
❑ 200 Corey Benjamin	.25	.60
❑ 201 Matt Harpring	.30	.75
❑ 202 Nick Van Exel	.30	.75
❑ 203 Vonteego Cummings	.25	.60
❑ 204 Ben Wallace	.30	.75
❑ 205 Karl Malone	.50	1.25
❑ 206 Jonathan Bender	.25	.60
❑ 207 Cuttino Mobley	.30	.75
❑ 208 Isaiah Rider	.30	.75
❑ 209 Tyrone Nesby	.25	.60
❑ 210 Jermaine O'Neal	.40	1.00
❑ 211 Corey Maggette	.30	.75
❑ 212 Anthony Carter	.25	.60
❑ 213 Horace Grant	.30	.75
❑ 214 Tim Thomas	.25	.60
❑ 215 Wally Szczerbiak	.30	.75
❑ 216 Stephon Marbury	.40	1.00
❑ 217 Charlie Ward	.25	.60
❑ 218 Bo Outlaw	.25	.60
❑ 219 Matt Geiger	.25	.60
❑ 220 Vlade Divac	.30	.75
❑ 221 Rasheed Wallace	.40	1.00
❑ 222 Derek Anderson	.30	.75
❑ 223 John Stockton	.50	1.25
❑ 224 Dikembe Mutombo	.30	.75
❑ 225 John Starks	.25	.60
❑ 226 Mike Bibby	.30	.75
❑ 227 Jahidi White	.25	.60
❑ 228 Jalen Rose	.30	.75
❑ 229 Glenn Robinson	.30	.75
❑ 230 Brevin Knight	.25	.60
❑ 231 Jerry Stackhouse	.30	.75
❑ 232 Raef LaFrentz	.25	.60
❑ 233 Brad Miller	.30	.75

2001-02 Topps Heritage

❑ COMPLETE SET (264)	125.00	250.00
❑ COMMON CARD (1-264)	.25	.60
❑ COMMON ROOKIE	.75	2.00
❑ 1 Shaquille O'Neal	1.00	2.50
❑ 2 Jalen Rose	.30	.75
❑ 3 Kwame Brown RC	1.00	2.50
❑ 4 Bryon Russell	.25	.60
❑ 5 Hakeem Olajuwon	.50	1.25
❑ 6 Shammond Williams	.25	.60
❑ 7 Aaron Mckie	.25	.60
❑ 8 Anfernee Hardaway	.40	1.00
❑ 9 Dale Davis	.25	.60
❑ 10 Tracy McGrady	.75	2.00
❑ 11 Speedy Claxton	.25	.60
❑ 12 Kurt Thomas	.25	.60
❑ 13 Keith Van Horn	.30	.75
❑ 14 Tyson Chandler RC	1.50	4.00
❑ 15 Andre Miller	.30	.75
❑ 16 Dirk Nowitzki	.60	1.50
❑ 17 Raef Lafrentz	.25	.60
❑ 18 Mateen Cleaves	.25	.60
❑ 19 Danny Fortson	.25	.60
❑ 20 Steve Francis	.40	1.00
❑ 21 Al Harrington	.30	.75
❑ 22 Keyon Dooling	.25	.60
❑ 23 Rick Fox	.30	.75
❑ 24 Michael Dickerson	.25	.60
❑ 25 Alonzo Mourning	.40	1.00
❑ 26 Glenn Robinson	.30	.75
❑ 27 Wally Szczerbiak	.30	.75
❑ 28 Todd MacCulloch	.25	.60
❑ 29 Shandon Anderson	.25	.60
❑ 30 Kobe Bryant	2.00	5.00
❑ 31 Tyrone Hill	.25	.60
❑ 32 Grant Hill	.40	1.00
❑ 33 Shawn Marion	.40	1.00
❑ 34 Derek Anderson	.30	.75
❑ 35 Hedo Turkoglu	.30	.75
❑ 36 David Robinson	.50	1.25
❑ 37 Gary Payton	.40	1.00

❑ 38 Alvin Williams	.25	.60
❑ 39 Pau Gasol RC	3.00	8.00
❑ 40 Tim Duncan	.75	2.00
❑ 41 Rashard Lewis	.40	1.00
❑ 42 Antonio Davis	.25	.60
❑ 43 Donyell Marshall	.25	.60
❑ 44 Jahidi White	.25	.60
❑ 45 Shareef Abdur-Rahim	.30	.75
❑ 46 Antoine Walker	.30	.75
❑ 47 P.J. Brown	.25	.60
❑ 48 Eddie Robinson	.25	.60
❑ 49 Chris Mihm	.25	.60
❑ 50 Kevin Garnett	.75	2.00
❑ 51 Marcus Camby	.30	.75
❑ 52 Mike Miller	.30	.75
❑ 53 Tony Delk	.25	.60
❑ 54 Mike Bibby	.30	.75
❑ 55 Dikembe Mutombo	.30	.75
❑ 56 Eddy Curry RC	1.25	3.00
❑ 57 Shawn Bradley	.25	.60
❑ 58 James Posey	.25	.60
❑ 59 Jason Richardson RC	1.50	4.00
❑ 60 Jason Kidd	.60	1.50
❑ 61 Eddie Griffin RC	.75	2.00
❑ 62 Larry Hughes	.30	.75
❑ 63 Ben Wallace	.30	.75
❑ 64 Antonio McDyess	.30	.75
❑ 65 Tim Hardaway	.30	.75
❑ 66 Shawn Kemp	.30	.75
❑ 67 Bobby Jackson	.25	.60
❑ 68 Tom Gugliotta	.25	.60
❑ 69 Antawn Jamison	.40	1.00
❑ 70 Lamar Odom	.40	1.00
❑ 71 Jamaal Tinsley RC	1.00	2.50
❑ 72 Moochie Norris	.25	.60
❑ 73 Marc Jackson	.25	.60
❑ 74 Andrei Kirilenko RC	2.00	5.00
❑ 75 Wang Zhizhi	.30	.75
❑ 76 Eric Snow	.25	.60
❑ 77 Rasheed Wallace	.40	1.00
❑ 78 Antonio Daniels	.25	.60
❑ 79 Vladimir Radmanovic RC	1.00	2.50
❑ 80 Morris Peterson	.30	.75
❑ 81 Terry/Terry/Mutombo/Terry	.40	1.00
❑ 82 Pierce/Pllcio/Walkr/Walkr	.25	.60
❑ 83 Mash/Hawkins/Brwn/Davis	.25	.60
❑ 84 Brand/Hoiberg/Brand/Hoiberg	.40	1.00
❑ 85 Millr/Lngdn/Wthrspoon/Millr	.25	.60
❑ 86 Nowitz/Nash/Nowitz/Nash	.40	1.00
❑ 87 McDys/McCld/McDys/VnEx	.25	.60
❑ 88 Stack/Barros/Wllce/Stack	.40	1.00
❑ 89 Jmisn/Jcksn/Jmisn/Blaylck	.40	1.00
❑ 90 Frncis/Mobly/Frncis/Frncis	.10	.30
❑ 91 Rose/Miller/O'Neal/Best	.40	1.00
❑ 92 Odm/Piatkow/Odm/McInns	.40	1.00
❑ 93 Shaq/Penbrthy/Shaq/Kobe	.60	1.50
❑ 94 Rahim/Rahim/Rahim/Bibby	.40	1.00
❑ 95 Jones/Jones/Masn/Hrdawy	.25	.60
❑ 96 Robnsn/Allen/Jhnsn/Cassll	.40	1.00
❑ 97 Grntt/Brandn/Grntt/Brandn	.50	1.25
❑ 98 Mrbry/Newmn/Wllams/Mrbry	.25	.60
❑ 99 Deshawn Stevenson	.25	.60
❑ 100 Allen Iverson	.75	2.00
❑ 101 Jeryl Sasser RC	.75	2.00
❑ 102 Jason Terry	.40	1.00
❑ 103 Vitaly Potapenko	.25	.60
❑ 104 Elden Campbell	.25	.60
❑ 105 Jamal Crawford	.30	.75
❑ 106 Michael Finley	.40	1.00
❑ 107 Earl Watson RC	1.00	2.50
❑ 108 Clifford Robinson	.25	.60
❑ 109 Chucky Atkins	.25	.60
❑ 110 Glen Rice	.30	.75
❑ 111 Jermaine O'Neal	.40	1.00
❑ 112 Jonathan Bender	.25	.60
❑ 113 Michael Olowokandi	.25	.60
❑ 114 Derek Fisher	.30	.75
❑ 115 Stromile Swift	.25	.60
❑ 116 Toni Kukoc	.30	.75
❑ 117 Samuel Dalembert RC	1.00	2.50
❑ 118 Paul Pierce	.40	1.00
❑ 119 Jamal Mashburn	.30	.75
❑ 120 Ron Mercer	.25	.60
❑ 121 Lamond Murray	.25	.60
❑ 122 Steve Nash	.60	1.50
❑ 123 Nick Van Exel	.30	.75
❑ 124 Desagana Diop RC	.75	2.00
❑ 125 Ron Artest	.30	.75
❑ 126 Marcus Fizer	.25	.60
❑ 127 Jumaine Jones	.25	.60
❑ 128 Corliss Williamson	.30	.75
❑ 129 Rodney White RC	.75	2.00
❑ 130 Cuttino Mobley	.30	.75
❑ 131 Reggie Miller	.40	1.00
❑ 132 Austin Croshere	.25	.60
❑ 133 Jeff Mcinnis	.25	.60
❑ 134 Joe Johnson RC	2.00	5.00
❑ 135 Kedrick Brown RC	.75	2.00
❑ 136 Theo Ratliff	.25	.60
❑ 137 Laphonso Ellis	.30	.75
❑ 138 Ervin Johnson	.25	.60
❑ 139 Terrell Brandon	.25	.60
❑ 140 Chauncey Billups	.30	.75
❑ 141 Kenyon Martin	.40	1.00
❑ 142 Richard Jefferson RC	2.00	5.00
❑ 143 Howard Eisley	.25	.60
❑ 144 Stackhouse/Iverson/Shaq	.50	1.25
❑ 145 Iverson/Stackhouse/Shaq	.60	1.50
❑ 146 Shaq/Wells/Camby	.40	1.00
❑ 147 Miller/Houston/Christie	.25	.60
❑ 148 Mutombo/Wallace/Shaq	.40	1.00
❑ 149 Kidd/Stockton/Van Exel	.40	1.00
❑ 150 Vince Carter	.75	2.00
❑ 151 Calvin Booth	.25	.60
❑ 152 Chris Whitney	.25	.60
❑ 153 John Amaechi	.25	.60
❑ 154 Keon Clark	.25	.60
❑ 155 Terry Porter	.25	.60
❑ 156 Doug Christie	.25	.60
❑ 157 Gerald Wallace RC	2.00	5.00
❑ 158 Zach Randolph RC	2.00	5.00
❑ 159 Iakovos Tsakalidis	.25	.60
❑ 160 Damone Brown RC	.75	2.00
❑ 161 Ivrsn/Miller/Grntt/Duncan	.50	1.25
❑ 162 Allen/T-Mac/Shaq/Smith	1.00	2.50
❑ 163 Mornig/Dvis/Wbber/Hrdway	.40	1.00
❑ 164 Houstn/Crtr/Nowitz/Malone	.60	1.50
❑ 165 Christian Laettner	.25	.60
❑ 166 John Starks	.25	.60
❑ 167 Jerome Williams	.25	.60
❑ 168 Brent Barry	.25	.60
❑ 169 Malik Rose	.25	.60
❑ 170 Vlade Divac	.30	.75
❑ 171 Damon Stoudamire	.30	.75
❑ 172 Rodney Rogers	.25	.60
❑ 173 Alvin Jones RC	.75	2.00
❑ 174 Darrell Armstrong	.25	.60
❑ 175 Mark Jackson	.30	.75
❑ 176 Kerry Kittles ERR	.30	.75
❑ 177 Radoslav Nesterovic	.25	.60
❑ 178 Brandon Armstrong RC	.75	2.00
❑ 179 Joe Smith	.25	.60
❑ 180 Ray Allen	.40	1.00
❑ 181 Anthony Mason	.25	.60
❑ 182 Bryant Reeves	.25	.60
❑ 183 Jason Williams	.30	.75
❑ 184 Terence Morris RC	.75	2.00
❑ 185 Travis Best	.25	.60
❑ 186 Troy Murphy RC	1.50	4.00
❑ 187 Gilbert Arenas RC	1.25	3.00
❑ 188 Avery Johnson	.30	.75
❑ 189 Juwan Howard	.30	.75
❑ 190 Checklist	.10	.30
❑ 191 Courtney Alexander	.25	.60
❑ 192 John Stockton	.50	1.25
❑ 193 Vin Baker	.30	.75
❑ 194 Desmond Mason	.30	.75
❑ 195 Steve Smith	.30	.75
❑ 196 Steven Hunter RC	.75	2.00
❑ 197 Stephon Marbury	.40	1.00
❑ 198 Patrick Ewing	.50	1.25
❑ 199 Allan Houston	.30	.75
❑ 200 Karl Malone	.50	1.25
❑ 201 Peja Stojakovic	.30	.75
❑ 202 Bonzi Wells	.30	.75
❑ 203 Latrell Sprewell	.30	.75
❑ 204 Rafer Alston	.25	.60
❑ 205 Tony Parker RC	3.00	8.00
❑ 206 Michael Bradley RC	.75	2.00
❑ 207 Richard Hamilton	.30	.75
❑ 208 Zeljko Rebraca RC	.75	2.00
❑ 209 Joel Przybilla	.25	.60
❑ 210 Tim Thomas	.25	.60
❑ 211 Eddie House	.25	.60
❑ 212 Brian Grant	.25	.60
❑ 213 Lindsey Hunter	.25	.60
❑ 214 Corey Maggette	.30	.75
❑ 215 Shane Battier RC	1.25	3.00
❑ 216 Will Solomon	.40	1.00
❑ 217 Mitch Richmond	.30	.75
❑ 218 Eddie Jones	.30	.75
❑ 219 Elton Brand	.40	1.00
❑ 220 Quentin Richardson	.30	.75
❑ 221 Hustn/Houstn/Cmby/Ward	.25	.60
❑ 222 T-Mc/Armstrong/Outlw/Arm	.40	1.00
❑ 223 Ivrsn/Ivrsn/Hill/McKie	.60	1.50
❑ 224 Mrion/Kidd/Mrion/Kidd	.40	1.00
❑ 225 Wllce/Smth/Davis/Stoudmr	.25	.60
❑ 226 Wbbr/Christi/Wbbr/Wllams	.40	1.00
❑ 227 Duncn/Andrsn/Duncn/Dnils	.40	1.00
❑ 228 Pytn/Williams/Ewing/Pytn	.25	.60
❑ 229 Cartr/Curry/Davis/Jackson	.40	1.00
❑ 230 Malon/Stock/Malon/Stock	.40	1.00
❑ 231 Hwrd/Whtny/White/Whtny	.25	.60
❑ 232 Brendan Haywood RC	1.00	2.50
❑ 233 Scottie Pippen	.60	1.50
❑ 234 Loren Woods RC	.75	2.00
❑ 235 Sam Cassell	.30	.75
❑ 236 Anthony Carter	.25	.60
❑ 237 Raja Bell RC	1.00	2.50
❑ 238 Robert Horry	.30	.75
❑ 239 Maurice Taylor	.25	.60
❑ 240 Zydrunas Ilgauskas	.30	.75
❑ 241 Derrick Coleman	.30	.75
❑ 242 Kenny Anderson	.30	.75
❑ 243 Joseph Forte RC	.75	2.00
❑ 244 Baron Davis	.40	1.00
❑ 245 Nazr Mohammed	.25	.60
❑ 246 Ivrsn/Cartr/Duncn/Bradly	.50	1.25
❑ 247 Allen/Davis/Kobe/Divac	.75	2.00
❑ 248 Mtmb/Robnsn/Robnsn/Lue	.40	1.00
❑ 249 Bryant/Iverson	.50	1.25
❑ 250 Darius Miles	.25	.60
❑ 251 Samaki Walker	.25	.60
❑ 252 Dermarr Johnson	.25	.60
❑ 253 David Wesley	.25	.60
❑ 254 Trenton Hassell RC	1.00	2.50
❑ 255 Jeff Trepagnier RC	.75	2.00
❑ 256 Jacque Vaughn	.25	.60
❑ 257 Kirk Haston RC	.75	2.00
❑ 258 Jamaal Magloire	.25	.60
❑ 259 Jason Collins RC	.75	2.00
❑ 260 Chris Webber	.40	1.00
❑ 261 Kenny Satterfield RC	.75	2.00
❑ 262 Horace Grant	.30	.75
❑ 263 Jerry Stackhouse	.30	.75
❑ 264 Michael Jordan	6.00	15.00

2001-02 Topps High Topps

❑ COMPLETE SET (164)	350.00	700.00
❑ COMP.SET w/o SP's (105)	30.00	60.00
❑ COMMON CARD (1-105)	.25	.60
❑ COMMON AU (106-113)	5.00	12.00
❑ COMMON JSY (114-129)	3.00	8.00
❑ COMMON AU RC (130-140)	5.00	12.00
❑ COMMON JSY RC (141-153)	4.00	10.00
❑ COMMON ROOKIE (154-164)	1.25	3.00
❑ 1 Shaquille O'Neal	1.00	2.50
❑ 2 Reggie Miller	.40	1.00
❑ 3 Steve Francis	.40	1.00
❑ 4 Jerry Stackhouse	.30	.75
❑ 5 Nick Van Exel	.30	.75
❑ 6 Dirk Nowitzki	.60	1.50
❑ 7 Dikembe Mutombo	.30	.75
❑ 8 Terrell Brandon	.25	.60
❑ 9 Allan Houston	.30	.75
❑ 10 Kevin Garnett	.75	2.00
❑ 11 Eric Snow	.25	.60
❑ 12 Stephon Marbury	.40	1.00
❑ 13 Jalen Rose	.30	.75
❑ 14 Rick Fox	.30	.75
❑ 15 Alonzo Mourning	.40	1.00

❑ 16 Tim Thomas .25 .60
❑ 17 Keith Van Horn .30 .75
❑ 18 Glen Rice .30 .75
❑ 19 Mike Miller .30 .75
❑ 20 Chris Webber .40 1.00
❑ 21 Larry Hughes .30 .75
❑ 22 Joe Smith .25 .60
❑ 23 Ron Mercer .25 .60
❑ 24 Jamal Mashburn .30 .75
❑ 25 Shareef Abdur-Rahim .30 .75
❑ 26 P.J. Brown .25 .60
❑ 27 Ben Wallace .30 .75
❑ 28 Wang Zhizhi .30 .75
❑ 29 Jermaine O'Neal .40 1.00
❑ 30 Lamar Odom .40 1.00
❑ 31 Stromile Swift .25 .60
❑ 32 Theo Ratliff .25 .60
❑ 33 Patrick Ewing .50 1.25
❑ 34 Antonio Davis .25 .60
❑ 35 John Stockton .50 1.25
❑ 36 Courtney Alexander .25 .60
❑ 37 Alvin Williams .25 .60
❑ 38 Rashard Lewis .40 1.00
❑ 39 Mike Bibby .30 .75
❑ 40 Scottie Pippen .60 1.50
❑ 41 Anfernee Hardaway .40 1.00
❑ 42 Marcus Camby .30 .75
❑ 43 Glenn Robinson .30 .75
❑ 44 Jason Williams .30 .75
❑ 45 Horace Grant .30 .75
❑ 46 Chris Mihm .25 .60
❑ 47 Paul Pierce .40 1.00
❑ 48 DerMarr Johnson .25 .60
❑ 49 Steve Nash .60 1.50
❑ 50 Vince Carter .75 2.00
❑ 51 Michael Jordan 6.00 15.00
❑ 52 Donyell Marshall .25 .60
❑ 53 Desmond Mason .30 .75
❑ 54 Tom Gugliotta .25 .60
❑ 55 Hedo Turkoglu .30 .75
❑ 56 Grant Hill .40 1.00
❑ 57 Kenyon Martin .40 1.00
❑ 58 Wally Szczerbiak .30 .75
❑ 59 Eddie Jones .30 .75
❑ 60 Kobe Bryant 2.00 5.00
❑ 61 Cuttino Mobley .30 .75
❑ 62 Michael Dickerson .25 .60
❑ 63 Clifford Robinson .25 .60
❑ 64 Raef LaFrentz .25 .60
❑ 65 Lamond Murray .25 .60
❑ 66 Kenny Anderson .30 .75
❑ 67 Antonio Daniels .25 .60
❑ 68 Hakeem Olajuwon .50 1.25
❑ 69 Eddie Robinson .25 .60
❑ 70 Karl Malone .50 1.25
❑ 71 Richard Hamilton .30 .75
❑ 72 Derek Anderson .30 .75
❑ 73 Bonzi Wells .30 .75
❑ 74 Darrell Armstrong .25 .60
❑ 75 Gary Payton .40 1.00
❑ 76 Bryon Russell .25 .60
❑ 77 Steve Smith .30 .75
❑ 78 Sam Cassell .30 .75
❑ 79 Brian Grant .25 .60
❑ 80 Antoine Walker .30 .75
❑ 81 Marcus Fizer .25 .60
❑ 82 Tim Duncan AN .75 2.00
❑ 83 Chris Webber AN .40 1.00
❑ 84 Shaquille O'Neal AN 1.00 2.50
❑ 85 Allen Iverson AN .75 2.00
❑ 86 Jason Kidd AN .60 1.50
❑ 87 Kevin Garnett AN .75 2.00
❑ 88 Vince Carter AN .75 2.00
❑ 89 Dikembe Mutombo AN .30 .75
❑ 90 Kobe Bryant AN 2.00 5.00
❑ 91 Tracy McGrady AN .75 2.00
❑ 92 Allen Iverson SL .50 1.25
❑ 93 Dikembe Mutombo SL .20 .50
❑ 94 Jason Kidd SL .40 1.00
❑ 95 Allen Iverson SL .50 1.25
❑ 96 Theo Ratliff SL .15 .40
❑ 97 Shaquille O'Neal SL .60 1.50
❑ 98 Reggie Miller SL .25 .60
❑ 99 Antoine Walker SL .20 .50
❑ 100 Michael Finley SL .25 .60
❑ 101 Jason Kidd SL .40 1.00
❑ 102 Shaquille O'Neal RTC .60 1.50
❑ 103 Kobe Bryant RTC 1.25 3.00
❑ 104 Derek Fisher RTC .20 .50
❑ 105 Shaquille O'Neal RTC .60 1.50
❑ 106 Shawn Marion AU 6.00 15.00
❑ 107 Antawn Jamison AU 8.00 20.00
❑ 108 Peja Stojakovic AU 15.00 40.00
❑ 109 Jason Terry AU 6.00 15.00
❑ 110 Aaron McKie AU 5.00 12.00
❑ 111 Keyon Dooling AU 5.00 12.00
❑ 112 Al Harrington AU 5.00 12.00
❑ 113 Chauncey Billups AU 5.00 12.00
❑ 114 Tim Duncan JSY 10.00 25.00
❑ 115 Tracy McGrady JSY 10.00 25.00
❑ 116 Jason Kidd JSY 8.00 20.00
❑ 117 Latrell Sprewell JSY 4.00 10.00
❑ 118 David Robinson JSY 6.00 15.00
❑ 119 Baron Davis JSY 5.00 12.00
❑ 120 Allen Iverson JSY 10.00 25.00
❑ 121 Ray Allen JSY 5.00 12.00
❑ 122 Rasheed Wallace JSY 5.00 12.00
❑ 123 Morris Peterson JSY 4.00 10.00
❑ 124 Darius Miles JSY 3.00 8.00
❑ 125 Marc Jackson JSY 3.00 8.00
❑ 126 Michael Finley JSY 5.00 12.00
❑ 127 Elton Brand JSY 5.00 12.00
❑ 128 Antonio McDyess JSY
❑ 129 Andre Miller JSY 4.00 10.00
❑ 130 Kwame Brown AU RC 5.00 12.00
❑ 131 Eddy Curry AU RC 6.00 15.00
❑ 132 Loren Woods AU RC 5.00 12.00
❑ 133 Joe Johnson AU RC 10.00 25.00
❑ 134 R.Jefferson AU RC 8.00 20.00
❑ 135 Z.Randolph AU RC 10.00 25.00
❑ 136 B.Haywood AU RC 5.00 12.00
❑ 137 Gilbert Arenas AU RC 20.00 40.00
❑ 138 Damone Brown AU RC 5.00 12.00
❑ 139 K.Satterfield AU RC 5.00 12.00
❑ 140 V.Radmanovic AU RC 5.00 12.00
❑ 141 Eddie Griffin JSY RC 5.00 12.00
❑ 142 Shane Battier JSY RC 5.00 12.00
❑ 143 M.Bradley JSY RC 4.00 10.00
❑ 144 Gerald Wallace JSY RC 6.00 15.00
❑ 145 S.Dalembert JSY RC 4.00 10.00
❑ 146 Tyson Chandler JSY RC 4.00 10.00
❑ 147 Pau Gasol JSY RC 8.00 20.00
❑ 148 Steven Hunter JSY RC 4.00 10.00
❑ 149 Rodney White JSY RC 4.00 10.00
❑ 150 Jeryl Sasser JSY RC 4.00 10.00
❑ 151 B.Armstrong JSY RC 5.00 12.00
❑ 152 Jamaal Tinsley JSY RC 5.00 12.00
❑ 153 DeSagana Diop JSY RC 4.00 10.00
❑ 154 Jason Richardson RC 2.50 6.00
❑ 155 Kirk Haston RC 1.25 3.00
❑ 156 Joseph Forte RC 1.25 3.00
❑ 157 Jason Collins RC 1.25 3.00
❑ 158 Kedrick Brown RC 1.25 3.00
❑ 159 Troy Murphy RC 2.50 6.00
❑ 160 Tony Parker RC 5.00 12.00
❑ 161 Raja Bell RC 1.50 4.00
❑ 162 Jeff Trepagnier RC 1.25 3.00
❑ 163 Terence Morris RC 1.25 3.00
❑ 164 Zeljko Rebraca RC 1.25 3.00

2002-03 Topps Jersey Edition

❑ ASTERISKS PERCIEVED AS SP VERSION
❑ JEAD Antonio Davis R UER 5.00 12.00
❑ JEAI Allen Iverson R * 8.00 20.00
❑ JEAJ Antawn Jamison R 5.00 12.00
❑ JEAK Andrei Kirilenko R 5.00 12.00
❑ JEAS A.Stoudemire R RC 10.00 25.00
❑ JEBD Baron Davis R 5.00 12.00
❑ JEBG Brian Grant R 5.00 12.00
❑ JEBW Ben Wallace R 5.00 12.00
❑ JECA Courtney Alexander R UER 5.0012.00
❑ JECB Carlos Boozer H RC 8.00 20.00
❑ JECJ Chris Jefferies H RC 5.00 12.00
❑ JECM Cuttino Mobley R 5.00 12.00
❑ JECW C.Wilcox R UER RC 6.00 15.00
❑ JEDD Dan Dickau R RC 5.00 12.00
❑ JEDF Derek Fisher R 5.00 12.00
❑ JEDN Dirk Nowitzki R 6.00 15.00
❑ JEDW DaJuan Wagner R 5.00 12.00
❑ JEEB Elton Brand R 5.00 12.00
❑ JEEC Eddy Curry R 5.00 12.00
❑ JEEG Eddie Griffin R UER 5.00 12.00
❑ JEEJ Eddie Jones R 5.00 12.00
❑ JEFJ Fred Jones R RC 5.00 12.00
❑ JEGA Gilbert Arenas R UER 5.00 12.00
❑ JEGG Gordan Giricek R RC 6.00 15.00
❑ JEJH Juwan Howard R 5.00 12.00
❑ JEJM Jamal Mashburn R 5.00 12.00
❑ JEJO Jermaine O'Neal R 5.00 12.00
❑ JEJR Jalen Rose R 5.00 12.00
❑ JEJS Joe Smith R 5.00 12.00
❑ JEJT Jamaal Tinsley R 5.00 12.00
❑ JEKG Kevin Garnett R 8.00 20.00
❑ JEKR Kareem Rush R RC 6.00 15.00
❑ JEKS Kenny Satterfield R 5.00 12.00
❑ JEKV Keith Van Horn R 5.00 12.00
❑ JEMD Mike Dunleavy H RC 8.00 20.00
❑ JEMF Michael Finley R 5.00 12.00
❑ JEMO Mehmet Okur R 5.00 12.00
❑ JEMP Morris Peterson R UER 5.00 12.00
❑ JENT N.Tskitishvili R RC 5.00 12.00
❑ JEPG Pau Gasol R 5.00 12.00
❑ JEPP Paul Pierce R 5.00 12.00
❑ JEQR Quentin Richardson R 5.00 12.00
❑ JEQW Qyntel Woods R RC 5.00 12.00
❑ JERB Rasual Butler R RC 5.00 12.00
❑ JERM Reggie Miller R 5.00 12.00
❑ JESA Shareef Abdur-Rahim R 5.00 12.00
❑ JESM Stephon Marbury R 5.00 12.00
❑ JESN Steve Nash R 5.00 12.00
❑ JESO Shaquille O'Neal R 10.00 25.00
❑ JETC Tyson Chandler R 5.00 12.00
❑ JETH Troy Hudson R 5.00 12.00
❑ JEWS Wally Szczerbiak R 5.00 12.00
❑ JEYM Yao Ming R RC 15.00 30.00
❑ JEAFM Aaron McKie R UER 5.00 12.00
❑ JEAHO Allan Houston H 5.00 12.00
❑ JEAIV Allen Iverson H 6.00 15.00
❑ JEALM Andre Miller R 5.00 12.00
❑ JEAMG Drew Gooden R 8.00 20.00
❑ JEAMI Andre Miller H 5.00 12.00
❑ JEAST Amare Stoudemire H 10.00 25.00
❑ JEBDA Baron Davis H 5.00 12.00
❑ JEBWA Ben Wallace H 5.00 12.00
❑ JECBU Caron Butler H RC 8.00 20.00
❑ JEDAS Damon Stoudamire H 5.00 12.00
❑ JEDDI Dan Dickau H UER 5.00 12.00
❑ JEDGO Drew Gooden H 8.00 20.00
❑ JEDJG Devean George R 5.00 12.00
❑ JEDLM Darius Miles R 5.00 12.00
❑ JEDMA Donyell Marshall R UER 5.00 12.00
❑ JEDNO Dirk Nowitzki H 6.00 15.00
❑ JEDWA DaJuan Wagner H RC 5.00 12.00
❑ JEEBR Elton Brand H 5.00 12.00
❑ JEECU Eddy Curry H 5.00 12.00
❑ JEECW Elden Campbell R UER 5.00 12.00
❑ JEGDW Bonzi Wells R 5.00 12.00
❑ JEGRO Glenn Robinson H 5.00 12.00
❑ JEJAR Jason Richardson R 5.00 12.00
❑ JEJAT Jason Terry R 5.00 12.00
❑ JEJCB Caron Butler R 8.00 20.00
❑ JEJDM Jamaal Magloire R UER 5.00 12.00
❑ JEJHS John Stockton R 5.00 12.00
❑ JEJKI Jason Kidd H 6.00 15.00
❑ JEJMJ Joe Johnson R 5.00 12.00
❑ JEJON Jermaine O'Neal H 5.00 12.00
❑ JEJOS John Stockton H 5.00 12.00
❑ JEJRI Jason Richardson H 5.00 12.00
❑ JEJRO Jalen Rose H 5.00 12.00
❑ JEJRS John Salmons R RC 6.00 15.00
❑ JEJWL Jerome Williams H 5.00 12.00
❑ JEKAM Karl Malone R 5.00 12.00
❑ JEKGA Kevin Garnett H 8.00 20.00
❑ JEKMA Karl Malone H 5.00 12.00
❑ JEKRU Kareem Rush H 6.00 15.00
❑ JEKVH Keith Van Horn H 5.00 12.00
❑ JELSP Latrell Sprewell H 5.00 12.00
❑ JEMAF Marcus Fizer R 5.00 12.00
❑ JEMOK Mehmet Okur H RC 5.00 12.00
❑ JENTS Nikoloz Tskitishvili H 5.00 12.00
❑ JEPGA Pau Gasol H 5.00 12.00
❑ JEQRI Quentin Richardson H 5.00 12.00

❑ JEQWO Qyntel Woods H	5.00	12.00
❑ JERAO Ron Artest R	5.00	12.00
❑ JERAW Rasheed Wallace R	5.00	12.00
❑ JERBU Rasual Butler H	5.00	12.00
❑ JERCH Richard Hamilton R	5.00	12.00
❑ JERHO Robert Horry R	5.00	12.00
❑ JERIH Richard Hamilton H	5.00	12.00
❑ JERWA Rasheed Wallace H	5.00	12.00
❑ JESCB Shane Battier R	5.00	12.00
❑ JESDM Shawn Marion R	5.00	12.00
❑ JESFR Steve Francis H	5.00	12.00
❑ JESMA Shawn Marion H	5.00	12.00
❑ JESNA Steve Nash H *	6.00	15.00
❑ JESON Shaquille O'Neal H	10.00	25.00
❑ JETCH Tyson Chandler H	5.00	12.00
❑ JETDU Tim Duncan H	10.00	25.00
❑ JETDU Tim Duncan R	8.00	20.00
❑ JETML Tracy McGrady R	10.00	25.00
❑ JETPA Tony Parker H	5.00	12.00
❑ JETPR Tayshaun Prince R RC	6.00	15.00
❑ JEWSZ Wally Szczerbiak H	5.00	12.00

2003-04 Topps Jersey Edition

❑ COMMON CARD	3.00	8.00
❑ COMMON ROOKIE	3.00	8.00
❑ COMMON SS RC	4.00	10.00
❑ AD Antonio Davis	3.00	8.00
❑ AH Allan Houston	3.00	8.00
❑ AI Allen Iverson	5.00	12.00
❑ AJ Antawn Jamison	3.00	8.00
❑ AK Andrei Kirilenko	3.00	8.00
❑ AM Andre Miller	3.00	8.00
❑ AP Aleksandar Pavlovic RC	4.00	10.00
❑ AS Amare Stoudemire	5.00	12.00
❑ BB Brent Barry	3.00	8.00
❑ BC Brian Cook RC	3.00	8.00
❑ BD Baron Davis	3.00	8.00
❑ BH Brandon Hunter RC	3.00	8.00
❑ BJ Bobby Jackson	3.00	8.00
❑ BM Brad Miller	3.00	8.00
❑ BW Ben Wallace	3.00	8.00
❑ CA Carmelo Anthony SS RC	10.00	25.00
❑ CB Caron Butler	3.00	8.00
❑ CK Chris Kaman RC	4.00	10.00
❑ CM Corey Maggette	3.00	8.00
❑ CW Chris Webber	3.00	8.00
❑ DC Derrick Coleman	3.00	8.00
❑ DG Drew Gooden	3.00	8.00
❑ DJ Dahntay Jones RC	3.00	8.00
❑ DM Desmond Mason	3.00	8.00
❑ DN Dirk Nowitzki	4.00	10.00
❑ DW Dwyane Wade SS RC	12.00	25.00
❑ EB Elton Brand AU	8.00	20.00
❑ EC Eddy Curry	3.00	8.00
❑ EG Manu Ginobili	3.00	8.00
❑ GA Gilbert Arenas	3.00	8.00
❑ GP Gary Payton	3.00	8.00
❑ GR Glenn Robinson	3.00	8.00
❑ HT Hedo Turkoglu	3.00	8.00
❑ JB Jerome Beasley RC	3.00	8.00
❑ JC Jamal Crawford	3.00	8.00
❑ JH Juwan Howard	3.00	8.00
❑ JJ James Jones RC	3.00	8.00
❑ JK Jason Kidd	4.00	10.00
❑ JM Jamal Mashburn	3.00	8.00
❑ JO Jermaine O'Neal	3.00	8.00
❑ JR Jalen Rose	3.00	8.00
❑ JS Jerry Stackhouse	3.00	8.00
❑ JT Jason Terry	3.00	8.00
❑ JW Jason Williams	3.00	8.00
❑ KB Kwame Brown	3.00	8.00
❑ KC Keon Clark	3.00	8.00
❑ KG Kevin Garnett	5.00	12.00
❑ KH Kirk Hinrich AU RC	20.00	40.00
❑ KM Karl Malone	3.00	8.00
❑ KP Kendrick Perkins RC	5.00	12.00
❑ KR Kareem Rush	3.00	8.00
❑ KT Kurt Thomas	3.00	8.00
❑ LB Leandro Barbosa SS RC	6.00	15.00
❑ LJ Lebron James SS RC	50.00	100.00
❑ LO Lamar Odom	3.00	8.00
❑ LR Luke Ridnour AU RC	10.00	25.00
❑ LS Latrell Sprewell	3.00	8.00
❑ LW Luke Walton SS RC	5.00	12.00
❑ MB Mike Bibby	3.00	8.00
❑ MC Marcus Camby	3.00	8.00
❑ MD Mike Dunleavy	3.00	8.00
❑ MJ Marko Jaric	3.00	8.00
❑ MM Mike Miller	3.00	8.00
❑ MO Michael Olowokandi	3.00	8.00
❑ MP Morris Peterson	3.00	8.00
❑ MR Michael Redd	3.00	8.00
❑ MS Mike Sweetney SS RC	4.00	10.00
❑ MT Maurice Taylor	3.00	8.00
❑ MW Maurice Williams RC	5.00	12.00
❑ NE Nduti Ebi RC	3.00	8.00
❑ NH Nene	3.00	8.00
❑ PG Pau Gasol	3.00	8.00
❑ PP Paul Pierce	3.00	8.00
❑ PS Peja Stojakovic	3.00	8.00
❑ QR Quentin Richardson	3.00	8.00
❑ QW Qyntel Woods	3.00	8.00
❑ RA Ray Allen	3.00	8.00
❑ RD Ricky Davis	3.00	8.00
❑ RG Reece Gaines SS RC	4.00	10.00
❑ RH Richard Hamilton	3.00	8.00
❑ RJ Richard Jefferson	3.00	8.00
❑ RL Raef LaFrentz	3.00	8.00
❑ RL Rashard Lewis	3.00	8.00
❑ RM Ron Mercer	3.00	8.00
❑ RN Radoslav Nesterovic	3.00	8.00
❑ RW Rasheed Wallace	3.00	8.00
❑ SB Steve Blake RC	3.00	8.00
❑ SC Sam Cassell	3.00	8.00
❑ SF Steve Francis	3.00	8.00
❑ SM Shawn Marion	3.00	8.00
❑ SN Steve Nash	3.00	8.00
❑ SO Shaquille O'Neal AU	40.00	80.00
❑ SP Scottie Pippen	4.00	10.00
❑ TB Troy Bell RC	3.00	8.00
❑ TC Tyson Chandler	3.00	8.00
❑ TD Tim Duncan	5.00	12.00
❑ TM Tracy McGrady	6.00	15.00
❑ TO Travis Outlaw RC	4.00	10.00
❑ TP Tony Parker	3.00	8.00
❑ TR Theo Ratliff	3.00	8.00
❑ TS Theron Smith RC	3.00	8.00
❑ TT Tim Thomas	3.00	8.00
❑ WG Willie Green RC	3.00	8.00
❑ YM Yao Ming	6.00	15.00
❑ ZC Zarko Cabarkapa RC	3.00	8.00
❑ ZI Zydrunas Ilgauskas	3.00	8.00
❑ ZP Zoran Planinic RC	3.00	8.00
❑ ZR Zach Randolph	3.00	8.00
❑ AHA Al Harrington	3.00	8.00
❑ BDR Boris Diaw RC	3.00	8.00
❑ CBI Chauncey Billups	3.00	8.00
❑ CBO Chris Bosh RC	6.00	15.00
❑ CBO Carlos Boozer	3.00	8.00
❑ CMO Cuttino Mobley	3.00	8.00
❑ CWI Corliss Williamson	3.00	8.00
❑ DAM Darko Milicic SS RC	5.00	12.00
❑ DCH Doug Christie	3.00	8.00
❑ DGE Devean George	3.00	8.00
❑ DMI Darius Miles	3.00	8.00
❑ DWA DaJuan Wagner	3.00	8.00
❑ DWE David West SS RC	8.00	20.00
❑ JHA Jarvis Hayes RC	3.00	8.00
❑ JHO Josh Howard RC	4.00	10.00
❑ JKA Jason Kapono SS RC	4.00	10.00
❑ JMA Jamaal Magloire	3.00	8.00
❑ JRI Jason Richardson	3.00	8.00
❑ JSM Joe Smith	3.00	8.00
❑ JWI Jerome Williams	3.00	8.00
❑ KMA Kenyon Martin	3.00	8.00
❑ KVH Keith Van Horn	3.00	8.00
❑ MBA Marcus Banks RC	3.00	8.00
❑ MJA Marc Jackson	3.00	8.00
❑ MPI Mickael Pietrus RC	3.00	8.00
❑ NVE Nick Van Exel	3.00	8.00
❑ RAR Ron Artest	3.00	8.00
❑ RHO Robert Horry	3.00	8.00
❑ RLO Raul Lopez	3.00	8.00
❑ RMI Reggie Miller	3.00	8.00
❑ SAR Shareef Abdur-Rahim	3.00	8.00
❑ SBA Shane Battier	3.00	8.00
❑ SCL Speedy Claxton	3.00	8.00
❑ SMA Stephon Marbury	3.00	8.00
❑ TMU Troy Murphy	3.00	8.00
❑ TPR Tayshaun Prince	3.00	8.00
❑ ZPA Zaur Pachulia RC	3.00	8.00

2007-08 Topps Letterman

❑ 1 Dwyane Wade	2.50	6.00
❑ 2 Kobe Bryant	5.00	12.00
❑ 3 Allen Iverson	2.00	5.00
❑ 4 Jason Kidd	1.50	4.00
❑ 5 Kevin Garnett	2.50	6.00
❑ 6 Tony Parker	1.00	2.50
❑ 7 Gilbert Arenas	1.00	2.50
❑ 8 Dwight Howard	2.00	5.00
❑ 9 Steve Nash	1.25	3.00
❑ 10 Carmelo Anthony	2.00	5.00
❑ 11 Tim Duncan	2.00	5.00
❑ 12 Chris Bosh	1.00	2.50
❑ 13 LeBron James	5.00	12.00
❑ 14 Tracy McGrady	2.00	5.00
❑ 15 Vince Carter	2.00	5.00
❑ 16 Amare Stoudemire	2.00	5.00
❑ 17 Shaquille O'Neal	2.50	6.00
❑ 18 Paul Pierce	1.00	2.50
❑ 19 Yao Ming	2.50	6.00
❑ 20 Dirk Nowitzki	1.50	4.00
❑ 21 Pau Gasol	1.00	2.50
❑ 22 Michael Redd	1.00	2.50
❑ 23 Carlos Boozer	1.00	2.50
❑ 24 Baron Davis	1.00	2.50
❑ 25 Caron Butler	1.00	2.50
❑ 26 Joe Johnson	1.00	2.50
❑ 27 Gerald Wallace	1.00	2.50
❑ 28 Al Jefferson	1.00	2.50
❑ 29 Chris Paul	2.00	5.00
❑ 30 Rudy Gay	.75	2.00
❑ 31 Manu Ginobili	1.00	2.50
❑ 32 Corey Maggette	.75	2.00
❑ 33 Ray Allen	1.00	2.50
❑ 34 Ben Gordon	1.25	3.00
❑ 35 Jamal Crawford	.60	1.50
❑ 36 David West	1.00	2.50
❑ 37 Andre Iguodala	1.00	2.50
❑ 38 Deron Williams	1.50	4.00
❑ 39 Brandon Roy	1.50	4.00
❑ 40 Richard Hamilton	.75	2.00
❑ 41 Larry Bird	4.00	10.00
❑ 42 John Stockton	2.00	5.00
❑ 43 Bill Russell	2.00	5.00
❑ 44 David Robinson	2.00	5.00
❑ 45 Isiah Thomas	1.25	3.00
❑ 46 Dennis Rodman	1.25	3.00
❑ 47 Jerry West	1.50	4.00
❑ 48 Moses Malone	1.25	3.00
❑ 49 Dominique Wilkins	1.50	4.00
❑ 50 Magic Johnson	2.50	6.00
❑ 51 Jamario Moon RC	4.00	10.00
❑ 52 Juan Carlos Navarro RC	2.50	6.00
❑ 53 Spencer Hawes RC	2.00	5.00
❑ 54 Glen Davis RC	4.00	10.00
❑ 55 Rodney Stuckey RC	4.00	10.00
❑ 56 Kevin Durant RC	15.00	40.00
❑ 57 Corey Brewer RC	2.50	6.00
❑ 58 Joakim Noah RC	2.50	6.00
❑ 59 Mike Conley RC	2.50	6.00
❑ 60 Al Horford RC	2.50	6.00
❑ 61 Julian Wright RC	2.50	6.00
❑ 62 Jeff Green RC	2.50	6.00
❑ 63 Luis Scola RC	3.00	8.00
❑ 64 Yi Jianlian RC	3.00	8.00
❑ 65 Sean Williams RC	2.00	5.00
❑ 66 Arron Afflalo RC	2.00	5.00

67 Al Thornton RC	2.00	5.00
68 Marco Belinelli RC	2.00	5.00
69 Javaris Crittenton RC	2.00	5.00
70 Thaddeus Young RC	2.50	6.00
71 Daequan Cook RC	2.50	6.00
72 Brandan Wright RC	2.50	6.00
73 Acie Law IV RC	2.50	6.00
74 Nick Young RC	2.00	5.00
75 Greg Oden RC	3.00	8.00
NNO Lottery Exchange	20.00	40.00

2004-05 Topps Luxury Box

COMMON CARD (1-100)	.25	.60
COMMON ROOKIE (101-130)	1.00	2.50
COMMON CARD (131-150)	1.25	3.00
1 Andrei Kirilenko	.40	1.00
2 Peja Stojakovic	.30	.75
3 Grant Hill	.40	1.00
4 Baron Davis	.40	1.00
5 Wally Szczerbiak	.30	.75
6 Ray Allen	.40	1.00
7 Shawn Marion	.40	1.00
8 Gilbert Arenas	.40	1.00
9 Keith Van Horn	.30	.75
10 Eddie Jones	.30	.75
11 Lamar Odom	.40	1.00
12 Stephen Jackson	.30	.75
13 Rasheed Wallace	.40	1.00
14 Steve Smith	.30	.75
15 Gary Payton	.40	1.00
16 Jason Terry	.30	.75
17 Eddy Curry	.30	.75
18 Yao Ming	1.00	2.50
19 Kenyon Martin	.40	1.00
20 Jason Richardson	.40	1.00
21 Bonzi Wells	.25	.60
22 Richard Jefferson	.40	1.00
23 LeBron James	2.50	6.00
24 Marko Jaric	.25	.60
25 Chauncey Billups	.40	1.00
26 Jamal Crawford	.30	.75
27 Willie Green	.25	.60
28 Zach Randolph	.40	1.00
29 Latrell Sprewell	.30	.75
30 Tim Duncan	.75	2.00
31 Cuttino Mobley	.30	.75
32 Shaquille O'Neal	1.00	2.50
33 Carlos Arroyo	.40	1.00
34 Jamaal Tinsley	.30	.75
35 Luke Ridnour	.25	.60
36 Kenny Anderson	.30	.75
37 Brad Miller	.30	.75
38 Caron Butler	.30	.75
39 Troy Murphy	.40	1.00
40 Vince Carter	.75	2.00
41 Shane Battier	.30	.75
42 Joe Johnson	.40	1.00
43 Jason Kapono	.25	.60
44 Juwan Howard	.30	.75
45 Zydrunas Ilgauskas	.30	.75
46 Jerry Stackhouse	.30	.75
47 Jamaal Magloire	.25	.60
48 Steve Francis	.40	1.00
49 Kwame Brown	.25	.60
50 Kevin Garnett	.75	2.00
51 Shareef Abdur-Rahim	.30	.75
52 Tony Parker	.40	1.00
53 Marcus Camby	.30	.75
54 Morris Peterson	.30	.75
55 Antoine Walker	.40	1.00
56 Elton Brand	.40	1.00
57 Paul Pierce	.40	1.00
58 Jason Kidd	.60	1.50
59 Gerald Wallace	.40	1.00
60 Jason Williams	.30	.75
61 Dwyane Wade	1.25	3.00
62 Amare Stoudemire	.75	2.00
63 T.J. Ford	.30	.75
64 Tyson Chandler	.30	.75
65 Alonzo Mourning	.40	1.00
66 Dirk Nowitzki	.60	1.50
67 Allan Houston	.30	.75
68 Andre Miller	.30	.75
69 Glenn Robinson	.30	.75
70 Richard Hamilton	.30	.75
71 Darius Miles	.30	.75
72 Mike Dunleavy	.30	.75
73 Mike Bibby	.30	.75
74 Tracy McGrady	.75	2.00
75 Manu Ginobili	.40	1.00
76 Jermaine O'Neal	.40	1.00
77 Rashard Lewis	.40	1.00
78 Corey Maggette	.30	.75
79 Chris Bosh	.40	1.00
80 Pau Gasol	.40	1.00
81 Carlos Boozer	.40	1.00
82 Desmond Mason	.30	.75
83 Antawn Jamison	.40	1.00
84 Sam Cassell	.30	.75
85 Al Harrington	.30	.75
86 Steve Nash	.60	1.50
87 Ricky Davis	.30	.75
88 Chris Andersen	.25	.60
89 Kirk Hinrich	.30	.75
90 Carmelo Anthony	1.25	3.00
91 Ron Mercer	.25	.60
92 Ben Wallace	.30	.75
93 Josh Howard	.40	1.00
94 Reggie Miller	.40	1.00
95 Chris Webber	.40	1.00
96 Drew Gooden	.25	.60
97 Michael Redd	.40	1.00
98 Allen Iverson	.75	2.00
99 Kobe Bryant	2.00	5.00
100 Stephon Marbury	.40	1.00
101 Dwight Howard RC	3.00	8.00
102 Emeka Okafor RC	2.00	5.00
103 Ben Gordon RC	1.25	3.00
104 Shaun Livingston RC	1.00	2.50
105 Devin Harris RC	2.00	5.00
106 Josh Childress RC	1.00	2.50
107 Luol Deng RC	1.25	3.00
108 Rafael Araujo RC	1.00	2.50
109 Andre Iguodala RC	2.50	6.00
110 Luke Jackson RC	1.00	2.50
111 Andris Biedrins RC	1.50	4.00
112 Robert Swift RC	1.00	2.50
113 Sebastian Telfair RC	1.00	2.50
114 Kris Humphries RC	1.50	4.00
115 Al Jefferson RC	2.00	5.00
116 Kirk Snyder RC	1.00	2.50
117 Josh Smith RC	2.50	6.00
118 J.R. Smith RC	2.00	5.00
119 Dorell Wright RC	1.25	3.00
120 Jameer Nelson RC	1.25	3.00
121 Andres Nocioni RC	1.25	3.00
122 Kevin Martin RC	1.25	3.00
123 Tony Allen RC	1.25	3.00
124 Anderson Varejao RC	1.25	3.00
125 Nenad Krstic RC	1.25	3.00
126 Sasha Vujacic RC	1.00	2.50
127 David Harrison RC	1.00	2.50
128 Pavel Podkolzin RC	1.00	2.50
129 Trevor Ariza RC	1.25	3.00
130 Delonte West RC	1.50	4.00
131 Rick Barry	1.25	3.00
132 Elgin Baylor	1.50	4.00
133 Larry Bird	3.00	8.00
134 Bob Cousy	1.25	3.00
135 Bill Russell	2.50	6.00
136 Walt Frazier	1.25	3.00
137 George Gervin	2.00	5.00
138 John Havlicek	2.00	5.00
139 James Worthy	2.00	5.00
140 Wilt Chamberlain	2.50	6.00
141 Dave Cowens	1.25	3.00
142 Moses Malone	1.50	4.00
143 Kevin McHale	1.50	4.00
144 Earl Monroe	1.25	3.00
145 Pete Maravich	5.00	12.00
146 Willis Reed	1.25	3.00
147 Oscar Robertson	2.00	5.00
148 Isiah Thomas	2.00	5.00
149 Bill Walton	1.50	4.00
150 Kareem Abdul-Jabbar	2.00	5.00

2005-06 Topps Luxury Box

COMP.SET w/o SP's (100)	20.00	50.00
COMMON CARD (1-100)	.10	.30
COMMON ROOKIE (101-145)	1.25	3.00
COMMON CELEB. (146-150)	1.50	4.00
1 Dwyane Wade	1.00	2.50
2 Joe Johnson	.40	1.00
3 Larry Hughes	.30	.75
4 Michael Finley	.40	1.00
5 Josh Howard	.40	1.00
6 Kenyon Martin	.40	1.00
7 Jermaine O'Neal	.40	1.00
8 Luke Ridnour	.30	.75
9 Andre Iguodala	.40	1.00
10 Wally Szczerbiak	.30	.75
11 Yao Ming	1.00	2.50
12 Dwight Howard	.75	2.00
13 Ricky Davis	.40	1.00
14 Baron Davis	.40	1.00
15 Carmelo Anthony	.75	2.00
16 Pau Gasol	.40	1.00
17 Robert Horry	.30	.75
18 Andres Nocioni	.25	.60
19 Sam Cassell	.40	1.00
20 Shareef Abdur-Rahim	.40	1.00
21 Gerald Wallace	.40	1.00
22 Vince Carter	.75	2.00
23 LeBron James	2.00	5.00
24 Richard Hamilton	.30	.75
25 Shawn Marion	.40	1.00
26 Stephon Marbury	.40	1.00
27 Chris Bosh	.40	1.00
28 Darius Miles	.40	1.00
29 Jamaal Magloire	.25	.60
30 Kevin Garnett	.75	2.00
31 Lamar Odom	.40	1.00
32 Shaquille O'Neal	1.00	2.50
33 Allen Iverson	.75	2.00
34 Paul Pierce	.40	1.00
35 Keith Van Horn	.30	.75
36 Damon Stoudamire	.30	.75
37 Jason Richardson	.40	1.00
38 Ben Gordon	.50	1.25
39 J.R. Smith	.30	.75
40 Brad Miller	.40	1.00
41 Dirk Nowitzki	.60	1.50
42 Bonzi Wells	.30	.75
43 Corey Maggette	.30	.75
44 Tracy McGrady	.75	2.00
45 T.J. Ford	.30	.75
46 Steve Francis	.40	1.00
47 Bobby Simmons	.25	.60
48 Eddy Curry	.30	.75
49 Antawn Jamison	.40	1.00
50 Emeka Okafor	.40	1.00
51 Tim Duncan	.75	2.00
52 Chauncey Billups	.40	1.00
53 Kwame Brown	.30	.75
54 Ray Allen	.40	1.00
55 Jason Kidd	.60	1.50
56 Marcus Camby	.30	.75
57 Stephen Jackson	.30	.75
58 Rasheed Wallace	.40	1.00
59 Rashard Lewis	.40	1.00
60 Sebastian Telfair	.30	.75
61 Manu Ginobili	.40	1.00
62 Kurt Thomas	.25	.60
63 Jamal Crawford	.30	.75
64 Jamaal Tinsley	.30	.75
65 Donyell Marshall	.25	.60
66 Chris Webber	.40	1.00

❑ 67 Peja Stojakovic	.40	1.00
❑ 68 P.J. Brown	.25	.60
❑ 69 Nenad Krstic	.30	.75
❑ 70 Ben Wallace	.40	1.00
❑ 71 Grant Hill	.40	1.00
❑ 72 Elton Brand	.40	1.00
❑ 73 Zach Randolph	.40	1.00
❑ 74 Josh Smith	.40	1.00
❑ 75 Samuel Dalembert	.25	.60
❑ 76 Andre Miller	.30	.75
❑ 77 Al Jefferson	.40	1.00
❑ 78 Caron Butler	.40	1.00
❑ 79 Shaun Livingston	.25	.60
❑ 80 Richard Jefferson	.30	.75
❑ 81 Rafer Alston	.25	.60
❑ 82 Antoine Walker	.30	.75
❑ 83 Zydrunas Ilgauskas	.30	.75
❑ 84 Morris Peterson	.30	.75
❑ 85 Marko Jaric	.25	.60
❑ 86 Steve Nash	.50	1.25
❑ 87 Kirk Hinrich	.40	1.00
❑ 88 Kobe Bryant	2.00	5.00
❑ 89 Eddie Jones	.25	.60
❑ 90 Luol Deng	.40	1.00
❑ 91 Ron Artest	.30	.75
❑ 92 Desmond Mason	.25	.60
❑ 93 Jason Terry	.40	1.00
❑ 94 Andrei Kirilenko	.40	1.00
❑ 95 Michael Redd	.40	1.00
❑ 96 Mehmet Okur	.25	.60
❑ 97 Mike Dunleavy	.30	.75
❑ 98 Mike Bibby	.40	1.00
❑ 99 Amare Stoudemire	.75	2.00
❑ 100 Gilbert Arenas	.40	1.00
❑ 101 Daniel Ewing RC	1.50	4.00
❑ 102 Andray Blatche RC	1.50	4.00
❑ 103 Jose Calderon RC	1.25	3.00
❑ 104 Shavlik Randolph RC	1.25	3.00
❑ 105 Travis Diener RC	1.25	3.00
❑ 106 Brandon Bass RC	1.25	3.00
❑ 107 Fabricio Oberto RC	1.25	3.00
❑ 108 Ryan Gomes RC	1.25	3.00
❑ 109 Gerald Fitch RC	1.25	3.00
❑ 110 James Singleton RC	1.25	3.00
❑ 111 Deron Williams RC	3.00	8.00
❑ 112 Gerald Green RC	1.25	3.00
❑ 113 C.J. Miles RC	1.25	3.00
❑ 114 Chris Paul RC	4.00	10.00
❑ 115 Julius Hodge RC	1.50	4.00
❑ 116 Salim Stoudamire RC	1.50	4.00
❑ 117 Raymond Felton RC	1.50	4.00
❑ 118 Nate Robinson RC	2.00	5.00
❑ 119 Sarunas Jasikevicius RC	1.50	4.00
❑ 120 Monta Ellis RC	3.00	8.00
❑ 121 Jarrett Jack RC	1.25	3.00
❑ 122 Orien Greene RC	1.25	3.00
❑ 123 Rashad McCants RC	1.50	4.00
❑ 124 Francisco Garcia RC	1.50	4.00
❑ 125 Antoine Wright RC	1.25	3.00
❑ 126 Luther Head RC	1.50	4.00
❑ 127 Martell Webster RC	1.25	3.00
❑ 128 Eddie Basden RC	1.25	3.00
❑ 129 Marvin Williams RC	2.00	5.00
❑ 130 Danny Granger RC	3.00	8.00
❑ 131 Charlie Villanueva RC	2.00	5.00
❑ 132 Hakim Warrick RC	2.00	5.00
❑ 133 Ike Diogu RC	1.50	4.00
❑ 134 Wayne Simien RC	1.50	4.00
❑ 135 Yaroslav Korolev RC	1.25	3.00
❑ 136 David Lee RC	2.50	6.00
❑ 137 Sean May RC	1.50	4.00
❑ 138 Linas Kleiza RC	1.50	4.00
❑ 139 Joey Graham RC	1.25	3.00
❑ 140 Jason Maxiell RC	1.50	4.00
❑ 141 Andrew Bogut RC	1.50	4.00
❑ 142 Channing Frye RC	1.50	4.00
❑ 143 Andrew Bynum RC	4.00	10.00
❑ 144 Martynas Andriuskevicius RC	1.25	3.00
❑ 145 Johan Petro RC	1.25	3.00
❑ 146 Christie Brinkley	1.50	4.00
❑ 147 Jenny McCarthy	1.50	4.00
❑ 148 Shannon Elizabeth	1.50	4.00
❑ 149 Carmen Electra	1.50	4.00
❑ 150 Jay-Z	1.50	4.00

2006-07 Topps Luxury Box

❑ COMP.SET w/o SP's (50)	20.00	50.00
❑ 1 Chris Bosh	.50	1.25
❑ 2 Dirk Nowitzki	.75	2.00
❑ 3 Ben Wallace	.50	1.25
❑ 4 Mike Bibby	.50	1.25
❑ 5 Josh Howard	.50	1.25
❑ 6 Vince Carter	1.00	2.50
❑ 7 Andrei Kirilenko	.50	1.25
❑ 8 Richard Hamilton	.40	1.00
❑ 9 Tony Parker	.50	1.25
❑ 10 Dwyane Wade	1.25	3.00
❑ 11 Amare Stoudemire	1.00	2.50
❑ 12 Tim Duncan	1.00	2.50
❑ 13 Steve Nash	.60	1.50
❑ 14 Dwight Howard	1.00	2.50
❑ 15 Carmelo Anthony	.60	1.50
❑ 16 Pau Gasol	.50	1.25
❑ 17 Zach Randolph	.50	1.25
❑ 18 Kirk Hinrich	.50	1.25
❑ 19 Stephon Marbury	.50	1.25
❑ 20 Tracy McGrady	1.00	2.50
❑ 21 Kevin Garnett	1.00	2.50
❑ 22 Michael Redd	.50	1.25
❑ 23 LeBron James	2.50	6.00
❑ 24 Kobe Bryant	2.50	6.00
❑ 25 Jason Kidd	.75	2.00
❑ 26 Baron Davis	.50	1.25
❑ 27 Jermaine O'Neal	.50	1.25
❑ 28 Ray Allen	.50	1.25
❑ 29 Joe Johnson	.40	1.00
❑ 30 Elton Brand	.50	1.25
❑ 31 Chris Paul	1.00	2.50
❑ 32 Shaquille O'Neal	1.25	3.00
❑ 33 Allen Iverson	1.00	2.50
❑ 34 Paul Pierce	.50	1.25
❑ 35 Chauncey Billups	.50	1.25
❑ 36 Gerald Wallace	.50	1.25
❑ 37 Jason Richardson	.50	1.25
❑ 38 Yao Ming	1.25	3.00
❑ 39 Andre Iguodala	.50	1.25
❑ 40 Gilbert Arenas	.50	1.25
❑ 41 Larry Bird	2.50	6.00
❑ 42 Isiah Thomas	.75	2.00
❑ 43 Dominique Wilkins	1.00	2.50
❑ 44 Moses Malone	.75	2.00
❑ 45 George Gervin	.75	2.00
❑ 46 Chris Mullin	.75	2.00
❑ 47 Karl Malone	1.00	2.50
❑ 48 Bob McAdoo	.75	2.00
❑ 49 James Worthy	.75	2.00
❑ 50 Walt Frazier	.75	2.00
❑ 51 J.J. Redick RC	1.25	3.00
❑ 52 Tyrus Thomas RC	1.50	4.00
❑ 53 Rodney Carney RC	1.25	3.00
❑ 54 Jorge Garbajosa RC	2.50	6.00
❑ 55 Shawne Williams RC	1.25	3.00
❑ 56 Renaldo Balkman RC	1.25	3.00
❑ 57 Chris Quinn RC	1.25	3.00
❑ 58 Solomon Jones RC	1.25	3.00
❑ 59 Maurice Ager RC	1.25	3.00
❑ 60 Rudy Gay RC	1.25	3.00
❑ 61 Hassan Adams RC	1.50	4.00
❑ 62 Sergio Rodriguez RC	1.25	3.00
❑ 63 Dee Brown RC	1.25	3.00
❑ 64 Saer Sene RC	1.25	3.00
❑ 65 Allan Ray RC	1.25	3.00
❑ 66 Damir Markota RC	1.25	3.00
❑ 67 Bobby Jones RC	1.25	3.00
❑ 68 Kyle Lowry RC	1.25	3.00
❑ 69 Cedric Simmons RC	1.25	3.00
❑ 70 LaMarcus Aldridge RC	1.50	4.00
❑ 71 Mardy Collins RC	1.25	3.00
❑ 72 Daniel Gibson RC	1.50	4.00
❑ 73 Patrick O'Bryant RC	1.25	3.00
❑ 74 Josh Boone RC	1.25	3.00
❑ 75 Paul Davis RC	1.25	3.00
❑ 76 Craig Smith RC	1.25	3.00
❑ 77 Andrea Bargnani RC	2.00	5.00
❑ 78 Alexander Johnson RC	1.25	3.00
❑ 79 James Augustine RC	1.25	3.00
❑ 80 Jordan Farmar RC	1.50	4.00
❑ 81 Marcus Vinicius RC	1.25	3.00
❑ 82 Ryan Hollins RC	1.25	3.00
❑ 83 Marcus Williams RC	1.50	4.00
❑ 84 Will Blalock RC	1.25	3.00
❑ 85 Shannon Brown RC	1.25	3.00
❑ 86 Pops Mensah-Bonsu RC	1.25	3.00
❑ 87 P.J. Tucker RC	1.25	3.00
❑ 88 Steve Novak RC	1.25	3.00
❑ 89 Quincy Douby RC	1.25	3.00
❑ 90 Rajon Rondo RC	5.00	12.00
❑ 91 David Noel RC	1.25	3.00
❑ 92 Mile Ilic RC	1.25	3.00
❑ 93 Ronnie Brewer RC	1.50	4.00
❑ 94 James White RC	1.25	3.00
❑ 95 Hilton Armstrong RC	1.25	3.00
❑ 96 Randy Foye RC	1.25	3.00
❑ 97 Shelden Williams RC	1.50	4.00
❑ 98 Thabo Sefolosha RC	1.50	4.00
❑ 99 Brandon Roy RC	3.00	8.00
❑ 100 Adam Morrison RC	1.50	4.00

2007-08 Topps Luxury Box

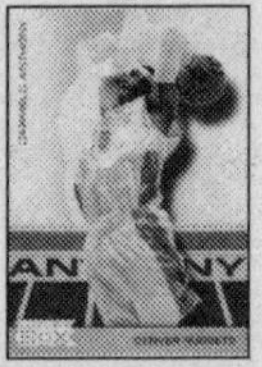

❑ COMP.SET w/o SPs (50)	20.00	40.00
❑ 1 Kevin Garnett	1.25	3.00
❑ 2 Kobe Bryant	2.50	6.00
❑ 3 Dwyane Wade	1.25	3.00
❑ 4 LeBron James	2.50	6.00
❑ 5 Baron Davis	.50	1.25
❑ 6 Dirk Nowitzki	.75	2.00
❑ 7 Jermaine O'Neal	.50	1.25
❑ 8 Jason Richardson	.50	1.25
❑ 9 Tony Parker	.50	1.25
❑ 10 Chris Bosh	.50	1.25
❑ 11 Yao Ming	1.25	3.00
❑ 12 Dwight Howard	1.00	2.50
❑ 13 Steve Nash	.60	1.50
❑ 14 Luol Deng	.50	1.25
❑ 15 Carmelo Anthony	1.00	2.50
❑ 16 Pau Gasol	.50	1.25
❑ 17 Carlos Boozer	.50	1.25
❑ 18 Vince Carter	1.00	2.50
❑ 19 Chauncey Billups	.50	1.25
❑ 20 Ray Allen	.50	1.25
❑ 21 Tim Duncan	1.00	2.50
❑ 22 Amare Stoudemire	1.00	2.50
❑ 23 Kevin Martin	.50	1.25
❑ 24 Michael Redd	.50	1.25
❑ 25 Corey Maggette	.40	1.00
❑ 26 Al Jefferson	.50	1.25
❑ 27 Brandon Roy	.75	2.00
❑ 28 Chris Paul	1.00	2.50
❑ 29 Andre Iguodala	.50	1.25
❑ 30 Gilbert Arenas	.50	1.25
❑ 31 Tracy McGrady	1.00	2.50
❑ 32 Shaquille O'Neal	1.25	3.00
❑ 33 Allen Iverson	1.00	2.50
❑ 34 Paul Pierce	.50	1.25
❑ 35 Jason Kidd	.75	2.00
❑ 36 John Stockton	1.25	3.00
❑ 37 Tim Hardaway	.75	2.00
❑ 38 Dennis Rodman	.75	2.00
❑ 39 Dominique Wilkins	1.00	2.50
❑ 40 David Thompson	1.00	2.50
❑ 41 Spencer Haywood	.75	2.00
❑ 42 Larry Bird	2.50	6.00

Card	Low	High
❑ 43 Isiah Thomas	.75	2.00
❑ 44 Magic Johnson	1.50	4.00
❑ 45 Bill Russell	1.25	3.00
❑ 46 Moses Malone	.75	2.00
❑ 47 Sidney Moncrief	.75	2.00
❑ 48 Bill Walton	.75	2.00
❑ 49 David Robinson	1.25	3.00
❑ 50 Jerry West	1.00	2.50
❑ 51 Thaddeus Young RC	1.50	4.00
❑ 52 Javaris Crittenton RC	1.25	3.00
❑ 53 Sean Williams RC	1.25	3.00
❑ 54 Jared Dudley RC	1.25	3.00
❑ 55 Wilson Chandler RC	1.25	3.00
❑ 56 Mario West RC	1.25	3.00
❑ 57 Chris Richard RC	1.25	3.00
❑ 58 Al Horford RC	1.50	4.00
❑ 59 Taurean Green RC	1.25	3.00
❑ 60 Corey Brewer RC	1.50	4.00
❑ 61 Joakim Noah RC	1.50	4.00
❑ 62 Al Thornton RC	1.25	3.00
❑ 63 Nick Young RC	1.25	3.00
❑ 64 Arron Afflalo RC	1.25	3.00
❑ 65 Juan Carlos Navarro RC	1.50	4.00
❑ 66 Marco Belinelli RC	1.25	3.00
❑ 67 Yi Jianlian RC	2.00	5.00
❑ 68 Luis Scola RC	2.00	5.00
❑ 69 Jeff Green RC	1.50	4.00
❑ 70 Herbert Hill RC	1.25	3.00
❑ 71 Aaron Gray RC	1.25	3.00
❑ 72 Kosta Perovic RC	1.25	3.00
❑ 73 Spencer Hawes RC	1.25	3.00
❑ 74 Aaron Brooks RC	2.00	5.00
❑ 75 Kevin Durant RC	10.00	25.00
❑ 76 Alando Tucker RC	1.25	3.00
❑ 77 Julian Wright RC	1.50	4.00
❑ 78 Carl Landry RC	1.25	3.00
❑ 79 Acie Law IV RC	1.50	4.00
❑ 80 Morris Almond RC	1.25	3.00
❑ 81 Nick Fazekas RC	1.25	3.00
❑ 82 Glen Davis RC	2.50	6.00
❑ 83 Jermareo Davidson RC	1.25	3.00
❑ 84 Jamario Moon RC	2.50	6.00
❑ 85 Jason Smith RC	1.25	3.00
❑ 86 Cheikh Samb RC	1.25	3.00
❑ 87 Coby Karl RC	1.25	3.00
❑ 88 Dominic McGuire RC	1.25	3.00
❑ 89 Ramon Sessions RC	1.50	4.00
❑ 90 Rodney Stuckey RC	2.50	6.00
❑ 91 JamesOn Curry RC	1.25	3.00
❑ 92 Gabe Pruitt RC	1.25	3.00
❑ 93 Adam Haluska RC	1.25	3.00
❑ 94 Kyrylo Fesenko RC	1.25	3.00
❑ 95 Josh McRoberts RC	1.50	4.00
❑ 96 D.J. Strawberry RC	1.25	3.00
❑ 97 Brandan Wright RC	1.50	4.00
❑ 98 Mike Conley RC	1.50	4.00
❑ 99 Daequan Cook RC	1.50	4.00
❑ 100 Greg Oden RC	2.00	5.00

2001-02 Topps Pristine

Card	Low	High
❑ COMPLETE SET (110)	200.00	400.00
❑ COMP.SET w/o SP's (50)	50.00	120.00
❑ COMMON CARD (1-50)	.60	1.50
❑ COMMON ROOKIE (51-110)	.75	2.00
❑ 1 Allen Iverson	2.00	5.00
❑ 2 Shawn Marion	1.00	2.50
❑ 3 Baron Davis	1.00	2.50
❑ 4 Peja Stojakovic	.75	2.00
❑ 5 Dirk Nowitzki	1.50	4.00
❑ 6 Michael Jordan	10.00	25.00
❑ 7 Dikembe Mutombo	.75	2.00
❑ 8 Antoine Walker	.75	2.00
❑ 9 David Robinson	1.25	3.00
❑ 10 Tracy McGrady	2.00	5.00
❑ 11 Rasheed Wallace	1.00	2.50
❑ 12 Kenyon Martin	1.00	2.50
❑ 13 Glenn Robinson	.75	2.00
❑ 14 Shareef Abdur-Rahim	.75	2.00
❑ 15 Lamar Odom	1.00	2.50
❑ 16 Alonzo Mourning	1.00	2.50
❑ 17 Latrell Sprewell	.75	2.00
❑ 18 Stephon Marbury	1.00	2.50
❑ 19 Chris Webber	1.00	2.50
❑ 20 Darius Miles	.60	1.50
❑ 21 Tim Duncan	2.00	5.00
❑ 22 Antawn Jamison	1.00	2.50
❑ 23 Jason Kidd	1.50	4.00
❑ 24 John Stockton	1.25	3.00
❑ 25 Michael Finley	1.00	2.50
❑ 26 Eddie Jones	.75	2.00
❑ 27 Jamal Mashburn	.75	2.00
❑ 28 Paul Pierce	1.00	2.50
❑ 29 Jason Terry	1.00	2.50
❑ 30 Kobe Bryant	5.00	12.00
❑ 31 Reggie Miller	1.00	2.50
❑ 32 Elton Brand	1.00	2.50
❑ 33 Antonio McDyess	.75	2.00
❑ 34 Ray Allen	1.00	2.50
❑ 35 Kevin Garnett	2.00	5.00
❑ 36 Allan Houston	.75	2.00
❑ 37 Grant Hill	1.00	2.50
❑ 38 Jalen Rose	.75	2.00
❑ 39 Gary Payton	1.00	2.50
❑ 40 Vince Carter	2.00	5.00
❑ 41 Jerry Stackhouse	.75	2.00
❑ 42 Karl Malone	1.25	3.00
❑ 43 Wang Zhizhi	.75	2.00
❑ 44 Marcus Fizer	.60	1.50
❑ 45 Marcus Camby	.75	2.00
❑ 46 Andre Miller	.75	2.00
❑ 47 Jason Williams	.75	2.00
❑ 48 Hakeem Olajuwon	1.25	3.00
❑ 49 Shaquille O'Neal	2.50	6.00
❑ 50 Steve Francis	1.00	2.50
❑ 51 Eddie Griffin C RC	.75	2.00
❑ 52 Eddie Griffin U	1.00	2.50
❑ 53 Eddie Griffin R	1.25	3.00
❑ 54 Kwame Brown C RC	1.00	2.50
❑ 55 Kwame Brown U	1.25	3.00
❑ 56 Kwame Brown R	1.50	4.00
❑ 57 Shane Battier C RC	1.25	3.00
❑ 58 Shane Battier U	1.50	4.00
❑ 59 Shane Battier R	2.00	5.00
❑ 60 Eddy Curry C RC	1.25	3.00
❑ 61 Eddy Curry U	1.50	4.00
❑ 62 Eddy Curry R	2.00	5.00
❑ 63 Tyson Chandler C RC	1.50	4.00
❑ 64 Tyson Chandler U	2.00	5.00
❑ 65 Tyson Chandler R	2.50	6.00
❑ 66 Rodney White C RC	.75	2.00
❑ 67 Rodney White U	1.00	2.50
❑ 68 Rodney White R	1.25	3.00
❑ 69 J.Richardson C RC	1.50	4.00
❑ 70 Jason Richardson U	2.00	5.00
❑ 71 Jason Richardson R	2.50	6.00
❑ 72 Joe Johnson C RC	2.00	5.00
❑ 73 Joe Johnson U	2.50	6.00
❑ 74 Joe Johnson R	3.00	8.00
❑ 75 Pau Gasol C RC	3.00	8.00
❑ 76 Pau Gasol U	4.00	10.00
❑ 77 Pau Gasol R	5.00	12.00
❑ 78 Desagana Diop C RC	.75	2.00
❑ 79 Desagana Diop U	1.00	2.50
❑ 80 Desagana Diop R	1.25	3.00
❑ 81 V.Radmanovic C RC	1.00	2.50
❑ 82 V.Radmanovic U	1.25	3.00
❑ 83 V.Radmanovic R	1.50	4.00
❑ 84 Troy Murphy C RC	1.50	4.00
❑ 85 Troy Murphy U	2.00	5.00
❑ 86 Troy Murphy R	2.50	6.00
❑ 87 Zach Randolph C RC	2.00	5.00
❑ 88 Zach Randolph U	2.50	6.00
❑ 89 Zach Randolph R	3.00	8.00
❑ 90 Jamaal Tinsley C RC	1.00	2.50
❑ 91 Jamaal Tinsley U	1.25	3.00
❑ 92 Jamaal Tinsley R	1.50	4.00
❑ 93 Richard Jefferson C RC	2.00	5.00
❑ 94 Richard Jefferson U	2.50	6.00
❑ 95 Richard Jefferson R	3.00	8.00
❑ 96 Loren Woods C RC	.75	2.00
❑ 97 Loren Woods U	1.00	2.50
❑ 98 Loren Woods R	1.25	3.00
❑ 99 Joseph Forte C RC	.75	2.00
❑ 100 Joseph Forte U	1.00	2.50
❑ 101 Joseph Forte R	1.25	3.00
❑ 102 Gerald Wallace C RC	2.00	5.00
❑ 103 Gerald Wallace U	2.50	6.00
❑ 104 Gerald Wallace R	3.00	8.00
❑ 105 Andrei Kirilenko C RC	2.00	5.00
❑ 106 Andrei Kirilenko U	2.50	6.00
❑ 107 Andrei Kirilenko R	3.00	8.00
❑ 108 Tony Parker C RC	3.00	8.00
❑ 109 Tony Parker U	4.00	10.00
❑ 110 Tony Parker R	5.00	12.00

2002-03 Topps Pristine

Card	Low	High
❑ COMMON CARD (1-50)	.40	1.00
❑ COMMON ROOKIE (51-125)	1.50	4.00
❑ 1 Shaquille O'Neal	1.50	4.00
❑ 2 Steve Nash	1.00	2.50
❑ 3 Vince Carter	1.25	3.00
❑ 4 Michael Jordan	4.00	10.00
❑ 5 Chris Webber	.60	1.50
❑ 6 Tim Duncan	1.25	3.00
❑ 7 Vladimir Radmanovic	.40	1.00
❑ 8 Kobe Bryant	3.00	8.00
❑ 9 Allan Houston	.50	1.25
❑ 10 Tracy McGrady	1.25	3.00
❑ 11 Allen Iverson	1.25	3.00
❑ 12 Scottie Pippen	1.00	2.50
❑ 13 Steve Francis	.60	1.50
❑ 14 Reggie Miller	.60	1.50
❑ 15 Antoine Walker	.50	1.25
❑ 16 Shawn Marion	.60	1.50
❑ 17 Wally Szczerbiak	.50	1.25
❑ 18 Elton Brand	.60	1.50
❑ 19 Jerry Stackhouse	.50	1.25
❑ 20 Andre Miller	.50	1.25
❑ 21 Gary Payton	.60	1.50
❑ 22 Richard Hamilton	.50	1.25
❑ 23 Pau Gasol	.60	1.50
❑ 24 Juwan Howard	.50	1.25
❑ 25 Jalen Rose	.50	1.25
❑ 26 Eddie Jones	.50	1.25
❑ 27 Baron Davis	.60	1.50
❑ 28 Darrell Armstrong	.40	1.00
❑ 29 John Stockton	.75	2.00
❑ 30 Mike Bibby	.50	1.25
❑ 31 Eddy Curry	.50	1.25
❑ 32 Kevin Garnett	1.25	3.00
❑ 33 Dikembe Mutombo	.50	1.25
❑ 34 Jason Kidd	1.00	2.50
❑ 35 Clifford Robinson	.40	1.00
❑ 36 Ray Allen	.60	1.50
❑ 37 Paul Pierce	.60	1.50
❑ 38 Shane Battier	.50	1.25
❑ 39 Kenyon Martin	.60	1.50
❑ 40 Rasheed Wallace	.60	1.50
❑ 41 Latrell Sprewell	.50	1.25
❑ 42 Cuttino Mobley	.50	1.25
❑ 43 Karl Malone	.60	1.50
❑ 44 Dirk Nowitzki	1.00	2.50
❑ 45 Antawn Jamison	.60	1.50
❑ 46 Elden Campbell	.40	1.00
❑ 47 Lamar Odom	.60	1.50
❑ 48 Jason Richardson	.60	1.50
❑ 49 Jermaine O'Neal	.60	1.50
❑ 50 Shareef Abdur-Rahim	.50	1.25
❑ 51 Yao Ming C RC	5.00	12.00
❑ 52 Yao Ming U	6.00	15.00
❑ 53 Yao Ming R	12.00	30.00
❑ 54 Jay Williams C RC	2.00	5.00
❑ 55 Jay Williams U	2.50	6.00
❑ 56 Jay Williams R	5.00	12.00
❑ 57 Mike Dunleavy C RC	2.00	5.00
❑ 58 Mike Dunleavy U	2.50	6.00
❑ 59 Mike Dunleavy R	5.00	12.00
❑ 60 Drew Gooden C RC	2.50	6.00
❑ 61 Drew Gooden U	3.00	8.00
❑ 62 Drew Gooden R	6.00	15.00
❑ 63 Nikoloz Tskitishvili C RC	1.50	4.00

❑ 64 Nikoloz Tskitishvili U	2.00	5.00
❑ 65 Nikoloz Tskitishvili R	4.00	10.00
❑ 66 DaJuan Wagner C RC	1.50	4.00
❑ 67 DaJuan Wagner U	2.00	5.00
❑ 68 DaJuan Wagner R	4.00	10.00
❑ 69 Nene Hilario C RC	2.00	5.00
❑ 70 Nene Hilario U	2.50	6.00
❑ 71 Nene Hilario R	5.00	12.00
❑ 72 Chris Wilcox C RC	2.00	5.00
❑ 73 Chris Wilcox U	2.50	6.00
❑ 74 Chris Wilcox R	5.00	12.00
❑ 75 Amare Stoudemire C RC	4.00	10.00
❑ 75A A.Stoudemire G.Ref ERR		
❑ 76 Amare Stoudemire U	5.00	12.00
❑ 77 Amare Stoudemire R	10.00	25.00
❑ 78 Caron Butler C RC	3.00	8.00
❑ 79 Caron Butler U	4.00	10.00
❑ 80 Caron Butler R	8.00	20.00
❑ 81 Jared Jeffries C RC	1.50	4.00
❑ 82 Jared Jeffries U	2.00	5.00
❑ 83 Jared Jeffries R	4.00	10.00
❑ 84 Melvin Ely C RC	1.50	4.00
❑ 85 Melvin Ely U	2.00	5.00
❑ 86 Melvin Ely R	4.00	10.00
❑ 87 Marcus Haislip C RC	1.50	4.00
❑ 88 Marcus Haislip U	2.00	5.00
❑ 89 Marcus Haislip R	4.00	10.00
❑ 90 Fred Jones C RC	2.00	5.00
❑ 91 Fred Jones U	2.50	6.00
❑ 92 Fred Jones R	5.00	12.00
❑ 93 Casey Jacobsen C RC	1.50	4.00
❑ 94 Casey Jacobsen U	2.00	5.00
❑ 95 Casey Jacobsen R	4.00	10.00
❑ 96 John Salmons C RC	2.50	6.00
❑ 97 John Salmons U	3.00	8.00
❑ 98 John Salmons R	6.00	15.00
❑ 99 Juan Dixon C RC	2.50	6.00
❑ 100 Juan Dixon U	3.00	8.00
❑ 101 Juan Dixon R	6.00	15.00
❑ 102 Chris Jefferies C RC	1.50	4.00
❑ 103 Chris Jefferies U	2.00	5.00
❑ 104 Chris Jefferies R	4.00	10.00
❑ 105 Ryan Humphrey C RC	1.50	4.00
❑ 106 Ryan Humphrey U	2.00	5.00
❑ 107 Ryan Humphrey R	4.00	10.00
❑ 108 Kareem Rush C RC	2.00	5.00
❑ 109 Kareem Rush U	2.50	6.00
❑ 110 Kareem Rush R	5.00	12.00
❑ 111 Qyntel Woods C RC	1.50	4.00
❑ 112 Qyntel Woods U	2.00	5.00
❑ 113 Qyntel Woods R	4.00	10.00
❑ 114 Frank Williams C RC	1.50	4.00
❑ 115 Frank Williams U	2.00	5.00
❑ 116 Frank Williams R	4.00	10.00
❑ 117 Tayshaun Prince C RC	2.50	6.00
❑ 118 Tayshaun Prince U	3.00	8.00
❑ 119 Tayshaun Prince R	6.00	15.00
❑ 120 Carlos Boozer C RC	3.00	8.00
❑ 121 Carlos Boozer U	4.00	10.00
❑ 122 Carlos Boozer R	8.00	20.00
❑ 123 Dan Dickau C RC	1.50	4.00
❑ 124 Dan Dickau U	2.00	5.00
❑ 125 Dan Dickau R	4.00	10.00

2003-04 Topps Pristine

❑ COMP.SET w/o RC's (100)	25.00	60.00
❑ COMMON CARD (1-100)	.30	.75
❑ COMMON ROOKIE (101-197)	2.00	5.00
❑ 1 Tracy McGrady	1.00	2.50
❑ 2 DaJuan Wagner	.30	.75
❑ 3 Allen Iverson	1.00	2.50
❑ 4 Chris Webber	.50	1.25
❑ 5 Jason Kidd	.75	2.00
❑ 6 Eddie Jones	.40	1.00
❑ 7 Jermaine O'Neal	.50	1.25
❑ 8 Kobe Bryant	2.50	6.00
❑ 9 Tony Parker	.50	1.25
❑ 10 Wally Szczerbiak	.40	1.00
❑ 11 Yao Ming	1.00	2.50
❑ 12 Amare Stoudemire	1.00	2.50
❑ 13 Steve Nash	.75	2.00
❑ 14 Baron Davis	.50	1.25
❑ 15 Vince Carter	1.00	2.50
❑ 16 Peja Stojakovic	.40	1.00
❑ 17 Desmond Mason	.40	1.00
❑ 18 Antoine Walker	.50	1.25
❑ 19 Steve Francis	.50	1.25
❑ 20 Gary Payton	.50	1.25
❑ 21 Tim Duncan	1.00	2.50
❑ 22 Jalen Rose	.40	1.00
❑ 23 Jason Richardson	.50	1.25
❑ 24 Andre Miller	.40	1.00
❑ 25 Allan Houston	.40	1.00
❑ 26 Ron Artest	.40	1.00
❑ 27 Andrei Kirilenko	.50	1.25
❑ 28 Kenyon Martin	.50	1.25
❑ 29 Kevin Garnett	1.00	2.50
❑ 30 Rasheed Wallace	.50	1.25
❑ 31 Shawn Marion	.50	1.25
❑ 32 Karl Malone	.50	1.25
❑ 33 Antawn Jamison	.50	1.25
❑ 34 Shaquille O'Neal	1.25	3.00
❑ 35 Paul Pierce	.50	1.25
❑ 36 Nene	.40	1.00
❑ 37 Ray Allen	.30	.75
❑ 38 Bonzi Wells	.30	.75
❑ 39 Ben Wallace	.40	1.00
❑ 40 Jerry Stackhouse	.40	1.00
❑ 41 Dirk Nowitzki	.75	2.00
❑ 42 Elton Brand	.50	1.25
❑ 43 Pau Gasol	.50	1.25
❑ 44 Richard Hamilton	.40	1.00
❑ 45 Shareef Abdur-Rahim	.40	1.00
❑ 46 Jason Terry	.40	1.00
❑ 47 Jamal Mashburn	.30	.75
❑ 48 Latrell Sprewell	.40	1.00
❑ 49 Keith Van Horn	.40	1.00
❑ 50 Mike Miller	.40	1.00
❑ 51 Theo Ratliff	.30	.75
❑ 52 Scottie Pippen	.75	2.00
❑ 53 Nick Van Exel	.40	1.00
❑ 54 Chauncey Billups	.50	1.25
❑ 55 Al Harrington	.40	1.00
❑ 56 Corey Maggette	.30	.75
❑ 57 Shane Battier	.40	1.00
❑ 58 Tim Thomas	.30	.75
❑ 59 Darius Miles	.40	1.00
❑ 60 Alonzo Mourning	.50	1.25
❑ 61 Jamaal Magloire	.30	.75
❑ 62 Antonio McDyess	.40	1.00
❑ 63 Juwan Howard	.40	1.00
❑ 64 Eric Snow	.30	.75
❑ 65 Anfernee Hardaway	.50	1.25
❑ 66 Tayshaun Prince	.40	1.00
❑ 67 Derek Anderson	.40	1.00
❑ 68 Mike Bibby	.40	1.00
❑ 69 Deshawn Stevenson	.30	.75
❑ 70 Kwame Brown	.30	.75
❑ 71 Jerome Williams	.30	.75
❑ 72 Radoslav Nesterovic	.30	.75
❑ 73 Stephon Marbury	.50	1.25
❑ 74 P.J. Brown	.30	.75
❑ 75 Sam Cassell	.40	1.00
❑ 76 Kenny Thomas	.30	.75
❑ 77 Jason Williams	.40	1.00
❑ 78 Jamaal Tinsley	.40	1.00
❑ 79 Nikoloz Tskitishvili	.30	.75
❑ 80 Michael Finley	.50	1.25
❑ 81 Jamal Crawford	.40	1.00
❑ 82 Brent Barry	.30	.75
❑ 83 Gilbert Arenas	.50	1.25
❑ 84 Morris Peterson	.40	1.00
❑ 85 Manu Ginobili	.50	1.25
❑ 86 Dale Davis	.30	.75
❑ 87 Aaron McKie	.30	.75
❑ 88 Richard Jefferson	.50	1.25
❑ 89 Michael Redd	.50	1.25
❑ 90 Reggie Miller	.50	1.25
❑ 91 Cuttino Mobley	.40	1.00
❑ 92 Marcus Camby	.40	1.00
❑ 93 Tony Delk	.30	.75
❑ 94 Tyson Chandler	.40	1.00
❑ 95 Caron Butler	.40	1.00
❑ 96 Kurt Thomas	.30	.75
❑ 97 Glenn Robinson	.40	1.00
❑ 98 Brad Miller	.40	1.00
❑ 99 Matt Harpring	.40	1.00
❑ 100 Alvin Williams	.30	.75
❑ 101 LeBron James C RC	30.00	60.00
❑ 102 LeBron James U	40.00	80.00
❑ 103 LeBron James R	75.00	150.00
❑ 104 Darko Milicic C RC	2.50	6.00
❑ 105 Darko Milicic U	3.00	8.00
❑ 106 Darko Milicic R	4.00	10.00
❑ 107 Carmelo Anthony C RC	5.00	12.00
❑ 108 Carmelo Anthony U	6.00	15.00
❑ 109 Carmelo Anthony R	8.00	20.00
❑ 110 Chris Bosh C RC	3.00	8.00
❑ 111 Chris Bosh U	4.00	10.00
❑ 112 Chris Bosh R	5.00	12.00
❑ 113 Dwyane Wade C RC	5.00	12.00
❑ 114 Dwyane Wade U	6.00	15.00
❑ 115 Dwyane Wade R	8.00	20.00
❑ 116 Chris Kaman C RC	2.50	6.00
❑ 117 Chris Kaman U	3.00	8.00
❑ 118 Chris Kaman R	4.00	10.00
❑ 119 Kirk Hinrich C RC	2.50	6.00
❑ 120 Kirk Hinrich U	3.00	8.00
❑ 121 Kirk Hinrich R	4.00	10.00
❑ 122 T.J. Ford C RC	2.50	6.00
❑ 123 T.J. Ford U	3.00	8.00
❑ 124 T.J. Ford R	4.00	10.00
❑ 125 Mike Sweetney C RC	2.00	5.00
❑ 126 Mike Sweetney U	2.50	6.00
❑ 127 Mike Sweetney R	3.00	8.00
❑ 128 Jarvis Hayes C RC	2.00	5.00
❑ 129 Jarvis Hayes U	2.50	6.00
❑ 130 Jarvis Hayes R	3.00	8.00
❑ 131 Mickael Pietrus C RC	2.50	6.00
❑ 132 Mickael Pietrus U	3.00	8.00
❑ 133 Mickael Pietrus R	4.00	10.00
❑ 134 Nick Collison C RC	2.00	5.00
❑ 135 Nick Collison U	2.50	6.00
❑ 136 Nick Collison R	3.00	8.00
❑ 137 Marcus Banks C RC	2.00	5.00
❑ 138 Marcus Banks U	2.50	6.00
❑ 139 Marcus Banks R	3.00	8.00
❑ 140 Luke Ridnour C RC	2.50	6.00
❑ 141 Luke Ridnour U	3.00	8.00
❑ 142 Luke Ridnour R	4.00	10.00
❑ 143 Reece Gaines C RC	2.00	5.00
❑ 144 Reece Gaines U	2.50	6.00
❑ 145 Reece Gaines R	3.00	8.00
❑ 146 Troy Bell C RC	2.00	5.00
❑ 147 Troy Bell U	2.50	6.00
❑ 148 Troy Bell R	3.00	8.00
❑ 149 Zarko Cabarkapa C RC	2.00	5.00
❑ 150 Zarko Cabarkapa U	2.50	6.00
❑ 151 Zarko Cabarkapa R	3.00	8.00
❑ 152 David West C RC	2.50	6.00
❑ 153 David West U	3.00	8.00
❑ 154 David West R	4.00	10.00
❑ 155 Aleksandar Pavlovic C RC	2.50	6.00
❑ 156 Aleksandar Pavlovic U	3.00	8.00
❑ 157 Aleksandar Pavlovic R	4.00	10.00
❑ 158 Dahntay Jones C RC	2.00	5.00
❑ 159 Dahntay Jones U	2.50	6.00
❑ 160 Dahntay Jones R	3.00	8.00
❑ 161 Boris Diaw C RC	2.50	6.00
❑ 162 Boris Diaw U	3.00	8.00
❑ 163 Boris Diaw R	4.00	10.00
❑ 164 Zoran Planinic C RC	2.00	5.00
❑ 165 Zoran Planinic U	2.50	6.00
❑ 166 Zoran Planinic R	3.00	8.00
❑ 167 Travis Outlaw C RC	2.50	6.00
❑ 168 Travis Outlaw U	3.00	8.00
❑ 169 Travis Outlaw R	4.00	10.00
❑ 170 Brian Cook C RC	2.00	5.00
❑ 171 Brian Cook U	2.50	6.00
❑ 172 Brian Cook R	3.00	8.00
❑ 173 Travis Hansen C RC	2.00	5.00
❑ 174 Travis Hansen U	2.50	6.00
❑ 175 Travis Hansen R	3.00	8.00
❑ 176 Ndudi Ebi C RC	2.00	5.00
❑ 177 Ndudi Ebi U	2.50	6.00
❑ 178 Ndudi Ebi R	3.00	8.00
❑ 179 Kendrick Perkins C RC	3.00	8.00
❑ 180 Kendrick Perkins U	4.00	10.00
❑ 181 Kendrick Perkins R	5.00	12.00
❑ 182 Leandro Barbosa C RC	2.50	6.00
❑ 183 Leandro Barbosa U	3.00	8.00
❑ 184 Leandro Barbosa R	4.00	10.00
❑ 185 Josh Howard C RC	2.50	6.00
❑ 186 Josh Howard U	3.00	8.00

187 Josh Howard R	4.00	10.00
188 Maciej Lampe C RC	2.00	5.00
189 Maciej Lampe U	2.50	6.00
190 Maciej Lampe R	3.00	8.00
191 Jason Kapono C RC	2.50	6.00
192 Jason Kapono U	3.00	8.00
193 Jason Kapono R	4.00	10.00
194 Luke Walton C RC	2.50	6.00
195 Luke Walton U	3.00	8.00
196 Luke Walton R	4.00	10.00
197 Jerome Beasley C RC	2.00	5.00
198 Jerome Beasley U	2.50	6.00
199 Jerome Beasley R	3.00	8.00

2004-05 Topps Pristine

COMPLETE SET (199)		
COMMON CARD (1-100)	.30	.75
COMMON ROOKIE (101-197)	1.50	4.00
1 Ben Wallace	.40	1.00
2 Michael Redd	.50	1.25
3 Dwyane Wade	1.50	4.00
4 Chris Webber	.50	1.25
5 Cuttino Mobley	.40	1.00
6 Bonzi Wells	.30	.75
7 Rashard Lewis	.50	1.25
8 Kobe Bryant	2.50	6.00
9 Gilbert Arenas	.50	1.25
10 Jeff Foster	.30	.75
11 Yao Ming	1.25	3.00
12 Ricky Davis	.40	1.00
13 Glenn Robinson	.40	1.00
14 Chauncey Billups	.50	1.25
15 Carmelo Anthony	1.50	4.00
16 Pau Gasol	.50	1.25
17 Erick Dampier	.30	.75
18 Jason Terry	.40	1.00
19 Corey Maggette	.40	1.00
20 Zach Randolph	.50	1.25
21 Kevin Garnett	1.00	2.50
22 Steve Nash	.75	2.00
23 LeBron James	3.00	8.00
24 Andre Miller	.40	1.00
25 Manu Ginobili	.50	1.25
26 Gordan Giricek	.30	.75
27 Juwan Howard	.40	1.00
28 Brad Miller	.40	1.00
29 Al Harrington	.40	1.00
30 Allen Iverson	1.00	2.50
31 Shawn Marion	.50	1.25
32 Elton Brand	.50	1.25
33 Steve Francis	.50	1.25
34 Shaquille O'Neal	1.25	3.00
35 Marcus Camby	.40	1.00
36 Tyson Chandler	.40	1.00
37 Dirk Nowitzki	.75	2.00
38 Damon Stoudamire	.40	1.00
39 Richard Hamilton	.40	1.00
40 Kurt Thomas	.30	.75
41 Paul Pierce	.50	1.25
42 Jarvis Hayes	.30	.75
43 Ray Allen	.50	1.25
44 Keith Van Horn	.40	1.00
45 Kirk Hinrich	.40	1.00
46 Caron Butler	.40	1.00
47 Andrei Kirilenko	.50	1.25
48 Jamaal Magloire	.30	.75
49 Chris Kaman	.40	1.00
50 Stephon Marbury	.50	1.25
51 Mike Miller	.40	1.00
52 Eddy Curry	.40	1.00
53 Sam Cassell	.40	1.00
54 Vince Carter	1.00	2.50
55 Jason Kidd	.75	2.00
56 Desmond Mason	.40	1.00
57 Nene	.40	1.00
58 Gerald Wallace	.50	1.25
59 Baron Davis	.50	1.25
60 Tim Duncan	1.00	2.50
61 Drew Gooden	.30	.75
62 Jason Williams	.40	1.00
63 Eddie Jones	.40	1.00
64 Michael Finley	.50	1.25
65 Gary Payton	.50	1.25
66 Kenyon Martin	.50	1.25
67 Mike Bibby	.40	1.00
68 Jason Kapono	.30	.75
69 Allan Houston	.40	1.00
70 Ron Artest	.40	1.00
71 Rasho Nesterovic	.30	.75
72 Kwame Brown	.30	.75
73 Wally Szczerbiak	.40	1.00
74 Joe Johnson	.50	1.25
75 Jamal Mashburn	.40	1.00
76 Peja Stojakovic	.40	1.00
77 Lamar Odom	.50	1.25
78 Jalen Rose	.40	1.00
79 Mike Dunleavy	.40	1.00
80 Rasheed Wallace	.50	1.25
81 Richard Jefferson	.50	1.25
82 Luke Ridnour	.30	.75
83 Samuel Dalembert	.30	.75
84 Zydrunas Ilgauskas	.40	1.00
85 Carlos Arroyo	.50	1.25
86 Primoz Brezec	.30	.75
87 Chris Bosh	.50	1.25
88 Antoine Walker	.50	1.25
89 Boris Diaw	.40	1.00
90 Tracy McGrady	1.00	2.50
91 Amare Stoudemire	1.00	2.50
92 Karl Malone	.50	1.25
93 Jamal Crawford	.40	1.00
94 Shareef Abdur-Rahim	.40	1.00
95 Jason Richardson	.50	1.25
96 Marcus Banks	.30	.75
97 Jermaine O'Neal	.50	1.25
98 Latrell Sprewell	.40	1.00
99 Tony Parker	.50	1.25
100 Carlos Boozer	.50	1.25
101 Dwight Howard C RC	5.00	12.00
102 Dwight Howard U	8.00	20.00
103 Dwight Howard R	10.00	25.00
104 Ben Gordon C RC	2.00	5.00
105 Ben Gordon U	3.00	8.00
106 Ben Gordon R	4.00	10.00
107 Devin Harris C RC	3.00	8.00
108 Devin Harris U	5.00	12.00
109 Devin Harris R	6.00	15.00
110 Rafael Araujo C RC	1.50	4.00
111 Rafael Araujo U	2.50	6.00
112 Rafael Araujo R	3.00	8.00
113 Luke Jackson C RC	1.50	4.00
114 Luke Jackson U	2.50	6.00
115 Luke Jackson R	3.00	8.00
116 Yuta Tabuse C RC	3.00	8.00
117 Yuta Tabuse U	5.00	12.00
118 Yuta Tabuse R	6.00	15.00
119 Kris Humphries C RC	2.50	6.00
120 Kris Humphries U	4.00	10.00
121 Kris Humphries R	5.00	12.00
122 Josh Smith C RC	4.00	10.00
123 Josh Smith U	6.00	15.00
124 Josh Smith R	8.00	20.00
125 Dorell Wright C RC	2.00	5.00
126 Dorell Wright U	3.00	8.00
127 Dorell Wright R	4.00	10.00
128 Jackson Vroman C RC	1.50	4.00
129 Jackson Vroman U	2.50	6.00
130 Jackson Vroman R	3.00	8.00
131 Sasha Vujacic C RC	1.50	4.00
132 Sasha Vujacic U	2.50	6.00
133 Sasha Vujacic R	3.00	8.00
134 David Harrison C RC	1.50	4.00
135 David Harrison U	2.50	6.00
136 David Harrison R	3.00	8.00
137 Blake Stepp C RC	1.50	4.00
138 Blake Stepp U	2.50	6.00
139 Blake Stepp R	3.00	8.00
140 Lionel Chalmers C RC	1.50	4.00
141 Lionel Chalmers U	2.50	6.00
142 Lionel Chalmers R	3.00	8.00
143 Delonte West C RC	2.50	6.00
144 Delonte West U	4.00	10.00
145 Delonte West R	5.00	12.00
146 Kevin Martin C RC	2.00	5.00
147 Kevin Martin U	3.00	8.00
148 Kevin Martin R	4.00	10.00
149 Robert Swift C RC	1.50	4.00
150 Robert Swift U	2.50	6.00
151 Robert Swift R	3.00	8.00
152 Trevor Ariza C RC	2.00	5.00
153 Trevor Ariza U	3.00	8.00
154 Trevor Ariza R	4.00	10.00
155 Peter John Ramos C RC	1.50	4.00
156 Peter John Ramos U	2.50	6.00
157 Peter John Ramos R	3.00	8.00
158 Anderson Varejao C RC	2.00	5.00
159 Anderson Varejao U	3.00	8.00
160 Anderson Varejao R	4.00	10.00
161 Andre Emmett C RC	1.50	4.00
162 Andre Emmett U	2.50	6.00
163 Andre Emmett R	3.00	8.00
164 Tony Allen C RC	2.00	5.00
165 Tony Allen U	3.00	8.00
166 Tony Allen R	4.00	10.00
167 Jameer Nelson C RC	2.00	5.00
168 Jameer Nelson U	3.00	8.00
169 Jameer Nelson R	4.00	10.00
170 J.R. Smith C RC	3.00	8.00
171 J.R. Smith U	5.00	12.00
172 J.R. Smith R	6.00	15.00
173 Kirk Snyder C RC	1.50	4.00
174 Kirk Snyder U	2.50	6.00
175 Kirk Snyder R	3.00	8.00
176 Al Jefferson C RC	3.00	8.00
177 Al Jefferson U	5.00	12.00
178 Al Jefferson R	6.00	15.00
179 Sebastian Telfair C RC	1.50	4.00
180 Sebastian Telfair U	2.50	6.00
181 Sebastian Telfair R	3.00	8.00
182 Andris Biedrins C RC	2.50	6.00
183 Andris Biedrins U	4.00	10.00
184 Andris Biedrins R	5.00	12.00
185 Andre Iguodala C RC	4.00	10.00
186 Andre Iguodala U	6.00	15.00
187 Andre Iguodala R	8.00	20.00
188 Luol Deng C RC	2.00	5.00
189 Luol Deng U	3.00	8.00
190 Luol Deng R	4.00	10.00
191 Josh Childress C RC	1.50	4.00
192 Josh Childress U	2.50	6.00
193 Josh Childress R	3.00	8.00
194 Shaun Livingston C RC	1.50	4.00
195 Shaun Livingston U	2.50	6.00
196 Shaun Livingston R	3.00	8.00
197 Emeka Okafor C RC	3.00	8.00
198 Emeka Okafor U	5.00	12.00
199 Emeka Okafor R	6.00	15.00

2005-06 Topps Pristine

COMP.SET w/o SP's	25.00	60.00
COMMON CARD (1-100)	.25	.60
SEMISTARS	.30	.75
UNLISTED STARS	.40	1.00
COMMON ROOKIE (101-130)	2.00	5.00
UNCOMMON RELIC (131-180)	3.00	8.00
SEMISTARS RELIC	3.00	8.00
UNLISTED STARS RELIC	3.00	8.00
RELIC PRINT RUN 500 SER.#'d SETS		
RARE AUTOGRAPH (181-205)	8.00	20.00
SEMISTARS AU	8.00	20.00
UNLISTED STARS AU	8.00	20.00
AUTO PRINT RUN 100 SER.#'d SETS		
UNLESS LISTED IN CHECKLIST		
SCARCE JSY AU (206-210)		
JSY AU PRINT RUN 50 SER.#'d SETS		
1 Ray Allen	.40	1.00
2 Cuttino Mobley	.30	.75
3 Sebastian Telfair	.30	.75
4 Dwight Howard	.75	2.00
5 Udonis Haslem	.40	1.00
6 Luol Deng	.40	1.00

❑ 7 Lamar Odom	.40	1.00
❑ 8 Paul Pierce	.40	1.00
❑ 9 Stephen Jackson	.30	.75
❑ 10 Mike Dunleavy	.30	.75
❑ 11 Andre Miller	.30	.75
❑ 12 Ben Gordon	.50	1.25
❑ 13 Caron Butler	.40	1.00
❑ 14 Al Jefferson	.40	1.00
❑ 15 Jamaal Tinsley	.30	.75
❑ 16 Josh Childress	.30	.75
❑ 17 Larry Hughes	.30	.75
❑ 18 Andrei Kirilenko	.40	1.00
❑ 19 Brad Miller	.40	1.00
❑ 20 Steve Nash	.50	1.25
❑ 21 Grant Hill	.40	1.00
❑ 22 Samuel Dalembert	.25	.60
❑ 23 Quentin Richardson	.30	.75
❑ 24 Wally Szczerbiak	.30	.75
❑ 25 Desmond Mason	.25	.60
❑ 26 Dwyane Wade	1.00	2.50
❑ 27 Richard Hamilton	.30	.75
❑ 28 Shane Battier	.40	1.00
❑ 29 Chauncey Billups	.40	1.00
❑ 30 Shawn Marion	.40	1.00
❑ 31 Kenyon Martin	.40	1.00
❑ 32 Marquis Daniels	.30	.75
❑ 33 Al Harrington	.25	.60
❑ 34 Brendan Haywood	.25	.60
❑ 35 Mehmet Okur	.25	.60
❑ 36 Rafer Alston	.25	.60
❑ 37 Luke Ridnour	.30	.75
❑ 38 Tim Duncan	.75	2.00
❑ 39 Mike Miller	.40	1.00
❑ 40 Allen Iverson	.75	2.00
❑ 41 Jamal Crawford	.30	.75
❑ 42 J.R. Smith	.30	.75
❑ 43 Kevin Garnett	.75	2.00
❑ 44 Baron Davis	.40	1.00
❑ 45 Corey Maggette	.30	.75
❑ 46 Jermaine O'Neal	.40	1.00
❑ 47 Yao Ming	1.00	2.50
❑ 48 Pau Gasol	.40	1.00
❑ 49 Devin Harris	.40	1.00
❑ 50 Emeka Okafor	.40	1.00
❑ 51 Zydrunas Ilgauskas	.30	.75
❑ 52 Vladimir Radmanovic	.25	.60
❑ 53 Tracy McGrady	.75	2.00
❑ 54 Steve Francis	.40	1.00
❑ 55 Stephon Marbury	.40	1.00
❑ 56 Shaun Livingston	.25	.60
❑ 57 Sam Cassell	.40	1.00
❑ 58 Rasheed Wallace	.40	1.00
❑ 59 Primoz Brezec	.25	.60
❑ 60 Nenad Krstic	.30	.75
❑ 61 Mike Bibby	.40	1.00
❑ 62 Marcus Camby	.30	.75
❑ 63 LeBron James	2.00	5.00
❑ 64 Kobe Bryant	2.00	5.00
❑ 65 Josh Smith	.40	1.00
❑ 66 Jason Richardson	.40	1.00
❑ 67 Jamaal Magloire	.25	.60
❑ 68 Gilbert Arenas	.40	1.00
❑ 69 Zach Randolph	.40	1.00
❑ 70 Vince Carter	.75	2.00
❑ 71 Tony Parker	.40	1.00
❑ 72 Shaquille O'Neal	1.00	2.50
❑ 73 Richard Jefferson	.30	.75
❑ 74 Rashard Lewis	.40	1.00
❑ 75 Peja Stojakovic	.40	1.00
❑ 76 Mike Sweetney	.30	.75
❑ 77 Elton Brand	.40	1.00
❑ 78 Drew Gooden	.30	.75
❑ 79 Chris Webber	.40	1.00
❑ 80 Carmelo Anthony	.75	2.00
❑ 81 Bobby Simmons	.25	.60
❑ 82 Bob Sura	.25	.60
❑ 83 Antoine Walker	.30	.75
❑ 84 Andre Iguodala	.40	1.00
❑ 85 Michael Redd	.40	1.00
❑ 86 Manu Ginobili	.40	1.00
❑ 87 Latrell Sprewell	.25	.60
❑ 88 Kirk Hinrich	.40	1.00
❑ 89 Josh Howard	.40	1.00
❑ 90 Jason Kidd	.60	1.50
❑ 91 Jalen Rose	.40	1.00
❑ 92 Gerald Wallace	.40	1.00
❑ 93 Eddy Curry	.30	.75
❑ 94 Dirk Nowitzki	.60	1.50
❑ 95 Joe Johnson	.40	1.00
❑ 96 Chris Bosh	.40	1.00
❑ 97 Carlos Boozer	.40	1.00
❑ 98 Ben Wallace	.40	1.00
❑ 99 Antawn Jamison	.40	1.00
❑ 100 Amare Stoudemire	.75	2.00
❑ 101 Andrew Bogut RC	2.50	6.00
❑ 102 Marvin Williams RC	3.00	8.00
❑ 103 Deron Williams RC	5.00	12.00
❑ 104 Chris Paul RC	6.00	15.00
❑ 105 Raymond Felton RC	2.50	6.00
❑ 106 Martell Webster RC	2.00	5.00
❑ 107 Charlie Villanueva RC	3.00	8.00
❑ 108 Channing Frye RC	2.50	6.00
❑ 109 Ike Diogu RC	2.50	6.00
❑ 110 Andrew Bynum RC	6.00	15.00
❑ 111 Monta Ellis RC	5.00	12.00
❑ 112 Yaroslav Korolev RC	2.00	5.00
❑ 113 Sean May RC	2.50	6.00
❑ 114 Rashad McCants RC	2.50	6.00
❑ 115 Antoine Wright RC	2.00	5.00
❑ 116 Joey Graham RC	2.00	5.00
❑ 117 Danny Granger RC	5.00	12.00
❑ 118 Gerald Green RC	2.00	5.00
❑ 119 Hakim Warrick RC	3.00	8.00
❑ 120 Julius Hodge RC	2.50	6.00
❑ 121 Nate Robinson RC	3.00	8.00
❑ 122 Jarrett Jack RC	2.00	5.00
❑ 123 Francisco Garcia RC	2.50	6.00
❑ 124 Luther Head RC	2.50	6.00
❑ 125 C.J. Miles RC	2.00	5.00
❑ 126 Salim Stoudamire RC	2.50	6.00
❑ 127 Sarunas Jasikevicius RC	2.50	6.00
❑ 128 Wayne Simien RC	2.50	6.00
❑ 129 David Lee RC	4.00	10.00
❑ 130 Jay-Z	3.00	8.00
❑ 131 Tim Duncan JSY	4.00	10.00
❑ 132 Ray Allen JSY	3.00	8.00
❑ 133 Grant Hill Warm	3.00	8.00
❑ 134 Dwyane Wade Shorts	6.00	15.00
❑ 135 Shawn Marion JSY	3.00	8.00
❑ 136 Jermaine O'Neal JSY	3.00	8.00
❑ 137 Emeka Okafor JSY	3.00	8.00
❑ 138 Tracy McGrady JSY	5.00	12.00
❑ 139 Chris Bosh Shorts	3.00	8.00
❑ 140 Dwight Howard JSY	3.00	8.00
❑ 141 Elton Brand JSY	3.00	8.00
❑ 142 Manu Ginobili JSY	3.00	8.00
❑ 143 Dirk Nowitzki JSY	3.00	8.00
❑ 144 Ben Wallace Warm	3.00	8.00
❑ 145 Steve Nash Warm	3.00	8.00
❑ 146 Allen Iverson Shirt	4.00	10.00
❑ 147 Kevin Garnett JSY	4.00	10.00
❑ 148 Corey Maggette JSY	3.00	8.00
❑ 149 Yao Ming JSY	5.00	12.00
❑ 150 Kobe Bryant Shorts	8.00	20.00
❑ 151 Rasheed Wallace JSY	3.00	8.00
❑ 152 Ben Gordon JSY	4.00	10.00
❑ 153 Gilbert Arenas Shirt	3.00	8.00
❑ 154 Shaquille O'Neal Warm	5.00	12.00
❑ 155 Peja Stojakovic JSY	3.00	8.00
❑ 156 Carmelo Anthony JSY	4.00	10.00
❑ 157 Kirk Hinrich JSY	3.00	8.00
❑ 158 Paul Pierce Shirt	3.00	8.00
❑ 159 Antawn Jamison JSY	3.00	8.00
❑ 160 Amare Stoudemire Shirt	4.00	10.00
❑ 161 Sarunas Jasikevicius Shorts	3.00	8.00
❑ 162 Wayne Simien JSY	3.00	8.00
❑ 163 Channing Frye JSY	5.00	12.00
❑ 164 Antoine Wright JSY	3.00	8.00
❑ 165 Sean May JSY	3.00	6.00
❑ 166 Rashad McCants JSY	3.00	8.00
❑ 167 Julius Hodge JSY	3.00	8.00
❑ 168 Nate Robinson JSY	4.00	10.00
❑ 169 Jarrett Jack JSY	3.00	8.00
❑ 170 Francisco Garcia JSY	3.00	8.00
❑ 171 Charlie Villanueva JSY	4.00	10.00
❑ 172 Andrew Bogut JSY	3.00	8.00
❑ 173 David Lee JSY	3.00	8.00
❑ 174 Deron Williams JSY	6.00	15.00
❑ 175 Chris Paul JSY	6.00	15.00
❑ 176 Raymond Felton JSY	4.00	10.00
❑ 177 Martell Webster JSY	3.00	8.00
❑ 178 Danny Granger JSY	4.00	10.00
❑ 179 Gerald Green JSY	4.00	10.00
❑ 180 Hakim Warrick JSY	4.00	10.00
❑ 181 Shaun Livingston AU	8.00	20.00
❑ 182 Danny Granger AU	10.00	25.00
❑ 183 Ryan Gomes AU RC	6.00	15.00
❑ 184 Jermaine O'Neal AU/75	10.00	25.00
❑ 185 George Gervin AU/60	12.50	30.00
❑ 186 Allen Iverson AU	100.00	200.00
❑ 187 Sean May AU	8.00	20.00
❑ 188 Andrew Bogut AU	10.00	25.00
❑ 189 Deron Williams AU	20.00	50.00
❑ 190 Stephon Marbury AU	10.00	25.00
❑ 191 Jason Kidd AU	12.50	30.00
❑ 192 Raymond Felton AU	10.00	25.00
❑ 193 Rashad McCants AU	12.50	30.00
❑ 194 Gerald Green AU	10.00	25.00
❑ 195 Andrew Bynum AU	30.00	60.00
❑ 196 Charlie Villanueva AU	15.00	40.00
❑ 197 Antoine Wright AU	8.00	20.00
❑ 198 Martell Webster AU	8.00	20.00
❑ 199 Francisco Garcia AU	8.00	20.00
❑ 200 Emeka Okafor AU	8.00	20.00
❑ 201 Hakim Warrick AU	12.50	30.00
❑ 202 Joey Graham AU	8.00	20.00
❑ 203 Julius Hodge AU	8.00	20.00
❑ 204 Ike Diogu AU	8.00	20.00
❑ 205 Johan Petro AU RC	8.00	20.00
❑ 206 Shaquille O'Neal JSY AU	40.00	80.00
❑ 207 Carmelo Anthony JSY AU		
❑ 208 Andrew Bogut JSY AU		
❑ 209 Deron Williams JSY AU	40.00	80.00
❑ 210 Jay-Z Jeans AU	75.00	150.00

2000-01 Topps Reserve

❑ COMPLETE SET (134)	125.00	250.00
❑ COMP.SET w/o SP's (100)	40.00	80.00
❑ COMMON CARD (1-100)	.30	.75
❑ COMMON ROOKIE/499	2.50	6.00
❑ COMMON ROOKIE/999	2.00	5.00
❑ COMMON ROOKIE/1499	1.50	4.00
❑ 1 Tim Duncan	1.00	2.50
❑ 2 Clifford Robinson	.30	.75
❑ 3 Allen Iverson	1.00	2.50
❑ 4 Marcus Camby	.40	1.00
❑ 5 Chauncey Billups	.50	1.25
❑ 6 Anthony Mason	.30	.75
❑ 7 Toni Kukoc	.40	1.00
❑ 8 Tim Thomas	.30	.75
❑ 9 Corey Maggette	.40	1.00
❑ 10 Steve Francis	.50	1.25
❑ 11 Larry Hughes	.40	1.00
❑ 12 Jerome Williams	.30	.75
❑ 13 Reggie Miller	.50	1.25
❑ 14 Chris Gatling	.30	.75
❑ 15 Ron Artest	.50	1.25
❑ 16 Derrick Coleman	.40	1.00
❑ 17 Paul Pierce	.50	1.25
❑ 18 Dikembe Mutombo	.40	1.00
❑ 19 Andre Miller	.40	1.00
❑ 20 Gary Payton	.50	1.25
❑ 21 Kevin Garnett	1.00	2.50
❑ 22 Allan Houston	.40	1.00
❑ 23 Rasheed Wallace	.50	1.25
❑ 24 Derek Anderson	.40	1.00
❑ 25 Vin Baker	.40	1.00
❑ 26 John Stockton	.60	1.50
❑ 27 Richard Hamilton	.40	1.00
❑ 28 Mike Bibby	.40	1.00
❑ 29 Dale Davis	.30	.75
❑ 30 Vince Carter	1.00	2.50
❑ 31 Shawn Marion	.50	1.25
❑ 32 Karl Malone	.60	1.50
❑ 33 Patrick Ewing	.60	1.50
❑ 34 Shaquille O'Neal	1.25	3.00
❑ 35 Jermaine O'Neal	.50	1.25
❑ 36 Danny Fortson	.30	.75
❑ 37 Steve Nash	.75	2.00
❑ 38 Antoine Walker	.40	1.00
❑ 39 Jason Terry	.50	1.25
❑ 40 Vlade Divac	.40	1.00
❑ 41 Avery Johnson	.40	1.00
❑ 42 Elton Brand	.50	1.25

❑	43 Mitch Richmond	.40	1.00
❑	44 Antonio Davis	.30	.75
❑	45 Shawn Kemp	.50	1.25
❑	46 Anfernee Hardaway	.50	1.25
❑	47 Kendall Gill	.30	.75
❑	48 Glen Rice	.40	1.00
❑	49 Tim Hardaway	.40	1.00
❑	50 Tracy McGrady	1.00	2.50
❑	51 Horace Grant	.40	1.00
❑	52 Hakeem Olajuwon	.60	1.50
❑	53 Antawn Jamison	.50	1.25
❑	54 Dirk Nowitzki	.75	2.00
❑	55 Antonio McDyess	.40	1.00
❑	56 Michael Dickerson	.30	.75
❑	57 Baron Davis	.50	1.25
❑	58 Nick Van Exel	.40	1.00
❑	59 Joe Smith	.30	.75
❑	60 Kobe Bryant	2.50	6.00
❑	61 Ray Allen	.50	1.25
❑	62 Keith Van Horn	.40	1.00
❑	63 Latrell Sprewell	.40	1.00
❑	64 Jason Kidd	.75	2.00
❑	65 Chris Webber	.50	1.25
❑	66 David Robinson	.60	1.50
❑	67 Mark Jackson	.40	1.00
❑	68 Bryon Russell	.30	.75
❑	69 Lamar Odom	.50	1.25
❑	70 Maurice Taylor	.30	.75
❑	71 Jonathan Bender	.30	.75
❑	72 Raef LaFrentz	.30	.75
❑	73 Sam Cassell	.40	1.00
❑	74 Wally Szczerbiak	.40	1.00
❑	75 Grant Hill	.50	1.25
❑	76 Theo Ratliff	.30	.75
❑	77 Rashard Lewis	.50	1.25
❑	78 Darrell Armstrong	.30	.75
❑	79 Glenn Robinson	.40	1.00
❑	80 Stephon Marbury	.50	1.25
❑	81 Michael Olowokandi	.30	.75
❑	82 Isaiah Rider	.40	1.00
❑	83 Jalen Rose	.40	1.00
❑	84 Cuttino Mobley	.40	1.00
❑	85 Jerry Stackhouse	.40	1.00
❑	86 Jamal Mashburn	.40	1.00
❑	87 Kenny Anderson	.40	1.00
❑	88 Michael Finley	.50	1.25
❑	89 Lamond Murray	.30	.75
❑	90 Eddie Jones	.40	1.00
❑	91 Eric Snow	.30	.75
❑	92 Terrell Brandon	.30	.75
❑	93 Jason Williams	.40	1.00
❑	94 Scottie Pippen	.75	2.00
❑	95 Rod Strickland	.40	1.00
❑	96 Jim Jackson	.30	.75
❑	97 Ron Mercer	.30	.75
❑	98 Juwan Howard	.40	1.00
❑	99 Brian Grant	.30	.75
❑	100 Shareef Abdur-Rahim	.40	1.00
❑	101 Kenyon Martin/499 RC	6.00	15.00
❑	102 Stromile Swift/999 RC	2.50	6.00
❑	103 Darius Miles/1499 RC	2.00	5.00
❑	104 Marcus Fizer/499 RC	2.50	6.00
❑	105 Mike Miller/999 RC	3.00	8.00
❑	106 DerMarr Johnson/1499 RC	1.50	4.00
❑	107 Chris Mihm/499 RC	2.50	6.00
❑	108 Jamal Crawford/999 RC	3.00	8.00
❑	109 Joel Przybilla/1499 RC	1.50	4.00
❑	110 Keyon Dooling/499 RC	2.50	6.00
❑	111 Jerome Moiso/999 RC	2.00	5.00
❑	112 Etan Thomas/1499 RC	1.50	4.00
❑	113 Courtney Alexander/499 RC	2.50	6.00
❑	114 Mateen Cleaves/999 RC	2.00	5.00
❑	115 Jason Collier/1499 RC	1.50	4.00
❑	116 Hedo Turkoglu/499 RC	6.00	15.00
❑	117 Desmond Mason/999 RC	2.50	6.00
❑	118 Quentin Richardson/1499 RC	2.00	5.00
❑	119 Jamaal Magloire/499 RC	2.50	6.00
❑	120 Speedy Claxton/999 RC	2.00	5.00
❑	121 Morris Peterson/1499 RC	2.50	6.00
❑	122 Donnell Harvey/499 RC	2.50	6.00
❑	123 DeShawn Stevenson/999 RC	2.00	5.00
❑	124 Dalibor Bagaric/1499 RC	1.50	4.00
❑	125 Iakovos Tsakalidis/499 RC	2.50	6.00
❑	126 Mamadou N'Diaye/999 RC	2.00	5.00
❑	127 Erick Barkley/1499 RC	1.50	4.00
❑	128 Mark Madsen/499 RC	2.50	6.00
❑	129 A.J. Guyton/999 RC	2.00	5.00
❑	130 Khalid El-Amin/1499 RC	1.50	4.00
❑	131 Lavor Postell/499 RC	2.50	6.00
❑	132 Marc Jackson/999 RC	2.50	6.00
❑	133 Stephen Jackson/1499 RC	2.50	6.00
❑	134 Wang Zhizhi/1499 RC	3.00	8.00

2003-04 Topps Rookie Matrix

❑	COMP.SET w/o RC's (110)	12.50	30.00
❑	COMMON CARD (1-110)	.20	.50
❑	COMMON TRI-RC	1.25	3.00
❑	1 Allen Iverson	.60	1.50
❑	2 Anfernee Hardaway	.30	.75
❑	3 Bonzi Wells	.20	.50
❑	4 Bobby Jackson	.20	.50
❑	5 Manu Ginobili	.30	.75
❑	6 Andrei Kirilenko	.30	.75
❑	7 Ray Allen	.20	.50
❑	8 Kwame Brown	.20	.50
❑	9 Jason Terry	.25	.60
❑	10 Paul Pierce	.30	.75
❑	11 Tyson Chandler	.25	.60
❑	12 Darius Miles	.25	.60
❑	13 Antoine Walker	.30	.75
❑	14 Antawn Jamison	.30	.75
❑	15 Steve Nash	.50	1.25
❑	16 Marcus Camby	.25	.60
❑	17 Chauncey Billups	.30	.75
❑	18 Jason Richardson	.30	.75
❑	19 Cuttino Mobley	.25	.60
❑	20 Yao Ming	.60	1.50
❑	21 Ron Artest	.25	.60
❑	22 Gary Payton	.30	.75
❑	23 Jason Williams	.25	.60
❑	24 Eddie Jones	.25	.60
❑	25 Kevin Garnett	.60	1.50
❑	26 Wally Szczerbiak	.25	.60
❑	27 Kenyon Martin	.30	.75
❑	28 Jamaal Magloire	.20	.50
❑	29 Keith Van Horn	.25	.60
❑	30 Tracy McGrady	.60	1.50
❑	31 Glenn Robinson	.25	.60
❑	32 Derek Anderson	.25	.60
❑	33 Chris Webber	.30	.75
❑	34 Tony Parker	.30	.75
❑	35 Morris Peterson	.25	.60
❑	36 Jerry Stackhouse	.25	.60
❑	37 Theo Ratliff	.20	.50
❑	38 Jalen Rose	.25	.60
❑	39 Dajuan Wagner	.20	.50
❑	40 Dirk Nowitzki	.50	1.25
❑	41 Nikoloz Tskitishvili	.20	.50
❑	42 Ben Wallace	.25	.60
❑	43 Tayshaun Prince	.25	.60
❑	44 Troy Murphy	.30	.75
❑	45 Jamaal Tinsley	.25	.60
❑	46 Corey Maggette	.20	.50
❑	47 Karl Malone	.30	.75
❑	48 Mike Miller	.25	.60
❑	49 Lamar Odom	.30	.75
❑	50 Shaquille O'Neal	.75	2.00
❑	51 Michael Redd	.30	.75
❑	52 Sam Cassell	.25	.60
❑	53 Raef LaFrentz	.20	.50
❑	54 Baron Davis	.30	.75
❑	55 Allan Houston	.25	.60
❑	56 Drew Gooden	.20	.50
❑	57 Eric Snow	.20	.50
❑	58 Stephon Marbury	.30	.75
❑	59 Zach Randolph	.30	.75
❑	60 Peja Stojakovic	.25	.60
❑	61 Brent Barry	.20	.50
❑	62 Radoslav Nesterovic	.20	.50
❑	63 Antonio Davis	.20	.50
❑	64 Gilbert Arenas	.30	.75
❑	65 Shareef Abdur-Rahim	.25	.60
❑	66 Scottie Pippen	.50	1.25
❑	67 Ronald Murray	.20	.50
❑	68 Zydrunas Ilgauskas	.25	.60
❑	69 Nene	.25	.60
❑	70 Steve Francis	.30	.75
❑	71 Mike Dunleavy	.25	.60
❑	72 Jermaine O'Neal	.30	.75
❑	73 Elton Brand	.30	.75
❑	74 Caron Butler	.25	.60
❑	75 Kobe Bryant	1.50	4.00
❑	76 Kenny Thomas	.20	.50
❑	77 Joe Smith	.20	.50
❑	78 Jason Kidd	.50	1.25
❑	79 Antonio McDyess	.25	.60
❑	80 Shawn Marion	.30	.75
❑	81 Rasheed Wallace	.30	.75
❑	82 Mike Bibby	.25	.60
❑	83 Tim Thomas	.20	.50
❑	84 Rashard Lewis	.30	.75
❑	85 Vince Carter	.60	1.50
❑	86 Matt Harpring	.25	.60
❑	87 Ricky Davis	.25	.60
❑	88 Michael Finley	.30	.75
❑	89 Andre Miller	.25	.60
❑	90 Pau Gasol	.30	.75
❑	91 Dion Glover	.20	.50
❑	92 Jamal Crawford	.25	.60
❑	93 Richard Hamilton	.25	.60
❑	94 Nick Van Exel	.25	.60
❑	95 Maurice Taylor	.20	.50
❑	96 Reggie Miller	.30	.75
❑	97 Marko Jaric	.20	.50
❑	98 Brian Grant	.20	.50
❑	99 Desmond Mason	.25	.60
❑	100 Tim Duncan	.60	1.50
❑	101 Latrell Sprewell	.25	.60
❑	102 Richard Jefferson	.30	.75
❑	103 David Wesley	.20	.50
❑	104 Kurt Thomas	.20	.50
❑	105 Juwan Howard	.25	.60
❑	106 Amare Stoudemire	.60	1.50
❑	107 Brad Miller	.25	.60
❑	108 Keon Clark	.20	.50
❑	109 Pat Garrity	.20	.50
❑	110 Jamal Mashburn	.20	.50
❑	AJF Carmelo/LeBron/Ford RC	4.00	10.00
❑	AKM Carmelo/Kaman/Darko RC	2.00	5.00
❑	AMB Carmelo/Darko/Bosh RC	3.00	8.00
❑	AWB Carmelo/Wade/Bosh RC	6.00	15.00
❑	BAH Bosh/Carmelo/Hinrich RC	2.50	6.00
❑	BAJ Bosh/Carmelo/LeBron RC	10.00	25.00
❑	BBG Barbosa/Bell/Gaines RC	1.50	4.00
❑	BBR Banks/Bell/Ridnour RC	1.25	3.00
❑	BCC Bell/Zarko/Collison RC	1.25	3.00
❑	BCG Bell/Collison/Gaines RC	1.25	3.00
❑	BCP Barbosa/Zarko/Pavlovic RC	2.00	5.00
❑	BCP Banks/Collison/Pietrus RC	1.25	3.00
❑	BHJ Bosh/Hinrich/LeBron RC	4.00	10.00
❑	BJP Bell/Jones/Planinic RC	1.25	3.00
❑	BKC Beasley/Kapono/Cook RC	1.25	3.00
❑	BKS Banks/Kaman/Sweetney RC	1.25	3.00
❑	BKW Bosh/Kaman/Wade RC	2.50	6.00
❑	BPH Banks/Pietrus/Hayes RC	1.25	3.00
❑	BPW Barbosa/Pavlovic/Williams RC	2.50	6.00
❑	BRG Banks/Ridnour/Gaines RC	1.25	3.00
❑	BWM Bosh/Wade/Darko RC	2.50	6.00
❑	CEK Cook/Ebi/Kapono RC	1.25	3.00
❑	CHB Collison/Hayes/Banks RC	1.25	3.00
❑	CHC Cook/Howard/Zarko RC	1.25	3.00
❑	CPD Zarko/Pietrus/Diaw RC	1.50	4.00
❑	CPS Collison/Pietrus/Sweetney RC	1.25	3.00
❑	CSH Collison/Sweetney/Hayes RC	1.25	3.00
❑	CWC Cook/West/Collison RC	2.50	6.00
❑	DPP Diaw/Pavlovic/Planinic RC	2.00	5.00
❑	DPW Diaw/Pavlovic/West RC	4.00	10.00
❑	EPW Ebi/Perkins/West RC	3.00	8.00
❑	EWC Ebi/West/Cook RC	2.50	6.00
❑	FAH Ford/Carmelo/Hinrich RC	1.25	3.00
❑	FBH Ford/Banks/Hinrich RC	1.25	3.00
❑	FBJ Ford/Bosh/LeBron RC	2.50	6.00
❑	FBR Ford/Banks/Ridnour RC	1.25	3.00
❑	FBW Ford/Bosh/Wade RC	1.25	3.00
❑	FCH Ford/Collison/Hinrich RC	1.25	3.00
❑	FGB Ford/Gaines/Banks RC	1.25	3.00
❑	FKW Ford/Kaman/Wade RC	1.25	3.00
❑	GBB Gaines/Banks/Bell RC	1.25	3.00
❑	GBR Gaines/Bell/Ridnour RC	1.25	3.00
❑	HAM Hinrich/Carmelo/Darko RC	2.50	6.00
❑	HBM Hinrich/Bosh/Darko RC	1.50	4.00
❑	HBS Hayes/Banks/Sweetney RC	1.25	3.00

HCJ Howard/Cook/Jones RC 1.25 3.00
HGP Hayes/Gaines/Pietrus RC 1.25 3.00
HJM Hinrich/LeBron/Darko RC 3.00 8.00
HKC Hayes/Kaman/Collison RC 1.25 3.00
HLC Howard/Lampe/Cook RC 1.25 3.00
HLK Howard/Lampe/Kapono RC 1.25 3.00
HPR Hayes/Peitrus/Ridnour RC 1.25 3.00
HSL Hayes/Sweetney/Lampe RC 1.25 3.00
HSP Hayes/Sweetney/Pietrus RC 1.25 3.00
HWS Hinrich/Wade/Sweetney RC 1.50 4.00
JAW LeBron/Carmelo/Wade RC 12.50 30.00
JBM LeBron/Bosh/Darko RC 4.00 10.00
JHA LeBron/Hinrich/Carmelo RC 6.00 15.00
JKA LeBron/Kaman/Carmelo RC 6.00 15.00
JMA LeBron/Darko/Carmelo RC 8.00 20.00
JMK LeBron/Darko/Kaman RC 3.00 8.00
JOB Jones/Outlaw/Barbosa RC 2.00 5.00
JWE Jones/Walton/Ebi RC 1.25 3.00
KCP Kaman/Zarko/Perkins RC 1.50 4.00
KEW Kapono/Ebi/Williams RC 1.50 4.00
KHW Kaman/Hinrich/Wade RC 1.50 4.00
KPH Kaman/Pietrus/Hayes RC 1.25 3.00
KSC Kaman/Sweetney/Collison RC 1.25 3.00
LBB Lampe/Barbosa/Beasley RC 1.50 4.00
LHC Lampe/Howard/Zarko RC 1.25 3.00
LSP Lampe/Sweetney/Planinic RC 1.25 3.00
MAF Darko/Carmelo/Ford RC 1.25 3.00
MBF Darko/Bosh/Ford RC 1.25 3.00
MFJ Darko/Ford/LeBron RC 1.50 4.00
MJW Darko/LeBron/Wade RC 5.00 12.00
OBD Outlaw/Barbosa/Diaw RC 2.00 5.00
OCB Outlaw/Cook/Beasley RC 1.50 4.00
OEJ Outlaw/Ebi/Jones RC 1.50 4.00
OPE Outlaw/Perkins/Ebi RC 2.00 5.00
PBE Perkins/Beasley/Ebi RC 1.50 4.00
PBG Perkins/Banks/Gaines RC 1.50 4.00
PBH Pietrus/Bell/Hayes RC 1.25 3.00
PCH Pietrus/Collison/Hayes RC 1.25 3.00
PCR Pietrus/Collison/Ridnour RC 1.25 3.00
PCW Perkins/Zarko/West RC 3.00 8.00
PDB Planinic/Diaw/Barbosa RC 2.00 5.00
PJD Pavlovic/Jones/Diaw RC 2.00 5.00
PLH Perkins/Lampe/Howard RC 1.50 4.00
POP Pavlovic/Outlaw/Planinic RC 2.00 5.00
PPC Pietrus/Pavlovic/Zarko RC 1.50 4.00
PSK Pietrus/Sweetney/Kaman RC 1.25 3.00
PWO Planinic/West/Outlaw RC 2.50 6.00
RFH Ridnour/Ford/Hinrich RC 1.25 3.00
RHC Ridnour/Hayes/Collison RC 1.25 3.00
SBC Sweetney/Banks/Collison RC 1.25 3.00
SHK Sweetney/Hayes/Kaman RC 1.25 3.00
SPB Sweetney/Pietrus/Banks RC 1.25 3.00
WBH Wade/Bosh/Hinrich RC 2.00 5.00
WBP Williams/Barbosa/Planinic RC 2.00 5.00
WDJ West/Diaw/Jones RC 4.00 10.00
WDP Williams/Diaw/Planinic RC 1.50 4.00
WFH Wade/Ford/Hinrich RC 1.25 3.00
WHL Walton/Howard/Lampe RC 1.25 3.00
WHO Walton/Outlaw/Howard RC 1.50 4.00
WJB Wade/LeBron/Bosh RC 8.00 20.00
WKP Walton/Kapono/Perkins RC 1.50 4.00
WKS Wade/Kaman/Sweetney RC 1.50 4.00
WMA Wade/Darko/Carmelo RC 5.00 12.00
WPJ West/Pavlovic/Jones RC 3.00 8.00
WWB Walton/Williams/Beasley RC 1.50 4.00

2008-09 Topps Signature

COMPLETE SET (85) 100.00 200.00
TSAA Arron Afflalo .60 1.50
TSAT Al Thornton 1.00 2.50
TSBD Baron Davis 1.00 2.50
TSBR Brandon Roy 1.25 3.00
TSBW Brandan Wright .75 2.00
TSCL Courtney Lee RC 2.50 6.00
TSCP Chris Paul 2.00 5.00
TSDC Daequan Cook .75 2.00
TSDE Dale Ellis 1.00 2.50
TSDH Dwight Howard 2.00 5.00
TSDJ DeAndre Jordan RC 1.50 4.00
TSDR Derrick Rose RC 6.00 15.00
TSDS Dolph Schayes 1.00 2.50
TSEB Elgin Baylor 1.00 2.50
TSEG Eric Gordon RC 2.00 5.00
TSEH Elvin Hayes 1.00 2.50
TSFL Fat Lever 1.00 2.50
TSGA Gilbert Arenas 1.00 2.50
TSGG George Gervin 1.25 3.00
TSGH George Hill RC 2.50 6.00
TSGP Gabe Pruitt .60 1.50
TSGW Gerald Wallace 1.00 2.50
TSIT Isiah Thomas 1.00 2.50
TSJA Joe Alexander RC 1.50 4.00
TSJD Joey Dorsey RC 1.50 4.00
TSJH Josh Howard 1.00 2.50
TSJM JaVale McGee RC 1.50 4.00
TSJS John Stockton 1.50 4.00
TSJW Jerry West 1.25 3.00
TSKW Kyle Weaver RC 1.50 4.00
TSLB Larry Bird 3.00 8.00
TSLW Lenny Wilkens 1.00 2.50
TSMA Morris Almond .60 1.50
TSME Mark Eaton 1.00 2.50
TSMJ Magic Johnson 2.00 5.00
TSML Maurice Lucas 1.00 2.50
TSMP Mickael Pietrus .60 1.50
TSMW Marcus Williams .60 1.50
TSNY Nick Young .60 1.50
TSOB Otis Birdsong 1.00 2.50
TSPP Paul Pierce 1.25 3.00
TSRA Ryan Anderson RC 1.50 4.00
TSRF Raymond Felton .75 2.00
TSRG Rudy Gay 1.00 2.50
TSRP Robert Parish 1.00 2.50
TSRR Rajon Rondo 1.00 2.50
TSRS Rodney Stuckey 1.25 3.00
TSRT Reggie Theus 1.00 2.50
TSRW Russell Westbrook RC 4.00 10.00
TSSC Speedy Claxton .60 1.50
TSSD Samuel Dalembert .60 1.50
TSSH Spencer Hawes .60 1.50
TSSO Shaquille O'Neal 2.00 5.00
TSSP Sam Perkins 1.00 2.50
TSSS Sean Singletary RC 1.50 4.00
TSSW Sonny Weems RC 1.50 4.00
TSTY Thaddeus Young .75 2.00
TSVC Vince Carter 1.25 3.00
TSWS Walter Sharpe RC 1.50 4.00
TSYJ Yi Jianlian 1.00 2.50
TSZR Zach Randolph 1.00 2.50
TSABR Aaron Brooks .75 2.00
TSATU Alando Tucker .60 1.50
TSBRU Bill Russell 1.50 4.00
TSBWA Bill Walker RC 1.50 4.00
TSBWI Buck Williams 1.00 2.50
TSCBU Caron Butler 1.00 2.50
TSDGA Danilo Gallinari RC 2.50 6.00
TSDGI Daniel Gibson 1.00 2.50
TSDGR Donte Greene RC 1.50 4.00
TSDRD Dennis Rodman 1.00 2.50
TSDRO David Robinson 1.50 4.00
TSDSC Danny Schayes 1.00 2.50
TSDWA Dwyane Wade 2.00 5.00
TSJHA John Havlicek 1.00 2.50
TSJJH J.J. Hickson RC 2.50 6.00
TSJJW Jo Jo White 1.00 2.50
TSJRG J.R. Giddens RC 1.50 4.00
TSMRR Micheal Ray Richardson 1.00 2.50
TSOJM O.J. Mayo RC 2.50 6.00
TSRAL Ray Allen 1.00 2.50
TSRPI Ricky Pierce 1.00 2.50
TSSHA Spencer Haywood 1.00 2.50
TSSWE Spud Webb 1.00 2.50
TSJHRW John "Hot Rod" Williams 1.00 2.50

2000-01 Topps Stars

COMPLETE SET (150) 30.00 60.00
COMMON CARD (1-150) .15 .40
COMMON ROOKIE (101-125) .25 .60
1 Elton Brand .25 .60
2 Paul Pierce .25 .60
3 Baron Davis .25 .60
4 Corey Benjamin .15 .40
5 Jason Kidd .40 1.00
6 Stephon Marbury .25 .60
7 Eric Snow .15 .40
8 Joe Smith .15 .40
9 Larry Hughes .20 .50
10 Tim Duncan .50 1.25
11 Theo Ratliff .15 .40
12 Dikembe Mutombo .20 .50
13 Tim Hardaway .20 .50
14 Glenn Robinson .20 .50
15 Grant Hill .25 .60
16 Patrick Ewing .30 .75
17 Ron Mercer .15 .40
18 Ron Artest .25 .60
19 Tom Gugliotta .15 .40
20 Steve Smith .20 .50
21 Vlade Divac .20 .50
22 Rashard Lewis .25 .60
23 Tracy McGrady .50 1.25
24 Bryon Russell .15 .40
25 Michael Dickerson .15 .40
26 Juwan Howard .20 .50
27 Damon Stoudamire .20 .50
28 Hakeem Olajuwon .30 .75
29 Antonio McDyess .20 .50
30 Kobe Bryant 1.25 3.00
31 Lindsey Hunter .15 .40
32 Magic Johnson 1.25 3.00
33 Alonzo Mourning .25 .60
34 Kenny Anderson .20 .50
35 Allan Houston .20 .50
36 Keith Van Horn .20 .50
37 Shawn Marion .25 .60
38 David Robinson .30 .75
39 Mitch Richmond .20 .50
40 Shaquille O'Neal .60 1.50
41 Gary Payton .25 .60
42 Sean Elliott .20 .50
43 Sam Cassell .20 .50
44 Dale Davis .15 .40
45 Derek Anderson .20 .50
46 Jonathan Bender .15 .40
47 Shandon Anderson .15 .40
48 Raef LaFrentz .15 .40
49 Michael Finley .25 .60
50 Toni Kukoc .20 .50
51 Anthony Mason .15 .40
52 Jim Jackson .15 .40
53 Glen Rice .20 .50
54 Jalen Rose .20 .50
55 Keon Clark .15 .40
56 Anfernee Hardaway .25 .60
57 Vin Baker .20 .50
58 Shawn Kemp .25 .60
59 John Stockton .30 .75
60 Shareef Abdur-Rahim .20 .50
61 Doug Christie .15 .40
62 Lamond Murray .15 .40
63 Scottie Pippen .40 1.00
64 Darrell Armstrong .15 .40
65 Marcus Camby .20 .50
66 Wally Szczerbiak .20 .50
67 Jamal Mashburn .20 .50
68 Antonio Davis .15 .40
69 Kevin Garnett .50 1.25
70 Cuttino Mobley .20 .50
71 Jerry Stackhouse .20 .50

72 Cedric Ceballos	.15	.40
73 Nick Van Exel	.20	.50
74 Latrell Sprewell	.20	.50
75 Antoine Walker	.20	.50
76 Allen Iverson	.50	1.25
77 Antawn Jamison	.25	.60
78 Derrick Coleman	.20	.50
79 Jason Terry	.25	.60
80 Steve Francis	.25	.60
81 Reggie Miller	.25	.60
82 Rasheed Wallace	.25	.60
83 Chris Webber	.25	.60
84 Donyell Marshall	.15	.40
85 Ruben Patterson	.15	.40
86 Terrell Brandon	.15	.40
87 Mike Bibby	.20	.50
88 Richard Hamilton	.20	.50
89 Jason Williams	.20	.50
90 Corey Maggette	.20	.50
91 Kerry Kittles	.20	.50
92 Karl Malone	.30	.75
93 Rod Strickland	.20	.50
94 Eddie Jones	.20	.50
95 Maurice Taylor	.15	.40
96 Dirk Nowitzki	.40	1.00
97 Andre Miller	.20	.50
98 Lamar Odom	.25	.60
99 Ray Allen	.25	.60
100 Vince Carter	.50	1.25
101 Chris Mihm RC	.25	.60
102 Kenyon Martin RC	.60	1.50
103 Stromile Swift RC	.30	.75
104 Joel Przybilla RC	.25	.60
105 Marcus Fizer RC	.25	.60
106 Mike Miller RC	.40	1.00
107 Darius Miles RC	.30	.75
108 Mark Madsen RC	.25	.60
109 Courtney Alexander RC	.25	.60
110 DeShawn Stevenson RC	.25	.60
111 DerMarr Johnson RC	.25	.60
112 Mamadou N'Diaye RC	.25	.60
113 Mateen Cleaves RC	.25	.60
114 Morris Peterson RC	.40	1.00
115 Etan Thomas RC	.25	.60
116 Erick Barkley RC	.25	.60
117 Quentin Richardson RC	.30	.75
118 Keyon Dooling RC	.25	.60
119 Jerome Moiso RC	.25	.60
120 Desmond Mason RC	.30	.75
121 Speedy Claxton RC	.25	.60
122 Jamaal Magloire RC	.25	.60
123 Donnell Harvey RC	.25	.60
124 Jamal Crawford RC	.40	1.00
125 Jason Collier RC	.25	.60
126 Tim Duncan SPOT	.25	.60
127 Shaquille O'Neal SPOT	.30	.75
128 Vince Carter SPOT	.25	.60
129 Allen Iverson SPOT	.25	.60
130 Jason Kidd SPOT	.20	.50
131 Kevin Garnett SPOT	.25	.60
132 Gary Payton SPOT	.15	.40
133 Tracy McGrady SPOT	.25	.60
134 Jason Williams SPOT	.15	.40
135 Kobe Bryant SPOT	.60	1.50
136 Elton Brand SPOT	.15	.40
137 Ray Allen SPOT	.15	.40
138 Grant Hill SPOT	.15	.40
139 Chris Webber SPOT	.15	.40
140 Latrell Sprewell SPOT	.15	.40
141 Alonzo Mourning SPOT	.15	.40
142 Lamar Odom SPOT	.15	.40
143 Shareef Abdur-Rahim SPOT	.15	.40
144 Steve Francis SPOT	.15	.40
145 Magic Johnson SPOT	.60	1.50
146 Darius Miles SPOT	.20	.50
147 Kenyon Martin SPOT	.40	1.00
148 Marcus Fizer SPOT	.15	.40
149 Mateen Cleaves SPOT	.15	.40
150 Stromile Swift SPOT	.20	.50

2005-06 Topps Style

COMPLETE SET (165)	40.00	80.00
COMMON CARD (1-130)	.15	.40
COMMON ROOKIE (131-160)	1.25	3.00
COMMON CELEBRITY (161-165)	2.00	5.00
1 Ben Wallace	.50	1.25
2 Joe Johnson	.50	1.25
3 Luol Deng	.50	1.25
4 Morris Peterson	.40	1.00
5 Jason Terry	.50	1.25
6 Carmelo Anthony	1.00	2.50
7 Mickey Mantle	3.00	8.00
8 Ron Artest	.40	1.00
9 Elton Brand	.50	1.25
10 Chris Mihm	.30	.75
11 Shane Battier	.50	1.25
12 Speedy Claxton	.30	.75
13 Baron Davis	.50	1.25
14 Damon Stoudamire	.40	1.00
15 Desmond Mason	.30	.75
16 Marko Jaric	.30	.75
17 Vince Carter	1.00	2.50
18 Sam Cassell	.50	1.25
19 J.R. Smith	.40	1.00
20 Trevor Ariza	.40	1.00
21 Quentin Richardson	.40	1.00
22 Jamal Crawford	.40	1.00
23 Dwight Howard	1.00	2.50
24 Kyle Korver	.50	1.25
25 Steve Nash	.60	1.50
26 Amare Stoudemire	1.00	2.50
27 Zach Randolph	.50	1.25
28 Brad Miller	.50	1.25
29 Tim Duncan	1.00	2.50
30 Michael Finley	.50	1.25
31 Ray Allen	.50	1.25
32 Luke Ridnour	.40	1.00
33 Andrei Kirilenko	.50	1.25
34 Tony Allen	.30	.75
35 Paul Pierce	.50	1.25
36 Al Jefferson	.50	1.25
37 Emeka Okafor	.50	1.25
38 Al Harrington	.30	.75
39 Ben Gordon	.60	1.50
40 Andres Nocioni	.30	.75
41 Zydrunas Ilgauskas	.40	1.00
42 Anderson Varejao	.40	1.00
43 Keith Van Horn	.40	1.00
44 Richard Hamilton	.40	1.00
45 Stromile Swift	.40	1.00
46 Dirk Nowitzki	.75	2.00
47 Stephen Jackson	.40	1.00
48 Pau Gasol	.50	1.25
49 Lamar Odom	.50	1.25
50 Kobe Bryant	2.50	6.00
51 Shaquille O'Neal	1.25	3.00
52 Jason Williams	.40	1.00
53 Dwyane Wade	1.25	3.00
54 Michael Redd	.50	1.25
55 Joe Smith	.40	1.00
56 Troy Hudson	.30	.75
57 Jameer Nelson	.40	1.00
58 Chris Webber	.50	1.25
59 Darius Miles	.50	1.25
60 Chris Wilcox	.30	.75
61 Rafer Alston	.30	.75
62 Kirk Hinrich	.50	1.25
63 Jalen Rose	.50	1.25
64 Matt Harpring	.40	1.00
65 Caron Butler	.50	1.25
66 Shareef Abdur-Rahim	.50	1.25
67 Josh Childress	.40	1.00
68 Delonte West	.40	1.00
69 Brevin Knight	.30	.75
70 Larry Hughes	.40	1.00
71 Dikembe Mutombo	.40	1.00
72 Kenyon Martin	.50	1.25
73 Earl Boykins	.30	.75
74 Tayshaun Prince	.50	1.25
75 Chauncey Billups	.50	1.25
76 Josh Smith	.50	1.25
77 Troy Murphy	.50	1.25
78 Jermaine O'Neal	.50	1.25
79 Corey Maggette	.40	1.00
80 Wally Szczerbiak	.40	1.00
81 Richard Jefferson	.40	1.00
82 Nenad Krstic	.40	1.00
83 Jason Kidd	.75	2.00
84 Jamaal Magloire	.30	.75
85 Stephon Marbury	.50	1.25
86 Samuel Dalembert	.30	.75
87 Andre Iguodala	.50	1.25
88 Yao Ming	1.25	3.00
89 Kurt Thomas	.30	.75
90 Brendan Haywood	.30	.75
91 Peja Stojakovic	.50	1.25
92 Mike Bibby	.50	1.25
93 Tony Parker	.50	1.25
94 Manu Ginobili	.50	1.25
95 Rashard Lewis	.50	1.25
96 Mehmet Okur	.30	.75
97 Gilbert Arenas	.50	1.25
98 Antawn Jamison	.50	1.25
99 Ricky Davis	.50	1.25
100 Shawn Marion	.50	1.25
101 Melvin Ely	.30	.75
102 Tyson Chandler	.50	1.25
103 Jason Richardson	.50	1.25
104 Drew Gooden	.40	1.00
105 Josh Howard	.50	1.25
106 Marcus Camby	.40	1.00
107 Jerry Stackhouse	.50	1.25
108 Andre Miller	.40	1.00
109 Rasheed Wallace	.50	1.25
110 Mike Dunleavy	.40	1.00
111 LeBron James	2.50	6.00
112 Allen Iverson	1.00	2.50
113 Tracy McGrady	1.00	2.50
114 Jamaal Tinsley	.40	1.00
115 Cuttino Mobley	.40	1.00
116 Kwame Brown	.40	1.00
117 Derek Anderson	.40	1.00
118 Eddie Jones	.30	.75
119 Antoine Walker	.40	1.00
120 Alonzo Mourning	.60	1.50
121 Bobby Simmons	.30	.75
122 Kevin Garnett	1.00	2.50
123 P.J. Brown	.30	.75
124 Steve Francis	.50	1.25
125 Grant Hill	.50	1.25
126 Primoz Brezec	.30	.75
127 Mike Miller	.50	1.25
128 Sebastian Telfair	.40	1.00
129 Chris Bosh	.50	1.25
130 Carlos Boozer	.50	1.25
131 Andrew Bogut RC	1.50	4.00
132 Raymond Felton RC	1.50	4.00
133 Ike Diogu RC	1.50	4.00
134 Rashad McCants RC	1.50	4.00
135 Gerald Green RC	1.25	3.00
136 Jarrett Jack RC	1.25	3.00
137 Linas Kleiza RC	1.50	4.00
138 Brandon Bass RC	1.25	3.00
139 Marvin Williams RC	2.00	5.00
140 Martell Webster RC	1.25	3.00
141 Sarunas Jasikevicius RC	1.50	4.00
142 Antoine Wright RC	1.25	3.00
143 Hakim Warrick RC	2.00	5.00
144 Francisco Garcia RC	1.50	4.00
145 Wayne Simien RC	1.50	4.00
146 Monta Ellis RC	3.00	8.00
147 Deron Williams RC	3.00	8.00
148 Charlie Villanueva RC	2.00	5.00
149 Chris Taft RC	1.25	3.00
150 Joey Graham RC	1.25	3.00
151 Julius Hodge RC	1.50	4.00
152 Luther Head RC	1.50	4.00
153 David Lee RC	2.50	6.00
154 Chris Paul RC	4.00	10.00
155 Channing Frye RC	1.50	4.00
156 Sean May RC	1.50	4.00
157 Danny Granger RC	3.00	8.00
158 Nate Robinson RC	2.00	5.00
159 Jason Maxiell RC	1.50	4.00

❑ 160 Salim Stoudamire RC 1.50 4.00
❑ 161 Christie Brinkley 2.00 5.00
❑ 162 Carmen Electra 2.00 5.00
❑ 163 Shannon Elizabeth 2.00 5.00
❑ 164 Jenny McCarthy 2.00 5.00
❑ 165 Jay-Z 2.00 5.00

2008-09 Topps T51 Murad

❑ COMPLETE SET (230) 100.00 200.00
❑ 1 Elton Brand .75 2.00
❑ 2 Ray Allen .50 1.25
❑ 3 Allen Iverson .60 1.50
❑ 4 Luis Scola .40 1.00
❑ 5 Jason Kidd .50 1.25
❑ 6 Lamar Odom .50 1.25
❑ 7 Yi Jianlian .50 1.25
❑ 8 Marcus Camby .30 .75
❑ 9 Jamal Crawford .30 .75
❑ 10 Steve Nash .50 1.25
❑ 11 Al Harrington .40 1.00
❑ 12 Carmelo Anthony .60 1.50
❑ 13 Peja Stojakovic .50 1.25
❑ 14 Mike Dunleavy .40 1.00
❑ 15 Larry Hughes .40 1.00
❑ 16 Josh Smith .50 1.25
❑ 17 Emeka Okafor .50 1.25
❑ 18 Ron Artest .50 1.25
❑ 19 Vince Carter .60 1.50
❑ 20 Jamario Moon .50 1.25
❑ 21 Mike Miller .50 1.25
❑ 22 Brendan Haywood .30 .75
❑ 23 Kirk Hinrich .50 1.25
❑ 24 Jason Terry .40 1.00
❑ 25 Brandan Wright .40 1.00
❑ 26 Derek Fisher .50 1.25
❑ 27 Desmond Mason .30 .75
❑ 28 Tyson Chandler .40 1.00
❑ 29 Mickael Pietrus .30 .75
❑ 30 Ronnie Brewer .40 1.00
❑ 31 Gerald Wallace .50 1.25
❑ 32 Daniel Gibson .50 1.25
❑ 33 J.R. Smith .40 1.00
❑ 34 Monta Ellis .50 1.25
❑ 35 Kobe Bryant 2.50 6.00
❑ 36 Ramon Sessions .50 1.25
❑ 37 Zach Randolph .50 1.25
❑ 38 Andre Miller .40 1.00
❑ 39 Tony Parker .50 1.25
❑ 40 Nick Young .30 .75
❑ 41 Kevin Garnett 1.00 2.50
❑ 42 Luol Deng .50 1.25
❑ 43 Josh Howard .50 1.25
❑ 44 Corey Maggette .50 1.25
❑ 45 Cuttino Mobley .40 1.00
❑ 46 James Posey .40 1.00
❑ 47 Hedo Turkoglu .50 1.25
❑ 48 Brad Miller .50 1.25
❑ 49 Andrei Kirilenko .50 1.25
❑ 50 Raymond Felton .40 1.00
❑ 51 Zydrunas Ilgauskas .40 1.00
❑ 52 Jason Maxiell .40 1.00
❑ 53 Yao Ming .60 1.50
❑ 54 Luke Walton .40 1.00
❑ 55 Mo Williams .40 1.00
❑ 56 David Lee .40 1.00
❑ 57 Thaddeus Young .40 1.00
❑ 58 Raja Bell .30 .75
❑ 59 Ime Udoka .30 .75
❑ 60 Gilbert Arenas .50 1.25
❑ 61 Glen Davis .40 1.00
❑ 62 Ben Wallace .50 1.25
❑ 63 Kenyon Martin .50 1.25
❑ 64 Stephen Jackson .40 1.00
❑ 65 Andrew Bynum .50 1.25
❑ 66 Richard Jefferson .50 1.25
❑ 67 Chris Duhon .30 .75
❑ 68 John Salmons .50 1.25
❑ 69 DeShawn Stevenson .30 .75
❑ 70 Zaza Pachulia .30 .75
❑ 71 Jason Richardson .50 1.25
❑ 72 Anderson Varejao .40 1.00
❑ 73 Rasheed Wallace .50 1.25
❑ 74 Rafer Alston .30 .75
❑ 75 Troy Murphy .50 1.25
❑ 76 T.J. Ford .30 .75
❑ 77 Chris Kaman .30 .75
❑ 78 Hakim Warrick .30 .75
❑ 79 Daequan Cook .40 1.00
❑ 80 Al Jefferson .50 1.25
❑ 81 Sean Williams .40 1.00
❑ 82 Eddy Curry .30 .75
❑ 83 Chris Wilcox .40 1.00
❑ 84 Willie Green .30 .75
❑ 85 Martell Webster .40 1.00
❑ 86 Travis Outlaw .50 1.25
❑ 87 Bruce Bowen .30 .75
❑ 88 Jermaine O'Neal .50 1.25
❑ 89 Ben Gordon .50 1.25
❑ 90 Antawn Jamison .50 1.25
❑ 91 Al Horford .50 1.25
❑ 92 Andres Nocioni .40 1.00
❑ 93 Rodney Stuckey .60 1.50
❑ 94 Shane Battier .40 1.00
❑ 95 Jarrett Jack .40 1.00
❑ 96 Al Thornton .50 1.25
❑ 97 Mike Conley .40 1.00
❑ 98 Udonis Haslem .50 1.25
❑ 99 Rashad McCants .40 1.00
❑ 100 Marcus Williams .30 .75
❑ 101 Jeff Green .40 1.00
❑ 102 Jameer Nelson .40 1.00
❑ 103 Shaquille O'Neal 1.00 2.50
❑ 104 LaMarcus Aldridge .50 1.25
❑ 105 Brandon Roy .60 1.50
❑ 106 Manu Ginobili .50 1.25
❑ 107 Jose Calderon .40 1.00
❑ 108 Jason Kapono .30 .75
❑ 109 Mike Bibby .50 1.25
❑ 110 Andrea Bargnani .40 1.00
❑ 111 Jerry Stackhouse .40 1.00
❑ 112 Richard Hamilton .40 1.00
❑ 113 Brent Barry .30 .75
❑ 114 Baron Davis .50 1.25
❑ 115 Darko Milicic .50 1.25
❑ 116 Ricky Davis .50 1.25
❑ 117 Corey Brewer .40 1.00
❑ 118 Nick Collison .30 .75
❑ 119 Rashard Lewis .50 1.25
❑ 120 Amare Stoudemire .60 1.50
❑ 121 Steve Blake .30 .75
❑ 122 Kevin Martin .50 1.25
❑ 123 Fabricio Oberto .30 .75
❑ 124 Mehmet Okur .50 1.25
❑ 125 Wally Szczerbiak .40 1.00
❑ 126 Mark Aguirre .75 2.00
❑ 127 Danny Ainge .75 2.00
❑ 128 Rick Barry .75 2.00
❑ 129 Elgin Baylor .75 2.00
❑ 130 Dave Bing .75 2.00
❑ 131 Otis Birdsong .75 2.00
❑ 132 Gail Goodrich .75 2.00
❑ 133 Bill Bradley 1.00 2.50
❑ 134 Bill Cartwright .75 2.00
❑ 135 James Worthy .75 2.00
❑ 136 Tom Chambers .75 2.00
❑ 137 Maurice Cheeks .75 2.00
❑ 138 Archie Clark .75 2.00
❑ 139 Michael Cooper .75 2.00
❑ 140 Bob Cousy 1.25 3.00
❑ 141 Dave Cowens .75 2.00
❑ 142 Billy Cunningham .75 2.00
❑ 143 Adrian Dantley .75 2.00
❑ 144 Darryl Dawkins .75 2.00
❑ 145 Clyde Drexler 1.00 2.50
❑ 146 Joe Dumars .75 2.00
❑ 147 Mario Elie .75 2.00
❑ 148 Walt Frazier .75 2.00
❑ 149 George Gervin 1.00 2.50
❑ 150 Tim Hardaway .75 2.00
❑ 151 John Havlicek .75 2.00
❑ 152 Bill Russell 1.25 3.00
❑ 153 Bill Laimbeer .75 2.00
❑ 154 Karl Malone 1.00 2.50
❑ 155 Bob McAdoo .75 2.00
❑ 156 Larry Bird 2.50 6.00
❑ 157 Magic Johnson 1.50 4.00
❑ 158 Willis Reed .75 2.00
❑ 159 Wilt Chamberlain 1.50 4.00
❑ 160 Pete Maravich 2.50 6.00
❑ 161 George Mikan 1.50 4.00
❑ 162 Hakeem Olajuwon 1.00 2.50
❑ 163 Patrick Ewing 1.00 2.50
❑ 164 Oscar Robertson .75 2.00
❑ 165 Bill Sharman .75 2.00
❑ 166 Dennis Rodman .75 2.00
❑ 167 David Robinson 1.25 3.00
❑ 168 Dominique Wilkins 1.00 2.50
❑ 169 Isiah Thomas .75 2.00
❑ 170 Jerry West 1.00 2.50
❑ 171A Derrick Rose Dribbling RC 4.00 10.00
❑ 171B Derrick Rose Standing 5.00 12.00
❑ 172A Michael Beasley 1BK RC 2.00 5.00
❑ 172B Michael Beasley 2BK 2.50 6.00
❑ 173A O.J. Mayo Dribbling RC 1.50 4.00
❑ 173B O.J. Mayo Standing 2.00 5.00
❑ 174A Russell Westbrook Red RC 2.50 6.00
❑ 174B Russell Westbrook Blue 3.00 8.00
❑ 175A Kevin Love Shooting RC 1.25 3.00
❑ 175B Kevin Love Standing 1.50 4.00
❑ 176A Danilo Gallinari Standing RC 1.50 4.00
❑ 176B Danilo Gallinari Dribbling 2.00 5.00
❑ 177A Eric Gordon Dribbling RC 1.25 3.00
❑ 177B Eric Gordon Standing 1.50 4.00
❑ 178A Joe Alexander Dribbling RC 1.00 2.50
❑ 178B Joe Alexander Standing 1.25 3.00
❑ 179A D.J. Augustin Dribbling RC 1.00 2.50
❑ 179B D.J. Augustin Standing 1.25 3.00
❑ 180A Brook Lopez Blue RC 2.00 5.00
❑ 180B Brook Lopez Red 2.50 6.00
❑ 181A Jerryd Bayless Layup RC 1.00 2.50
❑ 181B Jerryd Bayless Standing 1.25 3.00
❑ 182 Jason Thompson RC 1.00 2.50
❑ 183A A.Randolph Crouching RC 1.50 4.00
❑ 183B A.Randolph Standing 2.00 5.00
❑ 184A Robin Lopez Standing RC 1.00 2.50
❑ 184B Robin Lopez Crouching 1.25 3.00
❑ 185 Marreese Speights RC 1.00 2.50
❑ 186 Roy Hibbert RC 1.25 3.00
❑ 187 JaVale McGee RC 1.00 2.50
❑ 188A J.J. Hickson Dribbling RC 1.50 4.00
❑ 188B J.J. Hickson Standing 2.00 5.00
❑ 189A Brandon Rush Dribbling RC 1.00 2.50
❑ 189B Brandon Rush Standing 1.25 3.00
❑ 190 Ryan Anderson RC 1.00 2.50
❑ 191A Courtney Lee Dribbling RC 1.50 4.00
❑ 191B Courtney Lee Standing 2.00 5.00
❑ 192A Kosta Koufos Dribbling RC 1.00 2.50
❑ 192B Kosta Koufos Standing 1.25 3.00
❑ 193 Rudy Fernandez RC 2.00 5.00
❑ 194 George Hill RC 1.50 4.00
❑ 195 D.J. White RC 1.00 2.50
❑ 196 J.R. Giddens RC 1.00 2.50
❑ 197A C.Douglas-Roberts Red RC 1.25 3.00
❑ 197B C.Douglas-Roberts Blue 1.50 4.00
❑ 198A Mario Chalmers Dribbling RC 1.25 3.00
❑ 198B Mario Chalmers Standing 1.50 4.00
❑ 199 DeAndre Jordan RC 1.00 2.50
❑ 200A Darrell Arthur Blue RC 1.00 2.50
❑ 201 Joe Johnson SP 1.00 2.50
❑ 202 Paul Pierce SP 1.25 3.00
❑ 203 LeBron James SP 5.00 12.00
❑ 204 Tayshaun Prince SP 1.00 2.50
❑ 205 Danny Granger SP 1.00 2.50
❑ 206 Pau Gasol SP 1.00 2.50
❑ 207 Shawn Marion SP 1.00 2.50
❑ 208 Michael Redd SP 1.00 2.50
❑ 209 Devin Harris SP 1.00 2.50
❑ 210 David West SP 1.00 2.50
❑ 211 Kevin Durant SP 2.50 6.00
❑ 212 Dwight Howard SP 2.00 5.00
❑ 213 Samuel Dalembert SP 1.00 2.50
❑ 214 Greg Oden SP 1.00 2.50
❑ 215 Tim Duncan SP 1.50 4.00
❑ 216 Carlos Boozer SP 1.00 2.50
❑ 217 Caron Butler SP 1.00 2.50
❑ 218 Chris Bosh SP 1.00 2.50
❑ 219 Leandro Barbosa SP .75 2.00
❑ 220 Tracy McGrady SP 1.25 3.00
❑ 221 Andrew Bogut SP 1.00 2.50
❑ 222 Rudy Gay SP 1.00 2.50
❑ 223 Andre Iguodala SP 1.00 2.50
❑ 224 Dirk Nowitzki SP 1.25 3.00
❑ 225 Deron Williams SP 1.25 3.00
❑ 226 Chauncey Billups SP 1.00 2.50

❑ 227 Rajon Rondo SP	1.00	2.50
❑ 228 Beno Udrih SP	1.00	2.50
❑ 229 Dwyane Wade SP	2.00	5.00
❑ 230 Chris Paul SP	2.00	5.00

2001-02 Topps TCC

❑ COMPLETE SET (150)	30.00	80.00
❑ COMMON CARD	.15	.40
❑ COMMON ROOKIE (118-150)	.40	1.00
❑ 1 Shaquille O'Neal	.60	1.50
❑ 2 Jason Williams	.20	.50
❑ 3 Eddie Jones	.20	.50
❑ 4 Anthony Mason	.15	.40
❑ 5 Joe Smith	.15	.40
❑ 6 Kenyon Martin	.25	.60
❑ 7 Tracy McGrady	.50	1.25
❑ 8 Horace Grant	.20	.50
❑ 9 Andre Miller	.20	.50
❑ 10 Allen Iverson	.50	1.25
❑ 11 Shawn Marion	.25	.60
❑ 12 Derek Anderson	.20	.50
❑ 13 Chris Webber	.25	.60
❑ 14 Bruce Bowen	.15	.40
❑ 15 Alvin Williams	.15	.40
❑ 16 Brent Barry	.15	.40
❑ 17 Donyell Marshall	.15	.40
❑ 18 Richard Hamilton	.20	.50
❑ 19 Vlade Divac	.20	.50
❑ 20 Vince Carter	.50	1.25
❑ 21 Kevin Garnett	.50	1.25
❑ 22 Jason Terry	.25	.60
❑ 23 Antoine Walker	.20	.50
❑ 24 P.J. Brown	.15	.40
❑ 25 Baron Davis	.25	.60
❑ 26 Eddie Robinson	.15	.40
❑ 27 Chris Mihm	.15	.40
❑ 28 Michael Finley	.25	.60
❑ 29 Nick Van Exel	.20	.50
❑ 30 Steve Francis	.25	.60
❑ 31 Chucky Atkins	.15	.40
❑ 32 Raef LaFrentz	.15	.40
❑ 33 Antawn Jamison	.25	.60
❑ 34 Jalen Rose	.20	.50
❑ 35 Lamar Odom	.25	.60
❑ 36 Elton Brand	.25	.60
❑ 37 Derek Fisher	.20	.50
❑ 38 Alonzo Mourning	.25	.60
❑ 39 Ervin Johnson	.15	.40
❑ 40 Tim Duncan	.50	1.25
❑ 41 Kurt Thomas	.15	.40
❑ 42 Latrell Sprewell	.20	.50
❑ 43 Darrell Armstrong	.15	.40
❑ 44 Tom Gugliotta	.15	.40
❑ 45 Derrick Coleman	.20	.50
❑ 46 Dale Davis	.15	.40
❑ 47 David Robinson	.30	.75
❑ 48 Scottie Pippen	.40	1.00
❑ 49 Hakeem Olajuwon	.30	.75
❑ 50 Darius Miles	.15	.40
❑ 51 Greg Ostertag	.15	.40
❑ 52 Karl Malone	.30	.75
❑ 53 Morris Peterson	.20	.50
❑ 54 Shareef Abdur-Rahim	.20	.50
❑ 55 Dikembe Mutombo	.20	.50
❑ 56 Elden Campbell	.15	.40
❑ 57 Ron Mercer	.15	.40
❑ 58 Jumaine Jones	.15	.40
❑ 59 Wang ZhiZhi	.20	.50
❑ 60 Ray Allen	.25	.60
❑ 61 Marcus Camby	.20	.50
❑ 62 Jermaine O'Neal	.25	.60
❑ 63 Kenny Thomas	.15	.40
❑ 64 Danny Fortson	.15	.40
❑ 65 Ben Wallace	.20	.50
❑ 66 DeShawn Stevenson	.15	.40
❑ 67 Antonio Davis	.15	.40
❑ 68 Doug Christie	.15	.40
❑ 69 Rasheed Wallace	.25	.60
❑ 70 Stephon Marbury	.25	.60
❑ 71 Allan Houston	.20	.50
❑ 72 Kerry Kittles	.20	.50
❑ 73 Todd MacCulloch	.15	.40
❑ 74 Sam Cassell	.20	.50
❑ 75 Kobe Bryant	1.25	3.00
❑ 76 Aaron McKie	.15	.40
❑ 77 Terrell Brandon	.15	.40
❑ 78 Brian Grant	.15	.40
❑ 79 Michael Dickerson	.15	.40
❑ 80 Jerry Stackhouse	.20	.50
❑ 81 Antonio McDyess	.20	.50
❑ 82 Steve Nash	.40	1.00
❑ 83 Paul Pierce	.25	.60
❑ 84 Jamal Mashburn	.20	.50
❑ 85 Toni Kukoc	.20	.50
❑ 86 James Posey	.15	.40
❑ 87 Larry Hughes	.20	.50
❑ 88 Cuttino Mobley	.20	.50
❑ 89 Jeff Foster	.15	.40
❑ 90 Jason Kidd	.40	1.00
❑ 91 Keith Van Horn	.20	.50
❑ 92 Mike Miller	.20	.50
❑ 93 Anfernee Hardaway	.25	.60
❑ 94 Bonzi Wells	.20	.50
❑ 95 Mike Bibby	.20	.50
❑ 96 Steve Smith	.20	.50
❑ 97 Gary Payton	.25	.60
❑ 98 John Stockton	.30	.75
❑ 99 Peja Stojakovic	.20	.50
❑ 100 Michael Jordan	5.00	12.00
❑ 101 Iakovos Tsakalidis	.15	.40
❑ 102 Mark Jackson	.20	.50
❑ 103 Wally Szczerbiak	.20	.50
❑ 104 Rod Strickland	.20	.50
❑ 105 Rick Fox	.20	.50
❑ 106 Glenn Robinson	.20	.50
❑ 107 Michael Olowokandi	.15	.40
❑ 108 Reggie Miller	.25	.60
❑ 109 Kelvin Cato	.15	.40
❑ 110 Clifford Robinson	.15	.40
❑ 111 Dirk Nowitzki	.40	1.00
❑ 112 Brad Miller	.20	.50
❑ 113 David Wesley	.15	.40
❑ 114 Kenny Anderson	.20	.50
❑ 115 Theo Ratliff	.15	.40
❑ 116 Rashard Lewis	.25	.60
❑ 117 Matt Harpring	.20	.50
❑ 118 Eddie Griffin RC	.40	1.00
❑ 119 Brendan Haywood RC	.50	1.25
❑ 120 Steven Hunter RC	.40	1.00
❑ 121 Jamaal Tinsley RC	.50	1.25
❑ 122 Jason Richardson RC	.75	2.00
❑ 123 Tony Parker RC	1.50	4.00
❑ 124 Pau Gasol RC	1.50	4.00
❑ 125 Shane Battier RC	.60	1.50
❑ 126 Joe Johnson RC	1.00	2.50
❑ 127 Leon Smith RC	.40	1.00
❑ 128 Mengke Bateer RC	.40	1.00
❑ 129 Loren Woods RC	.40	1.00
❑ 130 Kwame Brown RC	.50	1.25
❑ 131 Tyson Chandler RC	.75	2.00
❑ 132 Eddy Curry RC	.60	1.50
❑ 133 Kedrick Brown RC	.40	1.00
❑ 134 Joseph Forte RC	.40	1.00
❑ 135 Troy Murphy RC	.75	2.00
❑ 136 Richard Jefferson RC	1.00	2.50
❑ 137 DeSagana Diop RC	.40	1.00
❑ 138 Vladimir Radmanovic RC	.50	1.25
❑ 139 Zach Randolph RC	1.00	2.50
❑ 140 Gerald Wallace RC	1.00	2.50
❑ 141 Brandon Armstrong RC	.40	1.00
❑ 142 Jeryl Sasser RC	.40	1.00
❑ 143 Rodney White RC	.40	1.00
❑ 144 Samuel Dalembert RC	.50	1.25
❑ 145 Jason Collins RC	.40	1.00
❑ 146 Michael Bradley RC	.40	1.00
❑ 147 Oscar Torres RC	.40	1.00
❑ 148 Zeljko Rebraca RC	.40	1.00
❑ 149 Andrei Kirilenko RC	1.00	2.50
❑ 150 Trenton Hassell RC	.50	1.25

2002-03 Topps Ten

❑ COMPLETE SET (150)	20.00	50.00
❑ COMMON CARD (1-121)	.15	.40
❑ COMMON ROOKIE (121-150)	.75	2.00
❑ 1 Allen Iverson	.50	1.25
❑ 2 Shaquille O'Neal	.60	1.50
❑ 3 Paul Pierce	.25	.60
❑ 4 Tracy McGrady	.50	1.25
❑ 5 Tim Duncan	.50	1.25
❑ 6 Kobe Bryant	1.25	3.00
❑ 7 Dirk Nowitzki	.40	1.00
❑ 8 Karl Malone	.25	.60
❑ 9 Antoine Walker	.20	.50
❑ 10 Gary Payton	.25	.60
❑ 11 Shaquille O'Neal	.60	1.50
❑ 12 Allen Iverson	.50	1.25
❑ 13 Tracy McGrady	.50	1.25
❑ 14 Kobe Bryant	1.25	3.00
❑ 15 Michael Jordan	1.50	4.00
❑ 16 Paul Pierce	.25	.60
❑ 17 Chris Webber	.25	.60
❑ 18 Tim Duncan	.50	1.25
❑ 19 Corliss Williamson	.20	.50
❑ 20 Dirk Nowitzki	.40	1.00
❑ 21 Ben Wallace	.20	.50
❑ 22 Tim Duncan	.50	1.25
❑ 23 Kevin Garnett	.50	1.25
❑ 24 Danny Fortson	.15	.40
❑ 25 Elton Brand	.25	.60
❑ 26 Dikembe Mutombo	.20	.50
❑ 27 Jermaine O'Neal	.25	.60
❑ 28 Dirk Nowitzki	.40	1.00
❑ 29 Shawn Marion	.25	.60
❑ 30 P.J. Brown	.15	.40
❑ 31 Andre Miller	.20	.50
❑ 32 Jason Kidd	.40	1.00
❑ 33 Gary Payton	.25	.60
❑ 34 Baron Davis	.25	.60
❑ 35 John Stockton	.30	.75
❑ 36 Stephon Marbury	.25	.60
❑ 37 Jamaal Tinsley	.20	.50
❑ 38 Jason Williams	.20	.50
❑ 39 Steve Nash	.40	1.00
❑ 40 Mark Jackson	.20	.50
❑ 41 Ben Wallace	.20	.50
❑ 42 Raef LaFrentz	.15	.40
❑ 43 Alonzo Mourning	.25	.60
❑ 44 Tim Duncan	.50	1.25
❑ 45 Dikembe Mutombo	.20	.50
❑ 46 Jermaine O'Neal	.25	.60
❑ 47 Erick Dampier	.15	.40
❑ 48 Adonal Foyle	.15	.40
❑ 49 Pau Gasol	.25	.60
❑ 50 Shaquille O'Neal	.60	1.50
❑ 51 Allen Iverson	.50	1.25
❑ 52 Ron Artest	.20	.50
❑ 53 Jason Kidd	.40	1.00
❑ 54 Baron Davis	.25	.60
❑ 55 Doug Christie	.15	.40
❑ 56 Darrell Armstrong	.15	.40
❑ 57 Karl Malone	.25	.60
❑ 58 Paul Pierce	.25	.60
❑ 59 Kenny Anderson	.20	.50
❑ 60 John Stockton	.30	.75
❑ 61 Shaquille O'Neal	.60	1.50
❑ 62 Elton Brand	.25	.60
❑ 63 Donyell Marshall	.15	.40
❑ 64 Pau Gasol	.25	.60
❑ 65 John Stockton	.30	.75
❑ 66 Alonzo Mourning	.25	.60
❑ 67 Ruben Patterson	.15	.40
❑ 68 Corliss Williamson	.20	.50
❑ 69 Tim Duncan	.50	1.25
❑ 70 Brent Barry	.15	.40
❑ 71 Steve Smith	.20	.50

❑ 72 Jon Barry	.15	.40
❑ 73 Eric Piatkowski	.15	.40
❑ 74 Wally Szczerbiak	.20	.50
❑ 75 Steve Nash	.40	1.00
❑ 76 Hubert Davis	.15	.40
❑ 77 Tyronn Lue	.15	.40
❑ 78 Michael Redd	.25	.60
❑ 79 Wesley Person	.15	.40
❑ 80 Ray Allen	.25	.60
❑ 81 Reggie Miller	.25	.60
❑ 82 Richard Hamilton	.20	.50
❑ 83 Darrell Armstrong	.15	.40
❑ 84 Damon Stoudamire	.20	.50
❑ 85 Steve Nash	.40	1.00
❑ 86 Chauncey Billups	.25	.60
❑ 87 Chris Whitney	.15	.40
❑ 88 Steve Smith	.20	.50
❑ 89 Peja Stojakovic	.20	.50
❑ 90 Troy Hudson	.15	.40
❑ 91 Allen Iverson	.50	1.25
❑ 92 Cuttino Mobley	.20	.50
❑ 93 Antoine Walker	.20	.50
❑ 94 Steve Francis	.25	.60
❑ 95 Latrell Sprewell	.20	.50
❑ 96 Tim Duncan	.50	1.25
❑ 97 Baron Davis	.25	.60
❑ 98 Paul Pierce	.25	.60
❑ 99 Gary Payton	.25	.60
❑ 100 Michael Finley	.25	.60
❑ 101 Tim Duncan	.50	1.25
❑ 102 Kevin Garnett	.50	1.25
❑ 103 Elton Brand	.25	.60
❑ 104 Jason Kidd	.40	1.00
❑ 105 Shawn Marion	.25	.60
❑ 106 Andre Miller	.20	.50
❑ 107 Shaquille O'Neal	.60	1.50
❑ 108 Jermaine O'Neal	.25	.60
❑ 109 Dirk Nowitzki	.40	1.00
❑ 110 Pau Gasol	.25	.60
❑ 111 Pau Gasol	.25	.60
❑ 112 Shane Battier	.20	.50
❑ 113 Jason Richardson	.25	.60
❑ 114 Gilbert Arenas	.25	.60
❑ 115 Andrei Kirilenko	.25	.60
❑ 116 Richard Jefferson	.25	.60
❑ 117 Jamaal Tinsley	.20	.50
❑ 118 Tony Parker	.25	.60
❑ 119 Eddie Griffin	.15	.40
❑ 120 Trenton Hassell	.15	.40
❑ 121 Jay Williams RC	1.00	2.50
❑ 122 DaJuan Wagner RC	.75	2.00
❑ 123 Fred Jones RC	1.00	2.50
❑ 124 Jiri Welsch RC	.75	2.00
❑ 125 Juan Dixon RC	1.25	3.00
❑ 126 Kareem Rush RC	1.00	2.50
❑ 127 Casey Jacobsen RC	.75	2.00
❑ 128 Frank Williams RC	.75	2.00
❑ 129 John Salmons RC	1.25	3.00
❑ 130 Dan Dickau RC	.75	2.00
❑ 131 Mike Dunleavy RC	1.00	2.50
❑ 132 Nikoloz Tskitishvili RC	.75	2.00
❑ 133 Caron Butler RC	1.50	4.00
❑ 134 Jared Jeffries RC	.75	2.00
❑ 135 Bostjan Nachbar RC	.75	2.00
❑ 136 Ryan Humphrey RC	.75	2.00
❑ 137 Qyntel Woods RC	.75	2.00
❑ 138 Tayshaun Prince RC	1.25	3.00
❑ 139 Chris Jefferies RC	.75	2.00
❑ 140 Vincent Yarbrough RC	.75	2.00
❑ 141 Yao Ming RC	2.50	6.00
❑ 142 Drew Gooden RC	1.25	3.00
❑ 143 Nene Hilario RC	1.00	2.50
❑ 144 Chris Wilcox RC	1.00	2.50
❑ 145 Amare Stoudemire RC	2.00	5.00
❑ 146 Melvin Ely RC	.75	2.00
❑ 147 Marcus Haislip RC	.75	2.00
❑ 148 Curtis Borchardt RC	.75	2.00
❑ 149 Robert Archibald RC	.75	2.00
❑ 150 Dan Gadzuric RC	.75	2.00

1999-00 Topps Tip-Off

❑ COMPLETE SET (132)	15.00	30.00
❑ 1 Steve Smith	.12	.30
❑ 2 Ron Harper	.12	.30
❑ 3 Michael Dickerson	.12	.30
❑ 4 LaPhonso Ellis	.12	.30
❑ 5 Chris Webber	.20	.50
❑ 6 Jason Caffey	.12	.30
❑ 7 Bryon Russell	.12	.30
❑ 8 Bison Dele	.12	.30
❑ 9 Isaiah Rider	.12	.30
❑ 10 Dean Garrett	.12	.30
❑ 11 Eric Murdock	.12	.30
❑ 12 Juwan Howard	.15	.40
❑ 13 Latrell Sprewell	.15	.40
❑ 14 Jalen Rose	.15	.40
❑ 15 Larry Johnson	.20	.50
❑ 16 Eric Williams	.12	.30
❑ 17 Bryant Reeves	.12	.30
❑ 18 Tony Battie	.15	.40
❑ 19 Luc Longley	.12	.30
❑ 20 Gary Payton	.20	.50
❑ 21 Tariq Abdul-Wahad	.12	.30
❑ 22 Armen Gilliam	.12	.30
❑ 23 Shaquille O'Neal	.50	1.25
❑ 24 Gary Trent	.12	.30
❑ 25 John Stockton	.25	.60
❑ 26 Mark Jackson	.20	.50
❑ 27 Cherokee Parks	.12	.30
❑ 28 Michael Olowokandi	.12	.30
❑ 29 Raef LaFrentz	.15	.40
❑ 30 Dell Curry	.12	.30
❑ 31 Travis Best	.12	.30
❑ 32 Shawn Kemp	.20	.50
❑ 33 Voshon Lenard	.12	.30
❑ 34 Brian Grant	.12	.30
❑ 35 Alvin Williams	.12	.30
❑ 36 Derek Fisher	.20	.50
❑ 37 Allan Houston	.15	.40
❑ 38 Arvydas Sabonis	.15	.40
❑ 39 Terry Cummings	.12	.30
❑ 40 Dale Ellis	.12	.30
❑ 41 Maurice Taylor	.15	.40
❑ 42 Grant Hill	.20	.50
❑ 43 Anthony Mason	.12	.30
❑ 44 John Wallace	.12	.30
❑ 45 David Wesley	.12	.30
❑ 46 Nick Van Exel	.15	.40
❑ 47 Cuttino Mobley	.15	.40
❑ 48 Anfernee Hardaway	.20	.50
❑ 49 Terry Porter	.12	.30
❑ 50 Brent Barry	.15	.40
❑ 51 Derek Harper	.15	.40
❑ 52 Antoine Walker	.20	.50
❑ 53 Karl Malone	.25	.60
❑ 54 Ben Wallace	.15	.40
❑ 55 Vlade Divac	.20	.50
❑ 56 Sam Mitchell	.12	.30
❑ 57 Joe Smith	.15	.40
❑ 58 Shawn Bradley	.12	.30
❑ 59 Darrell Armstrong	.12	.30
❑ 60 Kenny Anderson	.15	.40
❑ 61 Jason Williams	.20	.50
❑ 62 Alonzo Mourning	.20	.50
❑ 63 Matt Harpring	.15	.40
❑ 64 Antonio Davis	.12	.30
❑ 65 Lindsey Hunter	.12	.30
❑ 66 Allen Iverson	.40	1.00
❑ 67 Mookie Blaylock	.12	.30
❑ 68 Wesley Person	.12	.30
❑ 69 Bobby Phills	.12	.30
❑ 70 Theo Ratliff	.15	.40
❑ 71 Antonio Daniels	.12	.30
❑ 72 P.J. Brown	.12	.30
❑ 73 David Robinson	.25	.60
❑ 74 Sean Elliott	.20	.50
❑ 75 Zydrunas Ilgauskas	.15	.40
❑ 76 Kerry Kittles	.12	.30
❑ 77 Otis Thorpe	.12	.30
❑ 78 John Starks	.20	.50
❑ 79 Jaren Jackson	.12	.30
❑ 80 Hersey Hawkins	.12	.30
❑ 81 Glenn Robinson	.15	.40
❑ 82 Paul Pierce	.20	.50
❑ 83 Glen Rice	.20	.50
❑ 84 Charlie Ward	.12	.30
❑ 85 Dee Brown	.12	.30
❑ 86 Danny Fortson	.12	.30
❑ 87 Billy Owens	.12	.30
❑ 88 Jason Kidd	.30	.75
❑ 89 Brent Price	.12	.30
❑ 90 Don Reid	.12	.30
❑ 91 Mark Bryant	.12	.30
❑ 92 Vinny Del Negro	.12	.30
❑ 93 Stephon Marbury	.20	.50
❑ 94 Donyell Marshall	.15	.40
❑ 95 Jim Jackson	.15	.40
❑ 96 Horace Grant	.15	.40
❑ 97 Calbert Cheaney	.12	.30
❑ 98 Vince Carter	.40	1.00
❑ 99 Bobby Jackson	.15	.40
❑ 100 Alan Henderson	.12	.30
❑ 101 Mike Bibby	.20	.50
❑ 102 Cedric Henderson	.12	.30
❑ 103 Lamond Murray	.12	.30
❑ 104 A.C. Green	.20	.50
❑ 105 Hakeem Olajuwon	.20	.50
❑ 106 George Lynch	.12	.30
❑ 107 Kendall Gill	.12	.30
❑ 108 Rex Chapman	.12	.30
❑ 109 Eddie Jones	.20	.50
❑ 110 Kornel David RC	.50	1.25
❑ 111 Jason Terry RC	1.25	3.00
❑ 112 Corey Maggette RC	1.50	4.00
❑ 113 Ron Artest RC	2.00	5.00
❑ 114 Richard Hamilton RC	1.50	4.00
❑ 115 Elton Brand RC	1.50	4.00
❑ 116 Baron Davis RC	2.00	5.00
❑ 117 Wally Szczerbiak RC	1.50	4.00
❑ 118 Steve Francis RC	1.50	4.00
❑ 119 James Posey RC	.75	2.00
❑ 120 Shawn Marion RC	1.50	4.00
❑ 121 Tim Duncan	.40	1.00
❑ 122 Danny Manning	.12	.30
❑ 123 Chris Mullin	.20	.50
❑ 124 Antawn Jamison	.20	.50
❑ 125 Kobe Bryant	1.00	2.50
❑ 126 Matt Geiger	.12	.30
❑ 127 Rod Strickland	.12	.30
❑ 128 Howard Eisley	.12	.30
❑ 129 Steve Nash	.30	.75
❑ 130 Felipe Lopez	.12	.30
❑ 131 Ron Mercer	.12	.30
❑ 132 Checklist	.05	.15

2000-01 Topps Tip-Off

❑ COMPLETE SET (160)	25.00	50.00
❑ COMMON CARD (1-160)	.12	.30
❑ COMMON ROOKIE	.30	.75
❑ 1 Elton Brand	.20	.50
❑ 2 Marcus Camby	.15	.40
❑ 3 Jalen Rose	.15	.40
❑ 4 Jamie Feick	.12	.30
❑ 5 Toni Kukoc	.15	.40
❑ 6 Todd MacCulloch	.12	.30
❑ 7 Mario Elie	.12	.30
❑ 8 Doug Christie	.12	.30
❑ 9 Sam Cassell	.15	.40
❑ 10 Shaquille O'Neal	.50	1.25
❑ 11 Larry Hughes	.15	.40
❑ 12 Jerry Stackhouse	.15	.40

❑ 13 Rick Fox	.15	.40
❑ 14 Clifford Robinson	.12	.30
❑ 15 Felipe Lopez	.12	.30
❑ 16 Dirk Nowitzki	.30	.75
❑ 17 Cuttino Mobley	.15	.40
❑ 18 Latrell Sprewell	.15	.40
❑ 19 Nick Anderson	.12	.30
❑ 20 Kevin Garnett	.40	1.00
❑ 21 Rik Smits	.12	.30
❑ 22 Jerome Williams	.12	.30
❑ 23 Chris Webber	.20	.50
❑ 24 Jason Terry	.20	.50
❑ 25 Elden Campbell	.12	.30
❑ 26 Kelvin Cato	.12	.30
❑ 27 Tyrone Nesby	.12	.30
❑ 28 Jonathan Bender	.12	.30
❑ 29 Otis Thorpe	.15	.40
❑ 30 Scottie Pippen	.30	.75
❑ 31 Radoslav Nesterovic	.12	.30
❑ 32 P.J. Brown	.12	.30
❑ 33 Reggie Miller	.20	.50
❑ 34 Andre Miller	.15	.40
❑ 35 Tariq Abdul-Wahad	.12	.30
❑ 36 Michael Doleac	.12	.30
❑ 37 Rashard Lewis	.20	.50
❑ 38 Jacque Vaughn	.12	.30
❑ 39 Larry Johnson	.15	.40
❑ 40 Steve Francis	.20	.50
❑ 41 Arvydas Sabonis	.15	.40
❑ 42 Jaren Jackson	.12	.30
❑ 43 Howard Eisley	.12	.30
❑ 44 Rod Strickland	.15	.40
❑ 45 Tim Thomas	.12	.30
❑ 46 Robert Horry	.15	.40
❑ 47 Kenny Thomas	.12	.30
❑ 48 Anthony Peeler	.12	.30
❑ 49 Darrell Armstrong	.12	.30
❑ 50 Vince Carter	.40	1.00
❑ 51 Othella Harrington	.12	.30
❑ 52 Derek Anderson	.15	.40
❑ 53 Anthony Carter	.12	.30
❑ 54 Scott Burrell	.12	.30
❑ 55 Ray Allen	.20	.50
❑ 56 Jason Kidd	.30	.75
❑ 57 Sean Elliott	.15	.40
❑ 58 Muggsy Bogues	.15	.40
❑ 59 LaPhonso Ellis	.15	.40
❑ 60 Tim Duncan	.40	1.00
❑ 61 Adrian Griffin	.12	.30
❑ 62 Wally Szczerbiak	.15	.40
❑ 63 Austin Croshere	.12	.30
❑ 64 Wesley Person	.12	.30
❑ 65 James Posey	.12	.30
❑ 66 Alan Henderson	.12	.30
❑ 67 Ruben Patterson	.12	.30
❑ 68 Jahidi White	.12	.30
❑ 69 Shawn Marion	.20	.50
❑ 70 Lamar Odom	.20	.50
❑ 71 Lindsey Hunter	.12	.30
❑ 72 Keon Clark	.12	.30
❑ 73 Gary Trent	.12	.30
❑ 74 Lamond Murray	.12	.30
❑ 75 Paul Pierce	.20	.50
❑ 76 Charlie Ward	.12	.30
❑ 77 Matt Geiger	.12	.30
❑ 78 Greg Anthony	.12	.30
❑ 79 Horace Grant	.15	.40
❑ 80 John Stockton	.25	.60
❑ 81 Peja Stojakovic	.15	.40
❑ 82 William Avery	.12	.30
❑ 83 Dan Majerle	.15	.40
❑ 84 Christian Laettner	.12	.30
❑ 85 Dana Barros	.12	.30
❑ 86 Corey Benjamin	.12	.30
❑ 87 Keith Van Horn	.15	.40
❑ 88 Patrick Ewing	.25	.60
❑ 89 Steve Smith	.15	.40
❑ 90 Antonio Davis	.12	.30
❑ 91 Samaki Walker	.12	.30
❑ 92 Mitch Richmond	.15	.40
❑ 93 Michael Olowokandi	.12	.30
❑ 94 Baron Davis	.20	.50
❑ 95 Dikembe Mutombo	.15	.40
❑ 96 Andrew DeClercq	.12	.30
❑ 97 Raef LaFrentz	.12	.30
❑ 98 Trajan Langdon	.12	.30
❑ 99 Ervin Johnson	.12	.30
❑ 100 Alonzo Mourning	.20	.50
❑ 101 Kendall Gill	.12	.30
❑ 102 George Lynch	.12	.30
❑ 103 Detlef Schrempf	.15	.40
❑ 104 Donyell Marshall	.12	.30
❑ 105 Bo Outlaw	.12	.30
❑ 106 Kenny Anderson	.15	.40
❑ 107 Eddie Robinson	.12	.30
❑ 108 Jermaine O'Neal	.20	.50
❑ 109 John Amaechi	.12	.30
❑ 110 Glen Rice	.15	.40
❑ 111 Vlade Divac	.15	.40
❑ 112 Vin Baker	.15	.40
❑ 113 Mike Bibby	.15	.40
❑ 114 Richard Hamilton	.15	.40
❑ 115 Mookie Blaylock	.15	.40
❑ 116 Vitaly Potapenko	.12	.30
❑ 117 Anthony Mason	.12	.30
❑ 118 Robert Pack	.12	.30
❑ 119 Vonteego Cummings	.12	.30
❑ 120 Michael Finley	.20	.50
❑ 121 Ron Artest	.20	.50
❑ 122 Tyrone Hill	.12	.30
❑ 123 Rodney Rogers	.12	.30
❑ 124 Quincy Lewis	.12	.30
❑ 125 Kenyon Martin RC	.75	2.00
❑ 126 Stromile Swift RC	.40	1.00
❑ 127 Darius Miles RC	.40	1.00
❑ 128 Marcus Fizer RC	.30	.75
❑ 129 Mike Miller RC	.50	1.25
❑ 130 DerMarr Johnson RC	.30	.75
❑ 131 Chris Mihm RC	.30	.75
❑ 132 Jamal Crawford RC	.50	1.25
❑ 133 Joel Przybilla RC	.30	.75
❑ 134 Keyon Dooling RC	.30	.75
❑ 135 Shaq/Iverson/G.Hill SL	.15	.40
❑ 136 Kidd/Van Exel/Cassell SL	.20	.50
❑ 137 Mutombo/Shaq/Duncan SL	.25	.60
❑ 138 E.Jones/Pierce/Armstrong SL	.10	.30
❑ 139 Mourning/Mutombo/Shaq SL	.20	.50
❑ 140 Team Championship SL	.30	.75
❑ 141 Kobe Bryant	1.00	2.50
❑ 142 Stephon Marbury	.20	.50
❑ 143 Antoine Walker	.15	.40
❑ 144 Jason Williams	.15	.40
❑ 145 Shareef Abdur-Rahim	.15	.40
❑ 146 Gary Payton	.20	.50
❑ 147 Grant Hill	.20	.50
❑ 148 Allen Iverson	.40	1.00
❑ 149 Khalid El-Amin RC	.30	.75
❑ 150 Chris Carrawell RC	.30	.75
❑ 151 Shaquille O'Neal CS	.25	.60
❑ 152 Allen Iverson CS	.20	.50
❑ 153 Kevin Garnett CS	.20	.50
❑ 154 Vince Carter CS	.20	.50
❑ 155 Tim Duncan CS	.20	.50
❑ 156 Karl Malone CS	.12	.30
❑ 157 Chris Webber CS	.12	.30
❑ 158 Latrell Sprewell CS	.12	.30
❑ 159 Alonzo Mourning CS	.12	.30
❑ 160 Checklist	.05	.15

2008-09 Topps Tip-Off

❑ COMPLETE SET (143)	15.00	30.00
❑ 1 Kobe Bryant	1.00	2.50
❑ 2 Kevin Garnett	.40	1.00
❑ 3 Chris Paul	.40	1.00
❑ 4 Chris Bosh	.20	.50
❑ 5 Caron Butler	.20	.50
❑ 6 Andrew Bogut	.20	.50
❑ 7 Brandon Roy	.25	.60
❑ 8 Richard Hamilton	.15	.40
❑ 9 Tony Parker	.20	.50
❑ 10 Yao Ming	.25	.60
❑ 11 Jamal Crawford	.12	.30
❑ 12 Dwight Howard	.40	1.00
❑ 13 Steve Nash	.20	.50
❑ 14 Mike Miller	.20	.50
❑ 15 Vince Carter	.25	.60
❑ 16 Pau Gasol	.20	.50
❑ 17 Mike Dunleavy	.15	.40
❑ 18 Josh Smith	.20	.50
❑ 19 Kevin Martin	.20	.50
❑ 20 Ray Allen	.20	.50
❑ 21 Tim Duncan	.30	.75
❑ 22 Michael Redd	.20	.50
❑ 23 LeBron James	1.00	2.50
❑ 24 Richard Jefferson	.20	.50
❑ 25 Al Jefferson	.20	.50
❑ 26 Corey Maggette	.20	.50
❑ 27 Hedo Turkoglu	.20	.50
❑ 28 Mo Williams	.15	.40
❑ 29 Andre Iguodala	.20	.50
❑ 30 David West	.20	.50
❑ 31 Tracy McGrady	.25	.60
❑ 32 Shaquille O'Neal	.40	1.00
❑ 33 Dwyane Wade	.40	1.00
❑ 34 Paul Pierce	.25	.60
❑ 35 Kevin Durant	.50	1.25
❑ 36 Tayshaun Prince	.20	.50
❑ 37 Shawn Marion	.20	.50
❑ 38 Anderson Varejao	.15	.40
❑ 39 Stephen Jackson	.15	.40
❑ 40 Marcus Camby	.12	.30
❑ 41 Brad Miller	.20	.50
❑ 42 David Lee	.15	.40
❑ 43 Allen Iverson	.25	.60
❑ 44 Antawn Jamison	.20	.50
❑ 45 Peja Stojakovic	.20	.50
❑ 46 Rashad McCants	.15	.40
❑ 47 Andrei Kirilenko	.20	.50
❑ 48 Luol Deng	.20	.50
❑ 49 Hakim Warrick	.12	.30
❑ 50 Zach Randolph	.20	.50
❑ 51 Danny Granger	.20	.50
❑ 52 Greg Oden	.20	.50
❑ 53 Jason Kidd	.20	.50
❑ 54 Al Horford	.20	.50
❑ 55 Carlos Boozer	.20	.50
❑ 56 Jameer Nelson	.15	.40
❑ 57 Andre Miller	.15	.40
❑ 58 Ricky Davis	.20	.50
❑ 59 Elton Brand	.30	.75
❑ 60 Kirk Hinrich	.20	.50
❑ 61 Amare Stoudemire	.25	.60
❑ 62 Chris Wilcox	.15	.40
❑ 63 Baron Davis	.20	.50
❑ 64 Jason Richardson	.20	.50
❑ 65 Jamario Moon	.20	.50
❑ 66 LaMarcus Aldridge	.20	.50
❑ 67 Jermaine O'Neal	.20	.50
❑ 68 Joe Johnson	.20	.50
❑ 69 Ben Wallace	.20	.50
❑ 70 Carmelo Anthony	.25	.60
❑ 71 T.J. Ford	.12	.30
❑ 72 Dirk Nowitzki	.25	.60
❑ 73 Ryan Gomes	.15	.40
❑ 74 Ben Gordon	.20	.50
❑ 75 Gerald Wallace	.20	.50
❑ 76 Rudy Gay	.20	.50
❑ 77 Lamar Odom	.20	.50
❑ 78 Jeff Green	.15	.40
❑ 79 Devin Harris	.20	.50
❑ 80 Monta Ellis	.20	.50
❑ 81 Samuel Dalembert	.12	.30
❑ 82 Raymond Felton	.15	.40
❑ 83 Ron Artest	.20	.50
❑ 84 Chauncey Billups	.20	.50
❑ 85 Josh Howard	.20	.50
❑ 86 Rafer Alston	.12	.30
❑ 87 Chris Kaman	.12	.30
❑ 88 Deron Williams	.25	.60
❑ 89 Manu Ginobili	.20	.50
❑ 90 Gilbert Arenas	.20	.50
❑ 91 Bill Russell	.30	.75
❑ 92 David Robinson	.30	.75
❑ 93 Bill Cartwright	.20	.50
❑ 94 Dominique Wilkins	.25	.60
❑ 95 Larry Bird	.60	1.50
❑ 96 Dennis Rodman	.20	.50
❑ 97 Jerry West	.25	.60
❑ 98 George Gervin	.25	.60
❑ 99 Rick Barry	.20	.50
❑ 100 Bernard King	.20	.50
❑ 101 Karl Malone	.25	.60
❑ 102 Gail Goodrich	.20	.50
❑ 103 Bill Bradley	.25	.60

❑ 104 Adrian Dantley	.20	.50
❑ 105 Joe Dumars	.20	.50
❑ 106 Sam Jones	.25	.60
❑ 107 John Stockton	.30	.75
❑ 108 Magic Johnson	.40	1.00
❑ 109 Larry Nance	.20	.50
❑ 110 Dave Bing	.20	.50
❑ 111 Derrick Rose RC	1.50	4.00
❑ 112 Michael Beasley RC	.75	2.00
❑ 113 O.J. Mayo RC	.60	1.50
❑ 114 Russell Westbrook RC	1.00	2.50
❑ 115 Kevin Love RC	.50	1.25
❑ 116 Danilo Gallinari RC	.60	1.50
❑ 117 Eric Gordon RC	.50	1.25
❑ 118 Joe Alexander RC	.40	1.00
❑ 119 D.J. Augustin RC	.40	1.00
❑ 120 Brook Lopez RC	.75	2.00
❑ 121 Jerryd Bayless RC	.40	1.00
❑ 122 Jason Thompson RC	.40	1.00
❑ 123 Brandon Rush RC	.40	1.00
❑ 124 Anthony Randolph RC	.60	1.50
❑ 125 Robin Lopez RC	.40	1.00
❑ 126 Marreese Speights RC	.40	1.00
❑ 127 Roy Hibbert RC	.50	1.25
❑ 128 JaVale McGee RC	.40	1.00
❑ 129 J.J. Hickson RC	.60	1.50
❑ 130 Alexis Ajinca RC	.40	1.00
❑ 131 Ryan Anderson RC	.40	1.00
❑ 132 Courtney Lee RC	.60	1.50
❑ 133 Kosta Koufos RC	.40	1.00
❑ 134 Darrell Arthur RC	.40	1.00
❑ 135 Donte Greene RC	.40	1.00
❑ 136 Nicolas Batum RC	.50	1.25
❑ 137 George Hill RC	.60	1.50
❑ 138 D.J. White RC	.40	1.00
❑ 139 J.R. Giddens RC	.40	1.00
❑ 140 Walter Sharpe RC	.40	1.00
❑ 141 Joey Dorsey RC	.40	1.00
❑ 142 Mario Chalmers RC	.50	1.25
❑ 143 Chris Douglas-Roberts RC	.50	1.25

2004-05 Topps Total

❑ COMPLETE SET (440)	20.00	50.00
❑ COMMON CARD (1-311)	.12	.30
❑ COMMON ROOKIE (312-360)	.30	.75
❑ COMMON COACH (361-420)	.20	.50
❑ COMMON MASCOT (421-440)	.30	.75
❑ 1 Antoine Walker	.20	.50
❑ 2 Paul Pierce	.20	.50
❑ 3 Tyson Chandler	.15	.40
❑ 4 Lebron James	1.25	3.00
❑ 5 Dirk Nowitzki	.30	.75
❑ 6 Carmelo Anthony	.60	1.50
❑ 7 Chauncey Billups	.20	.50
❑ 8 Juwan Howard	.15	.40
❑ 9 Eddie Gill	.12	.30
❑ 10 Elton Brand	.20	.50
❑ 11 Chucky Atkins	.12	.30
❑ 12 Shane Battier	.15	.40
❑ 13 Shaquille O'Neal	.50	1.25
❑ 14 T.J. Ford	.15	.40
❑ 15 Sam Cassell	.15	.40
❑ 16 Rodney Buford	.12	.30
❑ 17 David West	.20	.50
❑ 18 Stephon Marbury	.20	.50
❑ 19 Steve Francis	.20	.50
❑ 20 Samuel Dalembert	.12	.30
❑ 21 Steve Nash	.30	.75
❑ 22 Shareef Abdur-Rahim	.15	.40
❑ 23 Mike Bibby	.15	.40
❑ 24 Tim Duncan	.40	1.00
❑ 25 Ray Allen	.20	.50
❑ 26 Vince Carter	.40	1.00
❑ 27 Carlos Arroyo	.20	.50
❑ 28 Gilbert Arenas	.20	.50
❑ 29 Mark Blount	.12	.30
❑ 30 Primoz Brezec	.12	.30
❑ 31 Eddy Curry	.15	.40
❑ 32 Lucious Harris	.12	.30
❑ 33 Shawn Bradley	.12	.30
❑ 34 Earl Boykins	.12	.30
❑ 35 Elden Campbell	.12	.30
❑ 36 Calbert Cheaney	.12	.30
❑ 37 Jim Jackson	.12	.30
❑ 38 Jonathan Bender	.12	.30
❑ 39 Kobe Bryant	1.00	2.50
❑ 40 Malik Allen	.12	.30
❑ 41 Dan Gadzuric	.12	.30
❑ 42 Eddie Griffin	.12	.30
❑ 43 Jason Collins	.12	.30
❑ 44 Chris Andersen	.12	.30
❑ 45 Marc Jackson	.12	.30
❑ 46 Leandro Barbosa	.20	.50
❑ 47 Derek Anderson	.15	.40
❑ 48 Doug Christie	.12	.30
❑ 49 Brent Barry	.12	.30
❑ 50 Nick Collison	.12	.30
❑ 51 Carlos Boozer	.20	.50
❑ 52 Steve Blake	.12	.30
❑ 53 Al Harrington	.15	.40
❑ 54 Melvin Ely	.12	.30
❑ 55 Zydrunas Ilgauskas	.15	.40
❑ 56 Erick Dampier	.12	.30
❑ 57 Marcus Camby	.15	.40
❑ 58 Derrick Coleman	.15	.40
❑ 59 Speedy Claxton	.12	.30
❑ 60 Tyronn Lue	.12	.30
❑ 61 Austin Croshere	.12	.30
❑ 62 Marko Jaric	.12	.30
❑ 63 Caron Butler	.15	.40
❑ 64 Pau Gasol	.20	.50
❑ 65 Christian Laettner	.12	.30
❑ 66 Daniel Santiago	.12	.30
❑ 67 Kevin Garnett	.40	1.00
❑ 68 Richard Jefferson	.20	.50
❑ 69 David Wesley	.12	.30
❑ 70 Vin Baker	.12	.30
❑ 71 Tony Battie	.12	.30
❑ 72 Allen Iverson	.40	1.00
❑ 73 Darius Miles	.15	.40
❑ 74 Bobby Jackson	.12	.30
❑ 75 Bruce Bowen	.12	.30
❑ 76 Antonio Daniels	.12	.30
❑ 77 Chris Bosh	.20	.50
❑ 78 Gordan Giricek	.12	.30
❑ 79 Kwame Brown	.12	.30
❑ 80 Raef Lafrentz	.12	.30
❑ 81 Jason Hart	.12	.30
❑ 82 Marquis Daniels	.12	.30
❑ 83 Francisco Elson	.12	.30
❑ 84 Carlos Delfino	.20	.50
❑ 85 Dale Davis	.12	.30
❑ 86 Tracy McGrady	.40	1.00
❑ 87 Jeff Foster	.12	.30
❑ 88 Chris Kaman	.15	.40
❑ 89 Brian Cook	.12	.30
❑ 90 Mike Miller	.15	.40
❑ 91 Rasual Butler	.12	.30
❑ 92 Mike James	.12	.30
❑ 93 Trenton Hassell	.12	.30
❑ 94 Jason Kidd	.30	.75
❑ 95 Lee Nailon	.12	.30
❑ 96 Jerome Williams	.12	.30
❑ 97 Stacey Augmon	.12	.30
❑ 98 Willie Green	.12	.30
❑ 99 Amare Stoudemire	.40	1.00
❑ 100 Ruben Patterson	.12	.30
❑ 101 Chris Webber	.20	.50
❑ 102 Manu Ginobili	.20	.50
❑ 103 Danny Fortson	.12	.30
❑ 104 Donyell Marshall	.12	.30
❑ 105 Matt Harpring	.15	.40
❑ 106 Juan Dixon	.12	.30
❑ 107 Boris Diaw	.15	.40
❑ 108 Ricky Davis	.15	.40
❑ 109 Eddie House	.12	.30
❑ 110 Kirk Hinrich	.15	.40
❑ 111 Jeff Mcinnis	.12	.30
❑ 112 Michael Finley	.20	.50
❑ 113 Voshon Lenard	.12	.30
❑ 114 Darvin Ham	.12	.30
❑ 115 Mike Dunleavy	.15	.40
❑ 116 Dikembe Mutombo	.15	.40
❑ 117 Kerry Kittles	.15	.40
❑ 118 Vlade Divac	.15	.40
❑ 119 James Posey	.12	.30
❑ 120 Michael Doleac	.12	.30
❑ 121 Toni Kukoc	.15	.40
❑ 122 Troy Hudson	.12	.30
❑ 123 Jamal Crawford	.15	.40
❑ 124 Grant Hill	.20	.50
❑ 125 Corliss Williamson	.12	.30
❑ 126 Quentin Richardson	.15	.40
❑ 127 Zach Randolph	.20	.50
❑ 128 Peja Stojakovic	.15	.40
❑ 129 Robert Horry	.15	.40
❑ 130 Jerome James	.12	.30
❑ 131 Morris Peterson	.15	.40
❑ 132 Jarvis Hayes	.12	.30
❑ 133 Tony Delk	.12	.30
❑ 134 Jason Kapono	.12	.30
❑ 135 Adrian Griffin	.12	.30
❑ 136 Aleksandar Pavlovic	.12	.30
❑ 137 Kenyon Martin	.20	.50
❑ 138 Richard Hamilton	.15	.40
❑ 139 Derek Fisher	.15	.40
❑ 140 Bob Sura	.12	.30
❑ 141 Stephen Jackson	.15	.40
❑ 142 Devean George	.12	.30
❑ 143 Stromile Swift	.12	.30
❑ 144 Keyon Dooling	.12	.30
❑ 145 Desmond Mason	.15	.40
❑ 146 Michael Olowokandi	.12	.30
❑ 147 Ron Mercer	.12	.30
❑ 148 P.J. Brown	.12	.30
❑ 149 Tim Thomas	.12	.30
❑ 150 Kelvin Cato	.12	.30
❑ 151 Kenny Thomas	.12	.30
❑ 152 Theo Ratliff	.12	.30
❑ 153 Rasho Nesterovic	.12	.30
❑ 154 Rashard Lewis	.20	.50
❑ 155 Jalen Rose	.15	.40
❑ 156 Brendan Haywood	.12	.30
❑ 157 Kevin Willis	.12	.30
❑ 158 Gary Payton	.20	.50
❑ 159 Brevin Knight	.12	.30
❑ 160 Othella Harrington	.12	.30
❑ 161 Eric Snow	.12	.30
❑ 162 Josh Howard	.20	.50
❑ 163 Andre Miller	.15	.40
❑ 164 Lindsey Hunter	.12	.30
❑ 165 Adonal Foyle	.12	.30
❑ 166 Maurice Taylor	.12	.30
❑ 167 Fred Jones	.12	.30
❑ 168 Corey Maggette	.15	.40
❑ 169 Brian Grant	.12	.30
❑ 170 Bonzi Wells	.12	.30
❑ 171 Michael Redd	.20	.50
❑ 172 Latrell Sprewell	.15	.40
❑ 173 Steven Hunter	.12	.30
❑ 174 Rodney Rogers	.12	.30
❑ 175 Anfernee Hardaway	.20	.50
❑ 176 Pat Garrity	.12	.30
❑ 177 Brian Skinner	.12	.30
❑ 178 Zarko Cabarkapa	.12	.30
❑ 179 Damon Stoudamire	.15	.40
❑ 180 Tony Parker	.20	.50
❑ 181 Ronald Murray	.12	.30
❑ 182 Alvin Williams	.12	.30
❑ 183 Raul Lopez	.12	.30
❑ 184 Larry Hughes	.15	.40
❑ 185 Predrag Drobnjak	.12	.30
❑ 186 Jiri Welsch	.12	.30
❑ 187 Robert Traylor	.12	.30
❑ 188 Nene	.15	.40
❑ 189 Antonio McDyess	.15	.40
❑ 190 Troy Murphy	.20	.50
❑ 191 Charlie Ward	.12	.30
❑ 192 Reggie Miller	.20	.50
❑ 193 Bobby Simmons	.12	.30
❑ 194 Stanislav Medvedenko	.12	.30
❑ 195 Jason Williams	.15	.40
❑ 196 Dwyane Wade	.60	1.50
❑ 197 Joe Smith	.12	.30
❑ 198 Wally Szczerbiak	.15	.40
❑ 199 Zoran Planinic	.12	.30
❑ 200 Baron Davis	.20	.50
❑ 201 Kurt Thomas	.12	.30
❑ 202 Deshawn Stevenson	.12	.30
❑ 203 John Salmons	.20	.50
❑ 204 Maciej Lampe	.12	.30
❑ 205 Greg Ostertag	.12	.30
❑ 206 Malik Rose	.12	.30
❑ 207 Matt Bonner	.12	.30

❑ 208 Keith McLeod	.12	.30
❑ 209 Antawn Jamison	.20	.50
❑ 210 Marcus Banks	.12	.30
❑ 211 Keith Bogans	.12	.30
❑ 212 Antonio Davis	.12	.30
❑ 213 Jerry Stackhouse	.15	.40
❑ 214 Nikoloz Tskitishvili	.12	.30
❑ 215 Darko Milicic	.12	.30
❑ 216 Eduardo Najera	.12	.30
❑ 217 Yao Ming	.50	1.25
❑ 218 Jermaine O'Neal	.20	.50
❑ 219 Chris Wilcox	.12	.30
❑ 220 Lamar Odom	.20	.50
❑ 221 Lorenzen Wright	.12	.30
❑ 222 Damon Jones	.12	.30
❑ 223 Keith Van Horn	.15	.40
❑ 224 Fred Hoiberg	.12	.30
❑ 225 Brian Scalabrine	.12	.30
❑ 226 Jamaal Magloire	.12	.30
❑ 227 Mike Sweetney	.12	.30
❑ 228 Hedo Turkoglu	.15	.40
❑ 229 Glenn Robinson	.15	.40
❑ 230 Casey Jacobsen	.12	.30
❑ 231 Nick Van Exel	.15	.40
❑ 232 Matt Barnes	.12	.30
❑ 233 Luke Ridnour	.12	.30
❑ 234 Loren Woods	.12	.30
❑ 235 Raja Bell	.15	.40
❑ 236 Walter McCarty	.12	.30
❑ 237 Steve Smith	.15	.40
❑ 238 Frank Williams	.12	.30
❑ 239 Dajuan Wagner	.12	.30
❑ 240 Jason Terry	.15	.40
❑ 241 Rodney White	.12	.30
❑ 242 Tayshaun Prince	.15	.40
❑ 243 Mickael Pietrus	.15	.40
❑ 244 Reece Gaines	.12	.30
❑ 245 Jamaal Tinsley	.15	.40
❑ 246 Zeljko Rebraca	.12	.30
❑ 247 Chris Mihm	.12	.30
❑ 248 Eddie Jones	.15	.40
❑ 249 Zaza Pachulia	.12	.30
❑ 250 Ervin Johnson	.12	.30
❑ 251 Jabari Smith	.12	.30
❑ 252 Nazr Mohammed	.12	.30
❑ 253 Andrew Declercq	.12	.30
❑ 254 Kyle Korver	.15	.40
❑ 255 Jake Voskuhl	.12	.30
❑ 256 Travis Outlaw	.12	.30
❑ 257 Vladimir Radmanovic	.12	.30
❑ 258 Lamond Murray	.12	.30
❑ 259 Jarron Collins	.12	.30
❑ 260 Jared Jeffries	.12	.30
❑ 261 Jason Collier	.12	.30
❑ 262 Tom Gugliotta	.12	.30
❑ 263 Gerald Wallace	.20	.50
❑ 264 Eric Piatkowski	.12	.30
❑ 265 Desagana Diop	.12	.30
❑ 266 Alan Henderson	.12	.30
❑ 267 Greg Buckner	.12	.30
❑ 268 Ben Wallace	.15	.40
❑ 269 Jason Richardson	.20	.50
❑ 270 Ryan Bowen	.12	.30
❑ 271 Mikki Moore	.12	.30
❑ 272 Brian Cardinal	.12	.30
❑ 273 Maurice Williams	.15	.40
❑ 274 Mark Madsen	.12	.30
❑ 275 Jacque Vaughn	.12	.30
❑ 276 George Lynch	.12	.30
❑ 277 Allan Houston	.15	.40
❑ 278 Aaron McKie	.12	.30
❑ 279 Joe Johnson	.20	.50
❑ 280 Qyntel Woods	.12	.30
❑ 281 Darius Songaila	.12	.30
❑ 282 Devin Brown	.12	.30
❑ 283 Mehmet Okur	.15	.40
❑ 284 Kenny Anderson	.15	.40
❑ 285 Jahidi White	.12	.30
❑ 286 Jon Barry	.12	.30
❑ 287 Drew Gooden	.12	.30
❑ 288 Wesley Person	.12	.30
❑ 289 Rasheed Wallace	.20	.50
❑ 290 Clifford Robinson	.12	.30
❑ 291 Bostjan Nachbar	.12	.30
❑ 292 Scot Pollard	.12	.30
❑ 293 Quinton Ross	.20	.50
❑ 294 Luke Walton	.15	.40
❑ 295 Earl Watson	.12	.30
❑ 296 Udonis Haslem	.15	.40

❑ 297 Erick Strickland	.12	.30
❑ 298 Eric Williams	.12	.30
❑ 299 Junior Harrington	.12	.30
❑ 300 Moochie Norris	.12	.30
❑ 301 Cuttino Mobley	.15	.40
❑ 302 Shawn Marion	.20	.50
❑ 303 Richie Frahm	.12	.30
❑ 304 Brad Miller	.15	.40
❑ 305 Michael Wilks	.12	.30
❑ 306 Rafer Alston	.12	.30
❑ 307 Andrei Kirilenko	.20	.50
❑ 308 Etan Thomas	.12	.30
❑ 309 Ndudi Ebi	.12	.30
❑ 310 Anthony Peeler	.12	.30
❑ 311 Pavel Podkolzine RC	.30	.75
❑ 312 Lionel Chalmers RC	.30	.75
❑ 313 Andre Emmett RC	.30	.75
❑ 314 Trevor Ariza RC	.40	1.00
❑ 315 Dwight Howard RC	1.00	2.50
❑ 316 Rafael Araujo RC	.30	.75
❑ 317 Tony Allen RC	.40	1.00
❑ 318 Luol Deng RC	.40	1.00
❑ 319 Jackson Vroman RC	.30	.75
❑ 320 Josh Smith RC	.75	2.00
❑ 321 Ben Gordon RC	.40	1.00
❑ 322 Luke Jackson RC	.30	.75
❑ 323 David Harrison RC	.30	.75
❑ 324 Nenad Krstic RC	.40	1.00
❑ 325 J.R. Smith RC	.60	1.50
❑ 326 Kris Humphries RC	.50	1.25
❑ 327 Al Jefferson RC	.60	1.50
❑ 328 Devin Harris RC	.60	1.50
❑ 329 Shaun Livingston RC	.30	.75
❑ 330 Kaniel Dickens RC	.30	.75
❑ 331 Kevin Martin RC	.40	1.00
❑ 332 Kirk Snyder RC	.30	.75
❑ 333 Josh Childress RC	.30	.75
❑ 334 Erik Daniels RC	.30	.75
❑ 335 Bernard Robinson RC	.30	.75
❑ 336 Andres Nocioni RC	.40	1.00
❑ 337 D.J. Mbenga RC	.30	.75
❑ 338 Sebastian Telfair RC	.30	.75
❑ 339 Robert Swift RC	.30	.75
❑ 340 Royal Ivey RC	.30	.75
❑ 341 Anderson Varejao RC	.40	1.00
❑ 342 Romain Sato RC	.30	.75
❑ 343 Peter John Ramos RC	.30	.75
❑ 344 Chris Duhon RC	.50	1.25
❑ 345 Emeka Okafor RC	.60	1.50
❑ 346 Matt Freije RC	.30	.75
❑ 347 Maurice Evans RC	.30	.75
❑ 348 Beno Udrih RC	.40	1.00
❑ 349 John Edwards RC	.30	.75
❑ 350 Sasha Vujacic RC	.30	.75
❑ 351 Dorell Wright RC	.40	1.00
❑ 352 Jameer Nelson RC	.40	1.00
❑ 353 Damien Wilkins RC	.30	.75
❑ 354 Pape Sow RC	.30	.75
❑ 355 Andris Biedrins RC	.50	1.25
❑ 356 Delonte West RC	.50	1.25
❑ 357 Arthur Johnson RC	.30	.75
❑ 358 Antonio Burks RC	.30	.75
❑ 359 Andre Iguodala RC	.75	2.00
❑ 360 Ibrahim Kutluay RC	.30	.75
❑ 361 Mike Woodson CO	.20	.50
❑ 362 Larry Drew CO	.20	.50
❑ 363 Doc Rivers CO	.40	1.00
❑ 364 Tony Brown CO	.20	.50
❑ 365 Bernie Bickerstaff CO	.20	.50
❑ 366 Gary Brokaw CO	.20	.50
❑ 367 Scott Skiles CO	.40	1.00
❑ 368 Ron Adams CO	.20	.50
❑ 369 Paul Silas CO	.20	.50
❑ 370 Brendan Malone CO	.20	.50
❑ 371 Don Nelson CO	.40	1.00
❑ 372 Donnie Nelson CO RC	.20	.50
❑ 373 Jeff Bzdelik CO	.20	.50
❑ 374 Michael Cooper CO	.20	.50
❑ 375 Larry Brown CO	.50	1.25
❑ 376 Dave Hanner CO	.20	.50
❑ 377 Mike Montgomery CO	.40	1.00
❑ 378 Terry Stotts CO	.20	.50
❑ 379 Jeff Van Gundy CO	.40	1.00
❑ 380 Tom Thibodeau CO	.20	.50
❑ 381 Rick Carlisle CO	.20	.50
❑ 382 Mike Brown CO	.20	.50
❑ 383 Mike Dunleavy Sr. CO	.40	1.00
❑ 384 Jim Eyen CO	.20	.50
❑ 385 Rudy Tomjanovich CO	.40	1.00

❑ 386 Frank Hamblen CO	.20	.50
❑ 387 Mike Fratello CO	.40	1.00
❑ 388 Eric Musselman CO	.20	.50
❑ 389 Stan Van Gundy CO	.40	1.00
❑ 390 Bob Mcadoo CO	.40	1.00
❑ 391 Terry Porter CO	.20	.50
❑ 392 Mike Schuler CO	.20	.50
❑ 393 Flip Saunders CO	.40	1.00
❑ 394 Jerry Sichting CO	.20	.50
❑ 395 Lawrence Frank CO	.40	1.00
❑ 396 Brian Hill CO	.20	.50
❑ 397 Byron Scott CO	.20	.50
❑ 398 Darrell Walker CO	.20	.50
❑ 399 Lenny Wilkens CO	.50	1.25
❑ 400 Mark Aguirre CO	.20	.50
❑ 401 Johnny Davis CO	.20	.50
❑ 402 Paul Westhead CO	.20	.50
❑ 403 Jim O'Brien CO	.40	1.00
❑ 404 Lester Conner CO	.20	.50
❑ 405 Mike D'Antoni CO	.40	1.00
❑ 406 Marc Iavaroni CO	.20	.50
❑ 407 Maurice Cheeks CO	.40	1.00
❑ 408 Jim Lynam CO	.20	.50
❑ 409 Rick Adelman CO	.40	1.00
❑ 410 Elston Turner CO	.20	.50
❑ 411 Gregg Popovich CO	.50	1.25
❑ 412 P.J. Carlesimo CO	.40	1.00
❑ 413 Nate Mcmillan CO	.20	.50
❑ 414 Dwane Casey CO	.20	.50
❑ 415 Sam Mitchell CO	.20	.50
❑ 416 Alex English CO	.40	1.00
❑ 417 Jerry Sloan CO	.40	1.00
❑ 418 Phil Johnson CO	.20	.50
❑ 419 Eddie Jordan CO	.20	.50
❑ 420 Mike O'Koren CO	.20	.50
❑ 421 Harry The Hawk	.30	.75
❑ 422 Blaze	.30	.75
❑ 423 Benny Da Bull	.30	.75
❑ 424 Slamson	.30	.75
❑ 425 Champ	.30	.75
❑ 426 Rocky	.30	.75
❑ 427 Clutch	.30	.75
❑ 428 Squatch	.30	.75
❑ 429 Boomer	.30	.75
❑ 430 The Raptor	.30	.75
❑ 431 Super Grizz	.30	.75
❑ 432 G-Wiz	.30	.75
❑ 433 Crunch	.30	.75
❑ 434 Sly The Fox	.30	.75
❑ 435 Hip Hop	.30	.75
❑ 436 The Gorilla	.30	.75
❑ 437 Skyhawk	.30	.75
❑ 438 Turbo	.30	.75
❑ 439 Bowser	.30	.75
❑ 440 Da Bull	.30	.75

2005-06 Topps Total

❑ COMPLETE SET (440)	20.00	50.00
❑ COMMON CARD (1-360)	.12	.30
❑ COMMON ROOKIE (1-360)	.20	.50
❑ COMMON COACH (361-420)	.20	.50
❑ COMMON MASCOTT (421-436)	.30	.75
❑ COMMON CELEBRITY (436-440)	.40	1.00
❑ 1 Josh Childress	.15	.40
❑ 2 Emeka Okafor	.20	.50
❑ 3 Luol Deng	.20	.50
❑ 4 Carmelo Anthony	.40	1.00
❑ 5 Carlos Arroyo	.20	.50
❑ 6 Shane Battier	.20	.50
❑ 7 Vince Carter	.40	1.00
❑ 8 Samuel Dalembert	.12	.30
❑ 9 Leandro Barbosa	.20	.50
❑ 10 Mike Bibby	.20	.50
❑ 11 Brent Barry	.12	.30
❑ 12 Ray Allen	.20	.50
❑ 13 Rafer Alston	.12	.30

❑ 14 Gilbert Arenas	.20	.50
❑ 15 Al Harrington	.12	.30
❑ 16 Primoz Brezec	.12	.30
❑ 17 Antonio Davis	.12	.30
❑ 18 Earl Boykins	.12	.30
❑ 19 Chauncey Billups	.20	.50
❑ 20 Antonio Burks	.12	.30
❑ 21 Jason Collins	.12	.30
❑ 22 P.J. Brown	.12	.30
❑ 23 Andre Iguodala	.20	.50
❑ 24 Bruce Bowen	.12	.30
❑ 25 Nick Collison	.12	.30
❑ 26 Rafael Araujo	.12	.30
❑ 27 Josh Smith	.20	.50
❑ 28 Melvin Ely	.12	.30
❑ 29 Ben Gordon	.25	.60
❑ 30 Zydrunas Ilgauskas	.15	.40
❑ 31 Marcus Camby	.15	.40
❑ 32 Carlos Delfino	.12	.30
❑ 33 Mike James	.12	.30
❑ 34 Brian Cardinal	.12	.30
❑ 35 Udonis Haslem	.20	.50
❑ 36 Toni Kukoc	.12	.30
❑ 37 Kevin Garnett	.40	1.00
❑ 38 Richard Jefferson	.15	.40
❑ 39 Jamal Crawford	.15	.40
❑ 40 Allen Iverson	.40	1.00
❑ 41 Tim Duncan	.40	1.00
❑ 42 Danny Fortson	.12	.30
❑ 43 Chris Bosh	.20	.50
❑ 44 Ricky Davis	.20	.50
❑ 45 LeBron James	1.00	2.50
❑ 46 Devin Harris	.20	.50
❑ 47 Tracy McGrady	.40	1.00
❑ 48 Chris Kaman	.12	.30
❑ 49 Pau Gasol	.20	.50
❑ 50 Jamaal Magloire	.12	.30
❑ 51 Trenton Hassell	.12	.30
❑ 52 Jason Kidd	.30	.75
❑ 53 Speedy Claxton	.12	.30
❑ 54 Kevin Martin	.20	.50
❑ 55 Manu Ginobili	.20	.50
❑ 56 Rashard Lewis	.20	.50
❑ 57 Matt Harpring	.15	.40
❑ 58 Kenyon Martin	.20	.50
❑ 59 Al Jefferson	.20	.50
❑ 60 Josh Howard	.20	.50
❑ 61 Bob Sura	.12	.30
❑ 62 David Harrison	.12	.30
❑ 63 Shaun Livingston	.12	.30
❑ 64 Alonzo Mourning	.25	.60
❑ 65 Michael Redd	.20	.50
❑ 66 Mark Madsen	.12	.30
❑ 67 Brad Miller	.20	.50
❑ 68 Robert Horry	.15	.40
❑ 69 Luke Ridnour	.15	.40
❑ 70 Paul Pierce	.20	.50
❑ 71 Anderson Varejao	.15	.40
❑ 72 Dirk Nowitzki	.30	.75
❑ 73 Stephen Jackson	.15	.40
❑ 74 Corey Maggette	.15	.40
❑ 75 Shaquille O'Neal	.50	1.25
❑ 76 Joe Smith	.15	.40
❑ 77 Troy Hudson	.12	.30
❑ 78 Steve Francis	.20	.50
❑ 79 Shawn Marion	.20	.50
❑ 80 Ruben Patterson	.12	.30
❑ 81 Morris Peterson	.15	.40
❑ 82 Jarvis Hayes	.12	.30
❑ 83 Derek Fisher	.12	.30
❑ 84 Fred Jones	.15	.40
❑ 85 Chris Mihm	.12	.30
❑ 86 Stephon Marbury	.20	.50
❑ 87 Grant Hill	.20	.50
❑ 88 Steve Nash	.25	.60
❑ 89 Joel Przybilla	.12	.30
❑ 90 Jalen Rose	.20	.50
❑ 91 Brendan Haywood	.12	.30
❑ 92 Jerry Stackhouse	.20	.50
❑ 93 Adonal Foyle	.12	.30
❑ 94 Lamar Odom	.20	.50
❑ 95 Dwight Howard	.40	1.00
❑ 96 Amare Stoudemire	.40	1.00
❑ 97 Zach Randolph	.20	.50
❑ 98 Peja Stojakovic	.20	.50
❑ 99 Mehmet Okur	.12	.30
❑ 100 Antawn Jamison	.20	.50
❑ 101 Jason Terry	.20	.50
❑ 102 Troy Murphy	.20	.50
❑ 103 Sasha Vujacic	.15	.40
❑ 104 Dwyane Wade	.50	1.25
❑ 105 Jameer Nelson	.15	.40
❑ 106 Jared Jeffries	.12	.30
❑ 107 J.R. Smith	.15	.40
❑ 108 Mike Sweetney	.15	.40
❑ 109 DeShawn Stevenson	.12	.30
❑ 110 Sebastian Telfair	.15	.40
❑ 111 Eddie Griffin	.12	.30
❑ 112 Tyronn Lue	.12	.30
❑ 113 Jon Barry	.12	.30
❑ 114 Eric Williams	.12	.30
❑ 115 Rasho Nesterovic	.12	.30
❑ 116 Keith Van Horn	.15	.40
❑ 117 Kenny Thomas	.12	.30
❑ 118 Chris Wilcox	.12	.30
❑ 119 Chris Webber	.20	.50
❑ 120 Nene	.12	.30
❑ 121 John Salmons	.20	.50
❑ 122 Chris Andersen	.15	.40
❑ 123 Lindsey Hunter	.12	.30
❑ 124 Matt Bonner	.12	.30
❑ 125 Darius Miles	.20	.50
❑ 126 Orien Greene RC	.20	.50
❑ 127 Jarron Collins	.12	.30
❑ 128 Trevor Ariza	.15	.40
❑ 129 Dan Gadzuric	.12	.30
❑ 130 Loren Woods	.12	.30
❑ 131 Jason Richardson	.20	.50
❑ 132 Corliss Williamson	.12	.30
❑ 133 Zeljko Rebraca	.12	.30
❑ 134 Othella Harrington	.12	.30
❑ 135 Theo Ratliff	.12	.30
❑ 136 David Wesley	.12	.30
❑ 137 Bostjan Nachbar	.12	.30
❑ 138 Eric Snow	.12	.30
❑ 139 Desmond Mason	.12	.30
❑ 140 Dahntay Jones	.12	.30
❑ 141 Andre Miller	.15	.40
❑ 142 Travis Outlaw	.12	.30
❑ 143 Jim Jackson	.12	.30
❑ 144 Gordan Giricek	.12	.30
❑ 145 Kelvin Cato	.12	.30
❑ 146 Michael Doleac	.12	.30
❑ 147 Lorenzen Wright	.12	.30
❑ 148 Vladimir Radmanovic	.12	.30
❑ 149 Maurice Evans	.12	.30
❑ 150 Hedo Turkoglu	.15	.40
❑ 151 Ryan Bowen	.12	.30
❑ 152 Brevin Knight	.12	.30
❑ 153 Jacque Vaughn	.12	.30
❑ 154 Tayshaun Prince	.20	.50
❑ 155 Clifford Robinson	.12	.30
❑ 156 Delonte West	.15	.40
❑ 157 Zoran Planinic	.12	.30
❑ 158 Slava Medvedenko	.12	.30
❑ 159 Andres Nocioni	.12	.30
❑ 160 Kyle Korver	.20	.50
❑ 161 Brian Cook	.12	.30
❑ 162 Viktor Khryapa	.12	.30
❑ 163 Malik Rose	.12	.30
❑ 164 Elton Brand	.20	.50
❑ 165 Gerald Wallace	.20	.50
❑ 166 Michael Bradley	.12	.30
❑ 167 DerMarr Johnson	.12	.30
❑ 168 Reece Gaines	.12	.30
❑ 169 Mickael Pietrus	.15	.40
❑ 170 Donta Smith	.12	.30
❑ 171 Wally Szczerbiak	.15	.40
❑ 172 Aleksandar Pavlovic	.12	.30
❑ 173 Michael Olowokandi	.12	.30
❑ 174 Jose Calderon RC	.20	.50
❑ 175 Jiri Welsch	.12	.30
❑ 176 Antonio McDyess	.12	.30
❑ 177 Andrei Kirilenko	.20	.50
❑ 178 Nenad Krstic	.15	.40
❑ 179 Richard Hamilton	.15	.40
❑ 180 Stacey Augmon	.12	.30
❑ 181 Kobe Bryant	1.00	2.50
❑ 182 Erick Dampier	.12	.30
❑ 183 Raef LaFrentz	.12	.30
❑ 184 Jackie Butler RC	.12	.30
❑ 185 Ira Newble	.12	.30
❑ 186 Luke Walton	.15	.40
❑ 187 Rasheed Wallace	.20	.50
❑ 188 Alvin Williams	.12	.30
❑ 189 Ben Wallace	.20	.50
❑ 190 Chris Duhon	.15	.40
❑ 191 Maurice Williams	.15	.40
❑ 192 Ronald Murray	.12	.30
❑ 193 Yao Ming	.50	1.25
❑ 194 Eduardo Najera	.20	.50
❑ 195 Nazr Mohammed	.12	.30
❑ 196 Devean George	.15	.40
❑ 197 Kirk Hinrich	.20	.50
❑ 198 Baron Davis	.20	.50
❑ 199 Juwan Howard	.15	.40
❑ 200 Drew Gooden	.15	.40
❑ 201 Carlos Boozer	.20	.50
❑ 202 Tony Delk	.12	.30
❑ 203 David West	.20	.50
❑ 204 Keith Bogans	.12	.30
❑ 205 Quinton Ross	.12	.30
❑ 206 Darrell Armstrong	.12	.30
❑ 207 Damien Wilkins	.12	.30
❑ 208 Voshon Lenard	.12	.30
❑ 209 Vitaly Potapenko	.12	.30
❑ 210 Mike Miller	.20	.50
❑ 211 Beno Udrih	.12	.30
❑ 212 Darko Milicic	.12	.30
❑ 213 Tony Parker	.20	.50
❑ 214 Brian Skinner	.12	.30
❑ 215 Mike Dunleavy	.15	.40
❑ 216 Kris Humphries	.12	.30
❑ 217 Mark Blount	.12	.30
❑ 218 Marquis Daniels	.15	.40
❑ 219 Tony Allen	.12	.30
❑ 220 Tony Battie	.12	.30
❑ 221 Luther Head RC	.25	.60
❑ 222 Richie Frahm	.12	.30
❑ 223 Arvydas Macijauskas RC	.20	.50
❑ 224 Eddie Jones	.12	.30
❑ 225 Dan Dickau	.12	.30
❑ 226 Marko Jaric	.12	.30
❑ 227 Daniel Ewing RC	.25	.60
❑ 228 Keyon Dooling	.12	.30
❑ 229 James Posey	.12	.30
❑ 230 Earl Watson	.12	.30
❑ 231 Juan Dixon	.12	.30
❑ 232 Rasual Butler	.12	.30
❑ 233 Bernard Robinson	.12	.30
❑ 234 Joe Johnson	.20	.50
❑ 235 Antoine Walker	.15	.40
❑ 236 Andris Biedrins	.15	.40
❑ 237 Gary Payton	.20	.50
❑ 238 Monta Ellis RC	.50	1.25
❑ 239 Quentin Richardson	.15	.40
❑ 240 Martynas Andriuskevicius RC	.20	.50
❑ 241 Kwame Brown	.15	.40
❑ 242 Travis Diener RC	.20	.50
❑ 243 Stromile Swift	.15	.40
❑ 244 Wayne Simien RC	.25	.60
❑ 245 Zaza Pachulia	.12	.30
❑ 246 Andrew Bogut RC	.25	.60
❑ 247 Marvin Williams RC	.30	.75
❑ 248 David Lee RC	.40	1.00
❑ 249 Nate Robinson RC	.30	.75
❑ 250 Jason Williams	.15	.40
❑ 251 Larry Hughes	.15	.40
❑ 252 Ike Diogu RC	.25	.60
❑ 253 Marc Jackson	.12	.30
❑ 254 Luke Jackson	.12	.30
❑ 255 Lee Nailon	.12	.30
❑ 256 T.J. Ford	.15	.40
❑ 257 Shavlik Randolph RC	.20	.50
❑ 258 Eddie Basden RC	.20	.50
❑ 259 Yaroslav Korolev RC	.20	.50
❑ 260 James Jones	.12	.30
❑ 261 Raja Bell	.12	.30
❑ 262 Salim Stoudamire RC	.25	.60
❑ 263 Cuttino Mobley	.15	.40
❑ 264 Kurt Thomas	.12	.30
❑ 265 D.J. Mbenga	.12	.30
❑ 266 Zarko Cabarkapa	.12	.30
❑ 267 Bobby Jackson	.12	.30
❑ 268 Rashad McCants RC	.25	.60
❑ 269 Antoine Wright RC	.20	.50
❑ 270 Josh Powell RC	.20	.50
❑ 271 Francisco Garcia RC	.25	.60
❑ 272 Robert Swift	.12	.30
❑ 273 Gerald Green RC	.20	.50
❑ 274 Peter John Ramos	.12	.30
❑ 275 Nick Van Exel	.20	.50
❑ 276 Jarrett Jack RC	.20	.50
❑ 277 Ronnie Price RC	.20	.50
❑ 278 Jamaal Tinsley	.15	.40
❑ 279 Jake Voskuhl	.12	.30
❑ 280 Devin Brown	.12	.30

❑ 281 James Singleton RC	.20	.50
❑ 282 C.J. Miles RC	.20	.50
❑ 283 Charlie Villanueva RC	.30	.75
❑ 284 Jeff McInnis	.12	.30
❑ 285 Eddie House	.12	.30
❑ 286 Rawle Marshall RC	.20	.50
❑ 287 Royal Ivey	.12	.30
❑ 288 Dikembe Mutombo	.15	.40
❑ 289 Fabricio Oberto RC	.20	.50
❑ 290 Damon Jones	.15	.40
❑ 291 Jason Hart	.12	.30
❑ 292 Jumaine Jones	.12	.30
❑ 293 Greg Ostertag	.12	.30
❑ 294 Ryan Gomes RC	.20	.50
❑ 295 Derek Anderson	.15	.40
❑ 296 Raymond Felton RC	.25	.60
❑ 297 Johan Petro RC	.20	.50
❑ 298 Bonzi Wells	.15	.40
❑ 299 Tyson Chandler	.20	.50
❑ 300 Sarunas Jasikevicius RC	.25	.60
❑ 301 Joey Graham RC	.20	.50
❑ 302 Alan Anderson RC	.20	.50
❑ 303 Steve Blake	.12	.30
❑ 304 Nikoloz Tskitishvili	.12	.30
❑ 305 Shareef Abdur-Rahim	.20	.50
❑ 306 Sean May RC	.25	.60
❑ 307 Julius Hodge RC	.25	.60
❑ 308 Deron Williams RC	.50	1.25
❑ 309 Michael Ruffin	.12	.30
❑ 310 Darius Songaila	.12	.30
❑ 311 Donyell Marshall	.12	.30
❑ 312 Jermaine O'Neal	.20	.50
❑ 313 Bracey Wright RC	.20	.50
❑ 314 Scot Pollard	.12	.30
❑ 315 Linas Kleiza RC	.25	.60
❑ 316 Jerome James	.12	.30
❑ 317 Brian Scalabrine	.12	.30
❑ 318 Tim Thomas	.12	.30
❑ 319 Reggie Evans	.12	.30
❑ 320 Jason Maxiell RC	.25	.60
❑ 321 Jannero Pargo	.12	.30
❑ 322 Michael Finley	.20	.50
❑ 323 Ersan Ilyasova RC	.20	.50
❑ 324 Robert Whaley RC	.20	.50
❑ 325 Chris Taft RC	.20	.50
❑ 326 Esteban Batista RC	.20	.50
❑ 327 Louis Williams RC	.30	.75
❑ 328 Austin Croshere	.12	.30
❑ 329 Martell Webster RC	.20	.50
❑ 330 Etan Thomas	.12	.30
❑ 331 Brandon Bass RC	.20	.50
❑ 332 Ron Artest	.15	.40
❑ 333 Gerald Fitch RC	.20	.50
❑ 334 Chucky Atkins	.12	.30
❑ 335 Jonathan Bender	.12	.30
❑ 336 Boris Diaw	.15	.40
❑ 337 Andray Blatche RC	.25	.60
❑ 338 Jeff Foster	.12	.30
❑ 339 Andrew Bynum RC	.60	1.50
❑ 340 Caron Butler	.20	.50
❑ 341 Danny Granger RC	.50	1.25
❑ 342 Channing Frye RC	.25	.60
❑ 343 Antonio Daniels	.12	.30
❑ 344 Brian Grant	.12	.30
❑ 345 Steven Hunter	.12	.30
❑ 346 Chris Paul RC	.60	1.50
❑ 347 Lawrence Roberts RC	.20	.50
❑ 348 Bobby Simmons	.12	.30
❑ 349 Dijon Thompson RC	.20	.50
❑ 350 Von Wafer RC	.20	.50
❑ 351 Damon Stoudamire	.15	.40
❑ 352 Kevin Ollie	.12	.30
❑ 353 Kirk Snyder	.12	.30
❑ 354 Hakim Warrick RC	.30	.75
❑ 355 Eddy Curry	.15	.40
❑ 356 Aaron McKie	.12	.30
❑ 357 Sam Cassell	.20	.50
❑ 358 Dorell Wright	.12	.30
❑ 359 Scott Padgett	.12	.30
❑ 360 Pat Garrity	.12	.30
❑ 361 Mike Woodson	.20	.50
❑ 362 Larry Drew	.20	.50
❑ 363 Doc Rivers	.20	.50
❑ 364 Tony Brown	.20	.50
❑ 365 Bernie Bickerstaff	.20	.50
❑ 366 Gary Brokaw	.20	.50
❑ 367 Scott Skiles	.20	.50
❑ 368 Ron Adams	.20	.50
❑ 369 Mike Brown	.20	.50
❑ 370 Kenny Natt	.20	.50
❑ 371 Avery Johnson	.20	.50
❑ 372 Del Harris	.20	.50
❑ 373 George Karl	.20	.50
❑ 374 Scott Brooks	.20	.50
❑ 375 Flip Saunders	.20	.50
❑ 376 Sid Lowe	.20	.50
❑ 377 Mike Montgomery	.20	.50
❑ 378 Mario Elie	.20	.50
❑ 379 Jeff Van Gundy	.20	.50
❑ 380 Tom Thibodeau	.20	.50
❑ 381 Rick Carlisle	.20	.50
❑ 382 Kevin O'Neill	.20	.50
❑ 383 Mike Dunleavy Sr.	.20	.50
❑ 384 Jim Eyen	.20	.50
❑ 385 Phil Jackson	.25	.60
❑ 386 Frank Hamblen	.20	.50
❑ 387 Mike Fratello	.25	.60
❑ 388 Eric Musselman	.20	.50
❑ 389 Pat Riley	.20	.50
❑ 390 Bob McAdoo	.20	.50
❑ 391 Terry Stotts	.20	.50
❑ 392 Lester Conner	.20	.50
❑ 393 Dwane Casey	.20	.50
❑ 394 Johnny Davis	.20	.50
❑ 395 Lawrence Frank	.20	.50
❑ 396 Bill Cartwright	.20	.50
❑ 397 Byron Scott	.20	.50
❑ 398 Darrell Walker	.20	.50
❑ 399 Larry Brown	.25	.60
❑ 400 Herb Williams	.20	.50
❑ 401 Brian Hill	.20	.50
❑ 402 Randy Ayers	.20	.50
❑ 403 Maurice Cheeks	.20	.50
❑ 404 John Kuester	.20	.50
❑ 405 Mike D'Antoni	.20	.50
❑ 406 Marc Iavaroni	.20	.50
❑ 407 Nate McMillan	.20	.50
❑ 408 Dean Demopoulos	.20	.50
❑ 409 Rick Adelman	.20	.50
❑ 410 Elston Turner	.20	.50
❑ 411 Gregg Popovich	.25	.60
❑ 412 P.J. Carlesimo	.20	.50
❑ 413 Bob Weiss	.20	.50
❑ 414 Jack Sikma	.20	.50
❑ 415 Sam Mitchell	.20	.50
❑ 416 Jim Todd	.20	.50
❑ 417 Jerry Sloan	.20	.50
❑ 418 Phil D. Johnson	.20	.50
❑ 419 Eddie Jordan	.20	.50
❑ 420 Mike O'Koren	.20	.50
❑ 421 The Gorilla	.30	.75
❑ 422 Rocky	.30	.75
❑ 423 Slamson	.30	.75
❑ 424 The Raptor	.30	.75
❑ 425 Squatch	.30	.75
❑ 426 Blaze	.30	.75
❑ 427 Crunch	.30	.75
❑ 428 Harry the Hawk	.30	.75
❑ 429 Champ	.30	.75
❑ 430 Hip Hop	.30	.75
❑ 431 Sly the Silver Fox	.30	.75
❑ 432 Benny the Bull	.30	.75
❑ 433 G-Wiz	.30	.75
❑ 434 Clutch	.30	.75
❑ 435 Boomer	.30	.75
❑ 436 Shannon Elizabeth	.40	1.00
❑ 437 Christie Brinkley	.40	1.00
❑ 438 Jenny McCarthy	.40	1.00
❑ 439 Carmen Electra	.40	1.00
❑ 440 Jay-Z	.60	1.50

2006-07 Topps Trademark Moves

❑ COMP.SET w/o SP's (100)	8.00	20.00
❑ 1 Dwyane Wade	.75	2.00
❑ 2 Richard Jefferson	.25	.60
❑ 3 Raymond Felton	.40	1.00
❑ 4 Ray Allen	.30	.75
❑ 5 Peja Stojakovic	.30	.75
❑ 6 Mike Miller	.30	.75
❑ 7 Mike Bibby	.30	.75
❑ 8 Marcus Camby	.25	.60
❑ 9 LeBron James	1.50	4.00
❑ 10 Joe Johnson	.25	.60
❑ 11 Corey Maggette	.25	.60
❑ 12 Charlie Villanueva	.30	.75
❑ 13 Caron Butler	.30	.75
❑ 14 Amare Stoudemire	.60	1.50
❑ 15 Vince Carter	.60	1.50
❑ 16 Tracy McGrady	.60	1.50
❑ 17 Shawn Marion	.30	.75
❑ 18 Ron Artest	.30	.75
❑ 19 Pau Gasol	.30	.75
❑ 20 Smush Parker	.20	.50
❑ 21 Josh Smith	.30	.75
❑ 22 Gilbert Arenas	.30	.75
❑ 23 Elton Brand	.30	.75
❑ 24 Dwight Howard	.60	1.50
❑ 25 Dirk Nowitzki	.50	1.25
❑ 26 Chris Bosh	.30	.75
❑ 27 Chauncey Billups	.30	.75
❑ 28 Ben Gordon	.40	1.00
❑ 29 Yao Ming	.75	2.00
❑ 30 Tyson Chandler	.30	.75
❑ 31 T.J. Ford	.25	.60
❑ 32 Steve Nash	.40	1.00
❑ 33 Sam Cassell	.30	.75
❑ 34 Speedy Claxton	.20	.50
❑ 35 Manu Ginobili	.30	.75
❑ 36 Kevin Garnett	.60	1.50
❑ 37 Jason Terry	.30	.75
❑ 38 Jameer Nelson	.25	.60
❑ 39 Ben Wallace	.30	.75
❑ 40 Antoine Walker	.25	.60
❑ 41 Al Jefferson	.30	.75
❑ 42 Tim Duncan	.60	1.50
❑ 43 Richard Hamilton	.25	.60
❑ 44 Paul Pierce	.30	.75
❑ 45 Mike James	.20	.50
❑ 46 Martell Webster	.25	.60
❑ 47 Kobe Bryant	1.50	4.00
❑ 48 Kirk Hinrich	.30	.75
❑ 49 Josh Howard	.30	.75
❑ 50 Bobby Simmons	.20	.50
❑ 51 Channing Frye	.25	.60
❑ 52 Andrei Kirilenko	.30	.75
❑ 53 Allen Iverson	.60	1.50
❑ 54 Al Harrington	.20	.50
❑ 55 Zach Randolph	.30	.75
❑ 56 Tony Parker	.30	.75
❑ 57 Stephon Marbury	.30	.75
❑ 58 Shaquille O'Neal	.75	2.00
❑ 59 Ricky Davis	.30	.75
❑ 60 Lamar Odom	.30	.75
❑ 61 Emeka Okafor	.30	.75
❑ 62 Raja Bell	.20	.50
❑ 63 Deron Williams	.50	1.25
❑ 64 Danny Granger	.25	.60
❑ 65 Baron Davis	.30	.75
❑ 66 Andre Miller	.25	.60
❑ 67 Andre Iguodala	.30	.75
❑ 68 Michael Redd	.30	.75
❑ 69 Rashard Lewis	.30	.75
❑ 70 Larry Hughes	.25	.60
❑ 71 Jermaine O'Neal	.30	.75
❑ 72 Jason Richardson	.30	.75
❑ 73 Jason Kidd	.50	1.25
❑ 74 Gerald Wallace	.30	.75
❑ 75 Leandro Barbosa	.30	.75
❑ 76 Chris Paul	.60	1.50
❑ 77 Carmelo Anthony	.40	1.00
❑ 78 Brad Miller	.30	.75
❑ 79 Antawn Jamison	.30	.75
❑ 80 Andrew Bogut	.30	.75
❑ 81 Dominique Wilkins	.60	1.50
❑ 82 Larry Bird	1.50	4.00
❑ 83 Clyde Drexler	.60	1.50
❑ 84 Dennis Rodman	.50	1.25
❑ 85 Isiah Thomas	.50	1.25
❑ 86 Rick Barry	.50	1.25
❑ 87 Hakeem Olajuwon	.60	1.50
❑ 88 George Gervin	.50	1.25

❑ 89 Spud Webb .50 1.25
❑ 90 Kareem Abdul-Jabbar .75 2.00
❑ 91 Oscar Robertson .50 1.25
❑ 92 Earl Monroe .50 1.25
❑ 93 Walt Frazier .50 1.25
❑ 94 Moses Malone .50 1.25
❑ 95 Wilt Chamberlain 1.00 2.50
❑ 96 Karl Malone .60 1.50
❑ 97 Manute Bol .50 1.25
❑ 98 Bill Walton .50 1.25
❑ 99 Maurice Cheeks .50 1.25
❑ 100 Bob Lanier .50 1.25
❑ 101 Solomon Jones AU/149 RC 3.00 8.00
❑ 102 Kyle Lowry AU/149 RC 3.00 8.00
❑ 103 Maurice Ager AU/149 RC 3.00 8.00
❑ 104 Patrick O'Bryant AU/75 RC 4.00 10.00
❑ 105 Pops Mensah-Bonsu AU/149 RC 3.00 8.00
❑ 106 Marcus Vinicius AU/149 RC 3.00 8.00
❑ 107 Josh Boone AU/149 RC 5.00 12.00
❑ 108 Mardy Collins AU/149 RC 3.00 8.00
❑ 109 Rodney Carney AU/75 RC 4.00 10.00
❑ 110 P.J. Tucker AU/149 RC 4.00 10.00
❑ 111 Shelden Williams AU/75 RC 6.00 15.00
❑ 112 Ryan Hollins AU/149 RC 3.00 8.00
❑ 113 Sergio Rodriguez AU/149 RC EXCH 3.00 8.00
❑ 114 Steve Novak AU/149 RC 3.00 8.00
❑ 115 Paul Davis AU/149 RC 3.00 8.00
❑ 116 David Noel AU/149 RC 3.00 8.00
❑ 117 Marcus Williams AU/75 RC 6.00 15.00
❑ 118 Renaldo Balkman AU/75 RC 4.00 10.00
❑ 119 Quincy Douby AU/149 RC EXCH 3.00 8.00
❑ 120 Andrea Bargnani AU/75 RC 6.00 15.00
❑ 121 Chris Quinn AU/149 RC 3.00 8.00
❑ 122 Thabo Sefolosha AU/75 RC 6.00 15.00
❑ 123 Hassan Adams AU/149 RC 3.00 8.00
❑ 124 James White AU/149 RC 4.00 10.00
❑ 125 Jordan Farmar AU/75 RC 8.00 20.00
❑ 126 Damir Markota AU/149 RC 3.00 8.00
❑ 127 Mile Ilic AU/149 RC 3.00 8.00
❑ 128 James Augustine AU/149 RC 3.00 8.00
❑ 129 Paul Millsap AU/149 RC 6.00 15.00
❑ 130 Jorge Garbajosa AU/149 RC 5.00 12.00
❑ 131 Allan Ray AU/75 RC EXCH 4.00 10.00
❑ 132 Shannon Brown AU/149 RC 3.00 8.00
❑ 133 Will Blalock AU/149 RC 3.00 8.00
❑ 134 Vassilis Spanoulis AU/149 RC 3.00 8.00
❑ 135 Adam Morrison AU/75 RC 15.00 30.00
❑ 136 Craig Smith AU/149 RC 3.00 8.00
❑ 137 Cedric Simmons AU/149 RC 3.00 8.00
❑ 138 J.J. Redick AU/75 RC 8.00 20.00
❑ 139 Rookie Exchange
❑ 140 Ronnie Brewer AU/75 RC 6.00 15.00
❑ 141 Rajon Rondo AU/149 RC 8.00 20.00
❑ 142 Daniel Gibson AU/149 RC 4.00 10.00
❑ 143 Mickael Gelabale AU/75 RC EXCH 4.00 10.00
❑ 144 Shawne Williams AU/75 RC 5.00 12.00
❑ 145 Alexander Johnson AU/149 RC 3.00 8.00
❑ 146 Randy Foye AU/75 RC 5.00 12.00
❑ 147 Hilton Armstrong AU RC
❑ 148 Bobby Jones AU/149 RC 3.00 8.00
❑ 149 Saer Sene AU/149 RC 3.00 8.00
❑ 150 Dee Brown AU/75 RC

2007-08 Topps Trademark Moves

❑ COMP.SET w/o SP's (50) 15.00 30.00
❑ 1 Amare Stoudemire 1.00 2.50
❑ 2 Elton Brand .50 1.25
❑ 3 Dwyane Wade 1.25 3.00
❑ 4 Dirk Nowitzki .75 2.00
❑ 5 Baron Davis .50 1.25
❑ 6 Brandon Roy .75 2.00
❑ 7 Ben Gordon .60 1.50
❑ 8 Richard Hamilton .40 1.00
❑ 9 Andre Iguodala .50 1.25
❑ 10 Tim Duncan 1.00 2.50
❑ 11 Yao Ming 1.25 3.00
❑ 12 Jason Kidd .75 2.00
❑ 13 Steve Nash .60 1.50
❑ 14 Chris Paul 1.00 2.50
❑ 15 Carmelo Anthony 1.00 2.50
❑ 16 Pau Gasol .50 1.25
❑ 17 Dwight Howard 1.00 2.50
❑ 18 Ray Allen .50 1.25
❑ 19 Deron Williams .75 2.00
❑ 20 Vince Carter 1.00 2.50
❑ 21 Kevin Garnett 1.25 3.00
❑ 22 Michael Redd .50 1.25
❑ 23 LeBron James 2.50 6.00
❑ 24 Kobe Bryant 2.50 6.00
❑ 25 Josh Smith .50 1.25
❑ 26 Gilbert Arenas .50 1.25
❑ 27 Jermaine O'Neal .50 1.25
❑ 28 Kirk Hinrich .50 1.25
❑ 29 Eddy Curry .30 .75
❑ 30 Chauncey Billups .50 1.25
❑ 31 Shawn Marion .50 1.25
❑ 32 Shaquille O'Neal 1.25 3.00
❑ 33 Allen Iverson 1.00 2.50
❑ 34 Paul Pierce .50 1.25
❑ 35 Tony Parker .50 1.25
❑ 36 Gerald Wallace .50 1.25
❑ 37 Carlos Boozer .50 1.25
❑ 38 Chris Bosh .50 1.25
❑ 39 Mike Bibby .50 1.25
❑ 40 Tracy McGrady 1.00 2.50
❑ 41 Rick Barry .50 1.25
❑ 42 David Robinson .75 2.00
❑ 43 John Stockton .75 2.00
❑ 44 Bill Walton .50 1.25
❑ 45 Larry Bird 1.50 4.00
❑ 46 Isiah Thomas .50 1.25
❑ 47 Magic Johnson 1.00 2.50
❑ 48 Dennis Rodman .50 1.25
❑ 49 Dominique Wilkins .60 1.50
❑ 50 Bill Russell .75 2.00
❑ 51 Yi Jianlian RC 1.50 4.00
❑ 52 Greg Oden RC 1.50 4.00
❑ 53 Michael Conley RC 1.25 3.00
❑ 54 Jeff Green RC 1.25 3.00
❑ 55 Corey Brewer RC 1.25 3.00
❑ 56 Joakim Noah RC 1.25 3.00
❑ 57 Julian Wright RC 1.25 3.00
❑ 58 Ramon Sessions RC 1.25 3.00
❑ 59 Sammy Mejia RC 1.00 2.50
❑ 60 Dominic McGuire RC 1.00 2.50
❑ 61 Kevin Durant RC 8.00 20.00
❑ 62 Arron Afflalo RC 1.00 2.50
❑ 63 Acie Law IV RC 1.25 3.00
❑ 64 Alando Tucker RC 1.00 2.50
❑ 65 Gabe Pruitt RC 1.00 2.50
❑ 66 Marcus Williams RC 1.00 2.50
❑ 67 Spencer Hawes RC 1.00 2.50
❑ 68 Carl Landry RC 1.00 2.50
❑ 69 Thaddeus Young RC 1.25 3.00
❑ 70 Nick Fazekas RC 1.00 2.50
❑ 71 Al Thornton RC 1.00 2.50
❑ 72 Rodney Stuckey RC 2.00 5.00
❑ 73 Nick Young RC 1.00 2.50
❑ 74 Glen Davis RC 2.00 5.00
❑ 75 Jermareo Davidson RC 1.00 2.50
❑ 76 Luis Scola RC 1.50 4.00
❑ 77 Jason Smith RC 1.00 2.50
❑ 78 Daequan Cook RC 1.25 3.00
❑ 79 Jared Dudley RC 1.00 2.50
❑ 80 Derrick Byars RC 1.00 2.50
❑ 81 Josh McRoberts RC 1.25 3.00
❑ 82 Adam Haluska RC 1.00 2.50
❑ 83 Juan Carlos Navarro RC 1.25 3.00
❑ 84 Aaron Gray RC 1.00 2.50
❑ 85 Herbert Hill RC 1.00 2.50
❑ 86 Jared Jordan RC 1.00 2.50
❑ 87 Wilson Chandler RC 1.00 2.50
❑ 88 Morris Almond RC 1.00 2.50
❑ 89 Aaron Brooks RC 1.50 4.00
❑ 90 Chris Richard RC 1.00 2.50
❑ 91 JamesOn Curry RC 1.00 2.50
❑ 92 Al Horford RC 1.25 3.00
❑ 93 Stephane Lasme RC 1.00 2.50
❑ 94 D.J. Strawberry RC 1.00 2.50
❑ 95 Sean Williams RC 1.00 2.50
❑ 96 Marco Belinelli RC 1.00 2.50
❑ 97 Javaris Crittenton RC 1.00 2.50
❑ 98 Demetris Nichols RC 1.00 2.50
❑ 99 Taurean Green RC 1.00 2.50
❑ 100 Brandan Wright RC 1.25 3.00

2008-09 Topps Treasury

❑ COMPLETE SET (120) 30.00 60.00
❑ 1 Kobe Bryant 2.50 6.00
❑ 2 Ray Allen .50 1.25
❑ 3 Chris Paul 1.00 2.50
❑ 4 Tim Duncan .75 2.00
❑ 5 Josh Smith .50 1.25
❑ 6 Luis Scola .40 1.00
❑ 7 Rashad McCants .40 1.00
❑ 8 Vince Carter .60 1.50
❑ 9 LeBron James 2.50 6.00
❑ 10 Mike Dunleavy .40 1.00
❑ 11 Chauncey Billups .50 1.25
❑ 12 Dwight Howard 1.00 2.50
❑ 13 Steve Nash .50 1.25
❑ 14 Monta Ellis .50 1.25
❑ 15 Carmelo Anthony .60 1.50
❑ 16 Pau Gasol .50 1.25
❑ 17 Anderson Varejao .40 1.00
❑ 18 Yi Jianlian .50 1.25
❑ 19 Deron Williams .60 1.50
❑ 20 Joe Johnson .50 1.25
❑ 21 Yao Ming .60 1.50
❑ 22 Rudy Gay .50 1.25
❑ 23 Jason Richardson .50 1.25
❑ 24 Andrew Bogut .50 1.25
❑ 25 Kevin Garnett 1.00 2.50
❑ 26 Chris Wilcox .40 1.00
❑ 27 Zach Randolph .50 1.25
❑ 28 Kirk Hinrich .50 1.25
❑ 29 Tony Parker .50 1.25
❑ 30 Allen Iverson .60 1.50
❑ 31 David West .50 1.25
❑ 32 Shaquille O'Neal 1.00 2.50
❑ 33 Dwyane Wade 1.00 2.50
❑ 34 Paul Pierce .60 1.50
❑ 35 Mike Miller .50 1.25
❑ 36 Hedo Turkoglu .50 1.25
❑ 37 LaMarcus Aldridge .50 1.25
❑ 38 Kevin Martin .50 1.25
❑ 39 Jamal Crawford .30 .75
❑ 40 Gilbert Arenas .50 1.25
❑ 41 Dirk Nowitzki .60 1.50
❑ 42 Amare Stoudemire .60 1.50
❑ 43 Danny Granger .50 1.25
❑ 44 Chris Bosh .50 1.25
❑ 45 Luol Deng .50 1.25
❑ 46 Al Thornton .50 1.25
❑ 47 Andrei Kirilenko .50 1.25
❑ 48 Tayshaun Prince .50 1.25
❑ 49 Gerald Wallace .50 1.25
❑ 50 Corey Maggette .50 1.25
❑ 51 Andre Iguodala .50 1.25
❑ 52 Greg Oden .50 1.25
❑ 53 Al Jefferson .50 1.25
❑ 54 Devin Harris .50 1.25
❑ 55 Baron Davis .50 1.25
❑ 56 Marcus Camby .30 .75
❑ 57 Udonis Haslem .50 1.25
❑ 58 Ron Artest .50 1.25
❑ 59 Jeff Green .40 1.00
❑ 60 Richard Hamilton .40 1.00
❑ 61 Samuel Dalembert .30 .75
❑ 62 Antawn Jamison .50 1.25
❑ 63 Mike Conley .40 1.00
❑ 64 Raymond Felton .40 1.00
❑ 65 Carlos Boozer .50 1.25

❑ 66 Ben Gordon	.50	1.25
❑ 67 Jermaine O'Neal	.50	1.25
❑ 68 Peja Stojakovic	.50	1.25
❑ 69 Ryan Gomes	.40	1.00
❑ 70 Michael Redd	.50	1.25
❑ 71 Manu Ginobili	.50	1.25
❑ 72 Elton Brand	.75	2.00
❑ 73 Josh Howard	.50	1.25
❑ 74 Stephen Jackson	.40	1.00
❑ 75 Richard Jefferson	.50	1.25
❑ 76 Andrew Bynum	.50	1.25
❑ 77 Shawn Marion	.50	1.25
❑ 78 David Lee	.40	1.00
❑ 79 Jamario Moon	.50	1.25
❑ 80 Caron Butler	.50	1.25
❑ 81 Tracy McGrady	.60	1.50
❑ 82 Al Horford	.50	1.25
❑ 83 Brandon Roy	.60	1.50
❑ 84 Ben Wallace	.50	1.25
❑ 85 Andre Miller	.40	1.00
❑ 86 Brad Miller	.50	1.25
❑ 87 Jameer Nelson	.40	1.00
❑ 88 Andrea Bargnani	.40	1.00
❑ 89 Kevin Durant	1.25	3.00
❑ 90 Jason Kidd	.50	1.25
❑ 91 Dennis Rodman	.50	1.25
❑ 92 Larry Bird	1.50	4.00
❑ 93 Moses Malone	.50	1.25
❑ 94 Jerry West	.60	1.50
❑ 95 Bill Russell	.75	2.00
❑ 96 David Robinson	.75	2.00
❑ 97 John Stockton	.75	2.00
❑ 98 Magic Johnson	1.00	2.50
❑ 99 George Gervin	.60	1.50
❑ 100 Dominique Wilkins	.60	1.50
❑ 101 Derrick Rose RC	3.00	8.00
❑ 102 Michael Beasley RC	1.50	4.00
❑ 103 O.J. Mayo RC	1.25	3.00
❑ 104 Russell Westbrook RC	2.00	5.00
❑ 105 Kevin Love RC	1.00	2.50
❑ 106 Danilo Gallinari RC	1.25	3.00
❑ 107 Eric Gordon RC	1.00	2.50
❑ 108 Joe Alexander RC	.75	2.00
❑ 109 D.J. Augustin RC	.75	2.00
❑ 110 Brook Lopez RC	1.50	4.00
❑ 111 Jerryd Bayless RC	.75	2.00
❑ 112 Brandon Rush RC	.75	2.00
❑ 113 Anthony Randolph RC	1.25	3.00
❑ 114 Robin Lopez RC	.75	2.00
❑ 115 Courtney Lee RC	1.25	3.00
❑ 116 Darrell Arthur RC	.75	2.00
❑ 117 Joey Dorsey RC	.75	2.00
❑ 118 Mario Chalmers RC	1.00	2.50
❑ 119 DeAndre Jordan RC	.75	2.00
❑ 120 Kosta Koufos RC	.75	2.00

2006-07 Topps Triple Threads

❑ 1 Amare Stoudemire	2.00	5.00
❑ 2 Dirk Nowitzki	1.50	4.00
❑ 3 Dwyane Wade	2.50	6.00
❑ 4 Allen Iverson	2.00	5.00
❑ 5 LeBron James	5.00	12.00
❑ 6 Tracy McGrady	2.00	5.00
❑ 7 Ben Wallace	1.00	2.50
❑ 8 Jason Richardson	1.00	2.50
❑ 9 Vince Carter	2.00	5.00
❑ 10 Joe Johnson	.75	2.00
❑ 11 Paul Pierce	1.00	2.50
❑ 12 Gerald Wallace	1.00	2.50
❑ 13 Elton Brand	1.00	2.50
❑ 14 Gilbert Arenas	1.00	2.50
❑ 15 Marcus Camby	.75	2.00
❑ 16 Andrew Bogut	1.00	2.50
❑ 17 Stephon Marbury	1.00	2.50
❑ 18 Kevin Garnett	2.00	5.00
❑ 19 Al Harrington	.60	1.50
❑ 20 Tim Duncan	2.00	5.00
❑ 21 Pau Gasol	1.00	2.50
❑ 22 Kobe Bryant	5.00	12.00
❑ 23 Dwight Howard	2.00	5.00
❑ 24 Jarrett Jack	.75	2.00
❑ 25 T.J. Ford	.75	2.00
❑ 26 Ron Artest	1.00	2.50
❑ 27 Deron Williams	1.50	4.00
❑ 28 Rasheed Wallace	1.00	2.50
❑ 29 Shaquille O'Neal	2.50	6.00
❑ 30 Ray Allen	1.00	2.50
❑ 31 Peja Stojakovic	1.00	2.50
❑ 32 Jermaine O'Neal	1.00	2.50
❑ 33 Larry Hughes	.75	2.00
❑ 34 Brad Miller	1.00	2.50
❑ 35 Caron Butler	1.00	2.50
❑ 36 Andre Miller	.75	2.00
❑ 37 Kirk Hinrich	1.00	2.50
❑ 38 Andrei Kirilenko	1.00	2.50
❑ 39 Charlie Villanueva	1.00	2.50
❑ 40 Sebastian Telfair	.75	2.00
❑ 41 Josh Howard	1.00	2.50
❑ 42 Emeka Okafor	1.00	2.50
❑ 43 Danny Granger	.75	2.00
❑ 44 Tony Parker	1.00	2.50
❑ 45 Zach Randolph	1.00	2.50
❑ 46 Ricky Davis	1.00	2.50
❑ 47 Chris Webber	1.00	2.50
❑ 48 Mike Bibby	1.00	2.50
❑ 49 Troy Murphy	1.00	2.50
❑ 50 Josh Smith	1.00	2.50
❑ 51 Steve Nash	1.25	3.00
❑ 52 Chris Paul	2.00	5.00
❑ 53 Rashard Lewis	1.00	2.50
❑ 54 Ben Gordon	1.25	3.00
❑ 55 Mehmet Okur	.60	1.50
❑ 56 Chris Bosh	1.00	2.50
❑ 57 Drew Gooden	.75	2.00
❑ 58 Corey Maggette	.75	2.00
❑ 59 Eddy Curry	.75	2.00
❑ 60 Yao Ming	2.50	6.00
❑ 61 Al Jefferson	1.00	2.50
❑ 62 Smush Parker	.60	1.50
❑ 63 Jason Kidd	1.50	4.00
❑ 64 Hakim Warrick	.75	2.00
❑ 65 Richard Hamilton	.75	2.00
❑ 66 Luke Ridnour	.75	2.00
❑ 67 Raymond Felton	1.25	3.00
❑ 68 Andre Iguodala	1.00	2.50
❑ 69 Jason Terry	1.00	2.50
❑ 70 Richard Jefferson	.75	2.00
❑ 71 Lamar Odom	1.00	2.50
❑ 72 Jameer Nelson	.75	2.00
❑ 73 Mike James	.60	1.50
❑ 74 Antawn Jamison	1.00	2.50
❑ 75 Shaun Livingston	.60	1.50
❑ 76 Manu Ginobili	1.00	2.50
❑ 77 Antoine Walker	.75	2.00
❑ 78 Desmond Mason	.60	1.50
❑ 79 Channing Frye	.75	2.00
❑ 80 Morris Peterson	.75	2.00
❑ 81 Michael Redd	1.00	2.50
❑ 82 Shawn Marion	1.00	2.50
❑ 83 Bonzi Wells	.75	2.00
❑ 84 Chauncey Billups	1.00	2.50
❑ 85 Baron Davis	1.00	2.50
❑ 86 Carmelo Anthony	1.25	3.00
❑ 87 Brandon Roy RC	4.00	10.00
❑ 88 Rudy Gay RC	1.50	4.00
❑ 89 Tyrus Thomas RC	2.00	5.00
❑ 90 LaMarcus Aldridge RC	2.00	5.00
❑ 91 Wilt Chamberlain	3.00	8.00
❑ 92 Larry Bird	5.00	12.00
❑ 93 Isiah Thomas	1.50	4.00
❑ 94 Bernard King	1.50	4.00
❑ 95 Elgin Baylor	1.50	4.00
❑ 96 Oscar Robertson	1.50	4.00
❑ 97 Walt Frazier	1.50	4.00
❑ 98 Chris Mullin	1.50	4.00
❑ 99 Bill Laimbeer	1.50	4.00
❑ 100 George Gervin	1.50	4.00
❑ 101 Dee Brown JSY AU RC	6.00	15.00
❑ 102 Renaldo Balkman JSY AU RC	6.00	15.00
❑ 103 Maurice Ager JSY AU RC	6.00	15.00
❑ 104 Shelden Williams JSY AU RC	8.00	20.00
❑ 105 Rodney Carney JSY AU RC	6.00	15.00
❑ 106 J.J. Redick JSY AU RC	6.00	15.00
❑ 107 Hilton Armstrong JSY AU RC	6.00	15.00
❑ 108 Craig Smith JSY AU RC	6.00	15.00
❑ 109 Kyle Lowry JSY AU RC	6.00	15.00
❑ 110 Josh Boone JSY AU RC	6.00	15.00
❑ 111 Saer Sene JSY AU RC	6.00	15.00
❑ 112 Jorge Garbajosa JSY AU RC	12.00	30.00
❑ 113 Paul Davis JSY AU RC	6.00	15.00
❑ 114 Thabo Sefolosha JSY AU RC	8.00	20.00
❑ 115 Shannon Brown JSY AU RC	6.00	15.00
❑ 116 Bobby Jones JSY AU RC	6.00	15.00
❑ 117 Jordan Farmar JSY AU RC	8.00	20.00
❑ 118 Allan Ray JSY AU RC	6.00	15.00
❑ 119 Randy Foye JSY AU RC	6.00	15.00
❑ 120 Marcus Williams JSY AU RC	8.00	20.00
❑ 121 Adam Morrison JSY AU RC	25.00	50.00
❑ 122 Cedric Simmons JSY AU RC	6.00	15.00
❑ 123 Rajon Rondo JSY AU RC	25.00	60.00
❑ 124 Patrick O'Bryant JSY AU RC	6.00	15.00
❑ 125 Shawne Williams JSY AU RC	6.00	15.00
❑ 126 Mardy Collins JSY AU RC	6.00	15.00
❑ 127 Steve Novak JSY AU RC	6.00	15.00
❑ 128 Ronnie Brewer JSY AU RC	8.00	20.00
❑ 129 Quincy Douby JSY AU RC	6.00	15.00
❑ 130 Andrea Bargnani JSY AU RC	10.00	25.00

2007-08 Topps Triple Threads

❑ 1 Yao Ming	2.00	5.00
❑ 2 Michael Redd	.75	2.00
❑ 3 Dwyane Wade	2.00	5.00
❑ 4 Chris Bosh	.75	2.00
❑ 5 Kevin Garnett	2.00	5.00
❑ 6 Sam Cassell	.75	2.00
❑ 7 Ben Gordon	1.00	2.50
❑ 8 Deron Williams	1.25	3.00
❑ 9 Andre Iguodala	.75	2.00
❑ 10 Mike Bibby	.75	2.00
❑ 11 Chauncey Billups	.75	2.00
❑ 12 Dwight Howard	1.50	4.00
❑ 13 Steve Nash	1.00	2.50
❑ 14 Raymond Felton	1.00	2.50
❑ 15 Carmelo Anthony	1.50	4.00
❑ 16 Pau Gasol	.75	2.00
❑ 17 Brandon Roy	1.25	3.00
❑ 18 Chris Wilcox	.60	1.50
❑ 19 Josh Howard	.75	2.00
❑ 20 Ray Allen	.75	2.00
❑ 21 Tim Duncan	1.50	4.00
❑ 22 Tayshaun Prince	.75	2.00
❑ 23 LeBron James	4.00	10.00
❑ 24 Kobe Bryant	4.00	10.00
❑ 25 Al Jefferson	.75	2.00
❑ 26 Stephon Marbury	.75	2.00
❑ 27 Mike Miller	.75	2.00
❑ 28 Jason Terry	.75	2.00
❑ 29 Corey Maggette	.60	1.50
❑ 30 Allen Iverson	1.50	4.00
❑ 31 Tracy McGrady	1.50	4.00
❑ 32 Shaquille O'Neal	2.00	5.00
❑ 33 Ben Wallace	.75	2.00
❑ 34 Paul Pierce	.75	2.00
❑ 35 Vince Carter	1.50	4.00
❑ 36 Chris Paul	1.50	4.00
❑ 37 Kyle Korver	.75	2.00
❑ 38 LaMarcus Aldridge	1.00	2.50
❑ 39 Al Harrington	.60	1.50
❑ 40 Gilbert Arenas	.75	2.00
❑ 41 Dirk Nowitzki	1.25	3.00
❑ 42 David Lee	.60	1.50
❑ 43 Gerald Wallace	.75	2.00
❑ 44 Luke Walton	.60	1.50
❑ 45 Manu Ginobili	.75	2.00

❑ 46 Charlie Villanueva	.75	2.00
❑ 47 Andrei Kirilenko	.75	2.00
❑ 48 Richard Jefferson	.75	2.00
❑ 49 Joe Johnson	.75	2.00
❑ 50 Zach Randolph	.75	2.00
❑ 51 Andrea Bargnani	1.00	2.50
❑ 52 Elton Brand	.75	2.00
❑ 53 Anderson Varejao	.60	1.50
❑ 54 Kirk Hinrich	.75	2.00
❑ 55 Baron Davis	.75	2.00
❑ 56 Shane Battier	.75	2.00
❑ 57 Jameer Nelson	.60	1.50
❑ 58 Antawn Jamison	.75	2.00
❑ 59 Andrew Bynum	.75	2.00
❑ 60 Kevin Martin	.75	2.00
❑ 61 Amare Stoudemire	1.50	4.00
❑ 62 Randy Foye	.75	2.00
❑ 63 Marcus Camby	.50	1.25
❑ 64 Larry Hughes	.60	1.50
❑ 65 Luol Deng	.75	2.00
❑ 66 Danny Granger	.60	1.50
❑ 67 Eddy Curry	.50	1.25
❑ 68 David West	.75	2.00
❑ 69 Tony Parker	.75	2.00
❑ 70 Jason Kidd	1.25	3.00
❑ 71 Monta Ellis	.60	1.50
❑ 72 Richard Hamilton	.60	1.50
❑ 73 Udonis Haslem	.75	2.00
❑ 74 Rudy Gay	.60	1.50
❑ 75 Carlos Boozer	.75	2.00
❑ 76 Luke Ridnour	.60	1.50
❑ 77 Jermaine O'Neal	.75	2.00
❑ 78 Ricky Davis	.75	2.00
❑ 79 Desmond Mason	.50	1.25
❑ 80 Lamar Odom	.75	2.00
❑ 81 T.J. Ford	.60	1.50
❑ 82 Jarrett Jack	.60	1.50
❑ 83 Ron Artest	.75	2.00
❑ 84 Sam Dalembert	.50	1.25
❑ 85 Josh Smith	.75	2.00
❑ 86 Tyson Chandler	.75	2.00
❑ 87 Shawn Marion	.75	2.00
❑ 88 Caron Butler	.75	2.00
❑ 89 Jason Richardson	.75	2.00
❑ 90 Rashard Lewis	.75	2.00
❑ 91 Larry Bird	2.50	6.00
❑ 92 Isiah Thomas	.75	2.00
❑ 93 Magic Johnson	1.50	4.00
❑ 94 John Stockton	1.25	3.00
❑ 95 Bill Russell	1.25	3.00
❑ 96 Dennis Rodman	.75	2.00
❑ 97 Dominique Wilkins	1.00	2.50
❑ 98 David Robinson	1.25	3.00
❑ 99 Bill Walton	.75	2.00
❑ 100 Jerry West	1.00	2.50
❑ 101 Greg Oden RC	4.00	10.00
❑ 102 Daequan Cook RC	3.00	8.00
❑ 103 Morris Almond RC	2.50	6.00
❑ 104 Sean Williams RC	2.50	6.00
❑ 105 Arron Afflalo RC	2.50	6.00
❑ 106 Coby Karl RC	2.50	6.00
❑ 107 Adam Haluska RC	2.50	6.00
❑ 108 Corey Brewer RC	3.00	8.00
❑ 109 Herbert Hill RC	2.50	6.00
❑ 110 Nick Young RC	2.50	6.00
❑ 111 Joakim Noah RC	3.00	8.00
❑ 112 Michael Conley RC	3.00	8.00
❑ 113 Kyrylo Fesenko RC	2.50	6.00
❑ 114 Aaron Brooks RC	4.00	10.00
❑ 115 Marco Belinelli RC	2.50	6.00
❑ 116 Juan Carlos Navarro RC	3.00	8.00
❑ 117 Jared Dudley RC	2.50	6.00
❑ 118 Rodney Stuckey RC	5.00	12.00
❑ 119 JamesOn Curry RC	2.50	6.00
❑ 120 Gabe Pruitt RC	2.50	6.00
❑ 121 Acie Law IV RC	3.00	8.00
❑ 122 Dominic McGuire RC	2.50	6.00
❑ 123 Ramon Sessions RC	3.00	8.00
❑ 124 Jeff Green RC	3.00	8.00
❑ 125 Wilson Chandler RC	2.50	6.00
❑ 126 Kosta Perovic RC	2.50	6.00
❑ 127 Josh McRoberts RC	3.00	8.00
❑ 128 Jason Smith RC	2.50	6.00
❑ 129 Cheik Samb RC	2.50	6.00
❑ 130 Stephane Lasme RC	2.50	6.00
❑ 131 Brandon Wallace RC	2.50	6.00
❑ 132 Alando Tucker RC	2.50	6.00
❑ 133 Javaris Crittenton RC	2.50	6.00
❑ 134 Chris Richard RC	2.50	6.00
❑ 135 Kevin Durant RC	20.00	50.00
❑ 136 Al Thornton RC	2.50	6.00
❑ 137 Carl Landry RC	2.50	6.00
❑ 138 Yi Jianlian RC	4.00	10.00
❑ 139 Brandan Wright RC	3.00	8.00
❑ 140 Nick Fazekas RC	2.50	6.00
❑ 141 Al Horford RC	3.00	8.00
❑ 142 Jermareo Davidson RC	2.50	6.00
❑ 143 D.J. Strawberry RC	2.50	6.00
❑ 144 Glen Davis RC	5.00	12.00
❑ 145 Julian Wright RC	3.00	8.00
❑ 146 Spencer Hawes RC	2.50	6.00
❑ 147 Taurean Green RC	2.50	6.00
❑ 148 Luis Scola RC	4.00	10.00
❑ 149 Aaron Gray RC	2.50	6.00
❑ 150 Thaddeus Young RC	3.00	8.00

2006-07 Topps Turkey Red

❑ COMPLETE SET (275)	60.00	120.00
❑ 1 Dwyane Wade SP	1.50	4.00
❑ 2 LeBron James	2.00	5.00
❑ 3 Allen Iverson SP	1.25	3.00
❑ 4 Sebastian Telfair	.30	.75
❑ 5 Bonzi Wells	.30	.75
❑ 6 Antawn Jamison	.40	1.00
❑ 7 Joe Johnson	.30	.75
❑ 8 DeSagana Diop	.25	.60
❑ 9 Stromile Swift	.30	.75
❑ 10 Shaun Livingston	.25	.60
❑ 11 Baron Davis	.40	1.00
❑ 12 Richard Hamilton	.30	.75
❑ 13 Andrei Kirilenko SP	.60	1.50
❑ 14 Richard Jefferson	.30	.75
❑ 15 T.J. Ford	.30	.75
❑ 16 Luke Ridnour	.30	.75
❑ 17 Carlos Boozer	.40	1.00
❑ 18 Al Jefferson	.40	1.00
❑ 19 Andrew Bogut SP	.60	1.50
❑ 20 Kobe Bryant	2.00	5.00
❑ 21 Tim Duncan	.75	2.00
❑ 22 Ben Gordon	.50	1.25
❑ 22B Ben Gordon Ad	.75	2.00
❑ 23 Stephen Jackson	.30	.75
❑ 24 Peja Stojakovic	.40	1.00
❑ 25 Mike Miller	.40	1.00
❑ 26 Ricky Davis SP	.60	1.50
❑ 27 Boris Diaw SP	.50	1.25
❑ 28 Shareef Abdur-Rahim	.40	1.00
❑ 29 Caron Butler	.40	1.00
❑ 30 Al Harrington	.25	.60
❑ 31 Ben Wallace SP	.60	1.50
❑ 32 Jason Richardson	.40	1.00
❑ 33 Channing Frye	.30	.75
❑ 34 Paul Pierce	.40	1.00
❑ 35 Andre Iguodala	.40	1.00
❑ 35B Andre Iguodala Ad	.60	1.50
❑ 36 Joey Graham	.30	.75
❑ 37 Corey Maggette	.30	.75
❑ 38 Sarunas Jasikevicius	.30	.75
❑ 39 Lamar Odom	.40	1.00
❑ 40 Shaquille O'Neal	1.00	2.50
❑ 40B Shaquille O'Neal Ad	1.50	4.00
❑ 41 Larry Hughes SP	.50	1.25
❑ 42 Darko Milicic SP	.60	1.50
❑ 43 Jerry Stackhouse	.40	1.00
❑ 44 Raymond Felton	.50	1.25
❑ 45 Nenad Krstic SP	.50	1.25
❑ 46 Michael Redd	.40	1.00
❑ 47 Shane Battier	.40	1.00
❑ 48 Kevin Garnett	.75	2.00
❑ 49 Deron Williams	.60	1.50
❑ 50 Chris Paul SP	1.25	3.00
❑ 51 Rashard Lewis	.40	1.00
❑ 52 Kevin Martin SP	.60	1.50

❑ 53 Zach Randolph	.40	1.00
❑ 54 Jared Jeffries	.25	.60
❑ 55 Donyell Marshall	.25	.60
❑ 56 Josh Howard SP	.60	1.50
❑ 57 Stephon Marbury	.40	1.00
❑ 58 Raja Bell	.25	.60
❑ 59 Tony Parker	.40	1.00
❑ 60 Dwight Howard	.75	2.00
❑ 61 Kirk Hinrich	.40	1.00
❑ 62 Emeka Okafor	.40	1.00
❑ 63 Zaza Pachulia	.25	.60
❑ 64 Troy Murphy	.40	1.00
❑ 65 Chris Duhon	.25	.60
❑ 65B Chris Duhon Ad	.40	1.00
❑ 66 Earl Boykins SP	.40	1.00
❑ 67 Tracy McGrady	.75	2.00
❑ 68 Hakim Warrick	.30	.75
❑ 69 Charlie Villanueva SP	.60	1.50
❑ 70 Jason Kidd	.60	1.50
❑ 71 Joel Przybilla SP	.40	1.00
❑ 72 Antonio Daniels	.25	.60
❑ 73 Wally Szczerbiak	.30	.75
❑ 74 Drew Gooden	.30	.75
❑ 75 Antonio McDyess	.25	.60
❑ 76 Ray Allen SP	.60	1.50
❑ 77 Rashad McCants	.30	.75
❑ 78 Eddy Curry	.30	.75
❑ 79 Chris Webber	.40	1.00
❑ 80 Yao Ming SP	1.50	4.00
❑ 81 Tyson Chandler	.40	1.00
❑ 82 Bobby Simmons	.25	.60
❑ 83 Jarrett Jack	.30	.75
❑ 84 Jameer Nelson SP	.50	1.25
❑ 85 Luol Deng	.40	1.00
❑ 86 Kurt Thomas	.25	.60
❑ 87 Mickael Pietrus	.30	.75
❑ 88 Chris Bosh SP	.60	1.50
❑ 89 Devin Harris	.40	1.00
❑ 90 Jermaine O'Neal	.40	1.00
❑ 91 Luther Head	.30	.75
❑ 92 Elton Brand SP	.60	1.50
❑ 93 Antoine Walker	.30	.75
❑ 94 Smush Parker	.25	.60
❑ 95 Nate Robinson SP	.60	1.50
❑ 96 Marvin Williams SP	.60	1.50
❑ 97 Primoz Brezec	.25	.60
❑ 98 Desmond Mason	.25	.60
❑ 99 Ron Artest SP	.60	1.50
❑ 100 Jason Terry	.40	1.00
❑ 101 Mehmet Okur	.25	.60
❑ 102 Kenyon Martin	.40	1.00
❑ 103 Ike Diogu SP	.50	1.25
❑ 104 Eddie Griffin	.25	.60
❑ 105 Amare Stoudemire	.75	2.00
❑ 106 Kwame Brown SP	.50	1.25
❑ 107 Hedo Turkoglu	.30	.75
❑ 108 Chauncey Billups	.40	1.00
❑ 108B Chauncey Billups Ad	.60	1.50
❑ 109 Rafer Alston	.25	.60
❑ 110 Dirk Nowitzki SP	1.00	2.50
❑ 111 Steve Francis	.40	1.00
❑ 112 Mike Bibby	.40	1.00
❑ 113 Kirk Snyder	.25	.60
❑ 114 Luke Walton	.30	.75
❑ 114B Luke Walton Ad	.50	1.25
❑ 115 Maurice Williams	.30	.75
❑ 116 Nick Collison	.25	.60
❑ 117 Brendan Haywood	.25	.60
❑ 118 Delonte West SP	.50	1.25
❑ 119 Mike Dunleavy	.30	.75
❑ 120 Vince Carter	.75	2.00
❑ 120B Vince Carter Ad	1.25	3.00
❑ 121 Juwan Howard	.30	.75
❑ 122 J.R. Smith	.30	.75
❑ 123 Gerald Wallace SP	.60	1.50
❑ 124 Cuttino Mobley	.30	.75
❑ 125 James Posey	.25	.60
❑ 126 Tayshaun Prince SP	.60	1.50
❑ 127 Anderson Varejao	.30	.75
❑ 128 Trenton Hassell	.25	.60
❑ 129 Matt Harpring	.30	.75
❑ 130 Gilbert Arenas SP	.60	1.50
❑ 131 Leandro Barbosa	.40	1.00
❑ 132 Bruce Bowen	.25	.60
❑ 133 Morris Peterson	.30	.75
❑ 134 David West SP	.60	1.50
❑ 135 Joe Smith	.30	.75
❑ 136 Rasheed Wallace	.40	1.00
❑ 137 Nene	.25	.60

❑ 138 Alonzo Mourning	.50	1.25
❑ 139 Jamal Crawford	.25	.60
❑ 140 Carmelo Anthony SP	.75	2.00
❑ 141 Brad Miller	.40	1.00
❑ 142 Tim Thomas	.25	.60
❑ 143 Jose Calderon	.30	.75
❑ 144 Sean May	.30	.75
❑ 145 Andres Nocioni SP	.40	1.00
❑ 146 Samuel Dalembert	.25	.60
❑ 147 Chris Wilcox	.25	.60
❑ 148 Jason Williams	.30	.75
❑ 149 DeShawn Stevenson	.25	.60
❑ 150 Josh Smith SP	.60	1.50
❑ 151 Andre Miller	.30	.75
❑ 152 Michael Finley	.40	1.00
❑ 153 Marquis Daniels	.30	.75
❑ 154 Martell Webster	.30	.75
❑ 155 Brevin Knight	.25	.60
❑ 156 Steve Nash SP	.75	2.00
❑ 157 Vladimir Radmanovic	.25	.60
❑ 158 Speedy Claxton	.25	.60
❑ 158B Speedy Claxton Ad	.40	1.00
❑ 159 Darius Miles	.25	.60
❑ 160 Pau Gasol SP	.60	1.50
❑ 161 Sam Cassell	.40	1.00
❑ 162 Nazr Mohammed	.25	.60
❑ 163 Shawn Marion	.40	1.00
❑ 164 Francisco Garcia	.25	.60
❑ 165 Kyle Korver	.40	1.00
❑ 166 Udonis Haslem	.40	1.00
❑ 167 Manu Ginobili SP	.60	1.50
❑ 168 Zydrunas Ilgauskas	.30	.75
❑ 169 Eddie Jones	.25	.60
❑ 170 Danny Granger SP	.50	1.25
❑ 171 Mike James	.25	.60
❑ 172 Ryan Gomes	.25	.60
❑ 173 Josh Childress	.30	.75
❑ 174 Marcus Camby	.30	.75
❑ 175 Chris Kaman SP	.40	1.00
❑ 176 Brandon Roy RC	3.00	8.00
❑ 177 Kyle Lowry RC	.60	1.50
❑ 178 Tyrus Thomas RC	1.50	4.00
❑ 179 Hilton Armstrong RC	1.00	2.50
❑ 180 LaMarcus Aldridge RC	1.25	3.00
❑ 181 Ronnie Brewer RC	1.25	3.00
❑ 182 Rajon Rondo RC	4.00	10.00
❑ 183 Marcus Vinicius RC	1.00	2.50
❑ 184 Solomon Jones RC	1.00	2.50
❑ 185 Leon Powe RC	1.00	2.50
❑ 186 Shawne Williams RC	1.00	2.50
❑ 187 Craig Smith RC	1.00	2.50
❑ 187B Craig Smith Ad RC	1.00	2.50
❑ 188 Patrick O'Bryant RC	1.00	2.50
❑ 189 James Augustine RC	1.00	2.50
❑ 190 Maurice Ager RC	1.00	2.50
❑ 191 Quincy Douby RC	1.00	2.50
❑ 192 Rudy Gay RC	1.00	2.50
❑ 193 Thabo Sefolosha RC	1.25	3.00
❑ 194 Bobby Jones RC	1.00	2.50
❑ 195 Shelden Williams RC	1.25	3.00
❑ 195B Shelden Williams Ad RC	1.25	3.00
❑ 196 Mile Ilic RC	1.00	2.50
❑ 197 Jorge Garbajosa RC	2.00	5.00
❑ 198 Cedric Simmons RC	1.00	2.50
❑ 199 Josh Boone RC	1.00	2.50
❑ 200 Adam Morrison RC	1.25	3.00
❑ 200B Adam Morrison Ad RC	1.50	4.00
❑ 201 Marcus Williams RC	1.25	3.00
❑ 201B Marcus Williams Ad RC	1.50	4.00
❑ 202 Steve Novak RC	1.00	2.50
❑ 203 Vassilis Spanoulis RC	1.00	2.50
❑ 204 Allan Ray RC	1.00	2.50
❑ 205 David Noel RC	1.00	2.50
❑ 206 Alexander Johnson RC	1.00	2.50
❑ 207 Mardy Collins RC	1.00	2.50
❑ 208 Dee Brown RC	1.00	2.50
❑ 209 P.J. Tucker RC	1.00	2.50
❑ 210 Paul Millsap RC	1.50	4.00
❑ 211 Paul Davis RC	1.00	2.50
❑ 212 Rodney Carney RC	1.00	2.50
❑ 212B Rodney Carney Ad RC	1.25	3.00
❑ 213 Saer Sene RC	1.00	2.50
❑ 214 Renaldo Balkman RC	1.00	2.50
❑ 215 Ryan Hollins RC	1.00	2.50
❑ 216 Will Blalock RC	1.00	2.50
❑ 217 Mickael Gelabale RC	1.00	2.50
❑ 218 Daniel Gibson RC	1.25	3.00
❑ 219 Hassan Adams RC	1.25	3.00
❑ 220 J.J. Redick RC	1.00	2.50
❑ 221 Jordan Farmar RC	1.25	3.00
❑ 221B Jordan Farmar Ad RC	1.50	4.00
❑ 222 Randy Foye RC	1.00	2.50
❑ 223 Shannon Brown RC	1.00	2.50
❑ 224 Sergio Rodriguez RC	1.00	2.50
❑ 225 Andrea Bargnani RC	1.50	4.00
❑ 225B Andrea Bargnani Ad RC	2.00	5.00
❑ 226 Larry Bird	3.00	8.00
❑ 227 George Gervin	1.00	2.50
❑ 228 Earl Monroe	1.00	2.50
❑ 229 Kareem Abdul-Jabbar	1.50	4.00
❑ 230 Wilt Chamberlain	2.00	5.00
❑ 231 Bill Walton	1.00	2.50
❑ 232 Isiah Thomas	1.00	2.50
❑ 233 Oscar Robertson	1.00	2.50
❑ 234 Pete Maravich	6.00	15.00
❑ 235 Bill Russell	2.00	5.00
❑ 236 James Worthy	1.00	2.50
❑ 237 Rick Barry	1.00	2.50
❑ 238 Walt Frazier	1.00	2.50
❑ 239 Elgin Baylor	1.00	2.50
❑ 240 Karl Malone	1.25	3.00
❑ 241 Connie Hawkins	1.00	2.50
❑ 242 Dennis Rodman	1.00	2.50
❑ 243 John Stockton	2.00	5.00
❑ 244 Jerry West	1.25	3.00
❑ 245 Bob Cousy	1.00	2.50
❑ 246 Hakeem Olajuwon	1.25	3.00
❑ 247 John Havlicek	1.00	2.50
❑ 248 Spencer Haywood	1.00	2.50
❑ 249 Moses Malone	1.00	2.50
❑ 250 Willis Reed	1.00	2.50
❑ 251 LeBron James CL	1.25	3.00
❑ 252 Shaquille O'Neal CL	.60	1.50
❑ 253 Dwyane Wade CL	.60	1.50
❑ 254 Y.Ming/T.McGrady CL	.60	1.50
❑ 255 Carmelo Anthony CL	.30	.75
❑ 256 K.Garnett/D.Howard CL	.75	2.00
❑ 257 Nate Robinson CL	.25	.60
❑ 258 Kobe Bryant/Team CL	1.00	2.50
❑ 259 Larry Bird CL	2.00	5.00
❑ 260 S.Nash/K.Thomas CL	.60	1.50

2001-02 Topps Xpectations

❑ COMP.SET w/o SP's (145)	50.00	120.00
❑ COMMON CARD (1-151)	.20	.50
❑ COMMON ROOKIE (101-150)	.75	2.00
❑ 1 Baron Davis	.30	.75
❑ 2 Jason Terry	.30	.75
❑ 3 Paul Pierce	.30	.75
❑ 4 Ron Mercer	.20	.50
❑ 5 Dirk Nowitzki	.50	1.25
❑ 6 Marc Jackson	.20	.50
❑ 7 Cuttino Mobley	.25	.60
❑ 8 Al Harrington	.25	.60
❑ 9 Keyon Dooling	.20	.50
❑ 10 Mark Madsen	.20	.50
❑ 11 Jumaine Jones	.20	.50
❑ 12 Shawn Marion	.30	.75
❑ 13 Mike Bibby	.25	.60
❑ 14 Antonio Daniels	.20	.50
❑ 15 Vince Carter	.60	1.50
❑ 16 Stromile Swift	.20	.50
❑ 17 Courtney Alexander	.20	.50
❑ 18 Desmond Mason	.25	.60
❑ 19 Hedo Turkoglu	.25	.60
❑ 20 Speedy Claxton	.20	.50
❑ 21 Lavor Postell	.20	.50
❑ 22 Chauncey Billups	.25	.60
❑ 23 Eddie House	.20	.50
❑ 24 Maurice Taylor	.20	.50
❑ 25 Lamar Odom	.30	.75
❑ 26 Antawn Jamison	.30	.75
❑ 27 Raef LaFrentz	.20	.50
❑ 28 Marcus Fizer	.20	.50
❑ 29 Chris Mihm	.20	.50
❑ 30 Eddie Robinson	.20	.50
❑ 31 Mark Blount	.20	.50
❑ 32 DerMarr Johnson	.20	.50
❑ 33 Wang Zhizhi	.25	.60
❑ 34 Danny Fortson	.20	.50
❑ 35 Elton Brand	.30	.75
❑ 36 Anthony Carter	.20	.50
❑ 37 Wally Szczerbiak	.25	.60
❑ 38 Mike Miller	.25	.60
❑ 39 Bonzi Wells	.25	.60
❑ 40 Tim Duncan	.60	1.50
❑ 41 Ruben Patterson	.20	.50
❑ 42 Keon Clark	.20	.50
❑ 43 Jason Williams	.25	.60
❑ 44 Richard Hamilton	.25	.60
❑ 45 Scott Padgett	.20	.50
❑ 46 Derek Anderson	.25	.60
❑ 47 Keith Van Horn	.25	.60
❑ 48 Tim Thomas	.20	.50
❑ 49 Jonathan Bender	.20	.50
❑ 50 Tracy McGrady	.60	1.50
❑ 51 Tyronn Lue	.20	.50
❑ 52 Austin Croshere	.20	.50
❑ 53 James Posey	.20	.50
❑ 54 Mateen Cleaves	.20	.50
❑ 55 Matt Harpring	.25	.60
❑ 56 Calvin Booth	.20	.50
❑ 57 Quentin Richardson	.25	.60
❑ 58 Joel Przybilla	.20	.50
❑ 59 Kenyon Martin	.30	.75
❑ 60 Iakovos Tsakalidis	.20	.50
❑ 61 Peja Stojakovic	.25	.60
❑ 62 Shammond Williams	.20	.50
❑ 63 Alvin Williams	.20	.50
❑ 64 Jahidi White	.20	.50
❑ 65 Morris Peterson	.25	.60
❑ 66 Larry Hughes	.25	.60
❑ 67 Andre Miller	.25	.60
❑ 68 Jamaal Magloire	.20	.50
❑ 69 Steve Francis	.30	.75
❑ 70 Todd MacCulloch	.20	.50
❑ 71 Rashard Lewis	.30	.75
❑ 72 Michael Dickerson	.20	.50
❑ 73 Nazr Mohammed	.20	.50
❑ 74 Jamal Crawford	.25	.60
❑ 75 Darius Miles	.20	.50
❑ 76 Allen Iverson	.60	1.50
❑ 77 Shaquille O'Neal	.75	2.00
❑ 78 Michael Finley	.30	.75
❑ 79 Antonio McDyess	.25	.60
❑ 80 Jerry Stackhouse	.25	.60
❑ 81 Chris Webber	.30	.75
❑ 82 Eddie Jones	.25	.60
❑ 83 Reggie Miller	.30	.75
❑ 84 Antoine Walker	.25	.60
❑ 85 Latrell Sprewell	.25	.60
❑ 86 Alonzo Mourning	.30	.75
❑ 87 Jalen Rose	.25	.60
❑ 88 Ray Allen	.30	.75
❑ 89 Gary Payton	.30	.75
❑ 90 Jason Kidd	.50	1.25
❑ 91 Stephon Marbury	.30	.75
❑ 92 Kobe Bryant	1.50	4.00
❑ 93 Grant Hill	.30	.75
❑ 94 Karl Malone	.40	1.00
❑ 95 John Stockton	.40	1.00
❑ 96 Anfernee Hardaway	.30	.75
❑ 97 Rasheed Wallace	.30	.75
❑ 98 Hakeem Olajuwon	.40	1.00
❑ 99 Shareef Abdur-Rahim	.25	.60
❑ 100 Kevin Garnett	.60	1.50
❑ 101 Kwame Brown/250 RC	8.00	20.00
❑ 102 Tyson Chandler RC	1.50	4.00
❑ 103 Pau Gasol RC	3.00	8.00
❑ 104 Eddy Curry RC	1.25	3.00
❑ 105 Jason Richardson/250 RC	12.00	30.00
❑ 106 Shane Battier/250 RC	10.00	25.00
❑ 107 Eddie Griffin RC	.75	2.00
❑ 108 DeSagana Diop RC	.75	2.00
❑ 109 Rodney White RC	.75	2.00
❑ 110 Joe Johnson/250 RC	15.00	40.00
❑ 111 Kedrick Brown RC	.75	2.00
❑ 112 Vladimir Radmanovic RC	1.00	2.50
❑ 113 Richard Jefferson RC	2.00	5.00
❑ 114 Troy Murphy/250 RC	12.00	30.00
❑ 115 Steven Hunter RC	.75	2.00
❑ 116 Kirk Haston RC	.75	2.00

❑ 117 Michael Bradley RC	.75	2.00
❑ 118 Jason Collins RC	.75	2.00
❑ 119 Zach Randolph/250 RC	15.00	40.00
❑ 120 Brendan Haywood RC	1.00	2.50
❑ 121 Joseph Forte RC	.75	2.00
❑ 122 Jeryl Sasser RC	.75	2.00
❑ 123 Brandon Armstrong RC	.75	2.00
❑ 124 Gerald Wallace RC	2.00	5.00
❑ 125 Samuel Dalembert RC	1.00	2.50
❑ 126 Jamaal Tinsley RC	1.00	2.50
❑ 127 Tony Parker RC	3.00	8.00
❑ 128 Trenton Hassell RC	1.00	2.50
❑ 129 Gilbert Arenas RC	1.25	3.00
❑ 130 Raja Bell RC	1.00	2.50
❑ 131 Will Solomon RC	.75	2.00
❑ 132 Terence Morris RC	.75	2.00
❑ 133 Brian Scalabrine RC	.75	2.00
❑ 134 Jeff Trepagnier RC	.75	2.00
❑ 135 Damone Brown RC	.75	2.00
❑ 136 Carlos Arroyo RC	6.00	15.00
❑ 137 Earl Watson RC	1.00	2.50
❑ 138 Jamison Brewer RC	.75	2.00
❑ 139 Bobby Simmons RC	.75	2.00
❑ 140 Andrei Kirilenko RC	2.00	5.00
❑ 141 Zeljko Rebraca RC	.75	2.00
❑ 142 Sean Lampley RC	.75	2.00
❑ 143 Loren Woods RC	.75	2.00
❑ 144 Alton Ford RC	.75	2.00
❑ 145 Antonis Fotsis RC	.75	2.00
❑ 146 Charlie Bell RC	.75	2.00
❑ 147 Ruben Boumtje-Boumtje RC	.75	2.00
❑ 148 Jarron Collins RC	.75	2.00
❑ 149 Kenny Satterfield RC	.75	2.00
❑ 150 Alvin Jones RC	.75	2.00
❑ 151 Michael Jordan	5.00	12.00

2002-03 Topps Xpectations

❑ COMPLETE SET (178)	125.00	300.00
❑ COMP.SET w/o SP's (100)	10.00	25.00
❑ COMMON CARD (1-100)	.15	.40
❑ COMMON ROOKIE (101-133)	.75	2.00
❑ COMMON ROOKIE (134-153)	2.50	6.00
❑ COMMON CARD (154-178)	.75	2.00
❑ 1 Darius Miles	.15	.40
❑ 2 Jason Williams	.20	.50
❑ 3 Speedy Claxton	.15	.40
❑ 4 Eduardo Najera	.15	.40
❑ 5 Chris Mihm	.15	.40
❑ 6 Eddie Robinson	.15	.40
❑ 7 Lee Nailon	.15	.40
❑ 8 Joseph Forte	.15	.40
❑ 9 Jason Terry	.25	.60
❑ 10 Vince Carter	.50	1.25
❑ 11 Matt Harpring	.20	.50
❑ 12 Bonzi Wells	.20	.50
❑ 13 Mike Bibby	.20	.50
❑ 14 Jerome James	.15	.40
❑ 15 Morris Peterson	.20	.50
❑ 16 Jarron Collins	.15	.40
❑ 17 Brendan Haywood	.15	.40
❑ 18 Dermarr Johnson	.15	.40
❑ 19 Kirk Haston	.15	.40
❑ 20 Paul Pierce	.25	.60
❑ 21 Eddy Curry	.20	.50
❑ 22 Ricky Davis	.20	.50
❑ 23 James Posey	.15	.40
❑ 24 Zeljko Rebraca	.15	.40
❑ 25 Jason Richardson	.25	.60
❑ 26 Ron Artest	.20	.50
❑ 27 Jonathan Bender	.15	.40
❑ 28 Elton Brand	.25	.60
❑ 29 Stromile Swift	.15	.40
❑ 30 Steve Francis	.25	.60
❑ 31 Devean George	.15	.40
❑ 32 Eddie House	.15	.40
❑ 33 Loren Woods	.15	.40
❑ 34 Richard Jefferson	.25	.60
❑ 35 Mike Miller	.20	.50
❑ 36 Joe Johnson	.25	.60
❑ 37 Zach Randolph	.25	.60
❑ 38 Peja Stojakovic	.20	.50
❑ 39 Predrag Drobnjak	.15	.40
❑ 40 Kwame Brown	.15	.40
❑ 41 DeShawn Stevenson	.15	.40
❑ 42 Desmond Mason	.20	.50
❑ 43 Stephen Jackson	.20	.50
❑ 44 Ruben Patterson	.15	.40
❑ 45 Samuel Dalembert	.15	.40
❑ 46 Pat Garrity	.15	.40
❑ 47 Jason Collins	.15	.40
❑ 48 Marc Jackson	.15	.40
❑ 49 Rafer Alston	.15	.40
❑ 50 Shawn Marion	.25	.60
❑ 51 Joel Przybilla	.15	.40
❑ 52 Shane Battier	.20	.50
❑ 53 Quentin Richardson	.20	.50
❑ 54 Jamaal Tinsley	.20	.50
❑ 55 Cuttino Mobley	.20	.50
❑ 56 Antawn Jamison	.25	.60
❑ 57 Chucky Atkins	.15	.40
❑ 58 Raef Lafrentz	.15	.40
❑ 59 Jumaine Jones	.15	.40
❑ 60 Dirk Nowitzki	.40	1.00
❑ 61 Marcus Fizer	.15	.40
❑ 62 Kedrick Brown	.15	.40
❑ 63 Nazr Mohammed	.15	.40
❑ 64 Jamaal Magloire	.15	.40
❑ 65 Tyson Chandler	.20	.50
❑ 66 Andre Miller	.20	.50
❑ 67 Wang Zhizhi	.15	.40
❑ 68 Mengke Bateer	.15	.40
❑ 69 Gilbert Arenas	.25	.60
❑ 70 Baron Davis	.25	.60
❑ 71 Lamar Odom	.25	.60
❑ 72 Mark Madsen	.15	.40
❑ 73 Pau Gasol	.25	.60
❑ 74 Anthony Carter	.15	.40
❑ 75 Wally Szczerbiak	.20	.50
❑ 76 Todd MacCulloch	.15	.40
❑ 77 Steven Hunter	.15	.40
❑ 78 Iakovos Tsakalidis	.15	.40
❑ 79 Ruben Boumtje-Boumtje	.15	.40
❑ 80 Gerald Wallace	.25	.60
❑ 81 Vladimir Radmanovic	.15	.40
❑ 82 Keon Clark	.15	.40
❑ 83 Andrei Kirilenko	.25	.60
❑ 84 Richard Hamilton	.20	.50
❑ 85 Trenton Hassell	.15	.40
❑ 86 Donnell Harvey	.15	.40
❑ 87 Rodney White	.15	.40
❑ 88 Troy Murphy	.25	.60
❑ 89 Terence Morris	.15	.40
❑ 90 Al Harrington	.20	.50
❑ 91 Michael Redd	.25	.60
❑ 92 Kenyon Martin	.25	.60
❑ 93 Lavor Postell	.15	.40
❑ 94 Jeryl Sasser	.15	.40
❑ 95 Hedo Turkoglu	.20	.50
❑ 96 Tony Parker	.25	.60
❑ 97 Rashard Lewis	.25	.60
❑ 98 Michael Bradley	.15	.40
❑ 99 Courtney Alexander	.15	.40
❑ 100 Eddie Griffin	.15	.40
❑ 101 Yao Ming RC	2.50	6.00
❑ 102 Dan Gadzuric RC	.75	2.00
❑ 103 Mike Dunleavy RC	1.00	2.50
❑ 104 Drew Gooden RC	1.25	3.00
❑ 105 Nikoloz Tskitishvili RC	.75	2.00
❑ 106 Roger Mason RC	.75	2.00
❑ 107 Nene Hilario RC	1.00	2.50
❑ 108 Chris Wilcox RC	1.00	2.50
❑ 109 Rod Grizzard RC	.75	2.00
❑ 110 Chris Owens RC	.75	2.00
❑ 111 Jared Jeffries RC	.75	2.00
❑ 112 Efthimios Rentzias RC	.75	2.00
❑ 113 Marcus Haislip RC	.75	2.00
❑ 114 Fred Jones RC	1.00	2.50
❑ 115 Bostjan Nachbar RC	.75	2.00
❑ 116 Jiri Welsch RC	.75	2.00
❑ 117 Jannero Pargo RC	.75	2.00
❑ 118 Curtis Borchardt RC	.75	2.00
❑ 119 Ryan Humphrey RC	.75	2.00
❑ 120 Raul Lopez RC	.75	2.00
❑ 121 Cezary Trybanski RC	.75	2.00
❑ 122 Predrag Savovic RC	.75	2.00
❑ 123 Tayshaun Prince RC	1.25	3.00
❑ 124 Frank Williams RC	.75	2.00
❑ 125 John Salmons RC	1.25	3.00
❑ 126 Chris Jefferies RC	.75	2.00
❑ 127 Luke Recker RC	.75	2.00
❑ 128 Tamar Slay RC	.75	2.00
❑ 129 Matt Barnes RC	1.00	2.50
❑ 130 Rasual Butler RC	.75	2.00
❑ 131 Vincent Yarbrough RC	.75	2.00
❑ 132 Junior Harrington RC	.75	2.00
❑ 133 Carlos Boozer RC	1.50	4.00
❑ 134 DaJuan Wagner/500 RC	2.50	6.00
❑ 135 Jay Williams/500 RC	3.00	8.00
❑ 136 Amare Stoudemire/500 RC	6.00	15.00
❑ 137 Caron Butler/500 RC	5.00	12.00
❑ 138 Melvin Ely/500 RC	2.50	6.00
❑ 139 Juan Dixon/500 RC	4.00	10.00
❑ 140 Kareem Rush/500 RC	3.00	8.00
❑ 141 Qyntel Woods/500 RC	2.50	6.00
❑ 142 Casey Jacobsen/500 RC	2.50	6.00
❑ 143 Robert Archibald/500 RC	2.50	6.00
❑ 144 Tito Maddox/500 RC	2.50	6.00
❑ 145 Ronald Murray/500 RC	4.00	10.00
❑ 146 Sam Clancy/500 RC	2.50	6.00
❑ 147 Dan Dickau/500 RC	2.50	6.00
❑ 148 Mehmet Okur/500 RC	3.00	8.00
❑ 149 Marko Jaric/500	2.50	6.00
❑ 150 Gordan Giricek/500 RC	2.50	6.00
❑ 151 Manu Ginobili/500 RC	6.00	15.00
❑ 152 J.R. Bremer/500 RC	2.50	6.00
❑ 153 Corsley Edwards/500 RC	2.50	6.00
❑ 154 Michael Jordan XX	10.00	25.00
❑ 155 Allen Iverson XX	2.00	5.00
❑ 156 Shaquille O'Neal XX	2.50	6.00
❑ 157 Tim Duncan XX	2.00	5.00
❑ 158 Tracy McGrady XX	2.00	5.00
❑ 159 Kevin Garnett XX	2.00	5.00
❑ 160 Chris Webber XX	1.00	2.50
❑ 161 Alonzo Mourning XX	1.00	2.50
❑ 162 Antoine Walker XX	.75	2.00
❑ 163 Latrell Sprewell XX	.75	2.00
❑ 164 Eddie Jones XX	.75	2.00
❑ 165 Kobe Bryant XX	5.00	12.00
❑ 166 Allan Houston XX	.75	2.00
❑ 167 Ray Allen XX	1.00	2.50
❑ 168 Gary Payton XX	1.00	2.50
❑ 169 Antonio McDyess XX	.75	2.00
❑ 170 Jason Kidd XX	1.50	4.00
❑ 171 Jerry Stackhouse XX	.75	2.00
❑ 172 Stephon Marbury XX	1.00	2.50
❑ 173 Karl Malone XX	1.00	2.50
❑ 174 Reggie Miller XX	1.00	2.50
❑ 175 S.Abdur-Rahim XX	.75	2.00
❑ 176 Rasheed Wallace XX	1.00	2.50
❑ 177 John Stockton XX	1.25	3.00
❑ 178 Grant Hill XX	1.00	2.50

1996-97 UD3

❑ COMPLETE SET (60)	30.00	50.00
❑ COMMON CARD (1-20)	.08	.25
❑ COMMON CARD (21-40)	.20	.50
❑ COMMON CARD (41-60)	.10	.30
❑ 1 Kerry Kittles RC	.30	.75
❑ 2 Stephon Marbury RC	.75	2.00
❑ 3 Jermaine O'Neal RC	.75	2.00
❑ 4 Shareef Abdur-Rahim RC	1.00	2.50
❑ 5 Ray Allen RC	1.00	2.50
❑ 6 Antoine Walker RC	.75	2.00
❑ 7 Erick Dampier RC	.30	.75
❑ 8 Walter McCarty RC	.08	.25
❑ 9 Todd Fuller RC	.08	.25
❑ 10 Tony Delk RC	.30	.75
❑ 11 Marcus Camby RC	.40	1.00
❑ 12 John Wallace RC	.30	.75

❑ 13 Vitaly Potapenko RC	.08	.25
❑ 14 Allen Iverson RC	1.00	2.50
❑ 15 Steve Nash RC	2.50	6.00
❑ 16 Derek Fisher RC	.50	1.25
❑ 17 Samaki Walker RC	.08	.25
❑ 18 Roy Rogers RC	.08	.25
❑ 19 Kobe Bryant RC	4.00	10.00
❑ 20 Lorenzen Wright RC	.20	.50
❑ 21 Kevin Garnett	1.25	3.00
❑ 22 Hakeem Olajuwon	.30	.75
❑ 23 Michael Jordan	4.00	10.00
❑ 24 John Stockton	.30	.75
❑ 25 Terrell Brandon	.40	1.00
❑ 26 Damon Stoudamire	.30	.75
❑ 27 Charles Barkley	.75	2.00
❑ 28 Dikembe Mutombo	.40	1.00
❑ 29 Gary Payton	.30	.75
❑ 30 Patrick Ewing	.60	1.50
❑ 31 Dennis Rodman	.20	.50
❑ 32 Joe Smith	.40	1.00
❑ 33 Grant Hill	.30	.75
❑ 34 Shaquille O'Neal	1.50	4.00
❑ 35 Kevin Johnson	.40	1.00
❑ 36 David Robinson	.30	.75
❑ 37 Juwan Howard	.40	1.00
❑ 38 Mitch Richmond	.40	1.00
❑ 39 Alonzo Mourning	.40	1.00
❑ 40 Reggie Miller	.60	1.50
❑ 41 Shawn Kemp	.20	.50
❑ 42 Scottie Pippen	.60	1.50
❑ 43 Kobe Bryant	3.00	8.00
❑ 44 Anfernee Hardaway	.30	.75
❑ 45 Brent Barry	.10	.30
❑ 46 Glenn Robinson	.40	1.00
❑ 47 Karl Malone	.30	.75
❑ 48 Chris Webber	.30	.75
❑ 49 Danny Manning	.25	.60
❑ 50 Antonio McDyess	.20	.50
❑ 51 Dominique Wilkins	.40	1.00
❑ 52 Vin Baker	.25	.60
❑ 53 Isaiah Rider	.25	.60
❑ 54 Eddie Jones	.30	.75
❑ 55 Glen Rice	.25	.60
❑ 56 Larry Johnson	.25	.60
❑ 57 Latrell Sprewell	.30	.75
❑ 58 Sean Elliott	.25	.60
❑ 59 Clyde Drexler	.40	1.00
❑ 60 Jerry Stackhouse	.50	1.25

1997-98 UD3

❑ COMPLETE SET (60)	25.00	50.00
❑ COMMON CARD (1-40)	.08	.25
❑ COMMON CARD (41-60)	.15	.40
❑ 1 Anfernee Hardaway JM	.30	.75
❑ 2 Alonzo Mourning JM	.20	.50
❑ 3 Grant Hill JM	.30	.75
❑ 4 Kerry Kittles JM	.30	.75
❑ 5 Latrell Sprewell JM	.30	.75
❑ 6 Rasheed Wallace JM	.30	.75
❑ 7 Jerry Stackhouse JM	.30	.75
❑ 8 Glen Rice JM	.20	.50
❑ 9 Marcus Camby JM	.30	.75
❑ 10 Scottie Pippen JM	.50	1.25
❑ 11 Patrick Ewing JM	.30	.75
❑ 12 Michael Finley JM	.30	.75
❑ 13 Karl Malone JM	.30	.75
❑ 14 Antonio McDyess JM	.20	.50
❑ 15 Michael Jordan JM	2.00	5.00
❑ 16 Clyde Drexler JM	.30	.75
❑ 17 Brent Barry JM	.20	.50
❑ 18 Glenn Robinson JM	.30	.75
❑ 19 Kobe Bryant JM	1.25	3.00
❑ 20 Reggie Miller JM	.30	.75
❑ 21 John Stockton AS	.30	.75
❑ 22 Gary Payton AS	.30	.75
❑ 23 Michael Jordan AS	2.00	5.00
❑ 24 Vin Baker AS	.20	.50
❑ 25 Karl Malone AS	.30	.75
❑ 26 Juwan Howard AS	.20	.50
❑ 27 Charles Barkley AS	.40	1.00
❑ 28 Jason Kidd AS	.50	1.25
❑ 29 Joe Dumars AS	.30	.75
❑ 30 Anfernee Hardaway AS	.20	.50
❑ 31 Mitch Richmond AS	.20	.50
❑ 32 Alonzo Mourning AS	.08	.25
❑ 33 Grant Hill AS	.30	.75
❑ 34 Shaquille O'Neal AS	.75	2.00
❑ 35 Scottie Pippen AS	.50	1.25
❑ 36 Reggie Miller AS	.30	.75
❑ 37 Hakeem Olajuwon AS	.20	.50
❑ 38 Tim Hardaway AS	.20	.50
❑ 39 David Robinson AS	.30	.75
❑ 40 Shawn Kemp AS	.20	.50
❑ 41 Allen Iverson BP	1.25	3.00
❑ 42 Stephon Marbury BP	.60	1.50
❑ 43 Dennis Rodman BP	.30	.75
❑ 44 Terrell Brandon BP	.30	.75
❑ 45 Michael Jordan BP	3.00	8.00
❑ 46 Kerry Kittles BP	.50	1.25
❑ 47 Hakeem Olajuwon BP	.30	.75
❑ 48 Loy Vaught BP	.15	.40
❑ 49 Antoine Walker BP	.60	1.50
❑ 50 Gary Payton BP	.30	.75
❑ 51 Kevin Johnson BP	.30	.75
❑ 52 Kevin Garnett BP	1.00	2.50
❑ 53 Shareef Abdur-Rahim BP	.75	2.00
❑ 54 Larry Johnson BP	.30	.75
❑ 55 Dikembe Mutombo BP	.15	.40
❑ 56 Chris Webber BP	.20	.50
❑ 57 Joe Smith BP	.30	.75
❑ 58 Kendall Gill BP	.15	.40
❑ 59 Kenny Anderson BP	.30	.75
❑ 60 Damon Stoudamire BP	.30	.75
❑ NNO Michael Jordan Promo		

2002-03 UD Authentics

❑ COMPLETE SET (132)	175.00	350.00
❑ COMP.SET w/o SP's (90)	15.00	40.00
❑ COMMON CARD (1-90)	.20	.50
❑ COMMON ROOKIE (91-123)	2.00	5.00
❑ COMMON ROOKIE (124-132)	2.50	6.00
❑ 1 Shareef Abdur-Rahim	.25	.60
❑ 2 Jason Terry	.30	.75
❑ 3 Glenn Robinson	.25	.60
❑ 4 Paul Pierce	.30	.75
❑ 5 Antoine Walker	.25	.60
❑ 6 Eric Williams	.20	.50
❑ 7 Kedrick Brown	.20	.50
❑ 8 Jalen Rose	.25	.60
❑ 9 Tyson Chandler	.25	.60
❑ 10 Eddy Curry	.25	.60
❑ 11 Darius Miles	.20	.50
❑ 12 Lamond Murray	.20	.50
❑ 13 Chris Mihm	.20	.50
❑ 14 Dirk Nowitzki	.50	1.25
❑ 15 Steve Nash	.50	1.25
❑ 16 Michael Finley	.30	.75
❑ 17 Raef LaFrentz	.20	.50
❑ 18 James Posey	.20	.50
❑ 19 Juwan Howard	.25	.60
❑ 20 Jerry Stackhouse	.25	.60
❑ 21 Ben Wallace	.25	.60
❑ 22 Clifford Robinson	.20	.50
❑ 23 Jason Richardson	.30	.75
❑ 24 Antawn Jamison	.30	.75
❑ 25 Gilbert Arenas	.30	.75
❑ 26 Steve Francis	.30	.75
❑ 27 Eddie Griffin	.20	.50
❑ 28 Cuttino Mobley	.25	.60
❑ 29 Reggie Miller	.30	.75
❑ 30 Jamaal Tinsley	.25	.60
❑ 31 Jermaine O'Neal	.30	.75
❑ 32 Elton Brand	.30	.75
❑ 33 Lamar Odom	.30	.75
❑ 34 Andre Miller	.25	.60
❑ 35 Kobe Bryant	1.50	4.00
❑ 36 Shaquille O'Neal	.75	2.00
❑ 37 Derek Fisher	.25	.60
❑ 38 Devean George	.20	.50
❑ 39 Pau Gasol	.30	.75
❑ 40 Shane Battier	.25	.60
❑ 41 Alonzo Mourning	.30	.75
❑ 42 Brian Grant	.20	.50
❑ 43 Eddie Jones	.25	.60
❑ 44 Ray Allen	.30	.75
❑ 45 Tim Thomas	.20	.50
❑ 46 Kevin Garnett	.60	1.50
❑ 47 Wally Szczerbiak	.25	.60
❑ 48 Terrell Brandon	.20	.50
❑ 49 Jason Kidd	.50	1.25
❑ 50 Dikembe Mutombo	.25	.60
❑ 51 Richard Jefferson	.30	.75
❑ 52 Baron Davis	.30	.75
❑ 53 Jamal Mashburn	.25	.60
❑ 54 David Wesley	.20	.50
❑ 55 P.J. Brown	.20	.50
❑ 56 Latrell Sprewell	.25	.60
❑ 57 Allan Houston	.25	.60
❑ 58 Antonio McDyess	.25	.60
❑ 59 Tracy McGrady	.60	1.50
❑ 60 Mike Miller	.25	.60
❑ 61 Darrell Armstrong	.20	.50
❑ 62 Allen Iverson	.60	1.50
❑ 63 Keith Van Horn	.25	.60
❑ 64 Stephon Marbury	.30	.75
❑ 65 Shawn Marion	.30	.75
❑ 66 Anfernee Hardaway	.30	.75
❑ 67 Rasheed Wallace	.30	.75
❑ 68 Bonzi Wells	.25	.60
❑ 69 Scottie Pippen	.50	1.25
❑ 70 Chris Webber	.30	.75
❑ 71 Peja Stojakovic	.25	.60
❑ 72 Mike Bibby	.25	.60
❑ 73 Hedo Turkoglu	.25	.60
❑ 74 Tim Duncan	.60	1.50
❑ 75 David Robinson	.40	1.00
❑ 76 Tony Parker	.30	.75
❑ 77 Malik Rose	.20	.50
❑ 78 Gary Payton	.30	.75
❑ 79 Rashard Lewis	.30	.75
❑ 80 Desmond Mason	.25	.60
❑ 81 Brent Barry	.20	.50
❑ 82 Vince Carter	.60	1.50
❑ 83 Morris Peterson	.25	.60
❑ 84 Antonio Davis	.20	.50
❑ 85 Karl Malone	.30	.75
❑ 86 John Stockton	.40	1.00
❑ 87 Andrei Kirilenko	.30	.75
❑ 88 Michael Jordan	2.00	5.00
❑ 89 Richard Hamilton	.25	.60
❑ 90 Kwame Brown	.20	.50
❑ 91 Efthimios Rentzias RC	2.00	5.00
❑ 92 Darius Songaila RC	2.00	5.00
❑ 93 Matt Barnes RC	2.50	6.00
❑ 94 Sam Clancy RC	2.00	5.00
❑ 95 Lonny Baxter RC	2.00	5.00
❑ 96 Manu Ginobili RC	5.00	12.00
❑ 97 Rod Grizzard RC	2.00	5.00
❑ 98 Tito Maddox RC	2.00	5.00
❑ 99 Predrag Savovic RC	2.00	5.00
❑ 100 Carlos Boozer RC	4.00	10.00
❑ 101 Dan Gadzuric RC	2.00	5.00
❑ 102 Vincent Yarbrough RC	2.00	5.00
❑ 103 Robert Archibald RC	2.00	5.00
❑ 104 Roger Mason RC	2.00	5.00
❑ 105 Steve Logan RC	2.00	5.00
❑ 106 Dan Dickau RC	2.00	5.00
❑ 107 Chris Jefferies RC	2.00	5.00
❑ 108 John Salmons RC	3.00	8.00
❑ 109 Frank Williams RC	2.00	5.00
❑ 110 Tayshaun Prince RC	3.00	8.00
❑ 111 Casey Jacobsen RC	2.00	5.00
❑ 112 Qyntel Woods RC	2.00	5.00
❑ 113 Kareem Rush RC	2.50	6.00
❑ 114 Ryan Humphrey RC	2.00	5.00
❑ 115 Curtis Borchardt RC	2.00	5.00
❑ 116 Juan Dixon RC	3.00	8.00
❑ 117 Jiri Welsch RC	2.00	5.00
❑ 118 Bostjan Nachbar RC	2.00	5.00
❑ 119 Fred Jones RC	2.50	6.00
❑ 120 Marcus Haislip RC	2.00	5.00

❑ 121 Melvin Ely RC	2.00	5.00
❑ 122 Jared Jeffries RC	2.00	5.00
❑ 123 Caron Butler RC	4.00	10.00
❑ 124 Amare Stoudemire RC	6.00	15.00
❑ 125 Chris Wilcox RC	3.00	8.00
❑ 126 Nene Hilario RC	3.00	8.00
❑ 127 DaJuan Wagner RC	2.50	6.00
❑ 128 Nikoloz Tskitishvili RC	2.50	6.00
❑ 129 Drew Gooden RC	4.00	10.00
❑ 130 Mike Dunleavy RC	3.00	8.00
❑ 131 Jay Williams RC	3.00	8.00
❑ 132 Yao Ming RC	8.00	20.00

2007-08 UD Black

❑ 1 Clyde Drexler JSY	35.00	75.00
❑ 2 Al Jefferson JSY	15.00	30.00
❑ 3 Allen Iverson JSY	25.00	50.00
❑ 4 Alonzo Mourning JSY	25.00	50.00
❑ 5 Amare Stoudemire JSY	25.00	50.00
❑ 6 Andre Iguodala JSY	20.00	40.00
❑ 7 Andrea Bargnani JSY	15.00	30.00
❑ 8 Andrew Bogut JSY	15.00	30.00
❑ 9 Antawn Jamison JSY	15.00	30.00
❑ 10 Baron Davis JSY	20.00	40.00
❑ 11 Ben Gordon JSY	20.00	40.00
❑ 12 Bernard King JSY	15.00	30.00
❑ 13 Bill Laimbeer JSY	12.50	25.00
❑ 14 Bill Russell JSY	25.00	50.00
❑ 15 Dwyane Wade JSY	20.00	40.00
❑ 16 Brandon Roy JSY	20.00	40.00
❑ 17 Carlos Arroyo JSY	15.00	30.00
❑ 18 Carlos Boozer JSY	15.00	30.00
❑ 19 Carmelo Anthony JSY	20.00	40.00
❑ 20 Chris Bosh JSY	20.00	40.00
❑ 21 Chris Mullin JSY	20.00	40.00
❑ 22 Chris Paul JSY	40.00	75.00
❑ 23 Corey Maggette JSY	12.50	25.00
❑ 24 Adrian Dantley JSY	12.50	25.00
❑ 25 Dennis Rodman JSY	25.00	50.00
❑ 26 Deron Williams JSY	20.00	40.00
❑ 27 Dirk Nowitzki JSY	20.00	40.00
❑ 28 Dominique Wilkins JSY	20.00	40.00
❑ 29 Dwight Howard JSY	20.00	40.00
❑ 30 Eddy Curry JSY	10.00	25.00
❑ 31 Elton Brand JSY	10.00	25.00
❑ 32 Emeka Okafor JSY	10.00	25.00
❑ 33 George Gervin JSY	15.00	30.00
❑ 34 Gilbert Arenas JSY	20.00	40.00
❑ 35 Hakeem Olajuwon JSY	20.00	40.00
❑ 36 Jamaal Tinsley JSY	10.00	25.00
❑ 37 James Worthy JSY	20.00	40.00
❑ 38 Jason Kidd JSY	15.00	30.00
❑ 39 Jason Richardson JSY	10.00	25.00
❑ 40 Jermaine O'Neal JSY	10.00	25.00
❑ 41 Jerry West JSY	40.00	75.00
❑ 42 Joe Dumars JSY	25.00	50.00
❑ 43 John Stockton JSY	20.00	40.00
❑ 44 Josh Howard JSY	15.00	30.00
❑ 45 Julius Erving JSY	25.00	50.00
❑ 46 Kareem Abdul-Jabbar JSY	30.00	60.00
❑ 47 Karl Malone JSY	20.00	40.00
❑ 48 Kevin Garnett JSY	30.00	60.00
❑ 49 Kevin McHale JSY	15.00	30.00
❑ 50 Kirk Hinrich JSY	15.00	30.00
❑ 51 Kobe Bryant JSY	60.00	120.00
❑ 52 Kyle Korver JSY	15.00	30.00
❑ 53 Lamar Odom JSY	10.00	25.00
❑ 54 LaMarcus Aldridge JSY	15.00	30.00
❑ 55 Larry Bird JSY	30.00	60.00
❑ 56 Larry Hughes JSY	10.00	25.00
❑ 57 LeBron James JSY	60.00	120.00
❑ 58 Magic Johnson JSY	40.00	75.00
❑ 59 Marvin Williams JSY	10.00	25.00
❑ 60 Michael Jordan JSY	125.00	225.00
❑ 61 Michael Redd JSY	10.00	25.00
❑ 62 Mike Bibby JSY	10.00	25.00
❑ 63 Oscar Robertson JSY	35.00	70.00
❑ 64 Pau Gasol JSY	10.00	25.00
❑ 65 Paul Pierce JSY	15.00	30.00
❑ 66 Pete Maravich JSY	60.00	120.00
❑ 67 Randy Foye JSY	10.00	25.00
❑ 68 Rashard Lewis JSY	10.00	25.00
❑ 69 Rasheed Wallace JSY	10.00	25.00
❑ 70 Ray Allen JSY	15.00	30.00
❑ 71 Ron Artest JSY	10.00	25.00
❑ 72 Rudy Gay JSY	10.00	25.00
❑ 73 Shaquille O'Neal JSY	25.00	50.00
❑ 74 Shelden Williams JSY	10.00	25.00
❑ 75 Stephon Marbury JSY	10.00	25.00
❑ 76 Steve Nash JSY	20.00	40.00
❑ 77 Tayshaun Prince JSY	15.00	30.00
❑ 78 Tim Duncan JSY	30.00	60.00
❑ 79 Tony Parker JSY	15.00	30.00
❑ 80 Tracy McGrady JSY	20.00	40.00
❑ 81 Vince Carter JSY	25.00	50.00
❑ 82 Walt Frazier JSY	10.00	25.00
❑ 83 Wilt Chamberlain JSY	50.00	100.00
❑ 84 Yao Ming JSY	20.00	40.00
❑ 85 Carl Landry JSY AU RC	15.00	30.00
❑ 86 Gabe Pruitt JSY AU RC	10.00	25.00
❑ 87 Marcus Williams JSY AU RC		
❑ 88 Nick Fazekas JSY AU RC	10.00	25.00
❑ 89 Glen Davis JSY AU RC	20.00	40.00
❑ 90 Jermareo Davidson JSY AU RC	10.00	25.00
❑ 91 Josh McRoberts JSY AU RC	10.00	25.00
❑ 92 Chris Richard JSY AU RC	10.00	25.00
❑ 93 Derrick Byars JSY AU RC		
❑ 94 Adam Haluska JSY AU RC	10.00	25.00
❑ 95 Reyshawn Terry JSY AU RC		
❑ 96 Jared Jordan JSY AU RC		
❑ 97 Stephane Lasme JSY AU RC		
❑ 98 Dominic McGuire JSY AU RC		
❑ 99 Al Horford JSY AU RC	40.00	80.00
❑ 100 Mike Conley JSY AU RC	25.00	50.00
❑ 101 Jeff Green JSY AU RC	25.00	50.00
❑ 102 Corey Brewer JSY AU RC	20.00	40.00
❑ 103 Joakim Noah JSY AU RC	20.00	40.00
❑ 104 Spencer Hawes JSY AU RC	15.00	30.00
❑ 105 Acie Law IV JSY AU RC	10.00	25.00
❑ 106 Kevin Durant JSY AU RC	250.00	450.00
❑ 107 Julian Wright JSY AU RC	25.00	50.00
❑ 108 Al Thornton JSY AU RC	25.00	50.00
❑ 109 Rodney Stuckey JSY AU RC	25.00	50.00
❑ 110 Sean Williams JSY AU RC	15.00	30.00
❑ 111 Marco Belinelli JSY AU RC		
❑ 112 Javaris Crittenton JSY AU RC	15.00	30.00
❑ 113 Jason Smith JSY AU RC	10.00	25.00
❑ 114 Daequan Cook JSY AU RC	20.00	40.00
❑ 115 Aaron Brooks JSY AU RC	10.00	25.00
❑ 116 Arron Afflalo JSY AU RC	10.00	25.00
❑ 117 Alando Tucker JSY AU RC	10.00	25.00
❑ 118 Jared Dudley JSY AU RC	10.00	25.00
❑ 119 Wilson Chandler JSY AU RC	10.00	25.00
❑ 120 Morris Almond JSY AU RC	10.00	25.00
❑ 121 Greg Oden RC		
❑ 122 Nick Young RC	8.00	20.00
❑ 123 Yi Jianlian RC		
❑ 124 Brandan Wright RC	10.00	25.00
❑ 125 Sun Yue RC		
❑ 126 Thaddeus Young RC	15.00	30.00

2008-09 UD Black

❑ COMMON CARD (1-42)	10.00	25.00
❑ 1 Al Horford	10.00	25.00
❑ 2 Allen Iverson	12.00	30.00
❑ 3 Amare Stoudemire	12.00	30.00
❑ 4 Baron Davis	10.00	25.00
❑ 5 Kirk Hinrich	10.00	25.00
❑ 6 Brandon Roy	12.00	30.00
❑ 7 Carmelo Anthony	30.00	60.00
❑ 8 Chauncey Billups	10.00	25.00
❑ 9 Chris Bosh	10.00	25.00
❑ 10 Peja Stojakovic	10.00	25.00
❑ 11 Corey Maggette	10.00	25.00
❑ 12 Danny Granger	10.00	25.00
❑ 13 Andrei Kirilenko	10.00	25.00
❑ 14 Dirk Nowitzki	12.00	30.00
❑ 15 Dwight Howard	20.00	40.00
❑ 16 Elton Brand	15.00	40.00
❑ 17 Gerald Wallace	10.00	25.00
❑ 18 Gilbert Arenas	10.00	25.00
❑ 19 Jason Kidd	10.00	25.00
❑ 20 Kevin Durant	25.00	60.00
❑ 21 Kevin Garnett	20.00	50.00
❑ 22 Kevin Martin	10.00	25.00
❑ 23 Kobe Bryant	50.00	100.00
❑ 24 LeBron James	50.00	100.00
❑ 25 Michael Redd	10.00	25.00
❑ 26 Mike Miller	10.00	25.00
❑ 27 Pau Gasol	10.00	25.00
❑ 28 Paul Pierce	12.00	30.00
❑ 29 Rudy Gay	10.00	25.00
❑ 30 Shawn Marion	10.00	25.00
❑ 31 Steve Nash	10.00	25.00
❑ 32 Tim Duncan	15.00	40.00
❑ 33 Tracy McGrady		
❑ 34 Vince Carter	12.00	30.00
❑ 35 Yao Ming	30.00	60.00
❑ 36 Zach Randolph	10.00	25.00
❑ 37 Julius Erving	15.00	30.00
❑ 38 Larry Bird	25.00	50.00
❑ 39 Magic Johnson	25.00	50.00
❑ 40 Michael Jordan	100.00	200.00
❑ 41 Oscar Robertson	25.00	50.00
❑ 42 Patrick Ewing	50.00	100.00
❑ 43 Derrick Rose JSY AU EXCH	100.00	200.00
❑ 44 M.Beasley JSY AU EXCH	30.00	60.00
❑ 45 O.J. Mayo JSY AU EXCH	25.00	50.00
❑ 46 R.Westbrook JSY AU RC	20.00	40.00
❑ 47 Kevin Love JSY AU RC	20.00	40.00
❑ 48 Eric Gordon JSY AU RC	20.00	40.00
❑ 49 Joe Alexander JSY AU RC	8.00	20.00
❑ 50 D.J. Augustin JSY AU EXCH	15.00	30.00
❑ 51 Brook Lopez JSY AU RC	15.00	30.00
❑ 52 Jerryd Bayless JSY AU RC	10.00	25.00
❑ 53 Jason Thompson JSY AU RC	8.00	20.00
❑ 54 Brandon Rush JSY AU RC	8.00	20.00
❑ 55 A.Randolph JSY AU RC	15.00	30.00
❑ 56 Robin Lopez JSY AU EXCH	8.00	20.00
❑ 57 Marreese Speights JSY AU RC	8.00	20.00
❑ 58 Roy Hibbert JSY AU RC	10.00	25.00
❑ 59 Javale McGee JSY AU RC	8.00	20.00
❑ 60 J.J. Hickson JSY AU RC	15.00	30.00
❑ 61 Ryan Anderson JSY AU RC	8.00	20.00
❑ 62 Kosta Koufos JSY AU RC	8.00	20.00
❑ 63 George Hill JSY AU RC	15.00	30.00
❑ 64 Darrell Arthur JSY AU EXCH	8.00	20.00
❑ 65 Donte Greene JSY AU RC	8.00	20.00
❑ 66 J.R. Giddens JSY AU EXCH	8.00	20.00
❑ 67 Walter Sharpe JSY AU RC	8.00	20.00
❑ 68 Joey Dorsey JSY AU RC	8.00	20.00
❑ 69 M.Chalmers JSY AU EXCH	15.00	30.00
❑ 70 Sonny Weems JSY AU RC	8.00	20.00
❑ 71 R.Fernandez JSY AU EXCH	20.00	40.00
❑ 72 Patrick Ewing Jr. JSY AU RC	8.00	20.00

1998-99 UD Choice Preview

❑ COMPLETE SET (55)	3.00	8.00
❑ 1 Dikembe Mutombo	.02	.10
❑ 3 Mookie Blaylock	.01	.05
❑ 7 Ron Mercer	.02	.10
❑ 9 Walter McCarty	.01	.05
❑ 13 Anthony Mason	.02	.10
❑ 14 Glen Rice	.02	.10
❑ 18 Toni Kukoc	.02	.10
❑ 23 Michael Jordan	.75	2.00
❑ 26 Zydrunas Ilgauskas	.02	.10
❑ 27 Cedric Henderson	.01	.05
❑ 29 Michael Finley	.05	.15
❑ 32 Hubert Davis	.01	.05
❑ 34 Bobby Jackson	.02	.10
❑ 37 Danny Fortson	.01	.05
❑ 41 Grant Hill	.05	.15
❑ 43 Jerome Williams	.01	.05

❑ 45 Erick Dampier	.02	.10
❑ 48 Donyell Marshall	.02	.10
❑ 50 Charles Barkley	.15	.40
❑ 51 Hakeem Olajuwon	.10	.30
❑ 56 Reggie Miller	.05	.15
❑ 60 Chris Mullin	.05	.15
❑ 64 Eric Piatkowski	.02	.10
❑ 65 Maurice Taylor	.02	.10
❑ 68 Shaquille O'Neal	.25	.60
❑ 69 Kobe Bryant	.50	1.25
❑ 74 Alonzo Mourning	.02	.10
❑ 75 Tim Hardaway	.02	.10
❑ 79 Ray Allen	.05	.15
❑ 80 Terrell Brandon	.02	.10
❑ 84 Stephon Marbury	.05	.15
❑ 85 Kevin Garnett	.25	.60
❑ 89 Keith Van Horn	.05	.15
❑ 90 Sam Cassell	.05	.15
❑ 95 Patrick Ewing	.05	.15
❑ 97 John Starks	.02	.10
❑ 100 Anfernee Hardaway	.05	.15
❑ 101 Nick Anderson	.01	.05
❑ 105 Allen Iverson	.25	.60
❑ 110 Jason Kidd	.15	.40
❑ 117 Isaiah Rider	.01	.05
❑ 118 Rasheed Wallace	.05	.15
❑ 121 Corliss Williamson	.02	.10
❑ 123 Billy Owens	.01	.05
❑ 126 Tim Duncan	.25	.60
❑ 127 Sean Elliott	.02	.10
❑ 131 Vin Baker	.02	.10
❑ 135 Gary Payton	.05	.15
❑ 137 Chauncey Billups	.02	.10
❑ 142 John Stockton	.05	.15
❑ 143 Karl Malone	.05	.15
❑ 148 Bryant Reeves	.01	.05
❑ 149 Shareef Abdur-Rahim	.05	.15
❑ 152 Harvey Grant	.01	.05
❑ 153 Juwan Howard	.02	.10

1998-99 UD Choice

❑ COMPLETE SET (200)	7.50	15.00
❑ 1 Dikembe Mutombo	.08	.25
❑ 2 Alan Henderson	.05	.15
❑ 3 Mookie Blaylock	.05	.15
❑ 4 Ed Gray	.05	.15
❑ 5 Eldridge Recasner	.05	.15
❑ 6 Kenny Anderson	.08	.25
❑ 7 Ron Mercer	.20	.50
❑ 8 Dana Barros	.05	.15
❑ 9 Walter McCarty	.05	.15
❑ 10 Travis Knight	.05	.15
❑ 11 Andrew DeClercq	.05	.15
❑ 12 David Wesley	.05	.15
❑ 13 Anthony Mason	.08	.25
❑ 14 Glen Rice	.08	.25
❑ 15 J.R. Reid	.05	.15
❑ 16 Bobby Phills	.05	.15
❑ 17 Dell Curry	.05	.15
❑ 18 Toni Kukoc	.08	.25
❑ 19 Randy Brown	.05	.15
❑ 20 Ron Harper	.08	.25
❑ 21 Keith Booth	.05	.15
❑ 22 Scott Burrell	.05	.15
❑ 23 Michael Jordan	1.00	2.50
❑ 24 Derek Anderson	.10	.30
❑ 25 Brevin Knight	.05	.15
❑ 26 Zydrunas Ilgauskas	.08	.25
❑ 27 Cedric Henderson	.05	.15
❑ 28 Vitaly Potapenko	.05	.15
❑ 29 Michael Finley	.15	.40
❑ 30 Erick Strickland	.05	.15
❑ 31 Shawn Bradley	.05	.15
❑ 32 Hubert Davis	.05	.15
❑ 33 Khalid Reeves	.05	.15
❑ 34 Bobby Jackson	.08	.25
❑ 35 Tony Battie	.05	.15
❑ 36 Bryant Stith	.05	.15
❑ 37 Danny Fortson	.05	.15
❑ 38 Dean Garrett	.05	.15
❑ 39 Eric Williams	.05	.15
❑ 40 Brian Williams	.05	.15
❑ 41 Grant Hill	.15	.40
❑ 42 Lindsey Hunter	.05	.15
❑ 43 Jerome Williams	.05	.15
❑ 44 Eric Montross	.05	.15
❑ 45 Erick Dampier	.08	.25
❑ 46 Muggsy Bogues	.08	.25
❑ 47 Tony Delk	.05	.15
❑ 48 Donyell Marshall	.08	.25
❑ 49 Bimbo Coles	.05	.15
❑ 50 Charles Barkley	.20	.50
❑ 51 Hakeem Olajuwon	.15	.40
❑ 52 Brent Price	.05	.15
❑ 53 Mario Elie	.05	.15
❑ 54 Rodrick Rhodes	.05	.15
❑ 55 Kevin Willis	.05	.15
❑ 56 Reggie Miller	.15	.40
❑ 57 Jalen Rose	.15	.40
❑ 58 Mark Jackson	.08	.25
❑ 59 Dale Davis	.08	.25
❑ 60 Chris Mullin	.15	.40
❑ 61 Derrick McKey	.05	.15
❑ 62 Lorenzen Wright	.05	.15
❑ 63 Rodney Rogers	.05	.15
❑ 64 Eric Piatkowski	.08	.25
❑ 65 Maurice Taylor	.07	.20
❑ 66 Isaac Austin	.05	.15
❑ 67 Corie Blount	.05	.15
❑ 68 Shaquille O'Neal	.40	1.00
❑ 69 Kobe Bryant	.60	1.50
❑ 70 Robert Horry	.08	.25
❑ 71 Sean Rooks	.05	.15
❑ 72 Derek Fisher	.15	.40
❑ 73 P.J. Brown	.05	.15
❑ 74 Alonzo Mourning	.08	.25
❑ 75 Tim Hardaway	.08	.25
❑ 76 Voshon Lenard	.05	.15
❑ 77 Dan Majerle	.08	.25
❑ 78 Ervin Johnson	.05	.15
❑ 79 Ray Allen	.15	.40
❑ 80 Terrell Brandon	.08	.25
❑ 81 Tyrone Hill	.05	.15
❑ 82 Elliot Perry	.05	.15
❑ 83 Anthony Peeler	.05	.15
❑ 84 Stephon Marbury	.15	.40
❑ 85 Kevin Garnett	.30	.75
❑ 86 Paul Grant	.05	.15
❑ 87 Chris Carr	.05	.15
❑ 88 Micheal Williams UER	.05	.15
❑ 89 Keith Van Horn	.15	.40
❑ 90 Sam Cassell	.15	.40
❑ 91 Kendall Gill	.05	.15
❑ 92 Chris Gatling	.05	.15
❑ 93 Kerry Kittles	.05	.15
❑ 94 Allan Houston	.08	.25
❑ 95 Patrick Ewing UER	.05	.15
❑ 96 Charles Oakley	.05	.15
❑ 97 John Starks	.08	.25
❑ 98 Charlie Ward	.05	.15
❑ 99 Chris Mills	.05	.15
❑ 100 Anfernee Hardaway	.15	.40
❑ 101 Nick Anderson	.05	.15
❑ 102 Mark Price	.08	.25
❑ 103 Horace Grant	.08	.25
❑ 104 David Benoit	.05	.15
❑ 105 Allen Iverson	.30	.75
❑ 106 Joe Smith	.08	.25
❑ 107 Tim Thomas	.08	.25
❑ 108 Brian Shaw	.05	.15
❑ 109 Aaron McKie	.08	.25
❑ 110 Jason Kidd	.25	.60
❑ 111 Danny Manning	.05	.15
❑ 112 Steve Nash	.15	.40
❑ 113 Rex Chapman	.05	.15
❑ 114 Dennis Scott	.05	.15
❑ 115 Antonio McDyess	.08	.25
❑ 116 Damon Stoudamire	.08	.25
❑ 117 Isaiah Rider	.05	.15
❑ 118 Rasheed Wallace	.15	.40
❑ 119 Kelvin Cato	.05	.15
❑ 120 Jermaine O'Neal	.15	.40
❑ 121 Corliss Williamson	.08	.25
❑ 122 Olden Polynice	.05	.15
❑ 123 Billy Owens	.05	.15
❑ 124 Lawrence Funderburke	.05	.15
❑ 125 Anthony Johnson	.05	.15
❑ 126 Tim Duncan	.25	.60
❑ 127 Sean Elliott	.08	.25
❑ 128 Avery Johnson	.05	.15
❑ 129 Vinny Del Negro	.05	.15
❑ 130 Monty Williams	.05	.15
❑ 131 Vin Baker	.08	.25
❑ 132 Hersey Hawkins	.05	.15
❑ 133 Nate McMillan	.05	.15
❑ 134 Detlef Schrempf	.08	.25
❑ 135 Gary Payton	.15	.40
❑ 136 Jim McIlvaine	.05	.15
❑ 137 Chauncey Billups	.08	.25
❑ 138 Doug Christie	.08	.25
❑ 139 John Wallace	.05	.15
❑ 140 Tracy McGrady	.40	1.00
❑ 141 Dee Brown	.05	.15
❑ 142 John Stockton	.15	.40
❑ 143 Karl Malone	.15	.40
❑ 144 Shandon Anderson	.05	.15
❑ 145 Jacque Vaughn	.05	.15
❑ 146 Bryon Russell	.05	.15
❑ 147 Lee Mayberry	.05	.15
❑ 148 Bryant Reeves	.05	.15
❑ 149 Shareef Abdur-Rahim	.15	.40
❑ 150 Michael Smith	.05	.15
❑ 151 Pete Chilcutt	.05	.15
❑ 152 Harvey Grant	.05	.15
❑ 153 Juwan Howard	.08	.25
❑ 154 Calbert Cheaney	.05	.15
❑ 155 Tracy Murray	.05	.15
❑ 156 Dikembe Mutombo FS	.05	.15
❑ 157 Antoine Walker FS	.15	.40
❑ 158 Glen Rice FS	.05	.15
❑ 159 Michael Jordan FS	.50	1.25
❑ 160 Wesley Person FS	.05	.15
❑ 161 Shawn Bradley FS	.05	.15
❑ 162 Dean Garrett FS	.05	.15
❑ 163 Jerry Stackhouse FS	.08	.25
❑ 164 Donyell Marshall FS	.08	.25
❑ 165 Hakeem Olajuwon FS	.08	.25
❑ 166 Chris Mullin FS	.08	.25
❑ 167 Isaac Austin FS	.05	.15
❑ 168 Shaquille O'Neal FS	.20	.50
❑ 169 Tim Hardaway FS	.08	.25
❑ 170 Glenn Robinson FS	.05	.15
❑ 171 Kevin Garnett FS	.15	.40
❑ 172 Keith Van Horn FS	.08	.25
❑ 173 Larry Johnson FS	.05	.15
❑ 174 Horace Grant FS	.05	.15
❑ 175 Derrick Coleman FS	.05	.15
❑ 176 Steve Nash FS	.08	.25
❑ 177 Arvydas Sabonis FS UER	.05	.15
❑ 178 Corliss Williamson FS	.05	.15
❑ 179 David Robinson FS	.15	.40
❑ 180 Vin Baker FS	.05	.15
❑ 181 Marcus Camby FS	.08	.25
❑ 182 John Stockton FS	.15	.40
❑ 183 Antonio Daniels FS	.05	.15
❑ 184 Rod Strickland FS	.05	.15
❑ 185 Michael Jordan FS	.50	1.25
❑ 186 Kobe Bryant YIR	.30	.75
❑ 187 Clyde Drexler YIR	.08	.25
❑ 188 Gary Payton YIR	.15	.40
❑ 189 Michael Jordan YIR	.50	1.25
❑ 190 D.Robinson/T.Duncan YIR	.10	.30
❑ 191 Attendance Record YIR	.05	.15
❑ 192 Karl Malone YIR	.15	.40
❑ 193 Dikembe Mutombo YIR	.05	.15
❑ 194 New Jersey Nets YIR	.15	.40
❑ 195 Ray Allen YIR	.15	.40
❑ 196 Michael Jordan YIR	.50	1.25
❑ 197 Los Angeles Lakers YIR	.30	.75
❑ 198 Michael Jordan YIR	.50	1.25
❑ 199 Michael Jordan CL	.25	.60
❑ 200 Michael Jordan CL	.25	.60

2002-03 UD Glass

COMP.SET w/o SP's (90)	15.00	40.00
COMMON CARD (1-90)	.25	.60
COMMON CW (91-110)	2.50	6.00
COMMON ROOKIE (111-120)	6.00	15.00
COMMON ROOKIE (121-130)	4.00	10.00
COMMON ROOKIE (131-150)	3.00	8.00
1 Shareef Abdur-Rahim	.30	.75
2 Glenn Robinson	.30	.75
3 Jason Terry	.40	1.00
4 Paul Pierce	.40	1.00
5 Antoine Walker	.30	.75
6 Vin Baker	.30	.75
7 Jalen Rose	.30	.75
8 Eddy Curry	.30	.75
9 Tyson Chandler	.30	.75
10 Darius Miles	.25	.60
11 Ricky Davis	.30	.75
12 Zydrunas Ilgauskas	.30	.75
13 Dirk Nowitzki	.60	1.50
14 Michael Finley	.40	1.00
15 Steve Nash	.60	1.50
16 Raef LaFrentz	.25	.60
17 Rodney White	.25	.60
18 Marcus Camby	.30	.75
19 Juwan Howard	.30	.75
20 Richard Hamilton	.30	.75
21 Ben Wallace	.30	.75
22 Chauncey Billups	.40	1.00
23 Jason Richardson	.40	1.00
24 Antawn Jamison	.40	1.00
25 Steve Francis	.40	1.00
26 Cuttino Mobley	.30	.75
27 Eddie Griffin	.25	.60
28 Jermaine O'Neal	.40	1.00
29 Reggie Miller	.40	1.00
30 Jamaal Tinsley	.30	.75
31 Andre Miller	.30	.75
32 Elton Brand	.40	1.00
33 Quentin Richardson	.30	.75
34 Kobe Bryant	2.00	5.00
35 Shaquille O'Neal	1.00	2.50
36 Robert Horry	.30	.75
37 Pau Gasol	.40	1.00
38 Shane Battier	.30	.75
39 Jason Williams	.30	.75
40 Eddie Jones	.30	.75
41 Brian Grant	.25	.60
42 Malik Allen	.25	.60
43 Ray Allen	.40	1.00
44 Tim Thomas	.25	.60
45 Sam Cassell	.30	.75
46 Kevin Garnett	.75	2.00
47 Wally Szczerbiak	.30	.75
48 Troy Hudson	.25	.60
49 Loren Woods	.25	.60
50 Jason Kidd	.60	1.50
51 Richard Jefferson	.40	1.00
52 Kenyon Martin	.40	1.00
53 Baron Davis	.40	1.00
54 Jamal Mashburn	.30	.75
55 David Wesley	.25	.60
56 P.J. Brown	.25	.60
57 Allan Houston	.30	.75
58 Kurt Thomas	.25	.60
59 Latrell Sprewell	.30	.75
60 Tracy McGrady	.75	2.00
61 Mike Miller	.30	.75
62 Grant Hill	.40	1.00
63 Allen Iverson	.75	2.00
64 Keith Van Horn	.30	.75
65 Aaron McKie	.25	.60
66 Stephon Marbury	.40	1.00
67 Shawn Marion	.40	1.00
68 Anfernee Hardaway	.40	1.00
69 Rasheed Wallace	.40	1.00
70 Damon Stoudamire	.30	.75
71 Bonzi Wells	.30	.75
72 Chris Webber	.40	1.00
73 Mike Bibby	.30	.75
74 Peja Stojakovic	.30	.75
75 Hedo Turkoglu	.30	.75
76 Tim Duncan	.75	2.00
77 David Robinson	.50	1.25
78 Tony Parker	.40	1.00
79 Gary Payton	.40	1.00
80 Rashard Lewis	.40	1.00
81 Desmond Mason	.30	.75
82 Vince Carter	.75	2.00
83 Antonio Davis	.25	.60
84 Morris Peterson	.30	.75
85 John Stockton	.50	1.25
86 Karl Malone	.40	1.00
87 Andrei Kirilenko	.40	1.00
88 Jerry Stackhouse	.30	.75
89 Larry Hughes	.30	.75
90 Michael Jordan	2.50	6.00
91 Kobe Bryant CW	15.00	40.00
92 Paul Pierce CW	3.00	8.00
93 Chris Webber CW	3.00	8.00
94 Vince Carter CW	6.00	15.00
95 Tracy McGrady CW	6.00	15.00
96 Allen Iverson CW	6.00	15.00
97 Pau Gasol CW	3.00	8.00
98 Steve Francis CW	3.00	8.00
99 Jason Kidd CW	5.00	12.00
100 Dirk Nowitzki CW	5.00	12.00
101 Antoine Walker CW	2.50	6.00
102 Jason Richardson CW	3.00	8.00
103 Baron Davis CW	3.00	8.00
104 Elton Brand CW	3.00	8.00
105 Stephon Marbury CW	3.00	8.00
106 Ray Allen CW	3.00	8.00
107 Shaquille O'Neal CW	8.00	20.00
108 Kevin Garnett CW	6.00	15.00
109 Tim Duncan CW	6.00	15.00
110 Mike Bibby CW	2.50	6.00
111 Jay Williams RC	8.00	20.00
112 Yao Ming RC	20.00	50.00
113 Mike Dunleavy RC	8.00	20.00
114 Drew Gooden RC	10.00	25.00
115 Nikoloz Tskitishvili RC	6.00	15.00
116 DaJuan Wagner RC	6.00	15.00
117 Nene Hilario RC	8.00	20.00
118 Amare Stoudemire RC	15.00	40.00
119 Caron Butler RC	12.00	30.00
120 Manu Ginobili RC	15.00	40.00
121 Juaquin Hawkins RC	4.00	10.00
122 Kareem Rush RC	5.00	12.00
123 Jiri Welsch RC	4.00	10.00
124 Chris Wilcox RC	5.00	12.00
125 Tayshaun Prince RC	6.00	15.00
126 Qyntel Woods RC	4.00	10.00
127 Jared Jeffries RC	4.00	10.00
128 Gordan Giricek RC	4.00	10.00
129 Ryan Humphrey RC	4.00	10.00
130 Marko Jaric	4.00	10.00
131 Casey Jacobsen RC	3.00	8.00
132 Dan Dickau RC	3.00	8.00
133 Juan Dixon RC	5.00	12.00
134 Melvin Ely RC	3.00	8.00
135 Fred Jones RC	4.00	10.00
136 John Salmons RC	5.00	12.00
137 Marcus Haislip RC	3.00	8.00
138 Carlos Boozer RC	6.00	15.00
139 Chris Jefferies RC	3.00	8.00
140 Smush Parker RC	3.00	8.00
141 Vincent Yarbrough RC	3.00	8.00
142 Pat Burke RC	3.00	8.00
143 Lonny Baxter RC	3.00	8.00
144 Bostjan Nachbar RC	3.00	8.00
145 Rasual Butler RC	3.00	8.00
146 Ronald Murray RC	5.00	12.00
147 J.R. Bremer RC	3.00	8.00
148 Reggie Evans RC	3.00	8.00
149 Sam Clancy RC	3.00	8.00
150 Tamar Slay RC	3.00	8.00
NNO K.Bryant AF Promo	4.00	10.00

2003-04 UD Glass

COMP.SET w/o SP's (60)	17.50	35.00
COMMON CARD (1-60)	.15	.40
COMMON LEV.3 RC (61-80)	2.00	5.00
COMMON LEV.2 RC (81-90)	3.00	8.00
COMMON LEV.1 RC (91-100)	6.00	15.00
1 Shareef Abdur-Rahim	.50	1.25
2 Jason Terry	.50	1.25
3 Paul Pierce	.50	1.25
4 Antoine Walker	.50	1.25
5 Scottie Pippen	.75	2.00
6 Jalen Rose	.50	1.25
7 Darius Miles	.50	1.25
8 Dajuan Wagner	.30	.75
9 Dirk Nowitzki	.75	2.00
10 Steve Nash	.50	1.25
11 Michael Finley	.50	1.25
12 Andre Miller	.30	.75
13 Nene	.30	.75
14 Richard Hamilton	.30	.75
15 Ben Wallace	.50	1.25
16 Jason Richardson	.50	1.25
17 Nick Van Exel	.50	1.25
18 Steve Francis	.50	1.25
19 Yao Ming	1.25	3.00
20 Jermaine O'Neal	.50	1.25
21 Reggie Miller	.50	1.25
22 Elton Brand	.50	1.25
23 Corey Maggette	.30	.75
24 Kobe Bryant	2.00	5.00
25 Shaquille O'Neal	1.25	3.00
26 Gary Payton	.50	1.25
27 Pau Gasol	.50	1.25
28 Shane Battier	.50	1.25
29 Caron Butler	.50	1.25
30 Eddie Jones	.50	1.25
31 Desmond Mason	.30	.75
32 Michael Redd	.50	1.25
33 Kevin Garnett	1.00	2.50
34 Latrell Sprewell	.50	1.25
35 Jason Kidd	.75	2.00
36 Richard Jefferson	.30	.75
37 Baron Davis	.50	1.25
38 Jamal Mashburn	.30	.75
39 Allan Houston	.30	.75
40 Keith Van Horn	.50	1.25
41 Tracy McGrady	1.25	3.00
42 Juwan Howard	.30	.75
43 Allen Iverson	1.00	2.50
44 Glenn Robinson	.50	1.25
45 Amare Stoudemire	1.00	2.50
46 Stephon Marbury	.50	1.25
47 Rasheed Wallace	.50	1.25
48 Bonzi Wells	.30	.75
49 Chris Webber	.50	1.25
50 Mike Bibby	.50	1.25
51 Tim Duncan	1.00	2.50
52 Tony Parker	.50	1.25
53 Ray Allen	.50	1.25
54 Rashard Lewis	.50	1.25
55 Vince Carter	1.25	3.00
56 Antonio Davis	.15	.40
57 Andrei Kirilenko	.50	1.25
58 Jarron Collins	.15	.40
59 Gilbert Arenas	.50	1.25
60 Jerry Stackhouse	.50	1.25
61 Kyle Korver RC	3.00	8.00
62 Travis Hansen RC	2.00	5.00
63 Willie Green RC	2.00	5.00
64 Keith Bogans RC	2.00	5.00
65 Theron Smith RC	2.00	5.00
66 Zaur Pachulia RC	2.00	5.00
67 Derrick Zimmerman RC	2.00	5.00
68 Jason Kapono RC	2.00	5.00
69 Steve Blake RC	2.00	5.00

70 Slavko Vranes RC	2.00	5.00
71 Jerome Beasley RC	2.00	5.00
72 Aleksandar Pavlovic RC	2.50	6.00
73 Boris Diaw RC	2.00	5.00
74 Kendrick Perkins RC	3.00	8.00
75 Leandro Barbosa RC	3.00	8.00
76 Josh Howard RC	2.50	6.00
77 Luke Walton RC	2.00	5.00
78 Maciej Lampe RC	2.00	5.00
79 Brian Cook RC	2.00	5.00
80 Zarko Cabarkapa RC	2.00	5.00
81 Travis Outlaw RC	4.00	10.00
82 Ndudi Ebi RC	3.00	8.00
83 David West RC	6.00	15.00
84 Reece Gaines RC	3.00	8.00
85 Dahntay Jones RC	3.00	8.00
86 Marcus Banks RC	3.00	8.00
87 Troy Bell RC	3.00	8.00
88 Luke Ridnour RC	3.00	8.00
89 Mickael Pietrus RC	3.00	8.00
90 Chris Kaman RC	4.00	10.00
91 Nick Collison RC	6.00	15.00
92 Mike Sweetney RC	6.00	15.00
93 Jarvis Hayes RC	6.00	15.00
94 T.J. Ford RC	6.00	15.00
95 Kirk Hinrich RC	6.00	15.00
96 Chris Bosh RC	10.00	25.00
97 Dwyane Wade RC	30.00	60.00
98 Carmelo Anthony RC	30.00	60.00
99 Darko Milicic RC	10.00	25.00
100 LeBron James RC	150.00	300.00

1998-99 UD Ionix

COMPLETE SET (80)	40.00	80.00
COMPLETE SET w/o RC (60)	15.00	30.00
COMMON MJ (1-6/13)	1.50	4.00
COMMON CARD (7-60)	.08	.25
COMMON ROOKIE (61-80)	.50	1.25
1 Michael Jordan	1.50	4.00
2 Michael Jordan	1.50	4.00
3 Michael Jordan	1.50	4.00
4 Michael Jordan	1.50	4.00
5 Michael Jordan	1.50	4.00
6 Michael Jordan	1.50	4.00
7 Steve Smith	.20	.50
8 Dikembe Mutombo	.20	.50
9 Ron Mercer	.15	.40
10 Antoine Walker	.30	.75
11 Derrick Coleman	.08	.25
12 Glen Rice	.20	.50
13 Michael Jordan	1.50	4.00
14 Toni Kukoc	.20	.50
15 Derek Anderson	.25	.60
16 Shawn Kemp	.20	.50
17 Michael Finley	.30	.75
18 Steve Nash	.30	.75
19 Antonio McDyess	.20	.50
20 Nick Van Exel	.30	.75
21 Grant Hill	.30	.75
22 Jerry Stackhouse	.30	.75
23 Donyell Marshall	.20	.50
24 John Starks	.20	.50
25 Charles Barkley	.40	1.00
26 Hakeem Olajuwon	.30	.75
27 Scottie Pippen	.50	1.25
28 Reggie Miller	.30	.75
29 Rik Smits	.20	.50
30 Maurice Taylor	.15	.40
31 Kobe Bryant	1.25	3.00
32 Shaquille O'Neal	.75	2.00
33 Tim Hardaway	.20	.50
34 Alonzo Mourning	.20	.50
35 Ray Allen	.30	.75
36 Glenn Robinson	.20	.50
37 Stephon Marbury	.30	.75
38 Kevin Garnett	.60	1.50
39 Jayson Williams	.08	.25
40 Keith Van Horn	.30	.75
41 Patrick Ewing	.30	.75
42 Allan Houston	.20	.50
43 Anfernee Hardaway	.30	.75
44 Isaac Austin	.08	.25
45 Tim Thomas	.20	.50
46 Allen Iverson	.60	1.50
47 Tom Gugliotta	.08	.25
48 Jason Kidd	.50	1.25
49 Damon Stoudamire	.20	.50
50 Chris Webber	.30	.75
51 Tim Duncan	.50	1.25
52 David Robinson	.30	.75
53 Gary Payton	.30	.75
54 Vin Baker	.20	.50
55 Tracy McGrady	.75	2.00
56 John Stockton	.30	.75
57 Karl Malone	.30	.75
58 Shareef Abdur-Rahim	.30	.75
59 Juwan Howard	.20	.50
60 Mitch Richmond	.20	.50
61 Michael Olowokandi RC	.75	2.00
62 Mike Bibby RC	1.50	4.00
63 Raef LaFrentz RC	.75	2.00
64 Antawn Jamison RC	2.00	5.00
65 Vince Carter RC	3.00	8.00
66 Robert Traylor RC	.50	1.25
67 Jason Williams RC	1.50	4.00
68 Larry Hughes RC	1.50	4.00
69 Dirk Nowitzki RC	6.00	12.00
70 Paul Pierce RC	4.00	10.00
71 Cuttino Mobley RC	2.00	5.00
72 Corey Benjamin RC	.50	1.25
73 Peja Stojakovic RC	2.00	5.00
74 Michael Dickerson RC	1.00	2.50
75 Matt Harpring RC	.75	2.00
76 Rashard Lewis RC	2.50	6.00
77 Pat Garrity RC	.50	1.25
78 Roshown McLeod RC	.50	1.25
79 Ricky Davis RC	1.50	4.00
80 Felipe Lopez RC	.60	1.50
J1A Michael Jordan AU	2500.00	4500.00

1999-00 UD Ionix

COMPLETE SET (90)	50.00	100.00
COMPLETE SET w/o SP (60)	10.00	25.00
COMMON CARD (1-60)	.20	.50
COMMON ROOKIE (61-90)	.75	2.00
1 Dikembe Mutombo	.25	.60
2 Isaiah Rider	.20	.50
3 Antoine Walker	.30	.75
4 Paul Pierce	.30	.75
5 Eddie Jones	.30	.75
6 Anthony Mason	.20	.50
7 Toni Kukoc	.30	.75
8 Hersey Hawkins	.20	.50
9 Shawn Kemp	.30	.75
10 Lamond Murray	.20	.50
11 Michael Finley	.30	.75
12 Cedric Ceballos	.20	.50
13 Antonio McDyess	.25	.60
14 Ron Mercer	.20	.50
15 Grant Hill	.30	.75
16 Jerry Stackhouse	.30	.75
17 Antawn Jamison	.30	.75
18 Mookie Blaylock	.20	.50
19 Charles Barkley	.40	1.00
20 Hakeem Olajuwon	.30	.75
21 Reggie Miller	.30	.75
22 Rik Smits	.30	.75
23 Maurice Taylor	.25	.60
24 Derek Anderson	.20	.50
25 Kobe Bryant	1.50	4.00
26 Shaquille O'Neal	.75	2.00
27 Tim Hardaway	.30	.75
28 Alonzo Mourning	.30	.75
29 Ray Allen	.30	.75
30 Glenn Robinson	.25	.60
31 Kevin Garnett	.60	1.50
32 Terrell Brandon	.20	.50
33 Stephon Marbury	.30	.75
34 Keith Van Horn	.25	.60
35 Allan Houston	.25	.60
36 Latrell Sprewell	.25	.60
37 Darrell Armstrong	.20	.50
38 Tariq Abdul-Wahad	.20	.50
39 Allen Iverson	.60	1.50
40 Larry Hughes	.25	.60
41 Anfernee Hardaway	.30	.75
42 Jason Kidd	.50	1.25
43 Tom Gugliotta	.20	.50
44 Scottie Pippen	.50	1.25
45 Damon Stoudamire	.30	.75
46 Rasheed Wallace	.30	.75
47 Jason Williams	.30	.75
48 Chris Webber	.30	.75
49 Tim Duncan	.60	1.50
50 David Robinson	.40	1.00
51 Gary Payton	.30	.75
52 Vin Baker	.30	.75
53 Vince Carter	.60	1.50
54 Tracy McGrady	.60	1.50
55 Karl Malone	.40	1.00
56 John Stockton	.40	1.00
57 Mike Bibby	.30	.75
58 Shareef Abdur-Rahim	.25	.60
59 Mitch Richmond	.25	.60
60 Juwan Howard	.25	.60
61 Elton Brand RC	2.50	6.00
62 Steve Francis RC	2.50	6.00
63 Baron Davis RC	3.00	8.00
64 Lamar Odom RC	2.50	6.00
65 Jonathan Bender RC	.75	2.00
66 Wally Szczerbiak RC	2.50	6.00
67 Richard Hamilton RC	2.50	6.00
68 Andre Miller RC	2.50	6.00
69 Shawn Marion RC	2.50	6.00
70 Jason Terry RC	2.00	5.00
71 Trajan Langdon RC	.75	2.00
72 A.Radojevic RC	.75	2.00
73 Corey Maggette RC	2.50	6.00
74 William Avery RC	.75	2.00
75 Ron Artest RC	3.00	8.00
76 Cal Bowdler RC	.75	2.00
77 James Posey RC	1.25	3.00
78 Quincy Lewis RC	.75	2.00
79 Dion Glover RC	.75	2.00
80 Jeff Foster RC	1.00	2.50
81 Kenny Thomas RC	.75	2.00
82 Devean George RC	1.25	3.00
83 Tim James RC	.75	2.00
84 Vonteego Cummings RC	.75	2.00
85 Jumaine Jones RC	.75	2.00
86 Scott Padgett RC	.75	2.00
87 Chucky Atkins RC	1.00	2.50
88 Adrian Griffin RC	.75	2.00
89 Todd MacCulloch RC	.75	2.00
90 Anthony Carter RC	1.50	4.00

2005-06 UD Portraits

COMP.SET w/o SP's (100)	50.00	125.00
COMMON CARD (1-100)	.25	.60
COMMON ROOKIE (101-136)	2.00	5.00
COMMON ROOKIE (137-142)	4.00	10.00
1 Al Harrington	.50	1.25
2 Al Jefferson	.75	2.00
3 Allen Iverson	1.50	4.00
4 Amare Stoudemire	1.50	4.00
5 Andre Iguodala	.75	2.00
6 Andre Miller	.60	1.50
7 Andrei Kirilenko	.75	2.00

❑ 8 Antawn Jamison	.75	2.00
❑ 9 Antoine Walker	.60	1.50
❑ 10 Baron Davis	.75	2.00
❑ 11 Ben Gordon	1.00	2.50
❑ 12 Ben Wallace	.75	2.00
❑ 13 Bob Sura	.50	1.25
❑ 14 Brevin Knight	.50	1.25
❑ 15 Carlos Boozer	.75	2.00
❑ 16 Carmelo Anthony	1.50	4.00
❑ 17 Caron Butler	.75	2.00
❑ 18 Chauncey Billups	.75	2.00
❑ 19 Chris Bosh	.75	2.00
❑ 20 Chris Webber	.75	2.00
❑ 21 Corey Maggette	.60	1.50
❑ 22 Cuttino Mobley	.60	1.50
❑ 23 Damon Jones	.60	1.50
❑ 24 Dan Dickau	.50	1.25
❑ 25 Desmond Mason	.50	1.25
❑ 26 Dirk Nowitzki	1.25	3.00
❑ 27 Donyell Marshall	.50	1.25
❑ 28 Drew Gooden	.60	1.50
❑ 29 Dwight Howard	1.50	4.00
❑ 30 Dwyane Wade	2.00	5.00
❑ 31 Elton Brand	.75	2.00
❑ 32 Emeka Okafor	.75	2.00
❑ 33 Gary Payton	.75	2.00
❑ 34 Gerald Wallace	.75	2.00
❑ 35 Gilbert Arenas	.75	2.00
❑ 36 Grant Hill	.75	2.00
❑ 37 J.R. Smith	.60	1.50
❑ 38 Jalen Rose	.75	2.00
❑ 39 Jamaal Magloire	.50	1.25
❑ 40 Jamaal Tinsley	.60	1.50
❑ 41 Jamal Crawford	.60	1.50
❑ 42 Jameer Nelson	.60	1.50
❑ 43 Jason Kidd	1.25	3.00
❑ 44 Jason Richardson	.75	2.00
❑ 45 Jason Terry	.75	2.00
❑ 46 Jason Williams	.60	1.50
❑ 47 Jermaine O'Neal	.75	2.00
❑ 48 Joe Johnson	.75	2.00
❑ 49 Josh Childress	.60	1.50
❑ 50 Josh Howard	.75	2.00
❑ 51 Josh Smith	.75	2.00
❑ 52 Kenyon Martin	.75	2.00
❑ 53 Kevin Garnett	1.50	4.00
❑ 54 Kirk Hinrich	.75	2.00
❑ 55 Kobe Bryant	4.00	10.00
❑ 56 Kurt Thomas	.50	1.25
❑ 57 Kyle Korver	.75	2.00
❑ 58 Lamar Odom	.75	2.00
❑ 59 Larry Hughes	.60	1.50
❑ 60 Eddie Griffin	.50	1.25
❑ 61 LeBron James	4.00	10.00
❑ 62 Luke Ridnour	.60	1.50
❑ 63 Luol Deng	.75	2.00
❑ 64 Manu Ginobili	.75	2.00
❑ 65 Marcus Camby	.60	1.50
❑ 66 Maurice Williams	.60	1.50
❑ 67 Michael Finley	.75	2.00
❑ 68 Michael Jordan	5.00	12.00
❑ 69 Michael Redd	.75	2.00
❑ 70 Mike Bibby	.75	2.00
❑ 71 Pau Gasol	.75	2.00
❑ 72 Paul Pierce	.75	2.00
❑ 73 Peja Stojakovic	.75	2.00
❑ 74 Raja Bell	.50	1.25
❑ 75 Rashard Lewis	.75	2.00
❑ 76 Rasheed Wallace	.75	2.00
❑ 77 Ray Allen	.75	2.00
❑ 78 Richard Hamilton	.60	1.50
❑ 79 Richard Jefferson	.60	1.50
❑ 80 Ron Artest	.60	1.50
❑ 81 Sam Cassell	.75	2.00
❑ 82 Sebastian Telfair	.60	1.50
❑ 83 Shaquille O'Neal	2.00	5.00
❑ 84 Shareef Abdur-Rahim	.75	2.00
❑ 85 Shaun Livingston	.50	1.25
❑ 86 Shawn Marion	.75	2.00
❑ 87 Stephon Marbury	.75	2.00
❑ 88 Steve Francis	.75	2.00
❑ 89 Steve Nash	1.00	2.50
❑ 90 Stromile Swift	.60	1.50
❑ 91 Tim Duncan	1.50	4.00
❑ 92 Tony Parker	.75	2.00
❑ 93 Tracy McGrady	1.50	4.00
❑ 94 Troy Murphy	.75	2.00
❑ 95 Tyronn Lue	.50	1.25
❑ 96 Vince Carter	1.50	4.00
❑ 97 Vladimir Radmanovic	.50	1.25
❑ 98 Yao Ming	2.00	5.00
❑ 99 Zach Randolph	.75	2.00
❑ 100 Zydrunas Ilgauskas	.60	1.50
❑ 101 Andray Blatche RC	2.50	6.00
❑ 102 Andrew Bynum RC	6.00	15.00
❑ 103 Antoine Wright RC	2.00	5.00
❑ 104 Brandon Bass RC	2.00	5.00
❑ 105 C.J. Miles RC	2.00	5.00
❑ 106 Channing Frye RC	2.50	6.00
❑ 107 Charlie Villanueva RC	3.00	8.00
❑ 108 Chris Taft RC	2.00	5.00
❑ 109 Daniel Ewing RC	2.50	6.00
❑ 110 Danny Granger RC	5.00	12.00
❑ 111 David Lee RC	4.00	10.00
❑ 112 Dijon Thompson RC	2.00	5.00
❑ 113 Ersan Ilyasova RC	2.00	5.00
❑ 114 Sarunas Jasikevicius RC	2.50	6.00
❑ 115 Francisco Garcia RC	2.50	6.00
❑ 116 Gerald Green RC	2.00	5.00
❑ 117 Hakim Warrick RC	3.00	8.00
❑ 118 Jose Calderon RC	2.00	5.00
❑ 119 Ike Diogu RC	2.50	6.00
❑ 120 Jarrett Jack RC	2.00	5.00
❑ 121 Jason Maxiell RC	2.50	6.00
❑ 122 Joey Graham RC	2.00	5.00
❑ 123 Julius Hodge RC	2.50	6.00
❑ 124 Linas Kleiza RC	2.50	6.00
❑ 125 Louis Williams RC	3.00	8.00
❑ 126 Luther Head RC	2.50	6.00
❑ 127 Martell Webster RC	2.00	5.00
❑ 128 Monta Ellis RC	5.00	12.00
❑ 129 Nate Robinson RC	3.00	8.00
❑ 130 Rashad McCants RC	2.50	6.00
❑ 131 James Singleton RC	2.00	5.00
❑ 132 Ryan Gomes RC	2.00	5.00
❑ 133 Salim Stoudamire RC	2.50	6.00
❑ 134 Travis Diener RC	2.00	5.00
❑ 135 Wayne Simien RC	2.50	6.00
❑ 136 Yaroslav Korolev RC	2.00	5.00
❑ 137 Andrew Bogut RC	4.00	10.00
❑ 138 Chris Paul RC	10.00	25.00
❑ 139 Deron Williams RC	8.00	20.00
❑ 140 Raymond Felton RC	4.00	10.00
❑ 141 Marvin Williams RC	5.00	12.00
❑ 142 Sean May RC	4.00	10.00

2000-01 UD Reserve

❑ COMP.SET w/o SP's (90)	10.00	25.00
❑ COMMON CARD (1-90)	.20	.50
❑ COMMON ROOKIE (91-120)	.40	1.00
❑ 1 Dikembe Mutombo	.25	.60
❑ 2 Jason Terry	.30	.75
❑ 3 Alan Henderson	.20	.50
❑ 4 Paul Pierce	.30	.75
❑ 5 Antoine Walker	.25	.60
❑ 6 Kenny Anderson	.25	.60
❑ 7 Derrick Coleman	.25	.60
❑ 8 Baron Davis	.30	.75
❑ 9 Jamal Mashburn	.25	.60
❑ 10 Elton Brand	.30	.75
❑ 11 Ron Mercer	.20	.50
❑ 12 Ron Artest	.30	.75
❑ 13 Lamond Murray	.20	.50
❑ 14 Andre Miller	.25	.60
❑ 15 Matt Harpring	.25	.60
❑ 16 Michael Finley	.30	.75
❑ 17 Dirk Nowitzki	.50	1.25
❑ 18 Steve Nash	.50	1.25
❑ 19 Antonio McDyess	.25	.60
❑ 20 James Posey	.20	.50
❑ 21 Nick Van Exel	.25	.60
❑ 22 Jerry Stackhouse	.25	.60
❑ 23 Jerome Williams	.20	.50
❑ 24 Chucky Atkins	.20	.50
❑ 25 Antawn Jamison	.30	.75
❑ 26 Larry Hughes	.25	.60
❑ 27 Chris Mills	.20	.50
❑ 28 Steve Francis	.30	.75
❑ 29 Hakeem Olajuwon	.40	1.00
❑ 30 Cuttino Mobley	.25	.60
❑ 31 Reggie Miller	.30	.75
❑ 32 Jalen Rose	.25	.60
❑ 33 Austin Croshere	.20	.50
❑ 34 Lamar Odom	.30	.75
❑ 35 Jeff McInnis	.20	.50
❑ 36 Corey Maggette	.25	.60
❑ 37 Shaquille O'Neal	.75	2.00
❑ 38 Kobe Bryant	1.50	4.00
❑ 39 Isaiah Rider	.25	.60
❑ 40 Horace Grant	.25	.60
❑ 41 Eddie Jones	.25	.60
❑ 42 Tim Hardaway	.25	.60
❑ 43 Brian Grant	.20	.50
❑ 44 Ray Allen	.30	.75
❑ 45 Tim Thomas	.20	.50
❑ 46 Glenn Robinson	.25	.60
❑ 47 Sam Cassell	.25	.60
❑ 48 Kevin Garnett	.60	1.50
❑ 49 Wally Szczerbiak	.25	.60
❑ 50 Terrell Brandon	.20	.50
❑ 51 Chauncey Billups	.30	.75
❑ 52 Stephon Marbury	.30	.75
❑ 53 Keith Van Horn	.25	.60
❑ 54 Kendall Gill	.20	.50
❑ 55 Latrell Sprewell	.25	.60
❑ 56 Marcus Camby	.25	.60
❑ 57 Allan Houston	.25	.60
❑ 58 Grant Hill	.30	.75
❑ 59 Tracy McGrady	.60	1.50
❑ 60 Darrell Armstrong	.20	.50
❑ 61 Allen Iverson	.60	1.50
❑ 62 Theo Ratliff	.20	.50
❑ 63 Toni Kukoc	.25	.60
❑ 64 Jason Kidd	.50	1.25
❑ 65 Clifford Robinson	.20	.50
❑ 66 Shawn Marion	.30	.75
❑ 67 Rasheed Wallace	.30	.75
❑ 68 Scottie Pippen	.50	1.25
❑ 69 Damon Stoudamire	.25	.60
❑ 70 Chris Webber	.30	.75
❑ 71 Jason Williams	.25	.60
❑ 72 Vlade Divac	.25	.60
❑ 73 Tim Duncan	.60	1.50
❑ 74 David Robinson	.40	1.00
❑ 75 Derek Anderson	.25	.60
❑ 76 Gary Payton	.30	.75
❑ 77 Patrick Ewing	.40	1.00
❑ 78 Rashard Lewis	.30	.75
❑ 79 Vince Carter	.60	1.50
❑ 80 Mark Jackson	.25	.60
❑ 81 Antonio Davis	.20	.50
❑ 82 Karl Malone	.40	1.00
❑ 83 John Stockton	.40	1.00
❑ 84 John Starks	.20	.50
❑ 85 Shareef Abdur-Rahim	.25	.60
❑ 86 Mike Bibby	.25	.60
❑ 87 Michael Dickerson	.20	.50
❑ 88 Mitch Richmond	.25	.60
❑ 89 Richard Hamilton	.25	.60
❑ 90 Juwan Howard	.25	.60
❑ 91 Kenyon Martin RC	1.00	2.50
❑ 92 Stromile Swift RC	.50	1.25
❑ 93 Darius Miles RC	.50	1.25
❑ 94 Marcus Fizer RC	.40	1.00
❑ 95 Mike Miller RC	.60	1.50
❑ 96 DerMarr Johnson RC	.40	1.00
❑ 97 Chris Mihm RC	.40	1.00
❑ 98 Jamal Crawford RC	.60	1.50
❑ 99 Joel Przybilla RC	.40	1.00
❑ 100 Keyon Dooling RC	.40	1.00
❑ 101 Jerome Moiso RC	.40	1.00
❑ 102 Etan Thomas RC	.40	1.00
❑ 103 Courtney Alexander RC	.40	1.00
❑ 104 Mateen Cleaves RC	.40	1.00
❑ 105 Hedo Turkoglu RC	1.00	2.50
❑ 106 Desmond Mason RC	.50	1.25
❑ 107 Quentin Richardson RC	.50	1.25
❑ 108 Jamaal Magloire RC	.40	1.00
❑ 109 Speedy Claxton RC	.40	1.00
❑ 110 Morris Peterson RC	.60	1.50
❑ 111 Donnell Harvey RC	.40	1.00
❑ 112 DeShawn Stevenson RC	.40	1.00
❑ 113 Mamadou N'Diaye RC	.40	1.00
❑ 114 Erick Barkley RC	.40	1.00

❑ 115 Mark Madsen RC .40 1.00
❑ 116 Eduardo Najera RC .40 1.00
❑ 117 Lavor Postell RC .40 1.00
❑ 118 Hanno Mottola RC .40 1.00
❑ 119 Stephen Jackson RC .60 1.50
❑ 120 Marc Jackson RC .50 1.25

2006-07 UD Reserve

❑ COMP.SET w/o SP's (200) 30.00 60.00
❑ 1 Josh Childress .50 1.25
❑ 2 Al Harrington .40 1.00
❑ 3 Joe Johnson .50 1.25
❑ 4 Josh Smith .60 1.50
❑ 5 Salim Stoudamire .50 1.25
❑ 6 Marvin Williams .60 1.50
❑ 7 Tony Allen .50 1.25
❑ 8 Dan Dickau .40 1.00
❑ 9 Al Jefferson .60 1.50
❑ 10 Raef LaFrentz .40 1.00
❑ 11 Michael Olowokandi .40 1.00
❑ 12 Paul Pierce .60 1.50
❑ 13 Wally Szczerbiak .50 1.25
❑ 14 Brevin Knight .40 1.00
❑ 15 Raymond Felton .75 2.00
❑ 16 Othella Harrington .40 1.00
❑ 17 Sean May .50 1.25
❑ 18 Emeka Okafor .60 1.50
❑ 19 Primoz Brezec .40 1.00
❑ 20 Gerald Wallace .60 1.50
❑ 21 Tyson Chandler .60 1.50
❑ 22 Michael Jordan 4.00 10.00
❑ 23 Luol Deng .60 1.50
❑ 24 Chris Duhon .40 1.00
❑ 25 Ben Gordon .75 2.00
❑ 26 Kirk Hinrich .60 1.50
❑ 27 Mike Sweetney .40 1.00
❑ 28 Drew Gooden .50 1.25
❑ 29 Larry Hughes .50 1.25
❑ 30 Zydrunas Ilgauskas .50 1.25
❑ 31 LeBron James 3.00 8.00
❑ 32 Damon Jones .50 1.25
❑ 33 Donyell Marshall .40 1.00
❑ 34 Anderson Varejao .50 1.25
❑ 35 Erick Dampier .40 1.00
❑ 36 Marquis Daniels .50 1.25
❑ 37 Devin Harris .60 1.50
❑ 38 Josh Howard .60 1.50
❑ 39 Dirk Nowitzki 1.00 2.50
❑ 40 Jerry Stackhouse .60 1.50
❑ 41 Jason Terry .60 1.50
❑ 42 Carmelo Anthony .75 2.00
❑ 43 Earl Boykins .40 1.00
❑ 44 Marcus Camby .50 1.25
❑ 45 Kenyon Martin .60 1.50
❑ 46 Andre Miller .50 1.25
❑ 47 Eduardo Najera .40 1.00
❑ 48 Nene .40 1.00
❑ 49 Chauncey Billups .60 1.50
❑ 50 Richard Hamilton .50 1.25
❑ 51 Lindsey Hunter .40 1.00
❑ 52 Antonio McDyess .40 1.00
❑ 53 Tayshaun Prince .60 1.50
❑ 54 Ben Wallace .60 1.50
❑ 55 Rasheed Wallace .60 1.50
❑ 56 Baron Davis .60 1.50
❑ 57 Ike Diogu .50 1.25
❑ 58 Mike Dunleavy .50 1.25
❑ 59 Derek Fisher .50 1.25
❑ 60 Troy Murphy .60 1.50
❑ 61 Mickael Pietrus .50 1.25
❑ 62 Jason Richardson .60 1.50
❑ 63 Rafer Alston .40 1.00
❑ 64 Luther Head .50 1.25
❑ 65 Juwan Howard .50 1.25
❑ 66 Tracy McGrady 1.25 3.00
❑ 67 Dikembe Mutombo .50 1.25
❑ 68 Stromile Swift .50 1.25
❑ 69 Yao Ming 1.50 4.00
❑ 70 Austin Croshere .40 1.00
❑ 71 Stephen Jackson .50 1.25
❑ 72 Sarunas Jasikevicius .50 1.25
❑ 73 Jermaine O'Neal .60 1.50
❑ 74 Peja Stojakovic .60 1.50
❑ 75 Jamaal Tinsley .50 1.25
❑ 76 Elton Brand .60 1.50
❑ 77 Sam Cassell .60 1.50
❑ 78 Chris Kaman .40 1.00
❑ 79 Shaun Livingston .40 1.00
❑ 80 Corey Maggette .50 1.25
❑ 81 Cuttino Mobley .50 1.25
❑ 82 Vladimir Radmanovic .40 1.00
❑ 83 Kwame Brown .50 1.25
❑ 84 Kobe Bryant 3.00 8.00
❑ 85 Devean George .50 1.25
❑ 86 Lamar Odom .60 1.50
❑ 87 Ronny Turiaf .50 1.25
❑ 88 Sasha Vujacic .40 1.00
❑ 89 Luke Walton .50 1.25
❑ 90 Shane Battier .60 1.50
❑ 91 Pau Gasol .60 1.50
❑ 92 Bobby Jackson .40 1.00
❑ 93 Eddie Jones .40 1.00
❑ 94 Mike Miller .60 1.50
❑ 95 Damon Stoudamire .50 1.25
❑ 96 Hakim Warrick .50 1.25
❑ 97 Alonzo Mourning .75 2.00
❑ 98 Shaquille O'Neal 1.50 4.00
❑ 99 Gary Payton .60 1.50
❑ 100 Wayne Simien .50 1.25
❑ 101 Dwyane Wade 1.50 4.00
❑ 102 Antoine Walker .50 1.25
❑ 103 Jason Williams .50 1.25
❑ 104 Andrew Bogut .60 1.50
❑ 105 T.J. Ford .50 1.25
❑ 106 Jamaal Magloire .40 1.00
❑ 107 Michael Redd .60 1.50
❑ 108 Bobby Simmons .40 1.00
❑ 109 Maurice Williams .50 1.25
❑ 110 Ricky Davis .60 1.50
❑ 111 Kevin Garnett 1.25 3.00
❑ 112 Kelenna Azubuike .75 2.00
❑ 113 Trenton Hassell .40 1.00
❑ 114 Troy Hudson .40 1.00
❑ 115 Rashad McCants .50 1.25
❑ 116 Vince Carter 1.25 3.00
❑ 117 Jason Collins .40 1.00
❑ 118 Richard Jefferson .50 1.25
❑ 119 Jason Kidd 1.00 2.50
❑ 120 Nenad Krstic .50 1.25
❑ 121 Jeff McInnis .40 1.00
❑ 122 Antoine Wright .40 1.00
❑ 123 P.J. Brown .40 1.00
❑ 124 Speedy Claxton .40 1.00
❑ 125 Desmond Mason .40 1.00
❑ 126 Chris Paul 1.25 3.00
❑ 127 J.R. Smith .50 1.25
❑ 128 Kirk Snyder .40 1.00
❑ 129 David West .60 1.50
❑ 130 Jamal Crawford .40 1.00
❑ 131 Eddy Curry .50 1.25
❑ 132 Channing Frye .50 1.25
❑ 133 Stephon Marbury .60 1.50
❑ 134 Quentin Richardson .50 1.25
❑ 135 Nate Robinson .60 1.50
❑ 136 David Lee .50 1.25
❑ 137 Carlos Arroyo .60 1.50
❑ 138 Tony Battie .40 1.00
❑ 139 Keyon Dooling .40 1.00
❑ 140 Grant Hill .60 1.50
❑ 141 Dwight Howard 1.25 3.00
❑ 142 Darko Milicic .60 1.50
❑ 143 Jameer Nelson .50 1.25
❑ 144 Samuel Dalembert .40 1.00
❑ 145 Steven Hunter .40 1.00
❑ 146 Andre Iguodala .60 1.50
❑ 147 Allen Iverson 1.25 3.00
❑ 148 Kyle Korver .60 1.50
❑ 149 Shavlik Randolph .40 1.00
❑ 150 Chris Webber .60 1.50
❑ 151 Raja Bell .40 1.00
❑ 152 Boris Diaw .50 1.25
❑ 153 Shawn Marion .60 1.50
❑ 154 Steve Nash .75 2.00
❑ 155 Amare Stoudemire 1.25 3.00
❑ 156 Kurt Thomas .40 1.00
❑ 157 Tim Thomas .40 1.00
❑ 158 Steve Blake .40 1.00
❑ 159 Juan Dixon .40 1.00
❑ 160 Zach Randolph .60 1.50
❑ 161 Joel Przybilla .40 1.00
❑ 162 Sebastian Telfair .50 1.25
❑ 163 Martell Webster .50 1.25
❑ 164 Shareef Abdur-Rahim .60 1.50
❑ 165 Ron Artest .60 1.50
❑ 166 Mike Bibby .60 1.50
❑ 167 Brad Miller .60 1.50
❑ 168 Kenny Thomas .40 1.00
❑ 169 Bonzi Wells .50 1.25
❑ 170 Bruce Bowen .40 1.00
❑ 171 Tim Duncan 1.25 3.00
❑ 172 Michael Finley .60 1.50
❑ 173 Manu Ginobili .60 1.50
❑ 174 Nazr Mohammed .40 1.00
❑ 175 Tony Parker .60 1.50
❑ 176 Ray Allen .60 1.50
❑ 177 Danny Fortson .40 1.00
❑ 178 Rashard Lewis .60 1.50
❑ 179 Luke Ridnour .50 1.25
❑ 180 Earl Watson .40 1.00
❑ 181 Chris Wilcox .40 1.00
❑ 182 Rafael Araujo .40 1.00
❑ 183 Chris Bosh .60 1.50
❑ 184 Joey Graham .50 1.25
❑ 185 Mike James .40 1.00
❑ 186 Morris Peterson .50 1.25
❑ 187 Charlie Villanueva .60 1.50
❑ 188 Carlos Boozer .60 1.50
❑ 189 Matt Harpring .50 1.25
❑ 190 Kris Humphries .40 1.00
❑ 191 Andrei Kirilenko .60 1.50
❑ 192 C.J. Miles .40 1.00
❑ 193 Paul Millsap 1.00 2.50
❑ 194 Deron Williams 1.00 2.50
❑ 195 Gilbert Arenas .60 1.50
❑ 196 Andray Blatche .40 1.00
❑ 197 Caron Butler .60 1.50
❑ 198 Antonio Daniels .40 1.00
❑ 199 Brendan Haywood .40 1.00
❑ 200 Antawn Jamison .60 1.50
❑ 201 Andrea Bargnani RC 2.00 5.00
❑ 202 LaMarcus Aldridge RC 1.50 4.00
❑ 203 Adam Morrison RC 1.50 4.00
❑ 204 Tyrus Thomas RC 1.50 4.00
❑ 205 Shelden Williams RC 1.50 4.00
❑ 206 Brandon Roy RC 3.00 8.00
❑ 207 Randy Foye RC 1.25 3.00
❑ 208 Rudy Gay RC 1.25 3.00
❑ 209 Patrick O'Bryant RC 1.25 3.00
❑ 210 Saer Sene RC 1.25 3.00
❑ 211 J.J. Redick RC 1.25 3.00
❑ 212 Hilton Armstrong RC 1.25 3.00
❑ 213 Thabo Sefolosha RC 1.50 4.00
❑ 214 Ronnie Brewer RC 1.50 4.00
❑ 215 Cedric Simmons RC 1.25 3.00
❑ 216 Rodney Carney RC 1.25 3.00
❑ 217 Shawne Williams RC 1.25 3.00
❑ 218 Quincy Douby RC 1.25 3.00
❑ 219 Renaldo Balkman RC 1.25 3.00
❑ 220 Rajon Rondo RC 5.00 12.00
❑ 221 Marcus Williams RC 1.50 4.00
❑ 222 Josh Boone RC 1.25 3.00
❑ 223 Kyle Lowry RC 1.25 3.00
❑ 224 Shannon Brown RC 1.25 3.00
❑ 225 Jordan Farmar RC 1.50 4.00
❑ 226 Maurice Ager RC 1.25 3.00
❑ 227 Mardy Collins RC 1.25 3.00
❑ 228 Jorge Garbajosa RC 2.50 6.00
❑ 229 James White RC 1.25 3.00
❑ 230 Steve Novak RC 1.25 3.00
❑ 231 Solomon Jones RC 1.25 3.00
❑ 232 Paul Davis RC 1.25 3.00
❑ 233 P.J. Tucker RC 1.25 3.00
❑ 234 Craig Smith RC 1.25 3.00
❑ 235 Bobby Jones RC 1.25 3.00
❑ 236 David Noel RC 1.25 3.00
❑ 237 Vassilis Spanoulis RC 1.25 3.00
❑ 238 James Augustine RC 1.25 3.00
❑ 239 Daniel Gibson RC 1.50 4.00
❑ 240 Alexander Johnson RC 1.25 3.00

2003 UD Superstars LeBron James

❑ COMPLETE SET (6)	10.00	25.00
❑ COMMON CARD (LBJ1-LBJ6)	2.00	5.00

2000-01 Ultimate Collection

❑ COMMON CARD (1-60)	1.50	4.00
❑ COMMON ROOKIE	3.00	8.00
❑ 1 Dikembe Mutombo	2.00	5.00
❑ 2 Hanno Mottola RC	3.00	8.00
❑ 3 Paul Pierce	2.50	6.00
❑ 4 Antoine Walker	2.00	5.00
❑ 5 Derrick Coleman	2.00	5.00
❑ 6 Baron Davis	2.50	6.00
❑ 7 Elton Brand	2.50	6.00
❑ 8 Michael Jordan	20.00	50.00
❑ 9 Andre Miller	2.00	5.00
❑ 10 Chris Mihm RC	3.00	8.00
❑ 11 Michael Finley	2.50	6.00
❑ 12 Donnell Harvey RC	3.00	8.00
❑ 13 Antonio McDyess	2.00	5.00
❑ 14 Nick Van Exel	2.00	5.00
❑ 15 Jerry Stackhouse	2.00	5.00
❑ 16 Jerome Williams	1.50	4.00
❑ 17 Larry Hughes	2.00	5.00
❑ 18 Antawn Jamison	2.50	6.00
❑ 19 Steve Francis	2.50	6.00
❑ 20 Hakeem Olajuwon	3.00	8.00
❑ 21 Reggie Miller	2.50	6.00
❑ 22 Jalen Rose	2.00	5.00
❑ 23 Lamar Odom	2.50	6.00
❑ 24 Michael Olowokandi	1.50	4.00
❑ 25 Shaquille O'Neal	6.00	15.00
❑ 26 Kobe Bryant	12.00	30.00
❑ 27 Ron Harper	2.00	5.00
❑ 28 Alonzo Mourning	2.50	6.00
❑ 29 Eddie House RC	3.00	8.00
❑ 30 Glenn Robinson	2.00	5.00
❑ 31 Ray Allen	2.50	6.00
❑ 32 Kevin Garnett	5.00	12.00
❑ 33 Wally Szczerbiak	2.00	5.00
❑ 34 Terrell Brandon	1.50	4.00
❑ 35 Stephon Marbury	2.50	6.00
❑ 36 Keith Van Horn	2.00	5.00
❑ 37 Allan Houston	2.00	5.00
❑ 38 Latrell Sprewell	2.00	5.00
❑ 39 Grant Hill	2.50	6.00
❑ 40 Tracy McGrady	5.00	12.00
❑ 41 Allen Iverson	5.00	12.00
❑ 42 Toni Kukoc	2.00	5.00
❑ 43 Jason Kidd	4.00	10.00
❑ 44 Anfernee Hardaway	2.50	6.00
❑ 45 Scottie Pippen	4.00	10.00
❑ 46 Rasheed Wallace	2.50	6.00
❑ 47 Chris Webber	2.50	6.00
❑ 48 Jason Williams	2.00	5.00
❑ 49 Tim Duncan	5.00	12.00
❑ 50 David Robinson	3.00	8.00
❑ 51 Gary Payton	2.50	6.00
❑ 52 Rashard Lewis	2.50	6.00
❑ 53 Vince Carter	5.00	12.00
❑ 54 Morris Peterson RC	5.00	12.00
❑ 55 Karl Malone	3.00	8.00
❑ 56 John Stockton	3.00	8.00
❑ 57 Shareef Abdur-Rahim	2.00	5.00
❑ 58 Mike Bibby	2.00	5.00
❑ 59 Mike Smith RC	3.00	8.00
❑ 60 Richard Hamilton	2.00	5.00
❑ P1 Kenyon Martin SAMPLE		

2001-02 Ultimate Collection

❑ COMPLETE SET (90)	1250.00	2500.00
❑ COMP.SET w/o SP's (60)	250.00	500.00
❑ COMMON CARD (1-60)	1.50	4.00
❑ COMMON ROOKIE (61-70)	3.00	8.00
❑ COMMON ROOKIE (71-84)	8.00	20.00
❑ 1 Jason Terry	2.50	6.00
❑ 2 Shareef Abdur-Rahim	2.00	5.00
❑ 3 Paul Pierce	2.50	6.00
❑ 4 Antoine Walker	2.00	5.00
❑ 5 Baron Davis	2.50	6.00
❑ 6 Jamal Mashburn	2.00	5.00
❑ 7 Ron Mercer	1.50	4.00
❑ 8 Marcus Fizer	1.50	4.00
❑ 9 Andre Miller	2.00	5.00
❑ 10 Lamond Murray	1.50	4.00
❑ 11 Dirk Nowitzki	4.00	10.00
❑ 12 Michael Finley	2.50	6.00
❑ 13 Antonio McDyess	2.00	5.00
❑ 14 Nick Van Exel	2.00	5.00
❑ 15 Jerry Stackhouse	2.00	5.00
❑ 16 Zeljko Rebraca RC	6.00	15.00
❑ 17 Antawn Jamison	2.50	6.00
❑ 18 Larry Hughes	2.00	5.00
❑ 19 Steve Francis	2.50	6.00
❑ 20 Cuttino Mobley	2.00	5.00
❑ 21 Reggie Miller	2.50	6.00
❑ 22 Jalen Rose	2.00	5.00
❑ 23 Darius Miles	1.50	4.00
❑ 24 Quentin Richardson	2.00	5.00
❑ 25 Kobe Bryant	12.00	30.00
❑ 26 Shaquille O'Neal	6.00	15.00
❑ 27 Mitch Richmond	2.00	5.00
❑ 28 Stromile Swift	1.50	4.00
❑ 29 Jason Williams	2.00	5.00
❑ 30 Alonzo Mourning	2.50	6.00
❑ 31 Eddie Jones	2.00	5.00
❑ 32 Ray Allen	2.50	6.00
❑ 33 Glenn Robinson	2.00	5.00
❑ 34 Kevin Garnett	5.00	12.00
❑ 35 Terrell Brandon	1.50	4.00
❑ 36 Wally Szczerbiak	2.00	5.00
❑ 37 Jason Kidd	4.00	10.00
❑ 38 Kenyon Martin	2.50	6.00
❑ 39 Latrell Sprewell	2.00	5.00
❑ 40 Allan Houston	2.00	5.00
❑ 41 Tracy McGrady	5.00	12.00
❑ 42 Grant Hill	2.50	6.00
❑ 43 Allen Iverson	5.00	12.00
❑ 44 Dikembe Mutombo	2.00	5.00
❑ 45 Stephon Marbury	2.50	6.00
❑ 46 Anfernee Hardaway	2.50	6.00
❑ 47 Rasheed Wallace	2.50	6.00
❑ 48 Derek Anderson	2.00	5.00
❑ 49 Chris Webber	2.50	6.00
❑ 50 Peja Stojakovic	2.00	5.00
❑ 51 Tim Duncan	5.00	12.00
❑ 52 David Robinson	3.00	8.00
❑ 53 Rashard Lewis	2.50	6.00
❑ 54 Desmond Mason	2.00	5.00
❑ 55 Vince Carter	5.00	12.00
❑ 56 Morris Peterson	2.00	5.00
❑ 57 Karl Malone	3.00	8.00
❑ 58 John Stockton	3.00	8.00
❑ 59 Richard Hamilton	2.00	5.00
❑ 60 Michael Jordan	30.00	60.00
❑ 61 Andrei Kirilenko RC	8.00	20.00
❑ 62 Gilbert Arenas RC	5.00	12.00
❑ 63 Trenton Hassell RC	4.00	10.00
❑ 64 Tony Parker RC	12.00	30.00
❑ 65 Jamaal Tinsley RC	4.00	10.00
❑ 66 Samuel Dalembert RC	4.00	10.00
❑ 67 Gerald Wallace RC	8.00	20.00
❑ 68 Brandon Armstrong RC	3.00	8.00
❑ 69 Jeryl Sasser RC	3.00	8.00
❑ 70 Joseph Forte RC	3.00	8.00
❑ 71 Pau Gasol RC	40.00	75.00
❑ 72 Brendan Haywood RC	10.00	25.00
❑ 73 Zach Randolph RC	20.00	50.00
❑ 74 Jason Collins RC	8.00	20.00
❑ 75 Michael Bradley RC	8.00	20.00
❑ 76 Kirk Haston RC	8.00	20.00
❑ 77 Steven Hunter RC	8.00	20.00
❑ 78 Troy Murphy RC	15.00	40.00
❑ 79 Richard Jefferson RC	20.00	50.00
❑ 80 Vladimir Radmanovic RC	10.00	25.00
❑ 81 Kedrick Brown RC	8.00	20.00
❑ 82 Joe Johnson RC	20.00	50.00
❑ 83 DeSagana Diop RC	8.00	20.00
❑ 84 Shane Battier RC	12.00	30.00
❑ 85 Rodney White AU RC	8.00	20.00
❑ 86 Eddie Griffin AU RC	8.00	20.00
❑ 87 Jason Richardson AU RC	15.00	40.00
❑ 88 Eddy Curry AU RC	12.00	30.00
❑ 89 Tyson Chandler AU RC	15.00	40.00
❑ 90 Kwame Brown AU RC	10.00	25.00

2002-03 Ultimate Collection

❑ COMP.SET w/o SP's (67)	150.00	350.00
❑ COMMON CARD (1-67)	1.50	4.00
❑ COMMON AU RC (68-79)	8.00	20.00
❑ COMMON ROOKIE (80-103)	5.00	12.00
❑ COMMON ROOKIE (104-120)	3.00	8.00
❑ 1 Shareef Abdur-Rahim	2.00	5.00
❑ 2 Glenn Robinson	2.00	5.00
❑ 3 Jason Terry	2.50	6.00
❑ 4 Paul Pierce	2.50	6.00
❑ 5 Antoine Walker	2.00	5.00
❑ 6 Vin Baker	2.00	5.00
❑ 7 Jalen Rose	2.00	5.00
❑ 8 Darius Miles	1.50	4.00
❑ 9 Dirk Nowitzki	4.00	10.00
❑ 10 Michael Finley	2.50	6.00
❑ 11 Steve Nash	4.00	10.00
❑ 12 Raef LaFrentz	1.50	4.00
❑ 13 Juwan Howard	2.00	5.00
❑ 14 Richard Hamilton	2.00	5.00
❑ 15 Chauncey Billups	2.50	6.00
❑ 16 Ben Wallace	2.00	5.00
❑ 17 Jason Richardson	2.50	6.00
❑ 18 Gilbert Arenas	2.50	6.00
❑ 19 Antawn Jamison	2.50	6.00
❑ 20 Steve Francis	2.50	6.00
❑ 21 Reggie Miller	2.50	6.00
❑ 22 Jamaal Tinsley	2.00	5.00
❑ 23 Jermaine O'Neal	2.50	6.00
❑ 24 Elton Brand	2.50	6.00
❑ 25 Andre Miller	2.00	5.00
❑ 26 Kobe Bryant	12.00	30.00
❑ 27 Shaquille O'Neal	6.00	15.00
❑ 28 Pau Gasol	2.50	6.00
❑ 29 Shane Battier	2.00	5.00
❑ 30 Eddie Jones	2.00	5.00
❑ 31 Brian Grant	1.50	4.00
❑ 32 Ray Allen	2.50	6.00
❑ 33 Kevin Garnett	5.00	12.00
❑ 34 Wally Szczerbiak	2.00	5.00

❑ 35 Troy Hudson	1.50	4.00
❑ 36 Jason Kidd	4.00	10.00
❑ 37 Richard Jefferson	2.50	6.00
❑ 38 Kenyon Martin	2.50	6.00
❑ 39 Baron Davis	2.50	6.00
❑ 40 Jamal Mashburn	2.00	5.00
❑ 41 David Wesley	1.50	4.00
❑ 42 P.J. Brown	1.50	4.00
❑ 43 Allan Houston	2.00	5.00
❑ 44 Latrell Sprewell	2.00	5.00
❑ 45 Kurt Thomas	1.50	4.00
❑ 46 Tracy McGrady	5.00	12.00
❑ 47 Grant Hill	2.50	6.00
❑ 48 Allen Iverson	5.00	12.00
❑ 49 Stephon Marbury	2.50	6.00
❑ 50 Shawn Marion	2.50	6.00
❑ 51 Rasheed Wallace	2.50	6.00
❑ 52 Derek Anderson	2.00	5.00
❑ 53 Bonzi Wells	2.00	5.00
❑ 54 Chris Webber	2.50	6.00
❑ 55 Mike Bibby	2.00	5.00
❑ 56 Peja Stojakovic	2.00	5.00
❑ 57 Tim Duncan	5.00	12.00
❑ 58 David Robinson	3.00	8.00
❑ 59 Tony Parker	2.50	6.00
❑ 60 Gary Payton	2.50	6.00
❑ 61 Rashard Lewis	2.50	6.00
❑ 62 Desmond Mason	2.00	5.00
❑ 63 Vince Carter	5.00	12.00
❑ 64 Morris Peterson	2.00	5.00
❑ 65 Karl Malone	2.50	6.00
❑ 66 John Stockton	3.00	8.00
❑ 67 Michael Jordan	15.00	40.00
❑ 68 Chris Wilcox AU RC	10.00	25.00
❑ 69 Drew Gooden AU RC	30.00	60.00
❑ 70 Marcus Haislip AU RC	8.00	20.00
❑ 71 Melvin Ely AU RC	8.00	20.00
❑ 72 Jared Jeffries AU RC	8.00	20.00
❑ 73 Caron Butler AU RC	30.00	60.00
❑ 74 A.Stoudemire AU RC	60.00	120.00
❑ 75 Nene Hilario AU RC	20.00	40.00
❑ 76 DaJuan Wagner AU RC	20.00	40.00
❑ 77 N.Tskitishvili AU RC	8.00	20.00
❑ 78 Jay Williams AU RC	20.00	40.00
❑ 79 Yao Ming AU RC	60.00	120.00
❑ 80 Predrag Savovic RC	5.00	12.00
❑ 81 Igor Rakocevic RC	5.00	12.00
❑ 82 Sam Clancy RC	5.00	12.00
❑ 83 Ronald Murray RC	8.00	20.00
❑ 84 Tito Maddox RC	5.00	12.00
❑ 85 Carlos Boozer RC	10.00	25.00
❑ 86 Dan Gadzuric RC	5.00	12.00
❑ 87 Vincent Yarbrough RC	5.00	12.00
❑ 88 Robert Archibald RC	5.00	12.00
❑ 89 Roger Mason RC	5.00	12.00
❑ 90 Juaquin Hawkins RC	5.00	12.00
❑ 91 Chris Jefferies RC	5.00	12.00
❑ 92 John Salmons RC	8.00	20.00
❑ 93 Manu Ginobili RC	12.00	30.00
❑ 94 Tayshaun Prince RC	8.00	20.00
❑ 95 Casey Jacobsen RC	5.00	12.00
❑ 96 Qyntel Woods RC	5.00	12.00
❑ 97 Kareem Rush RC	6.00	15.00
❑ 98 Ryan Humphrey RC	5.00	12.00
❑ 99 Juan Dixon RC	8.00	20.00
❑ 100 Fred Jones RC	6.00	15.00
❑ 101 Jiri Welsch RC	5.00	12.00
❑ 102 Bostjan Nachbar RC	5.00	12.00
❑ 103 Marko Jaric	5.00	12.00
❑ 104 Gordan Giricek RC	5.00	12.00
❑ 105 Frank Williams RC	5.00	12.00
❑ 106 Pat Burke RC	5.00	12.00
❑ 107 Junior Harrington RC	5.00	12.00
❑ 108 Rasual Butler RC	5.00	12.00
❑ 109 Raul Lopez RC	5.00	12.00
❑ 110 Cezary Trybanski RC	5.00	12.00
❑ 111 Dan Dickau RC	5.00	12.00
❑ 112 Efthimios Rentzias RC	5.00	12.00
❑ 113 Mehmet Okur RC	6.00	15.00
❑ 114 Curtis Borchardt RC	5.00	12.00
❑ 115 J.R. Bremer RC	5.00	12.00
❑ 116 Lonny Baxter RC	5.00	12.00
❑ 117 Jamal Sampson RC	5.00	12.00
❑ 118 Tamar Slay RC	5.00	12.00
❑ 119 Jannero Pargo RC	5.00	12.00
❑ 120 Smush Parker RC	5.00	12.00

2003-04 Ultimate Collection

❑ COMMON CARD (1-116)	.75	2.00
❑ COMMON ROOKIE (117-126)	5.00	12.00
❑ COMMON AU RC (127-164)	8.00	20.00
❑ COMMON US (165-190)	3.00	8.00
❑ LIMITED PRINT RUN 25 SER.#'d SETS		
❑ LIMITED NOT PRICED DUE TO SCARCITY		
❑ LIM.BLACK SER.#'D TO ONE EXIST		
❑ 1 Dominique Wilkins	4.00	10.00
❑ 2 Jason Terry	2.50	6.00
❑ 3 Dion Glover	.75	2.00
❑ 4 Stephen Jackson	.75	2.00
❑ 5 Bill Russell	4.00	10.00
❑ 6 Paul Pierce	2.50	6.00
❑ 7 Larry Bird	5.00	12.00
❑ 8 Ricky Davis	2.50	6.00
❑ 9 Antonio Davis	1.50	4.00
❑ 10 Michael Jordan	10.00	25.00
❑ 11 Scottie Pippen	4.00	10.00
❑ 12 Tyson Chandler	2.50	6.00
❑ 13 Jeff McInnis	.75	2.00
❑ 14 Dajuan Wagner	1.50	4.00
❑ 15 Carlos Boozer	2.50	6.00
❑ 16 Zydrunas Ilgauskas	1.50	4.00
❑ 17 Dirk Nowitzki	4.00	10.00
❑ 18 Steve Nash	2.50	6.00
❑ 19 Antoine Walker	2.50	6.00
❑ 20 Michael Finley	2.50	6.00
❑ 21 Andre Miller	1.50	4.00
❑ 22 Nene	1.50	4.00
❑ 23 Nikoloz Tskitishvili	.75	2.00
❑ 24 Marcus Camby	1.50	4.00
❑ 25 Richard Hamilton	1.50	4.00
❑ 26 Ben Wallace	2.50	6.00
❑ 27 Chauncey Billups	1.50	4.00
❑ 28 Rasheed Wallace	2.50	6.00
❑ 29 Jason Richardson	2.50	6.00
❑ 30 Nick Van Exel	2.50	6.00
❑ 31 Speedy Claxton	.75	2.00
❑ 32 Mike Dunleavy	1.50	4.00
❑ 33 Yao Ming	6.00	15.00
❑ 34 Steve Francis	2.50	6.00
❑ 35 Cuttino Mobley	1.50	4.00
❑ 36 Jim Jackson	.75	2.00
❑ 37 Reggie Miller	2.50	6.00
❑ 38 Jermaine O'Neal	2.50	6.00
❑ 39 Ron Artest	1.50	4.00
❑ 40 Al Harrington	1.50	4.00
❑ 41 Elton Brand	2.50	6.00
❑ 42 Corey Maggette	1.50	4.00
❑ 43 Quentin Richardson	1.50	4.00
❑ 44 Chris Wilcox	1.50	4.00
❑ 45 Kobe Bryant	8.00	20.00
❑ 46 Shaquille O'Neal	6.00	15.00
❑ 47 Gary Payton	2.50	6.00
❑ 48 Karl Malone	2.50	6.00
❑ 49 Pau Gasol	2.50	6.00
❑ 50 Bonzi Wells	1.50	4.00
❑ 51 Mike Miller	2.50	6.00
❑ 52 Jason Williams	1.50	4.00
❑ 53 Caron Butler	2.50	6.00
❑ 54 Lamar Odom	2.50	6.00
❑ 55 Eddie Jones	2.50	6.00
❑ 56 Brian Grant	1.50	4.00
❑ 57 Desmond Mason	1.50	4.00
❑ 58 Oscar Robertson	4.00	10.00
❑ 59 Michael Redd	2.50	6.00
❑ 60 Toni Kukoc	1.50	4.00
❑ 61 Latrell Sprewell	2.50	6.00
❑ 62 Kevin Garnett	5.00	12.00
❑ 63 Wally Szczerbiak	1.50	4.00
❑ 64 Sam Cassell	2.50	6.00
❑ 65 Kenyon Martin	2.50	6.00
❑ 66 Jason Kidd	4.00	10.00
❑ 67 Richard Jefferson	1.50	4.00
❑ 68 Alonzo Mourning	1.50	4.00
❑ 69 Jamal Mashburn	1.50	4.00
❑ 70 David Wesley	.75	2.00
❑ 71 Baron Davis	2.50	6.00
❑ 72 Jamaal Magloire	.75	2.00
❑ 73 Allan Houston	1.50	4.00
❑ 74 Patrick Ewing	2.50	6.00
❑ 75 Stephon Marbury	2.50	6.00
❑ 76 Dikembe Mutombo	1.50	4.00
❑ 77 Tracy McGrady	6.00	15.00
❑ 78 Drew Gooden	1.50	4.00
❑ 79 Juwan Howard	1.50	4.00
❑ 80 DeShawn Stevenson	.75	2.00
❑ 81 Julius Erving	4.00	10.00
❑ 82 Allen Iverson	5.00	12.00
❑ 83 Glenn Robinson	2.50	6.00
❑ 84 Eric Snow	1.50	4.00
❑ 85 Amare Stoudemire	6.00	15.00
❑ 86 Shawn Marion	2.50	6.00
❑ 87 Antonio McDyess	2.50	6.00
❑ 88 Joe Johnson	1.50	4.00
❑ 89 Shareef Abdur-Rahim	2.50	6.00
❑ 90 Derek Anderson	1.50	4.00
❑ 91 Damon Stoudamire	1.50	4.00
❑ 92 Zach Randolph	2.50	6.00
❑ 93 Mike Bibby	2.50	6.00
❑ 94 Chris Webber	2.50	6.00
❑ 95 Peja Stojakovic	2.50	6.00
❑ 96 Bobby Jackson	2.50	6.00
❑ 97 Manu Ginobili	2.50	6.00
❑ 98 Tim Duncan	5.00	12.00
❑ 99 Tony Parker	2.50	6.00
❑ 100 Radoslav Nesterovic	1.50	4.00
❑ 101 Rashard Lewis	2.50	6.00
❑ 102 Ray Allen	2.50	6.00
❑ 103 Vladimir Radmanovic	.75	
❑ 104 Brent Barry	1.50	4.00
❑ 105 Vince Carter	6.00	15.00
❑ 106 Morris Peterson	1.50	4.00
❑ 107 Jalen Rose	2.50	6.00
❑ 108 Donyell Marshall	2.50	6.00
❑ 109 John Stockton	2.50	6.00
❑ 110 Andrei Kirilenko	2.50	6.00
❑ 111 Matt Harpring	2.50	6.00
❑ 112 Carlos Arroyo	4.00	10.00
❑ 113 Gilbert Arenas	2.50	6.00
❑ 114 Jerry Stackhouse	2.50	6.00
❑ 115 Kwame Brown	2.50	6.00
❑ 116 Larry Hughes	1.50	4.00
❑ 117 T.J. Ford RC	5.00	10.00
❑ 118 Kirk Hinrich RC	6.00	15.00
❑ 119 Nick Collison RC	5.00	12.00
❑ 120 James Jones RC	5.00	12.00
❑ 121 Travis Hansen RC	5.00	12.00
❑ 122 Alex Garcia RC	5.00	12.00
❑ 123 Theron Smith RC	5.00	12.00
❑ 124 Francisco Elson RC	5.00	12.00
❑ 125 Jon Stefansson RC	5.00	12.00
❑ 126 Ronald Dupree RC	5.00	12.00
❑ 127 LeBron James AU RC	800.00	1100.00
❑ 128 Darko Milicic AU RC	40.00	80.00
❑ 129 Carmelo Anthony AU RC	200.00	350.00
❑ 130 Chris Bosh AU RC	60.00	120.00
❑ 131 Dwyane Wade AU RC	250.00	400.00
❑ 132 Chris Kaman AU RC	15.00	40.00
❑ 133 Jarvis Hayes AU RC	8.00	20.00
❑ 134 Mickael Pietrus AU RC	12.50	30.00
❑ 135 Dahntay Jones AU RC	8.00	20.00
❑ 136 Marcus Banks AU RC	8.00	20.00
❑ 137 Luke Ridnour AU RC	15.00	40.00
❑ 138 Reece Gaines AU RC	8.00	20.00
❑ 139 Troy Bell AU RC	8.00	20.00
❑ 140 Mike Sweetney AU RC	8.00	20.00
❑ 141 David West AU RC	25.00	50.00
❑ 142 Aleksandar Pavlovic AU RC	10.00	25.00
❑ 143 Steve Blake AU RC	12.50	30.00
❑ 144 Boris Diaw AU RC	25.00	50.00
❑ 145 Zoran Planinic AU RC	8.00	20.00
❑ 146 Travis Outlaw AU RC	25.00	50.00
❑ 147 Brian Cook AU RC	8.00	20.00
❑ 148 Jerome Beasley AU RC	8.00	20.00
❑ 149 Ndudi Ebi AU RC	8.00	20.00
❑ 150 Kendrick Perkins AU RC	15.00	30.00
❑ 151 Leandro Barbosa AU RC	25.00	60.00
❑ 152 Josh Howard AU RC	25.00	50.00
❑ 153 Maciej Lampe AU RC	8.00	20.00
❑ 154 Jason Kapono AU RC	10.00	25.00

❑ 155 Luke Walton AU RC	12.50	30.00
❑ 156 Kyle Korver AU RC	25.00	60.00
❑ 157 Zarko Cabarkapa AU RC	8.00	20.00
❑ 158 Zaur Pachulia AU RC	12.50	30.00
❑ 159 Maurice Williams AU RC	20.00	40.00
❑ 160 Brandon Hunter AU RC	8.00	20.00
❑ 161 Keith Bogans AU RC	8.00	20.00
❑ 162 Marquis Daniels AU RC	12.50	30.00
❑ 163 Willie Green AU RC	8.00	20.00
❑ 164 Udonis Haslem AU RC	15.00	40.00
❑ 165 Larry Bird US	6.00	15.00
❑ 166 Bill Russell US	5.00	12.00
❑ 167 Michael Jordan US	12.50	30.00
❑ 168 Steve Nash US	3.00	8.00
❑ 169 Michael Finley US	3.00	8.00
❑ 170 Ben Wallace US	3.00	8.00
❑ 171 Jason Richardson US	3.00	8.00
❑ 172 Yao Ming US	8.00	20.00
❑ 173 Reggie Miller US	3.00	8.00
❑ 174 Kobe Bryant US	10.00	25.00
❑ 175 Shaquille O'Neal US	8.00	20.00
❑ 176 Gary Payton US	3.00	8.00
❑ 177 Magic Johnson US	4.00	10.00
❑ 178 Pau Gasol US	3.00	8.00
❑ 179 Lamar Odom US	3.00	8.00
❑ 180 Oscar Robertson US	5.00	12.00
❑ 181 Kenyon Martin US	3.00	8.00
❑ 182 Baron Davis US	3.00	8.00
❑ 183 Julius Erving US	5.00	12.00
❑ 184 Amare Stoudemire US	8.00	20.00
❑ 185 Mike Bibby US	3.00	8.00
❑ 186 Tony Parker US	3.00	8.00
❑ 187 Rashard Lewis US	3.00	8.00
❑ 188 Vince Carter US	8.00	20.00
❑ 189 Andrei Kirilenko US	3.00	8.00
❑ 190 Gilbert Arenas US	3.00	8.00

2004-05 Ultimate Collection

❑ COMMON CARD (1-116)	.75	2.00
❑ COMMON ROOKIE (117-126)	4.00	10.00
❑ COMMON AU RC (127-168)	6.00	15.00
❑ 1 Tyronn Lue	.75	2.00
❑ 2 Tony Delk	.75	2.00
❑ 3 Al Harrington	1.50	4.00
❑ 4 Paul Pierce	2.50	6.00
❑ 5 Antoine Walker	2.50	6.00
❑ 6 Bill Russell	4.00	10.00
❑ 7 Larry Bird	6.00	15.00
❑ 8 Gerald Wallace	1.50	4.00
❑ 9 Jason Kapono	1.50	4.00
❑ 10 Primoz Brezec	1.50	4.00
❑ 11 Kirk Hinrich	2.50	6.00
❑ 12 Eddy Curry	1.50	4.00
❑ 13 Tyson Chandler	2.50	6.00
❑ 14 Michael Jordan	15.00	35.00
❑ 15 LeBron James	12.50	30.00
❑ 16 Drew Gooden	1.50	4.00
❑ 17 Jeff McInnis	.75	2.00
❑ 18 Zydrunas Ilgauskas	1.50	4.00
❑ 19 Dirk Nowitzki	4.00	10.00
❑ 20 Michael Finley	2.50	6.00
❑ 21 Josh Howard	1.50	4.00
❑ 22 Marquis Daniels	2.50	6.00
❑ 23 Carmelo Anthony	5.00	12.00
❑ 24 Kenyon Martin	2.50	6.00
❑ 25 Andre Miller	1.50	4.00
❑ 26 Nene	1.50	4.00
❑ 27 Ben Wallace	2.50	6.00
❑ 28 Richard Hamilton	1.50	4.00
❑ 29 Isiah Thomas	4.00	10.00
❑ 30 Chauncey Billups	1.50	4.00
❑ 31 Jason Richardson	2.50	6.00
❑ 32 Baron Davis	2.50	6.00
❑ 33 Derek Fisher	2.50	6.00
❑ 34 Tracy McGrady	6.00	15.00
❑ 35 Yao Ming	6.00	15.00
❑ 36 Hakeem Olajuwon	2.50	6.00
❑ 37 Jermaine O'Neal	2.50	6.00
❑ 38 Reggie Miller	2.50	6.00
❑ 39 Ron Artest	1.50	4.00
❑ 40 Stephen Jackson	.75	2.00
❑ 41 Elton Brand	2.50	6.00
❑ 42 Chris Kaman	1.50	4.00
❑ 43 Corey Maggette	1.50	4.00
❑ 44 Bobby Simmons	.75	2.00
❑ 45 Kobe Bryant	8.00	20.00
❑ 46 Magic Johnson	6.00	15.00
❑ 47 Wilt Chamberlain	4.00	10.00
❑ 48 Lamar Odom	2.50	6.00
❑ 49 Pau Gasol	2.50	6.00
❑ 50 Bonzi Wells	1.50	4.00
❑ 51 Jason Williams	1.50	4.00
❑ 52 Mike Miller	2.50	6.00
❑ 53 Shaquille O'Neal	6.00	15.00
❑ 54 Dwyane Wade	6.00	15.00
❑ 55 Eddie Jones	2.50	6.00
❑ 56 Udonis Haslem	.75	2.00
❑ 57 Oscar Robertson	4.00	10.00
❑ 58 Michael Redd	1.50	4.00
❑ 59 Desmond Mason	1.50	4.00
❑ 60 T.J. Ford	1.50	4.00
❑ 61 Kevin Garnett	5.00	12.00
❑ 62 Latrell Sprewell	2.50	6.00
❑ 63 Sam Cassell	2.50	6.00
❑ 64 Michael Olowokandi	.75	2.00
❑ 65 Jason Kidd	4.00	10.00
❑ 66 Richard Jefferson	1.50	4.00
❑ 67 Vince Carter	6.00	15.00
❑ 68 Ron Mercer	.75	2.00
❑ 69 Dan Dickau	.75	2.00
❑ 70 Jamaal Magloire	.75	2.00
❑ 71 P.J. Brown	.75	2.00
❑ 72 Lee Nailon	.75	2.00
❑ 73 Stephon Marbury	2.50	6.00
❑ 74 Allan Houston	1.50	4.00
❑ 75 Jamal Crawford	1.50	4.00
❑ 76 Bernard King	3.00	8.00
❑ 77 Steve Francis	2.50	6.00
❑ 78 Doug Christie	1.50	4.00
❑ 79 Grant Hill	2.50	6.00
❑ 80 Hedo Turkoglu	2.50	6.00
❑ 81 Allen Iverson	5.00	12.00
❑ 82 Julius Erving	4.00	10.00
❑ 83 Chris Webber	2.50	6.00
❑ 84 Kyle Korver	1.50	4.00
❑ 85 Amare Stoudemire	5.00	12.00
❑ 86 Steve Nash	2.50	6.00
❑ 87 Shawn Marion	2.50	6.00
❑ 88 Quentin Richardson	1.50	4.00
❑ 89 Shareef Abdur-Rahim	2.50	6.00
❑ 90 Darius Miles	2.50	6.00
❑ 91 Zach Randolph	2.50	6.00
❑ 92 Damon Stoudamire	1.50	4.00
❑ 93 Peja Stojakovic	2.50	6.00
❑ 94 Mike Bibby	2.50	6.00
❑ 95 Cuttino Mobley	1.50	4.00
❑ 96 Brad Miller	2.50	6.00
❑ 97 Tim Duncan	5.00	12.00
❑ 98 Manu Ginobili	2.50	6.00
❑ 99 Tony Parker	2.50	6.00
❑ 100 David Robinson	4.00	10.00
❑ 101 Ray Allen	2.50	6.00
❑ 102 Rashard Lewis	2.50	6.00
❑ 103 Ronald Murray	.75	2.00
❑ 104 Luke Ridnour	1.50	4.00
❑ 105 Rafer Alston	.75	2.00
❑ 106 Jalen Rose	2.50	6.00
❑ 107 Chris Bosh	2.50	6.00
❑ 108 Morris Peterson	1.50	4.00
❑ 109 Andrei Kirilenko	2.50	6.00
❑ 110 Carlos Boozer	2.50	6.00
❑ 111 John Stockton	4.00	10.00
❑ 112 Matt Harpring	2.50	6.00
❑ 113 Gilbert Arenas	2.50	6.00
❑ 114 Antawn Jamison	2.50	6.00
❑ 115 Jarvis Hayes	1.50	4.00
❑ 116 Larry Hughes	1.50	4.00
❑ 117 D.J. Mbenga RC	4.00	10.00
❑ 118 Damien Wilkins RC	4.00	10.00
❑ 119 Billy Thomas RC	4.00	10.00
❑ 120 Andre Barrett RC	4.00	10.00
❑ 121 Erik Daniels RC	4.00	10.00
❑ 122 Justin Reed RC	4.00	10.00
❑ 123 Viktor Khryapa RC	4.00	10.00
❑ 124 Mario Kasun RC	4.00	10.00
❑ 125 Luis Flores RC	4.00	10.00
❑ 126 Emeka Okafor RC	6.00	15.00
❑ 127 Dwight Howard AU RC	125.00	250.00
❑ 128 Ben Gordon AU RC	20.00	40.00
❑ 129 Shaun Livingston AU RC	10.00	25.00
❑ 130 Devin Harris AU RC	15.00	30.00
❑ 131 Josh Childress AU RC	8.00	20.00
❑ 132 Luol Deng AU RC	15.00	30.00
❑ 133 Rafael Araujo AU RC	6.00	15.00
❑ 134 Andre Iguodala AU RC	20.00	40.00
❑ 135 Luke Jackson AU RC	6.00	15.00
❑ 136 Andris Biedrins AU RC	10.00	25.00
❑ 137 Robert Swift AU RC	6.00	15.00
❑ 138 Sebastian Telfair AU RC	6.00	15.00
❑ 139 Kris Humphries AU RC	6.00	15.00
❑ 140 Al Jefferson AU RC	25.00	50.00
❑ 141 Kirk Snyder AU RC	6.00	15.00
❑ 142 Josh Smith AU RC	20.00	40.00
❑ 143 J.R. Smith AU RC	20.00	40.00
❑ 144 Dorell Wright AU RC	10.00	25.00
❑ 145 Jameer Nelson AU RC	8.00	20.00
❑ 146 Pavel Podkolzin AU RC	6.00	15.00
❑ 147 Delonte West AU RC	15.00	30.00
❑ 148 Tony Allen AU RC	8.00	20.00
❑ 149 Kevin Martin AU RC	8.00	20.00
❑ 150 Sasha Vujacic AU RC	6.00	15.00
❑ 151 Beno Udrih AU RC	8.00	20.00
❑ 152 David Harrison AU RC	6.00	15.00
❑ 153 Anderson Varejao AU RC	8.00	20.00
❑ 154 Jackson Vroman AU RC	6.00	15.00
❑ 155 Peter John Ramos AU RC	6.00	15.00
❑ 156 Lionel Chalmers AU RC	6.00	15.00
❑ 157 Donta Smith AU RC	6.00	15.00
❑ 158 Andre Emmett AU RC	6.00	15.00
❑ 159 Antonio Burks AU RC	6.00	15.00
❑ 160 Royal Ivey AU RC	6.00	15.00
❑ 161 Chris Duhon AU RC	8.00	20.00
❑ 162 Nenad Krstic AU RC	8.00	20.00
❑ 163 Trevor Ariza AU RC	10.00	25.00
❑ 164 Matt Freije AU RC	6.00	15.00
❑ 165 Bernard Robinson AU RC	6.00	15.00
❑ 166 Andres Nocioni AU RC	8.00	20.00
❑ 167 Pape Sow AU RC	6.00	15.00
❑ 168 Ha Seung-Jin AU RC	6.00	15.00

2005-06 Ultimate Collection

❑ COMMON CARD (1-130)	.60	1.50
❑ COMMON ROOKIE (131-142)	2.50	6.00
❑ COMMON AU RC (143-183)	4.00	10.00
❑ 1 Josh Smith	1.00	2.50
❑ 2 Josh Childress	.75	2.00
❑ 3 Joe Johnson	1.00	2.50
❑ 4 Al Harrington	.60	1.50
❑ 5 Tony Allen	.60	1.50
❑ 6 Ricky Davis	1.00	2.50
❑ 7 Al Jefferson	1.00	2.50
❑ 8 Paul Pierce	1.00	2.50
❑ 9 Delonte West	.75	2.00
❑ 10 Brevin Knight	.60	1.50
❑ 11 Emeka Okafor	1.00	2.50
❑ 12 Kareem Rush	.60	1.50
❑ 13 Gerald Wallace	1.00	2.50
❑ 14 Tyson Chandler	1.00	2.50
❑ 15 Luol Deng	1.00	2.50
❑ 16 Michael Jordan	6.00	15.00
❑ 17 Ben Gordon	1.25	3.00
❑ 18 Kirk Hinrich	1.00	2.50
❑ 19 LeBron James	5.00	12.00
❑ 20 Drew Gooden	.75	2.00
❑ 21 Larry Hughes	.75	2.00
❑ 22 Donyell Marshall	.60	1.50
❑ 23 Zydrunas Ilgauskas	.75	2.00

❑ 24 Marquis Daniels	.75	2.00
❑ 25 Josh Howard	1.00	2.50
❑ 26 Dirk Nowitzki	1.50	4.00
❑ 27 Jason Terry	1.00	2.50
❑ 28 Devin Harris	1.00	2.50
❑ 29 Carmelo Anthony	2.00	5.00
❑ 30 Marcus Camby	.75	2.00
❑ 31 Nene	.60	1.50
❑ 32 Kenyon Martin	1.00	2.50
❑ 33 Andre Miller	.75	2.00
❑ 34 Ben Wallace	1.00	2.50
❑ 35 Richard Hamilton	.75	2.00
❑ 36 Tayshaun Prince	1.00	2.50
❑ 37 Chauncey Billups	1.00	2.50
❑ 38 Rasheed Wallace	1.00	2.50
❑ 39 Baron Davis	1.00	2.50
❑ 40 Mike Dunleavy	.75	2.00
❑ 41 Troy Murphy	1.00	2.50
❑ 42 Jason Richardson	1.00	2.50
❑ 43 Tracy McGrady	2.00	5.00
❑ 44 Yao Ming	2.50	6.00
❑ 45 Stromile Swift	.75	2.00
❑ 46 Juwan Howard	.75	2.00
❑ 47 Bob Sura	.60	1.50
❑ 48 Ron Artest	.75	2.00
❑ 49 Stephen Jackson	.75	2.00
❑ 50 Jermaine O'Neal	1.00	2.50
❑ 51 Jamaal Tinsley	.75	2.00
❑ 52 Elton Brand	1.00	2.50
❑ 53 Corey Maggette	.75	2.00
❑ 54 Sam Cassell	1.00	2.50
❑ 55 Shaun Livingston	.60	1.50
❑ 56 Cuttino Mobley	.75	2.00
❑ 57 Kobe Bryant	5.00	12.00
❑ 58 Kwame Brown	.75	2.00
❑ 59 Lamar Odom	1.00	2.50
❑ 60 Devean George	.75	2.00
❑ 61 Pau Gasol	1.00	2.50
❑ 62 Damon Stoudamire	.75	2.00
❑ 63 Eddie Jones	.60	1.50
❑ 64 Bobby Jackson	.60	1.50
❑ 65 Shaquille O'Neal	2.50	6.00
❑ 66 Gary Payton	1.00	2.50
❑ 67 Antoine Walker	.75	2.00
❑ 68 Dwyane Wade	2.50	6.00
❑ 69 Jason Williams	.75	2.00
❑ 70 Jamaal Magloire	.60	1.50
❑ 71 Michael Redd	1.00	2.50
❑ 72 Bobby Simmons	.60	1.50
❑ 73 Maurice Williams	.75	2.00
❑ 74 Kevin Garnett	2.00	5.00
❑ 75 Marko Jaric	.60	1.50
❑ 76 Wally Szczerbiak	.75	2.00
❑ 77 Michael Olowokandi	.60	1.50
❑ 78 Vince Carter	2.00	5.00
❑ 79 Richard Jefferson	.75	2.00
❑ 80 Jason Kidd	1.50	4.00
❑ 81 Jeff McInnis	.60	1.50
❑ 82 J.R. Smith	.75	2.00
❑ 83 Desmond Mason	.60	1.50
❑ 84 Speedy Claxton	.60	1.50
❑ 85 David West	1.00	2.50
❑ 86 Stephon Marbury	1.00	2.50
❑ 87 Jamal Crawford	.75	2.00
❑ 88 Quentin Richardson	.75	2.00
❑ 89 Eddy Curry	.75	2.00
❑ 90 Steve Francis	1.00	2.50
❑ 91 Grant Hill	1.00	2.50
❑ 92 Dwight Howard	2.00	5.00
❑ 93 Jameer Nelson	.75	2.00
❑ 94 Hedo Turkoglu	.75	2.00
❑ 95 Allen Iverson	2.00	5.00
❑ 96 Andre Iguodala	1.00	2.50
❑ 97 Kyle Korver	1.00	2.50
❑ 98 Chris Webber	1.00	2.50
❑ 99 Steve Nash	1.25	3.00
❑ 100 Shawn Marion	1.00	2.50
❑ 101 Amare Stoudemire	2.00	5.00
❑ 102 Kurt Thomas	.60	1.50
❑ 103 Juan Dixon	.60	1.50
❑ 104 Darius Miles	1.00	2.50
❑ 105 Zach Randolph	1.00	2.50
❑ 106 Sebastian Telfair	.75	2.00
❑ 107 Shareef Abdur-Rahim	1.00	2.50
❑ 108 Mike Bibby	1.00	2.50
❑ 109 Brad Miller	1.00	2.50
❑ 110 Peja Stojakovic	1.00	2.50
❑ 111 Tim Duncan	2.00	5.00
❑ 112 Manu Ginobili	1.00	2.50

❑ 113 Tony Parker	1.00	2.50
❑ 114 Michael Finley	1.00	2.50
❑ 115 Ray Allen	1.00	2.50
❑ 116 Rashard Lewis	1.00	2.50
❑ 117 Vladimir Radmanovic	.60	1.50
❑ 118 Luke Ridnour	.75	2.00
❑ 119 Chris Bosh	1.00	2.50
❑ 120 Morris Peterson	.75	2.00
❑ 121 Jalen Rose	1.00	2.50
❑ 122 Alvin Williams	.60	1.50
❑ 123 Carlos Boozer	1.00	2.50
❑ 124 Matt Harpring	.75	2.00
❑ 125 Andrei Kirilenko	1.00	2.50
❑ 126 Mehmet Okur	.60	1.50
❑ 127 Gilbert Arenas	1.00	2.50
❑ 128 Caron Butler	1.00	2.50
❑ 129 Antawn Jamison	1.00	2.50
❑ 130 Brendan Haywood	.60	1.50
❑ 131 Von Wafer RC	2.50	6.00
❑ 132 Bracey Wright RC	2.50	6.00
❑ 133 Ryan Gomes RC	2.50	6.00
❑ 134 Robert Whaley RC	2.50	6.00
❑ 135 Orien Greene RC	2.50	6.00
❑ 136 Dijon Thompson RC	2.50	6.00
❑ 137 Lawrence Roberts RC	2.50	6.00
❑ 138 Amir Johnson RC	2.50	6.00
❑ 139 John Lucas III RC	2.50	6.00
❑ 140 Chuck Hayes RC	2.50	6.00
❑ 141 Alex Acker RC	2.50	6.00
❑ 142 Fabricio Oberto RC	2.50	6.00
❑ 143 Andrew Bogut AU RC	10.00	25.00
❑ 144 Marvin Williams AU RC	20.00	40.00
❑ 145 Deron Williams AU RC	40.00	80.00
❑ 146 Chris Paul AU RC	100.00	175.00
❑ 147 Raymond Felton AU RC	10.00	25.00
❑ 148 Martell Webster AU RC	15.00	30.00
❑ 149 Charlie Villanueva AU RC	20.00	40.00
❑ 150 Channing Frye AU RC	6.00	15.00
❑ 151 Ike Diogu AU RC	10.00	25.00
❑ 152 Andrew Bynum AU RC	50.00	100.00
❑ 153 Yaroslav Korolev AU RC	5.00	12.00
❑ 154 Sean May AU RC	6.00	15.00
❑ 155 Rashad McCants AU RC	10.00	25.00
❑ 156 Antoine Wright AU RC EXCH	5.00	12.00
❑ 157 Joey Graham AU RC	5.00	12.00
❑ 158 Danny Granger AU RC	30.00	60.00
❑ 159 Gerald Green AU RC	15.00	30.00
❑ 160 Hakim Warrick AU RC	10.00	25.00
❑ 161 Julius Hodge AU RC	5.00	12.00
❑ 162 Nate Robinson AU RC	10.00	25.00
❑ 163 Jarrett Jack AU RC	5.00	12.00
❑ 164 Francisco Garcia AU RC	5.00	12.00
❑ 165 Luther Head AU RC	6.00	15.00
❑ 166 Johan Petro AU RC	5.00	12.00
❑ 167 Jason Maxiell AU RC	6.00	15.00
❑ 168 Linas Kleiza AU RC	6.00	15.00
❑ 169 Wayne Simien AU RC	4.00	10.00
❑ 170 David Lee AU RC	10.00	25.00
❑ 171 Salim Stoudamire AU RC	4.00	10.00
❑ 172 Daniel Ewing AU RC	5.00	12.00
❑ 173 Brandon Bass AU RC	5.00	12.00
❑ 174 C.J. Miles AU RC	5.00	12.00
❑ 175 Ersan Ilyasova AU RC	5.00	12.00
❑ 176 Travis Diener AU RC	5.00	12.00
❑ 177 Chris Taft AU RC EXCH	5.00	12.00
❑ 178 Martynas Andriuskevicius AU RC	5.00	12.00
❑ 179 Louis Williams AU RC	8.00	20.00
❑ 180 Monta Ellis AU RC	30.00	60.00
❑ 181 Andray Blatche AU RC EXCH	15.00	30.00
❑ 182 Sarunas Jasikevicius AU RC	5.00	12.00
❑ 183 James Singleton AU RC	5.00	12.00

2006-07 Ultimate Collection

❑ 1 Josh Childress	1.25	3.00
❑ 2 Joe Johnson	1.25	3.00
❑ 3 Salim Stoudamire	1.25	3.00
❑ 4 Marvin Williams	1.50	4.00
❑ 5 Tony Allen	1.25	3.00
❑ 6 Al Jefferson	1.50	4.00
❑ 7 Paul Pierce	1.50	4.00
❑ 8 Wally Szczerbiak	1.25	3.00
❑ 9 Sebastian Telfair	1.25	3.00
❑ 10 Raymond Felton	2.00	5.00
❑ 11 Sean May	1.25	3.00
❑ 12 Emeka Okafor	1.50	4.00
❑ 13 Gerald Wallace	1.50	4.00
❑ 14 Luol Deng	1.50	4.00
❑ 15 Chris Duhon	1.00	2.50
❑ 16 Ben Gordon	2.00	5.00
❑ 17 Kirk Hinrich	1.50	4.00
❑ 18 Ben Wallace	1.50	4.00
❑ 19 Drew Gooden	1.25	3.00
❑ 20 Larry Hughes	1.25	3.00
❑ 21 Zydrunas Ilgauskas	1.25	3.00
❑ 22 LeBron James	8.00	20.00
❑ 23 Donyell Marshall	1.00	2.50
❑ 24 Devin Harris	1.50	4.00
❑ 25 Josh Howard	1.50	4.00
❑ 26 Dirk Nowitzki	2.50	6.00
❑ 27 Jerry Stackhouse	1.50	4.00
❑ 28 Jason Terry	1.50	4.00
❑ 29 Carmelo Anthony	2.00	5.00
❑ 30 Marcus Camby	1.25	3.00
❑ 31 Kenyon Martin	1.50	4.00
❑ 32 Andre Miller	1.25	3.00
❑ 33 J.R. Smith	1.25	3.00
❑ 34 Chauncey Billups	1.50	4.00
❑ 35 Richard Hamilton	1.25	3.00
❑ 36 Antonio McDyess	1.00	2.50
❑ 37 Tayshaun Prince	1.50	4.00
❑ 38 Rasheed Wallace	1.50	4.00
❑ 39 Baron Davis	1.50	4.00
❑ 40 Mike Dunleavy	1.25	3.00
❑ 41 Troy Murphy	1.50	4.00
❑ 42 Jason Richardson	1.50	4.00
❑ 43 Rafer Alston	1.00	2.50
❑ 44 Shane Battier	1.50	4.00
❑ 45 Tracy McGrady	3.00	8.00
❑ 46 Bonzi Wells	1.25	3.00
❑ 47 Yao Ming	4.00	10.00
❑ 48 Marquis Daniels	1.25	3.00
❑ 49 Al Harrington	1.00	2.50
❑ 50 Sarunas Jasikevicius	1.25	3.00
❑ 51 Jermaine O'Neal	1.50	4.00
❑ 52 Elton Brand	1.50	4.00
❑ 53 Sam Cassell	1.50	4.00
❑ 54 Chris Kaman	1.00	2.50
❑ 55 Shaun Livingston	1.00	2.50
❑ 56 Corey Maggette	1.25	3.00
❑ 57 Kobe Bryant	8.00	20.00
❑ 58 Andrew Bynum	1.50	4.00
❑ 59 Lamar Odom	1.50	4.00
❑ 60 Vladimir Radmanovic	1.00	2.50
❑ 61 Kwame Brown	1.25	3.00
❑ 62 Eddie Jones	1.00	2.50
❑ 63 Mike Miller	1.50	4.00
❑ 64 Hakim Warrick	1.25	3.00
❑ 65 Pau Gasol	1.50	4.00
❑ 66 Stromile Swift	1.25	3.00
❑ 67 Alonzo Mourning	2.00	5.00
❑ 68 Shaquille O'Neal	4.00	10.00
❑ 69 Gary Payton	1.50	4.00
❑ 70 Dwyane Wade	4.00	10.00
❑ 71 Jason Williams	1.25	3.00
❑ 72 Andrew Bogut	1.50	4.00

❑ 73 Michael Redd	1.50	4.00
❑ 74 Charlie Villanueva	1.50	4.00
❑ 75 Bobby Simmons	1.00	2.50
❑ 76 Ricky Davis	1.50	4.00
❑ 77 Kevin Garnett	3.00	8.00
❑ 78 Troy Hudson	1.00	2.50
❑ 79 Mike James	1.00	2.50
❑ 80 Rashad McCants	1.25	3.00
❑ 81 Vince Carter	3.00	8.00
❑ 82 Richard Jefferson	1.25	3.00
❑ 83 Jason Kidd	2.50	6.00
❑ 84 Nenad Krstic	1.25	3.00
❑ 85 Tyson Chandler	1.50	4.00
❑ 86 Bobby Jackson	1.00	2.50
❑ 87 Desmond Mason	1.00	2.50
❑ 88 Chris Paul	3.00	8.00
❑ 89 Peja Stojakovic	1.50	4.00
❑ 90 Steve Francis	1.50	4.00
❑ 91 Channing Frye	1.25	3.00
❑ 92 Stephon Marbury	1.50	4.00
❑ 93 Quentin Richardson	1.25	3.00
❑ 94 Nate Robinson	1.50	4.00
❑ 95 Carlos Arroyo	1.50	4.00
❑ 96 Grant Hill	1.50	4.00
❑ 97 Dwight Howard	3.00	8.00
❑ 98 Darko Milicic	1.50	4.00
❑ 99 Jameer Nelson	1.25	3.00
❑ 100 Samuel Dalembert	1.00	2.50
❑ 101 Andre Iguodala	1.50	4.00
❑ 102 Allen Iverson	3.00	8.00
❑ 103 Kyle Korver	1.50	4.00
❑ 104 Chris Webber	1.50	4.00
❑ 105 Leandro Barbosa	1.50	4.00
❑ 106 Boris Diaw	1.25	3.00
❑ 107 Shawn Marion	1.50	4.00
❑ 108 Steve Nash	2.00	5.00
❑ 109 Amare Stoudemire	3.00	8.00
❑ 110 Juan Dixon	1.00	2.50
❑ 111 Jarrett Jack	1.25	3.00
❑ 112 Jamaal Magloire	1.00	2.50
❑ 113 Zach Randolph	1.50	4.00
❑ 114 Martell Webster	1.25	3.00
❑ 115 Shareef Abdur-Rahim	1.50	4.00
❑ 116 Ron Artest	1.50	4.00
❑ 117 Brad Miller	1.50	4.00
❑ 118 Mike Bibby	1.50	4.00
❑ 119 Tim Duncan	3.00	8.00
❑ 120 Michael Finley	1.50	4.00
❑ 121 Manu Ginobili	1.50	4.00
❑ 122 Robert Horry	1.25	3.00
❑ 123 Tony Parker	1.50	4.00
❑ 124 Ray Allen	1.50	4.00
❑ 125 Rashard Lewis	1.50	4.00
❑ 126 Luke Ridnour	1.25	3.00
❑ 127 Chris Wilcox	1.00	2.50
❑ 128 Chris Bosh	1.50	4.00
❑ 129 T.J. Ford	1.25	3.00
❑ 130 Joey Graham	1.25	3.00
❑ 131 Morris Peterson	1.25	3.00
❑ 132 Carlos Boozer	1.50	4.00
❑ 133 Andrei Kirilenko	1.50	4.00
❑ 134 C.J. Miles	1.00	2.50
❑ 135 Mehmet Okur	1.00	2.50
❑ 136 Deron Williams	2.50	6.00
❑ 137 Gilbert Arenas	1.50	4.00
❑ 138 Caron Butler	1.50	4.00
❑ 139 Antonio Daniels	1.00	2.50
❑ 140 Antawn Jamison	1.50	4.00
❑ 141 David Robinson	5.00	12.00
❑ 142 Hakeem Olajuwon	5.00	12.00
❑ 143 Bill Russell	8.00	20.00
❑ 144 Walt Frazier	4.00	10.00
❑ 145 Nate Archibald	4.00	10.00
❑ 146 Spud Webb	4.00	10.00
❑ 147 Larry Bird	12.00	30.00
❑ 148 Michael Jordan	30.00	60.00
❑ 149 Magic Johnson	8.00	20.00
❑ 150 Julius Erving	8.00	20.00
❑ 151 Alvin Robertson	4.00	10.00
❑ 152 Bill Laimbeer	4.00	10.00
❑ 153 Bill Walton	4.00	10.00
❑ 154 Bob McAdoo	4.00	10.00
❑ 155 Clyde Drexler	5.00	12.00
❑ 156 Connie Hawkins	4.00	10.00
❑ 157 Dennis Rodman	4.00	10.00
❑ 158 Earl Monroe	4.00	10.00
❑ 159 Elvin Hayes	4.00	10.00
❑ 160 George Gervin	4.00	10.00
❑ 161 Kareem Abdul-Jabbar	6.00	15.00
❑ 162 Elgin Baylor	4.00	10.00
❑ 163 Rolando Blackman	4.00	10.00
❑ 164 Maurice Cheeks	4.00	10.00
❑ 165 Adrian Dantley	4.00	10.00
❑ 166 Joe Dumars	4.00	10.00
❑ 167 World B. Free	4.00	10.00
❑ 168 Robert Parish	4.00	10.00
❑ 169 Kevin McHale	5.00	12.00
❑ 170 Kevin Johnson	4.00	10.00
❑ 171 Bernard King	4.00	10.00
❑ 172 Moses Malone	4.00	10.00
❑ 173 Chris Mullin	4.00	10.00
❑ 174 Calvin Murphy	4.00	10.00
❑ 175 Oscar Robertson	4.00	10.00
❑ 176 Isiah Thomas	4.00	10.00
❑ 177 Reggie Theus	4.00	10.00
❑ 178 Rudy Tomjanovich	4.00	10.00
❑ 179 Wes Unseld	4.00	10.00
❑ 180 John Starks	4.00	10.00
❑ 181 Allan Ray AU RC	5.00	12.00
❑ 182 Andrea Bargnani AU RC	15.00	30.00
❑ 183 Bobby Jones AU RC	5.00	12.00
❑ 184 Brandon Roy AU RC	50.00	100.00
❑ 185 Cedric Simmons AU RC	5.00	12.00
❑ 186 Craig Smith AU RC	5.00	12.00
❑ 187 D.Markota AU RC EXCH	5.00	12.00
❑ 188 Daniel Gibson AU RC	10.00	25.00
❑ 189 David Noel AU RC	5.00	12.00
❑ 190 Dee Brown AU RC	6.00	15.00
❑ 191 Hassan Adams AU RC	5.00	12.00
❑ 192 Hilton Armstrong AU RC	5.00	12.00
❑ 193 James Augustine AU RC	5.00	12.00
❑ 194 James White AU RC	8.00	20.00
❑ 195 Jordan Farmar AU RC	10.00	25.00
❑ 196 Jorge Garbajosa AU RC	8.00	20.00
❑ 197 Josh Boone AU RC	6.00	15.00
❑ 198 Kyle Lowry AU RC	5.00	12.00
❑ 199 LaMarcus Aldridge AU RC	20.00	40.00
❑ 200 Marcus Williams AU RC	10.00	25.00
❑ 201 Mardy Collins AU RC	6.00	12.00
❑ 202 Maurice Ager AU RC	5.00	12.00
❑ 203 P.O'Bryant AU RC EXCH	5.00	12.00
❑ 204 Paul Davis AU RC EXCH	5.00	12.00
❑ 205 Paul Millsap AU RC	15.00	30.00
❑ 206 P.J. Tucker AU RC	5.00	12.00
❑ 207 Pops Mensah-Bonsu AU RC	5.00	12.00
❑ 208 Quincy Douby AU RC EXCH	5.00	12.00
❑ 209 Rajon Rondo AU RC	40.00	75.00
❑ 210 Randy Foye AU RC	10.00	25.00
❑ 211 Renaldo Balkman AU RC	5.00	12.00
❑ 212 R.Carney AU RC EXCH	6.00	15.00
❑ 213 Ronnie Brewer AU RC	6.00	15.00
❑ 214 Rudy Gay AU RC	10.00	25.00
❑ 215 Yakhouba Diawara AU	5.00	12.00
❑ 216 Saer Sene AU RC	5.00	12.00
❑ 217 Sergio Rodriguez AU RC	8.00	20.00
❑ 218 Shannon Brown AU RC	5.00	12.00
❑ 219 Shawne Williams AU RC	8.00	20.00
❑ 220 Shelden Williams AU RC	8.00	20.00
❑ 221 Solomon Jones AU RC	5.00	12.00
❑ 222 Steve Novak AU RC	5.00	12.00
❑ 223 Thabo Sefolosha AU RC	10.00	25.00
❑ 224 Tyrus Thomas AU RC	20.00	40.00
❑ 225 Will Blalock AU RC	5.00	12.00
❑ 226 Robert Hite AU RC	5.00	12.00
❑ 227 V.Spanoulis AU RC EXCH	5.00	12.00
❑ 228 Leon Powe AU RC EXCH	10.00	25.00
❑ 236 Adam Morrison RC	4.00	10.00
❑ 237 Alexander Johnson RC	3.00	8.00
❑ 238 J.J. Redick RC	3.00	8.00
❑ 239 Kelenna Azubuike RC	4.00	10.00
❑ 240 Chris Quinn RC	3.00	8.00
❑ 241 Tarence Kinsey RC	3.00	8.00
❑ 242 Vassilis Spanoulis RC	3.00	8.00
❑ 243 Yakhouba Diawara RC	3.00	8.00
❑ 244 Mike Hall RC	3.00	8.00
❑ 245 Randolph Morris RC	3.00	8.00
❑ 246 Walter Herrmann RC	4.00	10.00
❑ 247 Mickael Gelabale RC	3.00	8.00
❑ 248 Andre Brown RC	3.00	8.00
❑ 249 Justin Williams RC	3.00	8.00
❑ 250 Lynn Greer RC	3.00	8.00

2007-08 Ultimate Collection

❑ 1 LaMarcus Aldridge	1.50	4.00
❑ 2 Ray Allen	1.25	3.00
❑ 3 Carmelo Anthony	2.50	6.00
❑ 4 Gilbert Arenas	1.25	3.00
❑ 5 Ron Artest	1.25	3.00
❑ 6 Andrea Bargnani	1.50	4.00
❑ 7 Mike Bibby	1.25	3.00
❑ 8 Chauncey Billups	1.25	3.00
❑ 9 Andrew Bogut	1.25	3.00
❑ 10 Carlos Boozer	1.25	3.00
❑ 11 Chris Bosh	1.25	3.00
❑ 12 Elton Brand	1.25	3.00
❑ 13 Kobe Bryant	6.00	15.00
❑ 14 Caron Butler	1.25	3.00
❑ 15 Jorge Garbajosa	1.25	3.00
❑ 16 Marcus Camby	.75	2.00
❑ 17 Rodney Carney	.75	2.00
❑ 18 Vince Carter	2.50	6.00
❑ 19 Tyson Chandler	1.25	3.00
❑ 20 Damien Wilkins	.75	2.00
❑ 21 Eddy Curry	.75	2.00
❑ 22 Baron Davis	1.25	3.00
❑ 23 Ricky Davis	1.25	3.00
❑ 24 Luol Deng	1.25	3.00
❑ 25 Tim Duncan	2.50	6.00
❑ 26 Shawne Williams	1.00	2.50
❑ 27 Monta Ellis	1.00	2.50
❑ 28 Jordan Farmar	1.00	2.50
❑ 29 T.J. Ford	1.00	2.50
❑ 30 Randy Foye	1.25	3.00
❑ 31 Channing Frye	1.00	2.50
❑ 32 Al Jefferson	1.25	3.00
❑ 33 Pau Gasol	1.25	3.00
❑ 34 Rudy Gay	1.00	2.50
❑ 35 Manu Ginobili	1.25	3.00
❑ 36 Ben Gordon	1.50	4.00
❑ 37 Richard Hamilton	1.00	2.50
❑ 38 Luther Head	1.00	2.50
❑ 39 Grant Hill	1.25	3.00
❑ 40 Kirk Hinrich	1.25	3.00
❑ 41 Dwight Howard	2.50	6.00
❑ 42 Josh Howard	1.25	3.00
❑ 43 Larry Hughes	1.00	2.50
❑ 44 Andre Iguodala	1.25	3.00
❑ 45 Daniel Gibson	1.25	3.00
❑ 46 Allen Iverson	2.50	6.00
❑ 47 Morris Peterson	1.00	2.50
❑ 48 Stephen Jackson	1.00	2.50
❑ 49 LeBron James	6.00	15.00
❑ 50 Antawn Jamison	1.25	3.00
❑ 51 Kevin Garnett	3.00	8.00
❑ 52 Richard Jefferson	1.25	3.00
❑ 53 Joe Johnson	1.25	3.00
❑ 54 Jason Kidd	2.00	5.00
❑ 55 Andrei Kirilenko	1.25	3.00
❑ 56 David Lee	1.00	2.50
❑ 57 Rashard Lewis	1.25	3.00
❑ 58 Corey Maggette	1.00	2.50
❑ 59 Stephon Marbury	1.25	3.00
❑ 60 Shawn Marion	1.25	3.00
❑ 61 Kevin Martin	1.25	3.00
❑ 62 Tracy McGrady	2.50	6.00
❑ 63 Al Harrington	1.00	2.50
❑ 64 Andre Miller	1.00	2.50
❑ 65 Francisco Garcia	1.00	2.50
❑ 66 Yao Ming	3.00	8.00
❑ 67 Cuttino Mobley	1.00	2.50
❑ 68 Alonzo Mourning	1.50	4.00
❑ 69 Steve Nash	1.50	4.00
❑ 70 Dirk Nowitzki	2.00	5.00
❑ 71 Jermaine O'Neal	1.25	3.00
❑ 72 Shaquille O'Neal	3.00	8.00

❑ 73 Lamar Odom	1.25	3.00
❑ 74 Adam Morrison	1.25	3.00
❑ 75 Mehmet Okur	1.00	2.50
❑ 76 Tony Parker	1.25	3.00
❑ 77 Chris Paul	2.50	6.00
❑ 78 Johan Petro	.75	2.00
❑ 79 Paul Pierce	1.25	3.00
❑ 80 Tayshaun Prince	1.25	3.00
❑ 81 Zach Randolph	1.25	3.00
❑ 82 Michael Redd	1.25	3.00
❑ 83 Jason Richardson	1.25	3.00
❑ 84 Brandon Roy	2.00	5.00
❑ 85 Josh Smith	1.25	3.00
❑ 86 Amare Stoudemire	2.50	6.00
❑ 87 Jason Terry	1.25	3.00
❑ 88 Jamaal Tinsley	.75	2.00
❑ 89 Hedo Turkoglu	1.25	3.00
❑ 90 Desmond Mason	.75	2.00
❑ 91 Dwyane Wade	3.00	8.00
❑ 92 Ben Wallace	1.25	3.00
❑ 93 Gerald Wallace	1.25	3.00
❑ 94 Rasheed Wallace	1.25	3.00
❑ 95 Mike Miller	1.25	3.00
❑ 96 David West	1.25	3.00
❑ 97 Delonte West	1.00	2.50
❑ 98 Deron Williams	2.00	5.00
❑ 99 Marvin Williams	1.25	3.00
❑ 100 Raymond Felton	1.50	4.00
❑ 101 Arron Afflalo AU/99 RC	5.00	12.00
❑ 102 Morris Almond AU/99 RC	6.00	15.00
❑ 103 Marco Belinelli AU/99 RC	6.00	15.00
❑ 104 Corey Brewer AU/150 RC	8.00	20.00
❑ 105 Aaron Brooks AU/99 RC	8.00	20.00
❑ 106 Julian Wright AU/150 RC	6.00	15.00
❑ 107 Wilson Chandler AU/99 RC	6.00	15.00
❑ 108 Mike Conley AU/150 RC	10.00	25.00
❑ 109 Daequan Cook AU/99 RC	6.00	15.00
❑ 110 Javaris Crittenton AU/150 RC	5.00	12.00
❑ 111 JamesOn Curry AU/99 RC	5.00	12.00
❑ 112 Jermareo Davidson AU/99 RC	5.00	12.00
❑ 113 Glen Davis AU/150 RC	3.00	15.00
❑ 114 Jared Dudley AU/99 RC	5.00	12.00
❑ 115 Kevin Durant AU/150 RC	125.00	250.00
❑ 116 Nick Fazekas AU/99 RC	5.00	12.00
❑ 117 Aaron Gray AU/99 RC	5.00	12.00
❑ 118 Jeff Green AU/150 RC	8.00	20.00
❑ 119 Taurean Green AU/99 RC	5.00	12.00
❑ 120 Adam Haluska AU/99 RC	5.00	12.00
❑ 121 Spencer Hawes AU/99 RC	5.00	12.00
❑ 122 Herbert Hill AU/99 RC	5.00	12.00
❑ 123 Al Horford AU/150 RC	25.00	50.00
❑ 124 Louis Amundson AU/99 RC	5.00	12.00
❑ 125 Carl Landry AU/99 RC	6.00	15.00
❑ 126 Jamario Moon AU/150 RC	10.00	25.00
❑ 127 Acie Law IV AU/150 RC	5.00	12.00
❑ 129 Josh McRoberts AU/99 RC	5.00	12.00
❑ 130 Oleksiy Pecherov AU/99 RC	5.00	12.00
❑ 131 Coby Karl AU/99 RC	5.00	12.00
❑ 132 Joakim Noah AU/150 RC	10.00	25.00
❑ 133 Gabe Pruitt AU/99 RC	5.00	12.00
❑ 134 Chris Richard AU/99 RC	5.00	12.00
❑ 135 Juan Navarro AU/150 RC	6.00	15.00
❑ 136 Ramon Sessions AU/99 RC	15.00	30.00
❑ 137 Jason Smith AU/99 RC	5.00	12.00
❑ 138 D.J. Strawberry AU/99 RC	5.00	12.00
❑ 139 Rodney Stuckey AU/150 RC	25.00	50.00
❑ 140 Luis Scola AU/150 RC	10.00	25.00
❑ 141 Al Thornton AU/150 RC	10.00	25.00
❑ 142 Alando Tucker AU/99 RC	6.00	15.00
❑ 143 Sean Williams AU/99 RC	6.00	15.00
❑ 144 Cheikh Samb AU/99 RC	6.00	15.00
❑ 145 Yi Jianlian RC	6.00	15.00
❑ 146 Thaddeus Young RC	5.00	12.00
❑ 147 Nick Young RC	4.00	10.00
❑ 148 Kyrylo Fesenko RC	4.00	10.00
❑ 149 Greg Oden RC	6.00	15.00
❑ 150 Brandan Wright RC	5.00	12.00

2008-09 Ultimate Collection

❑ 1 LaMarcus Aldridge	2.00	5.00
❑ 2 Ray Allen	2.00	5.00
❑ 3 Carmelo Anthony	2.50	6.00
❑ 4 Gilbert Arenas	2.00	5.00
❑ 5 Ron Artest	2.00	5.00
❑ 6 Chauncey Billups	2.00	5.00
❑ 7 Carlos Boozer	2.00	5.00
❑ 8 Chris Bosh	2.00	5.00
❑ 9 Elton Brand	3.00	8.00
❑ 10 Kobe Bryant	10.00	25.00
❑ 11 Caron Butler	2.00	5.00
❑ 12 Andrew Bynum	2.00	5.00
❑ 13 Jose Calderon	1.50	4.00
❑ 14 Vince Carter	2.50	6.00
❑ 15 Tyson Chandler	1.50	4.00
❑ 16 Mike Conley	1.50	4.00
❑ 17 Jamal Crawford	1.25	3.00
❑ 18 Baron Davis	2.00	5.00
❑ 19 Luol Deng	2.00	5.00
❑ 20 Chris Duhon	1.25	3.00
❑ 21 Tim Duncan	3.00	8.00
❑ 22 Kevin Durant	5.00	12.00
❑ 23 Raymond Felton	1.50	4.00
❑ 24 T.J. Ford	1.25	3.00
❑ 25 Kevin Garnett	4.00	10.00
❑ 26 Pau Gasol	2.00	5.00
❑ 27 Rudy Gay	2.00	5.00
❑ 28 Manu Ginobili	2.00	5.00
❑ 29 Ben Gordon	2.00	5.00
❑ 30 Danny Granger	2.00	5.00
❑ 31 Jeff Green	1.50	4.00
❑ 32 Al Harrington	1.50	4.00
❑ 33 Devin Harris	2.00	5.00
❑ 34 Kirk Hinrich	2.00	5.00
❑ 35 Al Horford	2.00	5.00
❑ 36 Dwight Howard	4.00	10.00
❑ 37 Josh Howard	2.00	5.00
❑ 38 Andre Iguodala	2.00	5.00
❑ 39 Allen Iverson	2.50	6.00
❑ 40 Stephen Jackson	1.50	4.00
❑ 41 LeBron James	10.00	25.00
❑ 42 Antawn Jamison	2.00	5.00
❑ 43 Al Jefferson	2.00	5.00
❑ 44 Richard Jefferson	2.00	5.00
❑ 45 Yi Jianlian	2.00	5.00
❑ 46 Joe Johnson	2.00	5.00
❑ 47 Jason Kidd	2.00	5.00
❑ 48 David Lee	1.50	4.00
❑ 49 Rashard Lewis	2.00	5.00
❑ 50 Corey Maggette	2.00	5.00
❑ 51 Shawn Marion	2.00	5.00
❑ 52 Kevin Martin	2.00	5.00
❑ 53 Tracy McGrady	2.50	6.00
❑ 54 Andre Miller	1.50	4.00
❑ 55 Mike Miller	2.00	5.00
❑ 56 Paul Millsap	1.50	4.00
❑ 57 Yao Ming	2.50	6.00
❑ 58 Steve Nash	2.00	5.00
❑ 59 Jameer Nelson	1.50	4.00
❑ 60 Dirk Nowitzki	2.50	6.00
❑ 61 Greg Oden	2.00	5.00
❑ 62 Tony Parker	2.00	5.00
❑ 63 Chris Paul	4.00	10.00
❑ 64 Paul Pierce	2.50	6.00
❑ 65 Tayshaun Prince	2.00	5.00
❑ 66 Zach Randolph	2.00	5.00
❑ 67 Michael Redd	2.00	5.00
❑ 68 Jason Richardson	2.00	5.00
❑ 69 Brandon Roy	2.50	6.00
❑ 70 John Salmons	2.00	5.00
❑ 71 Josh Smith	2.00	5.00
❑ 72 Amare Stoudemire	2.50	6.00
❑ 73 Rodney Stuckey	2.50	6.00
❑ 74 Al Thornton	2.00	5.00
❑ 75 Dwyane Wade	4.00	10.00
❑ 76 Gerald Wallace	2.00	5.00
❑ 77 David West	2.00	5.00
❑ 78 Deron Williams	2.50	6.00
❑ 79 Mo Williams	1.50	4.00
❑ 80 Thaddeus Young	1.50	4.00
❑ 81 Sean Singletary RC	2.50	6.00
❑ 82 Luc Mbah A Moute RC	2.50	6.00
❑ 83 Darnell Jackson/491 RC	2.50	6.00
❑ 84 Nathan Jawai RC	2.50	6.00
❑ 85 Jawad Williams RC	2.50	6.00
❑ 86 Joey Dorsey RC	2.50	6.00
❑ 87 Alexis Ajinca RC	2.50	6.00
❑ 88 DeAndre Jordan/491 RC	2.50	6.00
❑ 89 Javale McGee RC	2.50	6.00
❑ 90 Hamed Haddadi RC	2.50	6.00
❑ 91 Roko Ukic RC	2.50	6.00
❑ 92 Kosta Koufos RC	2.50	6.00
❑ 93 Nicolas Batum RC	3.00	8.00
❑ 94 Ryan Anderson/491 RC	2.50	6.00
❑ 95 Joe Alexander RC	2.50	6.00
❑ 96 Chris Douglas-Roberts RC	3.00	8.00
❑ 97 Anthony Morrow RC	6.00	15.00
❑ 98 Darrell Arthur RC	2.50	6.00
❑ 99 Danilo Gallinari RC	4.00	10.00
❑ 100 Marc Gasol RC	4.00	10.00
❑ 101 Michael Jordan	12.00	30.00
❑ 102 Larry Bird	6.00	15.00
❑ 103 Magic Johnson	4.00	10.00
❑ 104 Oscar Robertson	2.00	5.00
❑ 105 John Stockton	3.00	8.00
❑ 106 Julius Erving	4.00	10.00
❑ 107 Manute Bol	2.00	5.00
❑ 108 Dee Brown	2.00	5.00
❑ 109 Joe Dumars	2.00	5.00
❑ 110 James Edwards	2.00	5.00
❑ 111 A.C. Green	2.00	5.00
❑ 112 Tim Hardaway	2.00	5.00
❑ 113 Kevin Johnson	2.00	5.00
❑ 114 Karl Malone	2.50	6.00
❑ 115 Danny Ainge	2.00	5.00
❑ 116 Kurt Rambis	2.50	6.00
❑ 117 Willis Reed	2.00	5.00
❑ 118 Scottie Pippen	2.50	6.00
❑ 119 Wilt Chamberlain	4.00	10.00
❑ 120 Drazen Petrovic	3.00	8.00
❑ 121 Kevin Love JSY AU RC	12.00	30.00
❑ 122 Michael Beasley JSY AU RC	30.00	60.00
❑ 123 Rudy Fernandez JSY AU RC	25.00	50.00
❑ 124 O.J. Mayo JSY AU RC	30.00	60.00
❑ 125 Derrick Rose JSY AU RC	80.00	160.00
❑ 126 Brook Lopez JSY AU RC	20.00	50.00
❑ 127 Russell Westbrk JSY AU RC	25.00	60.00
❑ 128 Courtney Lee JSY AU RC	15.00	40.00
❑ 129 Jerryd Bayless JSY AU RC	10.00	25.00
❑ 130 Marreese Speights JSY AU RC	10.00	25.00
❑ 131 Donte Greene JSY AU RC	10.00	25.00
❑ 132 J.J. Hickson JSY AU RC	15.00	40.00
❑ 133 D.J. Augustin JSY AU RC	10.00	25.00
❑ 134 Jason Thmpsn JSY AU RC	10.00	25.00
❑ 135 Robin Lopez JSY AU RC	10.00	25.00
❑ 136 A.Randolph JSY AU RC	15.00	40.00
❑ 137 Eric Gordon JSY AU RC	12.00	30.00
❑ 138 Brandon Rush JSY AU RC	10.00	25.00
❑ 139 Roy Hibbert JSY AU RC	12.00	30.00
❑ 140 Mario Chalmers JSY AU RC	12.00	30.00
❑ 141 George Hill JSY AU RC	15.00	40.00

1999-00 Ultimate Victory

❑ COMPLETE SET (150)	50.00	100.00
❑ COMP. SET w/o RC (120)	30.00	60.00

COMMON CARD (1-90)	.25	.60
COMMON ROOKIE (121-150)	.60	1.50
COMMON MJ GH (91-120)	.75	2.00
1 Dikembe Mutombo	.30	.75
2 Alan Henderson	.25	.60
3 LaPhonso Ellis	.25	.60
4 Kenny Anderson	.30	.75
5 Antoine Walker	.40	1.00
6 Paul Pierce	.40	1.00
7 Elden Campbell	.25	.60
8 Eddie Jones	.40	1.00
9 David Wesley	.25	.60
10 Michael Jordan	3.00	8.00
11 Kornel David RC	.40	1.00
12 Toni Kukoc	.40	1.00
13 Shawn Kemp	.40	1.00
14 Brevin Knight	.25	.60
15 Zydrunas Ilgauskas	.30	.75
16 Michael Finley	.40	1.00
17 Shawn Bradley	.25	.60
18 Dirk Nowitzki	.60	1.50
19 Antonio McDyess	.30	.75
20 Nick Van Exel	.30	.75
21 Ron Mercer	.25	.60
22 Grant Hill	.40	1.00
23 Lindsey Hunter	.25	.60
24 Jerry Stackhouse	.40	1.00
25 John Starks	.40	1.00
26 Antawn Jamison	.40	1.00
27 Mookie Blaylock	.25	.60
28 Hakeem Olajuwon	.40	1.00
29 Cuttino Mobley	.30	.75
30 Charles Barkley	.50	1.25
31 Reggie Miller	.40	1.00
32 Rik Smits	.40	1.00
33 Jalen Rose	.30	.75
34 Maurice Taylor	.30	.75
35 Tyrone Nesby RC	.40	1.00
36 Michael Olowokandi	.25	.60
37 Kobe Bryant	2.00	5.00
38 Shaquille O'Neal	1.00	2.50
39 Glen Rice	.40	1.00
40 Robert Horry	.40	1.00
41 Tim Hardaway	.40	1.00
42 Alonzo Mourning	.40	1.00
43 Jamal Mashburn	.25	.60
44 Ray Allen	.40	1.00
45 Glenn Robinson	.30	.75
46 Robert Traylor	.25	.60
47 Kevin Garnett	.75	2.00
48 Joe Smith	.30	.75
49 Bobby Jackson	.30	.75
50 Keith Van Horn	.30	.75
51 Stephon Marbury	.40	1.00
52 Jayson Williams	.30	.75
53 Patrick Ewing	.50	1.25
54 Allan Houston	.30	.75
55 Latrell Sprewell	.30	.75
56 Marcus Camby	.30	.75
57 Darrell Armstrong	.25	.60
58 Matt Harpring	.30	.75
59 Bo Outlaw	.25	.60
60 Allen Iverson	.75	2.00
61 Theo Ratliff	.30	.75
62 Larry Hughes	.30	.75
63 Jason Kidd	.60	1.50
64 Tom Gugliotta	.25	.60
65 Anfernee Hardaway	.40	1.00
66 Scottie Pippen	.60	1.50
67 Damon Stoudamire	.40	1.00
68 Brian Grant	.25	.60
69 Jason Williams	.40	1.00
70 Vlade Divac	.40	1.00
71 Chris Webber	.40	1.00
72 Tim Duncan	.75	2.00
73 Sean Elliott	.40	1.00
74 David Robinson	.50	1.25
75 Avery Johnson	.30	.75
76 Gary Payton	.40	1.00
77 Vin Baker	.40	1.00
78 Brent Barry	.30	.75
79 Vince Carter	.75	2.00
80 Doug Christie	.30	.75
81 Tracy McGrady	.75	2.00
82 Karl Malone	.50	1.25
83 John Stockton	.50	1.25
84 Bryon Russell	.25	.60
85 Shareef Abdur-Rahim	.30	.75
86 Mike Bibby	.40	1.00
87 Felipe Lopez	.25	.60
88 Juwan Howard	.30	.75
89 Rod Strickland	.25	.60
90 Mitch Richmond	.30	.75
91 Michael Jordan GH	.75	2.00
92 Michael Jordan GH	.75	2.00
93 Michael Jordan GH	.75	2.00
94 Michael Jordan GH	.75	2.00
95 Michael Jordan GH	.75	2.00
96 Michael Jordan GH	.75	2.00
97 Michael Jordan GH	.75	2.00
98 Michael Jordan GH	.75	2.00
99 Michael Jordan GH	.75	2.00
100 Michael Jordan GH	.75	2.00
101 Michael Jordan GH	.75	2.00
102 Michael Jordan GH	.75	2.00
103 Michael Jordan GH	.75	2.00
104 Michael Jordan GH	.75	2.00
105 Michael Jordan GH	.75	2.00
106 Michael Jordan GH	.75	2.00
107 Michael Jordan GH	.75	2.00
108 Michael Jordan GH	.75	2.00
109 Michael Jordan GH	.75	2.00
110 Michael Jordan GH	.75	2.00
111 Michael Jordan GH	.75	2.00
112 Michael Jordan GH	.75	2.00
113 Michael Jordan GH	.75	2.00
114 Michael Jordan GH	.75	2.00
115 Michael Jordan GH	.75	2.00
116 Michael Jordan GH	.75	2.00
117 Michael Jordan GH	.75	2.00
118 Michael Jordan GH	.75	2.00
119 Michael Jordan GH	.75	2.00
120 Michael Jordan GH	.75	2.00
121 Elton Brand RC	2.00	5.00
122 Steve Francis RC	2.00	5.00
123 Baron Davis RC	2.50	6.00
124 Lamar Odom RC	2.00	5.00
125 Jonathan Bender RC	.60	1.50
126 Wally Szczerbiak RC	2.00	5.00
127 Richard Hamilton RC	2.00	5.00
128 Andre Miller RC	2.00	5.00
129 Shawn Marion RC	2.00	5.00
130 Jason Terry RC	1.50	4.00
131 Trajan Langdon RC	.60	1.50
132 A.Radojevic RC	.60	1.50
133 Corey Maggette RC	2.00	5.00
134 William Avery RC	.60	1.50
135 Ron Artest RC	2.50	6.00
136 Cal Bowdler RC	.60	1.50
137 James Posey RC	1.00	2.50
138 Quincy Lewis RC	.60	1.50
139 Dion Glover RC	.60	1.50
140 Jeff Foster RC	.75	2.00
141 Kenny Thomas RC	.60	1.50
142 Devean George RC	1.00	2.50
143 Tim James RC	.60	1.50
144 Vonteego Cummings RC	.60	1.50
145 Jumaine Jones RC	.60	1.50
146 Scott Padgett RC	.60	1.50
147 John Celestand RC	.60	1.50
148 Adrian Griffin RC	.60	1.50
149 Chris Herren RC	.60	1.50
150 Anthony Carter RC	1.25	3.00

2000-01 Ultimate Victory

COMP.SET w/o SP (60)	12.50	25.00
COMMON CARD (1-60)	.20	.50
COMMON KOBE (61-75)	1.25	3.00
COMMON KG (76-90)	1.00	2.50
COMMON ROOKIE (91-120)	1.25	3.00
1 Dikembe Mutombo	.25	.60
2 Jim Jackson	.20	.50
3 Paul Pierce	.30	.75
4 Antoine Walker	.25	.60
5 Jamal Mashburn	.25	.60
6 Baron Davis	.30	.75
7 Elton Brand	.30	.75
8 Ron Artest	.30	.75
9 Lamond Murray	.20	.50
10 Andre Miller	.25	.60
11 Michael Finley	.30	.75
12 Dirk Nowitzki	.50	1.25
13 Antonio McDyess	.25	.60
14 Nick Van Exel	.25	.60
15 Jerry Stackhouse	.25	.60
16 Chucky Atkins	.20	.50
17 Antawn Jamison	.30	.75
18 Larry Hughes	.25	.60
19 Steve Francis	.30	.75
20 Hakeem Olajuwon	.40	1.00
21 Reggie Miller	.30	.75
22 Jalen Rose	.25	.60
23 Lamar Odom	.30	.75
24 Corey Maggette	.25	.60
25 Shaquille O'Neal	.75	2.00
26 Kobe Bryant	1.50	4.00
27 Ron Harper	.25	.60
28 Tim Hardaway	.25	.60
29 Eddie Jones	.25	.60
30 Ray Allen	.30	.75
31 Tim Thomas	.20	.50
32 Kevin Garnett	.60	1.50
33 Wally Szczerbiak	.25	.60
34 Terrell Brandon	.20	.50
35 Stephon Marbury	.30	.75
36 Keith Van Horn	.25	.60
37 Allan Houston	.25	.60
38 Latrell Sprewell	.25	.60
39 Grant Hill	.30	.75
40 Tracy McGrady	.60	1.50
41 Allen Iverson	.60	1.50
42 Toni Kukoc	.25	.60
43 Jason Kidd	.50	1.25
44 Anfernee Hardaway	.30	.75
45 Scottie Pippen	.50	1.25
46 Rasheed Wallace	.30	.75
47 Jason Williams	.25	.60
48 Chris Webber	.30	.75
49 Tim Duncan	.60	1.50
50 David Robinson	.40	1.00
51 Gary Payton	.30	.75
52 Rashard Lewis	.30	.75
53 Vince Carter	.60	1.50
54 Mark Jackson	.25	.60
55 Karl Malone	.40	1.00
56 John Stockton	.40	1.00
57 Shareef Abdur-Rahim	.25	.60
58 Mike Bibby	.25	.60
59 Mitch Richmond	.25	.60
60 Richard Hamilton	.25	.60
61 Kobe Bryant FLY	1.50	4.00
62 Kobe Bryant FLY	1.50	4.00
63 Kobe Bryant FLY	1.50	4.00
64 Kobe Bryant FLY	1.50	4.00
65 Kobe Bryant FLY	1.50	4.00
66 Kobe Bryant FLY	1.50	4.00
67 Kobe Bryant FLY	1.50	4.00
68 Kobe Bryant FLY	1.50	4.00
69 Kobe Bryant FLY	1.50	4.00
70 Kobe Bryant FLY	1.50	4.00
71 Kobe Bryant FLY	1.50	4.00
72 Kobe Bryant FLY	1.50	4.00
73 Kobe Bryant FLY	1.50	4.00
74 Kobe Bryant FLY	1.50	4.00
75 Kobe Bryant FLY	1.50	4.00
76 Kevin Garnett FLY	1.00	2.50
77 Kevin Garnett FLY	1.00	2.50
78 Kevin Garnett FLY	1.00	2.50
79 Kevin Garnett FLY	1.00	2.50
80 Kevin Garnett FLY	1.00	2.50
81 Kevin Garnett FLY	1.00	2.50
82 Kevin Garnett FLY	1.00	2.50
83 Kevin Garnett FLY	1.00	2.50
84 Kevin Garnett FLY	1.00	2.50
85 Kevin Garnett FLY	1.00	2.50
86 Kevin Garnett FLY	1.00	2.50
87 Kevin Garnett FLY	1.00	2.50
88 Kevin Garnett FLY	1.00	2.50
89 Kevin Garnett FLY	1.00	2.50
90 Kevin Garnett FLY	1.00	2.50
91 Kenyon Martin RC	3.00	8.00
92 Stromile Swift RC	1.50	4.00
93 Darius Miles RC	1.50	4.00
94 Marcus Fizer RC	1.25	3.00

❑ 95 Mike Miller RC	2.00	5.00
❑ 96 DerMarr Johnson RC	1.25	3.00
❑ 97 Chris Mihm RC	1.25	3.00
❑ 98 Jamal Crawford RC	2.00	5.00
❑ 99 Joel Przybilla RC	1.25	3.00
❑ 100 Keyon Dooling RC	1.25	3.00
❑ 101 Jerome Moiso RC	1.25	3.00
❑ 102 Etan Thomas RC	1.25	3.00
❑ 103 Courtney Alexander RC	1.25	3.00
❑ 104 Mateen Cleaves RC	1.25	3.00
❑ 105 Jason Collier RC	1.25	3.00
❑ 106 Hedo Turkoglu RC	3.00	8.00
❑ 107 Desmond Mason RC	1.50	4.00
❑ 108 Quentin Richardson RC	1.50	4.00
❑ 109 Jamaal Magloire RC	1.25	3.00
❑ 110 Speedy Claxton RC	1.25	3.00
❑ 111 Morris Peterson RC	2.00	5.00
❑ 112 Donnell Harvey RC	1.25	3.00
❑ 113 DeShawn Stevenson RC	1.25	3.00
❑ 114 Mamadou N'Diaye RC	1.25	3.00
❑ 115 Erick Barkley RC	1.25	3.00
❑ 116 Mike Smith RC	1.25	3.00
❑ 117 Eddie House RC	1.25	3.00
❑ 118 Eduardo Najera RC	1.25	3.00
❑ 119 Jason Hart RC	1.25	3.00
❑ 120 Chris Porter RC	1.25	3.00

1992-93 Ultra

❑ COMPLETE SET (375)	15.00	30.00
❑ COMPLETE SERIES 1 (200)	7.50	15.00
❑ COMPLETE SERIES 2 (175)	7.50	15.00
❑ COMMON CARD (1-200)	.02	.10
❑ COMMON CARD (201-375)	.01	.05
❑ 1 Stacey Augmon	.08	.25
❑ 2 Duane Ferrell	.02	.10
❑ 3 Paul Graham	.02	.10
❑ 4 Blair Rasmussen	.02	.10
❑ 5 Rumeal Robinson	.02	.10
❑ 6 Dominique Wilkins	.20	.50
❑ 7 Kevin Willis	.02	.10
❑ 8 John Bagley	.02	.10
❑ 9 Dee Brown	.02	.10
❑ 10 Rick Fox	.08	.25
❑ 11 Kevin Gamble	.02	.10
❑ 12 Joe Kleine	.02	.10
❑ 13 Reggie Lewis	.08	.25
❑ 14 Kevin McHale	.20	.50
❑ 15 Robert Parish	.08	.25
❑ 16 Ed Pinckney	.02	.10
❑ 17 Muggsy Bogues	.08	.25
❑ 18 Dell Curry	.02	.10
❑ 19 Kenny Gattison	.02	.10
❑ 20 Kendall Gill	.08	.25
❑ 21 Larry Johnson	.25	.60
❑ 22 Johnny Newman	.02	.10
❑ 23 J.R. Reid	.02	.10
❑ 24 B.J.Armstrong	.02	.10
❑ 25 Bill Cartwright	.02	.10
❑ 26 Horace Grant	.08	.25
❑ 27 Michael Jordan	2.50	6.00
❑ 28 Stacey King	.02	.10
❑ 29 John Paxson	.02	.10
❑ 30 Will Perdue	.02	.10
❑ 31 Scottie Pippen	.60	1.50
❑ 32 Scott Williams	.02	.10
❑ 33 John Battle	.02	.10
❑ 34 Terrell Brandon	.20	.50
❑ 35 Brad Daugherty	.02	.10
❑ 36 Craig Ehlo	.02	.10
❑ 37 Larry Nance	.02	.10
❑ 38 Mark Price	.02	.10
❑ 39 Mike Sanders	.02	.10
❑ 40 John Williams	.02	.10
❑ 41 Terry Davis	.02	.10
❑ 42 Derek Harper	.08	.25
❑ 43 Donald Hodge	.02	.10
❑ 44 Mike Iuzzolino	.02	.10
❑ 45 Fat Lever	.02	.10
❑ 46 Doug Smith	.02	.10
❑ 47 Randy White	.02	.10
❑ 48 Winston Garland	.02	.10
❑ 49 Chris Jackson	.02	.10
❑ 50 Marcus Liberty	.02	.10
❑ 51 Todd Lichti	.02	.10
❑ 52 Mark Macon	.02	.10
❑ 53 Dikembe Mutombo	.25	.60
❑ 54 Reggie Williams	.02	.10
❑ 55 Mark Aguirre	.02	.10
❑ 56 Joe Dumars	.20	.50
❑ 57 Bill Laimbeer	.08	.25
❑ 58 Dennis Rodman	.40	1.00
❑ 59 Isiah Thomas	.20	.50
❑ 60 Darrell Walker	.02	.10
❑ 61 Orlando Woolridge	.02	.10
❑ 62 Victor Alexander	.02	.10
❑ 63 Chris Gatling	.02	.10
❑ 64 Tim Hardaway	.25	.60
❑ 65 Tyrone Hill	.02	.10
❑ 66 Sarunas Marciulionis	.02	.10
❑ 67 Chris Mullin	.20	.50
❑ 68 Billy Owens	.08	.25
❑ 69 Sleepy Floyd	.02	.10
❑ 70 Avery Johnson	.02	.10
❑ 71 Vernon Maxwell	.02	.10
❑ 72 Hakeem Olajuwon	.30	.75
❑ 73 Kenny Smith	.02	.10
❑ 74 Otis Thorpe	.08	.25
❑ 75 Dale Davis	.02	.10
❑ 76 Vern Fleming	.02	.10
❑ 77 George McCloud	.02	.10
❑ 78 Reggie Miller	.20	.50
❑ 79 Detlef Schrempf	.08	.25
❑ 80 Rik Smits	.08	.25
❑ 81 LaSalle Thompson	.02	.10
❑ 82 Gary Grant	.02	.10
❑ 83 Ron Harper	.08	.25
❑ 84 Mark Jackson	.08	.25
❑ 85 Danny Manning	.08	.25
❑ 86 Ken Norman	.02	.10
❑ 87 Stanley Roberts	.02	.10
❑ 88 Loy Vaught	.02	.10
❑ 89 Elden Campbell	.08	.25
❑ 90 Vlade Divac	.08	.25
❑ 91 A.C. Green	.08	.25
❑ 92 Sam Perkins	.08	.25
❑ 93 Byron Scott	.08	.25
❑ 94 Tony Smith	.02	.10
❑ 95 Sedale Threatt	.02	.10
❑ 96 James Worthy	.20	.50
❑ 97 Willie Burton	.02	.10
❑ 98 Bimbo Coles	.02	.10
❑ 99 Kevin Edwards	.02	.10
❑ 100 Grant Long	.02	.10
❑ 101 Glen Rice	.20	.50
❑ 102 Rony Seikaly	.02	.10
❑ 103 Brian Shaw	.02	.10
❑ 104 Steve Smith	.25	.60
❑ 105 Frank Brickowski	.02	.10
❑ 106 Moses Malone	.20	.50
❑ 107 Fred Roberts	.02	.10
❑ 108 Alvin Robertson	.02	.10
❑ 109 Thurl Bailey	.02	.10
❑ 110 Gerald Glass	.02	.10
❑ 111 Luc Longley	.08	.25
❑ 112 Felton Spencer	.02	.10
❑ 113 Doug West	.02	.10
❑ 114 Kenny Anderson	.20	.50
❑ 115 Mookie Blaylock	.08	.25
❑ 116 Sam Bowie	.02	.10
❑ 117 Derrick Coleman	.08	.25
❑ 118 Chris Dudley	.02	.10
❑ 119 Chris Morris	.02	.10
❑ 120 Drazen Petrovic	.02	.10
❑ 121 Greg Anthony	.02	.10
❑ 122 Patrick Ewing	.20	.50
❑ 123 Anthony Mason	.20	.50
❑ 124 Charles Oakley	.08	.25
❑ 125 Doc Rivers	.08	.25
❑ 126 Charles Smith	.02	.10
❑ 127 John Starks	.08	.25
❑ 128 Nick Anderson	.08	.25
❑ 129 Anthony Bowie	.02	.10
❑ 130 Terry Catledge	.02	.10
❑ 131 Jerry Reynolds	.02	.10
❑ 132 Dennis Scott	.08	.25
❑ 133 Scott Skiles	.02	.10
❑ 134 Brian Williams	.02	.10
❑ 135 Ron Anderson	.02	.10
❑ 136 Manute Bol	.02	.10
❑ 137 Johnny Dawkins	.02	.10
❑ 138 Armon Gilliam	.02	.10
❑ 139 Hersey Hawkins	.08	.25
❑ 140 Jeff Ruland	.02	.10
❑ 141 Charles Shackleford	.02	.10
❑ 142 Cedric Ceballos	.08	.25
❑ 143 Tom Chambers	.02	.10
❑ 144 Kevin Johnson	.20	.50
❑ 145 Negele Knight	.02	.10
❑ 146 Dan Majerle	.08	.25
❑ 147 Mark West	.02	.10
❑ 148 Mark Bryant	.02	.10
❑ 149 Clyde Drexler	.20	.50
❑ 150 Kevin Duckworth	.02	.10
❑ 151 Jerome Kersey	.02	.10
❑ 152 Robert Pack	.02	.10
❑ 153 Terry Porter	.02	.10
❑ 154 Cliff Robinson	.08	.25
❑ 155 Buck Williams	.08	.25
❑ 156 Anthony Bonner	.02	.10
❑ 157 Duane Causwell	.02	.10
❑ 158 Mitch Richmond	.20	.50
❑ 159 Lionel Simmons	.02	.10
❑ 160 Wayman Tisdale	.02	.10
❑ 161 Spud Webb	.08	.25
❑ 162 Willie Anderson	.02	.10
❑ 163 Antoine Carr	.02	.10
❑ 164 Terry Cummings	.08	.25
❑ 165 Sean Elliott	.08	.25
❑ 166 Sidney Green	.02	.10
❑ 167 David Robinson	.30	.75
❑ 168 Dana Barros	.02	.10
❑ 169 Benoit Benjamin	.02	.10
❑ 170 Michael Cage	.02	.10
❑ 171 Eddie Johnson	.02	.10
❑ 172 Shawn Kemp	.40	1.00
❑ 173 Derrick McKey	.02	.10
❑ 174 Nate McMillan	.02	.10
❑ 175 Gary Payton	.40	1.00
❑ 176 Ricky Pierce	.02	.10
❑ 177 David Benoit	.02	.10
❑ 178 Mike Brown	.02	.10
❑ 179 Tyrone Corbin	.02	.10
❑ 180 Mark Eaton	.02	.10
❑ 181 Jeff Malone	.02	.10
❑ 182 Karl Malone	.30	.75
❑ 183 John Stockton	.20	.50
❑ 184 Michael Adams	.02	.10
❑ 185 Ledell Eackles	.02	.10
❑ 186 Pervis Ellison	.02	.10
❑ 187 A.J. English	.02	.10
❑ 188 Harvey Grant	.02	.10
❑ 189 Buck Johnson	.02	.10
❑ 190 LaBradford Smith	.02	.10
❑ 191 Larry Stewart	.02	.10
❑ 192 David Wingate	.02	.10
❑ 193 Alonzo Mourning RC	.75	2.00
❑ 194 Adam Keefe RC	.02	.10
❑ 195 Robert Horry RC	.20	.50
❑ 196 Anthony Peeler RC	.08	.25
❑ 197 Tracy Murray RC	.08	.25
❑ 198 Dave Johnson RC	.02	.10
❑ 199 Checklist 1-104	.02	.10
❑ 200 Checklist 105-200	.02	.10
❑ 201 David Robinson JS	.10	.30
❑ 202 Dikembe Mutombo JS	.10	.30
❑ 203 Otis Thorpe JS	.01	.05
❑ 204 Hakeem Olajuwon JS	.10	.30
❑ 205 Shawn Kemp JS	.20	.50
❑ 206 Charles Barkley JS	.10	.30
❑ 207 Pervis Ellison JS	.01	.05
❑ 208 Chris Morris JS	.01	.05
❑ 209 Brad Daugherty JS	.01	.05
❑ 210 Derrick Coleman JS	.01	.05
❑ 211 Tim Perry JS	.01	.05
❑ 212 Duane Causwell JS	.01	.05
❑ 213 Scottie Pippen JS	.20	.50
❑ 214 Robert Parish JS	.01	.05
❑ 215 Stacey Augmon JS	.01	.05
❑ 216 Michael Jordan JS	.75	2.00
❑ 217 Karl Malone JS	.10	.30
❑ 218 John Williams JS	.01	.05
❑ 219 Horace Grant JS	.01	.05
❑ 220 Orlando Woolridge JS	.01	.05
❑ 221 Mookie Blaylock	.05	.15

❑ 222 Greg Foster	.01	.05
❑ 223 Steve Henson	.01	.05
❑ 224 Adam Keefe	.01	.05
❑ 225 Jon Koncak	.01	.05
❑ 226 Travis Mays	.01	.05
❑ 227 Alaa Abdelnaby	.01	.05
❑ 228 Sherman Douglas	.01	.05
❑ 229 Xavier McDaniel	.01	.05
❑ 230 Marcus Webb RC	.01	.05
❑ 231 Tony Bennett RC	.01	.05
❑ 232 Mike Gminski	.01	.05
❑ 233 Kevin Lynch	.01	.05
❑ 234 Alonzo Mourning	.30	.75
❑ 235 David Wingate	.01	.05
❑ 236 Rodney McCray	.01	.05
❑ 237 Trent Tucker	.01	.05
❑ 238 Corey Williams RC	.01	.05
❑ 239 Danny Ferry	.01	.05
❑ 240 Jay Guidinger RC	.01	.05
❑ 241 Jerome Lane	.01	.05
❑ 242 Bobby Phills RC	.10	.30
❑ 243 Gerald Wilkins	.01	.05
❑ 244 Walter Bond RC	.01	.05
❑ 245 Dexter Cambridge RC	.01	.05
❑ 246 Radisav Curcic RC	.01	.05
❑ 247 Brian Howard RC	.01	.05
❑ 248 Tracy Moore RC	.01	.05
❑ 249 Sean Rooks RC	.01	.05
❑ 250 Kevin Brooks	.01	.05
❑ 251 LaPhonso Ellis RC	.10	.30
❑ 252 Scott Hastings	.01	.05
❑ 253 Robert Pack	.01	.05
❑ 254 Gary Plummer RC	.01	.05
❑ 255 Bryant Stith RC	.05	.15
❑ 256 Robert Werdann RC	.01	.05
❑ 257 Gerald Glass	.01	.05
❑ 258 Terry Mills	.01	.05
❑ 259 Olden Polynice	.01	.05
❑ 260 Danny Young	.01	.05
❑ 261 Jud Buechler	.01	.05
❑ 262 Jeff Grayer	.01	.05
❑ 263 Byron Houston RC	.01	.05
❑ 264 Keith Jennings RC	.01	.05
❑ 265 Ed Nealy	.01	.05
❑ 266 Latrell Sprewell RC	1.00	2.50
❑ 267 Scott Brooks	.01	.05
❑ 268 Matt Bullard	.01	.05
❑ 269 Winston Garland	.01	.05
❑ 270 Carl Herrera	.01	.05
❑ 271 Robert Horry	.10	.30
❑ 272 Tree Rollins	.01	.05
❑ 273 Greg Dreiling	.01	.05
❑ 274 Sean Green	.01	.05
❑ 275 Sam Mitchell	.01	.05
❑ 276 Pooh Richardson	.01	.05
❑ 277 Malik Sealy RC	.05	.15
❑ 278 Kenny Williams	.01	.05
❑ 279 Mark Jackson	.05	.15
❑ 280 Stanley Roberts	.01	.05
❑ 281 Elmore Spencer RC	.01	.05
❑ 282 Kiki Vandeweghe	.01	.05
❑ 283 John S. Williams	.01	.05
❑ 284 Randy Woods RC	.01	.05
❑ 285 Alex Blackwell RC	.01	.05
❑ 286 Duane Cooper RC	.01	.05
❑ 287 James Edwards	.01	.05
❑ 288 Jack Haley	.01	.05
❑ 289 Anthony Peeler	.05	.15
❑ 290 Keith Askins	.01	.05
❑ 291 Matt Geiger RC	.05	.15
❑ 292 Alec Kessler	.01	.05
❑ 293 Harold Miner with M.Jordan RC	.05	.15
❑ 294 John Salley	.01	.05
❑ 295 Anthony Avent RC	.01	.05
❑ 296 Jon Barry RC	.05	.15
❑ 297 Todd Day RC	.05	.15
❑ 298 Blue Edwards	.01	.05
❑ 299 Brad Lohaus	.01	.05
❑ 300 Lee Mayberry RC	.01	.05
❑ 301 Eric Murdock	.01	.05
❑ 302 Danny Schayes	.01	.05
❑ 303 Lance Blanks	.01	.05
❑ 304 Christian Laettner RC	.25	.60
❑ 305 Marlon Maxey RC	.01	.05
❑ 306 Bob McCann RC	.01	.05
❑ 307 Chuck Person	.01	.05
❑ 308 Brad Sellers	.01	.05
❑ 309 Chris Smith RC	.01	.05
❑ 310 Gundars Vetra RC	.01	.05
❑ 311 Micheal Williams	.01	.05
❑ 312 Rafael Addison	.01	.05
❑ 313 Chucky Brown	.01	.05
❑ 314 Maurice Cheeks	.01	.05
❑ 315 Tate George	.01	.05
❑ 316 Rick Mahorn	.01	.05
❑ 317 Rumeal Robinson	.01	.05
❑ 318 Eric Anderson RC	.01	.05
❑ 319 Rolando Blackman	.01	.05
❑ 320 Tony Campbell	.01	.05
❑ 321 Hubert Davis RC	.05	.15
❑ 322 Doc Rivers	.05	.15
❑ 323 Charles Smith	.01	.05
❑ 324 Herb Williams	.01	.05
❑ 325 Litterial Green RC	.01	.05
❑ 326 Steve Kerr	.05	.15
❑ 327 Greg Kite	.01	.05
❑ 328 Shaquille O'Neal RC	4.00	10.00
❑ 329 Tom Tolbert	.01	.05
❑ 330 Jeff Turner	.01	.05
❑ 331 Greg Grant	.01	.05
❑ 332 Jeff Hornacek	.05	.15
❑ 333 Andrew Lang	.01	.05
❑ 334 Tim Perry	.01	.05
❑ 335 C.Weatherspoon RC	.10	.30
❑ 336 Danny Ainge	.05	.15
❑ 337 Charles Barkley	.20	.50
❑ 338 Richard Dumas RC	.01	.05
❑ 339 Frank Johnson	.01	.05
❑ 340 Tim Kempton	.01	.05
❑ 341 Oliver Miller RC	.05	.15
❑ 342 Jerrod Mustaf	.01	.05
❑ 343 Mario Elie	.05	.15
❑ 344 Dave Johnson	.01	.05
❑ 345 Tracy Murray	.05	.15
❑ 346 Rod Strickland	.10	.30
❑ 347 Randy Brown	.01	.05
❑ 348 Pete Chilcutt	.01	.05
❑ 349 Marty Conlon	.01	.05
❑ 350 Jim Les	.01	.05
❑ 351 Kurt Rambis	.01	.05
❑ 352 Walt Williams RC	.10	.30
❑ 353 Lloyd Daniels RC	.01	.05
❑ 354 Vinny Del Negro	.01	.05
❑ 355 Dale Ellis	.01	.05
❑ 356 Avery Johnson	.01	.05
❑ 357 Sam Mack RC	.05	.15
❑ 358 J.R. Reid	.01	.05
❑ 359 David Wood	.01	.05
❑ 360 Vincent Askew	.01	.05
❑ 361 Isaac Austin RC	.05	.15
❑ 362 John Crotty RC	.01	.05
❑ 363 Stephen Howard RC	.01	.05
❑ 364 Jay Humphries	.01	.05
❑ 365 Larry Krystkowiak	.01	.05
❑ 366 Rex Chapman	.01	.05
❑ 367 Tom Gugliotta RC	.40	1.00
❑ 368 Buck Johnson	.01	.05
❑ 369 Charles Jones	.01	.05
❑ 370 Don MacLean RC	.01	.05
❑ 371 Doug Overton	.01	.05
❑ 372 Brent Price RC	.05	.15
❑ 373 Checklist 201-266	.01	.05
❑ 374 Checklist 267-330	.01	.05
❑ 375 Checklist 331-375	.01	.05
❑ JS207 Pervis Ellison AU	10.00	25.00
❑ JS212 Duane Causwell AU	10.00	25.00
❑ JS215 Stacey Augmon AU	15.00	30.00
❑ NNO Jam Session Rank 1-10	1.00	2.50
❑ NNO Jam Session Rank 11-20	1.00	2.50

1993-94 Ultra

❑ COMPLETE SET (375)	15.00	30.00
❑ COMPLETE SERIES 1 (200)	7.50	15.00
❑ COMPLETE SERIES 2 (175)	7.50	15.00
❑ 1 Stacey Augmon	.01	.05
❑ 2 Mookie Blaylock	.05	.15
❑ 3 Doug Edwards RC	.01	.05
❑ 4 Duane Ferrell	.01	.05
❑ 5 Paul Graham	.01	.05
❑ 6 Adam Keefe	.01	.05
❑ 7 Dominique Wilkins	.10	.30
❑ 8 Kevin Willis	.01	.05
❑ 9 Alaa Abdelnaby	.01	.05
❑ 10 Dee Brown	.01	.05
❑ 11 Sherman Douglas	.01	.05
❑ 12 Rick Fox	.01	.05
❑ 13 Kevin Gamble	.01	.05
❑ 14 Xavier McDaniel	.01	.05
❑ 15 Robert Parish	.05	.15
❑ 16 Muggsy Bogues	.05	.15
❑ 17 Scott Burrell RC	.10	.30
❑ 18 Dell Curry	.01	.05
❑ 19 Kenny Gattison	.01	.05
❑ 20 Hersey Hawkins	.05	.15
❑ 21 Eddie Johnson	.01	.05
❑ 22 Larry Johnson	.10	.30
❑ 23 Alonzo Mourning	.20	.50
❑ 24 Johnny Newman	.01	.05
❑ 25 David Wingate	.01	.05
❑ 26 B.J. Armstrong	.01	.05
❑ 27 Corie Blount RC	.01	.05
❑ 28 Bill Cartwright	.01	.05
❑ 29 Horace Grant	.05	.15
❑ 30 Michael Jordan	1.50	4.00
❑ 31 Stacey King	.01	.05
❑ 32 John Paxson	.01	.05
❑ 33 Will Perdue	.01	.05
❑ 34 Scottie Pippen	.40	1.00
❑ 35 Terrell Brandon	.05	.15
❑ 36 Brad Daugherty	.01	.05
❑ 37 Danny Ferry	.01	.05
❑ 38 Chris Mills RC	.10	.30
❑ 39 Larry Nance	.01	.05
❑ 40 Mark Price	.01	.05
❑ 41 Gerald Wilkins	.01	.05
❑ 42 John Williams	.01	.05
❑ 43 Terry Davis	.01	.05
❑ 44 Derek Harper	.05	.15
❑ 45 Donald Hodge	.01	.05
❑ 46 Jim Jackson	.05	.15
❑ 47 Sean Rooks	.01	.05
❑ 48 Doug Smith	.01	.05
❑ 49 Mahmoud Abdul-Rauf	.01	.05
❑ 50 LaPhonso Ellis	.01	.05
❑ 51 Mark Macon	.01	.05
❑ 52 Dikembe Mutombo	.10	.30
❑ 53 Bryant Stith	.01	.05
❑ 54 Reggie Williams	.01	.05
❑ 55 Mark Aguirre	.01	.05
❑ 56 Joe Dumars	.10	.30
❑ 57 Bill Laimbeer	.01	.05
❑ 58 Terry Mills	.01	.05
❑ 59 Olden Polynice	.01	.05
❑ 60 Alvin Robertson	.01	.05
❑ 61 Sean Elliott	.05	.15
❑ 62 Isiah Thomas	.10	.30
❑ 63 Victor Alexander	.01	.05
❑ 64 Chris Gatling	.01	.05
❑ 65 Tim Hardaway	.10	.30
❑ 66 Byron Houston	.01	.05
❑ 67 Sarunas Marciulionis	.01	.05
❑ 68 Chris Mullin	.10	.30
❑ 69 Billy Owens	.01	.05
❑ 70 Latrell Sprewell	.30	.75
❑ 71 Matt Bullard	.01	.05
❑ 72 Sam Cassell RC	.50	1.25
❑ 73 Carl Herrera	.01	.05
❑ 74 Robert Horry	.05	.15
❑ 75 Vernon Maxwell	.01	.05
❑ 76 Hakeem Olajuwon	.20	.50
❑ 77 Kenny Smith	.01	.05
❑ 78 Otis Thorpe	.05	.15
❑ 79 Dale Davis	.01	.05
❑ 80 Vern Fleming	.01	.05
❑ 81 Reggie Miller	.10	.30
❑ 82 Sam Mitchell	.01	.05
❑ 83 Pooh Richardson	.01	.05
❑ 84 Detlef Schrempf	.05	.15
❑ 85 Rik Smits	.05	.15
❑ 86 Ron Harper	.05	.15
❑ 87 Mark Jackson	.05	.15
❑ 88 Danny Manning	.05	.15
❑ 89 Stanley Roberts	.01	.05
❑ 90 Loy Vaught	.01	.05

❑ 91 John Williams	.01	.05
❑ 92 Sam Bowie	.01	.05
❑ 93 Doug Christie	.05	.15
❑ 94 Vlade Divac	.05	.15
❑ 95 George Lynch RC	.01	.05
❑ 96 Anthony Peeler	.01	.05
❑ 97 James Worthy	.10	.30
❑ 98 Bimbo Coles	.01	.05
❑ 99 Grant Long	.01	.05
❑ 100 Harold Miner	.01	.05
❑ 101 Glen Rice	.05	.15
❑ 102 Rony Seikaly	.01	.05
❑ 103 Brian Shaw	.01	.05
❑ 104 Steve Smith	.10	.30
❑ 105 Anthony Avent	.01	.05
❑ 106 Vin Baker RC	.30	.75
❑ 107 Frank Brickowski	.01	.05
❑ 108 Todd Day	.01	.05
❑ 109 Blue Edwards	.01	.05
❑ 110 Lee Mayberry	.01	.05
❑ 111 Eric Murdock	.01	.05
❑ 112 Orlando Woolridge	.01	.05
❑ 113 Thurl Bailey	.01	.05
❑ 114 Christian Laettner	.05	.15
❑ 115 Chuck Person	.01	.05
❑ 116 Doug West	.01	.05
❑ 117 Micheal Williams	.01	.05
❑ 118 Kenny Anderson	.05	.15
❑ 119 Derrick Coleman	.05	.15
❑ 120 Rick Mahorn	.01	.05
❑ 121 Chris Morris	.01	.05
❑ 122 Rumeal Robinson	.01	.05
❑ 123 Rex Walters RC	.01	.05
❑ 124 Greg Anthony	.01	.05
❑ 125 Rolando Blackman	.01	.05
❑ 126 Hubert Davis	.01	.05
❑ 127 Patrick Ewing	.10	.30
❑ 128 Anthony Mason	.05	.15
❑ 129 Charles Oakley	.05	.15
❑ 130 Doc Rivers	.05	.15
❑ 131 Charles Smith	.01	.05
❑ 132 John Starks	.05	.15
❑ 133 Nick Anderson	.05	.15
❑ 134 Anthony Bowie	.01	.05
❑ 135 Shaquille O'Neal	.60	1.50
❑ 136 Dennis Scott	.01	.05
❑ 137 Scott Skiles	.01	.05
❑ 138 Jeff Turner	.01	.05
❑ 139 Shawn Bradley RC	.10	.30
❑ 140 Johnny Dawkins	.01	.05
❑ 141 Jeff Hornacek	.05	.15
❑ 142 Tim Perry	.01	.05
❑ 143 Clarence Weatherspoon	.01	.05
❑ 144 Danny Ainge	.05	.15
❑ 145 Charles Barkley	.20	.50
❑ 146 Cedric Ceballos	.05	.15
❑ 147 Kevin Johnson	.05	.15
❑ 148 Negele Knight	.01	.05
❑ 149 Malcolm Mackey RC	.01	.05
❑ 150 Dan Majerle	.05	.15
❑ 151 Oliver Miller	.01	.05
❑ 152 Mark West	.01	.05
❑ 153 Mark Bryant	.01	.05
❑ 154 Clyde Drexler	.10	.30
❑ 155 Jerome Kersey	.01	.05
❑ 156 Terry Porter	.01	.05
❑ 157 Cliff Robinson	.05	.15
❑ 158 Rod Strickland	.05	.15
❑ 159 Buck Williams	.01	.05
❑ 160 Duane Causwell	.01	.05
❑ 161 Bobby Hurley RC	.05	.15
❑ 162 Mitch Richmond	.10	.30
❑ 163 Lionel Simmons	.01	.05
❑ 164 Wayman Tisdale	.01	.05
❑ 165 Spud Webb	.05	.15
❑ 166 Walt Williams	.01	.05
❑ 167 Willie Anderson	.01	.05
❑ 168 Antoine Carr	.01	.05
❑ 169 Lloyd Daniels	.01	.05
❑ 170 Dennis Rodman	.25	.60
❑ 171 Dale Ellis	.01	.05
❑ 172 Avery Johnson	.01	.05
❑ 173 J.R. Reid	.01	.05
❑ 174 David Robinson	.20	.50
❑ 175 Michael Cage	.01	.05
❑ 176 Kendall Gill	.05	.15
❑ 177 Ervin Johnson RC	.05	.15
❑ 178 Shawn Kemp	.20	.50
❑ 179 Derrick McKey	.01	.05
❑ 180 Nate McMillan	.01	.05
❑ 181 Gary Payton	.20	.50
❑ 182 Sam Perkins	.05	.15
❑ 183 Ricky Pierce	.01	.05
❑ 184 David Benoit	.01	.05
❑ 185 Tyrone Corbin	.01	.05
❑ 186 Mark Eaton	.01	.05
❑ 187 Jay Humphries	.01	.05
❑ 188 Jeff Malone	.01	.05
❑ 189 Karl Malone	.20	.50
❑ 190 John Stockton	.10	.30
❑ 191 Luther Wright RC	.01	.05
❑ 192 Michael Adams	.01	.05
❑ 193 Calbert Cheaney RC	.05	.15
❑ 194 Pervis Ellison	.01	.05
❑ 195 Tom Gugliotta	.10	.30
❑ 196 Buck Johnson	.01	.05
❑ 197 LaBradford Smith	.01	.05
❑ 198 Larry Stewart	.01	.05
❑ 199 Checklist	.01	.05
❑ 200 Checklist	.01	.05
❑ 201 Doug Edwards	.01	.05
❑ 202 Craig Ehlo	.01	.05
❑ 203 Jon Koncak	.01	.05
❑ 204 Andrew Lang	.01	.05
❑ 205 Ennis Whatley	.01	.05
❑ 206 Chris Corchiani	.01	.05
❑ 207 Acie Earl RC	.01	.05
❑ 208 Jimmy Oliver	.01	.05
❑ 209 Ed Pinckney	.01	.05
❑ 210 Dino Radja RC	.01	.05
❑ 211 Matt Wenstrom RC	.01	.05
❑ 212 Tony Bennett	.01	.05
❑ 213 Scott Burrell	.10	.30
❑ 214 LeRon Ellis	.01	.05
❑ 215 Hersey Hawkins	.05	.15
❑ 216 Eddie Johnson	.01	.05
❑ 217 Rumeal Robinson	.01	.05
❑ 218 Corie Blount	.01	.05
❑ 219 Dave Johnson	.01	.05
❑ 220 Steve Kerr	.05	.15
❑ 221 Toni Kukoc RC	.50	1.25
❑ 222 Pete Myers	.01	.05
❑ 223 Bill Wennington	.01	.05
❑ 224 Scott Williams	.01	.05
❑ 225 John Battle	.01	.05
❑ 226 Tyrone Hill	.01	.05
❑ 227 Gerald Madkins RC	.01	.05
❑ 228 Chris Mills	.10	.30
❑ 229 Bobby Phills	.01	.05
❑ 230 Greg Dreiling	.01	.05
❑ 231 Lucious Harris RC	.01	.05
❑ 232 Popeye Jones RC	.01	.05
❑ 233 Tim Legler RC	.01	.05
❑ 234 Fat Lever	.01	.05
❑ 235 Jamal Mashburn RC	.30	.75
❑ 236 Tom Hammonds	.01	.05
❑ 237 Darnell Mee RC	.01	.05
❑ 238 Robert Pack	.01	.05
❑ 239 Rodney Rogers RC	.10	.30
❑ 240 Brian Williams	.01	.05
❑ 241 Greg Anderson	.01	.05
❑ 242 Sean Elliott	.05	.15
❑ 243 Allan Houston RC	.50	1.25
❑ 244 Lindsey Hunter RC	.10	.30
❑ 245 Mark Macon	.01	.05
❑ 246 David Wood	.01	.05
❑ 247 Jud Buechler	.01	.05
❑ 248 Josh Grant RC	.01	.05
❑ 249 Jeff Grayer	.01	.05
❑ 250 Keith Jennings	.01	.05
❑ 251 Avery Johnson	.01	.05
❑ 252 Chris Webber RC	1.25	3.00
❑ 253 Scott Brooks	.01	.05
❑ 254 Sam Cassell	.10	.30
❑ 255 Mario Elie	.01	.05
❑ 256 Richard Petruska RC	.01	.05
❑ 257 Eric Riley RC	.01	.05
❑ 258 Antonio Davis RC	.15	.40
❑ 259 Scott Haskin RC	.01	.05
❑ 260 Derrick McKey	.01	.05
❑ 261 Byron Scott	.05	.15
❑ 262 Malik Sealy	.01	.05
❑ 263 Kenny Williams	.01	.05
❑ 264 Haywoode Workman	.01	.05
❑ 265 Mark Aguirre	.01	.05
❑ 266 Terry Dehere RC	.01	.05
❑ 267 Harold Ellis RC	.01	.05
❑ 268 Gary Grant	.01	.05
❑ 269 Bob Martin RC	.01	.05
❑ 270 Elmore Spencer	.01	.05
❑ 271 Tom Tolbert	.01	.05
❑ 272 Sam Bowie	.01	.05
❑ 273 Elden Campbell	.01	.05
❑ 274 Antonio Harvey RC	.01	.05
❑ 275 George Lynch	.01	.05
❑ 276 Tony Smith	.01	.05
❑ 277 Sedale Threatt	.01	.05
❑ 278 Nick Van Exel RC	.40	1.00
❑ 279 Willie Burton	.01	.05
❑ 280 Matt Geiger	.01	.05
❑ 281 John Salley	.01	.05
❑ 282 Vin Baker	.15	.40
❑ 283 Jon Barry	.01	.05
❑ 284 Brad Lohaus	.01	.05
❑ 285 Ken Norman	.01	.05
❑ 286 Derek Strong RC	.01	.05
❑ 287 Mike Brown	.01	.05
❑ 288 Brian Davis RC	.01	.05
❑ 289 Tellis Frank	.01	.05
❑ 290 Luc Longley	.05	.15
❑ 291 Marlon Maxey	.01	.05
❑ 292 Isaiah Rider RC	.25	.60
❑ 293 Chris Smith	.01	.05
❑ 294 P.J.Brown RC	.10	.30
❑ 295 Kevin Edwards	.01	.05
❑ 296 Armon Gilliam	.01	.05
❑ 297 Johnny Newman	.01	.05
❑ 298 Rex Walters	.01	.05
❑ 299 David Wesley RC	.10	.30
❑ 300 Jayson Williams	.05	.15
❑ 301 Anthony Bonner	.01	.05
❑ 302 Derek Harper	.05	.15
❑ 303 Herb Williams	.01	.05
❑ 304 Litterial Green	.01	.05
❑ 305 Anfernee Hardaway RC	1.00	2.50
❑ 306 Greg Kite	.01	.05
❑ 307 Larry Krystkowiak	.01	.05
❑ 308 Keith Tower RC	.01	.05
❑ 309 Dana Barros	.01	.05
❑ 310 Shawn Bradley	.10	.30
❑ 311 Greg Graham RC	.01	.05
❑ 312 Sean Green	.01	.05
❑ 313 Warren Kidd RC	.01	.05
❑ 314 Eric Leckner	.01	.05
❑ 315 Moses Malone	.10	.30
❑ 316 Orlando Woolridge	.01	.05
❑ 317 Duane Cooper	.01	.05
❑ 318 Joe Courtney RC	.01	.05
❑ 319 A.C. Green	.05	.15
❑ 320 Frank Johnson	.01	.05
❑ 321 Joe Kleine	.01	.05
❑ 322 Chris Dudley	.01	.05
❑ 323 Harvey Grant	.01	.05
❑ 324 Jaren Jackson	.01	.05
❑ 325 Tracy Murray	.01	.05
❑ 326 James Robinson RC	.01	.05
❑ 327 Reggie Smith	.01	.05
❑ 328 Kevin Thompson RC	.01	.05
❑ 329 Randy Brown	.01	.05
❑ 330 Evers Burns RC	.01	.05
❑ 331 Pete Chilcutt	.01	.05
❑ 332 Bobby Hurley	.05	.15
❑ 333 Mike Peplowski RC	.01	.05
❑ 334 LaBradford Smith	.01	.05
❑ 335 Trevor Wilson	.01	.05
❑ 336 Terry Cummings	.01	.05
❑ 337 Vinny Del Negro	.01	.05
❑ 338 Sleepy Floyd	.01	.05
❑ 339 Negele Knight	.01	.05
❑ 340 Dennis Rodman	.25	.60
❑ 341 Chris Whitney RC	.01	.05
❑ 342 Vincent Askew	.01	.05
❑ 343 Kendall Gill	.05	.15
❑ 344 Ervin Johnson	.05	.15
❑ 345 Chris King RC	.01	.05
❑ 346 Detlef Schrempf	.05	.15
❑ 347 Walter Bond	.01	.05
❑ 348 Tom Chambers	.01	.05
❑ 349 John Crotty	.01	.05
❑ 350 Bryon Russell RC	.10	.30
❑ 351 Felton Spencer	.01	.05
❑ 352 Mitchell Butler RC	.01	.05
❑ 353 Rex Chapman	.01	.05
❑ 354 Calbert Cheaney	.05	.15
❑ 355 Kevin Duckworth	.01	.05
❑ 356 Don MacLean	.01	.05
❑ 357 Gheorghe Muresan RC	.10	.30

❑ 358 Doug Overton	.01	.05
❑ 359 Brent Price	.01	.05
❑ 360 Kenny Walker	.01	.05
❑ 361 Derrick Coleman USA	.01	.05
❑ 362 Joe Dumars USA	.05	.15
❑ 363 Tim Hardaway USA	.05	.15
❑ 364 Larry Johnson USA	.05	.15
❑ 365 Shawn Kemp USA	.15	.40
❑ 366 Dan Majerle USA	.01	.05
❑ 367 Alonzo Mourning USA	.10	.30
❑ 368 Mark Price USA	.01	.05
❑ 369 Steve Smith USA	.05	.15
❑ 370 Isiah Thomas USA	.05	.15
❑ 371 Dominique Wilkins USA	.05	.15
❑ 372 Don Nelson	.05	.15
❑ 373 Jamal Mashburn CL	.10	.30
❑ 374 Checklist	.01	.05
❑ 375 Checklist	.01	.05
❑ M1 Reggie Miller USA	.30	.75
❑ M2 Shaquille O'Neal USA	2.50	6.00
❑ M3 Team Checklist USA	.75	2.00

1994-95 Ultra

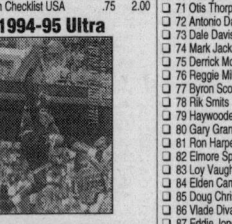

❑ COMPLETE SET (350)	17.50	35.00
❑ COMPLETE SERIES 1 (200)	10.00	20.00
❑ COMPLETE SERIES 2 (150)	7.50	15.00
❑ 1 Stacey Augmon	.02	.10
❑ 2 Mookie Blaylock	.02	.10
❑ 3 Craig Ehlo	.02	.10
❑ 4 Adam Keefe	.02	.10
❑ 5 Andrew Lang	.02	.10
❑ 6 Ken Norman	.02	.10
❑ 7 Kevin Willis	.02	.10
❑ 8 Dee Brown	.02	.10
❑ 9 Sherman Douglas	.02	.10
❑ 10 Acie Earl	.02	.10
❑ 11 Pervis Ellison	.02	.10
❑ 12 Rick Fox	.02	.10
❑ 13 Xavier McDaniel	.02	.10
❑ 14 Eric Montross RC	.02	.10
❑ 15 Dino Radja	.02	.10
❑ 16 Dominique Wilkins	.15	.40
❑ 17 Michael Adams	.02	.10
❑ 18 Muggsy Bogues	.05	.15
❑ 19 Dell Curry	.02	.10
❑ 20 Kenny Gattison	.02	.10
❑ 21 Hersey Hawkins	.05	.15
❑ 22 Larry Johnson	.05	.15
❑ 23 Alonzo Mourning	.20	.50
❑ 24 Robert Parish	.05	.15
❑ 25 B.J. Armstrong	.02	.10
❑ 26 Steve Kerr	.02	.10
❑ 27 Toni Kukoc	.25	.60
❑ 28 Luc Longley	.02	.10
❑ 29 Pete Myers	.02	.10
❑ 30 Will Perdue	.02	.10
❑ 31 Scottie Pippen	.50	1.25
❑ 32 Terrell Brandon	.05	.15
❑ 33 Brad Daugherty	.02	.10
❑ 34 Tyrone Hill	.02	.10
❑ 35 Chris Mills	.05	.15
❑ 36 Bobby Phills	.02	.10
❑ 37 Mark Price	.02	.10
❑ 38 Gerald Wilkins	.02	.10
❑ 39 John Williams	.02	.10
❑ 40 Terry Davis	.02	.10
❑ 41 Jim Jackson	.05	.15
❑ 42 Popeye Jones	.02	.10
❑ 43 Jason Kidd RC	1.50	4.00
❑ 44 Jamal Mashburn	.15	.40
❑ 45 Sean Rooks	.02	.10
❑ 46 Doug Smith	.02	.10
❑ 47 Mahmoud Abdul-Rauf	.02	.10
❑ 48 LaPhonso Ellis	.02	.10
❑ 49 Dikembe Mutombo	.05	.15
❑ 50 Robert Pack	.02	.10
❑ 51 Rodney Rogers	.02	.10
❑ 52 Bryant Stith	.02	.10
❑ 53 Brian Williams	.02	.10
❑ 54 Reggie Williams	.02	.10
❑ 55 Greg Anderson	.02	.10
❑ 56 Joe Dumars	.15	.40
❑ 57 Allan Houston	.25	.60
❑ 58 Lindsey Hunter	.05	.15
❑ 59 Terry Mills	.02	.10
❑ 60 Tim Hardaway	.15	.40
❑ 61 Chris Mullin	.15	.40
❑ 62 Billy Owens	.02	.10
❑ 63 Latrell Sprewell	.15	.40
❑ 64 Chris Webber	.40	1.00
❑ 65 Sam Cassell	.15	.40
❑ 66 Carl Herrera	.02	.10
❑ 67 Robert Horry	.05	.15
❑ 68 Vernon Maxwell	.02	.10
❑ 69 Hakeem Olajuwon	.25	.60
❑ 70 Kenny Smith	.02	.10
❑ 71 Otis Thorpe	.02	.10
❑ 72 Antonio Davis	.02	.10
❑ 73 Dale Davis	.02	.10
❑ 74 Mark Jackson	.02	.10
❑ 75 Derrick McKey	.02	.10
❑ 76 Reggie Miller	.15	.40
❑ 77 Byron Scott	.05	.15
❑ 78 Rik Smits	.02	.10
❑ 79 Haywoode Workman	.02	.10
❑ 80 Gary Grant	.02	.10
❑ 81 Ron Harper	.05	.15
❑ 82 Elmore Spencer	.02	.10
❑ 83 Loy Vaught	.02	.10
❑ 84 Elden Campbell	.02	.10
❑ 85 Doug Christie	.05	.15
❑ 86 Vlade Divac	.02	.10
❑ 87 Eddie Jones RC	.75	2.00
❑ 88 George Lynch	.02	.10
❑ 89 Anthony Peeler	.02	.10
❑ 90 Sedale Threatt	.02	.10
❑ 91 Nick Van Exel	.15	.40
❑ 92 James Worthy	.15	.40
❑ 93 Bimbo Coles	.02	.10
❑ 94 Matt Geiger	.02	.10
❑ 95 Grant Long	.02	.10
❑ 96 Harold Miner	.02	.10
❑ 97 Glen Rice	.05	.15
❑ 98 John Salley	.02	.10
❑ 99 Rony Seikaly	.02	.10
❑ 100 Brian Shaw	.02	.10
❑ 101 Steve Smith	.05	.15
❑ 102 Vin Baker	.15	.40
❑ 103 Jon Barry	.02	.10
❑ 104 Todd Day	.02	.10
❑ 105 Lee Mayberry	.02	.10
❑ 106 Eric Murdock	.02	.10
❑ 107 Thurl Bailey	.02	.10
❑ 108 Stacey King	.02	.10
❑ 109 Christian Laettner	.05	.15
❑ 110 Isaiah Rider	.05	.15
❑ 111 Chris Smith	.02	.10
❑ 112 Doug West	.02	.10
❑ 113 Micheal Williams	.02	.10
❑ 114 Kenny Anderson	.05	.15
❑ 115 Benoit Benjamin	.02	.10
❑ 116 P.J. Brown	.02	.10
❑ 117 Derrick Coleman	.05	.15
❑ 118 Yinka Dare RC	.02	.10
❑ 119 Kevin Edwards	.02	.10
❑ 120 Armon Gilliam	.02	.10
❑ 121 Chris Morris	.02	.10
❑ 122 Greg Anthony	.02	.10
❑ 123 Anthony Bonner	.02	.10
❑ 124 Hubert Davis	.02	.10
❑ 125 Patrick Ewing	.15	.40
❑ 126 Derek Harper	.02	.10
❑ 127 Anthony Mason	.05	.15
❑ 128 Charles Oakley	.02	.10
❑ 129 Doc Rivers	.05	.15
❑ 130 John Starks	.02	.10
❑ 131 Nick Anderson	.02	.10
❑ 132 Anthony Avent	.02	.10
❑ 133 Anthony Bowie	.02	.10
❑ 134 Anfernee Hardaway	.40	1.00
❑ 135 Shaquille O'Neal	.75	2.00
❑ 136 Dennis Scott	.02	.10
❑ 137 Jeff Turner	.02	.10
❑ 138 Dana Barros	.02	.10
❑ 139 Shawn Bradley	.02	.10
❑ 140 Greg Graham	.02	.10
❑ 141 Jeff Malone	.02	.10
❑ 142 Tim Perry	.02	.10
❑ 143 Clarence Weatherspoon	.02	.10
❑ 144 Scott Williams	.02	.10
❑ 145 Danny Ainge	.02	.10
❑ 146 Charles Barkley	.25	.60
❑ 147 Cedric Ceballos	.02	.10
❑ 148 A.C. Green	.05	.15
❑ 149 Frank Johnson	.02	.10
❑ 150 Kevin Johnson	.05	.15
❑ 151 Dan Majerle	.05	.15
❑ 152 Oliver Miller	.02	.10
❑ 153 Wesley Person RC	.15	.40
❑ 154 Mark Bryant	.02	.10
❑ 155 Clyde Drexler	.15	.40
❑ 156 Harvey Grant	.02	.10
❑ 157 Jerome Kersey	.02	.10
❑ 158 Tracy Murray	.02	.10
❑ 159 Terry Porter	.02	.10
❑ 160 Clifford Robinson	.05	.15
❑ 161 James Robinson	.02	.10
❑ 162 Rod Strickland	.05	.15
❑ 163 Buck Williams	.02	.10
❑ 164 Duane Causwell	.02	.10
❑ 165 Olden Polynice	.02	.10
❑ 166 Mitch Richmond	.15	.40
❑ 167 Lionel Simmons	.02	.10
❑ 168 Walt Williams	.02	.10
❑ 169 Willie Anderson	.02	.10
❑ 170 Terry Cummings	.02	.10
❑ 171 Sean Elliott	.05	.15
❑ 172 Avery Johnson	.02	.10
❑ 173 J.R. Reid	.02	.10
❑ 174 David Robinson	.25	.60
❑ 175 Dennis Rodman	.30	.75
❑ 176 Kendall Gill	.05	.15
❑ 177 Shawn Kemp	.25	.60
❑ 178 Nate McMillan	.02	.10
❑ 179 Gary Payton	.25	.60
❑ 180 Sam Perkins	.05	.15
❑ 181 Detlef Schrempf	.05	.15
❑ 182 David Benoit	.02	.10
❑ 183 Tyrone Corbin	.02	.10
❑ 184 Jeff Hornacek	.05	.15
❑ 185 Jay Humphries	.02	.10
❑ 186 Karl Malone	.25	.60
❑ 187 Bryon Russell	.02	.10
❑ 188 Felton Spencer	.02	.10
❑ 189 John Stockton	.15	.40
❑ 190 Mitchell Butler	.02	.10
❑ 191 Rex Chapman	.02	.10
❑ 192 Calbert Cheaney	.02	.10
❑ 193 Kevin Duckworth	.02	.10
❑ 194 Tom Gugliotta	.05	.15
❑ 195 Don MacLean	.02	.10
❑ 196 Gheorghe Muresan	.02	.10
❑ 197 Scott Skiles	.02	.10
❑ 198 Checklist	.02	.10
❑ 199 Checklist	.02	.10
❑ 200 Checklist	.02	.10
❑ 201 Tyrone Corbin	.02	.10
❑ 202 Doug Edwards	.02	.10
❑ 203 Jim Les	.02	.10
❑ 204 Grant Long	.02	.10
❑ 205 Ken Norman	.02	.10
❑ 206 Steve Smith	.05	.15
❑ 207 Blue Edwards	.02	.10
❑ 208 Greg Minor RC	.02	.10
❑ 209 Eric Montross	.02	.10
❑ 210 Derek Strong	.02	.10
❑ 211 David Wesley	.02	.10
❑ 212 Tony Bennett	.02	.10
❑ 213 Scott Burrell	.02	.10
❑ 214 Darrin Hancock	.02	.10
❑ 215 Greg Sutton	.02	.10
❑ 216 Corie Blount	.02	.10
❑ 217 Jud Buechler	.02	.10
❑ 218 Ron Harper	.05	.15
❑ 219 Larry Krystkowiak	.02	.10
❑ 220 Dickey Simpkins RC	.02	.10
❑ 221 Bill Wennington	.02	.10
❑ 222 Michael Cage	.02	.10
❑ 223 Tony Campbell	.02	.10
❑ 224 Steve Colter	.02	.10
❑ 225 Greg Dreiling	.02	.10
❑ 226 Danny Ferry	.02	.10
❑ 227 Tony Dumas RC	.02	.10
❑ 228 Lucious Harris	.02	.10

❑ 229 Donald Hodge	.02	.10
❑ 230 Jason Kidd	.75	2.00
❑ 231 Lorenzo Williams	.02	.10
❑ 232 Dale Ellis	.02	.10
❑ 233 Tom Hammonds	.02	.10
❑ 234 Jalen Rose RC	.60	1.50
❑ 235 Reggie Slater	.02	.10
❑ 236 Rafael Addison	.02	.10
❑ 237 Bill Curley RC	.02	.10
❑ 238 Johnny Dawkins	.02	.10
❑ 239 Grant Hill RC	.75	2.00
❑ 240 Eric Leckner	.02	.10
❑ 241 Mark Macon	.02	.10
❑ 242 Oliver Miller	.02	.10
❑ 243 Mark West	.02	.10
❑ 244 Victor Alexander	.02	.10
❑ 245 Chris Gatling	.02	.10
❑ 246 Tom Gugliotta	.05	.15
❑ 247 Keith Jennings	.02	.10
❑ 248 Ricky Pierce	.02	.10
❑ 249 Carlos Rogers RC	.02	.10
❑ 250 Clifford Rozier RC	.02	.10
❑ 251 Rony Seikaly	.02	.10
❑ 252 David Wood	.02	.10
❑ 253 Tim Breaux	.02	.10
❑ 254 Scott Brooks	.02	.10
❑ 255 Zan Tabak	.02	.10
❑ 256 Duane Ferrell	.02	.10
❑ 257 Mark Jackson	.02	.10
❑ 258 Sam Mitchell	.02	.10
❑ 259 John Williams	.02	.10
❑ 260 Terry Dehere	.02	.10
❑ 261 Harold Ellis	.02	.10
❑ 262 Matt Fish	.02	.10
❑ 263 Tony Massenburg	.02	.10
❑ 264 Lamond Murray RC	.05	.15
❑ 265 Bo Outlaw RC	.02	.10
❑ 266 Eric Piatkowski RC	.02	.10
❑ 267 Pooh Richardson	.02	.10
❑ 268 Malik Sealy	.02	.10
❑ 269 Randy Woods	.02	.10
❑ 270 Sam Bowie	.02	.10
❑ 271 Cedric Ceballos	.02	.10
❑ 272 Antonio Harvey	.02	.10
❑ 273 Eddie Jones	.40	1.00
❑ 274 Anthony Miller RC	.02	.10
❑ 275 Tony Smith	.02	.10
❑ 276 Ledell Eackles	.02	.10
❑ 277 Kevin Gamble	.02	.10
❑ 278 Brad Lohaus	.02	.10
❑ 279 Billy Owens	.02	.10
❑ 280 Khalid Reeves RC	.02	.10
❑ 281 Kevin Willis	.02	.10
❑ 282 Marty Conlon	.02	.10
❑ 283 Alton Lister	.02	.10
❑ 284 Eric Mobley RC	.02	.10
❑ 285 Johnny Newman	.02	.10
❑ 286 Ed Pinckney	.02	.10
❑ 287 Glenn Robinson RC	.50	1.25
❑ 288 Howard Eisley	.02	.10
❑ 289 Winston Garland	.02	.10
❑ 290 Andres Guibert	.02	.10
❑ 291 Donyell Marshall RC	.15	.40
❑ 292 Sean Rooks	.02	.10
❑ 293 Yinka Dare	.02	.10
❑ 294 Sleepy Floyd	.02	.10
❑ 295 Sean Higgins	.02	.10
❑ 296 Rex Walters	.02	.10
❑ 297 Jayson Williams	.05	.15
❑ 298 Charles Smith	.02	.10
❑ 299 Charlie Ward RC	.15	.40
❑ 300 Herb Williams	.02	.10
❑ 301 Monty Williams RC	.02	.10
❑ 302 Horace Grant	.05	.15
❑ 303 Geert Hammink	.02	.10
❑ 304 Tree Rollins	.02	.10
❑ 305 Donald Royal	.02	.10
❑ 306 Brian Shaw	.02	.10
❑ 307 Brooks Thompson RC	.02	.10
❑ 308 Derrick Alston RC	.02	.10
❑ 309 Willie Burton	.02	.10
❑ 310 Jaren Jackson	.02	.10
❑ 311 B.J.Tyler RC	.02	.10
❑ 312 Scott Williams	.02	.10
❑ 313 Sharone Wright RC	.02	.10
❑ 314 Joe Kleine	.02	.10
❑ 315 Danny Manning	.05	.15
❑ 316 Elliot Perry	.02	.10
❑ 317 Wesley Person	.05	.15
❑ 318 Trevor Ruffin RC	.02	.10
❑ 319 Danny Schayes	.02	.10
❑ 320 Wayman Tisdale	.02	.10
❑ 321 Chris Dudley	.02	.10
❑ 322 James Edwards	.02	.10
❑ 323 Alaa Abdelnaby	.02	.10
❑ 324 Randy Brown	.02	.10
❑ 325 Brian Grant RC	.40	1.00
❑ 326 Bobby Hurley	.02	.10
❑ 327 Michael Smith RC	.02	.10
❑ 328 Henry Turner	.02	.10
❑ 329 Trevor Wilson	.02	.10
❑ 330 Vinny Del Negro	.02	.10
❑ 331 Moses Malone	.15	.40
❑ 332 Julius Nwosu	.02	.10
❑ 333 Chuck Person	.02	.10
❑ 334 Chris Whitney	.02	.10
❑ 335 Vincent Askew	.02	.10
❑ 336 Bill Cartwright	.02	.10
❑ 337 Ervin Johnson	.02	.10
❑ 338 Sarunas Marciulionis	.02	.10
❑ 339 Antoine Carr	.02	.10
❑ 340 Tom Chambers	.02	.10
❑ 341 John Crotty	.02	.10
❑ 342 Jamie Watson RC	.02	.10
❑ 343 Juwan Howard RC	.40	1.00
❑ 344 Jim McIlvaine	.02	.10
❑ 345 Doug Overton	.02	.10
❑ 346 Scott Skiles	.02	.10
❑ 347 Anthony Tucker RC	.02	.10
❑ 348 Chris Webber	.40	1.00
❑ 349 Checklist	.02	.10
❑ 350 Checklist	.02	.10

1995-96 Ultra

❑ COMPLETE SET (350)	20.00	40.00
❑ COMPLETE SERIES 1 (200)	10.00	20.00
❑ COMPLETE SERIES 2 (150)	10.00	20.00
❑ 1 Stacey Augmon	.08	.25
❑ 2 Mookie Blaylock	.08	.25
❑ 3 Craig Ehlo	.08	.25
❑ 4 Andrew Lang	.08	.25
❑ 5 Grant Long	.08	.25
❑ 6 Ken Norman	.08	.25
❑ 7 Steve Smith	.20	.50
❑ 8 Spud Webb	.20	.50
❑ 9 Dee Brown	.08	.25
❑ 10 Sherman Douglas	.08	.25
❑ 11 Pervis Ellison	.08	.25
❑ 12 Rick Fox	.20	.50
❑ 13 Eric Montross	.08	.25
❑ 14 Dino Radja	.08	.25
❑ 15 David Wesley	.08	.25
❑ 16 Dominique Wilkins	.30	.75
❑ 17 Muggsy Bogues	.20	.50
❑ 18 Scott Burrell	.08	.25
❑ 19 Dell Curry	.08	.25
❑ 20 Kendall Gill	.08	.25
❑ 21 Larry Johnson	.20	.50
❑ 22 Alonzo Mourning	.20	.50
❑ 23 Robert Parish	.20	.50
❑ 24 Ron Harper	.20	.50
❑ 25 Michael Jordan	2.00	5.00
❑ 26 Toni Kukoc	.20	.50
❑ 27 Will Perdue	.08	.25
❑ 28 Scottie Pippen	.50	1.25
❑ 29 Terrell Brandon	.20	.50
❑ 30 Michael Cage	.08	.25
❑ 31 Tyrone Hill	.08	.25
❑ 32 Chris Mills	.08	.25
❑ 33 Bobby Phills	.08	.25
❑ 34 Mark Price	.20	.50
❑ 35 John Williams	.08	.25
❑ 36 Lucious Harris	.08	.25
❑ 37 Jim Jackson	.08	.25
❑ 38 Popeye Jones	.08	.25
❑ 39 Jason Kidd	1.00	2.50
❑ 40 Jamal Mashburn	.20	.50
❑ 41 George McCloud	.08	.25
❑ 42 Roy Tarpley	.08	.25
❑ 43 Lorenzo Williams	.08	.25
❑ 44 Mahmoud Abdul-Rauf	.08	.25
❑ 45 Dikembe Mutombo	.20	.50
❑ 46 Robert Pack	.08	.25
❑ 47 Jalen Rose	.40	1.00
❑ 48 Bryant Stith	.08	.25
❑ 49 Brian Williams	.08	.25
❑ 50 Reggie Williams	.08	.25
❑ 51 Joe Dumars	.30	.75
❑ 52 Grant Hill	.40	1.00
❑ 53 Allan Houston	.20	.50
❑ 54 Lindsey Hunter	.08	.25
❑ 55 Terry Mills	.08	.25
❑ 56 Mark West	.08	.25
❑ 57 Chris Gatling	.08	.25
❑ 58 Tim Hardaway	.20	.50
❑ 59 Donyell Marshall	.20	.50
❑ 60 Chris Mullin	.30	.75
❑ 61 Carlos Rogers	.08	.25
❑ 62 Clifford Rozier	.08	.25
❑ 63 Rony Seikaly	.08	.25
❑ 64 Latrell Sprewell	.30	.75
❑ 65 Sam Cassell	.30	.75
❑ 66 Clyde Drexler	.30	.75
❑ 67 Mario Elie	.08	.25
❑ 68 Carl Herrera	.08	.25
❑ 69 Robert Horry	.20	.50
❑ 70 Hakeem Olajuwon	.30	.75
❑ 71 Kenny Smith	.08	.25
❑ 72 Antonio Davis	.08	.25
❑ 73 Dale Davis	.08	.25
❑ 74 Mark Jackson	.20	.50
❑ 75 Derrick McKey	.08	.25
❑ 76 Reggie Miller	.30	.75
❑ 77 Rik Smits	.20	.50
❑ 78 Terry Dehere	.08	.25
❑ 79 Lamond Murray	.08	.25
❑ 80 Bo Outlaw	.08	.25
❑ 81 Pooh Richardson	.08	.25
❑ 82 Rodney Rogers	.08	.25
❑ 83 Malik Sealy	.08	.25
❑ 84 Loy Vaught	.08	.25
❑ 85 Sam Bowie	.08	.25
❑ 86 Elden Campbell	.08	.25
❑ 87 Cedric Ceballos	.08	.25
❑ 88 Vlade Divac	.20	.50
❑ 89 Eddie Jones	.40	1.00
❑ 90 Anthony Peeler	.08	.25
❑ 91 Sedale Threatt	.08	.25
❑ 92 Nick Van Exel	.30	.75
❑ 93 Rex Chapman	.08	.25
❑ 94 Bimbo Coles	.08	.25
❑ 95 Matt Geiger	.08	.25
❑ 96 Billy Owens	.08	.25
❑ 97 Khalid Reeves	.08	.25
❑ 98 Glen Rice	.20	.50
❑ 99 Kevin Willis	.20	.50
❑ 100 Vin Baker	.20	.50
❑ 101 Marty Conlon	.08	.25
❑ 102 Todd Day	.08	.25
❑ 103 Eric Murdock	.08	.25
❑ 104 Glenn Robinson	.30	.75
❑ 105 Winston Garland	.08	.25
❑ 106 Tom Gugliotta	.08	.25
❑ 107 Christian Laettner	.20	.50
❑ 108 Isaiah Rider	.08	.25
❑ 109 Sean Rooks	.08	.25
❑ 110 Doug West	.08	.25
❑ 111 Kenny Anderson	.20	.50
❑ 112 P.J. Brown	.08	.25
❑ 113 Derrick Coleman	.08	.25
❑ 114 Armon Gilliam	.08	.25
❑ 115 Chris Morris	.08	.25
❑ 116 Anthony Bonner	.08	.25
❑ 117 Patrick Ewing	.30	.75
❑ 118 Derek Harper	.20	.50
❑ 119 Anthony Mason	.20	.50
❑ 120 Charles Oakley	.08	.25
❑ 121 Charles Smith	.08	.25
❑ 122 John Starks	.20	.50
❑ 123 Nick Anderson	.08	.25
❑ 124 Horace Grant	.20	.50
❑ 125 Anfernee Hardaway	.30	.75
❑ 126 Shaquille O'Neal	.75	2.00
❑ 127 Donald Royal	.08	.25

❑ 128 Dennis Scott	.08	.25
❑ 129 Brian Shaw	.08	.25
❑ 130 Derrick Alston	.08	.25
❑ 131 Dana Barros	.08	.25
❑ 132 Shawn Bradley	.08	.25
❑ 133 Willie Burton	.08	.25
❑ 134 Jeff Malone	.08	.25
❑ 135 Clarence Weatherspoon	.08	.25
❑ 136 Scott Williams	.08	.25
❑ 137 Sharone Wright	.08	.25
❑ 138 Danny Ainge	.08	.25
❑ 139 Charles Barkley	.40	1.00
❑ 140 A.C. Green	.20	.50
❑ 141 Kevin Johnson	.20	.50
❑ 142 Dan Majerle	.20	.50
❑ 143 Danny Manning	.20	.50
❑ 144 Elliot Perry	.08	.25
❑ 145 Wesley Person	.08	.25
❑ 146 Wayman Tisdale	.08	.25
❑ 147 Chris Dudley	.08	.25
❑ 148 Harvey Grant	.08	.25
❑ 149 Aaron McKie	.20	.50
❑ 150 Terry Porter	.08	.25
❑ 151 Clifford Robinson	.08	.25
❑ 152 Rod Strickland	.08	.25
❑ 153 Otis Thorpe	.08	.25
❑ 154 Buck Williams	.08	.25
❑ 155 Brian Grant	.30	.75
❑ 156 Bobby Hurley	.08	.25
❑ 157 Olden Polynice	.08	.25
❑ 158 Mitch Richmond	.20	.50
❑ 159 Michael Smith	.08	.25
❑ 160 Walt Williams	.08	.25
❑ 161 Vinny Del Negro	.08	.25
❑ 162 Sean Elliott	.20	.50
❑ 163 Avery Johnson	.08	.25
❑ 164 Chuck Person	.08	.25
❑ 165 J.R. Reid	.08	.25
❑ 166 Doc Rivers	.20	.50
❑ 167 David Robinson	.30	.75
❑ 168 Dennis Rodman	.20	.50
❑ 169 Vincent Askew	.08	.25
❑ 170 Hersey Hawkins	.08	.25
❑ 171 Shawn Kemp	.20	.50
❑ 172 Sarunas Marciulionis	.08	.25
❑ 173 Nate McMillan	.08	.25
❑ 174 Gary Payton	.30	.75
❑ 175 Sam Perkins	.20	.50
❑ 176 Detlef Schrempf	.20	.50
❑ 177 B.J. Armstrong	.08	.25
❑ 178 Jerome Kersey	.08	.25
❑ 179 Tony Massenburg	.08	.25
❑ 180 Oliver Miller	.08	.25
❑ 181 John Salley	.08	.25
❑ 182 David Benoit	.08	.25
❑ 183 Antoine Carr	.08	.25
❑ 184 Jeff Hornacek	.20	.50
❑ 185 Karl Malone	.40	1.00
❑ 186 Felton Spencer	.08	.25
❑ 187 John Stockton	.40	1.00
❑ 188 Greg Anthony	.08	.25
❑ 189 Benoit Benjamin	.08	.25
❑ 190 Byron Scott	.08	.25
❑ 191 Calbert Cheaney	.08	.25
❑ 192 Juwan Howard	.30	.75
❑ 193 Don MacLean	.08	.25
❑ 194 Gheorghe Muresan	.08	.25
❑ 195 Doug Overton	.08	.25
❑ 196 Scott Skiles	.08	.25
❑ 197 Chris Webber	.40	1.00
❑ 198 Checklist (1-94)	.08	.25
❑ 199 Checklist (95-190)	.08	.25
❑ 200 Checklist (191-200)	.08	.25
❑ 201 Stacey Augmon	.08	.25
❑ 202 Mookie Blaylock	.08	.25
❑ 203 Grant Long	.08	.25
❑ 204 Steve Smith	.20	.50
❑ 205 Dana Barros	.08	.25
❑ 206 Kendall Gill	.08	.25
❑ 207 Khalid Reeves	.08	.25
❑ 208 Glen Rice	.20	.50
❑ 209 Luc Longley	.08	.25
❑ 210 Dennis Rodman	.20	.50
❑ 211 Dan Majerle	.20	.50
❑ 212 Tony Dumas	.08	.25
❑ 213 Elmore Spencer	.08	.25
❑ 214 Otis Thorpe	.08	.25
❑ 215 B.J. Armstrong	.08	.25
❑ 216 Sam Cassell	.30	.75
❑ 217 Clyde Drexler	.30	.75
❑ 218 Robert Horry	.20	.50
❑ 219 Hakeem Olajuwon	.30	.75
❑ 220 Eddie Johnson	.08	.25
❑ 221 Ricky Pierce	.08	.25
❑ 222 Eric Piatkowski	.20	.50
❑ 223 Rodney Rogers	.08	.25
❑ 224 Brian Williams	.08	.25
❑ 225 George Lynch	.08	.25
❑ 226 Alonzo Mourning	.20	.50
❑ 227 Benoit Benjamin	.08	.25
❑ 228 Terry Porter	.08	.25
❑ 229 Shawn Bradley	.08	.25
❑ 230 Kevin Edwards	.08	.25
❑ 231 Jayson Williams	.08	.25
❑ 232 Charlie Ward	.08	.25
❑ 233 Jon Koncak	.08	.25
❑ 234 Derrick Coleman	.08	.25
❑ 235 Richard Dumas	.08	.25
❑ 236 Vernon Maxwell	.08	.25
❑ 237 John Williams	.08	.25
❑ 238 Dontonio Wingfield	.08	.25
❑ 239 Tyrone Corbin	.08	.25
❑ 240 Will Perdue	.08	.25
❑ 241 Shawn Kemp	.20	.50
❑ 242 Gary Payton	.30	.75
❑ 243 Sam Perkins	.20	.50
❑ 244 Detlef Schrempf	.20	.50
❑ 245 Chris Morris	.08	.25
❑ 246 Robert Pack	.08	.25
❑ 247 Willie Anderson EXP	.08	.25
❑ 248 Oliver Miller EXP	.08	.25
❑ 249 Tracy Murray EXP	.08	.25
❑ 250 Alvin Robertson EXP	.08	.25
❑ 251 Carlos Rogers EXP	.08	.25
❑ 252 John Salley EXP	.08	.25
❑ 253 Damon Stoudamire EXP	.40	1.00
❑ 254 Zan Tabak EXP	.08	.25
❑ 255 Greg Anthony EXP	.08	.25
❑ 256 Blue Edwards EXP	.08	.25
❑ 257 Kenny Gattison EXP	.08	.25
❑ 258 Chris King EXP	.08	.25
❑ 259 Lawrence Moten EXP	.08	.25
❑ 260 Eric Murdock EXP	.08	.25
❑ 261 Bryant Reeves EXP	.20	.50
❑ 262 Byron Scott EXP	.08	.25
❑ 263 Cory Alexander RC	.08	.25
❑ 264 Brent Barry RC	.30	.75
❑ 265 Mario Bennett RC	.08	.25
❑ 266 Travis Best RC	.08	.25
❑ 267 Junior Burrough RC	.08	.25
❑ 268 Jason Caffey RC	.20	.50
❑ 269 Randolph Childress RC	.08	.25
❑ 270 Sasha Danilovic RC	.08	.25
❑ 271 Tyus Edney RC	.08	.25
❑ 272 Michael Finley RC	1.25	3.00
❑ 273 Sherrell Ford RC	.08	.25
❑ 274 Kevin Garnett RC	2.00	5.00
❑ 275 Alan Henderson RC	.30	.75
❑ 276 Donny Marshall RC	.08	.25
❑ 277 Antonio McDyess RC	.60	1.50
❑ 278 Loren Meyer RC	.08	.25
❑ 279 Lawrence Moten RC	.08	.25
❑ 280 Ed O'Bannon RC	.08	.25
❑ 281 Greg Ostertag RC	.08	.25
❑ 282 Cherokee Parks RC	.08	.25
❑ 283 Theo Ratliff RC	.40	1.00
❑ 284 Bryant Reeves RC	.30	.75
❑ 285 Shawn Respert RC	.08	.25
❑ 286 Lou Roe RC	.08	.25
❑ 287 Arvydas Sabonis RC	.40	1.00
❑ 288 Joe Smith RC	.50	1.25
❑ 289 Jerry Stackhouse RC	1.00	2.50
❑ 290 Damon Stoudamire RC	.60	1.50
❑ 291 Bob Sura RC	.20	.50
❑ 292 Kurt Thomas RC	.20	.50
❑ 293 Gary Trent RC	.08	.25
❑ 294 David Vaughn RC	.08	.25
❑ 295 Rasheed Wallace RC	.75	2.00
❑ 296 Eric Williams RC	.20	.50
❑ 297 Corliss Williamson RC	.30	.75
❑ 298 George Zidek RC	.08	.25
❑ 299 Mahmoud Abdul-Rauf ENC	.08	.25
❑ 300 Kenny Anderson ENC	.08	.25
❑ 301 Vin Baker ENC	.08	.25
❑ 302 Charles Barkley ENC	.30	.75
❑ 303 Mookie Blaylock ENC	.08	.25
❑ 304 Cedric Ceballos ENC	.08	.25
❑ 305 Vlade Divac ENC	.08	.25
❑ 306 Clyde Drexler ENC	.20	.50
❑ 307 Joe Dumars ENC	.20	.50
❑ 308 Sean Elliott ENC	.08	.25
❑ 309 Patrick Ewing ENC	.20	.50
❑ 310 Anfernee Hardaway ENC	.20	.50
❑ 311 Tim Hardaway ENC	.08	.25
❑ 312 Grant Hill ENC	.30	.75
❑ 313 Tyrone Hill ENC	.08	.25
❑ 314 Robert Horry ENC	.08	.25
❑ 315 Juwan Howard ENC	.20	.50
❑ 316 Jim Jackson ENC	.08	.25
❑ 317 Kevin Johnson ENC	.08	.25
❑ 318 Larry Johnson ENC	.08	.25
❑ 319 Eddie Jones ENC	.30	.75
❑ 320 Shawn Kemp ENC	.08	.25
❑ 321 Jason Kidd ENC	.50	1.25
❑ 322 Christian Laettner ENC	.08	.25
❑ 323 Karl Malone ENC	.30	.75
❑ 324 Jamal Mashburn ENC	.08	.25
❑ 325 Reggie Miller ENC	.20	.50
❑ 326 Alonzo Mourning ENC	.08	.25
❑ 327 Dikembe Mutombo ENC	.08	.25
❑ 328 Hakeem Olajuwon ENC	.20	.50
❑ 329 Gary Payton ENC	.20	.50
❑ 330 Scottie Pippen ENC	.20	.50
❑ 331 Dino Radja ENC	.08	.25
❑ 332 Glen Rice ENC	.08	.25
❑ 333 Mitch Richmond ENC	.08	.25
❑ 334 Clifford Robinson ENC	.08	.25
❑ 335 David Robinson ENC	.20	.50
❑ 336 Glenn Robinson ENC	.20	.50
❑ 337 Dennis Rodman ENC	.08	.25
❑ 338 Carlos Rogers ENC	.08	.25
❑ 339 Detlef Schrempf ENC	.08	.25
❑ 340 Byron Scott ENC	.08	.25
❑ 341 Rik Smits ENC	.08	.25
❑ 342 Latrell Sprewell ENC	.30	.75
❑ 343 John Stockton ENC	.30	.75
❑ 344 Nick Van Exel ENC	.08	.25
❑ 345 Loy Vaught ENC	.08	.25
❑ 346 Clarence Weatherspoon ENC	.08	.25
❑ 347 Chris Webber ENC	.30	.75
❑ 348 Kevin Willis ENC	.08	.25
❑ 349 Checklist (201-298)	.08	.25
❑ 350 Checklist (299-350/inserts)	.08	.25

1996-97 Ultra

❑ COMPLETE SET (300)	25.00	50.00
❑ COMPLETE SERIES 1 (150)	17.50	35.00
❑ COMPLETE SERIES 2 (150)	7.50	15.00
❑ 1 Mookie Blaylock	.08	.25
❑ 2 Alan Henderson	.08	.25
❑ 3 Christian Laettner	.20	.50
❑ 4 Dikembe Mutombo	.20	.50
❑ 5 Steve Smith	.20	.50
❑ 6 Dana Barros	.08	.25
❑ 7 Rick Fox	.08	.25
❑ 8 Dino Radja	.08	.25
❑ 9 Antoine Walker RC	.60	1.50
❑ 10 Eric Williams	.08	.25
❑ 11 Dell Curry	.08	.25
❑ 12 Tony Delk RC	.30	.75
❑ 13 Matt Geiger	.08	.25
❑ 14 Glen Rice	.20	.50
❑ 15 Ron Harper	.20	.50
❑ 16 Michael Jordan	2.00	5.00
❑ 17 Toni Kukoc	.20	.50
❑ 18 Scottie Pippen	.50	1.25
❑ 19 Dennis Rodman	.20	.50
❑ 20 Terrell Brandon	.20	.50
❑ 21 Chris Mills	.08	.25
❑ 22 Bobby Phills	.08	.25
❑ 23 Bob Sura	.08	.25
❑ 24 Jim Jackson	.08	.25
❑ 25 Jason Kidd	.50	1.25
❑ 26 Jamal Mashburn	.20	.50

❑ 27 George McCloud	.08	.25
❑ 28 Samaki Walker RC	.08	.25
❑ 29 LaPhonso Ellis	.08	.25
❑ 30 Antonio McDyess	.20	.50
❑ 31 Bryant Stith	.08	.25
❑ 32 Joe Dumars	.30	.75
❑ 33 Grant Hill	.30	.75
❑ 34 Theo Ratliff	.20	.50
❑ 35 Otis Thorpe	.08	.25
❑ 36 Chris Mullin	.30	.75
❑ 37 Joe Smith	.20	.50
❑ 38 Latrell Sprewell	.30	.75
❑ 39 Charles Barkley	.40	1.00
❑ 40 Clyde Drexler	.30	.75
❑ 41 Mario Elie	.08	.25
❑ 42 Hakeem Olajuwon	.30	.75
❑ 43 Erick Dampier RC	.30	.75
❑ 44 Dale Davis	.08	.25
❑ 45 Derrick McKey	.08	.25
❑ 46 Reggie Miller	.30	.75
❑ 47 Rik Smits	.20	.50
❑ 48 Brent Barry	.08	.25
❑ 49 Malik Sealy	.08	.25
❑ 50 Loy Vaught	.08	.25
❑ 51 Lorenzen Wright RC	.20	.50
❑ 52 Kobe Bryant RC	6.00	15.00
❑ 53 Cedric Ceballos	.08	.25
❑ 54 Eddie Jones	.30	.75
❑ 55 Shaquille O'Neal	.75	2.00
❑ 56 Nick Van Exel	.30	.75
❑ 57 Tim Hardaway	.20	.50
❑ 58 Alonzo Mourning	.20	.50
❑ 59 Kurt Thomas	.20	.50
❑ 60 Ray Allen RC	1.00	2.50
❑ 61 Vin Baker	.20	.50
❑ 62 Sherman Douglas	.08	.25
❑ 63 Glenn Robinson	.30	.75
❑ 64 Kevin Garnett	.60	1.50
❑ 65 Tom Gugliotta	.08	.25
❑ 66 Stephon Marbury RC	.75	2.00
❑ 67 Doug West	.08	.25
❑ 68 Shawn Bradley	.08	.25
❑ 69 Kendall Gill	.08	.25
❑ 70 Kerry Kittles RC	.30	.75
❑ 71 Ed O'Bannon	.08	.25
❑ 72 Patrick Ewing	.30	.75
❑ 73 Larry Johnson	.20	.50
❑ 74 Charles Oakley	.08	.25
❑ 75 John Starks	.20	.50
❑ 76 John Wallace RC	.30	.75
❑ 77 Nick Anderson	.08	.25
❑ 78 Horace Grant	.20	.50
❑ 79 Anfernee Hardaway	.30	.75
❑ 80 Dennis Scott	.08	.25
❑ 81 Derrick Coleman	.20	.50
❑ 82 Allen Iverson RC	2.00	5.00
❑ 83 Jerry Stackhouse	.40	1.00
❑ 84 Clarence Weatherspoon	.08	.25
❑ 85 Michael Finley	.40	1.00
❑ 86 Kevin Johnson	.20	.50
❑ 87 Steve Nash RC	2.00	5.00
❑ 88 Wesley Person	.08	.25
❑ 89 Jermaine O'Neal RC	.75	2.00
❑ 90 Clifford Robinson	.08	.25
❑ 91 Arvydas Sabonis	.20	.50
❑ 92 Gary Trent	.08	.25
❑ 93 Tyus Edney	.08	.25
❑ 94 Brian Grant	.30	.75
❑ 95 Olden Polynice	.08	.25
❑ 96 Mitch Richmond	.20	.50
❑ 97 Corliss Williamson	.20	.50
❑ 98 Vinny Del Negro	.08	.25
❑ 99 Sean Elliott	.20	.50
❑ 100 Avery Johnson	.08	.25
❑ 101 David Robinson	.30	.75
❑ 102 Hersey Hawkins	.20	.50
❑ 103 Shawn Kemp	.20	.50
❑ 104 Gary Payton	.30	.75
❑ 105 Sam Perkins	.20	.50
❑ 106 Detlef Schrempf	.20	.50
❑ 107 Marcus Camby RC	.40	1.00
❑ 108 Doug Christie	.20	.50
❑ 109 Damon Stoudamire	.30	.75
❑ 110 Sharone Wright	.08	.25
❑ 111 Jeff Hornacek	.20	.50
❑ 112 Karl Malone	.30	.75
❑ 113 Chris Morris	.08	.25
❑ 114 Bryon Russell	.08	.25
❑ 115 John Stockton	.30	.75
❑ 116 Shareef Abdur-Rahim RC	1.00	2.50
❑ 117 Greg Anthony	.08	.25
❑ 118 Blue Edwards	.08	.25
❑ 119 Bryant Reeves	.08	.25
❑ 120 Calbert Cheaney	.08	.25
❑ 121 Juwan Howard	.20	.50
❑ 122 Gheorghe Muresan	.08	.25
❑ 123 Chris Webber	.30	.75
❑ 124 Vin Baker OTB	.08	.25
❑ 125 Charles Barkley OTB	.30	.75
❑ 126 Kevin Garnett OTB	.30	.75
❑ 127 Juwan Howard OTB	.08	.25
❑ 128 Larry Johnson OTB	.08	.25
❑ 129 Shawn Kemp OTB	.08	.25
❑ 130 Karl Malone OTB	.30	.75
❑ 131 Anthony Mason OTB	.08	.25
❑ 132 Antonio McDyess OTB	.20	.50
❑ 133 Alonzo Mourning OTB	.08	.25
❑ 134 Hakeem Olajuwon OTB	.20	.50
❑ 135 Shaquille O'Neal OTB	.30	.75
❑ 136 David Robinson OTB	.20	.50
❑ 137 Dennis Rodman OTB	.08	.25
❑ 138 Joe Smith OTB	.08	.25
❑ 139 Mookie Blaylock UE	.08	.25
❑ 140 Terrell Brandon UE	.08	.25
❑ 141 Anfernee Hardaway UE	.20	.50
❑ 142 Grant Hill UE	.20	.50
❑ 143 Michael Jordan UE	1.00	2.50
❑ 144 Jason Kidd UE	.20	.50
❑ 145 Gary Payton UE	.20	.50
❑ 146 Jerry Stackhouse UE	.30	.75
❑ 147 Damon Stoudamire UE	.20	.50
❑ 148 H.Olajuwon/D.Robinson ME	.30	.75
❑ 149 Checklist	.08	.25
❑ 150 Checklist	.08	.25
❑ 151 Tyrone Corbin	.08	.25
❑ 152 Priest Lauderdale RC	.08	.25
❑ 153 Dikembe Mutombo	.20	.50
❑ 154 Eldridge Recasner RC	.08	.25
❑ 155 Todd Day	.08	.25
❑ 156 Greg Minor	.08	.25
❑ 157 David Wesley	.08	.25
❑ 158 Vlade Divac	.08	.25
❑ 159 Anthony Mason	.20	.50
❑ 160 Malik Rose RC	.20	.50
❑ 161 Jason Caffey	.08	.25
❑ 162 Steve Kerr	.20	.50
❑ 163 Luc Longley	.08	.25
❑ 164 Danny Ferry	.08	.25
❑ 165 Tyrone Hill	.08	.25
❑ 166 Vitaly Potapenko RC	.08	.25
❑ 167 Sam Cassell	.30	.75
❑ 168 Michael Finley	.40	1.00
❑ 169 Chris Gatling	.08	.25
❑ 170 A.C. Green	.20	.50
❑ 171 Oliver Miller	.08	.25
❑ 172 Eric Montross	.08	.25
❑ 173 Dale Ellis	.08	.25
❑ 174 Mark Jackson	.08	.25
❑ 175 Ervin Johnson	.08	.25
❑ 176 Sarunas Marciulionis	.08	.25
❑ 177 Stacey Augmon	.08	.25
❑ 178 Joe Dumars	.30	.75
❑ 179 Grant Hill	.30	.75
❑ 180 Lindsey Hunter	.08	.25
❑ 181 Grant Long	.08	.25
❑ 182 Terry Mills	.08	.25
❑ 183 Otis Thorpe	.08	.25
❑ 184 Jerome Williams RC	.30	.75
❑ 185 Todd Fuller RC	.08	.25
❑ 186 Ray Owes RC	.08	.25
❑ 187 Mark Price	.20	.50
❑ 188 Felton Spencer	.08	.25
❑ 189 Charles Barkley	.40	1.00
❑ 190 Emanual Davis RC	.08	.25
❑ 191 Othella Harrington RC	.30	.75
❑ 192 Matt Maloney RC	.20	.50
❑ 193 Brent Price	.08	.25
❑ 194 Kevin Willis	.08	.25
❑ 195 Travis Best	.08	.25
❑ 196 Antonio Davis	.08	.25
❑ 197 Jalen Rose	.30	.75
❑ 198 Pooh Richardson	.08	.25
❑ 199 Stanley Roberts	.08	.25
❑ 200 Rodney Rogers	.08	.25
❑ 201 Elden Campbell	.08	.25
❑ 202 Derek Fisher RC	.50	1.25
❑ 203 Travis Knight RC	.08	.25
❑ 204 Shaquille O'Neal	.75	2.00
❑ 205 Byron Scott	.08	.25
❑ 206 Sasha Danilovic	.08	.25
❑ 207 Dan Majerle	.20	.50
❑ 208 Martin Muursepp RC	.08	.25
❑ 209 Armon Gilliam	.08	.25
❑ 210 Andrew Lang	.08	.25
❑ 211 Johnny Newman	.08	.25
❑ 212 Kevin Garnett	.60	1.50
❑ 213 Tom Gugliotta	.08	.25
❑ 214 Shane Heal RC	.08	.25
❑ 215 Stojko Vrankovic	.08	.25
❑ 216 Robert Pack	.08	.25
❑ 217 Khalid Reeves	.08	.25
❑ 218 Jayson Williams	.20	.50
❑ 219 Chris Childs	.08	.25
❑ 220 Allan Houston	.20	.50
❑ 221 Larry Johnson	.20	.50
❑ 222 Walter McCarty RC	.08	.25
❑ 223 Charlie Ward	.08	.25
❑ 224 Brian Evans RC	.08	.25
❑ 225 Amal McCaskill RC	.08	.25
❑ 226 Rony Seikaly	.08	.25
❑ 227 Gerald Wilkins	.08	.25
❑ 228 Mark Davis	.08	.25
❑ 229 Lucious Harris	.08	.25
❑ 230 Don MacLean	.08	.25
❑ 231 Cedric Ceballos	.08	.25
❑ 232 Rex Chapman	.08	.25
❑ 233 Jason Kidd	.50	1.25
❑ 234 Danny Manning	.20	.50
❑ 235 Kenny Anderson	.08	.25
❑ 236 Aaron McKie	.20	.50
❑ 237 Isaiah Rider	.20	.50
❑ 238 Rasheed Wallace	.40	1.00
❑ 239 Mahmoud Abdul-Rauf	.08	.25
❑ 240 Billy Owens	.08	.25
❑ 241 Michael Smith	.08	.25
❑ 242 Vernon Maxwell	.08	.25
❑ 243 Charles Smith	.08	.25
❑ 244 Dominique Wilkins	.30	.75
❑ 245 Craig Ehlo	.08	.25
❑ 246 Jim McIlvaine	.08	.25
❑ 247 Nate McMillan	.08	.25
❑ 248 Hubert Davis	.08	.25
❑ 249 Carlos Rogers	.08	.25
❑ 250 Zan Tabak	.08	.25
❑ 251 Walt Williams	.08	.25
❑ 252 Jeff Hornacek	.20	.50
❑ 253 Karl Malone	.30	.75
❑ 254 Greg Ostertag	.08	.25
❑ 255 Bryon Russell	.08	.25
❑ 256 John Stockton	.30	.75
❑ 257 George Lynch	.08	.25
❑ 258 Lawrence Moten	.08	.25
❑ 259 Anthony Peeler	.08	.25
❑ 260 Roy Rogers RC	.08	.25
❑ 261 Tracy Murray	.08	.25
❑ 262 Rod Strickland	.08	.25
❑ 263 Ben Wallace RC	2.00	5.00
❑ 264 Shareef Abdur-Rahim RE	.50	1.25
❑ 265 Ray Allen RE	.60	1.50
❑ 266 Kobe Bryant RE	2.50	6.00
❑ 267 Marcus Camby RE	.20	.50
❑ 268 Erick Dampier RE	.08	.25
❑ 269 Tony Delk RE	.20	.50
❑ 270 Allen Iverson RE	.50	1.25
❑ 271 Kerry Kittles RE	.30	.75
❑ 272 Stephon Marbury RE	.50	1.25
❑ 273 Steve Nash RE	.40	1.00
❑ 274 Jermaine O'Neal RE	.60	1.50
❑ 275 Antoine Walker RE	.50	1.25
❑ 276 Samaki Walker RE	.08	.25
❑ 277 John Wallace RE	.20	.50
❑ 278 Lorenzen Wright RE	.08	.25
❑ 279 Anfernee Hardaway SU	.20	.50
❑ 280 Michael Jordan SU	1.00	2.50
❑ 281 Jason Kidd SU	.20	.50
❑ 282 Hakeem Olajuwon SU	.20	.50
❑ 283 Gary Payton SU	.20	.50
❑ 284 Mitch Richmond SU	.08	.25
❑ 285 David Robinson SU	.20	.50
❑ 286 John Stockton SU	.30	.75
❑ 287 Damon Stoudamire SU	.20	.50
❑ 288 Chris Webber SU	.30	.75
❑ 289 Clyde Drexler PG	.20	.50
❑ 290 Kevin Garnett PG	.30	.75
❑ 291 Grant Hill PG	.20	.50
❑ 292 Shawn Kemp PG	.08	.25
❑ 293 Karl Malone PG	.30	.75

❑ 294 Antonio McDyess PG	.20	.50
❑ 295 Alonzo Mourning PG	.08	.25
❑ 296 Shaquille O'Neal PG	.30	.75
❑ 297 Scottie Pippen PG	.30	.75
❑ 298 Jerry Stackhouse PG	.30	.75
❑ 299 Checklist (151-263)	.08	.25
❑ 300 Checklist (264-300/inserts)	.08	.25
❑ NNO Jerry Stackhouse Promo	1.25	3.00

1997-98 Ultra

❑ COMPLETE SET (275)	50.00	100.00
❑ COMPLETE SERIES 1 (150)	25.00	50.00
❑ COMPLETE SERIES 2 (125)	25.00	50.00
❑ COMMON CARD (1-275)	.08	.25
❑ COMMON ROOKIE (124-148)	.40	1.00
❑ 1 Kobe Bryant	1.25	3.00
❑ 2 Charles Barkley	.40	1.00
❑ 3 Joe Dumars	.30	.75
❑ 4 Wesley Person	.08	.25
❑ 5 Walt Williams	.08	.25
❑ 6 Vlade Divac	.20	.50
❑ 7 Mookie Blaylock	.08	.25
❑ 8 Jason Kidd	.50	1.25
❑ 9 Ron Harper	.20	.50
❑ 10 Sherman Douglas	.08	.25
❑ 11 Cedric Ceballos	.08	.25
❑ 12 Karl Malone	.30	.75
❑ 13 Antonio McDyess	.20	.50
❑ 14 Steve Kerr	.20	.50
❑ 15 Matt Maloney	.08	.25
❑ 16 Glenn Robinson	.30	.75
❑ 17 Rony Seikaly	.08	.25
❑ 18 Derrick Coleman	.08	.25
❑ 19 Jermaine O'Neal	.50	1.25
❑ 20 Scott Burrell	.08	.25
❑ 21 Glen Rice	.20	.50
❑ 22 Dale Ellis	.08	.25
❑ 23 Michael Jordan	2.00	5.00
❑ 24 Anfernee Hardaway	.30	.75
❑ 25 Bryon Russell	.08	.25
❑ 26 Toni Kukoc	.20	.50
❑ 27 Theo Ratliff	.08	.25
❑ 28 Tom Gugliotta	.20	.50
❑ 29 Dennis Rodman	.20	.50
❑ 30 John Stockton	.30	.75
❑ 31 Priest Lauderdale	.08	.25
❑ 32 Luc Longley	.08	.25
❑ 33 Grant Hill	.30	.75
❑ 34 Antonio Davis	.08	.25
❑ 35 Eddie Jones	.30	.75
❑ 36 Nick Anderson	.08	.25
❑ 37 Shareef Abdur-Rahim	.50	1.25
❑ 38 Stephon Marbury	.40	1.00
❑ 39 Todd Day	.08	.25
❑ 40 Tim Hardaway	.20	.50
❑ 41 Larry Johnson	.20	.50
❑ 42 Sam Perkins	.20	.50
❑ 43 Dikembe Mutombo	.20	.50
❑ 44 Bo Outlaw	.08	.25
❑ 45 Mitch Richmond	.20	.50
❑ 46 Bryant Reeves	.08	.25
❑ 47 P.J. Brown	.08	.25
❑ 48 Steve Smith	.20	.50
❑ 49 Martin Muursepp	.08	.25
❑ 50 Jamal Mashburn	.20	.50
❑ 51 Kendall Gill	.08	.25
❑ 52 Vinny Del Negro	.08	.25
❑ 53 Roy Rogers	.08	.25
❑ 54 Khalid Reeves	.08	.25
❑ 55 Scottie Pippen	.50	1.25
❑ 56 Joe Smith	.20	.50
❑ 57 Mark Jackson	.20	.50
❑ 58 Voshon Lenard	.08	.25
❑ 59 Dan Majerle	.20	.50
❑ 60 Alonzo Mourning	.20	.50
❑ 61 Kerry Kittles	.30	.75
❑ 62 Chris Childs	.08	.25
❑ 63 Patrick Ewing	.30	.75
❑ 64 Allan Houston	.20	.50
❑ 65 Marcus Camby	.30	.75
❑ 66 Christian Laettner	.20	.50
❑ 67 Loy Vaught	.08	.25
❑ 68 Jayson Williams	.08	.25
❑ 69 Avery Johnson	.08	.25
❑ 70 Damon Stoudamire	.20	.50
❑ 71 Kevin Johnson	.20	.50
❑ 72 Gheorghe Muresan	.08	.25
❑ 73 Reggie Miller	.30	.75
❑ 74 John Wallace	.08	.25
❑ 75 Terrell Brandon	.20	.50
❑ 76 Dale Davis	.08	.25
❑ 77 Latrell Sprewell	.30	.75
❑ 78 Lorenzen Wright	.08	.25
❑ 79 Rod Strickland	.08	.25
❑ 80 Kenny Anderson	.20	.50
❑ 81 Anthony Mason	.20	.50
❑ 82 Hakeem Olajuwon	.30	.75
❑ 83 Kevin Garnett	.60	1.50
❑ 84 Isaiah Rider	.20	.50
❑ 85 Mark Price	.20	.50
❑ 86 Shawn Bradley	.08	.25
❑ 87 Vin Baker	.20	.50
❑ 88 Steve Nash	.30	.75
❑ 89 Jeff Hornacek	.20	.50
❑ 90 Tony Delk	.08	.25
❑ 91 Horace Grant	.20	.50
❑ 92 Othella Harrington	.08	.25
❑ 93 Arvydas Sabonis	.20	.50
❑ 94 Antoine Walker	.40	1.00
❑ 95 Todd Fuller	.08	.25
❑ 96 John Starks	.20	.50
❑ 97 Olden Polynice	.08	.25
❑ 98 Sean Elliott	.20	.50
❑ 99 Travis Best	.08	.25
❑ 100 Chris Gatling	.08	.25
❑ 101 Derek Harper	.20	.50
❑ 102 LaPhonso Ellis	.08	.25
❑ 103 Dean Garrett	.08	.25
❑ 104 Hersey Hawkins	.08	.25
❑ 105 Jerry Stackhouse	.30	.75
❑ 106 Ray Allen	.30	.75
❑ 107 Allen Iverson	.75	2.00
❑ 108 Chris Webber	.30	.75
❑ 109 Robert Pack	.08	.25
❑ 110 Gary Payton	.30	.75
❑ 111 Mario Elie	.08	.25
❑ 112 Dell Curry	.08	.25
❑ 113 Lindsey Hunter	.08	.25
❑ 114 Robert Horry	.20	.50
❑ 115 David Robinson	.30	.75
❑ 116 Kevin Willis	.20	.50
❑ 117 Tyrone Hill	.08	.25
❑ 118 Vitaly Potapenko	.08	.25
❑ 119 Clyde Drexler	.30	.75
❑ 120 Derek Fisher	.30	.75
❑ 121 Detlef Schrempf	.20	.50
❑ 122 Gary Trent	.08	.25
❑ 123 Danny Ferry	.08	.25
❑ 124 Derek Anderson RC	1.50	4.00
❑ 125 Chris Anstey RC	.40	1.00
❑ 126 Tony Battie RC	.75	2.00
❑ 127 Chauncey Billups RC	5.00	12.00
❑ 128 Kelvin Cato RC	.75	2.00
❑ 129 Austin Croshere RC	1.25	3.00
❑ 130 Antonio Daniels RC	.75	2.00
❑ 131 Tim Duncan RC	4.00	10.00
❑ 132 Danny Fortson RC	1.00	2.50
❑ 133 Adonal Foyle RC	.60	1.50
❑ 134 Paul Grant RC	.40	1.00
❑ 135 Ed Gray RC	.40	1.00
❑ 136 Bobby Jackson RC	1.25	3.00
❑ 137 Brevin Knight RC	1.00	2.50
❑ 138 Tracy McGrady RC	4.00	10.00
❑ 139 Ron Mercer RC	1.50	4.00
❑ 140 Anthony Parker RC	.60	1.50
❑ 141 Scot Pollard RC	.60	1.50
❑ 142 Rodrick Rhodes RC	.40	1.00
❑ 143 Olivier Saint-Jean RC	.40	1.00
❑ 144 Maurice Taylor RC	1.25	3.00
❑ 145 Johnny Taylor RC	.40	1.00
❑ 146 Tim Thomas RC	2.50	6.00
❑ 147 Keith Van Horn RC	2.00	5.00
❑ 148 Jacque Vaughn RC	.60	1.50
❑ 149 Checklist	.08	.25
❑ 150 Checklist	.08	.25
❑ 151 Scott Burrell	.08	.25
❑ 152 Brian Williams	.08	.25
❑ 153 Terry Mills	.08	.25
❑ 154 Jim Jackson	.08	.25
❑ 155 Michael Finley	.30	.75
❑ 156 Jeff Nordgaard RC	.08	.25
❑ 157 Carl Herrera	.08	.25
❑ 158 Otis Thorpe	.08	.25
❑ 159 Wesley Person	.08	.25
❑ 160 Tyrone Hill	.08	.25
❑ 161 Charles O'Bannon RC	.08	.25
❑ 162 Greg Anthony	.08	.25
❑ 163 Rusty LaRue RC	.08	.25
❑ 164 David Wesley	.08	.25
❑ 165 Chris Garner RC	.08	.25
❑ 166 George McCloud	.08	.25
❑ 167 Mark Price	.20	.50
❑ 168 God Shammgod RC	.08	.25
❑ 169 Isaac Austin	.08	.25
❑ 170 Alan Henderson	.08	.25
❑ 171 Eric Washington RC	.30	.75
❑ 172 Darrell Armstrong	.08	.25
❑ 173 Calbert Cheaney	.08	.25
❑ 174 Cedric Henderson RC	.08	.25
❑ 175 Bryant Stith	.08	.25
❑ 176 Sean Rooks	.08	.25
❑ 177 Chris Mills	.08	.25
❑ 178 Eldridge Recasner	.08	.25
❑ 179 Priest Lauderdale	.08	.25
❑ 180 Rick Fox	.20	.50
❑ 181 Keith Closs RC	.08	.25
❑ 182 Chris Dudley	.08	.25
❑ 183 Lawrence Funderburke RC	.20	.50
❑ 184 Michael Stewart RC	.08	.25
❑ 185 Alvin Williams RC	.40	1.00
❑ 186 Adam Keefe	.08	.25
❑ 187 Chauncey Billups	.25	.60
❑ 188 Jon Barry	.08	.25
❑ 189 Bobby Jackson	.20	.50
❑ 190 Sam Cassell	.30	.75
❑ 191 Dee Brown	.08	.25
❑ 192 Travis Knight	.08	.25
❑ 193 Dean Garrett	.08	.25
❑ 194 David Benoit	.08	.25
❑ 195 Chris Morris	.08	.25
❑ 196 Bubba Wells RC	.08	.25
❑ 197 James Robinson	.08	.25
❑ 198 Anthony Johnson RC	.08	.25
❑ 199 Dennis Scott	.08	.25
❑ 200 DeJuan Wheat RC	.08	.25
❑ 201 Rodney Rogers	.08	.25
❑ 202 Tariq Abdul-Wahad	.08	.25
❑ 203 Cherokee Parks	.08	.25
❑ 204 Jacque Vaughn	.08	.25
❑ 205 Cory Alexander	.08	.25
❑ 206 Kevin Ollie RC	.08	.25
❑ 207 George Lynch	.08	.25
❑ 208 Lamond Murray	.08	.25
❑ 209 Jud Buechler	.08	.25
❑ 210 Erick Dampier	.20	.50
❑ 211 Malcolm Huckaby RC	.08	.25
❑ 212 Chris Webber	.30	.75
❑ 213 Chris Crawford RC	.08	.25
❑ 214 J.R. Reid	.08	.25
❑ 215 Eddie Johnson	.08	.25
❑ 216 Nick Van Exel	.30	.75
❑ 217 Antonio McDyess	.20	.50
❑ 218 David Wingate	.08	.25
❑ 219 Malik Sealy	.08	.25
❑ 220 Bo Outlaw	.08	.25
❑ 221 Serge Zwikker RC	.08	.25
❑ 222 Bobby Phills	.08	.25
❑ 223 Shea Seals RC	.08	.25
❑ 224 Clifford Robinson	.08	.25
❑ 225 Zydrunas Ilgauskas	.20	.50
❑ 226 John Thomas RC	.08	.25
❑ 227 Rik Smits	.20	.50
❑ 228 Rasheed Wallace	.30	.75
❑ 229 John Wallace	.08	.25
❑ 230 Bob Sura	.08	.25
❑ 231 Ervin Johnson	.08	.25
❑ 232 Keith Booth RC	.08	.25
❑ 233 Chuck Person	.08	.25
❑ 234 Brian Shaw	.08	.25
❑ 235 Todd Day	.08	.25
❑ 236 Clarence Weatherspoon	.08	.25
❑ 237 Charlie Ward	.08	.25
❑ 238 Rod Strickland	.08	.25
❑ 239 Shawn Kemp	.20	.50

240 Terrell Brandon	.20	.50
241 Corey Beck RC	.08	.25
242 Vin Baker	.20	.50
243 Fred Hoiberg	.08	.25
244 Chris Mullin	.30	.75
245 Brian Grant	.20	.50
246 Derek Anderson	.40	1.00
247 Zan Tabak	.08	.25
248 Charles Smith RC	.08	.25
249 Shareef Abdur-Rahim GRE	1.00	2.50
250 Ray Allen GRE	.60	1.50
251 Charles Barkley GRE	.75	2.00
252 Kobe Bryant GRE	2.50	6.00
253 Marcus Camby GRE	.60	1.50
254 Kevin Garnett GRE	1.25	3.00
255 Anfernee Hardaway GRE	.60	1.50
256 Grant Hill GRE	.60	1.50
257 Juwan Howard GRE	.30	.75
258 Allen Iverson GRE	1.50	4.00
259 Michael Jordan GRE	4.00	10.00
260 Shawn Kemp GRE	.40	1.00
261 Kerry Kittles GRE	.60	1.50
262 Karl Malone GRE	.60	1.50
263 Stephon Marbury GRE	.75	2.00
264 Hakeem Olajuwon GRE	.60	1.50
265 Shaquille O'Neal GRE	1.25	3.00
266 Gary Payton GRE	.60	1.50
267 Scottie Pippen GRE	1.00	2.50
268 David Robinson GRE	.60	1.50
269 Dennis Rodman GRE	.40	1.00
270 Joe Smith GRE	.40	1.00
271 Jerry Stackhouse GRE	.60	1.50
272 Damon Stoudamire GRE	.40	1.00
273 Antoine Walker GRE	.75	2.00
274 Checklist	.08	.25
275 Checklist	.08	.25
NNO Jerry Stackhouse Promo	.75	2.00

1998-99 Ultra

COMPLETE SET (125)	50.00	100.00
COMPLETE SET w/o SP (100)	12.50	25.00
COMMON CARD (1-100)	.08	.25
COMMON ROOKIE (101-125)	.20	.50
1 Keith Van Horn	.30	.75
1B K.Van Horn Promo	.30	.75
2 Antonio Daniels	.08	.25
3 Patrick Ewing	.30	.75
4 Alonzo Mourning	.20	.50
5 Isaac Austin	.08	.25
6 Bryant Reeves	.08	.25
7 Dennis Scott	.08	.25
8 Damon Stoudamire	.20	.50
9 Kenny Anderson	.20	.50
10 Mookie Blaylock	.08	.25
11 Mitch Richmond	.20	.50
12 Jalen Rose	.30	.75
13 Vin Baker	.20	.50
14 Donyell Marshall	.20	.50
15 Bryon Russell	.08	.25
16 Rasheed Wallace	.30	.75
17 Allan Houston	.20	.50
18 Shawn Kemp	.20	.50
19 Nick Van Exel	.30	.75
20 Theo Ratliff	.20	.50
21 Jayson Williams	.08	.25
22 Chauncey Billups	.20	.50
23 Brent Barry	.20	.50
24 David Wesley	.08	.25
25 Joe Dumars	.30	.75
26 Marcus Camby	.20	.50
27 Juwan Howard	.20	.50
28 Brevin Knight	.08	.25
29 Reggie Miller	.30	.75
30 Ray Allen	.30	.75
31 Michael Finley	.30	.75
32 Tom Gugliotta	.08	.25
33 Allen Iverson	.60	1.50
34 Toni Kukoc	.20	.50
35 Tim Thomas	.20	.50
36 Jeff Hornacek	.20	.50
37 Bobby Jackson	.20	.50
38 Bo Outlaw	.08	.25
39 Steve Smith	.20	.50
40 Terrell Brandon	.20	.50
41 Glen Rice	.20	.50
42 Rik Smits	.20	.50
43 Calbert Cheaney	.08	.25
44 Stephon Marbury	.30	.75
45 Glenn Robinson	.20	.50
46 Corliss Williamson	.20	.50
47 Larry Johnson	.20	.50
48 Antonio McDyess	.20	.50
49 Detlef Schrempf	.20	.50
50 Jerry Stackhouse	.30	.75
51 Doug Christie	.20	.50
52 Eddie Jones	.30	.75
53 Karl Malone	.30	.75
54 Anthony Mason	.20	.50
55 Tim Duncan	.50	1.25
56 Christian Laettner	.20	.50
57 Isaiah Rider	.08	.25
58 Shawn Bradley	.08	.25
59 Jim Jackson	.08	.25
60 Mark Jackson	.20	.50
61 Kobe Bryant	1.25	3.00
62 Zydrunas Ilgauskas	.20	.50
63 Ron Mercer	.15	.40
64 Hersey Hawkins	.08	.25
65 John Wallace	.08	.25
66 Avery Johnson	.08	.25
67 Dikembe Mutombo	.20	.50
68 Hakeem Olajuwon	.30	.75
69 Tony Battie	.08	.25
70 Jason Kidd	.50	1.25
71 Latrell Sprewell	.30	.75
72 Kevin Garnett	.60	1.50
73 Voshon Lenard	.08	.25
74 Gary Payton	.30	.75
75 Cherokee Parks	.08	.25
76 Antoine Walker	.30	.75
77 Anthony Johnson	.08	.25
78 Danny Fortson	.08	.25
79 Grant Hill	.30	.75
80 Dennis Rodman	.20	.50
81 Arvydas Sabonis	.20	.50
82 Tracy McGrady	.75	2.00
83 David Robinson	.30	.75
84 Tariq Abdul-Wahad	.08	.25
85 Michael Jordan	2.00	5.00
86 Kerry Kittles	.08	.25
87 Maurice Taylor	.15	.40
88 Cedric Ceballos	.08	.25
89 Anfernee Hardaway	.30	.75
90 John Stockton	.30	.75
91 Shareef Abdur-Rahim	.30	.75
92 Tim Hardaway	.20	.50
93 Shaquille O'Neal	.75	2.00
94 Rodney Rogers	.08	.25
95 Derek Anderson	.25	.60
96 Kendall Gill	.08	.25
97 Rod Strickland	.08	.25
98 Charles Barkley	.40	1.00
99 Chris Webber	.30	.75
100 Scottie Pippen	.50	1.25
101 Raef LaFrentz RC	.75	2.00
102 Ricky Davis RC	1.50	4.00
103 Robert Traylor RC	.50	1.25
104 Roshown McLeod RC	.25	.60
105 Tyronn Lue RC	.60	1.50
106 Vince Carter RC	3.00	8.00
107 Miles Simon RC	.20	.50
108 Paul Pierce RC	4.00	10.00
109 Pat Garrity RC	.25	.60
110 Nazr Mohammed RC	.25	.60
111 Mike Bibby RC	1.50	4.00
112 Michael Dickerson RC	1.00	2.50
113 Michael Doleac RC	.50	1.25
114 Matt Harpring RC	.75	2.00
115 Larry Hughes RC	1.50	4.00
116 Keon Clark RC	.75	2.00
117 Felipe Lopez RC	.60	1.50
118 Dirk Nowitzki RC	6.00	12.00
119 Corey Benjamin RC	.50	1.25
120 Bryce Drew RC	.50	1.25
121 Brian Skinner RC	.50	1.25
122 Bonzi Wells RC	2.00	5.00
123 Antawn Jamison RC	2.50	6.00
124 Al Harrington RC	1.25	3.00
125 Michael Olowokandi RC	.75	2.00

1999-00 Ultra

COMPLETE SET (150)	50.00	100.00
COMPLETE SET w/o RC (125)	12.50	25.00
COMMON CARD (1-125)	.20	.50
COMMON ROOKIE (126-150)	.60	1.50
1 Vince Carter	.60	1.50
2 Randell Jackson	.20	.50
3 Ray Allen	.30	.75
4 Corliss Williamson	.20	.50
5 Darrell Armstrong	.20	.50
6 Charles Oakley	.25	.60
7 Tyrone Nesby RC	.30	.75
8 Eddie Jones	.30	.75
9 Kerry Kittles	.20	.50
10 Jason Williams	.30	.75
11 Elden Campbell	.20	.50
12 Mookie Blaylock	.20	.50
13 Brent Barry	.25	.60
14 Mark Jackson	.30	.75
15 Tim Hardaway	.30	.75
16 Kendall Gill	.20	.50
17 Larry Johnson	.30	.75
18 Eric Snow	.25	.60
19 Raef LaFrentz	.25	.60
20 Allen Iverson	.60	1.50
21 Kenny Anderson	.25	.60
22 John Starks	.30	.75
23 Isaiah Rider	.20	.50
24 Tariq Abdul-Wahad	.20	.50
25 Vitaly Potapenko	.20	.50
26 Patrick Ewing	.40	1.00
27 Mitch Richmond	.25	.60
28 Steve Nash	.50	1.25
29 Dickey Simpkins	.20	.50
30 Grant Hill	.30	.75
31 Matt Geiger	.20	.50
32 John Stockton	.40	1.00
33 Jayson Williams	.25	.60
34 Reggie Miller	.30	.75
35 Eric Piatkowski	.25	.60
36 Jason Kidd	.50	1.25
37 Allan Houston	.25	.60
38 Christian Laettner	.25	.60
39 Marcus Camby	.25	.60
40 Shaquille O'Neal	.75	2.00
41 Derek Anderson	.20	.50
42 Gary Trent	.20	.50
43 Vin Baker	.30	.75
44 Alonzo Mourning	.30	.75
45 Latrell Sprewell	.25	.60
46 Rod Strickland	.20	.50
47 Bobby Jackson	.25	.60
48 Karl Malone	.40	1.00
49 Mario Elie	.20	.50
50 Kobe Bryant	1.50	4.00
51 Clifford Robinson	.20	.50
52 Jamal Mashburn	.20	.50
53 Dirk Nowitzki	.50	1.25
54 Rik Smits	.30	.75
55 Doug Christie	.25	.60
56 Ricky Davis	.30	.75
57 Jalen Rose	.25	.60
58 Michael Olowokandi	.20	.50
59 Cedric Ceballos	.20	.50
60 Ron Mercer	.20	.50
61 Brevin Knight	.20	.50
62 Rashard Lewis	.30	.75
63 Detlef Schrempf	.25	.60
64 Keith Van Horn	.25	.60
64B K.Van Horn Promo	.25	.60
65 Nick Anderson	.20	.50

❑ 66 Larry Hughes	.25	.60
❑ 67 Antonio McDyess	.25	.60
❑ 68 Terrell Brandon	.20	.50
❑ 69 Felipe Lopez	.20	.50
❑ 70 Scottie Pippen	.50	1.25
❑ 71 Erick Dampier	.25	.60
❑ 72 Arvydas Sabonis	.25	.60
❑ 73 Brian Grant	.20	.50
❑ 74 Nick Van Exel	.25	.60
❑ 75 Bryon Russell	.20	.50
❑ 76 Danny Fortson	.20	.50
❑ 77 Avery Johnson	.25	.60
❑ 78 Jerry Stackhouse	.30	.75
❑ 79 Robert Traylor	.20	.50
❑ 80 Tim Duncan	.60	1.50
❑ 81 Lindsey Hunter	.20	.50
❑ 82 Tyronn Lue	.20	.50
❑ 83 Michael Finley	.30	.75
❑ 84 Dikembe Mutombo	.25	.60
❑ 85 Zydrunas Ilgauskas	.25	.60
❑ 86 Pat Garrity	.20	.50
❑ 87 Damon Stoudamire	.30	.75
❑ 88 Shareef Abdur-Rahim	.25	.60
❑ 89 Matt Harpring	.25	.60
❑ 90 Michael Dickerson	.20	.50
❑ 91 Steve Smith	.20	.50
❑ 92 Bison Dele	.20	.50
❑ 93 Glenn Robinson	.25	.60
❑ 94 Antawn Jamison	.30	.75
❑ 95 Glen Rice	.30	.75
❑ 96 Vlade Divac	.30	.75
❑ 97 Vladimir Stepania	.20	.50
❑ 98 Kornel David RC	.30	.75
❑ 99 Shawn Kemp	.30	.75
❑ 100 Kevin Garnett	.60	1.50
❑ 101 Tim Thomas	.25	.60
❑ 102 Mike Bibby	.30	.75
❑ 103 Maurice Taylor	.25	.60
❑ 104 Gary Payton	.30	.75
❑ 105 Voshon Lenard	.20	.50
❑ 106 Theo Ratliff	.25	.60
❑ 107 Hakeem Olajuwon	.30	.75
❑ 108 Joe Smith	.25	.60
❑ 109 Toni Kukoc	.30	.75
❑ 110 Stephon Marbury	.30	.75
❑ 111 Anthony Mason	.20	.50
❑ 112 Anfernee Hardaway	.30	.75
❑ 113 Juwan Howard	.25	.60
❑ 114 Charles Barkley	.40	1.00
❑ 115 Antoine Walker	.30	.75
❑ 116 Donyell Marshall	.25	.60
❑ 117 Tom Gugliotta	.20	.50
❑ 118 Rasheed Wallace	.30	.75
❑ 119 Tracy McGrady	.60	1.50
❑ 120 Paul Pierce	.30	.75
❑ 121 Sean Elliott	.30	.75
❑ 122 Bryant Reeves	.20	.50
❑ 123 Michael Doleac	.20	.50
❑ 124 Chris Webber	.30	.75
❑ 125 David Robinson	.40	1.00
❑ 126 Steve Francis RC	2.00	5.00
❑ 127 Elton Brand RC	2.00	5.00
❑ 128 Wally Szczerbiak RC	2.00	5.00
❑ 129 Richard Hamilton RC	2.00	5.00
❑ 130 Shawn Marion RC	2.00	5.00
❑ 131 Trajan Langdon RC	.60	1.50
❑ 132 Corey Maggette RC	2.00	5.00
❑ 133 Dion Glover RC	.60	1.50
❑ 134 James Posey RC	1.00	2.50
❑ 135 Lamar Odom RC	2.00	5.00
❑ 136 A.Radojevic RC	.60	1.50
❑ 137 Cal Bowdler RC	.60	1.50
❑ 138 Scott Padgett RC	.60	1.50
❑ 139 Jumaine Jones RC	.60	1.50
❑ 140 Jonathan Bender RC	.60	1.50
❑ 141 Tim James RC	.60	1.50
❑ 142 Jason Terry RC	1.50	4.00
❑ 143 Quincy Lewis RC	.60	1.50
❑ 144 William Avery RC	.60	1.50
❑ 145 Galen Young RC	.60	1.50
❑ 146 Ron Artest RC	2.50	6.00
❑ 147 Kenny Thomas RC	.60	1.50
❑ 148 Devean George RC	1.00	2.50
❑ 149 Andre Miller RC	2.00	5.00
❑ 150 Baron Davis RC	2.50	6.00

2000-01 Ultra

❑ COMPLETE SET w/o RC (200)	20.00	40.00
❑ COMMON CARD (1-200)	.20	.50
❑ COMMON ROOKIE (201-225)	.75	2.00
❑ 1 Vince Carter	.60	1.50
❑ 2 Antawn Jamison	.30	.75
❑ 3 Shaquille O'Neal	.75	2.00
❑ 4 Paul Pierce	.30	.75
❑ 5 Antonio McDyess	.25	.60
❑ 6 Scott Burrell	.20	.50
❑ 7 Elton Brand	.30	.75
❑ 8 Lamar Odom	.30	.75
❑ 9 Nick Van Exel	.25	.60
❑ 10 Kobe Bryant	1.50	4.00
❑ 11 Reggie Miller	.30	.75
❑ 12 Sam Cassell	.25	.60
❑ 13 Darrell Armstrong	.20	.50
❑ 14 Rasheed Wallace	.30	.75
❑ 15 Charles Oakley	.25	.60
❑ 16 David Wesley	.20	.50
❑ 17 Al Harrington	.25	.60
❑ 18 Latrell Sprewell	.25	.60
❑ 19 Rick Brunson	.20	.50
❑ 20 Steve Smith	.25	.60
❑ 21 Antonio Davis	.20	.50
❑ 22 Michael Finley	.30	.75
❑ 23 Shandon Anderson	.20	.50
❑ 24 Danny Fortson	.20	.50
❑ 25 Kerry Kittles	.25	.60
❑ 26 Anfernee Hardaway	.30	.75
❑ 27 Vin Baker	.25	.60
❑ 28 Calvin Booth	.20	.50
❑ 29 Haywoode Workman	.20	.50
❑ 30 Dickey Simpkins	.20	.50
❑ 31 Jerome Williams	.20	.50
❑ 32 Ron Artest	.30	.75
❑ 33 Dennis Scott	.20	.50
❑ 34 Ron Mercer	.20	.50
❑ 35 Chris Webber	.30	.75
❑ 36 Bryon Russell	.20	.50
❑ 37 Dale Davis	.20	.50
❑ 38 Dirk Nowitzki	.50	1.25
❑ 39 Steve Francis	.30	.75
❑ 40 Glen Rice	.25	.60
❑ 41 Stephon Marbury	.30	.75
❑ 42 Jason Kidd	.50	1.25
❑ 43 Brent Barry	.20	.50
❑ 44 Richard Hamilton	.25	.60
❑ 45 Antoine Walker	.25	.60
❑ 46 Gary Trent	.20	.50
❑ 47 Cuttino Mobley	.25	.60
❑ 48 P.J. Brown	.20	.50
❑ 49 Elliot Perry	.20	.50
❑ 50 Shawn Marion	.30	.75
❑ 51 Horace Grant	.25	.60
❑ 52 Juwan Howard	.25	.60
❑ 53 Elden Campbell	.20	.50
❑ 54 Erick Strickland	.20	.50
❑ 55 Hakeem Olajuwon	.40	1.00
❑ 56 Anthony Carter	.20	.50
❑ 57 Keith Van Horn	.25	.60
❑ 58 Clifford Robinson	.20	.50
❑ 59 Ruben Patterson	.20	.50
❑ 60 Mitch Richmond	.25	.60
❑ 61 Jason Terry	.30	.75
❑ 62 Andre Miller	.25	.60
❑ 63 Vonteego Cummings	.20	.50
❑ 64 Joe Smith	.20	.50
❑ 65 Toni Kukoc	.25	.60
❑ 66 Sean Elliott	.25	.60
❑ 67 Michael Dickerson	.20	.50
❑ 68 Derrick Coleman	.25	.60
❑ 69 Shawn Bradley	.20	.50
❑ 70 Kenny Thomas	.20	.50
❑ 71 Tim Hardaway	.25	.60
❑ 72 Rex Chapman	.20	.50
❑ 73 Gary Payton	.30	.75
❑ 74 Jahidi White	.20	.50
❑ 75 Baron Davis	.30	.75
❑ 76 Chauncey Billups	.30	.75
❑ 77 Moochie Norris	.20	.50
❑ 78 Dan Majerle	.25	.60
❑ 79 Marcus Camby	.25	.60
❑ 80 Rodney Rogers	.20	.50
❑ 81 Rashard Lewis	.30	.75
❑ 82 Laron Profit	.20	.50
❑ 83 Ricky Davis	.25	.60
❑ 84 Keon Clark	.20	.50
❑ 85 Anthony Miller	.20	.50
❑ 86 Jamal Mashburn	.25	.60
❑ 87 Chris Childs	.20	.50
❑ 88 Brian Grant	.20	.50
❑ 89 Muggsy Bogues	.25	.60
❑ 90 Randy Brown	.20	.50
❑ 91 Tariq Abdul-Wahad	.20	.50
❑ 92 Lindsey Hunter	.20	.50
❑ 93 Rik Smits	.20	.50
❑ 94 Glenn Robinson	.25	.60
❑ 95 Michael Doleac	.20	.50
❑ 96 Quincy Lewis	.20	.50
❑ 97 Grant Hill	.30	.75
❑ 98 Jalen Rose	.25	.60
❑ 99 Ervin Johnson	.20	.50
❑ 100 Chucky Atkins	.20	.50
❑ 101 Jermaine O'Neal	.30	.75
❑ 102 Howard Eisley	.20	.50
❑ 103 Kenny Anderson	.25	.60
❑ 104 Lamond Murray	.20	.50
❑ 105 Adonal Foyle	.20	.50
❑ 106 Derek Fisher	.30	.75
❑ 107 Wally Szczerbiak	.25	.60
❑ 108 Todd MacCulloch	.20	.50
❑ 109 Avery Johnson	.25	.60
❑ 110 Othella Harrington	.20	.50
❑ 111 Tony Battie	.20	.50
❑ 112 Bob Sura	.20	.50
❑ 113 Larry Hughes	.25	.60
❑ 114 Rick Fox	.25	.60
❑ 115 Travis Best	.20	.50
❑ 116 Theo Ratliff	.20	.50
❑ 117 David Robinson	.40	1.00
❑ 118 Felipe Lopez	.20	.50
❑ 119 John Amaechi	.20	.50
❑ 120 George Lynch	.20	.50
❑ 121 Christian Laettner	.20	.50
❑ 122 Derek Anderson	.25	.60
❑ 123 Tim Thomas	.20	.50
❑ 124 Matt Harpring	.25	.60
❑ 125 Nick Anderson	.20	.50
❑ 126 Karl Malone	.40	1.00
❑ 127 Dion Glover	.20	.50
❑ 128 Wesley Person	.20	.50
❑ 129 Mikki Moore	.20	.50
❑ 130 Michael Olowokandi	.20	.50
❑ 131 William Avery	.20	.50
❑ 132 Bo Outlaw	.20	.50
❑ 133 Jason Williams	.25	.60
❑ 134 John Stockton	.40	1.00
❑ 135 Adrian Griffin	.20	.50
❑ 136 Hubert Davis	.20	.50
❑ 137 Donyell Marshall	.20	.50
❑ 138 Travis Knight	.20	.50
❑ 139 Kendall Gill	.20	.50
❑ 140 Tom Gugliotta	.20	.50
❑ 141 Malik Rose	.20	.50
❑ 142 Isaac Austin	.20	.50
❑ 143 Alan Henderson	.20	.50
❑ 144 Shawn Kemp	.30	.75
❑ 145 Terry Mills	.20	.50
❑ 146 Maurice Taylor	.20	.50
❑ 147 Terrell Brandon	.20	.50
❑ 148 Matt Geiger	.20	.50
❑ 149 Corliss Williamson	.25	.60
❑ 150 Jacque Vaughn	.20	.50
❑ 151 Dikembe Mutombo	.25	.60
❑ 152 Trajan Langdon	.20	.50
❑ 153 Jason Caffey	.20	.50
❑ 154 Tyrone Nesby	.20	.50
❑ 155 Bobby Jackson	.20	.50
❑ 156 Allen Iverson	.60	1.50
❑ 157 Mario Elie	.20	.50
❑ 158 Mike Bibby	.25	.60
❑ 159 Robert Horry	.25	.60
❑ 160 James Posey	.20	.50

❑ 161 Mark Jackson .25 .60
❑ 162 Ray Allen .30 .75
❑ 163 Charlie Ward .20 .50
❑ 164 Damon Stoudamire .25 .60
❑ 165 Tracy McGrady .60 1.50
❑ 166 Bimbo Coles .20 .50
❑ 167 Chucky Brown .20 .50
❑ 168 Jerry Stackhouse .25 .60
❑ 169 Greg Ostertag .20 .50
❑ 170 Radoslav Nesterovic .20 .50
❑ 171 Corey Maggette .25 .60
❑ 172 Vlade Divac .25 .60
❑ 173 Scott Padgett .20 .50
❑ 174 Anthony Mason .20 .50
❑ 175 Raef LaFrentz .20 .50
❑ 176 Austin Croshere .20 .50
❑ 177 Mark Strickland .20 .50
❑ 178 Allan Houston .25 .60
❑ 179 Arvydas Sabonis .25 .60
❑ 180 Doug Christie .20 .50
❑ 181 Jim Jackson .20 .50
❑ 182 Brevin Knight .20 .50
❑ 183 Mookie Blaylock .25 .60
❑ 184 Chris Herren .20 .50
❑ 185 Kevin Garnett .60 1.50
❑ 186 Tyrone Hill .20 .50
❑ 187 Tim Duncan .60 1.50
❑ 188 Shareef Abdur-Rahim .25 .60
❑ 189 Eddie Jones .25 .60
❑ 190 Jonathan Bender .20 .50
❑ 191 Alonzo Mourning .30 .75
❑ 192 Patrick Ewing .40 1.00
❑ 193 Scottie Pippen .50 1.25
❑ 194 Scot Pollard .20 .50
❑ 195 Cedric Ceballos .20 .50
❑ 196 Clarence Weatherspoon .20 .50
❑ 197 Jamie Feick .20 .50
❑ 198 Eric Snow .20 .50
❑ 199 Ron Harper .25 .60
❑ 200 Bryant Reeves .20 .50
❑ 201 Chris Mihm RC .75 2.00
❑ 202 Joel Przybilla RC .75 2.00
❑ 203 Kenyon Martin RC 2.00 5.00
❑ 204 Stromile Swift RC 1.00 2.50
❑ 205 Etan Thomas RC .75 2.00
❑ 206 Jason Collier RC .75 2.00
❑ 207 Marcus Fizer RC .75 2.00
❑ 208 Mateen Cleaves RC .75 2.00
❑ 209 Dan Langhi RC .75 2.00
❑ 210 Mike Miller RC 1.25 3.00
❑ 211 Jabari Smith RC .75 2.00
❑ 212 Hanno Mottola RC .75 2.00
❑ 213 Chris Porter RC .75 2.00
❑ 214 Desmond Mason RC 1.00 2.50
❑ 215 Erick Barkley RC .75 2.00
❑ 216 Donnell Harvey RC .75 2.00
❑ 217 DerMarr Johnson RC .75 2.00
❑ 218 Jerome Moiso RC .75 2.00
❑ 219 Quentin Richardson RC 1.00 2.50
❑ 220 Courtney Alexander RC .75 2.00
❑ 221 Michael Redd RC 2.00 5.00
❑ 222 Morris Peterson RC 1.25 3.00
❑ 223 Darius Miles RC 1.00 2.50
❑ 224 Jamal Crawford RC 1.25 3.00
❑ 225 Keyon Dooling RC .75 2.00

2001-02 Ultra

❑ COMP.SET w/o SP's (150) 20.00 40.00
❑ COMP.UPDATE SET (6) 15.00 40.00
❑ COMMON CARD (1-150) .20 .50
❑ COMMON ROOKIE (151-175) 1.25 3.00
❑ 151-175 PRINT RUN 2222 SERIAL #'d SETS
❑ COMMON UPDATE (1U-6U) 1.25 3.00
❑ 1 Vince Carter .60 1.50
❑ 2 Allen Iverson .60 1.50
❑ 3 Jerry Stackhouse .25 .60
❑ 4 Travis Best .20 .50
❑ 5 Eddie Jones .25 .60
❑ 6 Felipe Lopez .20 .50
❑ 7 Antonio Daniels .20 .50
❑ 8 A.J. Guyton .20 .50
❑ 9 Quentin Richardson .25 .60
❑ 10 Charlie Ward .20 .50
❑ 11 Ron Mercer .20 .50
❑ 12 Shandon Anderson .20 .50
❑ 13 Antawn Jamison .30 .75
❑ 14 Darius Miles .20 .50
❑ 15 Anthony Mason .20 .50
❑ 16 Latrell Sprewell .25 .60
❑ 17 Scottie Pippen .50 1.25
❑ 18 Shammond Williams .20 .50
❑ 19 P.J. Brown .20 .50
❑ 20 Dirk Nowitzki .50 1.25
❑ 21 Mateen Cleaves .20 .50
❑ 22 Tim Hardaway .25 .60
❑ 23 Christian Laettner .20 .50
❑ 24 Toni Kukoc .25 .60
❑ 25 Bob Sura .20 .50
❑ 26 Kobe Bryant 1.50 4.00
❑ 27 Wally Szczerbiak .25 .60
❑ 28 Darrell Armstrong .20 .50
❑ 29 Chris Webber .30 .75
❑ 30 David Wesley .20 .50
❑ 31 Michael Finley .30 .75
❑ 32 Jermaine O'Neal .30 .75
❑ 33 Jason Kidd .50 1.25
❑ 34 Tony Delk .20 .50
❑ 35 Avery Johnson .25 .60
❑ 36 Elden Campbell .20 .50
❑ 37 Lamond Murray .20 .50
❑ 38 Ben Wallace .25 .60
❑ 39 Jalen Rose .25 .60
❑ 40 Michael Dickerson .20 .50
❑ 41 Shawn Marion .30 .75
❑ 42 Jahidi White .20 .50
❑ 43 Jamal Mashburn .25 .60
❑ 44 Trajan Langdon .20 .50
❑ 45 Reggie Miller .30 .75
❑ 46 Stromile Swift .20 .50
❑ 47 Keith Van Horn .25 .60
❑ 48 Tom Gugliotta .20 .50
❑ 49 Brent Barry .20 .50
❑ 50 Courtney Alexander .20 .50
❑ 51 Antonio McDyess .25 .60
❑ 52 Robert Horry .25 .60
❑ 53 Ervin Johnson .20 .50
❑ 54 Speedy Claxton .20 .50
❑ 55 Bryon Russell .20 .50
❑ 56 Baron Davis .30 .75
❑ 57 Robert Traylor .20 .50
❑ 58 Chucky Atkins .20 .50
❑ 59 Stephon Marbury .30 .75
❑ 60 Desmond Mason .25 .60
❑ 61 Tyrone Nesby .20 .50
❑ 62 Brevin Knight .20 .50
❑ 63 Kenyon Martin .30 .75
❑ 64 Jumaine Jones .20 .50
❑ 65 Rashard Lewis .30 .75
❑ 66 Kenny Anderson .25 .60
❑ 67 Andre Miller .25 .60
❑ 68 Joe Smith .20 .50
❑ 69 Kelvin Cato .20 .50
❑ 70 Jason Williams .25 .60
❑ 71 Marcus Camby .25 .60
❑ 72 Eric Snow .20 .50
❑ 73 Gary Payton .30 .75
❑ 74 Robert Pack .20 .50
❑ 75 Brian Cardinal .20 .50
❑ 76 Sam Cassell .25 .60
❑ 77 Allan Houston .25 .60
❑ 78 Anfernee Hardaway .30 .75
❑ 79 Morris Peterson .25 .60
❑ 80 Chris Mihm .20 .50
❑ 81 Elton Brand .30 .75
❑ 82 Glenn Robinson .25 .60
❑ 83 Damon Stoudamire .25 .60
❑ 84 Alvin Williams .20 .50
❑ 85 Paul Pierce .30 .75
❑ 86 James Posey .20 .50
❑ 87 Cuttino Mobley .25 .60
❑ 88 Tim Thomas .20 .50
❑ 89 Dikembe Mutombo .25 .60
❑ 90 Tim Duncan .60 1.50
❑ 91 John Starks .20 .50
❑ 92 Antoine Walker .25 .60
❑ 93 Moochie Norris .20 .50
❑ 94 Dalibor Bagaric .20 .50
❑ 95 Ray Allen .30 .75
❑ 96 David Robinson .40 1.00
❑ 97 Shareef Abdur-Rahim .25 .60
❑ 98 Wang Zhizhi .25 .60
❑ 99 Chris Porter .20 .50
❑ 100 Chauncey Billups .25 .60
❑ 101 Tracy McGrady .60 1.50
❑ 102 Michael Jordan 5.00 12.00
❑ 103 Jerome Williams .20 .50
❑ 104 Jason Terry .30 .75
❑ 105 Calvin Booth .20 .50
❑ 106 Shaquille O'Neal .75 2.00
❑ 107 Kevin Garnett .60 1.50
❑ 108 Doug Christie .20 .50
❑ 109 Karl Malone .40 1.00
❑ 110 Steve Nash .50 1.25
❑ 111 Austin Croshere .20 .50
❑ 112 Alonzo Mourning .30 .75
❑ 113 Dan Majerle .25 .60
❑ 114 Malik Rose .20 .50
❑ 115 Richard Hamilton .25 .60
❑ 116 DerMarr Johnson .20 .50
❑ 117 Raef LaFrentz .20 .50
❑ 118 Derek Fisher .25 .60
❑ 119 Vlade Divac .25 .60
❑ 120 John Stockton .40 1.00
❑ 121 Dion Glover .20 .50
❑ 122 Voshon Lenard .20 .50
❑ 123 Steve Francis .30 .75
❑ 124 Darvin Ham .20 .50
❑ 125 Aaron McKie .20 .50
❑ 126 Peja Stojakovic .25 .60
❑ 127 Ron Artest .25 .60
❑ 128 Keyon Dooling .20 .50
❑ 129 Anthony Carter .20 .50
❑ 130 Kurt Thomas .20 .50
❑ 131 Rasheed Wallace .30 .75
❑ 132 Theo Ratliff .20 .50
❑ 133 Eric Piatkowski .20 .50
❑ 134 Terrell Brandon .20 .50
❑ 135 Mike Miller .25 .60
❑ 136 Mike Bibby .25 .60
❑ 137 Antonio Davis .20 .50
❑ 138 Lamar Odom .30 .75
❑ 139 Eddie House .20 .50
❑ 140 Nick Van Exel .25 .60
❑ 141 Rick Fox .25 .60
❑ 142 Juwan Howard .25 .60
❑ 143 Hedo Turkoglu .25 .60
❑ 144 Donyell Marshall .20 .50
❑ 145 Marcus Fizer .20 .50
❑ 146 Larry Hughes .25 .60
❑ 147 Steve Smith .25 .60
❑ 148 Brian Grant .20 .50
❑ 149 Grant Hill .30 .75
❑ 150 Derek Anderson .25 .60
❑ 151 Kwame Brown RC 1.50 4.00
❑ 152 Eddie Griffin RC 1.25 3.00
❑ 153 Eddy Curry RC 2.00 5.00
❑ 154 Jamaal Tinsley RC 1.50 4.00
❑ 155 Jason Richardson RC 2.50 6.00
❑ 156 Shane Battier RC 2.00 5.00
❑ 157 Troy Murphy RC 2.50 6.00
❑ 158 Richard Jefferson RC 3.00 8.00
❑ 159 DeSagana Diop RC 1.25 3.00
❑ 160 Tyson Chandler RC 2.50 6.00
❑ 161 Joe Johnson RC 3.00 8.00
❑ 162 Zach Randolph RC 3.00 8.00
❑ 163 Andrei Kirilenko RC 3.00 8.00
❑ 164 Loren Woods RC 1.25 3.00
❑ 165 Jason Collins RC 1.25 3.00
❑ 166 Rodney White RC 1.25 3.00
❑ 167 Jeryl Sasser RC 1.25 3.00
❑ 168 Kirk Haston RC 1.25 3.00
❑ 169 Pau Gasol RC 5.00 12.00
❑ 170 Kedrick Brown RC 1.25 3.00
❑ 171 Steven Hunter RC 1.25 3.00
❑ 172 Michael Bradley RC 1.25 3.00
❑ 173 Joseph Forte RC 1.25 3.00
❑ 174 Brandon Armstrong RC 1.25 3.00
❑ 175 Primoz Brezec RC 1.50 4.00
❑ 1U Gerald Wallace RC 2.50 6.00
❑ 2U Tony Parker RC 6.00 30.00
❑ 3U Vladimir Radmanovic RC 1.25 3.00
❑ 4U Trenton Hassell RC 1.50 4.00
❑ 5U Zeljko Rebraca RC 1.25 3.00
❑ 6U Oscar Torres RC 1.25 3.00

2002-03 Ultra

COMPLETET SET (210)	100.00	250.00
COMP.SET w/o RC's (180)	20.00	50.00
COMMON CARD (1-180)	.20	.50
COMMON ROOKIE (181-210)	1.25	3.00
1 Vince Carter	.60	1.50
2 Ben Wallace	.25	.60
3 Tim Thomas	.20	.50
4 Eric Snow	.20	.50
5 Peja Stojakovic	.25	.60
6 Andrei Kirilenko	.30	.75
7 Dion Glover	.20	.50
8 James Posey	.20	.50
9 Kenny Thomas	.20	.50
10 Michael Dickerson	.20	.50
11 Charlie Ward	.20	.50
12 Gary Payton	.30	.75
13 Eddy Curry	.25	.60
14 Rick Fox	.25	.60
15 Joel Przybilla	.20	.50
16 Aaron McKie	.20	.50
17 Hedo Turkoglu	.25	.60
18 Jarron Collins	.20	.50
19 Jason Collins	.20	.50
20 Nick Van Exel	.25	.60
21 Reggie Miller	.30	.75
22 Devean George	.20	.50
23 Michael Jordan	2.00	5.00
24 Tony Parker	.30	.75
25 Robert Horry	.25	.60
26 Wally Szczerbiak	.25	.60
27 Dikembe Mutombo	.25	.60
28 Scot Pollard	.20	.50
29 Darrell Armstrong	.20	.50
30 Jalen Rose	.25	.60
31 Antawn Jamison	.30	.75
32 Anfernee Hardaway	.30	.75
33 Paul Pierce	.30	.75
34 Juwan Howard	.25	.60
35 Eddie Griffin	.20	.50
36 Shane Battier	.25	.60
37 Shandon Anderson	.20	.50
38 Vladimir Radmanovic	.20	.50
39 DerMarr Johnson	.20	.50
40 Antonio McDyess	.25	.60
41 Cuttino Mobley	.25	.60
42 Stromile Swift	.20	.50
43 Tracy McGrady	.60	1.50
44 Charles Smith	.20	.50
45 Shawn Marion	.30	.75
46 P.J. Brown	.20	.50
47 Wang Zhizhi	.20	.50
48 Austin Croshere	.20	.50
49 Ervin Johnson	.20	.50
50 Jason Kidd	.50	1.25
51 Tom Gugliotta	.20	.50
52 Jamal Crawford	.25	.60
53 Toni Kukoc	.25	.60
54 Mengke Bateer	.20	.50
55 Moochie Norris	.20	.50
56 Jason Williams	.25	.60
57 Mike Miller	.25	.60
58 Steve Smith	.25	.60
59 Shareef Abdur-Rahim	.25	.60
60 Michael Finley	.30	.75
61 Jermaine O'Neal	.30	.75
62 Mark Madsen	.20	.50
63 Troy Hudson	.20	.50
64 David Robinson	.40	1.00
65 Corliss Williamson	.25	.60
66 Rodney Rogers	.20	.50
67 Derek Fisher	.25	.60
68 Anthony Carter	.20	.50
69 Allan Houston	.25	.60
70 Desmond Mason	.25	.60
71 Brendan Haywood	.20	.50
72 Tony Delk	.20	.50
73 Ryan Bowen	.20	.50
74 Danny Fortson	.20	.50
75 Alonzo Mourning	.30	.75
76 Latrell Sprewell	.25	.60
77 Rashard Lewis	.30	.75
78 Courtney Alexander	.20	.50
79 Marcus Fizer	.20	.50
80 Jason Richardson	.30	.75
81 Terrell Brandon	.20	.50
82 Allen Iverson	.60	1.50
83 Vlade Divac	.25	.60
84 Jahidi White	.20	.50
85 Eric Piatkowski	.20	.50
86 Marc Jackson	.20	.50
87 Pat Garrity	.20	.50
88 Tim Duncan	.60	1.50
89 Kwame Brown	.20	.50
90 Andre Miller	.25	.60
91 Troy Murphy	.30	.75
92 John Stockton	.40	1.00
93 Kenny Anderson	.25	.60
94 Chris Mihm	.20	.50
95 Larry Hughes	.25	.60
96 Lamar Odom	.30	.75
97 Brian Grant	.20	.50
98 Marcus Camby	.25	.60
99 Mike Bibby	.25	.60
100 Joseph Forte	.20	.50
101 Lamond Murray	.20	.50
102 Darius Miles	.20	.50
103 Eddie Jones	.25	.60
104 Aaron Williams	.20	.50
105 Derek Anderson	.25	.60
106 Karl Malone	.30	.75
107 Jon Barry	.20	.50
108 Tony Battie	.20	.50
109 Jumaine Jones	.20	.50
110 Corey Maggette	.25	.60
111 Eddie House	.20	.50
112 Theo Ratliff	.20	.50
113 Scottie Pippen	.50	1.25
114 Hakeem Olajuwon	.40	1.00
115 Antoine Walker	.25	.60
116 Tim Hardaway	.25	.60
117 Steve Francis	.30	.75
118 Lorenzen Wright	.20	.50
119 Howard Eisley	.20	.50
120 Brent Barry	.20	.50
121 Baron Davis	.30	.75
122 Michael Doleac	.20	.50
123 Quentin Richardson	.25	.60
124 LaPhonso Ellis	.25	.60
125 Richard Jefferson	.30	.75
126 Damon Stoudamire	.25	.60
127 Alvin Williams	.20	.50
128 Chucky Atkins	.20	.50
129 Jamal Mashburn	.25	.60
130 Wesley Person	.20	.50
131 Elton Brand	.30	.75
132 Ray Allen	.30	.75
133 Kerry Kittles	.25	.60
134 Rasheed Wallace	.30	.75
135 Antonio Davis	.20	.50
136 David Wesley	.20	.50
137 Dirk Nowitzki	.50	1.25
138 Rodney White	.20	.50
139 Jamaal Tinsley	.25	.60
140 Sam Cassell	.25	.60
141 Keith Van Horn	.25	.60
142 Ruben Patterson	.20	.50
143 Jerome Williams	.20	.50
144 Jason Terry	.30	.75
145 Eduardo Najera	.20	.50
146 Maurice Taylor	.20	.50
147 Pau Gasol	.30	.75
148 Grant Hill	.30	.75
149 Antonio Daniels	.20	.50
150 George Lynch	.20	.50
151 Steve Nash	.50	1.25
152 Al Harrington	.25	.60
153 Anthony Mason	.20	.50
154 Kenyon Martin	.30	.75
155 Bonzi Wells	.25	.60
156 Morris Peterson	.25	.60
157 Eddie Robinson	.20	.50
158 Kevin Garnett	.60	1.50
159 Chris Webber	.30	.75
160 John Amaechi	.20	.50
161 Kobe Bryant	1.50	4.00
162 Joe Smith	.20	.50
163 Speedy Claxton	.20	.50
164 Doug Christie	.20	.50
165 Richard Hamilton	.25	.60
166 Tyson Chandler	.25	.60
167 Gilbert Arenas	.30	.75
168 Stephon Marbury	.30	.75
169 Jamaal Magloire	.20	.50
170 Raef LaFrentz	.20	.50
171 Ron Mercer	.20	.50
172 Glenn Robinson	.25	.60
173 Chauncey Billups	.30	.75
174 Iakovos Tsakalidis	.20	.50
175 Vin Baker	.25	.60
176 Joe Johnson	.30	.75
177 Jerry Stackhouse	.25	.60
178 Shaquille O'Neal	.75	2.00
179 Derrick Coleman	.25	.60
180 Bryon Russell	.20	.50
181 Yao Ming RC	4.00	10.00
182 Jay Williams RC	1.50	4.00
183 Drew Gooden RC	2.00	5.00
184 DaJuan Wagner RC	1.25	3.00
185 Qyntel Woods RC	1.25	3.00
186 Chris Wilcox RC	1.50	4.00
187 Curtis Borchardt RC	1.25	3.00
188 Nikoloz Tskitishvili RC	1.25	3.00
189 Caron Butler RC	2.50	6.00
190 Nene Hilario RC	1.50	4.00
191 Jared Jeffries RC	1.25	3.00
192 Mike Dunleavy RC	1.50	4.00
193 Kareem Rush RC	1.50	4.00
194 Amare Stoudemire RC	3.00	8.00
195 Melvin Ely RC	1.25	3.00
196 Marcus Haislip RC	1.25	3.00
197 Jiri Welsch RC	1.25	3.00
198 Frank Williams RC	1.25	3.00
199 John Salmons RC	2.00	5.00
200 Gordan Giricek RC	1.25	3.00
201 Ryan Humphrey RC	1.25	3.00
202 Casey Jacobsen RC	1.25	3.00
203 Carlos Boozer RC	2.50	6.00
204 Manu Ginobili RC	3.00	8.00
205 Bostjan Nachbar RC	1.25	3.00
206 Fred Jones RC	1.50	4.00
207 Dan Dickau RC	1.25	3.00
208 Tayshaun Prince RC	2.00	5.00
209 Memo Okur RC	1.50	4.00
210 Juan Dixon RC	2.00	5.00

2003-04 Ultra

COMP. SET w/o SP's	12.50	30.00
COMMON CARD (1-170)	.08	.20
COMMON L13 RC (171-183)	4.00	10.00
COMMON ROOKIE (184-195)	1.50	4.00
1 Yao Ming	.75	2.00
2 DeShawn Stevenson	.08	.20
3 Malik Rose	.08	.20
4 DaJuan Wagner	.20	.50
5 Troy Murphy	.30	.75
6 Caron Butler	.30	.75
7 Radoslav Nesterovic	.20	.50
8 Joe Johnson	.20	.50
9 Al Harrington	.20	.50
10 Carlos Boozer	.30	.75
11 Morris Peterson	.20	.50
12 Malik Allen	.08	.20
13 Kurt Thomas	.20	.50
14 Derek Anderson	.20	.50
15 Zydrunas Ilgauskas	.20	.50
16 Jason Richardson	.30	.75
17 Brian Grant	.20	.50
18 Allan Houston	.20	.50
19 Bonzi Wells	.20	.50

❑ 20 Stephen Jackson	.08	.20
❑ 21 Eddy Curry	.30	.75
❑ 22 Tayshaun Prince	.20	.50
❑ 23 Brad Miller	.30	.75
❑ 24 Stromile Swift	.20	.50
❑ 25 Kendall Gill	.08	.20
❑ 26 Vladimir Radmanovic	.08	.20
❑ 27 Theo Ratliff	.20	.50
❑ 28 Nick Van Exel	.30	.75
❑ 29 Marko Jaric	.08	.20
❑ 30 Jason Collins	.08	.20
❑ 31 Darrell Armstrong	.08	.20
❑ 32 Vlade Divac	.20	.50
❑ 33 Juan Dixon	.20	.50
❑ 34 Calbert Cheaney	.08	.20
❑ 35 Tyson Chandler	.30	.75
❑ 36 Chauncey Billups	.20	.50
❑ 37 Reggie Miller	.30	.75
❑ 38 Mike Miller	.30	.75
❑ 39 Marc Jackson	.20	.50
❑ 40 Casey Jacobsen	.08	.20
❑ 41 Ray Allen	.30	.75
❑ 42 Mehmet Okur	.08	.20
❑ 43 Jermaine O'Neal	.30	.75
❑ 44 Lorenzen Wright	.08	.20
❑ 45 Wally Szczerbiak	.20	.50
❑ 46 Anfernee Hardaway	.30	.75
❑ 47 Matt Harpring	.30	.75
❑ 48 Jay Williams	.20	.50
❑ 49 Corliss Williamson	.20	.50
❑ 50 Jamaal Tinsley	.30	.75
❑ 51 Shane Battier	.30	.75
❑ 52 Kevin Garnett	.60	1.50
❑ 53 Shawn Marion	.30	.75
❑ 54 Alvin Williams	.08	.20
❑ 55 Juwan Howard	.20	.50
❑ 56 Shaquille O'Neal	.75	2.00
❑ 57 Jamal Mashburn	.20	.50
❑ 58 Kenny Thomas	.08	.20
❑ 59 Tim Duncan	.60	1.50
❑ 60 Predrag Drobnjak	.08	.20
❑ 61 Jalen Rose	.30	.75
❑ 62 Ben Wallace	.30	.75
❑ 63 James Posey	.20	.50
❑ 64 Pau Gasol	.30	.75
❑ 65 Michael Redd	.30	.75
❑ 66 Amare Stoudemire	.60	1.50
❑ 67 Karl Malone	.30	.75
❑ 68 Richard Hamilton	.20	.50
❑ 69 Eddie Griffin	.20	.50
❑ 70 Robert Horry	.20	.50
❑ 71 Tim Thomas	.20	.50
❑ 72 Eric Snow	.20	.50
❑ 73 Brent Barry	.20	.50
❑ 74 Jamal Crawford	.08	.20
❑ 75 Nikoloz Tskitishvili	.08	.20
❑ 76 Bostjan Nachbar	.08	.20
❑ 77 Devean George	.20	.50
❑ 78 Dan Gadzuric	.08	.20
❑ 79 Brian Skinner	.08	.20
❑ 80 Cuttino Mobley	.20	.50
❑ 81 Desmond Mason	.20	.50
❑ 82 Othella Harrington	.08	.20
❑ 83 Chris Webber	.30	.75
❑ 84 Dirk Nowitzki	.50	1.25
❑ 85 Steve Francis	.30	.75
❑ 86 Gary Payton	.30	.75
❑ 87 Howard Eisley	.08	.20
❑ 88 Zach Randolph	.30	.75
❑ 89 Sam Cassell	.30	.75
❑ 90 Tony Battie	.08	.20
❑ 91 Shammond Williams	.08	.20
❑ 92 Rick Fox	.20	.50
❑ 93 David Wesley	.08	.20
❑ 94 Frank Williams	.08	.20
❑ 95 Tony Delk	.08	.20
❑ 96 Troy Hudson	.08	.20
❑ 97 Donnell Harvey	.08	.20
❑ 98 Derek Fisher	.30	.75
❑ 99 Jamaal Magloire	.08	.20
❑ 100 Keith Van Horn	.30	.75
❑ 101 Tony Parker	.30	.75
❑ 102 Rashard Lewis	.30	.75
❑ 103 Shareef Abdur-Rahim	.30	.75
❑ 104 Michael Finley	.30	.75
❑ 105 Jason Kidd	.50	1.25
❑ 106 Drew Gooden	.20	.50
❑ 107 Mike Bibby	.30	.75
❑ 108 Jerry Stackhouse	.30	.75

❑ 109 Chris Jefferies	.08	.20
❑ 110 Glenn Robinson	.30	.75
❑ 111 Shawn Bradley	.08	.20
❑ 112 Corey Maggette	.20	.50
❑ 113 Richard Jefferson	.20	.50
❑ 114 Gordan Giricek	.20	.50
❑ 115 Bobby Jackson	.20	.50
❑ 116 Larry Hughes	.20	.50
❑ 117 Scott Padgett	.08	.20
❑ 118 Gilbert Arenas	.30	.75
❑ 119 Ron Artest	.20	.50
❑ 120 Jason Williams	.20	.50
❑ 121 Eric Williams	.08	.20
❑ 122 Stephon Marbury	.30	.75
❑ 123 Vince Carter	.75	2.00
❑ 124 Jason Terry	.30	.75
❑ 125 Raef LaFrentz	.20	.50
❑ 126 Michael Olowokandi	.08	.20
❑ 127 Kerry Kittles	.08	.20
❑ 128 Pat Garrity	.08	.20
❑ 129 Peja Stojakovic	.30	.75
❑ 130 Jared Jeffries	.08	.20
❑ 131 Antonio Davis	.08	.20
❑ 132 Rodney White	.08	.20
❑ 133 Kobe Bryant	1.25	3.00
❑ 134 Baron Davis	.30	.75
❑ 135 Derrick Coleman	.08	.20
❑ 136 Walter McCarty	.08	.20
❑ 137 Bruce Bowen	.08	.20
❑ 138 Mike Dunleavy	.20	.50
❑ 139 Rasual Butler	.20	.50
❑ 140 Latrell Sprewell	.30	.75
❑ 141 Rasheed Wallace	.30	.75
❑ 142 Andrei Kirilenko	.30	.75
❑ 143 Dan Dickau	.08	.20
❑ 144 Steve Nash	.30	.75
❑ 145 Elton Brand	.30	.75
❑ 146 Kenyon Martin	.30	.75
❑ 147 Jeryl Sasser	.08	.20
❑ 148 Doug Christie	.20	.50
❑ 149 Kwame Brown	.20	.50
❑ 150 Ricky Davis	.30	.75
❑ 151 Antawn Jamison	.30	.75
❑ 152 Travis Best	.08	.20
❑ 153 Courtney Alexander	.20	.50
❑ 154 Scottie Pippen	.50	1.25
❑ 155 Jerome Williams	.08	.20
❑ 156 Quentin Richardson	.20	.50
❑ 157 Lucious Harris	.08	.20
❑ 158 Allen Iverson	.60	1.50
❑ 159 Manu Ginobili	.30	.75
❑ 160 Bryon Russell	.08	.20
❑ 161 Paul Pierce	.30	.75
❑ 162 Nene	.20	.50
❑ 163 Darius Miles	.30	.75
❑ 164 Earl Boykins	.20	.50
❑ 165 Eddie Jones	.30	.75
❑ 166 P.J. Brown	.08	.20
❑ 167 Qyntel Woods	.08	.20
❑ 168 Andre Miller	.20	.50
❑ 169 Tracy McGrady	.75	2.00
❑ 170 Antoine Walker	.30	.75
❑ 171 LeBron James L13 RC	100.00	200.00
❑ 172 Darko Milicic L13 RC	8.00	20.00
❑ 173 Carmelo Anthony L13 RC	20.00	40.00
❑ 174 Chris Bosh L13 RC	10.00	25.00
❑ 175 Dwyane Wade L13 RC	20.00	40.00
❑ 176 Chris Kaman L13 RC	5.00	12.00
❑ 177 Kirk Hinrich L13 RC	10.00	25.00
❑ 178 T.J. Ford L13 RC	4.00	8.00
❑ 179 Mike Sweetney L13 RC	4.00	10.00
❑ 180 Jarvis Hayes L13 RC	4.00	10.00
❑ 181 Mickael Pietrus L13 RC	5.00	12.00
❑ 182 Nick Collison L13 RC	4.00	10.00
❑ 183 Marcus Banks L13 RC	4.00	10.00
❑ 184 Luke Ridnour RC	2.00	5.00
❑ 185 Troy Bell RC	1.50	4.00
❑ 186 Zarko Cabarkapa RC	1.50	4.00
❑ 187 David West RC	3.00	8.00
❑ 188 Sofoklis Schortsanitis RC	2.00	5.00
❑ 189 Travis Outlaw RC	2.00	5.00
❑ 190 Leandro Barbosa RC	2.50	6.00
❑ 191 Josh Howard RC	2.00	5.00
❑ 192 Maciej Lampe RC	1.50	4.00
❑ 193 Luke Walton RC	1.50	4.00
❑ 194 Travis Hansen RC	1.50	4.00
❑ 195 Rick Rickert RC	1.50	4.00

2004-05 Ultra

❑ COMP.SET w/o RC's (175)	15.00	40.00
❑ COMMON CARD (1-175)	.20	.50
❑ COMMON ROOKIE (189-199)	1.50	4.00
❑ COMMON RC UPDATE (200U-219U)	2.00	5.00
❑ AT THE RATE OF TWO PER BOX		
❑ 1 Ben Wallace	.25	.60
❑ 2 Chris Kaman	.25	.60
❑ 3 Steve Nash	.50	1.25
❑ 4 Al Harrington	.25	.60
❑ 5 T.J. Ford	.25	.60
❑ 6 Jason Collins	.20	.50
❑ 7 Theo Ratliff	.20	.50
❑ 8 Kobe Bryant	1.50	4.00
❑ 9 Kirk Hinrich	.25	.60
❑ 10 Darko Milicic	.20	.50
❑ 11 Karl Malone	.30	.75
❑ 12 Michael Olowokandi	.20	.50
❑ 13 Frank Williams	.20	.50
❑ 14 Vlade Divac	.25	.60
❑ 15 Vince Carter	.60	1.50
❑ 16 Eddy Curry	.25	.60
❑ 17 Keith Van Horn	.25	.60
❑ 18 Chris Wilcox	.20	.50
❑ 19 Tim Thomas	.20	.50
❑ 20 Shareef Abdur-Rahim	.25	.60
❑ 21 Carlos Arroyo	.30	.75
❑ 22 Jason Collier	.20	.50
❑ 23 Voshon Lenard	.20	.50
❑ 24 Reggie Miller	.30	.75
❑ 25 Dan Gadzuric	.20	.50
❑ 26 David Wesley	.20	.50
❑ 27 Vladimir Radmanovic	.20	.50
❑ 28 Derek Anderson	.25	.60
❑ 29 Zydrunas Ilgauskas	.25	.60
❑ 30 Nick Van Exel	.25	.60
❑ 31 Stromile Swift	.20	.50
❑ 32 Kerry Kittles	.25	.60
❑ 33 Zaza Pachulia	.20	.50
❑ 34 Brad Miller	.25	.60
❑ 35 Jerry Stackhouse	.25	.60
❑ 36 Jason Terry	.25	.60
❑ 37 Earl Boykins	.20	.50
❑ 38 Jermaine O'Neal	.30	.75
❑ 39 Joe Smith	.20	.50
❑ 40 Jamaal Magloire	.20	.50
❑ 41 Zarko Cabarkapa	.20	.50
❑ 42 Ronald Murray	.20	.50
❑ 43 Bob Sura	.20	.50
❑ 44 Andre Miller	.25	.60
❑ 45 Jamaal Tinsley	.25	.60
❑ 46 Michael Redd	.30	.75
❑ 47 Baron Davis	.30	.75
❑ 48 Amare Stoudemire	.60	1.50
❑ 49 Rashard Lewis	.30	.75
❑ 50 Jiri Welsch	.20	.50
❑ 51 Marcus Camby	.25	.60
❑ 52 Ron Artest	.25	.60
❑ 53 Eddie Jones	.25	.60
❑ 54 Darrell Armstrong	.20	.50
❑ 55 Shawn Marion	.30	.75
❑ 56 Brent Barry	.20	.50
❑ 57 Michael Finley	.30	.75
❑ 58 Jim Jackson	.20	.50
❑ 59 Jason Williams	.25	.60
❑ 60 Kenyon Martin	.30	.75
❑ 61 Kyle Korver	.25	.60
❑ 62 Marquis Daniels	.20	.50
❑ 63 Chucky Atkins	.20	.50
❑ 64 Nene	.25	.60
❑ 65 Marko Jaric	.20	.50
❑ 66 Dwyane Wade	1.00	2.50
❑ 67 P.J. Brown	.20	.50
❑ 68 Casey Jacobsen	.20	.50
❑ 69 Morris Peterson	.25	.60

❑ 70 Ricky Davis .25 .60
❑ 71 Tayshaun Prince .25 .60
❑ 72 Corey Maggette .25 .60
❑ 73 Udonis Haslem .25 .60
❑ 74 Kurt Thomas .20 .50
❑ 75 Leandro Barbosa .30 .75
❑ 76 Alvin Williams .20 .50
❑ 77 Mark Blount .20 .50
❑ 78 Chauncey Billups .30 .75
❑ 79 Boris Diaw .25 .60
❑ 80 Brian Grant .20 .50
❑ 81 Allan Houston .25 .60
❑ 82 Joe Johnson .30 .75
❑ 83 Donyell Marshall .20 .50
❑ 84 Jamal Crawford .25 .60
❑ 85 Jason Richardson .30 .75
❑ 86 Gary Payton .30 .75
❑ 87 Nazr Mohammed .20 .50
❑ 88 Mike Bibby .25 .60
❑ 89 Jalen Rose .25 .60
❑ 90 Scottie Pippen .50 1.25
❑ 91 Speedy Claxton .20 .50
❑ 92 Devean George .20 .50
❑ 93 Sam Cassell .25 .60
❑ 94 Mike Sweetney .20 .50
❑ 95 Chris Webber .30 .75
❑ 96 Chris Bosh .30 .75
❑ 97 Antoine Walker .30 .75
❑ 98 Cuttino Mobley .25 .60
❑ 99 Caron Butler .25 .60
❑ 100 John Salmons .30 .75
❑ 101 Bruce Bowen .20 .50
❑ 102 Josh Howard .30 .75
❑ 103 Steve Francis .30 .75
❑ 104 Lamar Odom .30 .75
❑ 105 Troy Hudson .20 .50
❑ 106 Allen Iverson .60 1.50
❑ 107 Dajuan Wagner .20 .50
❑ 108 Erick Dampier .20 .50
❑ 109 Luke Walton .25 .60
❑ 110 Aaron Williams .20 .50
❑ 111 Juwan Howard .25 .60
❑ 112 Bobby Jackson .20 .50
❑ 113 Andrei Kirilenko .30 .75
❑ 114 LeBron James 2.00 5.00
❑ 115 Brian Cardinal .20 .50
❑ 116 Mike Miller .25 .60
❑ 117 Tracy McGrady .60 1.50
❑ 118 Doug Christie .20 .50
❑ 119 Larry Hughes .25 .60
❑ 120 Stephen Jackson .25 .60
❑ 121 Carmelo Anthony 1.00 2.50
❑ 122 Fred Jones .20 .50
❑ 123 Desmond Mason .25 .60
❑ 124 Jamal Mashburn .25 .60
❑ 125 Ray Allen .30 .75
❑ 126 Jeff McInnis .20 .50
❑ 127 Yao Ming .75 2.00
❑ 128 Bonzi Wells .20 .50
❑ 129 Richard Jefferson .30 .75
❑ 130 Kenny Thomas .20 .50
❑ 131 Hedo Turkoglu .25 .60
❑ 132 Kwame Brown .20 .50
❑ 133 Dirk Nowitzki .50 1.25
❑ 134 Maurice Taylor .20 .50
❑ 135 Pau Gasol .30 .75
❑ 136 Jason Kidd .50 1.25
❑ 137 Samuel Dalembert .20 .50
❑ 138 Tim Duncan .60 1.50
❑ 139 Gilbert Arenas .30 .75
❑ 140 Tony Parker .30 .75
❑ 141 Tyson Chandler .25 .60
❑ 142 Richard Hamilton .25 .60
❑ 143 Shaquille O'Neal .75 2.00
❑ 144 Stephon Marbury .30 .75
❑ 145 Damon Stoudamire .25 .60
❑ 146 Gordan Giricek .20 .50
❑ 147 Latrell Sprewell .25 .60
❑ 148 Carlos Boozer .30 .75
❑ 149 Mike Dunleavy .25 .60
❑ 150 Luke Ridnour .20 .50
❑ 151 Reece Gaines .20 .50
❑ 152 Peja Stojakovic .25 .60
❑ 153 Juan Dixon .20 .50
❑ 154 Marcus Banks .20 .50
❑ 155 Rasheed Wallace .30 .75
❑ 156 Quentin Richardson .25 .60
❑ 157 Wally Szczerbiak .25 .60
❑ 158 Keith Bogans .20 .50
❑ 159 Darius Miles .25 .60
❑ 160 Matt Harpring .25 .60
❑ 161 Antawn Jamison .30 .75
❑ 162 Kelvin Cato .20 .50
❑ 163 James Posey .20 .50
❑ 164 Willie Green .20 .50
❑ 165 Rasho Nesterovic .20 .50
❑ 166 Jarvis Hayes .20 .50
❑ 167 Paul Pierce .30 .75
❑ 168 Mehmet Okur .25 .60
❑ 169 Elton Brand .30 .75
❑ 170 Kevin Garnett .60 1.50
❑ 171 Drew Gooden .20 .50
❑ 172 Zach Randolph .30 .75
❑ 173 Raul Lopez .20 .50
❑ 174 Manu Ginobili .30 .75
❑ 175 Raja Bell .25 .60
❑ 176 Dwight Howard L13 RC 10.00 25.00
❑ 177 Emeka Okafor L13 EXCH 6.00 15.00
❑ 178 Ben Gordon L13 RC 4.00 10.00
❑ 179 Shaun Livingston L13 RC 3.00 8.00
❑ 180 Devin Harris L13 RC 6.00 15.00
❑ 181 Josh Childress L13 RC 3.00 8.00
❑ 182 Luol Deng L13 RC 4.00 10.00
❑ 183 Rafael Araujo L13 RC 3.00 8.00
❑ 184 Andre Iguodala L13 RC 8.00 20.00
❑ 185 Luke Jackson L13 RC 3.00 8.00
❑ 186 Andris Biedrins L13 RC 5.00 12.00
❑ 187 Robert Swift L13 RC 3.00 8.00
❑ 188 Sebastian Telfair L13 RC 3.00 8.00
❑ 189 Kris Humphries RC 2.50 6.00
❑ 190 Al Jefferson RC 3.00 8.00
❑ 191 Kirk Snyder RC 1.50 4.00
❑ 192 Josh Smith RC 4.00 10.00
❑ 193 J.R. Smith RC 3.00 8.00
❑ 194 Dorell Wright RC 2.00 5.00
❑ 195 Jameer Nelson RC 2.00 5.00
❑ 196 Pavel Podkolzine RC 1.50 4.00
❑ 197 Ha Seung-Jin RC 1.50 4.00
❑ 198 Sasha Vujacic RC 1.50 4.00
❑ 199 Anderson Varejao RC 2.00 5.00
❑ 200U Bernard Robinson RC 2.00 5.00
❑ 201U Andres Nocioni RC 2.50 6.00
❑ 202U Delonte West RC 3.00 8.00
❑ 203U Tony Allen RC 2.50 6.00
❑ 204U Kevin Martin RC 2.50 6.00
❑ 205U Beno Udrih RC 2.50 6.00
❑ 206U David Harrison RC 2.00 5.00
❑ 207U Jackson Vroman RC 2.00 5.00
❑ 208U Peter John Ramos RC 2.00 5.00
❑ 209U Lionel Chalmers RC 2.00 5.00
❑ 210U Donta Smith RC 2.00 5.00
❑ 211U Andre Emmett RC 2.00 5.00
❑ 212U Antonio Burks RC 2.00 5.00
❑ 213U Royal Ivey RC 2.00 5.00
❑ 214U Chris Duhon RC 3.00 8.00
❑ 215U Damien Wilkins RC 2.00 5.00
❑ 216U Justin Reed RC 2.00 5.00
❑ 217U Trevor Ariza RC 2.50 6.00
❑ 218U Tim Pickett RC 2.00 5.00
❑ 219U Yuta Tabuse RC 4.00 10.00

2006-07 Ultra

❑ COMP.SET w/o SP's (170) 20.00 50.00
❑ 1 Josh Childress .25 .60
❑ 2 Al Harrington .20 .50
❑ 3 Joe Johnson .25 .60
❑ 4 Tyronn Lue .20 .50
❑ 5 Josh Smith .30 .75
❑ 6 Tony Allen .25 .60
❑ 7 Dan Dickau .20 .50
❑ 8 Al Jefferson .30 .75
❑ 9 Paul Pierce .30 .75
❑ 10 Wally Szczerbiak .25 .60
❑ 11 Raef LaFrentz .20 .50
❑ 12 Primoz Brezec .20 .50
❑ 13 Brevin Knight .20 .50
❑ 14 Emeka Okafor .30 .75
❑ 15 Kareem Rush .20 .50
❑ 16 Gerald Wallace .30 .75
❑ 17 Bernard Robinson .20 .50
❑ 18 Tyson Chandler .30 .75
❑ 19 Luol Deng .30 .75
❑ 20 Chris Duhon .20 .50
❑ 21 Ben Gordon .40 1.00
❑ 22 Kirk Hinrich .30 .75
❑ 23 Drew Gooden .25 .60
❑ 24 Larry Hughes .25 .60
❑ 25 Zydrunas Ilgauskas .25 .60
❑ 26 LeBron James 1.50 4.00
❑ 27 Luke Jackson .20 .50
❑ 28 Anderson Varejao .25 .60
❑ 29 Erick Dampier .20 .50
❑ 30 Marquis Daniels .25 .60
❑ 31 Devin Harris .30 .75
❑ 32 Josh Howard .30 .75
❑ 33 Dirk Nowitzki .50 1.25
❑ 34 Jason Terry .30 .75
❑ 35 Carmelo Anthony .40 1.00
❑ 36 Earl Boykins .20 .50
❑ 37 Marcus Camby .25 .60
❑ 38 Kenyon Martin .30 .75
❑ 39 Andre Miller .25 .60
❑ 40 Eduardo Najera .20 .50
❑ 41 Chauncey Billups .30 .75
❑ 42 Richard Hamilton .25 .60
❑ 43 Antonio McDyess .20 .50
❑ 44 Tayshaun Prince .30 .75
❑ 45 Ben Wallace .30 .75
❑ 46 Rasheed Wallace .30 .75
❑ 47 Baron Davis .30 .75
❑ 48 Mike Dunleavy .25 .60
❑ 49 Derek Fisher .25 .60
❑ 50 Troy Murphy .30 .75
❑ 51 Jason Richardson .30 .75
❑ 52 Rafer Alston .20 .50
❑ 53 Juwan Howard .25 .60
❑ 54 Tracy McGrady .60 1.50
❑ 55 Stromile Swift .25 .60
❑ 56 David Wesley .20 .50
❑ 57 Yao Ming .75 2.00
❑ 58 Austin Croshere .20 .50
❑ 59 Stephen Jackson .25 .60
❑ 60 Jermaine O'Neal .30 .75
❑ 61 Peja Stojakovic .30 .75
❑ 62 Jamaal Tinsley .25 .60
❑ 63 Elton Brand .30 .75
❑ 64 Sam Cassell .30 .75
❑ 65 Chris Kaman .20 .50
❑ 66 Shaun Livingston .20 .50
❑ 67 Corey Maggette .25 .60
❑ 68 Cuttino Mobley .25 .60
❑ 69 Kwame Brown .25 .60
❑ 70 Kobe Bryant 1.50 4.00
❑ 71 Devean George .25 .60
❑ 72 Lamar Odom .30 .75
❑ 73 Smush Parker .20 .50
❑ 74 Luke Walton .25 .60
❑ 75 Shane Battier .30 .75
❑ 76 Pau Gasol .30 .75
❑ 77 Bobby Jackson .20 .50
❑ 78 Mike Miller .30 .75
❑ 79 Damon Stoudamire .25 .60
❑ 80 Alonzo Mourning .40 1.00
❑ 81 Shaquille O'Neal .75 2.00
❑ 82 Gary Payton .30 .75
❑ 83 Dwyane Wade .75 2.00
❑ 84 Antoine Walker .25 .60
❑ 85 Jason Williams .25 .60
❑ 86 T.J. Ford .25 .60
❑ 87 Jamaal Magloire .20 .50
❑ 88 Michael Redd .30 .75
❑ 89 Bobby Simmons .20 .50
❑ 90 Maurice Williams .25 .60
❑ 91 Mark Blount .20 .50
❑ 92 Ricky Davis .30 .75
❑ 93 Kevin Garnett .60 1.50
❑ 94 Eddie Griffin .20 .50
❑ 95 Trenton Hassell .20 .50
❑ 96 Troy Hudson .20 .50
❑ 97 Vince Carter .60 1.50
❑ 98 Jason Collins .20 .50
❑ 99 Richard Jefferson .25 .60
❑ 100 Jason Kidd .50 1.25
❑ 101 Jeff McInnis .20 .50

❑ 102 Antoine Wright .20 .50
❑ 103 P.J. Brown .20 .50
❑ 104 Speedy Claxton .20 .50
❑ 105 Marc Jackson .20 .50
❑ 106 Desmond Mason .20 .50
❑ 107 J.R. Smith .25 .60
❑ 108 Eddy Curry .25 .60
❑ 109 Steve Francis .30 .75
❑ 110 Stephon Marbury .30 .75
❑ 111 Quentin Richardson .25 .60
❑ 112 Jalen Rose .25 .60
❑ 113 Maurice Taylor .20 .50
❑ 114 Carlos Arroyo .30 .75
❑ 115 Grant Hill .30 .75
❑ 116 Dwight Howard .60 1.50
❑ 117 Darko Milicic .30 .75
❑ 118 Jameer Nelson .25 .60
❑ 119 DeShawn Stevenson .20 .50
❑ 120 Samuel Dalembert .20 .50
❑ 121 Steven Hunter .20 .50
❑ 122 Andre Iguodala .30 .75
❑ 123 Allen Iverson .60 1.50
❑ 124 Kyle Korver .30 .75
❑ 125 Chris Webber .30 .75
❑ 126 Raja Bell .20 .50
❑ 127 Boris Diaw .25 .60
❑ 128 Shawn Marion .30 .75
❑ 129 Steve Nash .40 1.00
❑ 130 Amare Stoudemire .60 1.50
❑ 131 Kurt Thomas .20 .50
❑ 132 Darius Miles .20 .50
❑ 133 Joel Przybilla .20 .50
❑ 134 Zach Randolph .30 .75
❑ 135 Ha Seung-Jin .20 .50
❑ 136 Sebastian Telfair .25 .60
❑ 137 Shareef Abdur-Rahim .30 .75
❑ 138 Ron Artest .30 .75
❑ 139 Mike Bibby .30 .75
❑ 140 Brad Miller .30 .75
❑ 141 Vitaly Potapenko .20 .50
❑ 142 Bruce Bowen .20 .50
❑ 143 Tim Duncan .60 1.50
❑ 144 Michael Finley .30 .75
❑ 145 Manu Ginobili .30 .75
❑ 146 Robert Horry .25 .60
❑ 147 Tony Parker .30 .75
❑ 148 Ray Allen .30 .75
❑ 149 Rashard Lewis .30 .75
❑ 150 Luke Ridnour .25 .60
❑ 151 Robert Swift .20 .50
❑ 152 Earl Watson .20 .50
❑ 153 Chris Wilcox .20 .50
❑ 154 Rafael Araujo .20 .50
❑ 155 Chris Bosh .30 .75
❑ 156 Jose Calderon .25 .60
❑ 157 Mike James .20 .50
❑ 158 Morris Peterson .25 .60
❑ 159 Pape Sow .20 .50
❑ 160 Carlos Boozer .30 .75
❑ 161 Gordan Giricek .20 .50
❑ 162 Kris Humphries .20 .50
❑ 163 Andrei Kirilenko .30 .75
❑ 164 Mehmet Okur .20 .50
❑ 165 Greg Ostertag .20 .50
❑ 166 Gilbert Arenas .30 .75
❑ 167 Calvin Booth .30 .75
❑ 168 Caron Butler .50 1.25
❑ 169 Antonio Daniels .30 .75
❑ 170 Antawn Jamison .50 1.25
❑ 171 Andrew Bogut L14 Ret 1.25 3.00
❑ 172 Marvin Williams L14 Ret 1.25 3.00
❑ 173 Deron Williams L14 Ret 2.00 5.00
❑ 174 Chris Paul L14 Ret 2.50 6.00
❑ 175 Raymond Felton L14 Ret 1.50 4.00
❑ 176 Martell Webster L14 Ret 1.00 2.50
❑ 177 Charlie Villanueva L14 Ret 1.25 3.00
❑ 178 Channing Frye L14 Ret 1.00 2.50
❑ 179 Ike Diogu L14 Ret 1.00 2.50
❑ 180 Andrew Bynum L14 Ret 1.25 3.00
❑ 181 Yaroslav Korolev L14 Ret .50 1.25
❑ 182 Sean May L14 Ret 1.00 2.50
❑ 183 Rashad McCants L14 Ret 1.00 2.50
❑ 184 Antoine Wright L14 Ret .50 1.25
❑ 185 Nate Robinson WP Ret 1.25 3.00
❑ 186 Luther Head WP Ret 1.00 2.50
❑ 187 Joey Graham WP Ret 1.00 2.50
❑ 188 Johan Petro WP Ret .50 1.25
❑ 189 Wayne Simien WP Ret 1.00 2.50
❑ 190 David Lee WP Ret .50 1.25
❑ 191 Salim Stoudamire WP Ret 1.00 2.50
❑ 192 Travis Diener WP Ret .50 1.25
❑ 193 Monta Ellis WP Ret 1.25 3.00
❑ 194 M.Andriuskevicius WP Ret .75 2.00
❑ 195 Chuck Hayes WP Ret .50 1.25
❑ 196 Danny Granger WP Ret 1.00 2.50
❑ 197 Sarunas Jasikevicius WP Ret 1.00 2.50
❑ 198 Francisco Garcia WP Ret .50 1.25
❑ 199 Jarrett Jack WP Ret 1.00 2.50
❑ 200 Jose Calderon WP Ret 1.00 2.50
❑ 201 Andrea Bargnani L14/500 RC 6.00 15.00
❑ 202 LaMarcus Aldridge L14/500 RC 5.00 12.00
❑ 203 Adam Morrison L14/500 RC 5.00 12.00
❑ 204 Tyrus Thomas L14/500 RC 5.00 12.00
❑ 205 Shelden Williams L14/500 RC 5.00 12.00
❑ 206 Brandon Roy L14/500 RC 10.00 25.00
❑ 207 Randy Foye L14/500 RC 4.00 10.00
❑ 208 Rudy Gay L14/500 RC 4.00 10.00
❑ 209 Patrick O'Bryant L14/500 RC 4.00 10.00
❑ 210 Saer Sene L14/500 RC 4.00 10.00
❑ 211 J.J. Redick L14/500 RC 4.00 10.00
❑ 212 Hilton Armstrong L14/500 RC 4.00 10.00
❑ 213 Thabo Sefolosha L14/500 RC 5.00 12.00
❑ 214 Ronnie Brewer L14/500 RC 5.00 12.00
❑ 215 Allan Ray WP RC 1.00 2.50
❑ 216 Leon Powe WP RC 1.00 2.50
❑ 217 Joel Freeland WP RC 1.00 2.50
❑ 218 Shawne Williams WP RC 1.00 2.50
❑ 219 Kevin Pittsnogle WP RC 1.00 2.50
❑ 220 Shannon Brown WP RC 1.00 2.50
❑ 221 Kyle Lowry WP RC 1.00 2.50
❑ 222 Mardy Collins WP RC 1.00 2.50
❑ 223 Rodney Carney WP RC 1.00 2.50
❑ 224 Maurice Ager WP RC 1.00 2.50
❑ 225 Quincy Douby WP RC 1.00 2.50
❑ 226 Rajon Rondo WP RC 4.00 10.00
❑ 227 Jordan Farmar WP RC 1.25 3.00
❑ 228 Marcus Williams WP RC 1.25 3.00
❑ 229 Josh Boone WP RC 1.00 2.50
❑ 230 Solomon Jones WP RC 1.00 2.50
❑ 231 Denham Brown WP RC 1.00 2.50
❑ 232 Renaldo Balkman WP RC 1.00 2.50
❑ 233 Will Blalock WP RC 1.00 2.50
❑ 234 Bobby Jones WP RC 1.00 2.50
❑ 235 Steve Novak WP RC 1.00 2.50
❑ 236 James Augustine WP RC 1.00 2.50
❑ 237 Dee Brown WP RC 1.00 2.50
❑ 238 Hassan Adams WP RC 1.25 3.00
❑ 239 Alexander Johnson WP RC 1.00 2.50
❑ 240 Cedric Simmons WP RC 1.00 2.50
❑ 241 James White WP RC 1.00 2.50
❑ 242 Paul Davis WP RC 1.00 2.50
❑ 243 P.J. Tucker WP RC 1.00 2.50
❑ 244 Ryan Hollins WP RC 1.00 2.50

2007-08 Ultra SE

❑ COMP.SET w/o SP's (200) 25.00 50.00
❑ 1 Joe Johnson .40 1.00
❑ 2 Josh Smith .40 1.00
❑ 3 Josh Childress .30 .75
❑ 4 Marvin Williams .40 1.00
❑ 5 Anthony Johnson .25 .60
❑ 6 Shelden Williams .40 1.00
❑ 7 Tyronn Lue .25 .60
❑ 8 Al Jefferson .40 1.00
❑ 9 Paul Pierce .40 1.00
❑ 10 Wally Szczerbiak .30 .75
❑ 11 Sebastian Telfair .30 .75
❑ 12 Gerald Green .40 1.00
❑ 13 Rajon Rondo .40 1.00
❑ 14 Delonte West .30 .75
❑ 15 Adam Morrison .40 1.00
❑ 16 Emeka Okafor .40 1.00
❑ 17 Gerald Wallace .40 1.00
❑ 18 Raymond Felton .50 1.25
❑ 19 Sean May .30 .75
❑ 20 Matt Carroll .25 .60
❑ 21 Ben Wallace .40 1.00
❑ 22 Ben Gordon .50 1.25
❑ 23 Tyrus Thomas .50 1.25
❑ 24 Luol Deng .40 1.00
❑ 25 Kirk Hinrich .40 1.00
❑ 26 Andres Nocioni .25 .60
❑ 27 Thabo Sefolosha .40 1.00
❑ 28 LeBron James 2.00 5.00
❑ 29 Larry Hughes .30 .75
❑ 30 Zydrunas Ilgauskas .30 .75
❑ 31 Drew Gooden .30 .75
❑ 32 Daniel Gibson .40 1.00
❑ 33 Shannon Brown .25 .60
❑ 34 Dirk Nowitzki .60 1.50
❑ 35 Josh Howard .40 1.00
❑ 36 Jason Terry .40 1.00
❑ 37 Jerry Stackhouse .30 .75
❑ 38 Devin Harris .40 1.00
❑ 39 Erick Dampier .25 .60
❑ 40 Jose Barea .25 .60
❑ 41 Carmelo Anthony .75 2.00
❑ 42 Allen Iverson .75 2.00
❑ 43 J.R. Smith .30 .75
❑ 44 Yakhouba Diawara .25 .60
❑ 45 Marcus Camby .25 .60
❑ 46 Eduardo Najera .25 .60
❑ 47 Chauncey Billups .40 1.00
❑ 48 Richard Hamilton .30 .75
❑ 49 Tayshaun Prince .40 1.00
❑ 50 Chris Webber .40 1.00
❑ 51 Rasheed Wallace .40 1.00
❑ 52 Will Blalock .25 .60
❑ 53 Nazr Mohammed .25 .60
❑ 54 Baron Davis .40 1.00
❑ 55 Al Harrington .30 .75
❑ 56 Stephen Jackson .30 .75
❑ 57 Jason Richardson .40 1.00
❑ 58 Monta Ellis .30 .75
❑ 59 Mickael Pietrus .25 .60
❑ 60 Kelenna Azubuike .25 .60
❑ 61 Yao Ming 1.00 2.50
❑ 62 Tracy McGrady .75 2.00
❑ 63 Rafer Alston .25 .60
❑ 64 Luther Head .30 .75
❑ 65 Shane Battier .40 1.00
❑ 66 Juwan Howard .25 .60
❑ 67 Bonzi Wells .30 .75
❑ 68 Jermaine O'Neal .40 1.00
❑ 69 Danny Granger .30 .75
❑ 70 Jamaal Tinsley .25 .60
❑ 71 Mike Dunleavy .30 .75
❑ 72 Troy Murphy .40 1.00
❑ 73 Shawne Williams .30 .75
❑ 74 Elton Brand .40 1.00
❑ 75 Corey Maggette .30 .75
❑ 76 Sam Cassell .40 1.00
❑ 77 Cuttino Mobley .30 .75
❑ 78 Tim Thomas .25 .60
❑ 79 Chris Kaman .25 .60
❑ 80 Kobe Bryant 2.00 5.00
❑ 81 Jordan Farmar .30 .75
❑ 82 Lamar Odom .40 1.00
❑ 83 Andrew Bynum .40 1.00
❑ 84 Smush Parker .25 .60
❑ 85 Luke Walton .30 .75
❑ 86 Maurice Evans .25 .60
❑ 87 Rudy Gay .30 .75
❑ 88 Pau Gasol .40 1.00
❑ 89 Mike Miller .40 1.00
❑ 90 Hakim Warrick .30 .75
❑ 91 Kyle Lowry .25 .60
❑ 92 Damon Stoudamire .30 .75
❑ 93 Shaquille O'Neal 1.00 2.50
❑ 94 Dwyane Wade 1.00 2.50
❑ 95 Jason Williams .30 .75
❑ 96 Jason Kapono .25 .60
❑ 97 Alonzo Mourning .50 1.25
❑ 98 Udonis Haslem .40 1.00
❑ 99 Gary Payton .40 1.00
❑ 100 Michael Redd .40 1.00
❑ 101 Maurice Williams .30 .75
❑ 102 Andrew Bogut .40 1.00
❑ 103 Charlie Villanueva .40 1.00
❑ 104 Ruben Patterson .30 .75
❑ 105 Charlie Bell .25 .60
❑ 106 Kevin Garnett 1.00 2.50
❑ 107 Rashad McCants .30 .75

❑ 108 Ricky Davis	.40	1.00
❑ 109 Randy Foye	.40	1.00
❑ 110 Craig Smith	.40	1.00
❑ 111 Mike James	.25	.60
❑ 112 Jason Kidd	.60	1.50
❑ 113 Vince Carter	.75	2.00
❑ 114 Richard Jefferson	.40	1.00
❑ 115 Nenad Krstic	.30	.75
❑ 116 Bernard Robinson	.25	.60
❑ 117 Marcus Williams	.40	1.00
❑ 118 Josh Boone	.25	.60
❑ 119 Chris Paul	.75	2.00
❑ 120 Peja Stojakovic	.40	1.00
❑ 121 David West	.40	1.00
❑ 122 Desmond Mason	.25	.60
❑ 123 Cedric Simmons	.30	.75
❑ 124 Hilton Armstrong	.25	.60
❑ 125 Devin Brown	.25	.60
❑ 126 Nate Robinson	.40	1.00
❑ 127 Eddy Curry	.25	.60
❑ 128 Jamal Crawford	.25	.60
❑ 129 Stephon Marbury	.40	1.00
❑ 130 Quentin Richardson	.30	.75
❑ 131 David Lee	.30	.75
❑ 132 Channing Frye	.30	.75
❑ 133 Dwight Howard	.75	2.00
❑ 134 J.J. Redick	.40	1.00
❑ 135 Grant Hill	.40	1.00
❑ 136 Jameer Nelson	.30	.75
❑ 137 Hedo Turkoglu	.40	1.00
❑ 138 Tony Battie	.25	.60
❑ 139 Darko Milicic	.40	1.00
❑ 140 Carlos Arroyo	.40	1.00
❑ 141 Andre Iguodala	.40	1.00
❑ 142 Kyle Korver	.40	1.00
❑ 143 Samuel Dalembert	.25	.60
❑ 144 Rodney Carney	.25	.60
❑ 145 Willie Green	.25	.60
❑ 146 Andre Miller	.30	.75
❑ 147 Bobby Jones	.30	.75
❑ 148 Steve Nash	.50	1.25
❑ 149 Amare Stoudemire	.75	2.00
❑ 150 Shawn Marion	.40	1.00
❑ 151 Leandro Barbosa	.30	.75
❑ 152 Raja Bell	.25	.60
❑ 153 Boris Diaw	.30	.75
❑ 154 LaMarcus Aldridge	.50	1.25
❑ 155 Zach Randolph	.40	1.00
❑ 156 Brandon Roy	.60	1.50
❑ 157 Jarrett Jack	.30	.75
❑ 158 Ime Udoka	.30	.75
❑ 159 Martell Webster	.30	.75
❑ 160 Sergio Rodriguez	.30	.75
❑ 161 Fred Jones	.25	.60
❑ 162 Kevin Martin	.40	1.00
❑ 163 Ron Artest	.40	1.00
❑ 164 Mike Bibby	.40	1.00
❑ 165 Brad Miller	.40	1.00
❑ 166 Quincy Douby	.25	.60
❑ 167 Shareef Abdur-Rahim	.40	1.00
❑ 168 Radoslav Nesterovic	.25	.60
❑ 169 Tony Parker	.40	1.00
❑ 170 Tim Duncan	.75	2.00
❑ 171 Manu Ginobili	.40	1.00
❑ 172 Michael Finley	.40	1.00
❑ 173 Brent Barry	.25	.60
❑ 174 Bruce Bowen	.25	.60
❑ 175 Ray Allen	.40	1.00
❑ 176 Rashard Lewis	.40	1.00
❑ 177 Chris Wilcox	.30	.75
❑ 178 Luke Ridnour	.30	.75
❑ 179 Nick Collison	.25	.60
❑ 180 Earl Watson	.25	.60
❑ 181 Mickael Gelabale	.25	.60
❑ 182 Chris Bosh	.40	1.00
❑ 183 Andrea Bargnani	.50	1.25
❑ 184 T.J. Ford	.30	.75
❑ 185 Anthony Parker	.25	.60
❑ 186 Jorge Garbajosa	.40	1.00
❑ 187 Morris Peterson	.30	.75
❑ 188 Jose Calderon	.30	.75
❑ 189 Carlos Boozer	.40	1.00
❑ 190 Mehmet Okur	.30	.75
❑ 191 Deron Williams	.60	1.50
❑ 192 Paul Millsap	.30	.75
❑ 193 Ronnie Brewer	.30	.75
❑ 194 Andrei Kirilenko	.40	1.00
❑ 195 Gilbert Arenas	.40	1.00
❑ 196 Caron Butler	.40	1.00

❑ 197 Antawn Jamison	.40	1.00
❑ 198 DeShawn Stevenson	.25	.60
❑ 199 Brendan Haywood	.25	.60
❑ 200 Etan Thomas	.25	.60
❑ 201 Al Thornton RC	2.00	5.00
❑ 201B Al Thornton BB	5.00	12.00
❑ 202 Rodney Stuckey RC	4.00	10.00
❑ 203 Nick Young RC	2.00	5.00
❑ 204 Sean Williams RC	2.00	5.00
❑ 205 Marco Belinelli RC	2.00	5.00
❑ 206 Javaris Crittenton RC	2.00	5.00
❑ 206B Javaris Crittenton BB	4.00	10.00
❑ 207 Jason Smith RC	2.00	5.00
❑ 208 Daequan Cook RC	2.50	6.00
❑ 209 Jared Dudley RC	2.00	5.00
❑ 210 Wilson Chandler RC	2.00	5.00
❑ 211 Morris Almond RC	2.00	5.00
❑ 212 Aaron Brooks RC	3.00	8.00
❑ 213 Arron Afflalo RC	2.00	5.00
❑ 214 Alando Tucker RC	2.00	5.00
❑ 215 Petteri Koponen RC	2.00	5.00
❑ 216 Carl Landry RC	2.00	5.00
❑ 217 Gabe Pruitt RC	2.00	5.00
❑ 217B Gabe Pruitt BB	3.00	8.00
❑ 218 Marcus Williams RC	2.00	5.00
❑ 219 Nick Fazekas RC	2.00	5.00
❑ 220 Glen Davis RC	4.00	10.00
❑ 220B Glen Davis BB	3.00	8.00
❑ 221 Jermareo Davidson RC	2.00	5.00
❑ 222 Josh McRoberts RC	2.50	6.00
❑ 223 Kyrylo Fesenko RC	2.00	5.00
❑ 224 Stanko Barac RC	2.00	5.00
❑ 225 Sun Yue RC	2.00	5.00
❑ 225B Sun Yue BB	3.00	8.00
❑ 226 Chris Richard RC	2.00	5.00
❑ 227 Derrick Byars RC	2.00	5.00
❑ 227B Derrick Byars BB	3.00	8.00
❑ 228 Adam Haluska RC	2.00	5.00
❑ 229 Reyshawn Terry RC	2.00	5.00
❑ 230 Taurean Green RC	2.00	5.00
❑ 231 Greg Oden L13 RC	5.00	12.00
❑ 231B Greg Oden BB	40.00	75.00
❑ 232 Kevin Durant L13 RC	25.00	60.00
❑ 233 Al Horford L13 RC	4.00	10.00
❑ 233B Al Horford BB	10.00	25.00
❑ 234 Michael Conley L13 RC	4.00	10.00
❑ 235 Jeff Green L13 RC	4.00	10.00
❑ 236 Yi Jianlian L13 RC	5.00	12.00
❑ 236B Yi Jianlian BB	8.00	20.00
❑ 237 Corey Brewer L13 RC	4.00	10.00
❑ 238 Brandan Wright L13 RC	4.00	10.00
❑ 239 Joakim Noah L13 RC	4.00	10.00
❑ 239B Joakim Noah BB	10.00	25.00
❑ 240 Spencer Hawes L13 RC	3.00	8.00
❑ 241 Acie Law L13 RC	4.00	10.00
❑ 242 Thaddeus Young L13 RC	4.00	10.00
❑ 242B Thaddeus Young BB	6.00	15.00
❑ 243 Julian Wright L13 RC	4.00	10.00
❑ 243B Julian Wright BB	6.00	15.00
❑ 244 Michael Jordan L13	10.00	25.00
❑ 244B Michael Jordan BB	15.00	30.00
❑ 245 Larry Bird L13	5.00	12.00
❑ 246 Magic Johnson L13	3.00	8.00
❑ 246B Magic Johnson BB	6.00	15.00
❑ 247 Bill Russell L13	2.50	6.00
❑ 248 Dennis Rodman L13	1.50	4.00
❑ 248B Dennis Rodman BB	4.00	10.00
❑ 249 Kareem Abdul-Jabbar L13	2.50	6.00
❑ 249B Kareem Abdul-Jabbar BB	5.00	12.00
❑ 250 Clyde Drexler L13	2.00	5.00
❑ 251 Hakeem Olajuwon L13	2.00	5.00
❑ 252 John Havlicek L13	1.50	4.00
❑ 253 David Robinson L13	2.50	6.00
❑ 254 John Stockton L13	2.50	6.00
❑ 254B John Stockton BB	6.00	15.00
❑ 255 Jerry West L13	2.00	5.00
❑ 256 Julius Erving L13	3.00	8.00

1991-92 Upper Deck

❑ COMPLETE SET (500)	10.00	20.00
❑ COMPLETE FACT.SET (500)	10.00	20.00
❑ COMPLETE SERIES 1 (400)	6.00	12.00
❑ COMMON CARD (1-400)	.04	.10
❑ COMPLETE SERIES 2 (100)	4.00	8.00
❑ COMMON CARD (401-500)	.02	.10
❑ 1 S.Augmon/R.Monroe CL	.02	.10
❑ 2 Larry Johnson RC	.40	1.00
❑ 3 Dikembe Mutombo RC	.40	1.00
❑ 4 Steve Smith RC	.40	1.00
❑ 5 Stacey Augmon RC	.08	.25
❑ 6 Terrell Brandon RC	.30	.75
❑ 7 Greg Anthony RC	.08	.25
❑ 8 Rich King RC	.02	.10
❑ 9 Chris Gatling RC	.08	.25
❑ 10 Victor Alexander RC	.02	.10
❑ 11 John Turner RC	.02	.10
❑ 12 Eric Murdock RC	.02	.10
❑ 13 Mark Randall RC	.02	.10
❑ 14 Rodney Monroe RC	.02	.10
❑ 15 Myron Brown RC	.02	.10
❑ 16 Mike Iuzzolino RC	.02	.10
❑ 17 Chris Corchiani RC	.02	.10
❑ 18 Elliot Perry RC	.02	.10
❑ 19 Jimmy Oliver RC	.02	.10
❑ 20 Doug Overton RC	.02	.10
❑ 21 Steve Hood UER RC	.02	.10
❑ 22 Michael Jordan SCHOOL	.30	.75
❑ 23 Kevin Johnson School	.02	.10
❑ 24 Kurk Lee	.02	.10
❑ 25 Sean Higgins RC	.02	.10
❑ 26 Morlon Wiley	.02	.10
❑ 27 Derek Smith	.02	.10
❑ 28 Kenny Payne	.02	.10
❑ 29 Magic Johnson SPEC	.15	.40
❑ 30 L.Bird/C.Person CC	.08	.25
❑ 31 K.Malone/C.Barkley CC	.08	.25
❑ 32 K.Johnson/Stockton CC	.02	.10
❑ 33 H.Olajuwon/P.Ewing CC	.08	.25
❑ 34 M.Johnson/M.Jordan CC	.40	1.00
❑ 35 Derrick Coleman ART	.02	.10
❑ 36 Lionel Simmons ART	.02	.10
❑ 37 Dee Brown ART	.02	.10
❑ 38 Dennis Scott ART	.02	.10
❑ 39 Kendall Gill ART	.02	.10
❑ 40 Winston Garland	.02	.10
❑ 41 Danny Young	.02	.10
❑ 42 Rick Mahorn	.02	.10
❑ 43 Michael Adams	.02	.10
❑ 44 Michael Jordan	1.25	3.00
❑ 45 Magic Johnson	.30	.75
❑ 46 Doc Rivers	.02	.10
❑ 47 Moses Malone	.08	.25
❑ 48 Michael Jordan AS CL	.60	1.50
❑ 49 James Worthy AS	.02	.10
❑ 50 Tim Hardaway AS	.08	.25
❑ 51 Karl Malone AS	.08	.25
❑ 52 John Stockton AS	.02	.10
❑ 53 Clyde Drexler AS	.02	.10
❑ 54 Terry Porter AS	.02	.10
❑ 55 Kevin Duckworth AS	.02	.10
❑ 56 Tom Chambers AS	.02	.10
❑ 57 Magic Johnson AS	.15	.40
❑ 58 David Robinson AS	.08	.25
❑ 59 Kevin Johnson AS	.02	.10
❑ 60 Chris Mullin AS	.02	.10
❑ 61 Joe Dumars AS	.02	.10
❑ 62 Kevin McHale AS	.02	.10
❑ 63 Brad Daugherty AS	.02	.10
❑ 64 Alvin Robertson AS	.02	.10
❑ 65 Bernard King AS	.02	.10
❑ 66 Dominique Wilkins AS	.02	.10
❑ 67 Ricky Pierce AS	.02	.10
❑ 68 Patrick Ewing AS	.02	.10

❑ 69 Michael Jordan AS	.60	1.50
❑ 70 Charles Barkley AS	.08	.25
❑ 71 Hersey Hawkins AS	.02	.10
❑ 72 Robert Parish AS	.02	.10
❑ 73 Alvin Robertson TC	.02	.10
❑ 74 Bernard King TC	.02	.10
❑ 75 Michael Jordan TC	.60	1.50
❑ 76 Brad Daugherty TC	.02	.10
❑ 77 Larry Bird TC	.20	.50
❑ 78 Ron Harper TC	.02	.10
❑ 79 Dominique Wilkins TC	.02	.10
❑ 80 Rony Seikaly TC	.02	.10
❑ 81 Rex Chapman TC	.02	.10
❑ 82 Mark Eaton TC	.02	.10
❑ 83 Lionel Simmons TC	.02	.10
❑ 84 Gerald Wilkins TC	.02	.10
❑ 85 James Worthy TC	.02	.10
❑ 86 Scott Skiles TC	.02	.10
❑ 87 Rolando Blackman TC	.02	.10
❑ 88 Derrick Coleman TC	.02	.10
❑ 89 Chris Jackson TC	.02	.10
❑ 90 Reggie Miller TC	.02	.10
❑ 91 Isiah Thomas TC	.02	.10
❑ 92 Hakeem Olajuwon TC	.08	.25
❑ 93 Hersey Hawkins TC	.02	.10
❑ 94 David Robinson TC	.08	.25
❑ 95 Tom Chambers TC	.02	.10
❑ 96 Shawn Kemp TC	.08	.25
❑ 97 Pooh Richardson TC	.02	.10
❑ 98 Clyde Drexler TC	.02	.10
❑ 99 Chris Mullin TC	.02	.10
❑ 100 Checklist 1-100	.02	.10
❑ 101 John Shasky	.02	.10
❑ 102 Dana Barros	.02	.10
❑ 103 Stojko Vrankovic	.02	.10
❑ 104 Larry Drew	.02	.10
❑ 105 Randy White	.02	.10
❑ 106 Dave Corzine	.02	.10
❑ 107 Joe Kleine	.02	.10
❑ 108 Lance Blanks	.02	.10
❑ 109 Rodney McCray	.02	.10
❑ 110 Sedale Threatt	.02	.10
❑ 111 Ken Norman	.02	.10
❑ 112 Rickey Green	.02	.10
❑ 113 Andy Toolson	.02	.10
❑ 114 Bo Kimble	.02	.10
❑ 115 Mark West	.02	.10
❑ 116 Mark Eaton	.02	.10
❑ 117 John Paxson	.02	.10
❑ 118 Mike Brown	.02	.10
❑ 119 Brian Oliver	.02	.10
❑ 120 Will Perdue	.02	.10
❑ 121 Michael Smith	.02	.10
❑ 122 Sherman Douglas	.02	.10
❑ 123 Reggie Lewis	.02	.10
❑ 124 James Donaldson	.02	.10
❑ 125 Scottie Pippen	.30	.75
❑ 126 Elden Campbell	.02	.10
❑ 127 Michael Cage	.02	.10
❑ 128 Tony Smith	.02	.10
❑ 129 Ed Pinckney	.02	.10
❑ 130 Keith Askins RC	.02	.10
❑ 131 Darrell Griffith	.02	.10
❑ 132 Vinnie Johnson	.02	.10
❑ 133 Ron Harper	.02	.10
❑ 134 Andre Turner	.02	.10
❑ 135 Jeff Hornacek	.02	.10
❑ 136 John Stockton	.08	.25
❑ 137 Derek Harper	.02	.10
❑ 138 Loy Vaught	.02	.10
❑ 139 Thurl Bailey	.02	.10
❑ 140 Olden Polynice	.02	.10
❑ 141 Kevin Edwards	.02	.10
❑ 142 Byron Scott	.02	.10
❑ 143 Dee Brown	.02	.10
❑ 144 Sam Perkins	.02	.10
❑ 145 Rony Seikaly	.02	.10
❑ 146 James Worthy	.08	.25
❑ 147 Glen Rice	.08	.25
❑ 148 Craig Hodges	.02	.10
❑ 149 Bimbo Coles	.02	.10
❑ 150 Mychal Thompson	.02	.10
❑ 151 Xavier McDaniel	.02	.10
❑ 152 Roy Tarpley	.02	.10
❑ 153 Gary Payton	.25	.60
❑ 154 Rolando Blackman	.02	.10
❑ 155 Hersey Hawkins	.02	.10
❑ 156 Ricky Pierce	.02	.10
❑ 157 Fat Lever	.02	.10
❑ 158 Andrew Lang	.02	.10
❑ 159 Benoit Benjamin	.02	.10
❑ 160 Cedric Ceballos	.02	.10
❑ 161 Charles Smith	.02	.10
❑ 162 Jeff Martin	.02	.10
❑ 163 Robert Parish	.02	.10
❑ 164 Danny Manning	.02	.10
❑ 165 Mark Aguirre	.02	.10
❑ 166 Jeff Malone	.02	.10
❑ 167 Bill Laimbeer	.02	.10
❑ 168 Willie Burton	.02	.10
❑ 169 Dennis Hopson	.02	.10
❑ 170 Kevin Gamble	.02	.10
❑ 171 Terry Teagle	.02	.10
❑ 172 Dan Majerle	.02	.10
❑ 173 Shawn Kemp	.25	.60
❑ 174 Tom Chambers	.02	.10
❑ 175 Vlade Divac	.02	.10
❑ 176 Johnny Dawkins	.02	.10
❑ 177 A.C. Green	.02	.10
❑ 178 Manute Bol	.02	.10
❑ 179 Terry Davis	.02	.10
❑ 180 Ron Anderson	.02	.10
❑ 181 Horace Grant	.02	.10
❑ 182 Stacey King	.02	.10
❑ 183 William Bedford	.02	.10
❑ 184 B.J.Armstrong	.02	.10
❑ 185 Dennis Rodman	.20	.50
❑ 186 Nate McMillan	.02	.10
❑ 187 Cliff Levingston	.02	.10
❑ 188 Quintin Dailey	.02	.10
❑ 189 Bill Cartwright	.02	.10
❑ 190 John Salley	.02	.10
❑ 191 Jayson Williams	.08	.25
❑ 192 Grant Long	.02	.10
❑ 193 Negele Knight	.02	.10
❑ 194 Alec Kessler	.02	.10
❑ 195 Gary Grant	.02	.10
❑ 196 Billy Thompson	.02	.10
❑ 197 Delaney Rudd	.02	.10
❑ 198 Alan Ogg	.02	.10
❑ 199 Blue Edwards	.02	.10
❑ 200 Checklist 101-200	.02	.10
❑ 201 Mark Acres	.02	.10
❑ 202 Craig Ehlo	.02	.10
❑ 203 Anthony Cook	.02	.10
❑ 204 Eric Leckner	.02	.10
❑ 205 Terry Catledge	.02	.10
❑ 206 Reggie Williams	.02	.10
❑ 207 Greg Kite	.02	.10
❑ 208 Steve Kerr	.02	.10
❑ 209 Kenny Battle	.02	.10
❑ 210 John Morton	.02	.10
❑ 211 Kenny Williams	.02	.10
❑ 212 Mark Jackson	.02	.10
❑ 213 Alaa Abdelnaby	.02	.10
❑ 214 Rod Strickland	.08	.25
❑ 215 Micheal Williams	.02	.10
❑ 216 Kevin Duckworth	.02	.10
❑ 217 David Wingate	.02	.10
❑ 218 LaSalle Thompson	.02	.10
❑ 219 John Starks RC	.08	.25
❑ 220 Clifford Robinson	.02	.10
❑ 221 Jeff Grayer	.02	.10
❑ 222 Marcus Liberty	.02	.10
❑ 223 Larry Nance	.02	.10
❑ 224 Michael Ansley	.02	.10
❑ 225 Kevin McHale	.02	.10
❑ 226 Scott Skiles	.02	.10
❑ 227 Darnell Valentine	.02	.10
❑ 228 Nick Anderson	.02	.10
❑ 229 Brad Davis	.02	.10
❑ 230 Gerald Paddio	.02	.10
❑ 231 Sam Bowie	.02	.10
❑ 232 Sam Vincent	.02	.10
❑ 233 George McCloud	.02	.10
❑ 234 Gerald Wilkins	.02	.10
❑ 235 Mookie Blaylock	.02	.10
❑ 236 Jon Koncak	.02	.10
❑ 237 Danny Ferry	.02	.10
❑ 238 Vern Fleming	.02	.10
❑ 239 Mark Price	.02	.10
❑ 240 Sidney Moncrief	.02	.10
❑ 241 Jay Humphries	.02	.10
❑ 242 Muggsy Bogues	.02	.10
❑ 243 Tim Hardaway	.15	.40
❑ 244 Alvin Robertson	.02	.10
❑ 245 Chris Mullin	.08	.25
❑ 246 Pooh Richardson	.02	.10
❑ 247 Winston Bennett	.02	.10
❑ 248 Kelvin Upshaw	.02	.10
❑ 249 John Williams	.02	.10
❑ 250 Steve Alford	.02	.10
❑ 251 Spud Webb	.02	.10
❑ 252 Sleepy Floyd	.02	.10
❑ 253 Chuck Person	.02	.10
❑ 254 Hakeem Olajuwon	.15	.40
❑ 255 Dominique Wilkins	.08	.25
❑ 256 Reggie Miller	.08	.25
❑ 257 Dennis Scott	.02	.10
❑ 258 Charles Oakley	.02	.10
❑ 259 Sidney Green	.02	.10
❑ 260 Detlef Schrempf	.02	.10
❑ 261 Rod Higgins	.02	.10
❑ 262 J.R. Reid	.02	.10
❑ 263 Tyrone Hill	.02	.10
❑ 264 Reggie Theus	.02	.10
❑ 265 Mitch Richmond	.08	.25
❑ 266 Dale Ellis	.02	.10
❑ 267 Terry Cummings	.02	.10
❑ 268 Johnny Newman	.02	.10
❑ 269 Doug West	.02	.10
❑ 270 Jim Petersen	.02	.10
❑ 271 Otis Thorpe	.02	.10
❑ 272 John Williams	.02	.10
❑ 273 Kennard Winchester RC	.02	.10
❑ 274 Duane Ferrell	.02	.10
❑ 275 Vernon Maxwell	.02	.10
❑ 276 Kenny Smith	.02	.10
❑ 277 Jerome Kersey	.02	.10
❑ 278 Kevin Willis	.02	.10
❑ 279 Danny Ainge	.02	.10
❑ 280 Larry Smith	.02	.10
❑ 281 Maurice Cheeks	.02	.10
❑ 282 Willie Anderson	.02	.10
❑ 283 Tom Tolbert	.02	.10
❑ 284 Jerrod Mustaf	.02	.10
❑ 285 Randolph Keys	.02	.10
❑ 286 Jerry Reynolds	.02	.10
❑ 287 Sean Elliott	.02	.10
❑ 288 Otis Smith	.02	.10
❑ 289 Terry Mills RC	.08	.25
❑ 290 Kelly Tripucka	.02	.10
❑ 291 Jon Sundvold	.02	.10
❑ 292 Rumeal Robinson	.02	.10
❑ 293 Fred Roberts	.02	.10
❑ 294 Rik Smits	.02	.10
❑ 295 Jerome Lane	.02	.10
❑ 296 Dave Jamerson	.02	.10
❑ 297 Joe Wolf	.02	.10
❑ 298 David Wood RC	.02	.10
❑ 299 Todd Lichti	.02	.10
❑ 300 Checklist 201-300	.02	.10
❑ 301 Randy Breuer	.02	.10
❑ 302 Buck Johnson	.02	.10
❑ 303 Scott Brooks	.02	.10
❑ 304 Jeff Turner	.02	.10
❑ 305 Felton Spencer	.02	.10
❑ 306 Greg Dreiling	.02	.10
❑ 307 Gerald Glass	.02	.10
❑ 308 Tony Brown	.02	.10
❑ 309 Sam Mitchell	.02	.10
❑ 310 Adrian Caldwell	.02	.10
❑ 311 Chris Dudley	.02	.10
❑ 312 Blair Rasmussen	.02	.10
❑ 313 Antoine Carr	.02	.10
❑ 314 Greg Anderson	.02	.10
❑ 315 Drazen Petrovic	.02	.10
❑ 316 Alton Lister	.02	.10
❑ 317 Jack Haley	.02	.10
❑ 318 Bobby Hansen	.02	.10
❑ 319 Chris Jackson	.02	.10
❑ 320 Herb Williams	.02	.10
❑ 321 Kendall Gill	.02	.10
❑ 322 Tyrone Corbin	.02	.10
❑ 323 Kiki Vandeweghe	.02	.10
❑ 324 David Robinson	.20	.50
❑ 325 Rex Chapman	.02	.10
❑ 326 Tony Campbell	.02	.10
❑ 327 Dell Curry	.02	.10
❑ 328 Charles Jones	.02	.10
❑ 329 Kenny Gattison	.02	.10
❑ 330 Haywoode Workman RC	.02	.10
❑ 331 Travis Mays	.02	.10
❑ 332 Derrick Coleman	.02	.10
❑ 333 Isiah Thomas	.08	.25
❑ 334 Jud Buechler	.02	.10
❑ 335 Joe Dumars	.08	.25

❑ 336 Tate George	.02	.10
❑ 337 Mike Sanders	.02	.10
❑ 338 James Edwards	.02	.10
❑ 339 Chris Morris	.02	.10
❑ 340 Scott Hastings	.02	.10
❑ 341 Trent Tucker	.02	.10
❑ 342 Harvey Grant	.02	.10
❑ 343 Patrick Ewing	.08	.25
❑ 344 Larry Bird	.40	1.00
❑ 345 Charles Barkley	.15	.40
❑ 346 Brian Shaw	.02	.10
❑ 347 Kenny Walker	.02	.10
❑ 348 Danny Schayes	.02	.10
❑ 349 Tom Hammonds	.02	.10
❑ 350 Frank Brickowski	.02	.10
❑ 351 Terry Porter	.02	.10
❑ 352 Orlando Woolridge	.02	.10
❑ 353 Buck Williams	.02	.10
❑ 354 Sarunas Marciulionis	.02	.10
❑ 355 Karl Malone	.15	.40
❑ 356 Kevin Johnson	.08	.25
❑ 357 Clyde Drexler	.08	.25
❑ 358 Duane Causwell	.02	.10
❑ 359 Paul Pressey	.02	.10
❑ 360 Jim Les RC	.02	.10
❑ 361 Derrick McKey	.02	.10
❑ 362 Scott Williams RC	.02	.10
❑ 363 Mark Alarie	.02	.10
❑ 364 Brad Daugherty	.02	.10
❑ 365 Bernard King	.02	.10
❑ 366 Steve Henson	.02	.10
❑ 367 Darrell Walker	.02	.10
❑ 368 Larry Krystkowiak	.02	.10
❑ 369 Henry James UER	.02	.10
❑ 370 Jack Sikma	.02	.10
❑ 371 Eddie Johnson	.02	.10
❑ 372 Wayman Tisdale	.02	.10
❑ 373 Joe Barry Carroll	.02	.10
❑ 374 David Greenwood	.02	.10
❑ 375 Lionel Simmons	.02	.10
❑ 376 Dwayne Schintzius	.02	.10
❑ 377 Tod Murphy	.02	.10
❑ 378 Wayne Cooper	.02	.10
❑ 379 Anthony Bonner	.02	.10
❑ 380 Walter Davis	.02	.10
❑ 381 Lester Conner	.02	.10
❑ 382 Ledell Eackles	.02	.10
❑ 383 Brad Lohaus	.02	.10
❑ 384 Derrick Gervin	.02	.10
❑ 385 Pervis Ellison	.02	.10
❑ 386 Tim McCormick	.02	.10
❑ 387 A.J. English	.02	.10
❑ 388 John Battle	.02	.10
❑ 389 Roy Hinson	.02	.10
❑ 390 Armon Gilliam	.02	.10
❑ 391 Kurt Rambis	.02	.10
❑ 392 Mark Bryant	.02	.10
❑ 393 Chucky Brown	.02	.10
❑ 394 Avery Johnson	.02	.10
❑ 395 Rory Sparrow	.02	.10
❑ 396 Mario Elie RC	.08	.25
❑ 397 Ralph Sampson	.02	.10
❑ 398 Mike Gminski	.02	.10
❑ 399 Bill Wennington	.02	.10
❑ 400 Checklist 301-400	.02	.10
❑ 401 David Wingate	.02	.10
❑ 402 Moses Malone	.20	.50
❑ 403 Darrell Walker	.02	.10
❑ 404 Antoine Carr	.02	.10
❑ 405 Charles Shackleford	.02	.10
❑ 406 Orlando Woolridge	.02	.10
❑ 407 Robert Pack RC	.08	.25
❑ 408 Bobby Hansen	.02	.10
❑ 409 Dale Davis RC	.20	.50
❑ 410 Vincent Askew RC	.02	.10
❑ 411 Alexander Volkov	.02	.10
❑ 412 Dwayne Schintzius	.02	.10
❑ 413 Tim Perry	.02	.10
❑ 414 Tyrone Corbin	.02	.10
❑ 415 Pete Chilcutt RC	.02	.10
❑ 416 James Edwards	.02	.10
❑ 417 Jerrod Mustaf	.02	.10
❑ 418 Thurl Bailey	.02	.10
❑ 419 Spud Webb	.08	.25
❑ 420 Doc Rivers	.08	.25
❑ 421 Sean Green RC	.02	.10
❑ 422 Walter Davis	.02	.10
❑ 423 Terry Davis	.02	.10
❑ 424 John Battle	.02	.10
❑ 425 Vinnie Johnson	.02	.10
❑ 426 Sherman Douglas	.02	.10
❑ 427 Kevin Brooks RC	.02	.10
❑ 428 Greg Sutton RC	.02	.10
❑ 429 Rafael Addison RC	.02	.10
❑ 430 Anthony Mason RC	.40	1.00
❑ 431 Paul Graham RC	.02	.10
❑ 432 Anthony Frederick RC	.02	.10
❑ 433 Dennis Hopson	.02	.10
❑ 434 Rory Sparrow	.02	.10
❑ 435 Michael Adams	.02	.10
❑ 436 Kevin Lynch RC	.02	.10
❑ 437 Randy Brown RC	.02	.10
❑ 438 L.Johnson/B.Owens TP CL	.08	.25
❑ 439 Stacey Augmon TP	.02	.10
❑ 440 Larry Stewart TP RC	.02	.10
❑ 441 Terrell Brandon TP	.20	.50
❑ 442 Billy Owens TP RC	.02	.10
❑ 443 Rick Fox TP RC	.08	.25
❑ 444 Kenny Anderson TP RC	.40	1.00
❑ 445 Larry Johnson TP	.20	.50
❑ 446 Dikembe Mutombo TP	.20	.50
❑ 447 Steve Smith TP	.20	.50
❑ 448 Greg Anthony TP	.08	.25
❑ 449 East All-Star CL	.08	.25
❑ 450 West All-Star CL	.08	.25
❑ 451 Isiah Thomas AS w/Magic	.20	.50
❑ 452 Michael Jordan AS	1.25	3.00
❑ 453 Scottie Pippen AS	.30	.75
❑ 454 Charles Barkley AS	.20	.50
❑ 455 Patrick Ewing AS	.08	.25
❑ 456 Michael Adams AS	.02	.10
❑ 457 Dennis Rodman AS	.20	.50
❑ 458 Reggie Lewis AS	.02	.10
❑ 459 Joe Dumars AS	.08	.25
❑ 460 Mark Price AS	.02	.10
❑ 461 Brad Daugherty AS	.02	.10
❑ 462 Kevin Willis AS	.02	.10
❑ 463 Clyde Drexler AS	.08	.25
❑ 464 Magic Johnson AS	.30	.75
❑ 465 Chris Mullin AS	.08	.25
❑ 466 Karl Malone AS	.20	.50
❑ 467 David Robinson AS	.20	.50
❑ 468 Tim Hardaway AS	.20	.50
❑ 469 Jeff Hornacek AS	.02	.10
❑ 470 John Stockton AS	.08	.25
❑ 471 Dikembe Mutombo AS	.08	.25
❑ 472 Hakeem Olajuwon AS	.20	.50
❑ 473 James Worthy AS	.08	.25
❑ 474 Otis Thorpe AS	.02	.10
❑ 475 Dan Majerle AS	.02	.10
❑ 476 Cedric Ceballos SD CL	.02	.10
❑ 477 Nick Anderson SD	.02	.10
❑ 478 Stacey Augmon SD	.08	.25
❑ 479 Cedric Ceballos SD	.02	.10
❑ 480 Larry Johnson SD	.20	.50
❑ 481 Shawn Kemp SD	.25	.60
❑ 482 John Starks SD	.08	.25
❑ 483 Doug West SD	.02	.10
❑ 484 Craig Hodges	.02	.10
❑ 485 LaBradford Smith RC	.02	.10
❑ 486 Winston Garland	.02	.10
❑ 487 David Benoit RC	.08	.25
❑ 488 John Bagley	.02	.10
❑ 489 Mark Macon RC	.02	.10
❑ 490 Mitch Richmond	.08	.25
❑ 491 Luc Longley RC	.08	.25
❑ 492 Sedale Threatt	.02	.10
❑ 493 Doug Smith RC	.02	.10
❑ 494 Travis Mays	.02	.10
❑ 495 Xavier McDaniel	.02	.10
❑ 496 Brian Shaw	.02	.10
❑ 497 Stanley Roberts RC	.02	.10
❑ 498 Blair Rasmussen	.02	.10
❑ 499 Brian Williams RC	.20	.50
❑ 500 Checklist Card	.02	.10

1992-93 Upper Deck

❑ COMPLETE SET (514)	40.00	80.00
❑ COMPLETE LO SERIES (311)	10.00	20.00
❑ COMPLETE HI SERIES (203)	30.00	60.00
❑ 1 Shaquille O'Neal SP RC	10.00	25.00
❑ 1A Draft Trade Card	.10	.30
❑ 1B Shaquille O'Neal TRADE	6.00	15.00
❑ 1AX Draft Trade Stamped	.10	.30
❑ 2 Alonzo Mourning RC	.75	2.00
❑ 3 Christian Laettner RC	.25	.60
❑ 4 LaPhonso Ellis RC	.10	.30
❑ 5 C.Weatherspoon RC	.10	.30
❑ 6 Adam Keefe RC	.02	.10
❑ 7 Robert Horry RC	.10	.30
❑ 8 Harold Miner RC	.05	.15
❑ 9 Bryant Stith RC	.05	.15
❑ 10 Malik Sealy RC	.05	.15
❑ 11 Anthony Peeler RC	.05	.15
❑ 12 Randy Woods RC	.02	.10
❑ 13 Tracy Murray RC	.05	.15
❑ 14 Tom Gugliotta RC	.40	1.00
❑ 15 Hubert Davis RC	.05	.15
❑ 16 Don MacLean RC	.02	.10
❑ 17 Lee Mayberry RC	.02	.10
❑ 18 Corey Williams RC	.02	.10
❑ 19 Sean Rooks RC	.02	.10
❑ 20 Todd Day RC	.05	.15
❑ 21 B.Stith/L.Ellis CL	.10	.30
❑ 22 Jeff Hornacek	.05	.15
❑ 23 Michael Jordan	1.50	4.00
❑ 24 John Salley	.02	.10
❑ 25 Andre Turner	.02	.10
❑ 26 Charles Barkley	.20	.50
❑ 27 Anthony Frederick	.02	.10
❑ 28 Mario Elie	.05	.15
❑ 29 Olden Polynice	.02	.10
❑ 30 Rodney Monroe	.02	.10
❑ 31 Tim Perry	.02	.10
❑ 32 Doug Christie SP RC	.40	1.00
❑ 32A Magic Johnson SP	.75	2.00
❑ 33 Jim Jackson SP RC	1.00	2.50
❑ 33A Larry Bird SP	1.00	2.50
❑ 34 Randy White	.02	.10
❑ 35 Frank Brickowski TC	.02	.10
❑ 36 Michael Adams TC	.02	.10
❑ 37 Scottie Pippen TC	.20	.50
❑ 38 Mark Price TC	.02	.10
❑ 39 Robert Parish TC	.02	.10
❑ 40 Danny Manning TC	.02	.10
❑ 41 Kevin Willis TC	.02	.10
❑ 42 Glen Rice TC	.05	.15
❑ 43 Kendall Gill TC	.02	.10
❑ 44 Karl Malone TC	.10	.30
❑ 45 Mitch Richmond TC	.10	.30
❑ 46 Patrick Ewing TC	.10	.30
❑ 47 Sam Perkins TC	.02	.10
❑ 48 Dennis Scott TC	.02	.10
❑ 49 Derek Harper TC	.02	.10
❑ 50 Drazen Petrovic TC	.02	.10
❑ 51 Reggie Williams TC	.02	.10
❑ 52 Rik Smits TC	.02	.10
❑ 53 Joe Dumars TC	.05	.15
❑ 54 Otis Thorpe TC	.02	.10
❑ 55 Johnny Dawkins TC	.02	.10
❑ 56 Sean Elliott TC	.02	.10
❑ 57 Kevin Johnson TC	.05	.15
❑ 58 Ricky Pierce TC	.02	.10
❑ 59 Doug West TC	.02	.10
❑ 60 Terry Porter TC	.02	.10
❑ 61 Tim Hardaway TC	.10	.30
❑ 62 M.Jordan/S.Pippen ST	.40	1.00
❑ 63 K.Gill/L.Johnson ST	.10	.30
❑ 64 T.Chambers/K.Johnson ST	.05	.15
❑ 65 T.Hardaway/C.Mullin ST	.05	.15
❑ 66 K.Malone/J.Stockton ST	.10	.30

❑ 67 Michael Jordan MVP	.75	2.00
❑ 68 Stacey Augmon 6 MIL	.02	.10
❑ 69 Bob Lanier	.05	.15
❑ 70 Alaa Abdelnaby	.02	.10
❑ 71 Andrew Lang	.02	.10
❑ 72 Larry Krystkowiak	.02	.10
❑ 73 Gerald Wilkins	.02	.10
❑ 74 Rod Strickland	.10	.30
❑ 75 Danny Ainge	.05	.15
❑ 76 Chris Corchiani	.02	.10
❑ 77 Jeff Grayer	.02	.10
❑ 78 Eric Murdock	.02	.10
❑ 79 Rex Chapman	.02	.10
❑ 80 LaBradford Smith	.02	.10
❑ 81 Jay Humphries	.02	.10
❑ 82 David Robinson	.20	.50
❑ 83 William Bedford	.02	.10
❑ 84 James Edwards	.02	.10
❑ 85 Danny Schayes	.02	.10
❑ 86 Lloyd Daniels RC	.02	.10
❑ 87 Blue Edwards	.02	.10
❑ 88 Dale Ellis	.02	.10
❑ 89 Rolando Blackman	.02	.10
❑ 90 Form Checklist 1	.10	.30
❑ 91 Rik Smits	.05	.15
❑ 92 Terry Davis	.02	.10
❑ 93 Bill Cartwright	.02	.10
❑ 94 Avery Johnson	.02	.10
❑ 95 Micheal Williams	.02	.10
❑ 96 Spud Webb	.05	.15
❑ 97 Benoit Benjamin	.02	.10
❑ 98 Derek Harper	.05	.15
❑ 99 Matt Bullard	.02	.10
❑ 100A Tyrone Corbin ERR Heat	.40	1.00
❑ 100B Tyrone Corbin COR Jazz	.02	.10
❑ 101 Doc Rivers	.05	.15
❑ 102 Tony Smith	.02	.10
❑ 103 Doug West	.02	.10
❑ 104 Kevin Duckworth	.02	.10
❑ 105 Luc Longley	.05	.15
❑ 106 Antoine Carr	.02	.10
❑ 107 Cliff Robinson	.05	.15
❑ 108 Grant Long	.02	.10
❑ 109 Terry Porter	.02	.10
❑ 110A Steve Smith ERR Jazz	1.50	4.00
❑ 110B Steve Smith COR	.15	.40
❑ 111 Brian Williams	.02	.10
❑ 112 Karl Malone	.20	.50
❑ 113 Reggie Williams	.02	.10
❑ 114 Tom Chambers	.02	.10
❑ 115 Winston Garland	.02	.10
❑ 116 John Stockton	.10	.30
❑ 117 Chris Jackson	.02	.10
❑ 118 Mike Brown	.02	.10
❑ 119 Kevin Johnson	.10	.30
❑ 120 Reggie Lewis	.05	.15
❑ 121 Bimbo Coles	.02	.10
❑ 122 Drazen Petrovic	.02	.10
❑ 123 Reggie Miller	.10	.30
❑ 124 Derrick Coleman	.05	.15
❑ 125 Chuck Person	.02	.10
❑ 126 Glen Rice	.10	.30
❑ 127 Kenny Anderson	.10	.30
❑ 128 Willie Burton	.02	.10
❑ 129 Chris Morris	.02	.10
❑ 130 Patrick Ewing	.10	.30
❑ 131 Sean Elliott	.05	.15
❑ 132 Clyde Drexler	.10	.30
❑ 133 Scottie Pippen	.40	1.00
❑ 134 Pooh Richardson	.02	.10
❑ 135 Horace Grant	.05	.15
❑ 136 Hakeem Olajuwon	.20	.50
❑ 137 John Paxson	.02	.10
❑ 138 Kendall Gill	.05	.15
❑ 139 Michael Adams	.02	.10
❑ 140 Otis Thorpe	.05	.15
❑ 141 Dennis Scott	.05	.15
❑ 142 Stacey Augmon	.05	.15
❑ 143 Robert Pack	.02	.10
❑ 144 Kevin Willis	.02	.10
❑ 145 Jerome Kersey	.02	.10
❑ 146 Paul Graham	.02	.10
❑ 147 Stanley Roberts	.02	.10
❑ 148 Dominique Wilkins	.10	.30
❑ 149 Scott Skiles	.02	.10
❑ 150 Rumeal Robinson	.02	.10
❑ 151 Mookie Blaylock	.05	.15
❑ 152 Elden Campbell	.05	.15
❑ 153 Chris Dudley	.02	.10
❑ 154 Sedale Threatt	.02	.10
❑ 155 Tate George	.02	.10
❑ 156 James Worthy	.10	.30
❑ 157 B.J. Armstrong	.02	.10
❑ 158 Gary Payton	.25	.60
❑ 159 Ledell Eackles	.02	.10
❑ 160 Sam Perkins	.05	.15
❑ 161 Nick Anderson	.05	.15
❑ 162 Mitch Richmond	.10	.30
❑ 163 Buck Williams	.05	.15
❑ 164 Blair Rasmussen	.02	.10
❑ 165 Vern Fleming	.02	.10
❑ 166 Duane Ferrell	.02	.10
❑ 167 George McCloud	.02	.10
❑ 168 Terry Cummings	.05	.15
❑ 169 Detlef Schrempf	.05	.15
❑ 170 Willie Anderson	.02	.10
❑ 171 Scott Williams	.02	.10
❑ 172 Vernon Maxwell	.02	.10
❑ 173 Todd Lichti	.02	.10
❑ 174 David Benoit	.02	.10
❑ 175 Marcus Liberty	.02	.10
❑ 176 Kenny Smith	.02	.10
❑ 177 Dan Majerle	.05	.15
❑ 178 Jeff Malone	.02	.10
❑ 179 Robert Parish	.05	.15
❑ 180 Mark Eaton	.02	.10
❑ 181 Rony Seikaly	.02	.10
❑ 182 Tony Campbell	.02	.10
❑ 183 Kevin McHale	.10	.30
❑ 184 Thurl Bailey	.02	.10
❑ 185 Kevin Edwards	.02	.10
❑ 186 Gerald Glass	.02	.10
❑ 187 Hersey Hawkins	.05	.15
❑ 188 Sam Mitchell	.02	.10
❑ 189 Brian Shaw	.02	.10
❑ 190 Felton Spencer	.02	.10
❑ 191 Mark Macon	.02	.10
❑ 192 Jerry Reynolds	.02	.10
❑ 193 Dale Davis	.02	.10
❑ 194 Sleepy Floyd	.02	.10
❑ 195 A.C. Green	.05	.15
❑ 196 Terry Catledge	.02	.10
❑ 197 Byron Scott	.05	.15
❑ 198 Sam Bowie	.02	.10
❑ 199 Vlade Divac	.05	.15
❑ 200 Form Checklist 2	.10	.30
❑ 201 Brad Lohaus	.02	.10
❑ 202 Johnny Newman	.02	.10
❑ 203 Gary Grant	.02	.10
❑ 204 Sidney Green	.02	.10
❑ 205 Frank Brickowski	.02	.10
❑ 206 Anthony Bowie	.02	.10
❑ 207 Duane Causwell	.02	.10
❑ 208 A.J. English	.02	.10
❑ 209 Mark Aguirre	.02	.10
❑ 210 Jon Koncak	.02	.10
❑ 211 Kevin Gamble	.02	.10
❑ 212 Craig Ehlo	.02	.10
❑ 213 Herb Williams	.05	.15
❑ 214 Cedric Ceballos	.05	.15
❑ 215 Mark Jackson	.05	.15
❑ 216 John Bagley	.02	.10
❑ 217 Ron Anderson	.02	.10
❑ 218 John Battle	.02	.10
❑ 219 Kevin Lynch	.02	.10
❑ 220 Donald Hodge	.02	.10
❑ 221 Chris Gatling	.02	.10
❑ 222 Muggsy Bogues	.05	.15
❑ 223 Bill Laimbeer	.05	.15
❑ 224 Anthony Bonner	.02	.10
❑ 225 Fred Roberts	.02	.10
❑ 226 Larry Stewart	.02	.10
❑ 227 Darrell Walker	.02	.10
❑ 228 Larry Smith	.02	.10
❑ 229 Billy Owens	.05	.15
❑ 230 Vinnie Johnson	.02	.10
❑ 231 Johnny Dawkins	.02	.10
❑ 232 Rick Fox	.05	.15
❑ 233 Travis Mays	.02	.10
❑ 234 Mark Price	.02	.10
❑ 235 Derrick McKey	.02	.10
❑ 236 Greg Anthony	.02	.10
❑ 237 Doug Smith	.02	.10
❑ 238 Alec Kessler	.02	.10
❑ 239 Anthony Mason	.10	.30
❑ 240 Shawn Kemp	.25	.60
❑ 241 Jim Les	.02	.10
❑ 242 Dennis Rodman	.25	.60
❑ 243 Lionel Simmons	.02	.10
❑ 244 Pervis Ellison	.02	.10
❑ 245 Terrell Brandon	.10	.30
❑ 246 Mark Bryant	.02	.10
❑ 247 Brad Daugherty	.02	.10
❑ 248 Scott Brooks	.02	.10
❑ 249 Sarunas Marciulionis	.02	.10
❑ 250 Danny Ferry	.02	.10
❑ 251 Loy Vaught	.02	.10
❑ 252 Dee Brown	.02	.10
❑ 253 Alvin Robertson	.02	.10
❑ 254 Charles Smith	.02	.10
❑ 255 Dikembe Mutombo	.15	.40
❑ 256 Greg Kite	.02	.10
❑ 257 Ed Pinckney	.02	.10
❑ 258 Ron Harper	.05	.15
❑ 259 Elliot Perry	.02	.10
❑ 260 Rafael Addison	.02	.10
❑ 261 Tim Hardaway	.15	.40
❑ 262 Randy Brown	.02	.10
❑ 263 Isiah Thomas	.10	.30
❑ 264 Victor Alexander	.02	.10
❑ 265 Wayman Tisdale	.02	.10
❑ 266 Harvey Grant	.02	.10
❑ 267 Mike Iuzzolino	.02	.10
❑ 268 Joe Dumars	.10	.30
❑ 269 Xavier McDaniel	.02	.10
❑ 270 Jeff Sanders	.02	.10
❑ 271 Danny Manning	.05	.15
❑ 272 Jayson Williams	.05	.15
❑ 273 Ricky Pierce	.02	.10
❑ 274 Will Perdue	.02	.10
❑ 275 Dana Barros	.02	.10
❑ 276 Randy Breuer	.02	.10
❑ 277 Manute Bol	.02	.10
❑ 278 Negele Knight	.02	.10
❑ 279 Rodney McCray	.02	.10
❑ 280 Greg Sutton	.02	.10
❑ 281 Larry Nance	.02	.10
❑ 282 John Starks	.05	.15
❑ 283 Pete Chilcutt	.02	.10
❑ 284 Kenny Gattison	.02	.10
❑ 285 Stacey King	.02	.10
❑ 286 Bernard King	.02	.10
❑ 287 Larry Johnson	.15	.40
❑ 288 John Williams	.02	.10
❑ 289 Dell Curry	.02	.10
❑ 290 Orlando Woolridge	.02	.10
❑ 291 Nate McMillan	.02	.10
❑ 292 Terry Mills	.02	.10
❑ 293 Sherman Douglas	.02	.10
❑ 294 Charles Shackleford	.02	.10
❑ 295 Ken Norman	.02	.10
❑ 296 LaSalle Thompson	.02	.10
❑ 297 Chris Mullin	.10	.30
❑ 298 Eddie Johnson	.02	.10
❑ 299 Armon Gilliam	.02	.10
❑ 300 Michael Cage	.02	.10
❑ 301 Moses Malone	.10	.30
❑ 302 Charles Oakley	.05	.15
❑ 303 David Wingate	.02	.10
❑ 304 Steve Kerr	.05	.15
❑ 305 Tyrone Hill	.02	.10
❑ 306 Mark West	.02	.10
❑ 307 Fat Lever	.02	.10
❑ 308 J.R. Reid	.02	.10
❑ 309 Ed Nealy	.02	.10
❑ 310 Form Checklist 3	.10	.30
❑ 311 Alaa Abdelnaby	.02	.10
❑ 312 Stacey Augmon	.05	.15
❑ 313 Anthony Avent RC	.02	.10
❑ 314 Walter Bond RC	.02	.10
❑ 315 Byron Houston RC	.02	.10
❑ 316 Rick Mahorn	.02	.10
❑ 317 Sam Mitchell	.02	.10
❑ 318 Mookie Blaylock	.05	.15
❑ 319 Lance Blanks	.02	.10
❑ 320 John Williams	.02	.10
❑ 321 Rolando Blackman	.02	.10
❑ 322 Danny Ainge	.05	.15
❑ 323 Gerald Glass	.02	.10
❑ 324 Robert Pack	.02	.10
❑ 325 Oliver Miller RC	.05	.15
❑ 326 Charles Smith	.02	.10
❑ 327 Duane Ferrell	.02	.10
❑ 328 Pooh Richardson	.02	.10
❑ 329 Scott Brooks	.02	.10
❑ 330 Walt Williams RC	.10	.30
❑ 331 Andrew Lang	.02	.10

❑ 332 Eric Murdock	.02	.10
❑ 333 Vinny Del Negro	.02	.10
❑ 334 Charles Barkley	.20	.50
❑ 335 James Edwards	.02	.10
❑ 336 Xavier McDaniel	.02	.10
❑ 337 Paul Graham	.02	.10
❑ 338 David Wingate	.02	.10
❑ 339 Richard Dumas RC	.02	.10
❑ 340 Jay Humphries	.02	.10
❑ 341 Mark Jackson	.05	.15
❑ 342 John Salley	.02	.10
❑ 343 Jon Koncak	.02	.10
❑ 344 Rodney McCray	.02	.10
❑ 345 Chuck Person	.02	.10
❑ 346 Mario Elie	.05	.15
❑ 347 Frank Johnson	.02	.10
❑ 348 Rumeal Robinson	.02	.10
❑ 349 Terry Mills	.02	.10
❑ 350 Kevin Willis TFC	.02	.10
❑ 351 Dee Brown TFC	.02	.10
❑ 352 Muggsy Bogues TFC	.02	.10
❑ 353 B.J. Armstrong TFC	.02	.10
❑ 354 Larry Nance TFC	.02	.10
❑ 355 Doug Smith TFC	.02	.10
❑ 356 Robert Pack TFC	.02	.10
❑ 357 Joe Dumars TFC	.05	.15
❑ 358 Sarunas Marciulionis TFC	.02	.10
❑ 359 Kenny Smith TFC	.02	.10
❑ 360 Pooh Richardson TFC	.02	.10
❑ 361 Mark Jackson TFC	.02	.10
❑ 362 Sedale Threatt TFC	.02	.10
❑ 363 Grant Long TFC	.02	.10
❑ 364 Eric Murdock TFC	.02	.10
❑ 365 Doug West TFC	.02	.10
❑ 366 Kenny Anderson TFC	.05	.15
❑ 367 Anthony Mason TFC	.05	.15
❑ 368 Nick Anderson TFC	.02	.10
❑ 369 Jeff Hornacek TFC	.02	.10
❑ 370 Dan Majerle TFC	.02	.10
❑ 371 Cliff Robinson TFC	.02	.10
❑ 372 Lionel Simmons TFC	.02	.10
❑ 373 Dale Ellis TFC	.02	.10
❑ 374 Gary Payton TFC	.10	.30
❑ 375 David Benoit TFC	.02	.10
❑ 376 Harvey Grant TFC	.02	.10
❑ 377 Buck Johnson	.02	.10
❑ 378 Brian Howard RC	.02	.10
❑ 379 Travis Mays	.02	.10
❑ 380 Jud Buechler	.02	.10
❑ 381 Matt Geiger RC	.05	.15
❑ 382 Bob McCann RC	.02	.10
❑ 383 Cedric Ceballos	.05	.15
❑ 384 Rod Strickland	.10	.30
❑ 385 Kiki Vandeweghe	.02	.10
❑ 386 Latrell Sprewell RC	1.00	2.50
❑ 387 Larry Krystkowiak	.02	.10
❑ 388 Dale Ellis	.02	.10
❑ 389 Trent Tucker	.02	.10
❑ 390 Negele Knight	.02	.10
❑ 391 Stanley Roberts	.02	.10
❑ 392 Tony Campbell	.02	.10
❑ 393 Tim Perry	.02	.10
❑ 394 Doug Overton	.02	.10
❑ 395 Dan Majerle	.05	.15
❑ 396 Duane Cooper RC	.02	.10
❑ 397 Kevin Willis	.02	.10
❑ 398 Micheal Williams	.02	.10
❑ 399 Avery Johnson	.02	.10
❑ 400 Dominique Wilkins	.10	.30
❑ 401 Chris Smith RC	.02	.10
❑ 402 Blair Rasmussen	.02	.10
❑ 403 Jeff Hornacek	.05	.15
❑ 404 Blue Edwards	.02	.10
❑ 405 Olden Polynice	.02	.10
❑ 406 Jeff Grayer	.02	.10
❑ 407 Tony Bennett RC	.02	.10
❑ 408 Don MacLean	.02	.10
❑ 409 Tom Chambers	.02	.10
❑ 410 Keith Jennings RC	.02	.10
❑ 411 Gerald Wilkins	.02	.10
❑ 412 Kennard Winchester	.02	.10
❑ 413 Doc Rivers	.05	.15
❑ 414 Brent Price RC	.05	.15
❑ 415 Mark West	.02	.10
❑ 416 J.R. Reid	.02	.10
❑ 417 Jon Barry RC	.05	.15
❑ 418 Kevin Johnson	.10	.30
❑ 419 Form Checklist	.10	.30
❑ 420 Form Checklist	.10	.30
❑ 421 Daugh/Price/Nance AS CL	.02	.10
❑ 422 Scottie Pippen AS	.20	.50
❑ 423 Larry Johnson AS	.10	.30
❑ 424 Shaquille O'Neal AS	1.00	2.50
❑ 425 Michael Jordan AS	.75	2.00
❑ 426 Isiah Thomas AS	.05	.15
❑ 427 Brad Daugherty AS	.02	.10
❑ 428 Joe Dumars AS	.05	.15
❑ 429 Patrick Ewing AS	.05	.15
❑ 430 Larry Nance AS	.02	.10
❑ 431 Mark Price AS	.02	.10
❑ 432 Detlef Schrempf AS	.02	.10
❑ 433 Dominique Wilkins AS	.05	.15
❑ 434 Karl Malone AS	.10	.30
❑ 435 Charles Barkley AS	.10	.30
❑ 436 David Robinson AS	.10	.30
❑ 437 John Stockton AS	.05	.15
❑ 438 Clyde Drexler AS	.05	.15
❑ 439 Sean Elliott AS	.02	.10
❑ 440 Tim Hardaway AS	.10	.30
❑ 441 Shawn Kemp AS	.10	.30
❑ 442 Dan Majerle AS	.02	.10
❑ 443 Danny Manning AS	.02	.10
❑ 444 Hakeem Olajuwon AS	.10	.30
❑ 445 Terry Porter AS	.02	.10
❑ 446 Harold Miner FACE	.05	.15
❑ 447 David Benoit FACE	.02	.10
❑ 448 Cedric Ceballos FACE	.02	.10
❑ 449 Chris Jackson FACE	.02	.10
❑ 450 Tim Perry FACE	.02	.10
❑ 451 Kenny Smith FACE	.02	.10
❑ 452 Clar.Weatherspoon FACE	.10	.30
❑ 453A M.Jordan FACE 85 ERR	6.00	15.00
❑ 453B M.Jordan FACE 87 COR	.75	2.00
❑ 454A D.Wilkins FACE 87 ERR	.75	2.00
❑ 454B D.Wilkins FACE 85 COR	.10	.30
❑ 455 D.Cooper/A.Peeler TP CL	.02	.10
❑ 456 Adam Keefe TP	.02	.10
❑ 457 Alonzo Mourning TP	.20	.50
❑ 458 Jim Jackson TP	.10	.30
❑ 459 Sean Rooks TP	.02	.10
❑ 460 LaPhonso Ellis TP	.05	.15
❑ 461 Bryant Stith TP	.02	.10
❑ 462 Byron Houston TP	.02	.10
❑ 463 Latrell Sprewell TP	.10	.30
❑ 464 Robert Horry TP	.05	.15
❑ 465 Malik Sealy TP	.02	.10
❑ 466 Doug Christie TP	.10	.30
❑ 467 Duane Cooper TP	.02	.10
❑ 468 Anthony Peeler TP	.02	.10
❑ 469 Harold Miner TP	.02	.10
❑ 470 Todd Day TP	.02	.10
❑ 471 Lee Mayberry TP	.02	.10
❑ 472 Christian Laettner TP	.10	.30
❑ 473 Hubert Davis TP	.02	.10
❑ 474 Shaquille O'Neal TP	1.00	2.50
❑ 475 Clarence Weatherspoon TP	.10	.30
❑ 476 Richard Dumas TP	.02	.10
❑ 477 Oliver Miller TP	.02	.10
❑ 478 Tracy Murray TP	.02	.10
❑ 479 Walt Williams TP	.05	.15
❑ 480 Lloyd Daniels TP	.02	.10
❑ 481 Tom Gugliotta TP	.10	.30
❑ 482 Brent Price TP	.02	.10
❑ 483 Mark Aguirre GF	.02	.10
❑ 484 Frank Brickowski GF	.02	.10
❑ 485 Derrick Coleman GF	.02	.10
❑ 486 Clyde Drexler GF	.05	.15
❑ 487 Harvey Grant GF	.02	.10
❑ 488 Michael Jordan GF	.75	2.00
❑ 489 Karl Malone GF	.10	.30
❑ 490 Xavier McDaniel GF	.02	.10
❑ 491 Drazen Petrovic GF	.02	.10
❑ 492 John Starks GF	.02	.10
❑ 493 Robert Parish GF	.02	.10
❑ 494 Christian Laettner GF	.10	.30
❑ 495 Ron Harper GF	.02	.10
❑ 496 David Robinson GF	.10	.30
❑ 497 John Salley GF	.02	.10
❑ 498 B.Daugherty/M.Price ST	.02	.10
❑ 499 D.Mutombo/C.Jackson ST	.10	.30
❑ 500 I.Thomas/J.Dumars ST	.10	.30
❑ 501 H.Olajuwon/Thorpe ST	.10	.30
❑ 502 D.Coleman/D.Petrovic ST	.05	.15
❑ 503 T.Porter/C.Drexler ST	.10	.30
❑ 504 Lionel Simmons ST	.05	.15
❑ 505 D.Robinson/S.Elliott ST	.10	.30
❑ 506 Michael Jordan FAN	.75	2.00
❑ 507 Larry Bird FAN	.25	.60
❑ 508 Karl Malone FAN	.10	.30
❑ 509 Dikembe Mutombo FAN	.10	.30
❑ 510 L.Bird/M.Jordan FAN	.40	1.00
❑ SP1 L.Bird/M.Johnson Retire	1.25	3.00
❑ SP2 D.Wilkins/M.Jordan 20K	2.50	6.00

1993-94 Upper Deck

❑ COMPLETE SET (510)	15.00	30.00
❑ COMPLETE SERIES 1 (255)	7.50	15.00
❑ COMPLETE SERIES 2 (255)	7.50	15.00
❑ 1 Muggsy Bogues	.05	.15
❑ 2 Kenny Anderson	.05	.15
❑ 3 Dell Curry	.01	.05
❑ 4 Charles Smith	.01	.05
❑ 5 Chuck Person	.01	.05
❑ 6 Chucky Brown	.01	.05
❑ 7 Kevin Johnson	.05	.15
❑ 8 Winston Garland	.01	.05
❑ 9 John Salley	.01	.05
❑ 10 Dale Ellis	.01	.05
❑ 11 Otis Thorpe	.05	.15
❑ 12 John Stockton	.10	.30
❑ 13 Kendall Gill	.05	.15
❑ 14 Randy White	.01	.05
❑ 15 Mark Jackson	.05	.15
❑ 16 Vlade Divac	.05	.15
❑ 17 Scott Skiles	.01	.05
❑ 18 Xavier McDaniel	.01	.05
❑ 19 Jeff Hornacek	.05	.15
❑ 20 Stanley Roberts	.01	.05
❑ 21 Harold Miner	.01	.05
❑ 22 Terrell Brandon	.05	.15
❑ 23 Michael Jordan	1.50	4.00
❑ 24 Jim Jackson	.05	.15
❑ 25 Keith Askins	.01	.05
❑ 26 Corey Williams	.01	.05
❑ 27 David Benoit	.01	.05
❑ 28 Charles Oakley	.05	.15
❑ 29 Michael Adams	.01	.05
❑ 30 Clarence Weatherspoon	.01	.05
❑ 31 Jon Koncak	.01	.05
❑ 32 Gerald Wilkins	.01	.05
❑ 33 Anthony Bowie	.01	.05
❑ 34 Willie Burton	.01	.05
❑ 35 Stacey Augmon	.01	.05
❑ 36 Doc Rivers	.05	.15
❑ 37 Luc Longley	.05	.15
❑ 38 Dee Brown	.01	.05
❑ 39 Litterial Green	.01	.05
❑ 40 Dan Majerle	.05	.15
❑ 41 Doug West	.01	.05
❑ 42 Joe Dumars	.10	.30
❑ 43 Dennis Scott	.01	.05
❑ 44 Mahmoud Abdul-Rauf	.01	.05
❑ 45 Mark Eaton	.01	.05
❑ 46 Danny Ferry	.01	.05
❑ 47 Kenny Smith	.01	.05
❑ 48 Ron Harper	.05	.15
❑ 49 Adam Keefe	.01	.05
❑ 50 David Robinson	.20	.50
❑ 51 John Starks	.05	.15
❑ 52 Jeff Malone	.01	.05
❑ 53 Vern Fleming	.01	.05
❑ 54 Olden Polynice	.01	.05
❑ 55 Dikembe Mutombo	.10	.30
❑ 56 Chris Morris	.01	.05
❑ 57 Paul Graham	.01	.05
❑ 58 Richard Dumas	.01	.05
❑ 59 J.R. Reid	.01	.05
❑ 60 Brad Daugherty	.01	.05
❑ 61 Blue Edwards	.01	.05
❑ 62 Mark Macon	.01	.05
❑ 63 Latrell Sprewell	.30	.75
❑ 64 Mitch Richmond	.10	.30
❑ 65 David Wingate	.01	.05
❑ 66 LaSalle Thompson	.01	.05

❑ 67 Sedale Threatt	.01	.05
❑ 68 Larry Krystkowiak	.01	.05
❑ 69 John Paxson	.01	.05
❑ 70 Frank Brickowski	.01	.05
❑ 71 Duane Causwell	.01	.05
❑ 72 Fred Roberts	.01	.05
❑ 73 Rod Strickland	.05	.15
❑ 74 Willie Anderson	.01	.05
❑ 75 Thurl Bailey	.01	.05
❑ 76 Ricky Pierce	.01	.05
❑ 77 Todd Day	.01	.05
❑ 78 Hot Rod Williams	.01	.05
❑ 79 Danny Ainge	.05	.15
❑ 80 Mark West	.01	.05
❑ 81 Marcus Liberty	.01	.05
❑ 82 Keith Jennings	.01	.05
❑ 83 Derrick Coleman	.05	.15
❑ 84 Larry Stewart	.01	.05
❑ 85 Tracy Murray	.01	.05
❑ 86 Robert Horry	.05	.15
❑ 87 Derek Harper	.05	.15
❑ 88 Scott Hastings	.01	.05
❑ 89 Sam Perkins	.05	.15
❑ 90 Clyde Drexler	.10	.30
❑ 91 Brent Price	.01	.05
❑ 92 Chris Mullin	.10	.30
❑ 93 Rafael Addison	.01	.05
❑ 94 Tyrone Corbin	.01	.05
❑ 95 Sarunas Marciulionis	.01	.05
❑ 96 Antoine Carr	.01	.05
❑ 97 Tony Bennett	.01	.05
❑ 98 Sam Mitchell	.01	.05
❑ 99 Lionel Simmons	.01	.05
❑ 100 Tim Perry	.01	.05
❑ 101 Horace Grant	.05	.15
❑ 102 Tom Hammonds	.01	.05
❑ 103 Walter Bond	.01	.05
❑ 104 Detlef Schrempf	.05	.15
❑ 105 Terry Porter	.01	.05
❑ 106 Danny Schayes	.01	.05
❑ 107 Rumeal Robinson	.01	.05
❑ 108 Gerald Glass	.01	.05
❑ 109 Mike Gminski	.01	.05
❑ 110 Terry Mills	.01	.05
❑ 111 Loy Vaught	.01	.05
❑ 112 Jim Les	.01	.05
❑ 113 Byron Houston	.01	.05
❑ 114 Randy Brown	.01	.05
❑ 115 Anthony Avent	.01	.05
❑ 116 Donald Hodge	.01	.05
❑ 117 Kevin Willis	.01	.05
❑ 118 Robert Pack	.01	.05
❑ 119 Dale Davis	.01	.05
❑ 120 Grant Long	.01	.05
❑ 121 Anthony Bonner	.01	.05
❑ 122 Chris Smith	.01	.05
❑ 123 Elden Campbell	.01	.05
❑ 124 Cliff Robinson	.05	.15
❑ 125 Sherman Douglas	.01	.05
❑ 126 Alvin Robertson	.01	.05
❑ 127 Rolando Blackman	.01	.05
❑ 128 Malik Sealy	.01	.05
❑ 129 Ed Pinckney	.01	.05
❑ 130 Anthony Peeler	.01	.05
❑ 131 Scott Brooks	.01	.05
❑ 132 Rik Smits	.05	.15
❑ 133 Derrick McKey	.01	.05
❑ 134 Alaa Abdelnaby	.01	.05
❑ 135 Rex Chapman	.01	.05
❑ 136 Tony Campbell	.01	.05
❑ 137 John Williams	.01	.05
❑ 138 Vincent Askew	.01	.05
❑ 139 LaBradford Smith	.01	.05
❑ 140 Vinny Del Negro	.01	.05
❑ 141 Darrell Walker	.01	.05
❑ 142 James Worthy	.10	.30
❑ 143 Jeff Turner	.01	.05
❑ 144 Duane Ferrell	.01	.05
❑ 145 Larry Smith	.01	.05
❑ 146 Eddie Johnson	.01	.05
❑ 147 Chris Gatling	.01	.05
❑ 148 Buck Williams	.01	.05
❑ 149 Donald Royal	.01	.05
❑ 150 Dino Radja RC	.01	.05
❑ 151 Johnny Dawkins	.01	.05
❑ 152 Tim Legler RC	.01	.05
❑ 153 Bill Laimbeer	.01	.05
❑ 154 Glen Rice	.05	.15
❑ 155 Bill Cartwright	.01	.05
❑ 156 Luther Wright RC	.01	.05
❑ 157 Rex Walters RC	.01	.05
❑ 158 Doug Edwards RC	.01	.05
❑ 159 George Lynch RC	.01	.05
❑ 160 Chris Mills RC	.10	.30
❑ 161 Sam Cassell RC	.50	1.25
❑ 162 Nick Van Exel RC	.40	1.00
❑ 163 Shawn Bradley RC	.10	.30
❑ 164 Calbert Cheaney RC	.05	.15
❑ 165 Corie Blount RC	.01	.05
❑ 166 Michael Jordan SL	.75	2.00
❑ 167 Dennis Rodman SL	.10	.30
❑ 168 John Stockton SL	.05	.15
❑ 169 B.J. Armstrong SL	.01	.05
❑ 170 Hakeem Olajuwon SL	.10	.30
❑ 171 Michael Jordan SL	.75	2.00
❑ 172 Cedric Ceballos SL	.01	.05
❑ 173 Mark Price SL	.01	.05
❑ 174 Charles Barkley SL	.10	.30
❑ 175 Clifford Robinson SL	.01	.05
❑ 176 Hakeem Olajuwon SL	.10	.30
❑ 177 Shaquille O'Neal SL	.25	.60
❑ 178 R.Miller/C.Oakley PO	.05	.15
❑ 179 1st Round: Hornets 3&	.01	.05
❑ 180 M.Jordan/S.Augmon PO	.40	1.00
❑ 181 Brad Daugherty PO	.01	.05
❑ 182 O.Miller/B.Scott PO	.01	.05
❑ 183 D.Robinson/Elliott PO	.10	.30
❑ 184 1st Round: Rockets 3&	.01	.05
❑ 185 1st Round: Sonics	.01	.05
❑ 186 A.Mason/P.Ewing	.10	.30
❑ 187 M.Jordan/G.Wilkins PO	.40	1.00
❑ 188 Oliver Miller PO	.01	.05
❑ 189 West Semis: Sonics 4&	.10	.30
❑ 190 East Finals: Bulls 4&	.01	.05
❑ 191 K.Johnson PO	.05	.15
❑ 192 Dan Majerle PO	.01	.05
❑ 193 Michael Jordan PO	.75	2.00
❑ 194 L.Johnson/Bogues PO	.01	.05
❑ 195 Miller ties Playoffs	.05	.15
❑ 196 Bulls and Knicks	.10	.30
❑ 197 C.Barkley PO	.10	.30
❑ 198 Michael Jordan FIN	.75	2.00
❑ 199 Scottie Pippen FIN	.20	.50
❑ 200 Kevin Johnson G3	.01	.05
❑ 201 Michael Jordan FIN	.75	2.00
❑ 202 Richard Dumas FIN	.01	.05
❑ 203 Horace Grant G6	.01	.05
❑ 204 Michael Jordan FIN	.75	2.00
❑ 205 S.Pippen/C.Barkley FIN	.10	.30
❑ 206 John Paxson	.01	.05
❑ 207 B.J. Armstrong	.01	.05
❑ 208 1992-93 Bulls	.01	.05
❑ 209 1992-93 Suns	.01	.05
❑ 210 Atlanta Hawks Sked	.01	.05
❑ 211 Boston Celtics Sked	.01	.05
❑ 212 Charlotte Hornets Sked	.01	.05
❑ 213 M.Jordan/Group SKED	.40	1.00
❑ 214 Cleveland Cavaliers	.01	.05
❑ 215 J.Jackson/S.Rooks SKED	.01	.05
❑ 216 Denver Nuggets Sked	.05	.15
❑ 217 Detroit Pistons Sked	.05	.15
❑ 218 Golden State Warriors	.01	.05
❑ 219 H.Olajuwon/Group SKED	.10	.30
❑ 220 Indiana Pacers Sked	.01	.05
❑ 221 L.A. Clippers Sked	.01	.05
❑ 222 L.A. Lakers Sked	.01	.05
❑ 223 Smith/Miner/Seik SKED	.05	.15
❑ 224 Milwaukee Bucks Sked	.01	.05
❑ 225 Minnesota Timberwolves	.01	.05
❑ 226 New Jersey Nets Sked	.01	.05
❑ 227 New York Knicks Sked	.01	.05
❑ 228 S.O'Neal/Group SKED	.15	.40
❑ 229 Philadelphia 76ers	.01	.05
❑ 230 C.Barkley/Group SKED	.10	.30
❑ 231 Portland Trail Blazers	.01	.05
❑ 232 Sacramento Kings Sked	.01	.05
❑ 233 D.Robinson/Group SKED	.10	.30
❑ 234 S.Kemp/G.Payton SKED	.05	.15
❑ 235 Utah Jazz Sked	.01	.05
❑ 236 Gugliotta/Adams SKED	.05	.15
❑ 237 Michael Jordan SM	.75	2.00
❑ 238 Clyde Drexler SM	.05	.15
❑ 239 Tim Hardaway SM	.05	.15
❑ 240 Dominique Wilkins SM	.05	.15
❑ 241 Brad Daugherty SM	.01	.05
❑ 242 Chris Mullin SM	.05	.15
❑ 243 Kenny Anderson SM	.01	.05
❑ 244 Patrick Ewing SM	.05	.15
❑ 245 Isiah Thomas SM	.05	.15
❑ 246 Dikembe Mutombo SM	.05	.15
❑ 247 Danny Manning SM	.01	.05
❑ 248 David Robinson SM	.10	.30
❑ 249 Karl Malone SM	.10	.30
❑ 250 James Worthy SM	.05	.15
❑ 251 Shawn Kemp SM	.10	.30
❑ 252 Checklist 1-64	.01	.05
❑ 253 Checklist 65-128	.01	.05
❑ 254 Checklist 129-192	.01	.05
❑ 255 Checklist 193-255	.01	.05
❑ 256 Patrick Ewing	.10	.30
❑ 257 B.J. Armstrong	.01	.05
❑ 258 Oliver Miller	.01	.05
❑ 259 Jud Buechler	.01	.05
❑ 260 Pooh Richardson	.01	.05
❑ 261 Victor Alexander	.01	.05
❑ 262 Kevin Gamble	.01	.05
❑ 263 Doug Smith	.01	.05
❑ 264 Isiah Thomas	.10	.30
❑ 265 Doug Christie	.05	.15
❑ 266 Mark Bryant	.01	.05
❑ 267 Lloyd Daniels	.01	.05
❑ 268 Micheal Williams	.01	.05
❑ 269 Nick Anderson	.05	.15
❑ 270 Tom Gugliotta	.10	.30
❑ 271 Kenny Gattison	.01	.05
❑ 272 Vernon Maxwell	.01	.05
❑ 273 Terry Cummings	.01	.05
❑ 274 Karl Malone	.20	.50
❑ 275 Rick Fox	.01	.05
❑ 276 Matt Bullard	.01	.05
❑ 277 Johnny Newman	.01	.05
❑ 278 Mark Price	.01	.05
❑ 279 Mookie Blaylock	.05	.15
❑ 280 Charles Barkley	.20	.50
❑ 281 Larry Nance	.01	.05
❑ 282 Walt Williams	.01	.05
❑ 283 Brian Shaw	.01	.05
❑ 284 Robert Parish	.05	.15
❑ 285 Pervis Ellison	.01	.05
❑ 286 Spud Webb	.05	.15
❑ 287 Hakeem Olajuwon	.20	.50
❑ 288 Jerome Kersey	.01	.05
❑ 289 Carl Herrera	.01	.05
❑ 290 Dominique Wilkins	.10	.30
❑ 291 Billy Owens	.01	.05
❑ 292 Greg Anthony	.01	.05
❑ 293 Nate McMillan	.01	.05
❑ 294 Christian Laettner	.05	.15
❑ 295 Gary Payton	.20	.50
❑ 296 Steve Smith	.10	.30
❑ 297 Anthony Mason	.05	.15
❑ 298 Sean Rooks	.01	.05
❑ 299 Toni Kukoc RC	.50	1.25
❑ 300 Shaquille O'Neal	.60	1.50
❑ 301 Jay Humphries	.01	.05
❑ 302 Sleepy Floyd	.01	.05
❑ 303 Bimbo Coles	.01	.05
❑ 304 John Battle	.01	.05
❑ 305 Shawn Kemp	.20	.50
❑ 306 Scott Williams	.01	.05
❑ 307 Wayman Tisdale	.01	.05
❑ 308 Rony Seikaly	.01	.05
❑ 309 Reggie Miller	.10	.30
❑ 310 Scottie Pippen	.40	1.00
❑ 311 Chris Webber RC	1.25	3.00
❑ 312 Trevor Wilson	.01	.05
❑ 313 Derek Strong RC	.01	.05
❑ 314 Bobby Hurley RC	.05	.15
❑ 315 Herb Williams	.01	.05
❑ 316 Rex Walters	.01	.05
❑ 317 Doug Edwards	.01	.05
❑ 318 Ken Williams	.01	.05
❑ 319 Jon Barry	.01	.05
❑ 320 Joe Courtney RC	.01	.05
❑ 321 Ervin Johnson RC	.05	.15
❑ 322 Sam Cassell	.10	.30
❑ 323 Tim Hardaway	.10	.30
❑ 324 Ed Stokes	.01	.05
❑ 325 Steve Kerr	.05	.15
❑ 326 Doug Overton	.01	.05
❑ 327 Reggie Williams	.01	.05
❑ 328 Avery Johnson	.01	.05
❑ 329 Stacey King	.01	.05
❑ 330 Vin Baker RC	.30	.75
❑ 331 Greg Kite	.01	.05
❑ 332 Michael Cage	.01	.05
❑ 333 Alonzo Mourning	.20	.50

❑ 334 Acie Earl RC	.01	.05
❑ 335 Terry Dehere RC	.01	.05
❑ 336 Negele Knight	.01	.05
❑ 337 Gerald Madkins RC	.01	.05
❑ 338 Lindsey Hunter RC	.10	.30
❑ 339 Luther Wright	.01	.05
❑ 340 Mike Peplowski RC	.01	.05
❑ 341 Dino Radja	.01	.05
❑ 342 Danny Manning	.05	.15
❑ 343 Chris Mills	.10	.30
❑ 344 Kevin Lynch	.01	.05
❑ 345 Shawn Bradley	.10	.30
❑ 346 Evers Burns RC	.01	.05
❑ 347 Rodney Rogers RC	.10	.30
❑ 348 Cedric Ceballos	.05	.15
❑ 349 Warren Kidd RC	.01	.05
❑ 350 Darnell Mee RC	.01	.05
❑ 351 Matt Geiger	.01	.05
❑ 352 Jamal Mashburn RC	.30	.75
❑ 353 Antonio Davis RC	.15	.40
❑ 354 Calbert Cheaney	.05	.15
❑ 355 George Lynch	.01	.05
❑ 356 Derrick McKey	.01	.05
❑ 357 Jerry Reynolds	.01	.05
❑ 358 Don MacLean	.01	.05
❑ 359 Scott Haskin RC	.01	.05
❑ 360 Malcolm Mackey RC	.01	.05
❑ 361 Isaiah Rider RC	.25	.60
❑ 362 Detlef Schrempf	.05	.15
❑ 363 Josh Grant RC	.01	.05
❑ 364 Richard Petruska	.01	.05
❑ 365 Larry Johnson	.10	.30
❑ 366 Richard Petruska RC	.01	.05
❑ 367 Ken Norman	.01	.05
❑ 368 Anthony Cook	.01	.05
❑ 369 James Robinson RC	.01	.05
❑ 370 Kevin Duckworth	.01	.05
❑ 371 Chris Whitney RC	.01	.05
❑ 372 Moses Malone	.10	.30
❑ 373 Nick Van Exel	.20	.50
❑ 374 Scott Burrell RC	.10	.30
❑ 375 Harvey Grant	.01	.05
❑ 376 Benoit Benjamin	.01	.05
❑ 377 Henry James	.01	.05
❑ 378 Craig Ehlo	.01	.05
❑ 379 Ennis Whatley	.01	.05
❑ 380 Sean Green	.01	.05
❑ 381 Eric Murdock	.01	.05
❑ 382 Anfernee Hardaway RC	1.00	2.50
❑ 383 Gheorghe Muresan RC	.10	.30
❑ 384 Kendall Gill	.05	.15
❑ 385 David Wood	.01	.05
❑ 386 Mario Elie	.01	.05
❑ 387 Chris Corchiani	.01	.05
❑ 388 Greg Graham RC	.01	.05
❑ 389 Hersey Hawkins	.05	.15
❑ 390 Mark Aguirre	.01	.05
❑ 391 LaPhonso Ellis	.01	.05
❑ 392 Anthony Bonner	.01	.05
❑ 393 Lucious Harris RC	.01	.05
❑ 394 Andrew Lang	.01	.05
❑ 395 Chris Dudley	.01	.05
❑ 396 Dennis Rodman	.25	.60
❑ 397 Larry Krystkowiak	.01	.05
❑ 398 A.C. Green	.05	.15
❑ 399 Eddie Johnson	.01	.05
❑ 400 Kevin Edwards	.01	.05
❑ 401 Tyrone Hill	.01	.05
❑ 402 Greg Anderson	.01	.05
❑ 403 P.J.Brown RC	.25	.60
❑ 404 Dana Barros	.01	.05
❑ 405 Allan Houston RC	.50	1.25
❑ 406 Mike Brown	.01	.05
❑ 407 Lee Mayberry	.01	.05
❑ 408 Fat Lever	.01	.05
❑ 409 Tony Smith	.01	.05
❑ 410 Tom Chambers	.01	.05
❑ 411 Manute Bol	.01	.05
❑ 412 Joe Kleine	.01	.05
❑ 413 Bryant Stith	.01	.05
❑ 414 Eric Riley RC	.01	.05
❑ 415 Jo Jo English RC	.01	.05
❑ 416 Sean Elliott	.05	.15
❑ 417 Sam Bowie	.01	.05
❑ 418 Armon Gilliam	.01	.05
❑ 419 Brian Williams	.01	.05
❑ 420 Popeye Jones RC	.01	.05
❑ 421 Dennis Rodman EB	.10	.30
❑ 422 Karl Malone EB	.10	.30
❑ 423 Tom Gugliotta EB	.05	.15
❑ 424 Kevin Willis EB	.01	.05
❑ 425 Hakeem Olajuwon EB	.10	.30
❑ 426 Charles Oakley EB	.01	.05
❑ 427 Clarence Weatherspoon EB	.01	.05
❑ 428 Derrick Coleman EB	.01	.05
❑ 429 Buck Williams EB	.01	.05
❑ 430 Christian Laettner EB	.01	.05
❑ 431 Dikembe Mutombo EB	.05	.15
❑ 432 Rony Seikaly EB	.01	.05
❑ 433 Brad Daugherty EB	.01	.05
❑ 434 Horace Grant EB	.01	.05
❑ 435 Larry Johnson EB	.05	.15
❑ 436 Dee Brown BT	.01	.05
❑ 437 Muggsy Bogues BT	.01	.05
❑ 438 Michael Jordan BT	.75	2.00
❑ 439 Tim Hardaway BT	.05	.15
❑ 440 Micheal Williams BT	.01	.05
❑ 441 Gary Payton BT	.10	.30
❑ 442 Mookie Blaylock BT	.01	.05
❑ 443 Doc Rivers BT	.01	.05
❑ 444 Kenny Smith BT	.01	.05
❑ 445 John Stockton BT	.05	.15
❑ 446 Alvin Robertson BT	.01	.05
❑ 447 Mark Jackson BT	.01	.05
❑ 448 Kenny Anderson BT	.01	.05
❑ 449 Scottie Pippen BT	.20	.50
❑ 450 Isiah Thomas BT	.05	.15
❑ 451 Mark Price BT	.01	.05
❑ 452 Latrell Sprewell BT	.10	.30
❑ 453 Sedale Threatt BT	.01	.05
❑ 454 Nick Anderson BT	.01	.05
❑ 455 Rod Strickland BT	.01	.05
❑ 456 Oliver Miller GI	.01	.05
❑ 457 J.Worthy/V.Divac GI	.01	.05
❑ 458 Robert Horry GI	.01	.05
❑ 459 Rockets Shoot-Around GI	.01	.05
❑ 460 Rooks/Jackson/Legler GI	.01	.05
❑ 461 Mitch Richmond GI	.05	.15
❑ 462 Chris Morris GI	.01	.05
❑ 463 M.Jackson/G.Grant GI	.01	.05
❑ 464 David Robinson GI	.10	.30
❑ 465 Danny Ainge GI	.01	.05
❑ 466 Michael Jordan SKL	.75	2.00
❑ 467 Dominique Wilkins SKL	.05	.15
❑ 468 Alonzo Mourning SKL	.10	.30
❑ 469 Shaquille O'Neal SKL	.25	.60
❑ 470 Tim Hardaway SL	.05	.15
❑ 471 Patrick Ewing SKL	.05	.15
❑ 472 Kevin Johnson SL	.01	.05
❑ 473 Clyde Drexler SKL	.05	.15
❑ 474 David Robinson SKL	.10	.30
❑ 475 Shawn Kemp SKL	.10	.30
❑ 476 Dee Brown SL	.01	.05
❑ 477 Jim Jackson SKL	.01	.05
❑ 478 John Stockton SKL	.05	.15
❑ 479 Robert Horry SL	.01	.05
❑ 480 Glen Rice SL	.01	.05
❑ 481 Micheal Williams SIS	.01	.05
❑ 482 G.Lynch/T.Dehere CL	.01	.05
❑ 483 Chris Webber TP	.60	1.50
❑ 484 Anfernee Hardaway TP	.50	1.25
❑ 485 Shawn Bradley TP	.05	.15
❑ 486 Jamal Mashburn TP	.10	.30
❑ 487 Calbert Cheaney TP	.01	.05
❑ 488 Isaiah Rider TP	.10	.30
❑ 489 Bobby Hurley TP	.01	.05
❑ 490 Vin Baker TP	.10	.30
❑ 491 Rodney Rogers TP	.05	.15
❑ 492 Lindsey Hunter TP	.05	.15
❑ 493 Allan Houston TP	.10	.30
❑ 494 Terry Dehere TP	.01	.05
❑ 495 George Lynch TP	.01	.05
❑ 496 Toni Kukoc TP	.10	.30
❑ 497 Nick Van Exel TP	.10	.30
❑ 498 Charles Barkley MO	.10	.30
❑ 499 A.C. Green MO	.01	.05
❑ 500 Dan Majerle MO	.01	.05
❑ 501 Jerrod Mustaf MO	.01	.05
❑ 502 Kevin Johnson MO	.01	.05
❑ 503 Negele Knight MO	.01	.05
❑ 504 Danny Ainge MO	.01	.05
❑ 505 Oliver Miller MO	.01	.05
❑ 506 Joe Courtney MO	.01	.05
❑ 507 Checklist	.01	.05
❑ 508 Checklist	.01	.05
❑ 509 Checklist	.01	.05
❑ 510 Checklist	.01	.05
❑ SP3 M.Jordan/W.Chamberlain	3.00	8.00
❑ SP4 Chicago Bulls Third	3.00	8.00

1994-95 Upper Deck

❑ COMPLETE SET (360)	22.50	45.00
❑ COMPLETE SERIES 1 (180)	12.50	25.00
❑ COMPLETE SERIES 2 (180)	10.00	20.00
❑ 1 Chris Webber ART	.20	.50
❑ 2 Anfernee Hardaway ART	.20	.50
❑ 3 Vin Baker ART	.05	.15
❑ 4 Jamal Mashburn ART	.05	.15
❑ 5 Isaiah Rider ART	.02	.10
❑ 6 Dino Radja ART	.02	.10
❑ 7 Nick Van Exel ART	.05	.15
❑ 8 Shawn Bradley ART	.02	.10
❑ 9 Toni Kukoc ART	.15	.40
❑ 10 Lindsey Hunter ART	.02	.10
❑ 11 Scottie Pippen AN	.25	.60
❑ 12 Karl Malone AN	.15	.40
❑ 13 Hakeem Olajuwon AN	.15	.40
❑ 14 John Stockton AN	.05	.15
❑ 15 Latrell Sprewell AN	.15	.40
❑ 16 Shawn Kemp AN	.15	.40
❑ 17 Charles Barkley AN	.15	.40
❑ 18 David Robinson AN	.15	.40
❑ 19 Mitch Richmond AN	.05	.15
❑ 20 Kevin Johnson AN	.02	.10
❑ 21 Derrick Coleman AN	.02	.10
❑ 22 Dominique Wilkins AN	.05	.15
❑ 23 Shaquille O'Neal AN	.30	.75
❑ 24 Mark Price AN	.02	.10
❑ 25 Gary Payton AN	.15	.40
❑ 26 Dan Majerle	.05	.15
❑ 27 Vernon Maxwell	.02	.10
❑ 28 Matt Geiger	.02	.10
❑ 29 Jeff Turner	.02	.10
❑ 30 Vinny Del Negro	.02	.10
❑ 31 B.J. Armstrong	.02	.10
❑ 32 Chris Gatling	.02	.10
❑ 33 Tony Smith	.02	.10
❑ 34 Doug West	.02	.10
❑ 35 Clyde Drexler	.15	.40
❑ 36 Keith Jennings	.02	.10
❑ 37 Steve Smith	.05	.15
❑ 38 Kendall Gill	.05	.15
❑ 39 Bob Martin	.02	.10
❑ 40 Calbert Cheaney	.02	.10
❑ 41 Terrell Brandon	.05	.15
❑ 42 Pete Chilcutt	.02	.10
❑ 43 Avery Johnson	.02	.10
❑ 44 Tom Gugliotta	.05	.15
❑ 45 LaBradford Smith	.02	.10
❑ 46 Sedale Threatt	.02	.10
❑ 47 Chris Smith	.02	.10
❑ 48 Kevin Edwards	.02	.10
❑ 49 Lucious Harris	.02	.10
❑ 50 Tim Perry	.02	.10
❑ 51 Lloyd Daniels	.02	.10
❑ 52 Dee Brown	.02	.10
❑ 53 Sean Elliott	.05	.15
❑ 54 Tim Hardaway	.15	.40
❑ 55 Christian Laettner	.05	.15
❑ 56 Bo Outlaw RC	.02	.10
❑ 57 Kevin Johnson	.05	.15
❑ 58 Duane Ferrell	.02	.10
❑ 59 Jo Jo English	.02	.10
❑ 60 Stanley Roberts	.02	.10
❑ 61 Kevin Willis	.02	.10
❑ 62 Dana Barros	.02	.10
❑ 63 Gheorghe Muresan	.02	.10
❑ 64 Vern Fleming	.02	.10
❑ 65 Anthony Peeler	.02	.10
❑ 66 Negele Knight	.02	.10
❑ 67 Harold Ellis	.02	.10
❑ 68 Vincent Askew	.02	.10
❑ 69 Ennis Whatley	.02	.10

❑ 70 Elden Campbell	.02	.10
❑ 71 Sherman Douglas	.02	.10
❑ 72 Luc Longley	.02	.10
❑ 73 Lorenzo Williams	.02	.10
❑ 74 Jay Humphries	.02	.10
❑ 75 Chris King	.02	.10
❑ 76 Tyrone Corbin	.02	.10
❑ 77 Bobby Hurley	.02	.10
❑ 78 Dell Curry	.02	.10
❑ 79 Dino Radja	.02	.10
❑ 80 A.C. Green	.05	.15
❑ 81 Craig Ehlo	.02	.10
❑ 82 Gary Payton	.25	.60
❑ 83 Sleepy Floyd	.02	.10
❑ 84 Rodney Rogers	.02	.10
❑ 85 Brian Shaw	.02	.10
❑ 86 Kevin Gamble	.02	.10
❑ 87 John Stockton	.15	.40
❑ 88 Hersey Hawkins	.05	.15
❑ 89 Johnny Newman	.02	.10
❑ 90 Larry Johnson	.05	.15
❑ 91 Robert Pack	.02	.10
❑ 92 Willie Burton	.02	.10
❑ 93 Bobby Phills	.02	.10
❑ 94 David Benoit	.02	.10
❑ 95 Harold Miner	.02	.10
❑ 96 David Robinson	.25	.60
❑ 97 Nate McMillan	.02	.10
❑ 98 Chris Mills	.05	.15
❑ 99 Hubert Davis	.02	.10
❑ 100 Shaquille O'Neal	.75	2.00
❑ 101 Loy Vaught	.02	.10
❑ 102 Kenny Smith	.02	.10
❑ 103 Terry Dehere	.02	.10
❑ 104 Carl Herrera	.02	.10
❑ 105 LaPhonso Ellis	.02	.10
❑ 106 Armon Gilliam	.02	.10
❑ 107 Greg Graham	.02	.10
❑ 108 Eric Murdock	.02	.10
❑ 109 Ron Harper	.05	.15
❑ 110 Andrew Lang	.02	.10
❑ 111 Johnny Dawkins	.02	.10
❑ 112 David Wingate	.02	.10
❑ 113 Tom Hammonds	.02	.10
❑ 114 Brad Daugherty	.02	.10
❑ 115 Charles Smith	.02	.10
❑ 116 Dale Ellis	.02	.10
❑ 117 Bryant Stith	.02	.10
❑ 118 Lindsey Hunter	.05	.15
❑ 119 Patrick Ewing	.15	.40
❑ 120 Kenny Anderson	.05	.15
❑ 121 Charles Barkley	.25	.60
❑ 122 Harvey Grant	.02	.10
❑ 123 Anthony Bowie	.02	.10
❑ 124 Shawn Kemp	.25	.60
❑ 125 Lee Mayberry	.02	.10
❑ 126 Reggie Miller	.15	.40
❑ 127 Scottie Pippen	.50	1.25
❑ 128 Spud Webb	.02	.10
❑ 129 Antonio Davis	.02	.10
❑ 130 Greg Anderson	.02	.10
❑ 131 Jim Jackson	.05	.15
❑ 132 Dikembe Mutombo	.05	.15
❑ 133 Terry Porter	.02	.10
❑ 134 Mario Elie	.02	.10
❑ 135 Vlade Divac	.02	.10
❑ 136 Robert Horry	.05	.15
❑ 137 Popeye Jones	.02	.10
❑ 138 Brad Lohaus	.02	.10
❑ 139 Anthony Bonner	.02	.10
❑ 140 Doug Christie	.05	.15
❑ 141 Rony Seikaly	.02	.10
❑ 142 Allan Houston	.25	.60
❑ 143 Tyrone Hill	.02	.10
❑ 144 Latrell Sprewell	.15	.40
❑ 145 Andres Guibert	.02	.10
❑ 146 Dominique Wilkins	.15	.40
❑ 147 Jon Barry	.02	.10
❑ 148 Tracy Murray	.02	.10
❑ 149 Mike Peplowski	.02	.10
❑ 150 Mike Brown	.02	.10
❑ 151 Cedric Ceballos	.02	.10
❑ 152 Stacey King	.02	.10
❑ 153 Trevor Wilson	.02	.10
❑ 154 Anthony Avent	.02	.10
❑ 155 Horace Grant	.05	.15
❑ 156 Bill Curley RC	.02	.10
❑ 157 Grant Hill RC	.75	2.00
❑ 158 Charlie Ward RC	.15	.40
❑ 159 Jalen Rose RC	.60	1.50
❑ 160 Jason Kidd RC	1.50	4.00
❑ 161 Yinka Dare RC	.02	.10
❑ 162 Eric Montross RC	.02	.10
❑ 163 Donyell Marshall RC	.15	.40
❑ 164 Tony Dumas RC	.02	.10
❑ 165 Wesley Person RC	.15	.40
❑ 166 Eddie Jones RC	.75	2.00
❑ 167 Tim Hardaway USA	.05	.15
❑ 168 Isiah Thomas USA	.05	.15
❑ 169 Joe Dumars USA	.05	.15
❑ 170 Mark Price USA	.02	.10
❑ 171 Derrick Coleman USA	.02	.10
❑ 172 Shawn Kemp USA	.15	.40
❑ 173 Steve Smith USA	.02	.10
❑ 174 Dan Majerle USA	.02	.10
❑ 175 Reggie Miller USA	.05	.15
❑ 176 Kevin Johnson USA	.02	.10
❑ 177 Dominique Wilkins USA	.05	.15
❑ 178 Shaquille O'Neal USA	.30	.75
❑ 179 Alonzo Mourning USA	.15	.40
❑ 180 Larry Johnson USA	.02	.10
❑ 181 Brian Grant DA	.05	.15
❑ 182 Darrin Hancock DA	.02	.10
❑ 183 Grant Hill DA	.30	.75
❑ 184 Jalen Rose DA	.05	.15
❑ 185 Lamond Murray DA	.02	.10
❑ 186 Jason Kidd DA	.60	1.50
❑ 187 Donyell Marshall DA	.05	.15
❑ 188 Eddie Jones DA	.40	1.00
❑ 189 Eric Montross DA	.02	.10
❑ 190 Khalid Reeves DA	.02	.10
❑ 191 Sharone Wright DA	.02	.10
❑ 192 Wesley Person DA	.05	.15
❑ 193 Glenn Robinson DA	.25	.60
❑ 194 Carlos Rogers DA	.02	.10
❑ 195 Aaron McKie DA	.05	.15
❑ 196 Juwan Howard DA	.30	.75
❑ 197 Charlie Ward DA	.05	.15
❑ 198 Brooks Thompson DA	.02	.10
❑ 199 Tony Massenburg	.02	.10
❑ 200 James Robinson	.02	.10
❑ 201 Dickey Simpkins RC	.02	.10
❑ 202 Johnny Dawkins	.02	.10
❑ 203 Joe Kleine	.02	.10
❑ 204 Bill Wennington	.02	.10
❑ 205 Sean Higgins	.02	.10
❑ 206 Larry Krystkowiak	.02	.10
❑ 207 Winston Garland	.02	.10
❑ 208 Muggsy Bogues	.05	.15
❑ 209 Charles Oakley	.02	.10
❑ 210 Vin Baker	.15	.40
❑ 211 Malik Sealy	.02	.10
❑ 212 Willie Anderson	.02	.10
❑ 213 Dale Davis	.02	.10
❑ 214 Grant Long	.02	.10
❑ 215 Danny Ainge	.02	.10
❑ 216 Toni Kukoc	.25	.60
❑ 217 Doug Smith	.02	.10
❑ 218 Danny Manning	.05	.15
❑ 219 Otis Thorpe	.02	.10
❑ 220 Mark Price	.02	.10
❑ 221 Victor Alexander	.02	.10
❑ 222 Brent Price	.02	.10
❑ 223 Howard Eisley RC	.02	.10
❑ 224 Chris Mullin	.15	.40
❑ 225 Nick Van Exel	.15	.40
❑ 226 Xavier McDaniel	.02	.10
❑ 227 Khalid Reeves RC	.02	.10
❑ 228 Anfernee Hardaway	.40	1.00
❑ 229 B.J.Tyler RC	.02	.10
❑ 230 Elmore Spencer	.02	.10
❑ 231 Rick Fox	.02	.10
❑ 232 Alonzo Mourning	.20	.50
❑ 233 Hakeem Olajuwon	.25	.60
❑ 234 Blue Edwards	.02	.10
❑ 235 P.J. Brown	.02	.10
❑ 236 Ron Harper	.05	.15
❑ 237 Isaiah Rider	.05	.15
❑ 238 Eric Mobley RC	.02	.10
❑ 239 Brian Williams	.02	.10
❑ 240 Eric Piatkowski RC	.02	.10
❑ 241 Karl Malone	.25	.60
❑ 242 Wayman Tisdale	.02	.10
❑ 243 Sarunas Marciulionis	.02	.10
❑ 244 Sean Rooks	.02	.10
❑ 245 Ricky Pierce	.02	.10
❑ 246 Don MacLean	.02	.10
❑ 247 Aaron McKie RC	.30	.75
❑ 248 Kenny Gattison	.02	.10
❑ 249 Derek Harper	.02	.10
❑ 250 Michael Smith RC	.02	.10
❑ 251 John Williams	.02	.10
❑ 252 Pooh Richardson	.02	.10
❑ 253 Sergei Bazarevich RC	.02	.10
❑ 254 Brian Grant RC	.40	1.00
❑ 255 Ed Pinckney	.02	.10
❑ 256 Ken Norman	.02	.10
❑ 257 Marty Conlon	.02	.10
❑ 258 Matt Fish	.02	.10
❑ 259 Darrin Hancock RC	.02	.10
❑ 260 Mahmoud Abdul-Rauf	.02	.10
❑ 261 Roy Tarpley	.02	.10
❑ 262 Chris Morris	.02	.10
❑ 263 Sharone Wright RC	.02	.10
❑ 264 Jamal Mashburn	.15	.40
❑ 265 John Starks	.02	.10
❑ 266 Rod Strickland	.05	.15
❑ 267 Adam Keefe	.02	.10
❑ 268 Scott Burrell	.02	.10
❑ 269 Eric Riley	.02	.10
❑ 270 Sam Perkins	.05	.15
❑ 271 Stacey Augmon	.02	.10
❑ 272 Kevin Willis	.02	.10
❑ 273 Lamond Murray RC	.05	.15
❑ 274 Derrick Coleman	.05	.15
❑ 275 Scott Skiles	.02	.10
❑ 276 Buck Williams	.02	.10
❑ 277 Sam Cassell	.15	.40
❑ 278 Rik Smits	.02	.10
❑ 279 Dennis Rodman	.30	.75
❑ 280 Olden Polynice	.02	.10
❑ 281 Glenn Robinson RC	.50	1.25
❑ 282 Clarence Weatherspoon	.02	.10
❑ 283 Monty Williams RC	.02	.10
❑ 284 Terry Mills	.02	.10
❑ 285 Oliver Miller	.02	.10
❑ 286 Dennis Scott	.02	.10
❑ 287 Micheal Williams	.02	.10
❑ 288 Moses Malone	.15	.40
❑ 289 Donald Royal	.02	.10
❑ 290 Mark Jackson	.02	.10
❑ 291 Walt Williams	.02	.10
❑ 292 Bimbo Coles	.02	.10
❑ 293 Derrick Alston RC	.02	.10
❑ 294 Scott Williams	.02	.10
❑ 295 Acie Earl	.02	.10
❑ 296 Jeff Hornacek	.05	.15
❑ 297 Kevin Duckworth	.02	.10
❑ 298 Dontonio Wingfield RC	.02	.10
❑ 299 Danny Ferry	.02	.10
❑ 300 Mark West	.02	.10
❑ 301 Jayson Williams	.05	.15
❑ 302 David Wesley	.02	.10
❑ 303 Jim McIlvaine RC	.02	.10
❑ 304 Michael Adams	.02	.10
❑ 305 Greg Minor RC	.02	.10
❑ 306 Jeff Malone	.02	.10
❑ 307 Pervis Ellison	.02	.10
❑ 308 Clifford Rozier RC	.02	.10
❑ 309 Billy Owens	.02	.10
❑ 310 Duane Causwell	.02	.10
❑ 311 Rex Chapman	.02	.10
❑ 312 Detlef Schrempf	.05	.15
❑ 313 Mitch Richmond	.15	.40
❑ 314 Carlos Rogers RC	.02	.10
❑ 315 Byron Scott	.05	.15
❑ 316 Dwayne Morton	.02	.10
❑ 317 Bill Cartwright	.02	.10
❑ 318 J.R. Reid	.02	.10
❑ 319 Derrick McKey	.02	.10
❑ 320 Jamie Watson RC	.02	.10
❑ 321 Mookie Blaylock	.02	.10
❑ 322 Chris Webber	.40	1.00
❑ 323 Joe Dumars	.15	.40
❑ 324 Shawn Bradley	.02	.10
❑ 325 Chuck Person	.02	.10
❑ 326 Haywoode Workman	.02	.10
❑ 327 Benoit Benjamin	.02	.10
❑ 328 Will Perdue	.02	.10
❑ 329 Sam Mitchell	.02	.10
❑ 330 George Lynch	.02	.10
❑ 331 Juwan Howard RC	.40	1.00
❑ 332 Robert Parish	.05	.15
❑ 333 Glen Rice	.05	.15
❑ 334 Michael Cage	.02	.10
❑ 335 Brooks Thompson RC	.02	.10
❑ 336 Rony Seikaly	.02	.10

❑ 337 Steve Kerr	.02	.10
❑ 338 Anthony Miller RC	.02	.10
❑ 339 Nick Anderson	.02	.10
❑ 340 Clifford Robinson	.05	.15
❑ 341 Todd Day	.02	.10
❑ 342 Jon Koncak	.02	.10
❑ 343 Felton Spencer	.02	.10
❑ 344 Willie Burton	.02	.10
❑ 345 Ledell Eackles	.02	.10
❑ 346 Anthony Mason	.05	.15
❑ 347 Derek Strong	.02	.10
❑ 348 Reggie Williams	.02	.10
❑ 349 Johnny Newman	.02	.10
❑ 350 Terry Cummings	.02	.10
❑ 351 Anthony Tucker RC	.02	.10
❑ 352 Junior Bridgeman TN	.02	.10
❑ 353 Jerry West TN	.15	.40
❑ 354 Harvey Catchings TN	.02	.10
❑ 355 John Lucas TN	.05	.15
❑ 356 Bill Bradley TN	.05	.15
❑ 357 Bill Walton TN	.05	.15
❑ 358 Don Nelson TN	.05	.15
❑ 359 Michael Jordan TN	1.00	2.50
❑ 360 Tom(Satch) Sanders TN	.02	.10

1995-96 Upper Deck

❑ COMPLETE SET (360)	25.00	50.00
❑ COMPLETE SERIES 1 (180)	10.00	20.00
❑ COMPLETE SERIES 2 (180)	15.00	30.00
❑ 1 Eddie Jones	.40	1.00
❑ 2 Hubert Davis	.08	.25
❑ 3 Latrell Sprewell	.30	.75
❑ 4 Stacey Augmon	.08	.25
❑ 5 Mario Elie	.08	.25
❑ 6 Tyrone Hill	.08	.25
❑ 7 Dikembe Mutombo	.20	.50
❑ 8 Antonio Davis	.08	.25
❑ 9 Horace Grant	.20	.50
❑ 10 Ken Norman	.08	.25
❑ 11 Aaron McKie	.20	.50
❑ 12 Vinny Del Negro	.08	.25
❑ 13 Glenn Robinson	.30	.75
❑ 14 Allan Houston	.20	.50
❑ 15 Bryon Russell	.08	.25
❑ 16 Tony Dumas	.08	.25
❑ 17 Gary Payton	.30	.75
❑ 18 Rik Smits	.20	.50
❑ 19 Dino Radja	.08	.25
❑ 20 Robert Pack	.08	.25
❑ 21 Calbert Cheaney	.08	.25
❑ 22 Clarence Weatherspoon	.08	.25
❑ 23 Michael Jordan	2.00	5.00
❑ 24 Felton Spencer	.08	.25
❑ 25 J.R. Reid	.08	.25
❑ 26 Cedric Ceballos	.08	.25
❑ 27 Dan Majerle	.20	.50
❑ 28 Donald Hodge	.08	.25
❑ 29 Nate McMillan	.08	.25
❑ 30 Bimbo Coles	.08	.25
❑ 31 Mitch Richmond	.20	.50
❑ 32 Scott Brooks	.08	.25
❑ 33 Patrick Ewing	.30	.75
❑ 34 Carl Herrera	.08	.25
❑ 35 Rick Fox	.20	.50
❑ 36 James Robinson	.08	.25
❑ 37 Donald Royal	.08	.25
❑ 38 Joe Dumars	.30	.75
❑ 39 Rony Seikaly	.08	.25
❑ 40 Dennis Rodman	.20	.50
❑ 41 Muggsy Bogues	.20	.50
❑ 42 Gheorghe Muresan	.08	.25
❑ 43 Ervin Johnson	.08	.25
❑ 44 Todd Day	.08	.25
❑ 45 Rex Walters	.08	.25
❑ 46 Terrell Brandon	.20	.50
❑ 47 Wesley Person	.08	.25

❑ 48 Terry Dehere	.08	.25
❑ 49 Steve Smith	.20	.50
❑ 50 Brian Grant	.30	.75
❑ 51 Eric Piatkowski	.20	.50
❑ 52 Lindsey Hunter	.08	.25
❑ 53 Chris Webber	.30	.75
❑ 54 Antoine Carr	.08	.25
❑ 55 Chris Dudley	.08	.25
❑ 56 Clyde Drexler	.30	.75
❑ 57 P.J. Brown	.08	.25
❑ 58 Kevin Willis	.20	.50
❑ 59 Jeff Turner	.08	.25
❑ 60 Sean Elliott	.20	.50
❑ 61 Kevin Johnson	.20	.50
❑ 62 Scott Skiles	.08	.25
❑ 63 Charles Smith	.08	.25
❑ 64 Derrick McKey	.08	.25
❑ 65 Danny Ferry	.08	.25
❑ 66 Detlef Schrempf	.20	.50
❑ 67 Shawn Bradley	.08	.25
❑ 68 Isaiah Rider	.08	.25
❑ 69 Karl Malone	.40	1.00
❑ 70 Will Perdue	.08	.25
❑ 71 Terry Mills	.08	.25
❑ 72 Glen Rice	.20	.50
❑ 73 Tim Breaux	.08	.25
❑ 74 Malik Sealy	.08	.25
❑ 75 Walt Williams	.08	.25
❑ 76 Bobby Phills	.08	.25
❑ 77 Anthony Avent	.08	.25
❑ 78 Jamal Mashburn	.20	.50
❑ 79 Vlade Divac	.20	.50
❑ 80 Reggie Williams	.08	.25
❑ 81 Xavier McDaniel	.08	.25
❑ 82 Avery Johnson	.08	.25
❑ 83 Derek Harper	.20	.50
❑ 84 Don MacLean	.08	.25
❑ 85 Tom Gugliotta	.08	.25
❑ 86 Craig Ehlo	.08	.25
❑ 87 Robert Horry	.20	.50
❑ 88 Kevin Edwards	.08	.25
❑ 89 Chuck Person	.08	.25
❑ 90 Sharone Wright	.08	.25
❑ 91 Steve Kerr	.20	.50
❑ 92 Marty Conlon	.08	.25
❑ 93 Jalen Rose	.40	1.00
❑ 94 Bryant Reeves RC	.30	.75
❑ 95 Shaquille O'Neal	.75	2.00
❑ 96 David Wesley	.08	.25
❑ 97 Chris Mills	.08	.25
❑ 98 Rod Strickland	.08	.25
❑ 99 Pooh Richardson	.08	.25
❑ 100 Sam Perkins	.20	.50
❑ 101 Dell Curry	.08	.25
❑ 102 David Benoit	.08	.25
❑ 103 Christian Laettner	.20	.50
❑ 104 Duane Causwell	.08	.25
❑ 105 Jason Kidd	1.00	2.50
❑ 106 Mark West	.08	.25
❑ 107 Lee Mayberry	.08	.25
❑ 108 John Salley	.08	.25
❑ 109 Jeff Malone	.08	.25
❑ 110 George Zidek RC	.08	.25
❑ 111 Kenny Smith	.08	.25
❑ 112 George Lynch	.08	.25
❑ 113 Toni Kukoc	.20	.50
❑ 114 A.C. Green	.20	.50
❑ 115 Kenny Anderson	.20	.50
❑ 116 Robert Parish	.20	.50
❑ 117 Chris Mullin	.30	.75
❑ 118 Loy Vaught	.08	.25
❑ 119 Olden Polynice	.08	.25
❑ 120 Clifford Robinson	.08	.25
❑ 121 Eric Mobley	.08	.25
❑ 122 Doug West	.08	.25
❑ 123 Sam Cassell	.30	.75
❑ 124 Nick Anderson	.08	.25
❑ 125 Matt Geiger	.08	.25
❑ 126 Elden Campbell	.08	.25
❑ 127 Alonzo Mourning	.20	.50
❑ 128 Bryant Stith	.08	.25
❑ 129 Mark Jackson	.20	.50
❑ 130 Cherokee Parks RC	.08	.25
❑ 131 Shawn Respert RC	.08	.25
❑ 132 Alan Henderson RC	.30	.75
❑ 133 Jerry Stackhouse RC	1.00	2.50
❑ 134 Rasheed Wallace RC	.75	2.00
❑ 135 Antonio McDyess RC	.60	1.50
❑ 136 Charles Barkley ROO	.30	.75

❑ 137 Michael Jordan ROO	1.00	2.50
❑ 138 Hakeem Olajuwon ROO	.20	.50
❑ 139 Joe Dumars ROO	.20	.50
❑ 140 Patrick Ewing ROO	.20	.50
❑ 141 A.C. Green ROO	.08	.25
❑ 142 Karl Malone ROO	.30	.75
❑ 143 Detlef Schrempf ROO	.08	.25
❑ 144 Chuck Person ROO	.08	.25
❑ 145 Muggsy Bogues ROO	.08	.25
❑ 146 Horace Grant ROO	.08	.25
❑ 147 Mark Jackson ROO	.08	.25
❑ 148 Kevin Johnson ROO	.08	.25
❑ 149 Mitch Richmond ROO	.08	.25
❑ 150 Rik Smits ROO	.08	.25
❑ 151 Nick Anderson ROO	.08	.25
❑ 152 Tim Hardaway ROO	.08	.25
❑ 153 Shawn Kemp ROO	.08	.25
❑ 154 David Robinson ROO	.20	.50
❑ 155 Jason Kidd ART	.50	1.25
❑ 156 Grant Hill ART	.30	.75
❑ 157 Glenn Robinson ART	.20	.50
❑ 158 Eddie Jones ART	.30	.75
❑ 159 Brian Grant ART	.20	.50
❑ 160 Juwan Howard ART	.20	.50
❑ 161 Eric Montross ART	.08	.25
❑ 162 Wesley Person ART	.08	.25
❑ 163 Jalen Rose ART	.30	.75
❑ 164 Donyell Marshall ART	.20	.50
❑ 165 Sharone Wright ART	.08	.25
❑ 166 Karl Malone AN	.30	.75
❑ 167 Scottie Pippen AN	.20	.50
❑ 168 David Robinson AN	.20	.50
❑ 169 John Stockton AN	.30	.75
❑ 170 Anfernee Hardaway AN	.20	.50
❑ 171 Charles Barkley AN	.30	.75
❑ 172 Shawn Kemp AN	.08	.25
❑ 173 Shaquille O'Neal AN	.30	.75
❑ 174 Gary Payton AN	.20	.50
❑ 175 Mitch Richmond AN	.08	.25
❑ 176 Dennis Rodman AN	.08	.25
❑ 177 Detlef Schrempf AN	.08	.25
❑ 178 Hakeem Olajuwon AN	.20	.50
❑ 179 Reggie Miller AN	.20	.50
❑ 180 Clyde Drexler AN	.20	.50
❑ 181 Hakeem Olajuwon	.30	.75
❑ 182 Vin Baker	.20	.50
❑ 183 Jeff Hornacek	.20	.50
❑ 184 Popeye Jones	.08	.25
❑ 185 Sedale Threatt	.08	.25
❑ 186 Scottie Pippen	.50	1.25
❑ 187 Terry Porter	.08	.25
❑ 188 Dan Majerle	.20	.50
❑ 189 Clifford Rozier	.08	.25
❑ 190 Greg Minor	.08	.25
❑ 191 Dennis Scott	.08	.25
❑ 192 Hersey Hawkins	.08	.25
❑ 193 Chris Gatling	.08	.25
❑ 194 Charles Oakley	.08	.25
❑ 195 Dale Davis	.08	.25
❑ 196 Robert Pack	.08	.25
❑ 197 Lamond Murray	.08	.25
❑ 198 Mookie Blaylock	.08	.25
❑ 199 Dickey Simpkins	.08	.25
❑ 200 Kevin Gamble	.08	.25
❑ 201 Lorenzo Williams	.08	.25
❑ 202 Scott Burrell	.08	.25
❑ 203 Armon Gilliam	.08	.25
❑ 204 Doc Rivers	.20	.50
❑ 205 Blue Edwards	.08	.25
❑ 206 Billy Owens	.08	.25
❑ 207 Juwan Howard	.30	.75
❑ 208 Harvey Grant	.08	.25
❑ 209 Richard Dumas	.08	.25
❑ 210 Anthony Peeler	.08	.25
❑ 211 Matt Geiger	.08	.25
❑ 212 Lucious Harris	.08	.25
❑ 213 Grant Long	.08	.25
❑ 214 Sasha Danilovic RC	.08	.25
❑ 215 Chris Morris	.08	.25
❑ 216 Donyell Marshall	.20	.50
❑ 217 Alonzo Mourning	.20	.50
❑ 218 John Stockton	.40	1.00
❑ 219 Khalid Reeves	.08	.25
❑ 220 Mahmoud Abdul-Rauf	.08	.25
❑ 221 Sean Rooks	.08	.25
❑ 222 Shawn Kemp	.20	.50
❑ 223 John Williams	.08	.25
❑ 224 Dee Brown	.08	.25
❑ 225 Jim Jackson	.08	.25

❑ 226 Harold Miner	.08	.25
❑ 227 B.J. Armstrong	.08	.25
❑ 228 Elliot Perry	.08	.25
❑ 229 Anthony Miller	.08	.25
❑ 230 Donny Marshall RC	.08	.25
❑ 231 Tyrone Corbin	.08	.25
❑ 232 Anthony Mason	.20	.50
❑ 233 Grant Hill	.40	1.00
❑ 234 Buck Williams	.08	.25
❑ 235 Brian Shaw	.08	.25
❑ 236 Dale Ellis	.08	.25
❑ 237 Magic Johnson	.50	1.25
❑ 238 Eric Montross	.08	.25
❑ 239 Rex Chapman	.08	.25
❑ 240 Otis Thorpe	.08	.25
❑ 241 Tracy Murray	.08	.25
❑ 242 Sarunas Marciulionis	.08	.25
❑ 243 Luc Longley	.08	.25
❑ 244 Elmore Spencer	.08	.25
❑ 245 Terry Cummings	.08	.25
❑ 246 Sam Mitchell	.08	.25
❑ 247 Terrence Rencher RC	.08	.25
❑ 248 Byron Houston	.08	.25
❑ 249 Pervis Ellison	.08	.25
❑ 250 Carlos Rogers	.08	.25
❑ 251 Kendall Gill	.08	.25
❑ 252 Sherrell Ford RC	.08	.25
❑ 253 Michael Finley RC	1.25	3.00
❑ 254 Kurt Thomas RC	.20	.50
❑ 255 Joe Smith RC	.50	1.25
❑ 256 Bobby Hurley	.08	.25
❑ 257 Greg Anthony	.08	.25
❑ 258 Willie Anderson	.08	.25
❑ 259 Theo Ratliff RC	.40	1.00
❑ 260 Duane Ferrell	.08	.25
❑ 261 Antonio Harvey	.08	.25
❑ 262 Gary Grant	.08	.25
❑ 263 Brian Williams	.08	.25
❑ 264 Danny Manning	.20	.50
❑ 265 Micheal Williams	.08	.25
❑ 266 Dennis Rodman	.20	.50
❑ 267 Arvydas Sabonis RC	.40	1.00
❑ 268 Don MacLean	.08	.25
❑ 269 Keith Askins	.08	.25
❑ 270 Reggie Miller	.30	.75
❑ 271 Ed Pinckney	.08	.25
❑ 272 Bob Sura RC	.20	.50
❑ 273 Kevin Garnett RC	2.50	6.00
❑ 274 Byron Scott	.08	.25
❑ 275 Mario Bennett RC	.08	.25
❑ 276 Junior Burrough RC	.08	.25
❑ 277 Anfernee Hardaway	.30	.75
❑ 278 George McCloud	.08	.25
❑ 279 Loren Meyer RC	.08	.25
❑ 280 Ed O'Bannon RC	.08	.25
❑ 281 Lawrence Moten RC	.08	.25
❑ 282 Dana Barros	.08	.25
❑ 283 Damon Stoudamire RC	.60	1.50
❑ 284 Eric Williams RC	.20	.50
❑ 285 Wayman Tisdale	.08	.25
❑ 286 Rodney Rogers	.08	.25
❑ 287 Sherman Douglas	.08	.25
❑ 288 Greg Ostertag RC	.08	.25
❑ 289 Alvin Robertson	.08	.25
❑ 290 Tim Legler	.08	.25
❑ 291 Zan Tabak	.08	.25
❑ 292 Gary Trent RC	.08	.25
❑ 293 Haywoode Workman	.08	.25
❑ 294 Charles Barkley	.40	1.00
❑ 295 Derrick Coleman	.08	.25
❑ 296 Ricky Pierce	.08	.25
❑ 297 Benoit Benjamin	.08	.25
❑ 298 Larry Johnson	.20	.50
❑ 299 Travis Best RC	.08	.25
❑ 300 Jason Caffey RC	.20	.50
❑ 301 Cory Alexander RC	.08	.25
❑ 302 Nick Van Exel	.30	.75
❑ 303 Corliss Williamson RC	.30	.75
❑ 304 Eric Murdock	.08	.25
❑ 305 Tyus Edney RC	.08	.25
❑ 306 Lou Roe RC	.08	.25
❑ 307 John Salley	.08	.25
❑ 308 Spud Webb	.20	.50
❑ 309 Brent Barry RC	.30	.75
❑ 310 David Robinson	.30	.75
❑ 311 Glen Rice	.20	.50
❑ 312 Chris King	.08	.25
❑ 313 David Vaughn RC	.08	.25
❑ 314 Kenny Gattison	.08	.25
❑ 315 Randolph Childress RC	.08	.25
❑ 316 Anfernee Hardaway USA	.20	.50
❑ 317 Grant Hill USA	.30	.75
❑ 318 Karl Malone USA	.30	.75
❑ 319 Reggie Miller USA	.20	.50
❑ 320 Hakeem Olajuwon USA	.20	.50
❑ 321 Shaquille O'Neal USA	.30	.75
❑ 322 Scottie Pippen USA	.20	.50
❑ 323 David Robinson USA	.20	.50
❑ 324 Glenn Robinson USA	.20	.50
❑ 325 John Stockton USA	.30	.75
❑ 326 Cedric Ceballos I95	.08	.25
❑ 327 Shaquille O'Neal I95	.30	.75
❑ 328 Glenn Robinson I95	.20	.50
❑ 329 Shawn Kemp I95	.08	.25
❑ 330 Nick Anderson I95	.08	.25
❑ 331 Shawn Bradley I95	.08	.25
❑ 332 Orlando's Magic I95	.08	.25
❑ 333 1995 NBA Finals I95	.20	.50
❑ 334 NBA Expansion I95	.08	.25
❑ 335 Michael Jordan I95	1.00	2.50
❑ 336 N.Van Exel/D.Cannon MA	.08	.25
❑ 337 M.Jordan/D.Hanson MA	.50	1.25
❑ 338 S.Pippen/J.Von Oy MA	.30	.75
❑ 339 M.Jordan/C.Sheen MA	.50	1.25
❑ 340 J.Kidd/C.Reid MA	.30	.75
❑ 341 M.Jordan/Q.Latifah MA	.50	1.25
❑ 342 C.Barkley/D.Johnson MA	.30	.75
❑ 343 Olajuwon/C.Bernsen MA	.30	.75
❑ 344 Ahmad Rashad MA	.08	.25
❑ 345 Willow Bay MA	.08	.25
❑ 346 Mark Curry MA	.30	.75
❑ 347 Horace Grant SJ	.08	.25
❑ 348 Juwan Howard SJ	.20	.50
❑ 349 David Robinson SJ	.20	.50
❑ 350 Reggie Miller SJ	.20	.50
❑ 351 Brian Grant SJ	.20	.50
❑ 352 Michael Jordan SJ	1.00	2.50
❑ 353 Cedric Ceballos SJ	.08	.25
❑ 354 Blue Edwards SJ	.08	.25
❑ 355 Acie Earl SJ	.08	.25
❑ 356 Dennis Rodman SJ	.08	.25
❑ 357 Shawn Kemp SJ	.08	.25
❑ 358 Jerry Stackhouse SJ	.50	1.25
❑ 359 Jamal Mashburn SJ	.08	.25
❑ 360 Antonio McDyess SJ	.30	.75

1996-97 Upper Deck

❑ COMPLETE SET (360)	25.00	50.00
❑ COMPLETE SERIES 1 (180)	15.00	30.00
❑ COMPLETE SERIES 2 (180)	10.00	20.00
❑ 1 Mookie Blaylock	.08	.25
❑ 2 Alan Henderson	.08	.25
❑ 3 Christian Laettner	.20	.50
❑ 4 Ken Norman	.08	.25
❑ 5 Dee Brown	.08	.25
❑ 6 Todd Day	.08	.25
❑ 7 Rick Fox	.08	.25
❑ 8 Dino Radja	.08	.25
❑ 9 Dana Barros	.08	.25
❑ 10 Eric Williams	.08	.25
❑ 11 Scott Burrell	.08	.25
❑ 12 Dell Curry	.08	.25
❑ 13 Matt Geiger	.08	.25
❑ 14 Glen Rice	.20	.50
❑ 15 Ron Harper	.20	.50
❑ 16 Michael Jordan	2.00	5.00
❑ 17 Luc Longley	.08	.25
❑ 18 Toni Kukoc	.20	.50
❑ 19 Dennis Rodman	.20	.50
❑ 20 Danny Ferry	.08	.25
❑ 21 Tyrone Hill	.08	.25
❑ 22 Bobby Phills	.08	.25
❑ 23 Bob Sura	.08	.25
❑ 24 Tony Dumas	.08	.25
❑ 25 George McCloud	.08	.25
❑ 26 Jim Jackson	.08	.25
❑ 27 Jamal Mashburn	.20	.50
❑ 28 Loren Meyer	.08	.25
❑ 29 Dale Ellis	.08	.25
❑ 30 LaPhonso Ellis	.08	.25
❑ 31 Tom Hammonds	.08	.25
❑ 32 Antonio McDyess	.20	.50
❑ 33 Joe Dumars	.30	.75
❑ 34 Grant Hill	.30	.75
❑ 35 Lindsey Hunter	.08	.25
❑ 36 Terry Mills	.08	.25
❑ 37 Theo Ratliff	.20	.50
❑ 38 B.J. Armstrong	.08	.25
❑ 39 Donyell Marshall	.20	.50
❑ 40 Chris Mullin	.30	.75
❑ 41 Rony Seikaly	.08	.25
❑ 42 Joe Smith	.20	.50
❑ 43 Sam Cassell	.30	.75
❑ 44 Clyde Drexler	.30	.75
❑ 45 Mario Elie	.08	.25
❑ 46 Robert Horry	.20	.50
❑ 47 Travis Best	.08	.25
❑ 48 Antonio Davis	.08	.25
❑ 49 Dale Davis	.08	.25
❑ 50 Eddie Johnson	.08	.25
❑ 51 Derrick McKey	.08	.25
❑ 52 Reggie Miller	.30	.75
❑ 53 Brent Barry	.08	.25
❑ 54 Lamond Murray	.08	.25
❑ 55 Eric Piatkowski	.20	.50
❑ 56 Rodney Rogers	.08	.25
❑ 57 Loy Vaught	.08	.25
❑ 58 Kobe Bryant RC	6.00	15.00
❑ 59 Eddie Jones	.30	.75
❑ 60 Elden Campbell	.08	.25
❑ 61 Shaquille O'Neal	.75	2.00
❑ 62 Nick Van Exel	.30	.75
❑ 63 Keith Askins	.08	.25
❑ 64 Rex Chapman	.08	.25
❑ 65 Sasha Danilovic	.08	.25
❑ 66 Alonzo Mourning	.20	.50
❑ 67 Kurt Thomas	.20	.50
❑ 68 Tim Hardaway	.20	.50
❑ 69 Ray Allen RC	1.00	2.50
❑ 70 Johnny Newman	.08	.25
❑ 71 Shawn Respert	.08	.25
❑ 72 Glenn Robinson	.30	.75
❑ 73 Tom Gugliotta	.08	.25
❑ 74 Stephon Marbury RC	.60	1.50
❑ 75 Terry Porter	.08	.25
❑ 76 Doug West	.08	.25
❑ 77 Shawn Bradley	.08	.25
❑ 78 Kevin Edwards	.08	.25
❑ 79 Vern Fleming	.08	.25
❑ 80 Ed O'Bannon	.08	.25
❑ 81 Jayson Williams	.20	.50
❑ 82 John Starks	.20	.50
❑ 83 Patrick Ewing	.30	.75
❑ 84 Charlie Ward	.08	.25
❑ 85 Nick Anderson	.08	.25
❑ 86 Anfernee Hardaway	.30	.75
❑ 87 Jon Koncak	.08	.25
❑ 88 Donald Royal	.08	.25
❑ 89 Brian Shaw	.08	.25
❑ 90 Derrick Coleman	.20	.50
❑ 91 Allen Iverson RC	1.25	3.00
❑ 92 Jerry Stackhouse	.40	1.00
❑ 93 Clarence Weatherspoon	.08	.25
❑ 94 Charles Barkley	.40	1.00
❑ 95 Kevin Johnson	.20	.50
❑ 96 Danny Manning	.20	.50
❑ 97 Elliot Perry	.08	.25
❑ 98 Wayman Tisdale	.08	.25
❑ 99 Randolph Childress	.08	.25
❑ 100 Aaron McKie	.20	.50
❑ 101 Arvydas Sabonis	.20	.50
❑ 102 Gary Trent	.08	.25
❑ 103 Chris Dudley	.08	.25
❑ 104 Tyus Edney	.08	.25
❑ 105 Brian Grant	.30	.75
❑ 106 Bobby Hurley	.08	.25
❑ 107 Olden Polynice	.08	.25
❑ 108 Corliss Williamson	.20	.50
❑ 109 Vinny Del Negro	.08	.25
❑ 110 Avery Johnson	.08	.25
❑ 111 Will Perdue	.08	.25
❑ 112 David Robinson	.30	.75
❑ 113 Hersey Hawkins	.20	.50
❑ 114 Shawn Kemp	.20	.50

❑ 115 Nate McMillan	.08	.25
❑ 116 Detlef Schrempf	.20	.50
❑ 117 Gary Payton	.30	.75
❑ 118 Marcus Camby RC	.40	1.00
❑ 119 Zan Tabak	.08	.25
❑ 120 Damon Stoudamire	.30	.75
❑ 121 Carlos Rogers	.08	.25
❑ 122 Sharone Wright	.08	.25
❑ 123 Antoine Carr	.08	.25
❑ 124 Jeff Hornacek	.20	.50
❑ 125 Adam Keefe	.08	.25
❑ 126 Chris Morris	.08	.25
❑ 127 John Stockton	.30	.75
❑ 128 Blue Edwards	.08	.25
❑ 129 Shareef Abdur-Rahim RC	1.00	2.50
❑ 130 Bryant Reeves	.08	.25
❑ 131 Roy Rogers RC	.08	.25
❑ 132 Calbert Cheaney	.08	.25
❑ 133 Tim Legler	.08	.25
❑ 134 Gheorghe Muresan	.08	.25
❑ 135 Chris Webber	.30	.75
❑ 136 Mutombo/Blaylock/Smith BW	.30	.75
❑ 137 Barros/Radja/Williams BW	.08	.25
❑ 138 Rice/Geiger/Divac BW	.30	.75
❑ 139 Jordan/Pip/Rodman BW	.75	2.00
❑ 140 Brandon/Ferry/Hill BW	.20	.50
❑ 141 Kidd/Mash/Jackson BW	.20	.50
❑ 142 L.Ellis/McDyess/Jackson BW	.08	.25
❑ 143 Dumars/Hill/Augmon BW	.30	.75
❑ 144 Smith/Sprewell/Mullin BW	.30	.75
❑ 145 Olaj/Drexler/Barkley BW	.30	.75
❑ 146 R.Miller/Best/Smits BW	.20	.50
❑ 147 B.Barry/Murray/Rogers BW	.08	.25
❑ 148 O'Neal/Jones/Bryant BW	.60	1.50
❑ 149 ZO/Hardaway/Danilovic BW	.30	.75
❑ 150 Baker/Robinson/Douglas BW	.30	.75
❑ 151 Garnett/Gug/Parks BW	.30	.75
❑ 152 Bradley/Gill/O'Bannon BW	.20	.50
❑ 153 Ewing/Houston/L.Johnson BW	.30	.75
❑ 154 Hardaway/Scott/Grant BW	.20	.50
❑ 155 Stack/W'spoon/Cole BW	.20	.50
❑ 156 K.Johnson/Manning/Finley BW	.20	.50
❑ 157 Robinson/Rider/Sabonis BW	.20	.50
❑ 158 Richmond/Grant/Owens BW	.20	.50
❑ 159 D.Rob/Elliott/Johnson BW	.30	.75
❑ 160 Kemp/Payton/Schrem BW	.20	.50
❑ 161 Stoud/Tabak/Wright BW	.30	.75
❑ 162 Stockton/Malone/Hornacek BW	.30	.75
❑ 163 Reeves/Rahim/Edwards BW	.30	.75
❑ 164 Howard/Muresan/Web BW	.30	.75
❑ 165 Michael Jordan GP	1.00	2.50
❑ 166 Corliss Williamson GP	.08	.25
❑ 167 Dell Curry GP	.08	.25
❑ 168 John Starks GP	.08	.25
❑ 169 Dennis Rodman GP	.08	.25
❑ 170 C.Webber/L.Sprewell GP	.30	.75
❑ 171 Cedric Ceballos GP	.08	.25
❑ 172 Theo Ratliff GP	.08	.25
❑ 173 Anfernee Hardaway GP	.20	.50
❑ 174 Grant Hill GP	.30	.75
❑ 175 Alonzo Mourning GP	.08	.25
❑ 176 Shawn Kemp GP	.08	.25
❑ 177 Jason Kidd GP	.30	.75
❑ 178 Avery Johnson GP	.08	.25
❑ 179 Gary Payton GP	.20	.50
❑ 180 Michael Jordan CL	.08	.25
❑ 181 Priest Lauderdale RC	.08	.25
❑ 182 Dikembe Mutombo	.20	.50
❑ 183 Eldridge Recasner RC	.08	.25
❑ 184 Steve Smith	.20	.50
❑ 185 Pervis Ellison	.08	.25
❑ 186 Greg Minor	.08	.25
❑ 187 Antoine Walker RC	.75	2.00
❑ 188 David Wesley	.08	.25
❑ 189 Muggsy Bogues	.08	.25
❑ 190 Tony Delk RC	.30	.75
❑ 191 Vlade Divac	.08	.25
❑ 192 Anthony Mason	.20	.50
❑ 193 George Zidek	.08	.25
❑ 194 Jason Caffey	.08	.25
❑ 195 Steve Kerr	.20	.50
❑ 196 Robert Parish	.20	.50
❑ 197 Scottie Pippen	.50	1.25
❑ 198 Terrell Brandon	.20	.50
❑ 199 Antonio Lang	.08	.25
❑ 200 Chris Mills	.08	.25
❑ 201 Vitaly Potapenko RC	.08	.25
❑ 202 Mark West	.08	.25
❑ 203 Chris Gatling	.08	.25

❑ 204 Derek Harper	.08	.25
❑ 205 Sam Cassell	.30	.75
❑ 206 Eric Montross	.08	.25
❑ 207 Samaki Walker RC	.08	.25
❑ 208 Mark Jackson	.08	.25
❑ 209 Ervin Johnson	.08	.25
❑ 210 Sarunas Marciulionis	.08	.25
❑ 211 Ricky Pierce	.08	.25
❑ 212 Bryant Stith	.08	.25
❑ 213 Stacey Augmon	.08	.25
❑ 214 Grant Long	.08	.25
❑ 215 Rick Mahorn	.08	.25
❑ 216 Otis Thorpe	.08	.25
❑ 217 Jerome Williams RC	.30	.75
❑ 218 Bimbo Coles	.08	.25
❑ 219 Todd Fuller RC	.08	.25
❑ 220 Mark Price	.20	.50
❑ 221 Felton Spencer	.08	.25
❑ 222 Latrell Sprewell	.30	.75
❑ 223 Charles Barkley	.40	1.00
❑ 224 Othella Harrington RC	.30	.75
❑ 225 Hakeem Olajuwon	.30	.75
❑ 226 Matt Maloney RC	.20	.50
❑ 227 Kevin Willis	.08	.25
❑ 228 Erick Dampier RC	.30	.75
❑ 229 Duane Ferrell	.08	.25
❑ 230 Jalen Rose	.30	.75
❑ 231 Rik Smits	.20	.50
❑ 232 Terry Dehere	.08	.25
❑ 233 Bo Outlaw	.08	.25
❑ 234 Pooh Richardson	.08	.25
❑ 235 Malik Sealy	.08	.25
❑ 236 Lorenzen Wright RC	.20	.50
❑ 237 Cedric Ceballos	.08	.25
❑ 238 Derek Fisher RC	.50	1.25
❑ 239 Travis Knight RC	.08	.25
❑ 240 Sean Rooks	.08	.25
❑ 241 Byron Scott	.08	.25
❑ 242 P.J. Brown	.08	.25
❑ 243 Voshon Lenard RC	.20	.50
❑ 244 Dan Majerle	.20	.50
❑ 245 Martin Muursepp RC	.08	.25
❑ 246 Gary Grant	.08	.25
❑ 247 Vin Baker	.20	.50
❑ 248 Armon Gilliam	.08	.25
❑ 249 Andrew Lang	.08	.25
❑ 250 Elliot Perry	.08	.25
❑ 251 Kevin Garnett	.60	1.50
❑ 252 Shane Heal RC	.08	.25
❑ 253 Cherokee Parks	.08	.25
❑ 254 Stojko Vrankovic	.08	.25
❑ 255 Kendall Gill	.08	.25
❑ 256 Kerry Kittles RC	.30	.75
❑ 257 Xavier McDaniel	.08	.25
❑ 258 Robert Pack	.08	.25
❑ 259 Chris Childs	.08	.25
❑ 260 Allan Houston	.20	.50
❑ 261 Larry Johnson	.20	.50
❑ 262 Dontae' Jones RC	.08	.25
❑ 263 Walter McCarty RC	.08	.25
❑ 264 Charles Oakley	.08	.25
❑ 265 John Wallace RC	.30	.75
❑ 266 Buck Williams	.08	.25
❑ 267 Brian Evans RC	.08	.25
❑ 268 Horace Grant	.20	.50
❑ 269 Dennis Scott	.08	.25
❑ 270 Rony Seikaly	.08	.25
❑ 271 David Vaughn	.08	.25
❑ 272 Michael Cage	.08	.25
❑ 273 Lucious Harris	.08	.25
❑ 274 Don MacLean	.08	.25
❑ 275 Mark Davis	.08	.25
❑ 276 Jason Kidd	.50	1.25
❑ 277 Michael Finley	.40	1.00
❑ 278 A.C. Green	.20	.50
❑ 279 Robert Horry	.20	.50
❑ 280 Steve Nash RC	2.00	5.00
❑ 281 Wesley Person	.08	.25
❑ 282 Kenny Anderson	.08	.25
❑ 283 Aleksandar Djordjevic RC	.08	.25
❑ 284 Jermaine O'Neal RC	.75	2.00
❑ 285 Isaiah Rider	.20	.50
❑ 286 Clifford Robinson	.08	.25
❑ 287 Rasheed Wallace	.40	1.00
❑ 288 Mahmoud Abdul-Rauf	.08	.25
❑ 289 Billy Owens	.08	.25
❑ 290 Mitch Richmond	.20	.50
❑ 291 Michael Smith	.08	.25
❑ 292 Cory Alexander	.08	.25

❑ 293 Sean Elliott	.20	.50
❑ 294 Vernon Maxwell	.08	.25
❑ 295 Dominique Wilkins	.30	.75
❑ 296 Craig Ehlo	.08	.25
❑ 297 Jim McIlvaine	.08	.25
❑ 298 Sam Perkins	.20	.50
❑ 299 Steve Scheffler RC	.08	.25
❑ 300 Hubert Davis	.08	.25
❑ 301 Popeye Jones	.08	.25
❑ 302 Donald Whiteside RC	.08	.25
❑ 303 Walt Williams	.08	.25
❑ 304 Karl Malone	.30	.75
❑ 305 Greg Ostertag	.08	.25
❑ 306 Bryon Russell	.08	.25
❑ 307 Jamie Watson	.08	.25
❑ 308 Greg Anthony	.08	.25
❑ 309 George Lynch	.08	.25
❑ 310 Lawrence Moten	.08	.25
❑ 311 Anthony Peeler	.08	.25
❑ 312 Juwan Howard	.20	.50
❑ 313 Tracy Murray	.08	.25
❑ 314 Rod Strickland	.08	.25
❑ 315 Harvey Grant	.08	.25
❑ 316 Charles Barkley DN	.30	.75
❑ 317 Clyde Drexler DN	.20	.50
❑ 318 Dikembe Mutombo DN	.08	.25
❑ 319 Larry Johnson DN	.08	.25
❑ 320 Shaquille O'Neal DN	.30	.75
❑ 321 Mookie Blaylock DN	.08	.25
❑ 322 Tim Hardaway DN	.08	.25
❑ 323 Dennis Rodman DN	.08	.25
❑ 324 Dan Majerle DN	.08	.25
❑ 325 Stacey Augmon DN	.08	.25
❑ 326 Anthony Mason DN	.08	.25
❑ 327 Kenny Anderson DN	.08	.25
❑ 328 Mahmoud Abdul-Rauf DN	.08	.25
❑ 329 Chris Webber DN	.30	.75
❑ 330 Dominique Wilkins DN	.20	.50
❑ 331 Dikembe Mutombo WD	.08	.25
❑ 332 Dana Barros WD	.08	.25
❑ 333 Glen Rice WD	.08	.25
❑ 334 Dennis Rodman WD	.08	.25
❑ 335 Terrell Brandon WD	.08	.25
❑ 336 Jason Kidd WD	.30	.75
❑ 337 Antonio McDyess WD	.20	.50
❑ 338 Grant Hill WD	.30	.75
❑ 339 Joe Smith WD	.08	.25
❑ 340 Charles Barkley WD	.30	.75
❑ 341 Reggie Miller WD	.20	.50
❑ 342 Brent Barry WD	.08	.25
❑ 343 Shaquille O'Neal WD	.30	.75
❑ 344 Alonzo Mourning WD	.08	.25
❑ 345 Glenn Robinson WD	.20	.50
❑ 346 Stephon Marbury WD	.50	1.25
❑ 347 Kerry Kittles WD	.30	.75
❑ 348 Patrick Ewing WD	.20	.50
❑ 349 Anfernee Hardaway WD	.20	.50
❑ 350 Allen Iverson WD	.50	1.25
❑ 351 Danny Manning WD	.08	.25
❑ 352 Arvydas Sabonis WD	.08	.25
❑ 353 Mitch Richmond WD	.08	.25
❑ 354 David Robinson WD	.20	.50
❑ 355 Shawn Kemp WD	.08	.25
❑ 356 Marcus Camby WD	.20	.50
❑ 357 Karl Malone WD	.30	.75
❑ 358 Shareef Abdur-Rahim WD	.50	1.25
❑ 359 Gheorghe Muresan WD	.08	.25
❑ 360 Checklist	.08	.25

1997-98 Upper Deck

❑ COMPLETE SET (360)	30.00	50.00
❑ COMPLETE SERIES 1 (180)	15.00	25.00
❑ COMPLETE SERIES 2 (180)	15.00	25.00
❑ 1 Steve Smith	.20	.50
❑ 2 Christian Laettner	.20	.50
❑ 3 Alan Henderson	.08	.25

❑ 4 Dikembe Mutombo	.20	.50
❑ 5 Dana Barros	.08	.25
❑ 6 Antoine Walker	.40	1.00
❑ 7 Dee Brown	.08	.25
❑ 8 Eric Williams	.08	.25
❑ 9 Muggsy Bogues	.20	.50
❑ 10 Dell Curry	.08	.25
❑ 11 Vlade Divac	.20	.50
❑ 12 Anthony Mason	.20	.50
❑ 13 Glen Rice	.20	.50
❑ 14 Jason Caffey	.08	.25
❑ 15 Steve Kerr	.20	.50
❑ 16 Toni Kukoc	.20	.50
❑ 17 Luc Longley	.08	.25
❑ 18 Michael Jordan	2.00	5.00
❑ 19 Terrell Brandon	.20	.50
❑ 20 Danny Ferry	.08	.25
❑ 21 Tyrone Hill	.08	.25
❑ 22 Derek Anderson RC	.40	1.00
❑ 23 Bob Sura	.08	.25
❑ 24 Shawn Bradley	.08	.25
❑ 25 Michael Finley	.30	.75
❑ 26 Ed O'Bannon	.08	.25
❑ 27 Robert Pack	.08	.25
❑ 28 Samaki Walker	.08	.25
❑ 29 LaPhonso Ellis	.08	.25
❑ 30 Tony Battie RC	.30	.75
❑ 31 Antonio McDyess	.20	.50
❑ 32 Bryant Stith	.08	.25
❑ 33 Randolph Childress	.08	.25
❑ 34 Grant Hill	.30	.75
❑ 35 Lindsey Hunter	.08	.25
❑ 36 Grant Long	.08	.25
❑ 37 Theo Ratliff	.08	.25
❑ 38 B.J. Armstrong	.08	.25
❑ 39 Adonal Foyle RC	.20	.50
❑ 40 Mark Price	.20	.50
❑ 41 Felton Spencer	.08	.25
❑ 42 Latrell Sprewell	.30	.75
❑ 43 Clyde Drexler	.30	.75
❑ 44 Mario Elie	.08	.25
❑ 45 Hakeem Olajuwon	.30	.75
❑ 46 Brent Price	.08	.25
❑ 47 Kevin Willis	.20	.50
❑ 48 Erick Dampier	.20	.50
❑ 49 Antonio Davis	.08	.25
❑ 50 Dale Davis	.08	.25
❑ 51 Mark Jackson	.20	.50
❑ 52 Rik Smits	.20	.50
❑ 53 Brent Barry	.20	.50
❑ 54 Lamond Murray	.08	.25
❑ 55 Eric Piatkowski	.20	.50
❑ 56 Loy Vaught	.08	.25
❑ 57 Lorenzen Wright	.08	.25
❑ 58 Kobe Bryant	1.25	3.00
❑ 59 Elden Campbell	.08	.25
❑ 60 Derek Fisher	.30	.75
❑ 61 Eddie Jones	.30	.75
❑ 62 Nick Van Exel	.30	.75
❑ 63 Keith Askins	.08	.25
❑ 64 Isaac Austin	.08	.25
❑ 65 P.J. Brown	.08	.25
❑ 66 Tim Hardaway	.20	.50
❑ 67 Alonzo Mourning	.20	.50
❑ 68 Ray Allen	.30	.75
❑ 69 Vin Baker	.20	.50
❑ 70 Sherman Douglas	.08	.25
❑ 71 Armon Gilliam	.08	.25
❑ 72 Elliot Perry	.08	.25
❑ 73 Chris Carr	.08	.25
❑ 74 Tom Gugliotta	.20	.50
❑ 75 Kevin Garnett	.60	1.50
❑ 76 Doug West	.08	.25
❑ 77 Keith Van Horn RC	.40	1.00
❑ 78 Chris Gatling	.08	.25
❑ 79 Kendall Gill	.08	.25
❑ 80 Kerry Kittles	.30	.75
❑ 81 Jayson Williams	.08	.25
❑ 82 Chris Childs	.08	.25
❑ 83 Allan Houston	.20	.50
❑ 84 Larry Johnson	.20	.50
❑ 85 Charles Oakley	.20	.50
❑ 86 John Starks	.20	.50
❑ 87 Horace Grant	.20	.50
❑ 88 Anfernee Hardaway	.30	.75
❑ 89 Dennis Scott	.08	.25
❑ 90 Rony Seikaly	.08	.25
❑ 91 Brian Shaw	.08	.25
❑ 92 Derrick Coleman	.08	.25
❑ 93 Allen Iverson	.75	2.00
❑ 94 Tim Thomas RC	.50	1.25
❑ 95 Scott Williams	.08	.25
❑ 96 Cedric Ceballos	.08	.25
❑ 97 Kevin Johnson	.20	.50
❑ 98 Loren Meyer	.08	.25
❑ 99 Steve Nash	.30	.75
❑ 100 Wesley Person	.08	.25
❑ 101 Kenny Anderson	.20	.50
❑ 102 Jermaine O'Neal	.50	1.25
❑ 103 Isaiah Rider	.20	.50
❑ 104 Arvydas Sabonis	.20	.50
❑ 105 Gary Trent	.08	.25
❑ 106 Mahmoud Abdul-Rauf	.08	.25
❑ 107 Billy Owens	.08	.25
❑ 108 Olden Polynice	.08	.25
❑ 109 Mitch Richmond	.20	.50
❑ 110 Michael Smith	.08	.25
❑ 111 Cory Alexander	.08	.25
❑ 112 Vinny Del Negro	.08	.25
❑ 113 Carl Herrera	.08	.25
❑ 114 Tim Duncan RC	1.50	4.00
❑ 115 Hersey Hawkins	.08	.25
❑ 116 Shawn Kemp	.20	.50
❑ 117 Nate McMillan	.08	.25
❑ 118 Sam Perkins	.20	.50
❑ 119 Detlef Schrempf	.20	.50
❑ 120 Doug Christie	.20	.50
❑ 121 Popeye Jones	.08	.25
❑ 122 Carlos Rogers	.08	.25
❑ 123 Damon Stoudamire	.20	.50
❑ 124 Adam Keefe	.08	.25
❑ 125 Chris Morris	.08	.25
❑ 126 Greg Ostertag	.08	.25
❑ 127 John Stockton	.30	.75
❑ 128 Shareef Abdur-Rahim	.50	1.25
❑ 129 George Lynch	.08	.25
❑ 130 Lee Mayberry	.08	.25
❑ 131 Anthony Peeler	.08	.25
❑ 132 Calbert Cheaney	.08	.25
❑ 133 Tracy Murray	.08	.25
❑ 134 Rod Strickland	.08	.25
❑ 135 Chris Webber	.30	.75
❑ 136 Christian Laettner JAM	.08	.25
❑ 137 Eric Williams JAM	.08	.25
❑ 138 Vlade Divac JAM	.08	.25
❑ 139 Michael Jordan JAM	1.00	2.50
❑ 140 Tyrone Hill JAM	.08	.25
❑ 141 Michael Finley JAM	.20	.50
❑ 142 Tom Hammonds JAM	.08	.25
❑ 143 Theo Ratliff JAM	.08	.25
❑ 144 Latrell Sprewell JAM	.30	.75
❑ 145 Hakeem Olajuwon JAM	.20	.50
❑ 146 Reggie Miller JAM	.20	.50
❑ 147 Rodney Rogers JAM	.08	.25
❑ 148 Eddie Jones JAM	.20	.50
❑ 149 Jamal Mashburn JAM	.20	.50
❑ 150 Glenn Robinson JAM	.20	.50
❑ 151 Chris Carr JAM	.08	.25
❑ 152 Kendall Gill JAM	.08	.25
❑ 153 John Starks JAM	.08	.25
❑ 154 Anfernee Hardaway JAM	.20	.50
❑ 155 Derrick Coleman JAM	.08	.25
❑ 156 Cedric Ceballos JAM	.08	.25
❑ 157 Rasheed Wallace JAM	.20	.50
❑ 158 Corliss Williamson JAM	.08	.25
❑ 159 Sean Elliott JAM	.20	.50
❑ 160 Shawn Kemp JAM	.08	.25
❑ 161 Doug Christie JAM	.20	.50
❑ 162 Karl Malone JAM	.30	.75
❑ 163 Bryant Reeves JAM	.08	.25
❑ 164 Gheorghe Muresan JAM	.08	.25
❑ 165 Michael Jordan CP	1.00	2.50
❑ 166 Dikembe Mutombo CP	.08	.25
❑ 167 Glen Rice CP	.08	.25
❑ 168 Mitch Richmond CP	.08	.25
❑ 169 Juwan Howard CP	.08	.25
❑ 170 Clyde Drexler CP	.20	.50
❑ 171 Terrell Brandon CP	.08	.25
❑ 172 Jerry Stackhouse CP	.20	.50
❑ 173 Damon Stoudamire CP	.08	.25
❑ 174 Jayson Williams CP	.08	.25
❑ 175 P.J. Brown CP	.08	.25
❑ 176 Anfernee Hardaway CP	.20	.50
❑ 177 Vin Baker CP	.08	.25
❑ 178 LaPhonso Ellis CP	.08	.25
❑ 179 Shawn Kemp CP	.08	.25
❑ 180 Checklist	.08	.25
❑ 181 Mookie Blaylock	.08	.25
❑ 182 Tyrone Corbin	.08	.25
❑ 183 Chucky Brown	.08	.25
❑ 184 Ed Gray RC	.08	.25
❑ 185 Chauncey Billups RC	1.25	3.00
❑ 186 Tyus Edney	.08	.25
❑ 187 Travis Knight	.08	.25
❑ 188 Ron Mercer RC	.30	.75
❑ 189 Walter McCarty	.08	.25
❑ 190 B.J. Armstrong	.08	.25
❑ 191 Matt Geiger	.08	.25
❑ 192 Bobby Phills	.08	.25
❑ 193 David Wesley	.08	.25
❑ 194 Keith Booth RC	.08	.25
❑ 195 Randy Brown	.08	.25
❑ 196 Ron Harper	.20	.50
❑ 197 Scottie Pippen	.50	1.25
❑ 198 Dennis Rodman	.20	.50
❑ 199 Zydrunas Ilgauskas	.20	.50
❑ 200 Brevin Knight RC	.20	.50
❑ 201 Shawn Kemp	.20	.50
❑ 202 Vitaly Potapenko	.08	.25
❑ 203 Wesley Person	.08	.25
❑ 204 Erick Strickland RC	.20	.50
❑ 205 A.C. Green	.20	.50
❑ 206 Khalid Reeves	.08	.25
❑ 207 Hubert Davis	.08	.25
❑ 208 Dennis Scott	.08	.25
❑ 209 Danny Fortson RC	.20	.50
❑ 210 Bobby Jackson RC	.50	1.25
❑ 211 Eric Williams	.08	.25
❑ 212 Dean Garrett	.08	.25
❑ 213 Priest Lauderdale	.08	.25
❑ 214 Joe Dumars	.30	.75
❑ 215 Aaron McKie	.20	.50
❑ 216 Scot Pollard RC	.20	.50
❑ 217 Brian Williams	.08	.25
❑ 218 Malik Sealy	.08	.25
❑ 219 Duane Ferrell	.08	.25
❑ 220 Erick Dampier	.20	.50
❑ 221 Todd Fuller	.08	.25
❑ 222 Donyell Marshall	.20	.50
❑ 223 Joe Smith	.20	.50
❑ 224 Charles Barkley	.40	1.00
❑ 225 Matt Bullard	.08	.25
❑ 226 Othella Harrington	.08	.25
❑ 227 Rodrick Rhodes RC	.08	.25
❑ 228 Eddie Johnson	.08	.25
❑ 229 Matt Maloney	.08	.25
❑ 230 Travis Best	.08	.25
❑ 231 Reggie Miller	.30	.75
❑ 232 Chris Mullin	.30	.75
❑ 233 Fred Hoiberg	.08	.25
❑ 234 Austin Croshere RC	.25	.60
❑ 235 Keith Closs RC	.08	.25
❑ 236 Darrick Martin	.08	.25
❑ 237 Pooh Richardson	.08	.25
❑ 238 Rodney Rogers	.08	.25
❑ 239 Maurice Taylor RC	.25	.60
❑ 240 Robert Horry	.20	.50
❑ 241 Rick Fox	.20	.50
❑ 242 Shaquille O'Neal	.75	2.00
❑ 243 Corie Blount	.08	.25
❑ 244 Charles Smith RC	.08	.25
❑ 245 Voshon Lenard	.08	.25
❑ 246 Eric Murdock	.08	.25
❑ 247 Dan Majerle	.20	.50
❑ 248 Terry Mills	.08	.25
❑ 249 Terrell Brandon	.20	.50
❑ 250 Tyrone Hill	.08	.25
❑ 251 Ervin Johnson	.08	.25
❑ 252 Glenn Robinson	.30	.75
❑ 253 Terry Porter	.08	.25
❑ 254 Paul Grant RC	.08	.25
❑ 255 Stephon Marbury	.40	1.00
❑ 256 Sam Mitchell	.08	.25
❑ 257 Cherokee Parks	.08	.25
❑ 258 Sam Cassell	.30	.75
❑ 259 David Benoit	.08	.25
❑ 260 Kevin Edwards	.08	.25
❑ 261 Don MacLean	.08	.25
❑ 262 Patrick Ewing	.30	.75
❑ 263 Herb Williams	.08	.25
❑ 264 John Starks	.20	.50
❑ 265 Chris Mills	.08	.25
❑ 266 Chris Dudley	.08	.25
❑ 267 Darrell Armstrong	.08	.25
❑ 268 Nick Anderson	.08	.25
❑ 269 Derek Harper	.20	.50
❑ 270 Johnny Taylor RC	.08	.25

❑ 271 Mark Price	.20	.50
❑ 272 Clarence Weatherspoon	.08	.25
❑ 273 Jerry Stackhouse	.30	.75
❑ 274 Eric Montross	.08	.25
❑ 275 Anthony Parker RC	.20	.50
❑ 276 Antonio McDyess	.20	.50
❑ 277 Clifford Robinson	.08	.25
❑ 278 Jason Kidd	.50	1.25
❑ 279 Danny Manning	.20	.50
❑ 280 Rex Chapman	.08	.25
❑ 281 Stacey Augmon	.08	.25
❑ 282 Kelvin Cato RC	.30	.75
❑ 283 Brian Grant	.20	.50
❑ 284 Rasheed Wallace	.30	.75
❑ 285 Lawrence Funderburke RC	.20	.50
❑ 286 Anthony Johnson	.08	.25
❑ 287 Tariq Abdul-Wahad RC	.20	.50
❑ 288 Corliss Williamson	.20	.50
❑ 289 Sean Elliott	.20	.50
❑ 290 Avery Johnson	.08	.25
❑ 291 David Robinson	.30	.75
❑ 292 Will Perdue	.08	.25
❑ 293 Greg Anthony	.08	.25
❑ 294 Jim McIlvaine	.08	.25
❑ 295 Dale Ellis	.08	.25
❑ 296 Gary Payton	.30	.75
❑ 297 Aaron Williams	.08	.25
❑ 298 Marcus Camby	.30	.75
❑ 299 John Wallace	.08	.25
❑ 300 Tracy McGrady RC	.75	2.00
❑ 301 Walt Williams	.08	.25
❑ 302 Shandon Anderson	.08	.25
❑ 303 Antoine Carr	.08	.25
❑ 304 Jeff Hornacek	.20	.50
❑ 305 Karl Malone	.30	.75
❑ 306 Bryon Russell	.08	.25
❑ 307 Jacque Vaughn RC	.20	.50
❑ 308 Antonio Daniels RC	.30	.75
❑ 309 Blue Edwards	.08	.25
❑ 310 Bryant Reeves	.08	.25
❑ 311 Otis Thorpe	.08	.25
❑ 312 Harvey Grant	.08	.25
❑ 313 Terry Davis	.08	.25
❑ 314 Juwan Howard	.20	.50
❑ 315 Gheorghe Muresan	.08	.25
❑ 316 Michael Jordan OT	1.00	2.50
❑ 317 Allen Iverson OT	.30	.75
❑ 318 Karl Malone OT	.30	.75
❑ 319 Glen Rice OT	.08	.25
❑ 320 Dikembe Mutombo OT	.08	.25
❑ 321 Grant Hill OT	.20	.50
❑ 322 Hakeem Olajuwon OT	.20	.50
❑ 323 Stephon Marbury OT	.30	.75
❑ 324 Anfernee Hardaway OT	.20	.50
❑ 325 Eddie Jones OT	.20	.50
❑ 326 Mitch Richmond OT	.08	.25
❑ 327 Kevin Johnson OT	.08	.25
❑ 328 Kevin Garnett OT	.30	.75
❑ 329 Shareef Abdur-Rahim OT	.25	.60
❑ 330 Damon Stoudamire OT	.08	.25
❑ 331 Atlanta Hawks DM	.08	.25
❑ 332 Boston Celtics DM	.20	.50
❑ 333 Charlotte Hornets DM	.20	.50
❑ 334 Chicago Bulls DM	.40	1.00
❑ 335 Cleveland Cavaliers DM	.20	.50
❑ 336 Dallas Mavericks DM	.20	.50
❑ 337 Denver Nuggets DM	.30	.75
❑ 338 Detroit Pistons DM	.30	.75
❑ 339 Golden State Warriors DM	.30	.75
❑ 340 Houston Rockets DM	.30	.75
❑ 341 Indiana Pacers DM	.20	.50
❑ 342 Los Angeles Clippers DM	.08	.25
❑ 343 Los Angeles Lakers DM	.25	.60
❑ 344 Miami Heat DM	.30	.75
❑ 345 Milwaukee Bucks DM	.20	.50
❑ 346 Minnesota Timberwolves DM	.10	.30
❑ 347 New Jersey Nets DM	.20	.50
❑ 348 New York Knicks DM	.20	.50
❑ 349 Orlando Magic DM	.30	.75
❑ 350 Philadelphia 76ers DM	.10	.30
❑ 351 Phoenix Suns DM	.20	.50
❑ 352 Portland Trail Blazers DM	.08	.25
❑ 353 Sacramento Kings DM	.20	.50
❑ 354 San Antonio Spurs DM	.10	.25
❑ 355 Seattle Sonics DM	.30	.75
❑ 356 Toronto Raptors DM	.10	.25
❑ 357 Utah Jazz DM	.20	.50
❑ 358 Vancouver Grizzlies DM	.08	.25
❑ 359 Washington Wizards DM	.30	.75
❑ 360 Checklist	.08	.25
❑ NNO M.Jordan Red Audio	10.00	25.00
❑ NNO M.Jordan Black Audio	4.00	10.00

1998-99 Upper Deck

❑ COMPLETE SET (355)	90.00	180.00
❑ COMPLETE SERIES 1 (175)	50.00	100.00
❑ COMPLETE SERIES 2 (180)	40.00	80.00
❑ COMMON CARD (1-311)	.08	.25
❑ COMMON ROOKIE (312-333)	.25	.60
❑ COMMON JORDAN (230A-W)	1.25	3.00
❑ COMMON HS SUBSET	.30	.75
❑ COMMON TN SUBSET	.40	1.00
❑ 1 Mookie Blaylock	.08	.25
❑ 2 Ed Gray	.08	.25
❑ 3 Dikembe Mutombo	.20	.50
❑ 4 Steve Smith	.20	.50
❑ 5 D.Mutombo/S.Smith HS	.30	.75
❑ 6 Kenny Anderson	.20	.50
❑ 7 Dana Barros	.08	.25
❑ 8 Travis Knight	.08	.25
❑ 9 Walter McCarty	.08	.25
❑ 10 Ron Mercer	.15	.40
❑ 11 Greg Minor	.08	.25
❑ 12 A.Walker/R.Mercer HS	.25	.60
❑ 13 B.J. Armstrong	.08	.25
❑ 14 David Wesley	.08	.25
❑ 15 Anthony Mason	.20	.50
❑ 16 Glen Rice	.20	.50
❑ 17 J.R. Reid	.08	.25
❑ 18 Bobby Phills	.08	.25
❑ 19 G.Rice/A.Mason HS	.30	.75
❑ 20 Ron Harper	.20	.50
❑ 21 Toni Kukoc	.20	.50
❑ 22 Scottie Pippen	.50	1.25
❑ 23 Michael Jordan	2.00	5.00
❑ 24 Dennis Rodman	.20	.50
❑ 25 M.Jordan/S.Pippen HS	4.00	10.00
❑ 26 M.Jordan/M.Jordan HS	6.00	12.00
❑ 27 Shawn Kemp	.20	.50
❑ 28 Zydrunas Ilgauskas	.20	.50
❑ 29 Cedric Henderson	.08	.25
❑ 30 Vitaly Potapenko	.08	.25
❑ 31 Derek Anderson	.25	.60
❑ 32 S.Kemp/Z.Ilgauskas HS	.50	1.25
❑ 33 Shawn Bradley	.08	.25
❑ 34 Khalid Reeves	.08	.25
❑ 35 Robert Pack	.08	.25
❑ 36 Michael Finley	.30	.75
❑ 37 Erick Strickland	.08	.25
❑ 38 M.Finley/S.Bradley HS	.40	1.00
❑ 39 Bryant Stith	.08	.25
❑ 40 Dean Garrett	.08	.25
❑ 41 Eric Williams	.08	.25
❑ 42 Bobby Jackson	.20	.50
❑ 43 Danny Fortson	.08	.25
❑ 44 L.Ellis/B.Stith HS	.30	.75
❑ 45 Grant Hill	.30	.75
❑ 46 Lindsey Hunter	.08	.25
❑ 47 Brian Williams	.08	.25
❑ 48 Scot Pollard	.08	.25
❑ 49 G.Hill/B.Williams HS	.30	.75
❑ 50 Donyell Marshall	.20	.50
❑ 51 Tony Delk	.08	.25
❑ 52 Erick Dampier	.20	.50
❑ 53 Felton Spencer	.08	.25
❑ 54 Bimbo Coles	.08	.25
❑ 55 Muggsy Bogues	.20	.50
❑ 56 D.Marshall/M.Bogues HS	.30	.75
❑ 57 Charles Barkley	.40	1.00
❑ 58 Brent Price	.08	.25
❑ 59 Hakeem Olajuwon	.30	.75
❑ 60 Rodrick Rhodes	.08	.25
❑ 61 C.Barkley/H.Olaj HS	.75	2.00
❑ 62 Dale Davis	.20	.50
❑ 63 Antonio Davis	.08	.25
❑ 64 Chris Mullin	.30	.75
❑ 65 Jalen Rose	.30	.75
❑ 66 Reggie Miller	.30	.75
❑ 67 Mark Jackson	.20	.50
❑ 68 R.Miller/M.Jackson HS	.50	1.25
❑ 69 Rodney Rogers	.08	.25
❑ 70 Lamond Murray	.08	.25
❑ 71 Eric Piatkowski	.20	.50
❑ 72 Lorenzen Wright	.08	.25
❑ 73 Maurice Taylor	.15	.40
❑ 74 M.Taylor/L.Murray HS	.25	.60
❑ 75 Kobe Bryant	1.25	3.00
❑ 76 Shaquille O'Neal	.75	2.00
❑ 77 Derek Fisher	.30	.75
❑ 78 Elden Campbell	.08	.25
❑ 79 Corie Blount	.08	.25
❑ 80 S.O'Neal/K.Bryant HS	3.00	8.00
❑ 81 Jamal Mashburn	.20	.50
❑ 82 Alonzo Mourning	.20	.50
❑ 83 Tim Hardaway	.20	.50
❑ 84 Voshon Lenard	.08	.25
❑ 85 A.Mourning/T.Hard HS	.50	1.25
❑ 86 Ray Allen	.30	.75
❑ 87 Terrell Brandon	.20	.50
❑ 88 Elliot Perry	.08	.25
❑ 89 Ervin Johnson	.08	.25
❑ 90 R.Allen/G.Robinson HS	.30	.75
❑ 91 Micheal Williams	.08	.25
❑ 92 Anthony Peeler	.08	.25
❑ 93 Chris Carr	.08	.25
❑ 94 Kevin Garnett	.60	1.50
❑ 95 K.Garnett/S.Marbury HS	1.25	3.00
❑ 96 Keith Van Horn	.30	.75
❑ 97 Kerry Kittles	.08	.25
❑ 98 Kendall Gill	.08	.25
❑ 99 Sam Cassell	.30	.75
❑ 100 Chris Gatling	.08	.25
❑ 101 K.Van Horn/Cassell HS	.40	1.00
❑ 102 Patrick Ewing	.30	.75
❑ 103 John Starks	.20	.50
❑ 104 Allan Houston	.20	.50
❑ 105 Chris Mills	.08	.25
❑ 106 Chris Childs	.08	.25
❑ 107 Charlie Ward	.08	.25
❑ 108 P.Ewing/J.Starks HS	.50	1.25
❑ 109 Anfernee Hardaway	.30	.75
❑ 110 Horace Grant	.20	.50
❑ 111 Nick Anderson	.08	.25
❑ 112 Johnny Taylor	.08	.25
❑ 113 A.Hardaway/H.Grant HS	.75	2.00
❑ 114 Allen Iverson	.60	1.50
❑ 115 Scott Williams	.08	.25
❑ 116 Tim Thomas	.20	.50
❑ 117 Brian Shaw	.08	.25
❑ 118 Anthony Parker	.08	.25
❑ 119 A.Iverson/T.Thomas HS	.75	2.00
❑ 120 Jason Kidd	.50	1.25
❑ 121 Rex Chapman	.08	.25
❑ 122 Danny Manning	.08	.25
❑ 123 J.Kidd/D.Manning HS	1.00	2.50
❑ 124 Rasheed Wallace	.30	.75
❑ 125 Walt Williams	.08	.25
❑ 126 Kelvin Cato	.08	.25
❑ 127 Arvydas Sabonis	.20	.50
❑ 128 Brian Grant	.20	.50
❑ 129 R.Wallace/I.Rider HS	.30	.75
❑ 130 Tariq Abdul-Wahad	.08	.25
❑ 131 Corliss Williamson	.20	.50
❑ 132 Olden Polynice	.08	.25
❑ 133 Chris Robinson	.08	.25
❑ 134 T.Abdul-Wahad/O.Polynice HS	.30	.75
❑ 135 Tim Duncan	.50	1.25
❑ 136 Avery Johnson	.08	.25
❑ 137 David Robinson	.30	.75
❑ 138 Monty Williams	.08	.25
❑ 139 T.Duncan/D.Rob HS	1.00	2.50
❑ 140 Vin Baker	.20	.50
❑ 141 Hersey Hawkins	.08	.25
❑ 142 Detlef Schrempf	.20	.50
❑ 143 Jim McIlvaine	.08	.25
❑ 144 G.Payton/V.Baker HS	.40	1.00
❑ 145 Chauncey Billups	.20	.50
❑ 146 Tracy McGrady	.75	2.00
❑ 147 John Wallace	.08	.25
❑ 148 Doug Christie	.20	.50
❑ 149 Dee Brown	.08	.25
❑ 150 T.McGrady/C.Billups HS	.60	1.50
❑ 151 Karl Malone	.30	.75
❑ 152 John Stockton	.30	.75

❑ 153 Adam Keefe	.08	.25
❑ 154 Howard Eisley	.08	.25
❑ 155 K.Malone/J.Stockton HS	.30	.75
❑ 156 Bryant Reeves	.08	.25
❑ 157 Lee Mayberry	.08	.25
❑ 158 Michael Smith	.08	.25
❑ 159 Abdur-Rahim/Reeves HS	.75	2.00
❑ 160 Juwan Howard	.20	.50
❑ 161 Calbert Cheaney	.08	.25
❑ 162 Tracy Murray	.08	.25
❑ 163 J.Howard/C.Cheaney HS	.30	.75
❑ 164 Shaquille O'Neal TN	1.50	4.00
❑ 165 Maurice Taylor TN	.30	.75
❑ 166 Stephon Marbury TN	.30	.75
❑ 167 Tracy McGrady TN	1.50	4.00
❑ 168 Antoine Walker TN	.50	1.25
❑ 169 Michael Jordan TN	4.00	10.00
❑ 170 Keith Van Horn TN	.30	.75
❑ 171 S.Abdur-Rahim TN	.75	2.00
❑ 172 Kobe Bryant TN	2.50	6.00
❑ 173 Gary Payton TN	.60	1.50
❑ 174 Michael Jordan CL	.40	1.00
❑ 175 Michael Jordan CL	.40	1.00
❑ 176 Kevin Johnson	.20	.50
❑ 177 Glenn Robinson	.20	.50
❑ 178 Antoine Walker	.30	.75
❑ 179 Jerry Stackhouse	.30	.75
❑ 180 Mark Price	.20	.50
❑ 181 Stephon Marbury	.30	.75
❑ 182 Shareef Abdur-Rahim	.30	.75
❑ 183 Wesley Person	.08	.25
❑ 184 Keith Booth	.08	.25
❑ 185 Sean Elliott	.20	.50
❑ 186 Alan Henderson	.08	.25
❑ 187 Bryon Russell	.08	.25
❑ 188 Jermaine O'Neal	.30	.75
❑ 189 Steve Nash	.30	.75
❑ 190 Eldridge Recasner	.08	.25
❑ 191 Damon Stoudamire	.20	.50
❑ 192 Dell Curry	.08	.25
❑ 193 Michael Stewart	.08	.25
❑ 194 Bruce Bowen RC	.08	.25
❑ 195 Steve Kerr	.20	.50
❑ 196 Dale Ellis	.08	.25
❑ 197 Shandon Anderson	.08	.25
❑ 198 Larry Johnson	.20	.50
❑ 199 Chris Webber	.30	.75
❑ 200 Matt Geiger	.08	.25
❑ 201 Chris Anstey	.08	.25
❑ 202 Loy Vaught	.08	.25
❑ 203 Aaron McKie	.20	.50
❑ 204 A.C. Green	.20	.50
❑ 205 Bo Outlaw	.08	.25
❑ 206 Antonio McDyess	.20	.50
❑ 207 Priest Lauderdale	.08	.25
❑ 208 Greg Ostertag	.08	.25
❑ 209 Dan Majerle	.20	.50
❑ 210 Johnny Newman	.08	.25
❑ 211 Tyrone Corbin	.08	.25
❑ 212 Pervis Ellison	.08	.25
❑ 213 Shawnelle Scott	.08	.25
❑ 214 Travis Best	.08	.25
❑ 215 Stacey Augmon	.08	.25
❑ 216 Brevin Knight	.08	.25
❑ 217 Jerome Williams	.08	.25
❑ 218 Terry Mills	.08	.25
❑ 219 Matt Maloney	.08	.25
❑ 220 Dennis Scott	.08	.25
❑ 221 John Thomas	.08	.25
❑ 222 Nick Van Exel	.30	.75
❑ 223 Duane Ferrell	.08	.25
❑ 224 Chris Whitney	.08	.25
❑ 225 Luc Longley	.08	.25
❑ 226 Robert Horry	.20	.50
❑ 227 Clifford Robinson	.08	.25
❑ 228 Samaki Walker	.08	.25
❑ 229 Derrick McKey	.08	.25
❑ 230A Michael Jordan	1.25	3.00
❑ 230B Michael Jordan	1.25	3.00
❑ 230C Michael Jordan	1.25	3.00
❑ 230D Michael Jordan	1.25	3.00
❑ 230E Michael Jordan	1.25	3.00
❑ 230F Michael Jordan	1.25	3.00
❑ 230G Michael Jordan	1.25	3.00
❑ 230H Michael Jordan	1.25	3.00
❑ 230I Michael Jordan	1.25	3.00
❑ 230J Michael Jordan	1.25	3.00
❑ 230K Michael Jordan	1.25	3.00
❑ 230L Michael Jordan	1.25	3.00
❑ 230M Michael Jordan	1.25	3.00
❑ 230N Michael Jordan	1.25	3.00
❑ 230O Michael Jordan	1.25	3.00
❑ 230P Michael Jordan	1.25	3.00
❑ 230Q Michael Jordan	1.25	3.00
❑ 230R Michael Jordan	1.25	3.00
❑ 230S Michael Jordan	1.25	3.00
❑ 230T Michael Jordan	1.25	3.00
❑ 230U Michael Jordan	1.25	3.00
❑ 230V Michael Jordan	1.25	3.00
❑ 230W Michael Jordan	1.25	3.00
❑ 231 Armon Gilliam	.08	.25
❑ 232 Andrew DeClercq	.08	.25
❑ 233 Stojko Vrankovic	.08	.25
❑ 234 Jayson Williams	.08	.25
❑ 235 Vinny Del Negro	.08	.25
❑ 236 Theo Ratliff	.20	.50
❑ 237 Othella Harrington	.08	.25
❑ 238 Mitch Richmond	.20	.50
❑ 239 Vlade Divac	.20	.50
❑ 240 Duane Causwell	.08	.25
❑ 241 Todd Fuller	.08	.25
❑ 242 Tom Gugliotta	.08	.25
❑ 243 LaPhonso Ellis	.08	.25
❑ 244 Brian Evans	.08	.25
❑ 245 Jason Caffey	.08	.25
❑ 246 Pooh Richardson	.08	.25
❑ 247 George Lynch	.08	.25
❑ 248 Bill Wennington	.08	.25
❑ 249 Rik Smits	.20	.50
❑ 250 Kevin Willis	.08	.25
❑ 251 Mario Elie	.08	.25
❑ 252 Austin Croshere	.25	.60
❑ 253 Sharone Wright	.08	.25
❑ 254 Danny Ferry	.08	.25
❑ 255 Jacque Vaughn	.08	.25
❑ 256 Adonal Foyle	.08	.25
❑ 257 Billy Owens	.08	.25
❑ 258 Randy Brown	.08	.25
❑ 259 Joe Smith	.20	.50
❑ 260 Joe Dumars	.30	.75
❑ 261 Sean Rooks	.08	.25
❑ 262 Eric Montross	.08	.25
❑ 263 Hubert Davis	.08	.25
❑ 264 Gary Payton	.30	.75
❑ 265 Tyrone Hill	.08	.25
❑ 266 John Crotty	.08	.25
❑ 267 P.J. Brown	.08	.25
❑ 268 Michael Cage	.08	.25
❑ 269 Scott Burrell	.08	.25
❑ 270 Marcus Camby	.20	.50
❑ 271 Rod Strickland	.08	.25
❑ 272 Jim Jackson	.08	.25
❑ 273 Corey Beck	.08	.25
❑ 274 James Robinson	.08	.25
❑ 275 Cedric Ceballos	.08	.25
❑ 276 Charles Oakley	.08	.25
❑ 277 Anthony Johnson	.08	.25
❑ 278 Bob Sura	.08	.25
❑ 279 Isaiah Rider	.08	.25
❑ 280 Jeff Hornacek	.20	.50
❑ 281 Rony Seikaly	.08	.25
❑ 282 Charles Smith	.08	.25
❑ 283 Eddie Jones	.30	.75
❑ 284 Lucious Harris	.08	.25
❑ 285 Andrew Lang	.08	.25
❑ 286 Terry Cummings	.08	.25
❑ 287 Keith Closs	.08	.25
❑ 288 Chris Anstey	.08	.25
❑ 289 Clarence Weatherspoon	.08	.25
❑ 290 Michael Jordan H99	1.00	2.50
❑ 291 Shawn Kemp H99	.20	.50
❑ 292 Tracy McGrady H99	.40	1.00
❑ 293 Glen Rice H99	.08	.25
❑ 294 David Robinson H99	.30	.75
❑ 295 Antonio McDyess H99	.20	.50
❑ 296 Vin Baker H99	.08	.25
❑ 297 Juwan Howard H99	.08	.25
❑ 298 Ron Mercer H99	.15	.40
❑ 299 Michael Finley H99	.20	.50
❑ 300 Scottie Pippen H99	.25	.60
❑ 301 Tim Thomas H99	.20	.50
❑ 302 Rasheed Wallace H99	.20	.50
❑ 303 Alonzo Mourning H99	.20	.50
❑ 304 Dikembe Mutombo H99	.08	.25
❑ 305 Derek Anderson H99	.15	.40
❑ 306 Ray Allen H99	.30	.75
❑ 307 Patrick Ewing H99	.20	.50
❑ 308 Sean Elliott H99	.08	.25
❑ 309 Shaquille O'Neal H99	.40	1.00
❑ 310 Michael Jordan CL	.40	1.00
❑ 311 Michael Jordan CL	.40	1.00
❑ 312 Michael Olowokandi RC	1.00	2.50
❑ 313 Mike Bibby RC	2.00	5.00
❑ 314 Raef LaFrentz RC	1.00	2.50
❑ 315 Antawn Jamison RC	3.00	8.00
❑ 316 Vince Carter RC	4.00	10.00
❑ 317 Robert Traylor RC	.60	1.50
❑ 318 Jason Williams RC	2.50	6.00
❑ 319 Larry Hughes RC	2.00	5.00
❑ 320 Dirk Nowitzki RC	6.00	15.00
❑ 321 Paul Pierce RC	5.00	12.00
❑ 322 Bonzi Wells RC	2.50	6.00
❑ 323 Michael Doleac RC	.60	1.50
❑ 324 Keon Clark RC	1.00	2.50
❑ 325 Michael Dickerson RC	1.25	3.00
❑ 326 Matt Harpring RC	1.00	2.50
❑ 327 Bryce Drew RC	.60	1.50
❑ 328 Pat Garrity RC	.30	.75
❑ 329 Roshown McLeod RC	.25	.60
❑ 330 Ricky Davis RC	2.00	5.00
❑ 331 Peja Stojakovic RC	2.50	6.00
❑ 332 Felipe Lopez RC	.75	2.00
❑ 333 Al Harrington RC	1.50	4.00
❑ UDX M.Jordan Retires	1.25	3.00

1999-00 Upper Deck

❑ COMPLETE SET (360)	90.00	180.00
❑ COMPLETE SERIES 1 (180)	60.00	120.00
❑ COMPLETE SERIES 2 (180)	30.00	60.00
❑ COMP.SERIES 1 w/o RC (155)	25.00	50.00
❑ COMP.SERIES 2 w/o SP (133)	5.00	10.00
❑ COMMON CARD (1-133/181-315)	.20	.50
❑ COMMON RC (156-180/316-360)	.60	1.50
❑ COMMON MJ (134-153)	1.00	2.50
❑ 1 Roshown McLeod	.20	.50
❑ 2 Dikembe Mutombo	.25	.60
❑ 3 Alan Henderson	.20	.50
❑ 4 LaPhonso Ellis	.20	.50
❑ 5 Chris Crawford	.20	.50
❑ 6 Kenny Anderson	.25	.60
❑ 7 Antoine Walker	.30	.75
❑ 8 Paul Pierce	.30	.75
❑ 9 Vitaly Potapenko	.20	.50
❑ 10 Dana Barros	.20	.50
❑ 11 Elden Campbell	.20	.50
❑ 12 Eddie Jones	.30	.75
❑ 13 David Wesley	.20	.50
❑ 14 Derrick Coleman	.25	.60
❑ 15 Ricky Davis	.30	.75
❑ 16 Corey Benjamin	.20	.50
❑ 17 Randy Brown	.20	.50
❑ 18 Kornel David RC	.60	1.50
❑ 19 Toni Kukoc	.30	.75
❑ 20 Keith Booth	.20	.50
❑ 21 Shawn Kemp	.30	.75
❑ 22 Wesley Person	.20	.50
❑ 23 Brevin Knight	.20	.50
❑ 24 Bob Sura	.20	.50
❑ 25 Zydrunas Ilgauskas	.25	.60
❑ 26 Michael Finley	.30	.75
❑ 27 Shawn Bradley	.20	.50
❑ 28 Dirk Nowitzki	.50	1.25
❑ 29 Steve Nash	.50	1.25
❑ 30 Antonio McDyess	.25	.60
❑ 31 Nick Van Exel	.25	.60
❑ 32 Chauncey Billups	.30	.75
❑ 33 Bryant Stith	.20	.50
❑ 34 Raef LaFrentz	.25	.60
❑ 35 Grant Hill	.30	.75
❑ 36 Lindsey Hunter	.20	.50
❑ 37 Bison Dele	.20	.50
❑ 38 Jerry Stackhouse	.30	.75
❑ 39 John Starks	.30	.75
❑ 40 Antawn Jamison	.30	.75

❑ 41 Erick Dampier	.25	.60
❑ 42 Jason Caffey	.20	.50
❑ 43 Hakeem Olajuwon	.30	.75
❑ 44 Scottie Pippen	.50	1.25
❑ 45 Cuttino Mobley	.25	.60
❑ 46 Charles Barkley	.40	1.00
❑ 47 Bryce Drew	.20	.50
❑ 48 Reggie Miller	.30	.75
❑ 49 Jalen Rose	.25	.60
❑ 50 Mark Jackson	.30	.75
❑ 51 Dale Davis	.20	.50
❑ 52 Chris Mullin	.30	.75
❑ 53 Maurice Taylor	.25	.60
❑ 54 Tyrone Nesby RC	.60	1.50
❑ 55 Michael Olowokandi	.20	.50
❑ 56 Eric Piatkowski	.25	.60
❑ 57 Troy Hudson RC	.60	1.50
❑ 58 Kobe Bryant	1.50	4.00
❑ 59 Shaquille O'Neal	.75	2.00
❑ 60 Glen Rice	.30	.75
❑ 61 Robert Horry	.30	.75
❑ 62 Tim Hardaway	.30	.75
❑ 63 Alonzo Mourning	.30	.75
❑ 64 P.J. Brown	.20	.50
❑ 65 Dan Majerle	.30	.75
❑ 66 Ray Allen	.30	.75
❑ 67 Glenn Robinson	.25	.60
❑ 68 Sam Cassell	.25	.60
❑ 69 Robert Traylor	.20	.50
❑ 70 Kevin Garnett	.60	1.50
❑ 71 Sam Mitchell	.20	.50
❑ 72 Dean Garrett	.20	.50
❑ 73 Bobby Jackson	.25	.60
❑ 74 Radoslav Nesterovic RC	.75	2.00
❑ 75 Keith Van Horn	.25	.60
❑ 76 Stephon Marbury	.30	.75
❑ 77 Kendall Gill	.20	.50
❑ 78 Scott Burrell	.20	.50
❑ 79 Patrick Ewing	.40	1.00
❑ 80 Allan Houston	.25	.60
❑ 81 Latrell Sprewell	.25	.60
❑ 82 Larry Johnson	.30	.75
❑ 83 Marcus Camby	.25	.60
❑ 84 Darrell Armstrong	.20	.50
❑ 85 Derek Strong	.20	.50
❑ 86 Matt Harpring	.25	.60
❑ 87 Michael Doleac	.20	.50
❑ 88 Bo Outlaw	.20	.50
❑ 89 Allen Iverson	.60	1.50
❑ 90 Theo Ratliff	.25	.60
❑ 91 Larry Hughes	.25	.60
❑ 92 Eric Snow	.25	.60
❑ 93 Jason Kidd	.50	1.25
❑ 94 Clifford Robinson	.20	.50
❑ 95 Tom Gugliotta	.20	.50
❑ 96 Luc Longley	.20	.50
❑ 97 Rasheed Wallace	.30	.75
❑ 98 Arvydas Sabonis	.25	.60
❑ 99 Damon Stoudamire	.30	.75
❑ 100 Brian Grant	.20	.50
❑ 101 Jason Williams	.30	.75
❑ 102 Vlade Divac	.30	.75
❑ 103 Peja Stojakovic	.25	.60
❑ 104 Lawrence Funderburke	.20	.50
❑ 105 Tim Duncan	.60	1.50
❑ 106 Sean Elliott	.30	.75
❑ 107 David Robinson	.40	1.00
❑ 108 Mario Elie	.20	.50
❑ 109 Avery Johnson	.25	.60
❑ 110 Gary Payton	.30	.75
❑ 111 Vin Baker	.30	.75
❑ 112 Rashard Lewis	.30	.75
❑ 113 Jelani McCoy	.20	.50
❑ 114 Vladimir Stepania	.20	.50
❑ 115 Vince Carter	.60	1.50
❑ 116 Doug Christie	.25	.60
❑ 117 Kevin Willis	.20	.50
❑ 118 Dee Brown	.20	.50
❑ 119 John Thomas	.20	.50
❑ 120 Karl Malone	.40	1.00
❑ 121 John Stockton	.40	1.00
❑ 122 Howard Eisley	.20	.50
❑ 123 Bryon Russell	.20	.50
❑ 124 Greg Ostertag	.20	.50
❑ 125 Shareef Abdur-Rahim	.25	.60
❑ 126 Mike Bibby	.30	.75
❑ 127 Felipe Lopez	.20	.50
❑ 128 Cherokee Parks	.20	.50
❑ 129 Juwan Howard	.25	.60
❑ 130 Rod Strickland	.20	.50
❑ 131 Chris Whitney	.20	.50
❑ 132 Tracy Murray	.20	.50
❑ 133 Jahidi White	.20	.50
❑ 134 Michael Jordan AIR	1.00	2.50
❑ 135 Michael Jordan AIR	1.00	2.50
❑ 136 Michael Jordan AIR	1.00	2.50
❑ 137 Michael Jordan AIR	1.00	2.50
❑ 138 Michael Jordan AIR	1.00	2.50
❑ 139 Michael Jordan AIR	1.00	2.50
❑ 140 Michael Jordan AIR	1.00	2.50
❑ 141 Michael Jordan AIR	1.00	2.50
❑ 142 Michael Jordan AIR	1.00	2.50
❑ 143 Michael Jordan AIR	1.00	2.50
❑ 144 Michael Jordan AIR	1.00	2.50
❑ 145 Michael Jordan AIR	1.00	2.50
❑ 146 Michael Jordan AIR	1.00	2.50
❑ 147 Michael Jordan AIR	1.00	2.50
❑ 148 Michael Jordan AIR	1.00	2.50
❑ 149 Michael Jordan AIR	1.00	2.50
❑ 150 Michael Jordan AIR	1.00	2.50
❑ 151 Michael Jordan AIR	1.00	2.50
❑ 152 Michael Jordan AIR	1.00	2.50
❑ 153 Michael Jordan AIR	1.00	2.50
❑ 154 Michael Jordan CL	.75	2.00
❑ 155 Michael Jordan CL	.75	2.00
❑ 156 Elton Brand RC	2.00	5.00
❑ 157 Steve Francis RC	2.00	5.00
❑ 158 Baron Davis RC	2.50	6.00
❑ 159 Lamar Odom RC	2.00	5.00
❑ 160 Jonathan Bender RC	.60	1.50
❑ 161 Wally Szczerbiak RC	2.00	5.00
❑ 162 Richard Hamilton RC	2.00	5.00
❑ 163 Andre Miller RC	2.00	5.00
❑ 164 Shawn Marion RC	2.00	5.00
❑ 165 Jason Terry RC	1.50	4.00
❑ 166 Trajan Langdon RC	.60	1.50
❑ 167 Kenny Thomas RC	.60	1.50
❑ 168 Corey Maggette RC	2.00	5.00
❑ 169 William Avery RC	.60	1.50
❑ 170 Jumaine Jones RC	.60	1.50
❑ 171 Ron Artest RC	2.50	6.00
❑ 172 Cal Bowdler RC	.60	1.50
❑ 173 James Posey RC	1.00	2.50
❑ 174 Quincy Lewis RC	.60	1.50
❑ 175 Vonteego Cummings RC	.60	1.50
❑ 176 Jeff Foster RC	.75	2.00
❑ 177 Dion Glover RC	.60	1.50
❑ 178 Devean George RC	1.00	2.50
❑ 179 Evan Eschmeyer RC	.60	1.50
❑ 180 Tim James RC	.60	1.50
❑ 181 Jim Jackson	.25	.60
❑ 182 Isaiah Rider	.20	.50
❑ 183 Lorenzen Wright	.20	.50
❑ 184 Bimbo Coles	.20	.50
❑ 185 Anthony Johnson	.20	.50
❑ 186 Calbert Cheaney	.20	.50
❑ 187 Pervis Ellison	.20	.50
❑ 188 Walter McCarty	.20	.50
❑ 189 Eric Williams	.20	.50
❑ 190 Tony Battie	.25	.60
❑ 191 Anthony Mason	.20	.50
❑ 192 Bobby Phills	.20	.50
❑ 193 Todd Fuller	.20	.50
❑ 194 Brad Miller	.25	.60
❑ 195 Eldridge Recasner	.20	.50
❑ 196 Chris Anstey	.20	.50
❑ 197 Fred Hoiberg	.20	.50
❑ 198 Hersey Hawkins	.20	.50
❑ 199 Will Perdue	.20	.50
❑ 200 Mark Bryant	.20	.50
❑ 201 Lamond Murray	.20	.50
❑ 202 Cedric Henderson	.20	.50
❑ 203 Andrew DeClercq	.20	.50
❑ 204 Danny Ferry	.20	.50
❑ 205 Erick Strickland	.20	.50
❑ 206 Cedric Ceballos	.20	.50
❑ 207 Hubert Davis	.20	.50
❑ 208 Robert Pack	.20	.50
❑ 209 Gary Trent	.20	.50
❑ 210 Ron Mercer	.20	.50
❑ 211 George McCloud	.20	.50
❑ 212 Roy Rogers	.20	.50
❑ 213 Keon Clark	.20	.50
❑ 214 Terry Mills	.20	.50
❑ 215 Michael Curry	.20	.50
❑ 216 Christian Laettner	.25	.60
❑ 217 Jerome Williams	.20	.50
❑ 218 Loy Vaught	.20	.50
❑ 219 Jud Buechler	.20	.50
❑ 220 Mookie Blaylock	.20	.50
❑ 221 Terry Cummings	.20	.50
❑ 222 Donyell Marshall	.25	.60
❑ 223 Chris Mills	.20	.50
❑ 224 Adonal Foyle	.20	.50
❑ 225 Shandon Anderson	.20	.50
❑ 226 Kelvin Cato	.20	.50
❑ 227 Walt Williams	.20	.50
❑ 228 Al Harrington	.25	.60
❑ 229 Rik Smits	.30	.75
❑ 230 Derrick McKey	.20	.50
❑ 231 Sam Perkins	.20	.50
❑ 232 Austin Croshere	.20	.50
❑ 233 Derek Anderson	.20	.50
❑ 234 Keith Closs	.20	.50
❑ 235 Eric Murdock	.20	.50
❑ 236 Brian Skinner	.20	.50
❑ 237 Charles Jones	.20	.50
❑ 238 Ron Harper	.20	.50
❑ 239 Derek Fisher	.30	.75
❑ 240 Rick Fox	.20	.50
❑ 241 A.C. Green	.30	.75
❑ 242 Jamal Mashburn	.20	.50
❑ 243 Mark Strickland	.20	.50
❑ 244 Rex Walters	.20	.50
❑ 245 Clarence Weatherspoon	.20	.50
❑ 246 Ervin Johnson	.20	.50
❑ 247 J.R. Reid	.20	.50
❑ 248 Dale Ellis	.20	.50
❑ 249 Danny Manning	.20	.50
❑ 250 Tim Thomas	.25	.60
❑ 251 Terrell Brandon	.20	.50
❑ 252 Malik Sealy	.20	.50
❑ 253 Joe Smith	.25	.60
❑ 254 Anthony Peeler	.20	.50
❑ 255 Jayson Williams	.25	.60
❑ 256 Jamie Feick RC	.60	1.50
❑ 257 Kerry Kittles	.20	.50
❑ 258 Johnny Newman	.20	.50
❑ 259 Chris Childs	.20	.50
❑ 260 Kurt Thomas	.25	.60
❑ 261 Charlie Ward	.20	.50
❑ 262 Chris Dudley	.20	.50
❑ 263 John Wallace	.20	.50
❑ 264 Tariq Abdul-Wahad	.20	.50
❑ 265 John Amaechi RC	.60	1.50
❑ 266 Chris Gatling	.20	.50
❑ 267 Monty Williams	.20	.50
❑ 268 Ben Wallace	.25	.60
❑ 269 George Lynch	.20	.50
❑ 270 Tyrone Hill	.20	.50
❑ 271 Billy Owens	.20	.50
❑ 272 Anfernee Hardaway	.30	.75
❑ 273 Rex Chapman	.20	.50
❑ 274 Oliver Miller	.20	.50
❑ 275 Rodney Rogers	.20	.50
❑ 276 Randy Livingston	.20	.50
❑ 277 Scottie Pippen	.50	1.25
❑ 278 Detlef Schrempf	.25	.60
❑ 279 Steve Smith	.20	.50
❑ 280 Jermaine O'Neal	.30	.75
❑ 281 Bonzi Wells	.20	.50
❑ 282 Chris Webber	.30	.75
❑ 283 Nick Anderson	.20	.50
❑ 284 Darrick Martin	.20	.50
❑ 285 Corliss Williamson	.20	.50
❑ 286 Samaki Walker	.20	.50
❑ 287 Terry Porter	.20	.50
❑ 288 Malik Rose	.20	.50
❑ 289 Jaren Jackson	.20	.50
❑ 290 Antonio Daniels	.20	.50
❑ 291 Steve Kerr	.25	.60
❑ 292 Brent Barry	.25	.60
❑ 293 Horace Grant	.25	.60
❑ 294 Vernon Maxwell	.25	.60
❑ 295 Ruben Patterson	.20	.50
❑ 296 Shammond Williams	.20	.50
❑ 297 Antonio Davis	.20	.50
❑ 298 Tracy McGrady	.60	1.50
❑ 299 Dell Curry	.20	.50
❑ 300 Charles Oakley	.25	.60
❑ 301 Muggsy Bogues	.25	.60
❑ 302 Jeff Hornacek	.25	.60
❑ 303 Adam Keefe	.20	.50
❑ 304 Olden Polynice	.20	.50
❑ 305 Doug West	.20	.50
❑ 306 Michael Dickerson	.20	.50
❑ 307 Othella Harrington	.20	.50

❑ 308 Bryant Reeves	.20	.50
❑ 309 Brent Price	.20	.50
❑ 310 Mitch Richmond	.25	.60
❑ 311 Aaron Williams	.20	.50
❑ 312 Isaac Austin	.20	.50
❑ 313 Michael Smith	.20	.50
❑ 314 Michael Jordan CL	.75	2.00
❑ 315 Kevin Garnett CL	.20	.50
❑ 316 Elton Brand	1.00	2.50
❑ 317 Steve Francis	1.00	2.50
❑ 318 Baron Davis	1.25	3.00
❑ 319 Lamar Odom	1.00	2.50
❑ 320 Jonathan Bender	.30	.75
❑ 321 Wally Szczerbiak	1.00	2.50
❑ 322 Richard Hamilton	1.00	2.50
❑ 323 Andre Miller	1.00	2.50
❑ 324 Shawn Marion	1.00	2.50
❑ 325 Jason Terry	.75	2.00
❑ 326 Trajan Langdon	.30	.75
❑ 327 A.Radojevic RC	.60	1.50
❑ 328 Corey Maggette	1.00	2.50
❑ 329 William Avery	.30	.75
❑ 330 Ron Artest	1.25	3.00
❑ 331 Cal Bowdler	.30	.75
❑ 332 James Posey	.50	1.25
❑ 333 Quincy Lewis	.30	.75
❑ 334 Dion Glover	.30	.75
❑ 335 Jeff Foster	.40	1.00
❑ 336 Kenny Thomas	.30	.75
❑ 337 Devean George	.50	1.25
❑ 338 Tim James	.30	.75
❑ 339 Vonteego Cummings	.30	.75
❑ 340 Jumaine Jones	.30	.75
❑ 341 Scott Padgett RC	.60	1.50
❑ 342 John Celestand RC	.60	1.50
❑ 343 Adrian Griffin RC	.60	1.50
❑ 344 Michael Ruffin RC	.60	1.50
❑ 345 Chris Herren RC	.60	1.50
❑ 346 Evan Eschmeyer	.60	1.50
❑ 347 Eddie Robinson RC	.60	1.50
❑ 348 Obinna Ekezie RC	.60	1.50
❑ 349 Laron Profit RC	.60	1.50
❑ 350 Jermaine Jackson RC	.60	1.50
❑ 351 Lazaro Borrell RC	.60	1.50
❑ 352 Chucky Atkins RC	.75	2.00
❑ 353 Ryan Robertson RC	.60	1.50
❑ 354 Todd MacCulloch RC	.60	1.50
❑ 355 Rafer Alston RC	1.25	3.00
❑ 356 Mirsad Turkcan RC	.60	1.50
❑ 357 Anthony Carter RC	1.25	3.00
❑ 358 Ryan Bowen RC	.60	1.50
❑ 359 Rodney Buford RC	.60	1.50
❑ 360 Tim Young RC	.60	1.50

2000-01 Upper Deck

❑ COMPLETE SET (445)	100.00	200.00
❑ COMPLETE SERIES 1 (245)	60.00	120.00
❑ COMPLETE SER.1 w/o RC (200)	20.00	40.00
❑ COMPLETE SERIES 2 (200)	40.00	80.00
❑ COMMON CARD (1-445)	.20	.50
❑ COMMON ROOKIE	.40	1.00
❑ 1 Dikembe Mutombo	.25	.60
❑ 2 Jim Jackson	.20	.50
❑ 3 Alan Henderson	.20	.50
❑ 4 Jason Terry	.30	.75
❑ 5 Roshown McLeod	.20	.50
❑ 6 Lorenzen Wright	.20	.50
❑ 7 Paul Pierce	.30	.75
❑ 8 Antoine Walker	.25	.60
❑ 9 Vitaly Potapenko	.20	.50
❑ 10 Kenny Anderson	.25	.60
❑ 11 Tony Battie	.20	.50
❑ 12 Adrian Griffin	.20	.50
❑ 13 Eric Williams	.20	.50
❑ 14 Derrick Coleman	.25	.60
❑ 15 David Wesley	.20	.50
❑ 16 Baron Davis	.30	.75
❑ 17 Elden Campbell	.20	.50
❑ 18 Jamal Mashburn	.25	.60
❑ 19 Eddie Robinson	.20	.50
❑ 20 Elton Brand	.30	.75
❑ 21 Chris Carr	.20	.50
❑ 22 Ron Artest	.30	.75
❑ 23 Michael Ruffin	.20	.50
❑ 24 Fred Hoiberg	.20	.50
❑ 25 Corey Benjamin	.20	.50
❑ 26 Shawn Kemp	.30	.75
❑ 27 Lamond Murray	.20	.50
❑ 28 Andre Miller	.25	.60
❑ 29 Cedric Henderson	.20	.50
❑ 30 Wesley Person	.20	.50
❑ 31 Brevin Knight	.20	.50
❑ 32 Mark Bryant	.20	.50
❑ 33 Michael Finley	.30	.75
❑ 34 Cedric Ceballos	.20	.50
❑ 35 Dirk Nowitzki	.50	1.25
❑ 36 Hubert Davis	.20	.50
❑ 37 Steve Nash	.50	1.25
❑ 38 Gary Trent	.20	.50
❑ 39 Antonio McDyess	.25	.60
❑ 40 James Posey	.20	.50
❑ 41 Nick Van Exel	.25	.60
❑ 42 Raef LaFrentz	.20	.50
❑ 43 George McCloud	.20	.50
❑ 44 Keon Clark	.20	.50
❑ 45 Jerry Stackhouse	.25	.60
❑ 46 Christian Laettner	.20	.50
❑ 47 Loy Vaught	.20	.50
❑ 48 Jerome Williams	.20	.50
❑ 49 Michael Curry	.20	.50
❑ 50 Lindsey Hunter	.20	.50
❑ 51 Antawn Jamison	.30	.75
❑ 52 Larry Hughes	.25	.60
❑ 53 Chris Mills	.20	.50
❑ 54 Donyell Marshall	.20	.50
❑ 55 Mookie Blaylock		
❑ 56 Vonteego Cummings	.20	.50
❑ 57 Erick Dampier	.20	.50
❑ 58 Steve Francis	.30	.75
❑ 59 Shandon Anderson	.20	.50
❑ 60 Hakeem Olajuwon	.40	1.00
❑ 61 Walt Williams	.20	.50
❑ 62 Kenny Thomas	.20	.50
❑ 63 Kelvin Cato	.20	.50
❑ 64 Cuttino Mobley	.25	.60
❑ 65 Reggie Miller	.30	.75
❑ 66 Jalen Rose	.25	.60
❑ 67 Austin Croshere	.20	.50
❑ 68 Dale Davis	.20	.50
❑ 69 Travis Best	.20	.50
❑ 70 Jonathan Bender	.20	.50
❑ 71 Al Harrington	.25	.60
❑ 72 Lamar Odom	.30	.75
❑ 73 Tyrone Nesby	.20	.50
❑ 74 Michael Olowokandi	.20	.50
❑ 75 Brian Skinner	.20	.50
❑ 76 Eric Piatkowski	.20	.50
❑ 77 Keith Closs	.20	.50
❑ 78 Shaquille O'Neal	.75	2.00
❑ 79 Ron Harper	.25	.60
❑ 80 Kobe Bryant	1.50	4.00
❑ 81 Rick Fox	.25	.60
❑ 82 Robert Horry	.25	.60
❑ 83 Derek Fisher	.30	.75
❑ 84 Devean George	.20	.50
❑ 85 Alonzo Mourning	.30	.75
❑ 86 Eddie Jones	.25	.60
❑ 87 Anthony Carter	.20	.50
❑ 88 Bruce Bowen	.20	.50
❑ 89 Clarence Weatherspoon	.20	.50
❑ 90 Tim Hardaway	.25	.60
❑ 91 Ray Allen	.30	.75
❑ 92 Tim Thomas	.20	.50
❑ 93 Glenn Robinson	.25	.60
❑ 94 Scott Williams	.20	.50
❑ 95 Sam Cassell	.25	.60
❑ 96 Ervin Johnson	.20	.50
❑ 97 Darvin Ham	.20	.50
❑ 98 Kevin Garnett	.60	1.50
❑ 99 Wally Szczerbiak	.25	.60
❑ 100 Terrell Brandon	.20	.50
❑ 101 Joe Smith	.20	.50
❑ 102 Radoslav Nesterovic	.20	.50
❑ 103 William Avery	.20	.50
❑ 104 Stephon Marbury	.30	.75
❑ 105 Kerry Kittles	.25	.60
❑ 106 Keith Van Horn	.25	.60
❑ 107 Lucious Harris	.20	.50
❑ 108 Jamie Feick	.20	.50
❑ 109 Johnny Newman	.20	.50
❑ 110 Patrick Ewing	.40	1.00
❑ 111 Latrell Sprewell	.25	.60
❑ 112 Marcus Camby	.25	.60
❑ 113 Larry Johnson	.25	.60
❑ 114 Charlie Ward	.20	.50
❑ 115 Allan Houston	.25	.60
❑ 116 Chris Childs	.20	.50
❑ 117 Grant Hill	.30	.75
❑ 118 John Amaechi	.20	.50
❑ 119 Tracy McGrady	.60	1.50
❑ 120 Michael Doleac	.20	.50
❑ 121 Darrell Armstrong	.20	.50
❑ 122 Bo Outlaw	.20	.50
❑ 123 Allen Iverson	.60	1.50
❑ 124 Theo Ratliff	.20	.50
❑ 125 Matt Geiger	.20	.50
❑ 126 Tyrone Hill	.20	.50
❑ 127 George Lynch	.20	.50
❑ 128 Toni Kukoc	.25	.60
❑ 129 Jason Kidd	.50	1.25
❑ 130 Rodney Rogers	.20	.50
❑ 131 Anfernee Hardaway	.30	.75
❑ 132 Clifford Robinson	.20	.50
❑ 133 Tom Gugliotta	.20	.50
❑ 134 Shawn Marion	.30	.75
❑ 135 Luc Longley	.20	.50
❑ 136 Rasheed Wallace	.30	.75
❑ 137 Scottie Pippen	.50	1.25
❑ 138 Arvydas Sabonis	.25	.60
❑ 139 Steve Smith	.25	.60
❑ 140 Damon Stoudamire	.25	.60
❑ 141 Bonzi Wells	.20	.50
❑ 142 Jermaine O'Neal	.30	.75
❑ 143 Chris Webber	.30	.75
144 Jason Williams	.25	.60
❑ 145 Nick Anderson	.20	.50
❑ 146 Vlade Divac	.25	.60
❑ 147 Peja Stojakovic	.25	.60
❑ 148 Jon Barry	.20	.50
❑ 149 Corliss Williamson	.25	.60
❑ 150 Tim Duncan	.60	1.50
❑ 151 David Robinson	.40	1.00
❑ 152 Terry Porter	.25	.60
❑ 153 Malik Rose	.20	.50
❑ 154 Steve Kerr	.20	.50
❑ 155 Avery Johnson	.25	.60
❑ 156 Gary Payton	.30	.75
❑ 157 Brent Barry	.20	.50
❑ 158 Vin Baker	.25	.60
❑ 159 Rashard Lewis	.30	.75
❑ 160 Ruben Patterson	.20	.50
❑ 161 Shammond Williams	.20	.50
❑ 162 Vince Carter	.60	1.50
❑ 163 Dell Curry	.20	.50
❑ 164 Doug Christie	.20	.50
❑ 165 Antonio Davis	.20	.50
❑ 166 Kevin Willis	.20	.50
❑ 167 Charles Oakley	.25	.60
❑ 168 Karl Malone	.40	1.00
❑ 169 John Stockton	.40	1.00
❑ 170 Bryon Russell	.20	.50
❑ 171 Olden Polynice	.20	.50
❑ 172 Quincy Lewis	.20	.50
❑ 173 Scott Padgett	.20	.50
❑ 174 Shareef Abdur-Rahim	.25	.60
❑ 175 Mike Bibby	.25	.60
❑ 176 Michael Dickerson	.20	.50
❑ 177 Bryant Reeves	.20	.50
❑ 178 Othella Harrington	.20	.50
❑ 179 Grant Long	.20	.50
❑ 180 Mitch Richmond	.25	.60
❑ 181 Richard Hamilton	.25	.60
❑ 182 Juwan Howard	.25	.60
❑ 183 Rod Strickland	.25	.60
❑ 184 Tracy Murray	.20	.50
❑ 185 Chris Whitney	.20	.50
❑ 186 Kobe Bryant Y3K	.50	1.25
❑ 187 Kobe Bryant Y3K	.50	1.25
❑ 188 Kobe Bryant Y3K	.50	1.25
❑ 189 Kobe Bryant Y3K	.50	1.25
❑ 190 Kobe Bryant Y3K	.50	1.25
❑ 191 Kevin Garnett Y3K	.20	.50
❑ 192 Kevin Garnett Y3K	.20	.50
❑ 193 Kevin Garnett Y3K	.20	.50

❑ 194 Kevin Garnett Y3K .20 .50
❑ 195 Kevin Garnett Y3K .20 .50
❑ 196 Kenyon Martin Y3K .25 .60
❑ 197 Kenyon Martin Y3K .25 .60
❑ 198 Kenyon Martin Y3K .25 .60
❑ 199 Kenyon Martin Y3K .25 .60
❑ 200 Kenyon Martin Y3K .25 .60
❑ 201 Kenyon Martin RC 1.00 2.50
❑ 202 Stromile Swift RC .50 1.25
❑ 203 Chris Mihm RC .40 1.00
❑ 204 Marcus Fizer RC .40 1.00
❑ 205 Darius Miles RC .50 1.25
❑ 206 Joel Przybilla RC .40 1.00
❑ 207 Mike Miller RC .60 1.50
❑ 208 Courtney Alexander RC .40 1.00
❑ 209 DerMarr Johnson RC .40 1.00
❑ 210 Iakovos Tsakalidis RC .40 1.00
❑ 211 Jerome Moiso RC .40 1.00
❑ 212 Keyon Dooling RC .40 1.00
❑ 213 Erick Barkley RC .40 1.00
❑ 214 Jason Collier RC .40 1.00
❑ 215 Jamaal Magloire RC .40 1.00
❑ 216 DeShawn Stevenson RC .40 1.00
❑ 217 Hedo Turkoglu RC 1.00 2.50
❑ 218 Morris Peterson RC .60 1.50
❑ 219 Jamal Crawford RC .60 1.50
❑ 220 Etan Thomas RC .40 1.00
❑ 221 Quentin Richardson RC .50 1.25
❑ 222 Mateen Cleaves RC .40 1.00
❑ 223 Chris Carrawell RC .40 1.00
❑ 224 Corey Hightower RC .40 1.00
❑ 225 Donnell Harvey RC .40 1.00
❑ 226 Mark Madsen RC .40 1.00
❑ 227 Jake Voskuhl RC .40 1.00
❑ 228 Soumaila Samake RC .40 1.00
❑ 229 Mamadou N'Diaye RC .40 1.00
❑ 230 Dan Langhi RC .40 1.00
❑ 231 Hanno Mottola RC .40 1.00
❑ 232 Olumide Oyedeji RC .40 1.00
❑ 233 Jason Hart RC .40 1.00
❑ 234 Mike Smith RC .40 1.00
❑ 235 Chris Porter RC .40 1.00
❑ 236 Jabari Smith RC .40 1.00
❑ 237 Desmond Mason RC .50 1.25
❑ 238 Eddie House RC .40 1.00
❑ 239 A.J. Guyton RC .40 1.00
❑ 240 Speedy Claxton RC .40 1.00
❑ 241 Lavor Postell RC .40 1.00
❑ 242 Khalid El-Amin RC .40 1.00
❑ 243 Pepe Sanchez RC .40 1.00
❑ 244 Eduardo Najera RC .40 1.00
❑ 245 Michael Redd RC 1.00 2.50
❑ 246 DerMarr Johnson .30 .75
❑ 247 Hanno Mottola .30 .75
❑ 248 Dion Glover .20 .50
❑ 249 Matt Maloney .20 .50
❑ 250 Jason Terry .30 .75
❑ 251 Jerome Moiso .30 .75
❑ 252 Bryant Stith .20 .50
❑ 253 Randy Brown .20 .50
❑ 254 Mark Blount .30 .75
❑ 255 Chris Herren .20 .50
❑ 256 Jamal Mashburn .25 .60
❑ 257 P.J. Brown .20 .50
❑ 258 Lee Nailon .30 .75
❑ 259 Jamaal Magloire .30 .75
❑ 260 Otis Thorpe .25 .60
❑ 261 Ron Mercer .20 .50
❑ 262 Marcus Fizer .30 .75
❑ 263 Jamal Crawford .50 1.25
❑ 264 A.J. Guyton .30 .75
❑ 265 Dalibor Bagaric RC .40 1.00
❑ 266 Chris Mihm .30 .75
❑ 267 Robert Traylor .20 .50
❑ 268 Matt Harpring .25 .60
❑ 269 Clarence Weatherspoon .20 .50
❑ 270 Bimbo Coles .20 .50
❑ 271 Etan Thomas .30 .75
❑ 272 Courtney Alexander .30 .75
❑ 273 Donnell Harvey .30 .75
❑ 274 Eduardo Najera .30 .75
❑ 275 Christian Laettner .20 .50
❑ 276 Mamadou N'Diaye .30 .75
❑ 277 Tariq Abdul-Wahad .20 .50
❑ 278 Voshon Lenard .20 .50
❑ 279 Robert Pack .20 .50
❑ 280 Tracy Murray .20 .50
❑ 281 Mateen Cleaves .30 .75
❑ 282 Ben Wallace .25 .60
❑ 283 Chucky Atkins .20 .50
❑ 284 Billy Owens .20 .50
❑ 285 Brian Cardinal RC .40 1.00
❑ 286 Chris Porter .30 .75
❑ 287 Bob Sura .20 .50
❑ 288 Vinny Del Negro .20 .50
❑ 289 Marc Jackson RC .50 1.25
❑ 290 Danny Fortson .20 .50
❑ 291 Jason Collier .30 .75
❑ 292 Maurice Taylor .20 .50
❑ 293 Dan Langhi .30 .75
❑ 294 Carlos Rogers .20 .50
❑ 295 Moochie Norris .20 .50
❑ 296 Jermaine O'Neal .30 .75
❑ 297 Derrick McKey .20 .50
❑ 298 Sam Perkins .20 .50
❑ 299 Zan Tabak .20 .50
❑ 300 Jeff Foster .20 .50
❑ 301 Corey Maggette .25 .60
❑ 302 Darius Miles .40 1.00
❑ 303 Keyon Dooling .30 .75
❑ 304 Quentin Richardson .40 1.00
❑ 305 Jeff McInnis .20 .50
❑ 306 Isaiah Rider .25 .60
❑ 307 Mark Madsen .30 .75
❑ 308 Mike Penberthy RC .40 1.00
❑ 309 Brian Shaw .20 .50
❑ 310 Horace Grant .25 .60
❑ 311 Eddie Jones .25 .60
❑ 312 Brian Grant .20 .50
❑ 313 Anthony Mason .20 .50
❑ 314 Duane Causwell .20 .50
❑ 315 Eddie House .30 .75
❑ 316 Lindsey Hunter .20 .50
❑ 317 Jason Caffey .20 .50
❑ 318 Joel Przybilla .30 .75
❑ 319 Michael Redd .75 2.00
❑ 320 Rafer Alston .20 .50
❑ 321 Chauncey Billups .30 .75
❑ 322 LaPhonso Ellis .25 .60
❑ 323 Sam Mitchell .20 .50
❑ 324 Dean Garrett .20 .50
❑ 325 Tom Hammonds .20 .50
❑ 326 Kenyon Martin .75 2.00
❑ 327 Soumaila Samake .30 .75
❑ 328 Aaron Williams .20 .50
❑ 329 Kendall Gill .20 .50
❑ 330 Stephen Jackson RC .60 1.50
❑ 331 Lavor Postell .30 .75
❑ 332 Pete Mickeal RC .40 1.00
❑ 333 Kurt Thomas .20 .50
❑ 334 Erick Strickland .20 .50
❑ 335 Glen Rice .25 .60
❑ 336 Grant Hill .30 .75
❑ 337 Tracy McGrady .60 1.50
❑ 338 Pat Garrity .20 .50
❑ 339 Troy Hudson .20 .50
❑ 340 Mike Miller .50 1.25
❑ 341 Speedy Claxton .30 .75
❑ 342 Eric Snow .20 .50
❑ 343 Pepe Sanchez .30 .75
❑ 344 Aaron McKie .20 .50
❑ 345 Nazr Mohammed .20 .50
❑ 346 Ruben Garces RC .40 1.00
❑ 347 Daniel Santiago RC 1.00 2.50
❑ 348 Tony Delk .20 .50
❑ 349 Paul McPherson RC .40 1.00
❑ 350 Iakovos Tsakalidis .30 .75
❑ 351 Dale Davis .20 .50
❑ 352 Shawn Kemp .30 .75
❑ 353 Erick Barkley .30 .75
❑ 354 Greg Anthony .20 .50
❑ 355 Stacey Augmon .20 .50
❑ 356 Bobby Jackson .20 .50
❑ 357 Hedo Turkoglu .75 2.00
❑ 358 Jabari Smith .30 .75
❑ 359 Doug Christie .20 .50
❑ 360 Darrick Martin .20 .50
❑ 361 Sean Elliott .25 .60
❑ 362 Jaren Jackson .20 .50
❑ 363 Samaki Walker .20 .50
❑ 364 Derek Anderson .25 .60
❑ 365 Antonio Daniels .20 .50
❑ 366 Patrick Ewing .40 1.00
❑ 367 Desmond Mason .40 1.00
❑ 368 Jelani McCoy .20 .50
❑ 369 Ruben Wolkowyski RC .40 1.00
❑ 370 Emanual Davis .20 .50
❑ 371 Mark Jackson .25 .60
❑ 372 Morris Peterson .50 1.25
❑ 373 Muggsy Bogues .25 .60
❑ 374 Alvin Williams .20 .50
❑ 375 Corliss Williamson .25 .60
❑ 376 John Starks .20 .50
❑ 377 Danny Manning .20 .50
❑ 378 DeShawn Stevenson .30 .75
❑ 379 Donyell Marshall .20 .50
❑ 380 David Benoit .20 .50
❑ 381 Isaac Austin .20 .50
❑ 382 Mahmoud Abdul-Rauf .20 .50
❑ 383 Stromile Swift .40 1.00
❑ 384 Kevin Edwards .20 .50
❑ 385 Brent Price .20 .50
❑ 386 Popeye Jones .20 .50
❑ 387 Mike Smith .30 .75
❑ 388 Jahidi White .20 .50
❑ 389 Laron Profit .20 .50
❑ 390 Felipe Lopez .20 .50
❑ 391 Dikembe Mutombo MVP .25 .60
❑ 392 Paul Pierce MVP .30 .75
❑ 393 Derrick Coleman MVP .25 .60
❑ 394 Elton Brand MVP .30 .75
❑ 395 Andre Miller MVP .25 .60
❑ 396 Michael Finley MVP .30 .75
❑ 397 Antonio McDyess MVP .25 .60
❑ 398 Jerry Stackhouse MVP .25 .60
❑ 399 Larry Hughes MVP .25 .60
❑ 400 Steve Francis MVP .30 .75
❑ 401 Reggie Miller MVP .30 .75
❑ 402 Lamar Odom MVP .30 .75
❑ 403 Shaquille O'Neal MVP .75 2.00
❑ 404 Tim Hardaway MVP .25 .60
❑ 405 Ray Allen MVP .30 .75
❑ 406 Kevin Garnett MVP .60 1.50
❑ 407 Stephon Marbury MVP .30 .75
❑ 408 Allan Houston MVP .25 .60
❑ 409 Grant Hill MVP .30 .75
❑ 410 Allen Iverson MVP .60 1.50
❑ 411 Jason Kidd MVP .50 1.25
❑ 412 Rasheed Wallace MVP .30 .75
❑ 413 Chris Webber MVP .30 .75
❑ 414 Tim Duncan MVP .60 1.50
❑ 415 Gary Payton MVP .30 .75
❑ 416 Vince Carter MVP .60 1.50
❑ 417 Karl Malone MVP .40 1.00
❑ 418 Shareef Abdur-Rahim MVP .25 .60
❑ 419 Mitch Richmond MVP .25 .60
❑ 420 Kobe Bryant MVP 1.50 4.00
❑ 421 Mateen Cleaves ROC .30 .75
❑ 422 Speedy Claxton ROC .30 .75
❑ 423 Courtney Alexander ROC .30 .75
❑ 424 Desmond Mason ROC .40 1.00
❑ 425 Mike Miller ROC .50 1.25
❑ 426 DerMarr Johnson ROC .30 .75
❑ 427 Chris Mihm ROC .30 .75
❑ 428 Jamal Crawford ROC .50 1.25
❑ 429 Joel Przybilla ROC .30 .75
❑ 430 Keyon Dooling ROC .30 .75
❑ 431 Kobe Bryant PR .50 1.25
❑ 432 Kobe Bryant PR .50 1.25
❑ 433 Kobe Bryant PR .50 1.25
❑ 434 Kobe Bryant PR .50 1.25
❑ 435 Kobe Bryant PR .50 1.25
❑ 436 Kobe Bryant PR .50 1.25
❑ 437 Kobe Bryant PR .50 1.25
❑ 438 Kobe Bryant PR .50 1.25
❑ 439 Kobe Bryant PR .50 1.25
❑ 440 Kobe Bryant PR .50 1.25
❑ 441 Kobe Bryant PR .50 1.25
❑ 442 Kobe Bryant PR .50 1.25
❑ 443 Kobe Bryant PR .50 1.25
❑ 444 Kobe Bryant PR .50 1.25
❑ 445 Kobe Bryant PR .50 1.25
❑ CL1 Checklist .08 .25
❑ CL1 Checklist .08 .25
❑ CL2 Checklist .08 .25
❑ CL2 Checklist .08 .25
❑ CL3 Checklist .08 .25
❑ CL3 Checklist .08 .25

2001-02 Upper Deck

❑ COMP.SET w/o SP's (360)	60.00	120.00
❑ COMPLETE SER.1 (225)	100.00	200.00
❑ COMP.SER 1 w/o SP's (180)	20.00	40.00
❑ COMPLETE SER.2 (225)	100.00	200.00
❑ COMP.SER 2 w/o SP's (180)	40.00	80.00
❑ COMMON CARD (1-405)	.20	.50
❑ COMMON ROOKIE (181-225)	1.00	2.50
❑ COMMON CARD (406A-450B)	.50	1.25
❑ SEMISTARS 406-450	.50	1.25
❑ UNLISTED STARS 406-450	.60	1.50
❑ COMMON ROOKIE (406A-417B)	1.25	3.00
❑ 406B-450B NOT INCLUDED IN SET PRICES		
❑ 1 Jason Terry	.30	.75
❑ 2 Toni Kukoc	.25	.60
❑ 3 Alan Henderson	.20	.50
❑ 4 Theo Ratliff	.20	.50
❑ 5 Shareef Abdur-Rahim	.25	.60
❑ 6 DerMarr Johnson	.20	.50
❑ 7 Paul Pierce	.30	.75
❑ 8 Antoine Walker	.25	.60
❑ 9 Kenny Anderson	.25	.60
❑ 10 Vitaly Potapenko	.20	.50
❑ 11 Eric Williams	.20	.50
❑ 12 Jamal Mashburn	.25	.60
❑ 13 Baron Davis	.30	.75
❑ 14 David Wesley	.20	.50
❑ 15 P.J. Brown	.20	.50
❑ 16 Elden Campbell	.20	.50
❑ 17 Jamaal Magloire	.20	.50
❑ 18 Lee Nailon	.20	.50
❑ 19 A.J. Guyton	.20	.50
❑ 20 Ron Mercer	.20	.50
❑ 21 Jamal Crawford	.25	.60
❑ 22 Fred Hoiberg	.20	.50
❑ 23 Marcus Fizer	.20	.50
❑ 24 Ron Artest	.25	.60
❑ 25 Lamond Murray	.20	.50
❑ 26 Andre Miller	.25	.60
❑ 27 Jim Jackson	.20	.50
❑ 28 Chris Mihm	.20	.50
❑ 29 Trajan Langdon	.20	.50
❑ 30 Chris Gatling	.20	.50
❑ 31 Michael Finley	.30	.75
❑ 32 Dirk Nowitzki	.50	1.25
❑ 33 Steve Nash	.50	1.25
❑ 34 Juwan Howard	.25	.60
❑ 35 Wang Zhizhi	.25	.60
❑ 36 Eduardo Najera	.20	.50
❑ 37 Shawn Bradley	.20	.50
❑ 38 Antonio McDyess	.25	.60
❑ 39 Nick Van Exel	.25	.60
❑ 40 Raef LaFrentz	.20	.50
❑ 41 James Posey	.20	.50
❑ 42 Voshon Lenard	.20	.50
❑ 43 Ben Wallace	.25	.60
❑ 44 Jerry Stackhouse	.25	.60
❑ 45 Corliss Williamson	.25	.60
❑ 46 Chucky Atkins	.20	.50
❑ 47 Michael Curry	.20	.50
❑ 48 Dana Barros	.20	.50
❑ 49 Antawn Jamison	.30	.75
❑ 50 Larry Hughes	.25	.60
❑ 51 Bob Sura	.20	.50
❑ 52 Marc Jackson	.20	.50
❑ 53 Chris Porter	.20	.50
❑ 54 Vonteego Cummings	.20	.50
❑ 55 Steve Francis	.30	.75
❑ 56 Cuttino Mobley	.25	.60
❑ 57 Maurice Taylor	.20	.50
❑ 58 Kenny Thomas	.20	.50
❑ 59 Moochie Norris	.20	.50
❑ 60 Walt Williams	.20	.50
❑ 61 Reggie Miller	.30	.75
❑ 62 Jalen Rose	.25	.60
❑ 63 Jermaine O'Neal	.30	.75
❑ 64 Austin Croshere	.20	.50
❑ 65 Travis Best	.20	.50
❑ 66 Jonathan Bender	.20	.50
❑ 67 Eric Piatkowski	.20	.50
❑ 68 Darius Miles	.20	.50
❑ 69 Lamar Odom	.30	.75
❑ 70 Quentin Richardson	.25	.60
❑ 71 Corey Maggette	.25	.60
❑ 72 Elton Brand	.30	.75
❑ 73 Jeff McInnis	.20	.50
❑ 74 Kobe Bryant	1.50	4.00
❑ 75 Shaquille O'Neal	.75	2.00
❑ 76 Derek Fisher	.25	.60
❑ 77 Rick Fox	.25	.60
❑ 78 Mitch Richmond	.25	.60
❑ 79 Ron Harper	.25	.60
❑ 80 Brian Shaw	.20	.50
❑ 81 Stromile Swift	.20	.50
❑ 82 Michael Dickerson	.20	.50
❑ 83 Jason Williams	.25	.60
❑ 84 Grant Long	.20	.50
❑ 85 Bryant Reeves	.20	.50
❑ 86 Alonzo Mourning	.30	.75
❑ 87 Eddie Jones	.25	.60
❑ 88 Brian Grant	.20	.50
❑ 89 Anthony Mason	.20	.50
❑ 90 LaPhonso Ellis	.25	.60
❑ 91 Anthony Carter	.20	.50
❑ 92 Jason Caffey	.20	.50
❑ 93 Ray Allen	.30	.75
❑ 94 Glenn Robinson	.25	.60
❑ 95 Sam Cassell	.25	.60
❑ 96 Tim Thomas	.20	.50
❑ 97 Ervin Johnson	.20	.50
❑ 98 Joel Przybilla	.20	.50
❑ 99 Kevin Garnett	.60	1.50
❑ 100 Terrell Brandon	.20	.50
❑ 101 Wally Szczerbiak	.25	.60
❑ 102 Felipe Lopez	.20	.50
❑ 103 Chauncey Billups	.25	.60
❑ 104 Anthony Peeler	.20	.50
❑ 105 Kenyon Martin	.30	.75
❑ 106 Keith Van Horn	.25	.60
❑ 107 Jamie Feick	.20	.50
❑ 108 Aaron Williams	.20	.50
❑ 109 Lucious Harris	.20	.50
❑ 110 Jason Kidd	.50	1.25
❑ 111 Latrell Sprewell	.25	.60
❑ 112 Allan Houston	.25	.60
❑ 113 Marcus Camby	.25	.60
❑ 114 Mark Jackson	.25	.60
❑ 115 Othella Harrington	.20	.50
❑ 116 Kurt Thomas	.20	.50
❑ 117 Tracy McGrady	.60	1.50
❑ 118 Mike Miller	.25	.60
❑ 119 Darrell Armstrong	.20	.50
❑ 120 Grant Hill	.30	.75
❑ 121 Pat Garrity	.20	.50
❑ 122 Bo Outlaw	.20	.50
❑ 123 Allen Iverson	.60	1.50
❑ 124 Dikembe Mutombo	.25	.60
❑ 125 Aaron McKie	.20	.50
❑ 126 Matt Geiger	.20	.50
❑ 127 Eric Snow	.20	.50
❑ 128 George Lynch	.20	.50
❑ 129 Raja Bell RC	.75	2.00
❑ 130 Shawn Marion	.30	.75
❑ 131 Tom Gugliotta	.20	.50
❑ 132 Rodney Rogers	.20	.50
❑ 133 Anfernee Hardaway	.30	.75
❑ 134 Tony Delk	.20	.50
❑ 135 Stephon Marbury	.30	.75
❑ 136 Rasheed Wallace	.30	.75
❑ 137 Damon Stoudamire	.25	.60
❑ 138 Rod Strickland	.25	.60
❑ 139 Dale Davis	.20	.50
❑ 140 Scottie Pippen	.50	1.25
❑ 141 Bonzi Wells	.25	.60
❑ 142 Peja Stojakovic	.25	.60
❑ 143 Chris Webber	.30	.75
❑ 144 Doug Christie	.20	.50
❑ 145 Mike Bibby	.25	.60
❑ 146 Hedo Turkoglu	.25	.60
❑ 147 Scot Pollard	.20	.50
❑ 148 Vlade Divac	.25	.60
❑ 149 Tim Duncan	.60	1.50
❑ 150 David Robinson	.40	1.00
❑ 151 Antonio Daniels	.20	.50
❑ 152 Danny Ferry	.20	.50
❑ 153 Malik Rose	.20	.50
❑ 154 Terry Porter	.20	.50
❑ 155 Rashard Lewis	.30	.75
❑ 156 Gary Payton	.30	.75
❑ 157 Brent Barry	.20	.50
❑ 158 Vin Baker	.25	.60
❑ 159 Desmond Mason	.25	.60
❑ 160 Shammond Williams	.20	.50
❑ 161 Vince Carter	.60	1.50
❑ 162 Antonio Davis	.20	.50
❑ 163 Morris Peterson	.25	.60
❑ 164 Keon Clark	.20	.50
❑ 165 Chris Childs	.20	.50
❑ 166 Alvin Williams	.20	.50
❑ 167 Karl Malone	.40	1.00
❑ 168 John Stockton	.40	1.00
❑ 169 Donyell Marshall	.20	.50
❑ 170 John Starks	.20	.50
❑ 171 Bryon Russell	.20	.50
❑ 172 David Benoit	.20	.50
❑ 173 DeShawn Stevenson	.20	.50
❑ 174 Richard Hamilton	.25	.60
❑ 175 Jahidi White	.20	.50
❑ 176 Courtney Alexander	.20	.50
❑ 177 Chris Whitney	.20	.50
❑ 178 Michael Jordan	4.00	10.00
❑ 179 Kobe Bryant CL	.20	.50
❑ 180 Kevin Garnett CL	.30	.75
❑ 181 Sean Lampley RC	1.00	2.50
❑ 182 Andrei Kirilenko RC	2.50	6.00
❑ 183 Brandon Armstrong RC	1.00	2.50
❑ 184 Gerald Wallace RC	2.50	6.00
❑ 185 Tony Parker RC	4.00	10.00
❑ 186 Jeryl Sasser RC	1.00	2.50
❑ 187 Alton Ford RC	1.00	2.50
❑ 188 Kenny Satterfield RC	1.00	2.50
❑ 189 Will Solomon RC	1.00	2.50
❑ 190 Earl Watson RC	1.25	3.00
❑ 191 Michael Wright RC	1.00	2.50
❑ 192 Samuel Dalembert RC	1.25	3.00
❑ 193 Ousmane Cisse RC	1.00	2.50
❑ 194 R.Boumtje-Boumtje RC	1.00	2.50
❑ 195 Damone Brown RC	1.00	2.50
❑ 196 Jarron Collins RC	1.00	2.50
❑ 197 Terence Morris RC	1.00	2.50
❑ 198 Pau Gasol RC	4.00	10.00
❑ 199 Trenton Hassell RC	1.25	3.00
❑ 200 Kirk Haston RC	1.00	2.50
❑ 201 Brian Scalabrine RC	1.00	2.50
❑ 202 Gilbert Arenas RC	1.50	4.00
❑ 203 Jeff Trepagnier RC	1.00	2.50
❑ 204 Joseph Forte RC	1.00	2.50
❑ 205 Steven Hunter RC	1.00	2.50
❑ 206 Omar Cook RC	1.00	2.50
❑ 207 Jason Collins RC	1.00	2.50
❑ 208 Kedrick Brown RC	1.00	2.50
❑ 209 Michael Bradley RC	1.00	2.50
❑ 210 Zach Randolph RC	2.50	6.00
❑ 211 Richard Jefferson RC	2.50	6.00
❑ 212 Jamaal Tinsley RC	1.25	3.00
❑ 213 Vladimir Radmanovic RC	1.25	3.00
❑ 214 Brendan Haywood RC	1.25	3.00
❑ 215 Troy Murphy RC	2.00	5.00
❑ 216 DeSagana Diop RC	1.00	2.50
❑ 217 Jason Richardson RC	2.00	5.00
❑ 218 Joe Johnson RC	2.50	6.00
❑ 219 Rodney White RC	1.00	2.50
❑ 220 Loren Woods RC	1.00	2.50
❑ 221 Tyson Chandler RC	2.00	5.00
❑ 222 Eddy Curry RC	1.50	4.00
❑ 223 Shane Battier RC	1.50	4.00
❑ 224 Eddie Griffin RC	1.00	2.50
❑ 225 Kwame Brown RC	1.25	3.00
❑ 226 Shareef Abdur-Rahim	.25	.60
❑ 227 Nazr Mohammed	.20	.50
❑ 228 Hanno Mottola	.20	.50
❑ 229 Emanual Davis	.20	.50
❑ 230 Dion Glover	.20	.50
❑ 231 Chris Crawford	.20	.50
❑ 232 Mark Blount	.20	.50
❑ 233 Joe Johnson	.75	2.00
❑ 234 Milt Palacio	.20	.50
❑ 235 Kedrick Brown	.30	.75
❑ 236 Tony Battie	.20	.50
❑ 237 Erick Strickland	.20	.50
❑ 238 Kirk Haston	.30	.75
❑ 239 Stacey Augmon	.20	.50
❑ 240 Matt Bullard	.20	.50

❑ 241 Bryce Drew	.20	.50
❑ 242 Jerome Moiso	.20	.50
❑ 243 Robert Traylor	.20	.50
❑ 244 Tyson Chandler	.60	1.50
❑ 245 Eddy Curry	.50	1.25
❑ 246 Charles Oakley	.25	.60
❑ 247 Brad Miller	.25	.60
❑ 248 Kevin Ollie	.20	.50
❑ 249 Trenton Hassell	.40	1.00
❑ 250 Ricky Davis	.25	.60
❑ 251 Jumaine Jones	.20	.50
❑ 252 DeSagana Diop	.30	.75
❑ 253 Bryant Stith	.20	.50
❑ 254 Jeff Trepagnier	.30	.75
❑ 255 Michael Doleac	.20	.50
❑ 256 Tim Hardaway	.25	.60
❑ 257 Danny Manning	.20	.50
❑ 258 Johnny Newman	.20	.50
❑ 259 Adrian Griffin	.20	.50
❑ 260 Greg Buckner	.20	.50
❑ 261 Donnell Harvey	.20	.50
❑ 262 Evan Eschmeyer	.20	.50
❑ 263 Avery Johnson	.25	.60
❑ 264 Kenny Satterfield	.30	.75
❑ 265 Scott Williams	.20	.50
❑ 266 Tariq Abdul-Wahad	.20	.50
❑ 267 George McCloud	.20	.50
❑ 268 Clifford Robinson	.20	.50
❑ 269 Jon Barry	.20	.50
❑ 270 Brian Cardinal	.20	.50
❑ 271 Rodney White	.30	.75
❑ 272 Mikki Moore	.20	.50
❑ 273 Victor Alexander	.20	.50
❑ 274 Jason Richardson	.60	1.50
❑ 275 Adonal Foyle	.20	.50
❑ 276 Troy Murphy	.60	1.50
❑ 277 Chris Mills	.20	.50
❑ 278 Gilbert Arenas	.50	1.25
❑ 279 Erick Dampier	.20	.50
❑ 280 Glen Rice	.25	.60
❑ 281 Eddie Griffin	.30	.75
❑ 282 Kevin Willis	.20	.50
❑ 283 Terence Morris	.30	.75
❑ 284 Kelvin Cato	.20	.50
❑ 285 Dan Langhi	.20	.50
❑ 286 Jason Collier	.20	.50
❑ 287 Jamaal Tinsley	.40	1.00
❑ 288 Carlos Rogers	.20	.50
❑ 289 Jeff Foster	.20	.50
❑ 290 Al Harrington	.25	.60
❑ 291 Bruno Sundov	.20	.50
❑ 292 Elton Brand	.30	.75
❑ 293 Keyon Dooling	.20	.50
❑ 294 Michael Olowokandi	.20	.50
❑ 295 Obinna Ekezie	.20	.50
❑ 296 Earl Boykins	.25	.60
❑ 297 Harold Jamison	.20	.50
❑ 298 Sean Rooks	.20	.50
❑ 299 Lindsey Hunter	.20	.50
❑ 300 Samaki Walker	.20	.50
❑ 301 Mitch Richmond	.25	.60
❑ 302 Stanislav Medvedenko	.20	.50
❑ 303 Devean George	.20	.50
❑ 304 Robert Horry	.25	.60
❑ 305 Jelani McCoy	.20	.50
❑ 306 Pau Gasol	1.25	3.00
❑ 307 Shane Battier	.50	1.25
❑ 308 Jason Williams	.25	.60
❑ 309 Isaac Austin	.20	.50
❑ 310 Will Solomon	.30	.75
❑ 311 Lorenzen Wright	.20	.50
❑ 312 Kendall Gill	.20	.50
❑ 313 LaPhonso Ellis	.25	.60
❑ 314 Sean Marks	.20	.50
❑ 315 Rod Strickland	.25	.60
❑ 316 Jim Jackson	.20	.50
❑ 317 Eddie House	.20	.50
❑ 318 Jason Caffey	.20	.50
❑ 319 Rafer Alston	.20	.50
❑ 320 Anthony Mason	.20	.50
❑ 321 Mark Pope	.20	.50
❑ 322 Michael Redd	.30	.75
❑ 323 Darvin Ham	.20	.50
❑ 324 Joe Smith	.20	.50
❑ 325 William Avery	.20	.50
❑ 326 Sam Mitchell	.20	.50
❑ 327 Loren Woods	.30	.75
❑ 328 Dean Garrett	.20	.50
❑ 329 Gary Trent	.20	.50
❑ 330 Jason Kidd	.50	1.25
❑ 331 Todd MacCulloch	.20	.50
❑ 332 Richard Jefferson	.75	2.00
❑ 333 Brandon Armstrong	.30	.75
❑ 334 Jason Collins	.30	.75
❑ 335 Kerry Kittles	.25	.60
❑ 336 Shandon Anderson	.20	.50
❑ 337 Howard Eisley	.20	.50
❑ 338 Charlie Ward	.20	.50
❑ 339 Lavor Postell	.20	.50
❑ 340 Clarence Weatherspoon	.20	.50
❑ 341 Travis Knight	.20	.50
❑ 342 Horace Grant	.25	.60
❑ 343 Steven Hunter	.30	.75
❑ 344 Patrick Ewing	.40	1.00
❑ 345 Jeryl Sasser	.30	.75
❑ 346 Don Reid	.20	.50
❑ 347 Troy Hudson	.20	.50
❑ 348 Speedy Claxton	.20	.50
❑ 349 Derrick Coleman	.25	.60
❑ 350 Damone Brown	.30	.75
❑ 351 Samuel Dalembert	.40	1.00
❑ 352 Vonteego Cummings	.20	.50
❑ 353 Matt Harpring	.25	.60
❑ 354 Corie Blount	.20	.50
❑ 355 Stephon Marbury	.30	.75
❑ 356 Dan Majerle	.25	.60
❑ 357 Jake Voskuhl	.20	.50
❑ 358 Alton Ford	.30	.75
❑ 359 Iakovos Tsakalidis	.20	.50
❑ 360 John Wallace	.20	.50
❑ 361 Derek Anderson	.25	.60
❑ 362 Erick Barkley	.20	.50
❑ 363 R.Boumtje-Boumtje	.30	.75
❑ 364 Zach Randolph	.75	2.00
❑ 365 Steve Kerr	.20	.50
❑ 366 Shawn Kemp	.25	.60
❑ 367 Mateen Cleaves	.20	.50
❑ 368 Bobby Jackson	.20	.50
❑ 369 Mike Bibby	.25	.60
❑ 370 Gerald Wallace	.75	2.00
❑ 371 Jabari Smith	.20	.50
❑ 372 Lawrence Funderburke	.20	.50
❑ 373 Brent Price	.20	.50
❑ 374 Bruce Bowen	.20	.50
❑ 375 Stephen Jackson	.25	.60
❑ 376 Tony Parker	1.25	3.00
❑ 377 Steve Smith	.25	.60
❑ 378 Cherokee Parks	.20	.50
❑ 379 Mark Bryant	.20	.50
❑ 380 Jerome James	.20	.50
❑ 381 Earl Watson	.40	1.00
❑ 382 Vladimir Radmanovic	.40	1.00
❑ 383 Art Long	.20	.50
❑ 384 Calvin Booth	.20	.50
❑ 385 Olumide Oyedeji	.20	.50
❑ 386 Jerome Williams	.20	.50
❑ 387 Hakeem Olajuwon	.40	1.00
❑ 388 Dell Curry	.20	.50
❑ 389 Michael Bradley	.30	.75
❑ 390 Tracy Murray	.20	.50
❑ 391 Eric Montross	.20	.50
❑ 392 John Amaechi	.20	.50
❑ 393 John Crotty	.20	.50
❑ 394 Scott Padgett	.20	.50
❑ 395 Andrei Kirilenko	.75	2.00
❑ 396 Jarron Collins	.30	.75
❑ 397 Quincy Lewis	.20	.50
❑ 398 Kwame Brown	.40	1.00
❑ 399 Christian Laettner	.20	.50
❑ 400 Tyrone Nesby	.20	.50
❑ 401 Brendan Haywood	.40	1.00
❑ 402 Tyronn Lue	.20	.50
❑ 403 Michael Jordan	4.00	10.00
❑ 404 Kobe Bryant CL	.20	.50
❑ 405 Michael Jordan CL	1.50	4.00
❑ 406A Zeljko Rebraca RC	1.25	3.00
❑ 406B Zeljko Rebraca RC	1.25	3.00
❑ 407A Jamison Brewer RC	1.25	3.00
❑ 407B Jamison Brewer RC	1.25	3.00
❑ 408A Shawn Marion	.60	1.50
❑ 408B Shawn Marion	.60	1.50
❑ 409A Primoz Brezec RC	1.50	4.00
❑ 409B Primoz Brezec RC	1.50	4.00
❑ 410A Antonis Fotsis RC	1.25	3.00
❑ 410B Antonis Fotsis RC	1.25	3.00
❑ 411A Bobby Simmons RC	1.25	3.00
❑ 411B Bobby Simmons RC	1.25	3.00
❑ 412A Malik Allen RC	1.25	3.00
❑ 412B Malik Allen RC	1.25	3.00
❑ 413A Ratko Varda RC	1.25	3.00
❑ 413B Ratko Varda RC	1.25	3.00
❑ 414A Tierre Brown RC	1.25	3.00
❑ 414B Tierre Brown RC	1.25	3.00
❑ 415A Norm Richardson RC	1.25	3.00
❑ 415B Norm Richardson RC	1.25	3.00
❑ 416A Oscar Torres RC	1.25	3.00
❑ 416B Oscar Torres RC	1.25	3.00
❑ 417A Chris Anderson RC	5.00	12.00
❑ 417B Chris Anderson RC	5.00	12.00
❑ 418A Predrag Drobnjak	.60	1.50
❑ 418B Predrag Drobnjak	.60	1.50
❑ 419A Dirk Nowitzki	1.00	2.50
❑ 419B Dirk Nowitzki	1.00	2.50
❑ 420A Shareef Abdur-Rahim	.50	1.25
❑ 420B Shareef Abdur-Rahim	.50	1.25
❑ 421A Kenny Anderson	.50	1.25
❑ 421B Kenny Anderson	.50	1.25
❑ 422A Jamal Mashburn	.50	1.25
❑ 422B Jamal Mashburn	.50	1.25
❑ 423A Charles Oakley	.50	1.25
❑ 423B Charles Oakley	.50	1.25
❑ 424A Andre Miller	.50	1.25
❑ 424B Andre Miller	.50	1.25
❑ 425A Michael Finley	.60	1.50
❑ 425B Michael Finley	.60	1.50
❑ 426A Tim Hardaway	.50	1.25
❑ 426B Tim Hardaway	.50	1.25
❑ 427A Nick Van Exel	.50	1.25
❑ 427B Nick Van Exel	.50	1.25
❑ 428A Jerry Stackhouse	.50	1.25
❑ 428B Jerry Stackhouse	.50	1.25
❑ 429A Mookie Blaylock	.50	1.25
❑ 429B Mookie Blaylock	.50	1.25
❑ 430A Glen Rice	.50	1.25
❑ 430B Glen Rice	.50	1.25
❑ 431A Reggie Miller	.60	1.50
❑ 431B Reggie Miller	.60	1.50
❑ 432A Elton Brand	.60	1.50
❑ 432B Elton Brand	.60	1.50
❑ 433A Kobe Bryant	3.00	8.00
❑ 433B Kobe Bryant	3.00	8.00
❑ 434A Jason Williams	.50	1.25
❑ 434B Jason Williams	.50	1.25
❑ 435A Eddie Jones	.50	1.25
❑ 435B Eddie Jones	.50	1.25
❑ 436A Alonzo Mourning	.60	1.50
❑ 436B Alonzo Mourning	.60	1.50
❑ 437A Glenn Robinson	.50	1.25
❑ 437B Glenn Robinson	.50	1.25
❑ 438A Kevin Garnett	1.25	3.00
❑ 438B Kevin Garnett	1.25	3.00
❑ 439A Jason Kidd	1.00	2.50
❑ 439B Jason Kidd	1.00	2.50
❑ 440A Latrell Sprewell	.50	1.25
❑ 440B Latrell Sprewell	.50	1.25
❑ 441A Grant Hill	.60	1.50
❑ 441B Grant Hill	.60	1.50
❑ 442A Dikembe Mutombo	.50	1.25
❑ 442B Dikembe Mutombo	.50	1.25
❑ 443A Anfernee Hardaway	.60	1.50
❑ 443B Anfernee Hardaway	.60	1.50
❑ 444A Scottie Pippen	1.00	2.50
❑ 444B Scottie Pippen	1.00	2.50
❑ 445A Mike Bibby	.50	1.25
❑ 445B Mike Bibby	.50	1.25
❑ 446A David Robinson	.75	2.00
❑ 446B David Robinson	.75	2.00
❑ 447A Gary Payton	.60	1.50
❑ 447B Gary Payton	.60	1.50
❑ 448A Vince Carter	1.25	3.00
❑ 448B Vince Carter	1.25	3.00
❑ 449A John Stockton	.75	2.00
❑ 449B John Stockton	.75	2.00
❑ 450A Michael Jordan	8.00	20.00
❑ 450B Michael Jordan	8.00	20.00

2002-03 Upper Deck

❑ COMPLETE SER.1 (210)	80.00	160.00
❑ COMPLETE SER. 2 (220)	20.00	40.00
❑ COMP.SER.1 w/o SP's (180)	15.00	40.00
❑ COMMON CARD (1-420)	.20	.50
❑ COMMON ROOKIE	1.25	3.00
❑ 1 Shareef Abdur-Rahim	.25	.60
❑ 2 Jason Terry	.30	.75
❑ 3 Glenn Robinson	.25	.60
❑ 4 Nazr Mohammed	.20	.50
❑ 5 DerMarr Johnson	.20	.50
❑ 6 Dion Glover	.20	.50
❑ 7 Paul Pierce	.30	.75
❑ 8 Antoine Walker	.25	.60
❑ 9 Vin Baker	.25	.60
❑ 10 Eric Williams	.20	.50
❑ 11 Tony Delk	.20	.50
❑ 12 Kedrick Brown	.20	.50
❑ 13 Jalen Rose	.25	.60
❑ 14 Eddy Curry	.25	.60
❑ 15 Tyson Chandler	.25	.60
❑ 16 Jamal Crawford	.25	.60
❑ 17 Marcus Fizer	.20	.50
❑ 18 Trenton Hassell	.20	.50
❑ 19 Zydrunas Ilgauskas	.25	.60
❑ 20 Tyrone Hill	.20	.50
❑ 21 Darius Miles	.20	.50
❑ 22 Chris Mihm	.20	.50
❑ 23 Ricky Davis	.25	.60
❑ 24 Jumaine Jones	.20	.50
❑ 25 Dirk Nowitzki	.50	1.25
❑ 26 Michael Finley	.30	.75
❑ 27 Steve Nash	.50	1.25
❑ 28 Raef LaFrentz	.20	.50
❑ 29 Nick Van Exel	.25	.60
❑ 30 Adrian Griffin	.20	.50
❑ 31 Wang Zhizhi	.20	.50
❑ 32 Marcus Camby	.25	.60
❑ 33 Juwan Howard	.25	.60
❑ 34 James Posey	.20	.50
❑ 35 Donnell Harvey	.20	.50
❑ 36 Ryan Bowen	.20	.50
❑ 37 Zeljko Rebraca	.20	.50
❑ 38 Ben Wallace	.25	.60
❑ 39 Clifford Robinson	.20	.50
❑ 40 Corliss Williamson	.25	.60
❑ 41 Chucky Atkins	.20	.50
❑ 42 Michael Curry	.20	.50
❑ 43 Jason Richardson	.30	.75
❑ 44 Antawn Jamison	.30	.75
❑ 45 Troy Murphy	.30	.75
❑ 46 Gilbert Arenas	.30	.75
❑ 47 Danny Fortson	.20	.50
❑ 48 Steve Francis	.30	.75
❑ 49 Eddie Griffin	.20	.50
❑ 50 Cuttino Mobley	.25	.60
❑ 51 Kenny Thomas	.20	.50
❑ 52 Moochie Norris	.20	.50
❑ 53 Kelvin Cato	.20	.50
❑ 54 Reggie Miller	.30	.75
❑ 55 Jermaine O'Neal	.30	.75
❑ 56 Ron Mercer	.20	.50
❑ 57 Austin Croshere	.20	.50
❑ 58 Ron Artest	.25	.60
❑ 59 Jamaal Tinsley	.25	.60
❑ 60 Elton Brand	.30	.75
❑ 61 Andre Miller	.25	.60
❑ 62 Lamar Odom	.30	.75
❑ 63 Michael Olowokandi	.20	.50
❑ 64 Quentin Richardson	.25	.60
❑ 65 Corey Maggette	.25	.60
❑ 66 Kobe Bryant	1.50	4.00
❑ 67 Shaquille O'Neal	.75	2.00
❑ 68 Rick Fox	.25	.60
❑ 69 Robert Horry	.25	.60

❑ 70 Devean George	.20	.50
❑ 71 Samaki Walker	.20	.50
❑ 72 Brian Shaw	.20	.50
❑ 73 Pau Gasol	.30	.75
❑ 74 Jason Williams	.25	.60
❑ 75 Shane Battier	.25	.60
❑ 76 Stromile Swift	.20	.50
❑ 77 Lorenzen Wright	.20	.50
❑ 78 LaPhonso Ellis	.25	.60
❑ 79 Eddie Jones	.25	.60
❑ 80 Brian Grant	.20	.50
❑ 81 Vladimir Stepania	.20	.50
❑ 82 Eddie House	.20	.50
❑ 83 Anthony Carter	.20	.50
❑ 84 Ray Allen	.30	.75
❑ 85 Sam Cassell	.25	.60
❑ 86 Tim Thomas	.20	.50
❑ 87 Toni Kukoc	.25	.60
❑ 88 Jason Caffey	.20	.50
❑ 89 Anthony Mason	.20	.50
❑ 90 Joel Przybilla	.20	.50
❑ 91 Kevin Garnett	.60	1.50
❑ 92 Wally Szczerbiak	.25	.60
❑ 93 Terrell Brandon	.20	.50
❑ 94 Joe Smith	.20	.50
❑ 95 Felipe Lopez	.20	.50
❑ 96 Anthony Peeler	.20	.50
❑ 97 Radoslav Nesterovic	.20	.50
❑ 98 Jason Kidd	.50	1.25
❑ 99 Kenyon Martin	.30	.75
❑ 100 Dikembe Mutombo	.25	.60
❑ 101 Richard Jefferson	.30	.75
❑ 102 Kerry Kittles	.25	.60
❑ 103 Lucious Harris	.20	.50
❑ 104 Jason Collins	.20	.50
❑ 105 Baron Davis	.30	.75
❑ 106 Jamal Mashburn	.25	.60
❑ 107 Elden Campbell	.20	.50
❑ 108 David Wesley	.20	.50
❑ 109 P.J. Brown	.20	.50
❑ 110 Lee Nailon	.20	.50
❑ 111 Latrell Sprewell	.25	.60
❑ 112 Allan Houston	.25	.60
❑ 113 Kurt Thomas	.20	.50
❑ 114 Antonio McDyess	.25	.60
❑ 115 Othella Harrington	.20	.50
❑ 116 Clarence Weatherspoon	.20	.50
❑ 117 Tracy McGrady	.60	1.50
❑ 118 Mike Miller	.25	.60
❑ 119 Darrell Armstrong	.20	.50
❑ 120 Grant Hill	.30	.75
❑ 121 Pat Garrity	.20	.50
❑ 122 Steven Hunter	.20	.50
❑ 123 Allen Iverson	.60	1.50
❑ 124 Keith Van Horn	.25	.60
❑ 125 Aaron McKie	.20	.50
❑ 126 Eric Snow	.20	.50
❑ 127 Derrick Coleman	.25	.60
❑ 128 Samuel Dalembert	.20	.50
❑ 129 Stephon Marbury	.30	.75
❑ 130 Shawn Marion	.30	.75
❑ 131 Joe Johnson	.30	.75
❑ 132 Tom Gugliotta	.20	.50
❑ 133 Anfernee Hardaway	.30	.75
❑ 134 Iakovos Tsakalidis	.20	.50
❑ 135 Rasheed Wallace	.30	.75
❑ 136 Bonzi Wells	.25	.60
❑ 137 Damon Stoudamire	.25	.60
❑ 138 Scottie Pippen	.50	1.25
❑ 139 Derek Anderson	.25	.60
❑ 140 Ruben Patterson	.20	.50
❑ 141 Dale Davis	.20	.50
❑ 142 Mike Bibby	.25	.60
❑ 143 Chris Webber	.30	.75
❑ 144 Peja Stojakovic	.25	.60
❑ 145 Doug Christie	.20	.50
❑ 146 Hedo Turkoglu	.25	.60
❑ 147 Vlade Divac	.25	.60
❑ 148 Scot Pollard	.20	.50
❑ 149 Tim Duncan	.60	1.50
❑ 150 David Robinson	.40	1.00
❑ 151 Tony Parker	.30	.75
❑ 152 Malik Rose	.20	.50
❑ 153 Steve Smith	.25	.60
❑ 154 Bruce Bowen	.20	.50
❑ 155 Danny Ferry	.20	.50
❑ 156 Gary Payton	.30	.75
❑ 157 Rashard Lewis	.30	.75
❑ 158 Brent Barry	.20	.50

❑ 159 Kenny Anderson	.25	.60
❑ 160 Desmond Mason	.25	.60
❑ 161 Predrag Drobnjak	.20	.50
❑ 162 Vince Carter	.60	1.50
❑ 163 Morris Peterson	.25	.60
❑ 164 Antonio Davis	.20	.50
❑ 165 Alvin Williams	.20	.50
❑ 166 Jerome Williams	.20	.50
❑ 167 Michael Bradley	.20	.50
❑ 168 Karl Malone	.30	.75
❑ 169 John Stockton	.40	1.00
❑ 170 John Amaechi	.20	.50
❑ 171 Andrei Kirilenko	.30	.75
❑ 172 Greg Ostertag	.20	.50
❑ 173 Jarron Collins	.20	.50
❑ 174 DeShawn Stevenson	.20	.50
❑ 175 Christian Laettner	.20	.50
❑ 176 Brendan Haywood	.20	.50
❑ 177 Chris Whitney	.20	.50
❑ 178 Tyronn Lue	.20	.50
❑ 179 Kwame Brown	.20	.50
❑ 180 Michael Jordan	2.00	5.00
❑ 181 Jay Williams RC	1.50	4.00
❑ 182 Juan Dixon RC	2.00	5.00
❑ 183 Vincent Yarbrough RC	1.25	3.00
❑ 184 Casey Jacobsen RC	1.25	3.00
❑ 185 Chris Wilcox RC	1.50	4.00
❑ 186 John Salmons RC	2.00	5.00
❑ 187 Marcus Haislip RC	1.25	3.00
❑ 188 Robert Archibald RC	1.25	3.00
❑ 189 Jared Jeffries RC	1.25	3.00
❑ 190 Nikoloz Tskitishvili RC	1.25	3.00
❑ 191 Kareem Rush RC	1.50	4.00
❑ 192 Fred Jones RC	1.50	4.00
❑ 193 Caron Butler RC	2.50	6.00
❑ 194 Chris Jefferies RC	1.25	3.00
❑ 195 Ryan Humphrey RC	1.25	3.00
❑ 196 Frank Williams RC	1.25	3.00
❑ 197 DaJuan Wagner RC	1.25	3.00
❑ 198 Bostjan Nachbar RC	1.25	3.00
❑ 199 Mike Dunleavy RC	1.50	4.00
❑ 200 Roger Mason RC	1.25	3.00
❑ 201 Nene Hilario RC	1.50	4.00
❑ 202 Melvin Ely RC	1.25	3.00
❑ 203 Tayshaun Prince RC	2.00	5.00
❑ 204 Jiri Welsch RC	1.25	3.00
❑ 205 Dan Dickau RC	1.25	3.00
❑ 206 Qyntel Woods RC	1.25	3.00
❑ 207 Curtis Borchardt RC	1.25	3.00
❑ 208 Amare Stoudemire RC	3.00	8.00
❑ 209 Drew Gooden RC	2.00	5.00
❑ 210 Yao Ming RC	4.00	10.00
❑ 211 Glenn Robinson	.25	.60
❑ 212 Theo Ratliff	.20	.50
❑ 213 Emanual Davis	.20	.50
❑ 214 Dan Dickau	.60	1.50
❑ 215 Alan Henderson	.20	.50
❑ 216 Chris Crawford	.20	.50
❑ 217 Darvin Ham	.20	.50
❑ 218 Ira Newble	.20	.50
❑ 219 Vin Baker	.25	.60
❑ 220 Shammond Williams	.20	.50
❑ 221 Tony Battie	.20	.50
❑ 222 Walter McCarty	.20	.50
❑ 223 Bruno Sundov	.20	.50
❑ 224 Ruben Wolkowyski	.20	.50
❑ 225 Eddie Robinson	.20	.50
❑ 226 Jay Williams	.75	2.00
❑ 227 Fred Hoiberg	.20	.50
❑ 228 Donyell Marshall	.20	.50
❑ 229 Roger Mason	.60	1.50
❑ 230 Darius Miles	.20	.50
❑ 231 Michael Stewart	.20	.50
❑ 232 Tyrone Hill	.20	.50
❑ 233 DaJuan Wagner		
❑ 234 DeSagana Diop	.20	.50
❑ 235 Bimbo Coles	.20	.50
❑ 236 Milt Palacio	.20	.50
❑ 237 Avery Johnson	.25	.60
❑ 238 Evan Eschmeyer	.20	.50
❑ 239 Raja Bell	.25	.60
❑ 240 Shawn Bradley	.20	.50
❑ 241 Walt Williams	.20	.50
❑ 242 Eduardo Najera	.20	.50
❑ 243 Marcus Camby	.25	.60
❑ 244 Chris Whitney	.20	.50
❑ 245 Nikoloz Tskitishvili		
❑ 246 Kenny Satterfield	.20	.50
❑ 247 Nene Hilario		

❑ 248 Mark Blount	.20	.50
❑ 249 Richard Hamilton	.25	.60
❑ 250 Chauncey Billups	.30	.75
❑ 251 Tayshaun Prince		
❑ 252 Don Reid	.20	.50
❑ 253 Jon Barry	.20	.50
❑ 254 Hubert Davis	.20	.50
❑ 255 Pepe Sanchez	.20	.50
❑ 256 Chris Mills	.20	.50
❑ 257 Bob Sura	.20	.50
❑ 258 Mike Dunleavy		
❑ 259 Jiri Welsch		
❑ 260 Adonal Foyle	.20	.50
❑ 261 Erick Dampier	.20	.50
❑ 262 Maurice Taylor	.20	.50
❑ 263 Glen Rice	.25	.60
❑ 264 Yao Ming	2.00	5.00
❑ 265 Bostjan Nachbar	.60	1.50
❑ 266 Jason Collier	.20	.50
❑ 267 Terence Morris	.20	.50
❑ 268 Jonathan Bender	.20	.50
❑ 269 Jeff Foster	.20	.50
❑ 270 Fred Jones	.75	2.00
❑ 271 Al Harrington	.25	.60
❑ 272 Brad Miller	.25	.60
❑ 273 Jamison Brewer	.20	.50
❑ 274 Erick Strickland	.20	.50
❑ 275 Andre Miller	.25	.60
❑ 276 Melvin Ely	.60	1.50
❑ 277 Keyon Dooling	.20	.50
❑ 278 Chris Wilcox	.75	2.00
❑ 279 Eric Piatkowski	.20	.50
❑ 280 Sean Rooks	.20	.50
❑ 281 Wang Zhi Zhi	.20	.50
❑ 282 Mark Madsen	.20	.50
❑ 283 Kareem Rush	.75	2.00
❑ 284 Stanislav Medvedenko	.20	.50
❑ 285 Derek Fisher	.25	.60
❑ 286 Tracy Murray	.20	.50
❑ 287 Michael Dickerson	.20	.50
❑ 288 Wesley Person	.20	.50
❑ 289 Drew Gooden	1.00	2.50
❑ 290 Robert Archibald	.30	.75
❑ 291 Brevin Knight	.20	.50
❑ 292 Mike James	.20	.50
❑ 293 LaPhonso Ellis	.25	.60
❑ 294 Caron Butler	1.25	3.00
❑ 295 Malik Allen	.20	.50
❑ 296 Travis Best	.20	.50
❑ 297 Alonzo Mourning	.30	.75
❑ 298 Toni Kukoc	.25	.60
❑ 299 Michael Redd	.30	.75
❑ 300 Marcus Haislip	.60	1.50
❑ 301 Ervin Johnson	.20	.50
❑ 302 Kevin Ollie	.20	.50
❑ 303 Troy Hudson	.20	.50
❑ 304 Marc Jackson	.20	.50
❑ 305 Gary Trent	.20	.50
❑ 306 Kendall Gill	.20	.50
❑ 307 Loren Woods	.20	.50
❑ 308 Dikembe Mutombo	.25	.60
❑ 309 Anthony Johnson	.20	.50
❑ 310 Rodney Rogers	.20	.50
❑ 311 Brandon Armstrong	.20	.50
❑ 312 Brian Scalabrine	.20	.50
❑ 313 Aaron Williams	.20	.50
❑ 314 Courtney Alexander	.20	.50
❑ 315 Kirk Haston	.20	.50
❑ 316 George Lynch	.20	.50
❑ 317 Stacey Augmon	.20	.50
❑ 318 Robert Traylor	.20	.50
❑ 319 Jamaal Magloire	.20	.50
❑ 320 Lee Nailon	.20	.50
❑ 321 Frank Williams	.60	1.50
❑ 322 Michael Doleac	.20	.50
❑ 323 Shandon Anderson	.20	.50
❑ 324 Howard Eisley	.20	.50
❑ 325 Travis Knight	.20	.50
❑ 326 Lavor Postell	.20	.50
❑ 327 Charlie Ward	.20	.50
❑ 328 Mark Pope	.20	.50
❑ 329 Olumide Oyedeji	.20	.50
❑ 330 Shawn Kemp	.30	.75
❑ 331 Jacque Vaughn	.20	.50
❑ 332 Ryan Humphrey	.60	1.50
❑ 333 Andrew DeClercq	.20	.50
❑ 334 Jeryl Sasser	.20	.50
❑ 335 Keith Van Horn	.25	.60
❑ 336 Todd MacCulloch	.20	.50

❑ 337 Monty Williams	.20	.50
❑ 338 John Salmons	.50	1.25
❑ 339 Brian Skinner	.20	.50
❑ 340 Mark Bryant	.20	.50
❑ 341 Greg Buckner	.20	.50
❑ 342 Bo Outlaw	.20	.50
❑ 343 Amare Stoudemire	1.50	4.00
❑ 344 Casey Jacobsen	.60	1.50
❑ 345 Alton Ford	.20	.50
❑ 346 Scott Williams	.20	.50
❑ 347 Dan Langhi	.20	.50
❑ 348 Arvydas Sabonis	.25	.60
❑ 349 Antonio Daniels	.20	.50
❑ 350 Jeff McInnis	.20	.50
❑ 351 Qyntel Woods	.60	1.50
❑ 352 Zach Randolph	.30	.75
❑ 353 Ruben Boumtje-Boumtje	.20	.50
❑ 354 Chris Dudley	.20	.50
❑ 355 Charles Smith	.20	.50
❑ 356 Keon Clark	.20	.50
❑ 357 Bobby Jackson	.20	.50
❑ 358 Mateen Cleaves	.20	.50
❑ 359 Gerald Wallace	.30	.75
❑ 360 Lawrence Funderburke	.20	.50
❑ 361 Speedy Claxton	.20	.50
❑ 362 Stephen Jackson	.25	.60
❑ 363 Kevin Willis	.20	.50
❑ 364 Steve Kerr	.20	.50
❑ 365 Mengke Bateer	.20	.50
❑ 366 Kenny Anderson	.25	.60
❑ 367 Vladimir Radmanovic	.20	.50
❑ 368 Joseph Forte	.20	.50
❑ 369 Jerome James	.20	.50
❑ 370 Vitaly Potapenko	.20	.50
❑ 371 Calvin Booth	.20	.50
❑ 372 Ansu Sesay	.20	.50
❑ 373 Voshon Lenard	.20	.50
❑ 374 Lindsey Hunter	.20	.50
❑ 375 Mamadou N'Diaye	.20	.50
❑ 376 Chris Jefferies	.30	.75
❑ 377 Jelani McCoy	.20	.50
❑ 378 Lamond Murray	.20	.50
❑ 379 Eric Montross	.20	.50
❑ 380 Matt Harpring	.25	.60
❑ 381 Calbert Cheaney	.20	.50
❑ 382 Curtis Borchardt	.60	1.50
❑ 383 Mark Jackson	.25	.60
❑ 384 Scott Padgett	.20	.50
❑ 385 Jerry Stackhouse	.25	.60
❑ 386 Jared Jeffries	.60	1.50
❑ 387 Larry Hughes	.25	.60
❑ 388 Juan Dixon	1.00	2.50
❑ 389 Bryon Russell	.20	.50
❑ 390 Etan Thomas	.20	.50
❑ 391 Efthimios Rentzias RC	1.25	3.00
❑ 392 Manu Ginobili RC	3.00	8.00
❑ 393 Juaquin Hawkins RC	1.25	3.00
❑ 394 Rasual Butler RC	1.25	3.00
❑ 395 Ronald Murray RC	2.00	5.00
❑ 396 Igor Rakocevic RC	1.25	3.00
❑ 397 Tito Maddox RC	1.25	3.00
❑ 398 Mike Batiste RC	1.25	3.00
❑ 399 Sam Clancy RC	1.25	3.00
❑ 400 Tamar Slay RC	1.25	3.00
❑ 401 Lonny Baxter RC	1.25	3.00
❑ 402 Marko Jaric	1.25	3.00
❑ 403 Dan Gadzuric RC	1.25	3.00
❑ 404 Jannero Pargo RC	1.25	3.00
❑ 405 Pat Burke RC	1.25	3.00
❑ 406 Smush Parker RC	1.25	3.00
❑ 407 Reggie Evans RC	1.25	3.00
❑ 408 Gordan Giricek RC	1.25	3.00
❑ 409 Mehmet Okur RC	1.50	4.00
❑ 410 Jamal Sampson RC	1.25	3.00
❑ 411 Raul Lopez RC	1.25	3.00
❑ 412 Predrag Savovic RC	1.25	3.00
❑ 413 Carlos Boozer RC	2.50	6.00
❑ 414 Ken Johnson RC	1.25	3.00
❑ 415 Cezary Trybanski RC	1.25	3.00
❑ 416 Mike Wilks RC	1.25	3.00
❑ 417 J.R. Bremer RC	1.25	3.00
❑ 418 Junior Harrington RC	1.25	3.00
❑ 419 Nate Huffman RC	1.25	3.00
❑ 420 Michael Jordan	2.00	5.00

2003-04 Upper Deck

❑ COMP.SER.1 w/o SP's (300)	20.00	40.00
❑ COMMON CARD (1-300)	.08	.20
❑ COMMON ROOKIE (301-342)	1.25	3.00
❑ 1 Shareef Abdur-Rahim	.30	.75
❑ 2 Alan Henderson	.08	.20
❑ 3 Dan Dickau	.08	.20
❑ 4 Theo Ratliff	.20	.50
❑ 5 Terrell Brandon	.08	.20
❑ 6 Darvin Ham	.08	.20
❑ 7 Nazr Mohammed	.08	.20
❑ 8 Jason Terry	.30	.75
❑ 9 Dion Glover	.08	.20
❑ 10 Chris Crawford	.08	.20
❑ 11 Paul Pierce	.30	.75
❑ 12 Antoine Walker	.30	.75
❑ 13 Eric Williams	.08	.20
❑ 14 Kedrick Brown	.08	.20
❑ 15 Tony Battie	.08	.20
❑ 16 Vin Baker	.20	.50
❑ 17 Mark Blount	.08	.20
❑ 18 Tony Delk	.08	.20
❑ 19 Walter McCarty	.08	.20
❑ 20 Jumaine Jones	.20	.50
❑ 21 Jalen Rose	.30	.75
❑ 22 Marcus Fizer	.20	.50
❑ 23 Jamal Crawford	.08	.20
❑ 24 Donyell Marshall	.20	.50
❑ 25 Eddy Curry	.20	.50
❑ 26 Trenton Hassell	.08	.20
❑ 27 Michael Jordan	2.00	5.00
❑ 28 Tyson Chandler	.30	.75
❑ 29 Jay Williams	.20	.50
❑ 30 Scottie Pippen	.50	1.25
❑ 31 Eddie Robinson	.20	.50
❑ 32 Lonny Baxter	.08	.20
❑ 33 Darius Miles	.30	.75
❑ 34 DeSagana Diop	.08	.20
❑ 35 Ricky Davis	.30	.75
❑ 36 Chris Mihm	.08	.20
❑ 37 Carlos Boozer	.30	.75
❑ 38 Michael Stewart	.08	.20
❑ 39 Zydrunas Ilgauskas	.20	.50
❑ 40 Dajuan Wagner	.20	.50
❑ 41 J.R. Bremer	.08	.20
❑ 42 Kevin Ollie	.08	.20
❑ 43 Dirk Nowitzki	.50	1.25
❑ 44 Antawn Jamison	.30	.75
❑ 45 Shawn Bradley	.08	.20
❑ 46 Raef LaFrentz	.20	.50
❑ 47 Eduardo Najera	.20	.50
❑ 48 Travis Best	.08	.20
❑ 49 Danny Fortson	.08	.20
❑ 50 Michael Finley	.30	.75
❑ 51 Jiri Welsch	.20	.50
❑ 52 Steve Nash	.30	.75
❑ 53 Marcus Camby	.20	.50
❑ 54 Chris Anderson	.08	.20
❑ 55 Rodney White	.08	.20
❑ 56 Vincent Yarbrough	.08	.20
❑ 57 Nikoloz Tskitishvili	.08	.20
❑ 58 Nene	.20	.50
❑ 59 Andre Miller	.20	.50
❑ 60 Earl Boykins	.20	.50
❑ 61 Ryan Bowen	.08	.20
❑ 62 Ben Wallace	.30	.75
❑ 63 Tayshaun Prince	.20	.50
❑ 64 Richard Hamilton	.20	.50
❑ 65 Mehmet Okur	.08	.20
❑ 66 Bob Sura	.08	.20
❑ 67 Chucky Atkins	.08	.20
❑ 68 Chauncey Billups	.20	.50
❑ 69 Elden Campbell	.08	.20
❑ 70 Corliss Williamson	.20	.50
❑ 71 Zeljko Rebraca	.08	.20

❑ 72 Jason Richardson	.30	.75
❑ 73 Popeye Jones	.08	.20
❑ 74 Clifford Robinson	.08	.20
❑ 75 Mike Dunleavy	.20	.50
❑ 76 Troy Murphy	.30	.75
❑ 77 Speedy Claxton	.08	.20
❑ 78 Erick Dampier	.20	.50
❑ 79 Nick Van Exel	.30	.75
❑ 80 Avery Johnson	.08	.20
❑ 81 Adonal Foyle	.08	.20
❑ 82 Pepe Sanchez	.08	.20
❑ 83 Steve Francis	.30	.75
❑ 84 Glen Rice	.20	.50
❑ 85 Eddie Griffin	.20	.50
❑ 86 Moochie Norris	.08	.20
❑ 87 Maurice Taylor	.08	.20
❑ 88 Kelvin Cato	.08	.20
❑ 89 Jason Collier	.08	.20
❑ 90 Cuttino Mobley	.20	.50
❑ 91 Yao Ming	.75	2.00
❑ 92 Eric Piatkowski	.20	.50
❑ 93 Bostjan Nachbar	.08	.20
❑ 94 Adrian Griffin	.08	.20
❑ 95 Reggie Miller	.30	.75
❑ 96 Fred Jones	.08	.20
❑ 97 Scot Pollard	.08	.20
❑ 98 Jamaal Tinsley	.30	.75
❑ 99 Al Harrington	.20	.50
❑ 100 Jonathan Bender	.20	.50
❑ 101 Primoz Brezec	.08	.20
❑ 102 Ron Artest	.20	.50
❑ 103 Jermaine O'Neal	.30	.75
❑ 104 Kenny Anderson	.20	.50
❑ 105 Jeff Foster	.08	.20
❑ 106 Austin Croshere	.08	.20
❑ 107 Elton Brand	.30	.75
❑ 108 Tremaine Fowlkes	.08	.20
❑ 109 Quentin Richardson	.20	.50
❑ 110 Melvin Ely	.08	.20
❑ 111 Marko Jaric	.20	.50
❑ 112 Chris Wilcox	.08	.20
❑ 113 Wang Zhizhi	.30	.75
❑ 114 Corey Maggette	.20	.50
❑ 115 Keyon Dooling	.08	.20
❑ 116 Kobe Bryant	1.25	3.00
❑ 117 Shaquille O'Neal	.75	2.00
❑ 118 Slava Medvedenko	.08	.20
❑ 119 Gary Payton	.30	.75
❑ 120 Jannero Pargo	.08	.20
❑ 121 Kareem Rush	.20	.50
❑ 122 Karl Malone	.30	.75
❑ 123 Derek Fisher	.30	.75
❑ 124 Rick Fox	.20	.50
❑ 125 Devean George	.20	.50
❑ 126 Pau Gasol	.30	.75
❑ 127 Jason Williams	.20	.50
❑ 128 Stromile Swift	.20	.50
❑ 129 Wesley Person	.08	.20
❑ 130 Michael Dickerson	.08	.20
❑ 131 Lorenzen Wright	.08	.20
❑ 132 Earl Watson	.08	.20
❑ 133 Mike Miller	.30	.75
❑ 134 Shane Battier	.30	.75
❑ 135 Eddie Jones	.30	.75
❑ 136 Rasual Butler	.08	.20
❑ 137 Caron Butler	.30	.75
❑ 138 Brian Grant	.20	.50
❑ 139 Lamar Odom	.30	.75
❑ 140 Malik Allen	.08	.20
❑ 141 Ken Johnson	.08	.20
❑ 142 Samaki Walker	.08	.20
❑ 143 Sean Lampley	.08	.20
❑ 144 Vladimir Stepania	.08	.20
❑ 145 Erick Strickland	.08	.20
❑ 146 Toni Kukoc	.20	.50
❑ 147 Joel Przybilla	.08	.20
❑ 148 Tim Thomas	.20	.50
❑ 149 Dan Gadzuric	.08	.20
❑ 150 Joe Smith	.20	.50
❑ 151 Michael Redd	.30	.75
❑ 152 Desmond Mason	.20	.50
❑ 153 Brian Skinner	.08	.20
❑ 154 Kevin Garnett	.60	1.50
❑ 155 Michael Olowokandi	.08	.20
❑ 156 Troy Hudson	.08	.20
❑ 157 Latrell Sprewell	.30	.75
❑ 158 Wally Szczerbiak	.20	.50
❑ 159 Sam Cassell	.30	.75
❑ 160 Fred Hoiberg	.08	.20
❑ 161 Ervin Johnson	.08	.20
❑ 162 Mark Madsen	.08	.20
❑ 163 Gary Trent	.08	.20
❑ 164 Jason Kidd	.50	1.25
❑ 165 Dikembe Mutombo	.20	.50
❑ 166 Lucious Harris	.08	.20
❑ 167 Kerry Kittles	.08	.20
❑ 168 Brandon Armstrong	.08	.20
❑ 169 Jason Collins	.08	.20
❑ 170 Alonzo Mourning	.20	.50
❑ 171 Kenyon Martin	.30	.75
❑ 172 Richard Jefferson	.20	.50
❑ 173 Rodney Rogers	.08	.20
❑ 174 Aaron Williams	.08	.20
❑ 175 Jamal Mashburn	.20	.50
❑ 176 David Wesley	.08	.20
❑ 177 Kirk Haston	.08	.20
❑ 178 Courtney Alexander	.20	.50
❑ 179 Darrell Armstrong	.08	.20
❑ 180 Robert Traylor	.08	.20
❑ 181 George Lynch	.08	.20
❑ 182 Jamaal Magloire	.08	.20
❑ 183 Baron Davis	.30	.75
❑ 184 P.J. Brown	.08	.20
❑ 185 Sean Rooks	.08	.20
❑ 186 Stacey Augmon	.08	.20
❑ 187 Allan Houston	.20	.50
❑ 188 Antonio McDyess	.20	.50
❑ 189 Clarence Weatherspoon	.08	.20
❑ 190 Kurt Thomas	.20	.50
❑ 191 Shandon Anderson	.08	.20
❑ 192 Keith Van Horn	.30	.75
❑ 193 Michael Doleac	.08	.20
❑ 194 Othella Harrington	.08	.20
❑ 195 Charlie Ward	.08	.20
❑ 196 Lee Nailon	.08	.20
❑ 197 Tracy McGrady	.75	2.00
❑ 198 Pat Garrity	.08	.20
❑ 199 Grant Hill	.30	.75
❑ 200 Gordan Giricek	.20	.50
❑ 201 Steven Hunter	.08	.20
❑ 202 Jeryl Sasser	.08	.20
❑ 203 Andrew DeClercq	.08	.20
❑ 204 Juwan Howard	.20	.50
❑ 205 Tyronn Lue	.08	.20
❑ 206 Drew Gooden	.20	.50
❑ 207 Marc Jackson	.20	.50
❑ 208 Aaron McKie	.20	.50
❑ 209 Derrick Coleman	.08	.20
❑ 210 Eric Snow	.20	.50
❑ 211 Glenn Robinson	.30	.75
❑ 212 Greg Buckner	.08	.20
❑ 213 Allen Iverson	.60	1.50
❑ 214 Kenny Thomas	.08	.20
❑ 215 Sam Clancy	.08	.20
❑ 216 Monty Williams	.08	.20
❑ 217 Stephon Marbury	.30	.75
❑ 218 Shawn Marion	.30	.75
❑ 219 Joe Johnson	.20	.50
❑ 220 Bo Outlaw	.08	.20
❑ 221 Amare Stoudemire	.60	1.50
❑ 222 Casey Jacobsen	.08	.20
❑ 223 Tom Gugliotta	.08	.20
❑ 224 Scott Williams	.08	.20
❑ 225 Jake Tsakalidis	.08	.20
❑ 226 Damon Stoudamire	.20	.50
❑ 227 Arvydas Sabonis	.08	.20
❑ 228 Zach Randolph	.30	.75
❑ 229 Ruben Patterson	.20	.50
❑ 230 Derek Anderson	.20	.50
❑ 231 Dale Davis	.20	.50
❑ 232 Bonzi Wells	.20	.50
❑ 233 Rasheed Wallace	.30	.75
❑ 234 Jeff McInnis	.08	.20
❑ 235 Qyntel Woods	.08	.20
❑ 236 Chris Webber	.30	.75
❑ 237 Doug Christie	.20	.50
❑ 238 Vlade Divac	.20	.50
❑ 239 Bobby Jackson	.20	.50
❑ 240 Lawrence Funderburke	.08	.20
❑ 241 Peja Stojakovic	.30	.75
❑ 242 Gerald Wallace	.20	.50
❑ 243 Brad Miller	.30	.75
❑ 244 Mike Bibby	.30	.75
❑ 245 Anthony Peeler	.08	.20
❑ 246 Jim Jackson	.08	.20
❑ 247 David Robinson	.30	.75
❑ 248 Ron Mercer	.08	.20
❑ 249 Tony Parker	.30	.75
❑ 250 Malik Rose	.08	.20
❑ 251 Kevin Willis	.08	.20
❑ 252 Manu Ginobili	.30	.75
❑ 253 Bruce Bowen	.08	.20
❑ 254 Hedo Turkoglu	.30	.75
❑ 255 Tim Duncan	.60	1.50
❑ 256 Robert Horry	.20	.50
❑ 257 Radoslav Nesterovic	.20	.50
❑ 258 Ray Allen	.30	.75
❑ 259 Rashard Lewis	.30	.75
❑ 260 Reggie Evans	.08	.20
❑ 261 Brent Barry	.20	.50
❑ 262 Ronald Murray	.08	.20
❑ 263 Vladimir Radmanovic	.08	.20
❑ 264 Predrag Drobnjak	.08	.20
❑ 265 Antonio Daniels	.08	.20
❑ 266 Vitaly Potapenko	.08	.20
❑ 267 Calvin Booth	.08	.20
❑ 268 Vince Carter	.75	2.00
❑ 269 Chris Jefferies	.08	.20
❑ 270 Mengke Bateer	.08	.20
❑ 271 Alvin Williams	.08	.20
❑ 272 Jerome Williams	.08	.20
❑ 273 Michael Bradley	.08	.20
❑ 274 Lamond Murray	.08	.20
❑ 275 Antonio Davis	.08	.20
❑ 276 Morris Peterson	.20	.50
❑ 277 Jerome Moiso	.08	.20
❑ 278 Carlos Arroyo	.50	1.25
❑ 279 Matt Harpring	.30	.75
❑ 280 Andrei Kirilenko	.30	.75
❑ 281 Jarron Collins	.08	.20
❑ 282 Greg Ostertag	.08	.20
❑ 283 Curtis Borchardt	.08	.20
❑ 284 DeShawn Stevenson	.08	.20
❑ 285 Keon Clark	.20	.50
❑ 286 John Amaechi	.08	.20
❑ 287 Raul Lopez	.08	.20
❑ 288 Jerry Stackhouse	.30	.75
❑ 289 Kwame Brown	.30	.75
❑ 290 Larry Hughes	.20	.50
❑ 291 Brendan Haywood	.08	.20
❑ 292 Juan Dixon	.20	.50
❑ 293 Bryon Russell	.08	.20
❑ 294 Christian Laettner	.20	.50
❑ 295 Jahidi White	.08	.20
❑ 296 Jared Jeffries	.08	.20
❑ 297 Gilbert Arenas	.30	.75
❑ 298 Kobe Bryant CL	.60	1.50
❑ 299 Michael Jordan CL	1.00	2.50
❑ 300 Michael Jordan CL	1.00	2.50
❑ 301 LeBron James RC	25.00	50.00
❑ 302 Darko Milicic RC	1.50	4.00
❑ 303 Carmelo Anthony RC	4.00	10.00
❑ 304 Chris Bosh RC	2.50	6.00
❑ 305 Dwyane Wade RC	3.00	8.00
❑ 306 Chris Kaman RC	1.50	4.00
❑ 307 Kirk Hinrich RC	1.50	4.00
❑ 308 T.J. Ford RC	1.25	2.50
❑ 309 Mike Sweetney RC	1.25	3.00
❑ 310 Jarvis Hayes RC	1.25	3.00
❑ 311 Mickael Pietrus RC	1.25	3.00
❑ 312 Nick Collison RC	1.25	3.00
❑ 313 Marcus Banks RC	1.25	3.00
❑ 314 Luke Ridnour RC	1.50	4.00
❑ 315 Reece Gaines RC	1.25	3.00
❑ 316 Troy Bell RC	1.25	3.00
❑ 317 Zarko Cabarkapa RC	1.25	3.00
❑ 318 David West RC	2.50	6.00
❑ 319 Aleksandar Pavlovic RC	1.50	4.00
❑ 320 Dahntay Jones RC	1.25	3.00
❑ 321 Boris Diaw RC	1.25	3.00
❑ 322 Zoran Planinic RC	1.25	3.00
❑ 323 Travis Outlaw RC	1.50	4.00
❑ 324 Brian Cook RC	1.25	3.00
❑ 325 Kirk Penney RC	1.25	3.00
❑ 326 Ndudi Ebi RC	1.25	3.00
❑ 327 Kendrick Perkins RC	1.50	4.00
❑ 328 Leandro Barbosa RC	2.00	5.00
❑ 329 Josh Howard RC	1.50	4.00
❑ 330 Maciej Lampe RC	1.25	3.00
❑ 331 Jason Kapono RC	1.25	3.00
❑ 332 Luke Walton RC	1.25	3.00
❑ 333 Jerome Beasley RC	1.25	3.00
❑ 334 Brandon Hunter RC	1.25	3.00
❑ 335 Kyle Korver RC	2.00	5.00
❑ 336 Travis Hansen RC	1.25	3.00
❑ 337 Steve Blake RC	1.25	3.00
❑ 338 Slavko Vranes RC	1.25	3.00

❑ 339 Zaur Pachulia RC	1.25	3.00
❑ 340 Keith Bogans RC	1.25	3.00
❑ 341 Willie Green RC	1.25	3.00
❑ 342 Maurice Williams RC	2.00	5.00

2004-05 Upper Deck

❑ COMP.SET w/o SP's (200)	20.00	40.00
❑ COMMON CARD (1-200)	.08	.20
❑ COMMON ROOKIE (201-220)	1.25	3.00
❑ COMMON ROOKIE (221-230)		
❑ 1 Antoine Walker	.30	.75
❑ 2 Boris Diaw	.25	.60
❑ 3 Al Harrington	.25	.60
❑ 4 Tony Delk	.20	.50
❑ 5 Jason Collier	.20	.50
❑ 6 Chris Crawford	.20	.50
❑ 7 Ricky Davis	.25	.60
❑ 8 Paul Pierce	.30	.75
❑ 9 Jiri Welsch	.20	.50
❑ 10 Gary Payton	.30	.75
❑ 11 Rick Fox	.25	.60
❑ 12 Mark Blount	.20	.50
❑ 13 Adrian Griffin	.20	.50
❑ 14 Tyson Chandler	.25	.60
❑ 15 Eddy Curry	.25	.60
❑ 16 Kirk Hinrich	.25	.60
❑ 17 Scottie Pippen	.50	1.25
❑ 18 Jannero Pargo	.20	.50
❑ 19 Antonio Davis	.20	.50
❑ 20 Gerald Wallace	.30	.75
❑ 21 Eddie House	.20	.50
❑ 22 Steve Smith	.25	.60
❑ 23 Brandon Hunter	.20	.50
❑ 24 Theron Smith	.20	.50
❑ 25 Jahidi White	.20	.50
❑ 26 LeBron James	2.00	5.00
❑ 27 DeSagana Diop	.20	.50
❑ 28 Zydrunas Ilgauskas	.25	.60
❑ 29 Dajuan Wagner	.20	.50
❑ 30 Jeff McInnis	.20	.50
❑ 31 Eric Snow	.20	.50
❑ 32 Dirk Nowitzki	.50	1.25
❑ 33 Jason Terry	.25	.60
❑ 34 Michael Finley	.30	.75
❑ 35 Jerry Stackhouse	.25	.60
❑ 36 Erick Dampier	.20	.50
❑ 37 Josh Howard	.30	.75
❑ 38 Marquis Daniels	.20	.50
❑ 39 Carmelo Anthony	1.00	2.50
❑ 40 Nene	.25	.60
❑ 41 Andre Miller	.25	.60
❑ 42 Earl Boykins	.20	.50
❑ 43 Marcus Camby	.25	.60
❑ 44 Voshon Lenard	.20	.50
❑ 45 Kenyon Martin	.30	.75
❑ 46 Richard Hamilton	.25	.60
❑ 47 Chauncey Billups	.30	.75
❑ 48 Rasheed Wallace	.30	.75
❑ 49 Tayshaun Prince	.25	.60
❑ 50 Ben Wallace	.25	.60
❑ 51 Antonio McDyess	.25	.60
❑ 52 Carlos Delfino	.30	.75
❑ 53 Jason Richardson	.30	.75
❑ 54 Dale Davis	.20	.50
❑ 55 Adonal Foyle	.20	.50
❑ 56 Mickael Pietrus	.25	.60
❑ 57 Mike Dunleavy	.25	.60
❑ 58 Speedy Claxton	.20	.50
❑ 59 Derek Fisher	.25	.60
❑ 60 Yao Ming	.75	2.00
❑ 61 Jim Jackson	.20	.50
❑ 62 Tracy McGrady	.60	1.50
❑ 63 Maurice Taylor	.20	.50
❑ 64 Juwan Howard	.25	.60
❑ 65 Tyronn Lue	.20	.50
❑ 66 Dikembe Mutombo	.25	.60

❑ 67 Reggie Miller	.30	.75
❑ 68 Stephen Jackson	.25	.60
❑ 69 Jermaine O'Neal	.30	.75
❑ 70 Jamaal Tinsley	.25	.60
❑ 71 Ron Artest	.25	.60
❑ 72 Fred Jones	.20	.50
❑ 73 Jonathan Bender	.20	.50
❑ 74 Kerry Kittles	.25	.60
❑ 75 Chris Kaman	.25	.60
❑ 76 Elton Brand	.30	.75
❑ 77 Marko Jaric	.20	.50
❑ 78 Corey Maggette	.25	.60
❑ 79 Bobby Simmons	.20	.50
❑ 80 Chris Wilcox	.20	.50
❑ 81 Lamar Odom	.30	.75
❑ 82 Karl Malone	.30	.75
❑ 83 Kobe Bryant	1.50	4.00
❑ 84 Kareem Rush	.20	.50
❑ 85 Caron Butler	.25	.60
❑ 86 Devean George	.20	.50
❑ 87 Vlade Divac	.25	.60
❑ 88 Pau Gasol	.30	.75
❑ 89 Bonzi Wells	.20	.50
❑ 90 Mike Miller	.25	.60
❑ 91 Jason Williams	.25	.60
❑ 92 Shane Battier	.25	.60
❑ 93 James Posey	.20	.50
❑ 94 Stromile Swift	.20	.50
❑ 95 Shaquille O'Neal	.75	2.00
❑ 96 Dwyane Wade	1.00	2.50
❑ 97 Eddie Jones	.25	.60
❑ 98 Wang Zhizhi	.20	.50
❑ 99 Rasual Butler	.20	.50
❑ 100 Malik Allen	.20	.50
❑ 101 Udonis Haslem	.25	.60
❑ 102 Michael Redd	.30	.75
❑ 103 T.J. Ford	.25	.60
❑ 104 Keith Van Horn	.25	.60
❑ 105 Toni Kukoc	.25	.60
❑ 106 Desmond Mason	.25	.60
❑ 107 Mike James	.20	.50
❑ 108 Joe Smith	.20	.50
❑ 109 Kevin Garnett	.60	1.50
❑ 110 Michael Olowokandi	.20	.50
❑ 111 Sam Cassell	.25	.60
❑ 112 Troy Hudson	.20	.50
❑ 113 Latrell Sprewell	.25	.60
❑ 114 Fred Hoiberg	.20	.50
❑ 115 Wally Szczerbiak	.25	.60
❑ 116 Richard Jefferson	.30	.75
❑ 117 Alonzo Mourning	.30	.75
❑ 118 Jason Kidd	.50	1.25
❑ 119 Jacque Vaughn	.20	.50
❑ 120 Jason Collins	.20	.50
❑ 121 Aaron Williams	.20	.50
❑ 122 Zoran Planinic	.20	.50
❑ 123 Jamaal Magloire	.20	.50
❑ 124 P.J. Brown	.20	.50
❑ 125 Baron Davis	.30	.75
❑ 126 Darrell Armstrong	.20	.50
❑ 127 Jamal Mashburn	.25	.60
❑ 128 Rodney Rogers	.20	.50
❑ 129 David Wesley	.20	.50
❑ 130 Allan Houston	.25	.60
❑ 131 Jamal Crawford	.25	.60
❑ 132 Stephon Marbury	.30	.75
❑ 133 Tim Thomas	.20	.50
❑ 134 Anfernee Hardaway	.30	.75
❑ 135 Kurt Thomas	.20	.50
❑ 136 Mike Sweetney	.20	.50
❑ 137 Tony Battie	.20	.50
❑ 138 DeShawn Stevenson	.20	.50
❑ 139 Steve Francis	.30	.75
❑ 140 Cuttino Mobley	.25	.60
❑ 141 Hedo Turkoglu	.25	.60
❑ 142 Keith Bogans	.20	.50
❑ 143 Samuel Dalembert	.20	.50
❑ 144 Kenny Thomas	.20	.50
❑ 145 Allen Iverson	.60	1.50
❑ 146 Aaron McKie	.20	.50
❑ 147 Glenn Robinson	.25	.60
❑ 148 Willie Green	.20	.50
❑ 149 Corliss Williamson	.20	.50
❑ 150 Shawn Marion	.30	.75
❑ 151 Leandro Barbosa	.30	.75
❑ 152 Amare Stoudemire	.60	1.50
❑ 153 Quentin Richardson	.25	.60
❑ 154 Joe Johnson	.30	.75
❑ 155 Steve Nash	.50	1.25

❑ 156 Damon Stoudamire	.25	.60
❑ 157 Theo Ratliff	.20	.50
❑ 158 Shareef Abdur-Rahim	.25	.60
❑ 159 Derek Anderson	.25	.60
❑ 160 Zach Randolph	.30	.75
❑ 161 Nick Van Exel	.25	.60
❑ 162 Darius Miles	.25	.60
❑ 163 Mike Bibby	.25	.60
❑ 164 Brad Miller	.25	.60
❑ 165 Peja Stojakovic	.25	.60
❑ 166 Bobby Jackson	.20	.50
❑ 167 Chris Webber	.30	.75
❑ 168 Darius Songaila	.20	.50
❑ 169 Doug Christie	.20	.50
❑ 170 Manu Ginobili	.30	.75
❑ 171 Brent Barry	.20	.50
❑ 172 Tony Parker	.30	.75
❑ 173 Malik Rose	.20	.50
❑ 174 Tim Duncan	.60	1.50
❑ 175 Radoslav Nesterovic	.20	.50
❑ 176 Bruce Bowen	.20	.50
❑ 177 Rashard Lewis	.30	.75
❑ 178 Vladimir Radmanovic	.20	.50
❑ 179 Ray Allen	.30	.75
❑ 180 Antonio Daniels	.20	.50
❑ 181 Ronald Murray	.20	.50
❑ 182 Luke Ridnour	.20	.50
❑ 183 Vince Carter	.60	1.50
❑ 184 Donyell Marshall	.20	.50
❑ 185 Chris Bosh	.30	.75
❑ 186 Morris Peterson	.25	.60
❑ 187 Jalen Rose	.25	.60
❑ 188 Rafer Alston	.20	.50
❑ 189 Carlos Arroyo	.30	.75
❑ 190 Matt Harpring	.25	.60
❑ 191 Andrei Kirilenko	.30	.75
❑ 192 Carlos Boozer	.30	.75
❑ 193 Gordan Giricek	.20	.50
❑ 194 Mehmet Okur	.25	.60
❑ 195 Antawn Jamison	.30	.75
❑ 196 Larry Hughes	.25	.60
❑ 197 Gilbert Arenas	.30	.75
❑ 198 Kwame Brown	.20	.50
❑ 199 Jarvis Hayes	.20	.50
❑ 200 Juan Dixon	.20	.50
❑ 201 Rafael Araujo RC	1.25	3.00
❑ 202 Luke Jackson RC	1.25	3.00
❑ 203 Andris Biedrins RC	2.00	5.00
❑ 204 Robert Swift RC	1.25	3.00
❑ 205 Kris Humphries RC	2.00	5.00
❑ 206 Al Jefferson RC	2.50	6.00
❑ 207 Kirk Snyder RC	1.25	3.00
❑ 208 J.R. Smith RC	2.50	6.00
❑ 209 Dorell Wright RC	1.50	4.00
❑ 210 Jameer Nelson RC	1.50	4.00
❑ 211 Pavel Podkolzine RC	1.25	3.00
❑ 212 Viktor Khryapa RC	1.25	3.00
❑ 213 Sergei Monia RC	1.25	3.00
❑ 214 Delonte West RC	2.00	5.00
❑ 215 Tony Allen RC	1.50	4.00
❑ 216 Kevin Martin RC	1.50	4.00
❑ 217 Sasha Vujacic RC	1.25	3.00
❑ 218 Beno Udrih RC	1.50	4.00
❑ 219 David Harrison RC	1.25	3.00
❑ 220 Chris Duhon RC	2.00	5.00
❑ 221 Josh Smith SP RC	4.00	10.00
❑ 222 Sebastian Telfair SP RC	1.50	4.00
❑ 223 Andre Iguodala SP RC	4.00	10.00
❑ 224 Dwight Howard SP RC	5.00	12.00
❑ 225 Emeka Okafor SP RC	3.00	8.00
❑ 226 Ben Gordon SP RC	2.00	5.00
❑ 227 Shaun Livingston SP RC	1.50	4.00
❑ 228 Devin Harris SP RC	3.00	8.00
❑ 229 Josh Childress SP RC	1.50	4.00
❑ 230 Luol Deng SP RC	2.00	5.00

2005-06 Upper Deck

❑ COMP.SET w/o SP's (200)	20.00	40.00
❑ COMMON CARD (1-200)	.20	.50
❑ COMMON ROOKIE (201-220)	1.25	3.00
❑ COMMON ROOKIE (221-230)	2.00	5.00
❑ 1 Josh Childress	.25	.60
❑ 2 Josh Smith	.30	.75
❑ 3 Al Harrington	.20	.50
❑ 4 Tyronn Lue	.20	.50
❑ 5 Boris Diaw	.25	.60
❑ 6 Tony Delk	.20	.50
❑ 7 Paul Pierce	.30	.75
❑ 8 Antoine Walker	.25	.60
❑ 9 Gary Payton	.30	.75
❑ 10 Al Jefferson	.30	.75
❑ 11 Tony Allen	.20	.50
❑ 12 Ricky Davis	.30	.75
❑ 13 Delonte West	.25	.60
❑ 14 Emeka Okafor	.30	.75
❑ 15 Primoz Brezec	.20	.50
❑ 16 Kareem Rush	.20	.50
❑ 17 Gerald Wallace	.30	.75
❑ 18 Brevin Knight	.20	.50
❑ 19 Jason Kapono	.20	.50
❑ 20 Kirk Hinrich	.30	.75
❑ 21 Ben Gordon	.40	1.00
❑ 22 Eddy Curry	.25	.60
❑ 23 Michael Jordan	2.00	5.00
❑ 24 Andres Nocioni	.20	.50
❑ 25 Chris Duhon	.25	.60
❑ 26 Luol Deng	.30	.75
❑ 27 LeBron James	1.50	4.00
❑ 28 Zydrunas Ilgauskas	.25	.60
❑ 29 Drew Gooden	.25	.60
❑ 30 Jeff McInnis	.20	.50
❑ 31 Dajuan Wagner	.20	.50
❑ 32 Larry Hughes	.25	.60
❑ 33 Robert Traylor	.20	.50
❑ 34 Dirk Nowitzki	.50	1.25
❑ 35 Michael Finley	.30	.75
❑ 36 Jerry Stackhouse	.30	.75
❑ 37 Josh Howard	.30	.75
❑ 38 Marquis Daniels	.25	.60
❑ 39 Devin Harris	.30	.75
❑ 40 Jason Terry	.30	.75
❑ 41 Carmelo Anthony	.60	1.50
❑ 42 Kenyon Martin	.30	.75
❑ 43 Andre Miller	.25	.60
❑ 44 Earl Boykins	.20	.50
❑ 45 Nene	.20	.50
❑ 46 Marcus Camby	.25	.60
❑ 47 Ben Wallace	.30	.75
❑ 48 Richard Hamilton	.25	.60
❑ 49 Chauncey Billups	.30	.75
❑ 50 Rasheed Wallace	.30	.75
❑ 51 Tayshaun Prince	.30	.75
❑ 52 Carlos Arroyo	.30	.75
❑ 53 Antonio McDyess	.20	.50
❑ 54 Jason Richardson	.30	.75
❑ 55 Baron Davis	.30	.75
❑ 56 Troy Murphy	.30	.75
❑ 57 Mickael Pietrus	.25	.60
❑ 58 Derek Fisher	.20	.50
❑ 59 Mike Dunleavy	.25	.60
❑ 60 Yao Ming	.75	2.00
❑ 61 Tracy McGrady	.60	1.50
❑ 62 David Wesley	.20	.50
❑ 63 Bob Sura	.20	.50
❑ 64 Mike James	.20	.50
❑ 65 Jon Barry	.20	.50
❑ 66 Jermaine O'Neal	.30	.75
❑ 67 Ron Artest	.25	.60
❑ 68 Stephen Jackson	.25	.60
❑ 69 Jamaal Tinsley	.25	.60
❑ 70 Dale Davis	.20	.50
❑ 71 Anthony Johnson	.20	.50
❑ 72 Elton Brand	.30	.75
❑ 73 Corey Maggette	.25	.60
❑ 74 Bobby Simmons	.20	.50
❑ 75 Marko Jaric	.20	.50
❑ 76 Shaun Livingston	.20	.50
❑ 77 Chris Kaman	.20	.50
❑ 78 Chris Wilcox	.20	.50
❑ 79 Kobe Bryant	1.50	4.00
❑ 80 Caron Butler	.30	.75
❑ 81 Lamar Odom	.30	.75
❑ 82 Chucky Atkins	.20	.50
❑ 83 Brian Cook	.20	.50
❑ 84 Devean George	.25	.60
❑ 85 Sasha Vujacic	.25	.60
❑ 86 Pau Gasol	.30	.75
❑ 87 Mike Miller	.30	.75
❑ 88 Jason Williams	.25	.60
❑ 89 Shane Battier	.30	.75
❑ 90 Bonzi Wells	.25	.60
❑ 91 James Posey	.20	.50
❑ 92 Stromile Swift	.25	.60
❑ 93 Shaquille O'Neal	.75	2.00
❑ 94 Dwyane Wade	.75	2.00
❑ 95 Eddie Jones	.20	.50
❑ 96 Udonis Haslem	.30	.75
❑ 97 Damon Jones	.25	.60
❑ 98 Alonzo Mourning	.40	1.00
❑ 99 Keyon Dooling	.20	.50
❑ 100 Michael Redd	.30	.75
❑ 101 Desmond Mason	.20	.50
❑ 102 Maurice Williams	.25	.60
❑ 103 Joe Smith	.25	.60
❑ 104 Toni Kukoc	.20	.50
❑ 105 Dan Gadzuric	.20	.50
❑ 106 T.J. Ford	.25	.60
❑ 107 Kevin Garnett	.60	1.50
❑ 108 Sam Cassell	.30	.75
❑ 109 Latrell Sprewell	.20	.50
❑ 110 Wally Szczerbiak	.25	.60
❑ 111 Troy Hudson	.20	.50
❑ 112 Eddie Griffin	.20	.50
❑ 113 Jason Kidd	.50	1.25
❑ 114 Richard Jefferson	.25	.60
❑ 115 Vince Carter	.60	1.50
❑ 116 Nenad Krstic	.25	.60
❑ 117 Scott Padgett	.20	.50
❑ 118 Jason Collins	.20	.50
❑ 119 Jamaal Magloire	.20	.50
❑ 120 J.R. Smith	.25	.60
❑ 121 Speedy Claxton	.20	.50
❑ 122 Lee Nailon	.20	.50
❑ 123 P.J. Brown	.20	.50
❑ 124 Chris Andersen	.25	.60
❑ 125 Stephon Marbury	.30	.75
❑ 126 Jamal Crawford	.25	.60
❑ 127 Allan Houston	.20	.50
❑ 128 Trevor Ariza	.25	.60
❑ 129 Quentin Richardson	.25	.60
❑ 130 Tim Thomas	.20	.50
❑ 131 Michael Sweetney	.25	.60
❑ 132 Dwight Howard	.60	1.50
❑ 133 Steve Francis	.30	.75
❑ 134 Grant Hill	.30	.75
❑ 135 Jameer Nelson	.25	.60
❑ 136 Hedo Turkoglu	.25	.60
❑ 137 Doug Christie	.20	.50
❑ 138 DeShawn Stevenson	.20	.50
❑ 139 Allen Iverson	.60	1.50
❑ 140 Chris Webber	.30	.75
❑ 141 Andre Iguodala	.30	.75
❑ 142 Samuel Dalembert	.20	.50
❑ 143 Kyle Korver	.30	.75
❑ 144 Willie Green	.20	.50
❑ 145 Marc Jackson	.20	.50
❑ 146 Steve Nash	.40	1.00
❑ 147 Amare Stoudemire	.60	1.50
❑ 148 Joe Johnson	.30	.75
❑ 149 Shawn Marion	.30	.75
❑ 150 Kurt Thomas	.20	.50
❑ 151 Jim Jackson	.20	.50
❑ 152 Leandro Barbosa	.30	.75
❑ 153 Damon Stoudamire	.25	.60
❑ 154 Shareef Abdur-Rahim	.30	.75
❑ 155 Zach Randolph	.30	.75
❑ 156 Darius Miles	.30	.75
❑ 157 Sebastian Telfair	.25	.60
❑ 158 Theo Ratliff	.20	.50
❑ 159 Nick Van Exel	.30	.75
❑ 160 Peja Stojakovic	.30	.75
❑ 161 Mike Bibby	.30	.75
❑ 162 Brad Miller	.30	.75
❑ 163 Cuttino Mobley	.25	.60
❑ 164 Bobby Jackson	.20	.50
❑ 165 Kenny Thomas	.20	.50
❑ 166 Corliss Williamson	.20	.50
❑ 167 Tim Duncan	.60	1.50
❑ 168 Tony Parker	.30	.75
❑ 169 Manu Ginobili	.30	.75
❑ 170 Robert Horry	.25	.60
❑ 171 Beno Udrih	.20	.50
❑ 172 Nazr Mohammed	.20	.50
❑ 173 Brent Barry	.20	.50
❑ 174 Ray Allen	.30	.75
❑ 175 Rashard Lewis	.30	.75
❑ 176 Ronald Murray	.20	.50
❑ 177 Luke Ridnour	.25	.60
❑ 178 Vladimir Radmanovic	.20	.50
❑ 179 Antonio Daniels	.20	.50
❑ 180 Danny Fortson	.20	.50
❑ 181 Chris Bosh	.30	.75
❑ 182 Donyell Marshall	.20	.50
❑ 183 Jalen Rose	.30	.75
❑ 184 Morris Peterson	.25	.60
❑ 185 Rafer Alston	.20	.50
❑ 186 Matt Bonner	.20	.50
❑ 187 Aaron Williams	.20	.50
❑ 188 Andrei Kirilenko	.30	.75
❑ 189 Carlos Boozer	.30	.75
❑ 190 Matt Harpring	.25	.60
❑ 191 Keith McLeod	.20	.50
❑ 192 Raja Bell	.20	.50
❑ 193 Raul Lopez	.20	.50
❑ 194 Gordan Giricek	.20	.50
❑ 195 Gilbert Arenas	.30	.75
❑ 196 Antawn Jamison	.30	.75
❑ 197 Jarvis Hayes	.20	.50
❑ 198 Brendan Haywood	.20	.50
❑ 199 Juan Dixon	.20	.50
❑ 200 Etan Thomas	.20	.50
❑ 201 Daniel Ewing RC	1.50	4.00
❑ 202 Nate Robinson RC	2.00	5.00
❑ 203 C.J. Miles RC	1.25	3.00
❑ 204 Salim Stoudamire RC	1.50	4.00
❑ 205 Francisco Garcia RC	1.50	4.00
❑ 206 Julius Hodge RC	1.50	4.00
❑ 207 Andrew Bynum RC	4.00	10.00
❑ 208 Joey Graham RC	1.25	3.00
❑ 209 Johan Petro RC	1.25	3.00
❑ 210 Luther Head RC	1.50	4.00
❑ 211 Channing Frye RC	1.50	4.00
❑ 212 Sean May RC	1.50	4.00
❑ 213 Wayne Simien RC	1.50	4.00
❑ 214 Antoine Wright RC	1.25	3.00
❑ 215 Ike Diogu RC	1.50	4.00
❑ 216 Jarrett Jack RC	1.25	3.00
❑ 217 Jason Maxiell RC	1.50	4.00
❑ 218 David Lee RC	2.50	6.00
❑ 219 Travis Diener RC	1.25	3.00
❑ 220 Danny Granger RC	3.00	8.00
❑ 221 Charlie Villanueva SP RC	3.00	8.00
❑ 222 Hakim Warrick SP RC	3.00	8.00
❑ 223 Rashad McCants SP RC	2.50	6.00
❑ 224 Raymond Felton SP RC	2.50	6.00
❑ 225 Martell Webster SP RC	2.00	5.00
❑ 226 Gerald Green SP RC	2.00	5.00
❑ 227 Deron Williams SP RC	5.00	12.00
❑ 228 Andrew Bogut SP RC	2.50	6.00
❑ 229 Marvin Williams SP RC	3.00	8.00
❑ 230 Chris Paul SP RC	6.00	15.00

2006-07 Upper Deck

❑ COMP.SET w/o SP's (200)	15.00	40.00
❑ 1 Josh Childress	.25	.60
❑ 2 Al Harrington	.20	.50

❑ 3 Joe Johnson	.25	.60
❑ 4 Josh Smith	.30	.75
❑ 5 Salim Stoudamire	.25	.60
❑ 6 Marvin Williams	.30	.75
❑ 7 Tony Allen	.25	.60
❑ 8 Dan Dickau	.20	.50
❑ 9 Al Jefferson	.30	.75
❑ 10 Raef LaFrentz	.20	.50
❑ 11 Michael Olowokandi	.20	.50
❑ 12 Paul Pierce	.30	.75
❑ 13 Wally Szczerbiak	.25	.60
❑ 14 Alan Anderson	.20	.50
❑ 15 Raymond Felton	.40	1.00
❑ 16 Othella Harrington	.20	.50
❑ 17 Sean May	.25	.60
❑ 18 Emeka Okafor	.30	.75
❑ 19 Primoz Brezec	.20	.50
❑ 20 Gerald Wallace	.30	.75
❑ 21 Tyson Chandler	.30	.75
❑ 22 Michael Jordan	2.00	5.00
❑ 23 Luol Deng	.30	.75
❑ 24 Chris Duhon	.20	.50
❑ 25 Ben Gordon	.40	1.00
❑ 26 Kirk Hinrich	.30	.75
❑ 27 Mike Sweetney	.20	.50
❑ 28 Drew Gooden	.25	.60
❑ 29 Larry Hughes	.25	.60
❑ 30 Zydrunas Ilgauskas	.25	.60
❑ 31 LeBron James	1.50	4.00
❑ 32 Damon Jones	.25	.60
❑ 33 Donyell Marshall	.20	.50
❑ 34 Anderson Varejao	.25	.60
❑ 35 Erick Dampier	.20	.50
❑ 36 Marquis Daniels	.25	.60
❑ 37 Devin Harris	.30	.75
❑ 38 Josh Howard	.30	.75
❑ 39 Dirk Nowitzki	.50	1.25
❑ 40 Jerry Stackhouse	.30	.75
❑ 41 Jason Terry	.30	.75
❑ 42 Carmelo Anthony	.40	1.00
❑ 43 Earl Boykins	.20	.50
❑ 44 Marcus Camby	.25	.60
❑ 45 Kenyon Martin	.30	.75
❑ 46 Andre Miller	.25	.60
❑ 47 Eduardo Najera	.20	.50
❑ 48 Nene	.20	.50
❑ 49 Chauncey Billups	.30	.75
❑ 50 Richard Hamilton	.25	.60
❑ 51 Lindsey Hunter	.20	.50
❑ 52 Antonio McDyess	.20	.50
❑ 53 Tayshaun Prince	.30	.75
❑ 54 Ben Wallace	.30	.75
❑ 55 Rasheed Wallace	.30	.75
❑ 56 Baron Davis	.30	.75
❑ 57 Ike Diogu	.25	.60
❑ 58 Mike Dunleavy	.25	.60
❑ 59 Derek Fisher	.25	.60
❑ 60 Troy Murphy	.30	.75
❑ 61 Mickael Pietrus	.25	.60
❑ 62 Jason Richardson	.30	.75
❑ 63 Rafer Alston	.20	.50
❑ 64 Luther Head	.25	.60
❑ 65 Juwan Howard	.25	.60
❑ 66 Tracy McGrady	.60	1.50
❑ 67 Dikembe Mutombo	.25	.60
❑ 68 Stromile Swift	.25	.60
❑ 69 Yao Ming	.75	2.00
❑ 70 Austin Croshere	.20	.50
❑ 71 Stephen Jackson	.25	.60
❑ 72 Sarunas Jasikevicius	.25	.60
❑ 73 Jermaine O'Neal	.30	.75
❑ 74 Peja Stojakovic	.30	.75
❑ 75 Jamaal Tinsley	.25	.60
❑ 76 Elton Brand	.30	.75
❑ 77 Sam Cassell	.30	.75
❑ 78 Chris Kaman	.20	.50
❑ 79 Shaun Livingston	.20	.50
❑ 80 Corey Maggette	.25	.60
❑ 81 Cuttino Mobley	.25	.60
❑ 82 Vladimir Radmanovic	.20	.50
❑ 83 Kwame Brown	.25	.60
❑ 84 Kobe Bryant	1.50	4.00
❑ 85 Devean George	.25	.60
❑ 86 Lamar Odom	.30	.75
❑ 87 Ronny Turiaf	.25	.60
❑ 88 Sasha Vujacic	.20	.50
❑ 89 Luke Walton	.25	.60
❑ 90 Shane Battier	.30	.75
❑ 91 Pau Gasol	.30	.75
❑ 92 Bobby Jackson	.20	.50
❑ 93 Eddie Jones	.20	.50
❑ 94 Mike Miller	.30	.75
❑ 95 Damon Stoudamire	.25	.60
❑ 96 Hakim Warrick	.25	.60
❑ 97 Alonzo Mourning	.40	1.00
❑ 98 Shaquille O'Neal	.75	2.00
❑ 99 Gary Payton	.30	.75
❑ 100 Wayne Simien	.25	.60
❑ 101 Dwyane Wade	.75	2.00
❑ 102 Antoine Walker	.25	.60
❑ 103 Jason Williams	.25	.60
❑ 104 Andrew Bogut	.30	.75
❑ 105 T.J. Ford	.25	.60
❑ 106 Jamaal Magloire	.20	.50
❑ 107 Michael Redd	.30	.75
❑ 108 Bobby Simmons	.20	.50
❑ 109 Maurice Williams	.25	.60
❑ 110 Ricky Davis	.30	.75
❑ 111 Kevin Garnett	.60	1.50
❑ 112 Eddie Griffin	.20	.50
❑ 113 Trenton Hassell	.20	.50
❑ 114 Troy Hudson	.20	.50
❑ 115 Rashad McCants	.25	.60
❑ 116 Vince Carter	.60	1.50
❑ 117 Jason Collins	.20	.50
❑ 118 Richard Jefferson	.25	.60
❑ 119 Jason Kidd	.50	1.25
❑ 120 Nenad Krstic	.25	.60
❑ 121 Jeff McInnis	.20	.50
❑ 122 Antoine Wright	.20	.50
❑ 123 P.J. Brown	.20	.50
❑ 124 Speedy Claxton	.20	.50
❑ 125 Desmond Mason	.20	.50
❑ 126 Chris Paul	.60	1.50
❑ 127 J.R. Smith	.25	.60
❑ 128 Kirk Snyder	.20	.50
❑ 129 David West	.30	.75
❑ 130 Jamal Crawford	.20	.50
❑ 131 Steve Francis	.30	.75
❑ 132 Channing Frye	.25	.60
❑ 133 Stephon Marbury	.30	.75
❑ 134 Quentin Richardson	.25	.60
❑ 135 Nate Robinson	.30	.75
❑ 136 Maurice Taylor	.20	.50
❑ 137 Carlos Arroyo	.30	.75
❑ 138 Tony Battie	.20	.50
❑ 139 Keyon Dooling	.20	.50
❑ 140 Grant Hill	.30	.75
❑ 141 Dwight Howard	.60	1.50
❑ 142 Darko Milicic	.30	.75
❑ 143 Jameer Nelson	.25	.60
❑ 144 Samuel Dalembert	.20	.50
❑ 145 Steven Hunter	.20	.50
❑ 146 Andre Iguodala	.30	.75
❑ 147 Allen Iverson	.60	1.50
❑ 148 Kyle Korver	.30	.75
❑ 149 Shavlik Randolph	.20	.50
❑ 150 Chris Webber	.30	.75
❑ 151 Raja Bell	.20	.50
❑ 152 Boris Diaw	.25	.60
❑ 153 Shawn Marion	.30	.75
❑ 154 Steve Nash	.40	1.00
❑ 155 Amare Stoudemire	.60	1.50
❑ 156 Kurt Thomas	.20	.50
❑ 157 Tim Thomas	.20	.50
❑ 158 Steve Blake	.20	.50
❑ 159 Juan Dixon	.20	.50
❑ 160 Zach Randolph	.30	.75
❑ 161 Ha Seung-Jin	.20	.50
❑ 162 Sebastian Telfair	.25	.60
❑ 163 Martell Webster	.25	.60
❑ 164 Shareef Abdur-Rahim	.30	.75
❑ 165 Ron Artest	.30	.75
❑ 166 Mike Bibby	.30	.75
❑ 167 Brad Miller	.30	.75
❑ 168 Kenny Thomas	.20	.50
❑ 169 Bonzi Wells	.25	.60
❑ 170 Bruce Bowen	.20	.50
❑ 171 Tim Duncan	.60	1.50
❑ 172 Michael Finley	.30	.75
❑ 173 Manu Ginobili	.30	.75
❑ 174 Nazr Mohammed	.20	.50
❑ 175 Tony Parker	.30	.75
❑ 176 Ray Allen	.30	.75
❑ 177 Danny Fortson	.20	.50
❑ 178 Rashard Lewis	.30	.75
❑ 179 Luke Ridnour	.25	.60
❑ 180 Earl Watson	.20	.50
❑ 181 Chris Wilcox	.20	.50
❑ 182 Rafael Araujo	.20	.50
❑ 183 Chris Bosh	.30	.75
❑ 184 Joey Graham	.25	.60
❑ 185 Mike James	.20	.50
❑ 186 Morris Peterson	.25	.60
❑ 187 Charlie Villanueva	.30	.75
❑ 188 Carlos Boozer	.30	.75
❑ 189 Matt Harpring	.25	.60
❑ 190 Kris Humphries	.20	.50
❑ 191 Andrei Kirilenko	.30	.75
❑ 192 C.J. Miles	.20	.50
❑ 193 Chris Taft	.20	.50
❑ 194 Deron Williams	.50	1.25
❑ 195 Gilbert Arenas	.30	.75
❑ 196 Andray Blatche	.20	.50
❑ 197 Caron Butler	.30	.75
❑ 198 Antonio Daniels	.20	.50
❑ 199 Brendan Haywood	.20	.50
❑ 200 Antawn Jamison	.30	.75
❑ 201 Andrea Bargnani RC	1.50	4.00
❑ 202 LaMarcus Aldridge RC	1.25	3.00
❑ 203 Adam Morrison RC	1.25	3.00
❑ 204 Tyrus Thomas RC	1.25	3.00
❑ 205 Shelden Williams RC	1.25	3.00
❑ 206 Brandon Roy RC	2.50	6.00
❑ 207 Randy Foye RC	1.00	2.50
❑ 208 Rudy Gay RC	1.00	2.50
❑ 209 Patrick O'Bryant RC	1.00	2.50
❑ 210 Saer Sene RC	1.00	2.50
❑ 211 J.J. Redick RC	1.00	2.50
❑ 212 Hilton Armstrong RC	1.00	2.50
❑ 213 Thabo Sefolosha RC	1.25	3.00
❑ 214 Ronnie Brewer RC	1.25	3.00
❑ 215 Cedric Simmons RC	1.00	2.50
❑ 216 Rodney Carney RC	1.00	2.50
❑ 217 Shawne Williams RC	1.00	2.50
❑ 218 Quincy Douby RC	1.00	2.50
❑ 219 Renaldo Balkman RC	1.00	2.50
❑ 220 Rajon Rondo RC	4.00	10.00
❑ 221 Marcus Williams RC	1.25	3.00
❑ 222 Josh Boone RC	1.00	2.50
❑ 223 Kyle Lowry RC	1.00	2.50
❑ 224 Shannon Brown RC	1.00	2.50
❑ 225 Jordan Farmar RC	1.25	3.00
❑ 226 Maurice Ager RC	1.00	2.50
❑ 227 Mardy Collins RC	1.00	2.50
❑ 228 Jorge Garbajosa RC	2.00	5.00
❑ 229 James White RC	1.00	2.50
❑ 230 Steve Novak RC	1.00	2.50
❑ 231 Solomon Jones RC	1.00	2.50
❑ 232 Paul Davis RC	1.00	2.50
❑ 233 P.J. Tucker RC	1.00	2.50
❑ 234 Craig Smith RC	1.00	2.50
❑ 235 Bobby Jones RC	1.00	2.50
❑ 236 David Noel RC	1.00	2.50
❑ 237 Denham Brown RC	1.00	2.50
❑ 238 James Augustine RC	1.00	2.50
❑ 239 Daniel Gibson RC	1.25	3.00
❑ 240 Alexander Johnson RC	1.00	2.50

2007-08 Upper Deck

❑ COMPLETE SET (242)	125.00	200.00
❑ 1 Austin Croshere	.20	.50
❑ 2 Devean George	.20	.50
❑ 3 Devin Harris	.30	.75
❑ 4 Josh Howard	.30	.75
❑ 5 Jerry Stackhouse	.25	.60
❑ 6 Jason Terry	.30	.75
❑ 7 Rafer Alston	.20	.50
❑ 8 Shane Battier	.30	.75
❑ 9 Luther Head	.25	.60
❑ 10 Juwan Howard	.20	.50
❑ 11 Tracy McGrady	.60	1.50
❑ 12 Steve Novak	.20	.50
❑ 13 Rudy Gay	.25	.60

❑ 14 Eddie Jones	.20	.50
❑ 15 Kyle Lowry	.20	.50
❑ 16 Mike Miller	.30	.75
❑ 17 Damon Stoudamire	.25	.60
❑ 18 Hakim Warrick	.25	.60
❑ 19 Brandon Bass	.20	.50
❑ 20 Tyson Chandler	.30	.75
❑ 21 Bobby Jackson	.20	.50
❑ 22 Desmond Mason	.20	.50
❑ 23 Cedric Simmons	.25	.60
❑ 24 Peja Stojakovic	.30	.75
❑ 25 Bruce Bowen	.20	.50
❑ 26 Michael Finley	.30	.75
❑ 27 Manu Ginobili	.30	.75
❑ 28 Tony Parker	.30	.75
❑ 29 Beno Udrih	.20	.50
❑ 30 Monta Ellis	.25	.60
❑ 31 Al Harrington	.25	.60
❑ 32 Sarunas Jasikevicius	.20	.50
❑ 33 Stephen Jackson	.25	.60
❑ 34 Jason Richardson	.30	.75
❑ 35 Sam Cassell	.30	.75
❑ 36 Chris Kaman	.20	.50
❑ 37 Shaun Livingston	.20	.50
❑ 38 Corey Maggette	.25	.60
❑ 39 Cuttino Mobley	.25	.60
❑ 40 Tim Thomas	.20	.50
❑ 41 Kwame Brown	.20	.50
❑ 42 Andrew Bynum	.30	.75
❑ 43 Jordan Farmar	.25	.60
❑ 44 Lamar Odom	.30	.75
❑ 45 Ronny Turiaf	.25	.60
❑ 46 Luke Walton	.25	.60
❑ 47 Leandro Barbosa	.25	.60
❑ 48 Raja Bell	.20	.50
❑ 49 Boris Diaw	.25	.60
❑ 50 Shawn Marion	.30	.75
❑ 51 Amare Stoudemire	.60	1.50
❑ 52 Shareef Abdur-Rahim	.30	.75
❑ 53 Ron Artest	.30	.75
❑ 54 Quincy Douby	.20	.50
❑ 55 Kevin Martin	.30	.75
❑ 56 Brad Miller	.30	.75
❑ 57 Allen Iverson	.60	1.50
❑ 58 Kenyon Martin	.30	.75
❑ 59 Eduardo Najera	.20	.50
❑ 60 Nene	.20	.50
❑ 61 J.R. Smith	.25	.60
❑ 62 Ricky Davis	.30	.75
❑ 63 Randy Foye	.30	.75
❑ 64 Troy Hudson	.20	.50
❑ 65 Mike James	.20	.50
❑ 66 Rashad McCants	.25	.60
❑ 67 Craig Smith	.30	.75
❑ 68 LaMarcus Aldridge	.40	1.00
❑ 69 Jarrett Jack	.25	.60
❑ 70 Jamaal Magloire	.20	.50
❑ 71 Sergio Rodriguez	.25	.60
❑ 72 Brandon Roy	.50	1.25
❑ 73 Martell Webster	.25	.60
❑ 74 Rashard Lewis	.30	.75
❑ 75 Luke Ridnour	.25	.60
❑ 76 Danny Fortson	.20	.50
❑ 77 Chris Wilcox	.25	.60
❑ 78 Damien Wilkins	.20	.50
❑ 79 Ronnie Brewer	.25	.60
❑ 80 Derek Fisher	.25	.60
❑ 81 Matt Harpring	.25	.60
❑ 82 Andrei Kirilenko	.30	.75
❑ 83 Paul Millsap	.25	.60
❑ 84 Deron Williams	.50	1.25
❑ 85 Tony Allen	.20	.50
❑ 86 Gerald Green	.30	.75
❑ 87 Al Jefferson	.30	.75
❑ 88 Wally Szczerbiak	.25	.60
❑ 89 Allan Ray	.25	.60
❑ 90 Delonte West	.25	.60
❑ 91 Hassan Adams	.20	.50
❑ 92 Richard Jefferson	.30	.75
❑ 93 Jason Kidd	.50	1.25
❑ 94 Nenad Krstic	.25	.60
❑ 95 Marcus Williams	.30	.75
❑ 96 Renaldo Balkman	.20	.50
❑ 97 Jamal Crawford	.20	.50
❑ 98 Eddy Curry	.20	.50
❑ 99 Channing Frye	.25	.60
❑ 100 Quentin Richardson	.25	.60
❑ 101 Nate Robinson	.30	.75
❑ 102 Rodney Carney	.20	.50

❑ 103 Samuel Dalembert	.20	.50
❑ 104 Steven Hunter	.20	.50
❑ 105 Kyle Korver	.30	.75
❑ 106 Andre Miller	.25	.60
❑ 107 Shavlik Randolph	.20	.50
❑ 108 Andrea Bargnani	.40	1.00
❑ 109 Jose Calderon	.25	.60
❑ 110 T.J. Ford	.25	.60
❑ 111 Jorge Garbajosa	.30	.75
❑ 112 Joey Graham	.20	.50
❑ 113 Morris Peterson	.25	.60
❑ 114 Luol Deng	.30	.75
❑ 115 Ben Gordon	.40	1.00
❑ 116 Kirk Hinrich	.30	.75
❑ 117 Thabo Sefolosha	.30	.75
❑ 118 Tyrus Thomas	.40	1.00
❑ 119 Ben Wallace	.30	.75
❑ 120 Shannon Brown	.20	.50
❑ 121 Drew Gooden	.25	.60
❑ 122 Larry Hughes	.25	.60
❑ 123 Zydrunas Ilgauskas	.25	.60
❑ 124 Donyell Marshall	.20	.50
❑ 125 Richard Hamilton	.25	.60
❑ 126 Amir Johnson	.20	.50
❑ 127 Antonio McDyess	.20	.50
❑ 128 Tayshaun Prince	.30	.75
❑ 129 Rasheed Wallace	.30	.75
❑ 130 Chris Webber	.30	.75
❑ 131 Marquis Daniels	.25	.60
❑ 132 Ike Diogu	.20	.50
❑ 133 Mike Dunleavy	.25	.60
❑ 134 Jeff Foster	.20	.50
❑ 135 Troy Murphy	.30	.75
❑ 136 Jamaal Tinsley	.20	.50
❑ 137 Charlie Bell	.20	.50
❑ 138 Andrew Bogut	.30	.75
❑ 139 Earl Boykins	.20	.50
❑ 140 Bobby Simmons	.20	.50
❑ 141 Charlie Villanueva	.30	.75
❑ 142 Maurice Williams	.25	.60
❑ 143 Speedy Claxton	.20	.50
❑ 144 Solomon Jones	.20	.50
❑ 145 Tyronn Lue	.20	.50
❑ 146 Marvin Williams	.30	.75
❑ 147 Shelden Williams	.30	.75
❑ 148 Raymond Felton	.40	1.00
❑ 149 Othella Harrington	.20	.50
❑ 150 Sean May	.25	.60
❑ 151 Adam Morrison	.30	.75
❑ 152 Gerald Wallace	.30	.75
❑ 153 Udonis Haslem	.30	.75
❑ 154 Alonzo Mourning	.40	1.00
❑ 155 Shaquille O'Neal	.75	2.00
❑ 156 Gary Payton	.30	.75
❑ 157 Antoine Walker	.25	.60
❑ 158 Jason Williams	.25	.60
❑ 159 Carlos Arroyo	.30	.75
❑ 160 Travis Diener	.20	.50
❑ 161 Grant Hill	.30	.75
❑ 162 Darko Milicic	.30	.75
❑ 163 Jameer Nelson	.25	.60
❑ 164 J.J. Redick	.30	.75
❑ 165 Andray Blatche	.20	.50
❑ 166 Caron Butler	.30	.75
❑ 167 Antonio Daniels	.20	.50
❑ 168 Brendan Haywood	.20	.50
❑ 169 Antawn Jamison	.30	.75
❑ 170 DeShawn Stevenson	.20	.50
❑ 171 Dirk Nowitzki	.50	1.25
❑ 172 Yao Ming	.75	2.00
❑ 173 Pau Gasol	.30	.75
❑ 174 Chris Paul	.60	1.50
❑ 175 Tim Duncan	.60	1.50
❑ 176 Baron Davis	.30	.75
❑ 177 Elton Brand	.30	.75
❑ 178 Kobe Bryant	1.50	4.00
❑ 179 Steve Nash	.40	1.00
❑ 180 Mike Bibby	.30	.75
❑ 181 Carmelo Anthony	.60	1.50
❑ 182 Kevin Garnett	.75	2.00
❑ 183 Zach Randolph	.30	.75
❑ 184 Ray Allen	.30	.75
❑ 185 Carlos Boozer	.30	.75
❑ 186 Paul Pierce	.30	.75
❑ 187 Vince Carter	.60	1.50
❑ 188 Stephon Marbury	.30	.75
❑ 189 Andre Iguodala	.30	.75
❑ 190 Chris Bosh	.30	.75
❑ 191 Michael Jordan	2.00	5.00

❑ 192 LeBron James	1.50	4.00
❑ 193 Chauncey Billups	.30	.75
❑ 194 Jermaine O'Neal	.30	.75
❑ 195 Michael Redd	.30	.75
❑ 196 Joe Johnson	.30	.75
❑ 197 Emeka Okafor	.30	.75
❑ 198 Dwyane Wade	.75	2.00
❑ 199 Dwight Howard	.60	1.50
❑ 200 Gilbert Arenas	.30	.75
❑ 201 Acie Law RC	1.50	4.00
❑ 202 Thaddeus Young RC	1.50	4.00
❑ 203 Julian Wright RC	1.50	4.00
❑ 204 Al Thornton RC	1.25	3.00
❑ 205 Rodney Stuckey RC	2.50	6.00
❑ 206 Nick Young RC	1.25	3.00
❑ 207 Sean Williams RC	1.25	3.00
❑ 208 Marco Belinelli RC	1.25	3.00
❑ 209 Javaris Crittenton RC	1.25	3.00
❑ 210 Jason Smith RC	1.25	3.00
❑ 211 Daequan Cook RC	1.50	4.00
❑ 212 Jared Dudley RC	1.25	3.00
❑ 213 Wilson Chandler RC	1.25	3.00
❑ 214 Morris Almond RC	1.25	3.00
❑ 215 Aaron Brooks RC	2.00	5.00
❑ 216 Arron Afflalo RC	1.25	3.00
❑ 217 Alando Tucker RC	1.25	3.00
❑ 218 Petteri Koponen RC	1.25	3.00
❑ 219 Carl Landry RC	1.25	3.00
❑ 220 Gabe Pruitt RC	1.25	3.00
❑ 221 Marcus Williams RC	1.25	3.00
❑ 222 Nick Fazekas RC	1.25	3.00
❑ 223 Glen Davis RC	2.50	6.00
❑ 224 Jermareo Davidson RC	1.25	3.00
❑ 225 Josh McRoberts RC	1.50	4.00
❑ 226 Chris Richard RC	1.25	3.00
❑ 227 Derrick Byars RC	1.25	3.00
❑ 228 Adam Haluska RC	1.25	3.00
❑ 229 Reyshawn Terry RC	1.25	3.00
❑ 230 Jared Jordan RC	1.25	3.00
❑ 231 Stephane Lasme RC	1.25	3.00
❑ 232 Dominic McGuire RC	1.25	3.00
❑ 233 Greg Oden SP RC	2.00	5.00
❑ 234 Kevin Durant SP RC	10.00	25.00
❑ 235 Al Horford SP RC	1.50	4.00
❑ 236 Michael Conley SP RC	1.50	4.00
❑ 237 Jeff Green SP RC	1.50	4.00
❑ 238 Taurean Green SP RC	1.25	3.00
❑ 239 Corey Brewer SP RC	1.50	4.00
❑ 240 Brandan Wright SP RC	1.50	4.00
❑ 241 Joakim Noah SP RC	1.50	4.00
❑ 242 Spencer Hawes SP RC	1.25	3.00

2008-09 Upper Deck

❑ COMP.SET w/o SPs (200)	25.00	50.00
❑ 1 Mike Bibby	.30	.75
❑ 2 Al Horford	.30	.75
❑ 3 Joe Johnson	.30	.75
❑ 4 Josh Childress	.30	.75
❑ 5 Josh Smith	.30	.75
❑ 6 Marvin Williams	.30	.75
❑ 7 Eddie House	.20	.50
❑ 8 Glen Davis	.25	.60
❑ 9 Sam Cassell	.30	.75
❑ 10 Kevin Garnett	.60	1.50
❑ 11 Rajon Rondo	.30	.75
❑ 12 Ray Allen	.30	.75
❑ 13 Paul Pierce	.40	1.00
❑ 14 Adam Morrison	.30	.75
❑ 15 Emeka Okafor	.30	.75
❑ 16 Gerald Wallace	.30	.75
❑ 17 Jared Dudley	.30	.75
❑ 18 Jason Richardson	.30	.75
❑ 19 Nazr Mohammed	.20	.50
❑ 20 Raymond Felton	.25	.60
❑ 21 Andres Nocioni	.25	.60
❑ 22 Ben Gordon	.30	.75

23 Larry Hughes	.25	.60
24 Joakim Noah	.30	.75
25 Kirk Hinrich	.30	.75
26 Luol Deng	.30	.75
27 Tyrus Thomas	.25	.60
28 Aleksandar Pavlovic	.25	.60
29 Anderson Varejao	.25	.60
30 Daniel Gibson	.30	.75
31 Wally Szczerbiak	.25	.60
32 Ben Wallace	.30	.75
33 LeBron James	1.50	4.00
34 Zydrunas Ilgauskas	.25	.60
35 Jason Kidd	.30	.75
36 Dirk Nowitzki	.40	1.00
37 Jason Terry	.25	.60
38 Jerry Stackhouse	.25	.60
39 Jose Barea	.25	.60
40 Josh Howard	.30	.75
41 Allen Iverson	.40	1.00
42 Carmelo Anthony	.40	1.00
43 J.R. Smith	.25	.60
44 Kenyon Martin	.30	.75
45 Linas Kleiza	.20	.50
46 Marcus Camby	.20	.50
47 Antonio McDyess	.20	.50
48 Chauncey Billups	.30	.75
49 Jason Maxiell	.25	.60
50 Rasheed Wallace	.30	.75
51 Richard Hamilton	.25	.60
52 Rodney Stuckey	.40	1.00
53 Tayshaun Prince	.30	.75
54 Al Harrington	.25	.60
55 Baron Davis	.30	.75
56 Kelenna Azubuike	.20	.50
57 Matt Barnes	.20	.50
58 Monta Ellis	.30	.75
59 Stephen Jackson	.25	.60
60 Luis Scola	.25	.60
61 Luther Head	.25	.60
62 Rafer Alston	.20	.50
63 Shane Battier	.25	.60
64 Tracy McGrady	.40	1.00
65 Yao Ming	.40	1.00
66 Andre Owens	.20	.50
67 Danny Granger	.30	.75
68 Jamaal Tinsley	.20	.50
69 Jermaine O'Neal	.30	.75
70 Kareem Rush	.25	.60
71 Mike Dunleavy	.25	.60
72 Troy Murphy	.30	.75
73 Al Thornton	.30	.75
74 Chris Kaman	.20	.50
75 Corey Maggette	.30	.75
76 Cuttino Mobley	.25	.60
77 Elton Brand	.50	1.25
78 Tim Thomas	.20	.50
79 Andrew Bynum	.30	.75
80 Derek Fisher	.30	.75
81 Jordan Farmar	.25	.60
82 Kobe Bryant	1.50	4.00
83 Pau Gasol	.30	.75
84 Lamar Odom	.30	.75
85 Luke Walton	.25	.60
86 Darko Milicic	.30	.75
87 Javaris Crittenton	.20	.50
88 Kyle Lowry	.20	.50
89 Mike Conley	.25	.60
90 Mike Miller	.30	.75
91 Kwame Brown	.20	.50
92 Rudy Gay	.30	.75
93 Daequan Cook	.25	.60
94 Dorell Wright	.20	.50
95 Dwyane Wade	.60	1.50
96 Jason Williams	.25	.60
97 Ricky Davis	.30	.75
98 Shawn Marion	.30	.75
99 Udonis Haslem	.30	.75
100 Andrew Bogut	.30	.75
101 Charlie Villanueva	.30	.75
102 Desmond Mason	.20	.50
103 Michael Redd	.30	.75
104 Mo Williams	.25	.60
105 Yi Jianlian	.30	.75
106 Al Jefferson	.30	.75
107 Corey Brewer	.25	.60
108 Craig Smith	.30	.75
109 Randy Foye	.30	.75
110 Rashad McCants	.25	.60
111 Ryan Gomes	.25	.60

112 Sebastian Telfair	.25	.60
113 Bostjan Nachbar	.30	.75
114 Devin Harris	.30	.75
115 Josh Boone	.20	.50
116 Nenad Krstic	.25	.60
117 Richard Jefferson	.30	.75
118 Sean Williams	.25	.60
119 Vince Carter	.40	1.00
120 David Lee	.25	.60
121 Eddy Curry	.20	.50
122 Jamal Crawford	.20	.50
123 Nate Robinson	.30	.75
124 Quentin Richardson	.25	.60
125 Stephon Marbury	.30	.75
126 Zach Randolph	.30	.75
127 Chris Paul	.60	1.50
128 David West	.30	.75
129 Julian Wright	.25	.60
130 Morris Peterson	.25	.60
131 Peja Stojakovic	.30	.75
132 Tyson Chandler	.25	.60
133 Carlos Arroyo	.30	.75
134 Dwight Howard	.60	1.50
135 Hedo Turkoglu	.30	.75
136 J.J. Redick	.30	.75
137 Jameer Nelson	.25	.60
138 Maurice Evans	.20	.50
139 Rashard Lewis	.30	.75
140 Andre Iguodala	.30	.75
141 Andre Miller	.25	.60
142 Jason Smith	.20	.50
143 Louis Williams	.20	.50
144 Samuel Dalembert	.20	.50
145 Thaddeus Young	.25	.60
146 Willie Green	.20	.50
147 Amare Stoudemire	.40	1.00
148 Boris Diaw	.25	.60
149 Grant Hill	.30	.75
150 Leandro Barbosa	.25	.60
151 Raja Bell	.20	.50
152 Shaquille O'Neal	.60	1.50
153 Steve Nash	.30	.75
154 Brandon Roy	.40	1.00
155 Channing Frye	.25	.60
156 Greg Oden	.30	.75
157 LaMarcus Aldridge	.30	.75
158 Martell Webster	.25	.60
159 Steve Blake	.20	.50
160 Beno Udrih	.20	.50
161 Brad Miller	.30	.75
162 Francisco Garcia	.25	.60
163 John Salmons	.30	.75
164 Kevin Martin	.30	.75
165 Mikki Moore	.25	.60
166 Ron Artest	.30	.75
167 Brent Barry	.20	.50
168 Bruce Bowen	.20	.50
169 Manu Ginobili	.30	.75
170 Michael Finley	.30	.75
171 Robert Horry	.20	.50
172 Tim Duncan	.50	1.25
173 Tony Parker	.30	.75
174 Chris Wilcox	.25	.60
175 Damien Wilkins	.20	.50
176 Jeff Green	.25	.60
177 Kevin Durant	.75	2.00
178 Nick Collison	.20	.50
179 Earl Watson	.20	.50
180 Andrea Bargnani	.25	.60
181 Anthony Parker	.25	.60
182 Carlos Delfino	.20	.50
183 Chris Bosh	.30	.75
184 Jamario Moon	.30	.75
185 Jose Calderon	.25	.60
186 T.J. Ford	.20	.50
187 Andrei Kirilenko	.30	.75
188 Carlos Boozer	.30	.75
189 Deron Williams	.40	1.00
190 Kyle Korver	.30	.75
191 Mehmet Okur	.30	.75
192 Paul Millsap	.25	.60
193 Ronnie Brewer	.25	.60
194 Antawn Jamison	.30	.75
195 Antonio Daniels	.20	.50
196 Brendan Haywood	.20	.50
197 Caron Butler	.30	.75
198 DeShawn Stevenson	.20	.50
199 Gilbert Arenas	.30	.75
200 Nick Young	.20	.50

201 Spud Webb	.50	1.25
202 Bob Cousy	.75	2.00
203 Kevin McHale	.60	1.50
204 Larry Bird	1.50	4.00
205 Dennis Rodman	.50	1.25
206 Michael Jordan	4.00	10.00
207 Isiah Thomas	.50	1.25
208 Joe Dumars	.50	1.25
209 Nate Thurmond	.50	1.25
210 Hakeem Olajuwon	.60	1.50
211 Calvin Murphy	.50	1.25
212 Kareem Abdul-Jabbar	.75	2.00
213 Magic Johnson	1.00	2.50
214 Oscar Robertson	.50	1.25
215 Bill Bradley	.60	1.50
216 Earl Monroe	.50	1.25
217 Willis Reed	.50	1.25
218 Julius Erving	1.00	2.50
219 Clyde Drexler	.60	1.50
220 Bill Walton	.50	1.25
221 Maurice Lucas	.50	1.25
222 David Robinson	.75	2.00
223 John Stockton	.75	2.00
224 Karl Malone	.60	1.50
225 D.J. Augustin RC	1.00	2.50
226 Brook Lopez RC	2.00	5.00
227 Jerryd Bayless RC	1.00	2.50
228 Jason Thompson RC	1.00	2.50
229 Brandon Rush RC	1.00	2.50
230 Anthony Randolph RC	1.50	4.00
231 Robin Lopez RC	1.00	2.50
232 Marreese Speights RC	1.00	2.50
233 Roy Hibbert RC	1.25	3.00
234 Courtney Lee RC	1.50	4.00
235 J.J. Hickson RC	1.50	4.00
236 Ryan Anderson RC	1.00	2.50
237 Kosta Koufos RC	1.00	2.50
238 James Gist RC	1.00	2.50
239 Darrell Arthur RC	1.00	2.50
240 Donte Greene RC	1.00	2.50
241 D.J. White RC	1.00	2.50
242 J.R. Giddens RC	1.00	2.50
243 Deron Washington RC	1.00	2.50
244 Joey Dorsey RC	1.00	2.50
245 Mario Chalmers RC	1.25	3.00
246 DeAndre Jordan RC	1.00	2.50
247 Luc Richard Mbah A Moute RC	1.00	2.50
248 Kyle Weaver RC	1.00	2.50
249 Sonny Weems RC	1.00	2.50
250 Chris Douglas-Roberts RC	1.25	3.00
251 Sean Singletary RC	1.00	2.50
252 Patrick Ewing Jr. RC	1.00	2.50
253 Shan Foster RC	1.00	2.50
254 Bill Walker RC	1.00	2.50
255 Malik Hairston RC	1.00	2.50
256 Richard Hendrix RC	1.00	2.50
257 DeVon Hardin RC	1.00	2.50
258 Darnell Jackson RC	1.00	2.50
259 Derrick Rose RC	4.00	10.00
260 Michael Beasley RC	2.00	5.00
261 O.J. Mayo RC	1.50	4.00
262 Russell Westbrook RC	2.50	6.00
263 Kevin Love RC	1.25	3.00
264 Danilo Gallinari RC	1.50	4.00
265 Eric Gordon RC	1.25	3.00
266 Joe Alexander RC	1.00	2.50

2009-10 Upper Deck

1 Josh Smith	.30	.75
2 Al Horford	.30	.75
3 Mike Bibby	.20	.50
4 Joe Johnson	.30	.75
5 Marvin Williams	.25	.60
6 Maurice Evans	.20	.50
7 Kevin Garnett	.60	1.50
8 Paul Pierce	.40	1.00

❑ 9 Ray Allen	.30	.75
❑ 10 Rajon Rondo	.30	.75
❑ 11 Kendrick Perkins	.20	.50
❑ 12 Bill Walker	.20	.50
❑ 13 Leon Powe	.20	.50
❑ 14 Raymond Felton	.25	.60
❑ 15 Raja Bell	.25	.60
❑ 16 D.J. Augustin	.25	.60
❑ 17 Gerald Wallace	.30	.75
❑ 18 Boris Diaw	.25	.60
❑ 19 Emeka Okafor	.30	.75
❑ 20 Vladimir Radmanovic	.20	.50
❑ 21 Derrick Rose	.60	1.50
❑ 22 Luol Deng	.30	.75
❑ 23 Michael Jordan	2.00	5.00
❑ 24 John Salmons	.30	.75
❑ 25 Joakim Noah	.30	.75
❑ 26 Tyrus Thomas	.25	.60
❑ 27 Ben Gordon	.30	.75
❑ 28 LeBron James	1.50	4.00
❑ 29 Mo Williams	.25	.60
❑ 30 Ben Wallace	.30	.75
❑ 31 Delonte West	.20	.50
❑ 32 Zydrunas Ilgauskas	.20	.50
❑ 33 Daniel Gibson	.30	.75
❑ 34 Wally Szczerbiak	.25	.60
❑ 35 Josh Howard	.30	.75
❑ 36 Dirk Nowitzki	.40	1.00
❑ 37 Jason Kidd	.30	.75
❑ 38 Antoine Wright	.20	.50
❑ 39 Erick Dampier	.20	.50
❑ 40 Jason Terry	.25	.60
❑ 41 Chauncey Billups	.30	.75
❑ 42 Carmelo Anthony	.40	1.00
❑ 43 Kenyon Martin	.30	.75
❑ 44 Dahntay Jones	.20	.50
❑ 45 Nene	.25	.60
❑ 46 J.R. Smith	.25	.60
❑ 47 Allen Iverson	.40	1.00
❑ 48 Richard Hamilton	.25	.60
❑ 49 Tayshaun Prince	.30	.75
❑ 50 Rodney Stuckey	.30	.75
❑ 51 Amir Johnson	.20	.50
❑ 52 Rasheed Wallace	.30	.75
❑ 53 Monta Ellis	.30	.75
❑ 54 Stephen Jackson	.25	.60
❑ 55 Jamal Crawford	.20	.50
❑ 56 Kelenna Azubuike	.20	.50
❑ 57 Andris Biedrins	.20	.50
❑ 58 Anthony Morrow	.20	.50
❑ 59 Corey Maggette	.25	.60
❑ 60 Luis Scola	.20	.50
❑ 61 Tracy McGrady	.40	1.00
❑ 62 Yao Ming	.40	1.00
❑ 63 Ron Artest	.30	.75
❑ 64 Aaron Brooks	.25	.60
❑ 65 Shane Battier	.25	.60
❑ 66 Von Wafer	.20	.50
❑ 67 T.J. Ford	.20	.50
❑ 68 Danny Granger	.30	.75
❑ 69 Mike Dunleavy	.20	.50
❑ 70 Troy Murphy	.20	.50
❑ 71 Jeff Foster	.20	.50
❑ 72 Jarrett Jack	.25	.60
❑ 73 Eric Gordon	.30	.75
❑ 74 Baron Davis	.30	.75
❑ 75 Al Thornton	.30	.75
❑ 76 Zach Randolph	.20	.50
❑ 77 Chris Kaman	.30	.75
❑ 78 Mardy Collins	.20	.50
❑ 79 Kobe Bryant	1.50	4.00
❑ 80 Pau Gasol	.30	.75
❑ 81 Lamar Odom	.30	.75
❑ 82 Derek Fisher	.25	.60
❑ 83 Adam Morrison	.25	.60
❑ 84 Andrew Bynum	.30	.75
❑ 85 Sasha Vujacic	.20	.50
❑ 86 Trevor Ariza	.30	.75
❑ 87 O.J. Mayo	.40	1.00
❑ 88 Marc Gasol	.30	.75
❑ 89 Rudy Gay	.30	.75
❑ 90 Darrell Arthur	.25	.60
❑ 91 Marko Jaric	.20	.50
❑ 92 Mike Conley	.20	.50
❑ 93 Michael Beasley	.40	1.00
❑ 94 Mario Chalmers	.30	.75
❑ 95 Dwyane Wade	.60	1.50
❑ 96 Jermaine O'Neal	.30	.75
❑ 97 Udonis Haslem	.25	.60
❑ 98 Chris Quinn	.20	.50
❑ 99 Daequan Cook	.25	.60
❑ 100 Luke Ridnour	.20	.50
❑ 101 Michael Redd	.30	.75
❑ 102 Richard Jefferson	.30	.75
❑ 103 Charlie Villanueva	.25	.60
❑ 104 Andrew Bogut	.30	.75
❑ 105 Ramon Sessions	.20	.50
❑ 106 Joe Alexander	.30	.75
❑ 107 Kevin Love	.25	.60
❑ 108 Sebastian Telfair	.20	.50
❑ 109 Al Jefferson	.30	.75
❑ 110 Randy Foye	.20	.50
❑ 111 Ryan Gomes	.20	.50
❑ 112 Craig Smith	.20	.50
❑ 113 Mike Miller	.30	.75
❑ 114 Devin Harris	.30	.75
❑ 115 Vince Carter	.40	1.00
❑ 116 Yi Jianlian	.30	.75
❑ 117 Bobby Simmons	.25	.60
❑ 118 Brook Lopez	.20	.50
❑ 119 Chris Douglas-Roberts	.20	.50
❑ 120 Eduardo Najera	.20	.50
❑ 121 Chris Paul	.60	1.50
❑ 122 Peja Stojakovic	.20	.50
❑ 123 David West	.30	.75
❑ 124 Tyson Chandler	.25	.60
❑ 125 Rasual Butler	.20	.50
❑ 126 James Posey	.25	.60
❑ 127 Al Harrington	.25	.60
❑ 128 Chris Duhon	.20	.50
❑ 129 Quentin Richardson	.20	.50
❑ 130 David Lee	.25	.60
❑ 131 Jared Jeffries	.20	.50
❑ 132 Wilson Chandler	.20	.50
❑ 133 Danilo Gallinari	.30	.75
❑ 134 Russell Westbrook	.30	.75
❑ 135 Kevin Durant	.75	2.00
❑ 136 Jeff Green	.25	.60
❑ 137 Desmond Mason	.20	.50
❑ 138 Nick Collison	.20	.50
❑ 139 Earl Watson	.20	.50
❑ 140 Dwight Howard	.60	1.50
❑ 141 Courtney Lee	.25	.60
❑ 142 Hedo Turkoglu	.30	.75
❑ 143 Jameer Nelson	.25	.60
❑ 144 Rashard Lewis	.30	.75
❑ 145 Mickael Pietrus	.20	.50
❑ 146 Elton Brand	.30	.75
❑ 147 Andre Miller	.25	.60
❑ 148 Andre Iguodala	.30	.75
❑ 149 Thaddeus Young	.20	.50
❑ 150 Willie Green	.20	.50
❑ 151 Samuel Dalembert	.20	.50
❑ 152 Jason Richardson	.30	.75
❑ 153 Shaquille O'Neal	.60	1.50
❑ 154 Steve Nash	.30	.75
❑ 155 Grant Hill	.30	.75
❑ 156 Amare Stoudemire	.40	1.00
❑ 157 Leandro Barbosa	.25	.60
❑ 158 Robin Lopez	.20	.50
❑ 159 Brandon Roy	.40	1.00
❑ 160 LaMarcus Aldridge	.30	.75
❑ 161 Jerryd Bayless	.25	.60
❑ 162 Rudy Fernandez	.30	.75
❑ 163 Steve Blake	.20	.50
❑ 164 Martell Webster	.25	.60
❑ 165 Greg Oden	.25	.60
❑ 166 Spencer Hawes	.25	.60
❑ 167 Kevin Martin	.30	.75
❑ 168 Beno Udrih	.20	.50
❑ 169 Andres Nocioni	.25	.60
❑ 170 Jason Thompson	.20	.50
❑ 171 Rashad McCants	.20	.50
❑ 172 Francisco Garcia	.25	.60
❑ 173 Tim Duncan	.50	1.25
❑ 174 Tony Parker	.30	.75
❑ 175 Manu Ginobili	.30	.75
❑ 176 Roger Mason	.20	.50
❑ 177 Michael Finley	.20	.50
❑ 178 Matt Bonner	.20	.50
❑ 179 George Hill	.25	.60
❑ 180 Chris Bosh	.30	.75
❑ 181 Jose Calderon	.25	.60
❑ 182 Andrea Bargnani	.25	.60
❑ 183 Shawn Marion	.30	.75
❑ 184 Anthony Parker	.25	.60
❑ 185 Jason Kapono	.25	.60
❑ 186 Roko Leni Ukic	.20	.50
❑ 187 Deron Williams	.40	1.00
❑ 188 Carlos Boozer	.30	.75
❑ 189 Ronnie Brewer	.20	.50
❑ 190 C.J. Miles	.20	.50
❑ 191 Mehmet Okur	.20	.50
❑ 192 Kyle Korver	.25	.60
❑ 193 Andrei Kirilenko	.25	.60
❑ 194 Gilbert Arenas	.30	.75
❑ 195 Antawn Jamison	.30	.75
❑ 196 DeShawn Stevenson	.20	.50
❑ 197 Caron Butler	.30	.75
❑ 198 Brendan Haywood	.20	.50
❑ 199 Nick Young	.20	.50
❑ 200 Dominic McGuire	.20	.50
❑ 201 Toney Douglas RC	1.00	2.50
❑ 202 Taylor Griffin RC	1.00	2.50
❑ 203 DeJuan Blair RC	1.50	4.00
❑ 204 Darren Collison RC	1.50	4.00
❑ 205 Patrick Mills RC	1.25	3.00
❑ 206 DaJuan Summers RC	1.00	2.50
❑ 207 Austin Daye RC	1.25	3.00
❑ 208 Eric Maynor RC	1.50	4.00
❑ 209 DeMarre Carroll RC	1.25	3.00
❑ 210 Taj Gibson RC	1.50	4.00
❑ 211 Patrick Beverley RC	1.00	2.50
❑ 212 Dante Cunningham RC	1.00	2.50
❑ 213 Sam Young RC	1.50	4.00
❑ 214 Terrence Williams RC	2.00	5.00
❑ 215 Omri Casspi RC	1.50	4.00
❑ 216 Jeff Pendergraph RC	1.25	3.00
❑ 217 Jrue Holiday RC	1.50	4.00
❑ 218 Jeff Teague RC	1.25	3.00
❑ 219 James Johnson RC	1.50	4.00
❑ 220 B.J. Mullens RC	1.00	2.50
❑ 221 Nick Calathes RC	1.00	2.50
❑ 222 A.J. Price RC	1.00	2.50
❑ 223 Danny Green RC	1.25	3.00
❑ 224 Marcus Thornton RC	1.00	2.50
❑ 225 Chase Budinger RC	1.50	4.00
❑ 226 Blake Griffin SP RC	4.00	10.00
❑ 227 James Harden SP RC	3.00	8.00
❑ 228 Tyler Hansbrough SP RC	2.50	6.00
❑ 229 Gerald Henderson SP RC	2.50	6.00
❑ 230 Jordan Hill SP RC	2.00	5.00
❑ 231 Hasheem Thabeet SP RC	1.50	4.00
❑ 232 Earl Clark SP RC	2.50	6.00
❑ 233 Brandon Jennings SP RC	4.00	10.00
❑ 234 Stephen Curry SP RC	4.00	10.00
❑ 235 Ty Lawson SP RC	2.00	5.00
❑ 236 Wayne Ellington SP RC	2.50	6.00
❑ 237 Ricky Rubio SP RC	2.50	6.00
❑ 238 DeMar DeRozan SP RC	2.50	6.00
❑ 239 Jonny Flynn SP RC	2.50	6.00
❑ 240 Tyreke Evans SP RC	6.00	15.00
❑ 241 Michael Jordan	4.00	10.00
❑ 242 Larry Bird	2.00	5.00
❑ 243 Horace Grant	.60	1.50
❑ 244 Kiki Vandeweghe	.60	1.50
❑ 245 Michael Cooper	.60	1.50
❑ 246 Magic Johnson	.75	2.00
❑ 247 Kareem Abdul-Jabbar	1.00	2.50
❑ 248 Julius Erving	.75	2.00
❑ 249 Oscar Robertson	.60	1.50
❑ 250 Isiah Thomas	.60	1.50
❑ 251 Patrick Ewing	.60	1.50
❑ 252 A.C. Green	.60	1.50
❑ 253 Adrian Dantley	.60	1.50
❑ 254 Alex English	.60	1.50
❑ 255 Jerry West	.75	2.00
❑ 256 Bernard King	.60	1.50
❑ 257 Bill Laimbeer	.60	1.50
❑ 258 Bob McAdoo	.60	1.50
❑ 259 Byron Scott	.60	1.50
❑ 260 Calvin Murphy	.60	1.50
❑ 261 Clyde Drexler	.75	2.00
❑ 262 David Robinson	1.00	2.50
❑ 263 Dominique Wilkins	.75	2.00
❑ 264 Glen Rice	.60	1.50
❑ 265 Hakeem Olajuwon	.75	2.00
❑ 266 John Stockton	1.00	2.50
❑ 267 Robert Parish	.60	1.50
❑ 268 Scottie Pippen	.60	1.50
❑ 269 Sean Elliott	.60	1.50
❑ 270 Bill Walton	.60	1.50
❑ 271 Chris Mullin	.60	1.50
❑ 272 Dee Brown	.60	1.50
❑ 273 Dennis Rodman	1.00	2.50
❑ 274 Joe Dumars	.60	1.50
❑ 275 John Paxson	.60	1.50

276 Mark Price	.60	1.50
277 Maurice Cheeks	.60	1.50
278 Moses Malone	.60	1.50
279 Spud Webb	.60	1.50
280 Terry Porter	.30	.75
281 Darryl Dawkins	.60	1.50
282 Dino Radja	.60	1.50
283 Jamaal Wilkes	.60	1.50
284 John Salley	.60	1.50
285 Larry Johnson	.60	1.50
286 Larry Nance	.60	1.50
287 Pooh Richardson	.60	1.50
288 Reggie Theus	.60	1.50
289 Rick Mahorn	.60	1.50
290 Rick Barry	.60	1.50
291 Ron Harper	.60	1.50
292 Steve Kerr	.60	1.50
293 Tom Chambers	.60	1.50
294 Spencer Haywood	.60	1.50
295 Walt Frazier	.60	1.50

2004-05 Upper Deck All-Star Lineup

COMMON CARD (1-90)	.20	5.00
COMMON ROOKIE (91-132)	.75	2.00
1 Jason Terry	.25	.60
2 Al Harrington	.25	.60
3 Boris Diaw	.25	.60
4 Paul Pierce	.30	.75
5 Ricky Davis	.25	.60
6 Jiri Welsch	.20	.50
7 Marcus Fizer	.20	.50
8 Gerald Wallace	.30	.75
9 Jahidi White	.20	.50
10 Eddy Curry	.25	.60
11 Kirk Hinrich	.25	.60
12 Jamal Crawford	.25	.60
13 LeBron James	2.00	5.00
14 Dajuan Wagner	.20	.50
15 Jeff McInnis	.20	.50
16 Dirk Nowitzki	.50	1.25
17 Antoine Walker	.30	.75
18 Michael Finley	.30	.75
19 Carmelo Anthony	1.00	2.50
20 Andre Miller	.25	.60
21 Kenyon Martin	.30	.75
22 Chauncey Billups	.30	.75
23 Rasheed Wallace	.30	.75
24 Ben Wallace	.25	.60
25 Erick Dampier	.20	.50
26 Jason Richardson	.30	.75
27 Mike Dunleavy	.25	.60
28 Yao Ming	.75	2.00
29 Tracy McGrady	.60	1.50
30 Juwan Howard	.25	.60
31 Jermaine O'Neal	.30	.75
32 Reggie Miller	.30	.75
33 Ron Artest	.25	.60
34 Elton Brand	.30	.75
35 Corey Maggette	.25	.60
36 Quentin Richardson	.25	.60
37 Kobe Bryant	1.50	4.00
38 Gary Payton	.30	.75
39 Lamar Odom	.30	.75
40 Pau Gasol	.30	.75
41 Jason Williams	.25	.60
42 Bonzi Wells	.20	.50
43 Shaquille O'Neal	.75	2.00
44 Dwyane Wade	1.00	2.50
45 Eddie Jones	.25	.60
46 Michael Redd	.30	.75
47 Desmond Mason	.25	.60
48 T.J. Ford	.25	.60
49 Latrell Sprewell	.25	.60
50 Kevin Garnett	.60	1.50
51 Sam Cassell	.25	.60
52 Richard Jefferson	.30	.75
53 Kerry Kittles	.25	.60
54 Jason Kidd	.50	1.25
55 Jamal Mashburn	.25	.60
56 Baron Davis	.30	.75
57 Jamaal Magloire	.20	.50
58 Allan Houston	.25	.60
59 Kurt Thomas	.20	.50
60 Stephon Marbury	.30	.75
61 Cuttino Mobley	.25	.60
62 Drew Gooden	.20	.50
63 Steve Francis	.30	.75
64 Glenn Robinson	.25	.60
65 Allen Iverson	.60	1.50
66 Samuel Dalembert	.20	.50
67 Amare Stoudemire	.60	1.50
68 Steve Nash	.50	1.25
69 Shawn Marion	.30	.75
70 Shareef Abdur-Rahim	.25	.60
71 Damon Stoudamire	.25	.60
72 Zach Randolph	.30	.75
73 Peja Stojakovic	.25	.60
74 Chris Webber	.30	.75
75 Mike Bibby	.25	.60
76 Tony Parker	.30	.75
77 Tim Duncan	.60	1.50
78 Manu Ginobili	.30	.75
79 Ronald Murray	.20	.50
80 Ray Allen	.30	.75
81 Rashard Lewis	.30	.75
82 Chris Bosh	.30	.75
83 Vince Carter	.60	1.50
84 Jalen Rose	.25	.60
85 Andrei Kirilenko	.30	.75
86 Carlos Boozer	.30	.75
87 Carlos Arroyo	.30	.75
88 Gilbert Arenas	.30	.75
89 Jarvis Hayes	.20	.50
90 Antawn Jamison	.30	.75
91 Emeka Okafor RC	1.50	4.00
92 Dwight Howard RC	2.50	6.00
93 Shaun Livingston RC	.75	2.00
94 Luol Deng RC	1.00	2.50
95 Ben Gordon RC	1.00	2.50
96 Devin Harris RC	1.50	4.00
97 Andre Iguodala RC	2.00	5.00
98 Andris Biedrins RC	1.25	3.00
99 Josh Childress RC	.75	2.00
100 Josh Smith RC	2.00	5.00
101 Jameer Nelson RC	1.00	2.50
102 J.R. Smith RC	1.50	4.00
103 Sergei Monia RC	.75	2.00
104 Sebastian Telfair RC	.75	2.00
105 Pavel Podkolzine RC	.75	2.00
106 Luke Jackson RC	.75	2.00
107 Dorell Wright RC	1.00	2.50
108 Robert Swift RC	.75	2.00
109 Anderson Varejao RC	1.00	2.50
110 Sasha Vujacic RC	.75	2.00
111 Rafael Araujo RC	.75	2.00
112 Al Jefferson RC	1.50	4.00
113 Kris Humphries RC	1.25	3.00
114 Kirk Snyder RC	.75	2.00
115 Darius Rice RC	.75	2.00
116 Beno Udrih RC	1.00	2.50
117 Viktor Khryapa RC	.75	2.00
118 David Harrison RC	.75	2.00
119 Trevor Ariza RC	1.00	2.50
120 Ha Seung-Jin RC	.75	2.00
121 Kevin Martin RC	1.00	2.50
122 Delonte West RC	1.25	3.00
123 Rickey Paulding RC	.75	2.00
124 Chris Duhon RC	1.25	3.00
125 Tony Allen RC	1.00	2.50
126 Donta Smith RC	.75	2.00
127 Andre Emmett RC	.75	2.00
128 Royal Ivey RC	.75	2.00
129 Matt Freije RC	.75	2.00
130 Romain Sato RC	.75	2.00
131 Antonio Burks RC	.75	2.00
132 Lionel Chalmers RC	.75	2.00

1999 Upper Deck Century Legends

COMPLETE SET (89)	20.00	40.00
COMMON CARD (1-80)	.07	.20
COMMON MJ (81-90)	.75	2.00
1 Michael Jordan	2.00	5.00
2 Bill Russell	.40	1.00
3 Wilt Chamberlain	.50	1.25
4 George Mikan	.40	1.00
5 Oscar Robertson	.25	.60
6 Does not exist		
7 Larry Bird	.75	2.00
8 Karl Malone	.25	.60
9 Elgin Baylor	.25	.60
10 Kareem Abdul-Jabbar	.40	1.00
11 Jerry West	.40	1.00
12 Bob Cousy	.30	.75
13 Julius Erving	.40	1.00
14 Hakeem Olajuwon	.30	.75
15 John Havlicek	.25	.60
16 John Stockton	.40	1.00
17 Rick Barry	.25	.60
18 Moses Malone	.25	.60
19 Nate Thurmond	.25	.60
20 Bob Pettit	.25	.60
21 Pete Maravich	.75	2.00
22 Willis Reed	.25	.60
23 Isiah Thomas	.25	.60
24 Dolph Schayes	.25	.60
25 Walt Frazier	.25	.60
26 Wes Unseld	.25	.60
27 Bill Sharman	.25	.60
28 George Gervin	.30	.75
29 Hal Greer	.25	.60
30 Dave DeBusschere	.30	.75
31 Earl Monroe	.25	.60
32 Kevin McHale	.25	.60
33 Charles Barkley	.30	.75
34 Elvin Hayes	.25	.60
35 Scottie Pippen	.40	1.00
36 Jerry Lucas	.25	.60
37 Dave Bing	.25	.60
38 Lenny Wilkens	.25	.60
39 Paul Arizin	.25	.60
40 Nate Archibald	.25	.60
41 James Worthy	.25	.60
42 Patrick Ewing	.25	.60
43 Billy Cunningham	.25	.60
44 Sam Jones	.30	.75
45 Dave Cowens	.25	.60
46 Robert Parish	.25	.60
47 Bill Walton	.25	.60
48 Shaquille O'Neal	.50	1.25
49 David Robinson	.40	1.00
50 Dominique Wilkins	.30	.75
51 Kobe Bryant	1.25	3.00
52 Vince Carter	.50	1.25
53 Paul Pierce	.25	.60
54 Allen Iverson	.30	.75
55 Stephon Marbury	.25	.60
56 Mike Bibby	.25	.60
57 Jason Williams	.25	.60
58 Kevin Garnett	.50	1.25
59 Tim Duncan	.40	1.00
60 Antawn Jamison	.25	.60
61 Antoine Walker	.25	.60
62 Shareef Abdur-Rahim	.25	.60
63 Michael Olowokandi	.15	.40
64 Robert Traylor	.15	.40
65 Keith Van Horn	.20	.50
66 Shaquille O'Neal	.50	1.25
67 Ray Allen	.25	.60
68 Gary Payton	.25	.60
69 Raef LaFrentz	.15	.40

❑ 70 Grant Hill	.25	.60
❑ 71 Anfernee Hardaway	.25	.60
❑ 72 Maurice Taylor	.15	.40
❑ 73 Ron Mercer	.25	.60
❑ 74 Michael Finley	.25	.60
❑ 75 Jason Kidd	.25	.60
❑ 76 Allan Houston	.20	.50
❑ 77 Damon Stoudamire	.20	.50
❑ 78 Antonio McDyess	.20	.50
❑ 79 Eddie Jones	.20	.50
❑ 80 Michael Dickerson	.15	.40
❑ 81 Michael Jordan	1.00	2.50
❑ 82 Michael Jordan	1.00	2.50
❑ 83 Michael Jordan	1.00	2.50
❑ 84 Michael Jordan	1.00	2.50
❑ 85 Michael Jordan	1.00	2.50
❑ 86 Michael Jordan	1.00	2.50
❑ 87 Michael Jordan	1.00	2.50
❑ 88 Michael Jordan	1.00	2.50
❑ 89 Michael Jordan	1.00	2.50
❑ 90 Michael Jordan	1.00	2.50
❑ S1 Michael Jordan	1.00	2.50

2000 Upper Deck Century Legends

❑ COMPLETE SET (90)	10.00	25.00
❑ COMMON CARD (1-90)	.07	.20
❑ COMMON MJ (66-71/81-90)	.60	1.50
❑ 1 Michael Jordan	1.50	4.00
❑ 2 Magic Johnson	.75	2.00
❑ 3 Larry Bird	1.00	2.50
❑ 4 Bob Cousy	.25	.60
❑ 5 Bill Russell	.40	1.00
❑ 6 Julius Erving	.40	1.00
❑ 7 Nate Archibald	.25	.60
❑ 8 Oscar Robertson	.30	.75
❑ 9 Elgin Baylor	.25	.60
❑ 10 Jo Jo White	.07	.20
❑ 11 Hal Greer	.07	.20
❑ 12 Clyde Drexler	.25	.60
❑ 13 Wilt Chamberlain	.40	1.00
❑ 14 Walt Bellamy	.07	.20
❑ 15 Walt Frazier	.25	.60
❑ 16 Earl Monroe	.25	.60
❑ 17 John Havlicek	.30	.75
❑ 18 George Mikan	.40	1.00
❑ 19 George Karl	.15	.40
❑ 20 Tom Heinsohn	.07	.20
❑ 21 Kareem Abdul-Jabbar	.40	1.00
❑ 22 Bill Sharman	.07	.20
❑ 23 Elvin Hayes	.15	.40
❑ 24 Rick Barry	.25	.60
❑ 25 Paul Silas	.15	.40
❑ 26 Mitch Kupchak	.07	.20
❑ 27 Dave Cowens	.15	.40
❑ 28 Nate Thurmond	.07	.20
❑ 29 Dave DeBusschere	.07	.20
❑ 30 Jerry Lucas	.07	.20
❑ 31 Bill Walton	.25	.60
❑ 32 Jerry West	.25	.60
❑ 33 David Thompson	.07	.20
❑ 34 Spencer Haywood	.07	.20
❑ 35 Moses Malone	.25	.60
❑ 36 Alex English	.07	.20
❑ 37 Willis Reed	.15	.40
❑ 38 George Gervin	.25	.60
❑ 39 Dolph Schayes	.15	.40
❑ 40 Wes Unseld	.07	.20
❑ 41 Bob Lanier	.07	.20
❑ 42 James Worthy	.25	.60
❑ 43 Maurice Lucas	.07	.20
❑ 44 Pete Maravich	.30	.75
❑ 45 Isiah Thomas	.25	.60
❑ 46 Robert Parish	.25	.60
❑ 47 Dominique Wilkins	.25	.60
❑ 48 Walter Davis	.07	.20
❑ 49 Bob Pettit	.15	.40
❑ 50 Kevin McHale	.25	.60
❑ 51 Julius Erving HD	.25	.60
❑ 52 Dominique Wilkins HD	.15	.40
❑ 53 George Gervin HD	.15	.40
❑ 54 Kareem Abdul-Jabbar HD	.25	.60
❑ 55 Clyde Drexler HD	.15	.40
❑ 56 David Thompson HD	.07	.20
❑ 57 Walter Davis HD	.07	.20
❑ 58 James Worthy HD	.15	.40
❑ 59 Moses Malone HD	.15	.40
❑ 60 Bob Lanier HD	.07	.20
❑ 61 Robert Parish HD	.15	.40
❑ 62 Maurice Lucas HD	.07	.20
❑ 63 Wes Unseld HD	.07	.20
❑ 64 Ron Boone HD	.07	.20
❑ 65 Larry Nance HD	.07	.20
❑ 66 Michael Jordan HD	.60	1.50
❑ 67 Michael Jordan HD	.60	1.50
❑ 68 Michael Jordan HD	.60	1.50
❑ 69 Michael Jordan HD	.60	1.50
❑ 70 Michael Jordan HD	.60	1.50
❑ 71 Michael Jordan UDT	.60	1.50
❑ 72 Wilt Chamberlain UDT	.25	.60
❑ 73 Magic Johnson UDT	.40	1.00
❑ 74 Julius Erving UDT	.25	.60
❑ 75 Larry Bird UDT	.50	1.25
❑ 76 Bill Russell UDT	.25	.60
❑ 77 Jerry West UDT	.25	.60
❑ 78 Oscar Robertson UDT	.25	.60
❑ 79 John Havlicek UDT	.25	.60
❑ 80 Elgin Baylor UDT	.15	.40
❑ 81 Michael Jordan TB	.60	1.50
❑ 82 Michael Jordan TB	.60	1.50
❑ 83 Michael Jordan TB	.60	1.50
❑ 84 Michael Jordan TB	.60	1.50
❑ 85 Michael Jordan TB	.60	1.50
❑ 86 Michael Jordan TB	.60	1.50
❑ 87 Michael Jordan TB	.60	1.50
❑ 88 Michael Jordan TB	.60	1.50
❑ 89 Michael Jordan TB	.60	1.50
❑ 90 Michael Jordan TB	.60	1.50

2002-03 Upper Deck Championship Drive

❑ COMP.SET w/o SP's (100)	15.00	40.00
❑ COMMON CARD (1-100)	.25	.60
❑ COMMON JSY RC (101-130)	4.00	10.00
❑ COMMON ROOKIE (131-155)	2.00	5.00
❑ 1 Shareef Abdur-Rahim	.30	.75
❑ 2 Glenn Robinson	.30	.75
❑ 3 Jason Terry	.40	1.00
❑ 4 Dion Glover	.25	.60
❑ 5 Antoine Walker	.30	.75
❑ 6 Paul Pierce	.40	1.00
❑ 7 Vin Baker	.30	.75
❑ 8 Kedrick Brown	.25	.60
❑ 9 Jalen Rose	.30	.75
❑ 10 Tyson Chandler	.30	.75
❑ 11 Eddy Curry	.30	.75
❑ 12 Darius Miles	.25	.60
❑ 13 Ricky Davis	.30	.75
❑ 14 Zydrunas Ilgauskas	.30	.75
❑ 15 Dirk Nowitzki	.60	1.50
❑ 16 Michael Finley	.40	1.00
❑ 17 Steve Nash	.60	1.50
❑ 18 Raef LaFrentz	.25	.60
❑ 19 Nick Van Exel	.30	.75
❑ 20 James Posey	.25	.60
❑ 21 Juwan Howard	.30	.75
❑ 22 Chauncey Billups	.40	1.00
❑ 23 Ben Wallace	.30	.75
❑ 24 Richard Hamilton	.30	.75
❑ 25 Jason Richardson	.40	1.00
❑ 26 Antawn Jamison	.40	1.00
❑ 27 Gilbert Arenas	.40	1.00
❑ 28 Steve Francis	.40	1.00
❑ 29 Cuttino Mobley	.30	.75
❑ 30 Eddie Griffin	.25	.60
❑ 31 Reggie Miller	.40	1.00
❑ 32 Jermaine O'Neal	.40	1.00
❑ 33 Jamaal Tinsley	.30	.75
❑ 34 Ron Mercer	.25	.60
❑ 35 Elton Brand	.40	1.00
❑ 36 Andre Miller	.30	.75
❑ 37 Kobe Bryant	2.00	5.00
❑ 38 Shaquille O'Neal	1.00	2.50
❑ 39 Rick Fox	.30	.75
❑ 40 Devean George	.25	.60
❑ 41 Pau Gasol	.40	1.00
❑ 42 Shane Battier	.30	.75
❑ 43 Jason Williams	.30	.75
❑ 44 Eddie Jones	.30	.75
❑ 45 Brian Grant	.25	.60
❑ 46 Anthony Carter	.25	.60
❑ 47 Ray Allen	.40	1.00
❑ 48 Tim Thomas	.25	.60
❑ 49 Kevin Garnett	.75	2.00
❑ 50 Terrell Brandon	.25	.60
❑ 51 Wally Szczerbiak	.30	.75
❑ 52 Joe Smith	.25	.60
❑ 53 Jason Kidd	.60	1.50
❑ 54 Richard Jefferson	.40	1.00
❑ 55 Dikembe Mutombo	.30	.75
❑ 56 Kenyon Martin	.40	1.00
❑ 57 Baron Davis	.40	1.00
❑ 58 Jamal Mashburn	.30	.75
❑ 59 David Wesley	.25	.60
❑ 60 P.J. Brown	.25	.60
❑ 61 Courtney Alexander	.25	.60
❑ 62 Latrell Sprewell	.30	.75
❑ 63 Allan Houston	.30	.75
❑ 64 Kurt Thomas	.25	.60
❑ 65 Antonio McDyess	.30	.75
❑ 66 Tracy McGrady	.75	2.00
❑ 67 Mike Miller	.30	.75
❑ 68 Grant Hill	.40	1.00
❑ 69 Allen Iverson	.75	2.00
❑ 70 Keith Van Horn	.30	.75
❑ 71 Shawn Marion	.40	1.00
❑ 72 Stephon Marbury	.40	1.00
❑ 73 Anfernee Hardaway	.40	1.00
❑ 74 Rasheed Wallace	.40	1.00
❑ 75 Bonzi Wells	.30	.75
❑ 76 Scottie Pippen	.60	1.50
❑ 77 Mike Bibby	.30	.75
❑ 78 Peja Stojakovic	.30	.75
❑ 79 Chris Webber	.40	1.00
❑ 80 Hedo Turkoglu	.30	.75
❑ 81 Vlade Divac	.30	.75
❑ 82 Tim Duncan	.75	2.00
❑ 83 David Robinson	.50	1.25
❑ 84 Tony Parker	.40	1.00
❑ 85 Malik Rose	.25	.60
❑ 86 Gary Payton	.40	1.00
❑ 87 Rashard Lewis	.40	1.00
❑ 88 Brent Barry	.25	.60
❑ 89 Desmond Mason	.30	.75
❑ 90 Vladimir Radmanovic	.25	.60
❑ 91 Vince Carter	.75	2.00
❑ 92 Morris Peterson	.30	.75
❑ 93 Antonio Davis	.25	.60
❑ 94 Karl Malone	.40	1.00
❑ 95 John Stockton	.50	1.25
❑ 96 Andrei Kirilenko	.40	1.00
❑ 97 Matt Harpring	.30	.75
❑ 98 Jerry Stackhouse	.30	.75
❑ 99 Larry Hughes	.30	.75
❑ 100 Michael Jordan	2.50	6.00
❑ 101 Juan Dixon JSY RC	6.00	15.00
❑ 102 Carlos Boozer JSY RC	8.00	20.00
❑ 103 Dan Gadzuric JSY RC	4.00	10.00
❑ 104 V.Yarbrough JSY RC	4.00	10.00
❑ 105 R.Archibald JSY RC	4.00	10.00
❑ 106 Roger Mason JSY RC	4.00	10.00
❑ 107 Ronald Murray JSY RC	6.00	15.00
❑ 108 Chris Jefferies JSY RC	4.00	10.00
❑ 109 John Salmons JSY RC	6.00	15.00
❑ 110 Predrag Savovic JSY RC	4.00	10.00
❑ 111 Tayshaun Prince JSY RC	6.00	15.00
❑ 112 Casey Jacobsen JSY RC	4.00	10.00
❑ 113 Qyntel Woods JSY RC	4.00	10.00
❑ 114 Kareem Rush JSY RC	5.00	12.00

115 Ryan Humphrey JSY RC	4.00	10.00
116 Sam Clancy JSY RC	4.00	10.00
117 Lonny Baxter JSY RC	4.00	10.00
118 Fred Jones JSY RC	5.00	12.00
119 Marcus Haislip JSY RC	4.00	10.00
120 Melvin Ely JSY RC	4.00	10.00
121 Jared Jeffries JSY RC	4.00	10.00
122 Caron Butler JSY RC	8.00	20.00
123 A.Stoudemire JSY RC	10.00	25.00
124 Chris Wilcox JSY RC	5.00	12.00
125 Nene Hilario JSY RC	5.00	12.00
126 DaJuan Wagner JSY RC	4.00	10.00
127 N.Tskitishvili JSY RC	4.00	10.00
128 Drew Gooden JSY RC	6.00	15.00
129 Jay Williams JSY RC	5.00	12.00
130 Yao Ming JSY RC	12.00	30.00
131 Manu Ginobili RC	5.00	12.00
132 Efthimios Rentzias RC	2.00	5.00
133 Juaquin Hawkins RC	2.00	5.00
134 Marko Jaric	2.00	5.00
135 Dan Dickau RC	2.00	5.00
136 Frank Williams RC	2.00	5.00
137 Curtis Borchardt RC	2.00	5.00
138 Mike Dunleavy RC	2.50	6.00
139 Smush Parker RC	2.00	5.00
140 Tito Maddox RC	2.00	5.00
141 Jannero Pargo RC	2.00	5.00
142 Jiri Welsch RC	2.00	5.00
143 Bostjan Nachbar RC	2.00	5.00
144 Rasual Butler RC	2.00	5.00
145 Gordan Giricek RC	2.00	5.00
146 Igor Rakocevic RC	2.00	5.00
147 Tamar Slay RC	2.00	5.00
148 Junior Harrington RC	2.00	5.00
149 Nate Huffman RC	2.00	5.00
150 Jamal Sampson RC	2.00	5.00
151 Reggie Evans RC	2.00	5.00
152 Cezary Trybanski RC	2.00	5.00
153 Pat Burke RC	2.00	5.00
154 J.R. Bremer RC	2.00	5.00
155 Mehmet Okur RC	2.50	6.00

1997-98 Upper Deck Diamond Vision

COMPLETE SET (29)	75.00	125.00
1 Dikembe Mutombo	1.25	3.00
2 Dana Barros	.60	1.50
3 Glen Rice	1.25	3.00
4 Michael Jordan	10.00	25.00
5 Terrell Brandon	1.25	3.00
6 Michael Finley	1.50	4.00
7 Antonio McDyess	1.25	3.00
8 Grant Hill	1.50	4.00
9 Latrell Sprewell	1.50	4.00
10 Hakeem Olajuwon	1.50	4.00
11 Reggie Miller	1.50	4.00
12 Loy Vaught	.60	1.50
13 Shaquille O'Neal	5.00	12.00
14 Alonzo Mourning	1.25	3.00
15 Vin Baker	1.25	3.00
16 Kevin Garnett	4.00	10.00
17 Kerry Kittles	1.50	4.00
18 Patrick Ewing	1.50	4.00
19 Anfernee Hardaway	1.50	4.00
20 Allen Iverson	5.00	12.00
21 Jason Kidd	3.00	8.00
22 Isaiah Rider	1.25	3.00
23 Mitch Richmond	1.25	3.00
24 David Robinson	1.50	4.00
25 Gary Payton	1.50	4.00
26 Damon Stoudamire	1.25	3.00
27 Karl Malone	1.50	4.00
28 Shareef Abdur-Rahim	3.00	8.00
29 Chris Webber	1.50	4.00

1998-99 Upper Deck Encore

COMPLETE SET (150)	60.00	120.00
COMMON CARD (1-90)	.08	.25
COMMON MJ (91-113)	1.25	3.00
COMMON ROOKIE (114-143)	.25	.60
COMMON BONUS (144-150)	.50	1.25
1 Mookie Blaylock	.08	.25
2 Dikembe Mutombo	.20	.50
3 Steve Smith	.20	.50
4 Kenny Anderson	.20	.50
5 Antoine Walker	.30	.75
6 Ron Mercer	.15	.40
7 David Wesley	.08	.25
8 Elden Campbell	.08	.25
9 Eddie Jones	.30	.75
10 Ron Harper	.20	.50
11 Toni Kukoc	.20	.50
12 Brent Barry	.20	.50
13 Shawn Kemp	.20	.50
14 Brevin Knight	.08	.25
15 Derek Anderson	.25	.60
16 Shawn Bradley	.08	.25
17 Robert Pack	.08	.25
18 Michael Finley	.30	.75
19 Antonio McDyess	.20	.50
20 Nick Van Exel	.30	.75
21 Danny Fortson	.08	.25
22 Grant Hill	.30	.75
23 Jerry Stackhouse	.30	.75
24 Bison Dele	.08	.25
25 Donyell Marshall	.20	.50
26 Tony Delk	.08	.25
27 Erick Dampier	.20	.50
28 John Starks	.20	.50
29 Charles Barkley	.40	1.00
30 Hakeem Olajuwon	.30	.75
31 Othella Harrington	.08	.25
32 Scottie Pippen	.50	1.25
33 Rik Smits	.20	.50
34 Reggie Miller	.30	.75
35 Mark Jackson	.20	.50
36 Rodney Rogers	.08	.25
37 Lamond Murray	.08	.25
38 Maurice Taylor	.15	.40
39 Kobe Bryant	1.25	3.00
40 Shaquillie O'Neal	.75	2.00
41 Derek Fisher	.30	.75
42 Glen Rice	.20	.50
43 Jamal Mashburn	.20	.50
44 Alonzo Mourning	.20	.50
45 Tim Hardaway	.20	.50
46 Ray Allen	.30	.75
47 Vinny Del Negro	.08	.25
48 Glenn Robinson	.20	.50
49 Joe Smith	.20	.50
50 Terrell Brandon	.20	.50
51 Kevin Garnett	.60	1.50
52 Keith Van Horn	.30	.75
53 Stephon Marbury	.30	.75
54 Jayson Williams	.08	.25
55 Patrick Ewing	.30	.75
56 Allan Houston	.20	.50
57 Latrell Sprewell	.30	.75
58 Anfernee Hardaway	.30	.75
59 Horace Grant	.20	.50
60 Nick Anderson	.08	.25
61 Allen Iverson	.60	1.50
62 Matt Geiger	.08	.25
63 Theo Ratliff	.20	.50
64 Jason Kidd	.50	1.25
65 Rex Chapman	.08	.25
66 Tom Gugliotta	.08	.25
67 Rasheed Wallace	.30	.75
68 Arvydas Sabonis	.20	.50
69 Damon Stoudamire	.20	.50
70 Vlade Divac	.20	.50
71 Corliss Williamson	.20	.50
72 Chris Webber	.30	.75
73 Tim Duncan	.50	1.25
74 Sean Elliott	.20	.50
75 David Robinson	.30	.75
76 Vin Baker	.20	.50
77 Gary Payton	.30	.75
78 Detlef Schrempf	.20	.50
79 Tracy McGrady	.75	2.00
80 John Wallace	.08	.25
81 Doug Christie	.20	.50
82 Karl Malone	.30	.75
83 John Stockton	.30	.75
84 Jeff Hornacek	.20	.50
85 Bryant Reeves	.08	.25
86 Michael Smith	.08	.25
87 Shareef Abdur-Rahim	.30	.75
88 Juwan Howard	.20	.50
89 Rod Strickland	.08	.25
90 Mitch Richmond	.20	.50
91 Michael Jordan	1.25	3.00
92 Michael Jordan	1.25	3.00
93 Michael Jordan	1.25	3.00
94 Michael Jordan	1.25	3.00
95 Michael Jordan	1.25	3.00
96 Michael Jordan	1.25	3.00
97 Michael Jordan	1.25	3.00
98 Michael Jordan	1.25	3.00
99 Michael Jordan	1.25	3.00
100 Michael Jordan	1.25	3.00
101 Michael Jordan	1.25	3.00
102 Michael Jordan	1.25	3.00
103 Michael Jordan	1.25	3.00
104 Michael Jordan	1.25	3.00
105 Michael Jordan	1.25	3.00
106 Michael Jordan	1.25	3.00
107 Michael Jordan	1.25	3.00
108 Michael Jordan	1.25	3.00
109 Michael Jordan	1.25	3.00
110 Michael Jordan	1.25	3.00
111 Michael Jordan	1.25	3.00
112 Michael Jordan	1.25	3.00
113 Michael Jordan	1.25	3.00
114 Michael Olowokandi RC	1.00	2.50
115 Mike Bibby RC	1.50	4.00
116 Raef LaFrentz RC	1.00	2.50
117 Antawn Jamison RC	2.50	6.00
118 Vince Carter RC	4.00	10.00
119 Robert Traylor RC	.60	1.50
120 Jason Williams RC	2.50	6.00
121 Larry Hughes RC	2.00	5.00
122 Dirk Nowitzki RC	6.00	15.00
123 Paul Pierce RC	6.00	15.00
124 Michael Doleac RC	.60	1.50
125 Keon Clark RC	1.00	2.50
126 Michael Dickerson RC	1.25	3.00
127 Matt Harpring RC	1.00	2.50
128 Bryce Drew RC	.60	1.50
129 Pat Garrity RC	.30	.75
130 Roshown McLeod RC	.30	.75
131 Ricky Davis RC	2.00	5.00
132 Peja Stojakovic RC	2.50	6.00
133 Felipe Lopez RC	.75	2.00
134 Al Harrington RC	1.50	4.00
135 Ruben Patterson RC	1.25	3.00
136 Cuttino Mobley RC	3.00	8.00
137 Tyronn Lue RC	.40	1.00
138 Brian Skinner RC	.60	1.50
139 Nazr Mohammed RC	.30	.75
140 Toby Bailey RC	.25	.60
141 Casey Shaw RC	.25	.60
142 Corey Benjamin RC	.60	1.50
143 Rashard Lewis RC	2.50	6.00
144 Jason Williams BON	1.25	3.00
145 Paul Pierce BON	1.50	4.00
146 Vince Carter BON	3.00	8.00
147 Antawn Jamison BON	1.50	4.00
148 Raef LaFrentz BON	.50	1.25
149 Mike Bibby BON	1.50	4.00
150 Michael Olowokandi BON	.50	1.25
MJ Michael Jordan AU	1000.00	2000.00

1999-00 Upper Deck Encore

COMPLETE SET (120)	75.00	150.00
COMPLETE SET w/o RC (90)	12.50	25.00
COMMON CARD (1-90)	.20	.50
COMMON ROOKIE (91-120)	1.00	2.50
1 Dikembe Mutombo	.25	.60
2 Alan Henderson	.20	.50
3 Isaiah Rider	.20	.50
4 Kenny Anderson	.25	.60
5 Antoine Walker	.30	.75
6 Paul Pierce	.30	.75
7 Elden Campbell	.20	.50
8 Eddie Jones	.30	.75
9 David Wesley	.20	.50
10 Hersey Hawkins	.20	.50
11 Randy Brown	.20	.50
12 Toni Kukoc	.30	.75
13 Shawn Kemp	.30	.75
14 Bob Sura	.20	.50
15 Michael Finley	.30	.75
16 Dirk Nowitzki	.50	1.25
17 Gary Trent	.20	.50
18 Antonio McDyess	.25	.60
19 Nick Van Exel	.25	.60
20 Raef LaFrentz	.25	.60
21 Christian Laettner	.25	.60
22 Grant Hill	.30	.75
23 Lindsey Hunter	.20	.50
24 Jerry Stackhouse	.30	.75
25 John Starks	.30	.75
26 Antawn Jamison	.30	.75
27 Tony Farmer	.20	.50
28 Hakeem Olajuwon	.30	.75
29 Cuttino Mobley	.25	.60
30 Charles Barkley	.40	1.00
31 Reggie Miller	.30	.75
32 Jalen Rose	.25	.60
33 Mark Jackson	.30	.75
34 Maurice Taylor	.25	.60
35 Derek Anderson	.20	.50
36 Michael Olowokandi	.20	.50
37 Kobe Bryant	1.50	4.00
38 Shaquille O'Neal	.75	2.00
39 Glen Rice	.30	.75
40 Tim Hardaway	.30	.75
41 Alonzo Mourning	.30	.75
42 Ray Allen	.30	.75
43 Glenn Robinson	.25	.60
44 Sam Cassell	.25	.60
45 Tim Thomas	.25	.60
46 Kevin Garnett	.60	1.50
47 Terrell Brandon	.20	.50
48 Keith Van Horn	.25	.60
49 Stephon Marbury	.30	.75
50 Kendall Gill	.20	.50
51 Patrick Ewing	.40	1.00
52 Allan Houston	.25	.60
53 Latrell Sprewell	.25	.60
54 Darrell Armstrong	.20	.50
55 John Amaechi RC	.30	.75
56 Michael Doleac	.20	.50
57 Allen Iverson	.60	1.50
58 Theo Ratliff	.25	.60
59 Larry Hughes	.25	.60
60 Jason Kidd	.50	1.25
61 Tom Gugliotta	.20	.50
62 Anfernee Hardaway	.30	.75
63 Rasheed Wallace	.30	.75
64 Steve Smith	.20	.50
65 Damon Stoudamire	.30	.75
66 Scottie Pippen	.50	1.25
67 Corliss Williamson	.20	.50
68 Jason Williams	.30	.75
69 Vlade Divac	.30	.75
70 Chris Webber	.30	.75
71 Tim Duncan	.60	1.50
72 David Robinson	.40	1.00
73 Avery Johnson	.25	.60
74 Mario Elie	.20	.50
75 Gary Payton	.30	.75
76 Vin Baker	.30	.75
77 Ruben Patterson	.20	.50
78 Brent Barry	.25	.60
79 Vince Carter	.60	1.50
80 Antonio Davis	.20	.50
81 Tracy McGrady	.60	1.50
82 Karl Malone	.40	1.00
83 John Stockton	.40	1.00
84 Bryon Russell	.20	.50
85 Shareef Abdur-Rahim	.25	.60
86 Mike Bibby	.30	.75
87 Othella Harrington	.20	.50
88 Juwan Howard	.25	.60
89 Rod Strickland	.20	.50
90 Mitch Richmond	.25	.60
91 Elton Brand RC	3.00	8.00
92 Steve Francis RC	3.00	8.00
93 Baron Davis RC	4.00	10.00
94 Lamar Odom RC	3.00	8.00
95 Jonathan Bender RC	1.00	2.50
96 Wally Szczerbiak RC	3.00	8.00
97 Richard Hamilton RC	3.00	8.00
98 Andre Miller RC	3.00	8.00
99 Shawn Marion RC	3.00	8.00
100 Jason Terry RC	2.50	6.00
101 Trajan Langdon RC	1.00	2.50
102 Kenny Thomas RC	1.00	2.50
103 Corey Maggette RC	3.00	8.00
104 William Avery RC	1.00	2.50
105 Ron Artest RC	4.00	10.00
106 A.Radojevic RC	1.00	2.50
107 James Posey RC	1.50	4.00
108 Quincy Lewis RC	1.00	2.50
109 Vonteego Cummings RC	1.00	2.50
110 Jeff Foster RC	1.25	3.00
111 Dion Glover RC	1.00	2.50
112 Devean George RC	1.50	4.00
113 Evan Eschmeyer RC	1.00	2.50
114 Tim James RC	1.00	2.50
115 Adrian Griffin RC	1.00	2.50
116 Anthony Carter RC	2.00	5.00
117 Obinna Ekezie RC	1.00	2.50
118 Todd MacCulloch RC	1.00	2.50
119 Chucky Atkins RC	1.25	3.00
120 Lazaro Borrell RC	1.00	2.50

2000-01 Upper Deck Encore

COMPLETE SET w/o RC's	10.00	25.00
COMMON CARD (1-135)	.20	.50
COMMON ROOKIE (136-165)	1.25	3.00
1 Brevin Knight	.20	.50
2 Lorenzen Wright	.20	.50
3 Alan Henderson	.20	.50
4 Jason Terry	.30	.75
5 Paul Pierce	.30	.75
6 Antoine Walker	.25	.60
7 Kenny Anderson	.25	.60
8 Tony Battie	.20	.50
9 Adrian Griffin	.20	.50
10 Derrick Coleman	.25	.60
11 David Wesley	.20	.50
12 Baron Davis	.30	.75
13 Elden Campbell	.20	.50
14 Jamal Mashburn	.25	.60
15 Elton Brand	.30	.75
16 Ron Mercer	.20	.50
17 Ron Artest	.30	.75
18 Michael Ruffin	.20	.50
19 Lamond Murray	.20	.50
20 Andre Miller	.25	.60
21 Matt Harpring	.25	.60
22 Jim Jackson	.20	.50
23 Michael Finley	.30	.75
24 Dirk Nowitzki	.50	1.25
25 Steve Nash	.50	1.25
26 Howard Eisley	.20	.50
27 Antonio McDyess	.25	.60
28 James Posey	.20	.50
29 Nick Van Exel	.25	.60
30 Raef LaFrentz	.20	.50
31 Voshon Lenard	.20	.50
32 Jerry Stackhouse	.25	.60
33 Ben Wallace	.25	.60
34 Michael Curry	.20	.50
35 Joe Smith	.20	.50
36 Chucky Atkins	.20	.50
37 Antawn Jamison	.30	.75
38 Larry Hughes	.25	.60
39 Chris Mills	.20	.50
40 Mookie Blaylock	.25	.60
41 Vonteego Cummings	.20	.50
42 Steve Francis	.30	.75
43 Maurice Taylor	.20	.50
44 Hakeem Olajuwon	.40	1.00
45 Walt Williams	.20	.50
46 Cuttino Mobley	.25	.60
47 Reggie Miller	.30	.75
48 Jalen Rose	.25	.60
49 Austin Croshere	.20	.50
50 Travis Best	.20	.50
51 Jermaine O'Neal	.30	.75
52 Lamar Odom	.30	.75
53 Jeff McInnis	.20	.50
54 Michael Olowokandi	.20	.50
55 Brian Skinner	.20	.50
56 Corey Maggette	.25	.60
57 Shaquille O'Neal	.75	2.00
58 Ron Harper	.25	.60
59 Kobe Bryant	1.50	4.00
60 Robert Horry	.25	.60
61 Isaiah Rider	.25	.60
62 Eddie Jones	.25	.60
63 Anthony Carter	.20	.50
64 Tim Hardaway	.25	.60
65 Brian Grant	.20	.50
66 Anthony Mason	.20	.50
67 Ray Allen	.30	.75
68 Tim Thomas	.20	.50
69 Glenn Robinson	.25	.60
70 Sam Cassell	.25	.60
71 Lindsey Hunter	.20	.50
72 Kevin Garnett	.60	1.50
73 Wally Szczerbiak	.25	.60
74 Terrell Brandon	.20	.50
75 Chauncey Billups	.30	.75
76 Stephon Marbury	.30	.75
77 Keith Van Horn	.25	.60
78 Lucious Harris	.20	.50
79 Kendall Gill	.20	.50
80 Latrell Sprewell	.25	.60
81 Marcus Camby	.25	.60
82 Larry Johnson	.25	.60
83 Allan Houston	.25	.60
84 Glen Rice	.25	.60
85 Grant Hill	.30	.75
86 Tracy McGrady	.60	1.50
87 John Amaechi	.20	.50
88 Darrell Armstrong	.20	.50
89 Allen Iverson	.60	1.50
90 Dikembe Mutombo	.25	.60
91 George Lynch	.20	.50
92 Aaron McKie	.20	.50
93 Eric Snow	.20	.50
94 Jason Kidd	.50	1.25
95 Tony Delk	.20	.50
96 Clifford Robinson	.20	.50
97 Tom Gugliotta	.20	.50
98 Shawn Marion	.30	.75
99 Rasheed Wallace	.30	.75
100 Scottie Pippen	.50	1.25
101 Steve Smith	.25	.60
102 Damon Stoudamire	.25	.60
103 Bonzi Wells	.20	.50
104 Chris Webber	.30	.75
105 Jason Williams	.25	.60
106 Peja Stojakovic	.25	.60

❑ 107 Vlade Divac	.25	.60
❑ 108 Doug Christie	.20	.50
❑ 109 Tim Duncan	.60	1.50
❑ 110 David Robinson	.40	1.00
❑ 111 Derek Anderson	.25	.60
❑ 112 Antonio Daniels	.20	.50
❑ 113 Sean Elliott	.25	.60
❑ 114 Gary Payton	.30	.75
❑ 115 Patrick Ewing	.40	1.00
❑ 116 Vin Baker	.25	.60
❑ 117 Rashard Lewis	.30	.75
❑ 118 Vince Carter	.60	1.50
❑ 119 Alvin Williams	.20	.50
❑ 120 Antonio Davis	.20	.50
❑ 121 Charles Oakley	.25	.60
❑ 122 Karl Malone	.40	1.00
❑ 123 John Stockton	.40	1.00
❑ 124 Bryon Russell	.20	.50
❑ 125 John Starks	.20	.50
❑ 126 Shareef Abdur-Rahim	.25	.60
❑ 127 Mike Bibby	.25	.60
❑ 128 Michael Dickerson	.20	.50
❑ 129 Grant Long	.20	.50
❑ 130 Mitch Richmond	.25	.60
❑ 131 Richard Hamilton	.25	.60
❑ 132 Chris Whitney	.20	.50
❑ 133 Jahidi White	.20	.50
❑ 134 Checklist 1	.08	.25
❑ 135 Checklist 2	.08	.25
❑ 136 Kenyon Martin RC	3.00	8.00
❑ 137 Stromile Swift RC	1.50	4.00
❑ 138 Chris Mihm RC	1.25	3.00
❑ 139 Marcus Fizer RC	1.25	3.00
❑ 140 Darius Miles RC	1.50	4.00
❑ 141 Joel Przybilla RC	1.25	3.00
❑ 142 Mike Miller RC	2.00	5.00
❑ 143 Courtney Alexander RC	1.25	3.00
❑ 144 DerMarr Johnson RC	1.25	3.00
❑ 145 Stephen Jackson RC	2.00	5.00
❑ 146 Jerome Moiso RC	1.25	3.00
❑ 147 Keyon Dooling RC	1.25	3.00
❑ 148 Erick Barkley RC	1.25	3.00
❑ 149 Jason Collier RC	1.25	3.00
❑ 150 Jamaal Magloire RC	1.25	3.00
❑ 151 DeShawn Stevenson RC	1.25	3.00
❑ 152 Hedo Turkoglu RC	3.00	8.00
❑ 153 Morris Peterson RC	2.00	5.00
❑ 154 Jamal Crawford RC	2.00	5.00
❑ 155 Etan Thomas RC	1.25	3.00
❑ 156 Quentin Richardson RC	1.50	4.00
❑ 157 Mateen Cleaves RC	1.25	3.00
❑ 158 Donnell Harvey RC	1.25	3.00
❑ 159 Mark Madsen RC	1.25	3.00
❑ 160 Desmond Mason RC	1.50	4.00
❑ 161 Speedy Claxton RC	1.25	3.00
❑ 162 Hanno Mottola RC	1.25	3.00
❑ 163 Mamadou N'Diaye RC	1.25	3.00
❑ 164 Eduardo Najera RC	1.25	3.00
❑ 165 Khalid El-Amin RC	1.25	3.00

2005-06 Upper Deck ESPN

❑ COMPLETE SET (132)	15.00	40.00
❑ COMP.SET w/o SP's (90)	6.00	15.00
❑ COMMON CARD (1-90)	.12	.30
❑ COMMON ROOKIE (91-132)	.75	2.00
❑ 1 Josh Childress	.15	.40
❑ 2 Josh Smith	.20	.50
❑ 3 Al Harrington	.12	.30
❑ 4 Antoine Walker	.15	.40
❑ 5 Ricky Davis	.20	.50
❑ 6 Paul Pierce	.20	.50
❑ 7 Kareem Rush	.12	.30
❑ 8 Emeka Okafor	.20	.50
❑ 9 Gerald Wallace	.20	.50
❑ 10 Eddy Curry	.15	.40
❑ 11 Kirk Hinrich	.20	.50
❑ 12 Ben Gordon	.25	.60
❑ 13 Drew Gooden	.15	.40
❑ 14 LeBron James	1.00	2.50
❑ 15 Zydrunas Ilgauskas	.15	.40
❑ 16 Dirk Nowitzki	.30	.75
❑ 17 Jason Terry	.20	.50
❑ 18 Josh Howard	.20	.50
❑ 19 Carmelo Anthony	.40	1.00
❑ 20 Kenyon Martin	.20	.50
❑ 21 Andre Miller	.15	.40
❑ 22 Ben Wallace	.20	.50
❑ 23 Chauncey Billups	.20	.50
❑ 24 Richard Hamilton	.15	.40
❑ 25 Troy Murphy	.20	.50
❑ 26 Jason Richardson	.20	.50
❑ 27 Baron Davis	.20	.50
❑ 28 Tracy McGrady	.40	1.00
❑ 29 Yao Ming	.50	1.25
❑ 30 Juwan Howard	.15	.40
❑ 31 Jermaine O'Neal	.20	.50
❑ 32 Reggie Miller	.20	.50
❑ 33 Ron Artest	.15	.40
❑ 34 Corey Maggette	.15	.40
❑ 35 Elton Brand	.20	.50
❑ 36 Bobby Simmons	.12	.30
❑ 37 Caron Butler	.20	.50
❑ 38 Kobe Bryant	1.00	2.50
❑ 39 Lamar Odom	.20	.50
❑ 40 Mike Miller	.20	.50
❑ 41 Jason Williams	.15	.40
❑ 42 Pau Gasol	.20	.50
❑ 43 Dwyane Wade	.50	1.25
❑ 44 Eddie Jones	.12	.30
❑ 45 Shaquille O'Neal	.50	1.25
❑ 46 Desmond Mason	.12	.30
❑ 47 Maurice Williams	.15	.40
❑ 48 Michael Redd	.20	.50
❑ 49 Kevin Garnett	.40	1.00
❑ 50 Latrell Sprewell	.12	.30
❑ 51 Sam Cassell	.20	.50
❑ 52 Vince Carter	.40	1.00
❑ 53 Jason Kidd	.30	.75
❑ 54 Richard Jefferson	.15	.40
❑ 55 Dan Dickau	.12	.30
❑ 56 Jamaal Magloire	.12	.30
❑ 57 J.R. Smith	.15	.40
❑ 58 Jamal Crawford	.15	.40
❑ 59 Stephon Marbury	.20	.50
❑ 60 Allan Houston	.12	.30
❑ 61 Dwight Howard	.40	1.00
❑ 62 Grant Hill	.20	.50
❑ 63 Steve Francis	.20	.50
❑ 64 Allen Iverson	.40	1.00
❑ 65 Andre Iguodala	.20	.50
❑ 66 Chris Webber	.20	.50
❑ 67 Amare Stoudemire	.40	1.00
❑ 68 Shawn Marion	.20	.50
❑ 69 Steve Nash	.25	.60
❑ 70 Damon Stoudamire	.15	.40
❑ 71 Shareef Abdur-Rahim	.20	.50
❑ 72 Zach Randolph	.20	.50
❑ 73 Brad Miller	.20	.50
❑ 74 Mike Bibby	.20	.50
❑ 75 Peja Stojakovic	.20	.50
❑ 76 Manu Ginobili	.20	.50
❑ 77 Tim Duncan	.40	1.00
❑ 78 Tony Parker	.20	.50
❑ 79 Rashard Lewis	.20	.50
❑ 80 Ray Allen	.20	.50
❑ 81 Luke Ridnour	.15	.40
❑ 82 Rafer Alston	.12	.30
❑ 83 Jalen Rose	.20	.50
❑ 84 Chris Bosh	.20	.50
❑ 85 Andrei Kirilenko	.20	.50
❑ 86 Carlos Boozer	.20	.50
❑ 87 Matt Harpring	.15	.40
❑ 88 Antawn Jamison	.20	.50
❑ 89 Gilbert Arenas	.20	.50
❑ 90 Larry Hughes	.15	.40
❑ 91 Chris Taft RC	.75	2.00
❑ 92 Marvin Williams RC	1.25	3.00
❑ 93 Chris Paul RC	2.50	6.00
❑ 94 Andrew Bogut RC	1.00	2.50
❑ 95 Martynas Andriuskevicius RC	.75	2.00
❑ 96 Louis Williams RC	1.25	3.00
❑ 97 C.J. Miles RC	.75	2.00
❑ 98 Gerald Green RC	.75	2.00
❑ 99 Rashad McCants RC	1.00	2.50
❑ 100 Sarunas Jasikevicius RC	1.00	2.50
❑ 101 Andrew Bynum RC	2.50	6.00
❑ 102 Raymond Felton RC	1.00	2.50
❑ 103 Hakim Warrick RC	1.25	3.00
❑ 104 Deron Williams RC	2.00	5.00
❑ 105 Daniel Ewing RC	1.00	2.50
❑ 106 Martell Webster RC	.75	2.00
❑ 107 Johan Petro RC	.75	2.00
❑ 108 Travis Diener RC	.75	2.00
❑ 109 Joey Graham RC	.75	2.00
❑ 110 Antoine Wright RC	.75	2.00
❑ 111 Ersan Ilyasova RC	.75	2.00
❑ 112 Jason Maxiell RC	1.00	2.50
❑ 113 Linas Kleiza RC	1.00	2.50
❑ 114 Jarrett Jack RC	.75	2.00
❑ 115 Danny Granger RC	2.00	5.00
❑ 116 Monta Ellis RC	2.00	5.00
❑ 117 Francisco Garcia RC	1.00	2.50
❑ 118 Ryan Gomes RC	.75	2.00
❑ 119 Wayne Simien RC	1.00	2.50
❑ 120 Von Wafer RC	.75	2.00
❑ 121 Dijon Thompson RC	.75	2.00
❑ 122 Nate Robinson RC	1.25	3.00
❑ 123 Bracey Wright RC	.75	2.00
❑ 124 Andray Blatche RC	1.00	2.50
❑ 125 Channing Frye RC	1.00	2.50
❑ 126 Salim Stoudamire RC	1.00	2.50
❑ 127 Luther Head RC	1.00	2.50
❑ 128 Julius Hodge RC	1.00	2.50
❑ 129 David Lee RC	1.50	4.00
❑ 130 Ike Diogu RC	1.00	2.50
❑ 131 Sean May RC	1.00	2.50
❑ 132 Brandon Bass RC	.75	2.00

2002-03 Upper Deck Finite

❑ COMP.SET w/o SP's (100)	15.00	40.00
❑ COMMON CARD (1-100)	.40	1.00
❑ 181-200 NOT PRICED DUE TO SCARCITY		
❑ COMMON ROOKIE (201-221)	1.50	4.00
❑ COMMON ROOKIE (222-233)	1.50	4.00
❑ COMMON ROOKIE (234-242)	6.00	15.00
❑ 1 Shareef Abdur-Rahim	.50	1.25
❑ 2 Theo Ratliff	.40	1.00
❑ 3 Glenn Robinson	.50	1.25
❑ 4 Jason Terry	.60	1.50
❑ 5 Vin Baker	.50	1.25
❑ 6 Kedrick Brown	.40	1.00
❑ 7 Paul Pierce	.60	1.50
❑ 8 Antoine Walker	.50	1.25
❑ 9 Tyson Chandler	.50	1.25
❑ 10 Eddy Curry	.50	1.25
❑ 11 Jalen Rose	.50	1.25
❑ 12 Chris Mihm	.40	1.00
❑ 13 Darius Miles	.40	1.00
❑ 14 Ricky Davis	.50	1.25
❑ 15 Michael Finley	.60	1.50
❑ 16 Raef LaFrentz	.40	1.00
❑ 17 Steve Nash	1.00	2.50
❑ 18 Dirk Nowitzki	1.00	2.50
❑ 19 Nick Van Exel	.50	1.25
❑ 20 Marcus Camby	.50	1.25
❑ 21 Juwan Howard	.50	1.25
❑ 22 James Posey	.40	1.00
❑ 23 Chauncey Billups	.60	1.50
❑ 24 Richard Hamilton	.50	1.25
❑ 25 Ben Wallace	.50	1.25
❑ 26 Clifford Robinson	.40	1.00
❑ 27 Gilbert Arenas	.60	1.50
❑ 28 Antawn Jamison	.60	1.50
❑ 29 Jason Richardson	.60	1.50
❑ 30 Eddie Griffin	.40	1.00
❑ 31 Steve Francis	.60	1.50
❑ 32 Cuttino Mobley	.50	1.25
❑ 33 Reggie Miller	.60	1.50
❑ 34 Jermaine O'Neal	.60	1.50

❑ 35 Jamaal Tinsley	.50	1.25
❑ 36 Ron Mercer	.40	1.00
❑ 37 Elton Brand	.60	1.50
❑ 38 Andre Miller	.50	1.25
❑ 39 Lamar Odom	.60	1.50
❑ 40 Kobe Bryant	3.00	8.00
❑ 41 Rick Fox	.50	1.25
❑ 42 Devean George	.40	1.00
❑ 43 Shaquille O'Neal	1.50	4.00
❑ 44 Shane Battier	.50	1.25
❑ 45 Pau Gasol	.60	1.50
❑ 46 Jason Williams	.50	1.25
❑ 47 LaPhonso Ellis	.50	1.25
❑ 48 Eddie Jones	.50	1.25
❑ 49 Brian Grant	.40	1.00
❑ 50 Ray Allen	.60	1.50
❑ 51 Tim Thomas	.40	1.00
❑ 52 Sam Cassell	.50	1.25
❑ 53 Terrell Brandon	.40	1.00
❑ 54 Kevin Garnett	1.25	3.00
❑ 55 Wally Szczerbiak	.50	1.25
❑ 56 Marc Jackson	.40	1.00
❑ 57 Richard Jefferson	.60	1.50
❑ 58 Jason Kidd	1.00	2.50
❑ 59 Kenyon Martin	.60	1.50
❑ 60 Kerry Kittles	.50	1.25
❑ 61 Baron Davis	.60	1.50
❑ 62 Jamal Mashburn	.50	1.25
❑ 63 David Wesley	.40	1.00
❑ 64 P.J. Brown	.40	1.00
❑ 65 Latrell Sprewell	.50	1.25
❑ 66 Antonio McDyess	.50	1.25
❑ 67 Allan Houston	.50	1.25
❑ 68 Tracy McGrady	1.25	3.00
❑ 69 Mike Miller	.50	1.25
❑ 70 Darrell Armstrong	.40	1.00
❑ 71 Allen Iverson	1.25	3.00
❑ 72 Aaron McKie	.40	1.00
❑ 73 Keith Van Horn	.50	1.25
❑ 74 Stephon Marbury	.60	1.50
❑ 75 Shawn Marion	.60	1.50
❑ 76 Anfernee Hardaway	.60	1.50
❑ 77 Rasheed Wallace	.60	1.50
❑ 78 Bonzi Wells	.50	1.25
❑ 79 Scottie Pippen	1.00	2.50
❑ 80 Mike Bibby	.50	1.25
❑ 81 Peja Stojakovic	.50	1.25
❑ 82 Chris Webber	.60	1.50
❑ 83 Hedo Turkoglu	.50	1.25
❑ 84 Tim Duncan	1.25	3.00
❑ 85 David Robinson	.75	2.00
❑ 86 Tony Parker	.60	1.50
❑ 87 Malik Rose	.40	1.00
❑ 88 Gary Payton	.60	1.50
❑ 89 Rashard Lewis	.60	1.50
❑ 90 Brent Barry	.40	1.00
❑ 91 Desmond Mason	.50	1.25
❑ 92 Vince Carter	1.25	3.00
❑ 93 Morris Peterson	.50	1.25
❑ 94 Antonio Davis	.40	1.00
❑ 95 Karl Malone	.60	1.50
❑ 96 John Stockton	.75	2.00
❑ 97 Andrei Kirilenko	.60	1.50
❑ 98 Kwame Brown	.40	1.00
❑ 99 Jerry Stackhouse	.50	1.25
❑ 100 Michael Jordan	5.00	12.00
❑ 101 Kobe Bryant MF	6.00	15.00
❑ 102 Eddie Griffin MF	.75	2.00
❑ 103 Shawn Marion MF	1.25	3.00
❑ 104 Richard Jefferson MF	1.25	3.00
❑ 105 Jermaine O'Neal MF	1.25	3.00
❑ 106 Allan Houston MF	1.00	2.50
❑ 107 Shane Battier MF	1.00	2.50
❑ 108 Hedo Turkoglu MF	1.00	2.50
❑ 109 Michael Finley MF	1.25	3.00
❑ 110 Jamal Mashburn MF	1.00	2.50
❑ 111 Rashard Lewis MF	1.25	3.00
❑ 112 Tyson Chandler MF	1.00	2.50
❑ 113 Terrell Brandon MF	.75	2.00
❑ 114 Antonio Davis MF	.75	2.00
❑ 115 Jamaal Tinsley MF	1.00	2.50
❑ 116 Tony Parker MF	1.25	3.00
❑ 117 Ray Allen MF	1.25	3.00
❑ 118 Rasheed Wallace MF	1.25	3.00
❑ 119 Cuttino Mobley MF	1.00	2.50
❑ 120 Jason Terry MF	1.25	3.00
❑ 121 Mike Miller MF	1.00	2.50
❑ 122 Jalen Rose MF	1.00	2.50
❑ 123 Morris Peterson MF	1.00	2.50
❑ 124 Ricky Davis MF	1.00	2.50
❑ 125 Peja Stojakovic MF	1.00	2.50
❑ 126 Gary Payton MF	1.25	3.00
❑ 127 Andrei Kirilenko MF	1.25	3.00
❑ 128 Tim Duncan MF	2.50	6.00
❑ 129 Anfernee Hardaway MF	1.25	3.00
❑ 130 Shaquille O'Neal MF	3.00	8.00
❑ 131 Latrell Sprewell MF	1.00	2.50
❑ 132 Shareef Abdur-Rahim MF	1.00	2.50
❑ 133 Steve Nash MF	2.00	5.00
❑ 134 Lamar Odom MF	1.25	3.00
❑ 135 Antawn Jamison MF	1.25	3.00
❑ 136 Reggie Miller MF	1.25	3.00
❑ 137 Tim Thomas MF	.75	2.00
❑ 138 Eddy Curry MF	1.00	2.50
❑ 139 Jason Williams MF	1.00	2.50
❑ 140 John Stockton MF	1.50	4.00
❑ 141 Ben Wallace MF	1.00	2.50
❑ 142 Bonzi Wells MF	1.00	2.50
❑ 143 David Robinson MF	1.50	4.00
❑ 144 Stephon Marbury MF	1.25	3.00
❑ 145 Vince Carter MF	2.50	6.00
❑ 146 James Posey MF	.75	2.00
❑ 147 Wally Szczerbiak MF	1.00	2.50
❑ 148 Eddie Jones MF	1.00	2.50
❑ 149 Scottie Pippen MF	4.00	10.00
❑ 150 Michael Jordan MF	10.00	25.00
❑ 151 Kobe Bryant PP	15.00	40.00
❑ 152 Pau Gasol PP	3.00	8.00
❑ 153 Tim Duncan PP	6.00	15.00
❑ 154 Karl Malone PP	3.00	8.00
❑ 155 Allan Houston PP	2.50	6.00
❑ 156 Steve Nash PP	5.00	12.00
❑ 157 Shawn Marion PP	3.00	8.00
❑ 158 Jamal Mashburn PP	2.50	6.00
❑ 159 Shaquille O'Neal PP	8.00	20.00
❑ 160 Reggie Miller PP	3.00	8.00
❑ 161 Latrell Sprewell PP	2.50	6.00
❑ 162 Peja Stojakovic PP	2.50	6.00
❑ 163 Jalen Rose PP	2.50	6.00
❑ 164 Kenyon Martin PP	3.00	8.00
❑ 165 Baron Davis PP	3.00	8.00
❑ 166 Ray Allen PP	3.00	8.00
❑ 167 Vince Carter PP	6.00	15.00
❑ 168 Rashard Lewis PP	3.00	8.00
❑ 169 Steve Francis PP	3.00	8.00
❑ 170 Jermaine O'Neal PP	3.00	8.00
❑ 171 Shane Battier PP	2.50	6.00
❑ 172 Shareef Abdur-Rahim PP	2.50	6.00
❑ 173 Michael Finley PP	3.00	8.00
❑ 174 John Stockton PP	4.00	10.00
❑ 175 Jamaal Tinsley PP	2.50	6.00
❑ 176 Wally Szczerbiak PP	2.50	6.00
❑ 177 Antawn Jamison PP	3.00	8.00
❑ 178 Richard Jefferson PP	3.00	8.00
❑ 179 Rasheed Wallace PP	3.00	8.00
❑ 180 Michael Jordan PP	25.00	60.00
❑ 201 Marko Jaric	1.50	4.00
❑ 202 Dan Dickau RC	1.50	4.00
❑ 203 Tito Maddox RC	1.50	4.00
❑ 204 Predrag Savovic RC	1.50	4.00
❑ 205 Robert Archibald RC	1.50	4.00
❑ 206 Frank Williams RC	1.50	4.00
❑ 207 Ronald Murray RC	2.50	6.00
❑ 208 Lonny Baxter RC	1.50	4.00
❑ 209 Efthimios Rentzias RC	1.50	4.00
❑ 210 Vincent Yarbrough RC	1.50	4.00
❑ 211 Gordan Giricek RC	1.50	4.00
❑ 212 Carlos Boozer RC	3.00	8.00
❑ 213 John Salmons RC	2.50	6.00
❑ 214 Manu Ginobili RC	4.00	10.00
❑ 215 Roger Mason Jr. RC	1.50	4.00
❑ 216 Chris Jefferies RC	1.50	4.00
❑ 217 Sam Clancy RC	1.50	4.00
❑ 218 Rasual Butler RC	1.50	4.00
❑ 219 Dan Gadzuric RC	1.50	4.00
❑ 220 Tayshaun Prince RC	2.50	6.00
❑ 221 Casey Jacobsen RC	1.50	4.00
❑ 222 Qyntel Woods RC	1.50	4.00
❑ 223 Jiri Welsch RC	1.50	4.00
❑ 224 Curtis Borchardt RC	1.50	4.00
❑ 225 Marcus Haislip RC	1.50	4.00
❑ 226 Kareem Rush RC	2.00	5.00
❑ 227 Fred Jones RC	2.00	5.00
❑ 228 Caron Butler RC	3.00	8.00
❑ 229 Juan Dixon RC	2.50	6.00
❑ 230 Ryan Humphrey RC	1.50	4.00
❑ 231 Melvin Ely RC	1.50	4.00
❑ 232 Bostjan Nachbar RC	1.50	4.00
❑ 233 Jared Jeffries RC	1.50	4.00
❑ 234 Jay Williams RC	8.00	20.00
❑ 235 Nikoloz Tskitishvili RC	6.00	15.00
❑ 236 Chris Wilcox RC	8.00	20.00
❑ 237 Drew Gooden RC	10.00	25.00
❑ 238 Amare Stoudemire RC	15.00	40.00
❑ 239 DaJuan Wagner RC	6.00	15.00
❑ 240 Nene Hilario RC	8.00	20.00
❑ 241 Mike Dunleavy RC	8.00	20.00
❑ 242 Yao Ming RC	20.00	50.00

2003-04 Upper Deck Finite

❑ COMMON ODD (1-200)	.15	.40
❑ COMMON EVEN (1-200)	.25	.60
❑ COMMON ROOKIE (201-228)	2.00	5.00
❑ COMMON ROOKIE (229-236)	2.50	6.00
❑ COMMON ROOKIE (237-242)	8.00	20.00
❑ COMMON MAJ.FACT.(243-292)	1.25	3.00
❑ COMMON PROM.POW.(293-322)	2.00	5.00
❑ COMMON FIRST CLS.(323-342)	8.00	20.00
❑ 1 Shareef Abdur-Rahim	.50	1.25
❑ 2 Dominique Wilkins	.75	2.00
❑ 3 Theo Ratliff	.30	.75
❑ 4 Dan Dickau	.25	.60
❑ 5 Jason Terry	.50	1.25
❑ 6 Dion Glover	.25	.60
❑ 7 Alan Henderson	.15	.40
❑ 8 Paul Pierce	.75	2.00
❑ 9 Larry Bird	4.00	10.00
❑ 10 Raef LaFrentz	.50	1.25
❑ 11 Robert Parish	1.00	2.50
❑ 12 Jiri Welsch	.50	1.25
❑ 13 John Havlicek	1.00	2.50
❑ 14 Vin Baker	.50	1.25
❑ 15 Jamal Crawford	.15	.40
❑ 16 Michael Jordan	5.00	12.00
❑ 17 Scottie Pippen	.75	2.00
❑ 18 Reggie Theus	.75	2.00
❑ 19 Jalen Rose	.50	1.25
❑ 20 Tyson Chandler	.75	2.00
❑ 21 Eddy Curry	.50	1.25
❑ 22 Dajuan Wagner	.50	1.25
❑ 23 Lenny Wilkens	.75	2.00
❑ 24 Carlos Boozer	.75	2.00
❑ 25 World B. Free	.60	1.50
❑ 26 Darius Miles	.75	2.00
❑ 27 Craig Ehlo	.50	1.25
❑ 28 Ricky Davis	.75	2.00
❑ 29 Dirk Nowitzki	.75	2.00
❑ 30 Rolando Blackman	.75	2.00
❑ 31 Steve Nash	.50	1.25
❑ 32 Tony Delk	.25	.60
❑ 33 Antawn Jamison	.50	1.25
❑ 34 Antoine Walker	.75	2.00
❑ 35 Michael Finley	.50	1.25
❑ 36 Andre Miller	.50	1.25
❑ 37 David Thompson	.50	1.25
❑ 38 Nene	.50	1.25
❑ 39 Dan Issel	.50	1.25
❑ 40 Nikoloz Tskitishvili	.25	.60
❑ 41 Alex English	.60	1.50
❑ 42 Earl Boykins	.50	1.25
❑ 43 Richard Hamilton	.30	.75
❑ 44 Mehmet Okur	.25	.60
❑ 45 Ben Wallace	.50	1.25
❑ 46 Bob Lanier	1.00	2.50
❑ 47 Chauncey Billups	.30	.75
❑ 48 Dave Bing	.75	2.00
❑ 49 Tayshaun Prince	.30	.75
❑ 50 Nick Van Exel	.75	2.00
❑ 51 Erick Dampier	.30	.75
❑ 52 Jason Richardson	.75	2.00
❑ 53 Joe Barry Carroll	.50	1.25
❑ 54 Mike Dunleavy	.50	1.25

❑ 55 Wilt Chamberlain	2.00	5.00
❑ 56 Troy Murphy	.75	2.00
❑ 57 Steve Francis	.50	1.25
❑ 58 Maurice Taylor	.75	2.00
❑ 59 Yao Ming	1.25	3.00
❑ 60 Robert Reid	.75	2.00
❑ 61 Cuttino Mobley	.30	.75
❑ 62 Moses Malone	.75	2.00
❑ 63 Eddie Griffin	.30	.75
❑ 64 Jermaine O'Neal	.75	2.00
❑ 65 George McGinnis	.50	1.25
❑ 66 Reggie Miller	.75	2.00
❑ 67 Clark Kellogg	.50	1.25
❑ 68 Jamaal Tinsley	.75	2.00
❑ 69 Al Harrington	.30	.75
❑ 70 Ron Artest	.75	2.00
❑ 71 Elton Brand	.50	1.25
❑ 72 Corey Maggette	.50	1.25
❑ 73 Chris Wilcox	.15	.40
❑ 74 Quentin Richardson	.50	1.25
❑ 75 Bill Walton	1.00	2.50
❑ 76 Marko Jaric	.25	.60
❑ 77 Kobe Bryant	2.00	5.00
❑ 78 Kareem Abdul-Jabbar	1.50	4.00
❑ 79 Shaquille O'Neal	1.25	3.00
❑ 80 Michael Cooper	.75	2.00
❑ 81 Gary Payton	.50	1.25
❑ 82 James Worthy	1.00	2.50
❑ 83 Karl Malone	.50	1.25
❑ 84 Pau Gasol	.75	2.00
❑ 85 Michael Dickerson	.15	.40
❑ 86 Mike Miller	.75	2.00
❑ 87 Brevin Knight	.15	.40
❑ 88 Shane Battier	.75	2.00
❑ 89 Stromile Swift	.15	.40
❑ 90 Jason Williams	.50	1.25
❑ 91 Caron Butler	.50	1.25
❑ 92 Samaki Walker	.25	.60
❑ 93 Eddie Jones	.50	1.25
❑ 94 Rasual Butler	.50	1.25
❑ 95 Brian Grant	.30	.75
❑ 96 Loren Woods	.25	.60
❑ 97 Lamar Odom	.50	1.25
❑ 98 Desmond Mason	.50	1.25
❑ 99 Sidney Moncrief	.50	1.25
❑ 100 Toni Kukoc	.50	1.25
❑ 101 Oscar Robertson	1.25	3.00
❑ 102 Michael Redd	.75	2.00
❑ 103 Terry Cummings	.50	1.25
❑ 104 Tim Thomas	.50	1.25
❑ 105 Kevin Garnett	1.00	2.50
❑ 106 Troy Hudson	.25	.60
❑ 107 Sam Cassell	.50	1.25
❑ 108 Latrell Sprewell	.75	2.00
❑ 109 Michael Olowokandi	.15	.40
❑ 110 Wally Szczerbiak	.50	1.25
❑ 111 Jason Kidd	.75	2.00
❑ 112 Otis Birdsong	.75	2.00
❑ 113 Kenyon Martin	.50	1.25
❑ 114 Albert King	.75	2.00
❑ 115 Richard Jefferson	.30	.75
❑ 116 Kerry Kittles	.25	.60
❑ 117 Alonzo Mourning	.30	.75
❑ 118 Baron Davis	.75	2.00
❑ 119 Darrell Armstrong	.15	.40
❑ 120 Jamal Mashburn	.50	1.25
❑ 121 P.J. Brown	.15	.40
❑ 122 David Wesley	.25	.60
❑ 123 Courtney Alexander	.30	.75
❑ 124 Jamaal Magloire	.25	.60
❑ 125 Allan Houston	.30	.75
❑ 126 Willis Reed	1.00	2.50
❑ 127 Keith Van Horn	.50	1.25
❑ 128 Walt Frazier	1.00	2.50
❑ 129 Antonio McDyess	.30	.75
❑ 130 Earl Monroe	1.00	2.50
❑ 131 Kurt Thomas	.30	.75
❑ 132 Tracy McGrady	2.00	5.00
❑ 133 Pat Garrity	.15	.40
❑ 134 Grant Hill	.75	2.00
❑ 135 Tyronn Lue	.15	.40
❑ 136 Drew Gooden	.50	1.25
❑ 137 Juwan Howard	.30	.75
❑ 138 Gordan Giricek	.50	1.25
❑ 139 Allen Iverson	1.25	3.00
❑ 140 Julius Erving	2.00	5.00
❑ 141 Glenn Robinson	.30	.75
❑ 142 Maurice Cheeks	1.00	2.50
❑ 143 Aaron McKie	.30	.75
❑ 144 Billy Cunningham	.75	2.00
❑ 145 Eric Snow	.30	.75
❑ 146 Stephon Marbury	.75	2.00
❑ 147 Kevin Johnson	.50	1.25
❑ 148 Amare Stoudemire	1.50	4.00
❑ 149 Larry Nance	.50	1.25
❑ 150 Shawn Marion	.75	2.00
❑ 151 Walter Davis	.50	1.25
❑ 152 Anfernee Hardaway	.75	2.00
❑ 153 Rasheed Wallace	.50	1.25
❑ 154 Zach Randolph	.75	2.00
❑ 155 Derek Anderson	.30	.75
❑ 156 Dale Davis	.25	.60
❑ 157 Bonzi Wells	.30	.75
❑ 158 Jim Paxson	.75	2.00
❑ 159 Damon Stoudamire	.30	.75
❑ 160 Chris Webber	.75	2.00
❑ 161 Vlade Divac	.30	.75
❑ 162 Mike Bibby	.75	2.00
❑ 163 Bobby Jackson	.30	.75
❑ 164 Peja Stojakovic	.75	2.00
❑ 165 Doug Christie	.30	.75
❑ 166 Brad Miller	.75	2.00
❑ 167 Tim Duncan	1.00	2.50
❑ 168 Radoslav Nesterovic	.50	1.25
❑ 169 Tony Parker	.50	1.25
❑ 170 George Gervin	1.00	2.50
❑ 171 Manu Ginobili	.50	1.25
❑ 172 Artis Gilmore	.75	2.00
❑ 173 Ron Mercer	.15	.40
❑ 174 Ray Allen	.75	2.00
❑ 175 Spencer Haywood	.50	1.25
❑ 176 Rashard Lewis	.75	2.00
❑ 177 Fred Brown	.50	1.25
❑ 178 Vladimir Radmanovic	.25	.60
❑ 179 Jack Sikma	.50	1.25
❑ 180 Brent Barry	.75	2.00
❑ 181 Vince Carter	1.25	3.00
❑ 182 Antonio Davis	.25	.60
❑ 183 Morris Peterson	.30	.75
❑ 184 Alvin Williams	.25	.60
❑ 185 Chris Jefferies	.15	.40
❑ 186 Jerome Williams	.25	.60
❑ 187 Andrei Kirilenko	.50	1.25
❑ 188 Pete Maravich	5.00	12.00
❑ 189 Matt Harpring	.50	1.25
❑ 190 Mark Eaton	.75	2.00
❑ 191 Jarron Collins	.15	.40
❑ 192 Greg Ostertag	.25	.60
❑ 193 Carlos Arroyo	3.00	8.00
❑ 194 Jerry Stackhouse	.75	2.00
❑ 195 Wes Unseld	.50	1.25
❑ 196 Gilbert Arenas	.75	2.00
❑ 197 Larry Hughes	.30	.75
❑ 198 Kwame Brown	.50	1.25
❑ 199 Jeff Malone	.50	1.25
❑ 200 Jared Jeffries	.25	.60
❑ 201 Aleksandar Pavlovic RC	2.50	6.00
❑ 202 James Lang RC	2.00	5.00
❑ 203 Jason Kapono RC	2.00	5.00
❑ 204 Luke Walton RC	2.00	5.00
❑ 205 Jerome Beasley RC	2.00	5.00
❑ 206 Willie Green RC	2.00	5.00
❑ 207 Steve Blake RC	2.00	5.00
❑ 208 Slavko Vranes RC	2.00	5.00
❑ 209 Zaur Pachulia RC	2.00	5.00
❑ 210 Travis Hansen RC	2.00	5.00
❑ 211 Keith Bogans RC	2.00	5.00
❑ 212 Kyle Korver RC	3.00	8.00
❑ 213 Brandon Hunter RC	2.00	5.00
❑ 214 James Jones RC	2.00	5.00
❑ 215 Josh Howard RC	2.50	6.00
❑ 216 Leandro Barbosa RC	3.00	8.00
❑ 217 Kendrick Perkins RC	3.00	8.00
❑ 218 Ndudi Ebi RC	2.00	5.00
❑ 219 Brian Cook RC	2.00	5.00
❑ 220 Travis Outlaw RC	2.50	6.00
❑ 221 Zoran Planinic RC	2.00	5.00
❑ 222 Dahntay Jones RC	2.00	5.00
❑ 223 Boris Diaw RC	2.00	5.00
❑ 224 Zarko Cabarkapa RC	2.00	5.00
❑ 225 Troy Bell RC	2.00	5.00
❑ 226 Reece Gaines RC	2.00	5.00
❑ 227 Luke Ridnour RC	2.50	6.00
❑ 228 Chris Kaman RC	2.50	6.00
❑ 229 Marcus Banks RC	2.50	6.00
❑ 230 Maciej Lampe RC	2.50	6.00
❑ 231 David West RC	5.00	12.00
❑ 232 Mickael Pietrus RC	2.50	6.00
❑ 233 Jarvis Hayes RC	.25	.60
❑ 234 Mike Sweetney RC	2.50	6.00
❑ 235 Kirk Hinrich RC	3.00	8.00
❑ 236 Chris Bosh RC	5.00	12.00
❑ 237 Nick Collison RC	8.00	20.00
❑ 238 T.J. Ford RC	6.00	15.00
❑ 239 Dwyane Wade RC	25.00	50.00
❑ 240 Carmelo Anthony RC	40.00	80.00
❑ 241 Darko Milicic RC	8.00	20.00
❑ 242 LeBron James RC	150.00	300.00
❑ 243 Michael Jordan MF	6.00	15.00
❑ 244 Kobe Bryant MF	4.00	10.00
❑ 245 Michael Finley MF	1.25	3.00
❑ 246 Andrei Kirilenko MF	1.25	3.00
❑ 247 Desmond Mason MF	1.25	3.00
❑ 248 Kenyon Martin MF	1.25	3.00
❑ 249 Shaquille O'Neal MF	2.50	6.00
❑ 250 Jamal Mashburn MF	1.25	3.00
❑ 251 Jason Terry MF	1.25	3.00
❑ 252 Andre Miller MF	1.25	3.00
❑ 253 Keith Van Horn MF	1.25	3.00
❑ 254 Derek Anderson MF	1.25	3.00
❑ 255 Stephon Marbury MF	1.25	3.00
❑ 256 Glenn Robinson MF	1.25	3.00
❑ 257 Richard Hamilton MF	1.25	3.00
❑ 258 Lamar Odom MF	1.25	3.00
❑ 259 Bonzi Wells MF	1.25	3.00
❑ 260 Wally Szczerbiak MF	1.25	3.00
❑ 261 Alonzo Mourning MF	1.25	3.00
❑ 262 Gilbert Arenas MF	1.25	3.00
❑ 263 Mike Bibby MF	1.25	3.00
❑ 264 Antawn Jamison MF	1.25	3.00
❑ 265 Tony Parker MF	1.25	3.00
❑ 266 Reggie Miller MF	1.25	3.00
❑ 267 Vince Carter MF	2.50	6.00
❑ 268 Richard Jefferson MF	1.25	3.00
❑ 269 Nene MF	1.25	3.00
❑ 270 Grant Hill MF	1.25	3.00
❑ 271 Rashard Lewis MF	1.25	3.00
❑ 272 Shawn Marion MF	1.25	3.00
❑ 273 Morris Peterson MF	1.25	3.00
❑ 274 Chauncey Billups MF	1.25	3.00
❑ 275 Eddie Jones MF	1.25	3.00
❑ 276 Raef LaFrentz MF	1.25	3.00
❑ 277 Jerry Stackhouse MF	1.25	3.00
❑ 278 Pau Gasol MF	1.25	3.00
❑ 279 Darius Miles MF	1.25	3.00
❑ 280 Nick Van Exel MF	1.25	3.00
❑ 281 Gary Payton MF	1.25	3.00
❑ 282 Peja Stojakovic MF	1.25	3.00
❑ 283 Karl Malone MF	1.25	3.00
❑ 284 Mike Miller MF	1.25	3.00
❑ 285 Caron Butler MF	1.25	3.00
❑ 286 Cuttino Mobley MF	1.25	3.00
❑ 287 Zach Randolph MF	1.25	3.00
❑ 288 Scottie Pippen MF	1.50	4.00
❑ 289 Gordan Giricek MF	1.25	3.00
❑ 290 Ben Wallace MF	1.25	3.00
❑ 291 Manu Ginobili MF	1.25	3.00
❑ 292 Vladimir Radmanovic MF	1.25	3.00
❑ 293 Michael Jordan PP	10.00	25.00
❑ 294 Kobe Bryant PP	6.00	15.00
❑ 295 Vince Carter PP	4.00	10.00
❑ 296 Steve Nash PP	2.00	5.00
❑ 297 Shaquille O'Neal PP	4.00	10.00
❑ 298 Amare Stoudemire PP	3.00	8.00
❑ 299 Tracy McGrady PP	4.00	10.00
❑ 300 Gary Payton PP	2.00	5.00
❑ 301 Chris Bosh PP	2.50	6.00
❑ 302 Michael Finley PP	2.00	5.00
❑ 303 Caron Butler PP	2.00	5.00
❑ 304 Jarvis Hayes PP	2.50	6.00
❑ 305 Ben Wallace PP	2.00	5.00
❑ 306 Allan Houston PP	2.00	5.00
❑ 307 Mike Bibby PP	2.00	5.00
❑ 308 Antoine Walker PP	2.00	5.00
❑ 309 Dajuan Wagner PP	2.00	5.00
❑ 310 Kevin Garnett PP	3.00	8.00
❑ 311 Mickael Pietrus PP	2.00	5.00
❑ 312 Baron Davis PP	2.00	5.00
❑ 313 Paul Pierce PP	2.00	5.00
❑ 314 Rasheed Wallace PP	2.00	5.00
❑ 315 Chris Webber PP	2.00	5.00
❑ 316 Jermaine O'Neal PP	2.00	5.00
❑ 317 Shareef Abdur-Rahim PP	2.00	5.00
❑ 318 Ray Allen PP	2.00	5.00
❑ 319 Peja Stojakovic PP	2.00	5.00
❑ 320 Tim Duncan PP	3.00	8.00
❑ 321 Gilbert Arenas PP	2.00	5.00

❑ 322 Jason Richardson PP	2.00	5.00
❑ 323 Dwyane Wade FC	20.00	40.00
❑ 324 Gary Payton FC	8.00	20.00
❑ 325 Karl Malone FC	8.00	20.00
❑ 326 Jason Kidd FC	10.00	25.00
❑ 327 Darko Milicic FC	10.00	25.00
❑ 328 Steve Francis FC	8.00	20.00
❑ 329 Vince Carter FC	15.00	40.00
❑ 330 Elton Brand FC	8.00	20.00
❑ 331 Amare Stoudemire FC	15.00	40.00
❑ 332 Shaquille O'Neal FC	15.00	40.00
❑ 333 Carmelo Anthony FC	25.00	50.00
❑ 334 Tracy McGrady FC	15.00	40.00
❑ 335 Tim Duncan FC	15.00	40.00
❑ 336 Chris Webber FC	8.00	20.00
❑ 337 Allen Iverson FC	15.00	40.00
❑ 338 Dirk Nowitzki FC	12.50	30.00
❑ 339 Kevin Garnett FC	15.00	40.00
❑ 340 Kobe Bryant FC	20.00	50.00
❑ 341 LeBron James FC	150.00	300.00
❑ 342 Michael Jordan FC	50.00	100.00

2001-02 Upper Deck Flight Team

❑ COMPLETE SET (240)	250.00	600.00
❑ COMP.SET w/o SP's (90)	20.00	40.00
❑ COMMON CARD (1-90)	.08	.25
❑ COMMON ROOKIE (91-120)	.75	2.00
❑ COMMON ROOKIE (121-134)	1.00	2.50
❑ COMMON ROOKIE (135-140)	1.50	4.00
❑ 1 Michael Jordan	5.00	12.00
❑ 2 Dirk Nowitzki	.50	1.25
❑ 3 Antawn Jamison	.30	.75
❑ 4 Latrell Sprewell	.25	.60
❑ 5 Peja Stojakovic	.25	.60
❑ 6 Dikembe Mutombo	.25	.60
❑ 7 Jason Williams	.25	.60
❑ 8 Kobe Bryant	1.50	4.00
❑ 9 Baron Davis	.30	.75
❑ 10 Wally Szczerbiak	.25	.60
❑ 11 Reggie Miller	.30	.75
❑ 12 Marcus Fizer	.20	.50
❑ 13 Desmond Mason	.25	.60
❑ 14 Glenn Robinson	.25	.60
❑ 15 Vince Carter	.60	1.50
❑ 16 James Posey	.20	.50
❑ 17 Darius Miles	.20	.50
❑ 18 Jason Kidd	.50	1.25
❑ 19 Anfernee Hardaway	.30	.75
❑ 20 Karl Malone	.40	1.00
❑ 21 Kevin Garnett	.60	1.50
❑ 22 Shareef Abdur-Rahim	.25	.60
❑ 23 Steve Francis	.30	.75
❑ 24 Paul Pierce	.30	.75
❑ 25 Mike Miller	.25	.60
❑ 26 Tim Duncan	.60	1.50
❑ 27 Derek Anderson	.25	.60
❑ 28 Eddie Jones	.25	.60
❑ 29 Keith Van Horn	.25	.60
❑ 30 Chris Mihm	.20	.50
❑ 31 Clifford Robinson	.20	.50
❑ 32 Gary Payton	.30	.75
❑ 33 Courtney Alexander	.20	.50
❑ 34 Shaquille O'Neal	.75	2.00
❑ 35 Tim Thomas	.20	.50
❑ 36 Raef LaFrentz	.20	.50
❑ 37 Stromile Swift	.20	.50
❑ 38 Stephon Marbury	.30	.75
❑ 39 Morris Peterson	.25	.60
❑ 40 Donyell Marshall	.20	.50
❑ 41 Kenny Thomas	.20	.50
❑ 42 Juwan Howard	.25	.60
❑ 43 Tracy McGrady	.60	1.50
❑ 44 Kenny Anderson	.25	.60
❑ 45 Larry Hughes	.25	.60
❑ 46 Allan Houston	.25	.60
❑ 47 Chris Webber	.30	.75
❑ 48 Andre Miller	.25	.60
❑ 49 Corey Maggette	.25	.60
❑ 50 Sam Cassell	.25	.60
❑ 51 Steve Smith	.25	.60
❑ 52 Jamal Mashburn	.25	.60
❑ 53 Al Harrington	.25	.60
❑ 54 Brian Grant	.20	.50
❑ 55 Rasheed Wallace	.30	.75
❑ 56 Rick Fox	.25	.60
❑ 57 Jason Terry	.30	.75
❑ 58 Rashard Lewis	.30	.75
❑ 59 Joe Smith	.20	.50
❑ 60 Michael Dickerson	.20	.50
❑ 61 Michael Finley	.30	.75
❑ 62 Danny Fortson	.20	.50
❑ 63 Allen Iverson	.60	1.50
❑ 64 Richard Hamilton	.25	.60
❑ 65 Antonio McDyess	.25	.60
❑ 66 David Wesley	.20	.50
❑ 67 Ben Wallace	.25	.60
❑ 68 Mike Bibby	.25	.60
❑ 69 Antonio Davis	.20	.50
❑ 70 Cuttino Mobley	.25	.60
❑ 71 Lamond Murray	.20	.50
❑ 72 Antoine Walker	.25	.60
❑ 73 Jermaine O'Neal	.30	.75
❑ 74 Alonzo Mourning	.30	.75
❑ 75 Shawn Marion	.30	.75
❑ 76 John Stockton	.40	1.00
❑ 77 Marcus Camby	.25	.60
❑ 78 Derek Fisher	.25	.60
❑ 79 DerMarr Johnson	.20	.50
❑ 80 Aaron McKie	.20	.50
❑ 81 David Robinson	.40	1.00
❑ 82 Steve Nash	.50	1.25
❑ 83 Ray Allen	.30	.75
❑ 84 Elton Brand	.30	.75
❑ 85 Kenyon Martin	.30	.75
❑ 86 Bonzi Wells	.25	.60
❑ 87 Grant Hill	.30	.75
❑ 88 Terrell Brandon	.20	.50
❑ 89 Toni Kukoc	.25	.60
❑ 90 Jerry Stackhouse	.25	.60
❑ 91A Tierre Brown RC	.75	2.00
❑ 91B Tierre Brown RC	.75	2.00
❑ 91C Tierre Brown RC	.75	2.00
❑ 92A Jamison Brewer RC	.75	2.00
❑ 92B Jamison Brewer RC	.75	2.00
❑ 92C Jamison Brewer RC	.75	2.00
❑ 93A Antonis Fotsis RC	.75	2.00
❑ 93B Antonis Fotsis RC	.75	2.00
❑ 93C Antonis Fotsis RC	.75	2.00
❑ 94A Mike James RC	.75	2.00
❑ 94B Mike James RC	.75	2.00
❑ 94C Mike James RC	.75	2.00
❑ 95A Primoz Brezec RC	1.00	2.50
❑ 95B Primoz Brezec RC	1.00	2.50
❑ 95C Primoz Brezec RC	1.00	2.50
❑ 96A Jeryl Sasser RC	.75	2.00
❑ 96B Jeryl Sasser RC	.75	2.00
❑ 96C Jeryl Sasser RC	.75	2.00
❑ 97A DeSagana Diop RC	.75	2.00
❑ 97B DeSagana Diop RC	.75	2.00
❑ 97C DeSagana Diop RC	.75	2.00
❑ 98A Mengke Bateer RC	.75	2.00
❑ 98B Mengke Bateer RC	.75	2.00
❑ 98C Mengke Bateer RC	.75	2.00
❑ 99A Gerald Wallace RC	2.00	5.00
❑ 99B Gerald Wallace RC	2.00	5.00
❑ 99C Gerald Wallace RC	2.00	5.00
❑ 100A Kenny Satterfield RC	.75	2.00
❑ 100B Kenny Satterfield RC	.75	2.00
❑ 100C Kenny Satterfield RC	.75	2.00
❑ 101A R.Boumtje-Boumtje RC	.75	2.00
❑ 101B R.Boumtje-Boumtje RC	.75	2.00
❑ 101C R.Boumtje-Boumtje RC	.75	2.00
❑ 102A Brian Scalabrine RC	.75	2.00
❑ 102B Brian Scalabrine RC	.75	2.00
❑ 102C Brian Scalabrine RC	.75	2.00
❑ 103A Oscar Torres RC	.75	2.00
❑ 103B Oscar Torres RC	.75	2.00
❑ 103C Oscar Torres RC	.75	2.00
❑ 104A Jarron Collins RC	.75	2.00
❑ 104B Jarron Collins RC	.75	2.00
❑ 104C Jarron Collins RC	.75	2.00
❑ 105A Jeff Trepagnier RC	.75	2.00
❑ 105B Jeff Trepagnier RC	.75	2.00
❑ 105C Jeff Trepagnier RC	.75	2.00
❑ 106A Brendan Haywood RC	1.00	2.50
❑ 106B Brendan Haywood RC	1.00	2.50
❑ 106C Brendan Haywood RC	1.00	2.50
❑ 107A Vladimir Radmanovic RC	1.00	2.50
❑ 107B Vladimir Radmanovic RC	1.00	2.50
❑ 107C Vladimir Radmanovic RC	1.00	2.50
❑ 108A Loren Woods RC	.75	2.00
❑ 108B Loren Woods RC	.75	2.00
❑ 108C Loren Woods RC	.75	2.00
❑ 109A Terence Morris RC	.75	2.00
❑ 109B Terence Morris RC	.75	2.00
❑ 109C Terence Morris RC	.75	2.00
❑ 110A Kirk Haston RC	.75	2.00
❑ 110B Kirk Haston RC	.75	2.00
❑ 110C Kirk Haston RC	.75	2.00
❑ 111A Earl Watson RC	1.00	2.50
❑ 111B Earl Watson RC	1.00	2.50
❑ 111C Earl Watson RC	1.00	2.50
❑ 112A Brandon Armstrong RC	.75	2.00
❑ 112B Brandon Armstrong RC	.75	2.00
❑ 112C Brandon Armstrong RC	.75	2.00
❑ 113A Zach Randolph RC	2.00	5.00
❑ 113B Zach Randolph RC	2.00	5.00
❑ 113C Zach Randolph RC	2.00	5.00
❑ 114A Bobby Simmons RC	.75	2.00
❑ 114B Bobby Simmons RC	.75	2.00
❑ 114C Bobby Simmons RC	.75	2.00
❑ 115A Alton Ford RC	.75	2.00
❑ 115B Alton Ford RC	.75	2.00
❑ 115C Alton Ford RC	.75	2.00
❑ 116A Predrag Drobnjak RC	.75	2.00
❑ 116B Predrag Drobnjak RC	.75	2.00
❑ 116C Predrag Drobnjak RC	.75	2.00
❑ 117A Michael Bradley RC	.75	2.00
❑ 117B Michael Bradley RC	.75	2.00
❑ 117C Michael Bradley RC	.75	2.00
❑ 118A Samuel Dalembert RC	1.00	2.50
❑ 118B Samuel Dalembert RC	1.00	2.50
❑ 118C Samuel Dalembert RC	1.00	2.50
❑ 119A Gilbert Arenas RC	1.25	3.00
❑ 119B Gilbert Arenas RC	1.25	3.00
❑ 119C Gilbert Arenas RC	1.25	3.00
❑ 120A Kedrick Brown RC	.75	2.00
❑ 120B Kedrick Brown RC	.75	2.00
❑ 120C Kedrick Brown RC	.75	2.00
❑ 121A Trenton Hassell RC	1.25	3.00
❑ 121B Trenton Hassell RC	1.25	3.00
❑ 121C Trenton Hassell RC	1.25	3.00
❑ 122A Zeljko Rebraca RC	1.00	2.50
❑ 122B Zeljko Rebraca RC	1.00	2.50
❑ 122C Zeljko Rebraca RC	1.00	2.50
❑ 123A Jason Collins RC	1.00	2.50
❑ 123B Jason Collins RC	1.00	2.50
❑ 123C Jason Collins RC	1.00	2.50
❑ 124A Will Solomon RC	1.00	2.50
❑ 124B Will Solomon RC	1.00	2.50
❑ 124C Will Solomon RC	1.00	2.50
❑ 125A Joseph Forte RC	1.00	2.50
❑ 125B Joseph Forte RC	1.00	2.50
❑ 125C Joseph Forte RC	1.00	2.50
❑ 126A Steven Hunter RC	1.00	2.50
❑ 126B Steven Hunter RC	1.00	2.50
❑ 126C Steven Hunter RC	1.00	2.50
❑ 127A Eddy Curry RC	1.50	4.00
❑ 127B Eddy Curry RC	1.50	4.00
❑ 127C Eddy Curry RC	1.50	4.00
❑ 128A Troy Murphy RC	2.00	5.00
❑ 128B Troy Murphy RC	2.00	5.00
❑ 128C Troy Murphy RC	2.00	5.00
❑ 129A Shane Battier RC	1.50	4.00
❑ 129B Shane Battier RC	1.50	4.00
❑ 129C Shane Battier RC	1.50	4.00
❑ 130A Tyson Chandler RC	2.00	5.00
❑ 130B Tyson Chandler RC	2.00	5.00
❑ 130C Tyson Chandler RC	2.00	5.00
❑ 131A Joe Johnson RC	2.50	6.00
❑ 131B Joe Johnson RC	2.50	6.00
❑ 131C Joe Johnson RC	2.50	6.00
❑ 132A Richard Jefferson RC	2.50	6.00
❑ 132B Richard Jefferson RC	2.50	6.00
❑ 132C Richard Jefferson RC	2.50	6.00
❑ 133A Eddie Griffin RC	1.00	2.50
❑ 133B Eddie Griffin RC	1.00	2.50
❑ 133C Eddie Griffin RC	1.00	2.50
❑ 134A Rodney White RC	1.00	2.50
❑ 134B Rodney White RC	1.00	2.50
❑ 134C Rodney White RC	1.00	2.50
❑ 135A Andrei Kirilenko RC	3.00	8.00

❑ 135B Andrei Kirilenko RC	3.00	8.00
❑ 135C Andrei Kirilenko RC	3.00	8.00
❑ 136A Tony Parker RC	5.00	12.00
❑ 136B Tony Parker RC	5.00	12.00
❑ 136C Tony Parker RC	5.00	12.00
❑ 137A Jamaal Tinsley RC	1.50	4.00
❑ 137B Jamaal Tinsley RC	1.50	4.00
❑ 137C Jamaal Tinsley RC	1.50	4.00
❑ 138A Pau Gasol RC	5.00	12.00
❑ 138B Pau Gasol RC	5.00	12.00
❑ 138C Pau Gasol RC	5.00	12.00
❑ 139A Jason Richardson RC	2.50	6.00
❑ 139B Jason Richardson RC	2.50	6.00
❑ 139C Jason Richardson RC	2.50	6.00
❑ 140A Kwame Brown RC	1.50	4.00
❑ 140B Kwame Brown RC	1.50	4.00
❑ 140C Kwame Brown RC	1.50	4.00

2002-03 Upper Deck Generations

❑ COMP.SET w/o SP's (150)	25.00	60.00
❑ COMMON CARD (1-50)	.08	.20
❑ COMMON ROOKIE (51-92)	1.50	4.00
❑ COMMON CARD (93-192)	.30	.75
❑ COMMON CARD (193-234)	1.50	4.00
❑ 1 Shareef Abdur-Rahim	.25	.60
❑ 2 Paul Pierce	.30	.75
❑ 3 Antoine Walker	.25	.60
❑ 4 Jalen Rose	.25	.60
❑ 5 Tyson Chandler	.25	.60
❑ 6 Darius Miles	.20	.50
❑ 7 Dirk Nowitzki	.50	1.25
❑ 8 Steve Nash	.50	1.25
❑ 9 James Posey	.20	.50
❑ 10 Richard Hamilton	.25	.60
❑ 11 Ben Wallace	.25	.60
❑ 12 Antawn Jamison	.30	.75
❑ 13 Jason Richardson	.30	.75
❑ 14 Steve Francis	.30	.75
❑ 15 Eddie Griffin	.20	.50
❑ 16 Reggie Miller	.30	.75
❑ 17 Jamaal Tinsley	.25	.60
❑ 18 Elton Brand	.30	.75
❑ 19 Andre Miller	.25	.60
❑ 20 Kobe Bryant	1.50	4.00
❑ 21 Shaquille O'Neal	.75	2.00
❑ 22 Pau Gasol	.30	.75
❑ 23 Shane Battier	.25	.60
❑ 24 Alonzo Mourning	.30	.75
❑ 25 Ray Allen	.30	.75
❑ 26 Kevin Garnett	.60	1.50
❑ 27 Wally Szczerbiak	.25	.60
❑ 28 Jason Kidd	.50	1.25
❑ 29 Kenyon Martin	.30	.75
❑ 30 Jamal Mashburn	.25	.60
❑ 31 Baron Davis	.30	.75
❑ 32 Latrell Sprewell	.25	.60
❑ 33 Tracy McGrady	.60	1.50
❑ 34 Allen Iverson	.60	1.50
❑ 35 Stephon Marbury	.30	.75
❑ 36 Shawn Marion	.30	.75
❑ 37 Rasheed Wallace	.30	.75
❑ 38 Bonzi Wells	.25	.60
❑ 39 Chris Webber	.30	.75
❑ 40 Mike Bibby	.25	.60
❑ 41 Tim Duncan	.60	1.50
❑ 42 Tony Parker	.30	.75
❑ 43 Gary Payton	.30	.75
❑ 44 Rashard Lewis	.30	.75
❑ 45 Vince Carter	.60	1.50
❑ 46 Morris Peterson	.25	.60
❑ 47 Karl Malone	.30	.75
❑ 48 John Stockton	.40	1.00
❑ 49 Michael Jordan	3.00	8.00
❑ 50 Jerry Stackhouse	.25	.60
❑ 51 Yao Ming RC	5.00	12.00
❑ 52 Jay Williams RC	2.00	5.00
❑ 53 Mike Dunleavy RC	2.00	5.00
❑ 54 Drew Gooden RC	2.50	6.00
❑ 55 Nikoloz Tskitishvili RC	1.50	4.00
❑ 56 DaJuan Wagner RC	1.50	4.00
❑ 57 Nene Hilario RC	2.00	5.00
❑ 58 Chris Wilcox RC	2.00	5.00
❑ 59 Amare Stoudemire RC	4.00	10.00
❑ 60 Caron Butler RC	3.00	8.00
❑ 61 Jared Jeffries RC	1.50	4.00
❑ 62 Melvin Ely RC	1.50	4.00
❑ 63 Marcus Haislip RC	1.50	4.00
❑ 64 Fred Jones RC	2.00	5.00
❑ 65 Bostjan Nachbar RC	1.50	4.00
❑ 66 Jiri Welsch RC	1.50	4.00
❑ 67 Juan Dixon RC	2.50	6.00
❑ 68 Curtis Borchardt RC	1.50	4.00
❑ 69 Ryan Humphrey RC	1.50	4.00
❑ 70 Kareem Rush RC	2.00	5.00
❑ 71 Qyntel Woods RC	1.50	4.00
❑ 72 Casey Jacobsen RC	1.50	4.00
❑ 73 Tayshaun Prince RC	2.50	6.00
❑ 74 Predrag Savovic RC	1.50	4.00
❑ 75 Frank Williams RC	1.50	4.00
❑ 76 John Salmons RC	2.50	6.00
❑ 77 Chris Jefferies RC	1.50	4.00
❑ 78 Dan Dickau RC	1.50	4.00
❑ 79 Marcus Taylor RC	1.50	4.00
❑ 80 Roger Mason RC	1.50	4.00
❑ 81 Robert Archibald RC	1.50	4.00
❑ 82 Vincent Yarbrough RC	1.50	4.00
❑ 83 Dan Gadzuric RC	1.50	4.00
❑ 84 Carlos Boozer RC	3.00	8.00
❑ 85 Tito Maddox RC	1.50	4.00
❑ 86 Rod Grizzard RC	1.50	4.00
❑ 87 Ronald Murray RC	2.50	6.00
❑ 88 Marko Jaric	1.50	4.00
❑ 89 Lonny Baxter RC	1.50	4.00
❑ 90 Sam Clancy RC	1.50	4.00
❑ 91 Matt Barnes RC	2.00	5.00
❑ 92 Jamal Sampson RC	1.50	4.00
❑ 93 Oscar Robertson	.75	2.00
❑ 94 Moses Malone	.50	1.25
❑ 95 Earl Monroe	.30	.75
❑ 96 Pete Maravich	1.25	3.00
❑ 97 Artis Gilmore	.30	.75
❑ 98 Julius Erving	1.25	3.00
❑ 99 Nate Archibald	.30	.75
❑ 100 Wes Unseld	.30	.75
❑ 101 Willis Reed	.30	.75
❑ 102 Jo Jo White	.30	.75
❑ 103 Isiah Thomas	.50	1.25
❑ 104 Bill Sharman	.30	.75
❑ 105 Wilt Chamberlain	.75	2.00
❑ 106 Bob Cousy	.50	1.25
❑ 107 Tom Heinsohn	.30	.75
❑ 108 Terry Cummings	.30	.75
❑ 109 John Havlicek	.60	1.50
❑ 110 Bob Pettit	.30	.75
❑ 111 Drazen Petrovic	.30	.75
❑ 112 Dan Roundfield	.30	.75
❑ 113 David Thompson	.30	.75
❑ 114 Bobby Jones	.30	.75
❑ 115 Clyde Lovellette	.30	.75
❑ 116 Rick Barry	.50	1.25
❑ 117 K.C. Jones	.30	.75
❑ 118 Lionel Hollins	.30	.75
❑ 119 Bob Lanier	.30	.75
❑ 120 Al Attles	.30	.75
❑ 121 Jack Sikma	.30	.75
❑ 122 George McGinnis	.30	.75
❑ 123 Quinn Buckner	.30	.75
❑ 124 Magic Johnson	1.25	3.00
❑ 125 Larry Bird	1.50	4.00
❑ 126 Cliff Hagan	.30	.75
❑ 127 Jerry Lucas	.30	.75
❑ 128 Ricky Pierce	.30	.75
❑ 129 Walter Davis	.30	.75
❑ 130 Danny Ainge	.30	.75
❑ 131 Reggie Theus	.30	.75
❑ 132 Darryl Dawkins	.50	1.25
❑ 133 Tom Chambers	.30	.75
❑ 134 M.L. Carr	.30	.75
❑ 135 Kelly Tripucka	.30	.75
❑ 136 George Gervin	.50	1.25
❑ 137 Robert Parish	.50	1.25
❑ 138 Mitch Kupchak	.30	.75
❑ 139 Lou Hudson	.30	.75
❑ 140 Bill Cartwright	.30	.75
❑ 141 Lafayette Lever	.30	.75
❑ 142 Kevin Loughery	.30	.75
❑ 143 Hal Greer	.30	.75
❑ 144 Jamaal Wilkes	.30	.75
❑ 145 Alvan Adams	.30	.75
❑ 146 Thomas Sanders	.30	.75
❑ 147 Cazzie Russell	.50	1.25
❑ 148 Austin Carr	.30	.75
❑ 149 Gail Goodrich	.30	.75
❑ 150 Billy Knight	.30	.75
❑ 151 Dave Bing	.30	.75
❑ 152 Bill Walton	.75	2.00
❑ 153 Sam Jones	.30	.75
❑ 154 Swen Nater	.30	.75
❑ 155 Bobby Dandridge	.30	.75
❑ 156 Junior Bridgeman	.30	.75
❑ 157 Paul Silas	.50	1.25
❑ 158 John Kerr	.30	.75
❑ 159 Phil Chenier	.30	.75
❑ 160 Alex English	.30	.75
❑ 161 Geoff Petrie	.30	.75
❑ 162 Walt Bellamy	.30	.75
❑ 163 Don Nelson	.30	.75
❑ 164 Byron Scott	.30	.75
❑ 165 Harvey Catchings	.30	.75
❑ 166 Edward Macauley	.30	.75
❑ 167 John Drew	.30	.75
❑ 168 Detlef Schrempf	.30	.75
❑ 169 Rolando Blackman	.30	.75
❑ 170 Dave DeBusschere	.50	1.25
❑ 171 Marvin Barnes	.30	.75
❑ 172 Elgin Baylor	.50	1.25
❑ 173 Cedric Maxwell	.30	.75
❑ 174 Vern Mikkelsen	.30	.75
❑ 175 Larry Brown	.30	.75
❑ 176 Rick Mahorn	.30	.75
❑ 177 Dolph Schayes	.30	.75
❑ 178 Kevin McHale	.60	1.50
❑ 179 Clark Kellogg	.30	.75
❑ 180 Otis Birdsong	.30	.75
❑ 181 Michael Cooper	.30	.75
❑ 182 Mike Dunleavy	.30	.75
❑ 183 Spencer Haywood	.30	.75
❑ 184 Larry Nance	.30	.75
❑ 185 Maurice Lucas	.30	.75
❑ 186 Fred Brown	.30	.75
❑ 187 Jerry West	.60	1.50
❑ 188 Joe Barry Carroll	.30	.75
❑ 189 Dave Cowens	.30	.75
❑ 190 Sidney Moncrief	.50	1.25
❑ 191 Kiki Vandeweghe	.30	.75
❑ 192 Walt Frazier	.50	1.25
❑ 193 Y.Ming/W.Chamberlain	4.00	10.00
❑ 194 J.Williams/J.Erving	2.50	6.00
❑ 195 M.Dunleavy/M.Dunleavy	3.00	8.00
❑ 196 D.Gooden/J.Havlicek	4.00	10.00
❑ 197 N.Tskitishvili/K.McHale	1.50	4.00
❑ 198 D.Wagner/O.Robertson	1.50	4.00
❑ 199 N.Hilario/K.Vandeweghe	2.50	6.00
❑ 200 Chris Wilcox	2.00	5.00
❑ 201 A.Stoudamire/G.McGinnis	5.00	12.00
❑ 202 C.Butler/W.Reed	3.00	8.00
❑ 203 J.Jeffries/L.Bird	2.50	6.00
❑ 204 M.Ely/E.Baylor	1.50	4.00
❑ 205 M.Haislip/K.Abdul-Jabbar	1.50	4.00
❑ 206 F.Jones/K.C.Jones	1.50	4.00
❑ 207 Bostjan Nachbar	1.50	4.00
❑ 208 Jiri Welsch	1.50	4.00
❑ 209 Juan Dixon	2.50	6.00
❑ 210 Curtis Borchardt	1.50	4.00
❑ 211 R.Humphrey/B.Lanier	1.50	4.00
❑ 212 K.Rush/W.Frazier	2.00	5.00
❑ 213 Q.Woods/J.Wilkes	1.50	4.00
❑ 214 C.Jacobsen/T.Chambers	1.50	4.00
❑ 215 T.Prince/B.Scott	2.00	5.00
❑ 216 P.Savovic/D.Petrovic	1.50	4.00
❑ 217 Frank Williams	1.50	4.00
❑ 218 J.Salmons/E.Baylor	2.00	5.00
❑ 219 C.Jefferies/W.Davis	1.50	4.00
❑ 220 Dan Dickau	1.50	4.00
❑ 221 M.Taylor/O.Robertson	1.50	4.00
❑ 222 R.Mason/J.White	1.50	4.00
❑ 223 R.Archibald/S.Moncrief	1.50	4.00
❑ 224 V.Yarbrough/E.Monroe	1.50	4.00
❑ 225 D.Gadzuric/B.Walton	1.50	4.00
❑ 226 C.Boozer/R.Parish	3.00	8.00
❑ 227 Tito Maddox	1.50	4.00
❑ 228 R.Grizzard/G.Gervin	1.50	4.00

❑ 229 R.Murray/L.Lever	1.50	4.00
❑ 230 Marko Jaric	1.50	4.00
❑ 231 Lonny Baxter	1.50	4.00
❑ 232 S.Clancy/W.Unseld	1.50	4.00
❑ 233 Matt Barnes	1.50	4.00
❑ 234 Jamal Sampson	1.50	4.00

1999-00 Upper Deck Gold Reserve

❑ COMPLETE SET (270)	60.00	120.00
❑ COMPLETE SET w/o RC (240)	20.00	40.00
❑ COMMON CARD (1-240)	.20	.50
❑ COMMON ROOKIE (241-270)	1.00	2.50
❑ 1 Roshown McLeod	.20	.50
❑ 2 Dikembe Mutombo	.25	.60
❑ 3 Alan Henderson	.20	.50
❑ 4 Chris Crawford	.20	.50
❑ 5 Jim Jackson	.25	.60
❑ 6 Isaiah Rider	.20	.50
❑ 7 Lorenzen Wright	.20	.50
❑ 8 Bimbo Coles	.20	.50
❑ 9 Kenny Anderson	.25	.60
❑ 10 Antoine Walker	.30	.75
❑ 11 Paul Pierce	.30	.75
❑ 12 Vitaly Potapenko	.20	.50
❑ 13 Dana Barros	.20	.50
❑ 14 Calbert Cheaney	.20	.50
❑ 15 Pervis Ellison	.20	.50
❑ 16 Eric Williams	.20	.50
❑ 17 Tony Battie	.25	.60
❑ 18 Elden Campbell	.20	.50
❑ 19 Eddie Jones	.30	.75
❑ 20 David Wesley	.20	.50
❑ 21 Derrick Coleman	.25	.60
❑ 22 Ricky Davis	.30	.75
❑ 23 Anthony Mason	.20	.50
❑ 24 Todd Fuller	.20	.50
❑ 25 Brad Miller	.25	.60
❑ 26 Corey Benjamin	.20	.50
❑ 27 Randy Brown	.20	.50
❑ 28 Dickey Simpkins	.20	.50
❑ 29 Toni Kukoc	.30	.75
❑ 30 Fred Hoiberg	.20	.50
❑ 31 Hersey Hawkins	.20	.50
❑ 32 Will Perdue	.20	.50
❑ 33 Chris Anstey	.20	.50
❑ 34 Shawn Kemp	.30	.75
❑ 35 Wesley Person	.20	.50
❑ 36 Brevin Knight	.20	.50
❑ 37 Bob Sura	.20	.50
❑ 38 Danny Ferry	.20	.50
❑ 39 Lamond Murray	.20	.50
❑ 40 Cedric Henderson	.20	.50
❑ 41 Andrew DeClercq	.20	.50
❑ 42 Michael Finley	.30	.75
❑ 43 Shawn Bradley	.20	.50
❑ 44 Dirk Nowitzki	.50	1.25
❑ 45 Erick Strickland	.20	.50
❑ 46 Cedric Ceballos	.20	.50
❑ 47 Hubert Davis	.20	.50
❑ 48 Robert Pack	.20	.50
❑ 49 Gary Trent	.20	.50
❑ 50 Antonio McDyess	.25	.60
❑ 51 Nick Van Exel	.25	.60
❑ 52 Chauncey Billups	.30	.75
❑ 53 Bryant Stith	.20	.50
❑ 54 Raef LaFrentz	.25	.60
❑ 55 Ron Mercer	.20	.50
❑ 56 George McCloud	.20	.50
❑ 57 Roy Rogers	.20	.50
❑ 58 Keon Clark	.20	.50
❑ 59 Grant Hill	.30	.75
❑ 60 Lindsey Hunter	.20	.50
❑ 61 Jerry Stackhouse	.30	.75
❑ 62 Terry Mills	.20	.50
❑ 63 Michael Curry	.20	.50
❑ 64 Christian Laettner	.25	.60
❑ 65 Jerome Williams	.20	.50
❑ 66 Loy Vaught	.20	.50
❑ 67 John Starks	.30	.75
❑ 68 Antawn Jamison	.30	.75
❑ 69 Erick Dampier	.25	.60
❑ 70 Jason Caffey	.20	.50
❑ 71 Terry Cummings	.20	.50
❑ 72 Donyell Marshall	.25	.60
❑ 73 Chris Mills	.20	.50
❑ 74 Tony Farmer	.20	.50
❑ 75 Adonal Foyle	.20	.50
❑ 76 Hakeem Olajuwon	.30	.75
❑ 77 Cuttino Mobley	.25	.60
❑ 78 Charles Barkley	.40	1.00
❑ 79 Bryce Drew	.20	.50
❑ 80 Shandon Anderson	.20	.50
❑ 81 Kelvin Cato	.20	.50
❑ 82 Walt Williams	.20	.50
❑ 83 Carlos Rogers	.20	.50
❑ 84 Reggie Miller	.30	.75
❑ 85 Jalen Rose	.25	.60
❑ 86 Mark Jackson	.30	.75
❑ 87 Dale Davis	.20	.50
❑ 88 Chris Mullin	.30	.75
❑ 89 Al Harrington	.25	.60
❑ 90 Rik Smits	.30	.75
❑ 91 Sam Perkins	.20	.50
❑ 92 Austin Croshere	.20	.50
❑ 93 Maurice Taylor	.25	.60
❑ 94 Tyrone Nesby RC	.30	.75
❑ 95 Michael Olowokandi	.20	.50
❑ 96 Eric Piatkowski	.25	.60
❑ 97 Troy Hudson	.30	.75
❑ 98 Derek Anderson	.20	.50
❑ 99 Eric Murdock	.20	.50
❑ 100 Brian Skinner	.20	.50
❑ 101 Kobe Bryant	1.50	4.00
❑ 102 Shaquille O'Neal	.75	2.00
❑ 103 Glen Rice	.30	.75
❑ 104 Robert Horry	.30	.75
❑ 105 Ron Harper	.20	.50
❑ 106 Derek Fisher	.30	.75
❑ 107 Rick Fox	.20	.50
❑ 108 A.C. Green	.30	.75
❑ 109 Tim Hardaway	.30	.75
❑ 110 Alonzo Mourning	.30	.75
❑ 111 P.J. Brown	.20	.50
❑ 112 Dan Majerle	.30	.75
❑ 113 Jamal Mashburn	.20	.50
❑ 114 Voshon Lenard	.20	.50
❑ 115 Clarence Weatherspoon	.20	.50
❑ 116 Rex Walters	.20	.50
❑ 117 Ray Allen	.30	.75
❑ 118 Glenn Robinson	.25	.60
❑ 119 Sam Cassell	.25	.60
❑ 120 Robert Traylor	.20	.50
❑ 121 J.R. Reid	.20	.50
❑ 122 Ervin Johnson	.20	.50
❑ 123 Danny Manning	.20	.50
❑ 124 Tim Thomas	.25	.60
❑ 125 Kevin Garnett	.60	1.50
❑ 126 Sam Mitchell	.20	.50
❑ 127 Dean Garrett	.20	.50
❑ 128 Bobby Jackson	.25	.60
❑ 129 Radoslav Nesterovic	.40	1.00
❑ 130 Terrell Brandon	.20	.50
❑ 131 Joe Smith	.25	.60
❑ 132 Anthony Peeler	.20	.50
❑ 133 Keith Van Horn	.25	.60
❑ 134 Stephon Marbury	.30	.75
❑ 135 Kendall Gill	.20	.50
❑ 136 Scott Burrell	.20	.50
❑ 137 Jayson Williams	.25	.60
❑ 138 Jamie Feick RC	.30	.75
❑ 139 Kerry Kittles	.20	.50
❑ 140 Johnny Newman	.20	.50
❑ 141 Patrick Ewing	.40	1.00
❑ 142 Allan Houston	.25	.60
❑ 143 Latrell Sprewell	.25	.60
❑ 144 Larry Johnson	.30	.75
❑ 145 Marcus Camby	.25	.60
❑ 146 Chris Childs	.20	.50
❑ 147 Kurt Thomas	.25	.60
❑ 148 Charlie Ward	.20	.50
❑ 149 Darrell Armstrong	.20	.50
❑ 150 Matt Harpring	.25	.60
❑ 151 Michael Doleac	.20	.50
❑ 152 Bo Outlaw	.20	.50
❑ 153 Tariq Abdul-Wahad	.20	.50
❑ 154 John Amaechi RC	.30	.75
❑ 155 Ben Wallace	.25	.60
❑ 156 Monty Williams	.20	.50
❑ 157 Allen Iverson	.60	1.50
❑ 158 Theo Ratliff	.25	.60
❑ 159 Larry Hughes	.25	.60
❑ 160 Eric Snow	.25	.60
❑ 161 George Lynch	.20	.50
❑ 162 Tyrone Hill	.20	.50
❑ 163 Billy Owens	.20	.50
❑ 164 Aaron McKie	.25	.60
❑ 165 Jason Kidd	.50	1.25
❑ 166 Clifford Robinson	.20	.50
❑ 167 Tom Gugliotta	.20	.50
❑ 168 Luc Longley	.20	.50
❑ 169 Anfernee Hardaway	.30	.75
❑ 170 Rex Chapman	.20	.50
❑ 171 Oliver Miller	.20	.50
❑ 172 Rodney Rogers	.20	.50
❑ 173 Rasheed Wallace	.30	.75
❑ 174 Arvydas Sabonis	.25	.60
❑ 175 Damon Stoudamire	.30	.75
❑ 176 Brian Grant	.20	.50
❑ 177 Scottie Pippen	.50	1.25
❑ 178 Detlef Schrempf	.25	.60
❑ 179 Steve Smith	.20	.50
❑ 180 Jermaine O'Neal	.30	.75
❑ 181 Bonzi Wells	.20	.50
❑ 182 Jason Williams	.30	.75
❑ 183 Vlade Divac	.30	.75
❑ 184 Peja Stojakovic	.25	.60
❑ 185 Lawrence Funderburke	.20	.50
❑ 186 Chris Webber	.30	.75
❑ 187 Nick Anderson	.20	.50
❑ 188 Darrick Martin	.20	.50
❑ 189 Corliss Williamson	.20	.50
❑ 190 Tim Duncan	.60	1.50
❑ 191 Sean Elliott	.30	.75
❑ 192 David Robinson	.40	1.00
❑ 193 Mario Elie	.20	.50
❑ 194 Avery Johnson	.25	.60
❑ 195 Terry Porter	.20	.50
❑ 196 Malik Rose	.20	.50
❑ 197 Jaren Jackson	.20	.50
❑ 198 Gary Payton	.30	.75
❑ 199 Vin Baker	.30	.75
❑ 200 Rashard Lewis	.30	.75
❑ 201 Jelani McCoy	.20	.50
❑ 202 Brent Barry	.25	.60
❑ 203 Horace Grant	.25	.60
❑ 204 Vernon Maxwell UER	.25	.60
❑ 205 Ruben Patterson	.20	.50
❑ 206 Vince Carter	.60	1.50
❑ 207 Doug Christie	.25	.60
❑ 208 Kevin Willis	.20	.50
❑ 209 Dee Brown	.20	.50
❑ 210 Antonio Davis	.20	.50
❑ 211 Tracy McGrady	.60	1.50
❑ 212 Dell Curry	.20	.50
❑ 213 Charles Oakley	.25	.60
❑ 214 Karl Malone	.40	1.00
❑ 215 John Stockton	.40	1.00
❑ 216 Howard Eisley	.20	.50
❑ 217 Bryon Russell	.20	.50
❑ 218 Greg Ostertag	.20	.50
❑ 219 Jeff Hornacek	.25	.60
❑ 220 Olden Polynice	.20	.50
❑ 221 Adam Keefe	.20	.50
❑ 222 Shareef Abdur-Rahim	.25	.60
❑ 223 Mike Bibby	.30	.75
❑ 224 Felipe Lopez	.20	.50
❑ 225 Cherokee Parks	.20	.50
❑ 226 Michael Dickerson	.20	.50
❑ 227 Othella Harrington	.20	.50
❑ 228 Bryant Reeves	.20	.50
❑ 229 Brent Price	.20	.50
❑ 230 Michael Smith	.20	.50
❑ 231 Juwan Howard	.25	.60
❑ 232 Rod Strickland	.20	.50
❑ 233 Chris Whitney	.20	.50
❑ 234 Tracy Murray	.20	.50
❑ 235 Mitch Richmond	.25	.60
❑ 236 Aaron Williams	.20	.50
❑ 237 Isaac Austin	.20	.50
❑ 238 Kobe Bryant CL	1.50	4.00
❑ 239 Michael Jordan CL	2.00	5.00
❑ 240 Kevin Garnett CL	.60	1.50

❑ 241 Elton Brand RC	3.00	8.00
❑ 242 Steve Francis RC	3.00	8.00
❑ 243 Baron Davis RC	4.00	10.00
❑ 244 Lamar Odom RC	3.00	8.00
❑ 245 Jonathan Bender RC	1.00	2.50
❑ 246 Wally Szczerbiak RC	3.00	8.00
❑ 247 Richard Hamilton RC	3.00	8.00
❑ 248 Andre Miller RC	3.00	8.00
❑ 249 Shawn Marion RC	3.00	8.00
❑ 250 Jason Terry RC	2.50	6.00
❑ 251 Trajan Langdon RC	1.00	2.50
❑ 252 A.Radojevic RC	1.00	2.50
❑ 253 Corey Maggette RC	3.00	8.00
❑ 254 William Avery RC	1.00	2.50
❑ 255 Ron Artest RC	4.00	10.00
❑ 256 Cal Bowdler RC	1.00	2.50
❑ 257 James Posey RC	1.50	4.00
❑ 258 Quincy Lewis RC	1.00	2.50
❑ 259 Dion Glover RC	1.00	2.50
❑ 260 Jeff Foster RC	1.25	3.00
❑ 261 Kenny Thomas RC	1.00	2.50
❑ 262 Devean George RC	1.50	4.00
❑ 263 Tim James RC	1.00	2.50
❑ 264 Vonteego Cummings RC	1.00	2.50
❑ 265 Jumaine Jones RC	1.00	2.50
❑ 266 Scott Padgett RC	1.00	2.50
❑ 267 Rodney Buford RC	1.00	2.50
❑ 268 Adrian Griffin RC	1.00	2.50
❑ 269 Anthony Carter RC	2.00	5.00
❑ 270 Eddie Robinson RC	1.00	2.50

1998 Upper Deck Hardcourt

❑ COMPLETE SET (90)	40.00	75.00
❑ 1 Kobe Bryant	3.00	8.00
❑ 2 Donyell Marshall	.60	1.50
❑ 3 Bryant Reeves	.25	.60
❑ 4 Keith Van Horn	.75	2.00
❑ 5 David Robinson	.75	2.00
❑ 6 Nick Anderson	.25	.60
❑ 7 Nick Van Exel	.75	2.00
❑ 8 David Wesley	.25	.60
❑ 9 Alonzo Mourning	.60	1.50
❑ 10 Shawn Kemp	.60	1.50
❑ 11 Maurice Taylor	.50	1.25
❑ 12 Kenny Anderson	.60	1.50
❑ 13 Jason Kidd	1.25	3.00
❑ 14 Marcus Camby	.60	1.50
❑ 15 Tim Hardaway	.60	1.50
❑ 16 Damon Stoudamire	.60	1.50
❑ 17 Detlef Schrempf	.60	1.50
❑ 18 Dikembe Mutombo	.60	1.50
❑ 19 Charles Barkley	1.00	2.50
❑ 20 Ray Allen	.75	2.00
❑ 21 Ron Mercer	.50	1.25
❑ 22 Shawn Bradley	.25	.60
❑ 23 Michael Jordan	4.00	10.00
❑ 23A Michael Jordan Spec.	8.00	20.00
❑ 24 Antonio McDyess	.60	1.50
❑ 25 Stephon Marbury	.75	2.00
❑ 26 Rik Smits	.60	1.50
❑ 27 Michael Stewart	.25	.60
❑ 28 Steve Smith	.60	1.50
❑ 29 Glenn Robinson	.60	1.50
❑ 30 Chris Webber	.75	2.00
❑ 31 Antoine Walker	.75	2.00
❑ 32 Eddie Jones	.75	2.00
❑ 33 Mitch Richmond	.60	1.50
❑ 34 Kevin Garnett	1.50	4.00
❑ 35 Grant Hill	.75	2.00
❑ 36 John Stockton	.75	2.00
❑ 37 Allan Houston	.60	1.50
❑ 38 Bobby Jackson	.60	1.50
❑ 39 Sam Cassell	.75	2.00
❑ 40 Allen Iverson	1.50	4.00
❑ 41 LaPhonso Ellis	.25	.60
❑ 42 Lorenzen Wright	.25	.60
❑ 43 Gary Payton	.75	2.00
❑ 44 Patrick Ewing	.75	2.00
❑ 45 Scottie Pippen	1.25	3.00
❑ 46 Hakeem Olajuwon	.75	2.00
❑ 47 Glen Rice	.60	1.50
❑ 48 Antonio Daniels	.25	.60
❑ 49 Jayson Williams	.25	.60
❑ 50 Juwan Howard	.60	1.50
❑ 51 Reggie Miller	.75	2.00
❑ 52 Joe Smith	.60	1.50
❑ 53 Shaquille O'Neal	2.00	5.00
❑ 54 Dennis Rodman	.60	1.50
❑ 55 Vin Baker	.60	1.50
❑ 56 Rod Strickland	.25	.60
❑ 57 Anfernee Hardaway	.75	2.00
❑ 58 Zydrunas Ilgauskas	.60	1.50
❑ 59 Chris Mullin	.75	2.00
❑ 60 Rasheed Wallace	.75	2.00
❑ 61 Shareef Abdur-Rahim	.75	2.00
❑ 62 Tom Gugliotta	.25	.60
❑ 63 Tim Duncan	1.25	3.00
❑ 64 Michael Finley	.75	2.00
❑ 65 Jim Jackson	.25	.60
❑ 66 Chauncey Billups	.60	1.50
❑ 67 Jerry Stackhouse	.75	2.00
❑ 68 Jeff Hornacek	.60	1.50
❑ 69 Clyde Drexler	.75	2.00
❑ 70 Karl Malone	.75	2.00
❑ 71 Tim Duncan RE	.60	1.50
❑ 72 Keith Van Horn RE	.60	1.50
❑ 73 Chauncey Billups RE	.60	1.50
❑ 74 Antonio Daniels RE	.25	.60
❑ 75 Tony Battie RE	.25	.60
❑ 76 Ron Mercer RE	.50	1.25
❑ 77 Tim Thomas RE	.60	1.50
❑ 78 Tracy McGrady RE	2.00	5.00
❑ 79 Danny Fortson RE	.25	.60
❑ 80 Derek Anderson RE	.60	1.50
❑ 81 Maurice Taylor RE	.50	1.25
❑ 82 Kelvin Cato RE	.25	.60
❑ 83 Brevin Knight RE	.25	.60
❑ 84 Bobby Jackson RE	.25	.60
❑ 85 Rodrick Rhodes RE	.25	.60
❑ 86 Anthony Johnson RE	.25	.60
❑ 87 Cedric Henderson RE	.25	.60
❑ 88 Chris Anstey RE	.25	.60
❑ 89 Michael Stewart RE	.25	.60
❑ 90 Zydrunas Ilgauskas RE	.25	.60
❑ NNO Michael Jordan Jumbo	4.00	10.00

1999-00 Upper Deck Hardcourt

❑ COMPLETE SET (90)	50.00	100.00
❑ COMPLETE SET w/o RC (60)	12.50	25.00
❑ COMMON CARD (1-60)	.25	.60
❑ COMMON ROOKIE 61-90	.60	1.50
❑ 1 Dikembe Mutombo	.30	.75
❑ 2 Alan Henderson	.25	.60
❑ 3 Antoine Walker	.40	1.00
❑ 4 Paul Pierce	.40	1.00
❑ 5 Eddie Jones	.40	1.00
❑ 6 Elden Campbell	.25	.60
❑ 7 Toni Kukoc	.40	1.00
❑ 8 Randy Brown	.25	.60
❑ 9 Shawn Kemp	.40	1.00
❑ 10 Brevin Knight	.25	.60
❑ 11 Michael Finley	.40	1.00
❑ 12 Dirk Nowitzki	.60	1.50
❑ 13 Antonio McDyess	.30	.75
❑ 14 Nick Van Exel	.30	.75
❑ 15 Grant Hill	.40	1.00
❑ 16 Jerry Stackhouse	.40	1.00
❑ 17 Antawn Jamison	.40	1.00
❑ 18 John Starks	.40	1.00
❑ 19 Hakeem Olajuwon	.40	1.00
❑ 20 Scottie Pippen	.60	1.50
❑ 21 Reggie Miller	.40	1.00
❑ 22 Jalen Rose	.30	.75
❑ 23 Maurice Taylor	.30	.75
❑ 24 Michael Olowokandi	.25	.60
❑ 25 Shaquille O'Neal	1.00	2.50
❑ 26 Kobe Bryant	2.00	5.00
❑ 27 Tim Hardaway	.40	1.00
❑ 28 Alonzo Mourning	.40	1.00
❑ 29 Glenn Robinson	.30	.75
❑ 30 Ray Allen	.40	1.00
❑ 31 Kevin Garnett	.75	2.00
❑ 32 Terrell Brandon	.25	.60
❑ 33 Stephon Marbury	.40	1.00
❑ 34 Keith Van Horn	.30	.75
❑ 35 Latrell Sprewell	.30	.75
❑ 36 Allan Houston	.30	.75
❑ 37 Patrick Ewing	.50	1.25
❑ 38 Darrell Armstrong	.25	.60
❑ 39 Bo Outlaw	.25	.60
❑ 40 Allen Iverson	.75	2.00
❑ 41 Larry Hughes	.30	.75
❑ 42 Jason Kidd	.60	1.50
❑ 43 Tom Gugliotta	.25	.60
❑ 44 Brian Grant	.25	.60
❑ 45 Damon Stoudamire	.40	1.00
❑ 46 Jason Williams	.40	1.00
❑ 47 Vlade Divac	.40	1.00
❑ 48 Tim Duncan	.75	2.00
❑ 49 David Robinson	.50	1.25
❑ 50 Avery Johnson	.30	.75
❑ 51 Gary Payton	.40	1.00
❑ 52 Vin Baker	.40	1.00
❑ 53 Vince Carter	.75	2.00
❑ 54 Tracy McGrady	.75	2.00
❑ 55 Karl Malone	.50	1.25
❑ 56 John Stockton	.50	1.25
❑ 57 Shareef Abdur-Rahim	.30	.75
❑ 58 Mike Bibby	.40	1.00
❑ 59 Juwan Howard	.30	.75
❑ 60 Mitch Richmond	.30	.75
❑ 61 Elton Brand RC	2.00	5.00
❑ 62 Jason Terry RC	1.50	4.00
❑ 63 Kenny Thomas RC	.60	1.50
❑ 64 Jonathan Bender RC	.60	1.50
❑ 65 A.Radojevic RC	.60	1.50
❑ 66 Galen Young RC	.60	1.50
❑ 67 Baron Davis RC	2.50	6.00
❑ 68 Corey Maggette RC	2.00	5.00
❑ 69 Dion Glover RC	.60	1.50
❑ 70 Scott Padgett RC	.60	1.50
❑ 71 Steve Francis RC	2.00	5.00
❑ 72 Richard Hamilton RC	2.00	5.00
❑ 73 James Posey RC	1.00	2.50
❑ 74 Jumaine Jones RC	.60	1.50
❑ 75 Chris Herren RC	.60	1.50
❑ 76 Andre Miller RC	2.00	5.00
❑ 77 Lamar Odom RC	2.00	5.00
❑ 78 Wally Szczerbiak RC	2.00	5.00
❑ 79 William Avery RC	.60	1.50
❑ 80 Devean George RC	1.00	2.50
❑ 81 Trajan Langdon RC	.60	1.50
❑ 82 Cal Bowdler RC	.60	1.50
❑ 83 Kris Clack RC	.60	1.50
❑ 84 Tim James RC	.60	1.50
❑ 85 Shawn Marion RC	2.00	5.00
❑ 86 Ryan Robertson RC	.60	1.50
❑ 87 Quincy Lewis RC	.60	1.50
❑ 88 Vonteego Cummings RC	.60	1.50
❑ 89 Obinna Ekezie RC	.60	1.50
❑ 90 Jeff Foster RC	.75	2.00
❑ GF1 M.Jordan Floor	300.00	600.00
❑ GF6 W.Chamberlain Floor	100.00	200.00

2000-01 Upper Deck Hardcourt

❑ COMPLETE SET w/o RC (60)	10.00	25.00
❑ COMMON CARD (1-60)	.20	.50
❑ COMMON ROOKIE (61-102)	1.50	4.00
❑ 1 Dikembe Mutombo	.25	.60
❑ 2 Jason Terry	.30	.75
❑ 3 Antoine Walker	.25	.60
❑ 4 Paul Pierce	.30	.75
❑ 5 Eddie Jones	.25	.60
❑ 6 Baron Davis	.30	.75
❑ 7 Elton Brand	.30	.75
❑ 8 Ron Artest	.30	.75
❑ 9 Andre Miller	.25	.60
❑ 10 Shawn Kemp	.30	.75
❑ 11 Dirk Nowitzki	.50	1.25
❑ 12 Michael Finley	.30	.75
❑ 13 Antonio McDyess	.25	.60
❑ 14 Nick Van Exel	.25	.60
❑ 15 Grant Hill	.30	.75
❑ 16 Jerry Stackhouse	.25	.60
❑ 17 Antawn Jamison	.30	.75
❑ 18 Larry Hughes	.25	.60
❑ 19 Steve Francis	.30	.75
❑ 20 Hakeem Olajuwon	.40	1.00
❑ 21 Reggie Miller	.30	.75
❑ 22 Jalen Rose	.25	.60
❑ 23 Lamar Odom	.30	.75
❑ 24 Eric Piatkowski	.20	.50
❑ 25 Shaquille O'Neal	.75	2.00
❑ 26 Kobe Bryant	1.50	4.00
❑ 27 Alonzo Mourning	.30	.75
❑ 28 Jamal Mashburn	.25	.60
❑ 29 Ray Allen	.30	.75
❑ 30 Glenn Robinson	.25	.60
❑ 31 Kevin Garnett	.60	1.50
❑ 32 Wally Szczerbiak	.25	.60
❑ 33 Keith Van Horn	.25	.60
❑ 34 Stephon Marbury	.30	.75
❑ 35 Allan Houston	.25	.60
❑ 36 Latrell Sprewell	.25	.60
❑ 37 Darrell Armstrong	.20	.50
❑ 38 Ron Mercer	.20	.50
❑ 39 Allen Iverson	.60	1.50
❑ 40 Toni Kukoc	.25	.60
❑ 41 Jason Kidd	.50	1.25
❑ 42 Anfernee Hardaway	.30	.75
❑ 43 Shawn Marion	.30	.75
❑ 44 Scottie Pippen	.50	1.25
❑ 45 Damon Stoudamire	.25	.60
❑ 46 Chris Webber	.30	.75
❑ 47 Jason Williams	.25	.60
❑ 48 Tim Duncan	.60	1.50
❑ 49 David Robinson	.40	1.00
❑ 50 Gary Payton	.30	.75
❑ 51 Vin Baker	.25	.60
❑ 52 Rashard Lewis	.30	.75
❑ 53 Tracy McGrady	.60	1.50
❑ 54 Vince Carter	.60	1.50
❑ 55 Karl Malone	.40	1.00
❑ 56 John Stockton	.40	1.00
❑ 57 Shareef Abdur-Rahim	.25	.60
❑ 58 Mike Bibby	.25	.60
❑ 59 Mitch Richmond	.25	.60
❑ 60 Richard Hamilton	.25	.60
❑ 61 Kenyon Martin RC	4.00	10.00
❑ 62 Marcus Fizer RC	1.50	4.00
❑ 63 Chris Mihm RC	1.50	4.00
❑ 64 Chris Porter RC	1.50	4.00
❑ 65 Stromile Swift RC	2.00	5.00
❑ 66 Morris Peterson RC	2.50	6.00
❑ 67 Quentin Richardson RC	2.00	5.00
❑ 68 Courtney Alexander RC	1.50	4.00
❑ 69 Scoonie Penn RC	1.50	4.00
❑ 70 Mateen Cleaves RC	1.50	4.00
❑ 71 Erick Barkley RC	1.50	4.00
❑ 72 A.J. Guyton RC	1.50	4.00
❑ 73 Darius Miles RC	2.00	5.00
❑ 74 DerMarr Johnson RC	1.50	4.00
❑ 75 Hedo Turkoglu RC	4.00	10.00
❑ 76 Hanno Mottola RC	1.50	4.00
❑ 77 Mike Miller RC	2.50	6.00
❑ 78 Desmond Mason RC	2.00	5.00
❑ 79 Mark Madsen RC	1.50	4.00
❑ 80 Eduardo Najera RC	1.50	4.00
❑ 81 Speedy Claxton RC	1.50	4.00
❑ 82 Joel Przybilla RC	1.50	4.00
❑ 83 Brian Cardinal RC	1.50	4.00
❑ 84 Khalid El-Amin RC	1.50	4.00
❑ 85 Etan Thomas RC	1.50	4.00
❑ 86 Corey Hightower RC	1.50	4.00
❑ 87 Dan Langhi RC	1.50	4.00
❑ 88 Michael Redd RC	4.00	10.00
❑ 89 Pete Mickeal RC	1.50	4.00
❑ 90 Mamadou N'Diaye RC	1.50	4.00
❑ 91 Jerome Moiso RC	1.50	4.00
❑ 92 Chris Carrawell RC	1.50	4.00
❑ 93 Jason Collier RC	1.50	4.00
❑ 94 Keyon Dooling RC	1.50	4.00
❑ 95 Mark Karcher RC	1.50	4.00
❑ 96 Jamaal Magloire RC	1.50	4.00
❑ 97 Jason Hart RC	1.50	4.00
❑ 98 Jabari Smith RC	1.50	4.00
❑ 99 Donnell Harvey RC	1.50	4.00
❑ 100 Lavor Postell RC	1.50	4.00
❑ 101 Eddie House RC	1.50	4.00
❑ 102 Dan McClintock RC	1.50	4.00

2001-02 Upper Deck Hardcourt

❑ COMP.SET w/o SP's (90)	25.00	50.00
❑ COMMON CARD (1-121)	.10	.30
❑ COMMON ROOKIE (101-110)	2.00	5.00
❑ COMMON ROOKIE (111-120)	4.00	10.00
❑ 1 Jason Terry	.40	1.00
❑ 2 DerMarr Johnson	.25	.60
❑ 3 Toni Kukoc	.30	.75
❑ 4 Antoine Walker	.30	.75
❑ 5 Paul Pierce	.40	1.00
❑ 6 Kenny Anderson	.30	.75
❑ 7 Jamal Mashburn	.30	.75
❑ 8 Baron Davis	.40	1.00
❑ 9 David Wesley	.25	.60
❑ 10 Ron Artest	.30	.75
❑ 11 Jamal Crawford	.30	.75
❑ 12 Ron Mercer	.25	.60
❑ 13 Andre Miller	.30	.75
❑ 14 Lamond Murray	.25	.60
❑ 15 Matt Harpring	.30	.75
❑ 16 Michael Finley	.40	1.00
❑ 17 Dirk Nowitzki	.60	1.50
❑ 18 Steve Nash	.60	1.50
❑ 19 Antonio McDyess	.30	.75
❑ 20 Nick Van Exel	.30	.75
❑ 21 James Posey	.25	.60
❑ 22 Jerry Stackhouse	.30	.75
❑ 23 Chucky Atkins	.25	.60
❑ 24 Mateen Cleaves	.25	.60
❑ 25 Antawn Jamison	.40	1.00
❑ 26 Larry Hughes	.30	.75
❑ 27 Marc Jackson	.25	.60
❑ 28 Steve Francis	.40	1.00
❑ 29 Maurice Taylor	.25	.60
❑ 30 Cuttino Mobley	.30	.75
❑ 31 Reggie Miller	.40	1.00
❑ 32 Jalen Rose	.30	.75
❑ 33 Jermaine O'Neal	.40	1.00
❑ 34 Darius Miles	.25	.60
❑ 35 Lamar Odom	.40	1.00
❑ 36 Elton Brand	.40	1.00
❑ 37 Kobe Bryant	2.00	5.00
❑ 38 Shaquille O'Neal	1.00	2.50
❑ 39 Derek Fisher	.30	.75
❑ 40 Robert Horry	.30	.75
❑ 41 Alonzo Mourning	.40	1.00
❑ 42 Eddie Jones	.30	.75
❑ 43 Brian Grant	.25	.60
❑ 44 Anthony Mason	.25	.60
❑ 45 Ray Allen	.40	1.00
❑ 46 Glenn Robinson	.30	.75
❑ 47 Tim Thomas	.25	.60
❑ 48 Kevin Garnett	.75	2.00
❑ 49 Wally Szczerbiak	.30	.75
❑ 50 Terrell Brandon	.25	.60
❑ 51 Anthony Peeler	.25	.60
❑ 52 Jason Kidd	.60	1.50
❑ 53 Kenyon Martin	.40	1.00
❑ 54 Stephen Jackson	.30	.75
❑ 55 Latrell Sprewell	.30	.75
❑ 56 Allan Houston	.30	.75
❑ 57 Glen Rice	.30	.75
❑ 58 Tracy McGrady	.75	2.00
❑ 59 Darrell Armstrong	.25	.60
❑ 60 Mike Miller	.30	.75
❑ 61 Allen Iverson	.75	2.00
❑ 62 Dikembe Mutombo	.30	.75
❑ 63 Aaron McKie	.25	.60
❑ 64 Stephon Marbury	.40	1.00
❑ 65 Shawn Marion	.40	1.00
❑ 66 Tom Gugliotta	.25	.60
❑ 67 Rasheed Wallace	.40	1.00
❑ 68 Scottie Pippen	.60	1.50
❑ 69 Damon Stoudamire	.30	.75
❑ 70 Chris Webber	.40	1.00
❑ 71 Mike Bibby	.30	.75
❑ 72 Peja Stojakovic	.30	.75
❑ 73 Tim Duncan	.75	2.00
❑ 74 David Robinson	.50	1.25
❑ 75 Derek Anderson	.30	.75
❑ 76 Gary Payton	.40	1.00
❑ 77 Rashard Lewis	.40	1.00
❑ 78 Desmond Mason	.30	.75
❑ 79 Vince Carter	.75	2.00
❑ 80 Morris Peterson	.30	.75
❑ 81 Antonio Davis	.25	.60
❑ 82 Karl Malone	.50	1.25
❑ 83 John Stockton	.50	1.25
❑ 84 Donyell Marshall	.25	.60
❑ 85 Bryant Reeves	.25	.60
❑ 86 Jason Williams	.30	.75
❑ 87 Stromile Swift	.25	.60
❑ 88 Richard Hamilton	.30	.75
❑ 89 Courtney Alexander	.25	.60
❑ 90 Chris Whitney	.25	.60
❑ 91A Kenny Satterfield ON RC	1.50	4.00
❑ 91B Kenny Satterfield OFF RC	1.50	4.00
❑ 91C Kenny Satterfield HI RC	1.50	4.00
❑ 92A Jeff Trepagnier ON RC	1.50	4.00
❑ 92B Jeff Trepagnier OFF RC	1.50	4.00
❑ 92C Jeff Trepagnier HI RC	1.50	4.00
❑ 93A Michael Wright ON RC	1.50	4.00
❑ 93B Michael Wright OFF RC	1.50	4.00
❑ 93C Michael Wright HI RC	1.50	4.00
❑ 94A Terence Morris ON RC	1.50	4.00
❑ 94B Terence Morris OFF RC	1.50	4.00
❑ 94C Terence Morris HI RC	1.50	4.00
❑ 95A Omar Cook ON RC	1.50	4.00
❑ 95B Omar Cook OFF RC	1.50	4.00
❑ 95C Omar Cook HI RC	1.50	4.00
❑ 96A Gilbert Arenas ON RC	2.50	6.00
❑ 96B Gilbert Arenas OFF RC	2.50	6.00
❑ 96C Gilbert Arenas HI RC	2.50	6.00
❑ 97A Joseph Forte ON RC	1.50	4.00
❑ 97B Joseph Forte OFF RC	1.50	4.00
❑ 97C Joseph Forte HI RC	1.50	4.00
❑ 98A Jamaal Tinsley ON RC	2.00	5.00
❑ 98B Jamaal Tinsley OFF RC	2.00	5.00
❑ 98C Jamaal Tinsley HI RC	2.00	5.00
❑ 99A Samuel Dalembert ON RC	2.00	5.00
❑ 99B Samuel Dalembert OFF RC	2.00	5.00
❑ 99C Samuel Dalembert HI RC	2.00	5.00
❑ 100A Gerald Wallace ON RC	4.00	10.00
❑ 100B Gerald Wallace OFF RC	4.00	10.00
❑ 100C Gerald Wallace HI RC	4.00	10.00
❑ 101A Brendan Haywood ON RC	2.50	6.00
❑ 101B Brendan Haywood OFF RC	2.50	6.00
❑ 101C Brendan Haywood HI RC	2.50	6.00
❑ 102A Richard Jefferson ON RC	5.00	12.00

❑ 102B Richard Jefferson OFF RC 5.00 12.00
❑ 102C Richard Jefferson HI RC 5.00 12.00
❑ 103A Michael Bradley ON RC 2.00 5.00
❑ 103B Michael Bradley OFF RC 2.00 5.00
❑ 103C Michael Bradley HI RC 2.00 5.00
❑ 104A Loren Woods ON RC 2.00 5.00
❑ 104B Loren Woods OFF RC 2.00 5.00
❑ 104C Loren Woods HI RC 2.00 5.00
❑ 105A Jeryl Sasser ON RC 2.00 5.00
❑ 105B Jeryl Sasser OFF RC 2.00 5.00
❑ 105C Jeryl Sasser HI RC 2.00 5.00
❑ 106A Jason Collins ON RC 2.00 5.00
❑ 106B Jason Collins OFF RC 2.00 5.00
❑ 106C Jason Collins HI RC 2.00 5.00
❑ 107A Kirk Haston ON RC 2.00 5.00
❑ 107B Kirk Haston OFF RC 2.00 5.00
❑ 107C Kirk Haston HI RC 2.00 5.00
❑ 108A Steven Hunter ON RC 2.00 5.00
❑ 108B Steven Hunter OFF RC 2.00 5.00
❑ 108C Steven Hunter HI RC 2.00 5.00
❑ 109A Troy Murphy ON RC 4.00 10.00
❑ 109B Troy Murphy OFF RC 4.00 10.00
❑ 109C Troy Murphy HI RC 4.00 10.00
❑ 110A Vladimir Radmanovic ON RC 2.50 6.00
❑ 110B Vladimir Radmanovic OFF RC 2.50 6.00
❑ 110C Vladimir Radmanovic HI RC 2.50 6.00
❑ 111A Rodney White ON RC 4.00 10.00
❑ 111B Rodney White OFF RC 4.00 10.00
❑ 111C Rodney White HI RC 4.00 10.00
❑ 112A Kedrick Brown ON RC 4.00 10.00
❑ 112B Kedrick Brown OFF RC 4.00 10.00
❑ 112C Kedrick Brown HI RC 4.00 10.00
❑ 113A Joe Johnson ON RC 10.00 25.00
❑ 113B Joe Johnson OFF RC 10.00 25.00
❑ 113C Joe Johnson HI RC 10.00 25.00
❑ 114A Eddie Griffin ON RC 4.00 10.00
❑ 114B Eddie Griffin OFF RC 4.00 10.00
❑ 114C Eddie Griffin HI RC 4.00 10.00
❑ 115A Shane Battier ON RC 6.00 15.00
❑ 115B Shane Battier OFF RC 6.00 15.00
❑ 115C Shane Battier HI RC 6.00 15.00
❑ 116A Eddy Curry ON RC 6.00 15.00
❑ 116B Eddy Curry OFF RC 6.00 15.00
❑ 116C Eddy Curry HI RC 6.00 15.00
❑ 117A Jason Richardson ON RC 8.00 20.00
❑ 117B Jason Richardson OFF RC 8.00 20.00
❑ 117C Jason Richardson HI RC 8.00 20.00
❑ 118A DeSagana Diop ON RC 4.00 10.00
❑ 118B DeSagana Diop OFF RC 4.00 10.00
❑ 118C DeSagana Diop HI RC 4.00 10.00
❑ 119A Tyson Chandler ON RC 8.00 20.00
❑ 119B Tyson Chandler OFF RC 8.00 20.00
❑ 119C Tyson Chandler HI RC 8.00 20.00
❑ 120A Kwame Brown ON RC 5.00 12.00
❑ 120B Kwame Brown OFF RC 5.00 12.00
❑ 120C Kwame Brown HI RC 5.00 12.00
❑ 121 Michael Jordan 6.00 15.00

2002-03 Upper Deck Hardcourt

❑ COMP.SET w/o SP's (90) 20.00 50.00
❑ COMMON CARD (1-90) .25 .60
❑ COMMON ROOKIE (91-120) 1.25 3.00
❑ COMMON ROOKIE (121-129) 1.50 4.00
❑ 1 Shareef Abdur-Rahim .30 .75
❑ 2 Glenn Robinson .30 .75
❑ 3 Jason Terry .40 1.00
❑ 4 Antoine Walker .30 .75
❑ 5 Paul Pierce .40 1.00
❑ 6 Kedrick Brown .25 .60
❑ 7 Jalen Rose .30 .75
❑ 8 Eddy Curry .30 .75
❑ 9 Tyson Chandler .30 .75
❑ 10 Marcus Fizer .25 .60
❑ 11 Lamond Murray .25 .60
❑ 12 Darius Miles .25 .60
❑ 13 Chris Mihm .25 .60
❑ 14 Dirk Nowitzki .60 1.50
❑ 15 Michael Finley .40 1.00
❑ 16 Steve Nash .60 1.50
❑ 17 James Posey .25 .60
❑ 18 Juwan Howard .30 .75
❑ 19 Kenny Satterfield .25 .60
❑ 20 Jerry Stackhouse .30 .75
❑ 21 Clifford Robinson .25 .60
❑ 22 Ben Wallace .30 .75
❑ 23 Antawn Jamison .40 1.00
❑ 24 Jason Richardson .40 1.00
❑ 25 Gilbert Arenas .40 1.00
❑ 26 Steve Francis .40 1.00
❑ 27 Cuttino Mobley .30 .75
❑ 28 Eddie Griffin .25 .60
❑ 29 Reggie Miller .40 1.00
❑ 30 Jermaine O'Neal .40 1.00
❑ 31 Jamaal Tinsley .30 .75
❑ 32 Elton Brand .40 1.00
❑ 33 Andre Miller .30 .75
❑ 34 Lamar Odom .40 1.00
❑ 35 Kobe Bryant 2.00 5.00
❑ 36 Shaquille O'Neal 1.00 2.50
❑ 37 Derek Fisher .30 .75
❑ 38 Devean George .25 .60
❑ 39 Pau Gasol .40 1.00
❑ 40 Jason Williams .30 .75
❑ 41 Shane Battier .30 .75
❑ 42 Alonzo Mourning .40 1.00
❑ 43 Eddie Jones .30 .75
❑ 44 Brian Grant .25 .60
❑ 45 Ray Allen .40 1.00
❑ 46 Tim Thomas .25 .60
❑ 47 Sam Cassell .30 .75
❑ 48 Kevin Garnett .75 2.00
❑ 49 Wally Szczerbiak .30 .75
❑ 50 Terrell Brandon .25 .60
❑ 51 Jason Kidd .60 1.50
❑ 52 Richard Jefferson .40 1.00
❑ 53 Dikembe Mutombo .30 .75
❑ 54 Jamal Mashburn .30 .75
❑ 55 Baron Davis .40 1.00
❑ 56 David Wesley .25 .60
❑ 57 Allan Houston .30 .75
❑ 58 Latrell Sprewell .30 .75
❑ 59 Antonio McDyess .30 .75
❑ 60 Tracy McGrady .75 2.00
❑ 61 Mike Miller .30 .75
❑ 62 Darrell Armstrong .25 .60
❑ 63 Allen Iverson .75 2.00
❑ 64 Keith Van Horn .30 .75
❑ 65 Aaron McKie .25 .60
❑ 66 Stephon Marbury .40 1.00
❑ 67 Shawn Marion .40 1.00
❑ 68 Anfernee Hardaway .40 1.00
❑ 69 Rasheed Wallace .40 1.00
❑ 70 Damon Stoudamire .30 .75
❑ 71 Scottie Pippen .60 1.50
❑ 72 Chris Webber .40 1.00
❑ 73 Mike Bibby .30 .75
❑ 74 Peja Stojakovic .30 .75
❑ 75 Tim Duncan .75 2.00
❑ 76 David Robinson .50 1.25
❑ 77 Tony Parker .40 1.00
❑ 78 Gary Payton .40 1.00
❑ 79 Rashard Lewis .40 1.00
❑ 80 Desmond Mason .30 .75
❑ 81 Vince Carter .75 2.00
❑ 82 Morris Peterson .30 .75
❑ 83 Antonio Davis .25 .60
❑ 84 Karl Malone .40 1.00
❑ 85 John Stockton .50 1.25
❑ 86 Andrei Kirilenko .40 1.00
❑ 87 Richard Hamilton .30 .75
❑ 88 Michael Jordan 2.50 6.00
❑ 89 Chris Whitney .25 .60
❑ 90 Kwame Brown .25 .60
❑ 91 Efthimios Rentzias RC 1.25 3.00
❑ 92 Marko Jaric 1.25 3.00
❑ 93 Jiri Welsch RC 1.25 3.00
❑ 94 Carlos Boozer RC 2.50 6.00
❑ 95 Fred Jones RC 1.50 4.00
❑ 96 Sam Clancy RC 1.25 3.00
❑ 97 Predrag Savovic RC 1.25 3.00
❑ 98 Frank Williams RC 1.25 3.00
❑ 99 Rod Grizzard RC 1.25 3.00
❑ 100 Casey Jacobsen RC 1.25 3.00
❑ 101 Jamal Sampson RC 1.25 3.00
❑ 102 Lonny Baxter RC 1.25 3.00
❑ 103 Darius Songaila RC 1.25 3.00
❑ 104 Tito Maddox RC 1.25 3.00
❑ 105 Chris Owens RC 1.25 3.00
❑ 106 Juan Dixon RC 2.00 5.00
❑ 107 Chris Jefferies RC 1.25 3.00
❑ 108 Dan Dickau RC 1.25 3.00
❑ 109 Manu Ginobili RC 3.00 8.00
❑ 110 Tamar Slay RC 1.25 3.00
❑ 111 Matt Barnes RC 1.50 4.00
❑ 112 Vincent Yarbrough RC 1.25 3.00
❑ 113 Bostjan Nachbar RC 1.25 3.00
❑ 114 Dan Gadzuric RC 1.25 3.00
❑ 115 Robert Archibald RC 1.25 3.00
❑ 116 Ryan Humphrey RC 1.25 3.00
❑ 117 Tayshaun Prince RC 2.00 5.00
❑ 118 John Salmons RC 2.00 5.00
❑ 119 Steve Logan RC 1.25 3.00
❑ 120 Melvin Ely RC 1.25 3.00
❑ 121 Nikoloz Tskitishvili RC 1.50 4.00
❑ 122 Qyntel Woods RC 1.50 4.00
❑ 123 Marcus Haislip RC 1.50 4.00
❑ 124 Nene Hilario RC 2.00 5.00
❑ 125 Amare Stoudemire RC 4.00 10.00
❑ 126 Jared Jeffries RC 1.50 4.00
❑ 127 Kareem Rush RC 2.00 5.00
❑ 128 Chris Wilcox RC 2.00 5.00
❑ 129 Curtis Borchardt RC 1.50 4.00
❑ 130 Drew Gooden RC 3.00 8.00
❑ 131 Mike Dunleavy RC 2.50 6.00
❑ 132 DaJuan Wagner RC 2.00 5.00
❑ 133 Caron Butler RC 4.00 10.00
❑ 134 Yao Ming RC 6.00 15.00
❑ 135 Jay Williams RC 2.50 6.00

2003-04 Upper Deck Hardcourt

❑ COMP.SET w/o SP's (90) 15.00 40.00
❑ COMMON CARD (1-90) .08 .20
❑ COMMON ROOKIE (91-126) 2.00 5.00
❑ COMMON ROOKIE (127-132) 4.00 10.00
❑ 1 Shareef Abdur-Rahim .30 .75
❑ 2 Jason Terry .30 .75
❑ 3 Glenn Robinson .30 .75
❑ 4 Paul Pierce .30 .75
❑ 5 Antoine Walker .30 .75
❑ 6 Vin Baker .20 .50
❑ 7 Jalen Rose .30 .75
❑ 8 Tyson Chandler .30 .75
❑ 9 Michael Jordan 2.00 5.00
❑ 10 DaJuan Wagner .20 .50
❑ 11 Ricky Davis .30 .75
❑ 12 Darius Miles .30 .75
❑ 13 Dirk Nowitzki .50 1.25
❑ 14 Michael Finley .30 .75
❑ 15 Steve Nash .30 .75
❑ 16 Nene .20 .50
❑ 17 Marcus Camby .20 .50
❑ 18 Nikoloz Tskitishvili .08 .20
❑ 19 Richard Hamilton .20 .50
❑ 20 Ben Wallace .30 .75
❑ 21 Tayshaun Prince .20 .50
❑ 22 Antawn Jamison .30 .75
❑ 23 Jason Richardson .30 .75
❑ 24 Gilbert Arenas .30 .75
❑ 25 Steve Francis .30 .75
❑ 26 Yao Ming .75 2.00
❑ 27 Eddie Griffin .20 .50
❑ 28 Reggie Miller .30 .75
❑ 29 Jamaal Tinsley .30 .75
❑ 30 Jermaine O'Neal .30 .75
❑ 31 Elton Brand .30 .75
❑ 32 Andre Miller .20 .50

33 Lamar Odom	.30	.75
34 Kobe Bryant	1.25	3.00
35 Gary Payton	.30	.75
36 Shaquille O'Neal	.75	2.00
37 Karl Malone	.30	.75
38 Pau Gasol	.30	.75
39 Shane Battier	.30	.75
40 Mike Miller	.30	.75
41 Eddie Jones	.30	.75
42 Rasual Butler	.20	.50
43 Caron Butler	.30	.75
44 Michael Redd	.30	.75
45 Joe Smith	.20	.50
46 Desmond Mason	.20	.50
47 Kevin Garnett	.60	1.50
48 Wally Szczerbiak	.20	.50
49 Sam Cassell	.30	.75
50 Jason Kidd	.50	1.25
51 Richard Jefferson	.20	.50
52 Alonzo Mourning	.20	.50
53 Baron Davis	.30	.75
54 Jamal Mashburn	.20	.50
55 Jamaal Magloire	.08	.20
56 Allan Houston	.20	.50
57 Antonio McDyess	.20	.50
58 Latrell Sprewell	.30	.75
59 Tracy McGrady	.75	2.00
60 Grant Hill	.30	.75
61 Drew Gooden	.20	.50
62 Allen Iverson	.60	1.50
63 Keith Van Horn	.30	.75
64 Kenny Thomas	.08	.20
65 Stephon Marbury	.30	.75
66 Shawn Marion	.30	.75
67 Amare Stoudemire	.60	1.50
68 Rasheed Wallace	.30	.75
69 Bonzi Wells	.20	.50
70 Damon Stoudamire	.20	.50
71 Chris Webber	.30	.75
72 Mike Bibby	.30	.75
73 Peja Stojakovic	.30	.75
74 Bobby Jackson	.20	.50
75 Tim Duncan	.60	1.50
76 David Robinson	.30	.75
77 Tony Parker	.30	.75
78 Manu Ginobili	.30	.75
79 Ray Allen	.30	.75
80 Rashard Lewis	.30	.75
81 Reggie Evans	.08	.20
82 Vince Carter	.75	2.00
83 Morris Peterson	.20	.50
84 Antonio Davis	.08	.20
85 Matt Harpring	.30	.75
86 John Stockton	.30	.75
87 Andrei Kirilenko	.30	.75
88 Jerry Stackhouse	.30	.75
89 Kwame Brown	.20	.50
90 Larry Hughes	.20	.50
91 Kirk Hinrich RC	2.50	6.00
92 T.J. Ford RC	2.00	4.00
93 Mike Sweetney RC	2.00	5.00
94 Jarvis Hayes RC	2.00	5.00
95 Mickael Pietrus RC	2.00	5.00
96 Nick Collison RC	2.00	5.00
97 Marcus Banks RC	2.00	5.00
98 Luke Ridnour RC	2.50	6.00
99 Reece Gaines RC	2.00	5.00
100 Troy Bell RC	2.00	5.00
101 Zarko Cabarkapa RC	2.00	5.00
102 David West RC	4.00	10.00
103 Aleksandar Pavlovic RC	2.50	6.00
104 Dahntay Jones RC	2.00	5.00
105 Boris Diaw RC	2.00	5.00
106 Zoran Planinic RC	2.00	5.00
107 Travis Outlaw RC	2.50	6.00
108 Brian Cook RC	2.00	5.00
109 Carlos Delfino RC	2.00	5.00
110 Ndudi Ebi RC	2.00	5.00
111 Kendrick Perkins RC	3.00	8.00
112 Leandro Barbosa RC	3.00	8.00
113 Josh Howard RC	2.50	6.00
114 Maciej Lampe RC	2.00	5.00
115 Jason Kapono RC	2.00	5.00
116 Luke Walton RC	2.00	5.00
117 Jerome Beasley RC	2.00	5.00
118 Sofoklis Schortsanitis RC	2.50	6.00
119 Kyle Korver RC	3.00	8.00
120 Travis Hansen RC	2.00	5.00
121 Steve Blake RC	2.00	5.00
122 Slavko Vranes RC	2.00	5.00
123 Zaur Pachulia RC	2.00	5.00
124 Keith Bogans RC	2.00	5.00
125 Matt Bonner RC	2.00	5.00
126 Maurice Williams RC	3.00	8.00
127 Chris Kaman RC	6.00	15.00
128 Dwyane Wade RC	12.00	25.00
129 Chris Bosh RC	6.00	15.00
130 Carmelo Anthony RC	10.00	25.00
131 Darko Milicic RC	3.00	8.00
132 LeBron James RC	50.00	100.00

2004-05 Upper Deck Hardcourt

COMP.SET w/o SP's (90)	15.00	40.00
COMMON CARD (1-90)	.20	.50
COMMON ROOKIE (91-96)	2.50	6.00
COMMON ROOKIE (97-132)	2.00	5.00
1 Boris Diaw	.25	.60
2 Antoine Walker	.30	.75
3 Al Harrington	.25	.60
4 Jiri Welsch	.20	.50
5 Paul Pierce	.30	.75
6 Ricky Davis	.25	.60
7 Gerald Wallace	.30	.75
8 Eddie House	.20	.50
9 Jason Kapono	.20	.50
10 Tyson Chandler	.25	.60
11 Eddy Curry	.25	.60
12 Kirk Hinrich	.25	.60
13 Jeff McInnis	.20	.50
14 Dajuan Wagner	.20	.50
15 LeBron James	2.00	5.00
16 Michael Finley	.30	.75
17 Dirk Nowitzki	.50	1.25
18 Marquis Daniels	.20	.50
19 Kenyon Martin	.30	.75
20 Carmelo Anthony	1.00	2.50
21 Nene	.25	.60
22 Ben Wallace	.25	.60
23 Richard Hamilton	.25	.60
24 Rasheed Wallace	.30	.75
25 Mike Dunleavy	.25	.60
26 Jason Richardson	.30	.75
27 Derek Fisher	.25	.60
28 Tracy McGrady	.60	1.50
29 Tyronn Lue	.20	.50
30 Yao Ming	.75	2.00
31 Jermaine O'Neal	.30	.75
32 Reggie Miller	.30	.75
33 Stephen Jackson	.25	.60
34 Corey Maggette	.25	.60
35 Elton Brand	.30	.75
36 Marko Jaric	.20	.50
37 Karl Malone	.30	.75
38 Kobe Bryant	1.50	4.00
39 Lamar Odom	.30	.75
40 James Posey	.20	.50
41 Mike Miller	.25	.60
42 Pau Gasol	.30	.75
43 Dwyane Wade	1.00	2.50
44 Eddie Jones	.25	.60
45 Shaquille O'Neal	.75	2.00
46 Desmond Mason	.25	.60
47 Michael Redd	.30	.75
48 T.J. Ford	.25	.60
49 Kevin Garnett	.60	1.50
50 Latrell Sprewell	.25	.60
51 Sam Cassell	.25	.60
52 Jason Kidd	.50	1.25
53 Aaron Williams	.20	.50
54 Richard Jefferson	.30	.75
55 Baron Davis	.30	.75
56 Jamaal Magloire	.20	.50
57 Jamal Mashburn	.25	.60
58 Allan Houston	.25	.60
59 Jamal Crawford	.25	.60
60 Stephon Marbury	.30	.75
61 Hedo Turkoglu	.25	.60
62 Steve Francis	.30	.75
63 Cuttino Mobley	.25	.60
64 Allen Iverson	.60	1.50
65 Glenn Robinson	.25	.60
66 Kenny Thomas	.20	.50
67 Amare Stoudemire	.60	1.50
68 Quentin Richardson	.25	.60
69 Shawn Marion	.30	.75
70 Darius Miles	.25	.60
71 Shareef Abdur-Rahim	.25	.60
72 Zach Randolph	.30	.75
73 Chris Webber	.30	.75
74 Mike Bibby	.25	.60
75 Peja Stojakovic	.25	.60
76 Manu Ginobili	.30	.75
77 Tim Duncan	.60	1.50
78 Tony Parker	.30	.75
79 Rashard Lewis	.30	.75
80 Ray Allen	.30	.75
81 Ronald Murray	.20	.50
82 Chris Bosh	.30	.75
83 Jalen Rose	.25	.60
84 Vince Carter	.60	1.50
85 Andrei Kirilenko	.30	.75
86 Carlos Arroyo	.30	.75
87 Carlos Boozer	.30	.75
88 Gilbert Arenas	.30	.75
89 Jarvis Hayes	.20	.50
90 Antawn Jamison	.30	.75
91 Dwight Howard RC	8.00	20.00
92 Emeka Okafor RC	5.00	12.00
93 Ben Gordon RC	3.00	8.00
94 Shaun Livingston RC	2.50	6.00
95 Devin Harris RC	5.00	12.00
96 Josh Childress RC	2.50	6.00
97 Luol Deng RC	2.50	6.00
98 Andre Iguodala RC	5.00	12.00
99 Luke Jackson RC	2.00	5.00
100 Andris Biedrins RC	3.00	8.00
101 Sebastian Telfair RC	2.00	5.00
102 Josh Smith RC	5.00	12.00
103 Rafael Araujo RC	2.00	5.00
104 Robert Swift RC	2.00	5.00
105 Kris Humphries RC	3.00	8.00
106 Al Jefferson RC	4.00	10.00
107 Kirk Snyder RC	2.00	5.00
108 J.R. Smith RC	4.00	10.00
109 Dorell Wright RC	2.50	6.00
110 Jameer Nelson RC	2.50	6.00
111 Pavel Podkolzine RC	2.00	5.00
112 Justin Reed RC	2.00	5.00
113 Sergei Monia RC	2.00	5.00
114 Delonte West RC	3.00	8.00
115 Tony Allen RC	2.50	6.00
116 Kevin Martin RC	2.50	6.00
117 Sasha Vujacic RC	2.00	5.00
118 Beno Udrih RC	2.50	6.00
119 David Harrison RC	2.00	5.00
120 Anderson Varejao RC	2.50	6.00
121 Jackson Vroman RC	2.00	5.00
122 Peter John Ramos RC	2.00	5.00
123 Lionel Chalmers RC	2.00	5.00
124 Donta Smith RC	2.00	5.00
125 Andre Emmett RC	2.00	5.00
126 Antonio Burks RC	2.00	5.00
127 Royal Ivey RC	2.00	5.00
128 Chris Duhon RC	3.00	8.00
129 Trevor Ariza RC	2.50	6.00
130 Ha Seung-Jin RC	2.00	5.00
131 Romain Sato RC	2.00	5.00
132 Rickey Paulding RC	2.00	5.00

2005-06 Upper Deck Hardcourt

❑ COMP.SET w/o SP's (90)	15.00	40.00
❑ COMMON CARD (1-90)	.20	.50
❑ COMMON ROOKIE (91-140)	2.00	5.00
❑ 1 Tony Delk	.20	.50
❑ 2 Josh Smith	.30	.75
❑ 3 Al Harrington	.20	.50
❑ 4 Antoine Walker	.25	.60
❑ 5 Gary Payton	.30	.75
❑ 6 Paul Pierce	.30	.75
❑ 7 Kareem Rush	.20	.50
❑ 8 Emeka Okafor	.30	.75
❑ 9 Primoz Brezec	.20	.50
❑ 10 Eddy Curry	.25	.60
❑ 11 Kirk Hinrich	.30	.75
❑ 12 Ben Gordon	.40	1.00
❑ 13 Drew Gooden	.25	.60
❑ 14 LeBron James	1.50	4.00
❑ 15 Zydrunas Ilgauskas	.25	.60
❑ 16 Dirk Nowitzki	.50	1.25
❑ 17 Jason Terry	.30	.75
❑ 18 Jerry Stackhouse	.30	.75
❑ 19 Carmelo Anthony	.60	1.50
❑ 20 Kenyon Martin	.30	.75
❑ 21 Earl Boykins	.20	.50
❑ 22 Ben Wallace	.30	.75
❑ 23 Chauncey Billups	.30	.75
❑ 24 Richard Hamilton	.25	.60
❑ 25 Troy Murphy	.30	.75
❑ 26 Jason Richardson	.30	.75
❑ 27 Baron Davis	.30	.75
❑ 28 Tracy McGrady	.60	1.50
❑ 29 Yao Ming	.75	2.00
❑ 30 Juwan Howard	.25	.60
❑ 31 Jermaine O'Neal	.30	.75
❑ 32 Stephen Jackson	.25	.60
❑ 33 Ron Artest	.25	.60
❑ 34 Corey Maggette	.25	.60
❑ 35 Elton Brand	.30	.75
❑ 36 Bobby Simmons	.20	.50
❑ 37 Caron Butler	.30	.75
❑ 38 Kobe Bryant	1.50	4.00
❑ 39 Lamar Odom	.30	.75
❑ 40 Mike Miller	.30	.75
❑ 41 Jason Williams	.25	.60
❑ 42 Pau Gasol	.30	.75
❑ 43 Dwyane Wade	.75	2.00
❑ 44 Eddie Jones	.20	.50
❑ 45 Shaquille O'Neal	.75	2.00
❑ 46 Desmond Mason	.20	.50
❑ 47 Maurice Williams	.25	.60
❑ 48 Michael Redd	.30	.75
❑ 49 Kevin Garnett	.60	1.50
❑ 50 Latrell Sprewell	.20	.50
❑ 51 Sam Cassell	.30	.75
❑ 52 Vince Carter	.60	1.50
❑ 53 Jason Kidd	.50	1.25
❑ 54 Richard Jefferson	.25	.60
❑ 55 Dan Dickau	.20	.50
❑ 56 Jamaal Magloire	.20	.50
❑ 57 J.R. Smith	.25	.60
❑ 58 Jamal Crawford	.25	.60
❑ 59 Stephon Marbury	.30	.75
❑ 60 Allan Houston	.20	.50
❑ 61 Dwight Howard	.60	1.50
❑ 62 Grant Hill	.30	.75
❑ 63 Steve Francis	.30	.75
❑ 64 Allen Iverson	.60	1.50
❑ 65 Andre Iguodala	.30	.75
❑ 66 Chris Webber	.30	.75
❑ 67 Amare Stoudemire	.60	1.50
❑ 68 Shawn Marion	.30	.75
❑ 69 Steve Nash	.40	1.00
❑ 70 Damon Stoudamire	.25	.60
❑ 71 Shareef Abdur-Rahim	.30	.75
❑ 72 Zach Randolph	.30	.75
❑ 73 Mike Bibby	.30	.75
❑ 74 Peja Stojakovic	.30	.75
❑ 75 Brad Miller	.30	.75
❑ 76 Manu Ginobili	.30	.75
❑ 77 Tim Duncan	.60	1.50
❑ 78 Tony Parker	.30	.75
❑ 79 Rashard Lewis	.30	.75
❑ 80 Ray Allen	.30	.75
❑ 81 Ronald Murray	.20	.50
❑ 82 Rafer Alston	.20	.50
❑ 83 Jalen Rose	.30	.75
❑ 84 Chris Bosh	.30	.75
❑ 85 Andrei Kirilenko	.30	.75
❑ 86 Carlos Boozer	.30	.75
❑ 87 Matt Harpring	.25	.60
❑ 88 Antawn Jamison	.30	.75
❑ 89 Gilbert Arenas	.30	.75
❑ 90 Larry Hughes	.25	.60
❑ 91 Linas Kleiza RC	2.50	6.00
❑ 92 Julius Hodge RC	2.50	6.00
❑ 93 David Lee RC	4.00	10.00
❑ 94 Sarunas Jasikevicius RC	2.50	6.00
❑ 95 Jason Maxiell RC	2.50	6.00
❑ 96 Luther Head RC	2.50	6.00
❑ 97 Brandon Bass RC	2.00	5.00
❑ 98 Ricky Sanchez RC	2.00	5.00
❑ 99 Ersan Ilyasova RC	2.00	5.00
❑ 100 Andray Blatche RC	2.50	6.00
❑ 101 Sean May RC	2.50	6.00
❑ 102 Ike Diogu RC	2.50	6.00
❑ 103 Nate Robinson RC	3.00	8.00
❑ 105 Bracey Wright RC	2.00	5.00
❑ 106 Daniel Ewing RC	2.50	6.00
❑ 107 Salim Stoudamire RC	2.50	6.00
❑ 108 Dijon Thompson RC	2.00	5.00
❑ 109 Danny Granger RC	5.00	12.00
❑ 110 Raymond Felton RC	2.50	6.00
❑ 111 Louis Williams RC	3.00	8.00
❑ 112 Channing Frye RC	2.50	6.00
❑ 113 Francisco Garcia RC	2.50	6.00
❑ 114 Ryan Gomes RC	2.00	5.00
❑ 115 Travis Diener RC	2.00	5.00
❑ 116 Jarrett Jack RC	2.00	5.00
❑ 118 Von Wafer RC	2.00	5.00
❑ 119 C.J. Miles RC	2.00	5.00
❑ 120 Lawrence Roberts RC	2.00	5.00
❑ 121 Amir Johnson RC	2.00	5.00
❑ 122 Monta Ellis RC	5.00	12.00
❑ 123 Martell Webster RC	2.00	5.00
❑ 124 Johan Petro RC	2.00	5.00
❑ 126 Andrew Bynum RC	6.00	15.00
❑ 127 Martynas Andriuskevicius RC	2.00	5.00
❑ 128 Charlie Villanueva RC	3.00	8.00
❑ 129 Antoine Wright RC	2.00	5.00
❑ 130 Joey Graham RC	2.00	5.00
❑ 131 Wayne Simien RC	2.50	6.00
❑ 132 Hakim Warrick RC	3.00	8.00
❑ 133 Gerald Green RC	2.00	5.00
❑ 134 Marvin Williams RC	3.00	8.00
❑ 135 Deron Williams RC	5.00	12.00
❑ 136 Rashad McCants RC	2.50	6.00
❑ 137 Yaroslav Korolev RC	2.00	5.00
❑ 138 Chris Taft RC	2.00	5.00
❑ 139 Chris Paul RC	6.00	15.00
❑ 140 Andrew Bogut RC	2.50	6.00

2006-07 Upper Deck Hardcourt

❑ COMP.SET w/o SP's (100)	15.00	40.00
❑ 1 Joe Johnson	.25	.60
❑ 2 Salim Stoudamire	.25	.60
❑ 3 Marvin Williams	.30	.75
❑ 4 Dan Dickau	.20	.50
❑ 5 Paul Pierce	.30	.75
❑ 6 Wally Szczerbiak	.25	.60
❑ 7 Raymond Felton	.40	1.00
❑ 8 Emeka Okafor	.30	.75
❑ 9 Gerald Wallace	.30	.75
❑ 10 Tyson Chandler	.30	.75
❑ 11 Luol Deng	.30	.75
❑ 12 Ben Gordon	.40	1.00
❑ 13 Michael Jordan	2.00	5.00
❑ 14 Drew Gooden	.25	.60
❑ 15 Larry Hughes	.25	.60
❑ 16 Zydrunas Ilgauskas	.25	.60
❑ 17 LeBron James	1.50	4.00
❑ 18 Erick Dampier	.20	.50
❑ 19 Devin Harris	.30	.75
❑ 20 Dirk Nowitzki	.50	1.25
❑ 21 Jason Terry	.30	.75
❑ 22 Carmelo Anthony	.40	1.00
❑ 23 Earl Boykins	.20	.50
❑ 24 Marcus Camby	.25	.60
❑ 25 Kenyon Martin	.30	.75
❑ 26 Chauncey Billups	.30	.75
❑ 27 Richard Hamilton	.25	.60
❑ 28 Antonio McDyess	.20	.50
❑ 29 Ben Wallace	.30	.75
❑ 30 Baron Davis	.30	.75
❑ 31 Derek Fisher	.25	.60
❑ 32 Troy Murphy	.30	.75
❑ 33 Jason Richardson	.30	.75
❑ 34 Luther Head	.25	.60
❑ 35 Tracy McGrady	.60	1.50
❑ 36 Yao Ming	.75	2.00
❑ 37 Danny Granger	.25	.60
❑ 38 Jermaine O'Neal	.30	.75
❑ 39 Peja Stojakovic	.30	.75
❑ 40 Elton Brand	.30	.75
❑ 41 Sam Cassell	.30	.75
❑ 42 Chris Kaman	.20	.50
❑ 43 Shaun Livingston	.20	.50
❑ 44 Kwame Brown	.25	.60
❑ 45 Kobe Bryant	1.50	4.00
❑ 46 Andrew Bynum	.30	.75
❑ 47 Shane Battier	.30	.75
❑ 48 Pau Gasol	.30	.75
❑ 49 Mike Miller	.30	.75
❑ 50 Hakim Warrick	.25	.60
❑ 51 Shaquille O'Neal	.75	2.00
❑ 52 Dwyane Wade	.75	2.00
❑ 53 Jason Williams	.25	.60
❑ 54 Andrew Bogut	.30	.75
❑ 55 T.J. Ford	.25	.60
❑ 56 Jamaal Magloire	.20	.50
❑ 57 Michael Redd	.30	.75
❑ 58 Ricky Davis	.30	.75
❑ 59 Kevin Garnett	.60	1.50
❑ 60 Rashad McCants	.25	.60
❑ 61 Vince Carter	.60	1.50
❑ 62 Richard Jefferson	.25	.60
❑ 63 Jason Kidd	.50	1.25
❑ 64 Desmond Mason	.20	.50
❑ 65 Chris Paul	.60	1.50
❑ 66 J.R. Smith	.25	.60
❑ 67 Jamal Crawford	.20	.50
❑ 68 Channing Frye	.25	.60
❑ 69 Stephon Marbury	.30	.75
❑ 70 Quentin Richardson	.25	.60
❑ 71 Dwight Howard	.60	1.50
❑ 72 Darko Milicic	.30	.75
❑ 73 Jameer Nelson	.25	.60
❑ 74 Andre Iguodala	.30	.75
❑ 75 Allen Iverson	.60	1.50
❑ 76 Chris Webber	.30	.75
❑ 77 Shawn Marion	.30	.75
❑ 78 Steve Nash	.40	1.00
❑ 79 Amare Stoudemire	.60	1.50
❑ 80 Zach Randolph	.30	.75
❑ 81 Sebastian Telfair	.25	.60
❑ 82 Martell Webster	.25	.60
❑ 83 Ron Artest	.30	.75
❑ 84 Mike Bibby	.30	.75
❑ 85 Brad Miller	.30	.75
❑ 86 Tim Duncan	.60	1.50
❑ 87 Manu Ginobili	.30	.75
❑ 88 Tony Parker	.30	.75
❑ 89 Ray Allen	.30	.75
❑ 90 Danny Fortson	.20	.50
❑ 91 Rashard Lewis	.30	.75
❑ 92 Chris Bosh	.30	.75

❑ 93 Joey Graham	.25	.60
❑ 94 Charlie Villanueva	.30	.75
❑ 95 Carlos Boozer	.30	.75
❑ 96 Andrei Kirilenko	.30	.75
❑ 97 Deron Williams	.50	1.25
❑ 98 Gilbert Arenas	.30	.75
❑ 99 Caron Butler	.30	.75
❑ 100 Antawn Jamison	.30	.75
❑ 101 Adam Morrison RC	2.00	5.00
❑ 102 Randy Foye RC	1.50	4.00
❑ 103 Rudy Gay RC	1.50	4.00
❑ 104 Patrick O'Bryant RC	1.50	4.00
❑ 105 Saer Sene RC	1.50	4.00
❑ 106 J.J. Redick RC	1.50	4.00
❑ 107 Hilton Armstrong RC	1.50	4.00
❑ 108 Thabo Sefolosha RC	2.00	5.00
❑ 109 Cedric Simmons RC	1.50	4.00
❑ 110 Shawne Williams RC	1.50	4.00
❑ 111 Tarence Kinsey RC	1.50	4.00
❑ 112 Quincy Douby RC	1.50	4.00
❑ 113 Renaldo Balkman RC	1.50	4.00
❑ 114 Josh Boone RC	1.50	4.00
❑ 115 Kyle Lowry RC	1.50	4.00
❑ 116 Shannon Brown RC	1.50	4.00
❑ 117 Jordan Farmar RC	2.00	5.00
❑ 118 Joel Freeland RC	1.50	4.00
❑ 119 Paul Davis RC	1.50	4.00
❑ 120 P.J. Tucker RC	1.50	4.00
❑ 121 Craig Smith RC	1.50	4.00
❑ 122 Bobby Jones RC	1.50	4.00
❑ 123 David Noel RC	1.50	4.00
❑ 124 Denham Brown RC	1.50	4.00
❑ 125 James Augustine RC	1.50	4.00
❑ 126 Daniel Gibson RC	2.00	5.00
❑ 127 Allan Ray RC	1.50	4.00
❑ 128 Alexander Johnson RC	1.50	4.00
❑ 129 Dee Brown RC	1.50	4.00
❑ 130 Paul Millsap RC	2.50	6.00
❑ 131 Leon Powe RC	1.50	4.00
❑ 132 Ryan Hollins RC	1.50	4.00
❑ 133 Mike Gansey RC	1.50	4.00
❑ 134 Hassan Adams RC	2.00	5.00
❑ 135 Will Blalock RC	1.50	4.00
❑ 136 A.Bargnani AU RC EXCH	8.00	12.00
❑ 137 LaMarcus Aldridge AU RC	8.00	20.00
❑ 138 Tyrus Thomas AU RC	8.00	20.00
❑ 139 Shelden Williams AU RC	8.00	20.00
❑ 140 Brandon Roy AU RC	25.00	50.00
❑ 141 Ronnie Brewer AU RC	6.00	15.00
❑ 142 Rodney Carney AU RC	6.00	15.00
❑ 143 Rajon Rondo AU RC	25.00	50.00
❑ 144 Marc.Williams AU RC EXCH	10.00	25.00
❑ 145 Kevin Pittsnogle AU RC	8.00	20.00
❑ 146 Maurice Ager AU RC	6.00	15.00
❑ 147 Mardy Collins AU RC	8.00	20.00
❑ 148 James White AU RC	6.00	15.00
❑ 149 Steve Novak AU RC	8.00	20.00
❑ 150 Solomon Jones AU RC	6.00	15.00

1999-00 Upper Deck HoloGrFX

❑ COMPLETE SET (90)	30.00	60.00
❑ COMPLETE SET w/o RC (60)	10.00	20.00
❑ COMMON CARD (1-60)	.20	.50
❑ COMMON ROOKIE (61-90)	.40	1.00
❑ 1 Dikembe Mutombo	.25	.60
❑ 2 Alan Henderson	.20	.50
❑ 3 Antoine Walker	.30	.75
❑ 4 Paul Pierce	.30	.75
❑ 5 Eddie Jones	.30	.75
❑ 6 David Wesley	.20	.50
❑ 7 Dickey Simpkins	.20	.50
❑ 8 Toni Kukoc	.30	.75
❑ 9 Shawn Kemp	.30	.75
❑ 10 Zydrunas Ilgauskas	.25	.60
❑ 11 Michael Finley	.30	.75
❑ 12 Cedric Ceballos	.20	.50
❑ 13 Antonio McDyess	.25	.60
❑ 14 Nick Van Exel	.25	.60
❑ 15 Grant Hill	.30	.75
❑ 16 Bison Dele	.20	.50
❑ 17 Jerry Stackhouse	.30	.75
❑ 18 Antawn Jamison	.30	.75
❑ 19 John Starks	.30	.75
❑ 20 Scottie Pippen	.50	1.25
❑ 21 Charles Barkley	.40	1.00
❑ 22 Hakeem Olajuwon	.30	.75
❑ 23 Reggie Miller	.30	.75
❑ 24 Rik Smits	.30	.75
❑ 25 Michael Olowokandi	.20	.50
❑ 26 Maurice Taylor	.25	.60
❑ 27 Shaquille O'Neal	.75	2.00
❑ 28 Kobe Bryant	1.50	4.00
❑ 29 Tim Hardaway	.30	.75
❑ 30 Alonzo Mourning	.30	.75
❑ 31 Ray Allen	.30	.75
❑ 32 Glenn Robinson	.25	.60
❑ 33 Kevin Garnett	.60	1.50
❑ 34 Terrell Brandon	.20	.50
❑ 35 Stephon Marbury	.30	.75
❑ 36 Keith Van Horn	.25	.60
❑ 37 Allan Houston	.25	.60
❑ 38 Latrell Sprewell	.25	.60
❑ 39 Bo Outlaw	.20	.50
❑ 40 Darrell Armstrong	.20	.50
❑ 41 Allen Iverson	.60	1.50
❑ 42 Larry Hughes	.25	.60
❑ 43 Jason Kidd	.50	1.25
❑ 44 Tom Gugliotta	.20	.50
❑ 45 Damon Stoudamire	.30	.75
❑ 46 Rasheed Wallace	.30	.75
❑ 47 Jason Williams	.30	.75
❑ 48 Chris Webber	.30	.75
❑ 49 Tim Duncan	.60	1.50
❑ 50 David Robinson	.40	1.00
❑ 51 Gary Payton	.30	.75
❑ 52 Vin Baker	.30	.75
❑ 53 Vince Carter	.60	1.50
❑ 54 Tracy McGrady	.60	1.50
❑ 55 John Stockton	.40	1.00
❑ 56 Karl Malone	.40	1.00
❑ 57 Mike Bibby	.30	.75
❑ 58 Shareef Abdur-Rahim	.25	.60
❑ 59 Juwan Howard	.25	.60
❑ 60 Mitch Richmond	.25	.60
❑ 61 Elton Brand RC	1.25	3.00
❑ 62 Lamar Odom RC	1.25	3.00
❑ 63 Kenny Thomas RC	.40	1.00
❑ 64 Scott Padgett RC	.40	1.00
❑ 65 Trajan Langdon RC	.40	1.00
❑ 66 James Posey RC	.60	1.50
❑ 67 Shawn Marion RC	1.25	3.00
❑ 68 Chris Herren RC	.40	1.00
❑ 69 Tim James RC	.40	1.00
❑ 70 Evan Eschmeyer RC	.40	1.00
❑ 71 Corey Maggette RC	1.25	3.00
❑ 72 Richard Hamilton RC	1.25	3.00
❑ 73 Baron Davis RC	1.50	4.00
❑ 74 Galen Young RC	.40	1.00
❑ 75 Dion Glover RC	.40	1.00
❑ 76 Jumaine Jones RC	.40	1.00
❑ 77 Wally Szczerbiak RC	1.25	3.00
❑ 78 Andre Miller RC	1.25	3.00
❑ 79 Devean George RC	.60	1.50
❑ 80 Obinna Ekezie RC	.40	1.00
❑ 81 Steve Francis RC	1.25	3.00
❑ 82 Jason Terry RC	1.00	2.50
❑ 83 Quincy Lewis RC	.40	1.00
❑ 84 Ryan Robertson RC	.40	1.00
❑ 85 William Avery RC	.40	1.00
❑ 86 A.Radojevic RC	.40	1.00
❑ 87 Jonathan Bender RC	.40	1.00
❑ 88 Cal Bowdler RC	.40	1.00
❑ 89 Vonteego Cummings RC	.40	1.00
❑ 90 Jeff Foster RC	.50	1.25

2001-02 Upper Deck Honor Roll

❑ COMPLETE SET (130)	125.00	350.00
❑ COMP.SET w/o SP's (90)	20.00	40.00
❑ COMMON CARD (1-90)	.08	.25
❑ COMMON ROOKIE (91-120)	1.00	2.50
❑ COMMON JSY RC (121-130)	4.00	10.00
❑ 1 Shareef Abdur-Rahim	.25	.60
❑ 2 Jason Terry	.30	.75
❑ 3 Dion Glover	.20	.50
❑ 4 Paul Pierce	.30	.75
❑ 5 Antoine Walker	.25	.60
❑ 6 Kenny Anderson	.25	.60
❑ 7 Baron Davis	.30	.75
❑ 8 Jamal Mashburn	.25	.60
❑ 9 David Wesley	.20	.50
❑ 10 Ron Mercer	.20	.50
❑ 11 Brad Miller	.25	.60
❑ 12 Andre Miller	.25	.60
❑ 13 Lamond Murray	.20	.50
❑ 14 Chris Mihm	.20	.50
❑ 15 Michael Finley	.30	.75
❑ 16 Dirk Nowitzki	.50	1.25
❑ 17 Steve Nash	.50	1.25
❑ 18 Juwan Howard	.25	.60
❑ 19 Nick Van Exel	.25	.60
❑ 20 Raef LaFrentz	.20	.50
❑ 21 Antonio McDyess	.25	.60
❑ 22 James Posey	.20	.50
❑ 23 Jerry Stackhouse	.25	.60
❑ 24 Clifford Robinson	.20	.50
❑ 25 Ben Wallace	.25	.60
❑ 26 Antawn Jamison	.30	.75
❑ 27 Larry Hughes	.25	.60
❑ 28 Steve Francis	.30	.75
❑ 29 Cuttino Mobley	.25	.60
❑ 30 Glen Rice	.25	.60
❑ 31 Reggie Miller	.30	.75
❑ 32 Jalen Rose	.25	.60
❑ 33 Jermaine O'Neal	.30	.75
❑ 34 Darius Miles	.20	.50
❑ 35 Elton Brand	.30	.75
❑ 36 Lamar Odom	.30	.75
❑ 37 Corey Maggette	.25	.60
❑ 38 Kobe Bryant	1.50	4.00
❑ 39 Shaquille O'Neal	.75	2.00
❑ 40 Rick Fox	.25	.60
❑ 41 Lindsey Hunter	.20	.50
❑ 42 Stromile Swift	.20	.50
❑ 43 Jason Williams	.25	.60
❑ 44 Alonzo Mourning	.30	.75
❑ 45 Eddie Jones	.25	.60
❑ 46 Anthony Carter	.20	.50
❑ 47 Brian Grant	.20	.50
❑ 48 Ray Allen	.30	.75
❑ 49 Glenn Robinson	.25	.60
❑ 50 Sam Cassell	.25	.60
❑ 51 Kevin Garnett	.60	1.50
❑ 52 Terrell Brandon	.20	.50
❑ 53 Wally Szczerbiak	.25	.60
❑ 54 Joe Smith	.20	.50
❑ 55 Jason Kidd	.50	1.25
❑ 56 Kenyon Martin	.30	.75
❑ 57 Allan Houston	.25	.60
❑ 58 Latrell Sprewell	.25	.60
❑ 59 Marcus Camby	.25	.60
❑ 60 Mark Jackson	.25	.60
❑ 61 Tracy McGrady	.60	1.50
❑ 62 Grant Hill	.30	.75
❑ 63 Mike Miller	.25	.60
❑ 64 Allen Iverson	.60	1.50
❑ 65 Dikembe Mutombo	.25	.60
❑ 66 Aaron McKie	.20	.50
❑ 67 Stephon Marbury	.30	.75

❑ 68 Shawn Marion	.30	.75
❑ 69 Anfernee Hardaway	.30	.75
❑ 70 Tom Gugliotta	.20	.50
❑ 71 Rasheed Wallace	.30	.75
❑ 72 Damon Stoudamire	.25	.60
❑ 73 Derek Anderson	.25	.60
❑ 74 Chris Webber	.30	.75
❑ 75 Mike Bibby	.25	.60
❑ 76 Peja Stojakovic	.25	.60
❑ 77 Tim Duncan	.60	1.50
❑ 78 David Robinson	.40	1.00
❑ 79 Steve Smith	.25	.60
❑ 80 Gary Payton	.30	.75
❑ 81 Rashard Lewis	.30	.75
❑ 82 Desmond Mason	.25	.60
❑ 83 Vince Carter	.60	1.50
❑ 84 Morris Peterson	.25	.60
❑ 85 Antonio Davis	.20	.50
❑ 86 Karl Malone	.40	1.00
❑ 87 John Stockton	.40	1.00
❑ 88 Donyell Marshall	.20	.50
❑ 89 Richard Hamilton	.25	.60
❑ 90 Michael Jordan	5.00	12.00
❑ 91 Andrei Kirilenko RC	2.50	6.00
❑ 92 Gilbert Arenas RC	1.50	4.00
❑ 93 Earl Watson RC	1.25	3.00
❑ 94 Terence Morris RC	1.00	2.50
❑ 95 Kedrick Brown RC	1.00	2.50
❑ 96 Zach Randolph RC	2.50	6.00
❑ 97 Joe Johnson RC	2.50	6.00
❑ 98 Brandon Armstrong RC	1.00	2.50
❑ 99 DeSagana Diop RC	1.00	2.50
❑ 100 Joseph Forte RC	1.00	2.50
❑ 101 Brendan Haywood RC	1.25	3.00
❑ 102 Samuel Dalembert RC	1.25	3.00
❑ 103 Jason Collins RC	1.00	2.50
❑ 104 Michael Bradley RC	1.00	2.50
❑ 105 Gerald Wallace RC	2.50	6.00
❑ 106 Tierre Brown RC	1.00	2.50
❑ 107 Troy Murphy RC	2.00	5.00
❑ 108 Alton Ford RC	1.00	2.50
❑ 109 Vladimir Radmanovic RC	1.25	3.00
❑ 110 Ruben Boumtje-Boumtje RC	1.00	2.50
❑ 111 Bobby Simmons RC	1.00	2.50
❑ 112 Oscar Torres RC	1.00	2.50
❑ 113 Jeryl Sasser RC	1.00	2.50
❑ 114 Loren Woods RC	1.00	2.50
❑ 115 Shane Battier RC	1.50	4.00
❑ 116 Jamison Brewer RC	1.00	2.50
❑ 117 Richard Jefferson RC	2.50	6.00
❑ 118 Pau Gasol RC	4.00	10.00
❑ 119 Damone Brown RC	1.00	2.50
❑ 120 Rodney White RC	1.00	2.50
❑ 121 Kw.Brown RC/Garnett JSY	8.00	20.00
❑ 122 Chandler RC/Miles JSY	4.00	10.00
❑ 123 Curry RC/Malone JSY	8.00	20.00
❑ 124 Richardson RC/Kobe JSY	8.00	20.00
❑ 125 Parker RC/Kidd JSY	15.00	40.00
❑ 126 Griffin RC/A.Hardaway JSY	5.00	12.00
❑ 127 Haston RC/Mash JSY	5.00	12.00
❑ 128 Tinsley RC/A.Miller JSY	4.00	10.00
❑ 129 Hassell RC/Fizer JSY	4.00	10.00
❑ 130 Hunter RC/T-Mac JSY	8.00	20.00

2002-03 Upper Deck Honor Roll

❑ COMP.SET w/o SP's (90)	12.50	30.00
❑ COMMON CARD (1-90)	.08	.20
❑ COMMON JSY RC (91-105)	3.00	8.00
❑ COMMON ROOKIE (106-135)	2.00	5.00
❑ 1 Glenn Robinson	.25	.60
❑ 2 Shareef Abdur-Rahim	.25	.60
❑ 3 Jason Terry	.30	.75
❑ 4 Paul Pierce	.30	.75
❑ 5 Antoine Walker	.25	.60
❑ 6 Tony Delk	.20	.50
❑ 7 Jalen Rose	.25	.60
❑ 8 Tyson Chandler	.25	.60
❑ 9 Eddy Curry	.25	.60
❑ 10 Darius Miles	.20	.50
❑ 11 Zydrunas Ilgauskas	.25	.60
❑ 12 Ricky Davis	.25	.60
❑ 13 Dirk Nowitzki	.50	1.25
❑ 14 Michael Finley	.30	.75
❑ 15 Steve Nash	.50	1.25
❑ 16 Raef LaFrentz	.20	.50
❑ 17 Eduardo Najera	.20	.50
❑ 18 Rodney White	.20	.50
❑ 19 Juwan Howard	.25	.60
❑ 20 Chris Whitney	.20	.50
❑ 21 Ben Wallace	.25	.60
❑ 22 Richard Hamilton	.25	.60
❑ 23 Chauncey Billups	.30	.75
❑ 24 Chucky Atkins	.20	.50
❑ 25 Jason Richardson	.30	.75
❑ 26 Antawn Jamison	.30	.75
❑ 27 Gilbert Arenas	.30	.75
❑ 28 Steve Francis	.30	.75
❑ 29 Cuttino Mobley	.25	.60
❑ 30 Jermaine O'Neal	.30	.75
❑ 31 Reggie Miller	.30	.75
❑ 32 Jamaal Tinsley	.25	.60
❑ 33 Andre Miller	.25	.60
❑ 34 Elton Brand	.30	.75
❑ 35 Quentin Richardson	.25	.60
❑ 36 Shaquille O'Neal	.75	2.00
❑ 37 Kobe Bryant	1.50	4.00
❑ 38 Robert Horry	.25	.60
❑ 39 Shane Battier	.25	.60
❑ 40 Pau Gasol	.30	.75
❑ 41 Stromile Swift	.20	.50
❑ 42 Eddie Jones	.25	.60
❑ 43 Brian Grant	.20	.50
❑ 44 Malik Allen	.20	.50
❑ 45 Ray Allen	.30	.75
❑ 46 Tim Thomas	.20	.50
❑ 47 Kevin Garnett	.60	1.50
❑ 48 Wally Szczerbiak	.25	.60
❑ 49 Jason Kidd	.50	1.25
❑ 50 Kenyon Martin	.30	.75
❑ 51 Richard Jefferson	.30	.75
❑ 52 Baron Davis	.30	.75
❑ 53 Jamal Mashburn	.25	.60
❑ 54 David Wesley	.20	.50
❑ 55 P.J. Brown	.20	.50
❑ 56 Allan Houston	.25	.60
❑ 57 Latrell Sprewell	.25	.60
❑ 58 Kurt Thomas	.20	.50
❑ 59 Tracy McGrady	.60	1.50
❑ 60 Grant Hill	.30	.75
❑ 61 Mike Miller	.25	.60
❑ 62 Allen Iverson	.60	1.50
❑ 63 Keith Van Horn	.25	.60
❑ 64 Aaron McKie	.20	.50
❑ 65 Shawn Marion	.30	.75
❑ 66 Stephon Marbury	.30	.75
❑ 67 Rasheed Wallace	.30	.75
❑ 68 Derek Anderson	.25	.60
❑ 69 Bonzi Wells	.25	.60
❑ 70 Mike Bibby	.25	.60
❑ 71 Chris Webber	.30	.75
❑ 72 Peja Stojakovic	.25	.60
❑ 73 Hedo Turkoglu	.25	.60
❑ 74 Tim Duncan	.60	1.50
❑ 75 David Robinson	.40	1.00
❑ 76 Tony Parker	.30	.75
❑ 77 Gary Payton	.30	.75
❑ 78 Rashard Lewis	.30	.75
❑ 79 Brent Barry	.20	.50
❑ 80 Desmond Mason	.25	.60
❑ 81 Vince Carter	.60	1.50
❑ 82 Antonio Davis	.20	.50
❑ 83 Morris Peterson	.25	.60
❑ 84 John Stockton	.40	1.00
❑ 85 Karl Malone	.30	.75
❑ 86 Andrei Kirilenko	.30	.75
❑ 87 Matt Harpring	.25	.60
❑ 88 Jerry Stackhouse	.25	.60
❑ 89 Kwame Brown	.20	.50
❑ 90 Michael Jordan	2.00	5.00
❑ 91 R.Humphrey JSY RC	3.00	8.00
❑ 92 Juan Dixon JSY RC	5.00	12.00
❑ 93 Fred Jones JSY RC	4.00	10.00
❑ 94 Marcus Haislip JSY RC	3.00	8.00
❑ 95 Melvin Ely JSY RC	3.00	8.00
❑ 96 Jared Jeffries JSY RC	3.00	8.00
❑ 97 Caron Butler JSY RC	6.00	15.00
❑ 98 A.Stoudemire JSY RC	8.00	20.00
❑ 99 Chris Wilcox JSY RC	4.00	10.00
❑ 100 Nene Hilario JSY RC	4.00	10.00
❑ 101 Dajuan Wagner JSY RC	3.00	8.00
❑ 102 N.Tskitishvili JSY RC	3.00	8.00
❑ 103 Drew Gooden JSY RC	5.00	12.00
❑ 104 Jay Williams JSY RC	4.00	10.00
❑ 105 Yao Ming JSY RC	10.00	25.00
❑ 106 Mike Dunleavy RC	2.50	6.00
❑ 107 Bostjan Nachbar RC	2.00	5.00
❑ 108 Jiri Welsch RC	2.00	5.00
❑ 109 Rasual Butler RC	2.00	5.00
❑ 110 Kareem Rush RC	2.50	6.00
❑ 111 Qyntel Woods RC	2.00	5.00
❑ 112 Casey Jacobsen RC	2.00	5.00
❑ 113 Tayshaun Prince RC	3.00	8.00
❑ 114 Frank Williams RC	2.00	5.00
❑ 115 John Salmons RC	3.00	8.00
❑ 116 Chris Jefferies RC	2.00	5.00
❑ 117 Dan Dickau RC	2.00	5.00
❑ 118 Juaquin Hawkins RC	2.00	5.00
❑ 119 Roger Mason RC	2.00	5.00
❑ 120 Robert Archibald RC	2.00	5.00
❑ 121 Vincent Yarbrough RC	2.00	5.00
❑ 122 Dan Gadzuric RC	2.00	5.00
❑ 123 Carlos Boozer RC	4.00	10.00
❑ 124 Tito Maddox RC	2.00	5.00
❑ 125 Gordan Giricek RC	2.00	5.00
❑ 126 Ronald Murray RC	3.00	8.00
❑ 127 Lonny Baxter RC	2.00	5.00
❑ 128 Pat Burke RC	2.00	5.00
❑ 129 Manu Ginobili RC	5.00	12.00
❑ 130 Predrag Savovic RC	2.00	5.00
❑ 131 Marko Jaric	2.00	5.00
❑ 132 Efthimios Rentzias RC	2.00	5.00
❑ 133 J.R. Bremer RC	2.00	5.00
❑ 134 Igor Rakocevic RC	2.00	5.00
❑ 135 Tamar Slay RC	2.00	5.00

2003-04 Upper Deck Honor Roll

❑ COMP.SET w/o SP's (90)	15.00	40.00
❑ COMMON ROOKIE (91-105)	1.50	4.00
❑ COMMON JSY RC (106-130)	4.00	10.00
❑ JSY RC SWATCHES ARE EVENT WORN		
❑ 1 Shareef Abdur-Rahim	.30	.75
❑ 2 Dan Dickau	.08	.20
❑ 3 Jason Terry	.30	.75
❑ 4 Raef LaFrentz	.20	.50
❑ 5 Vin Baker	.08	.20
❑ 6 Paul Pierce	.30	.75
❑ 7 Antonio Davis	.20	.50
❑ 8 Scottie Pippen	.50	1.25
❑ 9 Jamal Crawford	.20	.50
❑ 10 Dajuan Wagner	.20	.50
❑ 11 Ricky Davis	.30	.75
❑ 12 Darius Miles	.30	.75
❑ 13 Dirk Nowitzki	.50	1.25
❑ 14 Antoine Walker	.30	.75
❑ 15 Steve Nash	.30	.75
❑ 16 Michael Finley	.30	.75
❑ 17 Nikoloz Tskitishvili	.08	.20
❑ 18 Andre Miller	.20	.50
❑ 19 Nene	.20	.50
❑ 20 Chauncey Billups	.20	.50
❑ 21 Richard Hamilton	.20	.50
❑ 22 Ben Wallace	.30	.75
❑ 23 Clifford Robinson	.08	.20
❑ 24 Jason Richardson	.30	.75
❑ 25 Mike Dunleavy	.20	.50
❑ 26 Yao Ming	.75	2.00
❑ 27 Cuttino Mobley	.20	.50

❑ 28 Steve Francis	.30	.75
❑ 29 Jermaine O'Neal	.30	.75
❑ 30 Reggie Miller	.30	.75
❑ 31 Al Harrington	.20	.50
❑ 32 Elton Brand	.30	.75
❑ 33 Corey Maggette	.20	.50
❑ 34 Quentin Richardson	.20	.50
❑ 35 Kobe Bryant	1.25	3.00
❑ 36 Karl Malone	.30	.75
❑ 37 Gary Payton	.30	.75
❑ 38 Shaquille O'Neal	.75	2.00
❑ 39 Pau Gasol	.30	.75
❑ 40 Jason Williams	.20	.50
❑ 41 Mike Miller	.30	.75
❑ 42 Lamar Odom	.30	.75
❑ 43 Eddie Jones	.30	.75
❑ 44 Caron Butler	.30	.75
❑ 45 Michael Redd	.30	.75
❑ 46 Desmond Mason	.20	.50
❑ 47 Tim Thomas	.20	.50
❑ 48 Latrell Sprewell	.30	.75
❑ 49 Kevin Garnett	.60	1.50
❑ 50 Wally Szczerbiak	.20	.50
❑ 51 Richard Jefferson	.20	.50
❑ 52 Kenyon Martin	.30	.75
❑ 53 Jason Kidd	.50	1.25
❑ 54 Jamal Mashburn	.20	.50
❑ 55 Baron Davis	.30	.75
❑ 56 Jamaal Magloire	.08	.20
❑ 57 Allan Houston	.20	.50
❑ 58 Antonio McDyess	.30	.75
❑ 59 Keith Van Horn	.30	.75
❑ 60 Grant Hill	.30	.75
❑ 61 Drew Gooden	.20	.50
❑ 62 Tracy McGrady	.75	2.00
❑ 63 Glenn Robinson	.30	.75
❑ 64 Allen Iverson	.60	1.50
❑ 65 Eric Snow	.20	.50
❑ 66 Amare Stoudemire	.60	1.50
❑ 67 Stephon Marbury	.30	.75
❑ 68 Shawn Marion	.30	.75
❑ 69 Derek Anderson	.20	.50
❑ 70 Damon Stoudamire	.20	.50
❑ 71 Rasheed Wallace	.30	.75
❑ 72 Peja Stojakovic	.30	.75
❑ 73 Chris Webber	.30	.75
❑ 74 Mike Bibby	.30	.75
❑ 75 Bobby Jackson	.20	.50
❑ 76 Tony Parker	.30	.75
❑ 77 Tim Duncan	.60	1.50
❑ 78 Manu Ginobili	.30	.75
❑ 79 Vladimir Radmanovic	.08	.20
❑ 80 Ray Allen	.30	.75
❑ 81 Rashard Lewis	.30	.75
❑ 82 Morris Peterson	.20	.50
❑ 83 Vince Carter	.75	2.00
❑ 84 Jalen Rose	.30	.75
❑ 85 Andrei Kirilenko	.30	.75
❑ 86 Matt Harpring	.30	.75
❑ 87 Greg Ostertag	.08	.20
❑ 88 Gilbert Arenas	.30	.75
❑ 89 Larry Hughes	.20	.50
❑ 90 Jerry Stackhouse	.30	.75
❑ 91 Kirk Hinrich RC	2.00	5.00
❑ 92 T.J. Ford RC	1.50	3.00
❑ 93 Nick Collison RC	1.50	4.00
❑ 94 Kendrick Perkins RC	2.50	6.00
❑ 95 Leandro Barbosa RC	2.50	6.00
❑ 96 Josh Howard RC	2.00	5.00
❑ 97 Jason Kapono RC	1.50	4.00
❑ 98 Jerome Beasley RC	1.50	4.00
❑ 99 Travis Hansen RC	1.50	4.00
❑ 100 Steve Blake RC	1.50	4.00
❑ 101 Willie Green RC	1.50	4.00
❑ 102 Zaur Pachulia RC	1.50	4.00
❑ 103 Keith Bogans RC	1.50	4.00
❑ 104 Kyle Korver RC	2.50	6.00
❑ 105 Brandon Hunter RC	1.50	4.00
❑ 106 LeBron James JSY RC	75.00	150.00
❑ 107 Darko Milicic JSY RC	4.00	10.00
❑ 108 Carmelo Anthony JSY RC	15.00	30.00
❑ 109 Chris Bosh JSY RC	8.00	20.00
❑ 110 Dwyane Wade JSY RC	15.00	30.00
❑ 111 Chris Kaman JSY RC	5.00	12.00
❑ 112 Mike Sweetney JSY RC	4.00	10.00
❑ 113 Jarvis Hayes JSY RC	4.00	10.00
❑ 114 Mickael Pietrus JSY RC	4.00	10.00
❑ 115 Marcus Banks JSY RC	4.00	10.00
❑ 116 Luke Ridnour JSY RC	5.00	12.00
❑ 117 Reece Gaines JSY RC	4.00	10.00
❑ 118 Troy Bell JSY RC	4.00	10.00
❑ 119 Z.Cabarkapa JSY RC	4.00	10.00
❑ 120 David West JSY RC	8.00	20.00
❑ 121 A.Pavlovic JSY RC	5.00	12.00
❑ 122 Dahntay Jones JSY RC	4.00	10.00
❑ 123 Boris Diaw JSY RC	4.00	10.00
❑ 124 Zoran Planinic JSY RC	4.00	10.00
❑ 125 Travis Outlaw JSY RC	5.00	12.00
❑ 126 Brian Cook JSY RC	4.00	10.00
❑ 127 Ndudi Ebi JSY RC	4.00	10.00
❑ 128 Maciej Lampe JSY RC	4.00	10.00
❑ 129 Slavko Vranes JSY RC	4.00	10.00
❑ 130 Luke Walton JSY RC	5.00	12.00

2001-02 Upper Deck Inspirations

❑ COMP.SET w/o SP's (90)	15.00	40.00
❑ COMMON CARD (1-90)	.08	.25
❑ COMMON ROOKIE (91-103)	2.50	6.00
❑ COMMON ROOKIE (104-109)	40.00	80.00
❑ COMMON ROOKIE (110-116)	8.00	20.00
❑ COMMON ROOKIE (117-124)	5.00	12.00
❑ COMMON ROOKIE (125-134)	6.00	15.00
❑ COMMON ROOKIE (135-140)	8.00	20.00
❑ COMMON XRC (141-152)	2.00	5.00
❑ COMMON XRC (153-164)	2.50	6.00
❑ COMMON XRC (165-176)	3.00	8.00
❑ COMMON XRC (177-182)		
❑ 1 Shareef Abdur-Rahim	.25	.60
❑ 2 Jason Terry	.30	.75
❑ 3 Dion Glover	.20	.50
❑ 4 Antoine Walker	.25	.60
❑ 5 Paul Pierce	.30	.75
❑ 6 Larry Bird	1.00	2.50
❑ 7 Baron Davis	.30	.75
❑ 8 Jamal Mashburn	.25	.60
❑ 9 David Wesley	.20	.50
❑ 10 Elden Campbell	.20	.50
❑ 11 Jalen Rose	.25	.60
❑ 12 Marcus Fizer	.20	.50
❑ 13 Andre Miller	.25	.60
❑ 14 Lamond Murray	.20	.50
❑ 15 Chris Mihm	.20	.50
❑ 16 Dirk Nowitzki	.50	1.25
❑ 17 Steve Nash	.50	1.25
❑ 18 Michael Finley	.30	.75
❑ 19 Nick Van Exel	.25	.60
❑ 20 Raef LaFrentz	.20	.50
❑ 21 Antonio McDyess	.25	.60
❑ 22 Juwan Howard	.25	.60
❑ 23 Tim Hardaway	.25	.60
❑ 24 James Posey	.20	.50
❑ 25 Jerry Stackhouse	.25	.60
❑ 26 Ben Wallace	.25	.60
❑ 27 Isiah Thomas	.50	1.25
❑ 28 Antawn Jamison	.30	.75
❑ 29 Larry Hughes	.25	.60
❑ 30 Steve Francis	.30	.75
❑ 31 Moses Malone	.40	1.00
❑ 32 Reggie Miller	.30	.75
❑ 33 Jermaine O'Neal	.30	.75
❑ 34 Elton Brand	.30	.75
❑ 35 Darius Miles	.20	.50
❑ 36 Lamar Odom	.30	.75
❑ 37 Quentin Richardson	.25	.60
❑ 38 Kobe Bryant	1.50	4.00
❑ 39 Shaquille O'Neal	.75	2.00
❑ 40 Derek Fisher	.25	.60
❑ 41 Devean George	.20	.50
❑ 42 Stromile Swift	.20	.50
❑ 43 Jason Williams	.25	.60
❑ 44 Alonzo Mourning	.30	.75
❑ 45 Eddie Jones	.25	.60
❑ 46 Anthony Carter	.20	.50
❑ 47 Ray Allen	.30	.75
❑ 48 Sam Cassell	.25	.60
❑ 49 Glenn Robinson	.25	.60
❑ 50 Tim Thomas	.20	.50
❑ 51 Oscar Robertson	.40	1.00
❑ 52 Kevin Garnett	.60	1.50
❑ 53 Wally Szczerbiak	.25	.60
❑ 54 Terrell Brandon	.20	.50
❑ 55 Chauncey Billups	.25	.60
❑ 56 Jason Kidd	.50	1.25
❑ 57 Kenyon Martin	.30	.75
❑ 58 Latrell Sprewell	.25	.60
❑ 59 Allan Houston	.25	.60
❑ 60 Marcus Camby	.25	.60
❑ 61 Kurt Thomas	.20	.50
❑ 62 Grant Hill	.30	.75
❑ 63 Mike Miller	.25	.60
❑ 64 Tracy McGrady	.60	1.50
❑ 65 Allen Iverson	.60	1.50
❑ 66 Julius Erving	.75	2.00
❑ 67 Bobby Jones	.20	.50
❑ 68 Stephon Marbury	.30	.75
❑ 69 Shawn Marion	.30	.75
❑ 70 Anfernee Hardaway	.30	.75
❑ 71 Rasheed Wallace	.30	.75
❑ 72 Bill Walton	.40	1.00
❑ 73 Chris Webber	.30	.75
❑ 74 Peja Stojakovic	.25	.60
❑ 75 Mike Bibby	.25	.60
❑ 76 Tim Duncan	.60	1.50
❑ 77 David Robinson	.40	1.00
❑ 78 George Gervin	.40	1.00
❑ 79 Gary Payton	.30	.75
❑ 80 Rashard Lewis	.30	.75
❑ 81 Desmond Mason	.25	.60
❑ 82 Vince Carter	.60	1.50
❑ 83 Morris Peterson	.25	.60
❑ 84 Antonio Davis	.20	.50
❑ 85 Hakeem Olajuwon	.40	1.00
❑ 86 Karl Malone	.40	1.00
❑ 87 John Stockton	.40	1.00
❑ 88 Donyell Marshall	.20	.50
❑ 89 Richard Hamilton	.25	.60
❑ 90 Michael Jordan	4.00	10.00
❑ 91 Z.Rebraca RC/S.O'Neal	2.50	6.00
❑ 92 O.Robertson/O.Torres RC	2.50	6.00
❑ 93 R.Miller/J.Brewer RC	2.50	6.00
❑ 94 P.Stojak/P.Drobnjak RC	2.50	6.00
❑ 95 M.Bateer RC/W.Zhi-Zhi	2.50	5.00
❑ 96 J.West/W.Solomon RC	2.50	6.00
❑ 97 T.Duncan/M.Allen RC	2.50	6.00
❑ 98 W.Frazier/D.Brown RC	2.50	6.00
❑ 99 S.Marion/A.Ford RC	2.50	6.00
❑ 100 T.Kukoc/A.Fotsis RC	2.50	6.00
❑ 101 B.Wallace/Z.Randolph RC	6.00	15.00
❑ 102 S.Marbury/J.Crispin RC	2.50	6.00
❑ 103 W.Unseld/B.Simmons RC	2.50	6.00
❑ 104 J.Kidd AU/J.Tinsley RC	12.50	30.00
❑ 105 K.Garnett AU/P.Gasol RC	20.00	50.00
❑ 106 K.Bryant AU/S.Battier RC	25.00	60.00
❑ 107 Carter/J.Trepagnier AU RC	6.00	15.00
❑ 108 J.Erving/Kw.Brown AU RC	12.50	30.00
❑ 109 T.Duncan/E.Curry AU RC	12.50	30.00
❑ 110 Odom AU/E.Griffin AU RC	10.00	25.00
❑ 111 Alexndr AU/Watson AU RC	6.00	15.00
❑ 112 MoPete AU/Arenas AU RC	15.00	30.00
❑ 113 Martin AU/Scalabrine AU RC	10.00	25.00
❑ 114 Chandler AU RC/Fizer AU	10.00	25.00
❑ 115 Mggtte AU/Boumtje AU RC	6.00	15.00
❑ 116 Jr.Collins AU RC/Madsen AU	6.00	15.00
❑ 117 V.Carter/J.Forte JSY RC	4.00	10.00
❑ 118 Jamison/Murphy JSY SP RC	10.00	25.00
❑ 119 Martin/Armstrong JSY RC	6.00	15.00
❑ 120 Francis/T.Morris JSY RC	5.00	12.00
❑ 121 G.Hill/S.Hunter JSY RC	5.00	12.00
❑ 122 Mourng/Radmnov JSY RC	5.00	12.00
❑ 123 Haywood JSY RC/Shaq	8.00	20.00
❑ 124 Dalmbrt JSY RC/M.Malone	5.00	12.00
❑ 125 Szczerbiak/P.Brezec RC	8.00	20.00
❑ 126 P.Stojakovic/M.Bradley RC	6.00	15.00
❑ 127 A.Hardaway/J.Johnson RC	6.00	15.00
❑ 128 L.Woods RC/T.Ratliff	6.00	15.00
❑ 129 C.Webber/G.Wallace RC	5.00	12.00
❑ 130 A.Walker/Ke.Brown RC	6.00	15.00
❑ 131 B.Davis/J.Brewer RC	8.00	20.00
❑ 132 D.Nowitzki/A.Kirilenko RC	10.00	25.00
❑ 133 J.Smith/A.Ford RC	6.00	15.00

❑ 134 J.Stockton/J.Crispin RC	6.00	15.00
❑ 135 K.Malone/R.White RC	8.00	20.00
❑ 136 T.McGrady/J.Sasser RC	15.00	40.00
❑ 137 E.Brand/Jas.Collins RC	8.00	20.00
❑ 138 K.Bryant/R.Jefferson RC	40.00	80.00
❑ 139 A.Iverson/T.Parker RC	20.00	50.00
❑ 140 Jordan/J.Richardson RC	40.00	80.00
❑ 141 Ronald Murray XRC	3.00	8.00
❑ 142 Pat Burke XRC	2.00	5.00
❑ 143 Manu Ginobili XRC	15.00	35.00
❑ 144 Gordan Giricek XRC	3.00	8.00
❑ 145 Tito Maddox XRC	2.00	5.00
❑ 146 Tamar Slay XRC	2.00	5.00
❑ 147 Rasual Butler XRC	2.00	5.00
❑ 148 Carlos Boozer XRC	5.00	12.00
❑ 149 Dan Gadzuric XRC	2.00	5.00
❑ 150 Vincent Yarbrough XRC	2.00	5.00
❑ 151 Robert Archibald XRC	2.00	5.00
❑ 152 Roger Mason XRC	2.00	5.00
❑ 153 Jamal Sampson XRC	2.50	6.00
❑ 154 Sam Clancy XRC	2.50	6.00
❑ 155 Dan Dickau XRC	2.50	6.00
❑ 156 Chris Jefferies XRC	2.50	6.00
❑ 157 John Salmons XRC	3.00	8.00
❑ 158 Frank Williams XRC	2.50	6.00
❑ 159 Lonny Baxter XRC	2.50	6.00
❑ 160 Tayshaun Prince XRC	2.50	6.00
❑ 161 Casey Jacobsen XRC	2.50	6.00
❑ 162 Qyntel Woods XRC	2.50	6.00
❑ 163 Kareem Rush XRC	2.50	6.00
❑ 164 Ryan Humphrey XRC	2.50	6.00
❑ 165 Curtis Borchardt XRC	3.00	8.00
❑ 166 Juan Dixon XRC	6.00	15.00
❑ 167 Jiri Welsch XRC	3.00	8.00
❑ 168 Bostjan Nachbar XRC		
❑ 169 Fred Jones XRC	3.00	8.00
❑ 170 Marcus Haislip XRC	3.00	8.00
❑ 171 Melvin Ely XRC	3.00	8.00
❑ 172 Jared Jeffries XRC		
❑ 173 Caron Butler XRC	6.00	15.00
❑ 174 Amare Stoudemire XRC	10.00	25.00
❑ 175 Chris Wilcox XRC	4.00	10.00
❑ 176 Nene Hilario XRC	4.00	10.00
❑ 177 Dajuan Wagner XRC	12.50	30.00
❑ 178 Nikoloz Tskitishvili XRC		
❑ 179 Drew Gooden XRC		
❑ 180 Mike Dunleavy XRC	10.00	25.00
❑ 181 Jay Williams XRC	12.50	30.00
❑ 182 Yao Ming XRC	25.00	50.00

2002-03 Upper Deck Inspirations

❑ COMP.SET w/o SP's (90)	12.50	30.00
❑ COMMON CARD (1-90)	.08	.20
❑ COMMON ROOKIE (91-104)	2.00	5.00
❑ COMMON ROOKIE (105-110)	6.00	15.00
❑ COMMON ROOKIE (111-127)	4.00	10.00
❑ 111-127 PRINT RUN 1500 SER.#'d SETS		
❑ 111-127 DUAL JERSEY CARDS		
❑ COMMON ROOKIE (128-133)	10.00	25.00
❑ 128-133 PRINT RUN 275 SER.#'d SETS		
❑ 128-133 DUAL AUTOGRAPH CARDS		
❑ COMMON ROOKIE (134-139)	6.00	15.00
❑ 134-139 PRINT RUN 1600 SER.#'d SETS		
❑ 134-139 DUAL AUTOGRAPH CARDS		
❑ COMMON ROOKIE (140-149)	4.00	10.00
❑ 140-149 PRINT RUN 1600 SER.#'d SETS		
❑ 140-149 ROOKIE AUTOGRAPH ONLY		
❑ COMMON DRAFT (156-161)	8.00	20.00
❑ 156-161 PRINT RUN 499 SER.#'d SETS		
❑ COMMON DRAFT (162-167)	5.00	12.00
❑ 162-167 PRINT RUN 799 SER.#'d SETS		
❑ COMMON DRAFT (168-175)	3.00	8.00
❑ 168-175 PRINT RUN 1499 SER.#'d SETS		
❑ COMMON DRAFT (176-197)	2.50	6.00
❑ 176-197 PRINT RUN 2999 SER.#'d SETS		
❑ 1 Shareef Abdur-Rahim	.25	.60
❑ 2 Jason Terry	.30	.75
❑ 3 Glenn Robinson	.25	.60
❑ 4 Paul Pierce	.30	.75
❑ 5 Antoine Walker	.25	.60
❑ 6 Bill Russell	.60	1.50
❑ 7 Vin Baker	.25	.60
❑ 8 Jalen Rose	.25	.60
❑ 9 Tyson Chandler	.25	.60
❑ 10 Eddy Curry	.25	.60
❑ 11 Ricky Davis	.25	.60
❑ 12 Zydrunas Ilgauskas	.25	.60
❑ 13 Darius Miles	.20	.50
❑ 14 Dirk Nowitzki	.50	1.25
❑ 15 Michael Finley	.30	.75
❑ 16 Steve Nash	.50	1.25
❑ 17 Nick Van Exel	.25	.60
❑ 18 Rodney White	.20	.50
❑ 19 Juwan Howard	.25	.60
❑ 20 Richard Hamilton	.25	.60
❑ 21 Ben Wallace	.25	.60
❑ 22 Isiah Thomas	.60	1.50
❑ 23 Antawn Jamison	.30	.75
❑ 24 Jason Richardson	.30	.75
❑ 25 Gilbert Arenas	.30	.75
❑ 26 Steve Francis	.30	.75
❑ 27 Eddie Griffin	.20	.50
❑ 28 Cuttino Mobley	.25	.60
❑ 29 Reggie Miller	.30	.75
❑ 30 Jamaal Tinsley	.25	.60
❑ 31 Jermaine O'Neal	.30	.75
❑ 32 Elton Brand	.30	.75
❑ 33 Andre Miller	.25	.60
❑ 34 Lamar Odom	.30	.75
❑ 35 Kobe Bryant	1.50	4.00
❑ 36 Shaquille O'Neal	.75	2.00
❑ 37 Wilt Chamberlain	1.00	2.50
❑ 38 Derek Fisher	.25	.60
❑ 39 Pau Gasol	.30	.75
❑ 40 Shane Battier	.25	.60
❑ 41 Stromile Swift	.20	.50
❑ 42 Eddie Jones	.25	.60
❑ 43 Alonzo Mourning	.30	.75
❑ 44 Travis Best	.20	.50
❑ 45 Gary Payton	.30	.75
❑ 46 Sam Cassell	.25	.60
❑ 47 Desmond Mason	.25	.60
❑ 48 Kevin Garnett	.60	1.50
❑ 49 Wally Szczerbiak	.25	.60
❑ 50 Joe Smith	.20	.50
❑ 51 Jason Kidd	.50	1.25
❑ 52 Richard Jefferson	.30	.75
❑ 53 Kenyon Martin	.30	.75
❑ 54 Baron Davis	.30	.75
❑ 55 Jamal Mashburn	.25	.60
❑ 56 David Wesley	.20	.50
❑ 57 Allan Houston	.25	.60
❑ 58 Antonio McDyess	.25	.60
❑ 59 Latrell Sprewell	.25	.60
❑ 60 Tracy McGrady	.60	1.50
❑ 61 Grant Hill	.30	.75
❑ 62 Pat Garrity	.20	.50
❑ 63 Allen Iverson	.60	1.50
❑ 64 Julius Erving	.75	2.00
❑ 65 Stephon Marbury	.30	.75
❑ 66 Shawn Marion	.30	.75
❑ 67 Anfernee Hardaway	.30	.75
❑ 68 Rasheed Wallace	.30	.75
❑ 69 Derek Anderson	.25	.60
❑ 70 Scottie Pippen	.50	1.25
❑ 71 Chris Webber	.30	.75
❑ 72 Mike Bibby	.25	.60
❑ 73 Peja Stojakovic	.25	.60
❑ 74 Hedo Turkoglu	.25	.60
❑ 75 Tim Duncan	.60	1.50
❑ 76 David Robinson	.40	1.00
❑ 77 Tony Parker	.30	.75
❑ 78 Ray Allen	.30	.75
❑ 79 Rashard Lewis	.30	.75
❑ 80 Brent Barry	.20	.50
❑ 81 Voshon Lenard	.20	.50
❑ 82 Vince Carter	.60	1.50
❑ 83 Morris Peterson	.25	.60
❑ 84 Antonio Davis	.20	.50
❑ 85 Karl Malone	.30	.75
❑ 86 John Stockton	.40	1.00
❑ 87 Andrei Kirilenko	.30	.75
❑ 88 Jerry Stackhouse	.25	.60
❑ 89 Michael Jordan	2.00	5.00
❑ 90 Kwame Brown	.20	.50
❑ 91 Mason RC/Jordan	2.50	6.00
❑ 92 Harrington RC/English	2.00	5.00
❑ 93 Dunleavy RC/R.Barry	2.00	5.00
❑ 94 Archibald RC/Swift	2.00	5.00
❑ 95 Maddox RC/Francis	2.00	4.00
❑ 96 Hawkins RC/M.Malone	2.00	5.00
❑ 97 Batiste RC/Jas.Williams	2.00	5.00
❑ 98 K.Johnson RC/Mourning	2.00	5.00
❑ 99 S.Parker RC/D.Miles	2.00	5.00
❑ 100 P.Burke RC/S.O'Neal	2.00	5.00
❑ 101 R.Lopez RC/J.Stockton	2.00	5.00
❑ 102 C.Owens RC/S.Battier	2.00	5.00
❑ 103 M.Wilks RC/E.Boykins	2.00	5.00
❑ 104 Rigadeau RC/Nowitzki	2.00	5.00
❑ 105 Butler JSY RC/Garnett JSY	10.00	25.00
❑ 106 Wagner JSY RC/Iversn JSY	8.00	20.00
❑ 107 Rush JSY RC/Bryant JSY	12.50	30.00
❑ 108 Hilario JSY RC/Duncan JSY	10.00	25.00
❑ 109 Ely JSY RC/E.Brand JSY	6.00	15.00
❑ 110 Hmphry JSY RC/T-Mac JSY	8.00	20.00
❑ 111 M.Jaric JSY/A.Miller JSY	4.00	10.00
❑ 112 Jones JSY RC/Miller JSY	4.00	10.00
❑ 113 Baxter JSY RC/Smith JSY	4.00	10.00
❑ 114 Bremer JSY RC/Pierce JSY	6.00	15.00
❑ 115 Boozer JSY RC/Hill JSY	6.00	15.00
❑ 116 Savovic JSY RC/Divac JSY	4.00	10.00
❑ 117 Okur JSY RC/Turkoglu JSY	5.00	12.00
❑ 118 Pargo JSY RC/Fisher JSY	4.00	10.00
❑ 119 Trybnski JSY RC/Swift JSY	4.00	10.00
❑ 120 Murray JSY RC/Lewis JSY	6.00	15.00
❑ 121 Evans JSY RC/Allen JSY	4.00	10.00
❑ 122 Butler JSY RC/Jones JSY	4.00	10.00
❑ 123 Smpsn JSY RC/A-Rahim JSY	4.00	10.00
❑ 124 Rakocv JSY RC/Brndn JSY	4.00	10.00
❑ 125 Slay JSY RC/Jefferson JSY	4.00	10.00
❑ 126 E.Rentz.JSY RC/V.Horn JSY	3.00	8.00
❑ 127 Yarbr.JSY RC/Howard JSY	4.00	10.00
❑ 128A JayWill AU RC/Kobe AU	75.00	150.00
❑ 128B JayWill AU RC/Jordan AU	200.00	400.00
❑ 129 Gooden AU RC/Garnett AU	25.00	60.00
❑ 130 A.Stoud AU RC/Marion AU	30.00	60.00
❑ 131 Tskitishv AU RC/Peja AU	6.00	15.00
❑ 132 Ming AU RC/Zhizhi AU	30.00	75.00
❑ 133 Dixon AU RC/Kidd AU	15.00	40.00
❑ 134 Jeffries AU RC/Stack AU	6.00	15.00
❑ 135 Haislip AU/K-Mart AU	6.00	15.00
❑ 136 Welsch AU RC/J-Rich AU	6.00	15.00
❑ 137 Salmons AU RC/Wallace AU	8.00	20.00
❑ 138 Ginobili AU RC/Parker AU	25.00	50.00
❑ 139 Dickau AU RC/Bibby AU	5.00	12.00
❑ 140 Clancy AU RC/J.Erving	4.00	10.00
❑ 141 Woods AU RC/Wallace	4.00	10.00
❑ 142 F.Williams AU RC/Houston	4.00	10.00
❑ 143 Jacobsen AU RC/Hardaway	4.00	10.00
❑ 144 Nachbar AU RC/Duncan	4.00	10.00
❑ 145 Gadzuric AU RC/S.O'Neal	4.00	10.00
❑ 146 Giricek AU RC/McGrady	5.00	12.00
❑ 147 Borchardt AU RC/Malone	4.00	10.00
❑ 148 Prince AU RC/Walker	6.00	15.00
❑ 149 Wilcox AU RC/Carter	3.00	8.00
❑ 150 W.Chamberlain/Y.Ming		
❑ 151 B.Russell/A.Stoudemire		
❑ 152 J.Erving/J.Williams		
❑ 153 L.Bird/M.Ginobili		
❑ 154 M.Jordan/D.Wagner		
❑ 155 K.Bryant/C.Butler		
❑ 156A LeBron James XRC	100.00	200.00
❑ 156B Draft Pick #1		
❑ 157A Darko Milicic XRC	8.00	20.00
❑ 157B Draft Pick #2		
❑ 158A Carmelo Anthony XRC	25.00	60.00
❑ 158B Draft Pick #3		
❑ 159A Chris Bosh XRC	12.50	30.00
❑ 159B Draft Pick #4		
❑ 160A Dwyane Wade XRC	20.00	40.00
❑ 160B Draft Pick #5		
❑ 161A Chris Kaman XRC	8.00	20.00
❑ 161B Draft Pick #6		
❑ 162A Kirk Hinrich XRC	8.00	20.00
❑ 162B Draft Pick #7		
❑ 163A T.J. Ford XRC	10.00	25.00
❑ 163B Draft Pick #8		
❑ 164A Mike Sweetney XRC	5.00	12.00
❑ 164B Draft Pick #9		
❑ 165A Jarvis Hayes XRC	5.00	12.00
❑ 165B Draft Pick #10		

❑ 166A Mickael Pietrus XRC	5.00	12.00
❑ 166B Draft Pick #11		
❑ 167A Nick Collison XRC	5.00	12.00
❑ 167B Draft Pick #12		
❑ 168A Marcus Banks XRC	3.00	8.00
❑ 168B Draft Pick #13		
❑ 169A Luke Ridnour XRC	4.00	10.00
❑ 169B Draft Pick #14		
❑ 170A Reece Gaines XRC	3.00	8.00
❑ 170B Draft Pick #15		
❑ 171A Troy Bell XRC	3.00	8.00
❑ 171B Draft Pick #16		
❑ 172A Zarko Cabarkapa XRC	3.00	8.00
❑ 172B Draft Pick #17		
❑ 173A David West XRC	4.00	10.00
❑ 173B Draft Pick #18		
❑ 174A Aleksandar Pavlovic XRC	3.00	8.00
❑ 174B Draft Pick #19		
❑ 175A Dahntay Jones XRC	3.00	8.00
❑ 175B Draft Pick #20		
❑ 176A Boris Diaw XRC	2.50	5.00
❑ 176B Draft Pick #21		
❑ 177A Zoran Planinic XRC	2.50	6.00
❑ 177B Draft Pick #22		
❑ 178A Travis Outlaw XRC	2.50	6.00
❑ 178B Draft Pick #23		
❑ 179A Brian Cook XRC	2.50	6.00
❑ 179B Draft Pick #24		
❑ 180A Udonis Haslem XRC	2.50	6.00
❑ 180B Draft Pick #25		
❑ 181A Ndudi Ebi XRC	2.50	6.00
❑ 181B Draft Pick #26		
❑ 182A Kendrick Perkins XRC	2.50	6.00
❑ 182B Draft Pick #27		
❑ 183A Leandro Barbosa XRC	4.00	10.00
❑ 183B Draft Pick #28		
❑ 184A Josh Howard XRC	4.00	10.00
❑ 184B Draft Pick #29		
❑ 185A Maciej Lampe XRC	2.50	6.00
❑ 185B Draft Pick #30		
❑ 186A Jason Kapono XRC	2.50	6.00
❑ 186B Draft Pick #31		
❑ 187B Draft Pick #32	2.50	6.00
❑ 188B Draft Pick #33	2.50	6.00
❑ 189B Draft Pick #34	2.50	6.00
❑ 190A Luke Walton XRC	2.50	6.00
❑ 190B Draft Pick #35		
❑ 191A Jerome Beasley XRC	2.50	6.00
❑ 191B Draft Pick #36		
❑ 192A Travis Hansen XRC	2.50	6.00
❑ 192B Draft Pick #37		
❑ 193A Steve Blake XRC	2.50	6.00
❑ 193B Draft Pick #38		
❑ 194A Slavko Vranes XRC	2.50	6.00
❑ 194B Draft Pick #39		
❑ 195A Keith Bogans XRC	2.50	6.00
❑ 195B Draft Pick #40		
❑ 196A Willie Green XRC	2.50	6.00
❑ 196B Draft Pick #41		
❑ 197A Zaur Pachulia XRC	2.50	6.00
❑ 197B Draft Pick #42		

2001-02 Upper Deck Legends

❑ COMP.SET w/o SP's (90)	10.00	25.00
❑ COMMON CARD	.07	.20
❑ SEMISTARS	.15	.40
❑ COMMON ROOKIE (91-110)	1.50	4.00
❑ COMMON ROOKIE (111-125)	4.00	10.00
❑ NOTE CARDS READ 2000-01		
❑ 1 Michael Jordan	1.50	4.00
❑ 2 Wilt Chamberlain	.40	1.00
❑ 3 Karl Malone	.25	.60
❑ 4 Steve Francis	.25	.60
❑ 5 George McGinnis	.15	.40
❑ 6 Julius Erving	.40	1.00
❑ 7 Alonzo Mourning	.15	.40
❑ 8 Kobe Bryant	1.00	2.50
❑ 9 Glen Rice	.15	.40
❑ 10 Mitch Kupchak	.07	.20
❑ 11 Isiah Thomas	.25	.60
❑ 12 Rick Barry	.25	.60
❑ 13 Moses Malone	.25	.60
❑ 14 Larry Bird	1.00	2.50
❑ 15 Vince Carter	.60	1.50
❑ 16 Jamaal Wilkes	.15	.40
❑ 17 John Havlicek	.30	.75
❑ 18 Elgin Baylor	.25	.60
❑ 19 Dave Bing	.15	.40
❑ 20 Steve Smith	.07	.20
❑ 21 Kevin Garnett	.50	1.25
❑ 22 Hakeem Olajuwon	.25	.60
❑ 23 Walt Bellamy	.07	.20
❑ 24 Kevin McHale	.25	.60
❑ 25 Kareem Abdul-Jabbar	.40	1.00
❑ 26 Chris Webber	.25	.60
❑ 27 Tom Heinsohn	.07	.20
❑ 28 Walt Frazier	.25	.60
❑ 29 Ron Boone	.15	.40
❑ 30 Gary Payton	.25	.60
❑ 31 Wes Unseld	.07	.20
❑ 32 Magic Johnson	.75	2.00
❑ 33 David Thompson	.07	.20
❑ 34 Maurice Lucas	.07	.20
❑ 35 Paul Pierce	.25	.60
❑ 36 Dikembe Mutombo	.15	.40
❑ 37 Gail Goodrich	.15	.40
❑ 38 Bob Lanier	.07	.20
❑ 39 Chris Mullin	.07	.20
❑ 40 Allen Iverson	.50	1.25
❑ 41 Sam Jones	.07	.20
❑ 42 James Worthy	.25	.60
❑ 43 Cedric Maxwell	.07	.20
❑ 44 George Gervin	.25	.60
❑ 45 Earl Monroe	.25	.60
❑ 46 Lenny Wilkens	.15	.40
❑ 47 Tracy McGrady	.60	1.50
❑ 48 Walter Davis	.07	.20
❑ 49 Stephon Marbury	.25	.60
❑ 50 Bob Cousy	.25	.60
❑ 51 Spencer Haywood	.07	.20
❑ 52 Dave Cowens	.15	.40
❑ 53 Scottie Pippen	.75	1.00
❑ 54 Hal Greer	.07	.20
❑ 55 Kiki Vandeweghe	.15	.40
❑ 56 Paul Silas	.15	.40
❑ 57 Elton Brand	.15	.40
❑ 58 John Stockton	.25	.60
❑ 59 Shareef Abdur-Rahim	.25	.60
❑ 60 Reggie Miller	.25	.60
❑ 61 Nate Thurmond	.07	.20
❑ 62 Billy Cunningham	.07	.20
❑ 63 Patrick Ewing	.25	.60
❑ 64 Nate Archibald	.25	.60
❑ 65 Tim Duncan	.50	1.25
❑ 66 Lafayette Lever	.15	.40
❑ 67 Willis Reed	.15	.40
❑ 68 Ray Allen	.25	.60
❑ 69 Jo Jo White	.07	.20
❑ 70 Pete Maravich	.30	.75
❑ 71 Grant Hill	.25	.60
❑ 72 Jerry West	.25	.60
❑ 73 George Karl	.15	.40
❑ 74 Bill Sharman	.07	.20
❑ 75 Dave DeBusschere	.07	.20
❑ 76 Tim Hardaway	.15	.40
❑ 77 Bill Walton	.25	.60
❑ 78 Jerry Lucas	.07	.20
❑ 79 Antonio McDyess	.15	.40
❑ 80 Robert Parish	.25	.60
❑ 81 Shaquille O'Neal	.60	1.50
❑ 82 Bill Russell	.40	1.00
❑ 83 Clyde Drexler	.25	.60
❑ 84 Dolph Schayes	.15	.40
❑ 85 K.C. Jones	.07	.20
❑ 86 Bob Pettit	.15	.40
❑ 87 Jason Kidd	.40	1.00
❑ 88 Mitch Richmond	.15	.40
❑ 89 Oscar Robertson	.30	.75
❑ 90 David Robinson	.25	.60
❑ 91 Bobby Simmons RC	1.50	4.00
❑ 92 Jamison Brewer RC	1.50	4.00
❑ 93 Earl Watson RC	1.50	4.00
❑ 94 Kenny Satterfield RC	1.50	4.00
❑ 95 Zeljko Rebraca RC	1.50	4.00
❑ 96 Damone Brown RC	1.50	4.00
❑ 97 R.Boumtje-Boumtje RC	1.50	4.00
❑ 98 Brian Scalabrine RC	1.50	4.00
❑ 99 Terence Morris RC	1.50	4.00
❑ 100 Willie Solomon RC	1.50	4.00
❑ 101 Primoz Brezec RC	2.00	5.00
❑ 102 Gilbert Arenas RC	4.00	10.00
❑ 103 Trenton Hassell RC	2.50	6.00
❑ 104 Loren Woods RC	1.50	4.00
❑ 105 Tony Parker RC	6.00	15.00
❑ 106 Jamaal Tinsley RC	2.50	6.00
❑ 107 Samuel Dalembert RC	1.50	4.00
❑ 108 Gerald Wallace RC	4.00	10.00
❑ 109 Andrei Kirilenko RC	5.00	12.00
❑ 110 Brandon Armstrong RC	2.50	6.00
❑ 111 Jeryl Sasser RC	4.00	10.00
❑ 112 Joseph Forte RC	4.00	8.00
❑ 113 Brendan Haywood RC	5.00	12.00
❑ 114 Zach Randolph RC	8.00	20.00
❑ 115 Jason Collins RC	4.00	10.00
❑ 116 Michael Bradley RC	4.00	10.00
❑ 117 Kirk Haston RC	4.00	10.00
❑ 118 Steven Hunter RC	4.00	10.00
❑ 119 Troy Murphy RC	6.00	15.00
❑ 120 Richard Jefferson RC	5.00	12.00
❑ 121 Vladimir Radmanovic RC	4.00	10.00
❑ 122 Kedrick Brown RC	4.00	10.00
❑ 123 Joe Johnson RC	8.00	20.00
❑ 124 Rodney White RC	5.00	12.00
❑ 125 DeSagana Diop RC	4.00	10.00
❑ 126 Eddie Griffin RC	5.00	12.00
❑ 127 Shane Battier RC	5.00	12.00
❑ 128 Jason Richardson RC	5.00	12.00
❑ 129 Eddy Curry RC	8.00	20.00
❑ 130 Pau Gasol RC	12.50	30.00
❑ 131 Tyson Chandler RC	6.00	15.00
❑ 132 Kwame Brown RC	6.00	15.00

2003-04 Upper Deck Legends

❑ COMP.SET w/o SP's (90)	12.50	30.00
❑ COMMON CARD (1-90)	.08	.20
❑ COMMON ROOKIE (91-125)	2.00	5.00
❑ COMMON ROOKIE (126-135)	2.50	6.00
❑ COMMON DRAFT (136-150)	3.00	8.00
❑ 1 Bob Sura	.08	.20
❑ 2 Stephen Jackson	.08	.20
❑ 3 Jason Terry	.30	.75
❑ 4 Ricky Davis	.30	.75
❑ 5 Jiri Welsch	.20	.50
❑ 6 Paul Pierce	.30	.75
❑ 7 Eddy Curry	.20	.50
❑ 8 Jamal Crawford	.20	.50
❑ 9 Tyson Chandler	.30	.75
❑ 10 Dajuan Wagner	.20	.50
❑ 11 Carlos Boozer	.30	.75
❑ 12 Zydrunas Ilgauskas	.20	.50
❑ 13 Dirk Nowitzki	.50	1.25
❑ 14 Antoine Walker	.30	.75
❑ 15 Steve Nash	.30	.75
❑ 16 Michael Finley	.30	.75
❑ 17 Jon Barry	.08	.20
❑ 18 Andre Miller	.20	.50
❑ 19 Nene	.20	.50
❑ 20 Rasheed Wallace	.30	.75
❑ 21 Richard Hamilton	.20	.50
❑ 22 Ben Wallace	.30	.75
❑ 23 Erick Dampier	.20	.50
❑ 24 Jason Richardson	.30	.75
❑ 25 Nick Van Exel	.30	.75
❑ 26 Yao Ming	.75	2.00
❑ 27 Cuttino Mobley	.20	.50
❑ 28 Steve Francis	.30	.75
❑ 29 Jermaine O'Neal	.30	.75

❑ 30 Reggie Miller	.30	.75
❑ 31 Ron Artest	.20	.50
❑ 32 Elton Brand	.30	.75
❑ 33 Corey Maggette	.20	.50
❑ 34 Quentin Richardson	.20	.50
❑ 35 Kobe Bryant	1.25	3.00
❑ 36 Karl Malone	.30	.75
❑ 37 Gary Payton	.30	.75
❑ 38 Shaquille O'Neal	.75	2.00
❑ 39 Pau Gasol	.30	.75
❑ 40 Bonzi Wells	.20	.50
❑ 41 Mike Miller	.30	.75
❑ 42 Lamar Odom	.30	.75
❑ 43 Eddie Jones	.30	.75
❑ 44 Caron Butler	.30	.75
❑ 45 Keith Van Horn	.30	.75
❑ 46 Desmond Mason	.20	.50
❑ 47 Michael Redd	.20	.50
❑ 48 Latrell Sprewell	.30	.75
❑ 49 Kevin Garnett	.60	1.50
❑ 50 Sam Cassell	.30	.75
❑ 51 Richard Jefferson	.20	.50
❑ 52 Kenyon Martin	.30	.75
❑ 53 Jason Kidd	.50	1.25
❑ 54 Jamal Mashburn	.20	.50
❑ 55 Baron Davis	.30	.75
❑ 56 David Wesley	.08	.20
❑ 57 Allan Houston	.20	.50
❑ 58 Stephon Marbury	.30	.75
❑ 59 Kurt Thomas	.20	.50
❑ 60 Juwan Howard	.20	.50
❑ 61 Drew Gooden	.20	.50
❑ 62 Tracy McGrady	.75	2.00
❑ 63 Zendon Hamilton RC	.40	1.00
❑ 64 Allen Iverson	.60	1.50
❑ 65 Eric Snow	.20	.50
❑ 66 Amare Stoudemire	.60	1.50
❑ 67 Joe Johnson	.20	.50
❑ 68 Shawn Marion	.30	.75
❑ 69 Zach Randolph	.30	.75
❑ 70 Darius Miles	.30	.75
❑ 71 Shareef Abdur-Rahim	.30	.75
❑ 72 Peja Stojakovic	.30	.75
❑ 73 Chris Webber	.30	.75
❑ 74 Mike Bibby	.30	.75
❑ 75 Brad Miller	.30	.75
❑ 76 Tony Parker	.30	.75
❑ 77 Tim Duncan	.60	1.50
❑ 78 Manu Ginobili	.30	.75
❑ 79 Ronald Murray	.08	.20
❑ 80 Ray Allen	.30	.75
❑ 81 Rashard Lewis	.30	.75
❑ 82 Donyell Marshall	.30	.75
❑ 83 Vince Carter	.75	2.00
❑ 84 Jalen Rose	.30	.75
❑ 85 Andrei Kirilenko	.30	.75
❑ 86 Matt Harpring	.30	.75
❑ 87 Carlos Arroyo	.50	1.25
❑ 88 Gilbert Arenas	.30	.75
❑ 89 Larry Hughes	.20	.50
❑ 90 Jerry Stackhouse	.30	.75
❑ 91 Devin Brown RC	2.00	5.00
❑ 92 Ronald Dupree RC	2.00	5.00
❑ 93 Alex Garcia RC	2.00	5.00
❑ 94 Udonis Haslem RC	2.00	5.00
❑ 95 Maurice Williams RC	3.00	8.00
❑ 96 Brandon Hunter RC	2.00	5.00
❑ 97 Keith Bogans RC	2.00	5.00
❑ 98 Willie Green RC	2.00	5.00
❑ 99 Zaza Pachulia RC	2.00	5.00
❑ 100 Zarko Cabarkapa RC	2.00	5.00
❑ 101 Kyle Korver RC	3.00	8.00
❑ 102 Luke Walton RC	2.00	5.00
❑ 103 Maciej Lampe RC	2.00	5.00
❑ 104 Josh Howard RC	2.50	6.00
❑ 105 Kendrick Perkins RC	3.00	8.00
❑ 106 Ndudi Ebi RC	2.00	5.00
❑ 107 Jerome Beasley RC	2.00	5.00
❑ 108 Brian Cook RC	2.00	5.00
❑ 109 Travis Outlaw RC	2.50	6.00
❑ 110 Zoran Planinic RC	2.00	5.00
❑ 111 Boris Diaw RC	2.00	5.00
❑ 112 Steve Blake RC	2.00	5.00
❑ 113 Aleksandar Pavlovic RC	2.50	6.00
❑ 114 David West RC	4.00	10.00
❑ 115 Mike Sweetney RC	2.00	5.00
❑ 116 Troy Bell RC	2.00	5.00
❑ 117 Reece Gaines RC	2.00	5.00
❑ 118 Marcus Banks RC	2.00	5.00
❑ 119 Dahntay Jones RC	2.00	5.00
❑ 120 Chris Kaman RC	2.50	6.00
❑ 121 Mickael Pietrus RC	2.00	5.00
❑ 122 Luke Ridnour RC	2.50	6.00
❑ 123 Jason Kapono RC	2.00	5.00
❑ 124 Marquis Daniels RC	2.00	5.00
❑ 125 Travis Hansen RC	2.00	5.00
❑ 126 Leandro Barbosa RC	4.00	10.00
❑ 127 Nick Collison RC	2.50	6.00
❑ 128 Kirk Hinrich RC	4.00	10.00
❑ 129 T.J. Ford RC	2.50	6.00
❑ 130 Jarvis Hayes RC	2.50	6.00
❑ 131 Dwyane Wade RC	6.00	15.00
❑ 132 Chris Bosh RC	5.00	12.00
❑ 133 Carmelo Anthony RC	6.00	15.00
❑ 134 Darko Milicic RC	3.00	8.00
❑ 135 LeBron James RC	40.00	80.00
❑ 136 Dwight Howard XRC	25.00	50.00
❑ 137 Emeka Okafor XRC	10.00	25.00
❑ 138 Ben Gordon XRC	6.00	15.00
❑ 139 Shaun Livingston XRC	5.00	12.00
❑ 140 Devin Harris XRC	6.00	15.00
❑ 141 Josh Childress XRC	4.00	10.00
❑ 142 Luol Deng XRC	5.00	12.00
❑ 143 Rafael Araujo XRC	4.00	10.00
❑ 144 Andre Iguodala XRC	4.00	10.00
❑ 145 Luke Jackson XRC	4.00	10.00
❑ 146 Andris Biedrins XRC	5.00	12.00
❑ 147 Robert Swift XRC	3.00	8.00
❑ 148 Sebastian Telfair XRC	3.00	8.00
❑ 149 Kris Humphries XRC	3.00	8.00
❑ 150 Al Jefferson XRC	5.00	12.00

2008-09 Upper Deck Lineage

❑ COMP.SET w/o RCs (200)	20.00	40.00
❑ 1 Bill Russell	.50	1.25
❑ 2 Sam Jones	.40	1.00
❑ 3 Oscar Robertson	.30	.75
❑ 4 Kareem Abdul-Jabbar	.50	1.25
❑ 5 Julius Erving	.60	1.50
❑ 6 George Gervin	.40	1.00
❑ 7 Bill Walton	.30	.75
❑ 8 Robert Parish	.30	.75
❑ 9 Larry Bird	1.00	2.50
❑ 10 Magic Johnson	.60	1.50
❑ 11 Isiah Thomas	.30	.75
❑ 12 James Worthy	.30	.75
❑ 13 Dominique Wilkins	.40	1.00
❑ 14 Clyde Drexler	.40	1.00
❑ 15 John Stockton	.50	1.25
❑ 16 Hakeem Olajuwon	.40	1.00
❑ 17 Michael Jordan	2.00	5.00
❑ 18 Tom Chambers	.30	.75
❑ 19 Adrian Dantley	.30	.75
❑ 20 David Robinson	.50	1.25
❑ 21 Shaquille O'Neal	.60	1.50
❑ 22 Alonzo Mourning	.30	.75
❑ 23 Jason Kidd	.30	.75
❑ 24 Grant Hill	.30	.75
❑ 25 Rasheed Wallace	.30	.75
❑ 26 Kevin Garnett	.60	1.50
❑ 27 Bruce Bowen	.20	.50
❑ 28 Steve Nash	.30	.75
❑ 29 Marcus Camby	.20	.50
❑ 30 Derek Fisher	.30	.75
❑ 31 Ben Wallace	.30	.75
❑ 32 Allen Iverson	.40	1.00
❑ 33 Ray Allen	.30	.75
❑ 34 Brad Miller	.30	.75
❑ 35 Kobe Bryant	1.50	4.00
❑ 36 Jermaine O'Neal	.30	.75
❑ 37 Tim Duncan	.50	1.25
❑ 38 Chauncey Billups	.30	.75
❑ 39 Tracy McGrady	.40	1.00
❑ 40 Zydrunas Ilgauskas	.25	.60
❑ 41 Javaris Crittenton	.20	.50
❑ 42 Antawn Jamison	.30	.75
❑ 43 Vince Carter	.40	1.00
❑ 44 Peja Stojakovic	.30	.75
❑ 45 Paul Pierce	.40	1.00
❑ 46 Mike Bibby	.30	.75
❑ 47 Dirk Nowitzki	.40	1.00
❑ 48 Rashard Lewis	.30	.75
❑ 49 Al Harrington	.25	.60
❑ 50 Andre Miller	.25	.60
❑ 51 Wally Szczerbiak	.25	.60
❑ 52 Jason Terry	.25	.60
❑ 53 Richard Hamilton	.25	.60
❑ 54 Shawn Marion	.30	.75
❑ 55 Elton Brand	.50	1.25
❑ 56 Baron Davis	.30	.75
❑ 57 Lamar Odom	.30	.75
❑ 58 Corey Maggette	.30	.75
❑ 59 Ron Artest	.30	.75
❑ 60 Morris Peterson	.25	.60
❑ 61 Desmond Mason	.20	.50
❑ 62 Kenyon Martin	.30	.75
❑ 63 Stephen Jackson	.25	.60
❑ 64 Hedo Turkoglu	.30	.75
❑ 65 Michael Redd	.30	.75
❑ 66 Mike Miller	.30	.75
❑ 67 Jamal Crawford	.20	.50
❑ 68 Quentin Richardson	.25	.60
❑ 69 Keyon Dooling	.20	.50
❑ 70 DeShawn Stevenson	.20	.50
❑ 71 Jamaal Tinsley	.20	.50
❑ 72 Shane Battier	.25	.60
❑ 73 Earl Watson	.20	.50
❑ 74 Richard Jefferson	.30	.75
❑ 75 Pau Gasol	.30	.75
❑ 76 Jason Richardson	.30	.75
❑ 77 Andrei Kirilenko	.30	.75
❑ 78 Joe Johnson	.30	.75
❑ 79 Zach Randolph	.30	.75
❑ 80 Gilbert Arenas	.30	.75
❑ 81 Tony Parker	.30	.75
❑ 82 Gerald Wallace	.30	.75
❑ 83 Tyson Chandler	.25	.60
❑ 84 Eddy Curry	.20	.50
❑ 85 Manu Ginobili	.30	.75
❑ 86 Marko Jaric	.25	.60
❑ 87 Mehmet Okur	.30	.75
❑ 88 John Salmons	.30	.75
❑ 89 Tayshaun Prince	.30	.75
❑ 90 Caron Butler	.30	.75
❑ 91 Yao Ming	.40	1.00
❑ 92 Mike Dunleavy	.25	.60
❑ 93 Samuel Dalembert	.20	.50
❑ 94 Carlos Boozer	.30	.75
❑ 95 Chris Wilcox	.25	.60
❑ 96 Nene	.25	.60
❑ 97 Amare Stoudemire	.40	1.00
❑ 98 Steve Blake	.20	.50
❑ 99 Luke Walton	.25	.60
❑ 100 Josh Howard	.30	.75
❑ 101 Keith Bogans	.20	.50
❑ 102 Udonis Haslem	.30	.75
❑ 103 David West	.30	.75
❑ 104 Kirk Hinrich	.30	.75
❑ 105 Kyle Korver	.30	.75
❑ 106 Willie Green	.20	.50
❑ 107 Dwyane Wade	.60	1.50
❑ 108 Boris Diaw	.25	.60
❑ 109 Chris Kaman	.20	.50
❑ 110 Leandro Barbosa	.25	.60
❑ 111 Mo Williams	.25	.60
❑ 112 Chris Bosh	.30	.75
❑ 113 Carmelo Anthony	.40	1.00
❑ 114 Kendrick Perkins	.25	.60
❑ 115 LeBron James	1.50	4.00
❑ 116 Andres Nocioni	.25	.60
❑ 117 Damien Wilkins	.20	.50
❑ 118 Jameer Nelson	.25	.60
❑ 119 Beno Udrih	.20	.50
❑ 120 Chris Duhon	.20	.50
❑ 121 Anderson Varejao	.25	.60
❑ 122 Emeka Okafor	.30	.75
❑ 123 Kevin Martin	.30	.75
❑ 124 Devin Harris	.30	.75
❑ 125 T.J. Ford	.20	.50
❑ 126 Ben Gordon	.30	.75
❑ 127 Andre Iguodala	.30	.75
❑ 128 Sasha Vujacic	.25	.60

❑ 129 Al Jefferson	.30	.75
❑ 130 Luol Deng	.30	.75
❑ 131 J.R. Smith	.25	.60
❑ 132 Josh Smith	.30	.75
❑ 133 Dwight Howard	.60	1.50
❑ 134 Fabricio Oberto	.20	.50
❑ 135 Jose Calderon	.25	.60
❑ 136 Francisco Garcia	.25	.60
❑ 137 Hakim Warrick	.20	.50
❑ 138 Luther Head	.25	.60
❑ 139 Jason Maxiell	.25	.60
❑ 140 Danny Granger	.30	.75
❑ 141 David Lee	.25	.60
❑ 142 Chuck Hayes	.20	.50
❑ 143 Jarrett Jack	.25	.60
❑ 144 Raymond Felton	.25	.60
❑ 145 Deron Williams	.40	1.00
❑ 146 Rashad McCants	.25	.60
❑ 147 Andrew Bogut	.30	.75
❑ 148 Brandon Bass	.25	.60
❑ 149 Chris Paul	.60	1.50
❑ 150 Shaun Livingston	.25	.60
❑ 151 Monta Ellis	.30	.75
❑ 152 Marvin Williams	.30	.75
❑ 153 Louis Williams	.20	.50
❑ 154 Martell Webster	.25	.60
❑ 155 Andrew Bynum	.30	.75
❑ 156 Randy Foye	.30	.75
❑ 157 Shelden Williams	.20	.50
❑ 158 Leon Powe	.20	.50
❑ 159 Rodney Carney	.20	.50
❑ 160 Jose Barea	.25	.60
❑ 161 Brandon Roy	.40	1.00
❑ 162 Josh Boone	.20	.50
❑ 163 Ronnie Brewer	.25	.60
❑ 164 LaMarcus Aldridge	.30	.75
❑ 165 Andrea Bargnani	.25	.60
❑ 166 Rajon Rondo	.30	.75
❑ 167 Daniel Gibson	.30	.75
❑ 168 Kyle Lowry	.20	.50
❑ 169 Sergio Rodriguez	.25	.60
❑ 170 Tyrus Thomas	.25	.60
❑ 171 Rudy Gay	.30	.75
❑ 172 Jordan Farmar	.25	.60
❑ 173 Luis Scola	.25	.60
❑ 174 Jamario Moon	.30	.75
❑ 175 Carl Landry	.20	.50
❑ 176 Al Thornton	.30	.75
❑ 177 C.J. Watson	.20	.50
❑ 178 Adam Morrison	.30	.75
❑ 179 Acie Law IV	.25	.60
❑ 180 Morris Almond	.20	.50
❑ 181 Joakim Noah	.30	.75
❑ 182 Nick Young	.20	.50
❑ 183 Arron Afflalo	.20	.50
❑ 184 Jared Dudley	.30	.75
❑ 185 Glen Davis	.25	.60
❑ 186 Corey Brewer	.25	.60
❑ 187 Marco Belinelli	.20	.50
❑ 188 Ramon Sessions	.30	.75
❑ 189 Rodney Stuckey	.40	1.00
❑ 190 Al Horford	.30	.75
❑ 191 Jeff Green	.25	.60
❑ 192 Sean Williams	.25	.60
❑ 193 Daequan Cook	.25	.60
❑ 194 Julian Wright	.25	.60
❑ 195 Brandan Wright	.25	.60
❑ 196 Mike Conley	.25	.60
❑ 197 Yi Jianlian	.30	.75
❑ 198 Thaddeus Young	.25	.60
❑ 199 Kevin Durant	.75	2.00
❑ 200 Greg Oden	.30	.75
❑ 201 Derrick Rose RC	3.00	8.00
❑ 202 Michael Beasley RC	1.50	4.00
❑ 203 O.J. Mayo RC	1.25	3.00
❑ 204 Russell Westbrook RC	2.00	5.00
❑ 205 Kevin Love RC	1.00	2.50
❑ 206 Danilo Gallinari RC	1.25	3.00
❑ 207 Eric Gordon RC	1.00	2.50
❑ 208 Joe Alexander RC	.75	2.00
❑ 209 D.J. Augustin RC	.75	2.00
❑ 210 Brook Lopez RC	1.50	4.00
❑ 211 Jerryd Bayless RC	.75	2.00
❑ 212 Jason Thompson RC	.75	2.00
❑ 213 Brandon Rush RC	.75	2.00
❑ 214 Anthony Randolph RC	1.25	3.00
❑ 215 Robin Lopez RC	.75	2.00
❑ 216 Marreese Speights RC	.75	2.00
❑ 217 Roy Hibbert RC	1.00	2.50
❑ 218 J.J. Hickson RC	1.25	3.00
❑ 219 Ryan Anderson RC	.75	2.00
❑ 220 George Hill RC	1.25	3.00
❑ 221 Darrell Arthur RC	.75	2.00
❑ 222 Donte Greene RC	.75	2.00
❑ 223 D.J. White RC	.75	2.00
❑ 224 J.R. Giddens RC	.75	2.00
❑ 225 Walter Sharpe RC	.75	2.00
❑ 226 Mario Chalmers RC	1.00	2.50
❑ 227 Sonny Weems RC	.75	2.00
❑ 228 Chris Douglas-Roberts RC	1.00	2.50
❑ 229 Sean Singletary RC	.75	2.00
❑ 230 Luc Richard Mbah A Moute RC	.75	2.00
❑ 231 Bill Walker RC	.75	2.00
❑ 232 Marc Gasol RC	1.25	3.00
❑ 233 Rudy Fernandez RC	1.50	4.00

1999-00 Upper Deck MVP

❑ COMPLETE SET (220)	20.00	40.00
❑ COMMON CARD (1-178)	.05	.15
❑ COMMON ROOKIE (209-218)	.30	.75
❑ COMMON MJ (179-208)	.75	2.00
❑ 1 Dikembe Mutombo	.15	.40
❑ 2 Steve Smith	.12	.30
❑ 3 Mookie Blaylock	.12	.30
❑ 4 Alan Henderson	.12	.30
❑ 5 LaPhonso Ellis	.12	.30
❑ 6 Grant Long	.12	.30
❑ 7 Kenny Anderson	.15	.40
❑ 8 Antoine Walker	.20	.50
❑ 9 Ron Mercer	.12	.30
❑ 10 Paul Pierce	.20	.50
❑ 11 Vitaly Potapenko	.12	.30
❑ 12 Dana Barros	.12	.30
❑ 13 Elden Campbell	.12	.30
❑ 14 Eddie Jones	.20	.50
❑ 15 David Wesley	.12	.30
❑ 16 Bobby Phills	.12	.30
❑ 17 Derrick Coleman	.15	.40
❑ 18 Ricky Davis	.20	.50
❑ 19 Toni Kukoc	.20	.50
❑ 20 Brent Barry	.15	.40
❑ 21 Ron Harper	.12	.30
❑ 22 Kornel David RC	.20	.50
❑ 23 Mark Bryant	.12	.30
❑ 24 Dickey Simpkins	.12	.30
❑ 25 Shawn Kemp	.20	.50
❑ 26 Derek Anderson	.12	.30
❑ 27 Brevin Knight	.12	.30
❑ 28 Andrew DeClercq	.12	.30
❑ 29 Zydrunas Ilgauskas	.15	.40
❑ 30 Cedric Henderson	.12	.30
❑ 31 Shawn Bradley	.12	.30
❑ 32 A.C. Green	.20	.50
❑ 33 Gary Trent	.12	.30
❑ 34 Michael Finley	.20	.50
❑ 35 Dirk Nowitzki	.30	.75
❑ 36 Steve Nash	.30	.75
❑ 37 Antonio McDyess	.15	.40
❑ 38 Nick Van Exel	.15	.40
❑ 39 Chauncey Billups	.20	.50
❑ 40 Danny Fortson	.12	.30
❑ 41 Eric Washington	.12	.30
❑ 42 Raef LaFrentz	.15	.40
❑ 43 Grant Hill	.20	.50
❑ 44 Bison Dele	.12	.30
❑ 45 Lindsey Hunter	.12	.30
❑ 46 Jerry Stackhouse	.20	.50
❑ 47 Don Reid	.12	.30
❑ 48 Christian Laettner	.15	.40
❑ 49 John Starks	.20	.50
❑ 50 Antawn Jamison	.20	.50
❑ 51 Erick Dampier	.15	.40
❑ 52 Donyell Marshall	.15	.40
❑ 53 Chris Mills	.12	.30
❑ 54 Bimbo Coles	.12	.30
❑ 55 Charles Barkley	.25	.60
❑ 56 Hakeem Olajuwon	.20	.50
❑ 57 Scottie Pippen	.30	.75
❑ 58 Othella Harrington	.12	.30
❑ 59 Bryce Drew	.12	.30
❑ 60 Michael Dickerson	.12	.30
❑ 61 Rik Smits	.20	.50
❑ 62 Reggie Miller	.20	.50
❑ 63 Mark Jackson	.20	.50
❑ 64 Antonio Davis	.12	.30
❑ 65 Jalen Rose	.15	.40
❑ 66 Dale Davis	.12	.30
❑ 67 Chris Mullin	.20	.50
❑ 68 Maurice Taylor	.15	.40
❑ 69 Lamond Murray	.12	.30
❑ 70 Rodney Rogers	.12	.30
❑ 71 Darrick Martin	.12	.30
❑ 72 Michael Olowokandi	.12	.30
❑ 73 Tyrone Nesby RC	.20	.50
❑ 74 Kobe Bryant	1.00	2.50
❑ 75 Shaquille O'Neal	.50	1.25
❑ 76 Robert Horry	.20	.50
❑ 77 Glen Rice	.20	.50
❑ 78 J.R. Reid	.12	.30
❑ 79 Rick Fox	.12	.30
❑ 80 Derek Fisher	.20	.50
❑ 81 Tim Hardaway	.20	.50
❑ 82 Alonzo Mourning	.20	.50
❑ 83 Jamal Mashburn	.12	.30
❑ 84 P.J. Brown	.12	.30
❑ 85 Terry Porter	.12	.30
❑ 86 Dan Majerle	.20	.50
❑ 87 Ray Allen	.20	.50
❑ 88 Vinny Del Negro	.12	.30
❑ 89 Glenn Robinson	.15	.40
❑ 90 Dell Curry	.12	.30
❑ 91 Sam Cassell	.15	.40
❑ 92 Robert Traylor	.12	.30
❑ 93 Kevin Garnett	.40	1.00
❑ 94 Terrell Brandon	.12	.30
❑ 95 Joe Smith	.15	.40
❑ 96 Sam Mitchell	.12	.30
❑ 97 Anthony Peeler	.12	.30
❑ 98 Bobby Jackson	.15	.40
❑ 99 Keith Van Horn	.15	.40
❑ 100 Stephon Marbury	.20	.50
❑ 101 Jayson Williams	.15	.40
❑ 102 Kendall Gill	.12	.30
❑ 103 Kerry Kittles	.12	.30
❑ 104 Scott Burrell	.12	.30
❑ 105 Patrick Ewing	.25	.60
❑ 106 Allan Houston	.15	.40
❑ 107 Latrell Sprewell	.15	.40
❑ 108 Larry Johnson	.20	.50
❑ 109 Marcus Camby	.15	.40
❑ 110 Charlie Ward	.12	.30
❑ 111 Anfernee Hardaway	.20	.50
❑ 112 Darrell Armstrong	.12	.30
❑ 113 Nick Anderson	.12	.30
❑ 114 Horace Grant	.15	.40
❑ 115 Isaac Austin	.12	.30
❑ 116 Matt Harpring	.15	.40
❑ 117 Michael Doleac	.12	.30
❑ 118 Allen Iverson	.40	1.00
❑ 119 Theo Ratliff	.15	.40
❑ 120 Matt Geiger	.12	.30
❑ 121 Larry Hughes	.15	.40
❑ 122 Tyrone Hill	.12	.30
❑ 123 George Lynch	.12	.30
❑ 124 Jason Kidd	.30	.75
❑ 125 Tom Gugliotta	.12	.30
❑ 126 Rex Chapman	.12	.30
❑ 127 Clifford Robinson	.12	.30
❑ 128 Luc Longley	.12	.30
❑ 129 Danny Manning	.12	.30
❑ 130 Rasheed Wallace	.20	.50
❑ 131 Arvydas Sabonis	.15	.40
❑ 132 Damon Stoudamire	.20	.50
❑ 133 Brian Grant	.12	.30
❑ 134 Isaiah Rider	.12	.30
❑ 135 Walt Williams	.12	.30
❑ 136 Jim Jackson	.15	.40
❑ 137 Jason Williams	.20	.50
❑ 138 Vlade Divac	.20	.50
❑ 139 Chris Webber	.20	.50
❑ 140 Corliss Williamson	.12	.30
❑ 141 Peja Stojakovic	.15	.40
❑ 142 Tariq Abdul-Wahad	.12	.30
❑ 143 Tim Duncan	.40	1.00

❑ 144 Sean Elliott	.20	.50
❑ 145 David Robinson	.25	.60
❑ 146 Mario Elie	.12	.30
❑ 147 Avery Johnson	.15	.40
❑ 148 Steve Kerr	.15	.40
❑ 149 Gary Payton	.20	.50
❑ 150 Vin Baker	.20	.50
❑ 151 Detlef Schrempf	.15	.40
❑ 152 Hersey Hawkins	.12	.30
❑ 153 Dale Ellis	.12	.30
❑ 154 Olden Polynice	.12	.30
❑ 155 Vince Carter	.40	1.00
❑ 156 John Wallace	.12	.30
❑ 157 Doug Christie	.15	.40
❑ 158 Tracy McGrady	.40	1.00
❑ 159 Kevin Willis	.12	.30
❑ 160 Charles Oakley	.15	.40
❑ 161 Karl Malone	.25	.60
❑ 162 John Stockton	.25	.60
❑ 163 Jeff Hornacek	.15	.40
❑ 164 Bryon Russell	.12	.30
❑ 165 Howard Eisley	.12	.30
❑ 166 Shandon Anderson	.12	.30
❑ 167 Shareef Abdur-Rahim	.15	.40
❑ 168 Mike Bibby	.20	.50
❑ 169 Bryant Reeves	.12	.30
❑ 170 Felipe Lopez	.12	.30
❑ 171 Cherokee Parks	.12	.30
❑ 172 Michael Smith	.12	.30
❑ 173 Juwan Howard	.15	.40
❑ 174 Rod Strickland	.12	.30
❑ 175 Mitch Richmond	.15	.40
❑ 176 Otis Thorpe	.12	.30
❑ 177 Calbert Cheaney	.12	.30
❑ 178 Tracy Murray	.12	.30
❑ 179 Michael Jordan	.75	2.00
❑ 180 Michael Jordan	.75	2.00
❑ 181 Michael Jordan	.75	2.00
❑ 182 Michael Jordan	.75	2.00
❑ 183 Michael Jordan	.75	2.00
❑ 184 Michael Jordan	.75	2.00
❑ 185 Michael Jordan	.75	2.00
❑ 186 Michael Jordan	.75	2.00
❑ 187 Michael Jordan	.75	2.00
❑ 188 Michael Jordan	.75	2.00
❑ 189 Michael Jordan	.75	2.00
❑ 190 Michael Jordan	.75	2.00
❑ 191 Michael Jordan	.75	2.00
❑ 192 Michael Jordan	.75	2.00
❑ 193 Michael Jordan	.75	2.00
❑ 194 Michael Jordan	.75	2.00
❑ 195 Michael Jordan	.75	2.00
❑ 196 Michael Jordan	.75	2.00
❑ 197 Michael Jordan	.75	2.00
❑ 198 Michael Jordan	.75	2.00
❑ 199 Michael Jordan	.75	2.00
❑ 200 Michael Jordan	.75	2.00
❑ 201 Michael Jordan	.75	2.00
❑ 202 Michael Jordan	.75	2.00
❑ 203 Michael Jordan	.75	2.00
❑ 204 Michael Jordan	.75	2.00
❑ 205 Michael Jordan	.75	2.00
❑ 206 Michael Jordan	.75	2.00
❑ 207 Michael Jordan	.75	2.00
❑ 208 Michael Jordan	.75	2.00
❑ 209 Elton Brand RC	1.00	2.50
❑ 210 Steve Francis RC	1.00	2.50
❑ 211 Baron Davis RC	1.25	3.00
❑ 212 Wally Szczerbiak RC	1.00	2.50
❑ 213 Richard Hamilton RC	1.00	2.50
❑ 214 Andre Miller RC	1.00	2.50
❑ 215 Jason Terry RC	.75	2.00
❑ 216 Corey Maggette RC	1.00	2.50
❑ 217 Shawn Marion RC	1.00	2.50
❑ 218 Lamar Odom RC	1.00	2.50
❑ 219 M.Jordan CL	.75	2.00
❑ 220 M.Jordan CL	.75	2.00

2000-01 Upper Deck MVP

❑ COMPLETE SET (220)	20.00	40.00
❑ COMMON CARD (1-190)	.12	.30
❑ COMMON ROOKIE (191-220)	.20	.50
❑ 1 Dikembe Mutombo	.15	.40
❑ 2 Jason Terry	.20	.50
❑ 3 Jim Jackson	.12	.30
❑ 4 Alan Henderson	.12	.30
❑ 5 Roshown McLeod	.12	.30
❑ 6 Bimbo Coles	.12	.30
❑ 7 Lorenzen Wright	.12	.30
❑ 8 Antoine Walker	.15	.40
❑ 9 Paul Pierce	.20	.50
❑ 10 Kenny Anderson	.15	.40
❑ 11 Adrian Griffin	.12	.30
❑ 12 Vitaly Potapenko	.12	.30
❑ 13 Dana Barros	.12	.30
❑ 14 Eric Williams	.12	.30
❑ 15 Eddie Jones	.15	.40
❑ 16 Eddie Robinson	.12	.30
❑ 17 Ricky Davis	.15	.40
❑ 18 Elden Campbell	.12	.30
❑ 19 Derrick Coleman	.15	.40
❑ 20 David Wesley	.12	.30
❑ 21 Baron Davis	.20	.50
❑ 22 Elton Brand	.20	.50
❑ 23 Ron Artest	.20	.50
❑ 24 Hersey Hawkins	.12	.30
❑ 25 Chris Carr	.12	.30
❑ 26 Corey Benjamin	.12	.30
❑ 27 Will Perdue	.12	.30
❑ 28 Andre Miller	.15	.40
❑ 29 Shawn Kemp	.20	.50
❑ 30 Wesley Person	.12	.30
❑ 31 Lamond Murray	.12	.30
❑ 32 Bob Sura	.12	.30
❑ 33 Andrew DeClercq	.12	.30
❑ 34 Dirk Nowitzki	.30	.75
❑ 35 Michael Finley	.20	.50
❑ 36 Cedric Ceballos	.12	.30
❑ 37 Shawn Bradley	.12	.30
❑ 38 Erick Strickland	.12	.30
❑ 39 Hubert Davis	.12	.30
❑ 40 Antonio McDyess	.15	.40
❑ 41 Raef LaFrentz	.12	.30
❑ 42 Keon Clark	.12	.30
❑ 43 Nick Van Exel	.15	.40
❑ 44 James Posey	.12	.30
❑ 45 Chris Gatling	.12	.30
❑ 46 George McCloud	.12	.30
❑ 47 Grant Hill	.20	.50
❑ 48 Jerry Stackhouse	.15	.40
❑ 49 Lindsey Hunter	.12	.30
❑ 50 Christian Laettner	.12	.30
❑ 51 Jerome Williams	.12	.30
❑ 52 Terry Mills	.12	.30
❑ 53 Antawn Jamison	.20	.50
❑ 54 Donyell Marshall	.12	.30
❑ 55 Chris Mills	.12	.30
❑ 56 Larry Hughes	.15	.40
❑ 57 Mookie Blaylock	.15	.40
❑ 58 Vonteego Cummings	.12	.30
❑ 59 Steve Francis	.20	.50
❑ 60 Shandon Anderson	.12	.30
❑ 61 Cuttino Mobley	.15	.40
❑ 62 Hakeem Olajuwon	.25	.60
❑ 63 Walt Williams	.12	.30
❑ 64 Kelvin Cato	.12	.30
❑ 65 Reggie Miller	.20	.50
❑ 66 Austin Croshere	.12	.30
❑ 67 Rik Smits	.12	.30
❑ 68 Jalen Rose	.15	.40
❑ 69 Dale Davis	.12	.30
❑ 70 Jonathan Bender	.12	.30
❑ 71 Michael Olowokandi	.12	.30

❑ 72 Lamar Odom	.20	.50
❑ 73 Tyrone Nesby	.12	.30
❑ 74 Etdrick Bohannon RC	.12	.30
❑ 75 Eric Piatkowski	.12	.30
❑ 76 Shaquille O'Neal	.50	1.25
❑ 77 Kobe Bryant	1.00	2.50
❑ 78 Robert Horry	.15	.40
❑ 79 Ron Harper	.15	.40
❑ 80 Rick Fox	.15	.40
❑ 81 Derek Fisher	.20	.50
❑ 82 Devean George	.12	.30
❑ 83 Alonzo Mourning	.20	.50
❑ 84 Clarence Weatherspoon	.12	.30
❑ 85 Anthony Carter	.12	.30
❑ 86 P.J. Brown	.12	.30
❑ 87 Tim Hardaway	.15	.40
❑ 88 Jamal Mashburn	.15	.40
❑ 89 Voshon Lenard	.12	.30
❑ 90 Ray Allen	.20	.50
❑ 91 Glenn Robinson	.15	.40
❑ 92 Tim Thomas	.12	.30
❑ 93 Sam Cassell	.15	.40
❑ 94 Robert Traylor	.12	.30
❑ 95 Ervin Johnson	.12	.30
❑ 96 Danny Manning	.12	.30
❑ 97 Kevin Garnett	.40	1.00
❑ 98 Wally Szczerbiak	.15	.40
❑ 99 Terrell Brandon	.12	.30
❑ 100 William Avery	.12	.30
❑ 101 Anthony Peeler	.12	.30
❑ 102 Radoslav Nesterovic	.12	.30
❑ 103 Dean Garrett	.12	.30
❑ 104 Keith Van Horn	.15	.40
❑ 105 Kerry Kittles	.15	.40
❑ 106 Stephon Marbury	.20	.50
❑ 107 Evan Eschmeyer	.12	.30
❑ 108 Jim McIlvaine	.12	.30
❑ 109 Lucious Harris	.12	.30
❑ 110 Jamie Feick	.12	.30
❑ 111 Allan Houston	.15	.40
❑ 112 Latrell Sprewell	.15	.40
❑ 113 Patrick Ewing	.25	.60
❑ 114 Chris Childs	.12	.30
❑ 115 Marcus Camby	.15	.40
❑ 116 Charlie Ward	.12	.30
❑ 117 Larry Johnson	.15	.40
❑ 118 Darrell Armstrong	.12	.30
❑ 119 Corey Maggette	.15	.40
❑ 120 Ron Mercer	.12	.30
❑ 121 Pat Garrity	.12	.30
❑ 122 Chucky Atkins	.12	.30
❑ 123 Ben Wallace	.15	.40
❑ 124 Michael Doleac	.12	.30
❑ 125 Allen Iverson	.40	1.00
❑ 126 Matt Geiger	.12	.30
❑ 127 Eric Snow	.12	.30
❑ 128 Toni Kukoc	.15	.40
❑ 129 Theo Ratliff	.12	.30
❑ 130 George Lynch	.12	.30
❑ 131 Jason Kidd	.30	.75
❑ 132 Tom Gugliotta	.12	.30
❑ 133 Rodney Rogers	.12	.30
❑ 134 Shawn Marion	.20	.50
❑ 135 Clifford Robinson	.12	.30
❑ 136 Kevin Johnson	.15	.40
❑ 137 Anfernee Hardaway	.20	.50
❑ 138 Scottie Pippen	.30	.75
❑ 139 Damon Stoudamire	.15	.40
❑ 140 Arvydas Sabonis	.15	.40
❑ 141 Jermaine O'Neal	.20	.50
❑ 142 Bonzi Wells	.12	.30
❑ 143 Rasheed Wallace	.20	.50
❑ 144 Detlef Schrempf	.15	.40
❑ 145 Chris Webber	.20	.50
❑ 146 Vlade Divac	.15	.40
❑ 147 Peja Stojakovic	.15	.40
❑ 148 Jason Williams	.15	.40
❑ 149 Corliss Williamson	.15	.40
❑ 150 Nick Anderson	.12	.30
❑ 151 Jon Barry	.12	.30
❑ 152 Tim Duncan	.40	1.00
❑ 153 David Robinson	.25	.60
❑ 154 Avery Johnson	.15	.40
❑ 155 Terry Porter	.15	.40
❑ 156 Mario Elie	.12	.30
❑ 157 Jaren Jackson	.12	.30
❑ 158 Steve Kerr	.12	.30
❑ 159 Gary Payton	.20	.50
❑ 160 Vin Baker	.15	.40

❑ 161 Brent Barry	.12	.30
❑ 162 Horace Grant	.15	.40
❑ 163 Ruben Patterson	.12	.30
❑ 164 Rashard Lewis	.20	.50
❑ 165 Tracy McGrady	.40	1.00
❑ 166 Charles Oakley	.15	.40
❑ 167 Doug Christie	.12	.30
❑ 168 Antonio Davis	.12	.30
❑ 169 Vince Carter	.40	1.00
❑ 170 Kevin Willis	.12	.30
❑ 171 Karl Malone	.25	.60
❑ 172 John Stockton	.25	.60
❑ 173 Bryon Russell	.12	.30
❑ 174 Quincy Lewis	.12	.30
❑ 175 Olden Polynice	.12	.30
❑ 176 Jacque Vaughn	.12	.30
❑ 177 Shareef Abdur-Rahim	.15	.40
❑ 178 Michael Dickerson	.12	.30
❑ 179 Bryant Reeves	.12	.30
❑ 180 Mike Bibby	.15	.40
❑ 181 Othella Harrington	.12	.30
❑ 182 Felipe Lopez	.12	.30
❑ 183 Mitch Richmond	.15	.40
❑ 184 Richard Hamilton	.15	.40
❑ 185 Jahidi White	.12	.30
❑ 186 Aaron Williams	.12	.30
❑ 187 Juwan Howard	.15	.40
❑ 188 Rod Strickland	.15	.40
❑ 189 Kobe Bryant CL	.50	1.25
❑ 190 Kevin Garnett CL	.20	.50
❑ 191 Kenyon Martin RC	.50	1.25
❑ 192 Marcus Fizer RC	.20	.50
❑ 193 Chris Mihm RC	.20	.50
❑ 194 Stromile Swift RC	.25	.60
❑ 195 Morris Peterson RC	.30	.75
❑ 196 Quentin Richardson RC	.25	.60
❑ 197 Courtney Alexander RC	.20	.50
❑ 198 Scoonie Penn RC	.20	.50
❑ 199 Mateen Cleaves RC	.20	.50
❑ 200 Erick Barkley RC	.20	.50
❑ 201 A.J. Guyton RC	.20	.50
❑ 202 Darius Miles RC	.25	.60
❑ 203 DerMarr Johnson RC	.20	.50
❑ 204 Jerome Moiso RC	.20	.50
❑ 205 Jamaal Magloire RC	.20	.50
❑ 206 Hanno Mottola RC	.20	.50
❑ 207 Mike Miller RC	.30	.75
❑ 208 Desmond Mason RC	.25	.60
❑ 209 Chris Carrawell RC	.20	.50
❑ 210 Eduardo Najera RC	.20	.50
❑ 211 Speedy Claxton RC	.20	.50
❑ 212 Joel Przybilla RC	.20	.50
❑ 213 Mark Madsen RC	.20	.50
❑ 214 Khalid El-Amin RC	.20	.50
❑ 215 Etan Thomas RC	.20	.50
❑ 216 Jason Collier RC	.20	.50
❑ 217 Jason Hart RC	.20	.50
❑ 218 Michael Redd RC	.50	1.25
❑ 219 Keyon Dooling RC	.20	.50
❑ 220 Mamadou N'Diaye RC	.20	.50

2001-02 Upper Deck MVP

❑ COMPLETE SET (220)	20.00	40.00
❑ COMMON CARD	.05	.15
❑ COMMON ROOKIE	.40	1.00
❑ 1 Jason Terry	.20	.50
❑ 2 Alan Henderson	.12	.30
❑ 3 Toni Kukoc	.15	.40
❑ 4 Hanno Mottola	.12	.30
❑ 5 Theo Ratliff	.12	.30
❑ 6 DerMarr Johnson	.12	.30
❑ 7 Paul Pierce	.20	.50
❑ 8 Antoine Walker	.15	.40
❑ 9 Bryant Stith	.12	.30
❑ 10 Kenny Anderson	.15	.40
❑ 11 Vitaly Potapenko	.12	.30
❑ 12 Eric Williams	.12	.30
❑ 13 Jamal Mashburn	.15	.40
❑ 14 David Wesley	.12	.30
❑ 15 Baron Davis	.20	.50
❑ 16 Elden Campbell	.12	.30
❑ 17 P.J. Brown	.12	.30
❑ 18 Jamaal Magloire	.12	.30
❑ 19 Eddie Robinson	.12	.30
❑ 20 Elton Brand	.20	.50
❑ 21 Ron Mercer	.12	.30
❑ 22 Fred Hoiberg	.12	.30
❑ 23 Jamal Crawford	.15	.40
❑ 24 Ron Artest	.15	.40
❑ 25 Marcus Fizer	.12	.30
❑ 26 Andre Miller	.15	.40
❑ 27 Lamond Murray	.12	.30
❑ 28 Jim Jackson	.12	.30
❑ 29 Chris Mihm	.12	.30
❑ 30 Matt Harpring	.15	.40
❑ 31 Chris Gatling	.12	.30
❑ 32 Michael Finley	.20	.50
❑ 33 Steve Nash	.30	.75
❑ 34 Dirk Nowitzki	.30	.75
❑ 35 Juwan Howard	.15	.40
❑ 36 Howard Eisley	.12	.30
❑ 37 Eduardo Najera	.12	.30
❑ 38 Wang Zhizhi	.15	.40
❑ 39 Antonio McDyess	.15	.40
❑ 40 Nick Van Exel	.15	.40
❑ 41 Raef LaFrentz	.12	.30
❑ 42 James Posey	.12	.30
❑ 43 George McCloud	.12	.30
❑ 44 Voshon Lenard	.12	.30
❑ 45 Jerry Stackhouse	.15	.40
❑ 46 Chucky Atkins	.12	.30
❑ 47 Corliss Williamson	.15	.40
❑ 48 Joe Smith	.12	.30
❑ 49 Mateen Cleaves	.12	.30
❑ 50 Ben Wallace	.15	.40
❑ 51 Antawn Jamison	.20	.50
❑ 52 Marc Jackson	.12	.30
❑ 53 Larry Hughes	.15	.40
❑ 54 Bob Sura	.12	.30
❑ 55 Chris Porter	.12	.30
❑ 56 Vonteego Cummings	.12	.30
❑ 57 Steve Francis	.20	.50
❑ 58 Hakeem Olajuwon	.25	.60
❑ 59 Cuttino Mobley	.15	.40
❑ 60 Maurice Taylor	.12	.30
❑ 61 Shandon Anderson	.12	.30
❑ 62 Walt Williams	.12	.30
❑ 63 Moochie Norris	.12	.30
❑ 64 Reggie Miller	.20	.50
❑ 65 Jalen Rose	.15	.40
❑ 66 Jermaine O'Neal	.20	.50
❑ 67 Austin Croshere	.12	.30
❑ 68 Travis Best	.12	.30
❑ 69 Al Harrington	.15	.40
❑ 70 Jonathan Bender	.12	.30
❑ 71 Darius Miles	.12	.30
❑ 72 Corey Maggette	.15	.40
❑ 73 Lamar Odom	.20	.50
❑ 74 Quentin Richardson	.15	.40
❑ 75 Keyon Dooling	.12	.30
❑ 76 Jeff McInnis	.12	.30
❑ 77 Eric Piatkowski	.12	.30
❑ 78 Kobe Bryant	1.00	2.50
❑ 79 Shaquille O'Neal	.50	1.25
❑ 80 Rick Fox	.15	.40
❑ 81 Derek Fisher	.15	.40
❑ 82 Robert Horry	.15	.40
❑ 83 Ron Harper	.15	.40
❑ 84 Brian Shaw	.12	.30
❑ 85 Alonzo Mourning	.20	.50
❑ 86 Eddie Jones	.15	.40
❑ 87 Tim Hardaway	.15	.40
❑ 88 Anthony Mason	.12	.30
❑ 89 Brian Grant	.12	.30
❑ 90 Anthony Carter	.12	.30
❑ 91 Bruce Bowen	.12	.30
❑ 92 Ray Allen	.20	.50
❑ 93 Glenn Robinson	.15	.40
❑ 94 Sam Cassell	.15	.40
❑ 95 Tim Thomas	.12	.30
❑ 96 Ervin Johnson	.12	.30
❑ 97 Joel Przybilla	.12	.30
❑ 98 Kevin Garnett	.40	1.00
❑ 99 Terrell Brandon	.12	.30
❑ 100 Wally Szczerbiak	.15	.40
❑ 101 Chauncey Billups	.15	.40
❑ 102 LaPhonso Ellis	.15	.40
❑ 103 Anthony Peeler	.12	.30
❑ 104 Stephon Marbury	.20	.50
❑ 105 Keith Van Horn	.15	.40
❑ 106 Kenyon Martin	.20	.50
❑ 107 Kendall Gill	.12	.30
❑ 108 Lucious Harris	.12	.30
❑ 109 Stephen Jackson	.15	.40
❑ 110 Latrell Sprewell	.15	.40
❑ 111 Allan Houston	.15	.40
❑ 112 Marcus Camby	.15	.40
❑ 113 Mark Jackson	.15	.40
❑ 114 Glen Rice	.15	.40
❑ 115 Kurt Thomas	.12	.30
❑ 116 Tracy McGrady	.40	1.00
❑ 117 Darrell Armstrong	.12	.30
❑ 118 Mike Miller	.15	.40
❑ 119 Grant Hill	.20	.50
❑ 120 Pat Garrity	.12	.30
❑ 121 John Amaechi	.12	.30
❑ 122 Allen Iverson	.40	1.00
❑ 123 Dikembe Mutombo	.15	.40
❑ 124 Aaron McKie	.12	.30
❑ 125 Tyrone Hill	.12	.30
❑ 126 George Lynch	.12	.30
❑ 127 Eric Snow	.12	.30
❑ 128 Matt Geiger	.12	.30
❑ 129 Jason Kidd	.30	.75
❑ 130 Shawn Marion	.20	.50
❑ 131 Tony Delk	.12	.30
❑ 132 Rodney Rogers	.12	.30
❑ 133 Tom Gugliotta	.12	.30
❑ 134 Anfernee Hardaway	.20	.50
❑ 135 Rasheed Wallace	.20	.50
❑ 136 Damon Stoudamire	.15	.40
❑ 137 Arvydas Sabonis	.15	.40
❑ 138 Scottie Pippen	.30	.75
❑ 139 Steve Smith	.15	.40
❑ 140 Stacey Augmon	.12	.30
❑ 141 Bonzi Wells	.15	.40
❑ 142 Jason Williams	.15	.40
❑ 143 Chris Webber	.20	.50
❑ 144 Peja Stojakovic	.15	.40
❑ 145 Doug Christie	.12	.30
❑ 146 Scot Pollard	.12	.30
❑ 147 Hedo Turkoglu	.15	.40
❑ 148 Vlade Divac	.15	.40
❑ 149 Tim Duncan	.40	1.00
❑ 150 David Robinson	.25	.60
❑ 151 Antonio Daniels	.12	.30
❑ 152 Sean Elliott	.12	.30
❑ 153 Derek Anderson	.15	.40
❑ 154 Avery Johnson	.15	.40
❑ 155 Malik Rose	.12	.30
❑ 156 Gary Payton	.20	.50
❑ 157 Rashard Lewis	.20	.50
❑ 158 Patrick Ewing	.25	.60
❑ 159 Vin Baker	.15	.40
❑ 160 Emanual Davis	.12	.30
❑ 161 Desmond Mason	.15	.40
❑ 162 Vince Carter	.40	1.00
❑ 163 Morris Peterson	.15	.40
❑ 164 Antonio Davis	.12	.30
❑ 165 Keon Clark	.12	.30
❑ 166 Chris Childs	.12	.30
❑ 167 Charles Oakley	.15	.40
❑ 168 Alvin Williams	.12	.30
❑ 169 Dell Curry	.12	.30
❑ 170 Karl Malone	.25	.60
❑ 171 John Stockton	.25	.60
❑ 172 Donyell Marshall	.12	.30
❑ 173 John Starks	.12	.30
❑ 174 Bryon Russell	.12	.30
❑ 175 David Benoit	.12	.30
❑ 176 Jacque Vaughn	.12	.30
❑ 177 Shareef Abdur-Rahim	.15	.40
❑ 178 Mike Bibby	.15	.40
❑ 179 Michael Dickerson	.12	.30
❑ 180 Bryant Reeves	.12	.30
❑ 181 Grant Long	.12	.30
❑ 182 Stromile Swift	.12	.30
❑ 183 Richard Hamilton	.15	.40
❑ 184 Tyrone Nesby	.12	.30
❑ 185 Jahidi White	.12	.30
❑ 186 Chris Whitney	.12	.30
❑ 187 Courtney Alexander	.12	.30
❑ 188 Christian Laettner	.12	.30
❑ 189 Kobe Bryant CL	.50	1.25

❑ 190 Kevin Garnett CL	.20	.50
❑ 191 Vladimir Radmanovic RC	.50	1.25
❑ 192 Alvin Jones RC	.40	1.00
❑ 193 Tyson Chandler RC	.75	2.00
❑ 194 Omar Cook RC	.40	1.00
❑ 195 Kedrick Brown RC	.40	1.00
❑ 196 DeSagana Diop RC	.40	1.00
❑ 197 Eddie Griffin RC	.40	1.00
❑ 198 Zach Randolph RC	1.00	2.50
❑ 199 Eddy Curry RC	.60	1.50
❑ 200 Jeryl Sasser RC	.40	1.00
❑ 201 Gerald Wallace RC	1.00	2.50
❑ 202 Jamaal Tinsley RC	.50	1.25
❑ 203 Kirk Haston RC	.40	1.00
❑ 204 Terence Morris RC	.40	1.00
❑ 205 Jarron Collins RC	.40	1.00
❑ 206 Joseph Forte RC	.40	1.00
❑ 207 Kenny Satterfield RC	.40	1.00
❑ 208 Michael Wright RC	.40	1.00
❑ 209 Jason Richardson RC	.75	2.00
❑ 210 Michael Bradley RC	.40	1.00
❑ 211 Gilbert Arenas RC	.60	1.50
❑ 212 Jeff Trepagnier RC	.40	1.00
❑ 213 Samuel Dalembert RC	.50	1.25
❑ 214 Troy Murphy RC	.75	2.00
❑ 215 Rodney White RC	.40	1.00
❑ 216 Joe Johnson RC	1.00	2.50
❑ 217 Richard Jefferson RC	1.00	2.50
❑ 218 Kwame Brown RC	.50	1.25
❑ 219 Jason Collins RC	.40	1.00
❑ 220 Steven Hunter RC	.40	1.00

2002-03 Upper Deck MVP

❑ COMPLETE SET (220)	20.00	50.00
❑ COMMON ROOKIE (191-220)	.50	1.25
❑ 1 Shareef Abdur-Rahim	.15	.40
❑ 2 Jason Terry	.20	.50
❑ 3 Toni Kukoc	.15	.40
❑ 4 DerMarr Johnson	.12	.30
❑ 5 Nazr Mohammed	.12	.30
❑ 6 Theo Ratliff	.12	.30
❑ 7 Dion Glover	.12	.30
❑ 8 Paul Pierce	.20	.50
❑ 9 Antoine Walker	.15	.40
❑ 10 Kenny Anderson	.15	.40
❑ 11 Tony Delk	.12	.30
❑ 12 Eric Williams	.12	.30
❑ 13 Rodney Rogers	.12	.30
❑ 14 Jamal Mashburn	.15	.40
❑ 15 Baron Davis	.20	.50
❑ 16 David Wesley	.12	.30
❑ 17 Elden Campbell	.12	.30
❑ 18 P.J. Brown	.12	.30
❑ 19 Jamaal Magloire	.12	.30
❑ 20 Stacey Augmon	.12	.30
❑ 21 Jalen Rose	.15	.40
❑ 22 Marcus Fizer	.12	.30
❑ 23 Tyson Chandler	.15	.40
❑ 24 Trenton Hassell	.12	.30
❑ 25 Eddy Curry	.15	.40
❑ 26 Travis Best	.12	.30
❑ 27 Andre Miller	.15	.40
❑ 28 Lamond Murray	.12	.30
❑ 29 Ricky Davis	.15	.40
❑ 30 Zydrunas Ilgauskas	.15	.40
❑ 31 Jumaine Jones	.12	.30
❑ 32 Chris Mihm	.12	.30
❑ 33 Dirk Nowitzki	.30	.75
❑ 34 Michael Finley	.20	.50
❑ 35 Steve Nash	.30	.75
❑ 36 Nick Van Exel	.15	.40
❑ 37 Raef LaFrentz	.12	.30
❑ 38 Adrian Griffin	.12	.30
❑ 39 Avery Johnson	.15	.40
❑ 40 Marcus Camby	.15	.40
❑ 41 Juwan Howard	.15	.40
❑ 42 James Posey	.12	.30
❑ 43 Ryan Bowen	.12	.30
❑ 44 Donnell Harvey	.12	.30
❑ 45 Voshon Lenard	.12	.30
❑ 46 Jerry Stackhouse	.15	.40
❑ 47 Clifford Robinson	.12	.30
❑ 48 Chucky Atkins	.12	.30
❑ 49 Ben Wallace	.15	.40
❑ 50 Jon Barry	.12	.30
❑ 51 Corliss Williamson	.15	.40
❑ 52 Antawn Jamison	.20	.50
❑ 53 Jason Richardson	.20	.50
❑ 54 Danny Fortson	.12	.30
❑ 55 Gilbert Arenas	.20	.50
❑ 56 Bob Sura	.12	.30
❑ 57 Troy Murphy	.20	.50
❑ 58 Steve Francis	.20	.50
❑ 59 Cuttino Mobley	.15	.40
❑ 60 Eddie Griffin	.12	.30
❑ 61 Kenny Thomas	.12	.30
❑ 62 Moochie Norris	.12	.30
❑ 63 Kelvin Cato	.12	.30
❑ 64 Glen Rice	.15	.40
❑ 65 Reggie Miller	.20	.50
❑ 66 Jermaine O'Neal	.20	.50
❑ 67 Ron Mercer	.12	.30
❑ 68 Jamaal Tinsley	.15	.40
❑ 69 Al Harrington	.15	.40
❑ 70 Ron Artest	.15	.40
❑ 71 Austin Croshere	.12	.30
❑ 72 Elton Brand	.20	.50
❑ 73 Darius Miles	.12	.30
❑ 74 Lamar Odom	.20	.50
❑ 75 Quentin Richardson	.15	.40
❑ 76 Corey Maggette	.15	.40
❑ 77 Jeff McInnis	.12	.30
❑ 78 Michael Olowokandi	.12	.30
❑ 79 Kobe Bryant	1.00	2.50
❑ 80 Shaquille O'Neal	.50	1.25
❑ 81 Derek Fisher	.15	.40
❑ 82 Rick Fox	.15	.40
❑ 83 Robert Horry	.15	.40
❑ 84 Devean George	.12	.30
❑ 85 Samaki Walker	.12	.30
❑ 86 Pau Gasol	.20	.50
❑ 87 Jason Williams	.15	.40
❑ 88 Shane Battier	.15	.40
❑ 89 Stromile Swift	.12	.30
❑ 90 Lorenzen Wright	.12	.30
❑ 91 Tony Massenburg	.12	.30
❑ 92 Eddie Jones	.15	.40
❑ 93 Alonzo Mourning	.20	.50
❑ 94 Brian Grant	.12	.30
❑ 95 Anthony Carter	.12	.30
❑ 96 LaPhonso Ellis	.15	.40
❑ 97 Jim Jackson	.12	.30
❑ 98 Ray Allen	.20	.50
❑ 99 Glenn Robinson	.15	.40
❑ 100 Sam Cassell	.15	.40
❑ 101 Tim Thomas	.12	.30
❑ 102 Anthony Mason	.12	.30
❑ 103 Joel Przybilla	.12	.30
❑ 104 Ervin Johnson	.12	.30
❑ 105 Kevin Garnett	.40	1.00
❑ 106 Wally Szczerbiak	.15	.40
❑ 107 Chauncey Billups	.20	.50
❑ 108 Terrell Brandon	.12	.30
❑ 109 Marc Jackson	.12	.30
❑ 110 Joe Smith	.12	.30
❑ 111 Jason Kidd	.30	.75
❑ 112 Keith Van Horn	.15	.40
❑ 113 Kenyon Martin	.20	.50
❑ 114 Kerry Kittles	.15	.40
❑ 115 Richard Jefferson	.20	.50
❑ 116 Jason Collins	.12	.30
❑ 117 Todd MacCulloch	.12	.30
❑ 118 Allan Houston	.15	.40
❑ 119 Latrell Sprewell	.15	.40
❑ 120 Kurt Thomas	.12	.30
❑ 121 Antonio McDyess	.15	.40
❑ 122 Othella Harrington	.12	.30
❑ 123 Clarence Weatherspoon	.12	.30
❑ 124 Tracy McGrady	.40	1.00
❑ 125 Mike Miller	.15	.40
❑ 126 Darrell Armstrong	.12	.30
❑ 127 Grant Hill	.20	.50
❑ 128 Horace Grant	.15	.40
❑ 129 Steven Hunter	.12	.30
❑ 130 Allen Iverson	.40	1.00
❑ 131 Dikembe Mutombo	.15	.40
❑ 132 Aaron McKie	.12	.30
❑ 133 Derrick Coleman	.15	.40
❑ 134 Eric Snow	.12	.30
❑ 135 Matt Harpring	.15	.40
❑ 136 Stephon Marbury	.20	.50
❑ 137 Shawn Marion	.20	.50
❑ 138 Joe Johnson	.20	.50
❑ 139 Anfernee Hardaway	.20	.50
❑ 140 Iakovos Tsakalidis	.12	.30
❑ 141 Tom Gugliotta	.12	.30
❑ 142 Bo Outlaw	.12	.30
❑ 143 Rasheed Wallace	.20	.50
❑ 144 Damon Stoudamire	.15	.40
❑ 145 Scottie Pippen	.30	.75
❑ 146 Ruben Patterson	.12	.30
❑ 147 Derek Anderson	.15	.40
❑ 148 Dale Davis	.12	.30
❑ 149 Bonzi Wells	.15	.40
❑ 150 Chris Webber	.20	.50
❑ 151 Peja Stojakovic	.15	.40
❑ 152 Mike Bibby	.15	.40
❑ 153 Doug Christie	.12	.30
❑ 154 Vlade Divac	.15	.40
❑ 155 Bobby Jackson	.12	.30
❑ 156 Hedo Turkoglu	.15	.40
❑ 157 Tim Duncan	.40	1.00
❑ 158 David Robinson	.25	.60
❑ 159 Steve Smith	.15	.40
❑ 160 Tony Parker	.20	.50
❑ 161 Antonio Daniels	.12	.30
❑ 162 Charles Smith	.12	.30
❑ 163 Bruce Bowen	.12	.30
❑ 164 Gary Payton	.20	.50
❑ 165 Rashard Lewis	.20	.50
❑ 166 Vin Baker	.15	.40
❑ 167 Brent Barry	.12	.30
❑ 168 Desmond Mason	.15	.40
❑ 169 Vladimir Radmanovic	.12	.30
❑ 170 Vince Carter	.40	1.00
❑ 171 Morris Peterson	.15	.40
❑ 172 Antonio Davis	.12	.30
❑ 173 Hakeem Olajuwon	.25	.60
❑ 174 Alvin Williams	.12	.30
❑ 175 Jerome Williams	.12	.30
❑ 176 Keon Clark	.12	.30
❑ 177 Karl Malone	.20	.50
❑ 178 John Stockton	.25	.60
❑ 179 Donyell Marshall	.12	.30
❑ 180 Andrei Kirilenko	.20	.50
❑ 181 Bryon Russell	.12	.30
❑ 182 Jarron Collins	.12	.30
❑ 183 DeShawn Stevenson	.12	.30
❑ 184 Michael Jordan	1.25	3.00
❑ 185 Richard Hamilton	.15	.40
❑ 186 Kwame Brown	.12	.30
❑ 187 Chris Whitney	.12	.30
❑ 188 Tyronn Lue	.12	.30
❑ 189 Brendan Haywood	.12	.30
❑ 190 Jahidi White	.12	.30
❑ 191 DaJuan Wagnerr RC	.50	1.25
❑ 192 Jay Williams RC	.60	1.50
❑ 193 Yao Ming RC	1.50	4.00
❑ 194 Drew Gooden RC	.75	2.00
❑ 195 Chris Jefferies RC	.50	1.25
❑ 196 Casey Jacobsen RC	.50	1.25
❑ 197 Juan Dixon RC	.75	2.00
❑ 198 Melvin Ely RC	.50	1.25
❑ 199 Curtis Borchardt RC	.50	1.25
❑ 200 John Salmons RC	.75	2.00
❑ 201 Carlos Boozer RC	1.00	2.50
❑ 202 Fred Jones RC	.60	1.50
❑ 203 Frank Williams RC	.50	1.25
❑ 204 Jamal Sampson RC	.50	1.25
❑ 205 Dan Dickau RC	.50	1.25
❑ 206 Marcus Haislip RC	.50	1.25
❑ 207 Jared Jeffries RC	.50	1.25
❑ 208 Amare Stoudemire RC	1.25	3.00
❑ 209 Caron Butler RC	1.00	2.50
❑ 210 Qyntel Woods RC	.50	1.25
❑ 211 Kareem Rush RC	.60	1.50
❑ 212 Ryan Humphrey RC	.50	1.25
❑ 213 Jiri Welsch RC	.50	1.25
❑ 214 Mike Dunleavy RC	.60	1.50
❑ 215 Tayshaun Prince RC	.75	2.00
❑ 216 Nene Hilario RC	.60	1.50
❑ 217 Nikoloz Tskitishvili RC	.50	1.25
❑ 218 Bostjan Nachbar RC	.50	1.25

❑ 219 Efthimios Rentzias RC	.50	1.25
❑ 220 Rod Grizzard RC	.50	1.25

2003-04 Upper Deck MVP

❑ COMP.SET w/o SP's		
❑ COMMON ROOKIE (201-230)	.60	1.50
❑ BLACK NOT PRICED DUE TO SCARCITY		
❑ *GOLD SINGLES: 8X TO 20X BASE CARD HI		
❑ *GOLD RC's: 4X TO 10X BASE CARD HI		
❑ *SILVER SINGLES: .75X TO 2X BASE CARD HI		
❑ 1 Shareef Abdur-Rahim	.20	.50
❑ 2 Jason Terry	.20	.50
❑ 3 Terrell Brandon	.06	.15
❑ 4 Alan Henderson	.06	.15
❑ 5 Dan Dickau	.06	.15
❑ 6 Theo Ratliff	.10	.25
❑ 7 Dion Glover	.06	.15
❑ 8 Paul Pierce	.20	.50
❑ 9 Antoine Walker	.20	.50
❑ 10 Eric Williams	.06	.15
❑ 11 Tony Delk	.06	.15
❑ 12 J.R. Bremer	.06	.15
❑ 13 Vin Baker	.10	.25
❑ 14 Jalen Rose	.20	.50
❑ 15 Marcus Fizer	.06	.15
❑ 16 Tyson Chandler	.20	.50
❑ 17 Jamal Crawford	.06	.15
❑ 18 Eddy Curry	.10	.25
❑ 19 Scottie Pippen	.30	.75
❑ 20 Darius Miles	.20	.50
❑ 21 Dajuan Wagner	.10	.25
❑ 22 Ricky Davis	.20	.50
❑ 23 Zydrunas Ilgauskas	.10	.25
❑ 24 Carlos Boozer	.20	.50
❑ 25 Chris Mihm	.06	.15
❑ 26 Dirk Nowitzki	.30	.75
❑ 27 Michael Finley	.20	.50
❑ 28 Steve Nash	.20	.50
❑ 29 Nick Van Exel	.20	.50
❑ 30 Raef LaFrentz	.10	.25
❑ 31 Eduardo Najera	.10	.25
❑ 32 Shawn Bradley	.06	.15
❑ 33 Marcus Camby	.10	.25
❑ 34 Vincent Yarbrough	.06	.15
❑ 35 Rodney White	.06	.15
❑ 36 Nene Hilario	.10	.25
❑ 37 Nikoloz Tskitishvili	.06	.15
❑ 38 Shammond Williams	.06	.15
❑ 39 Richard Hamilton	.10	.25
❑ 40 Clifford Robinson	.06	.15
❑ 41 Chauncey Billups	.10	.25
❑ 42 Ben Wallace	.20	.50
❑ 43 Elden Campbell	.06	.15
❑ 44 Corliss Williamson	.10	.25
❑ 45 Antawn Jamison	.20	.50
❑ 46 Jason Richardson	.20	.50
❑ 47 Danny Fortson	.06	.15
❑ 48 Speedy Claxton	.06	.15
❑ 49 Mike Dunleavy	.10	.25
❑ 50 Troy Murphy	.20	.50
❑ 51 Steve Francis	.20	.50
❑ 52 Cuttino Mobley	.10	.25
❑ 53 Eddie Griffin	.10	.25
❑ 54 Yao Ming	.50	1.25
❑ 55 Maurice Taylor	.06	.15
❑ 56 Kelvin Cato	.06	.15
❑ 57 Glen Rice	.10	.25
❑ 58 Reggie Miller	.20	.50
❑ 59 Jermaine O'Neal	.20	.50
❑ 60 Scot Pollard	.06	.15
❑ 61 Jamaal Tinsley	.20	.50
❑ 62 Al Harrington	.10	.25
❑ 63 Ron Artest	.10	.25
❑ 64 Danny Ferry	.06	.15
❑ 65 Elton Brand	.20	.50
❑ 66 Andre Miller	.10	.25
❑ 67 Lamar Odom	.20	.50
❑ 68 Quentin Richardson	.10	.25
❑ 69 Corey Maggette	.10	.25
❑ 70 Chris Wilcox	.10	.25
❑ 71 Marko Jaric	.10	.25
❑ 72 Kobe Bryant	.75	2.00
❑ 73 Shaquille O'Neal	.50	1.25
❑ 74 Derek Fisher	.20	.50
❑ 75 Karl Malone	.20	.50
❑ 76 Gary Payton	.20	.50
❑ 77 Devean George	.10	.25
❑ 78 Kareem Rush	.10	.25
❑ 79 Pau Gasol	.20	.50
❑ 80 Jason Williams	.10	.25
❑ 81 Shane Battier	.20	.50
❑ 82 Stromile Swift	.10	.25
❑ 83 Lorenzen Wright	.06	.15
❑ 84 Mike Miller	.20	.50
❑ 85 Eddie Jones	.20	.50
❑ 86 Ken Johnson	.06	.15
❑ 87 Brian Grant	.10	.25
❑ 88 Anthony Carter	.10	.25
❑ 89 Rasual Butler	.10	.25
❑ 90 Caron Butler	.20	.50
❑ 91 Marcus Haislip	.06	.15
❑ 92 Toni Kukoc	.10	.25
❑ 93 Joe Smith	.10	.25
❑ 94 Tim Thomas	.10	.25
❑ 95 Anthony Mason	.10	.25
❑ 96 Joel Przybilla	.06	.15
❑ 97 Desmond Mason	.10	.25
❑ 98 Kevin Garnett	.40	1.00
❑ 99 Wally Szczerbiak	.10	.25
❑ 100 Troy Hudson	.06	.15
❑ 101 Michael Olowokandi	.06	.15
❑ 102 Kendall Gill	.06	.15
❑ 103 Sam Cassell	.20	.50
❑ 104 Jason Kidd	.30	.75
❑ 105 Kenyon Martin	.20	.50
❑ 106 Alonzo Mourning	.10	.25
❑ 107 Kerry Kittles	.06	.15
❑ 108 Richard Jefferson	.10	.25
❑ 109 Jason Collins	.06	.15
❑ 110 Dikembe Mutombo	.10	.25
❑ 111 Jamal Mashburn	.10	.25
❑ 112 Baron Davis	.20	.50
❑ 113 David Wesley	.06	.15
❑ 114 Kenny Anderson	.10	.25
❑ 115 P.J. Brown	.06	.15
❑ 116 Jamaal Magloire	.06	.15
❑ 117 George Lynch	.06	.15
❑ 118 Courtney Alexander	.10	.25
❑ 119 Allan Houston	.10	.25
❑ 120 Keith Van Horn	.20	.50
❑ 121 Kurt Thomas	.10	.25
❑ 122 Antonio McDyess	.10	.25
❑ 123 Othella Harrington	.06	.15
❑ 124 Clarence Weatherspoon	.06	.15
❑ 125 Tracy McGrady	.50	1.25
❑ 126 Drew Gooden	.10	.25
❑ 127 Tyronn Lue	.06	.15
❑ 128 Pat Garrity	.06	.15
❑ 129 Grant Hill	.20	.50
❑ 130 Gordan Giricek	.10	.25
❑ 131 Juwan Howard	.10	.25
❑ 132 Allen Iverson	.40	1.00
❑ 133 Glenn Robinson	.10	.25
❑ 134 Aaron McKie	.10	.25
❑ 135 Derrick Coleman	.06	.15
❑ 136 Eric Snow	.10	.25
❑ 137 Kenny Thomas	.06	.15
❑ 138 Stephon Marbury	.20	.50
❑ 139 Shawn Marion	.20	.50
❑ 140 Joe Johnson	.10	.25
❑ 141 Anfernee Hardaway	.20	.50
❑ 142 Amare Stoudemire	.40	1.00
❑ 143 Casey Jacobsen	.06	.15
❑ 144 Tom Gugliotta	.06	.15
❑ 145 Bo Outlaw	.06	.15
❑ 146 Rasheed Wallace	.20	.50
❑ 147 Damon Stoudamire	.10	.25
❑ 148 Jeff McInnis	.06	.15
❑ 149 Ruben Patterson	.10	.25
❑ 150 Derek Anderson	.10	.25
❑ 151 Dale Davis	.10	.25
❑ 152 Bonzi Wells	.10	.25
❑ 153 Chris Webber	.20	.50
❑ 154 Peja Stojakovic	.20	.50
❑ 155 Mike Bibby	.20	.50
❑ 156 Doug Christie	.10	.25
❑ 157 Vlade Divac	.10	.25
❑ 158 Bobby Jackson	.10	.25
❑ 159 Brad Miller	.20	.50
❑ 160 Keon Clark	.10	.25
❑ 161 Tim Duncan	.40	1.00
❑ 162 David Robinson	.20	.50
❑ 163 Steve Smith	.10	.25
❑ 164 Tony Parker	.20	.50
❑ 165 Hedo Turkoglu	.20	.50
❑ 166 Radoslav Nesterovic	.10	.25
❑ 167 Manu Ginobili	.20	.50
❑ 168 Ron Mercer	.06	.15
❑ 169 Ray Allen	.20	.50
❑ 170 Rashard Lewis	.20	.50
❑ 171 Antonio Daniels	.06	.15
❑ 172 Brent Barry	.10	.25
❑ 173 Predrag Drobnjak	.06	.15
❑ 174 Vladimir Radmanovic	.06	.15
❑ 175 Vince Carter	.40	1.00
❑ 176 Morris Peterson	.10	.25
❑ 177 Antonio Davis	.06	.15
❑ 178 Chris Jefferies	.06	.15
❑ 179 Lindsey Hunter	.06	.15
❑ 180 Alvin Williams	.06	.15
❑ 181 Jerome Williams	.06	.15
❑ 182 Jerome Moiso	.06	.15
❑ 183 Greg Ostertag	.06	.15
❑ 184 John Stockton	.20	.50
❑ 185 Matt Harpring	.20	.50
❑ 186 Andrei Kirilenko	.20	.50
❑ 187 Calbert Cheaney	.06	.15
❑ 188 Jarron Collins	.06	.15
❑ 189 DeShawn Stevenson	.06	.15
❑ 190 Michael Jordan	1.25	3.00
❑ 191 Jerry Stackhouse	.20	.50
❑ 192 Kwame Brown	.10	.25
❑ 193 Larry Hughes	.10	.25
❑ 194 Gilbert Arenas	.20	.50
❑ 195 Brendan Haywood	.06	.15
❑ 196 Juan Dixon	.10	.25
❑ 197 Jahidi White	.06	.15
❑ 198 Etan Thomas	.06	.15
❑ 199 Michael Jordan - Checklist	.75	2.00
❑ 200 Michael Jordan - Checklist	.75	2.00
❑ 201 LeBron James RC	8.00	20.00
❑ 202 Darko Milicic RC	.60	1.50
❑ 203 Carmelo Anthony RC	2.00	5.00
❑ 204 Chris Bosh RC	1.00	2.50
❑ 205 Dwyane Wade RC	1.50	4.00
❑ 206 Chris Kaman RC	.75	2.00
❑ 207 Kirk Hinrich RC	.75	2.00
❑ 208 T.J. Ford RC	.60	1.25
❑ 209 Mike Sweetney RC	.60	1.50
❑ 210 Jarvis Hayes RC	.60	1.50
❑ 211 Mickael Pietrus RC	.60	1.50
❑ 212 Nick Collison RC	.60	1.50
❑ 213 Marcus Banks RC	.60	1.50
❑ 214 Luke Ridnour RC	.75	2.00
❑ 215 Reece Gaines RC	.60	1.50
❑ 216 Troy Bell RC	.60	1.50
❑ 217 Zarko Cabarkapa RC	.60	1.50
❑ 218 David West RC	1.25	3.00
❑ 219 Aleksandar Pavlovic RC	.75	2.00
❑ 220 Dahntay Jones RC	.60	1.50
❑ 221 Boris Diaw-Riffiod RC	.60	1.50
❑ 222 Zoran Planinic RC	.60	1.50
❑ 223 Travis Outlaw RC	.75	2.00
❑ 224 Brian Cook RC	.60	1.50
❑ 225 Carlos Delfino RC	.60	1.50
❑ 226 Ndudi Ebi RC	.60	1.50
❑ 227 Kendrick Perkins RC	1.00	2.50
❑ 228 Leandro Barbosa RC	1.00	2.50
❑ 229 Josh Howard RC	.75	2.00
❑ 230 Maciej Lampe RC	.60	1.50

2008-09 Upper Deck MVP

❑ COMPLETE SET (258)	30.00	60.00
❑ COMP.SET w/o SPs (200)	10.00	25.00
❑ 1 Joe Johnson	.20	.50
❑ 2 Marvin Williams	.20	.50
❑ 3 Acie Law IV	.15	.40
❑ 4 Al Horford	.20	.50
❑ 5 Mike Bibby	.20	.50
❑ 6 Josh Smith	.20	.50
❑ 7 Kendrick Perkins	.15	.40
❑ 8 Glen Davis	.15	.40
❑ 9 Rajon Rondo	.20	.50
❑ 10 Ray Allen	.20	.50
❑ 11 Paul Pierce	.25	.60
❑ 12 Kevin Garnett	.40	1.00
❑ 13 Adam Morrison	.20	.50
❑ 14 Raymond Felton	.15	.40
❑ 15 Jason Richardson	.20	.50
❑ 16 Emeka Okafor	.20	.50
❑ 17 Gerald Wallace	.20	.50
❑ 18 Tyrus Thomas	.15	.40
❑ 19 Andres Nocioni	.15	.40
❑ 20 Joakim Noah	.20	.50
❑ 21 Luol Deng	.20	.50
❑ 22 Kirk Hinrich	.20	.50
❑ 23 Ben Gordon	.20	.50
❑ 24 Zydrunas Ilgauskas	.15	.40
❑ 25 Anderson Varejao	.15	.40
❑ 26 Ben Wallace	.20	.50
❑ 27 Daniel Gibson	.20	.50
❑ 28 LeBron James	1.00	2.50
❑ 29 Wally Szczerbiak	.15	.40
❑ 30 Dirk Nowitzki	.25	.60
❑ 31 Josh Howard	.20	.50
❑ 32 Jason Kidd	.20	.50
❑ 33 Jerry Stackhouse	.15	.40
❑ 34 Jason Terry	.15	.40
❑ 35 Brandon Bass	.15	.40
❑ 36 Allen Iverson	.25	.60
❑ 37 Carmelo Anthony	.25	.60
❑ 38 Marcus Camby	.12	.30
❑ 39 Kenyon Martin	.20	.50
❑ 40 J.R. Smith	.15	.40
❑ 41 Linas Kleiza	.12	.30
❑ 42 Chauncey Billups	.20	.50
❑ 43 Richard Hamilton	.15	.40
❑ 44 Tayshaun Prince	.20	.50
❑ 45 Rasheed Wallace	.20	.50
❑ 46 Rodney Stuckey	.25	.60
❑ 47 Jason Maxiell	.15	.40
❑ 48 Baron Davis	.20	.50
❑ 49 Monta Ellis	.20	.50
❑ 50 Al Harrington	.15	.40
❑ 51 Stephen Jackson	.15	.40
❑ 52 Marco Belinelli	.12	.30
❑ 53 Yao Ming	.25	.60
❑ 54 Tracy McGrady	.25	.60
❑ 55 Luis Scola	.15	.40
❑ 56 Rafer Alston	.12	.30
❑ 57 Shane Battier	.15	.40
❑ 58 Mike Dunleavy	.15	.40
❑ 59 Danny Granger	.20	.50
❑ 60 Jermaine O'Neal	.20	.50
❑ 61 Jamaal Tinsley	.12	.30
❑ 62 David Harrison	.12	.30
❑ 63 Elton Brand	.30	.75
❑ 64 Chris Kaman	.12	.30
❑ 65 Corey Maggette	.20	.50
❑ 66 Al Thornton	.20	.50
❑ 67 Cuttino Mobley	.15	.40
❑ 68 Tim Thomas	.12	.30
❑ 69 Kobe Bryant	1.00	2.50
❑ 70 Pau Gasol	.20	.50
❑ 71 Andrew Bynum	.20	.50
❑ 72 Jordan Farmar	.15	.40
❑ 73 Luke Walton	.15	.40
❑ 74 Lamar Odom	.20	.50
❑ 75 Rudy Gay	.20	.50
❑ 76 Kyle Lowry	.12	.30
❑ 77 Mike Conley	.15	.40
❑ 78 Mike Miller	.20	.50
❑ 79 Hakim Warrick	.12	.30
❑ 80 Dwyane Wade	.40	1.00
❑ 81 Shawn Marion	.20	.50
❑ 82 Ricky Davis	.20	.50
❑ 83 Jason Williams	.15	.40
❑ 84 Daequan Cook	.15	.40
❑ 85 Michael Redd	.20	.50
❑ 86 Maurice Williams	.15	.40
❑ 87 Yi Jianlian	.20	.50
❑ 88 Charlie Villanueva	.20	.50
❑ 89 Andrew Bogut	.20	.50
❑ 90 Al Jefferson	.20	.50
❑ 91 Rashad McCants	.15	.40
❑ 92 Corey Brewer	.15	.40
❑ 93 Randy Foye	.20	.50
❑ 94 Ryan Gomes	.15	.40
❑ 95 Richard Jefferson	.20	.50
❑ 96 Vince Carter	.25	.60
❑ 97 Josh Boone	.12	.30
❑ 98 Bostjan Nachbar	.20	.50
❑ 99 Sean Williams	.15	.40
❑ 100 Chris Paul	.40	1.00
❑ 101 David West	.20	.50
❑ 102 Peja Stojakovic	.20	.50
❑ 103 Tyson Chandler	.15	.40
❑ 104 Morris Peterson	.15	.40
❑ 105 Julian Wright	.15	.40
❑ 106 Jamal Crawford	.12	.30
❑ 107 Zach Randolph	.20	.50
❑ 108 Stephon Marbury	.20	.50
❑ 109 Eddy Curry	.12	.30
❑ 110 Nate Robinson	.20	.50
❑ 111 David Lee	.15	.40
❑ 112 Dwight Howard	.40	1.00
❑ 113 Hedo Turkoglu	.20	.50
❑ 114 Rashard Lewis	.20	.50
❑ 115 Jameer Nelson	.15	.40
❑ 116 Keith Bogans	.12	.30
❑ 117 Carlos Arroyo	.20	.50
❑ 118 Andre Iguodala	.20	.50
❑ 119 Andre Miller	.15	.40
❑ 120 Willie Green	.12	.30
❑ 121 Samuel Dalembert	.12	.30
❑ 122 Reggie Evans	.12	.30
❑ 123 Thaddeus Young	.15	.40
❑ 124 Amare Stoudemire	.25	.60
❑ 125 Steve Nash	.20	.50
❑ 126 Leandro Barbosa	.15	.40
❑ 127 Shaquille O'Neal	.40	1.00
❑ 128 Grant Hill	.20	.50
❑ 129 Raja Bell	.12	.30
❑ 130 Brandon Roy	.25	.60
❑ 131 LaMarcus Aldridge	.20	.50
❑ 132 Travis Outlaw	.20	.50
❑ 133 Martell Webster	.15	.40
❑ 134 Greg Oden	.20	.50
❑ 135 Jarrett Jack	.15	.40
❑ 136 Kevin Martin	.20	.50
❑ 137 Ron Artest	.20	.50
❑ 138 Brad Miller	.20	.50
❑ 139 John Salmons	.20	.50
❑ 140 Mikki Moore	.15	.40
❑ 141 Francisco Garcia	.15	.40
❑ 142 Manu Ginobili	.20	.50
❑ 143 Tim Duncan	.30	.75
❑ 144 Tony Parker	.20	.50
❑ 145 Michael Finley	.20	.50
❑ 146 Bruce Bowen	.12	.30
❑ 147 Damon Stoudamire	.12	.30
❑ 148 Kevin Durant	.50	1.25
❑ 149 Chris Wilcox	.15	.40
❑ 150 Jeff Green	.15	.40
❑ 151 Damien Wilkins	.12	.30
❑ 152 Earl Watson	.12	.30
❑ 153 Chris Bosh	.20	.50
❑ 154 Jose Calderon	.15	.40
❑ 155 T.J. Ford	.12	.30
❑ 156 Andrea Bargnani	.15	.40
❑ 157 Jamario Moon	.20	.50
❑ 158 Jason Kapono	.12	.30
❑ 159 Carlos Boozer	.20	.50
❑ 160 Deron Williams	.25	.60
❑ 161 Kyle Korver	.20	.50
❑ 162 Andrei Kirilenko	.20	.50
❑ 163 Ronnie Brewer	.15	.40
❑ 164 Mehmet Okur	.20	.50
❑ 165 Gilbert Arenas	.20	.50
❑ 166 Caron Butler	.20	.50
❑ 167 Antawn Jamison	.20	.50
❑ 168 DeShawn Stevenson	.12	.30
❑ 169 Brendan Haywood	.12	.30
❑ 170 Nick Young	.12	.30
❑ 171 Joe Johnson	.20	.50
❑ 172 Kevin Garnett	.40	1.00
❑ 173 Gerald Wallace	.20	.50
❑ 174 Luol Deng	.20	.50
❑ 175 LeBron James	1.00	2.50
❑ 176 Dirk Nowitzki	.25	.60
❑ 177 Carmelo Anthony	.25	.60
❑ 178 Chauncey Billups	.20	.50
❑ 179 Monta Ellis	.20	.50
❑ 180 Tracy McGrady	.25	.60
❑ 181 Danny Granger	.20	.50
❑ 182 Chris Kaman	.12	.30
❑ 183 Kobe Bryant	1.00	2.50
❑ 184 Rudy Gay	.20	.50
❑ 185 Dwyane Wade	.40	1.00
❑ 186 Michael Redd	.20	.50
❑ 187 Al Jefferson	.20	.50
❑ 188 Vince Carter	.25	.60
❑ 189 Chris Paul	.40	1.00
❑ 190 Zach Randolph	.20	.50
❑ 191 Dwight Howard	.40	1.00
❑ 192 Andre Iguodala	.20	.50
❑ 193 Steve Nash	.20	.50
❑ 194 Brandon Roy	.25	.60
❑ 195 Kevin Martin	.20	.50
❑ 196 Tim Duncan	.30	.75
❑ 197 Kevin Durant	.50	1.25
❑ 198 Chris Bosh	.20	.50
❑ 199 Deron Williams	.25	.60
❑ 200 Antawn Jamison	.20	.50
❑ 201 Derrick Rose RC	2.50	6.00
❑ 202 Michael Beasley RC	1.25	3.00
❑ 203 O.J. Mayo RC	1.00	2.50
❑ 204 Russell Westbrook RC	1.50	4.00
❑ 205 Kevin Love RC	.75	2.00
❑ 206 Danilo Gallinari RC	1.00	2.50
❑ 207 Eric Gordon RC	.75	2.00
❑ 208 Joe Alexander RC	.60	1.50
❑ 209 D.J. Augustin RC	.60	1.50
❑ 210 Brook Lopez RC	1.25	3.00
❑ 211 Jerryd Bayless RC	.60	1.50
❑ 212 Jason Thompson RC	.60	1.50
❑ 213 Brandon Rush RC	.60	1.50
❑ 214 Anthony Randolph RC	1.00	2.50
❑ 215 Robin Lopez RC	.60	1.50
❑ 216 Marreese Speights RC	.60	1.50
❑ 217 Roy Hibbert RC	.75	2.00
❑ 218 Courtney Lee RC	1.00	2.50
❑ 219 J.J. Hickson RC	1.00	2.50
❑ 220 Ryan Anderson RC	.60	1.50
❑ 221 Kosta Koufos RC	.60	1.50
❑ 223 Darrell Arthur RC	.60	1.50
❑ 224 Donte Greene RC	.60	1.50
❑ 225 D.J. White RC	.60	1.50
❑ 226 Bill Walker RC	.60	1.50
❑ 227 James Gist RC	.60	1.50
❑ 228 Joey Dorsey RC	.60	1.50
❑ 229 Mario Chalmers RC	.75	2.00
❑ 230 DeAndre Jordan RC	.60	1.50
❑ 231 Luc Richard Mbah A Moute RC	.60	1.50
❑ 232 Kyle Weaver RC	.60	1.50
❑ 233 Sonny Weems RC	.60	1.50
❑ 234 Chris Douglas-Roberts RC	.75	2.00
❑ 235 Sean Singletary RC	.60	1.50
❑ 236 Patrick Ewing Jr. RC	.60	1.50
❑ 237 Darnell Jackson RC	.60	1.50
❑ 238 Maarty Leunen RC	.60	1.50
❑ 240 Deron Washington RC	.60	1.50
❑ 241 Spud Webb	1.00	2.50
❑ 242 Larry Bird	3.00	8.00
❑ 243 Bill Russell	1.50	4.00
❑ 244 Kevin McHale	1.25	3.00
❑ 245 Michael Jordan	8.00	20.00
❑ 246 Scottie Pippen	1.25	3.00
❑ 247 Joe Dumars	1.00	2.50
❑ 248 Isiah Thomas	1.00	2.50
❑ 249 Hakeem Olajuwon	1.25	3.00
❑ 250 Magic Johnson	2.00	5.00
❑ 251 Wilt Chamberlain	2.00	5.00
❑ 252 Kareem Abdul-Jabbar	1.50	4.00

❑ 253 Oscar Robertson	1.00	2.50
❑ 254 Pete Maravich	3.00	8.00
❑ 255 Patrick Ewing	1.25	3.00
❑ 256 Willis Reed	1.00	2.50
❑ 257 Julius Erving	2.00	5.00
❑ 258 David Robinson	1.50	4.00
❑ 259 Karl Malone	1.25	3.00
❑ 260 John Stockton	1.50	4.00

1998-99 Upper Deck Ovation

❑ COMPLETE SET (80)	60.00	120.00
❑ COMPLETE SET w/o RC (70)	20.00	40.00
❑ COMMON CARD (1-70)	.15	.40
❑ COMMON ROOKIE (71-80)	.60	1.50
❑ 1 Steve Smith	.30	.75
❑ 2 Dikembe Mutombo	.30	.75
❑ 3 Antoine Walker	.50	1.25
❑ 4 Ron Mercer	.25	.60
❑ 5 Glen Rice	.30	.75
❑ 6 Bobby Phills	.15	.40
❑ 7 Michael Jordan	3.00	8.00
❑ 8 Toni Kukoc	.30	.75
❑ 9 Dennis Rodman	.30	.75
❑ 10 Scottie Pippen	.75	2.00
❑ 11 Shawn Kemp	.30	.75
❑ 12 Derek Anderson	.40	1.00
❑ 13 Brevin Knight	.15	.40
❑ 14 Michael Finley	.50	1.25
❑ 15 Shawn Bradley	.15	.40
❑ 16 LaPhonso Ellis	.15	.40
❑ 17 Bobby Jackson	.30	.75
❑ 18 Grant Hill	.50	1.25
❑ 19 Jerry Stackhouse	.50	1.25
❑ 20 Donyell Marshall	.30	.75
❑ 21 Erick Dampier	.30	.75
❑ 22 Hakeem Olajuwon	.50	1.25
❑ 23 Charles Barkley	.60	1.50
❑ 24 Reggie Miller	.50	1.25
❑ 25 Chris Mullin	.50	1.25
❑ 26 Rik Smits	.30	.75
❑ 27 Maurice Taylor	.25	.60
❑ 28 Lorenzen Wright	.15	.40
❑ 29 Kobe Bryant	2.00	5.00
❑ 30 Eddie Jones	.50	1.25
❑ 31 Shaquille O'Neal	1.25	3.00
❑ 32 Alonzo Mourning	.30	.75
❑ 33 Tim Hardaway	.30	.75
❑ 34 Jamal Mashburn	.30	.75
❑ 35 Ray Allen	.50	1.25
❑ 36 Terrell Brandon	.30	.75
❑ 37 Glenn Robinson	.30	.75
❑ 38 Kevin Garnett	1.50	4.00
❑ 39 Tom Gugliotta	.15	.40
❑ 40 Stephon Marbury	.50	1.25
❑ 41 Keith Van Horn	.50	1.25
❑ 42 Kerry Kittles	.15	.40
❑ 43 Jayson Williams	.15	.40
❑ 44 Patrick Ewing	.50	1.25
❑ 45 Allan Houston	.30	.75
❑ 46 Larry Johnson	.30	.75
❑ 47 Anfernee Hardaway	.50	1.25
❑ 48 Nick Anderson	.15	.40
❑ 49 Allen Iverson	1.00	2.50
❑ 50 Joe Smith	.30	.75
❑ 51 Tim Thomas	.30	.75
❑ 52 Jason Kidd	.75	2.00
❑ 53 Antonio McDyess	.30	.75
❑ 54 Damon Stoudamire	.30	.75
❑ 55 Isaiah Rider	.15	.40
❑ 56 Rasheed Wallace	.50	1.25
❑ 57 Tariq Abdul-Wahad	.15	.40
❑ 58 Corliss Williamson	.30	.75
❑ 59 Tim Duncan	.75	2.00
❑ 60 David Robinson	.50	1.25
❑ 61 Vin Baker	.30	.75
❑ 62 Gary Payton	.50	1.25
❑ 63 Chauncey Billups	.30	.75
❑ 64 Tracy McGrady	1.25	3.00
❑ 65 Karl Malone	.50	1.25
❑ 66 John Stockton	.50	1.25
❑ 67 Shareef Abdur-Rahim	.50	1.25
❑ 68 Bryant Reeves	.15	.40
❑ 69 Juwan Howard	.30	.75
❑ 70 Rod Strickland	.15	.40
❑ 71 Michael Olowokandi RC	.60	1.50
❑ 72 Mike Bibby RC	1.50	4.00
❑ 73 Raef LaFrentz RC	.75	2.00
❑ 74 Antawn Jamison RC	2.00	5.00
❑ 75 Vince Carter RC	4.00	10.00
❑ 76 Robert Traylor RC	.60	1.50
❑ 77 Jason Williams RC	1.50	4.00
❑ 78 Larry Hughes RC	1.50	4.00
❑ 79 Dirk Nowitzki RC	5.00	12.00
❑ 80 Paul Pierce RC	4.00	10.00
❑ BK1 M.Jordan Ball/90	1000.00	1500.00

1999-00 Upper Deck Ovation

❑ COMPLETE SET (90)	50.00	100.00
❑ COMPLETE SET w/o RC (60)	12.50	25.00
❑ COMMON CARD (1-60)	.25	.60
❑ COMMON ROOKIE (61-90)	.60	1.50
❑ 1 Dikembe Mutombo	.30	.75
❑ 2 Alan Henderson	.25	.60
❑ 3 Antoine Walker	.40	1.00
❑ 4 Paul Pierce	.40	1.00
❑ 5 David Wesley	.25	.60
❑ 6 Eddie Jones	.40	1.00
❑ 7 Toni Kukoc	.40	1.00
❑ 8 Randy Brown	.25	.60
❑ 9 Shawn Kemp	.40	1.00
❑ 10 Zydrunas Ilgauskas	.30	.75
❑ 11 Michael Finley	.40	1.00
❑ 12 Dirk Nowitzki	.60	1.50
❑ 13 Nick Van Exel	.30	.75
❑ 14 Antonio McDyess	.30	.75
❑ 15 Grant Hill	.40	1.00
❑ 16 Jerry Stackhouse	.40	1.00
❑ 17 Antawn Jamison	.40	1.00
❑ 18 John Starks	.40	1.00
❑ 19 Hakeem Olajuwon	.40	1.00
❑ 20 Charles Barkley	.50	1.25
❑ 21 Cuttino Mobley	.30	.75
❑ 22 Reggie Miller	.40	1.00
❑ 23 Rik Smits	.40	1.00
❑ 24 Maurice Taylor	.30	.75
❑ 25 Michael Olowokandi	.25	.60
❑ 26 Kobe Bryant	2.00	5.00
❑ 27 Shaquille O'Neal	1.00	2.50
❑ 28 Tim Hardaway	.40	1.00
❑ 29 Alonzo Mourning	.40	1.00
❑ 30 Glenn Robinson	.30	.75
❑ 31 Ray Allen	.40	1.00
❑ 32 Kevin Garnett	.75	2.00
❑ 33 Joe Smith	.30	.75
❑ 34 Stephon Marbury	.40	1.00
❑ 35 Keith Van Horn	.30	.75
❑ 36 Patrick Ewing	.50	1.25
❑ 37 Latrell Sprewell	.30	.75
❑ 38 Darrell Armstrong	.25	.60
❑ 39 Bo Outlaw	.25	.60
❑ 40 Allen Iverson	.75	2.00
❑ 41 Larry Hughes	.30	.75
❑ 42 Jason Kidd	.60	1.50
❑ 43 Anfernee Hardaway	.40	1.00
❑ 44 Brian Grant	.25	.60
❑ 45 Damon Stoudamire	.40	1.00
❑ 46 Jason Williams	.40	1.00
❑ 47 Chris Webber	.40	1.00
❑ 48 Tim Duncan	.75	2.00
❑ 49 David Robinson	.50	1.25
❑ 50 Sean Elliott	.40	1.00
❑ 51 Gary Payton	.40	1.00
❑ 52 Vin Baker	.40	1.00
❑ 53 Vince Carter	.75	2.00
❑ 54 Tracy McGrady	.75	2.00
❑ 55 Karl Malone	.50	1.25
❑ 56 John Stockton	.50	1.25
❑ 57 Shareef Abdur-Rahim	.30	.75
❑ 58 Mike Bibby	.40	1.00
❑ 59 Juwan Howard	.30	.75
❑ 60 Mitch Richmond	.30	.75
❑ 61 Elton Brand RC	2.00	5.00
❑ 62 Steve Francis RC	2.00	5.00
❑ 63 Baron Davis RC	2.50	6.00
❑ 64 Lamar Odom RC	2.00	5.00
❑ 65 Jonathan Bender RC	.60	1.50
❑ 66 Wally Szczerbiak RC	2.00	5.00
❑ 67 Richard Hamilton RC	2.00	5.00
❑ 68 Andre Miller RC	2.00	5.00
❑ 69 Shawn Marion RC	2.00	5.00
❑ 70 Jason Terry RC	1.50	4.00
❑ 71 Trajan Langdon RC	.60	1.50
❑ 72 A.Radojevic RC	.60	1.50
❑ 73 Corey Maggette RC	2.00	5.00
❑ 74 William Avery RC	.60	1.50
❑ 75 Galen Young RC	.60	1.50
❑ 76 Chris Herren RC	.60	1.50
❑ 77 Cal Bowdler RC	.60	1.50
❑ 78 James Posey RC	1.00	2.50
❑ 79 Quincy Lewis RC	.60	1.50
❑ 80 Dion Glover RC	.60	1.50
❑ 81 Jeff Foster RC	.75	2.00
❑ 82 Kenny Thomas RC	.60	1.50
❑ 83 Devean George RC	1.00	2.50
❑ 84 Tim James RC	.60	1.50
❑ 85 Vonteego Cummings RC	.60	1.50
❑ 86 Jumaine Jones RC	.60	1.50
❑ 87 Scott Padgett RC	.60	1.50
❑ 88 Obinna Ekezie RC	.60	1.50
❑ 89 Ryan Robertson RC	.60	1.50
❑ 90 Evan Eschmeyer RC	.60	1.50
❑ MJS M.Jordan AU/23		

2000-01 Upper Deck Ovation

❑ COMPLETE SET w/o RC (60)	12.50	25.00
❑ COMMON CARD (1-60)	.20	.50
❑ COMMON ROOKIE (61-90)	1.25	3.00
❑ 1 Dikembe Mutombo	.25	.60
❑ 2 Jim Jackson	.20	.50
❑ 3 Paul Pierce	.30	.75
❑ 4 Antoine Walker	.25	.60
❑ 5 Derrick Coleman	.25	.60
❑ 6 Baron Davis	.30	.75
❑ 7 Elton Brand	.30	.75
❑ 8 Ron Artest	.30	.75
❑ 9 Lamond Murray	.20	.50
❑ 10 Andre Miller	.25	.60
❑ 11 Michael Finley	.30	.75
❑ 12 Dirk Nowitzki	.50	1.25
❑ 13 Antonio McDyess	.25	.60
❑ 14 Nick Van Exel	.25	.60
❑ 15 Jerry Stackhouse	.25	.60
❑ 16 Jerome Williams	.20	.50
❑ 17 Larry Hughes	.25	.60
❑ 18 Antawn Jamison	.30	.75
❑ 19 Steve Francis	.30	.75
❑ 20 Hakeem Olajuwon	.40	1.00
❑ 21 Reggie Miller	.30	.75
❑ 22 Jalen Rose	.25	.60
❑ 23 Lamar Odom	.30	.75
❑ 24 Michael Olowokandi	.20	.50
❑ 25 Shaquille O'Neal	.75	2.00

❑ 26 Kobe Bryant	1.50	4.00
❑ 27 Alonzo Mourning	.30	.75
❑ 28 Anthony Carter	.20	.50
❑ 29 Ray Allen	.30	.75
❑ 30 Tim Thomas	.20	.50
❑ 31 Kevin Garnett	.60	1.50
❑ 32 Wally Szczerbiak	.25	.60
❑ 33 Stephon Marbury	.30	.75
❑ 34 Keith Van Horn	.25	.60
❑ 35 Allan Houston	.25	.60
❑ 36 Latrell Sprewell	.25	.60
❑ 37 Grant Hill	.30	.75
❑ 38 Tracy McGrady	.60	1.50
❑ 39 Allen Iverson	.60	1.50
❑ 40 Toni Kukoc	.25	.60
❑ 41 Jason Kidd	.50	1.25
❑ 42 Anfernee Hardaway	.30	.75
❑ 43 Rasheed Wallace	.30	.75
❑ 44 Scottie Pippen	.50	1.25
❑ 45 Damon Stoudamire	.25	.60
❑ 46 Chris Webber	.30	.75
❑ 47 Jason Williams	.25	.60
❑ 48 Tim Duncan	.60	1.50
❑ 49 David Robinson	.40	1.00
❑ 50 Gary Payton	.30	.75
❑ 51 Brent Barry	.20	.50
❑ 52 Rashard Lewis	.30	.75
❑ 53 Vince Carter	.60	1.50
❑ 54 Antonio Davis	.20	.50
❑ 55 Karl Malone	.40	1.00
❑ 56 John Stockton	.40	1.00
❑ 57 Shareef Abdur-Rahim	.25	.60
❑ 58 Mike Bibby	.25	.60
❑ 59 Mitch Richmond	.25	.60
❑ 60 Richard Hamilton	.25	.60
❑ 61 Kenyon Martin RC	3.00	8.00
❑ 62 Stromile Swift RC	1.50	4.00
❑ 63 Darius Miles RC	1.50	4.00
❑ 64 Marcus Fizer RC	1.25	3.00
❑ 65 Mike Miller RC	2.00	5.00
❑ 66 DerMarr Johnson RC	1.25	3.00
❑ 67 Chris Mihm RC	1.25	3.00
❑ 68 Jamal Crawford RC	2.00	5.00
❑ 69 Joel Przybilla RC	1.25	3.00
❑ 70 Keyon Dooling RC	1.25	3.00
❑ 71 Jerome Moiso RC	1.25	3.00
❑ 72 Etan Thomas RC	1.25	3.00
❑ 73 Courtney Alexander RC	1.25	3.00
❑ 74 Mateen Cleaves RC	1.25	3.00
❑ 75 Jason Collier RC	1.25	3.00
❑ 76 Hedo Turkoglu RC	3.00	8.00
❑ 77 Desmond Mason RC	1.50	4.00
❑ 78 Quentin Richardson RC	1.50	4.00
❑ 79 Jamaal Magloire RC	1.25	3.00
❑ 80 Speedy Claxton RC	1.25	3.00
❑ 81 Morris Peterson RC	2.00	5.00
❑ 82 Donnell Harvey RC	1.25	3.00
❑ 83 DeShawn Stevenson RC	1.25	3.00
❑ 84 Mamadou N'Diaye RC	1.25	3.00
❑ 85 Erick Barkley RC	1.25	3.00
❑ 86 Mark Madsen RC	1.25	3.00
❑ 87 A.J. Guyton RC	1.25	3.00
❑ 88 Khalid El-Amin RC	1.25	3.00
❑ 89 Eddie House RC	1.25	3.00
❑ 90 Chris Porter RC	1.25	3.00

2001-02 Upper Deck Ovation

❑ COMP.SET w/o SP's (90)	20.00	40.00
❑ COMMON CARD (1-90)	.08	.25
❑ COMMON ROOKIE (91-110)	1.25	3.00
❑ COMMON ROOKIE (111-120)	2.50	6.00
❑ 1 Jason Terry	.30	.75
❑ 2 DerMarr Johnson	.20	.50
❑ 3 Shareef Abdur-Rahim	.25	.60
❑ 4 Paul Pierce	.30	.75
❑ 5 Antoine Walker	.25	.60
❑ 6 Kenny Anderson	.25	.60
❑ 7 Jamal Mashburn	.25	.60
❑ 8 David Wesley	.20	.50
❑ 9 Baron Davis	.30	.75
❑ 10 Ron Mercer	.20	.50
❑ 11 Marcus Fizer	.20	.50
❑ 12 Ron Artest	.25	.60
❑ 13 Andre Miller	.25	.60
❑ 14 Lamond Murray	.20	.50
❑ 15 Chris Mihm	.20	.50
❑ 16 Michael Finley	.30	.75
❑ 17 Steve Nash	.50	1.25
❑ 18 Dirk Nowitzki	.50	1.25
❑ 19 Antonio McDyess	.25	.60
❑ 20 Nick Van Exel	.25	.60
❑ 21 Raef LaFrentz	.20	.50
❑ 22 Jerry Stackhouse	.25	.60
❑ 23 Chucky Atkins	.20	.50
❑ 24 Corliss Williamson	.25	.60
❑ 25 Antawn Jamison	.30	.75
❑ 26 Chris Porter	.20	.50
❑ 27 Larry Hughes	.25	.60
❑ 28 Steve Francis	.30	.75
❑ 29 Cuttino Mobley	.25	.60
❑ 30 Maurice Taylor	.20	.50
❑ 31 Reggie Miller	.30	.75
❑ 32 Jalen Rose	.25	.60
❑ 33 Jermaine O'Neal	.30	.75
❑ 34 Darius Miles	.20	.50
❑ 35 Corey Maggette	.25	.60
❑ 36 Lamar Odom	.30	.75
❑ 37 Elton Brand	.30	.75
❑ 38 Kobe Bryant	1.50	4.00
❑ 39 Shaquille O'Neal	.75	2.00
❑ 40 Rick Fox	.25	.60
❑ 41 Derek Fisher	.25	.60
❑ 42 Stromile Swift	.20	.50
❑ 43 Michael Dickerson	.20	.50
❑ 44 Jason Williams	.25	.60
❑ 45 Alonzo Mourning	.30	.75
❑ 46 Eddie Jones	.25	.60
❑ 47 Anthony Carter	.20	.50
❑ 48 Ray Allen	.30	.75
❑ 49 Glenn Robinson	.25	.60
❑ 50 Sam Cassell	.25	.60
❑ 51 Kevin Garnett	.60	1.50
❑ 52 Terrell Brandon	.20	.50
❑ 53 Wally Szczerbiak	.25	.60
❑ 54 Joe Smith	.20	.50
❑ 55 Kenyon Martin	.30	.75
❑ 56 Keith Van Horn	.25	.60
❑ 57 Jason Kidd	.50	1.25
❑ 58 Latrell Sprewell	.25	.60
❑ 59 Allan Houston	.25	.60
❑ 60 Marcus Camby	.25	.60
❑ 61 Tracy McGrady	.60	1.50
❑ 62 Mike Miller	.25	.60
❑ 63 Grant Hill	.30	.75
❑ 64 Allen Iverson	.60	1.50
❑ 65 Dikembe Mutombo	.25	.60
❑ 66 Aaron McKie	.20	.50
❑ 67 Stephon Marbury	.30	.75
❑ 68 Shawn Marion	.30	.75
❑ 69 Tom Gugliotta	.20	.50
❑ 70 Rasheed Wallace	.30	.75
❑ 71 Damon Stoudamire	.25	.60
❑ 72 Bonzi Wells	.25	.60
❑ 73 Chris Webber	.30	.75
❑ 74 Peja Stojakovic	.25	.60
❑ 75 Mike Bibby	.25	.60
❑ 76 Tim Duncan	.60	1.50
❑ 77 David Robinson	.40	1.00
❑ 78 Antonio Daniels	.20	.50
❑ 79 Gary Payton	.30	.75
❑ 80 Rashard Lewis	.30	.75
❑ 81 Desmond Mason	.25	.60
❑ 82 Vince Carter	.60	1.50
❑ 83 Morris Peterson	.25	.60
❑ 84 Antonio Davis	.20	.50
❑ 85 Karl Malone	.40	1.00
❑ 86 John Stockton	.40	1.00
❑ 87 Donyell Marshall	.20	.50
❑ 88 Richard Hamilton	.25	.60
❑ 89 Courtney Alexander	.20	.50
❑ 90 Michael Jordan	6.00	15.00
❑ 91A Jeff Trepagnier P RC	1.25	3.00
❑ 91B Jeff Trepagnier S RC	1.25	3.00
❑ 91C Jeff Trepagnier SR RC	1.25	3.00
❑ 92A Pau Gasol P RC	5.00	12.00
❑ 92B Pau Gasol S RC	5.00	12.00
❑ 92C Pau Gasol SR RC	5.00	12.00
❑ 93A Will Solomon P RC	1.25	3.00
❑ 93B Will Solomon S RC	1.25	3.00
❑ 93C Will Solomon SP RC	1.25	3.00
❑ 94A Gilbert Arenas P RC	2.00	5.00
❑ 94B Gilbert Arenas S RC	2.00	5.00
❑ 94C Gilbert Arenas SR RC	2.00	5.00
❑ 95A Andrei Kirilenko P RC	3.00	8.00
❑ 95B Andrei Kirilenko S RC	3.00	8.00
❑ 95C Andrei Kirilenko SR RC	3.00	8.00
❑ 96A Jamaal Tinsley P RC	1.50	4.00
❑ 96B Jamaal Tinsley S RC	1.50	4.00
❑ 96C Jamaal Tinsley SR RC	1.50	4.00
❑ 97A Samuel Dalembert P RC	1.50	4.00
❑ 97B Samuel Dalembert S RC	1.50	4.00
❑ 97C Samuel Dalembert SR RC	1.50	4.00
❑ 98A Gerald Wallace P RC	3.00	8.00
❑ 98B Gerald Wallace S RC	3.00	8.00
❑ 98C Gerald Wallace SR RC	3.00	8.00
❑ 99A B.Armstrong P RC	1.25	3.00
❑ 99B B.Armstrong S RC	1.25	3.00
❑ 99C B.Armstrong SR RC	1.25	3.00
❑ 100A Jeryl Sasser P RC	1.25	3.00
❑ 100B Jeryl Sasser S RC	1.25	3.00
❑ 100C Jeryl Sasser SR RC	1.25	3.00
❑ 101A Joseph Forte P RC	1.25	3.00
❑ 101B Joseph Forte S RC	1.25	3.00
❑ 101C Joseph Forte SR RC	1.25	3.00
❑ 102A B.Haywood P RC	1.50	4.00
❑ 102B B.Haywood S RC	1.50	4.00
❑ 102C B.Haywood SR RC	1.50	4.00
❑ 103A Z.Randolph P RC	3.00	8.00
❑ 103B Z.Randolph S RC	3.00	8.00
❑ 103C Z.Randolph SR RC	3.00	8.00
❑ 104A Jason Collins P RC	1.25	3.00
❑ 104B Jason Collins S RC	1.25	3.00
❑ 104C Jason Collins SR RC	1.25	3.00
❑ 105A Michael Bradley P RC	1.25	3.00
❑ 105B Michael Bradley S RC	1.25	3.00
❑ 105C Michael Bradley SR RC	1.25	3.00
❑ 106A Kirk Haston P RC	1.25	3.00
❑ 106B Kirk Haston S RC	1.25	3.00
❑ 106C Kirk Haston SR RC	1.25	3.00
❑ 107A Steven Hunter P RC	1.25	3.00
❑ 107B Steven Hunter S RC	1.25	3.00
❑ 107C Steven Hunter SR RC	1.25	3.00
❑ 108A Troy Murphy P RC	2.50	6.00
❑ 108B Troy Murphy S RC	2.50	6.00
❑ 108C Troy Murphy SR RC	2.50	6.00
❑ 109A R.Jefferson P RC	3.00	8.00
❑ 109B R.Jefferson S RC	3.00	8.00
❑ 109C R.Jefferson SR RC	3.00	8.00
❑ 110A V.Radmanovic P RC	1.50	4.00
❑ 110B V.Radmanovic S RC	1.50	4.00
❑ 110C V.Radmanovic SR RC	1.50	4.00
❑ 111A Kedrick Brown P RC	2.50	6.00
❑ 111B Kedrick Brown S RC	2.50	6.00
❑ 111C Kedrick Brown SR RC	2.50	6.00
❑ 112A Joe Johnson P RC	6.00	15.00
❑ 112B Joe Johnson S RC	6.00	15.00
❑ 112C Joe Johnson SR RC	6.00	15.00
❑ 113A Rodney White P RC	2.50	6.00
❑ 113B Rodney White S RC	2.50	6.00
❑ 113C Rodney White SR RC	2.50	6.00
❑ 114A DeSagana Diop P RC	2.50	6.00
❑ 114B DeSagana Diop S RC	2.50	6.00
❑ 114C DeSagana Diop SR RC	2.50	6.00
❑ 115A Eddie Griffin P RC	2.50	6.00
❑ 115B Eddie Griffin S RC	2.50	6.00
❑ 115C Eddie Griffin SR RC	2.50	6.00
❑ 116A Shane Battier P RC	4.00	10.00
❑ 116B Shane Battier S RC	4.00	10.00
❑ 116C Shane Battier SR RC	4.00	10.00
❑ 117A J.Richardson P RC	5.00	12.00
❑ 117B J.Richardson S RC	5.00	12.00
❑ 117C J.Richardson SR RC	5.00	12.00
❑ 118A Eddy Curry P RC	4.00	10.00
❑ 118B Eddy Curry S RC	4.00	10.00
❑ 118C Eddy Curry SR RC	4.00	10.00
❑ 119A Tyson Chandler P RC	5.00	12.00
❑ 119B Tyson Chandler S RC	5.00	12.00
❑ 119C Tyson Chandler SR RC	5.00	12.00
❑ 120A Kwame Brown P RC	3.00	8.00
❑ 120B Kwame Brown S RC	3.00	8.00
❑ 120C Kwame Brown SR RC	3.00	8.00

2002-03 Upper Deck Ovation

❑ COMP.SET w/o SP's (90)	20.00	50.00
❑ COMMON CARD (1-90)	.08	.25
❑ COMMON ROOKIE (100-119)	2.50	6.00
❑ COMMON ROOKIE (120-134)	3.00	8.00
❑ 1 Shareef Abdur-Rahim	.25	.60
❑ 2 Jason Terry	.30	.75
❑ 3 Glenn Robinson	.25	.60
❑ 4 Paul Pierce	.30	.75
❑ 5 Antoine Walker	.25	.60
❑ 6 Vin Baker	.25	.60
❑ 7 Jalen Rose	.25	.60
❑ 8 Tyson Chandler	.25	.60
❑ 9 Eddy Curry	.25	.60
❑ 10 Marcus Fizer	.20	.50
❑ 11 Darius Miles	.20	.50
❑ 12 Lamond Murray	.20	.50
❑ 13 Chris Mihm	.20	.50
❑ 14 Dirk Nowitzki	.50	1.25
❑ 15 Michael Finley	.30	.75
❑ 16 Steve Nash	.50	1.25
❑ 17 Marcus Camby	.25	.60
❑ 18 Juwan Howard	.25	.60
❑ 19 James Posey	.20	.50
❑ 20 Jerry Stackhouse	.25	.60
❑ 21 Ben Wallace	.25	.60
❑ 22 Clifford Robinson	.20	.50
❑ 23 Antawn Jamison	.30	.75
❑ 24 Jason Richardson	.30	.75
❑ 25 Gilbert Arenas	.30	.75
❑ 26 Steve Francis	.30	.75
❑ 27 Eddie Griffin	.20	.50
❑ 28 Cuttino Mobley	.25	.60
❑ 29 Jermaine O'Neal	.30	.75
❑ 30 Reggie Miller	.30	.75
❑ 31 Jamaal Tinsley	.25	.60
❑ 32 Elton Brand	.30	.75
❑ 33 Andre Miller	.25	.60
❑ 34 Lamar Odom	.30	.75
❑ 35 Kobe Bryant	1.50	4.00
❑ 36 Shaquille O'Neal	.75	2.00
❑ 37 Derek Fisher	.25	.60
❑ 38 Devean George	.20	.50
❑ 39 Pau Gasol	.30	.75
❑ 40 Shane Battier	.25	.60
❑ 41 Jason Williams	.25	.60
❑ 42 Alonzo Mourning	.30	.75
❑ 43 Eddie Jones	.25	.60
❑ 44 Brian Grant	.20	.50
❑ 45 Ray Allen	.30	.75
❑ 46 Tim Thomas	.20	.50
❑ 47 Sam Cassell	.25	.60
❑ 48 Kevin Garnett	.60	1.50
❑ 49 Wally Szczerbiak	.25	.60
❑ 50 Terrell Brandon	.20	.50
❑ 51 Jason Kidd	.50	1.25
❑ 52 Kenyon Martin	.30	.75
❑ 53 Richard Jefferson	.30	.75
❑ 54 Jamal Mashburn	.25	.60
❑ 55 Baron Davis	.30	.75
❑ 56 David Wesley	.20	.50
❑ 57 Latrell Sprewell	.25	.60
❑ 58 Allan Houston	.25	.60
❑ 59 Antonio McDyess	.25	.60
❑ 60 Tracy McGrady	.60	1.50
❑ 61 Mike Miller	.25	.60
❑ 62 Darrell Armstrong	.20	.50
❑ 63 Allen Iverson	.60	1.50
❑ 64 Eric Snow	.20	.50
❑ 65 Aaron McKie	.20	.50
❑ 66 Stephon Marbury	.30	.75
❑ 67 Shawn Marion	.30	.75
❑ 68 Anfernee Hardaway	.30	.75
❑ 69 Rasheed Wallace	.30	.75
❑ 70 Bonzi Wells	.25	.60
❑ 71 Scottie Pippen	.50	1.25
❑ 72 Chris Webber	.30	.75
❑ 73 Mike Bibby	.25	.60
❑ 74 Peja Stojakovic	.25	.60
❑ 75 Tim Duncan	.60	1.50
❑ 76 David Robinson	.40	1.00
❑ 77 Tony Parker	.30	.75
❑ 78 Gary Payton	.30	.75
❑ 79 Rashard Lewis	.30	.75
❑ 80 Desmond Mason	.25	.60
❑ 81 Vince Carter	.60	1.50
❑ 82 Morris Peterson	.25	.60
❑ 83 Antonio Davis	.20	.50
❑ 84 Karl Malone	.30	.75
❑ 85 John Stockton	.40	1.00
❑ 86 Andrei Kirilenko	.30	.75
❑ 87 Michael Jordan	2.00	5.00
❑ 88 Richard Hamilton	.25	.60
❑ 89 Chris Whitney	.20	.50
❑ 90 Kwame Brown	.20	.50
❑ 91 Kevin Garnett/2999	3.00	8.00
❑ 92 Kevin Garnett/2999	3.00	8.00
❑ 93 Kevin Garnett/2999	3.00	8.00
❑ 94 Kobe Bryant/1999	5.00	12.00
❑ 95 Kobe Bryant/1999	5.00	12.00
❑ 96 Kobe Bryant/1999	5.00	12.00
❑ 97 Michael Jordan/499	20.00	50.00
❑ 98 Michael Jordan/499	20.00	50.00
❑ 99 Michael Jordan/499	20.00	50.00
❑ 100 Fred Jones RC	3.00	8.00
❑ 101 Jamal Sampson RC	2.50	6.00
❑ 102 John Salmons RC	4.00	10.00
❑ 103 Jiri Welsch RC	2.50	6.00
❑ 104 Dan Gadzuric RC	2.50	6.00
❑ 105 Vincent Yarbrough RC	2.50	6.00
❑ 106 Juan Dixon RC	4.00	10.00
❑ 107 Efthimios Rentzias RC	2.50	6.00
❑ 108 Predrag Savovic RC	2.50	6.00
❑ 109 Rod Grizzard RC	2.50	6.00
❑ 110 Bostjan Nachbar RC	2.50	6.00
❑ 111 Marko Jaric RC	2.50	6.00
❑ 112 Tayshaun Prince RC	4.00	10.00
❑ 113 Chris Jefferies RC	2.50	6.00
❑ 114 Casey Jacobsen RC	2.50	6.00
❑ 115 Carlos Boozer RC	5.00	12.00
❑ 116 Frank Williams RC	2.50	6.00
❑ 117 Dan Dickau RC	2.50	6.00
❑ 118 Ryan Humphrey RC	2.50	6.00
❑ 119 Melvin Ely RC	2.50	6.00
❑ 120 Nene Hilario RC	4.00	10.00
❑ 121 Nikoloz Tskitishvili RC	3.00	8.00
❑ 122 Marcus Haislip RC	3.00	8.00
❑ 123 Qyntol Woods RC	3.00	8.00
❑ 124 Caron Butler RC	6.00	15.00
❑ 125 Amare Stoudemire RC	8.00	20.00
❑ 126 Curtis Borchardt RC	3.00	8.00
❑ 127 Chris Wilcox RC	4.00	10.00
❑ 128 Drew Gooden RC	5.00	12.00
❑ 129 Jared Jeffries RC	3.00	8.00
❑ 130 Kareem Rush RC	4.00	10.00
❑ 131 Mike Dunleavy RC	4.00	10.00
❑ 132 Yao Ming RC	10.00	25.00
❑ 133 DaJuan Wagner RC	3.00	8.00
❑ 134 Jay Williams RC	4.00	10.00

2006-07 Upper Deck Ovation

❑ COMP.SET w/o SP's (90)	20.00	50.00
❑ 1 Joe Johnson	.30	.75
❑ 2 Marvin Williams	.40	1.00
❑ 3 Paul Pierce	.40	1.00
❑ 4 Wally Szczerbiak	.30	.75
❑ 5 Raymond Felton	.50	1.25
❑ 6 Emeka Okafor	.40	1.00
❑ 7 Gerald Wallace	.40	1.00
❑ 8 Tyson Chandler	.40	1.00
❑ 9 Ben Gordon	.50	1.25
❑ 10 Michael Jordan	2.50	6.00
❑ 11 Drew Gooden	.30	.75
❑ 12 Zydrunas Ilgauskas	.30	.75
❑ 13 LeBron James	2.00	5.00
❑ 14 Devin Harris	.40	1.00
❑ 15 Dirk Nowitzki	.60	1.50
❑ 16 Jason Terry	.40	1.00
❑ 17 Carmelo Anthony	.50	1.25
❑ 18 Marcus Camby	.30	.75
❑ 19 Kenyon Martin	.40	1.00
❑ 20 Chauncey Billups	.40	1.00
❑ 21 Richard Hamilton	.30	.75
❑ 22 Ben Wallace	.40	1.00
❑ 23 Baron Davis	.40	1.00
❑ 24 Jason Richardson	.40	1.00
❑ 25 Luther Head	.30	.75
❑ 26 Tracy McGrady	.75	2.00
❑ 27 Yao Ming	1.00	2.50
❑ 28 Austin Croshere	.25	.60
❑ 29 Jermaine O'Neal	.40	1.00
❑ 30 Peja Stojakovic	.40	1.00
❑ 31 Elton Brand	.40	1.00
❑ 32 Sam Cassell	.40	1.00
❑ 33 Cuttino Mobley	.30	.75
❑ 34 Kwame Brown	.30	.75
❑ 35 Kobe Bryant	2.00	5.00
❑ 36 Lamar Odom	.40	1.00
❑ 37 Pau Gasol	.40	1.00
❑ 38 Mike Miller	.40	1.00
❑ 39 Damon Stoudamire	.30	.75
❑ 40 Shaquille O'Neal	1.00	2.50
❑ 41 Wayne Simien	.30	.75
❑ 42 Dwyane Wade	1.00	2.50
❑ 43 Andrew Bogut	.40	1.00
❑ 44 T.J. Ford	.30	.75
❑ 45 Michael Redd	.40	1.00
❑ 46 Ricky Davis	.40	1.00
❑ 47 Kevin Garnett	.75	2.00
❑ 48 Rashad McCants	.30	.75
❑ 49 Vince Carter	.75	2.00
❑ 50 Richard Jefferson	.30	.75
❑ 51 Jason Kidd	.60	1.50
❑ 52 Desmond Mason	.25	.60
❑ 53 Chris Paul	.75	2.00
❑ 54 J.R. Smith	.30	.75
❑ 55 Steve Francis	.40	1.00
❑ 56 Stephon Marbury	.40	1.00
❑ 57 Nate Robinson	.40	1.00
❑ 58 Dwight Howard	.75	2.00
❑ 59 Darko Milicic	.40	1.00
❑ 60 Jameer Nelson	.30	.75
❑ 61 Andre Iguodala	.40	1.00
❑ 62 Allen Iverson	.75	2.00
❑ 63 Chris Webber	.40	1.00
❑ 64 Boris Diaw	.30	.75
❑ 65 Shawn Marion	.40	1.00
❑ 66 Steve Nash	.50	1.25
❑ 67 Zach Randolph	.40	1.00
❑ 68 Sebastian Telfair	.30	.75
❑ 69 Ron Artest	.40	1.00
❑ 70 Mike Bibby	.40	1.00
❑ 71 Bonzi Wells	.30	.75
❑ 72 Tim Duncan	.75	2.00
❑ 73 Manu Ginobili	.40	1.00
❑ 74 Tony Parker	.40	1.00
❑ 75 Ray Allen	.40	1.00
❑ 76 Rashard Lewis	.40	1.00
❑ 77 Luke Ridnour	.30	.75
❑ 78 Chris Bosh	.40	1.00
❑ 79 Joey Graham	.30	.75
❑ 80 Charlie Villanueva	.40	1.00
❑ 81 Carlos Boozer	.40	1.00
❑ 82 Andrei Kirilenko	.40	1.00
❑ 83 Gilbert Arenas	.40	1.00
❑ 84 Antawn Jamison	.40	1.00
❑ 85 Josh Childress	.30	.75
❑ 86 Al Jefferson	.40	1.00
❑ 87 Derek Fisher	.30	.75
❑ 88 Juan Dixon	.25	.60
❑ 89 Deron Williams	.60	1.50
❑ 90 Caron Butler	.40	1.00
❑ 91 Tyrus Thomas RC	2.00	5.00
❑ 92 Adam Morrison RC	2.00	5.00
❑ 93 LaMarcus Aldridge RC	2.00	5.00
❑ 94 Rudy Gay RC	1.50	4.00

❑ 95 Andrea Bargnani RC	2.50	6.00
❑ 96 Rodney Carney RC	1.50	4.00
❑ 97 Will Blalock RC	1.50	4.00
❑ 98 Brandon Roy RC	4.00	10.00
❑ 99 Patrick O'Bryant RC	1.50	4.00
❑ 100 Randy Foye RC	1.50	4.00
❑ 101 Ronnie Brewer RC	2.00	5.00
❑ 102 Mardy Collins RC	1.50	4.00
❑ 103 Shelden Williams RC	2.00	5.00
❑ 104 J.J. Redick RC	1.50	4.00
❑ 105 Hilton Armstrong RC	1.50	4.00
❑ 106 Marcus Williams RC	2.00	5.00
❑ 107 Rajon Rondo RC	6.00	15.00
❑ 108 Cedric Simmons RC	1.50	4.00
❑ 109 Alexander Johnson RC	1.50	4.00
❑ 110 Jordan Farmar RC	2.00	5.00
❑ 111 Maurice Ager RC	1.50	4.00
❑ 112 Renaldo Balkman RC	1.50	4.00
❑ 113 Leon Powe RC	1.50	4.00
❑ 114 Saer Sene RC	1.50	4.00
❑ 115 Paul Millsap RC	2.50	6.00
❑ 116 Josh Boone RC	1.50	4.00
❑ 117 Steve Novak RC	1.50	4.00
❑ 118 Daniel Gibson RC	2.00	5.00
❑ 119 Hassan Adams RC	2.00	5.00
❑ 120 Kyle Lowry RC	1.50	4.00
❑ 121 James White RC	1.50	4.00
❑ 122 Dee Brown RC	1.50	4.00
❑ 123 Shawne Williams RC	1.50	4.00
❑ 124 P.J. Tucker RC	1.50	4.00
❑ 125 Craig Smith RC	1.50	4.00
❑ 126 Paul Davis RC	1.50	4.00
❑ 127 Solomon Jones RC	1.50	4.00
❑ 128 Denham Brown RC	1.50	4.00
❑ 129 Thabo Sefolosha RC	2.00	5.00
❑ 130 Quincy Douby RC	1.50	4.00
❑ 131 Joel Freeland RC	1.50	4.00
❑ 132 Ryan Hollins RC	1.50	4.00

2001-02 Upper Deck Playmakers

❑ COMPLETE SET (145)	100.00	200.00
❑ COMP.SET w/o SP's (100)	20.00	40.00
❑ COMMON CARD (1-100)	.20	.50
❑ COMMON ROOKIE (101-130)	1.00	2.50
❑ COMMON ROOKIE (131-145)	1.50	4.00
❑ 1 Shareef Abdur-Rahim	.25	.60
❑ 2 Dion Glover	.20	.50
❑ 3 Jason Terry	.30	.75
❑ 4 Toni Kukoc	.25	.60
❑ 5 Theo Ratliff	.20	.50
❑ 6 Paul Pierce	.30	.75
❑ 7 Antoine Walker	.25	.60
❑ 8 Baron Davis	.30	.75
❑ 9 Jamal Mashburn	.25	.60
❑ 10 Ron Mercer	.20	.50
❑ 11 Brad Miller	.25	.60
❑ 12 Marcus Fizer	.20	.50
❑ 13 Andre Miller	.25	.60
❑ 14 Chris Mihm	.20	.50
❑ 15 Lamond Murray	.20	.50
❑ 16 Michael Finley	.30	.75
❑ 17 Dirk Nowitzki	.50	1.25
❑ 18 Steve Nash	.50	1.25
❑ 19 Tim Hardaway	.25	.60
❑ 20 Antonio McDyess	.25	.60
❑ 21 Nick Van Exel	.25	.60
❑ 22 Raef LaFrentz	.20	.50
❑ 23 Jerry Stackhouse	.25	.60
❑ 24 Clifford Robinson	.20	.50
❑ 25 Ben Wallace	.25	.60
❑ 26 Antawn Jamison	.30	.75
❑ 27 Larry Hughes	.25	.60
❑ 28 Danny Fortson	.20	.50
❑ 29 Steve Francis	.30	.75
❑ 30 Cuttino Mobley	.25	.60
❑ 31 Kenny Thomas	.20	.50
❑ 32 Jalen Rose	.25	.60
❑ 33 Reggie Miller	.30	.75
❑ 34 Jermaine O'Neal	.30	.75
❑ 35 Darius Miles	.20	.50
❑ 36 Elton Brand	.30	.75
❑ 37 Corey Maggette	.25	.60
❑ 38 Quentin Richardson	.25	.60
❑ 39 Kobe Bryant	1.50	4.00
❑ 40 Shaquille O'Neal	.75	2.00
❑ 41 Mitch Richmond	.25	.60
❑ 42 Derek Fisher	.25	.60
❑ 43 Lindsey Hunter	.20	.50
❑ 44 Stromile Swift	.20	.50
❑ 45 Jason Williams	.25	.60
❑ 46 Michael Dickerson	.20	.50
❑ 47 Eddie Jones	.25	.60
❑ 48 Alonzo Mourning	.30	.75
❑ 49 Anthony Carter	.20	.50
❑ 50 Brian Grant	.20	.50
❑ 51 Glenn Robinson	.25	.60
❑ 52 Ray Allen	.30	.75
❑ 53 Sam Cassell	.25	.60
❑ 54 Tim Thomas	.20	.50
❑ 55 Anthony Mason	.20	.50
❑ 56 Kevin Garnett	.60	1.50
❑ 57 Wally Szczerbiak	.25	.60
❑ 58 Terrell Brandon	.20	.50
❑ 59 Joe Smith	.20	.50
❑ 60 Jason Kidd	.50	1.25
❑ 61 Kenyon Martin	.30	.75
❑ 62 Allan Houston	.25	.60
❑ 63 Latrell Sprewell	.25	.60
❑ 64 Marcus Camby	.25	.60
❑ 65 Mark Jackson	.25	.60
❑ 66 Kurt Thomas	.20	.50
❑ 67 Tracy McGrady	.60	1.50
❑ 68 Grant Hill	.30	.75
❑ 69 Mike Miller	.25	.60
❑ 70 Allen Iverson	.60	1.50
❑ 71 Dikembe Mutombo	.25	.60
❑ 72 Aaron McKie	.20	.50
❑ 73 Stephon Marbury	.30	.75
❑ 74 Shawn Marion	.30	.75
❑ 75 Anfernee Hardaway	.30	.75
❑ 76 Tom Gugliotta	.20	.50
❑ 77 Rasheed Wallace	.30	.75
❑ 78 Derek Anderson	.25	.60
❑ 79 Bonzi Wells	.25	.60
❑ 80 Chris Webber	.30	.75
❑ 81 Peja Stojakovic	.25	.60
❑ 82 Mike Bibby	.25	.60
❑ 83 Doug Christie	.20	.50
❑ 84 Tim Duncan	.60	1.50
❑ 85 David Robinson	.40	1.00
❑ 86 Antonio Daniels	.20	.50
❑ 87 Steve Smith	.25	.60
❑ 88 Gary Payton	.30	.75
❑ 89 Rashard Lewis	.30	.75
❑ 90 Desmond Mason	.25	.60
❑ 91 Vince Carter	.60	1.50
❑ 92 Morris Peterson	.25	.60
❑ 93 Antonio Davis	.20	.50
❑ 94 Hakeem Olajuwon	.40	1.00
❑ 95 Karl Malone	.40	1.00
❑ 96 John Stockton	.40	1.00
❑ 97 Donyell Marshall	.20	.50
❑ 98 Michael Jordan	5.00	12.00
❑ 99 Courtney Alexander	.20	.50
❑ 100 Richard Hamilton	.25	.60
❑ 101 Jeryl Sasser RC	1.00	2.50
❑ 102 DeSagana Diop RC	1.00	2.50
❑ 103 Alvin Jones RC	1.00	2.50
❑ 104 Gerald Wallace RC	2.50	6.00
❑ 105 Kenny Satterfield RC	1.00	2.50
❑ 106 Ruben Boumtje-Boumtje RC	1.00	2.50
❑ 107 Brian Scalabrine RC	1.00	2.50
❑ 108 Oscar Torres RC	1.00	2.50
❑ 109 Jarron Collins RC	1.00	2.50
❑ 110 Jeff Trepagnier RC	1.00	2.50
❑ 111 Brendan Haywood RC	1.25	3.00
❑ 112 Vladimir Radmanovic RC	1.25	3.00
❑ 113 Loren Woods RC	1.00	2.50
❑ 114 Terence Morris RC	1.00	2.50
❑ 115 Kirk Haston RC	1.00	2.50
❑ 116 Earl Watson RC	1.25	3.00
❑ 117 Brandon Armstrong RC	1.00	2.50
❑ 118 Zach Randolph RC	2.50	6.00
❑ 119 Bobby Simmons RC	1.00	2.50
❑ 120 Alton Ford RC	1.00	2.50
❑ 121 Trenton Hassell RC	1.25	3.00
❑ 122 Damone Brown RC	1.00	2.50
❑ 123 Michael Bradley RC	1.00	2.50
❑ 124 Zeljko Rebraca RC	1.00	2.50
❑ 125 Jason Collins RC	1.00	2.50
❑ 126 Samuel Dalembert RC	1.25	3.00
❑ 127 Gilbert Arenas RC	1.50	4.00
❑ 128 Willie Solomon RC	1.00	2.50
❑ 129 Joseph Forte RC	1.00	2.50
❑ 130 Steven Hunter RC	1.00	2.50
❑ 131 Andrei Kirilenko RC	4.00	10.00
❑ 132 Eddy Curry RC	2.50	6.00
❑ 133 Tony Parker RC	6.00	15.00
❑ 134 Troy Murphy RC	3.00	8.00
❑ 135 Shane Battier RC	2.50	6.00
❑ 136 Kedrick Brown RC	1.50	4.00
❑ 137 Tyson Chandler RC	3.00	8.00
❑ 138 Jamaal Tinsley RC	2.00	5.00
❑ 139 Pau Gasol RC	6.00	15.00
❑ 140 Joe Johnson RC	4.00	10.00
❑ 141 Jason Richardson RC	3.00	8.00
❑ 142 Richard Jefferson RC	4.00	10.00
❑ 143 Eddie Griffin RC	1.50	4.00
❑ 144 Rodney White RC	1.50	4.00
❑ 145 Kwame Brown RC	2.00	5.00

2007-08 Upper Deck Premier

❑ 1 Bill Russell	5.00	12.00
❑ 2 Larry Bird	10.00	25.00
❑ 3 Paul Pierce	2.00	5.00
❑ 4 Ray Allen	2.00	5.00
❑ 5 Al Harrington	1.50	4.00
❑ 6 Baron Davis	2.00	5.00
❑ 7 Rick Barry	3.00	8.00
❑ 8 Earl Monroe	3.00	8.00
❑ 9 Eddy Curry	1.25	3.00
❑ 10 Stephon Marbury	2.00	5.00
❑ 11 Chauncey Billups	2.00	5.00
❑ 12 Dave Bing	3.00	8.00
❑ 13 Richard Hamilton	1.50	4.00
❑ 14 Kobe Bryant	10.00	25.00
❑ 15 Luke Walton	1.50	4.00
❑ 16 Magic Johnson	6.00	15.00
❑ 17 Kevin Martin	2.00	5.00
❑ 18 Mike Bibby	2.00	5.00
❑ 19 Ron Artest	2.00	5.00
❑ 20 Bob Pettit	4.00	10.00
❑ 21 Joe Johnson	2.00	5.00
❑ 22 Josh Smith	2.00	5.00
❑ 23 Andre Iguodala	2.00	5.00
❑ 24 Andre Miller	1.50	4.00
❑ 25 Julius Erving	6.00	15.00
❑ 26 Elvin Hayes	3.00	8.00
❑ 27 Caron Butler	2.00	5.00
❑ 28 Gilbert Arenas	2.00	5.00
❑ 29 Ben Gordon	2.50	6.00
❑ 30 Ben Wallace	2.00	5.00
❑ 31 Michael Jordan	12.00	30.00
❑ 32 Allen Iverson	4.00	10.00
❑ 33 Carmelo Anthony	4.00	10.00
❑ 34 Marcus Camby	1.25	3.00
❑ 35 Hakeem Olajuwon	2.50	6.00
❑ 36 Tracy McGrady	4.00	10.00
❑ 37 Yao Ming	5.00	12.00
❑ 38 Jamaal Tinsley	1.25	3.00
❑ 39 Jermaine O'Neal	2.00	5.00
❑ 40 Mike Dunleavy	1.50	4.00
❑ 41 Jason Kidd	3.00	8.00
❑ 42 Richard Jefferson	2.00	5.00
❑ 43 Vince Carter	4.00	10.00
❑ 44 Chris Wilcox	1.50	4.00
❑ 45 Delonte West	1.50	4.00

❑ 46 Detlef Schrempf	3.00	8.00
❑ 47 Andrew Bogut	2.00	5.00
❑ 48 Michael Redd	2.00	5.00
❑ 49 Oscar Robertson	2.00	5.00
❑ 50 Amare Stoudemire	4.00	10.00
❑ 51 Grant Hill	2.00	5.00
❑ 52 Shawn Marion	2.00	5.00
❑ 53 Steve Nash	2.50	6.00
❑ 54 Brad Daugherty	3.00	8.00
❑ 55 Larry Hughes	1.50	4.00
❑ 56 LeBron James	10.00	25.00
❑ 57 Cuttino Mobley	1.50	4.00
❑ 58 Elton Brand	2.00	5.00
❑ 59 Sam Cassell	2.00	5.00
❑ 60 Brandon Roy	3.00	8.00
❑ 61 Clyde Drexler	4.00	10.00
❑ 62 LaMarcus Aldridge	2.50	6.00
❑ 63 Sean Elliott	3.00	8.00
❑ 64 George Gervin	3.00	8.00
❑ 65 Tim Duncan	4.00	10.00
❑ 66 Tony Parker	2.00	5.00
❑ 67 Carlos Boozer	2.00	5.00
❑ 68 Deron Williams	3.00	8.00
❑ 69 Karl Malone	4.00	10.00
❑ 70 Mehmet Okur	1.50	4.00
❑ 71 Dirk Nowitzki	3.00	8.00
❑ 72 Jason Terry	2.00	5.00
❑ 73 Josh Howard	2.00	5.00
❑ 74 Alonzo Mourning	2.50	6.00
❑ 75 Dwyane Wade	5.00	12.00
❑ 76 Shaquille O'Neal	5.00	12.00
❑ 77 Chris Paul	4.00	10.00
❑ 78 David West	2.00	5.00
❑ 79 Tyson Chandler	2.00	5.00
❑ 80 Kevin Garnett	5.00	12.00
❑ 81 Randy Foye	2.00	5.00
❑ 82 Al Jefferson	2.00	5.00
❑ 83 Dwight Howard	4.00	10.00
❑ 84 Jameer Nelson	1.50	4.00
❑ 85 Rashard Lewis	2.00	5.00
❑ 86 Darko Milicic	2.00	5.00
❑ 87 Mike Miller	2.00	5.00
❑ 88 Pau Gasol	2.00	5.00
❑ 89 Andrea Bargnani	2.50	6.00
❑ 90 Chris Bosh	2.00	5.00
❑ 91 T.J. Ford	1.50	4.00
❑ 92 Emeka Okafor	2.00	5.00
❑ 93 Gerald Wallace	2.00	5.00
❑ 94 Jason Richardson	2.00	5.00
❑ 95 Yi Jianlian RC	6.00	15.00
❑ 96 Marco Belinelli RC	4.00	10.00
❑ 97 Greg Oden RC	6.00	15.00
❑ 98 Brandan Wright RC	5.00	12.00
❑ 99 Nick Young RC	4.00	10.00
❑ 100 Thaddeus Young RC	5.00	12.00
❑ 101 Kevin Durant JSY AU RC	125.00	250.00
❑ 102 Al Horford JSY AU RC	10.00	25.00
❑ 103 Mike Conley JSY AU RC	10.00	25.00
❑ 104 Jeff Green JSY AU RC	10.00	25.00
❑ 105 Corey Brewer JSY AU RC	10.00	25.00
❑ 106 Joakim Noah JSY AU RC	10.00	25.00
❑ 107 Spencer Hawes JSY AU RC	6.00	20.00
❑ 108 Acie Law IV JSY AU RC	10.00	25.00
❑ 109 Julian Wright JSY AU RC	10.00	25.00
❑ 111 Rodney Stuckey JSY AU RC	15.00	40.00
❑ 112 Sean Williams JSY AU RC	6.00	20.00
❑ 113 Javaris Crittenton JSY AU RC	6.00	20.00
❑ 114 Jason Smith JSY AU RC	6.00	20.00
❑ 115 Daequan Cook JSY AU RC	10.00	25.00
❑ 116 Jared Dudley JSY AU RC	6.00	15.00
❑ 117 Wilson Chandler JSY AU RC	6.00	15.00
❑ 120 Alando Tucker JSY AU RC	6.00	15.00
❑ 121 Carl Landry JSY AU RC	6.00	15.00
❑ 122 Gabe Pruitt JSY AU RC	6.00	15.00
❑ 126 Jermareo Davidson JSY AU RC	6.00	15.00
❑ 129 Adam Haluska JSY AU RC	6.00	15.00
❑ 133 Aaron Gray JSY AU RC	6.00	15.00
❑ 138 Herbert Hill JSY AU RC	6.00	15.00
❑ 139 Chris Richard JSY AU RC	6.00	15.00

2008-09 Upper Deck Premier

❑ 1 Kevin Garnett	4.00	10.00
❑ 2 Paul Pierce	2.50	6.00
❑ 3 Ray Allen	2.00	5.00
❑ 4 Larry Bird	6.00	15.00
❑ 5 Stephen Jackson	1.50	4.00
❑ 6 Monta Ellis	2.00	5.00
❑ 7 Mitch Richmond	2.00	5.00
❑ 8 Stephon Marbury	2.00	5.00
❑ 9 Jamal Crawford	1.25	3.00
❑ 10 Patrick Ewing	2.50	6.00
❑ 11 Chauncey Billups	2.00	5.00
❑ 12 Rasheed Wallace	2.00	5.00
❑ 13 Isiah Thomas	2.00	5.00
❑ 14 Kobe Bryant	10.00	25.00
❑ 15 Pau Gasol	2.00	5.00
❑ 16 Magic Johnson	4.00	10.00
❑ 17 Elgin Baylor	2.00	5.00
❑ 18 Kevin Martin	2.00	5.00
❑ 19 Beno Udrih	1.25	3.00
❑ 20 Oscar Robertson	2.00	5.00
❑ 21 Joe Johnson	2.00	5.00
❑ 22 Al Horford	2.00	5.00
❑ 23 Dominique Wilkins	2.50	6.00
❑ 24 Andre Iguodala	2.00	5.00
❑ 25 Elton Brand	3.00	8.00
❑ 26 Julius Erving	4.00	10.00
❑ 27 Wilt Chamberlain	4.00	10.00
❑ 28 Gilbert Arenas	2.00	5.00
❑ 29 Antawn Jamison	2.00	5.00
❑ 30 Elvin Hayes	2.00	5.00
❑ 31 Ben Gordon	2.00	5.00
❑ 32 Luol Deng	2.00	5.00
❑ 33 Michael Jordan	30.00	60.00
❑ 34 Scottie Pippen	2.50	6.00
❑ 35 Allen Iverson	2.50	6.00
❑ 36 Carmelo Anthony	2.50	6.00
❑ 37 Alex English	2.00	5.00
❑ 38 Tracy McGrady	2.50	6.00
❑ 39 Yao Ming	2.50	6.00
❑ 40 Hakeem Olajuwon	2.50	6.00
❑ 41 T.J. Ford	1.25	3.00
❑ 42 Danny Granger	2.00	5.00
❑ 43 Mike Dunleavy	1.50	4.00
❑ 44 Yi Jianlian	2.00	5.00
❑ 45 Vince Carter	2.50	6.00
❑ 46 Buck Williams	2.00	5.00
❑ 47 Kevin Durant	5.00	12.00
❑ 48 Jeff Green	1.50	4.00
❑ 49 Detlef Schrempf	2.00	5.00
❑ 50 Richard Jefferson	2.00	5.00
❑ 51 Andrew Bogut	2.00	5.00
❑ 52 Kareem Abdul-Jabbar	3.00	8.00
❑ 53 Steve Nash	2.00	5.00
❑ 54 Shaquille O'Neal	4.00	10.00
❑ 55 Kevin Johnson	2.00	5.00
❑ 56 LeBron James	10.00	25.00
❑ 57 Daniel Gibson	2.00	5.00
❑ 58 Mark Price	3.00	8.00
❑ 59 Baron Davis	2.00	5.00
❑ 60 Chris Kaman	1.25	3.00
❑ 61 World B. Free	2.00	5.00
❑ 62 Brandon Roy	2.50	6.00
❑ 63 LaMarcus Aldridge	2.00	5.00
❑ 64 Clyde Drexler	2.50	6.00
❑ 65 Tim Duncan	3.00	8.00
❑ 66 Tony Parker	2.00	5.00
❑ 67 David Robinson	3.00	8.00
❑ 68 Deron Williams	2.50	6.00
❑ 69 Carlos Boozer	2.00	5.00
❑ 70 Karl Malone	2.50	6.00
❑ 71 John Stockton	3.00	8.00
❑ 72 Dirk Nowitzki	2.50	6.00
❑ 73 Jason Kidd	2.00	5.00
❑ 74 Rolando Blackman	2.00	5.00
❑ 75 Dwyane Wade	4.00	10.00
❑ 76 Alonzo Mourning	2.00	5.00
❑ 77 Tim Hardaway	2.00	5.00
❑ 78 Chris Paul	4.00	10.00
❑ 79 David West	2.00	5.00
❑ 80 Larry Johnson	2.00	5.00
❑ 81 Al Jefferson	2.00	5.00
❑ 82 Corey Brewer	1.50	4.00
❑ 83 Dwight Howard	4.00	10.00
❑ 84 Hedo Turkoglu	2.00	5.00
❑ 85 Nick Anderson	2.00	5.00
❑ 86 Rudy Gay	2.00	5.00
❑ 87 Hakim Warrick	1.25	3.00
❑ 88 Mike Conley	1.50	4.00
❑ 89 Chris Bosh	2.00	5.00
❑ 90 Jermaine O'Neal	2.00	5.00
❑ 91 Jose Calderon	1.50	4.00
❑ 92 Emeka Okafor	2.00	5.00
❑ 93 Gerald Wallace	2.00	5.00
❑ 94 Raymond Felton	1.50	4.00
❑ 95 Courtney Lee RC	4.00	10.00
❑ 96 Chris Douglas-Roberts	3.00	8.00
❑ 97 Patrick Ewing Jr.	2.50	6.00
❑ 98 Alexis Ajinca RC	2.50	6.00
❑ 99 Bill Walker RC	2.50	6.00
❑ 100 Sonny Weems	2.50	6.00
❑ 101 Derrick Rose JSY AU RC	80.00	160.00
❑ 102 Michael Beasley JSY AU RC	25.00	50.00
❑ 103 O.J. Mayo JSY AU RC	25.00	50.00
❑ 104 R.Westbrook JSY AU RC	20.00	40.00
❑ 105 Kevin Love JSY AU RC	10.00	25.00
❑ 107 Eric Gordon JSY AU RC	10.00	25.00
❑ 108 Joe Alexander JSY AU RC	6.00	15.00
❑ 109 D.J. Augustin JSY AU RC	6.00	15.00
❑ 110 Brook Lopez JSY AU RC	8.00	20.00
❑ 111 Jerryd Bayless JSY AU RC	6.00	15.00
❑ 112 Jason Thompson JSY AU RC	5.00	12.00
❑ 113 Brandon Rush JSY AU RC	5.00	12.00
❑ 114 A.Randolph JSY AU RC	8.00	20.00
❑ 115 Robin Lopez JSY AU RC	5.00	12.00
❑ 116 Marreese Speights JSY AU RC	6.00	15.00
❑ 118 Javale McGee JSY AU RC	5.00	12.00
❑ 119 J.J. Hickson JSY AU RC	8.00	20.00
❑ 120 Ryan Anderson JSY AU RC	5.00	12.00
❑ 121 Kosta Koufos JSY AU RC	5.00	12.00
❑ 122 George Hill JSY AU RC	10.00	25.00
❑ 123 Darrell Arthur JSY AU RC	5.00	12.00
❑ 124 Donte Greene JSY AU RC	5.00	12.00
❑ 126 J.R. Giddens JSY AU RC	5.00	12.00
❑ 127 Walter Sharpe JSY AU RC	5.00	12.00
❑ 128 Joey Dorsey JSY AU RC	5.00	12.00
❑ 129 Mario Chalmers JSY AU RC	8.00	20.00
❑ 130 DeAndre Jordan JSY AU RC	5.00	12.00

2004-05 Upper Deck Pro Sigs

❑ COMP.SET w/o SP's	8.00	20.00
❑ COMMON CARD (1-90)	.15	.40
❑ COMMON ROOKIE (91-120)	1.00	2.50
❑ 1 Antoine Walker	.25	.60
❑ 2 Al Harrington	.20	.50
❑ 3 Boris Diaw	.20	.50
❑ 4 Paul Pierce	.25	.60
❑ 5 Ricky Davis	.20	.50
❑ 6 Gary Payton	.25	.60
❑ 7 Jahidi White	.15	.40
❑ 8 Jason Kapono	.15	.40
❑ 9 Gerald Wallace	.25	.60
❑ 10 Eddy Curry	.20	.50
❑ 11 Kirk Hinrich	.20	.50
❑ 12 Tyson Chandler	.20	.50

❑ 13 LeBron James	1.50	4.00
❑ 14 Dajuan Wagner	.15	.40
❑ 15 Drew Gooden	.15	.40
❑ 16 Dirk Nowitzki	.40	1.00
❑ 17 Michael Finley	.25	.60
❑ 18 Jerry Stackhouse	.20	.50
❑ 19 Carmelo Anthony	.75	2.00
❑ 20 Andre Miller	.20	.50
❑ 21 Kenyon Martin	.25	.60
❑ 22 Chauncey Billups	.25	.60
❑ 23 Rasheed Wallace	.25	.60
❑ 24 Ben Wallace	.20	.50
❑ 25 Derek Fisher	.20	.50
❑ 26 Jason Richardson	.25	.60
❑ 27 Mike Dunleavy	.20	.50
❑ 28 Yao Ming	.60	1.50
❑ 29 Jim Jackson	.15	.40
❑ 30 Tracy McGrady	.50	1.25
❑ 31 Jermaine O'Neal	.25	.60
❑ 32 Reggie Miller	.25	.60
❑ 33 Ron Artest	.20	.50
❑ 34 Elton Brand	.25	.60
❑ 35 Corey Maggette	.20	.50
❑ 36 Kerry Kittles	.20	.50
❑ 37 Kobe Bryant	1.25	3.00
❑ 38 Chris Mihm	.15	.40
❑ 39 Lamar Odom	.25	.60
❑ 40 Pau Gasol	.25	.60
❑ 41 Jason Williams	.20	.50
❑ 42 Bonzi Wells	.15	.40
❑ 43 Shaquille O'Neal	.60	1.50
❑ 44 Dwyane Wade	.75	2.00
❑ 45 Eddie Jones	.20	.50
❑ 46 Michael Redd	.25	.60
❑ 47 Desmond Mason	.20	.50
❑ 48 T.J. Ford	.20	.50
❑ 49 Latrell Sprewell	.20	.50
❑ 50 Kevin Garnett	.50	1.25
❑ 51 Sam Cassell	.20	.50
❑ 52 Richard Jefferson	.25	.60
❑ 53 Aaron Williams	.15	.40
❑ 54 Jason Kidd	.40	1.00
❑ 55 Jamal Mashburn	.20	.50
❑ 56 Baron Davis	.25	.60
❑ 57 Jamaal Magloire	.15	.40
❑ 58 Allan Houston	.20	.50
❑ 59 Jamal Crawford	.20	.50
❑ 60 Stephon Marbury	.25	.60
❑ 61 Cuttino Mobley	.20	.50
❑ 62 Kelvin Cato	.15	.40
❑ 63 Steve Francis	.25	.60
❑ 64 Glenn Robinson	.20	.50
❑ 65 Allen Iverson	.50	1.25
❑ 66 Samuel Dalembert	.15	.40
❑ 67 Amare Stoudemire	.50	1.25
❑ 68 Steve Nash	.40	1.00
❑ 69 Shawn Marion	.25	.60
❑ 70 Shareef Abdur-Rahim	.20	.50
❑ 71 Damon Stoudamire	.20	.50
❑ 72 Zach Randolph	.25	.60
❑ 73 Peja Stojakovic	.20	.50
❑ 74 Chris Webber	.25	.60
❑ 75 Mike Bibby	.20	.50
❑ 76 Tony Parker	.25	.60
❑ 77 Tim Duncan	.50	1.25
❑ 78 Manu Ginobili	.25	.60
❑ 79 Ronald Murray	.15	.40
❑ 80 Ray Allen	.25	.60
❑ 81 Rashard Lewis	.25	.60
❑ 82 Chris Bosh	.25	.60
❑ 83 Vince Carter	.50	1.25
❑ 84 Jalen Rose	.20	.50
❑ 85 Andrei Kirilenko	.25	.60
❑ 86 Carlos Boozer	.25	.60
❑ 87 Carlos Arroyo	.25	.60
❑ 88 Gilbert Arenas	.25	.60
❑ 89 Jarvis Hayes	.15	.40
❑ 90 Antawn Jamison	.25	.60
❑ 91 Dwight Howard RC	3.00	8.00
❑ 92 Emeka Okafor RC	2.00	5.00
❑ 93 Ben Gordon RC	1.25	3.00
❑ 94 Shaun Livingston RC	1.00	2.50
❑ 95 Devin Harris RC	2.00	5.00
❑ 96 Josh Childress RC	1.00	2.50
❑ 97 Luol Deng RC	1.25	3.00
❑ 98 Rafael Araujo RC	1.00	2.50
❑ 99 Andre Iguodala RC	2.50	6.00
❑ 100 Luke Jackson RC	1.00	2.50
❑ 101 Andris Biedrins RC	1.50	4.00
❑ 102 Robert Swift RC	1.00	2.50
❑ 103 Sebastian Telfair RC	1.00	2.50
❑ 104 Kris Humphries RC	1.50	4.00
❑ 105 Al Jefferson RC	2.00	5.00
❑ 106 Kirk Snyder RC	1.00	2.50
❑ 107 Josh Smith RC	2.50	6.00
❑ 108 J.R. Smith RC	2.00	5.00
❑ 109 Dorell Wright RC	1.25	3.00
❑ 110 Jameer Nelson RC	1.25	3.00
❑ 111 Pavel Podkolzine RC	1.00	2.50
❑ 112 Viktor Khryapa RC	1.00	2.50
❑ 113 Sergei Monia RC	1.00	2.50
❑ 114 Delonte West RC	1.50	4.00
❑ 115 Tony Allen RC	1.25	3.00
❑ 116 Kevin Martin RC	1.25	3.00
❑ 117 Sasha Vujacic RC	1.00	2.50
❑ 118 Beno Udrih RC	1.25	3.00
❑ 119 David Harrison RC	1.00	2.50
❑ 120 Lionel Chalmers RC	1.00	2.50

2000-01 Upper Deck Pros and Prospects

❑ COMPLETE SET (120)	100.00	200.00
❑ COMP.SET w/o RC (90)	10.00	25.00
❑ COMMON CARD (1-90)	.20	.50
❑ COMMON ROOKIE (91-120)	2.00	5.00
❑ 1 Dikembe Mutombo	.25	.60
❑ 2 Alan Henderson	.20	.50
❑ 3 Jim Jackson	.20	.50
❑ 4 Paul Pierce	.30	.75
❑ 5 Kenny Anderson	.25	.60
❑ 6 Antoine Walker	.25	.60
❑ 7 Baron Davis	.30	.75
❑ 8 Derrick Coleman	.25	.60
❑ 9 David Wesley	.20	.50
❑ 10 Elton Brand	.30	.75
❑ 11 Ron Artest	.30	.75
❑ 12 Hersey Hawkins	.20	.50
❑ 13 Andre Miller	.25	.60
❑ 14 Lamond Murray	.20	.50
❑ 15 Shawn Kemp	.30	.75
❑ 16 Michael Finley	.30	.75
❑ 17 Dirk Nowitzki	.50	1.25
❑ 18 Cedric Ceballos	.20	.50
❑ 19 Antonio McDyess	.25	.60
❑ 20 Nick Van Exel	.25	.60
❑ 21 Raef LaFrentz	.20	.50
❑ 22 Christian Laettner	.20	.50
❑ 23 Jerry Stackhouse	.25	.60
❑ 24 Lindsey Hunter	.20	.50
❑ 25 Antawn Jamison	.30	.75
❑ 26 Larry Hughes	.25	.60
❑ 27 Chris Mills	.20	.50
❑ 28 Steve Francis	.30	.75
❑ 29 Hakeem Olajuwon	.40	1.00
❑ 30 Shandon Anderson	.20	.50
❑ 31 Reggie Miller	.30	.75
❑ 32 Jonathan Bender	.20	.50
❑ 33 Jalen Rose	.25	.60
❑ 34 Lamar Odom	.30	.75
❑ 35 Michael Olowokandi	.20	.50
❑ 36 Tyrone Nesby	.20	.50
❑ 37 Kobe Bryant	1.50	4.00
❑ 38 Shaquille O'Neal	.75	2.00
❑ 39 Ron Harper	.25	.60
❑ 40 Robert Horry	.25	.60
❑ 41 Alonzo Mourning	.30	.75
❑ 42 P.J. Brown	.20	.50
❑ 43 Jamal Mashburn	.25	.60
❑ 44 Ray Allen	.30	.75
❑ 45 Glenn Robinson	.25	.60
❑ 46 Sam Cassell	.25	.60
❑ 47 Kevin Garnett	.60	1.50
❑ 48 Wally Szczerbiak	.25	.60
❑ 49 Terrell Brandon	.20	.50
❑ 50 William Avery	.20	.50
❑ 51 Stephon Marbury	.30	.75
❑ 52 Keith Van Horn	.25	.60
❑ 53 Kerry Kittles	.25	.60
❑ 54 Latrell Sprewell	.25	.60
❑ 55 Allan Houston	.25	.60
❑ 56 Patrick Ewing	.40	1.00
❑ 57 Darrell Armstrong	.20	.50
❑ 58 Pat Garrity	.20	.50
❑ 59 Michael Doleac	.20	.50
❑ 60 Allen Iverson	.60	1.50
❑ 61 Theo Ratliff	.20	.50
❑ 62 Tyrone Hill	.20	.50
❑ 63 Jason Kidd	.50	1.25
❑ 64 Anfernee Hardaway	.30	.75
❑ 65 Shawn Marion	.30	.75
❑ 66 Scottie Pippen	.50	1.25
❑ 67 Rasheed Wallace	.30	.75
❑ 68 Damon Stoudamire	.25	.60
❑ 69 Bonzi Wells	.20	.50
❑ 70 Chris Webber	.30	.75
❑ 71 Peja Stojakovic	.25	.60
❑ 72 Jason Williams	.25	.60
❑ 73 Tim Duncan	.60	1.50
❑ 74 David Robinson	.40	1.00
❑ 75 Terry Porter	.25	.60
❑ 76 Gary Payton	.30	.75
❑ 77 Rashard Lewis	.30	.75
❑ 78 Vin Baker	.25	.60
❑ 79 Vince Carter	.60	1.50
❑ 80 Doug Christie	.20	.50
❑ 81 Antonio Davis	.20	.50
❑ 82 Karl Malone	.40	1.00
❑ 83 John Stockton	.40	1.00
❑ 84 Bryon Russell	.20	.50
❑ 85 Shareef Abdur-Rahim	.25	.60
❑ 86 Mike Bibby	.25	.60
❑ 87 Michael Dickerson	.20	.50
❑ 88 Mitch Richmond	.25	.60
❑ 89 Richard Hamilton	.25	.60
❑ 90 Juwan Howard	.25	.60
❑ 91 Kenyon Martin JSY RC	15.00	30.00
❑ 92 Stromile Swift RC	2.50	6.00
❑ 93 Darius Miles RC	2.50	6.00
❑ 94 Marcus Fizer JSY RC	2.00	5.00
❑ 95 Mike Miller RC	3.00	8.00
❑ 96 DerMarr Johnson RC	2.00	5.00
❑ 97 Chris Mihm RC	2.00	5.00
❑ 98 Chris Porter RC	2.00	5.00
❑ 99 Joel Przybilla RC	2.00	5.00
❑ 100 Keyon Dooling RC	2.00	5.00
❑ 101 Jerome Moiso RC	2.00	5.00
❑ 102 Etan Thomas RC	2.00	5.00
❑ 103 Courtney Alexander RC	2.00	5.00
❑ 104 Mateen Cleaves RC	2.00	5.00
❑ 105 Jason Collier RC	2.00	5.00
❑ 106 Dan Langhi RC	2.00	5.00
❑ 107 Desmond Mason RC	2.50	6.00
❑ 108 Quentin Richardson RC	2.50	6.00
❑ 109 Jamaal Magloire RC	2.00	5.00
❑ 110 Speedy Claxton RC	2.00	5.00
❑ 111 Morris Peterson RC	3.00	8.00
❑ 112 Donnell Harvey RC	2.00	5.00
❑ 113 Hanno Mottola RC	2.00	5.00
❑ 114 Mamadou N'Diaye RC	2.00	5.00
❑ 115 Erick Barkley RC	2.00	5.00
❑ 116 Mark Madsen RC	2.00	5.00
❑ 117 A.J. Guyton RC	2.00	5.00
❑ 118 Khalid El-Amin RC	2.00	5.00
❑ 119 Lavor Postell RC	2.00	5.00
❑ 120 Eddie House RC	2.00	5.00

2001-02 Upper Deck Pros and Prospects

❑ COMP.SET w/o SP's (90)	10.00	25.00
❑ COMMON CARD (1-90)	.08	.25
❑ COMMON ROOKIE (91-125)	2.50	6.00
❑ COMMON ROOKIE (126-131)	4.00	10.00
❑ 1 Jason Terry	.30	.75
❑ 2 Toni Kukoc	.25	.60
❑ 3 DerMarr Johnson	.20	.50
❑ 4 Paul Pierce	.30	.75
❑ 5 Antoine Walker	.25	.60
❑ 6 Kenny Anderson	.25	.60
❑ 7 Jamal Mashburn	.25	.60
❑ 8 Baron Davis	.30	.75
❑ 9 David Wesley	.20	.50
❑ 10 Elton Brand	.30	.75
❑ 11 Ron Mercer	.20	.50
❑ 12 Jamal Crawford	.25	.60
❑ 13 Andre Miller	.25	.60
❑ 14 Lamond Murray	.20	.50
❑ 15 Chris Mihm	.20	.50
❑ 16 Michael Finley	.30	.75
❑ 17 Wang ZhiZHi	.25	.60
❑ 18 Dirk Nowitzki	.50	1.25
❑ 19 Antonio McDyess	.25	.60
❑ 20 Nick Van Exel	.25	.60
❑ 21 Raef LaFrentz	.20	.50
❑ 22 Jerry Stackhouse	.25	.60
❑ 23 Joe Smith	.20	.50
❑ 24 Mateen Cleaves	.20	.50
❑ 25 Antawn Jamison	.30	.75
❑ 26 Marc Jackson	.20	.50
❑ 27 Larry Hughes	.25	.60
❑ 28 Steve Francis	.30	.75
❑ 29 Maurice Taylor	.20	.50
❑ 30 Hakeem Olajuwon	.40	1.00
❑ 31 Reggie Miller	.30	.75
❑ 32 Jermaine O'Neal	.30	.75
❑ 33 Jalen Rose	.25	.60
❑ 34 Lamar Odom	.30	.75
❑ 35 Darius Miles	.20	.50
❑ 36 Quentin Richardson	.25	.60
❑ 37 Kobe Bryant	1.50	4.00
❑ 38 Shaquille O'Neal	.75	2.00
❑ 39 Derek Fisher	.25	.60
❑ 40 Rick Fox	.25	.60
❑ 41 Alonzo Mourning	.30	.75
❑ 42 Eddie Jones	.25	.60
❑ 43 Tim Hardaway	.25	.60
❑ 44 Brian Grant	.20	.50
❑ 45 Ray Allen	.30	.75
❑ 46 Glenn Robinson	.25	.60
❑ 47 Tim Thomas	.20	.50
❑ 48 Kevin Garnett	.60	1.50
❑ 49 Terrell Brandon	.20	.50
❑ 50 Wally Szczerbiak	.25	.60
❑ 51 Chauncey Billups	.25	.60
❑ 52 Stephon Marbury	.30	.75
❑ 53 Kenyon Martin	.30	.75
❑ 54 Keith Van Horn	.25	.60
❑ 55 Allan Houston	.25	.60
❑ 56 Latrell Sprewell	.25	.60
❑ 57 Glen Rice	.25	.60
❑ 58 Tracy McGrady	.60	1.50
❑ 59 Mike Miller	.25	.60
❑ 60 Darrell Armstrong	.20	.50
❑ 61 Allen Iverson	.60	1.50
❑ 62 Dikembe Mutombo	.25	.60
❑ 63 Aaron McKie	.20	.50
❑ 64 Jason Kidd	.50	1.25
❑ 65 Shawn Marion	.30	.75
❑ 66 Tom Gugliotta	.20	.50
❑ 67 Rasheed Wallace	.30	.75
❑ 68 Damon Stoudamire	.25	.60
❑ 69 Scottie Pippen	.50	1.25
❑ 70 Peja Stojakovic	.25	.60
❑ 71 Jason Williams	.25	.60
❑ 72 Chris Webber	.30	.75
❑ 73 Tim Duncan	.60	1.50
❑ 74 Derek Anderson	.25	.60
❑ 75 David Robinson	.40	1.00
❑ 76 Gary Payton	.30	.75
❑ 77 Rashard Lewis	.30	.75
❑ 78 Desmond Mason	.25	.60
❑ 79 Vince Carter	.60	1.50
❑ 80 Morris Peterson	.25	.60
❑ 81 Antonio Davis	.20	.50
❑ 82 Karl Malone	.40	1.00
❑ 83 John Stockton	.40	1.00
❑ 84 Donyell Marshall	.20	.50
❑ 85 Shareef Abdur-Rahim	.25	.60
❑ 86 Mike Bibby	.25	.60
❑ 87 Stromile Swift	.20	.50
❑ 88 Richard Hamilton	.25	.60
❑ 89 Courtney Alexander	.20	.50
❑ 90 Chris Whitney	.20	.50
❑ 91 Ruben Boumtje-Boumtje RC	2.00	5.00
❑ 92 Sean Lampley RC	2.00	5.00
❑ 93 Ken Johnson RC	2.00	5.00
❑ 94 Earl Watson RC	2.50	6.00
❑ 95 Jamaal Tinsley RC	2.50	6.00
❑ 96 Damone Brown RC	2.00	5.00
❑ 97 Michael Wright RC	2.00	5.00
❑ 98 Alvin Jones RC	2.00	5.00
❑ 99 Omar Cook RC	2.00	5.00
❑ 100 Jarron Collins RC	2.00	5.00
❑ 101 Brian Scalabrine RC	2.00	5.00
❑ 102 Jeryl Sasser RC	2.00	5.00
❑ 103 Samuel Dalembert RC	2.50	6.00
❑ 104 Terence Morris RC	2.00	5.00
❑ 105 Will Solomon RC	2.00	5.00
❑ 106 Kirk Haston RC	2.00	5.00
❑ 107 Richard Jefferson RC	5.00	12.00
❑ 108 Jason Collins RC	2.00	5.00
❑ 109 Troy Murphy RC	4.00	10.00
❑ 110 Gerald Wallace RC	5.00	12.00
❑ 111 Shane Battier RC	3.00	8.00
❑ 112 Jeff Trepagnier RC	2.00	5.00
❑ 113 Brandon Armstrong RC	2.00	5.00
❑ 114 Loren Woods RC	2.00	6.00
❑ 115 Joseph Forte RC	2.00	5.00
❑ 116 Michael Bradley RC	2.00	5.00
❑ 117 Joe Johnson RC	5.00	12.00
❑ 118 Gilbert Arenas RC	3.00	8.00
❑ 119 Ousmane Cisse RC	2.00	5.00
❑ 120 Kenny Satterfield RC	2.00	5.00
❑ 121 Vladimir Radmanovic RC	2.50	6.00
❑ 122 DeSagana Diop RC	2.00	5.00
❑ 123 Kedrick Brown RC	2.00	5.00
❑ 124 Trenton Hassell RC	2.50	6.00
❑ 125 Steven Hunter RC	2.00	5.00
❑ 126 Rodney White RC	2.00	5.00
❑ 127 Eddy Curry RC	3.00	8.00
❑ 128 Jason Richardson RC	4.00	10.00
❑ 129 Tyson Chandler RC	4.00	10.00
❑ 130 Eddie Griffin RC	2.00	5.00
❑ 131 Kwame Brown RC	2.50	6.00

2004-05 Upper Deck R-Class

❑ COMPLETE SET (132)	20.00	50.00
❑ COMP.SET w/o RC's (90)	8.00	20.00
❑ COMMON CARD (1-90)	.08	.20
❑ COMMON ROOKIE (91-132)	.60	1.50
❑ 1 Antoine Walker	.25	.60
❑ 2 Al Harrington	.20	.50
❑ 3 Boris Diaw	.20	.50
❑ 4 Paul Pierce	.25	.60
❑ 5 Gary Payton	.25	.60
❑ 6 Jiri Welsch	.15	.40
❑ 7 Gerald Wallace	.25	.60
❑ 8 Jason Kapono	.15	.40

❑ 9 Brandon Hunter	.15	.40
❑ 10 Eddy Curry	.20	.50
❑ 11 Kirk Hinrich	.20	.50
❑ 12 Tyson Chandler	.20	.50
❑ 13 LeBron James	1.50	4.00
❑ 14 Dajuan Wagner	.15	.40
❑ 15 Zydrunas Ilgauskas	.20	.50
❑ 16 Dirk Nowitzki	.40	1.00
❑ 17 Michael Finley	.25	.60
❑ 18 Jason Terry	.20	.50
❑ 19 Andre Miller	.20	.50
❑ 20 Carmelo Anthony	.75	2.00
❑ 21 Kenyon Martin	.25	.60
❑ 22 Chauncey Billups	.25	.60
❑ 23 Rasheed Wallace	.25	.60
❑ 24 Ben Wallace	.20	.50
❑ 25 Speedy Claxton	.15	.40
❑ 26 Jason Richardson	.25	.60
❑ 27 Mike Dunleavy	.20	.50
❑ 28 Yao Ming	.60	1.50
❑ 29 Tracy McGrady	.50	1.25
❑ 30 Juwan Howard	.20	.50
❑ 31 Jermaine O'Neal	.25	.60
❑ 32 Reggie Miller	.25	.60
❑ 33 Ron Artest	.20	.50
❑ 34 Elton Brand	.25	.60
❑ 35 Corey Maggette	.20	.50
❑ 36 Marko Jaric	.15	.40
❑ 37 Kobe Bryant	1.25	3.00
❑ 38 Devean George	.15	.40
❑ 39 Lamar Odom	.25	.60
❑ 40 Pau Gasol	.25	.60
❑ 41 Jason Williams	.20	.50
❑ 42 Bonzi Wells	.15	.40
❑ 43 Shaquille O'Neal	.60	1.50
❑ 44 Dwyane Wade	.75	2.00
❑ 45 Eddie Jones	.20	.50
❑ 46 Michael Redd	.25	.60
❑ 47 Desmond Mason	.20	.50
❑ 48 T.J. Ford	.20	.50
❑ 49 Latrell Sprewell	.20	.50
❑ 50 Kevin Garnett	.50	1.25
❑ 51 Sam Cassell	.20	.50
❑ 52 Richard Jefferson	.25	.60
❑ 53 Aaron Williams	.15	.40
❑ 54 Jason Kidd	.40	1.00
❑ 55 Jamal Mashburn	.20	.50
❑ 56 Baron Davis	.25	.60
❑ 57 Jamaal Magloire	.15	.40
❑ 58 Allan Houston	.20	.50
❑ 59 Jamal Crawford	.20	.50
❑ 60 Stephon Marbury	.25	.60
❑ 61 Steve Francis	.25	.60
❑ 62 Kelvin Cato	.15	.40
❑ 63 Cuttino Mobley	.20	.50
❑ 64 Glenn Robinson	.20	.50
❑ 65 Allen Iverson	.50	1.25
❑ 66 Willie Green	.15	.40
❑ 67 Amare Stoudemire	.50	1.25
❑ 68 Quentin Richardson	.20	.50
❑ 69 Steve Nash	.40	1.00
❑ 70 Shareef Abdur-Rahim	.20	.50
❑ 71 Damon Stoudamire	.20	.50
❑ 72 Zach Randolph	.25	.60
❑ 73 Peja Stojakovic	.20	.50
❑ 74 Chris Webber	.25	.60
❑ 75 Mike Bibby	.20	.50
❑ 76 Tony Parker	.25	.60
❑ 77 Tim Duncan	.50	1.25
❑ 78 Manu Ginobili	.25	.60

❑ 79 Ronald Murray .15 .40
❑ 80 Ray Allen .25 .60
❑ 81 Rashard Lewis .25 .60
❑ 82 Chris Bosh .25 .60
❑ 83 Vince Carter .50 1.25
❑ 84 Jalen Rose .20 .50
❑ 85 Andrei Kirilenko .25 .60
❑ 86 Carlos Boozer .25 .60
❑ 87 Carlos Arroyo .25 .60
❑ 88 Gilbert Arenas .25 .60
❑ 89 Jarvis Hayes .15 .40
❑ 90 Antawn Jamison .25 .60
❑ 91 Dwight Howard RC 2.00 5.00
❑ 92 Emeka Okafor RC 1.25 3.00
❑ 93 Ben Gordon RC .75 2.00
❑ 94 Shaun Livingston RC .60 1.50
❑ 95 Devin Harris RC 1.25 3.00
❑ 96 Josh Childress RC .60 1.50
❑ 97 Luol Deng RC .75 2.00
❑ 98 Andre Iguodala RC 1.50 4.00
❑ 99 Luke Jackson RC .60 1.50
❑ 100 Andris Biedrins RC 1.00 2.50
❑ 101 Sebastian Telfair RC .60 1.50
❑ 102 Josh Smith RC 1.50 4.00
❑ 103 Rafael Araujo RC .60 1.50
❑ 104 Robert Swift RC .60 1.50
❑ 105 Kris Humphries RC 1.00 2.50
❑ 106 Al Jefferson RC 1.25 3.00
❑ 107 Kirk Snyder RC .60 1.50
❑ 108 J.R. Smith RC 1.25 3.00
❑ 109 Dorell Wright RC .75 2.00
❑ 110 Jameer Nelson RC .75 2.00
❑ 111 Pavel Podkolzine RC .60 1.50
❑ 112 Bernard Robinson RC .60 1.50
❑ 113 Yuta Tabuse RC 1.25 3.00
❑ 114 Delonte West RC 1.00 2.50
❑ 115 Tony Allen RC .75 2.00
❑ 116 Kevin Martin RC .75 2.00
❑ 117 Sasha Vujacic RC .60 1.50
❑ 118 Beno Udrih RC .75 2.00
❑ 119 David Harrison RC .60 1.50
❑ 120 Anderson Varejao RC .75 2.00
❑ 121 Jackson Vroman RC .60 1.50
❑ 122 Peter John Ramos RC .60 1.50
❑ 123 Lionel Chalmers RC .60 1.50
❑ 124 Donta Smith RC .60 1.50
❑ 125 Andre Emmett RC .60 1.50
❑ 126 Antonio Burks RC .60 1.50
❑ 127 Royal Ivey RC .60 1.50
❑ 128 Chris Duhon RC 1.00 2.50
❑ 129 Trevor Ariza RC .75 2.00
❑ 130 Tim Pickett RC .60 1.50
❑ 131 Romain Sato RC .60 1.50
❑ 132 Nenad Krstic RC .75 2.00

2008-09 Upper Deck Radiance

❑ 1 LaMarcus Aldridge 1.50 4.00
❑ 2 Ray Allen 1.50 4.00
❑ 3 Carmelo Anthony 2.00 5.00
❑ 4 Ron Artest 1.50 4.00
❑ 5 Brandon Bass 1.25 3.00
❑ 6 Chauncey Billups 1.50 4.00
❑ 7 Carlos Boozer 1.50 4.00
❑ 8 Chris Bosh 1.50 4.00
❑ 9 Elton Brand 2.50 6.00
❑ 10 Kobe Bryant 8.00 20.00
❑ 11 Caron Butler 1.50 4.00
❑ 12 Andrew Bynum 1.50 4.00
❑ 13 Jose Calderon 1.25 3.00
❑ 14 Marcus Camby 1.00 2.50
❑ 15 Vince Carter 2.00 5.00
❑ 16 Tyson Chandler 1.25 3.00
❑ 17 Wilson Chandler 1.00 2.50
❑ 18 Mike Conley 1.25 3.00
❑ 19 Jamal Crawford 1.00 2.50
❑ 20 Eddy Curry 1.00 2.50
❑ 21 Baron Davis 1.50 4.00
❑ 22 Luol Deng 1.50 4.00
❑ 23 Michael Jordan 10.00 25.00
❑ 24 Tim Duncan 2.50 6.00
❑ 25 Kevin Durant 4.00 10.00
❑ 26 Monta Ellis 1.50 4.00
❑ 27 T.J. Ford 1.00 2.50
❑ 28 Francisco Garcia 1.25 3.00
❑ 29 Kevin Garnett 3.00 8.00
❑ 30 Rudy Gay 1.50 4.00
❑ 31 Manu Ginobili 1.50 4.00
❑ 32 Ben Gordon 1.50 4.00
❑ 33 Danny Granger 1.50 4.00
❑ 34 Devin Harris 1.50 4.00
❑ 35 Al Horford 1.50 4.00
❑ 36 Dwight Howard 3.00 8.00
❑ 37 Andre Iguodala 1.50 4.00
❑ 38 Allen Iverson 2.00 5.00
❑ 39 Stephen Jackson 1.25 3.00
❑ 40 LeBron James 8.00 20.00
❑ 41 Antawn Jamison 1.50 4.00
❑ 42 Al Jefferson 1.50 4.00
❑ 43 Richard Jefferson 1.50 4.00
❑ 44 Yi Jianlian 1.50 4.00
❑ 45 Jason Kidd 1.50 4.00
❑ 46 Andrei Kirilenko 1.50 4.00
❑ 47 David Lee 1.25 3.00
❑ 48 Corey Maggette 1.50 4.00
❑ 49 Shawn Marion 1.50 4.00
❑ 50 Kenyon Martin 1.50 4.00
❑ 51 Kevin Martin 1.50 4.00
❑ 52 Desmond Mason 1.00 2.50
❑ 53 Tracy McGrady 2.00 5.00
❑ 54 Brad Miller 1.50 4.00
❑ 55 Mike Miller 1.50 4.00
❑ 56 Yao Ming 2.00 5.00
❑ 57 Jamario Moon 1.50 4.00
❑ 58 Alonzo Mourning 1.50 4.00
❑ 59 Steve Nash 1.50 4.00
❑ 60 Joakim Noah 1.50 4.00
❑ 61 Dirk Nowitzki 2.00 5.00
❑ 62 Shaquille O'Neal 3.00 8.00
❑ 63 Greg Oden 1.50 4.00
❑ 64 Lamar Odom 1.50 4.00
❑ 65 Tony Parker 1.50 4.00
❑ 66 Chris Paul 3.00 8.00
❑ 67 Paul Pierce 2.00 5.00
❑ 68 Tayshaun Prince 1.50 4.00
❑ 69 Michael Redd 1.50 4.00
❑ 70 Jason Richardson 1.50 4.00
❑ 71 Brandon Roy 2.00 5.00
❑ 72 Luis Scola 1.25 3.00
❑ 73 Ramon Sessions 1.50 4.00
❑ 74 Josh Smith 1.50 4.00
❑ 75 Amare Stoudemire 2.00 5.00
❑ 76 Rodney Stuckey 2.00 5.00
❑ 77 Al Thornton 1.50 4.00
❑ 78 Hedo Turkoglu 1.50 4.00
❑ 79 Dwyane Wade 3.00 8.00
❑ 80 Ben Wallace 1.50 4.00
❑ 81 Gerald Wallace 1.50 4.00
❑ 82 Rasheed Wallace 1.50 4.00
❑ 83 David West 1.50 4.00
❑ 84 Chris Wilcox 1.25 3.00
❑ 85 Deron Williams 2.00 5.00
❑ 86 Louis Williams 1.00 2.50
❑ 87 Marvin Williams 1.50 4.00
❑ 88 Mo Williams 1.25 3.00
❑ 89 Brandan Wright 1.25 3.00
❑ 90 Thaddeus Young 1.25 3.00
❑ 91 Joe Alexander AU RC 6.00 15.00
❑ 92 Mario Chalmers AU RC 6.00 15.00
❑ 93 Joey Dorsey AU RC 5.00 12.00
❑ 94 Darrell Arthur AU RC 5.00 12.00
❑ 95 Rudy Fernandez AU RC 15.00 30.00
❑ 96 Marc Gasol AU RC EXCH 10.00 25.00
❑ 97 J.R. Giddens AU RC 5.00 12.00
❑ 98 Donte Greene AU RC 5.00 12.00
❑ 99 Roy Hibbert AU RC 6.00 15.00
❑ 100 J.J. Hickson AU RC 6.00 15.00
❑ 101 George Hill AU RC 10.00 25.00
❑ 102 Robin Lopez AU RC EXCH 5.00 12.00
❑ 103 A.Randolph AU RC 20.00 40.00
❑ 104 Brandon Rush AU RC 6.00 15.00
❑ 105 Walter Sharpe AU RC 5.00 12.00
❑ 106 Marreese Speights AU RC 5.00 12.00
❑ 107 Jason Thompson AU RC EXCH 5.00 12.00
❑ 108 Kyle Weaver AU RC 5.00 12.00
❑ 109 Sonny Weems AU RC 5.00 12.00
❑ 110 D.J. White AU RC 5.00 12.00
❑ 81RC D.J. Augustin AU RC 8.00 20.00
❑ 82RC Jerryd Bayless AU RC 10.00 25.00
❑ 83RC Michael Beasley AU RC 40.00 80.00
❑ 84RC Danilo Gallinari AU RC 8.00 20.00
❑ 85RC Eric Gordon AU RC 10.00 25.00
❑ 86RC Brook Lopez AU RC 15.00 30.00
❑ 87RC Kevin Love AU RC 10.00 25.00
❑ 88RC O.J. Mayo AU RC 20.00 40.00
❑ 89RC Derrick Rose AU RC 100.00 200.00
❑ 90RC Russell Westbrook AU RC 15.0030.00

1999-00 Upper Deck Retro

❑ COMPLETE SET (110) 20.00 40.00
❑ COMMON CARD (1-95) .15 .40
❑ COMMON ROOKIE (96-110) .40 1.00
❑ 1 Michael Jordan 2.00 5.00
❑ 2 John Havlicek .30 .75
❑ 3 Antawn Jamison .25 .60
❑ 4 Chris Webber .25 .60
❑ 5 Maurice Taylor .20 .50
❑ 6 Kevin Garnett .50 1.25
❑ 7 Walter Davis .25 .60
❑ 8 Kobe Bryant 1.25 3.00
❑ 9 Tim Duncan .50 1.25
❑ 10 Karl Malone .30 .75
❑ 11 Larry Bird .75 2.00
❑ 12 Juwan Howard .20 .50
❑ 13 Bill Walton .25 .60
❑ 14 Bob Cousy .30 .75
❑ 15 Dave DeBusschere .30 .75
❑ 16 Toni Kukoc .25 .60
❑ 17 Allan Houston .20 .50
❑ 18 Grant Hill .25 .60
❑ 19 Rik Smits .25 .60
❑ 20 Glenn Robinson .20 .50
❑ 21 Dave Cowens .25 .60
❑ 22 Isaac Austin .15 .40
❑ 23 Derek Anderson .15 .40
❑ 24 Tracy McGrady .50 1.25
❑ 25 Nate Thurmond .25 .60
❑ 26 Dikembe Mutombo .20 .50
❑ 27 Oscar Robertson .30 .75
❑ 28 Antonio McDyess .20 .50
❑ 29 Jamaal Wilkes .25 .60
❑ 30 Eddie Jones .25 .60
❑ 31 Nick Van Exel .20 .50
❑ 32 Reggie Miller .25 .60
❑ 33 David Thompson .30 .75
❑ 34 Ray Allen .25 .60
❑ 35 Anfernee Hardaway .25 .60
❑ 36 Brian Grant .15 .40
❑ 37 Allen Iverson .50 1.25
❑ 38 Vince Carter .50 1.25
❑ 39 Mitch Richmond .20 .50
❑ 40 Kareem Abdul-Jabbar .40 1.00
❑ 41 Alonzo Mourning .25 .60
❑ 42 Jonathan Bender RC .25 .60
❑ 43 Scottie Pippen .40 1.00
❑ 44 George Gervin .25 .60
❑ 45 Shawn Kemp .25 .60
❑ 46 Dave Bing .25 .60
❑ 47 John Starks .25 .60
❑ 48 Earl Monroe .25 .60
❑ 49 Stephon Marbury .25 .60
❑ 50 Cedric Maxwell .25 .60
❑ 51 Tom Gugliotta .15 .40

❑ 52 David Robinson	.30	.75
❑ 53 Shareef Abdur-Rahim	.20	.50
❑ 54 Elvin Hayes	.25	.60
❑ 55 Wilt Chamberlain	.50	1.25
❑ 56 Willis Reed	.25	.60
❑ 57 Kevin McHale	.30	.75
❑ 58 Elden Campbell	.15	.40
❑ 59 Steve Smith	.15	.40
❑ 60 Brent Barry	.20	.50
❑ 61 Jerry Stackhouse	.25	.60
❑ 62 Otis Birdsong	.25	.60
❑ 63 Michael Olowokandi	.15	.40
❑ 64 Joe Smith	.20	.50
❑ 65 Tim Thomas	.20	.50
❑ 66 Rick Barry	.25	.60
❑ 67 Jason Williams	.25	.60
❑ 68 Julius Erving	.40	1.00
❑ 69 John Stockton	.30	.75
❑ 70 Cal Bowdler RC	.25	.60
❑ 71 Nate Archibald	.25	.60
❑ 72 Elgin Baylor	.25	.60
❑ 73 Ron Mercer	.15	.40
❑ 74 Damon Stoudamire	.25	.60
❑ 75 Jerry West	.30	.75
❑ 76 Michael Finley	.25	.60
❑ 77 Charles Barkley	.30	.75
❑ 78 Shaquille O'Neal	.60	1.50
❑ 79 Paul Pierce	.25	.60
❑ 80 Keith Van Horn	.20	.50
❑ 81 Jason Kidd	.40	1.00
❑ 82 Gary Payton	.25	.60
❑ 83 James Worthy	.25	.60
❑ 84 Mike Bibby	.25	.60
❑ 85 Bill Russell	.40	1.00
❑ 86 Wes Unseld	.25	.60
❑ 87 Robert Parish	.25	.60
❑ 88 Walt Frazier	.25	.60
❑ 89 Antoine Walker	.25	.60
❑ 90 Steve Nash	.40	1.00
❑ 91 Moses Malone	.25	.60
❑ 92 Hakeem Olajuwon	.25	.60
❑ 93 Tim Hardaway	.25	.60
❑ 94 Patrick Ewing	.30	.75
❑ 95 Vin Baker	.25	.60
❑ 96 Trajan Langdon RC	.40	1.00
❑ 97 Ron Artest RC	1.50	4.00
❑ 98 James Posey RC	.60	1.50
❑ 99 Shawn Marion RC	1.25	3.00
❑ 100 Jumaine Jones RC	.40	1.00
❑ 101 William Avery RC	.40	1.00
❑ 102 Corey Maggette RC	1.25	3.00
❑ 103 Andre Miller RC	1.25	3.00
❑ 104 Jason Terry RC	1.00	2.50
❑ 105 Wally Szczerbiak RC	1.25	3.00
❑ 106 Richard Hamilton RC	1.25	3.00
❑ 107 Elton Brand RC	1.25	3.00
❑ 108 Baron Davis RC	1.50	4.00
❑ 109 Steve Francis RC	1.25	3.00
❑ 110 Lamar Odom RC	1.25	3.00

2005-06 Upper Deck Rookie Debut

❑ COMPLETE SET (150)	40.00	80.00
❑ COMP.SET w/o RC's (100)	15.00	40.00
❑ COMMON CARD (1-100)	.15	.40
❑ SEMISTARS	.20	.50
❑ UNLISTED STARS	.25	.60
❑ COMMON ROOKIE (101-150)	1.00	2.50
❑ 101-150 RC STATED ODDS 1:3		

❑ 1 Tony Delk	.15	.40
❑ 2 Josh Smith	.25	.60
❑ 3 Al Harrington	.15	.40
❑ 4 Antoine Walker	.20	.50
❑ 5 Ricky Davis	.25	.60
❑ 6 Paul Pierce	.25	.60
❑ 7 Kareem Rush	.15	.40
❑ 8 Emeka Okafor	.25	.60
❑ 9 Primoz Brezec	.15	.40
❑ 10 Eddy Curry	.20	.50
❑ 11 Kirk Hinrich	.25	.60
❑ 12 Ben Gordon	.30	.75
❑ 13 Luol Deng	.25	.60
❑ 14 Drew Gooden	.20	.50
❑ 15 LeBron James	1.25	3.00
❑ 16 Zydrunas Ilgauskas	.20	.50
❑ 17 Dirk Nowitzki	.40	1.00
❑ 18 Jason Terry	.25	.60
❑ 19 Josh Howard	.25	.60
❑ 20 Michael Finley	.25	.60
❑ 21 Carmelo Anthony	.50	1.25
❑ 22 Kenyon Martin	.25	.60
❑ 23 Andre Miller	.20	.50
❑ 24 Earl Boykins	.15	.40
❑ 25 Ben Wallace	.25	.60
❑ 26 Chauncey Billups	.25	.60
❑ 27 Richard Hamilton	.20	.50
❑ 28 Tayshaun Prince	.25	.60
❑ 29 Troy Murphy	.25	.60
❑ 30 Jason Richardson	.25	.60
❑ 31 Baron Davis	.25	.60
❑ 32 Tracy McGrady	.50	1.25
❑ 33 Yao Ming	.60	1.50
❑ 34 Juwan Howard	.20	.50
❑ 35 Jermaine O'Neal	.25	.60
❑ 36 Stephen Jackson	.20	.50
❑ 37 Ron Artest	.20	.50
❑ 38 Corey Maggette	.20	.50
❑ 39 Elton Brand	.25	.60
❑ 40 Bobby Simmons	.15	.40
❑ 41 Caron Butler	.25	.60
❑ 42 Kobe Bryant	1.25	3.00
❑ 43 Lamar Odom	.25	.60
❑ 44 Mike Miller	.25	.60
❑ 45 Jason Williams	.20	.50
❑ 46 Pau Gasol	.25	.60
❑ 47 Stromile Swift	.20	.50
❑ 48 Dwyane Wade	.60	1.50
❑ 49 Eddie Jones	.15	.40
❑ 50 Shaquille O'Neal	.60	1.50
❑ 51 Desmond Mason	.15	.40
❑ 52 Maurice Williams	.20	.50
❑ 53 Michael Redd	.25	.60
❑ 54 Kevin Garnett	.50	1.25
❑ 55 Latrell Sprewell	.15	.40
❑ 56 Sam Cassell	.25	.60
❑ 57 Vince Carter	.50	1.25
❑ 58 Jason Kidd	.40	1.00
❑ 59 Richard Jefferson	.20	.50
❑ 60 Dan Dickau	.15	.40
❑ 61 Jamaal Magloire	.15	.40
❑ 62 J.R. Smith	.20	.50
❑ 63 Jamal Crawford	.20	.50
❑ 64 Stephon Marbury	.25	.60
❑ 65 Allan Houston	.15	.40
❑ 66 Dwight Howard	.50	1.25
❑ 67 Grant Hill	.25	.60
❑ 68 Steve Francis	.25	.60
❑ 69 Allen Iverson	.50	1.25
❑ 70 Andre Iguodala	.25	.60
❑ 71 Chris Webber	.25	.60
❑ 72 Kyle Korver	.25	.60
❑ 73 Amare Stoudemire	.50	1.25
❑ 74 Shawn Marion	.25	.60
❑ 75 Steve Nash	.30	.75
❑ 76 Quentin Richardson	.20	.50
❑ 77 Damon Stoudamire	.20	.50
❑ 78 Shareef Abdur-Rahim	.25	.60
❑ 79 Zach Randolph	.25	.60
❑ 80 Brad Miller	.25	.60
❑ 81 Mike Bibby	.25	.60
❑ 82 Peja Stojakovic	.25	.60
❑ 83 Cuttino Mobley	.20	.50
❑ 84 Manu Ginobili	.25	.60
❑ 85 Tim Duncan	.50	1.25
❑ 86 Tony Parker	.25	.60
❑ 87 Rashard Lewis	.25	.60
❑ 88 Ray Allen	.25	.60
❑ 89 Luke Ridnour	.20	.50
❑ 90 Vladimir Radmanovic	.15	.40
❑ 91 Rafer Alston	.15	.40
❑ 92 Jalen Rose	.25	.60
❑ 93 Chris Bosh	.25	.60
❑ 94 Andrei Kirilenko	.25	.60
❑ 95 Carlos Boozer	.25	.60
❑ 96 Matt Harpring	.20	.50
❑ 97 Antawn Jamison	.25	.60
❑ 98 Gilbert Arenas	.25	.60
❑ 99 Larry Hughes	.20	.50
❑ 100 Jarvis Hayes	.15	.40
❑ 101 Andrew Bogut RC	1.00	2.50
❑ 102 Chris Taft RC	.75	2.00
❑ 103 Chris Paul RC	2.50	6.00
❑ 104 Martynas Andriuskevicius RC	.75	2.00
❑ 105 Amir Johnson RC	.75	2.00
❑ 106 Andrew Bynum RC	2.50	6.00
❑ 107 Gerald Green RC	.75	2.00
❑ 108 Rashad McCants RC	1.00	2.50
❑ 109 Fran Vazquez RC	.75	2.00
❑ 110 Ike Diogu RC	1.00	2.50
❑ 111 Raymond Felton RC	1.00	2.50
❑ 112 Hakim Warrick RC	1.25	3.00
❑ 113 Deron Williams RC	2.00	5.00
❑ 114 Daniel Ewing RC	1.00	2.50
❑ 115 Sean May RC	1.00	2.50
❑ 116 Johan Petro RC	.75	2.00
❑ 117 Erazem Lorbek RC		
❑ 118 Joey Graham RC	.75	2.00
❑ 119 Antoine Wright RC	.75	2.00
❑ 120 Ronny Turiaf RC	.75	2.00
❑ 121 Linas Kleiza RC	1.00	2.50
❑ 122 Alex Acker RC	.75	2.00
❑ 123 Jarrett Jack RC	.75	2.00
❑ 124 Danny Granger RC	2.00	5.00
❑ 125 Francisco Garcia RC	1.00	2.50
❑ 126 Ryan Gomes RC	.75	2.00
❑ 127 Wayne Simien RC	1.00	2.50
❑ 128 Robert Whaley RC	.75	2.00
❑ 129 Dijon Thompson RC	.75	2.00
❑ 130 Nate Robinson RC	1.25	3.00
❑ 131 Brandon Bass RC	.75	2.00
❑ 132 Andray Blatche RC	1.00	2.50
❑ 133 Channing Frye RC	1.00	2.50
❑ 134 Salim Stoudamire RC	1.00	2.50
❑ 135 Luther Head RC	1.00	2.50
❑ 136 Julius Hodge RC	1.00	2.50
❑ 137 David Lee RC	1.50	4.00
❑ 138 Travis Diener RC	.75	2.00
❑ 139 Marvin Williams RC	1.25	3.00
❑ 140 Lawrence Roberts RC	.75	2.00
❑ 141 C.J. Miles RC	.75	2.00
❑ 142 Ricky Sanchez RC	.75	2.00
❑ 143 Bracey Wright RC	.75	2.00
❑ 144 Jason Maxiell RC	1.00	2.50
❑ 145 Uros Slokar RC	.75	2.00
❑ 146 Martell Webster RC	.75	2.00
❑ 147 Orien Greene RC	.75	2.00
❑ 148 Charlie Villanueva RC	1.25	3.00
❑ 149 Monta Ellis RC	2.00	5.00
❑ 150 Von Wafer RC	.75	2.00

2006-07 Upper Deck Rookie Debut

COMPLETE SET (146)	40.00	80.00
1 Josh Childress	.20	.50
2 Joe Johnson	.20	.50
3 Marvin Williams	.25	.60
4 Gerald Green	.30	.75
5 Al Jefferson	.25	.60
6 Paul Pierce	.25	.60
7 Raymond Felton	.30	.75
8 Emeka Okafor	.25	.60
9 Gerald Wallace	.25	.60
10 Tyson Chandler	.25	.60
11 Luol Deng	.25	.60
12 Ben Gordon	.30	.75
13 Larry Hughes	.20	.50
14 Zydrunas Ilgauskas	.20	.50
15 LeBron James	1.25	3.00
16 Devin Harris	.25	.60
17 Josh Howard	.25	.60
18 Dirk Nowitzki	.40	1.00
19 Jason Terry	.25	.60
20 Carmelo Anthony	.30	.75
21 Marcus Camby	.20	.50
22 Kenyon Martin	.25	.60
23 Chauncey Billups	.25	.60
24 Richard Hamilton	.20	.50
25 Tayshaun Prince	.25	.60
26 Ben Wallace	.25	.60
27 Baron Davis	.25	.60
28 Troy Murphy	.25	.60
29 Jason Richardson	.25	.60
30 Rafer Alston	.15	.40
31 Tracy McGrady	.50	1.25
32 Stromile Swift	.20	.50
33 Yao Ming	.60	1.50
34 Jermaine O'Neal	.25	.60
35 Peja Stojakovic	.25	.60
36 Jamaal Tinsley	.20	.50
37 Elton Brand	.25	.60
38 Sam Cassell	.25	.60
39 Chris Kaman	.15	.40
40 Kobe Bryant	1.25	3.00
41 Devean George	.20	.50
42 Ronny Turiaf	.20	.50
43 Pau Gasol	.25	.60
44 Mike Miller	.25	.60
45 Damon Stoudamire	.20	.50
46 Shaquille O'Neal	.60	1.50
47 Gary Payton	.25	.60
48 Dwyane Wade	.60	1.50
49 Andrew Bogut	.25	.60
50 T.J. Ford	.20	.50
51 Jamaal Magloire	.15	.40
52 Michael Redd	.25	.60
53 Ricky Davis	.25	.60
54 Kevin Garnett	.50	1.25
55 Rashad McCants	.20	.50
56 Vince Carter	.50	1.25
57 Richard Jefferson	.20	.50
58 Jason Kidd	.40	1.00
59 P.J. Brown	.15	.40
60 Desmond Mason	.15	.40
61 Chris Paul	.50	1.25
62 J.R. Smith	.20	.50
63 Steve Francis	.25	.60
64 Channing Frye	.20	.50
65 Stephon Marbury	.25	.60
66 Nate Robinson	.25	.60
67 Grant Hill	.25	.60
68 Dwight Howard	.50	1.25
69 Jameer Nelson	.20	.50
70 Darko Milicic	.25	.60
71 Andre Iguodala	.25	.60
72 Allen Iverson	.50	1.25
73 Kyle Korver	.25	.60
74 Chris Webber	.25	.60
75 Boris Diaw	.20	.50
76 Shawn Marion	.25	.60
77 Steve Nash	.30	.75
78 Amare Stoudemire	.50	1.25
79 Juan Dixon	.15	.40
80 Joel Przybilla	.15	.40
81 Sebastian Telfair	.20	.50
82 Shareef Abdur-Rahim	.25	.60
83 Ron Artest	.25	.60
84 Mike Bibby	.25	.60
85 Tim Duncan	.50	1.25
86 Manu Ginobili	.25	.60
87 Robert Horry	.20	.50
88 Tony Parker	.25	.60
89 Ray Allen	.25	.60
90 Rashard Lewis	.25	.60
91 Luke Ridnour	.20	.50
92 Chris Bosh	.25	.60
93 Jose Calderon	.20	.50
94 Charlie Villanueva	.25	.60
95 Carlos Boozer	.25	.60
96 Andrei Kirilenko	.25	.60
97 Deron Williams	.40	1.00
98 Gilbert Arenas	.25	.60
99 Antawn Jamison	.25	.60
100 Caron Butler	.25	.60
101 Tyrus Thomas RC	.75	2.00
102 Adam Morrison RC	.75	2.00
103 LaMarcus Aldridge RC	.75	2.00
104 Rudy Gay RC	.60	1.50
105 Andrea Bargnani RC	1.00	2.50
106 Rodney Carney RC	.60	1.50
107 Mike Gansey RC	.60	1.50
108 Brandon Roy RC	1.50	4.00
109 Patrick O'Bryant RC	.60	1.50
110 Randy Foye RC	.60	1.50
111 Ronnie Brewer RC	.75	2.00
112 Mardy Collins RC	.60	1.50
113 Shelden Williams RC	.75	2.00
114 J.J. Redick RC	.60	1.50
115 Hilton Armstrong RC	.60	1.50
116 Marcus Williams RC	.75	2.00
117 Rajon Rondo RC	2.50	6.00
118 Cedric Simmons RC	.60	1.50
119 Ryan Hollins RC	.60	1.50
120 Jordan Farmar RC	.75	2.00
121 Maurice Ager RC	.60	1.50
122 Renaldo Balkman RC	.60	1.50
123 Leon Powe RC	.60	1.50
124 Solomon Jones RC	.60	1.50
125 Bobby Jones RC	.60	1.50
126 Josh Boone RC	.60	1.50
127 Saer Sene RC	.60	1.50
128 Daniel Gibson RC	.75	2.00
129 Hassan Adams RC	.75	2.00
130 Kyle Lowry RC	.60	1.50
131 Shannon Brown RC	.60	1.50
132 Dee Brown RC	.60	1.50
133 Shawne Williams RC	.60	1.50
134 P.J. Tucker RC	.60	1.50
135 Craig Smith RC	.60	1.50
136 Paul Davis RC	.60	1.50
137 Allan Ray RC	.60	1.50
138 Denham Brown RC	.60	1.50
139 Chris Quinn RC	.60	1.50
140 Joel Freeland RC	.60	1.50
141 James Augustine RC	.60	1.50
142 Thabo Sefolosha RC	.75	2.00
143 Quincy Douby RC	.60	1.50
144 James White RC	.60	1.50
145 David Noel RC	.60	1.50
146 Steve Novak RC	.60	1.50

2003-04 Upper Deck Rookie Exclusives

COMPLETE SET (60)	12.50	30.00
COMMON ROOKIE (1-30)	.40	1.00
COMMON CARD (31-60)	.08	.20
1 LeBron James RC	5.00	12.00
2 Darko Milicic RC	.40	1.00
3 Carmelo Anthony RC	1.25	3.00
4 Chris Bosh RC	.75	2.00
5 Dwyane Wade RC	1.50	4.00
6 Chris Kaman RC	.50	1.25
7 Jarvis Hayes RC	.40	1.00
8 Mickael Pietrus RC	.40	1.00
9 Marcus Banks RC	.40	1.00
10 Luke Ridnour RC	.50	1.25
11 Reece Gaines RC	.40	1.00
12 Troy Bell RC	.40	1.00
13 Zarko Cabarkapa RC	.40	1.00
14 David West RC	.75	2.00
15 Aleksandar Pavlovic RC	.50	1.25
16 Dahntay Jones RC	.40	1.00
17 Boris Diaw RC	.40	1.00
18 Zoran Planinic RC	.40	1.00
19 Travis Outlaw RC	.50	1.25
20 Brian Cook RC	.40	1.00
21 Ndudi Ebi RC	.40	1.00
22 Kendrick Perkins RC	.60	1.50
23 Leandro Barbosa RC	.60	1.50
24 Josh Howard RC	.50	1.25
25 Maciej Lampe RC	.40	1.00
26 Jason Kapono RC	.40	1.00
27 Luke Walton RC	.50	1.25
28 Travis Hansen RC	.40	1.00
29 Steve Blake RC	.40	1.00
30 Slavko Vranes RC	.40	1.00
31 Darius Miles	.40	1.00
32 Tony Parker	.40	1.00
33 Chauncey Billups	.40	1.00
34 Carlos Boozer	.40	1.00
35 Richard Hamilton	.40	1.00
36 Jamaal Tinsley	.40	1.00
37 Tracy McGrady	.60	1.50
38 Manu Ginobili	.40	1.00
39 Andre Miller	.40	1.00
40 Richard Jefferson	.40	1.00
41 Paul Pierce	.40	1.00
42 Peja Stojakovic	.40	1.00
43 Jason Richardson	.40	1.00
44 Shawn Marion	.40	1.00
45 Antawn Jamison	.40	1.00
46 Reggie Evans	.40	1.00
47 Earl Boykins	.40	1.00
48 Corey Maggette	.40	1.00
49 Cuttino Mobley	.40	1.00
50 Shane Battier	.40	1.00
51 Shareef Abdur-Rahim	.40	1.00
52 Chris Wilcox	.40	1.00
53 Steve Francis	.40	1.00
54 Mike Bibby	.40	1.00
55 Morris Peterson	.40	1.00
56 Nene	.40	1.00
57 Juan Dixon	.40	1.00
58 Yao Ming	.60	1.50
59 Kobe Bryant	1.00	2.50
60 Michael Jordan	2.00	5.00

1993-94 Upper Deck SE

COMPLETE SET (225)	7.50	15.00
1 Scottie Pippen	.40	1.00
2 Todd Day	.01	.05
3 Detlef Schrempf	.05	.15
4 Chris Webber RC	1.25	3.00
5 Michael Adams	.01	.05
6 Loy Vaught	.01	.05

❑ 7 Doug West	.01	.05
❑ 8 A.C. Green	.05	.15
❑ 9 Anthony Mason	.05	.15
❑ 10 Clyde Drexler	.10	.30
❑ 11 Popeye Jones RC	.01	.05
❑ 12 Vlade Divac	.05	.15
❑ 13 Armon Gilliam	.01	.05
❑ 14 Hersey Hawkins	.05	.15
❑ 15 Dennis Scott	.01	.05
❑ 16 Bimbo Coles	.01	.05
❑ 17 Blue Edwards	.01	.05
❑ 18 Negele Knight	.01	.05
❑ 19 Dale Davis	.01	.05
❑ 20 Isiah Thomas	.10	.30
❑ 21 Latrell Sprewell	.30	.75
❑ 22 Kenny Smith	.01	.05
❑ 23 Bryant Stith	.01	.05
❑ 24 Terry Porter	.01	.05
❑ 25 Spud Webb	.05	.15
❑ 26 John Battle	.01	.05
❑ 27 Jeff Malone	.01	.05
❑ 28 Olden Polynice	.01	.05
❑ 29 Kevin Willis	.01	.05
❑ 30 Robert Parish	.05	.15
❑ 31 Kevin Johnson	.05	.15
❑ 32 Shaquille O'Neal	.60	1.50
❑ 33 Willie Anderson	.01	.05
❑ 34 Micheal Williams	.01	.05
❑ 35 Steve Smith	.10	.30
❑ 36 Rik Smits	.05	.15
❑ 37 Pete Myers	.01	.05
❑ 38 Oliver Miller	.01	.05
❑ 39 Eddie Johnson	.01	.05
❑ 40 Calbert Cheaney RC	.05	.15
❑ 41 Vernon Maxwell	.01	.05
❑ 42 James Worthy	.10	.30
❑ 43 Dino Radja RC	.01	.05
❑ 44 Derrick Coleman	.05	.15
❑ 45 Reggie Williams	.01	.05
❑ 46 Dale Ellis	.01	.05
❑ 47 Clifford Robinson	.05	.15
❑ 48 Doug Christie	.05	.15
❑ 49 Ricky Pierce	.01	.05
❑ 50 Sean Elliott	.05	.15
❑ 51 Anfernee Hardaway RC	1.00	2.50
❑ 52 Dana Barros	.01	.05
❑ 53 Reggie Miller	.10	.30
❑ 54 Brian Williams	.01	.05
❑ 55 Otis Thorpe	.05	.15
❑ 56 Jerome Kersey	.01	.05
❑ 57 Larry Johnson	.10	.30
❑ 58 Rex Chapman	.01	.05
❑ 59 Kevin Edwards	.01	.05
❑ 60 Nate McMillan	.01	.05
❑ 61 Chris Mullin	.10	.30
❑ 62 Bill Cartwright	.01	.05
❑ 63 Dennis Rodman	.25	.60
❑ 64 Pooh Richardson	.01	.05
❑ 65 Tyrone Hill	.01	.05
❑ 66 Scott Brooks	.01	.05
❑ 67 Brad Daugherty	.01	.05
❑ 68 Joe Dumars	.10	.30
❑ 69 Vin Baker RC	.30	.75
❑ 70 Rod Strickland	.05	.15
❑ 71 Tom Chambers	.01	.05
❑ 72 Charles Oakley	.05	.15
❑ 73 Craig Ehlo	.01	.05
❑ 74 LaPhonso Ellis	.01	.05
❑ 75 Kevin Gamble	.01	.05
❑ 76 Shawn Bradley RC	.10	.30
❑ 77 Kendall Gill	.05	.15
❑ 78 Hakeem Olajuwon	.20	.50
❑ 79 Nick Anderson	.05	.15
❑ 80 Anthony Peeler	.01	.05
❑ 81 Wayman Tisdale	.01	.05
❑ 82 Danny Manning	.05	.15
❑ 83 John Starks	.05	.15
❑ 84 Jeff Hornacek	.05	.15
❑ 85 Victor Alexander	.01	.05
❑ 86 Mitch Richmond	.10	.30
❑ 87 Mookie Blaylock	.05	.15
❑ 88 Harvey Grant	.01	.05
❑ 89 Doug Smith	.01	.05

❑ 90 John Stockton	.10	.30
❑ 91 Charles Barkley	.20	.50
❑ 92 Gerald Wilkins	.01	.05
❑ 93 Mario Elie	.01	.05
❑ 94 Ken Norman	.01	.05
❑ 95 B.J. Armstrong	.01	.05
❑ 96 John Williams	.01	.05
❑ 97 Rony Seikaly	.01	.05
❑ 98 Sean Rooks	.01	.05
❑ 99 Shawn Kemp	.20	.50
❑ 100 Danny Ainge	.05	.15
❑ 101 Terry Mills	.01	.05
❑ 102 Doc Rivers	.05	.15
❑ 103 Chuck Person	.01	.05
❑ 104 Sam Cassell RC	.50	1.25
❑ 105 Kevin Duckworth	.01	.05
❑ 106 Dan Majerle	.05	.15
❑ 107 Mark Jackson	.05	.15
❑ 108 Steve Kerr	.05	.15
❑ 109 Sam Perkins	.05	.15
❑ 110 Clarence Weatherspoon	.01	.05
❑ 111 Felton Spencer	.01	.05
❑ 112 Greg Anthony	.01	.05
❑ 113 Pete Chilcutt	.01	.05
❑ 114 Malik Sealy	.01	.05
❑ 115 Horace Grant	.05	.15
❑ 116 Chris Morris	.01	.05
❑ 117 Xavier McDaniel	.01	.05
❑ 118 Lionel Simmons	.01	.05
❑ 119 Dell Curry	.01	.05
❑ 120 Moses Malone	.10	.30
❑ 121 Lindsey Hunter RC	.10	.30
❑ 122 Buck Williams	.01	.05
❑ 123 Mahmoud Abdul-Rauf	.01	.05
❑ 124 Rumeal Robinson	.01	.05
❑ 125 Chris Mills RC	.10	.30
❑ 126 Scott Skiles	.01	.05
❑ 127 Derrick McKey	.01	.05
❑ 128 Avery Johnson	.01	.05
❑ 129 Harold Miner	.01	.05
❑ 130 Frank Brickowski	.01	.05
❑ 131 Gary Payton	.20	.50
❑ 132 Don MacLean	.01	.05
❑ 133 Thurl Bailey	.01	.05
❑ 134 Nick Van Exel RC	.40	1.00
❑ 135 Matt Geiger	.01	.05
❑ 136 Stacey Augmon	.01	.05
❑ 137 Sedale Threatt	.01	.05
❑ 138 Patrick Ewing	.10	.30
❑ 130 Tyrone Corbin	.01	.05
❑ 140 Jim Jackson	.05	.15
❑ 141 Christian Laettner	.05	.15
❑ 142 Robert Horry	.05	.15
❑ 143 J.R. Reid	.01	.05
❑ 144 Eric Murdock	.01	.05
❑ 145 Alonzo Mourning	.20	.50
❑ 146 Sherman Douglas	.01	.05
❑ 147 Tom Gugliotta	.10	.30
❑ 148 Glen Rice	.05	.15
❑ 149 Mark Price	.01	.05
❑ 150 Dikembe Mutombo	.10	.30
❑ 151 Derek Harper	.05	.15
❑ 152 Karl Malone	.20	.50
❑ 153 Byron Scott	.05	.15
❑ 154 Reggie Jordan RC	.01	.05
❑ 155 Dominique Wilkins	.10	.30
❑ 156 Bobby Hurley RC	.05	.15
❑ 157 Ron Harper	.05	.15
❑ 158 Bryon Russell RC	.10	.30
❑ 159 Frank Johnson	.01	.05
❑ 160 Toni Kukoc RC	.50	1.25
❑ 161 Lloyd Daniels	.01	.05
❑ 162 Jeff Turner	.01	.05
❑ 163 Muggsy Bogues	.05	.15
❑ 164 Chris Gatling	.01	.05
❑ 165 Kenny Anderson	.05	.15
❑ 166 Elmore Spencer	.01	.05
❑ 167 Jamal Mashburn RC	.30	.75
❑ 168 Tim Perry	.01	.05
❑ 169 Antonio Davis RC	.15	.40
❑ 170 Isaiah Rider RC	.25	.60
❑ 171 Dee Brown	.01	.05
❑ 172 Walt Williams	.01	.05

❑ 173 Elden Campbell	.01	.05
❑ 174 Benoit Benjamin	.01	.05
❑ 175 Billy Owens	.01	.05
❑ 176 Andrew Lang	.01	.05
❑ 177 David Robinson	.20	.50
❑ 178 Checklist 1	.01	.05
❑ 179 Checklist 2	.01	.05
❑ 180 Checklist 3	.01	.05
❑ 181 Shawn Bradley ASW	.05	.15
❑ 182 Calbert Cheaney ASW	.01	.05
❑ 183 Toni Kukoc ASW	.10	.30
❑ 184 Popeye Jones ASW	.01	.05
❑ 185 Lindsey Hunter ASW	.05	.15
❑ 186 Chris Webber ASW	.60	1.50
❑ 187 Bryon Russell ASW	.05	.15
❑ 188 A.Hardaway ASW	.50	1.25
❑ 189 Nick Van Exel ASW	.10	.30
❑ 190 P.J.Brown ASW	.05	.15
❑ 191 Isaiah Rider ASW	.10	.30
❑ 192 Chris Mills ASW	.05	.15
❑ 193 Antonio Davis ASW	.05	.15
❑ 194 Jamal Mashburn ASW	.10	.30
❑ 195 Dino Radja ASW	.01	.05
❑ 196 Sam Cassell ASW	.10	.30
❑ 197 Isaiah Rider ASW SD	.10	.30
❑ 198 Mark Price LDS	.01	.05
❑ 199 Stacey Augmon TH	.01	.05
❑ 200 Celtics Team TH	.01	.05
❑ 201 Eddie Johnson TH	.01	.05
❑ 202 Scottie Pippen TH	.20	.50
❑ 203 Brad Daugherty TH	.01	.05
❑ 204 Jamal Mashburn TH	.10	.30
❑ 205 Dikembe Mutombo TH	.05	.15
❑ 206 Lindsey Hunter TH	.05	.15
❑ 207 Chris Webber TH	.40	1.00
❑ 208 Rockets Team TH	.01	.05
❑ 209 Derrick McKey TH	.01	.05
❑ 210 Danny Manning TH	.01	.05
❑ 211 Doug Christie TH	.05	.15
❑ 212 Glen Rice TH	.01	.05
❑ 213 Day/Norman/Barry/Baker T	.01	.05
❑ 214 Isaiah Rider TH	.10	.30
❑ 215 Kenny Anderson TH	.01	.05
❑ 216 Patrick Ewing TH	.05	.15
❑ 217 Anfernee Hardaway TH	.30	.75
❑ 218 Moses Malone TH	.05	.15
❑ 219 Kevin Johnson TH	.01	.05
❑ 220 Clifford Robinson TH	.01	.05
❑ 221 Wayman Tisdale TH	.01	.05
❑ 222 David Robinson TH	.10	.30
❑ 223 Sonics Team TH	.01	.05
❑ 224 John Stockton TH	.05	.15
❑ 225 Don MacLean TH	.01	.05
❑ JK1 Johnny Kilroy	1.50	4.00
❑ MJR1 M.Jordan Retirement	3.00	8.00

2000-01 Upper Deck Slam

❑ COMPLETE SET w/o RC (60)	10.00	20.00
❑ COMMON CARD (1-60)	.08	.25
❑ COMMON RC/2500 (61-100)	.50	1.25
❑ 1 Dikembe Mutombo	.25	.60
❑ 2 Jim Jackson	.20	.50
❑ 3 Paul Pierce	.30	.75
❑ 4 Antoine Walker	.25	.60
❑ 5 Eddie Jones	.25	.60
❑ 6 Baron Davis	.30	.75
❑ 7 Derrick Coleman	.25	.60
❑ 8 Elton Brand	.30	.75
❑ 9 Ron Artest	.30	.75
❑ 10 Andre Miller	.25	.60

❑ 11 Shawn Kemp	.30	.75
❑ 12 Michael Finley	.30	.75
❑ 13 Dirk Nowitzki	.50	1.25
❑ 14 Antonio McDyess	.25	.60
❑ 15 James Posey	.20	.50
❑ 16 Jerry Stackhouse	.25	.60
❑ 17 Jerome Williams	.20	.50
❑ 18 Larry Hughes	.25	.60
❑ 19 Antawn Jamison	.30	.75
❑ 20 Steve Francis	.30	.75
❑ 21 Hakeem Olajuwon	.40	1.00
❑ 22 Reggie Miller	.30	.75
❑ 23 Jalen Rose	.25	.60
❑ 24 Lamar Odom	.30	.75
❑ 25 Michael Olowokandi	.20	.50
❑ 26 Shaquille O'Neal	.75	2.00
❑ 27 Kobe Bryant	1.50	4.00
❑ 28 Alonzo Mourning	.30	.75
❑ 29 Jamal Mashburn	.25	.60
❑ 30 Ray Allen	.30	.75
❑ 31 Glenn Robinson	.25	.60
❑ 32 Kevin Garnett	.60	1.50
❑ 33 Wally Szczerbiak	.25	.60
❑ 34 Stephon Marbury	.30	.75
❑ 35 Keith Van Horn	.25	.60
❑ 36 Latrell Sprewell	.25	.60
❑ 37 Allan Houston	.25	.60
❑ 38 Darrell Armstrong	.20	.50
❑ 39 Ron Mercer	.20	.50
❑ 40 Allen Iverson	.60	1.50
❑ 41 Toni Kukoc	.25	.60
❑ 42 Jason Kidd	.50	1.25
❑ 43 Anfernee Hardaway	.30	.75
❑ 44 Shawn Marion	.30	.75
❑ 45 Scottie Pippen	.50	1.25
❑ 46 Rasheed Wallace	.30	.75
❑ 47 Chris Webber	.30	.75
❑ 48 Vlade Divac	.25	.60
❑ 49 Tim Duncan	.60	1.50
❑ 50 David Robinson	.40	1.00
❑ 51 Gary Payton	.30	.75
❑ 52 Rashard Lewis	.30	.75
❑ 53 Vince Carter	.60	1.50
❑ 54 Doug Christie	.20	.50
❑ 55 Karl Malone	.40	1.00
❑ 56 Bryon Russell	.20	.50
❑ 57 Shareef Abdur-Rahim	.25	.60
❑ 58 Michael Dickerson	.20	.50
❑ 59 Juwan Howard	.25	.60
❑ 60 Richard Hamilton	.25	.60
❑ 61 Jerome Moiso RC	.50	1.25
❑ 62 Etan Thomas RC	.50	1.25
❑ 63 Courtney Alexander RC	.50	1.25
❑ 64 Mateen Cleaves RC	.50	1.25
❑ 65 Jason Collier RC	.50	1.25
❑ 66 Hedo Turkoglu RC	6.00	15.00
❑ 67 Desmond Mason RC	.60	1.50
❑ 68 Quentin Richardson RC	.60	1.50
❑ 69 Jamaal Magloire RC	.50	1.25
❑ 70 Speedy Claxton RC	.50	1.25
❑ 71 Morris Peterson RC	.75	2.00
❑ 72 Donnell Harvey RC	.50	1.25
❑ 73 Ira Newble RC	.50	1.25
❑ 74 Mamadou N'Diaye RC	.50	1.25
❑ 75 Erick Barkley RC	.50	1.25
❑ 76 Mark Madsen RC	.50	1.25
❑ 77 Dan Langhi RC	.50	1.25
❑ 78 A.J. Guyton RC	.50	1.25
❑ 79 Olumide Oyedeji RC	2.50	6.00
❑ 80 Eddie House RC	2.50	6.00
❑ 81 Eduardo Najera RC	2.50	6.00
❑ 82 Lavor Postell RC	2.50	6.00
❑ 83 Hanno Mottola RC	2.50	6.00
❑ 84 Chris Carrawell RC	.50	1.25
❑ 85 Michael Redd RC	6.00	15.00
❑ 86 Jabari Smith RC	2.50	6.00
❑ 87 Jason Hart RC	2.50	6.00
❑ 88 Corey Hightower RC	.50	1.25
❑ 89 Chris Porter RC	.50	1.25
❑ 90 Justin Love RC	2.50	6.00
❑ 91 Kenyon Martin RC	1.25	3.00
❑ 92 Stromile Swift RC	.60	1.50
❑ 93 Darius Miles RC	.60	1.50
❑ 94 Marcus Fizer RC	.50	1.25
❑ 95 Mike Miller RC	.75	2.00
❑ 96 DerMarr Johnson RC	.50	1.25
❑ 97 Chris Mihm RC	.50	1.25
❑ 98 Jamal Crawford RC	.75	2.00
❑ 99 Joel Przybilla RC	.50	1.25
❑ 100 Keyon Dooling RC	.50	1.25
❑ P21 Kevin Garnett	1.00	2.50

2005-06 Upper Deck Slam

❑ COMPLETE SET (120)	15.00	40.00
❑ COMP.SET w/o SP's	6.00	15.00
❑ COMMON CARD (1-90)	.12	.30
❑ COMMON ROOKIE (91-120)	.60	1.50
❑ 1 Tony Delk	.12	.30
❑ 2 Josh Smith	.20	.50
❑ 3 Al Harrington	.12	.30
❑ 4 Antoine Walker	.15	.40
❑ 5 Gary Payton	.20	.50
❑ 6 Paul Pierce	.20	.50
❑ 7 Kareem Rush	.12	.30
❑ 8 Emeka Okafor	.20	.50
❑ 9 Primoz Brezec	.12	.30
❑ 10 Eddy Curry	.15	.40
❑ 11 Kirk Hinrich	.20	.50
❑ 12 Ben Gordon	.25	.60
❑ 13 Drew Gooden	.15	.40
❑ 14 LeBron James	1.00	2.50
❑ 15 Zydrunas Ilgauskas	.15	.40
❑ 16 Dirk Nowitzki	.30	.75
❑ 17 Jason Terry	.20	.50
❑ 18 Michael Finley	.20	.50
❑ 19 Carmelo Anthony	.40	1.00
❑ 20 Kenyon Martin	.20	.50
❑ 21 Earl Boykins	.12	.30
❑ 22 Ben Wallace	.20	.50
❑ 23 Chauncey Billups	.20	.50
❑ 24 Richard Hamilton	.15	.40
❑ 25 Troy Murphy	.20	.50
❑ 26 Jason Richardson	.20	.50
❑ 27 Baron Davis	.20	.50
❑ 28 Tracy McGrady	.40	1.00
❑ 29 Yao Ming	.50	1.25
❑ 30 Juwan Howard	.15	.40
❑ 31 Jermaine O'Neal	.20	.50
❑ 32 Stephen Jackson	.15	.40
❑ 33 Ron Artest	.15	.40
❑ 34 Corey Maggette	.15	.40
❑ 35 Elton Brand	.20	.50
❑ 36 Bobby Simmons	.12	.30
❑ 37 Caron Butler	.20	.50
❑ 38 Kobe Bryant	1.00	2.50
❑ 39 Lamar Odom	.20	.50
❑ 40 Mike Miller	.20	.50
❑ 41 Jason Williams	.15	.40
❑ 42 Pau Gasol	.20	.50
❑ 43 Dwyane Wade	.50	1.25
❑ 44 Eddie Jones	.12	.30
❑ 45 Shaquille O'Neal	.50	1.25
❑ 46 Desmond Mason	.12	.30
❑ 47 Maurice Williams	.15	.40
❑ 48 Michael Redd	.20	.50
❑ 49 Kevin Garnett	.40	1.00
❑ 50 Latrell Sprewell	.12	.30
❑ 51 Sam Cassell	.20	.50
❑ 52 Vince Carter	.40	1.00
❑ 53 Jason Kidd	.30	.75
❑ 54 Richard Jefferson	.15	.40
❑ 55 Dan Dickau	.12	.30
❑ 56 Jamaal Magloire	.12	.30
❑ 57 J.R. Smith	.15	.40
❑ 58 Jamal Crawford	.15	.40
❑ 59 Stephon Marbury	.20	.50
❑ 60 Allan Houston	.12	.30
❑ 61 Dwight Howard	.40	1.00
❑ 62 Grant Hill	.20	.50
❑ 63 Steve Francis	.20	.50
❑ 64 Allen Iverson	.40	1.00
❑ 65 Andre Iguodala	.20	.50
❑ 66 Chris Webber	.20	.50
❑ 67 Amare Stoudemire	.40	1.00
❑ 68 Shawn Marion	.20	.50
❑ 69 Steve Nash	.25	.60
❑ 70 Damon Stoudamire	.15	.40
❑ 71 Shareef Abdur-Rahim	.20	.50
❑ 72 Zach Randolph	.20	.50
❑ 73 Mike Bibby	.20	.50
❑ 74 Peja Stojakovic	.20	.50
❑ 75 Brad Miller	.20	.50
❑ 76 Manu Ginobili	.20	.50
❑ 77 Tim Duncan	.40	1.00
❑ 78 Tony Parker	.20	.50
❑ 79 Rashard Lewis	.20	.50
❑ 80 Ray Allen	.20	.50
❑ 81 Ronald Murray	.12	.30
❑ 82 Rafer Alston	.12	.30
❑ 83 Jalen Rose	.20	.50
❑ 84 Chris Bosh	.20	.50
❑ 85 Andrei Kirilenko	.20	.50
❑ 86 Carlos Boozer	.20	.50
❑ 87 Matt Harpring	.15	.40
❑ 88 Antawn Jamison	.20	.50
❑ 89 Gilbert Arenas	.20	.50
❑ 90 Larry Hughes	.15	.40
❑ 91 Andrew Bogut RC	.75	2.00
❑ 92 Martynas Andriuskevicius RC	.60	1.50
❑ 93 Chris Paul RC	2.00	5.00
❑ 94 Deron Williams RC	1.50	4.00
❑ 95 Luther Head RC	.75	2.00
❑ 96 Chris Taft RC	.60	1.50
❑ 97 David Lee RC	1.25	3.00
❑ 98 Gerald Green RC	.60	1.50
❑ 99 Andrew Bynum RC	2.00	5.00
❑ 100 Rashad McCants RC	.75	2.00
❑ 101 Raymond Felton RC	.75	2.00
❑ 102 Danny Granger RC	1.50	4.00
❑ 103 Johan Petro RC	.60	1.50
❑ 104 Antoine Wright RC	.60	1.50
❑ 105 Channing Frye RC	.75	2.00
❑ 106 Joey Graham RC	.60	1.50
❑ 107 Wayne Simien RC	.75	2.00
❑ 108 Monta Ellis RC	1.50	4.00
❑ 109 Charlie Villanueva RC	1.00	2.50
❑ 110 Martell Webster RC	.60	1.50
❑ 111 C.J. Miles RC	.60	1.50
❑ 112 Hakim Warrick RC	1.00	2.50
❑ 113 Ike Diogu RC	.75	2.00
❑ 114 Jarrett Jack RC	.60	1.50
❑ 115 Nate Robinson RC	1.00	2.50
❑ 116 Francisco Garcia RC	.75	2.00
❑ 117 Sarunas Jasikevicius RC	.75	2.00
❑ 118 Salim Stoudamire RC	.75	2.00
❑ 119 Marvin Williams RC	1.00	2.50
❑ 120 Sean May RC	.75	2.00

2003-04 Upper Deck Standing O

❑ COMP.SET w/o SP's	15.00	40.00
❑ COMMON ROOKIE (85-126)	1.50	4.00

*DIECUT SINGLES: .75X TO 2X BASE HI		
*EMBOSS RC's: .6X TO 1.5X BASE HI		
1 Shareef Abdur-Rahim	.30	.75
2 Jason Terry	.30	.75
3 Theo Ratliff	.20	.50
4 Paul Pierce	.30	.75
5 Antoine Walker	.30	.75
6 Vin Baker	.20	.50
7 Jalen Rose	.30	.75
8 Tyson Chandler	.30	.75
9 Michael Jordan	2.00	5.00
10 Dajuan Wagner	.20	.50
11 Zydrunas Ilgauskas	.20	.50
12 Darius Miles	.30	.75
13 Dirk Nowitzki	.50	1.25
14 Michael Finley	.30	.75
15 Steve Nash	.30	.75
16 Nene	.20	.50
17 Rodney White	.08	.20
18 Richard Hamilton	.20	.50
19 Ben Wallace	.30	.75
20 Chauncey Billups	.20	.50
21 Nick Van Exel	.30	.75
22 Jason Richardson	.30	.75
23 Mike Dunleavy	.20	.50
24 Steve Francis	.30	.75
25 Yao Ming	.75	2.00
26 Cuttino Mobley	.20	.50
27 Reggie Miller	.30	.75
28 Jamaal Tinsley	.30	.75
29 Jermaine O'Neal	.30	.75
30 Elton Brand	.30	.75
31 Corey Maggette	.20	.50
32 Quentin Richardson	.20	.50
33 Kobe Bryant	1.25	3.00
34 Shaquille O'Neal	.75	2.00
35 Gary Payton	.30	.75
36 Karl Malone	.30	.75
37 Pau Gasol	.30	.75
38 Mike Miller	.30	.75
39 Eddie Jones	.30	.75
40 Brian Grant	.20	.50
41 Caron Butler	.30	.75
42 Michael Redd	.30	.75
43 Joe Smith	.20	.50
44 Desmond Mason	.20	.50
45 Kevin Garnett	.60	1.50
46 Latrell Sprewell	.30	.75
47 Sam Cassell	.30	.75
48 Jason Kidd	.50	1.25
49 Richard Jefferson	.20	.50
50 Alonzo Mourning	.20	.50
51 Baron Davis	.30	.75
52 Jamal Mashburn	.20	.50
53 Jamaal Magloire	.08	.20
54 Allan Houston	.20	.50
55 Antonio McDyess	.20	.50
56 Keith Van Horn	.30	.75
57 Tracy McGrady	.75	2.00
58 Juwan Howard	.20	.50
59 Drew Gooden	.20	.50
60 Allen Iverson	.60	1.50
61 Glenn Robinson	.20	.50
62 Stephon Marbury	.30	.75
63 Shawn Marion	.30	.75
64 Amare Stoudemire	.60	1.50
65 Rasheed Wallace	.30	.75
66 Bonzi Wells	.20	.50
67 Chris Webber	.30	.75
68 Mike Bibby	.30	.75
69 Peja Stojakovic	.30	.75
70 Tim Duncan	.60	1.50
71 David Robinson	.30	.75
72 Tony Parker	.30	.75
73 Ray Allen	.30	.75
74 Rashard Lewis	.30	.75
75 Reggie Evans	.08	.20
76 Vince Carter	.75	2.00
77 Morris Peterson	.20	.50
78 Antonio Davis	.08	.20
79 Jarron Collins	.08	.20
80 John Stockton	.30	.75
81 Andrei Kirilenko	.30	.75
82 Jerry Stackhouse	.30	.75
83 Gilbert Arenas	.30	.75
84 Larry Hughes	.20	.50
85 LeBron James RC	25.00	50.00
86 Darko Milicic RC	2.00	5.00
87 Carmelo Anthony RC	4.00	10.00
88 Chris Bosh RC	3.00	8.00
89 Dwyane Wade RC	5.00	12.00
90 Chris Kaman RC	2.00	5.00
91 Kirk Hinrich RC	2.00	5.00
92 T.J. Ford RC	1.50	4.00
93 Mike Sweetney RC	1.50	4.00
94 Jarvis Hayes RC	1.50	4.00
95 Mickael Pietrus RC	1.50	4.00
96 Nick Collison RC	1.50	4.00
97 Marcus Banks RC	1.50	4.00
98 Luke Ridnour RC	2.00	5.00
99 Reece Gaines RC	1.50	4.00
100 Troy Bell RC	1.50	4.00
101 Zarko Cabarkapa RC	1.50	4.00
102 David West RC	3.00	8.00
103 Aleksandar Pavlovic RC	2.00	5.00
104 Dahntay Jones RC	1.50	4.00
105 Boris Diaw RC	1.50	4.00
106 Zoran Planinic RC	1.50	4.00
107 Travis Outlaw RC	2.00	5.00
108 Brian Cook RC	1.50	4.00
109 Carlos Delfino RC	1.50	4.00
110 Ndudi Ebi RC	1.50	4.00
111 Kendrick Perkins RC	2.50	6.00
112 Leandro Barbosa RC	2.50	6.00
113 Josh Howard RC	2.00	5.00
114 Maciej Lampe RC	1.50	4.00
115 Jason Kapono RC	1.50	4.00
116 Luke Walton RC	1.50	4.00
117 Jerome Beasley RC	1.50	4.00
118 Willie Green RC	1.50	4.00
119 Kyle Korver RC	2.50	6.00
120 Travis Hansen RC	1.50	4.00
121 Steve Blake RC	1.50	4.00
122 Slavko Vranes RC	1.50	4.00
123 Zaur Pachulia RC	1.50	4.00
124 Keith Bogans RC	1.50	4.00
125 Theron Smith RC	1.50	4.00
126 Brandon Hunter RC	1.50	4.00

2004-05 Upper Deck Trilogy

COMP.SET w/o SP's (100)	60.00	150.00
COMMON CARD (1-100)	.50	1.25
COMMON ROOKIE (101-140)	3.00	8.00
COMMON ROOKIE (141-150)	4.00	10.00
1 Antoine Walker	.75	2.00
2 Al Harrington	.60	1.50
3 Boris Diaw	.60	1.50
4 Paul Pierce	.75	2.00
5 Ricky Davis	.60	1.50
6 Gary Payton	.75	2.00
7 Gerald Wallace	.75	2.00
8 Emeka Okafor RC	1.50	4.00
9 Keith Bogans	.50	1.25
10 Eddy Curry	.60	1.50
11 Kirk Hinrich	.60	1.50
12 Michael Jordan	5.00	12.00
13 LeBron James	5.00	12.00
14 Dajuan Wagner	.50	1.25
15 Jeff McInnis	.50	1.25
16 Drew Gooden	.50	1.25
17 Dirk Nowitzki	1.25	3.00
18 Michael Finley	.75	2.00
19 Jerry Stackhouse	.60	1.50
20 Jason Terry	.60	1.50
21 Kenyon Martin	.75	2.00
22 Andre Miller	.60	1.50
23 Carmelo Anthony	2.50	6.00
24 Nene	.60	1.50
25 Chauncey Billups	.75	2.00
26 Rasheed Wallace	.75	2.00
27 Ben Wallace	.60	1.50
28 Richard Hamilton	.60	1.50
29 Derek Fisher	.60	1.50
30 Jason Richardson	.75	2.00
31 Mike Dunleavy	.60	1.50
32 Yao Ming	2.00	5.00
33 Tracy McGrady	1.50	4.00
34 Juwan Howard	.60	1.50
35 Jermaine O'Neal	.75	2.00
36 Reggie Miller	.75	2.00
37 Ron Artest	.60	1.50
38 Jamaal Tinsley	.60	1.50
39 Elton Brand	.75	2.00
40 Corey Maggette	.60	1.50
41 Marko Jaric	.50	1.25
42 Kerry Kittles	.60	1.50
43 Kobe Bryant	4.00	10.00
44 Caron Butler	.60	1.50
45 Lamar Odom	.75	2.00
46 Brian Cook	.50	1.25
47 Pau Gasol	.75	2.00
48 Jason Williams	.60	1.50
49 Bonzi Wells	.50	1.25
50 Shaquille O'Neal	2.00	5.00
51 Dwyane Wade	2.50	6.00
52 Eddie Jones	.60	1.50
53 Michael Redd	.75	2.00
54 Desmond Mason	.60	1.50
55 Maurice Williams	.60	1.50
56 Latrell Sprewell	.60	1.50
57 Kevin Garnett	1.50	4.00
58 Sam Cassell	.60	1.50
59 Troy Hudson	.50	1.25
60 Vince Carter	1.50	4.00
61 Richard Jefferson	.75	2.00
62 Jason Kidd	1.25	3.00
63 P.J. Brown	.50	1.25
64 Baron Davis	.75	2.00
65 Jamaal Magloire	.50	1.25
66 Allan Houston	.60	1.50
67 Jamal Crawford	.60	1.50
68 Stephon Marbury	.75	2.00
69 Grant Hill	.75	2.00
70 Cuttino Mobley	.60	1.50
71 Steve Francis	.75	2.00
72 Glenn Robinson	.60	1.50
73 Allen Iverson	1.50	4.00
74 Willie Green	.50	1.25
75 Amare Stoudemire	1.50	4.00
76 Steve Nash	1.25	3.00
77 Quentin Richardson	.60	1.50
78 Shawn Marion	.75	2.00
79 Shareef Abdur-Rahim	.60	1.50
80 Damon Stoudamire	.60	1.50
81 Zach Randolph	.75	2.00
82 Darius Miles	.60	1.50
83 Peja Stojakovic	.60	1.50
84 Chris Webber	.75	2.00
85 Mike Bibby	.60	1.50
86 Tony Parker	.75	2.00
87 Tim Duncan	1.50	4.00
88 Manu Ginobili	.75	2.00
89 Ronald Murray	.50	1.25
90 Ray Allen	.75	2.00
91 Rashard Lewis	.75	2.00
92 Chris Bosh	.75	2.00
93 Rafer Alston	.50	1.25
94 Jalen Rose	.60	1.50
95 Andrei Kirilenko	.75	2.00
96 Carlos Arroyo	.75	2.00
97 Carlos Boozer	.75	2.00
98 Gilbert Arenas	.75	2.00
99 Jarvis Hayes	.50	1.25
100 Antawn Jamison	.75	2.00

❑ 101 Rafael Araujo RC	3.00	8.00
❑ 102 Luke Jackson RC	3.00	8.00
❑ 103 Andris Biedrins RC	5.00	12.00
❑ 104 Robert Swift RC	3.00	8.00
❑ 105 Kris Humphries RC	5.00	12.00
❑ 106 Al Jefferson RC	6.00	15.00
❑ 107 Kirk Snyder RC	3.00	8.00
❑ 108 Josh Smith RC	8.00	20.00
❑ 109 Dorell Wright RC	4.00	10.00
❑ 110 Jameer Nelson RC	4.00	10.00
❑ 111 Pavel Podkolzine RC	3.00	8.00
❑ 112 Andres Nocioni RC	4.00	10.00
❑ 113 Luis Flores RC	3.00	8.00
❑ 114 Delonte West RC	5.00	12.00
❑ 115 Tony Allen RC	4.00	10.00
❑ 116 Kevin Martin RC	4.00	10.00
❑ 117 Sasha Vujacic RC	3.00	8.00
❑ 118 Beno Udrih RC	4.00	10.00
❑ 119 David Harrison RC	3.00	8.00
❑ 120 Anderson Varejao RC	4.00	10.00
❑ 121 Jackson Vroman RC	3.00	8.00
❑ 122 Peter John Ramos RC	3.00	8.00
❑ 123 Lionel Chalmers RC	3.00	8.00
❑ 124 Donta Smith RC	3.00	8.00
❑ 125 Andre Emmett RC	3.00	8.00
❑ 126 Antonio Burks RC	3.00	8.00
❑ 127 Royal Ivey RC	3.00	8.00
❑ 128 Chris Duhon RC	5.00	12.00
❑ 129 Nenad Krstic RC	4.00	10.00
❑ 130 Justin Reed RC	3.00	8.00
❑ 131 Pape Sow RC	3.00	8.00
❑ 132 Trevor Ariza RC	4.00	10.00
❑ 133 Tim Pickett RC	3.00	8.00
❑ 134 Bernard Robinson RC	3.00	8.00
❑ 135 John Edwards RC	3.00	8.00
❑ 136 Damien Wilkins RC	3.00	8.00
❑ 137 Romain Sato RC	3.00	8.00
❑ 138 Matt Freije RC	3.00	8.00
❑ 139 D.J. Mbenga RC	3.00	8.00
❑ 140 Yuta Tabuse RC	6.00	15.00
❑ 141 Dwight Howard RC	12.00	30.00
❑ 142 Emeka Okafor	8.00	20.00
❑ 143 Ben Gordon RC	5.00	12.00
❑ 144 Shaun Livingston RC	4.00	10.00
❑ 145 Devin Harris RC	8.00	20.00
❑ 146 Josh Childress RC	4.00	10.00
❑ 147 Luol Deng RC	5.00	12.00
❑ 148 Andre Iguodala RC	10.00	25.00
❑ 149 Sebastian Telfair RC	4.00	10.00
❑ 150 J.R. Smith RC	8.00	20.00

2005-06 Upper Deck Trilogy

❑ COMP.SET w/o SP's (90)	25.00	60.00
❑ COMMON CARD (1-90)	.60	1.50
❑ COMMON ROOKIE (91-130)	3.00	8.00
❑ COMMON ROOKIE (131-140)	4.00	10.00
❑ 1 Josh Smith	1.00	2.50
❑ 2 Josh Childress	.75	2.00
❑ 3 Al Harrington	.60	1.50
❑ 4 Paul Pierce	1.00	2.50
❑ 5 Ricky Davis	1.00	2.50
❑ 6 Al Jefferson	1.00	2.50
❑ 7 Emeka Okafor	1.00	2.50
❑ 8 Gerald Wallace	1.00	2.50
❑ 9 Kareem Rush	.60	1.50
❑ 10 Michael Jordan	6.00	15.00
❑ 11 Luol Deng	1.00	2.50
❑ 12 Ben Gordon	1.25	3.00
❑ 13 LeBron James	5.00	12.00
❑ 14 Larry Hughes	.75	2.00
❑ 15 Donyell Marshall	.60	1.50
❑ 16 Dirk Nowitzki	1.50	4.00
❑ 17 Josh Howard	1.00	2.50
❑ 18 Jason Terry	1.00	2.50
❑ 19 Carmelo Anthony	2.00	5.00
❑ 20 Kenyon Martin	1.00	2.50
❑ 21 Andre Miller	.75	2.00
❑ 22 Chauncey Billups	1.00	2.50
❑ 23 Richard Hamilton	.75	2.00
❑ 24 Ben Wallace	1.00	2.50
❑ 25 Jason Richardson	1.00	2.50
❑ 26 Baron Davis	1.00	2.50
❑ 27 Troy Murphy	1.00	2.50
❑ 28 Yao Ming	2.50	6.00
❑ 29 Tracy McGrady	2.00	5.00
❑ 30 Stromile Swift	.75	2.00
❑ 31 Ron Artest	.75	2.00
❑ 32 Jermaine O'Neal	1.00	2.50
❑ 33 Fred Jones	.75	2.00
❑ 34 Elton Brand	1.00	2.50
❑ 35 Shaun Livingston	.60	1.50
❑ 36 Corey Maggette	.75	2.00
❑ 37 Kobe Bryant	5.00	12.00
❑ 38 Kwame Brown	.75	2.00
❑ 39 Lamar Odom	1.00	2.50
❑ 40 Pau Gasol	1.00	2.50
❑ 41 Shane Battier	1.00	2.50
❑ 42 Mike Miller	1.00	2.50
❑ 43 Shaquille O'Neal	2.50	6.00
❑ 44 Dwyane Wade	2.50	6.00
❑ 45 Udonis Haslem	1.00	2.50
❑ 46 Michael Redd	1.00	2.50
❑ 47 Maurice Williams	.75	2.00
❑ 48 Desmond Mason	.60	1.50
❑ 49 Kevin Garnett	2.00	5.00
❑ 50 Wally Szczerbiak	.75	2.00
❑ 51 Marko Jaric	.60	1.50
❑ 52 Jason Kidd	1.50	4.00
❑ 53 Vince Carter	2.00	5.00
❑ 54 Richard Jefferson	.75	2.00
❑ 55 Jamaal Magloire	.60	1.50
❑ 56 J.R. Smith	.75	2.00
❑ 57 Speedy Claxton	.60	1.50
❑ 58 Stephon Marbury	1.00	2.50
❑ 59 Jamal Crawford	.75	2.00
❑ 60 Quentin Richardson	.75	2.00
❑ 61 Steve Francis	1.00	2.50
❑ 62 Dwight Howard	2.00	5.00
❑ 63 Grant Hill	1.00	2.50
❑ 64 Allen Iverson	2.00	5.00
❑ 65 Kyle Korver	1.00	2.50
❑ 66 Chris Webber	1.00	2.50
❑ 67 Steve Nash	1.25	3.00
❑ 68 Amare Stoudemire	2.00	5.00
❑ 69 Shawn Marion	1.00	2.50
❑ 70 Sebastian Telfair	.75	2.00
❑ 71 Zach Randolph	1.00	2.50
❑ 72 Travis Outlaw	.60	1.50
❑ 73 Peja Stojakovic	1.00	2.50
❑ 74 Mike Bibby	1.00	2.50
❑ 75 Brad Miller	1.00	2.50
❑ 76 Tim Duncan	2.00	5.00
❑ 77 Manu Ginobili	1.00	2.50
❑ 78 Tony Parker	1.00	2.50
❑ 79 Ray Allen	1.00	2.50
❑ 80 Rashard Lewis	1.00	2.50
❑ 81 Luke Ridnour	.75	2.00
❑ 82 Chris Bosh	1.00	2.50
❑ 83 Morris Peterson	.75	2.00
❑ 84 Jalen Rose	1.00	2.50
❑ 85 Carlos Boozer	1.00	2.50
❑ 86 Matt Harpring	.75	2.00
❑ 87 Andrei Kirilenko	1.00	2.50
❑ 88 Antawn Jamison	1.00	2.50
❑ 89 Gilbert Arenas	1.00	2.50
❑ 90 Caron Butler	1.00	2.50
❑ 91 Sarunas Jasikevicius RC	4.00	10.00
❑ 92 Alex Acker RC	3.00	8.00
❑ 93 Amir Johnson RC	3.00	8.00
❑ 94 Lawrence Roberts RC	3.00	8.00
❑ 95 Dijon Thompson RC	3.00	8.00
❑ 96 Orien Greene RC	3.00	8.00
❑ 97 Robert Whaley RC	3.00	8.00
❑ 98 Ryan Gomes RC	3.00	8.00
❑ 99 Andray Blatche RC	4.00	10.00
❑ 100 Yaroslav Korolev RC	3.00	8.00
❑ 101 Bracey Wright RC	3.00	8.00
❑ 102 Louis Williams RC	5.00	12.00
❑ 103 Martynas Andriuskevicius RC	3.00	8.00
❑ 104 Chris Taft RC	3.00	8.00
❑ 105 Monta Ellis RC	8.00	20.00
❑ 106 Von Wafer RC	3.00	8.00
❑ 107 Travis Diener RC	3.00	8.00
❑ 108 Ersan Ilyasova RC	3.00	8.00
❑ 109 Arvydas Macijauskas RC	3.00	8.00
❑ 110 C.J. Miles RC	3.00	8.00
❑ 111 Brandon Bass RC	3.00	8.00
❑ 112 Daniel Ewing RC	4.00	10.00
❑ 113 Salim Stoudamire RC	4.00	10.00
❑ 114 David Lee RC	6.00	15.00
❑ 115 Wayne Simien RC	4.00	10.00
❑ 116 Jason Maxiell RC	4.00	10.00
❑ 117 Johan Petro RC	3.00	8.00
❑ 118 Luther Head RC	4.00	10.00
❑ 119 Francisco Garcia RC	4.00	10.00
❑ 120 Jarrett Jack RC	3.00	8.00
❑ 121 Nate Robinson RC	5.00	12.00
❑ 122 Julius Hodge RC	4.00	10.00
❑ 123 Hakim Warrick RC	5.00	12.00
❑ 124 Gerald Green RC	3.00	8.00
❑ 125 Danny Granger RC	8.00	20.00
❑ 126 Joey Graham RC	3.00	8.00
❑ 127 Antoine Wright RC	3.00	8.00
❑ 128 Rashad McCants RC	4.00	10.00
❑ 129 Sean May RC	4.00	10.00
❑ 130 Linas Kleiza RC	4.00	10.00
❑ 131 Andrew Bynum RC	12.00	30.00
❑ 132 Ike Diogu RC	5.00	12.00
❑ 133 Channing Frye RC	5.00	12.00
❑ 134 Charlie Villanueva RC	6.00	15.00
❑ 135 Martell Webster RC	4.00	10.00
❑ 136 Raymond Felton RC	5.00	12.00
❑ 137 Chris Paul RC	15.00	30.00
❑ 138 Deron Williams RC	10.00	25.00
❑ 139 Marvin Williams RC	6.00	15.00
❑ 140 Andrew Bogut RC	5.00	12.00

2006-07 Upper Deck Trilogy

❑ COMP.SET w/o SP's (90)	20.00	50.00
❑ 1 Joe Johnson	.60	1.50
❑ 2 Marvin Williams	.75	2.00
❑ 3 Paul Pierce	.75	2.00
❑ 4 Wally Szczerbiak	.60	1.50
❑ 5 Emeka Okafor	.75	2.00
❑ 6 Raymond Felton	1.00	2.50
❑ 7 Ben Wallace	.75	2.00
❑ 8 Kirk Hinrich	.75	2.00
❑ 9 Ben Gordon	1.00	2.50
❑ 10 LeBron James	4.00	10.00
❑ 11 Larry Hughes	.60	1.50
❑ 12 Dirk Nowitzki	1.25	3.00
❑ 13 Jason Terry	.75	2.00
❑ 14 Carmelo Anthony	1.00	2.50
❑ 15 Andre Miller	.60	1.50
❑ 16 Chauncey Billups	.75	2.00
❑ 17 Richard Hamilton	.60	1.50
❑ 18 Jason Richardson	.75	2.00
❑ 19 Baron Davis	.75	2.00
❑ 20 Yao Ming	2.00	5.00

21 Tracy McGrady	1.50	4.00
22 Jermaine O'Neal	.75	2.00
23 Al Harrington	.50	1.25
24 Elton Brand	.75	2.00
25 Sam Cassell	.75	2.00
26 Kobe Bryant	4.00	10.00
27 Lamar Odom	.75	2.00
28 Pau Gasol	.75	2.00
29 Dwyane Wade	2.00	5.00
30 Shaquille O'Neal	2.00	5.00
31 Michael Redd	.75	2.00
32 Andrew Bogut	.75	2.00
33 Kevin Garnett	1.50	4.00
34 Mike James	.50	1.25
35 Vince Carter	1.50	4.00
36 Jason Kidd	1.25	3.00
37 Richard Jefferson	.60	1.50
38 Chris Paul	1.50	4.00
39 David West	.75	2.00
40 Stephon Marbury	.75	2.00
41 Steve Francis	.75	2.00
42 Dwight Howard	1.50	4.00
43 Jameer Nelson	.60	1.50
44 Allen Iverson	1.50	4.00
45 Chris Webber	.75	2.00
46 Steve Nash	1.00	2.50
47 Shawn Marion	.75	2.00
48 Zach Randolph	.75	2.00
49 Mike Bibby	.75	2.00
50 Ron Artest	.75	2.00
51 Tim Duncan	1.50	4.00
52 Tony Parker	.75	2.00
53 Ray Allen	.75	2.00
54 Rashard Lewis	.75	2.00
55 Chris Bosh	.75	2.00
56 T.J. Ford	.60	1.50
57 Mehmet Okur	.50	1.25
58 Andrei Kirilenko	.75	2.00
59 Gilbert Arenas	.75	2.00
60 Antawn Jamison	.75	2.00
61 Childress/Claxton/Smith	.75	2.00
62 Jefferson/West/Telfair	.75	2.00
63 Wallace/Brezec/Knight	.75	2.00
64 Nocioni/Deng/Brown	1.25	3.00
65 Gooden/Ilgauskas/Marshall	.75	2.00
66 Howard/Stackhouse/Harris	1.25	3.00
67 Martin/Camby/Smith	1.25	3.00
68 Wallace/Prince/Mohammed	1.25	3.00
69 Murphy/Dunleavy/Diogu	.75	2.00
70 Alston/Battier/Wells	.75	2.00
71 Granger/Tinsley/Dunleavy	.75	2.00
72 Kaman/Maggette/Livingston	.75	2.00
73 Parker/Radmanovic/Brown	1.25	3.00
74 Miller/Stoudamire/Warrick	.75	2.00
75 Walker/Haslem/Williams	1.25	3.00
76 Villanueva/Patterson/Williams	.75	2.00
77 Davis/Hassell/Blount	.75	2.00
78 Krstic/Collins/Robinson	.75	2.00
79 Chandler/Stojakovic/Mason	.75	2.00
80 Curry/Crawford/Frye	.75	2.00
81 Milicic/Turkoglu/Hill	1.00	2.50
82 Iguodala/Korver/Dalembert	.75	2.00
83 Stoudemire/Diaw/Bell	1.25	3.00
84 Jack/Randolph/Webster	.75	2.00
85 Miller/Abdur-Rahim/Martin	1.00	2.50
86 Ginobili/Finley/Bowen	1.50	4.00
87 Ridnour/Wilcox/Collison	.75	2.00
88 Peterson/Graham/Calderon	.75	2.00
89 Boozer/Williams/Giricek	1.25	3.00
90 Butler/Thomas/Stevenson	.75	2.00
91 Shelden Williams RC	4.00	10.00
92 Tyrus Thomas RC	4.00	10.00
93 Rudy Gay RC	3.00	8.00
94 Randy Foye RC	3.00	8.00
95 Rodney Carney RC	3.00	8.00
96 LaMarcus Aldridge RC	4.00	10.00
97 Brandon Roy RC	8.00	20.00
98 Andrea Bargnani RC	5.00	12.00
99 Solomon Jones RC	2.00	5.00
100 Rajon Rondo RC	8.00	20.00
101 Allan Ray RC	2.00	5.00
102 Thabo Sefolosha RC	2.50	6.00
103 Shannon Brown RC	2.00	5.00
104 Maurice Ager RC	2.00	5.00
105 Patrick O'Bryant RC	2.00	5.00
106 Steve Novak RC	2.00	5.00
107 Shawne Williams RC	2.00	5.00
108 Paul Davis RC	2.00	5.00
109 Jordan Farmar RC	2.50	6.00
110 Kyle Lowry RC	2.00	5.00
111 David Noel RC	2.00	5.00
112 Craig Smith RC	2.00	5.00
113 Marcus Williams RC	2.50	6.00
114 Josh Boone RC	2.00	5.00
115 Hilton Armstrong RC	2.00	5.00
116 Cedric Simmons RC	2.00	5.00
117 Renaldo Balkman RC	2.00	5.00
118 Mardy Collins RC	2.00	5.00
119 Bobby Jones RC	2.00	5.00
120 Quincy Douby RC	2.00	5.00
121 Saer Sene RC	2.00	5.00
122 P.J. Tucker RC	2.00	5.00
123 Jorge Garbajosa RC	4.00	10.00
124 Ronnie Brewer RC	2.50	6.00
125 Dee Brown RC	2.00	5.00
126 Leon Powe RC	2.00	5.00
127 Ryan Hollins RC	2.00	5.00
128 Adam Morrison RC	2.50	6.00
129 Daniel Gibson RC	2.50	6.00
130 Pops Mensah-Bonsu RC	2.00	5.00
131 Yakhouba Diawara RC	2.00	5.00
132 Will Blalock RC	2.00	5.00
133 Alexander Johnson RC	2.00	5.00
134 Damir Markota RC	2.00	5.00
135 Hassan Adams RC	2.50	6.00
136 Marcus Vinicius RC	2.00	5.00
137 James Augustine RC	2.00	5.00
138 J.J. Redick RC	2.00	5.00
139 Sergio Rodriguez RC	2.00	5.00
140 Paul Millsap RC	3.00	8.00

2003-04 Upper Deck Triple Dimensions

COMP.SET w/o SP's (90)	12.50	30.00
COMMON CARD (1-90)	.08	.20
COMMON ROOKIE (91-126)	2.00	5.00
1 Jason Terry	.30	.75
2 Theo Ratliff	.20	.50
3 Shareef Abdur-Rahim	.30	.75
4 Raef LaFrentz	.20	.50
5 Vin Baker	.20	.50
6 Paul Pierce	.30	.75
7 Eddy Curry	.20	.50
8 Tyson Chandler	.30	.75
9 Antonio Davis	.08	.20
10 Dajuan Wagner	.20	.50
11 Zydrunas Ilgauskas	.20	.50
12 Carlos Boozer	.30	.75
13 Steve Nash	.30	.75
14 Antoine Walker	.30	.75
15 Dirk Nowitzki	.50	1.25
16 Michael Finley	.30	.75
17 Andre Miller	.20	.50
18 Nene	.20	.50
19 Earl Boykins	.20	.50
20 Ben Wallace	.30	.75
21 Chauncey Billups	.20	.50
22 Richard Hamilton	.20	.50
23 Mike Dunleavy	.20	.50
24 Jason Richardson	.30	.75
25 Nick Van Exel	.30	.75
26 Cuttino Mobley	.20	.50
27 Yao Ming	.75	2.00
28 Steve Francis	.30	.75
29 Reggie Miller	.30	.75
30 Jamaal Tinsley	.30	.75
31 Jermaine O'Neal	.30	.75
32 Corey Maggette	.20	.50
33 Elton Brand	.30	.75
34 Quentin Richardson	.20	.50
35 Shaquille O'Neal	.75	2.00
36 Kobe Bryant	1.25	3.00
37 Karl Malone	.30	.75
38 Gary Payton	.30	.75
39 Mike Miller	.30	.75
40 Pau Gasol	.30	.75
41 Shane Battier	.30	.75
42 Eddie Jones	.30	.75
43 Caron Butler	.30	.75
44 Lamar Odom	.30	.75
45 Desmond Mason	.20	.50
46 Tim Thomas	.20	.50
47 Michael Redd	.30	.75
48 Latrell Sprewell	.30	.75
49 Kevin Garnett	.60	1.50
50 Wally Szczerbiak	.20	.50
51 Kenyon Martin	.30	.75
52 Jason Kidd	.50	1.25
53 Richard Jefferson	.20	.50
54 Jamal Mashburn	.20	.50
55 Baron Davis	.30	.75
56 Jamaal Magloire	.08	.20
57 Stephon Marbury	.30	.75
58 Allan Houston	.20	.50
59 Keith Van Horn	.30	.75
60 Drew Gooden	.20	.50
61 Tracy McGrady	.75	2.00
62 Gordan Giricek	.20	.50
63 Glenn Robinson	.30	.75
64 Allen Iverson	.60	1.50
65 Eric Snow	.20	.50
66 Antonio McDyess	.20	.50
67 Amare Stoudemire	.75	2.00
68 Shawn Marion	.30	.75
69 Zach Randolph	.30	.75
70 Rasheed Wallace	.30	.75
71 Damon Stoudamire	.20	.50
72 Mike Bibby	.30	.75
73 Chris Webber	.30	.75
74 Peja Stojakovic	.30	.75
75 Brad Miller	.30	.75
76 Tony Parker	.30	.75
77 Tim Duncan	.60	1.50
78 Manu Ginobili	.30	.75
79 Rashard Lewis	.30	.75
80 Ray Allen	.30	.75
81 Vladimir Radmanovic	.08	.20
82 Morris Peterson	.20	.50
83 Vince Carter	.75	2.00
84 Jalen Rose	.30	.75
85 Andrei Kirilenko	.30	.75
86 Matt Harpring	.30	.75
87 Carlos Arroyo	.50	1.25
88 Jerry Stackhouse	.30	.75
89 Gilbert Arenas	.30	.75
90 Larry Hughes	.20	.50
91 Udonis Haslem RC	2.00	5.00
92 Brandon Hunter RC	2.00	5.00
93 Maurice Williams RC	3.00	8.00
94 Keith Bogans RC	2.00	5.00
95 Zaur Pachulia RC	2.00	5.00
96 Willie Green RC	2.00	5.00
97 Kyle Korver RC	3.00	8.00
98 James Jones RC	2.00	5.00
99 Steve Blake RC	2.00	5.00
100 Travis Hansen RC	2.00	5.00
101 Jerome Beasley RC	2.00	5.00
102 Luke Walton RC	2.00	5.00
103 Jason Kapono RC	2.00	5.00
104 Maciej Lampe RC	2.00	5.00
105 Josh Howard RC	2.50	6.00
106 Leandro Barbosa RC	3.00	8.00
107 Kendrick Perkins RC	3.00	8.00
108 Ndudi Ebi RC	2.00	5.00
109 Brian Cook RC	2.00	5.00

❑ 110 Travis Outlaw RC	2.50	6.00
❑ 111 Zoran Planinic RC	2.00	5.00
❑ 112 Boris Diaw RC	2.00	5.00
❑ 113 Dahntay Jones RC	2.00	5.00
❑ 114 Aleksandar Pavlovic RC	2.50	6.00
❑ 115 David West RC	4.00	10.00
❑ 116 Zarko Cabarkapa RC	2.00	5.00
❑ 117 Troy Bell RC	2.00	5.00
❑ 118 Reece Gaines RC	2.00	5.00
❑ 119 Luke Ridnour RC	2.50	6.00
❑ 120 Marcus Banks RC	2.00	5.00
❑ 121 Nick Collison RC	2.00	5.00
❑ 122 Mickael Pietrus RC	2.00	5.00
❑ 123 Mike Sweetney RC	2.00	5.00
❑ 124 Chris Kaman RC	2.50	6.00
❑ 125 T.J. Ford RC	2.00	5.00
❑ 126 Kirk Hinrich RC	2.50	6.00
❑ 127 Jarvis Hayes RC	2.00	5.00
❑ 128 Dwyane Wade RC	6.00	15.00
❑ 129 Chris Bosh RC	5.00	12.00
❑ 130 Carmelo Anthony RC	8.00	20.00
❑ 131 Darko Milicic RC	4.00	10.00
❑ 132 LeBron James RC	40.00	80.00

1999-00 Upper Deck Victory

❑ COMPLETE SET (440)	35.00	60.00
❑ COMMON CARD (1-380)	.05	.15
❑ COMMON ROOKIE (431-440)	.50	1.25
❑ COMMON MJ HITS (381-430)	.40	1.00
❑ 1 Dikembe Mutombo CL	.12	.30
❑ 2 Steve Smith	.10	.25
❑ 3 Dikembe Mutombo	.12	.30
❑ 4 Ed Gray	.10	.25
❑ 5 Alan Henderson	.10	.25
❑ 6 LaPhonso Ellis	.10	.25
❑ 7 Roshown McLeod	.10	.25
❑ 8 Bimbo Coles	.10	.25
❑ 9 Chris Crawford	.10	.25
❑ 10 Anthony Johnson	.10	.25
❑ 11 Antoine Walker CL	.15	.40
❑ 12 Kenny Anderson	.12	.30
❑ 13 Antoine Walker	.15	.40
❑ 14 Greg Minor	.10	.25
❑ 15 Tony Battie	.12	.30
❑ 16 Ron Mercer	.10	.25
❑ 17 Paul Pierce	.15	.40
❑ 18 Vitaly Potapenko	.10	.25
❑ 19 Dana Barros	.10	.25
❑ 20 Walter McCarty	.10	.25
❑ 21 Elden Campbell CL	.10	.25
❑ 22 Elden Campbell	.10	.25
❑ 23 Eddie Jones	.15	.40
❑ 24 David Wesley	.10	.25
❑ 25 Bobby Phills	.10	.25
❑ 26 Derrick Coleman	.12	.30
❑ 27 Anthony Mason	.10	.25
❑ 28 Brad Miller	.12	.30
❑ 29 Eldridge Recasner	.10	.25
❑ 30 Ricky Davis	.15	.40
❑ 31 Toni Kukoc CL	.15	.40
❑ 32 Michael Jordan	1.00	2.50
❑ 33 Brent Barry	.12	.30
❑ 34 Randy Brown	.10	.25
❑ 35 Keith Booth	.10	.25
❑ 36 Kornel David RC	.15	.40
❑ 37 Mark Bryant	.10	.25
❑ 38 Toni Kukoc	.15	.40
❑ 39 Rusty LaRue	.10	.25
❑ 40 Brevin Knight CL	.10	.25
❑ 41 Shawn Kemp	.15	.40
❑ 42 Wesley Person	.10	.25
❑ 43 Johnny Newman	.10	.25
❑ 44 Derek Anderson	.10	.25
❑ 45 Brevin Knight	.10	.25
❑ 46 Bob Sura	.10	.25
❑ 47 Andrew DeClercq	.10	.25
❑ 48 Zydrunas Ilgauskas	.12	.30
❑ 49 Danny Ferry	.10	.25
❑ 50 Steve Nash CL	.25	.60
❑ 51 Michael Finley	.15	.40
❑ 52 Robert Pack	.10	.25
❑ 53 Shawn Bradley	.10	.25
❑ 54 John Williams	.10	.25
❑ 55 Hubert Davis	.10	.25
❑ 56 Dirk Nowitzki	.25	.60
❑ 57 Steve Nash	.25	.60
❑ 58 Chris Anstey	.10	.25
❑ 59 Erick Strickland	.10	.25
❑ 60 Nick Van Exel CL	.12	.30
❑ 61 Antonio McDyess	.12	.30
❑ 62 Nick Van Exel	.12	.30
❑ 63 Bryant Stith	.10	.25
❑ 64 Chauncey Billups	.15	.40
❑ 65 Danny Fortson	.10	.25
❑ 66 Eric Williams	.10	.25
❑ 67 Eric Washington	.10	.25
❑ 68 Raef LaFrentz	.12	.30
❑ 69 Johnny Taylor	.10	.25
❑ 70 Jerry Stackhouse CL	.15	.40
❑ 71 Grant Hill	.15	.40
❑ 72 Lindsey Hunter	.10	.25
❑ 73 Bison Dele	.10	.25
❑ 74 Loy Vaught	.10	.25
❑ 75 Jerome Williams	.10	.25
❑ 76 Jerry Stackhouse	.15	.40
❑ 77 Christian Laettner	.12	.30
❑ 78 Jud Buechler	.10	.25
❑ 79 Don Reid	.10	.25
❑ 80 Antawn Jamison CL	.15	.40
❑ 81 John Starks	.15	.40
❑ 82 Antawn Jamison	.15	.40
❑ 83 Adonal Foyle	.10	.25
❑ 84 Jason Caffey	.10	.25
❑ 85 Donyell Marshall	.12	.30
❑ 86 Chris Mills	.10	.25
❑ 87 Tony Delk	.10	.25
❑ 88 Mookie Blaylock	.10	.25
❑ 89 Charles Barkley CL	.20	.50
❑ 90 Hakeem Olajuwon	.15	.40
❑ 91 Scottie Pippen	.25	.60
❑ 92 Charles Barkley	.20	.50
❑ 93 Bryce Drew	.10	.25
❑ 94 Cuttino Mobley	.12	.30
❑ 95 Othella Harrington	.10	.25
❑ 96 Matt Maloney	.10	.25
❑ 97 Michael Dickerson	.10	.25
❑ 98 Matt Bullard	.10	.25
❑ 99 Jalen Rose CL	.12	.30
❑ 100 Reggie Miller	.15	.40
❑ 101 Rik Smits	.15	.40
❑ 102 Jalen Rose	.12	.30
❑ 103 Antonio Davis	.10	.25
❑ 104 Mark Jackson	.15	.40
❑ 105 Sam Perkins	.10	.25
❑ 106 Travis Best	.10	.25
❑ 107 Dale Davis	.10	.25
❑ 108 Chris Mullin	.15	.40
❑ 109 Michael Olowokandi CL	.10	.25
❑ 110 Maurice Taylor	.12	.30
❑ 111 Tyrone Nesby RC	.15	.40
❑ 112 Lamond Murray	.10	.25
❑ 113 Darrick Martin	.10	.25
❑ 114 Michael Olowokandi	.10	.25
❑ 115 Rodney Rogers	.10	.25
❑ 116 Eric Piatkowski	.12	.30
❑ 117 Lorenzen Wright	.10	.25
❑ 118 Brian Skinner	.10	.25
❑ 119 Kobe Bryant CL	.75	2.00
❑ 120 Kobe Bryant	.75	2.00
❑ 121 Shaquille O'Neal	.40	1.00
❑ 122 Derek Fisher	.15	.40
❑ 123 Tyronn Lue	.10	.25
❑ 124 Travis Knight	.10	.25
❑ 125 Glen Rice	.15	.40
❑ 126 Derek Harper	.12	.30
❑ 127 Robert Horry	.15	.40
❑ 128 Rick Fox	.10	.25
❑ 129 Tim Hardaway CL	.15	.40
❑ 130 Tim Hardaway	.15	.40
❑ 131 Alonzo Mourning	.15	.40
❑ 132 Keith Askins	.10	.25
❑ 133 Jamal Mashburn	.10	.25
❑ 134 P.J. Brown	.10	.25
❑ 135 Clarence Weatherspoon	.10	.25
❑ 136 Terry Porter	.10	.25
❑ 137 Dan Majerle	.15	.40
❑ 138 Voshon Lenard	.10	.25
❑ 139 Ray Allen CL	.15	.40
❑ 140 Ray Allen	.15	.40
❑ 141 Vinny Del Negro	.10	.25
❑ 142 Glenn Robinson	.12	.30
❑ 143 Dell Curry	.10	.25
❑ 144 Sam Cassell	.12	.30
❑ 145 Haywoode Workman	.10	.25
❑ 146 Armon Gilliam	.10	.25
❑ 147 Robert Traylor	.10	.25
❑ 148 Chris Gatling	.10	.25
❑ 149 Kevin Garnett CL	.30	.75
❑ 150 Kevin Garnett	.30	.75
❑ 151 Malik Sealy	.10	.25
❑ 152 Radoslav Nesterovic	.20	.50
❑ 153 Joe Smith	.12	.30
❑ 154 Sam Mitchell	.10	.25
❑ 155 Dean Garrett	.10	.25
❑ 156 Anthony Peeler	.10	.25
❑ 157 Tom Hammonds	.10	.25
❑ 158 Bobby Jackson	.12	.30
❑ 159 Jayson Williams CL	.12	.30
❑ 160 Keith Van Horn	.12	.30
❑ 161 Stephon Marbury	.15	.40
❑ 162 Jayson Williams	.12	.30
❑ 163 Kendall Gill	.10	.25
❑ 164 Kerry Kittles	.10	.25
❑ 165 Jamie Feick RC	.15	.40
❑ 166 Scott Burrell	.10	.25
❑ 167 Lucious Harris	.10	.25
❑ 168 Marcus Camby CL	.12	.30
❑ 169 Patrick Ewing	.20	.50
❑ 170 Allan Houston	.12	.30
❑ 171 Latrell Sprewell	.12	.30
❑ 172 Kurt Thomas	.12	.30
❑ 173 Larry Johnson	.15	.40
❑ 174 Chris Childs	.10	.25
❑ 175 Marcus Camby	.12	.30
❑ 176 Charlie Ward	.10	.25
❑ 177 Chris Dudley	.10	.25
❑ 178 Bo Outlaw CL	.10	.25
❑ 179 Anfernee Hardaway	.15	.40
❑ 180 Darrell Armstrong	.10	.25
❑ 181 Nick Anderson	.10	.25
❑ 182 Horace Grant	.12	.30
❑ 183 Isaac Austin	.10	.25
❑ 184 Matt Harpring	.12	.30
❑ 185 Michael Doleac	.10	.25
❑ 186 Bo Outlaw	.10	.25
❑ 187 Allen Iverson CL	.30	.75
❑ 188 Allen Iverson	.30	.75
❑ 189 Theo Ratliff	.12	.30
❑ 190 Matt Geiger	.10	.25
❑ 191 Larry Hughes	.12	.30
❑ 192 Tyrone Hill	.10	.25
❑ 193 George Lynch	.10	.25
❑ 194 Eric Snow	.12	.30
❑ 195 Aaron McKie	.12	.30
❑ 196 Harvey Grant	.10	.25
❑ 197 Jason Kidd CL	.25	.60
❑ 198 Jason Kidd	.25	.60
❑ 199 Tom Gugliotta	.10	.25
❑ 200 Rex Chapman	.10	.25
❑ 201 Clifford Robinson	.10	.25
❑ 202 Luc Longley	.10	.25
❑ 203 Danny Manning	.10	.25
❑ 204 Pat Garrity	.10	.25
❑ 205 George McCloud	.10	.25

❑ 206 Toby Bailey	.10	.25
❑ 207 Brian Grant CL	.10	.25
❑ 208 Rasheed Wallace	.15	.40
❑ 209 Arvydas Sabonis	.12	.30
❑ 210 Damon Stoudamire	.15	.40
❑ 211 Brian Grant	.10	.25
❑ 212 Isaiah Rider	.10	.25
❑ 213 Walt Williams	.10	.25
❑ 214 Jim Jackson	.12	.30
❑ 215 Greg Anthony	.10	.25
❑ 216 Stacey Augmon	.12	.30
❑ 217 Vlade Divac CL	.15	.40
❑ 218 Jason Williams	.15	.40
❑ 219 Vlade Divac	.15	.40
❑ 220 Chris Webber	.15	.40
❑ 221 Nick Anderson	.10	.25
❑ 222 Peja Stojakovic	.12	.30
❑ 223 Tariq Abdul-Wahad	.10	.25
❑ 224 Vernon Maxwell	.12	.30
❑ 225 Lawrence Funderburke	.10	.25
❑ 226 Jon Barry	.12	.30
❑ 227 David Robinson CL	.20	.50
❑ 228 Tim Duncan	.30	.75
❑ 229 Sean Elliott	.15	.40
❑ 230 David Robinson	.20	.50
❑ 231 Mario Elie	.10	.25
❑ 232 Avery Johnson	.12	.30
❑ 233 Steve Kerr	.12	.30
❑ 234 Malik Rose	.10	.25
❑ 235 Jaren Jackson	.10	.25
❑ 236 Vin Baker CL	.15	.40
❑ 237 Gary Payton	.15	.40
❑ 238 Vin Baker	.15	.40
❑ 239 Detlef Schrempf	.12	.30
❑ 240 Hersey Hawkins	.10	.25
❑ 241 Dale Ellis	.10	.25
❑ 242 Rashard Lewis	.15	.40
❑ 243 Billy Owens	.10	.25
❑ 244 Aaron Williams	.10	.25
❑ 245 Vince Carter CL	.30	.75
❑ 246 Vince Carter	.30	.75
❑ 247 John Wallace	.10	.25
❑ 248 Doug Christie	.12	.30
❑ 249 Tracy McGrady	.30	.75
❑ 250 Kevin Willis	.10	.25
❑ 251 Michael Stewart	.10	.25
❑ 252 Dee Brown	.10	.25
❑ 253 John Thomas	.10	.25
❑ 254 Alvin Williams	.10	.25
❑ 255 Karl Malone CL	.20	.50
❑ 256 Karl Malone	.20	.50
❑ 257 John Stockton	.20	.50
❑ 258 Jacque Vaughn	.10	.25
❑ 259 Bryon Russell	.10	.25
❑ 260 Howard Eisley	.10	.25
❑ 261 Greg Ostertag	.10	.25
❑ 262 Adam Keefe	.10	.25
❑ 263 Todd Fuller	.10	.25
❑ 264 Mike Bibby CL	.15	.40
❑ 265 Shareef Abdur-Rahim	.12	.30
❑ 266 Mike Bibby	.15	.40
❑ 267 Bryant Reeves	.10	.25
❑ 268 Felipe Lopez	.10	.25
❑ 269 Cherokee Parks	.10	.25
❑ 270 Michael Smith	.10	.25
❑ 271 Tony Massenburg	.10	.25
❑ 272 Rodrick Rhodes	.10	.25
❑ 273 Juwan Howard CL	.12	.30
❑ 274 Juwan Howard	.12	.30
❑ 275 Rod Strickland	.10	.25
❑ 276 Mitch Richmond	.12	.30
❑ 277 Otis Thorpe	.10	.25
❑ 278 Calbert Cheaney	.10	.25
❑ 279 Tracy Murray	.10	.25
❑ 280 Ben Wallace	.12	.30
❑ 281 Terry Davis	.10	.25
❑ 282 Michael Jordan RF	1.00	2.50
❑ 283 Reggie Miller RF	.15	.40
❑ 284 Dikembe Mutombo RF	.12	.30
❑ 285 Patrick Ewing RF	.20	.50
❑ 286 Allan Houston RF	.12	.30
❑ 287 Danny Manning RF	.10	.25
❑ 288 Jalen Rose RF	.12	.30
❑ 289 Rasheed Wallace RF	.15	.40
❑ 290 Jerry Stackhouse RF	.15	.40
❑ 291 Damon Stoudamire RF	.15	.40
❑ 292 Kenny Anderson RF	.12	.30
❑ 293 Shawn Kemp RF	.15	.40
❑ 294 Vlade Divac RF	.15	.40
❑ 295 Larry Johnson RF	.15	.40
❑ 296 Jamal Mashburn RF	.10	.25
❑ 297 Ron Harper RF	.10	.25
❑ 298 Steve Smith RF	.10	.25
❑ 299 Kendall Gill RF	.10	.25
❑ 300 Chris Mullin RF	.15	.40
❑ 301 Robert Horry RF	.15	.40
❑ 302 Dikembe Mutombo DD	.12	.30
❑ 303 Ron Mercer DD	.10	.25
❑ 304 Eddie Jones DD	.15	.40
❑ 305 Toni Kukoc DD	.15	.40
❑ 306 Derek Anderson DD	.10	.25
❑ 307 Shawn Bradley DD	.10	.25
❑ 308 Danny Fortson DD	.10	.25
❑ 309 Bison Dele DD	.10	.25
❑ 310 Antawn Jamison DD	.15	.40
❑ 311 Scottie Pippen DD	.25	.60
❑ 312 Reggie Miller DD	.15	.40
❑ 313 Maurice Taylor DD	.12	.30
❑ 314 Glen Rice DD	.15	.40
❑ 315 Alonzo Mourning DD	.15	.40
❑ 316 Glenn Robinson DD	.12	.30
❑ 317 Anthony Peeler DD	.10	.25
❑ 318 Kerry Kittles DD	.10	.25
❑ 319 Latrell Sprewell DD	.12	.30
❑ 320 Darrell Armstrong DD	.10	.25
❑ 321 Larry Hughes DD	.12	.30
❑ 322 Tom Gugliotta DD	.10	.25
❑ 323 Brian Grant DD	.10	.25
❑ 324 Chris Webber DD	.15	.40
❑ 325 David Robinson DD	.20	.50
❑ 326 Vin Baker DD	.15	.40
❑ 327 Vince Carter DD	.30	.75
❑ 328 Bryon Russell DD	.10	.25
❑ 329 Felipe Lopez DD	.10	.25
❑ 330 Juwan Howard DD	.12	.30
❑ 331 Michael Jordan DD	1.00	2.50
❑ 332 Jason Kidd CC	.25	.60
❑ 333 Rod Strickland CC	.10	.25
❑ 334 Stephon Marbury CC	.15	.40
❑ 335 Gary Payton CC	.15	.40
❑ 336 Mark Jackson CC	.15	.40
❑ 337 John Stockton CC	.20	.50
❑ 338 Brevin Knight CC	.10	.25
❑ 339 Bobby Jackson CC	.12	.30
❑ 340 Nick Van Exel CC	.12	.30
❑ 341 Tim Hardaway CC	.15	.40
❑ 342 Darrell Armstrong CC	.10	.25
❑ 343 Avery Johnson CC	.12	.30
❑ 344 Mike Bibby CC	.15	.40
❑ 345 Damon Stoudamire CC	.15	.40
❑ 346 Jason Williams CC	.15	.40
❑ 347 Allen Iverson PC	.30	.75
❑ 348 Kobe Bryant PC	.75	2.00
❑ 349 Karl Malone PC	.20	.50
❑ 350 Keith Van Horn PC	.12	.30
❑ 351 Kevin Garnett PC	.30	.75
❑ 352 Antoine Walker PC	.15	.40
❑ 353 Tim Duncan PC	.30	.75
❑ 354 Scottie Pippen PC	.25	.60
❑ 355 Paul Pierce PC	.15	.40
❑ 356 Michael Finley PC	.15	.40
❑ 357 Shaquille O'Neal PC	.40	1.00
❑ 358 Grant Hill PC	.15	.40
❑ 359 Jason Williams PC	.15	.40
❑ 360 Antonio McDyess PC	.12	.30
❑ 361 Shareef Abdur-Rahim PC	.12	.30
❑ 362 Allen Iverson SC	.30	.75
❑ 363 Shaquille O'Neal SC	.40	1.00
❑ 364 Karl Malone SC	.20	.50
❑ 365 Shareef Abdur-Rahim SC	.12	.30
❑ 366 Keith Van Horn SC	.12	.30
❑ 367 Tim Duncan SC	.30	.75
❑ 368 Gary Payton SC	.15	.40
❑ 369 Stephon Marbury SC	.15	.40
❑ 370 Antonio McDyess SC	.12	.30
❑ 371 Grant Hill SC	.15	.40
❑ 372 Kevin Garnett SC	.30	.75
❑ 373 Shawn Kemp SC	.15	.40
❑ 374 Kobe Bryant SC	.75	2.00
❑ 375 Michael Finley SC	.15	.40
❑ 376 Vince Carter SC	.30	.75
❑ 377 Checklist	.10	.15
❑ 378 Checklist	.10	.25
❑ 379 Checklist	.10	.15
❑ 380 Checklist	.10	.15
❑ 381 Michael Jordan GH	.40	1.00
❑ 382 Michael Jordan GH	.40	1.00
❑ 383 Michael Jordan GH	.40	1.00
❑ 384 Michael Jordan GH	.40	1.00
❑ 385 Michael Jordan GH	.40	1.00
❑ 386 Michael Jordan GH	.40	1.00
❑ 387 Michael Jordan GH	.40	1.00
❑ 388 Michael Jordan GH	.40	1.00
❑ 389 Michael Jordan GH	.40	1.00
❑ 390 Michael Jordan GH	.40	1.00
❑ 391 Michael Jordan GH	.40	1.00
❑ 392 Michael Jordan GH	.40	1.00
❑ 393 Michael Jordan GH	.40	1.00
❑ 394 Michael Jordan GH	.40	1.00
❑ 395 Michael Jordan GH	.40	1.00
❑ 396 Michael Jordan GH	.40	1.00
❑ 397 Michael Jordan GH	.40	1.00
❑ 398 Michael Jordan GH	.40	1.00
❑ 399 Michael Jordan GH	.40	1.00
❑ 400 Michael Jordan GH	.40	1.00
❑ 401 Michael Jordan GH	.40	1.00
❑ 402 Michael Jordan GH	.40	1.00
❑ 403 Michael Jordan GH	.40	1.00
❑ 404 Michael Jordan GH	.40	1.00
❑ 405 Michael Jordan GH	.40	1.00
❑ 406 Michael Jordan GH	.40	1.00
❑ 407 Michael Jordan GH	.40	1.00
❑ 408 Michael Jordan GH	.40	1.00
❑ 409 Michael Jordan GH	.40	1.00
❑ 410 Michael Jordan GH	.40	1.00
❑ 411 Michael Jordan GH	.40	1.00
❑ 412 Michael Jordan GH	.40	1.00
❑ 413 Michael Jordan GH	.40	1.00
❑ 414 Michael Jordan GH	.40	1.00
❑ 415 Michael Jordan GH	.40	1.00
❑ 416 Michael Jordan GH	.40	1.00
❑ 417 Michael Jordan GH	.40	1.00
❑ 418 Michael Jordan GH	.40	1.00
❑ 419 Michael Jordan GH	.40	1.00
❑ 420 Michael Jordan GH	.40	1.00
❑ 421 Michael Jordan GH	.40	1.00
❑ 422 Michael Jordan GH	.40	1.00
❑ 423 Michael Jordan GH	.40	1.00
❑ 424 Michael Jordan GH	.40	1.00
❑ 425 Michael Jordan GH	.40	1.00
❑ 426 Michael Jordan GH	.40	1.00
❑ 427 Michael Jordan GH	.40	1.00
❑ 428 Michael Jordan GH	.40	1.00
❑ 429 Michael Jordan GH	.40	1.00
❑ 430 Michael Jordan GH	.40	1.00
❑ 431 Elton Brand RC	.60	1.50
❑ 432 Steve Francis RC	.60	1.50
❑ 433 Baron Davis RC	.75	2.00
❑ 434 Lamar Odom RC	.60	1.50
❑ 435 Wally Szczerbiak RC	.60	1.50
❑ 436 Richard Hamilton RC	.60	1.50
❑ 437 Andre Miller RC	.60	1.50
❑ 438 Shawn Marion RC	.60	1.50
❑ 439 Jason Terry RC	.50	1.25
❑ 440 Corey Maggette RC	.60	1.50

2000-01 Upper Deck Victory

❑ COMPLETE SET (330)	30.00	60.00
❑ COMMON CARD (1-260)	.10	.25
❑ COMMON KOBE (281-305)	.25	.60
❑ COMMON KG (306-330)	.20	.50
❑ COMMON ROOKIE (261-280)	.25	.60
❑ 1 Dikembe Mutombo	.12	.30
❑ 2 Jim Jackson	.10	.25
❑ 3 Jason Terry	.15	.40
❑ 4 Roshown McLeod	.10	.25
❑ 5 Alan Henderson	.10	.25
❑ 6 Bimbo Coles	.10	.25
❑ 7 Dion Glover	.10	.25
❑ 8 Lorenzen Wright	.10	.25
❑ 9 Paul Pierce	.15	.40
❑ 10 Kenny Anderson	.12	.30
❑ 11 Antoine Walker	.12	.30
❑ 12 Adrian Griffin	.10	.25
❑ 13 Vitaly Potapenko	.10	.25
❑ 14 Dana Barros	.10	.25
❑ 15 Eric Williams	.10	.25
❑ 16 Calbert Cheaney	.10	.25
❑ 17 Derrick Coleman	.12	.30
❑ 18 Eddie Jones	.12	.30
❑ 19 Anthony Mason	.10	.25
❑ 20 Elden Campbell	.10	.25
❑ 21 Eddie Robinson	.10	.25
❑ 22 David Wesley	.10	.25
❑ 23 Baron Davis	.15	.40
❑ 24 Ricky Davis	.12	.30
❑ 25 Elton Brand	.15	.40
❑ 26 Ron Artest	.15	.40
❑ 27 Chris Carr	.10	.25
❑ 28 Fred Hoiberg	.10	.25
❑ 29 Hersey Hawkins	.10	.25
❑ 30 Dickey Simpkins	.10	.25
❑ 31 Corey Benjamin	.10	.25
❑ 32 Matt Maloney	.10	.25
❑ 33 Shawn Kemp	.15	.40
❑ 34 Lamond Murray	.10	.25
❑ 35 Wesley Person	.10	.25
❑ 36 Andre Miller	.12	.30
❑ 37 Bob Sura	.10	.25
❑ 38 Andrew DeClercq	.10	.25
❑ 39 Brevin Knight	.10	.25
❑ 40 Earl Boykins RC	.75	2.00
❑ 41 Michael Finley	.15	.40
❑ 42 Dirk Nowitzki	.25	.60
❑ 43 Cedric Ceballos	.10	.25
❑ 44 Robert Pack	.10	.25
❑ 45 Erick Strickland	.10	.25
❑ 46 Sean Rooks	.10	.25
❑ 47 Shawn Bradley	.10	.25
❑ 48 Steve Nash	.25	.60
❑ 49 Antonio McDyess	.12	.30
❑ 50 Nick Van Exel	.12	.30
❑ 51 Keon Clark	.10	.25
❑ 52 Raef LaFrentz	.10	.25
❑ 53 James Posey	.10	.25
❑ 54 Chris Gatling	.10	.25
❑ 55 George McCloud	.10	.25
❑ 56 Bryant Stith	.10	.25
❑ 57 Jerry Stackhouse	.12	.30
❑ 58 Lindsey Hunter	.10	.25
❑ 59 Christian Laettner	.10	.25
❑ 60 Jerome Williams	.10	.25
❑ 61 Michael Curry	.10	.25
❑ 62 Loy Vaught	.10	.25
❑ 63 Eric Montross	.10	.25
❑ 64 Grant Hill	.15	.40
❑ 65 Antawn Jamison	.15	.40
❑ 66 Chris Mills	.10	.25
❑ 67 Vonteego Cummings	.10	.25
❑ 68 Larry Hughes	.12	.30
❑ 69 Donyell Marshall	.10	.25
❑ 70 Mookie Blaylock	.12	.30
❑ 71 Erick Dampier	.10	.25
❑ 72 Jason Caffey	.10	.25
❑ 73 Steve Francis	.15	.40
❑ 74 Shandon Anderson	.10	.25
❑ 75 Hakeem Olajuwon	.20	.50
❑ 76 Walt Williams	.10	.25
❑ 77 Kenny Thomas	.10	.25
❑ 78 Carlos Rogers	.10	.25
❑ 79 Bryce Drew	.10	.25
❑ 80 Kelvin Cato	.10	.25
❑ 81 Reggie Miller	.15	.40
❑ 82 Austin Croshere	.10	.25
❑ 83 Rik Smits	.10	.25
❑ 84 Jalen Rose	.12	.30
❑ 85 Dale Davis	.10	.25
❑ 86 Jonathan Bender	.10	.25
❑ 87 Travis Best	.10	.25
❑ 88 Chris Mullin	.15	.40
❑ 89 Lamar Odom	.15	.40
❑ 90 Tyrone Nesby	.10	.25
❑ 91 Michael Olowokandi	.10	.25
❑ 92 Eric Piatkowski	.10	.25
❑ 93 Jeff McInnis	.10	.25
❑ 94 Brian Skinner	.10	.25
❑ 95 Pete Chilcutt	.10	.25
❑ 96 Eric Murdock	.10	.25
❑ 97 Shaquille O'Neal	.40	1.00
❑ 98 Kobe Bryant	.75	2.00
❑ 99 Ron Harper	.12	.30
❑ 100 Robert Horry	.12	.30
❑ 101 Rick Fox	.12	.30
❑ 102 Derek Fisher	.15	.40
❑ 103 Tyronn Lue	.10	.25
❑ 104 Devean George	.10	.25
❑ 105 Alonzo Mourning	.15	.40
❑ 106 Jamal Mashburn	.12	.30
❑ 107 Anthony Carter	.10	.25
❑ 108 P.J. Brown	.10	.25
❑ 109 Clarence Weatherspoon	.10	.25
❑ 110 Otis Thorpe	.12	.30
❑ 111 Voshon Lenard	.10	.25
❑ 112 Tim Hardaway	.12	.30
❑ 113 Ray Allen	.15	.40
❑ 114 Glenn Robinson	.12	.30
❑ 115 Sam Cassell	.12	.30
❑ 116 Robert Traylor	.10	.25
❑ 117 Ervin Johnson	.10	.25
❑ 118 Scott Williams	.10	.25
❑ 119 Tim Thomas	.10	.25
❑ 120 Vinny Del Negro	.10	.25
❑ 121 Kevin Garnett	.30	.75
❑ 122 Wally Szczerbiak	.12	.30
❑ 123 Terrell Brandon	.10	.25
❑ 124 Dean Garrett	.10	.25
❑ 125 William Avery	.10	.25
❑ 126 Sam Mitchell	.10	.25
❑ 127 Radoslav Nesterovic	.10	.25
❑ 128 Anthony Peeler	.10	.25
❑ 129 Stephon Marbury	.15	.40
❑ 130 Keith Van Horn	.12	.30
❑ 131 Kerry Kittles	.12	.30
❑ 132 Lucious Harris	.10	.25
❑ 133 Evan Eschmeyer	.10	.25
❑ 134 Jamie Feick	.10	.25
❑ 135 Jim McIlvaine	.10	.25
❑ 136 Kendall Gill	.10	.25
❑ 137 Allan Houston	.12	.30
❑ 138 Marcus Camby	.12	.30
❑ 139 Latrell Sprewell	.12	.30
❑ 140 Patrick Ewing	.20	.50
❑ 141 Larry Johnson	.12	.30
❑ 142 Charlie Ward	.10	.25
❑ 143 Chris Childs	.10	.25
❑ 144 John Wallace	.10	.25
❑ 145 Darrell Armstrong	.10	.25
❑ 146 Corey Maggette	.12	.30
❑ 147 Pat Garrity	.10	.25
❑ 148 John Amaechi	.10	.25
❑ 149 Matt Harpring	.12	.30
❑ 150 Michael Doleac	.10	.25
❑ 151 Ron Mercer	.10	.25
❑ 152 Chucky Atkins	.10	.25
❑ 153 Allen Iverson	.30	.75
❑ 154 Matt Geiger	.10	.25
❑ 155 Eric Snow	.10	.25
❑ 156 Tyrone Hill	.10	.25
❑ 157 Theo Ratliff	.10	.25
❑ 158 George Lynch	.10	.25
❑ 159 Kevin Ollie	.10	.25
❑ 160 Toni Kukoc	.12	.30
❑ 161 Jason Kidd	.25	.60
❑ 162 Anfernee Hardaway	.15	.40
❑ 163 Rodney Rogers	.10	.25
❑ 164 Shawn Marion	.15	.40
❑ 165 Clifford Robinson	.10	.25
❑ 166 Tom Gugliotta	.10	.25
❑ 167 Luc Longley	.10	.25
❑ 168 Randy Livingston	.10	.25
❑ 169 Scottie Pippen	.25	.60
❑ 170 Steve Smith	.12	.30
❑ 171 Damon Stoudamire	.12	.30
❑ 172 Bonzi Wells	.10	.25
❑ 173 Jermaine O'Neal	.15	.40
❑ 174 Arvydas Sabonis	.12	.30
❑ 175 Rasheed Wallace	.15	.40
❑ 176 Detlef Schrempf	.12	.30
❑ 177 Jason Williams	.12	.30
❑ 178 Chris Webber	.15	.40
❑ 179 Peja Stojakovic	.12	.30
❑ 180 Vlade Divac	.12	.30
❑ 181 Lawrence Funderburke	.10	.25
❑ 182 Tony Delk	.10	.25
❑ 183 Jon Barry	.10	.25
❑ 184 Tim Duncan	.30	.75
❑ 185 Sean Elliott	.12	.30
❑ 186 Terry Porter	.12	.30
❑ 187 David Robinson	.20	.50
❑ 188 Samaki Walker	.10	.25
❑ 189 Malik Rose	.10	.25
❑ 190 Jaren Jackson	.10	.25
❑ 191 Steve Kerr	.10	.25
❑ 192 Gary Payton	.15	.40
❑ 193 Brent Barry	.10	.25
❑ 194 Vin Baker	.12	.30
❑ 195 Horace Grant	.12	.30
❑ 196 Ruben Patterson	.10	.25
❑ 197 Vernon Maxwell	.10	.25
❑ 198 Shammond Williams	.10	.25
❑ 199 Rashard Lewis	.15	.40
❑ 200 Tracy McGrady	.30	.75
❑ 201 Charles Oakley	.12	.30
❑ 202 Doug Christie	.10	.25
❑ 203 Antonio Davis	.10	.25
❑ 204 Vince Carter	.30	.75
❑ 205 Kevin Willis	.10	.25
❑ 206 Dell Curry	.10	.25
❑ 207 Dee Brown	.10	.25
❑ 208 Karl Malone	.20	.50
❑ 209 John Stockton	.20	.50
❑ 210 Bryon Russell	.10	.25
❑ 211 Olden Polynice	.10	.25
❑ 212 Jacque Vaughn	.10	.25
❑ 213 Greg Ostertag	.10	.25
❑ 214 Quincy Lewis	.10	.25
❑ 215 Armon Gilliam	.10	.25
❑ 216 Shareef Abdur-Rahim	.12	.30
❑ 217 Michael Dickerson	.10	.25
❑ 218 Mike Bibby	.12	.30
❑ 219 Bryant Reeves	.10	.25
❑ 220 Othella Harrington	.10	.25
❑ 221 Grant Long	.10	.25
❑ 222 Felipe Lopez	.10	.25
❑ 223 Obinna Ekezie	.10	.25
❑ 224 Mitch Richmond	.12	.30
❑ 225 Richard Hamilton	.12	.30
❑ 226 Tracy Murray	.10	.25
❑ 227 Jahidi White	.10	.25
❑ 228 Aaron Williams	.10	.25

❑ 229 Juwan Howard	.12	.30
❑ 230 Rod Strickland	.12	.30
❑ 231 Isaac Austin	.10	.25
❑ 232 Dikembe Mutombo VL	.05	.15
❑ 233 Antoine Walker VL	.05	.15
❑ 234 Derrick Coleman VL	.05	.15
❑ 235 Elton Brand VL	.07	.20
❑ 236 Shawn Kemp VL	.07	.20
❑ 237 Michael Finley VL	.07	.20
❑ 238 Antonio McDyess VL	.05	.15
❑ 239 Grant Hill VL	.07	.20
❑ 240 Antawn Jamison VL	.07	.20
❑ 241 Steve Francis VL	.07	.20
❑ 242 Jalen Rose VL	.05	.15
❑ 243 Lamar Odom VL	.07	.20
❑ 244 Shaquille O'Neal VL	.20	.50
❑ 245 Alonzo Mourning VL	.07	.20
❑ 246 Ray Allen VL	.07	.20
❑ 247 Kevin Garnett VL	.15	.40
❑ 248 Stephon Marbury VL	.07	.20
❑ 249 Allan Houston VL	.05	.15
❑ 250 Darrell Armstrong VL	.05	.15
❑ 251 Allen Iverson VL	.15	.40
❑ 252 Jason Kidd VL	.12	.30
❑ 253 Rasheed Wallace VL	.07	.20
❑ 254 Chris Webber VL	.07	.20
❑ 255 Tim Duncan VL	.15	.40
❑ 256 Gary Payton VL	.07	.20
❑ 257 Vince Carter VL	.15	.40
❑ 258 Karl Malone VL	.10	.25
❑ 259 Shareef Abdur-Rahim VL	.05	.15
❑ 260 Mitch Richmond VL	.05	.15
❑ 261 Kenyon Martin RC	.60	1.50
❑ 262 Marcus Fizer RC	.25	.60
❑ 263 Chris Mihm RC	.25	.60
❑ 264 Stromile Swift RC	.30	.75
❑ 265 Keyon Dooling RC	.25	.60
❑ 266 Morris Peterson RC	.40	1.00
❑ 267 Quentin Richardson RC	.30	.75
❑ 268 Courtney Alexander RC	.25	.60
❑ 269 Desmond Mason RC	.30	.75
❑ 270 Mateen Cleaves RC	.25	.60
❑ 271 Erick Barkley RC	.25	.60
❑ 272 A.J. Guyton RC	.25	.60
❑ 273 Darius Miles RC	.30	.75
❑ 274 DerMarr Johnson RC	.25	.60
❑ 275 Joel Przybilla RC	.25	.60
❑ 276 Hanno Mottola RC	.25	.60
❑ 277 Mike Miller RC	.40	1.00
❑ 278 Donnell Harvey RC	.25	.60
❑ 279 Speedy Claxton RC	.25	.60
❑ 280 Khalid El-Amin RC	.25	.60

2003-04 Upper Deck Victory

❑ COMP.SET w/o SP's (100)	6.00	15.00
❑ COMMON ROOKIE (101-130)	.60	1.50
❑ COMMON POD (182-201)	.40	1.00
❑ 1 Shareef Abdur-Rahim	.10	.25
❑ 2 Jason Terry	.10	.25
❑ 3 Glenn Robinson	.10	.25
❑ 4 Paul Pierce	.10	.25
❑ 5 Antoine Walker	.10	.25
❑ 6 J.R.Bremer	.02	.10
❑ 7 Vin Baker	.08	.20
❑ 8 Jalen Rose	.10	.25
❑ 9 Tyson Chandler	.10	.25
❑ 10 Eddy Curry	.10	.25
❑ 11 Jay Williams	.08	.20
❑ 12 DaJuan Wagner	.08	.20
❑ 13 Ricky Davis	.10	.25
❑ 14 Zydrunas Ilgauskas	.08	.20
❑ 15 Darius Miles	.10	.25
❑ 16 Dirk Nowitzki	.20	.50
❑ 17A Michael Finley	.10	.25
❑ 17B Jermaine O'Neal	.10	.25
❑ 18 Steve Nash	.10	.25
❑ 19 Nick Van Exel	.10	.25
❑ 20 Rodney White	.02	.10
❑ 21 Juwan Howard	.08	.20
❑ 22 Marcus Camby	.08	.20
❑ 23 Nene Hilario	.08	.20
❑ 24 Richard Hamilton	.08	.20
❑ 25 Ben Wallace	.10	.25
❑ 26 Cliff Robinson	.02	.10
❑ 27 Antawn Jamison	.10	.25
❑ 28 Jason Richardson	.10	.25
❑ 29 Gilbert Arenas	.10	.25
❑ 30 Mike Dunleavy	.08	.20
❑ 31 Steve Francis	.10	.25
❑ 32 Eddie Griffin	.08	.20
❑ 33 Cuttino Mobley	.08	.20
❑ 34 Yao Ming	.60	1.50
❑ 35 Reggie Miller	.10	.25
❑ 36 Jamaal Tinsley	.10	.25
❑ 37 Does Not Exist		
❑ 38 Elton Brand	.10	.25
❑ 39 Andre Miller	.08	.20
❑ 40 Lamar Odom	.10	.25
❑ 41 Kobe Bryant	.50	1.25
❑ 42 Shaquille O'Neal	.30	.75
❑ 43 Derek Fisher	.10	.25
❑ 44 Pau Gasol	.10	.25
❑ 45 Shane Battier	.10	.25
❑ 46 Mike Miller	.10	.25
❑ 47 Eddie Jones	.10	.25
❑ 48 Alonzo Mourning	.08	.20
❑ 49 Caron Butler	.10	.25
❑ 50 Gary Payton	.10	.25
❑ 51 Desmond Mason	.08	.20
❑ 52 Sam Cassell	.10	.25
❑ 53 Toni Kukoc	.08	.20
❑ 54 Kevin Garnett	.25	.60
❑ 55 Wally Szczerbiak	.08	.20
❑ 56 Joe Smith	.08	.20
❑ 57 Jason Kidd	.20	.50
❑ 58 Richard Jefferson	.08	.20
❑ 59 Kenyon Martin	.10	.25
❑ 60 Baron Davis	.10	.25
❑ 61 Jamal Mashburn	.08	.20
❑ 62 Jamaal Magloire	.02	.10
❑ 63 Allan Houston	.08	.20
❑ 64 Antonio McDyess	.08	.20
❑ 65 Latrell Sprewell	.10	.25
❑ 66 Tracy McGrady	.40	1.00
❑ 67 Grant Hill	.10	.25
❑ 68 Drew Gooden	.08	.20
❑ 69 Gordan Giricek	.08	.20
❑ 70 Allen Iverson	.25	.60
❑ 71 Keth Van Horn	.10	.25
❑ 72 Aaron McKie	.08	.20
❑ 73 Stephon Marbury	.10	.25
❑ 74 Shawn Marion	.10	.25
❑ 75 Anfernee Hardaway	.10	.25
❑ 76 Amare Stoudemire	.25	.60
❑ 77 Rasheed Wallace	.10	.25
❑ 78 Derek Anderson	.08	.20
❑ 79 Scottie Pippen	.20	.50
❑ 80 Chris Webber	.10	.25
❑ 81 Mike Bibby	.10	.25
❑ 82 Peja Stojakovic	.10	.25
❑ 83 Hedo Turkoglu	.10	.25
❑ 84 Tim Duncan	.25	.60
❑ 85 David Robinson	.10	.25
❑ 86 Tony Parker	.10	.25
❑ 87 Manu Ginobili	.10	.25
❑ 88 Ray Allen	.10	.25
❑ 89 Rashard Lewis	.10	.25
❑ 90 Reggie Evans	.02	.10
❑ 91 Alvin Williams	.02	.10
❑ 92 Vince Carter	.30	.75
❑ 93 Morris Peterson	.08	.20
❑ 94 Antonio Davis	.02	.10
❑ 95 Karl Malone	.10	.25
❑ 96 John Stockton	.10	.25
❑ 97 Andrei Kirilenko	.10	.25
❑ 98 Jerry Stackhouse	.10	.25
❑ 99 Kwame Brown	.08	.20
❑ 100 Michael Jordan	1.25	3.00
❑ 101 Lebron James SP RC	8.00	20.00
❑ 102 Darko Milicic RC	.60	1.50
❑ 103 Carmelo Anthony RC	2.00	5.00
❑ 104 Chris Bosh RC	1.50	4.00
❑ 105 Dwyane Wade RC	1.50	4.00
❑ 106 Chris Kaman RC	.75	2.00
❑ 107 Kirk Hinrich RC	.75	2.00
❑ 108 T.J. Ford RC	.60	1.50
❑ 109 Mike Sweetney RC	.60	1.50
❑ 110 Jarvis Hayes RC	.60	1.50
❑ 111 Mickael Pietrus RC	.60	1.50
❑ 112 Nick Collison RC	.60	1.50
❑ 113 Marcus Banks RC	.60	1.50
❑ 114 Luke Ridnour RC	.75	2.00
❑ 115 Reece Gaines RC	.60	1.50
❑ 116 Troy Bell RC	.60	1.50
❑ 117 Zarko Cabarkapa RC	.60	1.50
❑ 118 David West RC	1.25	3.00
❑ 119 Aleksandar Pavlovic RC	.75	2.00
❑ 120 Dahntay Jones RC	.60	1.50
❑ 121 Boris Diaw RC	.60	1.50
❑ 122 Zoran Planinic RC	.60	1.50
❑ 123 Travis Outlaw RC	.75	2.00
❑ 124 Brian Cook RC	.60	1.50
❑ 125 Carlos Delfino RC	.60	1.50
❑ 126 Ndudi Ebi RC	.60	1.50
❑ 127 Kendrick Perkins RC	1.00	2.50
❑ 128 Leandro Barbosa RC	1.00	2.50
❑ 129 Josh Howard RC	.75	2.00
❑ 130 Maciej Lampe RC	.75	2.00
❑ 134 Michael Jordan AS	4.00	10.00
❑ 135 Kobe Bryant AS	2.00	5.00
❑ 136 Kevin Garnett AS	1.00	2.50
❑ 137 Yao Ming AS	1.25	3.00
❑ 138 Vince Carter AS	1.25	3.00
❑ 139 Dirk Nowitzki AS	.75	2.00
❑ 140 Antoine Walker AS	.40	1.00
❑ 141 Chris Webber AS	.40	
❑ 142 Ben Wallace AS	.40	1.00
❑ 143 Tracy McGrady AS	1.25	3.00
❑ 144 Jason Kidd AS	.75	2.00
❑ 145 Steve Francis AS	.30	
❑ 146 Gary Payton AS	.40	1.00
❑ 147 Peja Stojakovic AS	.40	1.00
❑ 148 Brad Miller AS	.50	1.25
❑ 149 Shawn Marion AS	.40	1.00
❑ 150 Zydrunas Ilgauskas AS	.30	.75
❑ 151 Stephon Marbury AS	.40	1.00
❑ 152 Jermaine O'Neal AS	.40	1.00
❑ 153 Desmond Mason AS	.30	.75
❑ 154 Jeson Richardson AS	.30	
❑ 155 Tony Parker AS	.40	1.00
❑ 156 Tim Duncan AS	1.00	2.50
❑ 157 Jamal Mashburn AS	.40	1.00
❑ 158 Allen Iverson AS	1.00	2.50
❑ 159 Shaquille O'Neal AS	1.25	3.00
❑ 160 Paul Pierce AS	.40	1.00
❑ 161 Steve Nash AS	.40	1.00
❑ 162 Michael Jordan CS	4.00	10.00
❑ 163 Mike Bibby CS	.40	1.00
❑ 164 Jay Williams CS	.30	.75
❑ 165 Richard Hamilton CS	.30	.75
❑ 166 Jerry Stackhouse CS	.40	1.00
❑ 167 Peja Stojakovic CS	.40	1.00
❑ 168 Reggie Miller CS	.40	1.00
❑ 169 Robert Horry CS	.40	1.00
❑ 170 Tim Duncan CS	1.00	2.50
❑ 171 Jalen Rose CS	.40	1.00
❑ 172 Jason Richardson CS	.75	2.00
❑ 173 Allen Iverson CS	1.00	2.50
❑ 174 Tracy McGrady CS	1.25	3.00
❑ 175 Paul Pierce CS	.40	1.00
❑ 176 Dirk Nowitzki CS	.75	2.00
❑ 177 Baron Davis CS	.40	1.00
❑ 178 Latrell Sprewell CS	.40	1.00
❑ 179 John Stockton CS	.40	1.00

❑ 180 Ray Allen CS	.40	1.00
❑ 181 Kobe Bryant CS	2.00	5.00
❑ 182 Mike Bibby POD	.40	1.00
❑ 183 Earl Boykins POD	.40	1.00
❑ 184 John Stockton POD	.40	1.00
❑ 185 Alvin Williams POD	.40	1.00
❑ 186 Darrell Armstrong POD	.40	1.00
❑ 187 Tony Parker POD	.40	1.00
❑ 188 Gary Payton POD	.40	1.00
❑ 189 Jalen Rose POD	.40	1.00
❑ 190 Jason Williams POD	.40	1.00
❑ 191 Derek Fisher POD	.40	1.00
❑ 192 Steve Nash POD	.40	1.00
❑ 193 Jamaal Tinsley POD	.40	1.00
❑ 194 Andre Miller POD	.40	1.00
❑ 195 Baron Davis POD	.40	1.00
❑ 196 Steve Francis POD	.40	1.00
❑ 197 DaJuan Wagner POD	.40	1.00
❑ 198 Stephon Marbury POD	.40	1.00
❑ 199 Jason Kidd POD	.75	2.00
❑ 200 Chauncey Billups POD	.40	1.00
❑ 201 Jay Williams POD	.40	1.00
❑ 202 Allen Iverson AKA	1.50	4.00
❑ 203 Steve Francis AKA	1.25	3.00
❑ 204 Kenyon Martin AKA	.60	1.50
❑ 205 Vince Carter AKA	1.25	3.00
❑ 206 Lebron James AKA	5.00	12.00
❑ 207 Julius Erving AKA	1.50	4.00
❑ 208 Tracy McGrady AKA	2.00	5.00
❑ 209 Jason Richardson AKA	1.25	3.00
❑ 210 Earvin Johnson AKA	1.50	4.00
❑ 211 Michael Jordan AKA	6.00	15.00
❑ 212 Michael Jordan MJ	6.00	15.00
❑ 213 Kobe Bryant MJ	3.00	8.00
❑ 214 Richard Jefferson MJ	.50	1.25
❑ 215 Desmond Mason MJ	.50	1.25
❑ 216 Vince Carter MJ	2.00	5.00
❑ 217 Amare Stoudemire MJ	1.50	4.00
❑ 218 Yao Ming MJ	2.00	5.00
❑ 219 Elton Brand MJ	.60	1.50
❑ 220 Kevin Garnett MJ	1.50	4.00
❑ 221 Shaquille O'Neal MJ	2.00	5.00
❑ 222 Lebron James HR	8.00	20.00
❑ 223 Kobe Bryant HR	4.00	10.00
❑ 224 Richard Jefferson HR	.60	1.50
❑ 225 Yao Ming HR	2.50	6.00
❑ 226 Amare Stoudemire HR	2.00	5.00
❑ 227 Michael Jordan HR	5.00	12.00
❑ 228 Michael Jordan FL	5.00	12.00
❑ 229 Michael Jordan FL	5.00	12.00
❑ 230 Michael Jordan FL	5.00	12.00
❑ 231 Michael Jordan FL	5.00	12.00
❑ 232 Michael Jordan FL	5.00	12.00
❑ 233 Michael Jordan FL	5.00	12.00

1996-97 Z-Force

❑ COMPLETE SET (200)	20.00	40.00
❑ COMPLETE SERIES 1 (100)	10.00	20.00
❑ COMPLETE SERIES 2 (100)	10.00	20.00
❑ 1 Mookie Blaylock	.07	.20
❑ 2 Alan Henderson	.07	.20
❑ 3 Christian Laettner	.15	.40
❑ 4 Steve Smith	.15	.40
❑ 5 Rick Fox	.07	.20
❑ 6 Dino Radja	.07	.20
❑ 7 Eric Williams	.07	.20
❑ 8 Muggsy Bogues	.07	.20
❑ 9 Larry Johnson	.15	.40
❑ 10 Glen Rice	.15	.40
❑ 11 Michael Jordan	1.50	4.00
❑ 12 Toni Kukoc	.15	.40
❑ 13 Scottie Pippen	.40	1.00
❑ 14 Dennis Rodman	.15	.40
❑ 15 Terrell Brandon	.15	.40
❑ 16 Bobby Phills	.07	.20
❑ 17 Bob Sura	.07	.20
❑ 18 Jim Jackson	.07	.20
❑ 19 Jason Kidd	.40	1.00
❑ 20 Jamal Mashburn	.15	.40
❑ 21 George McCloud	.07	.20
❑ 22 Mahmoud Abdul-Rauf	.07	.20
❑ 23 Antonio McDyess	.15	.40
❑ 24 Dikembe Mutombo	.15	.40
❑ 25 Joe Dumars	.25	.60
❑ 26 Grant Hill	.25	.60
❑ 27 Allan Houston	.15	.40
❑ 28 Otis Thorpe	.07	.20
❑ 29 Chris Mullin	.25	.60
❑ 30 Joe Smith	.15	.40
❑ 31 Latrell Sprewell	.25	.60
❑ 32 Sam Cassell	.25	.60
❑ 33 Clyde Drexler	.25	.60
❑ 34 Robert Horry	.15	.40
❑ 35 Hakeem Olajuwon	.25	.60
❑ 36 Travis Best	.07	.20
❑ 37 Dale Davis	.07	.20
❑ 38 Reggie Miller	.25	.60
❑ 39 Rik Smits	.15	.40
❑ 40 Brent Barry	.07	.20
❑ 41 Loy Vaught	.07	.20
❑ 42 Brian Williams	.07	.20
❑ 43 Cedric Ceballos	.07	.20
❑ 44 Eddie Jones	.25	.60
❑ 45 Nick Van Exel	.25	.60
❑ 46 Tim Hardaway	.15	.40
❑ 47 Alonzo Mourning	.15	.40
❑ 48 Kurt Thomas	.15	.40
❑ 49 Walt Williams	.07	.20
❑ 50 Vin Baker	.15	.40
❑ 51 Glenn Robinson	.25	.60
❑ 52 Kevin Garnett	.50	1.25
❑ 53 Tom Gugliotta	.07	.20
❑ 54 Isaiah Rider	.15	.40
❑ 55 Shawn Bradley	.07	.20
❑ 56 Chris Childs	.07	.20
❑ 57 Jayson Williams	.15	.40
❑ 58 Patrick Ewing	.25	.60
❑ 59 Anthony Mason	.15	.40
❑ 60 Charles Oakley	.07	.20
❑ 61 Nick Anderson	.07	.20
❑ 62 Horace Grant	.15	.40
❑ 63 Anfernee Hardaway	.25	.60
❑ 64 Shaquille O'Neal	.60	1.50
❑ 65 Dennis Scott	.07	.20
❑ 66 Jerry Stackhouse	.30	.75
❑ 67 Clarence Weatherspoon	.07	.20
❑ 68 Charles Barkley	.30	.75
❑ 69 Michael Finley	.30	.75
❑ 70 Kevin Johnson	.15	.40
❑ 71 Clifford Robinson	.07	.20
❑ 72 Arvydas Sabonis	.15	.40
❑ 73 Rod Strickland	.07	.20
❑ 74 Tyus Edney	.07	.20
❑ 75 Brian Grant	.25	.60
❑ 76 Billy Owens	.07	.20
❑ 77 Mitch Richmond	.15	.40
❑ 78 Vinny Del Negro	.07	.20
❑ 79 Sean Elliott	.15	.40
❑ 80 Avery Johnson	.07	.20
❑ 81 David Robinson	.25	.60
❑ 82 Hersey Hawkins	.15	.40
❑ 83 Shawn Kemp	.15	.40
❑ 84 Gary Payton	.25	.60
❑ 85 Detlef Schrempf	.15	.40
❑ 86 Doug Christie	.15	.40
❑ 87 Damon Stoudamire	.25	.60
❑ 88 Sharone Wright	.07	.20
❑ 89 Jeff Hornacek	.15	.40
❑ 90 Karl Malone	.25	.60
❑ 91 John Stockton	.25	.60
❑ 92 Greg Anthony	.07	.20
❑ 93 Bryant Reeves	.07	.20
❑ 94 Byron Scott	.07	.20
❑ 95 Juwan Howard	.15	.40
❑ 96 Gheorghe Muresan	.07	.20
❑ 97 Rasheed Wallace	.30	.75
❑ 98 Chris Webber	.25	.60
❑ 99 Checklist	.07	.20
❑ 100 Checklist	.07	.20
❑ 101 Dikembe Mutombo	.15	.40
❑ 102 Dee Brown	.07	.20
❑ 103 Dell Curry	.07	.20
❑ 104 Vlade Divac	.07	.20
❑ 105 Anthony Mason	.15	.40
❑ 106 Robert Parish	.15	.40
❑ 107 Oliver Miller	.07	.20
❑ 108 Eric Montross	.07	.20
❑ 109 Ervin Johnson	.07	.20
❑ 110 Stacey Augmon	.07	.20
❑ 111 Charles Barkley	.30	.75
❑ 112 Jalen Rose	.25	.60
❑ 113 Rodney Rogers	.07	.20
❑ 114 Shaquille O'Neal	.60	1.50
❑ 115 Dan Majerle	.15	.40
❑ 116 Kendall Gill	.07	.20
❑ 117 Khalid Reeves	.07	.20
❑ 118 Allan Houston	.15	.40
❑ 119 Larry Johnson	.15	.40
❑ 120 John Starks	.15	.40
❑ 121 Rony Seikaly	.07	.20
❑ 122 Gerald Wilkins	.07	.20
❑ 123 Michael Cage	.07	.20
❑ 124 Derrick Coleman	.15	.40
❑ 125 Sam Cassell	.25	.60
❑ 126 Danny Manning	.15	.40
❑ 127 Robert Horry	.15	.40
❑ 128 Kenny Anderson	.07	.20
❑ 129 Isaiah Rider	.15	.40
❑ 130 Rasheed Wallace	.30	.75
❑ 131 Mahmoud Abdul-Rauf	.07	.20
❑ 132 Vernon Maxwell	.07	.20
❑ 133 Dominique Wilkins	.25	.60
❑ 134 Hubert Davis	.07	.20
❑ 135 Popeye Jones	.07	.20
❑ 136 Anthony Peeler	.07	.20
❑ 137 Tracy Murray	.07	.20
❑ 138 Rod Strickland	.07	.20
❑ 139 Shareef Abdur-Rahim RC	.75	2.00
❑ 140 Ray Allen RC	.75	2.00
❑ 141 Shandon Anderson RC	.15	.40
❑ 142 Kobe Bryant RC	4.00	10.00
❑ 143 Marcus Camby RC	.30	.75
❑ 144 Erick Dampier RC	.25	.60
❑ 145 Emanual Davis RC	.07	.20
❑ 146 Tony Delk RC	.25	.60
❑ 147 Todd Fuller RC	.07	.20
❑ 148 Darvin Ham RC	.07	.20
❑ 149 Othella Harrington RC	.25	.60
❑ 150 Shane Heal RC	.07	.20
❑ 151 Allen Iverson RC	.75	2.00
❑ 152 Dontae' Jones RC	.07	.20
❑ 153 Kerry Kittles RC	.25	.60
❑ 154 Priest Lauderdale RC	.07	.20
❑ 155 Matt Maloney RC	.15	.40
❑ 156 Stephon Marbury RC	.60	1.50
❑ 157 Walter McCarty RC	.07	.20
❑ 158 Steve Nash RC	2.00	5.00
❑ 159 Jermaine O'Neal RC	.60	1.50
❑ 160 Ray Owes RC	.07	.20
❑ 161 Vitaly Potapenko RC	.07	.20
❑ 162 Roy Rogers RC	.07	.20
❑ 163 Antoine Walker RC	.60	1.50
❑ 164 Samaki Walker RC	.07	.20
❑ 165 Ben Wallace RC	1.50	4.00
❑ 166 John Wallace RC	.25	.60
❑ 167 Jerome Williams RC	.25	.60
❑ 168 Lorenzen Wright RC	.15	.40
❑ 169 Vin Baker ZUP	.07	.20
❑ 170 Charles Barkley ZUP	.25	.60
❑ 171 Patrick Ewing ZUP	.15	.40
❑ 172 Michael Finley ZUP	.25	.60
❑ 173 Kevin Garnett ZUP	.25	.60
❑ 174 Anfernee Hardaway ZUP	.15	.40
❑ 175 Grant Hill ZUP	.25	.60
❑ 176 Juwan Howard ZUP	.07	.20
❑ 177 Jim Jackson ZUP	.07	.20

❑ 178 Eddie Jones ZUP	.15	.40
❑ 179 Michael Jordan ZUP	.75	2.00
❑ 180 Shawn Kemp ZUP	.07	.20
❑ 181 Jason Kidd ZUP	.25	.60
❑ 182 Karl Malone ZUP	.25	.60
❑ 183 Antonio McDyess ZUP	.25	.60
❑ 184 Reggie Miller ZUP	.15	.40
❑ 185 Alonzo Mourning ZUP	.07	.20
❑ 186 Hakeem Olajuwon ZUP	.15	.40
❑ 187 Shaquille O'Neal ZUP	.25	.60
❑ 188 Gary Payton ZUP	.15	.40
❑ 189 Mitch Richmond ZUP	.07	.20
❑ 190 Clifford Robinson ZUP	.07	.20
❑ 191 David Robinson ZUP	.15	.40
❑ 192 Glenn Robinson ZUP	.15	.40
❑ 193 Dennis Rodman ZUP	.07	.20
❑ 194 Joe Smith ZUP	.07	.20
❑ 195 Jerry Stackhouse ZUP	.25	.60
❑ 196 John Stockton ZUP	.15	.40
❑ 197 Damon Stoudamire ZUP	.15	.40
❑ 198 Chris Webber ZUP	.25	.60
❑ 199 Checklist	.07	.20
❑ 200 Checklist	.07	.20
❑ NNO Grant Hill Promo	.75	2.00
❑ NNO Grant Hill Total Z	5.00	12.00
❑ NNO G.Hill/J.Stackhouse Promo	.75	2.00

1997-98 Z-Force

❑ COMPLETE SET (210)	12.50	25.00
❑ COMPLETE SERIES 1 (110)	5.00	10.00
❑ COMPLETE SERIES 2 (100)	7.50	15.00
❑ 1 Anfernee Hardaway	.20	.50
❑ 2 Mitch Richmond	.10	.30
❑ 3 Stephon Marbury	.25	.60
❑ 4 Charles Barkley	.25	.60
❑ 5 Juwan Howard	.10	.30
❑ 6 Avery Johnson	.05	.15
❑ 7 Rex Chapman	.05	.15
❑ 8 Antoine Walker	.25	.60
❑ 9 Nick Van Exel	.20	.50
❑ 10 Tim Hardaway	.10	.30
❑ 11 Clarence Weatherspoon	.05	.15
❑ 12 John Stockton	.20	.50
❑ 13 Glenn Robinson	.20	.50
❑ 14 Anthony Mason	.10	.30
❑ 15 Latrell Sprewell	.20	.50
❑ 16 Kendall Gill	.05	.15
❑ 17 Terry Mills	.05	.15
❑ 18 Mookie Blaylock	.05	.15
❑ 19 Michael Finley	.20	.50
❑ 20 Gary Payton	.20	.50
❑ 21 Kevin Garnett	.40	1.00
❑ 22 Clyde Drexler	.20	.50
❑ 23 Michael Jordan	1.25	3.00
❑ 24 Antonio McDyess	.10	.30
❑ 25 Nick Anderson	.05	.15
❑ 26 Patrick Ewing	.20	.50
❑ 27 Anthony Peeler	.05	.15
❑ 28 Doug Christie	.10	.30
❑ 29 Bobby Phills	.05	.15
❑ 30 Kerry Kittles	.20	.50
❑ 31 Reggie Miller	.20	.50
❑ 32 Karl Malone	.20	.50
❑ 33 Grant Hill	.20	.50
❑ 34 Shaquille O'Neal	.50	1.25
❑ 35 Loy Vaught	.05	.15
❑ 36 Kenny Anderson	.10	.30
❑ 37 Wesley Person	.05	.15
❑ 38 Jamal Mashburn	.10	.30
❑ 39 Christian Laettner	.10	.30
❑ 40 Shawn Kemp	.10	.30
❑ 41 Glen Rice	.10	.30
❑ 42 Vin Baker	.10	.30
❑ 43 Popeye Jones	.05	.15
❑ 44 Derrick Coleman	.05	.15
❑ 45 Rik Smits	.10	.30
❑ 46 Dale Ellis	.05	.15
❑ 47 Rod Strickland	.05	.15
❑ 48 Mark Price	.10	.30
❑ 49 Toni Kukoc	.10	.30
❑ 50 David Robinson	.20	.50
❑ 51 John Wallace	.05	.15
❑ 52 Samaki Walker	.05	.15
❑ 53 Shareef Abdur-Rahim	.30	.75
❑ 54 Rodney Rogers	.05	.15
❑ 55 Dikembe Mutombo	.10	.30
❑ 56 Rony Seikaly	.05	.15
❑ 57 Matt Maloney	.05	.15
❑ 58 Chris Webber	.20	.50
❑ 59 Robert Horry	.10	.30
❑ 60 Rasheed Wallace	.20	.50
❑ 61 Jeff Hornacek	.10	.30
❑ 62 Walt Williams	.05	.15
❑ 63 Detlef Schrempf	.10	.30
❑ 64 Dan Majerle	.10	.30
❑ 65 Dell Curry	.05	.15
❑ 66 Scottie Pippen	.30	.75
❑ 67 Greg Anthony	.05	.15
❑ 68 Mahmoud Abdul-Rauf	.05	.15
❑ 69 Cedric Ceballos	.05	.15
❑ 70 Terrell Brandon	.10	.30
❑ 71 Arvydas Sabonis	.10	.30
❑ 72 Malik Sealy	.05	.15
❑ 73 Dean Garrett	.05	.15
❑ 74 Joe Dumars	.20	.50
❑ 75 Joe Smith	.10	.30
❑ 76 Shawn Bradley	.05	.15
❑ 77 Gheorghe Muresan	.05	.15
❑ 78 Dale Davis	.05	.15
❑ 79 Bryant Stith	.05	.15
❑ 80 Lorenzen Wright	.05	.15
❑ 81 Chris Childs	.05	.15
❑ 82 Bryon Russell	.05	.15
❑ 83 Steve Smith	.10	.30
❑ 84 Jerry Stackhouse	.20	.50
❑ 85 Hersey Hawkins	.05	.15
❑ 86 Ray Allen	.20	.50
❑ 87 Dominique Wilkins	.20	.50
❑ 88 Kobe Bryant	.75	2.00
❑ 89 Tom Gugliotta	.10	.30
❑ 90 Dennis Scott	.05	.15
❑ 91 Dennis Rodman	.10	.30
❑ 92 Bryant Reeves	.05	.15
❑ 93 Vlade Divac	.10	.30
❑ 94 Jason Kidd	.30	75
❑ 95 Mario Elie	.05	.15
❑ 96 Lindsey Hunter	.05	.15
❑ 97 Olden Polynice	.05	.15
❑ 98 Allan Houston	.10	.30
❑ 99 Alonzo Mourning	.10	.30
❑ 100 Allen Iverson	.50	1.25
❑ 101 LaPhonso Ellis	.05	.15
❑ 102 Bob Sura	.05	.15
❑ 103 Chris Mullin	.20	.50
❑ 104 Sam Cassell	.20	.50
❑ 105 Eric Williams	.05	.15
❑ 106 Antonio Davis	.05	.15
❑ 107 Marcus Camby	.20	.50
❑ 108 Isaiah Rider	.10	.30
❑ 109 Checklist (Hawks/Suns)	.05	.15
❑ 110 Checklist (TrailBlazers/ Wizards/inserts)	.05	.15
❑ 111 Tim Duncan RC	.40	1.00
❑ 112 Joe Smith	.10	.30
❑ 113 Shawn Kemp	.10	.30
❑ 114 Terry Mills	.05	.15
❑ 115 Jacque Vaughn RC	.10	.30
❑ 116 Ron Mercer RC	.20	.50
❑ 117 Brian Williams	.05	.15
❑ 118 Rik Smits	.10	.30
❑ 119 Eric Williams	.05	.15
❑ 120 Tim Thomas RC	.30	.75
❑ 121 Damon Stoudamire	.10	.30
❑ 122 God Shammgod RC	.05	.15
❑ 123 Tyrone Hill	.05	.15
❑ 124 Elden Campbell	.05	.15
❑ 125 Keith Van Horn RC	.25	.60
❑ 126 Brian Grant	.10	.30
❑ 127 Antonio McDyess	.10	.30
❑ 128 Darrell Armstrong	.05	.15
❑ 129 Sam Perkins	.10	.30
❑ 130 Chris Mills	.05	.15
❑ 131 Reggie Miller	.20	.50
❑ 132 Chris Gatling	.05	.15
❑ 133 Ed Gray RC	.05	.15
❑ 134 Hakeem Olajuwon	.20	.50
❑ 135 Chris Webber	.20	.50
❑ 136 Kendall Gill	.05	.15
❑ 137 Wesley Person	.05	.15
❑ 138 Derrick Coleman	.05	.15
❑ 139 Dana Barros	.05	.15
❑ 140 Dennis Scott	.05	.15
❑ 141 Paul Grant RC	.05	.15
❑ 142 Scott Burrell	.05	.15
❑ 143 Does not Exist		
❑ 144 Austin Croshere RC	.15	.40
❑ 145 Maurice Taylor RC	.15	.40
❑ 146 Kevin Johnson	.10	.30
❑ 147 Tony Battie RC	.20	.50
❑ 148 Tariq Abdul-Wahad RC	.10	.30
❑ 149 Johnny Taylor RC	.05	.15
❑ 150 Allen Iverson	.50	1.25
❑ 151 Terrell Brandon	.10	.30
❑ 152 Derek Anderson RC	.20	.50
❑ 153 Calbert Cheaney	.05	.15
❑ 154 Jayson Williams	.05	.15
❑ 155 Rick Fox	.10	.30
❑ 156 John Thomas RC	.05	.15
❑ 157 David Wesley	.05	.15
❑ 158 Bobby Jackson RC	.40	1.00
❑ 159 Kelvin Cato RC	.20	.50
❑ 160 Vinny Del Negro	.05	.15
❑ 161 Adonal Foyle RC	.10	.30
❑ 162 Larry Johnson	.10	.30
❑ 163 Brevin Knight RC	.10	.30
❑ 164 Rod Strickland	.05	.15
❑ 165 Rodrick Rhodes RC	.05	.15
❑ 166 Scot Pollard RC	.10	.30
❑ 167 Sam Cassell	.20	.50
❑ 168 Jerry Stackhouse	.20	.50
❑ 169 Mark Jackson	.10	.30
❑ 170 John Wallace	.05	.15
❑ 171 Horace Grant	.10	.30
❑ 172A Vin Baker	.10	.30
❑ 172B Tracy McGrady ERR RC	.50	1.25
❑ 173 Eddie Jones	.20	.50
❑ 174 Kerry Kittles	.20	.50
❑ 175 Antonio Daniels RC	.20	.50
❑ 176 Alan Henderson	.05	.15
❑ 177 Sean Elliott	.10	.30
❑ 178 John Starks	.10	.30
❑ 179 Chauncey Billups RC	.75	2.00
❑ 180 Juwan Howard	.10	.30
❑ 181 Bobby Phills	.05	.15
❑ 182 Latrell Sprewell	.20	.50
❑ 183 Jim Jackson	.05	.15
❑ 184 Danny Fortson RC	.10	.30
❑ 185 Zydrunas Ilgauskas	.10	.30
❑ 186 Clifford Robinson	.05	.15
❑ 187 Chris Mullin	.20	.50
❑ 188 Greg Ostertag	.05	.15
❑ 189 Antoine Walker ZUP	.20	.50
❑ 190 Michael Jordan ZUP	.60	1.50
❑ 191 Scottie Pippen ZUP	.15	.40
❑ 192 Dennis Rodman ZUP	.05	.15
❑ 193 Grant Hill ZUP	.10	.30
❑ 194 Clyde Drexler ZUP	.10	.30
❑ 195 Kobe Bryant ZUP	.40	1.00
❑ 196 Shaquille O'Neal ZUP	.20	.50
❑ 197 Alonzo Mourning ZUP	.10	.30
❑ 198 Ray Allen ZUP	.20	.50
❑ 199 Kevin Garnett ZUP	.20	.50
❑ 200 Stephon Marbury ZUP	.20	.50
❑ 201 Anfernee Hardaway ZUP	.10	.30
❑ 202 Jason Kidd ZUP	.15	.40
❑ 203 David Robinson ZUP	.10	.30
❑ 204 Gary Payton ZUP	.10	.30
❑ 205 Marcus Camby ZUP	.10	.30
❑ 206 Karl Malone ZUP	.20	.50
❑ 207 John Stockton ZUP	.20	.50
❑ 208 S.Abdur-Rahim ZUP	.15	.40
❑ 209 Charles Barkley CL	.20	.50
❑ 210 Gary Payton CL	.10	.30

Acknowledgments

Each year we refine the process of developing the most accurate and up-to-date information for this book. We believe this year's price guide is our best yet. Thanks again to all the contributors nationwide (listed below) as well as our staff here in Dallas.

Those who have worked closely with us on this and many other books, have again proven themselves invaluable in every aspect of producing this book: Rich Altman, Randy Archer, Mike Aronstein, Jerry Bell, Chris Benjamin, Mike Blaisdell, Bill Bossert (Mid-Atlantic Coin Exchange), Todd Crosner (California Sports Card Exchange), Bud Darland, Bill and Diane Dodge, Rick Donohoo, Willie Erving, Fleer (Tim Franz), Gervise Ford, Steve Freedman, Larry and Jeff Fritsch, Jim Galusha, Dick Gariepy, Dick Gilkeson, Mike and Howard Gordon, Sally Grace, Oscar Gracia, George Grauer, John Greenwald, Jess Guffey, George Henn, Mike Hersh, John Inouye, Steven Judd, Edward J. Kabala, Judy Kaye, Lon Levitan, Lew Lipset, Dave Lucey, Paul Marchant, Brian Marcy (Scottsdale Baseball Cards), Dr. John McCue, Mike Mosier (Columbia City Collectibles Co.), Clark Muldavin, B.A. Murry, Steven Panet, Earl N. Petersen, J.C. (Boo) Phillips, Jack Pollard, Racing Champions (Bill Surdock), Pat Quinn, Henry M. Reizes, Gavin Riley, Rotman Productions, John Rumierz, Kevin Savage and Pat Blandford (Sports Gallery), Mike Schechter (MSA), Dan Sherlock, Bill Shonscheck, Glen J. Sidler, John Spalding, Spanky's, Nigel Spill (Oldies and Goodies), Rob Springs, Murvin Sterling, Dan Stickney, Steve Taft, Ed Taylor, Lee Temanson, Topps (Clay Luraschi), Upper Deck (Jake Gonzales), Bill Vizas, Bill Wesslund (Portland Sports Card Co.), Jim Woods, Kit Young, Robert Zanze, Bill Zimpleman, and Dean Zindler.

Many other individuals have provided price input, illustrative material, checklist verifications, errata, and/or background information. At the risk of inadvertently overlooking or omitting these many contributors, we should like to personally thank Joseph Abram, Darren Adams, Harry and Angela Agens, Brett Allen, Alan Applegate, Randy Archer, Jeremy Bachman, Fran Bailey, Dean Bedell, Bubba Bennett, Eric Berger, Stanley Bernstein, Mike Blair, Andrew Bosarge, Naed Bou, David Bowlby, Gary Boyd, Terry Boyd, Nelson Brewart, Ray Bright, Britt Britton, Jacey Buel, Terry Bunt, David Cadelina, Danny Cariseo, Sally Carves, Tom Cavalierre, Garrett Chan, Lance Churchill, Craig Coddling, H. William Cook, Dave Cooper, Ron Cornell, Paul Czuchna, Jeff Daniels, Robert DeSalvatore, Robert Dichiara, Pat Dorsey, Joe Drelich, Brad Drummond, Charles Easterday Jr., Al Eng, Brad Engelhardt, Darrell Ereth, F&F Fast Break Cards, Gary Farbstein, Anthony Fernando, Joe Filas, Tom Freeman, Bob Frye, Alex and Chris Gala, Greg George, Pete George, Arthur Goyette, Dina Gray, Bob Grissett, Jess Guffey, Simon Gutis, Steve Hart, John Haupt, Sol Hauptman, Brian Headrick, Steven Hecht, Rod Heffem, Kevin Heffner, Stephen Hils, Neil Hoppenworth, Bill Huggins, Wendell Hunter, Frank Hurtado, Brett Hyle, John Inouye, Brian Jaccoma, Mike Jardina, David Johnson, Craig Jones, Carmen Jordan, Loyd Jungling, Nick Kardoulias, Scott Kashner, Glenn Kasnuba, Jan Kemplin, Kal Kenfield, John Kilian, Tim Kirk, John Klassnik, Steve (DJ) Kluback, Mike Knoll, Don Knutsen, Mike Kohlhas, Bob and Bryan Kornfeld, George Kruk, Tom Kummer, Tim Landis, Jeff La Scala, Howard Lau, John Law, Ed Lim, Neil Lopez, Kendall Loyd, Fernando Mercado, Bruce Margulies, Scott Martinez, Bill McAvoy, Chris Merrill, Robert Merrill, Blake Meyer, Chad Meyer, Mark Meyer, Midwest Sports Cards, Jeff Mimick, Jeff Monaco, Jeff Morris, Michael Olsen, Don Olson Jr., Glenn Olson, Arto Paladian, Michael Parker, Jeff Patton, Jeff Prillaman, Paul Purves, Don Ras, Ron Resling, Carson Ritchey, Brent Ruland, Erik Runge, Mark Samarin, Bob Santos, Eric Shilito, Masa Shinohara, Bob Shurtleff, Sam Sliheet, Doug Smith, Doug Spooner, Dan Statman, Geoff Stevers, Brad Stiles, Andy Stoltz, Nick Teresi, Jim Tripodi, Rob Veres, Bill Vizas, Kevin Vo, Mark Watson, Brian Wentz, Brian White, Doc White, Jeff Wiedenfeld, Mike Wiggins, Douglas Wilding, Steve Yeh, Zario Zigler, and Mark Zubrensky.

Every year we make active solicitations for expert input. We are particularly appreciative of help (however extensive or cursory) provided for this volume. We receive many inquiries, comments, and questions regarding material within this book. In fact, each and every one is read and digested. Time constraints, however, prevent us from personally replying. But keep sharing your knowledge. Your letters and input are part of the "big picture" of hobby information we can pass along to readers in our books and magazines. Even though we cannot respond to each letter, you are making significant contributions to the hobby through your interest and comments.

The effort to continually refine and improve this book also involves a growing number of people and types of expertise on our home team. Our company boasts a substantial Sports Data Publishing team, which strengthens our ability to provide comprehensive analysis of the marketplace. Sports Data Publishing capably handled numerous technical details and provided able assistance and leadership in the preparation of this edition.

Our basketball analysts played a major part in compiling this year's book, traveling thousands of miles during the past year to attend sports card shows and visit card shops around the United States and Canada. The Beckett basketball specialist is Keith Hower (price guide editor). His gathering information, entering sets, pricing analysis, and careful proofreading were key contributions to the accuracy of this annual.

Also, key contributor to endless hours of information gathering, pricing, and analysis was Rich Klein.